Churches and Church Membership in the United States 1980

An Enumeration by Region, State and County
Based on Data Reported by 111 Church Bodies

Bernard Quinn, Herman Anderson
Martin Bradley, Paul Goetting
Peggy Shriver

GLENMARY RESEARCH CENTER / ATLANTA, GEORGIA

GRC A-68/P-250
International Standard Book Number: 0-914422-12-X
Library of Congress Catalog Card Number: 82-081978
Printed in the United States of America.

Cover design by Patricia Gotwols, Souder & Associates

Published by the Glenmary Research Center, 750 Piedmont
Ave., NE, Atlanta, Georgia 30308. Available also through the
Office of Research, Evaluation and Planning, National Council of
the Churches of Christ in the U.S.A., 475 Riverside Dr., New
York, N.Y. 10115. Book includes fold-out map, *Major Denominational Families, by Counties of the United States: 1980*. Map
is also available separately.

The authors gratefully acknowledge the generous grant from the members of AID ASSOCIATION FOR LUTHERANS, a fraternal insurance society based in Appleton, Wisconsin. Their generosity has made this study and its publication possible, as well as the distribution of this volume to participating church bodies.

Contents

Preface

This report contains statistics for 111 Judaeo-Christian church bodies, providing information on the number of their churches and members for regions, states and counties of the United States.

The study on which this report was based was sponsored jointly by the Department of Records and Research of the African Methodist Episcopal Zion Church, the Research Services Department of the Sunday School Board of the Southern Baptist Convention, the Office of Research, Evaluation and Planning of the National Council of the Churches of Christ in the U.S.A., the Lutheran Council in the U.S.A., and the Glenmary Research Center (a Catholic agency). The authors are the official representatives of the five sponsoring agencies on the study's executive committee. Herman Anderson represented the AME Zion; Martin Bradley, the SBC Sunday School Board; Peggy Shriver, the National Council; Paul Goetting, the Lutheran Council; and Bernard Quinn, the Glenmary Research Center.

A generous grant from the members of Aid Association for Lutherans covered major costs for the study and for the distribution of this report. Additional funds came from proceeds of the sale of books and tapes from the 1971 church membership study. The remaining costs were absorbed by the five sponsoring agencies and the denominational offices that furnished the data.

The authors wish to thank the members of the study's advisory committee: Jackson W. Carroll, John E. Dyble, Dean R. Hoge, Constant H. Jacquet, Jr., Douglas W. Johnson, William Kammrath, Mac Lynn, William McKinney, William Newman, Paul Picard, Edward A. Rauff, David Roozen, Herbert I. Sauer, James R. Shortridge, and Wilbur Zelinsky.

Special thanks are also due to those who served as denominational contact persons for furnishing the data:

Richard F. Amos, A. Ray Appelquist, Russell P. Baker, V. A. Ballantyne, Dennis Becker, Charles Beekley, Lowell Bennion, Clifford W. Bjorklund, James C. Blaylock, William Brink, Gordon M. Browne, Jr., Steve Burgess, Ralph S. Burns, Damon Burrows, Harvey H. Callies, K. Gene Carroll, Ronald Clark, Arthur M. Climenhaga, C. D. Coleman, C. Harmon Dickinson, Stanley Ditmer, Ronald Driggers, Elwyn Ewald, Joseph R. Flower, Julian B. Gamble, Kenneth E. Geiger, Walter Giffin, Hugh W. Good, Norman M. Green, Jr., Sona Hamalian, Edward A. Haug, Samuel T. Hemberger, Lucille S. Hicks, Marvin Hoff, Ed Hogan, Don Horath, James E. Horsch, Louis D. Hutmire, B. Edgar Johnson, Earl E. Johnson, Alice Jones, M. Joostens, Sheila M. Kelly, Reuben Koehn, Eugene S. Kreider, David Krogh, Jayne Kuryluk, B. W. Lanpher, James A. Lowry, Mac Lynn, James H. Martin, Alf Merseth, Walter H. Meyer, Bernard E. Michel, Arnold R. Mickelson, Audrey McClintic, M. E. Nicholls, Daniel A. Nielsen, John P. O'Hara, Paul Palmieri, Vinnia M. Pease, Roger Popplewell, Vern Preheim, Karl Pruter, Ben J. Raber, Karl Raudsepp, Clarence C. Reeder, William Regehr, Joseph D. Riser, Janis Robins, Andrew M. Rupp, Athanasius Y. Samuel, Don Sauls, Roberta Schott, John Schultz, Marie E. Schultz, Charles L. Selzer, Adrian B. Shepard, Earnest H. Skoog, Morton H. Smith, Ray E. Smith, R. Snipstead, Roscoe Snowden, Lorentz R. Soneson, John Springer, Everald H. Strom, Neal D. Sword, Ivan Tkaczuk, Walter G. Truesdell, John D. Tucker, Robert Uhrig, Vasile Vasilachi, Philip Walter, T. Warnick, Nancy Wilson, Lewis Wimberley, David Worgull and Steve Yoder.

The following offered assistance to the study in various ways: Terry M. Batts, Jr., Deirdre Gaquin, C. J. Malloy, Jr., Paul W. S. Schneirla, John E. Schweikert, Ishmael L. Shaw, and members of the U.S. Census Bureau staff.

William J. Goodwin, Research Technician of the Glenmary Research Center, served as manager of the data collection and checking process. Alexander Akalovsky, Jr. did the computer programming, James Kmetz did the graphics on the map, and Harry Wilson offered assistance with the analysis. Other members of the Glenmary staff who worked on the study were: Michael Hounslow, Peter Kreysa, Kathleen Goodwin, Apolo Kaggwa and John McAllister.

Statistics contained in this study are also available on computer tape, and, in combination with other data, in the form of Church Planning Data booklets for judicatories. Inquiries regarding the *computer tape* may be addressed to the Roper Center, Office of User Services, Box U-164R, University of Connecticut, Storrs, Connecticut 06268. Inquiries regarding *Catholic* Planning Data booklets may be addressed to the Glenmary Research Center, 750 Piedmont Ave., NE, Atlanta, Georgia 30308. Inquiries regarding *Protestant and other* Planning Data booklets may be addressed to the Office of Research, Evaluation and Planning, National Council of the Churches of Christ in the U.S.A., 475 Riverside Dr., New York, N.Y. 10115.

It is hoped that this report, despite its limitations, will stimulate ecumenical awareness at the judicatory and county level, aid in denominational planning, and contribute to the study of long-range religious trends in America.

Introduction

SCOPE OF THE STUDY

This publication presents data reported by the 111 church bodies who participated in a study sponsored jointly by the Department of Records and Research of the African Methodist Episcopal Zion Church, the Research Services Department of the Sunday School Board of the Southern Baptist Convention, the Office of Research, Evaluation and Planning of the National Council of the Churches of Christ in the U.S.A., the Lutheran Council in the U.S.A., and the Glenmary Research Center (a Catholic agency).

The sponsors invited all church bodies that could be identified as Judaeo-Christian to participate. The 111 groups that furnished data reported 231,708 congregations with 112,538,310 adherents.[1] No attempt was made to count strictly independent churches that have no connection with a denomination.

The present study is related to two previous studies.[2] The first reported 1952 statistics and was sponsored and published by the National Council of the Churches of Christ in the U.S.A. in 1956. The second reported 1971 statistics and was sponsored by the Office of Research, Evaluation and Planning of the National Council of the Churches of Christ in the U.S.A., the Department of Research and Statistics of the Lutheran Church—Missouri Synod, and the Glenmary Research Center. It was published in 1974 by the Glenmary Research Center.

---

1. For purposes of this study, adherents were defined as "all members, including full members, their children and the estimated number of other regular participants who are not considered as communicant, confirmed or full members, for example, the 'baptized,' 'those not confirmed,' 'those not eligible for communion,' and the like." See "Defining Membership," below.

2. Lauris B. Whitman and Glen W. Trimble, *Churches and Church Membership in the United States: An Enumeration and Analysis by Counties, States and Regions* (New York: National Council of the Churches of Christ in the U.S.A., 1956-1958), 80 bulletins; Douglas W. Johnson, Paul R. Picard and Bernard Quinn, *Churches and Church Membership in the United States 1971: An Enumeration by Region, State and County* (Washington, D.C.: Glenmary Research Center, 1974).

PARTICIPATING CHURCH BODIES

The 17 denominations with adherents of a million or more account for 91.9 percent of the reported adherents. The 25 groups with adherents of 100,000 to 999,999 account for an additional 6.9 percent. The remaining 69 groups comprise only 1.2 percent.

The following denominations participated in the 1980 study. The number of counties in which the groups report churches will provide a general idea of their geographic extension. (At the time of the study there were 3102 counties or county-equivalents in the United States.)

Communions with Adherents of 1,000,000 or More	Counties with Churches
1. African Methodist Episcopal Zion Church	407
2. American Baptist Churches in the U.S.A.	1106
3. American Lutheran Church	1029
4. Assemblies of God	2452
5. Catholic Church	2881
6. Christian Church (Disciples of Christ)	1424
7. Christian Churches and Churches of Christ	1590
8. Church of Jesus Christ of Latter-day Saints	1571
9. Churches of Christ	2364
10. Episcopal Church	2005
11. Lutheran Church in America	1181
12. Lutheran Church-Missouri Synod	1690
13. Presbyterian Church in the United States	1036
14. Southern Baptist Convention	2383
15. United Church of Christ	1283
16. United Methodist Church	2968
17. United Presbyterian Church in the U.S.A.	1874

Communions with Adherents of 100,000 to 999,999	Counties with Churches
18. American Baptist Association	496
19. Baptist General Conference	328
20. Baptist Missionary Association of America	375
21. Christian and Missionary Alliance	604
22. Christian Methodist Episcopal Church	552
23. Christian Reformed Church	223

Communions with Adherents Less than 100,000

Counties with Churches

PARTICIPATION IN 1971 AND 1980 COMPARED

There are 48 denominations that participated in both studies, 63 that participated in 1980 but not in 1971, and five that participated in 1971 but not in 1980.

Participants in Both Studies

1. American Baptist Churches in the U.S.A.
2. American Lutheran Church
3. Associate Reformed Presbyterian Church (General Synod)
4. Baptist Missionary Association of America
5. Brethren in Christ Church
6. Catholic Church
7. Christ Catholic Church
8. Christian Church (Disciples of Christ)
9. Christian Churches and Churches of Christ
10. Christian Reformed Church
11. Christian Union
12. Church of God General Conference (Abrahamic Faith), Oregon, Ill.
13. Church of God (Anderson, Indiana)
14. Church of God (Cleveland, Tennessee)
15. Church of Jesus Christ of Latter-day Saints
16. Church of the Brethren
17. Church of the Nazarene
18. Congregational Christian Churches, National Association of
19. Cumberland Presbyterian Church
20. Episcopal Church
21. Evangelical Church of North America
22. Evangelical Congregational Church
23. Evangelical Covenant Church of America
24. Evangelical Mennonite Brethren Conference
25. Free Methodist Church of North America
26. Friends
27. Lutheran Church in America
28. Lutheran Church-Missouri Synod
29. Mennonite Church
30. Mennonite Church, The General Conference
31. Moravian Church in America (Unitas Fratrum), Northern Province
32. Moravian Church in America (Unitas Fratrum), Southern Province
33. North American Baptist Conference
34. Orthodox Presbyterian Church
35. Pentecostal Holiness Church, Inc.
36. Christian Brethren (formerly Plymouth Brethren)
37. Presbyterian Church in the United States
38. Reformed Church in America
39. Reformed Presbyterian Church, Evangelical Synod
40. Salvation Army
41. Seventh-day Adventists
42. Seventh Day Baptist General Conference
43. Southern Baptist Convention
44. Unitarian Universalist Association
45. United Church of Christ
46. United Methodist Church
47. United Presbyterian Church in the U.S.A.
48. Wisconsin Evangelical Lutheran Synod

In the 1971 study the Christ Catholic Church was listed as the Christ Catholic Church—Diocese of Boston; the Friends were listed as the Friends World Committee, American Section; and the Christian Brethren were listed as the Plymouth Brethren.

In the 1971 study the Friends included the following groups: Religious Society of Friends (Conservative), Religious Society of Friends (General Conference), Five Year Meeting of Friends, Religious Society of Friends (Philadelphia and Vicinity), Central Yearly Meeting of Friends, Oregon Yearly Meeting of Friends Church. In the 1980 study the Friends comprise the following: Evangelical Friends Alliance, Friends General Conference, Friends United Meeting (formerly Five Year Meeting of Friends), Religious Society of Friends (Conservative), Religious Society of Friends (Unaffiliated Meetings.)

In 1980 the Moravian Church in America (Unitas Fratrum), Northern Province, includes statistics for Alaska, which is technically separate from the Northern Province.

Since the 1971 study was published, some congregations of the Lutheran Church-Missouri Synod became members of the newly-formed Association of Evangelical Lutheran Churches; and some congregations of the Presbyterian Church in the United States became members of the newly-formed Presbyterian Church in America.

New Participants in 1980

1. Advent Christian Church
2. African Methodist Episcopal Zion Church
3. Amana Church Society
4. American Baptist Association
5. Apostolic Christian Church (Nazarean)
6. Apostolic Lutheran Church of America
7. Armenian Apostolic Church of America (Eastern Prelacy)
8. Assemblies of God
9. Baptist General Conference
10. Beachy Amish Mennonite Churches
11. Berean Fundamental Church
12. Bethel Ministerial Association, Inc.
13. Bible Church of Christ, Inc.
14. Brethren Church (Ashland, Ohio)
15. Christian and Missionary Alliance
16. Christian Catholic Church
17. Christian Methodist Episcopal Church
18. Church of God (Seventh Day), Denver, Colorado
19. Church of God in Christ (Mennonite)
20. Church of Jesus Christ, The (Bickertonites)
21. Church of the Lutheran Brethren of America
22. Church of the Lutheran Confession
23. Churches of Christ
24. Congregational Holiness Church
25. Conservative Baptist Association of America
26. Conservative Congregational Christian Conference

27. Estonian Evangelical Lutheran Church
28. Evangelical Free Church of America
29. Evangelical Lutheran Churches, Association of
30. Evangelical Lutheran Synod
31. Evangelical Mennonite Church, Inc.
32. Evangelical Methodist Church
33. Fire Baptized Holiness Church, (Wesleyan)
34. Free Lutheran Congregations, The Association of
35. General Church of the New Jerusalem
36. General Conference of Mennonite Brethren Churches
37. General Convention of the New Jerusalem in the USA "The Swedenborgian Church"
38. Grace Brethren Churches, Fellowship of (formerly Fellowship of Brethren Churches)
39. Holiness Church of God, Inc.
40. International Church of the Foursquare Gospel
41. Conservative Judaism
42. Reform Judaism
43. Latvian Evangelical Lutheran Church in America (formerly Federation of Latvian Evangelical Churches in America)
44. Metropolitan Community Churches, Universal Fellowship of
45. Missionary Church
46. Old Order Amish Church
47. Open Bible Standard Churches, Inc.
48. Pentecostal Free Will Baptist Church, Inc.
49. Presbyterian Church in America
50. Primitive Advent Christian Church
51. Primitive Methodist Church, U.S.A.
52. The Protes'tant Conference of the Wisconsin Synod
53. Protestant Reformed Churches in America
54. Reformed Episcopal Church
55. Reformed Presbyterian Church of North America
56. Romanian Orthodox Church in America
57. Separate Baptists in Christ
58. Social Brethren
59. The Southern Methodist Church
60. Syrian Orthodox Church of Antioch (Archdiocese of the U.S.A. and Canada)
61. Ukrainian Orthodox Church of America (Ecumenical Patriarchate)
62. United Christian Church
63. United Zion Church

The 63 church bodies participating in 1980 but not in 1971 represent a total of 7.6 million adherents. The largest among the new participants are the African Methodist Episcopal Zion Church, with 1.1 million; the Assemblies of God, with 1.6 million; and the Churches of Christ, with 1.6 million.

Denominations Participating in 1971 but not 1980

1. Free Will Baptists
2. General Baptists (General Association of)

3. North American Old Roman Catholic Church (Brooklyn)
4. Unity of the Brethren
5. Wesleyan Church

INCLUSIVENESS OF THE STUDY

The study identified by county 112.5 million adherents, in 111 denominations. It is not known what percent of total Judaeo-Christian adherents this actually represents. The difficulty is in obtaining an agreed-upon basis for determining the total Judaeo-Christian adherents for the whole United States.

The *Yearbook of American and Canadian Churches*[3] lists 53.6 million "full, communicant or confirmed members" reported officially by U.S. church bodies. The present study reports 48.8 million full, communicant or confirmed members. From this perspective, the present study reported 91.0 percent of the U.S. communicant membership totals officially submitted to the *Yearbook of American and Canadian Churches.*

It is well known that there are independent and community churches, as well as religious movements and associations that might be considered churches, whose membership is not reported to the *Yearbook.* Because the membership of these groups is unknown, there is no way of determining the percent of church membership the present study would represent if these groups were included in the total. (Some members of such churches or groups do, of course, also belong to denominations participating in the study and, therefore, are accounted for in the CMS data reported.)

Jewish Bodies. With the assistance of the United Synagogue of America, the full members (individual adult members) of 793 Conservative synagogues were identified by county. For this group, the number of total adherents listed in Table 1 of this study should probably be increased, because the CMS method of estimating adherents adds children 13 and under to the full members; whereas in this case, 18 and under is probably a better basis. With the assistance of the Union of American Hebrew Congregations, the full members of 708 Reform congregations were also identified by county. No county information is available on either full members or adherents of Orthodox synagogues, although according to one estimate, their total number of adherents could be as high as 1.3 million.[4] The general Jewish population is, of course, considerably larger than

---

3. Constant H. Jacquet, Jr., ed., *Yearbook of American and Canadian Churches: 1981* (Nashville: Abingdon Press, 1981), pp. 225-232.

4. In a telephone conversation with the staff of the study, on April 20, 1982, Rabbi Arnie Rund of the Union of Orthodox Jewish Congregations of America stated that about 1.3 million persons identify with Orthodox synagogues or institutions.

the adherents of synagogues or congregations.[5]

Black Church Members. Four Black denominations, accounting for 1.8 million adherents, participated in the study.[6] The 107 other participants were asked to estimate the number of Blacks among their adherents. The 22 groups who responded reported a total of 1.8 million adherents.[7] There is no way of telling how many Blacks are adherents of the remaining 85 denominations who participated in the study.

The African Methodist Episcopal Church had hoped to participate, but their county statistics were not ready for release in time to meet the deadline. It is expected that their statistics will soon become available. The Progressive National Baptist Convention, Inc. and the National Primitive Baptist Convention, Inc. had also hoped to participate, but their records were only partially complete. Major efforts were made to enlist the participation of the four other large Black Churches,[8] but without success. The problem is the absence or incompleteness of membership figures. The 17 small non-participating Black denominations listed in the *Yearbook of American and Canadian Churches* were, of course, also invited to participate.

Orthodox Churches. Four Orthodox bodies, accounting for combined adherents of 55,000, participated in the study.[9] Although sizeable efforts were made to obtain data for the remaining 17 groups, both directly and with the assistance of the Standing Conference of Canonical Orthodox Bishops in the Americas (SCOBA), statistics were not actually obtained.

Other Groups. Besides the denominations mentioned above, there are 11 non-participating church bodies that reported more than 100,000 members to the *Yearbook of American and Canadi-*

an Churches: Jehovah's Witnesses, United Pentecostal Church International, Polish National Catholic Church of America, General Association of Regular Baptist Churches, Free Will Baptists, Church of God of Prophecy, National Council of Community Churches, Reorganized Church of Jesus Christ of Latter Day Saints, Independent Fundamental Churches of America, Pentecostal Church of God of America, Inc., and the Wesleyan Church.

PROBLEMS

Defining Membership. The most critical methodological problem was that of defining church membership. Since there is no generally acceptable statistical definition of church membership, it was felt that the designation of members rested finally with the denominations themselves.

In an effort to achieve comparability of data, however, two major categories were established:

COMMUNICANT, CONFIRMED, FULL MEMBERS: regular members with full membership status; and

TOTAL ADHERENTS: all members, including full members, their children and the estimated number of other regular participants who are not considered as communicant, confirmed or full members, for example, the "baptized," "those not confirmed," "those not eligible for communion," and the like.

Of the 111 participating denominations, 54 reported communicants *and* adherents; two (Catholics and Latter-day Saints) reported adherents only; and 55 reported communicants only.[10] For purposes of this report, the church membership study staff estimated the total adherents for the 55 groups that reported communicants only, according to a formula discussed below.

Participants were also requested to furnish descriptive definitions of the statistics they actually submitted. *Appendix A* contains the definitions submitted by the 67 groups that responded to this request.

Estimating Total Adherents. Since it was planned to use total adherents in computing percent of church membership to total population, for those 55 denominations that reported only communicant members, total adherents were estimated according to the following procedure. The total county population was divided by the total county population less children 13 years and under, and the resulting figure was multiplied by the communicant members.[11] The 1980 U.S. Census was used to

---

5. The *American Jewish Year Book 1981* (New York: American Jewish Committee, 1980), vol. 81, p. 173, reports 5.9 million.

6. The African Methodist Episcopal Zion Church, the Bible Church of Christ, Inc., the Christian Methodist Episcopal Church and the Fire Baptized Holiness Church (Wesleyan).

7. The following groups provided information on Black membership: American Baptist Association, Baptist General Conference, Baptist Missionary Association of America, Catholic Church, Christian and Missionary Alliance, Christian Church (Disciples), Christian Churches and Churches of Christ, Christian Reformed Church, Church of God (Cleveland, Tennessee), Church of the Nazarene, Churches of Christ, Congregational Christian Churches, Conservative Baptist Association of America, Episcopal Church, Lutheran Church in America, Lutheran Church—Missouri Synod, Mennonite Church, Presbyterian Church in the U.S., Reformed Church in America, Seventh-day Adventists, United Church of Christ, United Presbyterian Church in the U.S.A.

8. National Baptist Convention, U.S.A., Inc.; National Baptist Convention of America; Church of God in Christ, International; Church of God in Christ.

9. Armenian Apostolic Church of America (Eastern Prelacy), Romanian Orthodox Church in America, Syrian Orthodox Church of Antioch (Archdiocese of the U.S.A. and Canada), Ukrainian Orthodox Church of America (Ecumenical Patriarchate).

10. Consult Table 1 to learn which denominations reported what.

11. Thus the total adherents in a county with population of 1000 and 100 children 13 years and under would be the communicant members multiplied by 1.11; total adherents in a county with population of 1000 and 300 children would be the communicant members multiplied by 1.43; and total adherents in a county with population of 1000 and 500 children would be the confirmed members multiplied by 2.00.

determine for each county the population 13 years and under. An asterisk after a figure in the tables indicates that total adherents were estimated through use of this procedure, rather than reported directly by denominations.

The 55 denominations whose total adherents were estimated in this way were asked to comment on the procedure. Of the 32 who responded, 25 approved the formula, two had reservations, and five did not approve. The comments submitted are reproduced in *Appendix B*.

Locating Members by County. Membership statistics are generally reported for the county in which the church itself is located, rather than for the county in which the member resides.[12] In a majority of cases the county of residence will correspond to the county where the church is located, although modern mobility patterns suggest caution in accepting this assumption in every case.

County Listings. The church membership study employed the same counties or county-equivalents as the 1980 U.S. Census. Since the 1971 church membership study was published, the new county of Kalawao, Hawaii (formerly a part of Maui County) has been created; Washabaugh County, South Dakota has been absorbed into Jackson County; Nansemond County, Virginia has become Suffolk City; and Chesapeake City and Portsmouth City, Virginia are now part of Norfolk City. All of these changes have been incorporated into the 1980 church membership study.

In Virginia there are independent cities that are legally separate from the counties of that state. Since most denominations record location of churches within the counties from which these cities have been separated, it was decided to combine most of these cities with contiguous counties. A list of combinations and exceptions will be found in *Appendix C*.

Because Alaska has no counties, the 1980 census areas and boroughs that serve as county-equivalents for statistical reporting purposes were employed in this study. These 1980 county-equivalents differ from those used in the 1971 church membership study. *Appendix D* provides a comparative listing of the two. The change in geographic boundaries may be observed by comparing the fold-out maps of the 1971 and 1980 church membership studies.

Reporting Date. The study was designed to gather statistics as close as possible to the April 1, 1980 U.S. Census date. Accordingly, the request to the denominations stated: "We are asking that statistics be reported to us by the month of September, 1980. We hope to receive data from your *statistical year that ends anytime during*

1979; report earlier data only if that is all that is available by September, 1980."

Of the 90 denominations that stated that their statistics were valid as of a specific date, 40 gave December 31, 1979 or January 1, 1980 as the date. The dates for the other 50 ranged from October 31, 1978 to November 10, 1981. Seven groups did not indicate a specific date, but only the year (1979 or 1980).[13]

Accuracy of Reporting Procedures. Most large denominations maintain national offices that receive statistical reports from their individual congregations; these reports were combined to provide the membership data for this study. On the other hand, many smaller denominations, as well as those in which local churches have a great deal of autonomy, only request and do not require such reports. This means that data for a few denominations will not be as complete and current as might be desired.

During the course of the study, the denominational offices furnishing data were asked to comment on the accuracy of their own reporting procedures and to furnish copies of the forms they used to collect the data. Forms were received from 37 denominations, and these are available for study at the offices of the Glenmary Research Center.[14] Comments were received from 55 denominations; these comments will be found in *Appendix E*.

Dual Affiliation. In the 1980 church membership study some attempt was made to assess the extent of the practice whereby a local congregation affiliates with more than one denomination. The denominations were asked: "Do any local congregations of your denomination maintain affiliation with another denomination as well?" Of the 100 groups that replied, 72 responded No. The comments of the 28 denominations who responded Yes are contained in *Appendix F*. In many cases the comments will also reveal how dual membership statistics

---

12. Denominations were asked to state their general policy on reporting church members. Of the 82 who responded to the inquiry, all but one (Baptist General Conference) indicated county of membership rather than county of residence.

13. The following code numbers (see *Abbreviations* for code key) indicate the denominations who gave December 31, 1979 or January 1, 1980 as the date of their statistics: 001, 015, 019, 029, 053, 055, 063, 071, 081, 083, 093, 105, 123, 157, 163, 164, 185, 193, 201, 209, 221, 281, 283, 287, 293, 295, 313, 335, 356, 357, 367, 375, 381, 403, 413, 415, 419, 443, 449, 453. The following dates were given by other groups: 10-31-78: 211; 12-31-78: 371, 383; 6-1-79: 199; 6-30-79: 213, 217; 9-20-79: 091; 9-30-79: 237; 10-31-79: 059; 11-1-79: 271; 11-15-79: 165; 11-30-79: 167; 12-21-79: 347; 1-15-80: 195, 423; 1-31-80: 208; 2-19-80: 263; 3-12-80: 220; 3-14-80: 177; 3-22-80: 469; 3-31-80: 329; 4-30-80: 089, 363; 5-31-80: 133; 7-1-80: 421; 7-17-80: 459; 7-21-80: 323; 7-25-80: 107; 7-31-80: 097; 8-7-80: 149; 8-31-80: 233; 9-2-80: 290; 9-12-80: 291; 9-22-80: 203; 9-30-80: 127, 179, 353; 10-5-80: 247; 10-20-80: 049; 12-31-80: 274; 3-23-81: 065; 4-4-81: 075; 4-17-81: 017; 5-7-81: 181; 5-11-81: 359; 6-30-81: 270; 7-30-81: 409; 7-31-81: 395; 8-31-81: 349; 11-10-81: 101. The following groups did not report specific dates, but only years: 1979: 005, 175, 226, 285, 441; 1979-1980: 057; 1980: 197.

14. See *Appendix E* for a list of denominations furnishing data collection forms.

were handled for purposes of reporting to this study.

Membership Greater Than Population. There are 31 counties in this study reporting more church adherents than census population: GEORGIA: Franklin; HAWAII: Kalawao; KANSAS: Comanche, Morton, Wichita; KENTUCKY: Washington; MINNESOTA: Faribault, Traverse; NEBRASKA: Greeley; NEW MEXICO: Guadalupe, Harding, Mora, Taos; NORTH DAKOTA: Hettinger, LaMoure, Rolette; OKLAHOMA: Harmon; SOUTH DAKOTA: Douglas, Turner; TENNESSEE: Hancock; TEXAS: Cottle, Dallam, Haskell, Jeff Davis, Knox, Motley, Starr, Throckmorton, Willacy; UTAH: Morgan; VIRGINIA: Richmond. Reasons for the discrepancy will no doubt differ from county to county. But among the explanations the following might be suggested: U.S. Census undercount, church membership overcount, or county of residence differing from county of membership.

DATA PRESENTATION

This report consists of four tables and a fold-out map. The information is also available on computer tape and, in combination with other data, in the form of Church Planning Data booklets for judicatories.[15]

Table 1. The first table, "Churches and Church Membership by Denomination, for the United States: 1980," presents for each denomination the number of churches; the number of communicant, confirmed or full members; and the total adherents for the entire United States. It also indicates, for each denomination, what percent of the U.S. population and what percent of the total reported church membership its adherents comprise. Population figures are from the *U.S. Census 1980, Advance Reports.*

In all the tables, denominational names are abbreviated. A list of abbreviations will be found on the pages immediately preceding Table 1.

Table 2. The second table, "Churches and Church Membership by Region and Denomination: 1980," presents, for each of the nine census regions of the United States, the total of churches and members for each participating denomination. Both communicant, confirmed or full members and total

adherents are given, as well as the percent of regional population and of total adherents that each denomination represents.

A map displaying the nine census regions will be found on the page immediately preceding Table 2.

Table 3. The third table, "Churches and Church Membership by State and Denomination: 1980," presents for each state the total of churches and members for each participating denomination. Both communicant, confirmed or full members and total adherents are given, as well as the percent of state population and of total adherents that each denomination represents. States are arranged alphabetically within the table.

Table 4. The fourth table, "Churches and Church Membership by County and Denomination: 1980," provides the detailed data on which the totals in Tables 1-3 are based.

For each county of the United States, there is given the grand total of churches and members reported. Both communicant, confirmed or full members and total adherents are shown, as well as the percent of the county population that the combined total church adherents represent.

In addition, for each county there is a breakdown of data by denomination, showing for each communion the number of churches; the number of communicant, confirmed or full members; the number of total adherents; and the percent of county population and of total adherents its adherents comprise.

Fold-Out Map. Accompanying this report is a color map, 28″ × 41″, entitled *Major Denominational Families by Counties of the United States: 1980.* By means of a color code, this map indicates, for each county of the United States, the participating group that predominates. In consultation with the participating denominations, the various Adventist, Baptist, Brethren, Christian, Churches of God, Latter Day Saints, Lutheran, Mennonite, Methodist, Pentecostal, Presbyterian, and Reformed church bodies were grouped into families.[16] Catho-

---

15. Inquiries regarding the *computer tape* may be addressed to the Roper Center, Office of User Services, Box U-164R, University of Connecticut, Storrs, Connecticut 06268 (tel. 203-486-4440). Inquiries regarding *Catholic* Church Planning Data booklets may be addressed to the Glenmary Research Center, 750 Piedmont Ave., NE, Atlanta, Georgia 30308 (tel. 404-876-6518). Inquiries regarding *Protestant and other* Church Planning Data booklets may be addressed to the Office of Research, Evaluation and Planning, National Council of the Churches of Christ in the U.S.A., 475 Riverside Dr., New York, N.Y. 10115 (tel. 212-870-2561).

---

16. The family groups are as follows: ADVENTIST: Advent Christian Church, Primitive Advent Christian Church, Seventh-day Adventists; BAPTIST: American Baptist Association, American Baptist Churches in the U.S.A., Baptist General Conference, Baptist Missionary Association of America, Bethel Ministerial Association, Inc., Conservative Baptist Association of America, North American Baptist Conference, Separate Baptists in Christ, Seventh Day Baptist General Conference, Southern Baptist Convention; BRETHREN: Brethren Church (Ashland, Ohio), Church of the Brethren, Fellowship of Grace Brethren Churches; CHRISTIAN: Christian Church (Disciples of Christ), Christian Churches and Churches of Christ, Churches of Christ; CHURCHES OF GOD: Church of God General Conference (Abrahamic Faith) Oregon, Ill., Church of God (Anderson, Indiana), Church of God (Seventh Day) Denver, Colorado; LATTER DAY SAINTS: Church of Jesus Christ (Bickertonites), Church of Jesus Christ of Latter-day Saints; LUTHERAN: American Lutheran Church, Apostolic Lutheran Church of America, Church of the Lutheran Brethren of America, Church of the

lics, Congregational Christians, Episcopalians, Friends, Moravians, and members of the United Church of Christ were not grouped into families but were treated as separate units.

The number of counties in which the above mentioned families or units predominate is as follows:

Baptist	1164
Catholic	963
Methodist	374
Lutheran	227
Latter Day Saints	74
Christian	52
United Church of Christ	8
Churches of God	5
Reformed	5
Presbyterian	4
Mennonite	2
Moravian	2
Adventist	1
Brethren	1
Friends	1
Congregational Christian	1
Episcopal	1

A solid color on the map indicates that a group has 50 percent or more of the adherents in that county, as reported in the present study. When no group has 50 percent, a striped shading indicates the largest group with 25-49 percent of adherents in a county. The 217 counties where no group has 25 percent are left blank.

The percentages on which the map is based are taken from Table 4, Column 5 of this report.

Lutheran Confession, Estonian Evangelical Lutheran Church, Association of Evangelical Lutheran Churches, Evangelical Lutheran Synod, Association of Free Lutheran Congregations, Latvian Evangelical Lutheran Church in America, Lutheran Church in America, Lutheran Church—Missouri Synod, Protes'tant Conference of the Wisconsin Synod, Wisconsin Evangelical Lutheran Synod; MENNONITE: Beachy Amish Mennonite Churches, Church of God in Christ (Mennonite), Evangelical Mennonite Brethren Conference, Evangelical Mennonite Church, Inc., General Conference of Mennonite Brethren Churches, Mennonite Church, General Conference of the Mennonite Church, Old Order Amish Church; METHODIST: African Methodist Episcopal Zion Church, Christian Methodist Episcopal Church, Evangelical Methodist Church, Free Methodist Church of North America, Primitive Methodist Church in the U.S.A., The Southern Methodist Church, United Methodist Church; PENTECOSTAL: Assemblies of God, Bible Church of Christ, Inc., Church of God (Cleveland, Tennessee), Congregational Holiness Church, International Church of the Foursquare Gospel, Open Bible Standard Churches, Inc., Pentecostal Free Will Baptist Church, Inc., Pentecostal Holiness Church, Inc.; PRESBYTERIAN: Associate Reformed Presbyterian Church (General Synod), Cumberland Presbyterian Church, Orthodox Presbyterian Church, Presbyterian Church in America, Presbyterian Church in the United States, Reformed Presbyterian Church (Evangelical Synod), Reformed Presbyterian Church of North America, United Presbyterian Church in the U.S.A.; REFORMED: Christian Reformed Church, Protestant Reformed Churches in America, Reformed Church in America.

METHODOLOGY

The actual data collection was carried out in the offices of the Glenmary Research Center, which at that time was located in Washington, D.C. The data collection was managed by William J. Goodwin, staff person for the study's executive committee, under the supervision of Bernard Quinn, who served as committee liaison for that purpose. William Goodwin also assisted in enlisting denominational participation and in a variety of other administrative and editorial tasks.

On August 6, 1979 an invitation[17] to participate in the study was sent to all the Judaeo-Christian church bodies listed in the *Yearbook of American and Canadian Churches,* plus a few others for whom addresses could be found. Each denomination was assigned a member of the study's executive committee, whose responsibility was to encourage participation, by personal contact and other means, and to answer questions. The initial written invitation was followed by four additional general mailings and by special letters, personal visits and phone calls. As a result of these efforts, which extended over a two-year period, 228 denominations were invited, 111 actually participated, 21 expressed the intention to participate but were prevented from doing so, 36 declined to participate, and 60 did not respond.

Denominations agreeing to participate were asked to appoint a contact person, and signify their intentions on a special form. Three forms were then sent to the contact persons: instructions for reporting data; a transmittal sheet to be signed and sent with the data collected; and a state-county form for listing the statistics themselves. The contact persons were given the option of submitting their own computer print-out according to a prescribed format, or of using the forms provided by the study.

This process put the major burden of work on the denominational offices, since they were asked to compile data by county for all their congregations. In some cases, however, denominations were able to furnish information only in the form of yearbooks or other sources. Transferring yearbook information into county data then became the responsibility of the CMS staff. In a few cases the denominations instructed the CMS staff to estimate congregational membership according to a formula, and approved the result.[18] In all instances, however, the denominational contact person reviewed the statistics and signed the transmittal sheet.

---

17. Instruments for gathering the data will be found in *Appendix G.*

18. Apostolic Lutheran Church of America, Brethren in Christ Church, Conservative Baptist Association of America, General Convention of the New Jerusalem in the U.S.A. "The Swedenborgian Church", Old Order Amish Church, Social Brethren.

The CMS staff employed the following procedures for checking the data submitted. The state and national totals were first checked against the county data and discrepancies adjusted. A print-out was then made of all data. To insure the accuracy of data-entry into the computer, the state and national totals were then compared to the original documents, as checked and adjusted. If the denomination participated in 1971 and the difference in a given county's membership for 1980 was greater than 20 percent, this was noted on the print-out. The print-out was then sent back to the denominational contact person, along with the staff's comments and questions. Only after all problems raised by both the staff and the denominational contact person were solved were the statistics considered ready for publication.

When the 1980 U.S. county figures for persons 13 years of age or under were received from the Census Bureau on April 12, 1982, the total adherents for groups reporting only communicants were estimated, according to the formula described above. The final step was to run a series of computer edit tests to check for errors and to produce the print-out of tables for this report.

Abbreviations

```
001 ADVENT CHR CH.      ADVENT CHRISTIAN CHURCH
005 AME ZION......      AFRICAN METHODIST EPISCOPAL ZION CHURCH
015 AMANA CH SOC..      AMANA CHURCH SOCIETY
017 AMER BAPT ASSN      AMERICAN BAPTIST ASSOCIATION
019 AMER BAPT USA.      AMERICAN BAPTIST CHURCHES IN THE U.S.A.
029 AMER LUTH CH..      AMERICAN LUTHERAN CHURCH, THE
039 AP CHR CH(NAZ)      APOSTOLIC CHRISTIAN CHURCH (NAZAREAN)
045 APOSTOLIC LUTH      APOSTOLIC LUTHERAN CHURCH OF AMERICA
049 ARMEN AP CH AM      ARMENIAN APOSTOLIC CHURCH OF AMER, EASTERN PRELACY
053 ASSEMB OF GOD.      ASSEMBLIES OF GOD
055 AS REF PRES CH      ASSOCIATE REFORMED PRESBYTERIAN CHURCH (GEN SYNOD)
057 BAPT GEN CONF.      BAPTIST GENERAL CONFERENCE
059 BAPT MISS ASSN      BAPTIST MISSIONARY ASSOCIATION OF AMERICA
061 BEACHY AMISH..      BEACHY AMISH MENNONITE CHURCHES
063 BEREAN FUND CH      BEREAN FUNDAMENTAL CHURCH
065 BETHEL M ASSN.      BETHEL MINISTERIAL ASSOCIATION, INC.
066 BIBLE CH OF CR      BIBLE CHURCH OF CHRIST, INC., THE
071 BRETHREN (ASH)      BRETHREN CHURCH (ASHLAND, OHIO)
075 BRETHREN IN CR      BRETHREN IN CHRIST CHURCH
081 CATHOLIC......      CATHOLIC CHURCH
083 CHRIST CATH CH      CHRIST CATHOLIC CHURCH
089 CHR & MISS AL.      CHRISTIAN AND MISSIONARY ALLIANCE, THE
091 CHRISTIAN CATH      CHRISTIAN CATHOLIC CHURCH
093 CHR CH (DISC).      CHRISTIAN CHURCH (DISCIPLES OF CHRIST)
097 CHR CHS&CHS CR      CHRISTIAN CHURCHES AND CHURCHES OF CHRIST
101 C.M.E........      CHRISTIAN METHODIST EPISCOPAL CHURCH
105 CHRISTIAN REF.      CHRISTIAN REFORMED CHURCH
107 CHRISTIAN UN..      CHRISTIAN UNION
121 CH GOD (ABR)..      CHURCH OF GOD GENERAL CONFERENCE (ABRAHAMIC FAITH),
                            OREGON, ILL.
123 CH GOD (ANDER)      CHURCH OF GOD (ANDERSON, INDIANA)
127 CH GOD (CLEVE)      CHURCH OF GOD (CLEVELAND, TENNESSEE)
133 CH GOD(7TH)DEN      CHURCH OF GOD (SEVENTH DAY), DENVER, COLORADO, THE
143 CG IN CR(MENN)      CHURCH OF GOD IN CHRIST (MENNONITE)
149 CH OF JC (BIC)      CHURCH OF JESUS CHRIST, THE (BICKERTONITES)
151 L-D SAINTS....      CHURCH OF JESUS CHRIST OF LATTER-DAY SAINTS, THE
157 CH OF BRETHREN      CHURCH OF THE BRETHREN
163 CH OF LUTH BR.      CHURCH OF THE LUTHERAN BRETHREN OF AMERICA
164 CH LUTH CONF..      CHURCH OF THE LUTHERAN CONFESSION
165 CH OF NAZARENE      CHURCH OF THE NAZARENE
167 CHS OF CHRIST.      CHURCHES OF CHRIST
```

```
175 CONGR CHR CHS.      CONGREGATIONAL CHRISTIAN CHURCHES, NATL ASSOC OF
177 CONGR HOL CH..      CONGREGATIONAL HOLINESS CHURCH
179 CONSRV BAPT...      CONSERVATIVE BAPTIST ASSOCIATION OF AMERICA
181 CONSRV CONGR..      CONSERVATIVE CONGREGATIONAL CHRISTIAN CONFERENCE
185 CUMBER PRESB..      CUMBERLAND PRESBYTERIAN CHURCH
193 EPISCOPAL.....      EPISCOPAL CHURCH, THE
195 ESTONIAN ELC..      ESTONIAN EVANGELICAL LUTHERAN CHURCH
197 EVAN CH OF NA.      EVANGELICAL CHURCH OF NORTH AMERICA, THE
199 EVAN CONGR CH.      EVANGELICAL CONGREGATIONAL CHURCH
201 EVAN COV CH AM      EVANGELICAL COVENANT CHURCH OF AMERICA, THE
203 EVAN FREE CH..      EVANGELICAL FREE CHURCH OF AMERICA, THE
208 EVAN LUTH ASSN      EVANGELICAL LUTHERAN CHURCHES, ASSOCIATION OF
209 EVAN LUTH SYN.      EVANGELICAL LUTHERAN SYNOD
211 EVAN MENN BR..      EVANGELICAL MENNONITE BRETHREN CONFERENCE
213 EVAN MENN INC.      EVANGELICAL MENNONITE CHURCH INC.
215 EVAN METH CH..      EVANGELICAL METHODIST CHURCH
217 FIRE BAPTIZED.      FIRE BAPTIZED HOLINESS CHURCH, (WESLEYAN), THE
220 FREE LUTHERAN.      FREE LUTHERAN CONGREGATIONS, THE ASSOCIATION OF
221 FREE METHODIST      FREE METHODIST CHURCH OF NORTH AMERICA
226 FRIENDS-USA...      FRIENDS
233 GEN CH NEW JER      GENERAL CHURCH OF THE NEW JERUSALEM
237 GC MENN BR CHS      GENERAL CONFERENCE OF MENNONITE BRETHREN CHURCHES
239 SWEDENBORGIAN.      GENERAL CONVENTION OF THE NEW JERUSALEM IN THE
                           U.S.A. 'THE SWEDENBORGIAN CHURCH'
244 GRACE BRETHREN      GRACE BRETHREN CHURCHES, FELLOWSHIP OF
247 HOLINESS CH...      HOLINESS CHURCH OF GOD, INC., THE
263 INT FOURSQ GOS      INTERNATIONAL CHURCH OF THE FOURSQUARE GOSPEL
270 CONSRV JUDAISM      CONSERVATIVE JUDAISM
271 REFORM JUDAISM      REFORM JUDAISM
274 LAT EVAN LUTH.      LATVIAN EVANGELICAL LUTHERAN CHURCH IN AMERICA, THE
281 LUTH CH AMER..      LUTHERAN CHURCH IN AMERICA
283 LUTH---MO SYNOD     LUTHERAN CHURCH - MISSOURI SYNOD, THE
285 MENNONITE CH..      MENNONITE CHURCH
287 MENN GEN CONF.      MENNONITE CHURCH, THE GENERAL CONFERENCE
290 METRO COMM CHS      METROPOLITAN COMMUNITY CHURCHES, UNIVERSAL
                           FELLOWSHIP OF
291 MISSIONARY CH.      MISSIONARY CHURCH, THE
293 MORAV CH-NORTH      MORAVIAN CHURCH IN AMER (UNITAS FRATRUM),NO PROV
295 MORAV CH-SOUTH      MORAVIAN CHURCH IN AMER (UNITAS FRATRUM),SO PROV
313 N AM BAPT CONF      NORTH AMERICAN BAPTIST CONFERENCE
323 OLD ORD AMISH.      OLD ORDER AMISH CHURCH
329 OPEN BIBLE STD      OPEN BIBLE STANDARD CHURCHES, INC.
335 ORTH PRESB CH.      ORTHODOX PRESBYTERIAN CHURCH, THE
347 PENT FW BAPT..      PENTECOSTAL FREE WILL BAPTIST CHURCH, INC., THE
349 PENT HOLINESS.      PENTECOSTAL HOLINESS CHURCH, INC.
353 CHR BRETHREN..      CHRISTIAN BRETHREN
356 PRESB CH AMER.      PRESBYTERIAN CHURCH IN AMERICA
357 PRESB CH US...      PRESBYTERIAN CHURCH IN THE UNITED STATES
359 PRIM AD CHR CH      PRIMITIVE ADVENT CHRISTIAN CHURCH
363 PRIMITIVE METH      PRIMITIVE METHODIST CHURCH, U.S.A.
367 PROT CONF (WI)      THE PROTES'TANT CONFERENCE OF THE WISCONSIN SYNOD
369 PROT REF CHS..      PROTESTANT REFORMED CHURCHES IN AMERICA
371 REF CH IN AM..      REFORMED CHURCH IN AMERICA
375 REF EPISCOPAL.      REFORMED EPISCOPAL CHURCH
381 REF PRES-EVAN.      REFORMED PRESBYTERIAN CHURCH, EVANGELICAL SYNOD
```

383	REF PRES OF NA	REFORMED PRESBYTERIAN CHURCH OF NORTH AMERICA
395	ROMANIAN OR CH	ROMANIAN ORTHODOX CHURCH IN AMERICA, THE
403	SALVATION ARMY	SALVATION ARMY, THE
409	SEPARATE BAPT.	SEPARATE BAPTISTS IN CHRIST
413	S.D.A.........	SEVENTH-DAY ADVENTISTS
415	S-D BAPTIST GC	SEVENTH DAY BAPTIST GENERAL CONFERENCE
417	SOCIAL BRETH..	SOCIAL BRETHREN
419	SO BAPT CONV..	SOUTHERN BAPTIST CONVENTION
421	SO METHODIST..	THE SOUTHERN METHODIST CHURCH
423	SYRIAN ANTIOCH	SYRIAN ORTHODOX CHURCH OF ANTIOCH (ARCHDIOCESE OF THE U.S.A. AND CANADA)
431	UKRANIAN AMER.	UKRAINIAN ORTHODOX CHURCH OF AMER (ECUM PATR)
435	UNITARIAN-UNIV	UNITARIAN UNIVERSALIST ASSOCIATION
441	UN CHRISTIAN..	UNITED CHRISTIAN CHURCH
443	UN C OF CHRIST	UNITED CHURCH OF CHRIST
449	UN METHODIST..	UNITED METHODIST CHURCH, THE
453	UN PRES CH USA	UNITED PRESBYTERIAN CHURCH IN THE U.S.A., THE
459	UNITED ZION CH	UNITED ZION CHURCH
469	WELS..........	WISCONSIN EVANGELICAL LUTHERAN SYNOD

Table 1. Churches and Church Membership by Denomination, for the U.S.: 1980

County and Denomination	Number of churches	Communicant, confirmed, full members	Total adherents		
			Number	Percent of total population	Percent of total adherents
THE NATION	231 708	48 834 482	112 538 310*	49.7	100.0
001 ADVENT CHR CH.	358	29 228	35 448*	—	—
005 AME ZION......	1 801	897 441	1 092 723	0.5	1.0
015 AMANA CH SOC..	7	733	789	—	—
017 AMER BAPT ASSN	1 638	224 676	224 676	0.1	0.2
019 AMER BAPT USA.	5 792	1 595 448	1 922 467*	0.8	1.7
029 AMER LUTH CH..	4 845	1 767 551	2 361 845	1.0	2.1
039 AP CHR CH(NAZ)	42	2 419	2 915*	—	—
045 APOSTOLIC LUTH	50	6 509	7 807*	—	—
049 ARMEN AP CH AM	21	3 700	10 194	—	—
053 ASSEMB OF GOD.	9 447	945 726	1 612 655	0.7	1.4
055 AS REF PRES CH	159	28 513	31 984	—	—
057 BAPT GEN CONF.	701	125 082	151 201*	0.1	0.1
059 BAPT MISS ASSN	1 436	224 713	274 594*	0.1	0.2
061 BEACHY AMISH..	78	4 844	5 905*	—	—
063 BEREAN FUND CH	48	3 053	3 723*	—	—
065 BETHEL M ASSN.	21	4 820	5 785*	—	—
066 BIBLE CH OF CR	5	3 095	3 714*	—	—
071 BRETHREN (ASH)	120	15 162	18 372*	—	—
075 BRETHREN IN CR	166	12 911	18 443	—	—
081 CATHOLIC......	22 348	NA	47 502 152	21.0	42.2
083 CHRIST CATH CH	13	241	393	—	—
089 CHR & MISS AL.	1 258	92 905	170 643	0.1	0.2
091 CHRISTIAN CATH	6	1 435	2 560	—	—
093 CHR CH (DISC).	4 324	817 650	1 212 977	0.5	1.1
097 CHR CHS&CHS CR	5 293	929 650	1 127 925*	0.5	1.0
101 C.M.E........	1 780	560 012	681 391*	0.3	0.6
105 CHRISTIAN REF.	630	131 550	211 894	0.1	0.2
107 CHRISTIAN UN..	110	4 472	7 085	—	—
121 CH GOD (ABR)..	87	5 159	6 254*	—	—
123 CH GOD (ANDER)	2 259	178 550	535 647	0.2	0.5
127 CH GOD (CLEVE)	5 033	389 714	474 315*	0.2	0.4
133 CH GOD(7TH)DEN	131	3 246	3 957*	—	—
143 CG IN CR(MENN)	66	7 454	7 454	—	—
149 CH OF JC (BIC)	52	2 186	2 357	—	—
151 L-D SAINTS....	6 771	NA	2 684 744	1.2	2.4
157 CH OF BRETHREN	1 061	172 115	207 980*	0.1	0.2
163 CH OF LUTH BR.	102	6 402	10 935	—	—
164 CH LUTH CONF..	72	6 834	9 351	—	—

NA — Not applicable   *Total adherents estimated from known number of communicant, confirmed, full members.

Table 1. Churches and Church Membership by Denomination, for the U.S.: 1980

County and Denomination	Number of churches	Communicant, confirmed, full members	Total adherents		
			Number	Percent of total population	Percent of total adherents
165 CH OF NAZARENE	4 892	473 611	885 749	0.4	0.8
167 CHS OF CHRIST.	12 719	1 239 612	1 600 177	0.7	1.4
175 CONGR CHR CHS.	381	99 311	119 866*	0.1	0.1
177 CONGR HOL CH..	151	5 719	6 997*	—	—
179 CONSRV BAPT...	1 042	187 226	226 382*	0.1	0.2
181 CONSRV CONGR..	128	23 099	27 813*	—	—
185 CUMBER PRESB..	793	52 039	90 691	—	0.1
193 EPISCOPAL.....	7 291	2 070 422	2 823 399	1.2	2.5
195 ESTONIAN ELC..	25	2 480	8 692	—	—
197 EVAN CH OF NA.	145	13 238	13 238	—	—
199 EVAN CONGR CH.	163	28 522	34 085*	—	—
201 EVAN COV CH AM	545	76 980	92 765*	—	0.1
203 EVAN FREE CH..	649	58 883	71 134*	—	0.1
208 EVAN LUTH ASSN	235	77 389	106 281	—	0.1
209 EVAN LUTH SYN.	110	15 081	20 044	—	—
211 EVAN MENN BR..	16	2 115	2 750	—	—
213 EVAN MENN INC.	22	3 729	4 595*	—	—
215 EVAN METH CH..	127	9 695	11 788*	—	—
217 FIRE BAPTIZED.	48	751	907*	—	—
220 FREE LUTHERAN.	131	11 738	14 462	—	—
221 FREE METHODIST	1 021	50 934	204 576	0.1	0.2
226 FRIENDS—USA...	1 051	113 565	137 401*	0.1	0.1
233 GEN CH NEW JER	18	1 635	1 939*	—	—
237 GC MENN BR CHS	124	15 797	19 268*	—	—
239 SWEDENBORGIAN.	43	2 820	3 366*	—	—
244 GRACE BRETHREN	278	41 265	49 892*	—	—
247 HOLINESS CH...	23	1 399	1 413	—	—
263 INT FOURSQ GOS	832	132 291	160 074*	0.1	0.1
270 CONSRV JUDAISM	793	201 448	240 097*	0.1	0.2
271 REFORM JUDAISM	708	471 626	562 629*	0.2	0.5
274 LAT EVAN LUTH.	61	11 916	13 617	—	—
281 LUTH CH AMER..	5 762	2 171 848	2 911 817	1.3	2.6
283 LUTH——MO SYNOD	5 686	1 965 211	2 622 847	1.2	2.3
285 MENNONITE CH..	1 079	97 288	118 273*	0.1	0.1
287 MENN GEN CONF.	202	37 324	46 891	—	—
290 METRO COMM CHS	126	10 927	23 014	—	—
291 MISSIONARY CH.	277	22 084	31 493	—	—
293 MORAV CH—NORTH	116	28 009	36 961	—	—
295 MORAV CH—SOUTH	53	17 186	21 058	—	—

—Represents a percent less than 0.1.　　　　　　　　Percentages may not total due to rounding.

Table 1. Churches and Church Membership by Denomination, for the U.S.: 1980

County and Denomination	Number of churches	Communicant, confirmed, full members	Total adherents		
			Number	Percent of total population	Percent of total adherents
313 N AM BAPT CONF	254	42 779	51 726*	---	---
323 OLD ORD AMISH.	535	69 550	85 676*	---	0.1
329 OPEN BIBLE STD	267	29 506	46 549	---	
335 ORTH PRESB CH.	146	11 306	13 601*	---	---
347 PENT FW BAPT..	124	12 145	14 844*	---	---
349 PENT HOLINESS.	1 401	100 110	122 069*	0.1	0.1
353 CHR BRETHREN..	801	44 190	66 285	---	0.1
356 PRESB CH AMER.	505	76 816	86 631	---	0.1
357 PRESB CH US...	4 068	858 375	1 038 649*	0.5	0.9
359 PRIM AD CHR CH	10	542	542	---	---
363 PRIMITIVE METH	83	10 230	12 151*	---	---
367 PROT CONF (WI)	9	992	1 400	---	---
369 PROT REF CHS..	20	2 382	4 316	---	---
371 REF CH IN AM..	889	211 581	371 048	0.2	0.3
375 REF EPISCOPAL.	69	6 077	7 363*	---	---
381 REF PRES-EVAN.	186	20 052	26 495	---	---
383 REF PRES OF NA	66	3 694	4 733	---	---
395 ROMANIAN OR CH	13	12 835	15 365*	---	---
403 SALVATION ARMY	1 076	118 059	361 235	0.2	0.3
409 SEPARATE BAPT.	94	8 781	10 693*	---	---
413 S.D.A.........	3 676	553 099	668 611*	0.3	0.6
415 S-D BAPTIST GC	61	5 068	6 145*	---	---
417 SOCIAL BRETH..	28	1 655	1 990*	---	---
419 SO BAPT CONV..	35 552	13 369 848	16 281 692*	7.2	14.5
421 SO METHODIST..	155	8 361	10 818	---	---
423 SYRIAN ANTIOCH	14	20 200	23 980*	---	---
431 UKRANIAN AMER.	23	3 465	5 310	---	---
435 UNITARIAN-UNIV	932	130 603	156 286*	0.1	0.1
441 UN CHRISTIAN..	11	428	788	---	---
443 UN C OF CHRIST	6 405	1 740 202	2 096 014*	0.9	1.9
449 UN METHODIST..	38 465	9 534 803	11 552 111*	5.1	10.3
453 UN PRES CH USA	8 633	2 468 215	2 974 186*	1.3	2.6
459 UNITED ZION CH	13	936	936	---	---
469 WELS..........	1 127	306 185	404 377	0.2	0.4

NA—Not applicable

*Total adherents estimated from known number of communicant, confirmed, full members.

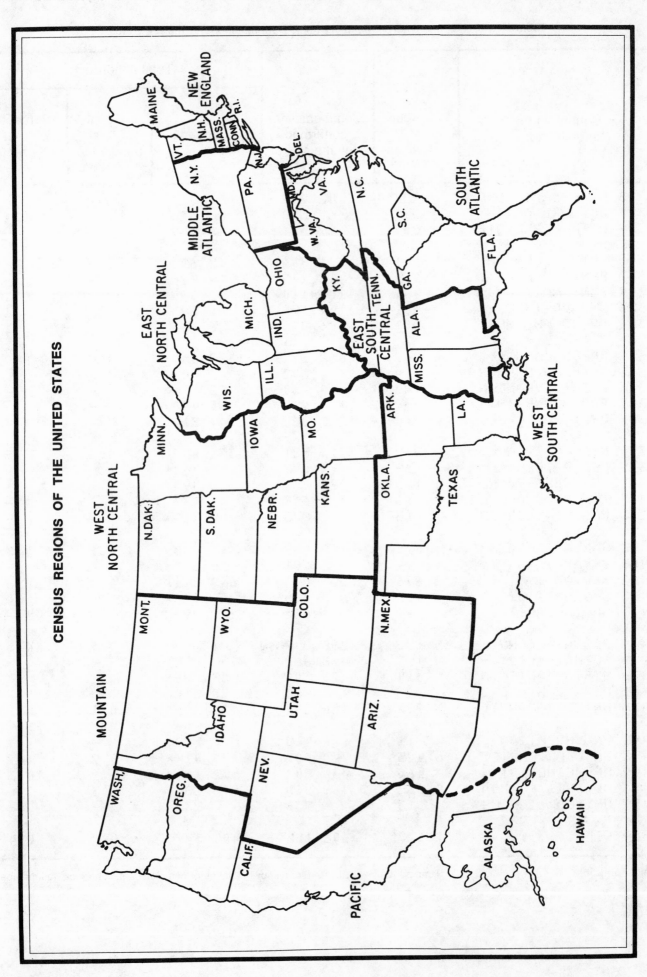

CENSUS REGIONS OF THE UNITED STATES

Table 2. Churches and Church Membership by Region and Denomination: 1980

County and Denomination	Number of churches	Communicant, confirmed, full members	Total adherents Number	Percent of total population	Percent of total adherents
NEW ENGLAND	7 948	1 304 182	7 451 972*	60.3	100.0
001 ADVENT CHR CH.	87	6 655	8 007*	0.1	0.1
005 AME ZION......	53	26 690	32 988	0.3	0.4
017 AMER BAPT ASSN	3	340	340	–	–
019 AMER BAPT USA.	816	176 502	210 923*	1.7	2.8
029 AMER LUTH CH..	19	2 314	3 474	–	–
039 AP CHR CH(NAZ)	1	17	20*	–	–
045 APOSTOLIC LUTH	1	600	730*	–	–
049 ARMEN AP CH AM	7	1 261	2 920	–	–
053 ASSEMB OF GOD.	206	18 575	33 799	0.3	0.5
057 BAPT GEN CONF.	41	5 783	6 915*	0.1	0.1
059 BAPT MISS ASSN	1	30	36*	–	–
081 CATHOLIC......	1 985	NA	5 751 857	46.6	77.2
083 CHRIST CATH CH	4	108	136	–	–
089 CHR & MISS AL.	51	2 976	5 381	–	0.1
093 CHR CH (DISC).	10	939	1 388	–	–
097 CHR CHS&CHS CR	30	967	1 155*	–	–
101 C.M.E.........	8	3 380	4 019*	–	0.1
105 CHRISTIAN REF.	5	1 078	1 733	–	–
123 CH GOD (ANDER)	12	498	1 494	–	–
127 CH GOD (CLEVE)	81	3 761	4 485*	–	0.1
151 L-D SAINTS....	75	NA	21 665	0.2	0.3
163 CH OF LUTH BR.	2	168	281	–	–
165 CH OF NAZARENE	125	9 437	21 631	0.2	0.3
167 CHS OF CHRIST.	111	5 324	7 548	0.1	0.1
175 CONGR CHR CHS.	95	21 271	25 368*	0.2	0.3
179 CONSRV BAPT...	76	11 749	14 166*	0.1	0.2
181 CONSRV CONGR..	26	5 791	6 825*	0.1	0.1
193 EPISCOPAL.....	673	229 829	339 425	2.7	4.6
195 ESTONIAN ELC..	1	113	578	–	–
201 EVAN COV CH AM	41	6 482	7 731*	0.1	0.1
203 EVAN FREE CH..	22	1 963	2 338*	–	–
208 EVAN LUTH ASSN	29	6 379	8 732	0.1	0.1
209 EVAN LUTH SYN.	2	145	184	–	–
220 FREE LUTHERAN.	1	17	19	–	–
221 FREE METHODIST	11	312	975	–	–
226 FRIENDS-USA...	62	4 126	4 913*	–	0.1
233 GEN CH NEW JER	1	20	24*	–	–
239 SWEDENBORGIAN.	11	700	842*	–	–
244 GRACE BRETHREN	2	75	92*	–	–
247 HOLINESS CH...	1	20	23	–	–
263 INT FOURSQ GOS	5	239	291*	–	–
270 CONSRV JUDAISM	103	22 064	26 218*	0.2	0.4
271 REFORM JUDAISM	57	38 138	45 198*	0.4	0.6
274 LAT EVAN LUTH.	7	1 593	1 814	–	–
281 LUTH CH AMER..	132	53 619	69 482	0.6	0.9
283 LUTH--MO SYNOD	71	21 166	27 679	0.2	0.4
285 MENNONITE CH..	6	259	310*	–	–
287 MENN GEN CONF.	1	40	50	–	–
290 METRO COMM CHS	5	391	832	–	–
313 N AM BAPT CONF	2	119	141*	–	–
335 ORTH PRESB CH.	12	619	742*	–	–
349 PENT HOLINESS.	1	47	55*	–	–
353 CHR BRETHREN..	49	2 435	3 995	–	0.1
356 PRESB CH AMER.	1	9	19	–	–
363 PRIMITIVE METH	11	1 293	1 537*	–	–
381 REF PRES-EVAN.	2	108	150	–	–
383 REF PRES OF NA	1	32	41	–	–
395 ROMANIAN OR CH	2	1 640	1 967*	–	–
403 SALVATION ARMY	77	7 441	23 449	0.2	0.3
413 S.D.A.........	131	14 287	17 052*	0.1	0.2
415 S-D BAPTIST GC	5	469	563*	–	–
419 SO BAPT CONV..	49	8 931	10 682*	0.1	0.1
423 SYRIAN ANTIOCH	2	2 300	2 742*	–	–
431 UKRANIAN AMER.	3	335	575	–	–
435 UNITARIAN-UNIV	261	37 421	44 636*	0.4	0.6
443 UN C OF CHRIST	1 210	320 638	382 645*	3.1	5.1
449 UN METHODIST..	862	191 829	229 630*	1.9	3.1
453 UN PRES CH USA	87	20 038	23 905*	0.2	0.3
469 WELS..........	5	287	412	–	–
MIDDLE ATLANTIC	25 083	5 248 172	19 941 403*	54.2	100.0
001 ADVENT CHR CH.	8	379	457*	–	–
005 AME ZION......	210	193 902	241 560	0.7	1.2
017 AMER BAPT ASSN	4	259	259	–	–
019 AMER BAPT USA.	1 249	350 581	419 149*	1.1	2.1
029 AMER LUTH CH..	138	37 751	51 903	0.1	0.3
039 AP CHR CH(NAZ)	8	288	342*	–	–
049 ARMEN AP CH AM	7	1 548	4 807	–	–
053 ASSEMB OF GOD.	735	82 061	139 232	0.4	0.7
055 AS REF PRES CH	2	173	211	–	–
057 BAPT GEN CONF.	26	3 615	4 318*	–	–
059 BAPT MISS ASSN	5	198	242*	–	–
061 BEACHY AMISH..	15	1 157	1 398*	–	–
065 BETHEL M ASSN.	1	150	181*	–	–
066 BIBLE CH OF CR	3	2 780	3 333*	–	–
071 BRETHREN (ASH)	20	2 093	2 518*	–	–

County and Denomination	Number of churches	Communicant, confirmed, full members	Total adherents Number	Percent of total population	Percent of total adherents
075 BRETHREN IN CR	89	8 162	11 716	–	0.1
081 CATHOLIC......	4 449	NA	13 097 729	35.6	65.7
089 CHR & MISS AL.	381	26 011	49 255	0.1	0.2
093 CHR CH (DISC).	146	22 889	34 279	0.1	0.2
097 CHR CHS&CHS CR	169	27 528	32 857*	0.1	0.2
101 C.M.E.........	40	25 208	29 902*	0.1	0.1
105 CHRISTIAN REF.	37	6 453	10 091	–	0.1
123 CH GOD (ANDER)	136	11 117	33 351	0.1	0.2
127 CH GOD (CLEVE)	253	15 237	18 316*	–	0.1
133 CH GOD(7TH)DEN	4	64	78*	–	–
143 CG IN CR(MENN)	3	171	171	–	–
149 CH OF JC (BIC)	20	808	891	–	–
151 L-D SAINTS....	183	NA	46 004	0.1	0.2
157 CH OF BRETHREN	227	52 913	63 754*	0.2	0.3
163 CH OF LUTH BR.	10	899	1 503	–	–
165 CH OF NAZARENE	284	25 664	51 755	0.1	0.3
167 CHS OF CHRIST.	232	15 417	21 148	0.1	0.1
175 CONGR CHR CHS.	32	6 250	7 458*	–	–
179 CONSRV BAPT...	193	27 618	33 172*	0.1	0.2
181 CONSRV CONGR..	20	2 417	2 905*	–	–
193 EPISCOPAL.....	1 459	439 933	622 472	1.7	3.1
195 ESTONIAN ELC..	10	1 107	5 232	–	–
197 EVAN CH OF NA.	16	1 534	1 534	–	–
199 EVAN CONGR CH.	135	25 861	30 858*	0.1	0.2
201 EVAN COV CH AM	31	3 387	4 076*	–	–
203 EVAN FREE CH..	54	5 385	6 445*	–	–
208 EVAN LUTH ASSN	54	17 001	24 505	0.1	0.1
209 EVAN LUTH SYN.	2	89	126	–	–
215 EVAN METH CH..	2	198	236*	–	–
221 FREE METHODIST	222	8 464	40 521	0.1	0.2
226 FRIENDS-USA...	180	19 454	23 253*	0.1	0.1
233 GEN CH NEW JER	5	975	1 150*	–	–
239 SWEDENBORGIAN.	4	320	374*	–	–
244 GRACE BRETHREN	51	8 125	9 780*	–	–
247 HOLINESS CH...	4	104	115	–	–
263 INT FOURSQ GOS	21	1 887	2 270*	–	–
270 CONSRV JUDAISM	362	92 375	109 655*	0.3	0.5
271 REFORM JUDAISM	215	154 654	182 962*	0.5	0.9
274 LAT EVAN LUTH.	11	1 303	1 428	–	–
281 LUTH CH AMER..	1 904	744 924	1 003 081	2.7	5.0
283 LUTH--MO SYNOD	363	113 966	159 096	0.4	0.8
285 MENNONITE CH..	354	34 290	41 412*	0.1	0.2
287 MENN GEN CONF.	27	4 744	6 382	–	–
290 METRO COMM CHS	11	677	1 354	–	–
291 MISSIONARY CH.	12	511	706	–	–
293 MORAV CH-NORTH	41	13 542	17 542	–	0.1
313 N AM BAPT CONF	24	3 182	3 785*	–	–
323 OLD ORD AMISH.	145	18 850	22 751*	0.1	0.1
329 OPEN BIBLE STD	9	705	1 225	–	–
335 ORTH PRESB CH.	40	3 895	4 663*	–	–
349 PENT HOLINESS.	19	1 191	1 424*	–	–
353 CHR BRETHREN..	134	8 305	11 455	–	0.1
356 PRESB CH AMER.	18	1 774	2 295	–	–
357 PRESB CH US...	1	143	176*	–	–
363 PRIMITIVE METH	52	7 472	8 839*	–	–
369 PROT REF CHS..	1	18	39	–	–
371 REF CH IN AM..	413	78 318	149 615	0.4	0.8
375 REF EPISCOPAL.	26	2 434	2 896*	–	–
381 REF PRES-EVAN.	43	4 406	5 866	–	–
383 REF PRES OF NA	25	1 462	1 901	–	–
395 ROMANIAN OR CH	2	1 910	2 199*	–	–
403 SALVATION ARMY	182	17 431	76 686	0.2	0.4
413 S.D.A.........	357	50 333	60 031*	0.2	0.3
415 S-D BAPTIST GC	19	1 589	1 926*	–	–
419 SO BAPT CONV..	224	34 135	40 906*	0.1	0.2
423 SYRIAN ANTIOCH	5	9 300	10 849*	–	0.1
431 UKRANIAN AMER.	12	2 040	3 140	–	–
435 UNITARIAN-UNIV	125	18 617	22 144*	0.1	0.1
441 UN CHRISTIAN..	11	428	788	–	–
443 UN C OF CHRIST	1 203	344 584	411 192*	1.1	2.1
449 UN METHODIST..	4 772	1 232 230	1 477 790*	4.0	7.4
453 UN PRES CH USA	2 307	755 081	901 989*	2.5	4.5
459 UNITED ZION CH	13	936	936	–	–
469 WELS..........	12	832	1 087	–	–
EAST NORTH CENTRAL	37 301	8 085 668	21 093 360*	50.6	100.0
001 ADVENT CHR CH.	28	2 554	3 118*	–	–
005 AME ZION......	84	99 663	123 017	0.3	0.6
017 AMER BAPT ASSN	62	5 112	5 112	–	–
019 AMER BAPT USA.	1 301	390 151	473 764*	1.1	2.2
029 AMER LUTH CH..	1 282	543 865	730 015	1.8	3.5
039 AP CHR CH(NAZ)	18	1 399	1 695*	–	–
045 APOSTOLIC LUTH	17	2 254	2 669*	–	–
049 ARMEN AP CH AM	6	741	2 017	–	–
053 ASSEMB OF GOD.	1 048	117 803	221 319	0.5	1.0
057 BAPT GEN CONF.	195	30 047	36 487*	0.1	0.2
059 BAPT MISS ASSN	40	3 156	3 871*	–	–
061 BEACHY AMISH..	29	1 855	2 296*	–	–

NA—Not applicable   *Total adherents estimated from known number of communicant, confirmed, full members.   —Represents a percent less than 0.1.   Percentages may not total due to rounding.

5

Table 2. Churches and Church Membership by Region and Denomination: 1980

County and Denomination	Number of churches	Communicant, confirmed, full members	Total adherents Number	Percent of total population	Percent of total adherents
065 BETHEL M ASSN.	16	4 005	4 790*	–	–
071 BRETHREN (ASH)	61	9 289	11 366*	–	0.1
075 BRETHREN IN CR	28	1 204	2 044	–	–
081 CATHOLIC......	4 789	NA	10 347 095	24.8	49.1
083 CHRIST CATH CH	4	57	128	–	–
089 CHR & MISS AL.	202	15 978	30 558	0.1	0.1
091 CHRISTIAN CATH	3	1 295	2 200	–	–
093 CHR CH (DISC).	716	183 097	277 504	0.7	1.3
097 CHR CHS&CHS CR	1 642	361 000	439 593*	1.1	2.1
101 C.M.E........	80	54 942	66 270*	0.2	0.3
105 CHRISTIAN REF.	316	79 489	126 508	0.3	0.6
107 CHRISTIAN UN..	69	2 649	3 765	–	–
121 CH GOD (ABR)..	38	2 380	2 885*	–	–
123 CH GOD (ANDER)	614	63 922	191 784	0.5	0.9
127 CH GOD (CLEVE)	615	51 346	63 060*	0.2	0.3
133 CH GOD(7TH)DEN	18	340	419*	–	–
143 CG IN CR(MENN)	8	721	721	–	–
149 CH OF JC (BIC)	13	700	698	–	–
151 L-D SAINTS....	287	NA	88 869	0.2	0.4
157 CH OF BRETHREN	287	43 718	53 478*	0.1	0.3
163 CH OF LUTH BR.	7	432	894	–	–
164 CH LUTH CONF..	17	1 960	2 708	–	–
165 CH OF NAZARENE	1 246	124 806	255 633	0.6	1.2
167 CHS OF CHRIST.	1 332	119 716	155 883	0.4	0.7
175 CONGR CHR CHS.	139	38 552	46 832*	0.1	0.2
177 CONGR HOL CH..	1	18	21*	–	–
179 CONSRV BAPT...	140	15 748	19 137*	–	0.1
181 CONSRV CONGR..	38	5 406	6 609*	–	–
185 CUMBER PRESB..	58	2 854	5 343	–	–
193 EPISCOPAL.....	874	243 768	325 490	0.8	1.5
195 ESTONIAN ELC..	6	494	1 075	–	–
197 EVAN CH OF NA.	13	699	699	–	–
199 EVAN CONGR CH.	25	2 576	3 120*	–	–
201 EVAN COV CH AM	139	20 658	25 066*	0.1	0.1
203 EVAN FREE CH..	139	14 595	17 754*	–	0.1
208 EVAN LUTH ASSN	74	31 892	43 084	0.1	0.2
209 EVAN LUTH SYN	28	5 729	7 494	–	–
211 EVAN MENN BR..	1	45	59	–	–
213 EVAN MENN INC.	21	3 511	4 332*	–	–
215 EVAN METH CH..	14	667	816*	–	–
217 FIRE BAPTIZED.	1	7	9*	–	–
220 FREE LUTHERAN.	17	1 276	1 691	–	–
221 FREE METHODIST	335	19 956	80 295	0.2	0.4
226 FRIENDS-USA...	289	32 833	40 055*	0.1	0.2
233 GEN CH NEW JER	3	305	368*	–	–
237 GC MENN BR CHS	1	41	49*	–	–
239 SWEDENBORGIAN.	8	480	580*	–	–
244 GRACE BRETHREN	79	12 685	15 458*	–	0.1
263 INT FOURSQ GOS	100	15 626	18 967*	–	0.1
270 CONSRV JUDAISM	86	23 198	28 026*	0.1	0.1
271 REFORM JUDAISM	107	79 576	95 932*	0.2	0.5
274 LAT EVAN LUTH.	21	5 428	6 259	–	–
281 LUTH CH AMER..	1 205	477 803	640 909	1.5	3.0
283 LUTH--MO SYNOD	1 697	769 240	1 024 504	2.5	4.9
285 MENNONITE CH..	302	33 712	41 632*	0.1	0.2
287 MENN GEN CONF.	47	8 862	10 975	–	0.1
290 METRO COMM CHS	10	1 252	2 504	–	–
291 MISSIONARY CH.	177	15 799	22 657	0.1	0.1
293 MORAV CH-NORTH	35	8 776	11 143	–	0.1
313 N AM BAPT CONF	59	13 040	15 858*	–	0.1
323 OLD ORD AMISH.	312	40 560	50 601*	0.1	0.2
329 OPEN BIBLE STD	57	5 234	8 729	–	–
335 ORTH PRESB CH.	17	1 749	2 137*	–	–
349 PENT HOLINESS.	25	1 178	1 447*	–	–
353 CHR BRETHREN..	145	7 650	11 380	–	0.1
356 PRESB CH AMER.	3	212	284	–	–
357 PRESB CH US...	1	67	83*	–	–
363 PRIMITIVE METH	17	1 308	1 588*	–	–
367 PROT CONF (WI)	8	842	1 200	–	–
369 PROT REF CHS..	10	1 737	3 059	–	–
371 REF CH IN AM..	257	75 453	123 870	0.3	0.6
375 REF EPISCOPAL.	4	384	464*	–	–
381 REF PRES-EVAN.	23	1 836	2 400	–	–
383 REF PRES OF NA	11	560	707	–	–
395 ROMANIAN OR CH	7	8 055	9 712*	–	–
403 SALVATION ARMY	227	29 516	80 846	0.2	0.4
409 SEPARATE BAPT.	38	2 602	3 194*	–	–
413 S.D.A.	562	73 445	89 343*	0.2	0.4
415 S-D BAPTIST GC	8	1 004	1 229*	–	–
417 SOCIAL BRETH..	28	1 655	1 990*	–	–
419 SO BAPT CONV..	1 844	471 621	572 127*	1.4	2.7
423 SYRIAN ANTIOCH	4	2 800	3 388*	–	–
431 UKRAINIAN AMER.	5	770	1 155	–	–
435 UNITARIAN-UNIV	142	20 883	25 228*	0.1	0.1
443 UN C OF CHRIST	1 596	534 503	650 436*	1.6	3.1
449 UN METHODIST.	6 667	1 715 236	2 087 957*	5.0	9.9
453 UN PRES CH USA	1 874	636 102	772 726*	1.9	3.7
469 WELS.........	602	219 495	287 045	0.7	1.4

County and Denomination	Number of churches	Communicant, confirmed, full members	Total adherents Number	Percent of total population	Percent of total adherents
WEST NORTH CENTRAL	26 801	5 263 298	10 271 622*	59.8	100.0
001 ADVENT CHR CH.	7	332	398*	–	–
005 AME ZION......	11	4 623	5 592	–	0.1
015 AMANA CH SOC..	7	733	789	–	–
017 AMER BAPT ASSN	37	3 908	3 908	–	–
019 AMER BAPT USA.	582	138 865	167 490*	1.0	1.6
029 AMER LUTH CH..	2 159	782 343	1 036 124	6.0	10.1
039 AP CHR CH(NAZ)	2	29	36*	–	–
045 APOSTOLIC LUTH	18	1 790	2 164*	–	–
053 ASSEMB OF GOD.	1 104	93 399	176 738	1.0	1.7
055 AS REF PRES CH	3	112	124	–	–
057 BAPT GEN CONF.	229	34 471	41 792*	0.2	0.4
059 BAPT MISS ASSN	109	10 448	12 762*	0.1	0.1
061 BEACHY AMISH..	7	576	688*	–	–
063 BEREAN FUND CH	35	2 445	2 985*	–	–
071 BRETHREN (ASH)	8	613	740*	–	–
075 BRETHREN IN CR	6	342	516	–	–
081 CATHOLIC......	3 298	NA	3 363 850	19.6	32.7
089 CHR & MISS AL.	110	7 386	15 955	0.1	0.2
093 CHR CH (DISC).	836	171 625	261 883	1.5	2.5
097 CHR CHS&CHS CR	868	123 798	149 362*	0.9	1.5
101 C.M.E........	15	6 741	8 058*	–	0.1
105 CHRISTIAN REF.	113	21 697	35 165	0.2	0.3
107 CHRISTIAN UN..	30	1 348	2 571	–	–
121 CH GOD (ABR)..	21	900	1 087*	–	–
123 CH GOD (ANDER)	199	12 895	38 676	0.2	0.4
127 CH GOD (CLEVE)	191	9 687	11 781*	0.1	0.1
133 CH GOD(7TH)DEN	19	436	526*	–	–
143 CG IN CR(MENN)	26	3 315	3 315	–	–
149 CH OF JC (BIC)	1	14	21	–	–
151 L-D SAINTS....	270	NA	58 137	0.3	0.6
157 CH OF BRETHREN	98	9 877	11 927*	0.1	0.1
163 CH OF LUTH BR.	55	3 117	4 945	–	–
164 CH LUTH CONF..	32	3 309	4 435	–	–
165 CH OF NAZARENE	524	44 752	89 117	0.5	0.9
167 CHS OF CHRIST.	918	61 506	80 370	0.5	0.8
175 CONGR CHR CHS.	31	11 755	14 246*	0.1	0.1
177 CONGR HOL CH..	1	12	14*	–	–
179 CONSRV BAPT...	65	8 097	9 802*	0.1	0.1
181 CONSRV CONGR..	25	3 292	4 009*	–	–
185 CUMBER PRESB..	51	1 842	3 475	–	–
193 EPISCOPAL.....	616	107 780	146 855	0.9	1.4
195 ESTONIAN ELC..	1	78	137	–	–
197 EVAN CH OF NA.	27	1 198	1 198	–	–
201 EVAN COV CH AM	177	23 192	28 008*	0.2	0.3
203 EVAN FREE CH..	217	16 034	19 389*	0.1	0.2
208 EVAN LUTH ASSN	49	17 573	23 381	0.1	0.2
209 EVAN LUTH SYN.	60	7 521	9 947	0.1	0.1
211 EVAN MENN BR..	10	1 262	1 641	–	–
213 EVAN MENN INC.	1	218	263*	–	–
215 EVAN METH CH..	6	627	778*	–	–
217 FIRE BAPTIZED.	30	596	720*	–	–
220 FREE LUTHERAN.	100	9 252	11 193	0.1	0.1
221 FREE METHODIST	109	3 655	13 404	0.1	0.1
226 FRIENDS-USA...	118	11 640	14 059*	0.1	0.1
237 GC MENN BR CHS	38	5 342	6 438*	–	0.1
239 SWEDENBORGIAN.	5	300	362*	–	–
244 GRACE BRETHREN	15	1 313	1 586*	–	–
263 INT FOURSQ GOS	74	8 036	9 704*	0.1	0.1
270 CONSRV JUDAISM	25	5 968	7 153*	–	0.1
271 REFORM JUDAISM	34	24 854	29 828*	0.2	0.3
274 LAT EVAN LUTH.	6	597	650	–	–
281 LUTH CH AMER..	867	383 942	516 910	3.0	5.0
283 LUTH--MO SYNOD	1 654	551 860	725 774	4.2	7.1
285 MENNONITE CH..	102	9 133	10 980*	0.1	0.1
287 MENN GEN CONF.	77	18 232	22 960	0.1	0.2
290 METRO COMM CHS	13	1 016	2 046	–	–
291 MISSIONARY CH.	22	870	1 125	–	–
293 MORAV CH-NORTH	12	1 717	2 117	–	–
313 N AM BAPT CONF	104	14 211	17 193*	0.1	0.2
323 OLD ORD AMISH.	50	6 500	7 896*	–	0.1
329 OPEN BIBLE STD	69	6 603	10 716	0.1	0.1
335 ORTH PRESB CH.	12	500	604*	–	–
349 PENT HOLINESS.	49	2 244	2 722*	–	–
353 CHR BRETHREN..	102	4 565	6 210	–	0.1
356 PRESB CH AMER.	2	594	817	–	–
357 PRESB CH US...	314	47 325	57 171*	0.3	0.6
363 PRIMITIVE METH	2	95	113*	–	–
367 PROT CONF (WI)	1	150	200	–	–
369 PROT REF CHS..	5	344	681	–	–
371 REF CH IN AM..	136	31 663	51 451	0.3	0.5
375 REF EPISCOPAL.	1	32	39*	–	–
381 REF PRES-EVAN.	17	1 471	1 907	–	–
383 REF PRES OF NA	18	1 062	1 359	–	–
395 ROMANIAN OR CH	1	380	463*	–	–
403 SALVATION ARMY	107	13 582	50 036	0.3	0.5
413 S.D.A........	408	37 546	45 361*	0.3	0.4

NA—Not applicable   *Total adherents estimated from known number of communicant, confirmed, full members.   —Represents a percent less than 0.1.   Percentages may not total due to rounding.

Table 2. Churches and Church Membership by Region and Denomination: 1980

County and Denomination	Number of churches	Communicant, confirmed, full members	Total adherents Number	Percent of total population	Percent of total adherents
415 S-D BAPTIST GC	4	451	550*	–	–
419 SO BAPT CONV..	2 150	665 468	803 794*	4.7	7.8
431 UKRANIAN AMER.	2	240	320	–	–
435 UNITARIAN-UNIV	54	7 491	8 975*	0.1	0.1
443 UN C OF CHRIST	942	225 708	272 847*	1.6	2.7
449 UN METHODIST..	4 008	1 014 931	1 225 424*	7.1	11.9
453 UN PRES CH USA	1 377	321 546	388 607*	2.3	3.8
469 WELS..........	280	62 360	81 987	0.5	0.8
SOUTH ATLANTIC	44 179	10 652 440	16 357 882*	44.3	100.0
001 ADVENT CHR CH.	180	16 195	19 701*	0.1	0.1
005 AME ZION......	890	365 299	462 174	1.3	2.8
017 AMER BAPT ASSN	159	19 092	19 092	0.1	0.1
019 AMER BAPT USA.	842	248 183	298 865*	0.8	1.8
029 AMER LUTH CH..	155	48 677	67 949	0.2	0.4
039 AP CHR CH(NAZ)	2	81	97*	–	–
045 APOSTOLIC LUTH	1	300	348*	–	–
049 ARMEN AP CH AM	1	150	450	–	–
053 ASSEMB OF GOD.	1 172	120 288	201 492	0.5	1.2
055 AS REF PRES CH	122	24 695	27 804	0.1	0.2
057 BAPT GEN CONF.	13	1 350	1 611*	–	–
059 BAPT MISS ASSN	17	2 216	2 686*	–	–
061 BEACHY AMISH..	18	902	1 094*	–	–
065 BETHEL M ASSN.	2	365	447*	–	–
066 BIBLE CH OF CR	2	315	381*	–	–
071 BRETHREN (ASH)	21	2 444	2 866*	–	–
075 BRETHREN IN CR	13	1 282	1 708	–	–
081 CATHOLIC......	1 573	NA	2 973 368	8.0	18.2
089 CHR & MISS AL.	192	16 570	27 784	0.1	0.2
093 CHR CH (DISC).	890	120 436	182 617	0.5	1.1
097 CHR CHS&CHS CR	786	134 071	161 680*	0.4	1.0
101 C.M.E.........	341	126 997	154 250*	0.4	0.9
105 CHRISTIAN REF.	18	2 153	3 317	–	–
121 CH GOD (ABR)..	9	618	747*	–	–
123 CH GOD (ANDER)	411	26 640	79 920	0.2	0.5
127 CH GOD (CLEVE)	2 000	179 290	217 634*	0.6	1.3
133 CH GOD(7TH)DEN	9	82	99*	–	–
143 CG IN CR(MENN)	2	279	279	–	–
149 CH OF JC (BIC)	5	220	251	–	–
151 L-D SAINTS....	447	NA	140 166	0.4	0.9
157 CH OF BRETHREN	330	52 346	62 739*	0.2	0.4
163 CH OF LUTH BR.	2	71	81	–	–
164 CH LUTH CONF..	3	394	559	–	–
165 CH OF NAZARENE	589	58 815	111 465	0.3	0.7
167 CHS OF CHRIST.	1 514	129 381	167 721	0.5	1.0
175 CONGR CHR CHS.	15	1 760	2 093*	–	–
177 CONGR HOL CH..	116	4 566	5 593*	–	–
179 CONSRV BAPT...	17	1 586	1 866*	–	–
181 CONSRV CONGR..	3	158	190*	–	–
185 CUMBER PRESB..	12	750	1 678	–	–
193 EPISCOPAL.....	1 551	460 332	617 111*	1.7	3.8
195 ESTONIAN ELC..	3	245	480	–	–
199 EVAN CONGR CH.	1	25	30*	–	–
201 EVAN COV CH AM	22	2 430	2 815*	–	–
203 EVAN FREE CH..	17	1 173	1 381*	–	–
208 EVAN LUTH ASSN	8	1 473	2 422	–	–
209 EVAN LUTH SYN.	3	360	444	–	–
215 EVAN METH CH..	45	3 759	4 553*	–	–
221 FREE METHODIST	63	2 469	11 996	–	0.1
226 FRIENDS-USA...	163	19 898	23 875*	0.1	0.1
233 GEN CH NEW JER	3	135	159*	–	–
237 GC MENN BR CHS	7	239	287*	–	–
239 SWEDENBORGIAN.	6	360	421*	–	–
244 GRACE BRETHREN	48	6 494	7 740*	–	–
247 HOLINESS CH...	18	1 275	1 275	–	–
263 INT FOURSQ GOS	69	6 598	7 966*	–	–
270 CONSRV JUDAISM	103	30 324	35 849*	0.1	0.2
271 REFORM JUDAISM	107	63 248	74 780*	0.2	0.5
274 LAT EVAN LUTH.	4	778	879	–	–
281 LUTH CH AMER..	929	294 211	384 065	1.0	2.3
283 LUTH--MO SYNOD	346	100 993	135 391	0.4	0.8
285 MENNONITE CH..	170	11 666	13 852*	–	0.1
287 MENN GEN CONF.	1	102	102	–	–
290 METRO COMM CHS	24	1 512	3 145	–	–
291 MISSIONARY CH.	6	356	521	–	–
293 MORAV CH-NORTH	3	644	875	–	–
295 MORAV CH-SOUTH	53	17 186	21 058	0.1	0.1
313 N AM BAPT CONF	2	95	110*	–	–
323 OLD ORD AMISH.	12	1 560	1 906*	–	–
329 OPEN BIBLE STD	29	2 922	4 187	–	–
335 ORTH PRESB CH.	22	1 634	1 952*	–	–
347 PENT FW BAPT..	124	12 145	14 844*	–	0.1
349 PENT HOLINESS.	840	68 411	83 383*	0.2	0.5
353 CHR BRETHREN..	162	8 985	14 880	–	0.1
356 PRESB CH AMER.	217	40 605	45 472	0.1	0.3
357 PRESB CH US...	2 212	533 725	642 293*	1.7	3.9
359 PRIM AD CHR CH	10	542	542	–	–
363 PRIMITIVE METH	1	62	74*	–	–

County and Denomination	Number of churches	Communicant, confirmed, full members	Total adherents Number	Percent of total population	Percent of total adherents
371 REF CH IN AM..	15	2 444	4 308	–	–
375 REF EPISCOPAL.	38	3 227	3 964*	–	–
381 REF PRES-EVAN.	59	8 319	10 805	–	0.1
383 REF PRES OF NA	1	76	104	–	–
403 SALVATION ARMY	169	18 707	51 105	0.1	0.3
413 S.D.A.........	586	90 484	108 478*	0.3	0.7
415 S-D BAPTIST GC	8	502	600*	–	–
419 SO BAPT CONV..	11 447	4 396 386	5 326 963*	14.4	32.6
421 SO METHODIST..	86	4 818	6 295	–	–
435 UNITARIAN-UNIV	110	15 706	18 582*	0.1	0.1
443 UN C OF CHRIST	580	126 589	151 008*	0.4	0.9
449 UN METHODIST..	10 118	2 426 281	2 927 538*	7.9	17.9
453 UN PRES CH USA	630	147 956	176 026*	0.5	1.1
469 WELS..........	34	2 957	4 129	–	–
EAST SOUTH CENTRAL	28 682	5 935 715	8 097 758*	55.2	100.0
001 ADVENT CHR CH.	13	707	868*	–	–
005 AME ZION......	457	178 553	191 573	1.3	2.4
017 AMER BAPT ASSN	102	14 178	14 178	0.1	0.2
019 AMER BAPT USA.	10	4 915	5 971*	–	0.1
029 AMER LUTH CH..	16	1 931	2 764	–	–
053 ASSEMB OF GOD.	801	68 570	110 753	0.8	1.4
055 AS REF PRES CH	25	2 960	3 213	–	–
059 BAPT MISS ASSN	221	33 528	41 418*	0.3	0.5
061 BEACHY AMISH..	6	272	331*	–	–
065 BETHEL M ASSN.	1	200	245*	–	–
071 BRETHREN (ASH)	3	100	126*	–	–
075 BRETHREN IN CR	8	344	584	–	–
081 CATHOLIC......	786	NA	681 412	4.6	8.4
089 CHR & MISS AL.	52	3 635	5 374	–	0.1
093 CHR CH (DISC).	512	79 918	114 084	0.8	1.4
097 CHR CHS&CHS CR	681	100 578	122 304*	0.8	1.5
101 C.M.E.........	642	168 137	206 184*	1.4	2.5
105 CHRISTIAN REF.	2	35	63	–	–
123 CH GOD (ANDER)	340	20 480	61 434	0.4	0.8
127 CH GOD (CLEVE)	1 032	81 457	99 697*	0.7	1.2
133 CH GOD(7TH)DEN	7	83	100*	–	–
143 CG IN CR(MENN)	9	841	841	–	–
151 L-D SAINTS....	163	NA	39 838	0.3	0.5
157 CH OF BRETHREN	30	1 933	2 345*	–	–
165 CH OF NAZARENE	481	39 520	65 416	0.4	0.8
167 CHS OF CHRIST.	3 266	336 204	433 830	3.0	5.4
175 CONGR CHR CHS.	4	284	350*	–	–
177 CONGR HOL CH..	31	1 063	1 296*	–	–
179 CONSRV BAPT...	4	325	396*	–	–
185 CUMBER PRESB..	512	35 725	61 770	0.4	0.8
193 EPISCOPAL.....	380	89 555	116 650*	0.8	1.4
197 EVAN CH OF NA.	4	147	147	–	–
199 EVAN CONGR CH.	1	22	27*	–	–
201 EVAN COV CH AM	3	139	170*	–	–
203 EVAN FREE CH..	7	191	239*	–	–
208 EVAN LUTH ASSN	3	132	164	–	–
215 EVAN METH CH..	12	1 099	1 344*	–	–
221 FREE METHODIST	25	678	3 084	–	–
226 FRIENDS-USA...	16	742	893*	–	–
239 SWEDENBORGIAN.	1	60	74*	–	–
244 GRACE BRETHREN	5	297	362*	–	–
263 INT FOURSQ GOS	23	1 528	1 877*	–	–
270 CONSRV JUDAISM	11	2 342	2 823*	–	–
271 REFORM JUDAISM	37	12 842	15 610*	0.1	0.2
274 LAT EVAN LUTH.	1	30	32	–	–
281 LUTH CH AMER..	100	22 030	28 722	0.2	0.4
283 LUTH--MO SYNOD	149	24 504	34 275	0.2	0.4
285 MENNONITE CH..	41	1 084	1 345*	–	–
287 MENN GEN CONF.	1	16	32	–	–
290 METRO COMM CHS	4	245	535	–	–
291 MISSIONARY CH.	2	122	115	–	–
323 OLD ORD AMISH.	11	1 430	1 733*	–	–
329 OPEN BIBLE STD	2	126	275	–	–
335 ORTH PRESB CH.	1	30	36*	–	–
349 PENT HOLINESS.	97	6 225	7 639*	0.1	0.1
353 CHR BRETHREN..	17	550	690	–	–
356 PRESB CH AMER.	214	29 317	32 686	0.2	0.4
357 PRESB CH US...	713	124 697	151 808*	1.0	1.9
371 REF CH IN AM..	4	196	543	–	–
381 REF PRES-EVAN.	7	735	942	–	–
383 REF PRES OF NA	1	77	81	–	–
403 SALVATION ARMY	57	5 825	11 490	0.1	0.1
409 SEPARATE BAPT.	56	6 179	7 499*	0.1	0.1
413 S.D.A.........	274	36 046	43 869*	0.3	0.5
415 S-D BAPTIST GC	3	71	87*	–	–
419 SO BAPT CONV..	9 868	3 302 117	4 034 138*	27.5	49.8
421 SO METHODIST..	41	2 229	2 827	–	–
435 UNITARIAN-UNIV	35	2 975	3 590*	–	0.3
443 UN C OF CHRIST	99	16 972	20 604*	0.1	0.3
449 UN METHODIST..	5 725	1 019 480	1 243 980*	8.5	15.4
453 UN PRES CH USA	416	45 759	55 390*	0.4	0.7

NA—Not applicable   *Total adherents estimated from known number of communicant, confirmed, full members.   —Represents a percent less than 0.1.   Percentages may not total due to rounding.

Table 2. Churches and Church Membership by Region and Denomination: 1980

County and Denomination	Number of churches	Communicant, confirmed, full members	Total adherents Number	Percent of total population	Percent of total adherents
469 WELS.........	7	398	573	-	-
WEST SOUTH CENTRAL	**30 893**	**7 466 148**	**13 233 197***	**55.7**	**100.0**
001 ADVENT CHR CH.	11	537	649*	-	-
005 AME ZION......	59	15 852	19 377	0.1	0.1
017 AMER BAPT ASSN	1 058	161 850	161 850	0.7	1.2
019 AMER BAPT USA.	74	20 226	24 739*	0.1	0.2
029 AMER LUTH CH..	281	90 221	113 278	0.5	0.9
053 ASSEMB OF GOD.	2 238	208 313	315 451	1.3	2.4
055 AS REF PRES CH		573	632	-	-
059 BAPT MISS ASSN	997	171 299	208 904*	0.9	1.6
061 BEACHY AMISH..	3	82	98*	-	-
065 BETHEL M ASSN.	1	100	122*	-	-
075 BRETHREN IN CR	4	228	344	-	-
081 CATHOLIC......	2 134	NA	3 810 354	16.0	28.8
083 CHRIST CATH CH	1	10	14	-	-
089 CHR & MISS AL.	34	1 461	2 924	-	-
093 CHR CH (DISC).	761	145 017	205 696	0.9	1.6
097 CHR CHS&CHS CR	437	65 528	79 994*	0.3	0.6
101 C.M.E.........	577	132 492	162 122*	0.7	1.2
105 CHRISTIAN REF.	3	105	165	-	-
107 CHRISTIAN UN..	11	475	749	-	-
121 CH GOD (ABR)..	12	579	712*	-	-
123 CH GOD (ANDER)	250	16 198	48 594	0.2	0.4
127 CH GOD (CLEVE)	432	26 382	32 379*	0.1	0.2
133 CH GOD(7TH)DEN	35	1 031	1 273*	-	-
143 CG IN CR(MENN)	10	987	987	-	-
149 CH OF JC (BIC)	1	13	13	-	-
151 L-D SAINTS....	343	NA	101 318	0.4	0.8
157 CH OF BRETHREN	13	929	1 121*	-	-
164 CH LUTH CONF..	3	147	201	-	-
165 CH OF NAZARENE	713	59 318	97 980	0.4	0.7
167 CHS OF CHRIST.	3 849	438 200	560 604	2.4	4.2
175 CONGR CHR CHS.	5	1 102	1 350*	-	-
177 CONGR HOL CH..	2	60	73*	-	-
181 CONSRV CONGR..	2	206	250*	-	-
185 CUMBER PRESB..	156	9 290	16 365	0.1	0.1
193 EPISCOPAL.....	623	197 352	252 155	1.1	1.9
197 EVAN CH OF NA.	1	46	46	-	-
199 EVAN CONGR CH.	1	38	50*	-	-
201 EVAN COV CH AM	1	59	77*	-	-
203 EVAN FREE CH..	18	1 217	1 484*	-	-
208 EVAN LUTH ASSN	16	2 590	3 594	-	-
209 EVAN LUTH SYN.	2	39	157	-	-
211 EVAN MENN BR..	1	103	134	-	-
215 EVAN METH CH..	22	2 033	2 475*	-	-
217 FIRE BAPTIZED.	7	80	96*	-	-
221 FREE METHODIST	51	1 789	6 072	-	-
226 FRIENDS-USA...	37	3 039	3 689*	-	-
237 GC MENN BR CHS	27	3 086	3 775*	-	-
244 GRACE BRETHREN	1	13	16*	-	-
263 INT FOURSQ GOS	68	7 535	9 251*	-	0.1
270 CONSRV JUDAISM	21	7 139	8 781*	-	0.1
271 REFORM JUDAISM	57	28 716	35 247*	0.1	0.3
281 LUTH CH AMER..	136	34 444	45 531	0.2	0.3
283 LUTH--MO SYNOD	492	130 536	172 273	0.7	1.3
285 MENNONITE CH..	23	1 368	1 690*	-	-
287 MENN GEN CONF.	19	1 670	1 958	-	-
290 METRO COMM CHS	12	1 277	2 618	-	-
313 N AM BAPT CONF	17	1 360	1 661*	-	-
323 OLD ORD AMISH.	5	650	789*	-	-
329 OPEN BIBLE STD	1	50	75	-	-
335 ORTH PRESB CH.	5	358	437*	-	-
349 PENT HOLINESS.	256	16 164	19 712*	0.1	0.1
353 CHR BRETHREN..	44	2 455	4 020	-	-
356 PRESB CH AMER.	35	3 053	3 642	-	-
357 PRESB CH US...	827	152 418	187 118*	0.8	1.4
369 PROT REF CHS..	1	10	26	-	-
371 REF CH IN AM..	3	592	1 092	-	-
381 REF PRES-EVAN.	9	741	923	-	-
403 SALVATION ARMY	81	8 209	22 931	0.1	0.2
413 S.D.A.........	346	36 080	44 546*	0.2	0.3
415 S-D BAPTIST GC	6	219	270*	-	-
419 SO BAPT CONV..	7 876	3 786 982	4 634 482*	19.5	35.0
421 SO METHODIST..	28	1 314	1 696	-	-
423 SYRIAN ANTIOCH	2	800	976*	-	-
431 UKRANIAN AMER.	1	80	120	-	-
435 UNITARIAN-UNIV	52	6 512	7 945*	-	0.1
443 UN C OF CHRIST	109	21 450	26 195*	0.1	0.2
449 UN METHODIST..	4 420	1 332 906	1 629 808*	6.9	12.3
453 UN PRES CH USA	590	98 469	119 872*	0.5	0.9
469 WELS.........	26	2 296	3 312	-	-
MOUNTAIN	**12 254**	**1 455 150**	**5 259 099***	**46.3**	**100.0**
001 ADVENT CHR CH.	3	203	253*	-	-
005 AME ZION......	2	290	336	-	-
017 AMER BAPT ASSN	35	2 993	2 993	-	0.1
019 AMER BAPT USA.	237	57 510	70 210*	0.6	1.3
029 AMER LUTH CH..	274	79 127	109 596	1.0	2.1
039 AP CHR CH(NAZ)	2	218	261*	-	-
045 APOSTOLIC LUTH	2	45	54*	-	-
053 ASSEMB OF GOD.	707	55 862	104 109	0.9	2.0
057 BAPT GEN CONF.	44	6 820	8 278*	0.1	0.2
059 BAPT MISS ASSN	16	1 097	1 365*	-	-
063 BEREAN FUND CH	9	374	457*	-	-
071 BRETHREN (ASH)	4	367	444*	-	-
075 BRETHREN IN CR	3	209	256	-	-
081 CATHOLIC......	1 410	NA	1 766 820	15.5	33.6
083 CHRIST CATH CH	2	47	73	-	-
089 CHR & MISS AL.	67	3 092	6 446	0.1	0.1
091 CHRISTIAN CATH	3	140	360	-	-
093 CHR CH (DISC).	133	30 238	44 395	0.4	0.8
097 CHR CHS&CHS CR	207	33 138	40 710*	0.4	0.8
101 C.M.E.........	15	2 629	3 227*	-	0.1
105 CHRISTIAN REF.	54	5 981	10 154	0.1	0.2
121 CH GOD (ABR)..	2	430	521*	-	-
123 CH GOD (ANDER)	74	5 269	15 807	0.1	0.3
127 CH GOD (CLEVE)	159	7 095	8 712*	0.1	0.2
133 CH GOD(7TH)DEN	11	282	339*	-	-
143 CG IN CR(MENN)	4	395	395	-	-
149 CH OF JC (BIC)	5	133	145	-	-
151 L-D SAINTS....	3 581	NA	1 567 330	13.8	29.8
157 CH OF BRETHREN	26	2 686	3 281*	-	0.1
163 CH OF LUTH BR.	8	307	495	-	-
164 CH LUTH CONF..	10	353	497	-	-
165 CH OF NAZARENE	316	34 915	59 702	0.5	1.1
167 CHS OF CHRIST.	556	43 972	57 210	0.5	1.1
175 CONGR CHR CHS.	13	2 615	3 228*	-	0.1
179 CONSRV BAPT...	149	35 402	43 208*	0.4	0.8
181 CONSRV CONGR..	2	316	405*	-	-
185 CUMBER PRESB..	1	777	1 033	-	-
193 EPISCOPAL.....	398	83 782	116 826	1.0	2.2
197 EVAN CH OF NA.	22	1 652	1 652	-	-
201 EVAN COV CH AM	18	2 350	2 854*	-	0.1
203 EVAN FREE CH..	47	4 397	5 324*	-	0.1
209 EVAN LUTH SYN.	2	81	109	-	-
211 EVAN MENN BR..	1	100	130	-	-
215 EVAN METH CH..	5	259	316*	-	-
217 FIRE BAPTIZED.	3	8	10*	-	-
220 FREE LUTHERAN.	5	285	386	-	-
221 FREE METHODIST	36	1 796	6 952	0.1	0.1
226 FRIENDS-USA...	54	3 753	4 589*	-	0.1
233 GEN CH NEW JER	2	45	54*	-	-
237 GC MENN BR CHS	8	679	843*	-	-
244 GRACE BRETHREN	12	806	989*	-	-
263 INT FOURSQ GOS	112	10 735	13 085*	0.1	0.2
270 CONSRV JUDAISM	14	2 404	2 900*	-	0.1
271 REFORM JUDAISM	18	12 492	15 032*	0.1	0.3
274 LAT EVAN LUTH.	2	226	264	-	-
281 LUTH CH AMER..	138	53 603	74 324	0.7	1.4
283 LUTH--MO SYNOD	327	87 561	117 989	1.0	2.2
285 MENNONITE CH..	40	2 433	2 979*	-	0.1
287 MENN GEN CONF.	13	1 182	1 568	-	-
290 METRO COMM CHS	11	635	1 345	-	-
291 MISSIONARY CH.	5	799	1 146	-	-
313 N AM BAPT CONF	11	1 028	1 256*	-	-
329 OPEN BIBLE STD	17	1 870	3 151	-	0.1
335 ORTH PRESB CH.	7	287	355*	-	-
349 PENT HOLINESS.	45	1 673	2 050*	-	-
353 CHR BRETHREN..	45	2 560	3 755	-	0.1
356 PRESB CH AMER.	5	342	438	-	-
369 PROT REF CHS..	1	100	173	-	-
371 REF CH IN AM..	17	3 258	6 071	0.1	0.1
381 REF PRES-EVAN.	9	1 232	1 774	-	-
383 REF PRES OF NA	4	163	210	-	-
403 SALVATION ARMY	53	4 730	12 429	0.1	0.2
413 S.D.A.........	288	35 698	43 631*	0.4	0.8
415 S-D BAPTIST GC	2	225	273*	-	-
419 SO BAPT CONV..	845	295 659	364 050*	3.2	6.9
435 UNITARIAN-UNIV	40	5 131	6 215*	0.1	0.1
443 UN C OF CHRIST	199	50 082	61 093*	0.5	1.2
449 UN METHODIST..	693	228 976	280 077*	2.5	5.3
453 UN PRES CH USA	449	125 601	153 616*	1.4	2.9
469 WELS.........	85	9 145	13 711	0.1	0.3
PACIFIC	**18 567**	**3 423 709**	**10 832 017***	**34.1**	**100.0**
001 ADVENT CHR CH.	21	1 666	1 997*	-	-
005 AME ZION......	35	12 569	16 106	0.1	0.1
017 AMER BAPT ASSN	178	16 944	16 944	0.1	0.2
019 AMER BAPT USA.	681	208 515	251 356*	0.8	2.3
029 AMER LUTH CH..	521	181 322	246 742	0.8	2.3
039 AP CHR CH(NAZ)	9	387	464*	-	-
045 APOSTOLIC LUTH	11	1 520	1 842*	-	-
053 ASSEMB OF GOD.	1 436	180 855	309 762	1.0	2.9
057 BAPT GEN CONF.	153	42 996	51 800*	0.2	0.5
059 BAPT MISS ASSN	30	2 741	3 310*	-	-

NA—Not applicable   *Total adherents estimated from known number of communicant, confirmed, full members.   —Represents a percent less than 0.1.   Percentages may not total due to rounding.

Table 2. Churches and Church Membership by Region and Denomination: 1980

County and Denomination	Number of churches	Communicant, confirmed, full members	Total adherents		
			Number	Percent of total population	Percent of total adherents
063 BEREAN FUND CH	4	234	281*	–	–
071 BRETHREN (ASH)	3	256	312*	–	–
075 BRETHREN IN CR	15	1 140	1 275	–	–
081 CATHOLIC......	1 924	NA	5 709 667	18.0	52.7
083 CHRIST CATH CH	2	19	42	–	–
089 CHR & MISS AL.	169	15 796	26 966	0.1	0.2
093 CHR CH (DISC).	320	63 491	91 131	0.3	0.8
097 CHR CHS&CHS CR	473	83 042	100 270*	0.3	0.9
101 C.M.E........	62	39 486	47 359*	0.1	0.4
105 CHRISTIAN REF.	82	14 559	24 698	0.1	0.2
121 CH GOD (ABR)..	5	252	302*	–	–
123 CH GOD (ANDER)	223	21 531	64 587	0.2	0.6
127 CH GOD (CLEVE)	270	15 001	18 251*	0.1	0.2
133 CH GOD(7TH)DEN	28	928	1 123*	–	–
143 CG IN CR(MENN)	4	745	745	–	–
149 CH OF JC (BIC)	7	298	338	–	–
151 L-D SAINTS....	1 422	NA	621 417	2.0	5.7
157 CH OF BRETHREN	50	7 713	9 335*	–	0.1
163 CH OF LUTH BR.	18	1 408	2 736	–	–
164 CH LUTH CONF..	7	671	951	–	–
165 CH OF NAZARENE	614	76 384	133 050	0.4	1.2
167 CHS OF CHRIST.	941	89 892	115 863	0.4	1.1
175 CONGR CHR CHS.	47	15 722	18 941*	0.1	0.2
179 CONSRV BAPT...	398	86 701	104 635*	0.3	1.0
181 CONSRV CONGR..	12	5 513	6 620*	–	0.1
185 CUMBER PRESB..	3	801	1 027	–	–
193 EPISCOPAL.....	717	218 091	286 415	0.9	2.6
195 ESTONIAN ELC..	4	443	1 190	–	–
197 EVAN CH OF NA.	62	7 962	7 962	–	0.1
201 EVAN COV CH AM	113	18 283	21 968*	0.1	0.2
203 EVAN FREE CH..	128	13 928	16 780*	0.1	0.2
208 EVAN LUTH ASSN	2	349	399	–	–
209 EVAN LUTH SYN.	11	1 117	1 583	–	–
211 EVAN MENN BR..	3	605	786	–	–
215 EVAN METH CH..	21	1 053	1 270*	–	–
217 FIRE BAPTIZED.	7	60	72*	–	–
220 FREE LUTHERAN.	8	908	1 173	–	–
221 FREE METHODIST	169	11 815	41 277	0.1	0.4
226 FRIENDS-USA...	132	18 080	22 075*	0.1	0.2
233 GEN CH NEW JER	4	155	184*	–	–
237 GC MENN BR CHS	43	6 410	7 876*	–	0.1
239 SWEDENBORGIAN.	8	600	713*	–	–
244 GRACE BRETHREN	65	11 457	13 869*	–	0.1
263 INT FOURSQ GOS	360	80 107	96 663*	0.3	0.9
270 CONSRV JUDAISM	68	15 634	18 692*	0.1	0.2
271 REFORM JUDAISM	76	57 106	68 040*	0.2	0.6
274 LAT EVAN LUTH.	9	1 961	2 291	–	–
281 LUTH CH AMER..	351	107 272	148 793	0.5	1.4
283 LUTH--MO SYNOD	587	165 385	225 866	0.7	2.1
285 MENNONITE CH..	41	3 343	4 073*	–	–
287 MENN GEN CONF.	16	2 476	2 864	–	–
290 METRO COMM CHS	36	3 922	8 635	–	0.1
291 MISSIONARY CH.	53	3 627	5 223	–	–
293 MORAV CH-NORTH	25	3 330	5 284	–	–
313 N AM BAPT CONF	35	9 744	11 722*	–	0.1
329 OPEN BIBLE STD	83	11 996	18 191	0.1	0.2
335 ORTH PRESB CH.	30	2 234	2 675*	–	–
349 PENT HOLINESS.	69	2 977	3 637*	–	–
353 CHR BRETHREN..	103	6 685	9 900	–	0.1
356 PRESB CH AMER.	10	910	978	–	–
369 PROT REF CHS..	2	173	338	–	–
371 REF CH IN AM..	44	19 657	34 098	0.1	0.3
381 REF PRES-EVAN.	17	1 204	1 728	–	–
383 REF PRES OF NA	5	262	330	–	–
395 ROMANIAN OR CH	1	850	1 024*	–	–
403 SALVATION ARMY	123	12 618	32 263	0.1	0.3
413 S.D.A.........	724	179 180	216 602*	0.7	2.0
415 S-D BAPTIST GC	6	538	647*	–	–
419 SO BAPT CONV..	1 249	408 549	494 550*	1.6	4.6
423 SYRIAN ANTIOCH	1	5 000	6 025*	–	0.1
435 UNITARIAN-UNIV	113	15 867	18 971*	0.1	0.2
443 UN C OF CHRIST	476	99 676	119 994*	0.4	1.1
449 UN METHODIST..	1 200	372 934	449 907*	1.4	4.2
453 UN PRES CH USA	903	317 663	382 055*	1.2	3.5
469 WELS..........	76	8 415	12 121	–	0.1

NA – Not applicable   *Total adherents estimated from known number of communicant, confirmed, full members.   –Represents a percent less than 0.1.   Percentages may not total due to rounding.

9

STATE SUMMARY

Table 3. Churches and Church Membership by State and Denomination: 1980

County and Denomination	Number of churches	Communicant, confirmed, full members	Total adherents — Number	Total adherents — Percent of total population	Total adherents — Percent of total adherents
ALABAMA	8 054	1 721 027	2 235 170*	57.5	100.0
001 ADVENT CHR CH.	6	354	431*	-	-
005 AME ZION......	315	134 644	139 714	3.6	6.3
017 AMER BAPT ASSN	38	4 476	4 476	0.1	0.2
019 AMER BAPT USA.	1	?	?	?	?
029 AMER LUTH CH..	5	368	595		
053 ASSEMB OF GOD.	345	27 075	48 610	1.2	2.2
055 AS REF PRES CH	4	328	349		
059 BAPT MISS ASSN	20	2 901	3 565*	0.1	0.2
061 BEACHY AMISH..	1	18	23*	-	-
081 CATHOLIC.....	169	NA	106 123	2.7	4.7
089 CHR & MISS AL.	24	2 114	2 940	0.1	0.1
093 CHR CH (DISC).	67	7 090	9 696	0.2	0.4
097 CHR CHS&CHS CR	28	3 304	4 067*	0.1	0.2
101 C.M.E.......	211	43 716	53 493*	1.4	2.4
123 CH GOD (ANDER)	81	3 620	10 854	0.3	0.5
127 CH GOD (CLEVE)	371	27 771	33 956*	0.9	1.5
133 CH GOD(7TH)DEN	3	36	44*	-	-
143 CG IN CR(MENN)	2	173	173	-	-
151 L-D SAINTS....	43	NA	10 973	0.3	0.5
157 CH OF BRETHREN	4	219	269*	-	-
165 CH OF NAZARENE	113	8 605	12 500	0.3	0.6
167 CHS OF CHRIST.	875	89 208	113 919	2.9	5.1
175 CONGR CHR CHS.	4	284	350*	-	-
177 CONGR HOL CH..	30	1 040	1 268*	-	0.1
179 CONSRV BAPT...	4	325	396*	-	-
185 CUMBER PRESB..	64	4 434	7 998	0.2	0.4
193 EPISCOPAL.....	115	25 430	34 608	0.9	1.5
197 EVAN CH OF NA.	2	110	110	-	-
201 EVAN COV CH AM	2	110	135*	-	-
215 EVAN METH CH..	2	261	321*	-	-
221 FREE METHODIST	3	30	156	-	-
226 FRIENDS-USA...	1	21	25*	-	-
263 INT FOURSQ GOS	6	164	201*	-	-
270 CONSRV JUDAISM	4	811	985*	-	-
271 REFORM JUDAISM	12	3 238	3 943*	0.1	0.2
281 LUTH CH AMER..	14	3 413	4 524	0.1	0.2
283 LUTH--MO SYNOD	54	9 460	13 448	0.3	0.6
285 MENNONITE CH..	10	191	234*	-	-
290 METRO COMM CHS	0	0	45	-	-
349 PENT HOLINESS.	53	3 483	4 275*	0.1	0.2
353 CHR BRETHREN..	6	155	205	-	-
356 PRESB CH AMER.	79	11 353	12 998	0.3	0.6
357 PRESB CH US..	150	28 484	34 775*	0.9	1.6
371 REF CH IN AM..	1	39	107	-	-
381 REF PRES-EVAN.	2	256	311	-	-
383 REF PRES OF NA	1	77	81	-	-
403 SALVATION ARMY	15	1 589	3 679	0.1	0.2
413 S.D.A........	63	9 875	12 053	0.3	0.5
415 S-D BAPTIST GC	1	43	53*	-	-
419 SO BAPT CONV..	3 005	966 464	1 182 018*	30.4	52.9
421 SO METHODIST..	10	427	551	-	-
435 UNITARIAN-UNIV	12	636	774*	-	-
443 UN C OF CHRIST	38	3 330	4 070*	0.1	0.2
449 UN METHODIST..	1 524	282 146	344 790*	8.9	15.4
453 UN PRES CH USA	38	7 142	8 665*	0.2	0.4
469 WELS.........	3	186	248	-	-
ALASKA	579	51 723	123 434*	30.8	100.0
005 AME ZION......	2	296	334	0.1	0.3
017 AMER BAPT ASSN	2	40	40	-	-
019 AMER BAPT USA.	5	815	1 014	0.3	0.8
029 AMER LUTH CH..	17	2 810	4 678	1.2	3.8
053 ASSEMB OF GOD.	74	3 656	6 560	1.6	5.3
057 BAPT GEN CONF.	5	476	592*	0.1	0.5
059 BAPT MISS ASSN	1	63	79*	-	0.1
081 CATHOLIC......	97	NA	39 678	9.9	32.1
089 CHR & MISS AL.	2	191	352	0.1	0.3
093 CHR CH (DISC).	1	238	450	0.1	0.4
097 CHR CHS&CHS CR	12	479	602*	0.2	0.5
101 C.M.E........	2	330	411*	0.1	0.3
105 CHRISTIAN REF.	1	123	216	0.1	0.2
123 CH GOD (ANDER)	8	784	2 346	0.6	1.9
127 CH GOD (CLEVE)	16	855	1 068*	0.3	0.9
151 L-D SAINTS....	36	NA	8 802	2.2	7.1
164 CH LUTH CONF..	1	19	31	-	-
165 CH OF NAZARENE	18	1 006	2 398	0.6	1.9
167 CHS OF CHRIST.	30	1 548	2 084	0.5	1.7
175 CONGR CHR CHS.	2	554	687*	0.2	0.6
179 CONSRV BAPT...	5	232	290*	0.1	0.2
193 EPISCOPAL.....	24	3 154	5 178	1.3	4.2
201 EVAN COV CH AM	7	356	458*	0.1	0.4
203 EVAN FREE CH..	2	42	53*	-	-
221 FREE METHODIST	1	80	240	0.1	0.2
226 FRIENDS-USA...	18	2 992	3 887*	1.0	3.1
244 GRACE BRETHREN	2	138	174*	-	0.1
271 REFORM JUDAISM	1	230	287*	0.1	0.2
281 LUTH CH AMER..	7	1 265	1 945	0.5	1.6
283 LUTH--MO SYNOD	8	1 742	2 560	0.6	2.1
285 MENNONITE CH..	1	27	34*	-	-
290 METRO COMM CHS	1	25	55	-	-
293 MORAV CH-NORTH	21	2 667	4 372	1.1	3.5
349 PENT HOLINESS.	5	148	190*	-	0.2
353 CHR BRETHREN..	5	200	445	0.1	0.4
403 SALVATION ARMY	13	822	1 573	0.4	1.3
413 S.D.A.........	20	1 187	1 481*	0.4	1.2
419 SO BAPT CONV..	40	13 696	17 088*	4.3	13.8
435 UNITARIAN-UNIV	4	214	267*	0.1	0.2
449 UN METHODIST..	22	3 411	4 262*	1.1	3.5
453 UN PRES CH USA	36	4 551	5 711*	1.4	4.6
469 WELS.........	4	261	462	0.1	0.4
ARIZONA	2 096	343 863	1 073 012*	39.5	100.0
017 AMER BAPT ASSN	8	600	600	-	0.1
019 AMER BAPT USA.	36	9 534	11 576*	0.4	1.1
029 AMER LUTH CH..	33	13 826	17 971	0.7	1.7
039 AP CHR CH(NAZ)	1	152	184*	-	-
045 APOSTOLIC LUTH	1	25	30*	-	-
053 ASSEMB OF GOD.	176	12 134	21 733	0.8	2.0
057 BAPT GEN CONF.	7	622	750*	-	0.1
059 BAPT MISS ASSN	3	186	232*	-	-
071 BRETHREN (ASH)	3	327	395*	-	-
081 CATHOLIC......	217	NA	485 025	17.8	45.2
083 CHRIST CATH CH	2	47	73	-	-
089 CHR & MISS AL.	12	421	710	-	0.1
091 CHRISTIAN CATH	3	140	360	-	-
093 CHR CH (DISC).	20	3 956	5 127	0.2	0.5
097 CHR CHS&CHS CR	37	4 494	5 507*	0.2	0.5
101 C.M.E.........	7	1 665	2 022*	0.1	0.2
105 CHRISTIAN REF.	9	886	1 506	0.1	0.1
121 CH GOD (ABR)	2	430	521*	-	-
123 CH GOD (ANDER)	14	1 519	4 557	0.2	0.4
127 CH GOD (CLEVE)	46	2 522	3 071*	0.1	0.3
133 CH GOD(7TH)DEN	3	44	53*	-	-
143 CG IN CR(MENN)	1	40	40	-	-
149 CH OF JC (BIC)	5	133	145	-	-
151 L-D SAINTS....	335	NA	139 178	5.1	13.0
157 CH OF BRETHREN	4	463	561*	-	0.1
163 CH OF LUTH BR.	2	68	89	-	-
164 CH LUTH CONF..	1	75	114	-	-
165 CH OF NAZARENE	74	8 002	12 618	0.5	1.2
167 CHS OF CHRIST.	124	10 461	13 648	0.5	1.3
175 CONGR CHR CHS.	1	146	177*	-	-
179 CONSRV BAPT...	70	17 479	21 314*	0.8	2.0
193 EPISCOPAL.....	63	18 219	23 027	0.8	2.1
201 EVAN COV CH AM	3	443	535*	-	-
203 EVAN FREE CH..	7	444	533*	-	-
209 EVAN LUTH SYN.	1	26	37	-	-
215 EVAN METH CH..	5	259	316*	-	-
217 FIRE BAPTIZED.	3	8	10*	-	-
220 FREE LUTHERAN.	1	45	56	-	-
221 FREE METHODIST	13	752	2 817	0.1	0.3
226 FRIENDS-USA...	6	309	375*	-	-
233 GEN CH NEW JER	1	30	36*	-	-
237 GC MENN BR CHS	1	38	46*	-	-
244 GRACE BRETHREN	4	223	270*	-	-
263 INT FOURSQ GOS	34	3 015	3 668*	0.1	0.3
270 CONSRV JUDAISM	5	1 162	1 404*	0.1	0.1
271 REFORM JUDAISM	6	5 850	7 073*	0.3	0.7
281 LUTH CH AMER..	31	14 824	19 903	0.7	1.9
283 LUTH--MO SYNOD	39	12 475	16 710	0.6	1.6
285 MENNONITE CH..	12	730	893*	-	0.1
287 MENN GEN CONF.	3	143	178	-	-
290 METRO COMM CHS	4	200	400	-	-
291 MISSIONARY CH.	2	748	1 058	-	0.1
313 N AM BAPT CONF	1	21	25*	-	-
349 PENT HOLINESS.	16	555	677*	-	0.1
353 CHR BRETHREN..	10	495	1 050	-	0.1
356 PRESB CH AMER.	4	189	240	-	-
371 REF CH IN AM..	5	1 440	2 540	0.1	0.2
381 REF PRES-EVAN.	1	10	16	-	-
383 REF PRES OF NA	1	41	65	-	-
403 SALVATION ARMY	14	1 389	6 369	0.2	0.6
413 S.D.A.........	47	6 880	8 377*	0.3	0.8
419 SO BAPT CONV..	230	90 688	110 849*	4.1	10.3
435 UNITARIAN-UNIV	8	1 290	1 561*	0.1	0.1
443 UN C OF CHRIST	31	14 290	17 304*	0.6	1.6
449 UN METHODIST..	94	43 039	52 271*	1.9	4.9
453 UN PRES CH USA	87	26 946	32 808*	1.2	3.1
469 WELS.........	46	6 250	9 628	0.4	0.9
ARKANSAS	5 493	989 400	1 284 100*	56.2	100.0
005 AME ZION......	27	4 132	5 092	0.2	0.4
017 AMER BAPT ASSN	534	88 528	88 528	3.9	6.9

NA—Not applicable *Total adherents estimated from known number of communicant, confirmed, full members. —Represents a percent less than 0.1. Percentages may not total due to rounding.

Table 3. Churches and Church Membership by State and Denomination: 1980

County and Denomination	Number of churches	Communicant, confirmed, full members	Total adherents Number	Percent of total population	Percent of total adherents
029 AMER LUTH CH..	3	303	406	–	–
053 ASSEMB OF GOD.	447	31 384	53 555	2.3	4.2
055 AS REF PRES CH	7	573	632	–	–
059 BAPT MISS ASSN	376	57 944	70 645*	3.1	5.5
061 BEACHY AMISH..	2	29	35*	–	–
065 BETHEL M ASSN.	1	100	122*	–	–
081 CATHOLIC......	122	NA	56 911	2.5	4.4
089 CHR & MISS AL.	5	149	306	–	–
093 CHR CH (DISC)	77	10 409	13 309	0.6	1.0
097 CHR CHS&CHS CR	56	6 291	7 621*	0.3	0.6
101 C.M.E.........	98	35 201	43 219*	1.9	3.4
107 CHRISTIAN UN..	3	42	42	–	–
121 CH GOD (ABR)..	5	275	332*	–	–
123 CH GOD (ANDER)	32	2 045	6 135	0.3	0.5
127 CH GOD (CLEVE)	91	4 524	5 568*	0.2	0.4
133 CH GOD(7TH)DEN	3	75	91*	–	–
151 L-D SAINTS....	35	NA	7 480	0.3	0.6
157 CH OF BRETHREN	1	63	79*	–	–
165 CH OF NAZARENE	116	9 405	14 829	0.6	1.2
167 CHS OF CHRIST.	763	70 139	90 671	4.0	7.1
185 CUMBER PRESB..	75	2 929	5 316	0.2	0.4
193 EPISCOPAL.....	55	13 185	16 790	0.7	1.3
203 EVAN FREE CH..	3	75	90*	–	–
215 EVAN METH CH..	1	131	159*	–	–
217 FIRE BAPTIZED.	1	10	12*	–	–
221 FREE METHODIST	2	26	90	–	–
226 FRIENDS-USA...	3	93	114*	–	–
237 GC MENN BR CHS	2	103	123*	–	–
263 INT FOURSQ GOS	5	499	611*	–	–
271 REFORM JUDAISM	9	1 484	1 828*	0.1	0.1
281 LUTH CH AMER..	11	1 963	2 493	0.1	0.2
283 LUTH--MO SYNOD	50	10 142	12 864	0.6	1.0
285 MENNONITE CH..	8	296	358*	–	–
290 METRO COMM CHS	2	55	160	–	–
323 OLD ORD AMISH.	2	260	314*	–	–
349 PENT HOLINESS.	9	360	433*	–	–
353 CHR BRETHREN..	2	25	25	–	–
356 PRESB CH AMER.	8	474	550	–	–
357 PRESB CH US...	147	15 875	19 361*	0.8	1.5
403 SALVATION ARMY	9	780	1 520	0.1	0.1
413 S.D.A.........	49	4 416	5 348*	0.2	0.4
415 S-D BAPTIST GC	4	201	248*	–	–
419 SO BAPT CONV..	1 242	428 386	522 985*	22.9	40.7
421 SO METHODIST..	2	116	142	–	–
435 UNITARIAN-UNIV	5	296	360*	–	–
443 UN C OF CHRIST	3	244	302*	–	–
449 UN METHODIST..	875	175 998	214 526*	9.4	16.7
453 UN PRES CH USA	104	9 312	11 293*	0.5	0.9
469 WELS..........	1	55	77	–	–
CALIFORNIA	11 421	2 313 529	8 157 906*	34.5	100.0
001 ADVENT CHR CH.	12	888	1 063*	–	–
005 AME ZION......	27	11 126	14 484	0.1	0.2
017 AMER BAPT ASSN	129	14 241	14 241	0.1	0.2
019 AMER BAPT USA.	492	161 392	194 594*	0.8	2.4
029 AMER LUTH CH..	254	91 062	122 795	0.5	1.5
039 AP CHR CH(NAZ)	7	232	279*	–	–
045 APOSTOLIC LUTH	2	125	148*	–	–
053 ASSEMB OF GOD.	864	115 056	189 577	0.8	2.3
057 BAPT GEN CONF.	100	33 292	40 088*	0.2	0.5
059 BAPT MISS ASSN	18	2 268	2 733*	–	–
063 BEREAN FUND CH	3	183	221*	–	–
071 BRETHREN (ASH)	3	256	312*	–	–
075 BRETHREN IN CR	13	988	1 105	–	–
081 CATHOLIC......	1 250	NA	4 759 250	20.1	58.3
083 CHRIST CATH CH	2	19	42	–	–
089 CHR & MISS AL.	87	9 297	14 991	0.1	0.2
093 CHR CH (DISC).	185	36 494	50 177	0.2	0.6
097 CHR CHS&CHS CR	223	43 785	52 761*	0.2	0.6
101 C.M.E.........	53	36 809	44 141*	0.2	0.5
105 CHRISTIAN REF.	45	9 015	15 097	0.1	0.2
121 CH GOD (ABR)..	3	117	141*	–	–
123 CH GOD (ANDER)	117	11 632	34 896	0.1	0.4
127 CH GOD (CLEVE)	162	9 704	11 776*	–	0.1
133 CH GOD(7TH)DEN	13	472	570*	–	–
143 CG IN CR(MENN)	3	685	685	–	–
149 CH OF JC (BIC)	7	298	338	–	–
151 L-D SAINTS....	884	NA	405 441	1.7	5.0
157 CH OF BRETHREN	32	5 351	6 490*	–	0.1
163 CH OF LUTH BR.	2	145	265	–	–
164 CH LUTH CONF..	2	145	187	–	–
165 CH OF NAZARENE	372	47 218	82 071	0.3	1.0
167 CHS OF CHRIST.	676	68 842	88 415	0.4	1.1
175 CONGR CHR CHS.	33	13 798	16 589*	0.1	0.2
179 CONSRV BAPT...	162	43 491	52 325*	0.2	0.6
181 CONSRV CONGR..	9	5 391	6 474*	–	0.1
185 CUMBER PRESB..	3	801	1 027	–	–

County and Denomination	Number of churches	Communicant, confirmed, full members	Total adherents Number	Percent of total population	Percent of total adherents
193 EPISCOPAL.....	426	144 078	184 330	0.8	2.3
195 ESTONIAN ELC..	2	303	780	–	–
201 EVAN COV CH AM	64	12 164	14 593*	0.1	0.2
203 EVAN FREE CH..	88	11 617	13 977*	0.1	0.2
208 EVAN LUTH ASSN	2	349	399	–	–
209 EVAN LUTH SYN.	4	221	285	–	–
211 EVAN MENN BR..	1	31	40	–	–
215 EVAN METH CH..	10	568	684*	–	–
217 FIRE BAPTIZED.	4	40	48*	–	–
221 FREE METHODIST	77	4 824	18 012	0.1	0.2
226 FRIENDS-USA...	65	8 234	9 910*	–	0.1
233 GEN CH NEW JER	3	95	113*	–	–
237 GC MENN BR CHS	36	5 560	6 848*	–	0.1
239 SWEDENBORGIAN.	6	480	571*	–	–
244 GRACE BRETHREN	47	9 809	11 850*	0.1	0.1
263 INT FOURSQ GOS	274	64 761	78 175*	0.3	1.0
270 CONSRV JUDAISM	62	14 087	16 856*	0.1	0.2
271 REFORM JUDAISM	68	50 080	59 683*	0.3	0.7
274 LAT EVAN LUTH.	5	1 043	1 214	–	–
281 LUTH CH AMER..	208	59 818	82 637	0.3	1.0
283 LUTH--MO SYNOD	376	110 073	148 292	0.6	1.8
285 MENNONITE CH..	9	664	806*	–	–
287 MENN GEN CONF.	6	1 030	1 243	–	–
290 METRO COMM CHS	29	3 180	7 180	–	0.1
291 MISSIONARY CH.	31	2 651	3 468	–	–
293 MORAV CH-NORTH	4	663	912	–	–
313 N AM BAPT CONF	13	6 056	7 310*	–	0.1
329 OPEN BIBLE STD	33	5 853	8 470	–	0.1
335 ORTH PRESB CH.	23	1 840	2 201*	–	–
349 PENT HOLINESS.	48	2 048	2 496*	–	–
353 CHR BRETHREN..	58	4 130	6 100	–	0.1
356 PRESB CH AMER.	7	302	338	–	–
369 PROT REF CHS..	1	91	148	–	–
371 REF CH IN AM..	36	17 836	30 778	0.1	0.4
381 REF PRES-EVAN.	8	471	767	–	–
383 REF PRES OF NA	4	192	236	–	–
395 ROMANIAN OR CH	1	850	1 024*	–	–
403 SALVATION ARMY	66	7 572	21 105	0.1	0.3
413 S.D.A.........	429	123 059	148 561*	0.6	1.8
415 S-D BAPTIST GC	4	458	552*	–	–
419 SO BAPT CONV..	937	324 546	392 451*	1.7	4.8
423 SYRIAN ANTIOCH	1	5 000	6 025*	–	0.1
435 UNITARIAN-UNIV	72	11 374	13 575*	0.1	0.2
443 UN C OF CHRIST	243	56 622	67 999*	0.3	0.8
449 UN METHODIST..	714	241 455	290 720*	1.2	3.6
453 UN PRES CH USA	526	217 577	261 279*	1.1	3.2
469 WELS..........	41	4 938	7 096	–	0.1
COLORADO	2 373	462 013	1 057 709*	36.6	100.0
005 AME ZION......	2	290	336	–	–
017 AMER BAPT ASSN	6	850	850	–	0.1
019 AMER BAPT USA.	83	24 097	29 041*	1.0	2.7
029 AMER LUTH CH..	55	19 642	26 711	0.9	2.5
039 AP CHR CH(NAZ)	1	66	77*	–	–
053 ASSEMB OF GOD.	147	16 340	28 786	1.0	2.7
057 BAPT GEN CONF.	22	4 505	5 436*	0.2	0.5
059 BAPT MISS ASSN	1	59	74*	–	–
063 BEREAN FUND CH	6	235	287*	–	–
075 BRETHREN IN CR	1	57	86	–	–
081 CATHOLIC......	289	NA	403 399	14.0	38.1
089 CHR & MISS AL.	5	576	1 064	–	0.1
093 CHR CH (DISC)	47	12 846	19 857	0.7	1.9
097 CHR CHS&CHS CR	61	12 005	14 630*	0.5	1.4
105 CHRISTIAN REF.	17	2 830	4 613	0.2	0.4
123 CH GOD (ANDER)	25	1 687	5 061	0.2	0.5
127 CH GOD (CLEVE)	20	1 520	1 851*	0.1	0.2
133 CH GOD(7TH)DEN	2	134	157*	–	–
151 L-D SAINTS....	132	NA	51 884	1.8	4.9
157 CH OF BRETHREN	9	1 007	1 207*	–	0.1
163 CH OF LUTH BR.	1	20	33	–	–
164 CH LUTH CONF..	3	103	144	–	–
165 CH OF NAZARENE	84	10 982	19 083	0.7	1.8
167 CHS OF CHRIST.	133	12 103	15 573	0.5	1.5
175 CONGR CHR CHS.	2	153	188*	–	–
179 CONSRV BAPT...	48	10 944	13 266*	0.5	1.3
193 EPISCOPAL.....	108	28 513	39 167	1.4	3.7
201 EVAN COV CH AM	8	1 400	1 698*	0.1	0.2
203 EVAN FREE CH..	21	3 018	3 635*	0.1	0.3
209 EVAN LUTH SYN.	1	55	72	–	–
221 FREE METHODIST	11	570	1 966	0.1	0.2
226 FRIENDS-USA...	22	1 481	1 781*	0.1	0.2
233 GEN CH NEW JER	1	15	18*	–	–
237 GC MENN BR CHS	4	451	560*	–	0.1
244 GRACE BRETHREN	3	247	298*	–	–
263 INT FOURSQ GOS	41	4 610	5 595*	0.2	0.5
270 CONSRV JUDAISM	4	545	647*	–	0.1
271 REFORM JUDAISM	6	4 334	5 101*	0.2	0.5
274 LAT EVAN LUTH.	2	226	264	–	–

NA— Not applicable   *Total adherents estimated from known number of communicant, confirmed, full members.   —Represents a percent less than 0.1.   Percentages may not total due to rounding.

11

Table 3. Churches and Church Membership by State and Denomination: 1980

County and Denomination	Number of churches	Communicant, confirmed, full members	Total adherents		
			Number	Percent of total population	Percent of total adherents
281 LUTH CH AMER..	45	20 064	27 969	1.0	2.6
283 LUTH--MO SYNOD	100	35 694	46 694	1.6	4.4
285 MENNONITE CH..	15	1 136	1 382*	-	0.1
287 MENN GEN CONF.	2	248	319	-	
290 METRO COMM CHS	3	255	585	-	0.1
291 MISSIONARY CH.	2	21	41	-	-
313 N AM BAPT CONF	5	338	416*	-	
329 OPEN BIBLE STD	4	660	1 163	-	0.1
335 ORTH PRESB CH.	3	207	257*	-	
349 PENT HOLINESS	24	891	1 090*	-	0.1
353 CHR BRETHREN..	22	1 665	2 145	0.1	0.2
369 PROT REF CHS..	1	100	173	-	-
371 REF CH IN AM..	8	1 485	2 578	0.1	0.2
381 REF PRES-EVAN.	4	899	1 304	-	0.1
383 REF PRES OF NA	2	116	139	-	
403 SALVATION ARMY	9	923	1 642	0.1	0.2
413 S.D.A........	72	12 863	15 552*	0.5	1.5
415 S-D BAPTIST GC	2	225	273*	-	
419 SO BAPT CONV..	156	54 807	66 560*	2.3	6.3
435 UNITARIAN-UNIV	13	2 065	2 465*	0.1	0.2
443 UN C OF CHRIST	76	18 456	22 322*	0.8	2.1
449 UN METHODIST..	224	82 069	99 445*	3.4	9.4
453 UN PRES CH USA	130	46 785	56 612*	2.0	5.4
469 WELS.........	17	1 525	2 087	0.1	0.2
CONNECTICUT	1 725	401 848	1 913 148*	61.6	100.0
001 ADVENT CHR CH.	10	935	1 112*	-	0.1
005 AME ZION......	29	17 457	21 468	0.7	1.1
019 AMER BAPT USA.	125	37 024	44 101*	1.4	2.3
039 AP CHR CH(NAZ)	1	17	20*	-	-
049 ARMEN AP CH AM	1	200	350	-	-
053 ASSEMB OF GOD.	51	5 695	9 859	0.3	0.5
057 BAPT GEN CONF.	12	1 652	1 962*	0.1	0.1
081 CATHOLIC.....	438	NA	1 390 607	44.7	72.7
089 CHR & MISS AL.	9	554	1 035	-	0.1
093 CHR CH (DISC).	5	513	758	-	-
097 CHR CHS&CHS CR	6	319	379*	-	-
101 C.M.E.......	7	3 095	3 678*	0.1	0.2
105 CHRISTIAN REF.	1	74	147	-	-
123 CH GOD (ANDER)	3	85	255	-	-
127 CH GOD (CLEVE)	18	1 097	1 305*	-	0.1
151 L-D SAINTS....	13	NA	4 798	0.2	0.3
163 CH OF LUTH BR.	1	130	216	-	-
165 CH OF NAZARENE	10	849	1 828	0.1	0.1
167 CHS OF CHRIST.	21	1 269	2 022	0.1	0.1
175 CONGR CHR CHS.	24	4 870	5 810*	0.2	0.3
179 CONSRV BAPT...	15	1 720	2 061*	0.1	0.1
181 CONSRV CONGR..	1	89	108*	-	-
193 EPISCOPAL.....	186	70 462	107 324	3.5	5.6
195 ESTONIAN ELC..	1	113	578	-	-
201 EVAN COV CH AM	15	2 605	3 101*	0.1	0.2
203 EVAN FREE CH..	12	1 039	1 236*	-	0.1
208 EVAN LUTH ASSN	12	3 121	4 375	0.1	0.2
226 FRIENDS--USA..	9	770	916*	-	-
233 GEN CH NEW JER	1	20	24*	-	-
270 CONSRV JUDAISM	40	7 301	8 683*	0.3	0.5
271 REFORM JUDAISM	18	12 250	14 565*	0.5	0.8
274 LAT EVAN LUTH.	4	513	561	-	-
281 LUTH CH AMER..	64	28 456	36 521	1.2	1.9
283 LUTH--MO SYNOD	35	12 565	16 204	0.5	0.8
285 MENNONITE CH..	1	78	93*	-	-
290 METRO COMM CHS	2	95	240	-	-
313 N AM BAPT CONF	2	119	141*	-	-
335 ORTH PRESB CH.	1	69	82*	-	-
353 CHR BRETHREN..	17	1 065	1 960	0.1	0.1
381 REF PRES-EVAN.	2	108	150	-	-
403 SALVATION ARMY	19	1 873	6 138	0.2	0.3
413 S.D.A.........	25	3 018	3 591*	0.1	0.2
415 S-D BAPTIST GC	2	74	89*	-	-
419 SO BAPT CONV..	18	3 862	4 615*	0.1	0.2
431 UKRANIAN AMER.	3	335	575	-	-
435 UNITARIAN-UNIV	19	3 598	4 279*	0.1	0.2
443 UN C OF CHRIST	262	110 038	130 993*	4.2	6.8
449 UN METHODIST..	136	51 413	61 196*	2.0	3.2
453 UN PRES CH USA	16	9 114	10 850*	0.3	0.6
469 WELS.........	2	130	189	-	-
DELAWARE	463	106 015	239 532*	40.2	100.0
005 AME ZION......	2	297	342	0.1	0.1
017 AMER BAPT ASSN	2	50	50	-	-
019 AMER BAPT USA.	10	2 924	3 524*	0.6	1.5
029 AMER LUTH CH..	1	212	304	0.1	0.1
053 ASSEMB OF GOD.	12	882	1 522	0.3	0.6
057 BAPT GEN CONF.	2	509	610*	0.1	0.3
061 BEACHY AMISH..	1	?	?	?	?
066 BIBLE CH OF CR	1	200	240*	-	0.1
071 BRETHREN (ASH)	1	53	64*	-	-
081 CATHOLIC......	45	NA	103 060	17.3	43.0

County and Denomination	Number of churches	Communicant, confirmed, full members	Total adherents		
			Number	Percent of total population	Percent of total adherents
089 CHR & MISS AL.	6	475	647	0.1	0.3
093 CHR CH (DISC).	1	117	241	-	0.1
097 CHR CHS&CHS CR	7	725	876*	0.1	0.4
123 CH GOD (ANDER)	5	248	744	0.1	0.3
127 CH GOD (CLEVE)	12	1 411	1 697*	0.3	0.7
151 L-D SAINTS....	3	NA	1 362	0.2	0.6
157 CH OF BRETHREN	2	205	248*	-	0.1
165 CH OF NAZARENE	10	743	1 885	0.3	0.8
167 CHS OF CHRIST.	9	740	1 155	0.2	0.5
179 CONSRV BAPT...	1	257	308*	0.1	0.1
193 EPISCOPAL.....	38	13 157	18 696	3.1	7.8
226 FRIENDS-USA...	8	767	921*	0.2	0.4
239 SWEDENBORGIAN.	1	60	72*	-	-
244 GRACE BRETHREN	1	13	16*	-	-
270 CONSRV JUDAISM	2	638	768*	0.1	0.3
271 REFORM JUDAISM	1	560	671*	0.1	0.3
274 LAT EVAN LUTH.	1	109	133	-	0.1
281 LUTH CH AMER..	10	5 378	7 518	1.3	3.1
283 LUTH--MO SYNOD	7	1 502	1 998	0.3	0.8
285 MENNONITE CH..	7	600	727*	0.1	0.3
290 METRO COMM CHS	0	0	25	-	-
323 OLD ORD AMISH.	6	780	958*	0.2	0.4
335 ORTH PRESB CH.	3	221	265*	-	0.1
353 CHR BRETHREN..	2	70	115	-	-
375 REF EPISCOPAL.	1	25	30*	-	-
381 REF PRES-EVAN.	7	1 352	1 829	0.3	0.8
403 SALVATION ARMY	2	186	959	0.2	0.4
413 S.D.A.........	11	1 159	1 403*	0.2	0.6
419 SO BAPT CONV..	9	3 539	4 279*	0.7	1.8
435 UNITARIAN-UNIV	2	922	1 105*	0.2	0.5
443 UN C OF CHRIST	2	516	633*	0.1	0.3
449 UN METHODIST..	170	50 213	60 489*	10.2	25.3
453 UN PRES CH USA	38	14 128	16 957*	2.8	7.1
469 WELS.........	1	72	86	-	-
DISTRICT OF COLUMBIA	376	167 523	312 444*	49.0	100.0
005 AME ZION......	12	31 450	39 183	6.1	12.5
019 AMER BAPT USA.	33	24 180	28 126*	4.4	9.0
029 AMER LUTH CH..	3	694	790	0.1	0.3
053 ASSEMB OF GOD.	2	375	625	0.1	0.2
061 BEACHY AMISH..	1	18	21*	-	-
071 BRETHREN (ASH)	1	171	199*	-	0.1
081 CATHOLIC......	44	NA	95 794	15.0	30.7
093 CHR CH (DISC).	5	1 179	2 009	0.3	0.6
101 C.M.E.......	6	6 436	7 486*	1.2	2.4
105 CHRISTIAN REF.	1	114	178	-	0.1
123 CH GOD (ANDER)	6	641	1 923	0.3	0.6
127 CH GOD (CLEVE)	2	170	198*	-	0.1
133 CH GOD(7TH)DEN	1	2	2*	-	-
157 CH OF BRETHREN	1	262	305*	-	0.1
165 CH OF NAZARENE	2	334	405	0.1	0.1
167 CHS OF CHRIST.	3	573	730	0.1	0.2
193 EPISCOPAL.....	93	30 550	49 861	7.8	16.0
208 EVAN LUTH ASSN	2	529	735	0.1	0.2
221 FREE METHODIST	2	117	489	0.1	0.2
226 FRIENDS--USA..	1	524	610*	0.1	0.2
233 GEN CH NEW JER	1	70	81*	-	-
239 SWEDENBORGIAN.	1	60	70*	-	-
270 CONSRV JUDAISM	2	999	1 162*	0.2	0.4
271 REFORM JUDAISM	3	6 064	7 053*	1.1	2.3
281 LUTH CH AMER..	10	3 442	4 436	0.7	1.4
283 LUTH--MO SYNOD	6	1 184	2 024	0.3	0.6
290 METRO COMM CHS	1	101	200	-	0.1
349 PENT HOLINESS.	2	103	120*	-	-
353 CHR BRETHREN..	4	130	200	-	0.1
357 PRESB CH US...	23	7 850	9 131*	1.4	2.9
403 SALVATION ARMY	3	403	1 537	0.2	0.5
413 S.D.A.........	10	3 371	3 921*	0.6	1.3
415 S-D BAPTIST GC	1	66	77*	-	-
419 SO BAPT CONV..	23	16 279	18 935*	3.0	6.1
435 UNITARIAN-UNIV	2	1 015	1 181*	0.2	0.4
443 UN C OF CHRIST	9	5 245	6 101*	1.0	2.0
449 UN METHODIST..	35	17 958	20 888*	3.3	6.7
453 UN PRES CH USA	19	4 864	5 658*	0.9	1.8
FLORIDA	6 818	1 926 628	3 753 873*	38.5	100.0
001 ADVENT CHR CH.	34	2 903	3 515*	-	0.1
005 AME ZION......	32	6 219	7 850	0.1	0.2
017 AMER BAPT ASSN	106	15 520	15 520	0.2	0.4
019 AMER BAPT USA.	24	11 430	13 397*	0.1	0.4
029 AMER LUTH CH..	48	14 851	19 309	0.2	0.5
045 APOSTOLIC LUTH	1	300	348*	-	-
053 ASSEMB OF GOD.	427	52 595	85 687	0.9	2.3
055 AS REF PRES CH	10	2 844	3 185	-	0.1
057 BAPT GEN CONF.	9	761	904*	-	-
059 BAPT MISS ASSN	13	1 308	1 589*	-	-
061 BEACHY AMISH..	1	43	48*	-	-

NA—Not applicable   *Total adherents estimated from known number of communicant, confirmed, full members.   —Represents a percent less than 0.1.   Percentages may not total due to rounding.

Table 3. Churches and Church Membership by State and Denomination: 1980

County and Denomination	Number of churches	Communicant, confirmed, full members	Total adherents Number	Percent of total population	Percent of total adherents
071 BRETHREN (ASH)	5	794	898*	-	-
075 BRETHREN IN CR	3	327	393	-	-
081 CATHOLIC......	399	NA	1 353 478	13.9	36.1
089 CHR & MISS AL.	76	7 105	11 661	0.1	0.3
093 CHR CH (DISC).	89	19 477	26 147	0.3	0.7
097 CHR CHS&CHS CR	132	28 191	33 139*	0.3	0.9
101 C.M.E......	50	9 435	11 141*	0.1	0.3
105 CHRISTIAN REF.	12	1 640	2 462	-	0.1
123 CH GOD (ANDER)	92	7 672	23 016	0.2	0.6
127 CH GOD (CLEVE)	403	36 575	43 386*	0.4	1.2
133 CH GOD(7TH)DEN	1	17	20*	-	-
143 CG IN CR(MENN)	1	137	137	-	-
149 CH OF JC (BIC)	4	184	214	-	-
151 L-D SAINTS....	116	NA	36 859	0.4	1.0
157 CH OF BRETHREN	15	1 838	2 155*	-	0.1
163 CH OF LUTH BR.	2	71	81	-	-
164 CH LUTH CONF..	1	110	169	-	-
165 CH OF NAZARENE	159	16 728	28 903	0.3	0.8
167 CHS OF CHRIST.	457	44 829	57 497	0.6	1.5
175 CONGR CHR CHS.	4	831	965*	-	-
177 CONGR HOL CH..	13	292	359*	-	-
179 CONSRV BAPT...	14	1 274	1 491*	-	-
181 CONSRV CONGR..	1	38	45*	-	-
185 CUMBER PRESB..	7	503	1 152	-	-
193 EPISCOPAL.....	302	120 332	145 443	1.5	3.9
195 ESTONIAN ELC..	1	38	53	-	-
199 EVAN CONGR CH.	1	25	30*	-	-
201 EVAN COV CH AM	17	2 168	2 496*	-	0.1
203 EVAN FREE CH..	12	806	930*	-	-
208 EVAN LUTH ASSN	4	649	1 314	-	-
209 EVAN LUTH SYN.	2	333	412	-	-
221 FREE METHODIST	20	854	4 161	-	0.1
226 FRIENDS-USA...	16	567	664*	-	-
239 SWEDENBORGIAN.	3	180	207*	-	-
244 GRACE BRETHREN	12	1 011	1 189*	-	-
263 INT FOURSQ GOS	13	772	922*	-	-
270 CONSRV JUDAISM	40	13 544	15 836*	0.2	0.4
271 REFORM JUDAISM	29	26 936	31 476*	0.3	0.8
274 LAT EVAN LUTH.	2	216	216	-	-
281 LUTH CH AMER..	120	43 208	53 769	0.6	1.4
283 LUTH--MO SYNOD	129	45 627	58 949	0.6	1.6
285 MENNONITE CH..	26	1 859	2 131*	-	0.1
290 METRO COMM CHS	12	726	1 550	-	-
291 MISSIONARY CH.	4	298	434	-	-
295 MORAV CH-SOUTH	4	510	651	-	-
313 N AM BAPT CONF	2	95	110*	-	-
323 OLD ORD AMISH.	1	130	146*	-	-
329 OPEN BIBLE STD	21	2 601	3 742	-	0.1
335 ORTH PRESB CH.	6	510	601*	-	-
349 PENT HOLINESS.	83	7 226	8 711*	0.1	0.2
353 CHR BRETHREN..	41	2 220	3 705	-	0.1
356 PRESB CH AMER.	50	16 034	17 726	0.2	0.5
357 PRESB CH US...	236	88 608	104 523*	1.1	2.8
363 PRIMITIVE METH	1	62	74*	-	-
371 REF CH IN AM..	15	2 444	4 308	-	0.1
375 REF EPISCOPAL.	3	44	52*	-	-
381 REF PRES-EVAN.	9	1 012	1 341	-	-
383 REF PRES OF NA	1	76	104	-	-
403 SALVATION ARMY	32	3 974	9 740	0.1	0.3
413 S.D.A.......	161	27 778	32 892*	0.3	0.9
415 S-D BAPTIST GC	2	110	129*	-	-
419 SO BAPT CONV..	1 537	786 276	937 719*	9.6	25.0
421 SO METHODIST..	9	249	392	-	-
435 UNITARIAN-UNIV	29	3 784	4 412*	-	0.1
443 UN C OF CHRIST	85	28 148	32 709*	0.3	0.9
449 UN METHODIST..	826	361 447	426 591*	4.4	11.4
453 UN PRES CH USA	116	44 196	51 351*	0.5	1.4
469 WELS.........	22	2 103	2 842	-	0.1
GEORGIA	7 485	1 942 558	2 570 084	47.0	100.0
001 ADVENT CHR CH.	17	1 498	1 839*	-	0.1
005 AME ZION......	32	5 651	6 750	0.1	0.3
017 AMER BAPT ASSN	20	1 400	1 400	-	0.1
019 AMER BAPT USA.	13	9 783	11 807*	0.2	0.5
029 AMER LUTH CH..	7	2 061	2 913	0.1	0:1
053 ASSEMB OF GOD.	180	17 317	28 074	0.5	1.1
055 AS REF PRES CH	11	1 920	2 138	-	0.1
057 BAPT GEN CONF.	1	15	18*	-	-
059 BAPT MISS ASSN	1	118	146*	-	-
061 BEACHY AMISH..	2	200	250*	-	-
065 BETHEL M ASSN	2	365	447*	-	-
081 CATHOLIC......	165	NA	141 145	2.6	5.5
089 CHR & MISS AL.	31	2 638	4 153	0.1	0.2
093 CHR CH (DISC).	80	11 826	17 571	0.3	0.7
097 CHR CHS&CHS CR	133	29 708	36 856*	0.7	1.4
101 C.M.E......	153	68 614	84 209*	1.5	3.3
105 CHRISTIAN REF.	1	32	51	-	-
123 CH GOD (ANDER)	48	1 975	5 925	0.1	0.2
127 CH GOD (CLEVE)	465	47 486	58 349*	1.1	2.3
143 CG IN CR(MENN)	1	142	142	-	-
151 L-D SAINTS....	67	NA	20 203	0.4	0.8
165 CH OF NAZARENE	86	7 493	13 040	0.2	0.5
167 CHS OF CHRIST.	351	27 776	35 757	0.7	1.4
175 CONGR CHR CHS.	3	253	313*	-	-
177 CONGR HOL CH..	74	3 108	3 803*	0.1	0.1
179 CONSRV BAPT...	2	55	67*	-	-
185 CUMBER PRESB..	5	247	526	-	-
193 EPISCOPAL.....	136	41 961	54 231	1.0	2.1
203 EVAN FREE CH..	1	45	55*	-	-
208 EVAN LUTH ASSN	1	256	323	-	-
209 EVAN LUTH SYN.	1	27	32	-	-
215 EVAN METH CH..	9	974	1 194*	-	-
221 FREE METHODIST	4	161	693	-	-
226 FRIENDS-USA...	2	80	97*	-	-
233 GEN CH NEW JER	1	40	48*	-	-
244 GRACE BRETHREN	1	110	134*	-	-
263 INT FOURSQ GOS	10	569	690*	-	-
270 CONSRV JUDAISM	6	1 744	2 108*	-	0.1
271 REFORM JUDAISM	12	6 264	7 582*	0.1	0.3
281 LUTH CH AMER..	50	15 276	20 102	0.4	0.8
283 LUTH--MO SYNOD	30	5 189	7 005	0.1	0.3
285 MENNONITE CH..	6	164	202*	-	-
290 METRO COMM CHS	1	190	380	-	-
295 MORAV CH-SOUTH	1	105	150	-	-
329 OPEN BIBLE STD	3	115	130	-	-
335 ORTH PRESB CH.	1	82	99*	-	-
349 PENT HOLINESS.	59	3 706	4 521*	0.1	0.2
353 CHR BRETHREN..	17	1 110	1 815	-	0.1
356 PRESB CH AMER.	35	6 011	6 878	0.1	0.3
357 PRESB CH US...	291	72 566	88 295*	1.6	3.4
403 SALVATION ARMY	23	2 357	4 919	0.1	0.2
413 S.D.A.........	93	14 459	17 672*	0.3	0.7
419 SO BAPT CONV..	2 958	1 120 472	1 374 905*	25.2	53.5
421 SO METHODIST..	15	724	907	-	-
435 UNITARIAN-UNIV	16	1 659	2 000*	-	0.1
443 UN C OF CHRIST	27	3 025	3 684*	0.1	0.1
449 UN METHODIST..	1 699	398 991	488 909*	8.9	19.0
453 UN PRES CH USA	22	2 308	2 807*	0.1	0.1
469 WELS.........	3	137	223	-	-
HAWAII	558	62 551	320 288*	33.2	100.0
017 AMER BAPT ASSN	8	450	450	-	0.1
019 AMER BAPT USA.	4	410	498*	0.1	0.2
029 AMER LUTH CH..	5	511	653	0.1	0.2
053 ASSEMB OF GOD.	41	4 641	7 132	0.7	2.2
057 BAPT GEN CONF.	1	81	100*	-	-
081 CATHOLIC......	64	NA	210 000	21.8	65.6
089 CHR & MISS AL.	7	619	832	0.1	0.3
093 CHR CH (DISC).	3	403	638	0.1	0.2
097 CHR CHS&CHS CR	8	678	823*	0.1	0.3
105 CHRISTIAN REF.	1	32	45	-	-
123 CH GOD (ANDER)	2	50	150	-	-
127 CH GOD (CLEVE)	14	708	864*	0.1	0.3
133 CH GOD(7TH)DEN	5	39	48*	-	-
151 L-D SAINTS....	80	NA	28 002	2.9	8.7
165 CH OF NAZARENE	14	1 002	1 946	0.2	0.6
167 CHS OF CHRIST.	12	691	904	0.1	0.3
175 CONGR CHR CHS.	5	145	177*	-	0.1
179 CONSRV BAPT...	4	897	1 089*	0.1	0.3
181 CONSRV CONGR..	1	26	32*	-	-
193 EPISCOPAL.....	42	6 729	10 077	1.0	3.1
203 EVAN FREE CH..	1	97	118*	-	-
226 FRIENDS-USA...	1	90	109*	-	-
244 GRACE BRETHREN	3	239	290*	-	0.1
270 CONSRV JUDAISM	1	35	42*	-	-
271 REFORM JUDAISM	1	720	874*	0.1	0.3
281 LUTH CH AMER..	5	810	1 208	0.1	0.4
283 LUTH--MO SYNOD	10	1 570	2 351	0.2	0.7
290 METRO COMM CHS	1	110	220	-	0.1
291 MISSIONARY CH.	8	336	796	0.1	0.2
353 CHR BRETHREN..	3	200	350	-	0.1
356 PRESB CH AMER.	1	?	?	?	?
403 SALVATION ARMY	9	1 068	1 779	0.2	0.6
413 S.D.A.........	21	3 995	4 869*	0.5	1.5
419 SO BAPT CONV..	38	10 978	13 336*	1.4	4.2
435 UNITARIAN-UNIV	2	190	231*	-	0.1
443 UN C OF CHRIST	96	17 052	20 787*	2.2	6.5
449 UN METHODIST..	31	5 943	7 233*	0.7	2.3
453 UN PRES CH USA	4	967	1 174*	0.1	0.4
469 WELS.........	1	39	61	-	-
IDAHO	1 393	114 350	472 497*	50.1	100.0
001 ADVENT CHR CH.	2	50	61*	-	-
017 AMER BAPT ASSN	4	225	225	-	-
019 AMER BAPT USA.	40	8 174	10 193*	1.1	2.2
029 AMER LUTH CH..	27	5 750	8 250	0.9	1.7

NA—Not applicable   *Total adherents estimated from known number of communicant, confirmed, full members.   —Represents a percent less than 0.1.   Percentages may not total due to rounding.

Table 3. Churches and Church Membership by State and Denomination: 1980

County and Denomination	Number of churches	Communicant, confirmed, full members	Total adherents			County and Denomination	Number of churches	Communicant, confirmed, full members	Total adherents		
			Number	Percent of total population	Percent of total adherents				Number	Percent of total population	Percent of total adherents
053 ASSEMB OF GOD.	78	6 243	13 102	1.4	2.8	195 ESTONIAN ELC..	3	320	742	–	–
						197 EVAN CH OF NA.	3	86	86	–	–
057 BAPT GEN CONF.	5	374	462*	–	0.1	199 EVAN CONGR CH.	12	1 111	1 349*	–	–
059 BAPT MISS ASSN	2	66	82*	–	–	201 EVAN COV CH AM	62	12 421	15 082*	0.1	0.2
081 CATHOLIC.....	106	NA	70 476	7.5	14.9	203 EVAN FREE CH..	68	9 579	11 650*	0.1	0.2
089 CHR & MISS AL.	5	260	401	–	0.1	208 EVAN LUTH ASSN	31	11 783	16 258	0.1	0.3
093 CHR CH (DISC).	20	4 844	7 342	0.8	1.6	209 EVAN LUTH SYN.	3	410	534	–	–
097 CHR CHS&CHS CR	23	4 950	6 135*	0.6	1.3	213 EVAN MENN INC.	6	919	1 120*	–	–
105 CHRISTIAN REF.	2	106	189	–	–	215 EVAN METH CH..	4	145	177*	–	–
123 CH GOD (ANDER)	10	633	1 899	0.2	0.4	217 FIRE BAPTIZED.	1	7	9*	–	–
127 CH GOD (CLEVE)	24	674	838*	0.1	0.2	220 FREE LUTHERAN.	1	113	152	–	–
133 CH GOD(7TH)DEN	1	57	71*	–	–	221 FREE METHODIST	81	4 475	17 670	0.2	0.3
143 CG IN CR(MENN)	3	355	355	–	0.1	226 FRIENDS-USA...	28	1 958	2 375*	–	–
151 L-D SAINTS....	560	NA	240 843	25.5	51.0	233 GEN CH NEW JER	1	215	259*	–	–
157 CH OF BRETHREN	8	929	1 154*	0.1	0.2	237 GC MENN BR CHS	1	41	49*	–	–
163 CH OF LUTH BR.	1	51	90	–	–	239 SWEDENBORGIAN.	2	120	145*	–	–
164 CH LUTH CONF..	1	26	32	–	–	263 INT FOURSQ GOS	32	7 704	9 342*	0.1	0.1
165 CH OF NAZARENE	52	8 407	14 395	1.5	3.0	270 CONSRV JUDAISM	31	8 343	10 094*	0.1	0.2
167 CHS OF CHRIST.	41	2 433	3 459	0.4	0.7	271 REFORM JUDAISM	37	29 746	35 937*	0.3	0.6
175 CONGR CHR CHS.	2	139	173*	–	–	274 LAT EVAN LUTH.	3	1 021	1 219	–	–
179 CONSRV BAPT...	11	2 475	3 074	0.3	0.7	281 LUTH CH AMER..	326	146 212	194 115	1.7	3.1
181 CONSRV CONGR..	1	289	372*	–	0.1	283 LUTH--MO SYNOD	506	236 692	313 425	2.7	5.0
193 EPISCOPAL.....	37	6 208	9 250	1.0	2.0	285 MENNONITE CH..	44	5 042	6 150*	0.1	0.1
201 EVAN COV CH AM	1	87	112*	–	–	287 MENN GEN CONF.	18	2 883	3 348	–	0.1
203 EVAN FREE CH..	2	99	123*	–	–	290 METRO COMM CHS	3	470	940	–	–
221 FREE METHODIST	8	416	1 887	0.2	0.4	291 MISSIONARY CH.	16	1 524	2 227	–	–
226 FRIENDS-USA...	13	1 725	2 142*	0.2	0.5	293 MORAV CH-NORTH	1	322	468	–	–
263 INT FOURSQ GOS	10	1 039	1 289*	0.1	0.3	313 N AM BAPT CONF	14	2 162	2 639*	–	–
270 CONSRV JUDAISM	1	23	28*	–	–	323 OLD ORD AMISH.	13	1 690	2 047*	–	–
271 REFORM JUDAISM	1	48	61*	–	–	329 OPEN BIBLE STD	22	2 117	3 451	–	0.1
281 LUTH CH AMER..	13	3 164	4 411	0.5	0.9	335 ORTH PRESB CH.	5	442	545*	–	–
283 LUTH--MO SYNOD	38	9 214	12 753	1.4	2.7	349 PENT HOLINESS.	4	91	112*	–	–
285 MENNONITE CH..	5	265	331*	–	0.1	353 CHR BRETHREN..	41	2 590	4 115	–	0.1
287 MENN GEN CONF.	1	330	520	0.1	0.1	356 PRESB CH AMER.	1	74	124	–	–
290 METRO COMM CHS	1	40	80	–	–	363 PRIMITIVE METH	1	161	194*	–	–
291 MISSIONARY CH.	1	30	47	–	–	369 PROT REF CHS..	1	242	435	–	–
313 N AM BAPT CONF	1	120	154*	–	–	371 REF CH IN AM..	54	13 022	21 288	0.2	0.3
329 OPEN BIBLE STD	2	85	135	–	–	375 REF EPISCOPAL.	2	312	377*	–	–
353 CHR BRETHREN..	2	70	120	–	–	381 REF PRES-EVAN.	11	961	1 180	–	–
371 REF CH IN AM..	1	99	249	–	0.1	383 REF PRES OF NA	3	116	138	–	–
403 SALVATION ARMY	7	565	1 216	0.1	0.3	395 ROMANIAN OR CH	1	2 450	2 957*	–	–
413 S.D.A........	45	5 400	6 692*	0.7	1.4	403 SALVATION ARMY	52	7 120	22 313	0.2	0.4
419 SO BAPT CONV..	35	7 269	9 085*	1.0	1.9	409 SEPARATE BAPT.	9	558	654*	–	–
435 UNITARIAN-UNIV	2	133	166*	–	–	413 S.D.A........	102	14 546	17 631*	0.2	0.3
443 UN C OF CHRIST	17	2 632	3 280*	0.3	0.7	415 S-D BAPTIST GC	2	71	85*	–	–
449 UN METHODIST..	65	17 883	22 303*	2.4	4.7	417 SOCIAL BRETH..	24	1 215	1 456*	–	–
453 UN PRES CH USA	53	9 775	12 205*	1.3	2.6	419 SO BAPT CONV..	890	219 108	264 480*	2.3	4.2
469 WELS..........	2	121	185	–	–	423 SYRIAN ANTIOCH	2	700	845*	–	–
ILLINOIS	9 358	2 054 178	6 297 355*	55.2	100.0	431 UKRANIAN AMER.	1	240	340	–	–
001 ADVENT CHR CH.	9	1 105	1 351*	–	–	435 UNITARIAN-UNIV	41	7 707	9 303*	0.1	0.1
005 AME ZION......	14	14 423	18 426	0.2	0.3	443 UN C OF CHRIST	429	157 763	191 865*	1.7	3.0
017 AMER BAPT ASSN	13	1 225	1 225	–	–	449 UN METHODIST..	1 534	417 399	505 406*	4.4	8.0
019 AMER BAPT USA.	299	86 761	104 795*	0.9	1.7	453 UN PRES CH USA	498	160 260	194 180*	1.7	3.1
029 AMER LUTH CH..	217	81 227	109 224	1.0	1.7	469 WELS..........	34	7 426	9 969	0.1	0.2
039 AP CHR CH(NAZ)	4	237	291*	–	–	INDIANA	6 590	1 290 569	2 458 653*	44.8	100.0
049 ARMEN AP CH AM	3	121	577	–	–	001 ADVENT CHR CH.	2	306	375*	–	–
053 ASSEMB OF GOD.	292	33 045	62 662	0.5	1.0	005 AME ZION......	19	18 257	23 286	0.4	0.9
057 BAPT GEN CONF.	70	13 513	16 404*	0.1	0.3	017 AMER BAPT ASSN	19	1 615	1 615	–	0.1
059 BAPT MISS ASSN	15	878	1 072*	–	–	019 AMER BAPT USA.	408	119 904	146 278*	2.7	5.9
061 BEACHY AMISH..	1	150	182*	–	–	029 AMER LUTH CH..	54	16 078	21 301	0.4	0.9
065 BETHEL M ASSN.	10	1 255	1 497*	–	–	053 ASSEMB OF GOD.	181	20 204	40 818	0.7	1.7
071 BRETHREN (ASH)	3	668	808*	–	–	057 BAPT GEN CONF.	6	724	891*	–	–
075 BRETHREN IN CR	1	43	73	–	–	059 BAPT MISS ASSN	4	225	276*	–	–
081 CATHOLIC......	1 235	NA	3 600 862	31.5	57.2	061 BEACHY AMISH..	11	767	948*	–	–
083 CHRIST CATH CH	2	41	106	–	–	065 BETHEL M ASSN.	6	2 750	3 293*	0.1	0.1
089 CHR & MISS AL.	31	2 087	3 349	–	0.1	071 BRETHREN (ASH)	36	5 331	6 544*	0.1	0.3
091 CHRISTIAN CATH	2	1 220	2 050	–	–	075 BRETHREN IN CR	4	172	292	–	–
093 CHR CH (DISC).	204	45 721	73 479	0.6	1.2	081 CATHOLIC......	497	NA	724 188	13.2	29.5
097 CHR CHS&CHS CR	469	91 880	110 783*	1.0	1.8	089 CHR & MISS AL.	26	1 790	3 349	0.1	0.1
101 C.M.E.........	27	18 113	21 877*	0.2	0.3	091 CHRISTIAN CATH	1	75	150	–	–
105 CHRISTIAN REF.	44	10 807	16 633	0.1	0.3	093 CHR CH (DISC).	250	70 084	104 662	1.9	4.3
121 CH GOD (ABR)..	11	630	759*	–	–	097 CHR CHS&CHS CR	556	136 515	166 973*	3.0	6.8
123 CH GOD (ANDER)	116	8 921	26 763	0.2	0.4	101 C.M.E.........	12	9 704	11 769*	0.2	0.5
127 CH GOD (CLEVE)	141	10 304	12 455*	0.1	0.2	105 CHRISTIAN REF.	15	3 328	5 606	0.1	0.2
133 CH GOD(7TH)DEN	2	40	47*	–	–	107 CHRISTIAN UN..	8	394	784	–	–
151 L-D SAINTS....	63	NA	23 671	0.2	0.4	121 CH GOD (ABR)..	8	431	523*	–	–
157 CH OF BRETHREN	42	5 944	7 236*	0.1	0.1	123 CH GOD (ANDER)	149	16 398	49 194	0.9	2.0
163 CH OF LUTH BR.	1	58	208	–	–	127 CH GOD (CLEVE)	102	5 913	7 229*	0.1	0.3
164 CH LUTH CONF..	1	45	63	–	–	151 L-D SAINTS....	55	NA	16 295	0.3	0.7
165 CH OF NAZARENE	259	22 088	48 677	0.4	0.8	157 CH OF BRETHREN	108	17 097	20 985*	0.4	0.9
167 CHS OF CHRIST.	306	24 419	31 644	0.3	0.5	165 CH OF NAZARENE	342	33 336	73 022	1.3	3.0
175 CONGR CHR CHS.	32	4 217	5 104*	–	0.1	167 CHS OF CHRIST.	335	29 883	39 122	0.7	1.6
177 CONGR HOL CH..	1	18	21*	–	–	175 CONGR CHR CHS.	12	2 832	3 428*	0.1	0.1
179 CONSRV BAPT...	40	8 920	10 804*	0.1	0.2	181 CONSRV CONGR..	2	330	402*	–	0.1
181 CONSRV CONGR..	7	1 183	1 445*	–	–	185 CUMBER PRESB..	9	944	1 623	–	0.1
185 CUMBER PRESB..	46	1 720	3 193	–	0.1	193 EPISCOPAL.....	81	18 021	25 428	0.5	1.0
193 EPISCOPAL.....	210	56 946	74 488	0.7	1.2						

NA—Not applicable   *Total adherents estimated from known number of communicant, confirmed, full members.   —Represents a percent less than 0.1.   Percentages may not total due to rounding.

Table 3. Churches and Church Membership by State and Denomination: 1980

County and Denomination	Number of churches	Communicant, confirmed, full members	Total adherents Number	Percent of total population	Percent of total adherents
195 ESTONIAN ELC..	1	48	52	–	–
197 EVAN CH OF NA.	4	360	360	–	–
201 EVAN COV CH AM	5	610	742*	–	–
203 EVAN FREE CH..	6	687	847*	–	–
208 EVAN LUTH ASSN	11	3 976	5 425	0.1	0.2
213 EVAN MENN INC.	9	1 217	1 502*	–	0.1
215 EVAN METH CH..	7	405	496*	–	–
221 FREE METHODIST	41	3 854	16 971	0.3	0.7
226 FRIENDS-USA...	136	17 536	21 468*	0.4	0.9
239 SWEDENBORGIAN.	1	60	73*	–	–
244 GRACE BRETHREN	18	3 038	3 734*	0.1	0.2
263 INT FOURSQ GOS	11	2 383	2 892*	0.1	0.1
270 CONSRV JUDAISM	3	1 048	1 274*	–	0.1
271 REFORM JUDAISM	13	5 248	6 365*	0.1	0.3
274 LAT EVAN LUTH.	2	512	581	–	–
281 LUTH CH AMER..	145	43 759	58 968	1.1	2.4
283 LUTH--MO SYNOD	211	81 850	110 408	2.0	4.5
285 MENNONITE CH..	88	11 813	14 645	0.3	0.6
287 MENN GEN CONF.	11	2 584	3 392	0.1	0.1
290 METRO COMM CHS	1	95	190	–	–
291 MISSIONARY CH.	59	7 392	9 873	0.2	0.4
293 MORAV CH-NORTH	4	634	857	–	–
313 N AM BAPT CONF	1	120	145*	–	–
323 OLD ORD AMISH.	102	13 260	16 631*	0.3	0.7
329 OPEN BIBLE STD	2	43	90	–	–
349 PENT HOLINESS.	3	69	87*	–	–
353 CHR BRETHREN..	13	325	605	–	–
356 PRESB CH AMER.	1	29	34	–	–
363 PRIMITIVE METH	1	84	104*	–	–
371 REF CH IN AM..	10	2 247	3 537	0.1	0.1
381 REF PRES-EVAN.	5	278	405	–	–
383 REF PRES OF NA	4	324	414	–	–
395 ROMANIAN OR CH	1	350	431*	–	–
403 SALVATION ARMY	40	4 491	7 526	0.1	0.3
409 SEPARATE BAPT.	27	1 905	2 372*	–	0.1
413 S.D.A........	85	8 275	10 087*	0.2	0.4
417 SOCIAL BRETH..	1	110	134*	–	–
419 SO BAPT CONV..	271	74 960	91 318*	1.7	3.7
431 UKRANIAN AMER.	1	150	270	–	–
435 UNITARIAN-UNIV	19	2 223	2 688*	–	0.1
443 UN C OF CHRIST	183	53 221	64 778*	1.2	2.6
449 UN METHODIST..	1 426	316 091	386 029*	7.0	15.7
453 UN PRES CH USA	282	88 804	108 255*	2.0	4.4
469 WELS..........	7	693	949	–	–
IOWA	4 534	940 758	1 783 704*	61.2	100.0
001 ADVENT CHR CH.	2	97	116*	–	–
005 AME ZION......	1	254	269	–	–
015 AMANA CH SOC..	7	733	789	–	–
017 AMER BAPT ASSN	1	50	50	–	–
019 AMER BAPT USA.	135	29 496	35 648*	1.2	2.0
029 AMER LUTH CH..	400	153 539	201 668	6.9	11.3
053 ASSEMB OF GOD.	121	12 863	24 743	0.8	1.4
057 BAPT GEN CONF.	31	4 667	5 665*	0.2	0.3
061 BEACHY AMISH..	2	185	217*	–	–
071 BRETHREN (ASH)	2	231	280*	–	–
075 BRETHREN IN CR	2	114	172	–	–
081 CATHOLIC......	589	NA	539 482	18.5	30.2
089 CHR & MISS AL.	17	1 080	2 349	0.1	0.1
093 CHR CH (DISC).	173	35 195	54 611	1.9	3.1
097 CHR CHS&CHS CR	136	19 394	23 432*	0.8	1.3
105 CHRISTIAN REF.	60	13 169	21 360	0.7	1.2
107 CHRISTIAN UN..	8	460	682	–	–
121 CH GOD (ABR)..	5	138	165*	–	–
123 CH GOD (ANDER)	14	558	1 674	0.1	0.1
127 CH GOD (CLEVE)	20	734	892*	–	0.1
133 CH GOD(7TH)DEN	2	41	50*	–	–
151 L-D SAINTS....	30	NA	8 088	0.3	0.5
157 CH OF BRETHREN	32	3 663	4 435*	0.2	0.2
163 CH OF LUTH BR.	7	417	550	–	–
165 CH OF NAZARENE	80	6 465	14 444	0.5	0.8
167 CHS OF CHRIST.	75	3 574	4 996	0.2	0.3
175 CONGR CHR CHS.	10	3 118	3 771*	0.1	0.2
179 CONSRV BAPT...	19	2 160	2 635*	0.1	0.1
181 CONSRV CONGR..	3	646	783*	–	–
185 CUMBER PRESB..	1	86	189	–	–
193 EPISCOPAL.....	70	12 878	17 905	0.6	1.0
197 EVAN CH OF NA.	5	254	254	–	–
201 EVAN COV CH AM	19	2 650	3 193*	0.1	0.2
203 EVAN FREE CH..	38	3 287	3 965*	0.1	0.2
208 EVAN LUTH ASSN	4	680	843	–	–
209 EVAN LUTH SYN.	19	1 753	2 236	0.1	0.1
215 EVAN METH CH..	1	16	20*	–	–
220 FREE LUTHERAN.	1	164	203	–	–
221 FREE METHODIST	28	977	3 446	0.1	0.2
226 FRIENDS-USA...	50	5 423	6 566*	0.2	0.4
244 GRACE BRETHREN	9	1 072	1 300*	–	0.1
263 INT FOURSQ GOS	21	2 078	2 518*	0.1	0.1

County and Denomination	Number of churches	Communicant, confirmed, full members	Total adherents Number	Percent of total population	Percent of total adherents
270 CONSRV JUDAISM	7	535	646*	–	–
271 REFORM JUDAISM	7	1 556	1 894*	0.1	0.1
274 LAT EVAN LUTH.	1	100	114	–	–
281 LUTH CH AMER..	128	62 124	82 280	2.8	4.6
283 LUTH--MO SYNOD	285	96 780	128 244	4.4	7.2
285 MENNONITE CH..	25	3 355	3 991*	0.1	0.2
287 MENN GEN CONF.	5	680	871	–	–
290 METRO COMM CHS	3	100	200	–	–
291 MISSIONARY CH.	7	266	313	–	–
313 N AM BAPT CONF	14	2 644	3 207*	0.1	0.2
323 OLD ORD AMISH.	19	2 470	2 983*	0.1	0.2
329 OPEN BIBLE STD	40	4 367	7 336	0.3	0.4
335 ORTH PRESB CH.	1	50	61*	–	–
353 CHR BRETHREN..	43	1 800	2 645	0.1	0.1
363 PRIMITIVE METH	2	95	113*	–	–
369 PROT REF CHS..	3	274	543	–	–
371 REF CH IN AM..	73	20 956	32 899	1.1	1.8
381 REF PRES-EVAN.	1	56	76	–	–
383 REF PRES OF NA	5	287	374	–	–
403 SALVATION ARMY	19	2 740	15 762	0.5	0.9
413 S.D.A........	65	4 699	5 679*	0.2	0.3
419 SO BAPT CONV..	55	8 739	10 564*	0.4	0.6
435 UNITARIAN-UNIV	10	1 378	1 660*	0.1	0.1
443 UN C OF CHRIST	217	50 840	61 585*	2.1	3.5
449 UN METHODIST..	911	261 613	316 303*	10.9	17.7
453 UN PRES CH USA	326	86 763	105 143*	3.6	5.9
469 WELS...,......	12	1 132	1 566	0.1	0.1
KANSAS	3 869	710 437	1 263 168*	53.5	100.0
001 ADVENT CHR CH.	1	12	15*	–	–
005 AME ZION......	2	165	189	–	–
017 AMER BAPT ASSN	15	2 220	2 220	0.1	0.2
019 AMER BAPT USA.	255	60 258	72 789*	3.1	5.8
029 AMER LUTH CH..	52	10 699	14 370	0.6	1.1
053 ASSEMB OF GOD.	154	13 498	24 735	1.0	2.0
057 BAPT GEN CONF.	1	34	42*	–	–
059 BAPT MISS ASSN	10	1 251	1 503*	0.1	0.1
061 BEACHY AMISH..	1	267	322*	–	–
063 BEREAN FUND CH	3	89	109*	–	–
071 BRETHREN (ASH)	4	307	371*	–	–
075 BRETHREN IN CR	4	228	344	–	–
081 CATHOLIC......	396	NA	337 077	14.3	26.7
089 CHR & MISS AL.	1	294	294	–	–
093 CHR CH (DISC).	178	45 304	68 858	2.9	5.5
097 CHR CHS&CHS CR	208	37 486	45 276*	1.9	3.6
101 C.M.E........	1	105	127*	–	–
105 CHRISTIAN REF.	2	314	463	–	–
121 CH GOD (ABR)..	1	16	19*	–	–
123 CH GOD (ANDER)	54	3 849	11 547	0.5	0.9
127 CH GOD (CLEVE)	28	1 376	1 662*	0.1	0.1
133 CH GOD(7TH)DEN	3	34	41*	–	–
143 CG IN CR(MENN)	20	2 835	2 835	0.1	0.2
149 CH OF JC (BIC)	1	14	21	–	–
151 L-D SAINTS....	48	NA	10 492	0.4	0.8
157 CH OF BRETHREN	33	3 903	4 709*	0.2	0.4
165 CH OF NAZARENE	138	16 137	31 322	1.3	2.5
167 CHS OF CHRIST.	183	13 544	17 258	0.7	1.4
175 CONGR CHR CHS.	7	3 516	4 342*	0.2	0.3
177 CONGR HOL CH..	1	12	14*	–	–
181 CONSRV CONGR..	1	44	51*	–	–
193 EPISCOPAL.....	82	17 272	21 763	0.9	1.7
201 EVAN COV CH AM	23	2 348	2 827*	0.1	0.2
203 EVAN FREE CH..	6	492	594*	–	–
208 EVAN LUTH ASSN	7	1 807	2 294	0.1	0.2
211 EVAN MENN BR..	1	170	221	–	–
213 EVAN MENN INC.	1	218	263*	–	–
215 EVAN METH CH..	3	170	206*	–	–
217 FIRE BAPTIZED.	16	350	422*	–	–
221 FREE METHODIST	29	1 408	4 914	0.2	0.4
226 FRIENDS-USA...	47	5 012	6 040*	0.3	0.5
237 GC MENN BR CHS	16	3 134	3 748*	0.2	0.3
239 SWEDENBORGIAN.	3	180	218*	–	–
244 GRACE BRETHREN	2	125	148*	–	–
263 INT FOURSQ GOS	17	1 875	2 262*	0.1	0.2
271 REFORM JUDAISM	4	968	1 173*	–	0.1
274 LAT EVAN LUTH.	1	18	20	–	–
281 LUTH CH AMER..	83	22 951	29 621	1.3	2.3
283 LUTH--MO SYNOD	162	44 645	58 218	2.5	4.6
285 MENNONITE CH..	24	2 566	3 084*	0.1	0.2
287 MENN GEN CONF.	44	11 595	14 478	0.6	1.1
290 METRO COMM CHS	1	155	310	–	–
291 MISSIONARY CH.	5	221	257	–	–
313 N AM BAPT CONF	12	1 614	1 920*	0.1	0.2
323 OLD ORD AMISH.	4	520	626*	–	–
329 OPEN BIBLE STD	2	110	150	–	–
335 ORTH PRESB CH.	1	30	36*	–	–
349 PENT HOLINESS.	23	1 157	1 398*	0.1	0.1
353 CHR BRETHREN..	17	630	830	–	0.1

Table 3. Churches and Church Membership by State and Denomination: 1980

County and Denomination	Number of churches	Communicant, confirmed, full members	Total adherents Number	Percent of total population	Percent of total adherents
356 PRESB CH AMER.	1	594	817	—	0.1
357 PRESB CH US..	50	15 564	18 917*	0.8	1.5
371 REF CH IN AM..	1	167	276	—	—
381 REF PRES-EVAN.	1	12	21	—	—
383 REF PRES OF NA	11	704	900	—	0.1
403 SALVATION ARMY	19	2 358	7 174	0.3	0.6
413 S.D.A.........	68	5 917	7 153*	0.3	0.6
415 S-D BAPTIST GC	1	97	118*	—	—
419 SO BAPT CONV..	184	60 528	73 306*	3.1	5.8
435 UNITARIAN-UNIV	7	562	674*	—	0.1
443 UN C OF CHRIST	86	17 426	20 934*	0.9	1.7
449 UN METHODIST..	775	217 728	262 082*	11.1	20.7
453 UN PRES CH USA	215	48 753	58 683*	2.5	4.6
469 WELS.........	8	475	655	—	0.1
KENTUCKY	6 704	1 276 494	1 982 830*	54.2	100.0
001 ADVENT CHR CH.	2	108	135*	—	—
005 AME ZION......	38	16 436	18 077	0.5	0.9
017 AMER BAPT ASSN	8	1 390	1 390	—	0.1
029 AMER LUTH CH..	3	442	660	—	—
053 ASSEMB OF GOD.	135	13 200	20 464	0.6	1.0
055 AS REF PRES CH	1	99	102	—	—
061 BEACHY AMISH..	2	131	160*	—	—
071 BRETHREN (ASH)	3	100	126*	—	—
075 BRETHREN IN CR	5	215	365	—	—
081 CATHOLIC......	331	NA	365 277	10.0	18.4
089 CHR & MISS AL.	17	893	1 417	—	0.1
093 CHR CH (DISC).	324	53 343	78 275	2.1	3.9
097 CHR CHS&CHS CR	470	67 134	81 787*	2.2	4.1
101 C.M.E........	51	10 659	12 949*	0.4	0.7
105 CHRISTIAN REF.	1	7	15	—	—
123 CH GOD (ANDER)	130	9 553	28 659	0.8	1.4
127 CH GOD (CLEVE)	177	13 320	16 390*	0.4	0.8
151 L-D SAINTS....	37	NA	10 680	0.3	0.5
157 CH OF BRETHREN	4	289	365*	—	—
165 CH OF NAZARENE	148	12 895	23 309	0.6	1.2
167 CHS OF CHRIST.	600	46 158	59 443	1.6	3.0
177 CONGR HOL CH..	1	23	28*	—	—
185 CUMBER PRESB..	128	8 141	13 959	0.4	0.7
193 EPISCOPAL.....	73	16 037	20 401	0.6	1.0
197 EVAN CH OF NA.	1	21	21	—	—
199 EVAN CONGR CH.	1	22	27*	—	—
203 EVAN FREE CH..	7	191	239*	—	—
215 EVAN METH CH..	3	181	219*	—	—
221 FREE METHODIST	12	422	1 926	0.1	0.1
226 FRIENDS-USA...	3	144	172*	—	—
244 GRACE BRETHREN	2	89	113*	—	—
263 INT FOURSQ GOS	3	69	87*	—	—
270 CONSRV JUDAISM	2	449	542*	—	—
271 REFORM JUDAISM	6	2 610	3 141*	0.1	0.2
281 LUTH CH AMER..	32	7 205	9 464	0.3	0.5
283 LUTH--MO SYNOD	22	4 049	5 326	0.1	0.3
285 MENNONITE CH..	14	277	346*	—	—
287 MENN GEN CONF.	1	16	32	—	—
290 METRO COMM CHS	1	83	166	—	—
291 MISSIONARY CH.	2	122	115	—	—
323 OLD ORD AMISH.	5	650	790*	—	—
329 OPEN BIBLE STD	2	126	275	—	—
349 PENT HOLINESS.	4	207	252*	—	—
353 CHR BRETHREN..	1	10	10	—	—
356 PRESB CH AMER.	5	345	397	—	—
357 PRESB CH US...	209	20 520	24 909*	0.7	1.3
371 REF CH IN AM..	3	157	436	—	—
381 REF PRES-EVAN.	1	15	21	—	—
403 SALVATION ARMY	16	1 472	2 476	0.1	0.1
409 SEPARATE BAPT.	51	5 666	6 861*	0.2	0.3
413 S.D.A.........	49	4 353	5 285*	0.1	0.3
419 SO BAPT CONV..	2 194	728 748	888 198*	24.3	44.8
435 UNITARIAN-UNIV	7	626	753*	—	—
443 UN C OF CHRIST	34	11 787	14 291*	0.4	0.7
449 UN METHODIST..	1 109	194 143	235 801*	6.4	11.9
453 UN PRES CH USA	212	21 110	25 636*	0.7	1.3
469 WELS.........	1	36	70	—	—
LOUISIANA	3 960	871 175	2 413 059*	57.4	100.0
001 ADVENT CHR CH.	1	30	37*	—	—
005 AME ZION......	20	8 463	10 369	0.2	0.4
017 AMER BAPT ASSN	85	15 140	15 140	0.4	0.6
019 AMER BAPT USA.	3	915	1 125*	—	—
029 AMER LUTH CH..	7	1 691	2 184	0.1	0.1
053 ASSEMB OF GOD.	186	18 183	29 975	0.7	1.2
059 BAPT MISS ASSN	51	8 978	11 067	0.3	0.5
081 CATHOLIC......	589	NA	1 304 084	31.0	54.0
089 CHR & MISS AL.	1	38	73	—	—
093 CHR CH (DISC).	25	4 115	5 667	0.1	0.2
097 CHR CHS&CHS CR	29	2 598	3 221*	0.1	0.1
101 C.M.E........	123	21 943	27 056*	0.6	1.1

County and Denomination	Number of churches	Communicant, confirmed, full members	Total adherents Number	Percent of total population	Percent of total adherents
121 CH GOD (ABR)..	4	218	273*	—	—
123 CH GOD (ANDER)	63	3 236	9 708	0.2	0.4
127 CH GOD (CLEVE)	68	4 637	5 750*	0.1	0.2
143 CG IN CR(MENN)	2	275	275	—	—
151 L-D SAINTS....	45	NA	11 581	0.3	0.5
157 CH OF BRETHREN	1	95	119*	—	—
165 CH OF NAZARENE	57	3 378	5 729	0.1	0.2
167 CHS OF CHRIST.	226	17 513	22 931	0.5	1.0
185 CUMBER PRESB..	7	442	779	—	—
193 EPISCOPAL.....	96	29 660	38 554	0.9	1.6
208 EVAN LUTH ASSN	3	960	1 272	—	0.1
215 EVAN METH CH..	3	137	171*	—	—
217 FIRE BAPTIZED.	1	2	2*	—	—
221 FREE METHODIST	14	492	1 722	—	0.1
226 FRIENDS-USA...	2	39	47*	—	—
263 INT FOURSQ GOS	2	224	277*	—	—
270 CONSRV JUDAISM	3	448	552*	—	—
271 REFORM JUDAISM	13	6 704	8 217*	0.2	0.3
281 LUTH CH AMER..	8	1 632	2 305	0.1	0.1
283 LUTH--MO SYNOD	58	15 237	20 429	0.5	0.8
285 MENNONITE CH..	1	95	120*	—	—
290 METRO COMM CHS	1	53	120	—	—
313 N AM BAPT CONF	1	68	85*	—	—
349 PENT HOLINESS.	2	125	154*	—	—
353 CHR BRETHREN..	6	310	330	—	—
356 PRESB CH AMER.	12	1 270	1 549	—	0.1
357 PRESB CH US...	129	25 733	31 717*	0.8	1.3
381 REF PRES-EVAN.	1	30	45	—	—
403 SALVATION ARMY	8	1 016	2 400	0.1	0.1
413 S.D.A.........	45	6 321	7 811*	0.2	0.3
419 SO BAPT CONV..	1 316	526 557	652 246*	15.5	27.0
421 SO METHODIST..	20	969	1 239	—	0.1
435 UNITARIAN-UNIV	7	724	885*	—	—
443 UN C OF CHRIST	18	2 899	3 545*	0.1	0.1
449 UN METHODIST..	590	136 971	169 328*	4.0	7.0
453 UN PRES CH USA	4	420	517*	—	—
469 WELS.........	3	191	277	—	—
MAINE	1 290	137 978	461 335*	41.0	100.0
001 ADVENT CHR CH.	30	2 298	2 789*	0.2	0.6
005 AME ZION......	1	209	254	—	0.1
017 AMER BAPT ASSN	1	20	20	—	—
019 AMER BAPT USA.	198	31 180	37 804*	3.4	8.2
029 AMER LUTH CH..	6	1 001	1 453	0.1	0.3
053 ASSEMB OF GOD.	36	2 506	4 266	0.4	0.9
057 BAPT GEN CONF.	2	188	232*	—	0.1
059 BAPT MISS ASSN	1	30	36*	—	—
081 CATHOLIC......	237	NA	275 876	24.5	59.8
083 CHRIST CATH CH	1	28	37	—	—
089 CHR & MISS AL.	10	497	1 030	0.1	0.2
093 CHR CH (DISC).	1	115	155	—	—
097 CHR CHS&CHS CR	2	55	66*	—	—
127 CH GOD (CLEVE)	26	1 091	1 323*	0.1	0.3
151 L-D SAINTS....	18	NA	4 449	0.4	1.0
165 CH OF NAZARENE	54	3 575	9 501	0.8	2.1
167 CHS OF CHRIST.	24	799	1 017	0.1	0.2
175 CONGR CHR CHS.	23	3 686	4 448*	0.4	1.0
179 CONSRV BAPT...	34	6 222	7 534*	0.7	1.6
181 CONSRV CONGR..	5	413	498*	—	0.1
193 EPISCOPAL.....	70	13 926	22 174	2.0	4.8
201 EVAN COV CH AM	3	213	260*	—	0.1
203 EVAN FREE CH..	2	158	191*	—	—
208 EVAN LUTH ASSN	1	185	251	—	0.1
221 FREE METHODIST	2	58	201	—	—
226 FRIENDS-USA...	14	606	731*	0.1	0.2
239 SWEDENBORGIAN.	3	180	219*	—	—
263 INT FOURSQ GOS	4	207	252*	—	0.1
270 CONSRV JUDAISM	2	462	556*	—	0.1
283 LUTH--MO SYNOD	2	278	369	—	0.1
285 MENNONITE CH..	1	9	11*	—	—
290 METRO COMM CHS	0	15	30	—	—
335 ORTH PRESB CH.	7	377	454*	—	0.1
353 CHR BRETHREN..	6	150	235	—	0.1
403 SALVATION ARMY	10	959	2 469	0.2	0.5
413 S.D.A.........	26	2 288	2 765*	0.2	0.6
419 SO BAPT CONV..	4	644	779*	0.1	0.2
435 UNITARIAN-UNIV	35	4 203	5 084*	0.5	1.1
443 UN C OF CHRIST	178	27 416	33 078*	2.9	7.2
449 UN METHODIST..	202	31 226	37 824*	3.4	8.2
453 UN PRES CH USA	8	505	614*	0.1	0.1
MARYLAND	3 107	744 742	1 695 948*	40.2	100.0
001 ADVENT CHR CH.	2	88	107*	—	—
005 AME ZION......	16	8 154	10 434	0.2	0.6
017 AMER BAPT ASSN	6	701	701	—	—
019 AMER BAPT USA.	52	28 760	34 564*	0.8	2.0
029 AMER LUTH CH..	46	16 322	24 629	0.6	1.5

NA—Not applicable *Total adherents estimated from known number of communicant, confirmed, full members. —Represents a percent less than 0.1. Percentages may not total due to rounding.

Table 3. Churches and Church Membership by State and Denomination: 1980

County and Denomination	Number of churches	Communicant, confirmed, full members	Total adherents: Number	Total adherents: Percent of total population	Total adherents: Percent of total adherents
039 AP CHR CH(NAZ)	1	37	45*	–	–
049 ARMEN AP CH AM	1	150	450	–	–
053 ASSEMB OF GOD.	86	8 557	15 881	0.4	0.9
061 BEACHY AMISH..	2	67	79*	–	–
071 BRETHREN (ASH)	4	628	750*	–	–
075 BRETHREN IN CR	4	328	528	–	–
081 CATHOLIC......	292	NA	736 361	17.5	43.4
089 CHR & MISS AL.	14	723	1 371	–	0.1
093 CHR CH (DISC).	36	5 738	8 132	0.2	0.5
097 CHR CHS&CHS CR	27	4 265	5 146*	0.1	0.3
101 C.M.E.........	4	1 527	1 837*	–	0.1
105 CHRISTIAN REF.	1	107	176	–	–
123 CH GOD (ANDER)	17	1 450	4 350	0.1	0.3
127 CH GOD (CLEVE)	85	8 103	9 701*	0.2	0.6
151 L-D SAINTS....	38	NA	13 484	0.3	0.8
157 CH OF BRETHREN	66	11 309	13 648*	0.3	0.8
165 CH OF NAZARENE	36	3 991	8 180	0.2	0.5
167 CHS OF CHRIST.	33	4 057	5 016	0.1	0.3
175 CONGR CHR CHS.	2	281	336*	–	–
181 CONSRV CONGR..	1	43	51*	–	–
193 EPISCOPAL.....	159	50 168	71 699	1.7	4.2
195 ESTONIAN ELC..	2	207	427	–	–
201 EVAN COV CH AM	2	142	172*	–	–
203 EVAN FREE CH..	1	15	18*	–	–
215 EVAN METH CH..	1	26	31*	–	–
221 FREE METHODIST	10	437	2 022	–	0.1
226 FRIENDS-USA...	14	1 624	1 942*	–	0.1
233 GEN CH NEW JER	1	25	30*	–	–
239 SWEDENBORGIAN.	1	60	72*	–	–
244 GRACE BRETHREN	9	2 012	2 410*	0.1	0.1
263 INT FOURSQ GOS	5	288	351*	–	–
270 CONSRV JUDAISM	22	7 945	9 468*	0.2	0.6
271 REFORM JUDAISM	13	11 052	13 228*	0.3	0.8
274 LAT EVAN LUTH.	1	453	530	–	–
281 LUTH CH AMER..	164	69 472	95 710	2.3	5.6
283 LUTH--MO SYNOD	65	22 227	30 883	0.7	1.8
285 MENNONITE CH..	48	2 782	3 343*	0.1	0.2
287 MENN GEN CONF.	1	102	102	–	–
290 METRO COMM CHS	2	110	220	–	–
291 MISSIONARY CH.	2	58	87	–	–
293 MORAV CH-NORTH	3	644	875	–	0.1
323 OLD ORD AMISH.	4	520	647*	–	–
329 OPEN BIBLE STD	2	85	115	–	–
335 ORTH PRESB CH.	5	434	519*	–	–
349 PENT HOLINESS.	10	816	969*	–	0.1
353 CHR BRETHREN..	17	890	1 245	–	0.1
356 PRESB CH AMER.	4	1 241	1 373	–	0.1
357 PRESB CH US...	46	6 218	7 482*	0.2	0.4
375 REF EPISCOPAL.	4	806	954*	–	0.1
381 REF PRES-EVAN.	15	2 427	3 329	0.1	0.2
403 SALVATION ARMY	13	1 726	4 518	0.1	0.3
413 S.D.A.........	72	15 620	18 711*	0.4	1.1
415 S-D BAPTIST GC	1	12	15*	–	–
419 SO BAPT CONV..	268	106 498	128 411*	3.0	7.6
435 UNITARIAN-UNIV	17	3 338	3 982*	0.1	0.2
443 UN C OF CHRIST	78	21 006	25 207*	0.6	1.5
449 UN METHODIST..	1 011	268 821	322 099*	7.6	19.0
453 UN PRES CH USA	140	38 870	46 527*	1.1	2.7
469 WELS..........	2	179	268	–	–
MASSACHUSETTS	2 945	516 218	3 709 251*	64.7	100.0
001 ADVENT CHR CH.	15	1 212	1 451*	–	–
005 AME ZION......	20	8 644	10 684	0.2	0.3
017 AMER BAPT ASSN	1	160	160	–	–
019 AMER BAPT USA.	256	63 835	75 749*	1.3	2.0
029 AMER LUTH CH..	7	804	1 204	–	–
049 ARMEN AP CH AM	5	711	1 620	–	–
053 ASSEMB OF GOD.	73	7 500	13 938	0.2	0.4
057 BAPT GEN CONF.	26	3 730	4 469*	0.1	0.1
081 CATHOLIC......	821	NA	3 040 435	53.0	82.0
083 CHRIST CATH CH	1	13	13	–	–
089 CHR & MISS AL.	16	1 174	2 084	–	0.1
093 CHR CH (DISC).	4	311	475	–	–
097 CHR CHS&CHS CR	11	105	124*	–	–
101 C.M.E.........	1	285	341*	–	–
105 CHRISTIAN REF.	3	836	1 266	–	–
123 CH GOD (ANDER)	4	212	636	–	–
127 CH GOD (CLEVE)	23	1 288	1 519*	–	–
151 L-D SAINTS....	21	NA	6 618	0.1	0.2
165 CH OF NAZARENE	38	3 722	7 838	0.1	0.2
167 CHS OF CHRIST.	33	1 797	2 507	–	0.1
175 CONGR CHR CHS.	29	10 263	12 158*	0.2	0.3
181 CONSRV CONGR..	19	5 055	5 943*	0.1	0.2
193 EPISCOPAL.....	249	96 847	141 060	2.5	3.8
201 EVAN COV CH AM	15	2 994	3 574*	0.1	0.1
203 EVAN FREE CH..	5	489	577*	–	–
208 EVAN LUTH ASSN	14	2 933	3 895	0.1	0.1
209 EVAN LUTH SYN.	2	145	184	–	–
220 FREE LUTHERAN.	1	17	19	–	–
221 FREE METHODIST	7	215	630	–	–
226 FRIENDS-USA...	21	1 818	2 153*	–	0.1
239 SWEDENBORGIAN.	7	460	550*	–	–
247 HOLINESS CH...	1	20	23	–	–
263 INT FOURSQ GOS	1	32	39*	–	–
270 CONSRV JUDAISM	50	11 789	13 994*	0.2	0.4
271 REFORM JUDAISM	32	22 224	26 281*	0.5	0.7
274 LAT EVAN LUTH.	3	1 080	1 253	–	–
281 LUTH CH AMER..	49	19 446	25 403	0.4	0.7
283 LUTH--MO SYNOD	24	5 878	7 826	0.1	0.2
285 MENNONITE CH..	1	43	51*	–	–
287 MENN GEN CONF.	1	40	50	–	–
290 METRO COMM CHS	2	199	398	–	–
335 ORTH PRESB CH.	3	145	172*	–	–
349 PENT HOLINESS.	1	47	55*	–	–
353 CHR BRETHREN..	19	995	1 445	–	–
363 PRIMITIVE METH	7	894	1 064*	–	–
383 REF PRES OF NA	1	32	41	–	–
395 ROMANIAN OR CH	2	1 640	1 967*	–	0.1
403 SALVATION ARMY	34	3 387	11 053	0.2	0.3
413 S.D.A.........	48	7 031	8 356*	0.1	0.2
419 SO BAPT CONV..	15	2 420	2 865*	–	0.1
423 SYRIAN ANTIOCH	1	1 500	1 799*	–	–
435 UNITARIAN-UNIV	161	24 646	29 292*	0.5	0.8
443 UN C OF CHRIST	451	126 007	149 739*	2.6	4.0
449 UN METHODIST..	256	63 623	75 653*	1.3	2.0
453 UN PRES CH USA	33	5 434	6 442*	0.1	0.2
469 WELS..........	1	91	116	–	–
MICHIGAN	6 595	1 390 586	3 952 916*	42.7	100.0
001 ADVENT CHR CH.	2	180	216*	–	–
005 AME ZION......	15	38 494	46 205	0.5	1.2
017 AMER BAPT ASSN	12	1 225	1 225	–	–
019 AMER BAPT USA.	178	59 605	72 712*	0.8	1.8
029 AMER LUTH CH..	147	54 212	74 092	0.8	1.9
039 AP CHR CH(NAZ)	2	78	94*	–	–
045 APOSTOLIC LUTH	17	2 254	2 669*	–	0.1
049 ARMEN AP CH AM	1	480	1 180	–	–
053 ASSEMB OF GOD.	257	25 631	45 959	0.5	1.2
057 BAPT GEN CONF.	51	8 276	10 074*	0.1	0.3
059 BAPT MISS ASSN	20	1 973	2 426*	–	0.1
061 BEACHY AMISH..	1	36	44*	–	–
071 BRETHREN (ASH)	1	23	28*	–	–
075 BRETHREN IN CR	8	344	584	–	–
081 CATHOLIC......	967	NA	2 043 483	22.1	51.7
089 CHR & MISS AL.	30	1 951	3 500	–	0.1
093 CHR CH (DISC).	44	8 531	12 271	0.1	0.3
097 CHR CHS&CHS CR	110	18 674	22 903*	0.2	0.6
105 CHRISTIAN REF.	230	60 712	96 740	1.0	2.4
121 CH GOD (ABR)..	6	541	656*	–	–
123 CH GOD (ANDER)	127	12 377	37 149	0.4	0.9
127 CH GOD (CLEVE)	122	12 037	14 739*	0.2	0.4
133 CH GOD(7TH)DEN	12	231	287*	–	–
143 CG IN CR(MENN)	3	313	313	–	–
149 CH OF JC (BIC)	6	385	397	–	–
151 L-D SAINTS....	75	NA	18 635	0.2	0.5
157 CH OF BRETHREN	24	2 253	2 741*	–	0.1
164 CH LUTH CONF..	6	790	1 138	–	–
165 CH OF NAZARENE	200	18 993	36 146	0.4	0.9
167 CHS OF CHRIST.	213	23 919	30 537	0.3	0.8
175 CONGR CHR CHS.	49	16 393	19 988*	0.2	0.5
179 CONSRV BAPT...	58	1 102	1 345*	–	–
181 CONSRV CONGR..	15	1 739	2 150*	–	0.1
185 CUMBER PRESB..	3	190	527	–	–
193 EPISCOPAL.....	256	75 215	100 078	1.1	2.5
195 ESTONIAN ELC..	1	72	123	–	–
197 EVAN CH OF NA.	2	110	110	–	–
201 EVAN COV CH AM	35	4 270	5 190*	0.1	0.1
203 EVAN FREE CH..	13	1 154	1 415*	–	–
208 EVAN LUTH ASSN	20	7 526	9 927	0.1	0.3
209 EVAN LUTH SYN.	6	523	744	–	–
211 EVAN MENN BR..	1	45	59	–	–
213 EVAN MENN INC.	3	168	209*	–	–
215 EVAN METH CH..	1	62	75*	–	–
220 FREE LUTHERAN.	6	426	585	–	–
221 FREE METHODIST	149	8 692	33 963	0.4	0.9
226 FRIENDS-USA...	19	1 811	2 198*	–	0.1
233 GEN CH NEW JER	1	60	73*	–	–
239 SWEDENBORGIAN.	1	60	73*	–	–
244 GRACE BRETHREN	8	522	638*	–	–
263 INT FOURSQ GOS	9	635	771*	–	–
270 CONSRV JUDAISM	18	5 691	6 900*	0.1	0.2
271 REFORM JUDAISM	18	11 342	13 775*	0.1	0.3
274 LAT EVAN LUTH.	7	1 894	2 147	–	0.1
281 LUTH CH AMER..	215	70 051	95 101	1.0	2.4
283 LUTH--MO SYNOD	384	191 466	258 937	2.8	6.6

NA—Not applicable *Total adherents estimated from known number of communicant, confirmed, full members. —Represents a percent less than 0.1. Percentages may not total due to rounding.

STATE SUMMARY

Table 3. Churches and Church Membership by State and Denomination: 1980

County and Denomination	Number of churches	Communicant, confirmed, full members	Total adherents Number	Percent of total population	Percent of total adherents
285 MENNONITE CH..	46	2 263	2 777*	–	0.1
287 MENN GEN CONF.	4	167	187	–	–
290 METRO COMM CHS	2	292	584	–	–
291 MISSIONARY CH..	64	4 233	7 135	0.1	0.2
293 MORAV CH-NORTH	3	677	886	–	–
313 N AM BAPT CONF	21	6 408	7 813*	0.1	0.2
323 OLD ORD AMISH.	12	1 560	1 912*	–	–
329 OPEN BIBLE STD	2	300	325	–	–
335 ORTH PRESB CH.	3	175	213*	–	–
349 PENT HOLINESS.	3	153	188*	–	–
353 CHR BRETHREN..	48	3 055	4 140	–	0.1
367 PROT CONF (WI)	1	100	150	–	–
369 PROT REF CHS..	8	1 434	2 503	–	0.1
371 REF CH IN AM..	160	50 811	83 904	0.9	2.1
381 REF PRES-EVAN.	2	176	260	–	–
383 REF PRES OF NA	3	91	122	–	–
395 ROMANIAN OR CH	2	3 005	3 638*	–	0.1
403 SALVATION ARMY	55	8 620	22 472	0.2	0.6
413 S.D.A.........	181	26 944	32 975*	0.4	0.8
415 S-D BAPT GC	2	292	357*	–	–
417 SOCIAL BRETH..	3	330	400*	–	–
419 SO BAPT CONV..	186	44 662	54 586*	0.6	1.4
423 SYRIAN ANTIOCH	2	2 100	2 543*	–	0.1
431 UKRANIAN AMER.	2	280	415	–	–
435 UNITARIAN-UNIV	26	3 271	3 966*	–	0.1
443 UN C OF CHRIST	203	70 450	85 917*	0.9	2.2
449 UN METHODIST..	945	237 728	290 570*	3.1	7.4
453 UN PRES CH USA	285	128 018	156 233*	1.7	4.0
469 WELS.........	136	37 254	49 501	0.5	1.3
MINNESOTA	4 818	1 210 803	2 653 161*	65.1	100.0
001 ADVENT CHR CH.	1	104	123*	–	–
017 AMER BAPT ASSN	1	10	10	–	–
019 AMER BAPT USA.	41	13 042	15 566*	0.4	0.6
029 AMER LUTH CH..	813	366 679	490 324	12.0	18.5
039 AP CHR CH(NAZ)	1	6	8*	–	–
045 APOSTOLIC LUTH	14	1 650	1 993*	–	0.1
053 ASSEMB OF GOD.	147	12 647	24 393	0.6	0.9
057 BAPT GEN CONF.	137	23 527	28 478*	0.7	1.1
061 BEACHY AMISH..	1	54	66*	–	–
063 BEREAN FUND CH	1	67	82*	–	–
081 CATHOLIC......	798	NA	1 041 781	25.6	39.3
089 CHR & MISS AL.	57	3 364	8 137	0.2	0.3
093 CHR CH (DISC).	10	1 893	2 749	0.1	0.1
097 CHR CHS&CHS CR	52	5 568	6 758*	0.2	0.3
101 C.M.E.........	1	380	449*	–	–
105 CHRISTIAN REF.	30	5 323	8 800	0.2	0.3
121 CH GOD (ABR)..	5	286	347*	–	–
123 CH GOD (ANDER)	9	551	1 653	–	0.1
127 CH GOD (CLEVE)	9	508	607*	–	–
133 CH GOD(7TH)DEN	1	40	48*	–	–
151 L-D SAINTS....	37	NA	9 700	0.2	0.4
157 CH OF BRETHREN	3	401	484*	–	–
163 CH OF LUTH BR.	27	1 739	2 600	0.1	0.1
164 CH LUTH CONF..	16	2 294	3 054	0.1	0.1
165 CH OF NAZARENE	37	2 428	4 786	0.1	0.2
167 CHS OF CHRIST.	32	1 269	1 861	–	0.1
175 CONGR CHR CHS.	5	3 560	4 259*	0.1	0.2
179 CONSRV BAPT...	45	5 720	6 906*	0.2	0.3
181 CONSRV CONGR..	9	1 044	1 268*	–	–
193 EPISCOPAL.....	131	28 481	38 868	1.0	1.5
195 ESTONIAN ELC..	1	78	137	–	–
197 EVAN CH OF NA.	8	308	308	–	–
201 EVAN COV CH AM	100	14 710	17 775*	0.4	0.7
203 EVAN FREE CH..	100	7 923	9 567*	0.2	0.4
208 EVAN LUTH ASSN	13	6 588	9 376	0.2	0.4
209 EVAN LUTH SYN.	32	5 130	6 875	0.2	0.3
211 EVAN MENN BR..	2	310	403	–	–
220 FREE LUTHERAN.	60	6 000	7 112	0.2	0.3
221 FREE METHODIST	14	376	1 461	–	0.1
226 FRIENDS-USA...	4	345	409*	–	–
237 GC MENN BR CHS	3	423	517*	–	–
239 SWEDENBORGIAN.	1	60	72*	–	–
244 GRACE BRETHREN	1	22	26*	–	–
263 INT FOURSQ GOS	3	167	200*	–	–
270 CONSRV JUDAISM	9	2 182	2 596*	0.1	0.1
271 REFORM JUDAISM	4	5 514	6 551*	0.2	0.2
281 LUTH CH AMER..	394	209 940	288 686	7.1	10.9
283 LUTH--MO SYNOD	436	167 321	220 316	5.4	8.3
285 MENNONITE CH..	15	338	412*	–	–
287 MENN GEN CONF.	7	1 517	1 774	–	0.1
290 METRO COMM CHS	2	103	220	–	–
293 MORAV CH-NORTH	6	1 067	1 301	–	–
313 N AM BAPT CONF	12	1 562	1 898*	–	0.1
323 OLD ORD AMISH.	5	650	804*	–	–
329 OPEN BIBLE STD	2	220	350	–	–
353 CHR BRETHREN..	12	680	780	–	–
367 PROT CONF (WI)	1	150	200	–	–
369 PROT REF CHS..	1	54	113	–	–
371 REF CH IN AM..	22	4 997	8 382	0.2	0.3
383 REF PRES OF NA	1	23	27	–	–
403 SALVATION ARMY	24	2 732	7 344	0.2	0.3
413 S.D.A.........	67	5 489	6 633*	0.2	0.3
415 S-D BAPTIST GC	1	135	168*	–	–
419 SO BAPT CONV..	20	2 095	2 547*	0.1	0.1
435 UNITARIAN-UNIV	21	3 048	3 640*	0.1	0.1
443 UN C OF CHRIST	154	45 371	54 787*	1.3	2.1
449 UN METHODIST..	439	120 941	146 422*	3.6	5.5
453 UN PRES CH USA	204	63 765	76 853*	1.9	2.9
469 WELS.........	146	45 834	59 961	1.5	2.3
MISSISSIPPI	5 395	1 026 216	1 387 371*	55.0	100.0
001 ADVENT CHR CH.	3	125	156*	–	–
005 AME ZION......	47	9 740	12 043	0.5	0.9
017 AMER BAPT ASSN	38	4 072	4 072	0.2	0.3
019 AMER BAPT USA.	3	700	887*	–	0.1
029 AMER LUTH CH..	2	156	216	–	–
053 ASSEMB OF GOD.	150	11 303	17 805	0.7	1.3
055 AS REF PRES CH	7	793	867	–	0.1
059 BAPT MISS ASSN	190	29 110	36 016*	1.4	2.6
081 CATHOLIC......	158	NA	95 096	3.8	6.9
089 CHR & MISS AL.	3	34	118	–	–
093 CHR CH (DISC).	52	4 698	6 716	0.3	0.5
097 CHR CHS&CHS CR	30	3 228	3 993*	0.2	0.3
101 C.M.E.........	227	37 874	47 209	1.9	3.4
105 CHRISTIAN REF.	1	28	48	–	–
123 CH GOD (ANDER)	61	2 522	7 566	0.3	0.5
127 CH GOD (CLEVE)	159	9 949	12 422*	0.5	0.9
143 CG IN CR(MENN)	6	648	648	–	–
151 L-D SAINTS....	34	NA	7 683	0.3	0.6
165 CH OF NAZARENE	52	3 618	5 656	0.2	0.4
167 CHS OF CHRIST.	347	26 483	34 148	1.4	2.5
185 CUMBER PRESB..	19	968	1 561	0.1	0.1
193 EPISCOPAL.....	82	15 973	20 098	0.8	1.4
197 EVAN CH OF NA.	1	16	16	–	–
208 EVAN LUTH ASSN	2	31	43	–	–
215 EVAN METH CH..	2	152	187*	–	–
239 SWEDENBORGIAN.	1	60	74*	–	–
263 INT FOURSQ GOS	7	440	545*	–	–
271 REFORM JUDAISM	12	1 658	2 075*	0.1	0.1
274 LAT EVAN LUTH.	1	30	32	–	–
281 LUTH CH AMER..	11	1 079	1 381	0.1	0.1
283 LUTH--MO SYNOD	28	3 110	4 344	0.2	0.3
285 MENNONITE CH..	13	497	623*	–	–
290 METRO COMM CHS	0	10	20	–	–
349 PENT HOLINESS.	17	1 052	1 307*	0.1	0.1
353 CHR BRETHREN..	4	75	75	–	–
356 PRESB CH AMER.	106	12 880	14 160	0.6	1.0
357 PRESB CH US...	139	21 164	26 257*	1.0	1.9
403 SALVATION ARMY	14	1 405	2 544	0.1	0.2
413 S.D.A.........	54	4 580	5 702*	0.2	0.4
415 S-D BAPTIST GC	1	13	16*	–	–
419 SO BAPT CONV..	1 915	612 517	760 385*	30.2	54.8
421 SO METHODIST..	11	491	632	–	–
435 UNITARIAN-UNIV	7	232	284*	–	–
443 UN C OF CHRIST	1	47	58*	–	–
449 UN METHODIST..	1 354	201 575	250 240*	9.9	18.0
453 UN PRES CH USA	23	1 080	1 347*	0.1	0.1
MISSOURI	7 571	1 418 794	2 634 435*	53.6	100.0
001 ADVENT CHR CH.	3	119	144*	–	–
005 AME ZION......	8	4 204	5 134	0.1	0.2
017 AMER BAPT ASSN	19	1 578	1 578	–	0.1
019 AMER BAPT USA.	17	11 365	13 564*	0.3	0.5
029 AMER LUTH CH..	29	5 000	6 485	0.1	0.2
039 AP CHR CH(NAZ)	1	23	28*	–	–
053 ASSEMB OF GOD.	494	40 620	77 158	1.6	2.9
055 AS REF PRES CH	3	112	124	–	–
057 BAPT GEN CONF.	4	407	493*	–	–
059 BAPT MISS ASSN	99	9 197	11 259*	0.2	0.4
061 BEACHY AMISH..	3	70	83*	–	–
081 CATHOLIC......	573	NA	800 228	16.3	30.4
089 CHR & MISS AL.	3	93	197	–	–
093 CHR CH (DISC).	415	78 118	116 875	2.4	4.4
097 CHR CHS&CHS CR	369	48 267	58 029*	1.2	2.2
101 C.M.E.........	13	6 256	7 482*	0.2	0.3
105 CHRISTIAN REF.	3	169	284	–	–
107 CHRISTIAN UN..	22	888	1 889	–	0.1
121 CH GOD (ABR)..	7	322	389*	–	–
123 CH GOD (ANDER)	87	6 377	19 122	0.4	0.7
127 CH GOD (CLEVE)	82	4 955	6 030*	0.1	0.2
133 CH GOD(7TH)DEN	5	184	220*	–	–
143 CG IN CR(MENN)	3	299	299	–	–
151 L-D SAINTS....	68	NA	18 908	0.4	0.7
157 CH OF BRETHREN	22	1 207	1 454*	–	0.1

NA—Not applicable *Total adherents estimated from known number of communicant, confirmed, full members. —Represents a percent less than 0.1. Percentages may not total due to rounding.

Table 3. Churches and Church Membership by State and Denomination: 1980

County and Denomination	Number of churches	Communicant, confirmed, full members	Total adherents Number	Percent of total population	Percent of total adherents
164 CH LUTH CONF..	1	50	74	–	–
165 CH OF NAZARENE	175	15 223	28 845	0.6	1.1
167 CHS OF CHRIST.	543	38 334	49 444	1.0	1.9
175 CONGR CHR CHS.	2	374	451*	–	–
185 CUMBER PRESB..	50	1 756	3 286	0.1	0.1
193 EPISCOPAL.....	103	26 180	35 939	0.7	1.4
197 EVAN CH OF NA.	5	229	229	–	–
201 EVAN COV CH AM	6	296	358*	–	–
203 EVAN FREE CH..	3	164	194*	–	–
208 EVAN LUTH ASSN	22	7 391	9 521	0.2	0.4
209 EVAN LUTH SYN.	1	36	44	–	–
215 EVAN METH CH..	2	441	552*	–	–
217 FIRE BAPTIZED.	14	246	298*	–	–
221 FREE METHODIST	20	465	2 009	–	0.1
226 FRIENDS-USA...	7	336	406*	–	–
239 SWEDENBORGIAN.	1	60	72*	–	–
244 GRACE BRETHREN	1	16	19*	–	–
263 INT FOURSQ GOS	14	1 909	2 292*	–	0.1
270 CONSRV JUDAISM	5	2 680	3 220*	0.1	0.1
271 REFORM JUDAISM	14	14 964	17 964*	0.4	0.7
274 LAT EVAN LUTH.	1	18	18	–	–
281 LUTH CH AMER..	35	10 247	13 099	0.3	0.5
283 LUTH--MO SYNOD	295	110 360	144 829	2.9	5.5
285 MENNONITE CH..	17	1 053	1 281*	–	–
287 MENN GEN CONF.	2	169	259	–	–
290 METRO COMM CHS	5	528	1 056	–	–
313 N AM BAPT CONF	2	190	228*	–	–
323 OLD ORD AMISH.	22	2 860	3 483*	0.1	0.1
329 OPEN BIBLE STD	3	255	360	–	–
349 PENT HOLINESS.	26	1 087	1 324*	–	0.1
353 CHR BRETHREN..	20	1 110	1 515	–	0.1
357 PRESB CH US...	264	31 761	38 254*	0.8	1.5
375 REF EPISCOPAL.	1	32	39*	–	–
381 REF PRES-EVAN.	11	1 196	1 558	–	0.1
403 SALVATION ARMY	23	2 932	10 147	0.2	0.4
413 S.D.A.........	77	9 357	11 264*	0.2	0.4
415 S-D BAPTIST GC	1	14	17*	–	–
419 SO BAPT CONV..	1 813	580 041	700 053*	14.2	26.6
435 UNITARIAN-UNIV	8	1 601	1 915*	–	0.1
443 UN C OF CHRIST	185	60 954	73 533*	1.5	2.8
449 UN METHODIST..	1 103	224 695	270 469*	5.5	10.3
453 UN PRES CH USA	307	46 726	56 176*	1.1	2.1
469 WELS..........	9	622	885	–	–
MONTANA	1 273	131 981	348 301*	44.3	100.0
017 AMER BAPT ASSN	8	500	500	0.1	0.1
019 AMER BAPT USA.	26	3 614	4 427*	0.6	1.3
029 AMER LUTH CH..	134	32 696	46 022	5.9	13.2
045 APOSTOLIC LUTH	1	20	24*	–	–
053 ASSEMB OF GOD.	73	5 739	10 866	1.4	3.1
057 BAPT GEN CONF.	3	394	478*	0.1	0.1
081 CATHOLIC......	229	NA	140 415	17.8	40.3
089 CHR & MISS AL.	32	1 387	3 424	0.4	1.0
093 CHR CH (DISC).	19	2 553	4 123	0.5	1.2
097 CHR CHS&CHS CR	20	1 987	2 439*	0.3	0.7
105 CHRISTIAN REF.	6	1 033	1 758	0.2	0.5
123 CH GOD (ANDER)	7	445	1 335	0.2	0.4
127 CH GOD (CLEVE)	15	517	627*	0.1	0.2
151 L-D SAINTS....	101	NA	26 035	3.3	7.5
157 CH OF BRETHREN	2	64	80*	–	–
163 CH OF LUTH BR.	4	168	283	–	0.1
164 CH LUTH CONF..	1	23	33	–	–
165 CH OF NAZARENE	24	1 368	2 770	0.4	0.8
167 CHS OF CHRIST.	38	1 721	2 189	0.3	0.6
175 CONGR CHR CHS.	4	175	212*	–	0.1
179 CONSRV BAPT...	4	332	406*	0.1	0.1
181 CONSRV CONGR..	1	27	33*	–	–
193 EPISCOPAL.....	46	5 103	8 279	1.1	2.4
197 EVAN CH OF NA.	20	1 599	1 599	0.2	0.5
201 EVAN COV CH AM	4	339	410*	0.1	0.1
203 EVAN FREE CH..	6	132	162*	–	–
211 EVAN MENN BR..	1	100	130	–	–
220 FREE LUTHERAN.	4	240	330	–	0.1
226 FRIENDS-USA...	1	11	13*	–	–
237 GC MENN BR CHS	3	190	237*	–	0.1
263 INT FOURSQ GOS	7	500	615*	0.1	0.2
271 REFORM JUDAISM	1	90	110*	–	–
281 LUTH CH AMER..	17	4 911	6 869	0.9	2.0
283 LUTH--MO SYNOD	58	11 757	16 149	2.1	4.6
285 MENNONITE CH..	4	204	251*	–	0.1
287 MENN GEN CONF.	7	461	551	0.1	0.2
290 METRO COMM CHS	0	20	40	–	–
313 N AM BAPT CONF	4	549	661*	0.1	0.2
329 OPEN BIBLE STD	4	330	640	0.1	0.2
335 ORTH PRESB CH.	3	56	69*	–	–
353 CHR BRETHREN..	6	170	215	–	0.1
371 REF CH IN AM..	1	97	217	–	0.1
403 SALVATION ARMY	8	582	1 237	0.2	0.4

County and Denomination	Number of churches	Communicant, confirmed, full members	Total adherents Number	Percent of total population	Percent of total adherents
413 S.D.A.........	37	2 941	3 571*	0.5	1.0
419 SO BAPT CONV..	46	6 954	8 515*	1.1	2.4
435 UNITARIAN-UNIV	5	188	227*	–	0.1
443 UN C OF CHRIST	41	7 576	9 268*	1.2	2.7
449 UN METHODIST..	121	20 287	24 767*	3.1	7.1
453 UN PRES CH USA	53	11 102	13 593*	1.7	3.9
469 WELS..........	13	729	1 097	0.1	0.3
NEBRASKA	2 604	503 490	992 303*	63.2	100.0
017 AMER BAPT ASSN	1	50	50	–	–
019 AMER BAPT USA.	72	14 973	18 072*	1.2	1.8
029 AMER LUTH CH..	115	37 509	49 169	3.1	5.0
053 ASSEMB OF GOD.	84	7 018	12 716	0.8	1.3
057 BAPT GEN CONF.	31	2 721	3 319*	0.2	0.3
063 BEREAN FUND CH	29	2 226	2 718*	0.2	0.3
071 BRETHREN (ASH)	2	75	89*	–	–
081 CATHOLIC......	382	NA	332 849	21.2	33.5
089 CHR & MISS AL.	15	1 863	3 574	0.2	0.4
093 CHR CH (DISC).	58	10 656	18 053	1.1	1.8
097 CHR CHS&CHS CR	83	11 713	14 200*	0.9	1.4
105 CHRISTIAN REF.	2	120	213	–	–
121 CH GOD (ABR)..	3	138	167*	–	–
123 CH GOD (ANDER)	24	992	2 976	0.2	0.3
127 CH GOD (CLEVE)	20	926	1 128*	0.1	0.1
133 CH GOD(7TH)DEN	3	20	25*	–	–
143 CG IN CR(MENN)	1	51	51	–	–
151 L-D SAINTS....	34	NA	6 971	0.4	0.7
157 CH OF BRETHREN	5	464	553*	–	0.1
164 CH LUTH CONF..	2	103	141	–	–
165 CH OF NAZARENE	44	2 437	5 382	0.3	0.5
167 CHS OF CHRIST.	51	3 709	5 343	0.3	0.5
175 CONGR CHR CHS.	7	1 187	1 423*	0.1	0.1
181 CONSRV CONGR..	4	912	1 119*	0.1	0.1
193 EPISCOPAL.....	72	11 557	15 286	1.0	1.5
197 EVAN CH OF NA.	1	38	38	–	–
201 EVAN COV CH AM	19	2 561	3 089*	0.2	0.3
203 EVAN FREE CH..	43	2 930	3 561*	0.2	0.4
208 EVAN LUTH ASSN	2	1 072	1 297	0.1	0.1
209 EVAN LUTH SYN.	4	305	411	–	–
211 EVAN MENN BR..	6	651	847	0.1	0.1
220 FREE LUTHERAN.	1	41	43	–	–
221 FREE METHODIST	9	235	870	0.1	0.1
226 FRIENDS-USA...	7	491	597*	–	0.1
237 GC MENN BR CHS	3	341	414*	–	–
244 GRACE BRETHREN	2	78	93*	–	–
263 INT FOURSQ GOS	12	1 701	2 059*	0.1	0.2
270 CONSRV JUDAISM	2	548	662*	–	0.1
271 REFORM JUDAISM	2	1 476	1 791*	0.1	0.2
274 LAT EVAN LUTH.	3	461	498	–	0.1
281 LUTH CH AMER..	163	62 116	81 941	5.2	8.3
283 LUTH--MO SYNOD	263	85 503	112 593	7.2	11.3
285 MENNONITE CH..	14	1 489	1 795*	0.1	0.2
287 MENN GEN CONF.	5	1 642	2 239	0.1	0.2
290 METRO COMM CHS	1	95	190	–	–
291 MISSIONARY CH.	8	269	390	–	–
313 N AM BAPT CONF	5	342	415*	–	–
329 OPEN BIBLE STD	8	350	625	–	0.1
335 ORTH PRESB CH.	2	73	87*	–	–
353 CHR BRETHREN..	5	220	275	–	–
356 PRESB CH AMER.	1	?	?	?	?
371 REF CH IN AM..	7	1 167	2 145	0.1	0.2
381 REF PRES-EVAN.	1	64	74	–	–
383 REF PRES OF NA	1	48	58	–	–
395 ROMANIAN OR CH	1	380	463*	–	–
403 SALVATION ARMY	10	1 667	5 711	0.4	0.6
413 S.D.A.........	61	6 694	8 062*	0.5	0.8
415 S-D BAPTIST GC	1	205	247*	–	–
419 SO BAPT CONV..	29	7 855	9 708*	0.6	1.0
431 UKRANIAN AMER.	2	240	320	–	–
435 UNITARIAN-UNIV	3	722	868*	0.1	0.1
443 UN C OF CHRIST	119	24 928	30 103*	1.9	3.0
449 UN METHODIST..	444	129 726	156 955*	10.0	15.8
453 UN PRES CH USA	155	48 451	58 702*	3.7	5.9
469 WELS..........	35	4 895	6 480	0.4	0.7
NEVADA	475	49 778	233 781*	29.3	100.0
019 AMER BAPT USA.	17	3 007	3 605*	0.5	1.5
029 AMER LUTH CH..	4	1 887	2 685	0.3	1.1
053 ASSEMB OF GOD.	28	2 194	7 163	0.9	3.1
059 BAPT MISS ASSN	1	65	79*	–	–
081 CATHOLIC......	72	NA	110 105	13.8	47.1
093 CHR CH (DISC).	3	763	986	0.1	0.4
097 CHR CHS&CHS CR	8	1 697	2 032*	0.3	0.9
123 CH GOD (ANDER)	4	267	801	0.1	0.3
127 CH GOD (CLEVE)	7	189	227*	–	0.1
133 CH GOD(7TH)DEN	1	8	10*	–	–
151 L-D SAINTS....	121	NA	55 148	6.9	23.6
165 CH OF NAZARENE	13	806	1 646	0.2	0.7

NA—Not applicable   *Total adherents estimated from known number of communicant, confirmed, full members.   —Represents a percent less than 0.1.   Percentages may not total due to rounding.

Table 3. Churches and Church Membership by State and Denomination: 1980

County and Denomination	Number of churches	Communicant, confirmed, full members	Total adherents			County and Denomination	Number of churches	Communicant, confirmed, full members	Total adherents		
			Number	Percent of total population	Percent of total adherents				Number	Percent of total population	Percent of total adherents
167 CHS OF CHRIST.	25	1 330	1 877	0.2	0.8	193 EPISCOPAL.....	308	102 970	146 990	2.0	3.7
193 EPISCOPAL.....	30	4 228	5 864	0.7	2.5	195 ESTONIAN ELC..	4	472	882	–	–
203 EVAN FREE CH..	2	182	214*	–	0.1	199 EVAN CONGR CH.	2	411	493*	–	–
						201 EVAN COV CH AM	4	504	604*	–	–
221 FREE METHODIST	1	8	39	–	–	203 EVAN FREE CH..	15	1 178	1 406*	–	–
226 FRIENDS-USA...	2	19	22*	–	–						
263 INT FOURSQ GOS	4	770	930*	0.1	0.4	208 EVAN LUTH ASSN	7	2 057	2 671	–	0.1
270 CONSRV JUDAISM	2	399	479*	0.1	0.2	221 FREE METHODIST	4	81	489	–	–
271 REFORM JUDAISM	2	620	746*	0.1	0.3	226 FRIENDS-USA...	35	3 895	4 700*	0.1	0.1
						233 GEN CH NEW JER	1	20	24*	–	–
281 LUTH CH AMER..	5	1 468	2 043	0.3	0.9	239 SWEDENBORGIAN.	1	60	72*	–	–
283 LUTH--MO SYNOD	16	3 421	5 020	0.6	2.1						
290 METRO COMM CHS	1	25	50	–	–	244 GRACE BRETHREN	2	124	150*	–	–
403 SALVATION ARMY	3	385	650	0.1	0.3	263 INT FOURSQ GOS	1	48	59*	–	–
413 S.D.A.........	12	1 640	1 963*	0.2	0.8	270 CONSRV JUDAISM	105	22 430	26 706*	0.4	0.7
						271 REFORM JUDAISM	45	32 032	38 196*	0.5	1.0
419 SO BAPT CONV..	44	13 499	16 276*	2.0	7.0	274 LAT EVAN LUTH.	1	137	153	–	–
435 UNITARIAN-UNIV	2	105	125*	–	0.1						
443 UN C OF CHRIST	3	514	617*	0.1	0.3	281 LUTH CH AMER..	179	62 723	88 739	1.2	2.2
449 UN METHODIST..	24	6 090	7 304*	0.9	3.1	283 LUTH--MO SYNOD	69	21 993	30 401	0.4	0.8
453 UN PRES CH USA	15	3 946	4 739*	0.6	2.0	285 MENNONITE CH..	8	256	308*	–	–
						290 METRO COMM CHS	2	72	144	–	–
469 WELS..........	3	246	336	–	0.1	293 MORAV CH-NORTH	4	953	1 162	–	–
NEW HAMPSHIRE	774	91 486	407 939*	44.3	100.0	313 N AM BAPT CONF	4	364	434*	–	–
						335 ORTH PRESB CH.	16	1 496	1 800*	–	–
001 ADVENT CHR CH.	20	1 309	1 574*	0.2	0.4	349 PENT HOLINESS.	1	68	80*	–	–
005 AME ZION......	1	50	87	–	–	353 CHR BRETHREN..	38	2 285	3 315	–	0.1
017 AMER BAPT ASSN	1	160	160	–	–	356 PRESB CH AMER.	2	163	200	–	–
019 AMER BAPT USA.	91	15 072	18 184*	2.0	4.5						
029 AMER LUTH CH..	4	385	609	0.1	0.1	363 PRIMITIVE METH	1	25	30*	–	–
						369 PROT REF CHS..	1	18	39	–	–
045 APOSTOLIC LUTH	1	600	730*	0.1	0.2	371 REF CH IN AM..	142	28 896	54 350	0.7	1.4
053 ASSEMB OF GOD.	22	1 502	2 846	0.3	0.7	375 REF EPISCOPAL.	7	552	658*	–	–
081 CATHOLIC......	170	NA	285 436	31.0	70.0	381 REF PRES-EVAN.	7	578	707	–	–
089 CHR & MISS AL.	4	180	302	–	0.1						
097 CHR CHS&CHS CR	6	320	384*	–	0.1	403 SALVATION ARMY	24	2 172	8 826	0.1	0.2
						413 S.D.A.........	70	7 767	9 321*	0.1	0.2
123 CH GOD (ANDER)	1	50	150	–	–	415 S-D BAPT GC	5	557	678*	–	–
127 CH GOD (CLEVE)	7	49	59*	–	–	419 SO BAPT CONV..	46	7 229	8 675*	0.1	0.2
151 L-D SAINTS....	12	NA	3 025	0.3	0.7	423 SYRIAN ANTIOCH	2	8 000	9 321*	0.1	0.2
165 CH OF NAZARENE	8	606	1 258	0.1	0.3						
167 CHS OF CHRIST.	16	603	909	0.1	0.2	431 UKRANIAN AMER.	1	170	210	–	–
						435 UNITARIAN-UNIV	20	3 676	4 375*	0.1	0.1
175 CONGR CHR CHS.	14	2 018	2 432*	0.3	0.6	443 UN C OF CHRIST	62	19 448	23 206*	0.3	0.6
179 CONSRV BAPT...	27	3 807	4 571*	0.5	1.1	449 UN METHODIST..	590	152 714	183 608*	2.5	4.6
193 EPISCOPAL.....	51	10 175	17 535	1.9	4.3	453 UN PRES CH USA	379	145 423	174 029*	2.4	4.4
201 EVAN COV CH AM	1	111	135*	–	–						
203 EVAN FREE CH..	1	47	56*	–	–	469 WELS..........	3	291	381	–	–
208 EVAN LUTH ASSN	1	102	155	–	–	NEW MEXICO	1 594	236 480	767 737*	59.1	100.0
221 FREE METHODIST	1	6	21	–	–						
226 FRIENDS-USA...	5	325	389*	–	0.1	001 ADVENT CHR CH.	1	153	192*	–	0.1
239 SWEDENBORGIAN.	1	60	73*	–	–	017 AMER BAPT ASSN	6	693	693	0.1	0.1
270 CONSRV JUDAISM	2	306	373*	–	0.1	019 AMER BAPT USA.	2	496	605*	–	0.1
						029 AMER LUTH CH..	6	1 466	2 098	0.2	0.3
271 REFORM JUDAISM	3	842	1 021*	0.1	0.3	053 ASSEMB OF GOD.	134	9 231	15 345	1.2	2.0
281 LUTH CH AMER..	4	937	1 240	0.1	0.3						
283 LUTH--MO SYNOD	6	1 230	1 764	0.2	0.4	059 BAPT MISS ASSN	9	721	898*	0.1	0.1
290 METRO COMM CHS	0	25	50	–	–	075 BRETHREN IN CR	2	152	170	–	–
353 CHR BRETHREN..	2	50	50	–	–	081 CATHOLIC......	375	NA	435 241	33.5	56.7
						089 CHR & MISS AL.	2	76	132	–	–
356 PRESB CH AMER.	1	9	19	–	–	093 CHR CH (DISC).	17	3 086	4 147	0.3	0.5
403 SALVATION ARMY	8	635	2 147	0.2	0.5						
413 S.D.A.........	14	836	1 005*	0.1	0.2	097 CHR CHS&CHS CR	33	5 829	7 224*	0.6	0.9
419 SO BAPT CONV..	2	744	907*	0.1	0.2	101 C.M.E.........	8	964	1 205*	0.1	0.2
435 UNITARIAN-UNIV	21	2 347	2 840*	0.3	0.7	105 CHRISTIAN REF.	15	835	1 561	0.1	0.2
						123 CH GOD (ANDER)	8	379	1 137	0.1	0.1
443 UN C OF CHRIST	136	28 099	33 871*	3.7	8.3	127 CH GOD (CLEVE)	41	1 361	1 710*	0.1	0.2
449 UN METHODIST..	100	16 472	19 837*	2.2	4.9						
453 UN PRES CH USA	8	1 391	1 695*	0.2	0.4	133 CH GOD(7TH)DEN	4	39	48*	–	–
469 WELS..........	1	26	40	–	–	151 L-D SAINTS....	90	NA	28 804	2.2	3.8
						157 CH OF BRETHREN	3	223	279*	–	–
NEW JERSEY	3 708	780 327	3 988 369*	54.2	100.0	164 CH LUTH CONF..	3	64	64	–	–
						165 CH OF NAZARENE	46	4 005	6 663	0.5	0.9
005 AME ZION......	37	32 836	40 368	0.5	1.0						
019 AMER BAPT USA.	225	61 446	73 691*	1.0	1.8	167 CHS OF CHRIST.	153	13 975	17 414	1.3	2.3
029 AMER LUTH CH..	17	4 651	6 346	0.1	0.2	179 CONSRV BAPT...	5	482	604*	–	0.1
039 AP CHR CH(NAZ)	3	112	132*	–	–	185 CUMBER PRESB..	1	777	1 033	0.1	0.1
049 ARMEN AP CH AM	1	350	1 900	–	–	193 EPISCOPAL.....	45	10 244	13 692	1.1	1.8
						197 EVAN CH OF NA.	2	53	53	–	–
053 ASSEMB OF GOD.	136	15 385	24 808	0.3	0.6						
057 BAPT GEN CONF.	1	205	248*	–	–	201 EVAN COV CH AM	1	40	49*	–	–
059 BAPT MISS ASSN	1	101	124*	–	–	203 EVAN FREE CH..	4	203	248*	–	–
071 BRETHREN (ASH)	1	43	52*	–	–	221 FREE METHODIST	2	39	153	–	–
081 CATHOLIC......	760	NA	2 958 499	40.2	74.2	226 FRIENDS-USA...	8	167	204*	–	–
						244 GRACE BRETHREN	4	324	406*	–	0.1
089 CHR & MISS AL.	36	2 217	4 052	0.1	0.1						
093 CHR CH (DISC).	7	753	1 181	–	–	263 INT FOURSQ GOS	11	662	817*	0.1	0.1
097 CHR CHS&CHS CR	9	409	489*	–	–	270 CONSRV JUDAISM	1	175	213*	–	–
101 C.M.E.........	8	3 186	3 830*	0.1	0.1	271 REFORM JUDAISM	1	760	924*	0.1	0.1
105 CHRISTIAN REF.	22	4 811	7 328	0.1	0.2	281 LUTH CH AMER..	14	4 948	7 139	0.5	0.9
						283 LUTH--MO SYNOD	24	4 309	5 543	0.4	0.7
123 CH GOD (ANDER)	16	883	2 649	–	0.1						
127 CH GOD (CLEVE)	46	2 448	2 956*	–	0.1	285 MENNONITE CH..	4	98	122*	–	–
149 CH OF JC (BIC)	5	189	223	–	–	290 METRO COMM CHS	1	50	100	–	–
151 L-D SAINTS....	30	NA	7 944	0.1	0.2	329 OPEN BIBLE STD	1	35	45	–	–
157 CH OF BRETHREN	1	120	145*	–	–	349 PENT HOLINESS.	5	227	283*	–	–
						353 CHR BRETHREN..	3	120	185	–	–
163 CH OF LUTH BR.	5	327	546	–	–						
165 CH OF NAZARENE	37	3 589	7 283	0.1	0.2	356 PRESB CH AMER.	1	153	198	–	–
167 CHS OF CHRIST.	34	2 986	4 181	0.1	0.1	371 REF CH IN AM..	2	137	487	–	0.1
175 CONGR CHR CHS.	4	763	920*	–	–	381 REF PRES-EVAN.	3	274	376	–	–
179 CONSRV BAPT...	48	8 209	9 882*	0.1	0.2	383 REF PRES OF NA	1	6	6	–	–
						403 SALVATION ARMY	6	402	601	–	0.1

NA—Not applicable   *Total adherents estimated from known number of communicant, confirmed, full members.   —Represents a percent less than 0.1.   Percentages may not total due to rounding.

Table 3. Churches and Church Membership by State and Denomination: 1980

County and Denomination	Number of churches	Communicant, confirmed, full members	Total adherents Number	Percent of total population	Percent of total adherents
413 S.D.A.........	41	2 863	3 555*	0.3	0.5
419 SO BAPT CONV..	251	105 778	131 575*	10.1	17.1
435 UNITARIAN-UNIV	7	971	1 189*	0.1	0.2
443 UN C OF CHRIST	10	1 856	2 273*	0.2	0.3
449 UN METHODIST..	110	42 960	53 185*	4.1	6.9
453 UN PRES CH USA	65	13 479	16 652*	1.3	2.2
469 WELS.........	2	155	197	–	–
NEW YORK	**8 989**	**1 862 886**	**8 721 200***	**49.7**	**100.0**
001 ADVENT CHR CH.	7	340	410*	–	–
005 AME ZION......	123	140 044	174 002	1.0	2.0
017 AMER BAPT ASSN	2	210	210	–	–
019 AMER BAPT USA.	562	181 119	216 552*	1.2	2.5
029 AMER LUTH CH..	67	16 077	23 064	0.1	0.3
039 AP CHR CH(NAZ)	3	134	159*	–	–
049 ARMEN AP CH AM	5	598	1 707	–	–
053 ASSEMB OF GOD.	307	36 035	58 419	0.3	0.7
055 AS REF PRES CH	2	173	211	–	–
057 BAPT GEN CONF.	11	1 422	1 701*	–	–
059 BAPT MISS ASSN	4	97	118*	–	–
061 BEACHY AMISH..	1	19	23*	–	–
066 BIBLE CH OF CR	3	2 780	3 333*	–	–
075 BRETHREN IN CR	3	300	394	–	–
081 CATHOLIC......	1 834	NA	6 257 786	35.6	71.8
089 CHR & MISS AL.	111	8 050	13 868	0.1	0.2
093 CHR CH (DISC).	68	9 898	14 270	0.1	0.2
097 CHR CHS&CHS CR	35	2 275	2 727*	–	–
101 C.M.E.........	18	13 912	16 469*	0.1	0.2
105 CHRISTIAN REF.	13	1 499	2 532	–	–
123 CH GOD (ANDER)	34	2 490	7 470	–	0.1
127 CH GOD (CLEVE)	117	5 575	6 681*	–	0.1
133 CH GOD(7TH)DEN	4	64	78*	–	–
149 CH OF JC (BIC)	4	91	103	–	–
151 L-D SAINTS....	77	NA	19 797	0.1	0.2
157 CH OF BRETHREN	1	92	112*	–	–
163 CH OF LUTH BR.	5	572	957	–	–
165 CH OF NAZARENE	89	6 936	14 801	0.1	0.2
167 CHS OF CHRIST.	77	5 431	7 413	–	0.1
175 CONGR CHR CHS.	8	2 376	2 843*	–	–
179 CONSRV BAPT...	86	12 874	15 469*	0.1	0.2
181 CONSRV CONGR..	16	2 092	2 520*	–	–
193 EPISCOPAL.....	735	211 160	307 481	1.8	3.5
195 ESTONIAN ELC..	5	557	4 218	–	–
201 EVAN COV CH AM	13	2 001	2 466*	–	–
203 EVAN FREE CH..	19	1 989	2 406*	–	–
208 EVAN LUTH ASSN	40	13 296	19 705	0.1	0.2
209 EVAN LUTH SYN.	2	89	126	–	–
215 EVAN METH CH..	1	20	24*	–	–
221 FREE METHODIST	86	4 115	17 799	0.1	0.2
226 FRIENDS-USA...	61	4 524	5 379*	–	0.1
239 SWEDENBORGIAN.	1	100	113*	–	–
247 HOLINESS CH...	4	104	115	–	–
263 INT FOURSQ GOS	5	249	301*	–	–
270 CONSRV JUDAISM	182	52 313	62 048*	0.4	0.7
271 REFORM JUDAISM	129	94 376	111 331*	0.6	1.3
274 LAT EVAN LUTH.	6	526	586	–	–
281 LUTH CH AMER..	349	124 720	172 257	1.0	2.0
283 LUTH--MO SYNOD	206	71 646	102 099	0.6	1.2
285 MENNONITE CH..	35	2 345	2 875*	–	–
290 METRO COMM CHS	6	378	756	–	–
293 MORAV CH-NORTH	10	2 830	3 879	–	–
313 N AM BAPT CONF	10	1 371	1 630*	–	–
323 OLD ORD AMISH.	12	1 560	1 881*	–	–
329 OPEN BIBLE STD	3	200	345	–	–
335 ORTH PRESB CH.	5	530	633*	–	–
349 PENT HOLINESS.	2	43	52*	–	–
353 CHR BRETHREN..	47	2 880	3 820	–	–
356 PRESB CH AMER.	1	16	23	–	–
363 PRIMITIVE METH	2	684	813*	–	–
371 REF CH IN AM..	261	46 555	90 134	0.5	1.0
375 REF EPISCOPAL.	3	281	335*	–	–
381 REF PRES-EVAN.	5	315	434	–	–
383 REF PRES OF NA	7	352	437	–	–
395 ROMANIAN OR CH	1	1 280	1 449*	–	–
403 SALVATION ARMY	76	6 863	25 908	0.1	0.3
413 S.D.A.........	173	30 509	36 329*	0.2	0.4
415 S-D BAPT GC	12	914	1 104*	–	–
419 SO BAPT CONV..	98	12 784	15 331*	0.1	0.2
423 SYRIAN ANTIOCH	2	900	1 052*	–	–
431 UKRANIAN AMER.	9	1 220	1 975	–	–
435 UNITARIAN-UNIV	67	10 632	12 627*	0.1	0.1
443 UN C OF CHRIST	311	71 462	85 424*	0.5	1.0
449 UN METHODIST..	1 519	422 697	508 029*	2.9	5.8
453 UN PRES CH USA	768	207 744	249 079*	1.4	2.9
469 WELS.........	3	181	253	–	–
NORTH CAROLINA	**10 281**	**2 470 569**	**3 173 793***	**54.0**	**100.0**
001 ADVENT CHR CH.	59	7 254	8 826*	0.2	0.3
005 AME ZION......	591	241 820	311 006	5.3	9.8
017 AMER BAPT ASSN	3	71	71	–	–
019 AMER BAPT USA.	20	11 486	13 787*	0.2	0.4
029 AMER LUTH CH..	13	3 998	5 351	0.1	0.2
053 ASSEMB OF GOD.	150	12 204	19 917	0.3	0.6
055 AS REF PRES CH	37	8 891	10 063	0.2	0.3
059 BAPT MISS ASSN	2	221	261*	–	–
066 BIBLE CH OF CR	1	115	141*	–	–
081 CATHOLIC......	155	NA	94 768	1.6	3.0
089 CHR & MISS AL.	33	3 272	4 826	0.1	0.2
093 CHR CH (DISC).	322	36 252	57 596	1.0	1.8
097 CHR CHS&CHS CR	152	21 832	26 573*	0.5	0.8
101 C.M.E.........	46	17 720	21 280*	0.4	0.7
105 CHRISTIAN REF.	1	120	211	–	–
121 CH GOD (ABR)..	2	143	173*	–	–
123 CH GOD (ANDER)	47	3 005	9 015	0.2	0.3
127 CH GOD (CLEVE)	414	31 420	38 213*	0.7	1.2
133 CH GOD(7TH)DEN	2	45	55*	–	–
151 L-D SAINTS....	80	NA	21 600	0.4	0.7
157 CH OF BRETHREN	19	1 782	2 139*	–	0.1
164 CH LUTH CONF.	1	38	46	–	–
165 CH OF NAZARENE	57	4 736	9 147	0.2	0.3
167 CHS OF CHRIST.	160	11 136	14 212	0.3	0.4
175 CONGR CHR CHS.	5	332	401*	–	–
177 CONGR HOL CH..	14	482	585*	–	–
193 EPISCOPAL.....	256	55 215	73 232	1.2	2.3
215 EVAN METH CH..	27	1 927	2 326*	–	0.1
221 FREE METHODIST	3	54	348	–	–
226 FRIENDS-USA...	92	14 336	17 230*	0.3	0.5
237 GC MENN BR CHS	7	239	287*	–	–
244 GRACE BRETHREN	1	14	17*	–	–
247 HOLINESS CH...	14	1 025	1 025	–	–
263 INT FOURSQ GOS	31	3 766	4 559*	0.1	0.1
270 CONSRV JUDAISM	11	981	1 173*	–	–
271 REFORM JUDAISM	14	2 900	3 485*	0.1	0.1
281 LUTH CH AMER..	210	64 802	82 439	1.4	2.6
283 LUTH--MO SYNOD	54	12 563	17 451	0.3	0.5
285 MENNONITE CH..	7	235	285*	–	–
290 METRO COMM CHS	3	130	260	–	–
295 MORAV CH-SOUTH	45	16 375	20 020	0.3	0.6
335 ORTH PRESB CH.	1	32	38*	–	–
347 PENT FW BAPT..	118	11 716	14 322*	0.2	0.5
349 PENT HOLINESS.	282	25 006	30 477*	0.5	1.0
353 CHR BRETHREN..	41	2 910	5 455	0.1	0.2
356 PRESB CH AMER.	38	4 381	4 944	0.1	0.2
357 PRESB CH US..	669	158 269	191 424*	3.3	6.0
381 REF PRES-EVAN.	6	686	800	–	–
403 SALVATION ARMY	37	4 312	12 514	0.2	0.4
413 S.D.A.........	85	12 539	15 104*	0.3	0.5
419 SO BAPT CONV..	3 460	1 108 773	1 341 047*	22.8	42.3
435 UNITARIAN-UNIV	14	1 561	1 874*	–	0.1
443 UN C OF CHRIST	251	45 268	54 489*	0.9	1.7
449 UN METHODIST..	2 016	490 407	592 967*	10.1	18.7
453 UN PRES CH USA	101	11 720	14 184*	0.2	0.4
469 WELS.........	1	52	74	–	–
NORTH DAKOTA	**1 695**	**233 749**	**482 574***	**73.9**	**100.0**
019 AMER BAPT USA.	18	2 047	2 496*	0.4	0.5
029 AMER LUTH CH..	500	124 849	163 956	25.1	34.0
045 APOSTOLIC LUTH	2	70	86*	–	–
053 ASSEMB OF GOD.	61	3 730	7 407	1.1	1.5
057 BAPT GEN CONF.	6	528	642*	0.1	0.1
081 CATHOLIC......	292	NA	174 046	26.7	36.1
089 CHR & MISS AL.	4	181	427	0.1	0.1
097 CHR CHS&CHS CR	3	109	133*	–	–
105 CHRISTIAN REF.	1	101	161	–	–
123 CH GOD (ANDER)	6	198	594	0.1	0.1
127 CH GOD (CLEVE)	18	707	870*	0.1	0.2
133 CH GOD(7TH)DEN	4	70	86*	–	–
143 CG IN CR(MENN)	1	57	57	–	–
151 L-D SAINTS....	21	NA	1 188	0.2	0.2
157 CH OF BRETHREN	3	239	292*	–	0.1
163 CH OF LUTH BR.	17	814	1 592	0.2	0.3
164 CH LUTH CONF.	1	156	210	–	–
165 CH OF NAZARENE	32	1 277	2 693	0.4	0.6
167 CHS OF CHRIST.	12	343	503	0.1	0.1
179 CONSRV BAPT...	1	217	261*	–	0.1
181 CONSRV CONGR..	6	606	739*	0.1	0.2
193 EPISCOPAL.....	29	2 558	3 899	0.6	0.8
197 EVAN CH OF NA.	8	369	369	0.1	0.1
201 EVAN COV CH AM	2	148	179*	–	–
203 EVAN FREE CH..	17	842	1 021*	0.2	0.2
208 EVAN LUTH ASSN	1	35	50	–	–
209 EVAN LUTH SYN.	2	162	214	–	–
220 FREE LUTHERAN.	26	2 248	2 806	0.4	0.6
221 FREE METHODIST	3	36	255	–	0.1

NA— Not applicable · *Total adherents estimated from known number of communicant, confirmed, full members. · —Represents a percent less than 0.1. · Percentages may not total due to rounding.

Table 3. Churches and Church Membership by State and Denomination: 1980

County and Denomination	Number of churches	Communicant, confirmed, full members	Total adherents		
			Number	Percent of total population	Percent of total adherents
226 FRIENDS-USA...	1	4	5*	–	–
237 GC MENN BR CHS	6	417	505*	0.1	0.1
270 CONSRV JUDAISM	1	15	19*	–	–
271 REFORM JUDAISM	1	208	250*	–	0.1
281 LUTH CH AMER..	38	11 423	14 620	2.2	3.0
283 LUTH--MO SYNOD	100	21 276	27 801	4.3	5.8
285 MENNONITE CH..	5	302	381*	0.1	0.1
287 MENN GEN CONF.	3	271	327	0.1	0.1
290 METRO COMM CHS	0	10	20	–	–
293 MORAV CH-NORTH	6	650	816	0.1	0.2
313 N AM BAPT CONF	36	4 533	5 492*	0.8	1.1
335 ORTH PRESB CH.	2	60	74*	–	–
353 CHR BRETHREN..	5	125	165	–	–
371 REF CH IN AM..	5	435	887	0.1	0.2
381 REF PRES-EVAN.	2	79	94	–	–
403 SALVATION ARMY	6	448	1 942	0.3	0.4
413 S.D.A.........	45	3 368	4 096*	0.6	0.8
419 SO BAPT CONV..	18	2 629	3 222*	0.5	0.7
435 UNITARIAN-UNIV	2	106	129*	–	–
443 UN C OF CHRIST	75	9 038	11 033*	1.7	2.3
449 UN METHODIST..	156	22 182	26 959*	4.1	5.6
453 UN PRES CH USA	73	11 986	14 609*	2.2	3.0
469 WELS.........	12	1 487	1 896	0.3	0.4
OHIO	10 060	2 212 329	5 346 227*	49.5	100.0
001 ADVENT CHR CH.	9	514	629*	–	–
005 AME ZION......	35	28 325	34 879	0.3	0.7
017 AMER BAPT ASSN	18	1 047	1 047	–	–
019 AMER BAPT USA.	325	107 063	129 650*	1.2	2.4
029 AMER LUTH CH..	320	132 361	177 807	1.6	3.3
039 AP CHR CH(NAZ)	12	1 084	1 310*	–	–
049 ARMEN AP CH AM	1	40	60	–	–
053 ASSEMB OF GOD.	190	26 239	49 445	0.5	0.9
057 BAPT GEN CONF.	17	2 442	2 943*	–	0.1
059 BAPT MISS ASSN	1	80	97*	–	–
061 BEACHY AMISH..	16	902	1 122*	–	–
071 BRETHREN (ASH)	21	3 267	3 986*	–	0.1
075 BRETHREN IN CR	14	602	1 022	–	–
081 CATHOLIC......	1 106	NA	2 433 745	22.5	45.5
083 CHRIST CATH CH	2	16	22	–	–
089 CHR & MISS AL.	90	8 737	17 238	0.2	0.3
093 CHR CH (DISC).	215	58 380	86 618	0.8	1.6
097 CHR CHS&CHS CR	472	109 203	133 183*	1.2	2.5
101 C.M.E........	34	21 902	26 353*	0.2	0.5
105 CHRISTIAN REF.	9	1 012	1 551	–	–
107 CHRISTIAN UN..	61	2 255	2 981	–	0.1
121 CH GOD (ABR)..	12	753	917*	–	–
123 CH GOD (ANDER)	206	25 227	75 681	0.7	1.4
127 CH GOD (CLEVE)	227	22 662	27 554*	0.3	0.5
133 CH GOD(7TH)DEN	3	48	59*	–	–
143 CG IN CR(MENN)	3	181	181	–	–
149 CH OF JC (BIC)	7	315	301	–	–
151 L-D SAINTS....	66	NA	22 613	0.2	0.4
157 CH OF BRETHREN	109	18 170	22 202*	0.2	0.4
163 CH OF LUTH BR.	1	29	57	–	–
165 CH OF NAZARENE	403	48 036	93 402	0.9	1.7
167 CHS OF CHRIST.	423	38 863	51 081	0.5	1.0
175 CONGR CHR CHS.	18	4 776	5 803*	0.1	0.1
179 CONSRV BAPT...	23	4 156	5 086*	–	0.1
181 CONSRV CONGR..	3	573	701*	–	–
193 EPISCOPAL.....	195	68 703	93 552	0.9	1.7
195 ESTONIAN ELC..	1	54	158	–	–
197 EVAN CH OF NA.	1	106	106	–	–
199 EVAN CONGR CH.	13	1 465	1 771*	–	–
201 EVAN COV CH AM	10	1 405	1 688*	–	–
203 EVAN FREE CH..	3	505	618*	–	–
208 EVAN LUTH ASSN	7	4 181	5 845	0.1	0.1
213 EVAN MENN INC.	3	1 207	1 501*	–	–
215 EVAN METH CH..	2	55	68*	–	–
220 FREE LUTHERAN.	1	30	40	–	–
221 FREE METHODIST	52	2 254	9 684	0.1	0.2
226 FRIENDS-USA...	97	11 085	13 482*	0.1	0.3
233 GEN CH NEW JER	1	30	36*	–	–
239 SWEDENBORGIAN.	4	240	289*	–	–
244 GRACE BRETHREN	53	9 125	11 086*	0.1	0.2
263 INT FOURSQ GOS	41	4 006	4 874*	–	0.1
270 CONSRV JUDAISM	25	6 491	7 805*	0.1	0.1
271 REFORM JUDAISM	31	27 014	32 401*	0.3	0.6
274 LAT EVAN LUTH.	4	1 033	1 213	–	–
281 LUTH CH AMER..	339	131 560	176 623	1.6	3.3
283 LUTH--MO SYNOD	182	65 064	87 051	0.8	1.6
285 MENNONITE CH..	112	14 228	17 614*	0.2	0.3
287 MENN GEN CONF.	13	3 207	4 012	–	0.1
290 METRO COMM CHS	3	330	660	–	–
291 MISSIONARY CH.	38	2 650	3 422	–	0.1
293 MORAV CH-NORTH	7	1 845	2 310	–	–
313 N AM BAPT CONF	9	1 858	2 232*	–	–
323 OLD ORD AMISH.	165	21 450	26 837*	0.2	0.5
329 OPEN BIBLE STD	29	2 634	4 613	–	0.1
335 ORTH PRESB CH.	3	84	102*	–	–
349 PENT HOLINESS.	14	837	1 026*	–	–
353 CHR BRETHREN..	27	1 135	1 740	–	–
356 PRESB CH AMER.	1	109	126	–	–
357 PRESB CH US...	1	67	83*	–	–
363 PRIMITIVE METH	4	399	481*	–	–
371 REF CH IN AM..	7	1 178	2 232	–	–
375 REF EPISCOPAL.	2	72	87*	–	–
381 REF PRES-EVAN.	4	351	456	–	–
383 REF PRES OF NA	1	29	33	–	–
395 ROMANIAN OR CH	2	2 225	2 656*	–	–
403 SALVATION ARMY	60	6 671	19 401	0.2	0.4
409 SEPARATE BAPT.	2	139	168*	–	–
413 S.D.A.........	116	16 919	20 465*	0.2	0.4
415 S-D BAPT GC	1	27	33*	–	–
419 SO BAPT CONV..	453	125 030	152 277*	1.4	2.8
431 UKRANIAN AMER.	1	100	130	–	–
435 UNITARIAN-UNIV	37	5 325	6 418*	0.1	0.1
443 UN C OF CHRIST	517	173 363	210 961*	2.0	3.9
449 UN METHODIST..	2 236	608 849	741 753*	6.9	13.9
453 UN PRES CH USA	635	213 160	258 476*	2.4	4.8
469 WELS.........	21	3 185	4 206	–	0.1
OKLAHOMA	5 329	1 294 314	1 754 071*	58.0	100.0
001 ADVENT CHR CH.	6	208	248*	–	–
005 AME ZION......	5	1 505	1 821	0.1	0.1
017 AMER BAPT ASSN	99	12 821	12 821	0.4	0.7
019 AMER BAPT USA.	12	1 524	1 844*	0.1	0.1
029 AMER LUTH CH..	14	2 941	4 031	0.1	0.2
053 ASSEMB OF GOD.	471	40 789	69 689	2.3	4.0
059 BAPT MISS ASSN	53	7 026	8 549*	0.3	0.5
061 BEACHY AMISH..	1	53	63*	–	–
075 BRETHREN IN CR	3	171	258	–	–
081 CATHOLIC......	196	NA	109 197	3.6	6.2
083 CHRIST CATH CH	1	10	14	–	–
089 CHR & MISS AL.	5	114	306	–	–
093 CHR CH (DISC).	211	46 198	66 424	2.2	3.8
097 CHR CHS&CHS CR	203	34 549	41 897*	1.4	2.4
101 C.M.E........	44	6 523	7 915*	0.3	0.5
107 CHRISTIAN UN..	8	433	707	–	–
123 CH GOD (ANDER)	71	5 367	16 101	0.5	0.9
127 CH GOD (CLEVE)	81	4 397	5 353*	0.2	0.3
133 CH GOD(7TH)DEN	12	312	378*	–	–
143 CG IN CR(MENN)	4	505	505	–	–
151 L-D SAINTS....	51	NA	13 882	0.5	0.8
157 CH OF BRETHREN	7	461	546*	–	–
165 CH OF NAZARENE	231	21 865	37 943	1.3	2.2
167 CHS OF CHRIST.	638	71 728	91 606	3.0	5.2
175 CONGR CHR CHS.	2	469	568*	–	–
181 CONSRV CONGR..	1	132	158*	–	–
185 CUMBER PRESB..	23	950	1 862	0.1	0.1
193 EPISCOPAL.....	77	18 091	22 230	0.7	1.3
208 EVAN LUTH ASSN	9	973	1 397	–	0.1
211 EVAN MENN BR..	1	103	134	–	–
215 EVAN METH CH..	1	79	95*	–	–
217 FIRE BAPTIZED.	5	68	82*	–	–
221 FREE METHODIST	17	707	2 403	0.1	0.1
226 FRIENDS-USA...	17	1 382	1 661*	0.1	0.1
237 GC MENN BR CHS	16	2 625	3 191*	0.1	0.2
263 INT FOURSQ GOS	12	1 138	1 375*	–	0.1
270 CONSRV JUDAISM	2	555	672*	–	–
271 REFORM JUDAISM	5	1 936	2 345*	0.1	0.1
281 LUTH CH AMER..	11	2 915	4 063	0.1	0.2
283 LUTH--MO SYNOD	73	16 780	21 906	0.7	1.2
285 MENNONITE CH..	4	413	500*	–	–
287 MENN GEN CONF.	18	1 610	1 874	0.1	0.1
290 METRO COMM CHS	2	165	330	–	–
313 N AM BAPT CONF	5	494	595*	–	–
323 OLD ORD AMISH.	3	390	475*	–	–
329 OPEN BIBLE STD	1	50	75	–	–
335 ORTH PRESB CH.	3	114	138*	–	–
349 PENT HOLINESS.	175	12 326	14 935*	0.5	0.9
353 CHR BRETHREN..	4	105	145	–	–
357 PRESB CH US...	32	4 244	5 145*	0.2	0.3
371 REF CH IN AM..	3	592	1 092	–	0.1
381 REF PRES-EVAN.	5	356	424	–	–
403 SALVATION ARMY	20	2 034	4 291	0.1	0.2
413 S.D.A.........	74	6 369	7 731*	0.3	0.4
419 SO BAPT CONV..	1 422	659 042	799 357*	26.4	45.6
431 UKRANIAN AMER.	1	80	120	–	–
435 UNITARIAN-UNIV	6	1 654	1 999*	0.1	0.1
443 UN C OF CHRIST	17	1 418	1 722*	0.1	0.1
449 UN METHODIST..	698	258 647	313 466*	10.4	17.9
453 UN PRES CH USA	134	35 459	42 712*	1.4	2.4
469 WELS.........	3	349	505		

NA—Not applicable   *Total adherents estimated from known number of communicant, confirmed, full members.   —Represents a percent less than 0.1.   Percentages may not total due to rounding.

Table 3. Churches and Church Membership by State and Denomination: 1980

County and Denomination	Number of churches	Communicant, confirmed, full members	Total adherents Number	Percent of total population	Percent of total adherents
OREGON	2 628	411 445	949 471*	36.1	100.0
001 ADVENT CHR CH.	3	148	177*	-	-
005 AME ZION......	3	470	518	-	0.1
017 AMER BAPT ASSN	27	1 692	1 692	0.1	0.2
019 AMER BAPT USA.	49	14 397	17 357*	0.7	1.8
029 AMER LUTH CH..	68	23 103	31 062	1.2	3.3
039 AP CHR CH(NAZ)	1	120	142*	-	-
045 APOSTOLIC LUTH	4	405	483*	-	0.1
053 ASSEMB OF GOD.	201	24 563	46 902	1.8	4.9
057 BAPT GEN CONF.	8	1 506	1 806*	0.1	0.2
059 BAPT MISS ASSN	4	135	164*	-	-
063 BEREAN FUND CH	1	51	60*	-	-
075 BRETHREN IN CR	2	152	170	-	-
081 CATHOLIC......	214	NA	320 716	12.2	33.8
089 CHR & MISS AL.	27	2 086	4 141	0.2	0.4
093 CHR CH (DISC).	51	12 092	18 736	0.7	2.0
097 CHR CHS&CHS CR	165	27 186	32 940*	1.3	3.5
101 C.M.E.........	2	1 153	1 365*	0.1	0.1
105 CHRISTIAN REF.	4	341	629	-	0.1
123 CH GOD (ANDER)	48	4 191	12 573	0.5	1.3
127 CH GOD (CLEVE)	38	1 784	2 157*	0.1	0.2
133 CH GOD(7TH)DEN	5	311	378*	-	-
143 CG IN CR(MENN)	1	60	60	-	-
151 L-D SAINTS....	184	NA	74 099	2.8	7.8
157 CH OF BRETHREN	6	536	648*	-	0.1
163 CH OF LUTH BR.	3	206	258	-	-
165 CH OF NAZARENE	85	12 783	21 573	0.8	2.3
167 CHS OF CHRIST.	116	8 647	11 146	0.4	1.2
175 CONGR CHR CHS.	2	221	270*	-	-
179 CONSRV BAPT...	167	32 621	39 412*	1.5	4.2
181 CONSRV CONGR..	2	96	114*	-	-
193 EPISCOPAL.....	99	25 964	35 476	1.3	3.7
195 ESTONIAN ELC..	1	52	160	-	-
197 EVAN CH OF NA.	46	6 307	6 307	0.2	0.7
201 EVAN COV CH AM	10	1 253	1 500*	0.1	0.2
203 EVAN FREE CH..	9	395	477*	-	0.1
209 EVAN LUTH SYN.	2	171	234	-	-
211 EVAN MENN BR..	2	574	746	-	0.1
215 EVAN METH CH..	5	211	250*	-	-
217 FIRE BAPTIZED.	2	11	13*	-	-
220 FREE LUTHERAN.	2	265	330	-	-
221 FREE METHODIST	36	1 958	7 620	0.3	0.8
226 FRIENDS-USA...	30	4 873	5 878*	0.2	0.6
237 GC MENN BR CHS	3	522	632*	-	0.1
239 SWEDENBORGIAN.	1	60	71*	-	-
244 GRACE BRETHREN	3	203	246*	-	-
263 INT FOURSQ GOS	57	12 652	15 204*	0.6	1.6
270 CONSRV JUDAISM	2	754	894*	-	0.1
271 REFORM JUDAISM	2	1 918	2 267*	0.1	0.2
274 LAT EVAN LUTH.	1	215	252	-	-
281 LUTH CH AMER..	41	14 205	19 639	0.7	2.1
283 LUTH--MO SYNOD	86	20 861	28 537	1.1	3.0
285 MENNONITE CH..	30	2 588	3 152*	0.1	0.3
287 MENN GEN CONF.	5	997	1 026	-	0.1
290 METRO COMM CHS	3	385	770	-	0.1
291 MISSIONARY CH.	7	361	608	-	0.1
313 N AM BAPT CONF	10	1 955	2 338*	0.1	0.2
329 OPEN BIBLE STD	29	3 205	5 471	0.2	0.6
335 ORTH PRESB CH	6	348	418*	-	-
349 PENT HOLINESS.	6	238	287*	-	-
353 CHR BRETHREN..	11	780	1 150	-	0.1
403 SALVATION ARMY	15	1 148	2 601	0.1	0.3
413 S.D.A.........	116	25 287	30 605*	1.2	3.2
415 S-D BAPTIST GC	1	10	12*	-	-
419 SO BAPT CONV..	87	21 808	26 369*	1.0	2.8
435 UNITARIAN-UNIV	12	1 849	2 208*	0.1	0.2
443 UN C OF CHRIST	42	9 206	11 056*	0.4	1.2
449 UN METHODIST..	180	41 007	49 578*	1.9	5.2
453 UN PRES CH USA	130	34 964	42 053*	1.6	4.4
469 WELS.........	7	829	1 288	-	0.1
PENNSYLVANIA	12 386	2 604 959	7 231 834*	60.9	100.0
001 ADVENT CHR CH.	1	39	47*	-	-
005 AME ZION......	50	21 022	27 190	0.2	0.4
017 AMER·BAPT ASSN	2	49	49	-	-
019 AMER BAPT USA.	462	108 016	128 906*	1.1	1.8
029 AMER LUTH CH..	54	17 023	22 493	0.2	0.3
039 AP CHR CH(NAZ)	2	42	51*	-	-
049 ARMEN AP CH AM	1	600	1 200	-	-
053 ASSEMB OF GOD.	292	30 641	56 005	0.5	0.8
057 BAPT GEN CONF.	14	1 988	2 369*	-	-
061 BEACHY AMISH..	14	1 138	1 375*	-	-
065 BETHEL M ASSN.	1	150	181*	-	-
071 BRETHREN (ASH)	19	2 050	2 466*	-	-
075 BRETHREN IN CR	86	7 862	11 322	0.1	0.2
081 CATHOLIC......	1 855	NA	3 881 444	32.7	53.7
089 CHR & MISS AL.	234	15 744	31 335	0.3	0.4
093 CHR CH (DISC).	71	12 238	18 828	0.2	0.3
097 CHR CHS&CHS CR	125	24 844	29 641*	0.2	0.4
101 C.M.E.........	14	8 110	9 603*	0.1	0.1
105 CHRISTIAN REF.	2	143	231	-	-
123 CH GOD (ANDER)	86	7 744	23 232	0.2	0.3
127 CH GOD (CLEVE)	90	7 214	8 679*	0.1	0.1
143 CG IN CR(MENN)	3	171	171	-	-
149 CH OF JC (BIC)	11	528	565	-	-
151 L-D SAINTS....	76	NA	18 263	0.2	0.3
157 CH OF BRETHREN	225	52 701	63 497*	0.5	0.9
165 CH OF NAZARENE	158	15 139	29 671	0.3	0.4
167 CHS OF CHRIST.	121	7 000	9 554	0.1	0.1
175 CONGR CHR CHS.	20	3 111	3 695*	-	0.1
179 CONSRV BAPT...	59	6 535	7 821*	0.1	0.1
181 CONSRV CONGR..	4	325	385*	-	-
193 EPISCOPAL.....	416	125 803	168 001	1.4	2.3
195 ESTONIAN ELC..	1	78	132	-	-
197 EVAN CH OF NA.	16	1 534	1 534	-	-
199 EVAN CONGR CH.	133	25 450	30 365*	0.3	0.4
201 EVAN COV CH AM	14	882	1 066*	-	-
203 EVAN FREE CH..	20	2 218	2 633*	-	-
208 EVAN LUTH ASSN	7	1 648	2 129	-	-
215 EVAN METH CH..	1	178	212*	-	-
221 FREE METHODIST	132	4 268	22 233	0.2	0.3
226 FRIENDS-USA...	84	11 035	13 174*	0.1	0.2
233 GEN CH-NEW JER	4	955	1 126*	-	-
239 SWEDENBORGIAN.	2	160	189*	-	-
244 GRACE BRETHREN	49	8 001	9 630*	0.1	0.1
263 INT FOURSQ GOS	15	1 590	1 910*	-	-
270 CONSRV JUDAISM	75	17 632	20 901*	0.2	0.3
271 REFORM JUDAISM	41	28 246	33 435*	0.3	0.5
274 LAT EVAN LUTH.	4	640	689	-	-
281 LUTH CH AMER..	1 376	557 481	742 085	6.3	10.3
283 LUTH--MO SYNOD	88	20 327	26 596	0.2	0.4
285 MENNONITE CH..	311	31 689	38 229*	0.3	0.5
287 MENN GEN CONF.	27	4 744	6 382	0.1	0.1
290 METRO COMM CHS	3	227	454	-	-
291 MISSIONARY CH.	12	511	706	-	-
293 MORAV CH-NORTH	27	9 759	12 501	0.1	0.2
313 N AM BAPT CONF	10	1 447	1 721*	-	-
323 OLD ORD AMISH.	133	17 290	20 870*	0.2	0.3
329 OPEN BIBLE STD	6	505	880	-	-
335 ORTH PRESB CH.	19	1 869	2 230*	-	-
349 PENT HOLINESS.	16	1 080	1 292*	-	-
353 CHR BRETHREN..	49	3 140	4 320	-	0.1
356 PRESB CH AMER.	15	1 595	2 072	-	-
357 PRESB CH US...	1	143	176*	-	-
363 PRIMITIVE METH	49	6 763	7 996*	0.1	0.1
371 REF CH IN AM..	10	2 867	5 131	-	0.1
375 REF EPISCOPAL.	16	1 601	1 903*	-	-
381 REF PRES-EVAN.	31	3 513	4 725	-	0.1
383 REF PRES OF NA	18	1 110	1 464	-	-
395 ROMANIAN OR CH	1	630	750*	-	-
403 SALVATION ARMY	82	8 396	41 952	0.4	0.6
413 S.D.A.........	114	12 057	14 381*	0.1	0.2
415 S-D BAPTIST GC	2	118	144*	-	-
419 SO BAPT CONV..	80	14 122	16 900*	0.1	0.2
423 SYRIAN ANTIOCH	1	400	476*	-	-
431 UKRANIAN AMER.	2	650	955	-	-
435 UNITARIAN-UNIV	38	4 309	5 142*	-	0.1
441 UN CHRISTIAN..	11	428	788	-	-
443 UN C OF CHRIST	830	253 674	302 562*	2.5	4.2
449 UN METHODIST..	2 663	656 819	786 153*	6.6	10.9
453 UN PRES CH USA	1 160	401 914	478 881*	4.0	6.6
459 UNITED ZION CH	13	936	936	-	-
469 WELS.........	6	360	453	-	-
RHODE ISLAND	498	88 129	715 569*	75.5	100.0
001 ADVENT CHR CH.	5	456	543*	0.1	0.1
005 AME ZION......	2	330	495	0.1	0.1
019 AMER BAPT USA.	79	20 377	24 183*	2.6	3.4
049 ARMEN AP CH AM	1	350	950	0.1	0.1
053 ASSEMB OF GOD.	9	569	1 183	0.1	0.2
057 BAPT GEN CONF.	1	213	252*	-	-
081 CATHOLIC......	174	NA	602 907	63.7	84.3
083 CHRIST CATH CH	2	67	86	-	-
089 CHR & MISS AL.	1	0	30	-	-
097 CHR CHS&CHS CR	1	21	25*	-	-
123 CH GOD (ANDER)	3	133	399	-	0.1
127 CH GOD (CLEVE)	6	217	256*	-	-
151 L-D SAINTS....	3	NA	1 051	0.1	0.1
163 CH OF LUTH BR.	1	38	65	-	-
165 CH OF NAZARENE	6	254	396	-	0.1
167 CHS OF CHRIST.	4	156	198	-	-
175 CONGR CHR CHS.	2	220	263*	-	-
181 CONSRV CONGR..	1	234	276*	-	-
193 EPISCOPAL.....	67	30 997	40 877	4.3	5.7
201 EVAN COV CH AM	5	549	649*	0.1	0.1

NA— Not applicable
*Total adherents estimated from known number of communicant, confirmed, full members.
—Represents a percent less than 0.1.
Percentages may not total due to rounding.

Table 3. Churches and Church Membership by State and Denomination: 1980

County and Denomination	Number of churches	Communicant, confirmed, full members	Total adherents Number	Percent of total population	Percent of total adherents
226 FRIENDS-USA...	5	400	474*	0.1	0.1
270 CONSRV JUDAISM	7	1 766	2 084*	0.2	0.3
271 REFORM JUDAISM	3	2 690	3 172*	0.3	0.4
281 LUTH CH AMER..	11	4 007	5 229	0.6	0.7
283 LUTH--MO SYNOD	3	972	1 215	0.1	0.2
290 METRO COMM CHS	1	57	114	–	–
353 CHR BRETHREN..	4	150	280	–	–
363 PRIMITIVE METH	4	399	473*	–	0.1
403 SALVATION ARMY	3	437	1 241	0.1	0.2
413 S.D.A.........	5	491	580*	0.1	0.1
415 S-D BAPTIST GC	3	395	474*	0.1	0.1
419 SO BAPT CONV..	4	847	1 015*	0.1	0.1
423 SYRIAN ANTIOCH	1	800	943*	0.1	0.1
435 UNITARIAN-UNIV	8	1 204	1 427*	0.2	0.2
443 UN C OF CHRIST	26	8 367	9 898*	1.0	1.4
449 UN METHODIST..	25	7 306	8 677*	0.9	1.2
453 UN PRES CH USA	11	2 620	3 122*	0.3	0.4
469 WELS.........	1	40	67	–	–
SOUTH CAROLINA	4 994	1 235 786	1 605 231*	51.5	100.0
001 ADVENT CHR CH.	10	973	1 207*	–	0.1
005 AME ZION......	132	45 641	55 344	1.8	3.4
017 AMER BAPT ASSN	10	545	545	–	–
053 ASSEMB OF GOD.	80	8 398	12 508	0.4	0.8
055 AS REF PRES CH	52	8 684	9 778	0.3	0.6
061 BEACHY AMISH..	2	132	163*	–	–
081 CATHOLIC.....	112	NA	59 027	1.9	3.7
089 CHR & MISS AL.	8	323	650	–	–
093 CHR CH (DISC).	49	4 663	6 473	0.2	0.4
097 CHR CHS&CHS CR	25	2 437	3 017*	0.1	0.2
101 C.M.E.........	56	17 215	21 060*	0.7	1.3
121 CH GOD (ABR)..	2	255	310*	–	–
123 CH GOD (ANDER)	46	2 912	8 736	0.3	0.5
127 CH GOD (CLEVE)	270	27 509	33 682*	1.1	2.1
133 CH GOD(7TH)DEN	3	12	15*	–	–
151 L-D SAINTS....	45	NA	12 506	0.4	0.8
157 CH OF BRETHREN	1	97	117*	–	–
164 CH LUTH CONF..	1	246	344	–	–
165 CH OF NAZARENE	56	5 941	11 189	0.4	0.7
167 CHS OF CHRIST.	95	6 691	8 680	0.3	0.5
177 CONGR HOL CH..	12	634	788*	–	–
193 EPISCOPAL.....	135	39 345	50 600	1.6	3.2
215 EVAN METH CH..	2	192	234*	–	–
226 FRIENDS-USA...	1	16	19*	–	–
244 GRACE BRETHREN	2	94	115*	–	–
263 INT FOURSQ GOS	5	268	331*	–	–
270 CONSRV JUDAISM	6	714	861*	–	0.1
271 REFORM JUDAISM	6	1 530	1 855*	0.1	0.1
281 LUTH CH AMER..	155	44 780	57 322	1.8	3.6
283 LUTH--MO SYNOD	11	1 570	2 146	0.1	0.1
285 MENNONITE CH..	5	198	242*	–	–
290 METRO COMM CHS	1	35	70	–	–
347 PENT FW BAPT..	1	35	43*	–	–
349 PENT HOLINESS.	245	18 525	22 843*	0.7	1.4
353 CHR BRETHREN..	19	770	1 095	–	0.1
356 PRESB CH AMER.	51	8 287	9 390	0.3	0.6
357 PRESB CH US...	294	69 700	85 185*	2.7	5.3
375 REF EPISCOPAL.	30	2 352	2 928*	0.1	0.2
381 REF PRES-EVAN.	10	1 724	2 037	0.1	0.1
403 SALVATION ARMY	15	1 561	6 031	0.2	0.4
413 S.D.A.........	41	3 865	4 734*	0.2	0.3
419 SO BAPT CONV..	1 674	655 646	802 152*	25.7	50.0
421 SO METHODIST..	60	3 746	4 860	0.2	0.3
435 UNITARIAN-UNIV	7	433	521*	–	–
443 UN C OF CHRIST	2	234	282*	–	–
449 UN METHODIST..	1 089	240 052	294 818*	9.5	18.4
453 UN PRES CH USA	58	6 739	8 269*	0.3	0.5
469 WELS.........	2	67	109	–	–
SOUTH DAKOTA	1 710	245 267	462 277*	67.0	100.0
019 AMER BAPT USA.	44	7 684	9 355*	1.4	2.0
029 AMER LUTH CH..	250	84 068	110 152	16.0	23.8
045 APOSTOLIC LUTH	2	70	85*	–	–
053 ASSEMB OF GOD.	43	3 023	5 586	0.8	1.2
057 BAPT GEN CONF.	19	2 587	3 153*	0.5	0.7
063 BEREAN FUND CH	2	63	76*	–	–
081 CATHOLIC.....	268	NA	138 387	20.1	29.9
089 CHR & MISS AL.	13	511	977	0.1	0.2
093 CHR CH (DISC).	2	459	737	0.1	0.2
097 CHR CHS&CHS CR	17	1 261	1 534*	0.2	0.3
105 CHRISTIAN REF.	15	2 501	3 884	0.6	0.8
123 CH GOD (ANDER)	5	370	1 110	0.2	0.2
127 CH GOD (CLEVE)	14	481	592*	0.1	0.1
133 CH GOD(7TH)DEN	1	47	56*	–	–
143 CG IN CR(MENN)	1	73	73	–	–
151 L-D SAINTS....	32	NA	2 790	0.4	0.6
163 CH OF LUTH BR.	4	147	203	–	–
164 CH LUTH CONF..	12	706	956	0.1	0.2
165 CH OF NAZARENE	18	785	1 645	0.2	0.4
167 CHS OF CHRIST.	22	733	965	0.1	0.2
181 CONSRV CONGR..	2	40	49*	–	–
193 EPISCOPAL.....	129	8 854	13 195	1.9	2.9
201 EVAN COV CH AM	8	479	587*	0.1	0.1
203 EVAN FREE CH..	10	396	487*	0.1	0.1
209 EVAN LUTH SYN.	2	135	167	–	–
211 EVAN MENN BR..	1	131	170	–	–
220 FREE LUTHERAN.	12	799	1 029	0.1	0.2
221 FREE METHODIST	6	158	451	0.1	0.1
226 FRIENDS-USA...	2	29	36*	–	–
237 GC MENN BR CHS	10	1 027	1 254*	0.2	0.3
263 INT FOURSQ GOS	7	306	373*	0.1	0.1
270 CONSRV JUDAISM	1	8	10*	–	–
271 REFORM JUDAISM	2	168	205*	–	–
281 LUTH CH AMER..	26	5 141	6 663	1.0	1.4
283 LUTH--MO SYNOD	113	25 975	33 773	4.9	7.3
285 MENNONITE CH..	2	30	36*	–	–
287 MENN GEN CONF.	11	2 358	3 012	0.4	0.7
290 METRO COMM CHS	1	25	50	–	–
291 MISSIONARY CH.	2	114	165	–	–
313 N AM BAPT CONF	23	3 326	4 033*	0.6	0.9
329 OPEN BIBLE STD	14	1 301	1 895	0.3	0.4
335 ORTH PRESB CH.	6	287	346*	0.1	0.1
369 PROT REF CHS..	1	16	25	–	–
371 REF CH IN AM..	28	3 941	6 862	1.0	1.5
381 REF PRES-EVAN.	1	64	84	–	–
403 SALVATION ARMY	6	705	1 956	0.3	0.4
413 S.D.A.........	25	2 022	2 474*	0.4	0.5
419 SO BAPT CONV..	31	3 575	4 394*	0.6	1.0
435 UNITARIAN-UNIV	3	74	89*	–	–
443 UN C OF CHRIST	106	17 151	20 872*	3.0	4.5
449 UN METHODIST..	180	38 046	46 234*	6.7	10.0
453 UN PRES CH USA	97	15 102	18 441*	2.7	4.0
469 WELS.........	58	7 915	10 544	1.5	2.3
TENNESSEE	8 529	1 911 978	2 492 387*	54.3	100.0
001 ADVENT CHR CH.	2	120	146*	–	–
005 AME ZION......	57	17 733	21 739	0.5	0.9
017 AMER BAPT ASSN	18	4 240	4 240	0.1	0.2
019 AMER BAPT USA.	6	4 215	5 084*	0.1	0.2
029 AMER LUTH CH..	6	965	1 293	–	0.1
053 ASSEMB OF GOD.	171	16 992	23 874	0.5	1.0
055 AS REF PRES CH	13	1 740	1 895	–	0.1
059 BAPT MISS ASSN	11	1 517	1 837*	–	0.1
061 BEACHY AMISH..	3	123	148*	–	–
065 BETHEL M ASSN.	1	200	245*	–	–
075 BRETHREN IN CR	3	129	219	–	–
081 CATHOLIC.....	128	NA	114 916	2.5	4.6
089 CHR & MISS AL.	8	594	899	–	–
093 CHR CH (DISC).	69	14 787	19 397	0.4	0.8
097 CHR CHS&CHS CR	153	26 912	32 457*	0.7	1.3
101 C.M.E.........	153	75 888	92 533*	2.0	3.7
123 CH GOD (ANDER)	68	4 785	14 355	0.3	0.6
127 CH GOD (CLEVE)	325	30 417	36 929*	0.8	1.5
133 CH GOD(7TH)DEN	4	47	56*	–	–
143 CG IN CR(MENN)	1	20	20	–	–
151 L-D SAINTS....	49	NA	10 502	0.2	0.4
157 CH OF BRETHREN	22	1 425	1 711*	–	0.1
165 CH OF NAZARENE	168	14 402	23 951	0.5	1.0
167 CHS OF CHRIST.	1 444	174 355	226 320	4.9	9.1
185 CUMBER PRESB..	301	22 182	38 252	0.8	1.5
193 EPISCOPAL.....	110	32 115	41 543	0.9	1.7
201 EVAN COV CH AM	1	29	35*	–	–
208 EVAN LUTH ASSN	1	101	121	–	–
215 EVAN METH CH..	5	505	617*	–	–
221 FREE METHODIST	10	226	1 002	–	–
226 FRIENDS-USA...	12	577	696*	–	–
244 GRACE BRETHREN	3	208	249*	–	–
263 INT FOURSQ GOS	7	855	1 044*	–	–
270 CONSRV JUDAISM	5	1 082	1 296*	–	0.1
271 REFORM JUDAISM	7	5 336	6 451*	0.1	0.3
281 LUTH CH AMER..	43	10 333	13 353	0.3	0.5
283 LUTH--MO SYNOD	45	7 885	11 157	0.2	0.4
285 MENNONITE CH..	4	119	142*	–	–
290 METRO COMM CHS	3	152	304	–	–
323 OLD ORD AMISH.	6	780	943*	–	–
335 ORTH PRESB CH.	1	30	36*	–	–
349 PENT HOLINESS.	23	1 483	1 805*	–	0.1
353 CHR BRETHREN..	6	310	400	–	–
356 PRESB CH AMER.	24	4 739	5 131	0.1	0.2
357 PRESB CH US...	215	54 529	65 867*	1.4	2.6
381 REF PRES-EVAN.	4	464	610	–	–
403 SALVATION ARMY	12	1 359	2 791	0.1	0.1
409 SEPARATE BAPT.	5	513	638*	–	–
413 S.D.A.........	108	17 238	20 829*	0.5	0.8
415 S-D BAPTIST GC	1	15	18*	–	–

NA—Not applicable   *Total adherents estimated from known number of communicant, confirmed, full members.   —Represents a percent less than 0.1.   Percentages may not total due to rounding.

Table 3. Churches and Church Membership by State and Denomination: 1980

County and Denomination	Number of churches	Communicant, confirmed, full members	Total adherents		
			Number	Percent of total population	Percent of total adherents
419 SO BAPT CONV..	2 754	994 388	1 203 537*	26.2	48.3
421 SO METHODIST..	20	1 311	1 644	–	0.1
435 UNITARIAN-UNIV	9	1 481	1 779*	–	0.1
443 UN C OF CHRIST	17	1 808	2 185*	–	0.1
449 UN METHODIST..	1 738	341 616	413 149*	9.0	16.6
453 UN PRES CH USA	143	16 427	19 742*	0.4	0.8
469 WELS.........	3	176	255	–	–
TEXAS	16 111	4 311 259	7 781 967*	54.7	100.0
001 ADVENT CHR CH.	4	299	364*	–	–
005 AME ZION......	7	1 752	2 095	–	–
017 AMER BAPT ASSN	340	45 361	45 361	0.3	0.6
019 AMER BAPT USA.	59	17 787	21 770*	0.2	0.3
029 AMER LUTH CH..	257	85 286	106 657	0.7	1.4
053 ASSEMB OF GOD.	1 134	117 957	162 232	1.1	2.1
059 BAPT MISS ASSN	517	97 351	118 643*	0.8	1.5
075 BRETHREN IN CR	1	57	86	–	–
081 CATHOLIC......	1 227	NA	2 340 162	16.4	30.1
089 CHR & MISS AL.	23	1 160	2 239	–	–
093 CHR CH (DISC).	448	84 295	120 296	0.8	1.5
097 CHR CHS&CHS CR	149	22 090	27 255*	0.2	0.4
101 C.M.E........	312	68 825	83 932*	0.6	1.1
105 CHRISTIAN REF.	3	105	165	–	–
121 CH GOD (ABR)..	3	86	107*	–	–
123 CH GOD (ANDER)	84	5 550	16 650	0.1	0.2
127 CH GOD (CLEVE)	192	12 824	15 708*	0.1	0.2
133 CH GOD(7TH)DEN	20	644	804*	–	–
143 CG IN CR(MENN)	4	207	207	–	–
149 CH OF JC (BIC)	1	13	13	–	–
151 L-D SAINTS....	212	NA	68 375	0.5	0.9
157 CH OF BRETHREN	4	310	377*	–	–
164 CH LUTH CONF..	3	147	201	–	–
165 CH OF NAZARENE	309	24 670	39 479	0.3	0.5
167 CHS OF CHRIST.	2 222	278 820	355 396	2.5	4.6
175 CONGR CHR CHS.	3	633	782*	–	–
177 CONGR HOL CH..	2	60	73*	–	–
181 CONSRV CONGR..	1	74	92*	–	–
185 CUMBER PRESB..	51	4 969	8 408	0.1	0.1
193 EPISCOPAL.....	395	136 416	174 581	1.2	2.2
197 EVAN CH OF NA.	1	46	46	–	–
199 EVAN CONGR CH.	1	38	50*	–	–
201 EVAN COV CH AM	1	59	77*	–	–
203 EVAN FREE CH..	15	1 142	1 394*	–	–
208 EVAN LUTH ASSN	4	657	925	–	–
209 EVAN LUTH SYN.	2	39	157	–	–
215 EVAN METH CH..	17	1 686	2 050*	–	–
221 FREE METHODIST	18	564	1 857	–	–
226 FRIENDS-USA...	15	1 525	1 867*	–	–
237 GC MENN BR CHS	9	358	461*	–	–
244 GRACE BRETHREN	1	13	16*	–	–
263 INT FOURSQ GOS	49	5 674	6 988*	–	0.1
270 CONSRV JUDAISM	16	6 136	7 557*	0.1	0.1
271 REFORM JUDAISM	30	18 592	22 857*	0.2	0.3
281 LUTH CH AMER..	106	27 934	36 670	0.3	0.5
283 LUTH--MO SYNOD	311	88 377	117 074	0.8	1.5
285 MENNONITE CH..	10	564	712*	–	–
287 MENN GEN CONF.	1	60	84	–	–
290 METRO COMM CHS	7	1 004	2 008	–	–
313 N AM BAPT CONF	11	798	981*	–	–
335 ORTH PRESB CH.	2	244	299*	–	–
349 PENT HOLINESS	70	3 353	4 190*	–	0.1
353 CHR BRETHREN..	32	2 015	3 520	–	–
356 PRESB CH AMER.	15	1 309	1 543	–	–
357 PRESB CH US...	519	106 566	130 895*	0.9	1.7
369 PROT REF CHS..	1	10	26	–	–
381 REF PRES-EVAN.	3	355	454	–	–
403 SALVATION ARMY	44	4 379	14 720	0.1	0.2
413 S.D.A........	178	18 974	23 354*	0.2	0.3
415 S-D BAPTIST GC	2	18	22*	–	–
419 SO BAPT CONV..	3 896	2 172 997	2 659 894*	18.7	34.2
421 SO METHODIST..	6	229	315	–	–
423 SYRIAN ANTIOCH	2	800	976*	–	–
435 UNITARIAN-UNIV	34	3 838	4 701*	–	0.1
443 UN C OF CHRIST	71	16 889	20 626*	0.1	0.3
449 UN METHODIST..	2 257	761 290	932 488*	6.6	12.0
453 UN PRES CH USA	348	53 278	65 150*	0.5	0.8
469 WELS.........	19	1 701	2 453	–	–
UTAH	2 422	39 496	1 098 578*	75.2	100.0
017 AMER BAPT ASSN	1	25	25	–	–
019 AMER BAPT USA.	10	2 759	3 580*	0.2	0.3
029 AMER LUTH CH..	4	962	1 485	0.1	0.1
053 ASSEMB OF GOD.	24	1 618	2 820	0.2	0.3
057 BAPT GEN CONF.	1	180	241*	–	–
081 CATHOLIC......	53	NA	59 844	4.1	5.4
089 CHR & MISS AL.	3	164	276	–	–
093 CHR CH (DISC).	3	579	732	0.1	0.1

County and Denomination	Number of churches	Communicant, confirmed, full members	Total adherents		
			Number	Percent of total population	Percent of total adherents
097 CHR CHS&CHS CR	5	666	856*	0.1	0.1
105 CHRISTIAN REF.	5	291	527	–	–
127 CH GOD (CLEVE)	4	80	102*	–	–
151 L-D SAINTS....	2 135	NA	985 070	67.4	89.7
165 CH OF NAZARENE	5	219	407	–	–
167 CHS OF CHRIST.	16	588	942	0.1	0.1
175 CONGR CHR CHS.	1	351	452*	–	–
179 CONSRV BAPT...	5	480	620*	–	0.1
193 EPISCOPAL.....	20	3 307	4 490	0.3	0.4
203 EVAN FREE CH..	2	190	246*	–	–
226 FRIENDS-USA...	2	41	52*	–	–
270 CONSRV JUDAISM	1	100	129*	–	–
271 REFORM JUDAISM	1	790	1 017*	0.1	0.1
281 LUTH CH AMER..	6	1 832	2 664	0.2	0.2
283 LUTH--MO SYNOD	13	3 082	4 480	0.3	0.4
290 METRO COMM CHS	1	25	50	–	–
403 SALVATION ARMY	2	207	290	–	–
413 S.D.A........	11	1 161	1 515*	0.1	0.1
419 SO BAPT CONV..	45	7 915	10 319*	0.7	0.9
435 UNITARIAN-UNIV	1	315	406*	–	–
443 UN C OF CHRIST	8	1 646	2 159*	0.1	0.2
449 UN METHODIST..	14	4 626	5 951*	0.4	0.5
453 UN PRES CH USA	19	5 239	6 742*	0.5	0.6
469 WELS.........	1	58	89	–	–
VERMONT	716	68 523	244 730*	47.8	100.0
001 ADVENT CHR CH.	7	445	538*	0.1	0.2
019 AMER BAPT USA.	67	9 014	10 902*	2.1	4.5
029 AMER LUTH CH..	2	124	208	–	0.1
053 ASSEMB OF GOD.	15	803	1 707	0.3	0.7
081 CATHOLIC......	145	NA	156 596	30.6	64.0
089 CHR & MISS AL.	11	571	900	0.2	0.4
097 CHR CHS&CHS CR	4	147	177*	–	0.1
105 CHRISTIAN REF.	1	168	320	0.1	0.1
123 CH GOD (ANDER)	1	18	54	–	–
127 CH GOD (CLEVE)	1	19	23*	–	–
151 L-D SAINTS....	8	NA	1 724	0.3	0.7
165 CH OF NAZARENE	9	431	810	0.2	0.3
167 CHS OF CHRIST.	13	700	895	0.2	0.4
175 CONGR CHR CHS.	3	214	257*	0.1	0.1
193 EPISCOPAL.....	50	7 422	10 455	2.0	4.3
201 EVAN COV CH AM	2	10	12*	–	–
203 EVAN FREE CH..	2	230	278*	0.1	0.1
208 EVAN LUTH ASSN	1	38	56	–	–
221 FREE METHODIST	1	33	123	–	0.1
226 FRIENDS-USA...	8	207	250*	–	0.1
244 GRACE BRETHREN	2	75	92*	–	–
270 CONSRV JUDAISM	2	440	528*	0.1	0.2
271 REFORM JUDAISM	1	132	159*	–	0.1
281 LUTH CH AMER..	4	773	1 089	0.2	0.4
283 LUTH--MO SYNOD	1	243	301	0.1	0.1
285 MENNONITE CH..	3	129	155*	–	0.1
335 ORTH PRESB CH.	1	28	34*	–	–
353 CHR BRETHREN..	1	25	25	–	–
403 SALVATION ARMY	3	150	401	0.1	0.2
413 S.D.A........	13	623	755*	0.1	0.3
419 SO BAPT CONV..	6	414	501*	0.1	0.2
435 UNITARIAN-UNIV	17	1 423	1 714*	0.3	0.7
443 UN C OF CHRIST	157	20 711	25 066*	4.9	10.2
449 UN METHODIST..	143	21 789	26 443*	5.2	10.8
453 UN PRES CH USA	11	974	1 182*	0.2	0.5
VIRGINIA	6 496	1 548 865	2 232 913*	41.8	100.0
001 ADVENT CHR CH.	16	1 530	1 838*	–	0.1
005 AME ZION......	64	24 791	29 776	0.6	1.3
017 AMER BAPT ASSN	3	376	376	–	–
019 AMER BAPT USA.	77	31 517	37 534*	0.7	1.7
029 AMER LUTH CH..	19	7 228	10 260	0.2	0.5
039 AP CHR CH(NAZ)	1	44	52*	–	–
053 ASSEMB OF GOD.	144	13 685	25 096	0.5	1.1
055 AS REF PRES CH	10	2 161	2 425	–	0.1
057 BAPT GEN CONF.	1	65	79*	–	–
059 BAPT MISS ASSN	1	569	690*	–	–
061 BEACHY AMISH..	8	413	498*	–	–
071 BRETHREN (ASH)	5	511	605*	–	–
075 BRETHREN IN CR	5	545	655	–	–
081 CATHOLIC......	186	NA	284 389	5.3	12.7
089 CHR & MISS AL.	14	1 314	2 791	0.1	0.1
093 CHR CH (DISC).	229	30 979	48 798	0.9	2.2
097 CHR CHS&CHS CR	209	33 575	40 456*	0.8	1.8
101 C.M.E........	24	5 942	7 107*	0.1	0.3
105 CHRISTIAN REF.	2	140	239	–	–
121 CH GOD (ABR)..	5	220	264*	–	–
123 CH GOD (ANDER)	55	3 167	9 501	0.2	0.4
127 CH GOD (CLEVE)	163	13 264	15 956*	0.3	0.7
133 CH GOD(7TH)DEN	1	5	6*	–	–
149 CH OF JC (BIC)	1	36	37	–	–
151 L-D SAINTS....	73	NA	26 137	0.5	1.2

NA— Not applicable   *Total adherents estimated from known number of communicant, confirmed, full members.   —Represents a percent less than 0.1.   Percentages may not total due to rounding.

Table 3. Churches and Church Membership by State and Denomination: 1980

County and Denomination	Number of churches	Communicant, confirmed, full members	Total adherents Number	Percent of total population	Percent of total adherents
157 CH OF BRETHREN	157	29 721	35 438*	0.7	1.6
165 CH OF NAZARENE	64	6 381	12 178	0.2	0.5
167 CHS OF CHRIST.	130	10 610	14 201	0.3	0.6
177 CONGR HOL CH..	3	50	58*	-	-
181 CONSRV CONGR..	1	77	94*	-	-
193 EPISCOPAL.....	347	95 865	134 258	2.5	6.0
201 EVAN COV CH AM	3	120	147*	-	-
203 EVAN FREE CH..	2	254	313*	-	-
208 EVAN LUTH ASSN	1	39	50	-	-
215 EVAN METH CH..	4	458	547*	-	-
221 FREE METHODIST	4	209	854	-	-
226 FRIENDS-USA...	28	1 978	2 385*	-	0.1
244 GRACE BRETHREN	19	2 829	3 357*	0.1	0.2
247 HOLINESS CH...	2	170	170	-	-
263 INT FOURSQ GOS	4	885	1 052*	-	-
270 CONSRV JUDAISM	12	3 177	3 772*	0.1	0.2
271 REFORM JUDAISM	18	6 534	7 740*	0.1	0.3
281 LUTH CH AMER..	168	38 372	50 368	0.9	2.3
283 LUTH--MO SYNOD	41	10 663	14 290	0.3	0.6
285 MENNONITE CH..	62	5 529	6 561*	0.1	0.3
290 METRO COMM CHS	3	175	350	-	-
295 MORAV CH-SOUTH	3	196	237	-	-
323 OLD ORD AMISH.	1	130	155*	-	-
329 OPEN BIBLE STD	1	30	60	-	-
335 ORTH PRESB CH.	6	355	430*	-	-
347 PENT FW BAPT..	5	394	479*	-	-
349 PENT HOLINESS.	115	10 261	12 342*	0.2	0.6
353 CHR BRETHREN..	15	675	945	-	-
356 PRESB CH AMER.	31	4 008	4 414	0.1	0.2
357 PRESB CH US...	490	105 289	125 715*	2.4	5.6
381 REF PRES-EVAN.	11	1 118	1 469	-	0.1
403 SALVATION ARMY	24	2 454	6 723	0.1	0.3
413 S.D.A.........	79	9 128	10 933*	0.2	0.5
419 SO BAPT CONV..	1 431	574 961	690 276*	12.9	30.9
421 SO METHODIST..	2	99	136	-	-
435 UNITARIAN-UNIV	17	2 830	3 312*	0.1	0.1
443 UN C OF CHRIST	117	21 659	26 117*	0.5	1.2
449 UN METHODIST..	1 688	417 433	501 217*	9.4	22.4
453 UN PRES CH USA	69	11 348	13 708*	0.3	0.6
469 WELS.........	2	324	497	-	-
WASHINGTON	3 381	584 461	1 280 918*	31.0	100.0
001 ADVENT CHR CH.	6	630	757*	-	0.1
005 AME ZION......	3	677	770	-	0.1
017 AMER BAPT ASSN	12	521	521	-	-
019 AMER BAPT USA.	131	31 501	37 893*	0.9	3.0
029 AMER LUTH CH..	177	63 836	87 554	2.1	6.8
039 AP CHR CH(NAZ)	1	35	43*	-	-
045 APOSTOLIC LUTH	5	990	1 211*	-	0.1
053 ASSEMB OF GOD.	256	32 939	59 591	1.4	4.7
057 BAPT GEN CONF.	39	7 641	9 214*	0.2	0.7
059 BAPT MISS ASSN	7	275	334*	-	-
081 CATHOLIC......	299	NA	380 023	9.2	29.7
089 CHR & MISS AL.	46	3 603	6 650	0.2	0.5
093 CHR CH (DISC).	80	14 264	21 130	0.5	1.6
097 CHR CHS&CHS CR	65	10 914	13 144*	0.3	1.0
101 C.M.E.........	5	1 194	1 442*	-	0.1
105 CHRISTIAN REF.	31	5 048	8 711	0.2	0.7
121 CH GOD (ABR)..	2	135	161*	-	-
123 CH GOD (ANDER)	48	4 874	14 622	0.4	1.1
127 CH GOD (CLEVE)	40	1 950	2 386*	0.1	0.2
133 CH GOD(7TH)DEN	5	106	127*	-	-
151 L-D SAINTS....	238	NA	105 073	2.5	8.2
157 CH OF BRETHREN	12	1 826	2 197*	0.1	0.2
163 CH OF LUTH BR.	13	1 057	2 213	0.1	0.2
164 CH LUTH CONF..	4	507	733	-	0.1
165 CH OF NAZARENE	125	14 375	25 062	0.6	2.0
167 CHS OF CHRIST.	107	10 164	13 314	0.3	1.0
175 CONGR CHR CHS.	5	1 004	1 218*	-	0.1
179 CONSRV BAPT...	60	9 460	11 519*	0.3	0.9
193 EPISCOPAL.....	126	38 166	51 354	1.2	4.0
195 ESTONIAN ELC..	1	88	250	-	-
197 EVAN CH OF NA.	16	1 655	1 655	-	0.1
201 EVAN COV CH AM	32	4 510	5 417*	0.1	0.4
203 EVAN FREE CH..	28	1 777	2 155*	0.1	0.2
209 EVAN LUTH SYN.	5	725	1 064	-	0.1
215 EVAN METH CH..	6	274	336*	-	-
217 FIRE BAPTIZED.	1	9	11*	-	-
220 FREE LUTHERAN.	6	643	843	-	0.1
221 FREE METHODIST	55	4 953	15 405	0.4	1.2
226 FRIENDS-USA...	18	1 891	2 291*	0.1	0.2
233 GEN CH NEW JER	1	60	71*	-	-
237 GC MENN BR CHS	4	328	396*	-	-
239 SWEDENBORGIAN.	1	60	71*	-	-
244 GRACE BRETHREN	10	1 068	1 309*	-	0.1
263 INT FOURSQ GOS	29	2 694	3 284*	0.1	0.3
270 CONSRV JUDAISM	3	758	900*	-	0.1
271 REFORM JUDAISM	4	4 158	4 929*	0.1	0.4
274 LAT EVAN LUTH.	3	703	825	-	0.1
281 LUTH CH AMER..	90	31 174	43 364	1.0	3.4
283 LUTH--MO SYNOD	107	31 139	44 126	1.1	3.4
285 MENNONITE CH..	1	64	81*	-	-
287 MENN GEN CONF.	5	449	595	-	-
290 METRO COMM CHS	2	222	410	-	-
291 MISSIONARY CH.	7	279	351	-	-
313 N AM BAPT CONF	12	1 733	2 074*	0.1	0.2
329 OPEN BIBLE STD	21	2 938	4 250	0.1	0.3
335 ORTH PRESB CH.	1	46	56*	-	-
349 PENT HOLINESS.	10	543	664*	-	0.1
353 CHR BRETHREN..	26	1 375	1 855	-	0.1
356 PRESB CH AMER.	2	608	640	-	-
369 PROT REF CHS..	1	82	190	-	-
371 REF CH IN AM..	8	1 821	3 320	0.1	0.3
381 REF PRES-EVAN.	9	733	961	-	0.1
383 REF PRES OF NA	1	70	94	-	-
403 SALVATION ARMY	20	2 008	5 205	0.1	0.4
413 S.D.A.........	138	25 652	31 086*	0.8	2.4
415 S-D BAPT GC	1	70	83*	-	-
419 SO BAPT CONV..	147	37 303	45 306*	1.1	3.5
435 UNITARIAN-UNIV	23	2 240	2 690*	0.1	0.2
443 UN C OF CHRIST	95	16 796	20 172*	0.5	1.6
449 UN METHODIST..	253	81 118	98 114*	2.4	7.7
453 UN PRES CH USA	207	59 604	71 838*	1.7	5.6
469 WELS.........	23	2 348	3 214	0.1	0.3
WEST VIRGINIA	4 159	509 754	774 064*	39.7	100.0
001 ADVENT CHR CH.	42	1 949	2 369*	0.1	0.3
005 AME ZION......	9	1 276	1 489	0.1	0.2
017 AMER BAPT ASSN	9	429	429	-	0.1
019 AMER BAPT USA.	613	128 103	156 126*	8.0	20.2
029 AMER LUTH CH..	18	3 311	4 393	0.2	0.6
053 ASSEMB OF GOD.	91	6 275	12 182	0.6	1.6
055 AS REF PRES CH	2	195	215	-	-
061 BEACHY AMISH..	1	29	35*	-	-
071 BRETHREN (ASH)	5	287	350*	-	-
075 BRETHREN IN CR	1	82	132	-	-
081 CATHOLIC......	175	NA	105 346	5.4	13.6
089 CHR & MISS AL.	10	720	1 685	0.1	0.2
093 CHR CH (DISC).	79	10 205	15 650	0.8	2.0
097 CHR CHS&CHS CR	101	13 338	16 215*	0.8	2.1
101 C.M.E.........	2	108	130*	-	-
123 CH GOD (ANDER)	95	5 570	16 710	0.9	2.2
127 CH GOD (CLEVE)	186	13 352	16 452*	0.8	2.1
133 CH GOD(7TH)DEN	1	1	1*	-	-
151 L-D SAINTS....	25	NA	8 015	0.4	1.0
157 CH OF BRETHREN	69	7 132	8 689*	0.4	1.1
165 CH OF NAZARENE	119	12 468	26 538	1.4	3.4
167 CHS OF CHRIST.	276	22 969	30 473	1.6	3.9
175 CONGR CHR CHS.	1	63	78*	-	-
193 EPISCOPAL.....	85	13 739	19 091	1.0	2.5
203 EVAN FREE CH..	1	53	65*	-	-
215 EVAN METH CH..	2	182	221*	-	-
221 FREE METHODIST	20	637	3 429	0.2	0.4
226 FRIENDS-USA...	1	6	7*	-	-
244 GRACE BRETHREN	3	411	502*	-	0.1
247 HOLINESS CH...	2	80	80	-	-
263 INT FOURSQ GOS	1	50	61*	-	-
270 CONSRV JUDAISM	2	582	701*	-	0.1
271 REFORM JUDAISM	11	1 408	1 690*	0.1	0.2
281 LUTH CH AMER..	42	9 481	12 401	0.6	1.6
283 LUTH--MO SYNOD	3	468	645	-	0.1
285 MENNONITE CH..	9	299	361*	-	-
290 METRO COMM CHS	1	45	90	-	-
329 OPEN BIBLE STD	2	91	140	-	-
349 PENT HOLINESS.	44	2 768	3 400*	0.2	0.4
353 CHR BRETHREN..	6	210	625	-	0.1
356 PRESB CH AMER.	8	643	747	-	0.1
357 PRESB CH US...	163	25 225	30 538*	1.6	3.9
359 PRIM AD CHR CH	10	542	542	-	0.1
381 REF PRES-EVAN.	1	?	?	?	?
403 SALVATION ARMY	20	1 734	4 164	0.2	0.5
413 S.D.A.........	34	2 565	3 108*	0.2	0.4
415 S-D BAPT GC	4	314	379*	-	-
419 SO BAPT CONV..	87	23 942	29 239*	1.5	3.8
435 UNITARIAN-UNIV	6	164	195*	-	-
443 UN C OF CHRIST	9	1 488	1 786*	0.1	0.2
449 UN METHODIST..	1 584	180 959	219 560*	11.3	28.4
453 UN PRES CH USA	67	13 783	16 565*	0.8	2.1
469 WELS.........	1	23	30	-	-
WISCONSIN	4 698	1 138 006	3 038 209*	64.6	100.0
001 ADVENT CHR CH.	6	449	547*	-	-
005 AME ZION......	1	164	221	-	-
019 AMER BAPT USA.	91	16 818	20 329*	0.4	0.7
029 AMER LUTH CH..	544	259 987	347 591	7.4	11.4

NA—Not applicable   *Total adherents estimated from known number of communicant, confirmed, full members.   —Represents a percent less than 0.1.   Percentages may not total due to rounding.

Table 3. Churches and Church Membership by State and Denomination: 1980

County and Denomination	Number of churches	Communicant, confirmed, full members	Total adherents Number	Percent of total population	Percent of total adherents
049 ARMEN AP CH AM	1	100	200	–	–
053 ASSEMB OF GOD.	128	12 684	22 435	0.5	0.7
057 BAPT GEN CONF.	51	5 092	6 175*	0.1	0.2
075 BRETHREN IN CR	1	43	73	–	–
081 CATHOLIC......	984	NA	1 544 817	32.8	50.8
089 CHR & MISS AL.	25	1 413	3 122	0.1	0.1
093 CHR CH (DISC).	3	381	474	–	–
097 CHR CHS&CHS CR	35	4 728	5 751*	0.1	0.2
101 C.M.E.........	7	5 223	6 271*	0.1	0.2
105 CHRISTIAN REF.	18	3 630	5 978	0.1	0.2
121 CH GOD (ABR)..	1	25	30*	–	–
123 CH GOD (ANDER)	16	999	2 997	0.1	0.1
127 CH GOD (CLEVE)	23	888	1 083*	–	–
133 CH GOD(7TH)DEN	1	21	26*	–	–
143 CG IN CR(MENN)	2	227	227	–	–
151 L-D SAINTS....	28	NA	7 655	0.2	0.3
157 CH OF BRETHREN	4	254	314*	–	–
163 CH OF LUTH BR.	5	345	629	–	–
164 CH LUTH CONF..	10	1 125	1 507	–	–
165 CH OF NAZARENE	42	2 353	4 386	0.1	0.1
167 CHS OF CHRIST.	55	2 632	3 499	0.1	0.1
175 CONGR CHR CHS.	28	10 334	12 509*	0.3	0.4
179 CONSRV BAPT...	19	1 570	1 902*	–	0.1
181 CONSRV CONGR..	11	1 581	1 911*	–	0.1
193 EPISCOPAL.....	132	24 883	31 944	0.7	1.1
197 EVAN CH OF NA.	1	37	37	–	–
201 EVAN COV CH AM	27	1 952	2 364*	0.1	0.1
203 EVAN FREE CH..	49	2 670	3 224*	0.1	0.1
208 EVAN LUTH ASSN	5	4 426	5 629	0.1	0.2
209 EVAN LUTH SYN	19	4 796	6 216	0.1	0.2
220 FREE LUTHERAN.	9	707	914	–	–
221 FREE METHODIST	12	681	2 007	–	0.1
226 FRIENDS-USA...	9	443	532*	–	–
263 INT FOURSQ GOS	7	898	1 088*	–	–
270 CONSRV JUDAISM	9	1 625	1 953*	–	0.1
271 REFORM JUDAISM	8	6 226	7 454*	0.2	0.2
274 LAT EVAN LUTH.	5	968	1 099	–	–
281 LUTH CH AMER..	180	86 221	116 102	2.5	3.8
283 LUTH--MO SYNOD	414	194 168	254 683	5.4	8.4
285 MENNONITE CH..	12	366	446*	–	–
287 MENN GEN CONF.	1	21	36	–	–
290 METRO COMM CHS	1	65	130	–	–
293 MORAV CH-NORTH	20	5 298	6 622	0.1	0.2
313 N AM BAPT CONF	14	2 492	3 029*	0.1	0.1
323 OLD ORD AMISH.	20	2 600	3 174*	0.1	0.1
329 OPEN BIBLE STD	2	140	250	–	–
335 ORTH PRESB CH.	6	1 048	1 277*	–	–
349 PENT HOLINESS.	1	28	34*	–	–
353 CHR BRETHREN..	16	545	780	–	–
363 PRIMITIVE METH	11	664	809*	–	–
367 PROT CONF (WI)	7	742	1 050	–	–
369 PROT REF CHS..	1	61	121	–	–
371 REF CH IN AM..	26	8 195	12 909	0.3	0.4
381 REF PRES-EVAN.	1	70	99	–	–
395 ROMANIAN OR CH	1	25	30*	–	–
403 SALVATION ARMY	20	2 614	9 134	0.2	0.3
413 S.D.A.........	78	6 761	8 185*	0.2	0.3
415 S-D BAPTIST GC	3	614	754*	–	–
419 SO BAPT CONV..	44	7 861	9 466*	0.2	0.3
435 UNITARIAN-UNIV	19	2 357	2 853*	0.1	0.1
443 UN C OF CHRIST	264	79 706	96 915*	2.1	3.2
449 UN METHODIST..	526	135 169	164 199*	3.5	5.4
453 UN PRES CH USA	174	45 860	55 582*	1.2	1.8
469 WELS.........	404	170 937	222 420	4.7	7.3
WYOMING	628	77 189	207 484*	44.1	100.0
017 AMER BAPT ASSN	2	100	100	–	–
019 AMER BAPT USA.	23	5 829	7 183*	1.5	3.5
029 AMER LUTH CH..	11	2 898	4 374	0.9	2.1
053 ASSEMB OF GOD.	47	2 363	4 294	0.9	2.1
057 BAPT GEN CONF.	6	745	911*	0.2	0.4
063 BEREAN FUND CH	3	139	170*	–	0.1
071 BRETHREN (ASH)	1	40	49*	–	–
081 CATHOLIC......	69	NA	62 315	13.2	30.0
089 CHR & MISS AL.	8	208	439	0.1	0.2
093 CHR CH (DISC).	4	1 611	2 081	0.4	1.0
097 CHR CHS&CHS CR	20	1 510	1 887*	0.4	0.9
123 CH GOD (ANDER)	6	339	1 017	0.2	0.5
127 CH GOD (CLEVE)	2	232	286*	0.1	0.1
151 L-D SAINTS....	107	NA	40 368	8.6	19.5
164 CH LUTH CONF..	1	77	110	–	0.1
165 CH OF NAZARENE	18	1 126	2 120	0.5	1.0
167 CHS OF CHRIST.	26	1 361	2 108	0.4	1.0
175 CONGR CHR CHS.	3	1 651	2 026*	0.4	1.0
179 CONSRV BAPT...	6	3 210	3 924*	0.8	1.9
193 EPISCOPAL.....	49	7 960	13 057	2.8	6.3
201 EVAN COV CH AM	1	41	50*	–	–
203 EVAN FREE CH..	3	129	163*	–	0.1
221 FREE METHODIST	1	11	90	–	–
244 GRACE BRETHREN	1	12	15*	–	–
263 INT FOURSQ GOS	5	139	171*	–	0.1
281 LUTH CH AMER..	7	2 392	3 326	0.7	1.6
283 LUTH--MO SYNOD	39	7 609	10 640	2.3	5.1
290 METRO COMM CHS	0	20	40	–	–
329 OPEN BIBLE STD	6	760	1 168	0.2	0.6
335 ORTH PRESB CH.	1	24	29*	–	–
353 CHR BRETHREN..	2	40	40	–	–
381 REF PRES-EVAN.	1	49	78	–	–
403 SALVATION ARMY	4	277	424	0.1	0.2
413 S.D.A.........	23	1 950	2 406*	0.5	1.2
419 SO BAPT CONV..	38	8 749	10 871*	2.3	5.2
435 UNITARIAN-UNIV	2	64	76*	–	–
443 UN C OF CHRIST	13	3 112	3 870*	0.8	1.9
449 UN METHODIST..	41	12 022	14 851*	3.2	7.2
453 UN PRES CH USA	27	8 329	10 265*	2.2	4.9
469 WELS.........	1	61	92	–	–

NA—Not applicable   *Total adherents estimated from known number of communicant, confirmed, full members.   —Represents a percent less than 0.1.   Percentages may not total due to rounding.

Table 4. Churches and Church Membership by County and Denomination: 1980

County and Denomination	Number of churches	Communicant, confirmed, full members	Total adherents Number	Percent of total population	Percent of total adherents
ALABAMA					
THE STATE.....	8 054	1 721 027	2 235 170*	57.5	100.0
AUTAUGA	64	12 619	16 039*	49.7	100.0
005 AME ZION......	7	1 548	1 914	5.9	11.9
017 AMER BAPT ASSN	1	95	95	0.3	0.6
053 ASSEMB OF GOD.	1	55	110	0.3	0.7
081 CATHOLIC......	1	NA	·43	0.1	0.3
089 CHR & MISS AL.	1	139	204	0.6	1.3
093 CHR CH (DISC).	1	20	45	0.1	0.3
097 CHR CHS&CHS CR	1	100	125*	0.4	0.8
101 C.M.E.........	1	320	399*	1.2	2.5
123 CH GOD (ANDER)	2	40	120	0.4	0.7
151 L-D SAINTS....	1	NA	200	0.6	1.2
167 CHS OF CHRIST.	5	248	302	0.9	1.9
175 CONGR CHR CHS.	1	79	99*	0.3	0.6
177 CONGR HOL CH..	1	10	12*	-	0.1
193 EPISCOPAL.....	1	123	169	0.5	1.1
281 LUTH CH AMER..	1	129	167	0.5	1.0
283 LUTH--MO SYNOD	1	79	125	0.4	0.8
356 PRESB CH AMER.	1	437	437	1.4	2.7
357 PRESB CH US...	1	10	12*	-	0.1
419 SO BAPT CONV..	24	7 090	8 845*	27.4	55.1
449 UN METHODIST..	11	2 097	2 616*	8.1	16.3
BALDWIN	164	28 969	41 628*	53.1	100.0
005 AME ZION......	9	1 599	2 132	2.7	5.1
017 AMER BAPT ASSN	1	50	50	0.1	0.1
053 ASSEMB OF GOD.	15	891	1 429	1.8	3.4
081 CATHOLIC......	12	NA	4 741	6.0	11.4
089 CHR & MISS AL.	2	97	211	0.3	0.5
093 CHR CH (DISC).	3	338	499	0.6	1.2
097 CHR CHS&CHS CR	1	150	185*	0.2	0.4
101 C.M.E.........	1	395	486*	0.6	1.2
123 CH GOD (ANDER)	1	84	252	0.3	0.6
127 CH GOD (CLEVE)	11	577	710*	0.9	1.7
151 L-D SAINTS....	1	NA	197	0.3	0.5
165 CH OF NAZARENE	1	30	28	-	0.1
167 CHS OF CHRIST.	8	994	1 144	1.5	2.7
193 EPISCOPAL.....	7	1 203	1 629	2.1	3.9
201 EVAN COV CH AM	2	110	135*	0.2	0.3
281 LUTH CH AMER..	1	37	45	0.1	0.1
283 LUTH--MO SYNOD	5	1 092	1 531	2.0	3.7
349 PENT HOLINESS.	5	429	528*	0.7	1.3
356 PRESB CH AMER.	2	71	71	0.1	0.2
357 PRESB CH US...	8	1 532	1 885*	2.4	4.5
413 S.D.A.........	2	51	63*	0.1	0.2
419 SO BAPT CONV..	43	14 760	18 165*	23.2	43.6
435 UNITARIAN-UNIV	1	41	50*	0.1	0.1
449 UN METHODIST..	22	4 438	5 462*	7.0	13.1
BARBOUR	68	9 515	12 157*	49.1	100.0
053 ASSEMB OF GOD.	8	588	806	3.3	6.6
081 CATHOLIC......	1	NA	130	0.5	1.1
127 CH GOD (CLEVE)	3	39	48*	0.2	0.4
151 L-D SAINTS....	1	NA	196	0.8	1.6
167 CHS OF CHRIST.	2	108	138	0.6	1.1
193 EPISCOPAL.....	1	107	146	0.6	1.2
356 PRESB CH AMER.	4	290	295	1.2	2.4
357 PRESB CH US...	2	303	376*	1.5	3.1
413 S.D.A.........	1	13	16*	0.1	0.1
419 SO BAPT CONV..	27	6 183	7 669*	31.0	63.1
443 UN C OF CHRIST	1	41	51*	0.2	0.4
449 UN METHODIST..	17	1 843	2 286*	9.2	18.8
BIBB	60	6 743	8 394*	53.4	100.0
005 AME ZION......	4	717	838	5.3	10.0
053 ASSEMB OF GOD.	1	30	50	0.3	0.6
081 CATHOLIC......	1	NA	37	0.2	0.4
127 CH GOD (CLEVE)	2	65	81*	0.5	1.0
165 CH OF NAZARENE	2	80	148	0.9	1.8
167 CHS OF CHRIST.	2	113	144	0.9	1.7
185 CUMBER PRESB..	1	22	30	0.2	0.4
356 PRESB CH AMER.	2	210	221	1.4	2.6
419 SO BAPT CONV..	38	5 208	6 472*	41.2	77.1
421 SO METHODIST..	1	42	55	0.3	0.7
449 UN METHODIST..	5	247	307*	2.0	3.7
453 UN PRES CH USA	1	9	11*	0.1	0.1
BLOUNT	129	17 996	22 191*	60.9	100.0
001 ADVENT CHR CH.	1	60	73*	0.2	0.3
053 ASSEMB OF GOD.	1	174	275	0.8	1.2
089 CHR & MISS AL.	1	60	70	0.2	0.3
127 CH GOD (CLEVE)	9	403	492*	1.3	2.2
157 CH OF BRETHREN	1	64	78*	0.2	0.4
165 CH OF NAZARENE	3	166	251	0.7	1.1
167 CHS OF CHRIST.	5	325	414	1.1	1.9
185 CUMBER PRESB..	4	114	228	0.6	1.0
285 MENNONITE CH..	1	14	17*	-	0.1
419 SO BAPT CONV..	72	13 257	16 191*	44.4	73.0
449 UN METHODIST..	31	3 359	4 102*	11.3	18.5
BULLOCK	31	4 683	5 727*	54.0	100.0
005 AME ZION......	6	1 860	2 178	20.6	38.0
053 ASSEMB OF GOD.	1	23	34	0.3	0.6
081 CATHOLIC......	1	NA	20	0.2	0.3
101 C.M.E.........	2	339	423*	4.0	7.4
127 CH GOD (CLEVE)	1	40	50*	0.5	0.9
167 CHS OF CHRIST.	2	81	103	1.0	1.8
193 EPISCOPAL.....	1	7	7	0.1	0.1
356 PRESB CH AMER.	1	29	39	0.4	0.7
357 PRESB CH US...	1	122	152*	1.4	2.7
419 SO BAPT CONV..	8	1 757	2 191*	20.7	38.3
449 UN METHODIST..	7	425	530*	5.0	9.3
BUTLER	109	16 610	20 498*	94.5	100.0
005 AME ZION......	22	7 458	8 944	41.3	43.6
053 ASSEMB OF GOD.	4	108	155	0.7	0.8
081 CATHOLIC......	1	NA	120	0.6	0.6
093 CHR CH (DISC).	1	74	115	0.5	0.6
101 C.M.E.........	1	53	66*	0.3	0.3
127 CH GOD (CLEVE)	2	100	124*	0.6	0.6
167 CHS OF CHRIST.	14	741	943	4.3	4.6
193 EPISCOPAL.....	1	146	237	1.1	1.2
349 PENT HOLINESS.	8	409	507*	2.3	2.5
413 S.D.A.........	1	18	22*	0.1	0.1
419 SO BAPT CONV..	32	5 878	7 282*	33.6	35.5
449 UN METHODIST..	21	1 498	1 856*	8.6	9.1
CALHOUN	214	54 331	69 119*	59.1	100.0
005 AME ZION......	5	2 106	2 592	2.2	3.8
029 AMER LUTH CH..	1	70	130	0.1	0.2
053 ASSEMB OF GOD.	6	350	718	0.6	1.0
081 CATHOLIC......	4	NA	1 460	1.2	2.1
093 CHR CH (DISC).	1	156	186	0.2	0.3
097 CHR CHS&CHS CR	3	282	344*	0.3	0.5
101 C.M.E.........	10	2 095	2 553*	2.2	3.7
123 CH GOD (ANDER)	3	75	225	0.2	0.3
127 CH GOD (CLEVE)	11	1 065	1 298*	1.1	1.9
151 L-D SAINTS....	1	NA	496	0.4	0.7
165 CH OF NAZARENE	2	131	178	0.2	0.3
167 CHS OF CHRIST.	19	1 995	2 540	2.2	3.7
177 CONGR HOL CH..	11	608	741*	0.6	1.1
185 CUMBER PRESB..	1	81	166	0.1	0.2
193 EPISCOPAL.....	3	703	837	0.7	1.2
263 INT FOURSQ GOS	2	60	73*	0.1	0.1
271 REFORM JUDAISM	1	94	115*	0.1	0.2
281 LUTH CH AMER..	1	164	227	0.2	0.3
349 PENT HOLINESS.	1	131	160*	0.1	0.2
356 PRESB CH AMER.	1	106	118	0.1	0.2
357 PRESB CH US...	7	1 320	1 608*	1.4	2.3
403 SALVATION ARMY	1	186	504	0.4	0.7
413 S.D.A.........	2	74	90*	0.1	0.1
419 SO BAPT CONV..	86	35 184	42 871*	36.7	62.0
449 UN METHODIST..	30	7 200	8 773*	7.5	12.7
453 UN PRES CH USA	1	95	116*	0.1	0.2
CHAMBERS	107	18 231	23 247*	59.3	100.0
053 ASSEMB OF GOD.	3	141	219	0.6	0.9
081 CATHOLIC......	1	NA	256	0.7	1.1
093 CHR CH (DISC).	5	529	749	1.9	3.2
097 CHR CHS&CHS CR	2	305	374*	1.0	1.6
101 C.M.E.........	7	1 380	1 693*	4.3	7.3
123 CH GOD (ANDER)	3	167	495	1.3	2.1
127 CH GOD (CLEVE)	1	91	112*	0.3	0.5
151 L-D SAINTS....	1	NA	52	0.1	0.2
165 CH OF NAZARENE	6	738	1 027	2.6	4.4
167 CHS OF CHRIST.	3	158	212	0.5	0.9
177 CONGR HOL CH..	1	23	28*	0.1	0.1
356 PRESB CH AMER.	1	10	10	-	-
357 PRESB CH US...	1	19	23*	0.1	0.1
419 SO BAPT CONV..	37	9 412	11 546*	29.5	49.7
435 UNITARIAN-UNIV	1	12	15*	-	0.1
443 UN C OF CHRIST	4	607	745*	1.9	3.2
449 UN METHODIST..	30	4 639	5 691*	14.5	24.5
CHEROKEE	94	10 443	12 762*	68.0	100.0
001 ADVENT CHR CH.	1	91	111*	0.6	0.9
053 ASSEMB OF GOD.	1	16	55	0.3	0.4
127 CH GOD (CLEVE)	3	68	83*	0.4	0.7
167 CHS OF CHRIST.	4	178	227	1.2	1.8
177 CONGR HOL CH..	3	103	125*	0.7	1.0
357 PRESB CH US...	1	37	45*	0.2	0.4
419 SO BAPT CONV..	54	7 601	9 256*	49.3	72.5
449 UN METHODIST..	27	2 349	2 860*	15.2	22.4
CHILTON	99	16 372	20 408*	66.7	100.0
017 AMER BAPT ASSN	2	150	150	0.5	0.7
053 ASSEMB OF GOD.	8	588	977	3.2	4.8
081 CATHOLIC......	1	NA	72	0.2	0.4
123 CH GOD (ANDER)	1	24	72	0.2	0.4
127 CH GOD (CLEVE)	8	558	685*	2.2	3.4
165 CH OF NAZARENE	1	22	33	0.1	0.2
167 CHS OF CHRIST.	7	255	310	1.0	1.5
197 EVAN CH OF NA.	1	60	60	0.2	0.3
356 PRESB CH AMER.	1	35	40	0.1	0.2
413 S.D.A.........	1	146	179*	0.6	0.9
419 SO BAPT CONV..	53	13 264	16 272*	53.2	79.7
449 UN METHODIST..	15	1 270	1 558*	5.1	7.6
CHOCTAW	90	8 312	11 089*	65.9	100.0
005 AME ZION......	4	1 209	1 612	9.6	14.5

NA— Not applicable   *Total adherents estimated from known number of communicant, confirmed, full members.   —Represents a percent less than 0.1.   Percentages may not total due to rounding.

28

Table 4. Churches and Church Membership by County and Denomination: 1980

County and Denomination	Number of churches	Communicant, confirmed, full members	Total adherents Number	Percent of total population	Percent of total adherents
053 ASSEMB OF GOD.	11	520	998	5.9	9.0
081 CATHOLIC......	1	NA	150	0.9	1.4
101 C.M.E.........	10	1 212	1 526*	9.1	13.8
123 CH GOD (ANDER)	1	5	15	0.1	0.1
127 CH GOD (CLEVE)	3	137	172*	1.0	1.6
151 L-D SAINTS....	1	NA	35	0.2	0.3
167 CHS OF CHRIST.	2	38	48	0.3	0.4
283 LUTH--MO SYNOD	1	35	42	0.2	0.4
349 PENT HOLINESS.	1	62	78*	0.5	0.7
357 PRESB CH US...	1	36	45*	0.3	0.4
413 S.D.A.........	1	45	57*	0.3	0.5
419 SO BAPT CONV..	31	3 761	4 735*	28.1	42.7
449 UN METHODIST..	22	1 252	1 576*	9.4	14.2
CLARKE	99	14 477	18 510*	66.8	100.0
005 AME ZION......	5	1 605	1 926	7.0	10.4
053 ASSEMB OF GOD.	2	258	358	1.3	1.9
081 CATHOLIC......	3	NA	189	0.7	1.0
101 C.M.E.........	10	897	1 127*	4.1	6.1
123 CH GOD (ANDER)	1	15	45	0.2	0.2
127 CH GOD (CLEVE)	2	77	97*	0.4	0.5
151 L-D SAINTS....	1	NA	109	0.4	0.6
165 CH OF NAZARENE	1	19	36	0.1	0.2
167 CHS OF CHRIST.	6	195	252	0.9	1.4
193 EPISCOPAL.....	1	55	90	0.3	0.5
283 LUTH--MO SYNOD	1	21	33	0.1	0.2
357 PRESB CH US...	1	76	96*	0.3	0.5
413 S.D.A.........	2	51	64*	0.2	0.3
419 SO BAPT CONV..	43	9 267	11 648*	42.0	62.9
449 UN METHODIST..	20	1 941	2 440*	8.8	13.2
CLAY	76	8 324	10 237*	74.7	100.0
053 ASSEMB OF GOD.	3	124	165	1.2	1.6
127 CH GOD (CLEVE)	1	49	60*	0.4	0.6
167 CHS OF CHRIST.	7	305	388	2.8	3.8
349 PENT HOLINESS.	2	95	117*	0.9	1.1
419 SO BAPT CONV..	44	5 915	7 255*	52.9	70.9
449 UN METHODIST..	19	1 836	2 252*	16.4	22.0
CLEBURNE	58	7 847	9 588*	76.1	100.0
127 CH GOD (CLEVE)	5	303	370*	2.9	3.9
167 CHS OF CHRIST.	2	108	137	1.1	1.4
419 SO BAPT CONV..	36	6 538	7 984*	63.4	83.3
449 UN METHODIST..	15	898	1 097*	8.7	11.4
COFFEE	93	19 919	25 498*	66.2	100.0
017 AMER BAPT ASSN	1	350	350	0.9	1.4
053 ASSEMB OF GOD.	16	1 518	2 240	5.8	8.8
081 CATHOLIC......	1	NA	670	1.7	2.6
127 CH GOD (CLEVE)	3	173	211*	0.5	0.8
151 L-D SAINTS....	1	NA	183	0.5	0.7
167 CHS OF CHRIST.	7	581	753	2.0	3.0
193 EPISCOPAL.....	1	135	151	0.4	0.6
283 LUTH--MO SYNOD	1	112	152	0.4	0.6
349 PENT HOLINESS.	1	35	43*	0.1	0.2
357 PRESB CH US...	2	193	235*	0.6	0.9
419 SO BAPT CONV..	46	13 881	16 924*	43.9	66.4
449 UN METHODIST..	13	2 941	3 586*	9.3	14.1
COLBERT	130	26 258	32 870*	60.3	100.0
017 AMER BAPT ASSN	3	343	343	0.6	1.0
053 ASSEMB OF GOD.	1	37	50	0.1	0.2
081 CATHOLIC......	1	NA	713	1.3	2.2
093 CHR CH (DISC).	1	43	66	0.1	0.2
101 C.M.E.........	6	585	709*	1.3	2.2
123 CH GOD (ANDER)	1	90	270	0.5	0.8
127 CH GOD (CLEVE)	5	320	388*	0.7	1.2
165 CH OF NAZARENE	4	390	400	0.7	1.2
167 CHS OF CHRIST.	40	4 524	5 758	10.6	17.5
185 CUMBER PRESB..	7	378	509	0.9	1.5
193 EPISCOPAL.....	1	234	250	0.5	0.8
283 LUTH--MO SYNOD	1	86	117	0.2	0.4
357 PRESB CH US...	1	222	269*	0.5	0.8
419 SO BAPT CONV..	38	15 007	18 183*	33.4	55.3
449 UN METHODIST..	18	3 879	4 700*	8.6	14.3
453 UN PRES CH USA	2	120	145*	0.3	0.4
CONECUH	79	8 879	11 013*	69.3	100.0
005 AME ZION......	9	2 430	2 919	18.4	26.5
053 ASSEMB OF GOD.	4	176	321	2.0	2.9
059 BAPT MISS ASSN	1	22	27*	0.2	0.2
127 CH GOD (CLEVE)	1	61	75*	0.5	0.7
167 CHS OF CHRIST.	6	325	426	2.7	3.9
349 PENT HOLINESS.	5	262	324*	2.0	2.9
357 PRESB CH US...	1	71	88*	0.6	0.8
419 SO BAPT CONV..	26	3 836	4 738*	29.8	43.0
449 UN METHODIST..	26	1 696	2 095*	13.2	19.0
COOSA	48	4 985	6 132*	53.9	100.0
059 BAPT MISS ASSN	1	30	37*	0.3	0.6
101 C.M.E.........	1	95	116*	1.0	1.9
123 CH GOD (ANDER)	1	13	39	0.3	0.6
127 CH GOD (CLEVE)	2	35	43*	0.4	0.7
167 CHS OF CHRIST.	2	170	216	1.9	3.5
357 PRESB CH US...	5	278	340*	3.0	5.5
419 SO BAPT CONV..	22	3 086	3 777*	33.2	61.6
449 UN METHODIST..	14	1 278	1 564*	13.7	25.5

County and Denomination	Number of churches	Communicant, confirmed, full members	Total adherents Number	Percent of total population	Percent of total adherents
COVINGTON	121	20 383	25 265*	68.6	100.0
053 ASSEMB OF GOD.	12	747	1 294	3.5	5.1
055 AS REF PRES CH	1	114	114	0.3	0.5
081 CATHOLIC......	1	NA	197	0.5	0.8
127 CH GOD (CLEVE)	6	178	214*	0.6	0.8
151 L-D SAINTS....	1	NA	136	0.4	0.5
165 CH OF NAZARENE	2	60	89	0.2	0.4
167 CHS OF CHRIST.	13	807	1 027	2.8	4.1
193 EPISCOPAL.....	1	34	45	0.1	0.2
283 LUTH--MO SYNOD	2	5	36	0.1	0.1
349 PENT HOLINESS.	1	56	67*	0.2	0.3
356 PRESB CH AMER.	1	84	90	0.2	0.4
357 PRESB CH US...	1	175	210*	0.6	0.8
413 S.D.A.........	1	63	76*	0.2	0.3
419 SO BAPT CONV..	60	15 958	19 148*	52.0	75.8
443 UN C OF CHRIST	2	82	98*	0.3	0.4
449 UN METHODIST..	16	2 020	2 424*	6.6	9.6
CRENSHAW	78	8 338	10 785*	76.4	100.0
005 AME ZION......	7	1 713	2 284	16.2	21.2
053 ASSEMB OF GOD.	7	269	509	3.6	4.7
101 C.M.E.........	2	114	139*	1.0	1.3
127 CH GOD (CLEVE)	2	39	48*	0.3	0.4
151 L-D SAINTS....	1	NA	200	1.4	1.9
167 CHS OF CHRIST.	12	765	973	6.9	9.0
419 SO BAPT CONV..	29	4 175	5 092*	36.1	47.2
443 UN C OF CHRIST	2	28	34*	0.2	0.3
449 UN METHODIST..	16	1 235	1 506*	10.7	14.0
CULLMAN	197	35 167	45 638*	74.0	100.0
053 ASSEMB OF GOD.	3	226	306	0.5	0.7
081 CATHOLIC......	2	NA	2 000	3.2	4.4
093 CHR CH (DISC).	1	78	89	0.1	0.2
097 CHR CHS&CHS CR	1	42	51*	0.1	0.1
123 CH GOD (ANDER)	1	80	240	0.4	0.5
127 CH GOD (CLEVE)	12	692	841*	1.4	1.8
151 L-D SAINTS....	1	NA	131	0.2	0.3
165 CH OF NAZARENE	2	233	393	0.6	0.9
167 CHS OF CHRIST.	27	2 000	2 546	4.1	5.6
185 CUMBER PRESB..	7	220	527	0.9	1.2
193 EPISCOPAL.....	2	191	278	0.5	0.6
281 LUTH CH AMER..	1	180	227	0.4	0.5
283 LUTH--MO SYNOD	2	992	1 264	2.1	2.8
357 PRESB CH US...	1	151	184*	0.3	0.4
413 S.D.A.........	1	106	129*	0.2	0.3
419 SO BAPT CONV..	104	25 167	31 443*	51.0	68.9
443 UN C OF CHRIST	3	695	845*	1.4	1.9
449 UN METHODIST..	26	3 410	4 144*	6.7	9.1
DALE	86	16 466	21 623*	45.2	100.0
053 ASSEMB OF GOD.	12	1 003	1 825	3.8	8.4
059 BAPT MISS ASSN	1	24	30*	0.1	0.1
081 CATHOLIC......	1	NA	260	0.5	1.2
127 CH GOD (CLEVE)	3	66	82*	0.2	0.4
151 L-D SAINTS....	1	NA	305	0.6	1.4
165 CH OF NAZARENE	1	15	47	0.1	0.2
167 CHS OF CHRIST.	2	151	192	0.4	0.9
193 EPISCOPAL.....	1	91	145	0.3	0.7
283 LUTH--MO SYNOD	1	57	80	0.2	0.4
356 PRESB CH AMER.	1	205	237	0.5	1.1
357 PRESB CH US...	1	15	19*	–	0.1
413 S.D.A.........	1	116	144*	0.3	0.7
419 SO BAPT CONV..	34	11 262	13 957*	29.2	64.5
421 SO METHODIST..	1	30	48	0.1	0.2
435 UNITARIAN-UNIV	1	20	25*	0.1	0.1
443 UN C OF CHRIST	2	35	43*	0.1	0.2
449 UN METHODIST..	22	3 376	4 184*	8.7	19.3
DALLAS	87	16 582	21 696*	40.2	100.0
005 AME ZION......	5	698	851	1.6	3.9
053 ASSEMB OF GOD.	1	80	154	0.3	0.7
055 AS REF PRES CH	1	50	50	0.1	0.2
061 BEACHY AMISH..	1	18	23*	–	0.1
081 CATHOLIC......	2	NA	600	1.1	2.8
089 CHR & MISS AL.	2	9	20	–	0.1
093 CHR CH (DISC).	2	171	214	0.4	1.0
097 CHR CHS&CHS CR	4	420	526*	1.0	2.4
101 C.M.E.........	2	190	238*	0.4	1.1
123 CH GOD (ANDER)	1	25	75	0.1	0.3
127 CH GOD (CLEVE)	4	188	236*	0.4	1.1
151 L-D SAINTS....	1	NA	104	0.2	0.5
165 CH OF NAZARENE	1	117	211	0.4	1.0
167 CHS OF CHRIST.	8	525	668	1.2	3.1
193 EPISCOPAL.....	2	516	611	1.1	2.8
271 REFORM JUDAISM	1	70	88*	0.2	0.4
283 LUTH--MO SYNOD	2	232	334	0.6	1.5
356 PRESB CH AMER.	2	389	436	0.8	2.0
357 PRESB CH US...	8	826	1 035*	1.9	4.8
383 REF PRES OF NA	1	77	81	0.2	0.4
403 SALVATION ARMY	1	98	245	0.5	1.1
413 S.D.A.........	2	139	174*	0.3	0.8
419 SO BAPT CONV..	21	9 737	12 206*	22.6	56.3
449 UN METHODIST..	12	2 007	2 516*	4.7	11.6
DE KALB	152	23 847	29 237*	54.5	100.0
005 AME ZION......	1	55	66	0.1	0.2
053 ASSEMB OF GOD.	1	8	15	–	0.1
081 CATHOLIC......	1	NA	112	0.2	0.4
089 CHR & MISS AL.	1	55	114	0.2	0.4

NA—Not applicable   *Total adherents estimated from known number of communicant, confirmed, full members.   —Represents a percent less than 0.1.   Percentages may not total due to rounding.

Table 4. Churches and Church Membership by County and Denomination: 1980

County and Denomination	Number of churches	Communicant, confirmed, full members	Total adherents Number	Percent of total population	Percent of total adherents
123 CH GOD (ANDER)	1	39	117	0.2	0.4
127 CH GOD (CLEVE)	15	1 093	1 337*	2.5	4.6
133 CH GOD(7TH)DEN	1	19	23*	-	0.1
167 CHS OF CHRIST.	12	755	760	1.4	2.6
193 EPISCOPAL.....	2	130	164	0.3	0.6
356 PRESB CH AMER.	1	?	?	?	?
357 PRESB CH US...	2	94	115*	0.2	0.4
413 S.D.A.........	1	104	127*	0.2	0.4
419 SO BAPT CONV..	73	17 435	21 322*	39.7	72.9
449 UN METHODIST..	40	4 060	4 965*	9.3	17.0
ELMORE	**107**	**19 643**	**25 738***	**59.3**	**100.0**
005 AME ZION......	9	2 703	3 604	8.3	14.0
017 AMER BAPT ASSN	1	175	175	0.4	0.7
053 ASSEMB OF GOD.	3	212	355	0.8	1.4
059 BAPT MISS ASSN	1	69	85*	0.2	0.3
081 CATHOLIC......	3	NA	1 035	2.4	4.0
093 CHR CH (DISC).	1	85	125	0.3	0.5
123 CH GOD (ANDER)	1	49	147	0.3	0.6
127 CH GOD (CLEVE)	3	209	256*	0.6	1.0
151 L-D SAINTS....	1	NA	87	0.2	0.3
167 CHS OF CHRIST.	12	775	985	2.3	3.8
175 CONGR CHR CHS.	3	205	251*	0.6	1.0
177 CONGR HOL CH..	1	29	36*	0.1	0.1
193 EPISCOPAL.....	2	158	208	0.5	0.8
356 PRESB CH AMER.	1	111	156	0.4	0.6
357 PRESB CH US...	1	85	104*	0.2	0.4
419 SO BAPT CONV..	38	11 633	14 271*	32.9	55.4
443 UN C OF CHRIST	2	93	114*	0.3	0.4
449 UN METHODIST..	24	3 052	3 744*	8.6	14.5
ESCAMBIA	**106**	**14 502**	**19 127***	**49.8**	**100.0**
005 AME ZION......	4	256	384	1.0	2.0
017 AMER BAPT ASSN	1	22	22	0.1	0.1
053 ASSEMB OF GOD.	11	712	1 109	2.9	5.8
081 CATHOLIC......	3	NA	485	1.3	2.5
101 C.M.E.........	1	25	31*	0.1	0.2
127 CH GOD (CLEVE)	3	160	197*	0.5	1.0
151 L-D SAINTS....	1	NA	157	0.4	0.8
165 CH OF NAZARENE	2	114	181	0.5	0.9
167 CHS OF CHRIST.	9	500	635	1.7	3.3
193 EPISCOPAL.....	4	300	488	1.3	2.6
283 LUTH--MO SYNOD	1	110	232	0.6	1.2
285 MENNONITE CH..	1	124	153*	0.4	0.8
349 PENT HOLINESS.	8	509	627*	1.6	3.3
357 PRESB CH US...	2	289	356*	0.9	1.9
371 REF CH IN AM..	1	39	107	0.3	0.6
413 S.D.A.........	1	39	48*	0.1	0.3
419 SO BAPT CONV..	32	9 136	11 247*	29.3	58.8
435 UNITARIAN-UNIV	1	30	37*	0.1	0.2
449 UN METHODIST..	15	2 137	2 631*	6.9	13.8
ETOWAH	**208**	**54 897**	**69 642***	**67.6**	**100.0**
001 ADVENT CHR CH.	2	108	131*	0.1	0.2
053 ASSEMB OF GOD.	4	247	404	0.4	0.6
081 CATHOLIC......	2	NA	1 772	1.7	2.5
089 CHR & MISS AL.	1	52	67	0.1	0.1
093 CHR CH (DISC).	1	126	159	0.2	0.2
101 C.M.E.........	2	732	890*	0.9	1.3
123 CH GOD (ANDER)	1	50	150	0.1	0.2
127 CH GOD (CLEVE)	16	1 552	1 888*	1.8	2.7
133 CH GOD(7TH)DEN	1	14	17*	-	-
151 L-D SAINTS....	1	NA	460	0.4	0.7
165 CH OF NAZARENE	2	149	230	0.2	0.3
167 CHS OF CHRIST.	17	1 520	1 935*	1.9	2.8
177 CONGR HOL CH..	3	92	112*	0.1	0.2
185 CUMBER PRESB..	4	421	818	0.8	1.2
193 EPISCOPAL.....	2	377	456	0.4	0.7
271 REFORM JUDAISM	1	100	122*	0.1	0.2
283 LUTH--MO SYNOD	2	300	375	0.4	0.5
356 PRESB CH AMER.	4	853	894	0.9	1.3
357 PRESB CH US...	1	92	112*	0.1	0.2
403 SALVATION ARMY	1	94	235	0.2	0.3
413 S.D.A.........	2	150	182*	0.2	0.3
419 SO BAPT CONV..	97	38 486	46 818*	45.4	67.2
421 SO METHODIST..	1	48	60	0.1	0.1
449 UN METHODIST..	40	9 334	11 355*	11.0	16.3
FAYETTE	**90**	**9 214**	**11 353***	**60.4**	**100.0**
005 AME ZION......	3	546	591	3.1	5.2
053 ASSEMB OF GOD.	1	63	100	0.5	0.9
059 BAPT MISS ASSN	1	92	112*	0.6	1.0
101 C.M.E.........	2	162	198*	1.1	1.7
127 CH GOD (CLEVE)	6	327	399*	2.1	3.5
165 CH OF NAZARENE	3	87	205	1.1	1.8
167 CHS OF CHRIST.	22	1 200	1 525	8.1	13.4
193 EPISCOPAL.....	1	24	34	0.2	0.3
419 SO BAPT CONV..	37	5 079	6 196*	32.9	54.6
449 UN METHODIST..	14	1 634	1 993*	10.6	17.6
FRANKLIN	**82**	**12 382**	**14 982***	**52.8**	**100.0**
017 AMER BAPT ASSN	5	819	819	2.9	5.5
101 C.M.E.........	1	278	337*	1.2	2.2
127 CH GOD (CLEVE)	2	171	207*	0.7	1.4
165 CH OF NAZARENE	1	49	95	0.3	0.6
167 CHS OF CHRIST.	26	2 000	2 545*	9.0	17.0
185 CUMBER PRESB..	1	18	26	0.1	0.2
357 PRESB CH US...	1	98	119*	0.4	0.8
413 S.D.A.........	1	10	12*	-	0.1
419 SO BAPT CONV..	32	7 481	9 057*	31.9	60.5
449 UN METHODIST..	11	1 445	1 749*	6.2	11.7
453 UN PRES CH USA	1	13	16*	0.1	0.1
GENEVA	**92**	**12 594**	**16 067***	**66.2**	**100.0**
053 ASSEMB OF GOD.	17	938	1 594	6.6	9.9
081 CATHOLIC......	1	NA	200	0.8	1.2
127 CH GOD (CLEVE)	2	94	115*	0.5	0.7
167 CHS OF CHRIST.	8	325	415	1.7	2.6
357 PRESB CH US...	3	97	119*	0.5	0.7
419 SO BAPT CONV..	39	8 629	10 553*	43.5	65.7
449 UN METHODIST..	22	2 511	3 071*	12.7	19.1
GREENE	**43**	**4 372**	**5 550***	**50.4**	**100.0**
005 AME ZION......	7	1 100	1 320	12.0	23.8
081 CATHOLIC......	1	NA	40	0.4	0.7
093 CHR CH (DISC)	2	113	201	1.8	3.6
101 C.M.E.........	8	927	1 171*	10.6	21.1
123 CH GOD (ANDER)	1	12	36	0.3	0.6
185 CUMBER PRESB..	1	53	87	0.8	1.6
193 EPISCOPAL.....	1	96	112	1.0	2.0
356 PRESB CH AMER.	3	211	233	2.1	4.2
419 SO BAPT CONV..	6	1 101	1 391*	12.6	25.1
449 UN METHODIST..	12	759	959*	8.7	17.3
HALE	**55**	**6 111**	**7 804***	**50.0**	**100.0**
005 AME ZION......	7	937	1 173	7.5	15.0
081 CATHOLIC......	1	NA	38	0.2	0.5
101 C.M.E.........	4	609	762*	4.9	9.8
123 CH GOD (ANDER)	3	72	216	1.4	2.8
165 CH OF NAZARENE	1	41	82	0.5	1.1
167 CHS OF CHRIST.	2	85	108	0.7	1.4
193 EPISCOPAL.....	3	208	266	1.7	3.4
356 PRESB CH AMER.	3	180	182	1.2	2.3
357 PRESB CH US...	2	28	35*	0.2	0.4
419 SO BAPT CONV..	14	2 571	3 216*	20.6	41.2
449 UN METHODIST..	14	1 380	1 726*	11.1	22.1
HENRY	**37**	**6 327**	**7 891***	**51.6**	**100.0**
053 ASSEMB OF GOD.	5	122	215	1.4	2.7
127 CH GOD (CLEVE)	1	?	?	?	?
167 CHS OF CHRIST.	2	70	89	0.6	1.1
419 SO BAPT CONV..	22	4 986	6 166*	40.3	78.1
449 UN METHODIST..	7	1 149	1 421*	9.3	18.0
HOUSTON	**115**	**32 071**	**43 048***	**57.7**	**100.0**
017 AMER BAPT ASSN	1	50	50	0.1	0.1
053 ASSEMB OF GOD.	15	1 221	1 924	2.6	4.5
081 CATHOLIC......	2	NA	2 430	3.3	5.6
093 CHR CH (DISC).	1	100	167	0.2	0.4
127 CH GOD (CLEVE)	1	79	98*	0.1	0.2
151 L-D SAINTS....	1	NA	380	0.5	0.9
165 CH OF NAZARENE	2	117	184	0.2	0.4
167 CHS OF CHRIST.	6	475	605	0.8	1.4
177 CONGR HOL CH..	1	21	26*	-	0.1
193 EPISCOPAL.....	1	519	620	0.8	1.4
263 INT FOURSQ GOS	1	50	62*	0.1	0.1
271 REFORM JUDAISM	1	80	99*	0.1	0.2
283 LUTH--MO SYNOD	1	187	294	0.4	0.7
357 PRESB CH US...	4	972	1 200*	1.6	2.8
403 SALVATION ARMY	1	91	195	0.3	0.5
413 S.D.A.........	2	268	331*	0.4	0.8
419 SO BAPT CONV..	50	22 234	27 458*	36.8	63.8
421 SO METHODIST..	1	12	15	-	-
449 UN METHODIST..	23	5 595	6 910*	9.3	16.1
JACKSON	**133**	**18 404**	**23 807***	**46.3**	**100.0**
001 ADVENT CHR CH.	1	53	65*	0.1	0.3
053 ASSEMB OF GOD.	1	54	90	0.2	0.4
081 CATHOLIC......	1	NA	610	1.2	2.6
101 C.M.E.........	1	35	43*	0.1	0.2
127 CH GOD (CLEVE)	8	550	679*	1.3	2.9
151 L-D SAINTS....	1	NA	152	0.3	0.6
165 CH OF NAZARENE	2	102	171	0.3	0.7
167 CHS OF CHRIST.	22	1 744	2 220	4.3	9.3
185 CUMBER PRESB..	5	375	632	1.2	2.7
283 LUTH--MO SYNOD	1	96	133	0.3	0.6
413 S.D.A.........	1	187	231*	0.4	1.0
415 S-D BAPTIST GC	1	43	53*	0.1	0.2
419 SO BAPT CONV..	61	12 572	15 526*	30.2	65.2
449 UN METHODIST..	26	2 580	3 186*	6.2	13.4
453 UN PRES CH USA	1	13	16*	-	0.1
JEFFERSON	**807**	**303 499**	**404 288***	**60.2**	**100.0**
001 ADVENT CHR CH.	1	42	51*	-	-
005 AME ZION......	25	17 540	21 048	3.1	5.2
017 AMER BAPT ASSN	2	200	200	-	-
029 AMER LUTH CH..	2	156	248	-	0.1
053 ASSEMB OF GOD.	26	3 733	8 888	1.3	2.2
059 BAPT MISS ASSN	2	363	438*	0.1	0.1
081 CATHOLIC......	37	NA	26 705	4.0	6.6
089 CHR & MISS AL.	9	1 426	1 879	0.3	0.5
093 CHR CH (DISC).	8	1 290	1 848	0.3	0.5
097 CHR CHS&CHS CR	3	265	319*	-	0.1
101 C.M.E.........	26	11 446	13 796*	2.1	3.4
123 CH GOD (ANDER)	19	1 011	3 033	0.5	0.8
127 CH GOD (CLEVE)	48	5 020	6 051*	0.9	1.5
133 CH GOD(7TH)DEN	1	3	4*	-	-
151 L-D SAINTS....	5	NA	2 076	0.3	0.5

NA—Not applicable   *Total adherents estimated from known number of communicant, confirmed, full members.   —Represents a percent less than 0.1.   Percentages may not total due to rounding.

Table 4. Churches and Church Membership by County and Denomination: 1980

County and Denomination	Number of churches	Communicant, confirmed, full members	Total adherents Number	Percent of total population	Percent of total adherents
157 CH OF BRETHREN	1	31	37*	–	–
165 CH OF NAZARENE	13	1 217	1 547	0.2	0.4
167 CHS OF CHRIST.	76	9 363	11 923	1.8	2.9
177 CONGR HOL CH..	1	51	61*	–	–
179 CONSRV BAPT...	1	50	60*	–	–
185 CUMBER PRESB..	7	894	1 576	0.2	0.4
193 EPISCOPAL.....	16	6 988	9 234	1.4	2.3
197 EVAN CH OF NA.	1	50	50	–	–
221 FREE METHODIST	1	4	15	–	–
226 FRIENDS-USA...	1	21	25*	–	–
270 CONSRV JUDAISM	1	511	616*	0.1	0.2
271 REFORM JUDAISM	1	1 300	1 567*	0.2	0.4
281 LUTH CH AMER..	3	863	1 172	0.2	0.3
283 LUTH--MO SYNOD	9	1 681	2 362	0.4	0.6
285 MENNONITE CH..	1	17	20*	–	–
290 METRO COMM CHS	0	0	25	–	–
349 PENT HOLINESS.	8	656	791*	0.1	0.2
353 CHR BRETHREN..	2	75	75	–	–
356 PRESB CH AMER.	7	2 885	3 792	0.6	0.9
357 PRESB CH US...	24	6 900	8 317*	1.2	2.1
403 SALVATION ARMY	3	333	569	0.1	0.1
413 S.D.A.........	8	2 130	2 567*	0.4	0.6
419 SO BAPT CONV..	262	160 163	193 050*	28.8	47.8
421 SO METHODIST..	2	158	187	–	–
435 UNITARIAN-UNIV	1	184	222*	–	0.1
443 UN C OF CHRIST	2	430	518*	0.1	0.1
449 UN METHODIST..	128	59 872	72 166*	10.8	17.9
453 UN PRES CH USA	12	4 184	5 043*	0.8	1.2
469 WELS..........	1	93	117	–	–
LAMAR	82	7 088	8 858*	53.8	100.0
017 AMER BAPT ASSN	1	100	100	0.6	1.1
053 ASSEMB OF GOD.	3	92	173	1.1	2.0
059 BAPT MISS ASSN	1	80	98*	0.6	1.1
101 C.M.E.........	8	707	866*	5.3	9.8
127 CH GOD (CLEVE)	10	351	430*	2.6	4.9
165 CH OF NAZARENE	2	54	61	0.4	0.7
167 CHS OF CHRIST.	13	737	1 007	6.1	11.4
185 CUMBER PRESB..	1	36	80	0.5	0.9
419 SO BAPT CONV..	23	3 250	3 983*	24.2	45.0
449 UN METHODIST..	20	1 681	2 060*	12.5	23.3
LAUDERDALE	160	34 477	45 119*	56.0	100.0
017 AMER BAPT ASSN	2	305	305	0.4	0.7
053 ASSEMB OF GOD.	1	65	138	0.2	0.3
081 CATHOLIC......	2	NA	1 840	2.3	4.1
093 CHR CH (DISC).	1	249	280	0.3	0.6
101 C.M.E.........	1	280	338*	0.4	0.7
123 CH GOD (ANDER)	2	54	162	0.2	0.4
127 CH GOD (CLEVE)	3	102	123*	0.2	0.3
151 L-D SAINTS....	1	NA	436	0.5	1.0
165 CH OF NAZARENE	3	297	403	0.5	0.9
167 CHS OF CHRIST.	59	10 700	13 620	16.9	30.2
185 CUMBER PRESB..	9	741	1 205	1.5	2.7
193 EPISCOPAL.....	2	523	662	0.8	1.5
271 REFORM JUDAISM	1	116	140*	0.2	0.3
281 LUTH CH AMER..	1	113	146	0.2	0.3
283 LUTH--MO SYNOD	1	93	117	0.1	0.3
357 PRESB CH US...	2	816	985*	1.2	2.2
403 SALVATION ARMY	1	127	194	0.2	0.4
413 S.D.A.........	2	156	188*	0.2	0.4
419 SO BAPT CONV..	32	11 776	14 220*	17.7	31.5
435 UNITARIAN-UNIV	1	34	41*	0.1	0.1
449 UN METHODIST..	32	7 893	9 531*	11.8	21.1
453 UN PRES CH USA	1	37	45*	0.1	0.1
LAWRENCE	75	12 647	15 818*	52.4	100.0
053 ASSEMB OF GOD.	1	32	44	0.1	0.3
101 C.M.E.........	5	956	1 194*	4.0	7.5
127 CH GOD (CLEVE)	1	180	225*	0.7	1.4
165 CH OF NAZARENE	1	27	44	0.1	0.3
167 CHS OF CHRIST.	19	1 230	1 565*	5.2	9.9
356 PRESB CH AMER.	1	70	70	0.2	0.4
419 SO BAPT CONV..	29	7 969	9 950*	33.0	62.9
443 UN C OF CHRIST	1	174	217*	0.7	1.4
449 UN METHODIST..	16	1 930	2 410*	8.0	15.2
453 UN PRES CH USA	1	79	99*	0.3	0.6
LEE	109	39 685	50 544*	66.3	100.0
005 AME ZION......	12	13 305	15 966	20.9	31.6
053 ASSEMB OF GOD.	7	356	691	0.9	1.4
081 CATHOLIC......	2	NA	2 666	3.5	5.3
093 CHR CH (DISC).	2	131	182	0.2	0.4
097 CHR CHS&CHS CR	1	50	59*	0.1	0.1
101 C.M.E.........	11	3 769	4 485*	5.9	8.9
123 CH GOD (ANDER)	2	35	105	0.1	0.2
127 CH GOD (CLEVE)	1	95	113*	0.1	0.2
151 L-D SAINTS....	1	NA	135	0.2	0.3
165 CH OF NAZARENE	1	67	64	0.1	0.1
167 CHS OF CHRIST.	6	1 035	1 215	1.6	2.4
193 EPISCOPAL.....	3	470	559	0.7	1.1
283 LUTH--MO SYNOD	1	183	254	0.3	0.5
356 PRESB CH AMER.	2	190	260	0.3	0.5
357 PRESB CH US...	2	861	1 025*	1.3	2.0
381 REF PRES-EVAN.	1	96	106	0.1	0.2
413 S.D.A.........	1	23	27*	–	0.1
419 SO BAPT CONV..	28	13 082	15 567*	20.4	30.8
435 UNITARIAN-UNIV	1	35	42*	0.1	0.1
449 UN METHODIST..	24	5 902	7 023*	9.2	13.9
LIMESTONE	118	19 620	25 642*	55.7	100.0

County and Denomination	Number of churches	Communicant, confirmed, full members	Total adherents Number	Percent of total population	Percent of total adherents
053 ASSEMB OF GOD.	1	95	138	0.3	0.5
081 CATHOLIC......	2	NA	700	1.5	2.7
093 CHR CH (DISC).	1	179	239	0.5	0.9
101 C.M.E.........	3	562	691*	1.5	2.7
123 CH GOD (ANDER)	3	277	831	1.8	3.2
127 CH GOD (CLEVE)	2	103	127*	0.3	0.5
165 CH OF NAZARENE	1	24	50	0.1	0.2
167 CHS OF CHRIST.	47	6 125	7 795	16.9	30.4
193 EPISCOPAL.....	1	98	120	0.3	0.5
413 S.D.A.........	1	42	52*	0.1	0.2
419 SO BAPT CONV..	29	9 092	11 181*	24.3	43.6
443 UN C OF CHRIST	1	24	30*	0.1	0.1
449 UN METHODIST..	22	2 596	3 192*	6.9	12.4
453 UN PRES CH USA	4	403	496*	1.1	1.9
LOWNDES	53	4 769	6 133*	46.3	100.0
005 AME ZION......	6	1 536	1 904	14.4	31.0
017 AMER BAPT ASSN	1	90	90	0.7	1.5
081 CATHOLIC......	1	NA	47	0.4	0.8
093 CHR CH (DISC).	11	569	814	6.1	13.3
101 C.M.E.........	7	655	846*	6.4	13.8
167 CHS OF CHRIST.	4	265	337	2.5	5.5
193 EPISCOPAL.....	1	45	53	0.4	0.9
356 PRESB CH AMER.	4	152	159	1.2	2.6
419 SO BAPT CONV..	9	822	1 062*	8.0	17.3
449 UN METHODIST..	9	635	821*	6.2	13.4
MACON	53	22 095	4 884*	18.2	100.0
005 AME ZION......	21	18 630	0		
053 ASSEMB OF GOD.	2	47	85	0.3	1.7
081 CATHOLIC......	1	NA	500	1.9	10.2
093 CHR CH (DISC).	2	167	291	1.1	6.0
167 CHS OF CHRIST.	2	100	127	0.5	2.6
193 EPISCOPAL.....	1	139	187	0.7	3.8
356 PRESB CH AMER.	2	86	124	0.5	2.5
357 PRESB CH US...	3	213	260*	1.0	5.3
413 S.D.A.........	1	95	116*	0.4	2.4
419 SO BAPT CONV..	8	1 478	1 803*	6.7	36.9
449 UN METHODIST..	10	1 140	1 391*	5.2	28.5
MADISON	228	73 575	100 180*	50.9	100.0
017 AMER BAPT ASSN	1	97	97	–	0.1
053 ASSEMB OF GOD.	5	399	749	0.4	0.7
059 BAPT MISS ASSN	1	136	165*	0.1	0.2
081 CATHOLIC......	4	NA	7 773	3.9	7.8
089 CHR & MISS AL.	1	25	47	–	–
093 CHR CH (DISC).	2	886	961	0.5	1.0
097 CHR CHS&CHS CR	2	249	302*	0.2	0.3
101 C.M.E.........	8	1 227	1 489*	0.8	1.5
123 CH GOD (ANDER)	3	216	648	0.3	0.6
127 CH GOD (CLEVE)	7	981	1 191*	0.6	1.2
151 L-D SAINTS....	2	NA	954	0.5	1.0
165 CH OF NAZARENE	5	482	821	0.4	0.8
167 CHS OF CHRIST.	37	7 075	9 005	4.6	9.0
179 CONSRV BAPT...	1	75	91*	–	0.1
185 CUMBER PRESB..	7	537	1 099	0.6	1.1
193 EPISCOPAL.....	4	1 587	2 145	1.1	2.1
221 FREE METHODIST	1	22	72	–	0.1
270 CONSRV JUDAISM	1	25	30*	–	–
271 REFORM JUDAISM	1	240	291*	0.1	0.3
281 LUTH CH AMER..	3	1 116	1 418	0.7	1.4
283 LUTH--MO SYNOD	2	713	978	0.5	1.0
349 PENT HOLINESS.	1	125	152*	0.1	0.2
353 CHR BRETHREN..	1	30	45	–	–
356 PRESB CH AMER.	2	114	136	0.1	0.1
357 PRESB CH US...	5	2 416	2 932*	1.5	2.9
381 REF PRES-EVAN.	1	160	205	0.1	0.2
403 SALVATION ARMY	1	102	175	0.1	0.2
413 S.D.A.........	3	2 199	2 669*	1.4	2.7
419 SO BAPT CONV..	69	37 411	45 404*	23.1	45.3
421 SO METHODIST..	1	32	46	–	–
435 UNITARIAN-UNIV	1	107	130*	0.1	0.1
443 UN C OF CHRIST	1	137	166*	0.1	0.2
449 UN METHODIST..	38	13 218	16 042*	8.1	16.0
453 UN PRES CH USA	5	1 394	1 692*	0.9	1.7
469 WELS..........	1	42	60	–	0.1
MARENGO	82	12 776	16 091*	64.2	100.0
005 AME ZION......	12	3 275	3 930	15.7	24.4
053 ASSEMB OF GOD.	2	159	202	0.8	1.3
081 CATHOLIC......	1	NA	210	0.8	1.3
097 CHR CHS&CHS CR	2	285	357*	1.4	2.2
101 C.M.E.........	1	322	403*	1.6	2.5
127 CH GOD (CLEVE)	4	98	123*	0.5	0.8
143 CG IN CR(MENN)	1	88	88	0.4	0.5
151 L-D SAINTS....	1	NA	89	0.4	0.6
167 CHS OF CHRIST.	3	93	118	0.5	0.7
193 EPISCOPAL.....	2	214	269	1.1	1.7
271 REFORM JUDAISM	1	24	30*	0.1	0.2
353 CHR BRETHREN..	1	30	50	0.2	0.3
356 PRESB CH AMER.	4	149	156	0.6	1.0
419 SO BAPT CONV..	30	6 117	7 659*	30.6	47.6
449 UN METHODIST..	16	1 908	2 389*	9.5	14.8
453 UN PRES CH USA	1	14	18*	0.1	0.1
MARION	79	10 481	13 247*	44.1	100.0
017 AMER BAPT ASSN	2	155	155	0.5	1.2
053 ASSEMB OF GOD.	2	123	171	0.6	1.3
059 BAPT MISS ASSN	1	80	98*	0.3	0.7
081 CATHOLIC......	1	NA	250	0.8	1.9

NA—Not applicable   *Total adherents estimated from known number of communicant, confirmed, full members.   —Represents a percent less than 0.1.   Percentages may not total due to rounding.

Table 4. Churches and Church Membership by County and Denomination: 1980

County and Denomination	Number of churches	Communicant, confirmed, full members	Total adherents Number	Percent of total population	Percent of total adherents
089 CHR & MISS AL.	1	71	91	0.3	0.7
127 CH GOD (CLEVE)	3	164	200*	0.7	1.5
151 L-D SAINTS....	1	NA	98	0.3	0.7
167 CHS OF CHRIST.	27	2 318	2 950	9.8	22.3
419 SO BAPT CONV	25	5 468	6 670*	22.2	50.4
443 UN C OF CHRIST	1	?	?	?	?
449 UN METHODIST..	15	2 102	2 564*	8.5	19.4
MARSHALL	**161**	**32 351**	**40 483***	**61.7**	**100.0**
053 ASSEMB OF GOD.	4	203	429	0.7	1.1
081 CATHOLIC......	1	NA	510	0.8	1.3
123 CH GOD (ANDER)	2	57	171	0.3	0.4
127 CH GOD (CLEVE)	12	1 033	1 253*	1.9	3.1
151 L-D SAINTS....	1	NA	189	0.3	0.5
165 CH OF NAZARENE	1	162	144	0.2	0.4
167 CHS OF CHRIST.	20	2 267	2 885	4.4	7.1
185 CUMBER PRESB..	1	0	14	-	-
193 EPISCOPAL.....	2	194	323	0.5	0.8
221 FREE METHODIST	1	4	69	0.1	0.2
357 PRESB CH US...	2	408	495*	0.8	1.2
413 S.D.A.........	1	50	61*	0.1	0.2
419 SO BAPT CONV..	81	22 507	27 308*	41.6	67.5
449 UN METHODIST..	32	5 466	6 632*	10.1	16.4
MOBILE	**369**	**129 713**	**199 174***	**54.7**	**100.0**
005 AME ZION......	20	12 245	14 694	4.0	7.4
017 AMER BAPT ASSN	8	1 030	1 030	0.3	0.5
029 AMER LUTH CH..	1	111	181	-	0.1
053 ASSEMB OF GOD.	36	3 725	6 845	1.9	3.4
059 BAPT MISS ASSN	8	1 425	1 762*	0.5	0.9
081 CATHOLIC......	38	NA	32 864	9.0	16.5
093 CHR CH (DISC).	3	258	379	0.1	0.2
097 CHR CHS&CHS CR	3	760	940*	0.3	0.5
101 C.M.E.........	2	1 270	1 571*	0.4	0.8
123 CH GOD (ANDER)	5	174	522	0.1	0.3
127 CH GOD (CLEVE)	23	2 987	3 694*	1.0	1.9
151 L-D SAINTS....	2	NA	1 080	0.3	0.5
157 CH OF BRETHREN	1	90	111*	-	0.1
165 CH OF NAZARENE	5	421	704	0.2	0.4
167 CHS OF CHRIST.	15	2 148	2 734	0.8	1.4
177 CONGR HOL CH..	1	12	15*	-	-
193 EPISCOPAL.....	15	4 854	7 553	2.1	3.8
215 EVAN METH CH..	1	128	158*	-	0.1
270 CONSRV JUDAISM	1	92	114*	-	0.1
271 REFORM JUDAISM	1	466	576*	0.2	0.3
281 LUTH CH AMER..	2	416	572	0.2	0.3
283 LUTH--MO SYNOD	7	1 653	2 438	0.7	1.2
285 MENNONITE CH..	1	5	6*	-	-
290 METRO COMM CHS	0	0	20	-	-
349 PENT HOLINESS.	7	440	544*	0.1	0.3
353 CHR BRETHREN..	1	10	20	-	-
356 PRESB CH AMER.	1	61	62	-	-
357 PRESB CH US...	13	3 984	4 927*	1.4	2.5
403 SALVATION ARMY	2	225	844	0.2	0.4
413 S.D.A.........	4	1 274	1 576*	0.4	0.8
419 SO BAPT CONV..	93	72 338	89 467*	24.6	44.9
421 SO METHODIST..	1	36	45	-	-
435 UNITARIAN-UNIV	1	46	57*	-	-
449 UN METHODIST..	46	16 978	20 998*	5.8	10.5
469 WELS..........	1	51	71	-	-
MONROE	**74**	**11 192**	**14 733***	**65.0**	**100.0**
005 AME ZION......	3	556	669	3.0	4.5
053 ASSEMB OF GOD.	9	440	901	4.0	6.1
081 CATHOLIC......	1	NA	89	0.4	0.6
101 C.M.E.........	5	911	1 149*	5.1	7.8
127 CH GOD (CLEVE)	3	38	48*	0.2	0.3
151 L-D SAINTS....	1	NA	188	0.8	1.3
165 CH OF NAZARENE	2	126	192	0.8	1.3
167 CHS OF CHRIST.	1	151	172	0.8	1.2
193 EPISCOPAL.....	1	82	92	0.4	0.6
283 LUTH--MO SYNOD	1	147	211	0.9	1.4
357 PRESB CH US...	2	197	248*	1.1	1.7
419 SO BAPT CONV..	31	7 175	9 048*	39.9	61.4
449 UN METHODIST..	14	1 369	1 726*	7.6	11.7
MONTGOMERY	**219**	**83 869**	**112 016***	**56.8**	**100.0**
005 AME ZION......	33	18 060	21 672	11.0	19.3
017 AMER BAPT ASSN	1	50	50	-	-
019 AMER BAPT USA.	1	?	?	?	?
053 ASSEMB OF GOD.	5	1 639	2 871	1.5	2.6
059 BAPT MISS ASSN	2	580	713*	0.4	0.6
081 CATHOLIC......	8	NA	7 467	3.8	6.7
089 CHR & MISS AL.	2	27	37	-	-
093 CHR CH (DISC).	6	559	754	0.4	0.7
097 CHR CHS&CHS CR	1	50	61*	-	0.1
101 C.M.E.........	3	987	1 213*	0.6	1.1
123 CH GOD (ANDER)	2	83	249	0.1	0.2
127 CH GOD (CLEVE)	3	192	236*	0.1	0.2
151 L-D SAINTS....	2	NA	747	0.4	0.7
165 CH OF NAZARENE	2	120	179	0.1	0.2
167 CHS OF CHRIST.	43	4 775	6 078	3.1	5.4
177 CONGR HOL CH..	2	58	71*	-	0.1
193 EPISCOPAL.....	6	2 311	2 972	1.5	2.7
215 EVAN METH CH..	1	133	163*	0.1	0.1
270 CONSRV JUDAISM	1	183	225*	0.1	0.2
271 REFORM JUDAISM	1	532	654*	0.3	0.6
281 LUTH CH AMER..	1	395	550	0.3	0.5
283 LUTH--MO SYNOD	4	491	695*	0.4	0.6
349 PENT HOLINESS.	1	46	57*	-	0.1
353 CHR BRETHREN..	1	10	15	-	-
356 PRESB CH AMER.	7	3 149	3 262	1.7	2.9
357 PRESB CH US...	3	1 132	1 391*	0.7	1.2
403 SALVATION ARMY	2	139	430	0.2	0.4
413 S.D.A.........	4	1 270	1 561*	0.8	1.4
419 SO BAPT CONV..	40	32 693	40 184*	20.4	35.9
435 UNITARIAN-UNIV	1	58	71*	-	0.1
443 UN C OF CHRIST	1	53	65*	-	0.1
449 UN METHODIST..	29	14 094	17 323*	8.8	15.5
MORGAN	**178**	**45 227**	**58 851***	**65.2**	**100.0**
005 AME ZION......	2	270	307	0.3	0.5
053 ASSEMB OF GOD.	1	216	275	0.3	0.5
081 CATHOLIC......	1	NA	1 624	1.8	2.8
093 CHR CH (DISC).	5	464	625	0.7	1.1
097 CHR CHS&CHS CR	1	100	122*	0.1	0.2
101 C.M.E.........	8	1 397	1 711*	1.9	2.9
123 CH GOD (ANDER)	3	186	558	0.6	0.9
127 CH GOD (CLEVE)	5	490	600*	0.7	1.0
151 L-D SAINTS....	1	NA	291	0.3	0.5
165 CH OF NAZARENE	3	352	591	0.7	1.0
167 CHS OF CHRIST.	23	2 820	4 302	4.8	7.3
179 CONSRV BAPT...	2	200	245*	0.3	0.4
193 EPISCOPAL.....	1	623	856	0.9	1.5
283 LUTH--MO SYNOD	1	412	539	0.6	0.9
349 PENT HOLINESS.	2	116	142*	0.2	0.2
356 PRESB CH AMER.	1	52	52	0.1	0.1
357 PRESB CH US...	3	781	957*	1.1	1.6
403 SALVATION ARMY	1	92	157	0.2	0.3
413 S.D.A.........	2	142	174*	0.2	0.3
419 SO BAPT CONV..	69	26 523	32 486*	36.0	55.2
449 UN METHODIST..	41	9 533	11 676*	12.9	19.8
453 UN PRES CH USA	2	458	561*	0.6	1.0
PERRY	**41**	**5 781**	**7 059***	**47.0**	**100.0**
005 AME ZION......	1	1 350	1 458	9.7	20.7
053 ASSEMB OF GOD.	2	70	127	0.8	1.8
127 CH GOD (CLEVE)	3	72	90*	0.6	1.3
165 CH OF NAZARENE	1	22	51	0.3	0.7
167 CHS OF CHRIST.	1	45	57	0.4	0.8
193 EPISCOPAL.....	2	62	90	0.6	1.3
356 PRESB CH AMER.	2	177	190	1.3	2.7
419 SO BAPT CONV..	16	2 694	3 379*	22.5	47.9
443 UN C OF CHRIST	1	16	20*	0.1	0.3
449 UN METHODIST..	12	1 273	1 597*	10.6	22.6
PICKENS	**87**	**11 512**	**14 322***	**66.7**	**100.0**
017 AMER BAPT ASSN	1	50	50	0.2	0.3
053 ASSEMB OF GOD.	2	98	196	0.9	1.4
101 C.M.E.........	13	1 812	2 245*	10.5	15.7
127 CH GOD (CLEVE)	3	116	144*	0.7	1.0
165 CH OF NAZARENE	1	?	?	?	?
167 CHS OF CHRIST.	2	110	140	0.7	1.0
356 PRESB CH AMER.	2	228	276	1.3	1.9
357 PRESB CH US...	3	88	109*	0.5	0.8
419 SO BAPT CONV..	35	5 940	7 359*	34.3	51.4
449 UN METHODIST..	25	3 070	3 803*	17.7	26.6
PIKE	**76**	**11 182**	**13 950***	**49.7**	**100.0**
005 AME ZION......	2	170	255	0.9	1.8
053 ASSEMB OF GOD.	4	247	450	1.6	3.2
081 CATHOLIC......	2	NA	118	0.4	0.8
101 C.M.E.........	1	142	171*	0.6	1.2
127 CH GOD (CLEVE)	1	45	54*	0.2	0.4
151 L-D SAINTS....	1	NA	79	0.3	0.6
167 CHS OF CHRIST.	8	460	585	2.1	4.2
193 EPISCOPAL.....	1	139	169	0.6	1.2
356 PRESB CH AMER.	1	232	300	1.1	2.2
357 PRESB CH US...	2	66	80*	0.3	0.6
413 S.D.A.........	2	60	72*	0.3	0.5
419 SO BAPT CONV..	32	7 804	9 423*	33.6	67.5
449 UN METHODIST..	19	1 817	2 194*	7.8	15.7
RANDOLPH	**105**	**10 113**	**12 605***	**62.8**	**100.0**
081 CATHOLIC......	1	NA	30	0.1	0.2
093 CHR CH (DISC).	2	71	109	0.5	0.9
097 CHR CHS&CHS CR	2	146	179*	0.9	1.4
101 C.M.E.........	1	97	119*	0.6	0.9
123 CH GOD (ANDER)	1	18	54	0.3	0.4
127 CH GOD (CLEVE)	7	291	357*	1.8	2.8
165 CH OF NAZARENE	2	89	207	1.0	1.6
167 CHS OF CHRIST.	10	529	678	3.4	5.4
177 CONGR HOL CH..	1	5	6*	-	-
193 EPISCOPAL.....	1	25	30	0.1	0.2
419 SO BAPT CONV..	34	4 859	5 955*	29.7	47.2
443 UN C OF CHRIST	8	488	598*	3.0	4.7
449 UN METHODIST..	35	3 495	4 283*	21.3	34.0
RUSSELL	**90**	**18 368**	**23 953***	**50.6**	**100.0**
005 AME ZION......	10	2 525	2 790	5.9	11.6
053 ASSEMB OF GOD.	10	853	1 500	3.2	6.3
081 CATHOLIC......	3	NA	980	2.1	4.1
093 CHR CH (DISC).	1	82	126	0.3	0.5
097 CHR CHS&CHS CR	1	100	123*	0.3	0.5
101 C.M.E.........	2	270	332*	0.7	1.4
123 CH GOD (ANDER)	1	15	45	0.1	0.2
127 CH GOD (CLEVE)	3	118	145*	0.3	0.6
151 L-D SAINTS....	1	NA	239	0.5	1.0
165 CH OF NAZARENE	1	94	93	0.2	0.4
167 CHS OF CHRIST.	5	336	428	0.9	1.8

NA—Not applicable   *Total adherents estimated from known number of communicant, confirmed, full members.   —Represents a percent less than 0.1.   Percentages may not total due to rounding.

Table 4. Churches and Church Membership by County and Denomination: 1980

County and Denomination	Number of churches	Communicant, confirmed, full members	Total adherents Number	Percent of total population	Percent of total adherents
193 EPISCOPAL.....	2	41	39	0.1	0.2
357 PRESB CH US...	1	109	134*	0.3	0.6
413 S.D.A.........	2	180	221*	0.5	0.9
419 SO BAPT CONV..	30	11 438	14 048*	29.7	58.6
443 UN C OF CHRIST	2	185	227*	0.5	0.9
449 UN METHODIST..	15	2 022	2 483*	5.2	10.4
ST CLAIR	112	18 269	23 338*	56.6	100.0
053 ASSEMB OF GOD.	2	155	309	0.7	1.3
081 CATHOLIC......	1	NA	450	1.1	1.9
101 C.M.E.........	2	469	581*	1.4	2.5
127 CH GOD (CLEVE)	8	309	383*	0.9	1.6
165 CH OF NAZARENE	1	44	63	0.2	0.3
167 CHS OF CHRIST.	7	241	325	0.8	1.4
185 CUMBER PRESB..	3	80	207	0.5	0.9
193 EPISCOPAL.....	1	93	125	0.3	0.5
285 MENNONITE CH..	1	31	38*	0.1	0.2
357 PRESB CH US...	1	17	21*	0.1	0.1
413 S.D.A.........	2	157	194*	0.5	0.8
419 SO BAPT CONV..	61	14 047	17 391*	42.2	74.5
443 UN C OF CHRIST	1	71	88*	0.2	0.4
449 UN METHODIST..	19	2 425	3 002*	7.3	12.9
453 UN PRES CH USA	2	130	161*	0.4	0.7
SHELBY	123	21 815	28 029*	42.3	100.0
005 AME ZION......	1	96	103	0.2	0.4
053 ASSEMB OF GOD.	10	1 040	1 492	2.3	5.3
081 CATHOLIC......	1	NA	250	0.4	0.9
123 CH GOD (ANDER)	2	200	600	0.9	2.1
127 CH GOD (CLEVE)	10	515	639*	1.0	2.3
165 CH OF NAZARENE	2	190	302	0.5	1.1
167 CHS OF CHRIST.	12	970	1 235	1.9	4.4
185 CUMBER PRESB..	3	359	518	0.8	1.8
193 EPISCOPAL.....	1	85	115	0.2	0.4
349 PENT HOLINESS	1	55	68*	0.1	0.2
356 PRESB CH AMER.	1	?	?	?	?
357 PRESB CH US...	2	127	158*	0.2	0.6
413 S.D.A.........	2	37	46*	0.1	0.2
419 SO BAPT CONV..	51	13 703	16 998*	25.6	60.6
449 UN METHODIST..	24	4 438	5 505*	8.3	19.6
SUMTER	70	6 235	7 842*	46.4	100.0
005 AME ZION......	17	1 550	1 860	11.0	23.7
017 AMER BAPT ASSN	1	275	275	1.6	3.5
081 CATHOLIC......	1	NA	118	0.7	1.5
101 C.M.E.........	4	1 101	1 388*	8.2	17.7
123 CH GOD (ANDER)	2	30	90	0.5	1.1
127 CH GOD (CLEVE)	1	15	19*	0.1	0.2
143 CG IN CR(MENN)	1	85	85	0.5	1.1
167 CHS OF CHRIST.	3	117	149	0.9	1.9
193 EPISCOPAL.....	2	74	100	0.6	1.3
356 PRESB CH AMER.	7	124	149	0.9	1.9
357 PRESB CH US...	5	378	476*	2.8	6.1
419 SO BAPT CONV..	12	1 705	2 149*	12.7	27.4
449 UN METHODIST..	14	781	984*	5.8	12.5
TALLADEGA	169	34 584	43 816*	59.4	100.0
005 AME ZION......	4	1 620	1 836	2.5	4.2
053 ASSEMB OF GOD.	8	468	721	1.0	1.6
081 CATHOLIC......	3	NA	300	0.4	0.7
089 CHR & MISS AL.	2	130	177	0.2	0.4
101 C.M.E.........	9	1 503	1 872*	2.5	4.3
123 CH GOD (ANDER)	2	153	459	0.6	1.0
127 CH GOD (CLEVE)	12	1 111	1 384*	1.9	3.2
151 L-D SAINTS....	2	NA	134	0.2	0.3
165 CH OF NAZARENE	3	300	376	0.5	0.9
167 CHS OF CHRIST.	9	1 260	1 603	2.2	3.7
177 CONGR HOL CH..	3	23	29*	–	0.1
193 EPISCOPAL.....	4	304	397	0.5	0.9
263 INT FOURSQ GOS	1	?	?	?	?
356 PRESB CH AMER.	1	58	79	0.1	0.2
357 PRESB CH US...	4	668	832*	1.1	1.9
413 S.D.A.........	2	103	128*	0.2	0.3
419 SO BAPT CONV..	70	21 333	26 576*	36.0	60.7
443 UN C OF CHRIST	1	91	113*	0.2	0.3
449 UN METHODIST..	28	5 430	6 764*	9.2	15.4
453 UN PRES CH USA	1	29	36*	–	0.1
TALLAPOOSA	109	19 875	24 477*	63.3	100.0
005 AME ZION......	6	2 430	2 754	7.1	11.3
053 ASSEMB OF GOD.	3	195	354	0.9	1.4
081 CATHOLIC......	1	NA	125	0.3	0.5
101 C.M.E.........	1	82	100*	0.3	0.4
123 CH GOD (ANDER)	2	32	96	0.2	0.4
127 CH GOD (CLEVE)	2	134	164*	0.4	0.7
165 CH OF NAZARENE	1	20	25	0.1	0.1
167 CHS OF CHRIST.	6	590	752	1.9	3.1
177 CONGR HOL CH..	1	5	6*	–	–
193 EPISCOPAL.....	1	72	115	0.3	0.5
263 INT FOURSQ GOS	2	54	66*	0.2	0.3
357 PRESB CH US...	6	528	647*	1.7	2.6
419 SO BAPT CONV..	46	11 683	14 312*	37.0	58.5
435 UNITARIAN-UNIV	1	30	37*	0.1	0.2
443 UN C OF CHRIST	2	80	98*	0.3	0.4
449 UN METHODIST..	28	3 940	4 826*	12.5	19.7
TUSCALOOSA	203	56 768	71 261*	51.8	100.0
005 AME ZION......	16	8 810	10 572	7.7	14.8
017 AMER BAPT ASSN	2	70	70	0.1	0.1

County and Denomination	Number of churches	Communicant, confirmed, full members	Total adherents Number	Percent of total population	Percent of total adherents
053 ASSEMB OF GOD.	3	243	463	0.3	0.6
081 CATHOLIC......	2	NA	1 520	1.1	2.1
089 CHR & MISS AL.	1	23	23	–	–
093 CHR CH (DISC)	2	265	367	0.3	0.5
101 C.M.E.........	8	2 243	2 707*	2.0	3.8
123 CH GOD (ANDER)	3	126	378	0.3	0.5
127 CH GOD (CLEVE)	8	785	947*	0.7	1.3
151 L-D SAINTS....	1	NA	323	0.2	0.5
165 CH OF NAZARENE	8	940	1 255	0.9	1.8
167 CHS OF CHRIST.	11	1 692	2 154	1.6	3.0
185 CUMBER PRESB..	2	105	276	0.2	0.4
193 EPISCOPAL.....	3	1 033	1 314	1.0	1.8
271 REFORM JUDAISM	1	170	205*	0.1	0.3
283 LUTH--MO SYNOD	3	332	462	0.3	0.6
356 PRESB CH AMER.	1	73	109	0.1	0.2
357 PRESB CH US...	5	1 556	1 878*	1.4	2.6
403 SALVATION ARMY	1	102	131	0.1	0.2
413 S.D.A.........	2	348	420*	0.3	0.6
419 SO BAPT CONV..	81	30 316	36 582*	26.6	51.3
421 SO METHODIST..	2	69	95	0.1	0.1
435 UNITARIAN-UNIV	1	39	47*	–	0.1
449 UN METHODIST..	36	7 428	8 963*	6.5	12.6
WALKER	214	32 005	40 629*	59.2	100.0
005 AME ZION......	1	132	147	0.2	0.4
029 AMER LUTH CH..	1	31	36	0.1	0.1
053 ASSEMB OF GOD.	4	263	454	0.7	1.1
081 CATHOLIC......	1	NA	398	0.6	1.0
093 CHR CH (DISC).	1	87	106	0.2	0.3
101 C.M.E.........	6	748	917*	1.3	2.3
123 CH GOD (ANDER)	3	105	315	0.5	0.8
127 CH GOD (CLEVE)	22	2 244	2 751*	4.0	6.8
151 L-D SAINTS....	1	NA	261	0.4	0.6
165 CH OF NAZARENE	10	759	1 113	1.6	2.7
167 CHS OF CHRIST.	50	5 400	6 875	10.0	16.9
193 EPISCOPAL.....	1	86	118	0.2	0.3
271 REFORM JUDAISM	1	46	56*	0.1	0.1
356 PRESB CH AMER.	1	77	81	0.1	0.2
357 PRESB CH US...	1	73	89*	0.1	0.2
413 S.D.A.........	1	29	36*	0.1	0.1
419 SO BAPT CONV..	80	18 645	22 855*	33.3	56.3
449 UN METHODIST..	29	3 280	4 021*	5.9	9.9
WASHINGTON	82	8 751	11 258*	66.9	100.0
005 AME ZION......	7	1 670	2 004	11.9	17.8
053 ASSEMB OF GOD.	12	483	870	5.2	7.7
081 CATHOLIC......	1	NA	47	0.3	0.4
101 C.M.E.........	1	90	113*	0.7	1.0
127 CH GOD (CLEVE)	1	23	29*	0.2	0.3
157 CH OF BRETHREN	1	34	43*	0.3	0.4
165 CH OF NAZARENE	3	124	186	1.1	1.7
193 EPISCOPAL.....	1	31	28	0.2	0.2
357 PRESB CH US...	1	5	6*	–	0.1
419 SO BAPT CONV..	33	4 592	5 790*	34.4	51.4
449 UN METHODIST..	21	1 699	2 142*	12.7	19.0
WILCOX	51	4 144	5 594*	37.9	100.0
005 AME ZION......	2	334	417	2.8	7.5
055 AS REF PRES CH	2	164	185	1.3	3.3
081 CATHOLIC......	1	NA	42	0.3	0.8
101 C.M.E.........	2	195	250*	1.7	4.5
123 CH GOD (ANDER)	1	8	24	0.2	0.4
127 CH GOD (CLEVE)	2	94	121*	0.8	2.2
151 L-D SAINTS....	1	NA	74	0.5	1.3
167 CHS OF CHRIST.	4	150	191	1.3	3.4
283 LUTH--MO SYNOD	3	351	644	4.4	11.5
356 PRESB CH AMER.	2	128	155	1.1	2.8
357 PRESB CH US...	1	20	26*	0.2	0.5
419 SO BAPT CONV..	13	1 785	2 291*	15.5	41.0
449 UN METHODIST..	14	751	964*	6.5	17.2
453 UN PRES CH USA	3	164	210*	1.4	3.8
WINSTON	74	11 748	14 616*	66.6	100.0
053 ASSEMB OF GOD.	1	137	220	1.0	1.5
081 CATHOLIC......	1	NA	120	0.5	0.8
101 C.M.E.........	1	32	39*	0.2	0.3
127 CH GOD (CLEVE)	6	506	619*	2.8	4.2
165 CH OF NAZARENE	1	14	40	0.2	0.3
167 CHS OF CHRIST.	9	967	1 231	5.6	8.4
349 PENT HOLINESS	1	57	70*	0.3	0.5
419 SO BAPT CONV..	44	8 825	10 797*	49.2	73.9
449 UN METHODIST..	10	1 210	1 480*	6.7	10.1

ALASKA

County and Denomination	Number of churches	Communicant, confirmed, full members	Total adherents Number	Percent of total population	Percent of total adherents
THE STATE.....	579	51 723	123 434*	30.8	100.0
ALEUTIAN ISLANDS	10	205	1 348*	17.4	100.0

NA—Not applicable   *Total adherents estimated from known number of communicant, confirmed, full members.   —Represents a percent less than 0.1.   Percentages may not total due to rounding.

Table 4. Churches and Church Membership by County and Denomination: 1980

County and Denomination	Number of churches	Communicant, confirmed, full members	Total adherents Number	Percent of total population	Percent of total adherents
053 ASSEMB OF GOD.	3	129	154	2.0	11.4
057 BAPT GEN CONF.	1	30	36*	0.5	2.7
081 CATHOLIC......	4	NA	1 100	14.2	81.6
151 L-D SAINTS....	1	NA	?	?	?
167 CHS OF CHRIST.	1	40	51	0.7	3.8
413 S.D.A.........	0	6	7*	0.1	0.5
ANCHORAGE	**125**	**21 484**	**49 202***	**28.4**	**100.0**
005 AME ZION......	1	242	280	0.2	0.6
017 AMER BAPT ASSN	1	30	30	-	0.1
019 AMER BAPT USA.	2	526	656*	0.4	1.3
029 AMER LUTH CH..	4	1 174	1 798	1.0	3.7
053 ASSEMB OF GOD.	14	1 176	2 022	1.2	4.1
057 BAPT GEN CONF.	4	446	556*	0.3	1.1
059 BAPT MISS ASSN	1	63	79*	-	0.2
081 CATHOLIC......	7	NA	15 175	8.8	30.8
093 CHR CH (DISC).	1	238	450	0.3	0.9
097 CHR CHS&CHS CR	3	140	175*	0.1	0.4
101 C.M.E.......	1	318	396*	0.2	0.8
105 CHRISTIAN REF.	1	123	216	0.1	0.4
127 CH GOD (CLEVE)	4	385	480*	0.3	1.0
151 L-D SAINTS....	11	NA	4 900	2.8	10.0
165 CH OF NAZARENE	4	382	732	0.4	1.5
167 CHS OF CHRIST.	6	735	922	0.5	1.9
175 CONGR CHR CHS.	1	225	280*	0.2	0.6
179 CONSRV BAPT...	2	82	102*	0.1	0.2
193 EPISCOPAL.....	3	1 000	1 431	0.8	2.9
201 EVAN COV CH AM	1	89	111*	0.1	0.2
203 EVAN FREE CH..	1	27	34*	-	0.1
221 FREE METHODIST	1	80	240	0.1	0.5
226 FRIENDS-USA...	2	272	339*	0.2	0.7
244 GRACE BRETHREN	1	45	56*	-	0.1
271 REFORM JUDAISM	1	230	287*	0.2	0.6
281 LUTH CH AMER..	3	568	892	0.5	1.8
283 LUTH--MO SYNOD	3	1 079	1 546	0.9	3.1
285 MENNONITE CH..	1	27	34*	-	0.1
290 METRO COMM CHS	1	25	50	-	0.1
349 PENT HOLINESS.	1	51	64*	-	0.1
353 CHR BRETHREN..	2	110	275	0.2	0.6
403 SALVATION ARMY	1	90	147	0.1	0.3
413 S.D.A.........	2	301	375*	0.2	0.8
419 SO BAPT CONV..	17	8 234	10 264*	5.9	20.9
435 UNITARIAN-UNIV	1	165	206*	0.1	0.4
449 UN METHODIST..	8	1 588	1 980*	1.1	4.0
453 UN PRES CH USA	5	1 027	1 280*	0.7	2.6
469 WELS..........	2	191	342	0.2	0.7
BETHEL	**28**	**2 318**	**5 925***	**53.9**	**100.0**
053 ASSEMB OF GOD.	2	77	124	1.1	2.1
081 CATHOLIC......	7	NA	2 200	20.0	37.1
151 L-D SAINTS....	1	NA	?	?	?
201 EVAN COV CH AM	1	33	43*	0.4	0.7
293 MORAV CH-NORTH	16	2 157	3 491	31.7	58.9
349 PENT HOLINESS.	1	44	58*	0.5	1.0
413 S.D.A.........	0	7	9*	0.1	0.2
BRISTOL BAY	**5**	**67**	**202***	**18.5**	**100.0**
081 CATHOLIC......	4	NA	125	11.4	61.9
413 S.D.A.........	1	67	77*	7.0	38.1
DILLINGHAM	**10**	**584**	**1 100***	**23.8**	**100.0**
081 CATHOLIC......	4	NA	125	2.7	11.4
293 MORAV CH-NORTH	5	510	881	19.1	80.1
413 S.D.A.........	1	74	94*	2.0	8.5
FAIRBANKS NORTH STAR	**69**	**7 156**	**15 407***	**28.5**	**100.0**
005 AME ZION......	1	54	54	0.1	0.4
019 AMER BAPT USA.	1	110	137*	0.3	0.9
029 AMER LUTH CH..	2	426	703	1.3	4.6
053 ASSEMB OF GOD.	12	540	921	1.7	6.0
081 CATHOLIC......	4	NA	4 000	7.4	26.0
097 CHR CHS&CHS CR	2	105	131*	0.2	0.9
101 C.M.E.........	1	12	15*	-	0.1
123 CH GOD (ANDER)	1	68	204	0.4	1.3
127 CH GOD (CLEVE)	1	42	52*	0.1	0.3
151 L-D SAINTS....	6	NA	1 724	3.2	11.2
165 CH OF NAZARENE	4	192	513	1.0	3.3
167 CHS OF CHRIST.	3	176	242	0.4	1.6
179 CONSRV BAPT...	1	76	95*	0.2	0.6
193 EPISCOPAL.....	2	854	713	1.3	4.6
201 EVAN COV CH AM	1	14	17*	-	0.1
203 EVAN FREE CH..	1	15	19*	-	0.1
226 FRIENDS-USA...	2	260	325*	0.6	2.1
281 LUTH CH AMER..	1	103	152	0.3	1.0
283 LUTH--MO SYNOD	1	251	416	0.8	2.7
349 PENT HOLINESS.	1	8	10*	-	0.1
353 CHR BRETHREN..	2	75	150	0.3	1.0
403 SALVATION ARMY	1	30	132	0.2	0.9
413 S.D.A.........	1	134	167*	0.3	1.1
419 SO BAPT CONV..	9	2 552	3 187*	5.9	20.7
435 UNITARIAN-UNIV	1	14	17*	-	0.1
449 UN METHODIST..	2	526	657*	1.2	4.3
453 UN PRES CH USA	4	479	598*	1.1	3.9
469 WELS..........	1	40	56	0.1	0.4
HAINES	**6**	**203**	**498***	**29.6**	**100.0**
017 AMER BAPT ASSN	1	10	10	0.6	2.0
081 CATHOLIC......	1	NA	148	8.8	29.7
151 L-D SAINTS....	1	NA	42	2.5	8.4
167 CHS OF CHRIST.	1	7	9	0.5	1.8
403 SALVATION ARMY	1	51	123	7.3	24.7
413 S.D.A.........	0	9	11*	0.7	2.2
453 UN PRES CH USA	1	126	155*	9.2	31.1
JUNEAU	**27**	**2 902**	**7 313***	**37.4**	**100.0**
053 ASSEMB OF GOD.	5	423	756	3.9	10.3
081 CATHOLIC......	3	NA	2 500	12.8	34.2
123 CH GOD (ANDER)	1	39	111	0.6	1.5
127 CH GOD (CLEVE)	1	36	44*	0.2	0.6
151 L-D SAINTS....	2	NA	596	3.1	8.1
165 CH OF NAZARENE	1	67	49	0.3	0.7
167 CHS OF CHRIST.	1	81	150	0.8	2.1
193 EPISCOPAL.....	1	166	310	1.6	4.2
281 LUTH CH AMER..	1	350	536	2.7	7.3
283 LUTH--MO SYNOD	1	111	163	0.8	2.2
290 METRO COMM CHS	0	0	5	-	0.1
403 SALVATION ARMY	2	168	298	1.5	4.1
413 S.D.A.........	1	102	125*	0.6	1.7
419 SO BAPT CONV..	2	512	629*	3.2	8.6
435 UNITARIAN-UNIV	1	25	31*	0.2	0.4
449 UN METHODIST..	2	305	375*	1.9	5.1
453 UN PRES CH USA	2	517	635*	3.3	8.7
KENAI PENINSULA	**51**	**2 559**	**5 434***	**21.5**	**100.0**
029 AMER LUTH CH..	3	203	335	1.3	6.2
053 ASSEMB OF GOD.	5	203	344	1.4	6.3
081 CATHOLIC......	6	NA	1 610	6.4	29.6
097 CHR CHS&CHS CR	4	171	216*	0.9	4.0
127 CH GOD (CLEVE)	3	41	52*	0.2	1.0
151 L-D SAINTS....	1	NA	55	0.2	1.0
165 CH OF NAZARENE	4	169	497	2.0	9.1
167 CHS OF CHRIST.	7	300	419	1.7	7.7
179 CONSRV BAPT...	1	41	52*	0.2	1.0
193 EPISCOPAL.....	2	62	94	0.4	1.7
244 GRACE BRETHREN	1	93	118*	0.5	2.2
283 LUTH--MO SYNOD	2	129	190	0.8	3.5
403 SALVATION ARMY	1	17	22	0.1	0.4
413 S.D.A.........	1	52	66*	0.3	1.2
419 SO BAPT CONV..	3	621	786*	3.1	14.5
449 UN METHODIST..	7	457	578*	2.3	10.6
KETCHIKAN GATEWAY	**19**	**2 328**	**4 781***	**42.2**	**100.0**
029 AMER LUTH CH..	1	220	364	3.2	7.6
053 ASSEMB OF GOD.	2	144	239	2.1	5.0
081 CATHOLIC......	1	NA	1 200	10.6	25.1
089 CHR & MISS AL.	1	123	214	1.9	4.5
127 CH GOD (CLEVE)	1	166	205*	1.8	4.3
151 L-D SAINTS....	1	NA	300	2.7	6.3
164 CH LUTH CONF..	1	19	31	0.3	0.6
165 CH OF NAZARENE	1	43	103	0.9	2.2
167 CHS OF CHRIST.	1	62	97	0.9	2.0
175 CONGR CHR CHS.	1	329	407*	3.6	8.5
193 EPISCOPAL.....	1	203	316	2.8	6.6
403 SALVATION ARMY	2	193	283	2.5	5.9
413 S.D.A.........	1	59	73*	0.6	1.5
419 SO BAPT CONV..	2	376	465*	4.1	9.7
449 UN METHODIST..	1	308	381*	3.4	8.0
453 UN PRES CH USA	1	83	103*	0.9	2.2
KOBUK	**17**	**2 621**	**3 678***	**76.1**	**100.0**
053 ASSEMB OF GOD.	1	8	14	0.3	0.4
081 CATHOLIC......	1	NA	240	5.0	6.5
127 CH GOD (CLEVE)	1	29	38*	0.8	1.0
167 CHS OF CHRIST.	1	11	14	0.3	0.4
226 FRIENDS-USA...	10	2 416	3 167*	65.6	86.1
413 S.D.A.........	2	11	14*	0.3	0.4
419 SO BAPT CONV..	1	146	191*	4.0	5.2
KODIAK ISLAND	**12**	**519**	**1 485***	**14.9**	**100.0**
019 AMER BAPT USA.	1	100	124*	1.2	8.4
029 AMER LUTH CH..	1	90	154	1.5	10.4
053 ASSEMB OF GOD.	1	50	104	1.0	7.0
081 CATHOLIC......	1	NA	600	6.0	40.4
089 CHR & MISS AL.	1	68	138	1.4	9.3
123 CH GOD (ANDER)	1	17	51	0.5	3.4
151 L-D SAINTS....	1	NA	?	?	?
165 CH OF NAZARENE	1	7	25	0.3	1.7
167 CHS OF CHRIST.	1	30	40	0.4	2.7
193 EPISCOPAL.....	1	55	122	1.2	8.2
413 S.D.A.........	1	41	51*	0.5	3.4
419 SO BAPT CONV..	1	61	76*	0.8	5.1
MATANUSKA-SUSITNA	**25**	**1 068**	**4 554***	**25.6**	**100.0**
029 AMER LUTH CH..	1	53	85	0.5	1.9
053 ASSEMB OF GOD.	2	194	389	2.2	8.5
081 CATHOLIC......	6	NA	2 000	11.3	43.9
097 CHR CHS&CHS CR	2	48	61*	0.3	1.3
123 CH GOD (ANDER)	2	121	363	2.0	8.0
127 CH GOD (CLEVE)	1	52	66*	0.4	1.4
151 L-D SAINTS....	3	NA	748	4.2	16.4
165 CH OF NAZARENE	1	18	31	0.2	0.7
167 CHS OF CHRIST.	1	23	32	0.2	0.7
193 EPISCOPAL.....	1	38	88	0.5	1.9
226 FRIENDS-USA...	1	11	14*	0.1	0.3
283 LUTH--MO SYNOD	1	172	245	1.4	5.4
413 S.D.A.........	1	60	77*	0.4	1.7
453 UN PRES CH USA	2	278	355*	2.0	7.8

NA—Not applicable   *Total adherents estimated from known number of communicant, confirmed, full members.   —Represents a percent less than 0.1.   Percentages may not total due to rounding.

Table 4. Churches and Church Membership by County and Denomination: 1980

County and Denomination	Number of churches	Communicant, confirmed, full members	Total adherents Number	Percent of total population	Percent of total adherents
NOME	23	1 429	3 235*	49.5	100.0
029 AMER LUTH CH..	4	411	920	14.1	28.4
053 ASSEMB OF GOD.	1	29	54	0.8	1.7
081 CATHOLIC.....	6	NA	900	13.8	27.8
165 CH OF NAZARENE	1	26	112	1.7	3.5
167 CHS OF CHRIST.	1	10	13	0.2	0.4
201 EVAN COV CH AM	3	185	240*	3.7	7.4
353 CHR BRETHREN..	1	15	20	0.3	0.6
413 S.D.A........	2	72	93*	1.4	2.9
449 UN METHODIST..	1	147	191*	2.9	5.9
453 UN PRES CH USA	3	534	692*	10.6	21.4
NORTH SLOPE	15	1 001	1 452*	34.6	100.0
053 ASSEMB OF GOD.	6	129	304	7.2	20.9
081 CATHOLIC......	1	NA	40	1.0	2.8
193 EPISCOPAL.....	2	141	195	4.6	13.4
226 FRIENDS-USA...	1	11	14*	0.3	1.0
413 S.D.A........	0	1	1*	–	0.1
453 UN PRES CH USA	5	719	898*	21.4	61.8
PR OF WALES-OUT KETC	18	388	710*	18.6	100.0
081 CATHOLIC......	9	NA	137	3.6	19.3
127 CH GOD (CLEVE)	2	92	116*	3.0	16.3
403 SALVATION ARMY	1	63	162	4.2	22.8
413 S.D.A........	3	74	94*	2.5	13.2
453 UN PRES CH USA	3	159	201*	5.3	28.3
SITKA	14	1 135	2 960*	37.9	100.0
053 ASSEMB OF GOD.	1	106	210	2.7	7.1
081 CATHOLIC......	1	NA	850	10.9	28.7
151 L-D SAINTS....	1	NA	170	2.2	5.7
165 CH OF NAZARENE	1	102	336	4.3	11.4
167 CHS OF CHRIST.	1	20	28	0.4	0.9
193 EPISCOPAL.....	1	108	255	3.3	8.6
281 LUTH CH AMER..	1	177	258	3.3	8.7
403 SALVATION ARMY	1	53	112	1.4	3.8
413 S.D.A........	1	57	72*	0.9	2.4
419 SO BAPT CONV..	1	196	246*	3.2	8.3
435 UNITARIAN-UNIV	1	10	13*	0.2	0.4
449 UN METHODIST..	1	80	100*	1.3	3.4
453 UN PRES CH USA	1	196	246*	3.2	8.3
469 WELS.........	1	30	64	0.8	2.2
SKAGWAY-YAKUTAT-ANGO	15	453	907*	26.1	100.0
053 ASSEMB OF GOD.	5	166	337	9.7	37.2
081 CATHOLIC......	3	NA	117	3.4	12.9
151 L-D SAINTS....	1	NA	68	2.0	7.5
403 SALVATION ARMY	1	42	74	2.1	8.2
453 UN PRES CH USA	5	245	311*	8.9	34.3
SOUTHEAST FAIRBANKS	9	420	1 038*	18.0	100.0
081 CATHOLIC......	2	NA	400	6.9	38.5
097 CHR CHS&CHS CR	1	15	19*	0.3	1.8
151 L-D SAINTS....	1	NA	101	1.8	9.7
167 CHS OF CHRIST.	1	8	10	0.2	1.0
349 PENT HOLINESS.	2	45	58*	1.0	5.6
413 S.D.A........	0	6	8*	0.1	0.8
419 SO BAPT CONV..	1	280	358*	6.2	34.5
453 UN PRES CH USA	1	66	84*	1.5	8.1
VALDEZ-CORDOVA	17	1 423	3 072*	36.8	100.0
019 AMER BAPT USA.	1	79	97*	1.2	3.2
081 CATHOLIC......	2	NA	391	4.7	12.7
123 CH GOD (ANDER)	2	510	1 530	18.3	49.8
127 CH GOD (CLEVE)	1	8	10*	0.1	0.3
151 L-D SAINTS....	2	NA	?	?	?
167 CHS OF CHRIST.	3	30	38	0.5	1.2
179 CONSRV BAPT...	1	33	41*	0.5	1.3
226 FRIENDS-USA...	1	11	14*	0.2	0.5
281 LUTH CH AMER..	1	67	107	1.3	3.5
413 S.D.A........	1	23	28*	0.3	0.9
419 SO BAPT CONV..	2	662	816*	9.8	26.6
WADE HAMPTON	14	62	3 702*	79.4	100.0
053 ASSEMB OF GOD.	2	27	55	1.2	1.5
081 CATHOLIC......	11	NA	3 600	77.2	97.2
201 EVAN COV CH AM	1	35	47*	1.0	1.3
WRANGELL-PETERSBURG	19	814	1 643*	26.6	100.0
029 AMER LUTH CH..	1	233	319	5.2	19.4
053 ASSEMB OF GOD.	2	90	133	2.2	8.1
081 CATHOLIC......	2	NA	320	5.2	19.5
123 CH GOD (ANDER)	1	29	87	1.4	5.3
127 CH GOD (CLEVE)	1	4	5*	0.1	0.3
151 L-D SAINTS....	2	NA	49	0.8	3.0
193 EPISCOPAL.....	2	128	240	3.9	14.6
226 FRIENDS-USA...	1	11	14*	0.2	0.9
403 SALVATION ARMY	2	115	220	3.6	13.4
413 S.D.A........	1	26	33*	0.5	2.0
419 SO BAPT CONV..	1	56	70*	1.1	4.3
453 UN PRES CH USA	3	122	153*	2.5	9.3
YUKON-KOYUKUK	31	584	3 788*	48.1	100.0
053 ASSEMB OF GOD.	10	165	400	5.1	10.6
081 CATHOLIC......	11	NA	1 900	24.1	50.2
151 L-D SAINTS....	1	NA	49	0.6	1.3
167 CHS OF CHRIST.	1	15	19	0.2	0.5
193 EPISCOPAL.....	8	399	1 414	18.0	37.3
413 S.D.A........	0	5	6*	0.1	0.2

ARIZONA

County and Denomination	Number of churches	Communicant, confirmed, full members	Total adherents Number	Percent of total population	Percent of total adherents
THE STATE.....	2 096	343 863	1 073 012*	39.5	100.0
APACHE	69	2 624	20 711*	39.8	100.0
029 AMER LUTH CH..	1	63	119	0.2	0.6
053 ASSEMB OF GOD.	7	283	722	1.4	3.5
081 CATHOLIC......	11	NA	7 884	15.1	38.1
097 CHR CHS&CHS CR	2	460	618*	1.2	3.0
105 CHRISTIAN REF.	3	150	379	0.7	1.8
123 CH GOD (ANDER)	1	100	300	0.6	1.4
149 CH OF JC (BIC)	1	25	25	–	0.1
151 L-D SAINTS....	20	NA	8 542	16.4	41.2
165 CH OF NAZARENE	3	197	288	0.6	1.4
167 CHS OF CHRIST.	3	102	132	0.3	0.6
263 INT FOURSQ GOS	1	30	40*	0.1	0.2
285 MENNONITE CH..	2	70	94*	0.2	0.5
353 CHR BRETHREN..	1	40	75	0.1	0.4
413 S.D.A........	1	36	48*	0.1	0.2
419 SO BAPT CONV..	5	562	755*	1.4	3.6
449 UN METHODIST..	1	4	5*	–	–
453 UN PRES CH USA	5	486	653*	1.3	3.2
469 WELS.........	1	16	32	0.1	0.2
COCHISE	119	10 087	32 885*	37.9	100.0
029 AMER LUTH CH..	3	460	582	0.7	1.8
053 ASSEMB OF GOD.	12	498	909	1.0	2.8
081 CATHOLIC......	15	NA	16 115	18.6	49.0
093 CHR CH (DISC).	2	52	206	0.2	0.6
097 CHR CHS&CHS CR	3	220	272*	0.3	0.8
127 CH GOD (CLEVE)	3	117	145*	0.2	0.4
151 L-D SAINTS....	9	NA	3 405	3.9	10.4
165 CH OF NAZARENE	5	200	442	0.5	1.3
167 CHS OF CHRIST.	10	540	775	0.9	2.4
179 CONSRV BAPT...	4	919	1 136*	1.3	3.5
193 EPISCOPAL.....	7	522	744	0.9	2.3
203 EVAN FREE CH..	1	19	23*	–	0.1
226 FRIENDS-USA...	1	8	10*	–	–
263 INT FOURSQ GOS	2	101	125*	0.1	0.4
349 PENT HOLINESS.	1	7	9*	–	–
403 SALVATION ARMY	1	45	104	0.1	0.3
413 S.D.A........	3	147	182*	0.2	0.6
419 SO BAPT CONV..	16	3 816	4 718*	5.4	14.3
435 UNITARIAN-UNIV	1	17	21*	–	0.1
443 UN C OF CHRIST	4	452	559*	0.6	1.7
449 UN METHODIST..	9	1 334	1 649*	1.9	5.0
453 UN PRES CH USA	3	448	554*	0.6	1.7
469 WELS.........	4	165	200	0.2	0.6
COCONINO	101	8 159	32 972*	44.0	100.0
019 AMER BAPT USA.	1	65	82*	0.1	0.2
053 ASSEMB OF GOD.	8	376	805	1.1	2.4
081 CATHOLIC......	7	NA	13 712	18.3	41.6
089 CHR & MISS AL.	1	0	29	–	0.1
091 CHRISTIAN CATH	2	90	235	0.3	0.7
097 CHR CHS&CHS CR	1	90	113*	0.2	0.3
105 CHRISTIAN REF.	1	34	52	0.1	0.2
127 CH GOD (CLEVE)	1	61	77*	0.1	0.2
151 L-D SAINTS....	24	NA	7 915	10.6	24.0
165 CH OF NAZARENE	7	507	810	1.1	2.5
167 CHS OF CHRIST.	6	230	293	0.4	0.9
179 CONSRV BAPT...	5	1 277	1 605*	2.1	4.9
193 EPISCOPAL.....	3	556	757	1.0	2.3
226 FRIENDS-USA...	1	20	25*	–	0.1
244 GRACE BRETHREN	1	?	?	?	?
263 INT FOURSQ GOS	5	336	422*	0.6	1.3
281 LUTH CH AMER..	1	348	571	0.8	1.7
283 LUTH--MO SYNOD	2	153	264	0.4	0.8
353 CHR BRETHREN..	2	25	125	0.2	0.4
403 SALVATION ARMY	1	28	80	0.1	0.2
413 S.D.A........	1	94	118*	0.2	0.4
419 SO BAPT CONV..	9	2 260	2 841*	3.8	8.6
435 UNITARIAN-UNIV	1	30	38*	0.1	0.1
443 UN C OF CHRIST	1	108	136*	0.2	0.4
449 UN METHODIST..	5	978	1 229*	1.6	3.7
453 UN PRES CH USA	3	363	456*	0.6	1.4
469 WELS.........	1	130	182	0.2	0.6
GILA	67	5 670	20 368*	54.9	100.0
019 AMER BAPT USA.	1	123	153*	0.4	0.8
053 ASSEMB OF GOD.	9	817	1 294	3.5	6.4
081 CATHOLIC......	11	NA	9 500	25.6	46.6
093 CHR CH (DISC).	1	110	125	0.3	0.6
097 CHR CHS&CHS CR	2	140	174*	0.5	0.9

NA—Not applicable   *Total adherents estimated from known number of communicant, confirmed, full members.   —Represents a percent less than 0.1.   Percentages may not total due to rounding.

Table 4. Churches and Church Membership by County and Denomination: 1980

County and Denomination	Number of churches	Communicant, confirmed, full members	Total adherents Number	Total adherents Percent of total population	Total adherents Percent of total adherents
127 CH GOD (CLEVE)	1	30	37*	0.1	0.2
151 L-D SAINTS....	8	NA	2 802	7.6	13.8
165 CH OF NAZARENE	2	126	194	0.5	1.0
167 CHS OF CHRIST.	4	138	176	0.5	0.9
179 CONSRV BAPT...	1	85	106*	0.3	0.5
193 EPISCOPAL.....	2	121	131	0.4	0.6
263 INT FOURSQ GOS	2	95	118*	0.3	0.6
281 LUTH CH AMER..	2	317	506	1.4	2.5
403 SALVATION ARMY	1	51	106	0.3	0.5
413 S.D.A.........	2	104	129*	0.3	0.6
419 SO BAPT CONV..	7	2 146	2 665*	7.2	13.1
449 UN METHODIST..	3	335	416*	1.1	2.0
453 UN PRES CH USA	5	474	589*	1.6	2.9
469 WELS.........	3	458	1 147	3.1	5.6
GRAHAM	33	1 765	16 481*	72.1	100.0
053 ASSEMB OF GOD.	2	88	164	0.7	1.0
081 CATHOLIC......	4	NA	8 000	35.0	48.5
097 CHR CHS&CHS CR	1	21	27*	0.1	0.2
151 L-D SAINTS....	15	NA	5 923	25.9	35.9
165 CH OF NAZARENE	1	?	?	?	?
167 CHS OF CHRIST.	1	35	45	0.2	0.3
179 CONSRV BAPT...	1	247	315*	1.4	1.9
193 EPISCOPAL.....	1	63	89	0.4	0.5
413 S.D.A.........	1	104	133*	0.6	0.8
419 SO BAPT CONV..	3	580	740*	3.2	4.5
449 UN METHODIST..	1	307	392*	1.7	2.4
469 WELS.........	2	320	653	2.9	4.0
GREENLEE	24	1 462	9 314*	81.7	100.0
019 AMER BAPT USA.	1	21	27*	0.2	0.3
053 ASSEMB OF GOD.	1	75	120	1.1	1.3
059 BAPT MISS ASSN	1	76	99*	0.9	1.1
081 CATHOLIC......	3	NA	6 000	52.6	64.4
127 CH GOD (CLEVE)	1	?	?	?	?
151 L-D SAINTS....	4	NA	1 313	11.5	14.1
167 CHS OF CHRIST.	3	129	227	2.0	2.4
179 CONSRV BAPT...	2	136	177*	1.6	1.9
193 EPISCOPAL.....	1	58	89	0.8	1.0
263 INT FOURSQ GOS	1	55	72*	0.6	0.8
419 SO BAPT CONV..	3	743	967*	8.5	10.4
449 UN METHODIST..	1	1	1*	–	–
453 UN PRES CH USA	1	157	204*	1.8	2.2
469 WELS.........	1	11	18	0.2	0.2
MARICOPA	871	201 024	572 500*	38.0	100.0
017 AMER BAPT ASSN	6	400	400	–	0.1
019 AMER BAPT USA.	26	8 618	10 447*	0.7	1.8
029 AMER LUTH CH..	19	9 896	12 904	0.9	2.3
039 AP CHR CH(NAZ)	1	152	184*	–	–
045 APOSTOLIC LUTH	1	25	30*	–	–
053 ASSEMB OF GOD.	61	5 446	9 285	0.6	1.6
057 BAPT GEN CONF.	3	314	381*	–	0.1
059 BAPT MISS ASSN	1	23	28*	–	–
071 BRETHREN (ASH)	1	111	135*	–	–
081 CATHOLIC......	64	NA	238 210	15.8	41.6
083 CHRIST CATH CH	2	47	73	–	–
089 CHR & MISS AL.	3	157	285	–	–
091 CHRISTIAN CATH	1	50	125	–	–
093 CHR CH (DISC)	10	2 392	3 139	0.2	0.5
097 CHR CHS&CHS CR	12	1 437	1 742*	0.1	0.3
101 C.M.E.........	3	1 291	1 565*	0.1	0.3
105 CHRISTIAN REF.	3	525	801	0.1	0.1
121 CH GOD (ABR)..	2	430	521*	–	0.1
123 CH GOD (ANDER)	6	907	2 721	0.2	0.5
127 CH GOD (CLEVE)	26	1 626	1 971*	0.1	0.3
133 CH GOD(7TH)DEN	1	29	35*	–	–
143 CG IN CR(MENN)	1	40	40	–	–
149 CH OF JC (BIC)	1	53	55	–	–
151 L-D SAINTS....	147	NA	73 602	4.9	12.9
157 CH OF BRETHREN	3	366	444*	–	0.1
163 CH OF LUTH BR.	2	68	89	–	–
164 CH LUTH CONF..	1	75	114	–	–
165 CH OF NAZARENE	24	4 319	6 268	0.4	1.1
167 CHS OF CHRIST.	47	5 410	6 885	0.5	1.2
175 CONGR CHR CHS.	1	146	177*	–	–
179 CONSRV BAPT...	25	6 692	8 112*	0.5	1.4
193 EPISCOPAL.....	25	10 404	12 855	0.9	2.2
201 EVAN COV CH AM	2	251	304*	–	0.1
203 EVAN FREE CH..	3	73	88*	–	–
215 EVAN METH CH..	3	134	162*	–	–
217 FIRE BAPTIZED.	3	8	10*	–	–
221 FREE METHODIST	10	618	2 430	0.2	0.4
226 FRIENDS-USA...	3	182	221*	–	–
237 GC MENN BR CHS	1	38	46*	–	–
244 GRACE BRETHREN	2	183	222*	–	–
263 INT FOURSQ GOS	8	680	824*	0.1	0.1
270 CONSRV JUDAISM	4	758	919*	0.1	0.2
271 REFORM JUDAISM	4	4 128	5 004*	0.3	0.9
281 LUTH CH AMER..	19	10 539	14 009	0.9	2.4
283 LUTH--MO SYNOD	21	8 270	10 826	0.7	1.9
285 MENNONITE CH..	8	624	756*	0.1	0.1
287 MENN GEN CONF.	2	117	138	–	–
290 METRO COMM CHS	2	150	300	–	0.1
291 MISSIONARY CH.	2	748	1 058	0.1	0.2
313 N AM BAPT CONF	1	21	25*	–	–
349 PENT HOLINESS	10	387	469*	–	0.1
353 CHR BRETHREN..	5	325	600	–	0.1
356 PRESB CH AMER.	2	61	85	–	–
371 REF CH IN AM..	4	1 213	2 104	0.1	0.4
381 REF PRES-EVAN.	1	10	16	–	–
383 REF PRES OF NA	1	41	65	–	–

County and Denomination	Number of churches	Communicant, confirmed, full members	Total adherents Number	Total adherents Percent of total population	Total adherents Percent of total adherents
403 SALVATION ARMY	7	889	5 556	0.4	1.0
413 S.D.A.........	19	4 036	4 893*	0.3	0.9
419 SO BAPT CONV..	87	48 871	59 243*	3.9	10.3
435 UNITARIAN-UNIV	3	752	912*	0.1	0.2
443 UN C OF CHRIST	15	10 660	12 922*	0.9	2.3
449 UN METHODIST..	40	26 614	32 262*	2.1	5.6
453 UN PRES CH USA	36	15 287	18 531*	1.2	3.2
469 WELS.........	14	2 907	3 877	0.3	0.7
MOHAVE	55	6 090	18 249*	32.8	100.0
029 AMER LUTH CH..	2	630	800	1.4	4.4
053 ASSEMB OF GOD.	6	325	624	1.1	3.4
057 BAPT GEN CONF.	1	188	225*	0.4	1.2
081 CATHOLIC......	5	NA	8 310	14.9	45.5
097 CHR CHS&CHS CR	3	362	432*	0.8	2.4
123 CH GOD (ANDER)	1	20	60	0.1	0.3
151 L-D SAINTS....	6	NA	2 106	3.8	11.5
165 CH OF NAZARENE	2	115	299	0.5	1.6
167 CHS OF CHRIST.	3	206	232	0.4	1.3
179 CONSRV BAPT...	1	335	400*	0.7	2.2
193 EPISCOPAL.....	2	224	345	0.6	1.9
209 EVAN LUTH SYN.	1	26	37	0.1	0.2
263 INT FOURSQ GOS	6	346	413*	0.7	2.3
283 LUTH--MO SYNOD	1	77	86	0.2	0.5
413 S.D.A.........	2	138	165*	0.3	0.9
419 SO BAPT CONV..	7	1 613	1 927*	3.5	10.6
449 UN METHODIST..	3	903	1 079*	1.9	5.9
453 UN PRES CH USA	2	544	650*	1.2	3.6
469 WELS.........	1	38	59	0.1	0.3
NAVAJO	126	6 822	30 689*	45.3	100.0
019 AMER BAPT USA.	3	134	178*	0.3	0.6
029 AMER LUTH CH..	2	202	281	0.4	0.9
053 ASSEMB OF GOD.	14	836	1 126	1.7	3.7
081 CATHOLIC......	10	NA	6 854	10.1	22.3
089 CHR & MISS AL.	2	80	80	0.1	0.3
149 CH OF JC (BIC)	2	40	50	0.1	0.2
151 L-D SAINTS....	45	NA	13 949	20.6	45.5
165 CH OF NAZARENE	7	333	577	0.9	1.9
167 CHS OF CHRIST.	6	260	331	0.5	1.1
193 EPISCOPAL.....	4	211	475	0.7	1.5
263 INT FOURSQ GOS	1	37	49*	0.1	0.2
353 CHR BRETHREN..	1	25	50	0.1	0.2
413 S.D.A.........	3	206	273*	0.4	0.9
419 SO BAPT CONV..	12	3 075	4 075*	6.0	13.3
449 UN METHODIST..	3	546	723*	1.1	2.4
453 UN PRES CH USA	3	199	264*	0.4	0.9
469 WELS.........	8	638	1 354	2.0	4.4
PIMA	296	63 310	203 325*	38.3	100.0
017 AMER BAPT ASSN	1	100	100	–	–
019 AMER BAPT USA.	2	477	573*	0.1	0.3
029 AMER LUTH CH..	4	1 714	2 259	0.4	1.1
053 ASSEMB OF GOD.	16	1 602	3 002	0.6	1.5
057 BAPT GEN CONF.	3	120	144*	–	0.1
059 BAPT MISS ASSN	1	87	105*	–	0.1
071 BRETHREN (ASH)	2	216	260*	–	0.1
081 CATHOLIC......	55	NA	113 100	21.3	55.6
089 CHR & MISS AL.	4	175	275	0.1	0.1
093 CHR CH (DISC)	5	1 223	1 420	0.3	0.7
097 CHR CHS&CHS CR	8	1 104	1 327*	0.2	0.7
101 C.M.E.........	1	208	250*	–	0.1
105 CHRISTIAN REF.	2	177	274	0.1	0.1
123 CH GOD (ANDER)	4	332	996	0.2	0.5
127 CH GOD (CLEVE)	6	405	487*	0.1	0.2
133 CH GOD(7TH)DEN	1	13	16*	–	–
149 CH OF JC (BIC)	1	15	15	–	–
151 L-D SAINTS....	23	NA	9 515	1.8	4.7
157 CH OF BRETHREN	1	97	117*	–	0.1
165 CH OF NAZARENE	11	1 043	1 876	0.4	0.9
167 CHS OF CHRIST.	14	1 907	2 633	0.5	1.3
179 CONSRV BAPT...	11	3 336	4 009*	0.8	2.0
193 EPISCOPAL.....	9	4 650	5 735	1.1	2.8
201 EVAN COV CH AM	1	192	231*	–	0.1
203 EVAN FREE CH..	2	322	387*	0.1	0.2
215 EVAN METH CH..	1	59	71*	–	–
226 FRIENDS-USA...	1	99	119*	–	0.1
233 GEN CH NEW JER	1	30	36*	–	–
244 GRACE BRETHREN	1	40	48*	–	–
263 INT FOURSQ GOS	2	394	473*	0.1	0.2
270 CONSRV JUDAISM	1	404	485*	0.1	0.2
271 REFORM JUDAISM	2	1 722	2 069*	0.4	1.0
281 LUTH CH AMER..	7	3 309	4 386	0.8	2.2
283 LUTH--MO SYNOD	7	2 662	3 730	0.7	1.8
285 MENNONITE CH..	1	18	22*	–	–
287 MENN GEN CONF.	1	26	40	–	–
290 METRO COMM CHS	2	50	100	–	–
349 PENT HOLINESS	2	60	72*	–	–
353 CHR BRETHREN..	1	80	200	–	0.1
356 PRESB CH AMER.	1	71	93	–	–
371 REF CH IN AM..	1	227	436	0.1	0.2
403 SALVATION ARMY	2	230	402	0.1	0.2
413 S.D.A.........	4	982	1 180*	0.2	0.6
419 SO BAPT CONV..	36	15 248	18 324*	3.4	9.0
435 UNITARIAN-UNIV	1	418	502*	0.1	0.2
443 UN C OF CHRIST	4	1 691	2 032*	0.4	1.0
449 UN METHODIST..	12	8 541	10 264*	1.9	5.0
453 UN PRES CH USA	11	6 300	7 571*	1.4	3.7
469 WELS.........	6	1 134	1 564	0.3	0.8
PINAL	135	13 372	42 844*	47.1	100.0

NA—Not applicable   *Total adherents estimated from known number of communicant, confirmed, full members.

—Represents a percent less than 0.1.   Percentages may not total due to rounding.

Table 4. Churches and Church Membership by County and Denomination: 1980

County and Denomination	Number of churches	Communicant, confirmed, full members	Total adherents		
			Number	Percent of total population	Percent of total adherents
029 AMER LUTH CH..	1	281	308	0.3	0.7
053 ASSEMB OF GOD.	20	748	1 630	1.8	3.8
081 CATHOLIC......	14	NA	21 600	23.8	50.4
089 CHR & MISS AL.	2	9	41	–	0.1
093 CHR CH (DISC).	1	40	60	0.1	0.1
097 CHR CHS&CHS CR	2	321	402*	0.4	0.9
101 C.M.E.........	2	108	135*	0.1	0.3
127 CH GOD (CLEVE)	6	199	249*	0.3	0.6
151 L-D SAINTS....	11	NA	3 598	4.0	8.4
165 CH OF NAZARENE	3	376	646	0.7	1.5
167 CHS OF CHRIST.	12	512	652	0.7	1.5
179 CONSRV BAPT..	5	402	503*	0.6	1.2
193 EPISCOPAL.....	4	309	390	0.4	0.9
215 EVAN METH CH..	1	66	83*	0.1	0.2
263 INT FOURSQ GOS	1	23	29*	–	0.1
281 LUTH CH AMER..	1	26	44	–	0.1
283 LUTH--MO SYNOD	2	258	329	0.4	0.8
349 PENT HOLINESS.	2	70	88*	0.1	0.2
413 S.D.A.........	3	144	180*	0.2	0.4
419 SO BAPT CONV..	24	6 684	8 369*	9.2	19.5
443 UN C OF CHRIST	1	207	259*	0.3	0.6
449 UN METHODIST..	5	897	1 123*	1.2	2.6
453 UN PRES CH USA	10	1 599	2 002*	2.2	4.7
469 WELS..........	2	93	124	0.1	0.3
SANTA CRUZ	24	1 216	11 205*	54.8	100.0
053 ASSEMB OF GOD.	2	163	455	2.2	4.1
081 CATHOLIC......	6	NA	9 000	44.0	80.3
127 CH GOD (CLEVE)	1	?	?	?	?
151 L-D SAINTS....	1	NA	223	1.1	2.0
167 CHS OF CHRIST.	1	35	50	0.2	0.4
179 CONSRV BAPT...	2	300	384*	1.9	3.4
193 EPISCOPAL.....	1	78	140	0.7	1.2
220 FREE LUTHERAN.	1	45	56	0.3	0.5
221 FREE METHODIST	2	84	243	1.2	2.2
263 INT FOURSQ GOS	1	161	206*	1.0	1.8
283 LUTH--MO SYNOD	1	33	43	0.2	0.4
413 S.D.A.........	2	78	100*	0.5	0.9
443 UN C OF CHRIST	1	134	171*	0.8	1.5
449 UN METHODIST..	2	105	134*	0.7	1.2
YAVAPAI	94	11 439	28 407*	41.7	100.0
019 AMER BAPT USA.	1	50	59*	0.1	0.2
029 AMER LUTH CH..	1	580	718	1.1	2.5
053 ASSEMB OF GOD.	8	422	782	1.1	2.8
081 CATHOLIC......	5	NA	10 740	15.8	37.8
093 CHR CH (DISC).	1	139	177	0.3	0.6
097 CHR CHS&CHS CR	3	339	400*	0.6	1.4
123 CH GOD (ANDER)	1	100	300	0.4	1.1
151 L-D SAINTS....	11	NA	3 254	4.8	11.5
165 CH OF NAZARENE	2	288	533	0.8	1.9
167 CHS OF CHRIST.	11	550	700	1.0	2.5
179 CONSRV BAPT...	6	1 682	1 985*	2.9	7.0
193 EPISCOPAL.....	2	527	722	1.1	2.5
203 EVAN FREE CH..	1	30	35*	0.1	0.1
221 FREE METHODIST	1	50	144	0.2	0.5
263 INT FOURSQ GOS	3	701	827*	1.2	2.9
283 LUTH--MO SYNOD	2	258	367	0.5	1.3
285 MENNONITE CH..	1	18	21*	–	0.1
356 PRESB CH AMER.	1	57	62	0.1	0.2
403 SALVATION ARMY	1	86	0	–	–
413 S.D.A.........	4	532	628*	0.9	2.2
419 SO BAPT CONV..	13	1 895	2 236*	3.3	7.9
435 UNITARIAN-UNIV	1	48	57*	0.1	0.2
443 UN C OF CHRIST	5	1 038	1 225*	1.8	4.3
449 UN METHODIST..	4	1 385	1 635*	2.4	5.8
453 UN PRES CH USA	3	386	456*	0.7	1.6
469 WELS..........	2	278	344	0.5	1.2
YUMA	82	10 823	33 062*	36.5	100.0
017 AMER BAPT ASSN	1	100	100	0.1	0.3
019 AMER BAPT USA.	1	46	57*	0.1	0.2
053 ASSEMB OF GOD.	10	455	815	0.9	2.5
081 CATHOLIC......	7	NA	16 000	17.7	48.4
101 C.M.E.........	1	58	72*	0.1	0.2
123 CH GOD (ANDER)	1	60	180	0.2	0.5
127 CH GOD (CLEVE)	1	84	105*	0.1	0.3
133 CH GOD(7TH)DEN	1	2	2*	–	–
151 L-D SAINTS....	11	NA	3 031	3.3	9.2
165 CH OF NAZARENE	7	498	685	0.8	2.1
167 CHS OF CHRIST.	3	407	517	0.6	1.6
179 CONSRV BAPT...	7	2 068	2 582*	2.9	7.8
193 EPISCOPAL.....	2	496	555	0.6	1.7
263 INT FOURSQ GOS	1	56	70*	0.1	0.2
281 LUTH CH AMER..	1	285	387	0.4	1.2
283 LUTH--MO SYNOD	3	764	1 065	1.2	3.2
349 PENT HOLINESS.	1	31	39*	–	0.1
403 SALVATION ARMY	1	60	121	0.1	0.4
413 S.D.A.........	2	279	348*	0.4	1.1
419 SO BAPT CONV..	8	3 195	3 989*	4.4	12.1
435 UNITARIAN-UNIV	1	25	31*	–	0.1
449 UN METHODIST..	5	1 089	1 359*	1.5	4.1
453 UN PRES CH USA	5	703	878*	1.0	2.7
469 WELS..........	1	62	74	0.1	0.2

County and Denomination	Number of churches	Communicant, confirmed, full members	Total adherents		
			Number	Percent of total population	Percent of total adherents
ARKANSAS					
THE STATE.....	5 493	989 400	1 284 100*	56.2	100.0
ARKANSAS	68	12 104	15 279*	63.2	100.0
017 AMER BAPT ASSN	11	1 803	1 803	7.5	11.8
029 AMER LUTH CH..	1	208	257	1.1	1.7
053 ASSEMB OF GOD.	4	310	535	2.2	3.5
059 BAPT MISS ASSN	8	552	672*	2.8	4.4
081 CATHOLIC......	2	NA	710	2.9	4.6
093 CHR CH (DISC).	1	238	286	1.2	1.9
097 CHR CHS&CHS CR	2	230	280*	1.2	1.8
165 CH OF NAZARENE	3	69	112	0.5	0.7
167 CHS OF CHRIST.	4	300	382	1.6	2.5
193 EPISCOPAL.....	1	92	119	0.5	0.8
215 EVAN METH CH..	1	131	159*	0.7	1.0
226 FRIENDS-USA...	1	13	16*	0.1	0.1
283 LUTH--MO SYNOD	3	887	1 095	4.5	7.2
357 PRESB CH US...	1	68	83*	0.3	0.5
419 SO BAPT CONV..	11	4 099	4 991*	20.6	32.7
449 UN METHODIST..	13	3 036	3 696*	15.3	24.2
453 UN PRES CH USA	1	68	83*	0.3	0.5
ASHLEY	79	14 830	18 432*	69.5	100.0
005 AME ZION......	8	969	1 282	4.8	7.0
017 AMER BAPT ASSN	12	2 197	2 197	8.3	11.9
053 ASSEMB OF GOD.	5	308	476	1.8	2.6
059 BAPT MISS ASSN	2	275	343*	1.3	1.9
081 CATHOLIC......	1	NA	137	0.5	0.7
101 C.M.E.........	2	390	486*	1.8	2.6
123 CH GOD (ANDER)	1	100	300	1.1	1.6
127 CH GOD (CLEVE)	1	26	32*	0.1	0.2
151 L-D SAINTS....	1	NA	34	0.1	0.2
165 CH OF NAZARENE	1	19	39	0.1	0.2
167 CHS OF CHRIST.	5	288	328	1.2	1.8
193 EPISCOPAL.....	1	132	157	0.6	0.9
283 LUTH--MO SYNOD	1	26	36	0.1	0.2
357 PRESB CH US...	2	152	189*	0.7	1.0
419 SO BAPT CONV..	26	8 271	10 306*	38.8	55.9
449 UN METHODIST..	10	1 677	2 090*	7.9	11.3
BAXTER	61	9 558	13 444*	49.0	100.0
017 AMER BAPT ASSN	2	100	100	0.4	0.7
053 ASSEMB OF GOD.	4	241	486	1.8	3.6
059 BAPT MISS ASSN	2	45	52*	0.2	0.4
081 CATHOLIC......	1	NA	1 825	6.7	13.6
093 CHR CH (DISC).	1	299	327	1.2	2.4
097 CHR CHS&CHS CR	2	185	214*	0.8	1.6
127 CH GOD (CLEVE)	1	24	28*	0.1	0.2
151 L-D SAINTS....	1	NA	240	0.9	1.8
165 CH OF NAZARENE	1	89	103	0.4	0.8
167 CHS OF CHRIST.	17	1 400	1 780	6.5	13.2
185 CUMBER PRESB..	1	99	154	0.6	1.1
193 EPISCOPAL.....	1	167	180	0.7	1.3
283 LUTH--MO SYNOD	1	1 061	1 180	4.3	8.8
357 PRESB CH US...	3	241	279*	1.0	2.1
413 S.D.A.........	1	110	127*	0.5	0.9
419 SO BAPT CONV..	13	3 465	4 015*	14.6	29.9
449 UN METHODIST..	6	1 792	2 076*	7.6	15.4
453 UN PRES CH USA	3	240	278*	1.0	2.1
BENTON	155	29 434	38 009*	48.7	100.0
017 AMER BAPT ASSN	4	593	593	0.8	1.6
053 ASSEMB OF GOD.	13	997	1 848	2.4	4.9
059 BAPT MISS ASSN	16	1 543	1 857*	2.4	4.9
081 CATHOLIC......	2	NA	1 100	1.4	2.9
093 CHR CH (DISC).	4	910	1 165	1.5	3.1
097 CHR CHS&CHS CR	7	820	987*	1.3	2.6
127 CH GOD (CLEVE)	2	146	176*	0.2	0.5
151 L-D SAINTS....	2	NA	282	0.4	0.7
165 CH OF NAZARENE	5	548	945	1.2	2.5
167 CHS OF CHRIST.	16	1 900	2 550	3.3	6.7
193 EPISCOPAL.....	3	475	514	0.7	1.4
203 EVAN FREE CH..	2	55	66*	0.1	0.2
217 FIRE BAPTIZED.	1	10	12*	–	–
221 FREE METHODIST	1	15	72	0.1	0.2
237 GC MENN BR CHS	1	61	73*	0.1	0.2
281 LUTH CH AMER..	2	549	672	0.9	1.8
283 LUTH--MO SYNOD	3	412	543	0.7	1.4
349 PENT HOLINESS.	4	174	209*	0.3	0.5
357 PRESB CH US...	6	599	721*	0.9	1.9
413 S.D.A.........	5	1 035	1 246*	1.6	3.3
419 SO BAPT CONV..	30	13 046	15 702*	20.1	41.3
449 UN METHODIST..	20	4 949	5 957*	7.6	15.7
453 UN PRES CH USA	6	597	719*	0.9	1.9
BOONE	79	10 965	14 474*	55.5	100.0
017 AMER BAPT ASSN	5	500	500	1.9	3.5
053 ASSEMB OF GOD.	7	496	1 017	3.9	7.0
061 BEACHY AMISH..	1	9	11*	–	0.1
081 CATHOLIC......	1	NA	540	2.1	3.7
089 CHR & MISS AL.	1	14	33	0.1	0.2
093 CHR CH (DISC).	3	417	554	2.1	3.8
123 CH GOD (ANDER)	1	90	270	1.0	1.9
127 CH GOD (CLEVE)	1	57	68*	0.3	0.5
151 L-D SAINTS....	1	NA	166	0.6	1.1

NA—Not applicable   *Total adherents estimated from known number of communicant, confirmed, full members.   —Represents a percent less than 0.1.   Percentages may not total due to rounding.

Table 4. Churches and Church Membership by County and Denomination: 1980

County and Denomination	Number of churches	Communicant, confirmed, full members	Total adherents		
			Number	Percent of total population	Percent of total adherents
165 CH OF NAZARENE	1	33	81	0.3	0.6
167 CHS OF CHRIST.	13	1 135	1 318	5.1	9.1
185 CUMBER PRESB..	1	31	58	0.2	0.4
193 EPISCOPAL.....	1	229	303	1.2	2.1
281 LUTH CH AMER..	1	54	57	0.2	0.4
283 LUTH--MO SYNOD	1	144	181	0.7	1.3
353 CHR BRETHREN..	1	15	15	0.1	0.1
357 PRESB CH US...	2	315	379*	1.5	2.6
413 S.D.A.........	1	170	204*	0.8	1.4
419 SO BAPT CONV..	24	5 330	6 405*	24.6	44.3
449 UN METHODIST..	10	1 612	1 937*	7.4	13.4
453 UN PRES CH USA	2	314	377*	1.4	2.6
BRADLEY	40	6 527	8 060*	58.4	100.0
005 AME ZION......	1	100	114	0.8	1.4
017 AMER BAPT ASSN	1	162	162	1.2	2.0
053 ASSEMB OF GOD.	1	221	428	3.1	5.3
055 AS REF PRES CH	1	31	31	0.2	0.4
059 BAPT MISS ASSN	7	1 063	1 285*	9.3	15.9
081 CATHOLIC......	1	NA	45	0.3	0.6
127 CH GOD (CLEVE)	1	27	33*	0.2	0.4
167 CHS OF CHRIST.	3	125	160	1.2	2.0
357 PRESB CH US...	3	357	432*	3.1	5.4
419 SO BAPT CONV..	13	3 371	4 076*	29.5	50.6
449 UN METHODIST..	8	1 070	1 294*	9.4	16.1
CALHOUN	28	2 468	3 102*	51.0	100.0
017 AMER BAPT ASSN	1	72	72	1.2	2.3
053 ASSEMB OF GOD.	3	163	243	4.0	7.8
059 BAPT MISS ASSN	10	621	747*	12.3	24.1
167 CHS OF CHRIST.	3	205	260	4.3	8.4
185 CUMBER PRESB..	1	110	220	3.6	7.1
419 SO BAPT CONV..	5	922	1 109*	18.2	35.8
449 UN METHODIST..	5	375	451*	7.4	14.5
CARROLL	42	5 215	6 679*	41.2	100.0
017 AMER BAPT ASSN	2	200	200	1.2	3.0
053 ASSEMB OF GOD.	5	509	761	4.7	11.4
059 BAPT MISS ASSN	1	38	45*	0.3	0.7
081 CATHOLIC......	2	NA	352	2.2	5.3
093 CHR CH (DISC).	1	181	219	1.4	3.3
097 CHR CHS&CHS CR	2	110	130*	0.8	1.9
165 CH OF NAZARENE	2	28	49	0.3	0.7
167 CHS OF CHRIST.	5	249	317	2.0	4.7
193 EPISCOPAL.....	1	92	100	0.6	1.5
283 LUTH--MO SYNOD	1	74	84	0.5	1.3
357 PRESB CH US...	2	54	64*	0.4	1.0
413 S.D.A.........	2	66	78*	0.5	1.2
419 SO BAPT CONV..	10	2 709	3 208*	19.8	48.0
449 UN METHODIST..	4	851	1 008*	6.2	15.1
453 UN PRES CH USA	2	54	64*	0.4	1.0
CHICOT	36	5 406	7 370*	41.4	100.0
005 AME ZION......	2	200	212	1.2	2.9
017 AMER BAPT ASSN	1	114	114	0.6	1.5
053 ASSEMB OF GOD.	3	136	245	1.4	3.3
059 BAPT MISS ASSN	1	123	156*	0.9	2.1
081 CATHOLIC......	2	NA	548	3.1	7.4
101 C.M.E.........	1	63	80*	0.4	1.1
127 CH GOD (CLEVE)	1	38	48*	0.3	0.7
167 CHS OF CHRIST.	3	175	183	1.0	2.5
193 EPISCOPAL.....	1	75	107	0.6	1.5
357 PRESB CH US...	3	170	215*	1.2	2.9
419 SO BAPT CONV..	13	3 476	4 403*	24.7	59.7
449 UN METHODIST..	5	836	1 059*	6.0	14.4
CLARK	77	11 516	14 105*	60.5	100.0
017 AMER BAPT ASSN	9	861	861	3.7	6.1
053 ASSEMB OF GOD.	6	301	584	2.5	4.1
059 BAPT MISS ASSN	5	855	1 015*	4.4	7.2
081 CATHOLIC......	1	NA	225	1.0	1.6
093 CHR CH (DISC).	3	108	140	0.6	1.0
123 CH GOD (ANDER)	2	54	162	0.7	1.1
165 CH OF NAZARENE	2	48	63	0.3	0.4
167 CHS OF CHRIST.	5	325	414	1.8	2.9
193 EPISCOPAL.....	1	45	55	0.2	0.4
357 PRESB CH US...	4	292	347*	1.5	2.5
419 SO BAPT CONV..	28	6 248	7 415*	31.8	52.6
449 UN METHODIST..	10	2 365	2 807*	12.0	19.9
453 UN PRES CH USA	1	14	17*	0.1	0.1
CLAY	82	9 355	11 447*	55.5	100.0
017 AMER BAPT ASSN	13	1 093	1 093	5.3	9.5
053 ASSEMB OF GOD.	3	109	146	0.7	1.3
059 BAPT MISS ASSN	6	504	602*	2.9	5.3
081 CATHOLIC......	3	NA	300	1.5	2.6
097 CHR CHS&CHS CR	2	275	329*	1.6	2.9
123 CH GOD (ANDER)	1	65	195	0.9	1.7
165 CH OF NAZARENE	1	13	45	0.2	0.4
167 CHS OF CHRIST.	16	1 280	1 538	7.5	13.4
283 LUTH--MO.SYNOD	1	86	113	0.5	1.0
419 SO BAPT CONV..	20	3 820	4 565*	22.1	39.9
449 UN METHODIST..	16	2 110	2 521*	12.2	22.0
CLEBURNE	46	6 286	7 867*	46.5	100.0
017 AMER BAPT ASSN	1	23	23	0.1	0.3
053 ASSEMB OF GOD.	2	185	274	1.6	3.5
059 BAPT MISS ASSN	5	731	869*	5.1	11.0
081 CATHOLIC......	1	NA	250	1.5	3.2
123 CH GOD (ANDER)	1	20	60	0.4	0.8
127 CH GOD (CLEVE)	2	60	71*	0.4	0.9
165 CH OF NAZARENE	2	44	60	0.4	0.8
167 CHS OF CHRIST.	5	437	556	3.3	7.1
193 EPISCOPAL.....	1	99	120	0.7	1.5
281 LUTH CH AMER..	1	159	200	1.2	2.5
357 PRESB CH US...	1	89	106*	0.6	1.3
419 SO BAPT CONV..	16	3 085	3 668*	21.7	46.6
449 UN METHODIST..	7	1 266	1 505*	8.9	19.1
453 UN PRES CH USA	1	88	105*	0.6	1.3
CLEVELAND	36	3 952	4 685*	59.5	100.0
017 AMER BAPT ASSN	10	1 704	1 704	21.7	36.4
053 ASSEMB OF GOD.	2	122	209	2.7	4.5
055 AS REF PRES CH	1	18	18	0.2	0.4
059 BAPT MISS ASSN	9	713	868*	11.0	18.5
123 CH GOD (ANDER)	1	100	300	3.8	6.4
167 CHS OF CHRIST.	2	54	75	1.0	1.6
419 SO BAPT CONV..	2	594	723*	9.2	15.4
449 UN METHODIST..	9	647	788*	10.0	16.8
COLUMBIA	88	14 506	17 970*	67.4	100.0
017 AMER BAPT ASSN	9	787	787	3.0	4.4
053 ASSEMB OF GOD.	3	168	307	1.2	1.7
059 BAPT MISS ASSN	21	4 195	5 060*	19.0	28.2
081 CATHOLIC......	1	NA	240	0.9	1.3
093 CHR CH (DISC).	1	5	8	-	-
101 C.M.E.........	6	1 912	2 306*	8.7	12.8
123 CH GOD (ANDER)	1	15	45	0.2	0.3
127 CH GOD (CLEVE)	1	10	12*	-	0.1
151 L-D SAINTS....	1	NA	163	0.6	0.9
165 CH OF NAZARENE	1	10	0	-	-
167 CHS OF CHRIST.	12	865	1 100	4.1	6.1
185 CUMBER PRESB..	2	52	89	0.3	0.5
193 EPISCOPAL.....	1	61	93	0.3	0.5
283 LUTH--MO SYNOD	1	74	97	0.4	0.5
357 PRESB CH US...	1	195	235*	0.9	1.3
419 SO BAPT CONV..	5	2 982	3 597*	13.5	20.0
421 SO METHODIST..	1	81	99	0.4	0.6
449 UN METHODIST..	20	3 094	3 732*	14.0	20.8
CONWAY	73	6 351	10 040*	51.5	100.0
017 AMER BAPT ASSN	11	1 316	1 316	6.7	13.1
053 ASSEMB OF GOD.	6	311	531	2.7	5.3
059 BAPT MISS ASSN	10	1 123	1 376*	7.1	13.7
081 CATHOLIC......	4	NA	2 038	10.4	20.3
121 CH GOD (ABR)..	1	40	49*	0.3	0.5
127 CH GOD (CLEVE)	1	?	?	?	?
151 L-D SAINTS....	1	NA	96	0.5	1.0
165 CH OF NAZARENE	1	86	230	1.2	2.3
167 CHS OF CHRIST.	17	1 210	1 587	8.1	15.8
185 CUMBER PRESB..	2	47	103	0.5	1.0
283 LUTH--MO SYNOD	1	17	17	0.1	0.2
357 PRESB CH US...	2	137	168*	0.9	1.7
419 SO BAPT CONV..	3	990	1 213*	6.2	12.1
449 UN METHODIST..	11	937	1 148*	5.9	11.4
453 UN PRES CH USA	2	137	168*	0.9	1.7
CRAIGHEAD	140	33 112	42 281*	66.9	100.0
017 AMER BAPT ASSN	1	260	260	0.4	0.6
053 ASSEMB OF GOD.	12	653	1 052	1.7	2.5
059 BAPT MISS ASSN	25	4 664	5 628*	8.9	13.3
081 CATHOLIC......	2	NA	1 607	2.5	3.8
093 CHR CH (DISC).	2	404	458	0.7	1.1
097 CHR CHS&CHS CR	3	443	535*	0.8	1.3
101 C.M.E.........	1	753	909*	1.4	2.1
127 CH GOD (CLEVE)	3	119	144*	0.2	0.3
151 L-D SAINTS....	1	NA	232	0.4	0.5
165 CH OF NAZARENE	4	395	589	0.9	1.4
167 CHS OF CHRIST.	20	3 182	4 010	6.3	9.5
271 REFORM JUDAISM	1	46	56*	0.1	0.1
283 LUTH--MO SYNOD	1	125	170	0.3	0.4
357 PRESB CH US...	1	228	275*	0.4	0.7
403 SALVATION ARMY	1	99	124	0.2	0.3
413 S.D.A.........	1	65	78*	0.1	0.2
419 SO BAPT CONV..	34	15 711	18 957*	30.0	44.8
435 UNITARIAN-UNIV	1	17	21*	-	-
449 UN METHODIST..	25	5 719	6 900*	10.9	16.3
453 UN PRES CH USA	1	229	276*	0.4	0.7
CRAWFORD	83	13 441	17 579*	47.6	100.0
017 AMER BAPT ASSN	9	1 293	1 293	3.5	7.4
053 ASSEMB OF GOD.	16	1 121	1 852	5.0	10.5
081 CATHOLIC......	1	NA	400	1.1	2.3
089 CHR & MISS AL.	1	37	87	0.2	0.5
093 CHR CH (DISC).	3	302	343	0.9	2.0
097 CHR CHS&CHS CR	1	36	45*	0.1	0.3
123 CH GOD (ANDER)	1	28	84	0.2	0.5
127 CH GOD (CLEVE)	4	349	432*	1.2	2.5
151 L-D SAINTS....	1	NA	101	0.3	0.6
165 CH OF NAZARENE	2	274	492	1.3	2.8
167 CHS OF CHRIST.	8	719	930	2.5	5.3
185 CUMBER PRESB..	1	4	7	-	-
193 EPISCOPAL.....	1	130	176	0.5	1.0
290 METRO COMM CHS	0	0	25	0.1	0.1
357 PRESB CH US...	3	202	250*	0.7	1.4
413 S.D.A.........	1	22	27*	0.1	0.2
419 SO BAPT CONV..	17	6 807	8 417*	22.8	47.9
449 UN METHODIST..	10	1 915	2 368*	6.4	13.5

NA—Not applicable   *Total adherents estimated from known number of communicant, confirmed, full members.   —Represents a percent less than 0.1.   Percentages may not total due to rounding.

Table 4. Churches and Church Membership by County and Denomination: 1980

County and Denomination	Number of churches	Communicant, confirmed, full members	Total adherents Number	Percent of total population	Percent of total adherents
453 UN PRES CH USA	3	202	250*	0.7	1.4
CRITTENDEN	55	14 827	20 260*	41.3	100.0
017 AMER BAPT ASSN	2	1 007	1 007	2.1	5.0
053 ASSEMB OF GOD.	4	387	647	1.3	3.2
059 BAPT MISS ASSN	2	527	671*	1.4	3.3
081 CATHOLIC......	3	NA	1 200	2.4	5.9
093 CHR CH (DISC).	1	48	71	0.1	0.4
101 C.M.E.	4	527	671*	1.4	3.3
127 CH GOD (CLEVE)	5	270	344*	0.7	1.7
151 L-D SAINTS....	1	NA	160	0.3	0.8
165 CH OF NAZARENE	1	145	239	0.5	1.2
167 CHS OF CHRIST.	7	1 054	1 368	2.8	6.8
193 EPISCOPAL.....	1	161	239	0.5	1.2
283 LUTH--MO SYNOD	1	56	90	0.2	0.4
357 PRESB CH US...	3	451	574*	1.2	2.8
413 S.D.A.	1	30	38*	0.1	0.2
419 SO BAPT CONV..	13	7 803	9 935*	20.2	49.0
449 UN METHODIST..	6	2 361	3 006*	6.1	14.8
CROSS	54	9 790	13 081*	64.0	100.0
017 AMER BAPT ASSN	4	348	348	1.7	2.7
053 ASSEMB OF GOD.	10	542	1 004	4.9	7.7
059 BAPT MISS ASSN	3	364	458*	2.2	3.5
081 CATHOLIC......	1	NA	460	2.3	3.5
093 CHR CH (DISC).	1	20	30	0.1	0.2
101 C.M.E.	4	1 271	1 600*	7.8	12.2
157 CH OF BRETHREN	1	63	79*	0.4	0.6
167 CHS OF CHRIST.	4	444	623	3.0	4.8
193 EPISCOPAL.....	1	20	22	0.1	0.2
357 PRESB CH US...	1	123	155*	0.8	1.2
419 SO BAPT CONV..	14	4 530	5 703*	27.9	43.6
449 UN METHODIST..	9	1 941	2 443*	12.0	18.7
453 UN PRES CH USA	1	124	156*	0.8	1.2
DALLAS	44	4 954	6 048*	57.5	100.0
017 AMER BAPT ASSN	3	616	616	5.9	10.2
053 ASSEMB OF GOD.	3	172	260	2.5	4.3
059 BAPT MISS ASSN	5	748	916*	8.7	15.1
151 L-D SAINTS....	1	NA	64	0.6	1.1
165 CH OF NAZARENE	1	?	?	?	?
167 CHS OF CHRIST.	3	115	146	1.4	2.4
357 PRESB CH US...	3	113	138*	1.3	2.3
419 SO BAPT CONV..	12	2 084	2 553*	24.3	42.2
449 UN METHODIST..	13	1 106	1 355*	12.9	22.4
DESHA	44	8 235	10 682*	54.1	100.0
005 AME ZION......	2	210	245	1.2	2.3
017 AMER BAPT ASSN	4	591	591	3.0	5.5
053 ASSEMB OF GOD.	7	502	804	4.1	7.5
059 BAPT MISS ASSN	2	434	547*	2.8	5.1
081 CATHOLIC......	2	NA	309	1.6	2.9
097 CHR CHS&CHS CR	1	115	145*	0.7	1.4
165 CH OF NAZARENE	1	44	73	0.4	0.7
167 CHS OF CHRIST.	2	165	195	1.0	1.8
193 EPISCOPAL.....	2	34	32	0.2	0.3
271 REFORM JUDAISM	1	130	164*	0.8	1.5
357 PRESB CH US...	1	145	183*	0.9	1.7
419 SO BAPT CONV..	13	4 340	5 471*	27.7	51.2
449 UN METHODIST..	6	1 525	1 923*	9.7	18.0
DREW	51	8 067	9 850*	55.0	100.0
005 AME ZION......	1	366	386	2.2	3.9
017 AMER BAPT ASSN	5	914	914	5.1	9.3
053 ASSEMB OF GOD.	5	258	400	2.2	4.1
055 AS REF PRES CH	1	111	121	0.7	1.2
059 BAPT MISS ASSN	1	288	352*	2.0	3.6
081 CATHOLIC......	1	NA	65	0.4	0.7
097 CHR CHS&CHS CR	1	42	51*	0.3	0.5
151 L-D SAINTS....	1	NA	99	0.6	1.0
167 CHS OF CHRIST.	1	130	145	0.8	1.5
185 CUMBER PRESB..	1	69	118	0.7	1.2
193 EPISCOPAL.....	1	48	57	0.3	0.6
283 LUTH--MO SYNOD	1	14	18	0.1	0.2
357 PRESB CH US...	2	272	333*	1.9	3.4
413 S.D.A.	1	42	51*	0.3	0.5
419 SO BAPT CONV..	14	4 167	5 094*	28.4	51.7
449 UN METHODIST..	13	1 311	1 603*	9.0	16.3
453 UN PRES CH USA	1	35	43*	0.2	0.4
FAULKNER	105	18 670	25 625*	55.5	100.0
005 AME ZION......	1	100	105	0.2	0.4
017 AMER BAPT ASSN	3	345	345	0.7	1.3
053 ASSEMB OF GOD.	5	211	328	0.7	1.3
059 BAPT MISS ASSN	18	3 851	4 647*	10.1	18.1
081 CATHOLIC......	1	NA	2 300	5.0	9.0
093 CHR CH (DISC).	1	32	40	0.1	0.2
121 CH GOD (ABR)..	1	75	90*	0.2	0.4
127 CH GOD (CLEVE)	1	26	31*	0.1	0.1
151 L-D SAINTS....	1	NA	461	1.0	1.8
165 CH OF NAZARENE	6	662	957	2.1	3.7
167 CHS OF CHRIST.	16	1 850	2 355	5.1	9.2
193 EPISCOPAL.....	1	145	228	0.5	0.9
283 LUTH--MO SYNOD	1	138	181	0.4	0.7
285 MENNONITE CH..	1	4	5*	-	-
357 PRESB CH US...	2	119	144*	0.3	0.6
413 S.D.A.	1	21	25*	0.1	0.1
419 SO BAPT CONV..	23	7 777	9 384*	20.3	36.6
449 UN METHODIST..	20	3 195	3 855*	8.3	15.0

County and Denomination	Number of churches	Communicant, confirmed, full members	Total adherents Number	Percent of total population	Percent of total adherents
453 UN PRES CH USA	2	119	144*	0.3	0.6
FRANKLIN	50	5 364	7 578*	51.5	100.0
017 AMER BAPT ASSN	6	569	569	3.9	7.5
053 ASSEMB OF GOD.	7	294	462	3.1	6.1
081 CATHOLIC......	2	NA	930	6.3	12.3
093 CHR CH (DISC).	2	155	235	1.6	3.1
101 C.M.E.	2	188	228*	1.6	3.0
165 CH OF NAZARENE	2	78	187	1.3	2.5
167 CHS OF CHRIST.	5	258	327	2.2	4.3
185 CUMBER PRESB..	1	6	20	0.1	0.3
221 FREE METHODIST	1	11	18	0.1	0.2
356 PRESB CH AMER.	1	8	8	0.1	0.1
357 PRESB CH US...	1	68	82*	0.6	1.1
419 SO BAPT CONV..	8	2 319	2 806*	19.1	37.0
449 UN METHODIST..	10	1 272	1 539*	10.5	20.3
453 UN PRES CH USA	2	138	167*	1.1	2.2
FULTON	55	4 062	5 075*	50.9	100.0
017 AMER BAPT ASSN	1	50	50	0.5	1.0
053 ASSEMB OF GOD.	3	150	252	2.5	5.0
059 BAPT MISS ASSN	1	41	49*	0.5	1.0
093 CHR CH (DISC).	1	70	80	0.8	1.6
127 CH GOD (CLEVE)	2	36	43*	0.4	0.8
165 CH OF NAZARENE	1	?	?	?	?
167 CHS OF CHRIST.	21	1 400	1 833	18.4	36.1
185 CUMBER PRESB..	2	39	66	0.7	1.3
283 LUTH--MO SYNOD	1	182	200	2.0	3.9
357 PRESB CH US...	1	16	19*	0.2	0.4
413 S.D.A.	1	53	63*	0.6	1.2
419 SO BAPT CONV..	11	1 635	1 954*	19.6	38.5
449 UN METHODIST..	8	374	447*	4.5	8.8
453 UN PRES CH USA	1	16	19*	0.2	0.4
GARLAND	122	32 163	40 316*	57.7	100.0
005 AME ZION......	1	98	113	0.2	0.3
017 AMER BAPT ASSN	29	4 823	4 823	6.9	12.0
053 ASSEMB OF GOD.	8	853	1 223	1.7	3.0
059 BAPT MISS ASSN	1	62	73*	0.1	0.2
081 CATHOLIC......	3	NA	1 767	2.5	4.4
093 CHR CH (DISC).	2	801	974	1.4	2.4
101 C.M.E.	1	1 195	1 411*	2.0	3.5
121 CH GOD (ABR)..	1	45	53*	0.1	0.1
123 CH GOD (ANDER)	4	259	777	1.1	1.9
127 CH GOD (CLEVE)	1	71	84*	0.1	0.2
151 L-D SAINTS....	1	NA	345	0.5	0.9
165 CH OF NAZARENE	3	478	641	0.9	1.6
167 CHS OF CHRIST.	7	693	856	1.2	2.1
193 EPISCOPAL.....	2	1 083	1 495	2.1	3.7
271 REFORM JUDAISM	1	128	151*	0.2	0.4
281 LUTH CH AMER..	2	335	372	0.5	0.9
283 LUTH--MO SYNOD	1	329	375	0.5	0.9
357 PRESB CH US...	4	621	733*	1.0	1.8
403 SALVATION ARMY	1	102	211	0.3	0.5
413 S.D.A.	1	269	318*	0.5	0.8
419 SO BAPT CONV..	29	13 806	16 303*	23.3	40.4
435 UNITARIAN-UNIV	1	22	26*	-	0.1
449 UN METHODIST..	14	5 471	6 461*	9.2	16.0
453 UN PRES CH USA	4	619	731*	1.0	1.8
GRANT	44	7 687	8 394*	64.5	100.0
017 AMER BAPT ASSN	23	5 067	5 067	39.0	60.4
053 ASSEMB OF GOD.	4	273	338	2.6	4.0
059 BAPT MISS ASSN	1	184	224*	1.7	2.7
081 CATHOLIC......	1	NA	100	0.8	1.2
093 CHR CH (DISC).	2	74	114	0.9	1.4
127 CH GOD (CLEVE)	1	42	51*	0.4	0.6
167 CHS OF CHRIST.	1	75	95	0.7	1.1
185 CUMBER PRESB..	1	37	47	0.4	0.6
419 SO BAPT CONV..	4	1 104	1 345*	10.3	16.0
449 UN METHODIST..	6	831	1 013*	7.8	12.1
GREENE	100	16 678	21 072*	68.5	100.0
017 AMER BAPT ASSN	5	333	333	1.1	1.6
053 ASSEMB OF GOD.	2	135	195	0.6	0.9
059 BAPT MISS ASSN	4	308	374*	1.2	1.8
081 CATHOLIC......	1	NA	425	1.4	2.0
097 CHR CHS&CHS CR	1	100	121*	0.4	0.6
123 CH GOD (ANDER)	1	102	306	1.0	1.5
127 CH GOD (CLEVE)	1	62	75*	0.2	0.4
133 CH GOD(7TH)DEN	1	2	2*	-	-
165 CH OF NAZARENE	3	132	232	0.8	1.1
167 CHS OF CHRIST.	23	2 960	3 787	12.3	18.0
193 EPISCOPAL.....	1	92	84	0.3	0.4
283 LUTH--MO SYNOD	2	223	297	1.0	1.4
357 PRESB CH US...	1	47	57*	0.2	0.3
419 SO BAPT CONV..	35	8 905	10 807*	35.2	51.3
449 UN METHODIST..	18	3 230	3 920*	12.8	18.6
453 UN PRES CH USA	1	47	57*	0.2	0.3
HEMPSTEAD	88	15 081	19 090*	80.8	100.0
017 AMER BAPT ASSN	2	230	230	1.0	1.2
053 ASSEMB OF GOD.	3	266	483	2.0	2.5
059 BAPT MISS ASSN	16	2 954	3 615*	15.3	18.9
065 BETHEL M ASSN	1	100	122*	0.5	0.6
081 CATHOLIC......	1	NA	286	1.2	1.5
093 CHR CH (DISC).	1	105	118	0.5	0.6
101 C.M.E.	18	5 555	6 798*	28.8	35.6
123 CH GOD (ANDER)	2	43	129	0.5	0.7

NA— Not applicable   *Total adherents estimated from known number of communicant, confirmed, full members.   —Represents a percent less than 0.1.   Percentages may not total due to rounding.

Table 4. Churches and Church Membership by County and Denomination: 1980

County and Denomination	Number of churches	Communicant, confirmed, full members	Total adherents Number	Percent of total population	Percent of total adherents
151 L-D SAINTS....	1	NA	87	0.4	0.5
165 CH OF NAZARENE	2	133	204	0.9	1.1
167 CHS OF CHRIST.	11	683	896	3.8	4.7
193 EPISCOPAL......	1	80	87	0.4	0.5
357 PRESB CH US...	2	234	286*	1.2	1.5
413 S.D.A.........	1	24	29*	0.1	0.2
419 SO BAPT CONV..	11	2 732	3 343*	14.1	17.5
449 UN METHODIST..	15	1 942	2 377*	10.1	12.5
HOT SPRING	96	13 179	15 373*	57.3	100.0
005 AME ZION......	1	102	119	0.4	0.8
017 AMER BAPT ASSN	39	6 677	6 677	24.9	43.4
053 ASSEMB OF GOD.	12	894	1 602	6.0	10.4
059 BAPT MISS ASSN	2	187	227*	0.8	1.5
081 CATHOLIC......	1	NA	195	0.7	1.3
097 CHR CHS&CHS CR	1	62	75*	0.3	0.5
123 CH GOD (ANDER)	1	16	48	0.2	0.3
127 CH GOD (CLEVE)	1	77	94*	0.4	0.6
165 CH OF NAZARENE	1	42	122	0.5	0.8
167 CHS OF CHRIST.	5	347	413	1.5	2.7
283 LUTH--MO SYNOD	1	62	76	0.3	0.5
357 PRESB CH US...	1	59	72*	0.3	0.5
413 S.D.A.........	3	297	361*	1.3	2.3
419 SO BAPT CONV..	7	2 102	2 553*	9.5	16.6
449 UN METHODIST..	19	2 196	2 667*	9.9	17.3
453 UN PRES CH USA	1	59	72*	0.3	0.5
HOWARD	61	9 241	11 791*	87.6	100.0
017 AMER BAPT ASSN	6	1 032	1 032	7.7	8.8
053 ASSEMB OF GOD.	2	144	340	2.5	2.9
059 BAPT MISS ASSN	13	1 747	2 132*	15.8	18.1
081 CATHOLIC......	1	NA	75	0.6	0.6
093 CHR CH (DISC).	1	48	74	0.5	0.6
097 CHR CHS&CHS CR	1	64	78*	0.6	0.7
101 C.M.E.........	5	1 771	2 161*	16.1	18.3
123 CH GOD (ANDER)	2	67	201	1.5	1.7
167 CHS OF CHRIST.	12	1 381	2 053	15.3	17.4
285 MENNONITE CH..	1	94	115*	0.9	1.0
413 S.D.A.........	1	24	29*	0.2	0.2
419 SO BAPT CONV..	5	1 793	2 188*	16.3	18.6
449 UN METHODIST..	11	1 076	1 313*	9.8	11.1
INDEPENDENCE	107	14 134	17 748*	58.9	100.0
017 AMER BAPT ASSN	12	1 359	1 359	4.5	7.7
053 ASSEMB OF GOD.	6	303	560	1.9	3.2
059 BAPT MISS ASSN	6	1 011	1 229*	4.1	6.9
081 CATHOLIC......	1	NA	280	0.9	1.6
123 CH GOD (ANDER)	1	13	39	0.1	0.2
127 CH GOD (CLEVE)	5	196	238*	0.8	1.3
151 L-D SAINTS....	1	NA	240	0.8	1.4
165 CH OF NAZARENE	1	137	176	0.6	1.0
167 CHS OF CHRIST.	17	1 491	1 879	6.2	10.6
185 CUMBER PRESB..	3	119	177	0.6	1.0
193 EPISCOPAL.....	1	173	219	0.7	1.2
283 LUTH--MO SYNOD	1	79	100	0.3	0.6
357 PRESB CH US...	2	363	441*	1.5	2.5
413 S.D.A.........	1	73	89*	0.3	0.5
419 SO BAPT CONV..	21	5 645	6 864*	22.8	38.7
449 UN METHODIST..	27	3 160	3 843*	12.7	21.7
453 UN PRES CH USA	1	12	15*	-	0.1
IZARD	67	5 389	6 729*	62.5	100.0
017 AMER BAPT ASSN	7	448	448	4.2	6.7
053 ASSEMB OF GOD.	4	144	254	2.4	3.8
059 BAPT MISS ASSN	1	145	169*	1.6	2.5
081 CATHOLIC......	1	NA	341	3.2	5.1
165 CH OF NAZARENE	1	30	35	0.3	0.5
167 CHS OF CHRIST.	9	457	503	4.7	7.5
185 CUMBER PRESB..	6	233	384	3.6	5.7
193 EPISCOPAL.....	1	28	32	0.3	0.5
285 MENNONITE CH..	1	36	42*	0.4	0.6
357 PRESB CH US...	2	110	129*	1.2	1.9
419 SO BAPT CONV..	16	2 467	2 883*	26.8	42.8
449 UN METHODIST..	15	1 007	1 177*	10.9	17.5
453 UN PRES CH USA	3	284	332*	3.1	4.9
JACKSON	77	9 754	12 318*	56.9	100.0
017 AMER BAPT ASSN	5	448	448	2.1	3.6
053 ASSEMB OF GOD.	7	255	490	2.3	4.0
059 BAPT MISS ASSN	4	657	801*	3.7	6.5
081 CATHOLIC......	1	NA	103	0.5	0.8
093 CHR CH (DISC).	1	104	150	0.7	1.2
101 C.M.E.........	1	128	156*	0.7	1.3
123 CH GOD (ANDER)	1	14	42	0.2	0.3
127 CH GOD (CLEVE)	1	23	28*	0.1	0.2
165 CH OF NAZARENE	1	35	70	0.3	0.6
167 CHS OF CHRIST.	31	2 900	3 700	17.1	30.0
193 EPISCOPAL.....	1	182	223	1.0	1.8
357 PRESB CH US...	1	75	91*	0.4	0.7
419 SO BAPT CONV..	14	3 336	4 069*	18.8	33.0
449 UN METHODIST..	7	1 522	1 856*	8.6	15.1
453 UN PRES CH USA	1	75	91*	0.4	0.7
JEFFERSON	114	34 119	44 261*	48.8	100.0
005 AME ZION......	1	192	267	0.3	0.6
017 AMER BAPT ASSN	14	4 571	4 571	5.0	10.3
029 AMER LUTH CH..	1	49	80	0.1	0.2
053 ASSEMB OF GOD.	6	876	1 581	1.7	3.6
059 BAPT MISS ASSN	7	1 092	1 345*	1.5	3.0
081 CATHOLIC......	4	NA	1 807	2.0	4.1
093 CHR CH (DISC).	2	346	554	0.6	1.3
097 CHR CHS&CHS CR	1	106	131*	0.1	0.3
101 C.M.E.........	4	1 371	1 689*	1.9	3.8
123 CH GOD (ANDER)	1	10	30	-	0.1
127 CH GOD (CLEVE)	2	112	138*	0.2	0.3
151 L-D SAINTS....	1	NA	274	0.3	0.6
165 CH OF NAZARENE	1	150	149	0.2	0.3
167 CHS OF CHRIST.	10	1 005	1 278	1.4	2.9
185 CUMBER PRESB..	2	177	408	0.4	0.9
193 EPISCOPAL.....	2	569	834	0.9	1.9
271 REFORM JUDAISM	1	116	143*	0.2	0.3
283 LUTH--MO SYNOD	1	265	343	0.4	0.8
290 METRO COMM CHS	0	0	25	-	0.1
357 PRESB CH US...	5	1 549	1 908*	2.1	4.3
403 SALVATION ARMY	1	82	240	0.3	0.5
413 S.D.A.........	3	188	232*	0.3	0.5
419 SO BAPT CONV..	25	15 109	18 615*	20.5	42.1
449 UN METHODIST..	18	6 158	7 587*	8.4	17.1
453 UN PRES CH USA	1	26	32*	-	0.1
JOHNSON	53	6 638	8 501*	48.8	100.0
017 AMER BAPT ASSN	2	684	684	3.9	8.0
053 ASSEMB OF GOD.	10	475	802	4.6	9.4
081 CATHOLIC......	2	NA	350	2.0	4.1
097 CHR CHS&CHS CR	1	23	28*	0.2	0.3
165 CH OF NAZARENE	1	35	68	0.4	0.8
167 CHS OF CHRIST.	5	487	609	3.5	7.2
185 CUMBER PRESB..	1	3	3	-	-
283 LUTH--MO SYNOD	1	59	71	0.4	0.8
357 PRESB CH US...	4	260	314*	1.8	3.7
413 S.D.A.........	1	27	33*	0.2	0.4
419 SO BAPT CONV..	13	2 778	3 356*	19.3	39.5
449 UN METHODIST..	8	1 548	1 870*	10.7	22.0
453 UN PRES CH USA	4	259	313*	1.8	3.7
LAFAYETTE	38	4 858	6 047*	59.2	100.0
017 AMER BAPT ASSN	2	230	230	2.3	3.8
053 ASSEMB OF GOD.	3	61	94	0.9	1.6
059 BAPT MISS ASSN	9	1 210	1 496*	14.6	24.7
093 CHR CH (DISC).	1	12	18	0.2	0.3
165 CH OF NAZARENE	1	28	92	0.9	1.5
167 CHS OF CHRIST.	6	400	510	5.0	8.4
356 PRESB CH AMER.	1	13	18	0.2	0.3
357 PRESB CH US...	1	23	28*	0.3	0.5
419 SO BAPT CONV..	6	1 883	2 327*	22.8	38.5
449 UN METHODIST..	8	998	1 234*	12.1	20.4
LAWRENCE	73	8 352	10 455*	56.7	100.0
017 AMER BAPT ASSN	10	981	981	5.3	9.4
053 ASSEMB OF GOD.	8	433	722	3.9	6.9
059 BAPT MISS ASSN	3	369	445*	2.4	4.3
081 CATHOLIC......	1	NA	105	0.6	1.0
127 CH GOD (CLEVE)	1	?	?	?	?
165 CH OF NAZARENE	1	12	57	0.3	0.5
167 CHS OF CHRIST.	17	1 505	2 043	11.1	19.5
185 CUMBER PRESB..	1	10	17	0.1	0.2
357 PRESB CH US...	1	23	28*	0.2	0.3
419 SO BAPT CONV..	14	3 245	3 916*	21.2	37.5
449 UN METHODIST..	15	1 751	2 113*	11.5	20.2
453 UN PRES CH USA	1	23	28*	0.2	0.3
LEE	31	4 470	5 701*	36.7	100.0
017 AMER BAPT ASSN	3	602	602	3.9	10.6
053 ASSEMB OF GOD.	1	88	136	0.9	2.4
059 BAPT MISS ASSN	2	226	287*	1.8	5.0
081 CATHOLIC......	1	NA	130	0.8	2.3
097 CHR CHS&CHS CR	1	200	254*	1.6	4.5
101 C.M.E.........	2	218	276*	1.8	4.8
127 CH GOD (CLEVE)	1	45	57*	0.4	1.0
167 CHS OF CHRIST.	4	211	269	1.7	4.7
193 EPISCOPAL.....	1	80	140	0.9	2.5
357 PRESB CH US...	1	50	63*	0.4	1.1
419 SO BAPT CONV..	5	1 869	2 370*	15.3	41.6
449 UN METHODIST..	8	831	1 054*	6.8	18.5
453 UN PRES CH USA	1	50	63*	0.4	1.1
LINCOLN	35	4 984	5 787*	43.3	100.0
005 AME ZION......	1	102	127	0.9	2.2
017 AMER BAPT ASSN	10	1 564	1 564	11.7	27.0
053 ASSEMB OF GOD.	2	131	224	1.7	3.9
059 BAPT MISS ASSN	1	75	91*	0.7	1.6
097 CHR CHS&CHS CR	1	74	90*	0.7	1.6
127 CH GOD (CLEVE)	1	13	16*	0.1	0.3
167 CHS OF CHRIST.	2	105	134	1.0	2.3
185 CUMBER PRESB..	1	17	24	0.2	0.4
357 PRESB CH US...	2	58	70*	0.5	1.2
419 SO BAPT CONV..	9	2 226	2 697*	20.2	46.6
449 UN METHODIST..	5	619	750*	5.6	13.0
LITTLE RIVER	39	6 067	7 791*	55.8	100.0
017 AMER BAPT ASSN	2	255	255	1.8	3.3
053 ASSEMB OF GOD.	3	183	361	2.6	4.6
059 BAPT MISS ASSN	2	522	653*	4.7	8.4
081 CATHOLIC......	1	NA	50	0.4	0.6
097 CHR CHS&CHS CR	1	40	50*	0.4	0.6
101 C.M.E.........	4	1 007	1 259*	9.0	16.2
165 CH OF NAZARENE	1	47	100	0.7	1.3
167 CHS OF CHRIST.	4	428	545	3.9	7.0

NA—Not applicable   *Total adherents estimated from known number of communicant, confirmed, full members.   —Represents a percent less than 0.1.   Percentages may not total due to rounding.

Table 4. Churches and Church Membership by County and Denomination: 1980

County and Denomination	Number of churches	Communicant, confirmed, full members	Total adherents Number	Total adherents Percent of total population	Total adherents Percent of total adherents
185 CUMBER PRESB..	3	68	137	1.0	1.8
193 EPISCOPAL......	1	90	97	0.7	1.2
357 PRESB CH US...	1	93	116*	0.8	1.5
419 SO BAPT CONV..	8	2 188	2 735*	19.6	35.1
449 UN METHODIST..	8	1 146	1 433*	10.3	18.4
LOGAN	74	8 776	13 280*	65.9	100.0
017 AMER BAPT ASSN	4	583	583	2.9	4.4
053 ASSEMB OF GOD.	12	761	1 361	6.8	10.2
059 BAPT MISS ASSN	1	52	63*	0.3	0.5
081 CATHOLIC......	9	NA	2 057	10.2	15.5
093 CHR CH (DISC).	1	206	216	1.1	1.6
101 C.M.E........	1	?	?	?	?
121 CH GOD (ABR)..	1	70	85*	0.4	0.6
127 CH GOD (CLEVE)	1	16	19*	0.1	0.1
151 L-D SAINTS....	1	NA	138	0.7	1.0
165 CH OF NAZARENE	1	10	10	–	0.1
167 CHS OF CHRIST.	6	555	706	3.5	5.3
185 CUMBER PRESB..	7	263	460	2.3	3.5
357 PRESB CH US...	1	21	25*	0.1	0.2
419 SO BAPT CONV..	15	4 345	5 263*	26.1	39.6
449 UN METHODIST..	12	1 872	2 267*	11.3	17.1
453 UN PRES CH USA	1	22	27*	0.1	0.2
LONOKE	97	17 151	21 243*	61.5	100.0
005 AME ZION......	1	80	98	0.3	0.5
017 AMER BAPT ASSN	12	2 313	2 313	6.7	10.9
053 ASSEMB OF GOD.	5	413	586	1.7	2.8
059 BAPT MISS ASSN	9	1 689	2 102*	6.1	9.9
081 CATHOLIC......	2	NA	340	1.0	1.6
093 CHR CH (DISC).	3	40	49	0.1	0.2
101 C.M.E........	1	148	184*	0.5	0.9
165 CH OF NAZARENE	3	85	147	0.4	0.7
167 CHS OF CHRIST.	7	653	831	2.4	3.9
185 CUMBER PRESB..	1	18	18	0.1	0.1
357 PRESB CH US...	3	201	250*	0.7	1.2
413 S.D.A........	1	160	199*	0.6	0.9
419 SO BAPT CONV..	26	8 226	10 237*	29.7	48.2
449 UN METHODIST..	21	3 039	3 782*	11.0	17.8
453 UN PRES CH USA	2	86	107*	0.3	0.5
MADISON	38	2 572	3 381*	29.7	100.0
017 AMER BAPT ASSN	1	50	50	0.4	1.5
053 ASSEMB OF GOD.	3	127	211	1.9	6.2
059 BAPT MISS ASSN	1	107	129*	1.1	3.8
081 CATHOLIC......	1	NA	80	0.7	2.4
097 CHR CHS&CHS CR	1	50	60*	0.5	1.8
107 CHRISTIAN UN..	1	12	12	0.1	0.4
151 L-D SAINTS....	1	NA	84	0.7	2.5
167 CHS OF CHRIST.	17	975	1 241	10.9	36.7
357 PRESB CH US...	2	37	45*	0.4	1.3
413 S.D.A........	1	70	85*	0.7	2.5
419 SO BAPT CONV..	5	886	1 072*	9.4	31.7
449 UN METHODIST..	2	220	266*	2.3	7.9
453 UN PRES CH USA	2	38	46*	0.4	1.4
MARION	38	3 804	4 720*	41.6	100.0
017 AMER BAPT ASSN	1	73	73	0.6	1.5
053 ASSEMB OF GOD.	3	129	277	2.4	5.9
093 CHR CH (DISC).	1	80	123	1.1	2.6
097 CHR CHS&CHS CR	2	220	264*	2.3	5.6
127 CH GOD (CLEVE)	2	82	98*	0.9	2.1
167 CHS OF CHRIST.	9	500	635	5.6	13.5
281 LUTH CH AMER..	1	73	76	0.7	1.6
357 PRESB CH US...	2	151	181*	1.6	3.8
419 SO BAPT CONV..	11	1 797	2 155*	19.0	45.7
449 UN METHODIST..	4	548	657*	5.8	13.9
453 UN PRES CH USA	2	151	181*	1.6	3.8
MILLER	79	19 137	24 595*	65.1	100.0
017 AMER BAPT ASSN	5	1 975	1 975	5.2	8.0
053 ASSEMB OF GOD.	6	392	569	1.5	2.3
059 BAPT MISS ASSN	3	336	415*	1.1	1.7
081 CATHOLIC......	1	NA	1 176	3.1	4.8
093 CHR CH (DISC).	1	652	752	2.0	3.1
101 C.M.E........	2	1 253	1 547*	4.1	6.3
165 CH OF NAZARENE	1	177	402	1.1	1.6
167 CHS OF CHRIST.	14	1 000	1 273	3.4	5.2
185 CUMBER PRESB..	1	7	9	–	–
357 PRESB CH US...	1	374	462*	1.2	1.9
413 S.D.A........	1	140	173*	0.5	0.7
415 S-D BAPTIST GC	2	137	169*	0.4	0.7
419 SO BAPT CONV..	28	9 687	11 960*	31.7	48.6
449 UN METHODIST..	13	3 007	3 713*	9.8	15.1
MISSISSIPPI	119	26 686	34 789*	58.5	100.0
053 ASSEMB OF GOD.	8	542	984*	1.7	2.8
059 BAPT MISS ASSN	8	1 702	2 142*	3.6	6.2
081 CATHOLIC......	2	NA	630	1.1	1.8
093 CHR CH (DISC).	2	355	462	0.8	1.3
101 C.M.E........	2	591	744*	1.3	2.1
127 CH GOD (CLEVE)	9	469	590*	1.0	1.7
165 CH OF NAZARENE	2	181	360	0.6	1.0
167 CHS OF CHRIST.	19	1 177	1 561	2.6	4.5
193 EPISCOPAL.....	2	219	324	0.5	0.9
271 REFORM JUDAISM	1	80	101*	0.2	0.3
283 LUTH--MO SYNOD	1	136	200	0.3	0.6
356 PRESB CH AMER.	2	204	224	0.4	0.6
357 PRESB CH US...	1	381	480*	0.8	1.4

County and Denomination	Number of churches	Communicant, confirmed, full members	Total adherents Number	Total adherents Percent of total population	Total adherents Percent of total adherents
419 SO BAPT CONV..	45	16 966	21 352*	35.9	61.4
449 UN METHODIST..	15	3 683	4 635*	7.8	13.3
MONROE	43	5 885	7 330*	52.2	100.0
017 AMER BAPT ASSN	7	938	938	6.7	12.8
053 ASSEMB OF GOD.	2	91	260	1.9	3.5
059 BAPT MISS ASSN	3	249	308*	2.2	4.2
081 CATHOLIC......	1	NA	83	0.6	1.1
101 C.M.E........	3	861	1 067*	7.6	14.6
123 CH GOD (ANDER)	1	11	33	0.2	0.5
127 CH GOD (CLEVE)	1	19	24*	0.2	0.3
165 CH OF NAZARENE	1	?	?	?	?
167 CHS OF CHRIST.	5	299	386	2.7	5.3
283 LUTH--MO SYNOD	1	109	142	1.0	1.9
356 PRESB CH AMER.	1	112	130	0.9	1.8
357 PRESB CH US...	2	67	83*	0.6	1.1
413 S.D.A........	1	105	130*	0.9	1.8
419 SO BAPT CONV..	6	2 055	2 546*	18.1	34.7
449 UN METHODIST..	6	902	1 117*	7.9	15.2
453 UN PRES CH USA	2	67	83*	0.6	1.1
MONTGOMERY	31	2 834	3 472*	44.7	100.0
017 AMER BAPT ASSN	4	300	300	3.9	8.6
053 ASSEMB OF GOD.	3	74	136	1.8	3.9
081 CATHOLIC......	1	NA	45	0.6	1.3
165 CH OF NAZARENE	1	86	166	2.1	4.8
167 CHS OF CHRIST.	2	95	119	1.5	3.4
357 PRESB CH US...	2	97	115*	1.5	3.3
419 SO BAPT CONV..	16	1 883	2 236*	28.8	64.4
449 UN METHODIST..	2	299	355*	4.6	10.2
NEVADA	55	5 828	7 250*	65.3	100.0
017 AMER BAPT ASSN	6	397	397	3.6	5.5
053 ASSEMB OF GOD.	1	99	152	1.4	2.1
059 BAPT MISS ASSN	18	2 272	2 783*	25.1	38.4
093 CHR CH (DISC).	1	49	80	0.7	1.1
101 C.M.E........	2	503	616*	5.6	8.5
123 CH GOD (ANDER)	1	30	90	0.8	1.2
165 CH OF NAZARENE	3	162	275	2.5	3.8
167 CHS OF CHRIST.	8	464	591	5.3	8.2
185 CUMBER PRESB..	1	9	9	0.1	0.1
357 PRESB CH US...	1	77	94*	0.8	1.3
419 SO BAPT CONV..	4	872	1 068*	9.6	14.7
449 UN METHODIST..	9	894	1 095*	9.9	15.1
NEWTON	22	1 442	1 937*	25.0	100.0
053 ASSEMB OF GOD.	3	179	323	4.2	16.7
089 CHR & MISS AL.	1	0	21	0.3	1.1
093 CHR CH (DISC).	1	80	123	1.6	6.4
097 CHR CHS&CHS CR	1	150	184*	2.4	9.5
107 CHRISTIAN UN..	1	20	20	0.3	1.0
167 CHS OF CHRIST.	8	488	621	8.0	32.1
419 SO BAPT CONV..	6	385	473*	6.1	24.4
449 UN METHODIST..	1	140	172*	2.2	8.9
OUACHITA	83	14 935	18 852*	61.7	100.0
017 AMER BAPT ASSN	4	401	401	1.3	2.1
053 ASSEMB OF GOD.	11	1 057	1 569	5.1	8.3
059 BAPT MISS ASSN	5	1 138	1 379*	4.5	7.3
081 CATHOLIC......	1	NA	380	1.2	2.0
093 CHR CH (DISC).	1	98	120	0.4	0.6
123 CH GOD (ANDER)	1	19	57	0.2	0.3
151 L-D SAINTS....	1	NA	36	0.1	0.2
165 CH OF NAZARENE	1	55	71	0.2	0.4
167 CHS OF CHRIST.	8	756	916	3.0	4.9
185 CUMBER PRESB..	5	169	315	1.0	1.7
193 EPISCOPAL.....	1	88	87	0.3	0.5
357 PRESB CH US...	4	380	461*	1.5	2.4
413 S.D.A........	1	52	64*	0.2	0.3
419 SO BAPT CONV..	20	7 264	8 805*	28.8	46.7
449 UN METHODIST..	17	3 432	4 160*	13.6	22.1
453 UN PRES CH USA	2	26	32*	0.1	0.2
PERRY	35	2 887	3 818*	52.5	100.0
017 AMER BAPT ASSN	5	426	426	5.9	11.2
053 ASSEMB OF GOD.	4	163	258	3.6	6.8
081 CATHOLIC......	1	NA	300	4.1	7.9
165 CH OF NAZARENE	1	42	63	0.9	1.7
167 CHS OF CHRIST.	5	228	282	3.9	7.4
419 SO BAPT CONV..	13	1 776	2 180*	30.0	57.1
449 UN METHODIST..	6	252	309*	4.3	8.1
PHILLIPS	54	12 602	16 670*	47.9	100.0
017 AMER BAPT ASSN	2	274	274	0.8	1.6
053 ASSEMB OF GOD.	2	156	329	0.9	2.0
059 BAPT MISS ASSN	6	1 087	1 381*	4.0	8.3
081 CATHOLIC......	1	NA	556	1.6	3.3
097 CHR CHS&CHS CR	1	50	64*	0.2	0.4
101 C.M.E........	2	763	970*	2.8	5.8
127 CH GOD (CLEVE)	2	185	235*	0.7	1.4
151 L-D SAINTS....	1	NA	120	0.3	0.7
165 CH OF NAZARENE	1	64	108	0.3	0.6
167 CHS OF CHRIST.	8	835	991	2.8	5.9
193 EPISCOPAL.....	1	360	425	1.2	2.5
271 REFORM JUDAISM	1	140	178*	0.5	1.1
283 LUTH--MO SYNOD	1	28	36	0.1	0.2
357 PRESB CH US...	3	195	248*	0.7	1.5
413 S.D.A........	1	34	43*	0.1	0.3

NA— Not applicable
*Total adherents estimated from known number of communicant, confirmed, full members.
—Represents a percent less than 0.1.
Percentages may not total due to rounding.

Table 4. Churches and Church Membership by County and Denomination: 1980

County and Denomination	Number of churches	Communicant, confirmed, full members	Total adherents Number	Percent of total population	Percent of total adherents
419 SO BAPT CONV..	12	6 256	7 949*	22.9	47.7
443 UN C OF CHRIST	1	70	89*	0.3	0.5
449 UN METHODIST..	6	1 934	2 457*	7.1	14.7
453 UN PRES CH USA	2	171	217*	0.6	1.3
PIKE	**55**	**4 669**	**5 593***	**53.9**	**100.0**
017 AMER BAPT ASSN	12	1 286	1 286	12.4	23.0
029 AMER LUTH CH..	1	46	69	0.7	1.2
053 ASSEMB OF GOD.	6	177	311	3.0	5.6
059 BAPT MISS ASSN	2	85	103*	1.0	1.8
081 CATHOLIC......	1	NA	55	0.5	1.0
093 CHR CH (DISC).	2	43	66	0.6	1.2
097 CHR CHS&CHS CR	2	412	499*	4.8	8.9
167 CHS OF CHRIST.	13	876	1 092	10.5	19.5
419 SO BAPT CONV..	5	1 041	1 261*	12.2	22.5
449 UN METHODIST..	11	703	851*	8.2	15.2
POINSETT	**76**	**13 776**	**17 491***	**64.7**	**100.0**
053 ASSEMB OF GOD.	6	320	677	2.5	3.9
059 BAPT MISS ASSN	3	531	652*	2.4	3.7
081 CATHOLIC......	2	NA	214	0.8	1.2
093 CHR CH (DISC).	3	160	237	0.9	1.4
097 CHR CHS&CHS CR	1	120	147*	0.5	0.8
127 CH GOD (CLEVE)	4	303	372*	1.4	2.1
167 CHS OF CHRIST.	10	1 092	1 362	5.0	7.8
283 LUTH--MO SYNOD	1	166	215	0.8	1.2
357 PRESB CH US...	1	6	7*	-	-
419 SO BAPT CONV..	33	9 061	11 131*	41.2	63.6
449 UN METHODIST..	11	2 011	2 470*	9.1	14.1
453 UN PRES CH USA	1	6	7*	-	-
POLK	**60**	**8 237**	**10 614***	**62.4**	**100.0**
017 AMER BAPT ASSN	3	252	252	1.5	2.4
053 ASSEMB OF GOD.	3	183	286	1.7	2.7
059 BAPT MISS ASSN	2	217	262*	1.5	2.5
081 CATHOLIC......	1	NA	300	1.8	2.8
097 CHR CHS&CHS CR	4	764	924*	5.4	8.7
101 C.M.E.........	1	703	850*	5.0	8.0
127 CH GOD (CLEVE)	2	89	108*	0.6	1.0
151 L-D SAINTS....	1	NA	126	0.7	1.2
165 CH OF NAZARENE	3	182	418	2.5	3.9
167 CHS OF CHRIST.	5	274	354	2.1	3.3
193 EPISCOPAL.....	1	56	73	0.4	0.7
283 LUTH--MO SYNOD	1	75	81	0.5	0.8
285 MENNONITE CH..	1	94	114*	0.7	1.1
357 PRESB CH US...	3	166	201*	1.2	1.9
413 S.D.A.........	1	52	63*	0.4	0.6
419 SO BAPT CONV..	18	3 970	4 800*	28.2	45.2
449 UN METHODIST..	8	1 134	1 371*	8.1	12.9
453 UN PRES CH USA	2	26	31*	0.2	0.3
POPE	**98**	**13 086**	**18 323***	**47.0**	**100.0**
017 AMER BAPT ASSN	4	534	534	1.4	2.9
053 ASSEMB OF GOD.	24	1 927	3 102	8.0	16.9
055 AS REF PRES CH	1	183	199	0.5	1.1
059 BAPT MISS ASSN	1	186	226*	0.6	1.2
081 CATHOLIC......	2	NA	929	2.4	5.1
089 CHR & MISS AL.	1	45	79	0.2	0.4
093 CHR CH (DISC).	2	111	135	0.3	0.7
097 CHR CHS&CHS CR	1	80	97*	0.2	0.5
101 C.M.E.........	1	253	307*	0.8	1.7
127 CH GOD (CLEVE)	1	32	39*	0.1	0.2
151 L-D SAINTS....	1	NA	398	1.0	2.2
165 CH OF NAZARENE	1	46	73	0.2	0.4
167 CHS OF CHRIST.	14	1 171	1 470	3.8	8.0
185 CUMBER PRESB..	8	402	858	2.2	4.7
193 EPISCOPAL.....	1	197	229	0.6	1.2
263 INT FOURSQ GOS	1	72	87*	0.2	0.5
283 LUTH--MO SYNOD	2	420	538	1.4	2.9
357 PRESB CH US...	2	303	368*	0.9	2.0
413 S.D.A.........	1	67	81*	0.2	0.4
419 SO BAPT CONV..	16	4 375	5 315*	13.6	29.0
449 UN METHODIST..	11	2 380	2 892*	7.4	15.8
453 UN PRES CH USA	2	302	367*	0.9	2.0
PRAIRIE	**39**	**5 033**	**6 118***	**60.3**	**100.0**
017 AMER BAPT ASSN	9	1 753	1 753	17.3	28.7
053 ASSEMB OF GOD.	3	133	224	2.2	3.7
059 BAPT MISS ASSN	1	57	69*	0.7	1.1
081 CATHOLIC......	2	NA	263	2.6	4.3
093 CHR CH (DISC).	1	24	37	0.4	0.6
097 CHR CHS&CHS CR	1	20	24*	0.2	0.4
167 CHS OF CHRIST.	5	290	369	3.6	6.0
193 EPISCOPAL.....	1	101	144	1.4	2.4
283 LUTH--MO SYNOD	1	260	316	3.1	5.2
357 PRESB CH US...	1	19	23*	0.2	0.4
419 SO BAPT CONV..	5	1 429	1 742*	17.2	28.5
449 UN METHODIST..	8	929	1 132*	11.2	18.5
453 UN PRES CH USA	1	18	22*	0.2	0.4
PULASKI	**362**	**140 862**	**191 658***	**56.3**	**100.0**
005 AME ZION......	7	1 613	2 024	0.6	1.1
017 AMER BAPT ASSN	30	8 596	8 596	2.5	4.5
053 ASSEMB OF GOD.	28	2 979	5 515	1.6	2.9
055 AS REF PRES CH	2	206	238	0.1	0.1
059 BAPT MISS ASSN	19	5 050	6 195*	1.8	3.2
081 CATHOLIC......	14	NA	14 691	4.3	7.7
089 CHR & MISS AL.	1	53	86	-	-
093 CHR CH (DISC).	10	1 787	2 378	0.7	1.2
097 CHR CHS&CHS CR	3	300	368*	0.1	0.2
101 C.M.E.........	11	6 797	8 338*	2.4	4.4
121 CH GOD (ABR)..	1	45	55*	-	-
123 CH GOD (ANDER)	2	252	756	0.2	0.4
127 CH GOD (CLEVE)	5	289	355*	0.1	0.2
151 L-D SAINTS....	4	NA	1 525	0.4	0.8
165 CH OF NAZARENE	13	2 536	3 327	1.0	1.7
167 CHS OF CHRIST.	30	7 338	9 813	2.9	5.1
185 CUMBER PRESB..	3	218	395	0.1	0.2
193 EPISCOPAL.....	7	4 768	6 219	1.8	3.2
226 FRIENDS-USA...	1	76	93*	-	-
263 INT FOURSQ GOS	2	272	334*	0.1	0.2
271 REFORM JUDAISM	1	770	945*	0.3	0.5
281 LUTH CH AMER..	2	329	465	0.1	0.2
283 LUTH--MO SYNOD	6	2 124	2 837	0.8	1.5
290 METRO COMM CHS	1	30	60	-	-
356 PRESB CH AMER.	1	90	122	-	0.1
357 PRESB CH US...	11	2 233	2 739*	0.8	1.4
403 SALVATION ARMY	2	167	396	0.1	0.2
413 S.D.A.........	2	308	378*	0.1	0.2
415 S-D BAPTIST GC	2	64	79*	-	-
419 SO BAPT CONV..	81	58 960	72 323*	21.2	37.7
435 UNITARIAN-UNIV	1	185	227*	0.1	0.1
443 UN C OF CHRIST	2	174	213*	0.1	0.1
449 UN METHODIST..	44	29 844	36 608*	10.7	19.1
453 UN PRES CH USA	12	2 354	2 888*	0.8	1.5
469 WELS..........	1	55	77	-	-
RANDOLPH	**51**	**5 587**	**8 522***	**50.6**	**100.0**
017 AMER BAPT ASSN	1	40	40	0.2	0.5
053 ASSEMB OF GOD.	1	114	225	1.3	2.6
081 CATHOLIC......	2	NA	1 456	8.6	17.1
127 CH GOD (CLEVE)	1	?	?	?	?
151 L-D SAINTS....	1	NA	97	0.6	1.1
167 CHS OF CHRIST.	25	1 760	2 237	13.3	26.2
357 PRESB CH US...	1	13	16*	0.1	0.2
413 S.D.A.........	1	29	35*	0.2	0.4
419 SO BAPT CONV..	9	2 702	3 286*	19.5	38.6
449 UN METHODIST..	8	915	1 113*	6.6	13.1
453 UN PRES CH USA	1	14	17*	0.1	0.2
ST FRANCIS	**67**	**12 431**	**16 030***	**51.9**	**100.0**
017 AMER BAPT ASSN	5	922	922	3.0	5.8
053 ASSEMB OF GOD.	2	178	260	0.8	1.6
059 BAPT MISS ASSN	4	530	678*	2.2	4.2
081 CATHOLIC......	1	NA	400	1.3	2.5
093 CHR CH (DISC).	1	65	79	0.3	0.5
101 C.M.E.........	6	1 709	2 185*	7.1	13.6
127 CH GOD (CLEVE)	3	251	321*	1.0	2.0
165 CH OF NAZARENE	1	37	58	0.2	0.4
167 CHS OF CHRIST.	5	427	555	1.8	3.5
185 CUMBER PRESB..	1	81	130	0.4	0.8
193 EPISCOPAL.....	2	233	220	0.7	1.4
283 LUTH--MO SYNOD	1	50	68	0.2	0.4
356 PRESB CH AMER.	1	34	35	0.1	0.2
357 PRESB CH US...	3	168	215*	0.7	1.3
413 S.D.A.........	1	55	55*	0.2	0.3
419 SO BAPT CONV..	16	5 755	7 358*	23.8	45.9
449 UN METHODIST..	11	1 781	2 277*	7.4	14.2
453 UN PRES CH USA	3	167	214*	0.7	1.3
SALINE	**97**	**22 988**	**27 860***	**52.7**	**100.0**
017 AMER BAPT ASSN	29	8 988	8 988	17.0	32.3
053 ASSEMB OF GOD.	7	449	836	1.6	3.0
059 BAPT MISS ASSN	2	392	483*	0.9	1.7
081 CATHOLIC......	1	NA	670	1.3	2.4
093 CHR CH (DISC).	1	92	104	0.2	0.4
123 CH GOD (ANDER)	2	175	525	1.0	1.9
127 CH GOD (CLEVE)	4	197	243*	0.5	0.9
151 L-D SAINTS....	1	NA	137	0.3	0.5
165 CH OF NAZARENE	4	276	497	0.9	1.8
167 CHS OF CHRIST.	10	950	1 209	2.3	4.3
193 EPISCOPAL.....	1	95	130	0.2	0.5
263 INT FOURSQ GOS	1	102	126*	0.2	0.5
283 LUTH--MO SYNOD	2	317	425	0.8	1.5
357 PRESB CH US...	1	103	127*	0.2	0.5
413 S.D.A.........	1	48	59*	0.1	0.2
419 SO BAPT CONV..	20	7 538	9 280*	17.5	33.3
449 UN METHODIST..	9	3 163	3 894*	7.4	14.0
453 UN PRES CH USA	1	103	127*	0.2	0.5
SCOTT	**43**	**3 852**	**4 901***	**50.6**	**100.0**
017 AMER BAPT ASSN	2	67	67	0.7	1.4
053 ASSEMB OF GOD.	5	248	419	4.3	8.5
081 CATHOLIC......	1	NA	35	0.4	0.7
165 CH OF NAZARENE	1	128	192	2.0	3.9
167 CHS OF CHRIST.	5	325	414	4.3	8.4
185 CUMBER PRESB..	2	85	165	1.7	3.4
419 SO BAPT CONV..	21	2 478	2 982*	30.8	60.8
449 UN METHODIST..	6	521	627*	6.5	12.8
SEARCY	**26**	**2 585**	**3 155***	**35.7**	**100.0**
017 AMER BAPT ASSN	5	360	360	4.1	11.4
053 ASSEMB OF GOD.	4	156	294	3.3	9.3
097 CHR CHS&CHS CR	1	250	300*	3.4	9.5
127 CH GOD (CLEVE)	1	20	24*	0.3	0.8
167 CHS OF CHRIST.	4	250	318	3.6	10.1
237 GC MENN BR CHS	1	42	50*	0.6	1.6
419 SO BAPT CONV..	7	1 256	1 508*	17.0	47.8
449 UN METHODIST..	3	251	301*	3.4	9.5

NA—Not applicable   *Total adherents estimated from known number of communicant, confirmed, full members.   —Represents a percent less than 0.1.   Percentages may not total due to rounding.

Table 4. Churches and Church Membership by County and Denomination: 1980

County and Denomination	Number of churches	Communicant, confirmed, full members	Total adherents		
			Number	Percent of total population	Percent of total adherents
SEBASTIAN	170	50 570	69 020*	72.7	100.0
017 AMER BAPT ASSN	9	2 105	2 105	2.2	3.0
053 ASSEMB OF GOD.	18	1 651	2 660	2.8	3.9
059 BAPT MISS ASSN	3	338	411*	0.4	0.6
081 CATHOLIC......	6	NA	5 399	5.7	7.8
093 CHR CH (DISC).	1	642	752	0.8	1.1
097 CHR CHS&CHS CR	3	440	535*	0.6	0.8
101 C.M.E.........	3	1 236	1 503*	1.6	2.2
123 CH GOD (ANDER)	2	480	1 440	1.5	2.1
127 CH GOD (CLEVE)	1	46	56*	0.1	0.1
133 CH GOD(7TH)DEN	2	73	89*	0.1	0.1
151 L-D SAINTS....	2	NA	623	0.7	0.9
165 CH OF NAZARENE	5	361	511	0.5	0.7
167 CHS OF CHRIST.	22	2 006	2 682	2.8	3.9
185 CUMBER PRESB..	1	131	200	0.2	0.3
193 EPISCOPAL.....	3	1 162	1 321	1.4	1.9
271 REFORM JUDAISM	1	58	71*	0.1	0.1
281 LUTH CH AMER..	1	294	402	0.4	0.6
283 LUTH--MO SYNOD	3	1 062	1 394	1.5	2.0
349 PENT HOLINESS.	1	37	45*	–	0.1
356 PRESB CH AMER.	1	13	13	–	–
357 PRESB CH US...	6	912	1 109*	1.2	1.6
403 SALVATION ARMY	1	184	309	0.3	0.4
413 S.D.A.........	1	135	164*	0.2	0.2
419 SO BAPT CONV..	44	26 794	32 572*	34.3	47.2
435 UNITARIAN-UNIV	1	10	12*	–	–
449 UN METHODIST..	23	9 494	11 541*	12.2	16.7
453 UN PRES CH USA	6	906	1 101*	1.2	1.6
SEVIER	52	6 596	8 365*	59.5	100.0
017 AMER BAPT ASSN	6	799	799	5.7	9.6
053 ASSEMB OF GOD.	3	118	224	1.6	2.7
059 BAPT MISS ASSN	3	363	444*	3.2	5.3
081 CATHOLIC......	1	NA	350	2.5	4.2
093 CHR CH (DISC).	1	55	80	0.6	1.0
097 CHR CHS&CHS CR	1	90	110*	0.8	1.3
165 CH OF NAZARENE	2	84	92	0.7	1.1
167 CHS OF CHRIST.	5	439	526	3.7	6.3
185 CUMBER PRESB..	5	122	209	1.5	2.5
357 PRESB CH US...	1	99	121*	0.9	1.4
413 S.D.A.........	1	204	249*	1.8	3.0
419 SO BAPT CONV..	10	2 905	3 550*	25.2	42.4
449 UN METHODIST..	13	1 318	1 611*	11.5	19.3
SHARP	60	6 416	8 100*	55.5	100.0
017 AMER BAPT ASSN	7	1 309	1 309	9.0	16.2
053 ASSEMB OF GOD.	3	130	271	1.9	3.3
059 BAPT MISS ASSN	5	433	513*	3.5	6.3
081 CATHOLIC......	1	NA	470	3.2	5.8
093 CHR CH (DISC).	1	29	35	0.2	0.4
127 CH GOD (CLEVE)	1	28	33*	0.2	0.4
165 CH OF NAZARENE	1	?	?	?	?
167 CHS OF CHRIST.	14	905	1 245	8.5	15.4
185 CUMBER PRESB..	1	15	33	0.2	0.4
193 EPISCOPAL.....	1	52	56	0.4	0.7
203 EVAN FREE CH..	1	20	24*	0.2	0.3
283 LUTH--MO SYNOD	1	337	372	2.5	4.6
357 PRESB CH US...	1	121	143*	1.0	1.8
419 SO BAPT CONV..	9	1 608	1 904*	13.0	23.5
449 UN METHODIST..	12	1 309	1 550*	10.6	19.1
453 UN PRES CH USA	1	120	142*	1.0	1.8
STONE	35	3 426	3 939*	43.7	100.0
017 AMER BAPT ASSN	11	1 430	1 430	15.9	36.3
053 ASSEMB OF GOD.	3	169	259	2.9	6.6
061 BEACHY AMISH..	1	20	24*	0.3	0.6
081 CATHOLIC......	1	NA	60	0.7	1.5
097 CHR CHS&CHS CR	1	45	54*	0.6	1.4
167 CHS OF CHRIST.	5	273	318	3.5	8.1
285 MENNONITE CH..	3	43	52*	0.6	1.3
413 S.D.A.........	1	32	39*	0.4	1.0
419 SO BAPT CONV..	7	1 049	1 263*	14.0	32.1
449 UN METHODIST..	2	365	440*	4.9	11.2
UNION	124	26 603	33 325*	66.7	100.0
017 AMER BAPT ASSN	8	626	626	1.3	1.9
053 ASSEMB OF GOD.	11	686	1 041	2.1	3.1
059 BAPT MISS ASSN	12	1 858	2 246*	4.5	6.7
081 CATHOLIC......	1	NA	450	0.9	1.4
093 CHR CH (DISC).	1	176	265	0.5	0.8
101 C.M.E.........	4	2 106	2 545*	5.1	7.6
123 CH GOD (ANDER)	1	82	246	0.5	0.7
127 CH GOD (CLEVE)	1	83	100*	0.2	0.3
151 L-D SAINTS....	1	NA	179	0.4	0.5
165 CH OF NAZARENE	2	116	204	0.4	0.6
167 CHS OF CHRIST.	13	975	1 240	2.5	3.7
185 CUMBER PRESB..	1	31	125	0.3	0.4
193 EPISCOPAL.....	1	382	450	0.9	1.4
271 REFORM JUDAISM	1	16	19*	–	0.1
283 LUTH--MO SYNOD	1	107	150	0.3	0.5
285 MENNONITE CH..	1	25	30*	0.1	0.1
357 PRESB CH US...	5	899	1 087*	2.2	3.3
403 SALVATION ARMY	1	49	100	0.2	0.3
413 S.D.A.........	1	58	70*	0.1	0.2
419 SO BAPT CONV..	35	13 752	16 621*	33.2	49.9
421 SO METHODIST..	1	35	43	0.1	0.1
449 UN METHODIST..	21	4 541	5 488*	11.0	16.5
VAN BUREN	55	5 425	6 747*	50.5	100.0

County and Denomination	Number of churches	Communicant, confirmed, full members	Total adherents		
			Number	Percent of total population	Percent of total adherents
017 AMER BAPT ASSN	3	136	136	1.0	2.0
053 ASSEMB OF GOD.	3	138	266	2.0	3.9
059 BAPT MISS ASSN	2	410	491*	3.7	7.3
081 CATHOLIC......	2	NA	140	1.0	2.1
165 CH OF NAZARENE	1	19	17	0.1	0.3
167 CHS OF CHRIST.	10	625	796	6.0	11.8
263 INT FOURSQ GOS	1	53	64*	0.5	0.9
283 LUTH--MO SYNOD	1	79	86	0.6	1.3
413 S.D.A.........	1	67	80*	0.6	1.2
419 SO BAPT CONV..	19	2 815	3 373*	25.3	50.0
449 UN METHODIST..	12	1 083	1 298*	9.7	19.2
WASHINGTON	169	33 984	46 142*	46.3	100.0
017 AMER BAPT ASSN	5	851	851	0.9	1.8
053 ASSEMB OF GOD.	14	1 643	2 491	2.5	5.4
059 BAPT MISS ASSN	12	1 989	2 377*	2.4	5.2
081 CATHOLIC......	5	NA	3 137	3.1	6.8
093 CHR CH (DISC).	4	764	948	1.0	2.1
097 CHR CHS&CHS CR	4	375	448*	0.4	1.0
107 CHRISTIAN UN..	1	10	10	–	–
127 CH GOD (CLEVE)	3	132	158*	0.2	0.3
151 L-D SAINTS....	2	NA	731	0.7	1.6
165 CH OF NAZARENE	5	439	847	0.8	1.8
167 CHS OF CHRIST.	24	2 272	3 439	3.4	7.5
185 CUMBER PRESB..	2	73	64	0.1	0.1
193 EPISCOPAL.....	2	974	1 247	1.3	2.7
226 FRIENDS-USA...	1	4	5*	–	–
281 LUTH CH AMER..	1	170	249	0.2	0.5
283 LUTH--MO SYNOD	2	559	737	0.7	1.6
290 METRO COMM CHS	1	25	50	0.1	0.1
349 PENT HOLINESS.	3	121	145*	0.1	0.3
353 CHR BRETHREN..	1	10	10	–	–
357 PRESB CH US...	10	749	895*	0.9	1.9
403 SALVATION ARMY	2	97	140	0.1	0.3
413 S.D.A.........	3	236	282*	0.3	0.6
419 SO BAPT CONV..	31	14 847	17 745*	17.8	38.5
435 UNITARIAN-UNIV	1	62	74*	0.1	0.2
449 UN METHODIST..	20	6 835	8 169*	8.2	17.7
453 UN PRES CH USA	10	747	893*	0.9	1.9
WHITE	172	25 714	32 376*	63.7	100.0
017 AMER BAPT ASSN	25	3 040	3 040	6.0	9.4
053 ASSEMB OF GOD.	10	942	1 796	3.5	5.5
059 BAPT MISS ASSN	16	2 654	3 209*	6.3	9.9
081 CATHOLIC......	1	NA	460	0.9	1.4
093 CHR CH (DISC).	3	222	310	0.6	1.0
101 C.M.E.........	4	1 929	2 333*	4.6	7.2
127 CH GOD (CLEVE)	6	406	491*	1.0	1.5
151 L-D SAINTS....	1	NA	242	0.5	0.7
165 CH OF NAZARENE	5	336	529	1.0	1.6
167 CHS OF CHRIST.	35	4 209	5 455	10.7	16.8
185 CUMBER PRESB..	5	114	156	0.3	0.5
193 EPISCOPAL.....	1	116	152	0.3	0.5
323 OLD ORD AMISH.	2	260	314*	0.6	1.0
349 PENT HOLINESS.	1	28	34*	0.1	0.1
357 PRESB CH US...	2	86	104*	0.2	0.3
413 S.D.A.........	1	31	37*	0.1	0.1
419 SO BAPT CONV..	27	7 557	9 160*	18.0	28.3
449 UN METHODIST..	25	3 679	4 449*	8.8	13.7
453 UN PRES CH USA	2	87	105*	0.2	0.3
WOODRUFF	35	4 825	6 008*	53.5	100.0
017 AMER BAPT ASSN	3	270	270	2.4	4.5
053 ASSEMB OF GOD.	3	72	102	0.9	1.7
059 BAPT MISS ASSN	1	51	63*	0.6	1.0
081 CATHOLIC......	1	NA	50	0.4	0.8
127 CH GOD (CLEVE)	2	48	59*	0.5	1.0
165 CH OF NAZARENE	1	102	180	1.6	3.0
167 CHS OF CHRIST.	4	389	468	4.2	7.8
419 SO BAPT CONV..	11	2 711	3 354*	29.9	55.8
449 UN METHODIST..	9	1 182	1 462*	13.0	24.3
YELL	63	6 407	8 080*	47.5	100.0
017 AMER BAPT ASSN	5	612	612	3.6	7.6
053 ASSEMB OF GOD.	7	407	725	4.3	9.0
055 AS REF PRES CH	1	24	25	0.1	0.3
059 BAPT MISS ASSN	2	121	145*	0.9	1.8
081 CATHOLIC......	1	NA	140	0.8	1.7
165 CH OF NAZARENE	1	37	72	0.4	0.9
167 CHS OF CHRIST.	12	875	1 106	6.5	13.7
185 CUMBER PRESB..	1	70	138	0.8	1.7
357 PRESB CH US...	1	46	55*	0.3	0.7
413 S.D.A.........	1	29	35*	0.2	0.4
419 SO BAPT CONV..	11	2 598	3 120*	18.3	38.6
449 UN METHODIST..	18	1 516	1 821*	10.7	22.5
453 UN PRES CH USA	2	72	86*	0.5	1.1

NA—Not applicable   *Total adherents estimated from known number of communicant, confirmed, full members.   —Represents a percent less than 0.1.   Percentages may not total due to rounding.

Table 4. Churches and Church Membership by County and Denomination: 1980

County and Denomination	Number of churches	Communicant, confirmed, full members	Total adherents Number	Percent of total population	Percent of total adherents
CALIFORNIA					
THE STATE.....	11 421	2 313 529	8 157 906*	34.5	100.0
ALAMEDA	468	101 577	393 520*	35.6	100.0
005 AME ZION......	2	599	899	0.1	0.2
017 AMER BAPT ASSN	1	201	201	–	0.1
019 AMER BAPT USA.	24	9 115	10 816*	1.0	2.7
029 AMER LUTH CH..	9	2 731	3 620	0.3	0.9
045 APOSTOLIC LUTH	1	100	119*	–	–
053 ASSEMB OF GOD.	29	4 161	6 261	0.6	1.6
057 BAPT GEN CONF.	3	558	662*	0.1	0.2
059 BAPT MISS ASSN	2	695	825*	0.1	0.2
081 CATHOLIC......	55	NA	249 745	22.6	63.5
089 CHR & MISS AL.	7	2 008	3 499	0.3	0.9
093 CHR CH (DISC).	9	1 071	1 311	0.1	0.3
097 CHR CHS&CHS CR	8	894	1 061*	0.1	0.3
101 C.M.E.........	5	5 392	6 398*	0.6	1.6
105 CHRISTIAN REF.	2	262	394	–	0.1
123 CH GOD (ANDER)	5	225	675	0.1	0.2
127 CH GOD (CLEVE)	4	97	115*	–	–
151 L-D SAINTS....	34	NA	17 339	1.6	4.4
157 CH OF BRETHREN	1	75	89*	–	–
165 CH OF NAZARENE	13	1 251	1 969	0.2	0.5
167 CHS OF CHRIST.	22	2 785	3 545	0.3	0.9
179 CONSRV BAPT...	6	1 600	1 899*	0.2	0.5
193 EPISCOPAL.....	21	8 443	9 211	0.8	2.3
201 EVAN COV CH AM	3	751	891*	0.1	0.2
203 EVAN FREE CH..	3	600	712*	0.1	0.2
215 EVAN METH CH..	1	70	83*	–	–
221 FREE METHODIST	2	62	315	–	0.1
226 FRIENDS-USA...	3	294	349*	–	0.1
237 GC MENN BR CHS	1	37	44*	–	–
263 INT FOURSQ GOS	3	467	554*	0.1	0.1
270 CONSRV JUDAISM	1	142	168*	–	–
271 REFORM JUDAISM	5	2 242	2 660*	0.2	0.7
274 LAT EVAN LUTH.	1	185	219	–	0.1
281 LUTH CH AMER..	12	3 775	5 529	0.5	1.4
283 LUTH--MO SYNOD	16	5 217	7 094	0.6	1.8
290 METRO COMM CHS	1	45	90	–	–
329 OPEN BIBLE STD	1	75	125	–	–
335 ORTH PRESB CH.	1	33	39*	–	–
353 CHR BRETHREN..	8	900	1 200	0.1	0.3
356 PRESB CH AMER.	1	36	62	–	–
371 REF CH IN AM..	1	105	138	–	–
403 SALVATION ARMY	2	390	505	–	0.1
413 S.D.A.........	10	2 747	3 260*	0.3	0.8
415 S-D BAPTIST GC	1	27	32*	–	–
419 SO BAPT CONV..	45	14 422	17 113*	1.5	4.3
435 UNITARIAN-UNIV	5	1 110	1 317*	0.1	0.3
443 UN C OF CHRIST	17	4 431	5 258*	0.5	1.3
449 UN METHODIST..	32	9 972	11 833*	1.1	3.0
453 UN PRES CH USA	27	11 144	13 223*	1.2	3.4
469 WELS..........	1	35	54	–	–
ALPINE	2	57	70*	6.4	100.0
053 ASSEMB OF GOD.	1	7	11	1.0	15.7
097 CHR CHS&CHS CR	1	50	59*	5.4	84.3
AMADOR	23	1 308	5 531*	28.6	100.0
053 ASSEMB OF GOD.	3	109	246	1.3	4.4
081 CATHOLIC......	6	NA	3 150	16.3	57.0
151 L-D SAINTS....	2	NA	608	3.1	11.0
165 CH OF NAZARENE	1	45	66	0.3	1.2
167 CHS OF CHRIST.	1	18	23	0.1	0.4
179 CONSRV BAPT...	2	200	234*	1.2	4.2
193 EPISCOPAL.....	1	193	230	1.2	4.2
221 FREE METHODIST	1	28	138	0.7	2.5
413 S.D.A.........	1	114	133*	0.7	2.4
419 SO BAPT CONV..	2	144	168*	0.9	3.0
449 UN METHODIST..	3	457	535*	2.8	9.7
BUTTE	110	16 193	36 734*	25.5	100.0
017 AMER BAPT ASSN	1	142	142	0.1	0.4
019 AMER BAPT USA.	3	935	1 096*	0.8	3.0
029 AMER LUTH CH..	2	572	779	0.5	2.1
045 APOSTOLIC LUTH	1	25	29*	–	0.1
053 ASSEMB OF GOD.	13	1 239	1 961	1.4	5.3
057 BAPT GEN CONF.	1	42	49*	–	0.1
081 CATHOLIC......	8	NA	9 773	6.8	26.6
089 CHR & MISS AL.	3	1 315	2 018	1.4	5.5
093 CHR CH (DISC).	2	533	698	0.5	1.9
097 CHR CHS&CHS CR	4	420	492*	0.3	1.3
101 C.M.E.........	1	137	161*	0.1	0.4
123 CH GOD (ANDER)	1	56	168	0.1	0.5
127 CH GOD (CLEVE)	2	52	61*	–	0.2
151 L-D SAINTS....	12	NA	5 544	3.9	15.1
157 CH OF BRETHREN	2	101	118*	0.1	0.3
165 CH OF NAZARENE	5	547	945	0.7	2.6
167 CHS OF CHRIST.	6	428	608	0.4	1.7
175 CONGR CHR CHS.	1	284	333*	0.2	0.9
193 EPISCOPAL.....	4	848	1 266	0.9	3.4
203 EVAN FREE CH..	2	149	175*	0.1	0.5
217 FIRE BAPTIZED	1	10	12*	–	–
221 FREE METHODIST	1	104	399	0.3	1.1
244 GRACE BRETHREN	1	50	59*	–	0.2
283 LUTH--MO SYNOD	4	876	1 160	0.8	3.2
353 CHR BRETHREN..	1	20	40	–	0.1
381 REF PRES-EVAN.	1	?	?	?	?
403 SALVATION ARMY	1	99	197	0.1	0.5
413 S.D.A.........	5	1 959	2 297*	1.6	6.3
419 SO BAPT CONV..	8	2 160	2 532*	1.8	6.9
435 UNITARIAN-UNIV	1	37	43*	–	0.1
443 UN C OF CHRIST	2	289	339*	0.2	0.9
449 UN METHODIST..	7	1 766	2 070*	1.4	5.6
453 UN PRES CH USA	3	998	1 170*	0.8	3.2
CALAVERAS	30	1 565	5 934*	28.7	100.0
053 ASSEMB OF GOD.	3	55	96	0.5	1.6
081 CATHOLIC......	6	NA	2 680	12.9	45.2
123 CH GOD (ANDER)	1	225	675	3.3	11.4
151 L-D SAINTS....	2	NA	893	4.3	15.0
165 CH OF NAZARENE	1	40	70	0.3	1.2
167 CHS OF CHRIST.	2	45	57	0.3	1.0
193 EPISCOPAL.....	1	90	96	0.5	1.6
201 EVAN COV CH AM	4	344	404*	2.0	6.8
281 LUTH CH AMER..	1	136	202	1.0	3.4
329 OPEN BIBLE STD	1	25	50	0.2	0.8
413 S.D.A.........	2	127	149*	0.7	2.5
419 SO BAPT CONV..	4	292	343*	1.7	5.8
443 UN C OF CHRIST	2	186	219*	1.1	3.7
COLUSA	25	1 672	4 153*	32.5	100.0
019 AMER BAPT USA.	1	141	172*	1.3	4.1
053 ASSEMB OF GOD.	4	202	286	2.2	6.9
081 CATHOLIC......	7	NA	1 850	14.5	44.5
089 CHR & MISS AL.	1	63	113	0.9	2.7
093 CHR CH (DISC).	1	50	70	0.5	1.7
151 L-D SAINTS....	1	NA	195	1.5	4.7
193 EPISCOPAL.....	1	123	149	1.2	3.6
283 LUTH--MO SYNOD	1	82	87	0.7	2.1
419 SO BAPT CONV..	2	213	259*	2.0	6.2
449 UN METHODIST..	5	699	851*	6.7	20.5
453 UN PRES CH USA	1	99	121*	0.9	2.9
CONTRA COSTA	321	69 136	243 841*	37.1	100.0
001 ADVENT CHR CH.	1	37	44*	–	–
017 AMER BAPT ASSN	6	815	815	0.1	0.3
019 AMER BAPT USA.	18	4 112	4 943*	0.8	2.0
029 AMER LUTH CH..	5	1 837	2 625	0.4	1.1
053 ASSEMB OF GOD.	17	1 801	3 482	0.5	1.4
057 BAPT GEN CONF.	1	850	1 022*	0.2	0.4
081 CATHOLIC......	35	NA	140 354	21.4	57.6
089 CHR & MISS AL.	4	374	500	0.1	0.2
093 CHR CH (DISC).	6	1 048	1 437	0.2	0.6
097 CHR CHS&CHS CR	3	260	313*	–	0.1
101 C.M.E.........	3	3 481	4 185*	0.6	1.7
105 CHRISTIAN REF.	1	167	275	–	0.1
123 CH GOD (ANDER)	1	40	120	–	–
127 CH GOD (CLEVE)	4	361	434*	0.1	0.2
151 L-D SAINTS....	27	NA	15 058	2.3	6.2
165 CH OF NAZARENE	8	903	1 634	0.2	0.7
167 CHS OF CHRIST.	20	2 300	2 882	0.4	1.2
175 CONGR CHR CHS.	2	286	344*	0.1	0.1
179 CONSRV BAPT...	4	250	301*	–	0.1
193 EPISCOPAL.....	17	5 224	6 351	1.0	2.6
201 EVAN COV CH AM	4	697	838*	0.1	0.3
203 EVAN FREE CH..	4	877	1 054*	0.2	0.4
221 FREE METHODIST	3	260	1 122	0.2	0.5
226 FRIENDS-USA...	1	89	107*	–	–
239 SWEDENBORGIAN.	1	100	120*	–	–
263 INT FOURSQ GOS	4	298	358*	0.1	0.1
270 CONSRV JUDAISM	1	166	200*	–	0.1
271 REFORM JUDAISM	2	1 222	1 469*	0.2	0.6
281 LUTH CH AMER..	11	3 565	5 145	0.8	2.1
283 LUTH--MO SYNOD	14	3 419	4 641	0.7	1.9
290 METRO COMM CHS	1	30	60	–	–
329 OPEN BIBLE STD	4	775	1 075	0.2	0.4
353 CHR BRETHREN..	4	200	300	–	0.1
403 SALVATION ARMY	2	122	323	–	0.1
413 S.D.A.........	7	1 807	2 172*	0.3	0.9
419 SO BAPT CONV..	30	11 101	13 345*	2.0	5.5
435 UNITARIAN-UNIV	1	400	481*	0.1	0.2
443 UN C OF CHRIST	9	2 783	3 346*	0.5	1.4
449 UN METHODIST..	19	7 050	8 475*	1.3	3.5
453 UN PRES CH USA	15	9 929	11 936*	1.8	4.9
469 WELS..........	1	100	155	–	0.1
DEL NORTE	19	2 778	6 566*	36.0	100.0
053 ASSEMB OF GOD.	2	124	193	1.1	2.9
081 CATHOLIC......	3	NA	2 356	12.9	35.9
097 CHR CHS&CHS CR	1	40	49*	0.3	0.7
151 L-D SAINTS....	1	NA	454	2.5	6.9
165 CH OF NAZARENE	1	80	274	1.5	4.2
167 CHS OF CHRIST.	1	60	76	0.4	1.2
193 EPISCOPAL.....	1	77	96	0.5	1.5
263 INT FOURSQ GOS	1	389	473*	2.6	7.2
283 LUTH--MO SYNOD	1	258	466	2.6	7.1
413 S.D.A.........	1	300	365*	2.0	5.6
419 SO BAPT CONV..	3	915	1 113*	6.1	17.0
449 UN METHODIST..	3	535	651*	3.6	9.9
EL DORADO	49	5 998	16 744*	19.5	100.0
017 AMER BAPT ASSN	1	41	41	–	0.2
019 AMER BAPT USA.	1	282	336*	0.4	2.0
029 AMER LUTH CH..	1	157	228	0.3	1.4
053 ASSEMB OF GOD.	3	577	1 040	1.2	6.2

NA—Not applicable   *Total adherents estimated from known number of communicant, confirmed, full members.   —Represents a percent less than 0.1.   Percentages may not total due to rounding.

Table 4. Churches and Church Membership by County and Denomination: 1980

County and Denomination	Number of churches	Communicant, confirmed, full members	Total adherents Number	Percent of total population	Percent of total adherents
081 CATHOLIC......	5	NA	6 500	7.6	38.8
097 CHR CHS&CHS CR	1	52	62*	0.1	0.4
127 CH GOD (CLEVE)	1	15	18*	-	0.1
151 L-D SAINTS....	5	NA	2 410	2.8	14.4
165 CH OF NAZARENE	2	142	222	0.3	1.3
167 CHS OF CHRIST.	3	125	155	0.2	0.9
179 CONSRV BAPT...	2	450	537*	0.6	3.2
193 EPISCOPAL.....	1	284	343	0.4	2.0
244 GRACE BRETHREN	1	11	13*	-	0.1
263 INT FOURSQ GOS	2	26	31*	-	0.2
281 LUTH CH AMER..	1	166	206	0.2	1.2
283 LUTH--MO SYNOD	1	387	686	0.8	4.1
313 N AM BAPT CONF	1	716	854*	1.0	5.1
413 S.D.A.........	4	917	1 094*	1.3	6.5
419 SO BAPT CONV..	6	648	773*	0.9	4.6
443 UN C OF CHRIST	2	136	162*	0.2	1.0
449 UN METHODIST..	3	426	508*	0.6	3.0
453 UN PRES CH USA	2	440	525*	0.6	3.1
FRESNO	**392**	**65 916**	**202 696***	**39.4**	**100.0**
001 ADVENT CHR CH.	1	23	28*	-	-
005 AME ZION.....	1	321	396	0.1	0.2
017 AMER BAPT ASSN	4	489	489	0.1	0.2
019 AMER BAPT USA.	18	5 813	7 122*	1.4	3.5
029 AMER LUTH CH..	8	1 959	2 451	0.5	1.2
039 AP CHR CH(NAZ)	1	15	18*	-	-
053 ASSEMB OF GOD.	43	7 063	11 270	2.2	5.6
057 BAPT GEN CONF.	2	563	690*	0.1	0.3
059 BAPT MISS ASSN	1	122	149*	-	0.1
081 CATHOLIC......	48	NA	107 396	20.9	53.0
089 CHR & MISS AL.	1	68	68	-	-
093 CHR CH (DISC).	5	787	1 260	0.2	0.6
097 CHR CHS&CHS CR	6	783	959*	0.2	0.5
101 C.M.E........	1	100	123*	-	0.1
105 CHRISTIAN REF.	1	61	108	-	0.1
123 CH GOD (ANDER)	5	395	1 185	0.2	0.6
127 CH GOD (CLEVE)	14	794	973*	0.2	0.5
151 L-D SAINTS....	19	NA	8 638	1.7	4.3
157 CH OF BRETHREN	3	713	874*	0.2	0.4
165 CH OF NAZARENE	14	1 443	2 673	0.5	1.3
167 CHS OF CHRIST.	35	3 500	4 457	0.9	2.2
179 CONSRV BAPT...	3	750	919*	0.2	0.5
185 CUMBER PRESB..	1	31	35	-	-
193 EPISCOPAL.....	9	1 789	2 554	0.5	1.3
201 EVAN COV CH AM	4	753	923*	0.2	0.5
203 EVAN FREE CH..	3	1 003	1 229*	0.2	0.6
211 EVAN MENN BR..	1	31	40	-	-
221 FREE METHODIST	2	45	228	-	0.1
226 FRIENDS-USA...	2	439	538*	0.1	0.3
237 GC MENN BR CHS	12	1 996	2 446*	0.5	1.2
263 INT FOURSQ GOS	4	1 163	1 425*	0.3	0.7
270 CONSRV JUDAISM	1	30	37*	-	-
271 REFORM JUDAISM	1	496	608*	0.1	0.3
281 LUTH CH AMER..	8	2 443	3 273	0.6	1.6
283 LUTH--MO SYNOD	5	1 425	2 118	0.4	1.0
285 MENNONITE CH..	1	126	154*	-	0.1
287 MENN GEN CONF.	2	612	768	0.1	0.4
290 METRO COMM CHS	1	20	40	-	-
349 PENT HOLINESS.	5	236	289*	0.1	0.1
353 CHR BRETHREN..	1	20	50	-	-
383 REF PRES OF NA	1	45	59	-	-
403 SALVATION ARMY	1	139	153	-	0.1
413 S.D.A.........	13	3 080	3 774*	0.7	1.9
419 SO BAPT CONV..	34	11 915	14 599*	2.8	7.2
435 UNITARIAN-UNIV	1	166	203*	-	0.1
443 UN C OF CHRIST	6	1 960	2 402*	0.5	1.2
449 UN METHODIST..	24	5 480	6 714*	1.3	3.3
453 UN PRES CH USA	14	4 622	5 663*	1.1	2.8
469 WELS.........	1	89	128	-	0.1
GLENN	**33**	**3 377**	**9 265***	**43.4**	**100.0**
019 AMER BAPT USA.	3	823	1 007*	4.7	10.9
029 AMER LUTH CH..	1	305	418	2.0	4.5
053 ASSEMB OF GOD.	3	138	221	1.0	2.4
081 CATHOLIC......	3	NA	4 482	21.0	48.4
097 CHR CHS&CHS CR	2	170	208*	1.0	2.2
143 CG IN CR(MENN)	1	142	142	0.7	1.5
151 L-D SAINTS....	2	NA	526	2.5	5.7
165 CH OF NAZARENE	2	45	97	0.5	1.0
167 CHS OF CHRIST.	1	46	50	0.2	0.5
193 EPISCOPAL.....	2	167	220	1.0	2.4
203 EVAN FREE CH..	2	136	166*	0.8	1.8
226 FRIENDS-USA...	1	53	65*	0.3	0.7
237 GC MENN BR CHS	1	46	56*	0.3	0.6
283 LUTH--MO SYNOD	2	193	245	1.1	2.6
413 S.D.A.........	2	111	136*	0.6	1.5
419 SO BAPT CONV..	2	407	498*	2.3	5.4
449 UN METHODIST..	2	523	640*	3.0	6.9
453 UN PRES CH USA	1	72	88*	0.4	0.9
HUMBOLDT	**130**	**14 308**	**33 318***	**30.8**	**100.0**
017 AMER BAPT ASSN	3	114	114	0.1	0.3
019 AMER BAPT USA.	3	902	1 076*	1.0	3.2
029 AMER LUTH CH..	5	882	1 172	1.1	3.5
053 ASSEMB OF GOD.	19	1 072	1 847	1.7	5.5
081 CATHOLIC......	14	NA	12 835	11.9	38.5
093 CHR CH (DISC).	1	89	93	0.1	0.3
097 CHR CHS&CHS CR	5	425	507*	0.5	1.5
127 CH GOD (CLEVE)	3	149	178*	0.2	0.5
151 L-D SAINTS....	6	NA	2 059	1.9	6.2
165 CH OF NAZARENE	7	599	1 272	1.2	3.8
167 CHS OF CHRIST.	5	260	330	0.3	1.0

County and Denomination	Number of churches	Communicant, confirmed, full members	Total adherents Number	Percent of total population	Percent of total adherents
179 CONSRV BAPT...	1	50	60*	0.1	0.2
193 EPISCOPAL.....	5	1 346	1 559	1.4	4.7
201 EVAN COV CH AM	1	164	196*	0.2	0.6
203 EVAN FREE CH..	2	89	106*	0.1	0.3
226 FRIENDS-USA...	1	42	50*	-	0.2
263 INT FOURSQ GOS	2	687	820*	0.8	2.5
271 REFORM JUDAISM	1	80	95*	0.1	0.3
281 LUTH CH AMER..	2	115	201	0.2	0.6
283 LUTH--MO SYNOD	4	449	610	0.6	1.8
403 SALVATION ARMY	1	73	117	0.1	0.4
413 S.D.A.........	6	1 251	1 493*	1.4	4.5
419 SO BAPT CONV..	16	2 782	3 320*	3.1	10.0
435 UNITARIAN-UNIV	1	120	143*	0.1	0.4
443 UN C OF CHRIST	1	92	110*	0.1	0.3
449 UN METHODIST..	3	1 164	1 389*	1.3	4.2
453 UN PRES CH USA	12	1 312	1 566*	1.4	4.7
IMPERIAL	**86**	**8 863**	**50 680***	**55.0**	**100.0**
017 AMER BAPT ASSN	1	76	76	0.1	0.1
019 AMER BAPT USA.	5	799	1 009*	1.1	2.0
053 ASSEMB OF GOD.	10	890	1 845	2.0	3.6
081 CATHOLIC......	13	NA	36 871	40.0	72.8
093 CHR CH (DISC).	1	164	249	0.3	0.5
097 CHR CHS&CHS CR	2	450	568*	0.6	1.1
101 C.M.E........	2	370	467*	0.5	0.9
127 CH GOD (CLEVE)	1	7	9*	-	-
151 L-D SAINTS....	6	NA	1 582	1.7	3.1
165 CH OF NAZARENE	5	274	444	0.5	0.9
167 CHS OF CHRIST.	10	650	827	0.9	1.6
193 EPISCOPAL.....	3	227	297	0.3	0.6
226 FRIENDS-USA...	1	31	39*	-	0.1
263 INT FOURSQ GOS	2	144	182*	0.2	0.4
283 LUTH--MO SYNOD	4	469	631	0.7	1.2
403 SALVATION ARMY	1	67	226	0.2	0.4
413 S.D.A.........	4	566	714*	0.8	1.4
419 SO BAPT CONV..	8	2 116	2 671*	2.9	5.3
449 UN METHODIST..	4	1 041	1 314*	1.4	2.6
453 UN PRES CH USA	3	522	659*	0.7	1.3
INYO	**34**	**2 466**	**8 234***	**46.0**	**100.0**
053 ASSEMB OF GOD.	2	213	378	2.1	4.6
081 CATHOLIC......	8	NA	4 179	23.4	50.8
097 CHR CHS&CHS CR	1	100	119*	0.7	1.4
151 L-D SAINTS....	2	NA	685	3.8	8.3
165 CH OF NAZARENE	2	157	277	1.5	3.4
167 CHS OF CHRIST.	2	150	191	1.1	2.3
179 CONSRV BAPT...	2	143	170*	0.9	2.1
193 EPISCOPAL.....	2	176	371	2.1	4.5
209 EVAN LUTH SYN.	1	48	57	0.3	0.7
263 INT FOURSQ GOS	2	291	346*	1.9	4.2
283 LUTH--MO SYNOD	1	167	246	1.4	3.0
413 S.D.A.........	2	190	226*	1.3	2.7
419 SO BAPT CONV..	2	128	152*	0.8	1.8
449 UN METHODIST..	3	372	443*	2.5	5.4
453 UN PRES CH USA	2	331	394*	2.2	4.8
KERN	**354**	**55 187**	**162 494***	**40.3**	**100.0**
017 AMER BAPT ASSN	13	1 204	1 204	0.3	0.7
019 AMER BAPT USA.	15	5 460	6 748*	1.7	4.2
029 AMER LUTH CH..	7	1 234	1 709	0.4	1.1
053 ASSEMB OF GOD.	37	4 367	8 364	2.1	5.1
057 BAPT GEN CONF.	1	248	307*	0.1	0.2
059 BAPT MISS ASSN	3	150	185*	-	0.1
081 CATHOLIC......	32	NA	79 888	19.8	49.2
089 CHR & MISS AL.	1	75	165	-	0.1
093 CHR CH (DISC).	2	582	708	0.2	0.4
097 CHR CHS&CHS CR	10	1 469	1 816*	0.5	1.1
101 C.M.E........	1	270	334*	0.1	0.2
105 CHRISTIAN REF.	1	94	167	-	0.1
123 CH GOD (ANDER)	2	250	750	0.2	0.5
127 CH GOD (CLEVE)	13	810	1 001*	0.2	0.6
151 L-D SAINTS....	21	NA	8 519	2.1	5.2
157 CH OF BRETHREN	2	442	546*	0.1	0.3
165 CH OF NAZARENE	16	1 691	3 705	0.9	2.3
167 CHS OF CHRIST.	35	3 240	4 207	1.0	2.6
179 CONSRV BAPT...	4	697	861*	0.2	0.5
193 EPISCOPAL.....	9	1 660	2 337	0.6	1.4
221 FREE METHODIST	1	35	177	-	0.1
263 INT FOURSQ GOS	9	1 279	1 581*	0.4	1.0
270 CONSRV JUDAISM	1	50	62*	-	-
271 REFORM JUDAISM	2	284	351*	0.1	0.2
281 LUTH CH AMER..	1	253	340	0.1	0.2
283 LUTH--MO SYNOD	10	1 703	2 193	0.5	1.3
290 METRO COMM CHS	1	35	70	-	-
349 PENT HOLINESS.	9	428	529*	0.1	0.3
356 PRESB CH AMER.	1	21	31	-	-
403 SALVATION ARMY	1	106	208	0.1	0.1
413 S.D.A.........	11	2 360	2 917*	0.7	1.8
419 SO BAPT CONV..	49	16 163	19 976*	5.0	12.3
435 UNITARIAN-UNIV	2	94	116*	-	0.1
443 UN C OF CHRIST	7	1 149	1 420*	0.4	0.9
449 UN METHODIST..	18	4 790	5 920*	1.5	3.6
453 UN PRES CH USA	6	2 494	3 082*	0.8	1.9
KINGS	**90**	**10 074**	**30 199***	**41.0**	**100.0**
017 AMER BAPT ASSN	4	653	653	0.9	2.2
019 AMER BAPT USA.	5	1 019	1 278*	1.7	4.2
053 ASSEMB OF GOD.	8	841	1 287	1.7	4.3
057 BAPT GEN CONF.	3	519	651*	0.9	2.2
081 CATHOLIC......	7	NA	15 607	21.2	51.7
093 CHR CH (DISC).	1	221	376	0.5	1.2

NA—Not applicable   *Total adherents estimated from known number of communicant, confirmed, full members.   —Represents a percent less than 0.1.   Percentages may not total due to rounding.

Table 4. Churches and Church Membership by County and Denomination: 1980

County and Denomination	Number of churches	Communicant, confirmed, full members	Total adherents Number	Percent of total population	Percent of total adherents
097 CHR CHS&CHS CR	1	230	288*	0.4	1.0
105 CHRISTIAN REF.	1	350	610	0.8	2.0
127 CH GOD (CLEVE)	1	79	99*	0.1	0.3
151 L-D SAINTS....	2	NA	963	1.3	3.2
165 CH OF NAZARENE	4	204	433	0.6	1.4
167 CHS OF CHRIST.	12	802	983	1.3	3.3
179 CONSRV BAPT...	3	150	188*	0.3	0.6
193 EPISCOPAL....	4	305	640	0.9	2.1
221 FREE METHODIST	1	11	24	-	0.1
237 GC MENN BR CHS	7	1 140	1 430*	1.9	4.7
263 INT FOURSQ GOS	1	24	30*	-	0.1
281 LUTH CH AMER..	1	165	260	0.4	0.9
283 LUTH--MO SYNOD	2	194	307	0.4	1.0
403 SALVATION ARMY	1	40	170	0.2	0.6
413 S.D.A.	5	656	823*	1.1	2.7
419 SO BAPT CONV..	6	825	1 035*	1.4	3.4
449 UN METHODIST..	6	905	1 135*	1.5	3.8
453 UN PRES CH USA	4	741	929*	1.3	3.1
LAKE	50	3 804	9 348*	25.7	100.0
017 AMER BAPT ASSN	2	162	162	0.4	1.7
019 AMER BAPT USA.	2	88	102*	0.3	1.1
053 ASSEMB OF GOD.	2	196	310	0.9	3.3
081 CATHOLIC......	9	NA	4 115	11.3	44.0
093 CHR CH (DISC).	1	77	113	0.3	1.2
097 CHR CHS&CHS CR	1	35	41*	0.1	0.4
151 L-D SAINTS....	2	NA	661	1.8	7.1
165 CH OF NAZARENE	1	30	59	0.2	0.6
167 CHS OF CHRIST.	3	143	182	0.5	1.9
179 CONSRV BAPT...	1	250	291*	0.8	3.1
193 EPISCOPAL.....	1	104	129	0.4	1.4
203 EVAN FREE CH..	1	34	40*	0.1	0.4
263 INT FOURSQ GOS	2	68	79*	0.2	0.8
281 LUTH CH AMER..	1	103	120	0.3	1.3
283 LUTH--MO SYNOD	2	197	246	0.7	2.6
413 S.D.A.	4	449	523*	1.4	5.6
419 SO BAPT CONV..	5	719	837*	2.3	9.0
449 UN METHODIST..	7	719	837*	2.3	9.0
453 UN PRES CH USA	3	430	501*	1.4	5.4
LASSEN	28	1 922	4 711*	21.7	100.0
019 AMER BAPT USA.	1	205	247*	1.1	5.2
053 ASSEMB OF GOD.	4	136	254	1.2	5.4
081 CATHOLIC......	5	NA	1 328	6.1	28.2
097 CHR CHS&CHS CR	1	50	60*	0.3	1.3
127 CH GOD (CLEVE)	1	13	16*	0.1	0.3
151 L-D SAINTS....	3	NA	857	4.0	18.2
165 CH OF NAZARENE	1	23	64	0.3	1.4
167 CHS OF CHRIST.	1	38	48	0.2	1.0
193 EPISCOPAL.....	1	130	165	0.8	3.5
226 FRIENDS-USA...	1	23	28*	0.1	0.6
263 INT FOURSQ GOS	1	?	?	?	?
283 LUTH--MO SYNOD	2	238	358	1.7	7.6
413 S.D.A.	1	149	180*	0.8	3.8
419 SO BAPT CONV..	4	597	720*	3.3	15.3
449 UN METHODIST..	1	320	386*	1.8	8.2
LOS ANGELES	2 837	727 165	2 928 140*	39.2	100.0
001 ADVENT CHR CH.	5	338	407*	-	-
005 AME ZION......	7	6 200	7 458	0.1	0.3
017 AMER BAPT ASSN	23	3 829	3 829	0.1	0.1
019 AMER BAPT USA.	151	65 576	79 014*	1.1	2.7
029 AMER LUTH CH..	72	28 137	38 041	0.5	1.3
039 AP CHR CH(NAZ)	3	126	152*	-	-
053 ASSEMB OF GOD.	150	25 679	40 123	0.5	1.4
057 BAPT GEN CONF.	23	12 323	14 848*	0.2	0.5
059 BAPT MISS ASSN	4	715	862*	-	-
075 BRETHREN IN CR	1	76	85	-	-
081 CATHOLIC......	262	NA	1 904 617	25.5	65.0
083 CHRIST CATH CH	1	3	10	-	-
089 CHR & MISS AL.	26	1 773	2 680	-	0.1
093 CHR CH (DISC).	68	14 118	19 495	0.3	0.7
097 CHR CHS&CHS CR	64	12 606	15 189*	0.2	0.5
101 C.M.E.........	15	18 777	22 625*	0.3	0.8
105 CHRISTIAN REF.	12	2 585	4 147	0.1	0.1
121 CH GOD (ABR)..	2	82	99*	-	-
123 CH GOD (ANDER)	30	3 841	11 523	0.2	0.4
127 CH GOD (CLEVE)	27	2 248	2 709*	-	0.1
133 CH GOD(7TH)DEN	4	148	178*	-	-
149 CH OF JC (BIC)	2	83	89	-	-
151 L-D SAINTS....	220	NA	96 962	1.3	3.3
157 CH OF BRETHREN	13	2 248	2 709*	-	0.1
163 CH OF LUTH BR.	1	65	145	-	-
165 CH OF NAZARENE	82	13 681	20 995	0.3	0.7
167 CHS OF CHRIST.	119	16 475	21 001	0.3	0.7
175 CONGR CHR CHS.	15	10 548	12 710*	0.2	0.4
179 CONSRV BAPT...	44	10 131	12 207*	0.2	0.4
181 CONSRV CONGR..	4	3 691	4 447*	0.1	0.2
193 EPISCOPAL.....	146	57 721	73 154	1.0	2.5
195 ESTONIAN ELC..	1	153	482	-	-
201 EVAN COV CH AM	12	2 793	3 365*	-	0.1
203 EVAN FREE CH..	19	1 770	2 133*	-	0.1
208 EVAN LUTH ASSN	1	119	137	-	-
209 EVAN LUTH SYN.	1	53	64	-	-
215 EVAN METH CH..	4	154	186*	-	-
217 FIRE BAPTIZED	1	12	14*	-	-
221 FREE METHODIST	23	1 703	5 886	0.1	0.2
226 FRIENDS-USA...	20	3 647	4 394*	0.1	0.2
233 GEN CH NEW JER	1	50	60*	-	-
237 GC MENN BR CHS	2	117	141*	-	-
239 SWEDENBORGIAN	2	160	193*	-	-
244 GRACE BRETHREN	17	6 243	7 522*	0.1	0.3
263 INT FOURSQ GOS	115	44 424	53 528*	0.7	1.8
270 CONSRV JUDAISM	30	8 187	9 865*	0.1	0.3
271 REFORM JUDAISM	25	22 176	26 720*	0.4	0.9
274 LAT EVAN LUTH.	2	419	505	-	-
281 LUTH CH AMER..	65	15 075	20 542	0.3	0.7
283 LUTH--MO SYNOD	90	27 209	35 607	0.5	1.2
285 MENNONITE CH..	4	281	339*	-	-
287 MENN GEN CONF.	1	20	20	-	-
290 METRO COMM CHS	8	1 590	4 000	0.1	0.1
291 MISSIONARY CH.	10	673	805	-	-
293 MORAV CH-NORTH	2	417	543	-	-
313 N AM BAPT CONF	1	56	67*	-	-
329 OPEN BIBLE STD	7	911	1 265	-	-
335 ORTH PRESB CH.	8	771	929*	-	-
349 PENT HOLINESS.	13	642	774*	-	-
353 CHR BRETHREN..	19	1 100	1 500	-	0.1
356 PRESB CH AMER.	1	216	216	-	-
371 REF CH IN AM..	12	4 424	7 703	0.1	0.3
381 REF PRES-EVAN.	5	449	737	-	-
383 REF PRES OF NA	1	92	107	-	-
395 ROMANIAN OR CH	1	850	1 024*	-	-
403 SALVATION ARMY	21	2 749	6 383	0.1	0.2
413 S.D.A.	102	30 862	37 186*	0.5	1.3
415 S-D BAPTIST GC	1	168	202*	-	-
419 SO BAPT CONV..	187	77 816	93 763*	1.3	3.2
423 SYRIAN ANTIOCH	1	5 000	6 025*	0.1	0.2
435 UNITARIAN-UNIV	17	2 926	3 526*	-	0.1
443 UN C OF CHRIST	57	13 306	16 033*	0.2	0.5
449 UN METHODIST..	179	70 407	84 835*	1.1	2.9
453 UN PRES CH USA	142	62 398	75 185*	1.0	2.6
469 WELS	10	754	1 119	-	-
MADERA	59	6 831	22 555*	35.7	100.0
005 AME ZION......	1	100	135	0.2	0.6
019 AMER BAPT USA.	4	672	839*	1.3	3.7
029 AMER LUTH CH..	1	165	203	0.3	0.9
053 ASSEMB OF GOD.	11	1 071	2 067	3.3	9.2
057 BAPT GEN CONF.	1	21	26*	-	0.1
081 CATHOLIC......	6	NA	11 491	18.2	50.9
093 CHR CH (DISC).	1	110	161	0.3	0.7
097 CHR CHS&CHS CR	1	163	204*	0.3	0.9
123 CH GOD (ANDER)	3	293	879	1.4	3.9
127 CH GOD (CLEVE)	1	80	100*	0.2	0.4
151 L-D SAINTS....	3	NA	952	1.5	4.2
165 CH OF NAZARENE	2	131	473	0.7	2.1
167 CHS OF CHRIST.	4	354	400	0.6	1.8
193 EPISCOPAL.....	2	220	314	0.5	1.4
203 EVAN FREE CH..	1	70	87*	0.1	0.4
237 GC MENN BR CHS	1	119	149*	0.2	0.7
413 S.D.A.	4	785	981*	1.6	4.3
419 SO BAPT CONV..	7	1 510	1 886*	3.0	8.4
443 UN C OF CHRIST	1	30	37*	0.1	0.2
449 UN METHODIST..	2	584	730*	1.2	3.2
453 UN PRES CH USA	2	353	441*	0.7	2.0
MARIN	106	17 866	60 306*	27.0	100.0
019 AMER BAPT USA.	6	723	839*	0.4	1.4
029 AMER LUTH CH..	5	1 307	1 749	0.8	2.9
053 ASSEMB OF GOD.	4	323	542	0.2	0.9
081 CATHOLIC......	20	NA	36 150	16.2	59.9
097 CHR CHS&CHS CR	2	1 137	1 319*	0.6	2.2
123 CH GOD (ANDER)	3	210	630	0.3	1.0
151 L-D SAINTS....	4	NA	1 991	0.9	3.3
165 CH OF NAZARENE	2	69	175	0.1	0.3
167 CHS OF CHRIST.	3	105	133	0.1	0.2
179 CONSRV BAPT...	1	350	406*	0.2	0.7
193 EPISCOPAL.....	11	3 684	4 695	2.1	7.8
201 EVAN COV CH AM	1	254	295*	0.1	0.5
203 EVAN FREE CH..	1	20	23*	-	-
226 FRIENDS-USA...	1	29	34*	-	0.1
271 REFORM JUDAISM	1	1 120	1 299*	0.6	2.2
281 LUTH CH AMER..	1	257	280	0.1	0.5
283 LUTH--MO SYNOD	4	919	1 188	0.5	2.0
290 METRO COMM CHS	1	25	50	-	0.1
335 ORTH PRESB CH.	1	39	45*	-	0.1
413 S.D.A.	2	188	218*	0.1	0.4
419 SO BAPT CONV..	6	1 350	1 566*	0.7	2.6
435 UNITARIAN-UNIV	1	331	384*	0.2	0.6
443 UN C OF CHRIST	4	700	812*	0.4	1.3
449 UN METHODIST..	5	1 117	1 296*	0.6	2.1
453 UN PRES CH USA	16	3 609	4 187*	1.9	6.9
MARIPOSA	17	906	1 790*	16.1	100.0
017 AMER BAPT ASSN	1	105	105	0.9	5.9
053 ASSEMB OF GOD.	1	43	39	0.4	2.2
081 CATHOLIC......	4	NA	636	5.7	35.5
151 L-D SAINTS....	1	NA	114	1.0	6.4
167 CHS OF CHRIST.	2	89	103	0.9	5.8
179 CONSRV BAPT...	1	150	175*	1.6	9.8
193 EPISCOPAL.....	1	41	60	0.5	3.4
413 S.D.A.	2	216	252*	2.3	14.1
419 SO BAPT CONV..	1	37	43*	0.4	2.4
449 UN METHODIST..	3	225	263*	2.4	14.7
MENDOCINO	72	7 100	16 877*	25.3	100.0
019 AMER BAPT USA.	3	936	1 139*	1.7	6.7
029 AMER LUTH CH..	1	146	193	0.3	1.1
053 ASSEMB OF GOD.	7	488	763	1.1	4.5
081 CATHOLIC......	9	NA	6 145	9.2	36.4
093 CHR CH (DISC).	1	42	65	0.1	0.4
151 L-D SAINTS....	4	NA	1 432	2.1	8.5

NA—Not applicable   *Total adherents estimated from known number of communicant, confirmed, full members.   —Represents a percent less than 0.1.   Percentages may not total due to rounding.

Table 4. Churches and Church Membership by County and Denomination: 1980

County and Denomination	Number of churches	Communicant, confirmed, full members	Total adherents		
			Number	Percent of total population	Percent of total adherents
165 CH OF NAZARENE	3	111	307	0.5	1.8
167 CHS OF CHRIST.	5	163	207	0.3	1.2
179 CONSRV BAPT...	1	100	122*	0.2	0.7
193 EPISCOPAL.....	2	336	538	0.8	3.2
203 EVAN FREE CH..	3	89	108*	0.2	0.6
263 INT FOURSQ GOS	2	88	107*	0.2	0.6
281 LUTH CH AMER..	1	179	320	0.5	1.9
283 LUTH--MO SYNOD	3	312	430	0.6	2.5
413 S.D.A.........	5	954	1 161*	1.7	6.9
419 SO BAPT CONV..	9	1 395	1 697*	2.5	10.1
449 UN METHODIST..	8	850	1 034*	1.5	6.1
453 UN PRES CH USA	5	911	1 109*	1.7	6.6
MERCED	103	14 010	59 888*	44.5	100.0
001 ADVENT CHR CH.	1	15	19*	—	—
005 AME ZION......	1	120	135	0.1	0.2
017 AMER BAPT ASSN	1	100	100	0.1	0.2
019 AMER BAPT USA.	4	977	1 221*	0.9	2.0
029 AMER LUTH CH..	1	74	99	0.1	0.2
053 ASSEMB OF GOD.	12	865	1 515	1.1	2.5
081 CATHOLIC......	15	NA	39 182	29.1	65.4
093 CHR CH (DISC).	2	217	296	0.2	0.5
097 CHR CHS&CHS CR	1	64	80*	0.1	0.1
123 CH GOD (ANDER)	2	176	528	0.4	0.9
127 CH GOD (CLEVE)	1	68	85*	0.1	0.1
143 CG IN CR(MENN)	2	543	543	0.4	0.9
151 L-D SAINTS....	4	NA	1 896	1.4	3.2
165 CH OF NAZARENE	3	298	551	0.4	0.9
167 CHS OF CHRIST.	10	765	974	0.7	1.6
179 CONSRV BAPT...	2	300	375*	0.3	0.6
193 EPISCOPAL.....	3	444	861	0.6	1.4
201 EVAN COV CH AM	1	307	384*	0.3	0.6
237 GC MENN BR CHS	1	56	70*	0.1	0.1
263 INT FOURSQ GOS	1	124	155*	0.1	0.3
281 LUTH CH AMER..	2	419	568	0.4	0.9
283 LUTH--MO SYNOD	2	492	628	0.5	1.0
285 MENNONITE CH..	1	63	79*	0.1	0.1
287 MENN GEN CONF.	1	53	68	0.1	0.1
403 SALVATION ARMY	1	31	181	0.1	0.3
413 S.D.A.........	3	321	401*	0.3	0.7
419 SO BAPT CONV..	16	4 355	5 442*	4.0	9.1
449 UN METHODIST..	5	1 780	2 224*	1.7	3.7
453 UN PRES CH USA	4	983	1 228*	0.9	2.1
MODOC	16	827	1 875*	21.8	100.0
081 CATHOLIC......	2	NA	558	6.5	29.8
151 L-D SAINTS....	2	NA	252	2.9	13.4
165 CH OF NAZARENE	1	21	51	0.6	2.7
167 CHS OF CHRIST.	2	73	91	1.1	4.9
193 EPISCOPAL.....	1	145	211	2.5	11.3
413 S.D.A.........	2	65	79*	0.9	4.2
419 SO BAPT CONV..	1	203	246*	2.9	13.1
443 UN C OF CHRIST	5	320	387*	4.5	20.6
MONO	11	236	638*	7.4	100.0
053 ASSEMB OF GOD.	2	91	191	2.2	29.9
081 CATHOLIC......	3	NA	60	0.7	9.4
151 L-D SAINTS....	2	NA	183	2.1	28.7
193 EPISCOPAL.....	1	28	37	0.4	5.8
283 LUTH--MO SYNOD	1	47	84	1.0	13.2
453 UN PRES CH USA	2	70	83*	1.0	13.0
MONTEREY	142	25 690	82 441*	28.4	100.0
017 AMER BAPT ASSN	2	346	346	0.1	0.4
019 AMER BAPT USA.	4	1 535	1 870*	0.6	2.3
029 AMER LUTH CH..	4	971	1 242	0.4	1.5
053 ASSEMB OF GOD.	14	1 163	2 286	0.8	2.8
081 CATHOLIC......	19	NA	46 212	15.9	56.1
093 CHR CH (DISC).	1	68	77	—	0.1
097 CHR CHS&CHS CR	1	300	366*	0.1	0.4
101 C.M.E.........	3	1 012	1 233*	0.4	1.5
123 CH GOD (ANDER)	1	45	135	—	0.2
127 CH GOD (CLEVE)	3	118	144*	—	0.2
151 L-D SAINTS....	7	NA	3 318	1.1	4.0
165 CH OF NAZARENE	2	173	338	0.1	0.4
167 CHS OF CHRIST.	11	1 000	1 273	0.4	1.5
179 CONSRV BAPT...	6	1 500	1 828*	0.6	2.2
193 EPISCOPAL.....	12	3 017	3 990	1.4	4.8
201 EVAN COV CH AM	1	64	78*	—	0.1
226 FRIENDS-USA...	1	22	27*	—	—
271 REFORM JUDAISM	2	572	697*	0.2	0.8
281 LUTH CH AMER..	3	908	1 176	0.4	1.4
283 LUTH--MO SYNOD	3	660	818	0.3	1.0
290 METRO COMM CHS	1	20	40	—	—
403 SALVATION ARMY	2	117	241	0.1	0.3
413 S.D.A.........	2	245	298*	0.1	0.4
419 SO BAPT CONV..	16	5 740	6 993*	2.4	8.5
435 UNITARIAN-UNIV	2	166	202*	0.1	0.2
449 UN METHODIST..	11	2 486	3 029*	1.0	3.7
453 UN PRES CH USA	8	3 442	4 194*	1.4	5.1
NAPA	58	13 842	35 049*	35.3	100.0
017 AMER BAPT ASSN	1	50	50	0.1	0.1
019 AMER BAPT USA.	3	657	773*	0.8	2.2
029 AMER LUTH CH..	1	213	272	0.3	0.8
053 ASSEMB OF GOD.	2	218	295	0.3	0.8
057 BAPT GEN CONF.	1	575	676*	0.7	1.9
081 CATHOLIC......	9	NA	15 947	16.1	45.5
089 CHR & MISS AL.	2	114	215	0.2	0.6
097 CHR CHS&CHS CR	1	850	1 000*	1.0	2.9

County and Denomination	Number of churches	Communicant, confirmed, full members	Total adherents		
			Number	Percent of total population	Percent of total adherents
123 CH GOD (ANDER)	2	101	303	0.3	0.9
151 L-D SAINTS....	5	NA	1 740	1.8	5.0
165 CH OF NAZARENE	1	152	371	0.4	1.1
167 CHS OF CHRIST.	3	149	187	0.2	0.5
193 EPISCOPAL.....	3	650	1 147	1.2	3.3
203 EVAN FREE CH..	1	81	95*	0.1	0.3
263 INT FOURSQ GOS	1	69	81*	0.1	0.2
281 LUTH CH AMER..	1	177	207	0.2	0.6
283 LUTH--MO SYNOD	2	757	1 020	1.0	2.9
353 CHR BRETHREN..	1	50	80	0.1	0.2
403 SALVATION ARMY	1	57	98	0.1	0.3
413 S.D.A.........	7	5 159	6 067*	6.1	17.3
419 SO BAPT CONV..	5	1 543	1 815*	1.8	5.2
449 UN METHODIST..	2	837	984*	1.0	2.8
453 UN PRES CH USA	3	1 383	1 626*	1.6	4.6
NEVADA	37	4 467	10 351*	20.0	100.0
019 AMER BAPT USA.	1	84	100*	0.2	1.0
029 AMER LUTH CH..	1	246	298	0.6	2.9
053 ASSEMB OF GOD.	2	406	616	1.2	6.0
081 CATHOLIC......	5	NA	3 205	6.2	31.0
089 CHR & MISS AL.	1	71	181	0.4	1.7
123 CH GOD (ANDER)	1	99	297	0.6	2.9
127 CH GOD (CLEVE)	1	23	27*	0.1	0.3
151 L-D SAINTS....	2	NA	1 370	2.7	13.2
165 CH OF NAZARENE	1	78	97	0.2	0.9
167 CHS OF CHRIST.	3	125	159	0.3	1.5
179 CONSRV BAPT...	1	150	178*	0.3	1.7
193 EPISCOPAL.....	2	637	805	1.6	7.8
226 FRIENDS-USA...	1	82	97*	0.2	0.9
244 GRACE BRETHREN	1	30	36*	0.1	0.3
263 INT FOURSQ GOS	1	46	55*	0.1	0.5
283 LUTH--MO SYNOD	2	156	179	0.3	1.7
413 S.D.A.........	3	473	561*	1.1	5.4
419 SO BAPT CONV..	3	836	992*	1.9	9.6
449 UN METHODIST..	4	685	813*	1.6	7.9
453 UN PRES CH USA	1	240	285*	0.6	2.8
ORANGE	617	173 893	620 464*	32.1	100.0
001 ADVENT CHR CH.	1	125	150*	—	—
017 AMER BAPT ASSN	5	595	595	—	0.1
019 AMER BAPT USA.	22	8 493	10 189*	0.5	1.6
029 AMER LUTH CH..	26	11 302	15 228	0.8	2.5
053 ASSEMB OF GOD.	35	5 037	8 348	0.4	1.3
057 BAPT GEN CONF.	7	1 711	2 053*	0.1	0.3
059 BAPT MISS ASSN	2	218	262*	—	—
075 BRETHREN IN CR	1	76	85	—	—
081 CATHOLIC......	51	NA	351 081	18.2	56.6
089 CHR & MISS AL.	4	349	517	—	0.1
093 CHR CH (DISC).	10	2 943	3 620	0.2	0.6
097 CHR CHS&CHS CR	17	9 116	10 937*	0.6	1.8
105 CHRISTIAN REF.	4	502	779	—	0.1
123 CH GOD (ANDER)	4	369	1 107	0.1	0.2
127 CH GOD (CLEVE)	8	818	981*	0.1	0.2
149 CH OF JC (BIC)	1	63	75	—	—
151 L-D SAINTS....	77	NA	41 300	2.1	6.7
157 CH OF BRETHREN	1	120	144*	—	—
163 CH OF LUTH BR.	1	80	120	—	—
165 CH OF NAZARENE	19	3 776	6 998	0.4	1.1
167 CHS OF CHRIST.	32	4 600	5 850	0.3	0.9
175 CONGR CHR CHS.	7	1 396	1 675*	0.1	0.3
179 CONSRV BAPT...	9	2 444	2 932*	0.2	0.5
201 EVAN COV CH AM	3	377	452*	—	0.1
203 EVAN FREE CH..	10	3 556	4 266*	0.2	0.7
217 FIRE BAPTIZED.	1	8	10*	—	—
221 FREE METHODIST	9	399	1 704	0.1	0.3
226 FRIENDS-USA...	8	1 906	2 287*	0.1	0.4
244 GRACE BRETHREN	7	1 104	1 325*	0.1	0.2
263 INT FOURSQ GOS	11	2 050	2 459*	0.1	0.4
270 CONSRV JUDAISM	6	783	939*	—	0.2
271 REFORM JUDAISM	5	3 078	3 693*	0.2	0.6
281 LUTH CH AMER..	14	6 890	9 637	0.5	1.6
283 LUTH--MO SYNOD	27	13 753	19 201	1.0	3.1
285 MENNONITE CH..	1	101	121*	—	—
290 METRO COMM CHS	2	80	160	—	—
293 MORAV CH-NORTH	1	182	258	—	—
313 N AM BAPT CONF	5	1 796	2 155*	0.1	0.3
329 OPEN BIBLE STD	2	1 250	2 075	0.1	0.3
335 ORTH PRESB CH.	1	98	118*	—	—
349 PENT HOLINESS.	4	84	101*	—	—
353 CHR BRETHREN..	4	550	1 000	0.1	0.2
356 PRESB CH AMER.	2	?	?	?	?
371 REF CH IN AM..	4	8 900	14 721	0.8	2.4
383 REF PRES OF NA	1	39	44	—	—
403 SALVATION ARMY	2	443	1 855	0.1	0.3
413 S.D.A.........	13	4 897	5 875*	0.3	0.9
415 S-D BAPTIST GC	1	15	18*	—	—
419 SO BAPT CONV..	37	21 246	25 490*	1.3	4.1
435 UNITARIAN-UNIV	8	541	649*	—	0.1
443 UN C OF CHRIST	11	2 137	2 564*	0.1	0.4
449 UN METHODIST..	40	20 953	25 138*	1.3	4.1
453 UN PRES CH USA	30	21 914	26 291*	1.4	4.2
469 WELS..........	3	630	832	—	0.1
PLACER	88	10 961	32 095*	27.4	100.0
019 AMER BAPT USA.	1	220	264*	0.2	0.8
029 AMER LUTH CH..	3	903	1 135	1.0	3.5
053 ASSEMB OF GOD.	8	913	1 957	1.7	6.1
081 CATHOLIC......	12	NA	12 800	10.9	39.9
089 CHR & MISS AL.	1	56	56	—	0.2
127 CH GOD (CLEVE)	1	11	13*	—	—
133 CH GOD(7TH)DEN	1	6	7*	—	—

NA—Not applicable   *Total adherents estimated from known number of communicant, confirmed, full members.   —Represents a percent less than 0.1.   Percentages may not total due to rounding.

47

Table 4. Churches and Church Membership by County and Denomination: 1980

County and Denomination	Number of churches	Communicant, confirmed, full members	Total adherents Number	Percent of total population	Percent of total adherents
151 L-D SAINTS....	9	NA	4 726	4.0	14.7
165 CH OF NAZARENE	4	416	735	0.6	2.3
167 CHS OF CHRIST.	3	354	444	0.4	1.4
179 CONSRV BAPT...	2	450	540*	0.5	1.7
193 EPISCOPAL.....	4	726	954	0.8	3.0
203 EVAN FREE CH..	1	32	38*	-	0.1
244 GRACE BRETHREN	1	12	14*	-	-
263 INT FOURSQ GOS	2	143	172*	0.1	0.5
281 LUTH CH AMER..	2	477	700	0.6	2.2
283 LUTH--MO SYNOD	1	108	146	0.1	0.5
291 MISSIONARY CH.	1	0	15	-	-
353 CHR BRETHREN..	1	25	40	-	0.1
413 S.D.A.........	6	998	1 198*	1.0	3.7
419 SO BAPT CONV..	12	2 249	2 700*	2.3	8.4
443 UN C OF CHRIST	2	505	606*	0.5	1.9
449 UN METHODIST..	8	1 741	2 090*	1.8	6.5
453 UN PRES CH USA	1	565	678*	0.6	2.1
469 WELS.........	1	51	67	0.1	0.2
PLUMAS	**31**	**1 641**	**4 636***	**26.7**	**100.0**
053 ASSEM OF GOD.	4	201	434	2.5	9.4
081 CATHOLIC......	5	NA	1 940	11.2	41.8
151 L-D SAINTS....	3	NA	441	2.5	9.5
165 CH OF NAZARENE	1	17	52	0.3	1.1
167 CHS OF CHRIST.	3	134	206	1.2	4.4
283 LUTH--MO SYNOD	4	141	182	1.0	3.9
413 S.D.A.........	2	75	90*	0.5	1.9
419 SO BAPT CONV..	4	523	629*	3.6	13.6
449 UN METHODIST..	5	550	662*	3.8	14.3
RIVERSIDE	**408**	**74 155**	**197 576***	**29.8**	**100.0**
017 AMER BAPT ASSN	1	90	90	-	-
019 AMER BAPT USA.	16	2 886	3 494*	0.5	1.8
029 AMER LUTH CH..	5	1 636	2 138	0.3	1.1
053 ASSEM OF GOD.	35	3 912	6 258	0.9	3.2
057 BAPT GEN CONF.	8	1 620	1 961*	0.3	1.0
075 BRETHREN IN CR	2	152	170	-	0.1
081 CATHOLIC......	34	NA	87 237	13.1	44.2
089 CHR & MISS AL.	1	31	46	-	-
093 CHR CH (DISC).	5	1 336	2 251	0.3	1.1
097 CHR CHS&CHS CR	8	1 560	1 888*	0.3	1.0
101 C.M.E.........	1	660	799*	0.1	0.4
105 CHRISTIAN REF.	1	73	124	-	0.1
123 CH GOD (ANDER)	4	375	1 125	0.2	0.6
127 CH GOD (CLEVE)	7	288	349*	0.1	0.2
149 CH OF JC (BIC)	1	17	19	-	-
151 L-D SAINTS....	33	NA	13 977	2.1	7.1
165 CH OF NAZARENE	18	1 662	2 961	0.4	1.5
167 CHS OF CHRIST.	32	2 000	2 545	0.4	1.3
179 CONSRV BAPT...	9	1 317	1 594*	0.2	0.8
181 CONSRV CONGR..	1	80	97*	-	-
193 EPISCOPAL.....	6	1 525	1 706	0.3	0.9
203 EVAN FREE CH..	3	259	314*	-	0.2
215 EVAN METH CH..	1	43	52*	-	-
221 FREE METHODIST	2	149	483	0.1	0.2
226 FRIENDS--USA..	1	19	23*	-	-
239 SWEDENBORGIAN.	1	60	73*	-	-
244 GRACE BRETHREN	3	203	246*	-	0.1
263 INT FOURSQ GOS	19	2 626	3 179*	0.5	1.6
270 CONSRV JUDAISM	2	729	883*	0.1	0.4
271 REFORM JUDAISM	2	1 868	2 261*	0.3	1.1
281 LUTH CH AMER..	6	2 195	3 128	0.5	1.6
283 LUTH--MO SYNOD	13	4 087	5 386	0.8	2.7
290 METRO COMM CHS	1	25	50	-	-
291 MISSIONARY CH.	4	240	253	-	0.1
293 MORAV CH-NORTH	1	64	111	-	0.1
329 OPEN BIBLE STD	2	850	1 025	0.2	0.5
349 PENT HOLINESS.	3	139	168*	-	0.1
353 CHR BRETHREN..	2	150	250	-	0.1
356 PRESB CH AMER.	1	29	29	-	-
371 REF CH IN AM..	5	1 199	2 309	0.3	1.2
403 SALVATION ARMY	1	139	525	0.1	0.3
413 S.D.A.........	22	9 557	11 569*	1.7	5.9
415 S-D BAPTIST GC	1	248	300*	-	0.2
419 SO BAPT CONV..	41	12 857	15 564*	2.3	7.9
435 UNITARIAN-UNIV	3	80	97*	-	-
443 UN C OF CHRIST	8	2 553	3 091*	0.5	1.6
449 UN METHODIST..	21	7 405	8 964*	1.4	4.5
453 UN PRES CH USA	10	5 047	6 110*	0.9	3.1
469 WELS.........	1	115	304	-	0.2
SACRAMENTO	**365**	**83 223**	**240 733***	**30.7**	**100.0**
005 AME ZION......	1	520	720	0.1	0.3
017 AMER BAPT ASSN	8	664	664	0.1	0.3
019 AMER BAPT USA.	16	4 644	5 572*	0.7	2.3
029 AMER LUTH CH..	12	4 598	5 996	0.8	2.5
053 ASSEM OF GOD.	25	5 479	9 946	1.3	4.1
057 BAPT GEN CONF.	2	137	164*	-	0.1
081 CATHOLIC......	35	NA	111 038	14.2	46.1
089 CHR & MISS AL.	1	120	212	-	0.1
093 CHR CH (DISC).	6	1 053	1 341	0.2	0.6
097 CHR CHS&CHS CR	4	600	720*	0.1	0.3
105 CHRISTIAN REF.	1	101	191	-	0.1
123 CH GOD (ANDER)	5	661	1 983	0.3	0.8
127 CH GOD (CLEVE)	4	368	442*	0.1	0.1
133 CH GOD(7TH)DEN	1	110	132*	-	0.1
151 L-D SAINTS....	38	NA	20 597	2.6	8.6
157 CH OF BRETHREN	1	176	211*	-	0.1
165 CH OF NAZARENE	12	2 144	3 762	0.5	1.6
167 CHS OF CHRIST.	21	2 400	3 055	0.4	1.3
179 CONSRV BAPT...	3	1 900	2.280*	0.3	0.9
193 EPISCOPAL.....	12	4 675	5 643	0.7	2.3
201 EVAN COV CH AM	4	769	923*	0.1	0.4
203 EVAN FREE CH..	3	414	497*	0.1	0.2
215 EVAN METH CH..	1	56	67*	-	-
221 FREE METHODIST	2	180	738	0.1	0.3
226 FRIENDS--USA..	3	359	431*	0.1	0.2
237 GC MENN BR CHS	1	42	50*	-	-
244 GRACE BRETHREN	1	110	132*	-	0.1
263 INT FOURSQ GOS	1	177	212*	-	0.1
270 CONSRV JUDAISM	1	313	376*	-	0.2
271 REFORM JUDAISM	1	854	1 025*	0.1	0.4
281 LUTH CH AMER..	8	3 232	4 173	0.5	1.7
283 LUTH--MO SYNOD	12	4 140	5 670	0.7	2.4
290 METRO COMM CHS	1	110	220	-	0.1
291 MISSIONARY CH.	2	21	95	-	-
313 N AM BAPT CONF	2	783	939*	0.1	0.4
329 OPEN BIBLE STD	2	300	375	-	0.2
353 CHR BRETHREN..	2	50	125	-	0.1
371 REF CH IN AM..	4	911	1 802	0.2	0.7
403 SALVATION ARMY	1	263	297	-	0.1
413 S.D.A.........	13	3 743	4 491*	0.6	1.9
419 SO BAPT CONV..	41	16 428	19 711*	2.5	8.2
435 UNITARIAN-UNIV	1	578	693*	0.1	0.3
443 UN C OF CHRIST	6	1 578	1 893*	0.2	0.8
449 UN METHODIST..	27	8 016	9 618*	1.2	4.0
453 UN PRES CH USA	15	8 857	10 627*	1.4	4.4
469 WELS.........	2	589	884	0.1	0.4
SAN BENITO	**16**	**1 349**	**6 783***	**27.1**	**100.0**
053 ASSEM OF GOD.	4	319	520	2.1	7.7
081 CATHOLIC......	3	NA	4 372	17.5	64.5
127 CH GOD (CLEVE)	1	41	51*	0.2	0.8
151 L-D SAINTS....	1	NA	532	2.1	7.8
167 CHS OF CHRIST.	1	45	60	0.2	0.9
193 EPISCOPAL.....	1	125	230	0.9	3.4
353 CHR BRETHREN..	1	25	25	0.1	0.4
413 S.D.A.........	1	132	165*	0.7	2.4
419 SO BAPT CONV..	1	155	194*	0.8	2.9
449 UN METHODIST..	1	267	334*	1.3	4.9
453 UN PRES CH USA	1	240	300*	1.2	4.4
SAN BERNARDINO	**554**	**97 682**	**300 820***	**33.7**	**100.0**
017 AMER BAPT ASSN	7	581	581	0.1	0.2
019 AMER BAPT USA.	26	5 655	6 964*	0.8	2.3
029 AMER LUTH CH..	8	3 076	4 242	0.5	1.4
053 ASSEM OF GOD.	49	5 064	8 644	1.0	2.9
057 BAPT GEN CONF.	5	2 051	2 526*	0.3	0.8
059 BAPT MISS ASSN	2	107	132*	-	-
075 BRETHREN IN CR	6	456	510	0.1	0.2
081 CATHOLIC......	55	NA	148 335	16.6	49.3
089 CHR & MISS AL.	4	380	634	0.1	0.2
093 CHR CH (DISC).	9	1 674	2 452	0.3	0.8
097 CHR CHS&CHS CR	14	1 981	2 440*	0.3	0.8
101 C.M.E.........	4	838	1 032*	0.1	0.3
105 CHRISTIAN REF.	5	1 759	3 148	0.4	1.0
123 CH GOD (ANDER)	9	756	2 268	0.3	0.8
127 CH GOD (CLEVE)	10	456	562*	0.1	0.2
133 CH GOD(7TH)DEN	1	49	60*	-	-
151 L-D SAINTS....	39	NA	20 641	2.3	6.9
165 CH OF NAZARENE	22	3 565	6 153	0.7	2.0
167 CHS OF CHRIST.	36	3 100	3 950	0.4	1.3
179 CONSRV BAPT...	13	2 578	3 175*	0.4	1.1
185 CUMBER PRESB..	1	70	92	-	-
201 EVAN COV CH AM	1	57	70*	-	-
203 EVAN FREE CH..	3	429	528*	0.1	0.2
217 FIRE BAPTIZED.	1	10	12*	-	-
221 FREE METHODIST	10	730	2 982	0.3	1.0
226 FRIENDS--USA..	1	10	12*	-	-
244 GRACE BRETHREN	5	438	539*	0.1	0.2
263 INT FOURSQ GOS	23	2 606	3 209*	0.4	1.1
270 CONSRV JUDAISM	1	50	62*	-	-
271 REFORM JUDAISM	2	954	1 175*	0.1	0.4
281 LUTH CH AMER..	7	1 601	2 328	0.3	0.8
283 LUTH--MO SYNOD	21	4 433	6 073	0.7	2.0
285 MENNONITE CH..	1	84	103*	-	-
287 MENN GEN CONF.	1	187	198	-	0.1
290 METRO COMM CHS	1	40	80	-	-
291 MISSIONARY CH.	2	0	133	-	-
329 OPEN BIBLE STD	3	152	235	-	0.1
349 PENT HOLINESS.	1	63	78*	-	-
353 CHR BRETHREN..	1	120	130	-	-
356 PRESB CH AMER.	1	?	?	?	?
369 PROT REF CHS..	1	91	148	-	-
371 REF CH IN AM..	2	881	1 562	0.2	0.5
381 REF PRES-EVAN.	1	12	13	-	-
403 SALVATION ARMY	3	302	741	0.1	0.2
413 S.D.A.........	28	13 896	17 113*	1.9	5.7
419 SO BAPT CONV..	45	19 436	23 936*	2.7	8.0
435 UNITARIAN-UNIV	3	204	251*	-	0.1
443 UN C OF CHRIST	15	2 658	3 273*	0.4	1.1
449 UN METHODIST..	26	8 813	10 854*	1.2	3.6
453 UN PRES CH USA	17	5 101	6 282*	0.7	2.1
469 WELS.........	2	128	159	-	0.1
SAN DIEGO	**752**	**167 476**	**555 224***	**29.8**	**100.0**
001 ADVENT CHR CH.	1	150	179*	-	-
005 AME ZION......	3	1 098	1 598	0.1	0.3
017 AMER BAPT ASSN	4	352	352	-	0.1
019 AMER BAPT USA.	25	5 966	7 112*	0.4	1.3
029 AMER LUTH CH..	21	8 278	11 025	0.6	2.0
039 AP CHR CH(NAZ)	1	47	56*	-	-
053 ASSEM OF GOD.	44	6 636	10 920	0.6	2.0
057 BAPT GEN CONF.	12	5 846	6 969*	0.4	1.3

NA—Not applicable   *Total adherents estimated from known number of communicant, confirmed, full members.   —Represents a percent less than 0.1.   Percentages may not total due to rounding.

Table 4. Churches and Church Membership by County and Denomination: 1980

County and Denomination	Number of churches	Communicant, confirmed, full members	Total adherents Number	Total adherents Percent of total population	Total adherents Percent of total adherents
081 CATHOLIC......	92	NA	308 464	16.6	55.6
089 CHR & MISS AL.	10	902	1 530	0.1	0.3
093 CHR CH (DISC).	13	3 412	4 703	0.3	0.8
097 CHR CHS&CHS CR	11	1 993	2 376*	0.1	0.4
101 C.M.E........	3	817	974*	0.1	0.2
105 CHRISTIAN REF.	4	661	1 101	0.1	0.2
123 CH GOD (ANDER)	7	855	2 565	0.1	0.5
127 CH GOD (CLEVE)	6	320	381*	–	0.1
133 CH GOD(7TH)DEN	1	11	13*	–	–
149 CH OF JC (BIC)	1	58	74	–	–
151 L-D SAINTS....	76	NA	31 872	1.7	5.7
157 CH OF BRETHREN	2	214	255*	–	–
165 CH OF NAZARENE	16	2 936	4 581	0.2	0.8
167 CHS OF CHRIST.	40	5 000	6 365	0.3	1.1
175 CONGR CHR CHS.	3	447	533*	–	0.1
179 CONSRV BAPT...	11	2 372	2 828*	0.2	0.5
181 CONSRV CONGR..	3	1 542	1 838*	0.1	0.3
193 EPISCOPAL.....	32	14 970	18 381	1.0	3.3
201 EVAN COV CH AM	4	772	920*	–	0.2
203 EVAN FREE CH..	6	216	257*	–	–
215 EVAN METH CH..	1	65	77*	–	–
221 FREE METHODIST	5	305	774	–	0.1
226 FRIENDS-USA...	6	341	407*	–	0.1
233 GEN CH NEW JER	1	25	30*	–	–
239 SWEDENBORGIAN.	1	60	72*	–	–
244 GRACE BRETHREN	2	164	196*	–	–
263 INT FOURSQ GOS	10	1 331	1 587*	0.1	0.3
270 CONSRV JUDAISM	5	815	972*	0.1	0.2
271 REFORM JUDAISM	3	2 930	3 493*	0.2	0.6
274 LAT EVAN LUTH.	1	46	47	–	–
281 LUTH CH AMER..	14	4 318	5 869	0.3	1.1
283 LUTH--MO SYNOD	31	10 175	13 486	0.7	2.4
290 METRO COMM CHS	3	375	750	–	0.1
291 MISSIONARY CH.	2	56	70	–	–
329 OPEN BIBLE STD	1	40	65	–	–
335 ORTH PRESB CH.	4	331	395*	–	0.1
349 PENT HOLINESS.	4	130	155*	–	–
353 CHR BRETHREN..	5	500	650	–	0.1
371 REF CH IN AM..	2	304	531	–	0.1
383 REF PRES OF NA	1	16	26	–	–
403 SALVATION ARMY	4	592	3 375	0.2	0.6
413 S.D.A.........	26	7 796	9 294*	0.5	1.7
419 SO BAPT CONV..	58	23 833	28 411*	1.5	5.1
435 UNITARIAN-UNIV	5	968	1 154*	0.1	0.2
443 UN C OF CHRIST	25	6 256	7 458*	0.4	1.3
449 UN METHODIST..	42	20 012	23 856*	1.3	4.3
453 UN PRES CH USA	31	18 971	22 615*	1.2	4.1
469 WELS..........	7	850	1 187	0.1	0.2
SAN FRANCISCO	254	49 626	208 142*	30.7	100.0
005 AME ZION......	1	570	770	0.1	0.4
019 AMER BAPT USA.	14	5 014	5 648*	0.8	2.7
029 AMER LUTH CH..	5	771	1 114	0.2	0.5
053 ASSEMB OF GOD.	14	2 154	2 544	0.4	1.2
075 BRETHREN IN CR	2	152	170	–	0.1
081 CATHOLIC......	60	NA	144 182	21.2	69.3
083 CHRIST CATH CH	1	16	32	–	–
089 CHR & MISS AL.	3	219	265	–	0.1
093 CHR CH (DISC).	2	341	404	0.1	0.2
097 CHR CHS&CHS CR	2	230	259*	–	0.1
101 C.M.E........	2	2 217	2 497*	0.4	1.2
105 CHRISTIAN REF.	2	136	191	–	0.1
127 CH GOD (CLEVE)	3	113	127*	–	0.1
151 L-D SAINTS....	4	NA	2 854	0.4	1.4
157 CH OF BRETHREN	1	50	56*	–	–
164 CH LUTH CONF..	2	145	187	–	0.1
165 CH OF NAZARENE	3	171	183	–	0.1
167 CHS OF CHRIST.	6	763	1 276	0.2	0.6
185 CUMBER PRESB..	1	700	900	0.1	0.4
193 EPISCOPAL.....	19	6 130	8 132	1.2	3.9
195 ESTONIAN ELC..	1	150	298	–	0.1
201 EVAN COV CH AM	3	482	543*	0.1	0.3
203 EVAN FREE CH..	1	57	64*	–	–
208 EVAN LUTH ASSN	1	230	262	–	0.1
221 FREE METHODIST	1	57	159	–	0.1
226 FRIENDS-USA...	1	80	90*	–	–
233 GEN CH NEW JER	1	20	23*	–	–
239 SWEDENBORGIAN.	1	100	113*	–	0.1
270 CONSRV JUDAISM	4	1 276	1 437*	0.2	0.7
271 REFORM JUDAISM	5	6 736	7 588*	1.1	3.6
274 LAT EVAN LUTH.	1	393	443	0.1	0.2
281 LUTH CH AMER..	4	913	1 325	0.2	0.6
283 LUTH--MO SYNOD	8	2 239	2 903	0.4	1.4
285 MENNONITE CH..	1	9	10*	–	–
290 METRO COMM CHS	1	500	1 000	0.1	0.5
329 OPEN BIBLE STD	2	175	350	0.1	0.2
335 ORTH PRESB CH.	1	44	50*	–	–
353 CHR BRETHREN..	1	60	100	–	–
371 REF CH IN AM..	1	100	141	–	0.1
403 SALVATION ARMY	4	712	2 103	0.3	1.0
413 S.D.A.........	7	1 353	1 524*	0.2	0.7
419 SO BAPT CONV..	15	2 564	2 888*	0.4	1.4
435 UNITARIAN-UNIV	1	789	889*	0.1	0.4
443 UN C OF CHRIST	6	1 155	1 301*	0.2	0.6
449 UN METHODIST..	17	4 803	5 411*	0.8	2.6
453 UN PRES CH USA	18	4 737	5 336*	0.8	2.6
SAN JOAQUIN	225	43 066	138 317*	39.8	100.0
005 AME ZION......	1	95	110	–	0.1
017 AMER BAPT ASSN	7	806	806	0.2	0.6
019 AMER BAPT USA.	6	1 427	1 740*	0.5	1.3
029 AMER LUTH CH..	3	1 663	2 133	0.6	1.5
053 ASSEMB OF GOD.	18	3 043	5 057	1.5	3.7

County and Denomination	Number of churches	Communicant, confirmed, full members	Total adherents Number	Total adherents Percent of total population	Total adherents Percent of total adherents
057 BAPT GEN CONF.	1	310	378*	0.1	0.3
059 BAPT MISS ASSN	1	79	96*	–	0.1
071 BRETHREN (ASH)	3	256	312*	0.1	0.2
081 CATHOLIC......	18	NA	75 545	21.7	54.6
089 CHR & MISS AL.	1	151	201	0.1	0.1
093 CHR CH (DISC).	5	558	847	0.2	0.6
097 CHR CHS&CHS CR	3	228	278*	0.1	0.2
101 C.M.E........	1	362	441*	0.1	0.3
105 CHRISTIAN REF.	3	959	1 490	0.4	1.1
123 CH GOD (ANDER)	4	242	726	0.2	0.5
127 CH GOD (CLEVE)	5	206	251*	0.1	0.2
133 CH GOD(7TH)DEN	2	105	128*	–	0.1
151 L-D SAINTS....	12	NA	5 876	1.7	4.2
165 CH OF NAZARENE	8	811	1 818	0.5	1.3
167 CHS OF CHRIST.	20	2 100	2 675	0.8	1.9
179 CONSRV BAPT...	3	950	1 158*	0.3	0.8
193 EPISCOPAL.....	4	1 748	2 307	0.7	1.7
201 EVAN COV CH AM	4	489	596*	0.2	0.4
215 EVAN METH CH..	1	109	133*	–	0.1
221 FREE METHODIST	2	85	354	0.1	0.3
226 FRIENDS-USA...	1	53	65*	–	–
237 GC MENN BR CHS	1	215	262*	0.1	0.2
244 GRACE BRETHREN	2	267	326*	0.1	0.2
263 INT FOURSQ GOS	4	602	734*	0.2	0.5
271 REFORM JUDAISM	1	612	746*	0.2	0.5
281 LUTH CH AMER..	4	745	1 005	0.3	0.7
283 LUTH--MO SYNOD	6	2 394	3 212	0.9	2.3
290 METRO COMM CHS	1	30	60	–	–
291 MISSIONARY CH.	1	45	46	–	–
313 N AM BAPT CONF	3	2 501	3 050*	0.9	2.2
329 OPEN BIBLE STD	2	625	750	0.2	0.5
371 REF CH IN AM..	1	536	958	0.3	0.7
403 SALVATION ARMY	1	106	267	0.1	0.2
413 S.D.A.........	10	3 048	3 717*	1.1	2.7
419 SO BAPT CONV..	21	5 253	6 405*	1.8	4.6
435 UNITARIAN-UNIV	1	219	267*	0.1	0.2
443 UN C OF CHRIST	4	1 496	1 824*	0.5	1.3
449 UN METHODIST..	14	5 198	6 338*	1.8	4.6
453 UN PRES CH USA	8	2 137	2 606*	0.8	1.9
469 WELS..........	1	202	223	0.1	0.2
SAN LUIS OBISPO	117	15 896	44 225*	28.5	100.0
019 AMER BAPT USA.	2	426	495*	0.3	1.1
029 AMER LUTH CH..	1	559	715	0.5	1.6
053 ASSEMB OF GOD.	12	1 055	1 819	1.2	4.1
057 BAPT GEN CONF.	4	552	642*	0.4	1.5
081 CATHOLIC......	12	NA	20 516	13.2	46.4
093 CHR CH (DISC).	3	228	302	0.2	0.7
097 CHR CHS&CHS CR	3	340	395*	0.3	0.9
123 CH GOD (ANDER)	2	52	156	0.1	0.4
127 CH GOD (CLEVE)	1	73	85*	0.1	0.2
151 L-D SAINTS....	6	NA	3 117	2.0	7.0
165 CH OF NAZARENE	5	737	1 680	1.1	3.8
167 CHS OF CHRIST.	10	650	830	0.5	1.9
193 EPISCOPAL.....	6	1 211	1 522	1.0	3.4
203 EVAN FREE CH..	1	86	100*	0.1	0.2
226 FRIENDS-USA...	1	13	15*	–	–
263 INT FOURSQ GOS	3	250	291*	0.2	0.7
271 REFORM JUDAISM	1	162	188*	0.1	0.4
281 LUTH CH AMER..	3	366	419	0.3	0.9
283 LUTH--MO SYNOD	4	1 251	1 548	1.0	3.5
287 MENN GEN. CONF.	1	158	189	0.1	0.4
290 METRO COMM CHS	1	20	40	–	0.1
291 MISSIONARY CH.	1	?	?	?	?
353 CHR BRETHREN..	1	90	300	0.2	0.7
403 SALVATION ARMY	1	27	34	–	0.1
413 S.D.A.........	5	899	1 046*	0.7	2.4
419 SO BAPT CONV..	8	2 093	2 434*	1.6	5.5
435 UNITARIAN-UNIV	1	88	102*	0.1	0.2
443 UN C OF CHRIST	3	725	843*	0.5	1.9
449 UN METHODIST..	8	1 858	2 161*	1.4	4.9
453 UN PRES CH USA	7	1 927	2 241*	1.4	5.1
SAN MATEO	226	42 641	194 241*	33.0	100.0
001 ADVENT CHR CH.	1	80	94*	–	–
005 AME ZION......	5	673	1 158	0.2	0.6
019 AMER BAPT USA.	15	4 129	4 835*	0.8	2.5
029 AMER LUTH CH..	7	1 963	2 520	0.4	1.3
053 ASSEMB OF GOD.	13	1 337	1 733	0.3	0.9
057 BAPT GEN CONF.	2	118	138*	–	0.1
081 CATHOLIC......	39	NA	133 320	22.7	68.6
093 CHR CH (DISC).	1	185	230	–	0.1
097 CHR CHS&CHS CR	4	590	691*	0.1	0.4
101 C.M.E........	2	267	313*	0.1	0.2
123 CH GOD (ANDER)	6	536	1 608	0.3	0.8
127 CH GOD (CLEVE)	2	57	67*	–	–
151 L-D SAINTS....	13	NA	7 026	1.2	3.6
165 CH OF NAZARENE	4	264	657	0.1	0.3
167 CHS OF CHRIST.	6	755	940	0.2	0.5
179 CONSRV BAPT...	3	450	527*	0.1	0.3
193 EPISCOPAL.....	15	6 309	8 322	1.4	4.3
201 EVAN COV CH AM	2	687	804*	0.1	0.4
203 EVAN FREE CH..	1	62	73*	–	–
221 FREE METHODIST	3	104	330	0.1	0.2
263 INT FOURSQ GOS	2	239	280*	–	0.1
270 CONSRV JUDAISM	2	453	530*	0.1	0.3
271 REFORM JUDAISM	1	1 120	1 311*	0.2	0.7
281 LUTH CH AMER..	4	1 159	1 595	0.3	0.8
283 LUTH--MO SYNOD	9	2 851	3 574	0.6	1.8
290 METRO COMM CHS	1	30	60	–	–
291 MISSIONARY CH.	2	51	96	–	–
329 OPEN BIBLE STD	1	100	175	–	0.1
335 ORTH PRESB CH.	1	52	61*	–	–

NA—Not applicable   *Total adherents estimated from known number of communicant, confirmed, full members.   —Represents a percent less than 0.1.   Percentages may not total due to rounding.

49

Table 4. Churches and Church Membership by County and Denomination: 1980

County and Denomination	Number of churches	Communicant, confirmed, full members	Total adherents Number	Total adherents Percent of total population	Total adherents Percent of total adherents
353 CHR BRETHREN..	1	45	60	—	—
403 SALVATION ARMY	1	65	116*	—	0.1
413 S.D.A.........	5	579	678*	0.1	0.3
419 SO BAPT CONV..	13	2 634	3 084*	0.5	1.6
435 UNITARIAN-UNIV	2	329	385*	0.1	0.2
443 UN C OF CHRIST	11	2 650	3 103*	0.5	1.6
449 UN METHODIST..	14	4 438	5 197*	0.9	2.7
453 UN PRES CH USA	11	7 183	8 411*	1.4	4.3
469 WELS..........	1	97	139	—	0.1
SANTA BARBARA	147	27 915	104 107*	34.9	100.0
017 AMER BAPT ASSN	1	100	100	—	0.1
019 AMER BAPT USA.	7	841	990*	0.3	1.0
029 AMER LUTH CH..	3	1 246	1 791	0.6	1.7
053 ASSEMB OF GOD.	9	923	1 595	0.5	1.5
057 BAPT GEN CONF.	3	1 975	2 325*	0.8	2.2
081 CATHOLIC......	15	NA	64 414	21.6	61.9
089 CHR & MISS AL.	1	44	104	—	0.1
093 CHR CH (DISC).	3	1 573	1 917	0.6	1.8
097 CHR CHS&CHS CR	1	120	141*	—	0.1
101 C.M.E.........	1	110	129*	—	0.1
123 CH GOD (ANDER)	1	79	237	0.1	0.2
127 CH GOD (CLEVE)	2	140	165*	0.1	0.2
151 L-D SAINTS....	13	NA	4 932	1.7	4.7
165 CH OF NAZARENE	6	376	710	0.2	0.7
167 CHS OF CHRIST.	10	810	1 030	0.3	1.0
179 CONSRV BAPT...	2	728	857*	0.3	0.8
181 CONSRV CONGR..	1	78	92*	—	0.1
201 EVAN COV CH AM	1	114	134*	—	0.1
203 EVAN FREE CH..	2	45	53*	—	0.1
221 FREE METHODIST	1	68	240	0.1	0.2
226 FRIENDS-USA...	1	49	58*	—	0.1
244 GRACE BRETHREN	2	67	79*	—	0.1
263 INT FOURSQ GOS	4	728	857*	0.3	0.8
271 REFORM JUDAISM	2	600	706*	0.2	0.7
281 LUTH CH AMER..	4	1 496	1 781	0.6	1.7
283 LUTH--MO SYNOD	7	2 057	2 613	0.9	2.5
290 METRO COMM CHS	1	45	90	—	0.1
291 MISSIONARY CH.	1	71	48	—	—
335 ORTH PRESB CH.	1	162	191*	0.1	0.2
403 SALVATION ARMY	2	118	212	0.1	0.2
413 S.D.A.........	4	784	923*	0.3	0.9
419 SO BAPT CONV..	10	3 585	4 220*	1.4	4.1
435 UNITARIAN-UNIV	1	512	603*	0.2	0.6
443 UN C OF CHRIST	3	556	655*	0.2	0.6
449 UN METHODIST..	8	3 011	3 544*	1.2	3.4
453 UN PRES CH USA	11	4 572	5 382*	1.8	5.2
469 WELS..........	2	132	189	0.1	0.2
SANTA CLARA	447	106 223	364 192*	28.1	100.0
005 AME ZION......	1	234	309	—	0.1
017 AMER BAPT ASSN	5	670	670	0.1	0.2
019 AMER BAPT USA.	13	3 188	3 836*	0.3	1.1
029 AMER LUTH CH..	13	6 243	8 726	0.7	2.4
053 ASSEMB OF GOD.	39	8 181	12 719	1.0	3.5
057 BAPT GEN CONF.	7	941	1 132*	0.1	0.3
059 BAPT MISS ASSN	1	44	53*	—	0.1
081 CATHOLIC......	53	NA	202 958	15.7	55.7
089 CHR & MISS AL.	4	314	518	—	0.1
093 CHR CH (DISC).	4	626	955	0.1	0.3
097 CHR CHS&CHS CR	10	1 661	1 999*	0.2	0.5
101 C.M.E.........	1	297	357*	—	0.1
105 CHRISTIAN REF.	2	328	513	—	0.1
121 CH GOD (ABR)..	1	35	42*	—	—
123 CH GOD (ANDER)	3	309	927	0.1	0.3
127 CH GOD (CLEVE)	7	296	356*	—	0.1
133 CH GOD(7TH)DEN	1	20	24*	—	—
151 L-D SAINTS....	49	NA	24 926	1.9	6.8
165 CH OF NAZARENE	13	1 471	1 940	0.1	0.5
167 CHS OF CHRIST.	17	2 425	3 080	0.2	0.8
175 CONGR CHR CHS.	1	156	188*	—	0.1
179 CONSRV BAPT...	7	6 700	8 062*	0.6	2.2
193 EPISCOPAL.....	19	9 274	11 664	0.9	3.2
201 EVAN COV CH AM	3	678	816*	0.1	0.2
203 EVAN FREE CH..	2	373	449*	—	0.1
221 FREE METHODIST	1	94	276	—	0.1
226 FRIENDS-USA...	2	185	223*	—	0.1
237 GC MENN BR CHS	3	665	800*	0.1	0.2
244 GRACE BRETHREN	1	63	76*	—	—
263 INT FOURSQ GOS	3	936	1 126*	0.1	0.3
270 CONSRV JUDAISM	3	610	734*	0.1	0.2
271 REFORM JUDAISM	2	1 424	1 713*	0.1	0.5
281 LUTH CH AMER..	12	3 844	5 447	0.4	1.5
283 LUTH--MO SYNOD	13	5 463	7 282	0.6	2.0
290 METRO COMM CHS	1	100	200	—	0.1
291 MISSIONARY CH.	1	57	45	—	—
313 N AM BAPT CONF	1	204	245*	—	0.1
329 OPEN BIBLE STD	1	200	250	—	0.1
335 ORTH PRESB CH.	2	153	184*	—	0.1
349 PENT HOLINESS.	2	47	57*	—	—
353 CHR BRETHREN..	1	150	150	—	—
371 REF CH IN AM..	1	177	328	—	0.1
381 REF PRES-EVAN.	1	10	17	—	—
403 SALVATION ARMY	2	299	974	0.1	0.3
413 S.D.A.........	16	4 851	5 837*	0.5	1.6
419 SO BAPT CONV..	28	12 933	15 561*	1.2	4.3
435 UNITARIAN-UNIV	4	761	916*	0.1	0.3
443 UN C OF CHRIST	11	4 293	5 165*	0.4	1.4
449 UN METHODIST..	31	13 859	16 676*	1.3	4.6
453 UN PRES CH USA	25	9 734	11 712*	0.9	3.2
469 WELS..........	3	647	979	0.1	0.3
SANTA CRUZ	108	19 042	49 824*	26.5	100.0

County and Denomination	Number of churches	Communicant, confirmed, full members	Total adherents Number	Total adherents Percent of total population	Total adherents Percent of total adherents
001 ADVENT CHR CH.	1	120	142*	0.1	0.3
017 AMER BAPT ASSN	4	490	490	0.3	1.0
019 AMER BAPT USA.	2	247	292*	0.2	0.6
029 AMER LUTH CH..	1	207	233	0.1	0.5
053 ASSEMB OF GOD.	14	1 755	2 632	1.4	5.3
081 CATHOLIC......	12	NA	23 176	12.3	46.5
089 CHR & MISS AL.	1	69	89	—	0.2
093 CHR CH (DISC).	2	535	535	0.3	1.1
097 CHR CHS&CHS CR	2	300	355*	0.2	0.7
127 CH GOD (CLEVE)	2	46	54*	—	0.1
151 L-D SAINTS....	6	NA	2 206	1.2	4.4
165 CH OF NAZARENE	2	395	460	0.2	0.9
167 CHS OF CHRIST.	4	236	351	0.2	0.7
175 CONGR CHR CHS.	1	546	645*	0.3	1.3
179 CONSRV BAPT...	3	3 900	4 609*	2.4	9.3
193 EPISCOPAL.....	4	1 318	1 924	1.0	3.9
201 EVAN COV CH AM	1	154	182*	0.1	0.4
203 EVAN FREE CH..	1	369	436*	0.2	0.9
221 FREE METHODIST	3	154	768	0.4	1.5
226 FRIENDS-USA...	1	43	51*	—	0.1
237 GC MENN BR CHS	1	100	118*	0.1	0.2
263 INT FOURSQ GOS	2	306	362*	0.2	0.7
271 REFORM JUDAISM	1	420	496*	0.3	1.0
281 LUTH CH AMER..	3	805	1 147	0.6	2.3
283 LUTH--MO SYNOD	3	728	1 009	0.5	2.0
290 METRO COMM CHS	0	20	40	—	0.1
335 ORTH PRESB CH.	1	47	56*	—	0.1
349 PENT HOLINESS.	1	42	50*	—	0.1
403 SALVATION ARMY	2	103	313	0.2	0.6
413 S.D.A.........	4	1 135	1 341*	0.7	2.7
419 SO BAPT CONV..	7	1 180	1 395*	0.7	2.8
435 UNITARIAN-UNIV	1	110	130*	0.1	0.3
443 UN C OF CHRIST	1	62	73*	—	0.1
449 UN METHODIST..	7	1 437	1 698*	0.9	3.4
453 UN PRES CH USA	7	1 663	1 966*	1.0	3.9
SHASTA	84	10 386	28 118*	24.3	100.0
017 AMER BAPT ASSN	1	37	37	—	0.1
019 AMER BAPT USA.	2	380	461*	0.4	1.6
053 ASSEMB OF GOD.	9	1 164	2 282	2.0	8.1
081 CATHOLIC......	10	NA	9 685	8.4	34.4
089 CHR & MISS AL.	1	50	210	0.2	0.7
093 CHR CH (DISC).	1	28	32	—	0.1
097 CHR CHS&CHS CR	1	130	158*	0.1	0.6
101 C.M.E.........	1	35	42*	—	0.1
123 CH GOD (ANDER)	1	55	165	0.1	0.6
133 CH GOD(7TH)DEN	1	5	6*	—	—
151 L-D SAINTS....	10	NA	3 997	3.5	14.2
165 CH OF NAZARENE	4	452	808	0.7	2.9
167 CHS OF CHRIST.	6	508	659	0.6	2.3
179 CONSRV BAPT...	1	150	182*	0.2	0.6
193 EPISCOPAL.....	2	568	798	0.7	2.8
203 EVAN FREE CH..	1	31	38*	—	0.1
263 INT FOURSQ GOS	4	213	259*	0.2	0.9
281 LUTH CH AMER..	1	380	496	0.4	1.8
283 LUTH--MO SYNOD	2	403	643	0.6	2.3
290 METRO COMM CHS	0	25	50	—	0.2
329 OPEN BIBLE STD	1	25	75	0.1	0.3
403 SALVATION ARMY	1	45	95	0.1	0.3
413 S.D.A.........	4	877	1 064*	0.9	3.8
419 SO BAPT CONV..	8	2 450	2 974*	2.6	10.6
435 UNITARIAN-UNIV	1	11	13*	—	—
443 UN C OF CHRIST	1	274	333*	0.3	1.2
449 UN METHODIST..	5	1 235	1 499*	1.3	5.3
453 UN PRES CH USA	2	521	632*	0.5	2.2
469 WELS..........	2	334	425	0.4	1.5
SIERRA	11	386	775*	25.2	100.0
019 AMER BAPT USA.	1	224	266*	8.7	34.3
053 ASSEMB OF GOD.	2	74	141	4.6	18.2
081 CATHOLIC......	5	NA	200	6.5	25.8
151 L-D SAINTS....	1	NA	64	2.1	8.3
449 UN METHODIST..	2	88	104	3.4	13.4
SISKIYOU	71	4 754	13 374*	33.7	100.0
019 AMER BAPT USA.	3	340	411*	1.0	3.1
029 AMER LUTH CH..	1	36	45	0.1	0.3
053 ASSEMB OF GOD.	8	471	874	2.2	6.5
057 BAPT GEN CONF.	1	24	29*	0.1	0.2
063 BEREAN FUND CH	3	183	221*	0.6	1.7
081 CATHOLIC......	14	NA	5 815	14.6	43.5
089 CHR & MISS AL.	1	20	35	0.1	0.3
097 CHR CHS&CHS CR	3	144	174*	0.4	1.3
151 L-D SAINTS....	4	NA	1 259	3.2	9.4
165 CH OF NAZARENE	3	116	303	0.8	2.3
167 CHS OF CHRIST.	4	125	159	0.4	1.2
179 CONSRV BAPT...	1	150	181*	0.5	1.4
193 EPISCOPAL.....	3	228	284	0.7	2.1
215 EVAN METH CH..	1	71	86*	0.2	0.6
281 LUTH CH AMER..	1	159	237	0.6	1.8
283 LUTH--MO SYNOD	1	162	206	0.5	1.5
413 S.D.A.........	2	188	227*	0.6	1.7
419 SO BAPT CONV..	7	1 060	1 283*	3.2	9.6
449 UN METHODIST..	3	925	1 119*	2.8	8.4
453 UN PRES CH USA	3	352	426*	1.1	3.2
SOLANO	121	22 766	69 976*	29.8	100.0
005 AME ZION......	1	350	475	0.2	0.7
017 AMER BAPT ASSN	3	252	252	0.1	0.4
019 AMER BAPT USA.	9	3 425	4 228*	1.8	6.0
029 AMER LUTH CH..	2	684	945	0.4	1.4

NA—Not applicable   *Total adherents estimated from known number of communicant, confirmed, full members.   —Represents a percent less than 0.1.   Percentages may not total due to rounding.

50

Table 4. Churches and Church Membership by County and Denomination: 1980

County and Denomination	Number of churches	Communicant, confirmed, full members	Total adherents		
			Number	Percent of total population	Percent of total adherents
053 ASSEMB OF GOD.	7	1 490	2 733	1.2	3.9
057 BAPT GEN CONF.	1	186	230*	0.1	0.3
059 BAPT MISS ASSN	1	27	33*	–	–
081 CATHOLIC......	10	NA	34 006	14.5	48.6
089 CHR & MISS AL.	1	59	119	0.1	0.2
093 CHR CH (DISC)	3	229	369	0.2	0.5
097 CHR CHS&CHS CR	2	91	112*	–	0.2
101 C.M.E.........	3	995	1 228*	0.5	1.8
105 CHRISTIAN REF.	1	2	5	–	–
127 CH GOD (CLEVE)	3	189	233*	0.1	0.3
151 L-D SAINTS....	13	NA	5 332	2.3	7.6
165 CH OF NAZARENE	5	472	881	0.4	1.3
167 CHS OF CHRIST.	9	1 040	1 325	0.6	1.9
179 CONSRV BAPT...	2	350	432*	0.2	0.6
193 EPISCOPAL.....	4	1 189	1 566	0.7	2.2
203 EVAN FREE CH..	2	29	36*	–	0.1
263 INT FOURSQ GOS	1	86	106*	–	0.2
281 LUTH CH AMER..	1	543	964	0.4	1.4
283 LUTH--MO SYNOD	5	854	1 687	0.7	2.4
329 OPEN BIBLE STD	1	100	150	0.1	0.2
403 SALVATION ARMY	1	43	85	–	0.1
413 S.D.A.........	3	557	688*	0.3	1.0
419 SO BAPT CONV..	14	5 718	7 058*	3.0	10.1
443 UN C OF CHRIST	3	385	475*	0.2	0.7
449 UN METHODIST..	6	1 746	2 155*	0.9	3.1
453 UN PRES CH USA	4	1 675	2 068*	0.9	3.0
SONOMA	172	24 824	86 762*	28.9	100.0
017 AMER BAPT ASSN	2	59	59	–	0.1
019 AMER BAPT USA.	1	496	593*	0.2	0.7
029 AMER LUTH CH..	3	1 071	1 767	0.6	2.0
039 AP CHR CH(NAZ)	1	32	38*	–	–
053 ASSEMB OF GOD.	13	1 886	2 944	1.0	3.4
057 BAPT GEN CONF.	1	337	403*	0.1	0.5
081 CATHOLIC......	21	NA	47 789	15.9	55.1
089 CHR & MISS AL.	5	576	858	0.3	1.0
093 CHR CH (DISC).	1	79	100	–	0.1
097 CHR CHS&CHS CR	6	1 280	1 531*	0.5	1.8
101 C.M.E.........	1	85	102*	–	0.1
123 CH GOD (ANDER)	1	34	102	–	0.1
127 CH GOD (CLEVE)	2	28	33*	–	–
151 L-D SAINTS....	15	NA	5 845	1.9	6.7
165 CH OF NAZARENE	3	422	813	0.3	0.9
167 CHS OF CHRIST.	14	816	1 156	0.4	1.3
175 CONGR CHR CHS.	3	135	161*	0.1	0.2
179 CONSRV BAPT...	1	350	419*	0.1	0.5
193 EPISCOPAL.....	8	1 721	2 529	0.8	2.9
203 EVAN FREE CH..	2	168	201*	0.1	0.2
221 FREE METHODIST	3	229	873	0.3	1.0
226 FRIENDS--USA...	1	41	49*	–	0.1
263 INT FOURSQ GOS	2	178	213*	0.1	0.2
270 CONSRV JUDAISM	1	99	118*	–	0.1
271 REFORM JUDAISM	1	120	143*	–	0.2
281 LUTH CH AMER..	1	294	445	0.1	0.5
283 LUTH--MO SYNOD	7	2 084	2 729	0.9	3.1
329 OPEN BIBLE STD	1	150	200	0.1	0.2
371 REF CH IN AM..	1	62	122	–	0.1
403 SALVATION ARMY	1	104	212	0.1	0.2
413 S.D.A.........	8	1 650	1 973*	0.7	2.3
419 SO BAPT CONV..	12	3 737	4 469*	1.5	5.2
435 UNITARIAN-UNIV	1	137	164*	0.1	0.2
443 UN C OF CHRIST	8	1 483	1 773*	0.6	2.0
449 UN METHODIST..	10	2 573	3 077*	1.0	3.5
453 UN PRES CH USA	9	2 260	2 703*	0.9	3.1
469 WELS..........	1	48	56	–	0.1
STANISLAUS	198	37 874	89 429*	33.6	100.0
005 AME ZION......	1	150	200	0.1	0.2
017 AMER BAPT ASSN	9	729	729	0.3	0.8
019 AMER BAPT USA.	7	4 216	5 170*	1.9	5.8
029 AMER LUTH CH..	2	485	620	0.2	0.7
053 ASSEMB OF GOD.	26	3 594	6 419	2.4	7.2
057 BAPT GEN CONF.	2	322	395*	0.1	0.4
059 BAPT MISS ASSN	1	111	136*	0.1	0.2
081 CATHOLIC......	13	NA	31 800	12.0	35.6
093 CHR CH (DISC).	4	731	1 185	0.4	1.3
097 CHR CHS&CHS CR	2	555	681*	0.3	0.8
101 C.M.E.........	1	137	168*	0.1	0.2
105 CHRISTIAN REF.	3	726	1 363	0.5	1.5
123 CH GOD (ANDER)	2	231	693	0.3	0.8
127 CH GOD (CLEVE)	4	313	384*	0.1	0.4
149 CH OF JC (BIC)	1	55	59	–	0.1
151 L-D SAINTS....	12	NA	5 484	2.1	6.1
157 CH OF BRETHREN	3	803	985*	0.4	1.1
165 CH OF NAZARENE	9	835	1 727	0.6	1.9
167 CHS OF CHRIST.	17	1 585	2 015	0.8	2.3
179 CONSRV BAPT....	3	400	491*	0.2	0.5
193 EPISCOPAL.....	5	1 223	2 155	0.8	2.4
201 EVAN COV CH AM	3	919	1 127*	0.4	1.3
203 EVAN FREE CH..	1	350	429*	0.2	0.5
226 FRIENDS--USA...	1	202	248*	0.1	0.3
244 GRACE BRETHREN	2	683	838*	0.3	0.9
263 INT FOURSQ GOS	2	347	426*	0.2	0.5
270 CONSRV JUDAISM	1	109	134*	0.1	0.1
281 LUTH CH AMER..	2	1 238	1 603	0.6	1.8
283 LUTH--MO SYNOD	5	1 476	2 239	0.8	2.5
291 MISSIONARY CH.	1	81	77	–	0.1
335 ORTH PRESB CH.	1	52	64*	–	0.1
353 CHR BRETHREN..	1	25	25	–	–
371 REF CH IN AM..	1	112	190	0.1	0.2
403 SALVATION ARMY	1	109	810	0.3	0.9
413 S.D.A.........	7	2 513	3 082*	1.2	3.4
419 SO BAPT CONV..	20	6 130	7 517*	2.8	8.4
435 UNITARIAN-UNIV	1	159	195*	0.1	0.2
443 UN C OF CHRIST	2	413	506*	0.2	0.6
449 UN METHODIST..	10	3 693	4 529*	1.7	5.1
453 UN PRES CH USA	8	2 017	2 473*	0.9	2.8
469 WELS..........	1	45	58	–	0.1
SUTTER	34	5 683	15 548*	29.8	100.0
053 ASSEMB OF GOD.	5	770	1 040	2.0	6.7
081 CATHOLIC......	1	NA	6 800	13.0	43.7
093 CHR CH (DISC).	1	75	90	0.2	0.6
097 CHR CHS&CHS CR	2	168	204*	0.4	1.3
123 CH GOD (ANDER)	1	134	402	0.8	2.6
151 L-D SAINTS....	4	NA	1 320	2.5	8.5
157 CH OF BRETHREN	2	249	303*	0.6	1.9
165 CH OF NAZARENE	3	270	444	0.8	2.9
167 CHS OF CHRIST.	3	308	399	0.8	2.6
203 EVAN FREE CH..	1	108	131*	0.3	0.8
283 LUTH--MO SYNOD	1	396	517	1.0	3.3
413 S.D.A.........	1	338	411*	0.8	2.6
419 SO BAPT CONV..	4	1 617	1 967*	3.8	12.7
449 UN METHODIST..	4	1 028	1 250*	2.4	8.0
453 UN PRES CH USA	1	222	270*	0.5	1.7
TEHAMA	41	4 503	10 033*	25.8	100.0
019 AMER BAPT USA.	3	412	496*	1.3	4.9
053 ASSEMB OF GOD.	3	473	679	1.7	6.8
057 BAPT GEN CONF.	1	24	29*	0.1	0.3
081 CATHOLIC......	3	NA	3 270	8.4	32.6
093 CHR CH (DISC).	2	100	138	0.4	1.4
123 CH GOD (ANDER)	1	260	780	2.0	7.8
127 CH GOD (CLEVE)	1	22	26*	0.1	0.3
151 L-D SAINTS....	1	NA	439	1.1	4.4
165 CH OF NAZARENE	2	209	428	1.1	4.3
167 CHS OF CHRIST.	4	192	244	0.6	2.4
179 CONSRV BAPT...	1	250	301*	0.8	3.0
193 EPISCOPAL.....	2	179	316	0.8	3.1
263 INT FOURSQ GOS	4	212	255*	0.7	2.5
283 LUTH--MO SYNOD	2	165	218	0.6	2.2
413 S.D.A.........	2	275	331*	0.9	3.3
419 SO BAPT CONV..	2	552	665*	1.7	6.6
449 UN METHODIST..	5	745	897*	2.3	8.9
453 UN PRES CH USA	2	433	521*	1.3	5.2
TRINITY	16	580	1 469*	12.4	100.0
053 ASSEMB OF GOD.	3	125	179	1.5	12.2
081 CATHOLIC......	3	NA	412	3.5	28.0
151 L-D SAINTS....	1	NA	264	2.2	18.0
165 CH OF NAZARENE	1	27	86	0.7	5.9
167 CHS OF CHRIST.	1	40	50	0.4	3.4
193 EPISCOPAL.....	1	10	20	0.2	1.4
263 INT FOURSQ GOS	1	24	29*	0.2	2.0
413 S.D.A.........	2	173	210*	1.8	14.3
419 SO BAPT CONV..	1	48	58*	0.5	3.9
443 UN C OF CHRIST	2	133	161*	1.4	11.0
TULARE	242	34 199	99 393*	40.4	100.0
005 AME ZION......	1	96	121	–	0.1
017 AMER BAPT ASSN	3	220	220	0.1	0.2
019 AMER BAPT USA.	10	3 448	4 305*	1.8	4.3
029 AMER LUTH CH..	3	717	980	0.4	1.0
039 AP CHR CH(NAZ)	1	12	15*	–	–
053 ASSEMB OF GOD.	28	2 595	4 451	1.8	4.5
057 BAPT GEN CONF.	4	499	623*	0.3	0.6
075 BRETHREN IN CR	1	76	85	–	0.1
081 CATHOLIC......	20	NA	48 600	19.8	48.9
089 CHR & MISS AL.	1	76	132	0.1	0.1
093 CHR CH (DISC).	4	839	1 235	0.5	1.2
097 CHR CHS&CHS CR	4	614	767*	0.3	0.8
105 CHRISTIAN REF.	1	249	491	0.2	0.5
123 CH GOD (ANDER)	7	683	2 049	0.8	2.1
127 CH GOD (CLEVE)	9	696	869*	0.4	0.9
133 CH GOD(7TH)DEN	1	18	22*	–	–
149 CH OF JC (BIC)	1	22	22	–	–
151 L-D SAINTS....	6	NA	3 181	1.3	3.2
157 CH OF BRETHREN	1	160	200*	0.1	0.2
165 CH OF NAZARENE	14	2 092	4 054	1.6	4.1
167 CHS OF CHRIST.	25	2 420	3 317	1.3	3.3
193 EPISCOPAL.....	5	959	1 374	0.6	1.4
201 EVAN COV CH AM	2	69	86*	–	0.1
203 EVAN FREE CH..	1	30	37*	–	–
226 FRIENDS--USA...	2	14	17*	–	–
237 GC MENN BR CHS	5	1 027	1 282*	0.5	1.3
263 INT FOURSQ GOS	6	561	700*	0.3	0.7
283 LUTH--MO SYNOD	6	1 141	1 460	0.6	1.5
349 PENT HOLINESS.	4	139	174*	0.1	0.2
353 CHR BRETHREN..	3	50	75	–	0.1
371 REF CH IN AM..	1	125	273	0.1	0.3
403 SALVATION ARMY	1	36	52	–	0.1
413 S.D.A.........	10	1 842	2 300*	0.9	2.3
419 SO BAPT CONV..	22	5 406	6 749*	2.7	6.8
435 UNITARIAN-UNIV	2	58	72*	–	0.1
443 UN C OF CHRIST	2	614	767*	0.3	0.8
449 UN METHODIST..	14	3 463	4 324*	1.8	4.4
453 UN PRES CH USA	11	3 133	3 912*	1.6	3.9
TUOLUMNE	30	3 233	6 492*	19.1	100.0
019 AMER BAPT USA.	1	287	341*	1.0	5.3
053 ASSEMB OF GOD.	2	233	292	0.9	4.5
081 CATHOLIC......	6	NA	2 525	7.4	38.9
165 CH OF NAZARENE	1	36	39	0.1	0.6

NA—Not applicable   *Total adherents estimated from known number of communicant, confirmed, full members.   —Represents a percent less than 0.1.   Percentages may not total due to rounding.

Table 4. Churches and Church Membership by County and Denomination: 1980

County and Denomination	Number of churches	Communicant, confirmed, full members	Total adherents		
			Number	Percent of total population	Percent of total adherents
167 CHS OF CHRIST.	3	175	244	0.7	3.8
193 EPISCOPAL.....	1	367	495	1.5	7.6
203 EVAN FREE CH..	2	45	53*	0.2	0.8
263 INT FOURSQ GOS	1	21	25*	0.1	0.4
281 LUTH CH AMER..	1	118	166	0.5	2.6
283 LUTH--MO SYNOD	1	206	240	0.7	3.7
291 MISSIONARY CH.	1	?	?	?	?
335 ORTH PRESB CH.	1	58	69*	0.2	1.1
413 S.D.A.........	1	486	577*	1.7	8.9
419 SO BAPT CONV..	3	450	534*	1.6	8.2
449 UN METHODIST..	4	432	513*	1.5	7.9
453 UN PRES CH USA	1	319	379*	1.1	5.8
VENTURA	238	49 975	185 076*	34.9	100.0
017 AMER BAPT ASSN	4	269	269	0.1	0.1
019 AMER BAPT USA.	11	3 798	4 686*	0.9	2.5
029 AMER LUTH CH..	7	3 742	5 122	1.0	2.8
053 ASSEMB OF GOD.	17	1 751	2 944	0.6	1.6
057 BAPT GEN CONF.	3	940	1 160*	0.2	0.6
081 CATHOLIC......	17	NA	107 558	20.3	58.1
089 CHR & MISS AL.	1	20	26	—	—
093 CHR CH (DISC).	3	697	957	0.2	0.5
097 CHR CHS&CHS CR	6	1 310	1 616*	0.3	0.9
123 CH GOD (ANDER)	1	13	39	—	—
127 CH GOD (CLEVE)	5	189	233*	—	0.1
151 L-D SAINTS....	28	NA	13 167	2.5	7.1
165 CH OF NAZARENE	8	824	1 171	0.2	0.6
167 CHS OF CHRIST.	17	1 640	2 085	0.4	1.1
179 CONSRV BAPT...	2	181	223*	—	0.1
201 EVAN COV CH AM	1	189	233*	—	0.1
203 EVAN FREE CH..	2	40	49*	—	—
209 EVAN LUTH SYN.	1	120	164	—	0.1
221 FREE METHODIST	1	22	42	—	—
226 FRIENDS-USA...	1	141	174*	—	0.1
244 GRACE BRETHREN	1	364	449*	0.1	0.2
263 INT FOURSQ GOS	13	1 652	1 652*	0.3	0.9
270 CONSRV JUDAISM	2	275	339*	0.1	0.2
271 REFORM JUDAISM	2	1 010	1 246*	0.2	0.7
281 LUTH CH AMER..	4	1 130	1 545	0.3	0.8
283 LUTH--MO SYNOD	9	3 131	4 414	0.8	2.4
290 METRO COMM CHS	1	15	30	—	—
291 MISSIONARY CH.	2	1 356	1 785	0.3	1.0
329 OPEN BIBLE STD	1	100	230	—	0.1
349 PENT HOLINESS.	2	98	121*	—	0.1
403 SALVATION ARMY	2	76	237	—	0.1
413 S.D.A.........	12	3 905	4 818*	0.9	2.6
419 SO BAPT CONV..	16	7 605	9 383*	1.8	5.1
435 UNITARIAN-UNIV	3	240	296*	0.1	0.2
443 UN C OF CHRIST	4	694	856*	0.2	0.5
449 UN METHODIST..	15	7 202	8 886*	1.7	4.8
453 UN PRES CH USA	11	5 457	6 733*	1.3	3.6
469 WELS..........	1	92	138	—	0.1
YOLO	69	9 095	34 092*	30.1	100.0
019 AMER BAPT USA.	2	123	146*	0.1	0.4
029 AMER LUTH CH..	3	628	822	0.7	2.4
053 ASSEMB OF GOD.	5	384	769	0.7	2.3
081 CATHOLIC......	11	NA	20 080	17.7	58.9
101 C.M.E.........	1	450	533*	0.5	1.6
123 CH GOD (ANDER)	1	32	96	0.1	0.3
127 CH GOD (CLEVE)	1	71	84*	0.1	0.2
151 L-D SAINTS....	6	NA	1 827	1.6	5.4
165 CH OF NAZARENE	3	309	705	0.6	2.1
167 CHS OF CHRIST.	6	340	430	0.4	1.3
179 CONSRV BAPT...	1	400	474*	0.4	1.4
193 EPISCOPAL.....	2	837	1 413	1.2	4.1
201 EVAN COV CH AM	1	281	333*	0.3	1.0
226 FRIENDS-USA...	1	27	32*	—	0.1
263 INT FOURSQ GOS	2	165	195*	0.2	0.6
281 LUTH CH AMER..	1	179	258	0.2	0.8
283 LUTH--MO SYNOD	2	409	612	0.5	1.8
413 S.D.A.........	2	226	268*	0.2	0.8
419 SO BAPT CONV..	5	985	1 167*	1.0	3.4
435 UNITARIAN-UNIV	2	240	284*	0.3	0.8
443 UN C OF CHRIST	2	620	734*	0.6	2.2
449 UN METHODIST..	4	774	917*	0.8	2.7
453 UN PRES CH USA	5	1 615	1 913*	1.7	5.6
YUBA	37	5 341	12 042*	24.2	100.0
019 AMER BAPT USA.	2	253	313*	0.6	2.6
029 AMER LUTH CH..	1	318	399	0.8	3.3
053 ASSEMB OF GOD.	5	499	915	1.8	7.6
081 CATHOLIC......	2	NA	4 020	8.1	33.4
093 CHR CH (DISC).	1	75	105	0.2	0.9
097 CHR CHS&CHS CR	1	226	279*	0.6	2.3
127 CH GOD (CLEVE)	1	49	61*	0.1	0.5
151 L-D SAINTS....	1	NA	1 038	2.1	8.6
165 CH OF NAZARENE	3	225	360	0.7	3.0
167 CHS OF CHRIST.	5	393	526	1.1	4.4
179 CONSRV BAPT...	2	250	309*	0.6	2.6
193 EPISCOPAL.....	2	677	779	1.6	6.5
263 INT FOURSQ GOS	1	34	42*	0.1	0.3
413 S.D.A.........	3	235	291*	0.6	2.4
419 SO BAPT CONV..	5	1 705	2 108*	4.2	17.5
453 UN PRES CH USA	1	402	497*	1.0	4.1

County and Denomination	Number of churches	Communicant, confirmed, full members	Total adherents		
			Number	Percent of total population	Percent of total adherents
COLORADO					
THE STATE.....	2 373	462 013	1 057 709*	36.6	100.0
ADAMS	100	27 750	68 929*	28.0	100.0
017 AMER BAPT ASSN	1	160	160	0.1	0.2
019 AMER BAPT USA.	2	875	1 086*	0.4	1.6
029 AMER LUTH CH..	3	1 093	1 470	0.6	2.1
053 ASSEMB OF GOD.	4	1 328	1 805	0.7	2.6
057 BAPT GEN CONF.	3	825	1 024*	0.4	1.5
081 CATHOLIC......	8	NA	28 500	11.6	41.3
089 CHR & MISS AL.	1	30	70	—	0.1
093 CHR CH (DISC).	2	544	803	0.3	1.2
097 CHR CHS&CHS CR	5	1 285	1 595*	0.6	2.3
105 CHRISTIAN REF.	1	60	90	—	0.1
123 CH GOD (ANDER)	1	39	117	—	0.2
151 L-D SAINTS....	7	NA	3 481	1.4	5.1
165 CH OF NAZARENE	4	447	836	0.3	1.2
167 CHS OF CHRIST.	5	464	595	0.2	0.9
179 CONSRV BAPT...	1	228	283*	0.1	0.4
193 EPISCOPAL.....	3	461	690	0.3	1.0
201 EVAN COV CH AM	1	471	585*	0.2	0.8
203 EVAN FREE CH..	1	166	206*	0.1	0.3
221 FREE METHODIST	1	93	285	0.1	0.4
281 LUTH CH AMER..	4	1 451	2 370	1.0	3.4
283 LUTH--MO SYNOD	4	3 408	4 928	2.0	7.1
313 N AM BAPT CONF	2	117	145*	0.1	0.2
335 ORTH PRESB CH.	2	172	214*	0.1	0.3
349 PENT HOLINESS.	1	30	37*	—	0.1
383 REF PRES OF NA	1	35	51	—	0.1
403 SALVATION ARMY	1	89	273	0.1	0.4
413 S.D.A.........	4	1 266	1 572*	0.6	2.3
419 SO BAPT CONV..	9	3 871	4 806*	2.0	7.0
443 UN C OF CHRIST	3	393	488*	0.2	0.7
449 UN METHODIST..	7	2 955	3 668*	1.5	5.3
453 UN PRES CH USA	8	5 394	6 696*	2.7	9.7
ALAMOSA	21	2 303	7 458*	63.2	100.0
019 AMER BAPT USA.	1	110	135*	1.1	1.8
053 ASSEMB OF GOD.	2	78	131	1.1	1.8
057 BAPT GEN CONF.	1	40	49*	0.4	0.7
081 CATHOLIC......	1	NA	3 500	29.7	46.9
093 CHR CH (DISC).	1	72	115	1.0	1.5
097 CHR CHS&CHS CR	1	145	178*	1.5	2.4
105 CHRISTIAN REF.	1	132	239	2.0	3.2
151 L-D SAINTS....	3	NA	964	8.2	12.9
167 CHS OF CHRIST.	1	90	95	0.8	1.3
179 CONSRV BAPT...	1	228	280*	2.4	3.8
193 EPISCOPAL.....	1	93	151	1.3	2.0
283 LUTH--MO SYNOD	1	169	236	2.0	3.2
353 CHR BRETHREN..	1	100	100	0.8	1.3
413 S.D.A.........	1	91	112*	0.9	1.5
419 SO BAPT CONV..	1	372	457*	3.9	6.1
449 UN METHODIST..	2	320	393*	3.3	5.3
453 UN PRES CH USA	1	263	323*	2.7	4.3
ARAPAHOE	132	37 753	91 412*	31.1	100.0
019 AMER BAPT USA.	5	857	1 051*	0.4	1.1
029 AMER LUTH CH..	6	2 038	2 798	1.0	3.1
053 ASSEMB OF GOD.	5	1 229	1 921	0.7	2.1
057 BAPT GEN CONF.	2	600	736*	0.3	0.8
081 CATHOLIC......	8	NA	33 000	11.2	36.1
089 CHR & MISS AL.	1	54	154	0.1	0.2
093 CHR CH (DISC).	1	555	763	0.3	0.8
097 CHR CHS&CHS CR	3	549	673*	0.2	0.7
105 CHRISTIAN REF.	1	205	358	0.1	0.4
123 CH GOD (ANDER)	6	576	1 728	0.6	1.9
127 CH GOD (CLEVE)	2	202	248*	0.1	0.3
151 L-D SAINTS....	11	NA	6 909	2.4	7.6
165 CH OF NAZARENE	4	1 841	3 314	1.1	3.6
167 CHS OF CHRIST.	6	1 181	1 627	0.6	1.8
175 CONGR CHR CHS.	1	52	64*	—	0.1
179 CONSRV BAPT...	5	1 140	1 398*	0.5	1.5
193 EPISCOPAL.....	8	1 790	2 547	0.9	2.8
203 EVAN FREE CH..	1	233	286*	0.1	0.3
221 FREE METHODIST	1	56	138	—	0.2
226 FRIENDS-USA...	1	55	67*	—	0.1
237 GC MENN BR CHS	1	180	221*	0.1	0.2
263 INT FOURSQ GOS	1	571	700*	0.2	0.8
270 CONSRV JUDAISM	1	31	38*	—	—
281 LUTH CH AMER..	5	3 124	4 391	1.5	4.8
283 LUTH--MO SYNOD	7	3 872	5 254	1.8	5.7
290 METRO COMM CHS	1	200	400	0.1	0.4
329 OPEN BIBLE STD	1	200	400	0.1	0.4
349 PENT HOLINESS.	2	74	91*	—	0.1
353 CHR BRETHREN..	3	350	350	0.1	0.4
371 REF CH IN AM.	1	184	389	0.1	0.4
403 SALVATION ARMY	2	170	284	0.1	0.3
413 S.D.A.........	3	867	1 063*	0.4	1.2
419 SO BAPT CONV..	7	4 379	5 371*	1.8	5.9
443 UN C OF CHRIST	5	1 262	1 548*	0.5	1.7
449 UN METHODIST..	7	6 248	7 663*	2.6	8.4
453 UN PRES CH USA	7	2 828	3 469*	1.2	3.8
ARCHULETA	13	673	2 297*	62.7	100.0
053 ASSEMB OF GOD.	1	33	64	1.7	2.8
081 CATHOLIC......	6	NA	1 295	35.3	56.4

NA—Not applicable   *Total adherents estimated from known number of communicant, confirmed, full members.   —Represents a percent less than 0.1.   Percentages may not total due to rounding.

Table 4. Churches and Church Membership by County and Denomination: 1980

County and Denomination	Number of churches	Communicant, confirmed, full members	Total adherents Number	Percent of total population	Percent of total adherents
151 L-D SAINTS....	1	NA	119	3.2	5.2
167 CHS OF CHRIST.	1	11	14	0.4	0.6
193 EPISCOPAL.....	1	38	72	2.0	3.1
283 LUTH--MO SYNOD	1	20	25	0.7	1.1
419 SO BAPT CONV..	1	351	435*	11.9	18.9
449 UN METHODIST..	1	220	273*	7.5	11.9
BACA	**20**	**866**	**1 460***	**26.9**	**100.0**
053 ASSEMB OF GOD.	2	62	101	1.9	6.9
081 CATHOLIC......	2	NA	275	5.1	18.8
123 CH GOD (ANDER)	2	58	174	3.2	11.9
167 CHS OF CHRIST.	3	56	71	1.3	4.9
226 FRIENDS-USA...	3	120	146*	2.7	10.0
349 PENT HOLINESS.	3	116	141*	2.6	9.7
413 S.D.A.........	1	35	43*	0.8	2.9
449 UN METHODIST..	4	419	509*	9.4	34.9
BENT	**17**	**1 380**	**4 091***	**68.8**	**100.0**
019 AMER BAPT USA.	1	237	289*	4.9	7.1
053 ASSEMB OF GOD.	1	7	17	0.3	0.4
081 CATHOLIC......	1	NA	2 200	37.0	53.8
093 CHR CH (DISC).	1	109	181	3.0	4.4
151 L-D SAINTS....	1	NA	53	0.9	1.3
165 CH OF NAZARENE	1	32	133	2.2	3.3
167 CHS OF CHRIST.	2	100	127	2.1	3.1
226 FRIENDS-USA...	2	112	137*	2.3	3.3
413 S.D.A.........	1	33	40*	0.7	1.0
419 SO BAPT CONV..	1	113	138*	2.3	3.4
449 UN METHODIST..	3	483	589*	9.9	14.4
453 UN PRES CH USA	1	128	156*	2.6	3.8
469 WELS.........	1	26	31	0.5	0.8
BOULDER	**125**	**33 024**	**69 588***	**36.7**	**100.0**
019 AMER BAPT USA.	3	743	881*	0.5	1.3
029 AMER LUTH CH..	3	1 733	2 492	1.3	3.6
053 ASSEMB OF GOD.	4	1 088	1 700	0.9	2.4
057 BAPT GEN CONF.	1	110	130*	0.1	0.2
081 CATHOLIC......	9	NA	24 100	12.7	34.6
093 CHR CH (DISC).	2	481	643	0.3	0.9
097 CHR CHS&CHS CR	5	1 858	2 204*	1.2	3.2
105 CHRISTIAN REF.	3	138	243	0.1	0.3
127 CH GOD (CLEVE)	1	49	58*	-	0.1
151 L-D SAINTS....	7	NA	3 644	1.9	5.2
165 CH OF NAZARENE	5	516	737	0.4	1.1
167 CHS OF CHRIST.	5	830	1 063	0.6	1.5
179 CONSRV BAPT...	3	684	811*	0.4	1.2
193 EPISCOPAL.....	5	2 090	2 880	1.5	4.1
203 EVAN FREE CH..	3	519	616*	0.3	0.9
221 FREE METHODIST	1	55	187	0.1	0.3
226 FRIENDS-USA...	1	66	78*	-	0.1
263 INT FOURSQ GOS	3	320	380*	0.2	0.5
281 LUTH CH AMER..	4	2 835	3 912	2.1	5.6
283 LUTH--MO SYNOD	7	2 496	3 296	1.7	4.7
290 METRO COMM CHS	1	30	60	-	0.1
291 MISSIONARY CH.	1	11	13	-	-
349 PENT HOLINESS.	1	40	47*	-	0.1
353 CHR BRETHREN.	3	130	175	0.1	0.3
413 S.D.A.........	3	1 050	1 246*	0.7	1.8
415 S-D BAPTIST GC	1	64	76*	-	0.1
419 SO BAPT CONV..	9	1 787	2 120*	1.1	3.0
435 UNITARIAN-UNIV	2	399	473*	0.2	0.7
443 UN C OF CHRIST	6	2 103	2 495*	1.3	3.6
449 UN METHODIST..	12	6 399	7 591*	4.0	10.9
453 UN PRES CH USA	9	4 247	5 038*	2.7	7.2
469 WELS.........	2	153	199	0.1	0.3
CHAFFEE	**27**	**2 761**	**6 094***	**46.1**	**100.0**
053 ASSEMB OF GOD.	2	89	187	1.4	3.1
081 CATHOLIC......	2	NA	2 257	17.1	37.0
093 CHR CH (DISC).	1	131	161	1.2	2.6
097 CHR CHS&CHS CR	1	100	121*	0.9	2.0
127 CH GOD (CLEVE)	1	45	55*	0.4	0.9
151 L-D SAINTS....	2	NA	269	2.0	4.4
165 CH OF NAZARENE	1	39	53	0.4	0.9
167 CHS OF CHRIST.	5	175	260	2.0	4.3
179 CONSRV BAPT...	2	456	553*	4.2	9.1
193 EPISCOPAL.....	2	258	366	2.8	6.0
263 INT FOURSQ GOS	1	24	29*	0.2	0.5
283 LUTH--MO SYNOD	1	167	235	1.8	3.9
413 S.D.A.........	1	17	21*	0.2	0.3
419 SO BAPT CONV..	2	784	950*	7.2	15.6
443 UN C OF CHRIST	1	160	194*	1.5	3.2
449 UN METHODIST..	1	181	219*	1.7	3.6
453 UN PRES CH USA	1	135	164*	1.2	2.7
CHEYENNE	**9**	**506**	**1 429***	**66.4**	**100.0**
029 AMER LUTH CH..	1	29	28	1.3	2.0
081 CATHOLIC......	2	NA	800	37.2	56.0
097 CHR CHS&CHS CR	1	100	123*	5.7	8.6
167 CHS OF CHRIST.	1	11	11	0.5	0.8
283 LUTH--MO SYNOD	2	154	207	9.6	14.5
449 UN METHODIST..	2	212	260*	12.1	18.2
CLEAR CREEK	**12**	**407**	**1 163***	**15.9**	**100.0**
081 CATHOLIC......	4	NA	500	6.8	43.0
151 L-D SAINTS....	1	NA	118	1.6	10.1
167 CHS OF CHRIST.	1	20	25	0.3	2.1
193 EPISCOPAL.....	1	7	7	0.1	0.6
281 LUTH CH AMER..	1	78	142	1.9	12.2
413 S.D.A.........	1	34	42*	0.6	3.6
449 UN METHODIST..	1	80	98*	1.3	8.4
453 UN PRES CH USA	2	188	231*	3.2	19.9
CONEJOS	**22**	**252**	**6 359***	**81.6**	**100.0**
053 ASSEMB OF GOD.	2	99	190	2.4	3.0
081 CATHOLIC......	10	NA	3 961	50.8	62.3
097 CHR CHS&CHS CR	1	40	51*	0.7	0.8
151 L-D SAINTS....	6	NA	2 013	25.8	31.7
285 MENNONITE CH..	1	30	38*	0.5	0.6
453 UN PRES CH USA	2	83	106*	1.4	1.7
COSTILLA	**10**	**13**	**2 516***	**81.9**	**100.0**
081 CATHOLIC......	9	NA	2 500	81.4	99.4
453 UN PRES CH USA	1	13	16*	0.5	0.6
CROWLEY	**11**	**589**	**1 511***	**50.6**	**100.0**
029 AMER LUTH CH..	1	50	53	1.8	3.5
053 ASSEMB OF GOD.	1	46	75	2.5	5.0
081 CATHOLIC......	3	NA	789	26.4	52.2
093 CHR CH (DISC).	1	90	120	4.0	7.9
226 FRIENDS-USA...	1	18	21*	0.7	1.4
283 LUTH--MO SYNOD	1	46	50	1.7	3.3
449 UN METHODIST..	2	307	366*	12.2	24.2
469 WELS.........	1	32	37	1.2	2.4
CUSTER	**6**	**408**	**541***	**35.4**	**100.0**
081 CATHOLIC......	1	NA	92	6.0	17.0
193 EPISCOPAL.....	2	94	70	4.6	12.9
283 LUTH--MO SYNOD	1	141	169	11.1	31.2
419 SO BAPT CONV..	1	57	69*	4.5	12.8
449 UN METHODIST..	1	116	141*	9.2	26.1
DELTA	**48**	**3 994**	**8 532***	**40.2**	**100.0**
019 AMER BAPT USA.	3	459	555*	2.6	6.5
053 ASSEMB OF GOD.	5	409	742	3.5	8.7
081 CATHOLIC......	4	NA	1 985	9.4	23.3
097 CHR CHS&CHS CR	2	375	453*	2.1	5.3
123 CH GOD (ANDER)	2	100	300	1.4	3.5
151 L-D SAINTS....	3	NA	1 055	5.0	12.4
165 CH OF NAZARENE	3	158	303	1.4	3.6
167 CHS OF CHRIST.	6	225	285	1.3	3.3
193 EPISCOPAL.....	2	134	248	1.2	2.9
226 FRIENDS-USA...	1	68	82*	0.4	1.0
263 INT FOURSQ GOS	1	18	22*	0.1	0.3
283 LUTH--MO SYNOD	2	223	295	1.4	3.5
349 PENT HOLINESS.	1	13	16*	0.1	0.2
413 S.D.A.........	3	256	310*	1.5	3.6
419 SO BAPT CONV..	3	454	549*	2.6	6.4
449 UN METHODIST..	5	839	1 014*	4.8	11.9
453 UN PRES CH USA	2	263	318*	1.5	3.7
DENVER	**284**	**88 513**	**213 831***	**43.5**	**100.0**
005 AME ZION......	2	290	336	0.1	0.2
019 AMER BAPT USA.	15	7 929	9 296*	1.9	4.3
029 AMER LUTH CH..	10	3 109	4 069	0.8	1.9
039 AP CHR CH(NAZ)	1	66	77*	-	-
053 ASSEMB OF GOD.	15	2 523	4 060	0.8	1.9
057 BAPT GEN CONF.	6	1 550	1 817*	0.4	0.8
081 CATHOLIC......	41	NA	98 497	20.0	46.1
089 CHR & MISS AL.	1	448	732	0.1	0.3
093 CHR CH (DISC).	12	2 898	4 247	0.9	2.0
097 CHR CHS&CHS CR	4	467	548*	0.1	0.3
105 CHRISTIAN REF.	6	1 641	2 587	0.5	1.2
127 CH GOD (CLEVE)	2	93	109*	-	0.1
133 CH GOD(7TH)DEN	1	133	156*	-	0.1
151 L-D SAINTS....	7	NA	3 635	0.7	1.7
157 CH OF BRETHREN	2	479	562*	0.1	0.3
164 CH LUTH CONF..	1	23	28	-	-
165 CH OF NAZARENE	6	880	1 450	0.3	0.7
167 CHS OF CHRIST.	7	1 660	2 112	0.4	1.0
179 CONSRV BAPT...	6	1 368	1 604*	0.3	0.8
193 EPISCOPAL.....	19	10 580	14 428	2.9	6.7
201 EVAN COV CH AM	1	246	288*	0.1	0.1
203 EVAN FREE CH..	2	633	742*	0.2	0.3
221 FREE METHODIST	1	166	534	0.1	0.2
226 FRIENDS-USA...	2	423	496*	0.1	0.2
233 GEN CH NEW JER	1	15	18*	-	-
244 GRACE BRETHREN	1	83	97*	-	-
263 INT FOURSQ GOS	2	110	129*	-	0.1
270 CONSRV JUDAISM	1	366	429*	0.1	0.2
271 REFORM JUDAISM	3	3 918	4 594*	0.9	2.1
274 LAT EVAN LUTH.	1	169	199	-	0.1
281 LUTH CH AMER..	7	4 021	5 248	1.1	2.5
283 LUTH--MO SYNOD	11	6 088	7 510	1.5	3.5
285 MENNONITE CH..	1	185	217*	-	0.1
291 MISSIONARY CH.	1	10	28	-	-
353 CHR BRETHREN.	3	450	600	0.1	0.3
371 REF CH IN AM..	7	1 301	2 189	0.4	1.0
403 SALVATION ARMY	1	113	121	-	0.1
413 S.D.A.........	5	2 522	2 957*	0.6	1.4
419 SO BAPT CONV..	10	7 526	8 824*	1.8	4.1
435 UNITARIAN-UNIV	2	720	844*	0.2	0.4
443 UN C OF CHRIST	11	3 364	3 944*	0.8	1.8
449 UN METHODIST..	25	10 824	12 691*	2.6	5.9
453 UN PRES CH USA	19	8 611	10 096*	2.1	4.7
469 WELS.........	2	512	686	0.1	0.3
DOLORES	**7**	**349**	**437***	**26.4**	**100.0**

NA—Not applicable   *Total adherents estimated from known number of communicant, confirmed, full members.   —Represents a percent less than 0.1.   Percentages may not total due to rounding.

Table 4. Churches and Church Membership by County and Denomination: 1980

County and Denomination	Number of churches	Communicant, confirmed, full members	Total adherents		
			Number	Percent of total population	Percent of total adherents
053 ASSEMB OF GOD.	1	33	43	2.6	9.8
167 CHS OF CHRIST.	2	22	28	1.7	6.4
413 S.D.A.	1	53	66*	4.0	15.1
419 SO BAPT CONV..	1	161	200*	12.1	45.8
449 UN METHODIST..	1	65	81*	4.9	18.5
453 UN PRES CH USA	1	15	19*	1.1	4.3
DOUGLAS	**20**	**2 982**	**6 124***	**24.3**	**100.0**
029 AMER LUTH CH..	1	353	554	2.2	9.0
053 ASSEMB OF GOD.	1	59	154	0.6	2.5
081 CATHOLIC......	1	NA	1 500	6.0	24.5
151 L-D SAINTS....	1	NA	618	2.5	10.1
167 CHS OF CHRIST.	1	55	70	0.3	1.1
179 CONSRV BAPT...	1	228	288*	1.1	4.7
193 EPISCOPAL.....	3	395	529	2.1	8.6
237 GC MENN BR CHS	1	166	210*	0.8	3.4
283 LUTH--MO SYNOD	1	317	427	1.7	7.0
329 OPEN BIBLE STD	1	47	53	0.2	0.9
349 PENT HOLINESS.	1	61	77*	0.3	1.3
413 S.D.A.	1	65	82*	0.3	1.3
419 SO BAPT CONV..	1	124	157*	0.6	2.6
443 UN C OF CHRIST	1	152	192*	0.8	3.1
449 UN METHODIST..	2	790	998*	4.0	16.3
453 UN PRES CH USA	2	170	215*	0.9	3.5
EAGLE	**17**	**726**	**1 706***	**13.0**	**100.0**
053 ASSEMB OF GOD.	2	45	111	0.8	6.5
081 CATHOLIC......	4	NA	550	4.2	32.2
151 L-D SAINTS....	1	NA	155	1.2	9.1
167 CHS OF CHRIST.	1	40	50	0.4	2.9
193 EPISCOPAL.....	1	66	104	0.8	6.1
281 LUTH CH AMER..	2	94	173	1.3	10.1
419 SO BAPT CONV..	2	161	189*	1.4	11.1
449 UN METHODIST..	3	259	303*	2.3	17.8
453 UN PRES CH USA	1	61	71*	0.5	4.2
ELBERT	**8**	**1 063**	**1 334***	**19.5**	**100.0**
019 AMER BAPT USA.	2	242	303*	4.4	22.7
097 CHR CHS&CHS CR	1	100	125*	1.8	9.4
165 CH OF NAZARENE	1	17	23	0.3	1.7
179 CONSRV BAPT...	1	228	286*	4.2	21.4
419 SO BAPT CONV..	1	74	93*	1.4	7.0
449 UN METHODIST..	1	100	125*	1.8	9.4
453 UN PRES CH USA	1	302	379*	5.5	28.4
EL PASO	**184**	**55 371**	**107 604***	**34.8**	**100.0**
017 AMER BAPT ASSN	2	320	320	0.1	0.3
019 AMER BAPT USA.	6	1 909	2 330*	0.8	2.2
029 AMER LUTH CH..	5	2 182	3 041	1.0	2.8
053 ASSEMB OF GOD.	8	1 403	2 751	0.9	2.6
057 BAPT GEN CONF.	1	100	122*	—	0.1
063 BEREAN FUND CH	1	67	82*	—	0.1
075 BRETHREN IN CR	1	57	86	—	0.1
081 CATHOLIC......	16	NA	30 250	9.8	28.1
089 CHR & MISS AL.	1	12	26	—	—
093 CHR CH (DISC).	2	1 369	2 114	0.7	2.0
097 CHR CHS&CHS CR	6	1 567	1 913*	0.6	1.8
105 CHRISTIAN REF.	1	229	422	0.1	0.4
123 CH GOD (ANDER)	2	181	543	0.2	0.5
127 CH GOD (CLEVE)	3	283	345*	0.1	0.3
151 L-D SAINTS....	11	NA	4 752	1.5	4.4
157 CH OF BRETHREN	2	65	79*	—	0.1
165 CH OF NAZARENE	11	2 737	4 657	1.5	4.3
167 CHS OF CHRIST.	8	1 310	1 679	0.5	1.6
179 CONSRV BAPT...	2	456	557*	0.2	0.5
193 EPISCOPAL.....	7	3 109	3 906	1.3	3.6
201 EVAN COV CH AM	1	58	71*	—	0.1
203 EVAN FREE CH..	2	328	400*	0.1	0.4
209 EVAN LUTH SYN.	1	55	72	—	0.1
221 FREE METHODIST	2	42	117	—	0.1
226 FRIENDS--USA...	1	149	182*	0.1	0.2
244 GRACE BRETHREN	1	134	164*	0.1	0.2
263 INT FOURSQ GOS	3	480	586*	0.2	0.5
270 CONSRV JUDAISM	1	115	140*	—	0.1
271 REFORM JUDAISM	1	316	386*	0.1	0.4
274 LAT EVAN LUTH.	1	57	65	—	0.1
281 LUTH CH AMER..	6	2 229	3 259	1.1	3.0
283 LUTH--MO SYNOD	4	2 747	3 451	1.1	3.2
285 MENNONITE CH..	2	184	225*	0.1	0.2
290 METRO COMM CHS	1	25	50	—	—
329 OPEN BIBLE STD	1	378	650	0.2	0.6
349 PENT HOLINESS.	3	81	99*	—	0.1
353 CHR BRETHREN..	2	325	450	0.1	0.4
381 REF PRES-EVAN.	2	777	1 122	0.4	1.0
403 SALVATION ARMY	1	162	267	0.1	0.2
413 S.D.A.	2	693	846*	0.3	0.8
419 SO BAPT CONV..	18	12 142	14 822*	4.8	13.8
435 UNITARIAN-UNIV	1	106	129*	—	0.1
443 UN C OF CHRIST	8	2 306	2 815*	0.9	2.6
449 UN METHODIST..	16	9 139	11 156*	3.6	10.4
453 UN PRES CH USA	6	4 885	5 963*	1.9	5.5
469 WELS..........	1	102	142	—	0.1
FREMONT	**41**	**6 158**	**11 359***	**39.6**	**100.0**
019 AMER BAPT USA.	2	582	694*	2.4	6.1
053 ASSEMB OF GOD.	2	154	300	1.0	2.6
081 CATHOLIC......	4	NA	2 880	10.0	25.4
093 CHR CH (DISC).	1	216	268	0.9	2.4
097 CHR CHS&CHS CR	2	210	250*	0.9	2.2
123 CH GOD (ANDER)	1	38	114	0.4	1.0

County and Denomination	Number of churches	Communicant, confirmed, full members	Total adherents		
			Number	Percent of total population	Percent of total adherents
127 CH GOD (CLEVE)	1	27	32*	0.1	0.3
151 L-D SAINTS....	2	NA	515	1.8	4.5
165 CH OF NAZARENE	3	225	416	1.5	3.7
167 CHS OF CHRIST.	2	202	262	0.9	2.3
193 EPISCOPAL.....	1	218	361	1.3	3.2
203 EVAN FREE CH..	1	39	47*	0.2	0.4
221 FREE METHODIST	1	28	108	0.4	1.0
226 FRIENDS--USA...	1	59	70*	0.2	0.6
263 INT FOURSQ GOS	2	273	326*	1.1	2.9
281 LUTH CH AMER..	1	177	240	0.8	2.1
283 LUTH--MO SYNOD	1	218	293	1.0	2.6
329 OPEN BIBLE STD	1	35	60	0.2	0.5
349 PENT HOLINESS.	1	35	42*	0.1	0.4
413 S.D.A.	2	261	311*	1.1	2.7
419 SO BAPT CONV..	4	1 343	1 602*	5.6	14.1
449 UN METHODIST..	2	1 154	1 376*	4.8	12.1
453 UN PRES CH USA	3	664	792*	2.8	7.0
GARFIELD	**40**	**3 507**	**8 278***	**36.8**	**100.0**
019 AMER BAPT USA.	2	220	268*	1.2	3.2
053 ASSEMB OF GOD.	2	254	661	2.9	8.0
057 BAPT GEN CONF.	1	95	116*	0.5	1.4
081 CATHOLIC......	4	NA	2 500	11.1	30.2
097 CHR CHS&CHS CR	1	275	335*	1.5	4.0
151 L-D SAINTS....	2	NA	883	3.9	10.7
165 CH OF NAZARENE	2	60	122	0.5	1.5
167 CHS OF CHRIST.	3	175	223	1.0	2.7
193 EPISCOPAL.....	2	261	459	2.0	5.5
263 INT FOURSQ GOS	2	56	68*	0.3	0.8
281 LUTH CH AMER..	1	65	100	0.4	1.2
283 LUTH--MO SYNOD	2	257	365	1.6	4.4
285 MENNONITE CH..	1	41	50*	0.2	0.6
349 PENT HOLINESS.	3	136	166*	0.7	2.0
413 S.D.A.	2	166	202*	0.9	2.4
419 SO BAPT CONV..	3	263	320*	1.4	3.9
443 UN C OF CHRIST	3	116	141*	0.6	1.7
449 UN METHODIST..	3	955	1 163*	5.2	14.0
453 UN PRES CH USA	1	112	136*	0.6	1.6
GILPIN	**3**	**88**	**203***	**8.3**	**100.0**
081 CATHOLIC......	1	NA	100	4.1	49.3
193 EPISCOPAL.....	1	14	14	0.6	6.9
449 UN METHODIST..	1	74	89*	3.6	43.8
GRAND	**15**	**616**	**1 479***	**19.8**	**100.0**
053 ASSEMB OF GOD.	1	35	96	1.3	6.5
081 CATHOLIC......	4	NA	550	7.4	37.2
151 L-D SAINTS....	1	NA	139	1.9	9.4
167 CHS OF CHRIST.	1	48	58	0.8	3.9
193 EPISCOPAL.....	2	88	94	1.3	6.4
413 S.D.A.	1	45	55*	0.7	3.7
419 SO BAPT CONV..	3	141	172*	2.3	11.6
453 UN PRES CH USA	2	259	315*	4.2	21.3
GUNNISON	**12**	**746**	**2 042***	**19.1**	**100.0**
053 ASSEMB OF GOD.	1	49	129	1.2	6.3
081 CATHOLIC......	3	NA	900	8.4	44.1
151 L-D SAINTS....	1	NA	113	1.1	5.5
167 CHS OF CHRIST.	1	49	62	0.6	3.0
193 EPISCOPAL.....	1	159	212	2.0	10.4
283 LUTH--MO SYNOD	1	151	239	2.2	11.7
413 S.D.A.	1	33	38*	0.4	1.9
419 SO BAPT CONV..	1	263	301*	2.8	14.7
443 UN C OF CHRIST	2	42	48*	0.4	2.4
HINSDALE	**3**	**58**	**69***	**16.9**	**100.0**
193 EPISCOPAL.....	1	11	13	3.2	18.8
419 SO BAPT CONV..	1	9	11*	2.7	15.9
453 UN PRES CH USA	1	38	45*	11.0	65.2
HUERFANO	**13**	**696**	**2 521***	**39.1**	**100.0**
019 AMER BAPT USA.	2	128	155*	2.4	6.1
053 ASSEMB OF GOD.	1	14	31	0.5	1.2
081 CATHOLIC......	3	NA	1 665	25.9	66.0
285 MENNONITE CH..	1	27	33*	0.5	1.3
413 S.D.A.	1	15	18*	0.3	0.7
419 SO BAPT CONV..	2	154	186*	2.9	7.4
449 UN METHODIST..	3	358	433*	6.7	17.2
JACKSON	**4**	**264**	**388***	**20.8**	**100.0**
053 ASSEMB OF GOD.	1	5	7	0.4	1.8
167 CHS OF CHRIST.	1	45	55	3.0	14.2
353 CHR BRETHREN..	1	50	125	6.7	32.2
449 UN METHODIST..	1	164	201*	10.8	51.8
JEFFERSON	**144**	**43 460**	**107 215***	**28.8**	**100.0**
017 AMER BAPT ASSN	1	160	160	—	0.1
019 AMER BAPT USA.	3	493	603*	0.2	0.6
029 AMER LUTH CH..	4	1 811	2 609	0.7	2.4
053 ASSEMB OF GOD.	4	874	1 385	0.4	1.3
057 BAPT GEN CONF.	4	550	673*	0.2	0.6
063 BEREAN FUND CH	1	38	74*	—	0.1
081 CATHOLIC......	12	NA	45 300	12.2	42.3
089 CHR & MISS AL.	1	32	82	—	0.1
093 CHR CH (DISC).	2	376	579	0.2	0.5
097 CHR CHS&CHS CR	2	409	501*	0.1	0.5
105 CHRISTIAN REF.	1	140	210	0.1	0.2

NA—Not applicable   *Total adherents estimated from known number of communicant, confirmed, full members.   —Represents a percent less than 0.1.   Percentages may not total due to rounding.

Table 4. Churches and Church Membership by County and Denomination: 1980

County and Denomination	Number of churches	Communicant, confirmed, full members	Total adherents Number	Total adherents Percent of total population	Total adherents Percent of total adherents
123 CH GOD (ANDER)	1	56	168	–	0.2
127 CH GOD (CLEVE)	3	389	476*	0.1	0.4
151 L-D SAINTS....	12	NA	6 060	1.6	5.7
163 CH OF LUTH BR.	1	20	33	–	–
165 CH OF NAZARENE	5	903	1 523	0.4	1.4
167 CHS OF CHRIST.	8	1 075	1 410	0.4	1.3
179 CONSRV BAPT...	12	2 736	3 348*	0.9	3.1
193 EPISCOPAL.....	9	3 010	4 360	1.2	4.1
201 EVAN COV CH AM	1	101	124*	–	0.1
203 EVAN FREE CH..	1	116	142*	–	0.1
244 GRACE BRETHREN	1	30	37*	–	0.1
263 INT FOURSQ GOS	2	186	228*	0.1	0.2
281 LUTH CH AMER..	5	2 750	3 702	1.0	3.5
283 LUTH--MO SYNOD	5	5 089	6 286	1.7	5.9
285 MENNONITE CH..	1	176	215*	0.1	0.2
287 MENN GEN CONF.	1	121	180	–	0.2
381 REF PRES-EVAN.	1	88	125	–	0.1
413 S.D.A.........	3	563	689*	0.2	0.6
415 S-D BAPTIST GC	1	161	197*	0.1	0.2
419 SO BAPT CONV..	8	4 820	5 899*	1.6	5.5
435 UNITARIAN-UNIV	2	418	512*	0.1	0.5
443 UN C OF CHRIST	5	1 479	1 810	0.5	1.7
449 UN METHODIST..	12	9 074	11 105*	3.0	10.4
453 UN PRES CH USA	8	5 061	6 194*	1.7	5.8
469 WELS.........	1	155	243	0.1	0.2
KIOWA	**6**	**559**	**708***	**36.6**	**100.0**
053 ASSEMB OF GOD.	1	37	90	4.6	12.7
097 CHR CHS&CHS CR	1	100	118*	6.1	16.7
226 FRIENDS-USA...	1	39	46*	2.4	6.5
419 SO BAPT CONV..	1	151	179*	9.2	25.3
449 UN METHODIST..	2	232	275*	14.2	38.8
KIT CARSON	**29**	**3 172**	**5 153***	**67.8**	**100.0**
019 AMER BAPT USA.	1	234	287*	3.8	5.6
029 AMER LUTH CH..	2	378	464	6.1	9.0
053 ASSEMB OF GOD.	1	173	312	4.1	6.1
081 CATHOLIC......	4	NA	850	11.2	16.5
093 CHR CH (DISC).	1	150	275	3.6	5.3
097 CHR CHS&CHS CR	1	85	104*	1.4	2.0
151 L-D SAINTS....	1	NA	113	1.5	2.2
165 CH OF NAZARENE	1	41	121	1.6	2.3
167 CHS OF CHRIST.	2	72	96	1.3	1.9
179 CONSRV BAPT...	1	228	280*	3.7	5.4
203 EVAN FREE CH..	1	39	48*	0.6	0.9
237 GC MENN BR CHS	1	55	68*	0.9	1.3
283 LUTH--MO SYNOD	3	369	495	6.5	9.6
287 MENN GEN CONF.	1	127	139	1.8	2.7
353 CHR BRETHREN..	1	40	50	0.7	1.0
413 S.D.A.........	1	34	42*	0.6	0.8
419 SO BAPT CONV..	1	210	258*	3.4	5.0
443 UN C OF CHRIST	2	257	316*	4.2	6.1
449 UN METHODIST..	3	680	835*	11.0	16.2
LAKE	**10**	**748**	**4 284***	**48.5**	**100.0**
053 ASSEMB OF GOD.	1	41	83	0.9	1.9
081 CATHOLIC......	2	NA	3 100	35.1	72.4
151 L-D SAINTS....	1	NA	151	1.7	3.5
167 CHS OF CHRIST.	1	60	76	0.9	1.8
193 EPISCOPAL.....	1	60	93	1.1	2.2
283 LUTH--MO SYNOD	1	133	212	2.4	4.9
413 S.D.A.........	1	36	45*	0.5	1.1
419 SO BAPT CONV..	1	217	272*	3.1	6.3
453 UN PRES CH USA	1	201	252*	2.9	5.9
LA PLATA	**34**	**3 929**	**9 419***	**34.3**	**100.0**
053 ASSEMB OF GOD.	3	89	166	0.6	1.8
081 CATHOLIC......	3	NA	3 355	12.2	35.6
097 CHR CHS&CHS CR	1	95	114*	0.4	1.2
151 L-D SAINTS....	4	NA	1 085	4.0	11.5
165 CH OF NAZARENE	1	44	74	0.3	0.8
167 CHS OF CHRIST.	2	260	331	1.2	3.5
179 CONSRV BAPT...	1	228	273*	1.0	2.9
193 EPISCOPAL.....	1	177	234	0.9	2.5
221 FREE METHODIST	1	26	105	0.4	1.1
226 FRIENDS-USA...	1	9	11*	–	0.1
263 INT FOURSQ GOS	1	450	538*	2.0	5.7
281 LUTH CH AMER..	1	187	240	0.9	2.5
283 LUTH--MO SYNOD	1	152	221	0.8	2.3
290 METRO COMM CHS	0	0	25	0.1	0.3
413 S.D.A.........	1	223	267*	1.0	2.8
419 SO BAPT CONV..	4	683	817*	3.0	8.7
435 UNITARIAN-UNIV	1	15	18*	0.1	0.2
449 UN METHODIST..	2	747	894*	3.3	9.5
453 UN PRES CH USA	5	544	651*	2.4	6.9
LARIMER	**106**	**27 486**	**50 222***	**33.7**	**100.0**
019 AMER BAPT USA.	2	505	604*	0.4	1.2
029 AMER LUTH CH..	4	2 941	3 979	2.7	7.9
053 ASSEMB OF GOD.	7	716	1 378	0.9	2.7
057 BAPT GEN CONF.	2	325	389*	0.3	0.8
081 CATHOLIC......	6	NA	11 000	7.4	21.9
093 CHR CH (DISC).	3	1 791	3 478	2.3	6.9
097 CHR CHS&CHS CR	1	100	120*	0.1	0.2
105 CHRISTIAN REF.	2	203	305	0.2	0.6
123 CH GOD (ANDER)	1	133	399	0.3	0.8
127 CH GOD (CLEVE)	1	22	26*	–	0.1
133 CH GOD(7TH)DEN	1	1	1*	–	–
151 L-D SAINTS....	7	NA	2 558	1.7	5.1
164 CH LUTH CONF..	1	10	11	–	–
165 CH OF NAZARENE	3	419	720	0.5	1.4
167 CHS OF CHRIST.	7	865	1 098	0.7	2.2
179 CONSRV BAPT...	2	456	546*	0.4	1.1
193 EPISCOPAL.....	5	1 327	1 577	1.1	3.1
201 EVAN COV CH AM	1	340	407*	0.3	0.8
203 EVAN FREE CH..	2	298	357*	0.2	0.7
221 FREE METHODIST	1	62	360	0.2	0.7
226 FRIENDS-USA...	2	24	29*	–	0.1
263 INT FOURSQ GOS	3	176	211*	0.1	0.4
281 LUTH CH AMER..	2	1 208	1 646	1.1	3.3
283 LUTH--MO SYNOD	7	2 387	3 065	2.1	6.1
353 CHR BRETHREN..	1	50	70	–	0.1
369 PROT REF CHS..	1	100	173	0.1	0.3
403 SALVATION ARMY	1	113	230	0.2	0.5
413 S.D.A.........	5	1 361	1 629*	1.1	3.2
419 SO BAPT CONV..	7	1 875	2 244*	1.5	4.5
435 UNITARIAN-UNIV	1	286	342*	0.2	0.7
443 UN C OF CHRIST	2	892	1 068*	0.7	2.1
449 UN METHODIST..	5	4 307	5 155*	3.5	10.3
453 UN PRES CH USA	9	4 083	4 887*	3.3	9.7
469 WELS.........	1	110	160	0.1	0.3
LAS ANIMAS	**32**	**1 459**	**7 565***	**50.8**	**100.0**
019 AMER BAPT USA.	1	45	54*	0.4	0.7
053 ASSEMB OF GOD.	2	20	35	0.2	0.5
081 CATHOLIC......	13	NA	5 543	37.2	73.3
093 CHR CH (DISC).	1	188	364	2.4	4.8
151 L-D SAINTS....	1	NA	76	0.5	1.0
165 CH OF NAZARENE	1	22	21	0.1	0.3
167 CHS OF CHRIST.	2	68	91	0.6	1.2
193 EPISCOPAL.....	1	66	70	0.5	0.9
263 INT FOURSQ GOS	2	85	103*	0.7	1.4
271 REFORM JUDAISM	1	20	24*	0.2	0.3
281 LUTH CH AMER..	1	79	139	0.9	1.8
413 S.D.A.........	1	62	75*	0.5	1.0
419 SO BAPT CONV..	2	414	499*	3.3	6.6
449 UN METHODIST..	1	295	356*	2.4	4.7
453 UN PRES CH USA	2	95	115*	0.8	1.5
LINCOLN	**21**	**1 369**	**2 311***	**49.6**	**100.0**
019 AMER BAPT USA.	1	166	196*	4.2	8.5
029 AMER LUTH CH..	2	138	195	4.2	8.4
081 CATHOLIC......	2	NA	589	12.6	25.5
157 CH OF BRETHREN	1	39	46*	1.0	2.0
165 CH OF NAZARENE	2	55	119	2.6	5.1
167 CHS OF CHRIST.	1	61	86	1.8	3.7
193 EPISCOPAL.....	1	31	33	0.7	1.4
283 LUTH--MO SYNOD	3	129	153	3.3	6.6
353 CHR BRETHREN..	2	65	85	1.8	3.7
413 S.D.A.........	1	29	34*	0.7	1.5
443 UN C OF CHRIST	1	78	92*	2.0	4.0
449 UN METHODIST..	4	578	683*	14.6	29.6
LOGAN	**36**	**6 087**	**14 004***	**70.7**	**100.0**
019 AMER BAPT USA.	2	425	517*	2.6	3.7
029 AMER LUTH CH..	1	334	466	2.4	3.3
053 ASSEMB OF GOD.	3	176	327	1.7	2.3
063 BEREAN FUND CH	1	24	29*	0.1	0.2
081 CATHOLIC......	4	NA	6 020	30.4	43.0
093 CHR CH (DISC).	1	249	366	1.8	2.6
151 L-D SAINTS....	1	NA	182	0.9	1.3
165 CH OF NAZARENE	1	113	183	0.9	1.3
167 CHS OF CHRIST.	1	40	51	0.3	0.4
193 EPISCOPAL.....	2	309	410	2.1	2.9
203 EVAN FREE CH..	1	41	50*	0.3	0.4
263 INT FOURSQ GOS	1	238	289*	1.5	2.1
283 LUTH--MO SYNOD	3	821	1 082	5.5	7.7
413 S.D.A.........	1	100	122*	0.6	0.9
419 SO BAPT CONV..	2	329	400*	2.0	2.9
443 UN C OF CHRIST	2	209	254*	1.3	1.8
449 UN METHODIST..	8	1 838	2 234*	11.3	16.0
453 UN PRES CH USA	1	841	1 022*	5.2	7.3
MESA	**70**	**13 275**	**28 691***	**35.2**	**100.0**
019 AMER BAPT USA.	4	887	1 081*	1.3	3.8
029 AMER LUTH CH..	1	493	691	0.8	2.4
053 ASSEMB OF GOD.	7	1 167	2 180	2.7	7.6
081 CATHOLIC......	4	NA	7 210	8.8	25.1
093 CHR CH (DISC).	1	377	460	0.6	1.6
097 CHR CHS&CHS CR	5	820	1 000*	1.2	3.5
123 CH GOD (ANDER)	1	80	240	0.3	0.8
127 CH GOD (CLEVE)	1	160	195*	0.2	0.7
151 L-D SAINTS....	7	NA	4 139	5.1	14.4
157 CH OF BRETHREN	1	166	202*	0.2	0.7
165 CH OF NAZARENE	2	266	349	0.4	1.2
167 CHS OF CHRIST.	4	355	452	0.6	1.6
179 CONSRV BAPT...	2	456	556*	0.7	1.9
193 EPISCOPAL.....	2	635	735	0.9	2.6
203 EVAN FREE CH..	2	120	146*	0.2	0.5
226 FRIENDS-USA...	1	59	72*	0.1	0.3
263 INT FOURSQ GOS	1	152	185*	0.2	0.6
283 LUTH--MO SYNOD	1	582	777	1.0	2.7
290 METRO COMM CHS	0	0	25	–	0.1
335 ORTH PRESB CH.	1	35	43*	0.1	0.1
349 PENT HOLINESS.	1	36	44*	0.1	0.2
403 SALVATION ARMY	1	115	181	0.2	0.6
413 S.D.A.........	3	725	884*	1.1	3.1
419 SO BAPT CONV..	5	1 712	2 087*	2.6	7.3
435 UNITARIAN-UNIV	1	30	37*	–	0.1
443 UN C OF CHRIST	2	664	809*	1.0	2.8
449 UN METHODIST..	7	2 417	2 946*	3.6	10.3

NA— Not applicable   *Total adherents estimated from known number of communicant, confirmed, full members.   —Represents a percent less than 0.1.   Percentages may not total due to rounding.

Table 4. Churches and Church Membership by County and Denomination: 1980

County and Denomination	Number of churches	Communicant, confirmed, full members	Total adherents Number	Total adherents Percent of total population	Total adherents Percent of total adherents
453 UN PRES CH USA	1	703	857*	1.1	3.0
469 WELS.........	1	63	108	0.1	0.4
MINERAL	3	91	130*	16.2	100.0
167 CHS OF CHRIST.	1	20	25	3.1	19.2
193 EPISCOPAL....	1	25	50	6.2	38.5
443 UN C OF CHRIST	1	46	55*	6.8	42.3
MOFFAT	17	1 470	3 397*	25.9	100.0
053 ASSEMB OF GOD.	1	87	128	1.0	3.8
081 CATHOLIC......	1	NA	600	4.6	17.7
097 CHR CHS&CHS CR	1	300	378*	2.9	11.1
127 CH GOD (CLEVE)	1	53	67*	0.5	2.0
151 L-D SAINTS....	2	NA	867	6.6	25.5
165 CH OF NAZARENE	1	38	75	0.6	2.2
167 CHS OF CHRIST.	2	80	102	0.8	3.0
193 EPISCOPAL.....	1	56	56	0.4	1.6
283 LUTH--MO SYNOD	1	117	194	1.5	5.7
413 S.D.A.........	1	50	63*	0.5	1.9
419 SO BAPT CONV..	2	347	437*	3.3	12.9
443 UN C OF CHRIST	2	264	332*	2.5	9.8
449 UN METHODIST..	1	78	98*	0.7	2.9
MONTEZUMA	30	3 201	7 133*	43.2	100.0
019 AMER BAPT USA.	2	306	383*	2.3	5.4
053 ASSEMB OF GOD.	2	183	304	1.8	4.3
059 BAPT MISS ASSN	1	59	74*	0.4	1.0
081 CATHOLIC......	3	NA	1 675	10.1	23.5
097 CHR CHS&CHS CR	1	70	88*	0.5	1.2
151 L-D SAINTS....	4	NA	1 218	7.4	17.1
165 CH OF NAZARENE	1	35	77	0.5	1.1
167 CHS OF CHRIST.	4	200	255	1.5	3.6
193 EPISCOPAL.....	1	219	371	2.2	5.2
263 INT FOURSQ GOS	1	49	61*	0.4	0.9
283 LUTH--MO SYNOD	1	120	173	1.0	2.4
413 S.D.A.........	1	261	327*	2.0	4.6
419 SO BAPT CONV..	2	985	1 233*	7.5	17.3
449 UN METHODIST..	3	500	626*	3.8	8.8
453 UN PRES CH USA	3	214	268*	1.6	3.8
MONTROSE	34	4 899	8 447*	34.7	100.0
019 AMER BAPT USA.	2	622	766*	3.1	9.1
053 ASSEMB OF GOD.	4	260	452	1.9	5.4
081 CATHOLIC......	2	NA	1 100	4.5	13.0
097 CHR CHS&CHS CR	1	1 031	1 270*	5.2	15.0
151 L-D SAINTS....	3	NA	1 064	4.4	12.6
165 CH OF NAZARENE	1	112	183	0.8	2.2
167 CHS OF CHRIST.	2	103	131	0.5	1.6
179 CONSRV BAPT...	1	228	281*	1.2	3.3
193 EPISCOPAL.....	2	129	193	0.8	2.3
283 LUTH--MO SYNOD	1	251	325	1.3	3.8
381 REF PRES-EVAN.	1	34	57	0.2	0.7
413 S.D.A.........	2	310	382*	1.6	4.5
419 SO BAPT CONV..	3	690	850*	3.5	10.1
443 UN C OF CHRIST	4	178	219*	0.9	2.6
449 UN METHODIST..	2	650	800*	3.3	9.5
453 UN PRES CH USA	2	251	309*	1.3	3.7
469 WELS.........	1	50	65	0.3	0.8
MORGAN	40	7 244	12 068*	53.6	100.0
019 AMER BAPT USA.	1	312	384*	1.7	3.2
029 AMER LUTH CH..	3	831	1 074	4.8	8.9
053 ASSEMB OF GOD.	3	190	439	1.9	3.6
063 BEREAN FUND CH	1	35	43*	0.2	0.4
081 CATHOLIC......	4	NA	2 400	10.7	19.9
093 CHR CH (DISC).	1	329	428	1.9	3.5
151 L-D SAINTS.....	1	NA	208	0.9	1.7
165 CH OF NAZARENE	3	232	439	1.9	3.6
167 CHS OF CHRIST.	2	170	217	1.0	1.8
193 EPISCOPAL.....	1	111	132	0.6	1.1
226 FRIENDS-USA...	1	70	86*	0.4	0.7
283 LUTH--MO SYNOD	1	551	786	3.5	6.5
349 PENT HOLINESS.	1	33	41*	0.2	0.3
413 S.D.A.........	1	51	63*	0.3	0.5
419 SO BAPT CONV..	3	725	892*	4.0	7.4
443 UN C OF CHRIST	3	1 055	1 298*	5.8	10.8
449 UN METHODIST..	5	1 562	1 922*	8.5	15.9
453 UN PRES CH USA	3	894	1 100*	4.9	9.1
469 WELS.........	2	93	116	0.5	1.0
OTERO	52	6 215	13 870*	61.5	100.0
017 AMER BAPT ASSN	1	50	50	0.2	0.4
019 AMER BAPT USA.	3	599	737*	3.3	5.3
029 AMER LUTH CH..	1	176	226	1.0	1.6
053 ASSEMB OF GOD.	4	188	357	1.6	2.6
081 CATHOLIC......	4	NA	5 500	24.4	39.7
093 CHR CH (DISC).	4	513	792	3.5	5.7
097 CHR CHS&CHS CR	1	22	27*	0.1	0.2
123 CH GOD (ANDER)	2	92	276	1.2	2.0
127 CH GOD (CLEVE)	1	49	60*	0.3	0.4
151 L-D SAINTS....	2	NA	154	0.7	1.1
165 CH OF NAZARENE	4	302	391	1.7	2.8
167 CHS OF CHRIST.	4	311	396	1.8	2.9
193 EPISCOPAL.....	1	128	227	1.0	1.6
226 FRIENDS-USA...	1	69	85*	0.4	0.6
263 INT FOURSQ GOS	1	28	34*	0.2	0.2
283 LUTH--MO SYNOD	2	243	321	1.4	2.3
285 MENNONITE CH..	4	315	387*	1.7	2.8
413 S.D.A.........	1	159	196*	0.9	1.4

County and Denomination	Number of churches	Communicant, confirmed, full members	Total adherents Number	Total adherents Percent of total population	Total adherents Percent of total adherents
419 SO BAPT CONV..	3	645	793*	3.5	5.7
449 UN METHODIST..	6	1 748	2 150*	9.5	15.5
453 UN PRES CH USA	2	578	711*	3.2	5.1
OURAY	5	281	726*	37.7	100.0
081 CATHOLIC......	1	NA	400	20.8	55.1
097 CHR CHS&CHS CR	1	55	67*	3.5	9.2
193 EPISCOPAL.....	1	75	76	3.9	10.5
419 SO BAPT CONV..	1	47	57*	3.0	7.9
453 UN PRES CH USA	1	104	126*	6.5	17.4
PARK	4	107	134*	2.5	100.0
097 CHR CHS&CHS CR	1	15	19*	0.4	14.2
413 S.D.A.........	1	12	15*	0.3	11.2
419 SO BAPT CONV..	1	52	65*	1.2	48.5
453 UN PRES CH USA	1	28	35*	0.7	26.1
PHILLIPS	20	2 392	3 452*	76.0	100.0
053 ASSEMB OF GOD.	2	77	180	4.0	5.2
063 BEREAN FUND CH	1	57	69*	1.5	2.0
081 CATHOLIC......	2	NA	400	8.8	11.6
097 CHR CHS&CHS CR	1	225	273*	6.0	7.9
157 CH OF BRETHREN	1	88	107*	2.4	3.1
165 CH OF NAZARENE	1	51	61	1.3	1.8
167 CHS OF CHRIST.	2	40	51	1.1	1.5
179 CONSRV BAPT...	1	228	276*	6.1	8.0
201 EVAN COV CH AM	1	78	95*	2.1	2.8
283 LUTH--MO SYNOD	3	600	783	17.2	22.7
353 CHR BRETHREN..	1	10	20	0.4	0.6
413 S.D.A.........	1	29	35*	0.8	1.0
419 SO BAPT CONV..	1	56	68*	1.5	2.0
449 UN METHODIST..	2	853	1 034*	22.8	30.0
PITKIN	12	595	1 856*	18.0	100.0
081 CATHOLIC......	5	NA	1 000	9.7	53.9
151 L-D SAINTS....	1	NA	144	1.4	7.8
179 CONSRV BAPT...	1	228	258*	2.5	13.9
193 EPISCOPAL.....	1	154	185	1.8	10.0
283 LUTH--MO SYNOD	1	18	23	0.2	1.2
290 METRO COMM CHS	0	0	25	0.2	1.3
435 UNITARIAN-UNIV	1	20	23*	0.2	1.2
449 UN METHODIST..	2	175	198*	1.9	10.7
PROWERS	34	4 399	8 062*	61.7	100.0
019 AMER BAPT USA.	2	787	983*	7.5	12.2
053 ASSEMB OF GOD.	2	59	93	0.7	1.2
081 CATHOLIC......	4	NA	2 020	15.5	25.1
097 CHR CHS&CHS CR	2	534	667*	5.1	8.3
123 CH GOD (ANDER)	2	106	318	2.4	3.9
151 L-D SAINTS....	1	NA	148	1.1	1.8
157 CH OF BRETHREN	1	113	141*	1.1	1.7
164 CH LUTH CONF..	1	70	105	0.8	1.3
165 CH OF NAZARENE	3	110	222	1.7	2.8
167 CHS OF CHRIST.	4	115	146	1.1	1.8
193 EPISCOPAL.....	1	81	146	1.1	1.8
263 INT FOURSQ GOS	1	206	257*	2.0	3.2
283 LUTH--MO SYNOD	1	129	208	1.6	2.6
413 S.D.A.........	1	69	86*	0.7	1.1
419 SO BAPT CONV..	1	381	476*	3.6	5.9
449 UN METHODIST..	5	1 457	1 819*	13.9	22.6
453 UN PRES CH USA	2	182	227*	1.7	2.8
PUEBLO	107	20 441	65 536*	52.0	100.0
019 AMER BAPT USA.	7	2 975	3 622*	2.9	5.5
053 ASSEMB OF GOD.	5	1 260	2 447	1.9	3.7
081 CATHOLIC......	22	NA	36 561	29.0	55.8
093 CHR CH (DISC).	4	1 482	2 235	1.8	3.4
097 CHR CHS&CHS CR	1	150	183*	0.1	0.3
123 CH GOD (ANDER)	1	57	171	0.1	0.3
127 CH GOD (CLEVE)	2	107	130*	0.1	0.2
151 L-D SAINTS....	4	NA	1 483	1.2	2.3
165 CH OF NAZARENE	4	583	1 293	1.0	2.0
167 CHS OF CHRIST.	5	732	922	0.7	1.4
179 CONSRV BAPT...	3	684	833*	0.7	1.3
193 EPISCOPAL.....	3	758	1 178	0.9	1.8
221 FREE METHODIST	1	24	72	0.1	0.1
226 FRIENDS-USA...	1	93	113*	0.1	0.2
263 INT FOURSQ GOS	2	416	506*	0.4	0.8
270 CONSRV JUDAISM	1	33	40*	–	0.1
271 REFORM JUDAISM	1	80	97*	0.1	0.1
281 LUTH CH AMER..	2	824	1 126	0.9	1.7
283 LUTH--MO SYNOD	3	554	734	0.6	1.1
285 MENNONITE CH..	1	27	33*	–	0.1
349 PENT HOLINESS.	1	42	51*	–	0.1
353 CHR BRETHREN..	1	10	15	–	–
403 SALVATION ARMY	1	77	139	0.1	0.2
413 S.D.A.........	3	455	554*	0.4	0.8
419 SO BAPT CONV..	9	2 611	3 179*	2.5	4.9
435 UNITARIAN-UNIV	1	21	26*	–	0.1
443 UN C OF CHRIST	2	357	435*	0.3	0.7
449 UN METHODIST..	12	4 203	5 117*	4.1	7.8
453 UN PRES CH USA	3	1 712	2 084*	1.7	3.2
469 WELS.........	1	114	157	0.1	0.2
RIO BLANCO	15	1 125	2 657*	42.5	100.0
019 AMER BAPT USA.	1	176	220*	3.5	8.3
053 ASSEMB OF GOD.	2	47	93	1.5	3.5
081 CATHOLIC......	2	NA	600	9.6	22.6

NA—Not applicable   *Total adherents estimated from known number of communicant, confirmed, full members.   —Represents a percent less than 0.1.   Percentages may not total due to rounding.

Table 4. Churches and Church Membership by County and Denomination: 1980

County and Denomination	Number of churches	Communicant, confirmed, full members	Total adherents		
			Number	Percent of total population	Percent of total adherents
097 CHR CHS&CHS CR	2	162	202*	3.2	7.6
151 L-D SAINTS....	2	NA	628	10.0	23.6
167 CHS OF CHRIST.	1	48	61	1.0	2.3
193 EPISCOPAL.....	2	269	322	5.1	12.1
283 LUTH--MO SYNOD	1	20	28	0.4	1.1
419 SO BAPT CONV..	1	174	217*	3.5	8.2
449 UN METHODIST..	1	229	286*	4.6	10.8
RIO GRANDE	29	2 243	5 998*	57.1	100.0
019 AMER BAPT USA.	1	97	120*	1.1	2.0
053 ASSEMB OF GOD.	3	68	131	1.2	2.2
081 CATHOLIC......	5	NA	2 700	25.7	45.0
093 CHR CH (DISC).	1	36	66	0.6	1.1
097 CHR CHS&CHS CR	1	85	105*	1.0	1.8
151 L-D SAINTS....	1	NA	344	3.3	5.7
165 CH OF NAZARENE	1	66	133	1.3	2.2
167 CHS OF CHRIST.	2	92	117	1.1	2.0
193 EPISCOPAL.....	1	129	172	1.6	2.9
226 FRIENDS-USA...	1	48	60*	0.6	1.0
283 LUTH--MO SYNOD	1	184	271	2.6	4.5
313 N AM BAPT CONF	1	34	42*	0.4	0.7
353 CHR BRETHREN..	1	30	30	0.3	0.5
413 S.D.A.........	1	68	84*	0.8	1.4
419 SO BAPT CONV..	2	339	421*	4.0	7.0
449 UN METHODIST..	3	660	819*	7.8	13.7
453 UN PRES CH USA	2	290	360*	3.4	6.0
469 WELS..........	1	17	23	0.2	0.4
ROUTT	13	1 049	2 202*	16.4	100.0
053 ASSEMB OF GOD.	1	56	77	0.6	3.5
081 CATHOLIC......	2	NA	750	5.6	34.1
151 L-D SAINTS....	1	NA	130	1.0	5.9
167 CHS OF CHRIST.	2	67	79	0.6	3.6
193 EPISCOPAL.....	1	100	149	1.1	6.8
283 LUTH--MO SYNOD	1	124	169	1.3	7.7
413 S.D.A.........	1	17	21*	0.2	1.0
419 SO BAPT CONV..	1	149	180*	1.3	8.2
443 UN C OF CHRIST	1	145	175*	1.3	7.9
449 UN METHODIST..	2	391	472*	3.5	21.4
SAGUACHE	12	812	3 846*	97.7	100.0
019 AMER BAPT USA.	1	135	166*	4.2	4.3
053 ASSEMB OF GOD.	1	77	122	3.1	3.2
081 CATHOLIC......	3	NA	2 700	68.6	70.2
123 CH GOD (ANDER)	1	25	75	1.9	2.0
151 L-D SAINTS....	1	NA	77	2.0	2.0
167 CHS OF CHRIST.	1	8	8	0.2	0.2
419 SO BAPT CONV..	2	187	230*	5.8	6.0
449 UN METHODIST..	2	380	468*	11.9	12.2
SAN JUAN	4	100	177*	21.2	100.0
151 L-D SAINTS....	1	NA	52	6.2	29.4
167 CHS OF CHRIST.	1	12	15	1.8	8.5
419 SO BAPT CONV..	1	35	44*	5.3	24.9
443 UN C OF CHRIST	1	53	66*	7.9	37.3
SAN MIGUEL	6	210	258*	8.1	100.0
097 CHR CHS&CHS CR	1	26	32*	1.0	12.4
167 CHS OF CHRIST.	1	30	38	1.2	14.7
349 PENT HOLINESS.	1	21	26*	0.8	10.1
419 SO BAPT CONV..	1	72	88*	2.8	34.1
449 UN METHODIST..	1	20	24*	0.8	9.3
453 UN PRES CH USA	1	41	50*	1.6	19.4
SEDGWICK	12	1 412	2 558*	78.3	100.0
053 ASSEMB OF GOD.	2	60	126	3.9	4.9
081 CATHOLIC......	2	NA	800	24.5	31.3
097 CHR CHS&CHS CR	1	220	266*	8.1	10.4
179 CONSRV BAPT...	1	228	276*	8.5	10.8
283 LUTH--MO SYNOD	1	254	304	9.3	11.9
285 MENNONITE CH..	1	29	35*	1.1	1.4
413 S.D.A.........	1	41	50*	1.5	2.0
449 UN METHODIST..	2	540	653*	20.0	25.5
453 UN PRES CH USA	1	40	48*	1.5	1.9
SUMMIT	10	532	1 250*	14.1	100.0
053 ASSEMB OF GOD.	1	21	52	0.6	4.2
081 CATHOLIC......	3	NA	450	5.1	36.0
151 L-D SAINTS....	1	NA	132	1.5	10.6
167 CHS OF CHRIST.	1	40	44	0.5	3.5
193 EPISCOPAL.....	1	90	107	1.2	8.6
201 EVAN COV CH AM	1	35	41*	0.5	3.3
281 LUTH CH AMER..	1	104	142	1.6	11.4
449 UN METHODIST..	1	242	282*	3.2	22.6
TELLER	15	1 387	2 432*	30.3	100.0
019 AMER BAPT USA.	1	78	95*	1.2	3.9
053 ASSEMB OF GOD.	1	19	22	0.3	0.9
081 CATHOLIC......	3	NA	550	6.8	22.6
151 L-D SAINTS....	1	NA	73	0.9	3.0
165 CH OF NAZARENE	1	82	141	1.8	5.8
167 CHS OF CHRIST.	1	65	69	0.9	2.8
193 EPISCOPAL.....	2	95	162	2.0	6.7
283 LUTH--MO SYNOD	1	259	343	4.3	14.1
353 CHR BRETHREN..	1	30	50	0.6	2.1
419 SO BAPT CONV..	1	578	706*	8.8	29.0
443 UN C OF CHRIST	1	44	54*	0.7	2.2

County and Denomination	Number of churches	Communicant, confirmed, full members	Total adherents		
			Number	Percent of total population	Percent of total adherents
449 UN METHODIST..	1	137	167*	2.1	6.9
WASHINGTON	15	1 495	2 491*	47.0	100.0
029 AMER LUTH CH..	2	239	365	6.9	14.7
053 ASSEMB OF GOD.	2	69	77	1.5	3.1
081 CATHOLIC......	2	NA	600	11.3	24.1
165 CH OF NAZARENE	1	19	29	0.5	1.2
167 CHS OF CHRIST.	1	40	46	0.9	1.8
263 INT FOURSQ GOS	1	124	150*	2.8	6.0
283 LUTH--MO SYNOD	1	76	103	1.9	4.1
413 S.D.A.........	1	24	29*	0.5	1.2
449 UN METHODIST..	2	478	577*	10.9	23.2
453 UN PRES CH USA	2	426	515*	9.7	20.7
WELD	140	21 939	44 207*	35.8	100.0
017 AMER BAPT ASSN	1	160	160	0.1	0.4
019 AMER BAPT USA.	4	964	1 180*	1.0	2.7
029 AMER LUTH CH..	5	1 714	2 137	1.7	4.8
053 ASSEMB OF GOD.	16	1 205	2 300	1.9	5.2
057 BAPT GEN CONF.	1	310	380*	0.3	0.9
063 BEREAN FUND CH	1	14	17*	-	-
081 CATHOLIC......	17	NA	14 230	11.5	32.2
093 CHR CH (DISC).	3	714	859	0.7	1.9
097 CHR CHS&CHS CR	2	430	527*	0.4	1.2
105 CHRISTIAN REF.	1	82	159	0.1	0.4
123 CH GOD (ANDER)	2	146	438	0.4	1.0
127 CH GOD (CLEVE)	1	41	50*	-	0.1
151 L-D SAINTS....	3	NA	1 306	1.1	3.0
157 CH OF BRETHREN	1	57	70*	0.1	0.2
165 CH OF NAZARENE	3	344	593	0.5	1.3
167 CHS OF CHRIST.	3	250	318	0.3	0.7
175 CONGR CHR CHS.	1	101	124*	0.1	0.3
179 CONSRV BAPT...	1	228	279*	0.2	0.6
193 EPISCOPAL.....	3	613	978	0.8	2.2
201 EVAN COV CH AM	1	71	87*	0.1	0.2
203 EVAN FREE CH..	4	486	595*	0.5	1.3
221 FREE METHODIST	1	18	60	-	0.1
263 INT FOURSQ GOS	8	620	759*	0.6	1.7
281 LUTH CH AMER..	2	838	1 139	0.9	2.6
283 LUTH--MO SYNOD	7	1 485	1 908	1.5	4.3
285 MENNONITE CH..	2	122	149*	0.1	0.3
313 N AM BAPT CONF	2	187	229*	0.2	0.5
349 PENT HOLINESS.	4	173	212*	0.2	0.5
353 CHR BRETHREN..	1	25	25	-	0.1
383 REF PRES OF NA	1	81	88	0.1	0.2
403 SALVATION ARMY	1	84	147	0.1	0.3
413 S.D.A.........	3	587	719*	0.6	1.6
419 SO BAPT CONV..	7	1 641	2 009*	1.6	4.5
435 UNITARIAN-UNIV	1	50	61*	-	0.1
443 UN C OF CHRIST	6	2 762	3 382*	2.7	7.7
449 UN METHODIST..	13	3 922	4 802*	3.9	10.9
453 UN PRES CH USA	6	1 316	1 611*	1.3	3.6
469 WELS..........	2	98	120	0.1	0.3
YUMA	32	3 014	4 495*	46.4	100.0
053 ASSEMB OF GOD.	2	79	154	1.6	3.4
081 CATHOLIC......	1	NA	250	2.6	5.6
093 CHR CH (DISC).	1	176	540	5.6	12.0
151 L-D SAINTS....	1	NA	57	0.6	1.3
165 CH OF NAZARENE	4	193	292	3.0	6.5
167 CHS OF CHRIST.	2	55	70	0.7	1.6
237 GC MENN BR CHS	1	50	61*	0.4	1.4
263 INT FOURSQ GOS	2	28	34*	0.4	0.8
283 LUTH--MO SYNOD	2	573	750	7.7	16.7
413 S.D.A.........	2	95	117*	1.2	2.6
419 SO BAPT CONV..	2	153	188*	1.9	4.2
443 UN C OF CHRIST	1	75	92*	1.0	2.0
449 UN METHODIST..	8	1 015	1 248*	12.9	27.8
453 UN PRES CH USA	3	522	642*	6.6	14.3

CONNECTICUT

County and Denomination	Number of churches	Communicant, confirmed, full members	Total adherents		
			Number	Percent of total population	Percent of total adherents
THE STATE.....	1 725	401 848	1 913 148*	61.6	100.0
FAIRFIELD	396	111 748	491 382*	60.9	100.0
001 ADVENT CHR CH.	3	196	233*	-	-
005 AME ZION......	6	1 050	1 980	0.2	0.4
019 AMER BAPT USA.	29	9 888	11 779*	1.5	2.4
053 ASSEMB OF GOD.	12	1 402	2 397	0.3	0.5
057 BAPT GEN CONF.	2	379	451*	0.1	0.1
081 CATHOLIC......	111	NA	345 244	42.8	70.3
089 CHR & MISS AL.	2	112	182	-	-
093 CHR CH (DISC).	3	323	465	0.1	0.1
097 CHR CHS&CHS CR	1	54	64*	-	-
101 C.M.E.........	2	1 446	1 722*	0.2	0.4
127 CH GOD (CLEVE)	4	209	249*	-	0.1
151 L-D SAINTS....	3	NA	1 381	0.3	0.3
165 CH OF NAZARENE	4	181	342	-	0.1
167 CHS OF CHRIST.	4	475	677	0.1	0.1

NA—Not applicable   *Total adherents estimated from known number of communicant, confirmed, full members.   —Represents a percent less than 0.1.   Percentages may not total due to rounding.

Table 4. Churches and Church Membership by County and Denomination: 1980

County and Denomination	Number of churches	Communicant, confirmed, full members	Total adherents Number	Percent of total population	Percent of total adherents
175 CONGR CHR CHS.	2	200	238*	–	–
179 CONSRV BAPT...	2	241	287*	–	0.1
193 EPISCOPAL.....	43	23 762	35 745	4.4	7.3
201 EVAN COV CH AM	3	420	500*	0.1	0.1
203 EVAN FREE CH..	4	537	640*	0.1	0.1
208 EVAN LUTH ASSN	2	878	1 283	0.2	0.3
226 FRIENDS-USA...	2	273	325*	–	0.1
233 GEN CH NEW JER	1	20	24*	–	–
270 CONSRV JUDAISM	8	1 620	1 930*	0.2	0.4
271 REFORM JUDAISM	7	4 942	5 887*	0.7	1.2
274 LAT EVAN LUTH.	1	34	34	–	–
281 LUTH CH AMER..	15	6 650	8 636	1.1	1.8
283 LUTH--MO SYNOD	10	4 744	6 031	0.7	1.2
290 METRO COMM CHS	0	0	50	–	–
313 N AM BAPT CONF	1	81	96*	–	–
353 CHR BRETHREN..	3	150	200	–	–
403 SALVATION ARMY	4	379	1 256	0.2	0.3
413 S.D.A.........	5	627	747*	0.1	0.2
419 SO BAPT CONV..	4	1 526	1 818*	0.2	0.4
431 UKRANIAN AMER.	3	335	575	0.1	0.1
435 UNITARIAN-UNIV	4	950	1 132*	0.1	0.2
443 UN C OF CHRIST	44	22 551	26 863*	3.3	5.5
449 UN METHODIST..	33	18 293	21 791*	2.7	4.4
453 UN PRES CH USA	8	6 802	8 103*	1.0	1.6
469 WELS..........	1	18	25	–	–
HARTFORD	**406**	**116 083**	**546 007***	**67.6**	**100.0**
001 ADVENT CHR CH.	3	321	381*	–	0.1
005 AME ZION......	9	5 739	6 984	0.9	1.3
019 AMER BAPT USA.	27	10 213	12 110*	1.5	2.2
049 ARMEN AP CH AM	1	200	350	–	0.1
053 ASSEMB OF GOD.	10	1 337	1 997	0.2	0.4
057 BAPT GEN CONF.	6	752	892*	0.1	0.2
081 CATHOLIC......	100	NA	398 533	49.3	73.0
089 CHR & MISS AL.	2	133	204	–	–
097 CHR CHS&CHS CR	3	143	170*	–	–
101 C.M.E.........	3	1 224	1 451*	0.2	0.3
105 CHRISTIAN REF.	1	74	147	–	–
123 CH GOD (ANDER)	1	25	75	–	–
127 CH GOD (CLEVE)	6	449	532*	0.1	0.1
151 L-D SAINTS....	3	NA	1 441	0.2	0.3
163 CH OF LUTH BR.	1	130	216	–	–
165 CH OF NAZARENE	3	438	1 008	0.1	0.2
167 CHS OF CHRIST.	5	338	516	0.1	0.1
175 CONGR CHR CHS.	1	1 555	1 844*	0.2	0.3
179 CONSRV BAPT...	1	60	71*	–	–
193 EPISCOPAL.....	38	16 830	23 800	2.9	4.4
195 ESTONIAN ELC..	1	113	578	0.1	0.1
201 EVAN COV CH AM	5	1 135	1 346*	0.2	0.2
203 EVAN FREE CH..	3	194	230*	–	–
208 EVAN LUTH ASSN	7	1 656	2 232	0.3	0.4
226 FRIENDS-USA...	1	238	282*	–	0.1
270 CONSRV JUDAISM	13	2 583	3 063*	0.4	0.6
271 REFORM JUDAISM	4	3 950	4 684*	0.6	0.9
274 LAT EVAN LUTH.	2	273	297	–	0.1
281 LUTH CH AMER..	14	9 684	12 321	1.5	2.3
283 LUTH--MO SYNOD	8	3 705	4 782	0.6	0.9
290 METRO COMM CHS	1	70	140	–	–
353 CHR BRETHREN..	4	150	200	–	–
381 REF PRES-EVAN.	1	47	61	–	–
403 SALVATION ARMY	6	729	1 861	0.2	0.3
413 S.D.A.........	6	1 020	1 209*	0.1	0.2
419 SO BAPT CONV..	5	520	617*	0.1	0.1
435 UNITARIAN-UNIV	5	1 441	1 709*	0.2	0.3
443 UN C OF CHRIST	58	33 150	39 306*	4.9	7.2
449 UN METHODIST..	33	13 672	16 211*	2.0	3.0
453 UN PRES CH USA	4	1 680	1 992*	0.2	0.4
469 WELS..........	1	112	164	–	–
LITCHFIELD	**137**	**23 433**	**98 432***	**62.8**	**100.0**
001 ADVENT CHR CH.	2	151	181*	0.1	0.2
019 AMER BAPT USA.	4	850	1 017*	0.6	1.0
053 ASSEMB OF GOD.	3	376	825	0.5	0.8
081 CATHOLIC......	31	NA	66 581	42.5	67.6
151 L-D SAINTS....	1	NA	266	0.2	0.3
167 CHS OF CHRIST.	2	58	83	0.1	0.1
175 CONGR CHR CHS.	4	514	615*	0.4	0.6
193 EPISCOPAL.....	24	5 532	9 650	6.2	9.8
201 EVAN COV CH AM	2	357	427*	0.3	0.4
226 FRIENDS-USA...	2	51	61*	–	0.1
270 CONSRV JUDAISM	1	85	102*	0.1	0.1
271 REFORM JUDAISM	1	240	287*	0.2	0.3
281 LUTH CH AMER..	5	1 838	2 222	1.4	2.3
283 LUTH--MO SYNOD	3	453	518	0.3	0.5
353 CHR BRETHREN..	3	75	100	0.1	0.1
403 SALVATION ARMY	1	37	155	0.1	0.2
413 S.D.A.........	1	52	62*	–	0.1
443 UN C OF CHRIST	33	8 818	10 556*	6.7	10.7
449 UN METHODIST..	14	3 946	4 724*	3.0	4.8
MIDDLESEX	**93**	**17 960**	**70 450***	**54.6**	**100.0**
005 AME ZION......	3	1 338	1 917	1.5	2.7
019 AMER BAPT USA.	5	1 017	1 207*	0.9	1.7
053 ASSEMB OF GOD.	2	71	110	0.1	0.2
081 CATHOLIC......	19	NA	48 212	37.4	68.4
089 CHR & MISS AL.	1	35	125	0.1	0.2
127 CH GOD (CLEVE)	1	13	15*	–	–
175 CONGR CHR CHS.	4	771	915*	0.7	1.3
179 CONSRV BAPT...	1	112	133*	0.1	0.2
193 EPISCOPAL.....	12	3 246	3 934	3.0	5.6
201 EVAN COV CH AM	2	241	286*	0.2	0.4
208 EVAN LUTH ASSN	1	67	100	0.1	0.1

County and Denomination	Number of churches	Communicant, confirmed, full members	Total adherents Number	Percent of total population	Percent of total adherents
226 FRIENDS-USA...	1	35	42*	–	0.1
270 CONSRV JUDAISM	3	315	374*	0.3	0.5
281 LUTH CH AMER..	7	1 897	2 455	1.9	3.5
283 LUTH--MO SYNOD	1	249	326	0.3	0.5
353 CHR BRETHREN..	1	20	40	–	0.1
403 SALVATION ARMY	1	72	213	0.2	0.3
413 S.D.A.........	1	66	78*	0.1	0.1
415 S-D BAPTIST GC	1	30	36*	–	0.1
419 SO BAPT CONV..	1	62	74*	0.1	0.1
443 UN C OF CHRIST	17	5 974	7 093*	5.5	10.1
449 UN METHODIST..	8	2 329	2 765*	2.1	3.9
NEW HAVEN	**374**	**82 659**	**493 580***	**64.8**	**100.0**
001 ADVENT CHR CH.	2	267	317*	–	0.1
005 AME ZION......	8	6 531	7 637	1.0	1.5
019 AMER BAPT USA.	22	8 343	9 910*	1.3	2.0
039 AP CHR CH(NAZ)	1	17	20*	–	–
053 ASSEMB OF GOD.	13	1 770	3 134	0.4	0.6
057 BAPT GEN CONF.	4	521	619*	0.1	0.1
081 CATHOLIC......	107	NA	383 554	50.4	77.7
089 CHR & MISS AL.	2	110	160	–	–
093 CHR CH (DISC).	2	190	293	–	0.1
097 CHR CHS&CHS CR	2	122	145*	–	–
101 C.M.E.........	2	425	505*	0.1	0.1
123 CH GOD (ANDER)	2	60	180	–	–
127 CH GOD (CLEVE)	5	213	253*	–	0.1
151 L-D SAINTS....	3	NA	557	0.1	0.1
165 CH OF NAZARENE	1	61	127	–	–
167 CHS OF CHRIST.	6	232	412	0.1	0.1
175 CONGR CHR CHS.	1	270	321*	–	0.1
179 CONSRV BAPT...	1	57	68*	–	–
193 EPISCOPAL.....	47	14 441	24 941	3.3	5.1
201 EVAN COV CH AM	2	260	309*	–	0.1
203 EVAN FREE CH..	5	308	366*	–	0.1
208 EVAN LUTH ASSN	1	145	190	–	–
226 FRIENDS-USA...	1	69	82*	–	–
270 CONSRV JUDAISM	9	2 071	2 460*	0.3	0.5
271 REFORM JUDAISM	5	2 802	3 328*	0.4	0.7
281 LUTH CH AMER..	16	6 292	8 024	1.1	1.6
283 LUTH--MO SYNOD	7	2 207	2 918	0.4	0.6
285 MENNONITE CH..	1	78	93*	–	–
290 METRO COMM CHS	1	25	50	–	–
313 N AM BAPT CONF	1	38	45*	–	–
335 ORTH PRESB CH.	1	69	82*	–	–
353 CHR BRETHREN..	3	400	550	0.1	0.1
403 SALVATION ARMY	4	424	1 733	0.2	0.4
413 S.D.A.........	6	819	973*	0.1	0.2
419 SO BAPT CONV..	2	86	102*	–	–
435 UNITARIAN-UNIV	4	576	684*	0.1	0.1
443 UN C OF CHRIST	49	23 370	27 759*	3.6	5.6
449 UN METHODIST..	23	8 694	10 327*	1.4	2.1
453 UN PRES CH USA	2	296	352*	–	0.1
NEW LONDON	**159**	**27 653**	**110 058***	**46.2**	**100.0**
005 AME ZION......	2	2 744	2 860	1.2	2.6
019 AMER BAPT USA.	20	4 706	5 649*	2.4	5.1
053 ASSEMB OF GOD.	7	498	862	0.4	0.8
081 CATHOLIC......	33	NA	73 413	30.8	66.7
089 CHR & MISS AL.	1	164	314	0.1	0.3
127 CH GOD (CLEVE)	2	213	256*	0.1	0.2
151 L-D SAINTS....	2	NA	950	0.4	0.9
165 CH OF NAZARENE	1	72	211	0.1	0.2
167 CHS OF CHRIST.	2	91	224	0.1	0.2
175 CONGR CHR CHS.	9	1 204	1 445*	0.6	1.3
179 CONSRV BAPT...	7	957	1 149*	0.5	1.0
193 EPISCOPAL.....	11	4 036	5 613	2.4	5.1
226 FRIENDS-USA...	1	29	35*	–	–
270 CONSRV JUDAISM	3	478	574*	0.2	0.5
271 REFORM JUDAISM	1	316	379*	0.2	0.3
281 LUTH CH AMER..	2	882	1 351	0.6	1.2
283 LUTH--MO SYNOD	4	906	1 271	0.5	1.2
353 CHR BRETHREN..	3	270	870	0.4	0.8
403 SALVATION ARMY	2	175	735	0.3	0.7
413 S.D.A.........	3	275	330*	0.1	0.3
415 S-D BAPTIST GC	1	44	53*	–	–
419 SO BAPT CONV..	4	1 280	1 536*	0.6	1.4
435 UNITARIAN-UNIV	2	231	277*	0.1	0.3
443 UN C OF CHRIST	22	5 469	6 565*	2.8	6.0
449 UN METHODIST..	12	2 277	2 733*	1.1	2.5
453 UN PRES CH USA	2	336	403*	0.2	0.4
TOLLAND	**58**	**12 389**	**43 082***	**37.5**	**100.0**
019 AMER BAPT USA.	3	418	499*	0.4	1.2
053 ASSEMB OF GOD.	1	45	95	0.1	0.2
081 CATHOLIC......	9	NA	27 906	24.3	64.8
167 CHS OF CHRIST.	1	35	50	–	0.1
179 CONSRV BAPT...	2	143	171*	0.1	0.4
193 EPISCOPAL.....	4	1 266	1 704	1.5	4.0
208 EVAN LUTH ASSN	1	375	570	0.5	1.3
226 FRIENDS-USA...	1	75	89*	0.1	0.2
270 CONSRV JUDAISM	1	70	84*	0.1	0.2
281 LUTH CH AMER..	2	705	857	0.7	2.0
283 LUTH--MO SYNOD	2	301	358	0.3	0.8
381 REF PRES-EVAN.	1	61	89	0.1	0.2
413 S.D.A.........	1	61	73*	0.1	0.2
419 SO BAPT CONV..	1	125	149*	0.1	0.3
435 UNITARIAN-UNIV	3	370	441*	0.4	1.0
443 UN C OF CHRIST	19	7 020	8 374*	7.3	19.4
449 UN METHODIST..	6	1 319	1 573*	1.4	3.7
WINDHAM	**102**	**9 923**	**60 157***	**65.2**	**100.0**

NA—Not applicable   *Total adherents estimated from known number of communicant, confirmed, full members.   —Represents a percent less than 0.1.   Percentages may not total due to rounding.

Table 4. Churches and Church Membership by County and Denomination: 1980

County and Denomination	Number of churches	Communicant, confirmed, full members	Total adherents Number	Percent of total population	Percent of total adherents
005 AME ZION......	1	55	90	0.1	0.1
019 AMER BAPT USA.	15	1 589	1 930*	2.1	3.2
053 ASSEMB OF GOD.	3	196	439	0.5	0.7
081 CATHOLIC......	28	NA	47 164	51.1	78.4
089 CHR & MISS AL.	1	0	50	0.1	0.1
151 L-D SAINTS....	1	NA	203	0.2	0.3
165 CH OF NAZARENE	1	97	140	0.2	0.2
167 CHS OF CHRIST.	1	40	60	0.1	0.1
175 CONGR CHR CHS.	3	356	432*	0.5	0.7
179 CONSRV BAPT...	1	150	182*	0.2	0.3
181 CONSRV CONGR..	1	89	108*	0.1	0.2
193 EPISCOPAL..	7	1 349	1 937	2.1	3.2
201 EVAN COV CH AM	1	192	233*	0.3	0.4
270 CONSRV JUDAISM	2	79	96*	0.1	0.2
274 LAT EVAN LUTH.	1	206	230	0.2	0.4
281 LUTH CH AMER..	3	508	655	0.7	1.1
403 SALVATION ARMY	1	57	185	0.2	0.3
413 S.D.A.........	2	98	119*	0.1	0.2
419 SO BAPT CONV..	1	263	319*	0.3	0.5
435 UNITARIAN-UNIV	1	30	36*	–	0.1
443 UN C OF CHRIST	20	3 686	4 477*	4.8	7.4
449 UN METHODIST..	7	883	1 072*	1.2	1.8

DELAWARE

County and Denomination	Number of churches	Communicant, confirmed, full members	Total adherents Number	Percent of total population	Percent of total adherents
THE STATE.....	463	106 015	239 532*	40.2	100.0
KENT	90	15 781	27 272*	27.8	100.0
017 AMER BAPT ASSN	2	50	50	0.1	0.2
019 AMER BAPT USA.	2	623	766*	0.8	2.8
053 ASSEMB OF GOD.	1	56	100	0.1	0.4
061 BEACHY AMISH..	1	?	?	?	?
081 CATHOLIC......	4	NA	6 024	6.1	22.1
097 CHR CHS&CHS CR	2	180	221*	0.2	0.8
123 CH GOD (ANDER)	1	25	75	0.1	0.3
127 CH GOD (CLEVE)	1	33	41*	–	0.2
151 L-D SAINTS....	1	NA	458	0.5	1.7
157 CH OF BRETHREN	1	79	97*	0.1	0.4
165 CH OF NAZARENE	6	346	823	0.8	3.0
167 CHS OF CHRIST.	2	86	165	0.2	0.6
193 EPISCOPAL.....	5	1 433	1 778	1.8	6.5
226 FRIENDS-USA...	1	75	92*	0.1	0.3
270 CONSRV JUDAISM	1	90	111*	0.1	0.4
281 LUTH CH AMER..	1	464	671	0.7	2.5
283 LUTH--MO SYNOD	2	320	414	0.4	1.5
285 MENNONITE CH..	3	178	219*	0.2	0.8
323 OLD ORD AMISH.	6	780	958*	1.0	3.5
353 CHR BRETHREN..	1	30	55	0.1	0.2
381 REF PRES-EVAN.	1	21	27	–	0.1
403 SALVATION ARMY	1	163	919	0.9	3.4
413 S.D.A.........	5	432	531*	0.5	1.9
419 SO BAPT CONV..	4	1 211	1 488*	1.5	5.5
443 UN C OF CHRIST	1	491	603*	0.6	2.2
449 UN METHODIST..	32	8 036	9 875*	10.1	36.2
453 UN PRES CH USA	2	579	711*	0.7	2.6
NEW CASTLE	229	66 922	179 253*	44.9	100.0
005 AME ZION......	1	192	222	0.1	0.1
019 AMER BAPT USA.	8	2 301	2 758*	0.7	1.5
029 AMER LUTH CH..	1	212	304	0.1	0.2
053 ASSEMB OF GOD.	8	582	944	0.2	0.5
057 BAPT GEN CONF.	2	509	610*	0.2	0.3
081 CATHOLIC......	35	NA	93 081	23.3	51.9
089 CHR & MISS AL.	2	165	270	0.1	0.2
093 CHR CH (DISC).	1	117	241	0.1	0.1
097 CHR CHS&CHS CR	2	55	66*	–	–
123 CH GOD (ANDER)	3	208	624	0.2	0.3
127 CH GOD (CLEVE)	4	307	368*	0.1	0.2
151 L-D SAINTS....	2	NA	904	0.2	0.5
157 CH OF BRETHREN	1	126	151*	–	0.1
165 CH OF NAZARENE	2	219	422	0.1	0.2
167 CHS OF CHRIST.	4	514	715	0.2	0.4
179 CONSRV BAPT....	1	257	308*	0.1	0.2
193 EPISCOPAL.....	22	9 798	14 378	3.6	8.0
226 FRIENDS-USA...	7	692	829*	0.2	0.5
239 SWEDENBORGIAN.	1	60	72*	–	–
244 GRACE BRETHREN	1	13	16*	–	–
270 CONSRV JUDAISM	1	548	657*	0.2	0.4
271 REFORM JUDAISM	1	560	671*	0.2	0.4
274 LAT EVAN LUTH.	1	109	133	–	0.1
281 LUTH CH AMER..	8	4 691	6 559	1.6	3.7
283 LUTH--MO SYNOD	3	933	1 248	0.3	0.7
285 MENNONITE CH..	1	19	23*	–	–
290 METRO COMM CHS	0	0	25	–	–
335 ORTH PRESB CH.	2	203	243*	0.1	0.1
353 CHR BRETHREN..	1	40	60	–	–
375 REF EPISCOPAL.	1	25	30*	–	–
381 REF PRES-EVAN.	6	1 331	1 802	0.5	1.0
403 SALVATION ARMY	1	23	40	–	–
413 S.D.A.........	4	577	692*	0.2	0.4
419 SO BAPT CONV..	4	2 049	2 456*	0.6	1.4

County and Denomination	Number of churches	Communicant, confirmed, full members	Total adherents Number	Percent of total population	Percent of total adherents
435 UNITARIAN-UNIV	2	922	1 105*	0.3	0.6
449 UN METHODIST..	57	26 258	31 474*	7.9	17.6
453 UN PRES CH USA	27	12 235	14 666*	3.7	8.2
469 WELS..........	1	72	86	–	–
SUSSEX	144	23 312	33 007*	33.7	100.0
005 AME ZION......	1	105	120	0.1	0.4
053 ASSEMB OF GOD.	3	244	478	0.5	1.4
066 BIBLE CH OF CR	1	200	240*	0.2	0.7
071 BRETHREN (ASH)	1	53	64*	0.1	0.2
081 CATHOLIC......	6	NA	3 955	4.0	12.0
089 CHR & MISS AL.	4	310	377	0.4	1.1
097 CHR CHS&CHS CR	3	490	589*	0.6	1.8
123 CH GOD (ANDER)	1	15	45	–	0.1
127 CH GOD (CLEVE)	7	1 071	1 288*	1.3	3.9
165 CH OF NAZARENE	2	178	640	0.7	1.9
167 CHS OF CHRIST.	3	140	275	0.3	0.8
193 EPISCOPAL.....	11	1 926	2 540	2.6	7.7
281 LUTH CH AMER..	1	223	288	0.3	0.9
283 LUTH--MO SYNOD	2	249	336	0.3	1.0
285 MENNONITE CH..	3	403	485*	0.5	1.5
335 ORTH PRESB CH.	1	18	22*	–	0.1
413 S.D.A.........	2	150	180*	0.2	0.5
419 SO BAPT CONV..	1	279	335*	0.3	1.0
443 UN C OF CHRIST	1	25	30*	–	0.1
449 UN METHODIST..	81	15 919	19 140*	19.5	58.0
453 UN PRES CH USA	9	1 314	1 580*	1.6	4.8

DISTRICT OF COLUMBIA

County and Denomination	Number of churches	Communicant, confirmed, full members	Total adherents Number	Percent of total population	Percent of total adherents
THE DISTRICT..	376	167 523	312 444*	49.0	100.0
DISTRICT OF COLUMBIA	376	167 523	312 444*	49.0	100.0
005 AME ZION......	12	31 450	39 183	6.1	12.5
019 AMER BAPT USA.	33	24 180	28 126*	4.4	9.0
029 AMER LUTH CH..	3	694	790	0.1	0.3
053 ASSEMB OF GOD.	2	375	625	0.1	0.2
061 BEACHY AMISH..	1	18	21*	–	–
071 BRETHREN (ASH)	1	171	199*	–	0.1
081 CATHOLIC......	44	NA	95 794	15.0	30.7
093 CHR CH (DISC).	5	1 179	2 009	0.3	0.6
101 C.M.E.........	6	6 436	7 486*	1.2	2.4
105 CHRISTIAN REF.	1	114	178	–	0.1
123 CH GOD (ANDER)	6	641	1 923	0.3	0.6
127 CH GOD (CLEVE)	2	170	198*	–	0.1
133 CH GOD(7TH)DEN	1	2	2*	–	–
157 CH OF BRETHREN	1	262	305*	–	0.1
165 CH OF NAZARENE	2	334	405	0.1	0.1
167 CHS OF CHRIST.	3	573	730	0.1	0.2
193 EPISCOPAL.....	93	30 550	49 861	7.8	16.0
208 EVAN LUTH ASSN	2	529	735	0.1	0.2
221 FREE METHODIST	2	117	489	0.1	0.2
226 FRIENDS-USA...	1	524	610*	0.1	0.2
233 GEN CH NEW JER	1	70	81*	–	–
239 SWEDENBORGIAN.	1	60	70*	–	–
270 CONSRV JUDAISM	2	999	1 162*	0.2	0.4
271 REFORM JUDAISM	3	6 064	7 053*	1.1	2.3
281 LUTH CH AMER..	10	3 442	4 436	0.7	1.4
283 LUTH--MO SYNOD	6	1 184	2 024	0.3	0.6
290 METRO COMM CHS	1	101	200	–	0.1
349 PENT HOLINESS.	2	103	120*	–	–
353 CHR BRETHREN..	4	130	200	–	0.1
357 PRESB CH US...	23	7 850	9 131*	1.4	2.9
403 SALVATION ARMY	3	403	1 537	0.2	0.5
413 S.D.A.........	10	3 371	3 921*	0.6	1.3
415 S-D BAPTIST GC	1	66	77*	–	–
419 SO BAPT CONV..	23	16 279	18 935*	3.0	6.1
435 UNITARIAN-UNIV	2	1 015	1 181*	0.2	0.4
443 UN C OF CHRIST	9	5 245	6 101*	1.0	2.0
449 UN METHODIST..	35	17 958	20 888*	3.3	6.7
453 UN PRES CH USA	19	4 864	5 658*	0.9	1.8

FLORIDA

County and Denomination	Number of churches	Communicant, confirmed, full members	Total adherents Number	Percent of total population	Percent of total adherents
THE STATE.....	6 818	1 926 628	3 753 873*	38.5	100.0
ALACHUA	155	36 091	52 964*	35.0	100.0
001 ADVENT CHR CH.	1	60	71*	–	0.1

NA—Not applicable   *Total adherents estimated from known number of communicant, confirmed, full members.

—Represents a percent less than 0.1.   Percentages may not total due to rounding.

FLORIDA

Table 4. Churches and Church Membership by County and Denomination: 1980

County and Denomination	Number of churches	Communicant, confirmed, full members	Total adherents Number	Total adherents Percent of total population	Total adherents Percent of total adherents
005 AME ZION......	1	160	160	0.1	0.3
017 AMER BAPT ASSN	3	320	320	0.2	0.6
053 ASSEMB OF GOD.	2	210	343	0.2	0.6
059 BAPT MISS ASSN	1	30	35*	–	0.1
081 CATHOLIC......	5	NA	9 053	6.0	17.1
089 CHR & MISS AL.	2	93	121	0.1	0.2
093 CHR CH (DISC)	1	126	194	0.1	0.4
097 CHR CHS&CHS CR	1	105	124*	0.1	0.2
101 C.M.E.........	1	60	71*	–	0.1
123 CH GOD (ANDER)	1	89	267	0.2	0.5
127 CH GOD (CLEVE)	7	517	608*	0.4	1.1
151 L-D SAINTS....	2	NA	906	0.6	1.7
165 CH OF NAZARENE	4	382	548	0.4	1.0
167 CHS OF CHRIST.	12	1 987	2 529	1.7	4.8
193 EPISCOPAL.....	8	1 621	1 793	1.2	3.4
203 EVAN FREE CH..	1	94	111*	0.1	0.2
226 FRIENDS-USA...	1	83	98*	0.1	0.2
270 CONSRV JUDAISM	1	179	211*	0.1	0.4
283 LUTH--MO SYNOD	1	488	619	0.4	1.2
290 METRO COMM CHS	0	0	25	–	–
349 PENT HOLINESS	4	234	275*	0.2	0.5
356 PRESB CH AMER.	1	76	96	0.1	0.2
357 PRESB CH US...	8	2 566	3 020*	2.0	5.7
403 SALVATION ARMY	1	51	96	0.1	0.2
413 S.D.A.........	2	385	453*	0.3	0.9
419 SO BAPT CONV..	38	17 287	20 344*	13.4	38.4
435 UNITARIAN-UNIV	1	198	233*	0.2	0.4
443 UN C OF CHRIST	1	154	181*	0.1	0.3
449 UN METHODIST..	41	8 382	9 864*	6.5	18.6
453 UN PRES CH USA	1	62	73*	–	0.1
469 WELS.........	1	92	122	0.1	0.2
BAKER	16	2 255	3 473*	22.7	100.0
053 ASSEMB OF GOD.	1	38	65	0.4	1.9
081 CATHOLIC......	1	NA	200	1.3	5.8
127 CH GOD (CLEVE)	4	394	493*	3.2	14.2
151 L-D SAINTS....	1	NA	370	2.4	10.7
167 CHS OF CHRIST.	2	115	201	1.3	5.8
177 CONGR HOL CH..	1	46	58*	0.4	1.7
193 EPISCOPAL.....	1	43	61	0.4	1.8
263 INT FOURSQ GOS	1	8	10*	0.1	0.3
419 SO BAPT CONV..	3	1 317	1 647*	10.8	47.4
449 UN METHODIST..	1	294	368*	2.4	10.6
BAY	96	31 461	42 478*	43.5	100.0
001 ADVENT CHR CH.	2	287	349*	0.4	0.8
017 AMER BAPT ASSN	1	283	283	0.3	0.7
029 AMER LUTH CH..	1	203	293	0.3	0.7
053 ASSEMB OF GOD.	15	1 783	3 121	3.2	7.3
081 CATHOLIC......	4	NA	1 652	1.7	3.9
097 CHR CHS&CHS CR	2	225	274*	0.3	0.6
123 CH GOD (ANDER)	2	64	192	0.2	0.5
127 CH GOD (CLEVE)	2	188	229*	0.2	0.5
151 L-D SAINTS....	3	NA	1 044	1.1	2.5
165 CH OF NAZARENE	2	208	329	0.3	0.8
167 CHS OF CHRIST.	8	791	1 040	1.1	2.4
193 EPISCOPAL.....	3	719	933	1.0	2.2
283 LUTH--MO SYNOD	3	629	921	0.9	2.2
349 PENT HOLINESS	1	59	72*	0.1	0.2
356 PRESB CH AMER.	1	143	171	0.2	0.4
357 PRESB CH US...	5	1 571	1 911*	2.0	4.5
403 SALVATION ARMY	1	92	212	0.2	0.5
413 S.D.A.........	2	262	319*	0.3	0.8
419 SO BAPT CONV..	24	17 746	21 583*	22.1	50.8
449 UN METHODIST..	14	6 208	7 550*	7.7	17.8
BRADFORD	35	5 280	7 090*	35.4	100.0
053 ASSEMB OF GOD.	1	20	57	0.3	0.8
059 BAPT MISS ASSN	1	50	61*	0.3	0.9
081 CATHOLIC......	1	NA	375	1.9	5.3
097 CHR CHS&CHS CR	2	180	218*	1.1	3.1
127 CH GOD (CLEVE)	2	200	243*	1.2	3.4
151 L-D SAINTS....	1	NA	197	1.0	2.8
167 CHS OF CHRIST.	3	98	131	0.7	1.8
177 CONGR HOL CH..	1	18	22*	0.1	0.3
193 EPISCOPAL.....	1	101	188	0.9	2.7
357 PRESB CH US...	2	254	308*	1.5	4.3
413 S.D.A.........	1	21	25*	0.1	0.4
419 SO BAPT CONV..	14	3 590	4 357*	21.8	61.5
449 UN METHODIST..	5	748	908*	4.5	12.8
BREVARD	188	56 897	104 878*	38.4	100.0
001 ADVENT CHR CH.	2	84	99*	–	0.1
005 AME ZION......	1	263	263	0.1	0.3
017 AMER BAPT ASSN	5	289	289	0.1	0.3
019 AMER BAPT USA.	1	200	235*	0.1	0.2
029 AMER LUTH CH..	4	1 243	1 613	0.6	1.5
053 ASSEMB OF GOD.	7	1 075	1 823	0.7	1.7
055 AS REF PRES CH	2	336	379	0.1	0.4
081 CATHOLIC......	11	NA	34 406	12.6	32.8
089 CHR & MISS AL.	3	109	207	0.1	0.2
093 CHR CH (DISC)	3	382	519	0.2	0.5
097 CHR CHS&CHS CR	8	1 227	1 440*	0.5	1.4
105 CHRISTIAN REF.	1	80	124	–	0.1
123 CH GOD (ANDER)	2	155	465	0.2	0.4
127 CH GOD (CLEVE)	12	944	1 108*	0.4	1.1
151 L-D SAINTS....	3	NA	1 386	0.5	1.3
165 CH OF NAZARENE	4	469	648	0.2	0.6
167 CHS OF CHRIST.	11	1 400	1 682	0.6	1.6
179 CONSRV BAPT...	1	91	107*	–	0.1
193 EPISCOPAL.....	10	4 208	5 346	2.0	5.1
203 EVAN FREE CH..	1	35	41*	–	–
221 FREE METHODIST	1	13	81	–	0.1
226 FRIENDS-USA...	1	18	21*	–	–
244 GRACE BRETHREN	1	11	13*	–	–
270 CONSRV JUDAISM	2	170	200*	0.1	0.2
271 REFORM JUDAISM	1	254	298*	0.1	0.3
281 LUTH CH AMER..	4	673	815	0.3	0.8
283 LUTH--MO SYNOD	6	2 162	2 735	1.0	2.6
290 METRO COMM CHS	0	0	25	–	–
349 PENT HOLINESS	3	157	184*	0.1	0.2
353 CHR BRETHREN..	1	80	180	0.1	0.2
356 PRESB CH AMER.	1	48	66	–	0.1
357 PRESB CH US...	5	2 299	2 699*	1.0	2.6
403 SALVATION ARMY	3	186	447	0.2	0.4
413 S.D.A.........	5	526	617*	0.2	0.6
419 SO BAPT CONV..	31	22 161	26 013*	9.5	24.8
435 UNITARIAN-UNIV	2	139	163*	0.1	0.2
443 UN C OF CHRIST	4	675	792*	0.3	0.8
449 UN METHODIST..	19	12 890	15 131*	5.5	14.4
453 UN PRES CH USA	5	1 767	2 074*	0.8	2.0
469 WELS..........	1	78	144	0.1	0.1
BROWARD	294	109 690	364 815*	36.0	100.0
005 AME ZION......	3	515	665	0.1	0.2
017 AMER BAPT ASSN	2	174	174	–	–
019 AMER BAPT ASSN	2	2 200	2 540*	0.3	0.7
029 AMER LUTH CH..	4	1 148	1 579	0.2	0.4
053 ASSEMB OF GOD.	12	1 221	2 386	0.2	0.7
081 CATHOLIC......	37	NA	231 300	22.8	63.4
089 CHR & MISS AL.	3	283	497	–	0.1
093 CHR CH (DISC)	8	3 492	4 175	0.4	1.1
097 CHR CHS&CHS CR	6	1 090	1 259*	0.1	0.3
101 C.M.E.........	1	845	976*	0.1	0.3
105 CHRISTIAN REF.	1	232	341	–	0.1
123 CH GOD (ANDER)	2	280	840	0.1	0.2
127 CH GOD (CLEVE)	16	1 531	1 768*	0.2	0.5
151 L-D SAINTS....	4	NA	1 388	0.1	0.4
157 CH OF BRETHREN	1	49	57*	–	–
165 CH OF NAZARENE	6	1 039	2 138	0.2	0.6
167 CHS OF CHRIST.	14	2 490	3 161	0.3	0.9
175 CONGR CHR CHS.	1	466	538*	0.1	0.1
193 EPISCOPAL.....	16	7 794	9 532	0.9	2.6
195 ESTONIAN ELC..	1	38	53	–	–
203 EVAN FREE CH..	1	40	46*	–	–
244 GRACE BRETHREN	3	269	311*	–	0.1
270 CONSRV JUDAISM	7	3 584	4 139*	0.4	1.1
271 REFORM JUDAISM	6	4 612	5 326*	0.5	1.5
281 LUTH CH AMER..	10	5 002	6 754	0.7	1.9
283 LUTH--MO SYNOD	11	4 340	5 799	0.6	1.6
290 METRO COMM CHS	1	126	250	–	0.1
295 MORAV CH-SOUTH	1	93	106	–	–
335 ORTH PRESB CH.	1	95	110*	–	–
349 PENT HOLINESS	1	50	58*	–	–
353 CHR BRETHREN..	4	265	450	–	0.1
356 PRESB CH AMER.	7	6 836	7 105	0.7	1.9
357 PRESB CH US...	4	1 536	1 774*	0.2	0.5
371 REF CH IN AM..	2	261	429	–	0.1
403 SALVATION ARMY	1	179	349	–	0.1
413 S.D.A.........	9	1 308	1 510*	0.1	0.4
419 SO BAPT CONV..	34	24 215	27 962*	2.8	7.7
435 UNITARIAN-UNIV	2	220	254*	–	0.1
443 UN C OF CHRIST	6	1 851	2 137*	0.2	0.6
449 UN METHODIST..	27	21 201	24 482*	2.4	6.7
453 UN PRES CH USA	15	8 557	9 881*	1.0	2.7
469 WELS..........	1	163	216	–	0.1
CALHOUN	31	3 158	4 133*	44.5	100.0
001 ADVENT CHR CH.	2	38	47*	0.5	1.1
017 AMER BAPT ASSN	2	100	100	1.1	2.4
053 ASSEMB OF GOD.	3	143	250	2.7	6.0
081 CATHOLIC......	1	NA	180	1.9	4.4
127 CH GOD (CLEVE)	2	46	56*	0.6	1.4
165 CH OF NAZARENE	1	53	91	1.0	2.2
285 MENNONITE CH..	2	110	135*	1.5	3.3
349 PENT HOLINESS	6	493	605*	6.5	14.6
357 PRESB CH US...	1	30	37*	0.4	0.9
419 SO BAPT CONV..	8	1 630	2 000*	21.5	48.4
449 UN METHODIST..	3	515	632*	6.8	15.3
CHARLOTTE	44	10 829	19 511*	33.0	100.0
053 ASSEMB OF GOD.	2	84	150	0.3	0.8
081 CATHOLIC......	4	NA	6 679	11.3	34.2
089 CHR & MISS AL.	1	122	447	0.8	2.3
097 CHR CHS&CHS CR	2	432	480*	0.8	2.5
123 CH GOD (ANDER)	1	28	84	0.1	0.4
127 CH GOD (CLEVE)	4	149	166*	0.3	0.9
151 L-D SAINTS....	1	NA	174	0.3	0.9
165 CH OF NAZARENE	1	102	379	0.6	1.9
167 CHS OF CHRIST.	3	200	255	0.4	1.3
193 EPISCOPAL.....	2	886	938	1.6	4.8
271 REFORM JUDAISM	1	212	235*	0.4	1.2
281 LUTH CH AMER..	2	821	877	1.5	4.5
283 LUTH--MO SYNOD	2	553	605	1.0	3.1
357 PRESB CH US...	1	1 355	1 505*	2.5	7.7
413 S.D.A.........	2	310	344*	0.6	1.8
419 SO BAPT CONV..	5	2 381	2 645*	4.5	13.6
435 UNITARIAN-UNIV	1	60	67*	0.1	0.3
443 UN C OF CHRIST	2	337	374*	0.6	1.9
449 UN METHODIST..	6	2 557	2 840*	4.8	14.6
453 UN PRES CH USA	1	240	267*	0.5	1.4
CITRUS	54	9 606	16 145*	29.5	100.0

NA—Not applicable   *Total adherents estimated from known number of communicant, confirmed, full members.   —Represents a percent less than 0.1.   Percentages may not total due to rounding.

Table 4. Churches and Church Membership by County and Denomination: 1980

County and Denomination	Number of churches	Communicant, confirmed, full members	Total adherents Number	Percent of total population	Percent of total adherents
017 AMER BAPT ASSN	3	333	333	0.6	2.1
053 ASSEMB OF GOD.	2	225	364	0.7	2.3
057 BAPT GEN CONF.	0	1	1*	-	-
081 CATHOLIC......	4	NA	4 736	8.7	29.3
097 CHR CHS&CHS CR	3	172	195*	0.4	1.2
123 CH GOD (ANDER)	1	60	180	0.3	1.1
127 CH GOD (CLEVE)	3	262	297*	0.5	1.8
151 L-D SAINTS....	1	NA	139	0.3	0.9
165 CH OF NAZARENE	1	130	231	0.4	1.4
167 CHS OF CHRIST.	6	280	368	0.7	2.3
193 EPISCOPAL.....	2	437	552	1.0	3.4
281 LUTH CH AMER..	2	392	455	0.8	2.8
283 LUTH--MO SYNOD	1	323	351	0.6	2.2
357 PRESB CH US...	1	512	581*	1.1	3.6
413 S.D.A.........	3	269	305*	0.6	1.9
419 SO BAPT CONV..	12	3 897	4 423*	8.1	27.4
449 UN METHODIST..	6	1 958	2 222*	4.1	13.8
453 UN PRES CH USA	2	255	289*	0.5	1.8
469 WELS..........	1	100	123	0.2	0.8
CLAY	**71**	**16 521**	**29 557***	**44.1**	**100.0**
029 AMER LUTH CH..	1	556	768	1.1	2.6
053 ASSEMB OF GOD.	4	545	1 112	1.7	3.8
081 CATHOLIC......	4	NA	6 374	9.5	21.6
089 CHR & MISS AL.	2	250	367	0.5	1.2
097 CHR CHS&CHS CR	1	208	260*	0.4	0.9
123 CH GOD (ANDER)	8	485	1 455	2.2	4.9
127 CH GOD (CLEVE)	3	163	204*	0.3	0.7
151 L-D SAINTS....	3	NA	972	1.4	3.3
157 CH OF BRETHREN	1	45	56*	0.1	0.2
165 CH OF NAZARENE	1	27	62	0.1	0.2
167 CHS OF CHRIST.	3	265	344	0.5	1.2
177 CONGR HOL CH..	1	30	37*	0.1	0.1
193 EPISCOPAL.....	5	1 145	1 487	2.2	5.0
353 CHR BRETHREN..	1	135	200	0.3	0.7
357 PRESB CH US...	2	836	1 044*	1.6	3.5
403 SALVATION ARMY	1	12	57	0.1	0.2
413 S.D.A.........	1	90	112*	0.2	0.4
419 SO BAPT CONV..	22	9 318	11 636*	17.4	39.4
449 UN METHODIST..	6	2 349	2 933*	4.4	9.9
453 UN PRES CH USA	1	62	77*	0.1	0.3
COLLIER	**57**	**13 869**	**33 386***	**38.9**	**100.0**
029 AMER LUTH CH..	1	149	180	0.2	0.5
053 ASSEMB OF GOD.	3	490	632	0.7	1.9
081 CATHOLIC......	6	NA	16 600	19.3	49.7
089 CHR & MISS AL.	1	50	50	0.1	0.1
093 CHR CH (DISC).	1	176	220	0.3	0.7
097 CHR CHS&CHS CR	1	160	187*	0.2	0.6
127 CH GOD (CLEVE)	5	503	589*	0.7	1.8
151 L-D SAINTS....	1	NA	243	0.3	0.7
165 CH OF NAZARENE	1	87	128	0.1	0.4
167 CHS OF CHRIST.	2	145	205	0.2	0.6
179 CONSRV BAPT...	1	91	107*	0.1	0.3
193 EPISCOPAL.....	5	1 144	1 366	1.6	4.1
209 EVAN LUTH SYN.	1	78	112	0.1	0.3
281 LUTH CH AMER..	2	468	588	0.7	1.8
283 LUTH--MO SYNOD	3	479	611	0.7	1.8
285 MENNONITE CH..	2	45	53*	0.1	0.2
357 PRESB CH US....	3	1 462	1 712*	2.0	5.1
381 REF PRES-EVAN.	1	227	302	0.4	0.9
413 S.D.A.........	1	140	164*	0.2	0.5
419 SO BAPT CONV..	6	3 373	3 949*	4.6	11.8
435 UNITARIAN-UNIV	1	62	73*	0.1	0.2
443 UN C OF CHRIST	2	684	801*	0.9	2.4
449 UN METHODIST..	6	2 849	3 335*	3.9	10.0
453 UN PRES CH USA	1	1 007	1 179*	1.4	3.5
COLUMBIA	**64**	**11 177**	**15 765***	**44.5**	**100.0**
001 ADVENT CHR CH.	7	389	481*	1.4	3.1
053 ASSEMB OF GOD.	3	366	541	1.5	3.4
081 CATHOLIC......	1	NA	1 000	2.8	6.3
097 CHR CHS&CHS CR	1	121	150*	0.4	1.0
127 CH GOD (CLEVE)	4	383	474*	1.3	3.0
151 L-D SAINTS....	2	NA	699	2.0	4.4
165 CH OF NAZARENE	2	168	248	0.7	1.6
167 CHS OF CHRIST.	4	261	371	1.0	2.4
177 CONGR HOL CH..	2	50	62*	0.2	0.4
193 EPISCOPAL.....	1	172	249	0.7	1.6
281 LUTH CH AMER..	2	216	269	0.8	1.7
283 LUTH--MO SYNOD	1	93	140	0.4	0.9
349 PENT HOLINESS.	1	202	250*	0.7	1.6
357 PRESB CH US...	2	609	753*	2.1	4.8
413 S.D.A.........	2	88	109*	0.3	0.7
419 SO BAPT CONV..	20	6 412	7 932*	22.4	50.3
449 UN METHODIST..	9	1 647	2 037*	5.8	12.9
DADE	**534**	**168 804**	**634 456***	**39.0**	**100.0**
001 ADVENT CHR CH.	2	110	129*	-	-
005 AME ZION......	5	546	946	0.1	0.1
017 AMER BAPT ASSN	3	935	935	0.1	0.1
019 AMER BAPT USA.	9	3 876	4 552*	0.3	0.7
029 AMER LUTH CH..	10	3 304	4 723	0.3	0.7
053 ASSEMB OF GOD.	27	2 992	4 508	0.3	0.7
081 CATHOLIC......	57	NA	426 437	26.2	67.2
089 CHR & MISS AL.	7	835	1 120	0.1	0.2
093 CHR CH (DISC).	8	1 594	2 095	0.1	0.3
097 CHR CHS&CHS CR	6	469	551*	-	0.1
101 C.M.E.........	3	1 312	1 541*	0.1	0.2
105 CHRISTIAN REF.	2	200	272	-	-
123 CH GOD (ANDER)	8	728	2 184	0.1	0.3
127 CH GOD (CLEVE)	20	1 524	1 790*	0.1	0.3
149 CH OF JC (BIC)	1	10	10	-	-
151 L-D SAINTS....	11	NA	2 896	0.2	0.5
157 CH OF BRETHREN	2	90	106*	-	-
165 CH OF NAZARENE	15	1 689	3 078	0.2	0.5
167 CHS OF CHRIST.	25	3 221	4 130	0.3	0.7
179 CONSRV BAPT...	4	364	427*	-	0.1
193 EPISCOPAL.....	29	14 093	16 278	1.0	2.6
201 EVAN COV CH AM	2	298	350*	-	0.1
208 EVAN LUTH ASSN	1	12	12	-	-
221 FREE METHODIST	3	51	219	-	-
226 FRIENDS-USA...	2	183	215*	-	-
239 SWEDENBORGIAN.	1	60	70*	-	-
263 INT FOURSQ GOS	1	4	5*	-	-
270 CONSRV JUDAISM	12	4 718	5 540*	0.3	0.9
271 REFORM JUDAISM	5	11 024	12 946*	0.8	2.0
274 LAT EVAN LUTH.	1	75	75	-	-
281 LUTH CH AMER..	13	3 550	4 659	0.3	0.7
283 LUTH--MO SYNOD	12	2 662	3 583	0.2	0.6
285 MENNONITE CH..	5	83	97*	-	-
290 METRO COMM CHS	2	65	130	-	-
329 OPEN BIBLE STD	4	530	950	0.1	0.1
335 ORTH PRESB CH.	2	241	283*	-	-
349 PENT HOLINESS.	2	111	130*	-	-
353 CHR BRETHREN..	10	450	740	-	0.1
356 PRESB CH AMER.	9	3 951	4 421	0.3	0.7
357 PRESB CH US...	17	6 801	7 986*	0.5	1.3
371 REF CH IN AM..	1	221	335	-	0.1
375 REF EPISCOPAL.	1	11	13*	-	-
403 SALVATION ARMY	3	381	904	0.1	0.1
413 S.D.A.........	16	4 618	5 423*	0.3	0.9
419 SO BAPT CONV..	78	57 047	66 991*	4.1	10.6
435 UNITARIAN-UNIV	2	470	552*	-	0.1
443 UN C OF CHRIST	14	6 197	7 277*	0.4	1.1
449 UN METHODIST..	48	24 314	28 552*	1.8	4.5
453 UN PRES CH USA	12	2 752	3 232*	0.2	0.5
469 WELS..........	1	32	58	-	-
DE SOTO	**33**	**5 312**	**6 839***	**35.9**	**100.0**
053 ASSEMB OF GOD.	1	137	198	1.0	2.9
081 CATHOLIC......	1	NA	337	1.8	4.9
097 CHR CHS&CHS CR	1	90	108*	0.6	1.6
101 C.M.E.........	1	42	50*	0.3	0.7
127 CH GOD (CLEVE)	5	284	341*	1.8	5.0
157 CH OF BRETHREN	1	51	61*	0.3	0.9
165 CH OF NAZARENE	1	109	241	1.3	3.5
167 CHS OF CHRIST.	2	135	172	0.9	2.5
193 EPISCOPAL.....	1	87	85	0.4	1.2
283 LUTH--MO SYNOD	1	35	40	0.2	0.6
285 MENNONITE CH..	1	25	30*	0.2	0.4
357 PRESB CH US...	1	263	315*	1.7	4.6
413 S.D.A.........	1	115	138*	0.7	2.0
419 SO BAPT CONV..	10	3 034	3 638*	19.1	53.2
449 UN METHODIST..	5	905	1 085*	5.7	15.9
DIXIE	**23**	**2 716**	**3 313***	**42.7**	**100.0**
053 ASSEMB OF GOD.	1	11	27	0.3	0.8
059 BAPT MISS ASSN	1	73	89*	1.1	2.7
081 CATHOLIC......	1	NA	?	?	?
127 CH GOD (CLEVE)	1	97	118*	1.5	3.6
167 CHS OF CHRIST.	1	60	76	1.0	2.3
349 PENT HOLINESS.	1	87	106*	1.4	3.2
413 S.D.A.........	1	45	55*	0.7	1.7
419 SO BAPT CONV..	13	2 082	2 525*	32.6	76.2
449 UN METHODIST..	3	261	317*	4.1	9.6
DUVAL	**402**	**162 283**	**242 707***	**42.5**	**100.0**
001 ADVENT CHR CH.	3	589	716*	0.1	0.3
005 AME ZION......	3	248	248	-	0.1
017 AMER BAPT ASSN	4	656	656	0.1	0.3
019 AMER BAPT USA.	3	1 278	1 554*	0.3	0.6
029 AMER LUTH CH..	3	321	422	0.1	0.2
053 ASSEMB OF GOD.	21	2 932	5 444	1.0	2.2
059 BAPT MISS ASSN	2	302	367*	0.1	0.2
081 CATHOLIC......	21	NA	37 674	6.6	15.5
089 CHR & MISS AL.	2	136	183	-	0.1
093 CHR CH (DISC).	12	2 273	3 397	0.6	1.4
097 CHR CHS&CHS CR	2	1 827	2 222*	0.4	0.9
101 C.M.E.........	5	596	725*	0.1	0.3
105 CHRISTIAN REF.	1	35	58	-	-
127 CH GOD (CLEVE)	26	2 786	3 388*	0.6	1.4
151 L-D SAINTS....	9	NA	3 271	0.6	1.3
157 CH OF BRETHREN	1	36	44*	-	-
165 CH OF NAZARENE	11	1 356	1 834	0.3	0.8
167 CHS OF CHRIST.	25	4 100	5 163	0.9	2.1
177 CONGR HOL CH..	4	61	74*	-	-
193 EPISCOPAL.....	23	11 116	14 109	2.5	5.8
203 EVAN FREE CH..	1	15	18*	-	-
226 FRIENDS-USA...	1	14	17*	-	-
263 INT FOURSQ GOS	1	167	203*	-	0.1
270 CONSRV JUDAISM	2	856	1 041*	0.2	0.4
271 REFORM JUDAISM	1	1 130	1 374*	0.2	0.6
281 LUTH CH AMER..	7	2 829	3 633	0.6	1.5
283 LUTH--MO SYNOD	6	1 545	2 068	0.4	0.9
290 METRO COMM CHS	1	75	150	-	0.1
349 PENT HOLINESS.	4	619	753*	0.1	0.3
353 CHR BRETHREN..	1	50	70	-	-
356 PRESB CH AMER.	1	82	120	-	-
357 PRESB CH US...	21	8 064	9 807*	1.7	4.0
403 SALVATION ARMY	1	174	738	0.1	0.3
413 S.D.A.........	3	1 284	1 561*	0.3	0.6
419 SO BAPT CONV..	110	86 777	105 531*	18.5	43.5

NA— Not applicable   *Total adherents estimated from known number of communicant, confirmed, full members.   —Represents a percent less than 0.1.   Percentages may not total due to rounding.

FLORIDA

Table 4. Churches and Church Membership by County and Denomination: 1980

County and Denomination	Number of churches	Communicant, confirmed, full members	Total adherents Number	Percent of total population	Percent of total adherents
421 SO METHODIST..	1	4	15	–	–
435 UNITARIAN-UNIV	1	318	387*	0.1	0.2
443 UN C OF CHRIST	2	476	579*	0.1	0.2
449 UN METHODIST..	51	25 836	31 419*	5.5	12.9
453 UN PRES CH USA	3	1 157	1 407*	0.2	0.6
469 WELS..........	2	163	267	–	0.1
ESCAMBIA	**214**	**67 725**	**98 779***	**42.3**	**100.0**
005 AME ZION......	11	2 990	3 990	1.7	4.0
017 AMER BAPT ASSN	5	802	802	0.3	0.8
053 ASSEMB OF GOD.	21	2 347	3 502	1.5	3.5
059 BAPT MISS ASSN	5	500	607*	0.3	0.6
081 CATHOLIC......	15	NA	13 808	5.9	14.0
089 CHR & MISS AL.	3	202	266	0.1	0.3
093 CHR CH (DISC).	4	495	641	0.3	0.6
097 CHR CHS&CHS CR	1	85	103*	–	0.1
127 CH GOD (CLEVE)	5	379	460*	0.2	0.5
143 CG IN CR(MENN)	1	137	137	0.1	0.1
151 L-D SAINTS....	3	NA	1 231	0.5	1.2
165 CH OF NAZARENE	2	425	520	0.2	0.5
167 CHS OF CHRIST.	17	2 139	2 741	1.2	2.8
193 EPISCOPAL.....	6	3 436	4 182	1.8	4.2
270 CONSRV JUDAISM	1	84	102*	–	0.1
271 REFORM JUDAISM	1	320	388*	0.2	0.4
281 LUTH CH AMER..	1	385	528	0.2	0.5
283 LUTH--MO SYNOD	7	1 806	2 297	1.0	2.3
285 MENNONITE CH..	1	15	18*	–	–
290 METRO COMM CHS	1	50	100	–	0.1
329 OPEN BIBLE STD	2	281	405	0.2	0.4
356 PRESB CH AMER.	5	1 322	1 535	0.7	1.6
357 PRESB CH US...	3	1 822	2 211*	0.9	2.2
403 SALVATION ARMY	1	133	480	0.2	0.5
413 S.D.A.........	1	104	126*	0.1	0.1
419 SO BAPT CONV..	61	35 361	42 911*	18.4	43.4
421 SO METHODIST..	1	66	78	–	0.1
435 UNITARIAN-UNIV	1	40	49*	–	–
443 UN C OF CHRIST	1	65	79*	–	0.1
449 UN METHODIST..	27	11 934	14 482*	6.2	14.7
FLAGLER	**12**	**1 935**	**4 122***	**37.8**	**100.0**
057 BAPT GEN CONF.	0	1	1*	–	–
081 CATHOLIC......	4	NA	1 732	15.9	42.0
151 L-D SAINTS....	1	NA	134	1.2	3.3
193 EPISCOPAL.....	1	67	80	0.7	1.9
281 LUTH CH AMER..	1	292	333	3.1	8.1
349 PENT HOLINESS.	1	54	63*	0.6	1.5
419 SO BAPT CONV..	2	1 046	1 223*	11.2	29.7
449 UN METHODIST..	2	475	556*	5.1	13.5
FRANKLIN	**20**	**2 357**	**3 928***	**51.3**	**100.0**
053 ASSEMB OF GOD.	3	252	457	6.0	11.6
081 CATHOLIC......	2	NA	879	11.5	22.4
127 CH GOD (CLEVE)	3	122	148*	1.9	3.8
151 L-D SAINTS....	1	NA	51	0.7	1.3
177 CONGR HOL CH..	1	16	19*	0.2	0.5
193 EPISCOPAL.....	2	140	152	2.0	3.9
349 PENT HOLINESS.	2	179	218*	2.8	5.5
419 SO BAPT CONV..	3	1 120	1 362*	17.8	34.7
449 UN METHODIST..	3	528	642*	8.4	16.3
GADSDEN	**55**	**10 141**	**13 054***	**31.4**	**100.0**
053 ASSEMB OF GOD.	7	304	455	1.1	3.5
081 CATHOLIC......	1	NA	75	0.2	0.6
101 C.M.E.	2	105	131*	0.3	1.0
127 CH GOD (CLEVE)	1	28	35*	0.1	0.3
151 L-D SAINTS....	1	NA	213	0.5	1.6
167 CHS OF CHRIST.	3	89	119	0.3	0.9
193 EPISCOPAL.....	2	155	195	0.5	1.5
349 PENT HOLINESS.	7	624	781*	1.9	6.0
356 PRESB CH AMER.	2	146	169	0.4	1.3
357 PRESB CH US...	5	648	811*	2.0	6.2
413 S.D.A.........	1	57	71*	0.2	0.5
419 SO BAPT CONV..	15	6 043	7 567*	18.2	58.0
449 UN METHODIST..	8	1 942	2 432*	5.9	18.6
GILCHRIST	**21**	**3 018**	**3 658***	**63.4**	**100.0**
001 ADVENT CHR CH.	1	34	41*	0.7	1.1
017 AMER BAPT ASSN	2	136	136	2.4	3.7
127 CH GOD (CLEVE)	2	97	117*	2.0	3.2
167 CHS OF CHRIST.	7	500	639	11.1	17.5
413 S.D.A.........	1	34	41*	0.7	1.1
419 SO BAPT CONV..	7	2 095	2 536*	44.0	69.3
449 UN METHODIST..	1	122	148*	2.6	4.0
GLADES	**8**	**1 047**	**2 667***	**44.5**	**100.0**
081 CATHOLIC......	1	NA	1 400	23.4	52.5
097 CHR CHS&CHS CR	1	90	109*	1.8	4.1
127 CH GOD (CLEVE)	1	62	75*	1.3	2.8
419 SO BAPT CONV..	4	781	945*	15.8	35.4
449 UN METHODIST..	1	114	138*	2.3	5.2
GULF	**28**	**4 181**	**5 552***	**52.1**	**100.0**
053 ASSEMB OF GOD.	4	433	626	5.9	11.3
081 CATHOLIC......	2	NA	300	2.8	5.4
127 CH GOD (CLEVE)	2	95	117*	1.1	2.1
165 CH OF NAZARENE	1	14	39	0.4	0.7
167 CHS OF CHRIST.	2	70	97	0.9	1.7
193 EPISCOPAL.....	2	133	145	1.4	2.6

County and Denomination	Number of churches	Communicant, confirmed, full members	Total adherents Number	Percent of total population	Percent of total adherents
349 PENT HOLINESS.	1	103	127*	1.2	2.3
357 PRESB CH US...	2	54	66*	0.6	1.2
419 SO BAPT CONV..	8	2 452	3 017*	28.3	54.3
449 UN METHODIST..	4	827	1 018*	9.6	18.3
HAMILTON	**28**	**2 981**	**3 907***	**44.6**	**100.0**
001 ADVENT CHR CH.	1	48	61*	0.7	1.6
053 ASSEMB OF GOD.	2	68	86	1.0	2.2
093 CHR CH (DISC).	1	160	325	3.7	8.3
097 CHR CHS&CHS CR	1	15	19*	0.2	0.5
101 C.M.E.	1	13	16*	0.2	0.4
127 CH GOD (CLEVE)	4	123	156*	1.8	4.0
165 CH OF NAZARENE	1	64	86	1.0	2.2
167 CHS OF CHRIST.	3	135	172	2.0	4.4
357 PRESB CH US...	2	122	155*	1.8	4.0
419 SO BAPT CONV..	9	1 782	2 259*	25.8	57.8
449 UN METHODIST..	3	451	572*	6.5	14.6
HARDEE	**47**	**8 231**	**11 289***	**58.3**	**100.0**
017 AMER BAPT ASSN	1	60	60	0.3	0.5
053 ASSEMB OF GOD.	2	99	130	0.7	1.2
081 CATHOLIC......	2	NA	741	3.8	6.6
097 CHR CHS&CHS CR	2	486	609*	3.1	5.4
101 C.M.E.	1	180	226*	1.2	2.0
123 CH GOD (ANDER)	1	30	90	0.5	0.8
127 CH GOD (CLEVE)	6	262	328*	1.7	2.9
151 L-D SAINTS....	1	NA	200	1.0	1.8
165 CH OF NAZARENE	1	34	46	0.2	0.4
167 CHS OF CHRIST.	3	145	185	1.0	1.6
193 EPISCOPAL.....	1	32	39	0.2	0.3
283 LUTH--MO SYNOD	1	37	43	0.2	0.4
356 PRESB CH AMER.	1	170	199	1.0	1.8
357 PRESB CH US...	1	89	112*	0.6	1.0
413 S.D.A.........	1	11	14*	0.1	0.1
419 SO BAPT CONV..	18	5 689	7 130*	36.8	63.2
449 UN METHODIST..	4	907	1 137*	5.9	10.1
HENDRY	**27**	**4 112**	**9 764***	**52.5**	**100.0**
017 AMER BAPT ASSN	1	51	51	0.3	0.5
053 ASSEMB OF GOD.	2	272	808	4.3	8.3
081 CATHOLIC......	2	NA	4 000	21.5	41.0
089 CHR & MISS AL.	1	0	28	0.2	0.3
093 CHR CH (DISC).	1	174	268	1.4	2.7
097 CHR CHS&CHS CR	2	100	126*	0.7	1.3
123 CH GOD (ANDER)	1	31	93	0.5	1.0
127 CH GOD (CLEVE)	2	180	227*	1.2	2.3
167 CHS OF CHRIST.	2	75	95	0.5	1.0
193 EPISCOPAL.....	1	120	144	0.8	1.5
349 PENT HOLINESS.	1	66	83*	0.4	0.9
413 S.D.A.........	1	26	33*	0.2	0.3
419 SO BAPT CONV..	7	2 328	2 939*	15.8	30.1
449 UN METHODIST..	2	596	752*	4.0	7.7
453 UN PRES CH USA	1	93	117*	0.6	1.2
HERNANDO	**46**	**9 270**	**16 666***	**37.5**	**100.0**
017 AMER BAPT ASSN	1	150	150	0.3	0.9
053 ASSEMB OF GOD.	1	73	111	0.2	0.7
081 CATHOLIC......	4	NA	5 571	12.5	33.4
097 CHR CHS&CHS CR	2	195	225*	0.5	1.4
123 CH GOD (ANDER)	2	58	174	0.4	1.0
127 CH GOD (CLEVE)	2	93	107*	0.2	0.6
151 L-D SAINTS....	1	NA	295	0.7	1.8
165 CH OF NAZARENE	2	129	209	0.5	1.3
167 CHS OF CHRIST.	4	155	199	0.4	1.2
193 EPISCOPAL.....	2	520	533	1.2	3.2
244 GRACE BRETHREN	1	50	58*	0.1	0.3
281 LUTH CH AMER..	2	520	590	1.3	3.5
283 LUTH--MO SYNOD	2	390	452	1.0	2.7
357 PRESB CH US...	1	219	252*	0.6	1.5
413 S.D.A.........	1	100	115*	0.3	0.7
419 SO BAPT CONV..	11	3 650	4 205*	9.5	25.2
443 UN C OF CHRIST	1	45	52*	0.1	0.3
449 UN METHODIST..	5	2 102	2 422*	5.4	14.5
453 UN PRES CH USA	1	821	946*	2.1	5.7
HIGHLANDS	**61**	**14 444**	**19 656***	**41.4**	**100.0**
017 AMER BAPT ASSN	1	46	46	0.1	0.2
053 ASSEMB OF GOD.	3	311	590	1.2	3.0
055 AS REF PRES CH	2	515	553	1.2	2.8
081 CATHOLIC......	3	NA	1 737	3.7	8.8
093 CHR CH (DISC).	1	250	284	0.6	1.4
097 CHR CHS&CHS CR	1	142	165*	0.3	0.8
123 CH GOD (ANDER)	3	147	441	0.9	2.2
127 CH GOD (CLEVE)	5	520	605*	1.3	3.1
151 L-D SAINTS....	1	NA	114	0.2	0.6
157 CH OF BRETHREN	2	559	650*	1.4	3.3
165 CH OF NAZARENE	2	204	574	1.2	2.9
167 CHS OF CHRIST.	4	320	405	0.9	2.1
193 EPISCOPAL.....	3	429	569	1.2	2.9
281 LUTH CH AMER..	2	345	378	0.8	1.9
283 LUTH--MO SYNOD	2	360	421	0.9	2.1
291 MISSIONARY CH.	1	25	57	0.1	0.3
357 PRESB CH US...	2	481	559*	1.2	2.8
403 SALVATION ARMY	1	56	189	0.4	1.0
413 S.D.A.........	5	630	733*	1.5	3.7
419 SO BAPT CONV..	9	5 189	6 034*	12.7	30.7
443 UN C OF CHRIST	1	214	249*	0.5	1.3
449 UN METHODIST..	7	3 701	4 303*	9.1	21.9
HILLSBOROUGH	**441**	**138 786**	**243 632***	**37.7**	**100.0**

NA— Not applicable *Total adherents estimated from known number of communicant, confirmed, full members.

—Represents a percent less than 0.1. Percentages may not total due to rounding.

Table 4. Churches and Church Membership by County and Denomination: 1980

County and Denomination	Number of churches	Communicant, confirmed, full members	Total adherents		
			Number	Percent of total population	Percent of total adherents
001 ADVENT CHR CH..	5	482	579*	0.1	0.2
005 AME ZION......	3	595	676	0.1	0.3
017 AMER BAPT ASSN	7	999	999	0.2	0.4
019 AMER BAPT USA.	1	75	90*	–	–
053 ASSEMB OF GOD.	35	3 903	7 565	1.2	3.1
055 AS REF PRES CH	2	390	473	0.1	0.2
057 BAPT GEN CONF.	2	152	183*	–	0.1
071 BRETHREN (ASH)	2	40	48*	–	–
081 CATHOLIC......	19	NA	68 242	10.5	28.0
089 CHR & MISS AL.	3	190	236	–	0.1
093 CHR CH (DISC).	6	1 152	1 654	0.3	0.7
097 CHR CHS&CHS CR	9	2 042	2 453*	0.4	1.0
101 C.M.E........	3	616	740*	0.1	0.3
123 CH GOD (ANDER)	1	60	180	–	0.1
127 CH GOD (CLEVE)	25	3 188	3 829*	0.6	1.6
149 CH OF JC (BIC)	1	42	42	–	–
151 L-D SAINTS....	5	NA	2 341	0.4	1.0
157 CH OF BRETHREN	1	56	67*	–	–
165 CH OF NAZARENE	11	1 009	1 666	0.3	0.7
167 CHS OF CHRIST.	43	3 675	4 678	0.7	1.9
179 CONSRV BAPT...	1	91	109*	–	–
185 CUMBER PRESB..	7	503	1 152	0.2	0.5
193 EPISCOPAL.....	14	5 269	6 641	1.0	2.7
208 EVAN LUTH ASSN	1	216	343	0.1	0.1
221 FREE METHODIST	2	143	648	0.1	0.3
263 INT FOURSQ GOS	1	171	205*	–	0.1
270 CONSRV JUDAISM	1	365	438*	0.1	0.2
271 REFORM JUDAISM	1	1 040	1 249*	0.2	0.5
281 LUTH CH AMER..	9	2 448	3 312	0.5	1.4
283 LUTH--MO SYNOD	6	1 987	2 816	0.4	1.2
285 MENNONITE CH..	2	106	127*	–	0.1
290 METRO COMM CHS	1	240	480	0.1	0.2
329 OPEN BIBLE STD	2	130	180	–	0.1
349 PENT HOLINESS.	4	322	387*	0.1	0.2
353 CHR BRETHREN..	3	125	150	–	0.1
356 PRESB CH AMER.	2	476	529	0.1	0.2
357 PRESB CH US...	16	6 581	7 904*	1.2	3.2
363 PRIMITIVE METH	1	62	74*	–	–
371 REF CH IN AM..	1	190	378	0.1	0.2
381 REF PRES-EVAN.	1	52	62	–	–
403 SALVATION ARMY	1	327	461	0.1	0.2
413 S.D.A........	10	2 611	3 136*	0.5	1.3
419 SO BAPT CONV..	113	68 265	81 993*	12.7	33.7
421 SO METHODIST..	2	58	84	–	–
435 UNITARIAN-UNIV	2	130	156*	–	0.1
443 UN C OF CHRIST	2	1 637	1 966*	0.3	0.8
449 UN METHODIST..	48	25 853	31 052*	4.8	12.7
453 UN PRES CH USA	2	648	778*	0.1	0.3
469 WELS.........	1	74	81	–	–
HOLMES	64	6 919	9 111*	61.9	100.0
053 ASSEMB OF GOD.	14	756	1 059	7.2	11.6
081 CATHOLIC......	1	NA	244	1.7	2.7
127 CH GOD (CLEVE)	2	116	141*	1.0	1.5
151 L-D SAINTS....	1	NA	283	1.9	3.1
165 CH OF NAZARENE	1	39	56	0.4	0.6
167 CHS OF CHRIST.	4	105	142	1.0	1.6
357 PRESB CH US...	1	15	18*	0.1	0.2
413 S.D.A........	1	20	24*	0.2	0.3
419 SO BAPT CONV..	28	5 118	6 231*	42.3	68.4
443 UN C OF CHRIST	1	11	13*	0.1	0.1
449 UN METHODIST..	10	739	900*	6.1	9.9
INDIAN RIVER	45	13 501	21 489*	35.9	100.0
029 AMER LUTH CH..	1	105	108	0.2	0.5
053 ASSEMB OF GOD.	3	470	839	1.4	3.9
081 CATHOLIC......	1	NA	4 540	7.6	21.1
093 CHR CH (DISC).	1	50	68	0.1	0.3
097 CHR CHS&CHS CR	1	215	251*	0.4	1.2
123 CH GOD (ANDER)	1	110	330	0.6	1.5
127 CH GOD (CLEVE)	7	672	784*	1.3	3.6
151 L-D SAINTS....	1	NA	170	0.3	0.8
165 CH OF NAZARENE	1	68	137	0.2	0.6
167 CHS OF CHRIST.	3	174	216	0.4	1.0
193 EPISCOPAL.....	1	880	1 480	2.5	6.9
201 EVAN COV CH AM	1	89	104*	0.2	0.5
209 EVAN LUTH SYN.	1	255	300	0.5	1.4
281 LUTH CH AMER..	1	310	371	0.6	1.7
283 LUTH--MO SYNOD	1	152	187	0.3	0.9
413 S.D.A........	1	97	113*	0.2	0.5
419 SO BAPT CONV..	10	5 175	6 035*	10.1	28.1
443 UN C OF CHRIST	1	791	922*	1.5	4.3
449 UN METHODIST..	7	2 985	3 481*	5.8	16.2
453 UN PRES CH USA	1	903	1 053*	1.8	4.9
JACKSON	93	14 691	19 224*	49.1	100.0
053 ASSEMB OF GOD.	15	1 177	1 743	4.5	9.1
081 CATHOLIC......	1	NA	408	1.0	2.1
101 C.M.E........	2	229	279*	0.7	1.5
127 CH GOD (CLEVE)	7	309	376*	1.0	2.0
151 L-D SAINTS....	1	NA	517	1.3	2.7
165 CH OF NAZARENE	1	47	60	0.2	0.3
167 CHS OF CHRIST.	2	163	219	0.6	1.1
193 EPISCOPAL.....	1	261	405	1.0	2.1
283 LUTH--MO SYNOD	1	63	79	0.2	0.4
349 PENT HOLINESS.	1	67	82*	0.2	0.4
357 PRESB CH US...	1	317	386*	1.0	2.0
413 S.D.A........	1	57	69*	0.2	0.4
419 SO BAPT CONV..	40	9 424	11 466*	29.3	59.6
449 UN METHODIST..	19	2 577	3 135*	8.0	16.3
JEFFERSON	20	2 748	3 612*	33.7	100.0

County and Denomination	Number of churches	Communicant, confirmed, full members	Total adherents		
			Number	Percent of total population	Percent of total adherents
053 ASSEMB OF GOD.	1	46	71	0.7	2.0
081 CATHOLIC......	1	NA	130	1.2	3.6
127 CH GOD (CLEVE)	1	19	24*	0.2	0.7
151 L-D SAINTS....	1	NA	39	0.4	1.1
165 CH OF NAZARENE	1	30	40	0.4	1.1
167 CHS OF CHRIST.	1	60	76	0.7	2.1
193 EPISCOPAL.....	1	92	107	1.0	3.0
349 PENT HOLINESS.	1	110	137*	1.3	3.8
357 PRESB CH US...	1	110	137*	1.3	3.8
419 SO BAPT CONV..	6	1 638	2 047*	19.1	56.7
449 UN METHODIST..	5	643	804*	7.5	22.3
LAFAYETTE	19	2 073	2 661*	65.9	100.0
053 ASSEMB OF GOD.	1	151	239	5.9	9.0
127 CH GOD (CLEVE)	2	97	121*	3.0	4.5
167 CHS OF CHRIST.	2	33	42	1.0	1.6
193 EPISCOPAL.....	1	13	41	1.0	1.5
419 SO BAPT CONV..	11	1 561	1 946*	48.2	73.1
449 UN METHODIST..	2	218	272*	6.7	10.2
LAKE	131	31 127	42 985*	41.0	100.0
017 AMER BAPT ASSN	6	927	927	0.9	2.2
053 ASSEMB OF GOD.	8	431	729	0.7	1.7
057 BAPT GEN CONF.	0	4	5*	–	–
081 CATHOLIC......	4	NA	5 604	5.3	13.0
089 CHR & MISS AL.	2	235	285	0.3	0.7
093 CHR CH (DISC).	1	121	121	0.1	0.3
097 CHR CHS&CHS CR	4	1 042	1 212*	1.2	2.8
123 CH GOD (ANDER)	5	308	924	0.9	2.1
127 CH GOD (CLEVE)	16	1 052	1 224*	1.2	2.8
151 L-D SAINTS....	1	NA	464	0.4	1.1
165 CH OF NAZARENE	3	205	408	0.4	0.9
167 CHS OF CHRIST.	11	896	1 150	1.1	2.7
175 CONGR CHR CHS.	1	193	225*	0.2	0.5
193 EPISCOPAL.....	5	2 096	2 266	2.2	5.3
201 EVAN COV CH AM	1	110	128*	0.1	0.3
203 EVAN FREE CH..	1	35	41*	–	0.1
281 LUTH CH AMER..	4	703	793	0.8	1.8
283 LUTH--MO SYNOD	2	700	806	0.8	1.9
357 PRESB CH US...	3	875	1 018*	1.0	2.4
413 S.D.A........	4	373	434*	0.4	1.0
419 SO BAPT CONV..	26	11 990	13 949*	13.3	32.5
443 UN C OF CHRIST	1	268	312*	0.3	0.7
449 UN METHODIST..	16	6 774	7 881*	7.5	18.3
453 UN PRES CH USA	5	1 746	2 031*	1.9	4.7
469 WELS.........	1	43	48	–	0.1
LEE	142	41 911	75 073*	36.6	100.0
001 ADVENT CHR CH..	1	14	16*	–	–
029 AMER LUTH CH..	1	135	147	0.1	0.2
053 ASSEMB OF GOD.	9	1 392	2 654	1.3	3.5
081 CATHOLIC......	11	NA	22 219	10.8	29.6
089 CHR & MISS AL.	4	898	1 848	0.9	2.5
093 CHR CH (DISC).	2	353	439	0.2	0.6
097 CHR CHS&CHS CR	3	1 403	1 630*	0.8	2.2
101 C.M.E........	1	517	601*	0.3	0.8
105 CHRISTIAN REF.	1	74	99	–	0.1
123 CH GOD (ANDER)	3	150	450	0.2	0.6
127 CH GOD (CLEVE)	8	775	900*	0.4	1.2
151 L-D SAINTS....	1	NA	507	0.2	0.7
157 CH OF BRETHREN	2	113	131*	0.1	0.2
163 CH OF LUTH BR.	1	61	71	–	0.1
165 CH OF NAZARENE	4	307	792	0.4	1.1
167 CHS OF CHRIST.	5	600	764	0.4	1.0
193 EPISCOPAL.....	8	2 815	3 721	1.8	5.0
221 FREE METHODIST	1	17	114	0.1	0.2
226 FRIENDS-USA...	1	34	40*	–	0.1
244 GRACE BRETHREN	1	114	132*	0.1	0.2
263 INT FOURSQ GOS	1	?	?	?	?
271 REFORM JUDAISM	1	398	462*	0.2	0.6
281 LUTH CH AMER..	5	2 006	2 425	1.2	3.2
283 LUTH--MO SYNOD	3	1 564	1 928	0.9	2.6
290 METRO COMM CHS	1	30	60	–	0.1
329 OPEN BIBLE STD	1	100	130	0.1	0.2
356 PRESB CH AMER.	1	60	69	–	0.1
357 PRESB CH US...	6	2 211	2 569*	1.3	3.4
381 REF PRES-EVAN.	1	21	26	–	–
403 SALVATION ARMY	1	154	379	0.2	0.5
413 S.D.A........	3	386	448*	0.2	0.6
419 SO BAPT CONV..	22	12 599	14 638*	7.1	19.5
435 UNITARIAN-UNIV	1	115	134*	0.1	0.2
443 UN C OF CHRIST	2	490	569*	0.3	0.8
449 UN METHODIST..	18	9 673	11 238*	5.5	15.0
453 UN PRES CH USA	5	2 181	2 534*	1.2	3.4
469 WELS.........	2	151	189	0.1	0.3
LEON	108	34 576	54 554*	36.7	100.0
017 AMER BAPT ASSN	3	407	407	0.3	0.7
053 ASSEMB OF GOD.	7	932	1 421	1.0	2.6
081 CATHOLIC......	5	NA	11 015	7.4	20.2
089 CHR & MISS AL.	1	78	119	0.1	0.2
093 CHR CH (DISC).	1	13	31	–	0.1
097 CHR CHS&CHS CR	2	500	597*	0.4	1.1
101 C.M.E........	3	176	210*	0.1	0.4
123 CH GOD (ANDER)	1	8	24	–	–
127 CH GOD (CLEVE)	2	352	420*	0.3	0.8
151 L-D SAINTS....	3	NA	924	0.6	1.7
165 CH OF NAZARENE	2	185	264	0.2	0.5
167 CHS OF CHRIST.	5	707	876	0.6	1.6
177 CONGR HOL CH..	1	9	11*	–	–
193 EPISCOPAL.....	6	2 632	3 714	2.5	6.8

NA—Not applicable   *Total adherents estimated from known number of communicant, confirmed, full members.   —Represents a percent less than 0.1.   Percentages may not total due to rounding.

FLORIDA

Table 4. Churches and Church Membership by County and Denomination: 1980

County and Denomination	Number of churches	Communicant, confirmed, full members	Total adherents Number	Percent of total population	Percent of total adherents
226 FRIENDS-USA...	1	6	7*	–	–
263 INT FOURSQ GOS	1	37	44*	–	0.1
270 CONSRV JUDAISM	1	37	44*	–	0.1
271 REFORM JUDAISM	1	422	504*	0.3	0.9
281 LUTH CH AMER..	1	276	474	0.3	0.9
283 LUTH--MO SYNOD	2	370	520	0.3	1.0
285 MENNONITE CH..	1	51	61*	–	0.1
290 METRO COMM CHS	1	25	50	–	0.1
329 OPEN BIBLE STD	1	50	60	–	0.1
335 ORTH PRESB CH.	1	65	78*	0.1	0.1
349 PENT HOLINESS.	4	683	816*	0.5	1.5
356 PRESB CH AMER.	2	261	282	0.2	0.5
357 PRESB CH US...	6	2 240	2 675*	1.8	4.9
403 SALVATION ARMY	1	59	256	0.2	0.5
413 S.D.A.........	2	341	407*	0.3	0.7
419 SO BAPT CONV..	21	16 144	19 276*	13.0	35.3
435 UNITARIAN-UNIV	1	115	137*	0.1	0.3
443 UN C OF CHRIST	1	61	73*	–	0.1
449 UN METHODIST..	16	7 238	8 642*	5.8	15.8
453 UN PRES CH USA	1	96	115*	0.1	0.2
LEVY	**44**	**6 458**	**8 623***	**43.4**	**100.0**
053 ASSEMB OF GOD.	2	57	101	0.5	1.2
081 CATHOLIC......	3	NA	450	2.3	5.2
127 CH GOD (CLEVE)	5	145	175*	0.9	2.0
151 L-D SAINTS....	1	NA	271	1.4	3.1
167 CHS OF CHRIST.	8	460	585	2.9	6.8
193 EPISCOPAL.....	3	132	218	1.1	2.5
203 EVAN FREE CH..	1	49	59*	0.3	0.7
357 PRESB CH US...	1	75	90*	0.5	1.0
419 SO BAPT CONV..	12	4 442	5 351*	26.9	62.1
449 UN METHODIST..	8	1 098	1 323*	6.7	15.3
LIBERTY	**17**	**1 550**	**2 580***	**60.6**	**100.0**
053 ASSEMB OF GOD.	4	176	250	5.9	9.7
081 CATHOLIC......	1	NA	118	2.8	4.6
097 CHR CHS&CHS CR	1	90	111*	2.6	4.3
127 CH GOD (CLEVE)	1	68	84*	2.0	3.3
151 L-D SAINTS....	1	NA	518	12.2	20.1
349 PENT HOLINESS.	1	125	154*	3.6	6.0
357 PRESB CH US...	1	9	11*	0.3	0.4
419 SO BAPT CONV..	5	946	1 166*	27.4	45.2
449 UN METHODIST..	2	136	168*	3.9	6.5
MADISON	**45**	**5 828**	**7 470***	**50.2**	**100.0**
017 AMER BAPT ASSN	1	222	222	1.5	3.0
053 ASSEMB OF GOD.	1	30	40	0.3	0.5
081 CATHOLIC......	1	NA	155	1.0	2.1
127 CH GOD (CLEVE)	3	113	141*	0.9	1.9
151 L-D SAINTS....	1	NA	97	0.7	1.3
165 CH OF NAZARENE	1	24	41	0.3	0.5
167 CHS OF CHRIST.	2	53	67	0.4	0.9
193 EPISCOPAL.....	1	44	57	0.4	0.8
356 PRESB CH AMER.	1	134	155	1.0	2.1
357 PRESB CH US...	1	33	41*	0.3	0.5
413 S.D.A.........	1	24	30*	0.2	0.4
419 SO BAPT CONV..	21	3 919	4 874*	32.7	65.2
421 SO METHODIST..	2	62	95	0.6	1.3
449 UN METHODIST..	8	1 170	1 455*	9.8	19.5
MANATEE	**106**	**33 188**	**51 696***	**34.8**	**100.0**
029 AMER LUTH CH..	1	261	305	0.2	0.6
053 ASSEMB OF GOD.	4	376	665	0.4	1.3
057 BAPT GEN CONF.	1	203	235*	0.2	0.5
071 BRETHREN (ASH)	1	45	52*	–	0.1
081 CATHOLIC......	5	NA	10 350	7.0	20.0
089 CHR & MISS AL.	1	103	163	0.3	0.3
093 CHR CH (DISC).	1	341	446	0.3	0.9
097 CHR CHS&CHS CR	4	468	541*	0.4	1.0
101 C.M.E.........	3	405	468*	0.3	0.9
105 CHRISTIAN REF.	1	416	556	0.4	1.1
123 CH GOD (ANDER)	1	218	654	0.4	1.3
127 CH GOD (CLEVE)	5	365	422*	0.3	0.8
151 L-D SAINTS....	1	NA	361	0.2	0.7
157 CH OF BRETHREN	1	143	165*	0.1	0.3
165 CH OF NAZARENE	3	768	1 674	1.1	3.2
167 CHS OF CHRIST.	8	850	1 080	0.7	2.1
179 CONSRV BAPT...	1	91	105*	0.1	0.2
193 EPISCOPAL.....	4	2 139	2 227	1.5	4.3
201 EVAN COV CH AM	2	426	492*	0.3	1.0
203 EVAN FREE CH..	1	25	29*	–	0.1
208 EVAN LUTH ASSN	1	350	865	0.6	1.7
270 CONSRV JUDAISM	1	57	66*	–	0.1
281 LUTH CH AMER..	2	1 052	1 311	0.9	2.5
283 LUTH--MO SYNOD	1	700	810	0.5	1.6
329 OPEN BIBLE STD	1	38	50	–	0.1
349 PENT HOLINESS.	1	74	86*	0.1	0.2
357 PRESB CH US...	4	2 525	2 919*	2.0	5.6
371 REF CH IN AM..	1	342	932	0.6	1.8
381 REF PRES-EVAN.	1	53	68	–	0.1
403 SALVATION ARMY	1	135	189	0.1	0.4
413 S.D.A.........	2	330	381*	0.3	0.7
419 SO BAPT CONV..	23	10 966	12 675*	8.5	24.5
435 UNITARIAN-UNIV	1	74	86*	0.1	0.2
443 UN C OF CHRIST	1	675	780*	0.5	1.5
449 UN METHODIST..	13	7 253	8 383*	5.6	16.2
453 UN PRES CH USA	2	761	880*	0.6	1.7
469 WELS..........	1	160	225	0.2	0.4
MARION	**123**	**28 684**	**42 892***	**35.0**	**100.0**
053 ASSEMB OF GOD.	3	282	507	0.4	1.2
057 BAPT GEN CONF.	1	32	38*	–	0.1
081 CATHOLIC......	3	NA	7 293	6.0	17.0
089 CHR & MISS AL.	1	45	99	0.1	0.2
093 CHR CH (DISC).	1	589	652	0.5	1.5
097 CHR CHS&CHS CR	3	340	405*	0.3	0.9
101 C.M.E.........	1	?	?	?	?
123 CH GOD (ANDER)	1	93	279	0.2	0.7
127 CH GOD (CLEVE)	5	502	598*	0.5	1.4
151 L-D SAINTS....	1	NA	456	0.4	1.1
165 CH OF NAZARENE	2	181	336	0.3	0.8
167 CHS OF CHRIST.	10	610	793	0.6	1.8
193 EPISCOPAL.....	3	1 139	1 549*	1.3	3.6
263 INT FOURSQ GOS	1	29	35*	–	0.1
281 LUTH CH AMER..	3	654	815	0.7	1.9
283 LUTH--MO SYNOD	2	870	1 248	1.0	2.9
335 ORTH PRESB CH.	1	26	31*	–	0.1
349 PENT HOLINESS.	2	171	204*	0.2	0.5
353 CHR BRETHREN..	1	40	70	0.1	0.2
356 PRESB CH AMER.	1	145	192	0.2	0.4
357 PRESB CH US...	7	2 000	2 381*	1.9	5.6
403 SALVATION ARMY	1	90	89	0.1	0.2
413 S.D.A.........	2	494	588*	0.5	1.4
419 SO BAPT CONV..	34	13 495	16 069*	13.1	37.5
449 UN METHODIST..	28	6 632	7 897*	6.4	18.4
453 UN PRES CH USA	1	225	268*	0.2	0.6
MARTIN	**51**	**11 311**	**25 949***	**40.5**	**100.0**
017 AMER BAPT ASSN	3	720	720	1.1	2.8
053 ASSEMB OF GOD.	1	55	101	0.2	0.4
081 CATHOLIC......	4	NA	12 400	19.4	47.8
089 CHR & MISS AL.	1	33	50	0.1	0.2
097 CHR CHS&CHS CR	2	200	230*	0.4	0.9
101 C.M.E.........	1	42	48*	0.1	0.2
127 CH GOD (CLEVE)	7	299	344*	0.5	1.3
151 L-D SAINTS....	1	NA	86	0.1	0.3
165 CH OF NAZARENE	2	45	191	0.3	0.7
167 CHS OF CHRIST.	4	276	352	0.5	1.4
193 EPISCOPAL.....	4	1 179	1 551	2.4	6.0
281 LUTH CH AMER..	1	357	440	0.7	1.7
283 LUTH--MO SYNOD	1	618	761	1.2	2.9
356 PRESB CH AMER.	1	70	99	0.2	0.4
413 S.D.A.........	2	49	56*	0.1	0.2
419 SO BAPT CONV..	8	3 518	4 051*	6.3	15.6
421 SO METHODIST..	1	26	65	0.1	0.3
443 UN C OF CHRIST	1	354	408*	0.6	1.6
449 UN METHODIST..	4	2 433	2 802*	4.4	10.8
453 UN PRES CH USA	2	1 037	1 194*	1.9	4.6
MONROE	**57**	**8 787**	**24 806***	**39.3**	**100.0**
053 ASSEMB OF GOD.	2	130	326	0.5	1.3
081 CATHOLIC......	6	NA	14 200	22.5	57.2
127 CH GOD (CLEVE)	3	203	233*	0.4	0.9
151 L-D SAINTS....	2	NA	194	0.3	0.8
165 CH OF NAZARENE	1	38	98	0.2	0.4
167 CHS OF CHRIST.	5	375	475	0.8	1.9
193 EPISCOPAL.....	5	1 188	1 258	2.0	5.1
281 LUTH CH AMER..	1	69	104	0.2	0.4
283 LUTH--MO SYNOD	3	380	501	0.8	2.0
290 METRO COMM CHS	1	30	60	0.1	0.2
353 CHR BRETHREN..	1	25	40	0.1	0.2
357 PRESB CH US...	1	161	184*	0.3	0.7
403 SALVATION ARMY	1	76	131	0.2	0.5
413 S.D.A.........	3	76	87*	0.1	0.4
419 SO BAPT CONV..	9	3 903	4 471*	7.1	18.0
443 UN C OF CHRIST	1	81	93*	0.1	0.4
449 UN METHODIST..	10	1 828	2 094*	3.3	8.4
453 UN PRES CH USA	2	224	257*	0.4	1.0
NASSAU	**46**	**9 102**	**12 945***	**39.4**	**100.0**
053 ASSEMB OF GOD.	4	250	362	1.1	2.8
081 CATHOLIC......	2	NA	1 144	3.5	8.8
089 CHR & MISS AL.	2	85	118	0.4	0.9
127 CH GOD (CLEVE)	6	443	551*	1.7	4.3
151 L-D SAINTS....	1	NA	171	0.5	1.3
167 CHS OF CHRIST.	2	105	118	0.4	0.9
193 EPISCOPAL.....	2	238	531	1.6	4.1
281 LUTH CH AMER..	1	89	130	0.4	1.0
357 PRESB CH US...	1	245	305*	0.9	2.4
419 SO BAPT CONV..	18	6 446	8 021*	24.4	62.0
449 UN METHODIST..	7	1 201	1 494*	4.5	11.5
OKALOOSA	**120**	**33 046**	**48 107***	**43.8**	**100.0**
053 ASSEMB OF GOD.	24	1 810	3 049	2.8	6.3
059 BAPT MISS ASSN	1	274	335*	0.3	0.7
081 CATHOLIC......	5	NA	4 987	4.5	10.4
093 CHR CH (DISC).	1	106	126	0.1	0.3
097 CHR CHS&CHS CR	3	746	911*	0.8	1.9
123 CH GOD (ANDER)	1	100	300	0.3	0.6
127 CH GOD (CLEVE)	3	232	283*	0.3	0.6
151 L-D SAINTS....	4	NA	1 345	1.2	2.8
165 CH OF NAZARENE	1	119	352	0.3	0.7
167 CHS OF CHRIST.	10	1 250	1 590	1.4	3.3
193 EPISCOPAL.....	4	1 578	2 049	1.9	4.3
281 LUTH CH AMER..	1	287	327	0.3	0.7
283 LUTH--MO SYNOD	2	481	609	0.6	1.3
285 MENNONITE CH..	1	10	12*	–	–
356 PRESB CH AMER.	2	268	286	0.3	0.6
357 PRESB CH US...	5	869	1 061*	1.0	2.2
403 SALVATION ARMY	1	60	138	0.1	0.3
413 S.D.A.........	2	114	139*	0.1	0.3

NA— Not applicable   *Total adherents estimated from known number of communicant, confirmed, full members.   —Represents a percent less than 0.1.   Percentages may not total due to rounding.

Table 4. Churches and Church Membership by County and Denomination: 1980

County and Denomination	Number of churches	Communicant, confirmed, full members	Total adherents Number	Percent of total population	Percent of total adherents
419 SO BAPT CONV..	38	18 435	22 508*	20.5	46.8
435 UNITARIAN-UNIV	1	24	29*	–	0.1
449 UN METHODIST..	10	6 283	7 671*	7.0	15.9
OKEECHOBEE	21	4 151	6 439*	31.8	100.0
017 AMER BAPT ASSN	1	192	192	0.9	3.0
053 ASSEMB OF GOD.	1	67	108	0.5	1.7
081 CATHOLIC......	1	NA	1 100	5.4	17.1
097 CHR CHS&CHS CR	1	13	16*	0.1	0.2
127 CH GOD (CLEVE)	3	260	321*	1.6	5.0
151 L-D SAINTS....	1	NA	105	0.5	1.6
165 CH OF NAZARENE	1	69	158	0.8	2.5
167 CHS OF CHRIST.	2	54	75	0.4	1.2
193 EPISCOPAL.....	1	152	212	1.0	3.3
244 GRACE BRETHREN	1	200	247*	1.2	3.8
283 LUTH--MO SYNOD	1	140	200	1.0	3.1
413 S.D.A.........	1	82	101*	0.5	1.6
419 SO BAPT CONV..	5	2 408	2 970*	14.7	46.1
449 UN METHODIST..	1	514	634*	3.1	9.8
ORANGE	320	123 689	194 363*	41.2	100.0
001 ADVENT CHR CH.	1	64	76*	–	–
017 AMER BAPT ASSN	10	1 363	1 363	0.3	0.7
019 AMER BAPT USA.	2	1 528	1 825*	0.4	0.9
029 AMER LUTH CH..	3	894	1 134	0.2	0.6
053 ASSEMB OF GOD.	11	5 437	7 229	1.5	3.7
055 AS REF PRES CH	1	24	30	–	–
057 BAPT GEN CONF.	3	255	305*	0.1	0.2
075 BRETHREN IN CR	1	109	131	–	0.1
081 CATHOLIC......	14	NA	39 886	8.5	20.5
089 CHR & MISS AL.	7	1 241	1 884	0.4	1.0
093 CHR CH (DISC).	4	1 035	1 530	0.3	0.8
097 CHR CHS&CHS CR	10	2 929	3 499*	0.7	1.8
101 C.M.E.........	2	1 268	1 515*	0.3	0.8
105 CHRISTIAN REF.	1	104	196	–	0.1
123 CH GOD (ANDER)	1	200	600	0.1	0.3
127 CH GOD (CLEVE)	19	2 744	3 278*	0.7	1.7
151 L-D SAINTS....	5	NA	2 568	0.5	1.3
157 CH OF BRETHREN	2	465	555*	0.1	0.3
165 CH OF NAZARENE	15	1 766	2 744	0.6	1.4
167 CHS OF CHRIST.	18	1 740	2 215	0.5	1.1
175 CONGR CHR CHS.	1	122	146*	–	0.1
179 CONSRV BAPT...	2	182	217*	–	0.1
181 CONSRV CONGR..	1	38	45*	–	–
193 EPISCOPAL.....	13	7 334	9 044	1.9	4.7
201 EVAN COV CH AM	1	79	94*	–	–
221 FREE METHODIST	2	29	111	–	0.1
226 FRIENDS-USA...	2	58	69*	–	–
244 GRACE BRETHREN	2	165	197*	–	0.1
263 INT FOURSQ GOS	2	170	203*	–	0.1
270 CONSRV JUDAISM	2	465	555*	0.1	0.3
271 REFORM JUDAISM	1	630	753*	0.2	0.4
281 LUTH CH AMER..	4	2 775	3 570	0.8	1.8
283 LUTH--MO SYNOD	7	3 226	4 391	0.9	2.3
290 METRO COMM CHS	1	25	50	–	–
329 OPEN BIBLE STD	1	20	30	–	–
335 ORTH PRESB CH.	1	83	99*	–	0.1
349 PENT HOLINESS.	2	224	268*	0.1	0.1
353 CHR BRETHREN..	5	250	450	0.1	0.2
356 PRESB CH AMER.	1	128	185	–	0.1
357 PRESB CH US...	17	11 111	13 273*	2.8	6.8
371 REF CH IN AM..	3	382	599	0.1	0.3
375 REF EPISCOPAL.	1	18	22*	–	–
381 REF PRES-EVAN.	1	60	97	–	–
383 REF PRES OF NA	1	76	104	–	0.1
403 SALVATION ARMY	1	394	618	0.1	0.3
413 S.D.A.........	14	3 481	4 158*	0.9	2.1
419 SO BAPT CONV..	62	44 999	53 755*	11.4	27.7
435 UNITARIAN-UNIV	1	234	280*	0.1	0.1
443 UN C OF CHRIST	4	1 406	1 680*	0.4	0.9
449 UN METHODIST..	33	22 198	26 517*	5.6	13.6
469 WELS..........	1	161	220	–	0.1
OSCEOLA	48	10 487	16 462*	33.4	100.0
005 AME ZION......	1	340	340	0.7	2.1
017 AMER BAPT ASSN	8	1 474	1 474	3.0	9.0
029 AMER LUTH CH..	1	322	387	0.8	2.4
053 ASSEMB OF GOD.	2	424	481	1.0	2.9
081 CATHOLIC......	2	NA	3 100	6.3	18.8
089 CHR & MISS AL.	1	35	83	0.2	0.5
097 CHR CHS&CHS CR	1	325	387*	0.8	2.4
123 CH GOD (ANDER)	1	80	240	0.5	1.5
127 CH GOD (CLEVE)	3	65	77*	0.2	0.5
151 L-D SAINTS....	2	NA	547	1.1	3.3
165 CH OF NAZARENE	3	220	530	1.1	3.2
167 CHS OF CHRIST.	4	235	300	0.6	1.8
179 CONSRV BAPT...	1	91	108*	0.2	0.7
193 EPISCOPAL.....	2	458	542	1.1	3.3
221 FREE METHODIST	1	50	255	0.5	1.5
283 LUTH--MO SYNOD	1	125	182	0.4	1.1
413 S.D.A.........	4	178	212*	0.4	1.3
419 SO BAPT CONV..	5	3 365	4 004*	8.1	24.3
449 UN METHODIST..	3	2 247	2 674*	5.4	16.2
453 UN PRES CH USA	2	453	539*	1.1	3.3
PALM BEACH	270	81 976	230 847*	40.3	100.0
017 AMER BAPT ASSN	4	402	402	0.1	0.2
019 AMER BAPT USA.	1	245	284*	–	0.1
029 AMER LUTH CH..	3	1 164	1 474	0.3	0.6
045 APOSTOLIC LUTH	1	300	348*	0.1	0.2
053 ASSEMB OF GOD.	7	1 130	1 818	0.3	0.8

County and Denomination	Number of churches	Communicant, confirmed, full members	Total adherents Number	Percent of total population	Percent of total adherents
081 CATHOLIC......	26	NA	127 750	22.3	55.3
089 CHR & MISS AL.	6	478	908	0.2	0.4
093 CHR CH (DISC).	5	883	1 378	0.2	0.6
097 CHR CHS&CHS CR	4	249	288*	0.1	0.1
101 C.M.E.........	4	702	813*	0.1	0.4
105 CHRISTIAN REF.	2	330	587	0.1	0.3
123 CH GOD (ANDER)	4	652	1 956	0.3	0.8
127 CH GOD (CLEVE)	22	1 962	2 273*	0.4	1.0
149 CH OF JC (BIC)	1	67	79	–	–
151 L-D SAINTS....	5	NA	1 577	0.3	0.7
165 CH OF NAZARENE	7	585	998	0.2	0.4
167 CHS OF CHRIST.	14	1 527	1 864	0.3	0.8
193 EPISCOPAL.....	23	8 945	11 291	2.0	4.9
201 EVAN COV CH AM	3	335	388*	0.1	0.2
221 FREE METHODIST	3	93	432	0.1	0.2
226 FRIENDS-USA...	1	32	37*	–	–
270 CONSRV JUDAISM	4	2 095	2 427*	0.4	1.1
271 REFORM JUDAISM	2	2 080	2 409*	0.4	1.0
281 LUTH CH AMER..	7	2 889	3 445	0.6	1.5
283 LUTH--MO SYNOD	7	2 872	4 651	0.8	2.0
290 METRO COMM CHS	0	0	25	–	–
295 MORAV CH-SOUTH	1	90	111	–	–
313 N AM BAPT CONF	2	95	110*	–	–
329 OPEN BIBLE STD	1	82	122	–	0.1
349 PENT HOLINESS.	2	311	360*	0.1	0.2
353 CHR BRETHREN..	4	350	625	0.1	0.3
356 PRESB CH AMER.	6	1 500	1 765	0.3	0.8
357 PRESB CH US...	3	1 190	1 378*	0.2	0.6
371 REF CH IN AM..	1	162	238	–	0.1
403 SALVATION ARMY	2	230	692	0.1	0.3
413 S.D.A.........	8	1 215	1 407*	0.2	0.6
419 SO BAPT CONV..	28	23 233	26 914*	4.7	11.7
435 UNITARIAN-UNIV	2	301	349*	0.1	0.2
443 UN C OF CHRIST	7	2 303	2 668*	0.5	1.2
449 UN METHODIST..	25	15 288	17 709*	3.1	7.7
453 UN PRES CH USA	11	5 558	6 438*	1.1	2.8
469 WELS..........	1	50	59	–	–
PASCO	123	29 261	54 989*	28.3	100.0
017 AMER BAPT ASSN	5	680	680	0.4	1.2
029 AMER LUTH CH..	2	90	105	0.1	0.2
053 ASSEMB OF GOD.	7	874	1 212	0.6	2.2
081 CATHOLIC......	8	NA	20 253	10.4	36.8
089 CHR & MISS AL.	2	133	175	0.1	0.3
093 CHR CH (DISC).	1	308	376	0.2	0.7
097 CHR CHS&CHS CR	4	550	624*	0.3	1.1
123 CH GOD (ANDER)	3	260	780	0.4	1.4
127 CH GOD (CLEVE)	8	976	1 107*	0.6	2.0
151 L-D SAINTS....	2	NA	528	0.3	1.0
163 CH OF LUTH BR.	1	10	10	–	–
165 CH OF NAZARENE	3	276	689	0.4	1.3
167 CHS OF CHRIST.	6	425	535	0.3	1.0
179 CONSRV BAPT...	1	91	103*	0.1	0.2
193 EPISCOPAL.....	4	1 844	1 883	1.0	3.4
203 EVAN FREE CH..	1	70	79*	–	0.1
221 FREE METHODIST	1	32	165	0.1	0.3
281 LUTH CH AMER..	3	1 610	1 743	0.9	3.2
283 LUTH--MO SYNOD	4	1 516	1 654	0.9	3.0
353 CHR BRETHREN..	3	100	200	0.1	0.4
357 PRESB CH US...	4	1 743	1 978*	1.0	3.6
371 REF CH IN AM..	2	201	253	0.1	0.5
413 S.D.A.........	3	458	520*	0.3	0.9
419 SO BAPT CONV..	27	9 844	11 168*	5.8	20.3
443 UN C OF CHRIST	3	679	770*	0.4	1.4
449 UN METHODIST..	11	6 007	6 815*	3.5	12.4
453 UN PRES CH USA	1	228	259*	0.1	0.5
469 WELS..........	3	256	325	0.2	0.6
PINELLAS	349	151 727	272 360*	37.4	100.0
001 ADVENT CHR CH.	4	148	168*	–	0.1
017 AMER BAPT ASSN	4	709	709	0.1	0.3
019 AMER BAPT USA.	3	1 418	1 613*	0.2	0.6
029 AMER LUTH CH..	5	2 808	3 579	0.5	1.3
053 ASSEMB OF GOD.	12	2 880	3 938	0.5	1.4
071 BRETHREN (ASH)	1	8	9*	–	–
075 BRETHREN IN CR	1	109	131	–	–
081 CATHOLIC......	25	NA	92 060	12.6	33.8
089 CHR & MISS AL.	6	413	771	0.1	0.3
093 CHR CH (DISC).	6	1 923	2 514	0.3	0.9
097 CHR CHS&CHS CR	7	5 893	6 702*	0.9	2.5
101 C.M.E.........	4	780	887*	0.1	0.3
105 CHRISTIAN REF.	1	130	173	–	0.1
123 CH GOD (ANDER)	12	1 068	3 204	0.4	1.2
127 CH GOD (CLEVE)	12	2 472	2 811*	0.4	1.0
151 L-D SAINTS....	3	NA	1 565	0.2	0.6
157 CH OF BRETHREN	1	231	263*	–	0.1
165 CH OF NAZARENE	10	1 272	2 267	0.3	0.8
167 CHS OF CHRIST.	20	2 650	3 375	0.5	1.2
179 CONSRV BAPT...	1	91	103*	–	–
193 EPISCOPAL.....	21	14 998	15 704	2.2	5.8
201 EVAN COV CH AM	3	370	421*	0.1	0.2
203 EVAN FREE CH..	1	42	48*	–	–
221 FREE METHODIST	2	268	1 026	0.1	0.4
226 FRIENDS-USA...	2	83	94*	–	–
239 SWEDENBORGIAN.	1	60	68*	–	–
244 GRACE BRETHREN	2	122	139*	–	0.1
263 INT FOURSQ GOS	1	95	108*	–	–
270 CONSRV JUDAISM	3	388	441*	0.1	0.2
271 REFORM JUDAISM	4	2 314	2 632*	0.4	1.0
274 LAT EVAN LUTH.	1	141	141	–	0.1
281 LUTH CH AMER..	12	6 400	7 557	1.0	2.8
283 LUTH--MO SYNOD	8	6 031	7 297	1.0	2.7
285 MENNONITE CH..	2	49	56*	–	–

NA– Not applicable

*Total adherents estimated from known number of communicant, confirmed, full members.

—Represents a percent less than 0.1.

Percentages may not total due to rounding.

Table 4. Churches and Church Membership by County and Denomination: 1980

County and Denomination	Number of churches	Communicant, confirmed, full members	Total adherents Number	Percent of total population	Percent of total adherents
290 METRO COMM CHS	1	30	60	–	–
291 MISSIONARY CH.	2	235	315	–	0.1
329 OPEN BIBLE STD	7	1 355	1 795	0.2	0.7
349 PENT HOLINESS	2	107	122*	–	–
353 CHR BRETHREN..	1	60	100	–	–
356 PRESB CH AMER.	1	?	?	?	?
357 PRESB CH US...	19	9 207	10 470*	1.4	3.8
371 REF CH IN AM..	2	434	681	0.1	0.3
375 REF EPISCOPAL.	1	15	17*	–	–
381 REF PRES-EVAN.	1	54	74	–	–
403 SALVATION ARMY	3	599	1 376	0.2	0.5
413 S.D.A.........	3	1 014	1 153*	0.2	0.4
419 SO BAPT CONV..	35	31 382	35 688*	4.9	13.1
435 UNITARIAN-UNIV	4	720	819*	0.1	0.3
443 UN C OF CHRIST	10	4 945	5 624*	0.8	2.1
449 UN METHODIST..	42	39 155	44 528*	6.1	16.3
453 UN PRES CH USA	14	5 555	6 317*	0.9	2.3
469 WELS..........	3	496	647	0.1	0.2
POLK	**332**	**99 719**	**142 571***	**44.3**	**100.0**
017 AMER BAPT ASSN	14	2 300	2 300	0.7	1.6
029 AMER LUTH CH..	1	264	364	0.1	0.3
053 ASSEMB OF GOD.	36	5 880	10 670	3.3	7.5
055 AS REF PRES CH	3	1 579	1 750	0.5	1.2
059 BAPT MISS ASSN	1	63	76*	–	0.1
081 CATHOLIC......	7	NA	15 467	4.8	10.8
089 CHR & MISS AL.	2	196	277	0.1	0.2
093 CHR CH (DISC).	4	918	1 101	0.3	0.8
097 CHR CHS&CHS CR	7	1 389	1 669*	0.5	1.2
101 C.M.E.........	3	314	377*	0.1	0.3
105 CHRISTIAN REF.	1	39	56	–	–
123 CH GOD (ANDER)	8	825	2 475	0.8	1.7
127 CH GOD (CLEVE)	28	3 662	4 399*	1.4	3.1
133 CH GOD(7TH)DEN	1	17	20*	–	–
151 L-D SAINTS....	4	NA	1 390	0.4	1.0
164 CH LUTH CONF..	1	110	169	0.1	0.1
165 CH OF NAZARENE	9	1 374	1 731	0.5	1.2
167 CHS OF CHRIST.	26	3 000	3 818	1.2	2.7
193 EPISCOPAL.....	11	3 983	4 655	1.4	3.3
203 EVAN FREE CH..	1	91	109*	–	0.1
221 FREE METHODIST	3	139	1 005	0.3	0.7
263 INT FOURSQ GOS	1	69	83*	–	0.1
270 CONSRV JUDAISM	1	163	196*	0.1	0.1
281 LUTH CH AMER..	2	711	835	0.3	0.6
283 LUTH--MO SYNOD	5	3 231	4 017	1.2	2.8
291 MISSIONARY CH.	1	38	62	–	–
349 PENT HOLINESS.	1	64	77*	–	0.1
356 PRESB CH AMER.	1	30	46	–	–
357 PRESB CH US...	10	2 655	3 190*	1.0	2.2
381 REF PRES-EVAN.	1	400	551	0.2	0.4
403 SALVATION ARMY	2	193	321	0.1	0.2
413 S.D.A.........	6	674	810*	0.3	0.6
419 SO BAPT CONV..	93	47 506	57 071*	17.7	40.0
435 UNITARIAN-UNIV	1	45	54*	–	–
449 UN METHODIST..	30	15 245	18 314*	5.7	12.8
453 UN PRES CH USA	6	2 552	3 066*	1.0	2.2
PUTNAM	**79**	**14 231**	**20 186***	**39.9**	**100.0**
005 AME ZION......	1	100	100	0.2	0.5
053 ASSEMB OF GOD.	1	114	152	0.3	0.8
059 BAPT MISS ASSN	1	16	19*	–	0.1
081 CATHOLIC......	3	NA	2 042	4.0	10.1
097 CHR CHS&CHS CR	1	50	60*	0.1	0.3
123 CH GOD*(ANDER)	2	130	390	0.8	1.9
127 CH GOD (CLEVE)	3	229	277*	0.5	1.4
151 L-D SAINTS....	3	NA	624	1.2	3.1
167 CHS OF CHRIST.	4	290	369	0.7	1.8
177 CONGR HOL CH..	1	19	23*	–	0.1
193 EPISCOPAL.....	7	558	718	1.4	3.6
208 EVAN LUTH ASSN	1	71	94	0.2	0.5
281 LUTH CH AMER..	1	36	58	0.1	0.3
349 PENT HOLINESS.	2	124	150*	0.3	0.7
357 PRESB CH US...	2	398	481*	1.0	2.4
413 S.D.A.........	2	191	231*	0.5	1.1
415 S-D BAPTIST GC	1	27	33*	0.1	0.2
419 SO BAPT CONV..	31	9 498	11 486*	22.7	56.9
443 UN C OF CHRIST	2	175	212*	0.4	1.1
449 UN METHODIST..	9	2 148	2 598*	5.1	12.9
453 UN PRES CH USA	1	57	69*	0.1	0.3
ST JOHNS	**46**	**9 498**	**17 292***	**33.7**	**100.0**
053 ASSEMB OF GOD.	2	70	136	0.3	0.8
081 CATHOLIC......	7	NA	5 374	10.5	31.1
089 CHR & MISS AL.	1	136	144	0.3	0.8
097 CHR CHS&CHS CR	1	161	192*	0.4	1.1
101 C.M.E.........	1	65	77*	0.2	0.4
123 CH GOD (ANDER)	2	55	165	0.3	1.0
127 CH GOD (CLEVE)	2	52	62*	0.1	0.4
151 L-D SAINTS....	1	NA	188	0.4	1.1
165 CH OF NAZARENE	1	108	163	0.3	0.9
167 CHS OF CHRIST.	2	200	255	0.5	1.5
193 EPISCOPAL.....	3	1 238	1 629	3.2	9.4
281 LUTH CH AMER..	1	224	280	0.5	1.6
283 LUTH--MO SYNOD	1	35	114	0.2	0.7
349 PENT HOLINESS.	5	376	447*	0.9	2.6
413 S.D.A.........	2	188	224*	0.4	1.3
419 SO BAPT CONV..	7	4 453	5 299*	10.3	30.6
449 UN METHODIST..	6	1 685	2 005*	3.9	11.6
453 UN PRES CH USA	1	452	538*	1.0	3.1
ST LUCIE	**59**	**14 884**	**26 181***	**30.0**	**100.0**

County and Denomination	Number of churches	Communicant, confirmed, full members	Total adherents Number	Percent of total population	Percent of total adherents
017 AMER BAPT ASSN	2	185	185	0.2	0.7
029 AMER LUTH CH..	1	337	373	0.4	1.4
053 ASSEMB OF GOD.	2	110	178	0.2	0.7
081 CATHOLIC......	3	NA	7 510	8.6	28.7
089 CHR & MISS AL.	1	57	76	0.1	0.3
093 CHR CH (DISC).	1	140	348	0.4	1.3
097 CHR CHS&CHS CR	2	400	481*	0.6	1.8
123 CH GOD (ANDER)	1	49	147	0.2	0.6
127 CH GOD (CLEVE)	4	351	422*	0.5	1.6
149 CH OF JC (BIC)	1	65	83	0.1	0.3
151 L-D SAINTS....	1	NA	232	0.3	0.9
165 CH OF NAZARENE	1	164	172	0.2	0.7
167 CHS OF CHRIST.	3	377	444	0.5	1.7
193 EPISCOPAL.....	3	949	1 355	1.6	5.2
226 FRIENDS-USA...	1	33	40*	–	0.2
263 INT FOURSQ GOS	1	22	26*	–	0.1
271 REFORM JUDAISM	1	920	1 105*	1.3	4.2
281 LUTH CH AMER..	1	340	422	0.5	1.6
283 LUTH--MO SYNOD	1	335	416	0.5	1.6
353 CHR BRETHREN..	2	100	175	0.2	0.7
357 PRESB CH US...	1	346	416*	0.5	1.6
403 SALVATION ARMY	1	56	105	0.1	0.4
413 S.D.A.........	2	360	432*	0.5	1.7
419 SO BAPT CONV..	11	5 086	6 110*	7.0	23.3
435 UNITARIAN-UNIV	1	25	30*	–	0.1
443 UN C OF CHRIST	1	?	?	?	?
449 UN METHODIST..	6	3 138	3 770*	4.3	14.4
453 UN PRES CH USA	3	939	1 128*	1.3	4.3
SANTA ROSA	**102**	**19 645**	**27 146***	**48.5**	**100.0**
005 AME ZION......	2	242	242	0.4	0.9
053 ASSEMB OF GOD.	20	2 837	3 343	6.0	12.3
081 CATHOLIC......	5	NA	2 179	3.9	8.0
101 C.M.E.........	3	721	885*	1.6	3.3
123 CH GOD (ANDER)	1	37	111	0.2	0.4
127 CH GOD (CLEVE)	1	18	22*	–	0.1
151 L-D SAINTS....	1	NA	259	0.5	1.0
165 CH OF NAZARENE	1	36	71	0.1	0.3
167 CHS OF CHRIST.	8	638	1 300	2.3	4.8
193 EPISCOPAL.....	2	497	767	1.4	2.8
283 LUTH--MO SYNOD	2	264	333	0.6	1.2
285 MENNONITE CH..	2	62	76*	0.1	0.3
349 PENT HOLINESS.	9	627	770*	1.4	2.8
356 PRESB CH AMER.	2	163	210	0.4	0.8
357 PRESB CH US...	3	418	513*	0.9	1.9
413 S.D.A.........	1	378	464*	0.8	1.7
419 SO BAPT CONV..	26	9 845	12 087*	21.6	44.5
449 UN METHODIST..	13	2 862	3 514*	6.3	12.9
SARASOTA	**142**	**44 264**	**74 307***	**36.7**	**100.0**
029 AMER LUTH CH..	5	1 547	1 755	0.9	2.4
053 ASSEMB OF GOD.	4	572	883	0.4	1.2
057 BAPT GEN CONF.	0	11	12*	–	–
061 BEACHY AMISH..	1	43	48*	–	0.1
071 BRETHREN (ASH)	1	701	789*	0.4	1.1
075 BRETHREN IN CR	1	109	131	0.1	0.2
081 CATHOLIC......	8	NA	21 573	10.7	29.0
089 CHR & MISS AL.	1	51	76	–	0.1
093 CHR CH (DISC).	3	972	1 233	0.6	1.7
097 CHR CHS&CHS CR	4	400	450*	0.2	0.6
101 C.M.E.........	2	370	416*	0.2	0.6
123 CH GOD (ANDER)	3	336	1 008	0.5	1.4
127 CH GOD (CLEVE)	4	294	331*	0.2	0.5
151 L-D SAINTS....	1	NA	354	0.2	0.5
165 CH OF NAZARENE	4	307	500	0.2	0.7
167 CHS OF CHRIST.	10	698	888	0.4	1.2
175 CONGR CHR CHS.	1	50	56*	–	0.1
193 EPISCOPAL.....	6	4 114	4 686	2.3	6.3
201 EVAN COV CH AM	4	461	519*	0.3	0.7
203 EVAN FREE CH..	2	310	349*	0.2	0.5
226 FRIENDS-USA...	3	23	26*	–	–
270 CONSRV JUDAISM	1	210	236*	0.1	0.3
271 REFORM JUDAISM	1	1 000	1 125*	0.6	1.5
281 LUTH CH AMER..	3	1 930	2 233	1.1	3.0
283 LUTH--MO SYNOD	2	1 229	1 363	0.7	1.8
285 MENNONITE CH..	7	1 303	1 466*	0.7	2.0
290 METRO COMM CHS	1	30	60	–	0.1
323 OLD ORD AMISH.	1	130	146*	0.1	0.2
353 CHR BRETHREN..	1	40	55	–	0.1
357 PRESB CH US...	8	4 807	5 409*	2.7	7.3
371 REF CH IN AM..	2	251	463	0.2	0.6
381 REF PRES-EVAN.	2	145	161	0.1	0.2
403 SALVATION ARMY	1	95	1 026	0.5	1.4
413 S.D.A.........	3	403	453*	0.2	0.6
419 SO BAPT CONV..	16	8 222	9 251*	4.6	12.4
421 SO METHODIST..	1	18	33	–	–
435 UNITARIAN-UNIV	1	350	394*	0.2	0.5
443 UN C OF CHRIST	4	1 570	1 767*	0.9	2.4
449 UN METHODIST..	12	8 727	9 820*	4.9	13.2
453 UN PRES CH USA	4	2 351	2 645*	1.3	3.6
469 WELS..........	2	84	118	0.1	0.2
SEMINOLE	**90**	**25 571**	**50 938***	**28.3**	**100.0**
053 ASSEMB OF GOD.	2	264	467	0.3	0.9
057 BAPT GEN CONF.	2	102	124*	0.1	0.2
081 CATHOLIC......	5	NA	18 243	10.1	35.8
089 CHR & MISS AL.	3	141	255	0.1	0.5
093 CHR CH (DISC).	1	96	174	0.1	0.3
097 CHR CHS&CHS CR	4	270	329*	0.2	0.6
123 CH GOD (ANDER)	1	20	60	–	0.1
127 CH GOD (CLEVE)	5	522	635*	0.4	1.2
151 L-D SAINTS....	1	NA	575	0.3	1.1

NA—Not applicable   *Total adherents estimated from known number of communicant, confirmed, full members.   —Represents a percent less than 0.1.   Percentages may not total due to rounding.

Table 4. Churches and Church Membership by County and Denomination: 1980

County and Denomination	Number of churches	Communicant, confirmed, full members	Total adherents		
			Number	Percent of total population	Percent of total adherents
165 CH OF NAZARENE	5	388	633	0.4	1.2
167 CHS OF CHRIST.	5	430	550	0.3	1.1
193 EPISCOPAL.....	4	1 380	1 893	1.1	3.7
199 EVAN CONGR CH.	1	25	30*	–	0.1
221 FREE METHODIST	1	19	105	0.1	0.2
281 LUTH CH AMER..	3	759	1 001	0.6	2.0
283 LUTH--MO SYNOD	3	1 673	2 050	1.1	4.0
295 MORAV CH-SOUTH	2	327	434	0.2	0.9
357 PRESB CH US...	5	1 399	1 703*	0.9	3.3
403 SALVATION ARMY	1	123	242	0.1	0.5
413 S.D.A.........	8	3 119	3 796*	2.1	7.5
419 SO BAPT CONV..	15	9 022	10 980*	6.1	21.6
443 UN C OF CHRIST	1	284	346*	0.2	0.7
449 UN METHODIST..	9	4 947	6 021*	3.3	11.8
453 UN PRES CH USA	3	261	318*	0.2	0.6
SUMTER	51	7 362	8 701*	35.8	100.0
005 AME ZION......	1	220	220	0.9	2.5
017 AMER BAPT ASSN	3	573	573	2.4	6.6
053 ASSEMB OF GOD.	5	531	707	2.9	8.1
081 CATHOLIC......	1	NA	?	?	?
127 CH GOD (CLEVE)	7	453	539*	2.2	6.2
167 CHS OF CHRIST.	5	202	261	1.1	3.0
193 EPISCOPAL.....	1	72	79	0.3	0.9
349 PENT HOLINESS.	1	67	80*	0.3	0.9
357 PRESB CH US...	2	184	219*	0.9	2.5
413 S.D.A.........	1	26	31*	0.1	0.4
419 SO BAPT CONV..	13	3 912	4 657*	19.2	53.5
449 UN METHODIST..	10	1 083	1 289*	5.3	14.8
453 UN PRES CH USA	1	39	46*	0.2	0.5
SUWANNEE	64	10 090	13 421*	60.2	100.0
001 ADVENT CHR CH.	4	529	649*	2.9	4.8
017 AMER BAPT ASSN	1	32	32	0.1	0.2
053 ASSEMB OF GOD.	3	146	277	1.2	2.1
081 CATHOLIC......	2	NA	650	2.9	4.8
097 CHR CHS&CHS CR	1	140	172*	0.8	1.3
123 CH GOD (ANDER)	1	20	60	0.3	0.4
127 CH GOD (CLEVE)	4	363	446*	2.0	3.3
151 L-D SAINTS....	1	NA	234	1.0	1.7
165 CH OF NAZARENE	1	50	65	0.3	0.5
167 CHS OF CHRIST.	6	390	496	2.2	3.7
193 EPISCOPAL.....	1	172	210	0.9	1.6
357 PRESB CH US...	2	254	312*	1.4	2.3
413 S.D.A.........	1	30	37*	0.2	0.3
419 SO BAPT CONV..	30	7 083	8 696*	39.0	64.8
421 SO METHODIST..	1	15	22	0.1	0.2
449 UN METHODIST..	5	866	1 063*	4.8	7.9
TAYLOR	39	6 110	8 162*	49.4	100.0
001 ADVENT CHR CH.	1	27	33*	0.2	0.4
053 ASSEMB OF GOD.	1	113	278	1.7	3.4
081 CATHOLIC......	1	NA	180	1.1	2.2
123 CH GOD (ANDER)	2	48	144	0.9	1.8
127 CH GOD (CLEVE)	1	150	185*	1.1	2.3
151 L-D SAINTS....	1	NA	149	0.9	1.8
165 CH OF NAZARENE	1	39	82	0.5	1.0
167 CHS OF CHRIST.	5	285	363	2.2	4.4
193 EPISCOPAL.....	1	133	198	1.2	2.4
349 PENT HOLINESS.	3	159	196*	1.2	2.4
357 PRESB CH US...	1	158	195*	1.2	2.4
413 S.D.A.........	1	30	37*	0.2	0.5
419 SO BAPT CONV..	14	4 199	5 174*	31.3	63.4
449 UN METHODIST..	6	769	948*	5.7	11.6
UNION	13	1 878	2 359*	23.2	100.0
097 CHR CHS&CHS CR	1	175	202*	2.0	8.6
127 CH GOD (CLEVE)	1	82	95*	0.9	4.0
151 L-D SAINTS....	1	NA	172	1.7	7.3
167 CHS OF CHRIST.	2	153	196	1.9	8.3
419 SO BAPT CONV..	5	1 273	1 469*	14.5	62.3
449 UN METHODIST..	3	195	225*	2.2	9.5
VOLUSIA	206	56 617	94 835*	36.6	100.0
019 AMER BAPT USA.	2	610	704*	0.3	0.7
053 ASSEMB OF GOD.	8	1 179	2 508	1.0	2.6
081 CATHOLIC......	10	NA	24 827	9.6	26.2
089 CHR & MISS AL.	6	477	808	0.3	0.9
093 CHR CH (DISC).	7	1 355	1 864	0.7	2.0
097 CHR CHS&CHS CR	6	782	903*	0.3	1.0
101 C.M.E........	2	77	89*	–	0.1
123 CH GOD (ANDER)	4	690	2 070	0.8	2.2
127 CH GOD (CLEVE)	14	820	947*	0.4	1.0
151 L-D SAINTS....	3	NA	888	0.3	0.9
165 CH OF NAZARENE	4	320	556	0.2	0.6
167 CHS OF CHRIST.	15	1 400	1 780	0.7	1.9
179 CONSRV BAPT...	1	91	105*	–	0.1
193 EPISCOPAL.....	8	3 157	3 756	1.5	4.0
239 SWEDENBORGIAN.	1	60	69*	–	0.1
244 GRACE BRETHREN	1	80	92*	–	0.1
263 INT FOURSQ GOS	1	?	?	?	?
270 CONSRV JUDAISM	1	173	200*	0.1	0.2
271 REFORM JUDAISM	2	580	670*	0.3	0.7
281 LUTH CH AMER..	5	1 790	2 244	0.9	2.4
283 LUTH--MO SYNOD	3	1 163	1 331	0.5	1.4
290 METRO COMM CHS	0	0	25	–	–
329 OPEN BIBLE STD	1	15	20	–	–
349 PENT HOLINESS.	6	527	608*	0.2	0.6
353 CHR BRETHREN..	3	150	200	0.1	0.2
356 PRESB CH AMER.	1	25	26	–	–

County and Denomination	Number of churches	Communicant, confirmed, full members	Total adherents		
			Number	Percent of total population	Percent of total adherents
357 PRESB CH US...	8	4 083	4 713*	1.8	5.0
403 SALVATION ARMY	1	119	245	0.1	0.3
413 S.D.A.........	5	498	575*	0.2	0.6
415 S-D BAPTIST GC	1	83	96*	–	0.1
419 SO BAPT CONV..	35	22 748	26 258*	10.1	27.7
435 UNITARIAN-UNIV	2	144	166*	0.1	0.2
443 UN C OF CHRIST	8	1 720	1 985*	0.8	2.1
449 UN METHODIST..	26	10 544	12 171*	4.7	12.8
453 UN PRES CH USA	5	1 157	1 336*	0.5	1.4
WAKULLA	24	2 644	3 539*	32.5	100.0
053 ASSEMB OF GOD.	2	176	269	2.5	7.6
081 CATHOLIC......	1	NA	100	0.9	2.8
151 L-D SAINTS....	1	NA	103	0.9	2.9
167 CHS OF CHRIST.	3	75	95	0.9	2.7
177 CONGR HOL CH..	1	43	53*	0.5	1.5
349 PENT HOLINESS.	1	50	62*	0.6	1.8
413 S.D.A.........	1	31	39*	0.4	1.1
419 SO BAPT CONV..	10	1 867	2 319*	21.3	65.5
449 UN METHODIST..	4	402	499*	4.6	14.1
WALTON	69	8 095	10 192*	47.8	100.0
053 ASSEMB OF GOD.	7	316	515	2.4	5.1
081 CATHOLIC......	1	NA	211	1.0	2.1
127 CH GOD (CLEVE)	3	158	189*	0.9	1.9
151 L-D SAINTS....	1	NA	134	0.6	1.3
167 CHS OF CHRIST.	6	400	510	2.4	5.0
193 EPISCOPAL.....	1	55	50	0.2	0.5
357 PRESB CH US...	6	609	729*	3.4	7.2
413 S.D.A.........	1	27	32*	0.2	0.3
419 SO BAPT CONV..	29	5 337	6 393*	30.0	62.7
449 UN METHODIST..	14	1 193	1 429*	6.7	14.0
WASHINGTON	35	5 052	6 622*	45.6	100.0
053 ASSEMB OF GOD.	6	620	1 011	7.0	15.3
081 CATHOLIC......	1	NA	228	1.6	3.4
127 CH GOD (CLEVE)	2	60	73*	0.5	1.1
167 CHS OF CHRIST.	2	92	105	0.7	1.6
357 PRESB CH US...	1	187	227*	1.6	3.4
419 SO BAPT CONV..	13	3 206	3 899*	26.9	58.9
449 UN METHODIST..	10	887	1 079*	7.4	16.3

GEORGIA

County and Denomination	Number of churches	Communicant, confirmed, full members	Total adherents		
			Number	Percent of total population	Percent of total adherents
THE STATE.....	7 485	1 942 558	2 570 084*	47.0	100.0
APPLING	39	7 709	9 739*	62.6	100.0
081 CATHOLIC......	1	NA	17	0.1	0.2
127 CH GOD (CLEVE)	4	673	849*	5.5	8.7
167 CHS OF CHRIST.	1	6	10	0.1	0.1
413 S.D.A.........	1	78	98*	0.6	1.0
419 SO BAPT CONV..	20	5 305	6 688*	43.0	68.7
449 UN METHODIST..	12	1 647	2 077*	13.3	21.3
ATKINSON	21	1 927	2 843*	46.3	100.0
053 ASSEMB OF GOD.	1	31	55	0.9	1.9
081 CATHOLIC......	1	NA	90	1.5	3.2
127 CH GOD (CLEVE)	1	58	72*	1.2	2.5
151 L-D SAINTS....	1	NA	335	5.5	11.8
349 PENT HOLINESS.	3	172	215*	3.5	7.6
353 CHR BRETHREN..	1	10	10	0.2	0.4
419 SO BAPT CONV..	5	1 021	1 274*	20.7	44.8
449 UN METHODIST..	8	635	792*	12.9	27.9
BACON	24	3 482	4 432*	47.3	100.0
081 CATHOLIC......	1	NA	40	0.4	0.9
127 CH GOD (CLEVE)	6	633	798*	8.5	18.0
167 CHS OF CHRIST.	1	30	38	0.4	0.9
413 S.D.A.........	1	31	39*	0.4	0.9
419 SO BAPT CONV..	11	2 103	2 653*	28.3	59.9
449 UN METHODIST..	4	685	864*	9.2	19.5
BAKER	13	1 731	2 163*	56.8	100.0
053 ASSEMB OF GOD.	1	34	47	1.2	2.2
101 C.M.E........	1	737	919*	24.1	42.5
357 PRESB CH US...	1	33	41*	1.1	1.9
419 SO BAPT CONV..	7	817	1 019*	26.8	47.1
449 UN METHODIST..	3	110	137*	3.6	6.3
BALDWIN	34	8 451	11 445*	33.0	100.0
053 ASSEMB OF GOD.	1	90	123	0.4	1.1
081 CATHOLIC......	1	NA	800	2.3	7.0
097 CHR CHS&CHS CR	1	160	192*	0.6	1.7
101 C.M.E........	1	315	378*	1.1	3.3
127 CH GOD (CLEVE)	1	84	101*	0.3	0.9

NA— Not applicable   *Total adherents estimated from known number of communicant, confirmed, full members.   —Represents a percent less than 0.1.   Percentages may not total due to rounding.

Table 4. Churches and Church Membership by County and Denomination: 1980

County and Denomination	Number of churches	Communicant, confirmed, full members	Total adherents Number	Percent of total population	Percent of total adherents
151 L-D SAINTS....	1	NA	264	0.8	2.3
167 CHS OF CHRIST.	2	35	50	0.1	0.4
193 EPISCOPAL.....	1	212	458	1.3	4.0
263 INT FOURSQ GOS	1	26	31*	0.1	0.3
283 LUTH--MO SYNOD	2	66	98	0.3	0.9
357 PRESB CH US...	1	387	464*	1.3	4.1
413 S.D.A.........	1	39	47*	0.1	0.4
419 SO BAPT CONV..	14	5 458	6 545*	18.9	57.2
449 UN METHODIST..	6	1 579	1 894*	5.5	16.5
BANKS	31	5 237	6 415*	73.7	100.0
097 CHR CHS&CHS CR	3	265	325*	3.7	5.1
101 C.M.E.........	1	392	480*	5.5	7.5
127 CH GOD (CLEVE)	2	204	250*	2.9	3.9
177 CONGR HOL CH..	2	76	93*	1.1	1.4
357 PRESB CH US...	1	73	89*	1.0	1.4
419 SO BAPT CONV..	16	3 870	4 741*	54.5	73.9
449 UN METHODIST..	6	357	437*	5.0	6.8
BARROW	44	9 074	11 355*	53.3	100.0
005 AME ZION......	1	188	218	1.0	1.9
053 ASSEMB OF GOD.	1	37	72	0.3	0.6
081 CATHOLIC......	1	NA	75	0.4	0.7
093 CHR CH (DISC).	4	524	668	3.1	5.9
097 CHR CHS&CHS CR	3	870	1 078*	5.1	9.5
127 CH GOD (CLEVE)	1	66	82*	0.4	0.7
167 CHS OF CHRIST.	1	43	61	0.3	0.5
177 CONGR HOL CH..	1	5	6*	-	0.1
193 EPISCOPAL.....	1	97	119	0.6	1.0
349 PENT HOLINESS.	1	18	22*	0.1	0.2
357 PRESB CH US...	2	255	316*	1.5	2.8
419 SO BAPT CONV..	14	4 501	5 578*	26.2	49.1
435 UNITARIAN-UNIV	1	10	12*	0.1	0.1
449 UN METHODIST..	12	2 460	3 048*	14.3	26.8
BARTOW	69	15 565	19 900*	48.8	100.0
053 ASSEMB OF GOD.	1	38	57	0.1	0.3
081 CATHOLIC......	1	NA	500	1.2	2.5
097 CHR CHS&CHS CR	2	271	337*	0.8	1.7
127 CH GOD (CLEVE)	4	752	934*	2.3	4.7
165 CH OF NAZARENE	1	16	52	0.1	0.3
167 CHS OF CHRIST.	2	175	223	0.5	1.1
185 CUMBER PRESB..	1	81	130	0.3	0.7
193 EPISCOPAL.....	1	245	290	0.7	1.5
215 EVAN METH CH..	1	108	134*	0.3	0.7
357 PRESB CH US...	2	503	625*	1.5	3.1
419 SO BAPT CONV..	36	10 846	13 475*	33.1	67.7
449 UN METHODIST..	17	2 530	3 143*	7.7	15.8
BEN HILL	29	7 731	9 771*	61.1	100.0
053 ASSEMB OF GOD.	1	53	140	0.9	1.4
081 CATHOLIC......	1	NA	150	0.9	1.5
093 CHR CH (DISC).	1	27	40	0.2	0.4
101 C.M.E.........	2	644	794*	5.0	8.1
127 CH GOD (CLEVE)	1	224	276*	1.7	2.8
165 CH OF NAZARENE	1	221	270	1.7	2.8
167 CHS OF CHRIST.	3	67	90	0.6	0.9
193 EPISCOPAL.....	1	62	74	0.5	0.8
357 PRESB CH US...	1	108	133*	0.8	1.4
419 SO BAPT CONV..	14	5 270	6 502*	40.6	66.5
449 UN METHODIST..	3	1 055	1 302*	8.1	13.3
BERRIEN	23	4 633	5 867*	43.4	100.0
081 CATHOLIC......	2	NA	138	1.0	2.4
093 CHR CH (DISC).	1	24	37	0.3	0.6
101 C.M.E.........	1	700	860*	6.4	14.7
127 CH GOD (CLEVE)	4	188	231*	1.7	3.9
165 CH OF NAZARENE	1	30	68	0.5	1.2
167 CHS OF CHRIST.	1	35	40	0.3	0.7
175 CONGR CHR CHS.	1	35	43*	0.3	0.7
419 SO BAPT CONV..	6	2 478	3 045*	22.5	51.9
449 UN METHODIST..	6	1 143	1 405*	10.4	23.9
BIBB	136	60 542	79 773*	52.8	100.0
053 ASSEMB OF GOD.	5	552	681	0.5	0.9
081 CATHOLIC......	3	NA	4 575	3.0	5.7
089 CHR & MISS AL.	1	156	206	0.1	0.3
093 CHR CH (DISC).	3	524	855	0.6	1.1
101 C.M.E.........	6	3 843	4 683*	3.1	5.9
123 CH GOD (ANDER)	1	200	600	0.4	0.8
127 CH GOD (CLEVE)	5	809	986*	0.7	1.2
151 L-D SAINTS....	2	NA	684	0.5	0.9
165 CH OF NAZARENE	2	166	341	0.2	0.4
167 CHS OF CHRIST.	8	665	845	0.6	1.1
177 CONGR HOL CH..	2	143	174*	0.1	0.2
193 EPISCOPAL.....	4	1 473	1 764	1.2	2.2
215 EVAN METH CH..	1	122	149*	0.1	0.2
221 FREE METHODIST	1	54	156	0.1	0.2
263 INT FOURSQ GOS	1	84	102*	0.1	0.1
270 CONSRV JUDAISM	1	113	138*	0.1	0.2
271 REFORM JUDAISM	1	260	317*	0.2	0.4
281 LUTH CH AMER..	1	598	807	0.5	1.0
283 LUTH--MO SYNOD	1	107	134	0.1	0.2
329 OPEN BIBLE STD	1	40	45	-	0.1
349 PENT HOLINESS.	2	169	206*	0.1	0.3
353 CHR BRETHREN..	1	80	110	0.1	0.1
356 PRESB CH AMER.	2	1 491	1 542	1.0	1.9
357 PRESB CH US...	5	808	985*	0.7	1.2
403 SALVATION ARMY	1	148	279	0.2	0.3
413 S.D.A.........	2	479	584*	0.4	0.7
419 SO BAPT CONV..	41	32 987	40 195*	26.6	50.4
421 SO METHODIST..	1	43	49	-	0.1
435 UNITARIAN-UNIV	1	30	37*	-	-
443 UN C OF CHRIST	1	?	?	?	?
449 UN METHODIST..	28	14 336	17 468*	11.6	21.9
453 UN PRES CH USA	1	62	76*	0.1	0.1
BLECKLEY	26	5 098	6 221*	57.8	100.0
053 ASSEMB OF GOD.	1	15	21	0.2	0.3
081 CATHOLIC......	1	NA	44	0.4	0.7
127 CH GOD (CLEVE)	1	104	125*	1.2	2.0
165 CH OF NAZARENE	2	101	136	1.3	2.2
167 CHS OF CHRIST.	1	49	62	0.6	1.0
193 EPISCOPAL.....	1	52	87	0.8	1.4
349 PENT HOLINESS.	3	153	184*	1.7	3.0
419 SO BAPT CONV..	13	3 908	4 701*	43.7	75.6
449 UN METHODIST..	3	716	861*	8.0	13.8
BRANTLEY	20	2 987	3 784*	43.5	100.0
001 ADVENT CHR CH.	2	62	79*	0.9	2.1
127 CH GOD (CLEVE)	4	128	162*	1.9	4.3
419 SO BAPT CONV..	13	2 780	3 521*	40.5	93.0
449 UN METHODIST..	1	17	22*	0.3	0.6
BROOKS	48	5 779	7 337*	48.1	100.0
053 ASSEMB OF GOD.	1	16	44	0.3	0.6
093 CHR CH (DISC).	2	149	195	1.3	2.7
101 C.M.E.........	2	305	383*	2.5	5.2
127 CH GOD (CLEVE)	3	76	95*	0.6	1.3
151 L-D SAINTS....	1	NA	43	0.3	0.6
165 CH OF NAZARENE	1	46	70	0.5	1.0
167 CHS OF CHRIST.	4	185	235	1.5	3.2
193 EPISCOPAL.....	1	35	37	0.2	0.5
357 PRESB CH US...	1	104	131*	0.9	1.8
413 S.D.A.........	2	70	88*	0.6	1.2
419 SO BAPT CONV..	20	3 612	4 534*	29.7	61.8
449 UN METHODIST..	10	1 181	1 482*	9.7	20.2
BRYAN	20	3 032	4 158*	40.9	100.0
001 ADVENT CHR CH.	1	39	50*	0.5	1.2
081 CATHOLIC......	2	NA	278	2.7	6.7
093 CHR CH (DISC).	1	116	178	1.7	4.3
097 CHR CHS&CHS CR	1	49	62*	0.6	1.5
127 CH GOD (CLEVE)	2	29	37*	0.4	0.9
357 PRESB CH US...	1	45	57*	0.6	1.4
419 SO BAPT CONV..	9	1 945	2 469*	24.3	59.4
449 UN METHODIST..	3	809	1 027*	10.1	24.7
BULLOCH	48	10 025	13 323*	37.2	100.0
053 ASSEMB OF GOD.	1	63	107	0.3	0.8
081 CATHOLIC......	1	NA	800	2.2	6.0
097 CHR CHS&CHS CR	1	60	72*	0.2	0.5
123 CH GOD (ANDER)	3	105	315	0.9	2.4
127 CH GOD (CLEVE)	2	203	245*	0.7	1.8
151 L-D SAINTS....	1	NA	168	0.5	1.3
167 CHS OF CHRIST.	1	40	51	0.1	0.4
193 EPISCOPAL.....	1	170	238	0.7	1.8
283 LUTH--MO SYNOD	1	88	115	0.3	0.9
357 PRESB CH US...	1	230	277*	0.8	2.1
413 S.D.A.........	1	70	84*	0.2	0.6
419 SO BAPT CONV..	22	6 100	7 358*	20.6	55.2
449 UN METHODIST..	12	2 896	3 493*	9.8	26.2
BURKE	41	5 810	7 489*	38.7	100.0
005 AME ZION......	3	414	519	2.7	6.9
055 AS REF PRES CH	1	90	107	0.6	1.4
081 CATHOLIC......	1	NA	90	0.5	1.2
093 CHR CH (DISC).	1	30	95	0.5	1.3
101 C.M.E.........	1	215	273*	1.4	3.6
127 CH GOD (CLEVE)	1	28	36*	0.2	0.5
167 CHS OF CHRIST.	1	35	40	0.2	0.5
193 EPISCOPAL.....	1	73	102	0.5	1.4
285 MENNONITE CH..	1	33	42*	0.2	0.6
353 CHR BRETHREN..	1	50	60	0.3	0.8
356 PRESB CH AMER.	1	106	120	0.6	1.6
419 SO BAPT CONV..	12	2 718	3 446*	17.8	46.0
449 UN METHODIST..	14	1 911	2 423*	12.5	32.4
453 UN PRES CH USA	2	107	136*	0.7	1.8
BUTTS	25	5 202	6 575*	48.1	100.0
053 ASSEMB OF GOD.	1	30	36	0.3	0.5
081 CATHOLIC......	1	NA	200	1.5	3.0
097 CHR CHS&CHS CR	1	35	43*	0.3	0.7
101 C.M.E.........	3	913	1 113*	8.1	16.9
165 CH OF NAZARENE	1	121	181	1.3	2.8
167 CHS OF CHRIST.	1	40	51	0.4	0.8
357 PRESB CH US...	2	129	157*	1.1	2.4
419 SO BAPT CONV..	10	3 192	3 890*	28.5	59.2
449 UN METHODIST..	5	742	904*	6.6	13.7
CALHOUN	15	2 104	2 603*	45.5	100.0
127 CH GOD (CLEVE)	2	48	59*	1.0	2.3
167 CHS OF CHRIST.	1	18	23	0.4	0.9
357 PRESB CH US...	1	17	21*	0.4	0.8
419 SO BAPT CONV..	6	1 499	1 854*	32.4	71.2
449 UN METHODIST..	5	522	646*	11.3	24.8

NA—Not applicable   *Total adherents estimated from known number of communicant, confirmed, full members.   —Represents a percent less than 0.1.   Percentages may not total due to rounding.

Table 4. Churches and Church Membership by County and Denomination: 1980

County and Denomination	Number of churches	Communicant, confirmed, full members	Total adherents Number	Percent of total population	Percent of total adherents
CAMDEN	37	5 182	6 884*	51.5	100.0
053 ASSEMB OF GOD.	1	32	46	0.3	0.7
081 CATHOLIC......	2	NA	175	1.3	2.5
127 CH GOD (CLEVE)	6	365	456*	3.4	6.6
151 L-D SAINTS....	1	NA	208	1.6	3.0
167 CHS OF CHRIST.	1	48	61	0.5	0.9
193 EPISCOPAL.....	2	75	112	0.8	1.6
357 PRESB CH US...	1	102	127*	0.9	1.8
419 SO BAPT CONV..	9	2 767	3 458*	25.9	50.2
449 UN METHODIST..	14	1 793	2 241*	16.8	32.6
CANDLER	15	2 284	2 897*	38.5	100.0
081 CATHOLIC......	1	NA	47	0.6	1.6
123 CH GOD (ANDER)	1	30	90	1.2	3.1
127 CH GOD (CLEVE)	1	112	137*	1.8	4.7
167 CHS OF CHRIST.	1	16	20	0.3	0.7
357 PRESB CH US...	1	75	92*	1.2	3.2
419 SO BAPT CONV..	8	1 633	1 999*	26.6	69.0
449 UN METHODIST..	2	418	512*	6.8	17.7
CARROLL	103	22 684	28 713*	51.0	100.0
053 ASSEMB OF GOD.	1	13	52	0.1	0.2
081 CATHOLIC......	1	NA	650	1.2	2.3
097 CHR CHS&CHS CR	8	1 390	1 705*	3.0	5.9
127 CH GOD (CLEVE)	9	701	860*	1.5	3.0
151 L-D SAINTS....	1	NA	121	0.2	0.4
167 CHS OF CHRIST.	6	305	420	0.7	1.5
177 CONGR HOL CH..	2	77	94*	0.2	0.3
193 EPISCOPAL.....	1	154	231	0.4	0.8
349 PENT HOLINESS.	2	91	112*	0.2	0.4
357 PRESB CH US...	2	354	434*	0.8	1.5
413 S.D.A.........	1	33	40*	0.1	0.1
419 SO BAPT CONV..	39	14 586	17 887*	31.7	62.3
449 UN METHODIST..	30	4 980	6 107*	10.8	21.3
CATOOSA	41	12 579	16 393*	44.3	100.0
081 CATHOLIC......	1	NA	850	2.3	5.2
127 CH GOD (CLEVE)	4	330	407*	1.1	2.5
165 CH OF NAZARENE	1	44	64	0.2	0.4
167 CHS OF CHRIST.	2	250	318	0.9	1.9
357 PRESB CH US...	2	91	112*	0.3	0.7
413 S.D.A.........	1	220	272*	0.7	1.7
419 SO BAPT CONV..	23	9 854	12 161*	32.9	74.2
449 UN METHODIST..	7	1 790	2 209*	6.0	13.5
CHARLTON	21	2 818	3 632*	49.5	100.0
053 ASSEMB OF GOD.	1	90	145	2.0	4.0
081 CATHOLIC......	1	NA	25	0.3	0.7
127 CH GOD (CLEVE)	3	143	181*	2.5	5.0
167 CHS OF CHRIST.	1	30	42	0.6	1.2
419 SO BAPT CONV..	8	1 857	2 354*	32.1	64.8
449 UN METHODIST..	7	698	885*	12.1	24.4
CHATHAM	188	61 246	91 250*	45.1	100.0
001 ADVENT CHR CH.	2	67	82*	–	0.1
017 AMER BAPT ASSN	3	300	300	0.1	0.3
053 ASSEMB OF GOD.	6	815	1 060	0.5	1.2
081 CATHOLIC......	13	NA	14 285	7.1	15.7
089 CHR & MISS AL.	5	379	629	0.3	0.7
093 CHR CH (DISC).	3	351	676	0.3	0.7
097 CHR CHS&CHS CR	6	1 220	1 493*	0.7	1.6
101 C.M.E........	2	980	1 200*	0.6	1.3
123 CH GOD (ANDER)	2	111	333	0.2	0.4
127 CH GOD (CLEVE)	7	1 292	1 581*	0.8	1.7
151 L-D SAINTS....	2	NA	913	0.5	1.0
165 CH OF NAZARENE	3	300	852	0.4	0.9
167 CHS OF CHRIST.	8	660	840	0.4	0.9
193 EPISCOPAL.....	13	4 106	4 774	2.4	5.2
209 EVAN LUTH SYN.	1	27	32	–	–
221 FREE METHODIST	1	31	69	–	0.1
263 INT FOURSQ GOS	1	33	40*	–	–
270 CONSRV JUDAISM	1	162	198*	0.1	0.2
271 REFORM JUDAISM	1	504	617*	0.3	0.7
281 LUTH CH AMER..	7	2 631	3 347	1.7	3.7
283 LUTH--MO SYNOD	1	219	314	0.2	0.3
349 PENT HOLINESS.	2	159	195*	0.1	0.2
353 CHR BRETHREN..	2	80	150	0.1	0.2
356 PRESB CH AMER.	5	637	697	0.3	0.8
357 PRESB CH US...	7	1 358	1 662*	0.8	1.8
403 SALVATION ARMY	1	101	165	0.1	0.2
413 S.D.A.........	2	1 004	1 229*	0.6	1.3
419 SO BAPT CONV..	46	28 897	35 370*	17.5	38.8
421 SO METHODIST..	1	20	30	–	–
435 UNITARIAN-UNIV	1	40	49*	–	0.1
443 UN C OF CHRIST	1	117	143*	0.1	0.2
449 UN METHODIST..	30	14 358	17 574*	8.7	19.3
453 UN PRES CH USA	2	287	351*	0.2	0.4
CHATTAHOOCHEE	10	840	2 455*	11.3	100.0
081 CATHOLIC......	2	NA	458	2.1	18.7
101 C.M.E........	1	347	414*	1.9	16.9
151 L-D SAINTS....	2	NA	993	4.6	40.4
167 CHS OF CHRIST.	1	25	32	0.1	1.3
419 SO BAPT CONV..	1	306	365*	1.7	14.9
449 UN METHODIST..	3	162	193*	0.9	7.9
CHATTOOGA	76	11 245	13 788*	63.1	100.0

County and Denomination	Number of churches	Communicant, confirmed, full members	Total adherents Number	Percent of total population	Percent of total adherents
005 AME ZION......	5	564	699	3.2	5.1
089 CHR & MISS AL.	1	115	137	0.6	1.0
127 CH GOD (CLEVE)	3	403	492*	2.3	3.6
165 CH OF NAZARENE	1	12	29	0.1	0.2
167 CHS OF CHRIST.	12	900	1 146	5.2	8.3
193 EPISCOPAL.....	1	40	42	0.2	0.3
357 PRESB CH US...	6	481	587*	2.7	4.3
413 S.D.A.........	1	21	26*	0.1	0.2
419 SO BAPT CONV..	35	7 723	9 427*	43.1	68.4
449 UN METHODIST..	11	986	1 203*	5.5	8.7
CHEROKEE	68	14 636	18 702*	36.2	100.0
053 ASSEMB OF GOD.	2	62	81	0.2	0.4
081 CATHOLIC......	1	NA	350	0.7	1.9
097 CHR CHS&CHS CR	2	351	440*	0.9	2.4
127 CH GOD (CLEVE)	3	372	466*	0.9	2.5
167 CHS OF CHRIST.	2	249	294	0.6	1.6
177 CONGR HOL CH..	1	9	11*	–	0.1
193 EPISCOPAL.....	1	41	57	0.1	0.3
283 LUTH--MO SYNOD	1	40	68	0.1	0.4
349 PENT HOLINESS.	1	20	25*	–	0.1
357 PRESB CH US...	3	204	256*	0.5	1.4
419 SO BAPT CONV..	32	10 501	13 161*	25.5	70.4
449 UN METHODIST..	19	2 787	3 493*	6.8	18.7
CLARKE	58	21 907	29 357*	39.4	100.0
005 AME ZION......	1	50	65	0.1	0.2
053 ASSEMB OF GOD.	1	113	245	0.3	0.8
081 CATHOLIC......	1	NA	2 930	3.9	10.0
089 CHR & MISS AL.	1	5	16	–	0.1
093 CHR CH (DISC).	2	514	723	1.0	2.5
097 CHR CHS&CHS CR	1	172	200*	0.3	0.7
101 C.M.E........	2	689	802*	1.1	2.7
127 CH GOD (CLEVE)	2	275	320*	0.4	1.1
151 L-D SAINTS....	1	NA	426	0.6	1.5
165 CH OF NAZARENE	1	89	102	0.1	0.3
167 CHS OF CHRIST.	3	295	375	0.5	1.3
177 CONGR HOL CH..	1	46	54*	0.1	0.2
193 EPISCOPAL.....	2	1 085	1 384	1.9	4.7
271 REFORM JUDAISM	1	180	210*	0.3	0.7
281 LUTH CH AMER..	1	192	253	0.3	0.9
283 LUTH--MO SYNOD	2	155	193	0.3	0.7
349 PENT HOLINESS.	1	195	227*	0.3	0.8
356 PRESB CH AMER.	1	80	80	0.1	0.3
357 PRESB CH US...	4	1 636	1 904*	2.6	6.5
403 SALVATION ARMY	1	99	181	0.2	0.6
413 S.D.A.........	2	190	221*	0.3	0.8
419 SO BAPT CONV..	14	10 357	12 055*	16.2	41.1
435 UNITARIAN-UNIV	1	102	119*	0.2	0.4
449 UN METHODIST..	11	5 388	6 272*	8.4	21.4
CLAY	13	1 300	1 591*	44.8	100.0
357 PRESB CH US...	1	26	32*	0.9	2.0
419 SO BAPT CONV..	7	840	1 028*	28.9	64.6
449 UN METHODIST..	5	434	531*	14.9	33.4
CLAYTON	88	38 888	53 361*	35.5	100.0
017 AMER BAPT ASSN	1	50	50	–	0.1
053 ASSEMB OF GOD.	4	390	630	0.4	1.2
081 CATHOLIC......	1	NA	3 100	2.1	5.8
093 CHR CH (DISC).	2	145	247	0.2	0.5
097 CHR CHS&CHS CR	4	1 434	1 791*	1.2	3.4
123 CH GOD (ANDER)	1	21	63	–	0.1
127 CH GOD (CLEVE)	8	970	1 211*	0.8	2.3
151 L-D SAINTS....	2	NA	1 193	0.8	2.2
165 CH OF NAZARENE	1	54	67	–	0.1
167 CHS OF CHRIST.	8	849	1 116	0.7	2.1
193 EPISCOPAL.....	1	90	180	0.1	0.3
281 LUTH CH AMER..	2	577	795	0.5	1.5
283 LUTH--MO SYNOD	1	276	400	0.3	0.7
356 PRESB CH AMER.	1	72	112	0.1	0.2
357 PRESB CH US...	5	1 262	1 576*	1.0	3.0
413 S.D.A.........	1	182	227*	0.2	0.4
419 SO BAPT CONV..	30	27 039	33 763*	22.5	63.3
435 UNITARIAN-UNIV	1	12	15*	–	–
443 UN C OF CHRIST	1	187	234*	0.2	0.4
449 UN METHODIST..	13	5 278	6 591*	4.4	12.4
CLINCH	12	1 432	1 833*	27.5	100.0
053 ASSEMB OF GOD.	1	35	71	1.1	3.9
127 CH GOD (CLEVE)	3	378	477*	7.2	26.0
167 CHS OF CHRIST.	1	20	25	0.4	1.4
419 SO BAPT CONV..	3	639	806*	12.1	44.0
449 UN METHODIST..	4	360	454*	6.8	24.8
COBB	213	94 333	131 827*	44.3	100.0
029 AMER LUTH CH..	2	332	455	0.2	0.3
053 ASSEMB OF GOD.	4	460	598	0.2	0.5
065 BETHEL M ASSN.	1	300	366*	0.1	0.3
081 CATHOLIC......	6	NA	13 589	4.6	10.3
089 CHR & MISS AL.	1	78	130	–	0.1
093 CHR CH (DISC).	2	284	465	0.2	0.4
097 CHR CHS&CHS CR	6	1 097	1 338*	0.4	1.0
101 C.M.E........	1	220	268*	0.1	0.2
105 CHRISTIAN REF.	1	32	51	–	–
123 CH GOD (ANDER)	1	9	27	–	–
127 CH GOD (CLEVE)	12	1 771	2 161*	0.7	1.6
151 L-D SAINTS....	4	NA	1 521	0.5	1.2
165 CH OF NAZARENE	2	281	631	0.2	0.5

NA— Not applicable   *Total adherents estimated from known number of communicant, confirmed, full members.   —Represents a percent less than 0.1.   Percentages may not total due to rounding.

Table 4. Churches and Church Membership by County and Denomination: 1980

County and Denomination	Number of churches	Communicant, confirmed, full members	Total adherents Number	Total adherents Percent of total population	Total adherents Percent of total adherents
167 CHS OF CHRIST.	11	1 525	1 940	0.7	1.5
193 EPISCOPAL.....	4	1 811	2 389	0.8	1.8
203 EVAN FREE CH..	1	45	55*	-	-
215 EVAN METH CH..	2	408	498*	0.2	0.4
244 GRACE BRETHREN	1	110	134*	-	0.1
263 INT FOURSQ GOS	1	25	30*	-	-
281 LUTH CH AMER..	2	851	1 208	0.4	0.9
283 LUTH--MO SYNOD	1	805	1 109	0.4	0.8
349 PENT HOLINESS.	1	38	46*	-	0.1
353 CHR BRETHREN..	1	50	80	-	0.1
356 PRESB CH AMER.	3	675	819	0.3	0.6
357 PRESB CH US...	11	3 967	4 840*	1.6	3.7
403 SALVATION ARMY	1	52	572	0.2	0.4
413 S.D.A.........	4	609	743*	0.2	0.6
419 SO BAPT CONV..	88	60 167	73 401*	24.7	55.7
421 SO METHODIST..	1	20	25	-	-
443 UN C OF CHRIST	1	34	41*	-	-
449 UN METHODIST..	36	18 277	22 297*	7.5	16.9
COFFEE	50	8 412	11 361*	42.2	100.0
053 ASSEMB OF GOD.	1	137	277	1.0	2.4
081 CATHOLIC......	1	NA	210	0.8	1.8
101 C.M.E........	1	257	321*	1.2	2.8
127 CH GOD (CLEVE)	7	674	842*	3.1	7.4
151 L-D SAINTS....	1	NA	518	1.9	4.6
165 CH OF NAZARENE	1	30	36	0.1	0.3
167 CHS OF CHRIST.	2	37	55	0.2	0.5
177 CONGR HOL CH..	2	106	132*	0.5	1.2
193 EPISCOPAL.....	1	94	129	0.5	1.1
357 PRESB CH US...	1	103	129*	0.5	1.1
419 SO BAPT CONV..	22	5 494	6 864*	25.5	60.4
443 UN C OF CHRIST	1	30	37*	0.1	0.3
449 UN METHODIST..	9	1 450	1 811*	6.7	15.9
COLQUITT	74	19 375	24 709*	69.8	100.0
017 AMER BAPT ASSN	1	30	30	0.1	0.1
053 ASSEMB OF GOD.	4	331	695	2.0	2.8
081 CATHOLIC......	1	NA	125	0.4	0.5
101 C.M.E........	1	362	448*	1.3	1.8
127 CH GOD (CLEVE)	6	326	404*	1.1	1.6
151 L-D SAINTS....	1	NA	209	0.6	0.8
165 CH OF NAZARENE	1	182	292	0.8	1.2
167 CHS OF CHRIST.	2	150	191	0.5	0.8
193 EPISCOPAL.....	1	88	136	0.4	0.6
357 PRESB CH US...	1	506	627*	1.8	2.5
413 S.D.A.........	1	77	95*	0.3	0.4
419 SO BAPT CONV..	41	14 997	18 573*	52.5	75.2
421 SO METHODIST..	1	22	31	0.1	0.1
449 UN METHODIST..	12	2 304	2 853*	8.1	11.5
COLUMBIA	38	8 402	10 767*	26.8	100.0
097 CHR CHS&CHS CR	2	285	358*	0.9	3.3
127 CH GOD (CLEVE)	2	188	236*	0.6	2.2
151 L-D SAINTS....	1	NA	138	0.3	1.3
165 CH OF NAZARENE	1	20	48	0.1	0.4
167 CHS OF CHRIST.	2	185	235	0.6	2.2
177 CONGR HOL CH..	2	37	46*	0.1	0.4
193 EPISCOPAL.....	2	236	360	0.9	3.3
271 REFORM JUDAISM	1	364	457*	1.1	4.2
356 PRESB CH AMER.	1	123	144	0.4	1.3
357 PRESB CH US...	2	125	157*	0.4	1.5
419 SO BAPT CONV..	13	5 332	6 696*	16.7	62.2
435 UNITARIAN-UNIV	1	20	25*	0.1	0.2
449 UN METHODIST..	8	1 487	1 867*	4.7	17.3
COOK	27	5 234	6 633*	49.2	100.0
053 ASSEMB OF GOD.	1	128	174	1.3	2.6
081 CATHOLIC......	1	NA	49	0.4	0.7
127 CH GOD (CLEVE)	2	223	280*	2.1	4.2
165 CH OF NAZARENE	1	33	41	0.3	0.6
167 CHS OF CHRIST.	2	107	136	1.0	2.1
357 PRESB CH US...	1	15	19*	0.1	0.3
419 SO BAPT CONV..	13	3 512	4 408*	32.7	66.5
449 UN METHODIST..	6	1 216	1 526*	11.3	23.0
COWETA	64	14 373	18 401*	46.9	100.0
053 ASSEMB OF GOD.	1	56	107	0.3	0.6
055 AS REF PRES CH	1	184	202	0.5	1.1
081 CATHOLIC......	1	NA	560	1.4	3.0
093 CHR CH (DISC).	1	40	60	0.2	0.3
097 CHR CHS&CHS CR	1	100	124*	0.3	0.7
127 CH GOD (CLEVE)	2	65	80*	0.2	0.4
167 CHS OF CHRIST.	3	210	267	0.7	1.5
193 EPISCOPAL.....	1	114	196	0.5	1.1
281 LUTH CH AMER..	1	39	44	0.1	0.2
283 LUTH--MO SYNOD	1	112	140	0.4	0.8
349 PENT HOLINESS.	1	154	190*	0.5	1.0
357 PRESB CH US...	2	314	388*	1.0	2.1
419 SO BAPT CONV..	24	8 964	11 075*	28.2	60.2
435 UNITARIAN-UNIV	1	13	16*	-	0.1
449 UN METHODIST..	22	4 008	4 952*	12.6	26.9
453 UN PRES CH USA	1	?	?	?	?
CRAWFORD	17	2 913	3 621*	47.1	100.0
101 C.M.E........	3	1 004	1 248*	16.2	34.5
127 CH GOD (CLEVE)	1	15	19*	0.2	0.5
175 CONGR CHR CHS.	1	110	137*	1.8	3.8
419 SO BAPT CONV..	5	1 313	1 632*	21.2	45.1
449 UN METHODIST..	7	471	585*	7.6	16.2
CRISP	36	7 175	9 127*	46.8	100.0
053 ASSEMB OF GOD.	1	33	29	0.1	0.3
081 CATHOLIC......	1	NA	150	0.8	1.6
101 C.M.E........	1	220	275*	1.4	3.0
127 CH GOD (CLEVE)	2	53	66*	0.3	0.7
167 CHS OF CHRIST.	3	125	178	0.9	2.0
193 EPISCOPAL.....	1	61	85	0.4	0.9
357 PRESB CH US...	1	51	64*	0.3	0.7
419 SO BAPT CONV..	18	5 031	6 281*	32.2	68.8
449 UN METHODIST..	7	1 541	1 924*	9.9	21.1
453 UN PRES CH USA	1	60	75*	0.4	0.8
DADE	31	3 206	4 213*	34.2	100.0
127 CH GOD (CLEVE)	5	257	317*	2.6	7.5
151 L-D SAINTS....	1	NA	248	2.0	5.9
167 CHS OF CHRIST.	4	300	380	3.1	9.0
413 S.D.A.........	2	365	450*	3.7	10.7
419 SO BAPT CONV..	10	1 493	1 842*	15.0	43.7
449 UN METHODIST..	9	791	976*	7.9	23.2
DAWSON	19	3 018	3 709*	77.7	100.0
127 CH GOD (CLEVE)	1	62	76*	1.6	2.0
419 SO BAPT CONV..	12	2 554	3 139*	65.8	84.6
449 UN METHODIST..	6	402	494*	10.3	13.3
DECATUR	51	8 572	11 050*	43.3	100.0
053 ASSEMB OF GOD.	3	144	233	0.9	2.1
081 CATHOLIC......	1	NA	70	0.3	0.6
097 CHR CHS&CHS CR	1	200	251*	1.0	2.3
123 CH GOD (ANDER)	1	18	54	0.2	0.5
127 CH GOD (CLEVE)	5	345	433*	1.7	3.9
151 L-D SAINTS....	1	NA	78	0.3	0.7
165 CH OF NAZARENE	1	73	147	0.6	1.3
167 CHS OF CHRIST.	2	150	191	0.7	1.7
193 EPISCOPAL.....	1	74	102	0.4	0.9
271 REFORM JUDAISM	1	22	28*	0.1	0.3
357 PRESB CH US...	1	259	325*	1.3	2.9
413 S.D.A.........	1	51	64*	0.3	0.6
419 SO BAPT CONV..	22	5 602	7 025*	27.6	63.6
449 UN METHODIST..	10	1 634	2 049*	8.0	18.5
DE KALB	242	143 792	199 267*	41.3	100.0
001 ADVENT CHR CH.	1	149	179*	-	0.1
019 AMER BAPT USA.	1	285	343*	0.1	0.2
029 AMER LUTH CH..	4	1 526	2 204	0.5	1.1
053 ASSEMB OF GOD.	9	1 428	1 988	0.4	1.0
055 AS REF PRES CH	4	1 208	1 331	0.3	0.7
081 CATHOLIC......	9	NA	22 600	4.7	11.3
089 CHR & MISS AL.	3	855	1 100	0.2	0.6
093 CHR CH (DISC).	3	1 926	2 530	0.5	1.3
097 CHR CHS&CHS CR	2	6 445	7 759*	1.6	3.9
123 CH GOD (ANDER)	5	413	1 239	0.3	0.6
127 CH GOD (CLEVE)	9	1 488	1 791*	0.4	0.9
151 L-D SAINTS....	3	NA	1 205	0.2	0.6
165 CH OF NAZARENE	3	562	675	0.1	0.3
167 CHS OF CHRIST.	10	1 785	2 272	0.5	1.1
177 CONGR HOL CH..	2	34	41*	-	-
185 CUMBER PRESB..	1	47	167	-	0.1
193 EPISCOPAL.....	9	5 157	6 547*	1.4	3.3
226 FRIENDS-USA...	1	62	75*	-	-
263 INT FOURSQ GOS	1	25	30*	-	-
281 LUTH CH AMER..	6	1 637	2 070	0.4	1.0
283 LUTH--MO SYNOD	2	655	874	0.2	0.4
285 MENNONITE CH..	1	43	52*	-	-
290 METRO COMM CHS	0	30	60	-	-
329 OPEN BIBLE STD	1	50	60	-	-
335 ORTH PRESB CH.	1	82	99*	-	-
349 PENT HOLINESS.	2	122	147*	-	0.1
353 CHR BRETHREN..	1	40	65	-	-
356 PRESB CH AMER.	4	488	605	0.1	0.3
357 PRESB CH US...	27	14 158	17 044*	3.5	8.6
413 S.D.A.........	3	664	799*	0.2	0.4
419 SO BAPT CONV..	61	64 195	77 279*	16.0	38.8
435 UNITARIAN-UNIV	4	1 218	1 466*	0.3	0.7
443 UN C OF CHRIST	1	492	592*	0.1	0.3
449 UN METHODIST..	46	36 377	43 791*	9.1	22.0
453 UN PRES CH USA	1	65	78*	-	-
469 WELS..........	1	81	110	-	0.1
DODGE	61	9 484	12 090*	71.3	100.0
081 CATHOLIC......	1	NA	47	0.3	0.4
093 CHR CH (DISC).	2	68	102	0.6	0.8
101 C.M.E........	2	365	451*	2.7	3.7
127 CH GOD (CLEVE)	3	191	236*	1.4	2.0
151 L-D SAINTS....	1	NA	282	1.7	2.3
165 CH OF NAZARENE	1	26	48	0.3	0.4
167 CHS OF CHRIST.	1	27	39	0.2	0.3
177 CONGR HOL CH..	2	46	57*	0.3	0.5
357 PRESB CH US...	2	208	257*	1.5	2.1
419 SO BAPT CONV..	39	7 603	9 397*	55.4	77.7
449 UN METHODIST..	7	950	1 174*	6.9	9.7
DOOLY	37	5 771	7 298*	67.4	100.0
017 AMER BAPT ASSN	1	30	30	0.3	0.4
101 C.M.E........	5	1 097	1 376*	12.7	18.9
123 CH GOD (ANDER)	2	38	114	1.1	1.6
177 CONGR HOL CH..	1	41	51*	0.5	0.7
419 SO BAPT CONV..	18	3 356	4 210*	38.9	57.7

NA—Not applicable   *Total adherents estimated from known number of communicant, confirmed, full members.   —Represents a percent less than 0.1   Percentages may not total due to rounding.

Table 4. Churches and Church Membership by County and Denomination: 1980

County and Denomination	Number of churches	Communicant, confirmed, full members	Total adherents		
			Number	Percent of total population	Percent of total adherents
449 UN METHODIST..	9	1 209	1 517*	14.0	20.8
453 UN PRES CH USA	1	?	?	?	?
DOUGHERTY	**70**	**29 980**	**41 360***	**41.0**	**100.0**
053 ASSEMB OF GOD.	2	651	791	0.8	1.9
081 CATHOLIC......	2	NA	2 646	2.6	6.4
089 CHR & MISS AL.	1	71	91	0.1	0.2
093 CHR CH (DISC).	1	114	198	0.2	0.5
097 CHR CHS&CHS CR	3	580	729*	0.7	1.8
101 C.M.E.........	2	900	1 131*	1.1	2.7
127 CH GOD (CLEVE)	4	774	973*	1.0	2.4
151 L-D SAINTS....	2	NA	688	0.7	1.7
165 CH OF NAZARENE	1	187	275	0.3	0.7
167 CHS OF CHRIST.	8	850	1 080	1.1	2.6
193 EPISCOPAL.....	4	1 061	1 303	1.3	3.2
271 REFORM JUDAISM	1	264	332*	0.3	0.8
281 LUTH CH AMER..	1	255	344	0.3	0.8
283 LUTH--MO SYNOD	1	137	172	0.2	0.4
349 PENT HOLINESS.	1	30	38*	-	0.1
353 CHR BRETHREN..	1	100	350	0.3	0.8
357 PRESB CH US...	4	1 247	1 567*	1.6	3.8
403 SALVATION ARMY	1	113	197	0.2	0.5
413 S.D.A.........	2	274	344*	0.3	0.8
419 SO BAPT CONV..	18	15 761	19 810*	19.6	47.9
421 SO METHODIST..	1	62	69	0.1	0.2
435 UNITARIAN-UNIV	1	10	13*	-	-
449 UN METHODIST..	7	6 493	8 161*	8.1	19.7
453 UN PRES CH USA	1	46	58*	0.1	0.1
DOUGLAS	**44**	**14 757**	**19 166***	**35.1**	**100.0**
053 ASSEMB OF GOD.	2	127	241	0.4	1.3
097 CHR CHS&CHS CR	2	185	234*	0.4	1.2
123 CH GOD (ANDER)	1	46	138	0.3	0.7
127 CH GOD (CLEVE)	4	257	325*	0.6	1.7
151 L-D SAINTS....	1	NA	260	0.5	1.4
165 CH OF NAZARENE	1	35	68	0.1	0.4
167 CHS OF CHRIST.	3	343	471	0.9	2.5
193 EPISCOPAL.....	1	126	159	0.3	0.8
283 LUTH--MO SYNOD	1	147	211	0.4	1.1
357 PRESB CH US...	1	328	415*	0.8	2.2
413 S.D.A.........	1	192	243*	0.4	1.3
419 SO BAPT CONV..	19	10 529	13 313*	24.4	69.5
449 UN METHODIST..	7	2 442	3 088*	5.7	16.1
EARLY	**33**	**5 251**	**6 674***	**50.7**	**100.0**
053 ASSEMB OF GOD.	3	136	162	1.2	2.4
081 CATHOLIC......	1	NA	50	0.4	0.7
101 C.M.E.........	3	1 107	1 395*	10.6	20.9
127 CH GOD (CLEVE)	2	47	59*	0.4	0.9
167 CHS OF CHRIST.	3	144	195	1.5	2.9
193 EPISCOPAL.....	1	32	42	0.3	0.6
357 PRESB CH US...	1	54	68*	0.5	1.0
413 S.D.A.........	1	41	52*	0.4	0.8
419 SO BAPT CONV..	12	2 769	3 490*	26.5	52.3
449 UN METHODIST..	6	921	1 161*	8.8	17.4
ECHOLS	**7**	**631**	**809***	**35.2**	**100.0**
123 CH GOD (ANDER)	1	8	24	1.0	3.0
127 CH GOD (CLEVE)	1	36	45*	2.0	5.6
167 CHS OF CHRIST.	1	62	79	3.4	9.8
419 SO BAPT CONV..	2	323	407*	17.7	50.3
449 UN METHODIST..	2	202	254*	11.1	31.4
EFFINGHAM	**41**	**6 740**	**8 591***	**46.9**	**100.0**
053 ASSEMB OF GOD.	1	70	114	0.6	1.3
089 CHR & MISS AL.	1	7	7	-	0.1
093 CHR CH (DISC).	1	100	158	0.9	1.8
097 CHR CHS&CHS CR	3	225	283*	1.5	3.3
127 CH GOD (CLEVE)	1	96	121*	0.7	1.4
151 L-D SAINTS....	1	NA	62	0.3	0.7
167 CHS OF CHRIST.	2	75	95	0.5	1.1
281 LUTH CH AMER..	7	1 051	1 306	7.1	15.2
419 SO BAPT CONV..	13	3 639	4 579*	25.0	53.3
421 SO METHODIST..	1	19	31	0.2	0.4
449 UN METHODIST..	10	1 458	1 835*	10.0	21.4
ELBERT	**57**	**10 869**	**13 615***	**72.6**	**100.0**
053 ASSEMB OF GOD.	1	29	54	0.3	0.4
081 CATHOLIC......	1	NA	70	0.4	0.5
097 CHR CHS&CHS CR	1	160	195*	1.0	1.4
101 C.M.E.........	3	1 324	1 618*	8.6	11.9
127 CH GOD (CLEVE)	2	213	260*	1.4	1.9
151 L-D SAINTS....	1	NA	108	0.6	0.8
167 CHS OF CHRIST.	2	60	76	0.4	0.6
193 EPISCOPAL.....	1	61	114	0.6	0.8
281 LUTH CH AMER..	1	110	132	0.7	1.0
349 PENT HOLINESS.	6	385	470*	2.5	3.5
357 PRESB CH US...	3	361	441*	2.4	3.2
403 SALVATION ARMY	1	26	131	0.7	1.0
419 SO BAPT CONV..	20	5 792	7 077*	37.7	52.0
443 UN C OF CHRIST	1	40	49*	0.3	0.4
449 UN METHODIST..	13	2 308	2 820*	15.0	20.7
EMANUEL	**48**	**6 924**	**8 830***	**42.5**	**100.0**
001 ADVENT CHR CH.	1	22	27*	0.1	0.3
053 ASSEMB OF GOD.	1	25	36	0.2	0.4
081 CATHOLIC......	1	NA	110	0.5	1.2
127 CH GOD (CLEVE)	4	242	302*	1.5	3.4

County and Denomination	Number of churches	Communicant, confirmed, full members	Total adherents		
			Number	Percent of total population	Percent of total adherents
165 CH OF NAZARENE	2	141	255	1.2	2.9
167 CHS OF CHRIST.	1	31	40	0.2	0.5
349 PENT HOLINESS.	2	84	105*	0.5	1.2
357 PRESB CH US...	1	57	71*	0.3	0.8
419 SO BAPT CONV..	20	4 339	5 411*	26.0	61.3
449 UN METHODIST..	15	1 983	2 473*	11.9	28.0
EVANS	**17**	**2 739**	**3 520***	**41.8**	**100.0**
081 CATHOLIC......	1	NA	130	1.5	3.7
127 CH GOD (CLEVE)	1	27	33*	0.4	0.9
165 CH OF NAZARENE	1	73	83	1.0	2.4
167 CHS OF CHRIST.	1	31	39	0.5	1.1
419 SO BAPT CONV..	6	1 203	1 492*	17.7	42.4
449 UN METHODIST..	7	1 405	1 743*	20.7	49.5
FANNIN	**49**	**9 462**	**11 422***	**77.4**	**100.0**
081 CATHOLIC......	1	NA	50	0.3	0.4
127 CH GOD (CLEVE)	2	218	261*	1.8	2.3
167 CHS OF CHRIST.	4	380	485	3.3	4.2
419 SO BAPT CONV..	36	8 160	9 782*	66.3	85.6
449 UN METHODIST..	6	704	844*	5.7	7.4
FAYETTE	**44**	**10 548**	**14 760***	**50.8**	**100.0**
053 ASSEMB OF GOD.	1	31	52	0.2	0.4
081 CATHOLIC......	1	NA	908	3.1	6.2
093 CHR CH (DISC).	1	18	28	0.1	0.2
097 CHR CHS&CHS CR	4	329	413*	1.4	2.8
151 L-D SAINTS....	1	NA	425	1.5	2.9
167 CHS OF CHRIST.	2	181	300	1.0	2.0
177 CONGR HOL CH..	2	35	44*	0.2	0.3
193 EPISCOPAL.....	1	79	107	0.4	0.7
281 LUTH CH AMER..	1	271	440	1.5	3.0
357 PRESB CH US...	2	661	829*	2.9	5.6
413 S.D.A.........	1	67	84*	0.3	0.6
419 SO BAPT CONV..	15	6 340	7 950*	27.4	53.9
449 UN METHODIST..	12	2 536	3 180*	10.9	21.5
FLOYD	**133**	**40 437**	**50 792***	**63.6**	**100.0**
005 AME ZION......	2	144	159	0.2	0.3
053 ASSEMB OF GOD.	2	144	214	0.3	0.4
081 CATHOLIC......	1	NA	1 375	1.7	2.7
089 CHR & MISS AL.	1	56	81	0.1	0.2
093 CHR CH (DISC).	1	183	243	0.3	0.5
097 CHR CHS&CHS CR	1	350	423*	0.5	0.8
101 C.M.E.........	2	767	926*	1.2	1.8
127 CH GOD (CLEVE)	8	1 337	1 615*	2.0	3.2
151 L-D SAINTS....	1	NA	303	0.4	0.6
165 CH OF NAZARENE	1	47	82	0.1	0.2
167 CHS OF CHRIST.	6	705	835	1.0	1.6
177 CONGR HOL CH..	2	68	82*	0.1	0.2
193 EPISCOPAL.....	2	529	718	0.9	1.4
271 REFORM JUDAISM	1	46	56*	0.1	0.1
283 LUTH--MO SYNOD	1	76	107	0.1	0.2
357 PRESB CH US...	4	1 412	1 705*	2.1	3.4
403 SALVATION ARMY	1	59	192	0.2	0.4
413 S.D.A.........	2	92	111*	0.1	0.2
419 SO BAPT CONV..	63	28 668	34 620*	43.4	68.2
421 SO METHODIST..	1	95	112	0.1	0.2
435 UNITARIAN-UNIV	1	14	17*	-	-
449 UN METHODIST..	28	5 633	6 802*	8.5	13.4
453 UN PRES CH USA	1	12	14*	-	-
FORSYTH	**60**	**16 505**	**20 840***	**74.5**	**100.0**
053 ASSEMB OF GOD.	1	14	20	0.1	0.1
081 CATHOLIC......	1	NA	345	1.2	1.7
097 CHR CHS&CHS CR	1	185	230*	0.8	1.1
127 CH GOD (CLEVE)	1	159	197*	0.7	0.9
167 CHS OF CHRIST.	1	30	38	0.1	0.2
177 CONGR HOL CH..	4	10	12*	-	0.1
179 CONSRV BAPT...	1	30	37*	0.1	0.2
193 EPISCOPAL.....	1	86	120	0.4	0.6
356 PRESB CH AMER.	1	?	?	?	?
357 PRESB CH US...	1	107	133*	0.5	0.6
413 S.D.A.........	1	112	139*	0.5	0.7
419 SO BAPT CONV..	37	14 463	17 945*	64.2	86.1
449 UN METHODIST..	9	1 309	1 624*	5.8	7.8
FRANKLIN	**67**	**14 188**	**17 171***	**113.1**	**100.0**
097 CHR CHS&CHS CR	2	160	194*	1.3	1.1
101 C.M.E.........	2	584	707*	4.7	4.1
127 CH GOD (CLEVE)	5	414	501*	3.3	2.9
167 CHS OF CHRIST.	2	20	25	0.2	0.1
349 PENT HOLINESS.	6	522	632*	4.2	3.7
357 PRESB CH US...	4	122	148*	1.0	0.9
413 S.D.A.........	10	4 255	5 149*	33.9	30.0
419 SO BAPT CONV..	24	6 468	7 827*	51.5	45.6
435 UNITARIAN-UNIV	1	20	24*	0.2	0.1
449 UN METHODIST..	11	1 623	1 964*	12.9	11.4
FULTON	**381**	**204 769**	**282 190***	**47.8**	**100.0**
005 AME ZION......	1	810	910	0.2	0.3
019 AMER BAPT USA.	6	7 273	8 747*	1.5	3.1
029 AMER LUTH CH..	1	203	254	-	0.1
053 ASSEMB OF GOD.	7	982	1 358	0.2	0.5
057 BAPT GEN CONF.	1	15	18*	-	-
081 CATHOLIC......	16	NA	30 420	5.2	10.8
089 CHR & MISS AL.	2	67	77	-	-
093 CHR CH (DISC).	5	2 076	3 388	0.6	1.2

NA— Not applicable   *Total adherents estimated from known number of communicant, confirmed, full members.   —Represents a percent less than 0.1.   Percentages may not total due to rounding.

Table 4. Churches and Church Membership by County and Denomination: 1980

County and Denomination	Number of churches	Communicant, confirmed, full members	Total adherents Number	Percent of total population	Percent of total adherents
097 CHR CHS&CHS CR	22	7 307	8 788*	1.5	3.1
101 C.M.E.........	7	6 538	7 863*	1.3	2.8
127 CH GOD (CLEVE)	12	5 617	6 756*	1.1	2.4
151 L-D SAINTS....	3	NA	1 480	0.3	0.5
165 CH OF NAZARENE	2	204	416	0.1	0.1
167 CHS OF CHRIST.	21	3 312	4 222	0.7	1.5
177 CONGR HOL CH..	2	75	90*	–	–
179 CONSRV BAPT...	1	25	30*	–	–
193 EPISCOPAL.....	15	12 444	16 529	2.8	5.9
208 EVAN LUTH ASSN	1	256	323	0.1	0.1
215 EVAN METH CH..	1	35	42*	–	–
221 FREE METHODIST	1	37	318	0.1	0.1
233 GEN CH NEW JER	1	40	48*	–	–
270 CONSRV JUDAISM	1	1 239	1 490*	0.3	0.5
271 REFORM JUDAISM	3	4 296	5 167*	0.9	1.8
281 LUTH CH AMER..	7	3 266	4 186	0.7	1.5
283 LUTH--MO SYNOD	4	714	927	0.2	0.3
285 MENNONITE CH..	1	?	?	?	?
290 METRO COMM CHS	1	150	300	0.1	0.1
353 CHR BRETHREN..	2	200	250	–	0.1
356 PRESB CH AMER.	6	627	755	0.1	0.3
357 PRESB CH US...	23	17 423	20 954*	3.6	7.4
403 SALVATION ARMY	5	698	1 128	0.2	0.4
413 S.D.A.........	1	140	168*	–	0.1
419 SO BAPT CONV..	102	79 440	95 542*	16.2	33.9
421 SO METHODIST..	1	15	20	–	–
443 UN C OF CHRIST	5	864	1 039*	0.2	0.4
449 UN METHODIST..	87	47 275	56 857*	9.6	20.1
453 UN PRES CH USA	4	1 106	1 330*	0.2	0.5
GILMER	26	3 744	4 539*	40.9	100.0
127 CH GOD (CLEVE)	1	82	99*	0.9	2.2
167 CHS OF CHRIST.	3	180	229	2.1	5.0
419 SO BAPT CONV..	16	2 954	3 572*	32.2	78.7
449 UN METHODIST..	6	528	639*	5.8	14.1
GLASCOCK	15	1 561	2 021*	84.8	100.0
123 CH GOD (ANDER)	1	18	54	2.3	2.7
127 CH GOD (CLEVE)	2	70	84*	3.5	4.2
151 L-D SAINTS....	1	NA	123	5.2	6.1
419 SO BAPT CONV..	7	1 123	1 342*	56.3	66.4
449 UN METHODIST..	4	350	418*	17.5	20.7
GLYNN	76	18 907	25 787*	46.9	100.0
001 ADVENT CHR CH.	1	139	169*	0.3	0.7
019 AMER BAPT USA.	1	150	183*	0.3	0.7
053 ASSEM OF GOD.	2	141	319	0.6	1.2
081 CATHOLIC......	4	NA	1 915	3.5	7.4
097 CHR CHS&CHS CR	1	25	30*	0.1	0.1
101 C.M.E.........	1	230	280*	0.5	1.1
123 CH GOD (ANDER)	1	16	48	0.1	0.2
127 CH GOD (CLEVE)	6	843	1 026*	1.9	4.0
151 L-D SAINTS....	1	NA	343	0.6	1.3
165 CH OF NAZARENE	3	200	390	0.7	1.5
167 CHS OF CHRIST.	5	400	509	0.9	2.0
193 EPISCOPAL.....	7	1 298	1 686	3.1	6.5
263 INT FOURSQ GOS	1	16	19*	–	0.1
271 REFORM JUDAISM	1	40	49*	0.1	0.2
281 LUTH CH AMER..	1	215	284	0.5	1.1
357 PRESB CH US...	4	1 303	1 586*	2.9	6.2
403 SALVATION ARMY	1	54	92	0.2	0.4
413 S.D.A.........	2	133	162*	0.3	0.6
419 SO BAPT CONV..	17	9 267	11 283*	20.5	43.8
421 SO METHODIST..	1	24	41	0.1	0.2
449 UN METHODIST..	14	4 354	5 301*	9.6	20.6
453 UN PRES CH USA	1	59	72*	0.1	0.3
GORDON	62	12 752	16 227*	54.0	100.0
053 ASSEM OF GOD.	2	54	83	0.3	0.5
081 CATHOLIC......	1	NA	400	1.3	2.5
127 CH GOD (CLEVE)	4	596	738*	2.5	4.5
167 CHS OF CHRIST.	3	275	353	1.2	2.2
185 CUMBER PRESB..	1	11	22	0.1	0.1
193 EPISCOPAL.....	1	58	81	0.3	0.5
357 PRESB CH US...	1	110	136*	0.5	0.8
413 S.D.A.........	3	1 204	1 490*	5.0	9.2
419 SO BAPT CONV..	31	8 983	11 116*	37.0	68.5
449 UN METHODIST..	15	1 461	1 808*	6.0	11.1
GRADY	48	8 858	11 279*	56.8	100.0
053 ASSEM OF GOD.	3	95	203	1.0	1.8
081 CATHOLIC......	1	NA	90	0.5	0.8
093 CHR CH (DISC).	1	31	48	0.2	0.4
101 C.M.E.........	1	362	451*	2.3	4.0
127 CH GOD (CLEVE)	1	113	141*	0.7	1.3
151 L-D SAINTS....	1	NA	65	0.3	0.6
165 CH OF NAZARENE	1	31	49	0.2	0.4
167 CHS OF CHRIST.	2	50	55	0.3	0.5
357 PRESB CH US...	1	133	166*	0.8	1.5
413 S.D.A.........	1	87	108*	0.5	1.0
419 SO BAPT CONV..	23	6 531	8 129*	41.0	72.1
449 UN METHODIST..	12	1 425	1 774*	8.9	15.7
GREENE	28	3 965	5 040*	44.2	100.0
127 CH GOD (CLEVE)	1	60	75*	1.5	1.5
167 CHS OF CHRIST.	1	27	150	1.3	3.0
177 CONGR HOL CH..	1	24	30*	0.3	0.6
193 EPISCOPAL.....	1	25	25	0.2	0.5
356 PRESB CH AMER.	2	43	43	0.4	0.9

County and Denomination	Number of churches	Communicant, confirmed, full members	Total adherents Number	Percent of total population	Percent of total adherents
357 PRESB CH US...	3	156	194*	1.7	3.8
419 SO BAPT CONV..	12	2 550	3 177*	27.9	63.0
449 UN METHODIST..	7	1 080	1 346*	11.8	26.7
GWINNETT	122	40 123	56 281*	33.7	100.0
005 AME ZION......	2	248	283	0.2	0.5
017 AMER BAPT ASSN	1	50	50	–	0.1
053 ASSEM OF GOD.	1	101	182	0.1	0.3
081 CATHOLIC......	4	NA	5 035	3.0	8.9
089 CHR & MISS AL.	2	228	351	0.2	0.6
093 CHR CH (DISC).	2	369	492	0.3	0.9
097 CHR CHS&CHS CR	5	1 048	1 313*	0.8	2.3
127 CH GOD (CLEVE)	7	1 798	2 253*	1.3	4.0
151 L-D SAINTS....	1	NA	409	0.2	0.7
165 CH OF NAZARENE	3	48	79	–	0.1
167 CHS OF CHRIST.	5	617	868	0.5	1.5
185 CUMBER PRESB..	1	15	15	–	–
193 EPISCOPAL.....	3	546	726	0.4	1.3
281 LUTH CH AMER..	2	819	1 286	0.8	2.3
295 MORAV CH-SOUTH	1	105	150	0.1	0.3
329 OPEN BIBLE STD	1	25	25	–	–
357 PRESB CH US...	8	1 781	2 231*	1.3	4.0
413 S.D.A.........	3	215	269*	0.2	0.5
419 SO BAPT CONV..	34	21 184	26 542*	15.9	47.2
443 UN C OF CHRIST	1	70	88*	0.1	0.2
449 UN METHODIST..	34	10 821	13 558*	8.1	24.1
469 WELS..........	1	35	76	–	0.1
HABERSHAM	58	11 858	14 538*	58.1	100.0
053 ASSEM OF GOD.	1	24	48	0.2	0.3
081 CATHOLIC......	1	NA	242	1.0	1.7
097 CHR CHS&CHS CR	2	280	336*	1.3	2.3
101 C.M.E.........	1	112	135*	0.5	0.9
127 CH GOD (CLEVE)	3	268	322*	1.3	2.2
167 CHS OF CHRIST.	2	50	64	0.3	0.4
177 CONGR HOL CH..	2	77	93*	0.4	0.6
193 EPISCOPAL.....	1	116	162	0.6	1.1
357 PRESB CH US...	2	357	429*	1.7	3.0
419 SO BAPT CONV..	32	9 244	11 108*	44.4	76.4
443 UN C OF CHRIST	1	33	40*	0.2	0.3
449 UN METHODIST..	10	1 297	1 559*	6.2	10.7
HALL	103	31 881	40 843*	54.0	100.0
053 ASSEM OF GOD.	2	654	1 113	1.5	2.7
081 CATHOLIC......	1	NA	1 000	1.3	2.4
089 CHR & MISS AL.	1	17	41	0.1	0.1
093 CHR CH (DISC).	1	76	86	0.1	0.2
097 CHR CHS&CHS CR	1	50	61*	0.1	0.1
101 C.M.E.........	1	125	153*	0.2	0.4
127 CH GOD (CLEVE)	4	173	211*	0.3	0.5
151 L-D SAINTS....	1	NA	289	0.4	0.7
165 CH OF NAZARENE	2	233	394	0.5	1.0
167 CHS OF CHRIST.	2	100	127	0.2	0.3
177 CONGR HOL CH..	5	533	651*	0.9	1.6
193 EPISCOPAL.....	1	547	679	0.9	1.7
221 FREE METHODIST	1	39	150	0.2	0.4
283 LUTH--MO SYNOD	1	109	138	0.2	0.3
356 PRESB CH AMER.	1	146	159	0.2	0.4
357 PRESB CH US...	2	1 198	1 464*	1.9	3.6
403 SALVATION ARMY	1	79	79	0.1	0.2
419 SO BAPT CONV..	51	23 103	28 225*	37.3	69.1
449 UN METHODIST..	24	4 699	5 741*	7.6	14.1
HANCOCK	29	2 531	3 199*	33.8	100.0
093 CHR CH (DISC).	1	37	57	0.6	1.8
101 C.M.E.........	2	647	813*	8.6	25.4
167 CHS OF CHRIST.	1	30	50	0.5	1.6
356 PRESB CH AMER.	1	38	45	0.5	1.4
419 SO BAPT CONV..	13	1 192	1 497*	15.8	46.8
449 UN METHODIST..	11	587	737*	7.8	23.0
HARALSON	47	8 787	10 934*	59.4	100.0
053 ASSEM OF GOD.	1	20	51	0.3	0.5
097 CHR CHS&CHS CR	3	227	278*	1.5	2.5
127 CH GOD (CLEVE)	3	197	241*	1.3	2.2
151 L-D SAINTS....	1	NA	158	0.9	1.4
167 CHS OF CHRIST.	3	268	330	1.8	3.0
349 PENT HOLINESS.	1	33	40*	0.2	0.4
357 PRESB CH US...	2	73	89*	0.5	0.8
419 SO BAPT CONV..	23	6 714	8 212*	44.6	75.1
449 UN METHODIST..	10	1 255	1 535*	8.3	14.0
HARRIS	39	5 447	6 648*	43.0	100.0
081 CATHOLIC......	1	NA	70	0.5	1.1
101 C.M.E.........	3	978	1 181*	7.6	17.8
127 CH GOD (CLEVE)	1	93	112*	0.7	1.7
167 CHS OF CHRIST.	1	25	30	0.2	0.5
413 S.D.A.........	1	72	87*	0.6	1.3
419 SO BAPT CONV..	20	2 907	3 511*	22.7	52.8
443 UN C OF CHRIST	1	98	118*	0.8	1.8
449 UN METHODIST..	11	1 274	1 539*	10.0	23.1
HART	47	10 952	13 573*	73.0	100.0
081 CATHOLIC......	1	NA	100	0.5	0.7
089 CHR & MISS AL.	1	6	27	0.1	0.2
097 CHR CHS&CHS CR	1	16	20*	0.1	0.1
101 C.M.E.........	3	1 790	2 196*	11.8	16.2
127 CH GOD (CLEVE)	3	262	321*	1.7	2.4

NA—Not applicable   *Total adherents estimated from known number of communicant, confirmed, full members.   —Represents a percent less than 0.1.   Percentages may not total due to rounding.

Table 4. Churches and Church Membership by County and Denomination: 1980

County and Denomination	Number of churches	Communicant, confirmed, full members	Total adherents		
			Number	Percent of total population	Percent of total adherents
167 CHS OF CHRIST.	1	29	37	0.2	0.3
177 CONGR HOL CH..	3	108	132*	0.7	1.0
193 EPISCOPAL.....	1	75	110	0.6	0.8
349 PENT HOLINESS.	2	111	136*	0.7	1.0
357 PRESB CH US...	2	114	140*	0.8	1.0
419 SO BAPT CONV..	19	6 837	8 386*	45.1	61.8
449 UN METHODIST..	10	1 604	1 968*	10.6	14.5
HEARD	29	2 583	3 178*	48.7	100.0
127 CH GOD (CLEVE)	2	158	194*	3.0	6.1
167 CHS OF CHRIST.	2	30	38	0.6	1.2
419 SO BAPT CONV..	11	1 571	1 932*	29.6	60.8
449 UN METHODIST..	14	824	1 014*	15.6	31.9
HENRY	53	11 733	15 051*	41.5	100.0
053 ASSEM OF GOD.	2	156	318	0.9	2.1
081 CATHOLIC......	1	NA	460	1.3	3.1
097 CHR CHS&CHS CR	3	537	663*	1.8	4.4
127 CH GOD (CLEVE)	4	133	164*	0.5	1.1
167 CHS OF CHRIST.	1	106	114	0.3	0.8
175 CONGR CHR CHS.	1	108	133*	0.4	0.9
177 CONGR HOL CH..	1	25	31*	0.1	0.2
357 PRESB CH US...	5	675	833*	2.3	5.5
413 S.D.A.........	1	39	48*	0.1	0.3
419 SO BAPT CONV..	16	6 261	7 728*	21.3	51.3
449 UN METHODIST..	18	3 693	4 559*	12.6	30.3
HOUSTON	74	28 896	39 966*	51.5	100.0
053 ASSEM OF GOD.	5	421	643	0.8	1.6
059 BAPT MISS ASSN	1	118	146*	0.2	0.4
081 CATHOLIC......	3	NA	3 273	4.2	8.2
089 CHR & MISS AL.	1	64	95	0.1	0.2
093 CHR CH (DISC).	1	153	235	0.3	0.6
097 CHR CHS&CHS CR	1	70	87*	0.1	0.2
101 C.M.E.........	3	2 377	2 942*	3.8	7.4
127 CH GOD (CLEVE)	4	558	691*	0.9	1.7
151 L-D SAINTS....	1	NA	583	0.8	1.5
165 CH OF NAZARENE	1	183	356	0.5	0.9
167 CHS OF CHRIST.	4	460	585	0.8	1.5
177 CONGR HOL CH..	1	20	25*	-	0.1
193 EPISCOPAL.....	2	466	556	0.7	1.4
263 INT FOURSQ GOS	1	25	31*	-	0.1
281 LUTH CH AMER..	1	418	534	0.7	1.3
349 PENT HOLINESS.	1	15	19*	-	-
356 PRESB CH AMER.	2	303	336	0.4	0.8
357 PRESB CH US...	2	296	366*	0.5	0.9
403 SALVATION ARMY	1	41	110	0.1	0.3
413 S.D.A.........	1	108	134*	0.2	0.3
419 SO BAPT CONV..	24	17 090	21 152*	27.3	52.9
449 UN METHODIST..	12	5 620	6 956*	9.0	17.4
453 UN PRES CH USA	1	90	111*	0.1	0.3
IRWIN	17	2 766	3 416*	38.0	100.0
127 CH GOD (CLEVE)	2	257	317*	3.5	9.3
167 CHS OF CHRIST.	1	8	12	0.1	0.4
413 S.D.A.........	2	67	83*	0.9	2.4
419 SO BAPT CONV..	10	2 075	2 561*	28.5	75.0
449 UN METHODIST..	2	359	443*	4.9	13.0
JACKSON	57	9 942	12 250*	48.3	100.0
053 ASSEM OF GOD.	1	14	27	0.1	0.2
093 CHR CH (DISC).	2	200	307	1.2	2.5
097 CHR CHS&CHS CR	2	380	465*	1.8	3.8
127 CH GOD (CLEVE)	1	93	114*	0.4	0.9
167 CHS OF CHRIST.	1	60	75	0.3	0.6
177 CONGR HOL CH..	4	287	352*	1.4	2.9
357 PRESB CH US...	5	294	360*	1.4	2.9
419 SO BAPT CONV..	24	6 718	8 228*	32.5	67.2
443 UN C OF CHRIST	1	46	56*	0.2	0.5
449 UN METHODIST..	16	1 850	2 266*	8.9	18.5
JASPER	21	3 240	3 973*	52.6	100.0
101 C.M.E.........	2	862	1 057*	14.0	26.6
127 CH GOD (CLEVE)	1	15	18*	0.2	0.5
357 PRESB CH US...	1	135	166*	2.2	4.2
419 SO BAPT CONV..	11	1 639	2 010*	26.6	50.6
449 UN METHODIST..	6	589	722*	9.6	18.2
JEFF DAVIS	34	5 624	7 381*	64.3	100.0
081 CATHOLIC......	1	NA	57	0.5	0.8
089 CHR & MISS AL.	1	78	128	1.1	1.7
093 CHR CH (DISC).	1	40	63	0.5	0.9
101 C.M.E.........	1	92	115*	1.0	1.6
127 CH GOD (CLEVE)	7	668	832*	7.3	11.3
151 L-D SAINTS....	1	NA	278	2.4	3.8
167 CHS OF CHRIST.	3	28	33	0.3	0.4
413 S.D.A.........	1	7	9*	0.1	0.1
419 SO BAPT CONV..	15	3 937	4 902*	42.7	66.4
449 UN METHODIST..	3	774	964*	8.4	13.1
JEFFERSON	44	7 300	9 279*	50.4	100.0
053 ASSEM OF GOD.	1	16	36	0.2	0.4
055 AS REF PRES CH	3	258	314	1.7	3.4
081 CATHOLIC......	1	NA	47	0.3	0.5
101 C.M.E.........	2	1 289	1 613*	8.8	17.4
123 CH GOD (ANDER)	2	75	225	1.2	2.4
127 CH GOD (CLEVE)	2	144	180*	1.0	1.9

County and Denomination	Number of churches	Communicant, confirmed, full members	Total adherents		
			Number	Percent of total population	Percent of total adherents
143 CG IN CR(MENN)	1	142	142	0.8	1.5
165 CH OF NAZARENE	2	78	96	0.5	1.0
167 CHS OF CHRIST.	1	10	15	0.1	0.2
353 CHR BRETHREN..	1	20	20	0.1	0.2
413 S.D.A.........	1	59	74*	0.4	0.8
419 SO BAPT CONV..	15	3 295	4 122*	22.4	44.4
449 UN METHODIST..	12	1 914	2 395*	13.0	25.8
JENKINS	18	3 556	4 465*	50.5	100.0
081 CATHOLIC......	1	NA	45	0.5	1.0
123 CH GOD (ANDER)	1	16	48	0.5	1.1
127 CH GOD (CLEVE)	1	68	84*	1.0	1.9
167 CHS OF CHRIST.	1	6	8	0.1	0.2
419 SO BAPT CONV..	10	2 904	3 586*	40.6	80.3
449 UN METHODIST..	4	562	694*	7.8	15.5
JOHNSON	36	3 674	4 741*	54.7	100.0
001 ADVENT CHR CH.	1	154	190*	2.2	4.0
053 ASSEM OF GOD.	2	88	156	1.8	3.3
097 CHR CHS&CHS CR	1	140	173*	2.0	3.6
127 CH GOD (CLEVE)	2	147	182*	2.1	3.8
165 CH OF NAZARENE	2	213	419	4.8	8.8
349 PENT HOLINESS.	1	19	23*	0.3	0.5
413 S.D.A.........	1	32	40*	0.5	0.8
419 SO BAPT CONV..	14	1 723	2 128*	24.6	44.9
449 UN METHODIST..	12	1 158	1 430*	16.5	30.2
JONES	23	4 181	5 176*	31.2	100.0
101 C.M.E.........	1	932	1 154*	7.0	22.3
127 CH GOD (CLEVE)	3	120	149*	0.9	2.9
167 CHS OF CHRIST.	1	25	30	0.2	0.6
357 PRESB CH US...	1	62	77*	0.5	1.5
419 SO BAPT CONV..	12	2 223	2 752*	16.6	53.2
449 UN METHODIST..	5	819	1 014*	6.1	19.6
LAMAR	34	5 681	7 147*	58.5	100.0
053 ASSEM OF GOD.	1	82	120	1.0	1.7
081 CATHOLIC......	1	NA	70	0.6	1.0
101 C.M.E.........	2	1 230	1 507*	12.3	21.1
127 CH GOD (CLEVE)	1	20	25*	0.2	0.3
165 CH OF NAZARENE	1	143	275	2.3	3.8
167 CHS OF CHRIST.	1	30	35	0.3	0.5
349 PENT HOLINESS.	4	191	234*	1.9	3.3
357 PRESB CH US...	1	51	62*	0.5	0.9
419 SO BAPT CONV..	9	2 519	3 086*	25.3	43.2
443 UN C OF CHRIST	1	55	67*	0.5	0.9
449 UN METHODIST..	12	1 360	1 666*	13.6	23.3
LANIER	11	1 909	2 460*	43.5	100.0
081 CATHOLIC......	1	NA	67	1.2	2.7
127 CH GOD (CLEVE)	2	90	113*	2.0	4.6
167 CHS OF CHRIST.	1	15	18	0.3	0.7
413 S.D.A.........	1	102	128*	2.3	5.2
419 SO BAPT CONV..	3	1 091	1 368*	24.2	55.6
449 UN METHODIST..	3	611	766*	13.5	31.1
LAURENS	93	16 734	21 456*	58.0	100.0
053 ASSEM OF GOD.	5	250	355	1.0	1.7
081 CATHOLIC......	1	NA	266	0.7	1.2
089 CHR & MISS AL.	1	0	20	0.1	0.1
093 CHR CH (DISC).	3	125	195	0.5	0.9
101 C.M.E.........	1	585	720*	1.9	3.4
123 CH GOD (ANDER)	3	97	291	0.8	1.4
127 CH GOD (CLEVE)	3	234	288*	0.8	1.3
151 L-D SAINTS....	1	NA	242	0.7	1.1
165 CH OF NAZARENE	3	292	424	1.1	2.0
167 CHS OF CHRIST.	3	97	140	0.4	0.7
193 EPISCOPAL.....	1	210	233	0.6	1.1
285 MENNONITE CH..	1	25	31*	0.1	0.1
357 PRESB CH US...	2	283	349*	0.9	1.6
413 S.D.A.........	2	69	85*	0.2	0.4
419 SO BAPT CONV..	40	10 605	13 061*	35.3	60.9
449 UN METHODIST..	23	3 862	4 756*	12.9	22.2
LEE	10	2 392	3 022*	25.9	100.0
127 CH GOD (CLEVE)	1	58	73*	0.6	2.4
167 CHS OF CHRIST.	1	38	48	0.4	1.6
357 PRESB CH US...	1	33	42*	0.4	1.4
419 SO BAPT CONV..	5	1 890	2 388*	20.4	79.0
449 UN METHODIST..	2	373	471*	4.0	15.6
LIBERTY	26	4 934	6 593*	17.5	100.0
053 ASSEM OF GOD.	1	144	208	0.6	3.2
081 CATHOLIC......	2	NA	171	0.5	2.6
123 CH GOD (ANDER)	1	44	132	0.4	2.0
127 CH GOD (CLEVE)	2	119	148*	0.4	2.2
151 L-D SAINTS....	1	NA	186	0.5	2.8
167 CHS OF CHRIST.	1	125	155	0.4	2.4
193 EPISCOPAL.....	1	91	121	0.3	1.8
357 PRESB CH US...	5	458	568*	1.5	8.6
419 SO BAPT CONV..	7	2 802	3 476*	9.2	52.7
443 UN C OF CHRIST	1	93	115*	0.3	1.7
449 UN METHODIST..	3	929	1 153*	3.1	17.5
453 UN PRES CH USA	1	129	160*	0.4	2.4
LINCOLN	21	3 766	4 593*	66.1	100.0

NA — Not applicable *Total adherents estimated from known number of communicant, confirmed, full members. —Represents a percent less than 0.1. Percentages may not total due to rounding.

Table 4. Churches and Church Membership by County and Denomination: 1980

County and Denomination	Number of churches	Communicant, confirmed, full members	Total adherents Number	Percent of total population	Percent of total adherents
101 C.M.E.........	1	755	921*	13.3	20.1
177 CONGR HOL CH..	1	89	109*	1.6	2.4
349 PENT HOLINESS.	2	64	78*	1.1	1.7
357 PRESB CH US...	1	25	30*	0.4	0.7
419 SO BAPT CONV..	9	2 040	2 488*	35.8	54.2
449 UN METHODIST..	7	793	967*	13.9	21.1
LONG	12	1 556	1 951*	43.1	100.0
017 AMER BAPT ASSN	2	50	50	1.1	2.6
127 CH GOD (CLEVE)	2	69	87*	1.9	4.5
167 CHS OF CHRIST.	1	2	10	0.2	0.5
419 SO BAPT CONV..	5	1 261	1 585*	35.0	81.2
449 UN METHODIST..	2	174	219*	4.8	11.2
LOWNDES	99	24 706	33 009*	48.6	100.0
005 AME ZION......	1	150	167	0.2	0.5
017 AMER BAPT ASSN	5	530	530	0.8	1.6
053 ASSEMB OF GOD.	3	374	646	1.0	2.0
081 CATHOLIC......	2	NA	1 700	2.5	5.2
089 CHR & MISS AL.	1	3	17	-	0.1
093 CHR CH (DISC).	3	295	463	0.7	1.4
097 CHR CHS&CHS CR	1	35	43*	0.1	0.1
101 C.M.E.........	2	290	359*	0.5	1.1
123 CH GOD (ANDER)	1	37	111	0.2	0.3
127 CH GOD (CLEVE)	10	947	1 172*	1.7	3.6
151 L-D SAINTS....	1	NA	273	0.4	0.8
165 CH OF NAZARENE	1	181	345	0.5	1.0
167 CHS OF CHRIST.	17	2 337	2 970	4.4	9.0
193 EPISCOPAL.....	1	502	523	0.8	1.6
270 CONSRV JUDAISM	1	32	40*	0.1	0.1
283 LUTH--MO SYNOD	1	148	204	0.3	0.6
356 PRESB CH AMER.	1	138	180	0.3	0.5
357 PRESB CH US...	3	653	808*	1.2	2.4
403 SALVATION ARMY	1	92	210	0.3	0.6
413 S.D.A.	2	185	229*	0.3	0.7
419 SO BAPT CONV..	24	11 921	14 753*	21.7	44.7
421 SO METHODIST..	1	83	121	0.2	0.4
435 UNITARIAN-UNIV	1	19	24*	-	0.1
449 UN METHODIST..	15	5 754	7 121*	10.5	21.6
LUMPKIN	15	2 221	3 042*	28.3	100.0
053 ASSEMB OF GOD.	1	43	111	1.0	3.6
081 CATHOLIC......	1	NA	250	2.3	8.2
127 CH GOD (CLEVE)	1	114	137*	1.3	4.5
151 L-D SAINTS....	1	NA	65	0.6	2.1
167 CHS OF CHRIST.	1	2	2	-	0.1
177 CONGR HOL CH..	1	11	13*	0.1	0.4
357 PRESB CH US...	1	39	47*	0.4	1.5
419 SO BAPT CONV..	6	1 715	2 060*	19.1	67.7
449 UN METHODIST..	2	297	357*	3.3	11.7
MC DUFFIE	27	6 486	8 082*	43.6	100.0
001 ADVENT CHR CH.	1	50	62*	0.3	0.8
081 CATHOLIC......	1	NA	70	0.4	0.9
101 C.M.E.........	3	620	766*	4.1	9.5
127 CH GOD (CLEVE)	2	86	106*	0.6	1.3
167 CHS OF CHRIST.	1	51	65	0.4	0.8
177 CONGR HOL CH..	1	47	58*	0.3	0.7
193 EPISCOPAL.....	1	37	47	0.3	0.6
357 PRESB CH US...	1	223	275*	1.5	3.4
419 SO BAPT CONV..	12	4 037	4 985*	26.9	61.7
449 UN METHODIST..	4	1 335	1 648*	8.9	20.4
MC INTOSH	18	1 939	2 549*	31.7	100.0
053 ASSEMB OF GOD.	1	13	26	0.3	1.0
081 CATHOLIC......	1	NA	35	0.4	1.4
127 CH GOD (CLEVE)	2	188	234*	2.9	9.2
151 L-D SAINTS....	1	NA	86	1.1	3.4
193 EPISCOPAL.....	2	165	218	2.7	8.6
353 CHR BRETHREN.	1	20	20	0.2	0.8
357 PRESB CH US...	2	152	189*	2.3	7.4
419 SO BAPT CONV..	6	1 159	1 440*	17.9	56.5
449 UN METHODIST..	2	242	301*	3.7	11.8
MACON	32	6 140	7 810*	55.8	100.0
061 BEACHY AMISH..	1	190	238*	1.7	3.0
081 CATHOLIC......	1	NA	45	0.3	0.6
101 C.M.E.........	5	1 907	2 384*	17.0	30.5
123 CH GOD (ANDER)	1	50	150	1.1	1.9
127 CH GOD (CLEVE)	2	165	206*	1.5	2.6
167 CHS OF CHRIST.	2	83	106	0.8	1.4
177 CONGR HOL CH..	1	27	34*	0.2	0.4
193 EPISCOPAL.....	1	31	34	0.2	0.4
281 LUTH CH AMER..	1	147	187	1.3	2.4
413 S.D.A.	1	48	60*	0.4	0.8
419 SO BAPT CONV..	10	2 406	3 008*	21.5	38.5
449 UN METHODIST..	6	1 086	1 358*	9.7	17.4
MADISON	38	7 277	8 996*	50.7	100.0
093 CHR CH (DISC).	1	20	31	0.2	0.3
097 CHR CHS&CHS CR	1	75	93*	0.5	1.0
127 CH GOD (CLEVE)	2	209	258*	1.5	2.9
177 CONGR HOL CH..	1	74	91*	0.5	1.0
215 EVAN METH CH..	1	112	138*	0.8	1.5
349 PENT HOLINESS.	1	22	27*	0.2	0.3
357 PRESB CH US...	2	101	125*	0.7	1.4
419 SO BAPT CONV..	22	5 440	6 721*	37.9	74.7
449 UN METHODIST..	7	1 224	1 512*	8.5	16.8

County and Denomination	Number of churches	Communicant, confirmed, full members	Total adherents Number	Percent of total population	Percent of total adherents
MARION	17	1 510	1 873*	35.4	100.0
053 ASSEM OF GOD.	1	12	26	0.5	1.4
127 CH GOD (CLEVE)	1	49	60*	1.1	3.2
167 CHS OF CHRIST.	1	16	19	0.4	1.0
419 SO BAPT CONV..	9	915	1 129*	21.3	60.3
449 UN METHODIST..	5	518	639*	12.1	34.1
MERIWETHER	59	9 621	12 272*	57.8	100.0
053 ASSEMB OF GOD.	1	63	135	0.6	1.1
081 CATHOLIC......	1	NA	75	0.4	0.6
101 C.M.E.........	5	1 694	2 105*	9.9	17.2
127 CH GOD (CLEVE)	5	134	167*	0.8	1.4
165 CH OF NAZARENE	2	134	340	1.6	2.8
167 CHS OF CHRIST.	2	50	60	0.3	0.5
177 CONGR HOL CH..	1	55	68*	0.3	0.6
193 EPISCOPAL.....	1	37	58	0.3	0.5
357 PRESB CH US...	2	116	144*	0.7	1.2
419 SO BAPT CONV..	19	4 869	6 051*	28.5	49.3
443 UN C OF CHRIST	1	122	152*	0.7	1.2
449 UN METHODIST..	19	2 347	2 917*	13.7	23.8
MILLER	15	2 119	2 657*	37.8	100.0
053 ASSEMB OF GOD.	1	28	55	0.8	2.1
127 CH GOD (CLEVE)	2	69	86*	1.2	3.2
167 CHS OF CHRIST.	3	70	90	1.3	3.4
285 MENNONITE CH..	1	25	31*	0.4	1.2
419 SO BAPT CONV..	5	1 216	1 511*	21.5	56.9
449 UN METHODIST..	3	711	884*	12.6	33.3
MITCHELL	36	7 841	10 138*	48.0	100.0
053 ASSEMB OF GOD.	3	188	369	1.7	3.6
081 CATHOLIC......	1	NA	65	0.3	0.6
097 CHR CHS&CHS CR	1	50	63*	0.3	0.6
101 C.M.E.........	1	120	152*	0.7	1.5
167 CHS OF CHRIST.	1	30	38	0.2	0.4
193 EPISCOPAL.....	1	24	28	0.1	0.3
357 PRESB CH US...	2	57	72*	0.3	0.7
419 SO BAPT CONV..	19	6 004	7 616*	36.1	75.1
449 UN METHODIST..	7	1 368	1 735*	8.2	17.1
MONROE	33	4 533	5 595*	38.3	100.0
005 AME ZION......	1	185	260	1.8	4.6
053 ASSEMB OF GOD.	1	16	23	0.2	0.4
081 CATHOLIC......	1	NA	40	0.3	0.7
167 CHS OF CHRIST.	1	23	29	0.2	0.5
177 CONGR HOL CH..	1	19	23*	0.2	0.4
357 PRESB CH US...	1	92	112*	0.8	2.0
419 SO BAPT CONV..	17	2 874	3 497*	23.9	62.5
449 UN METHODIST..	10	1 324	1 611*	11.0	28.8
MONTGOMERY	27	2 819	3 442*	49.1	100.0
001 ADVENT CHR CH.	1	?	?	?	?
127 CH GOD (CLEVE)	4	306	374*	5.3	10.9
357 PRESB CH US...	2	68	83*	1.2	2.4
419 SO BAPT CONV..	11	1 762	2 151*	30.7	62.5
449 UN METHODIST..	9	683	834*	11.9	24.2
MORGAN	25	3 778	4 771*	41.2	100.0
081 CATHOLIC......	1	NA	60	0.5	1.3
097 CHR CHS&CHS CR	1	50	62*	0.5	1.3
127 CH GOD (CLEVE)	1	63	79*	0.7	1.7
167 CHS OF CHRIST.	1	67	85	0.7	1.8
357 PRESB CH US...	1	101	126*	1.1	2.6
413 S.D.A.	1	36	45*	0.4	0.9
419 SO BAPT CONV..	9	2 443	3 045*	26.3	63.8
449 UN METHODIST..	10	1 018	1 269*	11.0	26.6
MURRAY	27	5 235	6 640*	33.7	100.0
127 CH GOD (CLEVE)	5	236	296*	1.5	4.5
167 CHS OF CHRIST.	1	119	151	0.8	2.3
185 CUMBER PRESB..	1	93	192	1.0	2.9
419 SO BAPT CONV..	12	4 090	5 127*	26.0	77.2
449 UN METHODIST..	8	697	874*	4.4	13.2
MUSCOGEE	142	62 190	83 836*	49.3	100.0
005 AME ZION......	1	492	542	0.3	0.6
019 AMER BAPT USA.	2	900	1 096*	0.6	1.3
053 ASSEMB OF GOD.	13	3 157	5 540	3.3	6.6
081 CATHOLIC......	3	NA	5 940	3.5	7.1
089 CHR & MISS AL.	1	46	56	-	0.1
093 CHR CH (DISC).	1	250	273	0.2	0.3
101 C.M.E.........	5	3 969	4 832*	2.8	5.8
123 CH GOD (ANDER)	2	41	123	0.1	0.1
127 CH GOD (CLEVE)	8	797	970*	0.6	1.2
165 CH OF NAZARENE	3	395	620	0.4	0.7
167 CHS OF CHRIST.	10	715	910	0.5	1.1
193 EPISCOPAL.....	3	1 497	1 821	1.1	2.2
263 INT FOURSQ GOS	1	151	184*	0.1	0.2
270 CONSRV JUDAISM	1	144	175*	0.1	0.2
281 LUTH CH AMER..	1	357	434	0.3	0.5
283 LUTH--MO SYNOD	3	615	858	0.5	1.0
356 PRESB CH AMER.	1	54	74	-	0.1
357 PRESB CH US...	8	2 021	2 460*	1.4	2.9
403 SALVATION ARMY	1	167	417	0.2	0.5
413 S.D.A.	2	756	920*	0.5	1.1
419 SO BAPT CONV..	45	32 131	39 114*	23.0	46.7

NA—Not applicable   *Total adherents estimated from known number of communicant, confirmed, full members.   —Represents a percent less than 0.1.   Percentages may not total due to rounding.

Table 4. Churches and Church Membership by County and Denomination: 1980

County and Denomination	Number of churches	Communicant, confirmed, full members	Total adherents Number	Percent of total population	Percent of total adherents
443 UN C OF CHRIST	2	100	122*	0.1	0.1
449 UN METHODIST..	24	13 393	16 304*	9.6	19.4
453 UN PRES CH USA	1	42	51*	–	0.1
NEWTON	59	13 560	17 323*	50.2	100.0
053 ASSEMB OF GOD.	1	57	62	0.2	0.4
055 AS REF PRES CH	1	104	104	0.3	0.6
065 BETHEL M ASSN.	1	65	81*	0.2	0.5
081 CATHOLIC......	1	NA	500	1.4	2.9
097 CHR CHS&CHS CR	1	223	276*	0.8	1.6
101 C.M.E........	2	537	666*	1.9	3.8
127 CH GOD (CLEVE)	1	24	30*	0.1	0.2
165 CH OF NAZARENE	1	69	144	0.4	0.8
167 CHS OF CHRIST.	2	77	93	0.3	0.5
193 EPISCOPAL.....	1	136	158	0.5	0.9
357 PRESB CH US...	6	549	681*	2.0	3.9
413 S.D.A.........	1	57	71*	0.2	0.4
419 SO BAPT CONV..	15	6 655	8 250*	23.9	47.6
449 UN METHODIST..	25	5 007	6 207*	18.0	35.8
OCONEE	25	4 259	5 404*	43.5	100.0
093 CHR CH (DISC).	6	611	896	7.2	16.6
167 CHS OF CHRIST.	1	78	99	0.8	1.8
177 CONGR HOL CH..	1	5	6*	–	0.1
357 PRESB CH US...	1	192	237*	1.9	4.4
419 SO BAPT CONV..	8	2 557	3 158*	25.4	58.4
449 UN METHODIST..	8	816	1 008*	8.1	18.7
OGLETHORPE	30	2 769	3 427*	38.4	100.0
005 AME ZION......	1	125	150	1.7	4.4
093 CHR CH (DISC).	1	50	77	0.9	2.2
177 CONGR HOL CH..	3	41	51*	0.6	1.5
357 PRESB CH US...	1	13	16*	0.2	0.5
419 SO BAPT CONV..	15	1 903	2 347*	26.3	68.5
449 UN METHODIST..	9	637	786*	8.8	22.9
PAULDING	42	8 942	11 183*	42.9	100.0
053 ASSEMB OF GOD.	1	121	156	0.6	1.4
097 CHR CHS&CHS CR	1	250	313*	1.2	2.8
127 CH GOD (CLEVE)	2	66	83*	0.3	0.7
167 CHS OF CHRIST.	1	45	47	0.2	0.4
419 SO BAPT CONV..	25	7 208	9 018*	34.6	80.6
449 UN METHODIST..	12	1 252	1 566*	6.0	14.0
PEACH	22	6 192	7 840*	40.9	100.0
053 ASSEMB OF GOD.	1	44	78	0.4	1.0
081 CATHOLIC......	1	NA	160	0.8	2.0
101 C.M.E........	3	2 147	2 656*	13.9	33.9
127 CH GOD (CLEVE)	1	34	42*	0.2	0.5
151 L-D SAINTS....	1	NA	56	0.3	0.7
165 CH OF NAZARENE	1	144	168	0.9	2.1
167 CHS OF CHRIST.	2	44	56	0.3	0.7
193 EPISCOPAL.....	2	177	168	0.9	2.1
357 PRESB CH US...	1	149	184*	1.0	2.3
413 S.D.A.........	1	11	14*	0.1	0.2
419 SO BAPT CONV..	4	2 024	2 504*	13.1	31.9
449 UN METHODIST..	4	1 418	1 754*	9.2	22.4
PICKENS	18	2 873	3 516*	30.2	100.0
053 ASSEMB OF GOD.	1	74	104	0.9	3.0
097 CHR CHS&CHS CR	1	70	85*	0.7	2.4
127 CH GOD (CLEVE)	2	111	135*	1.2	3.8
167 CHS OF CHRIST.	4	130	170	1.5	4.8
357 PRESB CH US...	1	53	64*	0.5	1.8
419 SO BAPT CONV..	6	2 015	2 448*	21.0	69.6
449 UN METHODIST..	3	420	510*	4.4	14.5
PIERCE	28	5 467	6 826*	57.4	100.0
127 CH GOD (CLEVE)	2	266	332*	2.8	4.9
167 CHS OF CHRIST.	1	14	21	0.2	0.3
357 PRESB CH US...	1	151	188*	1.6	2.8
419 SO BAPT CONV..	17	4 252	5 307*	44.6	77.7
449 UN METHODIST..	7	784	978*	8.2	14.3
PIKE	34	4 718	5 874*	65.7	100.0
053 ASSEMB OF GOD.	1	18	35	0.4	0.6
093 CHR CH (DISC).	1	26	40	0.4	0.7
097 CHR CHS&CHS CR	1	50	61*	0.7	1.0
101 C.M.E........	2	817	1 002*	11.2	17.1
165 CH OF NAZARENE	2	108	197	2.2	3.4
167 CHS OF CHRIST.	1	3	4	–	0.1
357 PRESB CH US...	1	47	58*	0.6	1.0
419 SO BAPT CONV..	15	2 884	3 538*	39.6	60.2
449 UN METHODIST..	10	765	939*	10.5	16.0
POLK	57	15 476	19 382*	59.8	100.0
053 ASSEMB OF GOD.	1	35	78	0.2	0.4
081 CATHOLIC......	1	NA	325	1.0	1.7
097 CHR CHS&CHS CR	1	50	61*	0.2	0.3
127 CH GOD (CLEVE)	3	322	392*	1.2	2.0
151 L-D SAINTS....	1	NA	115	0.4	0.6
167 CHS OF CHRIST.	3	252	375	1.2	1.9
177 CONGR HOL CH..	1	62	76*	0.2	0.4
193 EPISCOPAL.....	1	79	79	0.2	0.4
357 PRESB CH US...	2	390	475*	1.5	2.5
413 S.D.A.........	1	31	38*	0.1	0.2
419 SO BAPT CONV..	34	12 628	15 386*	47.5	79.4
449 UN METHODIST..	8	1 627	1 982*	6.1	10.2
PULASKI	17	4 619	5 673*	63.4	100.0
101 C.M.E........	2	187	230*	2.6	4.1
167 CHS OF CHRIST.	1	12	15	0.2	0.3
193 EPISCOPAL.....	1	66	79	0.9	1.4
349 PENT HOLINESS.	1	45	55*	0.6	1.0
419 SO BAPT CONV..	11	3 776	4 639*	51.8	81.8
449 UN METHODIST..	1	533	655*	7.3	11.5
PUTNAM	17	2 307	2 952*	28.7	100.0
123 CH GOD (ANDER)	1	45	135	1.3	4.6
127 CH GOD (CLEVE)	1	22	27*	0.3	0.9
167 CHS OF CHRIST.	1	200	300	2.9	10.2
349 PENT HOLINESS.	1	29	35*	0.3	1.2
357 PRESB CH US...	1	36	44*	0.4	1.5
419 SO BAPT CONV..	3	1 032	1 260*	12.2	42.7
449 UN METHODIST..	9	943	1 151*	11.2	39.0
QUITMAN	5	677	837*	35.5	100.0
419 SO BAPT CONV..	3	499	617*	26.2	73.7
449 UN METHODIST..	2	178	220*	9.3	26.3
RABUN	43	4 814	5 784*	55.3	100.0
081 CATHOLIC......	1	NA	42	0.4	0.7
127 CH GOD (CLEVE)	4	233	279*	2.7	4.8
167 CHS OF CHRIST.	1	25	30	0.3	0.5
193 EPISCOPAL.....	1	76	76	0.7	1.3
357 PRESB CH US...	6	249	298*	2.8	5.2
419 SO BAPT CONV..	23	3 515	4 203*	40.2	72.7
449 UN METHODIST..	7	716	856*	8.2	14.8
RANDOLPH	31	3 276	4 055*	42.2	100.0
053 ASSEMB OF GOD.	1	22	49	0.5	1.2
061 BEACHY AMISH..	1	10	12*	0.1	0.3
081 CATHOLIC......	1	NA	10	0.1	0.2
127 CH GOD (CLEVE)	1	47	58*	0.6	1.4
167 CHS OF CHRIST.	2	21	26	0.3	0.6
357 PRESB CH US...	1	101	124*	1.3	3.1
419 SO BAPT CONV..	14	2 383	2 926*	30.5	72.2
449 UN METHODIST..	10	692	850*	8.9	21.0
RICHMOND	137	62 623	86 234*	47.5	100.0
001 ADVENT CHR CH.	2	410	497*	0.3	0.6
005 AME ZION......	2	1 144	1 294	0.7	1.5
019 AMER BAPT USA.	2	650	788*	0.4	0.9
053 ASSEMB OF GOD.	3	179	362	0.2	0.4
055 AS REF PRES CH	1	76	80	–	0.1
081 CATHOLIC......	5	NA	8 175	4.5	9.5
089 CHR & MISS AL.	1	103	149	0.1	0.2
093 CHR CH (DISC).	3	753	1 119	0.6	1.3
097 CHR CHS&CHS CR	2	296	359*	0.2	0.4
101 C.M.E........	5	3 451	4 183*	2.3	4.9
123 CH GOD (ANDER)	1	50	150	0.1	0.2
127 CH GOD (CLEVE)	7	1 038	1 258*	0.7	1.5
151 L-D SAINTS....	1	NA	1 042	0.6	1.2
165 CH OF NAZARENE	1	202	655	0.4	0.8
167 CHS OF CHRIST.	3	410	508	0.3	0.6
193 EPISCOPAL.....	6	2 979	3 690*	2.0	4.3
226 FRIENDS-USA...	1	18	22*	–	–
263 INT FOURSQ GOS	1	148	179*	0.1	0.2
271 REFORM JUDAISM	1	288	349*	0.2	0.4
281 LUTH CH AMER..	3	1 439	1 898*	1.0	2.2
283 LUTH--MO SYNOD	1	424	547	0.3	0.6
285 MENNONITE CH..	1	38	46*	–	0.1
290 METRO COMM CHS	0	10	20	–	–
349 PENT HOLINESS.	1	213	258*	0.1	0.3
353 CHR BRETHREN..	4	360	500	0.3	0.6
356 PRESB CH AMER.	1	918	1 088	0.6	1.3
357 PRESB CH US...	6	2 302	2 790*	1.5	3.2
403 SALVATION ARMY	1	209	281	0.2	0.3
413 S.D.A.........	2	674	817*	0.4	0.9
419 SO BAPT CONV..	39	33 013	40 013*	22.0	46.4
421 SO METHODIST..	2	234	265	0.1	0.3
435 UNITARIAN-UNIV	1	151	183*	0.1	0.2
449 UN METHODIST..	23	10 193	12 354*	6.8	14.3
453 UN PRES CH USA	2	229	278*	0.2	0.3
469 WELS.........	1	21	37	–	–
ROCKDALE	32	9 292	13 189*	35.9	100.0
053 ASSEMB OF GOD.	2	69	140	0.4	1.1
081 CATHOLIC......	1	NA	1 000	2.7	7.6
089 CHR & MISS AL.	1	58	103	0.3	0.8
097 CHR CHS&CHS CR	3	507	634*	1.7	4.8
101 C.M.E........	1	225	281*	0.8	2.1
127 CH GOD (CLEVE)	2	229	286*	0.8	2.2
151 L-D SAINTS....	1	NA	450	1.2	3.4
167 CHS OF CHRIST.	1	148	188	0.5	1.4
193 EPISCOPAL.....	1	160	202	0.5	1.5
281 LUTH CH AMER..	1	116	153	0.4	1.2
283 LUTH--MO SYNOD	1	116	164	0.4	1.2
357 PRESB CH US...	3	1 019	1 275*	3.5	9.7
419 SO BAPT CONV..	8	4 323	5 408*	14.7	41.0
449 UN METHODIST..	6	2 322	2 905*	7.9	22.0
SCHLEY	8	1 183	1 492*	43.5	100.0

NA— Not applicable
*Total adherents estimated from known number of communicant, confirmed, full members.
—Represents a percent less than 0.1.
Percentages may not total due to rounding.

Table 4. Churches and Church Membership by County and Denomination: 1980

County and Denomination	Number of churches	Communicant, confirmed, full members	Total adherents		
			Number	Percent of total population	Percent of total adherents
127 CH GOD (CLEVE)	1	17	21*	0.6	1.4
419 SO BAPT CONV..	2	532	671*	19.5	45.0
449 UN METHODIST..	5	634	800*	23.3	53.6
SCREVEN	54	7 250	9 090*	64.7	100.0
053 ASSEMB OF GOD.	1	7	14	0.1	0.2
081 CATHOLIC......	1	NA	75	0.5	0.8
093 CHR CH (DISC).	2	68	95	0.7	1.0
097 CHR CHS&CHS CR	2	163	201*	1.4	2.2
101 C.M.E.........	1	252	311*	2.2	3.4
123 CH GOD (ANDER)	2	39	117	0.8	1.3
127 CH GOD (CLEVE)	1	19	23*	0.2	0.3
167 CHS OF CHRIST.	1	25	30	0.2	0.3
263 INT FOURSQ GOS	1	36	44*	0.3	0.5
356 PRESB CH AMER.	1	72	79	0.6	0.9
419 SO BAPT CONV..	19	3 568	4 400*	31.3	48.4
449 UN METHODIST..	22	3 001	3 701*	26.4	40.7
SEMINOLE	18	2 559	3 210*	35.4	100.0
053 ASSEMB OF GOD.	2	49	59	0.7	1.8
081 CATHOLIC......	1	NA	30	0.3	0.9
127 CH GOD (CLEVE)	4	289	358*	4.0	11.2
165 CH OF NAZARENE	1	45	64	0.7	2.0
167 CHS OF CHRIST.	1	64	81	0.9	2.5
357 PRESB CH US...	1	162	201*	2.2	6.3
419 SO BAPT CONV..	4	1 377	1 707*	18.8	53.2
449 UN METHODIST..	4	573	710*	7.8	22.1
SPALDING	79	21 217	27 693*	57.8	100.0
019 AMER BAPT USA.	1	525	650*	1.4	2.3
053 ASSEMB OF GOD.	5	960	1 684	3.5	6.1
081 CATHOLIC......	1	NA	300	0.6	1.1
089 CHR & MISS AL.	1	0	31	0.1	0.1
093 CHR CH (DISC).	3	288	452	0.9	1.6
097 CHR CHS&CHS CR	1	100	124*	0.3	0.4
101 C.M.E.........	1	312	386*	0.8	1.4
127 CH GOD (CLEVE)	3	797	986*	2.1	3.6
151 L-D SAINTS....	1	NA	276	0.6	1.0
165 CH OF NAZARENE	1	81	128	0.3	0.5
167 CHS OF CHRIST.	2	165	191	0.4	0.7
177 CONGR HOL CH..	5	239	296*	0.6	1.1
193 EPISCOPAL.....	2	436	647	1.4	2.3
281 LUTH CH AMER..	1	139	199	0.4	0.7
349 PENT HOLINESS.	1	30	37*	0.1	0.1
357 PRESB CH US...	1	488	604*	1.3	2.2
403 SALVATION ARMY	1	121	241	0.5	0.9
413 S.D.A.........	2	95	118*	0.2	0.4
419 SO BAPT CONV..	27	12 395	15 337*	32.0	55.4
449 UN METHODIST..	19	4 046	5 006*	10.5	18.1
STEPHENS	52	11 881	15 494*	71.2	100.0
017 AMER BAPT ASSN	1	30	30	0.1	0.2
053 ASSEMB OF GOD.	2	90	202	0.9	1.3
081 CATHOLIC......	1	NA	271	1.2	1.7
089 CHR & MISS AL.	2	246	661	3.0	4.3
097 CHR CHS&CHS CR	1	40	49*	0.2	0.3
101 C.M.E.........	2	910	1 105*	5.1	7.1
123 CH GOD (ANDER)	1	78	234	1.1	1.5
127 CH GOD (CLEVE)	4	252	306*	1.4	2.0
151 L-D SAINTS....	1	NA	110	0.5	0.7
165 CH OF NAZARENE	1	26	71	0.3	0.5
167 CHS OF CHRIST.	1	45	50	0.2	0.3
177 CONGR HOL CH..	2	39	47*	0.2	0.3
193 EPISCOPAL.....	1	86	86	0.4	0.6
283 LUTH--MO SYNOD	1	53	75	0.3	0.5
349 PENT HOLINESS.	1	114	138*	0.6	0.9
357 PRESB CH US...	1	309	375*	1.7	2.4
403 SALVATION ARMY	1	65	153	0.7	1.0
413 S.D.A.........	1	20	24*	0.1	0.2
419 SO BAPT CONV..	21	8 316	10 096*	46.4	65.2
449 UN METHODIST..	6	1 162	1 411*	6.5	9.1
STEWART	22	2 706	3 355*	56.9	100.0
053 ASSEMB OF GOD.	1	7	17	0.3	0.5
101 C.M.E.........	3	1 182	1 462*	24.8	43.6
127 CH GOD (CLEVE)	1	26	32*	0.5	1.0
167 CHS OF CHRIST.	1	11	14	0.2	0.4
419 SO BAPT CONV..	9	982	1 214*	20.6	36.2
443 UN C OF CHRIST	1	12	15*	0.3	0.4
449 UN METHODIST..	6	486	601*	10.2	17.9
SUMTER	46	9 814	12 864*	43.8	100.0
053 ASSEMB OF GOD.	2	135	185	0.6	1.4
081 CATHOLIC......	1	NA	360	1.2	2.8
127 CH GOD (CLEVE)	3	62	77*	0.3	0.6
151 L-D SAINTS....	1	NA	218	0.7	1.7
167 CHS OF CHRIST.	2	88	100	0.3	0.8
193 EPISCOPAL.....	1	199	386	1.3	3.0
281 LUTH CH AMER..	1	71	87	0.3	0.7
357 PRESB CH US...	2	300	371*	1.3	2.9
413 S.D.A.........	2	136	168*	0.6	1.3
419 SO BAPT CONV..	19	5 953	7 363*	25.1	57.2
421 SO METHODIST..	1	35	42	0.1	0.3
449 UN METHODIST..	11	2 835	3 507*	11.9	27.3
TALBOT	21	2 100	2 585*	39.6	100.0
101 C.M.E.........	2	705	867*	13.3	33.5
167 CHS OF CHRIST.	1	8	13	0.2	0.5

County and Denomination	Number of churches	Communicant, confirmed, full members	Total adherents		
			Number	Percent of total population	Percent of total adherents
357 PRESB CH US...	1	10	12*	0.2	0.5
419 SO BAPT CONV..	6	770	947*	14.5	36.6
449 UN METHODIST..	11	607	746*	11.4	28.9
TALIAFERRO	15	970	1 234*	60.7	100.0
081 CATHOLIC......	1	NA	70	3.4	5.7
101 C.M.E.........	1	130	156*	7.7	12.6
357 PRESB CH US...	2	29	35*	1.7	2.8
419 SO BAPT CONV..	7	650	780*	38.4	63.2
449 UN METHODIST..	4	161	193*	9.5	15.6
TATTNALL	41	5 549	7 045*	38.8	100.0
017 AMER BAPT ASSN	1	50	50	0.3	0.7
053 ASSEMB OF GOD.	1	45	70	0.4	1.0
081 CATHOLIC......	2	NA	120	0.7	1.7
093 CHR CH (DISC).	1	269	357	2.0	5.1
123 CH GOD (ANDER)	2	45	135	0.7	1.9
127 CH GOD (CLEVE)	5	160	194*	1.1	2.8
151 L-D SAINTS....	1	NA	94	0.5	1.3
167 CHS OF CHRIST.	2	19	25	0.1	0.4
349 PENT HOLINESS.	1	37	45*	0.2	0.6
419 SO BAPT CONV..	15	3 496	4 228*	23.3	60.0
449 UN METHODIST..	10	1 428	1 727*	9.5	24.5
TAYLOR	20	2 316	2 867*	36.3	100.0
127 CH GOD (CLEVE)	1	39	48*	0.6	1.7
165 CH OF NAZARENE	1	42	79	1.0	2.8
419 SO BAPT CONV..	9	1 349	1 654*	20.9	57.7
449 UN METHODIST..	9	886	1 086*	13.7	37.9
TELFAIR	45	6 527	8 122*	71.0	100.0
081 CATHOLIC......	1	NA	50	0.4	0.6
101 C.M.E.........	3	1 542	1 900*	16.6	23.4
123 CH GOD (ANDER)	1	17	51	0.4	0.6
127 CH GOD (CLEVE)	6	249	307*	2.7	3.8
167 CHS OF CHRIST.	1	15	18	0.2	0.2
177 CONGR HOL CH..	1	16	20*	0.2	0.2
357 PRESB CH US...	1	90	111*	1.0	1.4
419 SO BAPT CONV..	17	3 060	3 770*	32.9	46.4
449 UN METHODIST..	14	1 538	1 895*	16.6	23.3
TERRELL	25	3 579	4 552*	37.9	100.0
053 ASSEMB OF GOD.	1	89	187	1.6	4.1
101 C.M.E.........	1	207	258*	2.1	5.7
127 CH GOD (CLEVE)	1	38	47*	0.4	1.0
167 CHS OF CHRIST.	1	48	61	0.5	1.3
193 EPISCOPAL.....	1	61	89	0.7	2.0
357 PRESB CH US...	1	99	123*	1.0	2.7
419 SO BAPT CONV..	11	2 134	2 661*	22.1	58.5
449 UN METHODIST..	8	903	1 126*	9.4	24.7
THOMAS	76	16 343	21 072*	55.3	100.0
053 ASSEMB OF GOD.	2	139	199	0.5	0.9
081 CATHOLIC......	1	NA	400	1.0	1.9
093 CHR CH (DISC).	1	21	32	0.1	0.2
101 C.M.E.........	6	1 671	2 057*	5.4	9.8
127 CH GOD (CLEVE)	11	608	748*	2.0	3.5
151 L-D SAINTS....	1	NA	217	0.6	1.0
165 CH OF NAZARENE	1	139	149	0.4	0.7
167 CHS OF CHRIST.	4	150	176	0.5	0.8
193 EPISCOPAL.....	2	300	621	1.6	2.9
349 PENT HOLINESS.	1	102	126*	0.3	0.6
357 PRESB CH US...	5	812	999*	2.6	4.7
403 SALVATION ARMY	1	60	158	0.4	0.7
413 S.D.A.........	1	67	82*	0.2	0.4
419 SO BAPT CONV..	23	9 257	11 394*	29.9	54.1
443 UN C OF CHRIST	2	107	132*	0.3	0.6
449 UN METHODIST..	14	2 910	3 582*	9.4	17.0
TIFT	51	13 367	17 122*	52.1	100.0
017 AMER BAPT ASSN	2	150	150	0.5	0.9
053 ASSEMB OF GOD.	1	319	519	1.6	3.0
081 CATHOLIC......	1	NA	150	0.5	0.9
097 CHR CHS&CHS CR	2	200	248*	0.8	1.4
101 C.M.E.........	1	270	335*	1.0	2.0
127 CH GOD (CLEVE)	5	522	647*	2.0	3.8
151 L-D SAINTS....	1	NA	331	1.0	1.9
165 CH OF NAZARENE	1	160	174	0.5	1.0
167 CHS OF CHRIST.	2	79	91	0.3	0.5
193 EPISCOPAL.....	1	177	224	0.7	1.3
283 LUTH--MO SYNOD	1	109	134	0.4	0.8
357 PRESB CH US...	1	237	294*	0.9	1.7
413 S.D.A.........	1	24	30*	0.1	0.2
419 SO BAPT CONV..	20	8 670	10 751*	32.7	62.8
421 SO METHODIST..	1	23	35	0.1	0.2
449 UN METHODIST..	10	2 427	3 009*	9.2	17.6
TOOMBS	48	9 435	12 354*	54.7	100.0
053 ASSEMB OF GOD.	2	152	248	1.1	2.0
081 CATHOLIC......	1	NA	240	1.1	1.9
097 CHR CHS&CHS CR	1	312	389*	1.7	3.1
127 CH GOD (CLEVE)	4	155	193*	0.9	1.6
151 L-D SAINTS....	1	NA	238	1.1	1.9
165 CH OF NAZARENE	1	45	66	0.3	0.5
167 CHS OF CHRIST.	1	20	50	0.2	0.4
193 EPISCOPAL.....	1	92	131	0.6	1.1
357 PRESB CH US...	2	299	373*	1.7	3.0

NA—Not applicable   *Total adherents estimated from known number of communicant, confirmed, full members.   —Represents a percent less than 0.1.   Percentages may not total due to rounding.

Table 4. Churches and Church Membership by County and Denomination: 1980

County and Denomination	Number of churches	Communicant, confirmed, full members	Total adherents Number	Percent of total population	Percent of total adherents
419 SO BAPT CONV..	22	5 968	7 443*	32.9	60.2
449 UN METHODIST..	12	2 392	2 983*	13.2	24.1
TOWNS	19	3 426	3 966*	70.3	100.0
127 CH GOD (CLEVE)	2	56	65*	1.2	1.6
419 SO BAPT CONV..	14	2 989	3 460*	61.4	87.2
449 UN METHODIST..	3	381	441*	7.8	11.1
TREUTLEN	14	1 648	2 079*	34.2	100.0
001 ADVENT CHR CH.	2	163	204*	3.4	9.8
053 ASSEMB OF GOD.	1	22	33	0.5	1.6
127 CH GOD (CLEVE)	1	49	61*	1.0	2.9
165 CH OF NAZARENE	1	7	24	0.4	1.2
419 SO BAPT CONV..	6	1 057	1 320*	21.7	63.5
449 UN METHODIST..	3	350	437*	7.2	21.0
TROUP	112	24 857	31 717*	63.4	100.0
053 ASSEMB OF GOD.	2	253	510	1.0	1.6
081 CATHOLIC......	1	NA	565	1.1	1.8
097 CHR CHS&CHS CR	2	130	159*	0.3	0.5
101 C.M.E.........	4	2 524	3 096*	6.2	9.8
123 CH GOD (ANDER)	1	70	210	0.4	0.7
127 CH GOD (CLEVE)	7	514	631*	1.3	2.0
151 L-D SAINTS....	1	NA	130	0.3	0.4
165 CH OF NAZARENE	1	28	44	0.1	0.1
167 CHS OF CHRIST.	7	400	510	1.0	1.6
177 CONGR HOL CH..	1	30	37*	0.1	0.1
193 EPISCOPAL.....	2	321	569	1.1	1.8
349 PENT HOLINESS.	1	53	65*	0.1	0.2
357 PRESB CH US...	7	1 128	1 384*	2.8	4.4
413 S.D.A.........	2	104	128*	0.3	0.4
419 SO BAPT CONV..	34	12 729	15 616*	31.2	49.2
443 UN C OF CHRIST	3	525	644*	1.3	2.0
449 UN METHODIST..	36	6 048	7 419*	14.8	23.4
TURNER	22	4 318	5 479*	57.6	100.0
053 ASSEMB OF GOD.	1	52	86	0.9	1.6
127 CH GOD (CLEVE)	2	29	37*	0.4	0.7
167 CHS OF CHRIST.	1	54	61	0.6	1.1
419 SO BAPT CONV..	14	3 462	4 382*	46.1	80.0
449 UN METHODIST..	4	721	913*	9.6	16.7
TWIGGS	18	3 711	4 625*	49.4	100.0
017 AMER BAPT ASSN	2	130	130	1.4	2.8
053 ASSEMB OF GOD.	1	62	104	1.1	2.2
101 C.M.E.........	1	1 152	1 437*	15.4	31.1
127 CH GOD (CLEVE)	1	42	52*	0.6	1.1
419 SO BAPT CONV..	7	1 883	2 350*	25.1	50.8
449 UN METHODIST..	6	442	552*	5.9	11.9
UNION	34	4 872	5 991*	63.8	100.0
081 CATHOLIC......	1	NA	50	0.5	0.8
127 CH GOD (CLEVE)	3	133	160*	1.7	2.7
165 CH OF NAZARENE	1	65	154	1.6	2.6
167 CHS OF CHRIST.	1	50	59	0.6	1.0
419 SO BAPT CONV..	21	4 117	4 957*	52.8	82.7
449 UN METHODIST..	7	507	611*	6.5	10.2
UPSON	43	11 570	14 118*	54.3	100.0
053 ASSEMB OF GOD.	1	93	151	0.6	1.1
081 CATHOLIC......	1	NA	40	0.2	0.3
101 C.M.E.........	1	780	944*	3.6	6.7
127 CH GOD (CLEVE)	1	349	422*	1.6	3.0
165 CH OF NAZARENE	2	29	69	0.3	0.5
167 CHS OF CHRIST.	2	85	108	0.4	0.8
177 CONGR HOL CH..	1	30	36*	0.1	0.3
349 PENT HOLINESS.	1	28	34*	0.1	0.2
357 PRESB CH US...	1	333	403*	1.6	2.9
413 S.D.A.........	1	54	65*	0.3	0.5
419 SO BAPT CONV..	24	7 838	9 485*	36.5	67.2
449 UN METHODIST..	7	1 951	2 361*	9.1	16.7
WALKER	112	23 153	29 345*	52.0	100.0
005 AME ZION......	4	284	376	0.7	1.3
053 ASSEMB OF GOD.	2	219	374	0.7	1.3
081 CATHOLIC......	1	NA	400	0.7	1.4
123 CH GOD (ANDER)	3	121	363	0.7	1.2
127 CH GOD (CLEVE)	8	995	1 218*	2.2	4.2
165 CH OF NAZARENE	6	539	792	1.4	2.7
167 CHS OF CHRIST.	8	1 192	1 565	2.8	5.3
215 EVAN METH CH..	1	65	80*	0.1	0.3
281 LUTH CH AMER..	1	77	108	0.2	0.4
357 PRESB CH US...	3	344	421*	0.7	1.4
413 S.D.A.........	2	148	181*	0.3	0.6
419 SO BAPT CONV..	53	16 141	19 760*	35.0	67.3
449 UN METHODIST..	20	3 028	3 707*	6.6	12.6
WALTON	54	9 610	12 475*	40.0	100.0
005 AME ZION......	6	778	1 028	3.3	8.2
053 ASSEMB OF GOD.	2	23	47	0.2	0.4
081 CATHOLIC......	1	NA	175	0.6	1.4
093 CHR CH (DISC).	4	443	777	2.5	6.2
127 CH GOD (CLEVE)	2	405	505*	1.6	4.0
167 CHS OF CHRIST.	3	100	127	0.4	1.0
177 CONGR HOL CH..	3	150	187*	0.6	1.5
193 EPISCOPAL.....	1	101	132	0.4	1.1
349 PENT HOLINESS.	1	74	92*	0.3	0.7
357 PRESB CH US...	1	107	134*	0.4	1.1
419 SO BAPT CONV..	19	5 303	6 618*	21.2	53.1
449 UN METHODIST..	11	2 126	2 653*	8.5	21.3
WARE	58	14 045	18 624*	50.1	100.0
001 ADVENT CHR CH.	2	243	300*	0.8	1.6
053 ASSEMB OF GOD.	2	127	216	0.6	1.2
081 CATHOLIC......	1	NA	500	1.3	2.7
093 CHR CH (DISC).	1	355	407	1.1	2.2
101 C.M.E.........	1	202	250*	0.7	1.3
127 CH GOD (CLEVE)	7	531	656*	1.8	3.5
151 L-D SAINTS....	1	NA	681	1.8	3.7
165 CH OF NAZARENE	1	113	191	0.5	1.0
167 CHS OF CHRIST.	3	100	127	0.3	0.7
283 LUTH--MO SYNOD	1	18	23	0.1	0.1
349 PENT HOLINESS.	2	160	198*	0.5	1.1
357 PRESB CH US...	1	336	415*	1.1	2.2
403 SALVATION ARMY	1	113	142	0.4	0.8
413 S.D.A.........	1	95	117*	0.3	0.6
419 SO BAPT CONV..	20	7 913	9 780*	26.3	52.5
449 UN METHODIST..	12	3 679	4 547*	12.2	24.4
WARREN	18	3 252	4 006*	60.9	100.0
101 C.M.E.........	2	1 372	1 690*	25.7	42.2
419 SO BAPT CONV..	8	1 207	1 487*	22.6	37.1
449 UN METHODIST..	8	673	829*	12.6	20.7
WASHINGTON	54	7 557	9 649*	51.2	100.0
053 ASSEMB OF GOD.	1	12	28	0.1	0.3
081 CATHOLIC......	1	NA	30	0.2	0.3
093 CHR CH (DISC).	3	133	183	1.0	1.9
097 CHR CHS&CHS CR	3	265	327*	1.7	3.4
101 C.M.E.........	1	407	502*	2.7	5.2
123 CH GOD (ANDER)	1	15	45	0.2	0.5
127 CH GOD (CLEVE)	4	117	144*	0.8	1.5
165 CH OF NAZARENE	1	282	571	3.0	5.9
167 CHS OF CHRIST.	2	101	139	0.7	1.4
357 PRESB CH US...	1	21	26*	0.1	0.3
419 SO BAPT CONV..	23	4 410	5 441*	28.9	56.4
421 SO METHODIST..	1	29	36	0.2	0.4
449 UN METHODIST..	12	1 765	2 177*	11.6	22.6
WAYNE	54	8 923	11 511*	55.5	100.0
053 ASSEMB OF GOD.	1	97	112	0.5	1.0
081 CATHOLIC......	1	NA	242	1.2	2.1
097 CHR CHS&CHS CR	1	40	49*	0.2	0.4
123 CH GOD (ANDER)	1	60	180	0.9	1.6
127 CH GOD (CLEVE)	15	1 539	1 903*	9.2	16.5
151 L-D SAINTS....	1	NA	162	0.8	1.4
167 CHS OF CHRIST.	2	68	87	0.4	0.8
193 EPISCOPAL.....	1	254	288	1.4	2.5
357 PRESB CH US...	2	46	57*	0.3	0.5
419 SO BAPT CONV..	21	5 488	6 785*	32.7	58.9
449 UN METHODIST..	8	1 331	1 646*	7.9	14.3
WEBSTER	9	1 121	1 398*	59.7	100.0
357 PRESB CH US...	1	13	16*	0.7	1.1
419 SO BAPT CONV..	5	901	1 124*	48.0	80.4
449 UN METHODIST..	3	207	258*	11.0	18.5
WHEELER	22	2 311	2 959*	57.4	100.0
123 CH GOD (ANDER)	2	42	126	2.4	4.3
127 CH GOD (CLEVE)	4	165	206*	4.0	7.0
419 SO BAPT CONV..	8	1 227	1 532*	29.7	51.8
449 UN METHODIST..	8	877	1 095*	21.2	37.0
WHITE	31	3 634	4 412*	43.6	100.0
081 CATHOLIC......	1	NA	50	0.5	1.1
127 CH GOD (CLEVE)	1	13	16*	0.2	0.4
167 CHS OF CHRIST.	1	28	36	0.4	0.8
177 CONGR HOL CH..	4	292	350*	3.5	7.9
357 PRESB CH US...	2	117	140*	1.4	3.2
413 S.D.A.........	1	99	119*	1.2	2.7
419 SO BAPT CONV..	12	2 233	2 679*	26.5	60.7
449 UN METHODIST..	9	852	1 022*	10.1	23.2
WHITFIELD	88	24 258	30 995*	47.1	100.0
053 ASSEMB OF GOD.	1	102	234	0.4	0.8
081 CATHOLIC......	1	NA	780	1.2	2.5
097 CHR CHS&CHS CR	1	79	98*	0.1	0.3
127 CH GOD (CLEVE)	8	1 187	1 469*	2.2	4.7
151 L-D SAINTS....	1	NA	110	0.2	0.4
165 CH OF NAZARENE	2	144	184	0.3	0.6
167 CHS OF CHRIST.	5	659	839	1.3	2.7
193 EPISCOPAL.....	1	393	393	0.6	1.3
215 EVAN METH CH..	1	64	79*	0.1	0.3
270 CONSRV JUDAISM	1	54	67*	0.1	0.2
357 PRESB CH US...	2	881	1 091*	1.7	3.5
403 SALVATION ARMY	1	60	109	0.2	0.4
413 S.D.A.........	2	269	333*	0.5	1.1
419 SO BAPT CONV..	41	16 106	19 936*	30.3	64.3
449 UN METHODIST..	19	4 246	5 256*	8.0	17.0
453 UN PRES CH USA	1	14	17*	—	0.1
WILCOX	34	4 357	5 338*	69.5	100.0

NA— Not applicable   *Total adherents estimated from known number of communicant, confirmed, full members.   —Represents a percent less than 0.1.   Percentages may not total due to rounding.

Table 4. Churches and Church Membership by County and Denomination: 1980

County and Denomination	Number of churches	Communicant, confirmed, full members	Total adherents Number	Percent of total population	Percent of total adherents
101 C.M.E.........	2	157	192*	2.5	3.6
127 CH GOD (CLEVE)	3	107	131*	1.7	2.5
419 SO BAPT CONV..	22	3 535	4 331*	56.4	81.1
449 UN METHODIST..	7	558	684*	8.9	12.8
WILKES	32	4 680	5 966*	54.5	100.0
005 AME ZION......	1	75	80	0.7	1.3
081 CATHOLIC......	1	NA	200	1.8	3.4
101 C.M.E.........	1	430	521*	4.8	8.7
127 CH GOD (CLEVE)	1	12	15*	0.1	0.3
167 CHS OF CHRIST.	2	50	63	0.6	1.1
193 EPISCOPAL.....	1	80	120	1.1	2.0
353 CHR BRETHREN..	1	100	200	1.8	3.4
357 PRESB CH US...	2	142	172*	1.6	2.9
419 SO BAPT CONV..	14	2 901	3 516*	32.1	58.9
449 UN METHODIST..	8	890	1 079*	9.9	18.1
WILKINSON	29	4 648	5 818*	56.1	100.0
081 CATHOLIC......	1	NA	31	0.3	0.5
097 CHR CHS&CHS CR	1	65	81*	0.8	1.4
101 C.M.E.........	2	1 254	1 560*	15.0	26.8
167 CHS OF CHRIST.	2	90	115	1.1	2.0
419 SO BAPT CONV..	14	2 458	3 059*	29.5	52.6
449 UN METHODIST..	9	781	972*	9.4	16.7
WORTH	40	6 679	8 382*	46.4	100.0
053 ASSEMB OF GOD.	1	55	82	0.5	1.0
081 CATHOLIC......	1	NA	45	0.2	0.5
127 CH GOD (CLEVE)	1	6	7*	-	0.1
167 CHS OF CHRIST.	2	54	74	0.4	0.9
349 PENT HOLINESS.	1	54	67*	0.4	0.8
357 PRESB CH US...	1	93	116*	0.6	1.4
419 SO BAPT CONV..	26	5 299	6 599*	36.5	78.7
449 UN METHODIST..	7	1 118	1 392*	7.7	16.6

HAWAII

County and Denomination	Number of churches	Communicant, confirmed, full members	Total adherents Number	Percent of total population	Percent of total adherents
THE STATE.....	558	62 551	320 288*	33.2	100.0
HAWAII	91	5 405	49 442*	53.7	100.0
017 AMER BAPT ASSN	2	95	95	0.1	0.2
053 ASSEMB OF GOD.	9	505	770	0.8	1.6
057 BAPT GEN CONF.	1	81	100*	0.1	0.2
081 CATHOLIC......	13	NA	38 000	41.3	76.9
127 CH GOD (CLEVE)	2	127	157*	0.2	0.3
133 CH GOD(7TH)DEN	1	3	4*	-	-
151 L-D SAINTS....	13	NA	3 970	4.3	8.0
165 CH OF NAZARENE	2	114	302	0.3	0.6
167 CHS OF CHRIST.	3	40	57	0.1	0.1
193 EPISCOPAL.....	8	732	981	1.1	2.0
283 LUTH--MO SYNOD	2	113	157	0.2	0.3
291 MISSIONARY CH.	1	15	69	0.1	0.1
353 CHR BRETHREN..	1	75	100	0.1	0.2
403 SALVATION ARMY	3	208	589	0.6	1.2
413 S.D.A.........	4	487	602*	0.7	1.2
419 SO BAPT CONV..	4	657	813*	0.9	1.6
443 UN C OF CHRIST	17	1 747	2 161*	2.3	4.4
449 UN METHODIST..	4	367	454*	0.5	0.9
469 WELS..........	1	39	61	0.1	0.1
HONOLULU	338	49 431	232 304*	30.5	100.0
017 AMER BAPT ASSN	6	355	355	-	0.2
019 AMER BAPT USA.	4	410	498*	0.1	0.2
029 AMER LUTH CH..	5	511	653	0.1	0.3
053 ASSEMB OF GOD.	24	3 370	5 409	0.7	2.3
081 CATHOLIC......	32	NA	148 000	19.4	63.7
089 CHR & MISS AL.	7	619	832	0.1	0.4
093 CHR CH (DISC).	3	403	638	0.1	0.3
097 CHR CHS&CHS CR	8	678	823*	0.1	0.4
105 CHRISTIAN REF.	1	32	45	-	-
123 CH GOD (ANDER)	2	50	150	-	0.1
127 CH GOD (CLEVE)	9	476	578*	0.1	0.2
133 CH GOD(7TH)DEN	2	27	33*	-	-
151 L-D SAINTS....	52	NA	19 828	2.6	8.5
165 CH OF NAZARENE	10	807	1 497	0.2	0.6
167 CHS OF CHRIST.	7	625	811	0.1	0.3
175 CONGR CHR CHS.	4	100	121*	-	0.1
179 CONSRV BAPT...	1	800	971*	0.1	0.4
193 EPISCOPAL.....	23	4 982	7 378	1.0	3.2
203 EVAN FREE CH..	1	97	118*	-	0.1
226 FRIENDS-USA...	1	90	109*	-	-
244 GRACE BRETHREN	3	239	290*	-	0.1
270 CONSRV JUDAISM	1	35	42*	-	-
271 REFORM JUDAISM	1	720	874*	0.1	0.4
281 LUTH CH AMER..	4	742	1 080	0.1	0.5
283 LUTH--MO SYNOD	6	1 341	2 016	0.3	0.9
290 METRO COMM CHS	1	100	200	-	0.1
291 MISSIONARY CH.	4	171	384	0.1	0.2

County and Denomination	Number of churches	Communicant, confirmed, full members	Total adherents Number	Percent of total population	Percent of total adherents
353 CHR BRETHREN..	2	125	250	-	0.1
356 PRESB CH AMER.	1	?	?	?	?
403 SALVATION ARMY	3	468	609	0.1	0.3
413 S.D.A.........	12	2 983	3 622*	0.5	1.6
419 SO BAPT CONV..	26	9 456	11 482*	1.5	4.9
435 UNITARIAN-UNIV	2	190	231*	-	0.1
443 UN C OF CHRIST	45	12 445	15 111*	2.0	6.5
449 UN METHODIST..	21	5 017	6 092*	0.8	2.6
453 UN PRES CH USA	4	967	1 174*	0.2	0.5
KALAWAO	2	92	162*	112.5	100.0
081 CATHOLIC......	1	NA	70	48.6	43.2
419 SO BAPT CONV..	1	92	92*	63.9	56.8
KAUAI	51	3 179	17 586*	45.0	100.0
053 ASSEMB OF GOD.	4	223	290	0.7	1.6
081 CATHOLIC......	5	NA	11 500	29.4	65.4
127 CH GOD (CLEVE)	1	8	10*	-	0.1
151 L-D SAINTS....	6	NA	1 764	4.5	10.0
165 CH OF NAZARENE	1	52	102	0.3	0.6
167 CHS OF CHRIST.	1	14	18	-	0.1
175 CONGR CHR CHS.	1	45	56*	0.1	0.3
179 CONSRV BAPT...	1	2	2*	-	-
181 CONSRV CONGR..	1	26	32*	0.1	0.2
193 EPISCOPAL.....	6	338	655	1.7	3.7
281 LUTH CH AMER..	1	68	128	0.3	0.7
291 MISSIONARY CH.	3	150	343	0.9	2.0
403 SALVATION ARMY	2	302	280	0.7	1.6
413 S.D.A.........	2	222	274*	0.7	1.6
419 SO BAPT CONV..	2	302	372*	1.0	2.1
443 UN C OF CHRIST	11	1 204	1 485*	3.8	8.4
449 UN METHODIST..	3	223	275*	0.7	1.6
MAUI	76	4 444	20 794*	29.4	100.0
053 ASSEMB OF GOD.	4	543	663	0.9	3.2
081 CATHOLIC......	13	NA	12 430	17.5	59.8
127 CH GOD (CLEVE)	2	97	119*	0.2	0.6
133 CH GOD(7TH)DEN	2	9	11*	-	0.1
151 L-D SAINTS....	9	NA	2 440	3.4	11.7
165 CH OF NAZARENE	1	29	45	0.1	0.2
167 CHS OF CHRIST.	1	12	18	-	0.1
179 CONSRV BAPT...	2	95	116*	0.2	0.6
193 EPISCOPAL.....	5	677	1 063	1.5	5.1
283 LUTH--MO SYNOD	2	116	178	0.3	0.9
290 METRO COMM CHS	0	10	20	-	0.1
403 SALVATION ARMY	1	90	301	0.4	1.4
413 S.D.A.........	3	303	371*	0.5	1.8
419 SO BAPT CONV..	5	471	577*	0.8	2.8
443 UN C OF CHRIST	23	1 656	2 030*	2.9	9.8
449 UN METHODIST..	3	336	412*	0.6	2.0

IDAHO

County and Denomination	Number of churches	Communicant, confirmed, full members	Total adherents Number	Percent of total population	Percent of total adherents
THE STATE.....	1 393	114 350	472 497*	50.1	100.0
ADA	148	23 005	70 786*	40.9	100.0
017 AMER BAPT ASSN	1	50	50	-	0.1
019 AMER BAPT USA.	5	1 639	2 023*	1.2	2.9
029 AMER LUTH CH..	1	217	409	0.2	0.6
053 ASSEMB OF GOD.	6	1 550	3 362	1.9	4.7
059 BAPT MISS ASSN	1	18	22*	-	-
081 CATHOLIC......	8	NA	13 742	7.9	19.4
089 CHR & MISS AL.	1	35	46	-	0.1
093 CHR CH (DISC).	2	1 378	2 220	1.3	3.1
097 CHR CHS&CHS CR	6	753	930*	0.5	1.3
105 CHRISTIAN REF.	1	41	79	-	0.1
123 CH GOD (ANDER)	2	190	570	0.3	0.8
127 CH GOD (CLEVE)	3	122	151*	0.1	0.2
151 L-D SAINTS....	50	NA	24 600	14.2	34.8
157 CH OF BRETHREN	2	219	270*	0.2	0.4
165 CH OF NAZARENE	7	1 429	2 300	1.3	3.2
167 CHS OF CHRIST.	4	538	742	0.4	1.0
179 CONSRV BAPT...	4	225	278*	0.2	0.4
193 EPISCOPAL.....	4	1 838	2 519	1.5	3.6
203 EVAN FREE CH..	1	76	94*	0.1	0.1
226 FRIENDS-USA...	5	738	911*	0.5	1.3
263 INT FOURSQ GOS	2	263	325*	0.2	0.5
270 CONSRV JUDAISM	1	23	28*	-	-
281 LUTH CH AMER..	3	1 172	1 647	1.0	2.3
283 LUTH--MO SYNOD	3	1 385	1 898	1.1	2.7
285 MENNONITE CH..	1	28	35*	-	0.1
290 METRO COMM CHS	1	40	80	-	0.1
353 CHR BRETHREN..	1	45	70	-	0.1
403 SALVATION ARMY	1	151	469	0.3	0.7
413 S.D.A.........	5	865	1 068*	0.6	1.5
419 SO BAPT CONV..	4	1 220	1 506*	0.9	2.1
435 UNITARIAN-UNIV	1	109	135*	0.1	0.2
443 UN C OF CHRIST	2	715	883*	0.5	1.2
449 UN METHODIST..	8	4 087	5 045*	2.9	7.1

NA—Not applicable   *Total adherents estimated from known number of communicant, confirmed, full members.   —Represents a percent less than 0.1.   Percentages may not total due to rounding.

Table 4. Churches and Church Membership by County and Denomination: 1980

County and Denomination	Number of churches	Communicant, confirmed, full members	Total adherents		
			Number	Percent of total population	Percent of total adherents
453 UN PRES CH USA	4	1 846	2 279*	1.3	3.2
ADAMS	7	212	589*	17.6	100.0
053 ASSEMB OF GOD.	2	27	46	1.4	7.8
081 CATHOLIC	1	NA	120	3.6	20.4
151 L-D SAINTS	1	NA	184	5.5	31.2
165 CH OF NAZARENE	1	59	83	2.5	14.1
175 CONGR CHR CHS.	1	80	99*	3.0	16.8
449 UN METHODIST	1	46	57*	1.7	9.7
BANNOCK	89	4 836	38 874*	59.4	100.0
019 AMER BAPT USA.	1	198	250*	0.4	0.6
053 ASSEMB OF GOD.	3	225	578	0.9	1.5
081 CATHOLIC	5	NA	3 820	5.8	9.8
093 CHR CH (DISC).	1	499	649	1.0	1.7
097 CHR CHS&CHS CR	1	50	63*	0.1	0.2
123 CH GOD (ANDER)	1	14	42	0.1	0.1
127 CH GOD (CLEVE)	1	42	53*	0.1	0.1
151 L-D SAINTS	61	NA	28 323	43.3	72.9
165 CH OF NAZARENE	1	149	314	0.5	0.8
167 CHS OF CHRIST.	1	55	60	0.1	0.2
193 EPISCOPAL	1	386	455	0.7	1.2
271 REFORM JUDAISM	1	48	61*	0.1	0.2
281 LUTH CH AMER.	1	319	415	0.6	1.1
283 LUTH--MO SYNOD	2	500	733	1.1	1.9
403 SALVATION ARMY	1	47	126	0.2	0.3
413 S.D.A.	1	152	192*	0.3	0.5
419 SO BAPT CONV.	1	592	749*	1.1	1.9
443 UN C OF CHRIST	2	214	271*	0.4	0.7
449 UN METHODIST.	1	899	1 137*	1.7	2.9
453 UN PRES CH USA	1	423	535*	0.8	1.4
469 WELS	1	24	48	0.1	0.1
BEAR LAKE	17	31	5 814*	83.9	100.0
081 CATHOLIC	1	NA	135	1.9	2.3
151 L-D SAINTS	15	NA	5 638	81.3	97.0
453 UN PRES CH USA	1	31	41*	0.6	0.7
BENEWAH	17	955	2 921*	35.2	100.0
029 AMER LUTH CH.	1	167	247	3.0	8.5
053 ASSEMB OF GOD.	1	40	70	0.8	2.4
081 CATHOLIC	5	NA	1 295	15.6	44.3
151 L-D SAINTS	2	NA	262	3.2	9.0
165 CH OF NAZARENE	1	110	230	2.8	7.9
167 CHS OF CHRIST.	1	15	19	0.2	0.7
175 CONGR CHR CHS.	1	59	74*	0.9	2.5
221 FREE METHODIST	1	9	33	0.4	1.1
263 INT FOURSQ GOS	1	201	250*	3.0	8.6
413 S.D.A.	1	51	64*	0.8	2.2
419 SO BAPT CONV.	1	156	194*	2.3	6.6
453 UN PRES CH USA	1	147	183*	2.2	6.3
BINGHAM	71	1 792	28 330*	77.6	100.0
019 AMER BAPT USA.	1	212	280*	0.8	1.0
053 ASSEMB OF GOD.	3	119	266	0.7	0.9
081 CATHOLIC	4	NA	2 580	7.1	9.1
151 L-D SAINTS	50	NA	22 825	62.6	80.6
167 CHS OF CHRIST.	1	30	31	0.1	0.1
193 EPISCOPAL	2	133	530	1.5	1.9
281 LUTH CH AMER.	2	279	377	1.0	1.3
283 LUTH--MO SYNOD	1	69	102	0.3	0.4
287 MENN GEN CONF.	1	330	520	1.4	1.8
413 S.D.A.	1	16	21*	0.1	0.1
419 SO BAPT CONV.	1	88	116*	0.3	0.4
449 UN METHODIST.	3	492	650*	1.8	2.3
453 UN PRES CH USA	1	24	32*	0.1	0.1
BLAINE	11	446	2 577*	26.2	100.0
019 AMER BAPT USA.	1	128	153*	1.6	5.9
053 ASSEMB OF GOD.	1	38	54	0.5	2.1
081 CATHOLIC	2	NA	503	5.1	19.5
151 L-D SAINTS	3	NA	1 493	15.2	57.9
193 EPISCOPAL	2	110	172	1.7	6.7
283 LUTH--MO SYNOD	1	65	76	0.8	2.9
453 UN PRES CH USA	1	105	126*	1.3	4.9
BOISE	10	165	571*	19.0	100.0
053 ASSEMB OF GOD.	2	40	102	3.4	17.9
081 CATHOLIC	3	NA	115	3.8	20.1
151 L-D SAINTS	2	NA	156	5.2	27.3
281 LUTH CH AMER.	1	53	89	3.0	15.6
353 CHR BRETHREN.	1	25	50	1.7	8.8
419 SO BAPT CONV.	1	47	59*	2.0	10.3
BONNER	32	2 944	6 969*	28.8	100.0
017 AMER BAPT ASSN	1	50	50	0.2	0.7
019 AMER BAPT USA.	1	257	316*	1.3	4.5
029 AMER LUTH CH.	2	435	632	2.6	9.1
053 ASSEMB OF GOD.	2	113	202	0.8	2.9
081 CATHOLIC	4	NA	1 542	6.4	22.1
097 CHR CHS&CHS CR	1	224	275*	1.1	3.9
123 CH GOD (ANDER)	1	50	150	0.6	2.2
127 CH GOD (CLEVE)	1	50	61*	0.3	0.9
151 L-D SAINTS	4	NA	1 364	5.6	19.6
165 CH OF NAZARENE	1	62	82	0.3	1.2
167 CHS OF CHRIST.	1	40	51	0.2	0.7
179 CONSRV BAPT...	1	225	277*	1.1	4.0
193 EPISCOPAL	1	60	70	0.3	1.0
221 FREE METHODIST	1	35	216	0.9	3.1
403 SALVATION ARMY	1	113	168	0.7	2.4
413 S.D.A.	3	470	578*	2.4	8.3
419 SO BAPT CONV.	1	33	41*	0.2	0.6
443 UN C OF CHRIST	1	109	134*	0.6	1.9
449 UN METHODIST.	3	369	454*	1.9	6.5
453 UN PRES CH USA	1	249	306*	1.3	4.4
BONNEVILLE	86	5 870	44 405*	67.3	100.0
019 AMER BAPT USA.	1	454	587*	0.9	1.3
053 ASSEMB OF GOD.	1	56	181	0.3	0.4
081 CATHOLIC	2	NA	4 100	6.2	9.2
089 CHR & MISS AL.	1	87	128	0.2	0.3
093 CHR CH (DISC).	1	131	151	0.2	0.3
127 CH GOD (CLEVE)	1	12	16*	-	-
151 L-D SAINTS	64	NA	32 099	48.6	72.3
165 CH OF NAZARENE	1	79	174	0.3	0.4
167 CHS OF CHRIST.	2	180	229	0.3	0.5
193 EPISCOPAL	1	506	872	1.3	2.0
201 EVAN COV CH AM	1	87	112*	0.2	0.3
281 LUTH CH AMER.	1	574	826	1.3	1.9
283 LUTH--MO SYNOD	2	802	1 181	1.8	2.7
413 S.D.A.	1	66	85*	0.1	0.2
419 SO BAPT CONV.	1	570	736*	1.1	1.7
435 UNITARIAN-UNIV	1	24	31*	-	0.1
449 UN METHODIST.	2	1 123	1 451*	2.2	3.3
453 UN PRES CH USA	2	1 119	1 446*	2.2	3.3
BOUNDARY	13	1 202	2 615*	35.9	100.0
029 AMER LUTH CH.	1	244	394	5.4	15.1
053 ASSEMB OF GOD.	1	49	65	0.9	2.5
081 CATHOLIC	1	NA	450	6.2	17.2
127 CH GOD (CLEVE)	1	16	20*	0.3	0.8
143 CG IN CR(MENN)	1	204	204	2.8	7.8
151 L-D SAINTS	1	NA	510	7.0	19.5
167 CHS OF CHRIST.	2	38	61	0.8	2.3
193 EPISCOPAL	1	16	26	0.4	1.0
221 FREE METHODIST	1	22	114	1.6	4.4
413 S.D.A.	1	77	97*	1.3	3.7
419 SO BAPT CONV.	1	255	321*	4.4	12.3
449 UN METHODIST.	1	281	353*	4.8	13.5
BUTTE	9	134	1 909*	57.1	100.0
019 AMER BAPT USA.	1	52	67*	2.0	3.5
081 CATHOLIC	1	NA	121	3.6	6.3
151 L-D SAINTS	5	NA	1 605	48.0	84.1
167 CHS OF CHRIST.	1	65	83	2.5	4.3
193 EPISCOPAL	1	17	33	1.0	1.7
CAMAS	2	0	155	18.9	100.0
081 CATHOLIC	1	NA	25	3.1	16.1
151 L-D SAINTS	1	NA	130	15.9	83.9
CANYON	103	15 622	37 817*	45.2	100.0
019 AMER BAPT USA.	4	721	901*	1.1	2.4
053 ASSEMB OF GOD.	6	609	1 076	1.3	2.8
081 CATHOLIC	6	NA	6 404	7.6	16.9
093 CHR CH (DISC).	2	558	846	1.0	2.2
097 CHR CHS&CHS CR	1	859	1 073*	1.3	2.8
123 CH GOD (ANDER)	1	130	390	0.5	1.0
127 CH GOD (CLEVE)	4	99	124*	0.1	0.3
133 CH GOD(7TH)DEN	1	57	71*	0.1	0.2
151 L-D SAINTS	18	NA	8 871	10.6	23.5
157 CH OF BRETHREN	2	422	527*	0.6	1.4
163 CH OF LUTH BR.	1	51	90	0.1	0.2
165 CH OF NAZARENE	12	3 692	5 577	6.7	14.7
167 CHS OF CHRIST.	5	286	397	0.5	1.0
179 CONSRV BAPT...	3	675	843*	1.0	2.2
193 EPISCOPAL	2	507	810	1.0	2.1
221 FREE METHODIST	2	276	1 206	1.4	3.2
226 FRIENDS--USA...	2	228	285*	0.3	0.8
263 INT FOURSQ GOS	2	197	246*	0.3	0.7
281 LUTH CH AMER.	2	447	614	0.7	1.6
283 LUTH--MO SYNOD	4	862	1 194	1.4	3.2
285 MENNONITE CH.	1	109	136*	0.2	0.4
403 SALVATION ARMY	2	155	270	0.3	0.7
413 S.D.A.	4	843	1 053*	1.3	2.8
419 SO BAPT CONV.	3	598	747*	0.9	2.0
443 UN C OF CHRIST	1	182	227*	0.3	0.6
449 UN METHODIST.	6	1 549	1 936*	2.3	5.1
453 UN PRES CH USA	5	1 413	1 766*	2.1	4.7
469 WELS	1	97	137	0.2	0.4
CARIBOU	18	221	6 323*	72.7	100.0
053 ASSEMB OF GOD.	1	23	34	0.4	0.5
081 CATHOLIC	1	NA	215	2.5	3.4
151 L-D SAINTS	13	NA	5 801	66.7	91.7
283 LUTH--MO SYNOD	1	28	49	0.6	0.8
419 SO BAPT CONV.	1	59	78*	0.9	1.2
453 UN PRES CH USA	1	111	146*	1.7	2.3
CASSIA	34	1 736	18 624*	95.9	100.0
053 ASSEMB OF GOD.	3	172	349	1.8	1.9
081 CATHOLIC	1	NA	5 500	28.3	29.5
093 CHR CH (DISC).	1	252	316	1.6	1.7
151 L-D SAINTS	23	NA	10 650	54.8	57.2
167 CHS OF CHRIST.	1	19	20	0.1	0.1

NA—Not applicable   *Total adherents estimated from known number of communicant, confirmed, full members.   —Represents a percent less than 0.1.   Percentages may not total due to rounding.

Table 4. Churches and Church Membership by County and Denomination: 1980

County and Denomination	Number of churches	Communicant, confirmed, full members	Total adherents Number	Percent of total population	Percent of total adherents
193 EPISCOPAL.....	1	49	125	0.6	0.7
283 LUTH--MO SYNOD	1	283	407	2.1	2.2
419 SO BAPT CONV..	1	321	420*	2.2	2.3
449 UN METHODIST..	1	355	464*	2.4	2.5
453 UN PRES CH USA	1	285	373*	1.9	2.0
CLARK	**2**	**115**	**462***	**57.9**	**100.0**
019 AMER BAPT USA.	1	115	145*	18.2	31.4
151 L-D SAINTS....	1	NA	317	39.7	68.6
CLEARWATER	**20**	**1 163**	**2 916***	**28.1**	**100.0**
029 AMER LUTH CH..	2	188	270	2.6	9.3
053 ASSEMB OF GOD.	1	27	97	0.9	3.3
081 CATHOLIC......	3	NA	710	6.8	24.3
089 CHR & MISS AL.	1	27	38	0.4	1.3
093 CHR CH (DISC).	1	38	93	0.9	3.2
123 CH GOD (ANDER)	1	23	69	0.7	2.4
151 L-D SAINTS....	1	NA	437	4.2	15.0
164 CH LUTH CONF..	1	26	32	0.3	1.1
165 CH OF NAZARENE	2	79	232	2.2	8.0
413 S.D.A.........	2	189	235*	2.3	8.1
419 SO BAPT CONV..	2	268	333*	3.2	11.4
449 UN METHODIST..	2	289	359*	3.5	12.3
453 UN PRES CH USA	1	9	11*	0.1	0.4
CUSTER	**6**	**87**	**1 342***	**39.6**	**100.0**
081 CATHOLIC......	2	NA	213	6.3	15.9
151 L-D SAINTS....	3	NA	1 021	30.2	76.1
443 UN C OF CHRIST	1	87	108*	3.2	8.0
ELMORE	**24**	**2 260**	**6 906***	**32.0**	**100.0**
019 AMER BAPT USA.	1	112	141*	0.7	2.0
053 ASSEMB OF GOD.	2	89	200	0.9	2.9
081 CATHOLIC......	2	NA	1 492	6.9	21.6
089 CHR & MISS AL.	1	20	48	0.2	0.7
093 CHR CH (DISC).	1	116	169	0.8	2.4
127 CH GOD (CLEVE)	1	38	48*	0.2	0.7
151 L-D SAINTS....	4	NA	2 017	9.4	29.2
165 CH OF NAZARENE	1	86	226	1.0	3.3
167 CHS OF CHRIST.	1	50	80	0.4	1.2
193 EPISCOPAL.....	2	256	291	1.3	4.2
283 LUTH--MO SYNOD	1	0	316	1.5	4.6
285 MENNONITE CH..	1	61	77*	0.4	1.1
413 S.D.A.........	1	81	102*	0.5	1.5
419 SO BAPT CONV..	2	998	1 255*	5.8	18.2
443 UN C OF CHRIST	1	234	294*	1.4	4.3
449 UN METHODIST..	1	82	103*	0.5	1.5
453 UN PRES CH USA	1	37	47*	0.2	0.7
FRANKLIN	**22**	**53**	**8 516***	**95.7**	**100.0**
053 ASSEMB OF GOD.	1	22	23	0.3	0.3
081 CATHOLIC......	1	NA	60	0.7	0.7
151 L-D SAINTS....	19	NA	8 392	94.3	98.5
453 UN PRES CH USA	1	31	41*	0.5	0.5
FREMONT	**21**	**590**	**8 136***	**75.2**	**100.0**
081 CATHOLIC......	1	NA	110	1.0	1.4
151 L-D SAINTS....	16	NA	7 282	67.3	89.5
167 CHS OF CHRIST.	1	37	47	0.4	0.6
283 LUTH--MO SYNOD	1	266	321	3.0	3.9
449 UN METHODIST..	1	168	220*	2.0	2.7
453 UN PRES CH USA	1	119	156*	1.4	1.9
GEM	**23**	**2 163**	**5 588***	**46.7**	**100.0**
019 AMER BAPT USA.	1	156	194*	1.6	3.5
053 ASSEMB OF GOD.	2	49	73	0.6	1.3
081 CATHOLIC......	1	NA	724	6.0	13.0
097 CHR CHS&CHS CR	1	400	496*	4.1	8.9
127 CH GOD (CLEVE)	1	84	104*	0.9	1.9
151 L-D SAINTS....	5	NA	1 906	15.9	34.1
165 CH OF NAZARENE	1	230	536	4.5	9.6
167 CHS OF CHRIST.	1	35	45	0.4	0.8
179 CONSRV BAPT...	1	225	279*	2.3	5.0
193 EPISCOPAL.....	1	91	127	1.1	2.3
226 FRIENDS-USA...	1	27	34*	0.3	0.6
263 INT FOURSQ GOS	1	132	164*	1.4	2.9
283 LUTH--MO SYNOD	1	225	274*	2.3	4.9
413 S.D.A.........	1	64	79*	0.7	1.4
419 SO BAPT CONV..	1	73	91*	0.8	1.6
449 UN METHODIST..	2	247	307*	2.6	5.5
453 UN PRES CH USA	1	125	155*	1.3	2.8
GOODING	**25**	**1 886**	**5 567***	**46.9**	**100.0**
019 AMER BAPT USA.	1	32	40*	0.3	0.7
053 ASSEMB OF GOD.	1	44	125	1.1	2.2
081 CATHOLIC......	3	NA	624	5.3	11.2
097 CHR CHS&CHS CR	2	350	434*	3.7	7.8
151 L-D SAINTS....	5	NA	2 421	20.4	43.5
165 CH OF NAZARENE	1	46	74	0.6	1.3
167 CHS OF CHRIST.	2	60	89	0.7	1.6
193 EPISCOPAL.....	1	91	93	0.8	1.7
221 FREE METHODIST	1	20	123	1.0	2.2
283 LUTH--MO SYNOD	2	192	241	2.0	4.3
413 S.D.A.........	1	40	50*	0.4	0.9
419 SO BAPT CONV..	1	128	159*	1.3	2.9
449 UN METHODIST..	3	685	849*	7.2	15.3
453 UN PRES CH USA	1	198	245*	2.1	4.4
IDAHO	**30**	**1 969**	**5 591***	**37.9**	**100.0**
019 AMER BAPT USA.	1	95	117*	0.8	2.1
053 ASSEMB OF GOD.	3	129	207	1.4	3.7
057 BAPT GEN CONF.	1	111	137*	0.9	2.5
081 CATHOLIC......	5	NA	2 626	17.8	47.0
093 CHR CH (DISC).	1	231	355	2.4	6.3
097 CHR CHS&CHS CR	1	350	431*	2.9	7.7
105 CHRISTIAN REF.	1	65	110	0.7	2.0
127 CH GOD (CLEVE)	2	34	42*	0.3	0.8
151 L-D SAINTS....	2	NA	311	2.1	5.6
165 CH OF NAZARENE	1	133	268	1.8	4.8
193 EPISCOPAL.....	1	60	60	0.4	1.1
283 LUTH--MO SYNOD	1	122	140	0.9	2.5
413 S.D.A.........	1	40	49*	0.3	0.9
419 SO BAPT CONV..	3	224	276*	1.9	4.9
449 UN METHODIST..	2	333	410*	2.8	7.3
453 UN PRES CH USA	2	42	52*	0.4	0.9
JEFFERSON	**27**	**53**	**12 559***	**82.1**	**100.0**
019 AMER BAPT USA.	2	53	70*	0.5	0.6
081 CATHOLIC......	2	NA	171	1.1	1.4
151 L-D SAINTS....	23	NA	12 318	80.5	98.1
JEROME	**26**	**2 083**	**6 746***	**45.5**	**100.0**
019 AMER BAPT USA.	1	192	243*	1.6	3.6
053 ASSEMB OF GOD.	3	247	394	2.7	5.8
081 CATHOLIC......	1	NA	680	4.6	10.1
093 CHR CH (DISC).	1	146	213	1.4	3.2
123 CH GOD (ANDER)	1	60	180	1.2	2.7
127 CH GOD (CLEVE)	1	5	6*	-	0.1
151 L-D SAINTS....	7	NA	3 153	21.2	46.7
165 CH OF NAZARENE	1	87	99	0.7	1.5
167 CHS OF CHRIST.	2	120	160	1.1	2.4
193 EPISCOPAL.....	1	55	82	0.6	1.2
283 LUTH--MO SYNOD	2	401	561	3.8	8.3
413 S.D.A.........	2	91	115*	0.8	1.7
449 UN METHODIST..	1	326	413*	2.8	6.1
453 UN PRES CH USA	2	353	447*	3.0	6.6
KOOTENAI	**47**	**6 900**	**16 982***	**28.4**	**100.0**
019 AMER BAPT USA.	2	413	510*	0.9	3.0
029 AMER LUTH CH..	4	1 122	1 564	2.6	9.2
053 ASSEMB OF GOD.	2	280	585	1.0	3.4
057 BAPT GEN CONF.	2	263	325*	0.5	1.9
081 CATHOLIC......	5	NA	4 695	7.9	27.6
093 CHR CH (DISC).	1	126	177	0.3	1.0
123 CH GOD (ANDER)	1	78	234	0.4	1.4
127 CH GOD (CLEVE)	2	65	80*	0.1	0.5
151 L-D SAINTS....	7	NA	2 866	4.8	16.9
165 CH OF NAZARENE	2	347	598	1.0	3.5
167 CHS OF CHRIST.	2	200	439	0.7	2.6
193 EPISCOPAL.....	1	430	472	0.8	2.8
221 FREE METHODIST	1	9	30	0.1	0.2
226 FRIENDS-USA...	2	105	130*	0.2	0.8
263 INT FOURSQ GOS	1	95	117*	0.2	0.7
281 LUTH CH AMER..	1	74	113	0.2	0.7
283 LUTH--MO SYNOD	1	992	1 207	2.0	7.1
285 MENNONITE CH..	1	?	?	?	?
413 S.D.A.........	2	586	723*	1.2	4.3
419 SO BAPT CONV..	1	315	389*	0.7	2.3
449 UN METHODIST..	3	644	795*	1.3	4.7
453 UN PRES CH USA	3	756	933*	1.6	5.5
LATAH	**39**	**4 072**	**9 348***	**32.5**	**100.0**
019 AMER BAPT USA.	1	199	234*	0.8	2.5
029 AMER LUTH CH..	5	839	1 115	3.9	11.9
053 ASSEMB OF GOD.	2	117	185	0.6	2.0
081 CATHOLIC......	5	NA	2 659	9.2	28.4
093 CHR CH (DISC).	2	302	363	1.3	3.9
097 CHR CHS&CHS CR	1	20	24*	0.1	0.3
123 CH GOD (ANDER)	1	60	180	0.6	1.9
151 L-D SAINTS....	5	NA	1 366	4.8	14.6
165 CH OF NAZARENE	4	421	684	2.4	7.3
167 CHS OF CHRIST.	1	15	25	0.1	0.3
281 LUTH CH AMER..	2	246	330	1.1	3.5
413 S.D.A.........	4	309	364*	1.3	3.9
419 SO BAPT CONV..	1	265	312*	1.1	3.3
449 UN METHODIST..	2	836	985*	3.4	10.5
453 UN PRES CH USA	3	443	522*	1.8	5.6
LEMHI	**16**	**757**	**3 155***	**42.3**	**100.0**
053 ASSEMB OF GOD.	1	128	250	3.4	7.9
081 CATHOLIC......	2	NA	271	3.6	8.6
151 L-D SAINTS....	5	NA	1 815	24.3	57.5
167 CHS OF CHRIST.	1	32	47	0.6	1.5
193 EPISCOPAL.....	1	93	142	1.9	4.5
263 INT FOURSQ GOS	1	75	93*	1.2	2.9
283 LUTH--MO SYNOD	1	53	70	0.9	2.2
413 S.D.A.........	1	107	133*	1.8	4.2
449 UN METHODIST..	2	219	272*	3.6	8.6
453 UN PRES CH USA	1	50	62*	0.8	2.0
LEWIS	**25**	**1 143**	**2 550***	**61.9**	**100.0**
029 AMER LUTH CH..	3	198	260	6.3	10.2
053 ASSEMB OF GOD.	2	47	88	2.1	3.5
081 CATHOLIC......	3	NA	784	19.0	30.7
093 CHR CH (DISC).	2	218	335	8.1	13.1
097 CHR CHS&CHS CR	1	120	147*	3.6	5.8

NA—Not applicable   *Total adherents estimated from known number of communicant, confirmed, full members.   —Represents a percent less than 0.1.   Percentages may not total due to rounding.

Table 4. Churches and Church Membership by County and Denomination: 1980

County and Denomination	Number of churches	Communicant, confirmed, full members	Total adherents Number	Percent of total population	Percent of total adherents
151 L-D SAINTS....	1	NA	247	6.0	9.7
157 CH OF BRETHREN	1	9	11*	0.3	0.4
165 CH OF NAZARENE	1	?	?	?	?
167 CHS OF CHRIST.	1	20	25	0.6	1.0
226 FRIENDS-USA...	1	47	58*	1.4	2.3
413 S.D.A.........	1	54	66*	1.6	2.6
419 SO BAPT CONV..	1	34	42*	1.0	1.6
449 UN METHODIST..	1	103	127*	3.1	5.0
453 UN PRES CH USA	6	293	360*	8.7	14.1
LINCOLN	**10**	**340**	**1 835***	**53.4**	**100.0**
019 AMER BAPT USA.	1	80	101*	2.9	5.5
053 ASSEMB OF GOD.	2	81	174	5.1	9.5
081 CATHOLIC......	1	NA	300	8.7	16.3
151 L-D SAINTS....	3	NA	1 007	29.3	54.9
193 EPISCOPAL.....	1	51	92	2.7	5.0
449 UN METHODIST..	2	128	161*	4.7	8.8
MADISON	**63**	**129**	**17 856***	**91.7**	**100.0**
081 CATHOLIC......	1	NA	43	0.2	0.2
151 L-D SAINTS....	60	NA	17 649	90.6	98.8
453 UN PRES CH USA	2	129	164*	0.8	0.9
MINIDOKA	**29**	**2 220**	**11 759***	**59.6**	**100.0**
019 AMER BAPT USA.	1	197	253*	1.3	2.2
053 ASSEMB OF GOD.	1	53	90	0.5	0.8
081 CATHOLIC......	1	NA	1 600	8.1	13.6
127 CH GOD (CLEVE)	1	9	12*	0.1	0.1
151 L-D SAINTS....	16	NA	7 231	36.7	61.5
165 CH OF NAZARENE	1	88	210	1.1	1.8
167 CHS OF CHRIST.	1	62	82	0.4	0.7
181 CONSRV CONGR..	1	289	372*	1.9	3.2
193 EPISCOPAL.....	1	120	162	0.8	1.4
283 LUTH--MO SYNOD	1	572	680	3.4	5.8
313 N AM BAPT CONF	1	120	154*	0.8	1.3
413 S.D.A.........	1	33	42*	0.2	0.4
449 UN METHODIST..	2	677	871*	4.4	7.4
NEZ PERCE	**39**	**5 114**	**12 023***	**36.2**	**100.0**
001 ADVENT CHR CH.	1	34	41*	0.1	0.3
019 AMER BAPT USA.	1	149	181*	0.5	1.5
029 AMER LUTH CH..	4	1 096	1 550	4.7	12.9
053 ASSEMB OF GOD.	3	449	1 366	4.1	11.4
081 CATHOLIC......	4	NA	2 705	8.1	22.5
089 CHR & MISS AL.	1	91	141	0.4	1.2
093 CHR CH (DISC).	1	231	331	1.0	2.8
097 CHR CHS&CHS CR	1	50	61*	0.2	0.5
123 CH GOD (ANDER)	1	28	84	0.3	0.7
127 CH GOD (CLEVE)	1	13	16*	-	0.1
151 L-D SAINTS....	3	NA	1 366	4.1	11.4
165 CH OF NAZARENE	2	262	702	2.1	5.8
167 CHS OF CHRIST.	1	95	145	0.4	1.2
193 EPISCOPAL.....	1	339	455	1.4	3.8
283 LUTH--MO SYNOD	1	177	291	0.9	2.4
329 OPEN BIBLE STD	1	35	50	0.2	0.4
403 SALVATION ARMY	1	44	83	0.2	0.7
413 S.D.A.........	1	248	301*	0.9	2.5
419 SO BAPT CONV..	2	470	571*	1.7	4.7
443 UN C OF CHRIST	1	44	53*	0.2	0.4
449 UN METHODIST..	4	877	1 066*	3.2	8.9
453 UN PRES CH USA	3	382	464*	1.4	3.9
ONEIDA	**12**	**278**	**3 183***	**97.7**	**100.0**
081 CATHOLIC......	1	NA	15	0.5	0.5
151 L-D SAINTS....	9	NA	2 644	81.2	83.1
193 EPISCOPAL.....	1	224	455	14.0	14.3
453 UN PRES CH USA	1	54	69*	2.1	2.2
OWYHEE	**17**	**751**	**4 679***	**56.6**	**100.0**
017 AMER BAPT ASSN	1	100	100	1.2	2.1
053 ASSEMB OF GOD.	2	90	223	2.7	4.8
081 CATHOLIC......	2	NA	1 921	23.2	41.1
093 CHR CH (DISC).	1	56	154	1.9	3.3
143 CG IN CR(MENN)	1	29	29	0.4	0.6
151 L-D SAINTS....	3	NA	1 476	17.8	31.5
165 CH OF NAZARENE	2	117	308	3.7	6.6
167 CHS OF CHRIST.	1	20	30	0.4	0.6
226 FRIENDS-USA...	1	129	163*	2.0	3.5
283 LUTH--MO SYNOD	1	62	87	1.1	1.9
413 S.D.A.........	1	70	89*	1.1	1.9
453 UN PRES CH USA	1	78	99*	1.2	2.1
PAYETTE	**32**	**4 319**	**8 859***	**56.3**	**100.0**
019 AMER BAPT USA.	2	938	1 167*	7.4	13.2
053 ASSEMB OF GOD.	3	398	845	5.4	9.5
081 CATHOLIC......	2	NA	1 160	7.4	13.1
097 CHR CHS&CHS CR	1	175	218*	1.4	2.5
127 CH GOD (CLEVE)	1	14	17*	0.1	0.2
151 L-D SAINTS....	4	NA	1 758	11.2	19.8
157 CH OF BRETHREN	1	142	177*	1.1	2.0
165 CH OF NAZARENE	2	179	288	1.8	3.3
167 CHS OF CHRIST.	2	95	121	0.8	1.4
179 CONSRV BAPT...	2	450	560*	3.6	6.3
193 EPISCOPAL.....	1	147	210	1.3	2.4
221 FREE METHODIST	1	45	165	1.0	1.9
226 FRIENDS-USA...	1	451	561*	3.6	6.3
263 INT FOURSQ GOS	1	55	68*	0.4	0.8
283 LUTH--MO SYNOD	1	83	118	0.8	1.3

County and Denomination	Number of churches	Communicant, confirmed, full members	Total adherents Number	Percent of total population	Percent of total adherents
413 S.D.A.........	2	312	388*	2.5	4.4
419 SO BAPT CONV..	1	75	93*	0.6	1.0
443 UN C OF CHRIST	2	177	220*	1.4	2.5
449 UN METHODIST..	2	583	725*	4.6	8.2
POWER	**15**	**976**	**4 392***	**64.2**	**100.0**
019 AMER BAPT USA.	1	159	206*	3.0	4.7
029 AMER LUTH CH..	1	377	521	7.6	11.9
053 ASSEMB OF GOD.	1	166	252	3.7	5.7
081 CATHOLIC......	1	NA	350	5.1	8.0
151 L-D SAINTS....	7	NA	2 718	39.7	61.9
193 EPISCOPAL.....	1	36	36	0.5	0.8
443 UN C OF CHRIST	1	137	178*	2.6	4.1
449 UN METHODIST..	1	101	131*	1.9	3.0
SHOSHONE	**28**	**2 485**	**6 391***	**33.2**	**100.0**
019 AMER BAPT USA.	1	50	62*	0.3	1.0
029 AMER LUTH CH..	2	614	902	4.7	14.1
053 ASSEMB OF GOD.	3	210	537	2.8	8.4
081 CATHOLIC......	3	NA	1 889	9.8	29.6
097 CHR CHS&CHS CR	1	45	56*	0.3	0.9
127 CH GOD (CLEVE)	2	53	66*	0.3	1.0
151 L-D SAINTS....	2	NA	768	4.0	12.0
165 CH OF NAZARENE	1	130	283	1.5	4.4
167 CHS OF CHRIST.	1	15	19	0.1	0.3
193 EPISCOPAL.....	2	117	157	0.8	2.5
203 EVAN FREE CH..	1	23	29*	0.2	0.5
283 LUTH--MO SYNOD	2	186	298	1.5	4.7
329 OPEN BIBLE STD	1	50	85	0.4	1.3
413 S.D.A.........	1	69	86*	0.4	1.3
419 SO BAPT CONV..	1	185	231*	1.2	3.6
443 UN C OF CHRIST	2	383	479*	2.5	7.5
449 UN METHODIST..	2	355	444*	2.3	6.9
TETON	**9**	**254**	**2 681***	**92.5**	**100.0**
151 L-D SAINTS....	7	NA	2 353	81.2	87.8
413 S.D.A.........	2	254	328*	11.3	12.2
TWIN FALLS	**80**	**10 341**	**26 881***	**50.8**	**100.0**
017 AMER BAPT ASSN	1	25	25	-	0.1
019 AMER BAPT USA.	4	1 192	1 479*	2.8	5.5
029 AMER LUTH CH..	1	253	386	0.7	1.4
053 ASSEMB OF GOD.	6	378	723	1.4	2.7
059 BAPT MISS ASSN	1	48	60*	0.1	0.2
081 CATHOLIC......	3	NA	3 051	5.8	11.4
093 CHR CH (DISC).	2	562	970	1.8	3.6
097 CHR CHS&CHS CR	3	966	1 199*	2.3	4.5
127 CH GOD (CLEVE)	1	18	22*	-	0.1
143 CG IN CR(MENN)	1	122	122	0.2	0.5
151 L-D SAINTS....	23	NA	9 646	18.2	35.9
157 CH OF BRETHREN	1	110	136*	0.3	0.5
165 CH OF NAZARENE	4	480	862	1.6	3.2
167 CHS OF CHRIST.	2	245	321	0.6	1.2
179 CONSRV BAPT...	2	450	558*	1.1	2.1
193 EPISCOPAL.....	3	339	639	1.2	2.4
283 LUTH--MO SYNOD	5	1 763	2 308	4.4	8.6
285 MENNONITE CH..	1	67	83*	0.2	0.3
291 MISSIONARY CH.	1	30	47	0.1	0.2
371 REF CH IN AM..	1	99	249	0.5	0.9
403 SALVATION ARMY	1	55	100	0.2	0.4
413 S.D.A.........	1	56	69*	0.1	0.3
419 SO BAPT CONV..	3	295	366*	0.7	1.4
449 UN METHODIST..	6	2 029	2 518*	4.8	9.4
453 UN PRES CH USA	3	759	942*	1.8	3.5
VALLEY	**16**	**660**	**1 653***	**29.5**	**100.0**
053 ASSEMB OF GOD.	3	66	129	2.3	7.8
081 CATHOLIC......	3	NA	230	4.1	13.9
097 CHR CHS&CHS CR	1	63	77*	1.4	4.7
151 L-D SAINTS....	2	NA	494	8.8	29.9
165 CH OF NAZARENE	1	26	92	1.6	5.6
193 EPISCOPAL.....	1	74	70	1.2	4.2
283 LUTH--MO SYNOD	1	85	137	2.4	8.3
413 S.D.A.........	3	257	315*	5.6	19.1
443 UN C OF CHRIST	1	89	109*	1.9	6.6
WASHINGTON	**23**	**2 018**	**4 662***	**53.0**	**100.0**
001 ADVENT CHR CH.	1	16	20*	0.2	0.4
019 AMER BAPT USA.	3	381	473*	5.4	10.1
053 ASSEMB OF GOD.	2	112	151	1.7	3.2
081 CATHOLIC......	2	NA	726	8.2	15.6
097 CHR CHS&CHS CR	1	525	651*	7.4	14.0
151 L-D SAINTS....	4	NA	1 353	15.4	29.0
157 CH OF BRETHREN	1	27	33*	0.4	0.7
165 CH OF NAZARENE	1	116	173	2.0	3.7
167 CHS OF CHRIST.	2	66	91	1.0	2.0
179 CONSRV BAPT...	1	225	279*	3.2	6.0
193 EPISCOPAL.....	1	63	95	1.1	2.0
263 INT FOURSQ GOS	1	21	26*	0.3	0.6
283 LUTH--MO SYNOD	1	41	64	0.7	1.4
443 UN C OF CHRIST	1	261	324*	3.7	6.9
453 UN PRES CH USA	1	164	203*	2.3	4.4

NA—Not applicable
*Total adherents estimated from known number of communicant, confirmed, full members.
—Represents a percent less than 0.1.
Percentages may not total due to rounding.

Table 4. Churches and Church Membership by County and Denomination: 1980

County and Denomination	Number of churches	Communicant, confirmed, full members	Total adherents		
			Number	Percent of total population	Percent of total adherents
ILLINOIS					
THE STATE.....	9 358	2 054 178	6 297 355*	55.2	100.0
ADAMS	96	21 637	46 526*	65.0	100.0
019 AMER BAPT USA.	4	1 686	2 031*	2.8	4.4
029 AMER LUTH CH..	2	520	665	0.9	1.4
053 ASSEMB OF GOD.	5	674	1 323	1.8	2.8
081 CATHOLIC......	12	NA	17 964	25.1	38.6
093 CHR CH (DISC).	6	911	1 441	2.0	3.1
097 CHR CHS&CHS CR	9	2 200	2 651*	3.7	5.7
151 L-D SAINTS....	1	NA	369	0.5	0.8
157 CH OF BRETHREN	1	51	61*	0.1	0.1
165 CH OF NAZARENE	1	140	346	0.5	0.7
167 CHS OF CHRIST.	2	86	91	0.1	0.2
175 CONGR CHR CHS.	1	650	783*	1.1	1.7
193 EPISCOPAL.....	1	420	450	0.6	1.0
221 FREE METHODIST	1	36	162	0.2	0.3
226 FRIENDS-USA...	1	12	14*	-	-
281 LUTH CH AMER..	6	2 248	2 734	3.8	5.9
283 LUTH--MO SYNOD	5	2 231	2 738	3.8	5.9
290 METRO COMM CHS	1	40	80	0.1	0.2
403 SALVATION ARMY	1	235	1 180	1.6	2.5
413 S.D.A.........	1	76	92*	0.1	0.2
419 SO BAPT CONV..	2	406	489*	0.7	1.1
435 UNITARIAN-UNIV	1	69	83*	0.1	0.2
443 UN C OF CHRIST	9	3 721	4 483*	6.3	9.6
449 UN METHODIST..	19	4 324	5 210*	7.3	11.2
453 UN PRES CH USA	4	901	1 086*	1.5	2.3
ALEXANDER	34	3 480	5 035*	41.1	100.0
019 AMER BAPT USA.	1	250	306*	2.5	6.1
053 ASSEMB OF GOD.	3	151	216	1.8	4.3
081 CATHOLIC......	1	NA	676	5.5	13.4
093 CHR CH (DISC).	1	49	75	0.6	1.5
097 CHR CHS&CHS CR	1	87	106*	0.9	2.1
101 C.M.E.........	1	28	34*	0.3	0.7
167 CHS OF CHRIST.	1	60	76	0.6	1.5
181 CONSRV CONGR..	1	58	71*	0.6	1.4
193 EPISCOPAL.....	1	128	226	1.8	4.5
281 LUTH CH AMER..	1	130	145	1.2	2.9
413 S.D.A.........	1	8	10*	0.1	0.2
419 SO BAPT CONV..	10	1 909	2 334*	19.0	46.4
443 UN C OF CHRIST	1	26	32*	0.3	0.6
449 UN METHODIST..	9	450	550*	4.5	10.9
453 UN PRES CH USA	1	146	178*	1.5	3.5
BOND	41	5 058	8 007*	49.4	100.0
019 AMER BAPT USA.	1	406	485*	3.0	6.1
053 ASSEMB OF GOD.	4	199	408	2.5	5.1
081 CATHOLIC......	3	NA	1 097	6.8	13.7
097 CHR CHS&CHS CR	5	1 080	1 290*	8.0	16.1
157 CH OF BRETHREN	1	43	51*	0.3	0.6
167 CHS OF CHRIST.	1	88	95	0.6	1.2
185 CUMBER PRESB..	2	71	106	0.7	1.3
208 EVAN LUTH ASSN	1	36	45	0.3	0.6
221 FREE METHODIST	2	415	1 158	7.1	14.5
283 LUTH--MO SYNOD	1	157	210	1.3	2.6
419 SO BAPT CONV..	10	1 214	1 450*	8.9	18.1
449 UN METHODIST..	7	837	1 000*	6.2	12.5
453 UN PRES CH USA	3	512	612*	3.8	7.6
BOONE	26	7 322	12 983*	45.3	100.0
019 AMER BAPT USA.	1	335	415*	1.4	3.2
029 AMER LUTH CH..	1	220	289	1.0	2.2
053 ASSEMB OF GOD.	1	87	155	0.5	1.2
081 CATHOLIC......	1	NA	3 307	11.6	25.5
165 CH OF NAZARENE	1	10	34	0.1	0.3
167 CHS OF CHRIST.	1	150	185	0.6	1.4
175 CONGR CHR CHS.	1	110	136*	0.5	1.0
193 EPISCOPAL.....	1	131	317	1.1	2.4
201 EVAN COV CH AM	1	184	228*	0.8	1.8
221 FREE METHODIST	1	20	54	0.2	0.4
281 LUTH CH AMER..	1	769	1 093	3.8	8.4
283 LUTH--MO SYNOD	1	1 341	1 780	6.2	13.7
329 OPEN BIBLE STD	1	169	250	0.9	1.9
375 REF EPISCOPAL.	1	16	20*	0.1	0.2
403 SALVATION ARMY	1	86	116	0.4	0.9
419 SO BAPT CONV..	1	123	152*	0.5	1.2
443 UN C OF CHRIST	2	546	677*	2.4	5.2
449 UN METHODIST..	5	1 751	2 170*	7.6	16.7
453 UN PRES CH USA	2	1 157	1 434*	5.0	11.0
469 WELS..........	1	117	171	0.6	1.3
BROWN	17	1 853	3 384*	62.5	100.0
019 AMER BAPT USA.	3	498	598*	11.1	17.7
081 CATHOLIC......	1	NA	931	17.2	27.5
093 CHR CH (DISC).	2	245	410	7.6	12.1
097 CHR CHS&CHS CR	3	437	525*	9.7	15.5
121 CH GOD (ABR)..	1	75	90*	1.7	2.7
165 CH OF NAZARENE	1	68	181	3.3	5.3
283 LUTH--MO SYNOD	1	67	93	1.7	2.7
419 SO BAPT CONV..	1	55	66*	1.2	2.0
449 UN METHODIST..	1	270	324*	6.0	9.6
453 UN PRES CH USA	3	138	166*	3.1	4.9
BUREAU	72	10 592	24 604*	62.9	100.0
019 AMER BAPT USA.	5	635	770*	2.0	3.1
029 AMER LUTH CH..	4	1 014	1 333	3.4	5.4
081 CATHOLIC......	18	NA	11 343	29.0	46.1
093 CHR CH (DISC).	3	570	872	2.2	3.5
165 CH OF NAZARENE	2	68	119	0.3	0.5
167 CHS OF CHRIST.	1	35	45	0.1	0.2
175 CONGR CHR CHS.	3	356	431*	1.1	1.8
193 EPISCOPAL.....	2	171	218	0.6	0.9
201 EVAN COV CH AM	1	310	376*	1.0	1.5
281 LUTH CH AMER..	3	1 649	2 072	5.3	8.4
283 LUTH--MO SYNOD	1	93	127	0.3	0.5
285 MENNONITE CH..	2	162	196*	0.5	0.8
291 MISSIONARY CH.	1	62	76	0.2	0.3
413 S.D.A.........	2	15	18*	-	0.1
419 SO BAPT CONV..	1	169	205*	0.5	0.8
443 UN C OF CHRIST	8	1 694	2 053*	5.2	8.3
449 UN METHODIST..	13	3 218	3 900*	10.0	15.9
453 UN PRES CH USA	3	371	450*	1.2	1.8
CALHOUN	25	1 048	4 093*	69.8	100.0
081 CATHOLIC......	7	NA	2 821	48.1	68.9
097 CHR CHS&CHS CR	1	50	60*	1.0	1.5
165 CH OF NAZARENE	2	30	62	1.1	1.5
167 CHS OF CHRIST.	5	100	125	2.1	3.1
281 LUTH CH AMER..	1	70	74	1.3	1.8
283 LUTH--MO SYNOD	3	479	569	9.7	13.9
449 UN METHODIST..	3	91	109*	1.9	2.7
453 UN PRES CH USA	3	228	273*	4.7	6.7
CARROLL	35	6 369	9 519*	50.7	100.0
019 AMER BAPT USA.	2	211	255*	1.4	2.7
053 ASSEMB OF GOD.	1	45	108	0.6	1.1
071 BRETHREN (ASH)	2	531	641*	3.4	6.7
081 CATHOLIC......	3	NA	1 560	8.3	16.4
097 CHR CHS&CHS CR	1	40	48*	0.3	0.5
157 CH OF BRETHREN	3	445	537*	2.9	5.6
193 EPISCOPAL.....	1	72	80	0.4	0.8
281 LUTH CH AMER..	4	1 224	1 641	8.7	17.2
371 REF CH IN AM..	1	62	119	0.6	1.3
413 S.D.A.........	1	13	16*	0.1	0.2
419 SO BAPT CONV..	1	86	104*	0.6	1.1
443 UN C OF CHRIST	1	254	306*	1.6	3.2
449 UN METHODIST..	10	2 729	3 292*	17.5	34.6
453 UN PRES CH USA	2	297	358*	1.9	3.8
469 WELS..........	2	360	454	2.4	4.8
CASS	34	5 937	9 120*	60.5	100.0
019 AMER BAPT USA.	1	206	250*	1.7	2.7
053 ASSEMB OF GOD.	2	72	115	0.8	1.3
081 CATHOLIC......	5	NA	1 201	8.0	13.2
093 CHR CH (DISC).	2	211	322	2.1	3.5
097 CHR CHS&CHS CR	2	300	364*	2.4	4.0
165 CH OF NAZARENE	2	167	616	4.1	6.8
167 CHS OF CHRIST.	1	40	40	0.3	0.4
185 CUMBER PRESB..	1	62	112	0.7	1.2
281 LUTH CH AMER..	4	1 171	1 448	9.6	15.9
283 LUTH--MO SYNOD	4	1 180	1 583	10.5	17.4
419 SO BAPT CONV..	3	635	771*	5.1	8.5
443 UN C OF CHRIST	1	154	187*	1.2	2.1
449 UN METHODIST..	4	1 410	1 712*	11.3	18.8
453 UN PRES CH USA	2	329	399*	2.6	4.4
CHAMPAIGN	153	37 455	67 946*	40.3	100.0
017 AMER BAPT ASSN	1	50	50	-	0.1
019 AMER BAPT USA.	5	1 178	1 381*	0.8	2.0
029 AMER LUTH CH..	9	4 792	6 299	3.7	9.3
053 ASSEMB OF GOD.	4	366	575	0.3	0.8
065 BETHEL M ASSN.	1	125	147*	0.1	0.2
081 CATHOLIC......	21	NA	20 881	12.4	30.7
093 CHR CH (DISC).	3	1 071	1 266	0.8	1.9
097 CHR CHS&CHS CR	14	3 194	3 745*	2.2	5.5
101 C.M.E.........	1	771	904*	0.5	1.3
105 CHRISTIAN REF.	1	28	34	-	0.1
123 CH GOD (ANDER)	1	38	114	0.1	0.2
151 L-D SAINTS....	3	NA	780	0.5	1.1
157 CH OF BRETHREN	1	84	98*	0.1	0.1
165 CH OF NAZARENE	8	524	1 102	0.7	1.6
167 CHS OF CHRIST.	7	500	636	0.4	0.9
179 CONSRV BAPT...	1	223	261*	0.2	0.4
193 EPISCOPAL.....	3	1 148	1 379	0.8	2.0
221 FREE METHODIST	1	111	450	0.3	0.7
226 FRIENDS-USA...	1	71	83*	-	0.1
263 INT FOURSQ GOS	1	331	388*	0.2	0.6
271 REFORM JUDAISM	1	490	574*	0.3	0.8
281 LUTH CH AMER..	1	412	560	0.3	0.8
283 LUTH--MO SYNOD	6	2 491	3 260	1.9	4.8
285 MENNONITE CH..	3	156	183*	0.1	0.3
287 MENN GEN CONF.	1	61	95	0.1	0.1
290 METRO COMM CHS	0	10	20	-	-
353 CHR BRETHREN..	1	100	200	0.1	0.3
403 SALVATION ARMY	1	200	258	0.2	0.4
413 S.D.A.........	2	162	190*	0.1	0.3
419 SO BAPT CONV..	7	2 671	3 132*	1.9	4.6
435 UNITARIAN-UNIV	1	367	430*	0.3	0.6
443 UN C OF CHRIST	3	1 200	1 407*	0.8	2.1
449 UN METHODIST..	30	11 460	13 436*	8.0	19.8
453 UN PRES CH USA	8	2 990	3 506*	2.1	5.2
469 WELS..........	1	80	122	0.1	0.2

NA—Not applicable   *Total adherents estimated from known number of communicant, confirmed, full members.   —Represents a percent less than 0.1.   Percentages may not total due to rounding.

Table 4. Churches and Church Membership by County and Denomination: 1980

County and Denomination	Number of churches	Communicant, confirmed, full members	Total adherents Number	Percent of total population	Percent of total adherents
CHRISTIAN	60	10 971	21 787*	59.8	100.0
001 ADVENT CHR CH.	1	51	62*	0.2	0.3
019 AMER BAPT USA.	4	1 167	1 408*	3.9	6.5
053 ASSEMB OF GOD.	3	114	279	0.8	1.3
081 CATHOLIC......	6	NA	7 526	20.6	34.5
093 CHR CH (DISC).	2	841	1 108	3.0	5.1
097 CHR CHS&CHS CR	5	1 143	1 379*	3.8	6.3
127 CH GOD (CLEVE)	2	199	240*	0.7	1.1
165 CH OF NAZARENE	5	424	910	2.5	4.2
167 CHS OF CHRIST.	2	80	102	0.3	0.5
203 EVAN FREE CH..	1	107	129*	0.4	0.6
221 FREE METHODIST	2	70	303	0.8	1.4
283 LUTH--MO SYNOD	4	1 108	1 506	4.1	6.9
419 SO BAPT CONV..	2	365	440*	1.2	2.0
443 UN C OF CHRIST	1	340	410*	1.1	1.9
449 UN METHODIST..	15	3 717	4 483*	12.3	20.6
453 UN PRES CH USA	5	1 245	1 502*	4.1	6.9
CLARK	57	7 004	9 533*	56.4	100.0
081 CATHOLIC......	2	NA	626	3.7	6.6
093 CHR CH (DISC).	1	194	451	2.7	4.7
097 CHR CHS&CHS CR	5	912	1 091*	6.5	11.4
121 CH GOD (ABR)..	2	37	44*	0.3	0.5
127 CH GOD (CLEVE)	1	17	20*	0.1	0.2
165 CH OF NAZARENE	3	195	401	2.4	4.2
167 CHS OF CHRIST.	4	186	268	1.6	2.8
185 CUMBER PRESB..	3	122	215	1.3	2.3
283 LUTH--MO SYNOD	2	177	237	1.4	2.5
419 SO BAPT CONV..	14	2 504	2 997*	17.7	31.4
443 UN C OF CHRIST	1	107	128*	0.8	1.3
449 UN METHODIST..	18	2 435	2 914*	17.2	30.6
453 UN PRES CH USA	1	118	141*	0.8	1.5
CLAY	44	6 853	9 856*	64.5	100.0
019 AMER BAPT USA.	1	346	415*	2.7	4.2
053 ASSEMB OF GOD.	1	69	165	1.1	1.7
081 CATHOLIC......	2	NA	1 287	8.4	13.1
097 CHR CHS&CHS CR	10	2 627	3 149*	20.6	32.0
123 CH GOD (ANDER)	1	72	216	1.4	2.2
127 CH GOD (CLEVE)	1	41	49*	0.3	0.5
165 CH OF NAZARENE	1	116	260	1.7	2.6
167 CHS OF CHRIST.	1	60	76	0.5	0.8
283 LUTH--MO SYNOD	1	83	117	0.8	1.2
419 SO BAPT CONV..	10	1 671	2 003*	13.1	20.3
443 UN C OF CHRIST	1	62	74*	0.5	0.8
449 UN METHODIST..	13	1 605	1 924*	12.6	19.5
453 UN PRES CH USA	1	101	121*	0.8	1.2
CLINTON	43	4 748	21 765*	66.7	100.0
019 AMER BAPT USA.	1	146	180*	0.6	0.8
081 CATHOLIC......	15	NA	15 784	48.4	72.5
097 CHR CHS&CHS CR	2	105	129*	0.4	0.6
127 CH GOD (CLEVE)	1	?	?	?	?
165 CH OF NAZARENE	1	43	62	0.2	0.3
283 LUTH--MO SYNOD	4	1 159	1 547*	4.7	7.1
313 N AM BAPT CONF	1	149	184*	0.6	0.8
419 SO BAPT CONV..	4	710	875*	2.7	4.0
443 UN C OF CHRIST	4	1 035	1 276*	3.9	5.9
449 UN METHODIST..	10	1 401	1 728*	5.3	7.9
COLES	68	13 532	21 390*	40.4	100.0
019 AMER BAPT USA.	4	1 702	1 987*	3.7	9.3
029 AMER LUTH CH..	1	147	196	0.4	0.9
053 ASSEMB OF GOD.	2	152	225	0.4	1.1
081 CATHOLIC......	2	NA	3 600	6.8	16.8
089 CHR & MISS AL.	1	65	95	0.2	0.4
093 CHR CH (DISC).	3	1 372	2 297	4.3	10.7
097 CHR CHS&CHS CR	5	1 183	1 381*	2.6	6.5
123 CH GOD (ANDER)	2	97	291	0.5	1.4
151 L-D SAINTS....	1	NA	312	0.6	1.5
165 CH OF NAZARENE	3	350	739	1.4	3.5
167 CHS OF CHRIST.	4	358	427	0.8	2.0
185 CUMBER PRESB..	2	84	98	0.2	0.5
193 EPISCOPAL.....	1	111	145	0.3	0.7
221 FREE METHODIST	1	62	237	0.4	1.1
271 REFORM JUDAISM	1	32	37*	0.1	0.2
283 LUTH--MO SYNOD	3	1 387	1 815	3.4	8.5
323 OLD ORD AMISH.	1	130	152*	0.3	0.7
403 SALVATION ARMY	1	119	139	0.3	0.6
409 SEPARATE BAPT.	7	485	566*	1.1	2.6
413 S.D.A.........	1	43	50*	0.1	0.2
419 SO BAPT CONV..	5	1 037	1 211*	2.3	5.7
435 UNITARIAN-UNIV	1	23	27*	0.1	0.1
449 UN METHODIST..	11	3 362	3 926*	7.4	18.4
453 UN PRES CH USA	5	1 231	1 437*	2.7	6.7
COOK	2 012	510 220	2 967 455*	56.5	100.0
001 ADVENT CHR CH.	2	224	270*	—	—
005 AME ZION......	8	12 785	16 090	0.3	0.5
019 AMER BAPT USA.	59	18 902	22 812*	0.4	0.8
029 AMER LUTH CH..	56	25 734	34 906	0.7	1.2
049 ARMEN AP CH AM	1	37	437		
053 ASSEMB OF GOD.	48	5 163	7 891	0.2	0.3
057 BAPT GEN CONF.	34	6 715	8 104*	0.2	0.3
059 BAPT MISS ASSN	2	44	53*	—	—
081 CATHOLIC......	431	NA	2 303 743	43.9	77.6
083 CHRIST CATH CH	2	41	106	—	—
089 CHR & MISS AL.	12	928	1 223	—	—
091 CHRISTIAN CATH	1	20	50	—	—

County and Denomination	Number of churches	Communicant, confirmed, full members	Total adherents Number	Percent of total population	Percent of total adherents
093 CHR CH (DISC).	21	3 599	5 491	0.1	0.2
097 CHR CHS&CHS CR	22	3 042	3 671*	0.1	0.1
101 C.M.E.	11	14 628	17 654*	0.3	0.6
105 CHRISTIAN REF.	33	8 308	12 795	0.2	0.4
123 CH GOD (ANDER)	18	2 501	7 503	0.1	0.3
127 CH GOD (CLEVE)	41	2 994	3 613*	0.1	0.1
133 CH GOD(7TH)DEN	1	31	37*	—	—
151 L-D SAINTS....	15	NA	6 464	0.1	0.2
157 CH OF BRETHREN	3	262	316*	—	—
164 CH LUTH CONF.	1	45	63	—	—
165 CH OF NAZARENE	23	2 556	4 918	0.1	0.2
167 CHS OF CHRIST.	47	4 580	5 829	0.1	0.2
175 CONGR CHR CHS.	4	560	676*	—	—
179 CONSRV BAPT...	19	4 237	5 113*	0.1	0.2
185 CUMBER PRESB..	1	7	7	—	—
193 EPISCOPAL.....	80	23 834	31 430	0.6	1.1
195 ESTONIAN ELC..	2	195	428	—	—
199 EVAN CONGR CH.	3	126	152*	—	—
201 EVAN COV CH AM	31	5 740	6 927*	0.1	0.2
203 EVAN FREE CH..	23	2 725	3 289*	0.1	0.1
208 EVAN LUTH ASSN	17	7 697	10 937	0.2	0.4
209 EVAN LUTH SYN.	2	101	151	—	—
213 EVAN MENN INC.	1	63	76*	—	—
221 FREE METHODIST	4	246	846	—	—
226 FRIENDS-USA...	5	377	455*	—	—
233 GEN CH NEW JER	1	215	259*	—	—
237 GC MENN BR CHS	1	41	49*	—	—
239 SWEDENBORGIAN.	2	120	145*	—	—
263 INT FOURSQ GOS	2	581	701*	—	—
270 CONSRV JUDAISM	23	6 581	7 942*	0.2	0.3
271 REFORM JUDAISM	21	24 428	29 481*	0.6	1.0
274 LAT EVAN LUTH.	2	825	981	—	—
281 LUTH CH AMER..	114	43 722	57 212	1.1	1.9
283 LUTH--MO SYNOD	145	76 747	101 364	1.9	3.4
285 MENNONITE CH..	10	483	583*	—	—
287 MENN GEN CONF.	4	256	334	—	—
290 METRO COMM CHS	2	400	800	—	—
291 MISSIONARY CH.	3	156	271	—	—
313 N AM BAPT CONF	7	732	883*	—	—
329 OPEN BIBLE STD	3	410	535	—	—
335 ORTH PRESB CH.	1	37	45*	—	—
349 PENT HOLINESS.	2	54	65*	—	—
353 CHR BRETHREN..	24	1 600	2 400	—	0.1
369 PROT REF CHS..	1	242	435	—	—
371 REF CH IN AM..	24	7 208	11 600	0.2	0.4
375 REF EPISCOPAL.	1	296	357*	—	—
383 REF PRES OF NA	1	24	33	—	—
395 ROMANIAN OR CH	1	2 450	2 957*	0.1	0.1
403 SALVATION ARMY	14	2 138	4 394	0.1	0.1
409 SEPARATE BAPT.	2	73	88*	—	—
413 S.D.A.........	36	8 148	9 833*	0.2	0.3
419 SO BAPT CONV..	72	17 468	21 081*	0.4	0.7
423 SYRIAN ANTIOCH	2	700	845*	—	—
431 UKRANIAN AMER.	1	240	340	—	—
435 UNITARIAN-UNIV	14	3 796	4 581*	0.1	0.2
443 UN C OF CHRIST	119	47 408	57 214*	1.1	1.9
449 UN METHODIST..	154	58 871	71 048*	1.4	2.4
453 UN PRES CH USA	113	42 870	51 737*	1.0	1.7
469 WELS..........	6	1 853	2 336	—	0.1
CRAWFORD	69	8 782	12 356*	59.4	100.0
019 AMER BAPT USA.	2	725	866*	4.2	7.0
053 ASSEMB OF GOD.	2	219	403	1.9	3.3
081 CATHOLIC......	2	NA	930	4.5	7.5
093 CHR CH (DISC).	2	678	1 304	6.3	10.6
097 CHR CHS&CHS CR	8	1 622	1 939*	9.3	15.7
127 CH GOD (CLEVE)	1	58	69*	0.3	0.6
151 L-D SAINTS....	1	NA	61	0.3	0.5
157 CH OF BRETHREN	1	25	30*	0.1	0.2
165 CH OF NAZARENE	1	30	72	0.3	0.6
167 CHS OF CHRIST.	6	300	382	1.8	3.1
185 CUMBER PRESB..	2	59	83	0.4	0.7
193 EPISCOPAL.....	1	40	54	0.3	0.4
221 FREE METHODIST	2	53	219	1.1	1.8
226 FRIENDS-USA...	1	89	106*	0.5	0.9
419 SO BAPT CONV..	8	1 332	1 592*	7.6	12.9
435 UNITARIAN-UNIV	1	20	24*	0.1	0.2
443 UN C OF CHRIST	3	142	170*	0.8	1.4
449 UN METHODIST..	23	2 955	3 532*	17.0	28.6
453 UN PRES CH USA	2	435	520*	2.5	4.2
CUMBERLAND	28	2 325	3 953*	35.7	100.0
081 CATHOLIC......	3	NA	950	8.6	24.0
097 CHR CHS&CHS CR	2	510	624*	5.6	15.8
167 CHS OF CHRIST.	1	50	72	0.7	1.8
221 FREE METHODIST	2	66	228	2.1	5.8
226 FRIENDS-USA...	2	37	45*	0.4	1.1
419 SO BAPT CONV..	7	585	716*	6.5	18.1
449 UN METHODIST..	9	786	962*	8.7	24.3
453 UN PRES CH USA	2	291	356*	3.2	9.0
DE KALB	78	20 691	44 879*	60.1	100.0
001 ADVENT CHR CH.	1	71	83*	0.1	0.2
019 AMER BAPT USA.	3	900	1 055*	1.4	2.4
029 AMER LUTH CH..	4	1 233	1 605	2.2	3.6
053 ASSEMB OF GOD.	2	103	204	0.3	0.5
057 BAPT GEN CONF.	1	300	352*	0.5	0.8
081 CATHOLIC......	6	NA	18 458	24.7	41.1
097 CHR CHS&CHS CR	1	166	195*	0.3	0.4
127 CH GOD (CLEVE)	1	100	117*	0.2	0.3
151 L-D SAINTS....	1	NA	339	0.5	0.8
165 CH OF NAZARENE	2	164	457	0.6	1.0

NA—Not applicable *Total adherents estimated from known number of communicant, confirmed, full members. —Represents a percent less than 0.1. Percentages may not total due to rounding.

83

Table 4. Churches and Church Membership by County and Denomination: 1980

County and Denomination	Number of churches	Communicant, confirmed, full members	Total adherents Number	Total adherents Percent of total population	Total adherents Percent of total adherents
167 CHS OF CHRIST.	2	148	190	0.3	0.4
179 CONSRV BAPT...	1	223	261*	0.3	0.6
193 EPISCOPAL...	2	416	566	0.8	1.3
201 EVAN COV CH AM	1	116	136*	0.2	0.3
220 FREE LUTHERAN.	1	113	152	0.2	0.3
226 FRIENDS-USA...	1	7	8*	–	–
263 INT FOURSQ GOS	2	329	386*	0.5	0.9
281 LUTH CH AMER..	5	3 184	4 278	5.7	9.5
283 LUTH--MO SYNOD	4	1 964	2 524	3.4	5.6
403 SALVATION ARMY	1	113	568	0.8	1.3
413 S.D.A.........	1	37	43*	0.1	0.1
419 SO BAPT CONV..	5	894	1 048*	1.4	2.3
435 UNITARIAN-UNIV	2	599	702*	0.9	1.6
443 UN C OF CHRIST	8	2 717	3 186*	4.3	7.1
449 UN METHODIST..	16	6 021	7 060*	9.5	15.7
453 UN PRES CH USA	4	773	906*	1.2	2.0
DE WITT	36	6 401	9 602*	53.0	100.0
053 ASSEMB OF GOD.	1	234	412	2.3	4.3
081 CATHOLIC......	4	NA	1 456	8.0	15.2
097 CHR CHS&CHS CR	6	2 546	3 081*	17.0	32.1
123 CH GOD (ANDER)	1	16	48	0.3	0.5
127 CH GOD (CLEVE)	2	137	166*	0.9	1.7
165 CH OF NAZARENE	2	214	440	2.4	4.6
167 CHS OF CHRIST.	1	60	76	0.4	0.8
185 CUMBER PRESB..	2	47	64	0.4	0.7
193 EPISCOPAL.....	1	9	9	–	0.1
221 FREE METHODIST	1	16	60	0.3	0.6
283 LUTH--MO SYNOD	2	171	219	1.2	2.3
419 SO BAPT CONV..	3	404	489*	2.7	5.1
435 UNITARIAN-UNIV	1	30	36*	0.2	0.4
449 UN METHODIST..	8	2 240	2 711*	15.0	28.2
453 UN PRES CH USA	1	277	335*	1.9	3.5
DOUGLAS	55	8 221	12 281*	62.1	100.0
019 AMER BAPT USA.	5	655	796*	4.0	6.5
053 ASSEMB OF GOD.	1	42	57	0.3	0.5
061 BEACHY AMISH..	1	150	182*	0.9	1.5
081 CATHOLIC......	3	NA	1 600	8.1	13.0
093 CHR CH (DISC).	2	312	706	3.6	5.7
097 CHR CHS&CHS CR	4	1 256	1 527*	7.7	12.4
123 CH GOD (ANDER)	2	97	291	1.5	2.4
165 CH OF NAZARENE	3	200	291	1.5	2.4
167 CHS OF CHRIST.	3	205	261	1.3	2.1
221 FREE METHODIST	1	22	135	0.7	1.1
283 LUTH--MO SYNOD	1	334	421	2.1	3.4
285 MENNONITE CH..	3	400	486*	2.5	4.0
323 OLD ORD AMISH.	9	1 170	1 422*	7.2	11.6
419 SO BAPT CONV..	2	117	142*	0.7	1.2
443 UN C OF CHRIST	2	272	331*	1.7	2.7
449 UN METHODIST..	10	2 765	3 361*	17.0	27.4
453 UN PRES CH USA	3	224	272*	1.4	2.2
DU PAGE	287	102 878	376 398*	57.2	100.0
017 AMER BAPT ASSN	1	150	150	–	–
019 AMER BAPT USA.	3	607	742*	0.1	0.2
029 AMER LUTH CH..	7	2 553	3 382	0.5	0.9
053 ASSEMB OF GOD.	10	2 042	3 349	0.5	0.9
057 BAPT GEN CONF.	6	760	929*	0.1	0.2
059 BAPT MISS ASSN	1	7	9*	–	–
081 CATHOLIC......	40	NA	241 030	36.6	64.0
089 CHR & MISS AL.	7	615	1 101	0.2	0.3
093 CHR CH (DISC).	2	368	407	0.1	0.1
097 CHR CHS&CHS CR	5	871	1 065*	0.2	0.3
105 CHRISTIAN REF.	5	1 519	2 324	0.4	0.6
123 CH GOD (ANDER)	1	105	315	–	0.1
127 CH GOD (CLEVE)	1	20	24*	–	–
151 L-D SAINTS....	3	NA	1 688	0.3	0.4
157 CH OF BRETHREN	2	417	510*	0.1	0.1
165 CH OF NAZARENE	2	271	416	0.1	0.1
167 CH OF CHRIST.	6	619	788	0.1	0.2
175 CONGR CHR CHS.	4	477	583*	0.1	0.2
179 CONSRV BAPT...	4	892	1 090*	0.2	0.3
193 EPISCOPAL.....	12	6 657	8 532	1.3	2.3
201 EVAN COV CH AM	5	1 292	1 579*	0.2	0.4
203 EVAN FREE CH..	7	926	1 132*	0.2	0.3
208 EVAN LUTH ASSN	2	1 121	1 359	0.2	0.4
209 EVAN LUTH SYN.	1	309	383	0.1	0.1
221 FREE METHODIST	1	43	90	–	–
226 FRIENDS-USA...	1	62	76*	–	–
263 INT FOURSQ GOS	1	134	164*	–	–
271 REFORM JUDAISM	1	470	575*	0.1	0.2
274 LAT EVAN LUTH.	1	196	238	–	0.1
281 LUTH CH AMER..	20	11 008	15 650	2.4	4.2
283 LUTH--MO SYNOD	24	19 483	26 374	4.0	7.0
285 MENNONITE CH..	1	151	185*	–	–
291 MISSIONARY CH.	2	21	63	–	–
313 N AM BAPT CONF	3	562	687*	0.1	0.2
335 ORTH PRESB CH.	1	219	268*	–	0.1
353 CHR BRETHREN..	3	375	700	0.1	0.2
356 PRESB CH AMER.	1	74	124	–	–
371 REF CH IN AM..	3	360	643	0.1	0.2
403 SALVATION ARMY	1	189	273	–	0.1
413 S.D.A.........	6	2 133	2 607*	0.4	0.7
419 SO BAPT CONV..	10	2 694	3 293*	0.5	0.9
435 UNITARIAN-UNIV	2	450	550*	0.1	0.1
443 UN C OF CHRIST	23	12 201	14 914*	2.3	4.0
449 UN METHODIST..	28	18 859	23 053*	3.5	6.1
453 UN PRES CH USA	15	10 399	12 712*	1.9	3.4
469 WELS..........	2	197	272	–	0.1
EDGAR	58	7 471	11 376*	52.4	100.0
019 AMER BAPT USA.	2	467	565*	2.6	5.0
053 ASSEMB OF GOD.	1	64	165	0.8	1.5
081 CATHOLIC......	4	NA	1 547	7.1	13.6
093 CHR CH (DISC).	2	484	779	3.6	6.8
097 CHR CHS&CHS CR	13	1 863	2 254*	10.4	19.8
123 CH GOD (ANDER)	1	15	45	0.2	0.4
127 CH GOD (CLEVE)	1	93	112*	0.5	1.0
165 CH OF NAZARENE	3	246	723	3.3	6.4
167 CHS OF CHRIST.	3	111	136	0.6	1.2
193 EPISCOPAL.....	1	62	77	0.4	0.7
226 FRIENDS-USA...	1	141	171*	0.8	1.5
283 LUTH--MO SYNOD	1	304	422	1.9	3.7
413 S.D.A.........	1	48	58*	0.3	0.5
419 SO BAPT CONV..	1	80	97*	0.4	0.9
449 UN METHODIST..	20	3 044	3 682*	16.9	32.4
453 UN PRES CH USA	3	449	543*	2.5	4.8
EDWARDS	34	4 338	5 579*	70.1	100.0
081 CATHOLIC......	1	NA	157	2.0	2.8
093 CHR CH (DISC).	1	271	322	4.0	5.8
097 CHR CHS&CHS CR	6	1 297	1 567*	19.7	28.1
165 CH OF NAZARENE	1	?	?	?	?
167 CHS OF CHRIST.	1	38	50	0.6	0.9
175 CONGR CHR CHS.	2	101	122*	1.5	2.2
193 EPISCOPAL.....	1	37	39	0.5	0.7
221 FREE METHODIST	3	57	177	2.2	3.2
293 MORAV CH-NORTH	1	322	468	5.9	8.4
419 SO BAPT CONV..	3	797	963*	12.1	17.3
443 UN C OF CHRIST	1	56	68*	0.9	1.2
449 UN METHODIST..	10	1 154	1 395*	17.5	25.0
453 UN PRES CH USA	3	208	251*	3.2	4.5
EFFINGHAM	70	9 710	24 830*	80.2	100.0
029 AMER LUTH CH..	2	451	534	1.7	2.2
053 ASSEMB OF GOD.	1	58	172	0.6	0.7
081 CATHOLIC......	10	NA	11 794	38.1	47.5
093 CHR CH (DISC).	2	264	406	1.3	1.6
097 CHR CHS&CHS CR	10	1 151	1 420*	4.6	5.7
123 CH GOD (ANDER)	2	175	525	1.7	2.1
165 CH OF NAZARENE	2	111	289	0.9	1.2
167 CHS OF CHRIST.	2	150	191	0.6	0.8
185 CUMBER PRESB..	1	17	28	0.1	0.1
193 EPISCOPAL.....	1	40	56	0.2	0.2
221 FREE METHODIST	1	24	135	0.4	0.5
283 LUTH--MO SYNOD	9	2 652	3 583	11.6	14.4
419 SO BAPT CONV..	7	2 109	2 602*	8.4	10.5
443 UN C OF CHRIST	2	98	121*	0.4	0.5
449 UN METHODIST..	16	2 087	2 575*	8.3	10.4
453 UN PRES CH USA	2	323	399*	1.3	1.6
FAYETTE	77	9 899	13 718*	61.9	100.0
053 ASSEMB OF GOD.	2	105	206	0.9	1.5
065 BETHEL M ASSN.	2	225	271*	1.2	2.0
081 CATHOLIC......	4	NA	851	3.8	6.2
093 CHR CH (DISC).	1	153	338	1.5	2.5
097 CHR CHS&CHS CR	10	921	1 107*	5.0	8.1
123 CH GOD (ANDER)	4	184	552	2.5	4.0
127 CH GOD (CLEVE)	1	8	10*	–	0.1
157 CH OF BRETHREN	1	92	111*	0.5	0.8
167 CHS OF CHRIST.	3	88	112	0.5	0.8
221 FREE METHODIST	3	153	585	2.6	4.3
281 LUTH CH AMER..	2	374	449	2.0	3.3
283 LUTH--MO SYNOD	4	1 656	1 985	9.0	14.5
413 S.D.A.........	1	14	17*	0.1	0.1
415 S-D BAPTIST GC	1	33	40*	0.2	0.3
419 SO BAPT CONV..	18	3 903	4 692*	21.2	34.2
443 UN C OF CHRIST	1	111	133*	0.6	1.0
449 UN METHODIST..	18	1 710	2 056*	9.3	15.0
453 UN PRES CH USA	1	169	203*	0.9	1.5
FORD	39	7 031	10 658*	69.8	100.0
029 AMER LUTH CH..	5	1 108	1 446	9.5	13.6
053 ASSEMB OF GOD.	2	35	46	0.3	0.4
081 CATHOLIC......	6	NA	1 912	12.5	17.9
093 CHR CH (DISC).	2	447	603	4.0	5.7
097 CHR CHS&CHS CR	1	450	540*	3.5	5.1
165 CH OF NAZARENE	3	83	231	1.5	2.2
167 CHS OF CHRIST.	1	35	45	0.3	0.4
201 EVAN COV CH AM	1	275	330*	2.2	3.1
263 INT FOURSQ GOS	1	36	43*	0.3	0.4
281 LUTH CH AMER..	1	434	504	3.3	4.7
419 SO BAPT CONV..	2	502	603*	4.0	5.7
443 UN C OF CHRIST	1	71	85*	0.6	0.8
449 UN METHODIST..	10	2 965	3 561*	23.3	33.4
453 UN PRES CH USA	3	590	709*	4.6	6.7
FRANKLIN	111	18 894	27 300*	63.2	100.0
019 AMER BAPT USA.	6	1 500	1 799*	4.2	6.6
053 ASSEMB OF GOD.	2	126	228	0.5	0.8
065 BETHEL M ASSN.	1	100	120*	0.3	0.4
081 CATHOLIC......	6	NA	2 634	6.1	9.6
093 CHR CH (DISC).	1	298	403	0.9	1.5
097 CHR CHS&CHS CR	11	1 057	1 268*	2.9	4.6
123 CH GOD (ANDER)	4	640	1 920	4.4	7.0
127 CH GOD (CLEVE)	6	733	879*	2.0	3.2
151 L-D SAINTS....	1	NA	366	0.8	1.3
165 CH OF NAZARENE	3	213	407	0.9	1.5
167 CHS OF CHRIST.	7	275	375	0.9	1.4
185 CUMBER PRESB..	1	10	93	0.2	0.3
193 EPISCOPAL.....	1	84	103	0.2	0.4

NA—Not applicable   *Total adherents estimated from known number of communicant, confirmed, full members.   —Represents a percent less than 0.1.   Percentages may not total due to rounding.

Table 4. Churches and Church Membership by County and Denomination: 1980

County and Denomination	Number of churches	Communicant, confirmed, full members	Total adherents		
			Number	Percent of total population	Percent of total adherents
283 LUTH--MO SYNOD	1	157	209	0.5	0.8
381 REF PRES-EVAN.	1	18	23	0.1	0.1
403 SALVATION ARMY	1	45	112	0.3	0.4
413 S.D.A.........	1	84	101*	0.2	0.4
417 SOCIAL BRETH..	1	65	78*	0.2	0.3
419 SO BAPT CONV..	41	11 612	13 930*	32.2	51.0
449 UN METHODIST..	14	1 822	2 186*	5.1	8.0
453 UN PRES CH USA	1	55	66*	0.2	0.2
FULTON	81	11 053	17 754*	40.6	100.0
019 AMER BAPT USA.	2	771	934*	2.1	5.3
053 ASSEMB OF GOD.	3	235	384	0.9	2.2
081 CATHOLIC......	4	NA	2 191	5.0	12.3
093 CHR CH (DISC).	5	1 134	2 005	4.6	11.3
097 CHR CHS&CHS CR	6	470	569*	1.3	3.2
151 L-D SAINTS....	1	NA	135	0.3	0.8
157 CH OF BRETHREN	3	484	586*	1.3	3.3
165 CH OF NAZARENE	10	432	1 350	3.1	7.6
167 CHS OF CHRIST.	2	65	83	0.2	0.5
193 EPISCOPAL.....	2	172	258	0.6	1.5
203 EVAN FREE CH..	1	111	134*	0.3	0.8
221 FREE METHODIST	2	88	354	0.8	2.0
281 LUTH CH AMER..	2	431	565	1.3	3.2
371 REF CH IN AM..	1	180	263	0.6	1.5
403 SALVATION ARMY	1	127	250	0.6	1.4
413 S.D.A.........	1	69	84*	0.2	0.5
419 SO BAPT CONV..	1	199	241*	0.6	1.4
435 UNITARIAN-UNIV	1	30	36*	0.1	0.2
443 UN C OF CHRIST	3	673	815*	1.9	4.6
449 UN METHODIST..	26	4 405	5 334*	12.2	30.0
453 UN PRES CH USA	4	977	1 183*	2.7	6.7
GALLATIN	28	1 714	3 226*	42.5	100.0
081 CATHOLIC......	4	NA	1 087	14.3	33.7
097 CHR CHS&CHS CR	1	35	42*	0.6	1.3
123 CH GOD (ANDER)	1	21	63	0.8	2.0
127 CH GOD (CLEVE)	4	67	81*	1.1	2.5
165 CH OF NAZARENE	1	41	64	0.8	2.0
185 CUMBER PRESB..	1	16	40	0.5	1.2
417 SOCIAL BRETH..	5	247	298*	3.9	9.2
419 SO BAPT CONV..	3	741	893*	11.8	27.7
449 UN METHODIST..	3	318	383*	5.0	11.9
453 UN PRES CH USA	5	228	275*	3.6	8.5
GREENE	45	7 795	11 437*	68.6	100.0
019 AMER BAPT USA.	11	2 976	3 591*	21.6	31.4
053 ASSEMB OF GOD.	2	57	103	0.6	0.9
081 CATHOLIC......	3	NA	1 848	11.1	16.2
093 CHR CH (DISC).	2	338	526	3.2	4.6
167 CHS OF CHRIST.	2	60	76	0.5	0.7
283 LUTH--MO SYNOD	1	141	198	1.2	1.7
419 SO BAPT CONV..	16	2 791	3 367*	20.2	29.4
449 UN METHODIST..	5	1 110	1 339*	8.0	11.7
453 UN PRES CH USA	3	322	389*	2.3	3.4
GRUNDY	32	6 690	19 012*	62.2	100.0
019 AMER BAPT USA.	1	357	439*	1.4	2.3
029 AMER LUTH CH..	4	1 787	2 370	7.7	12.5
053 ASSEMB OF GOD.	1	71	103	0.3	0.5
081 CATHOLIC......	7	NA	10 404	34.0	54.7
097 CHR CHS&CHS CR	1	212	261*	0.9	1.4
165 CH OF NAZARENE	1	63	110	0.4	0.6
167 CHS OF CHRIST.	1	45	57	0.2	0.3
193 EPISCOPAL.....	1	173	164	0.5	0.9
221 FREE METHODIST	1	42	264	0.9	1.4
283 LUTH--MO SYNOD	1	70	77	0.3	0.4
419 SO BAPT CONV..	2	329	405*	1.3	2.1
443 UN C OF CHRIST	1	234	288*	0.9	1.5
449 UN METHODIST..	7	2 314	2 848*	9.3	15.0
453 UN PRES CH USA	3	993	1 222*	4.0	6.4
HAMILTON	42	3 867	5 853*	63.8	100.0
053 ASSEMB OF GOD.	1	83	160	1.7	2.7
081 CATHOLIC......	3	NA	1 153	12.6	19.7
097 CHR CHS&CHS CR	2	80	95*	1.0	1.6
127 CH GOD (CLEVE)	1	42	50*	0.5	0.9
167 CHS OF CHRIST.	2	135	172	1.9	2.9
175 CONGR CHR CHS.	1	110	130*	1.4	2.2
185 CUMBER PRESB..	1	28	60	0.7	1.0
193 EPISCOPAL.....	1	46	72	0.8	1.2
283 LUTH--MO SYNOD	1	59	72	0.8	1.2
419 SO BAPT CONV..	20	2 852	3 377*	36.8	57.7
449 UN METHODIST..	9	432	512*	5.6	8.7
HANCOCK	71	8 323	13 791*	57.8	100.0
019 AMER BAPT USA.	2	386	465*	1.9	3.4
029 AMER LUTH CH..	3	592	802	3.4	5.8
053 ASSEMB OF GOD.	6	260	519	2.2	3.8
081 CATHOLIC......	8	NA	2 531	10.6	18.4
093 CHR CH (DISC).	5	874	1 478	6.2	10.7
097 CHR CHS&CHS CR	10	1 282	1 544*	6.5	11.2
127 CH GOD (CLEVE)	1	23	28*	0.1	0.2
151 L-D SAINTS....	1	NA	405	1.7	2.9
165 CH OF NAZARENE	1	36	33	0.1	0.2
193 EPISCOPAL.....	2	120	134	0.6	1.0
221 FREE METHODIST	1	27	156	0.7	1.1
281 LUTH CH AMER..	1	365	425	1.8	3.1
283 LUTH--MO SYNOD	2	316	401	1.7	2.9
413 S.D.A.........	2	44	53*	0.2	0.4

County and Denomination	Number of churches	Communicant, confirmed, full members	Total adherents		
			Number	Percent of total population	Percent of total adherents
419 SO BAPT CONV..	1	20	24*	0.1	0.2
443 UN C OF CHRIST	2	395	476*	2.0	3.5
449 UN METHODIST..	16	2 612	3 147*	13.2	22.8
453 UN PRES CH USA	7	971	1 170*	4.9	8.5
HARDIN	17	1 373	1 832*	34.0	100.0
081 CATHOLIC......	1	NA	160	3.0	8.7
097 CHR CHS&CHS CR	2	290	348*	6.5	19.0
123 CH GOD (ANDER)	1	8	24	0.4	1.3
167 CHS OF CHRIST.	3	150	191	3.5	10.4
417 SOCIAL BRETH..	3	117	140*	2.6	7.6
419 SO BAPT CONV..	4	612	734*	13.6	40.1
449 UN METHODIST..	3	196	235*	4.4	12.8
HENDERSON	22	3 008	4 166*	45.7	100.0
019 AMER BAPT USA.	2	378	460*	5.0	11.0
081 CATHOLIC......	2	NA	350	3.8	8.4
093 CHR CH (DISC).	1	114	175	1.9	4.2
097 CHR CHS&CHS CR	2	210	255*	2.8	6.1
165 CH OF NAZARENE	1	34	35	0.4	0.8
193 EPISCOPAL.....	1	324	455	5.0	10.9
281 LUTH CH AMER..	1	166	222	2.4	5.3
371 REF CH IN AM..	1	62	122	1.3	2.9
449 UN METHODIST..	8	1 238	1 506*	16.5	36.1
453 UN PRES CH USA	3	482	586*	6.4	14.1
HENRY	89	19 384	37 175*	64.1	100.0
017 AMER BAPT ASSN	1	50	50	0.1	0.1
019 AMER BAPT USA.	5	1 740	2 134*	3.7	5.7
029 AMER LUTH CH..	1	96	117	0.2	0.3
053 ASSEMB OF GOD.	4	176	327	0.6	0.9
057 BAPT GEN CONF.	1	95	117*	0.2	0.3
081 CATHOLIC......	13	NA	12 093	20.9	32.5
097 CHR CHS&CHS CR	3	503	617*	1.1	1.7
127 CH GOD (CLEVE)	3	127	156*	0.3	0.4
151 L-D SAINTS....	1	NA	242	0.4	0.7
165 CH OF NAZARENE	2	135	373	0.6	1.0
167 CHS OF CHRIST.	3	122	154	0.3	0.4
179 CONSRV BAPT...	1	223	274*	0.5	0.7
193 EPISCOPAL.....	2	131	162	0.3	0.4
197 EVAN CH OF NA.	1	48	48	0.1	0.1
199 EVAN CONGR CH.	1	94	115*	0.2	0.3
203 EVAN FREE CH..	2	201	247*	0.4	0.7
221 FREE METHODIST	1	18	249	0.4	0.7
263 INT FOURSQ GOS	1	51	63*	0.1	0.2
281 LUTH CH AMER..	8	4 075	5 234	9.0	14.1
283 LUTH--MO SYNOD	3	1 601	2 119	3.7	5.7
285 MENNONITE CH..	2	396	486*	0.8	1.3
403 SALVATION ARMY	1	93	259	0.4	0.7
413 S.D.A.........	1	64	78*	0.1	0.2
419 SO BAPT CONV..	1	265	325*	0.6	0.9
443 UN C OF CHRIST	7	1 721	2 111*	3.6	5.7
449 UN METHODIST..	17	6 382	7 827*	13.5	21.1
453 UN PRES CH USA	3	977	1 198*	2.1	3.2
IROQUOIS	72	12 248	20 810*	63.1	100.0
029 AMER LUTH CH..	8	2 339	3 011	9.1	14.5
081 CATHOLIC......	10	NA	5 244	15.9	25.2
093 CHR CH (DISC).	2	377	591	1.8	2.8
097 CHR CHS&CHS CR	8	1 270	1 533*	4.6	7.4
123 CH GOD (ANDER)	1	32	96	0.3	0.5
165 CH OF NAZARENE	4	166	306	0.9	1.5
175 CONGR CHR CHS.	1	146	176*	0.5	0.8
193 EPISCOPAL.....	1	52	61	0.2	0.3
203 EVAN FREE CH..	1	16	19*	0.1	0.1
226 FRIENDS-USA...	1	12	14*	–	0.1
283 LUTH--MO SYNOD	9	3 048	3 896	11.8	18.7
371 REF CH IN AM..	1	145	256	0.8	1.2
419 SO BAPT CONV..	2	72	87*	0.3	0.4
443 UN C OF CHRIST	2	432	521*	1.6	2.5
449 UN METHODIST..	19	3 909	4 719*	14.3	22.7
453 UN PRES CH USA	2	232	280*	0.8	1.3
JACKSON	94	16 927	30 252*	49.2	100.0
019 AMER BAPT USA.	9	2 361	2 722*	4.4	9.0
053 ASSEMB OF GOD.	3	202	343	0.6	1.1
065 BETHEL M ASSN.	1	200	231*	0.4	0.8
081 CATHOLIC......	5	NA	9 405	15.3	31.1
093 CHR CH (DISC).	1	354	381	0.6	1.3
097 CHR CHS&CHS CR	5	1 083	1 249*	2.0	4.1
123 CH GOD (ANDER)	4	111	333	0.5	1.1
127 CH GOD (CLEVE)	2	65	75*	0.1	0.2
151 L-D SAINTS....	1	NA	318	0.5	1.1
165 CH OF NAZARENE	3	219	471	0.8	1.6
167 CHS OF CHRIST.	3	175	222	0.4	0.7
185 CUMBER PRESB..	1	7	18	–	0.1
193 EPISCOPAL.....	1	148	171	0.3	0.6
208 EVAN LUTH ASSN	1	57	83	0.1	0.3
226 FRIENDS-USA...	1	10	12*	–	–
281 LUTH CH AMER..	5	1 121	1 405	2.3	4.6
283 LUTH--MO SYNOD	5	1 605	2 169	3.5	7.2
353 CHR BRETHREN..	2	50	85	0.1	0.3
381 REF PRES-EVAN.	1	59	66	0.1	0.2
419 SO BAPT CONV..	17	5 206	6 003*	9.8	19.8
435 UNITARIAN-UNIV	1	97	112*	0.2	0.4
443 UN C OF CHRIST	2	246	284*	0.5	0.9
449 UN METHODIST..	16	2 888	3 330*	5.4	11.0
453 UN PRES CH USA	4	663	764*	1.2	2.5
JASPER	35	2 737	6 120*	54.1	100.0

NA—Not applicable   *Total adherents estimated from known number of communicant, confirmed, full members.   —Represents a percent less than 0.1.   Percentages may not total due to rounding.

Table 4. Churches and Church Membership by County and Denomination: 1980

County and Denomination	Number of churches	Communicant, confirmed, full members	Total adherents		
			Number	Percent of total population	Percent of total adherents
019 AMER BAPT USA.	1	200	242*	2.1	4.0
053 ASSEMB OF GOD.	1	30	44	0.4	0.7
081 CATHOLIC......	4	NA	2 645	23.4	43.2
097 CHR CHS&CHS CR	5	745	903*	8.0	14.8
167 CHS OF CHRIST.	2	95	121	1.1	2.0
175 CONGR CHR CHS.	1	25	30*	0.3	0.5
185 CUMBER PRESB..	1	29	61	0.5	1.0
221 FREE METHODIST	1	58	186	1.6	3.0
281 LUTH CH AMER..	1	53	67	0.6	1.1
419 SO BAPT CONV..	6	508	616*	5.4	10.1
443 UN C OF CHRIST	1	24	29*	0.3	0.5
449 UN METHODIST..	10	868	1 052*	9.3	17.2
453 UN PRES CH USA	1	102	124*	1.1	2.0
JEFFERSON	81	15 020	20 412*	56.1	100.0
005 AME ZION......	1	340	515	1.4	2.5
019 AMER BAPT USA.	3	458	556*	1.5	2.7
029 AMER LUTH CH..	1	217	333	0.9	1.6
053 ASSEMB OF GOD.	1	49	81	0.2	0.4
081 CATHOLIC......	2	NA	1 436	4.0	7.0
097 CHR CHS&CHS CR	7	1 618	1 964*	5.4	9.6
101 C.M.E.........	1	116	141*	0.4	0.7
123 CH GOD (ANDER)	3	153	459	1.3	2.2
127 CH GOD (CLEVE)	1	99	120*	0.3	0.6
165 CH OF NAZARENE	3	132	315	0.9	1.5
167 CHS OF CHRIST.	2	186	286	0.8	1.4
193 EPISCOPAL.....	1	151	203	0.6	1.0
221 FREE METHODIST	1	18	54	0.1	0.3
283 LUTH--MO SYNOD	1	227	288	0.8	1.4
413 S.D.A.........	1	25	30*	0.1	0.1
419 SO BAPT CONV..	32	8 078	9 804*	27.0	48.0
435 UNITARIAN-UNIV	1	47	57*	0.2	0.3
443 UN C OF CHRIST	1	159	193*	0.5	0.9
449 UN METHODIST..	16	2 171	2 635*	7.2	12.9
453 UN PRES CH USA	2	776	942*	2.6	4.6
JERSEY	32	4 676	10 252*	49.9	100.0
019 AMER BAPT USA.	4	1 336	1 618*	7.9	15.8
053 ASSEMB OF GOD.	5	230	419	2.0	4.1
081 CATHOLIC......	5	NA	4 324	21.1	42.2
097 CHR CHS&CHS CR	1	33	40*	0.2	0.4
165 CH OF NAZARENE	1	45	141	0.7	1.4
167 CHS OF CHRIST.	1	100	127	0.6	1.2
283 LUTH--MO SYNOD	1	208	283	1.4	2.8
419 SO BAPT CONV..	5	863	1 045*	5.1	10.2
443 UN C OF CHRIST	2	463	561*	2.7	5.5
449 UN METHODIST..	6	959	1 162*	5.7	11.3
453 UN PRES CH USA	1	439	532*	2.6	5.2
JO DAVIESS	40	5 389	15 272*	64.9	100.0
029 AMER LUTH CH..	8	1 810	2 391	10.2	15.7
053 ASSEMB OF GOD.	1	27	52	0.2	0.3
081 CATHOLIC......	10	NA	8 377	35.6	54.9
165 CH OF NAZARENE	1	49	117	0.5	0.8
193 EPISCOPAL.....	1	71	89	0.4	0.6
283 LUTH--MO SYNOD	1	212	293	1.2	1.9
435 UNITARIAN-UNIV	1	113	139*	0.6	0.9
449 UN METHODIST..	10	2 261	2 772*	11.8	18.2
453 UN PRES CH USA	6	760	932*	4.0	6.1
469 WELS..........	1	86	110	0.5	0.7
JOHNSON	41	3 676	4 678*	48.6	100.0
019 AMER BAPT USA.	1	132	156*	1.6	3.3
053 ASSEMB OF GOD.	2	52	70	0.7	1.5
081 CATHOLIC......	2	NA	197	2.0	4.2
097 CHR CHS&CHS CR	1	135	160*	1.7	3.4
123 CH GOD (ANDER)	1	15	45	0.5	1.0
167 CHS OF CHRIST.	7	325	414	4.3	8.8
185 CUMBER PRESB..	2	62	142	1.5	3.0
417 SOCIAL BRETH..	1	39	46*	0.5	1.0
419 SO BAPT CONV..	14	2 077	2 456*	25.5	52.5
449 UN METHODIST..	10	839	992*	10.3	21.2
KANE	194	61 156	154 362*	55.4	100.0
001 ADVENT CHR CH.	2	592	734*	0.3	0.5
019 AMER BAPT USA.	8	3 200	3 965*	1.4	2.6
029 AMER LUTH CH..	4	1 896	2 625	0.9	1.7
039 AP CHR CH(NAZ)	1	29	36*	-	-
053 ASSEMB OF GOD.	3	380	653	0.2	0.4
057 BAPT GEN CONF.	3	392	486*	0.2	0.3
081 CATHOLIC......	28	NA	71 348	25.6	46.2
097 CHR CHS&CHS CR	2	220	273*	0.1	0.2
123 CH GOD (ANDER)	1	93	279	0.1	0.2
127 CH GOD (CLEVE)	3	401	497*	0.2	0.3
151 L-D SAINTS....	2	NA	1 010	0.4	0.7
157 CH OF BRETHREN	2	692	857*	0.3	0.6
165 CH OF NAZARENE	4	182	337	0.1	0.2
167 CHS OF CHRIST.	4	273	391	0.1	0.3
179 CONSRV BAPT...	2	446	553*	0.2	0.4
193 EPISCOPAL.....	8	2 986	3 662*	1.3	2.4
201 EVAN COV CH AM	2	248	307*	0.1	0.2
203 EVAN FREE CH..	2	25	31*	-	-
208 EVAN LUTH ASSN	2	1 000	1 310	0.5	0.8
221 FREE METHODIST	3	212	768	0.3	0.5
263 INT FOURSQ GOS	3	413	512*	0.2	0.3
281 LUTH CH AMER..	11	7 559	10 035	3.6	6.5
283 LUTH--MO SYNOD	17	10 452	13 864	5.0	9.0
313 N AM BAPT CONF	1	121	150*	0.1	0.1
329 OPEN BIBLE STD	1	70	125	-	0.1
349 PENT HOLINESS.	1	15	19*	-	-

County and Denomination	Number of churches	Communicant, confirmed, full members	Total adherents		
			Number	Percent of total population	Percent of total adherents
353 CHR BRETHREN..	2	225	340	0.1	0.2
381 REF PRES-EVAN.	1	110	175	0.1	0.1
403 SALVATION ARMY	3	409	3 618	1.3	2.3
413 S.D.A.........	4	473	586*	0.2	0.4
419 SO BAPT CONV..	13	2 575	3 191*	1.1	2.1
435 UNITARIAN-UNIV	2	231	286*	0.1	0.2
443 UN C OF CHRIST	17	8 045	9 969*	3.6	6.5
449 UN METHODIST..	23	13 162	16 310*	5.9	10.6
453 UN PRES CH USA	7	3 856	4 778*	1.7	3.1
469 WELS..........	2	173	282	0.1	0.2
KANKAKEE	102	21 724	60 126*	58.4	100.0
005 AME ZION......	1	363	488	0.5	0.8
019 AMER BAPT USA.	2	802	988*	1.0	1.6
029 AMER LUTH CH..	2	572	740	0.7	1.2
053 ASSEMB OF GOD.	1	74	103	0.1	0.2
057 BAPT GEN CONF.	1	138	170*	0.2	0.3
081 CATHOLIC......	18	NA	30 148	29.3	50.1
093 LUTH CH (DISC)	2	417	849	0.8	1.4
097 CHR CHS&CHS CR	1	187	230*	0.2	0.4
105 CHRISTIAN REF.	1	154	260	0.3	0.4
123 CH GOD (ANDER)	2	72	216	0.2	0.4
127 CH GOD (CLEVE)	1	217	267*	0.3	0.4
151 L-D SAINTS....	1	NA	316	0.3	0.5
165 CH OF NAZARENE	10	1 918	3 364	3.3	5.6
167 CHS OF CHRIST.	3	175	223	0.2	0.4
179 CONSRV BAPT...	1	223	275*	0.3	0.5
193 EPISCOPAL.....	2	573	776	0.8	1.3
208 EVAN LUTH ASSN	1	568	701	0.7	1.2
263 INT FOURSQ GOS	1	69	85*	0.1	0.1
283 LUTH--MO SYNOD	8	3 527	4 788	4.7	8.0
285 MENNONITE CH..	1	38	47*	-	0.1
313 N AM BAPT CONF	1	490	604*	0.6	1.0
329 OPEN BIBLE STD	1	50	100	0.1	0.2
371 REF CH IN AM..	3	530	876	0.9	1.5
403 SALVATION ARMY	1	130	631	0.6	1.0
413 S.D.A.........	2	143	176*	0.2	0.3
417 SOCIAL BRETH..	1	110	136*	0.1	0.2
419 SO BAPT CONV..	3	899	1 108*	1.1	1.8
435 UNITARIAN-UNIV	1	13	16*	-	-
443 UN C OF CHRIST	4	1 304	1 607*	1.6	2.7
449 UN METHODIST..	20	6 704	8 261*	8.0	13.7
453 UN PRES CH USA	3	962	1 185*	1.2	2.0
469 WELS..........	2	302	392	0.4	0.7
KENDALL	36	8 164	18 904*	50.8	100.0
019 AMER BAPT USA.	1	388	487*	1.3	2.6
029 AMER LUTH CH..	7	2 249	3 047	8.2	16.1
053 ASSEMB OF GOD.	2	278	505	1.4	2.7
057 BAPT GEN CONF.	1	42	53*	0.1	0.3
059 BAPT MISS ASSN	1	114	143*	0.4	0.8
081 CATHOLIC......	3	NA	8 088	21.7	42.8
097 CHR CHS&CHS CR	1	57	71*	0.2	0.4
127 CH GOD (CLEVE)	1	?	?	?	?
157 CH OF BRETHREN	1	210	263*	0.7	1.4
167 CHS OF CHRIST.	1	50	64	0.2	0.3
283 LUTH--MO SYNOD	2	1 069	1 533	4.1	8.1
335 ORTH PRESB CH.	1	128	161*	0.4	0.9
413 S.D.A.........	1	48	60*	0.2	0.3
419 SO BAPT CONV..	2	337	423*	1.1	2.2
443 UN C OF CHRIST	1	558	700*	1.9	3.7
449 UN METHODIST..	8	1 843	2 311*	6.2	12.2
453 UN PRES CH USA	2	793	995*	2.7	5.3
KNOX	63	18 085	30 467*	49.5	100.0
001 ADVENT CHR CH.	1	60	72*	0.1	0.2
019 AMER BAPT USA.	1	570	684*	1.1	2.2
053 ASSEMB OF GOD.	2	293	494	0.8	1.6
057 BAPT GEN CONF.	1	664	797*	1.3	2.6
081 CATHOLIC......	5	NA	4 718	7.7	15.5
093 LUTH CH (DISC)	3	1 528	2 013	3.3	6.6
097 CHR CHS&CHS CR	2	110	132*	0.2	0.4
123 CH GOD (ANDER)	1	175	525	0.9	1.7
127 CH GOD (CLEVE)	1	72	86*	0.1	0.3
151 L-D SAINTS....	1	NA	300	0.5	1.0
165 CH OF NAZARENE	2	225	686	1.1	2.3
167 CHS OF CHRIST.	1	70	89	0.1	0.3
175 CONGR CHR CHS.	4	828	994*	1.6	3.3
193 EPISCOPAL.....	1	252	292	0.5	1.0
201 EVAN COV CH AM	1	446	536*	0.9	1.8
226 FRIENDS--USA..	1	21	25*	-	0.1
263 INT FOURSQ GOS	1	60	72*	0.1	0.2
271 REFORM JUDAISM	1	110	132*	0.2	0.4
281 LUTH CH AMER..	6	3 371	4 319	7.0	14.2
283 LUTH--MO SYNOD	1	382	540	0.9	1.8
329 OPEN BIBLE STD	1	425	600	1.0	2.0
403 SALVATION ARMY	1	108	2 377	3.9	7.8
413 S.D.A.........	1	73	88*	0.1	0.3
419 SO BAPT CONV..	1	173	208*	0.3	0.7
443 UN C OF CHRIST	2	346	415*	0.7	1.4
449 UN METHODIST..	15	5 828	6 998*	11.4	23.0
453 UN PRES CH USA	5	1 895	2 275*	3.7	7.5
LAKE	207	60 448	213 232*	48.4	100.0
019 AMER BAPT USA.	3	1 986	2 432*	0.6	1.1
029 AMER LUTH CH..	5	1 991	2 947	0.7	1.4
049 ARMEN AP CH AM	1	23	29	-	-
053 ASSEMB OF GOD.	8	1 175	2 338	0.5	1.1
057 BAPT GEN CONF.	10	1 964	2 405*	0.5	1.1
081 CATHOLIC......	30	NA	131 478	29.9	61.7
089 CHR & MISS AL.	2	35	93	-	-

NA— Not applicable   *Total adherents estimated from known number of communicant, confirmed, full members.   —Represents a percent less than 0.1.   Percentages may not total due to rounding.

86

Table 4. Churches and Church Membership by County and Denomination: 1980

County and Denomination	Number of churches	Communicant, confirmed, full members	Total adherents Number	Percent of total population	Percent of total adherents
091 CHRISTIAN CATH	1	1 200	2 000	0.5	0.9
093 CHR CH (DISC).	4	943	1 570	0.4	0.7
097 CHR CHS&CHS CR	3	440	539*	0.1	0.3
127 CH GOD (CLEVE)	7	468	573*	0.1	0.3
151 L-D SAINTS....	2	NA	1 181	0.3	0.6
165 CH OF NAZARENE	3	179	317	0.1	0.1
167 CHS OF CHRIST.	7	379	508	0.1	0.2
175 CONGR CHR CHS.	1	93	114*	-	0.1
193 EPISCOPAL.....	11	5 373	7 882	1.8	3.7
199 EVAN CONGR CH.	1	122	149*	-	0.1
201 EVAN COV CH AM	1	41	50*	-	-
203 EVAN FREE CH..	8	1 202	1 472*	0.3	0.7
208 EVAN LUTH ASSN	2	362	502	0.1	0.2
221 FREE METHODIST	1	137	750	0.2	0.4
226 FRIENDS--USA..	1	82	100*	-	-
263 INT FOURSQ GOS	1	26	32*	-	-
270 CONSRV JUDAISM	4	1 226	1 502*	0.3	0.7
271 REFORM JUDAISM	3	2 268	2 778*	0.6	1.3
281 LUTH CH AMER..	11	6 629	9 214	2.1	4.3
283 LUTH--MO SYNOD	7	3 423	4 590	1.0	2.2
291 MISSIONARY CH.	1	302	538	0.1	0.3
335 ORTH PRESB CH.	1	45	55*	-	-
353 CHR BRETHREN..	2	40	50	-	-
403 SALVATION ARMY	1	95	123	-	0.1
413 S.D.A.........	2	230	282*	0.1	0.1
419 SO BAPT CONV..	15	4 606	4 973*	1.1	2.3
435 UNITARIAN-UNIV	1	370	453*	0.1	0.2
443 UN C OF CHRIST	14	5 655	6 926	1.6	3.2
449 UN METHODIST..	19	8 342	10 217*	2.3	4.8
453 UN PRES CH USA	8	7 284	8 921*	2.0	4.2
469 WELS.........	5	2 258	3 149	0.7	1.5
LA SALLE	135	22 953	73 683*	67.5	100.0
001 ADVENT CHR CH.	1	26	31*	-	-
019 AMER BAPT USA.	3	822	992*	0.9	1.3
029 AMER LUTH CH..	14	5 702	7 696	7.1	10.4
053 ASSEMB OF GOD.	4	256	432	0.4	0.6
081 CATHOLIC......	30	NA	43 674	40.0	59.3
097 CHR CHS&CHS CR	2	210	253*	0.2	0.3
123 CH GOD (ANDER)	2	76	228	0.2	0.3
127 CH GOD (CLEVE)	2	37	45*	-	0.1
151 L-D SAINTS....	1	NA	221	0.2	0.3
163 CH OF LUTH BR.	1	58	208	0.2	0.3
165 CH OF NAZARENE	7	571	1 217	1.1	1.7
167 CHS OF CHRIST.	4	155	197	0.2	0.3
179 CONSRV BAPT...	1	223	269*	0.2	0.4
193 EPISCOPAL.....	3	509	730	0.7	1.0
197 EVAN CH OF NA.	1	11	11	-	-
203 EVAN FREE CH..	1	25	30*	-	-
281 LUTH CH AMER..	2	123	144	0.1	0.2
283 LUTH--MO SYNOD	3	1 466	1 856	1.7	2.5
329 OPEN BIBLE STD	1	40	80	0.1	0.1
363 PRIMITIVE METH	1	161	194*	0.2	0.3
403 SALVATION ARMY	2	173	320	0.3	0.4
413 S.D.A.........	3	164	198*	0.2	0.3
419 SO BAPT CONV..	7	737	889*	0.8	1.2
443 UN C OF CHRIST	7	2 286	2 759*	2.5	3.7
449 UN METHODIST..	25	7 127	8 601*	7.9	11.7
453 UN PRES CH USA	7	1 995	2 408*	2.2	3.3
LAWRENCE	52	5 873	8 873*	49.8	100.0
053 ASSEMB OF GOD.	1	45	178	1.0	2.0
081 CATHOLIC......	3	NA	847	4.8	9.5
093 CHR CH (DISC).	1	553	763	4.3	8.6
097 CHR CHS&CHS CR	4	658	788*	4.4	8.9
123 CH GOD (ANDER)	1	18	54	0.3	0.6
127 CH GOD (CLEVE)	3	189	226*	1.3	2.5
157 CH OF BRETHREN	1	87	104*	0.6	1.2
165 CH OF NAZARENE	1	11	86	0.5	1.0
167 CHS OF CHRIST.	2	34	39	0.2	0.4
221 FREE METHODIST	5	291	999	5.6	11.3
283 LUTH--MO SYNOD	1	157	205	1.2	2.3
419 SO BAPT CONV..	2	733	877*	4.9	9.9
443 UN C OF CHRIST	2	118	141*	0.8	1.6
449 UN METHODIST..	21	2 561	3 066*	17.2	34.6
453 UN PRES CH USA	4	418	500*	2.8	5.6
LEE	60	10 522	22 320*	61.4	100.0
019 AMER BAPT USA.	3	546	661*	1.8	3.0
029 AMER LUTH CH..	6	1 867	2 408	6.6	10.8
053 ASSEMB OF GOD.	1	80	139	0.4	0.6
081 CATHOLIC......	9	NA	8 814	24.3	39.5
089 CHR & MISS AL.	2	80	211	0.6	0.9
093 CHR CH (DISC).	1	147	147	0.4	0.7
097 CHR CHS&CHS CR	2	110	133*	0.4	0.6
121 CH GOD (ABR)..	1	19	23*	0.1	0.1
123 CH GOD (ANDER)	1	157	471	1.3	2.1
157 CH OF BRETHREN	2	427	517*	1.4	2.3
165 CH OF NAZARENE	1	68	138	0.4	0.6
167 CHS OF CHRIST.	1	90	115	0.3	0.5
193 EPISCOPAL.....	1	213	244	0.7	1.1
199 EVAN CONGR CH.	3	416	504*	1.4	2.3
263 INT FOURSQ GOS	1	61	74*	0.2	0.3
281 LUTH CH AMER..	2	1 106	1 505	4.1	6.7
419 SO BAPT CONV..	4	519	628*	1.7	2.8
443 UN C OF CHRIST	3	285	345*	0.9	1.5
449 UN METHODIST..	13	3 409	4 127*	11.4	18.5
453 UN PRES CH USA	3	922	1 116*	3.1	5.0
LIVINGSTON	77	13 455	22 728*	54.9	100.0
019 AMER BAPT USA.	5	1 086	1 300*	3.1	5.7
029 AMER LUTH CH..	9	2 838	3 685	8.9	16.2
053 ASSEMB OF GOD.	2	77	127	0.3	0.6
081 CATHOLIC......	11	NA	5 144	12.4	22.6
093 CHR CH (DISC).	4	296	512	1.2	2.3
097 CHR CHS&CHS CR	2	200	239*	0.6	1.1
123 CH GOD (ANDER)	1	30	90	0.2	0.4
127 CH GOD (CLEVE)	2	59	71*	0.2	0.3
151 L-D SAINTS....	1	NA	503	1.2	2.2
165 CH OF NAZARENE	4	172	394	1.0	1.7
167 CHS OF CHRIST.	3	95	121	0.3	0.5
193 EPISCOPAL.....	1	159	193	0.5	0.8
213 EVAN MENN INC.	1	251	300*	0.7	1.3
221 FREE METHODIST	1	16	114	0.3	0.5
281 LUTH CH AMER..	1	408	511	1.2	2.2
283 LUTH--MO SYNOD	2	588	735	1.8	3.2
285 MENNONITE CH..	1	146	175*	0.4	0.8
287 MENN GEN CONF.	1	86	102	0.2	0.4
403 SALVATION ARMY	1	63	170	0.4	0.7
419 SO BAPT CONV..	1	80	96*	0.2	0.4
443 UN C OF CHRIST	3	572	685*	1.7	3.0
449 UN METHODIST..	18	5 249	6 283*	15.2	27.6
453 UN PRES CH USA	2	984	1 178*	2.8	5.2
LOGAN	52	13 025	20 121*	63.3	100.0
019 AMER BAPT USA.	1	312	370*	1.2	1.8
029 AMER LUTH CH..	3	1 630	2 020	6.4	10.0
053 ASSEMB OF GOD.	1	53	98	0.3	0.5
059 BAPT MISS ASSN	1	31	37*	0.1	0.2
065 BETHEL M ASSN.	1	125	148*	0.5	0.7
081 CATHOLIC......	6	NA	4 142	13.0	20.6
093 CHR CH (DISC).	1	90	138	0.4	0.7
097 CHR CHS&CHS CR	10	3 686	4 366*	13.7	21.7
165 CH OF NAZARENE	1	74	99	0.3	0.5
167 CHS OF CHRIST.	1	60	76	0.2	0.4
185 CUMBER PRESB..	2	190	389	1.2	1.9
193 EPISCOPAL.....	1	186	240	0.8	1.2
221 FREE METHODIST	1	49	180	0.6	0.9
281 LUTH CH AMER..	1	312	358	1.1	1.8
283 LUTH--MO SYNOD	5	1 958	2 374	7.5	11.8
403 SALVATION ARMY	1	89	134	0.4	0.7
413 S.D.A.........	1	20	24*	0.1	0.1
443 UN C OF CHRIST	1	465	551*	1.7	2.7
449 UN METHODIST..	12	3 360	3 980*	12.5	19.8
453 UN PRES CH USA	1	335	397*	1.2	2.0
MC DONOUGH	64	10 797	20 805*	55.9	100.0
019 AMER BAPT USA.	4	1 204	1 393*	3.7	6.7
053 ASSEMB OF GOD.	4	317	585	1.6	2.8
081 CATHOLIC......	4	NA	6 842	18.4	32.9
093 CHR CH (DISC).	5	845	1 428	3.8	6.9
097 CHR CHS&CHS CR	5	855	989*	2.7	4.8
121 CH GOD (ABR)..	1	120	139*	0.4	0.7
123 CH GOD (ANDER)	1	14	42	0.1	0.2
133 CH GOD(7TH)DEN	1	9	10*	-	-
151 L-D SAINTS....	1	NA	182	0.5	0.9
165 CH OF NAZARENE	2	125	283	0.8	1.4
167 CHS OF CHRIST.	1	63	65	0.2	0.3
179 CONSRV BAPT...	1	223	258*	0.7	1.2
193 EPISCOPAL.....	1	160	198	0.5	1.0
221 FREE METHODIST	1	24	93	0.2	0.4
281 LUTH CH AMER..	1	228	321	0.9	1.5
283 LUTH--MO SYNOD	1	175	261	0.7	1.3
329 OPEN BIBLE STD	1	60	95	0.3	0.5
403 SALVATION ARMY	1	105	365	1.0	1.8
419 SO BAPT CONV..	1	99	115*	0.3	0.6
435 UNITARIAN-UNIV	1	20	23*	0.1	0.1
449 UN METHODIST..	19	4 390	5 080*	13.6	24.4
453 UN PRES CH USA	7	1 761	2 038*	5.5	9.8
MC HENRY	101	30 045	81 418*	55.1	100.0
019 AMER BAPT USA.	2	209	259*	0.2	0.3
029 AMER LUTH CH..	1	1 020	1 450	1.0	1.8
053 ASSEMB OF GOD.	4	379	729	0.5	0.9
057 BAPT GEN CONF.	1	140	173*	0.1	0.2
081 CATHOLIC......	16	NA	39 164	26.5	48.1
089 CHR & MISS AL.	1	95	143	0.1	0.2
097 CHR CHS&CHS CR	1	144	178*	0.1	0.2
127 CH GOD (CLEVE)	1	?	?	?	?
151 L-D SAINTS....	2	NA	565	0.4	0.7
165 CH OF NAZARENE	1	41	125	0.1	0.2
167 CHS OF CHRIST.	1	58	109	0.1	0.1
193 EPISCOPAL.....	4	747	1 067	0.7	1.3
195 ESTONIAN ELC..	1	125	314	0.2	0.4
201 EVAN COV CH AM	3	163	202*	0.1	0.2
203 EVAN FREE CH..	4	465	576*	0.4	0.7
221 FREE METHODIST	1	118	336	0.2	0.4
226 FRIENDS--USA..	1	29	36*	-	-
263 INT FOURSQ GOS	1	25	31*	-	-
281 LUTH CH AMER..	7	5 369	8 366	5.7	10.3
283 LUTH--MO SYNOD	11	8 146	11 743	7.9	14.4
419 SO BAPT CONV..	7	1 418	1 757*	1.2	2.2
435 UNITARIAN-UNIV	1	125	155*	0.1	0.2
443 UN C OF CHRIST	7	3 778	4 691*	3.2	5.7
449 UN METHODIST..	16	5 606	6 946*	4.7	8.5
453 UN PRES CH USA	5	1 750	2 168*	1.5	2.7
469 WELS.........	1	95	145	0.1	0.2
MC LEAN	122	32 056	60 295*	50.6	100.0
019 AMER BAPT USA.	6	1 133	1 344*	1.1	2.2
029 AMER LUTH CH..	4	1 003	1 366	1.1	2.3
053 ASSEMB OF GOD.	3	292	541	0.5	0.9

NA—Not applicable *Total adherents estimated from known number of communicant, confirmed, full members. —Represents a percent less than 0.1. Percentages may not total due to rounding.

Table 4. Churches and Church Membership by County and Denomination: 1980

County and Denomination	Number of churches	Communicant, confirmed, full members	Total adherents Number	Percent of total population	Percent of total adherents
065 BETHEL M ASSN.	2	180	214*	0.2	0.4
081 CATHOLIC......	10	NA	18 589	15.6	30.8
093 CHR CH (DISC).	14	2 683	4 304	3.6	7.1
097 CHR CHS&CHS CR	8	2 290	2 717*	2.3	4.5
123 CH GOD (ANDER)	4	242	726	0.6	1.2
127 CH GOD (CLEVE)	1	229	272*	0.2	0.5
151 L-D SAINTS....	1	NA	529	0.4	0.9
165 CH OF NAZARENE	2	208	260	0.2	0.4
167 CHS OF CHRIST.	3	293	373	0.3	0.6
193 EPISCOPAL.....	2	511	646	0.5	1.1
203 EVAN FREE CH..	1	161	191*	0.2	0.3
221 FREE METHODIST	1	45	222	0.2	0.4
271 REFORM JUDAISM	1	180	214*	0.2	0.4
281 LUTH CH AMER..	1	1 252	1 703	1.4	2.8
283 LUTH--MO SYNOD	7	3 945	5 106	4.3	8.5
285 MENNONITE CH..	1	350	415*	0.3	0.7
287 MENN GEN CONF.	4	898	1 059	0.9	1.8
329 OPEN BIBLE STD	1	35	70	0.1	0.1
403 SALVATION ARMY	1	171	502	0.4	0.8
413 S.D.A.........	1	45	53*	–	0.1
419 SO BAPT CONV..	4	1 134	1 345*	1.1	2.2
435 UNITARIAN-UNIV	1	161	191*	0.2	0.3
443 UN C OF CHRIST	2	380	451*	0.4	0.7
449 UN METHODIST..	27	9 626	11 420*	9.6	18.9
453 UN PRES CH USA	8	4 579	5 432*	4.6	9.0
469 WELS..........	1	30	40	–	0.1
MACON	118	35 745	63 689*	48.5	100.0
019 AMER BAPT USA.	1	937	1 143*	0.9	1.8
053 ASSEMB OF GOD.	6	516	1 044	0.8	1.6
065 BETHEL M ASSN.	2	300	366*	0.3	0.6
081 CATHOLIC......	8	NA	13 684	10.4	21.5
093 CHR CH (DISC).	9	2 953	5 411	4.1	8.5
097 CHR CHS&CHS CR	1	140	171*	0.1	0.3
101 C.M.E.........	1	240	293*	0.2	0.5
123 CH GOD (ANDER)	5	610	1 830	1.4	2.9
127 CH GOD (CLEVE)	3	259	316*	0.2	0.5
151 L-D SAINTS....	1	NA	553	0.4	0.9
157 CH OF BRETHREN	2	205	250*	0.2	0.4
165 CH OF NAZARENE	5	1 182	2 518	1.9	4.0
167 CHS OF CHRIST.	4	612	802	0.6	1.3
193 EPISCOPAL.....	1	341	460	0.4	0.7
221 FREE METHODIST	1	202	840	0.6	1.3
226 FRIENDS-USA...	1	15	18*	–	–
263 INT FOURSQ GOS	4	1 630	1 988*	1.5	3.1
271 REFORM JUDAISM	1	212	259*	0.2	0.4
281 LUTH CH AMER..	3	1 453	1 889	1.4	3.0
283 LUTH--MO SYNOD	8	5 414	7 040	5.4	11.1
335 ORTH PRESB CH.	1	13	16*	–	–
403 SALVATION ARMY	1	226	497	0.4	0.8
413 S.D.A.........	2	185	226*	0.2	0.4
419 SO BAPT CONV..	11	3 594	4 383*	3.3	6.9
435 UNITARIAN-UNIV	1	30	37*	–	0.1
443 UN C OF CHRIST	2	609	743*	0.6	1.2
449 UN METHODIST..	26	10 403	12 687*	9.7	19.9
453 UN PRES CH USA	7	3 464	4 225*	3.2	6.6
MACOUPIN	100	15 708	27 747*	56.2	100.0
019 AMER BAPT USA.	4	702	847*	1.7	3.1
029 AMER LUTH CH..	5	1 033	1 349	2.7	4.9
053 ASSEMB OF GOD.	5	415	714	1.4	2.6
081 CATHOLIC......	15	NA	7 753	15.7	27.9
093 CHR CH (DISC).	4	538	978	2.0	3.5
097 CHR CHS&CHS CR	1	861	1 039*	2.1	3.7
157 CH OF BRETHREN	2	287	346*	0.7	1.2
165 CH OF NAZARENE	2	165	284	0.6	1.0
167 CHS OF CHRIST.	3	140	178	0.4	0.6
193 EPISCOPAL.....	2	134	171	0.3	0.6
221 FREE METHODIST	1	17	84	0.2	0.3
283 LUTH--MO SYNOD	6	2 433	3 165	6.4	11.4
419 SO BAPT CONV..	23	3 607	4 352*	8.8	15.7
443 UN C OF CHRIST	4	1 179	1 423*	2.9	5.1
449 UN METHODIST..	19	3 765	4 543*	9.2	16.4
453 UN PRES CH USA	4	432	521*	1.1	1.9
MADISON	268	71 835	141 528*	57.1	100.0
017 AMER BAPT ASSN	1	200	200	0.1	0.1
019 AMER BAPT USA.	15	5 134	6 207*	2.5	4.4
029 AMER LUTH CH..	1	265	348	0.1	0.2
039 AP CHR CH(NAZ)	1	14	17*	–	–
049 ARMEN AP CH AM	1	61	111	–	0.1
053 ASSEMB OF GOD.	31	4 239	7 212	2.9	5.1
081 CATHOLIC......	29	NA	47 798	19.3	33.8
093 CHR CH (DISC).	3	573	879	0.4	0.6
097 CHR CHS&CHS CR	9	1 799	2 175*	0.9	1.5
101 C.M.E.........	1	30	36*	–	–
123 CH GOD (ANDER)	6	491	1 473	0.6	1.0
127 CH GOD (CLEVE)	4	415	502*	0.2	0.4
151 L-D SAINTS....	2	NA	431	0.2	0.3
165 CH OF NAZARENE	7	980	2 293	0.9	1.6
167 CHS OF CHRIST.	17	2 060	2 622	1.1	1.9
175 CONGR CHR CHS.	1	252	305*	0.1	0.2
181 CONSRV CONGR..	1	246	297*	0.1	0.2
193 EPISCOPAL.....	6	1 057	1 243	0.5	0.9
203 EVAN FREE CH..	1	65	79*	–	0.1
208 EVAN LUTH ASSN	1	193	274	0.1	0.2
221 FREE METHODIST	2	95	372	0.2	0.3
271 REFORM JUDAISM	1	72	87*	–	0.1
281 LUTH CH AMER..	1	185	262	0.1	0.2
283 LUTH--MO SYNOD	22	9 816	13 088	5.3	9.2
381 REF PRES-EVAN.	1	46	62	–	–
403 SALVATION ARMY	2	324	897	0.4	0.6

County and Denomination	Number of churches	Communicant, confirmed, full members	Total adherents Number	Percent of total population	Percent of total adherents
413 S.D.A.........	2	169	204*	0.1	0.1
419 SO BAPT CONV..	37	17 710	21 412*	8.6	15.1
435 UNITARIAN-UNIV	1	98	118*	–	0.1
443 UN C OF CHRIST	17	9 892	11 960*	4.8	8.5
449 UN METHODIST..	27	9 064	10 959*	4.4	7.7
453 UN PRES CH USA	17	6 290	7 605*	3.1	5.4
MARION	98	18 022	27 360*	62.9	100.0
005 AME ZION......	1	375	540	1.2	2.0
019 AMER BAPT USA.	1	1 608	1 945*	4.5	7.1
053 ASSEMB OF GOD.	1	62	103	0.2	0.4
059 BAPT MISS ASSN	1	24	29*	0.1	0.1
081 CATHOLIC......	4	NA	3 825	8.8	14.0
093 CHR CH (DISC).	3	659	1 081	2.5	4.0
097 CHR CHS&CHS CR	16	3 016	3 649*	8.4	13.3
123 CH GOD (ANDER)	2	120	360	0.8	1.3
127 CH GOD (CLEVE)	2	206	249*	0.6	0.9
151 L-D SAINTS....	1	NA	307	0.7	1.1
157 CH OF BRETHREN	1	50	60*	0.1	0.2
165 CH OF NAZARENE	1	104	417	1.0	1.5
167 CHS OF CHRIST.	5	465	592	1.4	2.2
193 EPISCOPAL.....	2	108	127	0.3	0.5
221 FREE METHODIST	2	123	480	1.1	1.8
271 REFORM JUDAISM	1	40	48*	0.1	0.2
281 LUTH CH AMER..	1	181	227	0.5	0.8
283 LUTH--MO SYNOD	3	1 220	1 556	3.6	5.7
403 SALVATION ARMY	1	123	226	0.5	0.8
413 S.D.A.........	1	28	34*	0.1	0.1
419 SO BAPT CONV..	22	5 431	6 570*	15.1	24.0
443 UN C OF CHRIST	2	497	601*	1.4	2.2
449 UN METHODIST..	20	3 203	3 875*	8.9	14.2
453 UN PRES CH USA	4	379	459*	1.1	1.7
MARSHALL	31	4 962	8 972*	62.0	100.0
019 AMER BAPT USA.	1	207	252*	1.7	2.8
029 AMER LUTH CH..	2	633	846	5.8	9.4
081 CATHOLIC......	6	NA	2 767	19.1	30.8
093 CHR CH (DISC).	1	190	238	1.6	2.7
097 CHR CHS&CHS CR	2	391	476*	3.3	5.3
165 CH OF NAZARENE	1	38	114	0.8	1.3
193 EPISCOPAL.....	1	61	78	0.5	0.9
281 LUTH CH AMER..	2	370	426	2.9	4.7
283 LUTH--MO SYNOD	3	567	694	4.8	7.7
329 OPEN BIBLE STD	1	40	80	0.6	0.9
443 UN C OF CHRIST	1	238	290*	2.0	3.2
449 UN METHODIST..	6	1 580	1 923*	13.3	21.4
453 UN PRES CH USA	4	647	788*	5.4	8.8
MASON	36	8 446	11 426*	58.6	100.0
019 AMER BAPT USA.	2	702	861*	4.4	7.5
053 ASSEMB OF GOD.	2	294	402	2.1	3.5
081 CATHOLIC......	2	NA	600	3.1	5.3
093 CHR CH (DISC).	2	569	881	4.5	7.7
097 CHR CHS&CHS CR	5	1 534	1 881*	9.7	16.5
165 CH OF NAZARENE	2	123	368	1.9	3.2
193 EPISCOPAL.....	1	152	141	0.7	1.2
283 LUTH--MO SYNOD	7	2 020	2 570	13.2	22.5
291 MISSIONARY CH.	1	137	147	0.8	1.3
419 SO BAPT CONV..	4	594	728*	3.7	6.4
449 UN METHODIST..	7	2 000	2 453*	12.6	21.5
453 UN PRES CH USA	1	321	394*	2.0	3.4
MASSAC	44	8 275	10 490*	70.0	100.0
029 AMER LUTH CH..	3	460	604	4.0	5.8
053 ASSEMB OF GOD.	1	107	206	1.4	2.0
081 CATHOLIC......	1	NA	225	1.5	2.1
093 CHR CH (DISC).	1	194	325	2.2	3.1
097 CHR CHS&CHS CR	4	224	267*	1.8	2.5
123 CH GOD (ANDER)	1	60	180	1.2	1.7
127 CH GOD (CLEVE)	2	182	217*	1.4	2.1
165 CH OF NAZARENE	1	38	54	0.4	0.5
167 CHS OF CHRIST.	6	620	789	5.3	7.5
177 CONGR HOL CH..	1	18	21*	0.1	0.2
185 CUMBER PRESB..	1	50	50	0.3	0.5
281 LUTH CH AMER..	1	287	337	2.2	3.2
290 METRO COMM CHS	0	10	20	0.1	0.2
413 S.D.A.........	1	30	36*	0.2	0.3
419 SO BAPT CONV..	12	4 621	5 518*	36.8	52.6
443 UN C OF CHRIST	2	323	386*	2.6	3.7
449 UN METHODIST..	5	924	1 103*	7.4	10.5
453 UN PRES CH USA	1	127	152*	1.0	1.4
MENARD	28	4 937	7 003*	59.9	100.0
017 AMER BAPT ASSN	1	50	50	0.4	0.7
081 CATHOLIC......	3	NA	842	7.2	12.0
093 CHR CH (DISC).	2	216	412	3.5	5.9
097 CHR CHS&CHS CR	4	823	999*	8.5	14.3
185 CUMBER PRESB..	1	16	22	0.2	0.3
263 INT FOURSQ GOS	1	101	123*	1.1	1.8
283 LUTH--MO SYNOD	2	681	852	7.3	12.2
413 S.D.A.........	1	9	11*	0.1	0.2
419 SO BAPT CONV..	3	868	1 054*	9.0	15.1
443 UN C OF CHRIST	1	297	361*	3.1	5.2
449 UN METHODIST..	3	852	1 034*	8.8	14.8
453 UN PRES CH USA	6	1 024	1 243*	10.6	17.7
MERCER	38	6 374	9 471*	49.1	100.0
019 AMER BAPT USA.	2	685	840*	4.4	8.9
053 ASSEMB OF GOD.	2	99	170	0.9	1.8

NA—Not applicable　　　　*Total adherents estimated from known number of communicant, confirmed, full members.　　　　—Represents a percent less than 0.1.　　　　Percentages may not total due to rounding.

Table 4. Churches and Church Membership by County and Denomination: 1980

County and Denomination	Number of churches	Communicant, confirmed, full members	Total adherents		
			Number	Percent of total population	Percent of total adherents
081 CATHOLIC......	5	NA	1 109	5.8	11.7
093 CHR CH (DISC).	1	61	307	1.6	3.2
165 CH OF NAZARENE	1	62	168	0.9	1.8
193 EPISCOPAL.....	1	79	82	0.4	0.9
281 LUTH CH AMER..	5	1 272	1 716	8.9	18.1
329 OPEN BIBLE STD	1	40	60	0.4	0.8
413 S.D.A.	1	33	40*	0.2	0.4
419 SO BAPT CONV..	1	40	49*	0.3	0.5
449 UN METHODIST..	8	2 032	2 492*	12.9	26.3
453 UN PRES CH USA	10	1 971	2 418*	12.5	25.5
MONROE	30	6 760	15 284*	76.0	100.0
053 ASSEMB OF GOD.	2	72	136	0.7	0.9
081 CATHOLIC......	7	NA	6 988	34.7	45.7
127 CH GOD (CLEVE)	1	14	17*	0.1	0.1
165 CH OF NAZARENE	1	14	0	-	-
167 CHS OF CHRIST.	1	18	35	0.2	0.2
283 LUTH--MO SYNOD	4	1 483	1 874	9.3	12.3
381 REF PRES-EVAN.	1	59	70	0.3	0.5
419 SO BAPT CONV..	3	857	1 036*	5.1	6.8
443 UN C OF CHRIST	9	4 151	5 017*	24.9	32.8
449 UN METHODIST..	1	92	111*	0.6	0.7
MONTGOMERY	83	11 390	19 940*	62.9	100.0
017 AMER BAPT ASSN	1	50	50	0.2	0.3
019 AMER BAPT USA.	3	650	782*	2.5	3.9
029 AMER LUTH CH..	1	173	232	0.7	1.2
053 ASSEMB OF GOD.	3	135	259	0.8	1.3
081 CATHOLIC......	9	NA	5 234	16.5	26.2
093 CHR CH (DISC).	6	714	1 186	3.7	5.9
097 CHR CHS&CHS CR	5	416	500*	1.6	2.5
151 L-D SAINTS....	1	NA	152	0.5	0.8
165 CH OF NAZARENE	1	4	0	-	-
167 CHS OF CHRIST.	2	65	83	0.3	0.4
221 FREE METHODIST	3	43	225	0.7	1.1
281 LUTH CH AMER..	8	1 477	1 878	5.9	9.4
283 LUTH--MO SYNOD	5	1 826	2 337	7.4	11.7
413 S.D.A.	1	30	36*	0.2	
419 SO BAPT CONV..	18	2 853	3 432*	10.8	17.2
435 UNITARIAN-UNIV	1	16	19*	0.1	0.1
443 UN C OF CHRIST	1	88	106*	0.3	0.5
449 UN METHODIST..	7	1 920	2 310*	7.3	11.6
453 UN PRES CH USA	7	930	1 119*	3.5	5.6
MORGAN	64	12 358	21 201*	56.5	100.0
019 AMER BAPT USA.	3	1 178	1 409*	3.8	6.6
053 ASSEMB OF GOD.	1	87	119	0.3	0.6
081 CATHOLIC......	6	NA	5 175	13.8	24.4
093 CHR CH (DISC).	7	1 685	2 345	6.3	11.1
097 CHR CHS&CHS CR	2	496	593*	1.6	2.8
123 CH GOD (ANDER)	1	30	90	0.2	0.4
151 L-D SAINTS....	1	NA	149	0.4	0.7
165 CH OF NAZARENE	1	56	112	0.3	0.5
167 CHS OF CHRIST.	2	110	188	0.5	0.9
193 EPISCOPAL.....	1	243	252	0.7	1.2
281 LUTH CH AMER..	3	430	562	1.5	2.7
283 LUTH--MO SYNOD	5	1 628	2 152	5.7	10.2
403 SALVATION ARMY	1	126	531	1.4	2.5
419 SO BAPT CONV..	8	1 584	1 894*	5.1	8.9
443 UN C OF CHRIST	2	318	380*	1.0	1.8
449 UN METHODIST..	16	3 534	4 226*	11.3	19.9
453 UN PRES CH USA	3	829	991*	2.6	4.7
469 WELS.........	1	24	33	0.1	0.2
MOULTRIE	35	4 543	6 938*	47.7	100.0
019 AMER BAPT USA.	1	175	212*	1.5	3.1
081 CATHOLIC......	4	NA	534	3.7	7.7
093 CHR CH (DISC).	6	1 174	2 060	14.2	29.7
097 CHR CHS&CHS CR	2	342	414*	2.8	6.0
123 CH GOD (ANDER)	2	110	330	2.3	4.8
167 CHS OF CHRIST.	3	135	157	1.1	2.3
221 FREE METHODIST	1	44	111	0.8	1.6
283 LUTH--MO SYNOD	1	188	245	1.7	3.5
323 OLD ORD AMISH.	2	260	315*	2.2	4.5
419 SO BAPT CONV..	4	589	713*	4.9	10.3
449 UN METHODIST..	7	1 344	1 627*	11.2	23.5
453 UN PRES CH USA	2	182	220*	1.5	3.2
OGLE	69	14 773	22 936*	49.5	100.0
029 AMER LUTH CH..	4	853	1 165	2.5	5.1
053 ASSEMB OF GOD.	2	137	299	0.6	1.3
057 BAPT GEN CONF.	1	173	212*	0.5	0.9
081 CATHOLIC......	3	NA	3 848	8.3	16.8
093 CHR CH (DISC).	1	60	112	0.2	0.5
097 CHR CHS&CHS CR	3	343	419*	0.9	1.8
121 CH GOD (ABR).	3	245	300*	0.6	1.3
123 CH GOD (ANDER)	1	15	45	0.1	0.2
127 CH GOD (CLEVE)	1	181	221*	0.5	1.0
157 CH OF BRETHREN	3	852	1 042*	2.2	4.5
165 CH OF NAZARENE	2	127	311	0.7	1.4
167 CHS OF CHRIST.	1	40	45	0.1	0.2
179 CONSRV BAPT...	1	223	273*	0.6	1.2
181 CONSRV CONGR..	1	67	82*	0.2	0.4
193 EPISCOPAL.....	2	195	259	0.6	1.1
201 EVAN COV CH AM	1	111	136*	0.3	0.6
203 EVAN FREE CH..	1	117	143*	0.3	0.6
263 INT FOURSQ GOS	2	175	214*	0.5	0.9
281 LUTH CH AMER..	5	2 004	2 637	5.7	11.5
283 LUTH--MO SYNOD	2	1 099	1 445	3.1	6.3
329 OPEN BIBLE STD	2	100	140	0.3	0.6
371 REF CH IN AM..	4	669	1 046	2.3	4.6
419 SO BAPT CONV..	2	753	921*	2.0	4.0
443 UN C OF CHRIST	2	980	1 198*	2.6	5.2
449 UN METHODIST..	12	3 927	4 801*	10.4	20.9
453 UN PRES CH USA	7	1 327	1 622*	3.5	7.1
PEORIA	158	43 799	91 837*	45.8	100.0
017 AMER BAPT ASSN	2	150	150	0.1	0.2
019 AMER BAPT USA.	3	1 610	1 957*	1.0	2.1
029 AMER LUTH CH..	7	4 109	5 462	2.7	5.9
039 AP CHR CH(NAZ)	1	59	72*	-	0.1
053 ASSEMB OF GOD.	4	448	959	0.5	1.0
057 BAPT GEN CONF.	1	57	69*	-	0.1
059 BAPT MISS ASSN	2	20	24*	-	-
081 CATHOLIC......	23	NA	33 095	16.5	36.0
089 CHR & MISS AL.	1	39	67	-	0.1
093 CHR CH (DISC).	5	1 796	3 135	1.6	3.4
097 CHR CHS&CHS CR	3	490	596*	0.3	0.6
123 CH GOD (ANDER)	3	257	771	0.4	0.8
127 CH GOD (CLEVE)	1	139	169*	0.1	0.2
151 L-D SAINTS....	1	NA	532	0.3	0.6
157 CH OF BRETHREN	1	150	182*	0.1	0.2
165 CH OF NAZARENE	7	378	1 230	0.6	1.3
167 CHS OF CHRIST.	6	310	430	0.2	0.5
179 CONSRV BAPT...	1	223	271*	0.1	0.3
193 EPISCOPAL.....	4	1 365	1 588	0.8	1.7
201 EVAN COV CH AM	1	93	113*	0.1	0.1
203 EVAN FREE CH..	1	55	67*	-	0.1
221 FREE METHODIST	2	220	1 254	0.6	1.4
271 REFORM JUDAISM	1	480	584*	0.3	0.6
281 LUTH CH AMER..	3	1 499	1 931	1.0	2.1
283 LUTH--MO SYNOD	8	4 347	5 694	2.8	6.2
285 MENNONITE CH..	2	117	142*	0.1	0.2
287 MENN GEN CONF.	1	79	79	-	0.1
291 MISSIONARY CH.	4	472	648	0.3	0.7
313 N AM BAPT CONF	1	108	131*	0.1	0.1
353 CHR BRETHREN..	1	5	10	-	-
371 REF CH IN AM..	1	55	109	0.1	0.1
381 REF PRES-EVAN.	2	177	202	0.1	0.2
403 SALVATION ARMY	1	170	546	0.3	0.6
413 S.D.A.	2	397	483*	0.2	0.5
419 SO BAPT CONV..	7	2 500	3 039*	1.5	3.3
435 UNITARIAN-UNIV	1	187	227*	0.1	0.2
443 UN C OF CHRIST	7	2 065	2 510*	1.3	2.7
449 UN METHODIST..	25	11 812	14 360*	7.2	15.6
453 UN PRES CH USA	11	7 361	8 949*	4.5	9.7
PERRY	49	9 640	15 764*	72.6	100.0
005 AME ZION......	1	150	235	1.1	1.5
019 AMER BAPT USA.	3	335	407*	1.9	2.6
053 ASSEMB OF GOD.	1	62	94	0.4	0.6
081 CATHOLIC......	5	NA	3 714	17.1	23.6
093 CHR CH (DISC).	1	325	660	3.0	4.2
097 CHR CHS&CHS CR	3	361	438*	2.0	2.8
127 CH GOD (CLEVE)	1	33	40*	0.2	0.3
165 CH OF NAZARENE	1	44	75	0.3	0.5
167 CHS OF CHRIST.	1	22	35	0.2	0.2
283 LUTH--MO SYNOD	3	321	380	1.8	2.4
381 REF PRES-EVAN.	1	124	141	0.6	0.9
413 S.D.A.	1	28	34*	0.2	0.2
419 SO BAPT CONV..	18	5 675	6 889*	31.7	43.7
443 UN C OF CHRIST	2	708	859*	4.0	5.4
449 UN METHODIST..	3	961	1 167*	5.4	7.4
453 UN PRES CH USA	4	491	596*	2.7	3.8
PIATT	38	6 701	9 347*	56.4	100.0
019 AMER BAPT USA.	1	202	246*	1.5	2.6
029 AMER LUTH CH..	1	222	317	1.9	3.4
071 BRETHREN (ASH)	1	137	167*	1.0	1.8
081 CATHOLIC......	2	NA	988	6.0	10.6
093 CHR CH (DISC).	1	162	249	1.5	2.7
097 CHR CHS&CHS CR	3	345	420*	2.5	4.5
123 CH GOD (ANDER)	1	25	75	0.5	0.8
157 CH OF BRETHREN	2	385	469*	2.8	5.0
165 CH OF NAZARENE	2	120	201	1.2	2.2
167 CHS OF CHRIST.	2	75	95	0.6	1.0
323 OLD ORD AMISH.	1	130	158*	1.0	1.7
419 SO BAPT CONV..	6	486	592*	3.6	6.3
443 UN C OF CHRIST	4	631	768*	4.6	8.2
449 UN METHODIST..	9	3 376	4 109*	24.8	44.0
453 UN PRES CH USA	2	405	493*	3.0	5.3
PIKE	59	6 615	9 659*	51.1	100.0
019 AMER BAPT USA.	3	550	660*	3.5	6.8
053 ASSEMB OF GOD.	2	161	251	1.3	2.6
081 CATHOLIC......	2	NA	955	5.1	9.9
093 CHR CH (DISC).	2	438	594	3.1	6.1
097 CHR CHS&CHS CR	9	1 129	1 354*	7.2	14.0
165 CH OF NAZARENE	6	423	1 089	5.8	11.3
167 CHS OF CHRIST.	7	400	520	2.8	5.4
193 EPISCOPAL.....	1	94	117	0.6	1.2
283 LUTH--MO SYNOD	1	127	169	0.9	1.7
419 SO BAPT CONV..	6	785	942*	5.0	9.8
443 UN C OF CHRIST	1	62	74*	0.4	0.8
449 UN METHODIST..	16	2 392	2 869*	15.2	29.7
453 UN PRES CH USA	2	54	65*	0.3	0.7
POPE	25	1 868	2 229*	50.6	100.0
167 CHS OF CHRIST.	2	90	115	2.6	5.2
283 LUTH--MO SYNOD	1	94	115	2.6	5.2

NA— Not applicable   *Total adherents estimated from known number of communicant, confirmed, full members.   —Represents a percent less than 0.1.   Percentages may not total due to rounding.

Table 4. Churches and Church Membership by County and Denomination: 1980

County and Denomination	Number of churches	Communicant, confirmed, full members	Total adherents		
			Number	Percent of total population	Percent of total adherents
417 SOCIAL BRETH..	4	156	185*	4.2	8.3
419 SO BAPT CONV..	12	1 207	1 433*	32.5	64.3
449 UN METHODIST..	5	269	319*	7.2	14.3
453 UN PRES CH USA	1	52	62*	1.4	2.8
PULASKI	33	3 177	4 313*	48.8	100.0
053 ASSEMB OF GOD.	1	62	151	1.7	3.5
081 CATHOLIC......	3	NA	389	4.4	9.0
093 CHR CH (DISC).	1	55	73	0.8	1.7
097 CHR CHS&CHS CR	1	115	140*	1.6	3.2
101 C.M.E........	3	51	62*	0.7	1.4
127 CH GOD (CLEVE)	1	11	13*	0.1	0.3
167 CHS OF CHRIST.	1	50	62	0.7	1.4
181 CONSRV CONGR..	2	247	301*	3.4	7.0
193 EPISCOPAL.....	1	32	25	0.3	0.6
283 LUTH--MO SYNOD	1	107	116	1.3	2.7
419 SO BAPT CONV..	8	1 797	2 189*	24.8	50.8
443 UN C OF CHRIST	2	109	133*	1.5	3.1
449 UN METHODIST..	8	541	659*	7.5	15.3
PUTNAM	15	1 755	3 435*	56.5	100.0
081 CATHOLIC......	4	NA	1 336	22.0	38.9
097 CHR CHS&CHS CR	1	85	104*	1.7	3.0
226 FRIENDS-USA...	1	78	96*	1.6	2.8
281 LUTH CH AMER..	2	222	342	5.6	10.0
287 MENN GEN CONF.	2	637	657	10.8	19.1
443 UN C OF CHRIST	1	276	339*	5.6	9.9
449 UN METHODIST..	4	457	561*	9.2	16.3
RANDOLPH	72	13 883	23 913*	67.2	100.0
019 AMER BAPT USA.	1	182	218*	0.6	0.9
053 ASSEMB OF GOD.	3	168	273	0.8	1.1
059 BAPT MISS ASSN	1	81	97*	0.3	0.4
081 CATHOLIC......	15	NA	6 671	18.8	27.9
097 CHR CHS&CHS CR	1	75	90*	0.3	0.4
165 CH OF NAZARENE	3	59	160	0.4	0.7
167 CHS OF CHRIST.	2	141	242	0.7	1.0
281 LUTH CH AMER..	5	1 607	2 051	5.8	8.6
283 LUTH--MO SYNOD	9	5 190	6 443	18.1	26.9
353 CHR BRETHREN..	1	25	50	0.1	0.2
381 REF PRES-EVAN.	2	368	441	1.2	1.8
383 REF PRES OF NA	1	40	47	0.1	0.2
419 SO BAPT CONV..	9	2 161	2 591*	7.3	10.8
443 UN C OF CHRIST	2	702	842*	2.4	3.5
449 UN METHODIST..	9	1 459	1 749*	4.9	7.3
453 UN PRES CH USA	8	1 625	1 948*	5.5	8.1
RICHLAND	41	5 804	9 945*	56.5	100.0
019 AMER BAPT USA.	1	415	497*	2.8	5.0
053 ASSEMB OF GOD.	1	115	224	1.3	2.3
081 CATHOLIC......	2	NA	2 157	12.3	21.7
093 CHR CH (DISC).	1	56	120	0.7	1.2
097 CHR CHS&CHS CR	5	820	982*	5.6	9.9
127 CH GOD (CLEVE)	1	26	31*	0.2	0.3
151 L-D SAINTS....	1	NA	84	0.5	0.8
157 CH OF BRETHREN	1	31	37*	0.2	0.4
165 CH OF NAZARENE	1	226	394	2.2	4.0
167 CHS OF CHRIST.	4	276	351	2.0	3.5
193 EPISCOPAL.....	1	48	72	0.4	0.7
215 EVAN METH CH..	1	9	11*	0.1	0.1
221 FREE METHODIST	1	134	564	3.2	5.7
281 LUTH CH AMER..	1	496	648	3.7	6.5
413 S.D.A.........	1	49	59*	0.3	0.6
419 SO BAPT CONV..	3	508	608*	3.5	6.1
443 UN C OF CHRIST	2	153	183*	1.0	1.8
449 UN METHODIST..	12	2 146	2 569*	14.6	25.8
453 UN PRES CH USA	1	296	354*	2.0	3.6
ROCK ISLAND	128	40 733	84 247*	50.8	100.0
017 AMER BAPT ASSN	2	200	200	0.1	0.2
019 AMER BAPT USA.	5	1 484	1 798*	1.1	2.1
053 ASSEMB OF GOD.	6	446	828	0.5	1.0
057 BAPT GEN CONF.	1	318	385*	0.2	0.5
059 BAPT MISS ASSN	2	125	151*	0.1	0.2
081 CATHOLIC......	16	NA	30 279	18.2	35.9
093 CHR CH (DISC).	4	2 084	3 734	2.2	4.4
097 CHR CHS&CHS CR	2	325	394*	0.2	0.5
151 L-D SAINTS....	1	NA	595	0.4	0.7
165 CH OF NAZARENE	5	413	974	0.6	1.2
167 CHS OF CHRIST.	4	410	522	0.3	0.6
175 CONGR CHR CHS.	1	51	62*	–	0.1
193 EPISCOPAL.....	3	872	1 137	0.7	1.3
201 EVAN COV CH AM	2	610	739*	0.4	0.9
203 EVAN FREE CH..	3	817	990*	0.6	1.2
221 FREE METHODIST	1	51	108	0.1	0.1
263 INT FOURSQ GOS	2	2 954	3 579*	2.2	4.2
270 CONSRV JUDAISM	1	300	364*	0.2	0.4
281 LUTH CH AMER..	12	7 287	9 779	5.9	11.6
283 LUTH--MO SYNOD	7	4 372	5 859	3.5	7.0
290 METRO COMM CHS	0	10	20	–	–
329 OPEN BIBLE STD	3	130	255	0.2	0.3
353 CHR BRETHREN..	1	25	50	–	0.1
403 SALVATION ARMY	2	225	545	0.3	0.6
413 S.D.A.........	1	123	149*	0.1	0.2
419 SO BAPT CONV..	4	492	596*	0.4	0.7
443 UN C OF CHRIST	4	2 912	3 528*	2.1	4.2
449 UN METHODIST..	20	8 485	10 281*	6.2	12.2
453 UN PRES CH USA	12	4 979	6 033*	3.6	7.2
469 WELS..........	1	233	313	0.2	0.4

County and Denomination	Number of churches	Communicant, confirmed, full members	Total adherents		
			Number	Percent of total population	Percent of total adherents
ST CLAIR	209	49 458	115 420*	43.5	100.0
005 AME ZION......	2	410	558	0.2	0.5
019 AMER BAPT USA.	4	1 007	1 244*	0.5	1.1
029 AMER LUTH CH..	1	221	316	0.1	0.3
053 ASSEMB OF GOD.	12	1 022	1 796	0.7	1.6
059 BAPT MISS ASSN	2	251	310*	0.1	0.3
081 CATHOLIC......	41	NA	50 425	19.0	43.7
089 CHR & MISS AL.	1	45	75	–	0.1
093 CHR CH (DISC).	2	247	501	0.2	0.4
097 CHR CHS&CHS CR	4	1 325	1 637*	0.6	1.4
101 C.M.E........	3	929	1 148*	0.4	1.0
123 CH GOD (ANDER)	5	371	1 113	0.4	1.0
127 CH GOD (CLEVE)	4	338	418*	0.2	0.4
151 L-D SAINTS....	2	NA	881	0.3	0.8
165 CH OF NAZARENE	7	509	1 290	0.5	1.1
167 CHS OF CHRIST.	6	1 181	1 711	0.6	1.5
193 EPISCOPAL.....	2	524	686	0.3	0.6
208 EVAN LUTH ASSN	4	749	1 047	0.4	0.9
215 EVAN METH CH..	1	36	44*	–	–
281 LUTH CH AMER..	1	297	364	0.1	0.3
283 LUTH--MO SYNOD	11	3 552	4 684	1.8	4.1
287 MENN GEN CONF.	1	24	25	–	–
353 CHR BRETHREN..	1	30	50	–	–
381 REF PRES-EVAN.	1	?	?	?	?
403 SALVATION ARMY	1	128	281	0.1	0.2
413 S.D.A.........	1	174	215*	0.1	0.2
419 SO BAPT CONV..	40	16 964	20 963*	7.9	18.2
443 UN C OF CHRIST	25	10 655	13 167*	5.0	11.4
449 UN METHODIST..	19	6 631	8 194*	3.1	7.1
453 UN PRES CH USA	4	1 796	2 219*	0.8	1.9
469 WELS..........	1	42	58	–	0.1
SALINE	90	14 040	18 833*	68.8	100.0
019 AMER BAPT USA.	1	211	251*	0.9	1.3
029 AMER LUTH CH..	1	75	105	0.4	0.6
053 ASSEMB OF GOD.	1	15	30	0.1	0.2
081 CATHOLIC......	2	NA	1 310	4.8	7.0
097 CHR CHS&CHS CR	2	521	621*	2.3	3.3
101 C.M.E........	1	12	14*	0.1	0.1
121 CH GOD (ABR)..	1	45	54*	0.2	0.3
123 CH GOD (ANDER)	3	205	615	2.2	3.3
127 CH GOD (CLEVE)	4	375	447*	1.6	2.4
151 L-D SAINTS....	1	NA	122	0.4	0.6
165 CH OF NAZARENE	3	59	144	0.5	0.8
167 CHS OF CHRIST.	2	185	235	0.9	1.2
185 CUMBER PRESB..	4	121	293	1.1	1.6
221 FREE METHODIST	1	10	51	0.2	0.3
413 S.D.A.........	1	47	56*	0.2	0.3
415 S-D BAPTIST GC	1	38	45*	0.2	0.2
417 SOCIAL BRETH..	9	481	573*	2.1	3.0
419 SO BAPT CONV..	35	9 595	11 431*	41.8	60.7
449 UN METHODIST..	15	1 678	1 999*	7.3	10.6
453 UN PRES CH USA	2	367	437*	1.6	2.3
SANGAMON	162	45 730	102 931*	58.5	100.0
019 AMER BAPT USA.	9	3 313	3 993*	2.3	3.9
029 AMER LUTH CH..	1	119	212	0.1	0.2
053 ASSEMB OF GOD.	5	4 195	11 424	6.5	11.1
081 CATHOLIC......	21	NA	37 711	21.4	36.6
093 CHR CH (DISC).	3	942	1 685	1.0	1.6
097 CHR CHS&CHS CR	16	4 357	5 251*	3.0	5.1
101 C.M.E........	1	15	18*	–	–
123 CH GOD (ANDER)	4	315	945	0.5	0.9
127 CH GOD (CLEVE)	2	147	177*	0.1	0.2
151 L-D SAINTS....	1	NA	541	0.3	0.5
157 CH OF BRETHREN	1	122	147*	0.1	0.1
165 CH OF NAZARENE	5	576	1 301	0.7	1.3
167 CHS OF CHRIST.	5	490	624	0.4	0.6
193 EPISCOPAL.....	3	1 653	1 819	1.0	1.8
203 EVAN FREE CH..	1	86	104*	0.1	0.1
221 FREE METHODIST	1	81	270	0.2	0.3
226 FRIENDS-USA...	1	4	5*	–	–
263 INT FOURSQ GOS	1	296	357*	0.2	0.3
270 CONSRV JUDAISM	1	142	171*	0.1	0.2
271 REFORM JUDAISM	1	480	579*	0.3	0.6
281 LUTH CH AMER..	4	2 574	3 374	1.9	3.3
283 LUTH--MO SYNOD	11	5 348	7 117	4.0	6.9
353 CHR BRETHREN..	1	70	100	0.1	0.1
403 SALVATION ARMY	1	158	600	0.3	0.6
413 S.D.A.........	2	119	143*	0.1	0.1
419 SO BAPT CONV..	9	2 793	3 366*	1.9	3.3
435 UNITARIAN-UNIV	1	69	83*	–	0.1
443 UN C OF CHRIST	2	697	840*	0.5	0.8
449 UN METHODIST..	34	11 367	13 700*	7.8	13.3
453 UN PRES CH USA	13	5 175	6 237*	3.5	6.1
469 WELS..........	1	27	37	–	–
SCHUYLER	27	2 609	3 830*	45.8	100.0
053 ASSEMB OF GOD.	3	56	125	1.5	3.3
081 CATHOLIC......	1	NA	200	2.4	5.2
093 CHR CH (DISC).	2	302	313	3.7	8.2
097 CHR CHS&CHS CR	2	100	120*	1.4	3.1
165 CH OF NAZARENE	1	31	80	1.0	2.1
167 CHS OF CHRIST.	1	59	75	0.9	2.0
221 FREE METHODIST	1	132	576	6.9	15.0
283 LUTH--MO SYNOD	1	92	134	1.6	3.5
419 SO BAPT CONV..	1	109	131*	1.6	3.4
449 UN METHODIST..	13	1 540	1 850*	22.1	48.3
453 UN PRES CH USA	1	188	226*	2.7	5.9
SCOTT	23	3 313	4 339*	70.6	100.0

NA–Not applicable   *Total adherents estimated from known number of communicant, confirmed, full members.   —Represents a percent less than 0.1.   Percentages may not total due to rounding.

Table 4. Churches and Church Membership by County and Denomination: 1980

County and Denomination	Number of churches	Communicant, confirmed, full members	Total adherents Number	Percent of total population	Percent of total adherents
019 AMER BAPT USA.	3	760	907*	14.8	20.9
053 ASSEMB OF GOD.	1	51	64	1.0	1.5
081 CATHOLIC......	2	NA	364	5.9	8.4
093 CHR CH (DISC).	2	273	326	5.3	7.5
097 CHR CHS&CHS	1	50	60*	1.0	1.4
281 LUTH CH AMER..	1	248	292	4.8	6.7
283 LUTH--MO SYNOD	2	435	542	8.8	12.5
419 SO BAPT CONV..	6	856	1 021*	16.6	23.5
449 UN METHODIST..	5	640	763*	12.4	17.6
SHELBY	**73**	**10 032**	**15 062***	**63.0**	**100.0**
019 AMER BAPT USA.	1	302	366*	1.5	2.4
029 AMER LUTH CH..	2	238	318	1.3	2.1
053 ASSEMB OF GOD.	1	32	76	0.3	0.5
081 CATHOLIC......	5	NA	1 757	7.3	11.7
089 CHR & MISS AL.	1	68	82	0.3	0.5
093 CHR CH (DISC).	2	424	855	3.6	5.7
097 CHR CHS&CHS CR	11	2 958	3 589*	15.0	23.8
165 CH OF NAZARENE	1	231	507	2.1	3.4
167 CHS OF CHRIST.	10	450	573	2.4	3.8
221 FREE METHODIST	3	141	570	2.4	3.8
283 LUTH--MO SYNOD	5	1 334	1 692	7.1	11.2
285 MENNONITE CH..	1	41	50*	0.2	0.3
413 S.D.A.........	1	45	55*	0.2	0.4
419 SO BAPT CONV..	6	596	723*	3.0	4.8
443 UN C OF CHRIST	1	74	90*	0.4	0.6
449 UN METHODIST..	21	2 961	3 593*	15.0	23.9
453 UN PRES CH USA	1	137	166*	0.7	1.1
STARK	**18**	**2 466**	**3 983***	**53.9**	**100.0**
019 AMER BAPT USA.	1	278	337*	4.6	8.5
029 AMER LUTH CH..	1	115	139	1.9	3.5
081 CATHOLIC......	3	NA	898	12.2	22.5
165 CH OF NAZARENE	1	59	164	2.2	4.1
175 CONGR CHR CHS.	1	167	203*	2.7	5.1
179 CONSRV BAPT...	1	223	271*	3.7	6.8
413 S.D.A.........	1	17	21*	0.3	0.5
419 SO BAPT CONV..	1	84	102*	1.4	2.6
443 UN C OF CHRIST	2	298	362*	4.9	9.1
449 UN METHODIST..	5	1 112	1 349*	18.3	33.9
453 UN PRES CH USA	1	113	137*	1.9	3.4
STEPHENSON	**78**	**16 225**	**27 192***	**54.9**	**100.0**
053 ASSEMB OF GOD.	1	42	129	0.3	0.5
081 CATHOLIC......	6	NA	6 144	12.4	22.6
101 C.M.E.........	1	372	450*	0.9	1.7
105 CHRISTIAN REF.	1	101	151	0.3	0.6
123 CH GOD (ANDER)	1	20	60	0.1	0.2
127 CH GOD (CLEVE)	1	5	6*	-	-
151 L-D SAINTS....	1	NA	208	0.4	0.8
157 CH OF BRETHREN	3	265	320*	0.6	1.2
165 CH OF NAZARENE	1	135	326	0.7	1.2
167 CHS OF CHRIST.	1	80	102	0.2	0.4
179 CONSRV BAPT...	1	223	269*	0.5	1.0
181 CONSRV CONGR..	1	330	399*	0.8	1.5
193 EPISCOPAL.....	1	410	477	1.0	1.8
199 EVAN CONGR CH.	2	242	292*	0.6	1.1
203 EVAN FREE CH..	3	456	551*	1.1	2.0
221 FREE METHODIST	3	66	387	0.8	1.4
263 INT FOURSQ GOS	1	10	12*	-	-
281 LUTH CH AMER..	6	2 226	2 809	5.7	10.3
283 LUTH--MO SYNOD	3	1 397	1 850	3.7	6.8
285 MENNONITE CH..	1	195	236*	0.5	0.9
329 OPEN BIBLE STD	1	175	300	0.6	1.1
371 REF CH IN AM..	2	426	681	1.4	2.5
403 SALVATION ARMY	1	103	214	0.4	0.8
413 S.D.A.........	1	65	79*	0.2	0.3
419 SO BAPT CONV..	1	9	11*	-	-
443 UN C OF CHRIST	6	2 245	2 713*	5.5	10.0
449 UN METHODIST..	22	5 454	6 591*	13.3	24.2
453 UN PRES CH USA	3	1 065	1 287*	2.6	4.7
469 WELS..........	2	108	138	0.3	0.5
TAZEWELL	**133**	**35 867**	**66 921***	**50.7**	**100.0**
017 AMER BAPT ASSN	3	325	325	0.2	0.5
019 AMER BAPT USA.	4	1 305	1 604*	1.2	2.4
029 AMER LUTH CH..	1	317	520	0.4	0.8
039 AP CHR CH(NAZ)	1	135	166*	0.1	0.2
053 ASSEMB OF GOD.	5	942	1 776	1.3	2.7
059 BAPT MISS ASSN	1	77	95*	0.1	0.1
081 CATHOLIC......	7	NA	17 967	13.6	26.8
093 CHR CH (DISC).	4	1 645	2 674	2.0	4.0
097 CHR CHS&CHS CR	8	2 636	3 240*	2.5	4.8
121 CH GOD (ABR).	1	35	43*	-	0.1
123 CH GOD (ANDER)	2	220	660	0.5	1.0
127 CH GOD (CLEVE)	2	36	44*	-	0.1
151 L-D SAINTS....	1	NA	549	0.4	0.8
165 CH OF NAZARENE	6	734	1 906	1.4	2.8
167 CHS OF CHRIST.	5	730	929	0.7	1.4
179 CONSRV BAPT...	2	446	548*	0.4	0.8
193 EPISCOPAL.....	2	372	480	0.4	0.7
213 EVAN MENN INC.	3	553	680*	0.5	1.0
217 FIRE BAPTIZED.	1	7	9*	-	-
221 FREE METHODIST	2	141	516	0.4	0.8
281 LUTH CH AMER..	3	1 798	2 344	1.8	3.5
283 LUTH--MO SYNOD	9	4 459	6 132	4.6	9.2
285 MENNONITE CH..	8	1 111	1 366*	1.0	2.0
287 MENN GEN CONF.	3	626	746	0.6	1.1
291 MISSIONARY CH.	4	374	484	0.4	0.7
329 OPEN BIBLE STD	2	75	135	0.1	0.2
371 REF CH IN AM..	2	360	626	0.5	0.9
403 SALVATION ARMY	1	120	316	0.2	0.5
419 SO BAPT CONV..	12	2 857	3 512*	2.7	5.2
443 UN C OF CHRIST	6	3 038	3 735*	2.8	5.6
449 UN METHODIST..	14	9 157	11 257*	8.5	16.8
453 UN PRES CH USA	7	1 201	1 476*	1.1	2.2
469 WELS..........	1	35	61	-	0.1
UNION	**52**	**9 654**	**12 405***	**73.6**	**100.0**
019 AMER BAPT USA.	2	183	216*	1.3	1.7
053 ASSEMB OF GOD.	1	54	68	0.4	0.5
081 CATHOLIC......	2	NA	603	3.6	4.9
097 CHR CHS&CHS CR	1	550	650*	3.9	5.2
123 CH GOD (ANDER)	1	12	36	0.2	0.3
127 CH GOD (CLEVE)	1	47	56*	0.3	0.5
165 CH OF NAZARENE	1	161	482	2.9	3.9
167 CHS OF CHRIST.	4	260	331	2.0	2.7
175 CONGR CHR CHS.	1	25	30*	0.2	0.2
185 CUMBER PRESB..	2	36	60	0.4	0.5
281 LUTH CH AMER..	4	669	814	4.8	6.6
283 LUTH--MO SYNOD	1	129	165	1.0	1.3
419 SO BAPT CONV..	22	6 554	7 744*	46.0	62.4
449 UN METHODIST..	7	691	816*	4.8	6.6
453 UN PRES CH USA	2	283	334*	2.0	2.7
VERMILION	**141**	**26 085**	**43 191***	**45.4**	**100.0**
019 AMER BAPT USA.	3	890	1 084*	1.1	2.5
053 ASSEMB OF GOD.	3	388	562	0.6	1.3
081 CATHOLIC......	6	NA	8 750	9.2	20.3
089 CHR & MISS AL.	1	40	85	0.1	0.2
093 CHR CH (DISC).	5	1 402	1 787	1.9	4.1
097 CHR CHS&CHS CR	25	5 659	6 896*	7.2	16.0
101 C.M.E.........	1	567	691*	0.7	1.6
123 CH GOD (ANDER)	4	131	393	0.4	0.9
127 CH GOD (CLEVE)	4	387	472*	0.5	1.1
151 L-D SAINTS....	1	NA	350	0.4	0.8
165 CH OF NAZARENE	17	1 612	3 193	3.4	7.4
167 CHS OF CHRIST.	3	345	439	0.5	1.0
175 CONGR CHR CHS.	2	75	91*	0.1	0.2
179 CONSRV BAPT...	1	223	272*	0.3	0.6
185 CUMBER PRESB..	2	49	80	0.1	0.2
193 EPISCOPAL.....	1	249	332	0.3	0.8
197 EVAN CH OF NA.	1	27	27	-	0.1
215 EVAN METH CH..	2	100	122*	0.1	0.3
221 FREE METHODIST	1	122	435	0.5	1.0
226 FRIENDS-USA...	5	878	1 070*	1.1	2.5
263 INT FOURSQ GOS	1	39	48*	0.1	0.1
270 CONSRV JUDAISM	1	37	45*	-	0.1
281 LUTH CH AMER..	2	409	516	0.5	1.2
283 LUTH--MO SYNOD	3	2 402	2 994	3.1	6.9
403 SALVATION ARMY	1	86	309	0.3	0.7
413 S.D.A.........	2	104	127*	0.1	0.3
419 SO BAPT CONV..	1	278	339*	0.4	0.8
443 UN C OF CHRIST	4	859	1 047*	1.1	2.4
449 UN METHODIST..	33	7 356	8 964*	9.4	20.8
453 UN PRES CH USA	5	1 371	1 671*	1.8	3.9
WABASH	**30**	**4 708**	**8 356***	**60.9**	**100.0**
081 CATHOLIC......	1	NA	1 590	11.6	19.0
093 CHR CH (DISC).	3	656	954	7.0	11.4
097 CHR CHS&CHS CR	6	1 252	1 517*	11.1	18.2
123 CH GOD (ANDER)	1	145	435	3.2	5.2
151 L-D SAINTS....	1	NA	142	1.0	1.7
165 CH OF NAZARENE	1	67	126	0.9	1.5
167 CHS OF CHRIST.	1	350	500	3.6	6.0
193 EPISCOPAL.....	1	87	86	0.6	1.0
221 FREE METHODIST	2	122	549	4.0	6.6
281 LUTH CH AMER..	1	230	274	2.0	3.3
283 LUTH--MO SYNOD	1	104	130	0.9	1.6
419 SO BAPT CONV..	1	403	488*	3.6	5.8
449 UN METHODIST..	10	1 292	1 565*	11.4	18.7
WARREN	**36**	**8 177**	**12 314***	**56.1**	**100.0**
019 AMER BAPT USA.	3	439	533*	2.4	4.3
053 ASSEMB OF GOD.	2	51	100	0.5	0.8
057 BAPT GEN CONF.	2	395	479*	2.2	3.9
081 CATHOLIC......	2	NA	1 879	8.6	15.3
093 CHR CH (DISC).	3	500	827	3.8	6.7
097 CHR CHS&CHS CR	2	1 060	1 287*	5.9	10.5
165 CH OF NAZARENE	2	107	326	1.5	2.6
193 EPISCOPAL.....	2	347	468	2.1	3.8
263 INT FOURSQ GOS	1	167	203*	0.9	1.6
281 LUTH CH AMER..	2	752	921	4.2	7.5
413 S.D.A.........	1	72	87*	0.4	0.7
419 SO BAPT CONV..	1	89	108*	0.5	0.9
449 UN METHODIST..	8	2 521	3 060*	13.9	24.8
453 UN PRES CH USA	6	1 677	2 036*	9.3	16.5
WASHINGTON	**43**	**6 590**	**12 080***	**78.1**	**100.0**
053 ASSEMB OF GOD.	2	86	156	1.0	1.3
081 CATHOLIC......	6	NA	3 927	25.4	32.5
097 CHR CHS&CHS CR	2	150	180*	1.2	1.5
193 EPISCOPAL.....	1	113	155	1.0	1.3
283 LUTH--MO SYNOD	7	2 265	2 887	18.7	23.9
383 REF PRES OF NA	1	52	58	0.4	0.5
419 SO BAPT CONV..	5	863	1 037*	6.7	8.6
443 UN C OF CHRIST	10	1 918	2 306*	14.9	19.1
449 UN METHODIST..	7	850	1 022*	6.6	8.5
453 UN PRES CH USA	2	293	352*	2.3	2.9
WAYNE	**65**	**7 809**	**9 979***	**55.3**	**100.0**

NA— Not applicable   *Total adherents estimated from known number of communicant, confirmed, full members.   —Represents a percent less than 0.1.   Percentages may not total due to rounding.

Table 4. Churches and Church Membership by County and Denomination: 1980

County and Denomination	Number of churches	Communicant, confirmed, full members	Total adherents		
			Number	Percent of total population	Percent of total adherents
053 ASSEMB OF GOD.	1	227	389	2.2	3.9
081 CATHOLIC......	1	NA	212	1.2	2.1
097 CHR CHS&CHS CR	11	1 856	2 220*	12.3	22.2
123 CH GOD (ANDER)	2	23	69	0.4	0.7
127 CH GOD (CLEVE)	1	82	98*	0.5	1.0
157 CH OF BRETHREN	1	24	29*	0.2	0.3
165 CH OF NAZARENE	2	108	153	0.8	1.5
167 CHS OF CHRIST.	2	125	159	0.9	1.6
175 CONGR CHR CHS.	1	25	30*	0.2	0.3
185 CUMBER PRESB..	5	305	571	3.2	5.7
283 LUTH--MO SYNOD	1	73	113	0.6	1.1
419 SO BAPT CONV..	20	3 456	4 135*	22.9	41.4
449 UN METHODIST..	17	1 505	1 801*	10.0	18.0
WHITE	61	8 952	11 521*	64.5	100.0
053 ASSEMB OF GOD.	1	44	149	0.8	1.3
081 CATHOLIC......	2	NA	629	3.5	5.5
097 CHR CHS&CHS CR	7	2 007	2 360*	13.2	20.5
123 CH GOD (ANDER)	1	25	75	0.4	0.7
127 CH GOD (CLEVE)	3	242	285*	1.6	2.5
165 CH OF NAZARENE	1	44	108	0.6	0.9
167 CHS OF CHRIST.	2	150	191	1.1	1.7
185 CUMBER PRESB..	7	232	416	2.3	3.6
283 LUTH--MO SYNOD	1	38	51	0.3	0.4
419 SO BAPT CONV..	13	3 134	3 686*	20.6	32.0
449 UN METHODIST..	19	2 476	2 912*	16.3	25.3
453 UN PRES CH USA	4	560	659*	3.7	5.7
WHITESIDE	96	22 730	43 023*	65.2	100.0
001 ADVENT CHR CH.	1	81	99*	0.2	0.2
019 AMER BAPT USA.	3	557	684*	1.0	1.6
029 AMER LUTH CH..	2	1 748	2 269	3.4	5.3
053 ASSEMB OF GOD.	2	299	670	1.0	1.6
075 BRETHREN IN CR	1	43	73	0.1	0.2
081 CATHOLIC......	9	NA	11 193	17.0	26.0
093 CHR CH (DISC).	2	651	1 433	2.2	3.3
097 CHR CHS&CHS CR	6	849	1 043*	1.6	2.4
105 CHRISTIAN REF.	3	697	1 069	1.6	2.5
123 CH GOD (ANDER)	1	40	120	0.2	0.3
127 CH GOD (CLEVE)	1	30	37*	0.1	0.1
151 L-D SAINTS....	1	NA	233	0.4	0.5
165 CH OF NAZARENE	3	509	1 471	2.2	3.4
167 CHS OF CHRIST.	1	190	242	0.4	0.6
179 CONSRV BAPT...	1	223	274*	0.4	0.6
193 EPISCOPAL.....	2	277	290	0.4	0.7
199 EVAN CONGR CH.	1	95	117*	0.2	0.3
203 EVAN FREE CH..	1	36	44*	0.1	0.1
221 FREE METHODIST	1	26	138	0.2	0.3
263 INT FOURSQ GOS	1	108	133*	0.2	0.3
271 REFORM JUDAISM	1	52	64*	0.1	0.1
281 LUTH CH AMER..	4	2 085	2 535	3.8	5.9
283 LUTH--MO SYNOD	4	1 534	2 000	3.0	4.6
285 MENNONITE CH..	4	425	522*	0.8	1.2
329 OPEN BIBLE STD	1	23	43	0.1	0.1
371 REF CH IN AM..	8	2 655	4 394	6.7	10.2
403 SALVATION ARMY	1	119	316	0.5	0.7
413 S.D.A.........	1	62	76*	0.1	0.2
419 SO BAPT CONV..	6	1 298	1 594*	2.4	3.7
443 UN C OF CHRIST	4	1 068	1 312*	2.0	3.0
449 UN METHODIST..	14	5 293	6 500*	9.9	15.1
453 UN PRES CH USA	5	1 657	2 035*	3.1	4.7
WILL	186	42 570	168 543*	51.9	100.0
019 AMER BAPT USA.	6	1 611	2 022*	0.6	1.2
029 AMER LUTH CH..	4	1 186	1 834	0.6	1.1
053 ASSEMB OF GOD.	5	549	945	0.3	0.6
057 BAPT GEN CONF.	4	347	436*	0.1	0.3
081 CATHOLIC......	38	NA	110 960	34.2	65.8
089 CHR & MISS AL.	1	50	136	—	0.1
097 CHR CHS&CHS CR	10	1 984	2 490*	0.8	1.5
123 CH GOD (ANDER)	2	127	381	0.1	0.2
127 CH GOD (CLEVE)	2	117	147*	—	0.1
151 L-D SAINTS....	1	NA	642	0.2	0.4
165 CH OF NAZARENE	6	463	1 146	0.4	0.7
167 CHS OF CHRIST.	4	340	433	0.1	0.3
175 CONGR CHR CHS.	1	141	177*	0.1	0.1
181 CONSRV CONGR..	1	235	295*	0.1	0.2
193 EPISCOPAL.....	5	693	969*	0.3	0.6
201 EVAN COV CH AM	2	383	481*	0.1	0.3
221 FREE METHODIST	1	61	228	0.1	0.1
226 FRIENDS-USA...	1	16	20*	—	—
263 INT FOURSQ GOS	1	53	67*	—	—
281 LUTH CH AMER..	6	3 488	4 836	1.5	2.9
283 LUTH--MO SYNOD	16	7 133	9 928	3.1	5.9
349 PENT HOLINESS	1	22	28*	—	—
353 CHR BRETHREN..	1	20	30	—	—
371 REF CH IN AM..	2	197	357	0.1	0.2
403 SALVATION ARMY	1	104	304	0.1	0.2
413 S.D.A.........	2	169	212*	0.1	0.1
419 SO BAPT CONV..	13	4 566	5 731*	1.8	3.4
435 UNITARIAN-UNIV	1	183	230*	0.1	0.1
443 UN C OF CHRIST	11	4 719	5 923*	1.8	3.5
449 UN METHODIST..	24	8 725	10 951*	3.4	6.5
453 UN PRES CH USA	11	3 539	4 442*	1.4	2.6
469 WELS..........	2	1 349	1 762	0.5	1.0
WILLIAMSON	108	19 734	29 213*	51.7	100.0
019 AMER BAPT USA.	10	1 662	1 987*	3.5	6.8
029 AMER LUTH CH..	1	92	133	0.2	0.5
053 ASSEMB OF GOD.	3	152	457	0.8	1.6
059 BAPT MISS ASSN	1	104	124*	0.2	0.4

County and Denomination	Number of churches	Communicant, confirmed, full members	Total adherents		
			Number	Percent of total population	Percent of total adherents
081 CATHOLIC......	6	NA	4 360	7.7	14.9
093 CHR CH (DISC).	1	198	285	0.5	1.0
097 CHR CHS&CHS CR	8	1 723	2 060*	3.6	7.1
123 CH GOD (ANDER)	3	348	1 044	1.8	3.6
127 CH GOD (CLEVE)	4	338	404*	0.7	1.4
165 CH OF NAZARENE	3	102	256	0.5	0.9
167 CHS OF CHRIST.	4	295	375	0.7	1.3
193 EPISCOPAL.....	1	35	42	0.1	0.1
221 FREE METHODIST	3	70	192	0.3	0.7
271 REFORM JUDAISM	1	92	110*	0.2	0.4
283 LUTH--MO SYNOD	1	119	166	0.3	0.6
413 S.D.A.........	1	98	117*	0.2	0.4
419 SO BAPT CONV..	32	10 338	12 358*	21.9	42.3
443 UN C OF CHRIST	2	614	734*	1.3	2.5
449 UN METHODIST..	19	2 804	3 352*	5.9	11.5
453 UN PRES CH USA	4	550	657*	1.2	2.2
WINNEBAGO	169	57 520	117 621*	46.9	100.0
019 AMER BAPT USA.	3	1 043	1 274*	0.5	1.1
029 AMER LUTH CH..	5	3 062	4 195	1.7	3.6
053 ASSEMB OF GOD.	4	1 852	3 943	1.6	3.4
057 BAPT GEN CONF.	2	1 013	1 237*	0.5	1.1
081 CATHOLIC......	16	NA	40 725	16.2	34.6
089 CHR & MISS AL.	1	27	38	—	—
093 CHR CH (DISC).	2	127	199	0.1	0.2
097 CHR CHS&CHS CR	4	1 400	1 710*	0.7	1.5
101 C.M.E........	1	354	432*	0.2	0.4
121 CH GOD (ABR)..	1	54	66*	—	0.1
123 CH GOD (ANDER)	2	64	192	0.1	0.2
127 CH GOD (CLEVE)	2	199	243*	0.1	0.2
151 L-D SAINTS....	2	NA	914	0.4	0.8
157 CH OF BRETHREN	1	112	137*	0.1	0.1
165 CH OF NAZARENE	5	441	747	0.3	0.6
167 CHS OF CHRIST.	7	1 315	1 674	0.7	1.4
175 CONGR CHR CHS.	1	25	31*	—	—
179 CONSRV BAPT...	1	223	272*	0.1	0.2
185 CUMBER PRESB..	1	100	185	0.1	0.2
193 EPISCOPAL.....	3	972	1 523	0.6	1.3
199 EVAN CONGR CH.	1	16	20*	—	—
201 EVAN COV CH AM	9	2 409	2 942*	1.2	2.5
203 EVAN FREE CH..	6	1 983	2 422*	1.0	2.1
221 FREE METHODIST	1	37	156	0.1	0.1
226 FRIENDS-USA...	1	17	21*	—	—
263 INT FOURSQ GOS	1	55	67*	—	0.1
270 CONSRV JUDAISM	1	57	70*	—	0.1
271 REFORM JUDAISM	1	340	415*	0.2	0.4
281 LUTH CH AMER..	17	13 703	18 097	7.2	15.4
283 LUTH--MO SYNOD	9	4 096	5 528	2.2	4.7
329 OPEN BIBLE STD	1	275	563	0.2	0.5
353 CHR BRETHREN..	1	25	50	—	—
371 REF CH IN AM..	1	113	196	0.1	0.2
403 SALVATION ARMY	2	420	942	0.4	0.8
413 S.D.A.........	1	314	384*	0.2	0.3
419 SO BAPT CONV..	10	2 125	2 595*	1.0	2.2
435 UNITARIAN-UNIV	1	563	688*	0.3	0.6
443 UN C OF CHRIST	8	3 604	4 402*	1.8	3.7
449 UN METHODIST..	24	10 473	12 791*	5.1	10.9
453 UN PRES CH USA	8	4 455	5 441*	2.2	4.6
469 WELS..........	1	57	94	—	0.1
WOODFORD	52	8 903	16 615*	49.9	100.0
019 AMER BAPT USA.	3	569	704*	2.1	4.2
029 AMER LUTH CH..	3	925	1 197	3.6	7.2
053 ASSEMB OF GOD.	1	72	130	0.4	0.8
081 CATHOLIC......	8	NA	5 185	15.6	31.2
093 CHR CH (DISC).	2	821	979	2.9	5.9
097 CHR CHS&CHS CR	2	70	87*	0.3	0.5
157 CH OF BRETHREN	2	142	176*	0.5	1.1
165 CH OF NAZARENE	2	235	492	1.5	3.0
167 CHS OF CHRIST.	2	180	242	0.7	1.5
193 EPISCOPAL.....	1	16	29	0.1	0.2
213 EVAN MENN INC.	1	52	64*	0.2	0.4
283 LUTH--MO SYNOD	5	1 053	1 444	4.3	8.7
285 MENNONITE CH..	4	871	1 078*	3.2	6.5
287 MENN GEN CONF.	1	216	251	0.8	1.5
443 UN C OF CHRIST	4	1 430	1 770*	5.3	10.7
449 UN METHODIST..	8	1 887	2 336*	7.0	14.1
453 UN PRES CH USA	3	364	451*	1.4	2.7

INDIANA

THE STATE.....	6 590	1 290 569	2 458 653*	44.8	100.0
ADAMS	65	13 142	21 129*	71.3	100.0
019 AMER BAPT USA.	2	176	222*	0.7	1.1
053 ASSEMB OF GOD.	1	45	70	0.2	0.3
081 CATHOLIC......	2	NA	3 748	12.7	17.7
093 CHR CH (DISC).	1	83	161	0.5	0.8
097 CHR CHS&CHS CR	4	270	341*	1.2	1.6
123 CH GOD (ANDER)	1	185	555	1.9	2.6

NA—Not applicable   *Total adherents estimated from known number of communicant, confirmed, full members.   —Represents a percent less than 0.1.   Percentages may not total due to rounding.

Table 4. Churches and Church Membership by County and Denomination: 1980

County and Denomination	Number of churches	Communicant, confirmed, full members	Total adherents Number	Percent of total population	Percent of total adherents
151 L-D SAINTS....	1	NA	111	0.4	0.5
157 CH OF BRETHREN	1	253	320*	1.1	1.5
165 CH OF NAZARENE	4	385	719	2.4	3.4
213 EVAN MENN INC.	1	275	347*	1.2	1.6
226 FRIENDS-USA...	1	17	21*	0.1	0.1
244 GRACE BRETHREN	1	150	190*	0.6	0.9
283 LUTH--MO SYNOD	7	2 747	3 654	12.3	17.3
287 MENN GEN CONF.	1	1 216	1 566	5.3	7.4
291 MISSIONARY CH.	4	844	897	3.0	4.2
323 OLD ORD AMISH.	14	1 820	2 299*	7.8	10.9
349 PENT HOLINESS.	1	29	37*	0.1	0.2
443 UN C OF CHRIST	5	1 639	2 071*	7.0	9.8
449 UN METHODIST..	12	2 851	3 602*	12.2	17.0
453 UN PRES CH USA	1	157	198*	0.7	0.9
ALLEN	249	77 786	152 541*	51.8	100.0
019 AMER BAPT USA.	7	2 673	3 289*	1.1	2.2
029 AMER LUTH CH..	6	2 571	3 282	1.1	2.2
053 ASSEMB OF GOD.	4	607	747	0.3	0.5
061 BEACHY AMISH..	1	19	23*	-	-
071 BRETHREN (ASH)	1	28	34*	-	-
081 CATHOLIC......	24	NA	49 780	16.9	32.6
089 CHR & MISS AL.	3	422	718	0.2	0.5
093 CHR CH (DISC).	4	1 478	2 311	0.8	1.5
097 CHR CHS&CHS CR	12	2 708	3 332*	1.1	2.2
105 CHRISTIAN REF.	1	96	152	0.1	0.1
107 CHRISTIAN UN..	1	26	56	-	-
123 CH GOD (ANDER)	5	565	1 695	0.6	1.1
127 CH GOD (CLEVE)	1	133	164*	0.1	0.1
151 L-D SAINTS....	2	NA	851	0.3	0.6
157 CH OF BRETHREN	3	774	952*	0.3	0.6
165 CH OF NAZARENE	11	1 403	2 421	0.8	1.6
167 CHS OF CHRIST.	9	820	1 044	0.4	0.7
193 EPISCOPAL.....	2	1 308	2 058	0.7	1.3
208 EVAN LUTH ASSN	3	818	1 206	0.4	0.8
213 EVAN MENN INC.	5	710	874*	0.3	0.6
221 FREE METHODIST	1	78	285	0.1	0.2
226 FRIENDS-USA...	3	50	62*	-	-
244 GRACE BRETHREN	2	377	464*	0.2	0.3
271 REFORM JUDAISM	1	526	647*	0.2	0.4
281 LUTH CH AMER..	13	7 507	9 801	3.3	6.4
283 LUTH--MO SYNOD	28	20 291	27 101	9.2	17.8
285 MENNONITE CH..	8	945	1 163*	0.4	0.8
287 MENN GEN CONF.	1	208	318	0.1	0.2
290 METRO COMM CHS	0	20	40	-	-
291 MISSIONARY CH.	14	2 345	2 852	1.0	1.9
323 OLD ORD AMISH.	11	1 430	1 759*	0.6	1.2
353 CHR BRETHREN..	1	10	25	-	-
395 ROMANIAN OR CH	1	350	431*	0.1	0.3
403 SALVATION ARMY	2	187	217	0.1	0.1
413 S.D.A.........	2	326	401*	0.1	0.3
419 SO BAPT CONV..	4	1 063	1 308*	0.4	0.9
435 UNITARIAN-UNIV	1	232	285*	0.1	0.2
443 UN C OF CHRIST	6	3 634	4 471*	1.5	2.9
449 UN METHODIST..	35	16 187	19 916*	6.8	13.1
453 UN PRES CH USA	8	4 662	5 736*	1.9	3.8
469 WELS.........	2	199	270	0.1	0.2
BARTHOLOMEW	78	22 147	31 738*	48.8	100.0
019 AMER BAPT USA.	5	3 251	4 010*	6.2	12.6
029 AMER LUTH CH..	1	50	65	0.1	0.2
053 ASSEMB OF GOD.	2	114	366	0.6	1.2
081 CATHOLIC......	2	NA	2 786	4.3	8.8
089 CHR & MISS AL.	1	8	8	-	-
093 CHR CH (DISC).	1	527	733	1.1	2.3
097 CHR CHS&CHS CR	9	4 966	6 126*	9.4	19.3
107 CHRISTIAN UN..	1	24	30	-	0.1
123 CH GOD (ANDER)	1	37	111	0.2	0.3
127 CH GOD (CLEVE)	2	134	165*	0.3	0.5
151 L-D SAINTS....	1	NA	588	0.9	1.9
165 CH OF NAZARENE	3	333	553	0.8	1.7
167 CHS OF CHRIST.	4	320	407	0.6	1.3
193 EPISCOPAL.....	1	207	289	0.4	0.9
215 EVAN METH CH..	1	36	44*	0.1	0.1
221 FREE METHODIST	1	113	279	0.4	0.9
226 FRIENDS-USA...	1	194	239*	0.4	0.8
281 LUTH CH AMER..	1	360	502	0.8	1.6
283 LUTH--MO SYNOD	7	3 755	4 904	7.5	15.5
293 MORAV CH-NORTH	1	347	449	0.7	1.4
383 REF PRES OF NA	1	34	34	0.1	0.1
409 SEPARATE BAPT.	4	295	364*	0.6	1.1
413 S.D.A.........	1	98	121*	0.2	0.4
419 SO BAPT CONV..	3	567	699*	1.1	2.2
435 UNITARIAN-UNIV	1	30	37*	0.1	0.1
449 UN METHODIST..	19	5 292	6 528*	10.0	20.6
453 UN PRES CH USA	3	1 055	1 301*	2.0	4.1
BENTON	28	3 398	7 286*	71.3	100.0
081 CATHOLIC......	6	NA	3 083	30.2	42.3
093 CHR CH (DISC).	1	69	102	1.0	1.4
097 CHR CHS&CHS CR	6	908	1 109*	10.9	15.2
165 CH OF NAZARENE	1	21	35	0.3	0.5
221 FREE METHODIST	1	11	39	0.4	0.5
419 SO BAPT CONV..	3	470	574*	5.6	7.9
449 UN METHODIST..	7	1 533	1 873*	18.3	25.7
453 UN PRES CH USA	3	386	471*	4.6	6.5
BLACKFORD	29	3 772	6 308*	40.5	100.0
019 AMER BAPT USA.	1	220	269*	1.7	4.3
029 AMER LUTH CH..	1	520	709	4.6	11.2
053 ASSEMB OF GOD.	2	49	79	0.5	1.3
081 CATHOLIC......	2	NA	1 118	7.2	17.7
093 CHR CH (DISC).	1	252	432	2.8	6.8
097 CHR CHS&CHS CR	2	175	214*	1.4	3.4
123 CH GOD (ANDER)	1	20	60	0.4	1.0
157 CH OF BRETHREN	1	149	182*	1.2	2.9
165 CH OF NAZARENE	3	350	752	4.8	11.9
226 FRIENDS-USA...	2	76	93*	0.6	1.5
413 S.D.A.........	1	25	31*	0.2	0.5
419 SO BAPT CONV..	1	49	60*	0.4	1.0
449 UN METHODIST..	10	1 665	2 037*	13.1	32.3
453 UN PRES CH USA	1	222	272*	1.7	4.3
BOONE	46	8 825	13 644*	37.4	100.0
019 AMER BAPT USA.	2	942	1 150*	3.2	8.4
053 ASSEMB OF GOD.	2	104	193	0.5	1.4
057 BAPT GEN CONF.	1	30	37*	0.1	0.3
081 CATHOLIC......	2	NA	2 043	5.6	15.0
093 CHR CH (DISC).	3	1 332	2 109	5.8	15.5
097 CHR CHS&CHS CR	5	1 528	1 865*	5.1	13.7
123 CH GOD (ANDER)	1	23	69	0.2	0.5
127 CH GOD (CLEVE)	1	7	9*	-	0.1
165 CH OF NAZARENE	1	66	297	0.8	2.2
167 CHS OF CHRIST.	3	180	229	0.6	1.7
193 EPISCOPAL.....	2	160	198	0.5	1.5
226 FRIENDS-USA...	1	52	63*	0.2	0.5
281 LUTH CH AMER..	2	305	383	1.1	2.8
419 SO BAPT CONV..	1	287	350*	1.0	2.6
443 UN C OF CHRIST	5	487	594*	1.6	4.4
449 UN METHODIST..	12	2 577	3 146*	8.6	23.1
453 UN PRES CH USA	2	745	909*	2.5	6.7
BROWN	17	1 464	2 307*	18.6	100.0
019 AMER BAPT USA.	1	180	219*	1.8	9.5
081 CATHOLIC......	1	NA	438	3.5	19.0
093 CHR CH (DISC).	1	14	22	0.2	1.0
097 CHR CHS&CHS CR	1	300	365*	2.9	15.8
165 CH OF NAZARENE	1	97	184	1.5	8.0
167 CHS OF CHRIST.	2	70	89	0.7	3.9
193 EPISCOPAL.....	1	60	82	0.7	3.6
283 LUTH--MO SYNOD	1	83	105	0.8	4.6
409 SEPARATE BAPT.	2	87	106*	0.9	4.6
449 UN METHODIST..	6	573	697*	5.6	30.2
CARROLL	36	6 265	8 876*	45.0	100.0
019 AMER BAPT USA.	3	549	669*	3.4	7.5
071 BRETHREN (ASH)	2	317	386*	2.0	4.3
081 CATHOLIC......	1	NA	906	4.6	10.2
093 CHR CH (DISC).	3	439	756	3.8	8.5
097 CHR CHS&CHS CR	3	654	797*	4.0	9.0
157 CH OF BRETHREN	5	663	808*	4.1	9.1
167 CHS OF CHRIST.	1	60	76	0.4	0.9
281 LUTH CH AMER..	3	574	810	4.1	9.1
443 UN C OF CHRIST	1	104	127*	0.6	1.4
449 UN METHODIST..	8	1 731	2 110*	10.7	23.8
453 UN PRES CH USA	6	1 174	1 431*	7.3	16.1
CASS	67	12 083	19 492*	47.6	100.0
019 AMER BAPT USA.	5	1 741	2 124*	5.2	10.9
053 ASSEMB OF GOD.	1	8	14	-	0.1
071 BRETHREN (ASH)	1	115	140*	0.3	0.7
081 CATHOLIC......	4	NA	3 796	9.3	19.5
089 CHR & MISS AL.	1	77	111	0.3	0.6
093 CHR CH (DISC).	3	668	1 020	2.5	5.2
097 CHR CHS&CHS CR	7	1 516	1 849*	4.5	9.5
123 CH GOD (ANDER)	1	126	378	0.9	1.9
127 CH GOD (CLEVE)	1	187	228*	0.6	1.2
151 L-D SAINTS....	1	NA	226	0.6	1.2
157 CH OF BRETHREN	1	158	193*	0.5	1.0
165 CH OF NAZARENE	1	148	319	0.8	1.6
167 CHS OF CHRIST.	2	290	369	0.9	1.9
175 CONGR CHR CHS.	1	216	263*	0.6	1.3
193 EPISCOPAL.....	1	149	226	0.6	1.2
263 INT FOURSQ GOS	1	19	23*	0.1	0.1
281 LUTH CH AMER..	2	526	703	1.7	3.6
283 LUTH--MO SYNOD	1	491	629	1.5	3.2
353 CHR BRETHREN..	1	30	40	0.1	0.2
403 SALVATION ARMY	1	126	141	0.3	0.7
413 S.D.A.........	1	15	18*	-	0.1
419 SO BAPT CONV..	1	202	246*	0.6	1.3
443 UN C OF CHRIST	2	253	309*	0.8	1.6
449 UN METHODIST..	21	3 709	4 525*	11.1	23.2
453 UN PRES CH USA	5	1 313	1 602*	3.9	8.2
CLARK	110	19 453	37 424*	42.1	100.0
001 ADVENT CHR CH.	1	124	153*	0.2	0.4
017 AMER BAPT ASSN	1	50	50	0.1	0.1
019 AMER BAPT USA.	5	1 322	1 629*	1.8	4.4
053 ASSEMB OF GOD.	4	185	270	0.3	0.7
081 CATHOLIC......	8	NA	10 966	12.3	29.3
093 CHR CH (DISC).	6	1 366	2 127	2.4	5.7
097 CHR CHS&CHS CR	9	1 394	1 717*	1.9	4.6
123 CH GOD (ANDER)	4	847	2 541	2.9	6.8
127 CH GOD (CLEVE)	3	120	148*	0.2	0.4
165 CH OF NAZARENE	5	209	653	0.7	1.7
167 CHS OF CHRIST.	13	1 461	1 846	2.1	4.9
193 EPISCOPAL.....	1	182	259	0.3	0.7
281 LUTH CH AMER..	1	165	235	0.3	0.6
283 LUTH--MO SYNOD	1	124	165	0.2	0.4
413 S.D.A.........	1	66	81*	0.1	0.2
419 SO BAPT CONV..	14	5 600	6 899*	7.8	18.4

NA—Not applicable   *Total adherents estimated from known number of communicant, confirmed, full members.   —Represents a percent less than 0.1.   Percentages may not total due to rounding.

Table 4. Churches and Church Membership by County and Denomination: 1980

County and Denomination	Number of churches	Communicant, confirmed, full members	Total adherents Number	Percent of total population	Percent of total adherents
443 UN C OF CHRIST	2	518	638*	0.7	1.7
449 UN METHODIST..	24	4 578	5 640*	6.3	15.1
453 UN PRES CH USA	7	1 142	1 407*	1.6	3.8
CLAY	60	8 899	12 108*	48.7	100.0
019 AMER BAPT USA.	5	1 351	1 634*	6.6	13.5
053 ASSEMB OF GOD.	2	153	278	1.1	2.3
081 CATHOLIC......	1	NA	550	2.2	4.5
093 CHR CH (DISC).	1	60	92	0.4	0.8
097 CHR CHS&CHS CR	4	2 260	2 733*	11.0	22.6
127 CH GOD (CLEVE)	1	26	31*	0.1	0.3
165 CH OF NAZARENE	4	470	1 159	4.7	9.6
167 CHS OF CHRIST.	8	375	477	1.9	3.9
175 CONGR CHR CHS.	1	25	30*	0.1	0.2
221 FREE METHODIST	1	36	132	0.5	1.1
283 LUTH--MO SYNOD	1	191	214	0.9	1.8
419 SO BAPT CONV..	1	54	65*	0.3	0.5
443 UN C OF CHRIST	4	727	879*	3.5	7.3
449 UN METHODIST..	24	2 789	3 372*	13.6	27.8
453 UN PRES CH USA	2	382	462*	1.9	3.8
CLINTON	55	10 496	14 290*	45.3	100.0
017 AMER BAPT ASSN	1	10	10	—	0.1
019 AMER BAPT USA.	5	1 630	1 990*	6.3	13.9
053 ASSEMB OF GOD.	1	59	110	0.3	0.8
081 CATHOLIC......	1	NA	912	2.9	6.4
093 CHR CH (DISC).	1	558	798	2.5	5.6
097 CHR CHS&CHS CR	7	1 631	1 991*	6.3	13.9
121 CH GOD (ABR).	1	51	62*	0.2	0.4
123 CH GOD (ANDER)	2	60	180	0.6	1.3
127 CH GOD (CLEVE)	1	19	23*	0.1	0.2
151 L-D SAINTS....	1	NA	104	0.3	0.7
157 CH OF BRETHREN	1	147	179*	0.6	1.3
165 CH OF NAZARENE	2	348	636	2.0	4.5
167 CHS OF CHRIST.	1	150	191	0.6	1.3
281 LUTH CH AMER..	2	433	512	1.6	3.6
413 S.D.A.........	1	56	68*	0.2	0.5
419 SO BAPT CONV..	3	255	311*	1.0	2.2
443 UN C OF CHRIST	3	512	625*	2.0	4.4
449 UN METHODIST..	16	3 328	4 063*	12.9	28.4
453 UN PRES CH USA	5	1 249	1 525*	4.8	10.7
CRAWFORD	32	3 729	5 108*	52.0	100.0
019 AMER BAPT USA.	3	196	241*	2.5	4.7
075 BRETHREN IN CR	1	43	73	0.7	1.4
081 CATHOLIC......	1	NA	152	1.5	3.0
093 CHR CH (DISC).	1	77	118	1.2	2.3
097 CHR CHS&CHS CR	9	2 230	2 745*	28.0	53.7
151 L-D SAINTS....	1	NA	194	2.0	3.8
165 CH OF NAZARENE	2	36	99	1.0	1.9
221 FREE METHODIST	1	24	105	1.1	2.1
419 SO BAPT CONV..	2	153	188*	1.9	3.7
449 UN METHODIST..	10	821	1 010*	10.3	19.8
453 UN PRES CH USA	1	149	183*	1.9	3.6
DAVIESS	69	10 071	17 723*	63.7	100.0
019 AMER BAPT USA.	4	1 312	1 609*	5.8	9.1
029 AMER LUTH CH..	1	194	251	0.9	1.4
053 ASSEMB OF GOD.	2	161	321	1.2	1.8
061 BEACHY AMISH..	2	68	83*	0.3	0.5
081 CATHOLIC......	7	NA	4 855	17.4	27.4
093 CHR CH (DISC).	2	428	461	1.7	2.6
097 CHR CHS&CHS CR	5	2 156	2 643*	9.5	14.9
123 CH GOD (ANDER)	1	30	90	0.3	0.5
151 L-D SAINTS....	1	NA	?	?	?
165 CH OF NAZARENE	2	123	244	0.9	1.4
167 CHS OF CHRIST.	6	265	337	1.2	1.9
185 CUMBER PRESB..	1	37	44	0.2	0.2
193 EPISCOPAL.....	1	84	84	0.3	0.5
221 FREE METHODIST	1	121	459	1.6	2.6
285 MENNONITE CH..	3	599	734*	2.6	4.1
323 OLD ORD AMISH.	8	1 040	1 275*	4.6	7.2
413 S.D.A.........	1	10	12*	—	0.1
419 SO BAPT CONV..	3	444	544*	2.0	3.1
449 UN METHODIST..	17	2 774	3 401*	12.2	19.2
453 UN PRES CH USA	1	225	276*	1.0	1.6
DEARBORN	57	9 730	17 671*	51.5	100.0
019 AMER BAPT USA.	8	2 456	3 042*	8.9	17.2
029 AMER LUTH CH..	4	769	981	2.9	5.6
081 CATHOLIC......	6	NA	5 177	15.1	29.3
089 CHR & MISS AL.	1	92	213	0.6	1.2
097 CHR CHS&CHS CR	8	1 740	2 155*	6.3	12.2
107 CHRISTIAN UN..	1	45	146	0.4	0.8
123 CH GOD (ANDER)	1	40	120	0.3	0.7
165 CH OF NAZARENE	1	19	106	0.3	0.6
193 EPISCOPAL.....	1	31	83	0.2	0.5
281 LUTH CH AMER..	1	244	310	0.9	1.8
283 LUTH--MO SYNOD	4	1 153	1 448*	4.2	8.2
419 SO BAPT CONV..	1	35	43*	0.1	0.2
435 UNITARIAN-UNIV	1	45	56*	0.2	0.3
443 UN C OF CHRIST	2	256	317*	0.9	1.8
449 UN METHODIST..	13	2 205	2 731*	8.0	15.5
453 UN PRES CH USA	4	600	743*	2.2	4.2
DECATUR	55	8 518	16 119*	67.6	100.0
019 AMER BAPT USA.	11	3 455	4 301*	18.0	26.7
053 ASSEMB OF GOD.	2	114	200	0.8	1.2
081 CATHOLIC......	5	NA	4 789	20.1	29.7
093 CHR CH (DISC).	2	505	905	3.8	5.6
097 CHR CHS&CHS CR	7	1 198	1 491*	6.3	9.2
123 CH GOD (ANDER)	1	152	456	1.9	2.8
127 CH GOD (CLEVE)	1	56	70*	0.3	0.4
165 CH OF NAZARENE	1	12	36	0.2	0.2
167 CHS OF CHRIST.	1	45	57	0.2	0.4
221 FREE METHODIST	1	49	120	0.5	0.7
281 LUTH CH AMER..	2	173	242	1.0	1.5
283 LUTH--MO SYNOD	1	106	149	0.6	0.9
409 SEPARATE BAPT.	1	81	101*	0.4	0.6
419 SO BAPT CONV..	2	235	293*	1.2	1.8
449 UN METHODIST..	13	1 806	2 248*	9.4	13.9
453 UN PRES CH USA	4	531	661*	2.8	4.1
DE KALB	61	10 001	17 347*	51.6	100.0
019 AMER BAPT USA.	1	380	472*	1.4	2.7
053 ASSEMB OF GOD.	2	62	120	0.4	0.7
075 BRETHREN IN CR	1	43	73	0.2	0.4
081 CATHOLIC......	3	NA	3 238	9.6	18.7
093 CHR CH (DISC).	1	291	448	1.3	2.6
097 CHR CHS&CHS CR	8	2 030	2 523*	7.5	14.5
123 CH GOD (ANDER)	4	421	1 263	3.8	7.3
151 L-D SAINTS....	1	NA	252	0.7	1.5
157 CH OF BRETHREN	4	480	596*	1.8	3.4
165 CH OF NAZARENE	4	378	640	1.9	3.7
167 CHS OF CHRIST.	2	125	159	0.5	0.9
226 FRIENDS-USA...	1	6	7*	—	—
281 LUTH CH AMER..	5	762	1 214	3.6	7.0
283 LUTH--MO SYNOD	3	727	985	2.9	5.7
291 MISSIONARY CH.	1	99	141	0.4	0.8
323 OLD ORD AMISH.	1	130	162*	0.5	0.9
419 SO BAPT CONV..	1	133	165*	0.5	1.0
449 UN METHODIST..	16	2 843	3 533*	10.5	20.4
453 UN PRES CH USA	2	1 091	1 356*	4.0	7.8
DELAWARE	123	23 643	40 890*	31.8	100.0
019 AMER BAPT USA.	3	1 306	1 569*	1.2	3.8
029 AMER LUTH CH..	1	112	178	0.1	0.4
053 ASSEMB OF GOD.	2	483	962	0.7	2.4
071 BRETHREN (ASH)	2	255	306*	0.2	0.7
081 CATHOLIC......	3	NA	8 374	6.5	20.5
089 CHR & MISS AL.	1	36	100	0.1	0.2
093 CHR CH (DISC).	5	1 048	1 354	1.1	3.3
097 CHR CHS&CHS CR	2	600	721*	0.6	1.8
123 CH GOD (ANDER)	7	603	1 809	1.4	4.4
127 CH GOD (CLEVE)	1	81	97*	0.1	0.2
151 L-D SAINTS....	2	NA	543	0.4	1.3
157 CH OF BRETHREN	3	358	430*	0.3	1.1
165 CH OF NAZARENE	16	1 898	3 517	2.7	8.6
167 CHS OF CHRIST.	9	964	1 310	1.0	3.2
193 EPISCOPAL.....	1	160	288	0.2	0.7
221 FREE METHODIST	1	4	39	—	0.1
226 FRIENDS-USA...	2	700	841*	0.7	2.1
263 INT FOURSQ GOS	1	253	304*	0.2	0.7
271 REFORM JUDAISM	1	114	137*	0.1	0.3
281 LUTH CH AMER..	2	695	1 145	0.9	2.8
283 LUTH--MO SYNOD	1	471	618	0.5	1.5
291 MISSIONARY CH.	1	34	33	—	0.1
381 REF PRES-EVAN.	1	111	163	0.1	0.4
403 SALVATION ARMY	1	89	109	0.1	0.3
409 SEPARATE BAPT.	3	276	332*	0.3	0.8
413 S.D.A.........	2	90	108*	0.1	0.3
419 SO BAPT CONV..	9	1 680	2 019*	1.6	4.9
435 UNITARIAN-UNIV	1	211	254*	0.2	0.6
443 UN C OF CHRIST	5	973	1 169*	0.9	2.9
449 UN METHODIST..	32	8 698	10 451*	8.1	25.6
453 UN PRES CH USA	2	1 340	1 610*	1.3	3.9
DUBOIS	40	5 991	30 185*	88.2	100.0
029 AMER LUTH CH..	5	1 351	1 795	5.2	5.9
081 CATHOLIC......	13	NA	22 593	66.0	74.8
093 CHR CH (DISC).	1	40	62	0.2	0.2
097 CHR CHS&CHS CR	3	581	713*	2.1	2.4
165 CH OF NAZARENE	1	69	139	0.4	0.5
167 CHS OF CHRIST.	1	40	50	0.1	0.2
281 LUTH CH AMER..	2	714	913	2.7	3.0
419 SO BAPT CONV..	2	255	313*	0.9	1.0
443 UN C OF CHRIST	6	1 756	2 154*	6.3	7.1
449 UN METHODIST..	4	1 000	1 226*	3.6	4.1
453 UN PRES CH USA	2	185	227*	0.7	0.8
ELKHART	189	40 551	63 576*	46.3	100.0
005 AME ZION......	1	60	72	0.1	0.1
017 AMER BAPT ASSN	1	50	50	—	0.1
029 AMER LUTH CH..	1	385	504	0.4	0.8
053 ASSEMB OF GOD.	4	716	1 422	1.0	2.2
061 BEACHY AMISH..	4	481	595*	0.4	0.9
071 BRETHREN (ASH)	6	1 669	2 063*	1.5	3.2
075 BRETHREN IN CR	2	86	146	0.1	0.2
081 CATHOLIC......	5	NA	9 242	6.7	14.5
093 CHR CH (DISC).	2	493	581	0.4	0.9
097 CHR CHS&CHS CR	1	65	80*	0.1	0.1
105 CHRISTIAN REF.	1	144	223	0.2	0.4
123 CH GOD (ANDER)	5	826	2 478	1.8	3.9
127 CH GOD (CLEVE)	3	186	230*	0.2	0.4
151 L-D SAINTS....	1	NA	461	0.3	0.7
157 CH OF BRETHREN	19	3 940	4 870*	3.5	7.7
165 CH OF NAZARENE	7	908	1 504	1.1	2.4
167 CHS OF CHRIST.	2	269	453	0.3	0.7
193 EPISCOPAL.....	4	1 024	1 349	1.0	2.1
221 FREE METHODIST	1	75	240	0.2	0.4

NA— Not applicable   *Total adherents estimated from known number of communicant, confirmed, full members.   —Represents a percent less than 0.1.   Percentages may not total due to rounding.

Table 4. Churches and Church Membership by County and Denomination: 1980

County and Denomination	Number of churches	Communicant, confirmed, full members	Total adherents Number	Percent of total population	Percent of total adherents
244 GRACE BRETHREN	2	262	324*	0.2	0.5
281 LUTH CH AMER..	9	2 878	3 809	2.8	6.0
283 LUTH--MO SYNOD	1	1 031	1 409	1.0	2.2
285 MENNONITE CH..	35	6 430	7 947*	5.8	12.5
287 MENN GEN CONF.	7	963	1 257	0.9	2.0
291 MISSIONARY CH.	12	2 087	2 595	1.9	4.1
323 OLD ORD AMISH.	11	1 430	1 767*	1.3	2.8
353 CHR BRETHREN..	1	15	50	—	0.1
403 SALVATION ARMY	2	308	835	0.6	1.3
413 S.D.A.........	2	152	188*	0.1	0.3
419 SO BAPT CONV..	1	73	90*	0.1	0.1
435 UNITARIAN-UNIV	1	92	114*	0.1	0.2
443 UN C OF CHRIST	8	1 946	2 405*	1.8	3.8
449 UN METHODIST..	24	9 572	11 831*	8.6	18.6
453 UN PRES CH USA	3	1 935	2 392*	1.7	3.8
FAYETTE	37	5 406	11 276*	39.9	100.0
019 AMER BAPT USA.	1	531	659*	2.3	5.8
053 ASSEMB OF GOD.	1	39	55	0.2	0.5
081 CATHOLIC......	1	NA	3 431	12.1	30.4
093 CHR CH (DISC).	5	773	1 256	4.4	11.1
097 CHR CHS&CHS CR	4	280	348*	1.2	3.1
123 CH GOD (ANDER)	1	148	444	1.6	3.9
127 CH GOD (CLEVE)	1	39	48*	0.2	0.4
151 L-D SAINTS....	1	NA	209	0.7	1.9
165 CH OF NAZARENE	2	181	566	2.0	5.0
167 CHS OF CHRIST.	3	100	127	0.4	1.1
193 EPISCOPAL.....	1	56	69	0.2	0.6
281 LUTH CH AMER..	2	195	255	0.9	2.3
283 LUTH--MO SYNOD	1	70	109	0.4	1.0
403 SALVATION ARMY	1	102	109	0.4	1.0
413 S.D.A.........	1	42	52*	0.2	0.5
419 SO BAPT CONV..	1	517	642*	2.3	5.7
449 UN METHODIST..	9	1 883	2 338*	8.3	20.7
453 UN PRES CH USA	1	450	559*	2.0	5.0
FLOYD	65	18 334	36 186*	59.2	100.0
001 ADVENT CHR CH.	1	182	222*	0.4	0.6
005 AME ZION......	2	500	625	1.0	1.7
019 AMER BAPT USA.	4	2 302	2 806*	4.6	7.8
053 ASSEMB OF GOD.	1	115	325	0.5	0.9
081 CATHOLIC......	5	NA	11 378	18.6	31.4
093 CHR CH (DISC).	6	1 339	2 013	3.3	5.6
097 CHR CHS&CHS CR	4	915	1 115*	1.8	3.1
123 CH GOD (ANDER)	2	297	891	1.5	2.5
127 CH GOD (CLEVE)	1	71	87*	0.1	0.2
151 L-D SAINTS....	1	NA	616	1.0	1.7
165 CH OF NAZARENE	3	434	1 077	1.8	3.0
167 CHS OF CHRIST.	4	376	499	0.8	1.4
193 EPISCOPAL.....	1	228	228	0.4	0.6
244 GRACE BRETHREN	1	15	18*	—	—
281 LUTH CH AMER..	1	84	142	0.2	0.4
283 LUTH--MO SYNOD	2	728	1 060	1.7	2.9
403 SALVATION ARMY	1	91	95	0.2	0.3
413 S.D.A.........	2	162	197*	0.3	0.5
419 SO BAPT CONV..	5	3 786	4 615*	7.5	12.8
443 UN C OF CHRIST	1	1 136	1 385*	2.3	3.8
449 UN METHODIST..	15	4 867	5 932*	9.7	16.4
453 UN PRES CH USA	2	706	860*	1.4	2.4
FOUNTAIN	39	4 689	7 271*	38.2	100.0
053 ASSEMB OF GOD.	2	188	362	1.9	5.0
081 CATHOLIC......	2	NA	762	4.0	10.5
093 CHR CH (DISC).	3	278	538	2.8	7.4
097 CHR CHS&CHS CR	7	1 497	1 818*	9.6	25.0
123 CH GOD (ANDER)	1	52	156	0.8	2.1
127 CH GOD (CLEVE)	2	40	49*	0.3	0.7
165 CH OF NAZARENE	5	177	354	1.9	4.9
167 CHS OF CHRIST.	1	70	89	0.5	1.2
221 FREE METHODIST	1	88	300	1.6	4.1
281 LUTH CH AMER..	2	226	325	1.7	4.5
443 UN C OF CHRIST	2	195	237*	1.2	3.3
449 UN METHODIST..	9	1 603	1 947*	10.2	26.8
453 UN PRES CH USA	2	275	334*	1.8	4.6
FRANKLIN	39	4 273	10 687*	54.5	100.0
029 AMER LUTH CH..	1	84	111	0.6	1.0
057 BAPT GEN CONF.	1	33	41*	0.2	0.4
081 CATHOLIC......	7	NA	5 174	26.4	48.4
093 CHR CH (DISC).	1	24	52	0.3	0.5
097 CHR CHS&CHS CR	6	1 099	1 380*	7.0	12.9
165 CH OF NAZARENE	1	31	112	0.6	1.0
167 CHS OF CHRIST.	1	12	25	0.1	0.2
281 LUTH CH AMER..	1	265	370	1.9	3.5
419 SO BAPT CONV..	6	1 075	1 350*	6.9	12.6
443 UN C OF CHRIST	2	448	563*	2.9	5.3
449 UN METHODIST..	11	1 146	1 439*	7.3	13.5
453 UN PRES CH USA	1	56	70*	0.4	0.7
FULTON	34	4 686	7 556*	39.1	100.0
019 AMER BAPT USA.	2	511	620*	3.2	8.2
053 ASSEMB OF GOD.	1	56	109	0.6	1.4
081 CATHOLIC......	2	NA	822	4.3	10.9
093 CHR CH (DISC).	1	361	568	2.9	7.5
097 CHR CHS&CHS CR	1	100	121*	0.6	1.6
123 CH GOD (ANDER)	3	423	1 269	6.6	16.8
127 CH GOD (CLEVE)	1	7	8*	—	0.1
157 CH OF BRETHREN	1	79	96*	0.5	1.3
165 CH OF NAZARENE	1	82	216	1.1	2.9
167 CHS OF CHRIST.	1	100	127	0.7	1.7

County and Denomination	Number of churches	Communicant, confirmed, full members	Total adherents Number	Percent of total population	Percent of total adherents
226 FRIENDS-USA...	1	436	529*	2.7	7.0
283 LUTH--MO SYNOD	1	217	264	1.4	3.5
413 S.D.A.........	1	9	11*	0.1	0.1
419 SO BAPT CONV..	1	64	78*	0.4	1.0
449 UN METHODIST..	15	2 048	2 484*	12.8	32.9
453 UN PRES CH USA	1	193	234*	1.2	3.1
GIBSON	57	6 648	14 999*	45.2	100.0
053 ASSEMB OF GOD.	1	213	300	0.9	2.0
081 CATHOLIC......	6	NA	6 036	18.2	40.2
093 CHR CH (DISC).	2	283	424	1.3	2.8
097 CHR CHS&CHS CR	3	438	528*	1.6	3.5
123 CH GOD (ANDER)	1	120	360	1.1	2.4
165 CH OF NAZARENE	7	594	1 284	3.9	8.6
167 CHS OF CHRIST.	2	102	126	0.4	0.8
185 CUMBER PRESB..	1	38	65	0.2	0.4
281 LUTH CH AMER..	1	135	193	0.6	1.3
403 SALVATION ARMY	1	81	85	0.3	0.6
419 SO BAPT CONV..	4	497	599*	1.8	4.0
443 UN C OF CHRIST	3	269	324*	1.0	2.2
449 UN METHODIST..	19	2 983	3 596*	10.8	24.0
453 UN PRES CH USA	6	895	1 079*	3.3	7.2
GRANT	101	15 907	27 689*	34.2	100.0
017 AMER BAPT ASSN	1	50	50	0.1	0.2
019 AMER BAPT USA.	3	781	952*	1.2	3.4
029 AMER LUTH CH..	1	493	661	0.8	2.4
053 ASSEMB OF GOD.	4	847	2 424	3.0	8.8
071 BRETHREN (ASH)	1	15	18*	—	0.1
081 CATHOLIC......	3	NA	4 440	5.5	16.0
089 CHR & MISS AL.	2	159	206	0.3	0.7
093 CHR CH (DISC).	6	1 476	2 406	3.0	8.7
097 CHR CHS&CHS CR	3	350	426*	0.5	1.5
123 CH GOD (ANDER)	4	244	732	0.9	2.6
127 CH GOD (CLEVE)	2	24	29*	—	0.1
151 L-D SAINTS....	1	NA	378	0.5	1.4
157 CH OF BRETHREN	1	158	193*	0.2	0.7
165 CH OF NAZARENE	7	473	1 272	1.6	4.6
167 CHS OF CHRIST.	4	242	375	0.5	1.4
193 EPISCOPAL.....	2	307	465	0.6	1.7
213 EVAN MENN INC.	1	156	190*	0.2	0.7
226 FRIENDS-USA...	11	1 881	2 292*	2.8	8.3
271 REFORM JUDAISM	1	86	105*	0.1	0.4
281 LUTH CH AMER..	1	100	172	0.2	0.6
283 LUTH--MO SYNOD	1	323	489	0.6	1.8
403 SALVATION ARMY	1	138	147	0.2	0.5
409 SEPARATE BAPT.	1	45	55*	0.1	0.2
413 S.D.A.........	2	131	160*	0.2	0.6
417 SOCIAL BRETH..	1	110	134*	0.2	0.5
419 SO BAPT CONV..	2	744	907*	1.1	3.3
443 UN C OF CHRIST	2	396	483*	0.6	1.7
449 UN METHODIST..	29	5 251	6 398*	7.9	23.1
453 UN PRES CH USA	3	927	1 130*	1.4	4.1
GREENE	78	9 813	13 597*	44.7	100.0
019 AMER BAPT USA.	9	2 670	3 225*	10.6	23.7
029 AMER LUTH CH..	1	85	139	0.5	1.0
053 ASSEMB OF GOD.	4	284	522	1.7	3.8
081 CATHOLIC......	3	NA	707	2.3	5.2
093 CHR CH (DISC).	7	922	1 416	4.7	10.4
097 CHR CHS&CHS CR	8	1 583	1 912*	6.3	14.1
123 CH GOD (ANDER)	2	75	225	0.7	1.7
127 CH GOD (CLEVE)	3	259	313*	1.0	2.3
151 L-D SAINTS....	1	NA	212	0.7	1.6
165 CH OF NAZARENE	4	99	197	0.6	1.4
167 CHS OF CHRIST.	12	665	846	2.8	6.2
221 FREE METHODIST	1	27	87	0.3	0.6
403 SALVATION ARMY	1	45	54	0.2	0.4
413 S.D.A.........	1	59	71*	0.2	0.5
443 UN C OF CHRIST	1	328	396*	1.3	2.9
449 UN METHODIST..	19	2 614	3 157*	10.4	23.2
453 UN PRES CH USA	1	98	118*	0.4	0.9
HAMILTON	85	20 212	33 688*	40.9	100.0
017 AMER BAPT ASSN	1	100	100	0.1	0.3
019 AMER BAPT USA.	1	63	78*	0.1	0.2
053 ASSEMB OF GOD.	1	300	450	0.5	1.3
057 BAPT GEN CONF.	1	18	22*	—	0.1
081 CATHOLIC......	3	NA	7 131	8.7	21.2
089 CHR & MISS AL.	1	333	538	0.7	1.6
093 CHR CH (DISC).	7	2 128	2 874	3.5	8.5
097 CHR CHS&CHS CR	15	3 623	4 496*	5.5	13.3
123 CH GOD (ANDER)	4	270	810	1.0	2.4
127 CH GOD (CLEVE)	1	66	82*	0.1	0.2
157 CH OF BRETHREN	1	130	161*	0.2	0.5
165 CH OF NAZARENE	3	201	381	0.5	1.1
167 CHS OF CHRIST.	3	300	382	0.5	1.1
193 EPISCOPAL.....	2	697	1 032	1.3	3.1
226 FRIENDS-USA...	10	1 761	2 186*	2.7	6.5
281 LUTH CH AMER..	2	903	1 297	1.6	3.9
283 LUTH--MO SYNOD	3	702	974	1.2	2.9
413 S.D.A.........	4	651	808*	1.0	2.4
419 SO BAPT CONV..	3	391	485*	0.6	1.4
443 UN C OF CHRIST	1	275	341*	0.4	1.0
449 UN METHODIST..	16	5 856	7 268*	8.8	21.6
453 UN PRES CH USA	2	1 444	1 792*	2.2	5.3
HANCOCK	54	11 432	17 443*	39.7	100.0
053 ASSEMB OF GOD.	1	40	101	0.2	0.6
081 CATHOLIC......	2	NA	2 210	5.0	12.7

NA—Not applicable   *Total adherents estimated from known number of communicant, confirmed, full members.   —Represents a percent less than 0.1.   Percentages may not total due to rounding.

Table 4. Churches and Church Membership by County and Denomination: 1980

County and Denomination	Number of churches	Communicant, confirmed, full members	Total adherents Number	Percent of total population	Percent of total adherents
093 CHR CH (DISC).	3	692	1 070	2.4	6.1
097 CHR CHS&CHS CR	7	2 963	3 685*	8.4	21.1
123 CH GOD (ANDER)	1	80	240	0.5	1.4
127 CH GOD (CLEVE)	1	168	209*	0.5	1.2
165 CH OF NAZARENE	6	434	1 018	2.3	5.8
167 CHS OF CHRIST.	2	170	216	0.5	1.2
226 FRIENDS-USA...	3	359	447*	1.0	2.6
281 LUTH CH AMER..	1	171	241	0.5	1.4
283 LUTH--MO SYNOD	2	686	955	2.2	5.5
413 S.D.A.........	1	50	62*	0.1	0.4
419 SO BAPT CONV..	2	737	917*	2.1	5.3
443 UN C OF CHRIST	1	202	251*	0.6	1.4
449 UN METHODIST..	20	4 479	5 571*	12.7	31.9
453 UN PRES CH USA	1	201	250*	0.6	1.4
HARRISON	**71**	**6 906**	**12 964***	**47.5**	**100.0**
019 AMER BAPT USA.	1	106	131*	0.5	1.0
053 ASSEMB OF GOD.	2	81	185	0.7	1.4
081 CATHOLIC......	6	NA	3 973	14.6	30.6
093 CHR CH (DISC).	1	306	471	1.7	3.6
097 CHR CHS&CHS CR	5	240	297*	1.1	2.3
127 CH GOD (CLEVE)	1	11	14*	0.1	0.1
165 CH OF NAZARENE	2	168	392	1.4	3.0
167 CHS OF CHRIST.	4	260	328	1.2	2.5
281 LUTH CH AMER..	2	341	428	1.6	3.3
283 LUTH--MO SYNOD	1	541	747	2.7	5.8
413 S.D.A.........	1	15	19*	0.1	0.1
419 SO BAPT CONV..	6	853	1 054*	3.9	8.1
443 UN C OF CHRIST	1	38	47*	0.2	0.4
449 UN METHODIST..	33	3 555	4 395*	16.1	33.9
453 UN PRES CH USA	5	391	483*	1.8	3.7
HENDRICKS	**72**	**15 059**	**25 752***	**36.9**	**100.0**
019 AMER BAPT USA.	5	1 467	1 815*	2.6	7.0
053 ASSEMB OF GOD.	3	179	374	0.5	1.5
081 CATHOLIC......	3	NA	5 264	7.5	20.4
089 CHR & MISS AL.	1	39	106	0.2	0.4
093 CHR CH (DISC).	8	1 757	2 614	3.7	10.2
097 CHR CHS&CHS CR	7	4 230	5 234*	7.5	20.3
121 CH GOD (ABR)..	1	46	57*	0.1	0.2
123 CH GOD (ANDER)	2	84	252	0.4	1.0
127 CH GOD (CLEVE)	1	17	21*	–	0.1
151 L-D SAINTS....	1	NA	494	0.7	1.9
165 CH OF NAZARENE	4	174	456	0.7	1.8
167 CHS OF CHRIST.	3	150	191	0.3	0.7
193 EPISCOPAL.....	2	219	457	0.7	1.8
226 FRIENDS-USA...	7	1 264	1 564*	2.2	6.1
281 LUTH CH AMER..	1	243	361	0.5	1.4
283 LUTH--MO SYNOD	2	370	527	0.8	2.0
413 S.D.A.........	1	72	89*	0.1	0.3
419 SO BAPT CONV..	4	946	1 171*	1.7	4.5
449 UN METHODIST..	12	3 326	4 116*	5.9	16.0
453 UN PRES CH USA	4	476	589*	0.8	2.3
HENRY	**77**	**12 578**	**20 401***	**38.2**	**100.0**
019 AMER BAPT USA.	1	757	927*	1.7	4.5
053 ASSEMB OF GOD.	1	73	131	0.2	0.6
081 CATHOLIC......	1	NA	1 445	2.7	7.1
089 CHR & MISS AL.	1	78	269	0.5	1.3
093 CHR CH (DISC).	4	1 200	1 840	3.4	9.0
097 CHR CHS&CHS CR	7	940	1 151*	2.2	5.6
123 CH GOD (ANDER)	2	310	930	1.7	4.6
127 CH GOD (CLEVE)	1	119	146*	0.3	0.7
151 L-D SAINTS....	1	NA	130	0.2	0.6
157 CH OF BRETHREN	4	265	324*	0.6	1.6
165 CH OF NAZARENE	9	1 025	3 139	5.9	15.4
167 CHS OF CHRIST.	5	296	377	0.7	1.8
193 EPISCOPAL.....	1	104	93	0.2	0.5
221 FREE METHODIST	1	86	480	0.9	2.4
226 FRIENDS-USA...	7	1 270	1 555*	2.9	7.6
263 INT FOURSQ GOS	1	723	885*	1.7	4.3
281 LUTH CH AMER..	1	305	416	0.8	2.0
403 SALVATION ARMY	1	76	102	0.2	0.5
413 S.D.A.........	1	42	51*	0.1	0.2
419 SO BAPT CONV..	7	1 265	1 549*	2.9	7.6
443 UN C OF CHRIST	1	154	189*	0.4	0.9
449 UN METHODIST..	15	2 601	3 184*	6.0	15.6
453 UN PRES CH USA	3	889	1 088*	2.0	5.3
HOWARD	**101**	**21 310**	**37 508***	**43.2**	**100.0**
005 AME ZION......	1	200	275	0.3	0.7
017 AMER BAPT ASSN	1	100	100	0.1	0.3
019 AMER BAPT USA.	4	1 296	1 598*	1.8	4.3
053 ASSEMB OF GOD.	3	439	1 070	1.2	2.9
061 BEACHY AMISH..	1	75	92*	0.1	0.2
071 BRETHREN (ASH)	1	53	65*	0.1	0.2
081 CATHOLIC......	4	NA	8 582	9.9	22.9
089 CHR & MISS AL.	1	78	157	0.2	0.4
093 CHR CH (DISC).	3	1 164	1 723	2.0	4.6
097 CHR CHS&CHS CR	7	2 278	2 809*	3.2	7.5
121 CH GOD (ABR)..	1	64	79*	0.1	0.2
123 CH GOD (ANDER)	1	114	342	0.4	0.9
127 CH GOD (CLEVE)	3	195	240*	0.3	0.6
151 L-D SAINTS....	1	NA	338	0.4	0.9
157 CH OF BRETHREN	2	286	353*	0.4	0.9
165 CH OF NAZARENE	4	628	1 571	1.8	4.2
167 CHS OF CHRIST.	2	325	414	0.5	1.1
193 EPISCOPAL.....	1	410	505	0.6	1.3
221 FREE METHODIST	1	100	396	0.5	1.1
226 FRIENDS-USA...	12	1 515	1 868*	2.1	5.0
244 GRACE BRETHREN	2	236	291*	0.3	0.8

County and Denomination	Number of churches	Communicant, confirmed, full members	Total adherents Number	Percent of total population	Percent of total adherents
263 INT FOURSQ GOS	1	441	544*	0.6	1.5
271 REFORM JUDAISM	1	76	94*	0.1	0.3
281 LUTH CH AMER..	2	551	705	0.8	1.9
283 LUTH--MO SYNOD	3	993	1 362	1.6	3.6
285 MENNONITE CH..	2	140	173*	0.2	0.5
323 OLD ORD AMISH.	2	260	321*	0.4	0.9
403 SALVATION ARMY	1	282	320	0.4	0.9
409 SEPARATE BAPT.	3	242	298*	0.3	0.8
413 S.D.A.........	2	145	179*	0.2	0.5
419 SO BAPT CONV..	4	1 231	1 518*	1.7	4.0
435 UNITARIAN-UNIV	1	20	25*	–	0.1
443 UN C OF CHRIST	2	575	709*	0.8	1.9
449 UN METHODIST..	18	5 235	6 455*	7.4	17.2
453 UN PRES CH USA	3	1 529	1 885*	2.2	5.0
469 WELS..........	1	34	52	0.1	0.1
HUNTINGTON	**64**	**11 135**	**20 261***	**56.9**	**100.0**
019 AMER BAPT USA.	3	421	516*	1.4	2.5
053 ASSEMB OF GOD.	1	59	130	0.4	0.6
071 BRETHREN (ASH)	1	167	205*	0.6	1.0
081 CATHOLIC......	3	NA	4 735	13.3	23.4
089 CHR & MISS AL.	1	29	64	0.2	0.3
093 CHR CH (DISC).	4	802	1 123	3.2	5.5
097 CHR CHS&CHS CR	4	788	965*	2.7	4.8
123 CH GOD (ANDER)	1	206	618	1.7	3.1
127 CH GOD (CLEVE)	1	?	?	?	?
151 L-D SAINTS....	1	NA	330	0.9	1.6
157 CH OF BRETHREN	6	784	960*	2.7	4.7
165 CH OF NAZARENE	5	600	1 359	3.8	6.7
167 CHS OF CHRIST.	1	150	191	0.5	0.9
193 EPISCOPAL.....	1	50	188	0.5	0.9
283 LUTH--MO SYNOD	1	912	1 317	3.7	6.5
291 MISSIONARY CH.	1	56	81	0.2	0.4
403 SALVATION ARMY	1	115	133	0.4	0.7
413 S.D.A.........	1	25	31*	0.1	0.2
443 UN C OF CHRIST	6	1 568	1 921*	5.4	9.5
449 UN METHODIST..	19	3 827	4 688*	13.2	23.1
453 UN PRES CH USA	1	576	706*	2.0	3.5
JACKSON	**71**	**15 413**	**22 656***	**62.0**	**100.0**
019 AMER BAPT USA.	7	2 277	2 799*	7.7	12.4
029 AMER LUTH CH..	1	321	454	1.2	2.0
053 ASSEMB OF GOD.	1	109	169	0.5	0.7
081 CATHOLIC......	2	NA	1 506	4.1	6.6
089 CHR & MISS AL.	1	37	103	0.3	0.5
093 CHR CH (DISC).	2	745	1 194	3.3	5.3
097 CHR CHS&CHS CR	12	2 396	2 945*	8.1	13.0
123 CH GOD (ANDER)	1	79	237	0.6	1.0
127 CH GOD (CLEVE)	1	110	135*	0.4	0.6
157 CH OF BRETHREN	1	53	65*	0.2	0.3
165 CH OF NAZARENE	7	1 157	2 543	7.0	11.2
167 CHS OF CHRIST.	1	66	93	0.3	0.4
193 EPISCOPAL.....	1	51	62	0.2	0.3
221 FREE METHODIST	1	22	96	0.3	0.4
283 LUTH--MO SYNOD	9	4 593	6 079	16.6	26.8
413 S.D.A.........	2	54	66*	0.2	0.3
419 SO BAPT CONV..	3	562	691*	1.9	3.0
443 UN C OF CHRIST	2	244	300*	0.8	1.3
449 UN METHODIST..	13	1 983	2 438*	6.7	10.8
453 UN PRES CH USA	3	554	681*	1.9	3.0
JASPER	**40**	**5 641**	**12 047***	**46.1**	**100.0**
019 AMER BAPT USA.	2	304	379*	1.4	3.1
053 ASSEMB OF GOD.	2	120	196	0.7	1.6
081 CATHOLIC......	5	NA	4 092	15.7	34.0
093 CHR CH (DISC).	4	721	942	3.6	7.8
097 CHR CHS&CHS CR	2	141	176*	0.7	1.5
105 CHRISTIAN REF.	2	652	1 120	4.3	9.3
123 CH GOD (ANDER)	1	12	36	0.1	0.3
165 CH OF NAZARENE	2	126	279	1.1	2.3
167 CHS OF CHRIST.	1	30	38	0.1	0.3
193 EPISCOPAL.....	1	27	27	0.1	0.2
203 EVAN FREE CH..	1	13	16*	0.1	0.1
283 LUTH--MO SYNOD	3	490	683	2.6	5.7
285 MENNONITE CH..	1	51	64*	0.2	0.5
371 REF CH IN AM..	2	989	1 552	5.9	12.9
449 UN METHODIST..	9	1 616	2 012*	7.7	16.7
453 UN PRES CH USA	2	349	435*	1.7	3.6
JAY	**58**	**7 105**	**10 955***	**47.1**	**100.0**
019 AMER BAPT USA.	1	100	123*	0.5	1.1
029 AMER LUTH CH..	1	76	89	0.4	0.8
053 ASSEMB OF GOD.	1	43	75	0.3	0.7
081 CATHOLIC......	3	NA	1 701	7.3	15.5
097 CHR CHS&CHS CR	10	1 685	2 064*	8.9	18.8
123 CH GOD (ANDER)	1	16	48	0.2	0.4
157 CH OF BRETHREN	2	97	119*	0.5	1.1
165 CH OF NAZARENE	6	493	1 004	4.3	9.2
167 CHS OF CHRIST.	1	100	127	0.5	1.2
197 EVAN CH OF NA.	1	40	40	0.2	0.4
215 EVAN METH CH..	1	45	55*	0.2	0.5
226 FRIENDS-USA...	3	468	573*	2.5	5.2
281 LUTH CH AMER..	2	560	772	3.3	7.0
329 OPEN BIBLE STD	1	23	50	0.2	0.5
413 S.D.A.........	1	14	17*	0.1	0.2
419 SO BAPT CONV..	1	365	447*	1.9	4.1
443 UN C OF CHRIST	1	206	252*	1.1	2.3
449 UN METHODIST..	19	2 344	2 872*	12.4	26.2
453 UN PRES CH USA	1	430	527*	2.3	4.8
JEFFERSON	**65**	**9 756**	**14 578***	**47.9**	**100.0**

NA—Not applicable   *Total adherents estimated from known number of communicant, confirmed, full members.   —Represents a percent less than 0.1.   Percentages may not total due to rounding.

Table 4. Churches and Church Membership by County and Denomination: 1980

County and Denomination	Number of churches	Communicant, confirmed, full members	Total adherents		
			Number	Percent of total population	Percent of total adherents
019 AMER BAPT USA.	17	4 367	5 316*	17.5	36.5
053 ASSEMB OF GOD.	1	42	42	0.1	0.3
081 CATHOLIC......	4	NA	2 255	7.4	15.5
089 CHR & MISS AL.	1	43	83	0.3	0.6
093 CHR CH (DISC).	2	403	522	1.7	3.6
097 CHR CHS&CHS CR	6	680	828*	2.7	5.7
123 CH GOD (ANDER)	1	51	153	0.5	1.0
127 CH GOD (CLEVE)	1	?	?	?	?
151 L-D SAINTS....	1	NA	171	0.6	1.2
165 CH OF NAZARENE	2	47	132	0.4	0.9
167 CHS OF CHRIST.	1	48	70	0.2	0.5
193 EPISCOPAL.....	1	166	186	0.6	1.3
281 LUTH CH AMER..	1	153	222	0.7	1.5
283 LUTH--MO SYNOD	1	110	152	0.5	1.0
285 MENNONITE CH..	1	11	13*	-	0.1
403 SALVATION ARMY	1	104	117	0.4	0.8
413 S.D.A.........	1	23	28*	0.1	0.2
419 SO BAPT CONV..	2	788	959*	3.2	6.6
443 UN C OF CHRIST	1	81	99*	0.3	0.7
449 UN METHODIST..	15	2 038	2 481*	8.2	17.0
453 UN PRES CH USA	4	615	749*	2.5	5.1
JENNINGS	49	5 996	10 524*	46.0	100.0
019 AMER BAPT USA.	14	2 900	3 592*	15.7	34.1
053 ASSEMB OF GOD.	1	30	117	0.5	1.1
081 CATHOLIC......	4	NA	2 094	9.2	19.9
097 CHR CHS&CHS CR	3	835	1 034*	4.5	9.8
107 CHRISTIAN UN..	1	52	86	0.4	0.8
123 CH GOD (ANDER)	3	207	621	2.7	5.9
127 CH GOD (CLEVE)	1	35	43*	0.2	0.4
165 CH OF NAZARENE	1	163	735	3.2	7.0
167 CHS OF CHRIST.	2	80	104	0.5	1.0
285 MENNONITE CH..	1	35	43*	0.2	0.4
413 S.D.A.........	1	39	48*	0.2	0.5
419 SO BAPT CONV..	1	217	269*	1.2	2.6
449 UN METHODIST..	11	1 074	1 330*	5.8	12.6
453 UN PRES CH USA	5	329	408*	1.8	3.9
JOHNSON	73	18 274	29 476*	38.2	100.0
019 AMER BAPT USA.	6	2 274	2 811*	3.6	9.5
053 ASSEMB OF GOD.	2	118	191	0.2	0.6
081 CATHOLIC......	3	NA	5 286	6.8	17.9
093 CHR CH (DISC).	9	1 844	2 849	3.7	9.7
097 CHR CHS&CHS CR	14	4 696	5 806*	7.5	19.7
123 CH GOD (ANDER)	1	40	120	0.2	0.4
127 CH GOD (CLEVE)	2	233	288*	0.4	1.0
151 L-D SAINTS....	1	NA	324	0.4	1.1
165 CH OF NAZARENE	4	339	876	1.1	3.0
167 CHS OF CHRIST.	2	330	420	0.5	1.4
175 CONGR CHR CHS.	1	356	440*	0.6	1.5
193 EPISCOPAL.....	1	101	122	0.2	0.4
215 EVAN METH CH..	1	48	59*	0.1	0.2
281 LUTH CH AMER..	2	434	578	0.7	2.0
283 LUTH--MO SYNOD	2	512	716	0.9	2.4
409 SEPARATE BAPT.	2	81	100*	0.1	0.3
419 SO BAPT CONV..	3	1 240	1 533*	2.0	5.2
443 UN C OF CHRIST	1	95	117*	0.2	0.4
449 UN METHODIST..	10	3 911	4 835*	6.3	16.4
453 UN PRES CH USA	6	1 622	2 005*	2.6	6.8
KNOX	85	12 474	23 467*	56.1	100.0
019 AMER BAPT USA.	5	1 517	1 800*	4.3	7.7
053 ASSEMB OF GOD.	2	151	375	0.9	1.6
081 CATHOLIC......	6	NA	6 307	15.1	26.9
093 CHR CH (DISC).	5	1 164	1 922	4.6	8.2
097 CHR CHS&CHS CR	9	1 124	1 334*	3.2	5.7
123 CH GOD (ANDER)	2	310	930	2.2	4.0
127 CH GOD (CLEVE)	2	40	47*	0.1	0.2
151 L-D SAINTS....	1	NA	181	0.4	0.8
165 CH OF NAZARENE	3	270	631	1.5	2.7
167 CHS OF CHRIST.	7	460	585	1.4	2.5
185 CUMBER PRESB..	1	74	129	0.3	0.5
193 EPISCOPAL.....	1	124	169	0.4	0.7
221 FREE METHODIST	3	268	696	1.7	3.0
263 INT FOURSQ GOS	1	119	141*	0.3	0.6
281 LUTH CH AMER..	1	135	194	0.5	0.8
283 LUTH--MO SYNOD	2	720	906	2.2	3.9
381 REF PRES-EVAN.	1	40	55	0.1	0.2
403 SALVATION ARMY	1	102	117	0.3	0.5
413 S.D.A.........	1	56	66*	0.2	0.3
419 SO BAPT CONV..	1	564	669*	1.6	2.9
443 UN C OF CHRIST	2	1 199	1 423*	3.4	6.1
449 UN METHODIST..	21	3 288	3 901*	9.3	16.6
453 UN PRES CH USA	7	749	889*	2.1	3.8
KOSCIUSKO	73	12 018	19 027*	31.9	100.0
019 AMER BAPT USA.	1	182	224*	0.4	1.2
053 ASSEMB OF GOD.	1	40	90	0.2	0.5
061 BEACHY AMISH..	2	87	107*	0.2	0.6
071 BRETHRN (ASH)	3	423	522*	0.9	2.7
081 CATHOLIC......	4	NA	2 096	3.5	11.0
097 CHR CHS&CHS CR	2	543	670*	1.1	3.5
123 CH GOD (ANDER)	2	388	1 164	2.0	6.1
127 CH GOD (CLEVE)	1	?	?	?	?
151 L-D SAINTS....	1	NA	194	0.3	1.0
157 CH OF BRETHREN	9	1 106	1 364*	2.3	7.2
165 CH OF NAZARENE	2	146	273	0.5	1.4
167 CHS OF CHRIST.	2	175	223	0.4	1.2
193 EPISCOPAL.....	2	252	335	0.6	1.8
221 FREE METHODIST	1	322	1 425	2.4	7.5
244 GRACE BRETHREN	4	1 087	1 341*	2.3	7.0

County and Denomination	Number of churches	Communicant, confirmed, full members	Total adherents		
			Number	Percent of total population	Percent of total adherents
281 LUTH CH AMER..	1	125	137	0.2	0.7
283 LUTH--MO SYNOD	1	440	574	1.0	3.0
285 MENNONITE CH..	3	233	287*	0.5	1.5
353 CHR BRETHREN..	1	25	50	0.1	0.3
403 SALVATION ARMY	1	30	40	0.1	0.2
443 UN C OF CHRIST	1	65	80*	0.1	0.4
449 UN METHODIST..	25	5 283	6 516*	10.9	34.2
453 UN PRES CH USA	3	1 066	1 315*	2.2	6.9
LAGRANGE	77	9 936	13 914*	54.5	100.0
019 AMER BAPT USA.	1	40	52*	0.2	0.4
061 BEACHY AMISH..	1	37	48*	0.2	0.3
071 BRETHREN (ASH)	1	120	155*	0.6	1.1
081 CATHOLIC......	2	NA	486	1.9	3.5
097 CHR CHS&CHS CR	1	200	258*	1.0	1.9
123 CH GOD (ANDER)	2	204	612	2.4	4.4
157 CH OF BRETHREN	1	73	94*	0.4	0.7
165 CH OF NAZARENE	2	117	248	1.0	1.8
167 CHS OF CHRIST.	1	115	235	0.9	1.7
193 EPISCOPAL.....	1	122	137	0.5	1.0
281 LUTH CH AMER..	1	401	546	2.1	3.9
283 LUTH--MO SYNOD	1	165	210	0.8	1.5
285 MENNONITE CH..	9	1 446	1 866*	7.3	13.4
287 MENN GEN CONF.	1	138	185	0.7	1.3
291 MISSIONARY CH.	2	123	220	0.9	1.6
323 OLD ORD AMISH.	33	4 290	5 536*	21.7	39.8
449 UN METHODIST..	15	1 913	2 469*	9.7	17.7
453 UN PRES CH USA	2	432	557*	2.2	4.0
LAKE	340	75 486	249 924*	47.8	100.0
005 AME ZION......	5	8 150	10 187	1.9	4.1
017 AMER BAPT ASSN	1	150	150	-	0.1
019 AMER BAPT USA.	8	3 123	3 861*	0.7	1.5
029 AMER LUTH CH..	2	1 167	1 727	0.3	0.7
053 ASSEMB OF GOD.	19	1 859	3 461	0.7	1.4
057 BAPT GEN CONF.	1	273	337*	0.1	0.1
059 BAPT MISS ASSN	3	80	99*	-	-
081 CATHOLIC......	68	NA	148 013	28.3	59.2
089 CHR & MISS AL.	1	25	25	-	-
093 CHR CH (DISC).	6	813	1 351	0.3	0.5
097 CHR CHS&CHS CR	18	5 950	7 356*	1.4	2.9
105 CHRISTIAN REF.	6	1 725	2 918	0.6	1.2
123 CH GOD (ANDER)	10	689	2 067	0.4	0.8
127 CH GOD (CLEVE)	14	700	865*	0.2	0.3
165 CH OF NAZARENE	17	1 911	3 684	0.7	1.5
167 CHS OF CHRIST.	10	839	1 232	0.2	0.5
175 CONGR CHR CHS.	2	210	260*	-	0.1
193 EPISCOPAL.....	6	1 351	1 713	0.3	0.7
201 EVAN COV CH AM	2	275	340*	0.1	0.1
203 EVAN FREE CH..	1	30	37*	-	-
208 EVAN LUTH ASSN	2	699	923	0.2	0.4
221 FREE METHODIST	2	145	606	0.1	0.2
263 INT FOURSQ GOS	1	25	31*	-	-
270 CONSRV JUDAISM	1	297	367*	0.1	0.1
271 REFORM JUDAISM	2	726	898*	0.2	0.4
281 LUTH CH AMER..	10	3 304	4 395	0.8	1.8
283 LUTH--MO SYNOD	25	9 227	12 171	2.3	4.9
290 METRO COMM CHS	0	30	60	-	-
349 PENT HOLINESS.	1	15	19*	-	-
371 REF CH IN AM..	4	766	1 120	0.2	0.4
403 SALVATION ARMY	3	428	1 930	0.4	0.8
413 S.D.A.........	6	1 216	1 503*	0.3	0.6
419 SO BAPT CONV..	30	10 455	12 925*	2.5	5.2
435 UNITARIAN-UNIV	2	136	168*	-	0.1
443 UN C OF CHRIST	8	1 910	2 361*	0.5	0.9
449 UN METHODIST..	24	10 214	12 627*	2.4	5.1
453 UN PRES CH USA	18	6 525	8 067*	1.5	3.2
469 WELS..........	1	48	70	-	-
LA PORTE	102	22 738	54 568*	50.2	100.0
017 AMER BAPT ASSN	1	50	50	-	0.1
019 AMER BAPT USA.	2	1 200	1 465*	1.3	2.7
029 AMER LUTH CH..	3	1 856	2 344	2.2	4.3
053 ASSEMB OF GOD.	3	455	1 011	0.9	1.9
057 BAPT GEN CONF.	1	255	311*	0.3	0.6
059 BAPT MISS ASSN	1	145	177*	0.2	0.3
081 CATHOLIC......	14	NA	24 606	22.7	45.1
091 CHRISTIAN CATH	1	75	150	0.1	0.3
093 CHR CH (DISC).	3	627	1 255	1.2	2.3
097 CHR CHS&CHS CR	11	1 843	2 251*	2.1	4.1
123 CH GOD (ANDER)	2	100	300	0.3	0.5
127 CH GOD (CLEVE)	2	74	90*	0.1	0.2
151 L-D SAINTS....	1	NA	280	0.3	0.5
157 CH OF BRETHREN	2	154	188*	0.2	0.3
165 CH OF NAZARENE	2	97	200	0.2	0.4
167 CHS OF CHRIST.	2	210	267	0.2	0.5
175 CONGR CHR CHS.	1	115	140*	0.1	0.3
193 EPISCOPAL.....	3	917	1 048	1.0	1.9
221 FREE METHODIST	2	135	408	0.4	0.7
239 SWEDENBORGIAN.	1	60	73*	0.1	0.1
271 REFORM JUDAISM	1	340	415*	0.4	0.8
281 LUTH CH AMER..	2	967	1 314	1.2	2.4
283 LUTH--MO SYNOD	9	3 212	4 066	3.7	7.5
285 MENNONITE CH..	1	?	?	?	?
291 MISSIONARY CH.	1	66	139	0.1	0.3
349 PENT HOLINESS.	1	25	31*	-	0.1
353 CHR BRETHREN..	1	25	50	-	0.1
403 SALVATION ARMY	1	256	278	0.3	0.5
413 S.D.A.........	2	157	192*	0.2	0.4
419 SO BAPT CONV..	3	295	360*	0.2	0.7
431 UKRANIAN AMER.	1	150	270	0.2	0.5
443 UN C OF CHRIST	4	2 127	2 597*	2.4	4.8

NA—Not applicable   *Total adherents estimated from known number of communicant, confirmed, full members.   —Represents a percent less than 0.1.   Percentages may not total due to rounding.

Table 4. Churches and Church Membership by County and Denomination: 1980

County and Denomination	Number of churches	Communicant, confirmed, full members	Total adherents		
			Number	Percent of total population	Percent of total adherents
449 UN METHODIST..	14	4 610	5 629*	5.2	10.3
453 UN PRES CH USA	3	2 140	2 613*	2.4	4.8
LAWRENCE	81	14 277	21 463*	50.5	100.0
017 AMER BAPT ASSN	1	30	30	0.1	0.1
019 AMER BAPT USA.	16	5 343	6 518*	15.3	30.4
053 ASSEMB OF GOD.	1	104	153	0.4	0.7
081 CATHOLIC......	2	NA	1 812	4.3	8.4
093 CHR CH (DISC).	3	956	1 561	3.7	7.3
097 CHR CHS&CHS CR	11	2 230	2 720*	6.4	12.7
123 CH GOD (ANDER)	5	483	1 449	3.4	6.8
127 CH GOD (CLEVE)	2	76	93*	0.2	0.4
151 L-D SAINTS....	1	NA	233	0.5	1.1
165 CH OF NAZARENE	4	546	938	2.2	4.4
167 CHS OF CHRIST.	13	1 250	1 440	3.4	6.7
193 EPISCOPAL.....	1	125	273	0.6	1.3
221 FREE METHODIST	1	398	912	2.1	4.2
283 LUTH--MO SYNOD	2	301	385	0.9	1.8
403 SALVATION ARMY	1	127	129	0.3	0.6
413 S.D.A.........	1	107	131*	0.3	0.6
419 SO BAPT CONV..	1	67	82*	0.2	0.4
449 UN METHODIST..	13	1 721	2 100*	4.9	9.8
453 UN PRES CH USA	2	413	504*	1.2	2.3
MADISON	141	31 873	58 817*	42.2	100.0
005 AME ZION......	1	292	438	0.3	0.7
017 AMER BAPT ASSN	2	150	150	0.1	0.3
019 AMER BAPT USA.	10	3 491	4 265*	3.1	7.3
053 ASSEMB OF GOD.	2	324	532	0.4	0.9
081 CATHOLIC......	6	NA	9 441	6.8	16.1
089 CHR & MISS AL.	2	82	172	0.1	0.3
093 CHR CH (DISC).	10	3 759	5 205	3.7	8.8
097 CHR CHS&CHS CR	9	1 466	1 791*	1.3	3.0
101 C.M.E.........	1	1 675	2 046*	1.5	3.5
123 CH GOD (ANDER)	14	3 665	10 995	7.9	18.7
127 CH GOD (CLEVE)	4	209	255*	0.2	0.4
151 L-D SAINTS....	1	NA	559	0.4	1.0
157 CH OF BRETHREN	2	614	750*	0.5	1.3
165 CH OF NAZARENE	10	1 727	3 586	2.6	6.1
167 CHS OF CHRIST.	7	625	1 190	0.9	2.0
193 EPISCOPAL.....	2	548	829	0.6	1.4
197 EVAN CH OF NA.	2	210	210	0.2	0.4
208 EVAN LUTH ASSN	1	273	376	0.3	0.6
221 FREE METHODIST	1	37	195	0.1	0.3
226 FRIENDS-USA...	5	328	401*	0.3	0.7
263 INT FOURSQ GOS	1	96	117*	0.1	0.2
281 LUTH CH AMER..	3	770	1 053	0.8	1.8
283 LUTH--MO SYNOD	1	493	737	0.5	1.3
353 CHR BRETHREN..	1	50	75	0.1	0.1
403 SALVATION ARMY	2	245	281	0.2	0.5
409 SEPARATE BAPT.	1	0	42	–	0.1
413 S.D.A.........	3	294	359*	0.3	0.6
419 SO BAPT CONV..	2	305	373*	0.3	0.6
443 UN C OF CHRIST	1	433	529*	0.4	0.9
449 UN METHODIST..	31	7 949	9 711*	7.0	16.5
453 UN PRES CH USA	3	1 763	2 154*	1.5	3.7
MARION	493	168 176	312 058*	40.8	100.0
005 AME ZION......	6	7 945	10 328	1.3	3.3
017 AMER BAPT ASSN	2	200	200	–	0.1
019 AMER BAPT USA.	35	13 580	16 446*	2.1	5.3
029 AMER LUTH CH..	5	1 448	1 916	0.3	0.6
053 ASSEMB OF GOD.	12	3 476	6 501	0.8	2.1
065 BETHEL M ASSN.	1	125	151*	–	–
081 CATHOLIC......	43	NA	84 935	11.1	27.2
089 CHR & MISS AL.	2	25	47	–	–
093 CHR CH (DISC).	31	15 483	22 874	3.0	7.3
097 CHR CHS&CHS CR	39	18 752	22 709*	3.0	7.3
101 C.M.E.........	10	7 999	9 687*	1.3	3.1
105 CHRISTIAN REF.	1	68	221	–	0.1
123 CH GOD (ANDER)	11	1 564	4 692	0.6	1.5
127 CH GOD (CLEVE)	9	764	925*	0.1	0.3
151 L-D SAINTS....	5	NA	2 462	0.3	0.8
157 CH OF BRETHREN	1	180	218*	–	0.1
165 CH OF NAZARENE	27	2 952	6 148	0.8	2.0
167 CHS OF CHRIST.	31	5 081	6 495	0.8	2.1
185 CUMBER PRESB..	1	66	154	–	–
193 EPISCOPAL.....	10	4 024	5 648	0.7	1.8
195 ESTONIAN ELC.	1	48	52	–	–
208 EVAN LUTH ASSN	2	1 566	2 052	0.3	0.7
221 FREE METHODIST	8	1 077	6 831	0.9	2.2
226 FRIENDS-USA...	6	1 412	1 710*	0.2	0.5
244 GRACE BRETHREN	1	125	151*	–	–
263 INT FOURSQ GOS	1	209	253*	–	0.1
270 CONSRV JUDAISM	1	600	727*	0.1	0.2
271 REFORM JUDAISM	1	1 930	2 337*	0.3	0.7
274 LAT EVAN LUTH.	2	512	581	0.1	0.2
281 LUTH CH AMER..	15	4 604	5 984	0.8	1.9
283 LUTH--MO SYNOD	14	5 437	7 339	1.0	2.4
285 MENNONITE CH..	1	95	115*	–	–
290 METRO COMM CHS	1	25	50	–	–
291 MISSIONARY CH.	1	50	32	–	–
293 MORAV CH-NORTH	3	287	408	0.1	0.1
313 N AM BAPT CONF	1	120	145*	–	–
329 OPEN BIBLE STD	1	20	40	–	–
356 PRESB CH AMER.	1	29	34	–	–
371 REF CH IN AM..	2	195	321	–	0.1
381 REF PRES-EVAN.	2	96	130	–	–
383 REF PRES OF NA	1	143	204	–	0.1
403 SALVATION ARMY	3	28	46	–	–
409 SEPARATE BAPT.	1	57	69*	–	–
413 S.D.A.........	6	1 792	2 170*	0.3	0.7

County and Denomination	Number of churches	Communicant, confirmed, full members	Total adherents		
			Number	Percent of total population	Percent of total adherents
419 SO BAPT CONV..	24	6 854	8 300*	1.1	2.7
435 UNITARIAN-UNIV	4	886	1 073*	0.1	0.3
443 UN C OF CHRIST	16	6 851	8 297*	1.1	2.7
449 UN METHODIST..	66	32 560	39 431*	5.2	12.6
453 UN PRES CH USA	23	16 576	20 074*	2.6	6.4
469 WELS..........	2	260	345	–	0.1
MARSHALL	72	10 762	16 982*	43.4	100.0
019 AMER BAPT USA.	1	103	126*	0.3	0.7
053 ASSEMB OF GOD.	4	182	267	0.7	1.6
071 BRETHREN (ASH)	2	170	209*	0.5	1.2
081 CATHOLIC......	3	NA	3 188	8.1	18.8
097 CHR CHS&CHS CR	2	100	123*	0.3	0.7
121 CH GOD (ABR)..	1	48	59*	0.2	0.3
123 CH GOD (ANDER)	2	93	279	0.7	1.6
151 L-D SAINTS....	1	NA	115	0.3	0.7
157 CH OF BRETHREN	6	1 024	1 257*	3.2	7.4
165 CH OF NAZARENE	1	84	167	0.4	1.0
167 CHS OF CHRIST.	2	35	45	0.1	0.3
181 CONSRV CONGR..	1	188	231*	0.6	1.4
193 EPISCOPAL.....	1	241	335	0.9	2.0
201 EVAN COV CH AM	1	99	122*	0.3	0.7
281 LUTH CH AMER..	1	222	318	0.8	1.9
283 LUTH--MO SYNOD	3	699	952	2.4	5.6
291 MISSIONARY CH.	1	62	88	0.2	0.5
323 OLD ORD AMISH.	16	2 080	2 554*	6.5	15.0
413 S.D.A.........	1	36	44*	0.1	0.3
419 SO BAPT CONV..	1	57	70*	0.2	0.4
443 UN C OF CHRIST	4	1 321	1 622*	4.1	9.6
449 UN METHODIST..	16	3 586	4 403*	11.2	25.9
453 UN PRES CH USA	1	332	408*	1.0	2.4
MARTIN	30	2 748	6 264*	56.9	100.0
029 AMER LUTH CH..	1	218	270	2.5	4.3
081 CATHOLIC......	4	NA	2 784	25.3	44.4
097 CHR CHS&CHS CR	5	1 055	1 299*	11.8	20.7
165 CH OF NAZARENE	2	9	89	0.8	1.4
167 CHS OF CHRIST.	3	142	188	1.7	3.0
283 LUTH--MO SYNOD	1	20	28	0.3	0.4
285 MENNONITE CH..	1	42	52*	0.5	0.8
419 SO BAPT CONV..	2	180	222*	2.0	3.5
449 UN METHODIST..	11	1 082	1 332*	12.1	21.3
MIAMI	59	11 157	17 136*	43.0	100.0
019 AMER BAPT USA.	7	2 409	2 992*	7.5	17.5
053 ASSEMB OF GOD.	1	194	335	0.8	2.0
071 BRETHREN (ASH)	5	548	681*	1.7	4.0
081 CATHOLIC......	1	NA	2 259	5.7	13.2
089 CHR & MISS AL.	1	32	56	0.1	0.3
093 CHR CH (DISC).	1	875	1 027	2.6	6.0
097 CHR CHS&CHS CR	3	733	910*	2.3	5.3
123 CH GOD (ANDER)	1	35	105	0.3	0.6
127 CH GOD (CLEVE)	1	17	21*	0.1	0.1
151 L-D SAINTS....	1	NA	453	1.1	2.6
157 CH OF BRETHREN	3	731	908*	2.3	5.3
165 CH OF NAZARENE	1	174	223	0.6	1.3
167 CHS OF CHRIST.	1	100	127	0.3	0.7
193 EPISCOPAL.....	1	108	477	1.2	2.8
244 GRACE BRETHREN	2	194	241*	0.6	1.4
263 INT FOURSQ GOS	1	76	94*	0.2	0.5
283 LUTH--MO SYNOD	1	806	1 114	2.8	6.5
285 MENNONITE CH..	2	296	368*	0.9	2.1
291 MISSIONARY CH.	1	28	30	0.1	0.2
403 SALVATION ARMY	1	90	105	0.3	0.6
419 SO BAPT CONV..	1	428	532*	1.3	3.1
449 UN METHODIST..	21	2 813	3 494*	8.8	20.4
453 UN PRES CH USA	1	470	584*	1.5	3.4
MONROE	87	18 298	33 297*	33.8	100.0
019 AMER BAPT USA.	9	3 239	3 756*	3.8	11.3
053 ASSEMB OF GOD.	7	967	1 734	1.8	5.2
081 CATHOLIC......	3	NA	8 823	9.0	26.5
093 CHR CH (DISC).	4	1 909	2 514	2.6	7.6
097 CHR CHS&CHS CR	6	1 427	1 655*	1.7	5.0
123 CH GOD (ANDER)	1	150	450	0.5	1.4
127 CH GOD (CLEVE)	1	27	31*	–	0.1
151 L-D SAINTS....	2	NA	680	0.7	2.0
165 CH OF NAZARENE	5	759	1 535	1.6	4.6
167 CHS OF CHRIST.	21	2 200	2 800	2.8	8.4
193 EPISCOPAL.....	1	328	491	0.5	1.5
221 FREE METHODIST	1	262	540	0.5	1.6
226 FRIENDS-USA...	1	107	124*	0.1	0.4
281 LUTH CH AMER..	1	365	521	0.5	1.6
283 LUTH--MO SYNOD	1	213	280	0.3	0.8
383 REF PRES OF NA	1	81	95	0.1	0.3
403 SALVATION ARMY	1	104	126	0.1	0.4
409 SEPARATE BAPT.	1	21	24*	–	0.1
413 S.D.A.........	1	165	191*	0.2	0.6
419 SO BAPT CONV..	2	456	529*	0.5	1.6
435 UNITARIAN-UNIV	1	215	249*	0.3	0.7
443 UN C OF CHRIST	1	369	428*	0.4	1.3
449 UN METHODIST..	13	4 292	4 977*	5.1	14.9
453 UN PRES CH USA	2	642	744*	0.8	2.2
MONTGOMERY	67	11 828	16 953*	47.8	100.0
019 AMER BAPT USA.	5	1 970	2 377*	6.7	14.0
053 ASSEMB OF GOD.	1	118	250	0.7	1.5
081 CATHOLIC......	2	NA	1 657	4.7	9.8
093 CHR CH (DISC).	4	918	1 365	3.8	8.1
097 CHR CHS&CHS CR	16	2 796	3 373*	9.5	19.9

NA—Not applicable   *Total adherents estimated from known number of communicant, confirmed, full members.   —Represents a percent less than 0.1.   Percentages may not total due to rounding.

Table 4. Churches and Church Membership by County and Denomination: 1980

County and Denomination	Number of churches	Communicant, confirmed, full members	Total adherents		
			Number	Percent of total population	Percent of total adherents
107 CHRISTIAN UN..	1	40	73	0.2	0.4
123 CH GOD (ANDER)	1	33	99	0.3	0.6
127 CH GOD (CLEVE)	1	35	42*	0.1	0.2
151 L-D SAINTS....	1	NA	162	0.5	1.0
165 CH OF NAZARENE	2	291	630	1.8	3.7
167 CHS OF CHRIST.	3	100	127	0.4	0.7
181 CONSRV CONGR..	1	142	171*	0.5	1.0
193 EPISCOPAL.....	1	121	184	0.5	1.1
226 FRIENDS-USA...	1	28	34*	0.1	0.2
281 LUTH CH AMER..	1	244	374	1.1	2.2
283 LUTH--MO SYNOD	1	166	213	0.6	1.3
413 S.D.A........	1	15	18*	0.1	0.1
419 SO BAPT CONV..	3	218	263*	0.7	1.6
443 UN C OF CHRIST	1	76	92*	0.3	0.5
449 UN METHODIST..	16	3 468	4 184*	11.8	24.7
453 UN PRES CH USA	4	1 049	1 265*	3.6	7.5
MORGAN	82	12 062	19 240*	37.0	100.0
019 AMER BAPT USA.	9	1 732	2 154*	4.1	11.2
053 ASSEMB OF GOD.	3	158	353	0.7	1.8
081 CATHOLIC......	2	NA	1 625	3.1	8.4
093 CHR CH (DISC).	4	1 093	1 952	3.8	10.1
097 CHR CHS&CHS CR	16	3 191	3 968*	7.6	20.6
123 CH GOD (ANDER)	3	285	855	1.6	4.4
127 CH GOD (CLEVE)	1	22	27*	0.1	0.1
151 L-D SAINTS....	2	NA	495	1.0	2.6
165 CH OF NAZARENE	6	411	1 211	2.3	6.3
167 CHS OF CHRIST.	6	350	445	0.9	2.3
193 EPISCOPAL.....	1	43	61	0.1	0.3
215 EVAN METH CH..	1	38	47*	0.1	0.2
221 FREE METHODIST	1	27	120	0.2	0.6
226 FRIENDS-USA...	4	676	841*	1.6	4.4
283 LUTH--MO SYNOD	1	145	236	0.5	1.2
285 MENNONITE CH..	2	56	70*	0.1	0.4
291 MISSIONARY CH.	2	179	233	0.4	1.2
409 SEPARATE BAPT.	1	79	98*	0.2	0.5
413 S.D.A........	1	32	40*	0.1	0.2
419 SO BAPT CONV..	6	1 243	1 546*	3.0	8.0
449 UN METHODIST..	9	2 041	2 538*	4.9	13.2
453 UN PRES CH USA	1	261	325*	0.6	1.7
NEWTON	26	3 994	6 800*	45.8	100.0
019 AMER BAPT USA.	2	518	645*	4.3	9.5
053 ASSEMB OF GOD.	1	23	31	0.2	0.5
057 BAPT GEN CONF.	1	115	143*	1.0	2.1
081 CATHOLIC......	3	NA	1 772	11.9	26.1
093 CHR CH (DISC).	2	466	581	3.9	8.5
097 CHR CHS&CHS CR	1	387	482*	3.2	7.1
105 CHRISTIAN REF.	1	76	121	0.8	1.8
123 CH GOD (ANDER)	1	13	39	0.3	0.6
283 LUTH--MO SYNOD	1	84	113	0.8	1.7
287 MENN GEN CONF.	1	59	66	0.4	1.0
419 SO BAPT CONV..	2	330	411*	2.8	6.0
449 UN METHODIST..	7	1 606	2 001*	13.5	29.4
453 UN PRES CH USA	3	317	395*	2.7	5.8
NOBLE	59	7 681	12 840*	36.2	100.0
019 AMER BAPT USA.	2	139	173*	0.5	1.3
053 ASSEMB OF GOD.	3	250	716	2.0	5.6
081 CATHOLIC......	6	NA	2 487	7.0	19.4
093 CHR CH (DISC).	1	270	303	0.9	2.4
097 CHR CHS&CHS CR	2	187	232*	0.7	1.8
157 CH OF BRETHREN	1	105	130*	0.4	1.0
165 CH OF NAZARENE	3	107	313	0.9	2.4
167 CHS OF CHRIST.	2	63	80	0.2	0.6
197 EVAN CH OF NA.	1	110	110	0.3	0.9
226 FRIENDS-USA...	1	9	11*	-	0.1
281 LUTH CH AMER..	4	597	878	2.5	6.8
283 LUTH--MO SYNOD	4	1 219	1 641	4.6	12.8
285 MENNONITE CH..	1	23	29*	0.1	0.2
291 MISSIONARY CH.	1	22	27	0.1	0.2
323 OLD ORD AMISH.	1	130	162*	0.5	1.3
353 CHR BRETHREN..	1	25	50	0.1	0.4
413 S.D.A........	1	39	48*	0.1	0.4
419 SO BAPT CONV..	2	92	114*	0.3	0.9
449 UN METHODIST..	18	3 690	4 585*	12.9	35.7
453 UN PRES CH USA	4	604	751*	2.1	5.8
OHIO	11	1 692	2 103*	41.1	100.0
019 AMER BAPT USA.	3	541	657*	12.8	31.2
029 AMER LUTH CH..	1	111	133	2.6	6.3
097 CHR CHS&CHS CR	1	365	443*	8.7	21.1
165 CH OF NAZARENE	1	65	129	2.5	6.1
443 UN C OF CHRIST	1	178	216*	4.2	10.3
449 UN METHODIST..	3	382	464*	9.1	22.1
453 UN PRES CH USA	1	50	61*	1.2	2.9
ORANGE	48	6 248	8 539*	45.7	100.0
019 AMER BAPT USA.	4	1 217	1 479*	7.9	17.3
053 ASSEMB OF GOD.	1	60	75	0.4	0.9
081 CATHOLIC......	2	NA	483	2.6	5.7
093 CHR CH (DISC).	2	173	256	1.4	3.0
097 CHR CHS&CHS CR	8	1 854	2 253*	12.1	26.4
165 CH OF NAZARENE	3	199	567	3.0	6.6
167 CHS OF CHRIST.	7	440	625	3.3	7.3
226 FRIENDS-USA...	3	348	423*	2.3	5.0
285 MENNONITE CH..	1	29	35*	0.2	0.4
413 S.D.A........	1	75	91*	0.5	1.1
419 SO BAPT CONV..	1	333	405*	2.2	4.7
449 UN METHODIST..	14	1 410	1 713*	9.2	20.1

County and Denomination	Number of churches	Communicant, confirmed, full members	Total adherents		
			Number	Percent of total population	Percent of total adherents
453 UN PRES CH USA	1	110	134*	0.7	1.6
OWEN	44	4 596	6 214*	39.2	100.0
019 AMER BAPT USA.	9	1 449	1 764*	11.1	28.4
029 AMER LUTH CH..	1	70	77	0.5	1.2
053 ASSEMB OF GOD.	3	431	556	3.5	8.9
081 CATHOLIC......	1	NA	216	1.4	3.5
093 CHR CH (DISC).	1	55	85	0.5	1.4
097 CHR CHS&CHS CR	1	75	91*	0.6	1.5
127 CH GOD (CLEVE)	1	7	9*	0.1	0.1
151 L-D SAINTS....	1	NA	107	0.7	1.7
165 CH OF NAZARENE	5	317	623	3.9	10.0
167 CHS OF CHRIST.	3	320	407	2.6	6.5
409 SEPARATE BAPT.	2	168	205*	1.3	3.3
413 S.D.A........	1	28	34*	0.2	0.5
443 UN C OF CHRIST	1	56	68*	0.4	1.1
449 UN METHODIST..	11	1 288	1 568*	9.9	25.2
453 UN PRES CH USA	3	332	404*	2.6	6.5
PARKE	41	4 792	6 427*	39.3	100.0
019 AMER BAPT USA.	6	881	1 065*	6.5	16.6
053 ASSEMB OF GOD.	2	39	82	0.5	1.3
081 CATHOLIC......	2	NA	358	2.2	5.6
093 CHR CH (DISC).	2	330	455	2.8	7.1
097 CHR CHS&CHS CR	9	1 320	1 596*	9.7	24.8
165 CH OF NAZARENE	3	121	327	2.0	5.1
167 CHS OF CHRIST.	2	70	89	0.5	1.4
226 FRIENDS-USA...	4	551	666*	4.1	10.4
449 UN METHODIST..	9	1 130	1 366*	8.3	21.3
453 UN PRES CH USA	2	350	423*	2.6	6.6
PERRY	35	3 422	10 979*	56.8	100.0
019 AMER BAPT USA.	4	745	907*	4.7	8.3
053 ASSEMB OF GOD.	1	9	25	0.1	0.2
081 CATHOLIC......	8	NA	6 387	33.0	58.2
093 CHR CH (DISC).	3	160	246	1.3	2.2
097 CHR CHS&CHS CR	2	200	244*	1.3	2.2
151 L-D SAINTS....	1	NA	70	0.4	0.6
165 CH OF NAZARENE	1	137	426	2.2	3.9
167 CHS OF CHRIST.	2	80	102	0.5	0.9
193 EPISCOPAL.....	1	32	33	0.2	0.3
283 LUTH--MO SYNOD	1	212	289	1.5	2.6
413 S.D.A........	1	49	60*	0.3	0.5
419 SO BAPT CONV..	1	92	112*	0.6	1.0
443 UN C OF CHRIST	2	940	1 145*	5.9	10.4
449 UN METHODIST..	7	766	933*	4.8	8.5
PIKE	36	3 133	5 344*	39.7	100.0
019 AMER BAPT USA.	1	230	277*	2.1	5.2
029 AMER LUTH CH..	1	211	277	2.1	5.2
053 ASSEMB OF GOD.	1	23	48	0.4	0.9
081 CATHOLIC......	1	NA	311	2.3	5.8
093 CHR CH (DISC).	1	80	123	0.9	2.3
097 CHR CHS&CHS CR	4	415	499*	3.7	9.3
123 CH GOD (ANDER)	5	164	492	3.7	9.2
165 CH OF NAZARENE	2	153	386	2.9	7.2
167 CHS OF CHRIST.	5	271	345	2.6	6.5
185 CUMBER PRESB..	2	63	71	0.5	1.3
221 FREE METHODIST	1	93	795	5.9	14.9
419 SO BAPT CONV..	1	150	180*	1.3	3.4
449 UN METHODIST..	9	1 019	1 226*	9.1	22.9
453 UN PRES CH USA	2	261	314*	2.3	5.9
PORTER	75	17 772	43 191*	36.0	100.0
029 AMER LUTH CH..	2	702	1 027	0.9	2.4
053 ASSEMB OF GOD.	4	221	506	0.4	1.2
081 CATHOLIC......	8	NA	17 503	14.6	40.5
093 CHR CH (DISC).	2	496	962	0.8	2.2
097 CHR CHS&CHS CR	2	453	563*	0.5	1.3
123 CH GOD (ANDER)	1	40	120	0.1	0.3
127 CH GOD (CLEVE)	1	119	148*	0.1	0.3
151 L-D SAINTS....	1	NA	604	0.5	1.4
165 CH OF NAZARENE	5	1 036	2 716	2.3	6.3
167 CHS OF CHRIST.	3	250	319	0.3	0.7
193 EPISCOPAL.....	2	179	312	0.3	0.7
203 EVAN FREE CH..	3	484	601*	0.5	1.4
281 LUTH CH AMER..	4	2 095	2 887	2.4	6.7
283 LUTH--MO SYNOD	8	4 237	5 585	4.7	12.9
285 MENNONITE CH..	2	388	482*	0.4	1.1
353 CHR BRETHREN..	1	10	15	-	-
363 PRIMITIVE METH	1	84	104*	0.1	0.2
381 REF PRES-EVAN.	1	31	57	-	0.1
403 SALVATION ARMY	2	211	311	0.3	0.7
413 S.D.A........	2	77	96*	0.1	0.2
419 SO BAPT CONV..	6	1 422	1 767*	1.5	4.1
435 UNITARIAN-UNIV	1	59	73*	0.1	0.2
443 UN C OF CHRIST	1	147	183*	0.2	0.4
449 UN METHODIST..	7	3 193	3 967*	3.3	9.2
453 UN PRES CH USA	5	1 838	2 283*	1.9	5.3
POSEY	50	6 500	14 176*	53.7	100.0
053 ASSEMB OF GOD.	1	45	85	0.3	0.6
081 CATHOLIC......	5	NA	5 123	19.4	36.1
093 CHR CH (DISC).	2	257	390	1.5	2.8
097 CHR CHS&CHS CR	4	755	930*	3.5	6.6
127 CH GOD (CLEVE)	1	64	79*	0.3	0.6
151 L-D SAINTS....	3	NA	412	1.6	2.9
165 CH OF NAZARENE	4	229	770	2.9	5.4
167 CHS OF CHRIST.	2	85	120	0.5	0.8

NA—Not applicable *Total adherents estimated from known number of communicant, confirmed, full members.

—Represents a percent less than 0.1.

Percentages may not total due to rounding.

Table 4. Churches and Church Membership by County and Denomination: 1980

County and Denomination	Number of churches	Communicant, confirmed, full members	Total adherents		
			Number	Percent of total population	Percent of total adherents
193 EPISCOPAL.....	2	167	236	0.9	1.7
413 S.D.A.........	1	10	12*	–	0.1
419 SO BAPT CONV..	2	640	788*	3.0	5.6
443 UN C OF CHRIST	7	1 918	2 362*	8.9	16.7
449 UN METHODIST..	14	2 171	2 673*	10.1	18.9
453 UN PRES CH USA	2	159	196*	0.7	1.4
PULASKI	29	3 367	6 923*	52.2	100.0
019 AMER BAPT USA.	1	43	53*	0.4	0.8
053 ASSEMB OF GOD.	2	36	88	0.7	1.3
081 CATHOLIC......	5	NA	2 269	17.1	32.8
093 CHR CH (DISC).	2	174	477	3.6	6.9
097 CHR CHS&CHS CR	3	725	894*	6.7	12.9
165 CH OF NAZARENE	1	131	328	2.5	4.7
167 CHS OF CHRIST.	1	40	50	0.4	0.7
283 LUTH--MO SYNOD	3	417	538	4.1	7.8
353 CHR BRETHREN..	1	20	30	0.2	0.4
443 UN C OF CHRIST	3	257	317*	2.4	4.6
449 UN METHODIST..	5	1 216	1 499*	11.3	21.7
453 UN PRES CH USA	2	308	380*	2.9	5.5
PUTNAM	47	6 971	10 625*	36.4	100.0
019 AMER BAPT USA.	7	1 547	1 835*	6.3	17.3
053 ASSEMB OF GOD.	1	68	200	0.7	1.9
081 CATHOLIC......	1	NA	772	2.6	7.3
093 CHR CH (DISC).	5	864	1 989	6.8	18.7
097 CHR CHS&CHS CR	4	606	719*	2.5	6.8
123 CH GOD (ANDER)	1	33	99	0.3	0.9
127 CH GOD (CLEVE)	1	82	97*	0.3	0.9
151 L-D SAINTS....	1	NA	105	0.4	1.0
165 CH OF NAZARENE	3	221	517	1.8	4.9
167 CHS OF CHRIST.	5	388	494	1.7	4.6
175 CONGR CHR CHS.	1	76	90*	0.3	0.8
193 EPISCOPAL.....	1	119	186	0.6	1.8
283 LUTH--MO SYNOD	1	88	106	0.4	1.0
419 SO BAPT CONV..	2	500	593*	2.0	5.6
443 UN C OF CHRIST	1	192	228*	0.8	2.1
449 UN METHODIST..	9	1 733	2 056*	7.1	19.4
453 UN PRES CH USA	3	454	539*	1.8	5.1
RANDOLPH	66	8 104	11 523*	38.4	100.0
029 AMER LUTH CH..	1	218	270	0.9	2.3
053 ASSEMB OF GOD.	1	106	187	0.6	1.6
081 CATHOLIC......	2	NA	741	2.5	6.4
093 CHR CH (DISC).	3	1 112	1 342	4.5	11.6
097 CHR CHS&CHS CR	6	1 226	1 504*	5.0	13.1
123 CH GOD (ANDER)	2	157	471	1.6	4.1
165 CH OF NAZARENE	7	849	1 549	5.2	13.4
167 CHS OF CHRIST.	3	200	255	0.9	2.2
175 CONGR CHR CHS.	1	25	31*	0.1	0.3
213 EVAN MENN INC.	1	25	31*	0.1	0.3
226 FRIENDS-USA...	16	1 373	1 685*	5.6	14.6
281 LUTH CH AMER..	1	93	119	0.4	1.0
409 SEPARATE BAPT.	1	106	130*	0.4	1.1
419 SO BAPT CONV..	1	69	85*	0.3	0.7
449 UN METHODIST..	18	2 265	2 779*	9.3	24.1
453 UN PRES CH USA	2	280	344*	1.1	3.0
RIPLEY	54	8 253	16 425*	67.3	100.0
019 AMER BAPT USA.	13	2 941	3 652*	15.0	22.2
029 AMER LUTH CH..	1	358	449	1.8	2.7
081 CATHOLIC......	8	NA	5 920	24.3	36.0
097 CHR CHS&CHS CR	6	905	1 124*	4.6	6.8
151 L-D SAINTS....	1	NA	87	0.4	0.5
165 CH OF NAZARENE	1	41	133	0.5	0.8
167 CHS OF CHRIST.	1	48	63	0.3	0.4
281 LUTH CH AMER..	5	1 406	1 791	7.3	10.9
283 LUTH--MO SYNOD	1	191	271	1.1	1.6
419 SO BAPT CONV..	3	271	337*	1.4	2.1
443 UN C OF CHRIST	3	377	468*	1.9	2.8
449 UN METHODIST..	11	1 715	2 130*	8.7	13.0
RUSH	51	7 734	11 664*	59.5	100.0
019 AMER BAPT USA.	1	902	1 109*	5.7	9.5
053 ASSEMB OF GOD.	1	34	100	0.5	0.9
081 CATHOLIC......	1	NA	1 445	7.4	12.4
093 CHR CH (DISC).	8	1 265	1 812	9.2	15.5
097 CHR CHS&CHS CR	13	2 216	2 725*	13.9	23.4
107 CHRISTIAN UN..	1	70	98	0.5	0.8
123 CH GOD (ANDER)	1	70	210	1.1	1.8
165 CH OF NAZARENE	3	110	376	1.9	3.2
167 CHS OF CHRIST.	1	70	89	0.5	0.8
193 EPISCOPAL.....	1	16	23	0.1	0.2
226 FRIENDS-USA...	3	271	333*	1.7	2.9
283 LUTH--MO SYNOD	1	48	88	0.4	0.8
323 OLD ORD AMISH.	2	260	320*	1.6	2.7
403 SALVATION ARMY	1	92	94	0.5	0.8
419 SO BAPT CONV..	2	468	576*	2.9	4.9
435 UNITARIAN-UNIV	1	16	20*	0.1	0.2
449 UN METHODIST..	7	1 321	1 625*	8.3	13.9
453 UN PRES CH USA	3	505	621*	3.2	5.3
ST JOSEPH	186	39 247	115 360*	47.7	100.0
005 AME ZION......	2	810	972	0.4	0.8
017 AMER BAPT ASSN	3	350	350	0.1	0.3
019 AMER BAPT USA.	4	777	936*	0.4	0.8
029 AMER LUTH CH..	1	322	516	0.2	0.4
053 ASSEMB OF GOD.	5	986	2 443	1.0	2.1
071 BRETHREN (ASH)	5	604	728*	0.3	0.6

County and Denomination	Number of churches	Communicant, confirmed, full members	Total adherents		
			Number	Percent of total population	Percent of total adherents
081 CATHOLIC......	30	NA	62 660	25.9	54.3
093 CHR CH (DISC).	4	1 173	1 618	0.7	1.4
097 CHR CHS&CHS CR	10	2 740	3 302*	1.4	2.9
105 CHRISTIAN REF.	1	122	194	0.1	0.2
121 CH GOD (ABR)..	2	134	161*	0.1	0.1
123 CH GOD (ANDER)	3	461	1 383	0.6	1.2
127 CH GOD (CLEVE)	2	121	146*	0.1	0.1
151 L-D SAINTS....	1	NA	519	0.2	0.4
157 CH OF BRETHREN	7	1 230	1 482*	0.6	1.3
165 CH OF NAZARENE	4	519	1 238	0.5	1.1
167 CHS OF CHRIST.	5	600	764	0.3	0.7
175 CONGR CHR CHS.	1	842	1 015*	0.4	0.9
193 EPISCOPAL.....	4	1 299	1 397	0.6	1.2
201 EVAN COV CH AM	1	114	137*	0.1	0.1
203 EVAN FREE CH..	1	160	193*	0.1	0.2
208 EVAN LUTH ASSN	1	390	560	0.2	0.5
244 GRACE BRETHREN	2	557	671*	0.3	0.6
271 REFORM JUDAISM	1	596	718*	0.3	0.6
281 LUTH CH AMER..	6	1 888	2 600	1.1	2.3
283 LUTH--MO SYNOD	7	2 311	3 224	1.3	2.8
285 MENNONITE CH..	10	838	1 010*	0.4	0.9
290 METRO COMM CHS	0	10	20	–	–
291 MISSIONARY CH.	12	1 099	2 036*	0.8	1.8
403 SALVATION ARMY	2	289	763	0.3	0.7
413 S.D.A.........	2	639	770*	0.3	0.7
419 SO BAPT CONV..	2	266	321*	0.1	0.3
435 UNITARIAN-UNIV	1	100	120*	–	0.1
443 UN C OF CHRIST	5	1 566	1 887*	0.8	1.6
449 UN METHODIST..	30	10 703	12 897*	5.3	11.2
453 UN PRES CH USA	8	4 479	5 397*	2.2	4.7
469 WELS..........	1	152	212	0.1	0.2
SCOTT	39	6 589	8 747*	42.8	100.0
019 AMER BAPT USA.	9	2 627	3 269*	16.0	37.4
081 CATHOLIC......	1	NA	439	2.1	5.0
097 CHR CHS&CHS CR	8	2 070	2 576*	12.6	29.5
127 CH GOD (CLEVE)	3	280	348*	1.7	4.0
165 CH OF NAZARENE	1	51	133	0.7	1.5
167 CHS OF CHRIST.	2	123	173	0.8	2.0
283 LUTH--MO SYNOD	1	65	100	0.5	1.1
285 MENNONITE CH..	1	27	34*	0.2	0.4
413 S.D.A.........	1	42	52*	0.3	0.6
419 SO BAPT CONV..	2	271	337*	1.7	3.9
449 UN METHODIST..	8	824	1 026*	5.0	11.7
453 UN PRES CH USA	2	209	260*	1.3	3.0
SHELBY	66	11 310	18 145*	45.5	100.0
019 AMER BAPT USA.	11	3 069	3 778*	9.5	20.8
053 ASSEMB OF GOD.	1	59	187	0.5	1.0
081 CATHOLIC......	2	NA	2 973	7.5	16.4
093 CHR CH (DISC).	2	761	1 170	2.9	6.4
097 CHR CHS&CHS CR	7	1 536	1 891*	4.7	10.4
107 CHRISTIAN UN..	2	137	295	0.7	1.6
123 CH GOD (ANDER)	1	40	120	0.3	0.7
127 CH GOD (CLEVE)	1	82	101*	0.3	0.6
151 L-D SAINTS....	1	NA	219	0.5	1.2
165 CH OF NAZARENE	4	364	900	2.3	5.0
167 CHS OF CHRIST.	2	100	127	0.3	0.7
193 EPISCOPAL.....	1	88	131	0.3	0.8
215 EVAN METH CH..	1	120	148*	0.4	0.8
281 LUTH CH AMER..	1	83	123	0.3	0.7
283 LUTH--MO SYNOD	1	126	157	0.4	0.9
403 SALVATION ARMY	1	112	123	0.3	0.7
409 SEPARATE BAPT.	2	105	129*	0.3	0.7
413 S.D.A.........	1	97	119*	0.3	0.7
419 SO BAPT CONV..	3	357	439*	1.1	2.4
443 UN C OF CHRIST	2	418	515*	1.3	2.8
449 UN METHODIST..	18	3 252	4 003*	10.0	22.1
453 UN PRES CH USA	1	404	497*	1.2	2.7
SPENCER	50	5 617	12 296*	63.5	100.0
019 AMER BAPT USA.	5	652	794*	4.1	6.5
065 BETHEL M ASSN.	2	400	487*	2.5	4.0
081 CATHOLIC......	8	NA	5 291	27.3	43.0
097 CHR CHS&CHS CR	3	950	1 157*	6.0	9.4
127 CH GOD (CLEVE)	1	9	11*	0.1	0.1
165 CH OF NAZARENE	3	149	343	1.8	2.8
244 GRACE BRETHREN	1	35	43*	0.2	0.3
281 LUTH CH AMER..	2	135	178	0.9	1.4
283 LUTH--MO SYNOD	1	311	368	1.9	3.0
419 SO BAPT CONV..	3	483	588*	3.0	4.8
443 UN C OF CHRIST	4	408	497*	2.6	4.0
449 UN METHODIST..	16	2 033	2 476*	12.8	20.1
453 UN PRES CH USA	1	52	63*	0.3	0.5
STARKE	22	2 479	6 751*	30.7	100.0
053 ASSEMB OF GOD.	2	68	148	0.7	2.2
081 CATHOLIC......	4	NA	3 378	15.4	50.0
097 CHR CHS&CHS CR	1	170	211*	1.0	3.1
127 CH GOD (CLEVE)	1	12	15*	0.1	0.2
165 CH OF NAZARENE	1	49	147	0.7	2.2
283 LUTH--MO SYNOD	3	1 038	1 399	6.4	20.7
285 MENNONITE CH..	2	117	145*	0.7	2.1
353 CHR BRETHREN..	2	50	100	0.5	1.5
413 S.D.A.........	1	35	43*	0.2	0.6
443 UN C OF CHRIST	1	120	149*	0.7	2.2
449 UN METHODIST..	4	820	1 016*	4.6	15.0
STEUBEN	38	4 983	8 292*	33.6	100.0
019 AMER BAPT USA.	2	153	185*	0.7	2.2

NA — Not applicable   *Total adherents estimated from known number of communicant, confirmed, full members.   — Represents a percent less than 0.1.   Percentages may not total due to rounding.

Table 4. Churches and Church Membership by County and Denomination: 1980

County and Denomination	Number of churches	Communicant, confirmed, full members	Total adherents Number	Percent of total population	Percent of total adherents
029 AMER LUTH CH..	1	408	537	2.2	6.5
053 ASSEMB OF GOD.	1	116	260	1.1	3.1
081 CATHOLIC......	2	NA	1 750	7.1	21.1
097 CHR CHS&CHS CR	4	1 158	1 403*	5.7	16.9
165 CH OF NAZARENE	4	215	499	2.0	6.0
167 CHS OF CHRIST.	1	24	31	0.1	0.4
193 EPISCOPAL.....	1	52	132	0.5	1.6
283 LUTH--MO SYNOD	2	254	295	1.2	3.6
291 MISSIONARY CH.	2	103	170	0.7	2.1
323 OLD ORD AMISH.	2	260	315*	1.3	3.8
413 S.D.A.........	1	36	44*	0.2	0.5
419 SO BAPT CONV..	1	83	101*	0.4	1.2
443 UN C OF CHRIST	1	211	256*	1.0	3.1
449 UN METHODIST..	12	1 786	2 164*	8.8	26.1
453 UN PRES CH USA	1	124	150*	0.6	1.8
SULLIVAN	**62**	**6 826**	**9 293***	**44.0**	**100.0**
019 AMER BAPT USA.	5	1 402	1 695*	8.0	18.2
053 ASSEMB OF GOD.	5	282	680	3.2	7.3
081 CATHOLIC......	2	NA	471	2.2	5.1
093 CHR CH (DISC).	1	51	57	0.3	0.6
097 CHR CHS&CHS CR	4	1 515	1 832*	8.7	19.7
127 CH GOD (CLEVE)	3	215	260*	1.2	2.8
165 CH OF NAZARENE	2	98	95	0.5	1.0
167 CHS OF CHRIST.	11	753	1 168	5.5	12.6
215 EVAN METH CH..	1	109	132*	0.6	1.4
226 FRIENDS-USA...	1	21	25*	0.1	0.3
413 S.D.A.........	1	10	12*	0.1	0.1
419 SO BAPT CONV..	1	52	63*	0.3	0.7
443 UN C OF CHRIST	1	65	79*	0.4	0.9
449 UN METHODIST..	22	2 009	2 429*	11.5	26.1
453 UN PRES CH USA	2	244	295*	1.4	3.2
SWITZERLAND	**28**	**2 310**	**2 909***	**40.7**	**100.0**
019 AMER BAPT USA.	12	1 646	2 005*	28.0	68.9
081 CATHOLIC......	1	NA	65	0.9	2.2
097 CHR CHS&CHS CR	4	135	164*	2.3	5.6
165 CH OF NAZARENE	1	5	37	0.5	1.3
449 UN METHODIST..	8	433	527*	7.4	18.1
453 UN PRES CH USA	2	91	111*	1.6	3.8
TIPPECANOE	**93**	**25 087**	**51 600***	**42.4**	**100.0**
019 AMER BAPT USA.	3	1 672	1 965*	1.6	3.8
053 ASSEMB OF GOD.	2	844	2 233	1.8	4.3
081 CATHOLIC......	8	NA	17 359	14.3	33.6
089 CHR & MISS AL.	1	0	20	-	-
093 CHR CH (DISC).	2	2 019	2 734	2.2	5.3
097 CHR CHS&CHS CR	3	854	1 004*	0.8	1.9
105 CHRISTIAN REF.	1	397	577	0.5	1.1
121 CH GOD (ABR)..	1	48	56*	-	0.1
123 CH GOD (ANDER)	2	125	375	0.3	0.7
127 CH GOD (CLEVE)	1	56	66*	0.1	0.1
151 L-D SAINTS....	2	NA	673	0.6	1.3
157 CH OF BRETHREN	1	106	125*	0.1	0.2
165 CH OF NAZARENE	2	258	504	0.4	1.0
167 CHS OF CHRIST.	3	500	636	0.5	1.2
193 EPISCOPAL.....	2	516	1 046	0.9	2.0
201 EVAN COV CH AM	1	122	143*	0.1	0.3
213 EVAN MENN INC.	1	51	60*	-	0.1
221 FREE METHODIST	1	44	357	0.3	0.7
226 FRIENDS-USA...	2	47	55*	-	0.1
263 INT FOURSQ GOS	1	74	87*	0.1	0.2
271 REFORM JUDAISM	1	214	251*	0.2	0.5
281 LUTH CH AMER..	4	1 503	2 112	1.7	4.1
283 LUTH--MO SYNOD	4	1 312	2 121	1.7	4.1
353 CHR BRETHREN..	1	25	50	-	0.1
371 REF CH IN AM..	2	297	544	0.4	1.1
383 REF PRES OF NA	1	66	81	0.1	0.2
403 SALVATION ARMY	1	135	146	0.1	0.3
413 S.D.A.........	1	183	215*	0.2	0.4
419 SO BAPT CONV..	7	1 089	1 280*	1.1	2.5
435 UNITARIAN-UNIV	1	100	118*	0.1	0.2
443 UN C OF CHRIST	1	827	972*	0.8	1.9
449 UN METHODIST..	21	7 162	8 416*	6.9	16.3
453 UN PRES CH USA	8	4 441	5 219*	4.3	10.1
TIPTON	**25**	**3 941**	**6 958***	**41.4**	**100.0**
019 AMER BAPT USA.	1	276	337*	2.0	4.8
053 ASSEMB OF GOD.	1	57	114	0.7	1.6
081 CATHOLIC......	2	NA	1 644	9.8	23.6
093 CHR CH (DISC).	2	863	1 377	8.2	19.8
097 CHR CHS&CHS CR	1	400	489*	2.9	7.0
127 CH GOD (CLEVE)	1	52	64*	0.4	0.9
157 CH OF BRETHREN	1	75	92*	0.5	1.3
165 CH OF NAZARENE	1	50	181	1.1	2.6
167 CHS OF CHRIST.	1	100	127	0.8	1.8
226 FRIENDS-USA...	3	193	236*	1.4	3.4
283 LUTH--MO SYNOD	1	339	419	2.5	6.0
409 SEPARATE BAPT.	1	141	172*	1.0	2.5
413 S.D.A.........	1	9	11*	0.1	0.2
419 SO BAPT CONV..	1	111	136*	0.8	2.0
449 UN METHODIST..	6	1 095	1 339*	8.0	19.2
453 UN PRES CH USA	1	180	220*	1.3	3.2
UNION	**13**	**1 562**	**2 465***	**35.9**	**100.0**
081 CATHOLIC......	1	NA	310	4.5	12.6
097 CHR CHS&CHS CR	1	250	309*	4.5	12.5
157 CH OF BRETHREN	1	46	57*	0.8	2.3
165 CH OF NAZARENE	2	97	346	5.0	14.0
226 FRIENDS-USA...	1	43	53*	0.8	2.2
419 SO BAPT CONV..	1	27	33*	0.5	1.3
443 UN C OF CHRIST	1	138	170*	2.5	6.9
449 UN METHODIST..	4	825	1 019*	14.9	41.3
453 UN PRES CH USA	1	136	168*	2.4	6.8
VANDERBURGH	**156**	**49 945**	**97 150***	**58.0**	**100.0**
005 AME ZION......	1	300	389	0.2	0.4
019 AMER BAPT USA.	4	2 044	2 432*	1.5	2.5
029 AMER LUTH CH..	3	577	728	0.4	0.7
053 ASSEMB OF GOD.	5	761	1 840	1.1	1.9
065 BETHEL M ASSN.	2	2 100	2 499*	1.5	2.6
081 CATHOLIC......	24	NA	33 868	20.2	34.9
093 CHR CH (DISC).	3	926	1 532	0.9	1.6
097 CHR CHS&CHS CR	2	1 440	1 713*	1.0	1.8
123 CH GOD (ANDER)	2	200	600	0.4	0.6
127 CH GOD (CLEVE)	2	81	96*	0.1	0.1
165 CH OF NAZARENE	6	562	1 071	0.6	1.1
167 CHS OF CHRIST.	7	1 097	1 372	0.8	1.4
185 CUMBER PRESB..	2	511	893	0.5	0.9
193 EPISCOPAL.....	2	479	551	0.3	0.6
208 EVAN LUTH ASSN	2	230	308	0.2	0.3
221 FREE METHODIST	1	74	360	0.2	0.4
226 FRIENDS-USA...	1	10	12*	-	-
270 CONSRV JUDAISM	1	151	180*	0.1	0.2
271 REFORM JUDAISM	1	256	305*	0.2	0.3
281 LUTH CH AMER..	3	736	951	0.6	1.0
283 LUTH--MO SYNOD	8	2 334	3 718	2.2	3.8
403 SALVATION ARMY	2	255	300	0.2	0.3
413 S.D.A.........	2	230	274*	0.2	0.3
419 SO BAPT CONV..	27	15 478	18 417*	11.0	19.0
435 UNITARIAN-UNIV	1	60	71*	-	0.1
443 UN C OF CHRIST	15	8 091	9 627*	5.7	9.9
449 UN METHODIST..	18	8 258	9 826*	5.9	10.1
453 UN PRES CH USA	9	2 704	3 217*	1.9	3.3
VERMILLION	**34**	**3 794**	**6 212***	**34.1**	**100.0**
019 AMER BAPT USA.	4	966	1 172*	6.4	18.9
053 ASSEMB OF GOD.	3	118	267	1.5	4.3
081 CATHOLIC......	2	NA	1 276	7.0	20.5
093 CHR CH (DISC).	2	433	536	2.9	8.6
097 CHR CHS&CHS CR	2	220	267*	1.5	4.3
127 CH GOD (CLEVE)	1	37	45*	0.2	0.7
165 CH OF NAZARENE	4	252	498	2.7	8.0
167 CHS OF CHRIST.	2	100	127	0.7	2.0
226 FRIENDS-USA...	2	133	161*	0.9	2.6
449 UN METHODIST..	10	1 312	1 592*	8.7	25.6
453 UN PRES CH USA	2	223	271*	1.5	4.4
VIGO	**105**	**20 567**	**35 203***	**31.3**	**100.0**
017 AMER BAPT ASSN	3	325	325	0.3	0.9
019 AMER BAPT USA.	9	2 718	3 226*	2.9	9.2
029 AMER LUTH CH..	1	114	162	0.1	0.5
053 ASSEMB OF GOD.	5	788	1 324	1.2	3.8
081 CATHOLIC......	9	NA	8 835	7.9	25.1
089 CHR & MISS AL.	1	45	55	-	0.2
093 CHR CH (DISC).	1	300	525	0.5	1.5
097 CHR CHS&CHS CR	8	2 870	3 406*	3.0	9.7
101 C.M.E........	1	30	36*	-	0.1
105 CHRISTIAN REF.	1	48	80	0.1	0.2
123 CH GOD (ANDER)	1	28	84	0.1	0.2
127 CH GOD (CLEVE)	1	92	109*	0.1	0.3
151 L-D SAINTS....	1	NA	555	0.5	1.6
165 CH OF NAZARENE	5	434	917	0.8	2.6
167 CHS OF CHRIST.	8	817	1 040	0.9	3.0
175 CONGR CHR CHS.	2	601	713*	0.6	2.0
193 EPISCOPAL.....	2	775	906	0.8	2.6
221 FREE METHODIST	1	50	288	0.3	0.8
226 FRIENDS-USA...	1	34	40*	-	0.1
263 INT FOURSQ GOS	1	348	413*	0.4	1.2
271 REFORM JUDAISM	1	300	356*	0.3	1.0
281 LUTH CH AMER..	2	438	581	0.5	1.7
283 LUTH--MO SYNOD	1	372	475	0.4	1.3
290 METRO COMM CHS	0	10	20	-	0.1
353 CHR BRETHREN..	1	40	70	0.1	0.2
403 SALVATION ARMY	1	71	76	0.1	0.2
413 S.D.A.........	3	212	252*	0.2	0.7
419 SO BAPT CONV..	3	616	731*	0.7	2.1
435 UNITARIAN-UNIV	1	21	25*	-	0.1
443 UN C OF CHRIST	2	706	838*	0.7	2.4
449 UN METHODIST..	25	6 379	7 571*	6.7	21.5
453 UN PRES CH USA	3	985	1 169*	1.0	3.3
WABASH	**67**	**11 997**	**16 999***	**46.4**	**100.0**
029 AMER LUTH CH..	1	120	183	0.5	1.1
053 ASSEMB OF GOD.	2	114	183	0.5	1.1
071 BRETHREN (ASH)	4	847	1 032*	2.8	6.1
081 CATHOLIC......	3	NA	1 614	4.4	9.5
089 CHR & MISS AL.	1	116	231	0.6	1.4
093 CHR CH (DISC).	2	644	912	2.5	5.4
097 CHR CHS&CHS CR	11	1 972	2 402*	6.6	14.1
123 CH GOD (ANDER)	1	70	210	0.6	1.2
127 CH GOD (CLEVE)	1	28	34*	0.1	0.2
157 CH OF BRETHREN	6	1 485	1 809*	4.9	10.6
165 CH OF NAZARENE	2	175	504	1.4	3.0
167 CHS OF CHRIST.	2	185	225	0.6	1.3
175 CONGR CHR CHS.	1	366	446*	1.2	2.6
226 FRIENDS-USA...	1	315	384*	1.0	2.3
281 LUTH CH AMER..	1	372	427	1.2	2.5
283 LUTH--MO SYNOD	1	273	378	1.0	2.2
291 MISSIONARY CH.	1	62	114	0.3	0.7
409 SEPARATE BAPT.	1	121	147*	0.4	0.9

NA— Not applicable   *Total adherents estimated from known number of communicant, confirmed, full members.   —Represents a percent less than 0.1.   Percentages may not total due to rounding.

Table 4. Churches and Church Membership by County and Denomination: 1980

County and Denomination	Number of churches	Communicant, confirmed, full members	Total adherents		
			Number	Percent of total population	Percent of total adherents
413 S.D.A.........	1	30	37*	0.1	0.2
443 UN C OF CHRIST	3	579	705*	1.9	4.1
449 UN METHODIST..	19	3 353	4 084*	11.1	24.0
453 UN PRES CH USA	2	770	938*	2.6	5.5
WARREN	21	2 557	3 202*	35.7	100.0
053 ASSEMB OF GOD.	1	38	48	0.5	1.5
097 CHR CHS&CHS CR	5	1 181	1 450*	16.2	45.3
121 CH GOD (ABR)..	1	40	49*	0.5	1.5
165 CH OF NAZARENE	2	99	145	1.6	4.5
221 FREE METHODIST	1	22	66	0.7	2.1
449 UN METHODIST..	9	977	1 199*	13.4	37.4
453 UN PRES CH USA	2	200	245*	2.7	7.7
WARRICK	45	6 815	15 214*	36.7	100.0
019 AMER BAPT USA.	1	355	442*	1.1	2.9
029 AMER LUTH CH..	1	26	32	0.1	0.2
065 BETHEL M ASSN.	1	125	156*	0.4	1.0
081 CATHOLIC......	4	NA	6 185	14.9	40.7
093 CHR CH (DISC).	1	112	172	0.4	1.1
097 CHR CHS&CHS CR	1	112	140*	0.3	0.9
151 L-D SAINTS....	1	NA	84	0.2	0.6
165 CH OF NAZARENE	3	236	506	1.2	3.3
167 CHS OF CHRIST.	1	50	75	0.2	0.5
185 CUMBER PRESB..	1	155	267	0.6	1.8
221 FREE METHODIST	1	28	93	0.2	0.6
283 LUTH--MO SYNOD	1	174	282	0.7	1.9
419 SO BAPT CONV..	4	1 397	1 741*	4.2	11.4
443 UN C OF CHRIST	6	1 456	1 814*	4.4	11.9
449 UN METHODIST..	16	2 026	2 524*	6.1	16.6
453 UN PRES CH USA	2	563	701*	1.7	4.6
WASHINGTON	60	7 122	9 782*	44.6	100.0
019 AMER BAPT USA.	10	1 698	2 099*	9.6	21.5
081 CATHOLIC......	1	NA	387	1.8	4.0
093 CHR CH (DISC).	1	736	1 082	4.9	11.1
097 CHR CHS&CHS CR	5	751	929*	4.2	9.5
123 CH GOD (ANDER)	1	25	75	0.3	0.8
127 CH GOD (CLEVE)	1	35	43*	0.2	0.4
151 L-D SAINTS....	1	NA	179	0.8	1.8
165 CH OF NAZARENE	2	120	295	1.3	3.0
167 CHS OF CHRIST.	15	1 341	1 696	7.7	17.3
226 FRIENDS-USA...	1	78	96*	0.4	1.0
283 LUTH--MO SYNOD	1	47	68	0.3	0.7
285 MENNONITE CH..	1	12	15*	0.1	0.2
323 OLD ORD AMISH.	1	130	161*	0.7	1.6
413 S.D.A.........	1	15	19*	0.1	0.2
419 SO BAPT CONV..	3	593	733*	3.3	7.5
449 UN METHODIST..	13	1 336	1 652*	7.5	16.9
453 UN PRES CH USA	2	205	253*	1.2	2.6
WAYNE	95	18 415	30 208*	39.7	100.0
019 AMER BAPT USA.	3	1 727	2 101*	2.8	7.0
029 AMER LUTH CH..	2	818	966	1.3	3.2
053 ASSEMB OF GOD.	3	266	532	0.7	1.8
081 CATHOLIC......	4	NA	6 250	8.2	20.7
089 CHR & MISS AL.	1	34	67	0.1	0.2
093 CHR CH (DISC).	2	931	1 140	1.5	3.8
097 CHR CHS&CHS CR	7	1 410	1 716*	2.3	5.7
123 CH GOD (ANDER)	1	40	120	0.2	0.4
127 CH GOD (CLEVE)	1	212	258*	0.3	0.9
151 L-D SAINTS....	1	NA	335	0.4	1.1
157 CH OF BRETHREN	2	325	395*	0.5	1.3
165 CH OF NAZARENE	7	921	1 749	2.3	5.8
167 CHS OF CHRIST.	5	470	598	0.8	2.0
193 EPISCOPAL.....	1	214	425	0.6	1.4
226 FRIENDS-USA...	13	1 493	1 817*	2.4	6.0
271 REFORM JUDAISM	1	84	102*	0.1	0.3
281 LUTH CH AMER..	4	1 759	2 267	3.0	7.5
283 LUTH--MO SYNOD	1	42	51	0.1	0.2
403 SALVATION ARMY	1	172	197	0.3	0.7
413 S.D.A.........	1	156	190*	0.2	0.6
419 SO BAPT CONV..	7	1 815	2 208*	2.9	7.3
443 UN C OF CHRIST	2	244	297*	0.4	1.0
449 UN METHODIST..	20	3 981	4 844*	6.4	16.0
453 UN PRES CH USA	5	1 301	1 583*	2.1	5.2
WELLS	49	7 460	10 486*	41.3	100.0
019 AMER BAPT USA.	3	698	860*	3.4	8.2
029 AMER LUTH CH..	1	323	468	1.8	4.5
081 CATHOLIC......	1	NA	832	3.3	7.9
097 CHR CHS&CHS CR	2	445	548*	2.2	5.2
127 CH GOD (CLEVE)	1	22	27*	0.1	0.3
165 CH OF NAZARENE	2	274	572	2.3	5.5
167 CHS OF CHRIST.	1	30	38	0.1	0.4
215 EVAN METH CH..	1	9	11*	—	0.1
226 FRIENDS-USA...	1	17	21*	0.1	0.2
281 LUTH CH AMER..	2	501	729	2.9	7.0
283 LUTH--MO SYNOD	2	420	542	2.1	5.2
291 MISSIONARY CH.	2	133	185	0.7	1.8
413 S.D.A.........	1	24	30*	0.1	0.3
443 UN C OF CHRIST	3	835	1 029*	4.1	9.8
449 UN METHODIST..	24	2 932	3 612*	14.2	34.4
453 UN PRES CH USA	2	797	982*	3.9	9.4
WHITE	39	7 125	10 905*	45.7	100.0
019 AMER BAPT USA.	7	1 899	2 327*	9.7	21.3
053 ASSEMB OF GOD.	1	102	293	1.2	2.7
081 CATHOLIC......	2	NA	1 625	6.8	14.9

County and Denomination	Number of churches	Communicant, confirmed, full members	Total adherents		
			Number	Percent of total population	Percent of total adherents
093 CHR CH (DISC).	2	761	1 079	4.5	9.9
097 CHR CHS&CHS CR	4	400	490*	2.1	4.5
157 CH OF BRETHREN	4	412	505*	2.1	4.6
165 CH OF NAZARENE	1	41	103	0.4	0.9
167 CHS OF CHRIST.	2	150	191	0.8	1.8
283 LUTH--MO SYNOD	2	648	968	4.1	8.9
413 S.D.A.........	2	38	47*	0.2	0.4
443 UN C OF CHRIST	1	126	154*	0.6	1.4
449 UN METHODIST..	8	1 836	2 250*	9.4	20.6
453 UN PRES CH USA	3	712	873*	3.7	8.0
WHITLEY	40	6 192	10 317*	39.4	100.0
019 AMER BAPT USA.	1	176	217*	0.8	2.1
053 ASSEMB OF GOD.	1	11	25	0.1	0.2
081 CATHOLIC......	3	NA	1 587	6.1	15.4
093 CHR CH (DISC).	2	129	194	0.7	1.9
097 CHR CHS&CHS CR	2	170	210*	0.8	2.0
123 CH GOD (ANDER)	2	170	510	1.9	4.9
157 CH OF BRETHREN	5	657	810*	3.1	7.9
165 CH OF NAZARENE	2	258	540	2.1	5.2
167 CHS OF CHRIST.	1	30	38	0.1	0.4
221 FREE METHODIST	1	38	222	0.8	2.2
281 LUTH CH AMER..	3	1 014	1 433	5.5	13.9
283 LUTH--MO SYNOD	3	827	1 186	4.5	11.5
449 UN METHODIST..	12	2 262	2 790*	10.6	27.0
453 UN PRES CH USA	2	450	555*	2.1	5.4

IOWA

THE STATE.....	4 534	940 758	1 783 704*	61.2	100.0
ADAIR	30	4 347	6 145*	64.6	100.0
029 AMER LUTH CH..	2	664	907	9.5	14.8
053 ASSEMB OF GOD.	1	36	69	0.7	1.1
081 CATHOLIC......	3	NA	673	7.1	11.0
093 CHR CH (DISC).	1	43	58	0.6	0.9
226 FRIENDS-USA...	2	129	155*	1.6	2.5
283 LUTH--MO SYNOD	2	722	942	9.9	15.3
353 CHR BRETHREN..	2	95	145	1.5	2.4
413 S.D.A.........	1	9	11*	0.1	0.2
443 UN C OF CHRIST	3	127	153*	1.6	2.5
449 UN METHODIST..	11	2 103	2 528*	26.6	41.1
453 UN PRES CH USA	2	419	504*	5.3	8.2
ADAMS	20	2 210	3 138*	54.8	100.0
019 AMER BAPT USA.	1	140	166*	2.9	5.3
081 CATHOLIC......	1	NA	401	7.0	12.8
093 CHR CH (DISC).	1	380	530	9.2	16.9
097 CHR CHS&CHS CR	1	50	59*	1.0	1.9
157 CH OF BRETHREN	2	74	88*	1.5	2.8
281 LUTH CH AMER..	1	84	116	2.0	3.7
283 LUTH--MO SYNOD	1	184	232	4.0	7.4
353 CHR BRETHREN..	1	10	15	0.3	0.5
443 UN C OF CHRIST	1	61	73*	1.3	2.3
449 UN METHODIST..	8	1 035	1 230*	21.5	39.2
453 UN PRES CH USA	1	192	228*	4.0	7.3
ALLAMAKEE	39	6 610	13 198*	87.4	100.0
029 AMER LUTH CH..	6	1 673	2 173	14.4	16.5
057 BAPT GEN CONF.	1	81	99*	0.7	0.8
081 CATHOLIC......	11	NA	4 945	32.7	37.5
179 CONSRV BAPT...	1	110	134*	0.9	1.0
209 EVAN LUTH SYN.	1	93	108	0.7	0.8
281 LUTH CH AMER..	1	1 449	1 829	12.1	13.9
413 S.D.A.........	1	80	98*	0.6	0.7
443 UN C OF CHRIST	5	1 154	1 408*	9.3	10.7
449 UN METHODIST..	5	630	769*	5.1	5.8
453 UN PRES CH USA	6	1 340	1 635*	10.8	12.4
APPANOOSE	38	4 003	6 775*	43.7	100.0
019 AMER BAPT USA.	2	738	891*	5.7	13.2
081 CATHOLIC......	4	NA	1 515	9.8	22.4
093 CHR CH (DISC).	6	626	1 044	6.7	15.4
097 CHR CHS&CHS CR	5	270	326*	2.1	4.8
157 CH OF BRETHREN	1	116	140*	0.9	2.1
165 CH OF NAZARENE	2	94	155	1.0	2.3
193 EPISCOPAL.....	1	50	52	0.3	0.8
201 EVAN COV CH AM	1	71	86*	0.6	1.3
244 GRACE BRETHREN	1	40	48*	0.3	0.7
281 LUTH CH AMER..	1	316	440	2.8	6.5
329 OPEN BIBLE STD	1	55	75	0.5	1.1
353 CHR BRETHREN..	1	50	100	0.6	1.5
413 S.D.A.........	1	32	39*	0.3	0.6
449 UN METHODIST..	10	1 331	1 606*	10.4	23.7
453 UN PRES CH USA	1	214	258*	1.7	3.8
AUDUBON	21	4 954	7 021*	82.0	100.0

NA—Not applicable   *Total adherents estimated from known number of communicant, confirmed, full members.   —Represents a percent less than 0.1.   Percentages may not total due to rounding.

Table 4. Churches and Church Membership by County and Denomination: 1980

County and Denomination	Number of churches	Communicant, confirmed, full members	Total adherents Number	Percent of total population	Percent of total adherents
029 AMER LUTH CH..	5	2 120	2 614	30.5	37.2
053 ASSEMB OF GOD.	1	16	17	0.2	0.2
081 CATHOLIC......	2	NA	765	8.9	10.9
093 CHR CH (DISC).	1	179	368	4.3	5.2
097 CHR CHS&CHS CR	1	40	48*	0.6	0.7
281 LUTH CH AMER..	2	699	865	10.1	12.3
283 LUTH--MO SYNOD	2	413	560	6.5	8.0
413 S.D.A.........	2	54	65*	0.8	0.9
443 UN C OF CHRIST	1	61	73*	0.9	1.0
449 UN METHODIST..	3	882	1 058*	12.4	15.1
453 UN PRES CH USA	1	490	588*	6.9	8.4
BENTON	51	8 613	14 536*	61.5	100.0
019 AMER BAPT USA.	2	224	273*	1.2	1.9
029 AMER LUTH CH..	1	142	200	0.8	1.4
053 ASSEMB OF GOD.	2	94	210	0.9	1.4
081 CATHOLIC......	8	NA	3 331	14.1	22.9
093 CHR CH (DISC).	4	539	738	3.1	5.1
151 L-D SAINTS....	1	NA	70	0.3	0.5
157 CH OF BRETHREN	1	35	43*	0.2	0.3
221 FREE METHODIST	2	23	105	0.4	0.7
263 INT FOURSQ GOS	1	58	71*	0.3	0.5
281 LUTH CH AMER..	1	160	211	0.9	1.5
283 LUTH--MO SYNOD	11	3 720	4 878	20.6	33.6
353 CHR BRETHREN..	1	20	20	0.1	0.1
443 UN C OF CHRIST	1	269	328*	1.4	2.3
449 UN METHODIST..	10	2 122	2 587*	10.9	17.8
453 UN PRES CH USA	5	1 207	1 471*	6.2	10.1
BLACK HAWK	125	37 697	79 460*	57.6	100.0
019 AMER BAPT USA.	4	1 394	1 691*	1.2	2.1
029 AMER LUTH CH..	15	9 158	12 158	8.8	15.3
053 ASSEMB OF GOD.	4	252	629	0.5	0.8
057 BAPT GEN CONF.	2	354	429*	0.3	0.5
071 BRETHREN (ASH)	2	231	280*	0.2	0.4
081 CATHOLIC......	14	NA	27 136	19.7	34.2
089 CHR & MISS AL.	1	22	37	–	–
093 CHR CH (DISC).	2	774	949	0.7	1.2
097 CHR CHS&CHS CR	3	298	362*	0.3	0.5
105 CHRISTIAN REF.	1	70	116	0.1	0.1
121 CH GOD (ABR)..	1	48	58*	–	0.1
123 CH GOD (ANDER)	1	16	48	–	0.1
151 L-D SAINTS....	1	NA	599	0.4	0.8
157 CH OF BRETHREN	2	513	622*	0.5	0.8
165 CH OF NAZARENE	2	145	222	0.2	0.3
167 CHS OF CHRIST.	2	145	195	0.1	0.2
193 EPISCOPAL.....	2	732	927	0.7	1.2
209 EVAN LUTH SYN.	1	117	163	0.1	0.2
221 FREE METHODIST	1	103	345	0.3	0.4
244 GRACE BRETHREN	1	439	533*	0.4	0.7
263 INT FOURSQ GOS	1	49	59*	–	0.1
270 CONSRV JUDAISM	1	45	55*	–	0.1
281 LUTH CH AMER..	3	1 614	2 105	1.5	2.6
283 LUTH--MO SYNOD	7	3 982	5 581	4.0	7.0
290 METRO COMM CHS	1	20	40	–	0.1
313 N AM BAPT CONF	1	98	119*	0.1	0.1
329 OPEN BIBLE STD	1	220	350	0.3	0.4
335 ORTH PRESB CH.	1	50	61*	–	0.1
353 CHR BRETHREN..	6	300	640	0.5	0.8
371 REF CH IN AM..	3	502	818	0.6	1.0
403 SALVATION ARMY	1	266	3 036	2.2	3.8
413 S.D.A.........	1	155	188*	0.1	0.2
419 SO BAPT CONV..	3	606	735*	0.5	0.9
435 UNITARIAN-UNIV	1	69	84*	0.1	0.1
443 UN C OF CHRIST	3	1 374	1 667*	1.2	2.1
449 UN METHODIST..	19	8 903	10 802*	7.8	13.6
453 UN PRES CH USA	10	4 633	5 621*	4.1	7.1
BOONE	49	9 968	16 009*	61.1	100.0
019 AMER BAPT USA.	2	846	1 008*	3.8	6.3
081 CATHOLIC......	4	NA	2 945	11.2	18.4
089 CHR & MISS AL.	2	113	214	0.8	1.3
093 CHR CH (DISC).	2	568	874	3.3	5.5
123 CH GOD (ANDER)	1	50	150	0.6	0.9
151 L-D SAINTS....	1	NA	200	0.8	1.2
157 CH OF BRETHREN	1	45	54*	0.2	0.3
165 CH OF NAZARENE	1	28	80	0.3	0.5
167 CHS OF CHRIST.	2	63	102	0.4	0.6
193 EPISCOPAL.....	1	73	96	0.4	0.6
201 EVAN COV CH AM	1	9	11*	–	0.1
203 EVAN FREE CH..	2	293	349*	1.3	2.2
221 FREE METHODIST	1	20	66	0.3	0.4
281 LUTH CH AMER..	5	2 044	2 686	10.3	16.8
283 LUTH--MO SYNOD	3	1 566	1 969	7.5	12.3
329 OPEN BIBLE STD	1	170	350	1.3	2.2
353 CHR BRETHREN..	1	60	60	0.2	0.4
363 PRIMITIVE METH	2	95	113*	0.4	0.7
403 SALVATION ARMY	1	84	103	0.4	0.6
413 S.D.A.........	1	27	32*	0.1	0.2
443 UN C OF CHRIST	2	375	447*	1.7	2.8
449 UN METHODIST..	11	3 051	3 637*	13.9	22.7
453 UN PRES CH USA	1	388	463*	1.8	2.9
BREMER	43	13 564	19 530*	78.7	100.0
019 AMER BAPT USA.	1	151	184*	0.7	0.9
029 AMER LUTH CH..	14	7 175	9 363	37.7	47.9
057 BAPT GEN CONF.	1	177	215*	0.9	1.1
081 CATHOLIC......	3	NA	2 270	9.1	11.6
193 EPISCOPAL.....	1	48	61	0.2	0.3
197 EVAN CH OF NA.	1	107	107	0.4	0.5
283 LUTH--MO SYNOD	8	1 998	2 579	10.4	13.2

County and Denomination	Number of churches	Communicant, confirmed, full members	Total adherents Number	Percent of total population	Percent of total adherents
313 N AM BAPT CONF	1	99	120*	0.5	0.6
353 CHR BRETHREN..	1	20	20	0.1	0.1
443 UN C OF CHRIST	5	1 518	1 847*	7.4	9.5
449 UN METHODIST..	7	2 271	2 764*	11.1	14.2
BUCHANAN	44	7 115	16 057*	70.1	100.0
019 AMER BAPT USA.	4	422	528*	2.3	3.3
029 AMER LUTH CH..	4	1 651	2 184	9.5	13.6
081 CATHOLIC......	8	NA	7 060	30.8	44.0
097 CHR CHS&CHS CR	1	80	100*	0.4	0.6
193 EPISCOPAL.....	1	62	70	0.3	0.4
263 INT FOURSQ GOS	1	104	130*	0.6	0.8
283 LUTH--MO SYNOD	2	542	663	2.9	4.1
323 OLD ORD AMISH.	6	780	976*	4.3	6.1
413 S.D.A.........	1	15	19*	0.1	0.1
443 UN C OF CHRIST	1	154	193*	0.8	1.2
449 UN METHODIST..	9	2 213	2 768*	12.1	17.2
453 UN PRES CH USA	6	1 092	1 366*	6.0	8.5
BUENA VISTA	46	11 325	16 913*	81.4	100.0
019 AMER BAPT USA.	1	312	372*	1.8	2.2
029 AMER LUTH CH..	6	1 543	2 067	9.9	12.2
053 ASSEMB OF GOD.	2	154	254	1.2	1.5
081 CATHOLIC......	2	NA	2 940	14.2	17.4
097 CHR CHS&CHS CR	2	300	358*	1.7	2.1
121 CH GOD (ABR)..	1	17	20*	0.1	0.1
165 CH OF NAZARENE	1	23	0	–	–
193 EPISCOPAL.....	1	40	47	0.2	0.3
201 EVAN COV CH AM	1	174	208*	1.0	1.2
203 EVAN FREE CH..	1	153	183*	0.9	1.1
281 LUTH CH AMER..	4	1 493	1 802	8.7	10.7
283 LUTH--MO SYNOD	7	2 518	3 176	15.3	18.8
419 SO BAPT CONV..	1	12	14*	0.1	0.1
443 UN C OF CHRIST	3	336	401*	1.9	2.4
449 UN METHODIST..	7	2 955	3 526*	17.0	20.8
453 UN PRES CH USA	3	1 295	1 545*	7.4	9.1
BUTLER	47	8 564	12 522*	70.9	100.0
029 AMER LUTH CH..	6	2 603	3 439	19.5	27.5
081 CATHOLIC......	6	NA	1 216	6.9	9.7
097 CHR CHS&CHS CR	2	120	146*	0.8	1.2
105 CHRISTIAN REF.	2	319	490	2.8	3.9
157 CH OF BRETHREN	1	72	88*	0.5	0.7
181 CONSRV CONGR..	1	292	356*	2.0	2.8
209 EVAN LUTH SYN.	1	137	165	0.9	1.3
215 EVAN METH CH..	1	16	20*	0.1	0.2
283 LUTH--MO SYNOD	1	108	138	0.8	1.1
313 N AM BAPT CONF	2	428	522*	3.0	4.2
353 CHR BRETHREN..	2	40	40	0.2	0.3
371 REF CH IN AM..	6	1 148	1 901	10.8	15.2
443 UN C OF CHRIST	3	760	927*	5.2	7.4
449 UN METHODIST..	8	1 737	2 118*	12.0	16.9
453 UN PRES CH USA	5	784	956*	5.4	7.6
CALHOUN	43	8 354	13 124*	96.9	100.0
019 AMER BAPT USA.	1	187	223*	1.6	1.7
029 AMER LUTH CH..	3	1 645	2 149	15.9	16.4
053 ASSEMB OF GOD.	1	25	25	0.2	0.2
057 BAPT GEN CONF.	1	34	41*	0.3	0.3
081 CATHOLIC......	5	NA	2 715	20.0	20.7
093 CHR CH (DISC).	2	463	651	4.8	5.0
097 CHR CHS&CHS CR	1	160	191*	1.4	1.5
165 CH OF NAZARENE	1	13	0	–	–
167 CHS OF CHRIST.	1	12	15	0.1	0.1
201 EVAN COV CH AM	1	206	246*	1.8	1.9
281 LUTH CH AMER..	2	439	558	4.1	4.3
283 LUTH--MO SYNOD	5	1 422	1 839	13.6	14.0
285 MENNONITE CH..	1	270	322*	2.4	2.5
413 S.D.A.........	1	26	31*	0.2	0.2
419 SO BAPT CONV..	1	57	68*	0.5	0.5
443 UN C OF CHRIST	3	368	439*	3.2	3.3
449 UN METHODIST..	10	2 265	2 702*	20.0	20.6
453 UN PRES CH USA	3	762	909*	6.7	6.9
CARROLL	39	5 804	22 736*	99.1	100.0
029 AMER LUTH CH..	2	396	525	2.3	2.3
053 ASSEMB OF GOD.	1	36	90	0.4	0.4
081 CATHOLIC......	15	NA	15 294	66.6	67.3
093 CHR CH (DISC).	1	115	299	1.3	1.3
193 EPISCOPAL.....	1	38	77	0.3	0.3
221 FREE METHODIST	1	6	30	0.1	0.1
226 FRIENDS-USA...	3	173	213*	0.9	0.9
283 LUTH--MO SYNOD	5	2 216	2 725	11.9	12.0
449 UN METHODIST..	5	1 919	2 367*	10.3	10.4
453 UN PRES CH USA	5	905	1 116*	4.9	4.9
CASS	44	8 221	12 154*	71.8	100.0
019 AMER BAPT USA.	1	197	236*	1.4	1.9
029 AMER LUTH CH..	1	776	1 029	6.1	8.5
053 ASSEMB OF GOD.	1	56	100	0.6	0.8
081 CATHOLIC......	5	NA	1 893	11.2	15.6
093 CHR CH (DISC).	3	553	688	4.1	5.7
097 CHR CHS&CHS CR	4	665	796*	4.7	6.5
165 CH OF NAZARENE	1	28	102	0.6	0.8
167 CHS OF CHRIST.	1	20	60	0.4	0.5
193 EPISCOPAL.....	1	12	12	0.1	0.1
281 LUTH CH AMER..	1	214	278	1.6	2.3
283 LUTH--MO SYNOD	3	1 328	1 786	10.5	14.7
353 CHR BRETHREN..	4	295	295	1.7	2.4

NA— Not applicable   *Total adherents estimated from known number of communicant, confirmed, full members.   —Represents a percent less than 0.1.   Percentages may not total due to rounding.

Table 4. Churches and Church Membership by County and Denomination: 1980

County and Denomination	Number of churches	Communicant, confirmed, full members	Total adherents Number	Percent of total population	Percent of total adherents
413 S.D.A.........	1	48	57*	0.3	0.5
443 UN C OF CHRIST	5	818	979*	5.8	8.1
449 UN METHODIST..	11	2 730	3 267*	19.3	26.9
453 UN PRES CH USA	1	481	576*	3.4	4.7
CEDAR	**31**	**7 318**	**10 392***	**55.8**	**100.0**
019 AMER BAPT USA.	1	70	85*	0.5	0.8
029 AMER LUTH CH..	1	135	167	0.9	1.6
081 CATHOLIC......	2	NA	1 360	7.3	13.1
157 CH OF BRETHREN	1	15	18*	0.1	0.2
193 EPISCOPAL.....	1	112	169	0.9	1.6
226 FRIENDS-USA...	2	199	242*	1.3	2.3
263 INT FOURSQ GOS	1	50	61*	0.3	0.6
281 LUTH CH AMER..	2	577	814	4.4	7.8
283 LUTH--MO SYNOD	3	1 057	1 280	6.9	12.3
443 UN C OF CHRIST	4	2 149	2 609*	14.0	25.1
449 UN METHODIST..	9	2 526	3 067*	16.5	29.5
453 UN PRES CH USA	4	428	520*	2.8	5.0
CERRO GORDO	**63**	**19 046**	**34 750***	**71.7**	**100.0**
019 AMER BAPT USA.	3	542	647*	1.3	1.9
029 AMER LUTH CH..	7	6 924	9 260	19.1	26.6
053 ASSEMB OF GOD.	1	104	190	0.4	0.5
081 CATHOLIC......	8	NA	9 818	20.3	28.3
089 CHR & MISS AL.	1	50	96	0.2	0.3
093 CHR CH (DISC).	2	603	846	1.7	2.4
097 CHR CHS&CHS CR	2	130	155*	0.3	0.4
105 CHRISTIAN REF.	1	62	115	0.2	0.3
127 CH GOD (CLEVE)	1	7	8*	-	-
151 L-D SAINTS....	1	NA	155	0.3	0.4
165 CH OF NAZARENE	1	59	112	0.2	0.3
167 CHS OF CHRIST.	1	24	34	0.1	0.1
175 CONGR CHR CHS.	2	478	570*	1.2	1.6
179 CONSRV BAPT...	1	30	36*	0.1	0.1
193 EPISCOPAL.....	2	251	486	1.0	1.4
201 EVAN COV CH AM	1	117	140*	0.3	0.4
203 EVAN FREE CH..	1	99	118*	0.2	0.3
209 EVAN LUTH SYN.	1	163	200	0.4	0.6
221 FREE METHODIST	1	40	213	0.4	0.6
281 LUTH CH AMER..	1	491	574	1.2	1.7
283 LUTH--MO SYNOD	2	963	1 249	2.6	3.6
329 OPEN BIBLE STD	2	167	240	0.5	0.7
353 CHR BRETHREN..	1	20	20	-	0.1
371 REF CH IN AM..	1	253	482	1.0	1.4
403 SALVATION ARMY	1	135	225	0.5	0.6
413 S.D.A.........	1	103	123*	0.3	0.4
419 SO BAPT CONV..	1	221	264*	0.5	0.8
435 UNITARIAN-UNIV	1	13	16*	-	-
443 UN C OF CHRIST	1	516	616*	1.3	1.8
449 UN METHODIST..	11	5 848	6 977*	14.4	20.1
453 UN PRES CH USA	1	555	662*	1.4	1.9
469 WELS.........	1	78	103	0.2	0.3
CHEROKEE	**32**	**6 876**	**12 373***	**76.2**	**100.0**
019 AMER BAPT USA.	2	157	189*	1.2	1.5
053 ASSEMB OF GOD.	1	35	47	0.3	0.4
081 CATHOLIC......	5	NA	3 739	23.0	30.2
093 CHR CH (DISC).	1	45	69	0.4	0.6
097 CHR CHS&CHS CR	1	375	452*	2.8	3.7
203 EVAN FREE CH..	2	234	282*	1.7	2.3
281 LUTH CH AMER..	2	1 017	1 354	8.3	10.9
283 LUTH--MO SYNOD	5	1 543	2 057	12.7	16.6
413 S.D.A.........	1	16	19*	0.1	0.2
419 SO BAPT CONV..	1	22	27*	0.2	0.2
443 UN C OF CHRIST	1	165	199*	1.2	1.6
449 UN METHODIST..	7	2 480	2 990*	18.4	24.2
453 UN PRES CH USA	3	787	949*	5.8	7.7
CHICKASAW	**34**	**5 102**	**12 957***	**83.9**	**100.0**
019 AMER BAPT USA.	2	337	415*	2.7	3.2
029 AMER LUTH CH..	6	1 937	2 579	16.7	19.9
057 BAPT GEN CONF.	1	23	28*	0.2	0.2
081 CATHOLIC......	9	NA	6 418	41.6	49.5
157 CH OF BRETHREN	1	189	233*	1.5	1.8
209 EVAN LUTH SYN.	3	393	542	3.5	4.2
283 LUTH--MO SYNOD	1	260	326	2.1	2.5
443 UN C OF CHRIST	5	909	1 119*	7.2	8.6
449 UN METHODIST..	6	1 054	1 297*	8.4	10.0
CLARKE	**20**	**2 465**	**4 047***	**47.0**	**100.0**
053 ASSEMB OF GOD.	1	97	256	3.0	6.3
081 CATHOLIC......	2	NA	596	6.9	14.7
093 CHR CH (DISC).	2	435	654	7.6	16.2
097 CHR CHS&CHS CR	1	350	423*	4.9	10.5
107 CHRISTIAN UN..	1	32	43	0.5	1.1
151 L-D SAINTS....	1	NA	157	1.8	3.9
167 CHS OF CHRIST.	1	64	71	0.8	1.8
226 FRIENDS-USA...	1	49	59*	0.7	1.5
263 INT FOURSQ GOS	1	43	52*	0.6	1.3
283 LUTH--MO SYNOD	1	247	348	4.0	8.6
413 S.D.A.........	1	55	67*	0.8	1.7
419 SO BAPT CONV..	1	45	54*	0.6	1.3
449 UN METHODIST..	5	974	1 178*	13.7	29.1
453 UN PRES CH USA	1	74	89*	1.0	2.2
CLAY	**35**	**8 284**	**13 377***	**68.3**	**100.0**
019 AMER BAPT USA.	1	103	125*	0.6	0.9
029 AMER LUTH CH..	3	1 630	2 077	10.6	15.5
053 ASSEMB OF GOD.	1	70	125	0.6	0.9
081 CATHOLIC......	3	NA	2 629	13.4	19.7
093 CHR CH (DISC).	1	392	536	2.7	4.0
151 L-D SAINTS....	1	NA	111	0.6	0.8
167 CHS OF CHRIST.	1	30	41	0.2	0.3
175 CONGR CHR CHS.	2	936	1 139*	5.8	8.5
193 EPISCOPAL.....	1	69	88	0.4	0.7
281 LUTH CH AMER..	1	305	441	2.3	3.3
283 LUTH--MO SYNOD	3	1 084	1 422	7.3	10.6
371 REF CH IN AM..	2	374	639	3.3	4.8
413 S.D.A.........	1	64	78*	0.4	0.6
419 SO BAPT CONV..	1	44	54*	0.3	0.4
443 UN C OF CHRIST	3	250	304*	1.6	2.3
449 UN METHODIST..	10	2 933	3 568*	18.2	26.7
CLAYTON	**43**	**7 949**	**15 268***	**72.4**	**100.0**
029 AMER LUTH CH..	17	4 238	5 330	25.3	34.9
081 CATHOLIC......	10	NA	5 323	25.2	34.9
203 EVAN FREE CH..	1	31	38*	0.2	0.2
281 LUTH CH AMER..	3	759	983	4.7	6.4
283 LUTH--MO SYNOD	2	251	324	1.5	2.1
353 CHR BRETHREN..	1	70	100	0.5	0.7
443 UN C OF CHRIST	2	945	1 152*	5.5	7.5
449 UN METHODIST..	7	1 655	2 018*	9.6	13.2
CLINTON	**77**	**17 531**	**35 089***	**61.4**	**100.0**
019 AMER BAPT USA.	2	622	759*	1.3	2.2
029 AMER LUTH CH..	10	4 165	5 415	9.5	15.4
053 ASSEMB OF GOD.	1	34	80	0.1	0.2
081 CATHOLIC......	17	NA	12 137	21.2	34.6
097 CHR CHS&CHS CR	2	280	342*	0.6	1.0
123 CH GOD (ANDER)	2	63	189	0.3	0.5
151 L-D SAINTS....	1	NA	246	0.4	0.7
165 CH OF NAZARENE	2	77	260	0.5	0.7
167 CHS OF CHRIST.	1	50	75	0.1	0.2
193 EPISCOPAL.....	2	550	936	1.6	2.7
203 EVAN FREE CH..	1	101	123*	0.2	0.4
263 INT FOURSQ GOS	2	150	183*	0.3	0.5
281 LUTH CH AMER..	4	1 549	1 983	3.5	5.7
283 LUTH--MO SYNOD	5	2 927	3 770	6.6	10.7
371 REF CH IN AM..	1	181	288	0.5	0.8
403 SALVATION ARMY	1	119	158	0.3	0.5
413 S.D.A.........	1	26	32*	0.1	0.1
419 SO BAPT CONV..	2	341	416*	0.7	1.2
443 UN C OF CHRIST	4	1 658	2 024*	3.5	5.8
449 UN METHODIST..	11	3 258	3 978*	7.0	11.3
453 UN PRES CH USA	4	1 354	1 653*	2.9	4.7
469 WELS.........	1	26	42	0.1	0.1
CRAWFORD	**38**	**8 875**	**15 003***	**79.2**	**100.0**
019 AMER BAPT USA.	1	147	180*	1.0	1.2
053 ASSEMB OF GOD.	1	24	87	0.5	0.6
057 BAPT GEN CONF.	2	240	294*	1.6	2.0
081 CATHOLIC......	6	NA	3 876	20.5	25.8
167 CHS OF CHRIST.	1	22	22	0.1	0.1
193 EPISCOPAL.....	1	50	50	0.3	0.3
281 LUTH CH AMER..	1	168	209	1.1	1.4
283 LUTH--MO SYNOD	12	5 327	6 733	35.6	44.9
419 SO BAPT CONV..	1	71	87*	0.5	0.6
443 UN C OF CHRIST	3	640	785*	4.1	5.2
449 UN METHODIST..	5	1 216	1 491*	7.9	9.9
453 UN PRES CH USA	4	970	1 189*	6.3	7.9
DALLAS	**51**	**8 279**	**14 598***	**49.5**	**100.0**
029 AMER LUTH CH..	3	595	818	2.8	5.6
053 ASSEMB OF GOD.	2	97	268	0.9	1.8
075 BRETHREN IN CR	1	57	86	0.3	0.6
081 CATHOLIC......	5	NA	2 857	9.7	19.6
093 CHR CH (DISC).	6	902	2 244	7.6	15.4
097 CHR CHS&CHS CR	2	110	135*	0.5	0.9
127 CH GOD (CLEVE)	1	8	10*	-	0.1
157 CH OF BRETHREN	2	503	616*	2.1	4.2
193 EPISCOPAL.....	1	125	223	0.8	1.5
244 GRACE BRETHREN	1	129	158*	0.5	1.1
283 LUTH--MO SYNOD	4	858	1 186	4.0	8.1
329 OPEN BIBLE STD	1	21	25	0.1	0.2
413 S.D.A.........	1	8	10*	-	0.1
419 SO BAPT CONV..	2	79	97*	0.3	0.7
449 UN METHODIST..	16	4 251	5 208*	17.6	35.7
453 UN PRES CH USA	3	536	657*	2.2	4.5
DAVIS	**22**	**2 535**	**3 808***	**41.8**	**100.0**
019 AMER BAPT USA.	1	167	203*	2.2	5.3
029 AMER LUTH CH..	1	76	125	1.4	3.3
081 CATHOLIC......	1	NA	225	2.5	5.9
093 CHR CH (DISC).	5	921	1 509	16.6	39.6
097 CHR CHS&CHS CR	2	70	85*	0.9	2.2
165 CH OF NAZARENE	1	63	126	1.4	3.3
167 CHS OF CHRIST.	3	36	36	0.4	0.9
287 MENN GEN CONF.	1	147	189	2.1	5.0
329 OPEN BIBLE STD	1	100	150	1.6	3.9
413 S.D.A.........	1	11	13*	0.1	0.3
449 UN METHODIST..	5	944	1 147*	12.6	30.1
DECATUR	**31**	**2 063**	**3 239***	**33.1**	**100.0**
019 AMER BAPT USA.	2	130	154*	1.6	4.8
053 ASSEMB OF GOD.	4	152	275	2.8	8.5
061 BEACHY AMISH..	1	71	84*	0.9	2.6
081 CATHOLIC......	2	NA	544	5.6	16.8
093 CHR CH (DISC).	1	40	120	1.2	3.7

NA—Not applicable
*Total adherents estimated from known number of communicant, confirmed, full members.
—Represents a percent less than 0.1.
Percentages may not total due to rounding.

Table 4. Churches and Church Membership by County and Denomination: 1980

County and Denomination	Number of churches	Communicant, confirmed, full members	Total adherents Number	Percent of total population	Percent of total adherents
097 CHR CHS&CHS CR	2	150	178*	1.8	5.5
157 CH OF BRETHREN	1	28	33*	0.3	1.0
165 CH OF NAZARENE	1	16	70	0.7	2.2
167 CHS OF CHRIST.	2	75	94	1.0	2.9
179 CONSRV BAPT...	1	70	83*	0.8	2.6
244 GRACE BRETHREN	1	99	117*	1.2	3.6
283 LUTH--MO SYNOD	1	117	167	1.7	5.2
419 SO BAPT CONV.	2	282	334*	3.4	10.3
449 UN METHODIST.	7	632	748*	7.6	23.1
453 UN PRES CH USA	3	201	238*	2.4	7.3
DELAWARE	35	4 586	13 564*	71.6	100.0
029 AMER LUTH CH..	6	1 166	1 500	7.9	11.1
053 ASSEMB OF GOD.	1	59	124	0.7	0.9
081 CATHOLIC......	11	NA	7 729	40.8	57.0
179 CONSRV BAPT...	1	110	137*	0.7	1.0
283 LUTH--MO SYNOD	2	363	483	2.6	3.6
353 CHR BRETHREN..	1	20	20	0.1	0.1
443 UN C OF CHRIST	3	384	478*	2.5	3.5
449 UN METHODIST.	8	2 077	2 586*	13.7	19.1
453 UN PRES CH USA	2	407	507*	2.7	3.7
DES MOINES	63	14 700	25 484*	55.2	100.0
019 AMER BAPT USA.	3	598	725*	1.6	2.8
029 AMER LUTH CH..	2	494	723	1.6	2.8
053 ASSEMB OF GOD.	1	273	592	1.3	2.3
057 BAPT GEN CONF.	1	276	335*	0.7	1.3
081 CATHOLIC......	7	NA	6 103	13.2	23.9
093 CHR CH (DISC).	1	709	888	1.9	3.5
097 CHR CHS&CHS CR	1	185	224*	0.5	0.9
127 CH GOD (CLEVE)	1	17	21*	-	0.1
151 L-D SAINTS....	1	NA	219	0.5	0.9
165 CH OF NAZARENE	2	279	632	1.4	2.5
167 CHS OF CHRIST.	1	50	64	0.1	0.3
175 CONGR CHR CHS.	1	401	486*	1.1	1.9
193 EPISCOPAL.....	1	272	334	0.7	1.3
221 FREE METHODIST	1	33	90	0.2	0.4
263 INT FOURSQ GOS	1	18	22*	-	0.1
271 REFORM JUDAISM	1	10	12*	-	-
281 LUTH CH AMER..	4	2 319	3 250	7.0	12.8
283 LUTH--MO SYNOD	1	69	101	0.2	0.4
313 N AM BAPT CONF	1	765	927*	2.0	3.6
329 OPEN BIBLE STD	2	270	375	0.8	1.5
403 SALVATION ARMY	1	86	162	0.4	0.6
413 S.D.A.........	2	298	361*	0.8	1.4
419 SO BAPT CONV..	1	308	373*	0.8	1.5
435 UNITARIAN-UNIV	1	55	67*	0.1	0.3
443 UN C OF CHRIST	7	1 767	2 142*	4.6	8.4
449 UN METHODIST.	12	3 899	4 726*	10.2	18.5
453 UN PRES CH USA	4	1 181	1 432*	3.1	5.6
469 WELS.........	1	68	98	0.2	0.4
DICKINSON	26	5 815	9 368*	59.9	100.0
019 AMER BAPT USA.	1	65	78*	0.5	0.8
029 AMER LUTH CH..	3	1 117	1 488	9.5	15.9
053 ASSEMB OF GOD.	1	17	57	0.4	0.6
057 BAPT GEN CONF.	1	78	94*	0.6	1.0
081 CATHOLIC......	2	NA	2 171	13.9	23.2
193 EPISCOPAL.....	1	81	104	0.7	1.1
203 EVAN FREE CH..	1	74	89*	0.6	1.0
226 FRIENDS-USA...	1	63	76*	0.5	0.8
283 LUTH--MO SYNOD	3	983	1 202*	7.7	12.8
413 S.D.A.........	1	20	24*	0.2	0.3
443 UN C OF CHRIST	1	264	317*	2.0	3.4
449 UN METHODIST.	8	2 429	2 918*	18.7	31.1
453 UN PRES CH USA	2	624	750*	4.8	8.0
DUBUQUE	75	9 891	73 650*	78.6	100.0
019 AMER BAPT USA.	1	74	91*	0.1	0.1
029 AMER LUTH CH..	8	2 506	3 656	3.9	5.0
053 ASSEMB OF GOD.	1	70	200	0.2	0.3
081 CATHOLIC......	33	NA	59 886	63.9	81.3
151 L-D SAINTS....	1	NA	314	0.3	0.4
165 CH OF NAZARENE	1	46	75	0.1	0.1
167 CHS OF CHRIST.	1	63	110	0.1	0.1
193 EPISCOPAL.....	1	420	500	0.5	0.7
203 EVAN FREE CH..	1	80	99*	0.1	0.1
271 REFORM JUDAISM	1	78	96*	0.1	0.1
281 LUTH CH AMER..	1	250	311	0.3	0.4
283 LUTH--MO SYNOD	3	932	1 416	1.5	1.9
403 SALVATION ARMY	1	63	349	0.4	0.5
413 S.D.A.........	1	53	65*	0.1	0.1
419 SO BAPT CONV..	1	83	102*	0.1	0.1
443 UN C OF CHRIST	4	1 085	1 337*	1.4	1.8
449 UN METHODIST..	9	2 419	2 981*	3.2	4.0
453 UN PRES CH USA	5	1 639	2 020*	2.2	2.7
469 WELS.........	1	30	42	-	0.1
EMMET	29	7 203	11 704*	87.8	100.0
029 AMER LUTH CH..	9	2 953	3 893	29.2	33.3
057 BAPT GEN CONF.	1	181	220*	1.6	1.9
081 CATHOLIC......	2	NA	2 420	18.1	20.7
093 CHR CH (DISC).	1	330	384	2.9	3.3
165 CH OF NAZARENE	1	38	97	0.7	0.8
167 CHS OF CHRIST.	1	29	48	0.4	0.4
193 EPISCOPAL.....	1	20	28	0.2	0.2
221 FREE METHODIST	1	25	138	1.0	1.2
281 LUTH CH AMER..	2	475	609	4.6	5.2
283 LUTH--MO SYNOD	1	490	624	4.7	5.3
413 S.D.A.........	1	26	32*	0.2	0.3

County and Denomination	Number of churches	Communicant, confirmed, full members	Total adherents Number	Percent of total population	Percent of total adherents
449 UN METHODIST..	4	1 442	1 757*	13.2	15.0
453 UN PRES CH USA	4	1 194	1 454*	10.9	12.4
FAYETTE	57	10 810	20 273*	79.5	100.0
019 AMER BAPT USA.	2	393	476*	1.9	2.3
029 AMER LUTH CH..	14	4 836	6 371	25.0	31.4
053 ASSEMB OF GOD.	1	35	46	0.2	0.2
081 CATHOLIC......	8	NA	6 448	25.3	31.8
097 CHR CHS&CHS CR	2	260	315*	1.2	1.6
151 L-D SAINTS....	1	NA	93	0.4	0.5
163 CH OF LUTH BR.	1	130	130	0.5	0.6
165 CH OF NAZARENE	1	24	55	0.2	0.3
167 CHS OF CHRIST.	1	21	34	0.1	0.2
193 EPISCOPAL.....	2	46	63	0.2	0.3
283 LUTH--MO SYNOD	4	785	1 057	4.1	5.2
313 N AM BAPT CONF	1	167	202*	0.8	1.0
353 CHR BRETHREN..	1	20	20	0.1	0.1
413 S.D.A.........	1	45	55*	0.2	0.3
443 UN C OF CHRIST	1	5	6*	-	-
449 UN METHODIST..	13	2 860	3 468*	13.6	17.1
453 UN PRES CH USA	4	1 183	1 434*	5.6	7.1
FLOYD	27	6 915	12 222*	62.4	100.0
019 AMER BAPT USA.	2	284	345*	1.8	2.8
029 AMER LUTH CH..	5	2 488	3 233	16.5	26.5
053 ASSEMB OF GOD.	1	25	44	0.2	0.4
081 CATHOLIC......	3	NA	3 423	17.5	28.0
089 CH & MISS AL.	1	88	218	1.1	1.8
093 CHR CH (DISC).	2	217	324	1.7	2.7
193 EPISCOPAL.....	1	59	70	0.4	0.6
413 S.D.A.........	1	17	21*	0.1	0.2
443 UN C OF CHRIST	2	653	794*	4.1	6.5
449 UN METHODIST..	7	2 797	3 400*	17.3	27.8
453 UN PRES CH USA	1	186	226*	1.2	1.8
469 WELS.........	1	101	124	0.6	1.0
FRANKLIN	35	7 427	9 753*	74.8	100.0
019 AMER BAPT USA.	2	162	194*	1.5	2.0
029 AMER LUTH CH..	3	1 133	1 444	11.1	14.8
053 ASSEMB OF GOD.	1	23	20	0.2	0.2
057 BAPT GEN CONF.	1	96	115*	0.9	1.2
081 CATHOLIC......	2	NA	660	5.1	6.8
093 CHR CH (DISC).	1	174	224	1.7	2.3
097 CHR CHS&CHS CR	1	310	372*	2.9	3.8
281 LUTH CH AMER..	1	187	224	1.7	2.3
283 LUTH--MO SYNOD	2	1 002	1 183	9.1	12.1
313 N AM BAPT CONF	1	107	128*	1.0	1.3
353 CHR BRETHREN..	1	20	20	0.2	0.2
371 REF CH IN AM.	2	371	564	4.3	5.8
413 S.D.A.........	1	32	38*	0.3	0.4
443 UN C OF CHRIST	4	1 509	1 809*	13.9	18.5
449 UN METHODIST..	12	2 301	2 758*	21.2	28.3
FREMONT	29	2 861	4 237*	45.1	100.0
019 AMER BAPT USA.	1	278	336*	3.6	7.9
053 ASSEMB OF GOD.	1	25	86	0.9	2.0
081 CATHOLIC......	2	NA	490	5.2	11.6
097 CHR CHS&CHS CR	4	230	278*	3.0	6.6
127 CH GOD (CLEVE)	1	14	17*	0.2	0.4
151 L-D SAINTS....	1	NA	151	1.6	3.6
165 CH OF NAZARENE	1	77	161	1.7	3.8
221 FREE METHODIST	1	26	42	0.4	1.0
281 LUTH CH AMER..	1	74	96	1.0	2.3
283 LUTH--MO SYNOD	1	?	?	?	?
443 UN C OF CHRIST	3	170	205*	2.2	4.8
449 UN METHODIST..	9	1 618	1 954*	20.8	46.1
453 UN PRES CH USA	3	349	421*	4.5	9.9
GREENE	29	5 223	8 963*	74.0	100.0
019 AMER BAPT USA.	2	470	564*	4.7	6.3
081 CATHOLIC......	6	NA	2 162	17.8	24.1
093 CHR CH (DISC).	1	318	697	5.8	7.8
097 CHR CHS&CHS CR	2	161	193*	1.6	2.2
127 CH GOD (CLEVE)	1	42	50*	0.4	0.6
167 CHS OF CHRIST.	1	50	85	0.7	0.9
203 EVAN FREE CH..	1	23	28*	0.2	0.3
283 LUTH--MO SYNOD	2	530	724	6.0	8.1
329 OPEN BIBLE STD	1	250	403	3.3	4.5
449 UN METHODIST..	9	2 887	3 466*	28.6	38.7
453 UN PRES CH USA	3	492	591*	4.9	6.6
GRUNDY	31	7 306	10 046*	69.9	100.0
029 AMER LUTH CH..	2	412	559	3.9	5.6
053 ASSEMB OF GOD.	1	52	86	0.6	0.9
081 CATHOLIC......	3	NA	714	5.0	7.1
105 CHRISTIAN REF.	4	650	930	6.5	9.3
157 CH OF BRETHREN	1	220	266*	1.9	2.6
281 LUTH CH AMER..	2	608	799	5.6	8.0
283 LUTH--MO SYNOD	2	367	475	3.3	4.7
371 REF CH IN AM.	3	713	1 030	7.2	10.3
443 UN C OF CHRIST	2	696	843*	5.9	8.4
449 UN METHODIST..	5	1 864	2 257*	15.7	22.5
453 UN PRES CH USA	6	1 724	2 087*	14.5	20.8
GUTHRIE	36	4 530	7 426*	62.0	100.0
081 CATHOLIC......	6	NA	1 709	14.3	23.0
093 CHR CH (DISC).	3	575	884	7.4	11.9
097 CHR CHS&CHS CR	4	220	263*	2.2	3.5

NA—Not applicable   *Total adherents estimated from known number of communicant, confirmed, full members.   —Represents a percent less than 0.1.   Percentages may not total due to rounding.

Table 4. Churches and Church Membership by County and Denomination: 1980

County and Denomination	Number of churches	Communicant, confirmed, full members	Total adherents		
			Number	Percent of total population	Percent of total adherents
157 CH OF BRETHREN	1	157	188*	1.6	2.5
167 CHS OF CHRIST.	1	25	48	0.4	0.6
283 LUTH--MO SYNOD	4	624	826	6.9	11.1
329 OPEN BIBLE STD	1	20	25	0.2	0.3
413 S.D.A.	1	38	45*	0.4	0.6
443 UN C OF CHRIST	2	383	459*	3.8	6.2
449 UN METHODIST..	12	2 362	2 828*	23.6	38.1
453 UN PRES CH USA	1	126	151*	1.3	2.0
HAMILTON	**43**	**9 658**	**13 738***	**76.9**	**100.0**
019 AMER BAPT USA.	1	290	349*	2.0	2.5
029 AMER LUTH CH..	6	1 999	2 456	13.7	17.9
053 ASSEMB OF GOD.	2	151	121	0.7	0.9
057 BAPT GEN CONF.	1	135	162*	0.9	1.2
081 CATHOLIC......	3	NA	1 608	9.0	11.7
089 CHR & MISS AL.	1	102	202	1.1	1.5
093 CHR CH (DISC).	1	145	255	1.4	1.9
097 CHR CHS&CHS CR	1	700	842*	4.7	6.1
121 CH GOD (ABR)..	1	16	19*	0.1	0.1
163 CH OF LUTH BR.	1	12	26	0.1	0.2
167 CHS OF CHRIST.	1	6	8	–	0.1
193 EPISCOPAL.....	1	47	87	0.5	0.6
201 EVAN COV CH AM	1	6	7*	–	0.1
281 LUTH CH AMER..	2	1 396	1 902	10.6	13.8
283 LUTH--MO SYNOD	1	535	709	4.0	5.2
353 CHR BRETHREN..	3	60	105	0.6	0.8
435 UNITARIAN-UNIV	1	10	12*	0.1	0.1
443 UN C OF CHRIST	3	928	1 116*	6.2	8.1
449 UN METHODIST..	11	2 699	3 246*	18.2	23.6
453 UN PRES CH USA	1	421	506*	2.8	3.7
HANCOCK	**34**	**6 488**	**10 718***	**77.5**	**100.0**
019 AMER BAPT USA.	1	91	111*	0.8	1.0
029 AMER LUTH CH..	7	1 432	1 947	14.1	18.2
081 CATHOLIC......	5	NA	2 331	16.9	21.7
105 CHRISTIAN REF.	3	416	586	4.2	5.5
165 CH OF NAZARENE	1	162	242	1.7	2.3
203 EVAN FREE CH..	2	137	167*	1.2	1.6
283 LUTH--MO SYNOD	2	632	915	6.6	8.5
443 UN C OF CHRIST	3	853	1 042*	7.5	9.7
449 UN METHODIST..	8	2 467	3 013*	21.8	28.1
453 UN PRES CH USA	2	298	364*	2.6	3.4
HARDIN	**44**	**11 003**	**15 872***	**72.9**	**100.0**
019 AMER BAPT USA.	1	178	212*	1.0	1.3
029 AMER LUTH CH..	3	651	845	3.9	5.3
053 ASSEMB OF GOD.	1	27	60	0.3	0.4
081 CATHOLIC......	3	NA	2 111	9.7	13.3
093 CHR CH (DISC).	3	361	606	2.8	3.8
097 CHR CHS&CHS CR	1	75	89*	0.4	0.6
105 CHRISTIAN REF.	2	190	288	1.3	1.8
165 CH OF NAZARENE	1	35	70	0.3	0.4
193 EPISCOPAL.....	1	47	45	0.2	0.3
220 FREE LUTHERAN.	1	164	203	0.9	1.3
226 FRIENDS-USA...	1	397	472*	2.2	3.0
281 LUTH CH AMER..	1	343	440	2.0	2.8
283 LUTH--MO SYNOD	5	2 188	2 780	12.8	17.5
313 N AM BAPT CONF	1	237	282*	1.3	1.8
329 OPEN BIBLE STD	1	85	100	0.5	0.6
371 REF CH IN AM..	1	237	383	1.8	2.4
443 UN C OF CHRIST	5	1 537	1 829*	8.4	11.5
449 UN METHODIST..	8	3 486	4 147*	19.0	26.1
453 UN PRES CH USA	4	765	910*	4.2	5.7
HARRISON	**38**	**5 266**	**9 163***	**56.0**	**100.0**
019 AMER BAPT USA.	1	34	41*	0.3	0.4
053 ASSEMB OF GOD.	1	54	200	1.2	2.2
081 CATHOLIC......	5	NA	2 329	14.2	25.4
093 CHR CH (DISC).	1	189	323	2.0	3.5
097 CHR CHS&CHS CR	6	1 120	1 361*	8.3	14.9
165 CH OF NAZARENE	1	41	91	0.6	1.0
179 CONSRV BAPT...	1	60	73*	0.4	0.8
181 CONSRV CONGR..	1	171	208*	1.3	2.3
281 LUTH CH AMER..	3	625	837	5.1	9.1
283 LUTH--MO SYNOD	4	820	1 086	6.6	11.9
413 S.D.A.	1	11	13*	0.1	0.1
449 UN METHODIST..	10	1 866	2 267*	13.9	24.7
453 UN PRES CH USA	3	275	334*	2.0	3.6
HENRY	**37**	**6 777**	**9 975***	**52.8**	**100.0**
019 AMER BAPT USA.	4	727	874*	4.6	8.8
053 ASSEMB OF GOD.	1	37	55	0.3	0.6
081 CATHOLIC......	1	NA	1 500	7.9	15.0
097 CHR CHS&CHS CR	2	75	90*	0.5	0.9
165 CH OF NAZARENE	1	35	90	0.5	0.9
175 CONGR CHR CHS.	1	61	73*	0.4	0.7
185 CUMBER PRESB..	1	86	189	1.0	1.9
193 EPISCOPAL.....	1	239	277	1.5	2.8
203 EVAN FREE CH..	1	45	54*	0.3	0.5
226 FRIENDS-USA...	2	265	319*	1.7	3.2
281 LUTH CH AMER..	1	420	525	2.8	5.3
283 LUTH--MO SYNOD	1	231	312	1.7	3.1
285 MENNONITE CH..	1	105	126*	0.7	1.3
287 MENN GEN CONF.	1	261	353	1.9	3.5
291 MISSIONARY CH.	2	52	63	0.3	0.6
329 OPEN BIBLE STD	2	205	345	1.8	3.5
419 SO BAPT CONV.	1	28	34*	0.2	0.3
443 UN C OF CHRIST	1	197	237*	1.3	2.4
449 UN METHODIST..	9	2 751	3 308*	17.5	33.2
453 UN PRES CH USA	3	957	1 151*	6.1	11.5
HOWARD	**28**	**3 584**	**10 407***	**93.6**	**100.0**
019 AMER BAPT USA.	1	90	108*	1.0	1.0
029 AMER LUTH CH..	6	1 889	2 443	22.0	23.5
053 ASSEMB OF GOD.	1	20	36	0.3	0.3
081 CATHOLIC......	9	NA	5 874	52.9	56.4
283 LUTH--MO SYNOD	1	144	210	1.9	2.0
443 UN C OF CHRIST	1	102	123*	1.1	1.2
449 UN METHODIST..	7	1 164	1 402*	12.6	13.5
453 UN PRES CH USA	2	175	211*	1.9	2.0
HUMBOLDT	**22**	**6 607**	**9 690***	**79.1**	**100.0**
019 AMER BAPT USA.	1	104	125*	1.0	1.3
029 AMER LUTH CH..	8	2 782	3 549	29.0	36.6
057 BAPT GEN CONF.	1	319	383*	3.1	4.0
081 CATHOLIC......	2	NA	1 449	11.8	15.0
283 LUTH--MO SYNOD	2	764	1 018	8.3	10.5
413 S.D.A.	1	44	53*	0.4	0.5
443 UN C OF CHRIST	1	356	427*	3.5	4.4
449 UN METHODIST..	6	2 238	2 686*	21.9	27.7
IDA	**14**	**4 847**	**7 097***	**79.7**	**100.0**
029 AMER LUTH CH..	1	900	1 117	12.5	15.7
081 CATHOLIC......	2	NA	1 045	11.7	14.7
203 EVAN FREE CH..	1	98	118*	1.3	1.7
283 LUTH--MO SYNOD	3	1 668	2 192	24.6	30.9
449 UN METHODIST..	5	1 598	1 923*	21.6	27.1
453 UN PRES CH USA	2	583	702*	7.9	9.9
IOWA	**43**	**6 934**	**11 610***	**75.2**	**100.0**
015 AMANA CH SOC..	7	733	789	5.1	6.8
029 AMER LUTH CH..	1	118	165	1.1	1.4
081 CATHOLIC......	6	NA	2 585	16.8	22.3
093 CHR CH (DISC).	1	150	300	1.9	2.6
121 CH GOD (ABR)..	1	37	44*	0.3	0.4
165 CH OF NAZARENE	1	31	133	0.9	1.1
203 EVAN FREE CH..	1	95	114*	0.7	1.0
244 GRACE BRETHREN	1	66	79*	0.5	0.7
283 LUTH--MO SYNOD	8	2 705	3 804	24.7	32.8
285 MENNONITE CH..	2	403	483*	3.1	4.2
313 N AM BAPT CONF	1	118	142*	0.9	1.2
443 UN C OF CHRIST	1	173	207*	1.3	1.8
449 UN METHODIST..	10	1 685	2 021*	13.1	17.4
453 UN PRES CH USA	2	620	744*	4.8	6.4
JACKSON	**37**	**5 148**	**15 964***	**70.9**	**100.0**
019 AMER BAPT USA.	1	136	168*	0.7	1.1
029 AMER LUTH CH..	8	2 937	4 017	17.9	25.2
053 ASSEMB OF GOD.	1	48	206	0.9	1.3
081 CATHOLIC......	14	NA	9 014	40.1	56.5
193 EPISCOPAL.....	1	152	244	1.1	1.5
443 UN C OF CHRIST	3	438	541*	2.4	3.4
449 UN METHODIST..	5	930	1 148*	5.1	7.2
453 UN PRES CH USA	4	507	626*	2.8	3.9
JASPER	**67**	**12 782**	**21 050***	**57.8**	**100.0**
019 AMER BAPT USA.	1	413	500*	1.4	2.4
029 AMER LUTH CH..	2	211	274	0.8	1.3
053 ASSEMB OF GOD.	2	282	616	1.7	2.9
081 CATHOLIC......	3	NA	2 515	6.9	11.9
089 CHR & MISS AL.	1	213	483	1.3	2.3
093 CHR CH (DISC).	6	885	1 736	4.8	8.2
105 CHRISTIAN REF.	3	883	1 544	4.2	7.3
127 CH GOD (CLEVE)	2	65	79*	0.2	0.4
151 L-D SAINTS....	1	NA	80	0.2	0.4
157 CH OF BRETHREN	1	146	177*	0.5	0.8
165 CH OF NAZARENE	1	157	325	0.9	1.5
167 CHS OF CHRIST.	4	85	108	0.3	0.5
179 CONSRV BAPT...	1	125	151*	0.4	0.7
193 EPISCOPAL.....	1	136	252	0.7	1.2
203 EVAN FREE CH..	1	58	70*	0.2	0.3
221 FREE METHODIST	1	1	12	–	0.1
226 FRIENDS-USA...	1	237	287*	0.8	1.4
263 INT FOURSQ GOS	1	266	322*	0.9	1.5
281 LUTH CH AMER..	2	1 068	1 376	3.8	6.5
283 LUTH--MO SYNOD	1	286	422	1.2	2.0
371 REF CH IN AM..	3	783	1 421	3.9	6.8
403 SALVATION ARMY	1	142	612	1.7	2.9
413 S.D.A.	1	69	84*	0.2	0.4
419 SO BAPT CONV.	1	44	53*	0.1	0.3
443 UN C OF CHRIST	5	1 139	1 380*	3.8	6.6
449 UN METHODIST..	14	3 901	4 725*	13.0	22.4
453 UN PRES CH USA	4	1 152	1 395*	3.8	6.6
469 WELS..........	1	35	51	0.1	0.2
JEFFERSON	**29**	**4 832**	**8 020***	**49.2**	**100.0**
019 AMER BAPT USA.	3	406	482*	3.0	6.0
029 AMER LUTH CH..	1	197	229	1.4	2.9
081 CATHOLIC......	2	NA	1 848	11.3	23.0
093 CHR CH (DISC).	2	552	676	4.1	8.4
097 CHR CHS&CHS CR	1	50	59*	0.4	0.7
157 CH OF BRETHREN	1	67	80*	0.5	1.0
165 CH OF NAZARENE	1	96	146	0.9	1.8
193 EPISCOPAL.....	1	30	42	0.3	0.5
221 FREE METHODIST	2	104	414	2.5	5.2
226 FRIENDS-USA...	2	176	209*	1.3	2.6
263 INT FOURSQ GOS	1	130	154*	0.9	1.9
281 LUTH CH AMER..	2	777	995	6.1	12.4
283 LUTH--MO SYNOD	1	107	143	0.9	1.8

NA— Not applicable   *Total adherents estimated from known number of communicant, confirmed, full members.   —Represents a percent less than 0.1.   Percentages may not total due to rounding.

Table 4. Churches and Church Membership by County and Denomination: 1980

County and Denomination	Number of churches	Communicant, confirmed, full members	Total adherents		
			Number	Percent of total population	Percent of total adherents
413 S.D.A.........	1	47	56*	0.3	0.7
443 UN C OF CHRIST	1	53	63*	0.4	0.8
449 UN METHODIST..	6	1 620	1 925*	11.8	24.0
453 UN PRES CH USA	1	420	499*	3.1	6.2
JOHNSON	**70**	**14 388**	**29 094***	**35.6**	**100.0**
019 AMER BAPT USA.	1	345	403*	0.5	1.4
029 AMER LUTH CH..	2	1 196	1 552	1.9	5.3
053 ASSEMB OF GOD.	1	74	150	0.2	0.5
057 BAPT GEN CONF.	1	233	272*	0.3	0.9
061 BEACHY AMISH..	1	114	133*	0.2	0.5
081 CATHOLIC......	13	NA	10 995	13.5	37.8
093 CHR CH (DISC).	1	241	281	0.3	1.0
097 CHR CHS&CHS CR	2	127	148*	0.2	0.5
105 CHRISTIAN REF.	1	116	183	0.2	0.6
151 L-D SAINTS....	1	NA	340	0.4	1.2
165 CH OF NAZARENE	1	157	326	0.4	1.1
167 CHS OF CHRIST.	1	92	125	0.2	0.4
193 EPISCOPAL.....	2	604	777	1.0	2.7
221 FREE METHODIST	1	58	126	0.2	0.4
226 FRIENDS-USA...	1	40	47*	0.1	0.2
263 INT FOURSQ GOS	1	27	32*	–	0.1
270 CONSRV JUDAISM	1	70	82*	0.1	0.3
281 LUTH CH AMER..	1	977	1 346	1.6	4.6
283 LUTH--MO SYNOD	2	790	1 106	1.4	3.8
285 MENNONITE CH..	8	1 487	1 739*	2.1	6.0
291 MISSIONARY CH.	1	36	40	–	0.1
323 OLD ORD AMISH.	7	910	1 064*	1.3	3.7
413 S.D.A.........	1	57	67*	0.1	0.2
419 SO BAPT CONV..	1	242	283*	0.3	1.0
435 UNITARIAN-UNIV	1	264	309*	0.4	1.1
443 UN C OF CHRIST	3	456	533*	0.7	1.8
449 UN METHODIST..	10	3 787	4 428*	5.4	15.2
453 UN PRES CH USA	3	1 888	2 207*	2.7	7.6
JONES	**37**	**7 022**	**12 451***	**61.0**	**100.0**
019 AMER BAPT USA.	1	170	207*	1.0	1.7
029 AMER LUTH CH..	6	2 590	3 522	17.3	28.3
053 ASSEMB OF GOD.	1	33	58	0.3	0.5
081 CATHOLIC......	6	NA	3 537	17.3	28.4
097 CHR CHS&CHS CR	1	150	182*	0.9	1.5
165 CH OF NAZARENE	1	39	54	0.3	0.4
193 EPISCOPAL.....	1	17	31	0.2	0.2
281 LUTH CH AMER..	1	197	251	1.2	2.0
283 LUTH--MO SYNOD	1	401	444	2.2	3.6
419 SO BAPT CONV..	1	156	190*	0.9	1.5
443 UN C OF CHRIST	3	624	759*	3.7	6.1
449 UN METHODIST..	9	1 801	2 190*	10.7	17.6
453 UN PRES CH USA	5	844	1 026*	5.0	8.2
KEOKUK	**49**	**4 334**	**8 568***	**66.3**	**100.0**
019 AMER BAPT USA.	3	318	380*	2.9	4.4
029 AMER LUTH CH..	1	69	81	0.6	0.9
053 ASSEMB OF GOD.	1	42	70	0.5	0.8
081 CATHOLIC......	8	NA	3 226	25.0	37.7
093 CHR CH (DISC).	7	454	645	5.0	7.5
097 CHR CHS&CHS CR	1	28	33*	0.3	0.4
107 CHRISTIAN UN..	1	39	39	0.3	0.5
157 CH OF BRETHREN	2	203	243*	1.9	2.8
226 FRIENDS-USA...	4	253	302*	2.3	3.5
283 LUTH--MO SYNOD	2	136	212	1.6	2.5
285 MENNONITE CH..	1	70	84*	0.7	1.0
449 UN METHODIST..	13	2 138	2 555*	19.8	29.8
453 UN PRES CH USA	5	584	698*	5.4	8.1
KOSSUTH	**48**	**9 297**	**20 309***	**92.8**	**100.0**
019 AMER BAPT USA.	1	80	98*	0.4	0.5
029 AMER LUTH CH..	4	1 004	1 224	5.6	6.0
053 ASSEMB OF GOD.	1	22	45	0.2	0.2
057 BAPT GEN CONF.	1	144	176*	0.8	0.9
081 CATHOLIC......	8	NA	8 768	40.1	43.2
165 CH OF NAZARENE	1	?	?	?	?
179 CONSRV BAPT...	1	100	122*	0.6	0.6
193 EPISCOPAL.....	1	131	155	0.7	0.8
203 EVAN FREE CH..	1	40	49*	0.2	0.2
281 LUTH CH AMER..	2	876	1 140	5.2	5.6
283 LUTH--MO SYNOD	7	2 349	2 923	13.4	14.4
329 OPEN BIBLE STD	1	60	75	0.3	0.4
371 REF CH IN AM..	1	330	449	2.1	2.2
443 UN C OF CHRIST	2	530	648*	3.0	3.2
449 UN METHODIST..	11	2 625	3 208*	14.7	15.8
453 UN PRES CH USA	5	1 006	1 229*	5.6	6.1
LEE	**63**	**11 083**	**26 201***	**60.8**	**100.0**
019 AMER BAPT USA.	2	999	1 206*	2.8	4.6
053 ASSEMB OF GOD.	3	543	884	2.1	3.4
081 CATHOLIC......	11	NA	11 753	27.3	44.9
093 CHR CH (DISC).	2	717	1 251	2.9	4.8
097 CHR CHS&CHS CR	1	320	386*	0.9	1.5
133 CH GOD(7TH)DEN	1	1	1*	–	–
165 CH OF NAZARENE	3	278	618	1.4	2.4
167 CHS OF CHRIST.	1	40	51	0.1	0.2
193 EPISCOPAL.....	2	410	442	1.0	1.7
203 EVAN FREE CH..	1	60	72*	0.2	0.3
281 LUTH CH AMER..	2	642	818	1.9	3.1
283 LUTH--MO SYNOD	2	193	261	0.6	1.0
285 MENNONITE CH..	1	15	18*	–	0.1
287 MENN GEN CONF.	1	164	202	0.5	0.8
403 SALVATION ARMY	1	88	257	0.6	1.0
413 S.D.A.........	2	106	128*	0.3	0.5
419 SO BAPT CONV..	2	439	530*	1.2	2.0
443 UN C OF CHRIST	6	1 934	2 334*	5.4	8.9
449 UN METHODIST..	10	2 877	3 472*	8.1	13.3
453 UN PRES CH USA	9	1 257	1 517*	3.5	5.8
LINN	**150**	**42 325**	**93 268***	**54.9**	**100.0**
019 AMER BAPT USA.	3	718	874*	0.5	0.9
029 AMER LUTH CH..	5	2 375	3 334	2.0	3.6
053 ASSEMB OF GOD.	3	285	462	0.3	0.5
057 BAPT GEN CONF.	2	251	306*	0.2	0.3
081 CATHOLIC......	17	NA	33 790	19.9	36.2
089 CHR & MISS AL.	1	53	132	0.1	0.1
093 CHR CH (DISC).	7	1 900	2 993	1.8	3.2
097 CHR CHS&CHS CR	4	302	368*	0.2	0.4
105 CHRISTIAN REF.	1	80	154	0.1	0.2
123 CH GOD (ANDER)	1	96	288	0.2	0.3
127 CH GOD (CLEVE)	1	36	44*	–	–
133 CH GOD(7TH)DEN	1	40	49*	–	0.1
151 L-D SAINTS....	2	NA	747	0.4	0.8
157 CH OF BRETHREN	2	107	130*	0.1	0.1
165 CH OF NAZARENE	3	648	1 844	1.1	2.0
167 CHS OF CHRIST.	4	337	480	0.3	0.5
175 CONGR CHR CHS.	1	110	134*	0.1	0.1
179 CONSRV BAPT...	3	500	609*	0.4	0.7
193 EPISCOPAL.....	3	935	1 222	0.7	1.3
201 EVAN COV CH AM	1	241	293*	0.2	0.3
203 EVAN FREE CH..	1	68	83*	–	0.1
208 EVAN LUTH ASSN	2	416	477	0.3	0.5
221 FREE METHODIST	3	96	366	0.2	0.4
226 FRIENDS-USA...	1	101	123*	0.1	0.1
244 GRACE BRETHREN	1	68	83*	–	0.1
263 INT FOURSQ GOS	2	362	441*	0.3	0.5
271 REFORM JUDAISM	1	164	200*	0.1	0.2
281 LUTH CH AMER..	6	4 101	5 852	3.4	6.3
283 LUTH--MO SYNOD	8	4 918	6 645	3.9	7.1
285 MENNONITE CH..	1	9	11*	–	–
290 METRO COMM CHS	0	10	20	–	–
313 N AM BAPT CONF	1	127	155*	0.1	0.2
329 OPEN BIBLE STD	1	150	250	0.1	0.3
353 CHR BRETHREN..	2	45	70	–	0.1
371 REF CH IN AM..	1	125	296	0.2	0.3
381 REF PRES-EVAN.	1	56	76	–	0.1
383 REF PRES OF NA	1	35	55	–	0.1
403 SALVATION ARMY	1	162	2 630	1.5	2.8
413 S.D.A.........	1	290	353*	0.2	0.4
419 SO BAPT CONV..	1	656	798*	0.5	0.9
435 UNITARIAN-UNIV	1	300	365*	0.2	0.4
443 UN C OF CHRIST	4	1 405	1 710*	1.0	1.8
449 UN METHODIST..	28	12 412	15 108*	8.9	16.2
453 UN PRES CH USA	15	7 043	8 573*	5.0	9.2
469 WELS..........	1	192	275	0.2	0.3
LOUISA	**20**	**3 123**	**4 349***	**36.1**	**100.0**
081 CATHOLIC......	2	NA	391	3.2	9.0
165 CH OF NAZARENE	1	20	45	0.4	1.0
221 FREE METHODIST	1	22	105	0.9	2.4
283 LUTH--MO SYNOD	1	84	129	1.1	3.0
383 REF PRES OF NA	2	136	161	1.3	3.7
419 SO BAPT CONV..	1	?	?	?	?
449 UN METHODIST..	7	1 990	2 447*	20.3	56.3
453 UN PRES CH USA	5	871	1 071*	8.9	24.6
LUCAS	**21**	**3 179**	**4 491***	**43.5**	**100.0**
019 AMER BAPT USA.	2	520	623*	6.0	13.9
053 ASSEMB OF GOD.	3	74	135	1.3	3.0
081 CATHOLIC......	1	NA	240	2.3	5.3
093 CHR CH (DISC).	2	359	552	5.4	12.3
107 CHRISTIAN UN..	2	68	92	0.9	2.0
165 CH OF NAZARENE	1	183	381	3.7	8.5
193 EPISCOPAL.....	1	54	60	0.6	1.3
281 LUTH CH AMER..	1	352	528	5.1	11.8
449 UN METHODIST..	6	1 331	1 595*	15.5	35.5
453 UN PRES CH USA	2	238	285*	2.8	6.3
LYON	**36**	**6 127**	**10 009***	**77.6**	**100.0**
029 AMER LUTH CH..	5	1 429	1 731	13.4	17.3
053 ASSEMB OF GOD.	1	42	60	0.5	0.6
081 CATHOLIC......	3	NA	1 419	11.0	14.2
093 CHR CH (DISC).	1	63	80	0.6	0.8
105 CHRISTIAN REF.	3	535	927	7.2	9.3
201 EVAN COV CH AM	1	55	68*	0.5	0.7
283 LUTH--MO SYNOD	2	447	613	4.8	6.1
313 N AM BAPT CONF	3	367	453*	3.5	4.5
369 PROT REF CHS..	1	101	208	1.6	2.1
371 REF CH IN AM..	6	1 270	2 206	17.1	22.0
443 UN C OF CHRIST	2	278	343*	2.7	3.4
449 UN METHODIST..	4	597	737*	5.7	7.4
453 UN PRES CH USA	4	943	1 164*	9.0	11.6
MADISON	**33**	**4 484**	**6 584***	**52.3**	**100.0**
029 AMER LUTH CH..	1	153	202	1.6	3.1
081 CATHOLIC......	2	NA	645	5.1	9.8
089 CHR & MISS AL.	1	18	51	0.4	0.8
093 CHR CH (DISC).	3	388	779	6.2	11.8
097 CHR CHS&CHS CR	1	120	146*	1.2	2.2
107 CHRISTIAN UN..	1	45	62	0.5	0.9
165 CH OF NAZARENE	1	43	123	1.0	1.9
193 EPISCOPAL.....	1	15	15	0.1	0.2
226 FRIENDS-USA...	3	471	574*	4.6	8.7
263 INT FOURSQ GOS	1	60	73*	0.6	1.1

NA—Not applicable   *Total adherents estimated from known number of communicant, confirmed, full members.   —Represents a percent less than 0.1.   Percentages may not total due to rounding.

Table 4. Churches and Church Membership by County and Denomination: 1980

County and Denomination	Number of churches	Communicant, confirmed, full members	Total adherents Number	Total adherents Percent of total population	Total adherents Percent of total adherents
283 LUTH--MO SYNOD	1	291	375	3.0	5.7
353 CHR BRETHREN..	1	60	100	0.8	1.5
413 S.D.A.........	1	53	65*	0.5	1.0
419 SO BAPT CONV..	1	215	262*	2.1	4.0
443 UN C OF CHRIST	1	111	135*	1.1	2.1
449 UN METHODIST..	10	2 069	2 523*	20.0	38.3
453 UN PRES CH USA	3	372	454*	3.6	6.9
MAHASKA	46	8 062	12 931*	57.5	100.0
019 AMER BAPT USA.	2	172	207*	0.9	1.6
053 ASSEMB OF GOD.	2	413	615	2.7	4.8
081 CATHOLIC......	1	NA	921	4.1	7.1
089 CHR & MISS AL.	1	20	40	0.2	0.3
093 CHR CH (DISC).	3	789	1 211	5.4	9.4
097 CHR CHS&CHS CR	2	146	176*	0.8	1.4
105 CHRISTIAN REF.	6	1 169	1 916	8.5	14.8
151 L-D SAINTS....	1	NA	138	0.6	1.1
165 CH OF NAZARENE	2	491	1 261	5.6	9.8
167 CHS OF CHRIST.	2	80	102	0.5	0.8
193 EPISCOPAL.....	1	140	308	1.4	2.4
197 EVAN CH OF NA.	1	53	53	0.2	0.4
221 FREE METHODIST	1	53	144	0.6	1.1
226 FRIENDS-USA...	2	419	504*	2.2	3.9
283 LUTH--MO SYNOD	1	240	329	1.5	2.5
329 OPEN BIBLE STD	1	56	75	0.3	0.6
353 CHR BRETHREN..	1	60	100	0.4	0.8
371 REF CH IN AM..	2	733	1 085	4.8	8.4
403 SALVATION ARMY	1	86	182	0.8	1.4
413 S.D.A.........	1	11	13*	0.1	0.1
443 UN C OF CHRIST	1	232	279*	1.2	2.2
449 UN METHODIST..	8	2 205	2 654*	11.8	20.5
453 UN PRES CH USA	2	411	495*	2.2	3.8
469 WELS.........	1	83	123	0.5	1.0
MARION	51	11 544	18 499*	62.4	100.0
019 AMER BAPT USA.	2	921	1 115*	3.8	6.0
029 AMER LUTH CH..	1	162	268	0.9	1.4
053 ASSEMB OF GOD.	3	219	429	1.4	2.3
081 CATHOLIC......	4	NA	2 026	6.8	11.0
093 CHR CH (DISC).	2	229	651	2.2	3.5
097 CHR CHS&CHS CR	3	1 331	1 611*	5.4	8.7
105 CHRISTIAN REF.	5	1 875	2 827	9.5	15.3
127 CH GOD (CLEVE)	2	73	88*	0.3	0.5
165 CH OF NAZARENE	1	120	305	1.0	1.6
167 CHS OF CHRIST.	1	55	60	0.2	0.3
221 FREE METHODIST	1	37	108	0.4	0.6
283 LUTH--MO SYNOD	3	517	702	2.4	3.8
329 OPEN BIBLE STD	2	235	450	1.5	2.4
353 CHR BRETHREN..	1	45	65	0.2	0.4
369 PROT REF CHS..	1	28	49	0.2	0.3
371 REF CH IN AM..	6	2 921	4 384	14.8	23.7
413 S.D.A.........	1	99	120*	0.4	0.6
419 SO BAPT CONV..	1	31	38*	0.1	0.2
449 UN METHODIST..	10	2 457	2 974*	10.0	16.1
453 UN PRES CH USA	1	189	229*	0.8	1.2
MARSHALL	67	15 212	24 378*	58.5	100.0
017 AMER BAPT ASSN	1	50	50	0.1	0.2
019 AMER BAPT USA.	1	1 137	1 377*	3.3	5.6
029 AMER LUTH CH..	3	1 306	1 738	4.2	7.1
053 ASSEMB OF GOD.	1	155	423	1.0	1.7
081 CATHOLIC......	5	NA	4 580	11.0	18.8
093 CHR CH (DISC).	3	802	1 184	2.8	4.9
097 CHR CHS&CHS CR	2	350	424*	1.0	1.7
123 CH GOD (ANDER)	1	19	57	0.1	0.2
151 L-D SAINTS....	1	NA	177	0.4	0.7
157 CH OF BRETHREN	1	203	246*	0.6	1.0
165 CH OF NAZARENE	1	170	351	0.8	1.4
167 CHS OF CHRIST.	1	60	76	0.2	0.3
175 CONGR CHR CHS.	2	993	1 202*	2.9	4.9
193 EPISCOPAL.....	1	248	359	0.9	1.5
197 EVAN CH OF NA.	1	42	42	0.1	0.2
208 EVAN LUTH ASSN	1	97	143	0.3	0.6
226 FRIENDS-USA...	5	962	1 165*	2.8	4.8
263 INT FOURSQ GOS	1	?	?	?	?
270 CONSRV JUDAISM	1	15	18*	-	0.1
281 LUTH CH AMER..	2	527	714	1.7	2.9
283 LUTH--MO SYNOD	4	1 492	1 890	4.5	7.8
329 OPEN BIBLE STD	1	45	50	0.1	0.2
403 SALVATION ARMY	1	162	390	0.9	1.6
413 S.D.A.........	1	100	121*	0.3	0.5
419 SO BAPT CONV..	1	166	201*	0.5	0.8
443 UN C OF CHRIST	8	985	1 193*	2.9	4.9
449 UN METHODIST..	13	4 364	5 284*	12.7	21.7
453 UN PRES CH USA	3	762	923*	2.2	3.8
MILLS	27	4 410	6 224*	46.4	100.0
019 AMER BAPT USA.	3	708	869*	6.5	14.0
029 AMER LUTH CH..	1	445	588	4.4	9.4
081 CATHOLIC......	1	NA	585	4.4	9.4
093 CHR CH (DISC).	1	331	444	3.3	7.1
097 CHR CHS&CHS CR	1	150	184*	1.4	3.0
165 CH OF NAZARENE	1	54	166	1.2	2.7
179 CONSRV BAPT...	1	40	49*	0.4	0.8
193 EPISCOPAL.....	1	14	16	0.1	0.3
283 LUTH--MO SYNOD	2	373	506	3.8	8.1
413 S.D.A.........	1	5	6*	-	0.1
419 SO BAPT CONV..	1	28	34*	0.3	0.5
443 UN C OF CHRIST	2	355	436*	3.3	7.0
449 UN METHODIST..	10	1 880	2 308*	17.2	37.1
453 UN PRES CH USA	1	27	33*	0.2	0.5
MITCHELL	33	5 846	11 406*	92.5	100.0
019 AMER BAPT USA.	3	229	276*	2.2	2.4
029 AMER LUTH CH..	7	2 437	3 109	25.2	27.3
081 CATHOLIC......	6	NA	3 907	31.7	34.3
089 CHR & MISS AL.	1	70	152	1.2	1.3
209 EVAN LUTH SYN.	1	29	42	0.3	0.4
221 FREE METHODIST	1	14	48	0.4	0.4
283 LUTH--MO SYNOD	4	1 359	1 814	14.7	15.9
323 OLD ORD AMISH.	3	390	470*	3.8	4.1
443 UN C OF CHRIST	3	440	530*	4.3	4.6
449 UN METHODIST..	4	878	1 058*	8.6	9.3
MONONA	30	5 105	7 567*	64.7	100.0
029 AMER LUTH CH..	4	1 257	1 627	13.9	21.5
081 CATHOLIC......	4	NA	1 103	9.4	14.6
093 CHR CH (DISC).	1	158	243	2.1	3.2
097 CHR CHS&CHS CR	4	893	1 064*	9.1	14.1
151 L-D SAINTS....	1	NA	44	0.4	0.6
203 EVAN FREE CH..	1	32	38*	0.3	0.5
283 LUTH--MO SYNOD	2	1 096	1 460	12.5	19.3
413 S.D.A.........	2	64	76*	0.7	1.0
443 UN C OF CHRIST	6	732	872*	7.5	11.5
449 UN METHODIST..	5	873	1 040*	8.9	13.7
MONROE	19	2 301	4 825*	52.4	100.0
019 AMER BAPT USA.	1	37	44*	0.5	0.9
081 CATHOLIC......	5	NA	2 007	21.8	41.6
093 CHR CH (DISC).	1	498	635	6.9	13.2
157 CH OF BRETHREN	1	37	44*	0.5	0.9
165 CH OF NAZARENE	1	22	43	0.5	0.9
193 EPISCOPAL.....	1	47	48	0.5	1.0
281 LUTH CH AMER..	1	128	154	1.7	3.2
329 OPEN BIBLE STD	1	36	60	0.7	1.2
353 CHR BRETHREN..	1	10	10	0.1	0.2
413 S.D.A.........	1	56	67*	0.7	1.4
419 SO BAPT CONV..	1	100	120*	1.3	2.5
449 UN METHODIST..	3	1 282	1 536*	16.7	31.8
453 UN PRES CH USA	1	48	57*	0.6	1.2
MONTGOMERY	30	5 787	7 946*	59.2	100.0
001 ADVENT CHR CH.	1	86	103*	0.8	1.3
019 AMER BAPT USA.	1	332	398*	3.0	5.0
053 ASSEMB OF GOD.	1	103	203	1.5	2.6
081 CATHOLIC......	2	NA	628	4.7	7.9
093 CHR CH (DISC).	1	220	384	2.9	4.8
097 CHR CHS&CHS CR	1	37	44*	0.3	0.6
127 CH GOD (CLEVE)	1	38	46*	0.3	0.6
165 CH OF NAZARENE	1	79	207	1.5	2.6
167 CHS OF CHRIST.	1	9	15	0.1	0.2
201 EVAN COV CH AM	2	365	437*	3.3	5.5
281 LUTH CH AMER..	3	1 333	1 641	12.2	20.7
283 LUTH--MO SYNOD	2	204	268	2.0	3.4
443 UN C OF CHRIST	1	134	161*	1.2	2.0
449 UN METHODIST..	8	2 094	2 509*	18.7	31.6
453 UN PRES CH USA	4	753	902*	6.7	11.4
MUSCATINE	63	11 171	21 989*	54.4	100.0
019 AMER BAPT USA.	1	720	888*	2.2	4.0
029 AMER LUTH CH..	3	1 154	1 658	4.1	7.5
053 ASSEMB OF GOD.	3	276	473	1.2	2.2
057 BAPT GEN CONF.	2	78	96*	0.2	0.4
081 CATHOLIC......	7	NA	6 868	17.0	31.2
093 CHR CH (DISC).	3	425	586	1.4	2.7
097 CHR CHS&CHS CR	1	80	99*	0.2	0.5
127 CH GOD (CLEVE)	1	27	33*	0.1	0.2
151 L-D SAINTS....	1	NA	207	0.5	0.9
165 CH OF NAZARENE	1	21	32	0.1	0.1
167 CHS OF CHRIST.	1	148	291	0.7	1.3
179 CONSRV BAPT...	2	290	358*	0.9	1.6
193 EPISCOPAL.....	1	175	302	0.7	1.4
203 EVAN FREE CH..	1	217	268*	0.7	1.2
226 FRIENDS-USA...	2	174	215*	0.5	1.0
281 LUTH CH AMER..	2	1 100	1 431	3.5	6.5
283 LUTH--MO SYNOD	2	620	946	2.3	4.3
285 MENNONITE CH..	1	29	36*	0.1	0.2
403 SALVATION ARMY	1	72	341	0.8	1.6
413 S.D.A.........	2	296	365*	0.9	1.7
419 SO BAPT CONV..	1	45	55*	0.1	0.3
443 UN C OF CHRIST	4	515	635*	1.6	2.9
449 UN METHODIST..	14	3 450	4 254*	10.5	19.3
453 UN PRES CH USA	5	1 259	1 552*	3.8	7.1
O'BRIEN	39	9 983	15 617*	92.0	100.0
029 AMER LUTH CH..	3	1 029	1 325	7.8	8.5
053 ASSEMB OF GOD.	1	151	264	1.6	1.7
081 CATHOLIC......	5	NA	2 138	12.6	13.7
097 CHR CHS&CHS CR	3	283	340*	2.0	2.2
105 CHRISTIAN REF.	4	986	1 666	9.8	10.7
226 FRIENDS-USA...	1	112	135*	0.8	0.9
283 LUTH--MO SYNOD	5	2 120	2 768	16.3	17.7
371 REF CH IN AM..	5	1 694	2 643	15.6	16.9
443 UN C OF CHRIST	4	1 032	1 241*	7.3	7.9
449 UN METHODIST..	6	1 976	2 376*	14.0	15.2
453 UN PRES CH USA	2	600	721*	4.2	4.6
OSCEOLA	21	4 221	6 933*	82.8	100.0
029 AMER LUTH CH..	2	784	993	11.9	14.3
081 CATHOLIC......	2	NA	1 328	15.9	19.2

NA-- Not applicable   *Total adherents estimated from known number of communicant, confirmed, full members.   --Represents a percent less than 0.1.   Percentages may not total due to rounding.

Table 4. Churches and Church Membership by County and Denomination: 1980

County and Denomination	Number of churches	Communicant, confirmed, full members	Total adherents Number	Total adherents Percent of total population	Total adherents Percent of total adherents
105 CHRISTIAN REF.	2	420	716	8.6	10.3
179 CONSRV BAPT...	1	150	182*	2.2	2.6
283 LUTH--MO SYNOD	4	722	905	10.8	13.1
371 REF CH IN AM..	3	533	855	10.2	12.3
443 UN C OF CHRIST	1	134	162*	1.9	2.3
449 UN METHODIST..	4	979	1 187*	14.2	17.1
453 UN PRES CH USA	2	499	605*	7.2	8.7
PAGE	47	8 539	11 912*	62.5	100.0
019 AMER BAPT USA.	2	380	455*	2.4	3.8
053 ASSEMB OF GOD.	2	150	262	1.4	2.2
081 CATHOLIC......	2	NA	1 070	5.6	9.0
093 CHR CH (DISC).	3	569	944	5.0	7.9
097 CHR CHS&CHS CR	1	50	60*	0.3	0.5
127 CH GOD (CLEVE)	1	35	42*	0.2	0.4
165 CH OF NAZARENE	2	131	168	0.9	1.4
193 EPISCOPAL.....	1	105	161	0.8	1.4
201 EVAN COV CH AM	2	195	234*	1.2	2.0
221 FREE METHODIST	1	21	72	0.4	0.6
281 LUTH CH AMER..	4	928	1 131	5.9	9.5
283 LUTH--MO SYNOD	4	1 464	1 914	10.0	16.1
291 MISSIONARY CH.	2	82	97	0.5	0.8
383 REF PRES OF NA	1	40	46	0.2	0.4
419 SO BAPT CONV..	1	244	292*	1.5	2.5
443 UN C OF CHRIST	1	211	253*	1.3	2.1
449 UN METHODIST..	11	2 603	3 117*	16.4	26.2
453 UN PRES CH USA	6	1 331	1 594*	8.4	13.4
PALO ALTO	31	5 551	11 144*	87.6	100.0
029 AMER LUTH CH..	5	1 774	2 316	18.2	20.8
053 ASSEMB OF GOD.	1	67	185	1.5	1.7
081 CATHOLIC......	6	NA	4 099	32.2	36.8
179 CONSRV BAPT...	1	10	12*	0.1	0.1
193 EPISCOPAL.....	1	45	49	0.4	0.4
226 FRIENDS-USA...	1	69	83*	0.7	0.7
283 LUTH--MO SYNOD	5	1 241	1 576	12.4	14.1
353 CHR BRETHREN..	1	20	20	0.2	0.2
413 S.D.A.........	1	37	45*	0.4	0.4
443 UN C OF CHRIST	1	102	123*	1.0	1.1
449 UN METHODIST..	8	2 186	2 636*	20.7	23.7
PLYMOUTH	51	9 194	19 524*	78.9	100.0
019 AMER BAPT USA.	2	212	260*	1.1	1.3
029 AMER LUTH CH..	8	3 308	4 238	17.1	21.7
053 ASSEMB OF GOD.	1	31	52	0.2	0.3
081 CATHOLIC......	11	NA	7 842	31.7	40.2
097 CHR CHS&CHS CR	3	205	251*	1.0	1.3
105 CHRISTIAN REF.	1	132	216	0.9	1.1
157 CH OF BRETHREN	1	63	77*	0.3	0.4
165 CH OF NAZARENE	1	30	102	0.4	0.5
193 EPISCOPAL.....	1	28	37	0.1	0.2
197 EVAN CH OF NA.	1	15	15	0.1	0.1
281 LUTH CH AMER..	2	683	823	3.3	4.2
283 LUTH--MO SYNOD	4	1 529	1 990	8.0	10.2
443 UN C OF CHRIST	3	256	313*	1.3	1.6
449 UN METHODIST..	9	2 188	2 679*	10.8	13.7
453 UN PRES CH USA	3	514	629*	2.5	3.2
POCAHONTAS	29	5 176	10 774*	94.8	100.0
019 AMER BAPT USA.	1	50	60*	0.5	0.6
029 AMER LUTH CH..	5	1 717	2 192	19.3	20.3
081 CATHOLIC......	7	NA	4 248	37.4	39.4
093 CHR CH (DISC).	1	191	350	3.1	3.2
097 CHR CHS&CHS CR	1	50	60*	0.5	0.6
281 LUTH CH AMER..	2	386	529	4.7	4.9
283 LUTH--MO SYNOD	1	57	75	0.7	0.7
443 UN C OF CHRIST	1	143	171*	1.5	1.6
449 UN METHODIST..	7	2 161	2 585*	22.7	24.0
453 UN PRES CH USA	3	421	504*	4.4	4.7
POLK	245	71 558	140 231*	46.3	100.0
005 AME ZION......	1	254	269	0.1	0.2
019 AMER BAPT USA.	6	1 652	1 995*	0.7	1.4
029 AMER LUTH CH..	11	4 891	6 705	2.2	4.8
053 ASSEMB OF GOD.	10	1 330	2 963	1.0	2.1
057 BAPT GEN CONF.	2	481	581*	0.2	0.4
075 BRETHREN IN CR	1	57	86	-	0.1
081 CATHOLIC......	22	NA	43 395	14.3	30.9
089 CHR & MISS AL.	1	31	88	-	0.1
093 CHR CH (DISC).	19	7 202	10 365	3.4	7.4
097 CHR CHS&CHS CR	8	1 673	2 021*	0.7	1.4
105 CHRISTIAN REF.	1	124	208	0.1	0.1
123 CH GOD (ANDER)	1	76	228	0.1	0.2
127 CH GOD (CLEVE)	3	125	151*	-	0.1
151 L-D SAINTS....	2	NA	981	0.3	0.7
157 CH OF BRETHREN	2	358	432*	0.1	0.3
165 CH OF NAZARENE	6	675	1 402	0.5	1.0
167 CHS OF CHRIST.	10	661	844	0.3	0.6
179 CONSRV BAPT...	1	100	121*	-	0.1
193 EPISCOPAL.....	6	2 122	2 906	1.0	2.1
201 EVAN COV CH AM	2	464	560*	0.2	0.4
203 EVAN FREE CH..	7	897	1 083*	0.4	0.8
208 EVAN LUTH ASSN	1	167	223	0.1	0.2
221 FREE METHODIST	2	120	363	0.1	0.3
226 FRIENDS-USA...	2	259	313*	0.1	0.2
244 GRACE BRETHREN	1	?	?	?	?
263 INT FOURSQ GOS	1	218	263*	0.1	0.2
270 CONSRV JUDAISM	1	225	272*	0.1	0.2
271 REFORM JUDAISM	1	554	669*	0.2	0.5
274 LAT EVAN LUTH.	1	100	114	-	0.1

County and Denomination	Number of churches	Communicant, confirmed, full members	Total adherents Number	Total adherents Percent of total population	Total adherents Percent of total adherents
281 LUTH CH AMER..	12	8 442	11 030	3.6	7.9
283 LUTH--MO SYNOD	10	3 526	4 859	1.6	3.5
285 MENNONITE CH..	1	32	39*	-	-
290 METRO COMM CHS	1	48	80	-	0.1
329 OPEN BIBLE STD	13	1 766	3 305	1.1	2.4
353 CHR BRETHREN..	3	230	320	0.1	0.2
371 REF CH IN AM..	3	717	1 266	0.4	0.9
403 SALVATION ARMY	2	468	1 647	0.5	1.2
413 S.D.A.........	2	717	866*	0.3	0.6
419 SO BAPT CONV..	5	1 214	1 466*	0.5	1.0
435 UNITARIAN-UNIV	1	276	333*	0.1	0.2
443 UN C OF CHRIST	6	3 561	4 301*	1.4	3.1
449 UN METHODIST..	37	17 265	20 853*	6.9	14.9
453 UN PRES CH USA	16	8 305	10 031*	3.3	7.2
469 WELS..........	1	183	234	0.1	0.2
POTTAWATTAMIE	84	22 100	39 425*	45.6	100.0
019 AMER BAPT USA.	2	807	988*	1.1	2.5
029 AMER LUTH CH..	6	3 105	4 254	4.9	10.8
053 ASSEMB OF GOD.	3	164	311	0.4	0.8
081 CATHOLIC......	9	NA	9 913	11.5	25.1
093 CHR CH (DISC).	2	510	728	0.8	1.8
097 CHR CHS&CHS CR	5	2 438	2 986*	3.5	7.6
127 CH GOD (CLEVE)	2	161	197*	0.2	0.5
151 L-D SAINTS....	1	NA	758	0.9	1.9
157 CH OF BRETHREN	1	142	174*	0.2	0.4
165 CH OF NAZARENE	3	457	891	1.0	2.3
167 CHS OF CHRIST.	1	144	228	0.3	0.6
179 CONSRV BAPT...	1	250	306*	0.4	0.8
193 EPISCOPAL.....	1	312	339	0.4	0.9
281 LUTH CH AMER..	2	1 216	1 603	1.9	4.1
283 LUTH--MO SYNOD	5	2 043	2 796	3.2	7.1
290 METRO COMM CHS	0	10	20	-	0.1
291 MISSIONARY CH.	1	48	56	0.1	0.1
329 OPEN BIBLE STD	1	60	67	0.1	0.2
403 SALVATION ARMY	1	195	493	0.6	1.3
413 S.D.A.........	1	169	207*	0.2	0.5
419 SO BAPT CONV..	1	248	304*	0.4	0.8
443 UN C OF CHRIST	9	2 325	2 848*	3.3	7.2
449 UN METHODIST..	13	4 469	5 474*	6.3	13.9
453 UN PRES CH USA	12	2 730	3 344*	3.9	8.5
469 WELS..........	1	97	140	0.2	0.4
POWESHIEK	38	6 081	9 780*	50.7	100.0
019 AMER BAPT USA.	1	287	343*	1.8	3.5
029 AMER LUTH CH..	2	660	908	4.7	9.3
053 ASSEMB OF GOD.	1	71	250	1.3	2.6
081 CATHOLIC......	2	NA	2 063	10.7	21.1
093 CHR CH (DISC).	2	83	127	0.7	1.3
097 CHR CHS&CHS CR	2	583	697*	3.6	7.1
157 CH OF BRETHREN	1	50	60*	0.3	0.6
165 CH OF NAZARENE	2	58	178	0.9	1.8
167 CHS OF CHRIST.	4	110	140	0.7	1.4
193 EPISCOPAL.....	1	77	93	0.5	1.0
226 FRIENDS-USA...	3	179	214*	1.1	2.2
283 LUTH--MO SYNOD	1	169	222	1.1	2.3
413 S.D.A.........	1	12	14*	0.1	0.1
443 UN C OF CHRIST	2	535	639*	3.3	6.5
449 UN METHODIST..	7	2 154	2 574*	13.3	26.3
453 UN PRES CH USA	6	1 053	1 258*	6.5	12.9
RINGGOLD	28	2 432	3 510*	57.4	100.0
001 ADVENT CHR CH.	1	11	13*	0.2	0.4
019 AMER BAPT USA.	1	230	272*	4.5	7.7
053 ASSEMB OF GOD.	3	127	153	2.5	4.4
081 CATHOLIC......	2	NA	328	5.4	9.3
093 CHR CH (DISC).	4	407	638	10.4	18.2
097 CHR CHS&CHS CR	1	50	59*	1.0	1.7
221 FREE METHODIST	1	45	171	2.8	4.9
283 LUTH--MO SYNOD	1	75	115	1.9	3.3
413 S.D.A.........	1	22	26*	0.4	0.7
449 UN METHODIST..	10	1 318	1 561*	25.5	44.5
453 UN PRES CH USA	3	147	174*	2.8	5.0
SAC	38	7 625	12 815*	90.8	100.0
019 AMER BAPT USA.	1	268	321*	2.3	2.5
029 AMER LUTH CH..	1	396	503	3.6	3.9
081 CATHOLIC......	6	NA	3 198	22.7	25.0
093 CHR CH (DISC).	1	402	558	4.0	4.4
167 CHS OF CHRIST.	1	10	14	0.1	0.1
193 EPISCOPAL.....	1	23	32	0.2	0.2
221 FREE METHODIST	1	22	150	1.1	1.2
281 LUTH CH AMER..	1	269	382	2.7	3.0
283 LUTH--MO SYNOD	9	2 393	3 053	21.6	23.8
443 UN C OF CHRIST	2	293	351*	2.5	2.7
449 UN METHODIST..	7	2 270	2 720*	19.3	21.2
453 UN PRES CH USA	7	1 279	1 533*	10.9	12.0
SCOTT	108	35 464	79 239*	49.5	100.0
019 AMER BAPT USA.	2	738	911*	0.6	1.1
029 AMER LUTH CH..	2	1 154	1 742	1.1	2.2
053 ASSEMB OF GOD.	6	3 065	6 473	4.0	8.2
057 BAPT GEN CONF.	3	901	1 112*	0.7	1.4
081 CATHOLIC......	17	NA	28 220	17.6	35.6
089 CHR & MISS AL.	1	35	110	0.1	0.1
093 CHR CH (DISC).	3	1 092	1 666	1.0	2.1
097 CHR CHS&CHS CR	3	360	444*	0.3	0.6
105 CHRISTIAN REF.	1	57	108	0.1	0.1
123 CH GOD (ANDER)	1	53	159	0.1	0.2
127 CH GOD (CLEVE)	2	86	106*	0.1	0.1

NA— Not applicable   *Total adherents estimated from known number of communicant, confirmed, full members.   —Represents a percent less than 0.1.   Percentages may not total due to rounding.

Table 4. Churches and Church Membership by County and Denomination: 1980

County and Denomination	Number of churches	Communicant, confirmed, full members	Total adherents Number	Total adherents Percent of total population	Total adherents Percent of total adherents
151 L-D SAINTS....	3	NA	1 107	0.7	1.4
165 CH OF NAZARENE	2	204	383	0.2	0.5
167 CHS OF CHRIST.	3	361	494	0.3	0.6
193 EPISCOPAL.....	3	1 243	1 629	1.0	2.1
203 EVAN FREE CH..	1	38	47*	-	0.1
226 FRIENDS-USA...	2	168	207*	0.1	0.3
244 GRACE BRETHREN	1	93	115*	0.1	0.1
263 INT FOURSQ GOS	1	112	138*	0.1	0.2
271 REFORM JUDAISM	1	416	514*	0.3	0.6
281 LUTH CH AMER..	11	10 200	14 235	8.9	18.0
283 LUTH--MO SYNOD	5	2 858	4 053	2.5	5.1
285 MENNONITE CH..	1	19	23*	-	-
290 METRO COMM CHS	1	20	40	-	0.1
353 CHR BRETHREN..	1	85	125	0.1	0.2
371 REF CH IN AM..	1	92	134	0.1	0.2
403 SALVATION ARMY	1	160	295	0.2	0.4
413 S.D.A.........	1	275	340*	0.2	0.4
419 SO BAPT CONV..	4	1 194	1 474*	0.9	1.9
435 UNITARIAN-UNIV	1	193	238*	0.1	0.3
443 UN C OF CHRIST	3	819	1 011*	0.6	1.3
449 UN METHODIST..	9	4 913	6 065	3.8	7.7
453 UN PRES CH USA	10	4 380	5 407*	3.4	6.8
469 WELS.........	1	80	114	0.1	0.1
SHELBY	**32**	**5 240**	**12 416***	**82.5**	**100.0**
019 AMER BAPT USA.	3	612	746*	5.0	6.0
029 AMER LUTH CH..	5	2 184	2 734	18.2	22.0
053 ASSEMB OF GOD.	1	13	35	0.2	0.3
081 CATHOLIC......	6	NA	5 898	39.2	47.5
097 CHR CHS&CHS CR	2	210	256*	1.7	2.1
165 CH OF NAZARENE	1	7	7	-	0.1
167 CHS OF CHRIST.	2	100	140	0.9	1.1
179 CONSRV BAPT...	1	75	91*	0.6	0.7
193 EPISCOPAL.....	1	33	65	0.4	0.5
413 S.D.A.........	1	27	33*	0.2	0.3
443 UN C OF CHRIST	1	274	334*	2.2	2.7
449 UN METHODIST..	7	1 596	1 944*	12.9	15.7
453 UN PRES CH USA	1	109	133*	0.9	1.1
SIOUX	**64**	**16 017**	**27 090***	**87.9**	**100.0**
019 AMER BAPT USA.	1	258	318*	1.0	1.2
029 AMER LUTH CH..	6	1 099	1 480	4.8	5.5
053 ASSEMB OF GOD.	1	18	22	0.1	0.1
081 CATHOLIC......	6	NA	3 101	10.1	11.4
089 CHR & MISS AL.	1	107	203	0.7	0.7
105 CHRISTIAN REF.	16	4 818	7 916	25.7	29.2
157 CH OF BRETHREN	1	55	68*	0.2	0.3
167 CHS OF CHRIST.	1	18	30	0.1	0.1
283 LUTH--MO SYNOD	4	1 065	1 353	4.4	5.0
369 PROT REF CHS..	1	145	286	0.9	1.1
371 REF CH IN AM..	18	7 056	10 615	34.4	39.2
413 S.D.A.........	1	16	20*	0.1	0.1
443 UN C OF CHRIST	1	86	106*	0.3	0.4
449 UN METHODIST..	2	589	726*	2.4	2.7
453 UN PRES CH USA	4	687	846*	2.7	3.1
STORY	**72**	**21 752**	**38 312***	**53.0**	**100.0**
019 AMER BAPT USA.	1	322	373*	0.5	1.0
029 AMER LUTH CH..	15	7 018	9 092	12.6	23.7
053 ASSEMB OF GOD.	2	270	627	0.9	1.6
081 CATHOLIC......	6	NA	10 309	14.3	26.9
093 CHR CH (DISC).	5	850	1 256	1.7	3.3
097 CHR CHS&CHS CR	1	150	174*	0.2	0.5
105 CHRISTIAN REF.	1	64	109	0.2	0.3
123 CH GOD (ANDER)	1	20	60	0.1	0.2
151 L-D SAINTS....	1	NA	404	0.6	1.1
157 CH OF BRETHREN	1	40	46*	0.1	0.1
165 CH OF NAZARENE	1	81	161	0.2	0.4
167 CHS OF CHRIST.	1	37	55	0.1	0.1
193 EPISCOPAL.....	1	1 050	1 485	2.1	3.9
203 EVAN FREE CH..	1	134	155*	0.2	0.4
209 EVAN LUTH SYN.	1	39	65	0.1	0.2
226 FRIENDS-USA...	1	28	32*	-	0.1
271 REFORM JUDAISM	1	78	90*	0.1	0.2
281 LUTH CH AMER..	2	1 104	1 496	2.1	3.9
283 LUTH--MO SYNOD	2	986	1 333	1.8	3.5
285 MENNONITE CH..	1	13	15*	-	-
287 MENN GEN CONF.	1	14	24	-	0.1
353 CHR BRETHREN..	1	10	10	-	-
413 S.D.A.........	2	400	463*	0.6	1.2
419 SO BAPT CONV..	2	445	516*	0.7	1.3
435 UNITARIAN-UNIV	1	95	110*	0.2	0.3
443 UN C OF CHRIST	1	461	534*	0.7	1.4
449 UN METHODIST..	13	6 093	7 059*	9.8	18.4
453 UN PRES CH USA	5	1 950	2 259*	3.1	5.9
TAMA	**40**	**6 398**	**11 871***	**60.8**	**100.0**
029 AMER LUTH CH..	4	1 178	1 508	7.7	12.7
053 ASSEMB OF GOD.	1	39	93	0.5	0.8
081 CATHOLIC......	8	NA	3 951	20.2	33.3
089 CHR & MISS AL.	1	46	84	0.4	0.7
093 CHR CH (DISC).	1	64	98	0.5	0.8
121 CH GOD (ABR)..	1	20	24*	0.1	0.2
244 GRACE BRETHREN	1	138	167*	0.9	1.4
283 LUTH--MO SYNOD	1	77	87	0.4	0.7
413 S.D.A.........	1	5	6*	-	0.1
443 UN C OF CHRIST	4	1 045	1 266*	6.5	10.7
449 UN METHODIST..	13	3 132	3 795*	19.4	32.0
453 UN PRES CH USA	4	654	792*	4.1	6.7
TAYLOR	**28**	**4 101**	**5 420***	**64.9**	**100.0**

County and Denomination	Number of churches	Communicant, confirmed, full members	Total adherents Number	Total adherents Percent of total population	Total adherents Percent of total adherents
019 AMER BAPT USA.	1	703	836*	10.0	15.4
081 CATHOLIC......	2	NA	425	5.1	7.8
093 CHR CH (DISC).	4	475	655	7.8	12.1
097 CHR CHS&CHS CR	4	470	559*	6.7	10.3
165 CH OF NAZARENE	1	18	40	0.5	0.7
167 CHS OF CHRIST.	1	37	47	0.6	0.9
283 LUTH--MO SYNOD	1	56	72	0.9	1.3
291 MISSIONARY CH.	1	48	57	0.7	1.1
413 S.D.A.........	1	61	73*	0.9	1.3
419 SO BAPT CONV..	1	50	59*	0.7	1.1
449 UN METHODIST..	8	1 898	2 258*	27.0	41.7
453 UN PRES CH USA	3	285	339*	4.1	6.3
UNION	**28**	**4 381**	**7 510***	**54.2**	**100.0**
019 AMER BAPT USA.	1	86	104*	0.8	1.4
053 ASSEMB OF GOD.	2	130	323	2.3	4.3
081 CATHOLIC......	2	NA	1 689	12.2	22.5
093 CHR CH (DISC).	2	418	633	4.6	8.4
097 CHR CHS&CHS CR	1	50	60*	0.4	0.8
123 CH GOD (ANDER)	1	27	81	0.6	1.1
165 CH OF NAZARENE	1	26	112	0.8	1.5
167 CHS OF CHRIST.	1	34	59	0.4	0.8
193 EPISCOPAL.....	1	21	25	0.2	0.3
281 LUTH CH AMER..	1	355	464	3.3	6.2
283 LUTH--MO SYNOD	1	312	433	3.1	5.8
413 S.D.A.........	1	9	11*	0.1	0.1
443 UN C OF CHRIST	3	479	578*	4.2	7.7
449 UN METHODIST..	8	1 978	2 388*	17.2	31.8
453 UN PRES CH USA	2	456	550*	4.0	7.3
VAN BUREN	**30**	**2 964**	**4 062***	**47.1**	**100.0**
019 AMER BAPT USA.	2	243	294*	3.4	7.2
053 ASSEMB OF GOD.	1	29	41	0.5	1.0
081 CATHOLIC......	1	NA	372	4.3	9.2
097 CHR CHS&CHS CR	3	435	527*	6.1	13.0
165 CH OF NAZARENE	1	50	91	1.1	2.2
221 FREE METHODIST	1	15	81	0.9	2.0
283 LUTH--MO SYNOD	1	35	41	0.5	1.0
323 OLD ORD AMISH.	3	390	473*	5.5	11.6
443 UN C OF CHRIST	1	70	85*	1.0	2.1
449 UN METHODIST..	13	1 579	1 914*	22.2	47.1
453 UN PRES CH USA	3	118	143*	1.7	3.5
WAPELLO	**71**	**10 514**	**18 925***	**47.0**	**100.0**
019 AMER BAPT USA.	3	649	776*	1.9	4.1
029 AMER LUTH CH..	1	196	268	0.7	1.4
053 ASSEMB OF GOD.	4	531	674	1.7	3.6
081 CATHOLIC......	5	NA	4 000	9.9	21.1
089 CHR & MISS AL.	1	61	178	0.4	0.9
093 CHR CH (DISC).	6	1 320	2 364	5.9	12.5
097 CHR CHS&CHS CR	2	100	120*	0.3	0.6
123 CH GOD (ANDER)	2	112	336	0.8	1.8
151 L-D SAINTS....	1	NA	150	0.4	0.8
157 CH OF BRETHREN	1	169	202*	0.5	1.1
165 CH OF NAZARENE	3	268	753	1.9	4.0
167 CHS OF CHRIST.	3	90	115	0.3	0.6
193 EPISCOPAL.....	1	167	193	0.5	1.0
203 EVAN FREE CH..	1	30	36*	0.1	0.2
221 FREE METHODIST	1	59	117	0.3	0.6
263 INT FOURSQ GOS	3	364	435*	1.1	2.3
270 CONSRV JUDAISM	1	17	20*	-	0.1
281 LUTH CH AMER..	2	1 087	1 477	3.7	7.8
283 LUTH--MO SYNOD	1	272	353	0.9	1.9
329 OPEN BIBLE STD	3	271	403	1.0	2.1
353 CHR BRETHREN..	2	50	60	0.1	0.3
371 REF CH IN AM..	1	34	70	0.2	0.4
403 SALVATION ARMY	1	131	398	1.0	2.1
413 S.D.A.........	1	125	150*	0.4	0.8
419 SO BAPT CONV..	1	246	294*	0.7	1.6
443 UN C OF CHRIST	4	130	156*	0.4	0.8
449 UN METHODIST..	13	2 920	3 493*	8.7	18.5
453 UN PRES CH USA	3	1 115	1 334*	3.3	7.0
WARREN	**50**	**7 966**	**13 875***	**39.8**	**100.0**
019 AMER BAPT USA.	1	385	481*	1.4	3.5
029 AMER LUTH CH..	3	636	973	2.8	7.0
053 ASSEMB OF GOD.	1	311	565	1.6	4.1
057 BAPT GEN CONF.	1	27	34*	0.1	0.2
081 CATHOLIC......	7	NA	3 194	9.2	23.0
093 CHR CH (DISC).	4	503	760	2.2	5.5
097 CHR CHS&CHS CR	1	50	62*	0.2	0.4
107 CHRISTIAN UN..	3	276	446	1.3	3.2
165 CH OF NAZARENE	2	125	226	0.6	1.6
167 CHS OF CHRIST.	2	52	77	0.2	0.6
226 FRIENDS-USA...	4	408	510*	1.5	3.7
283 LUTH--MO SYNOD	2	466	641	1.8	4.6
413 S.D.A.........	1	27	34*	0.1	0.2
419 SO BAPT CONV..	3	87	109*	0.3	0.8
449 UN METHODIST..	12	3 763	4 701*	13.5	33.9
453 UN PRES CH USA	3	850	1 062*	3.0	7.7
WASHINGTON	**40**	**6 793**	**13 014***	**64.6**	**100.0**
019 AMER BAPT USA.	3	704	854*	4.2	6.6
029 AMER LUTH CH..	3	293	407	2.0	3.1
053 ASSEMB OF GOD.	1	63	118	0.6	0.9
057 BAPT GEN CONF.	1	146	177*	0.9	1.4
081 CATHOLIC......	5	NA	4 472	22.2	34.4
093 CHR CH (DISC).	3	439	681	3.4	5.2
097 CHR CHS&CHS CR	1	30	36*	0.2	0.3
151 L-D SAINTS....	1	NA	39	0.2	0.3

NA—Not applicable   *Total adherents estimated from known number of communicant, confirmed, full members.   —Represents a percent less than 0.1.   Percentages may not total due to rounding.

Table 4. Churches and Church Membership by County and Denomination: 1980

County and Denomination	Number of churches	Communicant, confirmed, full members	Total adherents		
			Number	Percent of total population	Percent of total adherents
165 CH OF NAZARENE	1	36	48	0.2	0.4
226 FRIENDS-USA...	1	20	24*	0.1	0.2
283 LUTH--MO SYNOD	1	52	70	0.3	0.5
285 MENNONITE CH..	5	850	1 031*	5.1	7.9
287 MENN GEN CONF.	1	94	103	0.5	0.8
383 REF PRES OF NA	1	76	112	0.6	0.9
413 S.D.A..........	1	22	27*	0.1	0.2
449 UN METHODIST..	9	2 807	3 406*	16.9	26.2
453 UN PRES CH USA	4	1 161	1 409*	7.0	10.8
WAYNE	33	3 209	4 174*	50.9	100.0
019 AMER BAPT USA.	4	631	744*	9.1	17.8
053 ASSEMB OF GOD.	4	153	263	3.2	6.3
081 CATHOLIC......	1	NA	160	2.0	3.8
093 CHR CH (DISC).	4	292	485	5.9	11.6
097 CHR CHS&CHS CR	4	200	236*	2.9	5.7
165 CH OF NAZARENE	1	10	16	0.2	0.4
167 CHS OF CHRIST.	3	85	103	1.3	2.5
419 SO BAPT CONV..	1	300	354*	4.3	8.5
449 UN METHODIST..	10	1 488	1 754*	21.4	42.0
453 UN PRES CH USA	1	50	59*	0.7	1.4
WEBSTER	70	17 414	33 280*	72.4	100.0
019 AMER BAPT USA.	3	617	742*	1.6	2.2
029 AMER LUTH CH..	7	3 028	3 962	8.6	11.9
053 ASSEMB OF GOD.	1	300	350	0.8	1.1
057 BAPT GEN CONF.	1	97	117*	0.3	0.4
081 CATHOLIC......	11	NA	11 024	24.0	33.1
093 CHR CH (DISC).	2	226	303	0.7	0.9
097 CHR CHS&CHS CR	1	49	59*	0.1	0.2
123 CH GOD (ANDER)	1	10	30	0.1	0.1
151 L-D SAINTS....	1	NA	158	0.3	0.5
157 CH OF BRETHREN	1	56	67*	0.1	0.2
165 CH OF NAZARENE	1	111	233	0.5	0.7
167 CHS OF CHRIST.	1	51	78	0.2	0.2
193 EPISCOPAL.....	1	270	318	0.7	1.0
201 EVAN COV CH AM	3	456	548*	1.2	1.6
203 EVAN FREE CH..	1	150	180*	0.4	0.5
270 CONSRV JUDAISM	1	19	23*	0.1	0.1
281 LUTH CH AMER..	5	1 962	2 394	5.2	7.2
283 LUTH--MO SYNOD	6	3 174	4 349	9.5	13.1
285 MENNONITE CH..	1	53	64*	0.1	0.2
403 SALVATION ARMY	1	115	260	0.6	0.8
413 S.D.A..........	1	14	17*	-	0.1
419 SO BAPT CONV..	1	139	167*	0.4	0.5
443 UN C OF CHRIST	2	570	685*	1.5	2.1
449 UN METHODIST..	13	4 728	5 686*	12.4	17.1
453 UN PRES CH USA	3	1 219	1 466*	3.2	4.4
WINNEBAGO	36	8 589	12 000*	92.2	100.0
029 AMER LUTH CH..	12	5 389	6 753	51.9	56.3
057 BAPT GEN CONF.	2	239	286*	2.2	2.4
081 CATHOLIC......	3	NA	1 331	10.2	11.1
163 CH OF LUTH BR.	3	160	229	1.8	1.9
175 CONGR CHR CHS.	1	139	167*	1.3	1.4
181 CONSRV CONGR..	1	183	219*	1.7	1.8
209 EVAN LUTH SYN.	6	544	671	5.2	5.6
283 LUTH--MO SYNOD	1	?	?	?	?
313 N AM BAPT CONF	1	131	157*	1.2	1.3
371 REF CH IN AM..	1	320	409	3.1	3.4
413 S.D.A..........	1	12	14*	0.1	0.1
449 UN METHODIST..	4	1 472	1 764*	13.6	14.7
WINNESHIEK	39	7 901	16 834*	77.0	100.0
029 AMER LUTH CH..	20	6 580	8 466	38.7	50.3
053 ASSEMB OF GOD.	1	84	150	0.7	0.9
081 CATHOLIC......	8	NA	6 748	30.8	40.1
193 EPISCOPAL.....	1	30	33	0.2	0.2
209 EVAN LUTH SYN.	1	76	82	0.4	0.5
226 FRIENDS-USA...	1	72	86*	0.4	0.5
419 SO BAPT CONV..	1	26	31*	0.1	0.2
443 UN C OF CHRIST	1	170	204*	0.9	1.2
449 UN METHODIST..	4	747	895*	4.1	5.3
453 UN PRES CH USA	1	116	139*	0.6	0.8
WOODBURY	121	31 626	67 978*	67.4	100.0
019 AMER BAPT USA.	3	479	585*	0.6	0.9
029 AMER LUTH CH..	8	5 013	6 813	6.8	10.0
053 ASSEMB OF GOD.	4	941	1 175	1.2	1.7
057 BAPT GEN CONF.	1	76	93*	0.1	0.1
081 CATHOLIC......	16	NA	22 050	21.9	32.4
089 CHR & MISS AL.	1	51	61	0.1	0.1
093 CHR CH (DISC).	4	395	607	0.6	0.9
097 CHR CHS&CHS CR	4	546	667*	0.7	1.0
105 CHRISTIAN REF.	1	91	171	0.2	0.3
123 CH GOD (ANDER)	1	16	48	-	0.1
151 L-D SAINTS....	1	NA	443	0.4	0.7
165 CH OF NAZARENE	4	240	493	0.5	0.7
167 CHS OF CHRIST.	2	93	122	0.1	0.2
179 CONSRV BAPT...	1	140	171*	0.2	0.3
193 EPISCOPAL.....	3	801	1 465	1.5	2.2
197 EVAN CH OF NA.	1	37	37	-	0.1
201 EVAN COV CH AM	2	291	355*	0.4	0.5
203 EVAN FREE CH..	1	82	100*	0.1	0.1
221 FREE METHODIST	1	34	138	0.1	0.2
263 INT FOURSQ GOS	1	67	82*	0.1	0.1
270 CONSRV JUDAISM	1	144	176*	0.2	0.3
271 REFORM JUDAISM	1	256	313*	0.3	0.5
281 LUTH CH AMER..	5	2 868	3 626	3.6	5.3
283 LUTH--MO SYNOD	12	4 750	6 627	6.6	9.7

County and Denomination	Number of churches	Communicant, confirmed, full members	Total adherents		
			Number	Percent of total population	Percent of total adherents
329 OPEN BIBLE STD	2	125	163	0.2	0.2
353 CHR BRETHREN..	2	85	145	0.1	0.2
371 REF CH IN AM..	1	295	516	0.5	0.8
403 SALVATION ARMY	1	296	4 224	4.2	6.2
413 S.D.A..........	2	183	223*	0.2	0.3
419 SO BAPT CONV..	1	217	265*	0.3	0.4
435 UNITARIAN-UNIV	1	103	126*	0.1	0.2
443 UN C OF CHRIST	4	1 211	1 478*	1.5	2.2
449 UN METHODIST..	20	8 397	10 252*	10.2	15.1
453 UN PRES CH USA	7	3 234	3 948*	3.9	5.8
469 WELS..........	1	159	220	0.2	0.3
WORTH	24	5 981	8 035*	88.5	100.0
029 AMER LUTH CH..	13	4 104	5 131	56.5	63.9
081 CATHOLIC......	1	NA	570	6.3	7.1
097 CHR CHS&CHS CR	1	200	240*	2.6	3.0
163 CH OF LUTH BR.	1	45	95	1.0	1.2
209 EVAN LUTH SYN.	2	162	198	2.2	2.5
281 LUTH CH AMER..	1	471	603	6.6	7.5
419 SO BAPT CONV..	1	8	10*	0.1	0.1
449 UN METHODIST..	4	991	1 188*	13.1	14.8
WRIGHT	40	8 323	12 702*	77.8	100.0
019 AMER BAPT USA.	1	98	117*	0.7	0.9
029 AMER LUTH CH..	9	2 959	3 783	23.2	29.8
053 ASSEMB OF GOD.	2	64	116	0.7	0.9
081 CATHOLIC......	3	NA	2 212	13.6	17.4
097 CHR CHS&CHS CR	2	344	411*	2.5	3.2
105 CHRISTIAN REF.	1	112	174	1.1	1.4
163 CH OF LUTH BR.	1	70	70	0.4	0.6
165 CH OF NAZARENE	1	46	140	0.9	1.1
203 EVAN FREE CH..	1	18	22*	0.1	0.2
283 LUTH--MO SYNOD	3	250	324	2.0	2.6
371 REF CH IN AM..	2	274	445	2.7	3.5
443 UN C OF CHRIST	4	903	1 080*	6.6	8.5
449 UN METHODIST..	7	2 565	3 067*	18.8	24.1
453 UN PRES CH USA	3	620	741*	4.5	5.8

KANSAS

County and Denomination	Number of churches	Communicant, confirmed, full members	Total adherents		
			Number	Percent of total population	Percent of total adherents
THE STATE.....	3 869	710 437	1 263 168*	53.5	100.0
ALLEN	42	5 214	8 713*	55.7	100.0
019 AMER BAPT USA.	2	752	908*	5.8	10.4
053 ASSEMB OF GOD.	2	163	252	1.6	2.9
081 CATHOLIC......	2	NA	1 827	11.7	21.0
093 CHR CH (DISC).	1	200	340	2.2	3.9
097 CHR CHS&CHS CR	5	435	525*	3.4	6.0
133 CH GOD(7TH)DEN	1	12	14*	0.1	0.2
151 L-D SAINTS....	1	NA	217	1.4	2.5
165 CH OF NAZARENE	2	224	443	2.8	5.1
167 CHS OF CHRIST.	1	25	30	0.2	0.3
193 EPISCOPAL.....	1	108	129	0.8	1.5
201 EVAN COV CH AM	1	85	103*	0.7	1.2
281 LUTH CH AMER..	1	142	174	1.1	2.0
283 LUTH--MO SYNOD	2	482	627	4.0	7.2
357 PRESB CH US...	4	219	265*	1.7	3.0
413 S.D.A..........	1	120	145*	0.9	1.7
419 SO BAPT CONV..	1	115	139*	0.9	1.6
449 UN METHODIST..	10	1 915	2 313*	14.8	26.5
453 UN PRES CH USA	4	217	262*	1.7	3.0
ANDERSON	31	2 611	5 570*	63.7	100.0
019 AMER BAPT USA.	3	499	598*	6.8	10.7
053 ASSEMB OF GOD.	1	28	50	0.6	0.9
081 CATHOLIC......	5	NA	2 381	27.2	42.7
097 CHR CHS&CHS CR	3	555	665*	7.6	11.9
157 CH OF BRETHREN	1	49	59*	0.7	1.1
165 CH OF NAZARENE	1	41	99	1.1	1.8
167 CHS OF CHRIST.	1	15	19	0.2	0.3
215 EVAN METH CH..	1	33	40*	0.5	0.7
323 OLD ORD AMISH.	1	130	156*	1.8	2.8
353 CHR BRETHREN..	2	40	40	0.5	0.7
357 PRESB CH US...	1	38	46*	0.5	0.8
449 UN METHODIST..	10	1 136	1 361*	15.6	24.4
453 UN PRES CH USA	1	47	56*	0.6	1.0
ATCHISON	37	5 142	10 156*	55.2	100.0
019 AMER BAPT USA.	1	243	293*	1.6	2.9
053 ASSEMB OF GOD.	1	51	75	0.4	0.7
081 CATHOLIC......	6	NA	3 736	20.3	36.8
093 CHR CH (DISC).	4	1 020	1 322	7.2	13.0
097 CHR CHS&CHS CR	6	345	416*	2.3	4.1
165 CH OF NAZARENE	1	30	22	0.1	0.2
193 EPISCOPAL.....	1	207	226	1.2	2.2
281 LUTH CH AMER..	2	529	673	3.7	6.6
283 LUTH--MO SYNOD	1	719	956	5.2	9.4
357 PRESB CH US...	2	260	313*	1.7	3.1

NA— Not applicable   *Total adherents estimated from known number of communicant, Church, confirmed, full members.   —Represents a percent less than 0.1.   Percentages may not total due to rounding.

111

Table 4. Churches and Church Membership by County and Denomination: 1980

County and Denomination	Number of churches	Communicant, confirmed, full members	Total adherents		
			Number	Percent of total population	Percent of total adherents
403 SALVATION ARMY	1	121	175	1.0	1.7
413 S.D.A.........	1	97	117*	0.6	1.2
419 SO BAPT CONV..	1	83	100*	0.5	1.0
443 UN C OF CHRIST	1	110	133*	0.7	1.3
449 UN METHODIST..	6	1 067	1 286*	7.0	12.7
453 UN PRES CH USA	2	260	313*	1.7	3.1
BARBER	29	3 030	4 558*	69.6	100.0
019 AMER BAPT USA.	1	74	88*	1.3	1.9
053 ASSEMB OF GOD.	2	52	92	1.4	2.0
081 CATHOLIC......	3	NA	881	13.5	19.3
093 CHR CH (DISC).	1	45	77	1.2	1.7
097 CHR CHS&CHS CR	2	600	712*	10.9	15.6
165 CH OF NAZARENE	1	11	13	0.2	0.3
167 CHS OF CHRIST.	3	75	95	1.5	2.1
193 EPISCOPAL.....	1	44	56	0.9	1.2
283 LUTH--MO SYNOD	1	116	157	2.4	3.4
349 PENT HOLINESS.	1	19	23*	0.4	0.5
413 S.D.A.........	1	13	15*	0.2	0.3
443 UN C OF CHRIST	2	156	185*	2.8	4.1
449 UN METHODIST..	7	1 701	2 017*	30.8	44.3
453 UN PRES CH USA	3	124	147*	2.2	3.2
BARTON	56	10 604	24 976*	79.7	100.0
019 AMER BAPT USA.	1	350	422*	1.3	1.7
029 AMER LUTH CH..	1	89	101	0.3	0.4
053 ASSEMB OF GOD.	2	272	578	1.8	2.3
081 CATHOLIC......	10	NA	11 059	35.3	44.3
093 CHR CH (DISC).	2	471	782	2.5	3.1
097 CHR CHS&CHS CR	2	90	109*	0.3	0.4
123 CH GOD (ANDER)	1	40	120	0.4	0.5
151 L-D SAINTS....	1	NA	90	0.3	0.4
165 CH OF NAZARENE	2	414	848	2.7	3.4
167 CHS OF CHRIST.	1	135	195	0.6	0.8
193 EPISCOPAL.....	1	140	227	0.7	0.9
208 EVAN LUTH ASSN	1	990	1 245	4.0	5.0
226 FRIENDS-USA...	2	81	98*	0.3	0.4
239 SWEDENBORGIAN.	1	60	72*	0.2	0.3
281 LUTH CH AMER..	2	359	469	1.5	1.9
283 LUTH--MO SYNOD	4	850	1 035	3.3	4.1
287 MENN GEN CONF.	1	182	189	0.6	0.8
313 N AM BAPT CONF	1	222	268*	0.9	1.1
413 S.D.A.........	2	138	166*	0.5	0.7
419 SO BAPT CONV..	5	902	1 088*	3.5	4.4
443 UN C OF CHRIST	3	942	1 137*	3.6	4.6
449 UN METHODIST..	9	3 414	4 119*	13.1	16.5
453 UN PRES CH USA	1	463	559*	1.8	2.2
BOURBON	38	4 800	7 567*	47.4	100.0
019 AMER BAPT USA.	5	1 002	1 192*	7.5	15.8
053 ASSEMB OF GOD.	2	81	145	0.9	1.9
059 BAPT MISS ASSN	1	122	145*	0.9	1.9
071 BRETHREN (ASH)	1	56	67*	0.4	0.9
081 CATHOLIC......	3	NA	1 337	8.4	17.7
093 CHR CH (DISC).	2	333	512	3.2	6.8
097 CHR CHS&CHS CR	3	330	393*	2.5	5.2
157 CH OF BRETHREN	1	82	98*	0.6	1.3
165 CH OF NAZARENE	2	189	531	3.3	7.0
167 CHS OF CHRIST.	2	76	106	0.7	1.4
193 EPISCOPAL.....	1	54	83	0.5	1.1
283 LUTH--MO SYNOD	1	74	102	0.6	1.3
357 PRESB CH US...	1	220	262*	1.6	3.5
413 S.D.A.........	2	60	71*	0.4	0.9
419 SO BAPT CONV..	1	175	208*	1.3	2.7
449 UN METHODIST..	11	1 727	2 054*	12.9	27.1
453 UN PRES CH USA	1	219	261*	1.6	3.4
BROWN	37	5 325	8 200*	68.6	100.0
019 AMER BAPT USA.	5	649	782*	6.5	9.5
029 AMER LUTH CH..	3	477	601	5.0	7.3
053 ASSEMB OF GOD.	1	24	30	0.3	0.4
071 BRETHREN (ASH)	1	68	82*	0.7	1.0
081 CATHOLIC......	3	NA	1 537	12.9	18.7
093 CHR CH (DISC).	3	567	821	6.9	10.0
097 CHR CHS&CHS CR	2	193	233*	1.9	2.8
151 L-D SAINTS....	1	NA	74	0.6	0.9
157 CH OF BRETHREN	1	85	102*	0.9	1.2
167 CHS OF CHRIST.	1	29	43	0.4	0.5
283 LUTH--MO SYNOD	3	467	563	4.7	6.9
413 S.D.A.........	1	21	25*	0.2	0.3
443 UN C OF CHRIST	2	353	425*	3.6	5.2
449 UN METHODIST..	9	2 109	2 541*	21.3	31.0
453 UN PRES CH USA	1	283	341*	2.9	4.2
BUTLER	75	14 473	22 077*	49.3	100.0
019 AMER BAPT USA.	8	3 028	3 691*	8.2	16.7
053 ASSEMB OF GOD.	4	230	342	0.8	1.5
059 BAPT MISS ASSN	1	50	61*	0.1	0.3
081 CATHOLIC......	3	NA	2 894	6.5	13.1
093 CHR CH (DISC).	6	1 408	2 178	4.9	9.9
097 CHR CHS&CHS CR	6	490	597*	1.3	2.7
123 CH GOD (ANDER)	1	145	435	1.0	2.0
127 CH GOD (CLEVE)	2	38	46*	0.1	0.2
151 L-D SAINTS....	1	NA	266	0.6	1.2
165 CH OF NAZARENE	3	253	645	1.4	2.9
167 CHS OF CHRIST.	5	325	412	0.9	1.9
193 EPISCOPAL.....	1	380	489	1.1	2.2
263 INT FOURSQ GOS	1	165	201*	0.4	0.9
283 LUTH--MO SYNOD	2	436	553	1.2	2.5
287 MENN GEN CONF.	3	798	949	2.1	4.3

County and Denomination	Number of churches	Communicant, confirmed, full members	Total adherents		
			Number	Percent of total population	Percent of total adherents
403 SALVATION ARMY	1	49	178	0.4	0.8
413 S.D.A.........	1	35	43*	0.1	0.2
419 SO BAPT CONV..	6	1 354	1 650*	3.7	7.5
443 UN C OF CHRIST	2	382	466*	1.0	2.1
449 UN METHODIST..	16	4 543	5 537*	12.4	25.1
453 UN PRES CH USA	2	364	444*	1.0	2.0
CHASE	17	1 587	2 195*	66.3	100.0
081 CATHOLIC......	1	NA	278	8.4	12.7
093 CHR CH (DISC).	1	55	85	2.6	3.9
097 CHR CHS&CHS CR	2	81	96*	2.9	4.4
167 CHS OF CHRIST.	1	20	27	0.8	1.2
226 FRIENDS-USA...	1	96	114*	3.4	5.2
283 LUTH--MO SYNOD	1	58	78	2.4	3.6
419 SO BAPT CONV..	1	171	203*	6.1	9.2
443 UN C OF CHRIST	1	50	59*	1.8	2.7
449 UN METHODIST..	6	744	884*	26.7	40.3
453 UN PRES CH USA	2	312	371*	11.2	16.9
CHAUTAUQUA	24	2 103	2 696*	53.7	100.0
019 AMER BAPT USA.	2	668	780*	15.6	28.9
053 ASSEMB OF GOD.	3	91	172	3.4	6.4
081 CATHOLIC......	2	NA	102	2.0	3.8
093 CHR CH (DISC).	1	97	149	3.0	5.5
097 CHR CHS&CHS CR	3	195	228*	4.5	8.5
167 CHS OF CHRIST.	3	110	140	2.8	5.2
193 EPISCOPAL.....	2	135	184	3.7	6.8
413 S.D.A.........	1	32	37*	0.7	1.4
419 SO BAPT CONV..	1	180	210*	4.2	7.8
449 UN METHODIST..	6	595	694*	13.8	25.7
CHEROKEE	61	7 612	11 164*	50.1	100.0
019 AMER BAPT USA.	1	224	270*	1.2	2.4
053 ASSEMB OF GOD.	4	378	975	4.4	8.7
059 BAPT MISS ASSN	1	357	431*	1.9	3.9
081 CATHOLIC......	6	NA	1 046	4.7	9.4
093 CHR CH (DISC).	4	729	1 104	4.9	9.9
097 CHR CHS&CHS CR	4	551	665*	3.0	6.0
165 CH OF NAZARENE	3	193	414	1.9	3.7
167 CHS OF CHRIST.	2	80	102	0.5	0.9
193 EPISCOPAL.....	1	32	37	0.2	0.3
217 FIRE BAPTIZED.	1	16	19*	0.1	0.2
226 FRIENDS-USA...	4	291	351*	1.6	3.1
357 PRESB CH US...	4	229	277*	1.2	2.5
413 S.D.A.........	2	95	115*	0.5	1.0
419 SO BAPT CONV..	12	2 952	3 565*	16.0	31.9
449 UN METHODIST..	8	1 254	1 514*	6.8	13.6
453 UN PRES CH USA	4	231	279*	1.3	2.5
CHEYENNE	15	2 143	3 011*	81.9	100.0
029 AMER LUTH CH..	3	756	1 062	28.9	35.3
053 ASSEMB OF GOD.	1	46	82	2.2	2.7
081 CATHOLIC......	2	NA	252	6.9	8.4
093 CHR CH (DISC).	1	168	229	6.2	7.6
097 CHR CHS&CHS CR	1	40	47*	1.3	1.6
167 CHS OF CHRIST.	1	20	25	0.7	0.8
226 FRIENDS-USA...	1	18	21*	0.6	0.7
413 S.D.A.........	1	35	41*	1.1	1.4
419 SO BAPT CONV..	1	79	93*	2.5	3.1
449 UN METHODIST..	3	981	1 159*	31.5	38.5
CLARK	12	1 498	2 132*	82.0	100.0
019 AMER BAPT USA.	1	53	62*	2.4	2.9
053 ASSEMB OF GOD.	1	7	12	0.5	0.6
081 CATHOLIC......	1	NA	281	10.8	13.2
097 CHR CHS&CHS CR	3	430	505*	19.4	23.7
123 CH GOD (ANDER)	1	48	144	5.5	6.8
167 CHS OF CHRIST.	1	20	26	1.0	1.2
383 REF PRES OF NA	1	39	45	1.7	2.1
449 UN METHODIST..	2	732	859*	33.1	40.3
453 UN PRES CH USA	1	169	198*	7.6	9.3
CLAY	29	4 852	6 606*	67.4	100.0
005 AME ZION......	2	165	189	1.9	2.9
019 AMER BAPT USA.	1	255	305*	3.1	4.6
053 ASSEMB OF GOD.	1	34	75	0.8	1.1
081 CATHOLIC......	1	NA	674	6.9	10.2
093 CHR CH (DISC).	1	75	115	1.2	1.7
097 CHR CHS&CHS CR	2	240	287*	2.9	4.3
193 EPISCOPAL.....	2	167	181	1.8	2.7
201 EVAN COV CH AM	1	34	41*	0.4	0.6
281 LUTH CH AMER..	1	138	163	1.7	2.5
283 LUTH--MO SYNOD	1	561	770	7.9	11.7
383 REF PRES OF NA	1	55	67	0.7	1.0
443 UN C OF CHRIST	1	40	48*	0.5	0.7
449 UN METHODIST..	10	2 057	2 459*	25.1	37.2
453 UN PRES CH USA	4	1 031	1 232*	12.6	18.6
CLOUD	34	3 799	8 184*	65.5	100.0
019 AMER BAPT USA.	2	661	776*	6.2	9.5
029 AMER LUTH CH..	1	186	244	2.0	3.0
053 ASSEMB OF GOD.	1	34	59	0.5	0.7
081 CATHOLIC......	11	NA	3 587	28.7	43.8
097 CHR CHS&CHS CR	4	485	570*	4.6	7.0
151 L-D SAINTS....	1	NA	62	0.5	0.8
165 CH OF NAZARENE	1	?	?	?	?
167 CHS OF CHRIST.	2	39	57	0.5	0.7
221 FREE METHODIST	1	23	48	0.4	0.6

NA—Not applicable   *Total adherents estimated from known number of communicant, confirmed, full members.   —Represents a percent less than 0.1.   Percentages may not total due to rounding.

Table 4. Churches and Church Membership by County and Denomination: 1980

County and Denomination	Number of churches	Communicant, confirmed, full members	Total adherents Number	Percent of total population	Percent of total adherents
281 LUTH CH AMER..	1	173	199	1.6	2.4
449 UN METHODIST..	7	1 842	2 164*	17.3	26.4
453 UN PRES CH USA	2	356	418*	3.3	5.1
COFFEY	30	3 692	5 175*	55.2	100.0
019 AMER BAPT USA.	3	364	440*	4.7	8.5
053 ASSEMB OF GOD.	2	102	184	2.0	3.6
081 CATHOLIC......	2	NA	525	5.6	10.1
097 CHR CHS&CHS CR	4	815	986*	10.5	19.1
127 CH GOD (CLEVE)	1	13	16*	0.2	0.3
157 CH OF BRETHREN	1	22	27*	0.3	0.5
165 CH OF NAZARENE	1	24	115	1.2	2.2
167 CHS OF CHRIST.	3	92	126	1.3	2.4
283 LUTH--MO SYNOD	2	227	298	3.2	5.8
419 SO BAPT CONV..	1	168	203*	2.2	3.9
449 UN METHODIST..	10	1 865	2 255*	24.1	43.6
COMANCHE	15	1 906	2 577*	100.9	100.0
019 AMER BAPT USA.	1	172	204*	8.0	7.9
053 ASSEMB OF GOD.	1	42	208	8.1	8.1
081 CATHOLIC......	1	NA	54	2.1	2.1
093 CHR CH (DISC).	2	307	472	18.5	18.3
097 CHR CHS&CHS CR	2	398	471*	18.4	18.3
143 CG IN CR(MENN)	1	?	?	?	?
226 FRIENDS-USA...	1	39	46*	1.8	1.8
285 MENNONITE CH..	1	100	118*	4.6	4.6
449 UN METHODIST..	4	717	849*	33.2	32.9
453 UN PRES CH USA	1	131	155*	6.1	6.0
COWLEY	72	12 840	19 471*	52.9	100.0
019 AMER BAPT USA.	4	1 630	1 961*	5.3	10.1
053 ASSEMB OF GOD.	3	200	363	1.0	1.9
081 CATHOLIC......	2	NA	2 135	5.8	11.0
093 CHR CH (DISC).	4	1 312	1 934	5.3	9.9
097 CHR CHS&CHS CR	4	306	368*	1.0	1.9
121 CH GOD (ABR)..	1	16	19*	0.1	0.1
123 CH GOD (ANDER)	3	100	300	0.8	1.5
127 CH GOD (CLEVE)	1	17	20*	0.1	0.1
151 L-D SAINTS....	1	NA	278	0.8	1.4
165 CH OF NAZARENE	3	279	826	2.2	4.2
167 CHS OF CHRIST.	6	535	681	1.8	3.5
177 CONGR HOL CH..	1	12	14*	-	0.1
193 EPISCOPAL.....	2	322	486	1.3	2.5
203 EVAN FREE CH..	1	54	65*	0.2	0.3
221 FREE METHODIST	1	30	108	0.3	0.6
226 FRIENDS-USA...	3	189	227*	0.6	1.2
263 INT FOURSQ GOS	1	120	144*	0.4	0.7
283 LUTH--MO SYNOD	2	941	1 295	3.5	6.7
403 SALVATION ARMY	1	99	212	0.6	1.1
413 S.D.A.........	2	42	51*	0.1	0.3
419 SO BAPT CONV..	7	1 560	1 877*	5.1	9.6
443 UN C OF CHRIST	1	80	96*	0.3	0.5
449 UN METHODIST..	14	3 703	4 455*	12.1	22.9
453 UN PRES CH USA	4	1 293	1 556*	4.2	8.0
CRAWFORD	74	9 885	18 670*	49.2	100.0
019 AMER BAPT USA.	3	846	992*	2.6	5.3
029 AMER LUTH CH..	1	309	413	1.1	2.2
053 ASSEMB OF GOD.	2	93	277	0.7	1.5
059 BAPT MISS ASSN	2	170	199*	0.5	1.1
081 CATHOLIC......	10	NA	5 441	14.4	29.1
093 CHR CH (DISC).	4	1 018	1 970	5.2	10.6
097 CHR CHS&CHS CR	5	565	662*	1.7	3.5
127 CH GOD (CLEVE)	2	115	135*	0.4	0.7
151 L-D SAINTS....	1	NA	221	0.6	1.2
157 CH OF BRETHREN	1	138	162*	0.4	0.9
165 CH OF NAZARENE	3	220	443	1.2	2.4
167 CHS OF CHRIST.	2	80	102	0.3	0.5
193 EPISCOPAL.....	1	273	349	0.9	1.9
217 FIRE BAPTIZED.	1	12	14*	-	0.1
263 INT FOURSQ GOS	1	50	59*	0.2	0.3
283 LUTH--MO SYNOD	4	650	827	2.2	4.4
357 PRESB CH US...	5	444	521*	1.4	2.8
403 SALVATION ARMY	1	117	273	0.7	1.5
413 S.D.A.........	1	149	175*	0.5	0.9
419 SO BAPT CONV..	4	954	1 118*	2.9	6.0
435 UNITARIAN-UNIV	1	10	12*	-	0.1
449 UN METHODIST..	14	3 228	3 784*	10.0	20.3
453 UN PRES CH USA	5	444	521*	1.4	2.8
DECATUR	22	1 861	2 905*	64.4	100.0
019 AMER BAPT USA.	1	64	76*	1.7	2.6
029 AMER LUTH CH..	2	170	223	4.9	7.7
053 ASSEMB OF GOD.	1	29	52	1.2	1.8
081 CATHOLIC......	2	NA	633	14.0	21.8
093 CHR CH (DISC).	1	66	66	1.5	2.3
165 CH OF NAZARENE	2	23	49	1.1	1.7
167 CHS OF CHRIST.	1	50	54	1.2	1.9
201 EVAN COV CH AM	2	102	121*	2.7	4.2
283 LUTH--MO SYNOD	1	244	312	6.9	10.7
413 S.D.A.........	1	12	14*	0.3	0.5
419 SO BAPT CONV..	1	96	114*	2.5	3.9
449 UN METHODIST..	6	939	1 113*	24.7	38.3
453 UN PRES CH USA	1	66	78*	1.7	2.7
DICKINSON	61	9 440	13 331*	66.1	100.0
019 AMER BAPT USA.	4	762	912*	4.5	6.8
029 AMER LUTH CH..	2	389	524	2.6	3.9
053 ASSEMB OF GOD.	1	18	31	0.2	0.2

County and Denomination	Number of churches	Communicant, confirmed, full members	Total adherents Number	Percent of total population	Percent of total adherents
075 BRETHREN IN CR	3	171	258	1.3	1.9
081 CATHOLIC......	5	NA	1 805	8.9	13.5
093 CHR CH (DISC).	1	174	217	1.1	1.6
097 CHR CHS&CHS CR	3	667	798*	4.0	6.0
123 CH GOD (ANDER)	1	16	48	0.2	0.4
127 CH GOD (CLEVE)	1	21	25*	0.1	0.2
157 CH OF BRETHREN	2	108	129*	0.6	1.0
165 CH OF NAZARENE	1	28	56	0.3	0.4
167 CHS OF CHRIST.	2	57	71	0.4	0.5
193 EPISCOPAL.....	1	54	60	0.3	0.5
263 INT FOURSQ GOS	1	38	45*	0.2	0.3
281 LUTH CH AMER..	2	590	740	3.7	5.6
283 LUTH--MO SYNOD	4	882	1 057	5.2	7.9
313 N AM BAPT CONF	2	235	281*	1.4	2.1
353 CHR BRETHREN..	1	30	50	0.2	0.4
413 S.D.A.........	2	223	267*	1.3	2.0
419 SO BAPT CONV..	1	162	194*	1.0	1.5
443 UN C OF CHRIST	1	126	151*	0.7	1.1
449 UN METHODIST..	15	3 906	4 675*	23.2	35.1
453 UN PRES CH USA	5	783	937*	4.6	7.0
DONIPHAN	28	3 555	5 560*	60.0	100.0
019 AMER BAPT USA.	4	967	1 170*	12.6	21.0
053 ASSEMB OF GOD.	2	102	126	1.4	2.3
081 CATHOLIC......	5	NA	1 072	11.6	19.3
093 CHR CH (DISC).	3	355	603	6.5	10.8
097 CHR CHS&CHS CR	2	400	484*	5.2	8.7
281 LUTH CH AMER..	1	275	354	3.8	6.4
283 LUTH--MO SYNOD	1	209	243	2.6	4.4
413 S.D.A.........	1	35	42*	0.5	0.8
419 SO BAPT CONV..	1	84	102*	1.1	1.8
443 UN C OF CHRIST	1	120	145*	1.6	2.6
449 UN METHODIST..	6	887	1 073*	11.6	19.3
453 UN PRES CH USA	1	121	146*	1.6	2.6
DOUGLAS	71	13 570	22 237*	32.9	100.0
019 AMER BAPT USA.	1	401	465*	0.7	2.1
029 AMER LUTH CH..	1	150	224	0.3	1.0
053 ASSEMB OF GOD.	3	185	370	0.5	1.7
081 CATHOLIC......	4	NA	4 660	6.9	21.0
093 CHR CH (DISC).	3	517	807	1.2	3.6
097 CHR CHS&CHS CR	2	295	342*	0.5	1.5
123 CH GOD (ANDER)	1	99	297	0.4	1.3
151 L-D SAINTS....	1	NA	389	0.6	1.7
157 CH OF BRETHREN	2	116	134*	0.2	0.6
165 CH OF NAZARENE	2	292	362	0.5	1.6
167 CHS OF CHRIST.	8	500	636	0.9	2.9
193 EPISCOPAL.....	1	603	766	1.1	3.4
221 FREE METHODIST	1	126	564	0.8	2.5
226 FRIENDS-USA...	3	300	348*	0.5	1.6
281 LUTH CH AMER..	1	1 118	1 429	2.1	6.4
283 LUTH--MO SYNOD	3	481	625	0.9	2.8
285 MENNONITE CH..	1	?	?	?	?
349 PENT HOLINESS.	2	80	93*	0.1	0.4
353 CHR BRETHREN..	3	90	130	0.2	0.6
383 REF PRES OF NA	1	41	63	0.1	0.3
403 SALVATION ARMY	1	105	176	0.3	0.8
413 S.D.A.........	1	35	41*	0.1	0.2
419 SO BAPT CONV..	5	1 591	1 844*	2.7	8.3
435 UNITARIAN-UNIV	1	107	124*	0.2	0.6
443 UN C OF CHRIST	3	1 506	1 746*	2.6	7.9
449 UN METHODIST..	13	3 759	4 358*	6.4	19.6
453 UN PRES CH USA	3	1 073	1 244*	1.8	5.6
EDWARDS	20	1 867	3 453*	80.8	100.0
019 AMER BAPT USA.	2	122	144*	3.4	4.2
053 ASSEMB OF GOD.	1	37	55	1.3	1.6
081 CATHOLIC......	4	NA	1 162	27.2	33.7
093 CHR CH (DISC).	2	189	280	6.6	8.1
149 CH OF JC (BIC)	1	14	21	0.5	0.6
165 CH OF NAZARENE	1	30	37	0.9	1.1
193 EPISCOPAL.....	1	41	45	1.1	1.3
283 LUTH--MO SYNOD	1	160	201	4.7	5.8
443 UN C OF CHRIST	1	211	250*	5.9	7.2
449 UN METHODIST..	6	1 063	1 258*	29.5	36.4
ELK	17	1 818	2 493*	63.6	100.0
019 AMER BAPT USA.	3	542	634*	16.2	25.4
081 CATHOLIC......	1	NA	260	6.6	10.4
093 CHR CH (DISC).	1	65	100	2.6	4.0
097 CHR CHS&CHS CR	3	310	362*	9.2	14.5
151 L-D SAINTS....	1	NA	79	2.0	3.2
167 CHS OF CHRIST.	1	40	51	1.3	2.0
217 FIRE BAPTIZED.	1	6	7*	0.2	0.3
449 UN METHODIST..	5	832	973*	24.8	39.0
453 UN PRES CH USA	1	23	27*	0.7	1.1
ELLIS	33	4 020	19 445*	74.5	100.0
019 AMER BAPT USA.	2	196	234*	0.9	1.2
029 AMER LUTH CH..	1	164	224	0.9	1.2
053 ASSEMB OF GOD.	1	73	150	0.6	0.8
081 CATHOLIC......	14	NA	14 370	55.1	73.9
097 CHR CHS&CHS CR	1	70	84*	0.3	0.4
151 L-D SAINTS....	1	NA	?	?	?
165 CH OF NAZARENE	1	85	183	0.7	0.9
167 CHS OF CHRIST.	1	40	54	0.2	0.3
193 EPISCOPAL.....	2	147	151	0.6	0.8
237 GC MENN BR CHS	1	28	33*	0.1	0.2
281 LUTH CH AMER..	2	553	719	2.8	3.7
283 LUTH--MO SYNOD	1	227	323	1.2	1.7

NA — Not applicable   *Total adherents estimated from known number of communicant, confirmed, full members.   —Represents a percent less than 0.1.   Percentages may not total due to rounding.

Table 4. Churches and Church Membership by County and Denomination: 1980

County and Denomination	Number of churches	Communicant, confirmed, full members	Total adherents		
			Number	Percent of total population	Percent of total adherents
383 REF PRES OF NA	1	20	29	0.1	0.1
419 SO BAPT CONV..	1	167	200*	0.8	1.0
449 UN METHODIST..	2	1 741	2 082*	8.0	10.7
453 UN PRES CH USA	1	509	609*	2.3	3.1
ELLSWORTH	**19**	**2 897**	**4 752***	**71.6**	**100.0**
029 AMER LUTH CH..	1	160	192	2.9	4.0
053 ASSEMB OF GOD.	1	14	34	0.5	0.7
081 CATHOLIC......	4	NA	1 196	18.0	25.2
193 EPISCOPAL.....	1	55	59	0.9	1.2
281 LUTH CH AMER..	1	40	54	0.8	1.1
283 LUTH--MO SYNOD	3	866	1 122	16.9	23.6
313 N AM BAPT CONF	1	228	271*	4.1	5.7
443 UN C OF CHRIST	1	252	300*	4.5	6.3
449 UN METHODIST..	4	653	776*	11.7	16.3
453 UN PRES CH USA	2	629	748*	11.3	15.7
FINNEY	**24**	**6 381**	**14 650***	**61.5**	**100.0**
019 AMER BAPT USA.	1	298	376*	1.6	2.6
029 AMER LUTH CH..	1	281	375	1.6	2.6
053 ASSEMB OF GOD.	1	345	723	3.0	4.9
081 CATHOLIC......	2	NA	5 600	23.5	38.2
093 CHR CH (DISC).	1	430	647	2.7	4.4
097 CHR CHS&CHS CR	1	350	441*	1.9	3.0
123 CH GOD (ANDER)	1	68	204	0.9	1.4
151 L-D SAINTS....	1	NA	203	0.9	1.4
157 CH OF BRETHREN	1	249	314*	1.3	2.1
165 CH OF NAZARENE	2	324	602	2.5	4.1
167 CHS OF CHRIST.	1	75	95	0.4	0.6
193 EPISCOPAL.....	1	108	144	0.6	1.0
237 GC MENN BR CHS	1	210	265*	1.1	1.8
283 LUTH--MO SYNOD	1	497	694	2.9	4.7
413 S.D.A........	1	107	135*	0.6	0.9
419 SO BAPT CONV..	1	371	468*	2.0	3.2
443 UN C OF CHRIST	1	317	400*	1.7	2.7
449 UN METHODIST..	3	1 988	2 506*	10.5	17.1
453 UN PRES CH USA	2	363	458*	1.9	3.1
FORD	**37**	**7 509**	**15 647***	**64.4**	**100.0**
019 AMER BAPT USA.	1	740	903*	3.7	5.8
029 AMER LUTH CH..	1	325	484	2.0	3.1
053 ASSEMB OF GOD.	1	108	250	1.0	1.6
081 CATHOLIC......	6	NA	5 617	23.1	35.9
097 CHR CHS&CHS CR	4	1 445	1 764*	7.3	11.3
123 CH GOD (ANDER)	1	65	195	0.8	1.2
143 CG IN CR(MENN)	1	?	?	?	?
151 L-D SAINTS....	1	NA	251	1.0	1.6
165 CH OF NAZARENE	2	251	377	1.6	2.4
167 CHS OF CHRIST.	1	145	175	0.7	1.1
193 EPISCOPAL.....	1	203	275	1.1	1.8
221 FREE METHODIST	1	30	144	0.6	0.9
283 LUTH--MO SYNOD	3	544	695	2.9	4.4
291 MISSIONARY CH.	1	66	85	0.3	0.5
349 PENT HOLINESS	1	35	43*	0.2	0.3
403 SALVATION ARMY	1	51	115	0.5	0.7
413 S.D.A.	1	28	34*	0.1	0.2
419 SO BAPT CONV..	1	285	348*	1.4	2.2
443 UN C OF CHRIST	1	67	82*	0.3	0.5
449 UN METHODIST..	3	2 329	2 843*	11.7	18.2
453 UN PRES CH USA	4	792	967*	4.0	6.2
FRANKLIN	**45**	**6 642**	**10 345***	**47.4**	**100.0**
019 AMER BAPT USA.	8	2 010	2 424*	11.1	23.4
053 ASSEMB OF GOD.	3	222	390	1.8	3.8
081 CATHOLIC......	2	NA	1 811	8.3	17.5
093 CHR CH (DISC).	3	382	729	3.3	7.0
097 CHR CHS&CHS CR	2	40	48*	0.2	0.5
157 CH OF BRETHREN	1	142	171*	0.8	1.7
165 CH OF NAZARENE	1	100	123	0.6	1.2
167 CHS OF CHRIST.	2	90	115	0.5	1.1
193 EPISCOPAL.....	1	243	275	1.3	2.7
221 FREE METHODIST	2	35	144	0.7	1.4
263 INT FOURSQ GOS	2	87	105*	0.5	1.0
283 LUTH--MO SYNOD	1	313	423	1.9	4.1
353 CHR BRETHREN..	1	20	20	0.1	0.2
357 PRESB CH US...	3	230	277*	1.3	2.7
413 S.D.A.	1	53	64*	0.3	0.6
449 UN METHODIST..	9	2 445	2 949*	13.5	28.5
453 UN PRES CH USA	3	230	277*	1.3	2.7
GEARY	**25**	**5 535**	**11 071***	**37.1**	**100.0**
019 AMER BAPT USA.	1	504	618*	2.1	5.6
081 CATHOLIC......	2	NA	2 998	10.0	27.1
097 CHR CHS&CHS CR	1	500	613*	2.1	5.5
123 CH GOD (ANDER)	1	48	144	0.5	1.3
127 CH GOD (CLEVE)	1	51	63*	0.2	0.6
151 L-D SAINTS....	1	NA	536	1.8	4.8
165 CH OF NAZARENE	1	137	558	1.9	5.0
167 CHS OF CHRIST.	2	95	121	0.4	1.1
193 EPISCOPAL.....	1	352	457	1.5	4.1
221 FREE METHODIST	1	18	93	0.3	0.8
281 LUTH CH AMER..	1	142	189	0.6	1.7
283 LUTH--MO SYNOD	2	643	830	2.8	7.5
313 N AM BAPT CONF	1	84	103*	0.3	0.9
403 SALVATION ARMY	1	76	211	0.7	1.9
413 S.D.A.	1	17	21*	0.1	0.2
419 SO BAPT CONV..	1	668	819*	2.7	7.4
443 UN C OF CHRIST	3	397	487*	1.6	4.4
449 UN METHODIST..	2	1 156	1 417*	4.7	12.8
453 UN PRES CH USA	1	647	793*	2.7	7.2
GOVE	**9**	**1 101**	**2 869***	**77.0**	**100.0**
081 CATHOLIC......	3	NA	1 522	40.8	53.0
157 CH OF BRETHREN	1	396	483*	13.0	16.8
383 REF PRES OF NA	1	71	91	2.4	3.2
449 UN METHODIST..	4	634	773*	20.7	26.9
GRAHAM	**15**	**1 436**	**2 634***	**65.9**	**100.0**
019 AMER BAPT USA.	1	190	229*	5.7	8.7
053 ASSEMB OF GOD.	2	82	149	3.7	5.7
081 CATHOLIC......	2	NA	816	20.4	31.0
097 CHR CHS&CHS CR	1	300	361*	9.0	13.7
123 CH GOD (ANDER)	1	20	60	1.5	2.3
283 LUTH--MO SYNOD	1	71	89	2.2	3.4
449 UN METHODIST..	6	673	810*	20.3	30.8
453 UN PRES CH USA	1	100	120*	3.0	4.6
GRANT	**15**	**2 472**	**4 273***	**61.2**	**100.0**
019 AMER BAPT USA.	1	243	306*	4.4	7.2
053 ASSEMB OF GOD.	1	74	145	2.1	3.4
081 CATHOLIC......	1	NA	875	12.5	20.5
093 CHR CH (DISC).	1	167	248	3.6	5.8
123 CH GOD (ANDER)	1	60	180	2.6	4.2
127 CH GOD (CLEVE)	1	28	35*	0.5	0.8
143 CG IN CR(MENN)	1	132	132	1.9	3.1
151 L-D SAINTS....	1	NA	100	1.4	2.3
165 CH OF NAZARENE	1	22	20	0.3	0.5
167 CHS OF CHRIST.	1	103	157	2.3	3.7
193 EPISCOPAL.....	1	106	133	1.9	3.1
237 GC MENN BR CHS	1	132	166*	2.4	3.9
283 LUTH--MO SYNOD	1	117	153	2.2	3.6
419 SO BAPT CONV..	1	527	664*	9.5	15.5
449 UN METHODIST..	1	761	959*	13.7	22.4
GRAY	**18**	**2 466**	**3 385***	**65.9**	**100.0**
081 CATHOLIC......	1	NA	420	8.2	12.4
093 CHR CH (DISC).	1	110	233	4.5	6.9
097 CHR CHS&CHS CR	1	100	124*	2.4	3.7
143 CG IN CR(MENN)	3	723	723	14.1	21.4
165 CH OF NAZARENE	1	157	220	4.3	6.5
193 EPISCOPAL.....	1	165	165	3.2	4.9
237 GC MENN BR CHS	1	75	93*	1.8	2.7
239 SWEDENBORGIAN.	1	60	74*	1.4	2.2
285 MENNONITE CH..	1	23	29*	0.6	0.9
287 MENN GEN CONF.	1	6	6	0.1	0.2
419 SO BAPT CONV..	2	156	193*	3.8	5.7
449 UN METHODIST..	4	891	1 105*	21.5	32.6
GREELEY	**6**	**773**	**1 147***	**62.2**	**100.0**
019 AMER BAPT USA.	1	286	349*	18.9	30.4
053 ASSEMB OF GOD.	1	29	60	3.3	5.2
081 CATHOLIC......	1	NA	170	9.2	14.8
281 LUTH CH AMER..	1	100	131	7.1	11.4
449 UN METHODIST..	1	239	292*	15.8	25.5
453 UN PRES CH USA	1	119	145*	7.9	12.6
GREENWOOD	**30**	**3 252**	**4 413***	**50.4**	**100.0**
081 CATHOLIC......	3	NA	445	5.1	10.1
093 CHR CH (DISC).	3	428	555	6.3	12.6
097 CHR CHS&CHS CR	3	150	178*	2.0	4.0
123 CH GOD (ANDER)	1	30	90	1.0	2.0
165 CH OF NAZARENE	2	116	137	1.6	3.1
167 CHS OF CHRIST.	1	6	12	0.1	0.3
203 EVAN FREE CH..	1	40	47*	0.5	1.1
281 LUTH CH AMER..	1	295	361	4.1	8.2
413 S.D.A........	1	58	69*	0.8	1.6
419 SO BAPT CONV..	3	547	647*	7.4	14.7
443 UN C OF CHRIST	1	83	98*	1.1	2.2
449 UN METHODIST..	9	1 401	1 658*	18.9	37.6
453 UN PRES CH USA	1	98	116*	1.3	2.6
HAMILTON	**7**	**990**	**1 531***	**60.9**	**100.0**
081 CATHOLIC......	1	NA	227	9.0	14.8
097 CHR CHS&CHS CR	1	165	198*	7.9	12.9
151 L-D SAINTS....	1	NA	74	2.9	4.8
165 CH OF NAZARENE	1	0	44	1.8	2.9
449 UN METHODIST..	1	569	681*	27.1	44.5
453 UN PRES CH USA	2	256	307*	12.2	20.1
HARPER	**33**	**3 688**	**5 437***	**69.9**	**100.0**
019 AMER BAPT USA.	2	332	392*	5.0	7.2
053 ASSEMB OF GOD.	3	65	207	2.7	3.8
081 CATHOLIC......	3	NA	610	7.8	11.2
093 CHR CH (DISC).	2	504	775	10.0	14.3
097 CHR CHS&CHS CR	2	748	884*	11.4	16.3
123 CH GOD (ANDER)	1	40	120	1.5	2.2
165 CH OF NAZARENE	1	40	116	1.5	2.1
167 CHS OF CHRIST.	4	130	165	2.1	3.0
193 EPISCOPAL.....	1	22	34	0.4	0.6
285 MENNONITE CH..	1	211	249*	3.2	4.6
291 MISSIONARY CH.	1	12	13	0.2	0.2
413 S.D.A.........	1	38	45*	0.6	0.8
443 UN C OF CHRIST	1	104	123*	1.6	2.3
449 UN METHODIST..	5	1 132	1 338*	17.2	24.6
453 UN PRES CH USA	4	310	366*	4.7	6.7
HARVEY	**61**	**13 344**	**20 272***	**66.4**	**100.0**

NA—Not applicable
*Total adherents estimated from known number of communicant, confirmed, full members.
—Represents a percent less than 0.1.
Percentages may not total due to rounding.

Table 4. Churches and Church Membership by County and Denomination: 1980

County and Denomination	Number of churches	Communicant, confirmed, full members	Total adherents Number	Percent of total population	Percent of total adherents
019 AMER BAPT USA.	1	822	984*	3.2	4.9
029 AMER LUTH CH..	1	156	203	0.7	1.0
053 ASSEMB OF GOD.	1	39	93	0.3	0.5
081 CATHOLIC......	3	NA	3 326	10.9	16.4
093 CHR CH (DISC).	2	489	658	2.2	3.2
097 CHR CHS&CHS CR	1	250	299*	1.0	1.5
123 CH GOD (ANDER)	1	47	141	0.5	0.7
127 CH GOD (CLEVE)	1	11	13*	–	0.1
143 CG IN CR(MENN)	3	457	457	1.5	2.3
151 L-D SAINTS....	1	NA	209	0.7	1.0
157 CH OF BRETHREN	1	76	91*	0.3	0.4
165 CH OF NAZARENE	1	338	527	1.7	2.6
167 CHS OF CHRIST.	1	110	140	0.5	0.7
193 EPISCOPAL.....	1	181	220	0.7	1.1
221 FREE METHODIST	1	60	198	0.6	1.0
237 GC MENN BR CHS	1	28	34*	0.1	0.2
263 INT FOURSQ GOS	1	208	249*	0.8	1.2
283 LUTH--MO SYNOD	1	509	668	2.2	3.3
285 MENNONITE CH..	6	1 104	1 322*	4.3	6.5
287 MENN GEN CONF.	11	3 251	4 161	13.6	20.5
291 MISSIONARY CH.	1	32	43	0.1	0.2
403 SALVATION ARMY	1	64	116	0.4	0.6
413 S.D.A.........	1	31	37*	0.1	0.2
419 SO BAPT CONV..	3	273	327*	1.1	1.6
443 UN C OF CHRIST	3	457	547*	1.8	2.7
449 UN METHODIST..	9	3 680	4 406*	14.4	21.7
453 UN PRES CH USA	2	658	788*	2.6	3.9
469 WELS..........	1	13	15	–	0.1
HASKELL	12	1 766	2 676*	70.2	100.0
019 AMER BAPT USA.	1	73	92*	2.4	3.4
081 CATHOLIC......	1	NA	186	4.9	7.0
097 CHR CHS&CHS CR	1	300	377*	9.9	14.1
123 CH GOD (ANDER)	1	88	264	6.9	9.9
151 L-D SAINTS....	1	NA	36	0.9	1.3
165 CH OF NAZARENE	1	132	226	5.9	8.4
167 CHS OF CHRIST.	2	55	91	2.4	3.4
419 SO BAPT CONV..	2	450	565*	14.8	21.1
449 UN METHODIST..	2	668	839*	22.0	31.4
HODGEMAN	12	928	1 413*	62.3	100.0
019 AMER BAPT USA.	2	137	162*	7.1	11.5
053 ASSEMB OF GOD.	1	17	27	1.2	1.9
081 CATHOLIC......	3	NA	310	13.7	21.9
167 CHS OF CHRIST.	1	5	5	0.2	0.4
283 LUTH--MO SYNOD	1	32	39	1.7	2.8
287 MENN GEN CONF.	1	37	41	1.8	2.9
449 UN METHODIST..	2	454	538*	23.7	38.1
453 UN PRES CH USA	1	246	291*	12.8	20.6
JACKSON	27	3 654	5 517*	47.4	100.0
019 AMER BAPT USA.	3	413	507*	4.4	9.2
081 CATHOLIC......	3	NA	746	6.4	13.5
093 CHR CH (DISC).	2	190	377	3.2	6.8
097 CHR CHS&CHS CR	2	231	284*	2.4	5.1
151 L-D SAINTS....	1	NA	42	0.4	0.8
165 CH OF NAZARENE	1	12	40	0.3	0.7
283 LUTH--MO SYNOD	2	317	461	4.0	8.4
383 REF PRES OF NA	1	79	98	0.8	1.8
449 UN METHODIST..	10	2 062	2 532*	21.7	45.9
453 UN PRES CH USA	2	350	430*	3.7	7.8
JEFFERSON	36	4 437	8 092*	53.2	100.0
019 AMER BAPT USA.	2	183	223*	1.5	2.8
053 ASSEMB OF GOD.	2	115	177	1.2	2.2
081 CATHOLIC......	5	NA	2 288	15.0	28.3
097 CHR CHS&CHS CR	4	678	825*	5.4	10.2
123 CH GOD (ANDER)	3	148	444	2.9	5.5
165 CH OF NAZARENE	1	39	143	0.9	1.8
167 CHS OF CHRIST.	1	13	17	0.1	0.2
226 FRIENDS-USA...	1	40	49*	0.3	0.6
237 GC MENN BR CHS	1	65	79*	0.5	1.0
281 LUTH CH AMER..	1	85	115	0.8	1.4
283 LUTH--MO SYNOD	1	176	206	1.4	2.5
383 REF PRES OF NA	1	67	84	0.6	1.0
415 S-D BAPTIST GC	1	97	118*	0.8	1.5
419 SO BAPT CONV..	1	148	180*	1.2	2.2
449 UN METHODIST..	10	2 435	2 964*	19.5	36.6
453 UN PRES CH USA	1	148	180*	1.2	2.2
JEWELL	25	2 599	3 551*	67.8	100.0
019 AMER BAPT USA.	1	147	174*	3.3	4.9
029 AMER LUTH CH..	1	87	124	2.4	3.5
053 ASSEMB OF GOD.	2	23	33	0.6	0.9
081 CATHOLIC......	2	NA	371	7.1	10.4
093 CHR CH (DISC).	1	152	223	4.3	6.3
097 CHR CHS&CHS CR	2	308	365*	7.0	10.3
105 CHRISTIAN REF.	1	128	187	3.6	5.3
165 CH OF NAZARENE	1	67	75	1.4	2.1
167 CHS OF CHRIST.	1	20	25	0.5	0.7
226 FRIENDS-USA...	1	143	169*	3.2	4.8
419 SO BAPT CONV..	1	54	64*	1.2	1.8
449 UN METHODIST..	11	1 470	1 741*	33.2	49.0
JOHNSON	151	66 225	134 310*	49.7	100.0
017 AMER BAPT ASSN	1	160	160	0.1	0.1
019 AMER BAPT USA.	12	4 371	5 323*	2.0	4.0
029 AMER LUTH CH..	5	2 285	3 206	1.2	2.4
053 ASSEMB OF GOD.	5	596	1 412	0.5	1.1

County and Denomination	Number of churches	Communicant, confirmed, full members	Total adherents Number	Percent of total population	Percent of total adherents
057 BAPT GEN CONF.	1	30	37*	–	–
063 BEREAN FUND CH	1	58	71*	–	0.1
081 CATHOLIC......	12	NA	48 772	18.0	36.3
093 CHR CH (DISC).	8	4 560	6 249	2.3	4.7
097 CHR CHS&CHS CR	4	1 220	1 486*	0.5	1.1
151 L-D SAINTS....	2	NA	1 210	0.4	0.9
157 CH OF BRETHREN	1	28	34*	–	–
165 CH OF NAZARENE	8	2 590	4 589	1.7	3.4
167 CHS OF CHRIST.	5	1 129	1 168	0.4	0.9
193 EPISCOPAL.....	6	3 099	3 836	1.4	2.9
201 EVAN COV CH AM	3	709	863*	0.3	0.6
208 EVAN LUTH ASSN	1	505	633	0.2	0.5
226 FRIENDS-USA...	1	80	97*	–	0.1
237 GC MENN BR CHS	1	46	56*	–	–
271 REFORM JUDAISM	1	288	351*	0.1	0.3
281 LUTH CH AMER..	4	1 957	2 442	0.9	1.8
283 LUTH--MO SYNOD	5	3 599	4 827	1.8	3.6
353 CHR BRETHREN..	1	120	100	–	0.1
356 PRESB CH AMER.	1	594	817	0.3	0.6
357 PRESB CH US...	13	12 248	14 915*	5.5	11.1
383 REF PRES OF NA	1	103	131	–	0.1
413 S.D.A.........	2	543	661*	0.2	0.5
419 SO BAPT CONV..	12	5 438	6 622*	2.5	4.9
435 UNITARIAN-UNIV	1	158	192*	0.1	0.1
443 UN C OF CHRIST	3	1 027	1 251*	0.5	0.9
449 UN METHODIST..	17	12 437	15 145*	5.6	11.3
453 UN PRES CH USA	12	6 055	7 373*	2.7	5.5
469 WELS..........	1	192	281	0.1	0.2
KEARNY	14	1 298	2 105*	61.3	100.0
019 AMER BAPT USA.	1	105	133*	3.9	6.3
053 ASSEMB OF GOD.	1	101	90	2.6	4.3
081 CATHOLIC......	2	NA	483	14.1	22.9
093 CHR CH (DISC).	1	38	58	1.7	2.8
097 CHR CHS&CHS CR	1	34	43*	1.3	2.0
167 CHS OF CHRIST.	1	40	51	1.5	2.4
283 LUTH--MO SYNOD	1	141	188	5.5	8.9
419 SO BAPT CONV..	1	39	49*	1.4	2.3
449 UN METHODIST..	4	673	850*	24.7	40.4
453 UN PRES CH USA	1	127	160*	4.7	7.6
KINGMAN	29	3 083	6 502*	72.6	100.0
019 AMER BAPT USA.	2	414	496*	5.5	7.6
053 ASSEMB OF GOD.	1	28	25	0.3	0.4
081 CATHOLIC......	7	NA	2 661	29.7	40.9
093 CHR CH (DISC).	2	348	516	5.8	7.9
097 CHR CHS&CHS CR	2	150	180*	2.0	2.8
165 CH OF NAZARENE	1	48	84	0.9	1.3
167 CHS OF CHRIST.	3	70	89	1.0	1.4
193 EPISCOPAL.....	1	31	50	0.6	0.8
208 EVAN LUTH ASSN	1	34	45	0.5	0.7
283 LUTH--MO SYNOD	1	162	201	2.2	3.1
287 MENN GEN CONF.	1	179	217	2.4	3.3
449 UN METHODIST..	6	1 417	1 696*	18.9	26.1
453 UN PRES CH USA	1	202	242*	2.7	3.7
KIOWA	14	2 436	3 137*	77.5	100.0
019 AMER BAPT USA.	1	232	277*	6.8	8.8
053 ASSEMB OF GOD.	1	65	150	3.7	4.8
081 CATHOLIC......	1	NA	121	3.0	3.9
093 CHR CH (DISC).	1	196	278	6.9	8.9
097 CHR CHS&CHS CR	1	50	60*	1.5	1.9
143 CG IN CR(MENN)	1	80	80	2.0	2.6
167 CHS OF CHRIST.	1	25	30	0.7	1.0
226 FRIENDS-USA...	1	505	604*	14.9	19.3
283 LUTH--MO SYNOD	1	51	65	1.6	2.1
285 MENNONITE CH..	1	11	13*	0.3	0.4
449 UN METHODIST..	4	1 221	1 459*	36.1	46.5
LABETTE	65	9 026	14 315*	55.7	100.0
019 AMER BAPT USA.	5	1 348	1 632*	6.4	11.4
053 ASSEMB OF GOD.	4	409	630	2.5	4.4
081 CATHOLIC......	4	NA	2 800	10.9	19.6
093 CHR CH (DISC).	2	597	830	3.2	5.8
097 CHR CHS&CHS CR	7	779	943*	3.7	6.6
123 CH GOD (ANDER)	1	5	15	0.1	0.1
127 CH GOD (CLEVE)	3	162	196*	0.8	1.4
151 L-D SAINTS....	1	NA	63	0.2	0.4
157 CH OF BRETHREN	1	152	184*	0.7	1.3
165 CH OF NAZARENE	2	178	368	1.4	2.6
167 CHS OF CHRIST.	2	70	89	0.3	0.6
193 EPISCOPAL.....	1	261	348	1.4	2.4
217 FIRE BAPTIZED.	3	84	102*	0.4	0.7
263 INT FOURSQ GOS	1	180	218*	0.8	1.5
283 LUTH--MO SYNOD	2	245	360	1.4	2.5
329 OPEN BIBLE STD	1	85	125	0.5	0.9
357 PRESB CH US...	2	209	253*	1.0	1.8
413 S.D.A.........	1	36	44*	0.2	0.3
419 SO BAPT CONV..	4	1 149	1 391*	5.4	9.7
449 UN METHODIST..	16	2 867	3 470*	13.5	24.2
453 UN PRES CH USA	2	210	254*	1.0	1.8
LANE	7	1 321	2 227*	90.1	100.0
019 AMER BAPT USA.	1	26	31*	1.3	1.4
081 CATHOLIC......	1	NA	304	12.3	13.7
093 CHR CH (DISC).	1	483	893	36.1	40.1
283 LUTH--MO SYNOD	1	64	94	3.8	4.2
449 UN METHODIST..	3	748	905*	36.6	40.6
LEAVENWORTH	54	9 064	20 458*	37.3	100.0

NA—Not applicable   *Total adherents estimated from known number of communicant, confirmed, full members.   —Represents a percent less than 0.1.   Percentages may not total due to rounding.

Table 4. Churches and Church Membership by County and Denomination: 1980

County and Denomination	Number of churches	Communicant, confirmed, full members	Total adherents Number	Percent of total population	Percent of total adherents
017 AMER BAPT ASSN	1	160	160	0.3	0.8
019 AMER BAPT USA.	6	1 332	1 627*	3.0	8.0
053 ASSEMB OF GOD.	3	210	338	0.6	1.7
081 CATHOLIC......	9	NA	7 871	14.4	38.5
093 CHR CH (DISC).	1	467	744	1.4	3.6
097 CHR CHS&CHS CR	2	390	476*	0.9	2.3
123 CH GOD (ANDER)	1	10	30	0.1	0.1
151 L-D SAINTS....	1	NA	387	0.7	1.9
165 CH OF NAZARENE	1	68	143	0.3	0.7
167 CHS OF CHRIST.	1	150	191	0.3	0.9
193 EPISCOPAL.....	2	669	885	1.6	4.3
226 FRIENDS-USA...	2	174	213*	0.4	1.0
283 LUTH--MO SYNOD	3	1 094	1 470	2.7	7.2
357 PRESB CH US...	1	284	347*	0.6	1.7
403 SALVATION ARMY	1	154	810	1.5	4.0
413 S.D.A.........	2	138	169*	0.3	0.8
419 SO BAPT CONV..	3	728	889*	1.6	4.3
443 UN C OF CHRIST	2	218	266*	0.5	1.3
449 UN METHODIST..	11	2 534	3 095*	5.6	15.1
453 UN PRES CH USA	1	284	347*	0.6	1.7
LINCOLN	**17**	**2 286**	**3 020***	**72.9**	**100.0**
019 AMER BAPT USA.	1	125	146*	3.5	4.8
081 CATHOLIC......	1	NA	246	5.9	8.1
093 CHR CH (DISC).	1	40	62	1.5	2.1
097 CHR CHS&CHS CR	1	75	88*	2.1	2.9
181 CONSRV CONGR..	1	44	51*	1.2	1.7
281 LUTH CH AMER..	1	51	60	1.4	2.0
283 LUTH--MO SYNOD	3	992	1 246	30.1	41.3
443 UN C OF CHRIST	1	26	30*	0.7	1.0
449 UN METHODIST..	4	597	698*	16.8	23.1
453 UN PRES CH USA	3	336	393*	9.5	13.0
LINN	**22**	**2 471**	**3 499***	**42.5**	**100.0**
019 AMER BAPT USA.	3	227	272*	3.3	7.8
053 ASSEMB OF GOD.	1	63	76	0.9	2.2
059 BAPT MISS ASSN	1	157	188*	2.3	5.4
081 CATHOLIC......	1	NA	360	4.4	10.3
093 CHR CH (DISC).	2	337	541	6.6	15.5
097 CHR CHS&CHS CR	3	350	419*	5.1	12.0
165 CH OF NAZARENE	1	46	97	1.2	2.8
357 PRESB CH US...	1	49	59*	0.7	1.7
413 S.D.A.........	1	24	29*	0.4	0.8
449 UN METHODIST..	7	1 169	1 399*	17.0	40.0
453 UN PRES CH USA	1	49	59*	0.7	1.7
LOGAN	**11**	**1 351**	**2 904***	**83.5**	**100.0**
081 CATHOLIC......	1	NA	1 171	33.7	40.3
097 CHR CHS&CHS CR	1	350	420*	12.1	14.5
151 L-D SAINTS....	1	NA	86	2.5	3.0
165 CH OF NAZARENE	1	29	32	0.9	1.1
167 CHS OF CHRIST.	1	25	32	0.9	1.1
193 EPISCOPAL.....	1	31	51	1.5	1.8
281 LUTH CH AMER..	1	56	64	1.8	2.2
283 LUTH--MO SYNOD	1	149	195	5.6	6.7
449 UN METHODIST..	2	697	836*	24.0	28.8
453 UN PRES CH USA	1	14	17*	0.5	0.6
LYON	**45**	**8 767**	**15 785***	**45.0**	**100.0**
019 AMER BAPT USA.	2	506	606*	1.7	3.8
053 ASSEMB OF GOD.	2	281	448	1.3	2.8
081 CATHOLIC......	5	NA	4 192	11.9	26.6
093 CHR CH (DISC).	1	675	905	2.6	5.7
097 CHR CHS&CHS CR	2	185	222*	0.6	1.4
123 CH GOD (ANDER)	1	35	105	0.3	0.7
151 L-D SAINTS....	1	NA	200	0.6	1.3
157 CH OF BRETHREN	1	62	74*	0.2	0.5
165 CH OF NAZARENE	1	163	285	0.8	1.8
167 CHS OF CHRIST.	1	90	120	0.3	0.8
193 EPISCOPAL.....	1	204	250	0.7	1.6
221 FREE METHODIST	2	70	189	0.5	1.2
226 FRIENDS-USA...	3	266	319*	0.9	2.0
263 INT FOURSQ GOS	1	66	79*	0.2	0.5
281 LUTH CH AMER..	1	500	694	2.0	4.4
283 LUTH--MO SYNOD	1	554	795	2.3	5.0
403 SALVATION ARMY	1	128	335	1.0	2.1
413 S.D.A.........	1	21	25*	0.1	0.2
419 SO BAPT CONV..	2	460	551*	1.6	3.5
443 UN C OF CHRIST	1	?	?	?	?
449 UN METHODIST..	11	3 475	4 162*	11.9	26.4
453 UN PRES CH USA	3	1 026	1 229*	3.5	7.8
MC PHERSON	**62**	**14 760**	**20 280***	**75.5**	**100.0**
019 AMER BAPT USA.	3	1 211	1 440*	5.4	7.1
081 CATHOLIC......	1	NA	1 462	5.4	7.2
093 CHR CH (DISC).	3	625	900	3.4	4.4
097 CHR CHS&CHS CR	1	75	89*	0.3	0.4
123 CH GOD (ANDER)	1	30	90	0.3	0.4
127 CH GOD (CLEVE)	1	17	20*	0.1	0.1
143 CG IN CR(MENN)	4	904	904	3.4	4.5
157 CH OF BRETHREN	2	478	568*	2.1	2.8
165 CH OF NAZARENE	1	89	154	0.6	0.8
167 CHS OF CHRIST.	3	163	208	0.8	1.0
193 EPISCOPAL.....	1	50	90	0.3	0.4
201 EVAN COV CH AM	4	410	488*	1.8	2.4
221 FREE METHODIST	1	376	1 110	4.1	5.5
237 GC MENN BR CHS	1	294	350*	1.3	1.7
263 INT FOURSQ GOS	1	98	117*	0.4	0.6
281 LUTH CH AMER..	7	2 715	3 432	12.8	16.9
283 LUTH--MO SYNOD	3	570	724	2.7	3.6

County and Denomination	Number of churches	Communicant, confirmed, full members	Total adherents Number	Percent of total population	Percent of total adherents
285 MENNONITE CH..	1	72	86*	0.3	0.4
287 MENN GEN CONF.	8	2 764	3 506	13.1	17.3
413 S.D.A.........	1	12	14*	0.1	0.1
419 SO BAPT CONV..	2	58	69*	0.3	0.3
443 UN C OF CHRIST	2	572	680*	2.5	3.4
449 UN METHODIST..	8	2 724	3 240*	12.1	16.0
453 UN PRES CH USA	2	453	539*	2.0	2.7
MARION	**49**	**7 814**	**10 815***	**80.0**	**100.0**
019 AMER BAPT USA.	1	95	111*	0.8	1.0
029 AMER LUTH CH..	1	57	80	0.6	0.7
081 CATHOLIC......	4	NA	1 468	10.9	13.6
093 CHR CH (DISC).	2	425	637	4.7	5.9
097 CHR CHS&CHS CR	1	150	175*	1.3	1.6
123 CH GOD (ANDER)	1	14	42	0.3	0.4
143 CG IN CR(MENN)	3	286	286	2.1	2.6
165 CH OF NAZARENE	1	?	?	?	?
167 CHS OF CHRIST.	1	25	38	0.3	0.4
237 GC MENN BR CHS	4	1 405	1 643*	12.2	15.2
281 LUTH CH AMER..	1	60	86	0.6	0.8
283 LUTH--MO SYNOD	6	980	1 165	8.6	10.8
287 MENN GEN CONF.	7	2 054	2 438	18.0	22.5
313 N AM BAPT CONF	3	375	438*	3.2	4.0
413 S.D.A.........	2	39	46*	0.3	0.4
449 UN METHODIST..	10	1 711	2 001*	14.8	18.5
453 UN PRES CH USA	1	138	161*	1.2	1.5
MARSHALL	**43**	**5 033**	**9 685***	**76.1**	**100.0**
019 AMER BAPT USA.	1	180	211*	1.7	2.2
063 BEREAN FUND CH	1	5	6*	–	0.1
081 CATHOLIC......	8	NA	3 517	27.6	36.3
093 CHR CH (DISC).	1	198	302	2.4	3.1
097 CHR CHS&CHS CR	1	75	88*	0.7	0.9
151 L-D SAINTS....	1	NA	46	0.4	0.5
157 CH OF BRETHREN	1	50	59*	0.5	0.6
167 CHS OF CHRIST.	1	25	40	0.3	0.4
193 EPISCOPAL.....	2	35	81	0.6	0.8
201 EVAN COV CH AM	1	30	35*	0.3	0.4
221 FREE METHODIST	1	6	24	0.2	0.2
281 LUTH CH AMER..	3	655	764	6.0	7.9
283 LUTH--MO SYNOD	6	1 034	1 298	10.2	13.4
413 S.D.A.........	1	12	14*	0.1	0.1
419 SO BAPT CONV..	1	138	162*	1.3	1.7
443 UN C OF CHRIST	1	301	353*	2.8	3.6
449 UN METHODIST..	8	1 700	1 994*	15.7	20.6
453 UN PRES CH USA	4	589	691*	5.4	7.1
MEADE	**18**	**2 059**	**3 590***	**75.0**	**100.0**
019 AMER BAPT USA.	2	316	380*	7.9	10.6
081 CATHOLIC......	3	NA	900	18.8	25.1
097 CHR CHS&CHS CR	3	222	267*	5.6	7.4
165 CH OF NAZARENE	1	105	241	5.0	6.7
167 CHS OF CHRIST.	1	35	45	0.9	1.3
193 EPISCOPAL.....	1	19	19	0.4	0.5
211 EVAN MENN BR.	1	170	221	4.6	6.2
226 FRIENDS-USA...	1	89	107*	2.2	3.0
283 LUTH--MO SYNOD	1	162	277	5.8	7.7
449 UN METHODIST..	3	873	1 051*	22.0	29.3
453 UN PRES CH USA	1	68	82*	1.7	2.3
MIAMI	**46**	**6 194**	**10 510***	**48.6**	**100.0**
019 AMER BAPT USA.	5	1 191	1 443*	6.7	13.7
053 ASSEMB OF GOD.	3	306	581	2.7	5.5
057 BAPT GEN CONF.	0	4	5*	–	–
081 CATHOLIC......	4	NA	2 309	10.7	22.0
093 CHR CH (DISC).	3	468	722	3.3	6.9
097 CHR CHS&CHS CR	3	200	242*	1.1	2.3
151 L-D SAINTS....	1	NA	188	0.9	1.8
165 CH OF NAZARENE	1	119	199	0.9	1.9
167 CHS OF CHRIST.	4	100	127	0.6	1.2
226 FRIENDS-USA...	1	32	39*	0.2	0.4
283 LUTH--MO SYNOD	2	950	1 234	5.7	11.7
357 PRESB CH US...	5	333	403*	1.9	3.8
419 SO BAPT CONV..	1	309	374*	1.7	3.6
449 UN METHODIST..	8	1 846	2 237*	10.3	21.3
453 UN PRES CH USA	5	336	407*	1.9	3.9
MITCHELL	**26**	**3 376**	**6 992***	**86.1**	**100.0**
019 AMER BAPT USA.	3	340	407*	5.0	5.8
053 ASSEMB OF GOD.	1	161	225	2.8	3.2
081 CATHOLIC......	3	NA	2 835	34.9	40.5
093 CHR CH (DISC).	1	315	395	4.9	5.6
097 CHR CHS&CHS CR	2	173	207*	2.6	3.0
167 CHS OF CHRIST.	3	81	108	1.3	1.5
193 EPISCOPAL.....	1	15	20	0.2	0.3
226 FRIENDS-USA...	1	118	141*	1.7	2.0
281 LUTH CH AMER..	1	374	491	6.0	7.0
283 LUTH--MO SYNOD	1	121	154	1.9	2.2
313 N AM BAPT CONF	1	73	87*	1.1	1.2
449 UN METHODIST..	6	1 366	1 636*	20.2	23.4
453 UN PRES CH USA	2	239	286*	3.5	4.1
MONTGOMERY	**97**	**16 730**	**25 105***	**59.4**	**100.0**
017 AMER BAPT ASSN	2	100	100	0.2	0.4
019 AMER BAPT USA.	4	2 376	2 865*	6.8	11.4
053 ASSEMB OF GOD.	4	424	833	2.0	3.3
059 BAPT MISS ASSN	1	181	218*	0.5	0.9
081 CATHOLIC......	5	NA	3 059	7.2	12.2
093 CHR CH (DISC).	5	1 544	2 474	5.9	9.9

NA—Not applicable   *Total adherents estimated from known number of communicant, confirmed, full members.   —Represents a percent less than 0.1.   Percentages may not total due to rounding.

Table 4. Churches and Church Membership by County and Denomination: 1980

County and Denomination	Number of churches	Communicant, confirmed, full members	Total adherents		
			Number	Percent of total population	Percent of total adherents
097 CHR CHS&CHS CR	6	1 340	1 616*	3.8	6.4
101 C.M.E.........	1	105	127*	0.3	0.5
123 CH GOD (ANDER)	1	60	180	0.4	0.7
127 CH GOD (CLEVE)	3	216	260*	0.6	1.0
151 L-D SAINTS....	2	NA	206	0.5	0.8
157 CH OF BRETHREN	1	117	141*	0.3	0.6
165 CH OF NAZARENE	6	678	1 220	2.9	4.9
167 CHS OF CHRIST.	4	175	223	0.5	0.9
193 EPISCOPAL.....	2	360	473	1.1	1.9
217 FIRE BAPTIZED	5	163	197*	0.5	0.8
226 FRIENDS-USA...	3	90	109*	0.3	0.4
283 LUTH--MO SYNOD	3	1 105	1 380	3.3	5.5
335 ORTH PRESB CH.	1	30	36*	0.1	0.1
349 PENT HOLINESS.	6	268	323*	0.8	1.3
403 SALVATION ARMY	1	81	242	0.6	1.0
413 S.D.A.........	4	184	222*	0.5	0.9
419 SO BAPT CONV..	9	2 168	2 614*	6.2	10.4
443 UN C OF CHRIST	1	83	100*	0.2	0.4
449 UN METHODIST..	14	3 807	4 591*	10.9	18.3
453 UN PRES CH USA	3	1 075	1 296*	3.1	5.2
MORRIS	19	2 893	3 877*	60.4	100.0
019 AMER BAPT USA.	1	81	96*	1.5	2.5
081 CATHOLIC......	1	NA	268	4.2	6.9
093 CHR CH (DISC).	1	395	607	9.5	15.7
097 CHR CHS&CHS CR	3	610	721*	11.2	18.6
281 LUTH CH AMER..	2	267	346	5.4	8.9
283 LUTH--MO SYNOD	2	216	274	4.3	7.1
443 UN C OF CHRIST	1	166	196*	3.1	5.1
449 UN METHODIST..	7	1 065	1 259*	19.6	32.5
453 UN PRES CH USA	1	93	110*	1.7	2.8
MORTON	14	2 501	3 712*	107.5	100.0
019 AMER BAPT USA.	1	167	209*	6.1	5.6
053 ASSEMB OF GOD.	1	6	7	0.2	0.2
081 CATHOLIC......	1	NA	350	10.1	9.4
097 CHR CHS&CHS CR	2	1 025	1 283*	37.1	34.6
123 CH GOD (ANDER)	1	97	291	8.4	7.8
165 CH OF NAZARENE	1	123	210	6.1	5.7
167 CHS OF CHRIST.	1	35	36	1.0	1.0
283 LUTH--MO SYNOD	1	92	129	3.7	3.5
349 PENT HOLINESS.	1	26	33*	1.0	0.9
419 SO BAPT CONV..	1	231	289*	8.4	7.8
449 UN METHODIST..	3	699	875*	25.3	23.6
NEMAHA	25	3 170	8 526*	76.1	100.0
019 AMER BAPT USA.	2	228	276*	2.5	3.2
081 CATHOLIC......	7	NA	4 622	41.2	54.2
097 CHR CHS&CHS CR	1	135	163*	1.5	1.9
157 CH OF BRETHREN	1	84	102*	0.9	1.2
167 CHS OF CHRIST.	1	69	120	1.1	1.4
175 CONGR CHR CHS.	1	510	618*	5.5	7.2
283 LUTH--MO SYNOD	1	139	197*	1.8	2.3
443 UN C OF CHRIST	3	569	689*	6.1	8.1
449 UN METHODIST..	8	1 436	1 739*	15.5	20.4
NEOSHO	44	5 991	10 614*	56.0	100.0
019 AMER BAPT USA.	4	944	1 141*	6.0	10.7
053 ASSEMB OF GOD.	1	216	300	1.6	2.8
081 CATHOLIC......	4	NA	2 655	14.0	25.0
093 CHR CH (DISC).	3	670	1 142	6.0	10.8
097 CHR CHS&CHS CR	3	336	406*	2.1	3.8
123 CH GOD (ANDER)	1	21	63	0.3	0.6
127 CH GOD (CLEVE)	1	79	95*	0.5	0.9
165 CH OF NAZARENE	2	166	312	1.6	2.9
167 CHS OF CHRIST.	2	35	45	0.2	0.4
193 EPISCOPAL.....	1	235	441	2.3	4.2
226 FRIENDS-USA...	1	34	41*	0.2	0.4
281 LUTH CH AMER..	1	30	36	0.2	0.3
283 LUTH--MO SYNOD	1	493	635	3.3	6.0
349 PENT HOLINESS.	2	61	74*	0.4	0.7
357 PRESB CH US...	1	112	135*	0.7	1.3
413 S.D.A.........	2	90	109*	0.6	1.0
419 SO BAPT CONV..	2	268	324*	1.7	3.1
449 UN METHODIST..	9	1 997	2 413*	12.7	22.7
453 UN PRES CH USA	3	204	247*	1.3	2.3
NESS	22	2 381	4 294*	95.5	100.0
019 AMER BAPT USA.	2	337	398*	8.8	9.3
029 AMER LUTH CH..	1	104	126	2.8	2.9
053 ASSEMB OF GOD.	2	33	50	1.1	1.2
081 CATHOLIC......	2	NA	1 423	31.6	33.1
093 CHR CH (DISC).	1	112	167	3.7	3.9
167 CHS OF CHRIST.	2	85	100	2.2	2.3
283 LUTH--MO SYNOD	1	102	123	2.7	2.9
287 MENN GEN CONF.	1	135	166	3.7	3.9
413 S.D.A.........	1	47	56*	1.2	1.3
419 SO BAPT CONV..	1	41	48*	1.1	1.1
443 UN C OF CHRIST	1	?	?	?	?
449 UN METHODIST..	7	1 385	1 637*	36.4	38.1
NORTON	20	1 999	3 723*	55.7	100.0
019 AMER BAPT USA.	1	175	206*	3.1	5.5
081 CATHOLIC......	3	NA	1 107	16.5	29.7
097 CHR CHS&CHS CR	1	50	59*	0.9	1.6
123 CH GOD (ANDER)	2	132	396	5.9	10.6
157 CH OF BRETHREN	1	64	75*	1.1	2.0
167 CHS OF CHRIST.	1	30	45	0.7	1.2
175 CONGR CHR CHS.	1	90	106*	1.6	2.8

County and Denomination	Number of churches	Communicant, confirmed, full members	Total adherents		
			Number	Percent of total population	Percent of total adherents
193 EPISCOPAL.....	1	91	103	1.5	2.8
283 LUTH--MO SYNOD	1	135	176	2.6	4.7
413 S.D.A.........	1	8	9*	0.1	0.2
443 UN C OF CHRIST	1	97	114*	1.7	3.1
449 UN METHODIST..	5	1 068	1 257*	18.8	33.8
469 WELS..........	1	59	70	1.0	1.9
OSAGE	26	3 257	4 924*	32.1	100.0
053 ASSEMB OF GOD.	3	103	208	1.4	4.2
081 CATHOLIC......	2	NA	750	4.9	15.2
093 CHR CH (DISC).	1	162	168	1.1	3.4
097 CHR CHS&CHS CR	1	80	97*	0.6	2.0
123 CH GOD (ANDER)	1	50	150	1.0	3.0
167 CHS OF CHRIST.	2	46	65	0.4	1.3
201 EVAN COV CH AM	3	152	184*	1.2	3.7
221 FREE METHODIST	1	24	90	0.6	1.8
281 LUTH CH AMER..	1	129	161	1.1	3.3
283 LUTH--MO SYNOD	1	261	325	2.1	6.6
419 SO BAPT CONV..	1	124	150*	1.0	3.0
443 UN C OF CHRIST	1	199	241*	1.6	4.9
449 UN METHODIST..	6	1 644	1 992*	13.0	40.5
453 UN PRES CH USA	2	283	343*	2.2	7.0
OSBORNE	29	2 833	4 261*	71.5	100.0
019 AMER BAPT USA.	1	36	43*	0.7	1.0
029 AMER LUTH CH..	1	108	134	2.2	3.1
053 ASSEMB OF GOD.	1	106	151	2.5	3.5
081 CATHOLIC......	2	NA	577	9.7	13.5
093 CHR CH (DISC).	1	229	352	5.9	8.3
097 CHR CHS&CHS CR	1	125	148*	2.5	3.5
157 CH OF BRETHREN	1	19	22*	0.4	0.5
165 CH OF NAZARENE	1	43	50	0.8	1.2
221 FREE METHODIST	1	55	279	4.7	6.5
226 FRIENDS-USA...	1	57	67*	1.1	1.6
244 GRACE BRETHREN	1	115	136*	2.3	3.2
283 LUTH--MO SYNOD	2	429	514	8.6	12.1
413 S.D.A.........	1	20	24*	0.4	0.6
443 UN C OF CHRIST	2	188	222*	3.7	5.2
449 UN METHODIST..	10	1 240	1 467*	24.6	34.4
453 UN PRES CH USA	2	63	75*	1.3	1.8
OTTAWA	23	2 017	2 961*	49.6	100.0
019 AMER BAPT USA.	2	192	227*	3.8	7.7
029 AMER LUTH CH..	1	105	146	2.4	4.9
081 CATHOLIC......	3	NA	385	6.4	13.0
165 CH OF NAZARENE	1	35	112	1.9	3.8
193 EPISCOPAL.....	1	35	42	0.7	1.4
221 FREE METHODIST	1	43	147	2.5	5.0
349 PENT HOLINESS.	1	18	21*	0.4	0.7
449 UN METHODIST..	9	1 120	1 326*	22.2	44.8
453 UN PRES CH USA	4	469	555*	9.3	18.7
PAWNEE	20	3 342	5 285*	65.5	100.0
019 AMER BAPT USA.	2	305	361*	4.5	6.8
053 ASSEMB OF GOD.	1	58	136	1.7	2.6
081 CATHOLIC......	2	NA	946	11.7	17.9
093 CHR CH (DISC).	1	315	562	7.0	10.6
151 L-D SAINTS....	1	NA	73	0.9	1.4
165 CH OF NAZARENE	1	80	111	1.4	2.1
167 CHS OF CHRIST.	2	55	70	0.9	1.3
193 EPISCOPAL.....	1	45	67	0.8	1.3
281 LUTH CH AMER..	1	50	57	0.7	1.1
283 LUTH--MO SYNOD	1	295	372	4.6	7.0
349 PENT HOLINESS.	1	96	114*	1.4	2.2
419 SO BAPT CONV..	1	119	141*	1.7	2.7
449 UN METHODIST..	4	1 596	1 887*	23.4	35.7
453 UN PRES CH USA	1	328	388*	4.8	7.3
PHILLIPS	29	3 329	4 895*	66.1	100.0
019 AMER BAPT USA.	1	129	153*	2.1	3.1
029 AMER LUTH CH..	3	630	767	10.4	15.7
053 ASSEMB OF GOD.	1	32	51	0.7	1.0
081 CATHOLIC......	2	NA	468	6.3	9.6
093 CHR CH (DISC).	1	275	423	5.7	8.6
097 CHR CHS&CHS CR	1	130	155*	2.1	3.2
105 CHRISTIAN REF.	1	186	276	3.7	5.6
123 CH GOD (ANDER)	1	62	186	2.5	3.8
151 L-D SAINTS....	1	NA	81	1.1	1.7
165 CH OF NAZARENE	2	53	74	1.0	1.5
167 CHS OF CHRIST.	2	73	82	1.1	1.7
221 FREE METHODIST	1	11	24	0.3	0.5
283 LUTH--MO SYNOD	1	112	136	1.8	2.8
353 CH BRETHREN...	1	15	15	0.2	0.3
371 REF CH IN AM..	1	167	276	3.7	5.6
413 S.D.A.........	1	37	44*	0.6	0.9
449 UN METHODIST..	7	1 225	1 456*	19.7	29.7
453 UN PRES CH USA	1	192	228*	3.1	4.7
POTTAWATOMIE	36	3 788	8 073*	54.6	100.0
019 AMER BAPT USA.	3	292	356*	2.4	4.4
029 AMER LUTH CH..	1	25	34	0.2	0.4
053 ASSEMB OF GOD.	1	19	25	0.2	0.3
081 CATHOLIC......	7	NA	3 383	22.9	41.9
097 CHR CHS&CHS CR	2	230	280*	1.9	3.5
127 CH GOD (CLEVE)	1	13	16*	0.1	0.2
167 CHS OF CHRIST.	1	15	19	0.1	0.2
193 EPISCOPAL.....	1	112	122	0.8	1.5
237 GC MENN BR CHS	1	25	30*	0.2	0.4
281 LUTH CH AMER..	1	154	182	1.2	2.3

NA—Not applicable   *Total adherents estimated from known number of communicant, confirmed, full members.   —Represents a percent less than 0.1.   Percentages may not total due to rounding.

Table 4. Churches and Church Membership by County and Denomination: 1980

County and Denomination	Number of churches	Communicant, confirmed, full members	Total adherents Number	Percent of total population	Percent of total adherents
283 LUTH--MO SYNOD	3	733	982	6.6	12.2
443 UN C OF CHRIST	3	605	737*	5.0	9.1
449 UN METHODIST..	10	1 382	1 684*	11.4	20.9
453 UN PRES CH USA	1	183	223*	1.5	2.8
PRATT	31	3 802	5 996*	58.4	100.0
019 AMER BAPT USA.	2	287	340*	3.3	5.7
053 ASSEMB OF GOD.	1	133	247	2.4	4.1
081 CATHOLIC......	1	NA	854	8.3	14.2
093 CHR CH (DISC).	2	506	770	7.5	12.8
123 CH GOD (ANDER)	1	57	171	1.7	2.9
127 CH GOD (CLEVE)	1	?	?	?	?
151 L-D SAINTS....	1	NA	79	0.8	1.3
165 CH OF NAZARENE	1	86	127	1.2	2.1
167 CHS OF CHRIST.	3	100	127	1.2	2.1
193 EPISCOPAL.....	1	77	108	1.1	1.8
221 FREE METHODIST	1	46	135	1.3	2.3
226 FRIENDS-USA...	3	123	146*	1.4	2.4
283 LUTH--MO SYNOD	2	455	603	5.9	10.1
349 PENT HOLINESS	1	44	52*	0.5	0.9
419 SO BAPT CONV..	1	109	129*	1.3	2.2
449 UN METHODIST..	8	1 537	1 821*	17.7	30.4
453 UN PRES CH USA	1	242	287*	2.8	4.8
RAWLINS	10	1 316	2 963*	72.2	100.0
081 CATHOLIC......	3	NA	1 339	32.6	45.2
093 CHR CH (DISC).	1	180	250	6.1	8.4
165 CH OF NAZARENE	1	18	20	0.5	0.7
201 EVAN COV CH AM	1	68	82*	2.0	2.8
283 LUTH--MO SYNOD	2	323	397	9.7	13.4
443 UN C OF CHRIST	1	131	158*	3.8	5.3
449 UN METHODIST..	1	596	717*	17.5	24.2
RENO	97	22 470	35 210*	54.2	100.0
019 AMER BAPT USA.	5	1 364	1 643*	2.5	4.7
053 ASSEMB OF GOD.	3	342	556	0.9	1.6
061 BEACHY AMISH..	1	267	322*	0.5	0.9
081 CATHOLIC......	5	NA	5 358	8.2	15.2
093 CHR CH (DISC).	5	1 167	2 303	3.5	6.5
097 CHR CHS&CHS CR	3	315	379*	0.6	1.1
123 CH GOD (ANDER)	1	175	525	0.8	1.5
127 CH GOD (CLEVE)	1	46	55*	0.1	0.2
151 L-D SAINTS....	1	NA	252	0.4	0.7
157 CH OF BRETHREN	2	273	329*	0.5	0.9
165 CH OF NAZARENE	5	1 131	2 125	3.3	6.0
167 CHS OF CHRIST.	5	450	573	0.9	1.6
175 CONGR CHR CHS.	1	245	295*	0.5	0.8
193 EPISCOPAL.....	1	546	617	0.9	1.8
203 EVAN FREE CH..	1	37	45*	0.1	0.1
208 EVAN LUTH ASSN	1	42	52	0.1	0.1
213 EVAN MENN INC.	1	218	263*	0.4	0.7
221 FREE METHODIST	1	25	81	0.1	0.2
226 FRIENDS-USA...	1	129	155*	0.2	0.4
237 GC MENN BR CHS	1	400	482*	0.7	1.4
239 SWEDENBORGIAN.	1	60	72*	0.1	0.2
263 INT FOURSQ GOS	1	59	71*	0.1	0.2
281 LUTH CH AMER..	2	744	1 023	1.6	2.9
283 LUTH--MO SYNOD	3	1 145	1 468*	2.3	4.2
285 MENNONITE CH..	4	653	787*	1.2	2.2
287 MENN GEN CONF.	4	1 347	1 617	2.5	4.6
291 MISSIONARY CH.	1	35	41	0.1	0.1
323 OLD ORD AMISH.	3	390	470*	0.7	1.3
349 PENT HOLINESS	1	54	65*	0.1	0.2
353 CHR BRETHREN..	1	40	100	0.2	0.3
403 SALVATION ARMY	1	123	260	0.4	0.7
413 S.D.A.........	1	194	234*	0.4	0.7
419 SO BAPT CONV..	3	1 157	1 394*	2.1	4.0
435 UNITARIAN-UNIV	1	15	18*	-	0.1
443 UN C OF CHRIST	3	420	506*	0.8	1.4
449 UN METHODIST..	18	7 399	8 912*	13.7	25.3
453 UN PRES CH USA	4	1 463	1 762*	2.7	5.0
REPUBLIC	25	3 285	4 601*	60.8	100.0
019 AMER BAPT USA.	1	127	148*	2.0	3.2
029 AMER LUTH CH..	2	255	343	4.5	7.5
053 ASSEMB OF GOD.	1	34	57	0.8	1.2
081 CATHOLIC......	3	NA	657	8.7	14.3
097 CHR CHS&CHS CR	2	335	391*	5.2	8.5
201 EVAN COV CH AM	1	31	36*	0.5	0.8
226 FRIENDS-USA...	1	49	57*	0.8	1.2
281 LUTH CH AMER..	2	418	537	7.1	11.7
413 S.D.A.........	1	24	28*	0.4	0.6
449 UN METHODIST..	8	1 534	1 789*	23.6	38.9
453 UN PRES CH USA	3	478	558*	7.4	12.1
RICE	34	5 515	8 071*	67.8	100.0
019 AMER BAPT USA.	5	675	801*	6.7	9.9
053 ASSEMB OF GOD.	2	76	138	1.2	1.7
081 CATHOLIC......	4	NA	1 340	11.3	16.6
093 CHR CH (DISC).	1	425	529	4.4	6.6
097 CHR CHS&CHS CR	1	60	71*	0.6	0.9
151 L-D SAINTS....	1	NA	18	0.2	0.2
165 CH OF NAZARENE	2	42	108	0.9	1.3
167 CHS OF CHRIST.	1	60	100	0.8	1.2
193 EPISCOPAL.....	1	10	11	0.1	0.1
283 LUTH--MO SYNOD	1	232	280	2.4	3.5
383 REF PRES OF NA	1	83	105	0.9	1.3
419 SO BAPT CONV..	1	158	187*	1.6	2.3
443 UN C OF CHRIST	1	267	317*	2.7	3.9
449 UN METHODIST..	8	2 719	3 226*	27.1	40.0

County and Denomination	Number of churches	Communicant, confirmed, full members	Total adherents Number	Percent of total population	Percent of total adherents
453 UN PRES CH USA	4	708	840*	7.1	10.4
RILEY	47	10 777	18 606*	29.3	100.0
019 AMER BAPT USA.	1	456	537*	0.8	2.9
053 ASSEMB OF GOD.	2	273	353	0.6	1.9
059 BAPT MISS ASSN	1	17	20*	-	0.1
081 CATHOLIC......	3	NA	4 546	7.2	24.4
093 CHR CH (DISC).	1	729	1 019	1.6	5.5
097 CHR CHS&CHS CR	3	445	524*	0.8	2.8
123 CH GOD (ANDER)	1	6	18	-	0.1
151 L-D SAINTS....	2	NA	597	0.9	3.2
165 CH OF NAZARENE	1	54	124	0.2	0.7
167 CHS OF CHRIST.	3	185	233	0.4	1.3
193 EPISCOPAL.....	1	392	430	0.7	2.3
201 EVAN COV CH AM	1	54	64*	0.1	0.3
221 FREE METHODIST	1	25	90	0.1	0.5
226 FRIENDS-USA...	1	10	12*	-	0.1
271 REFORM JUDAISM	1	44	52*	0.1	0.3
281 LUTH CH AMER..	3	1 164	1 743	2.7	9.4
283 LUTH--MO SYNOD	1	526	718	1.1	3.9
285 MENNONITE CH..	1	23	27*	-	0.1
287 MENN GEN CONF.	1	30	30	-	0.2
413 S.D.A.........	1	61	72*	0.1	0.4
419 SO BAPT CONV..	1	590	695*	1.1	3.7
435 UNITARIAN-UNIV	1	45	53*	0.1	0.3
443 UN C OF CHRIST	1	259	305*	0.5	1.6
449 UN METHODIST..	9	3 689	4 343*	6.8	23.3
453 UN PRES CH USA	5	1 700	2 001*	3.2	10.8
ROOKS	21	2 638	5 239*	74.8	100.0
019 AMER BAPT USA.	1	68	82*	1.2	1.6
053 ASSEMB OF GOD.	2	80	169	2.4	3.2
081 CATHOLIC......	4	NA	1 834	26.2	35.0
097 CHR CHS&CHS CR	2	500	603*	8.6	11.5
123 CH GOD (ANDER)	1	46	138	2.0	2.6
165 CH OF NAZARENE	2	113	181	2.6	3.5
283 LUTH--MO SYNOD	1	83	113	1.6	2.2
413 S.D.A.........	1	36	43*	0.6	0.8
419 SO BAPT CONV..	1	251	303*	4.3	5.8
443 UN C OF CHRIST	1	250	302*	4.3	5.8
449 UN METHODIST..	4	1 179	1 422*	20.3	27.1
469 WELS..........	1	32	49	0.7	0.9
RUSH	18	2 095	4 070*	90.1	100.0
029 AMER LUTH CH..	4	673	828	18.3	20.3
081 CATHOLIC......	5	NA	1 573	34.8	38.6
097 CHR CHS&CHS CR	1	140	164*	3.6	4.0
313 N AM BAPT CONF	1	59	69*	1.5	1.7
413 S.D.A.........	2	115	135*	3.0	3.3
449 UN METHODIST..	5	1 108	1 301*	28.8	32.0
RUSSELL	29	3 995	6 756*	76.2	100.0
019 AMER BAPT USA.	2	250	295*	3.3	4.4
029 AMER LUTH CH..	2	294	336	3.8	5.0
053 ASSEMB OF GOD.	1	60	112	1.3	1.7
081 CATHOLIC......	3	NA	1 575	17.8	23.3
097 CHR CHS&CHS CR	1	60	71*	0.8	1.1
165 CH OF NAZARENE	1	26	37	0.4	0.5
167 CHS OF CHRIST.	1	30	56	0.6	0.8
193 EPISCOPAL.....	1	30	30	0.3	0.4
208 EVAN LUTH ASSN	1	132	182	2.1	2.7
281 LUTH CH AMER..	2	817	1 343	15.1	19.9
419 SO BAPT CONV..	1	268	316*	3.6	4.7
443 UN C OF CHRIST	2	308	364*	4.1	5.4
449 UN METHODIST..	10	1 685	1 989*	22.4	29.4
469 WELS..........	1	35	50	0.6	0.7
SALINE	55	14 849	27 739*	56.7	100.0
019 AMER BAPT USA.	2	573	690*	1.4	2.5
053 ASSEMB OF GOD.	2	142	354	0.7	1.3
081 CATHOLIC......	8	NA	7 784	15.9	28.1
093 CHR CH (DISC).	2	656	935	1.9	3.4
097 CHR CHS&CHS CR	1	120	145*	0.3	0.5
123 CH GOD (ANDER)	1	35	105	0.2	0.4
133 CH GOD(7TH)DEN	1	4	5*	-	-
151 L-D SAINTS....	1	NA	274	0.6	1.0
165 CH OF NAZARENE	2	387	969	2.0	3.5
167 CHS OF CHRIST.	1	100	127	0.3	0.5
193 EPISCOPAL.....	2	509	591	1.2	2.1
201 EVAN COV CH AM	1	289	348*	0.7	1.3
221 FREE METHODIST	1	53	156	0.3	0.6
263 INT FOURSQ GOS	1	219	264*	0.5	1.0
281 LUTH CH AMER..	7	2 612	3 273	6.7	11.8
283 LUTH--MO SYNOD	2	1 075	1 440	2.9	5.2
353 CHR BRETHREN..	1	30	45	0.1	0.2
403 SALVATION ARMY	1	135	700	1.4	2.5
413 S.D.A.........	1	137	165*	0.3	0.6
419 SO BAPT CONV..	2	959	1 156*	2.4	4.2
443 UN C OF CHRIST	1	121	146*	0.3	0.5
449 UN METHODIST..	9	4 795	5 778*	11.8	20.8
453 UN PRES CH USA	3	1 869	2 252*	4.6	8.1
469 WELS..........	1	29	37	0.1	0.1
SCOTT	16	3 331	4 999*	86.5	100.0
019 AMER BAPT USA.	1	617	764*	13.2	15.3
053 ASSEMB OF GOD.	1	28	50	0.9	1.0
081 CATHOLIC......	1	NA	591	10.2	11.8
093 CHR CH (DISC).	1	473	703	12.2	14.1
097 CHR CHS&CHS CR	1	150	186*	3.2	3.7

NA—Not applicable   *Total adherents estimated from known number of communicant, confirmed, full members.   —Represents a percent less than 0.1.   Percentages may not total due to rounding.

Table 4. Churches and Church Membership by County and Denomination: 1980

County and Denomination	Number of churches	Communicant, confirmed, full members	Total adherents Number	Total adherents Percent of total population	Total adherents Percent of total adherents
143 CG IN CR(MENN)	1	123	123	2.1	2.5
151 L-D SAINTS....	1	NA	86	1.5	1.7
157 CH OF BRETHREN	1	184	228*	3.9	4.6
165 CH OF NAZARENE	1	72	129	2.2	2.6
167 CHS OF CHRIST.	1	25	32	0.6	0.6
193 EPISCOPAL.....	1	94	94	1.6	1.9
283 LUTH--MO SYNOD	1	238	369	6.4	7.4
285 MENNONITE CH..	2	164	203*	3.5	4.1
419 SO BAPT CONV..	1	140	173*	3.0	3.5
449 UN METHODIST..	1	1 023	1 268*	21.9	25.4
SEDGWICK	323	99 044	181 811*	49.6	100.0
017 AMER BAPT ASSN	7	1 120	1 120	0.3	0.6
019 AMER BAPT USA.	21	5 561	6 753*	1.8	3.7
029 AMER LUTH CH..	2	428	614	0.2	0.3
053 ASSEMB OF GOD.	13	1 658	3 541	1.0	1.9
059 BAPT MISS ASSN	1	55	67*	-	-
071 BRETHREN (ASH)	1	134	163*	-	0.1
075 BRETHREN IN CR	1	57	86	-	-
081 CATHOLIC......	27	NA	51 056	13.9	28.1
093 CHR CH (DISC).	19	6 512	9 252	2.5	5.1
097 CHR CHS&CHS CR	14	6 829	8 292*	2.3	4.6
123 CH GOD (ANDER)	6	1 137	3 411	0.9	1.9
127 CH GOD (CLEVE)	5	469	569*	0.2	0.3
133 CH GOD(7TH)DEN	1	18	22*	-	-
151 L-D SAINTS....	4	NA	1 579	0.4	0.9
157 CH OF BRETHREN	1	475	577*	0.2	0.3
165 CH OF NAZARENE	15	2 556	4 718	1.3	2.6
167 CHS OF CHRIST.	20	3 588	4 567	1.2	2.5
193 EPISCOPAL.....	9	2 845	3 491	1.0	1.9
201 EVAN COV CH AM	1	87	106*	-	0.1
203 EVAN FREE CH..	2	281	341*	0.1	0.2
208 EVAN LUTH ASSN	1	50	58	-	-
215 EVAN METH CH..	2	137	166*	-	0.1
217 FIRE BAPTIZED.	1	16	19*	-	-
221 FREE METHODIST	2	130	435	0.1	0.2
226 FRIENDS-USA...	3	1 334	1 620*	0.4	0.9
237 GC MENN BR CHS	2	426	517*	0.1	0.3
244 GRACE BRETHREN	1	10	12*	-	-
263 INT FOURSQ GOS	3	400	486*	0.1	0.3
271 REFORM JUDAISM	1	404	491*	0.1	0.3
274 LAT EVAN LUTH.	1	18	20	-	-
281 LUTH CH AMER..	5	1 848	2 336	0.6	1.3
283 LUTH--MO SYNOD	11	4 743	6 108	1.7	3.4
285 MENNONITE CH..	2	34	41*	-	-
287 MENN GEN CONF.	2	530	762	0.2	0.4
290 METRO COMM CHS	1	100	200	0.1	0.1
291 MISSIONARY CH.	1	76	75	-	-
313 N AM BAPT CONF	1	137	166*	-	0.1
329 OPEN BIBLE STD	1	25	25	-	-
349 PENT HOLINESS.	3	356	432*	0.1	0.2
353 CHR BRETHREN..	2	125	200	0.1	0.1
383 REF PRES OF NA	1	21	34	-	-
403 SALVATION ARMY	4	754	2 248	0.6	1.2
413 S.D.A.........	2	1 027	1 247*	0.3	0.7
419 SO BAPT CONV..	29	20 048	24 344*	6.6	13.4
435 UNITARIAN-UNIV	1	155	188*	0.1	0.1
443 UN C OF CHRIST	6	1 191	1 446*	0.4	0.8
449 UN METHODIST..	45	23 564	28 613*	7.8	15.7
453 UN PRES CH USA	18	7 519	9 130*	2.5	5.0
469 WELS..........	1	56	67	-	-
SEWARD	28	5 335	9 392*	55.0	100.0
019 AMER BAPT USA.	2	801	998*	5.8	10.6
029 AMER LUTH CH..	1	113	154	0.9	1.6
053 ASSEMB OF GOD.	1	115	144	0.8	1.5
081 CATHOLIC......	1	NA	1 775	10.4	18.9
093 CHR CH (DISC).	1	270	420	2.5	4.5
097 CHR CHS&CHS CR	1	190	237*	1.4	2.5
123 CH GOD (ANDER)	3	201	603	3.5	6.4
151 L-D SAINTS....	1	NA	227	1.3	2.4
165 CH OF NAZARENE	1	137	274	1.6	2.9
167 CHS OF CHRIST.	2	328	524	3.1	5.6
193 EPISCOPAL.....	1	144	228	1.3	2.4
226 FRIENDS-USA...	2	256	319*	1.9	3.4
283 LUTH--MO SYNOD	1	244	331	1.9	3.5
287 MENN GEN CONF.	1	52	62	0.4	0.7
349 PENT HOLINESS.	1	31	39*	0.2	0.4
413 S.D.A.........	1	40	50*	0.3	0.5
419 SO BAPT CONV..	2	783	976*	5.7	10.4
449 UN METHODIST..	4	1 414	1 762*	10.3	18.8
453 UN PRES CH USA	1	216	269*	1.6	2.9
SHAWNEE	131	40 000	77 311*	49.9	100.0
017 AMER BAPT ASSN	2	320	320	0.2	0.4
019 AMER BAPT USA.	10	3 406	4 102*	2.6	5.3
029 AMER LUTH CH..	1	429	597	0.4	0.8
053 ASSEMB OF GOD.	5	708	1 169	0.8	1.5
081 CATHOLIC......	9	NA	24 915	16.1	32.2
093 CHR CH (DISC).	6	2 491	3 580	2.3	4.6
097 CHR CHS&CHS CR	8	1 223	1 473*	1.0	1.9
127 CH GOD (CLEVE)	1	27	33*	-	-
151 L-D SAINTS....	2	NA	880	0.6	1.1
157 CH OF BRETHREN	1	177	213*	0.1	0.3
165 CH OF NAZARENE	4	806	1 864	1.2	2.4
167 CHS OF CHRIST.	6	930	1 182	0.8	1.5
193 EPISCOPAL.....	3	2 125	2 697	1.7	3.5
201 EVAN COV CH AM	1	130	157*	0.1	0.2
203 EVAN FREE CH..	1	80	96*	0.1	0.1
221 FREE METHODIST	1	61	240	0.2	0.3
226 FRIENDS-USA...	1	122	147*	0.1	0.2
263 INT FOURSQ GOS	1	135	163*	0.1	0.2

County and Denomination	Number of churches	Communicant, confirmed, full members	Total adherents Number	Total adherents Percent of total population	Total adherents Percent of total adherents
271 REFORM JUDAISM	1	232	279*	0.2	0.4
281 LUTH CH AMER..	2	988	1 248	0.8	1.6
283 LUTH--MO SYNOD	6	3 015	4 062	2.6	5.3
287 MENN GEN CONF.	1	84	138	0.1	0.2
290 METRO COMM CHS	0	25	50	-	0.1
353 CHR BRETHREN..	1	30	40	-	0.1
381 REF PRES-EVAN.	1	12	21	-	-
383 REF PRES OF NA	1	125	153	0.1	0.2
403 SALVATION ARMY	1	130	755	0.5	1.0
413 S.D.A.........	3	593	714*	0.5	0.9
419 SO BAPT CONV..	9	3 166	3 813*	2.5	4.9
435 UNITARIAN-UNIV	1	72	87*	0.1	0.1
443 UN C OF CHRIST	5	2 458	2 960*	1.9	3.8
449 UN METHODIST..	22	11 209	13 499*	8.7	17.5
453 UN PRES CH USA	13	4 632	5 578*	3.6	7.2
469 WELS..........	1	59	86	0.1	0.1
SHERIDAN	12	993	2 678*	75.6	100.0
081 CATHOLIC......	4	NA	1 394	39.3	52.1
093 CHR CH (DISC).	1	191	294	8.3	11.0
167 CHS OF CHRIST.	2	80	102	2.9	3.8
283 LUTH--MO SYNOD	1	132	161	4.5	6.0
449 UN METHODIST..	3	378	466*	13.1	17.4
453 UN PRES CH USA	1	212	261*	7.4	9.7
SHERMAN	12	2 303	4 039*	52.1	100.0
019 AMER BAPT USA.	1	118	143*	1.8	3.5
029 AMER LUTH CH..	1	463	630	8.1	15.6
081 CATHOLIC......	1	NA	1 020	13.1	25.3
093 CHR CH (DISC).	1	220	365	4.7	9.0
165 CH OF NAZARENE	1	60	106	1.4	2.6
167 CHS OF CHRIST.	1	35	46	0.6	1.1
193 EPISCOPAL.....	1	79	120	1.5	3.0
353 CHR BRETHREN..	1	20	20	0.3	0.5
413 S.D.A.........	1	48	58*	0.7	1.4
419 SO BAPT CONV..	1	101	123*	1.6	3.0
449 UN METHODIST..	2	1 159	1 408*	18.1	34.9
SMITH	25	3 298	4 446*	74.8	100.0
029 AMER LUTH CH..	3	733	984	16.5	22.1
053 ASSEMB OF GOD.	1	38	55	0.9	1.2
081 CATHOLIC......	2	NA	194	3.3	4.4
093 CHR CH (DISC).	3	553	826	13.9	18.6
097 CHR CHS&CHS CR	1	60	70*	1.2	1.6
165 CH OF NAZARENE	2	124	185	3.1	4.2
221 FREE METHODIST	1	8	30	0.5	0.7
283 LUTH--MO SYNOD	1	156	199	3.3	4.5
443 UN C OF CHRIST	3	352	412*	6.9	9.3
449 UN METHODIST..	7	1 160	1 358*	22.8	30.5
453 UN PRES CH USA	1	114	133*	2.2	3.0
STAFFORD	28	3 272	4 387*	79.2	100.0
017 AMER BAPT ASSN	1	200	200	3.6	4.6
019 AMER BAPT USA.	2	268	316*	5.7	7.2
053 ASSEMB OF GOD.	1	14	26	0.5	0.6
081 CATHOLIC......	2	NA	275	5.0	6.3
093 CHR CH (DISC).	2	247	389	7.0	8.9
097 CHR CHS&CHS CR	1	50	59*	1.1	1.3
157 CH OF BRETHREN	1	75	88*	1.6	2.0
165 CH OF NAZARENE	1	119	269	4.9	6.1
167 CHS OF CHRIST.	2	250	326	5.9	7.4
208 EVAN LUTH ASSN	1	54	79	1.4	1.8
221 FREE METHODIST	1	16	24	0.4	0.5
226 FRIENDS-USA...	1	42	50*	0.9	1.1
313 N AM BAPT CONF	1	201	237*	4.3	5.4
419 SO BAPT CONV..	1	72	85*	1.5	1.9
443 UN C OF CHRIST	2	338	399*	7.2	9.1
449 UN METHODIST..	6	1 161	1 370*	24.7	31.2
453 UN PRES CH USA	2	165	195*	3.5	4.4
STANTON	5	711	997*	42.6	100.0
081 CATHOLIC......	1	NA	117	5.0	11.7
165 CH OF NAZARENE	1	76	85	3.6	8.5
167 CHS OF CHRIST.	1	20	25	1.1	2.5
449 UN METHODIST..	2	615	770*	32.9	77.2
STEVENS	16	2 308	3 530*	74.5	100.0
019 AMER BAPT USA.	1	148	185*	3.9	5.2
053 ASSEMB OF GOD.	1	55	122	2.6	3.5
081 CATHOLIC......	1	NA	272	5.7	7.7
097 CHR CHS&CHS CR	1	750	938*	19.8	26.6
123 CH GOD (ANDER)	1	92	276	5.8	7.8
151 L-D SAINTS....	1	NA	61	1.3	1.7
165 CH OF NAZARENE	1	38	95	2.0	2.7
167 CHS OF CHRIST.	1	40	51	1.1	1.4
193 EPISCOPAL.....	1	30	58	1.2	1.6
226 FRIENDS-USA...	1	136	170*	3.6	4.8
283 LUTH--MO SYNOD	1	90	140	3.0	4.0
349 PENT HOLINESS.	1	69	86*	1.8	2.4
419 SO BAPT CONV..	1	122	153*	3.2	4.3
449 UN METHODIST..	2	738	923*	19.5	26.1
SUMNER	69	10 761	18 814*	75.5	100.0
019 AMER BAPT USA.	6	1 029	1 244*	5.0	6.6
053 ASSEMB OF GOD.	3	150	357	1.4	1.9
071 BRETHREN (ASH)	1	49	59*	0.2	0.3
081 CATHOLIC......	6	NA	4 524	18.1	24.0
093 CHR CH (DISC).	7	1 093	1 909	7.7	10.1

NA— Not applicable *Total adherents estimated from known number of communicant, confirmed, full members. —Represents a percent less than 0.1. Percentages may not total due to rounding.

Table 4. Churches and Church Membership by County and Denomination: 1980

County and Denomination	Number of churches	Communicant, confirmed, full members	Total adherents Number	Percent of total population	Percent of total adherents
097 CHR CHS&CHS CR	1	100	121*	0.5	0.6
123 CH GOD (ANDER)	1	54	162	0.6	0.9
151 L-D SAINTS....	2	NA	276	1.1	1.5
165 CH OF NAZARENE	1	144	245	1.0	1.3
167 CHS OF CHRIST.	8	450	573	2.3	3.0
193 EPISCOPAL.....	1	20	27	0.1	0.1
221 FREE METHODIST	1	10	39	0.2	0.2
226 FRIENDS-USA...	1	169	204*	0.8	1.1
281 LUTH CH AMER..	1	146	167	0.7	0.9
283 LUTH--MO SYNOD	2	232	302	1.2	1.6
413 S.D.A........	1	41	50*	0.2	0.3
419 SO BAPT CONV..	7	1 900	2 298*	9.2	12.2
449 UN METHODIST..	14	4 495	5 436*	21.8	28.9
453 UN PRES CH USA	5	679	821*	3.3	4.4
THOMAS	15	2 646	4 789*	56.7	100.0
019 AMER BAPT USA.	2	232	283*	3.3	5.9
029 AMER LUTH CH..	1	54	75	0.9	1.6
053 ASSEMB OF GOD.	2	177	250	3.0	5.2
063 BEREAN FUND CH	1	26	32*	0.4	0.7
081 CATHOLIC......	1	NA	1 381	16.3	28.8
093 CHR CH (DISC).	1	223	343	4.1	7.2
167 CHS OF CHRIST.	1	24	39	0.5	0.8
193 EPISCOPAL.....	1	48	57	0.7	1.2
283 LUTH--MO SYNOD	1	294	414	4.9	8.6
449 UN METHODIST..	3	1 333	1 628*	19.3	34.0
453 UN PRES CH USA	1	235	287*	3.4	6.0
TREGO	14	1 745	3 250*	78.0	100.0
029 AMER LUTH CH..	1	88	128	3.1	3.9
053 ASSEMB OF GOD.	1	19	39	0.9	1.2
081 CATHOLIC......	2	NA	1 074	25.8	33.0
097 CHR CHS&CHS CR	1	119	143*	3.4	4.4
123 CH GOD (ANDER)	1	16	48	1.2	1.5
165 CH OF NAZARENE	1	?	?	?	?
281 LUTH CH AMER..	3	779	946	22.7	29.1
419 SO BAPT CONV..	1	23	28*	0.7	0.9
449 UN METHODIST..	2	440	530*	12.7	16.3
453 UN PRES CH USA	1	261	314*	7.5	9.7
WABAUNSEE	23	2 536	3 725*	54.2	100.0
019 AMER BAPT USA.	1	69	83*	1.2	2.2
081 CATHOLIC......	3	NA	668	9.7	17.9
097 CHR CHS&CHS CR	1	80	96*	1.4	2.6
167 CHS OF CHRIST.	3	55	70	1.0	1.9
175 CONGR CHR CHS.	1	150	180*	2.6	4.8
283 LUTH--MO SYNOD	3	859	1 043	15.2	28.0
419 SO BAPT CONV..	1	39	47*	0.7	1.3
443 UN C OF CHRIST	2	290	347*	5.1	9.3
449 UN METHODIST..	7	899	1 077*	15.7	28.9
453 UN PRES CH USA	1	95	114*	1.7	3.1
WALLACE	10	816	1 379*	67.4	100.0
019 AMER BAPT USA.	2	123	152*	7.4	11.0
053 ASSEMB OF GOD.	1	27	61	3.0	4.4
081 CATHOLIC......	2	NA	344	16.8	24.9
143 CG IN CR(MENN)	1	35	35	1.7	2.5
281 LUTH CH AMER..	2	175	224	11.0	16.2
449 UN METHODIST..	2	456	563*	27.5	40.8
WASHINGTON	37	4 564	7 638*	89.4	100.0
019 AMER BAPT USA.	1	101	120*	1.4	1.6
029 AMER LUTH CH..	1	156	194	2.3	2.5
081 CATHOLIC......	6	NA	1 990	23.3	26.1
097 CHR CHS&CHS CR	4	525	625*	7.3	8.2
157 CH OF BRETHREN	1	33	39*	0.5	0.5
201 EVAN COV CH AM	1	167	199*	2.3	2.6
281 LUTH CH AMER..	8	952	1 187	13.9	15.5
283 LUTH--MO SYNOD	6	1 408	1 829	21.4	23.9
449 UN METHODIST..	6	785	935*	10.9	12.2
453 UN PRES CH USA	3	437	520*	6.1	6.8
WICHITA	12	3 408	5 165*	169.8	100.0
019 AMER BAPT USA.	1	271	338*	11.1	6.5
053 ASSEMB OF GOD.	1	52	110	3.6	2.1
081 CATHOLIC......	2	NA	806	26.5	15.6
175 CONGR CHR CHS.	3	2 521	3 143*	103.4	60.9
221 FREE METHODIST	1	63	144	4.7	2.8
449 UN METHODIST..	2	342	426*	14.0	8.2
453 UN PRES CH USA	2	159	198*	6.5	3.8
WILSON	33	3 649	5 686*	46.9	100.0
019 AMER BAPT USA.	2	248	299*	2.5	5.3
053 ASSEMB OF GOD.	1	103	215	1.8	3.8
081 CATHOLIC......	2	NA	568	4.7	10.0
093 CHR CH (DISC).	2	701	1 013	8.4	17.8
097 CHR CHS&CHS CR	4	185	223*	1.8	3.9
123 CH GOD (ANDER)	1	24	72	0.6	1.3
143 CG IN CR(MENN)	1	95	95	0.8	1.7
157 CH OF BRETHREN	1	34	41*	0.3	0.7
165 CH OF NAZARENE	3	219	692	5.7	12.2
167 CHS OF CHRIST.	1	35	45	0.4	0.8
193 EPISCOPAL.....	1	51	69	0.6	1.2
217 FIRE BAPTIZED.	3	44	53*	0.4	0.9
413 S.D.A........	1	54	65*	0.5	1.1
419 SO BAPT CONV..	1	31	37*	0.3	0.7
449 UN METHODIST..	7	1 585	1 910*	15.7	33.6
453 UN PRES CH USA	2	240	289*	2.4	5.1

County and Denomination	Number of churches	Communicant, confirmed, full members	Total adherents Number	Percent of total population	Percent of total adherents
WOODSON	16	1 646	2 498*	54.3	100.0
053 ASSEMB OF GOD.	1	21	31	0.7	1.2
081 CATHOLIC......	2	NA	430	9.3	17.2
093 CHR CH (DISC)	2	296	475	10.3	19.0
097 CHR CHS&CHS CR	1	40	47*	1.0	1.9
165 CH OF NAZARENE	1	36	49	1.1	2.0
167 CHS OF CHRIST.	1	20	25	0.5	1.0
193 EPISCOPAL.....	1	61	76	1.7	3.0
419 SO BAPT CONV..	1	239	278*	6.0	11.1
449 UN METHODIST..	4	770	897*	19.5	35.9
453 UN PRES CH USA	2	163	190*	4.1	7.6
WYANDOTTE	164	35 417	70 202*	40.7	100.0
001 ADVENT CHR CH.	1	12	15*	-	-
017 AMER BAPT ASSN	1	160	160	0.1	0.2
019 AMER BAPT USA.	23	5 283	6 469*	3.8	9.2
053 ASSEMB OF GOD.	8	2 471	3 800	2.2	5.4
059 BAPT MISS ASSN	1	142	174*	0.1	0.2
081 CATHOLIC......	17	NA	21 835	12.7	31.1
089 CHR & MISS AL.	1	294	294	0.2	0.4
093 CHR CH (DISC).	12	2 874	4 948	2.9	7.0
097 CHR CHS&CHS CR	1	2 220	2 719*	1.6	3.9
123 CH GOD (ANDER)	4	428	1 284	0.7	1.8
127 CH GOD (CLEVE)	1	53	65*	-	0.1
151 L-D SAINTS....	1	NA	496	0.3	0.7
157 CH OF BRETHREN	2	135	165*	0.1	0.2
165 CH OF NAZARENE	10	1 209	2 345	1.4	3.3
167 CHS OF CHRIST.	7	883	1 124	0.7	1.6
193 EPISCOPAL.....	3	777	950	0.6	1.4
217 FIRE BAPTIZED.	1	9	11*	-	-
221 FREE METHODIST	2	64	378	0.2	0.5
263 INT FOURSQ GOS	1	50	61*	-	0.1
281 LUTH CH AMER..	3	771	1 009	0.6	1.4
283 LUTH--MO SYNOD	8	2 546	3 303	1.9	4.7
285 MENNONITE CH..	2	171	209*	0.1	0.3
287 MENN GEN CONF.	1	146	196	0.1	0.3
290 METRO COMM CHS	0	30	60	-	0.1
353 CHR BRETHREN..	2	70	70	-	0.1
357 PRESB CH US...	7	689	844*	0.5	1.2
403 SALVATION ARMY	1	171	368	0.2	0.5
413 S.D.A........	3	862	1 056*	0.6	1.5
419 SO BAPT CONV..	12	4 830	5 915*	3.4	8.4
443 UN C OF CHRIST	5	1 237	1 515*	0.9	2.2
449 UN METHODIST..	16	6 145	7 525*	4.4	10.7
453 UN PRES CH USA	7	685	839*	0.5	1.2

KENTUCKY

County and Denomination	Number of churches	Communicant, confirmed, full members	Total adherents Number	Percent of total population	Percent of total adherents
THE STATE.....	6 704	1 276 494	1 982 830*	54.2	100.0
ADAIR	77	7 549	9 402*	61.7	100.0
005 AME ZION......	1	75	82	0.5	0.9
053 ASSEMB OF GOD.	1	34	52	0.3	0.6
075 BRETHREN IN CR	4	172	292	1.9	3.1
081 CATHOLIC......	1	NA	58	0.4	0.6
093 CHR CH (DISC).	1	27	42	0.3	0.4
097 CHR CHS&CHS CR	10	881	1 048*	6.9	11.1
123 CH GOD (ANDER)	1	35	105	0.7	1.1
165 CH OF NAZARENE	3	247	453	3.0	4.8
167 CHS OF CHRIST.	1	120	153	1.0	1.6
185 CUMBER PRESB..	2	18	49	0.3	0.5
357 PRESB CH US...	1	53	63*	0.4	0.7
409 SEPARATE BAPT.	8	604	719*	4.7	7.6
413 S.D.A........	1	38	45*	0.3	0.5
419 SO BAPT CONV..	19	2 370	2 820*	18.5	30.0
449 UN METHODIST..	22	2 822	3 358*	22.0	35.7
453 UN PRES CH USA	1	53	63*	0.4	0.7
ALLEN	36	5 161	6 405*	45.3	100.0
053 ASSEMB OF GOD.	1	?	?	?	?
081 CATHOLIC......	1	NA	50	0.4	0.8
165 CH OF NAZARENE	1	53	100	0.7	1.6
167 CHS OF CHRIST.	2	215	274	1.9	4.3
221 FREE METHODIST	1	78	225	1.6	3.5
419 SO BAPT CONV..	17	3 076	3 677*	26.0	57.4
449 UN METHODIST..	13	1 739	2 079*	14.7	32.5
ANDERSON	33	6 922	8 630*	68.7	100.0
053 ASSEMB OF GOD.	1	72	102	0.8	1.2
081 CATHOLIC......	1	NA	250	2.0	2.9
093 CHR CH (DISC).	4	909	1 107	8.8	12.8
097 CHR CHS&CHS CR	6	1 022	1 232*	9.8	14.3
127 CH GOD (CLEVE)	1	66	80*	0.6	0.9
167 CHS OF CHRIST.	2	150	191	1.5	2.2
357 PRESB CH US...	1	50	60*	0.5	0.7
413 S.D.A........	1	14	17*	0.1	0.2
419 SO BAPT CONV..	12	4 118	4 963*	39.5	57.5
449 UN METHODIST..	3	472	569*	4.5	6.6

NA—Not applicable   *Total adherents estimated from known number of communicant, confirmed, full members.   —Represents a percent less than 0.1.   Percentages may not total due to rounding.

Table 4. Churches and Church Membership by County and Denomination: 1980

County and Denomination	Number of churches	Communicant, confirmed, full members	Total adherents		
			Number	Percent of total population	Percent of total adherents
453 UN PRES CH USA	1	49	59*	0.5	0.7
BALLARD	32	5 461	6 951*	79.0	100.0
081 CATHOLIC......	1	NA	210	2.4	3.0
093 CHR CH (DISC).	2	97	132	1.5	1.9
167 CHS OF CHRIST.	2	46	59	0.7	0.8
185 CUMBER PRESB..	2	163	287	3.3	4.1
419 SO BAPT CONV..	17	4 071	4 946*	56.2	71.2
449 UN METHODIST..	8	1 084	1 317*	15.0	18.9
BARREN	75	14 429	18 031*	53.0	100.0
053 ASSEMB OF GOD.	1	45	83	0.2	0.5
081 CATHOLIC......	1	NA	132	0.4	0.7
093 CHR CH (DISC).	2	546	804	2.4	4.5
097 CHR CHS&CHS CR	2	285	341*	1.0	1.9
101 C.M.E........	1	200	239*	0.7	1.3
123 CH GOD (ANDER)	1	25	75	0.2	0.4
127 CH GOD (CLEVE)	1	50	60*	0.2	0.3
165 CH OF NAZARENE	2	183	319	0.9	1.8
167 CHS OF CHRIST.	16	1 572	1 970	5.8	10.9
185 CUMBER PRESB..	3	235	507	1.5	2.8
193 EPISCOPAL.....	1	76	101	0.3	0.6
357 PRESB CH US...	1	128	153*	0.4	0.8
413 S.D.A.........	1	31	37*	0.1	0.2
419 SO BAPT CONV..	24	8 198	9 798*	28.8	54.3
449 UN METHODIST..	17	2 728	3 260*	9.6	18.1
453 UN PRES CH USA	1	127	152*	0.4	0.8
BATH	43	2 966	5 512*	55.0	100.0
081 CATHOLIC......	1	NA	52	0.5	0.9
093 CHR CH (DISC).	9	931	1 479	14.8	26.8
097 CHR CHS&CHS CR	9	716	875*	8.7	15.9
101 C.M.E........	1	38	46*	0.5	0.8
123 CH GOD (ANDER)	10	621	1 863	18.6	33.8
127 CH GOD (CLEVE)	1	?	?	?	?
151 L-D SAINTS....	1	NA	385	3.8	7.0
167 CHS OF CHRIST.	2	80	102	1.0	1.9
357 PRESB CH US...	2	39	48*	0.5	0.9
419 SO BAPT CONV..	2	228	279*	2.8	5.1
449 UN METHODIST..	3	274	335*	3.3	6.1
453 UN PRES CH USA	2	39	48*	0.5	0.9
BELL	81	13 887	17 571*	51.2	100.0
005 AME ZION......	1	240	265	0.8	1.5
053 ASSEMB OF GOD.	1	121	189	0.6	1.1
081 CATHOLIC......	2	NA	287	0.8	1.6
093 CHR CH (DISC).	2	329	383	1.1	2.2
127 CH GOD (CLEVE)	3	237	295*	0.9	1.7
165 CH OF NAZARENE	2	50	97	0.3	0.6
167 CHS OF CHRIST.	2	130	165	0.5	0.9
193 EPISCOPAL.....	1	94	120	0.3	0.7
357 PRESB CH US...	2	154	191*	0.6	1.1
403 SALVATION ARMY	1	76	91	0.3	0.5
419 SO BAPT CONV..	56	11 492	14 289*	41.6	81.3
449 UN METHODIST..	6	808	1 005*	2.9	5.7
453 UN PRES CH USA	2	156	194*	0.6	1.1
BOONE	51	14 113	25 873*	56.4	100.0
053 ASSEMB OF GOD.	1	495	676	1.5	2.6
081 CATHOLIC......	3	NA	7 332	16.0	28.3
093 CHR CH (DISC).	7	1 077	2 034	4.4	7.9
097 CHR CHS&CHS CR	5	1 191	1 495*	3.3	5.8
101 C.M.E........	1	113	142*	0.3	0.5
127 CH GOD (CLEVE)	2	215	270*	0.6	1.0
157 CH OF BRETHREN	1	87	109*	0.2	0.4
165 CH OF NAZARENE	2	90	116	0.3	0.4
167 CHS OF CHRIST.	3	298	381	0.8	1.5
193 EPISCOPAL.....	1	210	278	0.6	1.1
281 LUTH CH AMER..	2	733	981	2.1	3.8
357 PRESB CH US...	2	143	180*	0.4	0.7
419 SO BAPT CONV..	15	8 130	10 208*	22.3	39.5
449 UN METHODIST..	4	1 187	1 490*	3.3	5.8
453 UN PRES CH USA	2	144	181*	0.4	0.7
BOURBON	41	7 714	10 989*	56.6	100.0
053 ASSEMB OF GOD.	1	80	136	0.7	1.2
081 CATHOLIC......	1	NA	664	3.4	6.0
093 CHR CH (DISC).	8	1 411	2 093	10.8	19.0
097 CHR CHS&CHS CR	4	732	891*	4.6	8.1
101 C.M.E........	2	108	132*	0.7	1.2
123 CH GOD (ANDER)	1	210	630	3.2	5.7
165 CH OF NAZARENE	4	124	222	1.1	2.0
167 CHS OF CHRIST.	2	99	149	0.8	1.4
193 EPISCOPAL.....	1	205	294	1.5	2.7
357 PRESB CH US...	2	220	268*	1.4	2.4
419 SO BAPT CONV..	5	3 022	3 680*	19.0	33.5
449 UN METHODIST..	8	1 281	1 560*	8.0	14.2
453 UN PRES CH USA	2	222	270*	1.4	2.5
BOYD	79	22 540	32 153*	57.9	100.0
053 ASSEMB OF GOD.	1	41	69	0.1	0.2
081 CATHOLIC......	1	NA	2 097	3.8	6.5
093 CHR CH (DISC).	2	729	1 076	1.9	3.3
097 CHR CHS&CHS CR	5	968	1 169*	2.1	3.6
101 C.M.E........	1	188	227*	0.4	0.7
123 CH GOD (ANDER)	3	473	1 419	2.6	4.4
127 CH GOD (CLEVE)	2	256	309*	0.6	1.0
151 L-D SAINTS....	1	NA	574	1.0	1.8

County and Denomination	Number of churches	Communicant, confirmed, full members	Total adherents		
			Number	Percent of total population	Percent of total adherents
165 CH OF NAZARENE	10	1 413	2 836	5.1	8.8
167 CHS OF CHRIST.	3	160	204	0.4	0.6
193 EPISCOPAL.....	2	630	784	1.4	2.4
271 REFORM JUDAISM	1	48	58*	0.1	0.2
283 LUTH--MO SYNOD	2	233	288	0.5	0.9
357 PRESB CH US...	4	625	755*	1.4	2.3
403 SALVATION ARMY	1	94	141	0.3	0.4
413 S.D.A.........	1	127	153*	0.3	0.5
419 SO BAPT CONV..	20	10 893	13 156*	23.7	40.9
449 UN METHODIST..	15	5 036	6 082*	11.0	18.9
453 UN PRES CH USA	4	626	756*	1.4	2.4
BOYLE	50	13 902	18 982*	75.7	100.0
053 ASSEMB OF GOD.	1	38	83	0.3	0.4
081 CATHOLIC......	3	NA	1 381	5.5	7.3
093 CHR CH (DISC).	4	961	1 288	5.1	6.8
097 CHR CHS&CHS CR	3	575	695*	2.8	3.7
123 CH GOD (ANDER)	1	180	540	2.2	2.8
127 CH GOD (CLEVE)	4	254	307*	1.2	1.6
151 L-D SAINTS....	1	NA	237	0.9	1.2
165 CH OF NAZARENE	1	73	137	0.5	0.7
167 CHS OF CHRIST.	5	370	470	1.9	2.5
283 LUTH--MO SYNOD	1	87	107	0.4	0.6
357 PRESB CH US...	2	461	557*	2.2	2.9
403 SALVATION ARMY	1	71	85	0.3	0.4
419 SO BAPT CONV..	17	8 949	10 819*	43.2	57.0
449 UN METHODIST..	4	1 423	1 720*	6.9	9.1
453 UN PRES CH USA	2	460	556*	2.2	2.9
BRACKEN	42	4 177	6 135*	79.3	100.0
029 AMER LUTH CH..	1	85	142	1.8	2.3
053 ASSEMB OF GOD.	1	25	48	0.6	0.8
081 CATHOLIC......	2	NA	790	10.2	12.9
093 CHR CH (DISC).	2	157	264	3.4	4.3
097 CHR CHS&CHS CR	14	1 633	1 992*	25.7	32.5
165 CH OF NAZARENE	1	87	229	3.0	3.7
357 PRESB CH US...	2	70	85*	1.1	1.4
419 SO BAPT CONV..	7	1 230	1 500*	19.4	24.4
449 UN METHODIST..	10	821	1 001*	12.9	16.3
453 UN PRES CH USA	2	69	84*	1.1	1.4
BREATHITT	35	2 310	3 572*	21.0	100.0
053 ASSEMB OF GOD.	2	51	96	0.6	2.7
071 BRETHREN (ASH)	2	85	107*	0.6	3.0
081 CATHOLIC......	1	NA	94	0.6	2.6
093 CHR CH (DISC).	2	123	189	1.1	5.3
097 CHR CHS&CHS CR	1	220	277*	1.6	7.8
123 CH GOD (ANDER)	2	149	447	2.6	12.5
127 CH GOD (CLEVE)	1	60	76*	0.4	2.1
167 CHS OF CHRIST.	1	25	30	0.2	0.8
203 EVAN FREE CH..	1	62	78*	0.5	2.2
221 FREE METHODIST	2	82	318	1.9	8.9
244 GRACE BRETHREN	1	58	73*	0.4	2.0
285 MENNONITE CH..	5	81	102*	0.6	2.9
329 OPEN BIBLE STD	1	35	75	0.4	2.1
357 PRESB CH US...	3	105	132*	0.8	3.7
419 SO BAPT CONV..	2	722	909*	5.3	25.4
449 UN METHODIST..	5	344	433*	2.5	12.1
453 UN PRES CH USA	3	108	136*	0.8	3.8
BRECKINRIDGE	65	7 760	11 639*	69.0	100.0
053 ASSEMB OF GOD.	1	53	47	0.3	0.4
081 CATHOLIC......	5	NA	1 910	11.3	16.4
097 CHR CHS&CHS CR	1	75	92*	0.5	0.8
123 CH GOD (ANDER)	1	45	135	0.8	1.2
167 CHS OF CHRIST.	3	85	108	0.6	0.9
185 CUMBER PRESB..	6	255	494	2.9	4.2
291 MISSIONARY CH.	1	16	24	0.1	0.2
419 SO BAPT CONV..	20	4 480	5 470*	32.4	47.0
449 UN METHODIST..	26	2 729	3 332*	19.8	28.6
453 UN PRES CH USA	1	22	27*	0.2	0.2
BULLITT	50	11 593	19 489*	45.0	100.0
053 ASSEMB OF GOD.	1	121	156	0.4	0.8
081 CATHOLIC......	4	NA	4 401	10.2	22.6
093 CHR CH (DISC).	2	166	277	0.6	1.4
097 CHR CHS&CHS CR	2	294	377*	0.9	1.9
127 CH GOD (CLEVE)	2	123	158*	0.4	0.8
165 CH OF NAZARENE	1	51	113	0.3	0.6
167 CHS OF CHRIST.	5	275	350	0.8	1.8
185 CUMBER PRESB..	1	149	298	0.7	1.5
357 PRESB CH US...	1	59	76*	0.2	0.4
409 SEPARATE BAPT.	1	104	133*	0.3	0.7
419 SO BAPT CONV..	23	9 156	11 745*	27.1	60.3
449 UN METHODIST..	6	1 036	1 329*	3.1	6.8
453 UN PRES CH USA	1	59	76*	0.2	0.4
BUTLER	60	6 413	8 212*	74.2	100.0
081 CATHOLIC......	1	NA	50	0.5	0.6
093 CHR CH (DISC).	1	10	15	0.1	0.2
097 CHR CHS&CHS CR	3	250	304*	2.7	3.7
151 L-D SAINTS....	1	NA	191	1.7	2.3
165 CH OF NAZARENE	1	30	72	0.7	0.9
167 CHS OF CHRIST.	14	464	648	5.9	7.9
185 CUMBER PRESB..	1	52	110	1.0	1.3
285 MENNONITE CH..	1	9	11*	0.1	0.1
357 PRESB CH US...	1	8	10*	0.1	0.1
419 SO BAPT CONV..	25	5 029	6 119*	55.3	74.5
449 UN METHODIST..	7	481	585*	5.3	7.1

NA—Not applicable   *Total adherents estimated from known number of communicant, confirmed, full members.

—Represents a percent less than 0.1.   Percentages may not total due to rounding.

Table 4. Churches and Church Membership by County and Denomination: 1980

County and Denomination	Number of churches	Communicant, confirmed, full members	Total adherents Number	Percent of total population	Percent of total adherents
453 UN PRES CH USA	3	80	97*	0.9	1.2
CALDWELL	48	10 184	12 821*	95.2	100.0
053 ASSEMB OF GOD.	1	86	155	1.2	1.2
081 CATHOLIC......	1	NA	450	3.3	3.5
093 CHR CH (DISC).	2	279	361	2.7	2.8
097 CHR CHS&CHS CR	2	260	310*	2.3	2.4
101 C.M.E........	1	365	435*	3.2	3.4
167 CHS OF CHRIST.	1	100	127	0.9	1.0
185 CUMBER PRESB..	6	292	500	3.7	3.9
357 PRESB CH US...	1	99	118*	0.9	0.9
419 SO BAPT CONV..	25	7 614	9 068*	67.3	70.7
449 UN METHODIST..	7	990	1 179*	8.8	9.2
453 UN PRES CH USA	1	99	118*	0.9	0.9
CALLOWAY	78	15 509	19 116*	63.7	100.0
053 ASSEMB OF GOD.	1	78	111	0.4	0.6
081 CATHOLIC......	1	NA	567	1.9	3.0
093 CHR CH (DISC).	1	375	415	1.4	2.2
127 CH GOD (CLEVE)	1	38	44*	0.1	0.2
151 L-D SAINTS....	1	NA	110	0.4	0.6
165 CH OF NAZARENE	2	83	100	0.3	0.5
167 CHS OF CHRIST.	17	2 535	3 265	10.9	17.1
185 CUMBER PRESB..	3	68	152	0.5	0.8
193 EPISCOPAL.....	1	90	153	0.5	0.8
283 LUTH--MO SYNOD	1	78	103	0.3	0.5
357 PRESB CH US...	1	77	89*	0.3	0.5
419 SO BAPT CONV..	27	8 534	9 890*	32.9	51.7
449 UN METHODIST..	20	3 476	4 028*	13.4	21.1
453 UN PRES CH USA	1	77	89*	0.3	0.5
CAMPBELL	88	18 792	46 407*	55.7	100.0
053 ASSEMB OF GOD.	3	825	1 045	1.3	2.3
081 CATHOLIC......	16	NA	22 659	27.2	48.8
093 CHR CH (DISC).	3	374	514	0.6	1.1
097 CHR CHS&CHS CR	4	422	516*	0.6	1.1
127 CH GOD (CLEVE)	4	460	562*	0.7	1.2
165 CH OF NAZARENE	4	454	883	1.1	1.9
167 CHS OF CHRIST.	2	77	100	0.1	0.2
193 EPISCOPAL.....	3	609	970	1.2	2.1
281 LUTH CH AMER...	4	569	722	0.9	1.6
357 PRESB CH US...	1	265	324*	0.4	0.7
403 SALVATION ARMY	1	78	203	0.2	0.4
409 SEPARATE BAPT.	1	27	33*	-	0.1
419 SO BAPT CONV..	20	8 436	10 306*	12.4	22.2
443 UN C OF CHRIST	6	3 057	3 735*	4.5	8.0
449 UN METHODIST..	13	2 679	3 273*	3.9	7.1
453 UN PRES CH USA	3	460	562*	0.7	1.2
CARLISLE	29	3 774	4 921*	89.7	100.0
053 ASSEMB OF GOD.	2	73	97	1.8	2.0
081 CATHOLIC......	1	NA	350	6.4	7.1
093 CHR CH (DISC).	2	183	239	4.4	4.9
097 CHR CHS&CHS CR	2	125	150*	2.7	3.0
167 CHS OF CHRIST.	4	216	275	5.0	5.6
419 SO BAPT CONV..	12	2 690	3 226*	58.8	65.6
449 UN METHODIST..	6	487	584*	10.6	11.9
CARROLL	25	4 257	5 917*	63.8	100.0
053 ASSEMB OF GOD.	1	48	78	0.8	1.3
081 CATHOLIC......	1	NA	480	5.2	8.1
093 CHR CH (DISC).	5	384	697	7.5	11.8
097 CHR CHS&CHS CR	3	380	462*	5.0	7.8
101 C.M.E........	1	50	61*	0.7	1.0
281 LUTH CH AMER..	1	60	87	0.9	1.5
419 SO BAPT CONV..	10	2 852	3 465*	37.4	58.6
449 UN METHODIST..	3	483	587*	6.3	9.9
CARTER	38	3 631	5 023*	20.0	100.0
053 ASSEMB OF GOD.	1	16	50	0.2	1.0
081 CATHOLIC......	1	NA	98	0.4	2.0
093 CHR CH (DISC).	3	161	247	1.0	4.9
097 CHR CHS&CHS CR	11	1 072	1 337*	5.3	26.6
123 CH GOD (ANDER)	1	75	225	0.9	4.5
165 CH OF NAZARENE	4	134	353	1.4	7.0
167 CHS OF CHRIST.	1	40	51	0.2	1.0
357 PRESB CH US...	1	32	40*	0.2	0.8
419 SO BAPT CONV..	8	1 614	2 014*	8.0	40.1
449 UN METHODIST..	6	456	569*	2.3	11.3
453 UN PRES CH USA	1	31	39*	0.2	0.8
CASEY	59	6 058	8 438*	56.9	100.0
081 CATHOLIC......	1	NA	443	3.0	5.3
093 CHR CH (DISC).	2	254	602	4.1	7.1
097 CHR CHS&CHS CR	5	320	393*	2.7	4.7
123 CH GOD (ANDER)	3	137	411	2.8	4.9
127 CH GOD (CLEVE)	2	43	53*	0.4	0.6
165 CH OF NAZARENE	1	48	70	0.5	0.8
167 CHS OF CHRIST.	9	300	380	2.6	4.5
409 SEPARATE BAPT.	9	1 009	1 239*	8.4	14.7
413 S.D.A.........	1	40	49*	0.3	0.6
419 SO BAPT CONV..	14	2 496	3 065*	20.7	36.3
449 UN METHODIST..	12	1 411	1 733*	11.7	20.5
CHRISTIAN	106	21 876	28 992*	43.4	100.0
005 AME ZION......	1	75	90	0.1	0.3
053 ASSEMB OF GOD.	2	133	230	0.3	0.8
081 CATHOLIC......	2	NA	920	1.4	3.2
093 CHR CH (DISC).	8	1 151	1 832	2.7	6.3
101 C.M.E........	5	1 731	2 131*	3.2	7.4
123 CH GOD (ANDER)	1	26	78	0.1	0.3
127 CH GOD (CLEVE)	2	100	123*	0.2	0.4
151 L-D SAINTS....	1	NA	277	0.4	1.0
165 CH OF NAZARENE	1	37	114	0.2	0.4
167 CHS OF CHRIST.	8	1 023	1 304	1.9	4.5
185 CUMBER PRESB..	4	293	547	0.8	1.9
193 EPISCOPAL.....	1	289	343	0.5	1.2
283 LUTH--MO SYNOD	1	144	229	0.3	0.8
323 OLD ORD AMISH.	1	130	160*	0.2	0.6
349 PENT HOLINESS.	1	45	55*	0.1	0.2
357 PRESB CH US...	5	301	371*	0.6	1.3
403 SALVATION ARMY	1	138	166	0.2	0.6
413 S.D.A.........	2	89	110*	0.2	0.4
419 SO BAPT CONV..	35	12 829	15 797*	23.6	54.5
435 UNITARIAN-UNIV	1	10	12*	-	-
449 UN METHODIST..	18	3 018	3 716*	5.6	12.8
453 UN PRES CH USA	5	314	387*	0.6	1.3
CLARK	51	11 045	15 821*	55.9	100.0
053 ASSEMB OF GOD.	1	25	37	0.1	0.2
081 CATHOLIC......	1	NA	720	2.5	4.6
093 CHR CH (DISC).	6	678	1 237	4.4	7.8
097 CHR CHS&CHS CR	7	1 048	1 290*	4.6	8.2
101 C.M.E........	3	321	395*	1.4	2.5
123 CH GOD (ANDER)	2	390	1 170	4.1	7.4
127 CH GOD (CLEVE)	1	329	405*	1.4	2.6
151 L-D SAINTS....	1	NA	392	1.4	2.5
165 CH OF NAZARENE	2	26	0	-	-
167 CHS OF CHRIST.	3	240	305	1.1	1.9
193 EPISCOPAL.....	1	120	188	0.7	1.2
263 INT FOURSQ GOS	1	12	15*	0.1	0.1
356 PRESB CH AMER.	1	34	40	0.1	0.3
357 PRESB CH US...	2	189	233*	0.8	1.5
413 S.D.A.........	1	36	44*	0.2	0.3
419 SO BAPT CONV..	10	5 432	6 685*	23.6	42.3
449 UN METHODIST..	6	1 976	2 432*	8.6	15.4
453 UN PRES CH USA	2	189	233*	0.8	1.5
CLAY	49	6 456	8 329*	36.6	100.0
081 CATHOLIC......	1	NA	117	0.5	1.4
089 CHR & MISS AL.	1	23	44	0.2	0.5
093 CHR CH (DISC).	1	29	45	0.2	0.5
097 CHR CHS&CHS CR	5	250	317*	1.4	3.8
127 CH GOD (CLEVE)	2	194	246*	1.1	3.0
157 CH OF BRETHREN	1	165	209*	0.9	2.5
167 CHS OF CHRIST.	1	52	66	0.3	0.8
285 MENNONITE CH..	3	38	48*	0.2	0.6
357 PRESB CH US...	3	56	71*	0.3	0.9
413 S.D.A.........	1	93	118*	0.5	1.4
419 SO BAPT CONV..	23	5 239	6 646*	29.2	79.8
449 UN METHODIST..	4	261	331*	1.5	4.0
453 UN PRES CH USA	3	56	71*	0.3	0.9
CLINTON	29	3 826	4 955*	53.2	100.0
081 CATHOLIC......	1	NA	44	0.5	0.9
093 CHR CH (DISC).	1	55	88	0.9	1.8
097 CHR CHS&CHS CR	1	36	44*	0.5	0.9
165 CH OF NAZARENE	3	218	502	5.4	10.1
167 CHS OF CHRIST.	2	61	77	0.8	1.6
409 SEPARATE BAPT.	2	222	270*	2.9	5.4
419 SO BAPT CONV..	7	1 453	1 766*	18.9	35.6
449 UN METHODIST..	12	1 781	2 164*	23.2	43.7
CRITTENDEN	37	4 213	5 398*	58.6	100.0
053 ASSEMB OF GOD.	1	18	38	0.4	0.7
081 CATHOLIC......	1	NA	86	0.9	1.6
093 CHR CH (DISC).	2	48	72	0.8	1.3
123 CH GOD (ANDER)	1	50	150	1.6	2.8
167 CHS OF CHRIST.	1	25	32	0.3	0.6
185 CUMBER PRESB..	3	291	484	5.3	9.0
323 OLD ORD AMISH.	1	130	156*	1.7	2.9
357 PRESB CH US...	3	59	71*	0.8	1.3
419 SO BAPT CONV..	16	2 766	3 318*	36.0	61.5
449 UN METHODIST..	5	768	921*	10.0	17.1
453 UN PRES CH USA	3	58	70*	0.8	1.3
CUMBERLAND	46	3 220	4 017*	55.1	100.0
053 ASSEMB OF GOD.	1	34	62	0.9	1.5
081 CATHOLIC......	1	NA	41	0.6	1.0
093 CHR CH (DISC).	1	101	164	2.2	4.1
097 CHR CHS&CHS CR	2	45	54*	0.7	1.3
101 C.M.E........	1	150	179*	2.5	4.5
165 CH OF NAZARENE	1	79	107	1.5	2.7
167 CHS OF CHRIST.	12	635	810	11.1	20.2
185 CUMBER PRESB..	1	13	21	0.3	0.5
357 PRESB CH US...	1	41	49*	0.7	1.2
419 SO BAPT CONV..	4	485	578*	7.9	14.4
449 UN METHODIST..	21	1 637	1 952*	26.8	48.6
DAVIESS	123	34 999	63 867*	74.3	100.0
005 AME ZION......	1	67	82	0.1	0.1
053 ASSEMB OF GOD.	3	495	800	0.9	1.3
081 CATHOLIC......	17	NA	20 068	23.3	31.4
093 CHR CH (DISC).	4	1 426	1 860	2.2	2.9
097 CHR CHS&CHS CR	2	325	398*	0.5	0.6
123 CH GOD (ANDER)	1	16	48	0.1	0.1

NA— Not applicable   *Total adherents estimated from known number of communicant, confirmed, full members.   —Represents a percent less than 0.1.   Percentages may not total due to rounding.

Table 4. Churches and Church Membership by County and Denomination: 1980

County and Denomination	Number of churches	Communicant, confirmed, full members	Total adherents Number	Percent of total population	Percent of total adherents
127 CH GOD (CLEVE)	3	123	151*	0.2	0.2
151 L-D SAINTS....	1	NA	105	0.1	0.2
165 CH OF NAZARENE	2	239	317	0.4	0.5
167 CHS OF CHRIST.	5	596	856	1.0	1.3
185 CUMBER PRESB..	4	390	697	0.8	1.1
193 EPISCOPAL.....	1	333	406	0.5	0.6
221 FREE METHODIST	1	3	24	-	-
271 REFORM JUDAISM	1	30	37*	-	0.1
281 LUTH CH AMER..	1	131	191	0.2	0.3
283 LUTH--MO SYNOD	1	145	237	0.3	0.4
357 PRESB CH US...	3	484	593*	0.7	0.9
381 REF PRES-EVAN.	1	15	21	-	-
403 SALVATION ARMY	1	107	110	0.1	0.2
413 S.D.A.........	1	123	151*	0.2	0.2
419 SO BAPT CONV..	46	24 106	29 550*	34.4	46.3
443 UN C OF CHRIST	1	380	466*	0.5	0.7
449 UN METHODIST..	19	4 981	6 106*	7.1	9.6
453 UN PRES CH USA	3	484	593*	0.7	0.9
EDMONSON	20	2 834	3 679*	36.9	100.0
081 CATHOLIC......	1	NA	178	1.8	4.8
167 CHS OF CHRIST.	4	220	286	2.9	7.8
419 SO BAPT CONV..	14	2 511	3 088*	31.0	83.9
449 UN METHODIST..	1	103	127*	1.3	3.5
ELLIOTT	3	254	321*	4.6	100.0
419 SO BAPT CONV..	1	125	158*	2.3	49.2
449 UN METHODIST..	2	129	163*	2.4	50.8
ESTILL	45	4 662	6 627*	45.7	100.0
081 CATHOLIC......	1	NA	64	0.4	1.0
093 CHR CH (DISC).	2	259	571	3.9	8.6
097 CHR CHS&CHS CR	11	655	809*	5.6	12.2
123 CH GOD (ANDER)	4	185	555	3.8	8.4
127 CH GOD (CLEVE)	1	185	229*	1.6	3.5
165 CH OF NAZARENE	3	216	318	2.2	4.8
167 CHS OF CHRIST.	4	130	165	1.1	2.5
221 FREE METHODIST	1	30	207	1.4	3.1
419 SO BAPT CONV..	14	2 432	3 005*	20.7	45.3
449 UN METHODIST..	4	570	704*	4.9	10.6
FAYETTE	156	68 696	104 238*	51.1	100.0
017 AMER BAPT ASSN	1	200	200	0.1	0.2
029 AMER LUTH CH..	1	240	358	0.2	0.3
053 ASSEMB OF GOD.	5	682	1 187	0.6	1.1
081 CATHOLIC......	6	NA	18 077	8.9	17.3
089 CHR & MISS AL.	1	186	313	0.2	0.3
093 CHR CH (DISC).	11	5 905	7 451	3.6	7.1
097 CHR CHS&CHS CR	14	10 072	12 013*	5.9	11.5
101 C.M.E.........	1	528	630*	0.3	0.6
123 CH GOD (ANDER)	3	480	1 440	0.7	1.4
127 CH GOD (CLEVE)	4	721	860*	0.4	0.8
151 L-D SAINTS....	3	NA	1 159	0.6	1.1
165 CH OF NAZARENE	6	995	1 797	0.9	1.7
167 CHS OF CHRIST.	7	700	891	0.4	0.9
185 CUMBER PRESB..	1	76	185	0.1	0.2
193 EPISCOPAL.....	8	2 501	3 124	1.5	3.0
203 EVAN FREE CH..	1	23	27*	-	-
215 EVAN METH CH..	2	96	115*	0.1	0.1
221 FREE METHODIST	1	18	90	-	0.1
226 FRIENDS-USA...	1	26	31*	-	-
270 CONSRV JUDAISM	1	20	24*	-	-
271 REFORM JUDAISM	1	510	608*	0.3	0.6
281 LUTH CH AMER..	1	483	646	0.3	0.6
283 LUTH--MO SYNOD	3	582	747	0.4	0.7
290 METRO COMM CHS	0	15	30	-	-
357 PRESB CH US...	12	2 055	2 451*	1.2	2.4
403 SALVATION ARMY	1	143	356	0.2	0.3
413 S.D.A.........	2	430	513*	0.3	0.5
419 SO BAPT CONV..	30	28 079	33 492*	16.4	32.1
435 UNITARIAN-UNIV	1	170	203*	0.1	0.2
443 UN C OF CHRIST	1	112	134*	0.1	0.1
449 UN METHODIST..	14	10 592	12 634*	6.2	12.1
453 UN PRES CH USA	12	2 056	2 452*	1.2	2.4
FLEMING	55	4 127	5 814*	47.2	100.0
053 ASSEMB OF GOD.	2	94	163	1.3	2.8
081 CATHOLIC......	1	NA	205	1.7	3.5
093 CHR CH (DISC).	5	566	818	6.6	14.1
097 CHR CHS&CHS CR	14	583	712*	5.8	12.2
123 CH GOD (ANDER)	6	213	639	5.2	11.0
165 CH OF NAZARENE	1	25	48	0.4	0.8
357 PRESB CH US...	2	46	56*	0.5	1.0
419 SO BAPT CONV..	6	877	1 070*	8.7	18.4
449 UN METHODIST..	16	1 678	2 048*	16.6	35.2
453 UN PRES CH USA	2	45	55*	0.4	0.9
FLOYD	62	5 381	7 397*	15.2	100.0
053 ASSEMB OF GOD.	2	84	119	0.2	1.6
081 CATHOLIC......	2	NA	200	0.4	2.7
093 CHR CH (DISC).	4	186	286	0.6	3.9
097 CHR CHS&CHS CR	3	310	388*	0.8	5.2
123 CH GOD (ANDER)	1	52	156	0.3	2.1
127 CH GOD (CLEVE)	3	74	93*	0.2	1.3
151 L-D SAINTS....	1	NA	283	0.6	3.8
165 CH OF NAZARENE	1	22	30	0.1	0.4
167 CHS OF CHRIST.	10	650	825	1.7	11.2
193 EPISCOPAL.....	1	45	62	0.1	0.8
349 PENT HOLINESS.	1	25	31*	0.1	0.4
357 PRESB CH US...	2	72	90*	0.2	1.2
413 S.D.A.........	1	48	60*	0.1	0.8
419 SO BAPT CONV..	13	2 198	2 752*	5.6	37.2
449 UN METHODIST..	15	1 544	1 933*	4.0	26.1
453 UN PRES CH USA	2	71	89*	0.2	1.2
FRANKLIN	65	19 556	27 541*	65.8	100.0
017 AMER BAPT ASSN	1	40	40	0.1	0.1
053 ASSEMB OF GOD.	2	140	225	0.5	0.8
081 CATHOLIC......	1	NA	2 500	6.0	9.1
093 CHR CH (DISC).	4	1 562	2 564	6.1	9.3
097 CHR CHS&CHS CR	4	877	1 060*	2.5	3.8
123 CH GOD (ANDER)	1	85	255	0.6	0.9
127 CH GOD (CLEVE)	2	127	153*	0.4	0.6
151 L-D SAINTS....	1	NA	221	0.5	0.8
165 CH OF NAZARENE	2	268	332	0.8	1.2
167 CHS OF CHRIST.	5	320	407	1.0	1.5
193 EPISCOPAL.....	1	511	526	1.3	1.9
281 LUTH CH AMER..	1	155	213	0.5	0.8
329 OPEN BIBLE STD	1	91	200	0.5	0.7
357 PRESB CH US...	2	442	534*	1.3	1.9
403 SALVATION ARMY	1	91	375	0.9	1.4
413 S.D.A.........	1	107	129*	0.3	0.5
419 SO BAPT CONV..	27	12 464	15 058*	36.0	54.7
449 UN METHODIST..	6	1 833	2 214*	5.3	8.0
453 UN PRES CH USA	2	443	535*	1.3	1.9
FULTON	34	6 298	8 427*	93.9	100.0
053 ASSEMB OF GOD.	2	74	124	1.4	1.5
081 CATHOLIC......	2	NA	300	3.3	3.6
093 CHR CH (DISC).	1	130	143	1.6	1.7
097 CHR CHS&CHS CR	2	119	144*	1.6	1.7
101 C.M.E.........	1	202	244*	2.7	2.9
123 CH GOD (ANDER)	1	95	285	3.2	3.4
151 L-D SAINTS....	1	NA	264	2.9	3.1
165 CH OF NAZARENE	1	89	99	1.1	1.2
167 CHS OF CHRIST.	2	170	208	2.3	2.5
185 CUMBER PRESB..	2	294	418	4.7	5.0
193 EPISCOPAL.....	1	87	101	1.1	1.2
413 S.D.A.........	1	41	50*	0.6	0.6
419 SO BAPT CONV..	12	3 754	4 543*	50.6	53.9
449 UN METHODIST..	4	1 243	1 504*	16.8	17.8
GALLATIN	19	2 910	3 782*	78.1	100.0
081 CATHOLIC......	1	NA	124	2.6	3.3
093 CHR CH (DISC).	2	184	301	6.2	8.0
097 CHR CHS&CHS CR	1	125	154*	3.2	4.1
167 CHS OF CHRIST.	2	65	83	1.7	2.2
419 SO BAPT CONV..	7	1 825	2 245*	46.4	59.4
449 UN METHODIST..	6	711	875*	18.1	23.1
GARRARD	34	4 862	6 489*	59.8	100.0
081 CATHOLIC......	1	NA	102	0.9	1.6
093 CHR CH (DISC).	4	416	690	6.4	10.6
097 CHR CHS&CHS CR	4	175	210*	1.9	3.2
123 CH GOD (ANDER)	1	130	390	3.6	6.0
127 CH GOD (CLEVE)	1	73	88*	0.8	1.4
165 CH OF NAZARENE	1	171	318	2.9	4.9
167 CHS OF CHRIST.	1	50	64	0.6	1.0
357 PRESB CH US...	2	134	161*	1.5	2.5
419 SO BAPT CONV..	11	2 922	3 515*	32.4	54.2
449 UN METHODIST..	6	658	791*	7.3	12.2
453 UN PRES CH USA	2	133	160*	1.5	2.5
GRANT	40	6 275	8 224*	61.8	100.0
053 ASSEMB OF GOD.	1	27	42	0.3	0.5
081 CATHOLIC......	1	NA	190	1.4	2.3
093 CHR CH (DISC).	2	300	446	3.4	5.4
097 CHR CHS&CHS CR	9	824	1 021*	7.7	12.4
101 C.M.E.........	1	5	6*	-	0.1
123 CH GOD (ANDER)	2	98	294	2.2	3.6
357 PRESB CH US...	2	24	30*	0.2	0.4
419 SO BAPT CONV..	17	4 668	5 787*	43.5	70.4
449 UN METHODIST..	3	306	379*	2.8	4.6
453 UN PRES CH USA	2	23	29*	0.2	0.4
GRAVES	108	19 865	27 221*	79.9	100.0
053 ASSEMB OF GOD.	1	311	832	2.4	3.1
081 CATHOLIC......	2	NA	2 650	7.8	9.7
093 CHR CH (DISC).	2	547	654	1.9	2.4
097 CHR CHS&CHS CR	2	130	155*	0.5	0.6
127 CH GOD (CLEVE)	1	110	131*	0.4	0.5
165 CH OF NAZARENE	2	137	201	0.6	0.7
167 CHS OF CHRIST.	23	2 708	3 423	10.1	12.6
185 CUMBER PRESB..	8	425	706	2.1	2.6
193 EPISCOPAL.....	1	55	82	0.2	0.3
349 PENT HOLINESS.	1	88	105*	0.3	0.4
357 PRESB CH US...	1	104	124*	0.4	0.5
413 S.D.A.........	1	10	12*	-	-
419 SO BAPT CONV..	42	12 335	14 687*	43.1	54.0
449 UN METHODIST..	20	2 800	3 334*	9.8	12.2
453 UN PRES CH USA	1	105	125*	0.4	0.5
GRAYSON	63	5 884	9 350*	44.8	100.0
053 ASSEMB OF GOD.	1	9	20	0.1	0.2
081 CATHOLIC......	7	NA	1 960	9.4	21.0
093 CHR CH (DISC).	1	60	151	0.7	1.6
097 CHR CHS&CHS CR	6	554	679*	3.3	7.3

NA—Not applicable   *Total adherents estimated from known number of communicant, confirmed, full members.   —Represents a percent less than 0.1.   Percentages may not total due to rounding.

Table 4. Churches and Church Membership by County and Denomination: 1980

County and Denomination	Number of churches	Communicant, confirmed, full members	Total adherents — Number	Total adherents — Percent of total population	Total adherents — Percent of total adherents
127 CH GOD (CLEVE)	1	16	20*	0.1	0.2
165 CH OF NAZARENE	1	77	71	0.3	0.8
167 CHS OF CHRIST.	11	552	705	3.4	7.5
185 CUMBER PRESB..	6	216	347	1.7	3.7
413 S.D.A.........	1	35	43*	0.2	0.5
419 SO BAPT CONV..	18	3 294	4 040*	19.4	43.2
449 UN METHODIST..	10	1 071	1 314*	6.3	14.1
GREEN	**50**	**7 702**	**9 490***	**85.9**	**100.0**
053 ASSEMB OF GOD.	1	14	22	0.2	0.2
081 CATHOLIC......	1	NA	65	0.6	0.7
097 CHR CHS&CHS CR	2	110	132*	1.2	1.4
165 CH OF NAZARENE	1	114	176	1.6	1.9
167 CHS OF CHRIST.	2	14	28	0.3	0.3
185 CUMBER PRESB..	3	279	479	4.3	5.0
357 PRESB CH US...	2	102	122*	1.1	1.3
409 SEPARATE BAPT.	5	580	695*	6.3	7.3
419 SO BAPT CONV..	21	4 832	5 787*	52.4	61.0
449 UN METHODIST..	10	1 556	1 863*	16.9	19.6
453 UN PRES CH USA	2	101	121*	1.1	1.3
GREENUP	**58**	**9 364**	**12 542***	**32.1**	**100.0**
029 AMER LUTH CH..	1	117	160	0.4	1.3
053 ASSEMB OF GOD.	1	66	103	0.3	0.8
081 CATHOLIC......	1	NA	25	0.1	0.2
097 CHR CHS&CHS CR	10	2 235	2 766*	7.1	22.1
123 CH GOD (ANDER)	2	229	687	1.8	5.5
127 CH GOD (CLEVE)	4	207	256*	0.7	2.0
165 CH OF NAZARENE	5	524	1 123	2.9	9.0
167 CHS OF CHRIST.	4	375	477	1.2	3.8
357 PRESB CH US...	1	29	36*	0.1	0.3
419 SO BAPT CONV..	11	3 290	4 072*	10.4	32.5
449 UN METHODIST..	17	2 264	2 802*	7.2	22.3
453 UN PRES CH USA	1	28	35*	0.1	0.3
HANCOCK	**26**	**4 205**	**6 256***	**80.8**	**100.0**
081 CATHOLIC......	3	NA	969	12.5	15.5
097 CHR CHS&CHS CR	1	27	34*	0.4	0.5
185 CUMBER PRESB..	1	14	30	0.4	0.5
349 PENT HOLINESS.	1	49	61*	0.8	1.0
419 SO BAPT CONV..	13	3 059	3 837*	49.6	61.3
449 UN METHODIST..	7	1 056	1 325*	17.1	21.2
HARDIN	**93**	**24 883**	**37 437***	**42.1**	**100.0**
053 ASSEMB OF GOD.	3	474	653	0.7	1.7
081 CATHOLIC......	8	NA	6 106	6.9	16.3
093 CHR CH (DISC).	1	56	130	0.1	0.3
097 CHR CHS&CHS CR	8	1 932	2 345*	2.6	6.3
123 CH GOD (ANDER)	1	44	132	0.1	0.4
127 CH GOD (CLEVE)	3	227	275*	0.3	0.7
151 L-D SAINTS....	1	NA	578	0.7	1.5
165 CH OF NAZARENE	2	99	199	0.2	0.5
167 CHS OF CHRIST.	6	533	678	0.8	1.8
185 CUMBER PRESB..	3	52	183	0.2	0.5
193 EPISCOPAL.....	1	130	210	0.2	0.6
281 LUTH CH AMER..	1	114	152	0.2	0.4
283 LUTH--MO SYNOD	1	171	248	0.3	0.7
357 PRESB CH US...	1	161	195*	0.2	0.5
413 S.D.A.........	1	55	67*	0.1	0.2
419 SO BAPT CONV..	33	16 053	19 483*	21.9	52.0
449 UN METHODIST..	18	4 622	5 609*	6.3	15.0
453 UN PRES CH USA	1	160	194*	0.2	0.5
HARLAN	**106**	**15 102**	**19 723***	**47.1**	**100.0**
005 AME ZION......	2	216	281	0.7	1.4
053 ASSEMB OF GOD.	2	?	?	?	?
081 CATHOLIC......	1	NA	443	1.1	2.2
093 CHR CH (DISC).	3	275	534	1.3	2.7
097 CHR CHS&CHS CR	6	370	464*	1.1	2.4
123 CH GOD (ANDER)	1	78	234	0.6	1.2
127 CH GOD (CLEVE)	14	1 225	1 536*	3.7	7.8
151 L-D SAINTS....	1	NA	?	?	?
165 CH OF NAZARENE	3	71	93	0.2	0.5
167 CHS OF CHRIST.	7	350	445	1.1	2.3
193 EPISCOPAL.....	1	86	95	0.2	0.5
285 MENNONITE CH..	1	17	21*	0.1	0.1
287 MENN GEN CONF.	1	16	32	0.1	0.2
357 PRESB CH US...	4	129	162*	0.4	0.8
413 S.D.A.........	1	20	25*	0.1	0.1
419 SO BAPT CONV..	44	10 721	13 442*	32.1	68.2
449 UN METHODIST..	10	1 398	1 753*	4.2	8.9
453 UN PRES CH USA	4	130	163*	0.4	0.8
HARRISON	**54**	**7 487**	**10 007***	**66.0**	**100.0**
053 ASSEMB OF GOD.	1	55	50	0.3	0.5
081 CATHOLIC......	1	NA	500	3.3	5.0
093 CHR CH (DISC).	5	769	1 159	7.6	11.6
097 CHR CHS&CHS CR	11	1 280	1 549*	10.2	15.5
123 CH GOD (ANDER)	1	100	300	2.0	3.0
165 CH OF NAZARENE	1	18	28	0.2	0.3
167 CHS OF CHRIST.	1	145	185	1.2	1.8
193 EPISCOPAL.....	1	52	106	0.7	1.1
356 PRESB CH AMER.	1	180	216	1.4	2.2
357 PRESB CH US...	2	102	123*	0.8	1.2
413 S.D.A.........	1	31	38*	0.3	0.4
419 SO BAPT CONV..	9	2 111	2 554*	16.8	25.5
449 UN METHODIST..	17	2 543	3 077*	20.3	30.7
453 UN PRES CH USA	2	101	122*	0.8	1.2
HART	**57**	**8 417**	**10 423***	**67.7**	**100.0**
081 CATHOLIC......	1	NA	98	0.6	0.9
097 CHR CHS&CHS CR	1	75	91*	0.6	0.9
127 CH GOD (CLEVE)	2	50	61*	0.4	0.6
167 CHS OF CHRIST.	6	450	573	3.7	5.5
185 CUMBER PRESB..	4	188	315	2.0	3.0
357 PRESB CH US...	1	11	13*	0.1	0.1
409 SEPARATE BAPT.	3	505	613*	4.0	5.9
419 SO BAPT CONV..	25	5 635	6 835*	44.4	65.6
449 UN METHODIST..	13	1 491	1 809*	11.7	17.4
453 UN PRES CH USA	1	12	15*	0.1	0.1
HENDERSON	**59**	**17 561**	**25 633***	**62.8**	**100.0**
005 AME ZION......	1	255	270	0.7	1.1
053 ASSEMB OF GOD.	2	212	555	1.4	2.2
081 CATHOLIC......	2	NA	3 370	8.2	13.1
093 CHR CH (DISC).	2	544	820	2.0	3.2
097 CHR CHS&CHS CR	4	367	449*	1.1	1.8
151 L-D SAINTS....	1	NA	126	0.3	0.5
165 CH OF NAZARENE	2	191	454	1.1	1.8
167 CHS OF CHRIST.	1	250	300	0.7	1.2
193 EPISCOPAL.....	1	211	295	0.7	1.2
283 LUTH--MO SYNOD	1	110	135	0.3	0.5
357 PRESB CH US...	1	242	296*	0.7	1.2
403 SALVATION ARMY	1	91	109	0.3	0.4
413 S.D.A.........	1	73	89*	0.2	0.3
419 SO BAPT CONV..	25	10 881	13 309*	32.6	51.9
443 UN C OF CHRIST	1	64	78*	0.2	0.3
449 UN METHODIST..	12	3 827	4 681*	11.5	18.3
453 UN PRES CH USA	1	243	297*	0.7	1.2
HENRY	**42**	**6 763**	**8 815***	**69.2**	**100.0**
053 ASSEMB OF GOD.	1	15	34	0.3	0.4
081 CATHOLIC......	1	NA	160	1.3	1.8
093 CHR CH (DISC).	11	943	1 606	12.6	18.2
097 CHR CHS&CHS CR	1	170	205*	1.6	2.3
127 CH GOD (CLEVE)	1	57	69*	0.5	0.8
167 CHS OF CHRIST.	1	30	38	0.3	0.4
357 PRESB CH US...	1	43	52*	0.4	0.6
419 SO BAPT CONV..	15	4 295	5 189*	40.7	58.9
449 UN METHODIST..	9	1 167	1 410*	11.1	16.0
453 UN PRES CH USA	1	43	52*	0.4	0.6
HICKMAN	**30**	**3 903**	**5 023***	**82.8**	**100.0**
053 ASSEMB OF GOD.	1	69	147	2.4	2.9
081 CATHOLIC......	1	NA	282	4.6	5.6
093 CHR CH (DISC).	1	55	79	1.3	1.6
101 C.M.E.........	1	188	224*	3.7	4.5
167 CHS OF CHRIST.	1	46	59	1.0	1.2
419 SO BAPT CONV..	12	2 187	2 611*	43.1	52.0
449 UN METHODIST..	13	1 358	1 621*	26.7	32.3
HOPKINS	**84**	**18 575**	**24 964***	**54.1**	**100.0**
005 AME ZION......	2	314	384	0.8	1.5
053 ASSEMB OF GOD.	3	420	702	1.5	2.8
081 CATHOLIC......	2	NA	1 025	2.2	4.1
093 CHR CH (DISC).	6	1 028	1 592	3.4	6.4
097 CHR CHS&CHS CR	4	678	829*	1.8	3.3
123 CH GOD (ANDER)	1	121	363	0.8	1.5
127 CH GOD (CLEVE)	1	15	18*	—	0.1
151 L-D SAINTS....	1	NA	297	0.6	1.2
165 CH OF NAZARENE	1	36	63	0.1	0.3
167 CHS OF CHRIST.	3	325	413	0.9	1.7
185 CUMBER PRESB..	4	246	419	0.9	1.7
193 EPISCOPAL.....	1	165	200	0.4	0.8
281 LUTH CH AMER..	1	56	86	0.2	0.3
357 PRESB CH US...	1	189	231*	0.5	0.9
403 SALVATION ARMY	1	14	49	0.1	0.2
413 S.D.A.........	1	44	54*	0.1	0.2
419 SO BAPT CONV..	33	11 669	14 261*	30.9	57.1
449 UN METHODIST..	17	3 067	3 748*	8.1	15.0
453 UN PRES CH USA	1	188	230*	0.5	0.9
JACKSON	**34**	**3 208**	**4 433***	**37.0**	**100.0**
081 CATHOLIC......	1	NA	61	0.5	1.4
093 CHR CH (DISC).	1	123	189	1.6	4.3
097 CHR CHS&CHS CR	2	50	62*	0.5	1.4
123 CH GOD (ANDER)	1	50	150	1.3	3.4
127 CH GOD (CLEVE)	1	56	70*	0.6	1.6
167 CHS OF CHRIST.	3	103	131	1.1	3.0
371 REF CH IN AM..	3	157	436	3.6	9.8
419 SO BAPT CONV..	22	2 669	3 334*	27.8	75.2
JEFFERSON	**570**	**205 586**	**417 172***	**60.9**	**100.0**
005 AME ZION......	8	12 380	13 180	1.9	3.2
053 ASSEMB OF GOD.	15	4 508	5 826	0.9	1.4
055 AS REF PRES CH	1	99	102	—	—
081 CATHOLIC......	81	NA	164 321	24.0	39.4
089 CHR & MISS AL.	3	389	656	0.1	0.2
093 CHR CH (DISC).	17	6 192	8 748	1.3	2.1
097 CHR CHS&CHS CR	22	7 662	9 245*	1.4	2.2
101 C.M.E.........	7	2 633	3 177*	0.5	0.8
105 CHRISTIAN REF.	1	7	15	—	—
123 CH GOD (ANDER)	5	569	1 707	0.2	0.4
127 CH GOD (CLEVE)	15	1 735	2 093*	0.3	0.5
151 L-D SAINTS....	3	NA	1 694	0.2	0.4
165 CH OF NAZARENE	17	1 596	2 861	0.4	0.7
167 CHS OF CHRIST.	54	6 450	8 210	1.2	2.0

NA—Not applicable   *Total adherents estimated from known number of communicant, confirmed, full members.   —Represents a percent less than 0.1.   Percentages may not total due to rounding.

Table 4. Churches and Church Membership by County and Denomination: 1980

County and Denomination	Number of churches	Communicant, confirmed, full members	Total adherents Number	Percent of total population	Percent of total adherents
185 CUMBER PRESB..	1	183	370	0.1	0.1
193 EPISCOPAL.....	17	6 495	7 816	1.1	1.9
221 FREE METHODIST	1	21	60	-	-
226 FRIENDS-USA...	1	75	90*	-	-
270 CONSRV JUDAISM	1	429	518*	0.1	0.1
271 REFORM JUDAISM	2	1 890	2 280*	0.3	0.5
281 LUTH CH AMER..	15	4 102	5 260	0.8	1.3
283 LUTH--MO SYNOD	6	1 677	2 141	0.3	0.5
285 MENNONITE CH..	1	28	34*	-	-
290 METRO COMM CHS	1	40	80	-	-
353 CHR BRETHREN..	1	10	10	-	-
356 PRESB CH AMER.	2	58	58	-	-
357 PRESB CH US...	31	6 943	8 377*	1.2	2.0
403 SALVATION ARMY	3	280	336	-	0.1
409 SEPARATE BAPT.	3	589	711*	0.1	0.2
413 S.D.A.........	4	1 454	1 754*	0.3	0.4
419 SO BAPT CONV..	122	96 506	116 444*	17.0	27.9
435 UNITARIAN-UNIV	3	415	501*	0.1	0.1
443 UN C OF CHRIST	20	7 111	8 580*	1.3	2.1
449 UN METHODIST..	54	25 949	31 310*	4.6	7.5
453 UN PRES CH USA	31	7 075	8 537*	1.2	2.0
469 WELS.........	1	36	70	-	-
JESSAMINE	**41**	**6 295**	**8 947***	**33.6**	**100.0**
053 ASSEMB OF GOD.	1	74	133	0.5	1.5
081 CATHOLIC......	1	NA	350	1.3	3.9
093 CHR CH (DISC).	5	671	1 088	4.1	12.2
097 CHR CHS&CHS CR	3	87	107*	0.4	1.2
127 CH GOD (CLEVE)	1	116	143*	0.5	1.6
165 CH OF NAZARENE	2	83	140	0.5	1.6
167 CHS OF CHRIST.	4	200	255	1.0	2.9
193 EPISCOPAL.....	1	26	36	0.1	0.4
197 EVAN CH OF NA.	1	21	21	0.1	0.2
221 FREE METHODIST	2	96	651	2.4	7.3
291 MISSIONARY CH.	1	106	91	0.3	1.0
357 PRESB CH US...	4	152	187*	0.7	2.1
419 SO BAPT CONV..	5	2 857	3 520*	13.2	39.3
449 UN METHODIST..	6	1 654	2 038*	7.6	22.8
453 UN PRES CH USA	4	152	187*	0.7	2.1
JOHNSON	**30**	**3 066**	**4 652***	**19.0**	**100.0**
081 CATHOLIC......	1	NA	250	1.0	5.4
097 CHR CHS&CHS CR	5	403	498*	2.0	10.7
123 CH GOD (ANDER)	4	243	729	3.0	15.7
127 CH GOD (CLEVE)	1	21	26*	0.1	0.6
151 L-D SAINTS....	1	NA	124	0.5	2.7
167 CHS OF CHRIST.	9	491	668	2.7	14.4
419 SO BAPT CONV..	3	918	1 134*	4.6	24.4
449 UN METHODIST..	6	990	1 223*	5.0	26.3
KENTON	**123**	**28 881**	**75 968***	**55.4**	**100.0**
005 AME ZION......	1	150	195	0.1	0.3
081 CATHOLIC......	21	NA	37 693	27.5	49.6
093 CHR CH (DISC).	8	1 861	3 282	2.4	4.3
097 CHR CHS&CHS CR	11	2 260	2 775*	2.0	3.7
123 CH GOD (ANDER)	4	300	900	0.7	1.2
127 CH GOD (CLEVE)	4	312	383*	0.3	0.5
151 L-D SAINTS....	2	NA	746	0.5	1.0
165 CH OF NAZARENE	5	880	1 306	1.0	1.7
167 CHS OF CHRIST.	3	130	248	0.2	0.3
193 EPISCOPAL.....	2	589	781	0.6	1.0
215 EVAN METH CH..	1	85	104*	0.1	0.1
281 LUTH CH AMER..	2	290	389	0.3	0.5
283 LUTH--MO SYNOD	1	151	216	0.2	0.3
290 METRO COMM CHS	0	16	32	-	-
357 PRESB CH US...	3	685	841*	0.6	1.1
403 SALVATION ARMY	1	117	220	0.2	0.3
413 S.D.A.........	2	290	356*	0.3	0.5
419 SO BAPT CONV..	27	14 249	17 499*	12.8	23.0
443 UN C OF CHRIST	4	822	1 009*	0.7	1.3
449 UN METHODIST..	16	4 590	5 637*	4.1	7.4
453 UN PRES CH USA	5	1 104	1 356*	1.0	1.8
KNOTT	**12**	**1 720**	**2 180***	**12.2**	**100.0**
167 CHS OF CHRIST.	1	20	28	0.2	1.3
203 EVAN FREE CH..	1	31	39*	0.2	1.8
263 INT FOURSQ GOS	1	12	15*	0.1	0.7
285 MENNONITE CH..	2	49	62*	0.3	2.8
419 SO BAPT CONV..	6	1 451	1 837*	10.2	84.3
449 UN METHODIST..	1	157	199*	1.1	9.1
KNOX	**71**	**13 165**	**16 589***	**54.9**	**100.0**
001 ADVENT CHR CH.	2	108	135*	0.4	0.8
081 CATHOLIC......	1	NA	98	0.3	0.6
093 CHR CH (DISC).	1	113	135	0.4	0.8
097 CHR CHS&CHS CR	2	125	157*	0.5	0.9
127 CH GOD (CLEVE)	2	122	153*	0.5	0.9
419 SO BAPT CONV..	58	12 156	15 233*	50.4	91.8
449 UN METHODIST..	5	541	678*	2.2	4.1
LARUE	**33**	**6 983**	**8 716***	**72.7**	**100.0**
053 ASSEMB OF GOD.	3	87	123	1.0	1.4
081 CATHOLIC......	1	NA	270	2.3	3.1
093 CHR CH (DISC).	1	95	126	1.1	1.4
097 CHR CHS&CHS CR	2	375	451*	3.8	5.2
101 C.M.E........	1	255	307*	2.6	3.5
127 CH GOD (CLEVE)	1	45	54*	0.5	0.6
167 CHS OF CHRIST.	1	30	38	0.3	0.4
185 CUMBER PRESB..	1	92	118	1.0	1.4
409 SEPARATE BAPT.	2	461	555*	4.6	6.4
419 SO BAPT CONV..	16	5 014	6 037*	50.4	69.3
449 UN METHODIST..	4	529	637*	5.3	7.3
LAUREL	**82**	**12 552**	**16 150***	**41.4**	**100.0**
053 ASSEMB OF GOD.	3	378	745	1.9	4.6
081 CATHOLIC......	2	NA	214	0.5	1.3
093 CHR CH (DISC).	5	680	761	2.0	4.7
097 CHR CHS&CHS CR	9	801	995*	2.6	6.2
123 CH GOD (ANDER)	1	30	90	0.2	0.6
127 CH GOD (CLEVE)	2	112	139*	0.4	0.9
165 CH OF NAZARENE	1	45	117	0.3	0.7
167 CHS OF CHRIST.	5	373	474	1.2	2.9
193 EPISCOPAL.....	1	31	63	0.2	0.4
357 PRESB CH US...	1	82	102*	0.3	0.6
413 S.D.A.........	1	87	108*	0.3	0.7
419 SO BAPT CONV..	42	9 117	11 328*	29.1	70.1
449 UN METHODIST..	8	734	912*	2.3	5.6
453 UN PRES CH USA	1	82	102*	0.3	0.6
LAWRENCE	**24**	**1 797**	**2 243***	**15.9**	**100.0**
093 CHR CH (DISC).	1	63	89	0.6	4.0
097 CHR CHS&CHS CR	2	130	161*	1.1	7.2
127 CH GOD (CLEVE)	1	22	27*	0.2	1.2
167 CHS OF CHRIST.	1	35	45	0.3	2.0
419 SO BAPT CONV..	4	645	801*	5.7	35.7
449 UN METHODIST..	15	902	1 120*	7.9	49.9
LEE	**40**	**2 655**	**4 285***	**55.3**	**100.0**
081 CATHOLIC......	2	NA	151	1.9	3.5
093 CHR CH (DISC).	7	592	910	11.7	21.2
097 CHR CHS&CHS CR	3	300	368*	4.7	8.6
123 CH GOD (ANDER)	5	311	933	12.0	21.8
127 CH GOD (CLEVE)	1	73	90*	1.2	2.1
165 CH OF NAZARENE	1	59	158	2.0	3.7
167 CHS OF CHRIST.	7	275	350	4.5	8.2
193 EPISCOPAL.....	1	58	81	1.0	1.9
199 EVAN CONGR CH.	1	22	27*	0.3	0.6
221 FREE METHODIST	1	8	42	0.5	1.0
357 PRESB CH US...	2	45	55*	0.7	1.3
419 SO BAPT CONV..	6	803	986*	12.7	23.0
449 UN METHODIST..	1	63	77*	1.0	1.8
453 UN PRES CH USA	2	46	57*	0.7	1.3
LESLIE	**34**	**1 988**	**2 604***	**17.5**	**100.0**
081 CATHOLIC......	1	NA	25	0.2	1.0
089 CHR & MISS AL.	2	14	21	0.1	0.8
093 CHR CH (DISC).	2	160	246	1.7	9.4
127 CH GOD (CLEVE)	4	288	367*	2.5	14.1
167 CHS OF CHRIST.	6	200	255	1.7	9.8
244 GRACE BRETHREN	1	31	40*	0.3	1.5
357 PRESB CH US...	3	111	141*	0.9	5.4
419 SO BAPT CONV..	6	766	976*	6.6	37.5
449 UN METHODIST..	6	306	390*	2.6	15.0
453 UN PRES CH USA	3	112	143*	1.0	5.5
LETCHER	**37**	**3 505**	**4 737***	**15.4**	**100.0**
005 AME ZION......	1	85	98	0.3	2.1
081 CATHOLIC......	1	NA	174	0.6	3.7
089 CHR & MISS AL.	1	38	52	0.2	1.1
097 CHR CHS&CHS CR	1	60	76*	0.2	1.6
123 CH GOD (ANDER)	1	80	240	0.8	5.1
127 CH GOD (CLEVE)	3	126	159*	0.5	3.4
165 CH OF NAZARENE	1	7	19	0.1	0.4
167 CHS OF CHRIST.	5	150	191	0.6	4.0
263 INT FOURSQ GOS	1	45	57*	0.2	1.2
357 PRESB CH US...	4	149	188*	0.6	4.0
413 S.D.A.........	1	5	6*	-	0.1
419 SO BAPT CONV..	7	2 170	2 734*	8.9	57.7
449 UN METHODIST..	6	442	557*	1.8	11.8
453 UN PRES CH USA	4	148	186*	0.6	3.9
LEWIS	**39**	**3 322**	**4 261***	**29.3**	**100.0**
081 CATHOLIC......	1	NA	102	0.7	2.4
089 CHR & MISS AL.	1	136	136	0.9	3.2
093 CHR CH (DISC).	1	57	88	0.6	2.1
097 CHR CHS&CHS CR	14	1 260	1 582*	10.9	37.1
127 CH GOD (CLEVE)	2	151	190*	1.3	4.5
165 CH OF NAZARENE	1	50	68	0.5	1.6
357 PRESB CH US...	2	4	5*	-	0.1
419 SO BAPT CONV..	5	816	1 025*	7.0	24.1
449 UN METHODIST..	10	842	1 057*	7.3	24.8
453 UN PRES CH USA	2	6	8*	0.1	0.2
LINCOLN	**78**	**10 091**	**13 410***	**70.4**	**100.0**
081 CATHOLIC......	2	NA	146	0.8	1.1
093 CHR CH (DISC).	4	288	567	3.0	4.2
097 CHR CHS&CHS CR	8	657	809*	4.2	6.0
123 CH GOD (ANDER)	8	352	1 056	5.5	7.9
127 CH GOD (CLEVE)	5	254	313*	1.6	2.3
165 CH OF NAZARENE	2	89	105	0.6	0.8
167 CHS OF CHRIST.	9	250	320	1.7	2.4
283 LUTH--MO SYNOD	1	23	30	0.2	0.2
357 PRESB CH US...	1	67	82*	0.4	0.6
419 SO BAPT CONV..	28	7 206	8 868*	46.5	66.1
449 UN METHODIST..	9	837	1 030*	5.4	7.7
453 UN PRES CH USA	1	68	84*	0.4	0.6

NA—Not applicable   *Total adherents estimated from known number of communicant, confirmed, full members.   —Represents a percent less than 0.1.   Percentages may not total due to rounding.

Table 4. Churches and Church Membership by County and Denomination: 1980

County and Denomination	Number of churches	Communicant, confirmed, full members	Total adherents Number	Percent of total population	Percent of total adherents
LIVINGSTON	44	5 265	6 409*	69.5	100.0
093 CHR CH (DISC).	1	32	61	0.7	1.0
167 CHS OF CHRIST.	2	100	127	1.4	2.0
185 CUMBER PRESB..	2	70	109	1.2	1.7
419 SO BAPT CONV..	23	3 674	4 435*	48.1	69.2
449 UN METHODIST..	16	1 389	1 677*	18.2	26.2
LOGAN	82	14 652	18 414*	76.3	100.0
005 AME ZION......	4	432	560	2.3	3.0
061 BEACHY AMISH..	1	52	63*	0.3	0.3
081 CATHOLIC......	1	NA	325	1.3	1.8
093 CHR CH (DISC).	3	359	452	1.9	2.5
097 CHR CHS&CHS CR	2	270	328*	1.4	1.8
167 CHS OF CHRIST.	13	971	1 290	5.3	7.0
185 CUMBER PRESB..	5	235	388	1.6	2.1
193 EPISCOPAL.....	1	65	117	0.5	0.6
357 PRESB CH US...	2	108	131*	0.5	0.7
419 SO BAPT CONV..	32	10 138	12 306*	51.0	66.8
449 UN METHODIST..	16	1 914	2 323*	9.6	12.6
453 UN PRES CH USA	2	108	131*	0.5	0.7
LYON	20	3 625	4 204*	64.8	100.0
081 CATHOLIC......	1	NA	28	0.4	0.7
167 CHS OF CHRIST.	2	150	191	2.9	4.5
419 SO BAPT CONV..	11	2 686	3 080*	47.5	73.3
449 UN METHODIST..	6	789	905*	13.9	21.5
MC CRACKEN	95	29 772	41 732*	68.1	100.0
053 ASSEMB OF GOD.	1	56	77	0.1	0.2
081 CATHOLIC......	4	NA	4 408	7.2	10.6
093 CHR CH (DISC).	4	611	917	1.5	2.2
097 CHR CHS&CHS CR	1	100	120*	0.2	0.3
101 C.M.E........	2	423	508*	0.8	1.2
123 CH GOD (ANDER)	3	98	294	0.5	0.7
127 CH GOD (CLEVE)	1	37	44*	0.1	0.1
151 L-D SAINTS....	1	NA	419	0.7	1.0
165 CH OF NAZARENE	1	79	273	0.4	0.7
167 CHS OF CHRIST.	11	2 151	2 640	4.3	6.3
177 CONGR HOL CH..	1	23	28*	-	0.1
185 CUMBER PRESB..	4	991	1 618	2.6	3.9
193 EPISCOPAL.....	1	399	494	0.8	1.2
271 REFORM JUDAISM	1	132	158*	0.3	0.4
281 LUTH CH AMER..	1	302	417	0.7	1.0
283 LUTH--MO SYNOD	1	372	484	0.8	1.2
290 METRO COMM CHS	0	12	24	-	0.1
357 PRESB CH US...	3	382	459*	0.7	1.1
403 SALVATION ARMY	1	83	100	0.2	0.2
413 S.D.A........	2	180	216*	0.4	0.5
419 SO BAPT CONV..	30	17 516	21 031*	34.3	50.4
443 UN C OF CHRIST	1	241	289*	0.5	0.7
449 UN METHODIST..	17	5 204	6 248*	10.2	15.0
453 UN PRES CH USA	3	380	456*	0.7	1.1
MC CREARY	20	3 211	4 120*	26.4	100.0
081 CATHOLIC......	1	NA	35	0.2	0.8
093 CHR CH (DISC).	2	35	65	0.4	1.6
127 CH GOD (CLEVE)	1	34	43*	0.3	1.0
167 CHS OF CHRIST.	2	45	57	0.4	1.4
413 S.D.A........	1	77	97*	0.6	2.4
419 SO BAPT CONV..	10	2 789	3 531*	22.6	85.7
449 UN METHODIST..	3	231	292*	1.9	7.1
MC LEAN	34	5 094	6 610*	65.5	100.0
081 CATHOLIC......	2	NA	343	3.4	5.2
093 CHR CH (DISC).	1	64	74	0.7	1.1
097 CHR CHS&CHS CR	2	240	291*	2.9	4.4
167 CHS OF CHRIST.	1	100	127	1.3	1.9
185 CUMBER PRESB..	3	258	392	3.9	5.9
357 PRESB CH US...	1	17	21*	0.2	0.3
419 SO BAPT CONV..	13	2 741	3 329*	33.0	50.4
449 UN METHODIST..	10	1 656	2 011*	19.9	30.4
453 UN PRES CH USA	1	18	22*	0.2	0.3
MADISON	96	17 175	23 908*	44.8	100.0
053 ASSEMB OF GOD.	2	98	146	0.3	0.6
081 CATHOLIC......	3	NA	2 420	4.5	10.1
093 CHR CH (DISC).	9	1 640	2 399	4.5	10.0
097 CHR CHS&CHS CR	13	1 543	1 832*	3.4	7.7
101 C.M.E........	2	244	290*	0.5	1.2
123 CH GOD (ANDER)	1	70	210	0.4	0.9
127 CH GOD (CLEVE)	3	324	385*	0.7	1.6
151 L-D SAINTS....	1	NA	186	0.3	0.8
165 CH OF NAZARENE	4	439	786	1.5	3.3
167 CHS OF CHRIST.	4	230	293	0.5	1.2
185 CUMBER PRESB..	1	79	88	0.2	0.4
193 EPISCOPAL.....	1	89	130	0.2	0.5
226 FRIENDS-USA...	1	43	51*	0.1	0.2
357 PRESB CH US...	3	265	315*	0.6	1.3
413 S.D.A........	4	111	132*	0.2	0.6
419 SO BAPT CONV..	31	10 099	11 988*	22.5	50.1
435 UNITARIAN-UNIV	1	16	19*	-	0.1
449 UN METHODIST..	9	1 620	1 923*	3.6	8.0
453 UN PRES CH USA	3	265	315*	0.6	1.3
MAGOFFIN	8	797	1 039*	7.7	100.0
053 ASSEMB OF GOD.	1	7	17	0.1	1.6
097 CHR CHS&CHS CR	1	83	106*	0.8	10.2
167 CHS OF CHRIST.	2	70	100	0.7	9.6
419 SO BAPT CONV..	3	457	585*	4.3	56.3
449 UN METHODIST..	1	180	231*	1.7	22.2
MARION	39	5 370	16 218*	90.6	100.0
005 AME ZION......	1	175	210	1.2	1.3
081 CATHOLIC......	8	NA	9 145	51.1	56.4
093 CHR CH (DISC).	1	190	255	1.4	1.6
097 CHR CHS&CHS CR	3	175	218*	1.2	1.3
101 C.M.E........	1	38	47*	0.3	0.3
127 CH GOD (CLEVE)	1	45	56*	0.3	0.3
151 L-D SAINTS....	1	NA	372	2.1	2.3
167 CHS OF CHRIST.	2	100	127	0.7	0.8
357 PRESB CH US...	2	102	127*	0.7	0.8
419 SO BAPT CONV..	9	3 602	4 487*	25.1	27.7
449 UN METHODIST..	8	840	1 046*	5.8	6.4
453 UN PRES CH USA	2	103	128*	0.7	0.8
MARSHALL	64	12 456	15 745*	61.4	100.0
017 AMER BAPT ASSN	1	150	150	0.6	1.0
053 ASSEMB OF GOD.	1	28	55	0.2	0.3
081 CATHOLIC......	1	NA	427	1.7	2.7
093 CHR CH (DISC).	1	166	186	0.7	1.2
097 CHR CHS&CHS CR	1	23	27*	0.1	0.2
165 CH OF NAZARENE	1	44	64	0.2	0.4
167 CHS OF CHRIST.	12	2 026	2 790	10.9	17.7
185 CUMBER PRESB..	5	363	525	2.0	3.3
193 EPISCOPAL.....	1	35	50	0.2	0.3
357 PRESB CH US...	1	49	58*	0.2	0.4
419 SO BAPT CONV..	24	7 170	8 549*	33.3	54.3
449 UN METHODIST..	14	2 354	2 807*	10.9	17.8
453 UN PRES CH USA	1	48	57*	0.2	0.4
MARTIN	16	1 014	1 642*	11.8	100.0
053 ASSEMB OF GOD.	1	?	?	?	?
081 CATHOLIC......	1	NA	25	0.2	1.5
127 CH GOD (CLEVE)	3	117	151*	1.1	9.2
157 CH OF BRETHREN	1	14	18*	0.1	1.1
165 CH OF NAZARENE	3	162	476	3.4	29.0
167 CHS OF CHRIST.	3	120	195	1.4	11.9
419 SO BAPT CONV..	2	464	600*	4.3	36.5
449 UN METHODIST..	2	137	177*	1.3	10.8
MASON	55	7 612	12 527*	70.5	100.0
053 ASSEMB OF GOD.	1	52	200	1.1	1.6
081 CATHOLIC......	3	NA	2 682	15.1	21.4
093 CHR CH (DISC).	8	875	1 373	7.7	11.0
097 CHR CHS&CHS CR	6	610	740*	4.2	5.9
151 L-D SAINTS....	1	NA	197	1.1	1.6
165 CH OF NAZARENE	1	242	235	1.3	1.9
167 CHS OF CHRIST.	1	21	33	0.2	0.3
193 EPISCOPAL.....	1	128	169	1.0	1.3
283 LUTH--MO SYNOD	1	36	45	0.3	0.4
357 PRESB CH US...	3	149	181*	1.0	1.4
419 SO BAPT CONV..	8	2 039	2 474*	13.9	19.7
449 UN METHODIST..	18	3 312	4 018*	22.6	32.1
453 UN PRES CH USA	3	148	180*	1.0	1.4
MEADE	35	5 447	11 001*	48.1	100.0
053 ASSEMB OF GOD.	1	27	36	0.2	0.3
081 CATHOLIC......	4	NA	3 883	17.0	35.3
097 CHR CHS&CHS CR	2	110	142*	0.6	1.3
151 L-D SAINTS....	1	NA	80	0.4	0.7
165 CH OF NAZARENE	1	86	111	0.5	1.0
167 CHS OF CHRIST.	3	150	191	0.8	1.7
193 EPISCOPAL.....	1	43	53	0.2	0.5
357 PRESB CH US...	1	33	43*	0.2	0.4
419 SO BAPT CONV..	15	4 253	5 499*	24.1	50.0
449 UN METHODIST..	5	713	922*	4.0	8.4
453 UN PRES CH USA	1	32	41*	0.2	0.4
MENIFEE	8	448	790*	15.4	100.0
097 CHR CHS&CHS CR	1	25	31*	0.6	3.9
123 CH GOD (ANDER)	2	132	396	7.7	50.1
127 CH GOD (CLEVE)	1	25	31*	0.6	3.9
167 CHS OF CHRIST.	1	50	64	1.3	8.1
357 PRESB CH US...	1	15	19*	0.4	2.4
419 SO BAPT CONV..	1	187	232*	4.5	29.4
453 UN PRES CH USA	1	14	17*	0.3	2.2
MERCER	52	11 426	14 838*	78.0	100.0
053 ASSEMB OF GOD.	1	37	73	0.4	0.5
081 CATHOLIC......	1	NA	450	2.4	3.0
093 CHR CH (DISC).	5	929	1 433	7.5	9.7
097 CHR CHS&CHS CR	6	703	853*	4.5	5.7
127 CH GOD (CLEVE)	1	157	191*	1.0	1.3
165 CH OF NAZARENE	1	?	?	?	?
167 CHS OF CHRIST.	3	230	293	1.5	2.0
185 CUMBER PRESB..	2	134	285	1.5	1.9
193 EPISCOPAL.....	1	82	152	0.8	1.0
357 PRESB CH US...	3	160	194*	1.0	1.3
419 SO BAPT CONV..	17	7 861	9 539*	50.2	64.3
449 UN METHODIST..	8	972	1 180*	6.2	8.0
453 UN PRES CH USA	3	161	195*	1.0	1.3
METCALFE	39	3 287	4 467*	47.1	100.0
081 CATHOLIC......	1	NA	29	0.3	0.6

NA— Not applicable   *Total adherents estimated from known number of communicant, confirmed, full members.   —Represents a percent less than 0.1.   Percentages may not total due to rounding.

Table 4. Churches and Church Membership by County and Denomination: 1980

County and Denomination	Number of churches	Communicant, confirmed, full members	Total adherents Number	Percent of total population	Percent of total adherents
097 CHR CHS&CHS CR	1	107	130*	1.4	2.9
151 L-D SAINTS....	1	NA	244	2.6	5.5
167 CHS OF CHRIST.	8	434	528	5.6	11.8
185 CUMBER PRESB..	8	293	566	6.0	12.7
419 SO BAPT CONV..	11	1 591	1 927*	20.3	43.1
449 UN METHODIST..	8	841	1 018*	10.7	22.8
453 UN PRES CH USA	1	21	25*	0.3	0.6
MONROE	43	4 709	6 048*	49.0	100.0
081 CATHOLIC......	1	NA	30	0.2	0.5
151 L-D SAINTS....	1	NA	210	1.7	3.5
167 CHS OF CHRIST.	26	1 681	2 140	17.3	35.4
419 SO BAPT CONV..	10	2 560	3 101*	25.1	51.3
449 UN METHODIST..	5	468	567*	4.6	9.4
MONTGOMERY	41	6 882	10 066*	50.2	100.0
005 AME ZION......	1	120	150	0.7	1.5
053 ASSEMB OF GOD.	2	66	100	0.5	1.0
081 CATHOLIC......	1	NA	225	1.1	2.2
089 CHR & MISS AL.	1	9	17	0.1	0.2
093 CHR CH (DISC).	4	1 157	1 451	7.2	14.4
097 CHR CHS&CHS CR	4	345	430*	2.1	4.3
101 C.M.E.	1	795	992*	4.9	9.9
123 CH GOD (ANDER)	5	633	1 899	9.5	18.9
127 CH GOD (CLEVE)	1	112	140*	0.7	1.4
165 CH OF NAZARENE	1	180	325	1.6	3.2
167 CHS OF CHRIST.	7	525	670	3.3	6.7
193 EPISCOPAL.....	1	173	216	1.1	2.1
357 PRESB CH US...	1	86	107*	0.5	1.1
419 SO BAPT CONV..	7	2 022	2 522*	12.6	25.1
449 UN METHODIST..	3	572	713*	3.6	7.1
453 UN PRES CH USA	1	87	109*	0.5	1.1
MORGAN	20	1 546	2 326*	19.2	100.0
081 CATHOLIC......	1	NA	48	0.4	2.1
093 CHR CH (DISC).	6	405	593	4.9	25.5
097 CHR CHS&CHS CR	1	235	292*	2.4	12.6
123 CH GOD (ANDER)	3	150	450	3.7	19.3
127 CH GOD (CLEVE)	1	80	99*	0.8	4.3
167 CHS OF CHRIST.	3	140	178	1.5	7.7
285 MENNONITE CH..	1	55	68*	0.6	2.9
357 PRESB CH US...	1	33	41*	0.3	1.8
419 SO BAPT CONV..	1	240	298*	2.5	12.8
449 UN METHODIST..	1	176	219*	1.8	9.4
453 UN PRES CH USA	1	32	40*	0.3	1.7
MUHLENBERG	99	18 369	23 229*	72.1	100.0
005 AME ZION......	3	463	613	1.9	2.6
053 ASSEMB OF GOD.	2	51	109	0.3	0.5
081 CATHOLIC......	1	NA	277	0.9	1.2
093 CHR CH (DISC).	2	354	414	1.3	1.8
097 CHR CHS&CHS CR	2	203	248*	0.8	1.1
127 CH GOD (CLEVE)	1	54	66*	0.2	0.3
151 L-D SAINTS....	1	NA	180	0.6	0.8
165 CH OF NAZARENE	1	67	171	0.5	0.7
167 CHS OF CHRIST.	10	752	998	3.1	4.3
185 CUMBER PRESB..	4	228	344	1.1	1.5
357 PRESB CH US...	6	174	213*	0.7	0.9
413 S.D.A.	1	29	35*	0.1	0.2
419 SO BAPT CONV..	44	13 526	16 543*	51.3	71.2
449 UN METHODIST..	15	2 293	2 804*	8.7	12.1
453 UN PRES CH USA	6	175	214*	0.7	0.9
NELSON	57	8 404	19 998*	72.5	100.0
005 AME ZION......	3	538	623	2.3	3.1
053 ASSEMB OF GOD.	2	62	94	0.3	0.5
081 CATHOLIC......	10	NA	9 343	33.9	46.7
093 CHR CH (DISC).	5	474	757	2.7	3.8
097 CHR CHS&CHS CR	3	310	386*	1.4	1.9
127 CH GOD (CLEVE)	2	188	234*	0.8	1.2
167 CHS OF CHRIST.	5	250	320	1.2	1.6
185 CUMBER PRESB..	1	102	155	0.6	0.8
193 EPISCOPAL.....	1	20	37	0.1	0.2
357 PRESB CH US...	3	125	156*	0.6	0.8
419 SO BAPT CONV..	13	5 269	6 565*	23.8	32.8
449 UN METHODIST..	7	985	1 227*	4.4	6.1
453 UN PRES CH USA	2	81	101*	0.4	0.5
NICHOLAS	23	2 918	3 868*	54.0	100.0
053 ASSEMB OF GOD.	1	34	78	1.1	2.0
081 CATHOLIC......	1	NA	185	2.6	4.8
093 CHR CH (DISC).	3	171	305	4.3	7.9
097 CHR CHS&CHS CR	5	870	1 058*	14.8	27.4
101 C.M.E.	1	158	192*	2.7	5.0
357 PRESB CH US...	1	36	44*	0.6	1.1
419 SO BAPT CONV..	2	640	778*	10.9	20.1
449 UN METHODIST..	8	974	1 185*	16.6	30.6
453 UN PRES CH USA	1	35	43*	0.6	1.1
OHIO	91	11 826	14 924*	68.6	100.0
053 ASSEMB OF GOD.	3	113	224	1.0	1.5
081 CATHOLIC......	2	NA	240	1.1	1.6
097 CHR CHS&CHS CR	3	355	436*	2.0	2.9
123 CH GOD (ANDER)	1	20	60	0.3	0.4
127 CH GOD (CLEVE)	3	211	259*	1.2	1.7
167 CHS OF CHRIST.	8	450	572	2.6	3.8
185 CUMBER PRESB..	3	89	119	0.5	0.8
357 PRESB CH US...	1	23	28*	0.1	0.2
413 S.D.A.	1	38	47*	0.2	0.3
419 SO BAPT CONV..	43	8 635	10 614*	48.8	71.1
449 UN METHODIST..	22	1 869	2 297*	10.6	15.4
453 UN PRES CH USA	1	23	28*	0.1	0.2
OLDHAM	37	7 525	12 382*	44.1	100.0
053 ASSEMB OF GOD.	3	120	229	0.8	1.8
081 CATHOLIC......	2	NA	2 767	9.8	22.3
093 CHR CH (DISC).	2	675	910	3.2	7.3
097 CHR CHS&CHS CR	2	144	179*	0.6	1.4
101 C.M.E.	1	13	16*	0.1	0.1
123 CH GOD (ANDER)	1	51	153	0.5	1.2
127 CH GOD (CLEVE)	1	32	40*	0.1	0.3
167 CHS OF CHRIST.	2	80	102	0.4	0.8
193 EPISCOPAL.....	1	60	84	0.3	0.7
357 PRESB CH US...	2	116	144*	0.5	1.2
413 S.D.A.	1	151	188*	0.7	1.5
419 SO BAPT CONV..	10	4 248	5 287*	18.8	42.7
449 UN METHODIST..	7	1 719	2 139*	7.6	17.3
453 UN PRES CH USA	2	116	144*	0.5	1.2
OWEN	41	6 216	7 799*	87.4	100.0
053 ASSEMB OF GOD.	3	177	281	3.1	3.6
081 CATHOLIC......	2	NA	84	0.9	1.1
093 CHR CH (DISC).	3	267	393	4.4	5.0
097 CHR CHS&CHS CR	1	150	183*	2.1	2.3
413 S.D.A.	1	80	98*	1.1	1.3
419 SO BAPT CONV..	26	5 230	6 379*	71.5	81.8
449 UN METHODIST..	5	312	381*	4.3	4.9
OWSLEY	22	1 055	1 398*	24.5	100.0
053 ASSEMB OF GOD.	2	78	116	2.0	8.3
123 CH GOD (ANDER)	1	37	111	1.9	7.9
127 CH GOD (CLEVE)	1	37	46*	0.8	3.3
167 CHS OF CHRIST.	4	150	190	3.3	13.6
357 PRESB CH US...	3	104	129*	2.3	9.2
419 SO BAPT CONV..	5	311	386*	6.8	27.6
449 UN METHODIST..	3	231	287*	5.0	20.5
453 UN PRES CH USA	3	107	133*	2.3	9.5
PENDLETON	41	6 227	8 354*	76.0	100.0
053 ASSEMB OF GOD.	1	14	36	0.3	0.4
081 CATHOLIC......	1	NA	400	3.6	4.8
093 CHR CH (DISC).	6	707	1 101	10.0	13.2
097 CHR CHS&CHS CR	7	1 028	1 270*	11.6	15.2
127 CH GOD (CLEVE)	1	8	10*	0.1	0.1
165 CH OF NAZARENE	1	22	43	0.4	0.5
419 SO BAPT CONV..	17	3 670	4 533*	41.3	54.3
449 UN METHODIST..	7	778	961*	8.7	11.5
PERRY	72	7 858	10 102*	29.9	100.0
053 ASSEMB OF GOD.	1	27	53	0.2	0.5
071 BRETHREN (ASH)	1	15	19*	0.1	0.2
081 CATHOLIC......	1	NA	125	0.4	1.2
093 CHR CH (DISC).	4	347	467	1.4	4.6
101 C.M.E.	1	125	158*	0.5	1.6
127 CH GOD (CLEVE)	11	713	900*	2.7	8.9
167 CHS OF CHRIST.	11	450	575	1.7	5.7
193 EPISCOPAL.....	1	41	53	0.2	0.5
203 EVAN FREE CH..	4	75	95*	0.3	0.9
357 PRESB CH US...	5	287	362*	1.1	3.6
419 SO BAPT CONV..	24	5 162	6 518*	19.3	64.5
449 UN METHODIST..	3	329	415*	1.2	4.1
453 UN PRES CH USA	5	287	362*	1.1	3.6
PIKE	98	10 661	14 362*	17.7	100.0
053 ASSEMB OF GOD.	1	47	62	0.1	0.4
081 CATHOLIC......	1	NA	315	0.4	2.2
089 CHR & MISS AL.	7	98	178	0.2	1.2
093 CHR CH (DISC).	1	234	262	0.3	1.8
097 CHR CHS&CHS CR	18	1 645	2 073*	2.6	14.4
123 CH GOD (ANDER)	6	249	747	0.9	5.2
127 CH GOD (CLEVE)	7	499	629*	0.8	4.4
151 L-D SAINTS....	1	NA	138	0.2	1.0
157 CH OF BRETHREN	1	23	29*	-	0.2
167 CHS OF CHRIST.	13	575	732	0.9	5.1
185 CUMBER PRESB..	1	13	18	-	0.1
193 EPISCOPAL.....	1	63	84	0.1	0.6
357 PRESB CH US...	5	245	309*	0.4	2.2
413 S.D.A.	1	30	38*	-	0.3
419 SO BAPT CONV..	18	5 263	6 634*	8.2	46.2
449 UN METHODIST..	11	1 427	1 799*	2.2	12.5
453 UN PRES CH USA	5	250	315*	0.4	2.2
POWELL	31	2 714	4 425*	39.9	100.0
053 ASSEMB OF GOD.	1	46	73	0.7	1.6
093 CHR CH (DISC).	2	142	218	2.0	4.9
097 CHR CHS&CHS CR	2	247	311*	2.8	7.0
101 C.M.E.	1	38	48*	0.4	1.1
123 CH GOD (ANDER)	8	545	1 635	14.7	36.9
127 CH GOD (CLEVE)	1	95	120*	1.1	2.7
167 CHS OF CHRIST.	7	272	346	3.1	7.8
357 PRESB CH US...	1	80	101*	0.9	2.3
419 SO BAPT CONV..	3	875	1 102*	9.9	24.9
449 UN METHODIST..	4	293	369*	3.3	8.3
453 UN PRES CH USA	1	81	102*	0.9	2.3
PULASKI	124	21 638	27 806*	60.7	100.0

NA— Not applicable   *Total adherents estimated from known number of communicant, confirmed, full members.   —Represents a percent less than 0.1.   Percentages may not total due to rounding.

Table 4. Churches and Church Membership by County and Denomination: 1980

County and Denomination	Number of churches	Communicant, confirmed, full members	Total adherents		
			Number	Percent of total population	Percent of total adherents
017 AMER BAPT ASSN	5	1 000	1 000	2.2	3.6
053 ASSEMB OF GOD.	2	104	179	0.4	0.6
081 CATHOLIC......	1	NA	800	1.7	2.9
093 CHR CH (DISC).	2	475	668	1.5	2.4
097 CHR CHS&CHS CR	5	290	353*	0.8	1.3
123 CH GOD (ANDER)	2	125	375	0.8	1.3
127 CH GOD (CLEVE)	4	339	413*	0.9	1.5
165 CH OF NAZARENE	6	648	1 220	2.7	4.4
167 CHS OF CHRIST.	13	760	967	2.1	3.5
193 EPISCOPAL.....	1	122	160	0.3	0.6
281 LUTH CH AMER..	1	107	170	0.4	0.6
357 PRESB CH US...	2	152	185*	0.4	0.7
409 SEPARATE BAPT.	1	25	30*	0.1	0.1
419 SO BAPT CONV..	60	14 801	18 013*	39.3	64.8
449 UN METHODIST..	17	2 536	3 086*	6.7	11.1
453 UN PRES CH USA	2	154	187*	0.4	0.7
ROBERTSON	8	856	1 058*	46.6	100.0
053 ASSEMB OF GOD.	1	50	68	3.0	6.4
097 CHR CHS&CHS CR	3	545	651*	28.7	61.5
123 CH GOD (ANDER)	1	15	45	2.0	4.3
449 UN METHODIST..	3	246	294*	13.0	27.8
ROCKCASTLE	48	6 469	8 046*	57.6	100.0
053 ASSEMB OF GOD.	1	26	32	0.2	0.4
081 CATHOLIC......	1	NA	25	0.2	0.3
093 CHR CH (DISC).	1	15	23	0.2	0.3
097 CHR CHS&CHS CR	10	831	1 027*	7.3	12.8
127 CH GOD (CLEVE)	2	117	145*	1.0	1.8
165 CH OF NAZARENE	1	16	32	0.2	0.4
167 CHS OF CHRIST.	7	334	425	3.0	5.3
419 SO BAPT CONV..	24	5 116	6 320*	45.2	78.5
449 UN METHODIST..	1	14	17*	0.1	0.2
ROWAN	19	2 493	4 381*	23.0	100.0
053 ASSEMB OF GOD.	1	43	121	0.6	2.8
081 CATHOLIC......	1	NA	372	2.0	8.5
093 CHR CH (DISC).	1	298	312	1.6	7.1
097 CHR CHS&CHS CR	2	85	101*	0.5	2.3
123 CH GOD (ANDER)	5	510	1 530	8.0	34.9
127 CH GOD (CLEVE)	1	69	82*	0.4	1.9
165 CH OF NAZARENE	1	24	99	0.5	2.3
167 CHS OF CHRIST.	1	150	191	1.0	4.4
193 EPISCOPAL.....	1	26	38	0.2	0.9
357 PRESB CH US...	1	50	60*	0.3	1.4
419 SO BAPT CONV..	2	565	673*	3.5	15.4
449 UN METHODIST..	1	622	741*	3.9	16.9
453 UN PRES CH USA	1	51	61*	0.3	1.4
RUSSELL	57	5 800	7 150*	52.2	100.0
081 CATHOLIC......	1	NA	90	0.7	1.3
097 CHR CHS&CHS CR	5	455	549*	4.0	7.7
127 CH GOD (CLEVE)	6	287	346*	2.5	4.8
165 CH OF NAZARENE	2	85	149	1.1	2.1
167 CHS OF CHRIST.	5	221	281	2.0	3.9
409 SEPARATE BAPT.	11	1 078	1 301*	9.5	18.2
413 S.D.A.........	1	75	91*	0.7	1.3
419 SO BAPT CONV..	15	2 195	2 649*	19.3	37.0
449 UN METHODIST..	11	1 404	1 694*	12.4	23.7
SCOTT	48	8 727	11 496*	52.7	100.0
053 ASSEMB OF GOD.	1	81	156	0.7	1.4
081 CATHOLIC......	2	NA	437	2.0	3.8
093 CHR CH (DISC).	5	872	1 260	5.8	11.0
097 CHR CHS&CHS CR	8	1 053	1 291*	5.9	11.2
123 CH GOD (ANDER)	1	142	426	2.0	3.7
127 CH GOD (CLEVE)	1	71	87*	0.4	0.8
165 CH OF NAZARENE	1	411	404	1.9	3.5
167 CHS OF CHRIST.	3	125	159	0.7	1.4
193 EPISCOPAL.....	1	138	127	0.6	1.1
357 PRESB CH US...	4	170	208*	1.0	1.8
419 SO BAPT CONV..	12	4 652	5 701*	26.1	49.6
449 UN METHODIST..	5	840	1 029*	4.7	9.0
453 UN PRES CH USA	4	172	211*	1.0	1.8
SHELBY	44	12 489	15 877*	68.1	100.0
053 ASSEMB OF GOD.	1	177	242	1.0	1.5
081 CATHOLIC......	1	NA	450	1.9	2.8
093 CHR CH (DISC).	5	959	1 364	5.8	8.6
097 CHR CHS&CHS CR	2	600	724*	3.1	4.6
151 L-D SAINTS....	1	NA	62	0.3	0.4
165 CH OF NAZARENE	1	52	115	0.5	0.7
167 CHS OF CHRIST.	2	80	116	0.5	0.7
193 EPISCOPAL.....	1	70	70	0.3	0.4
357 PRESB CH US...	1	164	198*	0.8	1.2
419 SO BAPT CONV..	23	9 355	11 291*	48.4	71.1
449 UN METHODIST..	5	867	1 046*	4.5	6.6
453 UN PRES CH USA	1	165	199*	0.9	1.3
SIMPSON	36	6 273	8 154*	55.6	100.0
061 BEACHY AMISH..	1	79	97*	0.7	1.2
081 CATHOLIC......	1	NA	296	2.0	3.6
097 CHR CHS&CHS CR	1	25	31*	0.2	0.4
165 CH OF NAZARENE	1	52	74	0.5	0.9
167 CHS OF CHRIST.	7	747	1 046	7.1	12.8
185 CUMBER PRESB..	1	17	17	0.1	0.2
193 EPISCOPAL.....	1	35	42	0.3	0.5
281 LUTH CH AMER..	1	103	150	1.0	1.8

County and Denomination	Number of churches	Communicant, confirmed, full members	Total adherents		
			Number	Percent of total population	Percent of total adherents
357 PRESB CH US...	2	123	151*	1.0	1.9
413 S.D.A.........	1	21	26*	0.2	0.3
419 SO BAPT CONV..	10	3 770	4 627*	31.5	56.7
449 UN METHODIST..	7	1 177	1 445*	9.8	17.7
453 UN PRES CH USA	2	124	152*	1.0	1.9
SPENCER	17	3 912	5 120*	86.4	100.0
053 ASSEMB OF GOD.	1	125	260	4.4	5.1
081 CATHOLIC......	1	NA	140	2.4	2.7
093 CHR CH (DISC).	1	132	234	3.9	4.6
097 CHR CHS&CHS CR	4	570	699*	11.8	13.7
167 CHS OF CHRIST.	1	50	64	1.1	1.2
419 SO BAPT CONV..	8	2 973	3 647*	61.5	71.2
449 UN METHODIST..	1	62	76*	1.3	1.5
TAYLOR	63	12 002	16 028*	75.7	100.0
053 ASSEMB OF GOD.	1	27	52	0.2	0.3
075 BRETHREN IN CR	1	43	73	0.3	0.5
081 CATHOLIC......	3	NA	941	4.4	5.9
097 CHR CHS&CHS CR	5	662	798*	3.8	5.0
101 C.M.E.........	1	130	157*	0.7	1.0
123 CH GOD (ANDER)	3	212	636	3.0	4.0
165 CH OF NAZARENE	1	50	140	0.7	0.9
167 CHS OF CHRIST.	3	100	125	0.6	0.8
185 CUMBER PRESB..	5	345	527	2.5	3.3
357 PRESB CH US...	1	131	158*	0.7	1.0
409 SEPARATE BAPT.	2	287	346*	1.6	2.2
419 SO BAPT CONV..	19	6 993	8 431*	39.8	52.6
449 UN METHODIST..	17	2 892	3 487*	16.5	21.8
453 UN PRES CH USA	1	130	157*	0.7	1.0
TODD	53	7 081	9 213*	77.6	100.0
053 ASSEMB OF GOD.	2	54	77	0.6	0.8
081 CATHOLIC......	2	NA	127	1.1	1.4
093 CHR CH (DISC).	3	173	275	2.3	3.0
101 C.M.E.........	5	882	1 073*	9.0	11.6
151 L-D SAINTS....	1	NA	220	1.9	2.4
165 CH OF NAZARENE	1	71	177	1.5	1.9
167 CHS OF CHRIST.	8	468	625	5.3	6.8
185 CUMBER PRESB..	2	37	78	0.7	0.8
323 OLD ORD AMISH.	3	390	474*	4.0	5.1
357 PRESB CH US...	1	19	23*	0.2	0.2
419 SO BAPT CONV..	13	3 639	4 425*	37.3	48.0
449 UN METHODIST..	11	1 330	1 617*	13.6	17.6
453 UN PRES CH USA	1	18	22*	0.2	0.2
TRIGG	33	6 007	7 365*	78.5	100.0
081 CATHOLIC......	1	NA	125	1.3	1.7
093 CHR CH (DISC).	2	148	203	2.2	2.8
097 CHR CHS&CHS CR	1	50	60*	0.6	0.8
101 C.M.E.........	1	118	142*	1.5	1.9
167 CHS OF CHRIST.	2	190	235	2.5	3.2
419 SO BAPT CONV..	17	4 497	5 395*	57.5	73.3
449 UN METHODIST..	9	1 004	1 205*	12.8	16.4
TRIMBLE	18	2 830	3 641*	58.2	100.0
081 CATHOLIC......	1	NA	20	0.3	0.5
093 CHR CH (DISC).	1	85	235	3.8	6.5
097 CHR CHS&CHS CR	2	433	534*	8.5	14.7
419 SO BAPT CONV..	8	1 557	1 921*	30.7	52.8
449 UN METHODIST..	6	755	931*	14.9	25.6
UNION	49	7 424	12 803*	71.8	100.0
081 CATHOLIC......	6	NA	3 599	20.2	28.1
093 CHR CH (DISC).	4	332	507	2.8	4.0
097 CHR CHS&CHS CR	2	340	412*	2.3	3.2
101 C.M.E.........	4	557	675*	3.8	5.3
167 CHS OF CHRIST.	4	260	331	1.9	2.6
185 CUMBER PRESB..	3	182	304	1.7	2.4
193 EPISCOPAL.....	1	28	39	0.2	0.3
357 PRESB CH US...	2	83	101*	0.6	0.8
419 SO BAPT CONV..	14	4 517	5 472*	30.7	42.7
449 UN METHODIST..	7	1 042	1 262*	7.1	9.9
453 UN PRES CH USA	2	83	101*	0.6	0.8
WARREN	123	26 394	36 629*	51.0	100.0
005 AME ZION......	1	83	98	0.1	0.3
053 ASSEMB OF GOD.	1	129	234	0.3	0.6
081 CATHOLIC......	3	NA	3 636	5.1	9.9
093 CHR CH (DISC).	4	800	952	1.3	2.6
097 CHR CHS&CHS CR	4	267	320*	0.4	0.9
101 C.M.E.........	1	63	76*	0.1	0.2
123 CH GOD (ANDER)	1	33	99	0.1	0.3
127 CH GOD (CLEVE)	2	84	101*	0.1	0.3
151 L-D SAINTS....	1	NA	414	0.6	1.1
165 CH OF NAZARENE	3	248	358	0.5	1.0
167 CHS OF CHRIST.	22	2 650	3 375	4.7	9.2
185 CUMBER PRESB..	2	224	387	0.5	1.1
193 EPISCOPAL.....	1	410	669	0.9	1.8
221 FREE METHODIST	2	86	309	0.4	0.8
283 LUTH--MO SYNOD	1	240	316	0.4	0.9
356 PRESB CH AMER.	1	73	83	0.1	0.2
357 PRESB CH US...	6	606	726*	1.0	2.0
403 SALVATION ARMY	1	89	135	0.2	0.4
413 S.D.A.........	3	205	246*	0.3	0.7
419 SO BAPT CONV..	37	14 896	17 853*	24.9	48.7
435 UNITARIAN-UNIV	1	15	18*	—	—
449 UN METHODIST..	21	4 666	5 592*	7.8	15.3

NA—Not applicable   *Total adherents estimated from known number of communicant, confirmed, full members.   —Represents a percent less than 0.1.   Percentages may not total due to rounding.

Table 4. Churches and Church Membership by County and Denomination: 1980

County and Denomination	Number of churches	Communicant, confirmed, full members	Total adherents		
			Number	Percent of total population	Percent of total adherents
453 UN PRES CH USA	4	527	632*	0.9	1.7
WASHINGTON	37	5 943	11 313*	105.1	100.0
005 AME ZION......	3	393	478	4.4	4.2
081 CATHOLIC......	5	NA	4 025	37.4	35.6
097 CHR CHS&CHS CR	5	1 052	1 289*	12.0	11.4
127 CH GOD (CLEVE)	2	83	102*	0.9	0.9
167 CHS OF CHRIST.	3	151	193	1.8	1.7
357 PRESB CH US...	2	89	109*	1.0	1.0
419 SO BAPT CONV..	12	3 801	4 658*	43.3	41.2
449 UN METHODIST..	3	283	347*	3.2	3.1
453 UN PRES CH USA	2	91	112*	1.0	1.0
WAYNE	43	7 899	10 159*	59.7	100.0
053 ASSEMB OF GOD.	1	24	31	0.2	0.3
081 CATHOLIC......	1	NA	90	0.5	0.9
097 CHR CHS&CHS CR	2	370	457*	2.7	4.5
123 CH GOD (ANDER)	1	74	222	1.3	2.2
127 CH GOD (CLEVE)	1	59	73*	0.4	0.7
165 CH OF NAZARENE	1	138	312	1.8	3.1
167 CHS OF CHRIST.	4	170	245	1.4	2.4
409 SEPARATE BAPT.	3	175	216*	1.3	2.1
419 SO BAPT CONV..	20	5 763	7 122*	41.8	70.1
449 UN METHODIST..	9	1 126	1 391*	8.2	13.7
WEBSTER	51	6 905	8 704*	58.7	100.0
005 AME ZION......	3	375	418	2.8	4.8
081 CATHOLIC......	2	NA	199	1.3	2.3
093 CHR CH (DISC).	3	246	336	2.3	3.9
097 CHR CHS&CHS CR	4	290	353*	2.4	4.1
167 CHS OF CHRIST.	5	300	382	2.6	4.4
185 CUMBER PRESB..	5	197	323	2.2	3.7
419 SO BAPT CONV..	19	4 113	5 008*	33.8	57.5
449 UN METHODIST..	10	1 384	1 685*	11.4	19.4
WHITLEY	97	17 763	22 952*	68.7	100.0
053 ASSEMB OF GOD.	4	197	271	0.8	1.2
081 CATHOLIC......	3	NA	590	1.8	2.6
093 CHR CH (DISC).	3	452	700	2.1	3.0
097 CHR CHS&CHS CR	6	547	673*	2.0	2.9
127 CH GOD (CLEVE)	4	375	462*	1.4	2.0
151 L-D SAINTS....	1	NA	195	0.6	0.8
165 CH OF NAZARENE	1	108	250	0.7	1.1
167 CHS OF CHRIST.	4	200	255	0.8	1.1
357 PRESB CH US...	1	140	172*	0.5	0.7
413 S.D.A.........	1	28	34*	0.1	0.1
419 SO BAPT CONV..	59	14 486	17 836*	53.4	77.7
449 UN METHODIST..	10	1 230	1 514*	4.5	6.6
WOLFE	7	773	1 317*	19.7	100.0
093 CHR CH (DISC).	2	144	219	3.3	16.6
123 CH GOD (ANDER)	2	180	540	8.1	41.0
419 SO BAPT CONV..	1	250	311*	4.6	23.6
449 UN METHODIST..	2	199	247*	3.7	18.8
WOODFORD	39	8 138	11 335*	63.8	100.0
053 ASSEMB OF GOD.	3	223	437	2.5	3.9
081 CATHOLIC......	1	NA	817	4.6	7.2
093 CHR CH (DISC).	5	727	1 121	6.3	9.9
097 CHR CHS&CHS CR	1	185	227*	1.3	2.0
165 CH OF NAZARENE	2	90	231	1.3	2.0
167 CHS OF CHRIST.	2	150	191	1.1	1.7
193 EPISCOPAL.....	1	312	402	2.3	3.5
357 PRESB CH US...	4	363	445*	2.5	3.9
413 S.D.A.........	1	7	9*	0.1	0.1
419 SO BAPT CONV..	10	4 621	5 665*	31.9	50.0
449 UN METHODIST..	5	1 094	1 341*	7.5	11.8
453 UN PRES CH USA	4	366	449*	2.5	4.0

LOUISIANA

County and Denomination	Number of churches	Communicant, confirmed, full members	Total adherents		
			Number	Percent of total population	Percent of total adherents
THE STATE.....	3 960	871 175	2 413 059*	57.4	100.0
ACADIA	59	6 063	55 228*	97.9	100.0
053 ASSEMB OF GOD.	3	235	402	0.7	0.7
081 CATHOLIC......	24	NA	47 336	83.9	85.7
093 CHR CH (DISC).	1	83	120	0.2	0.2
097 CHR CHS&CHS CR	2	219	275*	0.5	0.5
101 C.M.E.........	3	968	1 216*	2.2	2.2
165 CH OF NAZARENE	3	208	354	0.6	0.6
167 CHS OF CHRIST.	2	75	95	0.2	0.2
193 EPISCOPAL.....	2	160	202	0.4	0.4
283 LUTH--MO SYNOD	2	77	157	0.3	0.4
357 PRESB CH US...	1	167	210*	0.4	0.4
419 SO BAPT CONV..	8	2 721	3 417*	6.1	6.2
449 UN METHODIST..	8	1 150	1 444*	2.6	2.6

County and Denomination	Number of churches	Communicant, confirmed, full members	Total adherents		
			Number	Percent of total population	Percent of total adherents
ALLEN	38	6 076	11 948*	55.9	100.0
053 ASSEMB OF GOD.	3	85	178	0.8	1.5
081 CATHOLIC......	7	NA	4 299	20.1	36.0
101 C.M.E.........	1	29	36*	0.2	0.3
165 CH OF NAZARENE	1	12	23	0.1	0.2
167 CHS OF CHRIST.	2	75	95	0.4	0.8
193 EPISCOPAL.....	1	24	30	0.1	0.3
357 PRESB CH US...	1	35	44*	0.2	0.4
419 SO BAPT CONV..	17	5 257	6 547*	30.6	54.8
449 UN METHODIST..	5	559	696*	3.3	5.8
ASCENSION	34	3 938	30 664*	61.2	100.0
053 ASSEMB OF GOD.	2	132	271	0.5	0.9
081 CATHOLIC......	10	NA	25 113	50.2	81.9
151 L-D SAINTS....	1	NA	381	0.8	1.2
167 CHS OF CHRIST.	3	135	172	0.3	0.6
193 EPISCOPAL.....	1	16	34	0.1	0.1
283 LUTH--MO SYNOD	1	57	112	0.2	0.4
413 S.D.A.........	1	67	85*	0.2	0.3
419 SO BAPT CONV..	8	2 676	3 407*	6.8	11.1
449 UN METHODIST..	7	855	1 089*	2.2	3.6
ASSUMPTION	13	515	12 348*	55.9	100.0
081 CATHOLIC......	7	NA	11 697	53.0	94.7
193 EPISCOPAL.....	1	21	21	0.1	0.2
419 SO BAPT CONV..	1	167	213*	1.0	1.7
449 UN METHODIST..	4	327	417*	1.9	3.4
AVOYELLES	64	4 020	27 842*	67.3	100.0
017 AMER BAPT ASSN	1	53	53	0.1	0.2
053 ASSEMB OF GOD.	2	33	60	0.1	0.2
081 CATHOLIC......	28	NA	22 804	55.1	81.9
097 CHR CHS&CHS CR	1	20	25*	0.1	0.1
165 CH OF NAZARENE	1	78	139	0.3	0.5
167 CHS OF CHRIST.	2	50	64	0.2	0.2
193 EPISCOPAL.....	1	67	74	0.2	0.3
215 EVAN METH CH..	2	117	146*	0.4	0.5
283 LUTH--MO SYNOD	1	54	62	0.1	0.2
419 SO BAPT CONV..	16	2 730	3 397*	8.2	12.2
449 UN METHODIST..	9	818	1 018*	2.5	3.7
BEAUREGARD	52	10 967	15 059*	50.7	100.0
017 AMER BAPT ASSN	1	83	83	0.3	0.6
053 ASSEMB OF GOD.	1	69	103	0.3	0.7
081 CATHOLIC......	2	NA	1 335	4.5	8.9
101 C.M.E.........	2	341	426*	1.4	2.8
123 CH GOD (ANDER)	1	20	60	0.2	0.4
143 CG IN CR(MENN)	1	215	215	0.7	1.4
165 CH OF NAZARENE	1	87	140	0.5	0.9
167 CHS OF CHRIST.	7	300	369	1.2	2.5
193 EPISCOPAL.....	1	144	189	0.6	1.3
283 LUTH--MO SYNOD	1	115	150	0.5	1.0
357 PRESB CH US...	1	137	171*	0.6	1.1
413 S.D.A.........	1	65	81*	0.3	0.5
419 SO BAPT CONV..	29	8 500	10 623*	35.8	70.5
449 UN METHODIST..	3	891	1 114*	3.8	7.4
BIENVILLE	47	7 662	9 343*	57.0	100.0
017 AMER BAPT ASSN	4	586	586	3.6	6.3
053 ASSEMB OF GOD.	4	101	153	0.9	1.6
059 BAPT MISS ASSN	2	325	397*	2.4	4.2
081 CATHOLIC......	1	NA	63	0.4	0.7
167 CHS OF CHRIST.	3	120	153	0.9	1.6
419 SO BAPT CONV..	23	5 593	6 838*	41.7	73.2
421 SO METHODIST..	1	10	20	0.1	0.2
449 UN METHODIST..	9	927	1 133*	6.9	12.1
BOSSIER	96	26 355	36 991*	45.8	100.0
017 AMER BAPT ASSN	4	1 296	1 296	1.6	3.5
053 ASSEMB OF GOD.	9	625	844	1.0	2.3
059 BAPT MISS ASSN	5	593	739*	0.9	2.0
081 CATHOLIC......	5	NA	3 664	4.5	9.9
093 CHR CH (DISC).	1	64	88	0.1	0.2
101 C.M.E.........	16	1 998	2 489*	3.1	6.7
123 CH GOD (ANDER)	1	55	165	0.2	0.4
127 CH GOD (CLEVE)	1	107	133*	0.2	0.4
151 L-D SAINTS....	1	NA	536	0.7	1.4
165 CH OF NAZARENE	2	108	165	0.2	0.4
167 CHS OF CHRIST.	5	1 214	1 633	2.0	4.4
193 EPISCOPAL.....	1	331	341	0.4	0.9
263 INT FOURSQ GOS	1	74	92*	0.1	0.2
281 AMER LUTH AMER..	1	118	144	0.2	0.4
283 LUTH--MO SYNOD	1	189	259	0.3	0.7
357 PRESB CH US...	6	633	788*	1.0	2.1
413 S.D.A.........	1	82	102*	0.1	0.3
419 SO BAPT CONV..	24	16 026	19 962*	24.7	54.0
421 SO METHODIST..	1	47	70	0.1	0.2
449 UN METHODIST..	10	2 795	3 481*	4.3	9.4
CADDO	237	96 483	138 091*	54.7	100.0
017 AMER BAPT ASSN	8	1 143	1 143	0.5	0.8
029 AMER LUTH CH..	2	431	594	0.2	0.4
053 ASSEMB OF GOD.	9	1 214	1 533	0.6	1.1
059 BAPT MISS ASSN	3	930	1 145*	0.5	0.8
081 CATHOLIC......	12	NA	16 686	6.6	12.1
093 CHR CH (DISC).	3	1 576	2 054	0.8	1.5
097 CHR CHS&CHS CR	5	535	659*	0.3	0.5

NA—Not applicable   *Total adherents estimated from known number of communicant, confirmed, full members.   —Represents a percent less than 0.1.   Percentages may not total due to rounding.

Table 4. Churches and Church Membership by County and Denomination: 1980

County and Denomination	Number of churches	Communicant, confirmed, full members	Total adherents Number	Percent of total population	Percent of total adherents
101 C.M.E.........	25	6 026	7 418*	2.9	5.4
123 CH GOD (ANDER)	4	359	1 077	0.4	0.8
151 L-D SAINTS....	2	NA	1 055	0.4	0.8
165 CH OF NAZARENE	9	820	1 272	0.5	0.9
167 CHS OF CHRIST.	18	2 084	2 653	1.1	1.9
193 EPISCOPAL.....	5	4 704	5 721	2.3	4.1
215 EVAN METH CH..	1	20	25*	-	-
221 FREE METHODIST	2	96	345	0.1	0.2
263 INT FOURSQ GOS	1	150	185*	0.1	0.1
270 CONSRV JUDAISM	1	155	191*	0.1	0.1
271 REFORM JUDAISM	1	688	847*	0.3	0.6
281 LUTH CH AMER..	1	114	189	0.1	0.1
283 LUTH--MO SYNOD	5	746	975	0.4	0.7
356 PRESB CH AMER.	1	116	132	0.1	0.1
357 PRESB CH US...	12	3 585	4 413*	1.7	3.2
403 SALVATION ARMY	1	207	647	0.3	0.5
413 S.D.A.........	5	1 108	1 364*	0.5	1.0
419 SO BAPT CONV..	58	52 033	64 052*	25.4	46.4
421 SO METHODIST..	1	258	315	0.1	0.2
435 UNITARIAN-UNIV	1	120	148*	0.1	0.1
449 UN METHODIST..	41	17 265	21 253*	8.4	15.4
CALCASIEU	149	42 496	104 360*	62.5	100.0
053 ASSEMB OF GOD.	9	775	1 521	0.9	1.5
081 CATHOLIC......	26	NA	49 177	29.4	47.1
093 CHR CH (DISC).	2	497	577	0.3	0.6
097 CHR CHS&CHS CR	3	526	651*	0.4	0.6
101 C.M.E........	6	1 231	1 524*	0.9	1.5
123 CH GOD (ANDER)	4	384	1 152	0.7	1.1
151 L-D SAINTS....	2	NA	560	0.3	0.5
165 CH OF NAZARENE	6	343	430	0.3	0.4
167 CHS OF CHRIST.	13	1 183	1 718	1.0	1.6
193 EPISCOPAL.....	4	1 499	2 137	1.3	2.0
271 REFORM JUDAISM	1	190	235*	0.1	0.2
281 LUTH CH AMER..	1	164	217	0.1	0.2
283 LUTH--MO SYNOD	3	565	857	0.5	0.8
356 PRESB CH AMER.	1	13	19	-	-
357 PRESB CH US...	3	1 017	1 259*	0.8	1.2
403 SALVATION ARMY	1	160	304	0.2	0.3
413 S.D.A.........	1	101	125*	0.1	0.1
419 SO BAPT CONV..	42	25 745	31 867*	19.1	30.5
421 SO METHODIST..	1	12	15	-	-
443 UN C OF CHRIST	1	70	87*	0.1	0.1
449 UN METHODIST..	19	8 021	9 928*	5.9	9.5
CALDWELL	29	3 643	4 655*	43.3	100.0
053 ASSEMB OF GOD.	2	72	114	1.1	2.4
081 CATHOLIC......	2	NA	61	0.6	1.3
123 CH GOD (ANDER)	2	40	120	1.1	2.6
127 CH GOD (CLEVE)	1	29	36*	0.3	0.8
167 CHS OF CHRIST.	2	62	80	0.7	1.7
419 SO BAPT CONV..	16	3 012	3 716*	34.5	79.8
449 UN METHODIST..	4	428	528*	4.9	11.3
CAMERON	13	1 116	4 535*	48.6	100.0
081 CATHOLIC......	6	NA	3 151	33.8	69.5
419 SO BAPT CONV..	5	918	1 138*	12.2	25.1
449 UN METHODIST..	2	198	246*	2.6	5.4
CATAHOULA	33	4 597	5 918*	48.2	100.0
053 ASSEMB OF GOD.	2	106	165	1.3	2.8
081 CATHOLIC......	2	NA	75	0.6	1.3
123 CH GOD (ANDER)	1	45	135	1.1	2.3
167 CHS OF CHRIST.	2	35	45	0.4	0.8
357 PRESB CH US...	1	101	126*	1.0	2.1
419 SO BAPT CONV..	22	3 833	4 777*	38.9	80.7
449 UN METHODIST..	3	477	595*	4.8	10.1
CLAIBORNE	60	9 345	11 666*	68.2	100.0
017 AMER BAPT ASSN	3	290	290	1.7	2.5
053 ASSEMB OF GOD.	2	98	219	1.3	1.9
081 CATHOLIC......	2	NA	201	1.2	1.7
101 C.M.E........	16	2 564	3 134*	18.3	26.9
167 CHS OF CHRIST.	5	345	421	2.5	3.6
357 PRESB CH US...	3	254	310*	1.8	2.7
419 SO BAPT CONV..	17	4 362	5 332*	31.2	45.7
421 SO METHODIST..	2	37	54	0.3	0.5
449 UN METHODIST..	10	1 395	1 705*	10.0	14.6
CONCORDIA	39	7 022	9 729*	42.3	100.0
017 AMER BAPT ASSN	1	46	46	0.2	0.5
053 ASSEMB OF GOD.	2	61	62	0.3	0.6
059 BAPT MISS ASSN	1	341	427*	1.9	4.4
081 CATHOLIC......	2	NA	648	2.8	6.7
093 CHR CH (DISC).	2	39	60	0.3	0.6
097 CHR CHS&CHS CR	2	250	313*	1.4	3.2
123 CH GOD (ANDER)	4	161	483	2.1	5.0
127 CH GOD (CLEVE)	2	104	130*	0.6	1.3
167 CHS OF CHRIST.	2	100	127	0.6	1.3
221 FREE METHODIST	1	16	36	0.2	0.4
357 PRESB CH US...	2	189	237*	1.0	2.4
419 SO BAPT CONV..	15	5 072	6 354*	27.6	65.3
449 UN METHODIST..	3	643	806*	3.5	8.3
DE SOTO	66	8 702	11 450*	44.6	100.0
017 AMER BAPT ASSN	3	480	480	1.9	4.2
053 ASSEMB OF GOD.	3	88	126	0.5	1.1
081 CATHOLIC......	5	NA	842	3.3	7.4
093 CHR CH (DISC).	1	10	15	0.1	0.1
167 CHS OF CHRIST.	5	250	318	1.2	2.8
185 CUMBER PRESB..	1	6	10	-	0.1
193 EPISCOPAL.....	1	164	174	0.7	1.5
357 PRESB CH US...	5	239	294*	1.1	2.6
413 S.D.A.........	2	49	60*	0.2	0.5
419 SO BAPT CONV..	27	6 252	7 694*	30.0	67.2
421 SO METHODIST..	1	27	38	0.1	0.3
449 UN METHODIST..	12	1 137	1 399*	5.5	12.2
EAST BATON ROUGE	191	84 139	186 501*	50.9	100.0
017 AMER BAPT ASSN	6	796	796	0.2	0.4
019 AMER BAPT USA.	3	915	1 125*	0.3	0.6
053 ASSEMB OF GOD.	5	775	1 239	0.3	0.7
059 BAPT MISS ASSN	4	810	996*	0.3	0.5
081 CATHOLIC......	24	NA	79 943	21.8	42.9
093 CHR CH (DISC).	1	307	581	0.2	0.3
097 CHR CHS&CHS CR	4	363	446*	0.1	0.2
101 C.M.E........	1	175	215*	0.1	0.1
121 CH GOD (ABR)..	1	18	22*	-	-
123 CH GOD (ANDER)	3	159	477	0.1	0.3
127 CH GOD (CLEVE)	5	808	993*	0.3	0.5
151 L-D SAINTS....	5	NA	1 600	0.4	0.9
165 CH OF NAZARENE	3	223	383	0.1	0.2
167 CHS OF CHRIST.	10	1 075	1 445	0.4	0.8
193 EPISCOPAL.....	8	4 695	6 256	1.7	3.4
226 FRIENDS-USA...	1	10	12*	-	-
271 REFORM JUDAISM	2	732	900*	0.2	0.5
281 LUTH CH AMER..	1	438	626	0.2	0.3
283 LUTH--MO SYNOD	6	1 403	1 841	0.5	1.0
290 METRO COMM CHS	0	10	20	-	-
349 PENT HOLINESS.	2	125	154*	-	0.1
356 PRESB CH AMER.	2	329	394	0.1	0.2
357 PRESB CH US...	10	4 488	5 518*	1.5	3.0
403 SALVATION ARMY	1	167	214	0.1	0.1
413 S.D.A.........	2	891	1 095*	0.3	0.6
419 SO BAPT CONV..	49	46 103	56 683*	15.5	30.4
421 SO METHODIST..	1	37	43	-	-
435 UNITARIAN-UNIV	1	216	266*	0.1	0.1
449 UN METHODIST..	30	18 071	22 218*	6.1	11.9
EAST CARROLL	21	3 666	5 150*	43.7	100.0
053 ASSEMB OF GOD.	1	98	219	1.9	4.3
081 CATHOLIC......	1	NA	360	3.1	7.0
097 CHR CHS&CHS CR	1	30	39*	0.3	0.8
143 CG IN CR(MENN)	1	60	60	0.5	1.2
167 CHS OF CHRIST.	3	125	159	1.4	3.1
193 EPISCOPAL.....	1	103	110	0.9	2.1
357 PRESB CH US...	1	77	100*	0.8	1.9
419 SO BAPT CONV..	10	2 835	3 666*	31.1	71.2
449 UN METHODIST..	2	338	437*	3.7	8.5
EAST FELICIANA	33	4 911	6 866*	36.1	100.0
081 CATHOLIC......	2	NA	591	3.1	8.6
101 C.M.E........	1	86	106*	0.6	1.5
151 L-D SAINTS....	1	NA	185	1.0	2.7
167 CHS OF CHRIST.	1	50	62	0.3	0.9
193 EPISCOPAL.....	1	115	161	0.8	2.3
283 LUTH--MO SYNOD	1	122	164	0.9	2.4
357 PRESB CH US...	3	99	122*	0.6	1.8
419 SO BAPT CONV..	10	3 108	3 833*	20.2	55.8
421 SO METHODIST..	1	8	10	0.1	0.1
449 UN METHODIST..	12	1 323	1 632*	8.6	23.8
EVANGELINE	29	2 817	24 226*	72.7	100.0
081 CATHOLIC......	11	NA	20 604	61.8	85.0
097 CHR CHS&CHS CR	1	15	19*	0.1	0.1
151 L-D SAINTS....	1	NA	87	0.3	0.4
167 CHS OF CHRIST.	2	30	38	0.1	0.2
419 SO BAPT CONV..	12	2 738	3 435*	10.3	14.2
449 UN METHODIST..	2	34	43*	0.1	0.2
FRANKLIN	56	10 782	14 017*	58.1	100.0
053 ASSEMB OF GOD.	3	106	190	0.8	1.4
081 CATHOLIC......	1	NA	287	1.2	2.0
097 CHR CHS&CHS CR	1	50	62*	0.3	0.4
127 CH GOD (CLEVE)	1	?	?	?	?
151 L-D SAINTS....	1	NA	36	0.1	0.3
165 CH OF NAZARENE	2	39	150	0.6	1.1
167 CHS OF CHRIST.	2	160	203	0.8	1.4
193 EPISCOPAL.....	1	25	26	0.1	0.2
221 FREE METHODIST	2	38	138	0.6	1.0
357 PRESB CH US...	3	111	138*	0.6	1.0
419 SO BAPT CONV..	32	9 414	11 741*	48.6	83.8
449 UN METHODIST..	6	839	1 046*	4.3	7.5
GRANT	42	7 536	10 092*	60.4	100.0
053 ASSEMB OF GOD.	1	49	95	0.6	0.9
081 CATHOLIC......	3	NA	726	4.3	7.2
127 CH GOD (CLEVE)	1	18	22*	0.1	0.2
165 CH OF NAZARENE	1	28	37	0.2	0.4
167 CHS OF CHRIST.	2	143	182	1.1	1.8
419 SO BAPT CONV..	25	6 613	8 182*	49.0	81.1
449 UN METHODIST..	9	685	848*	5.1	8.4
IBERIA	47	5 471	45 442*	71.3	100.0
053 ASSEMB OF GOD.	1	165	258	0.4	0.6
081 CATHOLIC......	17	NA	38 550	60.5	84.8

NA—Not applicable   *Total adherents estimated from known number of communicant, confirmed, full members.   —Represents a percent less than 0.1.   Percentages may not total due to rounding.

Table 4. Churches and Church Membership by County and Denomination: 1980

County and Denomination	Number of churches	Communicant, confirmed, full members	Total adherents Number	Percent of total population	Percent of total adherents
097 CHR CHS&CHS CR	1	9	11*	–	–
101 C.M.E.........	3	557	701*	1.1	1.5
151 L-D SAINTS....	1	NA	47	0.1	0.1
165 CH OF NAZARENE	1	29	39	0.1	0.1
167 CHS OF CHRIST.	3	211	269	0.4	0.6
193 EPISCOPAL.....	1	373	375	0.6	0.8
271 REFORM JUDAISM	1	58	73*	0.1	0.2
357 PRESB CH US...	2	88	111*	0.2	0.2
413 S.D.A.........	1	13	16*	–	–
419 SO BAPT CONV..	4	2 307	2 902*	4.6	6.4
443 UN C OF CHRIST	3	166	209*	0.3	0.5
449 UN METHODIST..	8	1 495	1 881*	3.0	4.1
IBERVILLE	**29**	**2 142**	**13 239***	**41.2**	**100.0**
053 ASSEMB OF GOD.	1	21	21	0.1	0.2
081 CATHOLIC......	7	NA	10 570	32.9	79.8
101 C.M.E.........	1	10	12*	–	0.1
123 CH GOD (ANDER)	1	20	60	0.2	0.5
193 EPISCOPAL.....	1	55	47	0.1	0.4
419 SO BAPT CONV..	9	1 206	1 498*	4.7	11.3
449 UN METHODIST..	9	830	1 031*	3.2	7.8
JACKSON	**48**	**7 803**	**10 071***	**58.1**	**100.0**
017 AMER BAPT ASSN	1	154	154	0.9	1.5
053 ASSEMB OF GOD.	2	287	489	2.8	4.9
081 CATHOLIC......	1	NA	195	1.1	1.9
101 C.M.E.........	2	365	448*	2.6	4.4
123 CH GOD (ANDER)	2	100	300	1.7	3.0
165 CH OF NAZARENE	1	12	13	0.1	0.1
167 CHS OF CHRIST.	2	80	102	0.6	1.0
185 CUMBER PRESB..	1	48	67	0.4	0.7
413 S.D.A.........	1	23	28*	0.2	0.3
419 SO BAPT CONV..	25	5 725	7 035*	40.6	69.9
449 UN METHODIST..	10	1 009	1 240*	7.2	12.3
JEFFERSON	**127**	**35 591**	**264 649***	**58.2**	**100.0**
005 AME ZION......	1	225	320	0.1	0.1
017 AMER BAPT ASSN	4	471	471	0.1	0.2
029 AMER LUTH CH..	2	445	633	0.1	0.2
053 ASSEMB OF GOD.	8	1 071	2 543	0.6	1.0
059 BAPT MISS ASSN	3	939	1 157*	0.3	0.4
081 CATHOLIC......	36	NA	217 348	47.8	82.1
093 CHR CH (DISC).	1	145	245	0.1	0.1
097 CHR CHS&CHS CR	1	75	92*	–	–
101 C.M.E.........	2	119	147*	–	0.1
127 CH GOD (CLEVE)	3	185	228*	0.1	0.1
151 L-D SAINTS....	3	NA	1 469	0.3	0.6
165 CH OF NAZARENE	1	116	342	0.1	0.1
167 CHS OF CHRIST.	6	490	656	0.1	0.2
185 CUMBER PRESB..	1	218	463	0.1	0.2
193 EPISCOPAL.....	4	1 736	1 955	0.4	0.7
208 EVAN LUTH ASSN	1	218	325	0.1	0.1
270 CONSRV JUDAISM	1	264	325*	0.1	0.1
271 REFORM JUDAISM	1	950	1 171*	0.3	0.4
283 LUTH--MO SYNOD	4	2 510	3 432	0.8	1.3
356 PRESB CH AMER.	1	62	72	–	–
357 PRESB CH US...	6	2 084	2 569*	0.6	1.0
381 REF PRES-EVAN.	1	30	45	–	–
413 S.D.A.........	1	304	375*	0.1	0.1
419 SO BAPT CONV..	23	16 951	20 892*	4.6	7.9
443 UN C OF CHRIST	1	182	224*	–	0.1
449 UN METHODIST..	11	5 801	7 150*	1.6	2.7
JEFFERSON DAVIS	**45**	**5 137**	**21 503***	**66.8**	**100.0**
053 ASSEMB OF GOD.	4	221	415	1.3	1.9
081 CATHOLIC......	11	NA	14 809	46.0	68.9
093 CHR CH (DISC).	1	20	27	0.1	0.1
097 CHR CHS&CHS CR	1	180	226*	0.7	1.1
101 C.M.E.........	2	90	113*	0.4	0.5
151 L-D SAINTS....	1	NA	42	0.1	0.2
157 CH OF BRETHREN	1	95	119*	0.4	0.6
167 CHS OF CHRIST.	2	87	179	0.6	0.8
193 EPISCOPAL.....	1	52	61	0.2	0.3
283 LUTH--MO SYNOD	1	73	87	0.3	0.4
357 PRESB CH US...	2	186	234*	0.7	1.1
413 S.D.A.........	2	223	280*	0.9	1.3
419 SO BAPT CONV..	5	2 243	2 817*	8.8	13.1
449 UN METHODIST..	11	1 667	2 094*	6.5	9.7
LAFAYETTE	**68**	**15 321**	**99 612***	**66.4**	**100.0**
053 ASSEMB OF GOD.	2	438	721	0.5	0.7
081 CATHOLIC......	29	NA	79 959	53.3	80.3
093 CHR CH (DISC).	1	140	206	0.1	0.2
097 CHR CHS&CHS CR	1	80	99*	0.1	0.1
101 C.M.E.........	3	240	296*	0.2	0.3
127 CH GOD (CLEVE)	2	55	68*	–	0.1
151 L-D SAINTS....	1	NA	396	0.3	0.4
165 CH OF NAZARENE	1	29	63	–	0.1
167 CHS OF CHRIST.	3	250	318	0.2	0.3
193 EPISCOPAL.....	2	1 222	1 395	0.9	1.4
271 REFORM JUDAISM	2	136	168*	0.1	0.2
281 LUTH CH AMER..	1	262	379	0.3	0.4
283 LUTH--MO SYNOD	1	172	229	0.2	0.2
353 CHR BRETHREN..	2	70	90	0.1	0.1
357 PRESB CH US...	2	769	947*	0.6	1.0
403 SALVATION ARMY	1	62	238	0.2	0.2
413 S.D.A.........	1	85	105*	0.1	0.1
419 SO BAPT CONV..	7	7 613	9 379*	6.3	9.4
435 UNITARIAN-UNIV	1	9	11*	–	–
449 UN METHODIST..	5	3 689	4 545*	3.0	4.6

County and Denomination	Number of churches	Communicant, confirmed, full members	Total adherents Number	Percent of total population	Percent of total adherents
LAFOURCHE	**45**	**4 509**	**61 960***	**75.1**	**100.0**
053 ASSEMB OF GOD.	4	278	449	0.5	0.7
081 CATHOLIC......	15	NA	55 991	67.9	90.4
127 CH GOD (CLEVE)	1	18	22*	–	–
151 L-D SAINTS....	1	NA	207	0.3	0.3
167 CHS OF CHRIST.	4	150	191	0.2	0.3
193 EPISCOPAL.....	1	154	218	0.3	0.4
357 PRESB CH US...	4	319	398*	0.5	0.6
419 SO BAPT CONV..	8	2 396	2 993*	3.6	4.8
449 UN METHODIST..	6	1 153	1 440*	1.7	2.3
453 UN PRES CH USA	1	41	51*	0.1	0.1
LA SALLE	**51**	**8 776**	**11 088***	**65.2**	**100.0**
053 ASSEMB OF GOD.	1	35	46	0.3	0.4
081 CATHOLIC......	2	NA	119	0.7	1.1
127 CH GOD (CLEVE)	2	63	78*	0.5	0.7
165 CH OF NAZARENE	2	49	65	0.4	0.6
167 CHS OF CHRIST.	2	50	64	0.4	0.6
221 FREE METHODIST	4	138	330	1.9	3.0
419 SO BAPT CONV..	31	7 745	9 530*	56.0	85.9
449 UN METHODIST..	7	696	856*	5.0	7.7
LINCOLN	**59**	**14 821**	**18 528***	**46.6**	**100.0**
017 AMER BAPT ASSN	1	72	72	0.2	0.4
053 ASSEMB OF GOD.	2	220	304	0.8	1.6
059 BAPT MISS ASSN	1	161	189*	0.5	1.0
081 CATHOLIC......	2	NA	695	1.7	3.8
101 C.M.E.........	4	846	993*	2.5	5.4
123 CH GOD (ANDER)	1	110	330	0.8	1.8
151 L-D SAINTS....	1	NA	86	0.2	0.5
165 CH OF NAZARENE	1	50	71	0.2	0.4
167 CHS OF CHRIST.	4	300	448	1.1	2.4
185 CUMBER PRESB..	1	6	12	–	0.1
193 EPISCOPAL.....	1	238	283	0.7	1.5
283 LUTH--MO SYNOD	1	51	65	0.2	0.4
356 PRESB CH AMER.	1	148	162	0.4	0.9
357 PRESB CH US...	3	575	675*	1.7	3.6
419 SO BAPT CONV..	21	9 144	10 737*	27.0	58.0
421 SO METHODIST..	1	25	31	0.1	0.2
435 UNITARIAN-UNIV	1	20	23*	0.1	0.1
449 UN METHODIST..	12	2 855	3 352*	8.4	18.1
LIVINGSTON	**74**	**20 634**	**41 281***	**70.4**	**100.0**
017 AMER BAPT ASSN	1	160	160	0.3	0.4
053 ASSEMB OF GOD.	1	93	124	0.2	0.3
059 BAPT MISS ASSN	4	451	572*	1.0	1.4
081 CATHOLIC......	4	NA	14 503	24.7	35.1
121 CH GOD (ABR)	1	99	126*	0.2	0.3
127 CH GOD (CLEVE)	2	34	43*	0.1	0.1
151 L-D SAINTS....	3	NA	624	1.1	1.5
167 CHS OF CHRIST.	1	70	89	0.2	0.2
193 EPISCOPAL.....	1	175	230	0.4	0.6
357 PRESB CH US...	3	261	331*	0.6	0.8
413 S.D.A.........	1	97	123*	0.2	0.3
419 SO BAPT CONV..	39	17 043	21 630*	36.9	52.4
421 SO METHODIST..	1	41	48	0.1	0.1
449 UN METHODIST..	12	2 110	2 678*	4.6	6.5
MADISON	**20**	**4 577**	**6 244***	**42.4**	**100.0**
005 AME ZION......	2	351	546	3.7	8.7
017 AMER BAPT ASSN	1	139	139	0.9	2.2
053 ASSEMB OF GOD.	1	40	62	0.4	1.0
081 CATHOLIC......	1	NA	175	1.2	2.8
127 CH GOD (CLEVE)	1	3	4*	–	0.1
167 CHS OF CHRIST.	1	35	45	0.3	0.7
193 EPISCOPAL.....	1	142	188	1.3	3.0
357 PRESB CH US...	1	106	139*	0.9	2.2
413 S.D.A.........	1	22	29*	0.2	0.5
419 SO BAPT CONV..	9	3 248	4 271*	29.0	68.4
449 UN METHODIST..	1	491	646*	4.4	10.3
MOREHOUSE	**77**	**14 012**	**19 261***	**55.3**	**100.0**
005 AME ZION......	2	162	347	1.0	1.8
017 AMER BAPT ASSN	1	525	525	1.5	2.7
053 ASSEMB OF GOD.	5	578	821	2.4	4.3
059 BAPT MISS ASSN	2	289	362*	1.0	1.9
081 CATHOLIC......	3	NA	925	2.7	4.8
101 C.M.E.........	8	1 330	1 668*	4.8	8.7
123 CH GOD (ANDER)	6	230	690	2.0	3.6
127 CH GOD (CLEVE)	2	183	229*	0.7	1.2
151 L-D SAINTS....	1	NA	107	0.3	0.6
167 CHS OF CHRIST.	3	450	573	1.6	3.0
193 EPISCOPAL.....	3	369	603	1.7	3.1
357 PRESB CH US...	2	193	242*	0.7	1.3
413 S.D.A.........	1	105	132*	0.4	0.7
419 SO BAPT CONV..	27	8 028	10 068*	28.9	52.3
449 UN METHODIST..	11	1 570	1 969*	5.7	10.2
NATCHITOCHES	**89**	**11 852**	**20 216***	**50.7**	**100.0**
001 ADVENT CHR CH.	1	30	37*	0.1	0.2
017 AMER BAPT ASSN	2	53	53	0.1	0.3
053 ASSEMB OF GOD.	3	335	400	1.0	2.0
059 BAPT MISS ASSN	1	131	161*	0.4	0.8
081 CATHOLIC......	16	NA	5 403	13.6	26.7
123 CH GOD (ANDER)	1	10	30	0.1	0.1
151 L-D SAINTS....	1	NA	102	0.3	0.5
165 CH OF NAZARENE	1	39	59	0.1	0.3
167 CHS OF CHRIST.	3	150	191	0.5	0.9

NA—Not applicable • *Total adherents estimated from known number of communicant, confirmed, full members. • —Represents a percent less than 0.1. • Percentages may not total due to rounding.

Table 4. Churches and Church Membership by County and Denomination: 1980

County and Denomination	Number of churches	Communicant, confirmed, full members	Total adherents		
			Number	Percent of total population	Percent of total adherents
193 EPISCOPAL.....	1	169	268	0.7	1.3
221 FREE METHODIST	1	24	60	0.2	0.3
283 LUTH--MO SYNOD	1	50	69	0.2	0.3
357 PRESB CH US...	1	137	169*	0.4	0.8
413 S.D.A.........	3	61	75*	0.2	0.4
419 SO BAPT CONV..	36	8 959	11 038*	27.7	54.6
421 SO METHODIST..	1	54	68	0.2	0.3
449 UN METHODIST..	16	1 650	2 033*	5.1	10.1
ORLEANS	235	64 673	260 352*	46.7	100.0
005 AME ZION......	3	1 985	2 280	0.4	0.9
029 AMER LUTH CH..	2	731	825	0.1	0.3
053 ASSEMB OF GOD.	7	2 854	5 174	0.9	2.0
081 CATHOLIC......	62	NA	177 978	31.9	68.4
093 CHR CH (DISC).	3	356	582	0.1	0.2
097 CHR CHS&CHS CR	1	50	61*	-	-
121 CH GOD (ABR)..	1	20	24*	-	-
123 CH GOD (ANDER)	2	122	366	0.1	0.1
127 CH GOD (CLEVE)	3	558	679*	0.1	0.3
151 L-D SAINTS....	1	NA	241	-	0.1
165 CH OF NAZARENE	3	132	194	-	0.1
167 CHS OF CHRIST.	6	500	720	0.1	0.3
193 EPISCOPAL.....	15	6 886	8 964	1.6	3.4
208 EVAN LUTH ASSN	1	227	300	0.1	0.1
226 FRIENDS-USA...	1	29	35*	-	-
271 REFORM JUDAISM	2	3 230	3 930*	0.7	1.5
281 LUTH CH AMER..	2	434	599	0.1	0.2
283 LUTH--MO SYNOD	19	7 014	9 210	1.7	3.5
290 METRO COMM CHS	1	43	100	-	-
357 PRESB CH US...	15	4 814	5 857*	1.1	2.2
403 SALVATION ARMY	2	149	193	-	0.1
413 S.D.A.........	2	273	332*	0.1	0.1
419 SO BAPT CONV..	31	19 645	23 903*	4.3	9.2
421 SO METHODIST..	1	39	43	-	-
435 UNITARIAN-UNIV	2	345	420*	0.1	0.2
443 UN C OF CHRIST	9	2 273	2 766*	0.5	1.1
449 UN METHODIST..	36	11 660	14 187*	2.5	5.4
453 UN PRES CH USA	1	249	303*	0.1	0.1
469 WELS..........	1	55	86	-	-
OUACHITA	153	56 563	77 657*	55.8	100.0
017 AMER BAPT ASSN	6	1 302	1 302	0.9	1.7
053 ASSEMB OF GOD.	17	1 910	2 998	2.2	3.9
059 BAPT MISS ASSN	3	588	732*	0.5	0.9
081 CATHOLIC......	8	NA	5 495	3.9	7.1
093 CHR CH (DISC).	1	309	356	0.3	0.5
101 C.M.E.........	4	1 227	1 527*	1.1	2.0
123 CH GOD (ANDER)	5	413	1 239	0.9	1.6
127 CH GOD (CLEVE)	7	461	574*	0.4	0.7
151 L-D SAINTS....	1	NA	435	0.3	0.6
165 CH OF NAZARENE	2	271	407	0.3	0.5
167 CHS OF CHRIST.	14	2 400	3 055	2.2	3.9
185 CUMBER PRESB..	1	69	98	0.1	0.1
193 EPISCOPAL.....	4	1 465	1 887	1.4	2.4
217 FIRE BAPTIZED.	1	2	2*	-	-
271 REFORM JUDAISM	1	332	413*	0.3	0.5
281 LUTH CH AMER..	1	102	151	0.1	0.2
283 LUTH--MO SYNOD	1	198	273	0.2	0.4
353 CHR BRETHREN..	1	30	30	-	-
356 PRESB CH AMER.	1	66	98	0.1	0.1
357 PRESB CH US...	6	1 482	1 845*	1.3	2.4
403 SALVATION ARMY	1	128	198	0.1	0.3
413 S.D.A.........	1	120	149*	0.1	0.2
419 SO BAPT CONV..	44	34 795	43 316*	31.1	55.8
421 SO METHODIST..	2	102	133	0.1	0.2
443 UN C OF CHRIST	1	88	110*	0.1	0.1
449 UN METHODIST..	19	8 703	10 834*	7.8	14.0
PLAQUEMINES	30	4 945	16 751*	64.3	100.0
017 AMER BAPT ASSN	1	160	160	0.6	1.0
053 ASSEMB OF GOD.	3	289	393	1.5	2.3
081 CATHOLIC......	4	NA	10 476	40.2	62.5
101 C.M.E.........	3	752	949*	3.6	5.7
165 CH OF NAZARENE	1	66	152	0.6	0.9
167 CHS OF CHRIST.	4	145	209	0.8	1.2
353 CHR BRETHREN..	2	180	180	0.7	1.1
357 PRESB CH US...	1	36	45*	0.2	0.3
419 SO BAPT CONV..	8	3 074	3 880*	14.9	23.2
449 UN METHODIST..	3	243	307*	1.2	1.8
POINTE COUPEE	19	1 231	14 847*	61.7	100.0
081 CATHOLIC......	5	NA	13 260	55.1	89.3
193 EPISCOPAL.....	3	260	377	1.6	2.5
419 SO BAPT CONV..	6	790	984*	4.1	6.6
449 UN METHODIST..	5	181	226*	0.9	1.5
RAPIDES	191	44 146	74 676*	55.2	100.0
017 AMER BAPT ASSN	4	920	920	0.7	1.2
053 ASSEMB OF GOD.	7	392	736	0.5	1.0
059 BAPT MISS ASSN	1	29	36*	-	-
081 CATHOLIC......	21	NA	17 800	13.2	23.8
093 CHR CH (DISC).	1	75	115	0.1	0.2
097 CHR CHS&CHS CR	2	91	113*	0.1	0.2
123 CH GOD (ANDER)	7	240	720	0.5	1.0
127 CH GOD (CLEVE)	1	81	100*	0.1	0.1
151 L-D SAINTS....	1	NA	509	0.4	0.7
165 CH OF NAZARENE	4	231	355	0.3	0.5
167 CHS OF CHRIST.	6	590	750	0.6	1.0
193 EPISCOPAL.....	6	1 255	1 790	1.3	2.4
221 FREE METHODIST	3	138	645	0.5	0.9

County and Denomination	Number of churches	Communicant, confirmed, full members	Total adherents		
			Number	Percent of total population	Percent of total adherents
270 CONSRV JUDAISM	1	29	36*	-	-
271 REFORM JUDAISM	1	348	430*	0.3	0.6
283 LUTH--MO SYNOD	2	299	437	0.3	0.6
356 PRESB CH AMER.	1	225	273	0.2	0.4
357 PRESB CH US...	2	454	561*	0.4	0.8
403 SALVATION ARMY	1	143	606	0.4	0.8
413 S.D.A.........	2	365	451*	0.3	0.6
419 SO BAPT CONV..	87	32 684	40 409*	29.9	54.1
435 UNITARIAN-UNIV	1	14	17*	-	-
449 UN METHODIST..	28	5 493	6 791*	5.0	9.1
469 WELS..........	1	50	76	0.1	0.1
RED RIVER	29	3 978	5 282*	50.6	100.0
053 ASSEMB OF GOD.	3	80	99	0.9	1.9
059 BAPT MISS ASSN	1	140	174*	1.7	3.3
081 CATHOLIC......	1	NA	101	1.0	1.9
123 CH GOD (ANDER)	1	15	45	0.4	0.9
151 L-D SAINTS....	1	NA	137	1.3	2.6
167 CHS OF CHRIST.	2	90	115	1.1	2.2
185 CUMBER PRESB..	1	69	129	1.2	2.4
413 S.D.A.........	1	57	71*	0.7	1.3
419 SO BAPT CONV..	12	2 971	3 697*	35.4	70.0
421 SO METHODIST..	1	62	99	0.9	1.9
449 UN METHODIST..	5	494	615*	5.9	11.6
RICHLAND	63	10 557	13 404*	60.4	100.0
053 ASSEMB OF GOD.	6	229	290	1.3	2.2
081 CATHOLIC......	2	NA	227	1.0	1.7
101 C.M.E.........	1	45	56*	0.3	0.4
123 CH GOD (ANDER)	1	18	54	0.2	0.4
127 CH GOD (CLEVE)	5	174	217*	1.0	1.6
167 CHS OF CHRIST.	5	250	318	1.4	2.4
193 EPISCOPAL.....	1	98	99	0.4	0.7
356 PRESB CH AMER.	1	159	182	0.8	1.4
357 PRESB CH US...	3	51	64*	0.3	0.5
419 SO BAPT CONV..	31	8 409	10 494*	47.3	78.3
449 UN METHODIST..	7	1 124	1 403*	6.3	10.5
SABINE	79	9 674	15 490*	61.3	100.0
017 AMER BAPT ASSN	1	30	30	0.1	0.2
053 ASSEMB OF GOD.	2	184	256	1.0	1.7
081 CATHOLIC......	6	NA	3 117	12.3	20.1
151 L-D SAINTS....	1	NA	330	1.3	2.1
165 CH OF NAZARENE	4	196	373	1.5	2.4
167 CHS OF CHRIST.	2	80	102	0.4	0.7
185 CUMBER PRESB..	1	26	0	-	-
419 SO BAPT CONV..	51	8 416	10 368*	41.0	66.9
449 UN METHODIST..	11	742	914*	3.6	5.9
ST BERNARD	28	4 774	62 772*	97.9	100.0
053 ASSEMB OF GOD.	2	471	644	1.0	1.0
059 BAPT MISS ASSN	2	263	323*	0.5	0.5
081 CATHOLIC......	8	NA	56 590	88.3	90.2
151 L-D SAINTS....	1	NA	193	0.3	0.3
167 CHS OF CHRIST.	2	101	158	0.2	0.3
193 EPISCOPAL.....	1	104	139	0.2	0.2
208 EVAN LUTH ASSN	1	515	647	1.0	1.0
357 PRESB CH US...	2	190	233*	0.4	0.4
413 S.D.A.........	3	1 406	1 727*	2.7	2.8
419 SO BAPT CONV..	4	1 211	1 488*	2.3	2.4
449 UN METHODIST..	2	513	630*	1.0	1.0
ST CHARLES	28	4 593	26 263*	70.5	100.0
053 ASSEMB OF GOD.	3	332	889	2.4	3.4
081 CATHOLIC......	7	NA	19 889	53.4	75.7
151 L-D SAINTS....	1	NA	102	0.3	0.4
167 CHS OF CHRIST.	1	60	76	0.2	0.3
193 EPISCOPAL.....	1	58	87	0.2	0.3
285 MENNONITE CH..	1	95	120*	0.3	0.5
357 PRESB CH US...	2	119	150*	0.4	0.6
413 S.D.A.........	1	69	87*	0.2	0.3
419 SO BAPT CONV..	7	3 398	4 281*	11.5	16.3
449 UN METHODIST..	3	382	481*	1.3	1.8
453 UN PRES CH USA	1	80	101*	0.3	0.4
ST HELENA	24	3 600	4 880*	49.7	100.0
081 CATHOLIC......	2	NA	330	3.4	6.8
419 SO BAPT CONV..	12	2 756	3 483*	35.4	71.4
449 UN METHODIST..	10	844	1 067*	10.9	21.9
ST JAMES	13	384	14 812*	68.9	100.0
081 CATHOLIC......	6	NA	14 329	66.7	96.7
413 S.D.A.........	1	20	25*	0.1	0.2
419 SO BAPT CONV..	1	182	229*	1.1	1.5
449 UN METHODIST..	5	182	229*	1.1	1.5
ST JOHN THE BAPTIST	12	1 260	18 460*	57.8	100.0
053 ASSEMB OF GOD.	1	70	74	0.2	0.4
081 CATHOLIC......	6	NA	16 760	52.5	90.8
151 L-D SAINTS....	1	NA	75	0.2	0.4
167 CHS OF CHRIST.	1	95	121	0.4	0.7
193 EPISCOPAL.....	1	65	119	0.4	0.6
419 SO BAPT CONV..	1	759	966*	3.0	5.2
449 UN METHODIST..	1	271	345*	1.1	1.9
ST LANDRY	74	6 847	65 074*	77.4	100.0

NA—Not applicable   *Total adherents estimated from known number of communicant, confirmed, full members.   —Represents a percent less than 0.1.   Percentages may not total due to rounding.

Table 4. Churches and Church Membership by County and Denomination: 1980

County and Denomination	Number of churches	Communicant, confirmed, full members	Total adherents Number	Percent of total population	Percent of total adherents
017 AMER BAPT ASSN	2	293	293	0.3	0.5
053 ASSEMB OF GOD.	2	125	158	0.2	0.2
081 CATHOLIC......	35	NA	56 484	67.1	86.8
123 CH GOD (ANDER)	1	40	120	0.1	0.2
127 CH GOD (CLEVE)	1	?	?	?	?
167 CHS OF CHRIST.	2	58	74	0.1	0.1
193 EPISCOPAL.....	2	187	224	0.3	0.3
313 N AM BAPT CONF	1	68	85*	0.1	0.1
356 PRESB CH AMER.	2	99	126	0.1	0.2
419 SO BAPT CONV..	14	4 607	5 789*	6.9	8.9
449 UN METHODIST..	12	1 370	1 721*	2.0	2.6
ST MARTIN	15	457	25 148*	62.5	100.0
081 CATHOLIC......	12	NA	24 567	61.1	97.7
419 SO BAPT CONV..	2	355	451*	1.1	1.8
449 UN METHODIST..	1	102	130*	0.3	0.5
ST MARY	52	7 731	39 269*	61.0	100.0
053 ASSEMB OF GOD.	2	208	242	0.4	0.6
081 CATHOLIC......	14	NA	29 398	45.7	74.9
089 CHR & MISS AL.	1	38	73	0.1	0.2
123 CH GOD (ANDER)	1	8	24	-	0.1
151 L-D SAINTS....	1	NA	89	0.1	0.2
167 CHS OF CHRIST.	5	400	509	0.8	1.3
193 EPISCOPAL.....	2	313	404	0.6	1.0
271 REFORM JUDAISM	1	40	50*	0.1	0.1
283 LUTH--MO SYNOD	1	57	86	0.1	0.2
357 PRESB CH US...	3	225	283*	0.4	0.7
419 SO BAPT CONV..	9	4 145	5 219*	8.1	13.3
449 UN METHODIST..	12	2 297	2 892*	4.5	7.4
ST TAMMANY	85	19 462	56 552*	51.2	100.0
005 AME ZION......	1	145	216	0.2	0.4
029 AMER LUTH CH..	1	84	132	0.1	0.2
053 ASSEMB OF GOD.	2	270	490	0.4	0.9
059 BAPT MISS ASSN	1	50	63*	0.1	0.1
081 CATHOLIC......	11	NA	30 665	27.7	54.2
093 CHR CH (DISC).	2	165	206	0.2	0.4
123 CH GOD (ANDER)	2	138	414	0.4	0.7
127 CH GOD (CLEVE)	7	796	998*	0.9	1.8
151 L-D SAINTS....	2	NA	681	0.6	1.2
165 CH OF NAZARENE	1	110	375	0.3	0.7
167 CHS OF CHRIST.	3	179	228	0.2	0.4
193 EPISCOPAL.....	2	743	928	0.8	1.6
283 LUTH--MO SYNOD	2	817	1 118	1.0	2.0
353 CHR BRETHREN..	1	30	30	-	0.1
356 PRESB CH AMER.	1	53	91	0.1	0.2
357 PRESB CH US...	4	1 010	1 266*	1.1	2.2
413 S.D.A.........	3	173	217*	0.2	0.4
419 SO BAPT CONV..	24	10 170	12 749*	11.5	22.5
449 UN METHODIST..	14	4 443	5 570*	5.0	9.8
469 WELS.........	1	86	115	0.1	0.2
TANGIPAHOA	112	25 275	36 649*	45.4	100.0
005 AME ZION......	11	5 595	6 660	8.3	18.2
017 AMER BAPT ASSN	8	985	985	1.2	2.7
053 ASSEMB OF GOD.	3	234	330	0.4	0.9
059 BAPT MISS ASSN	3	292	365*	0.5	1.0
081 CATHOLIC......	8	NA	5 156	6.4	14.1
093 CHR CH (DISC).	1	144	188	0.2	0.5
121 CH GOD (ABR)..	1	81	101*	0.1	0.3
123 CH GOD (ANDER)	2	96	288	0.4	0.8
127 CH GOD (CLEVE)	3	182	227*	0.3	0.6
151 L-D SAINTS....	1	NA	342	0.4	0.9
165 CH OF NAZARENE	1	8	0	-	-
167 CHS OF CHRIST.	11	500	636	0.8	1.7
193 EPISCOPAL.....	3	345	437	0.5	1.2
283 LUTH--MO SYNOD	1	200	200	0.2	0.5
357 PRESB CH US...	3	570	712*	0.9	1.9
413 S.D.A.........	2	287	358*	0.4	1.0
419 SO BAPT CONV..	35	13 168	16 440*	20.4	44.9
421 SO METHODIST..	2	165	199	0.2	0.5
449 UN METHODIST..	12	2 373	2 963*	3.7	8.1
453 UN PRES CH USA	1	50	62*	0.1	0.2
TENSAS	22	2 423	3 164*	37.1	100.0
081 CATHOLIC......	3	NA	109	1.3	3.4
123 CH GOD (ANDER)	1	8	24	0.3	0.8
167 CHS OF CHRIST.	2	80	102	1.2	3.2
193 EPISCOPAL.....	2	91	103	1.2	3.3
357 PRESB CH US...	3	92	116*	1.4	3.7
419 SO BAPT CONV..	8	1 921	2 419*	28.4	76.5
449 UN METHODIST..	3	231	291*	3.4	9.2
TERREBONNE	46	8 689	65 019*	68.9	100.0
053 ASSEMB OF GOD.	3	226	398	0.4	0.6
081 CATHOLIC......	16	NA	53 351	56.5	82.1
127 CH GOD (CLEVE)	7	247	314*	0.3	0.5
165 CH OF NAZARENE	1	21	54	0.1	0.1
167 CHS OF CHRIST.	1	175	205	0.2	0.3
193 EPISCOPAL.....	2	466	1 068	1.1	1.6
283 LUTH--MO SYNOD	1	215	306	0.3	0.5
357 PRESB CH US...	1	158	201*	0.3	0.3
413 S.D.A.........	1	121	154*	0.2	0.2
419 SO BAPT CONV..	6	5 277	6 703*	7.1	10.3
449 UN METHODIST..	7	1 783	2 265*	2.4	3.5
UNION	70	'10 541	13 258*	62.6	100.0
017 AMER BAPT ASSN	1	160	160	0.8	1.2
053 ASSEMB OF GOD.	5	295	514	2.4	3.9
059 BAPT MISS ASSN	5	707	866*	4.1	6.5
081 CATHOLIC......	1	NA	60	0.3	0.5
151 L-D SAINTS....	1	NA	138	0.7	1.0
167 CHS OF CHRIST.	11	600	764	3.6	5.8
419 SO BAPT CONV..	37	7 922	9 706*	45.9	73.2
449 UN METHODIST..	9	857	1 050*	5.0	7.9
VERMILION	29	2 545	29 896*	61.7	100.0
081 CATHOLIC......	12	NA	26 729	55.2	89.4
097 CHR CHS&CHS CR	1	60	75*	0.2	0.3
127 CH GOD (CLEVE)	1	22	27*	0.1	0.1
357 PRESB CH US...	1	66	82*	0.2	0.3
419 SO BAPT CONV..	5	1 328	1 653*	3.4	5.5
443 UN C OF CHRIST	3	120	149*	0.3	0.5
449 UN METHODIST..	6	949	1 181*	2.4	4.0
VERNON	78	14 286	20 006*	37.4	100.0
053 ASSEMB OF GOD.	4	315	478	0.9	2.4
081 CATHOLIC......	1	NA	1 520	2.8	7.6
093 CHR CH (DISC).	1	118	138	0.3	0.7
101 C.M.E.........	1	10	12*	-	0.1
123 CH GOD (ANDER)	3	151	453	0.8	2.3
127 CH GOD (CLEVE)	1	27	34*	0.1	0.2
151 L-D SAINTS....	2	NA	344	0.6	1.7
167 CHS OF CHRIST.	5	290	369	0.7	1.8
193 EPISCOPAL.....	1	53	82	0.2	0.4
283 LUTH--MO SYNOD	1	123	180	0.3	0.9
419 SO BAPT CONV..	52	12 538	15 575*	29.1	77.9
449 UN METHODIST..	6	661	821*	1.5	4.1
WASHINGTON	66	17 598	22 523*	50.9	100.0
017 AMER BAPT ASSN	7	2 324	2 324	5.3	10.3
053 ASSEMB OF GOD.	1	55	160	0.4	0.7
059 BAPT MISS ASSN	3	353	436*	1.0	1.9
081 CATHOLIC......	1	NA	1 100	2.5	4.9
127 CH GOD (CLEVE)	2	107	132*	0.3	0.6
151 L-D SAINTS....	1	NA	120	0.3	0.5
167 CHS OF CHRIST.	3	60	76	0.2	0.3
193 EPISCOPAL.....	1	147	187	0.4	0.8
283 LUTH--MO SYNOD	1	130	160	0.4	0.7
357 PRESB CH US...	1	153	189*	0.4	0.8
413 S.D.A.........	2	94	116*	0.3	0.5
419 SO BAPT CONV..	32	12 096	14 953*	33.8	66.4
449 UN METHODIST..	11	2 079	2 570*	5.8	11.4
WEBSTER	105	23 049	28 599*	65.5	100.0
017 AMER BAPT ASSN	11	2 365	2 365	5.4	8.3
053 ASSEMB OF GOD.	8	812	1 074	2.5	3.8
059 BAPT MISS ASSN	6	1 586	1 927*	4.4	6.7
081 CATHOLIC......	2	NA	833	1.9	2.9
093 CHR CH (DISC).	2	67	109	0.2	0.4
097 CHR CHS&CHS CR	1	45	55*	0.1	0.2
101 C.M.E.........	15	2 734	3 323*	7.6	11.6
123 CH GOD (ANDER)	1	14	42	0.1	0.1
127 CH GOD (CLEVE)	1	50	61*	0.1	0.2
151 L-D SAINTS....	1	NA	71	0.2	0.2
165 CH OF NAZARENE	2	43	45	0.1	0.2
167 CHS OF CHRIST.	9	676	869	2.0	3.0
193 EPISCOPAL.....	1	172	223	0.5	0.8
357 PRESB CH US...	2	323	393*	0.9	1.4
413 S.D.A.........	1	40	49*	0.1	0.2
419 SO BAPT CONV..	24	10 933	13 286*	30.5	46.5
421 SO METHODIST..	2	45	53	0.1	0.2
449 UN METHODIST..	16	3 144	3 821*	8.8	13.4
WEST BATON ROUGE	9	1 222	6 797*	35.6	100.0
081 CATHOLIC......	2	NA	5 260	27.6	77.4
167 CHS OF CHRIST.	1	20	25	0.1	0.4
357 PRESB CH US...	1	66	83*	0.4	1.2
419 SO BAPT CONV..	4	968	1 218*	6.4	17.9
449 UN METHODIST..	1	168	211*	1.1	3.1
WEST CARROLL	39	7 017	9 480*	73.4	100.0
053 ASSEMB OF GOD.	2	99	188	1.5	2.0
081 CATHOLIC......	1	NA	133	1.0	1.4
123 CH GOD (ANDER)	5	280	840	6.5	8.9
127 CH GOD (CLEVE)	4	278	343*	2.7	3.6
167 CHS OF CHRIST.	2	80	102	0.8	1.1
221 FREE METHODIST	1	42	168	1.3	1.8
419 SO BAPT CONV..	17	5 552	6 859*	53.1	72.4
449 UN METHODIST..	7	686	847*	6.6	8.9
WEST FELICIANA	10	1 120	4 729*	38.8	100.0
017 AMER BAPT ASSN	1	160	160	1.3	3.4
081 CATHOLIC......	2	NA	3 354	27.5	70.9
193 EPISCOPAL.....	1	135	261	2.1	5.5
419 SO BAPT CONV..	2	580	671*	5.5	14.2
449 UN METHODIST..	4	245	283*	2.3	6.0
WINN	64	9 038	11 477*	66.5	100.0
017 AMER BAPT ASSN	1	94	94	0.5	0.8
053 ASSEMB OF GOD.	5	229	243	1.4	2.1
081 CATHOLIC......	2	NA	108	0.6	0.9
101 C.M.E.........	3	200	247*	1.4	2.2
127 CH GOD (CLEVE)	1	47	58*	0.3	0.5

NA—Not applicable   *Total adherents estimated from known number of communicant, confirmed, full members.   —Represents a percent less than 0.1.   Percentages may not total due to rounding.

Table 4. Churches and Church Membership by County and Denomination: 1980

County and Denomination	Number of churches	Communicant, confirmed, full members	Total adherents Number	Percent of total population	Percent of total adherents
151 L-D SAINTS....	1	NA	254	1.5	2.2
165 CH OF NAZARENE	1	30	29	0.2	0.3
167 CHS OF CHRIST.	3	150	191	1.1	1.7
193 EPISCOPAL.....	1	64	76	0.4	0.7
357 PRESB CH US...	1	74	92*	0.5	0.8
419 SO BAPT CONV..	40	7 591	9 393*	54.4	81.8
449 UN METHODIST..	5	559	692*	4.0	6.0

MAINE

County and Denomination	Number of churches	Communicant, confirmed, full members	Total adherents Number	Percent of total population	Percent of total adherents
THE STATE.....	1 290	137 978	461 335*	41.0	100.0
ANDROSCOGGIN	69	7 617	49 068*	49.2	100.0
001 ADVENT CHR CH.	2	147	179*	0.2	0.4
019 AMER BAPT USA.	9	1 828	2 220*	2.2	4.5
053 ASSEMB OF GOD.	1	123	200	0.2	0.4
081 CATHOLIC......	17	NA	38 829	39.0	79.1
165 CH OF NAZARENE	5	282	707	0.7	1.4
167 CHS OF CHRIST.	1	15	19	–	–
175 CONGR CHR CHS.	1	75	91*	0.1	0.2
179 CONSRV BAPT...	3	549	667*	0.7	1.4
193 EPISCOPAL.....	3	557	822	0.8	1.7
208 EVAN LUTH ASSN	1	185	251	0.3	0.5
226 FRIENDS-USA...	1	135	164*	0.2	0.3
270 CONSRV JUDAISM	1	138	168*	0.2	0.3
335 ORTH PRESB CH.	1	23	28*	–	0.1
403 SALVATION ARMY	1	135	564	0.6	1.1
413 S.D.A.........	1	99	120*	0.1	0.2
419 SO BAPT CONV..	1	128	155*	0.2	0.3
435 UNITARIAN-UNIV	2	191	232*	0.2	0.5
443 UN C OF CHRIST	6	931	1 131*	1.1	2.3
449 UN METHODIST..	9	1 757	2 134*	2.1	4.3
453 UN PRES CH USA	3	319	387*	0.4	0.8
AROOSTOOK	120	11 243	54 584*	59.8	100.0
001 ADVENT CHR CH.	7	469	578*	0.6	1.1
019 AMER BAPT USA.	20	4 603	5 672*	6.2	10.4
053 ASSEMB OF GOD.	2	203	283	0.3	0.5
057 BAPT GEN CONF.	2	188	232*	0.3	0.4
081 CATHOLIC......	36	NA	39 630	43.4	72.6
089 CHR & MISS AL.	1	43	103	0.1	0.2
127 CH GOD (CLEVE)	3	221	272*	0.3	0.5
151 L-D SAINTS....	2	NA	685	0.8	1.3
165 CH OF NAZARENE	2	67	92	0.1	0.2
167 CHS OF CHRIST.	3	91	116	0.1	0.2
175 CONGR CHR CHS.	1	16	20*	–	–
179 CONSRV BAPT...	1	183	225*	0.2	0.4
193 EPISCOPAL.....	7	871	1 370	1.5	2.5
201 EVAN COV CH AM	1	121	149*	0.2	0.3
335 ORTH PRESB CH.	2	29	36*	–	0.1
403 SALVATION ARMY	1	57	91	0.1	0.2
413 S.D.A.........	2	84	104*	0.1	0.2
419 SO BAPT CONV..	1	171	211*	0.2	0.4
435 UNITARIAN-UNIV	3	225	277*	0.3	0.5
443 UN C OF CHRIST	9	696	858*	0.9	1.6
449 UN METHODIST..	14	2 905	3 580*	3.9	6.6
CUMBERLAND	198	30 130	93 005*	43.1	100.0
001 ADVENT CHR CH.	3	249	298*	0.1	0.3
005 AME ZION......	1	209	254	0.1	0.3
019 AMER BAPT USA.	15	3 546	4 243*	2.0	4.6
029 AMER LUTH CH..	4	709	1 018	0.5	1.1
053 ASSEMB OF GOD.	6	434	806	0.4	0.9
081 CATHOLIC......	37	NA	52 677	24.4	56.6
089 CHR & MISS AL.	4	290	639	0.3	0.7
097 CHR CHS&CHS CR	2	55	66*	–	0.1
127 CH GOD (CLEVE)	7	199	238*	0.1	0.3
151 L-D SAINTS....	4	NA	788	0.4	0.8
165 CH OF NAZARENE	9	897	1 599	0.7	1.7
167 CHS OF CHRIST.	4	90	114	0.1	0.1
175 CONGR CHR CHS.	2	733	877*	0.4	0.9
179 CONSRV BAPT...	6	1 098	1 314*	0.6	1.4
181 CONSRV CONGR..	2	202	242*	0.1	0.3
193 EPISCOPAL.....	10	3 321	5 940*	2.8	6.4
203 EVAN FREE CH..	1	105	126*	0.1	0.1
221 FREE METHODIST	1	25	45	–	–
226 FRIENDS-USA...	3	122	146*	0.1	0.2
239 SWEDENBORGIAN.	1	60	72*	–	0.1
270 CONSRV JUDAISM	1	324	388*	0.2	0.4
283 LUTH--MO SYNOD	1	203	264	0.1	0.3
290 METRO COMM CHS	0	15	30	–	–
335 ORTH PRESB CH.	1	176	211*	0.1	0.2
353 CHR BRETHREN..	2	40	40	–	–
403 SALVATION ARMY	1	203	437	0.2	0.5
413 S.D.A.........	4	794	950*	0.4	1.0
419 SO BAPT CONV..	2	345	413*	0.2	0.4
435 UNITARIAN-UNIV	6	941	1 126*	0.5	1.2
443 UN C OF CHRIST	34	9 517	11 388*	5.3	12.2
449 UN METHODIST..	24	5 228	6 256*	2.9	6.7
FRANKLIN	39	3 459	9 826*	36.3	100.0
019 AMER BAPT USA.	5	598	726*	2.7	7.4
053 ASSEMB OF GOD.	1	94	220	0.8	2.2
081 CATHOLIC......	8	NA	5 118	18.9	52.1
151 L-D SAINTS....	1	NA	238	0.9	2.4
165 CH OF NAZARENE	2	144	219	0.8	2.2
167 CHS OF CHRIST.	1	10	13	–	0.1
179 CONSRV BAPT...	1	183	222*	0.8	2.3
193 EPISCOPAL.....	2	628	882	3.3	9.0
413 S.D.A.........	1	53	64*	0.2	0.7
443 UN C OF CHRIST	7	750	911*	3.4	9.3
449 UN METHODIST..	8	915	1 111*	4.1	11.3
453 UN PRES CH USA	2	84	102*	0.4	1.0
HANCOCK	98	6 417	11 134*	26.6	100.0
001 ADVENT CHR CH.	2	136	163*	0.4	1.5
019 AMER BAPT USA.	20	1 606	1 919*	4.6	17.2
053 ASSEMB OF GOD.	1	56	86	0.2	0.8
081 CATHOLIC......	14	NA	2 535	6.1	22.8
127 CH GOD (CLEVE)	4	80	96*	0.2	0.9
151 L-D SAINTS....	1	NA	179	0.4	1.6
165 CH OF NAZARENE	2	55	158	0.4	1.4
167 CHS OF CHRIST.	1	19	24	0.1	0.2
175 CONGR CHR CHS.	1	328	392*	0.9	3.5
179 CONSRV BAPT...	1	183	219*	0.5	2.0
193 EPISCOPAL.....	8	964	1 791	4.3	16.1
226 FRIENDS-USA...	2	37	44*	0.1	0.4
413 S.D.A.........	1	33	39*	0.1	0.4
435 UNITARIAN-UNIV	2	130	155*	0.4	1.4
443 UN C OF CHRIST	19	1 801	2 152*	5.2	19.3
449 UN METHODIST..	19	989	1 182*	2.8	10.6
KENNEBEC	112	14 170	49 850*	45.4	100.0
001 ADVENT CHR CH.	2	292	354*	0.3	0.7
019 AMER BAPT USA.	23	3 665	4 443*	4.0	8.9
029 AMER LUTH CH..	1	257	369	0.3	0.7
053 ASSEMB OF GOD.	2	349	460	0.4	0.9
081 CATHOLIC......	23	NA	29 897	27.2	60.0
089 CHR & MISS AL.	1	20	40	–	0.1
127 CH GOD (CLEVE)	2	132	160*	0.1	0.3
151 L-D SAINTS....	1	NA	638	0.6	1.3
165 CH OF NAZARENE	3	338	1 245	1.1	2.5
167 CHS OF CHRIST.	2	43	55	0.1	0.1
179 CONSRV BAPT...	3	549	665*	0.6	1.3
193 EPISCOPAL.....	6	1 714	2 977	2.7	6.0
221 FREE METHODIST	1	33	156	0.1	0.3
226 FRIENDS-USA...	3	186	225*	0.2	0.5
263 INT FOURSQ GOS	1	119	144*	0.1	0.3
283 LUTH--MO SYNOD	1	75	105	0.1	0.2
285 MENNONITE CH..	1	9	11*	–	–
353 CHR BRETHREN..	2	35	80	0.1	0.2
403 SALVATION ARMY	2	104	250	0.2	0.5
413 S.D.A.........	2	162	196*	0.2	0.4
435 UNITARIAN-UNIV	4	480	582*	0.5	1.2
443 UN C OF CHRIST	9	1 724	2 090*	1.9	4.2
449 UN METHODIST..	17	3 884	4 708*	4.3	9.4
KNOX	47	5 959	10 286*	31.2	100.0
001 ADVENT CHR CH.	2	196	234*	0.7	2.3
019 AMER BAPT USA.	11	1 736	2 074*	6.3	20.2
053 ASSEMB OF GOD.	1	83	200	0.6	1.9
059 BAPT MISS ASSN	1	30	36*	0.1	0.3
081 CATHOLIC......	6	NA	2 233	6.8	21.7
151 L-D SAINTS....	1	NA	200	0.6	1.9
165 CH OF NAZARENE	2	172	751	2.3	7.3
175 CONGR CHR CHS.	2	698	834*	2.5	8.1
179 CONSRV BAPT...	1	183	219*	0.7	2.1
193 EPISCOPAL.....	3	956	1 152	3.5	11.2
335 ORTH PRESB CH.	1	23	27*	0.1	0.3
353 CHR BRETHREN..	2	75	115	0.3	1.1
403 SALVATION ARMY	1	60	124	0.4	1.2
413 S.D.A.........	1	95	114*	0.3	1.1
435 UNITARIAN-UNIV	1	150	179*	0.5	1.7
443 UN C OF CHRIST	3	572	683*	2.1	6.6
449 UN METHODIST..	8	930	1 111*	3.4	10.8
LINCOLN	40	4 094	6 657*	25.9	100.0
001 ADVENT CHR CH.	1	5	6*	–	0.1
019 AMER BAPT USA.	8	743	896*	3.5	13.5
053 ASSEMB OF GOD.	1	19	25	0.1	0.4
081 CATHOLIC......	4	NA	1 242	4.8	18.7
127 CH GOD (CLEVE)	1	76	92*	0.4	1.4
165 CH OF NAZARENE	2	87	366	1.4	5.5
179 CONSRV BAPT...	3	549	662*	2.6	9.9
193 EPISCOPAL.....	3	490	805	3.1	12.1
226 FRIENDS-USA...	1	39	47*	0.2	0.7
443 UN C OF CHRIST	8	1 039	1 253*	4.9	18.8
449 UN METHODIST..	8	1 047	1 263*	4.9	19.0
OXFORD	68	5 361	15 877*	32.4	100.0
001 ADVENT CHR CH.	1	47	57*	0.1	0.4
019 AMER BAPT USA.	8	549	664*	1.4	4.2
053 ASSEMB OF GOD.	2	68	175	0.4	1.1
081 CATHOLIC......	8	NA	8 604	17.6	54.2
089 CHR & MISS AL.	2	63	107	0.2	0.7
127 CH GOD (CLEVE)	1	35	42*	0.1	0.3
151 L-D SAINTS....	1	NA	374	0.8	2.4
165 CH OF NAZARENE	3	155	451	0.9	2.8
167 CHS OF CHRIST.	1	80	102	0.2	0.6

NA—Not applicable   *Total adherents estimated from known number of communicant, confirmed, full members.   —Represents a percent less than 0.1.   Percentages may not total due to rounding.

Table 4. Churches and Church Membership by County and Denomination: 1980

County and Denomination	Number of churches	Communicant, confirmed, full members	Total adherents		
			Number	Percent of total population	Percent of total adherents
175 CONGR CHR CHS.	2	507	614*	1.3	3.9
181 CONSRV CONGR..	1	34	41*	0.1	0.3
193 EPISCOPAL.....	2	342	433	0.9	2.7
239 SWEDENBORGIAN.	1	60	73*	0.1	0.5
413 S.D.A.........	4	390	472*	1.0	3.0
435 UNITARIAN—UNIV	6	318	385*	0.8	2.4
443 UN C OF CHRIST	15	1 343	1 625*	3.3	10.2
449 UN METHODIST..	9	1 329	1 608*	3.3	10.1
453 UN PRES CH USA	1	41	50*	0.1	0.3
PENOBSCOT	132	16 835	53 460*	39.0	100.0
001 ADVENT CHR CH.	1	93	112*	0.1	0.2
019 AMER BAPT USA.	22	4 394	5 292*	3.9	9.9
053 ASSEMB OF GOD.	5	282	467	0.3	0.9
081 CATHOLIC......	22	NA	31 639	23.1	59.2
089 CHR & MISS AL.	1	58	90	0.1	0.2
127 CH GOD (CLEVE)	4	169	204*	0.1	0.4
151 L-D SAINTS....	2	NA	500	0.4	0.9
165 CH OF NAZARENE	4	363	793	0.6	1.5
167 CHS OF CHRIST.	3	140	178	0.1	0.3
175 CONGR CHR CHS.	1	226	272*	0.2	0.5
179 CONSRV BAPT...	6	1 098	1 322*	1.0	2.5
181 CONSRV CONGR..	1	27	33*	–	0.1
193 EPISCOPAL.....	7	1 601	2 247	1.6	4.2
201 EVAN COV CH AM	2	92	111*	0.1	0.2
226 FRIENDS-USA...	1	24	29*	–	0.1
263 INT FOURSQ GOS	1	27	33*	–	0.1
335 ORTH PRESB CH.	1	112	135*	0.1	0.3
403 SALVATION ARMY	1	97	329	0.2	0.6
413 S.D.A.........	3	136	164*	0.1	0.3
435 UNITARIAN—UNIV	4	788	949*	0.7	1.8
443 UN C OF CHRIST	18	2 765	3 330*	2.4	6.2
449 UN METHODIST..	22	4 343	5 231*	3.8	9.8
PISCATAQUIS	32	2 913	6 533*	37.0	100.0
001 ADVENT CHR CH.	1	31	38*	0.2	0.6
017 AMER BAPT ASSN	1	20	20	0.1	0.3
019 AMER BAPT USA.	3	645	786*	4.5	12.0
053 ASSEMB OF GOD.	3	114	225	1.3	3.4
081 CATHOLIC......	6	NA	2 716	15.4	41.6
165 CH OF NAZARENE	2	59	193	1.1	3.0
193 EPISCOPAL.....	2	96	182	1.0	2.8
435 UNITARIAN—UNIV	1	13	16*	0.1	0.2
443 UN C OF CHRIST	6	630	767*	4.3	11.7
449 UN METHODIST..	7	1 305	1 590*	9.0	24.3
SAGADAHOC	37	3 629	8 129*	28.2	100.0
001 ADVENT CHR CH.	1	?	?	?	?
019 AMER BAPT USA.	8	962	1 181*	4.1	14.5
081 CATHOLIC......	3	NA	2 648	9.2	32.6
089 CHR & MISS AL.	1	23	51	0.2	0.6
151 L-D SAINTS....	1	NA	270	0.9	3.3
165 CH OF NAZARENE	5	181	688	2.4	8.5
179 CONSRV BAPT...	1	183	225*	0.8	2.8
193 EPISCOPAL.....	2	520	796	2.8	9.8
239 SWEDENBORGIAN.	1	60	74*	0.3	0.9
263 INT FOURSQ GOS	1	47	58*	0.2	0.7
403 SALVATION ARMY	1	39	157	0.5	1.9
413 S.D.A.........	2	110	135*	0.5	1.7
443 UN C OF CHRIST	4	755	927*	3.2	11.4
449 UN METHODIST..	6	749	919*	3.2	11.3
SOMERSET	60	5 170	17 470*	38.8	100.0
019 AMER BAPT USA.	6	1 099	1 352*	3.0	7.7
053 ASSEMB OF GOD.	3	232	450	1.0	2.6
081 CATHOLIC......	8	NA	9 922	22.0	56.8
127 CH GOD (CLEVE)	1	27	33*	0.1	0.2
151 L-D SAINTS....	1	NA	230	0.5	1.3
165 CH OF NAZARENE	6	511	1 435	3.2	8.2
167 CHS OF CHRIST.	1	50	64	0.1	0.4
175 CONGR CHR CHS.	2	257	316*	0.7	1.8
179 CONSRV BAPT...	4	732	901*	2.0	5.2
193 EPISCOPAL.....	3	255	299	0.7	1.7
203 EVAN FREE CH..	1	53	65*	0.1	0.4
226 FRIENDS-USA...	1	27	33*	0.1	0.2
263 INT FOURSQ GOS	1	14	17*	–	0.1
335 ORTH PRESB CH.	1	14	17*	–	0.1
413 S.D.A.........	1	174	214*	0.5	1.2
435 UNITARIAN—UNIV	1	180	221*	0.5	1.3
443 UN C OF CHRIST	6	514	632*	1.4	3.6
449 UN METHODIST..	11	970	1 194*	2.7	6.8
453 UN PRES CH USA	2	61	75*	–	0.4
WALDO	33	3 008	5 038*	17.7	100.0
019 AMER BAPT USA.	7	609	748*	2.6	14.8
081 CATHOLIC......	3	NA	1 279	4.5	25.4
127 CH GOD (CLEVE)	1	120	147*	0.5	2.9
165 CH OF NAZARENE	1	92	169	0.6	3.4
167 CHS OF CHRIST.	2	50	64	0.2	1.3
175 CONGR CHR CHS.	2	118	145*	0.5	2.9
179 CONSRV BAPT...	1	183	225*	0.8	4.5
193 EPISCOPAL.....	1	151	190	0.7	3.8
435 UNITARIAN—UNIV	1	402	494*	1.7	9.8
443 UN C OF CHRIST	7	558	686*	2.4	13.6
449 UN METHODIST..	7	725	891*	3.1	17.7
WASHINGTON	79	4 754	9 608*	27.5	100.0
001 ADVENT CHR CH.	4	283	345*	1.0	3.6
019 AMER BAPT USA.	10	796	970*	2.8	10.1

County and Denomination	Number of churches	Communicant, confirmed, full members	Total adherents		
			Number	Percent of total population	Percent of total adherents
053 ASSEMB OF GOD.	1	10	23	0.1	0.2
081 CATHOLIC......	12	NA	3 639	10.4	37.9
093 CHR CH (DISC).	1	115	155	0.4	1.6
127 CH GOD (CLEVE)	1	32	39*	0.1	0.4
151 L-D SAINTS....	1	NA	67	0.2	0.7
165 CH OF NAZARENE	2	15	49	0.1	0.5
167 CHS OF CHRIST.	3	86	109	0.3	1.1
175 CONGR CHR CHS.	8	581	708*	2.0	7.4
179 CONSRV BAPT...	1	183	223*	0.6	2.3
193 EPISCOPAL.....	4	435	579	1.7	6.0
226 FRIENDS-USA...	1	6	7*	–	0.1
413 S.D.A.........	2	76	93*	0.3	1.0
435 UNITARIAN—UNIV	1	26	32*	0.1	0.3
443 UN C OF CHRIST	9	599	730*	2.1	7.6
449 UN METHODIST..	18	1 511	1 840*	5.3	19.2
YORK	126	13 219	60 810*	43.5	100.0
001 ADVENT CHR CH.	3	350	425*	0.3	0.7
019 AMER BAPT USA.	23	3 801	4 618*	3.3	7.6
029 AMER LUTH CH..	1	35	66	–	0.1
053 ASSEMB OF GOD.	7	439	646	0.5	1.1
081 CATHOLIC......	30	NA	43 268	31.0	71.2
083 CHRIST CATH CH	1	28	37	–	0.1
127 CH GOD (CLEVE)	1	?	?	?	?
151 L-D SAINTS....	2	NA	280	0.2	0.5
165 CH OF NAZARENE	4	157	586	0.4	1.0
167 CHS OF CHRIST.	2	125	159	0.1	0.3
175 CONGR CHR CHS.	1	147	179*	0.1	0.3
179 CONSRV BAPT...	2	366	445*	0.3	0.7
181 CONSRV CONGR..	1	150	182*	0.1	0.3
193 EPISCOPAL.....	7	1 025	1 709	1.2	2.8
226 FRIENDS-USA...	1	30	36*	–	0.1
403 SALVATION ARMY	2	264	517	0.4	0.9
413 S.D.A.........	2	82	100*	0.1	0.2
435 UNITARIAN—UNIV	3	359	436*	0.3	0.7
443 UN C OF CHRIST	18	3 222	3 915*	2.8	6.4
449 UN METHODIST..	15	2 639	3 206*	2.3	5.3

MARYLAND

County and Denomination	Number of churches	Communicant, confirmed, full members	Total adherents		
			Number	Percent of total population	Percent of total adherents
THE STATE.....	3 107	744 742	1 695 948*	40.2	100.0
ALLEGANY	145	27 223	49 886*	61.9	100.0
053 ASSEMB OF GOD.	14	1 470	3 069	3.8	6.2
061 BEACHY AMISH..	1	16	19*	–	0.1
071 BRETHREN (ASH)	1	28	33*	–	0.1
081 CATHOLIC......	11	NA	14 297	17.7	28.7
093 CHR CH (DISC).	2	235	467	0.6	0.9
097 CH CHS&CHS CR	1	45	53*	0.1	0.1
123 CH GOD (ANDER)	1	52	156	0.2	0.3
127 CH GOD (CLEVE)	1	126	149*	0.2	0.3
151 L-D SAINTS....	1	NA	486	0.6	1.0
157 CH OF BRETHREN	6	1 088	1 283*	1.6	2.6
165 CH OF NAZARENE	4	493	972	1.2	1.9
167 CHS OF CHRIST.	1	75	95	0.1	0.2
175 CONGR CHR CHS.	1	205	242*	0.3	0.5
193 EPISCOPAL.....	6	1 275	1 968	2.4	3.9
244 GRACE BRETHREN	2	102	120*	0.1	0.2
270 CONSRV JUDAISM	1	30	35*	–	0.1
271 REFORM JUDAISM	1	110	130*	0.2	0.3
281 LUTH CH AMER..	6	3 498	4 334	5.4	8.7
283 LUTH--MO SYNOD	1	0	193	0.2	0.4
285 MENNONITE CH..	2	164	193*	0.2	0.4
349 PENT HOLINESS.	2	91	107*	0.1	0.2
353 CHR BRETHREN..	3	60	60	0.1	0.1
356 PRESB CH AMER.	1	36	48	0.1	0.1
403 SALVATION ARMY	1	162	313	0.4	0.6
413 S.D.A.........	2	219	258*	0.3	0.5
419 SO BAPT CONV..	10	3 083	3 636*	4.5	7.3
443 UN C OF CHRIST	7	855	1 008*	1.3	2.0
449 UN METHODIST..	49	12 374	14 592*	18.1	29.3
453 UN PRES CH USA	6	1 331	1 570*	1.9	3.1
ANNE ARUNDEL	199	55 774	133 282*	35.9	100.0
005 AME ZION......	1	124	189	0.1	0.1
017 AMER BAPT ASSN	1	7	7	–	–
019 AMER BAPT USA.	1	447	540*	0.1	0.4
029 AMER LUTH CH..	4	1 109	1 963	0.5	1.5
053 ASSEMB OF GOD.	4	272	540	0.1	0.4
081 CATHOLIC......	19	NA	58 480	15.8	43.9
089 CHR & MISS AL.	1	54	94	–	0.1
097 CH CHS&CHS CR	2	139	168*	–	0.1
123 CH GOD (ANDER)	2	129	387	0.1	0.3
127 CH GOD (CLEVE)	8	886	1 071*	0.3	0.8
151 L-D SAINTS....	3	NA	1 116	0.3	0.8
157 CH OF BRETHREN	1	112	135*	–	0.1
165 CH OF NAZARENE	4	370	1 007	0.3	0.8
167 CHS OF CHRIST.	3	310	395	0.1	0.3
193 EPISCOPAL.....	15	6 165	9 456*	2.6	7.1
226 FRIENDS-USA...	1	30	36*	–	0.1

NA— Not applicable   *Total adherents estimated from known number of communicant, confirmed, full members.   —Represents a percent less than 0.1.   Percentages may not total due to rounding.

Table 4. Churches and Church Membership by County and Denomination: 1980

County and Denomination	Number of churches	Communicant, confirmed, full members	Total adherents		
			Number	Percent of total population	Percent of total adherents
270 CONSRV JUDAISM	1	28	34*	–	–
271 REFORM JUDAISM	1	270	326*	0.1	0.2
281 LUTH CH AMER..	6	4 105	6 196	1.7	4.6
283 LUTH--MO SYNOD	5	2 565	3 998	1.1	3.0
285 MENNONITE CH..	1	36	44*	–	–
381 REF PRES-EVAN.	2	675	1 028	0.3	0.8
403 SALVATION ARMY	2	112	361	0.1	0.3
413 S.D.A.........	7	673	813*	0.2	0.6
419 SO BAPT CONV..	22	7 936	9 590*	2.6	7.2
435 UNITARIAN-UNIV	2	188	227*	0.1	0.2
443 UN C OF CHRIST	2	221	267*	0.1	0.2
449 UN METHODIST..	73	25 517	30 834*	8.3	23.1
453 UN PRES CH USA	5	3 294	3 980*	1.1	3.0
BALTIMORE	322	93 107	257 314*	39.2	100.0
005 AME ZION......	1	57	100	–	–
019 AMER BAPT USA.	1	518	607*	0.1	0.2
029 AMER LUTH CH..	6	2 204	3 854	0.6	1.5
053 ASSEMB OF GOD.	10	1 140	2 229	0.3	0.9
081 CATHOLIC......	32	NA	140 358	21.4	54.5
089 CHR & MISS AL.	5	291	422	0.1	0.2
093 CHR CH (DISC)	11	1 257	1 654	0.3	0.6
097 CHR CHS&CHS CR	2	333	391*	0.1	0.2
127 CH GOD (CLEVE)	7	928	1 088*	0.2	0.4
151 L-D SAINTS....	3	NA	1 166	0.2	0.5
157 CH OF BRETHREN	5	458	537*	0.1	0.2
165 CH OF NAZARENE	2	177	450	0.1	0.2
167 CHS OF CHRIST.	5	425	549	0.1	0.2
193 EPISCOPAL.....	19	10 956	14 432	2.2	5.6
221 FREE METHODIST	1	29	219	–	0.1
226 FRIENDS-USA...	1	44	52*	–	–
270 CONSRV JUDAISM	2	859	1 007*	0.2	0.4
281 LUTH CH AMER..	8	3 435	4 845	0.7	1.9
283 LUTH--MO SYNOD	14	5 648	7 207	1.1	2.8
285 MENNONITE CH..	2	66	77*	–	–
349 PENT HOLINESS	2	330	387*	0.1	0.2
353 CHR BRETHREN..	1	100	135	–	0.1
356 PRESB CH AMER.	2	578	679	0.1	0.3
375 REF EPISCOPAL.	3	645	756*	0.1	0.3
381 REF PRES-EVAN.	3	1 169	1 560	0.2	0.6
403 SALVATION ARMY	4	503	1 033	0.2	0.4
413 S.D.A.........	11	2 197	2 577*	0.4	1.0
419 SO BAPT CONV..	4	810	950*	0.1	0.4
435 UNITARIAN-UNIV	3	655	768*	0.1	0.3
443 UN C OF CHRIST	6	2 721	3 191*	0.5	1.2
449 UN METHODIST..	125	46 607	54 658*	8.3	21.2
453 UN PRES CH USA	20	7 858	9 215*	1.4	3.6
469 WELS..........	1	109	161	–	0.1
BALTIMORE CITY	403	137 020	308 159*	39.2	100.0
005 AME ZION......	4	5 175	5 817	0.7	1.9
019 AMER BAPT USA.	15	10 023	11 977*	1.5	3.9
029 AMER LUTH CH..	19	7 442	11 089	1.4	3.6
053 ASSEMB OF GOD.	3	514	950	0.1	0.3
075 BRETHREN IN CR	1	82	132	–	–
081 CATHOLIC......	64	NA	130 197	16.5	42.2
097 CHR CHS&CHS CR	6	655	783*	0.1	0.3
101 C.M.E.........	2	886	1 059*	0.1	0.3
123 CH GOD (ANDER)	5	645	1 935	0.2	0.6
127 CH GOD (CLEVE)	12	1 234	1 475*	0.2	0.5
157 CH OF BRETHREN	2	278	332*	–	0.1
165 CH OF NAZARENE	1	47	58	–	–
167 CHS OF CHRIST.	2	1 080	1 226	0.2	0.4
181 CONSRV CONGR..	1	43	51*	–	–
193 EPISCOPAL.....	40	16 051	23 590	3.0	7.7
195 ESTONIAN ELC..	1	165	298	–	0.1
221 FREE METHODIST	3	162	666	0.1	0.2
226 FRIENDS-USA...	3	589	704*	0.1	0.2
233 GEN CH NEW JER	1	25	30*	–	–
239 SWEDENBORGIAN.	1	60	72*	–	–
270 CONSRV JUDAISM	2	2 116	2 528*	0.3	0.8
271 REFORM JUDAISM	4	7 322	8 749*	1.1	2.8
281 LUTH CH AMER..	36	19 862	28 508	3.6	9.3
283 LUTH--MO SYNOD	11	4 231	6 170	0.8	2.0
290 METRO COMM CHS	1	75	150	–	–
335 ORTH PRESB CH.	1	57	68*	–	–
353 CHR BRETHREN..	6	420	535	0.1	0.2
381 REF PRES-EVAN.	4	372	412	0.1	0.1
413 S.D.A.........	2	377	450*	0.1	0.1
419 SO BAPT CONV..	55	23 502	28 083*	3.6	9.1
443 UN C OF CHRIST	14	3 859	4 611*	0.6	1.5
449 UN METHODIST..	61	21 984	26 269*	3.3	8.5
453 UN PRES CH USA	20	7 687	9 185*	1.2	3.0
CALVERT	36	5 932	9 469*	27.3	100.0
053 ASSEMB OF GOD.	1	158	317	0.9	3.3
081 CATHOLIC......	3	NA	1 621	4.7	17.1
151 L-D SAINTS....	1	NA	138	0.4	1.5
167 CHS OF CHRIST.	1	40	45	0.1	0.5
193 EPISCOPAL.....	3	902	1 273	3.7	13.4
283 LUTH--MO SYNOD	1	60	125	0.4	1.3
413 S.D.A.........	2	100	125*	0.4	1.3
419 SO BAPT CONV..	1	185	231*	0.7	2.4
449 UN METHODIST..	23	4 487	5 594*	16.1	59.1
CAROLINE	43	6 027	9 533*	41.2	100.0
081 CATHOLIC......	4	NA	1 763	7.6	18.5
123 CH GOD (ANDER)	1	98	294	1.3	3.1
127 CH GOD (CLEVE)	1	56	68*	0.3	0.7
151 L-D SAINTS....	1	NA	56	0.2	0.6
157 CH OF BRETHREN	2	187	226*	1.0	2.4

County and Denomination	Number of churches	Communicant, confirmed, full members	Total adherents		
			Number	Percent of total population	Percent of total adherents
165 CH OF NAZARENE	1	72	237	1.0	2.5
193 EPISCOPAL.....	1	119	230	1.0	2.4
283 LUTH--MO SYNOD	1	395	499	2.2	5.2
419 SO BAPT CONV..	2	255	308*	1.3	3.2
449 UN METHODIST..	29	4 845	5 852*	25.3	61.4
CARROLL	118	25 552	43 845*	45.5	100.0
053 ASSEMB OF GOD.	1	160	300	0.3	0.7
071 BRETHREN (ASH)	1	87	106*	0.1	0.2
081 CATHOLIC......	3	NA	10 690	11.1	24.4
127 CH GOD (CLEVE)	3	181	221*	0.2	0.5
151 L-D SAINTS....	2	NA	631	0.7	1.4
157 CH OF BRETHREN	6	1 348	1 643*	1.7	3.7
165 CH OF NAZARENE	2	77	207	0.2	0.5
167 CHS OF CHRIST.	1	30	38	–	0.1
193 EPISCOPAL.....	3	757	1 170	1.2	2.7
221 FREE METHODIST	1	29	99	0.1	0.2
226 FRIENDS-USA...	1	22	27*	–	0.1
281 LUTH CH AMER..	22	6 875	9 176	9.5	20.9
283 LUTH--MO SYNOD	1	67	105	0.1	0.2
285 MENNONITE CH..	2	64	78*	0.1	0.2
381 REF PRES-EVAN.	1	79	125	0.1	0.3
413 S.D.A.........	2	199	243*	0.3	0.6
419 SO BAPT CONV..	7	2 155	2 627*	2.7	6.0
443 UN C OF CHRIST	9	2 493	3 038*	3.2	6.9
449 UN METHODIST..	44	10 323	12 582*	13.1	28.7
453 UN PRES CH USA	6	606	739*	0.8	1.7
CECIL	75	11 702	19 684*	32.6	100.0
001 ADVENT CHR CH.	1	17	21*	–	0.1
029 AMER LUTH CH..	1	84	122	0.2	0.6
053 ASSEMB OF GOD.	1	228	450	0.7	2.3
081 CATHOLIC......	7	NA	4 745	7.9	24.1
127 CH GOD (CLEVE)	3	219	269*	0.4	1.4
151 L-D SAINTS....	1	NA	135	0.2	0.7
157 CH OF BRETHREN	1	38	47*	0.1	0.2
165 CH OF NAZARENE	3	224	544	0.9	2.8
167 CHS OF CHRIST.	2	82	106	0.2	0.5
193 EPISCOPAL.....	5	1 117	1 322	2.2	6.7
226 FRIENDS-USA...	1	18	22*	–	0.1
285 MENNONITE CH..	2	43	53*	0.1	0.3
381 REF PRES-EVAN.	1	40	60	0.1	0.3
413 S.D.A.........	3	324	398*	0.7	2.0
419 SO BAPT CONV..	8	3 205	3 939*	6.5	20.0
449 UN METHODIST..	29	5 192	6 381*	10.6	32.4
453 UN PRES CH USA	6	871	1 070*	1.8	5.4
CHARLES	50	7 567	28 978*	39.8	100.0
029 AMER LUTH CH..	1	62	104	0.1	0.4
053 ASSEMB OF GOD.	2	130	340	0.5	1.2
081 CATHOLIC......	13	NA	18 398	25.3	63.5
123 CH GOD (ANDER)	1	75	225	0.3	0.8
127 CH GOD (CLEVE)	1	88	111*	0.2	0.4
151 L-D SAINTS....	1	NA	245	0.3	0.8
165 CH OF NAZARENE	1	102	373	0.5	1.3
167 CHS OF CHRIST.	1	97	166	0.2	0.6
283 LUTH--MO SYNOD	2	488	762	1.0	2.6
357 PRESB CH US...	1	119	151*	0.2	0.5
413 S.D.A.........	2	148	187*	0.3	0.6
419 SO BAPT CONV..	10	3 364	4 255*	5.8	14.7
449 UN METHODIST..	14	2 894	3 661*	5.0	12.6
DORCHESTER	86	9 687	13 207*	43.1	100.0
081 CATHOLIC......	3	NA	1 208	3.9	9.1
089 CHR & MISS AL.	2	48	157	0.5	1.2
097 CHR CHS&CHS CR	1	100	119*	0.4	0.9
127 CH GOD (CLEVE)	5	319	379*	1.2	2.9
151 L-D SAINTS....	1	NA	117	0.4	0.9
165 CH OF NAZARENE	1	77	205	0.7	1.6
193 EPISCOPAL.....	7	708	952	3.1	7.2
283 LUTH--MO SYNOD	1	125	148	0.5	1.1
403 SALVATION ARMY	1	128	213	0.7	1.6
413 S.D.A.........	3	160	190*	0.6	1.4
419 SO BAPT CONV..	1	1 055	1 252*	4.1	9.5
443 UN C OF CHRIST	1	250	297*	1.0	2.2
449 UN METHODIST..	57	6 717	7 970*	26.0	60.3
FREDERICK	160	33 191	55 046*	48.2	100.0
017 AMER BAPT ASSN	2	129	129	0.1	0.2
053 ASSEMB OF GOD.	4	248	395	0.3	0.7
075 BRETHREN IN CR	1	82	132	0.1	0.2
081 CATHOLIC......	10	NA	11 271	9.9	20.5
089 CHR & MISS AL.	2	112	233	0.2	0.4
097 CHR CHS&CHS CR	1	155	190*	0.2	0.3
127 CH GOD (CLEVE)	3	137	168*	0.1	0.3
151 L-D SAINTS....	1	NA	435	0.4	0.8
157 CH OF BRETHREN	13	3 315	4 064*	3.6	7.4
165 CH OF NAZARENE	2	175	449	0.4	0.8
167 CHS OF CHRIST.	1	93	141	0.1	0.3
193 EPISCOPAL.....	7	641	1 279	1.1	2.3
203 EVAN FREE CH..	1	15	18*	–	–
263 INT FOURSQ GOS	1	71	87*	0.1	0.2
281 LUTH CH AMER..	30	10 354	14 327	12.5	26.0
283 LUTH--MO SYNOD	1	62	96	0.1	0.2
293 MORAV CH-NORTH	1	269	332	0.3	0.6
381 REF PRES-EVAN.	1	80	115	0.1	0.2
403 SALVATION ARMY	1	189	268	0.2	0.5
413 S.D.A.........	2	436	534*	0.5	1.0
419 SO BAPT CONV..	5	2 284	2 800*	2.5	5.1
435 UNITARIAN-UNIV	1	51	63*	0.1	0.1

NA—Not applicable   *Total adherents estimated from known number of communicant, confirmed, full members.   —Represents a percent less than 0.1.   Percentages may not total due to rounding.

Table 4. Churches and Church Membership by County and Denomination: 1980

County and Denomination	Number of churches	Communicant, confirmed, full members	Total adherents Number	Percent of total population	Percent of total adherents
443 UN C OF CHRIST	17	3 828	4 692*	4.1	8.5
449 UN METHODIST..	51	9 891	12 124*	10.6	22.0
453 UN PRES CH USA	2	574	704*	0.6	1.3
GARRETT	92	8 198	12 096*	45.6	100.0
019 AMER BAPT USA.	1	10	12*	-	0.1
053 ASSEMB OF GOD.	12	663	1 447	5.5	12.0
081 CATHOLIC......	3	NA	873	3.3	7.2
093 CHR CH (DISC)	1	62	95	0.4	0.8
097 CHR CHS&CHS CR	1	30	37*	0.1	0.3
123 CH GOD (ANDER)	1	52	156	0.6	1.3
127 CH GOD (CLEVE)	3	168	207*	0.8	1.7
151 L-D SAINTS....	1	NA	144	0.5	1.2
157 CH OF BRETHREN	10	966	1 190*	4.5	9.8
165 CH OF NAZARENE	1	91	175	0.7	1.4
175 CONGR CHR CHS.	1	76	94*	0.4	0.8
193 EPISCOPAL.....	2	236	332	1.3	2.7
244 GRACE BRETHREN	1	54	67*	0.3	0.6
281 LUTH CH AMER..	9	1 362	1 808	6.8	14.9
283 LUTH--MO SYNOD	2	429	520	2.0	4.3
285 MENNONITE CH..	8	496	611*	2.3	5.1
323 OLD ORD AMISH.	1	130	160*	0.6	1.3
381 REF PRES-EVAN.	1	12	29	0.1	0.2
413 S.D.A.........	1	82	101*	0.4	0.8
419 SO BAPT CONV..	4	385	474*	1.8	3.9
443 UN C OF CHRIST	2	256	315*	1.2	2.6
449 UN METHODIST..	26	2 638	3 249*	12.3	26.9
HARFORD	116	27 993	57 531*	39.4	100.0
029 AMER LUTH CH..	3	1 629	2 468	1.7	4.3
053 ASSEMB OF GOD.	4	266	430	0.3	0.7
081 CATHOLIC......	9	NA	21 383	14.7	37.2
089 CHR & MISS AL.	1	20	26	-	-
097 CHR CHS&CHS CR	4	1 553	1 906*	1.3	3.3
127 CH GOD (CLEVE)	3	128	157*	0.1	0.3
151 L-D SAINTS....	1	NA	464	0.3	0.8
165 CH OF NAZARENE	1	260	350	0.2	0.6
167 CHS OF CHRIST.	2	139	175	0.1	0.3
193 EPISCOPAL.....	8	1 948	2 745	1.9	4.8
226 FRIENDS-USA...	2	123	151*	0.1	0.3
271 REFORM JUDAISM	1	240	295*	0.2	0.5
281 LUTH CH AMER..	2	636	1 006	0.7	1.7
283 LUTH--MO SYNOD	1	706	954	0.7	1.7
291 MISSIONARY CH.	1	38	65	-	0.1
349 PENT HOLINESS.	1	51	63*	-	0.1
353 CHR BRETHREN..	2	75	90	0.1	0.2
375 REF EPISCOPAL.	1	161	198*	0.1	0.3
381 REF PRES-EVAN.	1	?	?	?	?
403 SALVATION ARMY	1	79	130	0.1	0.2
413 S.D.A.........	2	155	190*	0.1	0.3
419 SO BAPT CONV..	14	5 964	7 320*	5.0	12.7
435 UNITARIAN-UNIV	1	56	69*	-	0.1
443 UN C OF CHRIST	1	131	161*	0.1	0.3
449 UN METHODIST..	37	9 936	12 195*	8.4	21.2
453 UN PRES CH USA	12	3 699	4 540*	3.1	7.9
HOWARD	88	18 855	45 689*	38.5	100.0
019 AMER BAPT USA.	1	388	476*	0.4	1.0
029 AMER LUTH CH..	3	1 008	1 283	1.1	2.8
053 ASSEMB OF GOD.	2	134	300	0.3	0.7
081 CATHOLIC......	6	NA	20 049	16.9	43.9
093 CHR CH (DISC)	1	51	108	0.1	0.2
123 CH GOD (ANDER)	2	181	543	0.5	1.2
127 CH GOD (CLEVE)	2	8	10*	-	-
151 L-D SAINTS....	2	NA	1 057	0.9	2.3
157 CH OF BRETHREN	2	104	128*	0.1	0.3
165 CH OF NAZARENE	1	358	517	0.4	1.1
193 EPISCOPAL.....	10	2 390	3 636	3.1	8.0
263 INT FOURSQ GOS	1	57	70*	0.1	0.2
270 CONSRV JUDAISM	1	122	150*	0.1	0.3
271 REFORM JUDAISM	1	500	613*	0.5	1.3
281 LUTH CH AMER..	2	1 219	1 593	1.3	3.5
283 LUTH--MO SYNOD	1	266	399	0.3	0.9
285 MENNONITE CH..	1	26	32*	-	0.1
335 ORTH PRESB CH.	1	58	71*	0.1	0.2
353 CHR BRETHREN..	1	100	200	0.2	0.4
356 PRESB CH AMER.	1	627	646	0.5	1.4
357 PRESB CH US...	1	204	250*	0.2	0.5
413 S.D.A.........	3	412	505*	0.4	1.1
419 SO BAPT CONV..	10	2 968	3 640*	3.1	8.0
435 UNITARIAN-UNIV	1	61	75*	0.1	0.2
443 UN C OF CHRIST	1	65	80*	0.1	0.2
449 UN METHODIST..	26	6 131	7 520*	6.3	16.5
453 UN PRES CH USA	4	1 417	1 738*	1.5	3.8
KENT	48	5 235	8 187*	49.0	100.0
061 BEACHY AMISH..	1	51	60*	0.4	0.7
081 CATHOLIC......	4	NA	1 846	11.1	22.5
157 CH OF BRETHREN	1	79	93*	0.6	1.1
165 CH OF NAZARENE	1	42	121	0.7	1.5
193 EPISCOPAL.....	5	732	970	5.8	11.8
215 EVAN METH CH..	1	26	31*	0.2	0.4
226 FRIENDS-USA...	1	23	27*	0.2	0.3
283 LUTH--MO SYNOD	1	178	224	1.3	2.7
285 MENNONITE CH..	1	11	13*	0.1	0.2
413 S.D.A.........	2	200	235*	1.4	2.9
419 SO BAPT CONV..	1	75	88*	0.5	1.1
449 UN METHODIST..	29	3 818	4 479*	26.8	54.7
MONTGOMERY	302	92 413	251 899*	43.5	100.0

County and Denomination	Number of churches	Communicant, confirmed, full members	Total adherents Number	Percent of total population	Percent of total adherents
005 AME ZION......	5	1 195	1 985	0.3	0.8
017 AMER BAPT ASSN	1	60	60	-	-
019 AMER BAPT USA.	10	5 581	6 643*	1.1	2.6
029 AMER LUTH CH..	5	1 337	1 651	0.3	0.7
049 ARMEN AP CH AM	1	150	450	0.1	0.2
053 ASSEMB OF GOD.	7	724	980	0.2	0.4
081 CATHOLIC......	30	NA	134 537	23.2	53.4
089 CHR & MISS AL.	2	153	364	0.1	0.1
093 CHR CH (DISC)	6	1 177	1 687	0.3	0.7
097 CHR CHS&CHS CR	1	180	214*	-	0.1
105 CHRISTIAN REF.	1	107	176	-	0.1
123 CH GOD (ANDER)	2	146	438	0.1	0.2
127 CH GOD (CLEVE)	7	664	790*	0.1	0.3
151 L-D SAINTS....	8	NA	3 643	0.6	1.4
157 CH OF BRETHREN	2	299	356*	0.1	0.1
165 CH OF NAZARENE	2	186	253	-	0.1
167 CHS OF CHRIST.	4	490	545	0.1	0.2
195 ESTONIAN ELC..	1	42	129	-	0.1
201 EVAN COV CH AM	1	25	30*	-	-
221 FREE METHODIST	4	191	864	0.1	0.3
226 FRIENDS-USA...	2	525	625*	0.1	0.2
270 CONSRV JUDAISM	10	4 240	5 047*	0.9	2.0
271 REFORM JUDAISM	3	2 026	2 412*	0.4	1.0
274 LAT EVAN LUTH.	1	453	530	0.1	0.2
281 LUTH CH AMER..	10	5 663	7 644	1.3	3.0
283 LUTH--MO SYNOD	6	2 293	3 034	0.5	1.2
285 MENNONITE CH..	3	98	117*	-	-
290 METRO COMM CHS	1	15	30	-	-
335 ORTH PRESB CH.	3	319	380*	0.1	0.2
349 PENT HOLINESS.	3	236	281*	-	0.1
353 CHR BRETHREN..	2	45	70	-	-
357 PRESB CH US...	21	2 963	3 527*	0.6	1.4
413 S.D.A.........	4	956	1 138*	0.2	0.5
419 SO BAPT CONV..	39	18 669	22 222*	3.8	8.8
435 UNITARIAN-UNIV	4	1 816	2 162*	0.4	0.9
443 UN C OF CHRIST	4	1 917	2 282*	0.4	0.9
449 UN METHODIST..	63	32 000	38 090*	6.6	15.1
453 UN PRES CH USA	23	5 472	6 513*	1.1	2.6
PRINCE GEORGES	303	82 266	238 289*	35.8	100.0
001 ADVENT CHR CH.	1	71	86*	-	-
005 AME ZION......	2	471	767	0.1	0.3
017 AMER BAPT ASSN	2	505	505	0.1	0.2
019 AMER BAPT USA.	22	11 668	14 160*	2.1	5.9
029 AMER LUTH CH..	4	1 447	2 095	0.3	0.9
039 AP CHR CH(NAZ)	1	37	45*	-	-
053 ASSEMB OF GOD.	9	1 382	2 314	0.3	1.0
081 CATHOLIC......	36	NA	132 122	19.9	55.4
089 CHR & MISS AL.	1	45	75	-	-
093 CHR CH (DISC)	8	1 305	2 203	0.3	0.9
097 CHR CHS&CHS CR	1	190	231*	-	0.1
101 C.M.E........	2	641	778*	0.1	0.3
123 CH GOD (ANDER)	1	65	195	-	0.1
127 CH GOD (CLEVE)	8	664	806*	0.1	0.3
151 L-D SAINTS....	7	NA	2 452	0.4	1.0
157 CH OF BRETHREN	1	337	409*	0.1	0.2
165 CH OF NAZARENE	5	571	962	0.1	0.4
167 CHS OF CHRIST.	7	1 050	1 335	0.2	0.6
201 EVAN COV CH AM	1	117	142*	-	0.1
221 FREE METHODIST	1	26	174	-	0.1
226 FRIENDS-USA...	1	144	175*	-	0.1
244 GRACE BRETHREN	2	596	723*	0.1	0.3
263 INT FOURSQ GOS	2	152	184*	-	0.1
270 CONSRV JUDAISM	3	410	498*	0.1	0.2
271 REFORM JUDAISM	1	324	393*	0.1	0.2
281 LUTH CH AMER..	10	3 052	4 310	0.6	1.8
283 LUTH--MO SYNOD	9	3 404	4 584	0.7	1.9
285 MENNONITE CH..	2	149	181*	-	0.1
287 MENN GEN CONF.	1	102	102	-	-
290 METRO COMM CHS	0	20	40	-	-
293 MORAV CH-NORTH	2	375	543	0.1	0.2
329 OPEN BIBLE STD	2	85	115	-	-
349 PENT HOLINESS.	2	108	131*	-	0.1
353 CHR BRETHREN..	1	70	135	-	0.1
357 PRESB CH US...	19	2 559	3 106*	0.5	1.3
403 SALVATION ARMY	1	179	577	0.1	0.2
413 S.D.A.........	6	1 556	1 888*	0.3	0.8
415 S-D BAPTIST GC	1	12	15*	-	-
419 SO BAPT CONV..	44	22 059	26 771*	4.0	11.2
435 UNITARIAN-UNIV	2	424	515*	0.1	0.2
443 UN C OF CHRIST	3	565	686*	0.1	0.3
449 UN METHODIST..	47	22 256	27 010*	4.1	11.3
453 UN PRES CH USA	21	3 003	3 644*	0.5	1.5
469 WELS.........	1	70	107	-	-
QUEEN ANNES	49	11 041	15 083*	59.1	100.0
053 ASSEMB OF GOD.	2	41	86	0.3	0.6
081 CATHOLIC......	3	NA	1 715	6.7	11.4
127 CH GOD (CLEVE)	3	194	232*	0.9	1.5
193 EPISCOPAL.....	3	595	823	3.2	5.5
283 LUTH--MO SYNOD	1	100	129	0.5	0.9
413 S.D.A.........	11	6 357	7 606*	29.8	50.4
419 SO BAPT CONV..	1	85	102*	0.4	0.7
449 UN METHODIST..	25	3 669	4 390*	17.2	29.1
ST MARYS	46	4 853	23 178*	38.7	100.0
053 ASSEMB OF GOD.	1	66	92	0.2	0.4
081 CATHOLIC......	16	NA	16 760	28.0	72.3
127 CH GOD (CLEVE)	1	87	109*	0.2	0.5
151 L-D SAINTS....	1	NA	202	0.3	0.9
165 CH OF NAZARENE	1	174	198	0.3	0.9
167 CHS OF CHRIST.	1	63	86	0.1	0.4

NA— Not applicable *Total adherents estimated from known number of communicant, confirmed, full members.

—Represents a percent less than 0.1. Percentages may not total due to rounding.

Table 4. Churches and Church Membership by County and Denomination: 1980

County and Denomination	Number of churches	Communicant, confirmed, full members	Total adherents		
			Number	Percent of total population	Percent of total adherents
270 CONSRV JUDAISM	1	37	46*	0.1	0.2
283 LUTH--MO SYNOD	2	478	756	1.3	3.3
285 MENNONITE CH..	2	104	130*	0.2	0.6
323 OLD ORD AMISH.	3	390	487*	0.8	2.1
357 PRESB CH US...	1	65	81*	0.1	0.3
413 S.D.A.........	1	28	35*	0.1	0.2
419 SO BAPT CONV..	2	1 418	1 770*	3.0	7.6
449 UN METHODIST..	12	1 877	2 344*	3.9	10.1
453 UN PRES CH USA	1	66	82*	0.1	0.4
SOMERSET	61	7 383	8 920*	46.5	100.0
005 AME ZION......	1	225	373	1.9	4.2
053 ASSEMB OF GOD.	1	74	85	0.4	1.0
081 CATHOLIC......	1	NA	?	?	?
093 CHR CH (DISC).	1	34	52	0.3	0.6
127 CH GOD (CLEVE)	2	444	529*	2.8	5.9
157 CH OF BRETHREN	1	122	145*	0.8	1.6
193 EPISCOPAL.....	4	267	334	1.7	3.7
419 SO BAPT CONV..	4	1 032	1 229*	6.4	13.8
449 UN METHODIST..	44	4 914	5 850*	30.5	65.6
453 UN PRES CH USA	2	271	323*	1.7	3.6
TALBOT	49	7 772	12 129*	47.4	100.0
081 CATHOLIC......	3	NA	2 240	8.7	18.5
127 CH GOD (CLEVE)	1	341	397*	1.6	3.3
157 CH OF BRETHREN	2	344	400*	1.6	3.3
165 CH OF NAZARENE	1	153	337	1.3	2.8
193 EPISCOPAL.....	5	1 631	2 520	9.8	20.8
226 FRIENDS-USA...	1	106	123*	0.5	1.0
281 LUTH CH AMER..	2	426	533	2.1	4.4
283 LUTH--MO SYNOD	1	152	203	0.8	1.7
419 SO BAPT CONV..	2	374	435*	1.7	3.6
435 UNITARIAN-UNIV	1	18	21*	0.1	0.2
449 UN METHODIST..	29	3 963	4 613*	18.0	38.0
453 UN PRES CH USA	1	264	307*	1.2	2.5
WASHINGTON	161	38 292	54 784*	48.4	100.0
019 AMER BAPT USA.	1	125	149*	0.1	0.3
053 ASSEMB OF GOD.	6	710	1 270	1.1	2.3
071 BRETHREN (ASH)	2	513	611*	0.5	1.1
075 BRETHREN IN CR	2	164	264	0.2	0.5
081 CATHOLIC......	7	NA	6 913	6.1	12.6
093 CHR CH (DISC).	5	1 554	1 771	1.6	3.2
097 CHR CHS&CHS CR	2	460	548*	0.5	1.0
127 CH GOD (CLEVE)	8	793	944*	0.8	1.7
151 L-D SAINTS....	2	NA	640	0.6	1.2
157 CH OF BRETHREN	11	2 234	2 660*	2.4	4.9
165 CH OF NAZARENE	2	65	166	0.1	0.3
167 CHS OF CHRIST.	1	45	57	0.1	0.1
193 EPISCOPAL.....	7	1 653	2 119	1.9	3.9
244 GRACE BRETHREN	4	1 260	1 500*	1.3	2.7
271 REFORM JUDAISM	1	260	310*	0.3	0.6
281 LUTH CH AMER..	20	8 844	11 260	10.0	20.6
283 LUTH--MO SYNOD	2	274	362	0.3	0.7
285 MENNONITE CH..	19	1 247	1 485*	1.3	2.7
291 MISSIONARY CH.	1	20	22	–	–
353 CHR BRETHREN..	1	20	20	–	–
357 PRESB CH US...	3	308	367*	0.3	0.7
381 REF PRES-EVAN.	1	?	?	?	?
403 SALVATION ARMY	1	261	528	0.5	1.0
413 S.D.A.........	3	720	857*	0.8	1.6
419 SO BAPT CONV..	7	1 843	2 195*	1.9	4.0
435 UNITARIAN-UNIV	1	49	58*	0.1	0.1
443 UN C OF CHRIST	11	3 845	4 579*	4.0	8.4
449 UN METHODIST..	27	10 042	11 958*	10.6	21.8
453 UN PRES CH USA	3	983	1 171*	1.0	2.1
WICOMICO	88	17 653	26 365*	40.9	100.0
005 AME ZION......	2	907	1 203	1.9	4.6
053 ASSEMB OF GOD.	1	73	113	0.2	0.4
081 CATHOLIC......	3	NA	3 480	5.4	13.2
097 CHR CHS&CHS CR	3	355	423*	0.7	1.6
123 CH GOD (ANDER)	1	7	21	–	0.1
127 CH GOD (CLEVE)	2	387	461*	0.7	1.7
151 L-D SAINTS....	1	NA	357	0.6	1.4
165 CH OF NAZARENE	1	277	599	0.9	2.3
167 CHS OF CHRIST.	1	38	57	0.1	0.2
193 EPISCOPAL.....	5	1 366	1 675	2.6	6.4
263 INT FOURSQ GOS	1	8	10*	–	–
270 CONSRV JUDAISM	1	103	123*	0.2	0.5
281 LUTH CH AMER..	1	141	170	0.3	0.6
283 LUTH--MO SYNOD	1	306	415	0.6	1.6
285 MENNONITE CH..	1	35	42*	0.1	0.2
403 SALVATION ARMY	1	113	1 095	1.7	4.2
413 S.D.A.........	2	269	320*	0.5	1.2
419 SO BAPT CONV..	6	1 709	2 035*	3.2	7.7
435 UNITARIAN-UNIV	1	20	24*	–	0.1
449 UN METHODIST..	52	11 001	13 101*	20.3	49.7
453 UN PRES CH USA	1	538	641*	1.0	2.4
WORCESTER	67	10 006	13 395*	43.4	100.0
053 ASSEMB OF GOD.	1	104	174	0.6	1.3
081 CATHOLIC......	2	NA	1 415	4.6	10.6
093 CHR CH (DISC).	1	63	95	0.3	0.7
097 CHR CHS&CHS CR	2	70	83*	0.3	0.6
127 CH GOD (CLEVE)	1	51	60*	0.2	0.4
193 EPISCOPAL.....	4	659	873	2.8	6.5
285 MENNONITE CH..	2	243	287*	0.9	2.1
413 S.D.A.........	1	52	61*	0.2	0.5
419 SO BAPT CONV..	7	2 083	2 459*	8.0	18.4
449 UN METHODIST..	39	5 745	6 783*	22.0	50.6
453 UN PRES CH USA	7	936	1 105*	3.6	8.2

MASSACHUSETTS

County and Denomination	Number of churches	Communicant, confirmed, full members	Total adherents		
			Number	Percent of total population	Percent of total adherents
THE STATE.....	2 945	516 218	3 709 251*	64.7	100.0
BARNSTABLE	92	17 912	67 470*	45.6	100.0
019 AMER BAPT USA.	5	811	949*	0.6	1.4
053 ASSEMB OF GOD.	3	258	650	0.4	1.0
057 BAPT GEN CONF.	1	149	174*	0.1	0.3
081 CATHOLIC......	17	NA	44 000	29.7	65.2
089 CHR & MISS AL.	2	64	145	0.1	0.2
123 CH GOD (ANDER)	1	30	90	0.1	0.1
151 L-D SAINTS....	2	NA	308	0.2	0.5
165 CH OF NAZARENE	1	68	97	0.1	0.1
167 CHS OF CHRIST.	1	33	42	–	0.1
175 CONGR CHR CHS.	1	567	664*	0.4	1.0
193 EPISCOPAL.....	11	4 940	7 279	4.9	10.8
208 EVAN LUTH ASSN	1	100	123	0.1	0.2
209 EVAN LUTH SYN.	1	63	82	0.1	0.1
226 FRIENDS-USA...	1	107	125*	0.1	0.2
239 SWEDENBORGIAN.	1	60	70*	–	0.1
271 REFORM JUDAISM	1	552	646*	0.4	1.0
281 LUTH CH AMER..	1	520	748	0.5	1.1
290 METRO COMM CHS	0	20	40	–	0.1
335 ORTH PRESB CH.	1	41	48*	–	0.1
403 SALVATION ARMY	1	41	82	0.1	0.1
413 S.D.A.........	1	99	116*	0.1	0.2
435 UNITARIAN-UNIV	7	687	804*	0.5	1.2
443 UN C OF CHRIST	17	5 674	6 643*	4.5	9.8
449 UN METHODIST..	14	3 028	3 545*	2.4	5.3
BERKSHIRE	133	19 910	92 587*	63.8	100.0
001 ADVENT CHR CH.	1	158	187*	0.1	0.2
005 AME ZION......	4	413	855	0.6	0.9
019 AMER BAPT USA.	11	3 198	3 785*	2.6	4.1
053 ASSEMB OF GOD.	2	474	850	0.6	0.9
081 CATHOLIC......	42	NA	66 169	45.6	71.5
151 L-D SAINTS....	1	NA	183	0.1	0.2
165 CH OF NAZARENE	2	114	192	0.1	0.2
167 CHS OF CHRIST.	1	100	127	0.1	0.1
175 CONGR CHR CHS.	6	855	1 012*	0.7	1.1
181 CONSRV CONGR..	1	107	127*	0.1	0.1
193 EPISCOPAL.....	15	3 845	5 917	4.1	6.4
203 EVAN FREE CH..	1	35	41*	–	–
270 CONSRV JUDAISM	2	394	466*	0.3	0.5
271 REFORM JUDAISM	1	350	414*	0.3	0.4
281 LUTH CH AMER..	1	915	1 252	0.9	1.4
403 SALVATION ARMY	2	120	547	0.4	0.6
413 S.D.A.........	1	140	166*	0.1	0.2
419 SO BAPT CONV..	1	44	52*	–	0.1
435 UNITARIAN-UNIV	2	156	185*	0.1	0.2
443 UN C OF CHRIST	23	5 472	6 477*	4.5	7.0
449 UN METHODIST..	12	2 929	3 467*	2.4	3.7
469 WELS..........	1	91	116	0.1	0.1
BRISTOL	252	31 805	324 979*	68.5	100.0
001 ADVENT CHR CH.	3	158	191*	–	0.1
005 AME ZION......	2	210	348	0.1	0.1
019 AMER BAPT USA.	20	4 516	5 448*	1.1	1.7
029 AMER LUTH CH..	1	264	364	0.1	0.1
053 ASSEMB OF GOD.	5	753	1 811	0.4	0.6
057 BAPT GEN CONF.	3	237	286*	0.1	0.1
081 CATHOLIC......	92	NA	281 670	59.3	86.7
089 CHR & MISS AL.	3	141	211	–	0.1
127 CH GOD (CLEVE)	1	35	42*	–	–
151 L-D SAINTS....	1	NA	298	0.1	0.1
165 CH OF NAZARENE	5	556	994	0.2	0.3
167 CHS OF CHRIST.	4	236	294	0.1	0.1
175 CONGR CHR CHS.	6	1 924	2 321*	0.5	0.7
181 CONSRV CONGR..	2	725	875*	0.2	0.3
193 EPISCOPAL.....	19	7 879	11 820	2.5	3.6
201 EVAN COV CH AM	2	489	590*	0.1	0.2
220 FREE LUTHERAN.	1	17	19	–	–
221 FREE METHODIST	1	23	141	–	–
226 FRIENDS-USA...	7	388	468*	0.1	0.1
270 CONSRV JUDAISM	3	954	1 151*	0.2	0.4
281 LUTH CH AMER..	2	894	1 325	0.3	0.4
283 LUTH--MO SYNOD	1	32	52	–	–
335 ORTH PRESB CH.	1	21	25*	–	–
353 CHR BRETHREN..	4	345	520	0.1	0.2
363 PRIMITIVE METH	3	224	270*	0.1	0.1
403 SALVATION ARMY	2	237	722	0.2	0.2
413 S.D.A.........	5	551	665*	0.1	0.2
419 SO BAPT CONV..	1	26	31*	–	–
435 UNITARIAN-UNIV	9	1 579	1 905*	0.4	0.6
443 UN C OF CHRIST	21	4 467	5 389*	1.1	1.7
449 UN METHODIST..	19	3 607	4 351*	0.9	1.3
453 UN PRES CH USA	3	317	382*	0.1	0.1

NA—Not applicable

*Total adherents estimated from known number of communicant, confirmed, full members.

—Represents a percent less than 0.1.

Percentages may not total due to rounding.

Table 4. Churches and Church Membership by County and Denomination: 1980

County and Denomination	Number of churches	Communicant, confirmed, full members	Total adherents Number	Percent of total population	Percent of total adherents
DUKES	18	1 578	4 106*	45.9	100.0
019 AMER BAPT USA.	3	238	279*	3.1	6.8
053 ASSEMB OF GOD.	1	5	5	0.1	0.1
081 CATHOLIC......	3	NA	2 000	22.4	48.7
193 EPISCOPAL.....	2	523	871	9.7	21.2
271 REFORM JUDAISM	1	118	138*	1.5	3.4
435 UNITARIAN-UNIV	1	71	83*	0.9	2.0
443 UN C OF CHRIST	1	94	110*	1.2	2.7
449 UN METHODIST..	6	529	620*	6.9	15.1
ESSEX	334	62 435	359 977*	56.8	100.0
001 ADVENT CHR CH.	2	212	253*	–	0.1
019 AMER BAPT USA.	28	5 605	6 676*	1.1	1.9
049 ARMEN AP CH AM	1	151	200	–	0.1
053 ASSEMB OF GOD.	11	962	1 899	0.3	0.5
057 BAPT GEN CONF.	1	205	244*	–	0.1
081 CATHOLIC......	83	NA	276 556	43.6	76.8
083 CHRIST CATH CH	1	13	13	–	–
089 CHR & MISS AL.	1	76	126	–	–
093 CHR CH (DISC).	3	245	355	0.1	0.1
127 CH GOD (CLEVE)	3	159	189*	–	0.1
151 L-D SAINTS....	2	NA	881	0.1	0.2
165 CH OF NAZARENE	5	446	980	0.2	0.3
167 CHS OF CHRIST.	3	119	188	–	0.1
175 CONGR CHR CHS.	1	300	357*	0.1	0.1
181 CONSRV CONGR..	4	622	741*	0.1	0.2
193 EPISCOPAL.....	29	15 783	23 356	3.7	6.5
201 EVAN COV CH AM	1	245	292*	–	0.1
208 EVAN LUTH ASSN	1	235	285	–	0.1
221 FREE METHODIST	3	161	411	0.1	0.1
226 FRIENDS-USA...	3	94	112*	–	–
270 CONSRV JUDAISM	8	2 020	2 406*	0.4	0.7
271 REFORM JUDAISM	3	2 210	2 632*	0.4	0.7
281 LUTH CH AMER..	6	1 498	1 978	0.3	0.5
283 LUTH--MO SYNOD	2	435	610	0.1	0.2
290 METRO COMM CHS	0	20	40	–	–
335 ORTH PRESB CH.	1	83	99*	–	–
353 CHR BRETHREN..	4	175	165	–	–
363 PRIMITIVE METH	2	256	305*	–	0.1
403 SALVATION ARMY	5	563	2 440	0.4	0.7
413 S.D.A.........	6	316	376*	0.1	0.1
419 SO BAPT CONV..	1	116	138*	–	–
435 UNITARIAN-UNIV	16	2 627	3 129*	0.5	0.9
443 UN C OF CHRIST	54	16 371	19 500*	3.1	5.4
449 UN METHODIST..	36	9 228	10 992*	1.7	3.1
453 UN PRES CH USA	4	884	1 053*	0.2	0.3
FRANKLIN	78	8 593	27 861*	43.3	100.0
019 AMER BAPT USA.	8	940	1 121*	1.7	4.0
053 ASSEMB OF GOD.	2	142	275	0.4	1.0
057 BAPT GEN CONF.	1	104	124*	0.2	0.4
081 CATHOLIC......	14	NA	17 004	26.4	61.0
089 CHR & MISS AL.	1	236	436	0.7	1.6
193 EPISCOPAL.....	5	1 582	2 033	3.2	7.3
201 EVAN COV CH AM	1	56	67*	0.1	0.2
270 CONSRV JUDAISM	1	60	72*	0.1	0.3
281 LUTH CH AMER..	2	417	595	0.9	2.1
403 SALVATION ARMY	1	117	246	0.4	0.9
413 S.D.A.........	1	48	57*	0.1	0.2
435 UNITARIAN-UNIV	6	454	541*	0.8	1.9
443 UN C OF CHRIST	28	3 563	4 248*	6.6	15.2
449 UN METHODIST..	7	874	1 042*	1.6	3.7
HAMPDEN	226	40 309	290 716*	65.6	100.0
001 ADVENT CHR CH.	3	176	211*	–	0.1
005 AME ZION......	1	200	276	0.1	0.1
019 AMER BAPT USA.	20	6 254	7 482*	1.7	2.6
049 ARMEN AP CH AM	1	78	93	–	–
053 ASSEMB OF GOD.	6	1 026	1 891	0.4	0.7
057 BAPT GEN CONF.	1	51	61*	–	–
081 CATHOLIC......	84	NA	238 816	53.9	82.1
089 CHR & MISS AL.	1	98	185	–	0.1
101 C.M.E........	1	285	341*	0.1	0.1
123 CH GOD (ANDER)	1	9	27	–	–
127 CH GOD (CLEVE)	3	273	327*	0.1	0.1
151 L-D SAINTS....	1	NA	618	0.1	0.2
165 CH OF NAZARENE	1	126	552	0.1	0.2
167 CHS OF CHRIST.	2	123	221	–	0.1
175 CONGR CHR CHS.	2	498	596*	0.1	0.2
193 EPISCOPAL.....	13	4 528	6 341	1.4	2.2
201 EVAN COV CH AM	1	272	325*	0.1	0.1
208 EVAN LUTH ASSN	2	866	1 145	0.3	0.4
221 FREE METHODIST	1	10	39	–	–
270 CONSRV JUDAISM	3	845	1 011*	0.2	0.3
271 REFORM JUDAISM	1	928	1 110*	0.3	0.4
281 LUTH CH AMER..	3	1 049	1 317	0.3	0.5
283 LUTH--MO SYNOD	4	1 673	2 063	0.5	0.7
290 METRO COMM CHS	0	20	40	–	–
353 CHR BRETHREN..	1	25	25	–	–
403 SALVATION ARMY	3	296	960	0.2	0.3
413 S.D.A.........	3	430	514*	0.1	0.2
419 SO BAPT CONV..	1	197	236*	0.1	0.1
435 UNITARIAN-UNIV	3	392	469*	0.1	0.2
443 UN C OF CHRIST	37	14 088	16 853*	3.8	5.8
449 UN METHODIST..	18	5 014	5 998*	1.4	2.1
453 UN PRES CH USA	4	479	573*	0.1	0.2
HAMPSHIRE	73	11 236	41 008*	29.5	100.0
005 AME ZION......	1	201	289	0.2	0.7
019 AMER BAPT USA.	3	472	545*	0.4	1.3

County and Denomination	Number of churches	Communicant, confirmed, full members	Total adherents Number	Percent of total population	Percent of total adherents
029 AMER LUTH CH..	1	86	114	0.1	0.3
053 ASSEMB OF GOD.	2	113	221	0.2	0.5
081 CATHOLIC......	16	NA	27 190	19.6	66.3
151 L-D SAINTS....	1	NA	345	0.2	0.8
175 CONGR CHR CHS.	1	571	660*	0.5	1.6
193 EPISCOPAL.....	4	1 243	1 712	1.2	4.2
208 EVAN LUTH ASSN	1	175	200	0.1	0.5
226 FRIENDS-USA...	2	206	238*	0.2	0.6
270 CONSRV JUDAISM	1	115	133*	0.1	0.3
281 LUTH CH AMER..	1	286	377	0.3	0.9
283 LUTH--MO SYNOD	1	345	409	0.3	1.0
353 CHR BRETHREN..	1	20	20	–	–
413 S.D.A.........	1	32	37*	–	0.1
435 UNITARIAN-UNIV	3	250	289*	0.2	0.7
443 UN C OF CHRIST	28	5 849	6 759*	4.9	16.5
449 UN METHODIST..	5	1 272	1 470*	1.1	3.6
MIDDLESEX	585	118 204	1 017 236*	74.4	100.0
001 ADVENT CHR CH.	2	215	254*	–	–
005 AME ZION......	2	201	335	–	–
017 AMER BAPT ASSN	1	160	160	–	–
019 AMER BAPT USA.	61	15 871	18 747*	1.4	1.8
029 AMER LUTH CH..	2	161	268	–	–
049 ARMEN AP CH AM	1	250	450	–	–
053 ASSEMB OF GOD.	9	1 106	1 727	0.1	0.2
057 BAPT GEN CONF.	2	111	131*	–	–
081 CATHOLIC......	145	NA	863 634	63.2	84.9
089 CHR & MISS AL.	1	42	67	–	–
097 CHR CHS&CHS CR	11	105	124*	–	–
105 CHRISTIAN REF.	1	80	137	–	–
127 CH GOD (CLEVE)	5	76	90*	–	–
151 L-D SAINTS....	8	NA	2 448	0.2	0.2
165 CH OF NAZARENE	10	1 107	2 519	0.2	0.2
167 CHS OF CHRIST.	11	602	800	0.1	0.1
175 CONGR CHR CHS.	1	125	148*	–	–
181 CONSRV CONGR..	2	329	389*	–	–
193 EPISCOPAL.....	51	21 487	32 350	2.4	3.2
201 EVAN COV CH AM	4	516	609*	–	0.1
203 EVAN FREE CH..	3	286	338*	–	–
208 EVAN LUTH ASSN	4	733	1 059	0.1	0.1
209 EVAN LUTH SYN.	1	82	102	–	–
226 FRIENDS-USA...	3	749	885*	0.1	0.1
239 SWEDENBORGIAN.	2	120	142*	–	–
270 CONSRV JUDAISM	12	3 968	4 687*	0.3	0.5
271 REFORM JUDAISM	12	6 710	7 926*	0.6	0.8
281 LUTH CH AMER..	10	3 719	4 872	0.4	0.5
283 LUTH--MO SYNOD	2	611	887	0.1	0.1
285 MENNONITE CH..	1	43	51*	–	–
290 METRO COMM CHS	0	15	30	–	–
353 CHR BRETHREN..	4	275	495	–	–
363 PRIMITIVE METH	2	414	489*	–	–
383 REF PRES OF NA	1	32	41	–	–
403 SALVATION ARMY	7	685	2 260	0.2	0.2
413 S.D.A.........	8	1 271	1 501*	0.1	0.1
419 SO BAPT CONV..	4	1 127	1 331*	0.1	0.1
435 UNITARIAN-UNIV	39	7 477	8 832*	0.6	0.9
443 UN C OF CHRIST	82	28 275	33 398*	2.4	3.3
449 UN METHODIST..	50	17 523	20 698*	1.5	2.0
453 UN PRES CH USA	8	1 545	1 825*	0.1	0.2
NANTUCKET	9	1 623	3 825*	75.2	100.0
019 AMER BAPT USA.	1	81	93*	1.8	2.4
081 CATHOLIC......	1	NA	1 800	35.4	47.1
175 CONGR CHR CHS.	1	250	288*	5.7	7.5
193 EPISCOPAL.....	2	1 031	1 316	25.9	34.4
353 CHR BRETHREN..	2	85	125	2.5	3.3
435 UNITARIAN-UNIV	1	102	118*	2.3	3.1
449 UN METHODIST..	1	74	85*	1.7	2.2
NORFOLK	250	55 270	374 511*	61.7	100.0
019 AMER BAPT USA.	19	4 952	5 834*	1.0	1.6
029 AMER LUTH CH..	1	103	170	–	–
053 ASSEMB OF GOD.	4	449	890	0.1	0.2
057 BAPT GEN CONF.	5	811	955*	0.2	0.3
081 CATHOLIC......	64	NA	304 137	50.1	81.2
089 CHR & MISS AL.	1	82	132	–	–
151 L-D SAINTS....	1	NA	432	0.1	0.1
165 CH OF NAZARENE	4	537	855	0.1	0.2
167 CHS OF CHRIST.	4	87	114	–	–
175 CONGR CHR CHS.	3	989	1 165*	0.2	0.3
181 CONSRV CONGR..	1	98	115*	–	–
193 EPISCOPAL.....	31	12 395	17 955	3.0	4.8
201 EVAN COV CH AM	1	103	121*	–	–
203 EVAN FREE CH..	1	168	198*	–	0.1
208 EVAN LUTH ASSN	2	228	312	0.1	0.1
226 FRIENDS-USA...	1	163	192*	–	0.1
270 CONSRV JUDAISM	13	2 448	2 884*	0.5	0.8
271 REFORM JUDAISM	7	4 562	5 374*	0.9	1.4
274 LAT EVAN LUTH.	1	638	747	0.1	0.2
281 LUTH CH AMER..	5	1 838	2 282	0.4	0.6
283 LUTH--MO SYNOD	4	804	1 098	0.2	0.3
349 PENT HOLINESS.	1	47	55*	–	–
353 CHR BRETHREN..	3	70	95	–	–
403 SALVATION ARMY	1	111	612	0.1	0.2
413 S.D.A.........	1	44	52*	–	–
419 SO BAPT CONV..	1	103	121*	–	–
435 UNITARIAN-UNIV	18	4 006	4 719*	0.8	1.3
443 UN C OF CHRIST	31	13 154	15 496*	2.6	4.1
449 UN METHODIST..	17	5 109	6 019*	1.0	1.6
453 UN PRES CH USA	4	1 171	1 380*	0.2	0.4
PLYMOUTH	191	31 386	213 273*	52.6	100.0

NA—Not applicable *Total adherents estimated from known number of communicant, confirmed, full members. —Represents a percent less than 0.1. Percentages may not total due to rounding.

139

Table 4. Churches and Church Membership by County and Denomination: 1980

County and Denomination	Number of churches	Communicant, confirmed, full members	Total adherents		
			Number	Percent of total population	Percent of total adherents
001 ADVENT CHR CH.	2	105	129*	–	0.1
005 AME ZION......	1	150	208	0.1	0.1
019 AMER BAPT USA.	17	3 592	4 427*	1.1	2.1
029 AMER LUTH CH..	1	114	186	–	0.1
053 ASSEMB OF GOD.	6	437	801	0.2	0.4
057 BAPT GEN CONF.	3	884	1 090*	0.3	0.5
081 CATHOLIC......	39	NA	171 807	42.4	80.6
089 CHR & MISS AL.	3	279	586	0.1	0.3
151 L-D SAINTS....	2	NA	488	0.1	0.2
165 CH OF NAZARENE	4	489	1 051	0.3	0.5
175 CONGR CHR CHS.	5	1 419	1 749*	0.4	0.8
181 CONSRV CONGR..	2	185	228*	0.1	0.1
193 EPISCOPAL.....	12	5 569	7 727	1.9	3.6
201 EVAN COV CH AM	1	217	267*	0.1	0.1
221 FREE METHODIST	1	14	21	–	–
226 FRIENDS-USA...	3	14	17*	–	–
239 SWEDENBORGIAN.	3	180	222*	0.1	0.1
263 INT FOURSQ GOS	1	32	39*	–	–
270 CONSRV JUDAISM	2	310	382*	0.1	0.2
271 REFORM JUDAISM	3	954	1 176*	0.3	0.6
281 LUTH CH AMER..	4	1 909	2 475	0.6	1.2
283 LUTH--MO SYNOD	2	424	708	0.2	0.3
403 SALVATION ARMY	2	172	311	0.1	0.1
413 S.D.A.........	2	148	182*	–	0.1
435 UNITARIAN-UNIV	17	2 109	2 599*	0.6	1.2
443 UN C OF CHRIST	29	7 360	9 072*	2.2	4.3
449 UN METHODIST..	23	4 243	5 230*	1.3	2.5
453 UN PRES CH USA	1	77	95*	–	–
SUFFOLK	254	44 824	469 080*	72.2	100.0
005 AME ZION......	7	6 159	6 955	1.1	1.5
019 AMER BAPT USA.	29	9 255	10 706*	1.6	2.3
029 AMER LUTH CH..	1	76	102	–	–
053 ASSEMB OF GOD.	7	557	909	0.1	0.2
057 BAPT GEN CONF.	2	227	263*	–	0.1
081 CATHOLIC......	88	NA	414 332	63.7	88.3
089 CHR & MISS AL.	2	137	167	–	–
123 CH GOD (ANDER)	2	173	519	0.1	0.1
127 CH GOD (CLEVE)	5	529	612*	0.1	0.1
165 CH OF NAZARENE	2	53	139	–	–
167 CHS OF CHRIST.	2	250	325	–	0.1
175 CONGR CHR CHS.	2	2 765	3 198*	0.5	0.7
181 CONSRV CONGR..	5	2 732	3 160*	0.5	0.7
193 EPISCOPAL.....	23	6 483	8 687	1.3	1.9
201 EVAN COV CH AM	1	269	311*	–	0.1
208 EVAN LUTH ASSN	1	131	143	–	–
239 SWEDENBORGIAN.	1	100	116*	–	–
247 HOLINESS CH...	1	20	23	–	–
270 CONSRV JUDAISM	2	172	199*	–	–
271 REFORM JUDAISM	1	3 280	3 794*	0.6	0.8
274 LAT EVAN LUTH.	2	442	506	0.1	0.1
281 LUTH CH AMER..	3	471	776	0.1	0.2
283 LUTH--MO SYNOD	3	578	736	0.1	0.2
287 MENN GEN CONF.	1	40	50	–	–
290 METRO COMM CHS	1	100	200	–	–
403 SALVATION ARMY	5	506	1 373	0.2	0.3
413 S.D.A.........	6	1 181	1 366*	0.2	0.3
419 SO BAPT CONV..	1	275	318*	–	0.1
435 UNITARIAN-UNIV	9	1 450	1 677*	0.3	0.4
443 UN C OF CHRIST	21	3 837	4 438*	0.7	0.9
449 UN METHODIST..	12	2 125	2 458*	0.4	0.5
453 UN PRES CH USA	6	451	522*	0.1	0.1
WORCESTER	450	71 133	422 622*	65.4	100.0
001 ADVENT CHR CH.	2	188	226*	–	0.1
005 AME ZION......	2	1 110	1 418	0.2	0.3
019 AMER BAPT USA.	31	8 050	9 657*	1.5	2.3
049 ARMEN AP CH AM	2	232	877	0.1	0.2
053 ASSEMB OF GOD.	15	1 218	2 009	0.3	0.5
057 BAPT GEN CONF.	7	951	1 141*	0.2	0.3
081 CATHOLIC......	133	NA	331 320	51.3	78.4
089 CHR & MISS AL.	1	19	29	–	–
093 CHR CH (DISC).	1	66	120	–	–
105 CHRISTIAN REF.	2	756	1 129	0.2	0.3
127 CH GOD (CLEVE)	6	216	259*	–	0.1
151 L-D SAINTS....	2	NA	617	0.1	0.1
165 CH OF NAZARENE	4	226	459	0.1	0.1
167 CHS OF CHRIST.	5	247	396	0.1	0.1
181 CONSRV CONGR..	2	257	308*	–	0.1
193 EPISCOPAL.....	32	9 559	13 696	2.1	3.2
201 EVAN COV CH AM	3	827	992*	0.2	0.2
208 EVAN LUTH ASSN	2	465	628	0.1	0.1
221 FREE METHODIST	1	7	18	–	–
226 FRIENDS-USA...	1	97	116*	–	–
270 CONSRV JUDAISM	3	503	603*	0.1	0.1
271 REFORM JUDAISM	2	2 560	3 071*	0.5	0.7
281 LUTH CH AMER..	11	5 930	7 406	1.1	1.8
283 LUTH--MO SYNOD	5	976	1 263	0.2	0.3
290 METRO COMM CHS	1	24	48	–	–
395 ROMANIAN OR CH	2	1 640	1 967*	0.3	0.5
403 SALVATION ARMY	5	539	1 500	0.2	0.4
413 S.D.A.........	13	2 771	3 324*	0.5	0.8
419 SO BAPT CONV..	5	532	638*	0.1	0.2
423 SYRIAN ANTIOCH	1	1 500	1 799*	0.3	0.4
435 UNITARIAN-UNIV	30	3 286	3 942*	0.6	0.9
443 UN C OF CHRIST	79	17 803	21 356*	3.3	5.1
449 UN METHODIST..	36	8 068	9 678*	1.5	2.3
453 UN PRES CH USA	3	510	612*	0.1	0.1

County and Denomination	Number of churches	Communicant, confirmed, full members	Total adherents		
			Number	Percent of total population	Percent of total adherents
MICHIGAN					
THE STATE.....	6 595	1 390 586	3 952 916*	42.7	100.0
ALCONA	20	1 381	2 650*	27.2	100.0
019 AMER BAPT USA.	2	170	201*	2.1	7.6
029 AMER LUTH CH..	2	267	360	3.7	13.6
081 CATHOLIC......	4	NA	789	8.1	29.8
193 EPISCOPAL.....	2	183	271	2.8	10.2
221 FREE METHODIST	1	25	114	1.2	4.3
283 LUTH--MO SYNOD	1	23	27	0.3	1.0
413 S.D.A.........	1	20	24*	0.2	0.9
449 UN METHODIST..	4	393	465*	4.8	17.5
453 UN PRES CH USA	2	185	219*	2.2	8.3
469 WELS..........	1	115	180	1.8	6.8
ALGER	16	1 436	4 742*	51.4	100.0
081 CATHOLIC......	4	NA	2 869	31.1	60.5
193 EPISCOPAL.....	1	51	81	0.9	1.7
220 FREE LUTHERAN.	1	100	150	1.6	3.2
281 LUTH CH AMER..	3	550	721	7.8	15.2
283 LUTH--MO SYNOD	1	274	359	3.9	7.6
285 MENNONITE CH..	1	21	26*	0.3	0.5
413 S.D.A.........	1	87	106*	1.1	2.2
449 UN METHODIST..	3	267	325*	3.5	6.9
453 UN PRES CH USA	1	86	105*	1.1	2.2
ALLEGAN	100	12 769	28 292*	34.7	100.0
019 AMER BAPT USA.	1	100	124*	0.2	0.4
053 ASSEMB OF GOD.	4	212	350	0.4	1.2
081 CATHOLIC......	10	NA	8 517	10.4	30.1
093 CHR CH (DISC).	1	173	292	0.4	1.0
105 CHRISTIAN REF.	17	3 274	5 478	6.7	19.4
123 CH GOD (ANDER)	3	298	894	1.1	3.2
127 CH GOD (CLEVE)	2	70	87*	0.1	0.3
151 L-D SAINTS....	1	NA	50	0.1	0.2
165 CH OF NAZARENE	1	41	19	–	0.1
167 CHS OF CHRIST.	3	100	163	0.2	0.6
175 CONGR CHR CHS.	3	784	972*	1.2	3.4
179 CONSRV BAPT...	4	76	94*	0.1	0.3
193 EPISCOPAL.....	3	336	463	0.6	1.6
221 FREE METHODIST	1	9	54	0.1	0.2
281 LUTH CH AMER..	1	151	221	0.3	0.8
371 REF CH IN AM..	10	2 362	3 817	4.7	13.5
403 SALVATION ARMY	1	99	789	1.0	2.8
413 S.D.A.........	4	383	475*	0.6	1.7
419 SO BAPT CONV..	1	27	33*	–	0.1
443 UN C OF CHRIST	2	234	290*	0.4	1.0
449 UN METHODIST..	20	2 885	3 576*	4.4	12.6
453 UN PRES CH USA	2	399	495*	0.6	1.7
469 WELS..........	5	756	1 039	1.3	3.7
ALPENA	40	8 139	24 673*	76.4	100.0
019 AMER BAPT USA.	2	349	425*	1.3	1.7
029 AMER LUTH CH..	5	2 720	3 738	11.6	15.2
053 ASSEMB OF GOD.	1	100	160	0.5	0.6
081 CATHOLIC......	6	NA	13 355	41.3	54.1
123 CH GOD (ANDER)	1	118	354	1.1	1.4
151 L-D SAINTS....	1	NA	40	0.1	0.2
165 CH OF NAZARENE	1	33	83	0.3	0.3
167 CHS OF CHRIST.	1	26	33	0.1	0.1
193 EPISCOPAL.....	2	723	997	3.1	4.0
209 EVAN LUTH SYN.	1	15	18	0.1	0.1
221 FREE METHODIST	2	86	231	0.7	0.9
271 REFORM JUDAISM	1	16	19*	–	0.1
283 LUTH--MO SYNOD	3	1 805	2 454	7.6	9.9
313 N AM BAPT CONF	1	270	328*	1.0	1.3
353 CHR BRETHREN..	3	45	50	0.2	0.2
403 SALVATION ARMY	1	135	322	1.0	1.3
413 S.D.A.........	1	83	101*	0.3	0.4
443 UN C OF CHRIST	1	470	572*	1.8	2.3
449 UN METHODIST..	5	929	1 130*	3.5	4.6
453 UN PRES CH USA	1	216	263*	0.8	1.1
ANTRIM	27	2 183	5 007*	30.9	100.0
029 AMER LUTH CH..	1	125	190	1.2	3.8
053 ASSEMB OF GOD.	1	10	54	0.3	1.1
081 CATHOLIC......	5	NA	2 035	12.6	40.6
097 CHR CHS&CHS CR	1	140	170*	1.0	3.4
165 CH OF NAZARENE	1	24	60	0.4	1.2
175 CONGR CHR CHS.	1	195	237*	1.5	4.7
193 EPISCOPAL.....	1	95	95	0.6	1.9
221 FREE METHODIST	2	23	87	0.5	1.7
283 LUTH--MO SYNOD	3	299	386	2.4	7.7
291 MISSIONARY CH.	1	113	216	1.3	4.3
371 REF CH IN AM..	1	151	251	1.5	5.0
413 S.D.A.........	1	25	30*	0.2	0.6
449 UN METHODIST..	7	777	945*	5.8	18.9
453 UN PRES CH USA	1	206	251*	1.5	5.0
ARENAC	24	1 795	7 729*	52.6	100.0
053 ASSEMB OF GOD.	1	15	50	0.3	0.6
081 CATHOLIC......	5	NA	5 183	35.2	67.1
193 EPISCOPAL.....	2	113	165	1.1	2.1
221 FREE METHODIST	3	44	270	1.8	3.5

NA— Not applicable *Total adherents estimated from known number of communicant, confirmed, full members.

—Represents a percent less than 0.1.   Percentages may not total due to rounding.

Table 4. Churches and Church Membership by County and Denomination: 1980

County and Denomination	Number of churches	Communicant, confirmed, full members	Total adherents		
			Number	Percent of total population	Percent of total adherents
283 LUTH--MO SYNOD	2	515	705	4.8	9.1
285 MENNONITE CH..	1	131	160*	1.1	2.1
443 UN C OF CHRIST	1	48	59*	0.4	0.8
449 UN METHODIST..	6	723	886*	6.0	11.5
453 UN PRES CH USA	1	47	58*	0.4	0.8
469 WELS..........	2	159	193	1.3	2.5
BARAGA	18	2 192	6 240*	73.6	100.0
045 APOSTOLIC LUTH	1	50	61*	0.7	1.0
081 CATHOLIC......	4	NA	3 430	40.4	55.0
121 CH GOD (ABR)..	1	35	43*	0.5	0.7
193 EPISCOPAL.....	1	16	20	0.2	0.3
203 EVAN FREE CH..	1	71	87*	1.0	1.4
220 FREE LUTHERAN.	1	21	28	0.3	0.4
281 LUTH CH AMER..	5	1 484	1 924	22.7	30.8
283 LUTH--MO SYNOD	1	240	310	3.7	5.0
413 S.D.A.........	1	48	59*	0.7	0.9
449 UN METHODIST..	2	227	278*	3.3	4.5
BARRY	43	5 446	10 105*	22.1	100.0
029 AMER LUTH CH..	1	263	339	0.7	3.4
053 ASSEMB OF GOD.	2	139	277	0.6	2.7
081 CATHOLIC......	4	NA	2 295	5.0	22.7
093 CHR CH (DISC).	1	76	93	0.2	0.9
097 CHR CHS&CHS CR	1	44	54*	0.1	0.5
105 CHRISTIAN REF.	1	116	190	0.4	1.9
123 CH GOD (ANDER)	1	29	87	0.2	0.9
127 CH GOD (CLEVE)	1	22	27*	0.1	0.3
133 CH GOD(7TH)DEN	1	9	11*	-	0.1
151 L-D SAINTS....	1	NA	109	0.2	1.1
157 CH OF BRETHREN	1	88	108*	0.2	1.1
165 CH OF NAZARENE	2	208	468	1.0	4.6
167 CHS OF CHRIST.	1	16	43	0.1	0.4
193 EPISCOPAL.....	2	250	413	0.9	4.1
208 EVAN LUTH ASSN	1	327	450	1.0	4.5
221 FREE METHODIST	2	60	174	0.4	1.7
244 GRACE BRETHREN	1	25	31*	0.1	0.3
371 REF CH IN AM..	1	401	786	1.7	7.8
413 S.D.A.........	2	181	223*	0.5	2.2
449 UN METHODIST..	15	2 587	3 183*	7.0	31.5
453 UN PRES CH USA	1	605	744*	1.6	7.4
BAY	84	22 805	79 972*	66.7	100.0
019 AMER BAPT USA.	3	850	1 043*	0.9	1.3
053 ASSEMB OF GOD.	2	234	338	0.3	0.4
081 CATHOLIC......	21	NA	49 716	41.5	62.2
123 CH GOD (ANDER)	3	200	600	0.5	0.8
127 CH GOD (CLEVE)	3	366	449*	0.4	0.6
151 L-D SAINTS....	1	NA	190	0.2	0.2
165 CH OF NAZARENE	2	162	349	0.3	0.4
167 CHS OF CHRIST.	2	60	88	0.1	0.1
193 EPISCOPAL.....	2	1 359	1 665	1.4	2.1
203 EVAN FREE CH..	1	167	205*	0.2	0.3
221 FREE METHODIST	1	83	381	0.3	0.5
270 CONSRV JUDAISM	1	97	119*	0.1	0.1
281 LUTH CH AMER..	2	692	984	0.8	1.2
283 LUTH--MO SYNOD	12	9 292	12 398	10.3	15.5
291 MISSIONARY CH.	1	317	185	0.2	0.2
313 N AM BAPT CONF	1	216	265*	0.2	0.3
353 CHR BRETHREN..	1	20	20	-	-
403 SALVATION ARMY	1	188	259	0.2	0.3
413 S.D.A.........	1	59	72*	0.1	0.1
419 SO BAPT CONV..	1	129	158*	0.1	0.2
443 UN C OF CHRIST	2	249	305*	0.3	0.4
449 UN METHODIST..	11	2 893	3 549*	3.0	4.4
453 UN PRES CH USA	4	2 139	2 624*	2.2	3.3
469 WELS..........	5	3 033	4 010	3.3	5.0
BENZIE	19	2 139	3 302*	29.5	100.0
029 AMER LUTH CH..	1	301	390	3.5	11.8
053 ASSEMB OF GOD.	1	15	35	0.3	1.1
081 CATHOLIC......	1	NA	649	5.8	19.7
093 CHR CH (DISC).	2	204	240	2.1	7.3
097 CHR CHS&CHS CR	1	140	169*	1.5	5.1
175 CONGR CHR CHS.	1	200	241*	2.2	7.3
181 CONSRV CONGR..	2	142	171*	1.5	5.2
193 EPISCOPAL.....	1	70	90	0.8	2.7
221 FREE METHODIST	1	4	9	0.1	0.3
283 LUTH--MO SYNOD	1	155	213	1.9	6.5
413 S.D.A.........	1	26	31*	0.3	0.9
443 UN C OF CHRIST	1	346	417*	3.7	12.6
449 UN METHODIST..	5	536	647*	5.8	19.6
BERRIEN	177	42 601	77 382*	45.2	100.0
017 AMER BAPT ASSN	4	375	375	0.2	0.5
019 AMER BAPT USA.	3	1 106	1 360*	0.8	1.8
029 AMER LUTH CH..	1	382	613	0.4	0.8
053 ASSEMB OF GOD.	6	718	1 096	0.6	1.4
057 BAPT GEN CONF.	2	363	446*	0.3	0.6
059 BAPT MISS ASSN	1	50	61*	-	0.1
081 CATHOLIC......	15	NA	21 366	12.5	27.6
093 CHR CH (DISC).	1	143	228	0.1	0.3
097 CHR CHS&CHS CR	5	1 214	1 493*	0.9	1.9
105 CHRISTIAN REF.	1	149	266	0.2	0.3
123 CH GOD (ANDER)	7	680	2 040	1.2	2.6
127 CH GOD (CLEVE)	6	442	544*	0.3	0.7
151 L-D SAINTS....	1	NA	208	0.1	0.3
164 CH UN CONF....	1	240	363	0.2	0.5
165 CH OF NAZARENE	5	297	454	0.3	0.6
167 CHS OF CHRIST.	6	505	580	0.3	0.7

County and Denomination	Number of churches	Communicant, confirmed, full members	Total adherents		
			Number	Percent of total population	Percent of total adherents
175 CONGR CHR CHS.	1	133	164*	0.1	0.2
181 CONSRV CONGR..	1	165	203*	0.1	0.3
193 EPISCOPAL.....	4	953	1 286	0.8	1.7
201 EVAN COV CH AM	1	192	236*	0.1	0.3
203 EVAN FREE CH..	1	34	42*	-	0.1
221 FREE METHODIST	4	193	789	0.5	1.0
244 GRACE BRETHREN	2	119	146*	0.1	0.2
270 CONSRV JUDAISM	1	168	207*	0.1	0.3
281 LUTH CH AMER..	4	960	1 344	0.8	1.7
283 LUTH--MO SYNOD	10	7 229	9 483	5.5	12.3
291 MISSIONARY CH.	1	76	78	-	0.1
313 N AM BAPT CONF	5	1 402	1 724*	1.0	2.2
371 REF CH IN AM..	2	180	294	0.2	0.4
403 SALVATION ARMY	2	334	522	0.3	0.7
413 S.D.A.........	13	5 753	7 074*	4.1	9.1
419 SO BAPT CONV..	7	1 107	1 361*	0.8	1.8
435 UNITARIAN-UNIV	1	38	47*	-	0.1
443 UN C OF CHRIST	14	4 361	5 363*	3.1	6.9
449 UN METHODIST..	27	6 253	7 689*	4.5	9.9
453 UN PRES CH USA	5	2 258	2 777*	1.6	3.6
469 WELS..........	6	4 029	5 060	3.0	6.5
BRANCH	40	5 129	11 419*	28.4	100.0
019 AMER BAPT USA.	2	600	735*	1.8	6.4
053 ASSEMB OF GOD.	3	75	180	0.4	1.6
071 BRETHREN (ASH)	1	23	28*	0.1	0.2
081 CATHOLIC......	3	NA	4 147	10.3	36.3
097 CHR CHS&CHS CR	2	225	276*	0.7	2.4
123 CH GOD (ANDER)	1	30	90	0.2	0.8
165 CH OF NAZARENE	1	95	196	0.5	1.7
167 CHS OF CHRIST.	1	80	135	0.3	1.2
193 EPISCOPAL.....	1	240	354	0.9	3.1
221 FREE METHODIST	2	135	624	1.6	5.5
281 LUTH CH AMER..	1	157	203	0.5	1.8
283 LUTH--MO SYNOD	3	499	624	1.6	5.5
291 MISSIONARY CH.	3	194	387	1.0	3.4
323 OLD ORD AMISH.	3	390	478*	1.2	4.2
353 CHR BRETHREN..	1	50	100	0.2	0.9
413 S.D.A.........	1	130	159*	0.4	1.4
443 UN C OF CHRIST	3	418	512*	1.3	4.5
449 UN METHODIST..	6	1 278	1 566*	3.9	13.7
453 UN PRES CH USA	2	510	625*	1.6	5.5
CALHOUN	125	24 949	49 783*	35.2	100.0
005 AME ZION......	1	435	492	0.3	1.0
019 AMER BAPT USA.	7	1 396	1 699*	1.2	3.4
053 ASSEMB OF GOD.	8	976	1 768	1.2	3.6
059 BAPT MISS ASSN	2	50	61*	-	0.1
081 CATHOLIC......	7	NA	14 940	10.6	30.0
093 CHR CH (DISC).	1	58	76	0.1	0.2
097 CHR CHS&CHS CR	4	617	751*	0.5	1.5
105 CHRISTIAN REF.	1	261	440	0.3	0.9
123 CH GOD (ANDER)	5	301	903	0.6	1.8
127 CH GOD (CLEVE)	3	212	258*	0.2	0.5
133 CH GOD(7TH)DEN	1	1	1*	-	-
151 L-D SAINTS....	3	NA	670	0.5	1.3
157 CH OF BRETHREN	1	62	75*	0.1	0.2
165 CH OF NAZARENE	5	421	955	0.7	1.9
167 CHS OF CHRIST.	5	412	524	0.4	1.1
179 CONSRV BAPT...	1	19	23*	-	-
193 EPISCOPAL.....	4	1 281	1 677	1.2	3.4
221 FREE METHODIST	2	170	591	0.4	1.2
226 FRIENDS-USA...	1	181	220*	0.2	0.4
263 INT FOURSQ GOS	1	51	62*	-	0.1
271 REFORM JUDAISM	1	86	105*	0.1	0.2
281 LUTH CH AMER..	4	539	870	0.6	1.7
283 LUTH--MO SYNOD	6	3 049	4 234	3.0	8.5
285 MENNONITE CH..	1	38	46*	-	0.1
291 MISSIONARY CH.	1	145	258	0.2	0.5
323 OLD ORD AMISH.	2	260	316*	0.2	0.6
353 CHR BRETHREN..	1	10	10	-	-
371 REF CH IN AM..	1	123	196	0.1	0.4
403 SALVATION ARMY	1	258	1 070	0.8	2.1
413 S.D.A.........	5	1 517	1 846*	1.3	3.7
415 S-D BAPTIST GC	1	242	295*	0.2	0.6
419 SO BAPT CONV..	7	1 654	2 013*	1.4	4.0
443 UN C OF CHRIST	5	2 270	2 763*	2.0	5.6
449 UN METHODIST..	19	4 760	5 793*	4.1	11.6
453 UN PRES CH USA	6	2 976	3 622*	2.6	7.3
469 WELS..........	1	118	160	0.1	0.3
CASS	44	4 496	10 416*	21.0	100.0
019 AMER BAPT USA.	2	358	440*	0.9	4.2
053 ASSEMB OF GOD.	1	23	50	0.1	0.5
059 BAPT MISS ASSN	2	117	144*	0.3	1.4
075 BRETHREN IN CR	1	43	73	0.1	0.7
081 CATHOLIC......	4	NA	3 922	7.9	37.7
093 CHR CH (DISC).	1	194	394	0.8	3.8
097 CHR CHS&CHS CR	1	300	369*	0.7	3.5
123 CH GOD (ANDER)	4	218	654	1.3	6.3
151 L-D SAINTS....	1	NA	155	0.3	1.5
165 CH OF NAZARENE	1	71	187	0.4	1.8
167 CHS OF CHRIST.	1	40	57	0.1	0.5
193 EPISCOPAL.....	1	102	188	0.4	1.8
226 FRIENDS-USA...	1	72	89*	0.2	0.9
283 LUTH--MO SYNOD	1	154	210	0.4	2.0
285 MENNONITE CH..	1	35	43*	0.1	0.4
291 MISSIONARY CH.	2	50	85	0.2	0.8
413 S.D.A.........	4	399	491*	1.0	4.7
419 SO BAPT CONV..	1	73	90*	0.2	0.9
443 UN C OF CHRIST	2	340	418*	0.8	4.0
449 UN METHODIST..	9	1 406	1 729*	3.5	16.6

NA-- Not applicable   *Total adherents estimated from known number of communicant, confirmed, full members.   --Represents a percent less than 0.1.   Percentages may not total due to rounding.

Table 4. Churches and Church Membership by County and Denomination: 1980

County and Denomination	Number of churches	Communicant, confirmed, full members	Total adherents Number	Percent of total population	Percent of total adherents
453 UN PRES CH USA	2	275	338*	0.7	3.2
469 WELS.........	1	226	290	0.6	2.8
CHARLEVOIX	36	3 546	8 433*	42.4	100.0
019 AMER BAPT USA.	1	99	121*	0.6	1.4
029 AMER LUTH CH..	1	92	113	0.6	1.3
053 ASSEMB OF GOD.	2	237	360	1.8	4.3
081 CATHOLIC......	6	NA	3 145	15.8	37.3
105 CHRISTIAN REF.	3	235	390	2.0	4.6
123 CH GOD (ANDER)	1	176	528	2.7	6.3
165 CH OF NAZARENE	2	72	136	0.7	1.6
167 CHS OF CHRIST.	1	40	51	0.3	0.6
193 EPISCOPAL.....	1	154	208	1.0	2.5
209 EVAN LUTH SYN.	1	47	62	0.3	0.7
221 FREE METHODIST	1	46	183	0.9	2.2
283 LUTH--MO SYNOD	2	452	569	2.9	6.7
291 MISSIONARY CH.	1	85	269	1.4	3.2
371 REF CH IN AM..	1	160	282	1.4	3.3
413 S.D.A.........	1	67	82*	0.4	1.0
443 UN C OF CHRIST	1	371	453*	2.3	5.4
449 UN METHODIST..	8	774	945*	4.7	11.2
453 UN PRES CH USA	2	439	536*	2.7	6.4
CHEBOYGAN	27	2 635	8 456*	41.0	100.0
029 AMER LUTH CH..	1	608	886	4.3	10.5
053 ASSEMB OF GOD.	1	106	300	1.5	3.5
081 CATHOLIC......	6	NA	4 525	21.9	53.5
093 CHR CH (DISC).	1	153	186	0.9	2.2
151 L-D SAINTS....	1	NA	44	0.2	0.5
167 CHS OF CHRIST.	1	25	32	0.2	0.4
193 EPISCOPAL.....	2	282	466	2.3	5.5
201 EVAN COV CH AM	1	89	109*	0.5	1.3
221 FREE METHODIST	1	43	213	1.0	2.5
283 LUTH--MO SYNOD	1	213	311	1.5	3.7
403 SALVATION ARMY	1	74	110	0.5	1.3
413 S.D.A.........	1	25	31*	0.2	0.4
443 UN C OF CHRIST	3	211	258*	1.2	3.1
449 UN METHODIST..	3	620	759*	3.7	9.0
453 UN PRES CH USA	2	125	153*	0.7	1.8
469 WELS.........	1	61	73	0.4	0.9
CHIPPEWA	49	4 846	12 458*	42.9	100.0
019 AMER BAPT USA.	1	191	230*	0.8	1.8
053 ASSEMB OF GOD.	1	18	29	0.1	0.2
081 CATHOLIC......	14	NA	5 998	20.7	48.1
097 CHR CHS&CHS CR	1	350	421*	1.5	3.4
105 CHRISTIAN REF.	1	108	242	0.8	1.9
151 L-D SAINTS....	1	NA	72	0.2	0.6
165 CH OF NAZARENE	2	102	126	0.4	1.0
167 CHS OF CHRIST.	1	30	38	0.1	0.3
193 EPISCOPAL.....	3	416	543	1.9	4.4
221 FREE METHODIST	1	39	180	0.6	1.4
281 LUTH CH AMER..	2	620	768	2.6	6.2
285 MENNONITE CH..	1	32	38*	0.1	0.3
353 CHR BRETHREN..	1	15	30	0.1	0.2
403 SALVATION ARMY	1	97	312	1.1	2.5
413 S.D.A.........	1	34	41*	0.1	0.3
419 SO BAPT CONV..	2	556	669*	2.3	5.4
435 UNITARIAN-UNIV	1	15	18*	0.1	0.1
443 UN C OF CHRIST	1	52	63*	0.2	0.5
449 UN METHODIST..	4	767	923*	3.2	7.4
453 UN PRES CH USA	8	1 221	1 469*	5.1	11.8
469 WELS.........	1	183	248	0.9	2.0
CLARE	26	3 001	6 385*	26.8	100.0
053 ASSEMB OF GOD.	2	175	380	1.6	6.0
081 CATHOLIC......	2	NA	2 200	9.2	34.5
097 CHR CHS&CHS CR	2	435	527*	2.2	8.3
123 CH GOD (ANDER)	1	32	96	0.4	1.5
143 CG IN CR(MENN)	1	16	16	0.1	0.3
151 L-D SAINTS....	1	NA	98	0.4	1.5
165 CH OF NAZARENE	2	90	234	1.0	3.7
167 CHS OF CHRIST.	2	93	139	0.6	2.2
203 EVAN FREE CH..	1	42	51*	0.2	0.8
283 LUTH--MO SYNOD	2	244	318	1.3	5.0
291 MISSIONARY CH.	1	19	44	0.2	0.7
413 S.D.A.........	1	34	41*	0.2	0.6
419 SO BAPT CONV..	1	38	46*	0.2	0.7
443 UN C OF CHRIST	2	638	772*	3.2	12.1
449 UN METHODIST..	2	777	941*	4.0	14.7
469 WELS.........	3	368	482	2.0	7.5
CLINTON	46	6 899	21 284*	38.1	100.0
019 AMER BAPT USA.	3	297	373*	0.7	1.8
053 ASSEMB OF GOD.	1	73	175	0.3	0.8
081 CATHOLIC......	5	NA	11 615	20.8	54.6
097 CHR CHS&CHS CR	3	837	1 050*	1.9	4.9
123 CH GOD (ANDER)	1	109	327	0.6	1.5
127 CH GOD (CLEVE)	1	17	21*	-	0.1
165 CH OF NAZARENE	1	97	316	0.6	1.5
175 CONGR CHR CHS.	1	573	719*	1.3	3.4
181 CONSRV CONGR..	1	114	143*	0.3	0.7
193 EPISCOPAL.....	2	221	306	0.5	1.4
221 FREE METHODIST	2	80	441	0.8	2.1
263 INT FOURSQ GOS	1	22	28*	0.1	0.1
283 LUTH--MO SYNOD	4	1 298	1 805	3.2	8.5
285 MENNONITE CH..	1	157	197*	0.4	0.9
413 S.D.A.........	1	77	97*	0.2	0.5
419 SO BAPT CONV..	1	57	71*	0.1	0.3
443 UN C OF CHRIST	1	298	374*	0.7	1.8

County and Denomination	Number of churches	Communicant, confirmed, full members	Total adherents Number	Percent of total population	Percent of total adherents
449 UN METHODIST..	16	2 572	3 226*	5.8	15.2
CRAWFORD	11	1 306	3 166*	33.4	100.0
019 AMER BAPT USA.	1	25	30*	0.3	0.9
053 ASSEMB OF GOD.	1	88	156	1.6	4.9
081 CATHOLIC......	1	NA	1 182	12.5	37.3
123 CH GOD (ANDER)	1	18	54	0.6	1.7
167 CHS OF CHRIST.	1	16	20	0.2	0.6
193 EPISCOPAL.....	1	67	130	1.4	4.1
221 FREE METHODIST	1	44	258	2.7	8.1
281 LUTH CH AMER..	1	121	150	1.6	4.7
283 LUTH--MO SYNOD	1	372	502	5.3	15.9
290 METRO COMM CHS	0	10	20	0.2	0.6
413 S.D.A.........	1	37	45*	0.5	1.4
449 UN METHODIST..	1	508	619*	6.5	19.6
DELTA	61	7 190	27 253*	70.0	100.0
029 AMER LUTH CH..	1	437	583	1.5	2.1
053 ASSEMB OF GOD.	1	60	121	0.3	0.4
057 BAPT GEN CONF.	2	373	458*	1.2	1.7
059 BAPT MISS ASSN	1	9	11*	-	-
081 CATHOLIC......	15	NA	17 620	45.2	64.7
097 CHR CHS&CHS CR	1	75	92*	0.2	0.3
127 CH GOD (CLEVE)	1	35	43*	0.1	0.2
151 L-D SAINTS....	1	NA	?	?	?
167 CHS OF CHRIST.	1	22	35	0.1	0.1
175 CONGR CHR CHS.	1	153	188*	0.5	0.7
185 CUMBER PRESB..	1	41	169	0.4	0.6
193 EPISCOPAL.....	3	308	509	1.3	1.9
201 EVAN COV CH AM	2	126	155*	0.4	0.6
203 EVAN FREE CH..	1	70	86*	0.2	0.3
221 FREE METHODIST	1	8	84	0.2	0.3
281 LUTH CH AMER..	9	2 811	3 665	9.4	13.4
285 MENNONITE CH..	1	18	22*	0.1	0.1
353 CHR BRETHREN..	1	25	80	0.2	0.3
403 SALVATION ARMY	1	154	240	0.6	0.9
413 S.D.A.........	2	113	139*	0.4	0.5
419 SO BAPT CONV..	1	63	77*	0.2	0.3
435 UNITARIAN-UNIV	1	16	20*	0.1	0.1
443 UN C OF CHRIST	3	76	93*	0.2	0.3
449 UN METHODIST..	4	1 203	1 477*	3.8	5.4
453 UN PRES CH USA	1	436	535*	1.4	2.0
469 WELS.........	4	558	751	1.9	2.8
DICKINSON	35	5 669	17 704*	69.9	100.0
053 ASSEMB OF GOD.	1	65	160	0.6	0.9
057 BAPT GEN CONF.	3	516	619*	2.4	3.5
081 CATHOLIC......	10	NA	10 421	41.1	58.9
097 CHR CHS&CHS CR	1	60	72*	0.3	0.4
193 EPISCOPAL.....	2	193	402	1.6	2.3
201 EVAN COV CH AM	3	429	515*	2.0	2.9
211 EVAN MENN BR..	1	45	59	0.2	0.3
281 LUTH CH AMER..	5	2 166	2 781	11.0	15.7
283 LUTH--MO SYNOD	1	241	311	1.2	1.8
413 S.D.A.........	1	24	29*	0.1	0.2
449 UN METHODIST..	4	1 211	1 453*	5.7	8.2
453 UN PRES CH USA	2	619	742*	2.9	4.2
469 WELS.........	1	100	140	0.6	0.8
EATON	72	10 731	20 429*	23.1	100.0
019 AMER BAPT USA.	2	804	993*	1.1	4.9
029 AMER LUTH CH..	2	677	899	1.0	4.4
053 ASSEMB OF GOD.	6	390	713	0.8	3.5
081 CATHOLIC......	4	NA	5 312	6.0	26.0
097 CHR CHS&CHS CR	2	70	86*	0.1	0.4
105 CHRISTIAN REF.	1	46	95	0.1	0.5
123 CH GOD (ANDER)	1	113	339	0.4	1.7
127 CH GOD (CLEVE)	2	161	199*	0.2	1.0
151 L-D SAINTS....	1	NA	193	0.2	0.9
157 CH OF BRETHREN	1	56	69*	0.1	0.3
165 CH OF NAZARENE	5	635	1 117	1.3	5.5
167 CHS OF CHRIST.	2	90	161	0.2	0.8
175 CONGR CHR CHS.	2	520	642*	0.7	3.1
179 CONSRV BAPT...	1	19	23*	-	0.1
193 EPISCOPAL.....	3	471	845	1.0	4.1
221 FREE METHODIST	2	78	354	0.4	1.7
281 LUTH CH AMER..	1	167	259	0.3	1.3
283 LUTH--MO SYNOD	3	572	859	1.0	4.2
349 PENT HOLINESS.	1	47	58*	0.1	0.3
413 S.D.A.........	4	460	568*	0.6	2.8
419 SO BAPT CONV..	2	262	324*	0.4	1.6
443 UN C OF CHRIST	4	1 165	1 439*	1.6	7.0
449 UN METHODIST..	17	3 582	4 425*	5.0	21.7
453 UN PRES CH USA	1	201	248*	0.3	1.2
469 WELS.........	2	145	209	0.2	1.0
EMMET	38	3 720	11 791*	51.3	100.0
053 ASSEMB OF GOD.	1	96	210	0.9	1.8
081 CATHOLIC......	8	NA	6 445	28.0	54.7
093 CHR CH (DISC).	1	291	513	2.2	4.4
123 CH GOD (ANDER)	1	25	75	0.3	0.6
151 L-D SAINTS....	1	NA	183	0.8	1.6
165 CH OF NAZARENE	1	96	173	0.8	1.5
167 CHS OF CHRIST.	1	14	18	0.1	0.1
193 EPISCOPAL.....	1	230	351	1.5	3.0
263 INT FOURSQ GOS	1	186	226*	1.0	1.9
271 REFORM JUDAISM	1	50	61*	0.3	0.5
281 LUTH CH AMER..	1	87	116	0.5	1.0
283 LUTH--MO SYNOD	1	395	532	2.3	4.5
285 MENNONITE CH..	3	146	177*	0.8	1.5

NA—Not applicable *Total adherents estimated from known number of communicant, confirmed, full members. —Represents a percent less than 0.1. Percentages may not total due to rounding.

Table 4. Churches and Church Membership by County and Denomination: 1980

County and Denomination	Number of churches	Communicant, confirmed, full members	Total adherents — Number	Percent of total population	Percent of total adherents
291 MISSIONARY CH.	2	120	237	1.0	2.0
353 CHR BRETHREN..	1	10	20	0.1	0.2
403 SALVATION ARMY	1	78	151	0.7	1.3
413 S.D.A.........	2	103	125*	0.5	1.1
419 SO BAPT CONV..	1	65	79*	0.3	0.7
443 UN C OF CHRIST	1	71	86*	0.4	0.7
449 UN METHODIST..	6	1 016	1 234*	5.4	10.5
453 UN PRES CH USA	2	641	779*	3.4	6.6
GENESEE	**286**	**63 921**	**156 411***	**34.7**	**100.0**
005 AME ZION......	1	539	646	0.1	0.4
019 AMER BAPT USA.	10	3 549	4 396*	1.0	2.8
029 AMER LUTH CH..	2	315	515	0.1	0.3
053 ASSEMB OF GOD.	13	1 665	2 600	0.6	1.7
059 BAPT MISS ASSN	6	1 125	1 393*	0.3	0.9
075 BRETHREN IN CR	1	43	73	-	-
081 CATHOLIC......	31	NA	66 275	14.7	42.4
089 CHR & MISS AL.	1	80	97	-	0.1
093 CHR CH (DISC).	3	921	1 173	0.3	0.7
097 CHR CHS&CHS CR	3	524	649*	0.1	0.4
105 CHRISTIAN REF.	1	59	115	-	0.1
123 CH GOD (ANDER)	9	1 350	4 050	0.9	2.6
127 CH GOD (CLEVE)	4	779	965*	0.2	0.6
151 L-D SAINTS....	3	NA	1 011	0.2	0.6
157 CH OF BRETHREN	1	40	50*	-	-
165 CH OF NAZARENE	15	2 228	3 895	0.9	2.5
167 CHS OF CHRIST.	16	3 099	3 738	0.8	2.4
179 CONSRV BAPT...	6	114	141*	-	0.1
181 CONSRV CONGR..	2	428	530*	0.1	0.3
193 EPISCOPAL.....	9	3 049	4 749	1.1	3.0
221 FREE METHODIST	13	861	3 102	0.7	2.0
270 CONSRV JUDAISM	1	193	239*	0.1	0.2
271 REFORM JUDAISM	1	504	624*	0.1	0.4
281 LUTH CH AMER..	5	1 217	1 807	0.4	1.2
283 LUTH--MO SYNOD	18	8 868	12 263	2.7	7.8
285 MENNONITE CH..	2	81	100*	-	0.1
290 METRO COMM CHS	1	22	44	-	-
291 MISSIONARY CH.	4	401	630	0.1	0.4
353 CHR BRETHREN..	2	100	125	-	0.1
371 REF CH IN AM..	2	236	447	0.1	0.3
381 REF PRES-EVAN.	1	?	?	?	?
403 SALVATION ARMY	3	572	1 400	0.3	0.9
413 S.D.A.........	5	996	1 234*	0.3	0.8
419 SO BAPT CONV..	24	6 534	8 093*	1.8	5.2
435 UNITARIAN-UNIV	1	159	197*	-	0.1
443 UN C OF CHRIST	3	1 294	1 603*	0.4	1.0
449 UN METHODIST..	43	13 321	16 500*	3.7	10.5
453 UN PRES CH USA	14	7 231	8 957*	2.0	5.7
469 WELS.........	6	1 424	1 985	0.4	1.3
GLADWIN	**24**	**2 959**	**6 670***	**33.4**	**100.0**
029 AMER LUTH CH..	1	159	236	1.2	3.5
053 ASSEMB OF GOD.	2	147	270	1.4	4.0
057 BAPT GEN CONF.	1	73	89*	0.4	1.3
075 BRETHREN IN CR	1	43	73	0.4	1.1
081 CATHOLIC......	1	NA	2 000	10.0	30.0
123 CH GOD (ANDER)	1	35	105	0.5	1.6
157 CH OF BRETHREN	1	167	203*	1.0	3.0
165 CH OF NAZARENE	2	166	319	1.6	4.8
167 CHS OF CHRIST.	1	65	100	0.5	1.5
193 EPISCOPAL.....	1	120	280	1.4	4.2
221 FREE METHODIST	2	133	642	3.2	9.6
283 LUTH--MO SYNOD	1	681	889	4.5	13.3
291 MISSIONARY CH.	1	23	59	0.3	0.9
313 N AM BAPT CONF	1	205	250*	1.3	3.7
413 S.D.A.........	2	86	105*	0.5	1.6
449 UN METHODIST..	3	685	834*	4.2	12.5
453 UN PRES CH USA	1	94	114*	0.6	1.7
469 WELS.........	1	77	102	0.5	1.5
GOGEBIC	**34**	**5 828**	**13 584***	**69.0**	**100.0**
045 APOSTOLIC LUTH	1	200	235*	1.2	1.7
053 ASSEMB OF GOD.	1	98	145	0.7	1.1
057 BAPT GEN CONF.	1	108	127*	0.6	0.9
081 CATHOLIC......	8	NA	6 283	31.9	46.3
097 CHR CHS&CHS CR	1	150	176*	0.9	1.3
165 CH OF NAZARENE	1	20	50	0.3	0.4
193 EPISCOPAL.....	1	145	175	0.9	1.3
201 EVAN COV CH AM	1	80	94*	0.5	0.7
220 FREE LUTHERAN.	1	66	83	0.4	0.6
281 LUTH CH AMER..	8	3 043	3 780	19.2	27.8
283 LUTH--MO SYNOD	4	981	1 334	6.8	9.8
413 S.D.A.........	1	63	74*	0.4	0.5
449 UN METHODIST..	2	630	741*	3.8	5.5
453 UN PRES CH USA	3	244	287*	1.5	2.1
GRAND TRAVERSE	**51**	**8 441**	**24 303***	**44.3**	**100.0**
019 AMER BAPT USA.	1	153	187*	0.3	0.8
029 AMER LUTH CH..	1	39	67	0.1	0.3
053 ASSEMB OF GOD.	1	50	128	0.2	0.5
081 CATHOLIC......	5	NA	12 534	22.8	51.6
093 CHR CH (DISC).	1	193	193	0.4	0.8
097 CHR CHS&CHS CR	1	50	61*	0.1	0.3
123 CH GOD (ANDER)	1	49	147	0.3	0.6
127 CH GOD (CLEVE)	1	58	71*	0.1	0.3
151 L-D SAINTS....	1	NA	263	0.5	1.1
165 CH OF NAZARENE	1	114	204	0.4	0.8
167 CHS OF CHRIST.	1	87	132	0.2	0.5
175 CONGR CHR CHS.	2	195	238*	0.4	1.0
179 CONSRV BAPT...	1	19	23*	-	0.1
193 EPISCOPAL.....	1	503	704	1.3	2.9
201 EVAN COV CH AM	1	89	109*	0.2	0.4
221 FREE METHODIST	2	35	192	0.3	0.8
226 FRIENDS-USA...	2	189	230*	0.4	0.9
263 INT FOURSQ GOS	1	15	18*	-	0.1
271 REFORM JUDAISM	1	54	66*	0.1	0.3
281 LUTH CH AMER..	1	1 099	1 680	3.1	6.9
283 LUTH--MO SYNOD	4	933	1 399	2.5	5.8
285 MENNONITE CH..	1	12	15*	-	0.1
291 MISSIONARY CH.	1	15	33	0.1	0.1
371 REF CH IN AM..	1	313	500	0.9	2.1
403 SALVATION ARMY	1	157	208	0.4	0.9
413 S.D.A.........	2	143	174*	0.3	0.7
419 SO BAPT CONV..	1	79	96*	0.2	0.4
435 UNITARIAN-UNIV	1	82	100*	0.2	0.4
443 UN C OF CHRIST	1	1 056	1 288*	2.3	5.3
449 UN METHODIST..	10	2 220	2 707*	4.9	11.1
453 UN PRES CH USA	1	440	536*	1.0	2.2
GRATIOT	**58**	**8 159**	**16 724***	**41.3**	**100.0**
019 AMER BAPT USA.	1	198	244*	0.6	1.5
053 ASSEMB OF GOD.	2	86	190	0.5	1.1
081 CATHOLIC......	6	NA	4 515	11.2	27.0
097 CHR CHS&CHS CR	6	1 143	1 408*	3.5	8.4
123 CH GOD (ANDER)	4	548	1 644	4.1	9.8
143 CG IN CR(MENN)	1	194	194	0.5	1.2
157 CH OF BRETHREN	1	131	161*	0.4	1.0
165 CH OF NAZARENE	4	349	729	1.8	4.4
193 EPISCOPAL.....	1	501	688	1.7	4.1
221 FREE METHODIST	4	115	501	1.2	3.0
263 INT FOURSQ GOS	1	19	23*	0.1	0.1
283 LUTH--MO SYNOD	2	688	926	2.3	5.5
403 SALVATION ARMY	1	93	423	1.0	2.5
413 S.D.A.........	2	205	252*	0.6	1.5
443 UN C OF CHRIST	1	140	172*	0.4	1.0
449 UN METHODIST..	14	2 381	2 932*	7.2	17.5
453 UN PRES CH USA	5	1 057	1 302*	3.2	7.8
469 WELS.........	2	311	420	1.0	2.5
HILLSDALE	**46**	**5 864**	**10 574***	**25.1**	**100.0**
019 AMER BAPT USA.	4	778	953*	2.3	9.0
053 ASSEMB OF GOD.	2	104	250	0.6	2.4
081 CATHOLIC......	1	NA	2 400	5.7	22.7
097 CHR CHS&CHS CR	2	196	240*	0.6	2.3
123 CH GOD (ANDER)	1	9	27	0.1	0.3
151 L-D SAINTS....	1	NA	172	0.4	1.6
165 CH OF NAZARENE	2	148	296	0.7	2.8
167 CHS OF CHRIST.	1	60	76	0.2	0.7
175 CONGR CHR CHS.	2	208	255*	0.6	2.4
193 EPISCOPAL.....	1	251	375	0.9	3.5
221 FREE METHODIST	1	159	573	1.4	5.4
281 LUTH CH AMER..	1	206	264	0.6	2.5
283 LUTH--MO SYNOD	1	260	325	0.8	3.1
285 MENNONITE CH..	2	92	113*	0.3	1.1
323 OLD ORD AMISH.	1	130	159*	0.4	1.5
403 SALVATION ARMY	1	152	284	0.7	2.7
413 S.D.A.........	2	109	134*	0.3	1.3
419 SO BAPT CONV..	2	197	241*	0.6	2.3
443 UN C OF CHRIST	2	300	368*	0.9	3.5
449 UN METHODIST..	13	1 821	2 231*	5.3	21.1
453 UN PRES CH USA	3	684	838*	2.0	7.9
HOUGHTON	**57**	**7 256**	**18 804***	**49.7**	**100.0**
045 APOSTOLIC LUTH	8	1 304	1 524*	4.0	8.1
053 ASSEMB OF GOD.	1	67	160	0.4	0.9
081 CATHOLIC......	15	NA	9 671	25.5	51.4
151 L-D SAINTS....	1	NA	?	?	?
167 CHS OF CHRIST.	1	34	53	0.1	0.3
193 EPISCOPAL.....	3	230	360	1.0	1.9
281 LUTH CH AMER..	9	2 853	3 754	9.9	20.0
283 LUTH--MO SYNOD	3	640	743	2.0	4.0
353 CHR BRETHREN..	1	20	20	0.1	0.1
403 SALVATION ARMY	1	66	107	0.3	0.6
413 S.D.A.........	1	54	63*	0.2	0.3
443 UN C OF CHRIST	3	413	483*	1.3	2.6
449 UN METHODIST..	7	1 165	1 362*	3.6	7.2
453 UN PRES CH USA	2	198	231*	0.6	1.2
469 WELS.........	1	212	273	0.7	1.5
HURON	**68**	**9 435**	**27 492***	**75.4**	**100.0**
019 AMER BAPT USA.	2	317	388*	1.1	1.4
029 AMER LUTH CH..	1	400	520	1.4	1.9
053 ASSEMB OF GOD.	3	130	260	0.7	0.9
081 CATHOLIC......	17	NA	14 956	41.0	54.4
151 L-D SAINTS....	1	NA	33	0.1	0.1
165 CH OF NAZARENE	2	123	173	0.5	0.6
167 CHS OF CHRIST.	1	9	11	-	-
193 EPISCOPAL.....	3	101	222	0.6	0.8
221 FREE METHODIST	2	74	612	1.7	2.2
283 LUTH--MO SYNOD	9	4 402	5 527	15.2	20.1
285 MENNONITE CH..	3	410	502*	1.4	1.8
291 MISSIONARY CH.	2	112	143	0.4	0.5
353 CHR BRETHREN..	1	10	10	-	-
413 S.D.A.........	1	28	34*	0.1	0.1
449 UN METHODIST..	12	1 883	2 305*	6.3	8.4
453 UN PRES CH USA	5	732	896*	2.5	3.3
469 WELS.........	3	704	900	2.5	3.3
INGHAM	**191**	**48 132**	**105 998***	**38.9**	**100.0**
019 AMER BAPT USA.	12	4 863	5 850*	2.1	5.5
029 AMER LUTH CH..	4	1 970	2 583	0.9	2.4

NA—Not applicable   *Total adherents estimated from known number of communicant, confirmed, full members.   —Represents a percent less than 0.1.   Percentages may not total due to rounding.

Table 4. Churches and Church Membership by County and Denomination: 1980

County and Denomination	Number of churches	Communicant, confirmed, full members	Total adherents Number	Percent of total population	Percent of total adherents
053 ASSEMB OF GOD.	8	725	1 323	0.5	1.2
057 BAPT GEN CONF.	3	302	363*	0.1	0.3
059 BAPT MISS ASSN	2	212	255*	0.1	0.2
081 CATHOLIC......	14	NA	40 665	14.9	38.4
089 CHR & MISS AL.	1	28	50	-	0.1
093 CHR CH (DISC).	1	388	480	0.2	0.5
097 CHR CHS&CHS CR	4	872	1 049*	0.4	1.0
105 CHRISTIAN REF.	2	525	860	0.3	0.8
123 CH GOD (ANDER)	3	470	1 410	0.5	1.3
127 CH GOD (CLEVE)	7	467	562*	0.2	0.5
151 L-D SAINTS....	4	NA	1 518	0.6	1.4
157 CH OF BRETHREN	1	87	105*	-	0.1
165 CH OF NAZARENE	13	1 225	2 467	0.9	2.3
167 CHS OF CHRIST.	7	535	807	0.3	0.8
175 CONGR CHR CHS.	1	1 278	1 537*	0.6	1.5
179 CONSRV BAPT...	2	38	46*	-	-
193 EPISCOPAL.....	5	2 743	3 509	1.3	3.3
201 EVAN COV CH AM	1	130	156*	0.1	0.1
215 EVAN METH CH..	1	62	75*	-	0.1
221 FREE METHODIST	6	434	1 986	0.7	1.9
226 FRIENDS-USA...	1	27	32*	-	-
244 GRACE BRETHREN	1	36	43*	-	-
270 CONSRV JUDAISM	2	115	138*	0.1	0.1
271 REFORM JUDAISM	1	660	794*	0.3	0.7
274 LAT EVAN LUTH.	1	74	96	-	0.1
281 LUTH CH AMER..	4	1 150	1 502	0.6	1.4
283 LUTH--MO SYNOD	6	3 455	4 930	1.8	4.7
285 MENNONITE CH..	1	35	42*	-	-
287 MENN GEN CONF.	1	40	40	-	-
290 METRO COMM CHS	0	20	40	-	-
291 MISSIONARY CH.	1	34	81	-	0.1
313 N AM BAPT CONF	1	372	448*	0.2	0.4
353 CHR BRETHREN..	2	60	70	-	0.1
371 REF CH IN AM..	2	386	814	0.3	0.8
403 SALVATION ARMY	2	223	227	0.1	0.2
413 S.D.A.........	7	1 060	1 275*	0.5	1.2
419 SO BAPT CONV..	4	1 309	1 575*	0.6	1.5
435 UNITARIAN-UNIV	1	236	284*	0.1	0.3
443 UN C OF CHRIST	7	4 499	5 412*	2.0	5.1
449 UN METHODIST..	31	10 173	12 239*	4.5	11.5
453 UN PRES CH USA	10	4 811	5 788*	2.1	5.5
469 WELS.........	3	2 003	2 472	0.9	2.3
IONIA	**60**	**5 741**	**18 608***	**35.9**	**100.0**
019 AMER BAPT USA.	3	381	472*	0.9	2.5
053 ASSEMB OF GOD.	3	116	189	0.4	1.0
081 CATHOLIC......	8	NA	10 471	20.2	56.3
093 CHR CH (DISC).	3	223	470	0.9	2.5
097 CHR CHS&CHS CR	1	45	56*	0.1	0.3
105 CHRISTIAN REF.	4	284	505	1.0	2.7
123 CH GOD (ANDER)	1	103	327	0.6	1.8
127 CH GOD (CLEVE)	2	103	128*	0.2	0.7
165 CH OF NAZARENE	4	151	301	0.6	1.6
175 CONGR CHR CHS.	1	91	113*	0.2	0.6
179 CONSRV BAPT...	1	19	24*	-	0.1
193 EPISCOPAL.....	1	114	149	0.3	0.8
221 FREE METHODIST	3	69	270	0.5	1.5
244 GRACE BRETHREN	1	115	142*	0.3	0.8
283 LUTH--MO SYNOD	2	623	888	1.7	4.8
413 S.D.A.........	2	143	177*	0.3	1.0
443 UN C OF CHRIST	3	603	747*	1.4	4.0
449 UN METHODIST..	14	2 231	2 764*	5.3	14.9
453 UN PRES CH USA	2	274	339*	0.7	1.8
469 WELS.........	1	53	76	0.1	0.4
IOSCO	**38**	**4 902**	**11 173***	**39.4**	**100.0**
019 AMER BAPT USA.	2	134	163*	0.6	1.5
053 ASSEMB OF GOD.	3	198	365	1.3	3.3
057 BAPT GEN CONF.	1	162	197*	0.7	1.8
081 CATHOLIC......	5	NA	4 700	16.6	42.1
097 CHR CHS&CHS CR	1	30	36*	0.1	0.3
127 CH GOD (CLEVE)	1	34	41*	0.1	0.4
151 L-D SAINTS....	1	NA	91	0.3	0.8
165 CH OF NAZARENE	1	47	92	0.3	0.8
167 CHS OF CHRIST.	1	68	87	0.3	0.8
179 CONSRV BAPT...	1	19	23*	0.1	0.2
193 EPISCOPAL.....	2	354	567	2.0	5.1
221 FREE METHODIST	1	13	27	0.1	0.2
281 LUTH CH AMER..	2	393	475	1.9	4.8
283 LUTH--MO SYNOD	3	891	1 126	4.0	10.1
285 MENNONITE CH..	1	10	12*	-	0.1
413 S.D.A.........	2	64	78*	0.3	0.7
419 SO BAPT CONV..	2	528	642*	2.3	5.7
449 UN METHODIST..	7	1 473	1 791*	6.3	16.0
469 WELS.........	1	484	594	2.1	5.3
IRON	**28**	**3 008**	**8 753***	**64.2**	**100.0**
053 ASSEMB OF GOD.	1	62	93	0.7	1.1
057 BAPT GEN CONF.	2	177	207*	1.5	2.4
081 CATHOLIC......	8	NA	5 014	36.8	57.3
151 L-D SAINTS....	1	NA	?	?	?
164 CH LUTH CONF.	1	85	102	0.7	1.2
193 EPISCOPAL.....	2	102	108	0.8	1.2
201 EVAN COV CH AM	1	166	194*	1.4	2.2
281 LUTH CH AMER..	4	1 436	1 820	13.3	20.8
283 LUTH--MO SYNOD	2	123	212	1.6	2.4
413 S.D.A.........	1	33	39*	0.3	0.4
449 UN METHODIST..	3	383	448*	3.3	5.1
453 UN PRES CH USA	1	385	450*	3.3	5.1
469 WELS.........	1	56	66	0.5	0.8
ISABELLA	**48**	**5 871**	**20 590***	**38.1**	**100.0**
019 AMER BAPT USA.	1	69	82*	0.2	0.4
029 AMER LUTH CH..	1	133	212	0.4	1.0
053 ASSEMB OF GOD.	1	53	154	0.3	0.7
081 CATHOLIC......	7	NA	12 278	22.7	59.6
089 CHR & MISS AL.	1	49	64	0.1	0.3
097 CHR CHS&CHS CR	3	440	522*	1.0	2.5
105 CHRISTIAN REF.	1	55	109	0.2	0.5
121 CH GOD (ABR)	1	154	183*	0.3	0.9
123 CH GOD (ANDER)	1	98	294	0.5	1.4
151 L-D SAINTS....	1	NA	296	0.5	1.4
157 CH OF BRETHREN	1	109	129*	0.2	0.6
165 CH OF NAZARENE	3	184	460	0.9	2.2
167 CHS OF CHRIST.	2	120	135	0.2	0.7
179 CONSRV BAPT...	1	19	23*	-	0.1
193 EPISCOPAL.....	1	335	550	1.0	2.7
221 FREE METHODIST	1	42	180	0.3	0.9
226 FRIENDS-USA...	1	250	297*	0.5	1.4
270 CONSRV JUDAISM	1	20	24*	-	0.1
283 LUTH--MO SYNOD	2	709	986	1.8	4.8
413 S.D.A.........	1	67	79*	0.1	0.4
435 UNITARIAN-UNIV	1	14	17*	-	0.1
449 UN METHODIST..	11	1 717	2 037*	3.8	9.9
453 UN PRES CH USA	2	1 106	1 312*	2.4	6.4
469 WELS.........	2	128	167	0.3	0.8
JACKSON	**102**	**19 432**	**51 010***	**33.7**	**100.0**
019 AMER BAPT USA.	4	909	1 107*	0.7	2.2
029 AMER LUTH CH..	1	437	633	0.4	1.2
053 ASSEMB OF GOD.	4	257	484	0.3	0.9
081 CATHOLIC......	8	NA	23 886	15.8	46.8
089 CHR & MISS AL.	1	44	75	-	0.1
097 CHR CHS&CHS CR	2	475	578*	0.4	1.1
105 CHRISTIAN REF.	1	18	122	0.1	0.2
123 CH GOD (ANDER)	4	192	576	0.4	1.1
127 CH GOD (CLEVE)	2	82	100*	0.1	0.2
151 L-D SAINTS....	1	NA	492	0.3	1.0
165 CH OF NAZARENE	4	284	679	0.4	1.3
167 CHS OF CHRIST.	4	220	293	0.2	0.6
175 CONGR CHR CHS.	1	356	433*	0.3	0.8
179 CONSRV BAPT...	5	95	116*	0.1	0.2
193 EPISCOPAL.....	5	1 899	2 417	1.6	4.7
221 FREE METHODIST	3	656	1 977	1.3	3.9
244 GRACE BRETHREN	1	70	85*	0.1	0.2
271 REFORM JUDAISM	1	174	212*	0.1	0.4
281 LUTH CH AMER..	2	707	983	0.6	1.9
283 LUTH--MO SYNOD	2	1 859	2 481	1.6	4.9
285 MENNONITE CH..	1	39	47*	-	0.1
290 METRO COMM CHS	0	50	100	0.1	0.2
291 MISSIONARY CH.	4	130	240	0.2	0.5
353 CHR BRETHREN..	1	50	50	-	0.1
403 SALVATION ARMY	1	95	239	0.2	0.5
413 S.D.A.........	2	327	398*	0.3	0.8
419 SO BAPT CONV..	5	1 524	1 855*	1.2	3.6
435 UNITARIAN-UNIV	4	130	158*	0.1	0.3
443 UN C OF CHRIST	5	935	1 138*	0.8	2.2
449 UN METHODIST..	17	4 755	5 789*	3.8	11.3
453 UN PRES CH USA	4	2 434	2 963*	2.0	5.8
469 WELS.........	2	229	304	0.2	0.6
KALAMAZOO	**157**	**35 272**	**75 220***	**35.4**	**100.0**
017 AMER BAPT ASSN	1	150	150	0.1	0.2
019 AMER BAPT USA.	5	2 182	2 622*	1.2	3.5
029 AMER LUTH CH..	3	822	1 183	0.6	1.6
053 ASSEMB OF GOD.	7	709	1 270	0.6	1.7
057 BAPT GEN CONF.	2	257	309*	0.1	0.4
059 BAPT MISS ASSN	1	188	226*	0.1	0.3
081 CATHOLIC......	14	NA	25 360	11.9	33.7
093 CHR CH (DISC).	1	256	394	0.2	0.5
097 CHR CHS&CHS CR	2	309	371*	0.2	0.5
105 CHRISTIAN REF.	18	3 914	6 278	3.0	8.3
123 CH GOD (ANDER)	4	402	1 206	0.6	1.6
127 CH GOD (CLEVE)	1	55	66*	-	0.1
151 L-D SAINTS....	2	NA	693	0.3	0.9
157 CH OF BRETHREN	1	46	55*	-	0.1
165 CH OF NAZARENE	5	531	843	0.4	1.1
167 CHS OF CHRIST.	3	262	353	0.2	0.5
175 CONGR CHR CHS.	1	95	114*	0.1	0.2
179 CONSRV BAPT...	2	38	46*	-	0.1
193 EPISCOPAL.....	5	1 583	2 222	1.0	3.0
201 EVAN COV CH AM	2	279	335*	0.2	0.4
208 EVAN LUTH ASSN	1	216	340	0.2	0.5
221 FREE METHODIST	2	257	1 116	0.5	1.5
226 FRIENDS-USA...	1	50	60*	-	0.1
263 INT FOURSQ GOS	1	?	?	?	?
270 CONSRV JUDAISM	1	152	183*	0.1	0.2
271 REFORM JUDAISM	1	106	127*	0.1	0.2
274 LAT EVAN LUTH.	2	618	683	0.3	0.9
281 LUTH CH AMER..	2	781	1 102	0.5	1.5
283 LUTH--MO SYNOD	3	2 143	2 572	1.2	3.4
290 METRO COMM CHS	0	25	50	-	0.1
291 MISSIONARY CH.	1	58	88	-	0.1
313 N AM BAPT CONF	1	18	22*	-	-
335 ORTH PRESB CH.	1	34	41*	-	0.1
369 PROT REF CHS..	1	41	62	-	0.1
371 REF CH IN AM..	18	4 967	8 039	3.8	10.7
403 SALVATION ARMY	1	215	380	0.2	0.5
413 S.D.A.........	2	482	579*	0.3	0.8
419 SO BAPT CONV..	2	574	690*	0.3	0.9
435 UNITARIAN-UNIV	1	242	291*	0.1	0.4
443 UN C OF CHRIST	7	1 630	1 958*	0.9	2.6
449 UN METHODIST..	21	7 522	9 038*	4.3	12.0
453 UN PRES CH USA	5	2 910	3 496*	1.6	4.6
469 WELS.........	2	153	207	0.1	0.3

NA— Not applicable   *Total adherents estimated from known number of communicant, confirmed, full members.   —Represents a percent less than 0.1.   Percentages may not total due to rounding.

Table 4. Churches and Church Membership by County and Denomination: 1980

County and Denomination	Number of churches	Communicant, confirmed, full members	Total adherents Number	Percent of total population	Percent of total adherents
KALKASKA	16	1 301	2 886*	26.4	100.0
019 AMER BAPT USA.	1	116	145*	1.3	5.0
053 ASSEMB OF GOD.	2	124	250	2.3	8.7
081 CATHOLIC......	2	NA	1 145	10.5	39.7
097 CHR CHS&CHS CR	3	480	602*	5.5	20.9
127 CH GOD (CLEVE)	1	14	18*	0.2	0.6
167 CHS OF CHRIST.	1	12	15	0.1	0.5
283 LUTH--MO SYNOD	1	247	325	3.0	11.3
285 MENNONITE CH..	1	36	45*	0.4	1.6
413 S.D.A.........	1	51	64*	0.6	2.2
443 UN C OF CHRIST	1	149	187*	1.7	6.5
449 UN METHODIST..	2	72	90*	0.8	3.1
KENT	346	93 900	219 727*	49.4	100.0
005 AME ZION......	1	1 500	1 875	0.4	0.9
017 AMER BAPT ASSN	1	100	100	-	-
019 AMER BAPT USA.	1	369	451*	0.1	0.2
029 AMER LUTH CH..	1	164	239	0.1	0.1
053 ASSEMB OF GOD.	8	1 374	2 264	0.5	1.0
057 BAPT GEN CONF.	3	489	598*	0.1	0.3
081 CATHOLIC......	44	NA	84 869	19.1	38.6
093 CHR CH (DISC).	2	1 362	1 475	0.3	0.7
097 CHR CHS&CHS CR	5	1 926	2 353*	0.5	1.1
105 CHRISTIAN REF.	78	25 569	40 115	9.0	18.3
121 CH GOD (ABR)..	3	332	406*	0.1	0.2
123 CH GOD (ANDER)	4	311	933	0.2	0.4
127 CH GOD (CLEVE)	5	187	228*	0.1	0.1
133 CH GOD(7TH)DEN	1	21	26*	-	-
151 L-D SAINTS....	2	NA	888	0.2	0.4
157 CH OF BRETHREN	1	120	147*	-	0.1
165 CH OF NAZARENE	6	868	1 474	0.3	0.7
167 CHS OF CHRIST.	7	500	700	0.2	0.3
175 CONGR CHR CHS.	2	1 041	1 272*	0.3	0.6
179 CONSRV BAPT...	2	38	46*	-	-
193 EPISCOPAL.....	11	3 569	4 340	1.0	2.0
201 EVAN COV CH AM	2	638	780*	0.2	0.4
203 EVAN FREE CH..	2	99	121*	-	0.1
208 EVAN LUTH ASSN	2	575	841	0.2	0.4
221 FREE METHODIST	4	262	1 149	0.3	0.5
226 FRIENDS-USA...	1	32	39*	-	-
244 GRACE BRETHREN	1	98	120*	-	0.1
270 CONSRV JUDAISM	1	168	205*	-	0.1
271 REFORM JUDAISM	1	508	621*	0.1	0.3
274 LAT EVAN LUTH.	1	590	668	0.2	0.3
281 LUTH CH AMER..	9	5 183	7 611	1.7	3.5
283 LUTH--MO SYNOD	16	5 297	7 169	1.6	3.3
285 MENNONITE CH..	2	97	119*	-	0.1
290 METRO COMM CHS	0	20	40	-	-
291 MISSIONARY CH.	2	33	66	-	-
335 ORTH PRESB CH.	2	141	172*	-	0.1
353 CHR BRETHREN..	3	325	450	0.1	0.2
369 PROT REF CHS..	4	841	1 423	0.3	0.6
371 REF CH IN AM..	36	13 734	21 761	4.9	9.9
381 REF PRES-EVAN.	1	176	260	0.1	0.1
403 SALVATION ARMY	3	537	1 094	0.2	0.5
413 S.D.A.........	5	1 180	1 442*	0.3	0.7
419 SO BAPT CONV..	4	639	781*	0.2	0.4
423 SYRIAN ANTIOCH	1	100	122*	-	0.1
435 UNITARIAN-UNIV	1	14	17*	-	-
443 UN C OF CHRIST	15	8 735	10 673*	2.4	4.9
449 UN METHODIST..	30	9 697	11 849*	2.7	5.4
453 UN PRES CH USA	8	4 161	5 084*	1.1	2.3
469 WELS..........	1	180	251	0.1	0.1
KEWEENAW	5	323	698*	35.6	100.0
081 CATHOLIC......	2	NA	312	15.9	44.7
193 EPISCOPAL.....	1	1	1	0.1	0.1
281 LUTH CH AMER..	1	256	309	15.7	44.3
449 UN METHODIST..	1	66	76*	3.9	10.9
LAKE	14	549	1 451*	18.8	100.0
081 CATHOLIC......	4	NA	763	9.9	52.6
093 CHR CH (DISC).	1	50	75	1.0	5.2
167 CHS OF CHRIST.	1	45	60	0.8	4.1
201 EVAN COV CH AM	1	40	48*	0.6	3.3
283 LUTH--MO SYNOD	1	34	52	0.7	3.6
413 S.D.A.........	3	83	99*	1.3	6.8
443 UN C OF CHRIST	1	131	156*	2.0	10.8
449 UN METHODIST..	2	166	198*	2.6	13.6
LAPEER	42	5 856	17 286*	24.7	100.0
019 AMER BAPT USA.	2	258	327*	0.5	1.9
029 AMER LUTH CH..	1	513	757	1.1	4.4
053 ASSEMB OF GOD.	3	255	480	0.7	2.8
081 CATHOLIC......	7	NA	8 888	12.7	51.4
097 CHR CHS&CHS CR	3	574	728*	1.0	4.2
105 CHRISTIAN REF.	1	279	452	0.6	2.6
127 CH GOD (CLEVE)	1	103	131*	0.2	0.8
165 CH OF NAZARENE	4	257	517	0.7	3.0
167 CHS OF CHRIST.	1	103	131	0.2	0.8
179 CONSRV BAPT...	1	19	24*	-	0.1
193 EPISCOPAL.....	2	422	599	0.9	3.5
221 FREE METHODIST	1	40	114	0.2	0.7
283 LUTH--MO SYNOD	3	1 550	2 215	3.2	12.8
285 MENNONITE CH..	1	36	46*	0.1	0.3
413 S.D.A.........	2	131	166*	0.2	1.0
443 UN C OF CHRIST	1	187	237*	0.3	1.4
449 UN METHODIST..	5	462	586*	0.8	3.4
453 UN PRES CH USA	1	448	568*	0.8	3.3
469 WELS..........	2	219	320	0.5	1.9

County and Denomination	Number of churches	Communicant, confirmed, full members	Total adherents Number	Percent of total population	Percent of total adherents
LEELANAU	34	3 592	8 397*	59.9	100.0
029 AMER LUTH CH..	2	221	259	1.8	3.1
081 CATHOLIC......	8	NA	3 994	28.5	47.6
175 CONGR CHR CHS.	1	136	164*	1.2	2.0
193 EPISCOPAL.....	1	41	41	0.3	0.5
201 EVAN COV CH AM	1	50	60*	0.4	0.7
209 EVAN LUTH SYN.	1	85	107	0.8	1.3
283 LUTH--MO SYNOD	3	461	522	3.7	6.2
371 REF CH IN AM..	1	116	254	1.8	3.0
419 SO BAPT CONV..	1	50	60*	0.4	0.7
443 UN C OF CHRIST	2	197	238*	1.7	2.8
449 UN METHODIST..	12	2 222	2 682*	19.1	31.9
453 UN PRES CH USA	1	13	16*	0.1	0.2
LENAWEE	100	17 659	36 508*	40.6	100.0
019 AMER BAPT USA.	7	1 729	2 135*	2.4	5.8
029 AMER LUTH CH..	3	1 124	1 421	1.6	3.9
053 ASSEMB OF GOD.	4	683	1 266	1.4	3.5
081 CATHOLIC......	9	NA	11 659	13.0	31.9
089 CHR & MISS AL.	1	16	35	-	0.1
093 CHR CH (DISC).	1	116	181	0.2	0.5
123 CH GOD (ANDER)	3	113	339	0.4	0.9
127 CH GOD (CLEVE)	4	246	304*	0.3	0.8
151 L-D SAINTS....	1	NA	266	0.3	0.7
157 CH OF BRETHREN	2	104	128*	0.1	0.4
165 CH OF NAZARENE	5	539	1 242	1.4	3.4
167 CHS OF CHRIST.	2	259	348	0.4	1.0
175 CONGR CHR CHS.	2	373	460*	0.5	1.3
193 EPISCOPAL.....	4	684	1 106	1.2	3.0
213 EVAN MENN INC.	1	29	36*	-	0.1
221 FREE METHODIST	2	94	414	0.5	1.1
226 FRIENDS-USA...	4	544	672*	0.7	1.8
281 LUTH CH AMER..	2	655	886	1.0	2.4
283 LUTH--MO SYNOD	5	1 889	2 563	2.8	7.0
291 MISSIONARY CH.	1	0	9	-	-
403 SALVATION ARMY	1	121	635	0.7	1.7
413 S.D.A.........	1	156	193*	0.2	0.5
419 SO BAPT CONV..	5	639	789*	0.9	2.2
443 UN C OF CHRIST	5	995	1 228*	1.4	3.4
449 UN METHODIST..	15	3 531	4 359*	4.8	11.9
453 UN PRES CH USA	6	1 446	1 785*	2.0	4.9
469 WELS..........	4	1 574	2 049	2.3	5.6
LIVINGSTON	56	10 675	32 547*	32.5	100.0
019 AMER BAPT USA.	3	506	634*	0.6	1.9
029 AMER LUTH CH..	4	1 559	2 200	2.2	6.8
053 ASSEMB OF GOD.	3	147	269	0.3	0.8
081 CATHOLIC......	6	NA	17 004	17.0	52.2
097 CHR CHS&CHS CR	1	66	83*	0.1	0.3
123 CH GOD (ANDER)	1	121	363	0.4	1.1
127 CH GOD (CLEVE)	1	?	?	?	?
151 L-D SAINTS....	1	NA	320	0.3	1.0
165 CH OF NAZARENE	3	488	843	0.8	2.6
167 CHS OF CHRIST.	2	226	439	0.4	1.3
193 EPISCOPAL.....	3	700	1 141	1.1	3.5
203 EVAN FREE CH..	1	80	100*	0.1	0.3
221 FREE METHODIST	2	122	369	0.4	1.1
281 LUTH CH AMER..	1	201	339	0.3	1.0
283 LUTH--MO SYNOD	5	1 426	2 107	2.1	6.5
403 SALVATION ARMY	1	113	156	0.2	0.5
419 SO BAPT CONV..	2	225	282*	0.3	0.9
443 UN C OF CHRIST	1	206	258*	0.3	0.8
449 UN METHODIST..	10	2 751	3 447*	3.4	10.6
453 UN PRES CH USA	4	1 561	1 956*	2.0	6.0
469 WELS..........	1	177	237	0.2	0.7
LUCE	8	854	2 014*	30.2	100.0
081 CATHOLIC......	1	NA	932	14.0	46.3
193 EPISCOPAL.....	1	58	73	1.1	3.6
281 LUTH CH AMER..	1	243	313	4.7	15.5
283 LUTH--MO SYNOD	1	171	232	3.5	11.5
413 S.D.A.........	1	23	28*	0.4	1.4
449 UN METHODIST..	2	214	260*	3.9	12.9
453 UN PRES CH USA	1	145	176*	2.6	8.7
MACKINAC	28	1 667	4 794*	47.1	100.0
053 ASSEMB OF GOD.	1	32	95	0.9	2.0
081 CATHOLIC......	7	NA	2 595	25.5	54.1
167 CHS OF CHRIST.	1	6	8	0.1	0.2
175 CONGR CHR CHS.	1	8	10*	0.1	0.2
193 EPISCOPAL.....	3	262	295	2.9	6.2
221 FREE METHODIST	1	3	6	0.1	0.1
244 GRACE BRETHREN	1	59	71*	0.7	1.5
281 LUTH CH AMER..	4	535	789	7.8	16.5
283 LUTH-+MO SYNOD	1	222	272	2.7	5.7
285 MENNONITE CH..	3	69	83*	0.8	1.7
449 UN METHODIST..	2	365	441*	4.3	9.2
453 UN PRES CH USA	2	86	104*	1.0	2.2
469 WELS..........	1	20	25	0.2	0.5
MACOMB	240	62 307	371 603*	53.5	100.0
001 ADVENT CHR CH.	1	113	137*	-	-
005 AME ZION......	1	400	448	0.1	0.1
017 AMER BAPT ASSN	1	100	100	-	-
019 AMER BAPT USA.	3	988	1 201*	0.2	0.3
029 AMER LUTH CH..	15	7 961	11 351	1.6	3.1
053 ASSEMB OF GOD.	11	1 421	2 505	0.4	0.7
057 BAPT GEN CONF.	1	77	94*	-	-
081 CATHOLIC......	53	NA	285 652	41.1	76.9

NA—Not applicable   *Total adherents estimated from known number of communicant, confirmed, full members.   —Represents a percent less than 0.1.   Percentages may not total due to rounding.

Table 4. Churches and Church Membership by County and Denomination: 1980

County and Denomination	Number of churches	Communicant, confirmed, full members	Total adherents Number	Percent of total population	Percent of total adherents
089 CHR & MISS AL.	2	59	79	–	–
097 CHR CHS&CHS CR	1	100	122*	–	–
105 CHRISTIAN REF.	1	57	81	–	–
123 CH GOD (ANDER)	3	133	399	0.1	0.1
127 CH GOD (CLEVE)	4	1 202	1 462*	0.2	0.4
149 CH OF JC (BIC)	1	59	60	–	–
151 L-D SAINTS....	3	NA	1 348	0.2	0.4
165 CH OF NAZARENE	4	508	1 057	0.2	0.3
167 CHS OF CHRIST.	12	1 812	2 395	0.3	0.6
175 CONGR CHR CHS.	1	43	52*	–	–
179 CONSRV BAPT...	2	38	46*	–	–
181 CONSRV CONGR..	3	182	221*	–	0.1
185 CUMBER PRESB..	1	38	112	–	–
193 EPISCOPAL.....	6	1 832	2 423	0.3	0.7
195 ESTONIAN ELC..	1	72	123	–	–
281 LUTH CH AMER..	7	1 814	2 622	0.4	0.7
283 LUTH--MO SYNOD	22	20 259	27 940	4.0	7.5
285 MENNONITE CH..	1	15	18*	–	–
287 MENN GEN CONF.	1	15	15	–	–
291 MISSIONARY CH.	4	348	570	0.1	0.2
313 N AM BAPT CONF	8	2 367	2 878*	0.4	0.8
353 CHR BRETHREN..	2	155	180	–	–
371 REF CH IN AM..	1	173	318	–	0.1
403 SALVATION ARMY	3	273	1 556	0.2	0.4
413 S.D.A.........	1	240	292*	–	0.1
419 SO BAPT CONV..	13	4 478	5 446*	0.8	1.5
435 UNITARIAN-UNIV	1	26	32*	–	–
443 UN C OF CHRIST	11	3 990	4 852*	0.7	1.3
449 UN METHODIST..	18	5 895	7 169*	1.0	1.9
453 UN PRES CH USA	11	4 381	5 328*	0.8	1.4
469 WELS.........	5	683	919	0.1	0.2
MANISTEE	35	6 187	15 571*	67.6	100.0
053 ASSEMB OF GOD.	1	35	70	0.3	0.4
057 BAPT GEN CONF.	1	276	331*	1.4	2.1
081 CATHOLIC......	5	NA	7 780	33.8	50.0
097 CHR CHS&CHS CR	1	40	48*	0.2	0.3
127 CH GOD (CLEVE)	1	22	26*	0.1	0.2
157 CH OF BRETHREN	3	282	338*	1.5	2.2
165 CH OF NAZARENE	1	41	72	0.3	0.5
167 CHS OF CHRIST.	1	12	19	0.1	0.1
193 EPISCOPAL.....	1	166	215	0.9	1.4
201 EVAN COV CH AM	1	59	71*	0.3	0.5
281 LUTH CH AMER..	2	1 218	1 552	6.7	10.0
283 LUTH--MO SYNOD	3	1 410	1 854	8.1	11.9
403 SALVATION ARMY	1	81	132	0.6	0.8
413 S.D.A.........	1	56	67*	0.3	0.4
443 UN C OF CHRIST	2	356	427*	1.9	2.7
449 UN METHODIST..	9	1 975	2 370*	10.3	15.2
469 WELS.........	1	158	199	0.9	1.3
MARQUETTE	85	15 092	36 012*	48.6	100.0
019 AMER BAPT USA.	1	142	173*	0.2	0.5
029 AMER LUTH CH..	1	291	387	0.5	1.1
045 APOSTOLIC LUTH	3	300	365*	0.5	1.0
053 ASSEMB OF GOD.	1	136	250	0.3	0.7
057 BAPT GEN CONF.	4	395	481*	0.6	1.3
081 CATHOLIC......	16	NA	16 113	21.7	44.7
097 CHR CHS&CHS CR	1	100	122*	0.2	0.3
121 CH GOD (ABR)..	1	20	24*	–	0.1
127 CH GOD (CLEVE)	1	64	78*	0.1	0.2
151 L-D SAINTS....	1	NA	?	?	?
164 CH LUTH CH....	1	216	314	0.4	0.9
165 CH OF NAZARENE	1	0	10	–	–
167 CHS OF CHRIST.	1	70	100	0.1	0.3
193 EPISCOPAL.....	6	854	1 135	1.5	3.2
201 EVAN COV CH AM	2	138	168*	0.2	0.5
220 FREE LUTHERAN.	1	177	244	0.3	0.7
221 FREE METHODIST	1	11	69	0.1	0.2
226 FRIENDS-USA...	1	12	15*	–	–
271 REFORM JUDAISM	1	84	102*	0.1	0.3
281 LUTH CH AMER..	14	6 554	8 812	11.9	24.5
283 LUTH--MO SYNOD	2	712	933	1.3	2.6
290 METRO COMM CHS	0	10	20	–	0.1
291 MISSIONARY CH.	1	104	181	0.2	0.5
353 CHR BRETHREN..	1	30	70	0.1	0.2
403 SALVATION ARMY	2	153	318	0.4	0.9
413 S.D.A.........	1	51	62*	0.1	0.2
419 SO BAPT CONV..	3	515	627*	0.8	1.7
449 UN METHODIST..	11	3 156	3 842*	5.2	10.7
453 UN PRES CH USA	3	684	833*	1.1	2.3
469 WELS.........	2	113	164	0.2	0.5
MASON	33	4 643	11 845*	44.9	100.0
053 ASSEMB OF GOD.	1	95	175	0.7	1.5
057 BAPT GEN CONF.	2	283	341*	1.3	2.9
081 CATHOLIC......	7	NA	5 508	20.9	46.5
151 L-D SAINTS....	1	NA	84	0.3	0.7
157 CH OF BRETHREN	1	123	148*	0.6	1.2
165 CH OF NAZARENE	1	92	182	0.7	1.5
167 CHS OF CHRIST.	2	94	134	0.5	1.1
193 EPISCOPAL.....	1	101	121	0.5	1.0
201 EVAN COV CH AM	1	72	87*	0.3	0.7
203 EVAN FREE CH..	1	115	139*	0.5	1.2
221 FREE METHODIST	1	40	84	0.3	0.7
281 LUTH CH AMER..	3	1 031	1 397	5.3	11.8
283 LUTH--MO SYNOD	2	1 006	1 356	5.1	11.4
371 REF CH IN AM..	1	117	213	0.8	1.8
403 SALVATION ARMY	1	145	274	1.0	2.3
413 S.D.A.........	1	50	60*	0.2	0.5
449 UN METHODIST..	5	1 127	1 360*	5.2	11.5
469 WELS.........	1	152	182	0.7	1.5
MECOSTA	43	4 589	10 322*	27.9	100.0
001 ADVENT CHR CH.	1	67	79*	0.2	0.8
053 ASSEMB OF GOD.	1	63	120	0.3	1.2
081 CATHOLIC......	4	NA	3 575	9.7	34.6
097 CHR CHS&CHS CR	3	325	382*	1.0	3.7
105 CHRISTIAN REF.	1	128	195	0.5	1.9
123 CH GOD (ANDER)	3	276	828	2.2	8.0
127 CH GOD (CLEVE)	1	50	59*	0.2	0.6
151 L-D SAINTS....	1	NA	95	0.3	0.9
157 CH OF BRETHREN	1	26	31*	0.1	0.3
165 CH OF NAZARENE	1	37	60	0.2	0.6
179 CONSRV BAPT...	1	19	22*	0.1	0.2
193 EPISCOPAL.....	1	212	238	0.6	2.3
221 FREE METHODIST	5	153	660	1.8	6.4
281 LUTH CH AMER..	1	369	480	1.3	4.7
283 LUTH--MO SYNOD	1	808	1 053	2.8	10.2
413 S.D.A.........	1	54	64*	0.2	0.6
435 UNITARIAN-UNIV	1	31	36*	0.1	0.3
443 UN C OF CHRIST	1	242	285*	0.8	2.8
449 UN METHODIST..	11	1 265	1 488*	4.0	14.4
453 UN PRES CH USA	1	275	323*	0.9	3.1
469 WELS.........	2	189	249	0.7	2.4
MENOMINEE	40	5 010	17 740*	67.7	100.0
029 AMER LUTH CH..	1	87	119	0.5	0.7
053 ASSEMB OF GOD.	1	37	71	0.3	0.4
057 BAPT GEN CONF.	1	119	145*	0.6	0.8
081 CATHOLIC......	11	NA	11 168	42.6	63.0
127 CH GOD (CLEVE)	1	28	34*	0.1	0.2
151 L-D SAINTS....	1	NA	111	0.4	0.6
165 CH OF NAZARENE	1	17	38	0.1	0.2
167 CHS OF CHRIST.	1	22	35	0.1	0.2
193 EPISCOPAL.....	2	143	226	0.9	1.3
201 EVAN COV CH AM	4	334	408*	1.6	2.3
203 EVAN FREE CH..	1	174	212*	0.8	1.2
281 LUTH CH AMER..	4	1 812	2 412	9.2	13.6
293 MORAV CH-NORTH	1	140	178	0.7	1.0
413 S.D.A.........	2	269	328*	1.3	1.8
449 UN METHODIST..	3	491	599*	2.3	3.4
453 UN PRES CH USA	1	519	634*	2.4	3.6
469 WELS.........	4	818	1 022	3.9	5.8
MIDLAND	67	16 381	38 042*	51.7	100.0
019 AMER BAPT USA.	1	419	520*	0.7	1.4
029 AMER LUTH CH..	1	1 079	1 523	2.1	4.0
053 ASSEMB OF GOD.	4	433	954	1.3	2.5
081 CATHOLIC......	7	NA	14 092	19.2	37.0
097 CHR CHS&CHS CR	1	115	143*	0.2	0.4
123 CH GOD (ANDER)	6	585	1 755	2.4	4.6
151 L-D SAINTS....	2	NA	488	0.7	1.3
157 CH OF BRETHREN	1	141	175*	0.2	0.5
165 CH OF NAZARENE	3	590	735	1.0	1.9
167 CHS OF CHRIST.	1	80	100	0.1	0.3
193 EPISCOPAL.....	2	810	1 227	1.7	3.2
209 EVAN LUTH SYN.	1	170	235	0.3	0.6
213 EVAN MENN INC.	1	99	123*	0.2	0.3
221 FREE METHODIST	3	147	636	0.9	1.7
270 CONSRV JUDAISM	1	36	45*	0.1	0.1
281 LUTH CH AMER..	1	148	216	0.3	0.6
283 LUTH--MO SYNOD	4	2 542	3 662	5.0	9.6
285 MENNONITE CH..	1	145	180*	0.2	0.5
291 MISSIONARY CH.	1	85	80	0.1	0.2
371 REF CH IN AM..	1	237	441	0.6	1.2
403 SALVATION ARMY	1	155	279	0.4	0.7
413 S.D.A.........	2	250	310*	0.4	0.8
419 SO BAPT CONV..	2	376	467*	0.6	1.2
435 UNITARIAN-UNIV	1	115	143*	0.2	0.4
443 UN C OF CHRIST	1	478	593*	0.8	1.6
449 UN METHODIST..	13	4 702	5 835*	7.9	15.3
453 UN PRES CH USA	3	2 331	2 893*	3.9	7.6
469 WELS.........	1	113	192	0.3	0.5
MISSAUKEE	26	2 354	4 514*	45.1	100.0
053 ASSEMB OF GOD.	1	27	40	0.4	0.9
081 CATHOLIC......	2	NA	793	7.9	17.6
105 CHRISTIAN REF.	7	1 130	1 831	18.3	40.6
165 CH OF NAZARENE	2	32	74	0.7	1.6
221 FREE METHODIST	2	31	135	1.3	3.0
281 LUTH CH AMER..	1	152	202	2.0	4.5
371 REF CH IN AM..	3	369	681	6.8	15.1
413 S.D.A.........	1	69	85*	0.9	1.9
449 UN METHODIST..	5	320	396*	4.0	8.8
453 UN PRES CH USA	2	224	277*	2.8	6.1
MONROE	99	21 107	65 680*	48.8	100.0
019 AMER BAPT USA.	5	1 352	1 689*	1.3	2.6
029 AMER LUTH CH..	8	2 465	3 461	2.6	5.3
053 ASSEMB OF GOD.	3	184	424	0.3	0.6
057 BAPT GEN CONF.	1	74	92*	0.1	0.1
081 CATHOLIC......	13	NA	37 037	27.5	56.4
089 CHR & MISS AL.	2	162	324	0.2	0.5
097 CHR CHS&CHS CR	1	30	37*	–	0.1
123 CH GOD (ANDER)	1	55	165	0.1	0.3
127 CH GOD (CLEVE)	4	1 010	1 262*	0.9	1.9
133 CH GOD(7TH)DEN	1	31	39*	–	0.1
151 L-D SAINTS....	1	NA	223	0.2	0.3
165 CH OF NAZARENE	2	277	632	0.5	1.0
167 CHS OF CHRIST.	2	125	159	0.1	0.2
181 CONSRV CONGR..	1	120	150*	0.1	0.2
193 EPISCOPAL.....	2	419	632	0.5	1.0

NA—Not applicable   *Total adherents estimated from known number of communicant, confirmed, full members.   —Represents a percent less than 0.1.   Percentages may not total due to rounding.

Table 4. Churches and Church Membership by County and Denomination: 1980

County and Denomination	Number of churches	Communicant, confirmed, full members	Total adherents		
			Number	Percent of total population	Percent of total adherents
221 FREE METHODIST	2	131	495	0.4	0.8
281 LUTH CH AMER..	2	1 185	1 563	1.2	2.4
283 LUTH--MO SYNOD	6	3 985	5 262	3.9	8.0
291 MISSIONARY CH.	1	0	20	-	-
403 SALVATION ARMY	1	119	264	0.2	0.4
413 S.D.A.........	2	97	121*	0.1	0.2
419 SO BAPT CONV.	14	3 474	4 340*	3.2	6.6
449 UN METHODIST..	17	3 636	4 543*	3.4	6.9
453 UN PRES CH USA	4	1 098	1 372*	1.0	2.1
469 WELS.........	3	1 078	1 374	1.0	2.1
MONTCALM	75	8 628	16 946*	35.6	100.0
019 AMER BAPT USA.	2	186	230*	0.5	1.4
029 AMER LUTH CH..	4	894	1 319	2.8	7.8
053 ASSEMB OF GOD.	3	86	159	0.3	0.9
081 CATHOLIC......	7	NA	4 558	9.6	26.9
093 CHR CH (DISC).	1	85	97	0.2	0.6
097 CHR CHS&CHS CR	4	799	989*	2.1	5.8
105 CHRISTIAN REF.	1	60	96	0.2	0.6
123 CH GOD (ANDER)	4	338	1 014	2.1	6.0
127 CH GOD (CLEVE)	1	31	38*	0.1	0.2
143 CG IN CR(MENN)	1	103	103	0.2	0.6
151 L-D SAINTS....	1	NA	184	0.4	1.1
157 CH OF BRETHREN	1	58	72*	0.2	0.4
165 CH OF NAZARENE	1	37	68	0.1	0.4
167 CHS OF CHRIST.	1	20	40	0.1	0.2
175 CONGR CHR CHS.	2	814	1 008*	2.1	5.9
193 EPISCOPAL.....	1	50	74	0.2	0.4
203 EVAN FREE CH..	1	70	87*	0.2	0.5
221 FREE METHODIST	4	128	540	1.1	3.2
281 LUTH CH AMER..	2	309	430	0.9	2.5
283 LUTH--MO SYNOD	5	1 011	1 449	3.0	8.6
323 OLD ORD AMISH.	1	130	161*	0.3	1.0
353 CHR BRETHREN..	1	10	10	-	0.1
413 S.D.A.........	8	700	866*	1.8	5.1
443 UN C OF CHRIST	5	738	914*	1.9	5.4
449 UN METHODIST..	13	1 971	2 440*	5.1	14.4
MONTMORENCY	17	1 748	3 787*	50.5	100.0
053 ASSEMB OF GOD.	1	89	172	2.3	4.5
075 BRETHREN IN CR	1	43	73	1.0	1.9
081 CATHOLIC......	3	NA	1 382	18.4	36.5
193 EPISCOPAL.....	2	197	286	3.8	7.6
209 EVAN LUTH SYN.	1	53	89	1.2	2.4
221 FREE METHODIST	2	45	177	2.4	4.7
283 LUTH--MO SYNOD	2	753	926	12.4	24.5
443 UN C OF CHRIST	4	429	515*	6.9	13.6
449 UN METHODIST..	1	139	167*	2.2	4.4
MUSKEGON	128	29 480	61 733*	39.2	100.0
005 AME ZION......	1	1 510	1 812	1.1	2.9
019 AMER BAPT USA.	2	733	900*	0.6	1.5
029 AMER LUTH CH..	5	1 534	2 210	1.4	3.6
053 ASSEMB OF GOD.	6	841	1 280	0.8	2.1
057 BAPT GEN CONF.	8	2 101	2 579*	1.6	4.2
081 CATHOLIC......	13	NA	20 522	13.0	33.2
089 CHR & MISS AL.	1	55	108	0.1	0.2
093 CHR CH (DISC).	1	135	179	0.1	0.3
097 CHR CHS&CHS CR	2	280	344*	0.2	0.6
105 CHRISTIAN REF.	9	2 107	3 163	2.0	5.1
123 CH GOD (ANDER)	3	292	876	0.6	1.4
127 CH GOD (CLEVE)	2	139	171*	0.1	0.3
133 CH GOD(7TH)DEN	1	14	17*	-	-
151 L-D SAINTS....	1	NA	310	0.2	0.5
157 CH OF BRETHREN	1	116	142*	0.1	0.2
165 CH OF NAZARENE	2	264	547	0.3	0.9
167 CHS OF CHRIST.	3	254	430	0.3	0.7
175 CONGR CHR CHS.	1	122	150*	0.1	0.2
181 CONSRV CONGR..	1	139	171*	0.1	0.3
185 CUMBER PRESB..	1	111	246	0.2	0.4
193 EPISCOPAL.....	4	1 292	1 593	1.0	2.6
201 EVAN COV CH AM	4	613	752*	0.5	1.2
203 EVAN FREE CH..	1	169	207*	0.1	0.3
209 EVAN LUTH SYN.	1	153	233	0.1	0.4
221 FREE METHODIST	4	142	663	0.4	1.1
271 REFORM JUDAISM	1	220	270*	0.2	0.4
281 LUTH CH AMER..	5	1 808	2 417	1.5	3.9
283 LUTH--MO SYNOD	5	2 653	3 504	2.2	5.7
290 METRO COMM CHS	0	10	20	-	-
353 CHR BRETHREN..	1	75	95	0.1	0.2
371 REF CH IN AM..	15	3 548	5 744	3.6	9.3
403 SALVATION ARMY	1	219	425	0.3	0.7
413 S.D.A.........	2	315	387*	0.2	0.6
419 SO BAPT CONV..	1	40	49*	-	0.1
435 UNITARIAN-UNIV	1	45	55*	-	0.1
443 UN C OF CHRIST	3	2 079	2 552*	1.6	4.1
449 UN METHODIST..	13	4 621	5 672*	3.6	9.2
453 UN PRES CH USA	1	463	568*	0.4	0.9
469 WELS.........	1	268	370	0.2	0.6
NEWAYGO	39	6 141	11 737*	33.6	100.0
053 ASSEMB OF GOD.	3	137	262	0.8	2.2
081 CATHOLIC......	4	NA	3 050	8.7	26.0
093 CHR CH (DISC).	1	135	310	0.9	2.6
097 CHR CHS&CHS CR	1	145	178*	0.5	1.5
105 CHRISTIAN REF.	5	1 551	2 332	6.7	19.9
127 CH GOD (CLEVE)	2	150	185*	0.5	1.6
151 L-D SAINTS....	1	NA	145	0.4	1.2
167 CHS OF CHRIST.	2	41	60	0.2	0.5
193 EPISCOPAL.....	2	174	182	0.5	1.6
283 LUTH--MO SYNOD	2	565	744	2.1	6.3
285 MENNONITE CH..	1	43	53*	0.2	0.5
353 CHR BRETHREN..	1	25	25	0.1	0.2
371 REF CH IN AM..	3	859	1 360	3.9	11.6
413 S.D.A.........	1	70	86*	0.2	0.7
415 S-D BAPTIST GC	1	50	62*	0.2	0.5
443 UN C OF CHRIST	3	931	1 146*	3.3	9.8
449 UN METHODIST..	6	1 265	1 557*	4.5	13.3
OAKLAND	441	141 862	376 968*	37.3	100.0
017 AMER BAPT ASSN	2	250	250	-	0.1
019 AMER BAPT USA.	14	5 420	6 562*	0.6	1.7
029 AMER LUTH CH..	10	3 703	5 014	0.5	1.3
039 AP CHR CH(NAZ)	1	58	70*	-	-
045 APOSTOLIC LUTH	1	300	363*	-	0.1
053 ASSEMB OF GOD.	17	1 618	3 057	0.3	0.8
057 BAPT GEN CONF.	1	186	225*	-	0.1
075 BRETHREN IN CR	1	43	73	-	-
081 CATHOLIC......	52	NA	191 474	18.9	50.8
089 CHR & MISS AL.	5	651	1 301	0.1	0.3
093 CHR CH (DISC).	4	550	1 057	0.1	0.3
097 CHR CHS&CHS CR	6	627	759*	0.1	0.2
105 CHRISTIAN REF.	2	192	332	-	0.1
123 CH GOD (ANDER)	6	869	2 607	0.3	0.7
127 CH GOD (CLEVE)	12	1 660	2 010*	0.2	0.5
151 L-D SAINTS....	7	NA	2 848	0.3	0.8
157 CH OF BRETHREN	1	136	165*	-	-
165 CH OF NAZARENE	16	1 937	3 156	0.3	0.8
167 CHS OF CHRIST.	25	3 650	4 645	0.5	1.2
175 CONGR CHR CHS.	7	3 747	4 536*	0.4	1.2
179 CONSRV BAPT...	12	228	276*	-	0.1
193 EPISCOPAL.....	23	14 319	16 553	1.6	4.4
208 EVAN LUTH ASSN	4	1 490	1 916	0.2	0.5
221 FREE METHODIST	7	814	2 556	0.3	0.7
226 FRIENDS-USA...	1	51	62*	-	-
263 INT FOURSQ GOS	2	323	391*	-	0.1
270 CONSRV JUDAISM	6	4 351	5 267*	0.5	1.4
271 REFORM JUDAISM	4	5 410	6 550*	0.6	1.7
274 LAT EVAN LUTH.	1	384	450	-	0.1
281 LUTH CH AMER..	19	6 324	8 855	0.9	2.3
283 LUTH--MO SYNOD	30	16 960	23 314	2.3	6.2
291 MISSIONARY CH.	6	468	621	0.1	0.2
313 N AM BAPT CONF	1	375	454*	-	0.1
329 OPEN BIBLE STD	2	300	325	-	0.1
353 CHR BRETHREN..	3	405	650	0.1	0.2
371 REF CH IN AM..	1	112	175	-	-
383 REF PRES OF NA	1	39	44	-	-
395 ROMANIAN OR CH	2	3 005	3 638*	0.4	1.0
403 SALVATION ARMY	3	719	1 471	0.1	0.4
413 S.D.A.........	7	1 624	1 966*	0.2	0.5
417 SOCIAL BRETH..	3	330	400*	-	0.1
419 SO BAPT CONV..	18	5 482	6 637*	0.7	1.8
423 SYRIAN ANTIOCH	1	2 000	2 421*	0.2	0.6
435 UNITARIAN-UNIV	4	952	1 153*	0.1	0.3
443 UN C OF CHRIST	8	2 917	3 531*	0.3	0.9
449 UN METHODIST..	51	25 401	30 751*	3.0	8.2
453 UN PRES CH USA	29	21 197	25 662*	2.5	6.8
469 WELS.........	2	285	375	-	0.1
OCEANA	42	4 723	8 922*	40.6	100.0
029 AMER LUTH CH..	1	185	258	1.2	2.9
053 ASSEMB OF GOD.	1	19	30	0.1	0.3
057 BAPT GEN CONF.	1	114	141*	0.6	1.6
081 CATHOLIC......	8	NA	2 739	12.4	30.7
105 CHRISTIAN REF.	3	284	436	2.0	4.9
123 CH GOD (ANDER)	1	45	135	0.6	1.5
165 CH OF NAZARENE	1	33	34	0.2	0.4
167 CHS OF CHRIST.	1	22	28	0.1	0.3
193 EPISCOPAL.....	1	82	95	0.4	1.1
201 EVAN COV CH AM	1	7	9*	-	0.1
283 LUTH--MO SYNOD	1	268	347	1.6	3.9
371 REF CH IN AM..	1	277	468	2.1	5.2
413 S.D.A.........	1	41	51*	0.2	0.6
443 UN C OF CHRIST	2	551	683*	3.1	7.7
449 UN METHODIST..	16	2 589	3 208*	14.6	36.0
453 UN PRES CH USA	1	71	88*	0.4	1.0
469 WELS.........	1	135	172	0.8	1.9
OGEMAW	21	2 195	5 852*	35.5	100.0
053 ASSEMB OF GOD.	1	12	37	0.2	0.6
081 CATHOLIC......	3	NA	2 749	16.7	47.0
151 L-D SAINTS....	1	NA	174	1.1	3.0
157 CH OF BRETHREN	1	63	76*	0.5	1.3
165 CH OF NAZARENE	2	41	113	0.7	1.9
167 CHS OF CHRIST.	1	42	60	0.4	1.0
193 EPISCOPAL.....	2	365	376	2.3	6.4
221 FREE METHODIST	1	64	237	1.4	4.0
226 FRIENDS-USA...	1	86	104*	0.6	1.8
281 LUTH CH AMER..	1	158	186	1.1	3.2
283 LUTH--MO SYNOD	2	581	781	4.8	13.3
383 REF PRES OF NA	1	15	28	0.2	0.5
413 S.D.A.........	1	36	44*	0.3	0.8
449 UN METHODIST..	3	732	887*	5.4	15.2
ONTONAGON	32	2 269	5 535*	56.1	100.0
045 APOSTOLIC LUTH	3	100	121*	1.2	2.2
053 ASSEMB OF GOD.	2	63	75	0.8	1.4
081 CATHOLIC......	7	NA	2 552	25.9	46.1
193 EPISCOPAL.....	2	68	190	1.9	3.4
220 FREE LUTHERAN.	1	37	48	0.5	0.9
281 LUTH CH AMER..	7	1 024	1 316	13.3	23.8
283 LUTH--MO SYNOD	2	355	458	4.6	8.3

NA—Not applicable   *Total adherents estimated from known number of communicant, confirmed, full members.   —Represents a percent less than 0.1.   Percentages may not total due to rounding.

Table 4. Churches and Church Membership by County and Denomination: 1980

County and Denomination	Number of churches	Communicant, confirmed, full members	Total adherents		
			Number	Percent of total population	Percent of total adherents
449 UN METHODIST..	6	442	537*	5.4	9.7
453 UN PRES CH USA	1	62	75*	0.8	1.4
469 WELS.........	1	118	163	1.7	2.9
OSCEOLA	**41**	**3 523**	**6 676***	**35.3**	**100.0**
029 AMER LUTH CH..	2	518	690	3.6	10.3
053 ASSEMB OF GOD.	2	97	180	1.0	2.7
057 BAPT GEN CONF.	1	63	78*	0.4	1.2
081 CATHOLIC......	3	NA	1 510	8.0	22.6
105 CHRISTIAN REF.	1	156	287	1.5	4.3
123 CH GOD (ANDER)	1	57	171	0.9	2.6
127 CH GOD (CLEVE)	1	26	32*	0.2	0.5
165 CH OF NAZARENE	2	124	247	1.3	3.7
181 CONSRV CONGR..	1	72	89*	0.5	1.3
201 EVAN COV CH AM	1	46	57*	0.3	0.9
221 FREE METHODIST	4	99	498	2.6	7.5
281 LUTH CH AMER..	2	224	268	1.4	4.0
283 LUTH--MO SYNOD	1	421	569	3.0	8.5
413 S.D.A.........	3	72	89*	0.5	1.3
443 UN C OF CHRIST	2	146	180*	1.0	2.7
449 UN METHODIST..	12	1 362	1 682*	8.9	25.2
453 UN PRES CH USA	1	40	49*	0.3	0.7
OSCODA	**13**	**817**	**1 752***	**25.5**	**100.0**
053 ASSEMB OF GOD.	1	27	60	0.9	3.4
081 CATHOLIC......	1	NA	572	8.3	32.6
123 CH GOD (ANDER)	1	85	255	3.7	14.6
167 CHS OF CHRIST.	2	50	64	0.9	3.7
193 EPISCOPAL.....	1	34	44	0.6	2.5
285 MENNONITE CH..	2	47	56*	0.8	3.2
287 MENN GEN CONF.	1	98	118	1.7	6.7
323 OLD ORD AMISH.	1	130	156*	2.3	8.9
413 S.D.A.........	1	95	114*	1.7	6.5
449 UN METHODIST..	1	196	235*	3.4	13.4
469 WELS.........	1	55	78	1.1	4.5
OTSEGO	**16**	**1 708**	**8 922***	**59.5**	**100.0**
053 ASSEMB OF GOD.	1	89	175	1.2	2.0
081 CATHOLIC......	2	NA	6 600	44.0	74.0
105 CHRISTIAN REF.	1	12	25	0.2	0.3
165 CH OF NAZARENE	1	20	50	0.3	0.6
167 CHS OF CHRIST.	1	50	64	0.4	0.7
193 EPISCOPAL.....	1	133	179	1.2	2.0
203 EVAN FREE CH..	1	63	78*	0.5	0.9
281 LUTH CH AMER..	1	129	189	1.3	2.1
283 LUTH--MO SYNOD	1	278	390	2.6	4.4
383 REF PRES OF NA	1	37	50	0.3	0.6
413 S.D.A.........	1	48	60*	0.4	0.7
419 SO BAPT CONV..	1	45	56*	0.4	0.6
443 UN C OF CHRIST	1	207	257*	1.7	2.9
449 UN METHODIST..	1	572	711*	4.7	8.0
469 WELS.........	1	25	38	0.3	0.4
OTTAWA	**170**	**51 983**	**99 914***	**63.6**	**100.0**
053 ASSEMB OF GOD.	4	350	595	0.4	0.6
057 BAPT GEN CONF.	1	80	99*	0.1	0.1
081 CATHOLIC......	12	NA	18 003	11.5	18.0
089 CHR & MISS AL.	1	57	87	0.1	0.1
097 CHR CHS&CHS CR	1	36	45*	-	-
105 CHRISTIAN REF.	58	18 882	30 256	19.3	30.3
127 CH GOD (CLEVE)	2	214	265*	0.2	0.3
133 CH GOD(7TH)DEN	1	20	25*	-	-
151 L-D SAINTS....	1	NA	152	0.1	0.2
165 CH OF NAZARENE	2	216	374	0.2	0.4
167 CHS OF CHRIST.	4	171	295	0.2	0.3
179 CONSRV BAPT...	1	19	24*	-	-
193 EPISCOPAL.....	2	732	1 223	0.8	1.2
208 EVAN LUTH ASSN	1	400	650	0.4	0.7
221 FREE METHODIST	1	54	165	0.1	0.2
274 LAT EVAN LUTH.	1	27	27	-	-
283 LUTH--MO SYNOD	9	3 701	5 230	3.3	5.2
349 PENT HOLINESS.	1	23	29*	-	-
353 CHR BRETHREN..	2	145	195	0.1	0.2
369 PROT REF CHS..	3	552	1 018	0.6	1.0
371 REF CH IN AM..	44	20 156	33 382	21.2	33.4
403 SALVATION ARMY	1	159	334	0.2	0.3
413 S.D.A.........	3	230	285*	0.2	0.3
419 SO BAPT CONV..	3	193	239*	0.2	0.2
443 UN C OF CHRIST	2	781	968*	0.6	1.0
449 UN METHODIST..	5	2 533	3 139*	2.0	3.1
453 UN PRES CH USA	3	2 210	2 739*	1.7	2.7
469 WELS.........	1	42	71	-	0.1
PRESQUE ISLE	**22**	**3 433**	**9 361***	**65.6**	**100.0**
029 AMER LUTH CH..	4	372	482	3.4	5.1
053 ASSEMB OF GOD.	2	45	96	0.7	1.0
081 CATHOLIC......	4	NA	4 964	34.8	53.0
193 EPISCOPAL.....	1	43	56	0.4	0.6
283 LUTH--MO SYNOD	6	1 941	2 509	17.6	26.8
413 S.D.A.........	1	111	135*	0.9	1.4
443 UN C OF CHRIST	1	61	74*	0.5	0.8
449 UN METHODIST..	2	419	509*	3.6	5.4
453 UN PRES CH USA	1	441	536*	3.8	5.7
ROSCOMMON	**22**	**1 792**	**3 931***	**24.0**	**100.0**
019 AMER BAPT USA.	2	88	103*	0.6	2.6
053 ASSEMB OF GOD.	1	76	159	1.0	4.0
081 CATHOLIC......	5	NA	1 687	10.3	42.9
165 CH OF NAZARENE	1	27	89	0.5	2.3

County and Denomination	Number of churches	Communicant, confirmed, full members	Total adherents		
			Number	Percent of total population	Percent of total adherents
167 CHS OF CHRIST.	1	33	42	0.3	1.1
175 CONGR CHR CHS.	1	297	347*	2.1	8.8
179 CONSRV BAPT...	1	19	22*	0.1	0.6
193 EPISCOPAL.....	2	204	252	1.5	6.4
220 FREE LUTHERAN.	1	25	32	0.2	0.8
221 FREE METHODIST	1	11	39	0.2	1.0
281 LUTH CH AMER..	1	153	178	1.1	4.5
283 LUTH--MO SYNOD	2	405	451	2.8	11.5
413 S.D.A.........	1	44	51*	0.3	1.3
419 SO BAPT CONV..	1	43	50*	0.3	1.3
449 UN METHODIST..	1	367	429*	2.6	10.9
SAGINAW	**166**	**47 585**	**122 409***	**53.7**	**100.0**
019 AMER BAPT USA.	5	1 583	1 966*	0.9	1.6
029 AMER LUTH CH..	10	6 159	8 296	3.6	6.8
053 ASSEMB OF GOD.	11	1 060	2 357	1.0	1.9
059 BAPT MISS ASSN	2	70	87*	-	0.1
075 BRETHREN IN CR	1	43	73	-	0.1
081 CATHOLIC......	33	NA	58 219	25.5	47.6
089 CHR & MISS AL.	1	73	145	0.1	0.1
093 CHR CH (DISC).	3	1 153	1 671	0.7	1.4
097 CHR CHS&CHS CR	1	100	124*	0.1	0.1
105 CHRISTIAN REF.	1	81	150	0.1	0.1
123 CH GOD (ANDER)	1	89	267	0.1	0.2
127 CH GOD (CLEVE)	2	137	170*	0.1	0.1
133 CH GOD(7TH)DEN	3	52	65*	-	0.1
151 L-D SAINTS....	1	NA	322	0.1	0.3
164 CH LUTH CONF..	1	186	252	0.1	0.2
165 CH OF NAZARENE	7	709	1 107	0.5	0.9
167 CHS OF CHRIST.	3	157	208	0.1	0.2
175 CONGR CHR CHS.	1	252	313*	0.1	0.3
193 EPISCOPAL.....	7	1 760	2 378	1.0	1.9
221 FREE METHODIST	2	110	405	0.2	0.3
270 CONSRV JUDAISM	1	45	56*	-	-
271 REFORM JUDAISM	1	16	20*	-	-
274 LAT EVAN LUTH.	1	201	223	0.1	0.2
281 LUTH CH AMER..	1	464	619	0.3	0.5
283 LUTH--MO SYNOD	13	14 066	18 692	8.2	15.3
285 MENNONITE CH..	2	114	142*	0.1	0.1
353 CHR BRETHREN..	1	10	10	-	-
367 PROT CONF (WI)	1	100	150	0.1	0.1
403 SALVATION ARMY	1	176	376	0.2	0.3
413 S.D.A.........	4	486	604*	0.3	0.5
419 SO BAPT CONV..	1	151	188*	0.1	0.2
431 UKRANIAN AMER.	1	100	135	0.1	0.1
435 UNITARIAN-UNIV	1	25	31*	-	-
443 UN C OF CHRIST	4	2 040	2 534*	1.1	2.1
449 UN METHODIST..	18	6 353	7 892*	3.5	6.4
453 UN PRES CH USA	7	4 040	5 019*	2.2	4.1
469 WELS.........	12	5 424	7 143	3.1	5.8
ST CLAIR	**90**	**17 258**	**63 819***	**46.0**	**100.0**
019 AMER BAPT USA.	3	700	864*	0.6	1.4
029 AMER LUTH CH..	6	1 980	2 605	1.9	4.1
053 ASSEMB OF GOD.	3	349	585	0.4	0.9
081 CATHOLIC......	15	NA	39 529	28.5	61.9
089 CHR & MISS AL.	2	70	93	0.1	0.1
097 CHR CHS&CHS CR	2	320	395*	0.3	0.6
127 CH GOD (CLEVE)	2	118	146*	0.1	0.2
165 CH OF NAZARENE	4	473	1 016	0.7	1.6
167 CHS OF CHRIST.	2	113	128	0.1	0.2
175 CONGR CHR CHS.	1	102	126*	0.1	0.2
179 CONSRV BAPT...	1	19	23*	-	-
193 EPISCOPAL.....	7	2 439	3 637	2.6	5.7
208 EVAN LUTH ASSN	2	586	711	0.5	1.1
221 FREE METHODIST	3	188	738	0.5	1.2
283 LUTH--MO SYNOD	8	3 618	5 197	3.7	8.1
291 MISSIONARY CH.	3	360	780	0.6	1.2
413 S.D.A.........	2	119	147*	0.1	0.2
443 UN C OF CHRIST	3	1 492	1 841*	1.3	2.9
449 UN METHODIST..	15	2 722	3 360*	2.4	5.3
453 UN PRES CH USA	4	1 144	1 412*	1.0	2.2
469 WELS.........	2	346	486	0.4	0.8
ST JOSEPH	**78**	**12 401**	**23 280***	**41.5**	**100.0**
019 AMER BAPT USA.	2	374	462*	0.8	2.0
053 ASSEMB OF GOD.	3	345	625	1.1	2.7
057 BAPT GEN CONF.	1	53	65*	0.1	0.3
059 BAPT MISS ASSN	2	84	104*	0.2	0.4
061 BEACHY AMISH..	1	36	44*	0.1	0.2
081 CATHOLIC......	6	NA	5 811	10.4	25.0
097 CHR CHS&CHS CR	2	276	341*	0.6	1.5
123 CH GOD (ANDER)	3	177	531	0.9	2.3
127 CH GOD (CLEVE)	1	71	88*	0.2	0.4
151 L-D SAINTS....	1	NA	146	0.3	0.6
165 CH OF NAZARENE	1	448	1 281	2.3	5.5
167 CHS OF CHRIST.	1	40	56	0.1	0.2
179 CONSRV BAPT...	1	19	23*	-	0.1
193 EPISCOPAL.....	2	565	860	1.5	3.7
197 EVAN CH OF NA.	1	50	50	0.1	0.2
281 LUTH CH AMER..	3	915	1 238	2.2	5.3
283 LUTH--MO SYNOD	6	1 697	2 306	4.1	9.9
285 MENNONITE CH..	2	182	225*	0.4	1.0
291 MISSIONARY CH.	4	191	336	0.6	1.4
323 OLD ORD AMISH.	4	520	642*	1.1	2.8
353 CHR BRETHREN..	1	125	200	0.4	0.9
403 SALVATION ARMY	1	104	237	0.4	1.0
413 S.D.A.........	3	196	242*	0.4	1.0
443 UN C OF CHRIST	1	64	79*	0.1	0.3
449 UN METHODIST..	20	4 196	5 180*	9.2	22.3
453 UN PRES CH USA	3	1 448	1 788*	3.2	7.7
469 WELS.........	1	225	320	0.6	1.4

NA—Not applicable   *Total adherents estimated from known number of communicant, confirmed, full members.   —Represents a percent less than 0.1.   Percentages may not total due to rounding.

Table 4. Churches and Church Membership by County and Denomination: 1980

County and Denomination	Number of churches	Communicant, confirmed, full members	Total adherents Number	Total adherents Percent of total population	Total adherents Percent of total adherents
SANILAC	66	6 210	15 570*	38.2	100.0
019 AMER BAPT USA.	2	331	407*	1.0	2.6
053 ASSEMB OF GOD.	4	218	459	1.1	2.9
075 BRETHREN IN CR	1	43	73	0.2	0.5
081 CATHOLIC......	9	NA	6 273	15.4	40.3
089 CHR & MISS AL.	1	90	125	0.3	0.8
127 CH GOD (CLEVE)	1	96	118*	0.3	0.8
165 CH OF NAZARENE	2	89	202	0.5	1.3
167 CHS OF CHRIST.	1	10	13	–	0.1
179 CONSRV BAPT...	2	38	47*	0.1	0.3
193 EPISCOPAL.....	2	177	233	0.6	1.5
221 FREE METHODIST	2	177	699	1.7	4.5
281 LUTH CH AMER..	2	395	525	1.3	3.4
283 LUTH--MO SYNOD	6	1 410	1 781	4.4	11.4
291 MISSIONARY CH.	5	218	452	1.1	2.9
353 CHR BRETHREN..	1	10	10	–	0.1
403 SALVATION ARMY	1	354	1 013	2.5	6.5
413 S.D.A.........	1	20	25*	0.1	0.2
443 UN C OF CHRIST	1	49	60*	0.1	0.4
449 UN METHODIST..	16	1 405	1 727*	4.2	11.1
453 UN PRES CH USA	6	1 080	1 328*	3.3	8.5
SCHOOLCRAFT	31	2 851	7 233*	84.3	100.0
019 AMER BAPT USA.	1	297	361*	4.2	5.0
053 ASSEMB OF GOD.	1	60	102	1.2	1.4
057 BAPT GEN CONF.	1	240	292*	3.4	4.0
081 CATHOLIC......	4	NA	3 550	41.4	49.1
151 L-D SAINTS....	1	NA	?	?	?
193 EPISCOPAL.....	1	57	77	0.9	1.1
221 FREE METHODIST	1	13	69	0.8	1.0
263 INT FOURSQ GOS	1	19	23*	0.3	0.3
281 LUTH CH AMER..	1	515	756	8.8	10.5
283 LUTH--MO SYNOD	1	70	82	1.0	1.1
285 MENNONITE CH..	4	82	100*	1.2	1.4
413 S.D.A.........	1	12	15*	0.2	0.2
443 UN C OF CHRIST	1	42	51*	0.6	0.7
449 UN METHODIST..	11	1 296	1 575*	18.4	21.8
453 UN PRES CH USA	1	148	180*	2.1	2.5
SHIAWASSEE	79	11 397	28 597*	40.2	100.0
019 AMER BAPT USA.	2	427	535*	0.8	1.9
029 AMER LUTH CH..	1	176	271	0.4	0.9
053 ASSEMB OF GOD.	3	144	274	0.4	1.0
075 BRETHREN IN CR	1	43	73	0.1	0.3
081 CATHOLIC......	6	NA	11 405	16.0	39.9
097 CHR CHS&CHS CR	4	1 187	1 488*	2.1	5.2
123 CH GOD (ANDER)	2	140	420	0.6	1.5
127 CH GOD (CLEVE)	1	118	148*	0.2	0.5
133 CH GOD(7TH)DEN	1	47	59*	0.1	0.2
151 L-D SAINTS....	1	NA	201	0.3	0.7
165 CH OF NAZARENE	6	659	1 401	2.0	4.9
167 CHS OF CHRIST.	3	160	201	0.3	0.7
175 CONGR CHR CHS.	2	484	607*	0.9	2.1
179 CONSRV BAPT...	1	19	24*	–	0.1
181 CONSRV CONGR..	2	327	410*	0.6	1.4
193 EPISCOPAL.....	2	485	882	1.2	3.1
221 FREE METHODIST	4	297	999	1.4	3.5
353 CHR BRETHREN..	2	95	210	0.3	0.7
403 SALVATION ARMY	1	152	614	0.9	2.1
413 S.D.A.........	2	206	258*	0.4	0.9
419 SO BAPT CONV..	2	185	232*	0.3	0.8
443 UN C OF CHRIST	3	885	1 109*	1.6	3.9
449 UN METHODIST..	24	3 619	4 536*	6.4	15.9
469 WELS..........	3	1 542	2 240	3.1	7.8
TUSCOLA	75	12 471	24 853*	43.6	100.0
019 AMER BAPT USA.	1	75	94*	0.2	0.4
029 AMER LUTH CH..	2	312	484	0.8	1.9
053 ASSEMB OF GOD.	5	179	358	0.6	1.4
081 CATHOLIC......	8	NA	7 321	12.9	29.5
089 CHR & MISS AL.	1	44	76	0.1	0.3
097 CHR CHS&CHS CR	2	211	263*	0.5	1.1
123 CH GOD (ANDER)	1	70	210	0.4	0.8
127 CH GOD (CLEVE)	1	59	74*	0.1	0.3
151 L-D SAINTS....	1	NA	55	0.1	0.2
165 CH OF NAZARENE	9	466	910	1.6	3.7
167 CHS OF CHRIST.	3	143	191	0.3	0.8
221 FREE METHODIST	2	100	375	0.7	1.5
283 LUTH--MO SYNOD	7	4 799	6 682	11.7	26.9
285 MENNONITE CH..	1	45	56*	0.1	0.2
291 MISSIONARY CH.	4	337	570	1.0	2.3
293 MORAV CH-NORTH	1	363	447	0.8	1.8
353 CHR BRETHREN..	1	15	25	–	0.1
413 S.D.A.........	1	84	105*	0.2	0.4
449 UN METHODIST..	15	3 156	3 939*	6.9	15.8
453 UN PRES CH USA	7	1 278	1 595*	2.8	6.4
469 WELS..........	2	735	1 023	1.8	4.1
VAN BUREN	79	9 607	20 046*	30.0	100.0
017 AMER BAPT ASSN	2	150	150	0.2	0.7
019 AMER BAPT USA.	2	199	247*	0.4	1.2
053 ASSEMB OF GOD.	3	115	185	0.3	0.9
059 BAPT MISS ASSN	1	68	84*	0.1	0.4
081 CATHOLIC......	8	NA	7 072	10.6	35.3
093 CHR CH (DISC).	1	267	269	0.4	1.3
097 CHR CHS&CHS CR	1	360	446*	0.7	2.2
105 CHRISTIAN REF.	3	176	305	0.5	1.5
123 CH GOD (ANDER)	2	130	390	0.6	1.9
127 CH GOD (CLEVE)	2	85	105*	0.2	0.5
133 CH GOD(7TH)DEN	1	17	21*	–	0.1

County and Denomination	Number of churches	Communicant, confirmed, full members	Total adherents Number	Total adherents Percent of total population	Total adherents Percent of total adherents
151 L-D SAINTS....	1	NA	102	0.2	0.5
164 CH LUTH CONF..	1	44	81	0.1	0.4
167 CHS OF CHRIST.	2	350	445	0.7	2.2
175 CONGR CHR CHS.	3	350	434*	0.6	2.2
179 CONSRV BAPT...	1	19	24*	–	0.1
181 CONSRV CONGR..	1	50	62*	0.1	0.3
193 EPISCOPAL.....	2	286	455	0.7	2.3
213 EVAN MENN INC.	1	40	50*	0.1	0.2
221 FREE METHODIST	2	72	435	0.7	2.2
281 LUTH CH AMER..	1	480	590	0.9	2.9
283 LUTH--MO SYNOD	1	390	489	0.7	2.4
371 REF CH IN AM..	2	360	608	0.9	3.0
413 S.D.A.........	7	554	687*	1.0	3.4
419 SO BAPT CONV..	1	114	141*	0.2	0.7
443 UN C OF CHRIST	2	678	841*	1.3	4.2
449 UN METHODIST..	19	2 737	3 393*	5.1	16.9
453 UN PRES CH USA	3	845	1 048*	1.6	5.2
469 WELS..........	3	671	887	1.3	4.4
WASHTENAW	154	39 532	91 347*	34.5	100.0
019 AMER BAPT USA.	9	3 940	4 670*	1.8	5.1
029 AMER LUTH CH..	6	3 215	4 451	1.7	4.9
053 ASSEMB OF GOD.	5	474	854	0.3	0.9
057 BAPT GEN CONF.	1	159	188*	0.1	0.2
081 CATHOLIC......	14	NA	37 762	14.3	41.3
089 CHR & MISS AL.	1	33	85	–	0.1
093 CHR CH (DISC).	1	139	161	0.1	0.2
097 CHR CHS&CHS CR	1	198	235*	0.1	0.3
105 CHRISTIAN REF.	2	296	487	0.2	0.5
123 CH GOD (ANDER)	3	246	738	0.3	0.8
127 CH GOD (CLEVE)	2	190	225*	0.1	0.2
149 CH OF JC (BIC)	1	34	36	–	–
151 L-D SAINTS....	4	NA	1 172	0.4	1.3
165 CH OF NAZARENE	4	197	382	0.1	0.4
167 CHS OF CHRIST.	8	870	1 107	0.4	1.2
175 CONGR CHR CHS.	1	982	1 164*	0.4	1.3
193 EPISCOPAL.....	7	3 197	4 682	1.8	5.1
221 FREE METHODIST	4	360	1 503	0.6	1.6
226 FRIENDS-USA...	2	245	290*	0.1	0.3
270 CONSRV JUDAISM	1	171	203*	0.1	0.2
271 REFORM JUDAISM	1	340	403*	0.2	0.4
281 LUTH CH AMER..	3	1 212	1 741	0.7	1.9
283 LUTH--MO SYNOD	11	3 078	4 243	1.6	4.6
285 MENNONITE CH..	3	53	63*	–	0.1
287 MENN GEN CONF.	1	14	14	–	–
290 METRO COMM CHS	0	25	50	–	0.1
291 MISSIONARY CH.	1	25	36	–	–
371 REF CH IN AM..	1	120	402	0.2	0.4
403 SALVATION ARMY	2	171	536	0.2	0.6
413 S.D.A.........	3	383	454*	0.2	0.5
419 SO BAPT CONV..	7	1 897	2 248*	0.8	2.5
435 UNITARIAN-UNIV	2	380	450*	0.2	0.5
443 UN C OF CHRIST	11	5 111	6 058*	2.3	6.6
449 UN METHODIST..	18	6 766	8 020*	3.0	8.8
453 UN PRES CH USA	7	3 253	3 856*	1.5	4.2
469 WELS..........	6	1 758	2 378	0.9	2.6
WAYNE	912	270 820	1 000 615*	42.8	100.0
005 AME ZION......	10	34 110	40 932	1.8	4.1
017 AMER BAPT ASSN	1	100	100	–	–
019 AMER BAPT USA.	30	18 936	23 113*	1.0	2.3
029 AMER LUTH CH..	29	9 553	12 235	0.5	1.2
039 AP CHR CH(NAZ)	1	20	24*	–	–
049 ARMEN AP CH AM	1	480	1 180	0.1	0.1
053 ASSEMB OF GOD.	29	5 741	9 650	0.4	1.0
057 BAPT GEN CONF.	5	854	1 042*	–	0.1
081 CATHOLIC......	217	NA	644 216	27.6	64.4
089 CHR & MISS AL.	8	440	756	–	0.1
093 CHR CH (DISC).	6	1 076	1 634	0.1	0.2
097 CHR CHS&CHS CR	10	1 518	1 853*	0.1	0.2
105 CHRISTIAN REF.	3	549	860	–	0.1
123 CH GOD (ANDER)	16	2 580	7 740	0.3	0.8
127 CH GOD (CLEVE)	28	3 089	3 770*	0.2	0.4
133 CH GOD(7TH)DEN	1	19	23*	–	–
149 CH OF JC (BIC)	4	292	301	–	–
151 L-D SAINTS....	6	NA	2 295	0.1	0.2
157 CH OF BRETHREN	2	298	364*	–	–
164 CH LUTH CONF..	1	19	26	–	–
165 CH OF NAZARENE	13	1 355	2 539	0.1	0.3
167 CHS OF CHRIST.	44	8 190	9 825	0.4	1.0
175 CONGR CHR CHS.	5	2 861	3 492*	0.1	0.3
179 CONSRV BAPT...	7	133	162*	–	–
193 EPISCOPAL.....	48	18 022	23 223	1.0	2.3
197 EVAN CH OF NA.	1	60	60	–	–
201 EVAN COV CH AM	2	512	625*	–	0.1
208 EVAN LUTH ASSN	9	3 932	5 019	0.2	0.5
221 FREE METHODIST	7	905	3 159	0.1	0.3
226 FRIENDS-USA...	2	72	88*	–	–
233 GEN CH NEW JER	1	60	73*	–	–
239 SWEDENBORGIAN.	1	60	73*	–	–
270 CONSRV JUDAISM	1	175	214*	–	–
271 REFORM JUDAISM	3	3 114	3 801*	0.2	0.4
281 LUTH CH AMER..	34	10 600	14 244	0.6	1.4
283 LUTH--MO SYNOD	64	35 501	47 599	2.0	4.8
285 MENNONITE CH..	1	42	51*	–	–
290 METRO COMM CHS	1	100	200	–	–
291 MISSIONARY CH.	4	172	381	–	–
293 MORAV CH-NORTH	1	174	261	–	–
313 N AM BAPT CONF	2	1 183	1 444*	0.1	0.1
349 PENT HOLINESS.	1	83	101*	–	–
353 CHR BRETHREN..	12	1 215	1 425	0.1	0.1
371 REF CH IN AM..	11	1 354	2 671	0.1	0.3
403 SALVATION ARMY	8	1 712	5 468	0.2	0.5

NA—Not applicable   *Total adherents estimated from known number of communicant, confirmed, full members.   —Represents a percent less than 0.1.   Percentages may not total due to rounding.

Table 4. Churches and Church Membership by County and Denomination: 1980

County and Denomination	Number of churches	Communicant, confirmed, full members	Total adherents		
			Number	Percent of total population	Percent of total adherents
413 S.D.A.........	15	4 992	6 093*	0.3	0.6
419 SO BAPT CONV..	42	11 340	13 841*	0.6	1.4
431 UKRANIAN AMER.	1	180	280	—	—
435 UNITARIAN-UNIV	2	751	917*	—	0.1
443 UN C OF CHRIST	25	12 880	15 721*	0.7	1.6
449 UN METHODIST..	68	28 594	34 902*	1.5	3.5
453 UN PRES CH USA	57	36 356	44 376*	1.9	4.4
469 WELS..........	13	4 466	6 173	0.3	0.6
WEXFORD	43	4 882	10 489*	41.8	100.0
019 AMER BAPT USA.	2	559	685*	2.7	6.5
053 ASSEMB OF GOD.	1	59	97	0.4	0.9
057 BAPT GEN CONF.	1	382	468*	1.9	4.5
081 CATHOLIC......	3	NA	3 400	13.5	32.4
093 CHR CH (DISC).	4	190	430	1.7	4.1
097 CHR CHS&CHS CR	2	120	147*	0.6	1.4
105 CHRISTIAN REF.	1	159	247	1.0	2.4
123 CH GOD (ANDER)	2	62	186	0.7	1.8
127 CH GOD (CLEVE)	1	25	31*	0.1	0.3
151 L-D SAINTS....	1	NA	125	0.5	1.2
165 CH OF NAZARENE	2	138	313	1.2	3.0
167 CHS OF CHRIST.	2	59	90	0.4	0.9
193 EPISCOPAL.....	1	116	135	0.5	1.3
201 EVAN COV CH AM	1	181	222*	0.9	2.1
221 FREE METHODIST	4	61	360	1.4	3.4
281 LUTH CH AMER..	2	595	807	3.2	7.7
283 LUTH--MO SYNOD	2	349	466	1.9	4.4
403 SALVATION ARMY	1	167	247	1.0	2.4
413 S.D.A.........	3	201	246*	1.0	2.3
443 UN C OF CHRIST	1	215	263*	1.0	2.5
449 UN METHODIST..	5	858	1 051*	4.2	10.0
453 UN PRES CH USA		386	473*	1.9	4.5

MINNESOTA

County and Denomination	Number of churches	Communicant, confirmed, full members	Total adherents		
			Number	Percent of total population	Percent of total adherents
THE STATE.....	4 818	1 210 803	2 653 161*	65.1	100.0
AITKIN	44	4 274	6 957*	51.9	100.0
029 AMER LUTH CH..	2	231	310	2.3	4.5
053 ASSEMB OF GOD.	2	133	255	1.9	3.7
057 BAPT GEN CONF.	2	162	194*	1.4	2.8
081 CATHOLIC......	5	NA	1 458	10.9	21.0
089 CHR & MISS AL.	2	9	50	0.4	0.7
097 CHR CHS&CHS CR	1	45	54*	0.4	0.8
163 CH OF LUTH BR.	2	65	80	0.6	1.1
179 CONSRV BAPT...	1	75	90*	0.7	1.3
193 EPISCOPAL.....	1	36	45	0.3	0.6
220 FREE LUTHERAN.	1	35	30	0.2	0.4
281 LUTH CH AMER..	7	1 307	1 729	12.9	24.9
283 LUTH--MO SYNOD	4	891	1 106	8.3	15.9
413 S.D.A.........	1	52	62*	0.5	0.9
443 UN C OF CHRIST	1	93	112*	0.8	1.6
449 UN METHODIST..	7	928	1 113*	8.3	16.0
453 UN PRES CH USA	4	164	197*	1.5	2.8
469 WELS..........	1	48	72	0.5	1.0
ANOKA	74	34 502	102 430*	52.3	100.0
029 AMER LUTH CH..	8	8 972	13 495	6.9	13.2
053 ASSEMB OF GOD.	6	1 066	2 089	1.1	2.0
057 BAPT GEN CONF.	4	858	1 087*	0.6	1.1
081 CATHOLIC......	8	NA	50 027	25.5	48.8
089 CHR & MISS AL.	2	239	1 077	0.5	1.1
093 CHR CH (DISC).	1	135	184	0.1	0.2
097 CHR CHS&CHS CR	2	160	203*	0.1	0.2
151 L-D SAINTS....	2	NA	761	0.4	0.7
165 CH OF NAZARENE	1	77	144	0.1	0.1
179 CONSRV BAPT...	1	190	241*	0.1	0.2
193 EPISCOPAL.....	2	467	697	0.4	0.7
201 EVAN COV CH AM	2	344	436*	0.2	0.4
203 EVAN FREE CH..	2	214	271*	0.1	0.3
281 LUTH CH AMER..	7	10 143	15 009	7.7	14.7
283 LUTH--MO SYNOD	9	6 017	8 373	4.3	8.2
403 SALVATION ARMY	1	36	1 181	0.6	1.2
413 S.D.A.........	1	116	147*	0.1	0.1
419 SO BAPT CONV..	1	249	316*	0.2	0.3
435 UNITARIAN-UNIV	1	67	85*	—	0.1
443 UN C OF CHRIST	1	396	502*	0.3	0.5
449 UN METHODIST..	10	3 983	5 047*	2.6	4.9
453 UN PRES CH USA	1	367	465*	0.2	0.5
469 WELS..........	1	406	593	0.3	0.6
BECKER	58	9 815	19 373*	66.0	100.0
029 AMER LUTH CH..	11	4 357	5 716	19.5	29.5
053 ASSEMB OF GOD.	2	174	280	1.0	1.4
081 CATHOLIC......	10	NA	5 106	17.4	26.4
164 CH LUTH CONF..	2	144	187	0.6	1.0
165 CH OF NAZARENE	1	41	90	0.3	0.5
179 CONSRV BAPT...	3	200	247*	0.8	1.3
193 EPISCOPAL.....	3	333	564	1.9	2.9

County and Denomination	Number of churches	Communicant, confirmed, full members	Total adherents		
			Number	Percent of total population	Percent of total adherents
203 EVAN FREE CH..	2	25	31*	0.1	0.2
209 EVAN LUTH SYN.	1	200	276	0.9	1.4
281 LUTH CH AMER..	6	1 430	1 801	6.1	9.3
283 LUTH--MO SYNOD	10	1 886	3 814	13.0	19.7
285 MENNONITE CH..	2	63	78*	0.3	0.4
353 CHR BRETHREN..	1	20	20	0.1	0.1
413 S.D.A.........	1	189	233*	0.8	1.2
443 UN C OF CHRIST	1	57	70*	0.2	0.4
449 UN METHODIST..	2	696	860*	2.9	4.4
BELTRAMI	47	7 258	15 449*	49.9	100.0
029 AMER LUTH CH..	11	3 474	4 967	16.0	32.2
053 ASSEMB OF GOD.	1	69	132	0.4	0.9
057 BAPT GEN CONF.	1	18	22*	0.1	0.1
081 CATHOLIC......	8	NA	4 922	15.9	31.9
097 CHR CHS&CHS CR	2	50	61*	0.2	0.4
151 L-D SAINTS....	2	NA	262	0.8	1.7
165 CH OF NAZARENE	1	31	43	0.1	0.3
167 CHS OF CHRIST.	1	6	18	0.1	0.1
193 EPISCOPAL.....	3	507	935	3.0	6.1
201 EVAN COV CH AM	1	158	192*	0.6	1.2
203 EVAN FREE CH..	3	58	71*	0.2	0.5
220 FREE LUTHERAN.	2	76	110	0.4	0.7
221 FREE METHODIST	1	38	186	0.6	1.2
281 LUTH CH AMER..	3	536	735	2.4	4.8
283 LUTH--MO SYNOD	2	687	869	2.8	5.6
413 S.D.A.........	1	135	164*	0.5	1.1
449 UN METHODIST..	1	718	873*	2.8	5.7
453 UN PRES CH USA	3	652	793*	2.6	5.1
469 WELS..........	1	45	94	0.3	0.6
BENTON	27	4 227	19 406*	77.0	100.0
029 AMER LUTH CH..	1	217	262	1.0	1.4
081 CATHOLIC......	9	NA	13 805	54.8	71.1
089 CHR & MISS AL.	1	84	173	0.7	0.9
097 CHR CHS&CHS CR	1	50	62*	0.2	0.3
201 EVAN COV CH AM	1	66	82*	0.3	0.4
203 EVAN FREE CH..	1	102	127*	0.5	0.7
281 LUTH CH AMER..	3	1 245	1 731	6.9	8.9
283 LUTH--MO SYNOD	3	1 828	2 351	9.3	12.1
413 S.D.A.........	1	79	99*	0.4	0.5
443 UN C OF CHRIST	1	19	24*	0.1	0.1
449 UN METHODIST..	1	158	197*	0.8	1.0
453 UN PRES CH USA	3	325	406*	1.6	2.1
469 WELS..........	1	54	87	0.3	0.4
BIG STONE	27	4 308	7 565*	98.0	100.0
029 AMER LUTH CH..	4	1 248	1 575	20.4	20.8
053 ASSEMB OF GOD.	1	42	96	1.2	1.3
057 BAPT GEN CONF.	1	73	87*	1.1	1.2
081 CATHOLIC......	4	NA	2 108	27.3	27.9
179 CONSRV BAPT...	1	60	72*	0.9	1.0
281 LUTH CH AMER..	2	579	728	9.4	9.6
283 LUTH--MO SYNOD	4	1 233	1 592	20.6	21.0
413 S.D.A.........	1	22	26*	0.3	0.3
443 UN C OF CHRIST	2	194	232*	3.0	3.1
449 UN METHODIST..	5	629	753*	9.8	10.0
469 WELS..........	2	228	296	3.8	3.9
BLUE EARTH	71	19 111	37 581*	71.8	100.0
019 AMER BAPT USA.	2	667	791*	1.5	2.1
029 AMER LUTH CH..	9	5 180	6 956	13.3	18.5
053 ASSEMB OF GOD.	1	68	136	0.3	0.4
057 BAPT GEN CONF.	1	204	242*	0.5	0.6
081 CATHOLIC......	10	NA	12 467	23.8	33.2
093 CHR CH (DISC).	2	260	360	0.7	1.0
097 CHR CHS&CHS CR	1	130	154*	0.3	0.4
123 CH GOD (ANDER)	1	31	93	0.2	0.2
151 L-D SAINTS....	1	NA	195	0.4	0.5
164 CH LUTH CONF..	2	924	1 191	2.3	3.2
165 CH OF NAZARENE	1	25	28	0.1	0.1
167 CHS OF CHRIST.	1	63	108	0.2	0.3
179 CONSRV BAPT...	1	40	47*	0.1	0.1
193 EPISCOPAL.....	1	354	421	0.8	1.1
201 EVAN COV CH AM	1	287	340*	0.6	0.9
209 EVAN LUTH SYN.	1	378	544	1.0	1.4
281 LUTH CH AMER..	2	1 166	1 673	3.2	4.5
283 LUTH--MO SYNOD	12	4 055	5 339	10.2	14.2
403 SALVATION ARMY	1	80	220	0.4	0.6
413 S.D.A.........	1	92	109*	0.2	0.3
435 UNITARIAN-UNIV	1	42	50*	0.1	0.1
443 UN C OF CHRIST	2	362	429*	0.8	1.1
449 UN METHODIST..	9	2 058	2 440*	4.7	6.5
453 UN PRES CH USA	4	1 882	2 231*	4.3	5.9
469 WELS..........	3	763	1 017	1.9	2.7
BROWN	39	10 531	26 680*	93.1	100.0
029 AMER LUTH CH..	11	3 985	5 369	18.7	20.1
053 ASSEMB OF GOD.	2	38	66	0.2	0.2
081 CATHOLIC......	7	NA	12 944	45.2	48.5
097 CHR CHS&CHS CR	1	50	60*	0.2	0.2
164 CH LUTH CONF..	1	267	350	1.2	1.3
193 EPISCOPAL.....	1	56	56	0.2	0.2
197 EVAN CH OF NA.	1	37	37	0.1	0.1
281 LUTH CH AMER..	1	272	340	1.2	1.3
283 LUTH--MO SYNOD	2	791	1 062	3.7	4.0
435 UNITARIAN-UNIV	1	173	209*	0.7	0.8
443 UN C OF CHRIST	3	842	1 018*	3.6	3.8
449 UN METHODIST..	4	1 263	1 527*	5.3	5.7
469 WELS..........	3	2 757	3 642	12.7	13.7

NA— Not applicable   *Total adherents estimated from known number of communicant, confirmed, full members.   —Represents a percent less than 0.1.   Percentages may not total due to rounding.

Table 4. Churches and Church Membership by County and Denomination: 1980

County and Denomination	Number of churches	Communicant, confirmed, full members	Total adherents Number	Percent of total population	Percent of total adherents
CARLTON	50	8 294	17 035*	56.9	100.0
029 AMER LUTH CH..	5	2 223	3 035	10.1	17.8
045 APOSTOLIC LUTH	3	420	514*	1.7	3.0
053 ASSEMB OF GOD.	1	51	93	0.3	0.5
057 BAPT GEN CONF.	2	184	225*	0.8	1.3
081 CATHOLIC......	9	NA	6 315	21.1	37.1
097 CHR CHS&CHS CR	1	12	15*	0.1	0.1
151 L-D SAINTS....	1	NA	72	0.2	0.4
193 EPISCOPAL.....	2	138	195	0.7	1.1
201 EVAN COV CH AM	3	226	277*	0.9	1.6
203 EVAN FREE CH..	1	63	77*	0.3	0.5
220 FREE LUTHERAN.	1	750	500	1.7	2.9
281 LUTH CH AMER..	6	1 771	2 445	8.2	14.4
283 LUTH--MO SYNOD	7	1 426	2 016	6.7	11.8
353 CHR BRETHREN..	1	20	20	0.1	0.1
413 S.D.A.........	1	6	7*	-	-
449 UN METHODIST..	3	290	355*	1.2	2.1
453 UN PRES CH USA	3	714	874*	2.9	5.1
CARVER	43	12 117	25 374*	68.5	100.0
029 AMER LUTH CH..	1	602	1 030	2.8	4.1
057 BAPT GEN CONF.	1	44	55*	0.1	0.2
081 CATHOLIC......	9	NA	9 109	24.6	35.9
089 CHR & MISS AL.	1	55	116	0.3	0.5
203 EVAN FREE CH..	1	110	136*	0.4	0.5
237 GC MENN BR CHS	1	102	127*	0.3	0.5
281 LUTH CH AMER..	4	1 489	2 029	5.5	8.0
283 LUTH--MO SYNOD	12	7 352	9 826	26.5	38.7
293 MORAV CH-NORTH	3	678	825	2.2	3.3
443 UN C OF CHRIST	5	1 201	1 489*	4.0	5.9
449 UN METHODIST..	2	109	135*	0.4	0.5
453 UN PRES CH USA	2	295	366*	1.0	1.4
469 WELS.........	1	80	131	0.4	0.5
CASS	50	4 233	8 536*	40.6	100.0
029 AMER LUTH CH..	13	1 730	2 320	11.0	27.2
045 APOSTOLIC LUTH	1	50	60*	0.3	0.7
053 ASSEMB OF GOD.	4	200	322	1.5	3.8
057 BAPT GEN CONF.	1	150	181*	0.9	2.1
081 CATHOLIC......	9	NA	2 830	13.4	33.2
089 CHR & MISS AL.	3	88	190	0.9	2.2
165 CH OF NAZARENE	1	78	192	0.9	2.2
179 CONSRV BAPT...	1	90	109*	0.5	1.3
193 EPISCOPAL.....	2	285	373	1.8	4.4
203 EVAN FREE CH..	2	11	13*	0.1	0.2
221 FREE METHODIST	2	6	30	0.1	0.4
281 LUTH CH AMER..	1	184	249	1.2	2.9
283 LUTH--MO SYNOD	3	354	450	2.1	5.3
413 S.D.A.........	1	22	27*	0.1	0.3
443 UN C OF CHRIST	4	705	852*	4.0	10.0
449 UN METHODIST..	2	280	338*	1.6	4.0
CHIPPEWA	32	9 135	13 197*	88.3	100.0
029 AMER LUTH CH..	13	5 427	6 780	45.4	51.4
053 ASSEMB OF GOD.	1	15	25	0.2	0.2
057 BAPT GEN CONF.	2	136	164*	1.1	1.2
081 CATHOLIC......	2	NA	1 427	9.6	10.8
105 CHRISTIAN REF.	1	276	457	3.1	3.5
281 LUTH CH AMER..	1	413	575	3.8	4.4
283 LUTH--MO SYNOD	4	893	1 188	8.0	9.0
371 REF CH IN AM..	2	847	1 219	8.2	9.2
443 UN C OF CHRIST	2	404	488*	3.3	3.7
449 UN METHODIST..	3	646	780*	5.2	5.9
453 UN PRES CH USA	1	78	94*	0.6	0.7
CHISAGO	32	8 380	15 281*	59.4	100.0
053 ASSEMB OF GOD.	1	46	81	0.3	0.5
057 BAPT GEN CONF.	1	101	126*	0.5	0.8
081 CATHOLIC......	5	NA	4 074	15.8	26.7
179 CONSRV BAPT...	2	115	144*	0.6	0.9
201 EVAN COV CH AM	2	64	80*	0.3	0.5
203 EVAN FREE CH..	2	149	187*	0.7	1.2
208 EVAN LUTH ASSN	1	394	576	2.2	3.8
220 FREE LUTHERAN.	2	215	340	1.3	2.2
281 LUTH CH AMER..	11	6 272	8 389	32.6	54.9
283 LUTH--MO SYNOD	1	103	131	0.5	0.9
449 UN METHODIST..	4	921	1 153*	4.5	7.5
CLAY	62	19 339	32 238*	65.4	100.0
029 AMER LUTH CH..	24	13 628	17 963	36.4	55.7
053 ASSEMB OF GOD.	2	183	312	0.6	1.0
057 BAPT GEN CONF.	1	76	91*	0.2	0.3
081 CATHOLIC......	8	NA	7 067	14.3	21.9
089 CHR & MISS AL.	1	21	53	0.1	0.2
097 CHR CHS&CHS CR	1	70	83*	0.2	0.3
163 CH OF LUTH BR.	2	104	171	0.3	0.5
165 CH OF NAZARENE	1	13	61	0.1	0.2
193 EPISCOPAL.....	1	142	142	0.3	0.4
201 EVAN COV CH AM	1	13	15*	-	-
203 EVAN FREE CH..	1	84	100*	0.2	0.3
209 EVAN LUTH SYN.	2	253	350	0.7	1.1
281 LUTH CH AMER..	1	598	741	1.5	2.3
283 LUTH--MO SYNOD	4	1 620	2 043	4.1	6.3
353 CHR BRETHREN..	1	50	50	0.1	0.2
419 SO BAPT CONV..	1	35	42*	0.1	0.1
443 UN C OF CHRIST	3	1 078	1 284*	2.6	4.0
449 UN METHODIST..	2	654	779*	1.6	2.4
453 UN PRES CH USA	4	612	729*	1.5	2.3
469 WELS.........	1	105	162	0.3	0.5
CLEARWATER	25	3 028	4 769*	54.4	100.0
029 AMER LUTH CH..	11	2 096	2 829	32.3	59.3
057 BAPT GEN CONF.	1	112	138*	1.6	2.9
081 CATHOLIC......	3	NA	550	6.3	11.5
151 L-D SAINTS....	1	NA	34	0.4	0.7
163 CH OF LUTH BR.	1	97	136	1.6	2.9
193 EPISCOPAL.....	1	94	184	2.1	3.9
209 EVAN LUTH SYN.	1	94	122	1.4	2.6
220 FREE LUTHERAN.	4	271	415	4.7	8.7
283 LUTH--MO SYNOD	1	264	361	4.1	7.6
COOK	13	1 307	2 210*	54.0	100.0
029 AMER LUTH CH..	4	793	996	24.3	45.1
057 BAPT GEN CONF.	2	101	121*	3.0	5.5
081 CATHOLIC......	3	NA	600	14.7	27.1
203 EVAN FREE CH..	1	91	109*	2.7	4.9
413 S.D.A.........	1	14	17*	0.4	0.8
443 UN C OF CHRIST	1	290	346*	8.5	15.7
449 UN METHODIST..	1	18	21*	0.5	1.0
COTTONWOOD	39	9 538	13 429*	90.4	100.0
029 AMER LUTH CH..	9	3 855	4 955	33.4	36.9
053 ASSEMB OF GOD.	3	119	309	2.1	2.3
081 CATHOLIC......	3	NA	1 290	8.7	9.6
089 CHR & MISS AL.	1	97	173	1.2	1.3
105 CHRISTIAN REF.	1	46	72	0.5	0.5
179 CONSRV BAPT...	2	200	243*	1.6	1.8
193 EPISCOPAL.....	1	142	141	0.9	1.0
203 EVAN FREE CH..	1	21	26*	0.2	0.2
211 EVAN MENN BR..	1	282	367	2.5	2.7
237 GC MENN BR CHS	2	321	390*	2.6	2.9
283 LUTH--MO SYNOD	2	1 445	1 857	12.5	13.8
287 MENN GEN CONF.	4	1 291	1 516	10.2	11.3
413 S.D.A.........	1	22	27*	0.2	0.2
449 UN METHODIST..	5	1 128	1 371*	9.2	10.2
453 UN PRES CH USA	3	569	692*	4.7	5.2
CROW WING	55	11 402	24 612*	59.0	100.0
029 AMER LUTH CH..	5	2 910	3 954	9.5	16.1
053 ASSEMB OF GOD.	2	451	700	1.7	2.8
057 BAPT GEN CONF.	1	140	170*	0.4	0.7
081 CATHOLIC......	12	NA	9 032	21.6	36.7
089 CHR & MISS AL.	1	46	86	0.2	0.3
097 CHR CHS&CHS CR	1	85	103*	0.2	0.4
127 CH GOD (CLEVE)	1	16	19*	-	0.1
151 L-D SAINTS....	1	NA	234	0.6	1.0
165 CH OF NAZARENE	2	122	357	0.9	1.5
167 CHS OF CHRIST.	1	25	35	0.1	0.1
179 CONSRV BAPT...	1	75	91*	0.2	0.4
193 EPISCOPAL.....	1	238	358	0.9	1.5
201 EVAN COV CH AM	1	49	60*	0.1	0.2
203 EVAN FREE CH..	1	41	50*	0.1	0.2
281 LUTH CH AMER..	6	2 756	3 721	8.9	15.1
283 LUTH--MO SYNOD	5	1 831	2 301	5.5	9.3
403 SALVATION ARMY	1	127	312	0.7	1.3
413 S.D.A.........	1	173	210*	0.5	0.9
443 UN C OF CHRIST	1	348	423*	1.0	1.7
449 UN METHODIST..	6	1 093	1 327*	3.2	5.4
453 UN PRES CH USA	3	814	989*	2.4	4.0
469 WELS.........	1	62	80	0.2	0.3
DAKOTA	107	37 134	108 516*	55.9	100.0
019 AMER BAPT USA.	2	221	278*	0.1	0.3
029 AMER LUTH CH..	13	11 525	17 649	9.1	16.3
039 AP CHR CH(NAZ)	1	6	8*	-	-
053 ASSEMB OF GOD.	4	596	1 278	0.7	1.2
057 BAPT GEN CONF.	4	628	789*	0.4	0.7
081 CATHOLIC......	20	NA	55 377	28.5	51.0
089 CHR & MISS AL.	1	51	81	-	0.1
097 CHR CHS&CHS CR	1	85	107*	0.1	0.1
127 CH GOD (CLEVE)	1	33	41*	-	-
164 CH LUTH CONF.	1	100	146	0.1	0.1
167 CHS OF CHRIST.	1	71	134	0.1	0.1
181 CONSRV CONGR..	1	119	150*	0.1	0.1
193 EPISCOPAL.....	4	713	1 087	0.6	1.0
201 EVAN COV CH AM	1	258	324*	0.2	0.3
203 EVAN FREE CH..	2	105	132*	0.1	0.1
209 EVAN LUTH SYN.	1	93	172	0.1	0.2
281 LUTH CH AMER..	9	7 003	10 367	5.3	9.6
283 LUTH--MO SYNOD	9	4 628	6 329	3.3	5.8
313 N AM BAPT CONF	3	539	677*	0.3	0.6
419 SO BAPT CONV..	3	308	387*	0.2	0.4
443 UN C OF CHRIST	3	870	1 093*	0.6	1.0
449 UN METHODIST..	10	4 047	5 085*	2.6	4.7
453 UN PRES CH USA	4	1 771	2 225*	1.1	2.1
469 WELS.........	7	3 364	4 600	2.4	4.2
DODGE	29	6 206	10 012*	67.8	100.0
029 AMER LUTH CH..	5	2 733	3 640	24.6	36.4
053 ASSEMB OF GOD.	1	54	82	0.6	0.8
057 BAPT GEN CONF.	1	424	528*	3.6	5.3
081 CATHOLIC......	5	NA	1 983	13.4	19.8
097 CHR CHS&CHS CR	1	175	218*	1.5	2.2
179 CONSRV BAPT...	1	145	181*	1.2	1.8
193 EPISCOPAL.....	1	75	105	0.7	1.0
283 LUTH--MO SYNOD	3	621	809	5.5	8.1
285 MENNONITE CH..	1	?	?	?	?
413 S.D.A.........	1	73	91*	0.6	0.9
415 S-D BAPT GC	1	135	168*	1.1	1.7

NA—Not applicable   *Total adherents estimated from known number of communicant, confirmed, full members.   —Represents a percent less than 0.1.   Percentages may not total due to rounding.

Table 4. Churches and Church Membership by County and Denomination: 1980

County and Denomination	Number of churches	Communicant, confirmed, full members	Total adherents		
			Number	Percent of total population	Percent of total adherents
443 UN C OF CHRIST	2	443	552*	3.7	5.5
449 UN METHODIST..	3	654	815*	5.5	8.1
453 UN PRES CH USA	3	674	840*	5.7	8.4
DOUGLAS	50	11 206	20 738*	74.5	100.0
029 AMER LUTH CH..	11	4 751	6 321	22.7	30.5
053 ASSEMB OF GOD.	1	177	330	1.2	1.6
081 CATHOLIC......	6	NA	6 066	21.8	29.3
097 CHR CHS&CHS CR	1	45	54*	0.2	0.3
151 L-D SAINTS....	1	NA	121	0.4	0.6
163 CH OF LUTH BR.	1	42	54	0.2	0.3
193 EPISCOPAL.....	1	173	195	0.7	0.9
201 EVAN COV CH AM	4	327	396*	1.4	1.9
220 FREE LUTHERAN.	1	80	110	0.4	0.5
221 FREE METHODIST	1	45	129	0.5	0.6
281 LUTH CH AMER..	8	2 144	2 692	9.7	13.0
283 LUTH--MO SYNOD	8	2 097	2 629	9.4	12.7
371 REF CH IN AM..	1	40	68	0.2	0.3
443 UN C OF CHRIST	1	531	643*	2.3	3.1
449 UN METHODIST..	1	447	541*	1.9	2.6
453 UN PRES CH USA	2	203	246*	0.9	1.2
469 WELS.........	1	104	143	0.5	0.7
FARIBAULT	50	11 235	20 130*	102.1	100.0
019 AMER BAPT USA.	1	309	371*	1.9	1.8
029 AMER LUTH CH..	13	4 386	5 687	28.8	28.3
053 ASSEMB OF GOD.	2	105	178	0.9	0.9
081 CATHOLIC......	7	NA	5 949	30.2	29.6
163 CH OF LUTH BR.	1	58	106	0.5	0.5
179 CONSRV BAPT...	2	130	156*	0.8	0.8
281 LUTH CH AMER..	2	322	400	2.0	2.0
283 LUTH--MO SYNOD	7	2 268	2 894	14.7	14.4
419 SO BAPT CONV..	1	45	54*	0.3	0.3
443 UN C OF CHRIST	2	510	612*	3.1	3.0
449 UN METHODIST..	10	2 597	3 117*	15.8	15.5
453 UN PRES CH USA	2	505	606*	3.1	3.0
FILLMORE	59	12 928	19 771*	90.2	100.0
029 AMER LUTH CH..	25	8 372	10 989	50.1	55.6
053 ASSEMB OF GOD.	1	65	139	0.6	0.7
081 CATHOLIC......	8	NA	2 853	13.0	14.4
157 CH OF BRETHREN	1	133	162*	0.7	0.8
167 CHS OF CHRIST.	1	19	22	0.1	0.1
193 EPISCOPAL.....	2	100	121	0.6	0.6
221 FREE METHODIST	1	38	228	1.0	1.2
283 LUTH--MO SYNOD	4	1 394	1 809	8.2	9.1
285 MENNONITE CH..	1	26	32*	0.1	0.2
371 REF CH IN AM..	1	340	451	2.1	2.3
449 UN METHODIST..	11	2 112	2 565*	11.7	13.0
453 UN PRES CH USA	3	329	400*	1.8	2.0
FREEBORN	53	20 489	31 201*	85.9	100.0
019 AMER BAPT USA.	3	1 228	1 484*	4.1	4.8
029 AMER LUTH CH..	24	12 496	16 424	45.2	52.6
053 ASSEMB OF GOD.	1	78	116	0.3	0.4
081 CATHOLIC......	2	NA	4 369	12.0	14.0
097 CHR CHS&CHS CR	1	100	121*	0.3	0.4
167 CHS OF CHRIST.	1	18	23	0.1	0.1
181 CONSRV CONGR..	2	263	318*	0.9	1.0
193 EPISCOPAL.....	1	178	255	0.7	0.8
209 EVAN LUTH SYN.	3	699	1 085	3.0	3.5
221 FREE METHODIST	1	12	24	0.1	0.1
281 LUTH CH AMER..	2	1 499	1 990	5.5	6.4
283 LUTH--MO SYNOD	2	614	845	2.3	2.7
371 REF CH IN AM..	1	277	442	1.2	1.4
403 SALVATION ARMY	1	104	172	0.5	0.6
413 S.D.A.........	1	77	93*	0.3	0.3
443 UN C OF CHRIST	1	269	325*	0.9	1.0
449 UN METHODIST..	5	1 542	1 864*	5.1	6.0
453 UN PRES CH USA	1	1 035	1 251*	3.4	4.0
GOODHUE	74	21 514	33 894*	87.5	100.0
029 AMER LUTH CH..	17	7 136	9 121	23.5	26.9
053 ASSEMB OF GOD.	2	98	190	0.5	0.6
057 BAPT GEN CONF.	2	334	405*	1.0	1.2
081 CATHOLIC......	8	NA	6 404	16.5	18.9
097 CHR CHS&CHS CR	2	59	72*	0.2	0.2
151 L-D SAINTS....	1	NA	154	0.4	0.5
164 CH LUTH CONF..	1	116	147	0.4	0.4
165 CH OF NAZARENE	1	17	99	0.3	0.3
167 CHS OF CHRIST.	1	20	27	0.1	0.1
193 EPISCOPAL.....	5	725	996	2.6	2.9
201 EVAN COV CH AM	1	172	209*	0.5	0.6
220 FREE LUTHERAN.	3	650	550	1.4	1.6
281 LUTH CH AMER..	9	5 967	7 812	20.2	23.0
283 LUTH--MO SYNOD	3	783	938	2.4	2.8
413 S.D.A.........	1	48	58*	0.1	0.2
443 UN C OF CHRIST	2	383	465*	1.2	1.4
449 UN METHODIST..	5	1 889	2 293*	5.9	6.8
453 UN PRES CH USA	1	290	352*	0.9	1.0
469 WELS.........	9	2 827	3 602	9.3	10.6
GRANT	28	4 553	6 414*	89.4	100.0
029 AMER LUTH CH..	10	2 024	2 591	36.1	40.4
081 CATHOLIC......	2	NA	694	9.7	10.8
201 EVAN COV CH AM	1	10	12*	0.2	0.2
203 EVAN FREE CH..	1	52	62*	0.9	1.0
281 LUTH CH AMER..	5	1 170	1 412	19.7	22.0
283 LUTH--MO SYNOD	3	570	730	10.2	11.4

County and Denomination	Number of churches	Communicant, confirmed, full members	Total adherents		
			Number	Percent of total population	Percent of total adherents
371 REF CH IN AM..	1	62	117	1.6	1.8
449 UN METHODIST..	2	392	469*	6.5	7.3
453 UN PRES CH USA	3	273	327*	4.6	5.1
HENNEPIN	551	245 489	512 754*	54.5	100.0
001 ADVENT CHR CH.	1	104	123*	–	–
019 AMER BAPT USA.	13	5 106	6 036*	0.6	1.2
029 AMER LUTH CH..	59	50 826	66 997	7.1	13.1
045 APOSTOLIC LUTH	1	300	355*	–	0.1
053 ASSEMB OF GOD.	18	2 300	4 527	0.5	0.9
057 BAPT GEN CONF.	17	5 567	6 581*	0.7	1.3
081 CATHOLIC......	74	NA	192 288	20.4	37.5
089 CHR & MISS AL.	8	581	1 210	0.1	0.2
093 CHR CH (DISC).	3	892	1 340	0.1	0.3
097 CHR CHS&CHS CR	5	547	647*	0.1	0.1
101 C.M.E.........	1	380	449*	–	0.1
105 CHRISTIAN REF.	3	286	510	0.1	0.1
121 CH GOD (ABR)..	1	63	74*	–	–
123 CH GOD (ANDER)	1	70	210	–	–
127 CH GOD (CLEVE)	3	370	437*	–	0.1
151 L-D SAINTS....	6	NA	3 220	0.3	0.6
163 CH OF LUTH BR.	2	307	458	–	0.1
164 CH LUTH CONF..	1	164	267	–	0.1
165 CH OF NAZARENE	6	767	1 251	0.1	0.2
167 CHS OF CHRIST.	4	326	425	–	0.1
175 CONGR CHR CHS.	1	2 486	2 939*	0.3	0.6
179 CONSRV BAPT...	7	1 900	2 246*	0.2	0.4
193 EPISCOPAL.....	24	10 892	14 790	1.6	2.9
195 ESTONIAN ELC..	1	78	137	–	–
197 EVAN CH OF NA.	2	133	133	–	–
201 EVAN COV CH AM	14	4 305	5 089*	0.5	1.0
203 EVAN FREE CH..	20	3 259	3 853*	0.4	0.8
208 EVAN LUTH ASSN	4	1 826	2 344	0.2	0.5
209 EVAN LUTH SYN.	2	646	697	0.1	0.1
220 FREE LUTHERAN.	4	396	545	0.1	0.1
221 FREE METHODIST	2	55	246	–	–
226 FRIENDS-USA...	1	188	222*	–	–
263 INT FOURSQ GOS	1	65	77*	–	–
270 CONSRV JUDAISM	3	1 022	1 208*	0.1	0.2
271 REFORM JUDAISM	1	3 502	4 140*	0.4	0.8
281 LUTH CH AMER..	69	64 344	87 261	9.3	17.0
283 LUTH--MO SYNOD	34	20 338	26 254	2.8	5.1
285 MENNONITE CH..	1	68	80*	–	–
287 MENN GEN CONF.	1	62	94	–	–
290 METRO COMM CHS	1	40	80	–	–
313 N AM BAPT CONF	4	568	671*	0.1	0.1
353 CHR BRETHREN..	3	190	245	–	–
371 REF CH IN AM..	2	204	393	–	0.1
403 SALVATION ARMY	5	757	1 160	0.1	0.2
413 S.D.A.........	7	1 607	1 900*	0.2	0.4
419 SO BAPT CONV..	6	612	724*	0.1	0.1
435 UNITARIAN-UNIV	5	1 470	1 738*	0.2	0.3
443 UN C OF CHRIST	20	10 267	12 138*	1.3	2.4
449 UN METHODIST..	44	25 404	30 033*	3.2	5.9
453 UN PRES CH USA	26	16 494	19 499*	2.1	3.8
469 WELS.........	9	3 355	4 413	0.5	0.9
HOUSTON	34	7 243	15 221*	77.6	100.0
029 AMER LUTH CH..	8	4 174	5 423	27.6	35.6
057 BAPT GEN CONF.	1	54	65*	0.3	0.4
081 CATHOLIC......	5	NA	5 966	30.4	39.2
203 EVAN FREE CH..	2	86	104*	0.5	0.7
290 METRO COMM CHS	0	10	20	0.1	0.1
313 N AM BAPT CONF	1	9	11*	0.1	0.1
443 UN C OF CHRIST	1	450	544*	2.8	3.6
449 UN METHODIST..	7	912	1 103*	5.6	7.2
453 UN PRES CH USA	3	216	261*	1.3	1.7
469 WELS.........	6	1 332	1 724	8.8	11.3
HUBBARD	30	3 896	7 013*	49.7	100.0
029 AMER LUTH CH..	5	1 214	1 584	11.2	22.6
053 ASSEMB OF GOD.	1	41	87	0.6	1.2
081 CATHOLIC......	4	NA	1 747	12.4	24.9
089 CHR & MISS AL.	2	44	152	1.1	2.2
097 CHR CHS&CHS CR	1	85	104*	0.7	1.5
151 L-D SAINTS....	1	NA	47	0.3	0.7
163 CH OF LUTH BR.	1	16	29	0.2	0.4
167 CHS OF CHRIST.	1	57	76	0.5	1.1
179 CONSRV BAPT...	2	300	365*	2.6	5.2
193 EPISCOPAL.....	1	67	57	0.4	0.8
203 EVAN FREE CH..	2	26	32*	0.2	0.5
221 FREE METHODIST	2	73	255	1.8	3.6
283 LUTH--MO SYNOD	4	1 290	1 646	11.7	23.5
413 S.D.A.........	1	31	38*	0.3	0.5
449 UN METHODIST..	2	652	794*	5.6	11.3
ISANTI	34	7 792	12 543*	53.1	100.0
053 ASSEMB OF GOD.	1	56	100	0.4	0.8
057 BAPT GEN CONF.	10	1 833	2 302*	9.8	18.4
081 CATHOLIC......	2	NA	2 236	9.5	17.8
127 CH GOD (CLEVE)	1	38	48*	0.2	0.4
201 EVAN COV CH AM	2	176	221*	0.9	1.8
203 EVAN FREE CH..	2	55	69*	0.3	0.6
281 LUTH CH AMER..	8	3 885	5 253	22.3	41.9
283 LUTH--MO SYNOD	4	1 282	1 730	7.3	13.8
413 S.D.A.........	1	64	80*	0.3	0.6
449 UN METHODIST..	2	359	451*	1.9	3.6
469 WELS.........	1	44	53	0.2	0.4
ITASCA	68	8 866	20 720*	48.2	100.0

NA—Not applicable   *Total adherents estimated from known number of communicant, confirmed, full members.   —Represents a percent less than 0.1.   Percentages may not total due to rounding.

Table 4. Churches and Church Membership by County and Denomination: 1980

County and Denomination	Number of churches	Communicant, confirmed, full members	Total adherents Number	Total adherents Percent of total population	Total adherents Percent of total adherents
029 AMER LUTH CH..	5	796	1 037	2.4	5.0
045 APOSTOLIC LUTH	1	50	62*	0.1	0.3
053 ASSEMB OF GOD.	1	85	300	0.7	1.4
057 BAPT GEN CONF.	1	157	194*	0.5	0.9
081 CATHOLIC......	13	NA	8 483	19.7	40.9
089 CHR & MISS AL.	1	20	55	0.1	0.3
097 CHR CHS&CHS CR	1	100	123*	0.3	0.6
123 CH GOD (ANDER)	1	79	237	0.6	1.1
127 CH GOD (CLEVE)	1	45	55*	0.1	0.3
151 L-D SAINTS....	1	NA	240	0.6	1.2
163 CH OF LUTH BR.	2	45	104	0.2	0.5
165 CH OF NAZARENE	1	122	188	0.4	0.9
193 EPISCOPAL.....	3	232	278	0.6	1.3
201 EVAN COV CH AM	1	31	38*	0.1	0.2
281 LUTH CH AMER..	7	2 527	3 533	8.2	17.1
283 LUTH--MO SYNOD	6	1 577	2 086	4.9	10.1
285 MENNONITE CH..	3	54	67*	0.2	0.3
413 S.D.A........	1	86	106*	0.2	0.5
419 SO BAPT CONV..	1	22	27*	0.1	0.1
435 UNITARIAN-UNIV	1	15	18*	-	0.1
449 UN METHODIST..	5	1 075	1 325*	3.1	6.4
453 UN PRES CH USA	10	1 710	2 108*	4.9	10.2
469 WELS.........	1	38	56	0.1	0.3
JACKSON	29	6 541	10 797*	78.9	100.0
029 AMER LUTH CH..	8	2 068	2 665	19.5	24.7
081 CATHOLIC......	3	NA	2 504	18.3	23.2
164 CH LUTH CONF.	1	173	220	1.6	2.0
179 CONSRV BAPT...	1	120	145*	1.1	1.3
283 LUTH--MO SYNOD	9	2 699	3 476	25.4	32.2
285 MENNONITE CH..	1	40	48*	0.4	0.4
413 S.D.A........	1	11	13*	0.1	0.1
449 UN METHODIST..	4	890	1 074*	7.8	9.9
453 UN PRES CH USA	1	540	652*	4.8	6.0
KANABEC	22	4 081	7 461*	61.4	100.0
029 AMER LUTH CH..	1	366	497	4.1	6.7
053 ASSEMB OF GOD.	1	51	96	0.8	1.3
057 BAPT GEN CONF.	5	490	606*	5.0	8.1
081 CATHOLIC......	2	NA	1 988	16.3	26.6
105 CHRISTIAN REF.	1	126	213	1.8	2.9
165 CH OF NAZARENE	1	42	41	0.3	0.5
201 EVAN COV CH AM	1	70	87*	0.7	1.2
281 LUTH CH AMER..	3	1 184	1 624	13.4	21.8
283 LUTH--MO SYNOD	3	1 118	1 525	12.5	20.4
413 S.D.A........	1	22	27*	0.2	0.4
449 UN METHODIST..	2	324	401*	3.3	5.4
453 UN PRES CH USA	1	288	356*	2.9	4.8
KANDIYOHI	67	18 526	28 751*	78.2	100.0
029 AMER LUTH CH..	16	7 571	9 826	26.7	34.2
053 ASSEMB OF GOD.	1	375	500	1.4	1.7
057 BAPT GEN CONF.	3	545	660*	1.8	2.3
081 CATHOLIC......	6	NA	4 398	12.0	15.3
105 CHRISTIAN REF.	3	1 041	1 637	4.5	5.7
123 CH GOD (ANDER)	1	72	216	0.6	0.8
165 CH OF NAZARENE	1	76	135	0.4	0.5
167 CHS OF CHRIST.	1	18	27	0.1	0.1
179 CONSRV BAPT...	1	30	36*	0.1	0.1
193 EPISCOPAL.....	1	117	150	0.4	0.5
201 EVAN COV CH AM	3	806	977*	2.7	3.4
203 EVAN FREE CH..	1	82	99*	0.3	0.3
220 FREE LUTHERAN.	3	342	435	1.2	1.5
281 LUTH CH AMER..	7	3 228	4 209	11.4	14.6
283 LUTH--MO SYNOD	3	997	1 259	3.4	4.4
371 REF CH IN AM..	2	449	673	1.8	2.3
403 SALVATION ARMY	1	40	142	0.4	0.5
413 S.D.A........	1	61	74*	0.2	0.3
435 UNITARIAN-UNIV	1	35	42*	0.1	0.1
449 UN METHODIST..	7	1 378	1 670*	4.5	5.8
453 UN PRES CH USA	3	1 123	1 361*	3.7	4.7
469 WELS.........	1	140	225	0.6	0.8
KITTSON	22	3 170	4 526*	67.8	100.0
029 AMER LUTH CH..	3	703	961	14.4	21.2
053 ASSEMB OF GOD.	2	52	110	1.6	2.4
057 BAPT GEN CONF.	1	116	140*	2.1	3.1
081 CATHOLIC......	2	NA	374	5.6	8.3
201 EVAN COV CH AM	4	158	191*	2.9	4.2
281 LUTH CH AMER..	6	1 743	2 269	34.0	50.1
413 S.D.A........	2	37	45*	0.7	1.0
449 UN METHODIST..	1	86	104*	1.6	2.3
453 UN PRES CH USA	1	275	332*	5.0	7.3
KOOCHICHING	30	3 877	12 118*	69.0	100.0
029 AMER LUTH CH..	5	1 533	2 209	12.6	18.2
053 ASSEMB OF GOD.	1	101	210	1.2	1.7
057 BAPT GEN CONF.	1	68	84*	0.5	0.7
081 CATHOLIC......	4	NA	6 500	37.0	53.6
165 CH OF NAZARENE	1	48	114	0.6	0.9
193 EPISCOPAL.....	1	216	299	1.7	2.5
201 EVAN COV CH AM	3	187	230*	1.3	1.9
203 EVAN FREE CH..	1	41	50*	0.3	0.4
281 LUTH CH AMER..	2	635	993	5.7	8.2
283 LUTH--MO SYNOD	1	361	480	2.7	4.0
285 MENNONITE CH..	4	72	89*	0.5	0.7
403 SALVATION ARMY	1	64	182	1.0	1.5
413 S.D.A........	2	125	154*	0.9	1.3
443 UN C OF CHRIST	1	348	428*	2.4	3.5
449 UN METHODIST..	2	78	96*	0.5	0.8
LAC QUI PARLE	31	6 379	9 588*	90.5	100.0
029 AMER LUTH CH..	13	4 410	5 511	52.0	57.5
081 CATHOLIC......	4	NA	1 723	16.3	18.0
163 CH OF LUTH BR.	1	72	72	0.7	0.8
165 CH OF NAZARENE	1	17	23	0.2	0.2
201 EVAN COV CH AM	1	86	103*	1.0	1.1
281 LUTH CH AMER..	1	294	353	3.3	3.7
283 LUTH--MO SYNOD	4	779	951	9.0	9.9
443 UN C OF CHRIST	2	244	293*	2.8	3.1
449 UN METHODIST..	2	170	204*	1.9	2.1
453 UN PRES CH USA	1	214	257*	2.4	2.7
469 WELS.........	1	93	98	0.9	1.0
LAKE	21	3 952	7 881*	60.4	100.0
019 AMER BAPT USA.	1	445	539*	4.1	6.8
029 AMER LUTH CH..	5	1 690	2 352	18.0	29.8
053 ASSEMB OF GOD.	2	134	247	1.9	3.1
057 BAPT GEN CONF.	1	78	94*	0.7	1.2
081 CATHOLIC......	3	NA	2 489	19.1	31.6
179 CONSRV BAPT...	2	125	151*	1.2	1.9
203 EVAN FREE CH..	1	19	23*	0.2	0.3
281 LUTH CH AMER..	1	757	973	7.5	12.3
283 LUTH--MO SYNOD	2	263	325	2.5	4.1
403 SALVATION ARMY	1	42	205	1.6	2.6
449 UN METHODIST..	1	163	197*	1.5	2.5
453 UN PRES CH USA	1	236	286*	2.2	3.6
LAKE OF THE WOODS	18	1 437	2 542*	67.5	100.0
029 AMER LUTH CH..	3	552	768	20.4	30.2
053 ASSEMB OF GOD.	1	41	86	2.3	3.4
081 CATHOLIC......	2	NA	533	14.2	21.0
151 L-D SAINTS....	1	NA	57	1.5	2.2
201 EVAN COV CH AM	1	32	38*	1.0	1.5
203 EVAN FREE CH..	1	40	48*	1.3	1.9
281 LUTH CH AMER..	2	226	346	9.2	13.6
283 LUTH--MO SYNOD	1	113	145	3.9	5.7
285 MENNONITE CH..	1	10	12*	0.3	0.5
353 CHR BRETHREN..	1	125	150	4.0	5.9
413 S.D.A........	1	23	28*	0.7	1.1
443 UN C OF CHRIST	3	275	331*	8.8	13.0
LE SUEUR	40	6 222	18 032*	76.9	100.0
029 AMER LUTH CH..	4	1 543	2 010	8.6	11.1
053 ASSEMB OF GOD.	1	25	106	0.5	0.6
081 CATHOLIC......	13	NA	9 805	41.8	54.4
089 CHR & MISS AL.	1	45	200	0.9	1.1
097 CHR CHS&CHS CR	1	135	166*	0.7	0.9
163 CH OF LUTH BR.	1	18	30	0.1	0.2
193 EPISCOPAL.....	2	84	94	0.4	0.5
281 LUTH CH AMER..	1	553	814	3.5	4.5
283 LUTH--MO SYNOD	4	1 078	1 433	6.1	7.9
413 S.D.A........	1	16	20*	0.1	0.1
443 UN C OF CHRIST	1	784	967*	4.1	5.4
449 UN METHODIST..	6	1 128	1 391*	5.9	7.7
453 UN PRES CH USA	2	343	423*	1.8	2.3
469 WELS.........	2	470	573	2.4	3.2
LINCOLN	24	4 081	7 494*	91.3	100.0
029 AMER LUTH CH..	7	1 962	2 501	30.5	33.4
081 CATHOLIC......	4	NA	2 266	27.6	30.2
089 CHR & MISS AL.	1	38	104	1.3	1.4
163 CH OF LUTH BR.	1	22	41	0.5	0.5
193 EPISCOPAL.....	1	19	21	0.3	0.3
281 LUTH CH AMER..	3	1 044	1 315	16.0	17.5
449 UN METHODIST..	4	445	539*	6.6	7.2
469 WELS.........	3	551	707	8.6	9.4
LYON	43	8 508	19 878*	78.9	100.0
029 AMER LUTH CH..	9	3 845	5 173	20.5	26.0
053 ASSEMB OF GOD.	1	43	66	0.3	0.3
057 BAPT GEN CONF.	1	17	21*	0.1	0.1
081 CATHOLIC......	7	NA	8 816	35.0	44.4
089 CHR & MISS AL.	1	15	49	0.2	0.2
097 CHR CHS&CHS CR	2	25	30*	0.1	0.2
193 EPISCOPAL.....	1	81	115	0.5	0.6
203 EVAN FREE CH..	2	125	152*	0.6	0.8
209 EVAN LUTH SYN.	2	332	444	1.8	2.2
281 LUTH CH AMER..	2	390	491	1.9	2.5
283 LUTH--MO SYNOD	2	283	402	1.6	2.0
443 UN C OF CHRIST	1	92	112*	0.4	0.6
449 UN METHODIST..	5	1 502	1 823*	7.2	9.2
453 UN PRES CH USA	4	906	1 100*	4.4	5.5
469 WELS.........	3	852	1 084	4.3	5.5
MC LEOD	46	14 777	27 389*	92.4	100.0
029 AMER LUTH CH..	8	3 544	5 001	16.9	18.3
053 ASSEMB OF GOD.	1	64	150	0.5	0.5
057 BAPT GEN CONF.	1	132	162*	0.5	0.6
081 CATHOLIC......	7	NA	7 822	26.4	28.6
151 L-D SAINTS....	1	NA	83	0.3	0.3
193 EPISCOPAL.....	1	34	31	0.1	0.1
283 LUTH--MO SYNOD	9	6 309	8 335	28.1	30.4
313 N AM BAPT CONF	1	85	104*	0.4	0.4
413 S.D.A........	1	375	461*	1.6	1.7
443 UN C OF CHRIST	7	1 898	2 331*	7.9	8.5
449 UN METHODIST..	3	953	1 171*	3.9	4.3
453 UN PRES CH USA	2	400	491*	1.7	1.8
469 WELS.........	4	983	1 247	4.2	4.6

NA— Not applicable   *Total adherents estimated from known number of communicant, confirmed, full members.   —Represents a percent less than 0.1.   Percentages may not total due to rounding.

Table 4. Churches and Church Membership by County and Denomination: 1980

County and Denomination	Number of churches	Communicant, confirmed, full members	Total adherents Number	Percent of total population	Percent of total adherents
MAHNOMEN	18	1 868	5 131*	92.7	100.0
029 AMER LUTH CH..	6	1 444	1 967	35.5	38.3
053 ASSEMB OF GOD.	1	30	55	1.0	1.1
081 CATHOLIC......	5	NA	2 546	46.0	49.6
105 CHRISTIAN REF.	1	18	23	0.4	0.4
193 EPISCOPAL.....	1	91	183	3.3	3.6
283 LUTH--MO SYNOD	1	144	180	3.3	3.5
443 UN C OF CHRIST	2	124	156*	2.8	3.0
449 UN METHODIST..	1	17	21*	0.4	0.4
MARSHALL	51	5 504	11 081*	85.1	100.0
029 AMER LUTH CH..	15	3 218	4 350	33.4	39.3
053 ASSEMB OF GOD.	1	18	25	0.2	0.2
057 BAPT GEN CONF.	3	68	84*	0.6	0.8
081 CATHOLIC......	9	NA	3 771	28.9	34.0
163 CH OF LUTH BR.	1	17	27	0.2	0.2
167 CHS OF CHRIST.	1	3	5	-	-
201 EVAN COV CH AM	3	239	295*	2.3	2.7
203 EVAN FREE CH..	1	46	57*	0.4	0.5
209 EVAN LUTH SYN.	1	40	55	0.4	0.5
220 FREE LUTHERAN.	4	247	380	2.9	3.4
281 LUTH CH AMER..	6	838	1 056	8.1	9.5
283 LUTH--MO SYNOD	2	293	386	3.0	3.5
413 S.D.A.........	1	79	98*	0.8	0.9
449 UN METHODIST..	1	216	267*	2.0	2.4
453 UN PRES CH USA	2	182	225*	1.7	2.0
MARTIN	57	14 106	22 526*	91.2	100.0
019 AMER BAPT USA.	1	178	214*	0.9	1.0
029 AMER LUTH CH..	6	2 858	3 752	15.2	16.7
053 ASSEMB OF GOD.	3	213	390	1.6	1.7
081 CATHOLIC......	5	NA	4 534	18.4	20.1
097 CHR CHS&CHS CR	3	285	343*	1.4	1.5
151 L-D SAINTS....	1	NA	48	0.2	0.2
193 EPISCOPAL.....	1	139	186	0.8	0.8
201 EVAN COV CH AM	2	236	284*	1.2	1.3
203 EVAN FREE CH..	2	295	355*	1.4	1.6
281 LUTH CH AMER..	3	480	566	2.3	2.5
283 LUTH--MO SYNOD	12	5 715	7 297	29.6	32.4
403 SALVATION ARMY	1	44	135	0.5	0.6
413 S.D.A.........	1	5	6*	-	-
443 UN C OF CHRIST	7	1 810	2 179*	8.8	9.7
449 UN METHODIST..	8	1 816	2 186*	8.9	9.7
469 WELS.........	1	32	51	0.2	0.2
MEEKER	42	9 271	16 546*	80.3	100.0
029 AMER LUTH CH..	4	2 091	2 690	13.1	16.3
045 APOSTOLIC LUTH	1	50	61*	0.3	0.4
053 ASSEMB OF GOD.	1	54	97	0.5	0.6
057 BAPT GEN CONF.	2	273	335*	1.6	2.0
061 BEACHY AMISH..	1	54	66*	0.3	0.4
081 CATHOLIC......	6	NA	4 610	22.4	27.9
121 CH GOD (ABR)..	1	52	64*	0.3	0.4
165 CH OF NAZARENE	2	134	250	1.2	1.5
193 EPISCOPAL.....	1	134	163	0.8	1.0
201 EVAN COV CH AM	2	467	573*	2.8	3.5
203 EVAN FREE CH..	1	40	49*	0.2	0.3
281 LUTH CH AMER..	10	3 187	4 079	19.8	24.7
283 LUTH--MO SYNOD	3	891	1 209	5.9	7.3
413 S.D.A.........	1	32	39*	0.2	0.2
443 UN C OF CHRIST	1	191	234*	1.1	1.4
449 UN METHODIST..	2	585	718*	3.5	4.3
453 UN PRES CH USA	1	190	233*	1.1	1.4
469 WELS.........	2	846	1 076	5.2	6.5
MILLE LACS	41	7 190	13 854*	75.2	100.0
029 AMER LUTH CH..	3	1 292	1 687	9.2	12.2
053 ASSEMB OF GOD.	2	131	270	1.5	1.9
057 BAPT GEN CONF.	2	305	374*	2.0	2.7
081 CATHOLIC......	6	NA	3 778	20.5	27.3
089 CHR & MISS AL.	3	142	303	1.6	2.2
105 CHRISTIAN REF.	2	567	948	5.1	6.8
151 L-D SAINTS....	1	NA	211	1.1	1.5
203 EVAN FREE CH..	6	395	485*	2.6	3.5
209 EVAN LUTH SYN.	2	554	799	4.3	5.8
281 LUTH CH AMER..	5	2 054	2 816	15.3	20.3
283 LUTH--MO SYNOD	3	716	914	5.0	6.6
413 S.D.A.........	1	2	2*	-	-
443 UN C OF CHRIST	1	180	221*	1.2	1.6
449 UN METHODIST..	3	788	967*	5.2	7.0
453 UN PRES CH USA	1	64	79*	0.4	0.6
MORRISON	46	4 994	24 627*	84.0	100.0
029 AMER LUTH CH..	1	565	829	2.8	3.4
053 ASSEMB OF GOD.	1	69	90	0.3	0.4
057 BAPT GEN CONF.	1	47	59*	0.2	0.2
081 CATHOLIC......	19	NA	17 970	61.3	73.0
089 CHR & MISS AL.	2	72	173	0.6	0.7
181 CONSRV CONGR..	1	82	103*	0.4	0.4
193 EPISCOPAL.....	2	112	143	0.5	0.6
201 EVAN COV CH AM	2	243	304*	1.0	1.2
203 EVAN FREE CH..	1	30	38*	0.1	0.2
281 LUTH CH AMER..	4	916	1 205	4.1	4.9
283 LUTH--MO SYNOD	8	2 052	2 704	9.2	11.0
443 UN C OF CHRIST	1	247	309*	1.1	1.3
449 UN METHODIST..	2	393	492*	1.7	2.0
453 UN PRES CH USA	1	166	208*	0.7	0.8
MOWER	64	18 076	35 211*	87.2	100.0
029 AMER LUTH CH..	16	9 735	12 553	31.1	35.7
053 ASSEMB OF GOD.	1	69	91	0.2	0.3
081 CATHOLIC......	11	NA	12 040	29.8	34.2
089 CHR & MISS AL.	1	14	33	0.1	0.1
093 CHR CH (DISC).	1	64	106	0.3	0.3
097 CHR CHS&CHS CR	1	500	599*	1.5	1.7
151 L-D SAINTS....	1	NA	198	0.5	0.6
164 CH LUTH CONF..	1	202	262	0.6	0.7
179 CONSRV BAPT...	1	30	36*	0.1	0.1
193 EPISCOPAL.....	1	446	469	1.2	1.3
201 EVAN COV CH AM	1	46	55*	0.1	0.2
221 FREE METHODIST	1	39	117	0.3	0.3
283 LUTH--MO SYNOD	7	1 889	2 281	5.6	6.5
329 OPEN BIBLE STD	1	180	300	0.7	0.9
403 SALVATION ARMY	1	233	521	1.3	1.5
413 S.D.A.........	1	32	38*	0.1	0.1
435 UNITARIAN-UNIV	1	9	11*	-	-
443 UN C OF CHRIST	3	585	700*	1.7	2.0
449 UN METHODIST..	9	2 605	3 119*	7.7	8.9
453 UN PRES CH USA	2	1 141	1 366*	3.4	3.9
469 WELS.........	2	257	316	0.8	0.9
MURRAY	27	4 842	9 526*	82.8	100.0
029 AMER LUTH CH..	7	1 481	1 957	17.0	20.5
053 ASSEMB OF GOD.	1	65	76	0.7	0.8
057 BAPT GEN CONF.	1	149	182*	1.6	1.9
081 CATHOLIC......	5	NA	2 945	25.6	30.9
105 CHRISTIAN REF.	1	212	381	3.3	4.0
281 LUTH CH AMER..	2	507	683	5.9	7.2
283 LUTH--MO SYNOD	2	888	1 189	10.3	12.5
371 REF CH IN AM..	2	392	710	6.2	7.5
449 UN METHODIST..	2	487	595*	5.2	6.2
453 UN PRES CH USA	4	661	808*	7.0	8.5
NICOLLET	32	8 364	17 690*	65.7	100.0
029 AMER LUTH CH..	1	620	1 032	3.8	5.8
053 ASSEMB OF GOD.	1	72	150	0.6	0.8
081 CATHOLIC......	8	NA	6 600	24.5	37.3
089 CHR & MISS AL.	1	52	134	0.5	0.8
097 CHR CHS&CHS CR	1	50	61*	0.2	0.3
164 CH LUTH CONF..	1	42	52	0.2	0.3
193 EPISCOPAL.....	1	187	235	0.9	1.3
209 EVAN LUTH SYN.	1	248	297	1.1	1.7
263 INT FOURSQ GOS	1	53	64*	0.2	0.4
281 LUTH CH AMER..	6	3 077	3 977	14.8	22.5
283 LUTH--MO SYNOD	1	370	490	1.8	2.8
449 UN METHODIST..	3	640	775*	2.9	4.4
453 UN PRES CH USA	1	275	333*	1.2	1.9
469 WELS.........	5	2 678	3 490	13.0	19.7
NOBLES	46	10 478	20 360*	93.2	100.0
029 AMER LUTH CH..	3	1 212	1 746	8.0	8.6
053 ASSEMB OF GOD.	1	131	215	1.0	1.1
057 BAPT GEN CONF.	1	173	210*	1.0	1.0
081 CATHOLIC......	8	NA	6 516	29.8	32.0
097 CHR CHS&CHS CR	1	600	727*	3.3	3.6
105 CHRISTIAN REF.	3	612	1 006	4.6	4.9
157 CH OF BRETHREN	1	124	150*	0.7	0.7
179 CONSRV BAPT...	1	300	364*	1.7	1.8
201 EVAN COV CH AM	1	112	136*	0.6	0.7
281 LUTH CH AMER..	2	1 020	1 300	6.0	6.4
283 LUTH--MO SYNOD	4	2 109	2 699	12.4	13.3
371 REF CH IN AM..	3	551	1 009	4.6	5.0
435 UNITARIAN-UNIV	1	11	13*	0.1	0.1
443 UN C OF CHRIST	1	?	?	?	?
449 UN METHODIST..	4	1 060	1 284*	5.9	6.3
453 UN PRES CH USA	11	2 463	2 985*	13.7	14.7
NORMAN	33	6 630	9 125*	97.3	100.0
029 AMER LUTH CH..	25	5 784	7 236	77.2	79.3
081 CATHOLIC......	2	NA	757	8.1	8.3
281 LUTH CH AMER..	1	115	139	1.5	1.5
283 LUTH--MO SYNOD	3	635	877	9.4	9.6
443 UN C OF CHRIST	1	71	86*	0.9	0.9
453 UN PRES CH USA	1	25	30*	0.3	0.3
OLMSTED	78	28 871	59 409*	64.6	100.0
029 AMER LUTH CH..	8	9 329	13 190	14.3	22.2
053 ASSEMB OF GOD.	1	240	400	0.4	0.7
057 BAPT GEN CONF.	1	108	132*	0.1	0.2
063 BEREAN FUND CH	1	67	82*	0.1	0.1
081 CATHOLIC......	11	NA	19 978	21.7	33.6
089 CHR & MISS AL.	1	57	102	0.1	0.2
093 CHR CH (DISC).	1	165	248	0.3	0.4
097 CHR CHS&CHS CR	4	475	579*	0.6	1.0
151 L-D SAINTS....	1	NA	431	0.5	0.7
163 CH OF LUTH BR.	1	30	55	0.1	0.1
164 CH LUTH CONF..	1	24	35	-	0.1
165 CH OF NAZARENE	1	89	196	0.2	0.3
167 CHS OF CHRIST.	2	126	191	0.2	0.3
193 EPISCOPAL.....	2	1 005	1 731	1.9	2.9
201 EVAN COV CH AM	2	350	427*	0.5	0.7
203 EVAN FREE CH..	2	143	174*	0.2	0.3
226 FRIENDS-USA...	1	6	7*	-	-
271 REFORM JUDAISM	1	180	220*	0.2	0.4
281 LUTH CH AMER..	2	488	679	0.7	1.1
283 LUTH--MO SYNOD	9	5 095	6 632	7.2	11.2
329 OPEN BIBLE STD	1	40	50	0.1	0.1
371 REF CH IN AM..	1	175	294	0.3	0.5
403 SALVATION ARMY	1	116	493	0.5	0.8

NA—Not applicable   *Total adherents estimated from known number of communicant, confirmed, full members.   —Represents a percent less than 0.1.   Percentages may not total due to rounding.

Table 4. Churches and Church Membership by County and Denomination: 1980

County and Denomination	Number of churches	Communicant, confirmed, full members	Total adherents		
			Number	Percent of total population	Percent of total adherents
413 S.D.A.........	1	169	206*	0.2	0.3
419 SO BAPT CONV..	1	154	188*	0.2	0.3
435 UNITARIAN-UNIV	1	120	146*	0.2	0.2
443 UN C OF CHRIST	3	1 704	2 078*	2.3	3.5
449 UN METHODIST..	11	5 897	7 193*	7.8	12.1
453 UN PRES CH USA	2	1 831	2 233*	2.4	3.8
469 WELS.........	3	688	1 039	1.1	1.7
OTTER TAIL	**129**	**25 413**	**39 888***	**76.8**	**100.0**
019 AMER BAPT USA.	1	65	78*	0.2	0.2
029 AMER LUTH CH..	31	9 993	12 748	24.5	32.0
045 APOSTOLIC LUTH	1	500	600*	1.2	1.5
053 ASSEMB OF GOD.	3	113	257	0.5	0.6
057 BAPT GEN CONF.	4	542	651*	1.3	1.6
081 CATHOLIC......	14	NA	7 497	14.4	18.8
089 CHR & MISS AL.	1	76	176	0.3	0.4
151 L-D SAINTS....	1	NA	93	0.2	0.2
163 CH OF LUTH BR.	3	570	776	1.5	1.9
164 CH LUTH CONF..	1	17	20	-	0.1
165 CH OF NAZARENE	1	92	227	0.4	0.6
167 CHS OF CHRIST.	1	20	25	-	0.1
179 CONSRV BAPT...	1	90	108*	0.2	0.3
193 EPISCOPAL.....	1	145	188	0.4	0.5
197 EVAN CH OF NA.	1	14	14	-	-
203 EVAN FREE CH..	1	42	50*	0.1	0.1
208 EVAN LUTH ASSN	1	140	185	0.4	0.5
220 FREE LUTHERAN.	6	426	616	1.2	1.5
281 LUTH CH AMER..	10	2 971	3 792	7.3	9.5
283 LUTH--MO SYNOD	21	6 192	7 596	14.6	19.0
403 SALVATION ARMY	1	4	107	0.2	0.3
413 S.D.A.........	3	91	109*	0.2	0.3
435 UNITARIAN-UNIV	1	47	56*	0.1	0.1
443 UN C OF CHRIST	6	820	985*	1.9	2.5
449 UN METHODIST..	11	1 852	2 224*	4.3	5.6
453 UN PRES CH USA	3	591	710*	1.4	1.8
PENNINGTON	**24**	**6 846**	**11 461***	**75.1**	**100.0**
029 AMER LUTH CH..	9	4 057	5 429	35.6	47.4
053 ASSEMB OF GOD.	1	69	115	0.8	1.0
057 BAPT GEN CONF.	1	122	149*	1.0	1.3
081 CATHOLIC......	2	NA	2 097	13.7	18.3
163 CH OF LUTH BR.	2	114	194	1.3	1.7
201 EVAN COV CH AM	1	140	171*	1.1	1.5
203 EVAN FREE CH..	1	153	187*	1.2	1.6
220 FREE LUTHERAN.	2	246	379	2.5	3.3
281 LUTH CH AMER..	2	988	1 512	9.9	13.2
283 LUTH--MO SYNOD	1	418	569	3.7	5.0
413 S.D.A.........	1	143	175*	1.1	1.5
449 UN METHODIST..	1	396	484*	3.2	4.2
PINE	**47**	**4 845**	**10 740***	**54.0**	**100.0**
045 APOSTOLIC LUTH	1	25	31*	0.2	0.3
053 ASSEMB OF GOD.	2	79	203	1.0	1.9
081 CATHOLIC......	8	NA	4 095	20.6	38.1
151 L-D SAINTS....	1	NA	117	0.6	1.1
165 CH OF NAZARENE	1	51	51	0.3	0.5
167 CHS OF CHRIST.	1	15	26	0.1	0.2
193 EPISCOPAL.....	1	69	72	0.4	0.7
203 EVAN FREE CH..	2	204	250*	1.3	2.3
220 FREE LUTHERAN.	1	68	80	0.4	0.7
221 FREE METHODIST	1	38	120	0.6	1.1
281 LUTH CH AMER..	10	1 957	2 639	13.3	24.6
283 LUTH--MO SYNOD	5	1 330	1 818	9.1	16.9
413 S.D.A.........	2	82	101*	0.5	0.9
443 UN C OF CHRIST	1	131	161*	0.8	1.5
449 UN METHODIST..	3	402	493*	2.5	4.6
453 UN PRES CH USA	7	394	483*	2.4	4.5
PIPESTONE	**34**	**7 060**	**11 364***	**97.2**	**100.0**
029 AMER LUTH CH..	3	1 594	2 092	17.9	18.4
053 ASSEMB OF GOD.	1	39	68	0.6	0.6
057 BAPT GEN CONF.	1	117	141*	1.2	1.2
081 CATHOLIC......	3	NA	1 849	15.8	16.3
097 CHR CHS&CHS CR	1	15	18*	0.2	0.2
105 CHRISTIAN REF.	4	1 081	1 694	14.5	14.9
167 CHS OF CHRIST.	1	3	12	0.1	0.1
193 EPISCOPAL.....	1	23	32	0.3	0.3
209 EVAN LUTH SYN.	1	63	88	0.8	0.8
283 LUTH--MO SYNOD	6	1 747	2 132	18.2	18.8
369 PROT REF CHS..	1	54	113	1.0	1.0
371 REF CH IN AM..	2	548	984	8.4	8.7
413 S.D.A.........	1	53	64*	0.5	0.6
449 UN METHODIST..	5	977	1 178*	10.1	10.4
453 UN PRES CH USA	3	746	899*	7.7	7.9
POLK	**88**	**14 578**	**26 412***	**75.8**	**100.0**
029 AMER LUTH CH..	30	8 647	11 373	32.6	43.1
053 ASSEMB OF GOD.	1	45	75	0.2	0.3
057 BAPT GEN CONF.	3	226	275*	0.8	1.0
081 CATHOLIC......	11	NA	7 707	22.1	29.2
097 CHR CHS&CHS CR	1	95	116*	0.3	0.4
105 CHRISTIAN REF.	2	83	131	0.4	0.5
163 CH OF LUTH BR.	1	15	16	-	0.1
167 CHS OF CHRIST.	1	17	25	0.1	0.1
179 CONSRV BAPT...	1	100	122*	0.4	0.5
193 EPISCOPAL.....	1	26	30	0.1	0.1
201 EVAN COV CH AM	2	99	120*	0.3	0.5
209 EVAN LUTH SYN.	6	445	581	1.7	2.2
220 FREE LUTHERAN.	6	518	420	1.2	1.6
281 LUTH CH AMER..	6	763	979	2.8	3.7

County and Denomination	Number of churches	Communicant, confirmed, full members	Total adherents		
			Number	Percent of total population	Percent of total adherents
283 LUTH--MO SYNOD	7	1 883	2 476	7.1	9.4
413 S.D.A.........	1	9	11*	-	-
449 UN METHODIST..	4	631	768*	2.2	2.9
453 UN PRES CH USA	4	976	1 187*	3.4	4.5
POPE	**33**	**6 401**	**9 748***	**83.6**	**100.0**
029 AMER LUTH CH..	15	5 057	6 243	53.6	64.0
053 ASSEMB OF GOD.	1	27	53	0.5	0.5
081 CATHOLIC......	4	NA	1 809	15.5	18.6
167 CHS OF CHRIST.	1	13	21	0.2	0.2
201 EVAN COV CH AM	1	78	94*	0.8	1.0
220 FREE LUTHERAN.	1	115	139	1.2	1.4
281 LUTH CH AMER..	2	84	108	0.9	1.1
283 LUTH--MO SYNOD	2	409	529	4.5	5.4
383 REF PRES OF NA	1	23	27	0.2	0.3
413 S.D.A.........	1	50	60*	0.5	0.6
443 UN C OF CHRIST	1	167	202*	1.7	2.1
449 UN METHODIST..	2	303	366*	3.1	3.8
469 WELS.........	1	75	97	0.8	1.0
RAMSEY	**269**	**104 032**	**285 417***	**62.1**	**100.0**
019 AMER BAPT USA.	10	3 858	4 602*	1.0	1.6
029 AMER LUTH CH..	26	19 063	24 965	5.4	8.7
053 ASSEMB OF GOD.	9	1 020	1 801	0.4	0.6
057 BAPT GEN CONF.	13	4 351	5 190*	1.1	1.8
081 CATHOLIC......	49	NA	145 122	31.6	50.8
089 CHR & MISS AL.	5	549	938	0.2	0.3
093 CHR CH (DISC)	1	233	328	0.1	0.1
097 CHR CHS&CHS CR	2	245	292*	0.1	0.1
105 CHRISTIAN REF.	1	200	385	0.1	0.1
123 CH GOD (ANDER)	1	17	51	-	-
127 CH GOD (CLEVE)	1	?	?	?	?
133 CH GOD(7TH)DEN	1	40	48*	-	-
151 L-D SAINTS....	4	NA	1 842	0.4	0.6
165 CH OF NAZARENE	3	246	512	0.1	0.2
167 CHS OF CHRIST.	2	177	263	0.1	0.1
179 CONSRV BAPT...	3	490	585*	0.1	0.2
193 EPISCOPAL.....	14	4 714	6 096	1.3	2.1
201 EVAN COV CH AM	6	2 117	2 525*	0.5	0.9
203 EVAN FREE CH..	4	424	506*	0.1	0.2
208 EVAN LUTH ASSN	5	4 035	5 752	1.3	2.0
226 FRIENDS-USA...	1	140	167*	-	0.1
239 SWEDENBORGIAN.	1	60	72*	-	-
270 CONSRV JUDAISM	3	799	953*	0.2	0.3
271 REFORM JUDAISM	1	1 216	1 451*	0.3	0.5
281 LUTH CH AMER..	23	23 446	34 817	7.6	12.2
283 LUTH--MO SYNOD	15	9 273	12 508	2.7	4.4
290 METRO COMM CHS	1	43	100	-	-
313 N AM BAPT CONF	1	220	262*	0.1	0.1
353 CHR BRETHREN..	1	125	150	-	0.1
371 REF CH IN AM..	1	305	619	0.1	0.2
403 SALVATION ARMY	2	431	1 014	0.2	0.4
413 S.D.A.........	2	455	543*	0.1	0.2
419 SO BAPT CONV..	1	220	262*	0.1	0.1
435 UNITARIAN-UNIV	1	705	841*	0.2	0.3
443 UN C OF CHRIST	11	5 626	6 711*	1.5	2.4
449 UN METHODIST..	22	7 976	9 515*	2.1	3.3
453 UN PRES CH USA	15	7 525	8 977*	2.0	3.1
469 WELS.........	7	3 688	4 652	1.0	1.6
RED LAKE	**19**	**1 808**	**4 854***	**88.7**	**100.0**
029 AMER LUTH CH..	6	970	1 384	25.3	28.5
081 CATHOLIC......	6	NA	2 396	43.8	49.4
209 EVAN LUTH SYN.	3	317	421	7.7	8.7
283 LUTH--MO SYNOD	2	367	462	8.4	9.5
453 UN PRES CH USA	2	154	191*	3.5	3.9
REDWOOD	**57**	**9 206**	**18 030***	**93.2**	**100.0**
029 AMER LUTH CH..	12	3 561	4 680	24.2	26.0
053 ASSEMB OF GOD.	1	60	100	0.5	0.6
081 CATHOLIC......	12	NA	6 101	31.5	33.8
097 CHR CHS&CHS CR	2	375	457*	2.4	2.5
164 CH LUTH CONF..	1	71	112	0.6	0.6
165 CH OF NAZARENE	1	25	122	0.6	0.7
193 EPISCOPAL.....	1	88	150	0.8	0.8
197 EVAN CH OF NA.	1	25	25	0.1	0.1
209 EVAN LUTH SYN.	2	379	468	2.4	2.6
281 LUTH CH AMER..	1	295	353	1.8	2.0
283 LUTH--MO SYNOD	2	179	230	1.2	1.3
367 PROT CONF (WI)	1	150	200	1.0	1.1
413 S.D.A.........	1	35	43*	0.2	0.2
449 UN METHODIST..	9	1 590	1 937*	10.0	10.7
453 UN PRES CH USA	4	610	743*	3.8	4.1
469 WELS.........	6	1 763	2 309	11.9	12.8
RENVILLE	**55**	**10 368**	**18 584***	**91.1**	**100.0**
029 AMER LUTH CH..	13	4 280	5 395	26.4	29.0
045 APOSTOLIC LUTH	1	30	36*	0.2	0.2
081 CATHOLIC......	8	NA	5 556	27.2	29.9
089 CHR & MISS AL.	1	15	48	0.2	0.3
105 CHRISTIAN REF.	1	157	224	1.1	1.2
121 CH GOD (ABR)..	1	40	49*	0.2	0.3
163 CH OF LUTH BR.	1	25	43	0.2	0.2
165 CH OF NAZARENE	2	48	63	0.3	0.3
201 EVAN COV CH AM	1	61	74*	0.4	0.4
203 EVAN FREE CH..	1	33	40*	0.2	0.2
281 LUTH CH AMER..	4	1 405	1 837	9.0	9.9
449 UN METHODIST..	12	2 015	2 444*	12.0	13.2
453 UN PRES CH USA	1	238	289*	1.4	1.6
469 WELS.........	8	2 021	2 486	12.2	13.4

NA— Not applicable   *Total adherents estimated from known number of communicant, confirmed, full members.   —Represents a percent less than 0.1.   Percentages may not total due to rounding.

Table 4. Churches and Church Membership by County and Denomination: 1980

County and Denomination	Number of churches	Communicant, confirmed, full members	Total adherents		
			Number	Percent of total population	Percent of total adherents
RICE	49	13 608	31 310*	67.9	100.0
029 AMER LUTH CH..	10	5 406	7 319	15.9	23.4
053 ASSEMB OF GOD.	2	168	315	0.7	1.0
081 CATHOLIC......	8	NA	13 254	28.8	42.3
089 CHR & MISS AL.	1	62	219	0.5	0.7
097 CHR CHS&CHS CR	1	50	60*	0.1	0.2
151 L-D SAINTS....	1	NA	132	0.3	0.4
163 CH OF LUTH BR.	1	57	113	0.2	0.4
193 EPISCOPAL.....	3	589	810	1.8	2.6
283 LUTH--MO SYNOD	6	3 334	4 328	9.4	13.8
293 MORAV CH-NORTH	1	100	114	0.2	0.4
413 S.D.A.........	1	83	100*	0.2	0.3
435 UNITARIAN-UNIV	1	16	19*	—	0.1
443 UN C OF CHRIST	4	1 509	1 825*	4.0	5.8
449 UN METHODIST..	9	2 234	2 702*	5.9	8.6
ROCK	17	5 455	8 403*	78.5	100.0
029 AMER LUTH CH..	3	1 559	2 063	19.3	24.6
053 ASSEMB OF GOD.	1	16	27	0.3	0.3
081 CATHOLIC......	1	NA	1 000	9.3	11.9
105 CHRISTIAN REF.	2	307	563	5.3	6.7
179 CONSRV BAPT...	1	120	147*	1.4	1.7
209 EVAN LUTH SYN.	1	271	334	3.1	4.0
283 LUTH--MO SYNOD	2	1 134	1 374	12.8	16.4
371 REF CH IN AM..	2	655	1 187	11.1	14.1
449 UN METHODIST..	2	717	879*	8.2	10.5
453 UN PRES CH USA	2	676	829*	7.7	9.9
ROSEAU	45	5 200	9 363*	74.5	100.0
029 AMER LUTH CH..	12	2 455	3 329	26.5	35.6
053 ASSEMB OF GOD.	1	55	95	0.8	1.0
057 BAPT GEN CONF.	1	149	184*	1.5	2.0
081 CATHOLIC......	7	NA	2 352	18.7	25.1
175 CONGR CHR CHS.	1	160	198*	1.6	2.1
193 EPISCOPAL.....	1	54	62	0.5	0.7
201 EVAN COV CH AM	3	100	124*	1.0	1.3
203 EVAN FREE CH..	1	75	93*	0.7	1.0
220 FREE LUTHERAN.	10	1 085	1 435	11.4	15.3
281 LUTH CH AMER..	4	891	1 313	10.4	14.0
285 MENNONITE CH..	1	5	6*	—	0.1
353 CHR BRETHREN..	1	80	60	0.5	0.6
413 S.D.A.........	1	2	2*	—	—
449 UN METHODIST..	1	89	110*	0.9	1.2
ST LOUIS	248	53 940	131 764*	59.3	100.0
019 AMER BAPT USA.	3	309	371*	0.2	0.3
029 AMER LUTH CH..	19	10 840	14 659	6.6	11.1
045 APOSTOLIC LUTH	2	100	120*	0.1	0.1
053 ASSEMB OF GOD.	8	863	2 193	1.0	1.7
057 BAPT GEN CONF.	16	2 467	2 962*	1.3	2.2
081 CATHOLIC......	51	NA	59 778	26.9	45.4
089 CHR & MISS AL.	2	205	420	0.2	0.3
093 CHR CH (DISC).	1	144	183	0.1	0.1
097 CHR CHS&CHS CR	1	30	36*	—	—
123 CH GOD (ANDER)	1	40	120	0.1	0.1
151 L-D SAINTS....	2	NA	733	0.3	0.6
163 CH OF LUTH BR.	1	14	18	—	—
165 CH OF NAZARENE	2	23	116	0.1	0.1
167 CHS OF CHRIST.	4	152	229	0.1	0.2
175 CONGR CHR CHS.	1	307	369*	0.2	0.3
181 CONSRV CONGR..	3	563	676*	0.3	0.5
193 EPISCOPAL.....	10	1 840	2 342	1.1	1.8
197 EVAN CH OF NA.	1	46	46	—	—
201 EVAN COV CH AM	9	1 004	1 206*	0.5	0.9
203 EVAN FREE CH..	3	42	50*	—	—
208 EVAN LUTH ASSN	1	50	250	0.1	0.2
211 EVAN MENN BR..	1	28	36	—	—
220 FREE LUTHERAN.	2	115	140	0.1	0.1
226 FRIENDS-USA...	1	11	13*	—	—
263 INT FOURSQ GOS	1	49	59*	—	—
270 CONSRV JUDAISM	2	342	411*	0.2	0.3
271 REFORM JUDAISM	1	616	740*	0.3	0.6
281 LUTH CH AMER..	35	15 119	19 967	9.0	15.2
283 LUTH--MO SYNOD	12	3 654	4 895	2.2	3.7
353 CHR BRETHREN..	2	60	75	—	0.1
403 SALVATION ARMY	4	567	1 301	0.6	1.0
413 S.D.A.........	3	232	279*	0.1	0.2
419 SO BAPT CONV..	2	307	369*	0.2	0.3
435 UNITARIAN-UNIV	3	198	238*	0.1	0.2
443 UN C OF CHRIST	4	1 810	2 173*	1.0	1.6
449 UN METHODIST..	23	6 889	8 272*	3.7	6.3
453 UN PRES CH USA	10	4 820	5 788*	2.6	4.4
469 WELS..........	1	84	131	0.1	0.1
SCOTT	36	7 649	36 624*	83.6	100.0
029 AMER LUTH CH..	5	2 366	3 364	7.7	9.2
053 ASSEMB OF GOD.	2	93	245	0.6	0.7
057 BAPT GEN CONF.	1	34	43*	0.1	0.1
081 CATHOLIC......	13	NA	25 715	58.7	70.2
281 LUTH CH AMER..	2	1 247	1 956	4.5	5.3
283 LUTH--MO SYNOD	3	1 371	1 903	4.3	5.2
313 N AM BAPT CONF	1	32	40*	0.1	0.1
449 UN METHODIST..	4	800	1 010*	2.3	2.8
453 UN PRES CH USA	1	363	458*	1.0	1.3
469 WELS..........	4	1 343	1 890	4.3	5.2
SHERBURNE	32	5 695	15 199*	50.8	100.0
029 AMER LUTH CH..	5	1 878	2 956	9.9	19.4
053 ASSEMB OF GOD.	2	232	508	1.7	3.3

County and Denomination	Number of churches	Communicant, confirmed, full members	Total adherents		
			Number	Percent of total population	Percent of total adherents
057 BAPT GEN CONF.	2	108	137*	0.5	0.9
081 CATHOLIC......	5	NA	6 586	22.0	43.3
089 CHR & MISS AL.	2	192	485	1.6	3.2
203 EVAN FREE CH..	4	139	176*	0.6	1.2
281 LUTH CH AMER..	1	706	1 150	3.8	7.6
283 LUTH--MO SYNOD	4	1 029	1 404	4.7	9.2
290 METRO COMM CHS	0	10	20	0.1	0.1
443 UN C OF CHRIST	2	768	974*	3.3	6.4
449 UN METHODIST..	4	548	695*	2.3	4.6
453 UN PRES CH USA	1	85	108*	0.4	0.7
SIBLEY	37	8 274	13 072*	84.6	100.0
029 AMER LUTH CH..	7	1 774	2 344	15.2	17.9
057 BAPT GEN CONF.	1	41	50*	0.3	0.4
081 CATHOLIC......	8	NA	2 595	16.8	19.9
179 CONSRV BAPT...	1	10	12*	0.1	0.1
201 EVAN COV CH AM	1	73	89*	0.6	0.7
209 EVAN LUTH SYN.	1	118	142	0.9	1.1
281 LUTH CH AMER..	3	969	1 186	7.7	9.1
283 LUTH--MO SYNOD	7	2 211	2 838	18.4	21.7
413 S.D.A.........	1	14	17*	0.1	0.1
443 UN C OF CHRIST	3	783	957*	6.2	7.3
449 UN METHODIST..	1	198	242*	1.6	1.9
469 WELS..........	3	2 083	2 600	16.8	19.9
STEARNS	104	13 761	82 080*	75.9	100.0
029 AMER LUTH CH..	9	5 051	6 979	6.5	8.5
053 ASSEMB OF GOD.	3	255	502	0.5	0.6
057 BAPT GEN CONF.	2	330	404*	0.4	0.5
081 CATHOLIC......	51	NA	63 656	58.9	77.6
097 CHR CHS&CHS CR	2	180	220*	0.2	0.3
105 CHRISTIAN REF.	2	133	228	0.2	0.3
121 CH GOD (ABR)..	2	131	160*	0.1	0.2
151 L-D SAINTS....	1	NA	127	0.1	0.2
167 CHS OF CHRIST.	1	32	55	0.1	0.1
179 CONSRV BAPT...	1	180	220*	0.2	0.3
193 EPISCOPAL.....	3	288	362	0.3	0.4
197 EVAN CH OF NA.	1	9	9	—	—
201 EVAN COV CH AM	1	102	125*	0.1	0.2
203 EVAN FREE CH..	2	106	130*	0.1	0.2
220 FREE LUTHERAN.	2	124	134	0.1	0.2
283 LUTH--MO SYNOD	9	3 193	4 231	3.9	5.2
403 SALVATION ARMY	1	39	123	0.1	0.1
419 SO BAPT CONV..	1	34	42*	—	0.1
435 UNITARIAN-UNIV	1	60	73*	0.1	0.1
443 UN C OF CHRIST	1	219	268*	0.2	0.3
449 UN METHODIST..	6	2 123	2 598*	2.4	3.2
453 UN PRES CH USA	2	1 172	1 434*	1.3	1.7
STEELE	40	12 456	24 717*	81.5	100.0
019 AMER BAPT USA.	1	285	349*	1.2	1.4
029 AMER LUTH CH..	12	7 139	9 563	31.5	38.7
053 ASSEMB OF GOD.	2	188	253	0.8	1.0
057 BAPT GEN CONF.	1	106	130*	0.4	0.5
081 CATHOLIC......	8	NA	8 248	27.2	33.4
123 CH GOD (ANDER)	1	63	189	0.6	0.8
193 EPISCOPAL.....	1	121	165	0.5	0.7
201 EVAN COV CH AM	1	88	108*	0.4	0.4
283 LUTH--MO SYNOD	4	1 702	2 298	7.6	9.3
403 SALVATION ARMY	1	48	76	0.3	0.3
413 S.D.A.........	1	5	6*	—	—
443 UN C OF CHRIST	2	916	1 121*	3.7	4.5
449 UN METHODIST..	3	1 089	1 333*	4.4	5.4
453 UN PRES CH USA	1	636	778*	2.6	3.1
469 WELS..........	1	70	100	0.3	0.4
STEVENS	25	4 709	8 969*	79.2	100.0
029 AMER LUTH CH..	7	2 955	3 885	34.3	43.3
053 ASSEMB OF GOD.	1	29	50	0.4	0.6
081 CATHOLIC......	3	NA	2 818	24.9	31.4
105 CHRISTIAN REF.	1	88	166	1.5	1.9
164 CH LUTH CONF..	1	50	65	0.6	0.7
165 CH OF NAZARENE	1	73	90	0.8	1.0
203 EVAN FREE CH..	2	80	96*	0.8	1.1
281 LUTH CH AMER..	1	76	106	0.9	1.2
283 LUTH--MO SYNOD	1	249	348	3.1	3.9
443 UN C OF CHRIST	2	337	404*	3.6	4.5
449 UN METHODIST..	3	331	397*	3.5	4.4
469 WELS..........	2	441	544	4.8	6.1
SWIFT	39	6 945	12 078*	93.5	100.0
029 AMER LUTH CH..	8	3 487	4 432	34.3	36.7
053 ASSEMB OF GOD.	1	49	85	0.7	0.7
057 BAPT GEN CONF.	2	244	297*	2.3	2.5
081 CATHOLIC......	7	NA	3 249	25.1	26.9
193 EPISCOPAL.....	2	35	58	0.4	0.5
201 EVAN COV CH AM	2	32	39*	0.3	0.3
203 EVAN FREE CH..	3	176	214*	1.7	1.8
281 LUTH CH AMER..	4	773	1 027	7.9	8.5
283 LUTH--MO SYNOD	5	1 350	1 704	13.2	14.1
313 N AM BAPT CONF	1	109	133*	1.0	1.1
443 UN C OF CHRIST	2	411	501*	3.9	4.1
449 UN METHODIST..	1	167	203*	1.6	1.7
453 UN PRES CH USA	1	112	136*	1.1	1.1
TODD	63	7 895	18 670*	74.7	100.0
029 AMER LUTH CH..	8	2 162	2 981	11.9	16.0
053 ASSEMB OF GOD.	3	165	303	1.2	1.6
057 BAPT GEN CONF.	1	59	73*	0.3	0.4

NA—Not applicable *Total adherents estimated from known number of communicant, confirmed, full members. —Represents a percent less than 0.1. Percentages may not total due to rounding.

Table 4. Churches and Church Membership by County and Denomination: 1980

County and Denomination	Number of churches	Communicant, confirmed, full members	Total adherents Number	Total adherents Percent of total population	Total adherents Percent of total adherents
081 CATHOLIC......	11	NA	7 902	31.6	42.3
123 CH GOD (ANDER)	1	105	315	1.3	1.7
163 CH OF LUTH BR.	1	51	77	0.3	0.4
165 CH OF NAZARENE	2	80	191	0.8	1.0
179 CONSRV BAPT...	1	140	173*	0.7	0.9
181 CONSRV CONGR..	1	17	21*	0.1	0.1
201 EVAN COV CH AM	1	66	82*	0.3	0.4
203 EVAN FREE CH..	2	64	79*	0.3	0.4
221 FREE METHODIST	2	32	126	0.5	0.7
281 LUTH CH AMER..	3	344	439	1.8	2.4
283 LUTH--MO SYNOD	8	2 583	3 397	13.6	18.2
323 OLD ORD AMISH.	4	520	644*	2.6	3.4
413 S.D.A.........	2	77	95*	0.4	0.5
443 UN C OF CHRIST	3	418	518*	2.1	2.8
449 UN METHODIST..	9	1 012	1 254*	5.0	6.7
TRAVERSE	**18**	**2 923**	**5 578***	**100.6**	**100.0**
081 CATHOLIC......	5	NA	1 990	35.9	35.7
127 CH GOD (CLEVE)	1	6	7*	0.1	0.1
201 EVAN COV CH AM	1	111	133*	2.4	2.4
281 LUTH CH AMER..	2	707	899	16.2	16.1
283 LUTH--MO SYNOD	4	1 326	1 609	29.0	28.8
443 UN C OF CHRIST	1	85	102*	1.8	1.8
449 UN METHODIST..	1	129	154*	2.8	2.8
453 UN PRES CH USA	2	347	414*	7.5	7.4
469 WELS.........	1	212	270	4.9	4.8
WABASHA	**43**	**7 126**	**16 209***	**83.8**	**100.0**
029 AMER LUTH CH..	2	231	370	1.9	2.3
053 ASSEMB OF GOD.	1	26	35	0.2	0.2
057 BAPT GEN CONF.	1	84	103*	0.5	0.6
081 CATHOLIC......	11	NA	7 064	36.5	43.6
097 CHR CHS&CHS CR	1	60	74*	0.4	0.5
193 EPISCOPAL.....	2	247	345	1.8	2.1
281 LUTH CH AMER..	1	434	527	2.7	3.3
283 LUTH--MO SYNOD	4	2 028	2 607	13.5	16.1
353 CHR BRETHREN..	1	10	10	0.1	0.1
443 UN C OF CHRIST	4	643	790*	4.1	4.9
449 UN METHODIST..	7	818	1 005*	5.2	6.2
453 UN PRES CH USA	1	165	203*	1.0	1.3
469 WELS.........	7	2 380	3 076	15.9	19.0
WADENA	**41**	**5 246**	**10 487***	**73.9**	**100.0**
029 AMER LUTH CH..	2	1 005	1 285	9.1	12.3
045 APOSTOLIC LUTH	2	125	154*	1.1	1.5
053 ASSEMB OF GOD.	3	191	379	2.7	3.6
081 CATHOLIC......	5	NA	3 138	22.1	29.9
089 CHR & MISS AL.	5	226	731	5.2	7.0
151 L-D SAINTS....	1	NA	38	0.3	0.4
167 CHS OF CHRIST.	1	27	35	0.2	0.3
193 EPISCOPAL.....	1	48	56	0.4	0.5
197 EVAN CH OF NA.	1	44	44	0.3	0.4
220 FREE LUTHERAN.	2	153	226	1.6	2.2
281 LUTH CH AMER..	2	486	638	4.5	6.1
283 LUTH--MO SYNOD	6	1 605	2 118	14.9	20.2
323 OLD ORD AMISH.	1	130	160*	1.1	1.5
413 S.D.A.........	1	120	148*	1.0	1.4
443 UN C OF CHRIST	2	304	374*	2.6	3.6
449 UN METHODIST..	6	782	963*	6.8	9.2
WASECA	**29**	**8 355**	**15 512***	**84.1**	**100.0**
029 AMER LUTH CH..	8	3 272	4 282	23.2	27.6
081 CATHOLIC......	4	NA	4 837	26.2	31.2
175 CONGR CHR CHS.	1	357	438*	2.4	2.8
193 EPISCOPAL.....	2	57	75	0.4	0.5
201 EVAN COV CH AM	1	117	143*	0.8	0.9
203 EVAN FREE CH..	1	78	96*	0.5	0.6
281 LUTH CH AMER..	1	92	117	0.6	0.8
283 LUTH--MO SYNOD	5	2 740	3 499	19.0	22.6
443 UN C OF CHRIST	2	320	392*	2.1	2.5
449 UN METHODIST..	3	1 111	1 362*	7.4	8.8
469 WELS.........	1	211	271	1.5	1.7
WASHINGTON	**77**	**23 492**	**64 077***	**56.4**	**100.0**
019 AMER BAPT USA.	1	111	140*	0.1	0.2
029 AMER LUTH CH..	8	4 992	7 746	6.8	12.1
053 ASSEMB OF GOD.	2	145	265	0.2	0.4
057 BAPT GEN CONF.	2	267	336*	0.3	0.5
081 CATHOLIC......	10	NA	29 664	26.1	46.3
089 CHR & MISS AL.	2	194	379	0.3	0.6
097 CHR CHS&CHS CR	1	250	315*	0.3	0.5
105 CHRISTIAN REF.	1	90	162	0.1	0.3
123 CH GOD (ANDER)	1	74	222	0.2	0.3
167 CHS OF CHRIST.	1	10	17	–	–
175 CONGR CHR CHS.	1	250	315*	0.3	0.5
179 CONSRV BAPT...	2	260	327*	0.3	0.5
193 EPISCOPAL.....	5	1 023	1 398	1.2	2.2
201 EVAN COV CH AM	3	375	472*	0.4	0.7
208 EVAN LUTH ASSN	1	143	269	0.2	0.4
220 FREE LUTHERAN.	1	35	60	0.1	0.1
270 CONSRV JUDAISM	1	19	24*	–	–
281 LUTH CH AMER..	10	8 138	12 368	10.9	19.3
283 LUTH--MO SYNOD	6	2 177	3 196	2.8	5.0
413 S.D.A.........	2	87	110*	0.1	0.2
435 UNITARIAN-UNIV	1	80	101*	0.1	0.2
443 UN C OF CHRIST	3	697	877*	0.8	1.4
449 UN METHODIST..	5	1 964	2 472*	2.2	3.9
453 UN PRES CH USA	1	730	919*	0.8	1.4
469 WELS.........	6	1 381	1 923	1.7	3.0

County and Denomination	Number of churches	Communicant, confirmed, full members	Total adherents Number	Total adherents Percent of total population	Total adherents Percent of total adherents
WATONWAN	**31**	**7 123**	**10 949***	**88.6**	**100.0**
029 AMER LUTH CH..	7	2 640	3 375	27.3	30.8
053 ASSEMB OF GOD.	1	28	56	0.5	0.5
081 CATHOLIC......	2	NA	2 053	16.6	18.8
097 CHR CHS&CHS CR	1	122	147*	1.2	1.3
193 EPISCOPAL.....	1	23	23	0.2	0.2
203 EVAN FREE CH..	1	28	34*	0.3	0.3
281 LUTH CH AMER..	5	1 295	1 623	13.1	14.8
283 LUTH--MO SYNOD	4	935	1 170	9.5	10.7
287 MENN GEN CONF.	2	164	164	1.3	1.5
449 UN METHODIST..	2	374	450*	3.6	4.1
453 UN PRES CH USA	2	678	816*	6.6	7.5
469 WELS.........	3	836	1 038	8.4	9.5
WILKIN	**23**	**3 292**	**6 551***	**78.2**	**100.0**
019 AMER BAPT USA.	1	72	88*	1.0	1.3
029 AMER LUTH CH..	5	1 702	2 336	27.9	35.7
057 BAPT GEN CONF.	1	90	110*	1.3	1.7
081 CATHOLIC......	4	NA	2 271	27.1	34.7
179 CONSRV BAPT...	1	110	134*	1.6	2.0
203 EVAN FREE CH..	1	88	107*	1.3	1.6
220 FREE LUTHERAN.	1	28	38	0.5	0.6
283 LUTH--MO SYNOD	4	623	762	9.1	11.6
443 UN C OF CHRIST	1	72	88*	1.0	1.3
449 UN METHODIST..	3	428	521*	6.2	8.0
453 UN PRES CH USA	1	79	96*	1.1	1.5
WINONA	**74**	**13 669**	**34 925***	**75.5**	**100.0**
017 AMER BAPT ASSN	1	10	10	–	–
019 AMER BAPT USA.	1	188	225*	0.5	0.6
029 AMER LUTH CH..	3	2 177	2 965	6.4	8.5
053 ASSEMB OF GOD.	2	63	105	0.2	0.3
057 BAPT GEN CONF.	1	49	59*	0.1	0.2
081 CATHOLIC......	20	NA	17 122	37.0	49.0
097 CHR CHS&CHS CR	1	60	74*	0.2	0.2
151 L-D SAINTS....	1	NA	118	0.3	0.3
157 CH OF BRETHREN	1	144	172*	0.4	0.5
165 CH OF NAZARENE	1	91	202	0.4	0.6
167 CHS OF CHRIST.	2	51	62	0.1	0.2
179 CONSRV BAPT...	1	30	36*	0.1	0.1
193 EPISCOPAL.....	2	346	626	1.4	1.8
203 EVAN FREE CH..	1	96	115*	0.2	0.3
244 GRACE BRETHREN	1	22	26*	0.1	0.1
281 LUTH CH AMER..	1	285	370	0.8	1.1
283 LUTH--MO SYNOD	6	3 463	4 424	9.6	12.7
293 MORAV CH-NORTH	2	289	362	0.8	1.0
413 S.D.A.........	1	41	49*	0.1	0.1
419 SO BAPT CONV..	1	23	27*	0.1	0.1
443 UN C OF CHRIST	3	794	948*	2.0	2.7
449 UN METHODIST..	8	1 709	2 041*	4.4	5.8
453 UN PRES CH USA	3	353	422*	0.9	1.2
469 WELS.........	10	3 385	4 367	9.4	12.5
WRIGHT	**72**	**14 736**	**35 556***	**60.3**	**100.0**
029 AMER LUTH CH..	3	1 018	1 580	2.7	4.4
053 ASSEMB OF GOD.	4	237	427	0.7	1.2
057 BAPT GEN CONF.	2	216	274*	0.5	0.8
081 CATHOLIC......	11	NA	15 329	26.0	43.1
089 CHR & MISS AL.	1	39	114	0.2	0.3
097 CHR CHS&CHS CR	1	50	63*	0.1	0.2
193 EPISCOPAL.....	2	133	163	0.3	0.5
201 EVAN COV CH AM	4	629	799*	1.4	2.2
203 EVAN FREE CH..	4	287	364*	0.6	1.0
281 LUTH CH AMER..	10	4 423	6 109	10.4	17.2
283 LUTH--MO SYNOD	6	2 949	4 090	6.9	11.5
371 REF CH IN AM..	1	152	216	0.4	0.6
419 SO BAPT CONV..	1	86	109*	0.2	0.3
443 UN C OF CHRIST	2	276	350*	0.6	1.0
449 UN METHODIST..	10	1 784	2 265*	3.8	6.4
453 UN PRES CH USA	4	580	736*	1.2	2.1
469 WELS.........	6	1 877	2 568	4.4	7.2
YELLOW MEDICINE	**37**	**7 602**	**11 978***	**87.7**	**100.0**
029 AMER LUTH CH..	11	4 571	5 764	42.2	48.1
053 ASSEMB OF GOD.	2	104	225	1.6	1.9
081 CATHOLIC......	4	NA	2 122	15.5	17.7
089 CHR & MISS AL.	2	36	113	0.8	0.9
097 CHR CHS&CHS CR	1	118	142*	1.0	1.2
151 L-D SAINTS....	1	NA	132	1.0	1.1
179 CONSRV BAPT...	1	65	78*	0.6	0.7
220 FREE LUTHERAN.	1	25	30	0.2	0.3
281 LUTH CH AMER..	2	288	352	2.6	2.9
283 LUTH--MO SYNOD	4	932	1 234	9.0	10.3
413 S.D.A.........	1	13	16*	0.1	0.1
449 UN METHODIST..	2	228	274*	2.0	2.3
453 UN PRES CH USA	2	440	528*	3.9	4.4
469 WELS.........	3	782	968	7.1	8.1

NA— Not applicable.   *Total adherents estimated from known number of communicant, confirmed, full members.   —Represents a percent less than 0.1.   Percentages may not total due to rounding.

Table 4. Churches and Church Membership by County and Denomination: 1980

County and Denomination	Number of churches	Communicant, confirmed, full members	Total adherents Number	Percent of total population	Percent of total adherents
MISSISSIPPI					
THE STATE.....	5 395	1 026 216	1 387 371*	55.0	100.0
ADAMS	47	12 287	18 829*	49.5	100.0
053 ASSEMB OF GOD.	1	69	112	0.3	0.6
059 BAPT MISS ASSN	2	160	198*	0.5	1.1
081 CATHOLIC......	4	NA	3 375	8.9	17.9
123 CH GOD (ANDER)	1	50	150	0.4	0.8
127 CH GOD (CLEVE)	2	419	518*	1.4	2.8
151 L-D SAINTS....	1	NA	201	0.5	1.1
165 CH OF NAZARENE	1	41	54	0.1	0.3
167 CHS OF CHRIST.	3	426	532	1.4	2.8
193 EPISCOPAL.....	1	626	730	1.9	3.9
215 EVAN METH CH.	1	112	138*	0.4	0.7
271 REFORM JUDAISM	1	58	72*	0.2	0.4
283 LUTH--MO SYNOD	1	69	93	0.2	0.5
357 PRESB CH US...	4	1 052	1 299*	3.4	6.9
403 SALVATION ARMY	1	107	120	0.3	0.6
413 S.D.A.........	2	162	200*	0.5	1.1
419 SO BAPT CONV..	13	6 643	8 205	21.6	43.6
449 UN METHODIST..	8	2 293	2 832*	7.4	15.0
ALCORN	87	16 806	20 965*	63.5	100.0
017 AMER BAPT ASSN	2	300	300	0.9	1.4
053 ASSEMB OF GOD.	2	364	464	1.4	2.2
059 BAPT MISS ASSN	2	784	963*	2.9	4.6
081 CATHOLIC......	1	NA	347	1.1	1.7
097 CHR CHS&CHS CR	4	805	989*	3.0	4.7
101 C.M.E........	3	474	582*	1.8	2.8
127 CH GOD (CLEVE)	1	18	22*	0.1	0.1
167 CHS OF CHRIST.	19	1 476	1 822	5.5	8.7
193 EPISCOPAL.....	1	77	90	0.3	0.4
283 LUTH--MO SYNOD	1	69	105	0.3	0.5
357 PRESB CH US...	3	468	575*	1.7	2.7
413 S.D.A.........	1	28	34*	0.1	0.2
419 SO BAPT CONV..	31	9 322	11 452*	34.7	54.6
449 UN METHODIST..	15	2 612	3 209*	9.7	15.3
453 UN PRES CH USA	1	9	11*	-	0.1
AMITE	59	8 760	11 194*	83.7	100.0
053 ASSEMB OF GOD.	1	18	30	0.2	0.3
101 C.M.E........	6	1 309	1 633*	12.2	14.6
127 CH GOD (CLEVE)	4	88	110*	0.8	1.0
151 L-D SAINTS....	1	NA	257	1.9	2.3
165 CH OF NAZARENE	2	68	105	0.8	0.9
356 PRESB CH AMER.	3	72	72	0.5	0.6
357 PRESB CH US...	1	11	14*	0.1	0.1
419 SO BAPT CONV..	34	6 635	8 276*	61.9	73.9
449 UN METHODIST..	7	559	697*	5.2	6.2
ATTALA	78	9 734	12 137*	61.1	100.0
005 AME ZION......	1	126	173	0.9	1.4
053 ASSEMB OF GOD.	1	92	108	0.5	0.9
059 BAPT MISS ASSN	1	44	54*	0.3	0.4
081 CATHOLIC......	1	NA	94	0.5	0.8
123 CH GOD (ANDER)	3	60	180	0.9	1.5
127 CH GOD (CLEVE)	2	78	96*	0.5	0.8
165 CH OF NAZARENE	1	47	63	0.3	0.5
167 CHS OF CHRIST.	6	345	430	2.2	3.5
193 EPISCOPAL.....	1	29	35	0.2	0.3
281 LUTH CH AMER..	1	69	90	0.5	0.7
356 PRESB CH AMER.	2	321	321	1.6	2.6
357 PRESB CH US...	1	22	27*	0.1	0.2
419 SO BAPT CONV..	30	6 114	7 527*	37.9	62.0
449 UN METHODIST..	27	2 387	2 939*	14.8	24.2
BENTON	22	2 363	2 997*	36.8	100.0
097 CHR CHS&CHS CR	1	71	89*	1.1	3.0
101 C.M.E........	6	1 549	1 935*	23.7	64.6
167 CHS OF CHRIST.	5	302	416	5.1	13.9
193 EPISCOPAL.....	1	21	32	0.4	1.1
357 PRESB CH US...	1	23	29*	0.4	1.0
449 UN METHODIST..	8	397	496*	6.1	16.5
BOLIVAR	81	12 269	17 364*	37.8	100.0
017 AMER BAPT ASSN	1	30	30	0.1	0.2
019 AMER BAPT USA.	1	230	296*	0.6	1.7
053 ASSEMB OF GOD.	3	165	233	0.5	1.3
081 CATHOLIC......	6	NA	1 586	3.5	9.1
093 CHR CH (DISC).	3	147	232	0.5	1.3
127 CH GOD (CLEVE)	1	126	162*	0.4	0.9
165 CH OF NAZARENE	3	205	262	0.6	1.5
167 CHS OF CHRIST.	7	847	1 052	2.3	6.1
193 EPISCOPAL.....	2	198	249	0.5	1.4
263 INT FOURSQ GOS	1	113	145*	0.3	0.8
271 REFORM JUDAISM	1	112	144*	0.3	0.8
283 LUTH--MO SYNOD	1	12	12	-	0.1
357 PRESB CH US...	5	604	776*	1.7	4.5
413 S.D.A.........	2	51	66*	0.1	0.4
419 SO BAPT CONV..	26	7 220	9 280*	20.2	53.4
449 UN METHODIST..	18	2 209	2 839*	6.2	16.3
CALHOUN	70	10 468	13 000*	83.0	100.0
101 C.M.E........	4	438	539*	3.4	4.1
123 CH GOD (ANDER)	1	70	210	1.3	1.6
127 CH GOD (CLEVE)	1	20	25*	0.2	0.2
165 CH OF NAZARENE	1	29	35	0.2	0.3
167 CHS OF CHRIST.	3	59	74	0.5	0.6
419 SO BAPT CONV..	49	8 907	10 955*	69.9	84.3
449 UN METHODIST..	11	945	1 162*	7.4	8.9
CARROLL	56	6 243	7 751*	79.3	100.0
001 ADVENT CHR CH.	2	91	113*	1.2	1.5
093 CHR CH (DISC).	2	128	197	2.0	2.5
101 C.M.E........	7	1 132	1 401*	14.3	18.1
167 CHS OF CHRIST.	1	45	55	0.6	0.7
356 PRESB CH AMER.	3	220	259	2.6	3.3
419 SO BAPT CONV..	20	3 174	3 928*	40.2	50.7
449 UN METHODIST..	21	1 453	1 798*	18.4	23.2
CHICKASAW	70	8 405	10 735*	60.1	100.0
053 ASSEMB OF GOD.	1	30	29	0.2	0.3
081 CATHOLIC......	1	NA	150	0.8	1.4
097 CHR CHS&CHS CR	1	100	125*	0.7	1.2
101 C.M.E........	6	618	773*	4.3	7.2
127 CH GOD (CLEVE)	2	174	218*	1.2	2.0
143 CG IN CR(MENN)	1	79	79	0.4	0.7
165 CH OF NAZARENE	3	244	400	2.2	3.7
167 CHS OF CHRIST.	5	254	329	1.8	3.1
193 EPISCOPAL.....	2	29	30	0.2	0.3
356 PRESB CH AMER.	2	98	125	0.7	1.2
357 PRESB CH US...	3	168	210*	1.2	2.0
419 SO BAPT CONV..	19	4 576	5 722*	32.1	53.3
449 UN METHODIST..	24	2 035	2 545*	14.3	23.7
CHOCTAW	50	5 321	6 671*	74.2	100.0
005 AME ZION......	1	160	207	2.3	3.1
127 CH GOD (CLEVE)	1	51	63*	0.7	0.9
167 CHS OF CHRIST.	1	88	112	1.2	1.7
185 CUMBER PRESB..	1	100	173	1.9	2.6
357 PRESB CH US...	7	294	365*	4.1	5.5
419 SO BAPT CONV..	26	3 539	4 398*	48.9	65.9
449 UN METHODIST..	13	1 089	1 353*	15.0	20.3
CLAIBORNE	33	3 397	4 593*	37.4	100.0
005 AME ZION......	1	240	293	2.4	6.4
081 CATHOLIC......	1	NA	125	1.0	2.7
093 CHR CH (DISC).	13	999	1 536	12.5	33.4
167 CHS OF CHRIST.	2	50	54	0.4	1.2
193 EPISCOPAL.....	1	110	125	1.0	2.7
271 REFORM JUDAISM	1	8	10*	0.1	0.2
357 PRESB CH US...	1	204	251*	2.0	5.5
413 S.D.A.........	1	109	134*	1.1	2.9
419 SO BAPT CONV..	5	1 098	1 352*	11.0	29.4
449 UN METHODIST..	7	579	713*	5.8	15.5
CLARKE	82	9 327	11 605*	68.5	100.0
053 ASSEMB OF GOD.	5	375	360	2.1	3.1
081 CATHOLIC......	1	NA	22	0.1	0.2
123 CH GOD (ANDER)	5	69	207	1.2	1.8
127 CH GOD (CLEVE)	1	10	12*	0.1	0.1
167 CHS OF CHRIST.	2	60	76	0.4	0.7
193 EPISCOPAL.....	1	14	12	0.1	0.1
349 PENT HOLINESS.	5	349	433*	2.6	3.7
413 S.D.A.........	1	23	29*	0.2	0.2
419 SO BAPT CONV..	28	5 438	6 744*	39.8	58.1
421 SO METHODIST..	1	23	32	0.2	0.3
449 UN METHODIST..	32	2 966	3 678*	21.7	31.7
CLAY	45	8 262	10 665*	50.6	100.0
053 ASSEMB OF GOD.	1	24	32	0.2	0.3
059 BAPT MISS ASSN	1	92	116*	0.6	1.1
081 CATHOLIC......	1	NA	231	1.1	2.2
093 CHR CH (DISC).	3	359	479	2.3	4.5
101 C.M.E........	4	352	442*	2.1	4.1
127 CH GOD (CLEVE)	4	251	315*	1.5	3.0
143 CG IN CR(MENN)	1	103	103	0.5	1.0
167 CHS OF CHRIST.	4	250	337	1.6	3.2
185 CUMBER PRESB..	1	28	51	0.2	0.5
193 EPISCOPAL.....	1	88	124	0.6	1.2
357 PRESB CH US...	1	181	227*	1.1	2.1
413 S.D.A.........	1	22	28*	0.1	0.3
419 SO BAPT CONV..	11	4 611	5 792*	27.5	54.3
449 UN METHODIST..	10	1 865	2 343*	11.1	22.0
453 UN PRES CH USA	1	36	45*	0.2	0.4
COAHOMA	40	9 194	13 210*	35.8	100.0
053 ASSEMB OF GOD.	1	36	94	0.3	0.7
081 CATHOLIC......	3	NA	1 455	3.9	11.0
093 CHR CH (DISC).	1	74	114	0.3	0.9
097 CHR CHS&CHS CR	1	90	115*	0.3	0.9
127 CH GOD (CLEVE)	1	81	103*	0.3	0.8
143 CG IN CR(MENN)	1	116	116	0.3	0.9
165 CH OF NAZARENE	1	106	184	0.5	1.4
167 CHS OF CHRIST.	2	175	223	0.6	1.7
193 EPISCOPAL.....	1	588	683	1.9	5.2
271 REFORM JUDAISM	1	160	204*	0.6	1.5
357 PRESB CH US...	1	403	515*	1.4	3.9
413 S.D.A.........	1	47	60*	0.2	0.5
419 SO BAPT CONV..	11	5 223	6 669*	18.1	50.5
449 UN METHODIST..	14	2 095	2 675*	7.2	20.2

NA—Not applicable.   *Total adherents estimated from known number of communicant, confirmed, full members.   —Represents a percent less than 0.1.   Percentages may not total due to rounding.

Table 4. Churches and Church Membership by County and Denomination: 1980

County and Denomination	Number of churches	Communicant, confirmed, full members	Total adherents Number	Percent of total population	Percent of total adherents
COPIAH	76	12 617	15 804*	59.6	100.0
053 ASSEMB OF GOD.	1	29	32	0.1	0.2
081 CATHOLIC......	2	NA	182	0.7	1.2
093 CHR CH (DISC).	1	25	38	0.1	0.2
101 C.M.E........	2	239	296*	1.1	1.9
127 CH GOD (CLEVE)	1	43	53*	0.2	0.3
151 L-D SAINTS....	1	NA	60	0.2	0.4
165 CH OF NAZARENE	1	41	54	0.2	0.3
167 CHS OF CHRIST.	2	45	54	0.2	0.3
193 EPISCOPAL.....	2	48	49	0.2	0.3
283 LUTH--MO SYNOD	1	19	21	0.1	0.1
349 PENT HOLINESS.	1	80	99*	0.4	0.6
356 PRESB CH AMER.	3	372	418	1.6	2.6
413 S.D.A.........	1	105	130*	0.5	0.8
419 SO BAPT CONV..	30	8 713	10 778*	40.7	68.2
421 SO METHODIST.	1	15	23	0.1	0.1
449 UN METHODIST..	26	2 843	3 517*	13.3	22.3
COVINGTON	47	7 100	8 812*	55.3	100.0
053 ASSEMB OF GOD.	2	71	87	0.5	1.0
059 BAPT MISS ASSN	3	290	362*	2.3	4.1
101 C.M.E........	4	642	802*	5.0	9.1
151 L-D SAINTS....	1	NA	?	?	?
167 CHS OF CHRIST.	3	85	120	0.8	1.4
193 EPISCOPAL.....	1	39	42	0.3	0.5
356 PRESB CH AMER.	5	335	353	2.2	4.0
419 SO BAPT CONV..	18	4 737	5 920*	37.2	67.2
449 UN METHODIST..	10	901	1 126*	7.1	12.8
DE SOTO	103	21 056	28 393*	52.6	100.0
017 AMER BAPT ASSN	2	200	200	0.4	0.7
053 ASSEMB OF GOD.	6	391	441	0.8	1.6
055 AS REF PRES CH	1	24	29	0.1	0.1
059 BAPT MISS ASSN	1	121	153*	0.3	0.5
081 CATHOLIC......	4	NA	1 868	3.5	6.6
097 CHR CHS&CHS CR	1	90	114*	0.2	0.4
101 C.M.E........	12	2 391	3 025*	5.6	10.7
123 CH GOD (ANDER)	1	16	48	0.1	0.2
127 CH GOD (CLEVE)	6	280	354*	0.7	1.2
165 CH OF NAZARENE	1	30	54	0.1	0.2
167 CHS OF CHRIST.	9	1 210	1 458	2.7	5.1
193 EPISCOPAL.....	2	130	164	0.3	0.6
283 LUTH--MO SYNOD	1	102	152	0.3	0.5
357 PRESB CH US...	2	228	288*	0.5	1.0
413 S.D.A.........	1	73	92*	0.2	0.3
419 SO BAPT CONV..	29	12 635	15 986*	29.6	56.3
449 UN METHODIST..	19	2 903	3 673*	6.8	12.9
453 UN PRES CH USA	5	232	294*	0.5	1.0
FORREST	100	30 652	41 385*	62.7	100.0
017 AMER BAPT ASSN	2	150	150	0.2	0.4
053 ASSEMB OF GOD.	4	300	529	0.8	1.3
059 BAPT MISS ASSN	6	1 098	1 330*	2.0	3.2
081 CATHOLIC......	3	NA	3 182	4.8	7.7
093 CHR CH (DISC).	1	217	237	0.4	0.6
101 C.M.E........	1	210	254*	0.4	0.6
123 CH GOD (ANDER)	2	145	435	0.7	1.1
127 CH GOD (CLEVE)	1	137	166*	0.3	0.4
151 L-D SAINTS....	1	NA	599	0.9	1.4
165 CH OF NAZARENE	1	100	125	0.2	0.3
167 CHS OF CHRIST.	5	375	477	0.7	1.2
193 EPISCOPAL.....	2	637	837	1.3	2.0
263 INT FOURSQ GOS	2	30	36*	0.1	0.1
271 REFORM JUDAISM	1	128	155*	0.2	0.4
283 LUTH--MO SYNOD	1	118	171	0.3	0.4
356 PRESB CH AMER.	4	892	1 049	1.6	2.5
357 PRESB CH US...	3	337	408*	0.6	1.0
403 SALVATION ARMY	1	74	96	0.1	0.2
413 S.D.A.........	2	199	241*	0.4	0.6
419 SO BAPT CONV..	35	19 669	23 821*	36.1	57.6
421 SO METHODIST.	2	100	140	0.2	0.3
449 UN METHODIST..	20	5 736	6 947*	10.5	16.8
FRANKLIN	45	4 509	5 610*	68.3	100.0
081 CATHOLIC......	1	NA	18	0.2	0.3
127 CH GOD (CLEVE)	4	201	248*	3.0	4.4
167 CHS OF CHRIST.	3	86	149	1.8	2.7
215 EVAN METH CH..	1	40	49*	0.6	0.9
356 PRESB CH AMER.	2	59	61	0.7	1.1
419 SO BAPT CONV..	22	3 273	4 037*	49.2	72.0
449 UN METHODIST..	12	850	1 048*	12.8	18.7
GEORGE	47	7 762	10 150*	66.4	100.0
053 ASSEMB OF GOD.	4	183	298	1.9	2.9
059 BAPT MISS ASSN	9	1 234	1 566*	10.2	15.4
081 CATHOLIC......	1	NA	107	0.7	1.1
127 CH GOD (CLEVE)	3	232	294*	1.9	2.9
151 L-D SAINTS....	1	NA	90	0.6	0.9
165 CH OF NAZARENE	1	14	52	0.3	0.5
167 CHS OF CHRIST.	3	275	350	2.3	3.4
357 PRESB CH US...	1	55	70*	0.5	0.7
413 S.D.A.........	1	15	19*	0.1	0.2
419 SO BAPT CONV..	11	4 165	5 287*	34.6	52.1
449 UN METHODIST..	12	1 589	2 017*	13.2	19.9
GREENE	48	4 493	5 912*	60.2	100.0
053 ASSEMB OF GOD.	2	104	156	1.6	2.6
059 BAPT MISS ASSN	5	440	560*	5.7	9.5

County and Denomination	Number of churches	Communicant, confirmed, full members	Total adherents Number	Percent of total population	Percent of total adherents
081 CATHOLIC......	1	NA	29	0.3	0.5
123 CH GOD (ANDER)	1	9	27	0.3	0.5
127 CH GOD (CLEVE)	4	177	225*	2.3	3.8
151 L-D SAINTS....	1	NA	144	1.5	2.4
167 CHS OF CHRIST.	2	45	59	0.6	1.0
356 PRESB CH AMER.	1	122	138	1.4	2.3
357 PRESB CH US...	1	92	117*	1.2	2.0
419 SO BAPT CONV..	19	2 732	3 475*	35.4	58.8
449 UN METHODIST..	11	772	982*	10.0	16.6
GRENADA	33	6 911	9 015*	42.8	100.0
053 ASSEMB OF GOD.	1	38	55	0.3	0.6
081 CATHOLIC......	1	NA	345	1.6	3.8
127 CH GOD (CLEVE)	1	149	186*	0.9	2.1
165 CH OF NAZARENE	1	104	174	0.8	1.9
167 CHS OF CHRIST.	4	298	383	1.8	4.2
193 EPISCOPAL.....	1	160	188	0.9	2.1
357 PRESB CH US...	2	288	359*	1.7	4.0
413 S.D.A.........	1	18	22*	0.1	0.2
419 SO BAPT CONV..	12	4 540	5 662*	26.9	62.8
449 UN METHODIST..	9	1 316	1 641*	7.8	18.2
HANCOCK	40	3 458	13 643*	55.6	100.0
053 ASSEMB OF GOD.	1	117	178	0.7	1.3
059 BAPT MISS ASSN	9	870	1 074*	4.4	7.9
081 CATHOLIC......	11	NA	8 991	36.6	65.9
127 CH GOD (CLEVE)	1	25	31*	0.1	0.2
151 L-D SAINTS....	1	NA	304	1.2	2.2
167 CHS OF CHRIST.	1	20	40	0.2	0.3
283 LUTH--MO SYNOD	1	141	203	0.8	1.5
357 PRESB CH US...	1	79	98*	0.4	0.7
419 SO BAPT CONV..	8	1 573	1 942*	7.9	14.2
449 UN METHODIST..	6	633	782*	3.2	5.7
HARRISON	157	42 625	84 456*	53.6	100.0
017 AMER BAPT ASSN	2	50	50	–	0.1
029 AMER LUTH CH..	2	156	216	0.1	0.3
053 ASSEMB OF GOD.	6	663	1 220	0.8	1.4
059 BAPT MISS ASSN	9	1 837	2 259*	1.4	2.7
081 CATHOLIC......	22	NA	29 906	19.0	35.4
089 CHR & MISS AL.	1	0	15	–	–
093 CHR CH (DISC).	1	119	170	0.1	0.2
097 CHR CHS&CHS CR	1	65	80*	0.1	0.1
101 C.M.E........	1	402	494*	0.3	0.6
123 CH GOD (ANDER)	1	39	117	0.1	0.1
127 CH GOD (CLEVE)	4	196	241*	0.2	0.3
151 L-D SAINTS....	3	NA	974	0.6	1.2
165 CH OF NAZARENE	3	233	383	0.2	0.5
167 CHS OF CHRIST.	8	672	855	0.5	1.0
193 EPISCOPAL.....	5	1 767	2 407	1.5	2.9
239 SWEDENBORGIAN.	1	60	74*	–	0.1
283 LUTH--MO SYNOD	3	732	982	0.6	1.2
285 MENNONITE CH..	1	59	73*	–	0.1
356 PRESB CH AMER.	2	465	513	0.3	0.6
357 PRESB CH US...	6	1 731	2 128*	1.3	2.5
403 SALVATION ARMY	2	197	499	0.3	0.6
413 S.D.A.........	2	191	235*	0.1	0.3
419 SO BAPT CONV..	38	22 252	27 361*	17.4	32.4
435 UNITARIAN-UNIV	1	15	18*	–	–
449 UN METHODIST..	32	10 724	13 186*	8.4	15.6
HINDS	210	99 666	131 907*	52.6	100.0
005 AME ZION......	1	500	565	0.2	0.4
017 AMER BAPT ASSN	1	112	112	–	0.1
053 ASSEMB OF GOD.	5	1 147	1 799	0.7	1.4
059 BAPT MISS ASSN	5	1 004	1 233*	0.5	0.9
081 CATHOLIC......	9	NA	8 155	3.2	6.2
093 CHR CH (DISC).	5	892	1 155	0.5	0.9
097 CHR CHS&CHS CR	1	175	215*	0.1	0.2
101 C.M.E........	8	1 166	1 432*	0.6	1.1
105 CHRISTIAN REF.	1	28	48	–	–
123 CH GOD (ANDER)	3	252	756	0.3	0.6
151 L-D SAINTS....	2	NA	782	0.3	0.6
165 CH OF NAZARENE	4	405	601	0.2	0.5
167 CHS OF CHRIST.	13	1 330	1 696	0.7	1.3
185 CUMBER PRESB..	1	80	118	–	0.1
193 EPISCOPAL.....	13	4 162	5 034	2.0	3.8
197 EVAN CH OF NA.	1	16	16	–	–
263 INT FOURSQ GOS	1	111	136*	0.1	0.1
271 REFORM JUDAISM	1	426	523*	0.2	0.4
281 LUTH CH AMER..	2	293	356	0.1	0.3
283 LUTH--MO SYNOD	5	701	979	0.4	0.7
285 MENNONITE CH..	1	15	18*	–	–
349 PENT HOLINESS.	1	58	71*	–	0.1
356 PRESB CH AMER.	15	4 208	4 543	1.8	3.4
357 PRESB CH US...	7	2 724	3 346*	1.3	2.5
403 SALVATION ARMY	1	132	273	0.1	0.2
413 S.D.A.........	3	845	1 038*	0.4	0.8
419 SO BAPT CONV..	56	58 581	71 965*	28.7	54.6
435 UNITARIAN-UNIV	1	49	60*	–	–
443 UN C OF CHRIST	1	47	58*	–	–
449 UN METHODIST..	42	20 207	24 824*	9.9	18.8
HOLMES	72	7 583	9 660*	42.1	100.0
001 ADVENT CHR CH.	1	34	43*	0.2	0.4
005 AME ZION......	2	130	195	0.8	2.0
081 CATHOLIC......	1	NA	54	0.2	0.6
101 C.M.E........	10	1 465	1 858*	8.1	19.2
123 CH GOD (ANDER)	1	20	60	0.3	0.6
165 CH OF NAZARENE	1	56	35	0.2	0.4

NA—Not applicable   *Total adherents estimated from known number of communicant, confirmed, full members.   —Represents a percent less than 0.1.   Percentages may not total due to rounding.

Table 4. Churches and Church Membership by County and Denomination: 1980

County and Denomination	Number of churches	Communicant, confirmed, full members	Total adherents		
			Number	Percent of total population	Percent of total adherents
167 CHS OF CHRIST.	4	86	107	0.5	1.1
193 EPISCOPAL.....	2	115	161	0.7	1.7
271 REFORM JUDAISM	1	50	63*	0.3	0.7
356 PRESB CH AMER.	6	232	244	1.1	2.5
357 PRESB CH US..	2	83	105*	0.5	1.1
419 SO BAPT CONV..	18	3 259	4 132*	18.0	42.8
449 UN METHODIST..	23	2 053	2 603*	11.3	26.9
HUMPHREYS	**26**	**3 774**	**5 018***	**36.0**	**100.0**
059 BAPT MISS ASSN	2	182	234*	1.7	4.7
081 CATHOLIC......	1	NA	120	0.9	2.4
123 CH GOD (ANDER)	2	37	111	0.8	2.2
127 CH GOD (CLEVE)	2	108	139*	1.0	2.8
167 CHS OF CHRIST.	2	78	99	0.7	2.0
193 EPISCOPAL.....	1	24	33	0.2	0.7
356 PRESB CH AMER.	1	151	169	1.2	3.4
413 S.D.A.........	1	44	57*	0.4	1.1
419 SO BAPT CONV..	8	2 367	3 048*	21.9	60.7
449 UN METHODIST..	6	783	1 008*	7.2	20.1
ISSAQUENA	**4**	**403**	**513***	**20.4**	**100.0**
419 SO BAPT CONV..	2	354	451*	17.9	87.9
449 UN METHODIST..	2	49	62*	2.5	12.1
ITAWAMBA	**69**	**9 132**	**11 348***	**55.3**	**100.0**
059 BAPT MISS ASSN	17	2 976	3 618*	17.6	31.9
081 CATHOLIC......	1	NA	41	0.2	0.4
101 C.M.E.........	3	387	470*	2.3	4.1
127 CH GOD (CLEVE)	1	66	80*	0.4	0.7
167 CHS OF CHRIST.	13	900	1 300	6.3	11.5
419 SO BAPT CONV..	12	2 457	2 987*	14.6	26.3
449 UN METHODIST..	21	2 336	2 840*	13.8	25.0
453 UN PRES CH USA	1	10	12*	0.1	0.1
JACKSON	**144**	**37 215**	**56 184***	**47.6**	**100.0**
005 AME ZION......	2	1 000	1 115	0.9	2.0
017 AMER BAPT ASSN	5	200	200	0.2	0.4
053 ASSEMB OF GOD.	16	1 993	3 565	3.0	6.3
059 BAPT MISS ASSN	8	788	994*	0.8	1.8
081 CATHOLIC......	7	NA	7 725	6.5	13.7
093 CHR CH (DISC).	1	37	57	-	0.1
097 CHR CHS&CHS CR	1	11	14*	-	-
123 CH GOD (ANDER)	1	12	36	-	0.1
127 CH GOD (CLEVE)	5	232	293*	0.2	0.5
151 L-D SAINTS....	1	NA	295	0.2	0.5
165 CH OF NAZARENE	2	201	323	0.3	0.6
167 CHS OF CHRIST.	7	610	790	0.7	1.4
193 EPISCOPAL.....	2	766	1 074	0.9	1.9
208 EVAN LUTH ASSN	1	25	35	-	0.1
281 LUTH CH AMER..	2	387	540	0.5	1.0
283 LUTH--MO SYNOD	1	115	150	0.1	0.3
290 METRO COMM CHS	0	10	20	-	-
349 PENT HOLINESS	4	280	353*	0.3	0.6
356 PRESB CH AMER.	1	112	130	0.1	0.2
357 PRESB CH US...	4	901	1 136*	1.0	2.0
403 SALVATION ARMY	1	95	217	0.2	0.4
413 S.D.A.........	1	30	38*	-	0.1
419 SO BAPT CONV..	42	21 284	26 838*	22.7	47.8
449 UN METHODIST..	29	8 126	10 246*	8.7	18.2
JASPER	**72**	**7 930**	**10 289***	**59.6**	**100.0**
053 ASSEMB OF GOD.	3	46	131	0.8	1.3
059 BAPT MISS ASSN	6	951	1 196*	6.9	11.6
081 CATHOLIC......	1	NA	112	0.6	1.1
123 CH GOD (ANDER)	2	90	270	1.6	2.6
167 CHS OF CHRIST.	1	27	34	0.2	0.3
356 PRESB CH AMER.	2	156	169	1.0	1.6
357 PRESB CH US...	6	121	152*	0.9	1.5
419 SO BAPT CONV..	22	3 491	4 391*	25.4	42.7
449 UN METHODIST..	29	3 048	3 834*	22.2	37.3
JEFFERSON	**29**	**1 957**	**2 890***	**31.5**	**100.0**
081 CATHOLIC......	2	NA	390	4.2	13.5
093 CHR CH (DISC).	1	30	46	0.5	1.6
285 MENNONITE CH..	2	67	85*	0.9	2.9
357 PRESB CH US...	2	132	168*	1.8	5.8
413 S.D.A.........	1	19	24*	0.3	0.8
419 SO BAPT CONV..	7	629	801*	8.7	27.7
449 UN METHODIST..	14	1 080	1 376*	15.0	47.6
JEFFERSON DAVIS	**34**	**5 943**	**7 932***	**57.3**	**100.0**
017 AMER BAPT ASSN	1	100	100	0.7	1.3
059 BAPT MISS ASSN	2	338	429*	3.1	5.4
081 CATHOLIC......	3	NA	426	3.1	5.4
101 C.M.E.........	5	1 035	1 314*	9.5	16.6
165 CH OF NAZARENE	1	23	55	0.4	0.7
167 CHS OF CHRIST.	1	12	18	0.1	0.2
356 PRESB CH AMER.	1	152	152	1.1	1.9
419 SO BAPT CONV..	14	3 664	4 652*	33.6	58.6
449 UN METHODIST..	6	619	786*	5.7	9.9
JONES	**127**	**32 840**	**41 453***	**67.0**	**100.0**
005 AME ZION......	2	315	410	0.7	1.0
053 ASSEMB OF GOD.	7	733	1 028*	1.7	2.5
059 BAPT MISS ASSN	18	4 321	5 277*	8.5	12.7
081 CATHOLIC......	1	NA	693	1.1	1.7
123 CH GOD (ANDER)	4	168	504	0.8	1.2
127 CH GOD (CLEVE)	1	139	170*	0.3	0.4
151 L-D SAINTS....	1	NA	157	0.3	0.4
165 CH OF NAZARENE	2	136	162	0.3	0.4
167 CHS OF CHRIST.	4	251	317	0.5	0.8
193 EPISCOPAL.....	1	395	459	0.7	1.1
281 LUTH CH AMER..	1	120	158	0.3	0.4
356 PRESB CH AMER.	1	55	61	0.1	0.1
357 PRESB CH US...	4	753	920*	1.5	2.2
403 SALVATION ARMY	1	137	219	0.4	0.5
413 S.D.A.........	3	220	269*	0.4	0.6
419 SO BAPT CONV..	50	20 040	24 473*	39.5	59.0
435 UNITARIAN-UNIV	2	117	143*	0.2	0.3
449 UN METHODIST..	24	4 940	6 033*	9.7	14.6
KEMPER	**52**	**4 352**	**5 439***	**53.6**	**100.0**
053 ASSEMB OF GOD.	1	95	114	1.1	2.1
123 CH GOD (ANDER)	1	15	45	0.4	0.8
356 PRESB CH AMER.	5	209	226	2.2	4.2
419 SO BAPT CONV..	15	1 707	2 139*	21.1	39.3
449 UN METHODIST..	30	2 326	2 915*	28.7	53.6
LAFAYETTE	**65**	**12 761**	**16 682***	**53.8**	**100.0**
017 AMER BAPT ASSN	1	400	400	1.3	2.4
053 ASSEMB OF GOD.	1	35	86	0.3	0.5
081 CATHOLIC......	1	NA	1 400	4.5	8.4
101 C.M.E.........	6	1 668	1 972*	6.4	11.8
151 L-D SAINTS....	1	NA	121	0.4	0.7
165 CH OF NAZARENE	1	26	55	0.2	0.3
167 CHS OF CHRIST.	5	508	643	2.1	3.9
193 EPISCOPAL.....	1	313	386	1.2	2.3
283 LUTH--MO SYNOD	1	44	71	0.2	0.4
357 PRESB CH US...	4	676	799*	2.6	4.8
419 SO BAPT CONV..	22	6 757	7 988*	25.7	47.9
421 SO METHODIST..	1	44	54	0.2	0.3
449 UN METHODIST..	20	2 290	2 707*	8.7	16.2
LAMAR	**46**	**8 349**	**10 655***	**44.7**	**100.0**
017 AMER BAPT ASSN	1	50	50	0.2	0.5
059 BAPT MISS ASSN	6	1 108	1 384*	5.8	13.0
081 CATHOLIC......	1	NA	207	0.9	1.9
123 CH GOD (ANDER)	1	15	45	0.2	0.4
127 CH GOD (CLEVE)	6	355	443*	1.9	4.2
167 CHS OF CHRIST.	2	37	55	0.2	0.5
413 S.D.A.........	1	182	227*	1.0	2.1
419 SO BAPT CONV..	15	5 218	6 516*	27.4	61.2
449 UN METHODIST..	13	1 384	1 728*	7.3	16.2
LAUDERDALE	**155**	**36 568**	**48 939***	**63.3**	**100.0**
005 AME ZION......	3	540	681	0.9	1.4
053 ASSEMB OF GOD.	6	529	721	0.9	1.5
059 BAPT MISS ASSN	1	59	72*	0.1	0.1
081 CATHOLIC......	2	NA	1 825	2.4	3.7
093 CHR CH (DISC).	1	350	539	0.7	1.1
097 CHR CHS&CHS CR	1	35	43*	0.1	0.1
101 C.M.E.........	5	607	746*	1.0	1.5
123 CH GOD (ANDER)	11	717	2 151	2.8	4.4
127 CH GOD (CLEVE)	2	125	154*	0.2	0.3
151 L-D SAINTS....	1	NA	339	0.4	0.7
165 CH OF NAZARENE	3	389	752	1.0	1.5
167 CHS OF CHRIST.	4	325	414	0.5	0.8
193 EPISCOPAL.....	2	842	1 062	1.4	2.2
263 INT FOURSQ GOS	2	186	228*	0.3	0.5
271 REFORM JUDAISM	1	134	165*	0.2	0.3
283 LUTH--MO SYNOD	2	155	245	0.3	0.5
285 MENNONITE CH..	1	21	26*	-	0.1
349 PENT HOLINESS	4	227	279*	0.4	0.6
356 PRESB CH AMER.	4	184	202	0.3	0.4
357 PRESB CH US...	6	1 154	1 418*	1.8	2.9
403 SALVATION ARMY	1	128	205	0.3	0.4
413 S.D.A.........	2	357	439*	0.6	0.9
419 SO BAPT CONV..	48	20 773	25 518*	33.0	52.1
421 SO METHODIST..	2	139	160	0.2	0.3
449 UN METHODIST..	39	8 524	10 471*	13.5	21.4
453 UN PRES CH USA	1	68	84*	0.1	0.2
LAWRENCE	**34**	**5 860**	**7 443***	**59.5**	**100.0**
053 ASSEMB OF GOD.	1	14	41	0.3	0.6
059 BAPT MISS ASSN	1	25	31*	0.2	0.4
123 CH GOD (ANDER)	1	42	126	1.0	1.7
127 CH GOD (CLEVE)	1	16	20*	0.2	0.3
165 CH OF NAZARENE	1	36	50	0.4	0.7
167 CHS OF CHRIST.	2	47	64	0.5	0.9
356 PRESB CH AMER.	1	21	32	0.3	0.4
419 SO BAPT CONV..	21	5 148	6 440*	51.4	86.5
449 UN METHODIST..	5	511	639*	5.1	8.6
LEAKE	**73**	**7 853**	**10 207***	**54.3**	**100.0**
005 AME ZION......	2	140	195	1.0	1.9
053 ASSEMB OF GOD.	1	38	69	0.4	0.7
081 CATHOLIC......	1	NA	247	1.3	2.4
093 CHR CH (DISC).	1	72	111	0.6	1.1
097 CHR CHS&CHS CR	1	50	62*	0.3	0.6
123 CH GOD (ANDER)	2	70	210	1.1	2.1
127 CH GOD (CLEVE)	2	202	249*	1.3	2.4
167 CHS OF CHRIST.	1	30	65	0.3	0.6
185 CUMBER PRESB..	2	51	135	0.7	1.3
356 PRESB CH AMER.	2	158	180	1.0	1.8
419 SO BAPT CONV..	38	5 738	7 076*	37.7	69.3
449 UN METHODIST..	20	1 304	1 608*	8.6	15.8

NA—Not applicable   *Total adherents estimated from known number of communicant, confirmed, full members.   —Represents a percent less than 0.1.   Percentages may not total due to rounding.

Table 4. Churches and Church Membership by County and Denomination: 1980

County and Denomination	Number of churches	Communicant, confirmed, full members	Total adherents		
			Number	Percent of total population	Percent of total adherents
LEE	134	30 293	38 515*	67.5	100.0
017 AMER BAPT ASSN	1	200	200	0.4	0.5
019 AMER BAPT USA.	1	211	260*	0.5	0.7
053 ASSEMB OF GOD.	4	185	318	0.6	0.8
055 AS REF PRES CH	1	127	168	0.3	0.4
059 BAPT MISS ASSN	10	1 640	2 023*	3.5	5.3
081 CATHOLIC......	2	NA	793	1.4	2.1
093 CHR CH (DISC)	2	191	271	0.5	0.7
097 CHR CHS&CHS CR	5	160	197*	0.3	0.5
101 C.M.E........	11	1 817	2 241*	3.9	5.8
127 CH GOD (CLEVE)	1	99	122*	0.2	0.3
151 L-D SAINTS....	1	NA	235	0.4	0.6
165 CH OF NAZARENE	1	54	79	0.1	0.2
167 CHS OF CHRIST.	11	1 424	1 727	3.0	4.5
193 EPISCOPAL.....	1	224	302	0.5	0.8
283 LUTH--MO SYNOD	1	126	172	0.3	0.4
357 PRESB CH US...	6	953	1 175*	2.1	3.1
403 SALVATION ARMY	1	49	73	0.1	0.2
413 S.D.A.........	1	22	27*	-	0.1
419 SO BAPT CONV..	44	17 502	21 585*	37.8	56.0
449 UN METHODIST..	28	5 296	6 531*	11.4	17.0
453 UN PRES CH USA	1	13	16*	-	-
LEFLORE	51	13 250	17 889*	43.1	100.0
017 AMER BAPT ASSN	1	30	30	0.1	0.2
053 ASSEMB OF GOD.	2	80	122	0.3	0.7
081 CATHOLIC......	3	NA	1 090	2.6	6.1
093 CHR CH (DISC).	3	359	515	1.2	2.9
101 C.M.E........	4	631	796*	1.9	4.4
127 CH GOD (CLEVE)	2	219	276*	0.7	1.5
151 L-D SAINTS....	1	NA	60	0.1	0.3
167 CHS OF CHRIST.	2	220	332	0.8	1.9
193 EPISCOPAL.....	1	474	512	1.2	2.9
271 REFORM JUDAISM	1	28	35*	0.1	0.2
283 LUTH--MO SYNOD	1	57	79	0.2	0.4
356 PRESB CH AMER.	2	97	106	0.3	0.6
357 PRESB CH US...	1	890	1 123*	2.7	6.3
403 SALVATION ARMY	1	116	132	0.3	0.7
413 S.D.A.........	1	191	241*	0.6	1.3
419 SO BAPT CONV..	12	7 239	9 135*	22.0	51.1
449 UN METHODIST..	13	2 619	3 305*	8.0	18.5
LINCOLN	84	16 866	21 733*	72.0	100.0
053 ASSEMB OF GOD.	2	83	129	0.4	0.6
081 CATHOLIC......	1	NA	402	1.3	1.8
123 CH GOD (ANDER)	1	24	72	0.2	0.3
127 CH GOD (CLEVE)	1	66	82*	0.3	0.4
151 L-D SAINTS....	1	NA	274	0.9	1.3
165 CH OF NAZARENE	1	67	140	0.5	0.6
167 CHS OF CHRIST.	16	600	764	2.5	3.5
193 EPISCOPAL.....	1	92	115	0.4	0.5
356 PRESB CH AMER.	1	378	378	1.3	1.7
357 PRESB CH US...	1	42	52*	0.2	0.2
413 S.D.A.........	2	75	93*	0.3	0.4
419 SO BAPT CONV..	39	13 199	16 442*	54.5	75.7
449 UN METHODIST..	17	2 240	2 790*	9.2	12.8
LOWNDES	90	20 208	26 546*	46.3	100.0
053 ASSEMB OF GOD.	4	406	570	1.0	2.1
059 BAPT MISS ASSN	2	224	279*	0.5	1.1
081 CATHOLIC......	1	NA	952	1.7	3.6
089 CHR & MISS AL.	1	0	35	0.1	0.1
097 CHR CHS&CHS CR	1	200	249*	0.4	0.9
101 C.M.E........	9	1 600	1 989*	3.5	7.5
127 CH GOD (CLEVE)	1	56	70*	0.1	0.3
151 L-D SAINTS....	1	NA	324	0.6	1.2
165 CH OF NAZARENE	2	127	199	0.3	0.7
167 CHS OF CHRIST.	8	1 140	1 451	2.5	5.5
185 CUMBER PRESB..	4	281	437	0.8	1.6
193 EPISCOPAL.....	2	651	703	1.2	2.6
271 REFORM JUDAISM	1	44	55*	0.1	0.2
283 LUTH--MO SYNOD	1	118	161	0.3	0.6
356 PRESB CH AMER.	1	323	370	0.6	1.4
357 PRESB CH US...	4	408	507*	0.9	1.9
403 SALVATION ARMY	1	103	133	0.2	0.5
413 S.D.A.........	2	193	240*	0.4	0.9
419 SO BAPT CONV..	22	10 780	13 403*	23.4	50.5
435 UNITARIAN-UNIV	1	?	?	?	?
449 UN METHODIST..	21	3 554	4 419*	7.7	16.6
MADISON	66	12 490	16 472*	39.6	100.0
005 AME ZION......	10	3 225	3 706	8.9	22.5
053 ASSEMB OF GOD.	2	68	105	0.3	0.6
081 CATHOLIC......	4	NA	871	2.1	5.3
093 CHR CH (DISC).	1	45	69	0.2	0.4
101 C.M.E........	4	334	422*	1.0	2.6
123 CH GOD (ANDER)	1	60	180	0.4	1.1
165 CH OF NAZARENE	1	30	0	-	-
167 CHS OF CHRIST.	3	164	257	0.6	1.6
193 EPISCOPAL.....	2	167	253	0.6	1.5
356 PRESB CH AMER.	3	139	169	0.4	1.0
357 PRESB CH US...	1	302	382*	0.9	2.3
413 S.D.A.........	1	83	105*	0.3	0.6
419 SO BAPT CONV..	16	5 575	7 048*	16.9	42.8
449 UN METHODIST..	17	2 298	2 905*	7.0	17.6
MARION	62	12 501	16 056*	62.5	100.0
017 AMER BAPT ASSN	1	100	100	0.4	0.6
053 ASSEMB OF GOD.	1	77	135	0.5	0.8
059 BAPT MISS ASSN	2	403	503*	2.0	3.1
081 CATHOLIC.....	1	NA	192	0.7	1.2
101 C.M.E.......	3	483	602*	2.3	3.7
127 CH GOD (CLEVE)	8	488	609*	2.4	3.8
151 L-D SAINTS....	1	NA	222	0.9	1.4
165 CH OF NAZARENE	1	42	84	0.3	0.5
167 CHS OF CHRIST.	2	50	73	0.3	0.5
193 EPISCOPAL.....	1	27	29	0.1	0.2
285 MENNONITE CH..	1	45	56*	0.2	0.3
357 PRESB CH US...	1	103	128*	0.5	0.8
413 S.D.A.........	2	43	54*	0.2	0.3
419 SO BAPT CONV..	22	8 524	10 630*	41.3	66.2
449 UN METHODIST..	15	2 116	2 639*	10.3	16.4
MARSHALL	81	11 448	14 707*	50.2	100.0
053 ASSEMB OF GOD.	1	13	22	0.1	0.1
081 CATHOLIC.....	1	NA	270	0.9	1.8
101 C.M.E........	24	4 345	5 476*	18.7	37.2
127 CH GOD (CLEVE)	1	29	37*	0.1	0.3
167 CHS OF CHRIST.	7	309	393	1.3	2.7
193 EPISCOPAL.....	1	111	134	0.5	0.9
208 EVAN LUTH ASSN	1	6	8	-	0.1
283 LUTH--MO SYNOD	1	33	48	0.2	0.3
357 PRESB CH US...	5	232	292*	1.0	2.0
419 SO BAPT CONV..	18	4 848	6 109*	20.9	41.5
449 UN METHODIST..	21	1 522	1 918*	6.5	13.0
MONROE	97	15 211	19 185*	52.7	100.0
017 AMER BAPT ASSN	3	350	350	1.0	1.8
053 ASSEMB OF GOD.	2	123	200	0.5	1.0
059 BAPT MISS ASSN	1	396	493*	1.4	2.6
081 CATHOLIC......	2	NA	197	0.5	1.0
089 CHR & MISS AL.	1	34	68	0.2	0.4
093 CHR CH (DISC)	1	31	48	0.1	0.3
097 CHR CHS&CHS CR	2	475	592*	1.6	3.1
101 C.M.E........	6	718	894*	2.5	4.7
127 CH GOD (CLEVE)	3	61	76*	0.2	0.4
167 CHS OF CHRIST.	11	1 018	1 296	3.6	6.8
193 EPISCOPAL.....	1	60	95	0.3	0.5
285 MENNONITE CH..	1	37	46*	0.1	0.2
357 PRESB CH US...	3	308	384*	1.1	2.0
413 S.D.A.........	2	69	86*	0.2	0.4
419 SO BAPT CONV..	29	7 425	9 247*	25.4	48.2
449 UN METHODIST..	28	4 048	5 041*	13.8	26.3
453 UN PRES CH USA	1	58	72*	0.2	0.4
MONTGOMERY	48	6 978	8 670*	64.9	100.0
081 CATHOLIC......	1	NA	58	0.4	0.7
101 C.M.E........	4	472	579*	4.3	6.7
127 CH GOD (CLEVE)	3	143	175*	1.3	2.0
167 CHS OF CHRIST.	4	209	329	2.5	3.8
193 EPISCOPAL.....	1	21	20	0.1	0.2
356 PRESB CH AMER.	1	127	144	1.1	1.7
357 PRESB CH US...	1	7	9*	0.1	0.1
419 SO BAPT CONV..	20	4 421	5 421*	40.6	62.5
449 UN METHODIST..	13	1 578	1 935*	14.5	22.3
NESHOBA	91	11 346	15 348*	64.5	100.0
053 ASSEMB OF GOD.	2	66	146	0.6	1.0
059 BAPT MISS ASSN	1	173	216*	0.9	1.4
081 CATHOLIC......	3	NA	853	3.6	5.6
123 CH GOD (ANDER)	4	113	339	1.4	2.2
127 CH GOD (CLEVE)	2	68	85*	0.4	0.6
151 L-D SAINTS....	1	NA	116	0.5	0.8
167 CHS OF CHRIST.	2	87	110	0.5	0.7
185 CUMBER PRESB..	1	25	41	0.2	0.3
193 EPISCOPAL.....	1	29	37	0.2	0.2
285 MENNONITE CH..	2	69	86*	0.4	0.6
356 PRESB CH AMER.	2	213	213	0.9	1.4
419 SO BAPT CONV..	41	7 525	9 390*	39.5	61.2
449 UN METHODIST..	28	2 947	3 677*	15.5	24.0
453 UN PRES CH USA	1	31	39*	0.2	0.3
NEWTON	63	9 362	11 917*	59.8	100.0
081 CATHOLIC......	2	NA	233	1.2	2.0
097 CHR CHS&CHS CR	2	200	244*	1.2	2.0
123 CH GOD (ANDER)	3	118	354	1.8	3.0
127 CH GOD (CLEVE)	2	179	218*	1.1	1.8
167 CHS OF CHRIST.	3	135	172	0.9	1.4
185 CUMBER PRESB..	2	108	215	1.1	1.8
193 EPISCOPAL.....	1	26	27	0.1	0.2
356 PRESB CH AMER.	3	192	201	1.0	1.7
357 PRESB CH US...	1	19	23*	0.1	0.2
413 S.D.A.........	1	62	76*	0.4	0.6
419 SO BAPT CONV..	29	6 533	7 970*	40.0	66.9
449 UN METHODIST..	13	1 790	2 184*	11.0	18.3
NOXUBEE	55	5 284	6 785*	51.4	100.0
005 AME ZION......	1	83	148	1.1	2.2
081 CATHOLIC......	1	NA	28	0.2	0.4
101 C.M.E........	6	1 145	1 454*	11.0	21.4
123 CH GOD (ANDER)	2	39	117	0.9	1.7
143 CG IN CR(MENN)	2	259	259	2.0	3.8
167 CHS OF CHRIST.	2	63	89	0.7	1.3
185 CUMBER PRESB..	2	55	109	0.8	1.6
193 EPISCOPAL.....	2	57	67	0.5	1.0
285 MENNONITE CH..	3	152	193*	1.5	2.8
356 PRESB CH AMER.	3	132	132	1.0	1.9
419 SO BAPT CONV..	11	1 765	2 241*	17.0	33.0

NA— Not applicable   *Total adherents estimated from known number of communicant, confirmed, full members.   —Represents a percent less than 0.1.   Percentages may not total due to rounding.

Table 4. Churches and Church Membership by County and Denomination: 1980

County and Denomination	Number of churches	Communicant, confirmed, full members	Total adherents Number	Percent of total population	Percent of total adherents
449 UN METHODIST..	20	1 534	1 948*	14.7	28.7
OKTIBBEHA	60	13 992	18 521*	51.4	100.0
053 ASSEMB OF GOD.	1	29	62	0.2	0.3
059 BAPT MISS ASSN	1	45	54*	0.1	0.3
081 CATHOLIC......	1	NA	1 540	4.3	8.3
093 CHR CH (DISC).	1	5	5	-	-
123 CH GOD (ANDER)	1	10	30	0.1	0.2
127 CH GOD (CLEVE)	2	132	158*	0.4	0.9
151 L-D SAINTS....	1	NA	96	0.3	0.5
167 CHS OF CHRIST.	4	305	405	1.1	2.2
193 EPISCOPAL.....	1	236	298	0.8	1.6
283 LUTH--MO SYNOD	1	79	98	0.3	0.5
356 PRESB CH AMER.	1	40	40	0.1	0.2
357 PRESB CH US...	3	954	1 145*	3.2	6.2
419 SO BAPT CONV..	18	7 785	9 343*	25.9	50.4
435 UNITARIAN-UNIV	1	16	19*	0.1	0.1
449 UN METHODIST..	22	4 337	5 205*	14.5	28.1
453 UN PRES CH USA	1	19	23*	0.1	0.1
PANOLA	97	14 836	19 074*	67.7	100.0
005 AME ZION......	12	1 902	2 478	8.8	13.0
053 ASSEMB OF GOD.	3	93	144	0.5	0.8
081 CATHOLIC......	2	NA	150	0.5	0.8
101 C.M.E........	13	2 446	3 076*	10.9	16.1
123 CH GOD (ANDER)	1	88	264	0.9	1.4
127 CH GOD (CLEVE)	2	39	49*	0.2	0.3
165 CH OF NAZARENE	1	21	19	0.1	0.1
167 CHS OF CHRIST.	7	589	750	2.7	3.9
193 EPISCOPAL.....	1	57	82	0.3	0.4
356 PRESB CH AMER.	1	91	101	0.4	0.5
357 PRESB CH US...	1	359	452*	1.6	2.4
419 SO BAPT CONV..	24	6 077	7 643*	27.1	40.1
449 UN METHODIST..	26	2 871	3 611*	12.8	18.9
453 UN PRES CH USA	3	203	255*	0.9	1.3
PEARL RIVER	70	16 792	21 995*	65.1	100.0
017 AMER BAPT ASSN	2	150	150	0.4	0.7
053 ASSEMB OF GOD.	3	146	270	0.8	1.2
059 BAPT MISS ASSN	16	2 613	3 263*	9.7	14.8
081 CATHOLIC......	2	NA	692	2.0	3.1
127 CH GOD (CLEVE)	3	243	303*	0.9	1.4
151 L-D SAINTS....	1	NA	245	0.7	1.1
167 CHS OF CHRIST.	2	112	150	0.4	0.7
193 EPISCOPAL.....	1	81	111	0.3	0.5
283 LUTH--MO SYNOD	1	138	194	0.6	0.9
356 PRESB CH AMER.	1	96	118	0.3	0.5
357 PRESB CH US...	1	25	31*	0.1	0.1
419 SO BAPT CONV..	29	11 513	14 376*	42.5	65.4
449 UN METHODIST..	8	1 675	2 092*	6.2	9.5
PERRY	37	4 928	6 270*	63.6	100.0
059 BAPT MISS ASSN	6	599	755*	7.7	12.0
123 CH GOD (ANDER)	1	32	96	1.0	1.5
127 CH GOD (CLEVE)	4	150	189*	1.9	3.0
357 PRESB CH US...	1	21	26*	0.3	0.4
419 SO BAPT CONV..	17	3 433	4 330*	43.9	69.1
449 UN METHODIST..	8	693	874*	8.9	13.9
PIKE	68	16 250	21 485*	59.4	100.0
005 AME ZION......	1	75	113	0.3	0.5
053 ASSEMB OF GOD.	2	138	171	0.5	0.8
059 BAPT MISS ASSN	1	85	106*	0.3	0.5
081 CATHOLIC......	3	NA	841	2.3	3.9
093 CHR CH (DISC).	1	107	137	0.4	0.6
127 CH GOD (CLEVE)	1	53	66*	0.2	0.3
151 L-D SAINTS....	1	NA	104	0.3	0.5
165 CH OF NAZARENE	2	374	637	1.8	3.0
167 CHS OF CHRIST.	2	155	215	0.6	1.0
193 EPISCOPAL.....	1	137	196	0.5	0.9
283 LUTH--MO SYNOD	1	53	75	0.2	0.3
353 CHR BRETHREN..	1	20	20	0.1	0.1
357 PRESB CH US...	4	546	682*	1.9	3.2
403 SALVATION ARMY	1	40	69	0.2	0.3
413 S.D.A........	2	57	71*	0.2	0.3
415 S-D BAPTIST GC	1	13	16*	-	0.1
419 SO BAPT CONV..	28	11 526	14 386*	39.8	67.0
421 SO METHODIST..	1	50	59	0.2	0.3
449 UN METHODIST..	14	2 821	3 521*	9.7	16.4
PONTOTOC	72	12 016	14 769*	70.6	100.0
053 ASSEMB OF GOD.	1	?	?	?	?
081 CATHOLIC......	1	NA	20	0.1	0.1
101 C.M.E........	2	559	686*	3.3	4.6
165 CH OF NAZARENE	1	70	80	0.4	0.5
167 CHS OF CHRIST.	4	240	307	1.5	2.1
357 PRESB CH US...	3	140	172*	0.8	1.2
419 SO BAPT CONV..	43	9 531	11 693*	55.9	79.2
449 UN METHODIST..	17	1 476	1 811*	8.7	12.3
PRENTISS	65	9 380	11 976*	49.8	100.0
053 ASSEMB OF GOD.	1	32	45	0.2	0.4
055 AS REF PRES CH	1	110	110	0.5	0.9
059 BAPT MISS ASSN	2	228	279*	1.2	2.3
081 CATHOLIC......	1	NA	59	0.2	0.5
097 CHR CHS&CHS CR	2	245	300*	1.2	2.5
101 C.M.E........	2	206	252*	1.0	2.1
127 CH GOD (CLEVE)	2	55	67*	0.3	0.6
151 L-D SAINTS....	1	NA	370	1.5	3.1
167 CHS OF CHRIST.	15	1 009	1 326	5.5·	11.1
357 PRESB CH US,..	1	45	55*	0.2	0.5
419 SO BAPT CONV..	20	4 924	6 023*	25.1	50.3
449 UN METHODIST..	17	2 526	3 090*	12.9	25.8
QUITMAN	35	5 804	7 478*	59.2	100.0
005 AME ZION......	4	561	749	5.9	10.0
019 AMER BAPT USA.	1	259	331*	2.6	4.4
053 ASSEMB OF GOD.	1	53	89	0.7	1.2
093 CHR CH (DISC).	1	31	48	0.4	0.6
127 CH GOD (CLEVE)	4	218	279*	2.2	3.7
165 CH OF NAZARENE	1	12	19	0.2	0.3
167 CHS OF CHRIST.	2	80	102	0.8	1.4
356 PRESB CH AMER.	1	84	99	0.8	1.3
419 SO BAPT CONV..	12	3 678	4 703*	37.2	62.9
449 UN METHODIST..	8	828	1 059*	8.4	14.2
RANKIN	112	27 436	35 910*	51.7	100.0
053 ASSEMB OF GOD.	4	213	280	0.4	0.8
059 BAPT MISS ASSN	3	441	550*	0.8	1.5
081 CATHOLIC......	3	NA	1 350	1.9	3.8
101 C.M.E........	4	479	598*	0.9	1.7
127 CH GOD (CLEVE)	8	1 095	1 366*	2.0	3.8
151 L-D SAINTS....	1	NA	324	0.5	0.9
167 CHS OF CHRIST.	2	282	415	0.6	1.2
185 CUMBER PRESB..	1	61	86	0.1	0.2
193 EPISCOPAL.....	1	178	178	0.3	0.5
349 PENT HOLINESS.	1	42	52*	0.1	0.1
353 CHR BRETHREN..	1	15	15	-	-
356 PRESB CH AMER.	2	437	513	0.7	1.4
357 PRESB CH US...	1	207	258*	0.4	0.7
413 S.D.A........	1	149	186*	0.3	0.5
419 SO BAPT CONV..	50	18 740	23 380*	33.7	65.1
449 UN METHODIST..	29	5 097	6 359*	9.2	17.7
SCOTT	76	11 355	14 313*	58.3	100.0
053 ASSEMB OF GOD.	2	108	186	0.8	1.3
059 BAPT MISS ASSN	2	51	64*	0.3	0.4
081 CATHOLIC......	1	NA	82	0.3	0.6
097 CHR CHS&CHS CR	2	56	70*	0.3	0.5
127 CH GOD (CLEVE)	2	123	154*	0.6	1.1
167 CHS OF CHRIST.	2	111	141	0.6	1.0
185 CUMBER PRESB..	3	116	98	0.4	0.7
356 PRESB CH AMER.	1	53	74	0.3	0.5
419 SO BAPT CONV..	37	7 619	9 540*	38.8	66.7
449 UN METHODIST..	24	3 118	3 904*	15.9	27.3
SHARKEY	16	2 549	3 404*	42.7	100.0
059 BAPT MISS ASSN	1	59	77*	1.0	2.3
081 CATHOLIC......	1	NA	105	1.3	3.1
101 C.M.E........	1	50	65*	0.8	1.9
167 CHS OF CHRIST.	1	115	146	1.8	4.3
356 PRESB CH AMER.	1	33	33	0.4	1.0
413 S.D.A........	1	67	87*	1.1	2.6
419 SO BAPT CONV..	6	1 688	2 193*	27.5	64.4
449 UN METHODIST..	4	537	698*	8.8	20.5
SIMPSON	66	13 752	17 257*	73.6	100.0
017 AMER BAPT ASSN	1	150	150	0.6	0.9
053 ASSEMB OF GOD.	1	37	65	0.3	0.4
059 BAPT MISS ASSN	1	79	98*	0.4	0.6
081 CATHOLIC......	1	NA	150	0.6	0.9
101 C.M.E........	3	605	754*	3.2	4.4
127 CH GOD (CLEVE)	3	236	294*	1.3	1.7
167 CHS OF CHRIST.	2	70	100	0.4	0.6
356 PRESB CH AMER.	2	225	249	1.1	1.4
419 SO BAPT CONV..	44	11 074	13 806*	58.9	80.0
449 UN METHODIST..	8	1 276	1 591*	6.8	9.2
SMITH	68	9 130	11 395*	75.6	100.0
059 BAPT MISS ASSN	5	553	687*	4.6	6.0
081 CATHOLIC......	1	NA	63	0.4	0.6
101 C.M.E........	1	42	52*	0.3	0.5
127 CH GOD (CLEVE)	2	100	124*	0.8	1.1
167 CHS OF CHRIST.	1	12	15	0.1	0.1
281 LUTH CH AMER..	2	62	78	0.5	0.7
356 PRESB CH AMER.	2	121	142	0.9	1.2
419 SO BAPT CONV..	41	6 851	8 509*	56.4	74.7
449 UN METHODIST..	13	1 389	1 725*	11.4	15.1
STONE	25	4 125	5 221*	53.7	100.0
017 AMER BAPT ASSN	2	350	350	3.6	6.7
059 BAPT MISS ASSN	6	1 251	1 536*	15.8	29.4
081 CATHOLIC......	1	NA	96	1.0	1.8
101 C.M.E........	1	28	34*	0.3	0.7
127 CH GOD (CLEVE)	1	20	25*	0.3	0.5
151 L-D SAINTS....	1	NA	139	1.4	2.7
357 PRESB CH US...	1	83	102*	1.0	2.0
419 SO BAPT CONV..	5	1 604	1 970*	20.3	37.7
449 UN METHODIST..	7	789	969*	10.0	18.6
SUNFLOWER	59	10 507	13 947*	40.0	100.0
053 ASSEMB OF GOD.	1	32	50	0.1	0.4
059 BAPT MISS ASSN	1	77	98*	0.3	0.7
081 CATHOLIC......	3	NA	495	1.4	3.5
093 CHR CH (DISC).	4	125	186	0.5	1.3

NA— Not applicable   *Total adherents estimated from known number of communicant, confirmed, full members.   —Represents a percent less than 0.1.   Percentages may not total due to rounding.

Table 4. Churches and Church Membership by County and Denomination: 1980

County and Denomination	Number of churches	Communicant, confirmed, full members	Total adherents			County and Denomination	Number of churches	Communicant, confirmed, full members	Total adherents		
			Number	Percent of total population	Percent of total adherents				Number	Percent of total population	Percent of total adherents
097 CHR CHS&CHS CR	1	50	64*	0.2	0.5	127 CH GOD (CLEVE)	1	51	64*	0.1	0.2
101 C.M.E........	1	180	229*	0.7	1.6	151 L-D SAINTS....	1	NA	268	0.5	1.0
123 CH GOD (ANDER)	1	42	126	0.4	0.9	165 CH OF NAZARENE	2	115	162	0.3	0.6
127 CH GOD (CLEVE)	7	331	421*	1.2	3.0	167 CHS OF CHRIST.	5	616	663	1.3	2.5
167 CHS OF CHRIST.	5	513	653	1.9	4.7	193 EPISCOPAL.....	4	806	987	1.9	3.7
193 EPISCOPAL.....	2	203	267	0.8	1.9	271 REFORM JUDAISM	1	190	238*	0.5	0.9
353 CHR BRETHREN..	1	20	20	0.1	0.1	283 LUTH--MO SYNOD	1	146	210	0.4	0.8
356 PRESB CH AMER.	1	175	204	0.6	1.5	356 PRESB CH AMER.	1	278	299	0.6	1.1
413 S.D.A........	1	104	132*	0.4	0.9	357 PRESB CH US...	2	734	918*	1.8	3.5
419 SO BAPT CONV..	17	6 477	8 233*	23.6	59.0	403 SALVATION ARMY	1	107	152	0.3	0.6
449 UN METHODIST..	13	2 178	2 769*	7.9	19.9	413 S.D.A........	2	176	220*	0.4	0.8
						419 SO BAPT CONV..	13	9 739	12 187*	23.6	46.2
TALLAHATCHIE	51	6 331	8 083*	47.1	100.0	449 UN METHODIST..	12	4 019	5 029*	9.7	19.1
005 AME ZION......	1	200	243	1.4	3.0	WASHINGTON	65	20 076	30 538*	42.2	100.0
053 ASSEMB OF GOD.	1	55	60	0.3	0.7						
081 CATHOLIC......	1	NA	42	0.2	0.5	053 ASSEMB OF GOD.	3	364	505	0.7	1.7
101 C.M.E........	3	507	645*	3.8	8.0	059 BAPT MISS ASSN	3	315	405*	0.6	1.3
127 CH GOD (CLEVE)	5	386	491*	2.9	6.1	081 CATHOLIC......	4	NA	4 152	5.7	13.6
165 CH OF NAZARENE	1	55	90	0.5	1.1	093 CHR CH (DISC).	1	124	191	0.3	0.6
167 CHS OF CHRIST.	6	213	273	1.6	3.4	127 CH GOD (CLEVE)	3	380	488*	0.7	1.6
193 EPISCOPAL.....	1	79	86	0.5	1.1	143 CG IN CR(MENN)	1	91	91	0.1	0.3
357 PRESB CH US...	5	259	330*	1.9	4.1	151 L-D SAINTS....	1	NA	227	0.3	0.7
419 SO BAPT CONV..	17	3 719	4 731*	27.6	58.5	165 CH OF NAZARENE	1	67	80	0.1	0.3
449 UN METHODIST..	8	830	1 056*	6.2	13.1	167 CHS OF CHRIST.	4	591	773	1.1	2.5
453 UN PRES CH USA	2	28	36*	0.2	0.4	193 EPISCOPAL.....	4	706	1 003	1.4	3.3
						271 REFORM JUDAISM	1	320	411*	0.6	1.3
TATE	57	8 803	11 388*	56.6	100.0	283 LUTH--MO SYNOD	1	83	123	0.2	0.4
						357 PRESB CH US...	4	1 009	1 296*	1.8	4.2
081 CATHOLIC......	1	NA	150	0.7	1.3	403 SALVATION ARMY	1	120	356	0.5	1.2
097 CHR CHS&CHS CR	1	50	62*	0.3	0.5	413 S.D.A........	4	444	570*	0.8	1.9
101 C.M.E........	5	431	533*	2.6	4.7	419 SO BAPT CONV..	19	12 320	15 830*	21.9	51.8
127 CH GOD (CLEVE)	2	23	28*	0.1	0.2	449 UN METHODIST..	10	3 142	4 037*	5.6	13.2
151 L-D SAINTS....	1	NA	285	1.4	2.5						
167 CHS OF CHRIST.	14	1 501	1 934*	9.6	17.0	WAYNE	61	7 116	9 390*	49.1	100.0
274 LAT EVAN LUTH.	1	30	32	0.2	0.3						
281 LUTH CH AMER..	1	31	33	0.2	0.3	053 ASSEMB OF GOD.	10	527	984	5.1	10.5
349 PENT HOLINESS.	1	16	20*	0.1	0.2	059 BAPT MISS ASSN	1	111	140*	0.7	1.5
357 PRESB CH US...	1	126	156*	0.8	1.4	081 CATHOLIC......	1	NA	72	0.4	0.8
419 SO BAPT CONV..	19	5 176	6 400*	31.8	56.2	127 CH GOD (CLEVE)	1	164	207*	1.1	2.2
449 UN METHODIST..	10	1 419	1 755*	8.7	15.4	167 CHS OF CHRIST.	2	78	112	0.6	1.2
						356 PRESB CH AMER.	3	176	206	1.1	2.2
TIPPAH	70	10 289	12 703*	67.8	100.0	419 SO BAPT CONV..	22	4 381	5 535*	28.9	58.9
						421 SO METHODIST..	3	120	164	0.9	1.7
017 AMER BAPT ASSN	1	150	150	0.8	1.2	449 UN METHODIST..	18	1 559	1 970*	10.3	21.0
053 ASSEMB OF GOD.	2	96	138	0.7	1.1						
055 AS REF PRES CH	2	156	158	0.8	1.2	WEBSTER	50	6 431	7 796*	75.7	100.0
167 CHS OF CHRIST.	8	709	945	5.0	7.4						
185 CUMBER PRESB..	1	63	98	0.5	0.8	127 CH GOD (CLEVE)	5	174	210*	2.0	2.7
357 PRESB CH US...	6	384	472*	2.5	3.7	167 CHS OF CHRIST.	3	156	224	2.2	2.9
419 SO BAPT CONV..	29	6 835	8 409*	44.9	66.2	419 SO BAPT CONV..	29	5 082	6 132*	59.5	78.7
449 UN METHODIST..	21	1 896	2 333*	12.4	18.4	449 UN METHODIST..	13	1 019	1 230*	11.9	15.8
TISHOMINGO	66	8 187	9 929*	53.9	100.0	WILKINSON	33	3 662	4 818*	48.1	100.0
017 AMER BAPT ASSN	3	300	300	1.6	3.0	081 CATHOLIC......	2	NA	195	1.9	4.0
059 BAPT MISS ASSN	7	481	580*	3.1	5.8	093 CHR CH (DISC).	1	63	148	1.5	3.1
081 CATHOLIC......	1	NA	20	0.1	0.2	101 C.M.E........	7	781	962*	9.6	20.0
101 C.M.E........	1	73	88*	0.5	0.9	151 L-D SAINTS....	1	NA	?	?	?
127 CH GOD (CLEVE)	2	98	118*	0.6	1.2	167 CHS OF CHRIST.	3	211	311	3.1	6.5
167 CHS OF CHRIST.	9	665	907	4.9	9.1	193 EPISCOPAL.....	1	117	138	1.4	2.9
419 SO BAPT CONV..	24	4 916	5 923*	32.1	59.7	356 PRESB CH AMER.	2	144	176	1.8	3.7
449 UN METHODIST..	19	1 654	1 993*	10.8	20.1	413 S.D.A........	1	7	9*	0.1	0.2
						419 SO BAPT CONV..	5	1 204	1 482*	14.8	30.8
TUNICA	18	2 695	3 615*	37.5	100.0	449 UN METHODIST..	10	1 135	1 397*	13.9	29.0
081 CATHOLIC......	1	NA	80	0.8	2.2	WINSTON	71	10 453	13 165*	67.6	100.0
101 C.M.E........	5	863	1 126*	11.7	31.1						
127 CH GOD (CLEVE)	2	?	?	?	?	053 ASSEMB OF GOD.	4	184	285	1.5	2.2
167 CHS OF CHRIST.	1	50	64	0.7	1.8	081 CATHOLIC......	1	NA	154	0.8	1.2
193 EPISCOPAL.....	1	54	91	0.9	2.5	101 C.M.E........	3	574	714*	3.7	5.4
357 PRESB CH US...	1	137	179*	1.9	5.0	127 CH GOD (CLEVE)	1	9	11*	0.1	0.1
419 SO BAPT CONV..	4	916	1 195*	12.4	33.1	167 CHS OF CHRIST.	2	92	119	0.6	0.9
449 UN METHODIST..	3	675	880*	9.1	24.3	281 LUTH CH AMER..	2	117	126	0.6	1.0
						285 MENNONITE CH..	1	32	40*	0.2	0.3
UNION	75	15 500	19 196*	88.3	100.0	356 PRESB CH AMER.	1	205	227	1.2	1.7
						357 PRESB CH US...	1	87	108*	0.6	0.8
053 ASSEMB OF GOD.	3	151	254	1.2	1.3	419 SO BAPT CONV..	29	6 229	7 745*	39.8	58.8
055 AS REF PRES CH	2	376	402	1.8	2.1	435 UNITARIAN--UNIV	1	35	44*	0.2	0.3
081 CATHOLIC......	1	NA	145	0.7	0.8	449 UN METHODIST..	23	2 712	3 372*	17.3	25.6
101 C.M.E........	3	784	961*	4.4	5.0	453 UN PRES CH USA	2	177	220*	1.1	1.7
127 CH GOD (CLEVE)	2	130	159*	0.7	0.8						
165 CH OF NAZARENE	1	30	60	0.3	0.3	YALOBUSHA	55	8 860	11 055*	84.1	100.0
167 CHS OF CHRIST.	5	387	493	2.3	2.6						
419 SO BAPT CONV..	39	11 152	13 670*	62.9	71.2	005 AME ZION......	3	543	772	5.9	7.0
449 UN METHODIST..	18	2 369	2 904*	13.4	15.1	017 AMER BAPT ASSN	1	200	200	1.5	1.8
453 UN PRES CH USA	1	121	148*	0.7	0.8	053 ASSEMB OF GOD.	1	77	216	1.6	2.0
						097 CHR CHS&CHS CR	1	300	369*	2.8	3.3
WALTHALL	27	5 269	6 831*	49.6	100.0	101 C.M.E........	8	1 637	2 013*	15.3	18.2
						127 CH GOD (CLEVE)	3	246	303*	2.3	2.7
081 CATHOLIC......	1	NA	116	0.8	1.7	167 CHS OF CHRIST.	4	306	368	2.8	3.3
151 L-D SAINTS....	1	NA	71	0.5	1.0	193 EPISCOPAL.....	1	13	13	0.1	0.1
167 CHS OF CHRIST.	1	27	34	0.2	0.5	356 PRESB CH AMER.	2	136	158	1.2	1.4
353 CHR BRETHREN..	1	20	20	0.1	0.3	419 SO BAPT CONV..	20	4 446	5 468*	41.6	49.5
419 SO BAPT CONV..	13	4 300	5 426*	39.4	79.4	449 UN METHODIST..	9	881	1 083*	8.2	9.8
449 UN METHODIST..	10	922	1 164*	8.5	17.0	453 UN PRES CH USA	2	75	92*	0.7	0.8
WARREN	56	17 743	26 373*	51.1	100.0	YAZOO	64	10 507	14 198*	51.9	100.0
017 AMER BAPT ASSN	1	150	150	0.3	0.6	017 AMER BAPT ASSN	3	350	350	1.3	2.5
053 ASSEMB OF GOD.	1	119	193	0.4	0.7	053 ASSEMB OF GOD.	1	49	49	0.2	0.3
059 BAPT MISS ASSN	2	319	399*	0.8	1.5	059 BAPT MISS ASSN	2	245	308*	1.1	2.2
081 CATHOLIC......	3	NA	4 017	7.8	15.2	081 CATHOLIC......	2	NA	963	3.5	6.8
093 CHR CH (DISC).	2	168	187	0.4	0.7	123 CH GOD (ANDER)	1	90	270	1.0	1.9
123 CH GOD (ANDER)	1	10	30	0.1	0.1	127 CH GOD (CLEVE)	1	86	108*	0.4	0.8

NA— Not applicable   *Total adherents estimated from known number of communicant, confirmed, full members.   —Represents a percent less than 0.1.   Percentages may not total due to rounding.

Table 4. Churches and Church Membership by County and Denomination: 1980

County and Denomination	Number of churches	Communicant, confirmed, full members	Total adherents		
			Number	Percent of total population	Percent of total adherents
165 CH OF NAZARENE	1	20	29	0.1	0.2
167 CHS OF CHRIST.	1	140	151	0.6	1.1
193 EPISCOPAL.....	1	189	348	1.3	2.5
263 INT FOURSQ GOS	1	?	?	?	?
356 PRESB CH AMER.	2	391	391	1.4	2.8
413 S.D.A.........	1	98	123*	0.4	0.9
419 SO BAPT CONV..	24	5 990	7 519*	27.5	53.0
449 UN METHODIST..	23	2 859	3 589*	13.1	25.3

MISSOURI

County and Denomination	Number of churches	Communicant, confirmed, full members	Total adherents		
			Number	Percent of total population	Percent of total adherents
THE STATE.....	7 571	1 418 794	2 634 435*	53.6	100.0
ADAIR	36	6 247	9 361*	37.6	100.0
053 ASSEMB OF GOD.	2	122	260	1.0	2.8
081 CATHOLIC......	2	NA	1 200	4.8	12.8
093 CHR CH (DISC).	3	518	763	3.1	8.2
097 CHR CHS&CHS CR	1	50	58*	0.2	0.6
123 CH GOD (ANDER)	1	87	261	1.0	2.8
151 L-D SAINTS....	1	NA	259	1.0	2.8
165 CH OF NAZARENE	1	135	209	0.8	2.2
167 CHS OF CHRIST.	2	120	149	0.6	1.6
193 EPISCOPAL.....	1	64	91	0.4	1.0
197 EVAN CH OF NA.	3	169	169	0.7	1.8
283 LUTH--MO SYNOD	1	249	326	1.3	3.5
357 PRESB CH US...	1	178	208*	0.8	2.2
403 SALVATION ARMY	1	66	160	0.6	1.7
413 S.D.A.........	1	57	67*	0.3	0.7
419 SO BAPT CONV..	5	2 805	3 279*	13.2	35.0
449 UN METHODIST..	9	1 449	1 694*	6.8	18.1
453 UN PRES CH USA	1	178	208*	0.8	2.2
ANDREW	31	4 245	6 152*	44.0	100.0
053 ASSEMB OF GOD.	1	19	30	0.2	0.5
081 CATHOLIC......	1	NA	540	3.9	8.8
093 CHR CH (DISC).	4	889	1 441	10.3	23.4
097 CHR CHS&CHS CR	3	180	219*	1.6	3.6
123 CH GOD (ANDER)	1	37	111	0.8	1.8
185 CUMBER PRESB..	1	4	15	0.1	0.2
357 PRESB CH US...	2	19	23*	0.2	0.4
419 SO BAPT CONV..	7	1 434	1 747*	12.5	28.4
443 UN C OF CHRIST	2	398	485*	3.5	7.9
449 UN METHODIST..	6	1 184	1 442*	10.3	23.4
453 UN PRES CH USA	3	81	99*	0.7	1.6
ATCHISON	26	4 342	5 851*	68.0	100.0
053 ASSEMB OF GOD.	2	111	165	1.9	2.8
081 CATHOLIC......	2	NA	425	4.9	7.3
093 CHR CH (DISC).	3	311	543	6.3	9.3
097 CHR CHS&CHS CR	1	71	84*	1.0	1.4
127 CH GOD (CLEVE)	1	38	45*	0.5	0.8
185 CUMBER PRESB..	1	8	31	0.4	0.5
193 EPISCOPAL.....	1	19	23	0.3	0.4
281 LUTH CH AMER..	2	763	945	11.0	16.2
357 PRESB CH US...	2	207	246*	2.9	4.2
419 SO BAPT CONV..	4	1 179	1 401*	16.3	23.9
449 UN METHODIST..	5	1 428	1 697*	19.7	29.0
453 UN PRES CH USA	2	207	246*	2.9	4.2
AUDRAIN	76	12 950	18 329*	69.3	100.0
053 ASSEMB OF GOD.	2	90	161	0.6	0.9
081 CATHOLIC......	4	NA	1 754	6.6	9.6
093 CHR CH (DISC).	8	1 137	1 956	7.4	10.7
097 CHR CHS&CHS CR	10	1 775	2 149*	8.1	11.7
151 L-D SAINTS....	1	NA	106	0.4	0.6
165 CH OF NAZARENE	2	88	223	0.8	1.2
167 CHS OF CHRIST.	2	80	92	0.3	0.5
193 EPISCOPAL.....	1	94	119	0.4	0.6
217 FIRE BAPTIZED.	1	10	12*	-	0.1
283 LUTH--MO SYNOD	2	301	404	1.5	2.2
323 OLD ORD AMISH.	4	520	630*	2.4	3.4
357 PRESB CH US...	7	726	879*	3.3	4.8
413 S.D.A.........	2	308	373*	1.4	2.0
419 SO BAPT CONV..	15	5 334	6 459*	24.4	35.2
443 UN C OF CHRIST	1	108	131*	0.5	0.7
449 UN METHODIST..	8	1 712	2 073*	7.8	11.3
453 UN PRES CH USA	6	667	808*	3.1	4.4
BARRY	84	12 017	16 747*	68.6	100.0
053 ASSEMB OF GOD.	8	288	494	2.0	2.9
059 BAPT MISS ASSN	3	170	204*	0.8	1.2
081 CATHOLIC......	3	NA	1 333	5.5	8.0
093 CHR CH (DISC).	1	179	211	0.9	1.3
097 CHR CHS&CHS CR	5	667	800*	3.3	4.8
151 L-D SAINTS....	1	NA	534	2.2	3.2
165 CH OF NAZARENE	2	142	412	1.7	2.5
167 CHS OF CHRIST.	12	700	891	3.7	5.3
193 EPISCOPAL.....	1	74	87	0.4	0.5

County and Denomination	Number of churches	Communicant, confirmed, full members	Total adherents		
			Number	Percent of total population	Percent of total adherents
283 LUTH--MO SYNOD	3	404	511	2.1	3.1
285 MENNONITE CH..	1	22	26*	0.1	0.2
413 S.D.A.........	1	70	84*	0.3	0.5
419 SO BAPT CONV..	31	7 406	8 886*	36.4	53.1
449 UN METHODIST..	10	1 732	2 078*	8.5	12.4
453 UN PRES CH USA	2	163	196*	0.8	1.2
BARTON	39	4 998	6 724*	59.5	100.0
053 ASSEMB OF GOD.	3	128	250	2.2	3.7
061 BEACHY AMISH..	1	32	38*	0.3	0.6
081 CATHOLIC......	2	NA	448	4.0	6.7
093 CHR CH (DISC).	2	287	392	3.5	5.8
097 CHR CHS&CHS CR	3	1 100	1 311*	11.6	19.5
151 L-D SAINTS....	1	NA	97	0.9	1.4
165 CH OF NAZARENE	1	82	150	1.3	2.2
167 CHS OF CHRIST.	1	50	64	0.6	1.0
185 CUMBER PRESB..	1	93	112	1.0	1.7
283 LUTH--MO SYNOD	1	172	222	2.0	3.3
357 PRESB CH US...	1	31	37*	0.3	0.6
413 S.D.A.........	1	20	24*	0.2	0.4
419 SO BAPT CONV..	11	1 797	2 142*	19.0	31.9
449 UN METHODIST..	9	1 176	1 401*	12.4	20.8
453 UN PRES CH USA	1	30	36*	0.3	0.5
BATES	72	7 519	9 888*	62.3	100.0
029 AMER LUTH CH..	3	70	97	0.6	1.0
053 ASSEMB OF GOD.	4	193	385	2.4	3.9
081 CATHOLIC......	2	NA	375	2.4	3.8
093 CHR CH (DISC).	3	651	1 085	6.8	11.0
097 CHR CHS&CHS CR	11	1 310	1 564*	9.9	15.8
143 CG IN CR(MENN)	1	139	139	0.9	1.4
165 CH OF NAZARENE	1	47	98	0.6	1.0
167 CHS OF CHRIST.	6	260	331	2.1	3.3
283 LUTH--MO SYNOD	1	231	302	1.9	3.1
357 PRESB CH US...	5	185	221*	1.4	2.2
419 SO BAPT CONV..	15	2 545	3 038*	19.1	30.7
443 UN C OF CHRIST	1	57	68*	0.4	0.7
449 UN METHODIST..	14	1 648	1 967*	12.4	19.9
453 UN PRES CH USA	5	183	218*	1.4	2.2
BENTON	48	5 833	7 676*	63.0	100.0
029 AMER LUTH CH..	2	396	515	4.2	6.7
053 ASSEMB OF GOD.	3	132	203	1.7	2.6
081 CATHOLIC......	2	NA	500	4.1	6.5
093 CHR CH (DISC).	2	75	127	1.0	1.7
097 CHR CHS&CHS CR	1	50	59*	0.5	0.8
157 CH OF BRETHREN	1	19	22*	0.2	0.3
165 CH OF NAZARENE	1	39	102	0.8	1.3
167 CHS OF CHRIST.	3	100	127	1.0	1.7
281 LUTH CH AMER..	1	110	134	1.1	1.7
283 LUTH--MO SYNOD	8	1 492	1 855	15.2	24.2
285 MENNONITE CH..	1	29	34*	0.3	0.4
419 SO BAPT CONV..	13	2 158	2 544*	20.9	33.1
449 UN METHODIST..	10	1 233	1 45**	11.9	18.9
BOLLINGER	40	2 734	4 178*	40.6	100.0
053 ASSEMB OF GOD.	2	60	160	1.6	3.8
059 BAPT MISS ASSN	1	11	13*	0.1	0.3
081 CATHOLIC......	2	NA	766	7.4	18.3
123 CH GOD (ANDER)	1	20	60	0.6	1.4
127 CH GOD (CLEVE)	1	31	37*	0.4	0.9
167 CHS OF CHRIST.	4	150	191	1.9	4.6
281 LUTH CH AMER..	2	185	209	2.0	5.0
353 CHR BRETHREN..	1	50	50	0.5	1.2
419 SO BAPT CONV..	11	1 392	1 683*	16.3	40.3
449 UN METHODIST..	12	658	795*	7.7	19.0
453 UN PRES CH USA	3	177	214*	2.1	5.1
BOONE	93	24 879	41 932*	41.8	100.0
017 AMER BAPT ASSN	2	85	85	0.1	0.2
019 AMER BAPT USA.	2	1 495	1 748*	1.7	4.2
053 ASSEMB OF GOD.	4	443	994	1.0	2.4
081 CATHOLIC......	4	NA	10 266	10.2	24.5
093 CHR CH (DISC).	11	3 382	4 749	4.7	11.3
097 CHR CHS&CHS CR	3	572	669*	0.7	1.6
105 CHRISTIAN REF.	1	34	59	0.1	0.1
123 CH GOD (ANDER)	1	50	150	0.1	0.4
151 L-D SAINTS....	2	NA	583	0.6	1.4
165 CH OF NAZARENE	1	135	280	0.3	0.7
167 CHS OF CHRIST.	8	540	687	0.7	1.6
193 EPISCOPAL.....	1	649	922	0.9	2.2
203 EVAN FREE CH..	1	132	154*	0.2	0.4
226 FRIENDS-USA...	1	11	13*	-	-
281 LUTH CH AMER..	1	445	638	0.6	1.5
283 LUTH--MO SYNOD	3	872	1 127	1.1	2.7
290 METRO COMM CHS	1	15	30	-	0.1
357 PRESB CH US...	2	531	621*	0.6	1.5
403 SALVATION ARMY	1	48	98	0.1	0.2
413 S.D.A.........	1	364	426*	0.4	1.0
419 SO BAPT CONV..	22	9 080	10 615*	10.6	25.3
435 UNITARIAN-UNIV	1	127	148*	0.1	0.4
443 UN C OF CHRIST	2	589	689*	0.7	1.6
449 UN METHODIST..	14	4 727	5 526*	5.5	13.2
453 UN PRES CH USA	2	531	621*	0.6	1.5
469 WELS..........	1	22	34	-	0.1
BUCHANAN	110	28 525	48 546*	55.2	100.0
053 ASSEMB OF GOD.	3	557	1 462	1.7	3.0
081 CATHOLIC......	9	NA	11 787	13.4	24.3

NA—Not applicable   *Total adherents estimated from known number of communicant, confirmed, full members.   —Represents a percent less than 0.1.   Percentages may not total due to rounding.

Table 4. Churches and Church Membership by County and Denomination: 1980

County and Denomination	Number of churches	Communicant, confirmed, full members	Total adherents Number	Percent of total population	Percent of total adherents
093 CHR CH (DISC).	5	2 398	3 526	4.0	7.3
097 CHR CHS&CHS CR	6	1 301	1 563*	1.8	3.2
123 CH GOD (ANDER)	1	27	81	0.1	0.2
127 CH GOD (CLEVE)	3	201	241*	0.3	0.5
133 CH GOD(7TH)DEN	1	35	42*	–	0.1
151 L-D SAINTS....	1	NA	531	0.6	1.1
157 CH OF BRETHREN	1	104	125*	0.1	0.3
165 CH OF NAZARENE	3	217	524	0.6	1.1
167 CHS OF CHRIST.	2	180	229	0.3	0.5
185 CUMBER PRESB..	2	63	147	0.2	0.3
193 EPISCOPAL.....	1	521	516	0.6	1.1
221 FREE METHODIST	1	4	39	–	0.1
263 INT FOURSQ GOS	2	361	434*	0.5	0.9
270 CONSRV JUDAISM	1	50	60*	0.1	0.1
271 REFORM JUDAISM	1	270	324*	0.4	0.7
281 LUTH CH AMER..	1	658	765	0.9	1.6
283 LUTH--MO SYNOD	2	966	1 270	1.4	2.6
329 OPEN BIBLE STD	1	35	60	0.1	0.1
357 PRESB CH US...	8	1 118	1 343*	1.5	2.8
403 SALVATION ARMY	1	176	304	0.3	0.6
413 S.D.A.........	2	443	532*	0.6	1.1
419 SO BAPT CONV..	19	10 919	13 117*	14.9	27.0
443 UN C OF CHRIST	2	788	947*	1.1	2.0
449 UN METHODIST..	22	5 972	7 174*	8.2	14.8
453 UN PRES CH USA	8	1 123	1 349*	1.5	2.8
469 WELS..........	1	38	54	0.1	0.1
BUTLER	75	10 684	15 394*	40.8	100.0
017 AMER BAPT ASSN	1	24	24	0.1	0.2
053 ASSEMB OF GOD.	4	371	623	1.7	4.0
059 BAPT MISS ASSN	12	685	828*	2.2	5.4
081 CATHOLIC......	2	NA	1 346	3.6	8.7
093 CHR CH (DISC).	1	694	847	2.2	5.5
123 CH GOD (ANDER)	3	260	780	2.1	5.1
127 CH GOD (CLEVE)	1	24	29*	0.1	0.2
151 L-D SAINTS....	1	NA	239	0.6	1.6
165 CH OF NAZARENE	3	163	369	1.0	2.4
167 CHS OF CHRIST.	12	785	1 000	2.7	6.5
193 EPISCOPAL.....	1	107	135	0.4	0.9
263 INT FOURSQ GOS	1	20	24*	0.1	0.2
283 LUTH--MO SYNOD	1	304	389	1.0	2.5
349 PENT HOLINESS	3	130	157*	0.4	1.0
413 S.D.A.........	1	149	180*	0.5	1.2
419 SO BAPT CONV..	18	5 122	6 192*	16.4	40.2
449 UN METHODIST..	8	1 549	1 873*	5.0	12.2
453 UN PRES CH USA	2	297	359*	1.0	2.3
CALDWELL	38	4 397	6 067*	70.1	100.0
053 ASSEMB OF GOD.	3	63	131	1.5	2.2
081 CATHOLIC......	2	NA	483	5.6	8.0
093 CHR CH (DISC).	5	411	632	7.3	10.4
097 CHR CHS&CHS CR	1	47	56*	0.6	0.9
107 CHRISTIAN UN..	2	73	147	1.7	2.4
165 CH OF NAZARENE	1	88	155	1.8	2.6
167 CHS OF CHRIST.	5	200	255	2.9	4.2
419 SO BAPT CONV..	9	1 918	2 296*	26.5	37.8
443 UN C OF CHRIST	1	121	145*	1.7	2.4
449 UN METHODIST..	9	1 476	1 767*	20.4	29.1
CALLAWAY	73	9 555	13 404*	41.6	100.0
053 ASSEMB OF GOD.	2	129	308	1.0	2.3
081 CATHOLIC......	3	NA	1 236	3.8	9.2
093 CHR CH (DISC).	12	1 514	2 192	6.8	16.4
097 CHR CHS&CHS CR	1	60	73*	0.2	0.5
151 L-D SAINTS....	1	NA	?	?	?
167 CHS OF CHRIST.	1	100	148	0.5	1.1
193 EPISCOPAL.....	2	98	158	0.5	1.2
283 LUTH--MO SYNOD	1	116	155	0.5	1.2
357 PRESB CH US...	6	416	504*	1.6	3.8
419 SO BAPT CONV..	19	4 841	5 866*	18.2	43.8
443 UN C OF CHRIST	1	123	149*	0.5	1.1
449 UN METHODIST..	18	1 746	2 116*	6.6	15.8
453 UN PRES CH USA	6	412	499*	1.5	3.7
CAMDEN	41	6 190	8 577*	43.0	100.0
019 AMER BAPT USA.	1	173	203*	1.0	2.4
053 ASSEMB OF GOD.	4	148	260	1.3	3.0
081 CATHOLIC......	1	NA	600	3.0	7.0
093 CHR CH (DISC).	3	506	851	4.3	9.9
097 CHR CHS&CHS CR	1	375	439*	2.2	5.1
151 L-D SAINTS....	1	NA	279	1.4	3.3
165 CH OF NAZARENE	1	16	66	0.3	0.8
167 CHS OF CHRIST.	5	225	286	1.4	3.3
193 EPISCOPAL.....	1	75	89	0.4	1.0
281 LUTH CH AMER..	2	622	760	3.8	8.9
283 LUTH--MO SYNOD	1	98	116	0.6	1.4
357 PRESB CH US...	1	58	68*	0.3	0.8
413 S.D.A.........	1	47	55*	0.3	0.6
419 SO BAPT CONV..	14	2 998	3 511*	17.6	40.9
449 UN METHODIST..	4	849	994*	5.0	11.6
CAPE GIRARDEAU	85	25 077	38 099*	64.8	100.0
001 ADVENT CHR CH.	1	3	4*	–	–
017 AMER BAPT ASSN	1	34	34	0.1	0.1
029 AMER LUTH CH..	1	199	244	0.4	0.6
053 ASSEMB OF GOD.	4	422	759	1.3	2.0
059 BAPT MISS ASSN	1	44	52*	0.1	0.1
081 CATHOLIC......	3	NA	6 623	11.3	17.4
093 CHR CH (DISC).	1	448	490	0.8	1.3
097 CHR CHS&CHS CR	1	130	154*	0.3	0.4

County and Denomination	Number of churches	Communicant, confirmed, full members	Total adherents Number	Percent of total population	Percent of total adherents
123 CH GOD (ANDER)	2	155	465	0.8	1.2
127 CH GOD (CLEVE)	1	43	51*	0.1	0.1
151 L-D SAINTS....	1	NA	286	0.5	0.8
165 CH OF NAZARENE	1	246	458	0.8	1.2
167 CHS OF CHRIST.	2	259	330	0.6	0.9
193 EPISCOPAL.....	1	133	217	0.4	0.6
263 INT FOURSQ GOS	1	110	131*	0.2	0.3
281 LUTH CH AMER..	1	117	156	0.3	0.4
283 LUTH--MO SYNOD	14	6 040	7 637	13.0	20.0
353 CHR BRETHREN..	2	225	300	0.5	0.8
357 PRESB CH US...	4	1 156	1 372*	2.3	3.6
403 SALVATION ARMY	1	104	279	0.5	0.7
413 S.D.A.........	1	37	44*	0.1	0.1
419 SO BAPT CONV..	17	8 925	10 592*	18.0	27.8
443 UN C OF CHRIST	4	1 124	1 334*	2.3	3.5
449 UN METHODIST..	18	5 089	6 040*	10.3	15.9
469 WELS..........	1	34	47	0.1	0.1
CARROLL	52	7 095	9 928*	81.8	100.0
053 ASSEMB OF GOD.	1	57	100	0.8	1.0
081 CATHOLIC......	2	NA	960	7.9	9.7
093 CHR CH (DISC).	8	662	1 127	9.3	11.4
097 CHR CHS&CHS CR	1	75	90*	0.7	0.9
165 CH OF NAZARENE	1	57	84	0.7	0.8
167 CHS OF CHRIST.	6	190	242	2.0	2.4
193 EPISCOPAL.....	1	6	6	–	0.1
283 LUTH--MO SYNOD	2	769	956	7.9	9.6
357 PRESB CH US...	1	42	51*	0.4	0.5
419 SO BAPT CONV..	16	3 560	4 291*	35.4	43.2
449 UN METHODIST..	12	1 636	1 972*	16.3	19.9
453 UN PRES CH USA	1	41	49*	0.4	0.5
CARTER	19	1 436	1 970*	36.3	100.0
053 ASSEMB OF GOD.	2	144	233	4.3	11.8
059 BAPT MISS ASSN	3	101	124*	2.3	6.3
081 CATHOLIC......	2	NA	149	2.7	7.6
167 CHS OF CHRIST.	2	75	95	1.8	4.8
285 MENNONITE CH..	1	47	58*	1.1	2.9
419 SO BAPT CONV..	4	836	1 025*	18.9	52.0
443 UN C OF CHRIST	1	16	20*	0.4	1.0
449 UN METHODIST..	4	217	266*	4.9	13.5
CASS	82	16 135	23 527*	46.1	100.0
017 AMER BAPT ASSN	1	47	47	0.1	0.2
029 AMER LUTH CH..	2	229	326	0.6	1.4
053 ASSEMB OF GOD.	5	381	687	1.3	2.9
081 CATHOLIC......	3	NA	2 723	5.3	11.6
093 CHR CH (DISC).	10	1 434	2 164	4.2	9.2
097 CHR CHS&CHS CR	2	180	223*	0.4	0.9
121 CH GOD (ABR)..	1	65	81*	0.2	0.3
165 CH OF NAZARENE	3	170	364	0.7	1.5
167 CHS OF CHRIST.	5	289	363	0.7	1.5
193 EPISCOPAL.....	1	282	290	0.6	1.2
203 EVAN FREE CH..	1	15	19*	–	0.1
221 FREE METHODIST	1	8	36	0.1	0.2
283 LUTH--MO SYNOD	2	139	203	0.4	0.9
285 MENNONITE CH..	3	347	430*	0.8	1.8
357 PRESB CH US...	4	185	229*	0.4	1.0
419 SO BAPT CONV..	22	8 919	11 057*	21.7	47.0
449 UN METHODIST..	11	3 130	3 880*	7.6	16.5
453 UN PRES CH USA	4	187	232*	0.5	1.0
469 WELS..........	1	128	173	0.3	0.7
CEDAR	28	3 571	4 896*	41.2	100.0
053 ASSEMB OF GOD.	2	101	177	1.5	3.6
081 CATHOLIC......	2	NA	216	1.8	4.4
093 CHR CH (DISC).	1	189	324	2.7	6.6
097 CHR CHS&CHS CR	5	637	751*	6.3	15.3
151 L-D SAINTS....	1	NA	131	1.1	2.7
165 CH OF NAZARENE	1	26	111	0.9	2.3
167 CHS OF CHRIST.	2	170	216	1.8	4.4
221 FREE METHODIST	1	9	75	0.6	1.5
283 LUTH--MO SYNOD	1	53	81	0.7	1.7
357 PRESB CH US...	2	59	70*	0.6	1.4
413 S.D.A.........	1	48	57*	0.5	1.2
419 SO BAPT CONV..	4	1 567	1 847*	15.5	37.7
449 UN METHODIST..	3	653	770*	6.5	15.7
453 UN PRES CH USA	2	59	70*	0.6	1.4
CHARITON	40	4 729	7 502*	71.5	100.0
053 ASSEMB OF GOD.	2	17	24	0.2	0.3
081 CATHOLIC......	5	NA	1 682	16.0	22.4
093 CHR CH (DISC).	6	411	684	6.5	9.1
097 CHR CHS&CHS CR	2	120	142*	1.4	1.9
165 CH OF NAZARENE	1	11	0	–	–
283 LUTH--MO SYNOD	3	974	1 184	11.3	15.8
419 SO BAPT CONV..	8	1 430	1 694*	16.2	22.6
449 UN METHODIST..	13	1 766	2 092*	19.9	27.9
CHRISTIAN	62	7 711	11 332*	50.6	100.0
053 ASSEMB OF GOD.	4	372	849	3.8	7.5
081 CATHOLIC......	2	NA	998	4.5	8.8
093 CHR CH (DISC).	6	546	875	3.9	7.7
097 CHR CHS&CHS CR	2	100	123*	0.5	1.1
107 CHRISTIAN UN..	2	0	40	0.2	0.4
165 CH OF NAZARENE	1	109	315	1.4	2.8
167 CHS OF CHRIST.	9	650	827	3.7	7.3
357 PRESB CH US...	1	29	36*	0.2	0.3
419 SO BAPT CONV..	28	5 088	6 263*	28.0	55.3

NA—Not applicable   *Total adherents estimated from known number of communicant, confirmed, full members.

—Represents a percent less than 0.1.   Percentages may not total due to rounding.

Table 4. Churches and Church Membership by County and Denomination: 1980

County and Denomination	Number of churches	Communicant, confirmed, full members	Total adherents		
			Number	Percent of total population	Percent of total adherents
443 UN C OF CHRIST	1	128	158*	0.7	1.4
449 UN METHODIST..	5	660	812*	3.6	7.2
453 UN PRES CH USA	1	29	36*	0.2	0.3
CLARK	33	3 726	5 525*	65.1	100.0
081 CATHOLIC......	3	NA	858	10.1	15.5
093 CHR CH (DISC).	3	331	531	6.3	9.6
097 CHR CHS&CHS CR	1	100	122*	1.4	2.2
167 CHS OF CHRIST.	1	35	45	0.5	0.8
357 PRESB CH US...	2	64	78*	0.9	1.4
413 S.D.A.........	1	71	86*	1.0	1.6
419 SO BAPT CONV..	11	1 696	2 065*	24.3	37.4
443 UN C OF CHRIST	1	438	533*	6.3	9.6
449 UN METHODIST..	8	928	1 130*	13.3	20.5
453 UN PRES CH USA	2	63	77*	0.9	1.4
CLAY	134	40 396	70 160*	51.4	100.0
019 AMER BAPT USA.	1	235	284*	0.2	0.4
029 AMER LUTH CH..	1	167	220	0.2	0.3
053 ASSEMB OF GOD.	13	1 048	2 043	1.5	2.9
081 CATHOLIC......	8	NA	16 422	12.0	23.4
093 CHR CH (DISC).	11	3 948	6 206	4.5	8.8
097 CHR CHS&CHS CR	4	870	1 052*	0.8	1.5
107 CHRISTIAN UN..	3	218	437	0.3	0.6
127 CH GOD (CLEVE)	2	172	208*	0.2	0.3
151 L-D SAINTS....	3	NA	1 459	1.1	2.1
165 CH OF NAZARENE	4	379	647	0.5	0.9
167 CHS OF CHRIST.	9	800	1 018	0.7	1.5
193 EPISCOPAL.....	3	862	1 165	0.9	1.7
226 FRIENDS-USA...	2	106	128*	0.1	0.2
281 LUTH CH AMER..	3	926	1 267	0.9	1.8
283 LUTH--MO SYNOD	5	1 841	2 715	2.0	3.9
290 METRO COMM CHS	0	40	80	0.1	0.1
357 PRESB CH US...	8	2 704	3 269*	2.4	4.7
413 S.D.A.........	1	94	114*	0.1	0.2
419 SO BAPT CONV..	33	16 736	20 233*	14.8	28.8
449 UN METHODIST..	14	8 336	10 078*	7.4	14.4
453 UN PRES CH USA	5	859	1 038*	0.8	1.5
469 WELS..........	1	55	77	0.1	0.1
CLINTON	33	5 575	8 448*	53.1	100.0
053 ASSEMB OF GOD.	3	136	270	1.7	3.2
081 CATHOLIC......	3	NA	1 100	6.9	13.0
093 CHR CH (DISC).	4	1 021	1 503	9.4	17.8
097 CHR CHS&CHS CR	1	11	13*	0.1	0.2
151 L-D SAINTS....	1	NA	184	1.2	2.2
157 CH OF BRETHREN	1	39	48*	0.3	0.6
167 CHS OF CHRIST.	1	130	140	0.9	1.7
185 CUMBER PRESB..	1	4	5	-	0.1
357 PRESB CH US...	2	24	29*	0.2	0.3
419 SO BAPT CONV..	7	2 746	3 363*	21.1	39.8
449 UN METHODIST..	6	1 386	1 697*	10.7	20.1
453 UN PRES CH USA	3	78	96*	0.6	1.1
COLE	60	16 991	39 359*	69.5	100.0
005 AME ZION......	1	150	183	0.3	0.5
029 AMER LUTH CH..	3	638	802	1.4	2.0
053 ASSEMB OF GOD.	3	198	403	0.7	1.0
059 BAPT MISS ASSN	1	25	30*	0.1	0.1
081 CATHOLIC......	8	NA	17 630	31.1	44.8
093 CHR CH (DISC).	3	1 046	1 429	2.5	3.6
097 CHR CHS&CHS CR	2	566	681*	1.2	1.7
123 CH GOD (ANDER)	1	90	270	0.5	0.7
151 L-D SAINTS....	1	NA	209	0.4	0.5
165 CH OF NAZARENE	1	54	65	0.2	0.3
167 CHS OF CHRIST.	2	289	340	0.6	0.9
193 EPISCOPAL.....	1	346	449	0.8	1.1
221 FREE METHODIST	1	30	57	0.1	0.1
271 REFORM JUDAISM	1	16	19*	-	-
283 LUTH--MO SYNOD	5	2 655	3 556	6.3	9.0
357 PRESB CH US...	1	532	640*	1.1	1.6
403 SALVATION ARMY	1	108	188	0.3	0.5
413 S.D.A.........	1	93	112*	0.2	0.3
419 SO BAPT CONV..	16	6 306	7 591*	13.4	19.3
443 UN C OF CHRIST	2	1 058	1 274*	2.2	3.2
449 UN METHODIST..	4	2 260	2 721*	4.8	6.9
453 UN PRES CH USA	1	531	639*	1.1	1.6
COOPER	52	6 352	10 107*	69.0	100.0
053 ASSEMB OF GOD.	1	31	82	0.6	0.8
081 CATHOLIC......	2	NA	2 137	14.6	21.1
093 CHR CH (DISC).	4	376	698	4.8	6.9
151 L-D SAINTS....	1	NA	75	0.5	0.7
167 CHS OF CHRIST.	3	100	127	0.9	1.3
193 EPISCOPAL.....	1	53	53	0.4	0.5
283 LUTH--MO SYNOD	4	824	996	6.8	9.9
357 PRESB CH US...	5	166	198*	1.4	2.0
419 SO BAPT CONV..	14	2 920	3 491*	23.8	34.5
443 UN C OF CHRIST	5	694	830*	5.7	8.2
449 UN METHODIST..	7	1 023	1 223*	8.4	12.1
453 UN PRES CH USA	5	165	197*	1.3	1.9
CRAWFORD	48	6 392	9 116*	49.8	100.0
053 ASSEMB OF GOD.	10	736	1 242	6.8	13.6
059 BAPT MISS ASSN	2	544	664*	3.6	7.3
081 CATHOLIC......	4	NA	938	5.1	10.3
097 CHR CHS&CHS CR	3	150	183*	1.0	2.0
127 CH GOD (CLEVE)	4	157	192*	1.0	2.1
167 CHS OF CHRIST.	2	198	254	1.4	2.8

County and Denomination	Number of churches	Communicant, confirmed, full members	Total adherents		
			Number	Percent of total population	Percent of total adherents
185 CUMBER PRESB..	1	6	6	-	0.1
283 LUTH--MO SYNOD	2	349	443	2.4	4.9
413 S.D.A.........	1	145	177*	1.0	1.9
419 SO BAPT CONV..	13	3 246	3 965*	21.7	43.5
449 UN METHODIST..	3	368	450*	2.5	4.9
453 UN PRES CH USA	3	493	602*	3.3	6.6
DADE	47	4 500	5 621*	76.1	100.0
053 ASSEMB OF GOD.	2	69	108	1.5	1.9
093 CHR CH (DISC).	7	580	892	12.1	15.9
097 CHR CHS&CHS CR	5	325	383*	5.2	6.8
121 CH GOD (ABR)..	1	40	47*	0.6	0.8
167 CHS OF CHRIST.	5	300	382	5.2	6.8
185 CUMBER PRESB..	2	18	41	0.6	0.7
283 LUTH--MO SYNOD	1	505	633	8.6	11.3
357 PRESB CH US...	4	91	107*	1.4	1.9
419 SO BAPT CONV..	13	2 193	2 582*	35.0	45.9
449 UN METHODIST..	3	289	340*	4.6	6.0
453 UN PRES CH USA	4	90	106*	1.4	1.9
DALLAS	33	3 499	4 652*	38.5	100.0
029 AMER LUTH CH..	1	90	108	0.9	2.3
053 ASSEMB OF GOD.	3	70	98	0.8	2.1
081 CATHOLIC......	1	NA	230	1.9	4.9
093 CHR CH (DISC).	4	491	787	6.5	16.9
097 CHR CHS&CHS CR	3	185	222*	1.8	4.8
167 CHS OF CHRIST.	2	85	108	0.9	2.3
285 MENNONITE CH..	2	161	194*	1.6	4.2
419 SO BAPT CONV..	14	1 965	2 362*	19.5	50.8
449 UN METHODIST..	3	452	543*	4.5	11.7
DAVIESS	43	4 674	6 047*	67.9	100.0
053 ASSEMB OF GOD.	1	38	60	0.7	1.0
081 CATHOLIC......	1	NA	171	1.9	2.8
093 CHR CH (DISC).	4	508	776	8.7	12.8
097 CHR CHS&CHS CR	3	90	108*	1.2	1.8
151 L-D SAINTS....	1	NA	58	0.7	1.0
167 CHS OF CHRIST.	3	113	144	1.6	2.4
323 OLD ORD AMISH.	6	780	940*	10.6	15.5
357 PRESB CH US...	2	47	57*	0.6	0.9
413 S.D.A.........	1	57	69*	0.8	1.1
419 SO BAPT CONV..	9	1 962	2 364*	26.5	39.1
449 UN METHODIST..	10	1 031	1 242*	13.9	20.5
453 UN PRES CH USA	2	48	58*	0.7	1.0
DE KALB	36	3 897	4 880*	59.4	100.0
081 CATHOLIC......		NA	80	1.0	1.6
093 CHR CH (DISC).	2	185	284	3.5	5.8
097 CHR CHS&CHS CR	1	270	324*	3.9	6.6
127 CH GOD (CLEVE)	1	20	24*	0.3	0.5
165 CH OF NAZARENE	1	69	83	1.0	1.7
185 CUMBER PRESB..	1	30	65	0.8	1.3
283 LUTH--MO SYNOD	1	137	197	2.4	4.0
357 PRESB CH US...	4	172	206*	2.5	4.2
419 SO BAPT CONV..	10	1 819	2 183*	26.6	44.7
449 UN METHODIST..	10	1 135	1 362*	16.6	27.9
453 UN PRES CH USA	2	60	72*	0.9	1.5
DENT	40	6 560	8 678*	59.8	100.0
053 ASSEMB OF GOD.	3	349	643	4.4	7.4
059 BAPT MISS ASSN	1	42	51*	0.4	0.6
081 CATHOLIC......	1	NA	431	3.0	5.0
097 CHR CHS&CHS CR	2	350	423*	2.9	4.9
123 CH GOD (ANDER)	1	22	66	0.5	0.8
165 CH OF NAZARENE	1	19	19	0.1	0.2
167 CHS OF CHRIST.	4	271	345	2.4	4.0
185 CUMBER PRESB..	2	26	61	0.4	0.7
283 LUTH--MO SYNOD	1	57	80	0.6	0.9
349 PENT HOLINESS.	1	24	29*	0.2	0.3
413 S.D.A.........	1	52	63*	0.4	0.7
419 SO BAPT CONV..	14	4 674	5 652*	38.9	65.1
443 UN C OF CHRIST	1	36	44*	0.3	0.5
449 UN METHODIST..	5	638	771*	5.3	8.9
DOUGLAS	23	1 771	2 877*	24.8	100.0
029 AMER LUTH CH..	1	76	91	0.8	3.2
053 ASSEMB OF GOD.	1	60	90	0.8	3.1
081 CATHOLIC......	2	NA	230	2.0	8.0
123 CH GOD (ANDER)	1	15	45	0.4	1.6
151 L-D SAINTS....	1	NA	194	1.7	6.7
165 CH OF NAZARENE	2	304	611	5.3	21.2
167 CHS OF CHRIST.	8	300	382	3.3	13.3
349 PENT HOLINESS.	1	18	22*	0.2	0.8
413 S.D.A.........	1	74	90*	0.8	3.1
419 SO BAPT CONV..	3	636	772*	6.7	26.8
449 UN METHODIST..	1	288	350*	3.0	12.2
DUNKLIN	96	15 365	20 609*	56.7	100.0
017 AMER BAPT ASSN	1	41	41	0.1	0.2
053 ASSEMB OF GOD.	11	595	1 120*	3.1	5.4
059 BAPT MISS ASSN	2	82	100*	0.3	0.5
081 CATHOLIC......	3	NA	774	2.1	3.8
093 CHR CH (DISC).	1	140	171	0.5	0.8
097 CHR CHS&CHS CR	2	358	438*	1.2	2.1
123 CH GOD (ANDER)	1	88	264	0.7	1.3
127 CH GOD (CLEVE)	1	97	119*	0.3	0.6
165 CH OF NAZARENE	3	261	735	2.0	3.6
167 CHS OF CHRIST.	13	1 338	1 703	4.7	8.3

NA—Not applicable   *Total adherents estimated from known number of communicant, confirmed, full members.   —Represents a percent less than 0.1.   Percentages may not total due to rounding.

Table 4. Churches and Church Membership by County and Denomination: 1980

County and Denomination	Number of churches	Communicant, confirmed, full members	Total adherents Number	Percent of total population	Percent of total adherents
185 CUMBER PRESB..	1	4	0	–	–
193 EPISCOPAL.....	1	17	17	–	0.1
283 LUTH--MO SYNOD	2	85	125	0.3	0.6
349 PENT HOLINESS.	4	266	326*	0.9	1.6
357 PRESB CH US...	3	279	341*	0.9	1.7
413 S.D.A.........	1	34	42*	0.1	0.2
419 SO BAPT CONV..	32	9 773	11 959*	32.9	58.0
449 UN METHODIST..	13	1 907	2 334*	6.4	11.3
FRANKLIN	**135**	**21 483**	**47 661***	**66.9**	**100.0**
017 AMER BAPT ASSN	1	536	536	0.8	1.1
053 ASSEMB OF GOD.	8	446	719	1.0	1.5
059 BAPT MISS ASSN	7	1 157	1 434*	2.0	3.0
081 CATHOLIC......	18	NA	20 490	28.8	43.0
093 CHR CH (DISC).	2	54	83	0.1	0.2
097 CHR CHS&CHS CR	7	757	938*	1.3	2.0
127 CH GOD (CLEVE)	2	97	120*	0.2	0.3
151 L-D SAINTS....	1	NA	289	0.4	0.6
165 CH OF NAZARENE	3	279	426	0.6	0.9
167 CHS OF CHRIST.	5	200	246	0.3	0.5
193 EPISCOPAL.....	2	88	122	0.2	0.3
208 EVAN LUTH ASSN	1	129	166	0.2	0.3
283 LUTH--MO SYNOD	8	2 179	2 805	3.9	5.9
349 PENT HOLINESS.	1	16	20*	–	0.1
353 CHR BRETHREN..	1	35	35	–	0.1
357 PRESB CH US...	2	243	301*	0.4	0.6
381 REF PRES-EVAN.	1	26	46	0.1	0.1
413 S.D.A.........	1	128	159*	0.2	0.3
419 SO BAPT CONV..	30	8 224	10 190*	14.3	21.4
443 UN C OF CHRIST	14	3 554	4 404*	6.2	9.2
449 UN METHODIST..	15	2 414	2 991*	4.2	6.3
453 UN PRES CH USA	5	921	1 141*	1.6	2.4
GASCONADE	**46**	**5 946**	**8 905***	**67.6**	**100.0**
053 ASSEMB OF GOD.	1	68	137	1.0	1.5
081 CATHOLIC......	4	NA	1 765	13.4	19.8
097 CHR CHS&CHS CR	3	205	243*	1.8	2.7
167 CHS OF CHRIST.	1	35	45	0.3	0.5
283 LUTH--MO SYNOD	3	519	645	4.9	7.2
313 N AM BAPT CONF	1	53	63*	0.5	0.7
413 S.D.A.........	1	27	32*	0.2	0.4
419 SO BAPT CONV..	8	1 632	1 934*	14.7	21.7
443 UN C OF CHRIST	12	2 366	2 803*	21.3	31.5
449 UN METHODIST..	9	892	1 057*	8.0	11.9
453 UN PRES CH USA	2	109	129*	1.0	1.4
469 WELS..........	1	40	52	0.4	0.6
GENTRY	**43**	**4 871**	**6 532***	**82.8**	**100.0**
053 ASSEMB OF GOD.	2	38	89	1.1	1.4
081 CATHOLIC......	2	NA	503	6.4	7.7
093 CHR CH (DISC).	4	626	911	11.6	13.9
097 CHR CHS&CHS CR	2	150	177*	2.2	2.7
127 CH GOD (CLEVE)	1	8	9*	0.1	0.1
133 CH GOD(7TH)DEN	2	50	59*	0.7	0.9
151 L-D SAINTS....	1	NA	45	0.6	0.7
167 CHS OF CHRIST.	3	110	140	1.8	2.1
185 CUMBER PRESB..	1	12	12	0.2	0.2
357 PRESB CH US...	3	141	167*	2.1	2.6
413 S.D.A.........	1	10	12*	0.2	0.2
419 SO BAPT CONV..	12	2 618	3 097*	39.3	47.4
449 UN METHODIST..	6	968	1 145*	14.5	17.5
453 UN PRES CH USA	3	140	166*	2.1	2.5
GREENE	**219**	**66 708**	**96 330***	**52.0**	**100.0**
019 AMER BAPT USA.	1	1 333	1 593*	0.9	1.7
029 AMER LUTH CH..	1	86	108	0.1	0.1
053 ASSEMB OF GOD.	31	5 120	9 479	5.1	9.8
059 BAPT MISS ASSN	2	142	170*	0.1	0.2
081 CATHOLIC......	5	NA	10 269	5.5	10.7
093 CHR CH (DISC).	9	3 539	4 725	2.5	4.9
097 CHR CHS&CHS CR	8	1 383	1 653*	0.9	1.7
123 CH GOD (ANDER)	3	246	738	0.4	0.8
127 CH GOD (CLEVE)	4	263	314*	0.2	0.3
151 L-D SAINTS....	3	NA	962	0.5	1.0
157 CH OF BRETHREN	1	60	72*	–	0.1
165 CH OF NAZARENE	6	808	1 396	0.8	1.4
167 CHS OF CHRIST.	19	3 378	4 224	2.3	4.4
185 CUMBER PRESB..	1	75	102	0.1	0.1
193 EPISCOPAL.....	4	1 574	1 941	1.0	2.0
221 FREE METHODIST	1	16	48	–	–
271 REFORM JUDAISM	1	114	136*	0.1	0.1
281 LUTH CH AMER..	1	467	670	0.4	0.7
283 LUTH--MO SYNOD	3	1 560	1 985	1.1	2.1
290 METRO COMM CHS	1	38	76	–	0.1
349 PENT HOLINESS.	2	73	87*	–	0.1
353 CHR BRETHREN..	1	55	70	–	0.1
357 PRESB CH US...	10	2 035	2 432*	1.3	2.5
403 SALVATION ARMY	1	115	231	0.1	0.2
413 S.D.A.........	3	325	388*	0.2	0.4
419 SO BAPT CONV..	57	31 471	37 605*	20.3	39.0
435 UNITARIAN-UNIV	1	159	190*	0.1	0.2
443 UN C OF CHRIST	2	544	650*	0.4	0.7
449 UN METHODIST..	27	9 694	11 584*	6.3	12.0
453 UN PRES CH USA	10	2 035	2 432*	1.3	2.5
GRUNDY	**44**	**6 487**	**8 329***	**69.6**	**100.0**
053 ASSEMB OF GOD.	5	233	345	2.9	4.1
081 CATHOLIC......	1	NA	230	1.9	2.8
093 CHR CH (DISC).	3	563	794	6.6	9.5
097 CHR CHS&CHS CR	4	367	436*	3.6	5.2

County and Denomination	Number of churches	Communicant, confirmed, full members	Total adherents Number	Percent of total population	Percent of total adherents
165 CH OF NAZARENE	1	95	286	2.4	3.4
167 CHS OF CHRIST.	2	130	165	1.4	2.0
185 CUMBER PRESB..	1	8	8	0.1	0.1
193 EPISCOPAL.....	1	42	57	0.5	0.7
283 LUTH--MO SYNOD	1	93	126	1.1	1.5
357 PRESB CH US...	1	77	91*	0.8	1.1
419 SO BAPT CONV..	14	3 779	4 485*	37.5	53.8
449 UN METHODIST..	9	1 022	1 213*	10.1	14.6
453 UN PRES CH USA	1	78	93*	0.8	1.1
HARRISON	**63**	**5 759**	**7 565***	**76.5**	**100.0**
053 ASSEMB OF GOD.	6	146	279	2.8	3.7
081 CATHOLIC......	3	NA	175	1.8	2.3
093 CHR CH (DISC).	9	817	1 420	14.4	18.8
097 CHR CHS&CHS CR	1	70	82*	0.8	1.1
107 CHRISTIAN UN..	1	71	105	1.1	1.4
127 CH GOD (CLEVE)	1	?	?	?	?
167 CHS OF CHRIST.	6	200	255	2.6	3.4
283 LUTH--MO SYNOD	1	28	42	0.4	0.6
357 PRESB CH US...	1	21	25*	0.3	0.3
419 SO BAPT CONV..	13	2 171	2 553*	25.8	33.7
449 UN METHODIST..	20	2 214	2 604*	26.3	34.4
453 UN PRES CH USA	1	21	25*	0.3	0.3
HENRY	**71**	**10 737**	**14 862***	**75.5**	**100.0**
053 ASSEMB OF GOD.	3	210	363	1.8	2.4
081 CATHOLIC......	5	NA	1 486	7.6	10.0
093 CHR CH (DISC).	4	1 039	1 495	7.6	10.1
097 CHR CHS&CHS CR	4	265	316*	1.6	2.1
123 CH GOD (ANDER)	1	20	60	0.3	0.4
151 L-D SAINTS....	1	NA	?	?	?
157 CH OF BRETHREN	1	44	53*	0.3	0.4
165 CH OF NAZARENE	2	50	140	0.7	0.9
167 CHS OF CHRIST.	2	141	179	0.9	1.2
185 CUMBER PRESB..	2	62	112	0.6	0.8
193 EPISCOPAL.....	1	26	34	0.2	0.2
283 LUTH--MO SYNOD	1	149	197	1.0	1.3
357 PRESB CH US...	4	265	316*	1.6	2.1
413 S.D.A.........	1	87	104*	0.5	0.7
419 SO BAPT CONV..	21	5 967	7 126*	36.2	47.9
443 UN C OF CHRIST	1	58	69*	0.4	0.5
449 UN METHODIST..	13	2 088	2 494*	12.7	16.8
453 UN PRES CH USA	4	266	318*	1.6	2.1
HICKORY	**23**	**1 806**	**2 443***	**38.4**	**100.0**
053 ASSEMB OF GOD.	2	57	100	1.6	4.1
081 CATHOLIC......	1	NA	162	2.5	6.6
093 CHR CH (DISC).	6	382	587	9.2	24.0
121 CH GOD (ABR)..	1	35	41*	0.6	1.7
263 INT FOURSQ GOS	1	23	27*	0.4	1.1
419 SO BAPT CONV..	5	958	1 117*	17.5	45.7
443 UN C OF CHRIST	1	16	19*	0.3	0.8
449 UN METHODIST..	6	335	390*	6.1	16.0
HOLT	**42**	**3 431**	**4 564***	**66.3**	**100.0**
081 CATHOLIC......	1	NA	148	2.2	3.2
093 CHR CH (DISC).	4	366	556	8.1	12.2
097 CHR CHS&CHS CR	3	562	668*	9.7	14.6
123 CH GOD (ANDER)	1	40	120	1.7	2.6
157 CH OF BRETHREN	1	14	17*	0.2	0.4
165 CH OF NAZARENE	3	149	282	4.1	6.2
283 LUTH--MO SYNOD	3	340	442	6.4	9.7
357 PRESB CH US...	7	210	250*	3.6	5.5
419 SO BAPT CONV..	4	327	389*	5.7	8.5
449 UN METHODIST..	8	1 212	1 441*	20.9	31.6
453 UN PRES CH USA	7	211	251*	3.6	5.5
HOWARD	**37**	**4 162**	**6 842***	**68.4**	**100.0**
053 ASSEMB OF GOD.	1	50	66	0.7	1.0
081 CATHOLIC......	2	NA	1 501	15.0	21.9
093 CHR CH (DISC).	7	644	1 177	11.8	17.2
097 CHR CHS&CHS CR	2	200	236*	2.4	3.4
167 CHS OF CHRIST.	1	25	32	0.3	0.5
193 EPISCOPAL.....	1	26	26	0.3	0.4
263 INT FOURSQ GOS	2	305	361*	3.6	5.3
419 SO BAPT CONV..	10	1 260	1 490*	14.9	21.8
443 UN C OF CHRIST	1	320	378*	3.8	5.5
449 UN METHODIST..	10	1 332	1 575*	15.7	23.0
HOWELL	**90**	**11 083**	**15 895***	**55.2**	**100.0**
053 ASSEMB OF GOD.	8	545	892	3.1	5.6
059 BAPT MISS ASSN	3	144	174*	0.6	1.1
081 CATHOLIC......	4	NA	1 080	3.7	6.8
093 CHR CH (DISC).	1	552	662	2.3	4.2
097 CHR CHS&CHS CR	5	556	673*	2.3	4.2
123 CH GOD (ANDER)	6	384	1 152	4.0	7.2
127 CH GOD (CLEVE)	1	4	5*	–	–
151 L-D SAINTS....	1	NA	285	1.0	1.8
157 CH OF BRETHREN	1	75	91*	0.3	0.6
165 CH OF NAZARENE	3	121	204	0.7	1.3
167 CHS OF CHRIST.	14	1 405	1 788	6.2	11.2
185 CUMBER PRESB..	1	42	93	0.3	0.6
193 EPISCOPAL.....	1	158	203	0.7	1.3
208 EVAN LUTH ASSN	2	197	244*	0.8	1.5
217 FIRE BAPTIZED.	1	4	5*	–	–
283 LUTH--MO SYNOD	1	44	54	0.2	0.3
349 PENT HOLINESS.	1	12	15*	0.1	0.1
357 PRESB CH US...	3	252	305*	1.1	1.9
413 S.D.A.........	2	124	150*	0.5	0.9

NA— Not applicable   *Total adherents estimated from known number of communicant, confirmed, full members.   —Represents a percent less than 0.1.   Percentages may not total due to rounding.

Table 4. Churches and Church Membership by County and Denomination: 1980

County and Denomination	Number of churches	Communicant, confirmed, full members	Total adherents Number	Percent of total population	Percent of total adherents
419 SO BAPT CONV..	19	5 395	6 527*	22.7	41.1
449 UN METHODIST..	9	943	1 141*	4.0	7.2
453 UN PRES CH USA	3	126	152*	0.5	1.0
IRON	34	3 518	5 208*	47.0	100.0
053 ASSEMB OF GOD.	6	243	521	4.7	10.0
059 BAPT MISS ASSN	2	46	56*	0.5	1.1
081 CATHOLIC....	2	NA	551	5.0	10.6
165 CH OF NAZARENE	3	158	289	2.6	5.5
167 CHS OF CHRIST.	1	45	58	0.5	1.1
193 EPISCOPAL.....	1	48	67	0.6	1.3
283 LUTH--MO SYNOD	2	136	183	1.7	3.5
419 SO BAPT CONV..	10	2 174	2 664*	24.0	51.2
449 UN METHODIST..	5	554	679*	6.1	13.0
453 UN PRES CH USA	2	114	140*	1.3	2.7
JACKSON	485	156 304	291 932*	46.4	100.0
005 AME ZION......	4	1 720	2 150	0.3	0.7
017 AMER BAPT ASSN	2	90	90	-	-
019 AMER BAPT USA.	4	2 396	2 885*	0.5	1.0
029 AMER LUTH CH..	4	1 236	1 578	0.3	0.5
053 ASSEMB OF GOD.	32	4 941	8 595	1.4	2.9
057 BAPT GEN CONF.	1	64	77*	-	-
059 BAPT MISS ASSN	5	1 410	1 698*	0.3	0.6
081 CATHOLIC.....	47	NA	85 996	13.7	29.5
093 CHR CH (DISC).	32	14 458	21 578	3.4	7.4
097 CHR CHS&CHS CR	8	1 195	1 439*	0.2	0.5
105 CHRISTIAN REF.	1	51	83	-	-
107 CHRISTIAN UN..	1	47	115	-	-
123 CH GOD (ANDER)	5	581	1 743	0.3	0.6
127 CH GOD (CLEVE)	4	63	76*	-	-
133 CH GOD(7TH)DEN	1	54	65*	-	-
151 L-D SAINTS....	7	NA	3 047	0.5	1.0
157 CH OF BRETHREN	1	188	226*	-	0.1
165 CH OF NAZARENE	15	2 379	3 460	0.5	1.2
167 CHS OF CHRIST.	26	3 037	4 130	0.7	1.4
175 CONGR CHR CHS.	1	239	288*	-	0.1
185 CUMBER PRESB..	3	172	351	0.1	0.1
193 EPISCOPAL.....	14	7 998	11 808	1.9	4.0
201 EVAN COV CH AM	2	115	138*	-	-
221 FREE METHODIST	1	45	120	-	-
244 GRACE BRETHREN	1	16	19*	-	-
263 INT FOURSQ GOS	1	242	291*	-	0.1
270 CONSRV JUDAISM	1	1 375	1 655*	0.3	0.6
271 REFORM JUDAISM	2	3 388	4 079*	0.6	1.4
281 LUTH CH AMER..	7	1 726	2 118	0.3	0.7
283 LUTH--MO SYNOD	18	6 126	8 762	1.4	3.0
290 METRO COMM CHS	1	300	600	0.1	0.2
313 N AM BAPT CONF	1	137	165*	-	0.1
349 PENT HOLINESS	1	23	28*	-	-
353 CHR BRETHREN..	2	40	40	-	-
357 PRESB CH US...	28	4 280	5 153*	0.8	1.8
403 SALVATION ARMY	4	443	2 012	0.3	0.7
413 S.D.A.........	8	2 265	2 727*	0.4	0.9
415 S-D BAPTIST GC	1	14	17*	-	-
419 SO BAPT CONV..	87	58 094	69 943*	11.1	24.0
435 UNITARIAN-UNIV	1	451	543*	0.1	0.2
443 UN C OF CHRIST	10	3 063	3 688*	0.6	1.3
449 UN METHODIST..	58	25 692	30 932*	4.9	10.6
453 UN PRES CH USA	31	6 115	7 362*	1.2	2.5
469 WELS.........	1	35	62	-	-
JASPER	154	34 223	51 618*	59.4	100.0
017 AMER BAPT ASSN	1	38	38	-	0.1
029 AMER LUTH CH..	1	132	179	0.2	0.3
053 ASSEMB OF GOD.	13	2 652	6 866	7.9	13.3
059 BAPT MISS ASSN	1	125	151*	0.2	0.3
081 CATHOLIC.....	5	NA	4 375	5.0	8.5
093 CHR CH (DISC).	4	805	1 140	1.3	2.2
097 CHR CHS&CHS CR	13	3 275	3 948*	4.5	7.6
123 CH GOD (ANDER)	2	75	225	0.3	0.4
127 CH GOD (CLEVE)	3	281	339*	0.4	0.7
133 CH GOD(7TH)DEN	1	45	54*	0.1	0.1
151 L-D SAINTS....	1	NA	514	0.6	1.0
157 CH OF BRETHREN	1	20	24*	-	-
165 CH OF NAZARENE	6	1 066	1 935	2.2	3.7
167 CHS OF CHRIST.	5	618	763	0.9	1.5
185 CUMBER PRESB..	1	133	244	0.3	0.5
193 EPISCOPAL.....	2	1 122	1 276	1.5	2.5
217 FIRE BAPTIZED.	1	12	14*	-	-
221 FREE METHODIST	2	27	152	0.2	0.3
226 FRIENDS-USA...	1	71	86*	0.1	0.2
263 INT FOURSQ GOS	1	123	148*	0.2	0.3
271 REFORM JUDAISM	1	116	140*	0.2	0.3
283 LUTH--MO SYNOD	3	991	1 358	1.6	2.6
290 METRO COMM CHS	1	35	70	0.1	0.1
357 PRESB CH US...	9	988	1 191*	1.4	2.3
375 REF EPISCOPAL.	1	32	39*	-	0.1
403 SALVATION ARMY	2	210	754	0.9	1.5
413 S.D.A.........	1	23	28*	-	0.1
419 SO BAPT CONV..	34	14 610	17 613*	20.3	34.1
435 UNITARIAN-UNIV	1	12	14*	-	-
443 UN C OF CHRIST	1	14	17*	-	-
449 UN METHODIST..	26	5 579	6 726*	7.7	13.0
453 UN PRES CH USA	9	993	1 197*	1.4	2.3
JEFFERSON	120	30 183	66 823*	45.5	100.0
017 AMER BAPT ASSN	1	40	40	-	0.1
053 ASSEMB OF GOD.	10	1 599	3 240	2.2	4.8
059 BAPT MISS ASSN	6	516	646*	0.4	1.0
081 CATHOLIC......	11	NA	26 562	18.1	39.7

County and Denomination	Number of churches	Communicant, confirmed, full members	Total adherents Number	Percent of total population	Percent of total adherents
093 CHR CH (DISC).	2	287	436	0.3	0.7
097 CHR CHS&CHS CR	5	776	971*	0.7	1.5
121 CH GOD (ABR)..	1	43	54*	-	0.1
123 CH GOD (ANDER)	1	145	435	0.3	0.7
127 CH GOD (CLEVE)	4	326	408*	0.3	0.6
151 L-D SAINTS....	1	NA	257	0.2	0.4
165 CH OF NAZARENE	4	351	645	0.4	1.0
167 CHS OF CHRIST.	6	682	922	0.6	1.4
193 EPISCOPAL.....	1	81	90	0.1	0.1
263 INT FOURSQ GOS	1	?	?	?	?
283 LUTH--MO SYNOD	8	3 701	5 049	3.4	7.6
357 PRESB CH US...	2	437	547*	0.4	0.8
419 SO BAPT CONV..	33	15 737	19 688*	13.4	29.5
443 UN C OF CHRIST	5	1 881	2 353*	1.6	3.5
449 UN METHODIST..	15	3 340	4 178*	2.8	6.3
453 UN PRES CH USA	3	241	302*	0.2	0.5
JOHNSON	80	11 439	16 015*	41.0	100.0
053 ASSEMB OF GOD.	3	120	279	0.7	1.7
081 CATHOLIC......	3	NA	1 277	3.3	8.0
093 CHR CH (DISC).	6	832	1 306	3.3	8.2
097 CHR CHS&CHS CR	4	530	632*	1.6	3.9
151 L-D SAINTS....	1	NA	313	0.8	2.0
157 CH OF BRETHREN	2	92	110*	0.3	0.7
165 CH OF NAZARENE	2	86	105	0.3	0.7
167 CHS OF CHRIST.	2	121	186	0.5	1.2
185 CUMBER PRESB..	5	141	313	0.8	1.3
193 EPISCOPAL.....	1	125	201	0.5	1.3
221 FREE METHODIST	1	19	66	0.2	0.4
283 LUTH--MO SYNOD	1	315	429	1.1	2.7
357 PRESB CH US...	6	331	395*	1.0	2.5
413 S.D.A.........	1	86	103*	0.3	0.6
419 SO BAPT CONV..	21	6 165	7 349*	18.8	45.9
449 UN METHODIST..	13	2 142	2 553*	6.5	15.9
453 UN PRES CH USA	7	334	398*	1.0	2.5
KNOX	29	2 314	3 756*	68.2	100.0
053 ASSEMB OF GOD.	3	146	319	5.8	8.5
081 CATHOLIC......	2	NA	747	13.6	19.9
093 CHR CH (DISC).	2	228	347	6.3	9.2
097 CHR CHS&CHS CR	5	390	468*	8.5	12.5
165 CH OF NAZARENE	1	30	61	1.1	1.6
167 CHS OF CHRIST.	1	25	32	0.6	0.9
197 EVAN CH OF NA.	1	55	55	1.0	1.5
419 SO BAPT CONV..	8	764	916*	16.6	24.4
449 UN METHODIST..	6	676	811*	14.7	21.6
LACLEDE	61	8 766	12 495*	51.4	100.0
053 ASSEMB OF GOD.	4	211	326	1.3	2.6
081 CATHOLIC......	2	NA	1 155	4.7	9.2
093 CHR CH (DISC).	1	294	445	1.8	3.6
097 CHR CHS&CHS CR	5	766	930*	3.8	7.4
123 CH GOD (ANDER)	2	140	420	1.7	3.4
165 CH OF NAZARENE	1	152	336	1.4	2.7
167 CHS OF CHRIST.	6	400	509	2.1	4.1
185 CUMBER PRESB..	3	258	381	1.6	3.0
193 EPISCOPAL.....	1	52	67	0.3	0.5
283 LUTH--MO SYNOD	1	230	324	1.3	2.6
413 S.D.A.........	1	74	90*	0.4	0.7
419 SO BAPT CONV..	23	4 710	5 717*	23.5	45.8
443 UN C OF CHRIST	1	180	218*	0.9	1.7
449 UN METHODIST..	10	1 299	1 577*	6.5	12.6
LAFAYETTE	77	15 032	20 391*	68.1	100.0
053 ASSEMB OF GOD.	4	213	437	1.5	2.1
081 CATHOLIC......	5	NA	1 539	5.1	7.5
093 CHR CH (DISC).	7	1 136	1 532	5.1	7.5
097 CHR CHS&CHS CR	1	50	60*	0.2	0.3
151 L-D SAINTS....	1	NA	160	0.5	0.8
167 CHS OF CHRIST.	4	116	170	0.6	0.8
193 EPISCOPAL.....	2	148	192	0.6	0.9
283 LUTH--MO SYNOD	8	3 762	4 748	15.9	23.3
353 CHR BRETHREN..	1	20	20	0.1	0.1
357 PRESB CH US...	5	209	251*	0.8	1.2
419 SO BAPT CONV..	16	4 672	5 621*	18.8	27.6
443 UN C OF CHRIST	7	2 256	2 714*	9.1	13.3
449 UN METHODIST..	13	2 242	2 697*	9.0	13.2
453 UN PRES CH USA	4	208	250*	0.8	1.2
LAWRENCE	97	12 146	17 487*	60.4	100.0
053 ASSEMB OF GOD.	6	462	791	2.7	4.5
081 CATHOLIC......	2	NA	1 857	6.4	10.6
093 CHR CH (DISC).	4	585	762	2.6	4.4
097 CHR CHS&CHS CR	7	413	501*	1.7	2.9
107 CHRISTIAN UN..	3	0	30	0.1	0.2
127 CH GOD (CLEVE)	1	17	21*	0.1	0.1
151 L-D SAINTS....	1	NA	213	0.7	1.2
165 CH OF NAZARENE	5	140	258	0.9	1.5
167 CHS OF CHRIST.	7	400	550	1.9	3.1
185 CUMBER PRESB..	4	146	279	1.0	1.6
203 EVAN FREE CH..	1	17	21*	0.1	0.1
221 FREE METHODIST	2	32	123	0.4	0.7
283 LUTH--MO SYNOD	7	1 037	1 285	4.4	7.3
357 PRESB CH US...	7	590	716*	2.5	4.1
419 SO BAPT CONV..	21	6 306	7 652*	26.4	43.8
443 UN C OF CHRIST	3	216	262*	0.9	1.5
449 UN METHODIST..	12	1 495	1 814*	6.3	10.4
453 UN PRES CH USA	6	290	352*	1.2	2.0
LEWIS	43	5 188	7 284*	66.8	100.0

NA— Not applicable   *Total adherents estimated from known number of communicant, confirmed, full members.   —Represents a percent less than 0.1.   Percentages may not total due to rounding.

Table 4. Churches and Church Membership by County and Denomination: 1980

County and Denomination	Number of churches	Communicant, confirmed, full members	Total adherents — Number	Percent of total population	Percent of total adherents
053 ASSEMB OF GOD.	2	149	226	2.1	3.1
081 CATHOLIC......	3	NA	763	7.0	10.5
093 CHR CH (DISC).	6	607	947	8.7	13.0
097 CHR CHS&CHS CR	4	290	349*	3.2	4.8
167 CHS OF CHRIST.	2	100	127	1.2	1.7
283 LUTH--MO SYNOD	1	303	371	3.4	5.1
357 PRESB CH US...	1	3	4*	–	0.1
419 SO BAPT CONV..	13	2 981	3 588*	32.9	49.3
449 UN METHODIST..	9	747	899*	8.2	12.3
453 UN PRES CH USA	2	8	10*	0.1	0.1
LINCOLN	63	7 510	13 355*	60.2	100.0
053 ASSEMB OF GOD.	4	246	375	1.7	2.8
055 AS REF PRES CH	2	112	124	0.6	0.9
081 CATHOLIC......	5	NA	3 865	17.4	28.9
093 CHR CH (DISC).	4	445	761	3.4	5.7
097 CHR CHS&CHS CR	3	344	420*	1.9	3.1
165 CH OF NAZARENE	1	20	30	0.1	0.2
167 CHS OF CHRIST.	1	50	64	0.3	0.5
217 FIRE BAPTIZED.	4	132	161*	0.7	1.2
283 LUTH--MO SYNOD	1	240	332	1.5	2.5
357 PRESB CH US...	4	125	152*	0.7	1.1
419 SO BAPT CONV..	13	3 476	4 240*	19.1	31.7
443 UN C OF CHRIST	3	504	615*	2.8	4.6
449 UN METHODIST..	14	1 690	2 062*	9.3	15.4
453 UN PRES CH USA	4	126	154*	0.7	1.2
LINN	56	7 969	11 363*	73.3	100.0
053 ASSEMB OF GOD.	3	152	361	2.3	3.2
061 BEACHY AMISH..	1	27	32*	0.2	0.3
081 CATHOLIC......	2	NA	1 566	10.1	13.8
093 CHR CH (DISC).	4	800	1 114	7.2	9.8
097 CHR CHS&CHS CR	3	200	236*	1.5	2.1
165 CH OF NAZARENE	1	58	74	0.5	0.7
167 CHS OF CHRIST.	8	350	445	2.9	3.9
193 EPISCOPAL.....	1	17	29	0.2	0.3
283 LUTH--MO SYNOD	1	13	15	0.1	0.1
357 PRESB CH US...	1	66	78*	0.5	0.7
413 S.D.A........	1	59	70*	0.5	0.6
419 SO BAPT CONV..	15	3 549	4 185*	27.0	36.8
449 UN METHODIST..	14	2 612	3 080*	19.9	27.1
453 UN PRES CH USA	1	66	78*	0.5	0.7
LIVINGSTON	49	7 874	12 163*	77.3	100.0
019 AMER BAPT USA.	1	145	174*	1.1	1.4
029 AMER LUTH CH..	1	28	46	0.3	0.4
053 ASSEMB OF GOD.	2	122	214	1.4	1.8
081 CATHOLIC......	3	NA	1 660	10.5	13.6
093 CHR CH (DISC).	4	555	783	5.0	6.4
097 CHR CHS&CHS CR	3	150	180*	1.1	1.5
127 CH GOD (CLEVE)	1	72	86*	0.5	0.7
151 L-D SAINTS....	1	NA	114	0.7	0.9
167 CHS OF CHRIST.	1	250	325	2.1	2.7
193 EPISCOPAL.....	1	69	69	0.4	0.6
221 FREE METHODIST	1	101	636	4.0	5.2
283 LUTH--MO SYNOD	1	110	130	0.8	1.1
357 PRESB CH US...	3	187	225*	1.4	1.8
403 SALVATION ARMY	1	79	308	2.0	2.5
419 SO BAPT CONV..	13	3 736	4 487*	28.5	36.9
443 UN C OF CHRIST	1	130	156*	1.0	1.3
449 UN METHODIST..	8	1 955	2 348*	14.9	19.3
453 UN PRES CH USA	3	185	222*	1.4	1.8
MC DONALD	48	4 733	6 033*	40.4	100.0
053 ASSEMB OF GOD.	2	51	82	0.5	1.4
081 CATHOLIC......	1	NA	200	1.3	3.3
093 CHR CH (DISC).	1	89	137	0.9	2.3
097 CHR CHS&CHS CR	3	239	290*	1.9	4.8
165 CH OF NAZARENE	1	65	90	0.6	1.5
167 CHS OF CHRIST.	12	415	528	3.5	8.8
193 EPISCOPAL.....	1	68	80	0.5	1.3
208 EVAN LUTH ASSN	1	42	58	0.4	1.0
285 MENNONITE CH..	1	13	16*	0.1	0.3
357 PRESB CH US...	2	34	41*	0.3	0.7
413 S.D.A........	1	30	36*	0.2	0.6
419 SO BAPT CONV..	14	3 016	3 661*	24.5	60.7
449 UN METHODIST..	7	656	796*	5.3	13.2
453 UN PRES CH USA	1	15	18*	0.1	0.3
MACON	67	8 193	11 025*	67.6	100.0
053 ASSEMB OF GOD.	3	140	173	1.1	1.6
061 BEACHY AMISH..	1	11	13*	0.1	0.1
081 CATHOLIC......	3	NA	800	4.9	7.3
093 CHR CH (DISC).	4	677	1 067	6.5	9.7
097 CHR CHS&CHS CR	8	932	1 116*	6.8	10.1
165 CH OF NAZARENE	1	70	189	1.2	1.7
167 CHS OF CHRIST.	4	200	255	1.6	2.3
193 EPISCOPAL.....	1	20	21	0.1	0.2
283 LUTH--MO SYNOD	1	208	284	1.7	2.6
323 OLD ORD AMISH.	2	260	311*	1.9	2.8
357 PRESB CH US...	5	290	347*	2.1	3.1
413 S.D.A........	2	92	110*	0.7	1.0
419 SO BAPT CONV..	16	3 593	4 303*	26.4	39.0
443 UN C OF CHRIST	2	177	212*	1.3	1.9
449 UN METHODIST..	9	1 236	1 480*	9.1	13.4
453 UN PRES CH USA	5	287	344*	2.1	3.1
MADISON	35	3 869	5 450*	50.8	100.0
053 ASSEMB OF GOD.	2	106	161	1.5	3.0
059 BAPT MISS ASSN	1	43	51*	0.5	0.9
081 CATHOLIC......	1	NA	545	5.1	10.0
093 CHR CH (DISC).	1	219	389	3.6	7.1
097 CHR CHS&CHS CR	1	50	60*	0.6	1.1
121 CH GOD (ABR).	1	56	67*	0.6	1.2
165 CH OF NAZARENE	1	119	240	2.2	4.4
167 CHS OF CHRIST.	3	75	95	0.9	1.7
283 LUTH--MO SYNOD	1	149	207	1.9	3.8
413 S.D.A........	1	50	60*	0.6	1.1
419 SO BAPT CONV..	12	2 174	2 589*	24.1	47.5
449 UN METHODIST..	8	743	885*	8.3	16.2
453 UN PRES CH USA	2	85	101*	0.9	1.9
MARIES	33	2 969	4 485*	59.4	100.0
053 ASSEMB OF GOD.	4	675	1 790	6.3	8.9
081 CATHOLIC......	3	NA	3 310	11.6	16.4
093 CHR CH (DISC).	6	911	1 419	5.0	7.0
097 CHR CHS&CHS CR	1	50	60*	0.2	0.3
151 L-D SAINTS....	1	NA	164	0.6	0.8
165 CH OF NAZARENE	1	236	582	2.0	2.9
167 CHS OF CHRIST.	2	113	144	0.5	0.7
193 EPISCOPAL.....	2	295	403	1.4	2.0
221 FREE METHODIST	1	49	45*	0.2	0.2
283 LUTH--MO SYNOD	3	1 582	2 153	7.5	10.7
285 MENNONITE CH..	2	84	102*	0.4	0.5
357 PRESB CH US...	2	360	435*	1.5	2.2
403 SALVATION ARMY	1	90	142	0.5	0.7
413 S.D.A........	1	44	53*	0.2	0.3
419 SO BAPT CONV..	17	5 324	6 440*	22.5	31.9
449 UN METHODIST..	11	2 067	2 500*	8.7	12.4
453 UN PRES CH USA	3	361	437*	1.5	2.2
MARION	61	12 211	20 179*	70.5	100.0
053 ASSEMB OF GOD.	2	123	240	5.1	7.5
081 CATHOLIC......	1	NA	60	1.3	1.9
093 CHR CH (DISC).	2	218	316	6.7	9.9
097 CHR CHS&CHS CR	2	110	129*	2.8	4.0
167 CHS OF CHRIST.	1	25	32	0.7	1.0
283 LUTH--MO SYNOD	1	59	88	1.9	2.7
419 SO BAPT CONV..	9	1 448	1 692*	36.1	52.8
449 UN METHODIST..	5	554	647*	13.8	20.2
MERCER	23	2 537	3 204*	68.4	100.0
001 ADVENT CHR CH.	1	84	102*	0.6	0.8
053 ASSEMB OF GOD.	5	337	654	3.5	5.4
081 CATHOLIC......	5	NA	2 591	14.0	21.5
093 CHR CH (DISC).	3	577	783	4.2	6.5
097 CHR CHS&CHS CR	6	785	955*	5.2	7.9
165 CH OF NAZARENE	2	225	303	1.6	2.5
167 CHS OF CHRIST.	13	525	668	3.6	5.5
283 LUTH--MO SYNOD	1	154	172	0.9	1.4
419 SO BAPT CONV..	18	4 234	5 150*	27.8	42.6
443 UN C OF CHRIST	1	45	55*	0.3	0.5
449 UN METHODIST..	2	531	646*	3.5	5.3
MILLER	57	7 497	12 079*	65.2	100.0
053 ASSEMB OF GOD.	2	131	310	2.0	3.3
081 CATHOLIC......	1	NA	746	4.7	7.9
093 CHR CH (DISC).	1	71	104	0.7	1.1
097 CHR CHS&CHS CR	3	430	532*	3.4	5.6
123 CH GOD (ANDER)	2	302	906	5.8	9.6
127 CH GOD (CLEVE)	1	60	61*	0.4	0.6
165 CH OF NAZARENE	2	67	87	0.6	0.9
167 CHS OF CHRIST.	4	250	400	2.5	4.2
185 CUMBER PRESB.	1	100	224	1.4	2.4
349 PENT HOLINESS.	1	32	40*	0.3	0.4
413 S.D.A........	4	197	244*	1.6	2.6
419 SO BAPT CONV..	13	3 693	4 568*	29.0	48.3
449 UN METHODIST..	7	997	1 233*	7.8	13.0
MISSISSIPPI	42	6 319	9 455*	60.1	100.0
053 ASSEMB OF GOD.	3	115	202	1.7	2.0
081 CATHOLIC......	3	NA	2 318	19.2	22.7
093 CHR CH (DISC).	3	292	473	3.9	4.6
167 CHS OF CHRIST.	1	37	47	0.4	0.5
283 LUTH--MO SYNOD	1	383	496	4.1	4.9
287 MENN GEN CONF.	1	159	235	1.9	2.3
357 PRESB CH US...	1	4	5*	–	–
419 SO BAPT CONV..	18	3 810	4 602*	38.1	45.0
443 UN C OF CHRIST	4	827	999*	8.3	9.8
449 UN METHODIST..	7	694	838*	6.9	8.2
453 UN PRES CH USA	1	5	6*	–	0.1
MONITEAU	43	6 326	10 221*	84.7	100.0
053 ASSEMB OF GOD.	1	31	47	0.5	0.7
081 CATHOLIC......	4	NA	1 653	17.0	24.6
093 CHR CH (DISC).	10	1 049	1 783	18.4	26.5

NA—Not applicable   *Total adherents estimated from known number of communicant, confirmed, full members.   —Represents a percent less than 0.1.   Percentages may not total due to rounding.

Table 4. Churches and Church Membership by County and Denomination: 1980

County and Denomination	Number of churches	Communicant, confirmed, full members	Total adherents		
			Number	Percent of total population	Percent of total adherents
123 CH GOD (ANDER)	1	30	90	0.9	1.3
193 EPISCOPAL.....	1	16	18	0.2	0.3
357 PRESB CH US...	3	93	112*	1.2	1.7
419 SO BAPT CONV..	11	1 624	1 963*	20.2	29.2
449 UN METHODIST..	6	806	974*	10.0	14.5
453 UN PRES CH USA	2	73	88*	0.9	1.3
MONTGOMERY	50	5 100	7 653*	66.3	100.0
053 ASSEMB OF GOD.	1	32	72	0.6	0.9
081 CATHOLIC......	3	NA	1 109	9.6	14.5
093 CHR CH (DISC).	3	289	573	5.0	7.5
097 CHR CHS&CHS CR	3	213	256*	2.2	3.3
165 CH OF NAZARENE	1	35	83	0.7	1.1
167 CHS OF CHRIST.	2	80	102	0.9	1.3
217 FIRE BAPTIZED.	3	36	43*	0.4	0.6
283 LUTH--MO SYNOD	3	476	673	5.8	8.8
357 PRESB CH US...	3	71	85*	0.7	1.1
419 SO BAPT CONV..	11	1 862	2 242*	19.4	29.3
443 UN C OF CHRIST	2	292	352*	3.1	4.6
449 UN METHODIST..	12	1 644	1 979*	17.2	25.9
453 UN PRES CH USA	3	70	84*	0.7	1.1
MORGAN	43	5 582	7 368*	53.4	100.0
029 AMER LUTH CH..	2	365	458	3.3	6.2
053 ASSEMB OF GOD.	4	351	626	4.5	8.5
081 CATHOLIC......	2	NA	429	3.1	5.8
093 CHR CH (DISC).	1	26	40	0.3	0.5
097 CHR CHS&CHS CR	4	215	255*	1.8	3.5
123 CH GOD (ANDER)	1	27	81	0.6	1.1
127 CH GOD (CLEVE)	1	?	?	?	?
143 CG IN CR(MENN)	1	73	73	0.5	1.0
167 CHS OF CHRIST.	2	25	32	0.2	0.4
283 LUTH--MO SYNOD	2	414	529	3.8	7.2
285 MENNONITE CH..	1	75	89*	0.6	1.2
357 PRESB CH US...	2	88	104*	0.8	1.4
419 SO BAPT CONV..	10	2 377	2 819*	20.4	38.3
443 UN C OF CHRIST	1	120	142*	1.0	1.9
449 UN METHODIST..	6	1 281	1 519*	11.0	20.6
453 UN PRES CH USA	3	145	172*	1.2	2.3
NEW MADRID	57	8 049	11 863*	51.7	100.0
017 AMER BAPT ASSN	1	115	115	0.5	1.0
053 ASSEMB OF GOD.	8	316	676	2.9	5.7
059 BAPT MISS ASSN	3	310	387*	1.7	3.3
081 CATHOLIC......	2	NA	1 180	5.1	9.9
093 CHR CH (DISC).	1	110	125	0.5	1.1
097 CHR CHS&CHS CR	0	105	131*	0.6	1.1
101 C.M.E........	1	98	122*	0.5	1.0
123 CH GOD (ANDER)	3	237	711	3.1	6.0
127 CH GOD (CLEVE)	1	34	42*	0.2	0.4
157 CH OF BRETHREN	1	18	22*	0.1	0.2
165 CH OF NAZARENE	2	57	56	0.2	0.5
167 CHS OF CHRIST.	8	425	541	2.4	4.6
283 LUTH--MO SYNOD	1	29	29	0.1	0.2
349 PENT HOLINESS.	1	24	30*	0.1	0.3
357 PRESB CH US...	2	110	137*	0.6	1.2
419 SO BAPT CONV..	13	4 966	6 193*	27.0	52.2
449 UN METHODIST..	9	1 095	1 366*	6.0	11.5
NEWTON	89	15 029	20 038*	49.4	100.0
053 ASSEMB OF GOD.	7	508	777	1.9	3.9
081 CATHOLIC......	2	NA	870	2.1	4.3
093 CHR CH (DISC).	1	469	509	1.3	2.5
097 CHR CHS&CHS CR	6	1 114	1 349*	3.3	6.7
123 CH GOD (ANDER)	1	60	180	0.4	0.9
127 CH GOD (CLEVE)	1	?	?	?	?
151 L-D SAINTS....	1	NA	391	1.0	2.0
157 CH OF BRETHREN	1	26	31*	0.1	0.2
165 CH OF NAZARENE	2	159	439	1.1	2.2
167 CHS OF CHRIST.	12	1 170	1 485	3.7	7.4
175 CONGR CHR CHS.	1	135	163*	0.4	0.8
185 CUMBER PRESB..	1	15	15	–	0.1
193 EPISCOPAL.....	1	70	98	0.2	0.5
217 FIRE BAPTIZED.	2	32	39*	0.1	0.2
283 LUTH--MO SYNOD	1	237	304	0.7	1.5
329 OPEN BIBLE STD	1	60	100	0.2	0.5
357 PRESB CH US...	2	149	180*	0.4	0.9
413 S.D.A.........	2	233	282*	0.7	1.4
419 SO BAPT CONV..	34	8 962	10 852*	26.8	54.2
449 UN METHODIST..	9	1 509	1 827*	4.5	9.1
453 UN PRES CH USA	1	121	147*	0.4	0.7
NODAWAY	50	7 868	13 439*	61.1	100.0
053 ASSEMB OF GOD.	1	100	172	0.8	1.3
081 CATHOLIC......	4	NA	3 435	15.6	25.6
093 CHR CH (DISC).	6	1 181	1 819	8.3	13.5
097 CHR CHS&CHS CR	10	912	1 078*	4.9	8.0
151 L-D SAINTS....	1	NA	143	0.7	1.1
165 CH OF NAZARENE	1	21	70	0.3	0.5
167 CHS OF CHRIST.	3	150	191	0.9	1.4
193 EPISCOPAL.....	1	57	74	0.3	0.6
283 LUTH--MO SYNOD	1	159	206	0.9	1.5
357 PRESB CH US...	1	89	105*	0.5	0.8
419 SO BAPT CONV..	4	1 746	2 064*	9.4	15.4
449 UN METHODIST..	16	3 364	3 977*	18.1	29.6
453 UN PRES CH USA	1	89	105*	0.5	0.8
OREGON	33	2 931	3 972*	38.8	100.0
053 ASSEMB OF GOD.	6	298	453	4.4	11.4

County and Denomination	Number of churches	Communicant, confirmed, full members	Total adherents		
			Number	Percent of total population	Percent of total adherents
059 BAPT MISS ASSN	1	43	52*	0.5	1.3
081 CATHOLIC......	1	NA	127	1.2	3.2
093 CHR CH (DISC).	1	34	59	0.6	1.5
123 CH GOD (ANDER)	1	95	285	2.8	7.2
167 CHS OF CHRIST.	6	400	509	5.0	12.8
185 CUMBER PRESB..	1	12	22	0.2	0.6
419 SO BAPT CONV..	11	1 658	1 995*	19.5	50.2
449 UN METHODIST..	5	391	470*	4.6	11.8
OSAGE	32	2 008	9 939*	82.7	100.0
053 ASSEMB OF GOD.	1	15	23	0.2	0.2
081 CATHOLIC......	12	NA	7 458	62.1	75.0
097 CHR CHS&CHS CR	5	374	461*	3.8	4.6
283 LUTH--MO SYNOD	2	91	112	0.9	1.1
357 PRESB CH US...	1	43	53*	0.4	0.5
419 SO BAPT CONV..	6	896	1 105*	9.2	11.1
443 UN C OF CHRIST	1	144	178*	1.5	1.8
449 UN METHODIST..	3	401	495*	4.1	5.0
453 UN PRES CH USA	1	44	54*	0.4	0.5
OZARK	38	2 143	3 236*	40.6	100.0
053 ASSEMB OF GOD.	4	260	570	7.2	17.6
081 CATHOLIC......	1	NA	225	2.8	7.0
097 CHR CHS&CHS CR	1	50	60*	0.8	1.9
123 CH GOD (ANDER)	2	55	165	2.1	5.1
165 CH OF NAZARENE	1	18	34	0.4	1.1
167 CHS OF CHRIST.	24	1 000	1 273	16.0	39.3
283 LUTH--MO SYNOD	1	49	60	0.8	1.9
419 SO BAPT CONV..	3	516	616*	7.7	19.0
449 UN METHODIST..	1	195	233*	2.9	7.2
PEMISCOT	65	10 127	13 467*	53.9	100.0
017 AMER BAPT ASSN	1	96	96	0.4	0.7
053 ASSEMB OF GOD.	5	210	412	1.6	3.1
081 CATHOLIC......	2	NA	353	1.4	2.6
097 CHR CHS&CHS CR	1	225	281*	1.1	2.1
127 CH GOD (CLEVE)	5	274	343*	1.4	2.5
151 L-D SAINTS....	1	NA	295	1.2	2.2
165 CH OF NAZARENE	3	140	188	0.8	1.4
167 CHS OF CHRIST.	11	750	955	3.8	7.1
193 EPISCOPAL.....	1	29	34	0.1	0.3
349 PENT HOLINESS.	2	110	138*	0.6	1.0
357 PRESB CH US...	1	309	386*	1.5	2.9
419 SO BAPT CONV..	22	6 892	8 620*	34.5	64.0
449 UN METHODIST..	10	1 092	1 366*	5.5	10.1
PERRY	32	4 905	15 023*	89.5	100.0
029 AMER LUTH CH..	1	190	232	1.4	1.5
081 CATHOLIC......	10	NA	8 905	53.1	59.3
093 CHR CH (DISC).	1	151	232	1.4	1.5
097 CHR CHS&CHS CR	1	50	61*	0.4	0.4
165 CH OF NAZARENE	1	33	47	0.3	0.3
283 LUTH--MO SYNOD	9	3 408	4 233	25.2	28.2
357 PRESB CH US...	2	153	187*	1.1	1.2
419 SO BAPT CONV..	4	628	769*	4.6	5.1
449 UN METHODIST..	3	292	357*	2.1	2.4
PETTIS	79	17 355	25 154*	69.1	100.0
017 AMER BAPT ASSN	1	20	20	0.1	0.1
029 AMER LUTH CH..	1	132	169	0.5	0.7
053 ASSEMB OF GOD.	3	284	466	1.3	1.9
081 CATHOLIC......	4	NA	3 618	9.9	14.4
093 CHR CH (DISC).	1	1 398	1 630	4.5	6.5
097 CHR CHS&CHS CR	4	516	620*	1.7	2.5
127 CH GOD (CLEVE)	1	51	61*	0.2	0.2
151 L-D SAINTS....	1	NA	351	1.0	1.4
165 CH OF NAZARENE	1	54	111	0.3	0.4
167 CHS OF CHRIST.	2	97	136	0.4	0.5
185 CUMBER PRESB..	1	7	7	–	–
193 EPISCOPAL.....	1	254	338	0.9	1.3
221 FREE METHODIST	1	26	90	0.2	0.4
271 REFORM JUDAISM	1	28	34*	0.1	0.1
281 LUTH CH AMER..	1	168	222	0.6	0.9
283 LUTH--MO SYNOD	2	1 404	1 629	4.5	6.5
329 OPEN BIBLE STD	1	160	200	0.5	0.8
357 PRESB CH US...	4	453	545*	1.5	2.2
403 SALVATION ARMY	1	125	264	0.7	1.0
413 S.D.A.........	2	116	139*	0.4	0.6
419 SO BAPT CONV..	25	8 176	9 832*	27.0	39.1
443 UN C OF CHRIST	1	337	405*	1.1	1.6
449 UN METHODIST..	16	3 133	3 767*	10.4	15.0
453 UN PRES CH USA	3	416	500*	1.4	2.0
PHELPS	55	11 393	17 487*	52.0	100.0
017 AMER BAPT ASSN	1	48	48	0.1	0.3
053 ASSEMB OF GOD.	5	390	854	2.5	4.9
059 BAPT MISS ASSN	1	29	34*	0.1	0.2
081 CATHOLIC......	3	NA	2 282	6.8	13.0
097 CHR CHS&CHS CR	4	1 408	1 670*	5.0	9.5
123 CH GOD (ANDER)	3	409	1 218	3.6	7.0
127 CH GOD (CLEVE)	1	32	38*	0.1	0.2
151 L-D SAINTS....	1	NA	286	0.9	1.6
165 CH OF NAZARENE	1	60	66	0.2	0.4
167 CHS OF CHRIST.	5	210	267	0.8	1.5
193 EPISCOPAL.....	1	397	579	1.7	3.3
226 FRIENDS-USA...	1	4	5*	–	–
283 LUTH--MO SYNOD	4	882	1 217	3.6	7.0
357 PRESB CH US...	1	337	400*	1.2	2.3
413 S.D.A.........	1	74	88*	0.3	0.5

NA— Not applicable   *Total adherents estimated from known number of communicant, confirmed, full members.   —Represents a percent less than 0.1.   Percentages may not total due to rounding.

Table 4. Churches and Church Membership by County and Denomination: 1980

County and Denomination	Number of churches	Communicant, confirmed, full members	Total adherents		
			Number	Percent of total population	Percent of total adherents
419 SO BAPT CONV..	15	5 649	6 699*	19.9	38.3
435 UNITARIAN-UNIV	1	20	24*	0.1	0.1
449 UN METHODIST..	4	1 108	1 314*	3.9	7.5
453 UN PRES CH USA	1	336	398*	1.2	2.3
PIKE	86	7 019	10 781*	61.4	100.0
053 ASSEMB OF GOD.	2	62	87	0.5	0.8
081 CATHOLIC......	3	NA	1 900	10.8	17.6
093 CHR CH (DISC).	11	658	1 044	5.9	9.7
167 CHS OF CHRIST.	6	210	267	1.5	2.5
193 EPISCOPAL.....	3	113	125	0.7	1.2
217 FIRE BAPTIZED.	1	11	13*	0.1	0.1
221 FREE METHODIST	1	6	21	0.1	0.2
283 LUTH--MO SYNOD	1	151	209	1.2	1.9
323 OLD ORD AMISH.	4	520	637*	3.6	5.9
357 PRESB CH US...	13	456	559*	3.2	5.2
419 SO BAPT CONV..	20	3 671	4 497*	25.6	41.7
449 UN METHODIST..	8	711	871*	5.0	8.1
453 UN PRES CH USA	13	450	551*	3.1	5.1
PLATTE	57	11 013	20 504*	44.2	100.0
053 ASSEMB OF GOD.	2	321	565	1.2	2.8
081 CATHOLIC......	2	NA	5 740	12.4	28.0
093 CHR CH (DISC).	13	1 877	3 188	6.9	15.5
097 CHR CHS&CHS CR	5	400	493*	1.1	2.4
127 CH GOD (CLEVE)	1	28	35*	0.1	0.2
165 CH OF NAZARENE	1	65	107	0.2	0.5
167 CHS OF CHRIST.	4	136	173	0.4	0.8
193 EPISCOPAL.....	1	219	278	0.6	1.4
281 LUTH CH AMER..	1	290	392	0.8	1.9
283 LUTH--MO SYNOD	2	659	880	1.9	4.3
357 PRESB CH US...	2	363	448*	1.0	2.2
419 SO BAPT CONV..	14	4 131	5 093*	11.0	24.8
443 UN C OF CHRIST	1	67	83*	0.2	0.4
449 UN METHODIST..	6	2 095	2 583*	5.6	12.6
453 UN PRES CH USA	2	362	446*	1.0	2.2
POLK	48	6 770	9 200*	48.9	100.0
053 ASSEMB OF GOD.	9	661	1 224	6.5	13.3
081 CATHOLIC......	2	NA	489	2.6	5.3
093 CHR CH (DISC).	3	375	485	2.6	5.3
097 CHR CHS&CHS CR	3	265	316*	1.7	3.4
123 CH GOD (ANDER)	1	30	90	0.5	1.0
165 CH OF NAZARENE	1	49	125	0.7	1.4
167 CHS OF CHRIST.	1	75	95	0.5	1.0
185 CUMBER PRESB..	2	56	84	0.4	0.9
283 LUTH--MO SYNOD	1	57	82	0.4	0.9
419 SO BAPT CONV..	14	4 063	4 850*	25.8	52.7
449 UN METHODIST..	11	1 139	1 360*	7.2	14.8
PULASKI	63	10 632	14 437*	34.4	100.0
053 ASSEMB OF GOD.	5	302	508	1.2	3.5
081 CATHOLIC......	5	NA	757	1.8	5.2
093 CHR CH (DISC).	1	80	222	0.5	1.5
097 CHR CHS&CHS CR	7	1 175	1 401*	3.3	9.7
107 CHRISTIAN UN..	2	0	81	0.2	0.6
123 CH GOD (ANDER)	3	102	306	0.7	2.1
151 L-D SAINTS....	1	NA	198	0.5	1.4
165 CH OF NAZARENE	1	52	253	0.6	1.8
167 CHS OF CHRIST.	5	313	398	0.9	2.8
217 FIRE BAPTIZED.	1	9	11*	—	0.1
283 LUTH--MO SYNOD	1	246	340	0.8	2.4
357 PRESB CH US...	1	57	68*	0.2	0.5
413 S.D.A.........	1	29	35*	0.1	0.2
419 SO BAPT CONV..	25	7 563	9 019*	21.5	62.5
449 UN METHODIST..	3	647	772*	1.8	5.3
453 UN PRES CH USA	1	57	68*	0.2	0.5
PUTNAM	24	2 201	2 783*	45.7	100.0
053 ASSEMB OF GOD.	1	44	83	1.4	3.0
081 CATHOLIC......	1	NA	101	1.7	3.6
097 CHR CHS&CHS CR	3	600	714*	11.7	25.7
151 L-D SAINTS....	1	NA	19	0.3	0.7
167 CHS OF CHRIST.	6	150	191	3.1	6.9
419 SO BAPT CONV..	6	1 065	1 268*	20.8	45.6
449 UN METHODIST..	6	342	407*	6.7	14.6
RALLS	34	3 122	4 610*	51.7	100.0
081 CATHOLIC......	2	NA	390	4.4	8.5
093 CHR CH (DISC).	11	798	1 303	14.6	28.3
097 CHR CHS&CHS CR	2	175	214*	2.4	4.6
165 CH OF NAZARENE	1	52	140	1.6	3.0
357 PRESB CH US...	3	607	742*	8.3	16.1
419 SO BAPT CONV..	10	1 265	1 546*	17.3	33.5
449 UN METHODIST..	3	154	188*	2.1	4.1
453 UN PRES CH USA	2	71	87*	1.0	1.9
RANDOLPH	60	10 402	14 754*	57.9	100.0
053 ASSEMB OF GOD.	3	136	263	1.0	1.8
081 CATHOLIC......	2	NA	1 455	5.7	9.9
093 CHR CH (DISC).	8	1 394	2 007	7.9	13.6
097 CHR CHS&CHS CR	3	555	669*	2.6	4.5
123 CH GOD (ANDER)	1	50	150	0.6	1.0
127 CH GOD (CLEVE)	1	30	36*	0.1	0.2
151 L-D SAINTS....	1	NA	137	0.5	0.9
165 CH OF NAZARENE	1	86	158	0.6	1.1
167 CHS OF CHRIST.	3	150	183	0.7	1.2
185 CUMBER PRESB..	2	70	111	0.4	0.8

County and Denomination	Number of churches	Communicant, confirmed, full members	Total adherents		
			Number	Percent of total population	Percent of total adherents
193 EPISCOPAL.....	1	47	65	0.3	0.4
283 LUTH--MO SYNOD	1	244	310	1.2	2.1
357 PRESB CH US...	3	216	260*	1.0	1.8
413 S.D.A.........	1	92	111*	0.4	0.8
419 SO BAPT CONV..	15	5 085	6 130*	24.1	41.5
449 UN METHODIST..	11	2 033	2 451*	9.6	16.6
453 UN PRES CH USA	3	214	258*	1.0	1.7
RAY	59	10 045	13 568*	63.5	100.0
053 ASSEMB OF GOD.	4	249	485	2.3	3.6
081 CATHOLIC......	1	NA	300	1.4	2.2
093 CHR CH (DISC).	4	618	1 117	5.2	8.2
097 CHR CHS&CHS CR	1	100	122*	0.6	0.9
107 CHRISTIAN UN..	6	479	877	4.1	6.5
157 CH OF BRETHREN	2	155	189*	0.9	1.4
165 CH OF NAZARENE	2	129	285	1.3	2.1
167 CHS OF CHRIST.	3	120	164	0.8	1.2
283 LUTH--MO SYNOD	1	118	158	0.7	1.2
357 PRESB CH US...	2	149	182*	0.9	1.3
419 SO BAPT CONV..	17	5 783	7 067*	33.1	52.1
449 UN METHODIST..	14	1 997	2 441*	11.4	18.0
453 UN PRES CH USA	2	148	181*	0.8	1.3
REYNOLDS	28	2 300	3 088*	42.7	100.0
053 ASSEMB OF GOD.	4	133	235	3.3	7.6
059 BAPT MISS ASSN	5	255	312*	4.3	10.1
081 CATHOLIC......	3	NA	139	1.9	4.5
165 CH OF NAZARENE	2	49	113	1.6	3.7
167 CHS OF CHRIST.	4	140	178	2.5	5.8
419 SO BAPT CONV..	9	1 545	1 893*	26.2	61.3
449 UN METHODIST..	1	178	218*	3.0	7.1
RIPLEY	45	3 460	5 253*	42.2	100.0
053 ASSEMB OF GOD.	1	59	86	0.7	1.6
059 BAPT MISS ASSN	8	362	436*	3.5	8.3
081 CATHOLIC......	1	NA	306	2.5	5.8
093 CHR CH (DISC).	1	60	89	0.7	1.7
097 CHR CHS&CHS CR	1	60	72*	0.6	1.4
121 CH GOD (ABR)..	1	40	48*	0.4	0.9
123 CH GOD (ANDER)	4	296	888	7.1	16.9
151 L-D SAINTS....	1	NA	51	0.4	1.0
167 CHS OF CHRIST.	10	515	775	6.2	14.8
283 LUTH--MO SYNOD	1	73	102	0.8	1.9
413 S.D.A.........	1	40	48*	0.4	0.9
419 SO BAPT CONV..	7	1 570	1 889*	15.2	36.0
449 UN METHODIST..	7	306	368*	3.0	7.0
453 UN PRES CH USA	1	79	95*	0.8	1.8
ST CHARLES	103	27 529	71 510*	49.8	100.0
053 ASSEMB OF GOD.	5	607	1 082	0.8	1.5
055 AS REF PRES CH	1	?	?	?	?
057 BAPT GEN CONF.	1	86	108*	0.1	0.2
059 BAPT MISS ASSN	3	310	389*	0.3	0.5
081 CATHOLIC......	18	NA	34 549	24.1	48.3
093 CHR CH (DISC).	2	614	704	0.5	1.0
097 CHR CHS&CHS CR	5	875	1 099*	0.8	1.5
123 CH GOD (ANDER)	3	120	360	0.3	0.5
127 CH GOD (CLEVE)	2	163	205*	0.1	0.3
151 L-D SAINTS....	1	NA	709	0.5	1.0
165 CH OF NAZARENE	3	200	647	0.5	0.9
167 CHS OF CHRIST.	6	535	750	0.5	1.0
193 EPISCOPAL.....	1	247	440	0.3	0.6
201 EVAN COV CH AM	1	54	68*	—	0.1
215 EVAN METH CH..	1	312	392*	0.3	0.5
263 INT FOURSQ GOS	1	133	167*	0.1	0.2
281 LUTH CH AMER..	1	285	439	0.3	0.6
283 LUTH--MO SYNOD	9	6 381	8 492	5.9	11.9
353 CHR BRETHREN..	2	50	75	0.1	0.1
357 PRESB CH US...	1	404	508*	0.4	0.7
403 SALVATION ARMY	1	124	187	0.1	0.3
413 S.D.A.........	1	116	146*	0.1	0.2
419 SO BAPT CONV..	13	7 577	9 520*	6.6	13.3
443 UN C OF CHRIST	12	3 752	4 714*	3.3	6.6
449 UN METHODIST..	7	3 790	4 762*	3.3	6.7
453 UN PRES CH USA	2	794	998*	0.7	1.4
ST CLAIR	27	3 415	4 234*	49.1	100.0
053 ASSEMB OF GOD.	1	63	130	1.5	3.1
081 CATHOLIC......	1	NA	85	1.0	2.0
093 CHR CH (DISC).	1	130	166	1.9	3.9
097 CHR CHS&CHS CR	4	225	268*	3.1	6.3
157 CH OF BRETHREN	1	47	56*	0.6	1.3
185 CUMBER PRESB..	1	14	25	0.3	0.6
283 LUTH--MO SYNOD	1	149	186	2.2	4.4
419 SO BAPT CONV..	10	2 098	2 498*	29.0	59.0
449 UN METHODIST..	7	689	820*	9.5	19.4
ST FRANCOIS	86	16 568	25 166*	59.1	100.0
053 ASSEMB OF GOD.	12	792	1 423	3.3	5.7
059 BAPT MISS ASSN	1	59	72*	0.2	0.3
081 CATHOLIC......	5	NA	3 636	8.5	14.4
093 CHR CH (DISC).	3	354	529	1.2	2.1
097 CHR CHS&CHS CR	2	135	164*	0.4	0.7
123 CH GOD (ANDER)	3	220	660	1.5	2.6
127 CH GOD (CLEVE)	6	524	636*	1.5	2.5
151 L-D SAINTS....	1	NA	299	0.7	1.2
165 CH OF NAZARENE	3	306	471	1.1	1.9
167 CHS OF CHRIST.	5	249	313	0.7	1.2
193 EPISCOPAL.....	2	40	51	0.1	0.2

NA—Not applicable   *Total adherents estimated from known number of communicant, confirmed, full members.   —Represents a percent less than 0.1.   Percentages may not total due to rounding.

Table 4. Churches and Church Membership by County and Denomination: 1980

County and Denomination	Number of churches	Communicant, confirmed, full members	Total adherents Number	Percent of total population	Percent of total adherents
283 LUTH--MO SYNOD	4	946	1 208	2.8	4.8
357 PRESB CH US...	1	250	303*	0.7	1.2
413 S.D.A.	1	131	159*	0.4	0.6
419 SO BAPT CONV..	21	9 061	10 994*	25.8	43.7
443 UN C OF CHRIST	1	195	237*	0.6	0.9
449 UN METHODIST..	14	3 194	3 875*	9.1	15.4
453 UN PRES CH USA	1	112	136*	0.3	0.5
ST LOUIS	**503**	**187 228**	**548 715***	**56.3**	**100.0**
005 AME ZION......	3	2 334	2 801	0.3	0.5
017 AMER BAPT ASSN	1	88	88	-	-
029 AMER LUTH CH..	3	865	1 183	0.1	0.2
039 AP CHR CH(NAZ)	1	23	28*	-	-
053 ASSEMB OF GOD.	21	2 382	3 710	0.4	0.7
057 BAPT GEN CONF.	2	257	308*	-	0.1
059 BAPT MISS ASSN	8	833	999*	0.1	0.2
081 CATHOLIC.....	102	NA	311 770	32.0	56.8
089 CHR & MISS AL.	2	77	116	-	-
093 CHR CH (DISC).	3	580	898	0.1	0.2
097 CHR CHS&CHS CR	8	1 577	1 892*	0.2	0.3
101 C.M.E......	6	573	687*	0.1	0.1
105 CHRISTIAN REF.	1	84	142	-	-
123 CH GOD (ANDER)	1	41	123	-	-
127 CH GOD (CLEVE)	3	177	212*	-	-
151 L-D SAINTS....	5	NA	2 360	0.2	0.4
165 CH OF NAZARENE	13	1 923	3 434	0.4	0.6
167 CHS OF CHRIST.	17	3 494	4 634	0.5	0.8
185 CUMBER PRESB..	1	4	5	-	-
193 EPISCOPAL.....	16	6 223	8 746	0.9	1.6
201 EVAN COV CH AM	3	127	152*	-	-
208 EVAN LUTH ASSN	8	4 983	6 534	0.7	1.2
226 FRIENDS-USA...	1	125	150*	-	-
263 INT FOURSQ GOS	2	304	365*	-	0.1
270 CONSRV JUDAISM	3	1 255	1 505*	0.2	0.3
271 REFORM JUDAISM	7	11 032	13 232*	1.4	2.4
281 LUTH CH AMER..	4	1 437	1 874	0.2	0.3
283 LUTH--MO SYNOD	46	32 955	43 438	4.5	7.9
285 MENNONITE CH..	2	131	157*	-	-
287 MENN GEN CONF.	1	10	24	-	-
290 METRO COMM CHS	1	100	200	-	-
349 PENT HOLINESS	2	71	85*	-	-
353 CHR BRETHREN..	9	605	875	0.1	0.2
357 PRESB CH US...	9	5 515	6 615*	0.7	1.2
381 REF PRES-EVAN.	3	366	561	0.1	0.1
403 SALVATION ARMY	2	370	1 239	0.1	0.2
413 S.D.A.......	6	1 494	1 792*	0.2	0.3
419 SO BAPT CONV..	73	45 618	54 717*	5.6	10.0
435 UNITARIAN-UNIV	2	413	495*	0.1	0.1
443 UN C OF CHRIST	29	18 007	21 599*	2.2	3.9
449 UN METHODIST..	43	24 060	28 859*	3.0	5.3
453 UN PRES CH USA	28	16 445	19 725*	2.0	3.6
469 WELS.......	2	270	386	-	0.1
ST LOUIS CITY	**321**	**87 205**	**223 209***	**49.3**	**100.0**
001 ADVENT CHR CH.	1	32	38*	-	-
017 AMER BAPT ASSN	1	14	14	-	-
019 AMER BAPT USA.	7	5 588	6 677*	1.5	3.0
053 ASSEMB OF GOD.	10	1 144	2 228	0.5	1.0
081 CATHOLIC.....	69	NA	107 840	23.8	48.3
093 CHR CH (DISC).	12	3 733	5 806	1.3	2.6
097 CHR CHS&CHS CR	10	1 547	1 848*	0.4	0.8
101 C.M.E......	6	5 585	6 673*	1.5	3.0
121 CH GOD (ABR)..	1	43	51*	-	-
123 CH GOD (ANDER)	12	1 221	3 663	0.8	1.6
127 CH GOD (CLEVE)	6	835	998*	0.2	0.4
151 L-D SAINTS....	3	NA	1 150	0.3	0.5
164 CH LUTH CONF.	1	50	74	-	-
165 CH OF NAZARENE	5	501	920	0.2	0.4
167 CHS OF CHRIST.	7	1 041	1 290	0.3	0.6
193 EPISCOPAL.....	11	2 541	3 311	0.7	1.5
208 EVAN LUTH ASSN	10	2 040	2 519	0.6	1.1
221 FREE METHODIST	4	115	465*	0.1	0.2
239 SWEDENBORGIAN.	1	60	72*	-	-
263 INT FOURSQ GOS	1	288	344*	0.1	0.2
274 LAT EVAN LUTH.	1	18	18	-	-
281 LUTH CH AMER..	6	1 941	2 380	0.5	1.1
283 LUTH--MO SYNOD	30	13 151	17 280	3.8	7.7
381 REF PRES-EVAN.	7	804	951	0.2	0.4
403 SALVATION ARMY	5	874	3 981	0.9	1.8
413 S.D.A.......	1	693	828*	0.2	0.4
419 SO BAPT CONV..	20	17 201	20 552*	4.5	9.2
435 UNITARIAN-UNIV	1	419	501*	0.1	0.2
443 UN C OF CHRIST	34	14 004	16 732*	3.7	7.5
449 UN METHODIST..	18	6 402	7 649*	1.7	3.4
453 UN PRES CH USA	20	5 320	6 356*	1.4	2.8
STE GENEVIEVE	**26**	**2 392**	**12 359***	**81.4**	**100.0**
081 CATHOLIC.....	9	NA	9 429	62.1	76.3
127 CH GOD (CLEVE)	1	41	50*	0.3	0.4
167 CHS OF CHRIST.	1	45	57	0.4	0.5
283 LUTH--MO SYNOD	1	141	158	1.0	1.3
357 PRESB CH US...	1	238	293*	1.9	2.4
419 SO BAPT CONV..	12	1 895	2 333*	15.4	18.9
449 UN METHODIST..	1	32	39*	0.3	0.3
SALINE	**87**	**11 773**	**17 164***	**68.9**	**100.0**
053 ASSEMB OF GOD.	5	305	439	1.8	2.6
081 CATHOLIC.....	3	NA	2 300	9.2	13.4
093 CHR CH (DISC).	9	1 385	1 913	7.7	11.1
097 CHR CHS&CHS CR	1	50	60*	0.2	0.3
123 CH GOD (ANDER)	1	32	96	0.4	0.6
151 L-D SAINTS....	1	NA	48	0.2	0.3
165 CH OF NAZARENE	1	105	200	0.8	1.2
167 CHS OF CHRIST.	3	57	76	0.3	0.4
185 CUMBER PRESB.	3	86	229	0.9	1.3
193 EPISCOPAL.....	1	110	181	0.7	1.1
283 LUTH--MO SYNOD	7	1 449	1 797	7.2	10.5
357 PRESB CH US...	6	363	435*	1.7	2.5
419 SO BAPT CONV..	19	4 841	5 805*	23.3	33.8
443 UN C OF CHRIST	4	434	520*	2.1	3.0
449 UN METHODIST..	16	2 154	2 583*	10.4	15.0
453 UN PRES CH USA	7	402	482*	1.9	2.8
SCHUYLER	**21**	**2 041**	**2 507***	**50.4**	**100.0**
053 ASSEMB OF GOD.	1	20	42	0.8	1.7
093 CHR CH (DISC).	1	61	117	2.3	4.7
097 CHR CHS&CHS CR	6	822	984*	19.8	39.3
281 LUTH CH AMER..	1	107	130	2.6	5.2
419 SO BAPT CONV..	5	731	875*	17.6	34.9
449 UN METHODIST..	6	300	359*	7.2	14.3
SCOTLAND	**29**	**3 140**	**4 049***	**74.8**	**100.0**
053 ASSEMB OF GOD.	1	20	50	0.9	1.2
081 CATHOLIC.....	1	NA	158	2.9	3.9
093 CHR CH (DISC).	1	52	121	2.2	3.0
097 CHR CHS&CHS CR	4	871	1 044*	19.3	25.8
151 L-D SAINTS....	1	NA	42	0.8	1.0
167 CHS OF CHRIST.	1	25	32	0.6	0.8
283 LUTH--MO SYNOD	1	44	51	0.9	1.3
357 PRESB CH US...	2	89	107*	2.0	2.6
419 SO BAPT CONV..	7	948	1 136*	21.0	28.1
449 UN METHODIST..	8	1 001	1 200*	22.2	29.6
453 UN PRES CH USA	2	90	108*	2.0	2.7
SCOTT	**72**	**13 001**	**23 046***	**58.1**	**100.0**
017 AMER BAPT ASSN	1	234	234	0.6	1.0
053 ASSEMB OF GOD.	4	347	794	2.0	3.4
059 BAPT MISS ASSN	2	326	403*	1.0	1.7
081 CATHOLIC.....	7	NA	5 937	15.0	25.8
093 CHR CH (DISC).	2	437	517	1.3	2.2
123 CH GOD (ANDER)	3	311	933	2.4	4.0
127 CH GOD (CLEVE)	1	213	263*	0.7	1.1
165 CH OF NAZARENE	2	500	500	1.3	2.2
167 CHS OF CHRIST.	11	850	1 075	2.7	4.7
193 EPISCOPAL.....	1	121	165	0.4	0.7
283 LUTH--MO SYNOD	3	617	772	1.9	3.3
357 PRESB CH US...	1	185	229*	0.6	1.0
413 S.D.A.......	1	24	30*	0.1	0.1
419 SO BAPT CONV..	22	6 813	8 421*	21.2	36.5
449 UN METHODIST..	10	2 214	2 737*	6.9	11.9
453 UN PRES CH USA	1	29	36*	0.1	0.2
SHANNON	**25**	**2 350**	**3 064***	**38.9**	**100.0**
053 ASSEMB OF GOD.	3	151	354	4.5	11.6
081 CATHOLIC.....	1	NA	31	0.4	1.0
097 CHR CHS&CHS CR	2	285	346*	4.4	11.3
165 CH OF NAZARENE	1	27	41	0.5	1.3
167 CHS OF CHRIST.	3	75	95	1.2	3.1
285 MENNONITE CH..	1	9	11*	0.1	0.4
419 SO BAPT CONV..	6	1 439	1 745*	22.1	57.0
449 UN METHODIST..	8	364	441*	5.6	14.4
SHELBY	**46**	**4 630**	**6 503***	**83.1**	**100.0**
053 ASSEMB OF GOD.	2	17	31	0.4	0.5
081 CATHOLIC.....	3	NA	880	11.2	13.5
093 CHR CH (DISC).	4	95	169	2.2	2.6
097 CHR CHS&CHS CR	11	1 690	2 005*	25.6	30.8
157 CH OF BRETHREN	1	45	53*	0.7	0.8
165 CH OF NAZARENE	1	37	70	0.9	1.1
167 CHS OF CHRIST.	1	25	35	0.5	0.5
221 FREE METHODIST	1	8	36	0.5	0.6
283 LUTH--MO SYNOD	1	98	121	1.5	1.9
285 MENNONITE CH..	1	55	65*	0.8	1.0
419 SO BAPT CONV..	11	1 455	1 727*	22.1	26.6
449 UN METHODIST..	9	1 105	1 311*	16.8	20.2
STODDARD	**71**	**8 601**	**11 982***	**41.3**	**100.0**
017 AMER BAPT ASSN	1	28	28	0.1	0.2
053 ASSEMB OF GOD.	8	617	1 014	3.5	8.5
059 BAPT MISS ASSN	1	108	130*	0.4	1.1
081 CATHOLIC.....	2	NA	737	2.5	6.2
089 CHR & MISS AL.	1	16	81	0.3	0.7
093 CHR CH (DISC).	1	255	327	1.1	2.7
097 CHR CHS&CHS CR	4	200	241*	0.8	2.0
123 CH GOD (ANDER)	1	30	90	0.3	0.8
127 CH GOD (CLEVE)	2	79	95*	0.3	0.8
151 L-D SAINTS....	1	NA	71	0.2	0.6
157 CH OF BRETHREN	1	66	79*	0.3	0.7
165 CH OF NAZARENE	4	302	713	2.5	6.0
167 CHS OF CHRIST.	13	890	1 133	3.9	9.5
283 LUTH--MO SYNOD	1	91	115	0.4	1.0
419 SO BAPT CONV..	18	4 163	5 013*	17.3	41.8
449 UN METHODIST..	11	1 679	2 022*	7.0	16.9
453 UN PRES CH USA	1	77	93*	0.3	0.8
STONE	**41**	**3 777**	**4 928***	**31.6**	**100.0**
053 ASSEMB OF GOD.	4	184	346	2.2	7.0
081 CATHOLIC.....	1	NA	278	1.8	5.6
097 CHR CHS&CHS CR	3	237	279*	1.8	5.7

NA—Not applicable   *Total adherents estimated from known number of communicant, confirmed, full members.   —Represents a percent less than 0.1.   Percentages may not total due to rounding.

Table 4. Churches and Church Membership by County and Denomination: 1980

County and Denomination	Number of churches	Communicant, confirmed, full members	Total adherents		
			Number	Percent of total population	Percent of total adherents
107 CHRISTIAN UN..	2	0	57	0.4	1.2
127 CH GOD (CLEVE)	2	86	101*	0.6	2.0
165 CH OF NAZARENE	1	24	31	0.2	0.6
167 CHS OF CHRIST.	4	200	255	1.6	5.2
283 LUTH--MO SYNOD	1	172	197	1.3	4.0
357 PRESB CH US...	3	115	135*	0.9	2.7
413 S.D.A........	1	21	25*	0.2	0.5
419 SO BAPT CONV..	14	1 788	2 106*	13.5	42.7
449 UN METHODIST..	2	836	984*	6.3	20.0
453 UN PRES CH USA	3	114	134*	0.9	2.7
SULLIVAN	36	3 458	4 562*	61.4	100.0
053 ASSEMB OF GOD.	2	50	78	1.0	1.7
081 CATHOLIC......	1	NA	254	3.4	5.6
093 CHR CH (DISC).	1	115	193	2.6	4.2
097 CHR CHS&CHS CR	4	665	785*	10.6	17.2
123 CH GOD (ANDER)	1	44	132	1.8	2.9
151 L-D SAINTS....	1	NA	50	0.7	1.1
167 CHS OF CHRIST.	2	67	76	1.0	1.7
283 LUTH--MO SYNOD	1	44	72	1.0	1.6
357 PRESB CH US...	2	60	71*	1.0	1.6
419 SO BAPT CONV..	10	1 582	1 869*	25.1	41.0
449 UN METHODIST..	7	771	911*	12.3	20.0
453 UN PRES CH USA	2	60	71*	1.0	1.6
TANEY	35	4 637	8 223*	40.2	100.0
053 ASSEMB OF GOD.	3	176	520	2.5	6.3
081 CATHOLIC......	2	NA	2 189	10.7	26.6
093 CHR CH (DISC).	1	271	327	1.6	4.0
097 CHR CHS&CHS CR	3	275	318*	1.6	3.9
127 CH GOD (CLEVE)	1	16	19*	0.1	0.2
151 L-D SAINTS....	1	NA	126	0.6	1.5
165 CH OF NAZARENE	3	159	367	1.8	4.5
167 CHS OF CHRIST.	4	246	292	1.4	3.6
193 EPISCOPAL.....	1	186	229	1.1	2.8
283 LUTH--MO SYNOD	1	374	443	2.2	5.4
357 PRESB CH US...	4	456	527*	2.6	6.4
413 S.D.A........	1	36	42*	0.2	0.5
419 SO BAPT CONV..	5	1 285	1 486*	7.3	18.1
449 UN METHODIST..	1	699	808*	3.9	9.8
453 UN PRES CH USA	4	458	530*	2.6	6.4
TEXAS	65	8 789	11 570*	54.9	100.0
053 ASSEMB OF GOD.	6	211	405	1.9	3.5
081 CATHOLIC......	4	NA	463	2.2	4.0
093 CHR CH (DISC).	1	25	38	0.2	0.3
097 CHR CHS&CHS CR	5	900	1 086*	5.2	9.4
123 CH GOD (ANDER)	2	100	300	1.4	2.6
127 CH GOD (CLEVE)	1	?	?	?	?
151 L-D SAINTS....	1	NA	163	0.8	1.4
157 CH OF BRETHREN	2	117	141*	0.7	1.2
167 CHS OF CHRIST.	6	230	282	1.3	2.4
283 LUTH--MO SYNOD	1	71	85	0.4	0.7
349 PENT HOLINESS	6	288	347*	1.6	3.0
419 SO BAPT CONV..	23	5 868	7 079*	33.6	61.2
449 UN METHODIST..	7	979	1 181*	5.6	10.2
VERNON	54	6 786	9 760*	49.3	100.0
029 AMER LUTH CH..	1	101	129	0.7	1.3
053 ASSEMB OF GOD.	2	112	290	1.5	3.0
081 CATHOLIC......	1	NA	854	4.3	8.7
093 CHR CH (DISC).	2	610	923	4.7	9.5
097 CHR CHS&CHS CR	8	705	845*	4.3	8.7
143 CG IN CR(MENN)	1	87	87	0.4	0.9
151 L-D SAINTS....	1	NA	257	1.3	2.6
165 CH OF NAZARENE	1	109	288	1.5	3.0
167 CHS OF CHRIST.	4	120	153	0.8	1.6
193 EPISCOPAL.....	1	121	149	0.8	1.5
283 LUTH--MO SYNOD	1	67	84	0.4	0.9
357 PRESB CH US...	1	58	70*	0.4	0.7
413 S.D.A........	1	134	161*	0.8	1.6
419 SO BAPT CONV..	18	3 323	3 984*	20.1	40.8
449 UN METHODIST..	10	1 181	1 416*	7.1	14.5
453 UN PRES CH USA	1	58	70*	0.4	0.7
WARREN	22	3 963	7 798*	52.3	100.0
053 ASSEMB OF GOD.	2	108	51	0.3	0.7
081 CATHOLIC......	4	NA	2 961	19.9	38.0
165 CH OF NAZARENE	1	49	138	0.9	1.8
167 CHS OF CHRIST.	1	25	32	0.2	0.4
283 LUTH--MO SYNOD	1	292	382	2.6	4.9
419 SO BAPT CONV..	3	801	972*	6.5	12.5
443 UN C.OF CHRIST	5	1 773	2 152*	14.4	27.6
449 UN METHODIST..	5	915	1 110*	7.4	14.2
WASHINGTON	45	3 782	7 892*	43.9	100.0
053 ASSEMB OF GOD.	6	298	567	3.2	7.2
059 BAPT MISS ASSN	13	1 275	1 599*	8.9	20.3
081 CATHOLIC......	4	NA	2 930	16.3	37.1
097 CHR CHS&CHS CR	1	121	152*	0.8	1.9
127 CH GOD (CLEVE)	5	325	407*	2.3	5.2
165 CH OF NAZARENE	2	67	112	0.6	1.4
167 CHS OF CHRIST.	1	43	54	0.3	0.7
283 LUTH--MO SYNOD	1	46	56	0.3	0.7
357 PRESB CH US...	2	118	148*	0.8	1.9
419 SO BAPT CONV..	5	1 076	1 349*	7.5	17.1
449 UN METHODIST..	5	413	518*	2.9	6.6
WAYNE	41	3 253	4 532*	40.2	100.0

County and Denomination	Number of churches	Communicant, confirmed, full members	Total adherents		
			Number	Percent of total population	Percent of total adherents
053 ASSEMB OF GOD.	4	116	263	2.3	5.8
081 CATHOLIC......	2	NA	353	3.1	7.8
097 CHR CHS&CHS CR	3	241	287*	2.5	6.3
165 CH OF NAZARENE	2	177	393	3.5	8.7
167 CHS OF CHRIST.	2	70	89	0.8	2.0
209 EVAN LUTH SYN.	1	36	44	0.4	1.0
283 LUTH--MO SYNOD	1	45	46	0.4	1.0
413 S.D.A........	1	28	33*	0.3	0.7
419 SO BAPT CONV..	15	1 963	2 337*	20.7	51.6
449 UN METHODIST..	10	577	687*	6.1	15.2
WEBSTER	83	9 115	12 202*	59.8	100.0
053 ASSEMB OF GOD.	5	234	429	2.1	3.5
081 CATHOLIC......	1	NA	497	2.4	4.1
093 CHR CH (DISC).	3	495	589	2.9	4.8
097 CHR CHS&CHS CR	3	150	186*	0.9	1.5
127 CH GOD (CLEVE)	1	84	104*	0.5	0.9
151 L-D SAINTS....	1	NA	175	0.9	1.4
165 CH OF NAZARENE	3	81	182	0.9	1.5
167 CHS OF CHRIST.	13	615	783	3.8	6.4
185 CUMBER PRESB..	1	48	81	0.4	0.7
197 EVAN CH OF NA.	1	5	5	–	–
215 EVAN METH CH.	1	129	160*	0.8	1.3
226 FRIENDS-USA...	1	19	24*	0.1	0.2
283 LUTH--MO SYNOD	3	395	499	2.4	4.1
285 MENNONITE CH..	1	80	99*	0.5	0.8
323 OLD ORD AMISH.	6	780	965*	4.7	7.9
413 S.D.A........	3	241	298*	1.5	2.4
419 SO BAPT CONV..	24	4 226	5 229*	25.6	42.9
449 UN METHODIST..	12	1 533	1 897*	9.3	15.5
WORTH	15	1 764	2 357*	78.4	100.0
053 ASSEMB OF GOD.	1	25	33	1.1	1.4
093 CHR CH (DISC).	2	258	576	19.1	24.4
097 CHR CHS&CHS CR	2	200	236*	7.8	10.0
167 CHS OF CHRIST.	1	25	32	1.1	1.4
419 SO BAPT CONV..	5	757	892*	29.7	37.8
449 UN METHODIST..	4	499	588*	19.5	24.9
WRIGHT	53	6 261	8 650*	53.4	100.0
053 ASSEMB OF GOD.	7	328	619	3.8	7.2
081 CATHOLIC......	2	NA	336	2.1	3.9
093 CHR CH (DISC).	2	145	232	1.4	2.7
097 CHR CHS&CHS CR	2	269	326*	2.0	3.8
123 CH GOD (ANDER)	2	83	249	1.5	2.9
157 CH OF BRETHREN	2	78	95*	0.6	1.1
165 CH OF NAZARENE	3	211	469	2.9	5.4
167 CHS OF CHRIST.	7	451	574	3.5	6.6
185 CUMBER PRESB..	1	39	105	0.6	1.2
193 EPISCOPAL.....	1	32	35	0.2	0.4
413 S.D.A........	2	71	86*	0.5	1.0
419 SO BAPT CONV..	18	3 978	4 825*	29.8	55.8
449 UN METHODIST..	4	576	699*	4.3	8.1

MONTANA

County and Denomination	Number of churches	Communicant, confirmed, full members	Total adherents		
			Number	Percent of total population	Percent of total adherents
THE STATE.....	1 273	131 981	348 301*	44.3	100.0
BEAVERHEAD	14	1 070	3 480*	42.5	100.0
017 AMER BAPT ASSN	1	100	100	1.2	2.9
029 AMER LUTH CH..	1	199	235	2.9	6.8
053 ASSEMB OF GOD.	1	79	82	1.0	2.4
081 CATHOLIC......	1	NA	1 200	14.7	34.5
151 L-D SAINTS....	3	NA	958	11.7	27.5
167 CHS OF CHRIST.	1	28	36	0.4	1.0
193 EPISCOPAL.....	1	101	183	2.2	5.3
413 S.D.A........	1	25	30*	0.4	0.9
419 SO BAPT CONV..	1	21	26*	0.3	0.7
449 UN METHODIST..	1	137	167*	2.0	4.8
453 UN PRES CH USA	2	380	463*	5.7	13.3
BIG HORN	30	1 502	4 496*	40.5	100.0
019 AMER BAPT USA.	6	409	522*	4.7	11.6
029 AMER LUTH CH..	1	132	181	1.6	4.0
053 ASSEMB OF GOD.	1	30	45	0.4	1.0
081 CATHOLIC......	5	NA	1 586	14.3	35.3
123 CH GOD (ANDER)	1	40	120	1.1	2.7
151 L-D SAINTS....	5	NA	644	5.8	14.3
193 EPISCOPAL.....	1	32	130	1.2	2.9
263 INT FOURS♀ GOS	1	104	133*	1.2	3.0
283 LUTH--MO SYNOD	2	131	205	1.8	4.6
287 MENN GEN CONF.	1	51	101	0.9	2.2
329 OPEN BIBLE STD	1	120	250	2.3	5.6
413 S.D.A........	1	17	22*	0.2	0.5
419 SO BAPT CONV..	1	25	32*	0.3	0.7
443 UN C OF CHRIST	2	286	365*	3.3	8.1
449 UN METHODIST..	1	125	160*	1.4	3.6

NA— Not applicable   *Total adherents estimated from known number of communicant, confirmed, full members.   —Represents a percent less than 0.1.   Percentages may not total due to rounding.

MONTANA

Table 4. Churches and Church Membership by County and Denomination: 1980

County and Denomination	Number of churches	Communicant, confirmed, full members	Total adherents Number	Percent of total population	Percent of total adherents
BLAINE	26	1 385	4 146*	59.2	100.0
029 AMER LUTH CH..	4	560	748	10.7	18.0
053 ASSEMB OF GOD.	4	172	308	4.4	7.4
081 CATHOLIC......	6	NA	2 010	28.7	48.5
089 CHR & MISS AL.	1	4	4	0.1	0.1
097 CHR CHS&CHS CR	1	86	108*	1.5	2.6
151 L-D SAINTS....	2	NA	240	3.4	5.8
165 CH OF NAZARENE	1	13	32	0.5	0.8
167 CHS OF CHRIST.	1	15	19	0.3	0.5
197 EVAN CH OF NA.	1	29	29	0.4	0.7
283 LUTH--MO SYNOD	1	111	151	2.2	3.6
449 UN METHODIST..	2	225	283*	4.0	6.8
453 UN PRES CH USA	2	170	214*	3.1	5.2
BROADWATER	8	381	1 269*	38.8	100.0
029 AMER LUTH CH..	1	84	130	4.0	10.2
081 CATHOLIC......	1	NA	445	13.6	35.1
089 CHR & MISS AL.	1	22	71	2.2	5.6
151 L-D SAINTS....	1	NA	284	8.7	22.4
167 CHS OF CHRIST.	1	10	13	0.4	1.0
193 EPISCOPAL.....	1	44	53	1.6	4.2
419 SO BAPT CONV..	1	80	99*	3.0	7.8
449 UN METHODIST..	1	141	174*	5.3	13.7
CARBON	27	1 235	2 745*	33.9	100.0
029 AMER LUTH CH..	2	151	192	2.4	7.0
053 ASSEMB OF GOD.	1	?	?	?	?
081 CATHOLIC......	5	NA	950	11.7	34.6
089 CHR & MISS AL.	1	30	70	0.9	2.6
093 CHR CH (DISC).	1	59	99	1.2	3.6
151 L-D SAINTS....	2	NA	204	2.5	7.4
167 CHS OF CHRIST.	1	28	36	0.4	1.3
193 EPISCOPAL.....	3	72	109	1.3	4.0
283 LUTH--MO SYNOD	2	256	314*	3.9	11.4
413 S.D.A.........	1	61	74*	0.9	2.7
419 SO BAPT CONV..	1	28	34*	0.4	1.2
443 UN C OF CHRIST	1	225	271*	3.3	9.9
449 UN METHODIST..	6	325	392*	4.8	14.3
CARTER	8	167	404*	22.5	100.0
029 AMER LUTH CH..	1	35	45	2.5	11.1
081 CATHOLIC......	2	NA	184	10.2	45.5
175 CONGR CHR CHS.	1	70	84*	4.7	20.8
329 OPEN BIBLE STD	1	10	30	1.7	7.4
413 S.D.A.........	1	13	16*	0.9	4.0
443 UN C OF CHRIST	1	25	30*	1.7	7.4
469 WELS.........	1	14	15	0.8	3.7
CASCADE	70	11 921	34 888*	43.2	100.0
017 AMER BAPT ASSN	1	75	75	0.1	0.2
019 AMER BAPT USA.	1	277	337*	0.4	1.0
029 AMER LUTH CH..	3	2 863	4 022	5.0	11.5
053 ASSEMB OF GOD.	2	191	358	0.4	1.0
057 BAPT GEN CONF.	1	192	234*	0.3	0.7
081 CATHOLIC......	14	NA	16 005	19.8	45.9
089 CHR & MISS AL.	2	85	260	0.3	0.7
093 CHR CH (DISC).	1	216	280	0.3	0.8
097 CHR CHS&CHS CR	1	20	24*	—	0.1
123 CH GOD (ANDER)	1	60	180	0.2	0.5
127 CH GOD (CLEVE)	1	99	121*	0.1	0.3
151 L-D SAINTS....	7	NA	2 630	3.3	7.5
163 CH OF LUTH BR.	1	15	30	—	0.1
165 CH OF NAZARENE	1	181	383	0.5	1.1
167 CHS OF CHRIST.	1	150	180	0.2	0.5
181 CONSRV CONGR..	1	27	33*	—	0.1
193 EPISCOPAL.....	2	534	709	0.9	2.0
197 EVAN CH OF NA.	1	198	198	0.2	0.6
263 INT FOURSQ GOS	1	?	?	?	?
281 LUTH CH AMER..	3	828	1 100	1.4	3.2
283 LUTH--MO SYNOD	3	884	1 184	1.5	3.4
371 REF CH IN AM..	1	97	217	0.3	0.6
403 SALVATION ARMY	1	99	419	0.5	1.2
413 S.D.A.........	1	191	232*	0.3	0.7
419 SO BAPT CONV..	4	1 122	1 366*	1.7	3.9
435 UNITARIAN-UNIV	1	20	24*	—	0.1
443 UN C OF CHRIST	1	430	523*	0.6	1.5
449 UN METHODIST..	9	1 627	1 980*	2.5	5.7
453 UN PRES CH USA	2	1 373	1 671*	2.1	4.8
469 WELS.........	1	67	113	0.1	0.3
CHOUTEAU	17	1 769	5 371*	88.2	100.0
029 AMER LUTH CH..	1	240	322	5.3	6.0
081 CATHOLIC......	5	NA	2 823	46.3	52.6
093 CHR CH (DISC).	1	275	423	6.9	7.9
097 CHR CHS&CHS CR	1	321	392*	6.4	7.3
123 CH GOD (ANDER)	1	70	210	3.4	3.9
151 L-D SAINTS....	1	NA	138	2.3	2.6
193 EPISCOPAL.....	1	37	60	1.0	1.1
283 LUTH--MO SYNOD	1	98	114	1.9	2.1
449 UN METHODIST..	5	728	889*	14.6	16.6
CUSTER	15	2 780	7 686*	58.6	100.0
019 AMER BAPT USA.	1	313	381*	2.9	5.0
029 AMER LUTH CH..	1	562	794	6.1	10.3
053 ASSEMB OF GOD.	1	125	200	1.5	2.6
081 CATHOLIC......	1	NA	3 750	28.6	48.8
093 CHR CH (DISC).	1	54	85	0.6	1.1
151 L-D SAINTS....	1	NA	203	1.5	2.6
167 CHS OF CHRIST.	1	26	39	0.3	0.5
193 EPISCOPAL.....	1	117	255	1.9	3.3
263 INT FOURSQ GOS	1	96	117*	0.9	1.5
283 LUTH--MO SYNOD	1	449	597	4.6	7.8
413 S.D.A.........	1	91	111*	0.8	1.4
419 SO BAPT CONV..	1	161	196*	1.5	2.6
443 UN C OF CHRIST	1	53	65*	0.5	0.8
449 UN METHODIST..	1	379	462*	3.5	6.0
453 UN PRES CH USA	1	354	431*	3.3	5.6
DANIELS	11	1 161	2 412*	85.1	100.0
029 AMER LUTH CH..	4	934	1 295	45.7	53.7
053 ASSEMB OF GOD.	1	39	55	1.9	2.3
081 CATHOLIC......	2	NA	822	29.0	34.1
089 CHR & MISS AL.	1	11	32	1.1	1.3
193 EPISCOPAL.....	1	14	11	0.4	0.5
449 UN METHODIST..	2	163	197*	6.9	8.2
DAWSON	24	2 757	8 293*	70.2	100.0
029 AMER LUTH CH..	3	782	1 167	9.9	14.1
053 ASSEMB OF GOD.	1	125	150	1.3	1.8
081 CATHOLIC......	1	NA	4 200	35.6	50.6
089 CHR & MISS AL.	1	119	263	2.2	3.2
151 L-D SAINTS....	1	NA	263	2.2	3.2
167 CHS OF CHRIST.	1	40	60	0.5	0.7
193 EPISCOPAL.....	1	28	51	0.4	0.6
197 EVAN CH OF NA.	1	122	122	1.0	1.5
283 LUTH--MO SYNOD	1	409	614	5.2	7.4
285 MENNONITE CH..	2	88	109*	0.9	1.3
287 MENN GEN CONF.	2	169	203	1.7	2.4
413 S.D.A.........	1	34	42*	0.4	0.5
419 SO BAPT CONV..	1	174	216*	1.8	2.6
443 UN C OF CHRIST	2	263	326*	2.8	3.9
449 UN METHODIST..	2	380	471*	4.0	5.7
469 WELS.........	1	24	36	0.3	0.4
DEER LODGE	13	1 291	4 801*	38.4	100.0
029 AMER LUTH CH..	1	138	199	1.6	4.1
053 ASSEMB OF GOD.	1	74	250	2.0	5.2
057 BAPT GEN CONF.	1	163	196*	1.6	4.1
081 CATHOLIC......	1	NA	2 119	16.9	44.1
093 CHR CH (DISC).	1	21	21	0.2	0.4
151 L-D SAINTS....	2	NA	888	7.1	18.5
167 CHS OF CHRIST.	1	20	25	0.2	0.5
281 LUTH CH AMER..	1	286	390	3.1	8.1
283 LUTH--MO SYNOD	1	56	71	0.6	1.5
419 SO BAPT CONV..	1	140	169*	1.4	3.5
449 UN METHODIST..	1	162	195*	1.6	4.1
453 UN PRES CH USA	1	231	278*	2.2	5.8
FALLON	10	953	2 298*	61.1	100.0
029 AMER LUTH CH..	2	443	734	19.5	31.9
053 ASSEMB OF GOD.	1	95	180	4.8	7.8
081 CATHOLIC......	2	NA	800	21.3	34.8
151 L-D SAINTS....	1	NA	69	1.8	3.0
203 EVAN FREE CH..	1	35	43*	1.1	1.9
313 N AM BAPT CONF	1	116	144*	3.8	6.3
419 SO BAPT CONV..	1	139	173*	4.6	7.5
443 UN C OF CHRIST	1	125	155*	4.1	6.7
FERGUS	32	2 593	6 195*	47.4	100.0
029 AMER LUTH CH..	3	566	739	5.7	11.9
053 ASSEMB OF GOD.	1	89	200	1.5	3.2
081 CATHOLIC......	8	NA	2 275	17.4	36.7
089 CHR & MISS AL.	1	30	145	1.1	2.3
097 CHR CHS&CHS CR	1	175	211*	1.6	3.4
127 CH GOD (CLEVE)	1	5	6*	—	0.1
151 L-D SAINTS....	1	NA	344	2.6	5.6
165 CH OF NAZARENE	1	29	49	0.4	0.8
167 CHS OF CHRIST.	1	36	45	0.3	0.7
179 CONSRV BAPT...	1	83	100*	0.8	1.6
193 EPISCOPAL.....	1	97	300	2.3	4.8
283 LUTH--MO SYNOD	2	236	276	2.1	4.5
413 S.D.A.........	1	65	78*	0.6	1.3
419 SO BAPT CONV..	1	117	141*	1.1	2.3
449 UN METHODIST..	5	651	786*	6.0	12.7
453 UN PRES CH USA	3	414	500*	3.8	8.1
FLATHEAD	70	8 954	20 927*	40.3	100.0
017 AMER BAPT ASSN	2	150	150	0.3	0.7
019 AMER BAPT USA.	1	177	217*	0.4	1.0
029 AMER LUTH CH..	7	2 388	3 397	6.5	16.2
053 ASSEMB OF GOD.	6	639	1 290	2.5	6.2
057 BAPT GEN CONF.	1	39	48*	0.1	0.2
081 CATHOLIC......	6	NA	6 054	11.6	28.9
089 CHR & MISS AL.	4	369	661	1.3	3.2
093 CHR CH (DISC).	3	356	572	1.1	2.7
097 CHR CHS&CHS CR	2	93	114*	0.2	0.5
123 CH GOD (ANDER)	1	150	450	0.9	2.2
127 CH GOD (CLEVE)	1	14	17*	—	0.1
151 L-D SAINTS....	7	NA	1 935	3.7	9.2
165 CH OF NAZARENE	2	345	601	1.2	2.9
167 CHS OF CHRIST.	3	120	153	0.3	0.7
193 EPISCOPAL.....	3	361	485	0.9	2.3
197 EVAN CH OF NA.	1	9	9	—	—
220 FREE LUTHERAN.	2	170	250	0.5	1.2
283 LUTH--MO SYNOD	3	852	1 094	2.1	5.2
285 MENNONITE CH..	1	95	117*	0.2	0.6
335 ORTH PRESB CH.	1	12	15*	—	0.1

NA—Not applicable *Total adherents estimated from known number of communicant, confirmed, full members. —Represents a percent less than 0.1. Percentages may not total due to rounding.

Table 4. Churches and Church Membership by County and Denomination: 1980

County and Denomination	Number of churches	Communicant, confirmed, full members	Total adherents		
			Number	Percent of total population	Percent of total adherents
403 SALVATION ARMY	1	83	190	0.4	0.9
413 S.D.A.........	1	182	223*	0.4	1.1
419 SO BAPT CONV..	2	398	489*	0.9	2.3
435 UNITARIAN-UNIV	1	54	66*	0.1	0.3
449 UN METHODIST..	6	1 213	1 489*	2.9	7.1
453 UN PRES CH USA	2	685	841*	1.6	4.0
GALLATIN	55	7 563	16 618*	38.8	100.0
017 AMER BAPT ASSN	1	50	50	0.1	0.3
019 AMER BAPT USA.	2	165	195*	0.5	1.2
029 AMER LUTH CH..	1	708	1 165	2.7	7.0
053 ASSEMB OF GOD.	3	539	1 051	2.5	6.3
081 CATHOLIC......	5	NA	4 770	11.1	28.7
089 CHR & MISS AL.	1	80	105	0.2	0.6
093 CHR CH (DISC).	1	266	496	1.2	3.0
097 CHR CHS&CHS CR	1	60	71*	0.2	0.4
105 CHRISTIAN REF.	4	951	1 625	3.8	9.8
127 CH GOD (CLEVE)	2	84	99*	0.2	0.6
151 L-D SAINTS....	5	NA	1 130	2.6	6.8
165 CH OF NAZARENE	1	63	146	0.3	0.9
167 CHS OF CHRIST.	3	281	316	0.7	1.9
193 EPISCOPAL.....	2	263	417	1.0	2.5
197 EVAN CH OF NA.	1	16	16	–	0.1
263 INT FOURSQ GOS	1	?	?	?	?
281 LUTH CH AMER..	1	260	402	0.9	2.4
283 LUTH--MO SYNOD	2	531	699	1.6	4.2
403 SALVATION ARMY	1	44	68	0.2	0.4
413 S.D.A.........	2	567	671*	1.6	4.0
419 SO BAPT CONV..	4	450	532*	1.2	3.2
435 UNITARIAN-UNIV	1	24	28*	0.1	0.2
443 UN C OF CHRIST	1	145	172*	0.4	1.0
449 UN METHODIST..	3	1 012	1 197*	2.8	7.2
453 UN PRES CH USA	5	970	1 148*	2.7	6.9
469 WELS..........	1	34	49	0.1	0.3
GARFIELD	7	226	630*	38.0	100.0
029 AMER LUTH CH..	1	69	96	5.8	15.2
053 ASSEMB OF GOD.	1	21	45	2.7	7.1
081 CATHOLIC......	1	NA	260	15.7	41.3
151 L-D SAINTS....	1	NA	64	3.9	10.2
353 CHR BRETHREN..	1	10	10	0.6	1.6
413 S.D.A.........	1	43	53*	3.2	8.4
453 UN PRES CH USA	1	83	102*	6.2	16.2
GLACIER	11	1 013	6 738*	63.4	100.0
029 AMER LUTH CH..	1	436	623	5.9	9.2
053 ASSEMB OF GOD.	1	63	137	1.3	2.0
081 CATHOLIC......	5	NA	5 021	47.2	74.5
151 L-D SAINTS....	1	NA	305	2.9	4.5
449 UN METHODIST..	2	112	142*	1.3	2.1
453 UN PRES CH USA	1	402	510*	4.8	7.6
GOLDEN VALLEY	9	185	422*	41.1	100.0
029 AMER LUTH CH..	2	47	74	7.2	17.5
053 ASSEMB OF GOD.	1	21	40	3.9	9.5
081 CATHOLIC......	3	NA	160	15.6	37.9
449 UN METHODIST..	2	92	113*	11.0	26.8
469 WELS..........	1	25	35	3.4	8.3
GRANITE	8	105	901*	33.4	100.0
081 CATHOLIC......	3	NA	493	18.3	54.7
151 L-D SAINTS....	2	NA	280	10.4	31.1
449 UN METHODIST..	2	73	89*	3.3	9.9
453 UN PRES CH USA	1	32	39*	1.4	4.3
HILL	32	4 036	8 301*	46.2	100.0
019 AMER BAPT USA.	2	84	103*	0.6	1.2
029 AMER LUTH CH..	7	1 661	2 366	13.2	28.5
053 ASSEMB OF GOD.	2	152	280	1.6	3.4
081 CATHOLIC......	4	NA	2 212	12.3	26.6
089 CHR & MISS AL.	1	21	51	0.3	0.6
097 CHR CHS&CHS CR	1	350	431*	2.4	5.2
151 L-D SAINTS....	1	NA	287	1.6	3.5
157 CH OF BRETHREN	1	27	33*	0.2	0.4
165 CH OF NAZARENE	1	10	17	0.1	0.2
167 CHS OF CHRIST.	1	39	50	0.3	0.6
193 EPISCOPAL.....	1	91	310	1.7	3.7
197 EVAN CH OF NA.	1	29	29	0.2	0.3
281 LUTH CH AMER..	1	181	368	2.0	4.4
283 LUTH--MO SYNOD	1	249	332	1.8	4.0
403 SALVATION ARMY	1	32	66	0.4	0.8
413 S.D.A.........	1	81	100*	0.6	1.2
419 SO BAPT CONV..	1	280	345*	1.9	4.2
449 UN METHODIST..	3	574	706*	3.9	8.5
453 UN PRES CH USA	1	175	215*	1.2	2.6
JEFFERSON	17	980	2 242*	31.9	100.0
081 CATHOLIC......	5	NA	694	9.9	31.0
093 CHR CH (DISC).	1	34	47	0.7	2.1
151 L-D SAINTS....	2	NA	285	4.1	12.7
165 CH OF NAZARENE	1	13	30	0.4	1.3
283 LUTH--MO SYNOD	2	156	224	3.2	10.0
413 S.D.A.........	1	17	21*	0.3	0.9
419 SO BAPT CONV..	1	81	100*	1.4	4.5
449 UN METHODIST..	3	180	223*	3.2	9.9
453 UN PRES CH USA	1	499	618*	8.8	27.6
JUDITH BASIN	6	306	747*	28.2	100.0

County and Denomination	Number of churches	Communicant, confirmed, full members	Total adherents		
			Number	Percent of total population	Percent of total adherents
081 CATHOLIC......	3	NA	375	14.2	50.2
449 UN METHODIST..	1	149	181*	6.8	24.2
453 UN PRES CH USA	2	157	191*	7.2	25.6
LAKE	37	2 739	7 716*	40.5	100.0
029 AMER LUTH CH..	2	585	825	4.3	10.7
053 ASSEMB OF GOD.	1	35	80	0.4	1.0
081 CATHOLIC......	6	NA	2 900	15.2	37.6
089 CHR & MISS AL.	3	41	179	0.9	2.3
093 CHR CH (DISC).	1	85	110	0.6	1.4
097 CHR CHS&CHS CR	3	275	341*	1.8	4.4
151 L-D SAINTS....	3	NA	1 057	5.5	13.7
165 CH OF NAZARENE	1	45	116	0.6	1.5
167 CHS OF CHRIST.	2	70	89	0.5	1.2
193 EPISCOPAL.....	2	140	189	1.0	2.4
283 LUTH--MO SYNOD	3	424	542	2.8	7.0
335 ORTH PRESB CH.	1	30	37*	0.2	0.5
413 S.D.A.........	1	117	145*	0.8	1.9
419 SO BAPT CONV..	1	41	51*	0.3	0.7
449 UN METHODIST..	5	545	676*	3.5	8.8
453 UN PRES CH USA	2	306	379*	2.0	4.9
LEWIS AND CLARK	39	6 943	19 662*	45.7	100.0
017 AMER BAPT ASSN	1	25	25	0.1	0.1
019 AMER BAPT USA.	1	210	256*	0.6	1.3
029 AMER LUTH CH..	1	612	902	2.1	4.6
053 ASSEMB OF GOD.	1	354	700	1.6	3.6
081 CATHOLIC......	8	NA	8 142	18.9	41.4
089 CHR & MISS AL.	1	54	114	0.3	0.6
093 CHR CH (DISC).	1	170	313	0.7	1.6
105 CHRISTIAN REF.	1	18	25	0.1	0.1
127 CH GOD (CLEVE)	1	60	73*	0.2	0.4
151 L-D SAINTS....	4	NA	1 579	3.7	8.0
165 CH OF NAZARENE	1	52	121	0.3	0.6
167 CHS OF CHRIST.	1	95	160	0.4	0.8
193 EPISCOPAL.....	2	554	948	2.2	4.8
201 EVAN COV CH AM	1	93	113*	0.3	0.6
263 INT FOURSQ GOS	1	125	152*	0.4	0.8
281 LUTH CH AMER..	1	869	1 372	3.2	7.0
283 LUTH--MO SYNOD	1	695	1 004	2.3	5.1
353 CHR BRETHREN..	1	30	50	0.1	0.3
403 SALVATION ARMY	1	57	112	0.3	0.6
413 S.D.A.........	1	79	96*	0.2	0.5
419 SO BAPT CONV..	2	349	426*	1.0	2.2
443 UN C OF CHRIST	1	524	639*	1.5	3.2
449 UN METHODIST..	4	1 302	1 588*	3.7	8.1
453 UN PRES CH USA	1	616	752*	1.7	3.8
LIBERTY	9	768	1 425*	61.2	100.0
029 AMER LUTH CH..	4	564	701	30.1	49.2
053 ASSEMB OF GOD.	1	22	29	1.2	2.0
081 CATHOLIC......	1	NA	433	18.6	30.4
089 CHR & MISS AL.	1	22	67	2.9	4.7
449 UN METHODIST..	1	129	157*	6.7	11.0
453 UN PRES CH USA	1	31	38*	1.6	2.7
LINCOLN	29	2 638	5 783*	32.6	100.0
019 AMER BAPT USA.	1	200	251*	1.4	4.3
029 AMER LUTH CH..	1	433	622	3.5	10.8
053 ASSEMB OF GOD.	3	204	404	2.3	7.0
081 CATHOLIC......	3	NA	1 230	6.9	21.3
089 CHR & MISS AL.	1	34	53	0.3	0.9
097 CHR CHS&CHS CR	1	250	314*	1.8	5.4
123 CH GOD (ANDER)	2	70	210	1.2	3.6
151 L-D SAINTS....	3	NA	604	3.4	10.4
165 CH OF NAZARENE	1	88	213	1.2	3.7
167 CHS OF CHRIST.	1	54	56	0.3	1.0
193 EPISCOPAL.....	2	76	186	1.0	3.2
203 EVAN FREE CH..	1	23	29*	0.2	0.5
283 LUTH--MO SYNOD	2	501	725	4.1	12.5
413 S.D.A.........	3	116	146*	0.8	2.5
419 SO BAPT CONV..	1	179	225*	1.3	3.9
449 UN METHODIST..	2	286	359*	2.0	6.2
453 UN PRES CH USA	1	124	156*	0.9	2.7
MC CONE	13	624	1 342*	49.7	100.0
019 AMER BAPT USA.	1	44	55*	2.0	4.1
029 AMER LUTH CH..	1	307	406	15.0	30.3
053 ASSEMB OF GOD.	1	39	90	3.3	6.7
081 CATHOLIC......	4	NA	500	18.5	37.3
151 L-D SAINTS....	1	NA	?	?	?
197 EVAN CH OF NA.	1	70	70	2.6	5.2
419 SO BAPT CONV..	1	89	112*	4.1	8.3
443 UN C OF CHRIST	2	22	28*	1.0	2.1
469 WELS..........	1	53	81	3.0	6.0
MADISON	13	356	1 128*	20.7	100.0
053 ASSEMB OF GOD.	1	46	99	1.8	8.8
081 CATHOLIC......	4	NA	400	7.3	35.5
151 L-D SAINTS....	1	NA	211	3.9	18.7
167 CHS OF CHRIST.	1	8	10	0.2	0.9
193 EPISCOPAL.....	3	106	173	3.2	15.3
449 UN METHODIST..	2	162	194*	3.6	17.2
453 UN PRES CH USA	1	34	41*	0.8	3.6
MEAGHER	8	243	524*	24.3	100.0
029 AMER LUTH CH..	2	118	197	9.1	37.6
053 ASSEMB OF GOD.	1	11	22	1.0	4.2

NA—Not applicable   *Total adherents estimated from known number of communicant, confirmed, full members.   —Represents a percent less than 0.1.   Percentages may not total due to rounding.

Table 4. Churches and Church Membership by County and Denomination: 1980

County and Denomination	Number of churches	Communicant, confirmed, full members	Total adherents Number	Total adherents Percent of total population	Total adherents Percent of total adherents
081 CATHOLIC......	1	NA	120	5.6	22.9
089 CHR & MISS AL.	1	37	77	3.6	14.7
193 EPISCOPAL.....	1	7	24	1.1	4.6
413 S.D.A.........	1	14	17*	0.8	3.2
453 UN PRES CH USA	1	56	67*	3.1	12.8
MINERAL	7	268	513*	14.0	100.0
053 ASSEMB OF GOD.	1	38	100	2.7	19.5
151 L-D SAINTS....	1	NA	113	3.1	22.0
167 CHS OF CHRIST.	1	10	13	0.4	2.5
283 LUTH--MO SYNOD	1	62	92	2.5	17.9
449 UN METHODIST..	3	158	195*	5.3	38.0
MISSOULA	54	8 917	23 609*	31.1	100.0
019 AMER BAPT USA.	1	250	300*	0.4	1.3
029 AMER LUTH CH..	4	1 709	2 592	3.4	11.0
053 ASSEMB OF GOD.	2	551	1 186	1.6	5.0
081 CATHOLIC......	8	NA	8 527	11.2	36.1
089 CHR & MISS AL.	1	89	259	0.3	1.1
093 CHR CH (DISC).	1	230	345	0.5	1.5
097 CHR CHS&CHS CR	3	137	164*	0.2	0.7
127 CH GOD (CLEVE)	1	45	54*	0.1	0.2
151 L-D SAINTS....	8	NA	2 486	3.3	10.5
164 CH LUTH CONF..	1	23	33	-	0.1
165 CH OF NAZARENE	1	84	152	0.2	0.6
167 CHS OF CHRIST.	1	150	191	0.3	0.8
193 EPISCOPAL.....	1	470	838	1.1	3.5
197 EVAN CH OF NA.	1	106	106	0.1	0.4
201 EVAN COV CH AM	1	149	179*	0.2	0.8
263 INT FOURSQ GOS	1	74	89*	0.1	0.4
281 LUTH CH AMER.	2	654	853	1.1	3.6
283 LUTH--MO SYNOD	4	999	1 391	1.8	5.9
290 METRO COMM CHS	0	10	20	-	0.1
313 N AM BAPT CONF	1	288	346*	0.5	1.5
353 CHR BRETHREN..	1	20	40	0.1	0.2
403 SALVATION ARMY	1	127	146	0.2	0.6
413 S.D.A.........	1	247	297*	0.4	1.3
419 SO BAPT CONV..	1	324	389*	0.5	1.6
435 UNITARIAN-UNIV	1	30	36*	-	0.2
443 UN C OF CHRIST	1	413	496*	0.7	2.1
449 UN METHODIST..	2	1 040	1 249*	1.6	5.3
453 UN PRES CH USA	2	669	803*	1.1	3.4
469 WELS..........	1	29	42	0.1	0.2
MUSSELSHELL	16	731	1 532*	34.6	100.0
019 AMER BAPT USA.	1	113	139*	3.1	9.1
029 AMER LUTH CH..	1	123	159	3.6	10.4
053 ASSEMB OF GOD.	1	51	100	2.3	6.5
081 CATHOLIC......	3	NA	460	10.4	30.0
151 L-D SAINTS....	1	NA	95	2.1	6.2
167 CHS OF CHRIST.	1	9	11	0.2	0.7
175 CONGR CHR CHS	2	51	63*	1.4	4.1
193 EPISCOPAL.....	1	28	42	0.9	2.7
203 EVAN FREE CH..	1	19	23*	0.5	1.5
283 LUTH--MO SYNOD	1	81	101	2.3	6.6
413 S.D.A.........	1	18	22*	0.5	1.4
449 UN METHODIST..	1	193	237*	5.4	15.5
469 WELS..........	1	45	80	1.8	5.2
PARK	24	2 607	4 145*	32.7	100.0
019 AMER BAPT USA.	1	341	411*	3.2	9.9
029 AMER LUTH CH..	2	606	798	6.3	19.3
053 ASSEMB OF GOD.	1	56	146	1.2	3.5
081 CATHOLIC......	4	NA	540	4.3	13.0
127 CH GOD (CLEVE)	1	27	33*	0.3	0.8
151 L-D SAINTS....	1	NA	265	2.1	6.4
165 CH OF NAZARENE	1	39	62	0.5	1.5
167 CHS OF CHRIST.	1	50	55	0.4	1.3
175 CONGR CHR CHS	1	54	65*	0.5	1.6
193 EPISCOPAL.....	2	215	276	2.2	6.7
281 LUTH CH AMER.	1	142	182	1.4	4.4
413 S.D.A.........	1	65	78*	0.6	1.9
419 SO BAPT CONV..	1	43	52*	0.4	1.3
449 UN METHODIST..	5	885	1 066*	8.4	25.7
469 WELS..........	1	84	116	0.9	2.8
PETROLEUM	4	84	186*	28.4	100.0
081 CATHOLIC......	2	NA	50	7.6	26.9
449 UN METHODIST..	1	41	51*	7.8	27.4
469 WELS..........	1	43	85	13.0	45.7
PHILLIPS	20	1 222	2 833*	52.8	100.0
029 AMER LUTH CH..	5	744	1 022	19.0	36.1
053 ASSEMB OF GOD.	2	92	178	3.3	6.3
081 CATHOLIC......	4	NA	1 025	19.1	36.2
097 CHR CHS&CHS CR	2	70	86*	1.6	3.0
151 L-D SAINTS....	1	NA	113	2.1	4.0
163 CH OF LUTH BR.	1	33	66	1.2	2.3
167 CHS OF CHRIST.	1	9	10	0.2	0.4
193 EPISCOPAL.....	1	27	28	0.5	1.0
419 SO BAPT CONV..	1	20	25*	0.5	0.9
443 UN C OF CHRIST	1	154	190*	3.5	6.7
449 UN METHODIST..	1	73	90*	1.7	3.2
PONDERA	13	1 598	3 647*	54.2	100.0
029 AMER LUTH CH..	3	837	1 095	16.3	30.0
053 ASSEMB OF GOD.	1	39	110	1.6	3.0
081 CATHOLIC......	2	NA	1 318	19.6	36.1

County and Denomination	Number of churches	Communicant, confirmed, full members	Total adherents Number	Total adherents Percent of total population	Total adherents Percent of total adherents
093 CHR CH (DISC).	1	88	121	1.8	3.3
105 CHRISTIAN REF.	1	64	108	1.6	3.0
151 L-D SAINTS....	1	NA	187	2.8	5.1
419 SO BAPT CONV..	1	99	123*	1.8	3.4
449 UN METHODIST..	2	174	216*	3.2	5.9
453 UN PRES CH USA	1	297	369*	5.5	10.1
POWDER RIVER	9	290	787*	31.2	100.0
029 AMER LUTH CH..	1	88	138	5.5	17.5
053 ASSEMB OF GOD.	1	14	23	0.9	2.9
081 CATHOLIC......	3	NA	350	13.9	44.5
089 CHR & MISS AL.	1	0	43	1.7	5.5
179 CONSRV BAPT...	1	83	103*	4.1	13.1
443 UN C OF CHRIST	2	105	130*	5.2	16.5
POWELL	12	724	2 400*	34.5	100.0
053 ASSEMB OF GOD.	1	76	150	2.2	6.3
081 CATHOLIC......	3	NA	1 421	20.4	59.2
093 CHR CH (DISC).	1	87	107	1.5	4.5
167 CHS OF CHRIST.	1	20	25	0.4	1.0
193 EPISCOPAL.....	2	87	114	1.6	4.7
226 FRIENDS-USA...	1	11	13*	0.2	0.5
283 LUTH--MO SYNOD	1	191	267	3.8	11.1
419 SO BAPT CONV..	1	95	114*	1.6	4.7
453 UN PRES CH USA	1	157	189*	2.7	7.9
PRAIRIE	6	503	950*	51.7	100.0
029 AMER LUTH CH..	1	87	117	6.4	12.3
081 CATHOLIC......	1	NA	300	16.3	31.6
197 EVAN CH OF NA.	1	97	97	5.3	10.2
283 LUTH--MO SYNOD	1	159	228	12.4	24.0
453 UN PRES CH USA	1	104	127*	6.9	13.4
469 WELS..........	1	56	81	4.4	8.5
RAVALLI	34	2 659	6 760*	30.1	100.0
019 AMER BAPT USA.	3	189	231*	1.0	3.4
029 AMER LUTH CH..	1	314	402	1.8	5.9
053 ASSEMB OF GOD.	2	277	421	1.9	6.2
081 CATHOLIC......	3	NA	1 775	7.9	26.3
093 CHR CH (DISC).	1	67	110	0.5	1.6
127 CH GOD (CLEVE)	1	24	29*	0.1	0.4
151 L-D SAINTS....	5	NA	1 520	6.8	22.5
165 CH OF NAZARENE	1	3	0	-	-
167 CHS OF CHRIST.	2	50	64	0.3	0.9
193 EPISCOPAL.....	1	101	116	0.5	1.7
203 EVAN FREE CH..	1	23	28*	0.1	0.4
283 LUTH--MO SYNOD	2	391	569	2.5	8.4
353 CHR BRETHREN..	2	50	65	0.3	1.0
413 S.D.A.........	3	257	314*	1.4	4.6
419 SO BAPT CONV..	1	215	263*	1.2	3.9
449 UN METHODIST..	3	360	440*	2.0	6.5
453 UN PRES CH USA	2	338	413*	1.8	6.1
RICHLAND	29	3 364	7 059*	57.7	100.0
029 AMER LUTH CH..	5	1 449	2 224	18.2	31.5
053 ASSEMB OF GOD.	1	188	300	2.5	4.2
081 CATHOLIC......	5	NA	1 978	16.2	28.0
089 CHR & MISS AL.	4	133	289	2.4	4.1
127 CH GOD (CLEVE)	1	?	?	?	?
151 L-D SAINTS....	1	NA	181	1.5	2.6
163 CH OF LUTH BR.	1	57	96	0.8	1.4
165 CH OF NAZARENE	2	88	143	1.2	2.0
167 CHS OF CHRIST.	1	60	80	0.7	1.1
283 LUTH--MO SYNOD	2	550	724	5.9	10.3
313 N AM BAPT CONF	1	48	60*	0.5	0.8
413 S.D.A.........	1	21	26*	0.2	0.4
443 UN C OF CHRIST	2	242	301*	2.5	4.3
449 UN METHODIST..	1	375	467*	3.8	6.6
453 UN PRES CH USA	1	153	190*	1.6	2.7
ROOSEVELT	40	2 927	6 967*	66.6	100.0
019 AMER BAPT USA.	1	29	37*	0.4	0.5
029 AMER LUTH CH..	8	1 414	1 721	16.4	24.7
053 ASSEMB OF GOD.	2	80	156	1.5	2.2
081 CATHOLIC......	7	NA	2 763	26.4	39.7
151 L-D SAINTS....	2	NA	466	4.5	6.7
157 CH OF BRETHREN	1	37	47*	0.4	0.7
165 CH OF NAZARENE	1	24	70	0.7	1.0
167 CHS OF CHRIST.	2	16	20	0.2	0.3
220 FREE LUTHERAN.	1	70	80	0.8	1.1
237 GC MENN BR CHS	1	61	77*	0.7	1.1
283 LUTH--MO SYNOD	1	160	224	2.1	3.2
287 MENN GEN CONF.	1	63	69	0.7	1.0
419 SO BAPT CONV..	2	268	338*	3.2	4.9
443 UN C OF CHRIST	1	61	77*	0.7	1.1
449 UN METHODIST..	2	57	72*	0.7	1.0
453 UN PRES CH USA	5	552	696*	6.6	10.0
469 WELS..........	1	35	54	0.5	0.8
ROSEBUD	31	1 164	4 833*	48.8	100.0
029 AMER LUTH CH..	1	19	29	0.3	0.6
053 ASSEMB OF GOD.	1	28	51	0.5	1.1
081 CATHOLIC......	8	NA	2 578	26.0	53.3
089 CHR & MISS AL.	1	9	26	0.3	0.5
127 CH GOD (CLEVE)	1	16	21*	0.2	0.4
151 L-D SAINTS....	4	NA	610	6.2	12.6
167 CHS OF CHRIST.	2	21	34	0.4	0.7
193 EPISCOPAL.....	1	14	41	0.4	0.8

NA—Not applicable   *Total adherents estimated from known number of communicant, confirmed, full members.   —Represents a percent less than 0.1.   Percentages may not total due to rounding.

Table 4. Churches and Church Membership by County and Denomination: 1980

County and Denomination	Number of churches	Communicant, confirmed, full members	Total adherents Number	Percent of total population	Percent of total adherents
283 LUTH--MO SYNOD	3	351	583	5.9	12.1
287 MENN GEN CONF.	3	178	178	1.8	3.7
419 SO BAPT CONV..	2	194	251*	2.5	5.2
443 UN C OF CHRIST	1	21	27*	0.3	0.6
449 UN METHODIST..	1	15	19*	0.2	0.4
453 UN PRES CH USA	2	298	385*	3.9	8.0
SANDERS	25	1 069	2 453*	28.3	100.0
017 AMER BAPT ASSN	1	50	50	0.6	2.0
029 AMER LUTH CH..	3	314	512	5.9	20.9
053 ASSEMB OF GOD.	2	58	138	1.6	5.6
081 CATHOLIC......	4	NA	514	5.9	21.0
089 CHR & MISS AL.	1	30	98	1.1	4.0
097 CHR CHS&CHS CR	1	50	62*	0.7	2.5
123 CH GOD (ANDER)	1	55	165	1.9	6.7
151 L-D SAINTS....	1	NA	278	3.2	11.3
165 CH OF NAZARENE	1	0	27	0.3	1.1
353 CHR BRETHREN..	1	60	50	0.6	2.0
413 S.D.A.........	2	61	75*	0.9	3.1
443 UN C OF CHRIST	2	143	177*	2.0	7.2
449 UN METHODIST..	4	164	203*	2.3	8.3
453 UN PRES CH USA	1	84	104*	1.2	4.2
SHERIDAN	28	2 124	4 060*	75.0	100.0
029 AMER LUTH CH..	10	1 215	1 491	27.5	36.7
053 ASSEMB OF GOD.	2	87	130	2.4	3.2
081 CATHOLIC......	5	NA	1 426	26.3	35.1
151 L-D SAINTS....	1	NA	?	?	?
167 CHS OF CHRIST.	1	8	10	0.2	0.2
197 EVAN CH OF NA.	1	33	33	0.6	0.8
281 LUTH CH AMER..	2	370	475	8.8	11.7
283 LUTH--MO SYNOD	1	79	100	1.8	2.5
285 MENNONITE CH..	1	21	25*	0.5	0.6
413 S.D.A.........	1	37	44*	0.8	1.1
443 UN C OF CHRIST	2	210	250*	4.6	6.2
449 UN METHODIST..	1	64	76*	1.4	1.9
SILVER BOW	33	3 649	21 463*	56.3	100.0
019 AMER BAPT USA.	2	177	214*	0.6	1.0
029 AMER LUTH CH..	1	469	677	1.8	3.2
045 APOSTOLIC LUTH	1	20	24*	0.1	0.1
053 ASSEMB OF GOD.	2	94	223	0.6	1.0
081 CATHOLIC......	9	NA	15 588	40.9	72.6
093 CHR CH (DISC).	1	46	105	0.3	0.5
097 CHR CHS&CHS CR	1	50	60*	0.2	0.3
127 CH GOD (CLEVE)	1	43	52*	0.1	0.2
151 L-D SAINTS....	2	NA	1 002	2.6	4.7
165 CH OF NAZARENE	1	32	59	0.2	0.3
167 CHS OF CHRIST.	1	85	108	0.3	0.5
193 EPISCOPAL.....	1	527	595	1.6	2.8
201 EVAN COV CH AM	1	15	18*	–	0.1
281 LUTH CH AMER..	1	394	559	1.5	2.6
283 LUTH--MO SYNOD	1	168	293	0.8	1.4
403 SALVATION ARMY	1	37	83	0.2	0.4
413 S.D.A.........	1	74	89*	0.2	0.4
419 SO BAPT CONV..	1	337	407*	1.1	1.9
443 UN C OF CHRIST	1	219	265*	0.7	1.2
449 UN METHODIST..	3	862	1 042*	2.7	4.9
STILLWATER	17	1 088	1 646*	29.4	100.0
029 AMER LUTH CH..	1	165	203	3.6	12.3
053 ASSEMB OF GOD.	1	41	60	1.1	3.6
081 CATHOLIC......	3	NA	336	6.0	20.4
193 EPISCOPAL.....	1	54	74	1.3	4.5
197 EVAN CH OF NA.	4	183	183	3.3	11.1
281 LUTH CH AMER..	1	145	165	2.9	10.0
283 LUTH--MO SYNOD	2	193	254	4.5	15.4
443 UN C OF CHRIST	3	266	321*	5.7	19.5
449 UN METHODIST..	1	41	50*	0.9	3.0
SWEET GRASS	11	881	1 560*	48.5	100.0
029 AMER LUTH CH..	2	546	778	24.2	49.9
053 ASSEMB OF GOD.	1	16	37	1.2	2.4
081 CATHOLIC......	2	NA	349	10.9	22.4
127 CH GOD (CLEVE)	1	25	30*	0.9	1.9
193 EPISCOPAL.....	1	42	77	2.4	4.9
197 EVAN CH OF NA.	1	75	75	2.3	4.8
203 EVAN FREE CH..	1	18	22*	0.7	1.4
413 S.D.A.........	1	27	33*	1.0	2.1
443 UN C OF CHRIST	1	132	159*	4.9	10.2
TETON	19	1 927	3 608*	55.6	100.0
029 AMER LUTH CH..	4	758	972	15.0	26.9
053 ASSEMB OF GOD.	1	23	35	0.5	1.0
081 CATHOLIC......	4	NA	675	10.4	18.7
151 L-D SAINTS....	2	NA	513	7.9	14.2
283 LUTH--MO SYNOD	2	191	241	3.7	6.7
413 S.D.A.........	1	56	69*	1.1	1.9
443 UN C OF CHRIST	2	278	341*	5.3	9.5
449 UN METHODIST..	3	621	762*	11.7	21.1
TOOLE	20	1 550	3 104*	55.8	100.0
029 AMER LUTH CH..	5	864	1 296	23.3	41.8
053 ASSEMB OF GOD.	1	29	44	0.8	1.4
081 CATHOLIC......	7	NA	814	14.6	26.2
151 L-D SAINTS....	1	NA	145	2.6	4.7
413 S.D.A.........	1	65	80*	1.4	2.6
419 SO BAPT CONV..	1	246	301*	5.4	9.7
449 UN METHODIST..	4	346	424*	7.6	13.7
TREASURE	3	144	343*	35.0	100.0
081 CATHOLIC......	1	NA	156	15.9	45.5
283 LUTH--MO SYNOD	1	30	48	4.9	14.0
453 UN PRES CH USA	1	114	139*	14.2	40.5
VALLEY	35	2 651	5 147*	50.2	100.0
029 AMER LUTH CH..	9	1 332	1 800	17.6	35.0
053 ASSEMB OF GOD.	1	91	156	1.5	3.0
081 CATHOLIC......	7	NA	1 430	14.0	27.8
151 L-D SAINTS....	2	NA	249	2.4	4.8
165 CH OF NAZARENE	1	15	31	0.3	0.6
167 CHS OF CHRIST.	1	28	36	0.4	0.7
193 EPISCOPAL.....	1	40	44	0.4	0.9
197 EVAN CH OF NA.	1	79	79	0.8	1.5
211 EVAN MENN BR..	1	100	130	1.3	2.5
237 GC MENN BR CHS	2	129	160*	1.6	3.1
283 LUTH--MO SYNOD	1	52	57	0.6	1.1
413 S.D.A.........	1	39	48*	0.5	0.9
419 SO BAPT CONV..	2	164	204*	2.0	4.0
443 UN C OF CHRIST	1	95	118*	1.2	2.3
449 UN METHODIST..	3	400	497*	4.8	9.7
453 UN PRES CH USA	1	87	108*	1.1	2.1
WHEATLAND	12	515	985*	41.8	100.0
029 AMER LUTH CH..	1	126	155	6.6	15.7
053 ASSEMB OF GOD.	1	26	49	2.1	5.0
081 CATHOLIC......	3	NA	280	11.9	28.4
151 L-D SAINTS....	1	NA	42	1.8	4.3
193 EPISCOPAL.....	1	29	42	1.8	4.3
283 LUTH--MO SYNOD	1	94	124	5.3	12.6
419 SO BAPT CONV..	1	14	17*	0.7	1.7
449 UN METHODIST..	2	136	166*	7.0	16.9
453 UN PRES CH USA	1	90	110*	4.7	11.2
WIBAUX	5	220	768*	52.0	100.0
029 AMER LUTH CH..	1	114	140	9.5	18.2
053 ASSEMB OF GOD.	1	39	61	4.1	7.9
081 CATHOLIC......	2	NA	484	32.8	63.0
449 UN METHODIST..	1	67	83*	5.6	10.8
YELLOWSTONE	94	20 364	53 242*	49.3	100.0
017 AMER BAPT ASSN	1	50	50		0.1
019 AMER BAPT USA.	1	636	778*	0.7	1.5
029 AMER LUTH CH..	7	3 786	5 524	5.1	10.4
053 ASSEMB OF GOD.	6	580	917	0.8	1.7
081 CATHOLIC......	10	NA	22 345	20.7	42.0
089 CHR & MISS AL.	1	167	557	0.5	1.0
093 CHR CH (DISC).	2	499	889	0.8	1.7
097 CHR CHS&CHS CR	1	50	61*	0.1	0.1
127 CH GOD (CLEVE)	2	75	92*	0.1	0.2
151 L-D SAINTS....	8	NA	3 168	2.9	6.0
163 CH OF LUTH BR.	1	63	91	0.1	0.2
165 CH OF NAZARENE	4	244	518	0.5	1.0
167 CHS OF CHRIST.	1	185	245	0.2	0.5
179 CONSRV BAPT...	2	166	203*	0.2	0.4
193 EPISCOPAL.....	3	795	1 399	1.3	2.6
197 EVAN CH OF NA.	4	553	553	0.5	1.0
201 EVAN COV CH AM	1	82	100*	0.1	0.2
203 EVAN FREE CH..	1	14	17*		–
263 INT FOURSQ GOS	1	101	124*	0.1	0.2
271 REFORM JUDAISM	1	90	110*	0.1	0.2
281 LUTH CH AMER..	3	782	1 003	0.9	1.9
283 LUTH--MO SYNOD	5	1 968	2 707	2.5	5.1
290 METRO COMM CHS	0	10	20	–	–
329 OPEN BIBLE STD	2	200	360	0.3	0.7
335 ORTH PRESB CH.	1	14	17*	–	–
403 SALVATION ARMY	1	103	153	0.1	0.3
413 S.D.A.........	2	261	319*	0.3	0.6
419 SO BAPT CONV..	5	1 061	1 299*	1.2	2.4
435 UNITARIAN-UNIV	1	60	73*	0.1	0.1
443 UN C OF CHRIST	8	3 139	3 842*	3.6	7.2
449 UN METHODIST..	5	3 343	4 092*	3.8	7.7
453 UN PRES CH USA	2	1 067	1 306*	1.2	2.5
469 WELS..........	1	220	310	0.3	0.6
YELLOWSTONE NATIONAL	4	97	111*	40.4	100.0
081 CATHOLIC......	3	NA	?	?	?
313 N AM BAPT CONF	1	97	111*	40.4	100.0

NEBRASKA

County and Denomination	Number of churches	Communicant, confirmed, full members	Total adherents Number	Percent of total population	Percent of total adherents
THE STATE.....	2 604	503 490	992 303*	63.2	100.0
ADAMS	43	12 524	21 040*	68.6	100.0

NA—Not applicable   *Total adherents estimated from known number of communicant, confirmed, full members.   —Represents a percent less than 0.1.   Percentages may not total due to rounding.

Table 4. Churches and Church Membership by County and Denomination: 1980

County and Denomination	Number of churches	Communicant, confirmed, full members	Total adherents			County and Denomination	Number of churches	Communicant, confirmed, full members	Total adherents		
			Number	Percent of total population	Percent of total adherents				Number	Percent of total population	Percent of total adherents
019 AMER BAPT USA.	2	598	709*	2.3	3.4	019 AMER BAPT USA.	2	594	715*	2.1	3.5
029 AMER LUTH CH..	1	346	442	1.4	2.1	053 ASSEMB OF GOD.	3	180	365	1.0	1.8
053 ASSEMB OF GOD.	1	258	464	1.5	2.2	063 BEREAN FUND CH	1	18	22*	0.1	0.1
063 BEREAN FUND CH	1	33	39*	0.1	0.2	081 CATHOLIC......	7	NA	4 529	13.0	22.4
081 CATHOLIC......	5	NA	4 840	15.8	23.0	093 CHR CH (DISC).	2	495	777	2.2	3.8
093 CHR CH (DISC).	1	241	328	1.1	1.6	097 CHR CHS&CHS CR	3	160	193*	0.6	1.0
097 CHR CHS&CHS CR	1	45	53*	0.2	0.3	123 CH GOD (ANDER)	1	101	303	0.9	1.5
123 CH GOD (ANDER)	1	59	177	0.6	0.8	127 CH GOD (CLEVE)	1	?	?	?	?
151 L-D SAINTS....	1	NA	201	0.7	1.0	151 L-D SAINTS....	1	NA	159	0.5	0.8
165 CH OF NAZARENE	2	205	478	1.6	2.3	165 CH OF NAZARENE	1	108	250	0.7	1.2
167 CHS OF CHRIST.	1	110	160	0.5	0.8	167 CHS OF CHRIST.	1	130	160	0.5	0.8
193 EPISCOPAL.....	1	406	438	1.4	2.1	193 EPISCOPAL.....	1	348	445	1.3	2.2
203 EVAN FREE CH..	1	11	13*	–	0.1	203 EVAN FREE CH..	1	130	156*	0.4	0.8
281 LUTH CH AMER..	3	2 266	2 849	9.3	13.5	281 LUTH CH AMER..	1	1 136	1 527	4.4	7.5
283 LUTH--MO SYNOD	7	2 525	3 344	10.9	15.9	283 LUTH--MO SYNOD	8	2 420	3 292	9.5	16.3
403 SALVATION ARMY	1	94	176	0.6	0.8	329 OPEN BIBLE STD	2	105	180	0.5	0.9
413 S.D.A.........	1	72	85*	0.3	0.4	381 REF PRES-EVAN.	1	64	74	0.2	0.4
443 UN C OF CHRIST	2	406	481*	1.6	2.3	403 SALVATION ARMY	1	101	264	0.8	1.3
449 UN METHODIST..	6	2 990	3 543*	11.6	16.8	413 S.D.A.........	2	146	176*	0.5	0.9
453 UN PRES CH USA	3	1 730	2 050*	6.7	9.7	419 SO BAPT CONV..	1	63	76*	0.2	0.4
469 WELS.........	1	129	170	0.6	0.8	443 UN C OF CHRIST	1	119	143*	0.4	0.7
						449 UN METHODIST..	13	4 721	5 681*	16.3	28.1
ANTELOPE	25	3 322	6 062*	69.9	100.0	453 UN PRES CH USA	1	623	750*	2.2	3.7
081 CATHOLIC......	4	NA	1 882	21.7	31.0	BURT	26	5 260	7 165*	81.3	100.0
089 CHR & MISS AL.	1	71	101	1.2	1.7	019 AMER BAPT USA.	2	515	614*	7.0	8.6
097 CHR CHS&CHS CR	3	259	319*	3.7	5.3	053 ASSEMB OF GOD.	1	96	160	1.8	2.2
193 EPISCOPAL.....	1	80	93	1.1	1.5	057 BAPT GEN CONF.	1	60	72*	0.8	1.0
283 LUTH--MO SYNOD	5	1 364	1 760	20.3	29.0	081 CATHOLIC......	3	NA	587	6.7	8.2
413 S.D.A.........	1	80	99*	1.1	1.6	201 EVAN COV CH AM	2	145	173*	2.0	2.4
443 UN C OF CHRIST	5	600	739*	8.5	12.2	203 EVAN FREE CH..	1	45	54*	0.6	0.8
449 UN METHODIST..	5	868	1 069*	12.3	17.6	281 LUTH CH AMER..	3	1 461	1 955	22.2	27.3
						283 LUTH--MO SYNOD	2	319	426	4.8	5.9
ARTHUR	2	234	275*	53.6	100.0	413 S.D.A.........	1	21	25*	0.3	0.3
019 AMER BAPT USA.	2	234	275*	53.6	100.0	449 UN METHODIST..	7	1 692	2 018*	22.9	28.2
						453 UN PRES CH USA	3	906	1 081*	12.3	15.1
BANNER	2	126	160*	17.4	100.0	BUTLER	25	1 657	6 447*	69.1	100.0
193 EPISCOPAL.....	1	25	37	4.0	23.1	019 AMER BAPT USA.	2	123	149*	1.6	2.3
449 UN METHODIST..	1	101	123*	13.4	76.9	081 CATHOLIC......	11	NA	4 407	47.2	68.4
						093 CHR CH (DISC).	1	14	18	0.2	0.3
BLAINE	5	244	366*	42.2	100.0	281 LUTH CH AMER..	1	161	214	2.3	3.3
329 OPEN BIBLE STD	1	30	100	11.5	27.3	283 LUTH--MO SYNOD	2	319	384	4.1	6.0
443 UN C OF CHRIST	3	148	182*	21.0	49.7	443 UN C OF CHRIST	1	53	64*	0.7	1.0
469 WELS.........	1	66	84	9.7	23.0	449 UN METHODIST..	5	812	981*	10.5	15.2
						469 WELS.........	2	175	230	2.5	3.6
BOONE	26	2 704	6 387*	86.4	100.0	CASS	39	5 711	9 603*	47.3	100.0
019 AMER BAPT USA.	1	148	179*	2.4	2.8	019 AMER BAPT USA.	1	49	60*	0.3	0.6
029 AMER LUTH CH..	2	958	1 202	16.3	18.8	081 CATHOLIC......	5	NA	2 052	10.1	21.4
053 ASSEMB OF GOD.	1	17	30	0.4	0.5	093 CHR CH (DISC).	5	471	925	4.6	9.6
081 CATHOLIC......	6	NA	3 028	41.0	47.4	097 CHR CHS&CHS CR	1	75	92*	0.5	1.0
165 CH OF NAZARENE	2	5	16	0.2	0.3	127 CH GOD (CLEVE)	1	15	18*	0.1	0.2
167 CHS OF CHRIST.	1	30	38	0.5	0.6	167 CHS OF CHRIST.	1	80	140	0.7	1.5
193 EPISCOPAL.....	1	25	31	0.4	0.5	193 EPISCOPAL.....	1	40	71	0.3	0.7
209 EVAN LUTH SYN.	3	203	269	3.6	4.2	281 LUTH CH AMER..	1	238	297	1.5	3.1
413 S.D.A.........	1	29	35*	0.5	0.5	283 LUTH--MO SYNOD	5	1 089	1 446	7.1	15.1
443 UN C OF CHRIST	1	97	117*	1.6	1.8	291 MISSIONARY CH.	1	41	71	0.3	0.7
449 UN METHODIST..	4	890	1 077*	14.6	16.9	419 SO BAPT CONV..	1	311	381*	1.9	4.0
453 UN PRES CH USA	3	302	365*	4.9	5.7	443 UN C OF CHRIST	3	479	587*	2.9	6.1
						449 UN METHODIST..	11	2 295	2 815*	13.9	29.3
BOX BUTTE	21	4 140	7 535*	55.0	100.0	453 UN PRES CH USA	2	528	648*	3.2	6.7
019 AMER BAPT USA.	1	253	313*	2.3	4.2	CEDAR	31	3 471	10 649*	98.1	100.0
053 ASSEMB OF GOD.	1	62	125	0.9	1.7	019 AMER BAPT USA.	1	49	61*	0.6	0.6
063 BEREAN FUND CH	1	37	46*	0.3	0.6	029 AMER LUTH CH..	6	1 641	2 111	19.5	19.8
081 CATHOLIC......	2	NA	2 046	14.9	27.2	053 ASSEMB OF GOD.	1	21	35	0.3	0.3
093 CHR CH (DISC).	1	209	319	2.3	4.2	081 CATHOLIC......	12	NA	6 230	57.4	58.5
123 CH GOD (ANDER)	2	30	90	0.7	1.2	097 CHR CHS&CHS CR	1	40	50*	0.5	0.5
151 L-D SAINTS....	1	NA	?	?	?	283 LUTH--MO SYNOD	1	242	315	2.9	3.0
165 CH OF NAZARENE	2	49	86	0.6	1.1	443 UN C OF CHRIST	2	378	472*	4.3	4.4
167 CHS OF CHRIST.	1	56	86	0.6	1.1	449 UN METHODIST..	5	757	946*	8.7	8.9
193 EPISCOPAL.....	1	241	330	2.4	4.4	453 UN PRES CH USA	2	343	429*	4.0	4.0
281 LUTH CH AMER..	1	379	531	3.9	7.0	CHASE	17	1 870	2 844*	59.8	100.0
283 LUTH--MO SYNOD	1	574	776	5.7	10.3	063 BEREAN FUND CH	1	24	30*	0.6	1.1
413 S.D.A.........	2	143	177*	1.3	2.3	081 CATHOLIC......	2	NA	426	9.0	15.0
443 UN C OF CHRIST	1	103	128*	0.9	1.7	097 CHR CHS&CHS CR	1	50	62*	1.3	2.2
449 UN METHODIST..	2	1 392	1 724*	12.6	22.9	151 L-D SAINTS....	1	NA	22	0.5	0.8
453 UN PRES CH USA	1	612	758*	5.5	10.1	157 CH OF BRETHREN	1	54	67*	1.4	2.4
						165 CH OF NAZARENE	1	16	54	1.1	1.9
BOYD	17	1 131	2 601*	78.1	100.0	167 CHS OF CHRIST.	3	98	122	2.6	4.3
081 CATHOLIC......	4	NA	1 195	35.9	45.9	193 EPISCOPAL.....	1	34	48	1.0	1.7
201 EVAN COV CH AM	2	65	76*	2.3	2.9	283 LUTH--MO SYNOD	2	568	752	15.8	26.4
281 LUTH CH AMER..	2	256	300	9.0	11.5	291 MISSIONARY CH.	1	53	54	1.1	1.9
283 LUTH--MO SYNOD	3	265	372	11.2	14.3	449 UN METHODIST..	3	973	1 207*	25.4	42.4
413 S.D.A.........	1	21	25*	0.8	1.0	CHERRY	26	1 997	4 083*	60.4	100.0
443 UN C OF CHRIST	1	127	149*	4.5	5.7	019 AMER BAPT USA.	1	48	58*	0.9	1.4
449 UN METHODIST..	3	257	301*	9.0	11.6	053 ASSEMB OF GOD.	1	73	125	1.8	3.1
469 WELS.........	1	140	183	5.5	7.0	063 BEREAN FUND CH	1	21	25*	0.4	0.6
						081 CATHOLIC......	5	NA	1 426	21.1	34.9
BROWN	11	1 316	2 243*	51.2	100.0	105 CHRISTIAN REF.	1	46	84	1.2	2.1
053 ASSEMB OF GOD.	2	95	176	4.0	7.8	151 L-D SAINTS....	1	NA	?	?	?
063 BEREAN FUND CH	1	30	36*	0.8	1.6	164 CH LUTH CONF.	1	94	132	2.0	3.2
081 CATHOLIC......	1	NA	476	10.9	21.2	165 CH OF NAZARENE	1	29	116	1.7	2.8
151 L-D SAINTS....	1	NA	?	?	?	193 EPISCOPAL.....	3	161	200	3.0	4.9
165 CH OF NAZARENE	1	107	197	4.5	8.8	283 LUTH--MO SYNOD	3	187	273	4.0	6.7
283 LUTH--MO SYNOD	1	279	382	8.7	17.0	413 S.D.A.........	1	54	65*	1.0	1.6
443 UN C OF CHRIST	1	225	273*	6.2	12.2						
449 UN METHODIST..	3	580	703*	16.1	31.3						
BUFFALO	56	11 762	20 237*	58.2	100.0						

NA—Not applicable   *Total adherents estimated from known number of communicant, confirmed, full members.   —Represents a percent less than 0.1.   Percentages may not total due to rounding.

Table 4. Churches and Church Membership by County and Denomination: 1980

County and Denomination	Number of churches	Communicant, confirmed, full members	Total adherents Number	Percent of total population	Percent of total adherents
419 SO BAPT CONV..	1	83	101*	1.5	2.5
449 UN METHODIST..	4	641	777*	11.5	19.0
453 UN PRES CH USA	1	377	457*	6.8	11.2
469 WELS..........	1	183	244	3.6	6.0
CHEYENNE	29	4 542	8 447*	84.0	100.0
029 AMER LUTH CH..	1	169	207	2.1	2.5
053 ASSEMB OF GOD.	2	44	84	0.8	1.0
081 CATHOLIC......	3	NA	2 420	24.1	28.6
093 CHR CH (DISC).	1	80	230	2.3	2.7
151 L-D SAINTS....	1	NA	105	1.0	1.2
165 CH OF NAZARENE	1	41	112	1.1	1.3
167 CHS OF CHRIST.	1	41	56	0.6	0.7
193 EPISCOPAL.....	1	151	163	1.6	1.9
263 INT FOURSQ GOS	1	87	105*	1.0	1.2
281 LUTH CH AMER..	5	1 261	1 664	16.5	19.7
283 LUTH--MO SYNOD	4	687	916	9.1	10.8
413 S.D.A.........	2	50	60*	0.6	0.7
419 SO BAPT CONV..	1	133	160*	1.6	1.9
449 UN METHODIST..	3	1 356	1 633*	16.2	19.3
453 UN PRES CH USA	2	442	532*	5.3	6.3
CLAY	31	3 619	5 539*	68.3	100.0
029 AMER LUTH CH..	2	528	696	8.6	12.6
081 CATHOLIC......	3	NA	1 009	12.4	18.2
093 CHR CH (DISC).	1	49	75	0.9	1.4
097 CHR CHS&CHS CR	3	190	231*	2.8	4.2
123 CH GOD (ANDER)	1	20	60	0.7	1.1
193 EPISCOPAL.....	1	9	12	0.1	0.2
203 EVAN FREE CH..	1	31	38*	0.5	0.7
281 LUTH CH AMER..	3	305	378	4.7	6.8
419 SO BAPT CONV..	1	33	40*	0.5	0.7
443 UN C OF CHRIST	3	804	978*	12.1	17.7
449 UN METHODIST..	8	998	1 214*	15.0	21.9
453 UN PRES CH USA	3	587	714*	8.8	12.9
469 WELS..........	1	65	94	1.2	1.7
COLFAX	21	2 698	8 192*	82.8	100.0
081 CATHOLIC......	9	NA	4 744	48.0	57.9
193 EPISCOPAL.....	1	13	23	0.2	0.3
281 LUTH CH AMER..	2	582	783	7.9	9.6
283 LUTH--MO SYNOD	4	677	918	9.3	11.2
443 UN C OF CHRIST	1	78	94*	1.0	1.1
449 UN METHODIST..	2	349	422*	4.3	5.2
453 UN PRES CH USA	2	999	1 208*	12.2	14.7
CUMING	26	5 266	10 238*	87.8	100.0
057 BAPT GEN CONF.	1	33	40*	0.3	0.4
081 CATHOLIC......	7	NA	3 501	30.0	34.2
281 LUTH CH AMER..	2	1 048	1 316	11.3	12.9
283 LUTH--MO SYNOD	9	3 244	4 231	36.3	41.3
285 MENNONITE CH..	1	175	214*	1.8	2.1
443 UN C OF CHRIST	2	275	336*	2.9	3.3
449 UN METHODIST..	3	346	423*	3.6	4.1
453 UN PRES CH USA	1	145	177*	1.5	1.7
CUSTER	56	5 120	8 406*	60.6	100.0
019 AMER BAPT USA.	4	777	937*	6.8	11.1
053 ASSEMB OF GOD.	2	56	98	0.7	1.2
057 BAPT GEN CONF.	1	64	77*	0.6	0.9
063 BEREAN FUND CH	2	71	86*	0.6	1.0
081 CATHOLIC......	9	NA	1 870	13.5	22.2
093 CHR CH (DISC).	1	108	155	1.1	1.8
097 CHR CHS&CHS CR	4	609	735*	5.3	8.7
123 CH GOD (ANDER)	1	60	180	1.3	2.1
127 CH GOD (CLEVE)	1	?	?	?	?
165 CH OF NAZARENE	2	34	61	0.4	0.7
167 CHS OF CHRIST.	1	37	53	0.4	0.6
193 EPISCOPAL.....	2	102	168	1.2	2.0
203 EVAN FREE CH..	2	25	30*	0.2	0.4
221 FREE METHODIST	1	25	54	0.4	0.6
281 LUTH CH AMER..	2	175	244	1.8	2.9
283 LUTH--MO SYNOD	3	180	261	1.9	3.1
285 MENNONITE CH..	1	40	48*	0.3	0.6
329 OPEN BIBLE STD	1	12	25	0.2	0.3
413 S.D.A.........	1	87	105*	0.8	1.2
449 UN METHODIST..	13	2 332	2 813*	20.3	33.5
453 UN PRES CH USA	1	190	229*	1.7	2.7
469 WELS..........	1	136	177	1.3	2.1
DAKOTA	19	3 503	8 809*	53.2	100.0
053 ASSEMB OF GOD.	1	57	150	0.9	1.7
081 CATHOLIC......	5	NA	4 162	25.1	47.2
097 CHR CHS&CHS CR	1	50	63*	0.4	0.7
197 EVAN CH OF NA.	1	38	38	0.2	0.4
281 LUTH CH AMER..	4	1 659	2 198*	13.3	25.0
283 LUTH--MO SYNOD	1	494	688	4.2	7.8
313 N AM BAPT CONF	1	19	24*	0.1	0.3
413 S.D.A.........	1	66	83*	0.5	0.9
449 UN METHODIST..	3	696	872*	5.3	9.9
453 UN PRES CH USA	1	424	531*	3.2	6.0
DAWES	26	2 861	4 343*	45.2	100.0
019 AMER BAPT USA.	2	399	473*	4.9	10.9
029 AMER LUTH CH..	1	263	359	3.7	8.3
053 ASSEMB OF GOD.	1	176	182	1.9	4.2
063 BEREAN FUND CH	1	23	27*	0.3	0.6
081 CATHOLIC......	2	NA	843	8.8	19.4

County and Denomination	Number of churches	Communicant, confirmed, full members	Total adherents Number	Percent of total population	Percent of total adherents
097 CHR CHS&CHS CR	1	75	89*	0.9	2.0
123 CH GOD (ANDER)	1	25	75	0.8	1.7
151 L-D SAINTS....	2	NA	?	?	?
165 CH OF NAZARENE	2	44	85	0.9	2.0
167 CHS OF CHRIST.	1	17	20	0.2	0.5
175 CONGR CHR CHS.	1	94	111*	1.2	2.6
193 EPISCOPAL.....	1	208	227	2.4	5.2
283 LUTH--MO SYNOD	2	283	365	3.8	8.4
413 S.D.A.........	2	102	121*	1.3	2.8
419 SO BAPT CONV..	1	47	56*	0.6	1.3
443 UN C OF CHRIST	2	214	254*	2.6	5.8
449 UN METHODIST..	3	891	1 056*	11.0	24.3
DAWSON	52	10 342	16 207*	73.1	100.0
019 AMER BAPT USA.	2	225	278*	1.3	1.7
029 AMER LUTH CH..	3	1 640	2 302	10.4	14.2
053 ASSEMB OF GOD.	2	187	335	1.5	2.1
057 BAPT GEN CONF.	1	118	146*	0.7	0.9
063 BEREAN FUND CH	2	217	268*	1.2	1.7
081 CATHOLIC......	6	NA	2 580	11.6	15.9
093 CHR CH (DISC).	1	48	86	0.4	0.5
097 CHR CHS&CHS CR	3	755	933*	4.2	5.8
123 CH GOD (ANDER)	2	70	210	0.9	1.3
133 CH GOD(7TH)DEN	1	5	6*	–	–
151 L-D SAINTS....	1	NA	37	0.2	0.2
165 CH OF NAZARENE	3	192	346	1.6	2.1
167 CHS OF CHRIST.	2	59	114	0.5	0.7
193 EPISCOPAL.....	1	12	34	0.2	0.2
203 EVAN FREE CH..	4	309	382*	1.7	2.4
281 LUTH CH AMER..	2	337	440	2.0	2.7
283 LUTH--MO SYNOD	3	922	1 226	5.5	7.6
413 S.D.A.........	1	92	114*	0.5	0.7
419 SO BAPT CONV..	1	73	90*	0.4	0.6
449 UN METHODIST..	7	3 690	4 561*	20.6	28.1
453 UN PRES CH USA	4	1 391	1 719*	7.8	10.6
DEUEL	10	1 565	2 178*	88.5	100.0
053 ASSEMB OF GOD.	2	107	199	8.1	9.1
081 CATHOLIC......	1	NA	211	8.6	9.7
263 INT FOURSQ GOS	1	120	144*	5.8	6.6
281 LUTH CH AMER..	2	225	286	11.6	13.1
283 LUTH--MO SYNOD	2	346	419	17.0	19.2
449 UN METHODIST..	2	767	919*	37.3	42.2
DIXON	26	4 227	6 378*	89.4	100.0
029 AMER LUTH CH..	1	83	105	1.5	1.6
081 CATHOLIC......	4	NA	1 160	16.3	18.2
097 CHR CHS&CHS CR	1	150	184*	2.6	2.9
203 EVAN FREE CH..	2	119	146*	2.0	2.3
226 FRIENDS-USA...	1	89	109*	1.5	1.7
281 LUTH CH AMER..	6	2 327	2 856	40.0	44.8
283 LUTH--MO SYNOD	5	740	938	13.1	14.7
443 UN C OF CHRIST	1	57	70*	1.0	1.1
449 UN METHODIST..	4	572	700*	9.8	11.0
453 UN PRES CH USA	1	90	110*	1.5	1.7
DODGE	57	15 001	31 492*	87.9	100.0
019 AMER BAPT USA.	1	607	734*	2.0	2.3
029 AMER LUTH CH..	2	1 252	1 635	4.6	5.2
053 ASSEMB OF GOD.	1	33	58	0.2	0.2
057 BAPT GEN CONF.	0	13	16*	–	0.1
081 CATHOLIC......	6	NA	12 071	33.7	38.3
089 CHR & MISS AL.	1	222	417	1.2	1.3
093 CHR CH (DISC).	1	299	480	1.3	1.5
097 CHR CHS&CHS CR	1	30	36*	0.1	0.1
121 CH GOD (ABR)..	1	25	30*	0.1	0.1
127 CH GOD (CLEVE)	1	16	19*	0.1	0.1
151 L-D SAINTS....	1	NA	245	0.7	0.8
167 CHS OF CHRIST.	1	55	70	0.2	0.2
193 EPISCOPAL.....	1	360	488	1.4	1.5
203 EVAN FREE CH..	1	43	52*	0.1	0.2
221 FREE METHODIST	1	22	87	0.2	0.3
263 INT FOURSQ GOS	1	112	135*	0.4	0.4
281 LUTH CH AMER..	13	3 934	4 919	13.7	15.6
283 LUTH--MO SYNOD	8	3 004	3 903	10.9	12.4
403 SALVATION ARMY	1	156	267	0.7	0.8
413 S.D.A.........	1	47	57*	0.2	0.2
419 SO BAPT CONV..	1	47	57*	0.2	0.2
443 UN C OF CHRIST	3	995	1 203*	3.4	3.8
449 UN METHODIST..	6	2 236	2 704*	7.5	8.6
453 UN PRES CH USA	2	1 474	1 782*	5.0	5.7
469 WELS..........	1	19	27	0.1	0.1
DOUGLAS	261	79 408	233 379*	58.7	100.0
017 AMER BAPT ASSN	1	50	50	–	–
019 AMER BAPT USA.	11	2 801	3 409*	0.9	1.5
029 AMER LUTH CH..	11	5 735	7 513	1.9	3.2
053 ASSEMB OF GOD.	4	997	1 370	0.3	0.6
057 BAPT GEN CONF.	5	759	924*	0.2	0.4
063 BEREAN FUND CH	2	118	144*	–	0.1
081 CATHOLIC......	52	NA	125 492	31.5	53.8
089 CHR & MISS AL.	2	776	1 377	0.3	0.6
093 CHR CH (DISC).	4	1 280	2 179	0.5	0.9
097 CHR CHS&CHS CR	6	1 394	1 697*	0.4	0.7
105 CHRISTIAN REF.	1	74	129	–	0.1
121 CH GOD (ABR)..	1	77	94*	–	–
123 CH GOD (ANDER)	2	110	330	0.1	0.1
127 CH GOD (CLEVE)	4	425	517*	0.1	0.2
133 CH GOD(7TH)DEN	1	8	10*	–	–
151 L-D SAINTS....	5	NA	2 126	0.5	0.9

NA – Not applicable   *Total adherents estimated from known number of communicant, confirmed, full members.   —Represents a percent less than 0.1.   Percentages may not total due to rounding.

Table 4. Churches and Church Membership by County and Denomination: 1980

County and Denomination	Number of churches	Communicant, confirmed, full members	Total adherents Number	Percent of total population	Percent of total adherents
165 CH OF NAZARENE	3	346	837	0.2	0.4
167 CHS OF CHRIST.	5	739	1 145	0.3	0.5
193 EPISCOPAL.....	12	2 984	3 942	1.0	1.7
201 EVAN COV CH AM	2	667	812*	0.2	0.3
203 EVAN FREE CH..	1	125	152*	—	0.1
208 EVAN LUTH ASSN	1	1 000	1 200	0.3	0.5
211 EVAN MENN BR..	2	273	355	0.1	0.2
221 FREE METHODIST	1	42	126	—	0.1
226 FRIENDS-USA...	1	110	134*	—	0.1
237 GC MENN BR CHS	1	28	34*	—	—
244 GRACE BRETHREN	1	48	58*	—	—
263 INT FOURSQ GOS	3	519	632*	0.2	0.3
270 CONSRV JUDAISM	1	383	466*	0.1	0.2
271 REFORM JUDAISM	1	1 314	1 599*	0.4	0.7
274 LAT EVAN LUTH.	1	95	105	—	—
281 LUTH CH AMER..	18	12 798	17 747	4.5	7.6
283 LUTH--MO SYNOD	18	9 126	12 580	3.2	5.4
285 MENNONITE CH..	2	20	24*	—	—
290 METRO COMM CHS	1	75	150	—	0.1
291 MISSIONARY CH.	1	?	?	?	?
329 OPEN BIBLE STD	1	100	150	—	0.1
335 ORTH PRESB CH.	1	23	28*	—	—
353 CHR BRETHREN..	2	130	155	—	0.1
371 REF CH IN AM..	1	274	485	0.1	0.2
395 ROMANIAN OR CH	1	380	463*	0.1	0.2
403 SALVATION ARMY	3	610	2 830	0.7	1.2
413 S.D.A.........	3	1 350	1 643*	0.4	0.7
419 SO BAPT CONV..	4	1 646	2 003*	0.5	0.9
431 UKRANIAN AMER.	1	80	110	—	—
435 UNITARIAN-UNIV	2	358	436*	0.1	0.2
443 UN C OF CHRIST	5	3 937	4 792*	1.2	2.1
449 UN METHODIST..	19	12 576	15 306*	3.8	6.6
453 UN PRES CH USA	27	12 124	14 756*	3.7	6.3
469 WELS.........	3	524	763	0.2	0.3
DUNDY	**15**	**1 460**	**1 960***	**68.5**	**100.0**
019 AMER BAPT USA.	1	41	49*	1.7	2.5
029 AMER LUTH CH..	2	356	456	15.9	23.3
081 CATHOLIC......	1	NA	178	6.2	9.1
167 CHS OF CHRIST.	1	8	15	0.5	0.8
226 FRIENDS-USA...	1	64	76*	2.7	3.9
283 LUTH--MO SYNOD	1	130	162	5.7	8.3
413 S.D.A.........	2	32	38*	1.3	1.9
419 SO BAPT CONV..	1	69	82*	2.9	4.2
449 UN METHODIST..	4	690	821*	28.7	41.9
453 UN PRES CH USA	1	70	83*	2.9	4.2
FILLMORE	**24**	**3 211**	**5 277***	**66.6**	**100.0**
029 AMER LUTH CH..	1	175	267	3.4	5.1
081 CATHOLIC......	5	NA	1 367	17.3	25.9
167 CHS OF CHRIST.	1	7	12	0.2	0.2
203 EVAN FREE CH..	1	35	42*	0.5	0.8
281 LUTH CH AMER..	3	334	366	4.6	6.9
283 LUTH--MO SYNOD	1	133	170	2.1	3.2
285 MENNONITE CH..	1	218	261*	3.3	4.9
287 MENN GEN CONF.	1	44	44	0.6	0.8
443 UN C OF CHRIST	2	502	600*	7.6	11.4
449 UN METHODIST..	6	1 594	1 907*	24.1	36.1
469 WELS.........	2	169	241	3.0	4.6
FRANKLIN	**23**	**2 652**	**3 619***	**82.7**	**100.0**
029 AMER LUTH CH..	3	559	697	15.9	19.3
053 ASSEMB OF GOD.	2	59	115	2.6	3.2
081 CATHOLIC......	4	NA	343	7.8	9.5
093 CHR CH (DISC).	1	39	60	1.4	1.7
281 LUTH CH AMER..	1	299	355	8.1	9.8
283 LUTH--MO SYNOD	3	422	534	12.2	14.8
291 MISSIONARY CH.	2	42	61	1.4	1.7
443 UN C OF CHRIST	2	266	314*	7.2	8.7
449 UN METHODIST..	4	765	903*	20.6	25.0
453 UN PRES CH USA	1	201	237*	5.4	6.5
FRONTIER	**14**	**1 654**	**2 205***	**60.5**	**100.0**
029 AMER LUTH CH..	1	451	547	15.0	24.8
063 BEREAN FUND CH	1	32	39*	1.1	1.8
081 CATHOLIC......	2	NA	156	4.3	7.1
097 CHR CHS&CHS CR	1	65	78*	2.1	3.5
165 CH OF NAZARENE	1	11	43	1.2	2.0
283 LUTH--MO SYNOD	1	258	334	9.2	15.1
413 S.D.A.........	1	19	23*	0.6	1.0
443 UN C OF CHRIST	2	68	82*	2.2	3.7
449 UN METHODIST..	4	750	903*	24.8	41.0
FURNAS	**31**	**3 907**	**5 404***	**83.3**	**100.0**
019 AMER BAPT USA.	3	504	596*	9.2	11.0
029 AMER LUTH CH..	1	54	61	0.9	1.1
053 ASSEMB OF GOD.	2	44	75	1.2	1.4
057 BAPT GEN CONF.	1	96	114*	1.8	2.1
081 CATHOLIC......	3	NA	616	9.5	11.4
093 CHR CH (DISC).	1	71	115	1.8	2.1
097 CHR CHS&CHS CR	3	318	376*	5.8	7.0
121 CH GOD (ABR)..	1	36	43*	0.7	0.8
193 EPISCOPAL.....	1	54	93	1.4	1.7
221 FREE METHODIST	1	13	42	0.6	0.8
244 GRACE BRETHREN	1	30	35*	0.5	0.6
283 LUTH--MO SYNOD	2	776	978	15.1	18.1
413 S.D.A.........	1	33	39*	0.6	0.7
443 UN C OF CHRIST	1	217	257*	4.0	4.8
449 UN METHODIST..	8	1 509	1 784*	27.5	33.0
453 UN PRES CH USA	1	152	180*	2.8	3.3

County and Denomination	Number of churches	Communicant, confirmed, full members	Total adherents Number	Percent of total population	Percent of total adherents
GAGE	**64**	**13 549**	**19 649***	**80.3**	**100.0**
019 AMER BAPT USA.	2	309	366*	1.5	1.9
029 AMER LUTH CH..	10	4 223	5 566	22.8	28.3
053 ASSEMB OF GOD.	1	30	54	0.2	0.3
081 CATHOLIC......	5	NA	2 040	8.3	10.4
093 CHR CH (DISC).	3	561	835	3.4	4.2
097 CHR CHS&CHS CR	4	1 250	1 480*	6.1	7.5
123 CH GOD (ANDER)	1	30	90	0.4	0.5
127 CH GOD (CLEVE)	1	37	44*	0.2	0.2
151 L-D SAINTS....	1	NA	?	?	?
157 CH OF BRETHREN	2	185	219*	0.9	1.1
165 CH OF NAZARENE	1	77	219	0.9	1.1
167 CHS OF CHRIST.	2	135	157	0.6	0.8
193 EPISCOPAL.....	2	181	294	1.2	1.5
281 LUTH CH AMER..	1	220	289	1.2	1.5
283 LUTH--MO SYNOD	4	1 235	1 789	7.3	9.1
287 MENN GEN CONF.	2	406	531	2.2	2.7
313 N AM BAPT CONF	1	170	201*	0.8	1.0
371 REF CH IN AM..	1	161	247	1.0	1.3
403 SALVATION ARMY	1	120	184	0.8	0.9
413 S.D.A.........	1	51	60*	0.2	0.3
443 UN C OF CHRIST	1	144	171*	0.7	0.9
449 UN METHODIST..	10	2 755	3 262*	13.3	16.6
453 UN PRES CH USA	4	857	1 015*	4.2	5.2
469 WELS.........	3	412	536	2.2	2.7
GARDEN	**11**	**1 040**	**1 562***	**55.7**	**100.0**
053 ASSEMB OF GOD.	1	26	61	2.2	3.9
081 CATHOLIC......	2	NA	289	10.3	18.5
167 CHS OF CHRIST.	1	3	3	0.1	0.2
193 EPISCOPAL.....	1	26	29	1.0	1.9
281 LUTH CH AMER..	2	438	541	19.3	34.6
413 S.D.A.........	1	17	20*	0.7	1.3
449 UN METHODIST..	2	468	547*	19.5	35.0
453 UN PRES CH USA	1	62	72*	2.6	4.6
GARFIELD	**8**	**902**	**1 443***	**61.1**	**100.0**
053 ASSEMB OF GOD.	1	46	87	3.7	6.0
057 BAPT GEN CONF.	0	1	1*	—	0.1
063 BEREAN FUND CH	2	62	74*	3.1	5.1
081 CATHOLIC......	1	NA	296	12.5	20.5
097 CHR CHS&CHS CR	1	164	197*	8.3	13.7
283 LUTH--MO SYNOD	1	157	221	9.4	15.3
443 UN C OF CHRIST	1	193	232*	9.8	16.1
449 UN METHODIST..	1	279	335*	14.2	23.2
GOSPER	**5**	**1 018**	**1 362***	**63.6**	**100.0**
029 AMER LUTH CH..	1	310	385	18.0	28.3
081 CATHOLIC......	1	NA	72	3.4	5.3
093 CHR CH (DISC).	1	96	153	7.1	11.2
283 LUTH--MO SYNOD	1	305	383	17.9	28.1
449 UN METHODIST..	1	307	369*	17.2	27.1
GRANT	**8**	**413**	**680***	**77.5**	**100.0**
081 CATHOLIC......	2	NA	70	8.0	10.3
193 EPISCOPAL.....	1	73	163	18.6	24.0
283 LUTH--MO SYNOD	2	62	108	12.3	15.9
413 S.D.A.........	1	17	21*	2.4	3.1
443 UN C OF CHRIST	2	261	318*	36.3	46.8
GREELEY	**13**	**1 068**	**3 693***	**106.7**	**100.0**
057 BAPT GEN CONF.	1	57	70*	2.0	1.9
081 CATHOLIC......	5	NA	2 341	67.6	63.4
281 LUTH CH AMER..	1	271	356	10.3	9.6
283 LUTH--MO SYNOD	1	211	278	8.0	7.5
449 UN METHODIST..	4	504	617*	17.8	16.7
453 UN PRES CH USA	1	25	31*	0.9	0.8
HALL	**50**	**17 692**	**35 729***	**74.9**	**100.0**
019 AMER BAPT USA.	1	515	635*	1.3	1.8
029 AMER LUTH CH..	1	288	396	0.8	1.1
053 ASSEMB OF GOD.	2	385	1 226	2.6	3.4
057 BAPT GEN CONF.	2	100	123*	0.3	0.3
081 CATHOLIC......	6	NA	11 626	24.4	32.5
089 CHR & MISS AL.	1	15	100	0.2	0.3
093 CHR CH (DISC).	1	347	597	1.3	1.7
097 CHR CHS&CHS CR	2	169	208*	0.4	0.6
127 CH GOD (CLEVE)	1	122	150*	0.3	0.4
151 L-D SAINTS....	1	NA	508	1.1	1.4
165 CH OF NAZARENE	2	149	305	0.6	0.9
167 CHS OF CHRIST.	1	50	64	0.1	0.2
193 EPISCOPAL.....	1	537	583	1.2	1.6
203 EVAN FREE CH..	1	141	174*	0.4	0.5
281 LUTH CH AMER..	2	3 069	3 991	8.4	11.2
283 LUTH--MO SYNOD	6	3 215	4 435	9.3	12.4
285 MENNONITE CH..	3	101	124*	0.3	0.3
403 SALVATION ARMY	1	111	132	0.3	0.4
413 S.D.A.........	2	236	291*	0.6	0.8
419 SO BAPT CONV..	1	68	84*	0.2	0.2
443 UN C OF CHRIST	2	175	216*	0.5	0.6
449 UN METHODIST..	8	6 221	7 665*	16.1	21.5
453 UN PRES CH USA	2	1 491	1 837*	3.9	5.1
469 WELS.........	1	187	259	0.5	0.7
HAMILTON	**24**	**4 095**	**5 745***	**61.8**	**100.0**
029 AMER LUTH CH..	2	308	417	4.5	7.3
053 ASSEMB OF GOD.	1	78	115	1.2	2.0

NA—Not applicable   *Total adherents estimated from known number of communicant, confirmed, full members.   —Represents a percent less than 0.1.   Percentages may not total due to rounding.

Table 4. Churches and Church Membership by County and Denomination: 1980

County and Denomination	Number of churches	Communicant, confirmed, full members	Total adherents		
			Number	Percent of total population	Percent of total adherents
057 BAPT GEN CONF.	1	66	81*	0.9	1.4
081 CATHOLIC......	2	NA	528	5.7	9.2
093 CHR CH (DISC).	1	176	356	3.8	6.2
167 CHS OF CHRIST.	1	17	33	0.4	0.6
201 EVAN COV CH AM	1	151	185*	2.0	3.2
203 EVAN FREE CH..	3	214	262*	2.8	4.6
281 LUTH CH AMER..	2	399	472	5.1	8.2
283 LUTH--MO SYNOD	3	769	943	10.1	16.4
413 S.D.A.........	1	42	52*	0.6	0.9
443 UN C OF CHRIST	1	113	139*	1.5	2.4
449 UN METHODIST..	3	1 569	1 924*	20.7	33.5
453 UN PRES CH USA	1	103	126*	1.4	2.2
469 WELS..........	1	90	112	1.2	1.9
HARLAN	**18**	**1 984**	**2 874***	**67.0**	**100.0**
029 AMER LUTH CH..	2	254	309	7.2	10.8
053 ASSEMB OF GOD.	1	58	60	1.4	2.1
081 CATHOLIC......	2	NA	358	8.3	12.5
093 CHR CH (DISC).	1	159	224	5.2	7.8
203 EVAN FREE CH..	3	95	113*	2.6	3.9
221 FREE METHODIST	1	21	69	1.6	2.4
281 LUTH CH AMER..	1	205	290	6.8	10.1
283 LUTH--MO SYNOD	1	258	344	8.0	12.0
449 UN METHODIST..	4	666	789*	18.4	27.5
453 UN PRES CH USA	2	268	318*	7.4	11.1
HAYES	**5**	**280**	**495***	**36.5**	**100.0**
057 BAPT GEN CONF.	1	65	79*	5.8	16.0
081 CATHOLIC......	1	NA	107	7.9	21.6
089 CHR & MISS AL.	1	42	90	6.6	18.2
167 CHS OF CHRIST.	1	14	26	1.9	5.3
443 UN C OF CHRIST	1	159	193*	14.2	39.0
HITCHCOCK	**16**	**1 655**	**2 563***	**62.8**	**100.0**
081 CATHOLIC......	3	NA	365	8.9	14.2
089 CHR & MISS AL.	1	39	114	2.8	4.4
123 CH GOD (ANDER)	1	52	156	3.8	6.1
167 CHS OF CHRIST.	2	54	73	1.8	2.8
283 LUTH--MO SYNOD	2	309	371	9.1	14.5
291 MISSIONARY CH.	1	17	55	1.3	2.1
353 CHR BRETHREN..	1	25	25	0.6	1.0
443 UN C OF CHRIST	1	89	108*	2.6	4.2
449 UN METHODIST..	4	1 070	1 296*	31.8	50.6
HOLT	**33**	**3 394**	**9 569***	**70.6**	**100.0**
029 AMER LUTH CH..	1	175	231	1.7	2.4
053 ASSEMB OF GOD.	2	116	200	1.5	2.1
063 BEREAN FUND CH	1	34	42*	0.3	0.4
081 CATHOLIC......	7	NA	5 161	38.1	53.9
097 CHR CHS&CHS CR	2	120	148*	1.1	1.5
151 L-D SAINTS....	1	NA	?	?	?
165 CH OF NAZARENE	1	?	?	?	?
221 FREE METHODIST	1	36	90	0.7	0.9
283 LUTH--MO SYNOD	3	638	885	6.5	9.2
449 UN METHODIST..	7	1 550	1 906*	14.1	19.9
453 UN PRES CH USA	6	703	864*	6.4	9.0
469 WELS..........	1	22	42	0.3	0.4
HOOKER	**4**	**369**	**603***	**60.9**	**100.0**
053 ASSEMB OF GOD.	1	20	49	4.9	8.1
081 CATHOLIC......	1	NA	96	9.7	15.9
193 EPISCOPAL.....	1	110	174	17.6	28.9
449 UN METHODIST..	1	239	284*	28.7	47.1
HOWARD	**17**	**1 861**	**4 162***	**61.4**	**100.0**
029 AMER LUTH CH..	2	492	624	9.2	15.0
057 BAPT GEN CONF.	2	146	179*	2.6	4.3
081 CATHOLIC......	5	NA	1 844	27.2	44.3
220 FREE LUTHERAN.	1	41	43	0.6	1.0
283 LUTH--MO SYNOD	1	232	305	4.5	7.3
449 UN METHODIST..	5	663	814*	12.0	19.6
453 UN PRES CH USA	1	287	353*	5.2	8.5
JEFFERSON	**32**	**5 807**	**7 798***	**79.4**	**100.0**
019 AMER BAPT USA.	1	294	345*	3.5	4.4
029 AMER LUTH CH..	3	760	945	9.6	12.1
053 ASSEMB OF GOD.	1	30	75	0.8	1.0
081 CATHOLIC......	1	NA	676	6.9	8.7
093 CHR CH (DISC).	1	372	430	4.4	5.5
123 CH GOD (ANDER)	1	39	117	1.2	1.5
165 CH OF NAZARENE	1	71	67	0.7	0.9
167 CHS OF CHRIST.	1	17	18	0.2	0.2
193 EPISCOPAL.....	1	57	75	0.8	1.0
211 EVAN MENN BR..	1	89	116	1.2	1.5
263 INT FOURSQ GOS	1	108	127*	1.3	1.6
281 LUTH CH AMER..	1	194	262	2.7	3.4
283 LUTH--MO SYNOD	5	1 335	1 638	16.7	21.0
413 S.D.A.........	1	45	53*	0.5	0.7
443 UN C OF CHRIST	5	460	540*	5.5	6.9
449 UN METHODIST..	4	1 090	1 280*	13.0	16.4
453 UN PRES CH USA	2	535	628*	6.4	8.1
469 WELS..........	1	311	406	4.1	5.2
JOHNSON	**19**	**2 686**	**4 124***	**78.0**	**100.0**
019 AMER BAPT USA.	1	243	290*	5.5	7.0
029 AMER LUTH CH..	2	788	966	18.3	23.4
081 CATHOLIC......	2	NA	825	15.6	20.0
127 CH GOD (CLEVE)	1	15	18*	0.3	0.4
193 EPISCOPAL.....	1	0	16	0.3	0.4
281 LUTH CH AMER..	1	37	37	0.7	0.9
283 LUTH--MO SYNOD	2	516	676	12.8	16.4
443 UN C OF CHRIST	1	137	163*	3.1	4.0
449 UN METHODIST..	7	767	915*	17.3	22.2
453 UN PRES CH USA	1	183	218*	4.1	5.3
KEARNEY	**19**	**3 386**	**4 689***	**66.5**	**100.0**
029 AMER LUTH CH..	3	538	652	9.2	13.9
081 CATHOLIC......	2	NA	441	6.3	9.4
093 CHR CH (DISC).	1	149	274	3.9	5.8
203 EVAN FREE CH..	3	64	77*	1.1	1.6
263 INT FOURSQ GOS	1	84	101*	1.4	2.2
281 LUTH CH AMER..	2	488	605	8.6	12.9
283 LUTH--MO SYNOD	3	664	858	12.2	18.3
413 S.D.A.........	1	15	18*	0.3	0.4
449 UN METHODIST..	1	790	949*	13.5	20.2
453 UN PRES CH USA	2	594	714*	10.1	15.2
KEITH	**20**	**3 667**	**6 632***	**70.8**	**100.0**
053 ASSEMB OF GOD.	1	71	167	1.8	2.5
063 BEREAN FUND CH	1	195	238*	2.5	3.6
081 CATHOLIC......	2	NA	1 851	19.8	27.9
123 CH GOD (ANDER)	1	22	66	0.7	1.0
151 L-D SAINTS....	1	NA	36	0.4	0.5
165 CH OF NAZARENE	1	?	?	?	?
167 CHS OF CHRIST.	1	95	120	1.3	1.8
193 EPISCOPAL.....	1	134	152	1.6	2.3
281 LUTH CH AMER..	1	202	256	2.7	3.9
283 LUTH--MO SYNOD	3	1 017	1 392	14.9	21.0
413 S.D.A.........	1	20	24*	0.3	0.4
443 UN C OF CHRIST	2	674	822*	8.8	12.4
449 UN METHODIST..	2	1 177	1 435*	15.3	21.6
453 UN PRES CH USA	2	60	73*	0.8	1.1
KEYA PAHA	**6**	**556**	**726***	**55.8**	**100.0**
053 ASSEMB OF GOD.	1	53	100	7.7	13.8
283 LUTH--MO SYNOD	2	184	236	18.1	32.5
413 S.D.A.........	1	32	39*	3.0	5.4
449 UN METHODIST..	2	287	351*	27.0	48.3
KIMBALL	**12**	**1 811**	**3 165***	**64.8**	**100.0**
029 AMER LUTH CH..	1	398	517	10.6	16.3
053 ASSEMB OF GOD.	1	31	67	1.4	2.1
081 CATHOLIC......	1	NA	730	15.0	23.1
165 CH OF NAZARENE	1	44	174	3.6	5.5
167 CHS OF CHRIST.	1	16	25	0.5	0.8
193 EPISCOPAL.....	1	62	78	1.6	2.5
283 LUTH--MO SYNOD	1	232	324	6.6	10.2
419 SO BAPT CONV..	1	205	249*	5.1	7.9
449 UN METHODIST..	2	560	681*	13.9	21.5
453 UN PRES CH USA	2	263	320*	6.6	10.1
KNOX	**34**	**5 076**	**9 405***	**82.1**	**100.0**
029 AMER LUTH CH..	2	567	812	7.1	8.6
081 CATHOLIC......	5	NA	2 855	24.9	30.4
151 L-D SAINTS....	1	NA	?	?	?
193 EPISCOPAL.....	4	139	263	2.3	2.8
201 EVAN COV CH AM	1	189	228*	2.0	2.4
281 LUTH CH AMER..	4	1 564	1 998	17.4	21.2
283 LUTH--MO SYNOD	5	1 146	1 470	12.8	15.6
353 CHR BRETHREN..	1	15	20	0.2	0.2
443 UN C OF CHRIST	4	356	430*	3.8	4.6
449 UN METHODIST..	5	969	1 171*	10.2	12.5
453 UN PRES CH USA	2	131	158*	1.4	1.7
LANCASTER	**171**	**58 243**	**99 741***	**51.7**	**100.0**
019 AMER BAPT USA.	4	1 477	1 753*	0.9	1.8
029 AMER LUTH CH..	7	3 215	4 744	2.5	4.8
053 ASSEMB OF GOD.	6	764	1 194	0.6	1.2
057 BAPT GEN CONF.	1	99	117*	0.1	0.1
063 BEREAN FUND CH	1	232	275*	0.1	0.3
081 CATHOLIC......	14	NA	23 464	12.2	23.5
089 CHR & MISS AL.	5	567	1 164	0.6	1.2
093 CHR CH (DISC).	6	1 791	2 804	1.5	2.8
097 CHR CHS&CHS CR	3	915	1 086*	0.6	1.1
123 CH GOD (ANDER)	3	82	246	0.1	0.2
127 CH GOD (CLEVE)	3	114	135*	0.1	0.1
151 L-D SAINTS....	2	NA	1 167	0.6	1.2
157 CH OF BRETHREN	1	119	141*	0.1	0.1
165 CH OF NAZARENE	3	221	424	0.2	0.4
167 CHS OF CHRIST.	2	445	762	0.4	0.8
175 CONGR CHR CHS.	1	100	119*	0.1	0.1
193 EPISCOPAL.....	4	2 051	2 527	1.3	2.5
201 EVAN COV CH AM	2	515	611*	0.3	0.6
203 EVAN FREE CH..	1	178	211*	0.1	0.2
208 EVAN LUTH ASSN	1	72	97	0.1	0.1
211 EVAN MENN BR..	2	135	176	0.1	0.2
221 FREE METHODIST	1	21	105	0.1	0.1
226 FRIENDS-USA...	1	26	31*	-	-
263 INT FOURSQ GOS	1	259	307*	0.2	0.3
270 CONSRV JUDAISM	1	165	196*	0.1	0.2
271 REFORM JUDAISM	1	162	192*	0.1	0.2
274 LAT EVAN LUTH.	2	366	393	0.2	0.4
281 LUTH CH AMER..	8	4 434	5 694	3.0	5.7
283 LUTH--MO SYNOD	13	7 794	10 507	5.4	10.5
285 MENNONITE CH..	1	30	36*	-	-
287 MENN GEN CONF.	1	10	18	-	-

NA—Not applicable   *Total adherents estimated from known number of communicant, confirmed, full members.   —Represents a percent less than 0.1.   Percentages may not total due to rounding.

Table 4. Churches and Church Membership by County and Denomination: 1980

County and Denomination	Number of churches	Communicant, confirmed, full members	Total adherents		
			Number	Percent of total population	Percent of total adherents
290 METRO COMM CHS	0	20	40	–	–
291 MISSIONARY CH.	1	78	92	–	0.1
329 OPEN BIBLE STD	1	36	60	–	0.1
335 ORTH PRESB CH.	1	50	59*	–	0.1
353 CHR BRETHREN..	1	50	75	–	0.1
356 PRESB CH AMER.	1	?	?	?	?
371 REF CH IN AM..	3	635	940	0.5	0.9
403 SALVATION ARMY	1	266	1 233	0.6	1.2
413 S.D.A.........	7	2 863	3 397*	1.8	3.4
419 SO BAPT CONV..	2	975	1 157*	0.6	1.2
431 UKRANIAN AMER.	1	160	210	0.1	0.2
435 UNITARIAN-UNIV	1	364	432*	0.2	0.4
443 UN C OF CHRIST	10	4 144	4 917*	2.5	4.9
449 UN METHODIST..	27	14 510	17 217*	8.9	17.3
453 UN PRES CH USA	10	7 395	8 775*	4.5	8.8
469 WELS.........	2	338	441	0.2	0.4
LINCOLN	44	10 008	20 149*	55.3	100.0
019 AMER BAPT USA.	2	540	667*	1.8	3.3
053 ASSEMB OF GOD.	3	187	498	1.4	2.5
057 BAPT GEN CONF.	1	18	22*	0.1	0.1
063 BEREAN FUND CH	2	612	756*	2.1	3.8
081 CATHOLIC......	6	NA	5 518	15.1	27.4
093 CHR CH (DISC).	1	545	1 087	3.0	5.4
097 CHR CHS&CHS CR	1	125	154*	0.4	0.8
123 CH GOD (ANDER)	1	20	60	0.2	0.3
127 CH GOD (CLEVE)	1	66	82*	0.2	0.4
151 L-D SAINTS....	1	NA	371	1.0	1.8
165 CH OF NAZARENE	1	221	348	1.0	1.7
167 CHS OF CHRIST.	1	140	159	0.4	0.8
193 EPISCOPAL.....	1	373	536	1.5	2.7
201 EVAN COV CH AM	1	29	36*	0.1	0.2
203 EVAN FREE CH..	1	207	256*	0.7	1.3
263 INT FOURSQ GOS	1	232	287*	0.8	1.4
281 LUTH CH AMER..	4	1 518	2 298	6.3	11.4
283 LUTH--MO SYNOD	2	985	1 441	4.0	7.2
329 OPEN BIBLE STD	1	45	65	0.2	0.3
403 SALVATION ARMY	1	209	625	1.7	3.1
413 S.D.A.........	1	158	195*	0.5	1.0
419 SO BAPT CONV..	1	161	199*	0.5	1.0
449 UN METHODIST..	6	2 398	2 963*	8.1	14.7
453 UN PRES CH USA	2	1 103	1 363*	3.7	6.8
469 WELS..........	1	116	163	0.4	0.8
LOGAN	4	196	491*	49.9	100.0
053 ASSEMB OF GOD.	1	8	27	2.7	5.5
063 BEREAN FUND CH	1	23	29*	3.0	5.9
081 CATHOLIC......	1	NA	230	23.4	46.8
453 UN PRES CH USA	1	165	205*	20.9	41.8
LOUP	2	100	145*	16.9	100.0
053 ASSEMB OF GOD.	1	34	65	7.6	44.8
449 UN METHODIST..	1	66	80*	9.3	55.2
MC PHERSON	2	76	182*	30.7	100.0
221 FREE METHODIST	1	14	108	18.2	59.3
449 UN METHODIST..	1	62	74*	12.5	40.7
MADISON	53	14 851	26 088*	83.1	100.0
019 AMER BAPT USA.	1	450	545*	1.7	2.1
029 AMER LUTH CH..	3	670	864	2.8	3.3
053 ASSEMB OF GOD.	1	34	200	0.6	0.8
081 CATHOLIC......	5	NA	7 017	22.4	26.9
089 CHR & MISS AL.	2	56	110	0.4	0.4
097 CHR CHS&CHS CR	3	820	992*	3.2	3.8
127 CH GOD (CLEVE)	1	9	11*	–	–
151 L-D SAINTS....	1	NA	145	0.5	0.6
165 CH OF NAZARENE	2	28	51	0.2	0.2
167 CHS OF CHRIST.	1	30	48	0.2	0.2
181 CONSRV CONGR..	1	12	15*	–	0.1
193 EPISCOPAL.....	1	309	360	1.1	1.4
203 EVAN FREE CH..	2	60	73*	0.2	0.3
281 LUTH CH AMER..	3	1 229	1 638	5.2	6.3
283 LUTH--MO SYNOD	9	5 888	7 610	24.2	29.2
413 S.D.A.........	1	40	48*	0.2	0.2
419 SO BAPT CONV..	1	161	195*	0.6	0.7
443 UN C OF CHRIST	2	578	700*	2.2	2.7
449 UN METHODIST..	9	3 051	3 692*	11.8	14.2
453 UN PRES CH USA	2	645	781*	2.5	3.0
469 WELS..........	2	781	993	3.2	3.8
MERRICK	27	3 735	6 048*	67.6	100.0
019 AMER BAPT USA.	1	121	149*	1.7	2.5
057 BAPT GEN CONF.	0	10	12*	0.1	0.2
063 BEREAN FUND CH	1	34	42*	0.5	0.7
081 CATHOLIC......	3	NA	1 239	13.9	20.5
097 CHR CHS&CHS CR	2	210	258*	2.9	4.3
133 CH GOD(7TH)DEN	1	7	9*	0.1	0.1
165 CH OF NAZARENE	1	7	30	0.1	0.5
167 CHS OF CHRIST.	1	6	13	0.1	0.2
181 CONSRV CONGR..	1	70	86*	1.0	1.4
193 EPISCOPAL.....	1	56	140	1.6	2.3
203 EVAN FREE CH..	1	60	74*	0.8	1.2
226 FRIENDS-USA...	1	110	135*	1.5	2.2
281 LUTH CH AMER..	1	200	272	3.0	4.5
283 LUTH--MO SYNOD	3	806	1 083	12.1	17.9
449 UN METHODIST..	8	1 858	2 285*	25.5	37.8
453 UN PRES CH USA	1	180	221*	2.5	3.7
MORRILL	21	2 532	3 661*	60.2	100.0
019 AMER BAPT USA.	1	184	225*	3.7	6.1
053 ASSEMB OF GOD.	3	251	331	5.4	9.0
081 CATHOLIC......	3	NA	394	6.5	10.8
097 CHR CHS&CHS CR	2	302	369*	6.1	10.1
151 L-D SAINTS....	1	NA	76	1.2	2.1
165 CH OF NAZARENE	1	?	?	?	?
181 CONSRV CONGR..	1	165	201*	3.3	5.5
281 LUTH CH AMER..	1	182	252	4.1	6.9
283 LUTH--MO SYNOD	2	434	575	9.4	15.7
413 S.D.A.........	1	19	23*	0.4	0.6
443 UN C OF CHRIST	1	303	370*	6.1	10.1
449 UN METHODIST..	1	139	170*	2.8	4.6
453 UN PRES CH USA	3	553	675*	11.1	18.4
NANCE	14	1 660	3 893*	82.1	100.0
081 CATHOLIC......	3	NA	1 859	39.2	47.8
175 CONGR CHR CHS.	1	95	115*	2.4	3.0
203 EVAN FREE CH..	1	20	24*	0.5	0.6
209 EVAN LUTH SYN.	1	102	142	3.0	3.6
281 LUTH CH AMER..	1	334	400	8.4	10.3
283 LUTH--MO SYNOD	1	190	239	5.0	6.1
413 S.D.A.........	1	15	18*	0.4	0.5
449 UN METHODIST..	4	711	862*	18.2	22.1
453 UN PRES CH USA	1	193	234*	4.9	6.0
NEMAHA	27	4 111	5 550*	66.3	100.0
029 AMER LUTH CH..	4	840	1 003	12.0	18.1
053 ASSEMB OF GOD.	1	53	76	0.9	1.4
063 BEREAN FUND CH	1	45	54*	0.6	1.0
081 CATHOLIC......	3	NA	451	5.4	8.1
093 CHR CH (DISC).	4	453	577	6.9	10.4
097 CHR CHS&CHS CR	1	580	691*	8.3	12.5
167 CHS OF CHRIST.	1	26	46	0.5	0.8
281 LUTH CH AMER..	3	866	1 135	13.6	20.5
283 LUTH--MO SYNOD	1	177	241	2.9	4.3
419 SO BAPT CONV..	1	50	60*	0.7	1.1
449 UN METHODIST..	6	884	1 053*	12.6	19.0
453 UN PRES CH USA	1	137	163*	1.9	2.9
NUCKOLLS	25	2 969	5 250*	78.1	100.0
019 AMER BAPT USA.	1	246	295*	4.4	5.6
029 AMER LUTH CH..	2	463	601	8.9	11.4
053 ASSEMB OF GOD.	1	19	35	0.5	0.7
081 CATHOLIC......	4	NA	1 463	21.8	27.9
093 CHR CH (DISC).	1	88	146	2.2	2.8
097 CHR CHS&CHS CR	2	120	144*	2.1	2.7
165 CH OF NAZARENE	1	28	79	1.2	1.5
167 CHS OF CHRIST.	1	34	49	0.7	0.9
281 LUTH CH AMER..	2	198	262	3.9	5.0
283 LUTH--MO SYNOD	2	453	595	8.8	11.3
383 REF PRES OF NA	1	48	58	0.9	1.1
413 S.D.A.........	1	36	43*	0.6	0.8
449 UN METHODIST..	4	875	1 048*	15.6	20.0
453 UN PRES CH USA	2	361	432*	6.4	8.2
OTOE	40	7 214	11 723*	77.2	100.0
029 AMER LUTH CH..	5	2 055	2 473	16.3	21.1
053 ASSEMB OF GOD.	1	88	100	0.7	0.9
081 CATHOLIC......	7	NA	2 346	15.5	20.0
093 CHR CH (DISC).	2	390	917	6.0	7.8
097 CHR CHS&CHS CR	2	125	150*	1.0	1.3
151 L-D SAINTS....	1	NA	166	1.1	1.4
167 CHS OF CHRIST.	1	18	36	0.2	0.3
193 EPISCOPAL.....	1	143	198	1.3	1.7
281 LUTH CH AMER..	2	762	971	6.4	8.3
283 LUTH--MO SYNOD	1	58	84	0.6	0.7
413 S.D.A.........	1	30	36*	0.2	0.3
419 SO BAPT CONV..	1	41	49*	0.3	0.4
443 UN C OF CHRIST	5	1 359	1 628*	10.7	13.9
449 UN METHODIST..	6	1 392	1 667*	11.0	14.2
453 UN PRES CH USA	4	753	902*	5.9	7.7
PAWNEE	15	1 829	2 739*	69.6	100.0
019 AMER BAPT USA.	1	164	191*	4.9	7.0
029 AMER LUTH CH..	1	21	30	0.8	1.1
081 CATHOLIC......	2	NA	529	13.4	19.3
093 CHR CH (DISC).	1	137	211	5.4	7.7
097 CHR CHS&CHS CR	1	55	64*	1.6	2.3
283 LUTH--MO SYNOD	2	373	459	11.7	16.8
443 UN C OF CHRIST	1	237	276*	7.0	10.1
449 UN METHODIST..	5	632	735*	18.7	26.8
453 UN PRES CH USA	1	210	244*	6.2	8.9
PERKINS	14	1 929	2 800*	77.0	100.0
081 CATHOLIC......	2	NA	457	12.6	16.3
143 CG IN CR(MENN)	1	51	51	1.4	1.8
237 GC MENN BR CHS	1	76	93*	2.6	3.3
263 INT FOURSQ GOS	1	32	39*	1.1	1.4
283 LUTH--MO SYNOD	3	371	456	12.5	16.3
443 UN C OF CHRIST	1	289	352*	9.7	12.6
449 UN METHODIST..	5	1 110	1 352*	37.2	48.3
PHELPS	26	5 526	7 423*	76.0	100.0
019 AMER BAPT USA.	1	405	488*	5.0	6.6
053 ASSEMB OF GOD.	1	93	176	1.8	2.4
057 BAPT GEN CONF.	0	4	5*	0.1	0.1

NA— Not applicable   *Total adherents estimated from known number of communicant, confirmed, full members.   —Represents a percent less than 0.1.   Percentages may not total due to rounding.

Table 4. Churches and Church Membership by County and Denomination: 1980

County and Denomination	Number of churches	Communicant, confirmed, full members	Total adherents		
			Number	Percent of total population	Percent of total adherents
081 CATHOLIC......	1	NA	563	5.8	7.6
167 CHS OF CHRIST.	1	58	73	0.7	1.0
193 EPISCOPAL.....	1	100	107	1.1	1.4
201 EVAN COV CH AM	1	67	81*	0.8	1.1
203 EVAN FREE CH..	5	627	756*	7.7	10.2
281 LUTH CH AMER..	4	1 270	1 596	16.3	21.5
283 LUTH--MO SYNOD	2	669	887	9.1	11.9
413 S.D.A........	1	47	57*	0.6	0.8
449 UN METHODIST..	7	1 756	2 116*	21.7	28.5
453 UN PRES CH USA	1	430	518*	5.3	7.0
PIERCE	**20**	**4 557**	**7 153***	**84.3**	**100.0**
029 AMER LUTH CH..	1	376	485	5.7	6.8
081 CATHOLIC......	3	NA	1 493	17.6	20.9
226 FRIENDS-USA...	1	48	58*	0.7	0.8
281 LUTH CH AMER..	1	227	309	3.6	4.3
283 LUTH--MO SYNOD	5	2 285	2 840	33.5	39.7
443 UN C OF CHRIST	2	504	611*	7.2	8.5
449 UN METHODIST..	6	859	1 041*	12.3	14.6
469 WELS..........	1	258	316	3.7	4.4
PLATTE	**43**	**8 980**	**25 712***	**89.1**	**100.0**
019 AMER BAPT USA.	3	343	425*	1.5	1.7
053 ASSEMB OF GOD.	1	85	185	0.6	0.7
057 BAPT GEN CONF.	0	2	2*	-	-
081 CATHOLIC......	8	NA	13 941	48.3	54.2
097 CHR CHS&CHS CR	1	40	50*	0.2	0.2
165 CH OF NAZARENE	1	26	63	0.2	0.2
167 CHS OF CHRIST.	1	21	36	0.1	0.1
193 EPISCOPAL.....	1	127	206	0.7	0.8
203 EVAN FREE CH..	1	118	146*	0.5	0.6
281 LUTH CH AMER..	7	2 557	3 506	12.2	13.6
283 LUTH--MO SYNOD	6	2 691	3 464	12.0	13.5
313 N AM BAPT CONF	3	153	190*	0.7	0.7
413 S.D.A........	1	27	33*	0.1	0.1
419 SO BAPT CONV..	1	80	99*	0.3	0.4
443 UN C OF CHRIST	2	700	867*	3.0	3.4
449 UN METHODIST..	4	1 405	1 741*	6.0	6.8
453 UN PRES CH USA	1	578	716*	2.5	2.8
469 WELS..........	1	27	42	0.1	0.2
POLK	**21**	**3 391**	**5 314***	**84.1**	**100.0**
019 AMER BAPT USA.	1	236	286*	4.5	5.4
057 BAPT GEN CONF.	2	362	439*	6.9	8.3
081 CATHOLIC......	4	NA	1 138	18.0	21.4
201 EVAN COV CH AM	1	128	155*	2.5	2.9
203 EVAN FREE CH..	2	138	167*	2.6	3.1
281 LUTH CH AMER..	4	1 067	1 357	21.5	25.5
449 UN METHODIST..	7	1 460	1 772*	28.0	33.3
RED WILLOW	**27**	**4 684**	**8 518***	**67.5**	**100.0**
019 AMER BAPT USA.	1	244	295*	2.3	3.5
029 AMER LUTH CH..	1	216	346	2.7	4.1
053 ASSEMB OF GOD.	1	135	250	2.0	2.9
063 BEREAN FUND CH	1	72	87*	0.7	1.0
081 CATHOLIC......	2	NA	2 183	17.3	25.6
093 CHR CH (DISC).	1	114	329	2.6	3.9
097 CHR CHS&CHS CR	3	307	371*	2.9	4.4
123 CH GOD (ANDER)	1	54	162	1.3	1.9
127 CH GOD (CLEVE)	1	23	28*	0.2	0.3
151 L-D SAINTS....	1	NA	101	0.8	1.2
165 CH OF NAZARENE	1	12	25	0.2	0.3
167 CHS OF CHRIST.	1	81	128	1.0	1.5
175 CONGR CHR CHS.	1	481	581*	4.6	6.8
193 EPISCOPAL.....	1	364	443	3.5	5.2
283 LUTH--MO SYNOD	2	835	1 078	8.5	12.7
413 S.D.A........	1	65	78*	0.6	0.9
419 SO BAPT CONV..	1	86	104*	0.8	1.2
449 UN METHODIST..	3	1 490	1 799*	14.3	21.1
453 UN PRES CH USA	2	80	97*	0.8	1.1
469 WELS..........	1	25	33	0.3	0.4
RICHARDSON	**38**	**4 857**	**8 031***	**71.0**	**100.0**
019 AMER BAPT USA.	1	110	130*	1.1	1.6
053 ASSEMB OF GOD.	1	38	40	0.4	0.5
063 BEREAN FUND CH	1	24	28*	0.2	0.3
071 BRETHREN (ASH)	1	75	89*	0.8	1.1
081 CATHOLIC......	5	NA	1 584	14.0	19.7
093 CHR CH (DISC).	4	628	1 024	9.0	12.8
097 CHR CHS&CHS CR	1	50	59*	0.5	0.7
127 CH GOD (CLEVE)	1	?	?	?	?
165 CH OF NAZARENE	1	119	361	3.2	4.5
167 CHS OF CHRIST.	1	73	142	1.3	1.8
175 CONGR CHR CHS.	2	282	333*	2.9	4.1
193 EPISCOPAL.....	1	67	130	1.1	1.6
281 LUTH CH AMER..	3	801	1 014	9.0	12.6
283 LUTH--MO SYNOD	3	710	875	7.7	10.9
413 S.D.A........	1	36	43*	0.4	0.5
443 UN C OF CHRIST	2	191	226*	2.0	2.8
449 UN METHODIST..	7	1 322	1 562*	13.8	19.4
453 UN PRES CH USA	2	331	391*	3.5	4.9
ROCK	**8**	**602**	**1 009***	**42.3**	**100.0**
029 AMER LUTH CH..	1	126	189	7.9	18.7
053 ASSEMB OF GOD.	1	47	70	2.9	6.9
081 CATHOLIC......	1	NA	190	8.0	18.8
097 CHR CHS&CHS CR	1	26	32*	1.3	3.2
193 EPISCOPAL.....	1	44	88	3.7	8.7
449 UN METHODIST..	3	359	440*	18.5	43.6
SALINE	**24**	**4 357**	**6 649***	**50.6**	**100.0**
019 AMER BAPT USA.	1	28	33*	0.3	0.5
029 AMER LUTH CH..	1	408	523	4.0	7.9
081 CATHOLIC......	4	NA	1 310	10.0	19.7
193 EPISCOPAL.....	2	68	78	0.6	1.2
281 LUTH CH AMER..	1	242	323	2.5	4.9
283 LUTH--MO SYNOD	2	1 007	1 290	9.8	19.4
443 UN C OF CHRIST	5	875	1 039*	7.9	15.6
449 UN METHODIST..	8	1 729	2 053*	15.6	30.9
SARPY	**39**	**13 147**	**32 545***	**37.8**	**100.0**
019 AMER BAPT USA.	1	137	174*	0.2	0.5
029 AMER LUTH CH..	2	509	723	0.8	2.2
053 ASSEMB OF GOD.	1	538	1 200	1.4	3.7
057 BAPT GEN CONF.	2	226	287*	0.3	0.9
081 CATHOLIC......	3	NA	13 396	15.6	41.2
089 CHR & MISS AL.	1	75	101	0.1	0.3
093 CHR CH (DISC).	1	178	495	0.6	1.5
097 CHR CHS&CHS CR	2	591	751*	0.9	2.3
127 CH GOD (CLEVE)	1	64	81*	0.1	0.2
151 L-D SAINTS....	2	NA	908	1.1	2.8
167 CHS OF CHRIST.	1	296	407	0.5	1.3
193 EPISCOPAL.....	2	503	701	0.8	2.2
221 FREE METHODIST	1		189	0.2	0.6
281 LUTH CH AMER..	3	1 746	2 467	2.9	7.6
283 LUTH--MO SYNOD	3	1 390	1 952	2.3	6.0
413 S.D.A........	1	99	126*	0.1	0.4
419 SO BAPT CONV..	4	3 209	4 080*	4.7	12.5
449 UN METHODIST..	5	2 115	2 689*	3.1	8.3
453 UN PRES CH USA	3	1 430	1 818*	2.1	5.6
SAUNDERS	**47**	**5 587**	**12 870***	**68.8**	**100.0**
019 AMER BAPT USA.	1	127	155*	0.8	1.2
029 AMER LUTH CH..	2	309	429	2.3	3.3
057 BAPT GEN CONF.	3	121	147*	0.8	1.1
081 CATHOLIC......	12	NA	5 473	29.2	42.5
093 CHR CH (DISC).	1	225	626	3.3	4.9
097 CHR CHS&CHS CR	1	40	49*	0.3	0.4
175 CONGR CHR CHS.	1	135	164*	0.9	1.3
193 EPISCOPAL.....	1	2	1	-	-
201 EVAN COV CH AM	4	344	419*	2.2	3.3
281 LUTH CH AMER..	6	1 580	2 083	11.1	16.2
283 LUTH--MO SYNOD	2	389	505	2.7	3.9
443 UN C OF CHRIST	2	193	235*	1.3	1.8
449 UN METHODIST..	7	1 277	1 555*	8.3	12.1
453 UN PRES CH USA	4	845	1 029*	5.5	8.0
SCOTTS BLUFF	**63**	**12 071**	**21 588***	**56.3**	**100.0**
019 AMER BAPT USA.	2	389	478*	1.2	2.2
029 AMER LUTH CH..	1	649	893	2.3	4.1
053 ASSEMB OF GOD.	6	710	1 182	3.1	5.5
057 BAPT GEN CONF.	1	74	91*	0.2	0.4
063 BEREAN FUND CH	3	269	331*	0.9	1.5
081 CATHOLIC......	7	NA	5 554	14.5	25.7
093 CHR CH (DISC).	2	333	524	1.4	2.4
097 CHR CHS&CHS CR	7	805	990*	2.6	4.6
123 CH GOD (ANDER)	2	115	345	0.9	1.6
127 CH GOD (CLEVE)	1	20	25*	0.1	0.1
151 L-D SAINTS....	1	NA	281	0.7	1.3
165 CH OF NAZARENE	1	108	256	0.7	1.2
167 CHS OF CHRIST.	1	47	53	0.1	0.2
181 CONSRV CONGR..	1	665	817*	2.1	3.8
193 EPISCOPAL.....	2	571	713	1.9	3.3
263 INT FOURSQ GOS	1	148	182*	0.5	0.8
283 LUTH--MO SYNOD	4	1 361	1 723	4.5	8.0
413 S.D.A........	3	256	315*	0.8	1.5
419 SO BAPT CONV..	1	264	325*	0.8	1.5
443 UN C OF CHRIST	4	722	888*	2.3	4.1
449 UN METHODIST..	8	3 247	4 041*	10.5	18.7
453 UN PRES CH USA	3	1 248	1 534*	4.0	7.1
469 WELS..........	1	30	47	0.1	0.2
SEWARD	**39**	**8 090**	**11 716***	**74.2**	**100.0**
029 AMER LUTH CH..	1	195	262	1.7	2.2
053 ASSEMB OF GOD.	1	69	133	0.8	1.1
057 BAPT GEN CONF.	0	1	1*	-	-
081 CATHOLIC......	4	NA	1 552	9.8	13.2
093 CHR CH (DISC).	1	26	57	0.4	0.5
167 CHS OF CHRIST.	1	20	30	0.2	0.3
193 EPISCOPAL.....	1	26	69	0.4	0.6
203 EVAN FREE CH..	1	48	58*	0.4	0.5
281 LUTH CH AMER..	1	309	389	2.5	3.3
283 LUTH--MO SYNOD	9	3 980	5 039	31.9	43.0
285 MENNONITE CH..	5	905	1 088*	6.9	9.3
291 MISSIONARY CH.	1	38	57	0.4	0.5
413 S.D.A........	1	8	10*	0.1	0.1
443 UN C OF CHRIST	2	323	388*	2.5	3.3
449 UN METHODIST..	6	1 838	2 209*	14.0	18.9
453 UN PRES CH USA	2	191	230*	1.5	2.0
469 WELS..........	2	113	144	0.9	1.2
SHERIDAN	**24**	**2 556**	**4 309***	**57.1**	**100.0**
029 AMER LUTH CH..	1	118	145	1.9	3.4
081 CATHOLIC......	4	NA	962	12.8	22.3
123 CH GOD (ANDER)	2	103	309	4.1	7.2
151 L-D SAINTS....	1	NA	?	?	?
193 EPISCOPAL.....	2	141	233	3.1	5.4
226 FRIENDS-USA...	1	44	54*	0.7	1.3
281 LUTH CH AMER..	1	184	220	2.9	5.1

NA—Not applicable   *Total adherents estimated from known number of communicant, confirmed, full members.   —Represents a percent less than 0.1.   Percentages may not total due to rounding.

Table 4. Churches and Church Membership by County and Denomination: 1980

County and Denomination	Number of churches	Communicant, confirmed, full members	Total adherents		
			Number	Percent of total population	Percent of total adherents
283 LUTH--MO SYNOD	3	578	696	9.2	16.2
413 S.D.A.........	2	42	51*	0.7	1.2
443 UN C OF CHRIST	1	30	37*	0.5	0.9
449 UN METHODIST..	5	1 013	1 233*	16.3	28.6
453 UN PRES CH USA	1	303	369*	4.9	8.6
SHERMAN	13	776	3 332*	78.8	100.0
029 AMER LUTH CH..	1	112	144	3.4	4.3
057 BAPT GEN CONF.	0	3	4*	0.1	0.1
081 CATHOLIC......	4	NA	2 340	55.4	70.2
097 CHR CHS&CHS CR	1	80	98*	2.3	2.9
165 CH OF NAZARENE	1	?	?	?	?
283 LUTH--MO SYNOD	1	166	240	5.7	7.2
413 S.D.A.........	1	11	13*	0.3	0.4
443 UN C OF CHRIST	1	48	59*	1.4	1.8
449 UN METHODIST..	2	261	318*	7.5	9.5
453 UN PRES CH USA	1	95	116*	2.7	3.5
SIOUX	3	244	490*	26.6	100.0
081 CATHOLIC......	1	NA	191	10.4	39.0
283 LUTH--MO SYNOD	1	37	51	2.8	10.4
449 UN METHODIST..	1	207	248*	13.4	50.6
STANTON	10	1 663	2 596*	39.6	100.0
081 CATHOLIC......	1	NA	485	7.4	18.7
203 EVAN FREE CH..	1	25	31*	0.5	1.2
281 LUTH CH AMER..	2	278	361	5.5	13.9
283 LUTH--MO SYNOD	2	528	656	10.0	25.3
443 UN C OF CHRIST	1	252	317*	4.8	12.2
449 UN METHODIST..	2	294	370*	5.6	14.3
469 WELS.........	1	286	376	5.7	14.5
THAYER	32	5 447	7 321*	96.6	100.0
029 AMER LUTH CH..	8	2 351	2 899	38.2	39.6
053 ASSEMB OF GOD.	1	31	40	0.5	0.5
071 BRETHREN (ASH)	1	?	?	?	?
081 CATHOLIC......:	3	NA	678	8.9	9.3
093 CHR CH (DISC).	1	165	193	2.5	2.6
097 CHR CHS&CHS CR	1	100	119*	1.6	1.6
157 CH OF BRETHREN	1	106	126*	1.7	1.7
167 CHS OF CHRIST.	1	40	55	0.7	0.8
281 LUTH CH AMER..	1	284	342	4.5	4.7
283 LUTH--MO SYNOD	5	1 100	1 359	17.9	18.6
443 UN C OF CHRIST	1	79	94*	1.2	1.3
449 UN METHODIST..	5	920	1 094*	14.4	14.9
453 UN PRES CH USA	3	271	322*	4.2	4.4
THOMAS	8	369	571*	58.7	100.0
053 ASSEMB OF GOD.	1	59	95	9.8	16.6
081 CATHOLIC......	1	NA	66	6.8	11.6
164 CH LUTH CONF..	1	9	9	0.9	1.6
283 LUTH--MO SYNOD	1	47	68	7.0	11.9
329 OPEN BIBLE STD	1	22	45	4.6	7.9
443 UN C OF CHRIST	3	232	288*	29.6	50.4
THURSTON	24	2 533	4 707*	65.5	100.0
053 ASSEMB OF GOD.	2	81	115	1.6	2.4
081 CATHOLIC......	4	NA	755	10.5	16.0
151 L-D SAINTS....	2	NA	317	4.4	6.7
193 EPISCOPAL.....	1	26	50	0.7	1.1
201 EVAN COV CH AM	1	67	84*	1.2	1.8
281 LUTH CH AMER..	3	1 022	1 301	18.1	27.6
283 LUTH--MO SYNOD	1	282	409	5.7	8.7
371 REF CH IN AM..	2	97	473	6.6	10.0
449 UN METHODIST..	3	532	668*	9.3	14.2
453 UN PRES CH USA	5	426	535*	7.4	11.4
VALLEY	19	2 325	4 043*	71.8	100.0
029 AMER LUTH CH..	1	129	171	3.0	4.2
053 ASSEMB OF GOD.	1	35	60	1.1	1.5
057 BAPT GEN CONF.	2	116	140*	2.5	3.5
081 CATHOLIC......	4	NA	1 266	22.5	31.3
097 CHR CHS&CHS CR	1	154	186*	3.3	4.6
203 EVAN FREE CH..	1	40	48*	0.9	1.2
283 LUTH--MO SYNOD	1	288	288	5.1	7.1
415 S-D BAPTIST GC	1	205	247*	4.4	6.1
443 UN C OF CHRIST	1	18	22*	0.4	0.5
449 UN METHODIST..	5	1 210	1 458*	25.9	36.1
453 UN PRES CH USA	1	130	157*	2.8	3.9
WASHINGTON	23	5 747	8 784*	56.6	100.0
019 AMER BAPT USA.	2	225	275*	1.8	3.1
029 AMER LUTH CH..	4	1 436	1 825	11.8	20.8
053 ASSEMB OF GOD.	1	41	58	0.4	0.7
057 BAPT GEN CONF.	1	22	27*	0.2	0.3
081 CATHOLIC......	2	NA	1 481	9.5	16.9
093 CHR CH (DISC).	1	166	255	1.6	2.9
097 CHR CHS&CHS CR	1	200	245*	1.6	2.8
167 CHS OF CHRIST.	1	26	36	0.2	0.4
281 LUTH CH AMER..	1	290	379	2.4	4.3
283 LUTH--MO SYNOD	3	1 068	1 423	9.2	16.2
443 UN C OF CHRIST	2	608	744*	4.8	8.5
449 UN METHODIST..	3	1 453	1 777*	11.5	20.2
453 UN PRES CH USA	1	212	259*	1.7	2.9
WAYNE	26	4 952	6 868*	69.7	100.0

County and Denomination	Number of churches	Communicant, confirmed, full members	Total adherents		
			Number	Percent of total population	Percent of total adherents
019 AMER BAPT USA.	1	83	98*	1.0	1.4
053 ASSEMB OF GOD.	1	36	65	0.7	0.9
081 CATHOLIC......	1	NA	685	6.9	10.0
097 CHR CHS&CHS CR	1	35	41*	0.4	0.6
193 EPISCOPAL.....	1	10	14	0.1	0.2
201 EVAN COV CH AM	1	194	229*	2.3	3.3
203 EVAN FREE CH..	1	22	26*	0.3	0.4
281 LUTH CH AMER..	3	1 367	1 862	18.9	27.1
283 LUTH--MO SYNOD	6	1 529	1 861	18.9	27.1
443 UN C OF CHRIST	2	73	86*	0.9	1.3
449 UN METHODIST..	3	884	1 042*	10.6	15.2
453 UN PRES CH USA	3	426	502*	5.1	7.3
469 WELS.........	2	293	357	3.6	5.2
WEBSTER	19	2 413	3 361*	69.2	100.0
019 AMER BAPT USA.	1	66	78*	1.6	2.3
053 ASSEMB OF GOD.	1	39	56	1.2	1.7
081 CATHOLIC......	2	NA	402	8.3	12.0
097 CHR CHS&CHS CR	2	65	77*	1.6	2.3
167 CHS OF CHRIST.	1	20	25	0.5	0.7
281 LUTH CH AMER..	1	246	329	6.8	9.8
283 LUTH--MO SYNOD	3	668	845	17.4	25.1
443 UN C OF CHRIST	1	153	181*	3.7	5.4
449 UN METHODIST..	7	1 156	1 368*	28.2	40.7
WHEELER	3	180	351*	33.1	100.0
081 CATHOLIC......	1	NA	125	11.8	35.6
449 UN METHODIST..	2	180	226*	21.3	64.4
YORK	35	8 169	12 144*	82.1	100.0
019 AMER BAPT USA.	1	72	87*	0.6	0.7
053 ASSEMB OF GOD.	1	37	58	0.4	0.5
057 BAPT GEN CONF.	1	85	103*	0.7	0.8
081 CATHOLIC......	2	NA	1 651	11.2	13.6
093 CHR CH (DISC).	1	153	192	1.3	1.6
165 CH OF NAZARENE	1	139	299	2.0	2.5
167 CHS OF CHRIST.	1	460	535	3.6	4.4
193 EPISCOPAL.....	1	4	22	0.1	0.2
211 EVAN MENN BR..	1	154	200	1.4	1.6
237 GC MENN BR CHS	1	237	287*	1.9	2.4
281 LUTH CH AMER..	3	655	859	5.8	7.1
283 LUTH--MO SYNOD	6	2 308	2 953	20.0	24.3
287 MENN GEN CONF.	1	1 182	1 646	11.1	13.6
413 S.D.A.........	1	23	28*	0.2	0.2
419 SO BAPT CONV..	1	50	61*	0.4	0.5
443 UN C OF CHRIST	2	108	131*	0.9	1.1
449 UN METHODIST..	8	2 014	2 441*	16.5	20.1
453 UN PRES CH USA	2	488	591*	4.0	4.9

NEVADA

County and Denomination	Number of churches	Communicant, confirmed, full members	Total adherents		
			Number	Percent of total population	Percent of total adherents
THE STATE.....	475	49 778	233 781*	29.3	100.0
CARSON CITY	23	3 466	10 325*	32.2	100.0
019 AMER BAPT USA.	1	11	13*	-	0.1
053 ASSEMB OF GOD.	1	132	280	0.9	2.7
081 CATHOLIC......	4	NA	4 250	13.3	41.2
097 CHR CHS&CHS CR	1	55	65*	0.2	0.6
127 CH GOD (CLEVE)	1	14	17*	0.1	0.2
151 L-D SAINTS....	4	NA	1 715	5.4	16.6
165 CH OF NAZARENE	1	37	95	0.3	0.9
167 CHS OF CHRIST.	1	50	82	0.3	0.8
193 EPISCOPAL.....	1	348	400	1.2	3.9
281 LUTH CH AMER..	1	192	269	0.8	2.6
283 LUTH--MO SYNOD	1	179	250	0.8	2.4
413 S.D.A.........	1	114	135*	0.4	1.3
419 SO BAPT CONV..	2	856	1 010*	3.2	9.8
449 UN METHODIST..	2	878	1 036*	3.2	10.0
453 UN PRES CH USA	1	600	708*	2.2	6.9
CHURCHILL	12	1 079	4 851*	34.9	100.0
053 ASSEMB OF GOD.	1	94	129	0.9	2.7
081 CATHOLIC......	1	NA	2 100	15.1	43.3
151 L-D SAINTS....	3	NA	1 239	8.9	25.5
165 CH OF NAZARENE	1	108	169	1.2	3.5
167 CHS OF CHRIST.	1	50	68	0.5	1.4
193 EPISCOPAL.....	1	95	150	1.1	3.1
283 LUTH--MO SYNOD	1	83	205	1.5	4.2
413 S.D.A.........	1	154	188*	1.4	3.9
419 SO BAPT CONV..	1	208	253*	1.8	5.2
449 UN METHODIST..	1	287	350*	2.5	7.2
CLARK	181	27 298	136 959*	29.7	100.0
019 AMER BAPT USA.	8	1 924	2 325*	0.5	1.7
029 AMER LUTH CH..	3	1 595	2 295	0.5	1.7
053 ASSEMB OF GOD.	5	1 001	5 194	1.1	3.8
059 BAPT MISS ASSN	1	65	79*	-	0.1

NA— Not applicable   *Total adherents estimated from known number of communicant, confirmed, full members.   —Represents a percent less than 0.1.   Percentages may not total due to rounding.

Table 4. Churches and Church Membership by County and Denomination: 1980

County and Denomination	Number of churches	Communicant, confirmed, full members	Total adherents		
			Number	Percent of total population	Percent of total adherents
081 CATHOLIC......	16	NA	63 262	13.7	46.2
093 CHR CH (DISC).	1	454	479	0.1	0.3
097 CHR CHS&CHS CR	2	1 105	1 335*	0.3	1.0
123 CH GOD (ANDER)	2	62	186	–	0.1
127 CH GOD (CLEVE)	4	136	164*	–	0.1
133 CH GOD(7TH)DEN	1	8	10*	–	–
151 L-D SAINTS....	67	NA	35 293	7.6	25.8
165 CH OF NAZARENE	3	311	649	0.1	0.5
167 CHS OF CHRIST.	11	882	1 250	0.3	0.9
193 EPISCOPAL.....	6	1 540	1 887	0.4	1.4
226 FRIENDS-USA...	1	7	8*	–	–
263 INT FOURSQ GOS	4	770	930*	0.2	0.7
270 CONSRV JUDAISM	1	300	363*	0.1	0.3
271 REFORM JUDAISM	1	514	621*	0.1	0.5
281 LUTH CH AMER..	2	561	765	0.2	0.6
283 LUTH--MO SYNOD	5	1 864	2 587	0.6	1.9
290 METRO COMM CHS	1	15	30	–	–
403 SALVATION ARMY	2	258	391	0.1	0.3
413 S.D.A.........	3	568	686*	0.1	0.5
419 SO BAPT CONV..	17	8 642	10 443*	2.3	7.6
435 UNITARIAN-UNIV	1	47	57*	–	–
443 UN C OF CHRIST	2	372	450*	0.1	0.3
449 UN METHODIST..	6	2 561	3 095*	0.7	2.3
453 UN PRES CH USA	4	1 618	1 955*	0.4	1.4
469 WELS..........	1	118	170	–	0.1
DOUGLAS	14	1 010	4 142*	21.3	100.0
053 ASSEMB OF GOD.	1	115	180	0.9	4.3
081 CATHOLIC......	2	NA	2 214	11.4	53.5
097 CHR CHS&CHS CR	1	20	24*	0.1	0.6
151 L-D SAINTS....	1	NA	456	2.3	11.0
193 EPISCOPAL.....	2	175	318	1.6	7.7
283 LUTH--MO SYNOD	1	307	481	2.5	11.6
419 SO BAPT CONV..	2	222	265*	1.4	6.4
449 UN METHODIST..	3	129	154*	0.8	3.7
453 UN PRES CH USA	1	42	50*	0.3	1.2
ELKO	36	1 630	7 014*	40.6	100.0
019 AMER BAPT USA.	1	115	141*	0.8	2.0
053 ASSEMB OF GOD.	4	173	181	1.0	2.6
081 CATHOLIC......	11	NA	2 620	15.2	37.4
151 L-D SAINTS....	8	NA	2 233	12.9	31.8
165 CH OF NAZARENE	1	20	37	0.2	0.5
167 CHS OF CHRIST.	1	8	13	0.1	0.2
193 EPISCOPAL.....	2	182	358	2.1	5.1
283 LUTH--MO SYNOD	1	83	142	0.8	2.0
413 S.D.A.........	1	34	42*	0.2	0.6
419 SO BAPT CONV..	1	279	343*	2.0	4.9
449 UN METHODIST..	1	45	55*	0.3	0.8
453 UN PRES CH USA	4	691	849*	4.9	12.1
ESMERALDA	0	0	125	16.1	100.0
081 CATHOLIC......	0	NA	125	16.1	100.0
EUREKA	5	55	258*	21.5	100.0
081 CATHOLIC......	1	NA	94	7.8	36.4
151 L-D SAINTS....	1	NA	94	7.8	36.4
193 EPISCOPAL.....	1	19	26	2.2	10.1
419 SO BAPT CONV..	2	36	44*	3.7	17.1
HUMBOLDT	16	559	2 845*	30.2	100.0
053 ASSEMB OF GOD.	2	69	154	1.6	5.4
081 CATHOLIC......	6	NA	1 314	13.9	46.2
151 L-D SAINTS....	2	NA	710	7.5	25.0
167 CHS OF CHRIST.	1	5	8	0.1	0.3
193 EPISCOPAL.....	1	31	46	0.5	1.6
283 LUTH--MO SYNOD	1	56	123	1.3	4.3
413 S.D.A.........	1	42	52*	0.6	1.8
419 SO BAPT CONV..	1	147	181*	1.9	6.4
449 UN METHODIST..	1	209	257*	2.7	9.0
LANDER	10	230	1 412*	34.6	100.0
053 ASSEMB OF GOD.	1	56	80	2.0	5.7
081 CATHOLIC......	2	NA	571	14.0	40.4
151 L-D SAINTS....	2	NA	530	13.0	37.5
193 EPISCOPAL.....	2	23	36	0.9	2.5
283 LUTH--MO SYNOD	1	22	33	0.8	2.3
419 SO BAPT CONV..	1	111	139*	3.4	9.8
449 UN METHODIST..	1	18	23*	0.6	1.6
LINCOLN	8	65	1 972*	52.8	100.0
081 CATHOLIC......	1	NA	474	12.7	24.0
151 L-D SAINTS....	4	NA	1 376	36.9	69.8
193 EPISCOPAL.....	1	20	66	1.8	3.3
419 SO BAPT CONV..	1	36	45*	1.2	2.3
449 UN METHODIST..	1	9	11*	0.3	0.6
LYON	22	969	4 082*	30.0	100.0
053 ASSEMB OF GOD.	2	47	90	0.7	2.2
081 CATHOLIC......	5	NA	1 850	13.6	45.3
151 L-D SAINTS....	4	NA	917	6.7	22.5
165 CH OF NAZARENE	1	21	24	0.2	0.6
167 CHS OF CHRIST.	2	24	34	0.3	0.8
193 EPISCOPAL.....	1	25	90	0.7	2.2
221 FREE METHODIST	1	8	39	0.3	1.0
283 LUTH--MO SYNOD	1	23	35	0.3	0.9
413 S.D.A.........	2	86	105*	0.8	2.6
419 SO BAPT CONV..	2	583	712*	5.2	17.4
449 UN METHODIST..	1	152	186*	1.4	4.6
MINERAL	11	744	2 351*	37.8	100.0
053 ASSEMB OF GOD.	1	32	55	0.9	2.3
081 CATHOLIC......	1	NA	974	15.7	41.4
151 L-D SAINTS....	1	NA	417	6.7	17.7
165 CH OF NAZARENE	1	26	39	0.6	1.7
167 CHS OF CHRIST.	1	8	9	0.1	0.4
193 EPISCOPAL.....	1	29	36	0.6	1.5
283 LUTH--MO SYNOD	1	50	85	1.4	3.6
419 SO BAPT CONV..	2	460	565*	9.1	24.0
449 UN METHODIST..	1	42	52*	0.8	2.2
453 UN PRES CH USA	1	97	119*	1.9	5.1
NYE	21	409	2 369*	26.2	100.0
019 AMER BAPT USA.	2	30	36*	0.4	1.5
053 ASSEMB OF GOD.	2	26	48	0.5	2.0
081 CATHOLIC......	4	NA	1 034	11.4	43.6
151 L-D SAINTS....	4	NA	824	9.1	34.8
167 CHS OF CHRIST.	2	40	54	0.6	2.3
193 EPISCOPAL.....	3	143	167	1.8	7.0
419 SO BAPT CONV..	3	134	162*	1.8	6.8
453 UN PRES CH USA	1	36	44*	0.5	1.9
PERSHING	9	333	1 077*	31.6	100.0
053 ASSEMB OF GOD.	1	27	35	1.0	3.2
081 CATHOLIC......	2	NA	375	11.0	34.8
151 L-D SAINTS....	1	NA	304	8.9	28.2
167 CHS OF CHRIST.	1	10	13	0.4	1.2
193 EPISCOPAL.....	1	47	47	1.4	4.4
419 SO BAPT CONV..	1	143	173*	5.1	16.1
449 UN METHODIST..	1	78	95*	2.8	8.8
469 WELS..........	1	28	35	1.0	3.2
STOREY	1	0	192	13.2	100.0
081 CATHOLIC......	1	NA	192	13.2	100.0
WASHOE	92	11 402	49 173*	25.4	100.0
019 AMER BAPT USA.	5	927	1 090*	0.6	2.2
029 AMER LUTH CH..	1	292	390	0.2	0.8
053 ASSEMB OF GOD.	6	399	662	0.3	1.3
081 CATHOLIC......	13	NA	27 191	14.0	55.3
093 CHR CH (DISC).	2	309	507	0.3	1.0
097 CHR CHS&CHS CR	4	517	608*	0.3	1.2
123 CH GOD (ANDER)	2	205	615	0.3	1.3
127 CH GOD (CLEVE)	2	39	46*	–	0.1
151 L-D SAINTS....	14	NA	6 616	3.4	13.5
165 CH OF NAZARENE	4	260	583	0.3	1.2
167 CHS OF CHRIST.	4	253	346	0.2	0.7
193 EPISCOPAL.....	6	1 494	2 138	1.1	4.3
203 EVAN FREE CH..	2	182	214*	0.1	0.4
226 FRIENDS-USA...	1	12	14*	–	–
270 CONSRV JUDAISM	1	99	116*	0.1	0.2
271 REFORM JUDAISM	1	106	125*	0.1	0.3
281 LUTH CH AMER..	2	715	1 009	0.5	2.1
283 LUTH--MO SYNOD	2	738	1 061	0.5	2.2
290 METRO COMM CHS	0	10	20	–	–
403 SALVATION ARMY	1	127	259	0.1	0.5
413 S.D.A.........	3	642	755*	0.4	1.5
419 SO BAPT CONV..	7	1 448	1 703*	0.9	3.5
435 UNITARIAN-UNIV	1	58	68*	–	0.1
443 UN C OF CHRIST	1	142	167*	0.1	0.3
449 UN METHODIST..	3	1 466	1 725*	0.9	3.5
453 UN PRES CH USA	3	862	1 014*	0.5	2.1
469 WELS..........	1	100	131	0.1	0.3
WHITE PINE	14	529	4 634*	56.7	100.0
053 ASSEMB OF GOD.	1	23	75	0.9	1.6
081 CATHOLIC......	2	NA	1 465	17.9	31.6
151 L-D SAINTS....	5	NA	2 424	29.7	52.3
165 CH OF NAZARENE	1	23	50	0.6	1.1
193 EPISCOPAL.....	1	57	99	1.2	2.1
283 LUTH--MO SYNOD	1	16	18	0.2	0.4
419 SO BAPT CONV..	1	194	238*	2.9	5.1
449 UN METHODIST..	2	216	265*	3.2	5.7

NEW HAMPSHIRE

County and Denomination	Number of churches	Communicant, confirmed, full members	Total adherents		
			Number	Percent of total population	Percent of total adherents
THE STATE.....	774	91 486	407 939*	44.3	100.0
BELKNAP	49	4 941	16 005*	37.3	100.0
001 ADVENT CHR CH.	3	210	253*	0.6	1.6
019 AMER BAPT USA.	11	1 553	1 871*	4.4	11.7
053 ASSEMB OF GOD.	1	51	75	0.2	0.5
081 CATHOLIC......	11	NA	9 344	21.8	58.4

NA— Not applicable   *Total adherents estimated from known number of communicant, confirmed, full members.   —Represents a percent less than 0.1.   Percentages may not total due to rounding.

Table 4. Churches and Church Membership by County and Denomination: 1980

County and Denomination	Number of churches	Communicant, confirmed, full members	Total adherents — Number	Percent of total population	Percent of total adherents
089 CHR & MISS AL.	1	53	75	0.2	0.5
151 L-D SAINTS....	1	NA	375	0.9	2.3
167 CHS OF CHRIST.	1	10	15	–	0.1
175 CONGR CHR CHS.	3	175	211*	0.5	1.3
179 CONSRV BAPT...	1	141	170*	0.4	1.1
193 EPISCOPAL.....	3	366	665	1.6	4.2
271 REFORM JUDAISM	1	130	157*	0.4	1.0
403 SALVATION ARMY	1	52	144	0.3	0.9
413 S.D.A.........	1	36	43*	0.1	0.3
435 UNITARIAN-UNIV	1	95	114*	0.3	0.7
443 UN C OF CHRIST	6	1 372	1 653*	3.9	10.3
449 UN METHODIST..	3	697	840*	2.0	5.2
CARROLL	**45**	**4 044**	**7 967***	**28.5**	**100.0**
001 ADVENT CHR CH.	2	55	65*	0.2	0.8
017 AMER BAPT ASSN	1	160	160	0.6	2.0
019 AMER BAPT USA.	6	716	846*	3.0	10.6
081 CATHOLIC......	7	NA	2 868	10.3	36.0
089 CHR & MISS AL.	1	77	144	0.5	1.8
151 L-D SAINTS....	1	NA	?	?	?
165 CH OF NAZARENE	1	35	75	0.3	0.9
167 CHS OF CHRIST.	1	47	62	0.2	0.8
175 CONGR CHR CHS.	2	306	361*	1.3	4.5
179 CONSRV BAPT...	2	282	333*	1.2	4.2
193 EPISCOPAL.....	4	655	1 032	3.7	13.0
443 UN C OF CHRIST	9	1 133	1 338*	4.8	16.8
449 UN METHODIST..	8	578	683*	2.4	8.6
CHESHIRE	**70**	**7 242**	**22 792***	**36.7**	**100.0**
019 AMER BAPT USA.	5	815	977*	1.6	4.3
053 ASSEMB OF GOD.	2	66	178	0.3	0.8
081 CATHOLIC......	16	NA	13 228	21.3	58.0
151 L-D SAINTS....	1	NA	385	0.6	1.7
165 CH OF NAZARENE	1	61	124	0.2	0.5
167 CHS OF CHRIST.	2	50	68	0.1	0.3
175 CONGR CHR CHS.	2	369	443*	0.7	1.9
193 EPISCOPAL.....	2	596	911	1.5	4.0
283 LUTH--MO SYNOD	2	547	739	1.2	3.2
403 SALVATION ARMY	1	92	168	0.3	0.7
413 S.D.A.........	3	161	193*	0.3	0.8
435 UNITARIAN-UNIV	6	478	573*	0.9	2.5
443 UN C OF CHRIST	17	3 277	3 930*	6.3	17.2
449 UN METHODIST..	10	730	875*	1.4	3.8
COOS	**52**	**3 495**	**22 165***	**63.1**	**100.0**
001 ADVENT CHR CH.	1	70	84*	0.2	0.4
019 AMER BAPT USA.	3	242	291*	0.8	1.3
029 AMER LUTH CH..	2	246	389	1.1	1.8
053 ASSEMB OF GOD.	3	123	305	0.9	1.4
081 CATHOLIC......	15	NA	17 465	49.7	78.8
151 L-D SAINTS....	1	NA	104	0.3	0.5
167 CHS OF CHRIST.	1	9	18	0.1	0.1
193 EPISCOPAL.....	4	463	655	1.9	3.0
403 SALVATION ARMY	1	55	101	0.3	0.5
413 S.D.A.........	1	23	28*	0.1	0.1
443 UN C OF CHRIST	7	736	886*	2.5	4.0
449 UN METHODIST..	13	1 528	1 839*	5.2	8.3
GRAFTON	**96**	**8 767**	**22 035***	**33.5**	**100.0**
001 ADVENT CHR CH.	2	40	47*	0.1	0.2
019 AMER BAPT USA.	10	1 224	1 447*	2.2	6.6
029 AMER LUTH CH..	1	76	113	0.2	0.5
053 ASSEMB OF GOD.	6	191	341	0.5	1.5
081 CATHOLIC......	19	NA	10 620	16.1	48.2
151 L-D SAINTS....	2	NA	263	0.4	1.2
165 CH OF NAZARENE	1	64	167	0.3	0.8
167 CHS OF CHRIST.	1	20	28	–	0.1
175 CONGR CHR CHS.	1	56	66*	0.1	0.3
179 CONSRV BAPT...	3	423	500*	0.8	2.3
193 EPISCOPAL.....	7	933	1 653	2.5	7.5
226 FRIENDS-USA...	2	119	141*	0.2	0.6
283 LUTH--MO SYNOD	1	132	162	0.2	0.7
413 S.D.A.........	2	161	190*	0.3	0.9
443 UN C OF CHRIST	19	2 743	3 242*	4.9	14.7
449 UN METHODIST..	19	2 585	3 055*	4.6	13.9
HILLSBOROUGH	**148**	**22 039**	**150 455***	**54.4**	**100.0**
001 ADVENT CHR CH.	1	70	85*	–	0.1
019 AMER BAPT USA.	10	1 904	2 318*	0.8	1.5
045 APOSTOLIC LUTH	1	600	730*	0.3	0.5
053 ASSEMB OF GOD.	1	192	293	0.1	0.2
081 CATHOLIC......	44	NA	120 454	43.5	80.1
089 CHR & MISS AL.	1	35	50	–	–
097 CHR CHS&CHS CR	1	20	24*	–	–
127 CH GOD (CLEVE)	1	9	11*	–	–
151 L-D SAINTS....	2	NA	761	0.3	0.5
165 CH OF NAZARENE	1	195	372	0.1	0.2
167 CHS OF CHRIST.	4	166	232	0.1	0.2
175 CONGR CHR CHS.	2	246	300*	0.1	0.2
179 CONSRV BAPT...	6	846	1 030*	0.4	0.7
193 EPISCOPAL.....	8	2 581	4 389	1.6	2.9
201 EVAN COV CH AM	1	111	135*	–	0.1
226 FRIENDS-USA...	2	93	113*	–	0.1
239 SWEDENBORGIAN.	1	60	73*	–	–
270 CONSRV JUDAISM	2	306	373*	0.1	0.2
271 REFORM JUDAISM	1	502	611*	0.2	0.4
281 LUTH CH AMER..	1	283	322	0.1	0.2
283 LUTH--MO SYNOD	3	551	863	0.3	0.6
290 METRO COMM CHS	0	25	50	–	–
356 PRESB CH AMER.	1	9	19	–	–
403 SALVATION ARMY	2	214	985	0.4	0.7
413 S.D.A.........	2	228	278*	0.1	0.2
419 SO BAPT CONV..	1	211	257*	0.1	0.2
435 UNITARIAN-UNIV	5	885	1 077*	0.4	0.7
443 UN C OF CHRIST	24	7 254	8 832*	3.2	5.9
449 UN METHODIST..	11	3 356	4 086*	1.5	2.7
453 UN PRES CH USA	6	1 061	1 292*	0.5	0.9
469 WELS.........	1	26	40	–	–
MERRIMACK	**89**	**13 090**	**39 271***	**39.9**	**100.0**
001 ADVENT CHR CH.	3	182	219*	0.2	0.6
019 AMER BAPT USA.	13	3 342	4 019*	4.1	10.2
053 ASSEMB OF GOD.	1	55	100	0.1	0.3
081 CATHOLIC......	14	NA	22 472	22.9	57.2
097 CHR CHS&CHS CR	2	150	180*	0.2	0.5
127 CH GOD (CLEVE)	2	?	?	?	?
151 L-D SAINTS....	1	NA	188	0.2	0.5
165 CH OF NAZARENE	2	144	239	0.2	0.6
167 CHS OF CHRIST.	2	116	155	0.2	0.4
175 CONGR CHR CHS.	1	290	349*	0.4	0.9
179 CONSRV BAPT...	5	705	848*	0.9	2.2
193 EPISCOPAL.....	9	1 604	2 555	2.6	6.5
221 FREE METHODIST	1	6	21	–	0.1
271 REFORM JUDAISM	1	210	253*	0.3	0.6
281 LUTH CH AMER..	1	197	257	0.3	0.7
403 SALVATION ARMY	1	86	196	0.2	0.5
413 S.D.A.........	1	53	64*	0.1	0.2
435 UNITARIAN-UNIV	3	368	443*	0.5	1.1
443 UN C OF CHRIST	19	3 791	4 559*	4.6	11.6
449 UN METHODIST..	7	1 791	2 154*	2.2	5.5
ROCKINGHAM	**120**	**16 654**	**76 093***	**40.0**	**100.0**
001 ADVENT CHR CH.	4	301	367*	0.2	0.5
005 AME ZION.....	1	50	87	–	0.1
019 AMER BAPT USA.	21	3 719	4 537*	2.4	6.0
053 ASSEMB OF GOD.	4	572	1 093	0.6	1.4
081 CATHOLIC......	25	NA	53 940	28.3	70.9
097 CHR CHS&CHS CR	1	35	43*	–	0.1
127 CH GOD (CLEVE)	2	27	33*	–	–
151 L-D SAINTS....	1	NA	366	0.2	0.5
165 CH OF NAZARENE	1	50	91	–	0.1
167 CHS OF CHRIST.	1	65	150	0.1	0.2
175 CONGR CHR CHS.	2	474	578*	0.3	0.8
179 CONSRV BAPT...	2	282	344*	0.2	0.5
193 EPISCOPAL.....	7	1 933	3 061	1.6	4.0
281 LUTH CH AMER..	2	457	661	0.3	0.9
403 SALVATION ARMY	1	88	249	0.1	0.3
413 S.D.A.........	1	21	26*	–	–
419 SO BAPT CONV..	1	533	650*	0.3	0.9
435 UNITARIAN-UNIV	4	406	495*	0.3	0.7
443 UN C OF CHRIST	21	4 394	5 360*	2.8	7.0
449 UN METHODIST..	16	2 917	3 559*	1.9	4.7
453 UN PRES CH USA	2	330	403*	0.2	0.5
STRAFFORD	**61**	**7 278**	**33 603***	**39.3**	**100.0**
001 ADVENT CHR CH.	1	18	22*	0.1	0.1
019 AMER BAPT USA.	7	1 079	1 309*	3.6	7.5
053 ASSEMB OF GOD.	1	86	200	0.6	1.1
081 CATHOLIC......	5	NA	11 799	32.7	67.2
089 CHR & MISS AL.	1	15	33	0.1	0.2
151 L-D SAINTS....	1	NA	270	0.7	1.5
165 CH OF NAZARENE	1	57	190	0.5	1.1
167 CHS OF CHRIST.	1	20	25	0.1	0.1
175 CONGR CHR CHS.	1	102	124*	0.3	0.7
179 CONSRV BAPT...	1	141	171*	0.5	1.0
193 EPISCOPAL.....	4	289	806	2.2	4.6
208 EVAN LUTH ASSN	1	102	155	0.4	0.9
353 CHR BRETHREN..	1	50	50	0.1	0.3
413 S.D.A.........	2	58	70*	0.2	0.4
435 UNITARIAN-UNIV	1	60	73*	0.2	0.4
443 UN C OF CHRIST	5	1 016	1 233*	3.4	7.0
449 UN METHODIST..	9	843	1 023*	2.8	5.8
SULLIVAN	**44**	**3 936**	**17 553***	**48.7**	**100.0**

NA—Not applicable   *Total adherents estimated from known number of communicant, confirmed, full members.   —Represents a percent less than 0.1.   Percentages may not total due to rounding.

Table 4. Churches and Church Membership by County and Denomination: 1980

County and Denomination	Number of churches	Communicant, confirmed, full members	Total adherents		
			Number	Percent of total population	Percent of total adherents

NEW JERSEY

THE STATE.....	3 708	780 327	3 988 369*	54.2	100.0
ATLANTIC	129	18 723	79 577*	41.0	100.0
005 AME ZION......	1	340	510	0.3	0.6
019 AMER BAPT USA.	4	1 177	1 405*	0.7	1.8
053 ASSEMB OF GOD.	7	484	959	0.5	1.2
081 CATHOLIC......	23	NA	54 934	28.3	69.0
089 CHR & MISS AL.	2	85	286	0.1	0.4
101 C.M.E.........	1	118	141*	0.1	0.2
123 CH GOD (ANDER)	2	54	162	0.1	0.2
127 CH GOD (CLEVE)	3	96	115*	0.1	0.1
151 L-D SAINTS....	1	NA	251	0.1	0.3
165 CH OF NAZARENE	3	167	225	0.1	0.3
167 CHS OF CHRIST.	2	75	93	-	0.1
175 CONGR CHR CHS.	1	50	60*	-	0.1
193 EPISCOPAL.....	9	2 464	3 197	1.6	4.0
226 FRIENDS-USA...	2	74	88*	-	0.1
270 CONSRV JUDAISM	3	684	816*	0.4	1.0
271 REFORM JUDAISM	2	1 354	1 616*	0.8	2.0
281 LUTH CH AMER..	7	2 066	3 109	1.6	3.9
285 MENNONITE CH..	1	6	7*	-	-
290 METRO COMM CHS	1	17	34	-	-
293 MORAV CH-NORTH	1	323	395	0.2	0.5
353 CHR BRETHREN..	2	100	110	0.1	0.1
375 REF EPISCOPAL.	2	99	118*	0.1	0.1
381 REF PRES-EVAN.	1	45	71	-	0.1
403 SALVATION ARMY	1	78	411	0.2	0.5
413 S.D.A.........	5	285	340*	0.2	0.4
419 SO BAPT CONV..	1	168	201*	0.1	0.3
435 UNITARIAN-UNIV	1	11	13*	-	-
443 UN C OF CHRIST	4	1 348	1 609*	0.8	2.0
449 UN METHODIST..	27	4 941	5 897*	3.0	7.4
453 UN PRES CH USA	9	2 014	2 404*	1.2	3.0
BERGEN	386	101 342	587 532*	69.5	100.0
005 AME ZION......	7	6 275	8 158	1.0	1.4
019 AMER BAPT USA.	17	3 529	4 112*	0.5	0.7
029 AMER LUTH CH..	4	1 324	1 631	0.2	0.3
039 AP CHR CH(NAZ)	1	73	85*	-	-
049 ARMEN AP CH AM	1	350	1 900	0.2	0.3
053 ASSEMB OF GOD.	6	624	1 014	0.1	0.2
081 CATHOLIC......	77	NA	451 753	53.4	76.9
089 CHR & MISS AL.	1	19	22	-	-
097 CHR CHS&CHS CR	1	21	24*	-	-
105 CHRISTIAN REF.	6	1 744	2 682	0.3	0.5
151 L-D SAINTS....	2	NA	776	0.1	0.1
163 CH OF LUTH BR.	2	134	190	-	-
165 CH OF NAZARENE	3	459	381	-	0.1
167 CHS OF CHRIST.	2	116	156	-	-
179 CONSRV BAPT...	2	342	398*	-	0.1
193 EPISCOPAL.....	41	13 649	19 607	2.3	3.3
195 ESTONIAN ELC..	1	33	160	-	-
203 EVAN FREE CH..	5	276	322*	-	0.1
208 EVAN LUTH ASSN	3	1 180	1 498	0.2	0.3
226 FRIENDS-USA...	1	167	195*	-	-
270 CONSRV JUDAISM	24	5 346	6 229*	0.7	1.1
271 REFORM JUDAISM	10	5 350	6 234*	0.7	1.1
281 LUTH CH AMER..	24	8 314	11 893	1.4	2.0
283 LUTH--MO SYNOD	13	5 952	7 948	0.9	1.4
335 ORTH PRESB CH.	2	130	151*	-	-
353 CHR BRETHREN..	5	500	575	-	0.1
369 PROT REF CHS..	1	18	39	-	-
371 REF CH IN AM..	38	9 593	17 221	2.0	2.9
403 SALVATION ARMY	2	69	506	0.1	0.1
413 S.D.A.........	3	441	514*	0.1	0.1
419 SO BAPT CONV..	4	478	557*	0.1	0.1
423 SYRIAN ANTIOCH	2	8 000	9 321*	1.1	1.6
435 UNITARIAN-UNIV	3	603	703*	0.1	0.1
443 UN C OF CHRIST	12	3 118	3 633*	0.4	0.6
449 UN METHODIST..	29	9 890	11 523*	1.4	2.0
453 UN PRES CH USA	30	13 193	15 372*	1.8	2.6
469 WELS..........	1	32	49	-	-
BURLINGTON	165	35 622	154 002*	42.5	100.0
005 AME ZION......	1	400	475	0.1	0.3
019 AMER BAPT USA.	14	3 730	4 530*	1.2	2.9
053 ASSEMB OF GOD.	5	1 495	2 580	0.7	1.7
081 CATHOLIC......	22	NA	107 362	29.6	69.7
097 CHR CHS&CHS CR	1	25	30*	-	-
101 C.M.E.........	1	193	234*	0.1	0.2
127 CH GOD (CLEVE)	2	111	135*	-	0.1
151 L-D SAINTS....	2	NA	790	0.2	0.5
165 CH OF NAZARENE	2	280	567	0.2	0.4
167 CHS OF CHRIST.	2	258	290	0.1	0.2
179 CONSRV BAPT...	1	171	208*	0.1	0.1
193 EPISCOPAL.....	19	6 790	9 189	2.5	6.0
203 EVAN FREE CH..	1	14	17*	-	-
226 FRIENDS-USA...	10	1 266	1 538*	0.4	1.0
244 GRACE BRETHREN	1	90	109*	-	0.1
270 CONSRV JUDAISM	4	367	446*	0.1	0.3
271 REFORM JUDAISM	1	622	755*	0.2	0.5
281 LUTH CH AMER..	9	4 790	6 454	1.8	4.2
283 LUTH--MO SYNOD	2	445	570	0.2	0.4
293 MORAV CH-NORTH	2	502	610	0.2	0.4
363 PRIMITIVE METH	1	25	30*	-	-
371 REF CH IN AM..	1	177	235	0.1	0.2

County and Denomination	Number of churches	Communicant, confirmed, full members	Total adherents		
			Number	Percent of total population	Percent of total adherents
375 REF EPISCOPAL.	1	68	83*	-	0.1
413 S.D.A.........	3	182	221*	0.1	0.1
419 SO BAPT CONV..	4	1 511	1 835*	0.5	1.2
435 UNITARIAN-UNIV	1	20	24*	-	-
443 UN C OF CHRIST	2	470	571*	0.2	0.4
449 UN METHODIST..	42	9 949	12 084*	3.3	7.8
453 UN PRES CH USA	8	1 671	2 030*	0.6	1.3
CAMDEN	248	54 306	249 192*	52.8	100.0
005 AME ZION......	2	1 161	1 548	0.3	0.6
019 AMER BAPT USA.	24	6 425	7 809*	1.7	3.1
053 ASSEMB OF GOD.	9	1 318	1 892	0.4	0.8
081 CATHOLIC......	52	NA	177 808	37.7	71.4
089 CHR & MISS AL.	2	92	247	0.1	0.1
101 C.M.E.........	3	229	278*	0.1	0.1
123 CH GOD (ANDER)	2	130	390	0.1	0.2
151 L-D SAINTS....	2	NA	505	0.1	0.2
165 CH OF NAZARENE	1	35	131	-	0.1
167 CHS OF CHRIST.	2	132	195	-	0.1
179 CONSRV BAPT...	2	343	417*	0.1	0.2
193 EPISCOPAL.....	21	6 723	9 206	2.0	3.7
203 EVAN FREE CH..	1	28	34*	-	-
226 FRIENDS-USA...	2	234	284*	0.1	0.1
270 CONSRV JUDAISM	3	1 367	1 662*	0.4	0.7
271 REFORM JUDAISM	1	1 374	1 670*	0.4	0.7
281 LUTH CH AMER..	22	8 052	11 647	2.5	4.7
283 LUTH--MO SYNOD	2	783	1 192	0.3	0.5
335 ORTH PRESB CH.	3	230	280*	0.1	0.1
353 CHR BRETHREN..	5	115	135	-	0.1
381 REF PRES-EVAN.	2	375	429	0.1	0.2
403 SALVATION ARMY	1	107	981	0.2	0.4
413 S.D.A.........	4	492	598*	0.1	0.2
419 SO BAPT CONV..	1	317	385*	0.1	0.2
435 UNITARIAN-UNIV	1	249	303*	0.1	0.1
449 UN METHODIST..	53	13 295	16 160*	3.4	6.5
453 UN PRES CH USA	25	10 700	13 006*	2.8	5.2
CAPE MAY	75	10 647	30 426*	37.0	100.0
019 AMER BAPT USA.	6	1 257	1 471*	1.8	4.8
053 ASSEMB OF GOD.	2	116	164	0.2	0.5
081 CATHOLIC......	16	NA	17 442	21.2	57.3
151 L-D SAINTS....	1	NA	67	0.1	0.2
165 CH OF NAZARENE	2	108	281	0.3	0.9
167 CHS OF CHRIST.	1	10	13	-	-
193 EPISCOPAL.....	7	1 384	1 625	2.0	5.3
281 LUTH CH AMER..	6	1 512	2 038	2.5	6.7
335 ORTH PRESB CH.	2	81	95*	0.1	0.3
413 S.D.A.........	2	101	118*	0.1	0.4
419 SO BAPT CONV..	1	120	140*	0.2	0.5
449 UN METHODIST..	25	4 934	5 774*	7.0	19.0
453 UN PRES CH USA	4	1 024	1 198*	1.5	3.9
CUMBERLAND	122	20 235	61 849*	46.5	100.0
005 AME ZION......	2	418	507	0.4	0.8
019 AMER BAPT USA.	6	1 989	2 435*	1.8	3.9
053 ASSEMB OF GOD.	7	1 086	2 198	1.7	3.6
081 CATHOLIC......	18	NA	33 838	25.5	54.7
089 CHR & MISS AL.	2	69	150	0.1	0.2
127 CH GOD (CLEVE)	7	735	900*	0.7	1.5
151 L-D SAINTS....	1	NA	282	0.2	0.5
165 CH OF NAZARENE	4	614	1 769	1.3	2.9
167 CHS OF CHRIST.	1	114	168	0.1	0.3
193 EPISCOPAL.....	4	1 317	1 999	1.5	3.2
195 ESTONIAN ELC..	1	105	259	0.2	0.4
226 FRIENDS-USA...	1	55	67*	0.1	0.1
270 CONSRV JUDAISM	2	416	509*	0.4	0.8
281 LUTH CH AMER..	3	1 032	1 417	1.1	2.3
283 LUTH--MO SYNOD	1	362	463	0.3	0.7
285 MENNONITE CH..	2	29	35*	-	0.1
335 ORTH PRESB CH.	2	317	388*	0.3	0.6
356 PRESB CH AMER.	1	101	123	0.1	0.2
403 SALVATION ARMY	1	84	396	0.3	0.6
413 S.D.A.........	4	408	499*	0.4	0.8
415 S-D BAPTIST GC	2	440	539*	0.4	0.9
419 SO BAPT CONV..	1	115	141*	0.1	0.2
443 UN C OF CHRIST	1	65	80*	0.1	0.1
449 UN METHODIST..	38	8 000	9 793*	7.4	15.8
453 UN PRES CH USA	10	2 364	2 894*	2.2	4.7
ESSEX	347	80 695	453 759*	53.4	100.0
005 AME ZION......	4	8 265	10 575	1.2	2.3
019 AMER BAPT USA.	28	9 890	11 947*	1.4	2.6
053 ASSEMB OF GOD.	12	1 349	1 785	0.2	0.4
057 BAPT GEN CONF.	1	205	248*	-	0.1
081 CATHOLIC......	72	NA	349 258	41.1	77.0
089 CHR & MISS AL.	2	52	88	-	-
093 CHR CH (DISC).	5	550	869	0.1	0.2
097 CHR CHS&CHS CR	2	80	97*	-	-
101 C.M.E.........	1	1 408	1 701*	0.2	0.4
123 CH GOD (ANDER)	1	60	180	-	-
127 CH GOD (CLEVE)	8	283	342*	-	0.1
151 L-D SAINTS....	3	NA	923	0.1	0.2
163 CH OF LUTH BR.	1	31	50	-	-
165 CH OF NAZARENE	1	96	194	-	-
167 CHS OF CHRIST.	4	812	1 055	0.1	0.2
179 CONSRV BAPT...	4	684	826*	0.1	0.2
193 EPISCOPAL.....	32	9 924	14 470	1.7	3.2
201 EVAN COV CH AM	2	291	352*	-	0.1
203 EVAN FREE CH..	2	453	547*	0.1	0.1
226 FRIENDS-USA...	1	161	194*	-	-
239 SWEDENBORGIAN.	1	60	72*	-	-

NA—Not applicable   *Total adherents estimated from known number of communicant, confirmed, full members.   —Represents a percent less than 0.1.   Percentages may not total due to rounding.

Table 4. Churches and Church Membership by County and Denomination: 1980

County and Denomination	Number of churches	Communicant, confirmed, full members	Total adherents Number	Total adherents Percent of total population	Total adherents Percent of total adherents
270 CONSRV JUDAISM	12	2 930	3 539*	0.4	0.8
271 REFORM JUDAISM	6	6 204	7 494*	0.9	1.7
281 LUTH CH AMER..	7	1 805	2 436	0.3	0.5
283 LUTH--MO SYNOD	7	1 395	1 854	0.2	0.4
313 N AM BAPT CONF	1	82	99*	–	–
353 CHR BRETHREN..	6	360	520	0.1	0.1
356 PRESB CH AMER.	1	62	77	–	–
371 REF CH IN AM..	11	1 417	2 637	0.3	0.6
403 SALVATION ARMY	6	559	1 609	0.2	0.4
413 S.D.A.........	6	1 179	1 424*	0.2	0.3
415 S-D BAPTIST GC	1	13	16*	–	–
419 SO BAPT CONV..	6	746	901*	0.1	0.2
435 UNITARIAN-UNIV	2	603	728*	0.1	0.2
443 UN C OF CHRIST	16	6 506	7 859*	0.9	1.7
449 UN METHODIST..	23	7 223	8 725*	1.0	1.9
453 UN PRES CH USA	49	14 957	18 068*	2.1	4.0
GLOUCESTER	136	23 252	89 435*	44.7	100.0
019 AMER BAPT USA.	5	1 081	1 324*	0.7	1.5
053 ASSEMB OF GOD.	8	743	1 222	0.6	1.4
059 BAPT MISS ASSN	1	101	124*	0.1	0.1
081 CATHOLIC......	23	NA	58 221	29.1	65.1
089 CHR & MISS AL.	2	75	182	0.1	0.2
127 CH GOD (CLEVE)	4	58	71*	–	0.1
151 L-D SAINTS....	1	NA	461	0.2	0.5
165 CH OF NAZARENE	2	117	275	0.1	0.3
167 CHS OF CHRIST.	2	170	218	0.1	0.2
179 CONSRV BAPT...	8	1 368	1 676*	0.8	1.9
193 EPISCOPAL.....	8	2 014	3 215	1.6	3.6
226 FRIENDS-USA...	3	331	405*	0.2	0.5
263 INT FOURSQ GOS	1	48	59*	–	0.1
270 CONSRV JUDAISM	1	60	73*	–	0.1
281 LUTH CH AMER..	6	2 108	3 553	1.8	4.0
381 REF PRES-EVAN.	1	33	49	–	0.1
413 S.D.A.........	2	338	414*	0.2	0.5
419 SO BAPT CONV..	1	51	62*	–	0.1
443 UN C OF CHRIST	1	115	141*	0.1	0.2
449 UN METHODIST..	44	10 889	13 339*	6.7	14.9
453 UN PRES CH USA	12	3 552	4 351*	2.2	4.9
HUDSON	223	26 152	370 752*	66.6	100.0
005 AME ZION......	2	2 476	2 579	0.5	0.7
019 AMER BAPT USA.	10	4 192	5 000*	0.9	1.3
029 AMER LUTH CH..	1	140	211	–	0.1
039 AP CHR CH(NAZ)	1	30	36*	–	–
053 ASSEMB OF GOD.	12	814	1 092	0.2	0.3
081 CATHOLIC......	64	NA	335 641	60.3	90.5
089 CHR & MISS AL.	3	94	126	–	–
101 C.M.E.........	2	1 238	1 476*	0.3	0.4
123 CH GOD (ANDER)	3	177	531	0.1	0.1
127 CH GOD (CLEVE)	3	158	188*	–	0.1
151 L-D SAINTS....	2	NA	350	0.1	0.1
165 CH OF NAZARENE	2	156	564	0.1	0.2
179 CONSRV BAPT...	2	342	408*	0.1	0.1
193 EPISCOPAL.....	19	2 447	4 554	0.8	1.2
203 EVAN FREE CH..	2	124	148*	–	–
208 EVAN LUTH ASSN	1	156	182	–	–
270 CONSRV JUDAISM	3	373	445*	0.1	0.1
271 REFORM JUDAISM	2	1 082	1 290*	0.2	0.3
281 LUTH CH AMER..	15	3 474	4 441	0.8	1.2
283 LUTH--MO SYNOD	7	1 184	1 421	0.3	0.4
290 METRO COMM CHS	0	30	60	–	–
313 N AM BAPT CONF	2	97	116*	–	–
353 CHR BRETHREN..	5	165	190	–	0.1
371 REF CH IN AM..	16	1 851	3 111	0.6	0.8
375 REF EPISCOPAL.	1	130	155*	–	–
403 SALVATION ARMY	2	73	306	0.1	0.1
413 S.D.A.........	6	574	685*	0.1	0.2
419 SO BAPT CONV..	4	401	478*	0.1	0.1
443 UN C OF CHRIST	1	56	67*	–	–
449 UN METHODIST..	18	2 447	2 918*	0.5	0.8
453 UN PRES CH USA	12	1 671	1 993*	0.4	0.5
HUNTERDON	86	13 168	38 579*	44.2	100.0
019 AMER BAPT USA.	6	1 271	1 539*	1.8	4.0
053 ASSEMB OF GOD.	3	273	475	0.5	1.2
071 BRETHREN (ASH)	1	43	52*	0.1	0.1
081 CATHOLIC......	9	NA	20 026	22.9	51.9
097 CHR CHS&CHS CR	1	20	24*	–	0.1
151 L-D SAINTS....	1	NA	?	?	?
157 CH OF BRETHREN	1	120	145*	0.2	0.4
165 CH OF NAZARENE	1	34	53	0.1	0.1
179 CONSRV BAPT...	2	342	414*	0.5	1.1
193 EPISCOPAL.....	4	530	1 036	1.2	2.7
226 FRIENDS-USA...	1	52	63*	0.1	0.2
270 CONSRV JUDAISM	1	100	121*	0.1	0.3
281 LUTH CH AMER..	2	474	650	0.7	1.7
283 LUTH--MO SYNOD	1	648	1 437	1.6	3.7
335 ORTH PRESB CH.	1	56	68*	0.1	0.2
371 REF CH IN AM..	8	1 227	2 816	3.2	7.3
443 UN C OF CHRIST	1	188	228*	0.3	0.6
449 UN METHODIST..	26	3 607	4 367*	5.0	11.3
453 UN PRES CH USA	16	4 183	5 065*	5.8	13.1
MERCER	166	41 827	157 073*	51.0	100.0
005 AME ZION......	1	2 340	2 495	0.8	1.6
019 AMER BAPT USA.	16	4 648	5 514*	1.8	3.5
053 ASSEMB OF GOD.	9	875	1 485	0.5	0.9
081 CATHOLIC......	36	NA	103 902	33.7	66.1
089 CHR & MISS AL.	1	58	98	–	0.1
123 CH GOD (ANDER)	2	85	255	0.1	0.2

County and Denomination	Number of churches	Communicant, confirmed, full members	Total adherents Number	Total adherents Percent of total population	Total adherents Percent of total adherents
127 CH GOD (CLEVE)	4	124	147*	–	0.1
151 L-D SAINTS....	1	NA	280	0.1	0.2
165 CH OF NAZARENE	1	145	164	0.1	0.1
167 CHS OF CHRIST.	3	403	595	0.2	0.4
179 CONSRV BAPT...	1	171	203*	0.1	0.1
193 EPISCOPAL.....	12	6 371	8 947	2.9	5.7
208 EVAN LUTH ASSN	2	496	671	0.2	0.4
226 FRIENDS-USA...	3	406	482*	0.2	0.3
270 CONSRV JUDAISM	3	662	785*	0.3	0.5
271 REFORM JUDAISM	2	1 666	1 976*	0.6	1.3
281 LUTH CH AMER..	11	3 282	4 557	1.5	2.9
283 LUTH--MO SYNOD	3	734	960	0.3	0.6
285 MENNONITE CH..	1	45	53*	–	–
290 METRO COMM CHS	1	15	30	–	–
335 ORTH PRESB CH.	1	53	63*	–	–
353 CHR BRETHREN..	1	70	100	–	0.1
381 REF PRES-EVAN.	1	46	64	–	–
403 SALVATION ARMY	1	140	717	0.2	0.5
413 S.D.A.........	5	829	983*	0.3	0.6
419 SO BAPT CONV..	1	197	234*	0.1	0.1
435 UNITARIAN-UNIV	2	531	630*	0.2	0.4
443 UN C OF CHRIST	1	79	94*	–	0.1
449 UN METHODIST..	18	5 878	6 973*	2.3	4.4
453 UN PRES CH USA	21	11 478	13 616*	4.4	8.7
MIDDLESEX	233	45 750	350 537*	58.8	100.0
005 AME ZION......	2	592	717	0.1	0.2
019 AMER BAPT USA.	13	2 441	2 895*	0.5	0.8
029 AMER LUTH CH..	1	348	456	0.1	0.1
053 ASSEMB OF GOD.	7	648	875	0.1	0.2
081 CATHOLIC......	67	NA	290 514	48.8	82.9
089 CHR & MISS AL.	1	97	177	–	0.1
093 CHR CH (DISC)	2	203	312	0.1	0.1
127 CH GOD (CLEVE)	1	94	111*	–	–
149 CH OF JC (BIC)	4	166	178	–	0.1
151 L-D SAINTS....	1	NA	406	0.1	0.1
165 CH OF NAZARENE	1	92	139	–	–
167 CHS OF CHRIST.	2	69	105	–	–
179 CONSRV BAPT...	3	513	608*	0.1	0.2
193 EPISCOPAL.....	18	5 255	7 946	1.3	2.3
201 EVAN COV CH AM	1	150	178*	–	0.1
226 FRIENDS-USA...	1	60	71*	–	–
270 CONSRV JUDAISM	12	2 612	3 098*	0.5	0.9
271 REFORM JUDAISM	3	2 590	3 072*	0.5	0.9
281 LUTH CH AMER..	13	4 114	5 770	1.0	1.6
283 LUTH--MO SYNOD	3	1 601	2 205	0.4	0.6
313 N AM BAPT CONF	1	185	219*	–	0.1
353 CHR BRETHREN..	2	100	180	–	0.1
371 REF CH IN AM..	11	2 332	4 550	0.8	1.3
403 SALVATION ARMY	2	104	355	0.1	0.1
413 S.D.A.........	6	476	564*	0.1	0.2
419 SO BAPT CONV..	3	565	670*	0.1	0.2
431 UKRAINIAN AMER.	1	170	210	–	0.1
435 UNITARIAN-UNIV	1	159	189*	–	0.1
443 UN C OF CHRIST	7	2 477	2 938*	0.5	0.8
449 UN METHODIST..	19	6 326	7 502*	1.3	2.1
453 UN PRES CH USA	23	11 094	13 157*	2.2	3.8
469 WELS..........	1	117	170	–	–
MONMOUTH	254	62 228	236 978*	47.1	100.0
005 AME ZION......	8	5 935	7 716	1.5	3.3
019 AMER BAPT USA.	22	5 697	6 873*	1.4	2.9
029 AMER LUTH CH..	2	583	885	0.2	0.4
053 ASSEMB OF GOD.	7	656	1 022	0.2	0.4
081 CATHOLIC......	48	NA	153 409	30.5	64.7
089 CHR & MISS AL.	1	12	12	–	–
097 CHR CHS&CHS CR	1	34	41*	–	–
127 CH GOD (CLEVE)	3	195	235*	–	0.1
149 CH OF JC (BIC)	1	23	45	–	–
151 L-D SAINTS....	2	NA	469	0.1	0.2
165 CH OF NAZARENE	1	2	16	–	–
167 CHS OF CHRIST.	1	150	199	–	0.1
179 CONSRV BAPT...	4	684	825*	0.2	0.3
193 EPISCOPAL.....	30	8 970	13 189	2.6	5.6
221 FREE METHODIST	1	5	30	–	–
226 FRIENDS-USA...	2	153	185*	–	0.1
270 CONSRV JUDAISM	6	1 941	2 342*	0.5	1.0
271 REFORM JUDAISM	4	3 178	3 834*	0.8	1.6
281 LUTH CH AMER..	9	3 687	5 481	1.1	2.3
283 LUTH--MO SYNOD	3	797	1 275	0.3	0.5
290 METRO COMM CHS	0	10	20	–	–
335 ORTH PRESB CH.	1	49	59*	–	–
353 CHR BRETHREN..	3	185	380	0.1	0.2
371 REF CH IN AM..	10	2 229	4 354	0.9	1.8
403 SALVATION ARMY	2	494	2 041	0.4	0.9
413 S.D.A.........	2	229	276*	0.1	0.1
419 SO BAPT CONV..	5	732	883*	0.2	0.4
435 UNITARIAN-UNIV	1	273	329*	0.1	0.1
443 UN C OF CHRIST	2	250	302*	0.1	0.1
449 UN METHODIST..	52	16 417	19 806*	3.9	8.4
453 UN PRES CH USA	20	8 658	10 445*	2.1	4.4
MORRIS	202	44 627	193 238*	47.4	100.0
019 AMER BAPT USA.	5	785	945*	0.2	0.5
029 AMER LUTH CH..	5	1 600	2 332	0.6	1.2
053 ASSEMB OF GOD.	5	295	340	0.1	0.2
081 CATHOLIC......	45	NA	132 476	32.5	68.6
089 CHR & MISS AL.	7	950	1 607	0.4	0.8
097 CHR CHS&CHS CR	1	109	131*	–	0.1
105 CHRISTIAN REF.	1	84	143	–	0.1
123 CH GOD (ANDER)	1	38	114	–	0.1
127 CH GOD (CLEVE)	1	73	88*	–	–

NA—Not applicable   *Total adherents estimated from known number of communicant, confirmed, full members.   —Represents a percent less than 0.1.   Percentages may not total due to rounding.

Table 4. Churches and Church Membership by County and Denomination: 1980

County and Denomination	Number of churches	Communicant, confirmed, full members	Total adherents		
			Number	Percent of total population	Percent of total adherents
151 L-D SAINTS....	2	NA	851	0.2	0.4
163 CH OF LUTH BR..	1	118	210	0.1	0.1
165 CH OF NAZARENE	2	356	719	0.2	0.4
167 CHS OF CHRIST.	6	296	599	0.1	0.3
175 CONGR CHR CHS.	1	202	243*	0.1	0.1
193 EPISCOPAL.....	17	7 040	10 721	2.6	5.5
203 EVAN FREE CH..	1	45	54*	–	–
221 FREE METHODIST	1	41	93	–	–
226 FRIENDS-USA...	2	217	261*	0.1	0.1
233 GEN CH NEW JER	1	20	24*	–	–
270 CONSRV JUDAISM	7	1 206	1 452*	0.4	0.8
271 REFORM JUDAISM	3	1 652	1 988*	0.5	1.0
281 LUTH CH AMER..	7	2 098	2 996	0.7	1.6
283 LUTH--MO SYNOD	3	1 077	1 375	0.3	0.7
285 MENNONITE CH..	1	13	16*	–	–
335 ORTH PRESB CH.	1	91	110*	–	0.1
371 REF CH IN AM..	5	1 363	3 237	0.8	1.7
403 SALVATION ARMY	1	50	263	0.1	0.1
413 S.D.A........	3	202	243*	0.1	0.1
419 SO BAPT CONV..	3	774	932*	0.2	0.5
435 UNITARIAN-UNIV	2	355	427*	0.1	0.2
443 UN C OF CHRIST	3	1 237	1 489*	0.4	0.8
449 UN METHODIST..	32	10 984	13 220*	3.2	6.8
453 UN PRES CH USA	25	11 114	13 377*	3.3	6.9
469 WELS..........	1	142	162	–	0.1
OCEAN	**136**	**29 092**	**139 950***	**40.4**	**100.0**
005 AME ZION......	1	204	272	0.1	0.2
019 AMER BAPT USA.	5	1 106	1 327*	0.4	0.9
029 AMER LUTH CH..	1	218	220	0.1	0.2
053 ASSEMB OF GOD.	6	862	1 928	0.6	1.4
081 CATHOLIC......	28	NA	100 943	29.2	72.1
089 CHR & MISS AL.	1	31	49	–	–
097 CHR CHS&CHS CR	1	50	60*	–	–
127 CH GOD (CLEVE)	2	143	172*	–	0.1
151 L-D SAINTS....	3	NA	660	0.2	0.5
165 CH OF NAZARENE	2	112	298	0.1	0.2
167 CHS OF CHRIST.	2	116	148	–	0.1
179 CONSRV BAPT...	6	1 026	1 231*	0.4	0.9
193 EPISCOPAL.....	10	3 781	5 433	1.6	3.9
195 ESTONIAN ELC..	1	295	415	0.1	0.3
199 EVAN CONGR CH.	2	411	493*	0.1	0.4
203 EVAN FREE CH..	1	55	66*	–	–
226 FRIENDS-USA...	2	13	16*	–	–
270 CONSRV JUDAISM	3	515	618*	0.2	0.4
271 REFORM JUDAISM	1	640	768*	0.2	0.5
281 LUTH CH AMER..	10	4 370	6 222	1.8	4.4
283 LUTH--MO SYNOD	2	723	1 011	0.3	0.7
353 CHR BRETHREN..	2	170	245	0.1	0.2
371 REF CH IN AM..	1	406	551	0.2	0.4
381 REF PRES-EVAN.	2	79	94	–	0.1
403 SALVATION ARMY	1	105	318	0.1	0.2
413 S.D.A........	2	142	170*	–	0.1
419 SO BAPT CONV..	2	384	461*	0.1	0.3
435 UNITARIAN-UNIV	1	30	36*	–	–
449 UN METHODIST..	26	7 302	8 762*	2.5	6.3
453 UN PRES CH USA	9	5 803	6 963*	2.0	5.0
PASSAIC	**207**	**38 237**	**217 002***	**48.5**	**100.0**
005 AME ZION......	2	2 775	2 870	0.6	1.3
019 AMER BAPT USA.	14	3 267	3 928*	0.9	1.8
029 AMER LUTH CH..	1	115	152	–	0.1
053 ASSEMB OF GOD.	12	1 244	1 842	0.4	0.8
081 CATHOLIC......	53	NA	166 041	37.1	76.5
105 CHRISTIAN REF.	13	2 632	3 804	0.8	1.8
123 CH GOD (ANDER)	3	189	567	0.1	0.3
127 CH GOD (CLEVE)	5	283	340*	0.1	0.2
165 CH OF NAZARENE	2	352	439	0.1	0.2
193 EPISCOPAL.....	14	5 194	6 820	1.5	3.1
195 ESTONIAN ELC..	1	39	48	–	–
221 FREE METHODIST	1	21	330	0.1	0.2
270 CONSRV JUDAISM	5	1 060	1 274*	0.3	0.6
271 REFORM JUDAISM	3	2 198	2 643*	0.6	1.2
281 LUTH CH AMER..	3	1 758	2 451	0.5	1.1
283 LUTH--MO SYNOD	7	1 723	2 385	0.5	1.1
371 REF CH IN AM..	18	4 300	7 410	1.7	3.4
403 SALVATION ARMY	2	190	556	0.1	0.3
413 S.D.A........	4	484	582*	0.1	0.3
419 SO BAPT CONV..	3	152	183*	–	0.1
435 UNITARIAN-UNIV	1	61	73*	–	–
443 UN C OF CHRIST	3	1 110	1 335*	0.3	0.6
449 UN METHODIST..	19	4 710	5 663*	1.3	2.6
453 UN PRES CH USA	18	4 380	5 266*	1.2	2.4
SALEM	**66**	**11 232**	**23 236***	**35.9**	**100.0**
019 AMER BAPT USA.	5	1 486	1 810*	2.8	7.8
029 AMER LUTH CH..	1	237	340	0.5	1.5
053 ASSEMB OF GOD.	4	618	1 260	1.9	5.4
081 CATHOLIC......	6	NA	8 241	12.7	35.5
151 L-D SAINTS....	1	NA	50	0.1	0.2
165 CH OF NAZARENE	3	290	729	1.1	3.1
179 CONSRV BAPT...	4	684	833*	1.3	3.6
193 EPISCOPAL.....	4	703	1 147	1.8	4.9
226 FRIENDS-USA...	2	494	602*	0.9	2.6
281 LUTH CH AMER..	1	246	320	0.5	1.4
283 LUTH--MO SYNOD	1	200	262	0.4	1.1
285 MENNONITE CH..	1	32	39*	0.1	0.2
335 ORTH PRESB CH.	1	81	99*	0.2	0.4
413 S.D.A........	3	197	240*	0.4	1.0
449 UN METHODIST..	24	4 490	5 469*	8.5	23.5
453 UN PRES CH USA	5	1 474	1 795*	2.8	7.7

County and Denomination	Number of churches	Communicant, confirmed, full members	Total adherents		
			Number	Percent of total population	Percent of total adherents
SOMERSET	**121**	**26 678**	**112 968***	**55.6**	**100.0**
005 AME ZION......	1	525	590	0.3	0.5
019 AMER BAPT USA.	1	404	479*	0.2	0.4
053 ASSEMB OF GOD.	2	199	330	0.2	0.3
081 CATHOLIC......	25	NA	77 094	38.0	68.2
089 CHR & MISS AL.	2	65	113	0.1	0.1
151 L-D SAINTS....	1	NA	356	0.2	0.3
163 CH OF LUTH BR.	1	44	96	–	0.1
167 CHS OF CHRIST.	1	177	224	0.1	0.2
175 CONGR CHR CHS.	1	336	399*	0.2	0.4
179 CONSRV BAPT...	4	684	812*	0.4	0.7
193 EPISCOPAL.....	8	5 132	6 274	3.1	5.6
203 EVAN FREE CH..	1	130	154*	0.1	0.1
226 FRIENDS-USA...	1	28	33*	–	–
270 CONSRV JUDAISM	4	454	539*	0.3	0.5
271 REFORM JUDAISM	1	456	541*	0.3	0.5
281 LUTH CH AMER..	4	1 315	1 718	0.8	1.5
283 LUTH--MO SYNOD	4	1 485	1 922	0.9	1.7
353 CHR BRETHREN..	1	25	50	–	–
371 REF CH IN AM..	21	3 701	7 577	3.7	6.7
375 REF EPISCOPAL.	2	200	237*	0.1	0.2
415 S-D BAPTIST GC	1	21	25*	–	–
419 SO BAPT CONV..	3	280	332*	0.2	0.3
435 UNITARIAN-UNIV	1	40	47*	–	–
443 UN C OF CHRIST	2	231	274*	0.1	0.2
449 UN METHODIST..	17	4 884	5 796*	2.9	5.1
453 UN PRES CH USA	11	5 862	6 956*	3.4	6.2
SUSSEX	**75**	**12 516**	**43 111***	**37.1**	**100.0**
019 AMER BAPT USA.	4	545	678*	0.6	1.6
029 AMER LUTH CH..	1	86	119	0.1	0.3
053 ASSEMB OF GOD.	2	198	275	0.2	0.6
081 CATHOLIC......	15	NA	26 000	22.4	60.3
089 CHR & MISS AL.	1	0	36	–	0.1
105 CHRISTIAN REF.	2	351	699	0.6	1.6
151 L-D SAINTS....	1	NA	41	–	0.1
165 CH OF NAZARENE	1	75	126	0.1	0.3
167 CHS OF CHRIST.	1	20	25	–	0.1
175 CONGR CHR CHS.	1	175	218*	0.2	0.5
179 CONSRV BAPT...	1	171	213*	0.2	0.5
193 EPISCOPAL.....	5	1 319	2 108	1.8	4.9
270 CONSRV JUDAISM	2	162	202*	0.2	0.5
271 REFORM JUDAISM	1	90	112*	0.1	0.3
281 LUTH CH AMER..	2	409	716	0.6	1.7
283 LUTH--MO SYNOD	3	968	1 534	1.3	3.6
353 CHR BRETHREN..	1	15	15	–	–
371 REF CH IN AM..	1	64	200	0.2	0.5
413 S.D.A........	2	267	332*	0.3	0.8
435 UNITARIAN-UNIV	1	31	39*	–	0.1
449 UN METHODIST..	14	3 464	4 312*	3.7	10.0
453 UN PRES CH USA	14	4 106	5 111*	4.4	11.9
UNION	**235**	**65 029**	**345 919***	**68.6**	**100.0**
005 AME ZION......	3	1 130	1 356	0.3	0.4
019 AMER BAPT USA.	20	6 526	7 670*	1.5	2.2
053 ASSEMB OF GOD.	9	1 171	1 516	0.3	0.4
081 CATHOLIC......	49	NA	264 833	52.5	76.6
089 CHR & MISS AL.	4	347	542*	0.1	0.2
097 CHR CHS&CHS CR	1	70	82*	–	–
123 CH GOD (ANDER)	2	150	450	0.1	0.1
127 CH GOD (CLEVE)	3	95	112*	–	–
151 L-D SAINTS....	1	NA	360	0.1	0.1
165 CH OF NAZARENE	2	57	171	–	–
167 CHS OF CHRIST.	1	38	48	–	–
179 CONSRV BAPT...	4	513	603*	0.1	0.2
193 EPISCOPAL.....	20	10 433	14 048	2.8	4.1
201 EVAN COV CH AM	1	63	74*	–	–
208 EVAN LUTH ASSN	1	225	320	0.1	0.1
226 FRIENDS-USA...	1	184	216*	–	0.1
270 CONSRV JUDAISM	10	2 175	2 556*	0.5	0.7
271 REFORM JUDAISM	5	3 576	4 203*	0.8	1.2
274 LAT EVAN LUTH.	1	137	153	–	–
281 LUTH CH AMER..	13	4 657	6 368	1.3	1.8
283 LUTH--MO SYNOD	5	1 521	2 016	0.4	0.6
293 MORAV CH-NORTH	1	128	157	–	–
335 ORTH PRESB CH.	1	178	209*	–	0.1
349 PENT HOLINESS	1	68	80*	–	–
353 CHR BRETHREN..	5	480	815	0.2	0.2
371 REF CH IN AM..	1	236	451	0.1	0.1
375 REF EPISCOPAL.	1	55	65*	–	–
403 SALVATION ARMY	2	119	367	0.1	0.1
413 S.D.A........	5	583	685*	0.1	0.2
415 S-D BAPTIST GC	1	83	98*	–	–
419 SO BAPT CONV..	3	238	280*	0.1	0.1
435 UNITARIAN-UNIV	2	710	834*	0.2	0.2
443 UN C OF CHRIST	5	2 118	2 489*	0.5	0.7
449 UN METHODIST..	21	8 625	10 137*	2.0	2.9
453 UN PRES CH USA	31	18 340	21 555*	4.3	6.2
WARREN	**96**	**18 969**	**53 254***	**63.1**	**100.0**
039 AP CHR CH(NAZ)	1	9	11*	–	–
053 ASSEMB OF GOD.	3	317	554*	0.7	1.0
081 CATHOLIC......	12	NA	28 763	34.1	54.0
089 CHR & MISS AL.	4	171	317	0.4	0.6
151 L-D SAINTS....	1	NA	66	0.1	0.1
165 CH OF NAZARENE	1	42	42	–	0.1
167 CHS OF CHRIST.	1	30	50	0.1	0.1
179 CONSRV BAPT...	1	171	207*	0.2	0.4
193 EPISCOPAL.....	6	1 530	2 269	2.7	4.3
203 EVAN FREE CH..	1	53	64*	0.1	0.1
221 FREE METHODIST	1	14	36	–	0.1

NA— Not applicable   *Total adherents estimated from known number of communicant, confirmed, full members.   —Represents a percent less than 0.1.   Percentages may not total due to rounding.

Table 4. Churches and Church Membership by County and Denomination: 1980

County and Denomination	Number of churches	Communicant, confirmed, full members	Total adherents		
			Number	Percent of total population	Percent of total adherents
244 GRACE BRETHREN	1	34	41*	–	0.1
281 LUTH CH AMER..	5	3 160	4 502	5.3	8.5
283 LUTH--MO SYNOD	1	395	571	0.7	1.1
285 MENNONITE CH..	2	131	158*	0.2	0.3
335 ORTH PRESB CH.	1	230	278*	0.3	0.5
413 S.D.A.........	3	358	433*	0.5	0.8
443 UN C OF CHRIST	1	80	97*	0.1	0.2
449 UN METHODIST..	23	4 459	5 388*	6.4	10.1
453 UN PRES CH USA	27	7 785	9 407*	11.1	17.7

NEW MEXICO

County and Denomination	Number of churches	Communicant, confirmed, full members	Total adherents		
			Number	Percent of total population	Percent of total adherents
THE STATE.....	1 594	236 480	767 737*	59.1	100.0
BERNALILLO	216	63 316	223 578*	53.3	100.0
017 AMER BAPT ASSN	1	92	92	–	–
019 AMER BAPT USA.	1	324	394*	0.1	0.2
029 AMER LUTH CH..	2	941	1 354	0.3	0.6
053 ASSEMB OF GOD.	15	2 114	3 232	0.8	1.4
075 BRETHREN IN CR	1	76	85	–	–
081 CATHOLIC......	36	NA	137 852	32.8	61.7
089 CHR & MISS AL.	1	23	33	–	–
093 CHR CH (DISC).	3	1 095	1 557	0.4	0.7
097 CHR CHS&CHS CR	7	1 711	2 080*	0.5	0.9
101 C.M.E........	1	148	180*	–	0.1
105 CHRISTIAN REF.	2	130	210	0.1	0.1
123 CH GOD (ANDER)	2	223	669	0.2	0.3
127 CH GOD (CLEVE)	2	127	154*	–	0.1
133 CH GOD(7TH)DEN	1	21	26*	–	–
151 L-D SAINTS....	14	NA	5 933	1.4	2.7
165 CH OF NAZARENE	9	1 317	1 767	0.4	0.8
167 CHS OF CHRIST.	12	2 565	2 739	0.7	1.2
179 CONSRV BAPT...	2	218	265*	0.1	0.1
185 CUMBER PRESB..	1	777	1 033	0.2	0.5
193 EPISCOPAL.....	8	4 483	5 884	1.4	2.6
201 EVAN COV CH AM	1	40	49*	–	–
203 EVAN FREE CH..	2	161	196*	–	0.1
226 FRIENDS-USA...	2	113	137*	–	0.1
244 GRACE BRETHREN	2	69	84*	–	–
263 INT FOURSQ GOS	3	427	519*	0.1	0.2
270 CONSRV JUDAISM	1	175	213*	0.1	0.1
271 REFORM JUDAISM	1	760	924*	0.2	0.4
281 LUTH CH AMER..	6	3 170	4 724	1.1	2.1
283 LUTH--MO SYNOD	6	2 115	2 643	0.6	1.2
285 MENNONITE CH..	1	32	39*	–	–
290 METRO COMM CHS	1	40	80	–	–
329 OPEN BIBLE STD	1	35	45	–	–
349 PENT HOLINESS.	1	43	52*	–	–
353 CHR BRETHREN..	2	70	85	–	–
403 SALVATION ARMY	1	84	117	–	0.1
413 S.D.A.........	5	1 096	1 332*	0.3	0.6
419 SO BAPT CONV..	27	19 886	24 170*	5.8	10.8
435 UNITARIAN-UNIV	1	532	647*	0.2	0.3
443 UN C OF CHRIST	4	988	1 201*	0.3	0.5
449 UN METHODIST..	16	12 071	14 671*	3.5	6.6
453 UN PRES CH USA	10	4 905	5 962*	1.4	2.7
469 WELS..........	1	119	149	–	0.1
CATRON	14	486	1 294*	47.6	100.0
053 ASSEMB OF GOD.	1	6	8	0.3	0.6
081 CATHOLIC......	2	NA	495	18.2	38.3
151 L-D SAINTS....	1	NA	197	7.2	15.2
167 CHS OF CHRIST.	1	20	25	0.9	1.9
413 S.D.A.........	1	7	9*	0.3	0.7
419 SO BAPT CONV..	4	318	393*	14.4	30.4
453 UN PRES CH USA	4	135	167*	6.1	12.9
CHAVES	80	16 042	30 089*	58.9	100.0
017 AMER BAPT ASSN	1	145	145	0.3	0.5
053 ASSEMB OF GOD.	8	662	1 071	2.1	3.6
059 BAPT MISS ASSN	1	175	215*	0.4	0.7
081 CATHOLIC......	5	NA	9 535	18.7	31.7
093 CHR CH (DISC).	1	380	410	0.8	1.4
097 CHR CHS&CHS CR	1	86	105*	0.2	0.3
101 C.M.E........	1	33	40*	0.1	0.1
123 CH GOD (ANDER)	1	14	42	0.1	0.1
127 CH GOD (CLEVE)	5	117	143*	0.3	0.5
133 CH GOD(7TH)DEN	1	12	15*	–	–
151 L-D SAINTS....	2	NA	559	1.1	1.9
165 CH OF NAZARENE	3	252	387	0.8	1.3
167 CHS OF CHRIST.	12	1 265	1 610	3.2	5.4
193 EPISCOPAL.....	2	583	709	1.4	2.4
203 EVAN FREE CH..	1	18	22*	–	0.1
263 INT FOURSQ GOS	1	?	?	?	?
281 LUTH CH AMER..	1	213	251	0.5	0.8
283 LUTH--MO SYNOD	1	245	283	0.6	0.9
403 SALVATION ARMY	1	135	192	0.4	0.6
413 S.D.A.........	3	184	226*	0.4	0.8
419 SO BAPT CONV..	16	7 811	9 577*	18.7	31.8
435 UNITARIAN-UNIV	1	21	26*	0.1	0.1

County and Denomination	Number of churches	Communicant, confirmed, full members	Total adherents		
			Number	Percent of total population	Percent of total adherents
449 UN METHODIST..	7	2 763	3 388*	6.6	11.3
453 UN PRES CH USA	4	928	1 138*	2.2	3.8
COLFAX	31	2 329	10 497*	76.6	100.0
053 ASSEMB OF GOD.	2	115	200	1.5	1.9
081 CATHOLIC......	8	NA	7 385	53.9	70.4
093 CHR CH (DISC).	1	69	146	1.1	1.4
127 CH GOD (CLEVE)	1	3	4*	–	–
151 L-D SAINTS....	1	NA	90	0.7	0.9
165 CH OF NAZARENE	1	19	36	0.3	0.3
167 CHS OF CHRIST.	3	91	127	0.9	1.2
193 EPISCOPAL.....	1	55	65	0.5	0.6
283 LUTH--MO SYNOD	1	16	28	0.2	0.3
413 S.D.A.........	1	9	11*	0.1	0.1
419 SO BAPT CONV..	5	1 136	1 400*	10.2	13.3
449 UN METHODIST..	4	664	818*	6.0	7.8
453 UN PRES CH USA	2	152	187*	1.4	1.8
CURRY	58	16 246	29 856*	71.1	100.0
001 ADVENT CHR CH.	1	153	192*	0.5	0.6
017 AMER BAPT ASSN	1	50	50	0.1	0.2
029 AMER LUTH CH..	1	114	167	0.4	0.6
053 ASSEMB OF GOD.	3	411	615	1.5	2.1
059 BAPT MISS ASSN	1	54	68*	0.2	0.2
081 CATHOLIC......	3	NA	8 223	19.6	27.5
097 CHR CHS&CHS CR	2	1 023	1 281*	3.0	4.3
101 C.M.E........	2	85	106*	0.3	0.4
123 CH GOD (ANDER)	1	53	159	0.4	0.5
127 CH GOD (CLEVE)	1	48	60*	0.1	0.2
151 L-D SAINTS....	1	NA	282	0.7	0.9
157 CH OF BRETHREN	1	93	116*	0.3	0.4
165 CH OF NAZARENE	3	621	1 351	3.2	4.5
167 CHS OF CHRIST.	8	1 301	1 780	4.2	6.0
193 EPISCOPAL.....	1	324	400	1.0	1.3
283 LUTH--MO SYNOD	1	248	342	0.8	1.1
353 CHR BRETHREN..	1	50	100	0.2	0.3
403 SALVATION ARMY	1	47	78	0.2	0.3
413 S.D.A.........	2	99	124*	0.3	0.4
419 SO BAPT CONV..	16	8 613	10 783*	25.7	36.1
449 UN METHODIST..	5	2 489	3 116*	7.4	10.4
453 UN PRES CH USA	2	370	463*	1.1	1.6
DE BACA	7	995	2 211*	90.1	100.0
053 ASSEMB OF GOD.	1	11	32	1.3	1.4
081 CATHOLIC......	1	NA	1 000	40.7	45.2
165 CH OF NAZARENE	1	29	27	1.1	1.2
167 CHS OF CHRIST.	1	95	140	5.7	6.3
193 EPISCOPAL.....	1	24	25	1.0	1.1
419 SO BAPT CONV..	1	552	652*	26.6	29.5
449 UN METHODIST..	1	284	335*	13.7	15.2
DONA ANA	107	13 583	45 918*	47.7	100.0
029 AMER LUTH CH..	1	197	304	0.3	0.7
053 ASSEMB OF GOD.	9	583	964	1.0	2.1
059 BAPT MISS ASSN	1	49	61*	0.1	0.1
081 CATHOLIC......	30	NA	27 167	28.2	59.2
093 CHR CH (DISC).	1	178	204	0.2	0.4
097 CHR CHS&CHS CR	2	80	100*	0.1	0.2
101 C.M.E........	1	33	41*	–	0.1
123 CH GOD (ANDER)	2	70	210	0.2	0.5
127 CH GOD (CLEVE)	1	40	50*	0.1	0.1
133 CH GOD(7TH)DEN	1	4	5*	–	–
151 L-D SAINTS....	5	NA	1 250	1.3	2.7
165 CH OF NAZARENE	2	106	224	0.2	0.5
167 CHS OF CHRIST.	10	985	1 254	1.3	2.7
193 EPISCOPAL.....	5	990	1 229	1.3	2.7
203 EVAN FREE CH..	1	24	30*	–	0.1
226 FRIENDS-USA...	1	5	6*	–	–
263 INT FOURSQ GOS	1	18	22*	–	–
281 LUTH CH AMER..	1	103	140	–	0.3
349 PENT HOLINESS.	1	18	22*	–	–
381 REF PRES-EVAN.	2	145	217	0.2	0.5
403 SALVATION ARMY	1	27	68	0.1	0.1
413 S.D.A.........	3	147	183*	0.2	0.4
419 SO BAPT CONV..	17	6 010	7 476*	7.8	16.3
435 UNITARIAN-UNIV	1	105	131*	0.1	0.3
449 UN METHODIST..	6	2 845	3 539*	3.7	7.7
453 UN PRES CH USA	1	821	1 021*	1.1	2.2
EDDY	84	16 605	36 088*	75.4	100.0
017 AMER BAPT ASSN	1	73	73	0.2	0.2
053 ASSEMB OF GOD.	7	687	1 104	2.3	3.1
059 BAPT MISS ASSN	2	288	358*	0.7	1.0
081 CATHOLIC......	10	NA	14 260	29.8	39.5
093 CHR CH (DISC).	2	284	517	1.1	1.4
097 CHR CHS&CHS CR	2	185	230*	0.5	0.6
101 C.M.E........	1	220	273*	0.6	0.8
127 CH GOD (CLEVE)	5	212	263*	0.5	0.7
151 L-D SAINTS....	2	NA	610	1.3	1.7
164 CH LUTH CONF..	1	21	22	–	0.1
165 CH OF NAZARENE	3	262	534	1.1	1.5
167 CHS OF CHRIST.	9	1 593	1 987	4.2	5.5
193 EPISCOPAL.....	2	316	320	0.7	0.9
281 LUTH CH AMER..	1	149	207	0.4	0.6
283 LUTH--MO SYNOD	2	186	272	0.6	0.8
285 MENNONITE CH..	2	53	66*	0.1	0.2
413 S.D.A.........	1	30	37*	0.1	0.1
419 SO BAPT CONV..	18	8 123	10 085*	21.1	27.9
449 UN METHODIST..	10	3 170	3 935*	8.2	10.9
453 UN PRES CH USA	2	753	935*	2.0	2.6

NA— Not applicable *Total adherents estimated from known number of communicant, confirmed, full members. —Represents a percent less than 0.1. Percentages may not total due to rounding.

Table 4. Churches and Church Membership by County and Denomination: 1980

County and Denomination	Number of churches	Communicant, confirmed, full members	Total adherents Number	Percent of total population	Percent of total adherents
GRANT	39	3 829	19 302*	73.7	100.0
053 ASSEMB OF GOD.	2	246	360	1.4	1.9
081 CATHOLIC......	12	NA	13 141	50.1	68.1
127 CH GOD (CLEVE)	1	44	55*	0.2	0.3
151 L-D SAINTS....	3	NA	1 050	4.0	5.4
167 CHS OF CHRIST.	4	210	267	1.0	1.4
179 CONSRV BAPT...	1	116	146*	0.6	0.8
193 EPISCOPAL.....	1	147	409	1.6	2.1
263 INT FOURSQ GOS	1	110	139*	0.5	0.7
283 LUTH--MO SYNOD	1	100	134	0.5	0.7
413 S.D.A.........	1	31	39*	0.1	0.2
419 SO BAPT CONV..	5	1 529	1 928*	7.4	10.0
443 UN C OF CHRIST	3	139	175*	0.7	0.9
449 UN METHODIST..	2	901	1 136*	4.3	5.9
453 UN PRES CH USA	2	256	323*	1.2	1.7
GUADALUPE	16	393	6 234*	138.7	100.0
053 ASSEMB OF GOD.	1	12	24	0.5	0.4
081 CATHOLIC......	9	NA	5 735	127.6	92.0
167 CHS OF CHRIST.	2	50	64	1.4	1.0
419 SO BAPT CONV..	3	218	271*	6.0	4.3
449 UN METHODIST..	1	113	140*	3.1	2.2
HARDING	9	222	1 483*	136.1	100.0
081 CATHOLIC......	6	NA	1 200	110.1	80.9
093 CHR CH (DISC).	1	50	77	7.1	5.2
419 SO BAPT CONV..	1	138	165*	15.1	11.1
449 UN METHODIST..	1	34	41*	3.8	2.8
HIDALGO	17	1 079	4 430*	73.2	100.0
053 ASSEMB OF GOD.	2	70	142	2.3	3.2
081 CATHOLIC......	5	NA	2 312	38.2	52.2
097 CHR CHS&CHS CR	1	150	193*	3.2	4.4
151 L-D SAINTS....	3	NA	678	11.2	15.3
167 CHS OF CHRIST.	1	70	89	1.5	2.0
419 SO BAPT CONV..	3	543	699*	11.6	15.8
449 UN METHODIST..	1	174	224*	3.7	5.1
453 UN PRES CH USA	1	72	93*	1.5	2.1
LEA	99	24 565	39 714*	71.4	100.0
017 AMER BAPT ASSN	1	243	243	0.4	0.6
029 AMER LUTH CH..	1	66	91	0.2	0.2
053 ASSEMB OF GOD.	9	617	1 123	2.0	2.8
059 BAPT MISS ASSN	2	92	117*	0.2	0.3
081 CATHOLIC......	6	NA	7 660	13.8	19.3
093 CHR CH (DISC).	1	70	108	0.2	0.3
097 CHR CHS&CHS CR	3	715	908*	1.6	2.3
101 C.M.E.	1	445	565*	1.0	1.4
127 CH GOD (CLEVE)	5	121	154*	0.3	0.4
151 L-D SAINTS....	2	NA	488	0.9	1.2
165 CH OF NAZARENE	3	308	407	0.7	1.0
167 CHS OF CHRIST.	16	1 725	2 195	3.9	5.5
193 EPISCOPAL.....	2	270	379	0.7	1.0
281 LUTH CH AMER..	1	65	84	0.2	0.2
283 LUTH--MO SYNOD	2	147	186	0.3	0.5
349 PENT HOLINESS.	2	132	168*	0.3	0.4
403 SALVATION ARMY	1	72	116	0.2	0.3
413 S.D.A.........	2	57	72*	0.1	0.2
419 SO BAPT CONV..	30	15 344	19 476*	35.0	49.0
449 UN METHODIST..	6	3 579	4 543*	8.2	11.4
453 UN PRES CH USA	3	497	631*	1.1	1.6
LINCOLN	28	2 385	5 273*	47.9	100.0
053 ASSEMB OF GOD.	2	61	120	1.1	2.3
081 CATHOLIC......	5	NA	2 235	20.3	42.4
093 CHR CH (DISC).	1	313	342	3.1	6.5
151 L-D SAINTS....	1	NA	82	0.7	1.6
165 CH OF NAZARENE	1	27	24	0.2	0.5
167 CHS OF CHRIST.	3	140	178	1.6	3.4
193 EPISCOPAL.....	1	119	203	1.8	3.8
413 S.D.A.........	1	19	23*	0.2	0.4
419 SO BAPT CONV..	6	1 147	1 389*	12.6	26.3
449 UN METHODIST..	3	374	453*	4.1	8.6
453 UN PRES CH USA	4	185	224*	2.0	4.2
LOS ALAMOS	23	5 325	11 834*	67.2	100.0
019 AMER BAPT USA.	1	172	211*	1.2	1.8
053 ASSEMB OF GOD.	1	77	175	1.0	1.5
081 CATHOLIC......	2	NA	4 500	25.6	38.0
089 CHR & MISS AL.	1	53	99	0.6	0.8
093 CHR CH (DISC).	1	172	173	1.0	1.5
097 CHR CHS&CHS CR	1	300	367*	2.1	3.1
151 L-D SAINTS....	2	NA	600	3.4	5.1
165 CH OF NAZARENE	1	39	72	0.4	0.6
167 CHS OF CHRIST.	1	153	195	1.1	1.6
193 EPISCOPAL.....	1	584	673	3.8	5.7
281 LUTH CH AMER..	1	682	967	5.5	8.2
356 PRESB CH AMER.	1	153	198	1.1	1.7
419 SO BAPT CONV..	2	745	912*	5.2	7.7
435 UNITARIAN-UNIV	1	135	165*	0.9	1.4
443 UN C OF CHRIST	1	689	844*	4.8	7.1
449 UN METHODIST..	2	970	1 188*	6.8	10.0
453 UN PRES CH USA	2	365	447*	2.5	3.8
469 WELS.........	1	36	48	0.3	0.4
LUNA	25	2 958	6 840*	43.9	100.0
053 ASSEMB OF GOD.	2	68	88	0.6	1.3
059 BAPT MISS ASSN	1	12	15*	0.1	0.2
081 CATHOLIC......	5	NA	2 800	18.0	40.9
097 CHR CHS&CHS CR	1	157	193*	1.2	2.8
123 CH GOD (ANDER)	1	11	33	0.2	0.5
151 L-D SAINTS....	1	NA	286	1.8	4.2
165 CH OF NAZARENE	1	39	60	0.4	0.9
167 CHS OF CHRIST.	1	80	102	0.7	1.5
193 EPISCOPAL.....	1	118	219	1.4	3.2
263 INT FOURSQ GOS	1	5	6*	-	0.1
283 LUTH--MO SYNOD	1	116	146	0.9	2.1
413 S.D.A.........	1	55	68*	0.4	1.0
419 SO BAPT CONV..	5	1 391	1 710*	11.0	25.0
449 UN METHODIST..	2	758	932*	6.0	13.6
453 UN PRES CH USA	1	148	182*	1.2	2.7
MC KINLEY	76	4 421	20 653*	37.6	100.0
053 ASSEMB OF GOD.	8	334	585	1.1	2.8
081 CATHOLIC......	14	NA	9 792	17.8	47.4
097 CHR CHS&CHS CR	1	50	67*	0.1	0.3
105 CHRISTIAN REF.	8	464	841	1.5	4.1
127 CH GOD (CLEVE)	6	193	257*	0.5	1.2
151 L-D SAINTS....	13	NA	4 546	8.3	22.0
165 CH OF NAZARENE	3	224	352	0.6	1.7
167 CHS OF CHRIST.	5	220	280	0.5	1.4
179 CONSRV BAPT...	1	39	52*	0.1	0.3
193 EPISCOPAL.....	1	120	188	0.3	0.9
197 EVAN CH OF NA.	2	53	53	0.1	0.3
226 FRIENDS-USA...	1	3	4*	-	-
263 INT FOURSQ GOS	1	?	?	?	?
283 LUTH--MO SYNOD	2	149	213	0.4	1.0
413 S.D.A.........	1	22	29*	0.1	0.1
419 SO BAPT CONV..	6	1 787	2 378*	4.3	11.5
443 UN C OF CHRIST	1	40	53*	0.1	0.3
449 UN METHODIST..	1	615	819*	1.5	4.0
453 UN PRES CH USA	1	108	144*	0.3	0.7
MORA	25	185	5 219*	124.1	100.0
081 CATHOLIC......	18	NA	5 000	118.9	95.8
133 CH GOD(7TH)DEN	1	2	2*	-	-
167 CHS OF CHRIST.	3	54	57	1.4	1.1
419 SO BAPT CONV..	1	76	94*	2.2	1.8
453 UN PRES CH USA	2	53	66*	1.6	1.3
OTERO	65	10 138	20 668*	46.3	100.0
053 ASSEMB OF GOD.	5	319	612	1.4	3.0
059 BAPT MISS ASSN	1	51	64*	0.1	0.3
081 CATHOLIC......	9	NA	6 738	15.1	32.6
093 CHR CH (DISC).	1	88	105	0.2	0.5
097 CHR CHS&CHS CR	1	125	156*	0.3	0.8
127 CH GOD (CLEVE)	1	54	67*	0.2	0.3
151 L-D SAINTS....	4	NA	718	1.6	3.5
157 CH OF BRETHREN	1	106	132*	0.3	0.6
165 CH OF NAZARENE	2	85	244	0.5	1.2
167 CHS OF CHRIST.	11	560	713	1.6	3.4
193 EPISCOPAL.....	1	126	177	0.4	0.9
281 LUTH CH AMER..	1	189	236	0.5	1.1
283 LUTH--MO SYNOD	1	277	363	0.8	1.8
371 REF CH IN AM..	1	65	232	0.5	1.1
381 REF PRES-EVAN.	1	129	159	0.4	0.8
413 S.D.A.........	1	58	72*	0.2	0.3
419 SO BAPT CONV..	15	5 306	6 631*	14.8	32.1
435 UNITARIAN-UNIV	1	25	31*	0.1	0.1
449 UN METHODIST..	6	2 379	2 973*	6.7	14.4
453 UN PRES CH USA	1	196	245*	0.5	1.2
QUAY	37	4 619	9 371*	88.6	100.0
053 ASSEMB OF GOD.	4	162	262	2.5	2.8
081 CATHOLIC......	5	NA	3 511	33.2	37.5
097 CHR CHS&CHS CR	1	150	184*	1.7	2.0
127 CH GOD (CLEVE)	1	19	23*	0.2	0.2
151 L-D SAINTS....	1	NA	90	0.9	1.0
164 CH LUTH CONF..	1	11	16	0.2	0.2
165 CH OF NAZARENE	1	25	56	0.5	0.6
167 CHS OF CHRIST.	5	150	191	1.8	2.0
193 EPISCOPAL.....	1	34	42	0.4	0.4
263 INT FOURSQ GOS	1	21	26*	0.2	0.3
413 S.D.A.........	1	31	38*	0.4	0.4
419 SO BAPT CONV..	9	3 119	3 831*	36.2	40.9
449 UN METHODIST..	5	790	970*	9.2	10.4
453 UN PRES CH USA	1	107	131*	1.2	1.4
RIO ARRIBA	73	1 803	27 042*	92.4	100.0
053 ASSEMB OF GOD.	11	501	864	3.0	3.2
081 CATHOLIC......	39	NA	23 840	81.4	88.2
151 L-D SAINTS....	3	NA	510	1.7	1.9
157 CH OF BRETHREN	1	24	31*	0.1	0.1
167 CHS OF CHRIST.	4	225	286	1.0	1.1
193 EPISCOPAL.....	1	47	68	0.2	0.3
371 REF CH IN AM..	1	72	255	0.9	0.9
413 S.D.A.........	3	122	155*	0.5	0.6
419 SO BAPT CONV..	2	264	336*	1.1	1.2
449 UN METHODIST..	5	316	402*	1.4	1.5
453 UN PRES CH USA	3	232	295*	1.0	1.1
ROOSEVELT	39	7 491	12 692*	80.9	100.0
053 ASSEMB OF GOD.	1	113	160	1.0	1.3
081 CATHOLIC......	1	NA	3 300	21.0	26.0
097 CHR CHS&CHS CR	1	180	216*	1.4	1.7
127 CH GOD (CLEVE)	1	47	56*	0.4	0.4

NA— Not applicable   *Total adherents estimated from known number of communicant, confirmed, full members.   —Represents a percent less than 0.1.   Percentages may not total due to rounding.

Table 4. Churches and Church Membership by County and Denomination: 1980

County and Denomination	Number of churches	Communicant, confirmed, full members	Total adherents		
			Number	Percent of total population	Percent of total adherents
151 L-D SAINTS....	1	NA	159	1.0	1.3
165 CH OF NAZARENE	1	116	221	1.4	1.7
167 CHS OF CHRIST.	12	882	1 174	7.5	9.2
193 EPISCOPAL.....	1	46	68	0.4	0.5
413 S.D.A.........	1	42	50*	0.3	0.4
419 SO BAPT CONV..	14	5 032	6 047*	38.5	47.6
449 UN METHODIST..	4	897	1 078*	6.9	8.5
453 UN PRES CH USA	1	136	163*	1.0	1.3
SANDOVAL	32	1 007	22 209*	63.8	100.0
053 ASSEMB OF GOD.	5	111	198	0.6	0.9
081 CATHOLIC......	12	NA	20 700	59.5	93.2
097 CHR CHS&CHS CR	1	200	251*	0.7	1.1
151 L-D SAINTS....	2	NA	201	0.6	0.9
167 CHS OF CHRIST.	1	25	32	0.1	0.1
193 EPISCOPAL.....	1	68	68	0.2	0.3
244 GRACE BRETHREN	1	18	23*	0.1	0.1
413 S.D.A.........	1	85	107*	0.3	0.5
419 SO BAPT CONV..	3	331	416*	1.2	1.9
449 UN METHODIST..	1	34	43*	0.1	0.2
453 UN PRES CH USA	4	135	170*	0.5	0.8
SAN JUAN	94	14 265	36 159*	44.7	100.0
017 AMER BAPT ASSN	1	90	90	0.1	0.2
053 ASSEMB OF GOD.	9	732	1 397	1.7	3.9
075 BRETHREN IN CR	1	76	85	0.1	0.2
081 CATHOLIC......	7	NA	9 280	11.5	25.7
093 CHR CH (DISC).	1	178	274	0.3	0.8
097 CHR CHS&CHS CR	3	205	265*	0.3	0.7
105 CHRISTIAN REF.	5	241	510	0.6	1.4
123 CH GOD (ANDER)	1	8	24	–	0.1
127 CH GOD (CLEVE)	4	115	149*	0.2	0.4
151 L-D SAINTS....	16	NA	7 350	9.1	20.3
165 CH OF NAZARENE	2	173	323	0.4	0.9
167 CHS OF CHRIST.	8	400	509	0.6	1.4
179 CONSRV BAPT...	1	109	141*	0.2	0.4
193 EPISCOPAL.....	5	477	803	1.0	2.2
221 FREE METHODIST	2	39	153	0.2	0.4
226 FRIENDS-USA...	1	4	5*	–	–
263 INT FOURSQ GOS	1	43	56*	0.1	0.2
281 LUTH CH AMER..	1	202	298	0.4	0.8
283 LUTH--MO SYNOD	1	226	305	0.4	0.8
285 MENNONITE CH..	1	13	17*	–	–
403 SALVATION ARMY	1	37	30	–	0.1
413 S.D.A.........	4	443	573*	0.7	1.6
419 SO BAPT CONV..	11	7 614	9 849*	12.2	27.2
435 UNITARIAN-UNIV	1	32	41*	0.1	0.1
449 UN METHODIST..	4	2 195	2 839*	3.5	7.9
453 UN PRES CH USA	2	613	793*	1.0	2.2
SAN MIGUEL	42	1 412	16 699*	73.4	100.0
053 ASSEMB OF GOD.	4	90	210	0.9	1.3
081 CATHOLIC......	25	NA	14 741	64.8	88.3
093 CHR CH (DISC).	1	29	29	0.1	0.2
151 L-D SAINTS....	1	NA	106	0.5	0.6
167 CHS OF CHRIST.	5	200	255	1.1	1.5
193 EPISCOPAL.....	1	73	94	0.4	0.6
283 LUTH--MO SYNOD	1	77	100	0.4	0.6
419 SO BAPT CONV..	2	486	600*	2.6	3.6
449 UN METHODIST..	1	257	317*	1.4	1.9
453 UN PRES CH USA	1	200	247*	1.1	1.5
SANTA FE	56	7 474	46 006*	61.1	100.0
053 ASSEMB OF GOD.	3	346	550	0.7	1.2
081 CATHOLIC......	26	NA	36 138	48.0	78.6
093 CHR CH (DISC).	1	150	165	0.2	0.4
097 CHR CHS&CHS CR	1	200	245*	0.3	0.5
127 CH GOD (CLEVE)	1	19	23*	–	–
151 L-D SAINTS....	1	NA	500	0.7	1.1
165 CH OF NAZARENE	1	37	62	0.1	0.1
167 CHS OF CHRIST.	1	109	133	0.2	0.3
193 EPISCOPAL.....	2	887	1 120	1.5	2.4
226 FRIENDS-USA...	1	31	38*	0.1	0.1
281 LUTH CH AMER..	1	175	232	0.3	0.5
283 LUTH--MO SYNOD	1	176	247	0.3	0.5
290 METRO COMM CHS	0	10	20	–	–
413 S.D.A.........	2	87	107*	0.1	0.2
419 SO BAPT CONV..	7	2 069	2 534*	3.4	5.5
435 UNITARIAN-UNIV	1	121	148*	0.2	0.3
443 UN C OF CHRIST	1	?	?	?	?
449 UN METHODIST..	2	1 873	2 294*	3.0	5.0
453 UN PRES CH USA	3	1 184	1 450*	1.9	3.2
SIERRA	22	1 338	3 635*	43.0	100.0
053 ASSEMB OF GOD.	2	87	111	1.3	3.1
081 CATHOLIC......	6	NA	1 904	22.5	52.4
093 CHR CH (DISC).	1	30	40	0.5	1.1
097 CHR CHS&CHS CR	1	112	129*	1.5	3.5
127 CH GOD (CLEVE)	1	15	17*	0.2	0.5
151 L-D SAINTS....	1	NA	95	1.1	2.6
165 CH OF NAZARENE	1	29	51	0.6	1.4
167 CHS OF CHRIST.	3	150	191	2.3	5.3
193 EPISCOPAL.....	1	56	108	1.3	3.0
283 LUTH--MO SYNOD	1	82	92	1.1	2.5
383 REF PRES OF NA	1	6	6	0.1	0.2
413 S.D.A.........	1	32	37*	0.4	1.0
419 SO BAPT CONV..	1	379	438*	5.2	12.0
449 UN METHODIST..	1	360	416*	4.9	11.4
SOCORRO	27	1 461	9 676*	74.6	100.0

County and Denomination	Number of churches	Communicant, confirmed, full members	Total adherents		
			Number	Percent of total population	Percent of total adherents
053 ASSEMB OF GOD.	2	20	26	0.2	0.3
081 CATHOLIC......	11	NA	7 662	59.1	79.2
097 CHR CHS&CHS CR	1	50	62*	0.5	0.6
127 CH GOD (CLEVE)	1	5	6*	–	0.1
151 L-D SAINTS....	1	NA	134	1.0	1.4
167 CHS OF CHRIST.	1	56	78	0.6	0.8
193 EPISCOPAL.....	1	36	95	0.7	1.0
226 FRIENDS-USA...	1	8	10*	0.1	0.1
413 S.D.A.........	1	37	46*	0.4	0.5
419 SO BAPT CONV..	3	854	1 065*	8.2	11.0
449 UN METHODIST..	2	171	213*	1.6	2.2
453 UN PRES CH USA	2	224	279*	2.2	2.9
TAOS	45	1 350	20 944*	111.0	100.0
053 ASSEMB OF GOD.	4	169	285	1.5	1.4
081 CATHOLIC......	27	NA	18 800	99.7	89.8
151 L-D SAINTS....	2	NA	370	2.0	1.8
167 CHS OF CHRIST.	2	90	115	0.6	0.5
193 EPISCOPAL.....	1	127	156	0.8	0.7
226 FRIENDS-USA...	1	3	4*	–	–
244 GRACE BRETHREN	1	237	299*	1.6	1.4
419 SO BAPT CONV..	3	338	427*	2.3	2.0
449 UN METHODIST..	1	75	95*	0.5	0.5
453 UN PRES CH USA	3	311	393*	2.1	1.9
TORRANCE	29	1 605	4 226*	56.4	100.0
053 ASSEMB OF GOD.	4	161	229	3.1	5.4
081 CATHOLIC......	10	NA	1 983	26.5	46.9
151 L-D SAINTS....	2	NA	162	2.2	3.8
164 CH LUTH CONF..	1	17	26	0.3	0.6
165 CH OF NAZARENE	2	81	139	1.9	3.3
167 CHS OF CHRIST.	3	150	191	2.5	4.5
419 SO BAPT CONV..	3	872	1 091*	14.6	25.8
449 UN METHODIST..	4	324	405*	5.4	9.6
UNION	16	1 551	3 201*	67.7	100.0
053 ASSEMB OF GOD.	1	31	50	1.1	1.6
081 CATHOLIC......	2	NA	1 300	27.5	40.6
127 CH GOD (CLEVE)	2	60	73*	1.5	2.3
167 CHS OF CHRIST.	2	96	120	2.5	3.7
349 PENT HOLINESS.	1	34	41*	0.9	1.3
413 S.D.A.........	1	17	21*	0.4	0.7
419 SO BAPT CONV..	4	705	857*	18.1	26.8
449 UN METHODIST..	3	608	739*	15.6	23.1
VALENCIA	63	6 002	34 696*	57.0	100.0
029 AMER LUTH CH..	1	148	182	0.3	0.5
053 ASSEMB OF GOD.	6	315	548	0.9	1.6
081 CATHOLIC......	18	NA	25 052	41.2	72.2
097 CHR CHS&CHS CR	2	150	192*	0.3	0.6
127 CH GOD (CLEVE)	2	122	156*	0.3	0.4
151 L-D SAINTS....	4	NA	1 758	2.9	5.1
165 CH OF NAZARENE	5	216	326	0.5	0.9
167 CHS OF CHRIST.	3	265	337	0.6	1.0
193 EPISCOPAL.....	2	134	190	0.3	0.5
263 INT FOURSQ GOS	1	38	49*	0.1	0.1
283 LUTH--MO SYNOD	2	149	189	0.3	0.5
413 S.D.A.........	3	153	196*	0.3	0.6
419 SO BAPT CONV..	8	3 042	3 895*	6.4	11.2
449 UN METHODIST..	3	877	1 123*	1.8	3.2
453 UN PRES CH USA	3	393	503*	0.8	1.4

NEW YORK

County and Denomination	Number of churches	Communicant, confirmed, full members	Total adherents		
			Number	Percent of total population	Percent of total adherents
THE STATE.....	8 989	1 862 886	8 721 200*	49.7	100.0
ALBANY	172	38 020	163 983*	57.4	100.0
005 AME ZION......	2	2 017	2 723	1.0	1.7
019 AMER BAPT USA.	7	1 334	1 568*	0.5	1.0
053 ASSEMB OF GOD.	2	204	384	0.1	0.2
057 BAPT GEN CONF.	2	321	377*	0.1	0.2
059 BAPT MISS ASSN	1	29	34*	–	–
081 CATHOLIC......	44	NA	111 760	39.1	68.2
089 CHR & MISS AL.	3	468	691	0.2	0.4
127 CH GOD (CLEVE)	1	40	47*	–	–
151 L-D SAINTS....	1	NA	485	0.2	0.3
165 CH OF NAZARENE	1	42	93	–	0.1
167 CHS OF CHRIST.	1	99	137	–	0.1
193 EPISCOPAL.....	16	4 646	6 487	2.3	4.0
195 ESTONIAN ELC..	1	16	89	–	0.1
208 EVAN LUTH ASSN	1	43	80	–	–
226 FRIENDS-USA...	1	90	106*	–	0.1
270 CONSRV JUDAISM	2	1 124	1 321*	0.5	0.8
271 REFORM JUDAISM	2	2 414	2 838*	1.0	1.7
281 LUTH CH AMER..	7	3 002	4 209	1.5	2.6
283 LUTH--MO SYNOD	6	2 183	3 479	1.2	2.1
290 METRO COMM CHS	1	15	30	–	–
371 REF CH IN AM..	23	4 152	8 021	2.8	4.9

NA—Not applicable   *Total adherents estimated from known number of communicant, confirmed, full members.   —Represents a percent less than 0.1.   Percentages may not total due to rounding.

Table 4. Churches and Church Membership by County and Denomination: 1980

County and Denomination	Number of churches	Communicant, confirmed, full members	Total adherents Number	Total adherents Percent of total population	Total adherents Percent of total adherents
403 SALVATION ARMY	2	139	635	0.2	0.4
413 S.D.A.........	2	307	361*	0.1	0.2
435 UNITARIAN-UNIV	1	325	382*	0.1	0.2
443 UN C OF CHRIST	5	1 092	1 284*	0.4	0.8
449 UN METHODIST..	21	9 623	11 313*	4.0	6.9
453 UN PRES CH USA	16	4 295	5 049*	1.8	3.1
ALLEGANY	84	7 474	17 871*	34.5	100.0
019 AMER BAPT USA.	6	754	913*	1.8	5.1
053 ASSEMB OF GOD.	2	166	263	0.5	1.5
081 CATHOLIC......	15	NA	7 782	15.0	43.5
089 CHR & MISS AL.	3	157	304	0.6	1.7
093 CHR CH (DISC).	1	405	683	1.3	3.8
097 CHR CHS&CHS CR	1	145	176*	0.3	1.0
151 L-D SAINTS....	1	NA	87	0.2	0.5
193 EPISCOPAL.....	6	406	755	1.5	4.2
215 EVAN METH CH..	1	20	24*	–	0.1
221 FREE METHODIST	2	48	165	0.3	0.9
226 FRIENDS-USA...	1	34	41*	0.1	0.2
283 LUTH--MO SYNOD	2	542	769	1.5	4.3
285 MENNONITE CH..	3	107	130*	0.3	0.7
403 SALVATION ARMY	1	78	198	0.4	1.1
413 S.D.A.........	1	45	54*	0.1	0.3
415 S-D BAPTIST GC	4	519	628*	1.2	3.5
435 UNITARIAN-UNIV	1	10	12*	–	0.1
443 UN C OF CHRIST	1	248	300*	0.6	1.7
449 UN METHODIST..	28	3 443	4 167*	8.1	23.3
453 UN PRES CH USA	4	347	420*	0.8	2.4
BRONX	314	56 018	569 983*	48.8	100.0
005 AME ZION......	11	12 869	15 623	1.3	2.7
019 AMER BAPT USA.	20	7 053	8 581*	0.7	1.5
029 AMER LUTH CH..	8	964	1 360	0.1	0.2
053 ASSEMB OF GOD.	33	4 775	6 617	0.6	1.2
057 BAPT GEN CONF.	4	177	215*	–	–
066 BIBLE CH OF CR	1	1 500	1 825*	0.2	0.3
075 BRETHREN IN CR	1	109	131	–	–
081 CATHOLIC......	70	NA	496 690	42.5	87.1
089 CHR & MISS AL.	5	516	551	–	0.1
093 CHR CH (DISC).	5	804	1 156	0.1	0.2
101 C.M.E.........	3	1 613	1 962*	0.2	0.3
123 CH GOD (ANDER)	1	50	150	–	–
127 CH GOD (CLEVE)	15	823	1 001*	0.1	0.2
133 CH GOD(7TH)DEN	1	29	35*	–	–
151 L-D SAINTS....	2	NA	347	–	0.1
165 CH OF NAZARENE	1	106	167	–	–
167 CHS OF CHRIST.	3	31	50	–	–
181 CONSRV CONGR..	1	19	23*	–	–
193 EPISCOPAL.....	22	4 719	8 146	0.7	1.4
201 EVAN COV CH AM	2	128	156*	–	–
270 CONSRV JUDAISM	4	1 044	1 270*	0.1	0.2
271 REFORM JUDAISM	3	1 728	2 102*	0.2	0.4
281 LUTH CH AMER..	12	1 911	3 024	0.3	0.5
283 LUTH--MO SYNOD	6	1 229	1 591	0.1	0.3
285 MENNONITE CH..	9	245	298*	–	0.1
293 MORAV CH-NORTH	2	731	1 023	0.1	0.2
353 CHR BRETHREN..	4	155	265	–	–
383 REF PRES OF NA	1	77	86	–	–
403 SALVATION ARMY	2	109	327	–	0.1
413 S.D.A.........	12	2 690	3 273*	0.3	0.6
419 SO BAPT CONV..	4	971	1 181*	0.1	0.2
443 UN C OF CHRIST	10	1 364	1 659*	0.1	0.3
449 UN METHODIST..	15	3 691	4 490*	0.4	0.8
453 UN PRES CH USA	21	3 788	4 608*	0.4	0.8
BROOME	160	37 946	116 401*	54.5	100.0
005 AME ZION......	1	432	512	0.2	0.4
019 AMER BAPT USA.	6	1 786	2 121*	1.0	1.8
053 ASSEMB OF GOD.	3	801	1 390	0.7	1.2
081 CATHOLIC......	33	NA	68 252	31.9	58.6
089 CHR & MISS AL.	5	280	515	0.2	0.4
093 CHR CH (DISC).	1	192	223	0.1	0.2
097 CHR CHS&CHS CR	3	335	398*	0.2	0.3
105 CHRISTIAN REF.	1	110	222	0.1	0.2
151 L-D SAINTS....	1	NA	523	0.2	0.4
165 CH OF NAZARENE	2	338	447	0.2	0.4
167 CHS OF CHRIST.	1	91	168	0.1	0.1
179 CONSRV BAPT...	1	225	267*	0.1	0.2
193 EPISCOPAL.....	9	3 517	4 580	2.1	3.9
203 EVAN FREE CH..	1	43	51*	–	–
221 FREE METHODIST	3	114	567	0.3	0.5
270 CONSRV JUDAISM	1	265	315*	0.1	0.3
271 REFORM JUDAISM	1	500	594*	0.3	0.5
281 LUTH CH AMER..	6	1 862	2 660	1.2	2.3
283 LUTH--MO SYNOD	2	486	651	0.3	0.6
363 PRIMITIVE METH	1	620	736*	0.3	0.6
381 REF PRES-EVAN.	1	34	42	–	–
403 SALVATION ARMY	1	83	494	0.2	0.4
413 S.D.A.........	2	223	265*	0.1	0.2
419 SO BAPT CONV..	1	270	321*	0.2	0.3
435 UNITARIAN-UNIV	2	244	290*	0.1	0.2
443 UN C OF CHRIST	6	1 315	1 561*	0.7	1.3
449 UN METHODIST..	48	18 336	21 772*	10.2	18.7
453 UN PRES CH USA	17	5 444	6 464*	3.0	5.6
CATTARAUGUS	120	13 052	42 545*	49.6	100.0
019 AMER BAPT USA.	4	1 107	1 355*	1.6	3.2
053 ASSEMB OF GOD.	1	34	76	0.1	0.2
081 CATHOLIC......	29	NA	23 915	27.9	56.2
089 CHR & MISS AL.	3	143	240	0.3	0.6
151 L-D SAINTS....	2	NA	438	0.5	1.0

County and Denomination	Number of churches	Communicant, confirmed, full members	Total adherents Number	Total adherents Percent of total population	Total adherents Percent of total adherents
165 CH OF NAZARENE	1	28	71	0.1	0.2
193 EPISCOPAL.....	6	1 212	1 805	2.1	4.2
221 FREE METHODIST	7	337	1 494	1.7	3.5
263 INT FOURSQ GOS	1	48	59*	0.1	0.1
271 REFORM JUDAISM	1	96	117*	0.1	0.3
281 LUTH CH AMER..	2	314	441	0.5	1.0
283 LUTH--MO SYNOD	7	1 760	2 555	3.0	6.0
329 OPEN BIBLE STD	1	80	130	0.2	0.3
403 SALVATION ARMY	2	126	343	0.4	0.8
413 S.D.A.........	4	192	235*	0.3	0.6
419 SO BAPT CONV..	1	16	20*	–	–
443 UN C OF CHRIST	4	646	791*	0.9	1.9
449 UN METHODIST..	36	4 947	6 054*	7.1	14.2
453 UN PRES CH USA	8	1 966	2 406*	2.8	5.7
CAYUGA	101	11 558	46 206*	57.8	100.0
005 AME ZION......	1	299	339	0.4	0.7
019 AMER BAPT USA.	11	1 298	1 578*	2.0	3.4
053 ASSEMB OF GOD.	3	108	174	0.2	0.4
081 CATHOLIC......	21	NA	31 243	39.1	67.6
089 CHR & MISS AL.	1	48	93	0.1	0.2
093 CHR CH (DISC).	2	170	306	0.4	0.7
151 L-D SAINTS....	2	NA	165	0.2	0.4
165 CH OF NAZARENE	1	150	182	0.2	0.4
179 CONSRV BAPT...	2	471	572*	0.7	1.2
193 EPISCOPAL.....	6	1 109	1 623	2.0	3.5
221 FREE METHODIST	1	20	138	0.2	0.3
226 FRIENDS-USA...	2	103	125*	0.2	0.3
270 CONSRV JUDAISM	1	55	67*	0.1	0.1
283 LUTH--MO SYNOD	1	155	221	0.3	0.5
371 REF CH IN AM..	2	114	259	0.3	0.6
403 SALVATION ARMY	1	126	211	0.3	0.5
413 S.D.A.........	2	285	346*	0.4	0.7
435 UNITARIAN-UNIV	1	29	35*	–	0.1
443 UN C OF CHRIST	4	469	570*	0.7	1.2
449 UN METHODIST..	21	4 296	5 221*	6.5	11.3
453 UN PRES CH USA	15	2 253	2 738*	3.4	5.9
CHAUTAUQUA	179	31 458	87 878*	59.8	100.0
005 AME ZION......	1	524	630	0.4	0.7
019 AMER BAPT USA.	7	1 709	2 054*	1.4	2.3
053 ASSEMB OF GOD.	5	403	678	0.5	0.8
057 BAPT GEN CONF.	2	595	715*	0.5	0.8
081 CATHOLIC......	26	NA	46 115	31.4	52.5
089 CHR & MISS AL.	3	124	267	0.2	0.3
093 CHR CH (DISC).	1	40	62	–	0.1
123 CH GOD (ANDER)	4	222	666	0.5	0.8
127 CH GOD (CLEVE)	2	61	73*	–	0.1
151 L-D SAINTS....	2	NA	433	0.3	0.5
165 CH OF NAZARENE	2	145	283	0.2	0.3
167 CHS OF CHRIST.	1	84	105	0.1	0.1
181 CONSRV CONGR..	5	583	701*	0.5	0.8
193 EPISCOPAL.....	7	1 946	2 669	1.8	3.0
201 EVAN COV CH AM	2	1 146	1 377*	0.9	1.6
221 FREE METHODIST	4	281	879	0.6	1.0
226 FRIENDS-USA...	1	29	35*	–	–
263 INT FOURSQ GOS	2	76	91*	0.1	0.1
270 CONSRV JUDAISM	1	41	49*	–	0.1
271 REFORM JUDAISM	1	138	166*	0.1	0.2
281 LUTH CH AMER..	12	5 243	7 017	4.8	8.0
283 LUTH--MO SYNOD	3	561	736	0.5	0.8
323 OLD ORD AMISH.	7	910	1 093*	0.7	1.2
329 OPEN BIBLE STD	1	20	75	0.1	0.1
349 PENT HOLINESS.	1	19	23*	–	–
353 CHR BRETHREN..	1	20	75	0.1	0.1
371 REF CH IN AM..	2	471	685	0.5	0.8
403 SALVATION ARMY	2	308	1 190	0.8	1.4
413 S.D.A.........	2	199	239*	0.2	0.3
419 SO BAPT CONV..	1	104	125*	0.1	0.1
435 UNITARIAN-UNIV	2	110	132*	0.1	0.2
443 UN C OF CHRIST	4	1 114	1 339*	0.9	1.5
449 UN METHODIST..	54	11 527	13 851*	9.4	15.8
453 UN PRES CH USA	8	2 705	3 250*	2.2	3.7
CHEMUNG	83	19 204	53 693*	55.0	100.0
005 AME ZION......	2	683	827	0.8	1.5
019 AMER BAPT USA.	6	1 593	1 920*	2.0	3.6
053 ASSEMB OF GOD.	4	679	1 395	1.4	2.6
081 CATHOLIC......	11	NA	28 202	28.9	52.5
089 CHR & MISS AL.	2	154	258	0.3	0.5
093 CHR CH (DISC).	1	149	175	0.2	0.3
097 CHR CHS&CHS CR	1	26	31*	–	0.1
151 L-D SAINTS....	1	NA	423	0.4	0.8
165 CH OF NAZARENE	3	267	457	0.5	0.9
167 CHS OF CHRIST.	1	76	109	0.1	0.2
193 EPISCOPAL.....	6	1 431	2 419	2.5	4.5
203 EVAN FREE CH..	2	389	469*	0.5	0.9
221 FREE METHODIST	1	24	63	0.1	0.1
226 FRIENDS-USA...	1	33	40*	–	0.1
270 CONSRV JUDAISM	1	164	198*	0.2	0.4
271 REFORM JUDAISM	1	310	374*	0.4	0.7
281 LUTH CH AMER..	3	1 099	1 546	1.6	2.9
403 SALVATION ARMY	1	110	301	0.3	0.6
413 S.D.A.........	1	306	369*	0.4	0.7
419 SO BAPT CONV..	1	240	289*	0.3	0.5
435 UNITARIAN-UNIV	1	52	63*	0.1	0.1
443 UN C OF CHRIST	1	404	487*	0.5	0.9
449 UN METHODIST..	24	8 249	9 944*	10.2	18.5
453 UN PRES CH USA	6	2 766	3 334*	3.4	6.2
CHENANGO	70	9 422	19 628*	39.8	100.0

NA—Not applicable   *Total adherents estimated from known number of communicant, confirmed, full members.   —Represents a percent less than 0.1.   Percentages may not total due to rounding.

Table 4. Churches and Church Membership by County and Denomination: 1980

County and Denomination	Number of churches	Communicant, confirmed, full members	Total adherents		
			Number	Percent of total population	Percent of total adherents
005 AME ZION......	1	179	220	0.4	1.1
019 AMER BAPT USA.	10	1 710	2 101*	4.3	10.7
053 ASSEMB OF GOD.	4	207	300	0.6	1.5
081 CATHOLIC......	7	NA	6 842	13.9	34.9
089 CHR & MISS AL.	1	68	178	0.4	0.9
151 L-D SAINTS....	1	NA	94	0.2	0.5
193 EPISCOPAL.....	9	1 272	2 242	4.5	11.4
221 FREE METHODIST	2	65	303	0.6	1.5
226 FRIENDS-USA...	1	9	11*	–	0.1
281 LUTH CH AMER..	1	296	438	0.9	2.2
285 MENNONITE CH..	1	31	38*	0.1	0.2
413 S.D.A.........	1	105	129*	0.3	0.7
443 UN C OF CHRIST	6	1 120	1 376*	2.8	7.0
449 UN METHODIST..	20	3 738	4 592*	9.3	23.4
453 UN PRES CH USA	5	622	764*	1.5	3.9
CLINTON	69	5 596	54 591*	67.6	100.0
019 AMER BAPT USA.	1	165	199*	0.2	0.4
053 ASSEMB OF GOD.	1	152	303	0.4	0.6
081 CATHOLIC......	32	NA	47 191	58.4	86.4
127 CH GOD (CLEVE)	1	47	57*	0.1	0.1
151 L-D SAINTS....	1	NA	222	0.3	0.4
165 CH OF NAZARENE	2	166	391	0.5	0.7
167 CHS OF CHRIST.	1	50	64	0.1	0.1
193 EPISCOPAL.....	2	556	602	0.7	1.1
208 EVAN LUTH ASSN	1	63	119	0.1	0.2
271 REFORM JUDAISM	1	160	193*	0.2	0.4
403 SALVATION ARMY	1	55	210	0.3	0.4
413 S.D.A.........	2	39	47*	0.1	0.1
419 SO BAPT CONV..	1	170	205*	0.3	0.4
435 UNITARIAN-UNIV	1	39	47*	0.1	0.1
449 UN METHODIST..	15	3 187	3 841*	4.8	7.0
453 UN PRES CH USA	6	747	900*	1.1	1.6
COLUMBIA	82	10 116	28 708*	48.3	100.0
005 AME ZION......	1	275	323	0.5	1.1
019 AMER BAPT USA.	2	288	344*	0.6	1.2
053 ASSEMB OF GOD.	1	102	152	0.3	0.5
081 CATHOLIC......	14	NA	13 440	22.6	46.8
151 L-D SAINTS....	1	NA	129	0.2	0.4
193 EPISCOPAL.....	7	1 208	1 800	3.0	6.3
221 FREE METHODIST	1	17	105	0.2	0.4
226 FRIENDS-USA...	1	14	17*	–	0.1
281 LUTH CH AMER..	12	1 929	2 623	4.4	9.1
283 LUTH--MO SYNOD	2	332	567	1.0	2.0
371 REF CH IN AM..	14	2 115	4 629	7.8	16.1
413 S.D.A.........	1	175	209*	0.4	0.7
443 UN C OF CHRIST	2	287	343*	0.6	1.2
449 UN METHODIST..	19	2 836	3 385*	5.7	11.8
453 UN PRES CH USA	4	538	642*	1.1	2.2
CORTLAND	51	8 474	20 872*	42.8	100.0
019 AMER BAPT USA.	4	1 517	1 828*	3.7	8.8
053 ASSEMB OF GOD.	2	158	265	0.5	1.3
081 CATHOLIC......	5	NA	9 830	20.1	47.1
089 CHR & MISS AL.	1	79	107	0.2	0.5
097 CHR CHS&CHS CR	1	18	22*	–	0.1
151 L-D SAINTS....	1	NA	269	0.6	1.3
165 CH OF NAZARENE	1	62	88	0.2	0.4
193 EPISCOPAL.....	4	651	946	1.9	4.5
221 FREE METHODIST	1	44	114	0.2	0.5
281 LUTH CH AMER..	1	105	205	0.4	1.0
283 LUTH--MO SYNOD	1	151	235	0.5	1.1
353 CHR BRETHREN..	1	10	10	–	–
403 SALVATION ARMY	1	75	199	0.4	1.0
413 S.D.A.........	1	169	204*	0.4	1.0
435 UNITARIAN-UNIV	1	50	60*	0.1	0.3
443 UN C OF CHRIST	4	1 074	1 294*	2.7	6.2
449 UN METHODIST..	17	3 191	3 846*	7.9	18.4
453 UN PRES CH USA	4	1 120	1 350*	2.8	6.5
DELAWARE	91	10 245	18 018*	38.4	100.0
001 ADVENT CHR CH.	1	92	110*	0.2	0.6
019 AMER BAPT USA.	8	828	992*	2.1	5.5
053 ASSEMB OF GOD.	3	170	369	0.8	2.0
081 CATHOLIC......	7	NA	4 800	10.2	26.6
089 CHR & MISS AL.	6	177	374	0.8	2.1
179 CONSRV BAPT...	2	223	267*	0.6	1.5
193 EPISCOPAL.....	11	1 041	1 517	3.2	8.4
208 EVAN LUTH ASSN	1	131	172	0.4	1.0
221 FREE METHODIST	3	41	174	0.4	1.0
281 LUTH CH AMER..	1	216	334	0.7	1.9
283 LUTH--MO SYNOD	1	40	55	0.1	0.3
371 REF CH IN AM..	1	173	326	0.7	1.8
383 REF PRES OF NA	1	84	111	0.2	0.6
443 UN C OF CHRIST	3	588	704*	1.5	3.9
449 UN METHODIST..	20	3 746	4 486*	9.6	24.9
453 UN PRES CH USA	22	2 695	3 227*	6.9	17.9
DUTCHESS	152	28 750	121 847*	49.7	100.0
005 AME ZION......	3	1 550	1 755	0.7	1.4
019 AMER BAPT USA.	11	1 655	1 989*	0.8	1.6
053 ASSEMB OF GOD.	3	592	1 283	0.5	1.1
081 CATHOLIC......	23	NA	81 900	33.4	67.2
089 CHR & MISS AL.	3	133	281	0.1	0.2
097 CHR CHS&CHS CR	1	27	32*	–	–
105 CHRISTIAN REF.	1	83	142	0.1	0.1
127 CH GOD (CLEVE)	1	18	22*	–	–
151 L-D SAINTS....	1	NA	393	0.2	0.3
165 CH OF NAZARENE	2	147	616	0.3	0.5

County and Denomination	Number of churches	Communicant, confirmed, full members	Total adherents		
			Number	Percent of total population	Percent of total adherents
167 CHS OF CHRIST.	1	63	80	–	0.1
179 CONSRV BAPT...	1	188	226*	0.1	0.2
193 EPISCOPAL.....	22	4 078	6 029	2.5	4.9
226 FRIENDS-USA...	6	369	443*	0.2	0.4
270 CONSRV JUDAISM	2	738	887*	0.4	0.7
271 REFORM JUDAISM	2	628	755*	0.3	0.6
274 LAT EVAN LUTH.	1	82	93	–	0.1
281 LUTH CH AMER..	6	2 102	2 861	1.2	2.3
283 LUTH--MO SYNOD	3	868	1 232	0.5	1.0
353 CHR BRETHREN..	1	20	20	–	–
363 PRIMITIVE METH	1	64	77*	–	0.1
371 REF CH IN AM..	10	2 810	5 339	2.2	4.4
403 SALVATION ARMY	2	100	450	0.2	0.4
413 S.D.A.........	3	261	314*	0.1	0.3
419 SO BAPT CONV..	1	287	345*	0.1	0.3
435 UNITARIAN-UNIV	1	157	189*	0.1	0.2
443 UN C OF CHRIST	2	473	568*	0.2	0.5
449 UN METHODIST..	24	7 541	9 061*	3.7	7.4
453 UN PRES CH USA	14	3 716	4 465*	1.8	3.7
ERIE	561	136 970	700 519*	69.0	100.0
005 AME ZION......	10	11 652	13 909	1.4	2.0
019 AMER BAPT USA.	34	9 913	11 820*	1.2	1.7
029 AMER LUTH CH..	12	2 772	4 055	0.4	0.6
053 ASSEMB OF GOD.	16	2 861	4 477	0.4	0.6
075 BRETHREN IN CR	1	82	132	–	–
081 CATHOLIC......	161	NA	523 531	51.6	74.7
089 CHR & MISS AL.	4	334	497	–	0.1
093 CHR CH (DISC).	7	1 158	1 490	0.1	0.2
097 CHR CHS&CHS CR	3	416	496*	–	0.1
101 C.M.E.	3	1 350	1 610*	0.2	0.2
123 CH GOD (ANDER)	2	167	501	–	0.1
127 CH GOD (CLEVE)	4	93	111*	–	–
151 L-D SAINTS....	4	NA	1 056	0.1	0.2
165 CH OF NAZARENE	2	143	231	–	0.1
167 CHS OF CHRIST.	4	448	570	0.1	0.1
179 CONSRV BAPT...	3	431	514*	0.1	0.1
181 CONSRV CONGR..	1	175	209*	–	–
193 EPISCOPAL.....	34	13 221	17 436	1.7	2.5
195 ESTONIAN ELC..	1	85	337	–	–
201 EVAN COV CH AM	1	78	93*	–	–
208 EVAN LUTH ASSN	4	780	989	0.1	0.1
221 FREE METHODIST	8	418	2 574	0.3	0.4
226 FRIENDS-USA...	3	207	247*	–	–
270 CONSRV JUDAISM	3	2 011	2 398*	0.2	0.3
271 REFORM JUDAISM	4	4 432	5 284*	0.5	0.8
274 LAT EVAN LUTH.	1	51	58	–	–
281 LUTH CH AMER..	31	14 265	19 711	1.9	2.8
283 LUTH--MO SYNOD	26	10 222	13 697	1.3	2.0
285 MENNONITE CH..	3	361	430*	–	0.1
290 METRO COMM CHS	0	15	30	–	–
313 N AM BAPT CONF	4	618	737*	0.1	0.1
353 CHR BRETHREN..	7	310	480	–	0.1
371 REF CH IN AM..	1	35	66	–	–
403 SALVATION ARMY	2	403	2 170	0.2	0.3
413 S.D.A.........	4	919	1 096*	0.1	0.2
419 SO BAPT CONV..	6	924	1 102*	0.1	0.2
431 UKRANIAN AMER.	1	90	165	–	–
435 UNITARIAN-UNIV	4	770	918*	0.1	0.1
443 UN C OF CHRIST	43	13 997	16 689*	1.6	2.4
449 UN METHODIST..	54	21 338	25 442*	2.5	3.6
453 UN PRES CH USA	43	19 425	23 161*	2.3	3.3
ESSEX	70	6 257	20 673*	57.1	100.0
019 AMER BAPT USA.	4	408	491*	1.4	2.4
053 ASSEMB OF GOD.	1	45	63	0.2	0.3
081 CATHOLIC......	19	NA	12 822	35.4	62.0
165 CH OF NAZARENE	3	201	332	0.9	1.6
193 EPISCOPAL.....	9	808	1 198	3.3	5.8
419 SO BAPT CONV..	2	220	265*	0.7	1.3
443 UN C OF CHRIST	9	680	818*	2.3	4.0
449 UN METHODIST..	20	3 781	4 547*	12.6	22.0
453 UN PRES CH USA	3	114	137*	0.4	0.7
FRANKLIN	68	4 432	34 756*	77.4	100.0
019 AMER BAPT USA.	1	180	219*	0.5	0.6
053 ASSEMB OF GOD.	1	37	60	0.1	0.2
081 CATHOLIC......	28	NA	29 126	64.8	83.8
151 L-D SAINTS....	1	NA	55	0.1	0.2
165 CH OF NAZARENE	1	47	75	0.2	0.2
193 EPISCOPAL.....	5	466	667	1.5	1.9
221 FREE METHODIST	2	14	60	0.1	0.2
413 S.D.A.........	3	44	54*	0.1	0.2
419 SO BAPT CONV..	2	317	386*	0.9	1.1
443 UN C OF CHRIST	1	360	439*	1.0	1.3
449 UN METHODIST..	14	2 331	2 840*	6.3	8.2
453 UN PRES CH USA	8	636	775*	1.7	2.2
FULTON	52	10 599	30 198*	54.8	100.0
005 AME ZION......	2	438	573	1.0	1.9
019 AMER BAPT USA.	1	518	628*	1.1	2.1
053 ASSEMB OF GOD.	2	127	206	0.4	0.7
055 AS REF PRES CH	1	50	78	0.1	0.3
081 CATHOLIC......	9	NA	15 512	28.1	51.4
093 CHR CH (DISC).	1	56	86	0.2	0.3
151 L-D SAINTS....	1	NA	251	0.5	0.8
167 CHS OF CHRIST.	1	30	38	0.1	0.1
179 CONSRV BAPT...	1	116	141*	0.3	0.5
193 EPISCOPAL.....	2	760	1 178	2.1	3.9
221 FREE METHODIST	2	70	318	0.6	1.1
270 CONSRV JUDAISM	1	174	211*	0.4	0.7

NA—Not applicable   *Total adherents estimated from known number of communicant, confirmed, full members.   —Represents a percent less than 0.1.   Percentages may not total due to rounding.

Table 4. Churches and Church Membership by County and Denomination: 1980

County and Denomination	Number of churches	Communicant, confirmed, full members	Total adherents Number	Percent of total population	Percent of total adherents
281 LUTH CH AMER..	3	1 235	2 051	3.7	6.8
371 REF CH IN AM..	2	207	540	1.0	1.8
381 REF PRES-EVAN.	1	34	41	0.1	0.1
403 SALVATION ARMY	1	70	212	0.4	0.7
413 S.D.A.........	1	20	24*	–	0.1
443 UN C OF CHRIST	1	121	147*	0.3	0.5
449 UN METHODIST..	14	5 264	6 377*	11.6	21.1
453 UN PRES CH USA	5	1 309	1 586*	2.9	5.3
GENESEE	**72**	**12 006**	**39 177***	**66.0**	**100.0**
019 AMER BAPT USA.	10	2 138	2 611*	4.4	6.7
053 ASSEMB OF GOD.	1	127	253	0.4	0.6
081 CATHOLIC......	18	NA	23 705	39.9	60.5
089 CHR & MISS AL.	1	45	60	0.1	0.2
093 CHR CH (DISC).	1	165	254	0.4	0.6
151 L-D SAINTS....	1	NA	95	0.2	0.2
179 CONSRV BAPT...	1	225	275*	0.5	0.7
193 EPISCOPAL.....	4	1 301	1 727	2.9	4.4
221 FREE METHODIST	1	88	264	0.4	0.7
270 CONSRV JUDAISM	1	43	53*	0.1	0.1
283 LUTH--MO SYNOD	1	585	777	1.3	2.0
353 CHR BRETHREN..	1	25	25	–	0.1
403 SALVATION ARMY	1	119	353	0.6	0.9
413 S.D.A.........	1	44	54*	0.1	0.1
435 UNITARIAN-UNIV	1	15	18*	–	–
443 UN C OF CHRIST	3	318	388*	0.7	1.0
449 UN METHODIST..	13	3 219	3 931*	6.6	10.0
453 UN PRES CH USA	12	3 549	4 334*	7.3	11.1
GREENE	**66**	**6 141**	**17 357***	**42.5**	**100.0**
005 AME ZION......	1	308	353	0.9	2.0
019 AMER BAPT USA.	2	69	82*	0.2	0.5
081 CATHOLIC......	10	NA	8 600	21.0	49.5
193 EPISCOPAL.....	8	676	1 031	2.5	5.9
208 EVAN LUTH ASSN	1	91	113	0.3	0.7
221 FREE METHODIST	1	49	315	0.8	1.8
271 REFORM JUDAISM	1	98	117*	0.3	0.7
281 LUTH CH AMER..	1	384	419	1.0	2.4
283 LUTH--MO SYNOD	1	323	499	1.2	2.9
353 CHR BRETHREN..	1	20	20	–	0.1
371 REF CH IN AM..	8	783	1 836	4.5	10.6
443 UN C OF CHRIST	2	238	283*	0.7	1.6
449 UN METHODIST..	26	2 929	3 483*	8.5	20.1
453 UN PRES CH USA	3	173	206*	0.5	1.2
HAMILTON	**17**	**778**	**2 755***	**54.7**	**100.0**
081 CATHOLIC......	7	NA	1 843	36.6	66.9
179 CONSRV BAPT...	1	184	218*	4.3	7.9
193 EPISCOPAL.....	2	46	45	0.9	1.6
449 UN METHODIST..	6	519	615*	12.2	22.3
453 UN PRES CH USA	1	29	34*	0.7	1.2
HERKIMER	**84**	**12 188**	**40 048***	**60.0**	**100.0**
019 AMER BAPT USA.	12	2 007	2 427*	3.6	6.1
053 ASSEMB OF GOD.	3	85	192	0.3	0.5
081 CATHOLIC......	16	NA	23 732	35.6	59.3
089 CHR & MISS AL.	2	58	90	0.1	0.2
179 CONSRV BAPT...	1	168	203*	0.3	0.5
193 EPISCOPAL.....	4	1 003	1 841	2.8	4.6
221 FREE METHODIST	1	48	195	0.3	0.5
263 INT FOURSQ GOS	1	27	33*	–	0.1
270 CONSRV JUDAISM	1	51	62*	0.1	0.2
281 LUTH CH AMER..	5	1 290	1 676	2.5	4.2
371 REF CH IN AM..	2	574	1 159	1.7	2.9
403 SALVATION ARMY	1	73	211	0.3	0.5
413 S.D.A.........	1	34	41*	0.1	0.1
435 UNITARIAN-UNIV	4	295	357*	0.5	0.9
443 UN C OF CHRIST	1	533	644*	1.0	1.6
449 UN METHODIST..	24	4 828	5 883*	8.8	14.6
453 UN PRES CH USA	5	1 114	1 347*	2.0	3.4
JEFFERSON	**130**	**16 323**	**48 102***	**54.6**	**100.0**
005 AME ZION......	1	37	54	0.1	0.1
019 AMER BAPT USA.	8	1 402	1 719*	2.0	3.6
053 ASSEMB OF GOD.	3	331	571	0.6	1.2
081 CATHOLIC......	25	NA	25 463	28.9	52.9
089 CHR & MISS AL.	1	54	93	0.1	0.2
093 CHR CH (DISC).	1	100	154	0.2	0.3
151 L-D SAINTS....	1	NA	262	0.3	0.5
165 CH OF NAZARENE	2	259	496	0.6	1.0
167 CHS OF CHRIST.	1	30	38	–	0.1
193 EPISCOPAL.....	17	2 875	4 335	4.9	9.0
221 FREE METHODIST	1	74	264	0.3	0.5
270 CONSRV JUDAISM	1	90	110*	0.1	0.2
281 LUTH CH AMER..	3	525	708	0.8	1.5
285 MENNONITE CH..	3	104	127*	0.1	0.3
371 REF CH IN AM..	1	82	279	0.3	0.6
403 SALVATION ARMY	1	93	844	1.0	1.8
413 S.D.A.........	2	78	96*	0.1	0.2
415 S-D BAPTIST GC	1	58	71*	0.1	0.1
419 SO BAPT CONV..	2	247	303*	0.3	0.6
435 UNITARIAN-UNIV	3	164	201*	0.2	0.4
443 UN C OF CHRIST	4	901	1 104*	1.3	2.3
449 UN METHODIST..	38	6 719	8 236*	9.3	17.1
453 UN PRES CH USA	10	2 100	2 574*	2.9	5.4
KINGS	**519**	**120 028**	**861 606***	**38.6**	**100.0**
019 AMER BAPT USA.	44	43 349	52 618*	2.4	6.1
029 AMER LUTH CH..	5	1 080	1 476	0.1	0.2
053 ASSEMB OF GOD.	31	4 711	6 537	0.3	0.8
075 BRETHREN IN CR	1	109	131	–	–
081 CATHOLIC......	127	NA	702 298	31.5	81.5
089 CHR & MISS AL.	4	277	491	–	0.1
093 CHR CH (DISC).	24	4 067	6 066	0.3	0.7
097 CHR CHS&CHS CR	1	32	39*	–	–
101 C.M.E........	1	13	16*	–	–
123 CH GOD (ANDER)	7	511	1 533	0.1	0.2
127 CH GOD (CLEVE)	17	1 141	1 385*	0.1	0.2
133 CH GOD(7TH)DEN	1	27	33*	–	–
151 L-D SAINTS....	3	NA	625	–	0.1
157 CH OF BRETHREN	1	92	112*	–	–
163 CH OF LUTH BR.	1	367	423	–	–
165 CH OF NAZARENE	8	738	2 670	0.1	0.3
167 CHS OF CHRIST.	2	150	200	–	–
175 CONGR CHR CHS.	5	1 309	1 589*	0.1	0.2
179 CONSRV BAPT...	7	712	864*	–	0.1
193 EPISCOPAL.....	36	15 364	22 492	1.0	2.6
201 EVAN COV CH AM	1	111	135*	–	–
203 EVAN FREE CH..	4	326	396*	–	–
208 EVAN LUTH ASSN	3	948	1 003	–	0.1
221 FREE METHODIST	2	66	369	–	–
226 FRIENDS-USA...	2	244	296*	–	–
247 HOLINESS CH...	1	25	25	–	–
270 CONSRV JUDAISM	14	3 336	4 049*	0.2	0.5
271 REFORM JUDAISM	8	4 082	4 955*	0.2	0.6
281 LUTH CH AMER..	29	6 415	9 013	0.4	1.0
283 LUTH--MO SYNOD	8	1 669	2 354	0.1	0.3
285 MENNONITE CH..	1	46	56*	–	–
290 METRO COMM CHS	1	30	60	–	–
293 MORAV CH-NORTH	1	412	669	–	0.1
329 OPEN BIBLE STD	1	100	140	–	–
353 CHR BRETHREN..	6	665	870	–	0.1
375 REF EPISCOPAL.	1	27	33*	–	–
403 SALVATION ARMY	6	578	2 875	0.1	0.3
413 S.D.A.........	23	7 637	9 270*	0.4	1.1
419 SO BAPT CONV..	12	1 131	1 373*	0.1	0.2
431 UKRANIAN AMER.	1	100	180	–	–
435 UNITARIAN-UNIV	3	717	870*	–	0.1
443 UN C OF CHRIST	9	1 219	1 480*	0.1	0.2
449 UN METHODIST..	30	10 555	12 812*	0.6	1.5
453 UN PRES CH USA	26	5 540	6 725*	0.3	0.8
LEWIS	**51**	**4 870**	**15 116***	**60.4**	**100.0**
019 AMER BAPT USA.	2	205	255*	1.0	1.7
053 ASSEMB OF GOD.	1	87	116	0.5	0.8
081 CATHOLIC......	17	NA	8 725	34.9	57.7
093 CHR CH (DISC).	1	55	85	0.3	0.6
165 CH OF NAZARENE	1	108	213	0.9	1.4
181 CONSRV CONGR..	1	157	196*	0.8	1.3
193 EPISCOPAL.....	4	336	655	2.6	4.3
285 MENNONITE CH..	6	1 209	1 506*	6.0	10.0
371 REF CH IN AM..	1	64	65	0.3	0.4
413 S.D.A.........	1	47	59*	0.2	0.4
443 UN C OF CHRIST	2	193	240*	1.0	1.6
449 UN METHODIST..	12	1 828	2 277*	9.1	15.1
453 UN PRES CH USA	2	581	724*	2.9	4.8
LIVINGSTON	**65**	**7 014**	**21 625***	**37.9**	**100.0**
019 AMER BAPT USA.	2	86	104*	0.2	0.5
053 ASSEMB OF GOD.	3	170	292	0.5	1.4
081 CATHOLIC......	14	NA	12 310	21.6	56.9
093 CHR CH (DISC).	1	31	48	0.1	0.2
123 CH GOD (ANDER)	1	15	45	0.1	0.2
127 CH GOD (CLEVE)	1	71	86*	0.2	0.4
193 EPISCOPAL.....	4	616	993	1.7	4.6
221 FREE METHODIST	1	71	333	0.6	1.5
281 LUTH CH AMER..	1	347	571	1.0	2.6
283 LUTH--MO SYNOD	1	209	338	0.6	1.6
435 UNITARIAN-UNIV	1	18	22*	–	0.1
443 UN C OF CHRIST	2	286	345*	0.6	1.6
449 UN METHODIST..	16	2 122	2 557*	4.5	11.8
453 UN PRES CH USA	17	2 972	3 581*	6.3	16.6
MADISON	**75**	**12 020**	**31 740***	**48.7**	**100.0**
019 AMER BAPT USA.	13	2 169	2 635*	4.0	8.3
053 ASSEMB OF GOD.	3	331	394	0.6	1.2
081 CATHOLIC......	8	NA	15 326	23.5	48.3
089 CHR & MISS AL.	1	52	70	0.1	0.2
151 L-D SAINTS....	1	NA	225	0.3	0.7
165 CH OF NAZARENE	1	63	55	0.1	0.2
167 CHS OF CHRIST.	1	8	14	–	–
193 EPISCOPAL.....	5	977	2 378	3.7	7.5
221 FREE METHODIST	2	69	342	0.5	1.1
226 FRIENDS-USA...	1	17	21*	–	0.1
283 LUTH--MO SYNOD	1	184	243	0.4	0.8
403 SALVATION ARMY	1	59	209	0.3	0.7
415 S-D BAPTIST GC	3	134	163*	0.3	0.5
443 UN C OF CHRIST	3	373	453*	0.7	1.4
449 UN METHODIST..	25	5 665	6 881*	10.6	21.7
453 UN PRES CH USA	6	1 919	2 331*	3.6	7.3
MONROE	**354**	**98 375**	**360 038***	**51.3**	**100.0**
005 AME ZION......	2	1 205	1 338	0.2	0.4
019 AMER BAPT USA.	35	12 908	15 493*	2.2	4.3
029 AMER LUTH CH..	4	1 045	1 393	0.2	0.4
039 AP CHR CH(NAZ)	1	32	38*	–	–
053 ASSEMB OF GOD.	10	1 269	2 401	0.3	0.7
081 CATHOLIC......	76	NA	229 097	32.7	63.9
089 CHR & MISS AL.	2	182	296	–	0.1
093 CHR CH (DISC).	3	180	247	–	0.1

NA—Not applicable *Total adherents estimated from known number of communicant, confirmed, full members. —Represents a percent less than 0.1. Percentages may not total due to rounding.

Table 4. Churches and Church Membership by County and Denomination: 1980

County and Denomination	Number of churches	Communicant, confirmed, full members	Total adherents Number	Percent of total population	Percent of total adherents
097 CHR CHS&CHS CR	1	75	90*	-	-
101 C.M.E.........	1	4 058	4 871*	0.7	1.4
105 CHRISTIAN REF.	2	365	610	0.1	0.2
123 CH GOD (ANDER)	1	135	405	0.1	0.1
127 CH GOD (CLEVE)	7	332	398*	0.1	0.1
149 CH OF JC (BIC)	1	15	20	-	-
151 L-D SAINTS....	4	NA	1 932	0.3	0.5
165 CH OF NAZARENE	5	762	1 435	0.2	0.4
167 CHS OF CHRIST.	7	1 117	1 437	0.2	0.4
179 CONSRV BAPT...	1	44	53*	-	-
193 EPISCOPAL.....	24	9 671	13 528	1.9	3.8
201 EVAN COV CH AM	2	197	236*	-	0.1
208 EVAN LUTH ASSN	1	528	894	0.1	0.2
209 EVAN LUTH SYN.	2	89	126	-	-
221 FREE METHODIST	7	1 059	3 510	0.5	1.0
226 FRIENDS-USA...	2	217	260*	-	0.1
263 INT FOURSQ GOS	1	98	118*	-	-
270 CONSRV JUDAISM	4	1 448	1 738*	0.2	0.5
271 REFORM JUDAISM	3	3 416	4 100*	0.6	1.1
274 LAT EVAN LUTH.	1	164	184	-	0.1
281 LUTH CH AMER..	17	8 673	11 733	1.7	3.3
283 LUTH--MO SYNOD	13	5 193	7 921	1.1	2.2
290 METRO COMM CHS	0	20	40	-	-
313 N AM BAPT CONF	2	277	332*	-	0.1
335 ORTH PRESB CH.	2	215	258*	-	0.1
349 PENT HOLINESS.	1	24	29*	-	-
353 CHR BRETHREN..	3	475	505	0.1	0.1
371 REF CH IN AM..	4	943	1 636	0.2	0.5
383 REF PRES OF NA	1	?	?	?	?
403 SALVATION ARMY	2	257	419	0.1	0.1
413 S.D.A.........	4	1 173	1 408*	0.2	0.4
419 SO BAPT CONV..	6	623	748*	0.1	0.2
435 UNITARIAN-UNIV	2	880	1 056*	0.2	0.3
443 UN C OF CHRIST	19	6 472	7 768*	1.1	2.2
449 UN METHODIST..	33	13 144	15 776*	2.2	4.4
453 UN PRES CH USA	35	19 395	23 279*	3.3	6.5
MONTGOMERY	67	9 032	36 973*	69.2	100.0
005 AME ZION......	1	27	34	0.1	0.1
019 AMER BAPT USA.	1	319	381*	0.7	1.0
053 ASSEMB OF GOD.	1	27	40	0.1	0.1
081 CATHOLIC......	15	NA	23 870	44.7	64.6
089 CHR & MISS AL.	1	18	43	0.1	0.1
193 EPISCOPAL.....	3	632	878	1.6	2.4
221 FREE METHODIST	1	31	123	0.2	0.3
270 CONSRV JUDAISM	1	50	60*	0.1	0.2
271 REFORM JUDAISM	1	24	29*	0.1	0.1
281 LUTH CH AMER..	7	2 159	3 224	6.0	8.7
285 MENNONITE CH..	1	28	33*	0.1	0.1
371 REF CH IN AM..	15	1 688	3 449	6.5	9.3
413 S.D.A.........	1	16	19*	-	0.1
435 UNITARIAN-UNIV	1	85	101*	0.2	0.3
443 UN C OF CHRIST	1	91	109*	0.2	0.3
449 UN METHODIST..	12	2 650	3 163*	5.9	8.6
453 UN PRES CH USA	4	1 187	1 417*	2.7	3.8
NASSAU	409	142 668	726 782*	55.0	100.0
005 AME ZION......	10	7 373	8 216	0.6	1.1
019 AMER BAPT USA.	8	2 724	3 208*	0.2	0.4
029 AMER LUTH CH..	9	2 401	3 389	0.3	0.5
053 ASSEMB OF GOD.	10	1 112	1 576	0.1	0.2
081 CATHOLIC......	68	NA	547 818	41.5	75.4
089 CHR & MISS AL.	3	85	153	-	-
093 CHR CH (DISC).	1	80	123	-	-
097 CHR CHS&CHS CR	3	130	153*	-	-
123 CH GOD (ANDER)	1	121	363	-	-
127 CH GOD (CLEVE)	4	48	57*	-	-
151 L-D SAINTS....	3	NA	971	0.1	0.1
165 CH OF NAZARENE	6	492	1 146	0.1	0.2
167 CHS OF CHRIST.	4	338	433	-	0.1
179 CONSRV BAPT...	7	1 271	1 497*	0.1	0.2
193 EPISCOPAL.....	45	22 405	28 710	2.2	4.0
201 EVAN COV CH AM	1	67	79*	-	-
203 EVAN FREE CH..	3	195	230*	-	-
208 EVAN LUTH ASSN	7	3 319	4 677	0.4	0.6
226 FRIENDS-USA...	3	552	650*	-	0.1
270 CONSRV JUDAISM	44	15 536	18 294*	1.4	2.5
271 REFORM JUDAISM	30	26 410	31 098*	2.4	4.3
281 LUTH CH AMER..	23	13 280	17 545	1.3	2.4
283 LUTH--MO SYNOD	9	5 118	6 335	0.5	0.9
290 METRO COMM CHS	0	50	100	-	-
313 N AM BAPT CONF	1	92	108*	-	-
335 ORTH PRESB CH.	1	105	124*	-	-
353 CHR BRETHREN..	4	280	370	-	0.1
371 REF CH IN AM..	11	2 054	4 636	0.4	0.6
403 SALVATION ARMY	2	318	1 391	0.1	0.2
413 S.D.A.........	9	1 394	1 641*	0.1	0.2
419 SO BAPT CONV..	3	230	271*	-	-
431 UKRANIAN AMER.	1	120	245	-	-
435 UNITARIAN-UNIV	4	844	994*	0.1	0.1
443 UN C OF CHRIST	10	5 064	5 963*	0.5	0.8
449 UN METHODIST..	38	20 956	24 676*	1.9	3.4
453 UN PRES CH USA	23	8 104	9 542*	0.7	1.3
NEW YORK	492	187 521	539 769*	37.8	100.0
005 AME ZION......	19	62 581	80 018	5.6	14.8
019 AMER BAPT USA.	36	22 702	25 700*	1.8	4.8
049 ARMEN AP CH AM	1	300	1 300	0.1	0.2
053 ASSEMB OF GOD.	25	2 464	3 365	0.2	0.6
057 BAPT GEN CONF.	1	102	115*	-	-
081 CATHOLIC......	107	NA	295 040	20.7	54.7
089 CHR & MISS AL.	6	619	674	-	0.1
093 CHR CH (DISC).	7	930	1 311	0.1	0.2
097 CHR CHS&CHS CR	1	45	51*	-	-
101 C.M.E.........	2	2 433	2 754*	0.2	0.5
105 CHRISTIAN REF.	1	42	79	-	-
123 CH GOD (ANDER)	5	485	1 455	0.1	0.3
127 CH GOD (CLEVE)	10	813	920*	0.1	0.2
151 L-D SAINTS....	4	NA	1 210	0.1	0.2
165 CH OF NAZARENE	2	210	233	-	-
167 CHS OF CHRIST.	6	431	531	-	0.1
179 CONSRV BAPT...	2	314	355*	-	0.1
193 EPISCOPAL.....	42	18 119	26 859	1.9	5.0
195 ESTONIAN ELC..	1	330	2 720	0.2	0.5
208 EVAN LUTH ASSN	2	432	525	-	0.1
221 FREE METHODIST	2	84	138	-	-
226 FRIENDS-USA...	2	540	611*	-	0.1
239 SWEDENBORGIAN.	1	100	113*	-	-
247 HOLINESS CH...	1	34	40	-	-
270 CONSRV JUDAISM	12	2 814	3 186*	0.2	0.6
271 REFORM JUDAISM	14	16 528	18 711*	1.3	3.5
281 LUTH CH AMER..	14	3 629	5 135	0.4	1.0
283 LUTH--MO SYNOD	6	1 980	3 924	0.3	0.7
285 MENNONITE CH..	1	32	36*	-	-
290 METRO COMM CHS	2	150	300	-	0.1
293 MORAV CH-NORTH	1	133	200	-	-
353 CHR BRETHREN..	1	50	50	-	-
371 REF CH IN AM..	56	9 808	17 995	1.3	3.3
375 REF EPISCOPAL.	1	104	118*	-	-
395 ROMANIAN OR CH	1	1 280	1 449*	0.1	0.3
403 SALVATION ARMY	5	761	1 462	0.1	0.3
413 S.D.A.........	14	4 633	5 245*	0.4	1.0
415 S-D BAPT GC	1	27	31*	-	-
419 SO BAPT CONV..	6	691	782*	0.1	0.1
423 SYRIAN ANTIOCH	1	500	566*	-	0.1
431 UKRANIAN AMER.	2	600	850	0.1	0.2
435 UNITARIAN-UNIV	3	1 568	1 775*	0.1	0.3
443 UN C OF CHRIST	10	4 101	4 643	0.3	0.9
449 UN METHODIST..	23	13 561	15 352*	1.1	2.8
453 UN PRES CH USA	32	10 461	11 842*	0.8	2.2
NIAGARA	183	41 196	141 796*	62.4	100.0
005 AME ZION......	1	620	667	0.3	0.5
017 AMER BAPT ASSN	1	50	50	-	-
019 AMER BAPT USA.	10	2 356	2 839*	1.3	2.0
029 AMER LUTH CH..	9	2 465	3 198	1.4	2.3
049 ARMEN AP CH AM	1	33	47	-	-
053 ASSEMB OF GOD.	6	790	1 355	0.6	1.0
081 CATHOLIC......	35	NA	85 328	37.6	60.2
089 CHR & MISS AL.	3	228	525	0.2	0.4
093 CHR CH (DISC).	2	644	725	0.3	0.5
123 CH GOD (ANDER)	1	90	270	0.1	0.2
127 CH GOD (CLEVE)	1	88	106*	-	0.1
149 CH OF JC (BIC)	1	24	24	-	-
151 L-D SAINTS....	2	NA	464	0.2	0.3
165 CH OF NAZARENE	3	201	429	0.2	0.3
167 CHS OF CHRIST.	3	225	286	0.1	0.2
193 EPISCOPAL.....	11	3 647	5 716	2.5	4.0
221 FREE METHODIST	7	342	1 935	0.9	1.4
226 FRIENDS-USA...	1	27	33*	-	-
270 CONSRV JUDAISM	1	121	146*	0.1	0.1
271 REFORM JUDAISM	1	136	164*	0.1	0.1
281 LUTH CH AMER..	5	2 337	3 073	1.4	2.2
283 LUTH--MO SYNOD	20	9 161	12 186	5.4	8.6
353 CHR BRETHREN..	2	65	150	0.1	0.1
403 SALVATION ARMY	2	257	1 249	0.5	0.9
413 S.D.A.........	4	172	207*	0.1	0.1
419 SO BAPT CONV..	3	319	384*	0.2	0.3
435 UNITARIAN-UNIV	1	127	153*	0.1	0.1
443 UN C OF CHRIST	8	2 578	3 106*	1.4	2.2
449 UN METHODIST..	24	8 274	9 970*	4.4	7.0
453 UN PRES CH USA	14	5 819	7 011*	3.1	4.9
ONEIDA	218	36 732	153 799*	60.7	100.0
005 AME ZION......	1	619	697	0.3	0.5
017 AMER BAPT ASSN	1	160	160	0.1	0.1
019 AMER BAPT USA.	15	2 828	3 400*	1.3	2.2
053 ASSEMB OF GOD.	3	378	588	0.2	0.4
081 CATHOLIC......	51	NA	104 276	41.1	67.8
089 CHR & MISS AL.	3	185	336	0.1	0.2
127 CH GOD (CLEVE)	1	63	76*	-	-
151 L-D SAINTS....	1	NA	475	0.2	0.3
165 CH OF NAZARENE	2	69	108	-	0.1
167 CHS OF CHRIST.	2	146	206	0.1	0.1
179 CONSRV BAPT...	3	675	812*	0.3	0.5
193 EPISCOPAL.....	20	4 600	8 092	3.2	5.3
221 FREE METHODIST	1	15	102	-	0.1
226 FRIENDS-USA...	1	22	26*	-	-
270 CONSRV JUDAISM	2	390	469*	0.2	0.3
271 REFORM JUDAISM	1	392	471*	0.2	0.3
281 LUTH CH AMER..	4	1 974	2 598	1.0	1.7
283 LUTH--MO SYNOD	4	2 291	4 080	1.6	2.7
293 MORAV CH-NORTH	1	200	253	0.1	0.2
371 REF CH IN AM..	1	140	365	0.1	0.2
403 SALVATION ARMY	2	268	579	0.2	0.4
413 S.D.A.........	4	316	380*	0.1	0.2
415 S-D BAPT GC	1	104	125*	-	0.1
419 SO BAPT CONV..	4	731	879*	0.3	0.6
435 UNITARIAN-UNIV	2	152	183*	0.1	0.1
443 UN C OF CHRIST	12	1 675	2 014*	0.8	1.3
449 UN METHODIST..	46	11 953	14 371*	5.7	9.5
453 UN PRES CH USA	29	6 386	7 678*	3.0	5.0
ONONDAGA	265	67 632	257 112*	55.5	100.0

NA—Not applicable   *Total adherents estimated from known number of communicant, confirmed, full members.   —Represents a percent less than 0.1.   Percentages may not total due to rounding.

Table 4. Churches and Church Membership by County and Denomination: 1980

County and Denomination	Number of churches	Communicant, confirmed, full members	Total adherents Number	Total adherents Percent of total population	Total adherents Percent of total adherents
005 AME ZION......	3	859	1 036	0.2	0.4
019 AMER BAPT USA.	21	5 402	6 489*	1.4	2.5
039 AP CHR CH(NAZ)	1	56	67*	–	–
049 ARMEN AP CH AM	1	38	58	–	–
053 ASSEMB OF GOD.	8	1 261	2 865	0.6	1.1
081 CATHOLIC......	56	NA	168 035	36.3	65.4
089 CHR & MISS AL.	1	408	658	0.1	0.3
093 CHR CH (DISC).	2	122	188	–	0.1
097 CHR CHS&CHS CR	4	332	399*	0.1	0.2
101 C.M.E........	1	1 225	1 472*	0.3	0.6
105 CHRISTIAN REF.	1	56	103	–	–
127 CH GOD (CLEVE)	1	42	50*	–	–
151 L-D SAINTS....	3	NA	763	0.2	0.3
165 CH OF NAZARENE	3	279	418	0.1	0.2
167 CHS OF CHRIST.	3	215	274	0.1	0.1
193 EPISCOPAL.....	24	8 505	13 466	2.9	5.2
195 ESTONIAN ELC.	1	20	32	–	–
201 EVAN COV CH AM	1	103	124*	–	–
208 EVAN LUTH ASSN	1	233	314	0.1	0.1
221 FREE METHODIST	1	82	258	0.1	0.1
226 FRIENDS-USA...	1	143	172*	–	0.1
270 CONSRV JUDAISM	2	990	1 189*	0.3	0.5
271 REFORM JUDAISM	1	1 512	1 816*	0.4	0.7
274 LAT EVAN LUTH.	2	159	181	–	0.1
281 LUTH CH AMER..	15	5 908	7 679	1.7	3.0
283 LUTH--MO SYNOD	1	401	495	0.1	0.2
285 MENNONITE CH..	1	11	13*	–	–
290 METRO COMM CHS	1	23	46	–	–
371 REF CH IN AM..	2	511	816	0.2	0.3
383 REF PRES OF NA	1	74	90	–	–
403 SALVATION ARMY	1	120	1 240	0.3	0.5
413 S.D.A........	4	606	728*	0.2	0.3
419 SO BAPT CONV..	5	530	637*	0.1	0.2
435 UNITARIAN-UNIV	2	637	765*	0.2	0.3
443 UN C OF CHRIST	8	2 021	2 428*	0.5	0.9
449 UN METHODIST..	54	26 866	32 273*	7.0	12.6
453 UN PRES CH USA	25	7 840	9 418*	2.0	3.7
469 WELS..........	1	42	57	–	–
ONTARIO	80	15 743	42 024*	47.3	100.0
019 AMER BAPT USA.	9	1 667	2 012*	2.3	4.8
053 ASSEMB OF GOD.	2	122	197	0.2	0.5
081 CATHOLIC......	13	NA	21 345	24.0	50.8
089 CHR & MISS AL.	1	22	59	0.1	0.1
097 CHR CHS&CHS CR	2	70	84*	0.1	0.2
151 L-D SAINTS....	2	NA	568	0.6	1.4
165 CH OF NAZARENE	1	53	82	0.1	0.2
179 CONSRV BAPT...	2	206	249*	0.3	0.6
193 EPISCOPAL.....	6	1 349	2 018	2.3	4.8
208 EVAN LUTH ASSN	1	223	296	0.3	0.7
281 LUTH CH AMER..	1	309	467	0.5	1.1
283 LUTH--MO SYNOD	2	562	835	0.9	2.0
285 MENNONITE CH..	1	16	19*	–	–
403 SALVATION ARMY	2	152	526	0.6	1.3
419 SO BAPT CONV..	1	94	113*	0.1	0.3
443 UN C OF CHRIST	8	1 353	1 633*	1.8	3.9
449 UN METHODIST..	17	6 319	7 627*	8.6	18.1
453 UN PRES CH USA	9	3 226	3 894*	4.4	9.3
ORANGE	178	31 046	136 578*	52.6	100.0
005 AME ZION......	4	2 038	2 713	1.0	2.0
019 AMER BAPT USA.	5	888	1 090*	0.4	0.8
053 ASSEMB OF GOD.	5	454	842	0.3	0.6
081 CATHOLIC......	28	NA	94 330	36.3	69.1
089 CHR & MISS AL.	1	33	47	–	–
093 CHR CH (DISC).	1	160	246	0.1	0.2
105 CHRISTIAN REF.	1	268	460	0.2	0.3
127 CH GOD (CLEVE)	2	191	234*	0.1	0.2
151 L-D SAINTS....	3	NA	354	0.1	0.3
165 CH OF NAZARENE	3	134	272	0.1	0.2
167 CHS OF CHRIST.	2	87	133	0.1	0.1
179 CONSRV BAPT...	4	731	897*	0.3	0.7
181 CONSRV CONGR..	1	435	534*	0.2	0.4
193 EPISCOPAL.....	19	3 089	4 403	1.7	3.2
221 FREE METHODIST	1	15	66	–	–
226 FRIENDS-USA...	1	68	83*	–	0.1
270 CONSRV JUDAISM	3	617	757*	0.3	0.6
271 REFORM JUDAISM	4	1 490	1 829*	0.7	1.3
281 LUTH CH AMER..	5	1 568	2 344	0.9	1.7
283 LUTH--MO SYNOD	5	1 273	1 941	0.7	1.4
371 REF CH IN AM..	7	1 399	3 088	1.2	2.3
381 REF PRES-EVAN.	1	104	140	0.1	0.1
383 REF PRES OF NA	1	77	102	–	0.1
403 SALVATION ARMY	1	94	237	0.1	0.2
413 S.D.A........	4	329	404*	0.2	0.3
419 SO BAPT CONV..	1	190	233*	0.1	0.2
435 UNITARIAN-UNIV	2	99	122*	–	0.1
443 UN C OF CHRIST	4	942	1 156*	0.4	0.8
449 UN METHODIST..	30	8 313	10 205*	3.9	7.5
453 UN PRES CH USA	29	5 960	7 316*	2.8	5.4
ORLEANS	49	6 900	20 811*	54.1	100.0
005 AME ZION......	1	75	83	0.2	0.4
019 AMER BAPT USA.	7	909	1 111*	2.9	5.3
029 AMER LUTH CH..	2	344	504	1.3	2.4
053 ASSEMB OF GOD.	2	358	606	1.6	2.9
081 CATHOLIC......	6	NA	11 137	28.9	53.5
089 CHR & MISS AL.	2	91	249	0.6	1.2
151 L-D SAINTS....	1	NA	163	0.4	0.8
193 EPISCOPAL.....	3	503	964	2.5	4.6
221 FREE METHODIST	1	45	234	0.6	1.1
281 LUTH CH AMER..	1	294	367	1.0	1.8

County and Denomination	Number of churches	Communicant, confirmed, full members	Total adherents Number	Total adherents Percent of total population	Total adherents Percent of total adherents
283 LUTH--MO SYNOD	1	143	315	0.8	1.5
431 UKRANIAN AMER.	1	80	120	0.3	0.6
435 UNITARIAN-UNIV	1	35	43*	0.1	0.2
443 UN C OF CHRIST	1	109	133*	0.3	0.6
449 UN METHODIST..	14	2 575	3 146*	8.2	15.1
453 UN PRES CH USA	5	1 339	1 636*	4.2	7.9
OSWEGO	111	16 553	46 582*	40.9	100.0
019 AMER BAPT USA.	9	1 506	1 853*	1.6	4.0
053 ASSEMB OF GOD.	3	164	267	0.2	0.6
081 CATHOLIC......	19	NA	24 789	21.8	53.2
089 CHR & MISS AL.	2	242	652	0.6	1.4
097 CHR CHS&CHS CR	2	148	182*	0.2	0.4
127 CH GOD (CLEVE)	1	48	59*	0.1	0.1
151 L-D SAINTS....	1	NA	287	0.3	0.6
165 CH OF NAZARENE	2	139	240	0.2	0.5
167 CHS OF CHRIST.	1	70	89	0.1	0.2
179 CONSRV BAPT...	1	225	277*	0.2	0.6
193 EPISCOPAL.....	6	1 395	1 841	1.6	4.0
221 FREE METHODIST	1	28	207	0.2	0.4
270 CONSRV JUDAISM	1	26	32*	–	0.1
281 LUTH CH AMER..	1	649	920	0.8	2.0
283 LUTH--MO SYNOD	1	150	209	0.2	0.4
403 SALVATION ARMY	2	178	421	0.4	0.9
413 S.D.A........	3	204	251*	0.2	0.5
419 SO BAPT CONV..	1	116	143*	0.1	0.3
435 UNITARIAN-UNIV	1	75	92*	0.1	0.2
443 UN C OF CHRIST	9	1 357	1 670*	1.5	3.6
449 UN METHODIST..	37	8 975	11 045*	9.7	23.7
453 UN PRES CH USA	7	858	1 056*	0.9	2.3
OTSEGO	95	13 295	27 069*	45.8	100.0
019 AMER BAPT USA.	10	1 454	1 713*	2.9	6.3
053 ASSEMB OF GOD.	2	163	307	0.5	1.1
081 CATHOLIC......	6	NA	10 300	17.4	38.1
089 CHR & MISS AL.	1	0	18	–	0.1
105 CHRISTIAN REF.	1	50	89	0.2	0.3
151 L-D SAINTS....	1	NA	248	0.4	0.9
167 CHS OF CHRIST.	1	20	25	–	0.1
179 CONSRV BAPT...	4	736	867*	1.5	3.2
193 EPISCOPAL.....	11	1 903	2 580	4.4	9.5
226 FRIENDS-USA...	2	59	70*	0.1	0.3
270 CONSRV JUDAISM	1	58	68*	0.1	0.3
281 LUTH CH AMER..	4	808	1 129	1.9	4.2
403 SALVATION ARMY	1	83	275	0.5	1.0
413 S.D.A........	1	33	39*	0.1	0.1
419 SO BAPT CONV..	1	55	65*	0.1	0.2
435 UNITARIAN-UNIV	2	129	152*	0.3	0.6
449 UN METHODIST..	33	5 605	6 604*	11.2	24.4
453 UN PRES CH USA	13	2 139	2 520*	4.3	9.3
PUTNAM	37	6 085	36 627*	47.4	100.0
001 ADVENT CHR CH.	1	15	18*	–	–
005 AME ZION......	1	282	339	0.4	0.9
019 AMER BAPT USA.	4	903	1 113*	1.4	3.0
081 CATHOLIC......	5	NA	28 620	37.1	78.1
167 CHS OF CHRIST.	1	20	36	–	0.1
179 CONSRV BAPT...	2	202	249*	0.3	0.7
193 EPISCOPAL.....	5	708	1 103	1.4	3.0
270 CONSRV JUDAISM	1	132	163*	0.2	0.4
271 REFORM JUDAISM	2	184	227*	0.3	0.6
281 LUTH CH AMER..	1	586	922	1.2	2.5
283 LUTH--MO SYNOD	1	366	526	0.7	1.4
449 UN METHODIST..	8	1 758	2 166*	2.8	5.9
453 UN PRES CH USA	5	929	1 145*	1.5	3.1
QUEENS	445	88 386	760 165*	40.2	100.0
005 AME ZION......	4	5 444	7 247	0.4	1.0
019 AMER BAPT USA.	24	9 408	11 008*	0.6	1.4
029 AMER LUTH CH..	2	172	232	–	–
039 AP CHR CH(NAZ)	1	46	54*	–	–
049 ARMEN AP CH AM	1	175	225	–	–
053 ASSEMB OF GOD.	11	2 118	3 357	0.2	0.4
081 CATHOLIC......	105	NA	644 207	34.1	84.7
089 CHR & MISS AL.	4	192	282	–	–
093 CHR CH (DISC).	1	95	146	–	–
097 CHR CHS&CHS CR	3	160	187*	–	–
101 C.M.E........	4	985	1 153*	0.1	0.2
105 CHRISTIAN REF.	1	48	70	–	–
123 CH GOD (ANDER)	5	511	1 533	0.1	0.2
127 CH GOD (CLEVE)	21	480	562*	–	0.1
151 L-D SAINTS....	3	NA	869	–	0.1
165 CH OF NAZARENE	4	164	503	–	0.1
167 CHS OF CHRIST.	6	240	440	–	0.1
175 CONGR CHR CHS.	1	850	995*	0.1	0.1
179 CONSRV BAPT...	6	873	1 021*	0.1	0.1
181 CONSRV CONGR..	1	81	95*	–	–
193 EPISCOPAL.....	33	12 411	17 204	0.9	2.3
195 ESTONIAN ELC..	1	106	1 040	0.1	0.1
203 EVAN FREE CH..	1	83	97*	–	–
208 EVAN LUTH ASSN	6	1 583	2 291	0.1	0.3
226 FRIENDS-USA...	2	77	90*	–	–
270 CONSRV JUDAISM	29	9 750	11 408*	0.6	1.5
271 REFORM JUDAISM	8	3 630	4 247*	0.2	0.6
281 LUTH CH AMER..	32	9 394	12 876	0.7	1.7
283 LUTH--MO SYNOD	23	6 305	9 113	0.5	1.2
290 METRO COMM CHS	1	20	40	–	–
313 N AM BAPT CONF	2	308	360*	–	–
353 CHR BRETHREN..	1	140	140	–	–
403 SALVATION ARMY	3	173	878	–	0.1
413 S.D.A........	15	3 862	4 519*	0.2	0.6

NA—Not applicable   *Total adherents estimated from known number of communicant, confirmed, full members.

—Represents a percent less than 0.1.   Percentages may not total due to rounding.

Table 4. Churches and Church Membership by County and Denomination: 1980

County and Denomination	Number of churches	Communicant, confirmed, full members	Total adherents Number	Percent of total population	Percent of total adherents
419 SO BAPT CONV..	9	1 754	2 052*	0.1	0.3
431 UKRANIAN AMER.	1	70	110	–	–
435 UNITARIAN-UNIV	2	173	202*	–	–
443 UN C OF CHRIST	14	3 104	3 632*	0.2	0.5
449 UN METHODIST..	29	8 445	9 881*	0.5	1.3
453 UN PRES CH USA	25	4 956	5 799*	0.3	0.8
RENSSELAER	**137**	**20 964**	**86 022***	**56.6**	**100.0**
005 AME ZION......	1	656	741	0.5	0.9
019 AMER BAPT USA.	9	1 739	2 090*	1.4	2.4
049 ARMEN AP CH AM	1	52	77	0.1	0.1
053 ASSEMB OF GOD.	2	118	159	0.1	0.2
081 CATHOLIC.....	31	NA	58 388	38.4	67.9
089 CHR & MISS AL.	2	72	117	0.1	0.1
093 CHR CH (DISC)	2	118	223	0.1	0.3
097 CHR CHS&CHS CR	1	30	36*	–	–
123 CH GOD (ANDER)	1	40	120	0.1	0.1
167 CHS OF CHRIST.	1	18	30	–	–
179 CONSRV BAPT...	6	297	357*	0.2	0.4
193 EPISCOPAL.....	12	2 826	3 957	2.6	4.6
201 EVAN COV CH AM	1	43	52*	–	0.1
208 EVAN LUTH ASSN	1	262	480	0.3	0.6
226 FRIENDS-USA...	1	26	31*	–	–
270 CONSRV JUDAISM	1	195	234*	0.2	0.3
271 REFORM JUDAISM	1	244	293*	0.2	0.3
281 LUTH CH AMER..	10	2 129	3 078	2.0	3.6
283 LUTH--MO SYNOD	1	182	237	0.2	0.3
371 REF CH IN AM..	8	1 650	2 790	1.8	3.2
403 SALVATION ARMY	1	102	318	0.2	0.4
413 S.D.A.........	1	51	61*	–	0.1
415 S-D BAPTIST GC	1	51	61*	–	0.1
443 UN C OF CHRIST	4	229	275*	0.2	0.3
449 UN METHODIST..	27	7 427	8 925*	5.9	10.4
453 UN PRES CH USA	10	2 407	2 892*	1.9	3.4
RICHMOND	**109**	**16 671**	**204 286***	**58.0**	**100.0**
005 AME ZION......	2	637	819	0.2	0.4
019 AMER BAPT USA.	1	200	243*	0.1	0.1
029 AMER LUTH CH..	4	1 568	2 113	0.6	1.0
053 ASSEMB OF GOD.	5	379	547	0.2	0.3
081 CATHOLIC.....	35	NA	182 010	51.7	89.1
097 CHR CHS&CHS CR	1	50	61*	–	–
151 L-D SAINTS....	1	NA	143	–	0.1
163 CH OF LUTH BR.	1	48	127	–	0.1
165 CH OF NAZARENE	2	38	217	0.1	0.1
167 CHS OF CHRIST.	2	55	85	–	–
179 CONSRV BAPT...	2	372	452*	0.1	0.2
193 EPISCOPAL.....	10	2 118	2 899	0.8	1.4
203 EVAN FREE CH..	3	230	280*	0.1	0.1
226 FRIENDS-USA...	1	3	4*	–	–
270 CONSRV JUDAISM	3	615	748*	0.2	0.4
271 REFORM JUDAISM	1	622	756*	0.2	0.4
281 LUTH CH AMER..	5	2 503	3 372	1.0	1.7
283 LUTH--MO SYNOD	2	1 200	1 760	0.5	0.9
285 MENNONITE CH..	1	18	22*	–	–
293 MORAV CH-NORTH	5	1 354	1 734	0.5	0.8
403 SALVATION ARMY	2	104	353	0.1	0.2
413 S.D.A.........	2	240	292*	0.1	0.1
419 SO BAPT CONV..	2	112	136*	–	0.1
423 SYRIAN ANTIOCH	1	400	486*	0.1	0.2
435 UNITARIAN-UNIV	1	146	178*	0.1	0.1
443 UN C OF CHRIST	3	568	691*	0.2	0.3
449 UN METHODIST..	8	2 321	2 822*	0.8	1.4
453 UN PRES CH USA	3	770	936*	0.3	0.5
ROCKLAND	**113**	**21 076**	**125 027***	**48.2**	**100.0**
005 AME ZION......	8	1 640	2 221	0.9	1.8
019 AMER BAPT USA.	1	107	131*	0.1	0.1
053 ASSEMB OF GOD.	3	171	277	0.1	0.2
081 CATHOLIC.....	19	NA	96 826	37.3	77.4
089 CHR & MISS AL.	4	616	1 027	0.4	0.8
105 CHRISTIAN REF.	1	51	98	–	0.1
127 CH GOD (CLEVE)	1	113	138*	0.1	0.1
163 CH OF LUTH BR.	1	26	66	–	0.1
165 CH OF NAZARENE	1	42	193	0.1	0.2
179 CONSRV BAPT...	2	578	706*	0.3	0.6
181 CONSRV CONGR..	1	44	54*	–	–
193 EPISCOPAL.....	9	2 337	3 353	1.3	2.7
203 EVAN FREE CH..	1	100	122*	–	0.1
208 EVAN LUTH ASSN	1	300	400	0.2	0.3
226 FRIENDS-USA...	1	80	98*	–	0.1
270 CONSRV JUDAISM	7	1 713	2 092*	0.8	1.7
271 REFORM JUDAISM	5	3 332	4 070*	1.6	3.3
281 LUTH CH AMER..	3	2 260	3 113	1.2	2.5
283 LUTH--MO SYNOD	2	436	600	0.2	0.5
353 CHR BRETHREN..	1	20	20	–	–
371 REF CH IN AM..	6	906	1 764	0.7	1.4
403 SALVATION ARMY	1	53	145	0.1	0.1
413 S.D.A.........	4	424	518*	0.2	0.4
419 SO BAPT CONV..	1	60	73*	–	0.1
435 UNITARIAN-UNIV	1	125	153*	0.1	0.1
443 UN C OF CHRIST	1	64	78*	–	0.1
449 UN METHODIST..	14	3 093	3 778*	1.5	3.0
453 UN PRES CH USA	13	2 385	2 913*	1.1	2.3
ST LAWRENCE	**155**	**14 601**	**64 605***	**56.5**	**100.0**
001 ADVENT CHR CH.	1	109	132*	0.1	0.2
019 AMER BAPT USA.	5	619	751*	0.7	1.2
053 ASSEMB OF GOD.	4	113	281	0.2	0.4
081 CATHOLIC.....	36	NA	44 793	39.2	69.3
089 CHR & MISS AL.	1	14	26	–	–
127 CH GOD (CLEVE)	1	11	13*	–	–
133 CH GOD(7TH)DEN	2	8	10*	–	–
151 L-D SAINTS....	1	NA	220	0.2	0.3
165 CH OF NAZARENE	3	129	268	0.2	0.4
167 CHS OF CHRIST.	1	12	13	–	–
179 CONSRV BAPT...	1	105	127*	0.1	0.2
193 EPISCOPAL.....	10	1 666	2 860	2.5	4.4
221 FREE METHODIST	2	28	123	0.1	0.2
283 LUTH--MO SYNOD	2	154	269	0.2	0.4
323 OLD ORD AMISH.	5	650	788*	0.7	1.2
335 ORTH PRESB CH.	1	50	61*	0.1	0.1
383 REF PRES OF NA	1	25	32	–	–
403 SALVATION ARMY	2	76	700	0.6	1.1
413 S.D.A.........	2	80	97*	0.1	0.2
419 SO BAPT CONV..	5	449	545*	0.5	0.8
435 UNITARIAN-UNIV	1	200	243*	0.2	0.4
443 UN C OF CHRIST	9	1 252	1 518*	1.3	2.3
449 UN METHODIST..	39	6 285	7 623*	6.7	11.8
453 UN PRES CH USA	20	2 566	3 112*	2.7	4.8
SARATOGA	**99**	**19 233**	**61 408***	**39.9**	**100.0**
005 AME ZION......	1	186	229	0.1	0.4
019 AMER BAPT USA.	7	1 961	2 410*	1.6	3.9
053 ASSEMB OF GOD.	3	126	231	0.2	0.4
055 AS REF PRES CH	1	123	133	0.1	0.2
059 BAPT MISS ASSN	3	68	84*	0.1	0.1
081 CATHOLIC......	16	NA	35 675	23.2	58.1
089 CHR & MISS AL.	2	207	339	0.2	0.6
151 L-D SAINTS....	1	NA	251	0.2	0.4
165 CH OF NAZARENE	1	66	143	0.1	0.2
167 CHS OF CHRIST.	1	130	233	0.2	0.4
193 EPISCOPAL.....	9	3 140	4 393	2.9	7.2
221 FREE METHODIST	2	85	486	0.3	0.8
226 FRIENDS-USA...	2	140	172*	0.1	0.3
270 CONSRV JUDAISM	1	66	81*	0.1	0.1
271 REFORM JUDAISM	1	74	91*	0.1	0.1
281 LUTH CH AMER..	1	240	375	0.2	0.6
283 LUTH--MO SYNOD	1	378	507	0.3	0.8
353 CHR BRETHREN..	1	80	90	0.1	0.1
371 REF CH IN AM..	4	588	1 052	0.7	1.7
381 REF PRES-EVAN.	1	66	95	0.1	0.2
403 SALVATION ARMY	1	89	280	0.2	0.5
413 S.D.A.........	1	77	95*	0.1	0.2
419 SO BAPT CONV..	1	91	112*	0.1	0.2
443 UN C OF CHRIST	1	83	102*	0.1	0.2
449 UN METHODIST..	27	9 531	11 715*	7.6	19.1
453 UN PRES CH USA	8	1 522	1 871*	1.2	3.0
469 WELS..........	1	116	163	0.1	0.3
SCHENECTADY	**100**	**25 043**	**113 916***	**76.0**	**100.0**
001 ADVENT CHR CH.	1	54	64*	–	0.1
005 AME ZION......	1	498	645	0.4	0.6
019 AMER BAPT USA.	8	1 736	2 059*	1.4	1.8
053 ASSEMB OF GOD.	2	919	2 222	1.5	2.0
081 CATHOLIC......	22	NA	77 810	51.9	68.3
151 L-D SAINTS....	1	NA	535	0.4	0.5
165 CH OF NAZARENE	1	103	151	0.1	0.1
167 CHS OF CHRIST.	1	90	140	0.1	0.1
181 CONSRV CONGR..	3	496	588*	0.4	0.5
193 EPISCOPAL.....	4	2 372	4 091	2.7	3.6
208 EVAN LUTH ASSN	1	142	194	0.1	0.2
226 FRIENDS-USA...	2	100	119*	0.1	0.1
270 CONSRV JUDAISM	1	368	436*	0.3	0.4
271 REFORM JUDAISM	1	840	996*	0.7	0.9
274 LAT EVAN LUTH.	1	70	70	–	0.1
281 LUTH CH AMER..	4	1 728	2 305	1.5	2.0
283 LUTH--MO SYNOD	3	1 448	1 982	1.3	1.7
335 ORTH PRESB CH.	1	160	190*	0.1	0.2
353 CHR BRETHREN..	1	75	90	0.1	0.1
371 REF CH IN AM..	12	4 600	8 151	5.4	7.2
381 REF PRES-EVAN.	1	77	116	0.1	0.1
403 SALVATION ARMY	1	114	225	0.2	0.2
413 S.D.A.........	1	93	110*	0.1	0.1
415 S-D BAPTIST GC	1	21	25*	–	–
419 SO BAPT CONV..	1	142	168*	0.1	0.1
435 UNITARIAN-UNIV	1	528	626*	0.4	0.5
443 UN C OF CHRIST	2	206	244*	0.2	0.2
449 UN METHODIST..	15	6 437	7 635*	5.1	6.7
453 UN PRES CH USA	6	1 626	1 929*	1.3	1.7
SCHOHARIE	**55**	**6 395**	**11 816***	**39.8**	**100.0**
019 AMER BAPT USA.	2	221	264*	0.9	2.2
053 ASSEMB OF GOD.	1	70	122	0.4	1.0
081 CATHOLIC......	4	NA	2 900	9.8	24.5
089 CHR & MISS AL.	1	25	43	0.1	0.4
151 L-D SAINTS....	1	NA	225	0.8	1.9
193 EPISCOPAL.....	3	156	182	0.6	1.5
281 LUTH CH AMER..	7	1 425	2 040	6.9	17.3
371 REF CH IN AM..	6	386	1 133	3.8	9.6
443 UN C OF CHRIST	2	50	60*	0.2	0.5
449 UN METHODIST..	23	3 659	4 366*	14.7	36.9
453 UN PRES CH USA	5	403	481*	1.6	4.1
SCHUYLER	**27**	**3 282**	**9 190***	**52.0**	**100.0**
019 AMER BAPT USA.	6	730	891*	5.0	9.7
053 ASSEMB OF GOD.	1	19	25	0.1	0.3
081 CATHOLIC......	1	NA	4 982	28.2	54.2
165 CH OF NAZARENE	1	20	37	0.2	0.4
193 EPISCOPAL.....	3	358	623	3.5	6.8
449 UN METHODIST..	11	1 609	1 965*	11.1	21.4
453 UN PRES CH USA	4	546	667*	3.8	7.3

NA– Not applicable   *Total adherents estimated from known number of communicant, confirmed, full members.   –Represents a percent less than 0.1.   Percentages may not total due to rounding.

Table 4. Churches and Church Membership by County and Denomination: 1980

County and Denomination	Number of churches	Communicant, confirmed, full members	Total adherents Number	Total adherents Percent of total population	Total adherents Percent of total adherents
SENECA	38	5 275	14 827*	44.0	100.0
019 AMER BAPT USA.	2	188	226*	0.7	1.5
053 ASSEMB OF GOD.	2	181	291	0.9	2.0
081 CATHOLIC......	4	NA	7 808	23.1	52.7
089 CHR & MISS AL.	1	16	51	0.2	0.3
127 CH GOD (CLEVE)	1	17	20*	0.1	0.1
151 L-D SAINTS....	1	NA	81	0.2	0.5
165 CH OF NAZARENE	1	31	55	0.2	0.4
179 CONSRV BAPT...	3	675	813*	2.4	5.5
193 EPISCOPAL.....	4	833	1 121	3.3	7.6
281 LUTH CH AMER..	1	?	?	?	?
283 LUTH--MO SYNOD	2	280	482	1.4	3.3
371 REF CH IN AM..	2	303	565	1.7	3.8
443 UN C OF CHRIST	1	81	98*	0.3	0.7
449 UN METHODIST..	5	1 277	1 538*	4.6	10.4
453 UN PRES CH USA	8	1 393	1 678*	5.0	11.3
STEUBEN	130	17 407	39 152*	39.5	100.0
001 ADVENT CHR CH.	1	26	32*	-	0.1
019 AMER BAPT USA.	12	2 020	2 464*	2.5	6.3
053 ASSEMB OF GOD.	4	405	692	0.7	1.8
081 CATHOLIC......	19	NA	16 795	16.9	42.9
089 CHR & MISS AL.	4	293	407	0.4	1.0
127 CH GOD (CLEVE)	1	?	?	?	?
151 L-D SAINTS....	1	NA	220	0.2	0.6
165 CH OF NAZARENE	2	146	297	0.3	0.8
179 CONSRV BAPT...	1	52	63*	0.1	0.2
193 EPISCOPAL.....	7	1 568	1 901	1.9	4.9
208 EVAN LUTH ASSN	1	88	128	0.1	0.3
221 FREE METHODIST	2	26	138	0.1	0.4
270 CONSRV JUDAISM	2	32	39*	-	0.1
281 LUTH CH AMER..	2	299	428	0.4	1.1
283 LUTH--MO SYNOD	2	182	263	0.3	0.7
285 MENNONITE CH..	3	128	156*	0.2	0.4
353 CHR BRETHREN..	1	20	20	-	0.1
403 SALVATION ARMY	2	133	483	0.5	1.2
413 S.D.A.........	2	159	194*	0.2	0.5
419 SO BAPT CONV..	1	19	23*	-	0.1
443 UN C OF CHRIST	5	647	789*	0.8	2.0
449 UN METHODIST..	38	7 915	9 656*	9.7	24.7
453 UN PRES CH USA	17	3 249	3 964*	4.0	10.1
SUFFOLK	412	108 420	642 340*	50.0	100.0
005 AME ZION......	11	6 212	7 513	0.6	1.2
019 AMER BAPT USA.	8	2 343	2 878*	0.2	0.4
029 AMER LUTH CH..	9	2 746	4 632	0.4	0.7
053 ASSEMB OF GOD.	20	2 852	4 437	0.3	0.7
057 BAPT GEN CONF.	2	227	279*	-	-
081 CATHOLIC......	78	NA	495 624	38.6	77.2
089 CHR & MISS AL.	2	77	182	-	-
097 CHR CHS&CHS CR	6	236	290*	-	-
105 CHRISTIAN REF.	2	257	405	-	0.1
123 CH GOD (ANDER)	1	37	111	-	-
127 CH GOD (CLEVE)	16	799	982*	0.1	0.2
151 L-D SAINTS....	3	NA	460	-	0.1
163 CH OF LUTH BR.	1	77	162	-	-
165 CH OF NAZARENE	3	209	259	-	-
167 CHS OF CHRIST.	7	620	859	0.1	0.1
179 CONSRV BAPT...	7	694	853*	0.1	0.1
193 EPISCOPAL.....	43	17 565	25 125	2.0	3.9
201 EVAN COV CH AM	1	46	57*	-	-
203 EVAN FREE CH..	3	503	618*	-	0.1
208 EVAN LUTH ASSN	4	3 287	5 892	0.5	0.9
226 FRIENDS-USA...	5	173	213*	-	-
247 HOLINESS CH...	2	45	50	-	-
270 CONSRV JUDAISM	14	3 727	4 578*	0.4	0.7
271 REFORM JUDAISM	8	4 710	5 786*	0.5	0.9
281 LUTH CH AMER..	15	9 527	14 043	1.1	2.2
283 LUTH--MO SYNOD	15	8 693	12 439	1.0	1.9
290 METRO COMM CHS	0	25	50	-	-
353 CHR BRETHREN..	5	205	350	-	0.1
371 REF CH IN AM..	3	603	1 189	0.1	0.2
375 REF EPISCOPAL.	1	150	184*	-	-
403 SALVATION ARMY	1	100	565	-	0.1
413 S.D.A.........	7	647	795*	0.1	0.1
419 SO BAPT CONV..	6	1 295	1 591*	0.1	0.2
431 UKRANIAN AMER.	1	110	210	-	-
435 UNITARIAN-UNIV	5	679	834*	0.1	0.1
443 UN C OF CHRIST	13	3 087	3 792	0.3	0.6
449 UN METHODIST..	47	23 239	28 548*	2.2	4.4
453 UN PRES CH USA	36	12 595	15 472*	1.2	2.4
469 WELS..........	1	23	33	-	-
SULLIVAN	79	6 669	23 821*	36.6	100.0
005 AME ZION......	2	258	410	0.6	1.7
053 ASSEMB OF GOD.	3	168	269	0.4	1.1
066 BIBLE CH OF CR	1	80	95*	0.1	0.4
081 CATHOLIC......	12	NA	14 742	22.6	61.9
123 CH GOD (ANDER)	1	28	84	0.1	0.4
193 EPISCOPAL.....	3	175	229	0.4	1.0
221 FREE METHODIST	2	49	297	0.5	1.2
226 FRIENDS-USA...	1	14	18*	-	0.1
271 REFORM JUDAISM	1	410	487*	0.7	2.0
281 LUTH CH AMER..	4	530	814*	1.2	3.4
353 CHR BRETHREN..	1	15	15	-	0.1
371 REF CH IN AM..	6	353	741	1.1	3.1
383 REF PRES OF NA	1	15	16	-	0.1
403 SALVATION ARMY	1	83	276	0.4	1.2
413 S.D.A.........	1	27	32*	-	0.1
443 UN C OF CHRIST	1	144	171*	0.3	0.7
449 UN METHODIST..	29	3 155	3 744*	5.7	15.7
453 UN PRES CH USA	9	1 164	1 381*	2.1	5.8
TIOGA	54	9 917	16 700*	33.5	100.0
019 AMER BAPT USA.	3	904	1 119*	2.2	6.7
053 ASSEMB OF GOD.	2	47	61	0.1	0.4
081 CATHOLIC......	4	NA	3 410	6.8	20.4
089 CHR & MISS AL.	4	436	852	1.7	5.1
151 L-D SAINTS....	1	NA	153	0.3	0.9
165 CH OF NAZARENE	2	333	772	1.5	4.6
167 CHS OF CHRIST.	1	30	38	0.1	0.2
179 CONSRV BAPT...	1	125	155*	0.3	0.9
193 EPISCOPAL.....	3	815	1 123	2.3	6.7
281 LUTH CH AMER..	1	125	191	0.4	1.1
283 LUTH--MO SYNOD	1	276	377	0.8	2.3
419 SO BAPT CONV..	2	76	94*	0.2	0.6
443 UN C OF CHRIST	3	472	584*	1.2	3.5
449 UN METHODIST..	22	5 156	6 382*	12.8	38.2
453 UN PRES CH USA	4	1 122	1 389*	2.8	8.3
TOMPKINS	61	11 338	27 633*	31.7	100.0
005 AME ZION......	1	556	701	0.8	2.5
019 AMER BAPT USA.	5	894	1 035*	1.2	3.7
053 ASSEMB OF GOD.	4	297	472	0.5	1.7
081 CATHOLIC......	6	NA	12 273	14.1	44.4
089 CHR & MISS AL.	1	112	198	0.2	0.7
151 L-D SAINTS....	1	NA	404	0.5	1.5
165 CH OF NAZARENE	2	60	68	0.1	0.2
167 CHS OF CHRIST.	3	127	172	0.2	0.6
193 EPISCOPAL.....	5	728	1 824	2.1	6.6
226 FRIENDS-USA...	3	147	170*	0.2	0.6
281 LUTH CH AMER..	1	516	696	0.8	2.5
283 LUTH--MO SYNOD	1	209	280	0.3	1.0
403 SALVATION ARMY	1	96	546	0.6	2.0
413 S.D.A.........	1	80	93*	0.1	0.3
435 UNITARIAN-UNIV	1	214	248*	0.3	0.9
443 UN C OF CHRIST	7	1 324	1 533*	1.8	5.5
449 UN METHODIST..	15	4 142	4 795*	5.5	17.4
453 UN PRES CH USA	3	1 836	2 125*	2.4	7.7
ULSTER	150	20 419	85 129*	53.8	100.0
005 AME ZION......	3	1 614	1 840	1.2	2.2
019 AMER BAPT USA.	2	584	696*	0.4	0.8
053 ASSEMB OF GOD.	5	228	485	0.3	0.6
081 CATHOLIC......	21	NA	54 330	34.4	63.8
089 CHR & MISS AL.	1	56	112	0.1	0.1
127 CH GOD (CLEVE)	1	?	?	?	?
151 L-D SAINTS....	1	NA	450	0.3	0.5
165 CH OF NAZARENE	3	175	339	0.2	0.4
167 CHS OF CHRIST.	1	48	61	-	0.1
175 CONGR CHR CHS.	2	217	259*	0.2	0.3
179 CONSRV BAPT...	1	225	268*	0.2	0.3
181 CONSRV CONGR..	1	49	58*	-	0.1
193 EPISCOPAL.....	9	1 147	1 898	1.2	2.2
203 EVAN FREE CH..	1	120	143*	0.1	0.2
208 EVAN LUTH ASSN	1	450	519	0.3	0.6
221 FREE METHODIST	1	6	18	-	-
226 FRIENDS-USA...	3	169	202*	0.1	0.2
270 CONSRV JUDAISM	2	147	175*	0.1	0.2
271 REFORM JUDAISM	2	640	763*	0.5	0.9
281 LUTH CH AMER..	9	2 451	3 433	2.2	4.0
283 LUTH--MO SYNOD	1	65	67	-	0.1
371 REF CH IN AM..	30	3 900	9 049	5.7	10.6
403 SALVATION ARMY	2	163	430	0.3	0.5
413 S.D.A.........	3	228	272*	0.2	0.3
419 SO BAPT CONV..	2	144	172*	0.1	0.2
431 UKRANIAN AMER.	1	50	95	0.1	0.1
435 UNITARIAN-UNIV	1	80	95*	0.1	0.1
443 UN C OF CHRIST	1	94	112*	0.1	0.1
449 UN METHODIST..	35	6 567	7 832*	5.0	9.2
453 UN PRES CH USA	4	802	956*	0.6	1.1
WARREN	60	9 077	25 372*	46.3	100.0
019 AMER BAPT USA.	5	781	952*	1.7	3.8
053 ASSEMB OF GOD.	3	146	314	0.6	1.2
081 CATHOLIC......	10	NA	12 680	23.1	50.0
089 CHR & MISS AL.	1	22	48	0.1	0.2
127 CH GOD (CLEVE)	1	71	87*	0.2	0.3
151 L-D SAINTS....	1	NA	275	0.5	1.1
167 CHS OF CHRIST.	1	43	43	0.1	0.2
193 EPISCOPAL.....	9	1 382	2 517	4.6	9.9
221 FREE METHODIST	2	57	180	0.3	0.7
270 CONSRV JUDAISM	1	139	169*	0.3	0.7
271 REFORM JUDAISM	1	246	300*	0.5	1.2
283 LUTH--MO SYNOD	1	437	582	1.1	2.3
403 SALVATION ARMY	1	114	331	0.6	1.3
413 S.D.A.........	2	141	172*	0.3	0.7
435 UNITARIAN-UNIV	1	40	49*	0.1	0.2
449 UN METHODIST..	14	3 388	4 128*	7.5	16.3
453 UN PRES CH USA	6	2 089	2 545*	4.6	10.0
WASHINGTON	77	9 859	26 684*	48.7	100.0
001 ADVENT CHR CH.	1	25	31*	0.1	0.1
019 AMER BAPT USA.	11	1 611	1 972*	3.6	7.4
053 ASSEMB OF GOD.	3	314	717	1.3	2.7
081 CATHOLIC......	13	NA	14 128	25.8	52.9
179 CONSRV BAPT...	2	450	551*	1.0	2.1
193 EPISCOPAL.....	8	873	1 174	2.1	4.4
285 MENNONITE CH..	1	9	11*	-	-
371 REF CH IN AM..	1	101	174	0.3	0.7
413 S.D.A.........	1	78	95*	0.2	0.4

NA—Not applicable   *Total adherents estimated from known number of communicant, confirmed, full members.   —Represents a percent less than 0.1.   Percentages may not total due to rounding.

Table 4. Churches and Church Membership by County and Denomination: 1980

County and Denomination	Number of churches	Communicant, confirmed, full members	Total adherents		
			Number	Percent of total population	Percent of total adherents
443 UN C OF CHRIST	1	46	56*	0.1	0.2
449 UN METHODIST..	20	4 389	5 372*	9.8	20.1
453 UN PRES CH USA	15	1 963	2 403*	4.4	9.0
WAYNE	103	16 596	29 920*	35.1	100.0
001 ADVENT CHR CH.	1	19	23*	–	0.1
019 AMER BAPT USA.	13	2 607	3 206*	3.8	10.7
053 ASSEMB OF GOD.	6	301	588	0.7	2.0
081 CATHOLIC.....	10	NA	6 916	8.1	23.1
089 CHR & MISS AL.	1	34	53	0.1	0.2
093 CHR CH (DISC).	1	137	211	0.2	0.7
105 CHRISTIAN REF.	1	169	254	0.3	0.8
123 CH GOD (ANDER)	2	53	159	0.2	0.5
127 CH GOD (CLEVE)	1	31	38*	–	0.1
151 L-D SAINTS....	2	NA	465	0.5	1.6
167 CHS OF CHRIST.	1	40	51	0.1	0.2
179 CONSRV BAPT...	1	28	34*	–	0.1
193 EPISCOPAL.....	6	1 144	1 560	1.8	5.2
221 FREE METHODIST	4	161	594	0.7	2.0
226 FRIENDS-USA...	2	254	312*	0.4	1.0
281 LUTH CH AMER..	2	726	1 185	1.4	4.0
283 LUTH--MO SYNOD	2	241	385	0.5	1.3
371 REF CH IN AM..	9	1 237	2 309	2.7	7.7
413 S.D.A.........	2	105	129*	0.2	0.4
443 UN C OF CHRIST	2	88	108*	0.1	0.4
449 UN METHODIST..	22	6 572	8 082*	9.5	27.0
453 UN PRES CH USA	12	2 649	3 258*	3.8	10.9
WESTCHESTER	394	111 189	570 051*	65.8	100.0
005 AME ZION......	9	15 401	18 654	2.2	3.3
019 AMER BAPT USA.	20	9 201	10 833*	1.3	1.9
029 AMER LUTH CH..	2	270	346	–	0.1
053 ASSEMB OF GOD.	12	954	1 501	0.2	0.3
066 BIBLE CH OF CR	1	1 200	1 413*	0.2	0.2
081 CATHOLIC.....	89	NA	429 268	49.5	75.3
089 CHR & MISS AL.	6	540	1 186	0.1	0.2
093 CHR CH (DISC).	1	40	62	–	–
101 C.M.E.........	3	2 235	2 631*	0.3	0.5
123 CH GOD (ANDER)	1	25	75	–	–
127 CH GOD (CLEVE)	3	101	119*	–	–
149 CH OF JC (BIC)	2	52	59	–	–
151 L-D SAINTS....	2	NA	763	0.1	0.1
163 CH OF LUTH BR.	1	54	179	–	–
165 CH OF NAZARENE	1	41	230	–	–
167 CHS OF CHRIST.	3	168	225	–	–
179 CONSRV BAPT...	4	505	595*	0.1	0.1
181 CONSRV CONGR..	1	53	62*	–	–
193 EPISCOPAL.....	54	14 274	20 819	2.4	3.7
201 EVAN COV CH AM	1	82	97*	–	–
208 EVAN LUTH ASSN	2	393	619	0.1	0.1
226 FRIENDS-USA...	5	563	663*	0.1	0.1
270 CONSRV JUDAISM	16	4 243	4 996*	0.6	0.9
271 REFORM JUDAISM	18	14 950	17 602*	2.0	3.1
281 LUTH CH AMER..	17	6 009	7 482	0.9	1.3
283 LUTH--MO SYNOD	11	2 826	3 739	0.4	0.7
290 METRO COMM CHS	0	30	60	–	–
353 CHR BRETHREN..	4	230	255	–	–
356 PRESB CH AMER.	1	16	23	–	–
371 REF CH IN AM..	11	3 805	6 028	0.7	1.1
403 SALVATION ARMY	5	217	953	0.1	0.2
413 S.D.A.........	8	1 454	1 712*	0.2	0.3
419 SO BAPT CONV..	2	166	195*	–	–
435 UNITARIAN-UNIV	5	821	967*	0.1	0.2
443 UN C OF CHRIST	11	3 386	3 987*	0.5	0.7
449 UN METHODIST..	33	12 804	15 075*	1.7	2.6
453 UN PRES CH USA	29	14 080	16 578*	1.9	2.9
WYOMING	59	6 085	22 561*	56.6	100.0
019 AMER BAPT USA.	6	624	764*	1.9	3.4
053 ASSEMB OF GOD.	1	84	152	0.4	0.7
081 CATHOLIC.....	16	NA	14 455	36.2	64.1
089 CHR & MISS AL.	1	58	75	0.2	0.3
127 CH GOD (CLEVE)	1	33	40*	0.1	0.2
151 L-D SAINTS....	2	NA	271	0.7	1.2
179 CONSRV BAPT...	3	548	671*	1.7	3.0
193 EPISCOPAL.....	3	303	392	1.0	1.7
221 FREE METHODIST	2	44	354	0.9	1.6
283 LUTH--MO SYNOD	1	197	251	0.6	1.1
313 N AM BAPT CONF	1	76	93*	0.2	0.4
413 S.D.A.........	1	13	16*	–	0.1
443 UN C OF CHRIST	6	1 265	1 549*	3.9	6.9
449 UN METHODIST..	10	1 957	2 397*	6.0	10.6
453 UN PRES CH USA	5	883	1 081*	2.7	4.8
YATES	36	5 247	8 719*	40.6	100.0
019 AMER BAPT USA.	6	834	1 006*	4.7	11.5
029 AMER LUTH CH..	1	250	366	1.7	4.2
061 BEACHY AMISH..	1	19	23*	0.1	0.3
081 CATHOLIC.....	2	NA	1 944	9.1	22.3
165 CH OF NAZARENE	1	30	39	0.2	0.4
193 EPISCOPAL.....	2	202	482	2.2	5.5
281 LUTH CH AMER..	1	144	183	0.9	2.1
403 SALVATION ARMY	1	54	194	0.9	2.2
413 S.D.A.........	1	55	66*	0.3	0.8
443 UN C OF CHRIST	2	96	116*	0.5	1.3
449 UN METHODIST..	13	2 931	3 537*	16.5	40.6
453 UN PRES CH USA	5	632	763*	3.6	8.8

NORTH CAROLINA

County and Denomination	Number of churches	Communicant, confirmed, full members	Total adherents		
			Number	Percent of total population	Percent of total adherents
THE STATE.....	10 281	2 470 569	3 173 793*	54.0	100.0
ALAMANCE	162	43 170	54 581*	55.1	100.0
005 AME ZION......	1	75	83	0.1	0.2
053 ASSEMB OF GOD.	1	375	750	0.8	1.4
055 AS REF PRES CH	1	288	319	0.3	0.6
059 BAPT MISS ASSN	1	170	202*	0.2	0.4
081 CATHOLIC.....	1	NA	1 653	1.7	3.0
089 CHR & MISS AL.	1	34	49	–	0.1
093 CHR CH (DISC).	1	63	111	0.1	0.2
097 CHR CHS&CHS CR	1	48	57*	0.1	0.1
127 CH GOD (CLEVE)	3	177	211*	0.2	0.4
151 L-D SAINTS....	1	NA	348	0.4	0.6
165 CH OF NAZARENE	3	479	715	0.7	1.3
167 CHS OF CHRIST.	1	116	169	0.2	0.3
175 CONGR CHR CHS.	1	25	30*	–	0.1
193 EPISCOPAL.....	3	489	661	0.7	1.2
215 EVAN METH CH..	2	179	213*	0.2	0.4
226 FRIENDS-USA...	9	1 362	1 621*	1.6	3.0
247 HOLINESS CH...	3	61	61	0.1	0.1
281 LUTH CH AMER..	6	1 747	2 228	2.2	4.1
283 LUTH--MO SYNOD	1	104	130	0.1	0.2
349 PENT HOLINESS.	5	442	526*	0.5	1.0
353 CHR BRETHREN..	4	250	525	0.5	1.0
356 PRESB CH AMER.	2	493	599	0.6	1.1
357 PRESB CH US...	12	4 264	5 075*	5.1	9.3
403 SALVATION ARMY	1	111	374	0.4	0.7
413 S.D.A.........	2	74	88*	0.1	0.2
419 SO BAPT CONV..	30	12 537	14 922	15.1	27.3
443 UN C OF CHRIST	36	7 011	8 345	8.4	15.3
449 UN METHODIST..	28	12 147	14 458	14.6	26.5
453 UN PRES CH USA	1	49	58*	0.1	0.1
ALEXANDER	62	14 296	17 697*	70.8	100.0
001 ADVENT CHR CH.	1	150	184*	0.7	1.0
029 AMER LUTH CH..	1	153	201	0.8	1.1
055 AS REF PRES CH	3	451	517	2.1	2.9
097 CHR CHS&CHS CR	1	50	61*	0.2	0.3
127 CH GOD (CLEVE)	2	80	98*	0.4	0.6
167 CHS OF CHRIST.	1	41	51	0.2	0.3
281 LUTH CH AMER..	4	1 235	1 712	6.8	9.7
283 LUTH--MO SYNOD	2	271	350	1.4	2.0
357 PRESB CH US...	2	288	353*	1.4	2.0
419 SO BAPT CONV..	34	9 915	12 136*	48.5	68.6
449 UN METHODIST..	11	1 662	2 034*	8.1	11.5
ALLEGHANY	25	2 331	2 833*	29.6	100.0
081 CATHOLIC......	1	NA	45	0.5	1.6
127 CH GOD (CLEVE)	1	14	17*	0.2	0.6
157 CH OF BRETHREN	2	141	169*	1.8	6.0
167 CHS OF CHRIST.	1	11	14	0.1	0.5
349 PENT HOLINESS.	1	34	41*	0.4	1.4
357 PRESB CH US...	2	144	172*	1.8	6.1
419 SO BAPT CONV..	12	1 584	1 893*	19.7	66.8
449 UN METHODIST..	5	403	482*	5.0	17.0
ANSON	82	16 117	20 352*	79.6	100.0
005 AME ZION......	15	6 281	8 040	31.5	39.5
081 CATHOLIC......	1	NA	50	0.2	0.2
127 CH GOD (CLEVE)	1	83	103*	0.4	0.5
151 L-D SAINTS....	1	NA	105	0.4	0.5
167 CHS OF CHRIST.	1	30	38	0.1	0.2
193 EPISCOPAL.....	2	239	281	1.1	1.4
349 PENT HOLINESS.	1	61	75*	0.3	0.4
357 PRESB CH US...	4	366	453*	1.8	2.2
419 SO BAPT CONV..	28	6 024	7 454*	29.2	36.6
449 UN METHODIST..	26	2 951	3 652*	14.3	17.9
453 UN PRES CH USA	2	82	101*	0.4	0.5
ASHE	99	10 497	12 626*	56.6	100.0
053 ASSEMB OF GOD.	1	6	11	–	0.1
081 CATHOLIC......	1	NA	90	0.4	0.7
093 CHR CH (DISC).	1	75	115	0.5	0.9
097 CHR CHS&CHS CR	2	130	156*	0.7	1.2
157 CH OF BRETHREN	3	103	124*	0.6	1.0
167 CHS OF CHRIST.	2	75	95	0.4	0.8
193 EPISCOPAL.....	1	246	198	0.9	1.6
283 LUTH--MO SYNOD	1	24	33	0.1	0.3
285 MENNONITE CH..	2	66	79*	0.4	0.6
357 PRESB CH US...	6	379	455*	2.0	3.6
419 SO BAPT CONV..	56	7 330	8 795*	39.4	69.7
449 UN METHODIST..	23	2 063	2 475*	11.1	19.6
AVERY	68	6 566	8 035*	55.8	100.0
081 CATHOLIC......	1	NA	27	0.2	0.3
093 CHR CH (DISC).	2	130	200	1.4	2.5
097 CHR CHS&CHS CR	3	245	295*	2.0	3.7
127 CH GOD (CLEVE)	1	47	57*	0.4	0.7
151 L-D SAINTS....	1	NA	62	0.4	0.8
167 CHS OF CHRIST.	2	20	25	0.2	0.3
193 EPISCOPAL.....	1	1	1	–	–
215 EVAN METH CH..	1	20	24*	0.1	0.3
237 GC MENN BR CHS	1	7	8*	0.1	0.1

NA— Not applicable   *Total adherents estimated from known number of communicant, confirmed, full members.   —Represents a percent less than 0.1.   Percentages may not total due to rounding.

Table 4. Churches and Church Membership by County and Denomination: 1980

County and Denomination	Number of churches	Communicant, confirmed, full members	Total adherents Number	Percent of total population	Percent of total adherents
356 PRESB CH AMER.	2	117	142	1.0	1.8
357 PRESB CH US...	9	684	823*	5.7	10.2
413 S.D.A.........	1	189	227*	1.6	2.8
419 SO BAPT CONV..	31	4 514	5 432*	37.7	67.6
449 UN METHODIST..	12	592	712*	4.9	8.9
BEAUFORT	120	21 547	28 314*	70.3	100.0
005 AME ZION......	21	7 640	9 168	22.8	32.4
053 ASSEMB OF GOD.	2	96	158	0.4	0.6
081 CATHOLIC......	1	NA	279	0.7	1.0
093 CHR CH (DISC).	24	2 001	4 151	10.3	14.7
097 CHR CHS&CHS CR	20	4 204	5 145*	12.8	18.2
101 C.M.E.........	3	1 061	1 298*	3.2	4.6
105 CHRISTIAN REF.	1	120	211	0.5	0.7
127 CH GOD (CLEVE)	8	444	543*	1.3	1.9
167 CHS OF CHRIST.	2	120	152	0.4	0.5
347 PENT FW BAPT..	1	75	92*	0.2	0.3
349 PENT HOLINESS.	9	481	589*	1.5	2.1
356 PRESB CH AMER.	1	71	77	0.2	0.3
357 PRESB CH US...	2	409	501*	1.2	1.8
403 SALVATION ARMY	1	126	200	0.5	0.7
413 S.D.A.........	1	23	28*	0.1	0.1
419 SO BAPT CONV..	10	2 132	2 609*	6.5	9.2
449 UN METHODIST..	13	2 544	3 113*	7.7	11.0
BERTIE	42	7 920	9 741*	46.3	100.0
005 AME ZION......	1	130	199	0.9	2.0
053 ASSEMB OF GOD.	5	582	609	2.9	6.3
093 CHR CH (DISC).	2	107	211	1.0	2.2
349 PENT HOLINESS.	4	296	364*	1.7	3.7
419 SO BAPT CONV..	24	6 394	7 853*	37.4	80.6
449 UN METHODIST..	6	411	505*	2.4	5.2
BLADEN	96	18 149	22 725*	74.6	100.0
005 AME ZION......	20	6 582	8 401*	27.6	37.0
053 ASSEMB OF GOD.	1	7	18	0.1	0.1
081 CATHOLIC......	1	NA	44	0.1	0.2
123 CH GOD (ANDER)	1	20	60	0.2	0.3
127 CH GOD (CLEVE)	2	83	102*	0.3	0.4
167 CHS OF CHRIST.	1	25	32	0.1	0.1
347 PENT FW BAPT..	8	776	955*	3.1	4.2
349 PENT HOLINESS.	2	89	110*	0.4	0.5
357 PRESB CH US...	7	789	971*	3.2	4.3
413 S.D.A.........	1	61	75*	0.2	0.3
419 SO BAPT CONV..	37	7 748	9 534*	31.3	42.0
449 UN METHODIST..	14	1 930	2 375*	7.8	10.5
453 UN PRES CH USA	1	39	48*	0.2	0.2
BRUNSWICK	80	13 033	16 379*	45.8	100.0
001 ADVENT CHR CH.	1	42	52*	0.1	0.3
005 AME ZION......	9	2 430	2 916	8.2	17.8
053 ASSEMB OF GOD.	1	23	50	0.1	0.3
081 CATHOLIC......	1	NA	271	0.8	1.7
127 CH GOD (CLEVE)	2	107	132*	0.4	0.8
151 L-D SAINTS....	1	NA	133	0.4	0.8
167 CHS OF CHRIST.	1	10	13	-	0.1
281 LUTH CH AMER..	1	114	140	0.4	0.9
347 PENT FW BAPT..	3	174	214*	0.6	1.3
357 PRESB CH US...	5	571	702*	2.0	4.3
419 SO BAPT CONV..	44	7 569	9 306*	26.0	56.8
449 UN METHODIST..	11	1 993	2 450*	6.8	15.0
BUNCOMBE	282	74 271	93 866*	58.3	100.0
005 AME ZION......	8	2 479	3 180	2.0	3.4
017 AMER BAPT ASSN	1	26	26	-	-
019 AMER BAPT USA.	2	575	685*	0.4	0.7
053 ASSEMB OF GOD.	2	392	490	0.3	0.5
081 CATHOLIC......	5	NA	3 320	2.1	3.5
089 CHR & MISS AL.	3	286	456	0.3	0.5
093 CHR CH (DISC).	7	486	659	0.4	0.7
097 CHR CHS&CHS CR	5	263	313*	0.2	0.3
101 C.M.E.........	1	425	506*	0.3	0.5
123 CH GOD (ANDER)	3	99	297	0.2	0.3
127 CH GOD (CLEVE)	12	951	1 132*	0.7	1.2
151 L-D SAINTS....	2	NA	489	0.3	0.5
165 CH OF NAZARENE	2	261	406	0.3	0.4
167 CHS OF CHRIST.	6	385	490	0.3	0.5
193 EPISCOPAL.....	12	2 877	3 818	2.4	4.1
215 EVAN METH CH..	1	64	76*	-	0.1
221 FREE METHODIST	1	10	102	0.1	0.1
226 FRIENDS-USA...	1	57	68*	-	0.1
263 INT FOURSQ GOS	1	?	?	?	?
270 CONSRV JUDAISM	1	79	94*	0.1	0.1
271 REFORM JUDAISM	1	258	307*	0.2	0.3
281 LUTH CH AMER..	2	767	984	0.6	1.0
283 LUTH--MO SYNOD	1	381	468	0.3	0.5
290 METRO COMM CHS	0	10	20	-	-
349 PENT HOLINESS.	3	68	81*	0.1	0.1
353 CHR BRETHREN..	2	150	210	0.1	0.2
356 PRESB CH AMER.	3	321	382	0.2	0.4
357 PRESB CH US...	17	5 069	6 036*	3.8	6.4
403 SALVATION ARMY	1	168	469	0.3	0.5
413 S.D.A.........	4	1 320	1 572*	1.0	1.7
419 SO BAPT CONV..	110	42 716	50 861*	31.6	54.2
435 UNITARIAN-UNIV	1	287	342*	0.2	0.4
443 UN C OF CHRIST	1	130	155*	0.1	0.2
449 UN METHODIST..	56	12 363	14 720*	9.1	15.7
453 UN PRES CH USA	4	548	652*	0.4	0.7
BURKE	152	36 741	45 839*	63.2	100.0

County and Denomination	Number of churches	Communicant, confirmed, full members	Total adherents Number	Percent of total population	Percent of total adherents
001 ADVENT CHR CH.	1	72	87*	0.1	0.2
005 AME ZION......	1	234	349	0.5	0.8
053 ASSEMB OF GOD.	5	339	522	0.7	1.1
081 CATHOLIC......	1	NA	365	0.5	0.8
097 CHR CHS&CHS CR	1	16	19*	-	-
123 CH GOD (ANDER)	3	361	1 083	1.5	2.4
127 CH GOD (CLEVE)	6	870	1 050*	1.4	2.3
151 L-D SAINTS....	1	NA	154	0.2	0.3
167 CHS OF CHRIST.	1	60	80	0.1	0.2
193 EPISCOPAL.....	4	501	703	1.0	1.5
215 EVAN METH CH..	3	233	281*	0.4	0.6
281 LUTH CH AMER..	3	726	913	1.3	2.0
349 PENT HOLINESS.	1	23	28*	-	0.1
356 PRESB CH AMER.	1	11	20	-	-
357 PRESB CH US...	6	1 513	1 826*	2.5	4.0
413 S.D.A.........	3	245	296*	0.4	0.6
419 SO BAPT CONV..	80	25 397	30 653*	42.3	66.9
449 UN METHODIST..	30	6 090	7 350*	10.1	16.0
453 UN PRES CH USA	1	50	60*	0.1	0.1
CABARRUS	201	52 843	67 420*	78.5	100.0
001 ADVENT CHR CH.	2	102	123*	0.1	0.2
005 AME ZION......	26	9 758	12 734	14.8	18.9
053 ASSEMB OF GOD.	2	1 068	2 095	2.4	3.1
055 AS REF PRES CH	1	126	142	0.2	0.2
081 CATHOLIC......	2	NA	837	1.0	1.2
093 CHR CH (DISC).	3	305	470	0.5	0.7
123 CH GOD (ANDER)	2	140	420	0.5	0.6
127 CH GOD (CLEVE)	11	1 191	1 436*	1.7	2.1
165 CH OF NAZARENE	3	291	571	0.7	0.8
167 CHS OF CHRIST.	3	220	280	0.3	0.4
177 CONGR HOL CH..	1	20	24*	-	-
193 EPISCOPAL.....	1	356	451	0.5	0.7
215 EVAN METH CH..	2	222	268*	0.3	0.4
263 INT FOURSQ GOS	2	570	687*	0.8	1.0
281 LUTH CH AMER..	16	4 199	5 396	6.3	8.0
283 LUTH--MO SYNOD	2	450	639	0.7	0.9
349 PENT HOLINESS.	2	92	111*	0.1	0.2
357 PRESB CH US...	15	3 797	4 579*	5.3	6.8
381 REF PRES-EVAN.	1	71	78	0.1	0.1
403 SALVATION ARMY	1	86	167	0.2	0.2
413 S.D.A.........	1	51	62*	0.1	0.1
419 SO BAPT CONV..	58	17 766	21 425*	24.9	31.8
443 UN C OF CHRIST	9	1 584	1 910*	2.2	2.8
449 UN METHODIST..	30	9 698	11 695*	13.6	17.3
453 UN PRES CH USA	5	680	820*	1.0	1.2
CALDWELL	136	32 465	40 332*	59.5	100.0
001 ADVENT CHR CH.	8	1 261	1 539*	2.3	3.8
053 ASSEMB OF GOD.	1	23	40	0.1	0.1
081 CATHOLIC......	1	NA	294	0.4	0.7
097 CHR CHS&CHS CR	1	45	55*	0.1	0.1
121 CH GOD (ABR)..	1	105	128*	0.2	0.3
123 CH GOD (ANDER)	1	100	300	0.4	0.7
127 CH GOD (CLEVE)	8	492	601*	0.9	1.5
151 L-D SAINTS....	1	NA	122	0.2	0.3
167 CHS OF CHRIST.	1	28	36	0.1	0.1
193 EPISCOPAL.....	2	225	307	0.5	0.8
237 GC MENN BR CHS	4	150	183*	0.3	0.5
281 LUTH CH AMER..	5	892	1 153	1.7	2.9
349 PENT HOLINESS.	3	154	188*	0.3	0.5
357 PRESB CH US...	4	979	1 195*	1.8	3.0
413 S.D.A.........	1	62	76*	0.1	0.2
419 SO BAPT CONV..	69	23 041	28 124*	41.5	69.7
443 UN C OF CHRIST	1	154	188*	0.3	0.5
449 UN METHODIST..	23	4 611	5 628*	8.3	14.0
453 UN PRES CH USA	1	143	175*	0.3	0.4
CAMDEN	10	2 109	2 565*	44.0	100.0
097 CHR CHS&CHS CR	1	50	61*	1.0	2.4
419 SO BAPT CONV..	4	1 374	1 671*	28.7	65.1
449 UN METHODIST..	5	685	833*	14.3	32.5
CARTERET	66	13 514	18 293*	44.5	100.0
005 AME ZION......	7	1 786	2 256	5.5	12.3
053 ASSEMB OF GOD.	1	13	20	-	0.1
081 CATHOLIC......	1	NA	1 181	2.9	6.5
093 CHR CH (DISC).	2	169	343	0.8	1.9
127 CH GOD (CLEVE)	4	187	223*	0.5	1.2
151 L-D SAINTS....	2	NA	706	1.7	3.9
167 CHS OF CHRIST.	3	125	159	0.4	0.9
281 LUTH CH AMER..	1	106	115	0.3	0.6
349 PENT HOLINESS.	4	389	465*	1.1	2.5
357 PRESB CH US...	3	605	723*	1.8	3.9
419 SO BAPT CONV..	15	4 809	5 743*	14.0	31.4
443 UN C OF CHRIST	1	58	69*	0.2	0.4
449 UN METHODIST..	22	5 267	6 290*	15.3	34.4
CASWELL	42	4 627	5 817*	28.1	100.0
053 ASSEMB OF GOD.	1	26	40	0.2	0.7
151 L-D SAINTS....	1	NA	192	0.9	3.3
193 EPISCOPAL.....	1	7	10	-	0.2
349 PENT HOLINESS.	1	26	32*	0.2	0.6
357 PRESB CH US...	7	352	427*	2.1	7.3
419 SO BAPT CONV..	13	2 038	2 473*	11.9	42.5
443 UN C OF CHRIST	1	118	143*	0.7	2.5
449 UN METHODIST..	17	2 060	2 500*	12.1	43.0
CATAWBA	187	56 991	74 591*	70.9	100.0

NA—Not applicable *Total adherents estimated from known number of communicant, confirmed, full members. —Represents a percent less than 0.1. Percentages may not total due to rounding.

Table 4. Churches and Church Membership by County and Denomination: 1980

County and Denomination	Number of churches	Communicant, confirmed, full members	Total adherents		
			Number	Percent of total population	Percent of total adherents
001 ADVENT CHR CH.	2	173	210*	0.2	0.3
005 AME ZION......	11	2 140	3 022	2.9	4.1
017 AMER BAPT ASSN	1	30	30	–	–
019 AMER BAPT USA.	1	588	715*	0.7	1.0
029 AMER LUTH CH..	6	2 946	3 974	3.8	5.3
053 ASSEMB OF GOD.	3	106	227	0.2	0.3
081 CATHOLIC......	2	NA	1 273	1.2	1.7
123 CH GOD (ANDER)	2	362	1 086	1.0	1.5
127 CH GOD (CLEVE)	3	246	299*	0.3	0.4
133 CH GOD(7TH)DEN	1	12	15*	–	–
151 L-D SAINTS....	2	NA	615	0.6	0.8
165 CH OF NAZARENE	1	20	64	0.1	0.1
167 CHS OF CHRIST.	3	203	258	0.2	0.3
193 EPISCOPAL.....	3	708	930	0.9	1.2
215 EVAN METH CH..	1	44	54*	0.1	0.1
281 LUTH CH AMER..	21	8 488	10 694	10.2	14.3
283 LUTH--MO SYNOD	13	5 293	7 661	7.3	10.3
285 MENNONITE CH..	3	78	95*	0.1	0.1
349 PENT HOLINESS.	5	452	550*	0.5	0.7
353 CHR BRETHREN..	1	25	25	–	–
357 PRESB CH US...	6	1 847	2 246*	2.1	3.0
403 SALVATION ARMY	1	150	314	0.3	0.4
413 S.D.A.........	1	270	328*	0.3	0.4
419 SO BAPT CONV..	47	19 383	23 575*	22.4	31.6
435 UNITARIAN-UNIV	1	15	18*	–	–
443 UN C OF CHRIST	12	2 732	3 323*	3.2	4.5
449 UN METHODIST..	34	10 680	12 990*	12.3	17.4
CHATHAM	105	19 339	23 878*	71.5	100.0
005 AME ZION......	16	4 708	6 152	18.4	25.8
053 ASSEMB OF GOD.	1	20	28	0.1	0.1
081 CATHOLIC......	1	NA	75	0.2	0.3
101 C.M.E........	2	746	893*	2.7	3.7
123 CH GOD (ANDER)	1	37	111	0.3	0.5
127 CH GOD (CLEVE)	3	76	91*	0.3	0.4
167 CHS OF CHRIST.	1	20	25	0.1	0.1
175 CONGR CHR CHS.	1	72	86*	0.3	0.4
193 EPISCOPAL.....	1	43	71	0.2	0.3
226 FRIENDS-USA...	3	419	501*	1.5	2.1
349 PENT HOLINESS.	1	119	142*	0.4	0.6
353 CHR BRETHREN..	4	210	305	0.9	1.3
357 PRESB CH US...	3	250	299*	0.9	1.3
413 S.D.A.........	1	57	68*	0.2	0.3
419 SO BAPT CONV..	32	7 687	9 198*	27.5	38.5
443 UN C OF CHRIST	5	693	829*	2.5	3.5
449 UN METHODIST..	29	4 182	5 004*	15.0	21.0
CHEROKEE	75	12 149	15 167*	80.1	100.0
081 CATHOLIC......	2	NA	221	1.2	1.5
123 CH GOD (ANDER)	1	63	189	1.0	1.2
127 CH GOD (CLEVE)	3	91	110*	0.6	0.7
167 CHS OF CHRIST.	1	11	14	0.1	0.1
193 EPISCOPAL.....	1	79	123	0.6	0.8
221 FREE METHODIST	1	14	105	0.6	0.7
281 LUTH CH AMER..	1	97	112	0.6	0.7
349 PENT HOLINESS.	1	58	70*	0.4	0.5
357 PRESB CH US...	3	134	162*	0.9	1.1
413 S.D.A.........	1	129	156*	0.8	1.0
419 SO BAPT CONV..	50	10 213	12 378*	65.4	81.6
449 UN METHODIST..	10	1 260	1 527*	8.1	10.1
CHOWAN	35	7 672	9 875*	78.6	100.0
005 AME ZION......	14	2 650	3 408	27.1	34.5
053 ASSEMB OF GOD.	1	78	130	1.0	1.3
081 CATHOLIC......	1	NA	230	1.8	2.3
093 CHR CH (DISC).	2	362	556	4.4	5.6
097 CHR CHS&CHS CR	2	95	115*	0.9	1.2
127 CH GOD (CLEVE)	1	52	63*	0.5	0.6
167 CHS OF CHRIST.	1	40	51	0.4	0.5
349 PENT HOLINESS.	2	166	201*	1.6	2.0
357 PRESB CH US...	1	83	101*	0.8	1.0
419 SO BAPT CONV..	7	3 737	4 525*	36.0	45.8
449 UN METHODIST..	3	409	495*	3.9	5.0
CLAY	35	3 424	4 191*	63.3	100.0
053 ASSEMB OF GOD.	1	41	97	1.5	2.3
081 CATHOLIC......	1	NA	62	0.9	1.5
127 CH GOD (CLEVE)	3	254	303*	4.6	7.2
167 CHS OF CHRIST.	2	43	50	0.8	1.2
193 EPISCOPAL.....	1	57	65	1.0	1.6
357 PRESB CH US...	1	32	38*	0.6	0.9
419 SO BAPT CONV..	17	2 347	2 800*	42.3	66.8
449 UN METHODIST..	9	650	776*	11.7	18.5
CLEVELAND	163	45 940	57 175*	68.5	100.0
005 AME ZION......	5	1 974	2 632	3.2	4.6
053 ASSEMB OF GOD.	1	48	79	0.1	0.1
055 AS REF PRES CH	1	337	385	0.5	0.7
081 CATHOLIC......	2	NA	504	0.6	0.9
101 C.M.E........	1	370	452*	0.5	0.8
127 CH GOD (CLEVE)	3	220	269*	0.3	0.5
151 L-D SAINTS....	1	NA	86	0.1	0.2
165 CH OF NAZARENE	2	132	227	0.3	0.4
167 CHS OF CHRIST.	1	90	115	0.1	0.2
193 EPISCOPAL.....	2	222	376	0.5	0.7
215 EVAN METH CH..	1	69	84*	0.1	0.1
263 INT FOURSQ GOS	1	59	72*	0.1	0.1
281 LUTH CH AMER..	3	923	1 161	1.4	2.0
349 PENT HOLINESS.	1	57	70*	0.1	0.1
357 PRESB CH US...	5	1 242	1 517*	1.8	2.7

County and Denomination	Number of churches	Communicant, confirmed, full members	Total adherents		
			Number	Percent of total population	Percent of total adherents
403 SALVATION ARMY	1	123	194	0.2	0.3
413 S.D.A.........	1	66	81*	0.1	0.1
419 SO BAPT CONV..	88	31 854	38 910*	46.6	68.1
443 UN C OF CHRIST	1	71	87*	0.1	0.2
449 UN METHODIST..	40	7 985	9 754*	11.7	17.1
453 UN PRES CH USA	2	98	120*	0.1	0.2
COLUMBUS	125	26 442	32 713*	64.1	100.0
001 ADVENT CHR CH.	1	60	74*	0.1	0.2
005 AME ZION......	9	4 715	5 658	11.1	17.3
081 CATHOLIC......	2	NA	215	0.4	0.7
089 CHR & MISS AL.	1	54	100	0.2	0.3
127 CH GOD (CLEVE)	7	420	515*	1.0	1.6
151 L-D SAINTS....	1	NA	149	0.3	0.5
167 CHS OF CHRIST.	1	72	92	0.2	0.3
347 PENT FW BAPT..	5	504	618*	1.2	1.9
349 PENT HOLINESS.	2	291	357*	0.7	1.1
357 PRESB CH US...	7	904	1 109*	2.2	3.4
413 S.D.A.........	3	94	115*	0.2	0.4
419 SO BAPT CONV..	65	15 748	19 319*	37.9	59.1
449 UN METHODIST..	20	3 533	4 334*	8.5	13.2
453 UN PRES CH USA	1	47	58*	0.1	0.2
CRAVEN	110	27 829	37 616*	52.9	100.0
005 AME ZION......	15	11 495	13 794	19.4	36.7
053 ASSEMB OF GOD.	2	161	380	0.5	1.0
081 CATHOLIC......	2	NA	2 675	3.8	7.1
093 CHR CH (DISC).	17	1 642	2 485	3.5	6.6
097 CHR CHS&CHS CR	5	305	376*	0.5	1.0
127 CH GOD (CLEVE)	5	222	274*	0.4	0.7
151 L-D SAINTS....	1	NA	329	0.5	0.9
165 CH OF NAZARENE	3	48	87	0.1	0.2
167 CHS OF CHRIST.	3	169	205	0.3	0.5
263 INT FOURSQ GOS	1	13	16*	–	–
271 REFORM JUDAISM	1	32	39*	0.1	0.1
281 LUTH CH AMER..	2	154	189	0.3	0.5
283 LUTH--MO SYNOD	1	134	173	0.2	0.5
347 PENT FW BAPT..	1	64	79*	0.1	0.2
349 PENT HOLINESS.	6	479	590*	0.8	1.6
356 PRESB CH AMER.	1	242	274	0.4	0.7
357 PRESB CH US...	5	1 063	1 310*	1.8	3.5
403 SALVATION ARMY	1	114	181	0.3	0.5
413 S.D.A.........	2	317	391*	0.6	1.0
419 SO BAPT CONV..	12	5 079	6 258*	8.8	16.6
443 UN C OF CHRIST	3	400	493*	0.7	1.3
449 UN METHODIST..	20	5 629	6 935*	9.8	18.4
453 UN PRES CH USA	1	67	83*	0.1	0.2
CUMBERLAND	200	59 540	81 769*	33.1	100.0
001 ADVENT CHR CH.	3	384	476*	0.2	0.6
005 AME ZION......	21	11 701	15 122	6.1	18.5
053 ASSEMB OF GOD.	4	688	707	0.3	0.9
081 CATHOLIC......	3	NA	5 100	2.1	6.2
089 CHR & MISS AL.	1	94	139	0.1	0.2
093 CHR CH (DISC).	8	527	735	0.3	0.9
127 CH GOD (CLEVE)	23	1 813	2 246*	0.9	2.7
151 L-D SAINTS....	3	NA	1 617	0.7	2.0
165 CH OF NAZARENE	1	130	229	0.1	0.3
167 CHS OF CHRIST.	3	400	509	0.2	0.6
281 LUTH CH AMER..	2	645	977	0.4	1.2
283 LUTH--MO SYNOD	1	0	292	0.1	0.4
290 METRO COMM CHS	1	35	70	–	0.1
347 PENT FW BAPT..	3	185	229*	0.1	0.3
349 PENT HOLINESS.	8	1 414	1 752*	0.7	2.1
353 CHR BRETHREN..	2	65	125	0.1	0.2
356 PRESB CH AMER.	1	29	33	–	–
357 PRESB CH US...	22	5 117	6 339*	2.6	7.8
403 SALVATION ARMY	1	133	251	0.1	0.3
413 S.D.A.........	1	129	160*	0.1	0.2
419 SO BAPT CONV..	57	25 554	31 657*	12.8	38.7
443 UN C OF CHRIST	3	261	323*	0.1	0.4
449 UN METHODIST..	26	10 061	12 464*	5.0	15.2
453 UN PRES CH USA	2	175	217*	0.1	0.3
CURRITUCK	27	4 146	5 316*	47.9	100.0
005 AME ZION......	4	765	1 020	9.2	19.2
053 ASSEMB OF GOD.	2	79	167	1.5	3.1
093 CHR CH (DISC).	3	53	105	0.9	2.0
097 CHR CHS&CHS CR	2	250	303*	2.7	5.7
151 L-D SAINTS....	1	NA	91	0.8	1.7
419 SO BAPT CONV..	8	1 880	2 276*	20.5	42.8
449 UN METHODIST..	7	1 119	1 354*	12.2	25.5
DARE	32	4 015	11 871*	88.7	100.0
005 AME ZION......	0	0	6 535	48.9	55.1
053 ASSEMB OF GOD.	8	548	887	6.6	7.5
081 CATHOLIC......	1	NA	218	1.6	1.8
093 CHR CH (DISC).	1	120	200	1.5	1.7
097 CHR CHS&CHS CR	1	50	59*	0.4	0.5
127 CH GOD (CLEVE)	1	31	36*	0.3	0.3
151 L-D SAINTS....	1	NA	103	0.8	0.9
357 PRESB CH US...	1	42	49*	0.4	0.4
419 SO BAPT CONV..	4	615	722*	5.4	6.1
449 UN METHODIST..	14	2 609	3 062*	22.9	25.8
DAVIDSON	174	45 921	56 944*	50.3	100.0
005 AME ZION......	5	1 248	1 667	1.5	2.9
053 ASSEMB OF GOD.	2	115	193	0.2	0.3
081 CATHOLIC......	2	NA	494	0.4	0.9

NA— Not applicable   *Total adherents estimated from known number of communicant, confirmed, full members.   —Represents a percent less than 0.1.   Percentages may not total due to rounding.

Table 4. Churches and Church Membership by County and Denomination: 1980

County and Denomination	Number of churches	Communicant, confirmed, full members	Total adherents Number	Percent of total population	Percent of total adherents
089 CHR & MISS AL.	2	254	299	0.3	0.5
101 C.M.E.........	1	68	83*	0.1	0.1
127 CH GOD (CLEVE)	5	458	556*	0.5	1.0
157 CH OF BRETHREN	1	87	106*	0.1	0.2
165 CH OF NAZARENE	1	24	28	–	–
167 CHS OF CHRIST.	2	255	325	0.3	0.6
177 CONGR HOL CH.	3	93	113*	0.1	0.2
193 EPISCOPAL.....	2	250	487	0.4	0.9
215 EVAN METH CH..	2	43	52*	–	0.1
263 INT FOURSQ GOS	2	55	67*	0.1	0.1
281 LUTH CH AMER..	9	2 087	2 678	2.4	4.7
295 MORAV CH–SOUTH	2	206	247	0.2	0.4
349 PENT HOLINESS.	2	156	189*	0.2	0.3
357 PRESB CH US...	4	1 174	1 426*	1.3	2.5
381 REF PRES–EVAN.	1	103	118	0.1	0.2
403 SALVATION ARMY	2	142	328	0.3	0.6
413 S.D.A.........	2	276	335*	0.3	0.6
419 SO BAPT CONV..	43	16 065	19 510*	17.2	34.3
443 UN C OF CHRIST	17	5 665	6 875*	6.1	12.1
449 UN METHODIST..	61	16 991	20 634*	18.2	36.2
453 UN PRES CH USA	1	110	134*	0.1	0.2
DAVIE	59	11 004	13 716*	55.8	100.0
005 AME ZION......	4	720	960	3.9	7.0
053 ASSEMB OF GOD.	1	11	17	0.1	0.1
081 CATHOLIC......	1	NA	192	0.8	1.4
101 C.M.E.........	1	405	493*	2.0	3.6
127 CH GOD (CLEVE)	2	65	79*	0.3	0.6
167 CHS OF CHRIST.	3	340	433	1.8	3.2
193 EPISCOPAL.....	2	126	138	0.6	1.0
247 HOLINESS CH...	1	10	10	–	0.1
281 LUTH CH AMER..	1	80	113	0.5	0.8
295 MORAV CH–SOUTH	1	283	380	1.5	2.8
357 PRESB CH US...	4	988	1 202*	4.9	8.8
413 S.D.A.........	1	38	46*	0.2	0.3
419 SO BAPT CONV..	15	4 333	5 269*	21.4	38.4
449 UN METHODIST..	21	3 560	4 329*	17.6	31.6
453 UN PRES CH USA	1	45	55*	0.2	0.4
DUPLIN	108	15 756	20 267*	49.5	100.0
005 AME ZION......	5	655	786	1.9	3.9
053 ASSEMB OF GOD.	1	98	140	0.3	0.7
081 CATHOLIC......	1	NA	103	0.3	0.5
093 CHR CH (DISC).	8	600	923	2.3	4.6
127 CH GOD (CLEVE)	4	186	228*	0.6	1.1
151 L–D SAINTS....	3	NA	673	1.6	3.3
167 CHS OF CHRIST.	1	30	38	0.1	0.2
226 FRIENDS–USA...	1	107	131*	0.3	0.6
347 PENT FW BAPT..	19	1 793	2 196*	5.4	10.8
349 PENT HOLINESS.	4	494	605*	1.5	3.0
357 PRESB CH US...	17	2 098	2 570*	6.3	12.7
419 SO BAPT CONV..	27	7 215	8 837*	21.6	43.6
449 UN METHODIST..	17	2 480	3 037*	7.4	15.0
DURHAM	135	55 039	71 040*	46.5	100.0
001 ADVENT CHR CH.	1	127	151*	0.1	0.2
005 AME ZION......	5	5 228	6 535	4.3	9.2
019 AMER BAPT USA.	4	2 506	2 987*	2.0	4.2
029 AMER LUTH CH..	1	111	168	0.1	0.2
053 ASSEMB OF GOD.	2	180	351	0.2	0.5
081 CATHOLIC......	3	NA	2 994	2.0	4.2
089 CHR & MISS AL.	2	222	315	0.2	0.4
093 CHR CH (DISC).	2	171	240	0.2	0.3
097 CHR CHS&CHS CR	1	150	179*	0.1	0.3
101 C.M.E.........	2	1 740	2 074*	1.4	2.9
123 CH GOD (ANDER)	1	12	36	–	0.1
127 CH GOD (CLEVE)	2	254	303*	0.2	0.4
151 L–D SAINTS....	1	NA	486	0.3	0.7
165 CH OF NAZARENE	1	54	86	0.1	0.1
167 CHS OF CHRIST.	3	263	330	0.2	0.5
193 EPISCOPAL.....	7	1 653	2 091*	1.4	2.9
226 FRIENDS–USA...	1	33	39*	–	0.1
270 CONSRV JUDAISM	1	110	131*	0.1	0.2
271 REFORM JUDAISM	1	372	443*	0.3	0.6
281 LUTH CH AMER..	3	670	918	0.6	1.3
283 LUTH––MO SYNOD	1	223	271	0.2	0.4
285 MENNONITE CH..	1	29	35*	–	–
290 METRO COMM CHS	0	10	20	–	–
349 PENT HOLINESS.	2	324	386*	0.3	0.5
353 CHR BRETHREN..	2	305	715	0.5	1.0
356 PRESB CH AMER.	1	155	160	0.1	0.2
357 PRESB CH US...	7	2 577	3 072*	2.0	4.3
381 REF PRES–EVAN.	1	45	55	–	0.1
403 SALVATION ARMY	1	137	916	0.6	1.3
413 S.D.A.........	2	292	348*	0.2	0.5
419 SO BAPT CONV..	37	24 022	28 633*	18.7	40.3
435 UNITARIAN–UNIV	1	141	168*	0.1	0.2
443 UN C OF CHRIST	5	1 087	1 296*	0.8	1.8
449 UN METHODIST..	29	11 627	13 859*	9.1	19.5
453 UN PRES CH USA	1	209	249*	0.2	0.4
EDGECOMBE	79	16 710	21 312*	38.1	100.0
001 ADVENT CHR CH.	1	23	28*	0.1	0.1
005 AME ZION......	4	2 425	3 108	5.6	14.6
019 AMER BAPT USA.	1	380	468*	0.8	2.2
053 ASSEMB OF GOD.	2	152	170	0.3	0.8
081 CATHOLIC......	1	NA	84	0.2	0.4
093 CHR CH (DISC).	4	740	1 040	1.9	4.9
097 CHR CHS&CHS CR	2	185	228*	0.4	1.1
127 CH GOD (CLEVE)	6	402	495*	0.9	2.3
151 L–D SAINTS....	2	NA	313	0.6	1.5

County and Denomination	Number of churches	Communicant, confirmed, full members	Total adherents Number	Percent of total population	Percent of total adherents
167 CHS OF CHRIST.	2	61	78	0.1	0.4
193 EPISCOPAL.....	7	936	1 197	2.1	5.6
271 REFORM JUDAISM	1	72	89*	0.2	0.4
281 LUTH CH AMER..	1	283	375	0.7	1.8
349 PENT HOLINESS.	4	633	780*	1.4	3.7
353 CHR BRETHREN..	1	25	50	0.1	0.2
357 PRESB CH US...	8	1 305	1 608*	2.9	7.5
413 S.D.A.........	1	33	41*	0.1	0.2
419 SO BAPT CONV..	21	7 129	8 786*	15.7	41.2
435 UNITARIAN–UNIV	1	60	74*	0.1	0.3
449 UN METHODIST..	9	1 866	2 300*	4.1	10.8
FORSYTH	292	100 746	129 493*	53.1	100.0
005 AME ZION......	11	8 140	9 768	4.0	7.5
019 AMER BAPT USA.	1	715	854*	0.4	0.7
029 AMER LUTH CH..	1	68	95	–	0.1
053 ASSEMB OF GOD.	4	387	520	0.2	0.4
055 AS REF PRES CH	1	28	33	–	–
081 CATHOLIC......	3	NA	6 660	2.7	5.1
089 CHR & MISS AL.	3	621	737	0.3	0.6
093 CHR CH (DISC).	10	2 068	3 110	1.3	2.4
097 CHR CHS&CHS CR	10	1 858	2 219*	0.9	1.7
101 C.M.E.........	6	3 710	4 431*	1.8	3.4
123 CH GOD (ANDER)	2	52	156	0.1	0.1
127 CH GOD (CLEVE)	3	288	344*	0.1	0.3
151 L–D SAINTS....	2	NA	789	0.3	0.6
157 CH OF BRETHREN	1	264	315*	0.1	0.2
165 CH OF NAZARENE	2	103	123	0.1	0.1
167 CHS OF CHRIST.	15	1 498	1 907	0.8	1.5
193 EPISCOPAL.....	5	2 459	3 177	1.3	2.5
215 EVAN METH CH..	1	55	66*	–	0.1
226 FRIENDS–USA...	4	856	1 022*	0.4	0.8
247 HOLINESS CH...	4	547	547	0.2	0.4
270 CONSRV JUDAISM	1	18	21*	–	–
271 REFORM JUDAISM	1	196	234*	0.1	0.2
281 LUTH CH AMER..	5	1 773	2 137	0.9	1.7
283 LUTH––MO SYNOD	3	613	809	0.3	0.6
295 MORAV CH–SOUTH	31	13 184	16 023	6.6	12.4
349 PENT HOLINESS.	8	664	793*	0.3	0.6
353 CHR BRETHREN..	3	170	310	0.1	0.2
357 PRESB CH US...	12	5 437	6 493*	2.7	5.0
403 SALVATION ARMY	2	176	355	0.1	0.3
413 S.D.A.........	3	1 005	1 200*	0.5	0.9
419 SO BAPT CONV..	60	29 961	35 783*	14.7	27.6
435 UNITARIAN–UNIV	1	104	124*	0.1	0.1
443 UN C OF CHRIST	10	1 309	1 563*	0.6	1.2
449 UN METHODIST..	61	21 863	26 111*	10.7	20.2
453 UN PRES CH USA	2	556	664*	0.3	0.5
FRANKLIN	61	12 975	15 803*	52.6	100.0
005 AME ZION......	3	298	451	1.5	2.9
093 CHR CH (DISC).	2	185	284	0.9	1.8
127 CH GOD (CLEVE)	1	71	85*	0.3	0.5
193 EPISCOPAL.....	2	134	209	0.7	1.3
349 PENT HOLINESS.	1	78	94*	0.3	0.6
419 SO BAPT CONV..	31	9 459	11 374*	37.8	72.0
443 UN C OF CHRIST	9	999	1 201*	4.0	7.6
449 UN METHODIST..	10	1 621	1 949*	6.5	12.3
453 UN PRES CH USA	2	130	156*	0.5	1.0
GASTON	272	79 794	102 399*	63.0	100.0
005 AME ZION......	26	7 676	9 714	6.0	9.5
053 ASSEMB OF GOD.	6	721	1 215	0.7	1.2
055 AS REF PRES CH	6	1 631	1 870	1.2	1.8
081 CATHOLIC......	3	NA	2 224	1.4	2.2
127 CH GOD (CLEVE)	33	3 631	4 441*	2.7	4.3
151 L–D SAINTS....	1	NA	398	0.2	0.4
165 CH OF NAZARENE	2	130	309	0.2	0.3
167 CHS OF CHRIST.	2	170	216	0.1	0.2
177 CONGR HOL CH.	2	57	70*	–	0.1
193 EPISCOPAL.....	4	602	806	0.5	0.8
263 INT FOURSQ GOS	4	862	1 054*	0.6	1.0
271 REFORM JUDAISM	1	170	208*	0.1	0.2
281 LUTH CH AMER..	15	4 742	5 995	3.7	5.9
283 LUTH––MO SYNOD	1	90	110	0.1	0.1
347 PENT FW BAPT..	1	85	104*	0.1	0.1
349 PENT HOLINESS.	3	336	411*	0.3	0.4
353 CHR BRETHREN..	1	25	25	–	–
356 PRESB CH AMER.	5	716	770	0.5	0.8
357 PRESB CH US...	18	5 167	6 320*	3.9	6.2
403 SALVATION ARMY	1	209	1 586	1.0	1.5
419 SO BAPT CONV..	97	41 303	50 522*	31.1	49.3
449 UN METHODIST..	38	11 242	13 751*	8.5	13.4
453 UN PRES CH USA	2	229	280*	0.2	0.3
GATES	19	3 896	4 753*	53.6	100.0
005 AME ZION......	1	208	323	3.6	6.8
053 ASSEMB OF GOD.	1	25	28	0.3	0.6
419 SO BAPT CONV..	9	2 526	3 036*	34.2	63.9
443 UN C OF CHRIST	2	378	454*	5.1	9.6
449 UN METHODIST..	6	759	912*	10.3	19.2
GRAHAM	20	4 385	5 353*	74.2	100.0
127 CH GOD (CLEVE)	2	43	53*	0.7	1.0
193 EPISCOPAL.....	1	31	31	0.4	0.6
419 SO BAPT CONV..	16	4 114	5 028*	69.7	93.9
449 UN METHODIST..	1	197	241*	3.3	4.5
GRANVILLE	64	14 902	18 224*	53.6	100.0

NA–Not applicable   *Total adherents estimated from known number of communicant, confirmed, full members.   –Represents a percent less than 0.1.   Percentages may not total due to rounding.

Table 4. Churches and Church Membership by County and Denomination: 1980

County and Denomination	Number of churches	Communicant, confirmed, full members	Total adherents		
			Number	Percent of total population	Percent of total adherents
005 AME ZION......	5	1 140	1 520	4.5	8.3
081 CATHOLIC......	2	NA	136	0.4	0.7
127 CH GOD (CLEVE)	2	66	79*	0.2	0.4
193 EPISCOPAL.....	2	339	429	1.3	2.4
357 PRESB CH US...	6	425	511*	1.5	2.8
419 SO BAPT CONV..	28	9 987	12 008*	35.3	65.9
443 UN C OF CHRIST	3	162	195*	0.6	1.1
449 UN METHODIST..	15	2 683	3 226*	9.5	17.7
453 UN PRES CH USA	1	100	120*	0.4	0.7
GREENE	31	4 627	5 738*	35.6	100.0
005 AME ZION......	3	965	1 158	7.2	20.2
066 BIBLE CH OF CR	1	115	141*	0.9	2.5
093 CHR CH (DISC).	5	295	445	2.8	7.8
127 CH GOD (CLEVE)	1	?	?	?	?
347 PENT FW BAPT..	2	533	655*	4.1	11.4
349 PENT HOLINESS.	6	435	534*	3.3	9.3
357 PRESB CH US...	1	45	55*	0.3	1.0
419 SO BAPT CONV..	2	505	620*	3.8	10.8
449 UN METHODIST..	9	1 684	2 069*	12.8	36.1
453 UN PRES CH USA	1	50	61*	0.4	1.1
GUILFORD	335	131 675	170 911*	53.9	100.0
001 ADVENT CHR CH.	1	41	49*	-	-
005 AME ZION......	8	13 345	16 014	5.0	9.4
029 AMER LUTH CH..	1	171	212	0.1	0.1
053 ASSEMB OF GOD.	6	364	610	0.2	0.4
055 AS REF PRES CH	1	?	?	?	?
081 CATHOLIC......	7	NA	7 466	2.4	4.4
089 CHR & MISS AL.	3	340	498	0.2	0.3
093 CHR CH (DISC).	4	654	988	0.3	0.6
097 CHR CHS&CHS CR	4	940	1 125*	0.4	0.7
101 C.M.E........	2	1 281	1 534*	0.5	0.9
123 CH GOD (ANDER)	3	215	645	0.2	0.4
127 CH GOD (CLEVE)	9	606	725*	0.2	0.4
151 L-D SAINTS....	4	NA	1 707	0.5	1.0
165 CH OF NAZARENE	8	662	1 065	0.3	0.6
167 CHS OF CHRIST.	6	666	857	0.3	0.5
193 EPISCOPAL.....	9	3 976	5 553	1.8	3.2
215 EVAN METH CH..	3	167	200*	0.1	0.1
226 FRIENDS-USA...	17	4 241	5 077*	1.6	3.0
247 HOLINESS CH...	3	297	297	0.1	0.2
263 INT FOURSQ GOS	1	268	321*	0.1	0.2
270 CONSRV JUDAISM	3	322	385*	0.1	0.2
271 REFORM JUDAISM	1	640	766*	0.2	0.4
281 LUTH CH AMER..	10	3 434	4 495	1.4	2.6
283 LUTH--MO SYNOD	6	872	1 132	0.4	0.7
290 METRO COMM CHS	0	20	40	-	-
295 MORAV CH-SOUTH	2	552	700	0.2	0.4
349 PENT HOLINESS.	8	808	967*	0.3	0.6
353 CHR BRETHREN..	1	450	650	0.2	0.4
356 PRESB CH AMER.	1	25	42	-	-
357 PRESB CH US...	24	12 723	15 231*	4.8	8.9
403 SALVATION ARMY	1	333	1 885	0.6	1.1
413 S.D.A........	3	1 109	1 328*	0.4	0.8
419 SO BAPT CONV..	73	41 433	49 600*	15.6	29.0
435 UNITARIAN-UNIV	1	143	171*	0.1	0.1
443 UN C OF CHRIST	16	4 229	5 063*	1.6	3.0
449 UN METHODIST..	82	35 731	42 774*	13.5	25.0
453 UN PRES CH USA	3	617	739*	0.2	0.4
HALIFAX	84	17 097	21 358*	38.6	100.0
053 ASSEMB OF GOD.	1	6	6	-	-
081 CATHOLIC......	2	NA	289	0.5	1.4
097 CHR CHS&CHS CR	6	1 163	1 425*	2.6	6.7
127 CH GOD (CLEVE)	4	346	424*	0.8	2.0
151 L-D SAINTS....	1	NA	187	0.3	0.9
165 CH OF NAZARENE	2	?	?	?	?
167 CHS OF CHRIST.	1	25	32	0.1	0.1
193 EPISCOPAL.....	7	697	792	1.4	3.7
271 REFORM JUDAISM	1	42	51*	0.1	0.2
349 PENT HOLINESS.	6	733	898*	1.6	4.2
357 PRESB CH US...	3	410	502*	0.9	2.4
413 S.D.A........	1	55	67*	0.1	0.3
419 SO BAPT CONV..	24	8 210	10 058*	18.2	47.1
443 UN C OF CHRIST	2	157	192*	0.3	0.9
449 UN METHODIST..	23	5 253	6 435*	11.6	30.1
HARNETT	119	25 510	31 984*	53.7	100.0
001 ADVENT CHR CH.	3	488	593*	1.0	1.9
005 AME ZION......	17	4 415	5 876	9.9	18.4
053 ASSEMB OF GOD.	2	205	310	0.5	1.0
081 CATHOLIC......	1	NA	213	0.4	0.7
093 CHR CH (DISC).	3	297	382	0.6	1.2
101 C.M.E........	1	158	192*	0.3	0.6
127 CH GOD (CLEVE)	6	646	786*	1.3	2.5
151 L-D SAINTS....	1	NA	169	0.3	0.5
193 EPISCOPAL.....	1	176	205	0.3	0.6
226 FRIENDS-USA...	1	151	184*	0.3	0.6
347 PENT FW BAPT..	10	1 314	1 598*	2.7	5.0
349 PENT HOLINESS.	3	336	409*	0.7	1.3
357 PRESB CH US...	18	2 623	3 190*	5.4	10.0
413 S.D.A........	2	84	102*	0.2	0.3
419 SO BAPT CONV..	30	10 815	13 152*	22.1	41.1
443 UN C OF CHRIST	1	139	169*	0.3	0.5
449 UN METHODIST..	16	3 527	4 289*	7.2	13.4
453 UN PRES CH USA	3	136	165*	0.3	0.5
HAYWOOD	113	26 611	32 552*	70.0	100.0
053 ASSEMB OF GOD.	1	42	60	0.1	0.2
081 CATHOLIC......	3	NA	393	0.8	1.2
127 CH GOD (CLEVE)	5	279	332*	0.7	1.0
151 L-D SAINTS....	1	NA	132	0.3	0.4
165 CH OF NAZARENE	1	35	82	0.2	0.3
167 CHS OF CHRIST.	2	52	66	0.1	0.2
193 EPISCOPAL.....	2	285	432	0.9	1.3
221 FREE METHODIST	1	30	141	0.3	0.4
283 LUTH--MO SYNOD	1	82	106	0.2	0.3
353 CHR BRETHREN..	1	80	90	0.2	0.3
356 PRESB CH AMER.	2	298	301	0.6	0.9
357 PRESB CH US...	3	314	374*	0.8	1.1
403 SALVATION ARMY	2	103	279	0.6	0.9
413 S.D.A........	1	88	105*	0.2	0.3
419 SO BAPT CONV..	59	19 433	23 126*	49.7	71.0
449 UN METHODIST..	28	5 490	6 533*	14.1	20.1
HENDERSON	96	26 369	33 415*	57.0	100.0
053 ASSEM OF GOD.	1	51	75	0.1	0.2
055 AS REF PRES CH	1	181	204	0.3	0.6
081 CATHOLIC......	1	NA	1 250	2.1	3.7
089 CHR & MISS AL.	1	75	117	0.2	0.4
121 CH GOD (ABR).	1	38	45*	0.1	0.1
127 CH GOD (CLEVE)	3	131	156*	0.3	0.5
151 L-D SAINTS....	1	NA	279	0.5	0.8
164 CH LUTH CONF..	1	38	46	0.1	0.1
165 CH OF NAZARENE	1	370	684	1.2	2.0
167 CHS OF CHRIST.	1	150	191	0.3	0.6
193 EPISCOPAL.....	5	1 622	2 181	3.7	6.5
263 INT FOURSQ GOS	1	11	13*	-	-
270 CONSRV JUDAISM	1	59	70*	0.1	0.2
281 LUTH CH AMER..	1	259	296	0.5	0.9
283 LUTH--MO SYNOD	1	100	125	0.2	0.4
349 PENT HOLINESS.	1	91	108*	0.2	0.3
356 PRESB CH AMER.	1	392	392	0.7	1.2
357 PRESB CH US...	5	1 677	1 995*	3.4	6.0
403 SALVATION ARMY	1	55	118	0.2	0.4
413 S.D.A........	3	1 284	1 528*	2.6	4.6
419 SO BAPT CONV..	50	15 885	18 901*	32.3	56.6
443 UN C OF CHRIST	1	361	430*	0.7	1.3
449 UN METHODIST..	13	3 539	4 211*	7.2	12.6
HERTFORD	40	7 794	9 586*	41.0	100.0
005 AME ZION......	1	105	138	0.6	1.4
053 ASSEMB OF GOD.	2	75	120	0.5	1.3
081 CATHOLIC......	1	NA	76	0.3	0.8
097 CHR CHS&CHS CR	1	72	87*	0.4	0.9
127 CH GOD (CLEVE)	1	13	16*	0.1	0.2
349 PENT HOLINESS.	8	484	588*	2.5	6.1
357 PRESB CH US...	1	129	157*	0.7	1.6
419 SO BAPT CONV..	19	5 835	7 090*	30.3	74.0
449 UN METHODIST..	6	1 081	1 314*	5.6	13.7
HOKE	35	6 631	8 864*	43.5	100.0
005 AME ZION......	5	1 646	2 469	12.1	27.9
081 CATHOLIC......	1	NA	70	0.3	0.8
127 CH GOD (CLEVE)	1	70	89*	0.4	1.0
215 EVAN METH CH..	1	72	91*	0.4	1.0
263 INT FOURSQ GOS	1	23	29*	0.1	0.3
349 PENT HOLINESS.	1	29	37*	0.2	0.4
357 PRESB CH US...	5	1 030	1 307*	6.4	14.7
413 S.D.A........	2	289	367*	1.8	4.1
419 SO BAPT CONV..	12	2 390	3 032*	14.9	34.2
449 UN METHODIST..	5	1 063	1 349*	6.6	15.2
453 UN PRES CH USA	1	19	24*	0.1	0.3
HYDE	38	2 192	2 798*	47.6	100.0
053 ASSEMB OF GOD.	2	34	62	1.1	2.2
093 CHR CH (DISC).	12	351	531	9.0	19.0
097 CHR CHS&CHS CR	6	488	595*	10.1	21.3
167 CHS OF CHRIST.	1	25	32	0.5	1.1
285 MENNONITE CH..	1	62	76*	1.3	2.7
349 PENT HOLINESS.	1	41	50*	0.9	1.8
357 PRESB CH US...	1	53	65*	1.1	2.3
419 SO BAPT CONV..	4	230	280*	4.8	10.0
449 UN METHODIST..	10	908	1 107*	18.8	39.6
IREDELL	195	44 147	55 199*	66.9	100.0
005 AME ZION......	15	4 147	5 404	6.5	9.8
053 ASSEMB OF GOD.	3	102	182	0.3	0.3
055 AS REF PRES CH	7	2 205	2 537	3.1	4.6
081 CATHOLIC......	2	NA	802	1.0	1.5
097 CHR CHS&CHS CR	1	11	13*	-	-
101 C.M.E........	1	373	452*	0.5	0.8
127 CH GOD (CLEVE)	8	584	708*	0.9	1.3
151 L-D SAINTS....	1	NA	340	0.4	0.6
157 CH OF BRETHREN	1	29	35*	-	0.1
165 CH OF NAZARENE	2	179	309	0.4	0.6
167 CHS OF CHRIST.	5	581	719	0.9	1.3
193 EPISCOPAL.....	2	353	426	0.5	0.8
215 EVAN METH CH..	2	122	148*	0.2	0.3
226 FRIENDS-USA...	2	172	209*	0.3	0.4
263 INT FOURSQ GOS	2	212	257*	0.3	0.5
270 CONSRV JUDAISM	1	21	25*	-	-
281 LUTH CH AMER..	7	2 309	2 825	3.4	5.1
283 LUTH--MO SYNOD	1	117	164	0.2	0.3
356 PRESB CH AMER.	2	36	41*	0.1	0.1
357 PRESB CH US...	18	3 416	4 142*	5.0	7.5
403 SALVATION ARMY	1	44	135	0.2	0.2
413 S.D.A........	1	45	55*	0.1	0.1
419 SO BAPT CONV..	53	17 621	21 365*	25.9	38.7

NA—Not applicable   *Total adherents estimated from known number of communicant, confirmed, full members.   —Represents a percent less than 0.1.   Percentages may not total due to rounding.

Table 4. Churches and Church Membership by County and Denomination: 1980

County and Denomination	Number of churches	Communicant, confirmed, full members	Total adherents Number	Percent of total population	Percent of total adherents
443 UN C OF CHRIST	5	312	378*	0.5	0.7
449 UN METHODIST..	47	10 563	12 807*	15.5	23.2
453 UN PRES CH USA	5	593	719*	0.9	1.3
JACKSON	84	12 952	15 591*	60.4	100.0
005 AME ZION......	1	150	223	0.9	1.4
081 CATHOLIC......	3	NA	211	0.8	1.4
127 CH GOD (CLEVE)	5	218	257*	1.0	1.6
167 CHS OF CHRIST.	2	132	168	0.7	1.1
193 EPISCOPAL.....	3	245	314	1.2	2.0
281 LUTH CH AMER..	1	127	173	0.7	1.1
349 PENT HOLINESS.	2	54	64*	0.2	0.4
357 PRESB CH US...	2	168	198*	0.8	1.3
413 S.D.A.........	1	54	64*	0.2	0.4
419 SO BAPT CONV..	51	10 184	12 012*	46.5	77.0
449 UN METHODIST..	13	1 617	1 907*	7.4	12.2
JOHNSTON	165	25 738	32 477*	46.0	100.0
001 ADVENT CHR CH.	10	1 664	2 024*	2.9	6.2
005 AME ZION......	3	158	239	0.3	0.7
053 ASSEMB OF GOD.	1	29	60	0.1	0.2
081 CATHOLIC......	2	NA	358	0.5	1.1
093 CHR CH (DISC).	19	1 849	2 751	3.9	8.5
123 CH GOD (ANDER)	1	120	360	0.5	1.1
127 CH GOD (CLEVE)	13	718	873*	1.2	2.7
167 CHS OF CHRIST.	1	9	11	–	–
193 EPISCOPAL.....	1	169	215	0.3	0.7
226 FRIENDS-USA...	1	178	216*	0.3	0.7
347 PENT FW BAPT..	14	1 279	1 555*	2.2	4.8
349 PENT HOLINESS.	11	935	1 137*	1.6	3.5
356 PRESB CH AMER.	1	126	131	0.2	0.4
357 PRESB CH US...	15	1 211	1 473*	2.1	4.5
403 SALVATION ARMY	1	74	134	0.2	0.4
419 SO BAPT CONV..	46	12 636	15 367*	21.8	47.3
443 UN C OF CHRIST	4	566	688*	1.0	2.1
449 UN METHODIST..	20	3 992	4 855*	6.9	14.9
453 UN PRES CH USA	1	25	30*	–	0.1
JONES	32	3 350	4 324*	44.6	100.0
081 CATHOLIC......	1	NA	25	0.3	0.6
093 CHR CH (DISC).	5	453	755	7.8	17.5
097 CHR CHS&CHS CR	1	50	61*	0.6	1.4
347 PENT FW BAPT..	1	46	56*	0.6	1.3
349 PENT HOLINESS.	7	455	557*	5.7	12.9
357 PRESB CH US...	1	103	126*	1.3	2.9
419 SO BAPT CONV..	5	1 141	1 396*	14.4	32.3
443 UN C OF CHRIST	3	148	181*	1.9	4.2
449 UN METHODIST..	8	954	1 167*	12.0	27.0
LEE	76	18 182	23 632*	64.4	100.0
005 AME ZION......	17	4 651	6 076	16.5	25.7
053 ASSEMB OF GOD.	1	71	250	0.7	1.1
081 CATHOLIC......	1	NA	626	1.7	2.6
093 CHR CH (DISC).	2	136	209	0.6	0.9
127 CH GOD (CLEVE)	1	304	370*	1.0	1.6
165 CH OF NAZARENE	1	13	60	0.2	0.3
167 CHS OF CHRIST.	1	30	38	0.1	0.2
175 CONGR CHR CHS.	1	150	183*	0.5	0.8
193 EPISCOPAL.....	1	278	424	1.2	1.8
281 LUTH CH AMER..	1	187	248	0.7	1.0
347 PENT FW BAPT..	1	161	196*	0.5	0.8
349 PENT HOLINESS.	2	209	255*	0.7	1.1
353 CHR BRETHREN..	1	150	275	0.7	1.2
357 PRESB CH US...	13	2 295	2 795*	7.6	11.8
419 SO BAPT CONV..	13	5 015	6 107*	16.6	25.8
443 UN C OF CHRIST	7	875	1 066*	2.9	4.5
449 UN METHODIST..	11	3 345	4 074*	11.1	17.2
453 UN PRES CH USA	1	312	380*	1.0	1.6
LENOIR	98	19 865	27 898*	46.6	100.0
001 ADVENT CHR CH.	1	154	188*	0.3	0.7
005 AME ZION......	10	3 863	5 150	8.6	18.5
053 ASSEMB OF GOD.	1	122	130	0.2	0.5
081 CATHOLIC......	1	NA	741	1.2	2.7
089 CHR & MISS AL.	1	35	50	0.1	0.2
093 CHR CH (DISC).	23	3 654	5 401	9.0	19.4
127 CH GOD (CLEVE)	4	244	298*	0.5	1.1
151 L-D SAINTS....	3	NA	1 097	1.8	3.9
165 CH OF NAZARENE	1	27	73	0.1	0.3
167 CHS OF CHRIST.	1	87	120	0.2	0.4
271 REFORM JUDAISM	1	82	100*	0.2	0.4
281 LUTH CH AMER..	2	141	174	0.3	0.6
283 LUTH--MO SYNOD	1	119	160	0.3	0.6
347 PENT FW BAPT..	1	57	70*	0.1	0.3
349 PENT HOLINESS.	4	515	629*	1.1	2.3
357 PRESB CH US...	8	1 274	1 556*	2.6	5.6
403 SALVATION ARMY	1	184	594	1.0	2.1
413 S.D.A.........	3	339	414*	0.7	1.5
419 SO BAPT CONV..	14	4 859	5 934*	9.9	21.3
435 UNITARIAN-UNIV	1	30	37*	0.1	0.1
443 UN C OF CHRIST	1	111	136*	0.2	0.5
449 UN METHODIST..	14	3 908	4 773*	8.0	17.1
453 UN PRES CH USA	1	60	73*	0.1	0.3
LINCOLN	99	21 854	27 149*	64.1	100.0
005 AME ZION......	3	977	1 178	2.8	4.3
053 ASSEMB OF GOD.	1	25	54	0.1	0.2
081 CATHOLIC......	1	NA	375	0.9	1.4
093 CHR CH (DISC).	1	76	117	0.3	0.4

County and Denomination	Number of churches	Communicant, confirmed, full members	Total adherents Number	Percent of total population	Percent of total adherents
127 CH GOD (CLEVE)	2	218	266*	0.6	1.0
167 CHS OF CHRIST.	1	30	38	0.1	0.1
193 EPISCOPAL.....	3	201	355	0.8	1.3
215 EVAN METH CH..	1	32	39*	0.1	0.1
263 INT FOURSQ GOS	1	30	37*	0.1	0.1
281 LUTH CH AMER..	9	2 369	2 834	6.7	10.4
283 LUTH--MO SYNOD	1	24	49	0.1	0.2
349 PENT HOLINESS.	1	69	84*	0.2	0.3
356 PRESB CH AMER.	1	220	248	0.6	0.9
357 PRESB CH US...	3	579	707*	1.7	2.6
419 SO BAPT CONV..	33	9 878	12 065*	28.5	44.4
443 UN C OF CHRIST	1	219	267*	0.6	1.0
449 UN METHODIST..	35	6 890	8 415*	19.9	31.0
453 UN PRES CH USA	1	17	21*	–	0.1
MC DOWELL	89	15 081	18 905*	53.8	100.0
005 AME ZION......	1	272	408	1.2	2.2
053 ASSEMB OF GOD.	1	18	39	0.1	0.2
081 CATHOLIC......	1	NA	206	0.6	1.1
097 CHR CHS&CHS CR	1	75	92*	0.3	0.5
127 CH GOD (CLEVE)	5	324	395*	1.1	2.1
151 L-D SAINTS....	1	180	180	0.5	1.0
167 CHS OF CHRIST.	3	120	153	0.4	0.8
193 EPISCOPAL.....	1	47	85	0.2	0.4
283 LUTH--MO SYNOD	1	75	98	0.3	0.5
349 PENT HOLINESS.	5	334	408*	1.2	2.2
356 PRESB CH AMER.	3	222	252	0.7	1.3
357 PRESB CH US...	5	530	647*	1.8	3.4
413 S.D.A.........	1	104	127*	0.4	0.7
419 SO BAPT CONV..	41	10 449	12 751*	36.3	67.4
449 UN METHODIST..	19	2 511	3 064*	8.7	16.2
MACON	88	12 483	15 228*	75.5	100.0
053 ASSEMB OF GOD.	4	304	638	3.2	4.2
081 CATHOLIC......	2	NA	342	1.7	2.2
127 CH GOD (CLEVE)	6	284	333*	1.7	2.2
151 L-D SAINTS....	2	NA	161	0.8	1.1
167 CHS OF CHRIST.	2	41	55	0.3	0.4
193 EPISCOPAL.....	4	462	350	1.7	2.3
283 LUTH--MO SYNOD	1	68	71	0.4	0.5
357 PRESB CH US...	3	474	556*	2.8	3.7
413 S.D.A.........	1	80	94*	0.5	0.6
419 SO BAPT CONV..	45	8 680	10 178*	50.4	66.8
435 UNITARIAN-UNIV	1	26	30*	0.1	0.2
449 UN METHODIST..	17	2 064	2 420*	12.0	15.9
MADISON	80	9 998	12 666*	75.3	100.0
081 CATHOLIC......	2	NA	45	0.3	0.4
097 CHR CHS&CHS CR	2	53	63*	0.4	0.5
123 CH GOD (ANDER)	8	386	1 158	6.9	9.1
127 CH GOD (CLEVE)	1	16	19*	0.1	0.2
403 SALVATION ARMY	1	75	109	0.6	0.9
419 SO BAPT CONV..	52	8 625	10 269*	61.0	81.1
449 UN METHODIST..	10	636	757*	4.5	6.0
453 UN PRES CH USA	4	207	246*	1.5	1.9
MARTIN	71	11 055	15 565*	60.0	100.0
005 AME ZION......	5	1 095	1 460	5.6	9.4
053 ASSEMB OF GOD.	1	33	60	0.2	0.4
081 CATHOLIC......	1	NA	56	0.2	0.4
093 CHR CH (DISC).	17	1 585	3 774	14.5	24.2
097 CHR CHS&CHS CR	13	2 597	3 180*	12.3	20.4
127 CH GOD (CLEVE)	3	77	94*	0.4	0.6
347 PENT FW BAPT..	1	55	67*	0.3	0.4
349 PENT HOLINESS.	6	582	713*	2.7	4.6
357 PRESB CH US...	3	283	347*	1.3	2.2
419 SO BAPT CONV..	11	3 402	4 166*	16.1	26.8
449 UN METHODIST..	10	1 346	1 648*	6.4	10.6
MECKLENBURG	385	185 742	245 505*	60.7	100.0
001 ADVENT CHR CH.	2	357	431*	0.1	0.2
005 AME ZION......	37	32 680	39 794	9.8	16.2
017 AMER BAPT ASSN	1	15	15	–	–
019 AMER BAPT USA.	7	4 992	6 031*	1.5	2.5
029 AMER LUTH CH..	1	141	189	–	0.1
053 ASSEMB OF GOD.	6	1 210	1 826	0.5	0.7
055 AS REF PRES CH	13	3 410	3 803	0.9	1.5
081 CATHOLIC......	9	NA	14 891	3.7	6.1
089 CHR & MISS AL.	3	280	425	0.1	0.2
093 CHR CH (DISC).	3	562	922	0.2	0.4
097 CHR CHS&CHS CR	2	256	309*	0.1	0.1
101 C.M.E.	3	2 132	2 576*	0.6	1.0
123 CH GOD (ANDER)	3	290	870	0.2	0.4
127 CH GOD (CLEVE)	14	1 974	2 385*	0.6	1.0
151 L-D SAINTS....	3	NA	1 189	0.3	0.5
165 CH OF NAZARENE	5	796	1 863	0.5	0.8
167 CHS OF CHRIST.	8	890	1 133	0.3	0.5
193 EPISCOPAL.....	12	6 331	9 317	2.3	3.8
226 FRIENDS-USA...	1	50	60*	–	–
244 GRACE BRETHREN	1	14	17*	–	–
263 INT FOURSQ GOS	7	480	580*	0.1	0.2
270 CONSRV JUDAISM	1	193	233*	0.1	0.1
271 REFORM JUDAISM	2	550	664*	0.2	0.3
281 LUTH CH AMER..	12	5 132	6 741	1.7	2.7
283 LUTH--MO SYNOD	4	2 062	2 708	0.7	1.1
290 METRO COMM CHS	1	25	50	–	–
295 MORAV CH-SOUTH	2	497	590	0.1	0.2
349 PENT HOLINESS.	1	103	124*	–	0.1
353 CHR BRETHREN..	1	60	85	–	–
356 PRESB CH AMER.	2	214	259	0.1	0.1

NA— Not applicable   *Total adherents estimated from known number of communicant, confirmed, full members.   —Represents a percent less than 0.1.   Percentages may not total due to rounding.

Table 4. Churches and Church Membership by County and Denomination: 1980

County and Denomination	Number of churches	Communicant, confirmed, full members	Total adherents		
			Number	Percent of total population	Percent of total adherents
357 PRESB CH US...	57	30 061	36 318*	9.0	14.8
381 REF PRES-EVAN.	1	137	176	–	0.1
403 SALVATION ARMY	2	237	669	0.2	0.3
413 S.D.A.......	3	1 899	2 294*	0.6	0.9
419 SO BAPT CONV..	80	51 860	62 654*	15.5	25.5
435 UNITARIAN-UNIV	1	437	528*	0.1	0.2
443 UN C OF CHRIST	5	571	690*	0.2	0.3
449 UN METHODIST..	52	31 219	37 717*	9.3	15.4
453 UN PRES CH USA	17	3 625	4 379*	1.1	1.8
MITCHELL	**61**	**9 435**	**11 338***	**78.6**	**100.0**
053 ASSEMB OF GOD.	1	28	35	0.2	0.3
081 CATHOLIC.....	1	NA	87	0.6	0.8
093 CHR CH (DISC).	1	126	194	1.3	1.7
097 CHR CHS&CHS CR	2	50	59*	0.4	0.5
127 CH GOD (CLEVE)	3	79	94*	0.7	0.8
157 CH OF BRETHREN	3	134	159*	1.1	1.4
167 CHS OF CHRIST.	1	30	38	0.3	0.3
193 EPISCOPAL.....	2	126	173	1.2	1.5
357 PRESB CH US...	6	324	384*	2.7	3.4
419 SO BAPT CONV..	36	8 015	9 495*	65.8	83.7
449 UN METHODIST..	5	523	620*	4.3	5.5
MONTGOMERY	**76**	**11 499**	**14 240***	**63.4**	**100.0**
005 AME ZION......	12	2 861	3 689	16.4	25.9
127 CH GOD (CLEVE)	4	166	203*	0.9	1.4
167 CHS OF CHRIST.	1	15	19	0.1	0.1
349 PENT HOLINESS	3	128	156*	0.7	1.1
357 PRESB CH US...	6	686	838*	3.7	5.9
419 SO BAPT CONV..	26	4 635	5 661*	25.2	39.8
443 UN C OF CHRIST	4	236	288*	1.3	2.0
449 UN METHODIST..	20	2 772	3 386*	15.1	23.8
MOORE	**83**	**13 518**	**18 046***	**35.7**	**100.0**
005 AME ZION......	12	2 887	3 724	7.4	20.6
053 ASSEMB OF GOD.	1	78	135	0.3	0.7
081 CATHOLIC......	2	NA	1 383	2.7	7.7
127 CH GOD (CLEVE)	4	121	145*	0.3	0.8
151 L-D SAINTS....	1	NA	99	0.2	0.5
167 CHS OF CHRIST.	1	24	31	0.1	0.2
175 CONGR CHR CHS.	2	85	102*	0.2	0.6
193 EPISCOPAL.....	2	679	878	1.7	4.9
226 FRIENDS-USA...	6	303	362*	0.7	2.0
247 HOLINESS CH...	3	110	110	0.2	0.6
281 LUTH CH AMER..	1	240	292	0.6	1.6
283 LUTH--MO SYNOD	1	46	80	0.2	0.4
349 PENT HOLINESS.	1	61	73*	0.1	0.4
353 CHR BRETHREN..	1	10	30	0.1	0.2
357 PRESB CH US...	17	3 393	4 054*	8.0	22.5
419 SO BAPT CONV..	2	526	628*	1.2	3.5
443 UN C OF CHRIST	3	541	646*	1.3	3.6
449 UN METHODIST..	18	4 243	5 070*	10.0	28.1
453 UN PRES CH USA	5	171	204*	0.4	1.1
NASH	**103**	**25 514**	**32 288***	**48.1**	**100.0**
005 AME ZION......	2	382	571	0.9	1.8
029 AMER LUTH CH..	1	58	75	0.1	0.2
053 ASSEMB OF GOD.	1	57	60	0.1	0.2
081 CATHOLIC......	2	NA	856	1.3	2.7
093 CHR CH (DISC).	4	676	979	1.5	3.0
097 CHR CHS&CHS CR	2	386	470*	0.7	1.5
101 C.M.E........	1	88	107*	0.2	0.3
127 CH GOD (CLEVE)	10	1 106	1 348*	2.0	4.2
165 CH OF NAZARENE	1	14	38	0.1	0.1
193 EPISCOPAL.....	2	982	1 156	1.7	3.6
347 PENT FW BAPT..	3	183	223*	0.3	0.7
349 PENT HOLINESS.	6	364	444*	0.7	1.4
357 PRESB CH US...	5	1 077	1 312*	2.0	4.1
403 SALVATION ARMY	1	80	202	0.3	0.6
413 S.D.A........	1	62	76*	0.1	0.2
419 SO BAPT CONV..	40	14 660	17 865*	26.6	55.3
449 UN METHODIST..	20	5 156	6 283*	9.4	19.5
453 UN PRES CH USA	1	183	223*	0.3	0.7
NEW HANOVER	**189**	**54 905**	**73 083***	**70.6**	**100.0**
001 ADVENT CHR CH.	5	670	809*	0.8	1.1
005 AME ZION......	11	8 390	10 068	9.7	13.8
053 ASSEMB OF GOD.	3	205	310	0.3	0.4
081 CATHOLIC......	5	NA	3 439	3.3	4.7
089 CHR & MISS AL.	2	113	161	0.2	0.2
093 CHR CH (DISC).	1	363	527	0.5	0.7
097 CHR CHS&CHS CR	1	60	72*	0.1	0.1
127 CH GOD (CLEVE)	6	681	822*	0.8	1.1
151 L-D SAINTS....	2	NA	918	0.9	1.3
165 CH OF NAZARENE	1	97	226	0.2	0.3
167 CHS OF CHRIST.	3	385	490	0.5	0.7
193 EPISCOPAL.....	73	12 532	17 085	16.5	23.4
271 REFORM JUDAISM	1	90	109*	0.1	0.1
281 LUTH CH AMER..	3	1 483	1 918	1.9	2.6
283 LUTH--MO SYNOD	1	104	134	0.1	0.2
295 MORAV CH-SOUTH	1	58	79	0.1	0.1
347 PENT FW BAPT..	1	173	209*	0.2	0.3
349 PENT HOLINESS.	2	358	432*	0.4	0.6
353 CHR BRETHREN..	1	75	150	0.1	0.2
357 PRESB CH US...	14	4 738	5 722*	5.5	7.8
381 REF PRES-EVAN.	1	24	29	–	–
403 SALVATION ARMY	1	128	173	0.2	0.2
413 S.D.A........	4	595	719*	0.7	1.0
419 SO BAPT CONV..	30	17 037	20 576*	19.9	28.2
435 UNITARIAN-UNIV	1	85	103*	0.1	0.1
443 UN C OF CHRIST	1	125	151*	0.1	0.2
449 UN METHODIST..	13	6 204	7 493*	7.2	10.3
453 UN PRES CH USA	1	132	159*	0.2	0.2
NORTHAMPTON	**40**	**6 945**	**8 386***	**37.1**	**100.0**
053 ASSEMB OF GOD.	1	28	57	0.3	0.7
193 EPISCOPAL.....	2	47	47	0.2	0.6
226 FRIENDS-USA...	1	72	87*	0.4	1.0
419 SO BAPT CONV..	18	4 233	5 103*	22.6	60.9
449 UN METHODIST..	18	2 565	3 092*	13.7	36.9
ONSLOW	**81**	**20 840**	**30 382***	**26.9**	**100.0**
005 AME ZION......	6	2 652	3 536	3.1	11.6
053 ASSEMB OF GOD.	3	364	601	0.5	2.0
081 CATHOLIC......	2	NA	3 369	3.0	11.1
093 CHR CH (DISC).	4	570	804	0.7	2.6
097 CHR CHS&CHS CR	1	138	167*	0.1	0.5
123 CH GOD (ANDER)	4	185	555	0.5	1.8
127 CH GOD (CLEVE)	4	165	200*	0.2	0.7
151 L-D SAINTS....	3	NA	738	0.7	2.4
165 CH OF NAZARENE	1	23	93	0.1	0.3
167 CHS OF CHRIST.	4	300	382	0.3	1.3
263 INT FOURSQ GOS	1	99	120*	0.1	0.4
281 LUTH CH AMER..	1	280	359	0.3	1.2
283 LUTH--MO SYNOD	1	124	180	0.2	0.6
347 PENT FW BAPT..	1	59	71*	0.1	0.2
349 PENT HOLINESS	5	306	370*	0.3	1.2
357 PRESB CH US...	2	448	542*	0.5	1.8
413 S.D.A........	2	68	82*	0.1	0.3
419 SO BAPT CONV..	23	10 447	12 635*	11.2	41.6
443 UN C OF CHRIST	1	13	16*	–	0.1
449 UN METHODIST..	12	4 599	5 562*	4.9	18.3
ORANGE	**90**	**24 676**	**31 500***	**40.9**	**100.0**
005 AME ZION......	1	76	109	0.1	0.3
019 AMER BAPT USA.	2	825	953*	1.2	3.0
059 BAPT MISS ASSN	1	51	59*	0.1	0.2
081 CATHOLIC......	2	NA	2 909	3.8	9.2
101 C.M.E........	1	929	1 073*	1.4	3.4
123 CH GOD (ANDER)	1	75	225	0.3	0.7
127 CH GOD (CLEVE)	2	164	189*	0.2	0.6
151 L-D SAINTS....	1	NA	288	0.4	0.9
167 CHS OF CHRIST.	1	29	41	0.1	0.1
193 EPISCOPAL.....	2	2 259	2 190	2.8	7.0
226 FRIENDS-USA...	1	39	45*	0.1	0.1
281 LUTH CH AMER..	1	435	551	0.7	1.7
347 PENT FW BAPT..	1	20	23*	–	0.1
349 PENT HOLINESS.	1	32	37*	–	0.1
357 PRESB CH US...	9	1 505	1 739*	2.3	5.5
419 SO BAPT CONV..	40	12 912	14 917*	19.4	47.4
443 UN C OF CHRIST	3	258	298*	0.4	0.9
449 UN METHODIST..	19	5 067	5 854*	7.6	18.6
PAMLICO	**27**	**2 673**	**3 630***	**34.9**	**100.0**
005 AME ZION......	2	542	813	7.8	22.4
053 ASSEMB OF GOD.	1	27	46	0.4	1.3
093 CHR CH (DISC).	7	662	1 026	9.9	28.3
097 CHR CHS&CHS CR	1	50	61*	0.6	1.7
127 CH GOD (CLEVE)	2	89	108*	1.0	3.0
349 PENT HOLINESS.	1	48	58*	0.6	1.6
419 SO BAPT CONV..	3	268	324*	3.1	8.9
443 UN C OF CHRIST	2	135	163*	1.6	4.5
449 UN METHODIST..	8	852	1 031*	9.9	28.4
PASQUOTANK	**44**	**13 750**	**18 327***	**64.4**	**100.0**
005 AME ZION......	11	5 500	6 781	23.8	37.0
053 ASSEMB OF GOD.	1	110	200	0.7	1.1
081 CATHOLIC......	1	NA	742	2.6	4.0
093 CHR CH (DISC).	3	342	662	2.3	3.6
097 CHR CHS&CHS CR	1	210	253*	0.9	1.4
127 CH GOD (CLEVE)	1	29	35*	0.1	0.2
151 L-D SAINTS....	1	NA	449	1.6	2.4
167 CHS OF CHRIST.	1	30	38	0.1	0.2
215 EVAN METH CH.	2	264	318*	1.1	1.7
349 PENT HOLINESS.	1	185	223*	0.8	1.2
357 PRESB CH US...	1	223	268*	0.9	1.5
403 SALVATION ARMY	1	106	231	0.8	1.3
413 S.D.A........	1	70	84*	0.3	0.5
419 SO BAPT CONV..	8	4 077	4 908*	17.2	26.8
449 UN METHODIST..	9	2 586	3 113*	10.9	17.0
453 UN PRES CH USA	1	18	22*	0.1	0.1
PENDER	**53**	**7 213**	**8 962***	**40.3**	**100.0**
001 ADVENT CHR CH.	2	154	188*	0.8	2.1
005 AME ZION......	1	10	12	0.1	0.1
053 ASSEMB OF GOD.	1	68	84	0.4	0.9
081 CATHOLIC......	1	NA	148	0.7	1.7
093 CHR CH (DISC).	1	36	55	0.2	0.6
127 CH GOD (CLEVE)	1	?	?	?	?
347 PENT FW BAPT..	6	419	511*	2.3	5.7
357 PRESB CH US...	10	1 144	1 396*	6.3	15.6
413 S.D.A........	1	16	20*	0.1	0.2
419 SO BAPT CONV..	19	4 163	5 080*	22.9	56.7
449 UN METHODIST..	9	1 203	1 468*	6.6	16.4
PERQUIMANS	**28**	**4 903**	**6 010***	**63.4**	**100.0**
005 AME ZION......	4	1 408	1 760	18.6	29.3
053 ASSEMB OF GOD.	2	92	119	1.3	2.0

NA—Not applicable   *Total adherents estimated from known number of communicant, confirmed, full members.   —Represents a percent less than 0.1.   Percentages may not total due to rounding.

Table 4. Churches and Church Membership by County and Denomination: 1980

County and Denomination	Number of churches	Communicant, confirmed, full members	Total adherents		
			Number	Percent of total population	Percent of total adherents
081 CATHOLIC......	1	NA	30	0.3	0.5
093 CHR CH (DISC).	1	13	24	0.3	0.4
097 CHR CHS&CHS CR	2	260	313*	3.3	5.2
226 FRIENDS-USA...	2	319	384*	4.0	6.4
419 SO BAPT CONV..	8	1 525	1 834*	19.3	30.5
449 UN METHODIST..	8	1 286	1 546*	16.3	25.7
PERSON	**43**	**11 157**	**13 783***	**47.3**	**100.0**
081 CATHOLIC......	1	NA	126	0.4	0.9
127 CH GOD (CLEVE)	1	150	182*	0.6	1.3
151 L-D SAINTS....	1	NA	141	0.5	1.0
167 CHS OF CHRIST.	1	32	41	0.1	0.3
193 EPISCOPAL.....	1	62	71	0.2	0.5
349 PENT HOLINESS.	1	31	38*	0.1	0.3
357 PRESB CH US...	1	173	210*	0.7	1.5
419 SO BAPT CONV..	22	7 206	8 730*	29.9	63.3
449 UN METHODIST..	14	3 503	4 244*	14.6	30.8
PITT	**102**	**18 255**	**24 120***	**28.8**	**100.0**
001 ADVENT CHR CH.	1	67	81*	0.1	0.3
005 AME ZION......	2	310	465	0.6	1.9
053 ASSEMB OF GOD.	1	35	50	0.1	0.2
081 CATHOLIC......	4	NA	815	1.0	3.4
093 CHR CH (DISC).	20	2 917	4 144	5.0	17.2
097 CHR CHS&CHS CR	4	605	733*	0.9	3.0
101 C.M.E.........	2	248	300*	0.4	1.2
127 CH GOD (CLEVE)	5	341	413*	0.5	1.7
133 CH GOD(7TH)DEN	1	33	40*	-	0.2
151 L-D SAINTS....	1	NA	281	0.3	1.2
167 CHS OF CHRIST.	1	45	57	0.1	0.2
226 FRIENDS-USA...	1	44	53*	0.1	0.2
281 LUTH CH AMER..	1	197	257	0.3	1.1
283 LUTH--MO SYNOD	1	19	25	-	0.1
347 PENT FW BAPT..	2	275	333*	0.4	1.4
349 PENT HOLINESS.	14	1 139	1 380*	1.6	5.7
356 PRESB CH AMER.	1	20	25	-	0.1
357 PRESB CH US...	10	1 452	1 759*	2.1	7.3
403 SALVATION ARMY	1	121	325	0.4	1.3
413 S.D.A.........	2	138	167*	0.2	0.7
419 SO BAPT CONV..	13	4 396	5 326*	6.4	22.1
435 UNITARIAN-UNIV	1	24	29*	-	0.1
449 UN METHODIST..	13	5 829	7 062*	8.4	29.3
POLK	**52**	**8 391**	**10 156***	**78.2**	**100.0**
055 AS REF PRES CH	1	105	116	0.9	1.1
081 CATHOLIC......	1	NA	204	1.6	2.0
101 C.M.E.........	2	361	424*	3.3	4.2
127 CH GOD (CLEVE)	1	23	27*	0.2	0.3
157 CH OF BRETHREN	2	242	284*	2.2	2.8
167 CHS OF CHRIST.	1	29	37	0.3	0.4
177 CONGR HOL CH..	4	45	53*	0.4	0.5
193 EPISCOPAL.....	3	415	589	4.5	5.8
357 PRESB CH US...	3	518	608*	4.7	6.0
413 S.D.A.........	1	162	190*	1.5	1.9
419 SO BAPT CONV..	25	5 496	6 455*	49.7	63.6
443 UN C OF CHRIST	1	359	422*	3.3	4.2
449 UN METHODIST..	7	636	747*	5.8	7.4
RANDOLPH	**188**	**32 619**	**41 132***	**44.8**	**100.0**
005 AME ZION......	2	654	1 031	1.1	2.5
053 ASSEMB OF GOD.	2	207	435	0.5	1.1
081 CATHOLIC......	1	NA	419	0.5	1.0
089 CHR & MISS AL.	2	13	59	0.1	0.1
097 CHR CHS&CHS CR	1	20	24*	-	0.1
123 CH GOD (ANDER)	1	95	285	0.3	0.7
127 CH GOD (CLEVE)	8	719	870*	0.9	2.1
151 L-D SAINTS....	1	NA	137	0.1	0.3
165 CH OF NAZARENE	2	88	387	0.4	0.9
167 CHS OF CHRIST.	1	75	95	0.1	0.2
193 EPISCOPAL.....	1	259	425	0.5	1.0
215 EVAN METH CH..	2	171	207*	0.2	0.5
226 FRIENDS-USA...	12	2 381	2 880*	3.1	7.0
281 LUTH CH AMER..	3	422	543	0.6	1.3
349 PENT HOLINESS.	3	205	248*	0.3	0.6
353 CHR BRETHREN..	1	15	35	-	0.1
357 PRESB CH US...	4	700	847*	0.9	2.1
403 SALVATION ARMY	1	24	61	0.1	0.1
413 S.D.A.........	1	92	111*	0.1	0.3
419 SO BAPT CONV..	48	12 676	15 335*	16.7	37.3
443 UN C OF CHRIST	16	2 235	2 704*	2.9	6.6
449 UN METHODIST..	75	11 568	13 994*	15.2	34.0
RICHMOND	**104**	**24 387**	**29 979***	**65.9**	**100.0**
005 AME ZION......	18	7 570	9 084	20.0	30.3
053 ASSEMB OF GOD.	1	38	62	0.1	0.2
081 CATHOLIC......	1	NA	232	0.5	0.8
097 CHR CHS&CHS CR	1	50	61*	0.1	0.2
101 C.M.E.........	2	545	667*	1.5	2.2
127 CH GOD (CLEVE)	3	137	168*	0.4	0.6
151 L-D SAINTS....	1	NA	85	0.2	0.3
167 CHS OF CHRIST.	2	84	107	0.2	0.4
177 CONGR HOL CH..	3	106	130*	0.3	0.4
193 EPISCOPAL.....	2	233	276	0.6	0.9
281 LUTH CH AMER..	1	148	180	0.4	0.6
349 PENT HOLINESS.	7	565	691*	1.5	2.3
357 PRESB CH US...	12	1 718	2 101*	4.6	7.0
419 SO BAPT CONV..	27	7 404	9 055*	19.9	30.2
443 UN C OF CHRIST	1	99	121*	0.3	0.4
449 UN METHODIST..	22	5 690	6 959*	15.3	23.2
ROBESON	**207**	**37 109**	**47 911***	**47.2**	**100.0**
005 AME ZION......	15	1 195	1 434	1.4	3.0
053 ASSEM OF GOD.	4	323	609	0.6	1.3
081 CATHOLIC......	2	NA	470	0.5	1.0
089 CHR & MISS AL.	2	220	282	0.3	0.6
093 CHR CH (DISC).	1	34	52	0.1	0.1
127 CH GOD (CLEVE)	16	1 306	1 650*	1.6	3.4
151 L-D SAINTS....	1	NA	350	0.3	0.7
167 CHS OF CHRIST.	2	110	140	0.1	0.3
281 LUTH CH AMER..	1	139	192	0.2	0.4
347 PENT FW BAPT..	2	125	158*	0.2	0.3
349 PENT HOLINESS.	6	749	946*	0.9	2.0
353 CHR BRETHREN..	1	75	150	0.1	0.3
357 PRESB CH US...	17	2 681	3 387*	3.3	7.1
419 SO BAPT CONV..	96	22 712	28 692*	28.2	59.9
449 UN METHODIST..	36	7 043	8 897*	8.8	18.6
453 UN PRES CH USA	5	397	502*	0.5	1.0
ROCKINGHAM	**143**	**26 673**	**33 148***	**39.7**	**100.0**
053 ASSEMB OF GOD.	3	131	190	0.2	0.6
081 CATHOLIC......	2	NA	462	0.2	1.4
089 CHR & MISS AL.	1	92	148	0.2	0.4
093 CHR CH (DISC).	7	845	1 275	1.5	3.8
097 CHR CHS&CHS CR	9	1 524	1 846*	2.2	5.6
127 CH GOD (CLEVE)	5	257	311*	0.4	0.9
157 CH OF BRETHREN	1	383	464*	0.6	1.4
167 CHS OF CHRIST.	1	15	19	-	0.1
193 EPISCOPAL.....	5	714	888	1.1	2.7
215 EVAN METH CH..	1	120	145*	0.2	0.4
226 FRIENDS-USA...	2	105	127*	0.2	0.4
281 LUTH CH AMER..	1	109	143	0.2	0.4
295 MORAV CH-SOUTH	2	461	577	0.7	1.7
347 PENT FW BAPT..	1	81	98*	0.1	0.3
349 PENT HOLINESS.	8	795	963*	1.2	2.9
357 PRESB CH US...	11	1 688	2 044*	2.5	6.2
403 SALVATION ARMY	2	133	172	0.2	0.5
419 SO BAPT CONV..	36	10 925	13 231*	15.9	39.9
443 UN C OF CHRIST	4	770	932*	1.1	2.8
449 UN METHODIST..	41	7 525	9 113*	10.9	27.5
ROWAN	**189**	**55 395**	**69 050***	**69.6**	**100.0**
005 AME ZION......	11	6 851	8 724	8.8	12.6
053 ASSEMB OF GOD.	2	315	417	0.4	0.6
055 AS REF PRES CH	1	129	137	0.1	0.2
081 CATHOLIC......	1	NA	1 120	1.1	1.6
097 CHR CHS&CHS CR	2	106	126*	0.1	0.2
101 C.M.E.........	1	170	203*	0.2	0.3
123 CH GOD (ANDER)	1	22	66	0.1	0.1
127 CH GOD (CLEVE)	7	417	498*	0.5	0.7
151 L-D SAINTS....	2	NA	498	0.5	0.7
165 CH OF NAZARENE	1	79	104	0.1	0.2
167 CHS OF CHRIST.	4	330	420	0.4	0.6
193 EPISCOPAL.....	5	1 068	1 243	1.3	1.8
263 INT FOURSQ GOS	3	494	590*	0.6	0.9
270 CONSRV JUDAISM	1	26	31*	-	-
281 LUTH CH AMER..	33	12 909	16 013	16.1	23.2
283 LUTH--MO SYNOD	1	153	175	0.2	0.3
349 PENT HOLINESS.	2	249	297*	0.3	0.4
353 CHR BRETHREN..	1	20	30	-	-
356 PRESB CH AMER.	1	146	174	0.2	0.3
357 PRESB CH US...	12	2 660	3 174*	3.2	4.6
403 SALVATION ARMY	1	96	219	0.2	0.3
413 S.D.A.........	2	137	163*	0.2	0.2
419 SO BAPT CONV..	46	15 564	18 573*	18.7	26.9
443 UN C OF CHRIST	11	2 784	3 322*	3.3	4.8
449 UN METHODIST..	33	10 066	12 012*	12.1	17.4
453 UN PRES CH USA	4	604	721*	0.7	1.0
RUTHERFORD	**148**	**34 946**	**42 889***	**79.7**	**100.0**
005 AME ZION......	5	328	492	0.9	1.1
053 ASSEMB OF GOD.	1	30	35	0.1	0.1
081 CATHOLIC......	1	NA	279	0.5	0.7
089 CHR & MISS AL.	1	57	57	0.1	0.1
097 CHR CHS&CHS CR	1	200	243*	0.5	0.6
101 C.M.E.........	7	1 160	1 408*	2.6	3.3
127 CH GOD (CLEVE)	3	150	182*	0.3	0.4
151 L-D SAINTS....	1	NA	155	0.3	0.4
157 CH OF BRETHREN	1	156	189*	0.4	0.4
167 CHS OF CHRIST.	1	16	20	-	-
177 CONGR HOL CH..	1	161	195*	0.4	0.5
193 EPISCOPAL.....	2	342	378	0.7	0.9
281 LUTH CH AMER..	1	108	129	0.2	0.3
357 PRESB CH US...	8	882	1 070*	2.0	2.5
413 S.D.A.........	1	58	70*	0.1	0.2
419 SO BAPT CONV..	85	26 741	32 456*	60.3	75.7
449 UN METHODIST..	28	4 557	5 531*	10.3	12.9
SAMPSON	**143**	**26 064**	**33 189***	**66.8**	**100.0**
005 AME ZION......	11	4 060	4 872	9.8	14.7
019 AMER BAPT USA.	1	455	556*	1.1	1.7
053 ASSEMB OF GOD.	1	17	27	0.1	0.1
081 CATHOLIC......	2	NA	499	1.0	1.5
093 CHR CH (DISC).	18	2 505	3 859	7.8	11.6
127 CH GOD (CLEVE)	6	273	333*	0.7	1.0
151 L-D SAINTS....	1	NA	143	0.3	0.4
167 CHS OF CHRIST.	1	13	17	-	0.1
347 PENT FW BAPT..	19	1 625	1 984*	4.0	6.0
349 PENT HOLINESS.	7	779	951*	1.9	2.9
357 PRESB CH US...	4	698	852*	1.7	2.6
413 S.D.A.........	1	13	16*	-	-

NA—Not applicable   *Total adherents estimated from known number of communicant, confirmed, full members.   —Represents a percent less than 0.1.   Percentages may not total due to rounding.

Table 4. Churches and Church Membership by County and Denomination: 1980

County and Denomination	Number of churches	Communicant, confirmed, full members	Total adherents Number	Percent of total population	Percent of total adherents
419 SO BAPT CONV..	44	11 464	13 998*	28.2	42.2
449 UN METHODIST..	26	4 143	5 059*	10.2	15.2
453 UN PRES CH USA	1	19	23*	–	0.1
SCOTLAND	67	13 228	17 192*	53.3	100.0
005 AME ZION......	9	3 589	4 660	14.4	27.1
053 ASSEMB OF GOD.	1	49	97	0.3	0.6
081 CATHOLIC......	1	NA	310	1.0	1.8
097 CHR CHS&CHS CR	1	64	80*	0.2	0.5
127 CH GOD (CLEVE)	4	588	736*	2.3	4.3
193 EPISCOPAL.....	1	85	111	0.3	0.6
281 LUTH CH AMER..	1	91	110	0.3	0.6
349 PENT HOLINESS.	8	605	758*	2.3	4.4
353 CHR BRETHREN..	2	115	260	0.8	1.5
357 PRESB CH US...	9	1 927	2 413*	7.5	14.0
413 S.D.A.........	1	76	95*	0.3	0.6
419 SO BAPT CONV..	12	2 523	3 159*	9.8	18.4
449 UN METHODIST..	15	3 311	4 146*	12.8	24.1
453 UN PRES CH USA	2	205	257*	0.8	1.5
STANLY	118	27 456	33 906*	69.9	100.0
005 AME ZION......	7	1 842	2 456	5.1	7.2
053 ASSEMB OF GOD.	1	17	35	0.1	0.1
081 CATHOLIC......	1	NA	490	1.0	1.4
127 CH GOD (CLEVE)	5	342	411*	0.8	1.2
165 CH OF NAZARENE	2	135	250	0.5	0.7
167 CHS OF CHRIST.	1	40	51	0.1	0.2
193 EPISCOPAL.....	1	251	338	0.7	1.0
281 LUTH CH AMER..	4	1 000	1 222	2.5	3.6
349 PENT HOLINESS.	1	30	36*	0.1	0.1
356 PRESB CH AMER.	1	151	204	0.4	0.6
357 PRESB CH US...	7	1 270	1 527*	3.1	4.5
381 REF PRES-EVAN.	1	306	344	0.7	1.0
413 S.D.A.........	1	99	119*	0.2	0.4
419 SO BAPT CONV..	54	16 045	19 294*	39.8	56.9
443 UN C OF CHRIST	1	235	283*	0.6	0.8
449 UN METHODIST..	30	5 693	6 846*	14.1	20.2
STOKES	62	10 623	13 186*	39.9	100.0
093 CHR CH (DISC).	2	265	383	1.2	2.9
097 CHR CHS&CHS CR	7	1 672	2 053*	6.2	15.6
127 CH GOD (CLEVE)	3	61	75*	0.2	0.6
167 CHS OF CHRIST.	1	80	102	0.3	0.8
193 EPISCOPAL.....	2	64	108	0.3	0.8
226 FRIENDS-USA...	2	104	128*	0.4	1.0
295 MORAV CH-SOUTH	2	403	547	1.7	4.1
349 PENT HOLINESS.	2	103	126*	0.4	1.0
357 PRESB CH US...	6	362	444*	1.3	3.4
419 SO BAPT CONV..	19	5 453	6 695*	20.2	50.8
443 UN C OF CHRIST	1	86	106*	0.3	0.8
449 UN METHODIST..	15	1 970	2 419*	7.3	18.3
SURRY	146	26 370	32 890*	55.3	100.0
053 ASSEMB OF GOD.	1	25	38	0.1	0.1
081 CATHOLIC......	2	NA	240	0.4	0.7
093 CHR CH (DISC).	1	135	171	0.3	0.5
097 CHR CHS&CHS CR	7	499	602*	1.0	1.8
101 C.M.E.........	1	75	90*	0.2	0.3
127 CH GOD (CLEVE)	2	208	251*	0.4	0.8
151 L-D SAINTS....	2	NA	645	1.1	2.0
157 CH OF BRETHREN	2	136	164*	0.3	0.5
167 CHS OF CHRIST.	3	103	132	0.2	0.4
193 EPISCOPAL.....	2	199	318	0.5	1.0
226 FRIENDS-USA...	8	1 018	1 228*	2.1	3.7
281 LUTH CH AMER..	1	108	137	0.2	0.4
295 MORAV CH-SOUTH	1	506	601	1.0	1.8
349 PENT HOLINESS.	6	385	465*	0.8	1.4
357 PRESB CH US...	6	908	1 096*	1.8	3.3
403 SALVATION ARMY	1	108	217	0.4	0.7
419 SO BAPT CONV..	70	17 852	21 541*	36.2	65.5
449 UN METHODIST..	29	4 087	4 932*	8.3	15.0
453 UN PRES CH USA	1	18	22*	–	0.1
SWAIN	38	4 258	5 495*	53.4	100.0
053 ASSEMB OF GOD.	1	46	66	0.6	1.2
081 CATHOLIC......	2	NA	167	1.6	3.0
127 CH GOD (CLEVE)	3	127	154*	1.5	2.8
151 L-D SAINTS....	1	NA	156	1.5	2.8
167 CHS OF CHRIST.	1	30	38	0.4	0.7
193 EPISCOPAL.....	1	15	15	0.1	0.3
357 PRESB CH US...	1	93	113*	1.1	2.1
419 SO BAPT CONV..	26	3 699	4 485*	43.6	81.6
449 UN METHODIST..	2	248	301*	2.9	5.5
TRANSYLVANIA	50	10 718	13 341*	57.0	100.0
053 ASSEMB OF GOD.	1	39	75	0.3	0.6
081 CATHOLIC......	1	NA	466	2.0	3.5
127 CH GOD (CLEVE)	4	240	288*	1.2	2.2
165 CH OF NAZARENE	1	20	38	0.2	0.3
167 CHS OF CHRIST.	2	80	102	0.4	0.8
193 EPISCOPAL.....	1	352	378	1.6	2.8
281 LUTH CH AMER..	1	237	305	1.3	2.3
356 PRESB CH AMER.	1	27	37	0.2	0.3
413 S.D.A.........	1	32	38*	0.2	0.3
419 SO BAPT CONV..	31	8 301	9 948*	42.5	74.6
449 UN METHODIST..	6	1 390	1 666*	7.1	12.5
TYRRELL	21	1 897	2 746*	69.1	100.0
053 ASSEMB OF GOD.	1	21	50	1.3	1.8
081 CATHOLIC......	1	NA	24	0.6	0.9
093 CHR CH (DISC).	9	680	1 217	30.6	44.3
097 CHR CHS&CHS CR	3	437	532*	13.4	19.4
127 CH GOD (CLEVE)	1	2	2*	0.1	0.1
419 SO BAPT CONV..	2	392	477*	12.0	17.4
449 UN METHODIST..	4	365	444*	11.2	16.2
UNION	149	32 361	41 377*	58.8	100.0
001 ADVENT CHR CH.	2	405	501*	0.7	1.2
005 AME ZION......	17	3 388	4 367	6.2	10.6
053 ASSEMB OF GOD.	1	61	233	0.3	0.6
081 CATHOLIC......	1	NA	439	0.6	1.1
101 C.M.E.........	1	535	662*	0.9	1.6
123 CH GOD (ANDER)	3	125	375	0.5	0.9
127 CH GOD (CLEVE)	2	121	150*	0.2	0.4
151 L-D SAINTS....	1	NA	154	0.2	0.4
165 CH OF NAZARENE	1	106	172	0.2	0.4
167 CHS OF CHRIST.	2	37	47	0.1	0.1
193 EPISCOPAL.....	1	235	406	0.6	1.0
263 INT FOURSQ GOS	1	207	256*	0.4	0.6
281 LUTH CH AMER..	1	205	284	0.4	0.7
349 PENT HOLINESS.	1	56	69*	0.1	0.2
357 PRESB CH US...	19	2 454	3 037*	4.3	7.3
419 SO BAPT CONV..	58	17 505	21 661*	30.8	52.4
449 UN METHODIST..	35	6 702	8 293*	11.8	20.0
453 UN PRES CH USA	2	219	271*	0.4	0.7
VANCE	74	15 247	19 212*	52.3	100.0
005 AME ZION......	3	478	707	1.9	3.7
081 CATHOLIC......	1	NA	172	0.5	0.9
127 CH GOD (CLEVE)	4	522	641*	1.7	3.3
151 L-D SAINTS....	1	NA	70	0.2	0.4
165 CH OF NAZARENE	1	48	70	0.2	0.4
167 CHS OF CHRIST.	2	60	76	0.2	0.4
193 EPISCOPAL.....	4	344	399	1.1	2.1
349 PENT HOLINESS.	4	463	569*	1.5	3.0
357 PRESB CH US...	5	597	734*	2.0	3.8
403 SALVATION ARMY	1	125	278	0.8	1.4
419 SO BAPT CONV..	19	6 069	7 458*	20.3	38.8
443 UN C OF CHRIST	10	2 002	2 460*	6.7	12.8
449 UN METHODIST..	18	4 356	5 353*	14.6	27.9
453 UN PRES CH USA	1	183	225*	0.6	1.2
WAKE	278	110 943	149 406*	49.7	100.0
001 ADVENT CHR CH.	2	236	282*	0.1	0.2
005 AME ZION......	7	7 306	9 270	3.1	6.2
019 AMER BAPT USA.	1	450	538*	0.2	0.4
029 AMER LUTH CH..	1	350	437	0.1	0.3
053 ASSEMB OF GOD.	6	439	805	0.3	0.5
081 CATHOLIC......	9	NA	11 956	4.0	8.0
089 CHR & MISS AL.	3	421	729	0.2	0.5
093 CHR CH (DISC).	10	1 442	1 850	0.6	1.2
097 CHR CHS&CHS CR	2	222	265*	0.1	0.2
101 C.M.E.........	4	1 140	1 362*	0.5	0.9
123 CH GOD (ANDER)	3	192	576	0.2	0.4
127 CH GOD (CLEVE)	9	724	865*	0.3	0.6
151 L-D SAINTS....	3	NA	1 359	0.5	0.9
165 CH OF NAZARENE	2	240	498	0.2	0.3
167 CHS OF CHRIST.	4	786	1 000	0.3	0.7
193 EPISCOPAL.....	13	5 438	6 933	2.3	4.6
226 FRIENDS-USA...	1	34	41*	–	–
263 INT FOURSQ GOS	1	258	308*	0.1	0.2
270 CONSRV JUDAISM	1	153	183*	0.1	0.1
271 REFORM JUDAISM	1	342	409*	0.1	0.3
281 LUTH CH AMER..	4	1 781	2 434	0.8	1.6
283 LUTH--MO SYNOD	2	583	735	0.2	0.5
290 METRO COMM CHS	1	30	60	–	–
295 MORAV CH-SOUTH	1	225	276	0.1	0.2
335 ORTH PRESB CH.	1	32	38*	–	–
347 PENT FW BAPT.	1	75	90*	–	0.1
349 PENT HOLINESS.	6	612	731*	0.2	0.5
353 CHR BRETHREN..	8	580	1 015	0.3	0.7
356 PRESB CH AMER.	1	169	192	0.1	0.1
357 PRESB CH US...	19	10 172	12 156*	4.0	8.1
403 SALVATION ARMY	1	206	810	0.3	0.5
413 S.D.A.........	2	368	440*	0.1	0.3
419 SO BAPT CONV..	87	47 294	56 521*	18.8	37.8
435 UNITARIAN-UNIV	1	160	191*	0.1	0.1
443 UN C OF CHRIST	21	3 822	4 568*	1.5	3.1
449 UN METHODIST..	35	24 412	29 174*	9.7	19.5
453 UN PRES CH USA	2	197	235*	0.1	0.2
469 WELS.........	1	52	74	–	–
WARREN	38	6 557	8 039*	49.5	100.0
081 CATHOLIC......	1	NA	48	0.3	0.6
127 CH GOD (CLEVE)	1	66	80*	0.5	1.0
193 EPISCOPAL.....	3	118	156	1.0	1.9
283 LUTH--MO SYNOD	1	214	295	1.8	3.7
349 PENT HOLINESS.	1	67	81*	0.5	1.0
357 PRESB CH US...	2	109	132*	0.8	1.6
419 SO BAPT CONV..	14	3 243	3 928*	24.2	48.9
443 UN C OF CHRIST	4	917	1 111*	6.8	13.8
449 UN METHODIST..	11	1 823	2 208*	13.6	27.5
WASHINGTON	36	4 851	7 605*	51.4	100.0
053 ASSEMB OF GOD.	1	39	60	0.4	0.8
081 CATHOLIC......	1	NA	90	0.6	1.2
093 CHR CH (DISC).	4	496	1 905	12.9	25.0
097 CHR CHS&CHS CR	8	1 600	1 985*	13.4	26.1

NA— Not applicable   *Total adherents estimated from known number of communicant, confirmed, full members.   —Represents a percent less than 0.1.   Percentages may not total due to rounding.

Table 4. Churches and Church Membership by County and Denomination: 1980

County and Denomination	Number of churches	Communicant, confirmed, full members	Total adherents		
			Number	Percent of total population	Percent of total adherents
127 CH GOD (CLEVE)	2	129	160*	1.1	2.1
151 L-D SAINTS....	1	NA	82	0.6	1.1
165 CH OF NAZARENE	1	94	228	1.5	3.0
167 CHS OF CHRIST.	2	65	83	0.6	1.1
349 PENT HOLINESS.	2	149	185*	1.2	2.4
357 PRESB CH US...	1	85	105*	0.7	1.4
413 S.D.A.........	1	32	40*	0.3	0.5
419 SO BAPT CONV..	6	1 192	1 479*	10.0	19.4
449 UN METHODIST..	6	970	1 203*	8.1	15.8
WATAUGA	89	13 327	16 390*	51.7	100.0
001 ADVENT CHR CH.	2	88	102*	0.3	0.6
053 ASSEMB OF GOD.	3	62	148	0.5	0.9
081 CATHOLIC......	2	NA	409	1.3	2.5
089 CHR & MISS AL.	1	61	205	0.6	1.3
127 CH GOD (CLEVE)	2	74	86*	0.3	0.5
151 L-D SAINTS....	1	NA	75	0.2	0.5
167 CHS OF CHRIST.	1	55	70	0.2	0.4
193 EPISCOPAL.....	3	384	610	1.9	3.7
237 GC MENN BR CHS	1	57	66*	0.2	0.4
281 LUTH CH AMER..	3	681	878	2.8	5.4
357 PRESB CH US...	3	561	650*	2.1	4.0
413 S.D.A.........	2	49	57*	0.2	0.3
419 SO BAPT CONV..	52	9 674	11 203*	35.4	68.4
435 UNITARIAN-UNIV	1	24	28*	0.1	0.2
449 UN METHODIST..	12	1 557	1 803*	5.7	11.0
WAYNE	140	27 007	35 818*	36.9	100.0
001 ADVENT CHR CH.	2	220	270*	0.3	0.8
005 AME ZION......	11	2 565	3 078	3.2	8.6
053 ASSEMB OF GOD.	1	71	111	0.1	0.3
081 CATHOLIC......	2	NA	1 270	1.3	3.5
093 CHR CH (DISC).	22	2 697	3 921	4.0	10.9
127 CH GOD (CLEVE)	7	637	781*	0.8	2.2
151 L-D SAINTS....	3	NA	914	0.9	2.6
165 CH OF NAZARENE	1	38	62	0.1	0.2
167 CHS OF CHRIST.	1	145	185	0.2	0.5
226 FRIENDS-USA...	6	936	1 148*	1.2	3.2
271 REFORM JUDAISM	1	54	66*	0.1	0.2
281 LUTH CH AMER..	1	188	247	0.3	0.7
283 LUTH--MO SYNOD	1	55	79	0.1	0.2
347 PENT FW BAPT..	10	1 580	1 938*	2.0	5.4
349 PENT HOLINESS.	10	1 059	1 299*	1.3	3.6
353 CHR BRETHREN..	1	30	50	0.1	0.1
356 PRESB CH AMER.	1	138	145	0.1	0.4
357 PRESB CH US...	4	1 462	1 793*	1.8	5.0
403 SALVATION ARMY	1	194	137	0.1	0.4
413 S.D.A.........	2	124	152*	0.2	0.4
419 SO BAPT CONV..	18	6 751	8 281*	8.5	23.1
435 UNITARIAN-UNIV	1	25	31*	—	0.1
443 UN C OF CHRIST	1	114	140*	0.1	0.4
449 UN METHODIST..	29	7 833	9 608*	9.9	26.8
453 UN PRES CH USA	3	91	112*	0.1	0.3
WILKES	131	29 754	36 824*	62.8	100.0
001 ADVENT CHR CH.	3	142	172*	0.3	0.5
005 AME ZION......	2	356	534	0.9	1.5
081 CATHOLIC......	1	NA	201	0.3	0.5
093 CHR CH (DISC).	1	74	114	0.2	0.3
127 CH GOD (CLEVE)	2	75	91*	0.2	0.2
151 L-D SAINTS....	1	NA	281	0.5	0.8
157 CH OF BRETHREN	2	107	130*	0.2	0.4
167 CHS OF CHRIST.	3	129	165	0.3	0.4
193 EPISCOPAL.....	1	154	262	0.4	0.7
237 GC MENN BR CHS	1	25	30*	0.1	0.1
281 LUTH CH AMER..	1	171	217	0.4	0.6
349 PENT HOLINESS.	3	194	236*	0.4	0.6
357 PRESB CH US...	3	621	754*	1.3	2.0
413 S.D.A.........	1	43	52*	0.1	0.1
419 SO BAPT CONV..	90	25 032	30 391*	51.8	82.5
449 UN METHODIST..	16	2 631	3 194*	5.4	8.7
WILSON	74	16 831	21 810*	34.5	100.0
001 ADVENT CHR CH.	2	174	212*	0.3	1.0
005 AME ZION......	5	2 182	2 784	4.4	12.8
053 ASSEMB OF GOD.	1	38	45	0.1	0.2
081 CATHOLIC......	2	NA	512	0.8	2.3
093 CHR CH (DISC).	12	1 658	2 221	3.5	10.2
097 CHR CHS&CHS CR	1	30	37*	0.1	0.2
123 CH GOD (ANDER)	1	25	75	0.1	0.3
127 CH GOD (CLEVE)	4	399	486*	0.8	2.2
151 L-D SAINTS....	1	NA	181	0.3	0.8
167 CHS OF CHRIST.	1	55	70	0.1	0.3
193 EPISCOPAL.....	2	436	590	0.9	2.7
263 INT FOURSQ GOS	1	125	152*	0.2	0.7
281 LUTH CH AMER..	1	98	131	0.2	0.6
283 LUTH--MO SYNOD	1	163	199	0.3	0.9
349 PENT HOLINESS.	8	806	982*	1.6	4.5
353 CHR BRETHREN..	1	25	25	—	0.1
357 PRESB CH US...	5	1 132	1 379*	2.2	6.3
403 SALVATION ARMY	1	211	431	0.7	2.0
413 S.D.A.........	2	144	175*	0.3	0.8
419 SO BAPT CONV..	10	4 858	5 919*	9.4	27.1
449 UN METHODIST..	11	4 124	5 024*	8.0	23.0
453 UN PRES CH USA	1	148	180*	0.3	0.8
YADKIN	75	14 145	16 998*	59.8	100.0
005 AME ZION......	4	552	690	2.4	4.1
053 ASSEMB OF GOD.	1	45	61	0.2	0.4
127 CH GOD (CLEVE)	2	65	78*	0.3	0.5

County and Denomination	Number of churches	Communicant, confirmed, full members	Total adherents		
			Number	Percent of total population	Percent of total adherents
167 CHS OF CHRIST.	3	127	189	0.7	1.1
215 EVAN METH CH..	1	50	60*	0.2	0.4
226 FRIENDS-USA...	8	1 299	1 552*	5.5	9.1
281 LUTH CH AMER..	1	86	121	0.4	0.7
349 PENT HOLINESS.	3	394	471*	1.7	2.8
357 PRESB CH US...	1	55	66*	0.2	0.4
419 SO BAPT CONV..	28	8 680	10 373*	36.5	61.0
443 UN C OF CHRIST	1	41	49*	0.2	0.3
449 UN METHODIST..	21	2 721	3 252*	11.4	19.1
453 UN PRES CH USA	1	30	36*	0.1	0.2
YANCEY	46	6 365	7 783*	52.1	100.0
005 AME ZION......	1	136	207	1.4	2.7
081 CATHOLIC......	1	NA	34	0.2	0.4
123 CH GOD (ANDER)	1	29	87	0.6	1.1
167 CHS OF CHRIST.	1	13	17	0.1	0.2
226 FRIENDS-USA...	1	56	67*	0.4	0.9
356 PRESB CH AMER.	1	42	42	0.3	0.5
357 PRESB CH US...	6	261	314*	2.1	4.0
419 SO BAPT CONV..	26	4 940	5 946*	39.8	76.4
449 UN METHODIST..	7	801	964*	6.5	12.4
453 UN PRES CH USA	1	87	105*	0.7	1.3

NORTH DAKOTA

County and Denomination	Number of churches	Communicant, confirmed, full members	Total adherents		
			Number	Percent of total population	Percent of total adherents
THE STATE.....	1 695	233 749	482 574*	73.9	100.0
ADAMS	14	1 590	2 621*	73.1	100.0
029 AMER LUTH CH..	6	1 225	1 606	44.8	61.3
053 ASSEMB OF GOD.	1	52	111	3.1	4.2
081 CATHOLIC......	2	NA	528	14.7	20.1
313 N AM BAPT CONF	1	15	18*	0.5	0.7
443 UN C OF CHRIST	2	153	185*	5.2	7.1
449 UN METHODIST..	1	100	121*	3.4	4.6
469 WELS..........	1	45	52	1.5	2.0
BARNES	47	6 449	11 430*	81.9	100.0
029 AMER LUTH CH..	17	3 621	4 642	33.3	40.6
053 ASSEMB OF GOD.	2	90	122	0.9	1.1
081 CATHOLIC......	6	NA	3 131	22.4	27.4
165 CH OF NAZARENE	1	85	255	1.8	2.2
167 CHS OF CHRIST.	1	3	9	0.1	0.1
193 EPISCOPAL.....	1	41	57	0.4	0.5
203 EVAN FREE CH..	2	28	33*	0.2	0.3
220 FREE LUTHERAN.	2	383	485	3.5	4.2
281 LUTH CH AMER..	1	299	377	2.7	3.3
283 LUTH--MO SYNOD	1	223	290	2.1	2.5
313 N AM BAPT CONF	1	60	72*	0.5	0.6
353 CHR BRETHREN..	2	60	75	0.5	0.7
371 REF CH IN AM..	1	51	67	0.5	0.6
413 S.D.A.........	1	12	14*	0.1	0.1
443 UN C OF CHRIST	1	378	451*	3.2	3.9
449 UN METHODIST..	5	1 005	1 200*	8.6	10.5
453 UN PRES CH USA	1	32	38*	0.3	0.3
469 WELS..........	1	78	112	0.8	1.0
BENSON	38	2 939	7 009*	88.2	100.0
029 AMER LUTH CH..	16	2 253	2 901	36.5	41.4
081 CATHOLIC......	11	NA	3 219	40.5	45.9
157 CH OF BRETHREN	1	53	67*	0.8	1.0
163 CH OF LUTH BR.	1	27	59	0.7	0.8
193 EPISCOPAL.....	2	60	91	1.1	1.3
203 EVAN FREE CH..	1	52	66*	0.8	0.9
220 FREE LUTHERAN.	2	225	280	3.5	4.0
281 LUTH CH AMER..	2	183	217	2.7	3.1
453 UN PRES CH USA	2	86	109*	1.4	1.6
BILLINGS	5	35	435*	38.2	100.0
029 AMER LUTH CH..	1	26	33	2.9	7.6
081 CATHOLIC......	3	NA	391	34.4	89.9
443 UN C OF CHRIST	1	9	11*	1.0	2.5
BOTTINEAU	38	4 530	7 072*	75.7	100.0
019 AMER BAPT USA.	1	108	131*	1.4	1.9
029 AMER LUTH CH..	13	2 579	3 479	37.3	49.2
081 CATHOLIC......	5	NA	997	10.7	14.1
163 CH OF LUTH BR.	4	138	345	3.7	4.9
167 CHS OF CHRIST.	1	2	3	—	—
281 LUTH CH AMER..	1	143	198	2.1	2.8
283 LUTH--MO SYNOD	5	850	1 059	11.3	15.0
413 S.D.A.........	1	38	46*	0.5	0.7
449 UN METHODIST..	4	255	309*	3.3	4.4
453 UN PRES CH USA	3	417	505*	5.4	7.1
BOWMAN	19	1 771	3 456*	81.7	100.0
029 AMER LUTH CH..	7	1 275	1 668	39.4	48.3

NA—Not applicable   *Total adherents estimated from known number of communicant, confirmed, full members.   —Represents a percent less than 0.1.   Percentages may not total due to rounding.

209

Table 4. Churches and Church Membership by County and Denomination: 1980

County and Denomination	Number of churches	Communicant, confirmed, full members	Total adherents Number	Percent of total population	Percent of total adherents
053 ASSEMB OF GOD.	3	155	270	6.4	7.8
081 CATHOLIC......	3	NA	1 095	25.9	31.7
151 L-D SAINTS....	1	NA	?	?	?
193 EPISCOPAL.....	1	10	13	0.3	0.4
413 S.D.A.........	1	66	82*	1.9	2.4
443 UN C OF CHRIST	1	100	124*	2.9	3.6
449 UN METHODIST..	1	151	187*	4.4	5.4
453 UN PRES CH USA	1	14	17*	0.4	0.5
BURKE	23	2 078	3 325*	87.0	100.0
019 AMER BAPT USA.	1	250	299*	7.8	9.0
029 AMER LUTH CH..	7	1 350	1 788	46.8	53.8
053 ASSEMB OF GOD.	1	23	45	1.2	1.4
081 CATHOLIC......	5	NA	657	17.2	19.8
127 CH GOD (CLEVE)	1	20	24*	0.6	0.7
283 LUTH--MO SYNOD	2	130	147	3.8	4.4
449 UN METHODIST..	4	222	266*	7.0	8.0
453 UN PRES CH USA	2	83	99*	2.6	3.0
BURLEIGH	59	16 466	37 212*	67.9	100.0
019 AMER BAPT USA.	1	336	413*	0.8	1.1
029 AMER LUTH CH..	6	6 822	9 215	16.8	24.8
053 ASSEMB OF GOD.	2	285	605	1.1	1.6
081 CATHOLIC......	8	NA	15 247	27.8	41.0
089 CHR & MISS AL.	1	10	40	0.1	0.1
097 CHR CHS&CHS CR	1	19	23*	-	0.1
127 CH GOD (CLEVE)	1	61	75*	0.1	0.2
151 L-D SAINTS....	2	NA	?	?	?
163 CH OF LUTH BR.	1	72	134	0.2	0.4
165 CH OF NAZARENE	1	74	85	0.2	0.2
167 CHS OF CHRIST.	1	45	57	0.1	0.2
193 EPISCOPAL.....	1	404	549	1.0	1.5
203 EVAN FREE CH..	1	71	87*	0.2	0.2
226 FRIENDS-USA...	1	4	5*	-	-
237 GC MENN BR CHS	1	31	38*	0.1	0.1
281 LUTH CH AMER..	4	1 406	1 784	3.3	4.8
283 LUTH--MO SYNOD	4	1 183	1 593	2.9	4.3
287 MENN GEN CONF.	1	30	30	0.1	0.1
313 N AM BAPT CONF	2	566	696*	1.3	1.9
371 REF CH IN AM.	1	153	327	0.6	0.9
403 SALVATION ARMY	1	124	321	0.6	0.9
413 S.D.A.........	4	460	565*	1.0	1.5
419 SO BAPT CONV..	1	76	93*	0.2	0.2
435 UNITARIAN-UNIV	1	52	64*	0.1	0.2
443 UN C OF CHRIST	2	302	371*	0.7	1.0
449 UN METHODIST..	6	2 408	2 960*	5.4	8.0
453 UN PRES CH USA	2	1 309	1 609*	2.9	4.3
469 WELS.........	1	163	226	0.4	0.6
CASS	113	31 719	61 854*	70.1	100.0
019 AMER BAPT USA.	1	291	350*	0.4	0.6
029 AMER LUTH CH..	27	15 743	21 155	24.0	34.2
053 ASSEMB OF GOD.	1	411	1 000	1.1	1.6
081 CATHOLIC......	14	NA	19 045	21.6	30.8
123 CH GOD (ANDER)	2	35	105	0.1	0.2
127 CH GOD (CLEVE)	1	40	48*	0.1	0.1
133 CH GOD(7TH)DEN	1	8	10*	-	-
151 L-D SAINTS....	2	NA	548	0.6	0.9
163 CH OF LUTH BR.	1	4	77	0.1	0.1
165 CH OF NAZARENE	2	41	75	0.1	0.1
167 CHS OF CHRIST.	1	77	111	0.1	0.2
179 CONSRV BAPT...	1	217	261*	0.3	0.4
193 EPISCOPAL.....	2	545	682	0.8	1.1
201 EVAN COV CH AM	1	94	113*	0.1	0.2
203 EVAN FREE CH..	2	209	251*	0.3	0.4
220 FREE LUTHERAN.	1	90	105	0.1	0.2
221 FREE METHODIST	1	14	75	0.1	0.1
271 REFORM JUDAISM	1	208	250*	0.3	0.4
281 LUTH CH AMER..	7	4 328	5 456	6.2	8.8
283 LUTH--MO SYNOD	4	2 054	2 837	3.2	4.6
285 MENNONITE CH..	2	76	91*	0.1	0.1
290 METRO COMM CHS	0	10	20	-	-
293 MORAV CH-NORTH	6	650	816	0.9	1.3
313 N AM BAPT CONF	2	165	198*	0.2	0.3
353 CHR BRETHREN..	1	40	60	0.1	0.1
403 SALVATION ARMY	1	28	497	0.6	0.8
413 S.D.A.........	1	123	148*	0.2	0.2
419 SO BAPT CONV..	1	214	257*	0.3	0.4
435 UNITARIAN-UNIV	1	54	65*	0.1	0.1
443 UN C OF CHRIST	4	788	947*	1.1	1.5
449 UN METHODIST..	12	2 722	3 270*	3.7	5.3
453 UN PRES CH USA	9	2 440	2 931*	3.3	4.7
CAVALIER	39	2 870	6 451*	84.5	100.0
029 AMER LUTH CH..	10	1 178	1 516	19.9	23.5
053 ASSEMB OF GOD.	1	22	35	0.5	0.5
081 CATHOLIC......	9	NA	2 927	38.3	45.4
193 EPISCOPAL.....	1	23	23	0.3	0.4
197 EVAN CH OF NA.	1	138	138	1.8	2.1
220 FREE LUTHERAN.	1	50	55	0.7	0.9
237 GC MENN BR CHS	1	65	78*	1.0	1.2
281 LUTH CH AMER..	1	44	46	0.6	0.7
283 LUTH--MO SYNOD	2	205	246	3.2	3.8
287 MENN GEN CONF.	2	241	297	3.9	4.6
419 SO BAPT CONV..	1	110	133*	1.7	2.1
449 UN METHODIST..	3	316	381*	5.0	5.9
453 UN PRES CH USA	6	478	576*	7.5	8.9
DICKEY	24	3 189	5 367*	74.5	100.0
019 AMER BAPT USA.	1	148	180*	2.5	3.4
029 AMER LUTH CH..	3	685	888	12.3	16.5
053 ASSEMB OF GOD.	1	55	80	1.1	1.5
081 CATHOLIC......	3	NA	1 232	17.1	23.0
165 CH OF NAZARENE	2	134	277	3.8	5.2
193 EPISCOPAL.....	2	47	100	1.4	1.9
283 LUTH--MO SYNOD	4	1 229	1 524	21.1	28.4
413 S.D.A.........	1	142	173*	2.4	3.2
443 UN C OF CHRIST	1	27	33*	0.5	0.6
449 UN METHODIST..	4	520	634*	8.8	11.8
453 UN PRES CH USA	2	202	246*	3.4	4.6
DIVIDE	23	1 603	2 576*	73.7	100.0
029 AMER LUTH CH..	12	1 324	1 809	51.8	70.2
053 ASSEMB OF GOD.	2	62	145	4.1	5.6
081 CATHOLIC......	4	NA	358	10.2	13.9
163 CH OF LUTH BR.	1	21	31	0.9	1.2
283 LUTH--MO SYNOD	1	23	29	0.8	1.1
419 SO BAPT CONV.	1	24	28*	0.8	1.1
449 UN METHODIST..	1	12	14*	0.4	0.5
453 UN PRES CH USA	1	137	162*	4.6	6.3
DUNN	18	1 545	3 536*	76.4	100.0
019 AMER BAPT USA.	1	22	27*	0.6	0.8
029 AMER LUTH CH..	5	624	844	18.2	23.9
057 BAPT GEN CONF.	1	36	45*	1.0	1.3
081 CATHOLIC......	6	NA	1 510	32.6	42.7
281 LUTH CH AMER.	1	432	574	12.4	16.2
283 LUTH--MO SYNOD	1	133	160	3.5	4.5
381 REF PRES-EVAN.	1	16	27	0.6	0.8
443 UN C OF CHRIST	2	282	349*	7.5	9.9
EDDY	13	1 598	2 823*	79.4	100.0
029 AMER LUTH CH..	4	898	1 166	32.8	41.3
081 CATHOLIC......	1	NA	775	21.8	27.5
165 CH OF NAZARENE	1	31	73	2.1	2.6
181 CONSRV CONGR.	1	117	140*	3.9	5.0
203 EVAN FREE CH..	1	19	23*	0.6	0.8
281 LUTH CH AMER.	2	223	263	7.4	9.3
283 LUTH--MO SYNOD	1	108	141	4.0	5.0
449 UN METHODIST..	2	202	242*	6.8	8.6
EMMONS	20	1 324	5 351*	91.0	100.0
029 AMER LUTH CH..	2	388	509	8.7	9.5
053 ASSEMB OF GOD.	1	21	35	0.6	0.7
081 CATHOLIC......	8	NA	3 479	59.2	65.0
105 CHRISTIAN REF.	1	101	161	2.7	3.0
313 N AM BAPT CONF	1	108	132*	2.2	2.5
371 REF CH IN AM.	2	151	373	6.3	7.0
413 S.D.A.........	1	14	17*	0.3	0.3
449 UN METHODIST..	2	240	294*	5.0	5.5
453 UN PRES CH USA	1	84	103*	1.8	1.9
469 WELS.........	1	217	248	4.2	4.6
FOSTER	15	2 317	4 071*	88.3	100.0
029 AMER LUTH CH..	5	1 314	1 741	37.8	42.8
081 CATHOLIC......	3	NA	1 011	21.9	24.8
165 CH OF NAZARENE	1	36	127	2.8	3.1
283 LUTH--MO SYNOD	1	257	323	7.0	7.9
313 N AM BAPT CONF	1	148	181*	3.9	4.4
413 S.D.A.........	1	73	89*	1.9	2.2
443 UN C OF CHRIST	1	196	240*	5.2	5.9
449 UN METHODIST..	2	293	359*	7.8	8.8
GOLDEN VALLEY	12	698	1 916*	80.1	100.0
029 AMER LUTH CH..	2	307	405	16.9	21.1
081 CATHOLIC......	3	NA	1 019	42.6	53.2
197 EVAN CH OF NA.	2	63	63	2.6	3.3
283 LUTH--MO SYNOD	1	168	233	9.7	12.2
413 S.D.A.........	1	48	59*	2.5	3.1
443 UN C OF CHRIST	2	89	109*	4.6	5.7
449 UN METHODIST..	1	23	28*	1.2	1.5
GRAND FORKS	82	18 880	40 719*	61.6	100.0
019 AMER BAPT USA.	1	55	67*	0.1	0.2
029 AMER LUTH CH..	28	10 289	13 790	20.9	33.9
053 ASSEMB OF GOD.	3	267	1 186	1.8	2.9
081 CATHOLIC......	8	NA	14 554	22.0	35.7
097 CHR CHS&CHS CR	1	50	61*	0.1	0.1
123 CH GOD (ANDER)	1	82	246	0.4	0.6
127 CH GOD (CLEVE)	1	80	98*	0.1	0.2
151 L-D SAINTS....	2	NA	386	0.6	0.9
163 CH OF LUTH BR.	1	147	217	0.3	0.5
165 CH OF NAZARENE	2	83	158	0.2	0.4
167 CHS OF CHRIST.	2	62	86	0.1	0.2
193 EPISCOPAL.....	1	430	475	0.7	1.2
203 EVAN FREE CH..	2	116	141*	0.2	0.3
220 FREE LUTHERAN.	1	95	120	0.2	0.3
221 FREE METHODIST	1	3	6	-	-
281 LUTH CH AMER..	2	1 350	1 803	2.7	4.4
283 LUTH--MO SYNOD	4	1 006	1 385	2.1	3.4
313 N AM BAPT CONF	1	370	451*	0.7	1.1
353 CHR BRETHREN..	1	15	15	-	-
403 SALVATION ARMY	1	63	210	0.3	0.5
413 S.D.A.........	2	174	212*	0.3	0.5
419 SO BAPT CONV..	3	1 132	1 380*	2.1	3.4
443 UN C OF CHRIST	2	240	293*	0.4	0.7
449 UN METHODIST..	6	1 510	1 841*	2.8	4.5
453 UN PRES CH USA	5	1 261	1 538*	2.3	3.8

NA—Not applicable   *Total adherents estimated from known number of communicant, confirmed, full members.   —Represents a percent less than 0.1.   Percentages may not total due to rounding.

Table 4. Churches and Church Membership by County and Denomination: 1980

County and Denomination	Number of churches	Communicant, confirmed, full members	Total adherents		
			Number	Percent of total population	Percent of total adherents
GRANT	25	1 944	3 548*	83.0	100.0
029 AMER LUTH CH..	3	865	1 146	26.8	32.3
053 ASSEMB OF GOD.	1	34	62	1.5	1.7
081 CATHOLIC.....	6	NA	1 069	25.0	30.1
181 CONSRV CONGR..	2	239	294*	6.9	8.3
313 N AM BAPT CONF	1	100	123*	2.9	3.5
335 ORTH PRESB CH.	2	60	74*	1.7	2.1
443 UN C OF CHRIST	4	186	229*	5.4	6.5
449 UN METHODIST..	2	145	178*	4.2	5.0
453 UN PRES CH USA	1	74	91*	2.1	2.6
469 WELS.........	3	241	282	6.6	7.9
GRIGGS	21	1 900	2 810*	75.7	100.0
029 AMER LUTH CH..	9	1 339	1 643	44.2	58.5
053 ASSEMB OF GOD.	1	33	50	1.3	1.8
081 CATHOLIC.....	2	NA	416	11.2	14.8
163 CH OF LUTH BR.	1	43	101	2.7	3.6
203 EVAN FREE CH..	3	102	122*	3.3	4.3
220 FREE LUTHERAN.	1	81	101	2.7	3.6
283 LUTH--MO SYNOD	2	184	236	6.4	8.4
449 UN METHODIST..	1	35	42*	1.1	1.5
453 UN PRES CH USA	1	83	99*	2.7	3.5
HETTINGER	18	1 498	4 393*	102.8	100.0
029 AMER LUTH CH..	5	877	1 095	25.6	24.9
053 ASSEMB OF GOD.	2	51	125	2.9	2.8
081 CATHOLIC.....	3	NA	2 480	58.0	56.5
165 CH OF NAZARENE	1	26	35	0.8	0.8
181 CONSRV CONGR..	1	143	173*	4.0	3.9
413 S.D.A.........	1	15	18*	0.4	0.4
443 UN C OF CHRIST	4	275	333*	7.8	7.6
449 UN METHODIST..	1	111	134*	3.1	3.1
KIDDER	23	1 664	2 799*	73.0	100.0
029 AMER LUTH CH..	6	752	955	24.9	34.1
081 CATHOLIC.....	3	NA	504	13.1	18.0
165 CH OF NAZARENE	1	33	80	2.1	2.9
197 EVAN CH OF NA.	1	46	46	1.2	1.6
283 LUTH--MO SYNOD	1	41	186	4.9	6.6
443 UN C OF CHRIST	4	108	133*	3.5	4.8
449 UN METHODIST..	5	356	438*	11.4	15.6
453 UN PRES CH USA	1	74	91*	2.4	3.3
469 WELS.........	1	254	366	9.5	13.1
LA MOURE	38	3 757	6 560*	101.3	100.0
029 AMER LUTH CH..	10	1 159	1 522	23.5	23.2
053 ASSEMB OF GOD.	1	75	130	2.0	2.0
057 BAPT GEN CONF.	1	90	109*	1.7	1.7
081 CATHOLIC.....	6	NA	1 722	26.6	26.2
133 CH GOD(7TH)DEN	2	54	66*	1.0	1.0
165 CH OF NAZARENE	1	43	114	1.8	1.7
283 LUTH--MO SYNOD	4	805	1 013	15.6	15.4
371 REF CH IN AM..	1	80	120	1.9	1.8
413 S.D.A.........	2	122	148*	2.3	2.3
443 UN C OF CHRIST	2	370	450*	7.0	6.9
449 UN METHODIST..	6	729	886*	13.7	13.5
453 UN PRES CH USA	2	230	280*	4.3	4.3
LOGAN	19	1 529	3 246*	92.9	100.0
029 AMER LUTH CH..	3	691	873	25.0	26.9
045 APOSTOLIC LUTH	1	20	24*	0.7	0.7
053 ASSEMB OF GOD.	2	44	50	1.4	1.5
081 CATHOLIC.....	4	NA	1 368	39.2	42.1
283 LUTH--MO SYNOD	1	81	99	2.8	3.0
313 N AM BAPT CONF	3	244	293*	8.4	9.0
413 S.D.A.........	2	84	101*	2.9	3.1
443 UN C OF CHRIST	2	231	277*	7.9	8.5
449 UN METHODIST..	1	134	161*	4.6	5.0
MC HENRY	37	3 769	7 225*	91.9	100.0
019 AMER BAPT USA.	2	57	69*	0.9	1.0
029 AMER LUTH CH..	13	2 436	3 221	41.0	44.6
081 CATHOLIC.....	7	NA	2 336	29.7	32.3
127 CH GOD (CLEVE)	1	23	28*	0.4	0.4
165 CH OF NAZARENE	1	28	38	0.5	0.5
197 EVAN CH OF NA.	1	11	11	0.1	0.2
237 GC MENN BR CHS	1	68	83*	1.1	1.1
283 LUTH--MO SYNOD	4	551	717	9.1	9.9
313 N AM BAPT CONF	2	109	132*	1.7	1.8
413 S.D.A.........	1	72	87*	1.1	1.2
443 UN C OF LUTHERAN	1	93	113*	1.4	1.6
449 UN METHODIST..	2	182	221*	2.8	3.1
453 UN PRES CH USA	1	139	169*	2.2	2.3
MC INTOSH	20	3 688	4 761*	99.2	100.0
029 AMER LUTH CH..	3	1 929	2 287	47.6	48.0
053 ASSEMB OF GOD.	1	35	39	0.8	0.8
057 BAPT GEN CONF.	1	25	29*	0.6	0.6
081 CATHOLIC.....	3	NA	438	9.1	9.2
127 CH GOD (CLEVE)	1	6	7*	0.1	0.1
283 LUTH--MO SYNOD	1	108	128	2.7	2.7
313 N AM BAPT CONF	4	635	735*	15.3	15.4
413 S.D.A.........	1	69	80*	1.7	1.7
443 UN C OF CHRIST	1	282	327*	6.8	6.9
449 UN METHODIST..	3	433	501*	10.4	10.5
469 WELS.........	1	166	190	4.0	4.0

County and Denomination	Number of churches	Communicant, confirmed, full members	Total adherents		
			Number	Percent of total population	Percent of total adherents
MC KENZIE	28	2 147	3 478*	48.8	100.0
029 AMER LUTH CH..	13	1 768	2 448	34.3	70.4
053 ASSEMB OF GOD.	1	23	41	0.6	1.2
081 CATHOLIC.....	4	NA	541	7.6	15.6
151 L-D SAINTS....	1	NA	?	?	?
165 CH OF NAZARENE	1	15	17	0.2	0.5
193 EPISCOPAL.....	1	42	54	0.8	1.6
283 LUTH--MO SYNOD	2	116	147	2.1	4.2
413 S.D.A.........	1	28	35*	0.5	1.0
443 UN C OF CHRIST	2	82	103*	1.4	3.0
449 UN METHODIST..	1	18	23*	0.3	0.7
453 UN PRES CH USA	1	55	69*	1.0	2.0
MC LEAN	59	5 078	8 674*	70.6	100.0
029 AMER LUTH CH..	16	2 387	3 092	25.2	35.6
053 ASSEMB OF GOD.	3	99	165	1.3	1.9
081 CATHOLIC.....	10	NA	1 984	16.1	22.9
127 CH GOD (CLEVE)	2	35	43*	0.3	0.5
165 CH OF NAZARENE	2	41	150	1.2	1.7
181 CONSRV CONGR..	1	46	57*	0.5	0.7
193 EPISCOPAL.....	1	51	132	1.1	1.5
203 EVAN FREE CH..	1	54	67*	0.5	0.8
281 LUTH CH AMER..	3	296	407	3.3	4.7
283 LUTH--MO SYNOD	3	508	657	5.3	7.6
313 N AM BAPT CONF	4	412	510*	4.2	5.9
381 REF PRES-EVAN.	1	63	67	0.5	0.8
413 S.D.A.........	2	89	110*	0.9	1.3
443 UN C OF CHRIST	3	415	513*	4.2	5.9
449 UN METHODIST..	6	373	461*	3.8	5.3
453 UN PRES CH USA	1	209	259*	2.1	3.0
MERCER	25	4 043	6 434*	68.6	100.0
029 AMER LUTH CH..	7	2 337	3 043	32.4	47.3
053 ASSEMB OF GOD.	2	59	88	0.9	1.4
081 CATHOLIC.....	4	NA	1 196	12.8	18.6
127 CH GOD (CLEVE)	1	103	128*	1.4	2.0
283 LUTH--MO SYNOD	5	1 033	1 345	14.3	20.9
313 N AM BAPT CONF	1	78	97*	1.0	1.5
413 S.D.A.........	2	50	62*	0.7	1.0
443 UN C OF CHRIST	1	187	232*	2.5	3.6
449 UN METHODIST..	2	196	243*	2.6	3.8
MORTON	43	6 294	21 038*	83.6	100.0
029 AMER LUTH CH..	4	1 863	2 531	10.1	12.0
053 ASSEMB OF GOD.	2	207	414	1.6	2.0
057 BAPT GEN CONF.	1	14	17*	0.1	0.1
081 CATHOLIC.....	12	NA	12 733	50.6	60.5
151 L-D SAINTS....	1	NA	?	?	?
165 CH OF NAZARENE	1	35	68	0.3	0.3
167 CHS OF CHRIST.	1	15	19	0.1	0.1
193 EPISCOPAL.....	1	54	68	0.3	0.3
283 LUTH--MO SYNOD	3	631	842	3.3	4.0
313 N AM BAPT CONF	1	196	244*	1.0	1.2
413 S.D.A.........	1	11	14*	0.1	0.1
419 SO BAPT CONV..	1	145	181*	0.7	0.9
443 UN C OF CHRIST	6	1 734	2 162*	8.6	10.3
449 UN METHODIST..	4	700	873*	3.5	4.1
453 UN PRES CH USA	2	391	487*	1.9	2.3
469 WELS.........	2	298	385	1.5	1.8
MOUNTRAIL	42	3 276	5 316*	69.2	100.0
019 AMER BAPT USA.	1	80	99*	1.3	1.9
029 AMER LUTH CH..	18	2 518	3 313	43.1	62.3
045 APOSTOLIC LUTH	1	50	62*	0.8	1.2
053 ASSEMB OF GOD.	2	126	135	1.8	2.5
081 CATHOLIC.....	5	NA	1 093	14.2	20.6
127 CH GOD (CLEVE)	2	13	16*	0.2	0.3
151 L-D SAINTS....	1	NA	?	?	?
193 EPISCOPAL.....	1	10	15	0.2	0.3
197 EVAN CH OF NA.	1	9	9	0.1	0.2
220 FREE LUTHERAN.	1	66	80	1.0	1.5
283 LUTH--MO SYNOD	1	41	45	0.6	0.8
413 S.D.A.........	1	21	26*	0.3	0.5
419 SO BAPT CONV..	1	15	19*	0.2	0.4
443 UN C OF CHRIST	5	244	301*	3.9	5.7
453 UN PRES CH USA	1	83	103*	1.3	1.9
NELSON	28	3 276	5 013*	95.8	100.0
029 AMER LUTH CH..	18	2 887	3 573	68.3	71.3
081 CATHOLIC.....	4	NA	973	18.6	19.4
193 EPISCOPAL.....	1	24	33	0.6	0.7
220 FREE LUTHERAN.	1	141	170	3.2	3.4
283 LUTH--MO SYNOD	2	85	100	1.9	2.0
443 UN C OF CHRIST	2	139	164*	3.1	3.3
OLIVER	6	601	1 452*	58.2	100.0
029 AMER LUTH CH..	2	273	370	14.8	25.5
081 CATHOLIC.....	1	NA	651	26.1	44.8
165 CH OF NAZARENE	1	17	52	2.1	3.6
283 LUTH--MO SYNOD	1	264	320	12.8	22.0
449 UN METHODIST..	1	47	59*	2.4	4.1
PEMBINA	52	4 844	8 276*	79.6	100.0
029 AMER LUTH CH..	6	1 159	1 485	14.3	17.9
053 ASSEMB OF GOD.	3	108	246	2.4	3.0
081 CATHOLIC.....	9	NA	2 100	20.2	25.4
151 L-D SAINTS....	2	NA	28	0.3	0.3

NA—Not applicable.   *Total adherents estimated from known number of communicant, confirmed, full members.   —Represents a percent less than 0.1.   Percentages may not total due to rounding.

Table 4. Churches and Church Membership by County and Denomination: 1980

County and Denomination	Number of churches	Communicant, confirmed, full members	Total adherents		
			Number	Percent of total population	Percent of total adherents
193 EPISCOPAL.....	1	34	51	0.5	0.6
201 EVAN COV CH AM	1	54	66*	0.6	0.8
203 EVAN FREE CH..	1	82	100*	1.0	1.2
220 FREE LUTHERAN.	1	27	35	0.3	0.4
281 LUTH CH AMER..	7	1 068	1 345	12.9	16.3
283 LUTH--MO SYNOD	4	655	803	7.7	9.7
419 SO BAPT CONV..	1	21	26*	0.3	0.3
449 UN METHODIST..	12	1 097	1 335*	12.8	16.1
453 UN PRES CH USA	4	539	656*	6.3	7.9
PIERCE	22	1 778	5 125*	83.1	100.0
029 AMER LUTH CH..	6	1 334	1 698	27.5	33.1
053 ASSEMB OF GOD.	1	48	80	1.3	1.6
081 CATHOLIC......	5	NA	2 844	46.1	55.5
127 CH GOD (CLEVE)	1	?	?	?	?
193 EPISCOPAL.....	1	23	30	0.5	0.6
203 EVAN FREE CH..	1	18	22*	0.4	0.4
220 FREE LUTHERAN.	1	15	20	0.3	0.4
283 LUTH--MO SYNOD	1	147	195	3.2	3.8
449 UN METHODIST..	3	121	148*	2.4	2.9
453 UN PRES CH USA	2	72	88*	1.4	1.7
RAMSEY	40	5 001	10 736*	82.3	100.0
029 AMER LUTH CH..	13	3 384	4 269	32.7	39.8
053 ASSEMB OF GOD.	2	58	250	1.9	2.3
081 CATHOLIC......	6	NA	4 198	32.2	39.1
133 CH GOD(7TH)DEN	1	8	10*	0.1	0.1
151 L-D SAINTS....	1	NA	89	0.7	0.8
167 CHS OF CHRIST.	1	8	25	0.2	0.2
193 EPISCOPAL.....	1	25	35	0.3	0.3
203 EVAN FREE CH..	1	38	46*	0.4	0.4
220 FREE LUTHERAN.	3	160	190	1.5	1.8
283 LUTH--MO SYNOD	2	374	483	3.7	4.5
413 S.D.A.........	1	7	8*	0.1	0.1
419 SO BAPT CONV..	1	98	118*	0.9	1.1
449 UN METHODIST..	5	606	731*	5.6	6.8
453 UN PRES CH USA	2	235	284*	2.2	2.6
RANSOM	21	3 757	6 018*	89.8	100.0
019 AMER BAPT USA.	1	92	111*	1.7	1.8
029 AMER LUTH CH..	8	2 701	3 634	54.3	60.4
053 ASSEMB OF GOD.	1	36	34	0.5	0.6
081 CATHOLIC......	3	NA	1 103	16.5	18.3
193 EPISCOPAL.....	1	16	22	0.3	0.4
220 FREE LUTHERAN.	1	43	54	0.8	0.9
283 LUTH--MO SYNOD	1	281	348	5.2	5.8
413 S.D.A.........	1	35	42*	0.6	0.7
449 UN METHODIST..	3	430	521*	7.8	8.7
453 UN PRES CH USA	1	123	149*	2.2	2.5
RENVILLE	17	1 832	3 024*	83.8	100.0
019 AMER BAPT USA.	1	129	157*	4.4	5.2
029 AMER LUTH CH..	5	912	1 197	33.2	39.6
081 CATHOLIC......	4	NA	702	19.5	23.2
165 CH OF NAZARENE	1	48	72	2.0	2.4
281 LUTH CH AMER..	3	389	469	13.0	15.5
283 LUTH--MO SYNOD	1	127	150	4.2	5.0
449 UN METHODIST..	2	227	277*	7.7	9.2
RICHLAND	54	7 811	16 739*	87.2	100.0
029 AMER LUTH CH..	19	3 469	4 497	23.4	26.9
053 ASSEMB OF GOD.	1	46	71	0.4	0.4
081 CATHOLIC......	8	NA	6 975	36.3	41.7
127 CH GOD (CLEVE)	1	41	49*	0.3	0.3
163 CH OF LUTH BR.	1	17	31	0.2	0.2
193 EPISCOPAL.....	1	88	111	0.6	0.7
220 FREE LUTHERAN.	1	102	112	0.6	0.7
283 LUTH--MO SYNOD	9	2 421	2 957	15.4	17.7
413 S.D.A.........	1	205	244*	1.3	1.5
443 UN C OF CHRIST	4	519	618*	3.2	3.7
449 UN METHODIST..	8	903	1 074*	5.6	6.4
ROLETTE	27	1 919	14 874*	122.1	100.0
029 AMER LUTH CH..	6	1 015	1 401	11.5	9.4
053 ASSEMB OF GOD.	3	65	157	1.3	1.1
081 CATHOLIC......	6	NA	12 020	98.7	80.8
089 CHR & MISS AL.	1	45	51	0.4	0.3
127 CH GOD (CLEVE)	1	6	8*	0.1	0.1
151 L-D SAINTS....	1	NA	?	?	?
163 CH OF LUTH BR.	1	31	91	0.7	0.6
193 EPISCOPAL.....	1	36	223	1.8	1.5
283 LUTH--MO SYNOD	1	171	210	1.7	1.4
285 MENNONITE CH..	2	167	217*	1.8	1.5
449 UN METHODIST..	2	132	171*	1.4	1.1
453 UN PRES CH USA	2	251	325*	2.7	2.2
SARGENT	21	2 615	4 393*	79.7	100.0
019 AMER BAPT USA.	1	40	49*	0.9	1.1
029 AMER LUTH CH..	8	1 575	2 055	37.3	46.8
081 CATHOLIC......	5	NA	1 011	18.3	23.0
097 CHR CHS&CHS CR	1	40	49*	0.9	1.1
281 LUTH CH AMER..	1	404	507	9.2	11.5
283 LUTH--MO SYNOD	2	353	473	8.6	10.8
443 UN C OF CHRIST	1	17	21*	0.4	0.5
449 UN METHODIST..	2	186	228*	4.1	5.2
SHERIDAN	17	1 524	2 075*	73.6	100.0

County and Denomination	Number of churches	Communicant, confirmed, full members	Total adherents		
			Number	Percent of total population	Percent of total adherents
029 AMER LUTH CH..	3	438	575	20.4	27.7
053 ASSEMB OF GOD.	1	53	70	2.5	3.4
081 CATHOLIC......	1	NA	123	4.4	5.9
123 CH GOD (ANDER)	1	22	66	2.3	3.2
165 CH OF NAZARENE	1	9	20	0.7	1.0
237 GC MENN BR CHS	1	10	12*	0.4	0.6
283 LUTH--MO SYNOD	1	251	319	11.3	15.4
313 N AM BAPT CONF	3	404	485*	17.2	23.4
413 S.D.A.........	2	123	148*	5.3	7.1
449 UN METHODIST..	3	214	257*	9.1	12.4
SIOUX	12	263	3 409*	94.2	100.0
053 ASSEMB OF GOD.	2	43	76	2.1	2.2
081 CATHOLIC......	4	NA	2 735	75.6	80.2
193 EPISCOPAL.....	2	90	425	11.7	12.5
419 SO BAPT CONV..	2	58	77*	2.1	2.3
443 UN C OF CHRIST	2	72	96*	2.7	2.8
SLOPE	3	67	276	23.9	100.0
029 AMER LUTH CH..	1	67	89	7.7	32.2
081 CATHOLIC......	2	NA	187	16.2	67.8
STARK	32	2 777	16 846*	71.1	100.0
029 AMER LUTH CH..	5	1 482	2 009	8.5	11.9
053 ASSEMB OF GOD.	1	59	92	0.4	0.5
081 CATHOLIC......	12	NA	13 135	55.4	78.0
151 L-D SAINTS....	1	NA	?	?	?
165 CH OF NAZARENE	1	35	81	0.3	0.5
167 CHS OF CHRIST.	1	18	23	0.1	0.1
181 CONSRV CONGR..	1	61	75*	0.3	0.4
193 EPISCOPAL.....	1	76	101	0.4	0.6
220 FREE LUTHERAN.	1	60	80	0.3	0.5
283 LUTH--MO SYNOD	2	280	380	1.6	2.3
313 N AM BAPT CONF	1	54	67*	0.3	0.4
413 S.D.A.........	1	95	117*	0.5	0.7
419 SO BAPT CONV..	1	83	102*	0.4	0.6
443 UN C OF CHRIST	1	65	80*	0.3	0.5
449 UN METHODIST..	1	335	413*	1.7	2.5
453 UN PRES CH USA	1	74	91*	0.4	0.5
STEELE	22	2 057	2 855*	91.9	100.0
029 AMER LUTH CH..	12	1 653	2 045	65.8	71.6
053 ASSEMB OF GOD.	1	39	67	2.2	2.3
081 CATHOLIC......	2	NA	294	9.5	10.3
283 LUTH--MO SYNOD	1	86	111	3.6	3.9
419 SO BAPT CONV..	1	?	?	?	?
443 UN C OF CHRIST	1	58	70*	2.3	2.5
449 UN METHODIST..	2	146	177*	5.7	6.2
453 UN PRES CH USA	2	75	91*	2.9	3.2
STUTSMAN	52	9 839	17 158*	71.0	100.0
029 AMER LUTH CH..	9	4 134	5 515	22.8	32.1
053 ASSEMB OF GOD.	2	391	420	1.7	2.4
057 BAPT GEN CONF.	1	281	340*	1.4	2.0
081 CATHOLIC......	8	NA	4 067	16.8	23.7
127 CH GOD (CLEVE)	1	3	4*	–	–
151 L-D SAINTS....	1	NA	118	0.5	0.7
164 CH LUTH CONF..	1	156	210	0.9	1.2
165 CH OF NAZARENE	1	117	253	1.0	1.5
167 CHS OF CHRIST.	1	10	25	0.1	0.1
193 EPISCOPAL.....	1	123	180	0.7	1.0
197 EVAN CH OF NA.	1	81	81	0.3	0.5
208 EVAN LUTH ASSN	1	35	50	0.2	0.3
221 FREE METHODIST	1	19	174	0.7	1.0
281 LUTH CH AMER..	1	203	278	1.2	1.6
283 LUTH--MO SYNOD	3	694	955	4.0	5.6
313 N AM BAPT CONF	3	206	249*	1.0	1.5
403 SALVATION ARMY	1	75	228	0.9	1.3
413 S.D.A.........	2	419	507*	2.1	3.0
443 UN C OF CHRIST	3	667	807*	3.3	4.7
449 UN METHODIST..	7	1 532	1 854*	7.7	10.8
453 UN PRES CH USA	2	668	808*	3.3	4.7
469 WELS..........	1	25	35	0.1	0.2
TOWNER	16	1 955	3 531*	87.1	100.0
029 AMER LUTH CH..	4	965	1 268	31.3	35.9
053 ASSEMB OF GOD.	1	77	124	3.1	3.5
081 CATHOLIC......	4	NA	1 022	25.2	28.9
157 CH OF BRETHREN	1	132	158*	3.9	4.5
283 LUTH--MO SYNOD	2	408	511	12.6	14.5
449 UN METHODIST..	2	320	384*	9.5	10.9
453 UN PRES CH USA	2	53	64*	1.6	1.8
TRAILL	35	5 931	8 374*	87.0	100.0
029 AMER LUTH CH..	21	4 790	6 040	62.8	72.1
081 CATHOLIC......	2	NA	806	8.4	9.6
163 CH OF LUTH BR.	2	87	197	2.0	2.4
203 EVAN FREE CH..	1	53	63*	0.7	0.8
209 EVAN LUTH SYN.	1	130	160	1.7	1.9
220 FREE LUTHERAN.	3	160	230	2.4	2.7
283 LUTH--MO SYNOD	1	263	343	3.6	4.1
443 UN C OF CHRIST	2	240	287*	3.0	3.4
449 UN METHODIST..	1	89	106*	1.1	1.3
453 UN PRES CH USA	1	119	142*	1.5	1.7
WALSH	47	5 364	10 372*	67.5	100.0
029 AMER LUTH CH..	19	4 137	5 238	34.1	50.5

NA— Not applicable   *Total adherents estimated from known number of communicant, confirmed, full members.   —Represents a percent less than 0.1.   Percentages may not total due to rounding.

Table 4. Churches and Church Membership by County and Denomination: 1980

County and Denomination	Number of churches	Communicant, confirmed, full members	Total adherents Number	Percent of total population	Percent of total adherents
053 ASSEMB OF GOD.	1	47	130	0.8	1.3
081 CATHOLIC......	11	NA	3 530	23.0	34.0
143 CG IN CR(MENN)	1	57	57	0.4	0.5
151 L-D SAINTS....	1	NA	19	0.1	0.2
165 CH OF NAZARENE	1	7	15	0.1	0.1
193 EPISCOPAL.....	1	23	44	0.3	0.4
220 FREE LUTHERAN.	2	115	154	1.0	1.5
281 LUTH CH AMER..	1	31	38	0.2	0.4
283 LUTH--MO SYNOD	1	188	234	1.5	2.3
449 UN METHODIST..	3	237	285*	1.9	2.7
453 UN PRES CH USA	5	522	628*	4.1	6.1
WARD	81	16 444	32 230*	55.2	100.0
019 AMER BAPT USA.	5	439	544*	0.9	1.7
029 AMER LUTH CH..	18	7 612	10 117	17.3	31.4
053 ASSEMB OF GOD.	2	340	495	0.8	1.5
057 BAPT GEN CONF.	1	82	102*	0.2	0.3
081 CATHOLIC......	13	NA	9 874	16.9	30.6
089 CHR & MISS AL.	1	115	303	0.5	0.9
123 CH GOD (ANDER)	1	17	51	0.1	0.2
127 CH GOD (CLEVE)	3	276	342*	0.6	1.1
151 L-D SAINTS....	3	NA	?	?	?
157 CH OF BRETHREN	1	54	67*	0.1	0.2
163 CH OF LUTH BR.	1	142	170	0.3	0.5
165 CH OF NAZARENE	4	215	354	0.6	1.1
167 CHS OF CHRIST.	1	79	108	0.2	0.3
193 EPISCOPAL.....	1	146	240	0.4	0.7
209 EVAN LUTH SYN.	1	32	54	0.1	0.2
220 FREE LUTHERAN.	1	55	85	0.1	0.3
237 GC MENN BR CHS	1	55	68*	0.1	0.2
270 CONSRV JUDAISM	1	15	19*	–	0.1
281 LUTH CH AMER..	1	624	858	1.5	2.7
283 LUTH--MO SYNOD	4	2 114	2 927	5.0	9.1
285 MENNONITE CH..	1	59	73*	0.1	0.2
313 N AM BAPT CONF	1	335	415*	0.7	1.3
403 SALVATION ARMY	1	94	569	1.0	1.8
413 S.D.A.........	2	295	366*	0.6	1.1
419 SO BAPT CONV..	2	499	619*	1.1	1.9
443 UN C OF CHRIST	2	286	355*	0.6	1.1
449 UN METHODIST..	6	1 235	1 531*	2.6	4.8
453 UN PRES CH USA	2	1 229	1 524*	2.6	4.7
WELLS	38	3 261	6 170*	88.4	100.0
029 AMER LUTH CH..	11	1 821	2 300	33.0	37.3
053 ASSEMB OF GOD.	1	14	30	0.4	0.5
081 CATHOLIC......	5	NA	1 983	28.4	32.1
123 CH GOD (ANDER)	1	42	126	1.8	2.0
163 CH OF LUTH BR.	1	15	22	0.3	0.4
165 CH OF NAZARENE	2	85	165	2.4	2.7
237 GC MENN BR CHS	1	188	226*	3.2	3.7
283 LUTH--MO SYNOD	2	119	141	2.0	2.3
313 N AM BAPT CONF	3	328	394*	5.6	6.4
353 CHR BRETHREN..	1	10	15	0.2	0.2
413 S.D.A.........	5	341	410*	5.9	6.6
443 UN C OF CHRIST	2	60	72*	1.0	1.2
449 UN METHODIST..	3	238	286*	4.1	4.6
WILLIAMS	52	8 645	16 122*	72.5	100.0
029 AMER LUTH CH..	25	6 219	8 257	37.1	51.2
053 ASSEMB OF GOD.	2	77	132	0.6	0.8
081 CATHOLIC......	6	NA	4 658	20.9	28.9
089 CHR & MISS AL.	1	11	33	0.1	0.2
151 L-D SAINTS....	1	NA	?	?	?
163 CH OF LUTH BR.	1	70	117	0.5	0.7
165 CH OF NAZARENE	2	39	129	0.6	0.8
167 CHS OF CHRIST.	1	24	37	0.2	0.2
193 EPISCOPAL.....	1	137	145	0.7	0.9
197 EVAN CH OF NA.	1	21	21	0.1	0.1
220 FREE LUTHERAN.	2	380	450	2.0	2.8
283 LUTH--MO SYNOD	1	327	459	2.1	2.8
403 SALVATION ARMY	1	64	117	0.5	0.7
413 S.D.A.........	2	137	168*	0.8	1.0
419 SO BAPT CONV..	1	154	189*	0.8	1.2
443 UN C OF CHRIST	1	144	177*	0.8	1.1
449 UN METHODIST..	2	696	855*	3.8	5.3
453 UN PRES CH USA	1	145	178*	0.8	1.1

OHIO

County and Denomination	Number of churches	Communicant, confirmed, full members	Total adherents Number	Percent of total population	Percent of total adherents
THE STATE.....	10 060	2 212 329	5 346 227*	49.5	100.0
ADAMS	64	6 216	9 036*	37.1	100.0
019 AMER BAPT USA.	2	200	249*	1.0	2.8
029 AMER LUTH CH..	4	1 748	2 489	10.2	27.5
081 CATHOLIC......	4	NA	777	3.2	8.6
097 CHR CHS&CHS CR	8	945	1 175*	4.8	13.0
107 CHRISTIAN UN..	9	349	381	1.6	4.2
123 CH GOD (ANDER)	1	55	165	0.7	1.8
157 CH OF BRETHREN	3	62	77*	0.3	0.9

County and Denomination	Number of churches	Communicant, confirmed, full members	Total adherents Number	Percent of total population	Percent of total adherents
165 CH OF NAZARENE	2	186	369	1.5	4.1
167 CHS OF CHRIST.	2	36	76	0.3	0.8
323 OLD ORD AMISH.	1	130	162*	0.7	1.8
413 S.D.A.........	1	32	40*	0.2	0.4
419 SO BAPT CONV..	2	122	152*	0.6	1.7
449 UN METHODIST..	18	1 634	2 032*	8.4	22.5
453 UN PRES CH USA	7	717	892*	3.7	9.9
ALLEN	126	26 731	57 566*	51.3	100.0
019 AMER BAPT USA.	3	939	1 156*	1.0	2.0
029 AMER LUTH CH..	3	1 039	1 461	1.3	2.5
053 ASSEMB OF GOD.	2	266	489	0.4	0.8
081 CATHOLIC......	8	NA	21 696	19.3	37.7
089 CHR & MISS AL.	2	335	878	0.8	1.5
093 CHR CH (DISC).	2	1 293	1 853	1.7	3.2
097 CHR CHS&CHS CR	4	395	486*	0.4	0.8
101 C.M.E.........	1	195	240*	0.2	0.4
107 CHRISTIAN UN..	3	151	221	0.2	0.4
123 CH GOD (ANDER)	2	400	1 200	1.1	2.1
127 CH GOD (CLEVE)	1	73	90*	0.1	0.2
151 L-D SAINTS....	1	NA	373	0.3	0.6
157 CH OF BRETHREN	4	836	1 029*	0.9	1.8
165 CH OF NAZARENE	4	595	1 181	1.1	2.1
167 CHS OF CHRIST.	2	190	242	0.2	0.4
175 CONGR CHR CHS.	1	282	347*	0.3	0.6
221 FREE METHODIST	1	49	153	0.1	0.3
226 FRIENDS-USA...	1	32	39*	–	0.1
244 GRACE BRETHREN	1	32	39*	–	0.1
263 INT FOURSQ GOS	1	41	50*	–	0.1
271 REFORM JUDAISM	1	188	231*	0.2	0.4
281 LUTH CH AMER..	4	1 282	1 532	1.4	2.7
283 LUTH--MO SYNOD	1	321	441	0.4	0.8
285 MENNONITE CH..	4	405	498*	0.4	0.9
287 MENN GEN CONF.	3	1 246	1 516	1.4	2.6
291 MISSIONARY CH.	5	267	398	0.4	0.7
329 OPEN BIBLE STD	1	30	40	–	0.1
403 SALVATION ARMY	1	178	403	0.4	0.7
413 S.D.A.........	2	162	199*	0.2	0.3
419 SO BAPT CONV..	4	782	962*	0.9	1.7
435 UNITARIAN-UNIV	1	30	37*	–	0.1
443 UN C OF CHRIST	11	2 936	3 613*	3.2	6.3
449 UN METHODIST..	34	10 237	12 599*	11.2	21.9
453 UN PRES CH USA	6	1 506	1 853*	1.7	3.2
469 WELS..........	1	18	21	–	–
ASHLAND	78	15 266	21 635*	46.9	100.0
019 AMER BAPT USA.	2	552	674*	1.5	3.1
053 ASSEMB OF GOD.	1	104	192	0.4	0.9
071 BRETHREN (ASH)	2	597	729*	1.6	3.4
075 BRETHREN IN CR	1	43	73	0.2	0.3
081 CATHOLIC......	4	NA	2 081	4.5	9.6
089 CHR & MISS AL.	2	67	157	0.3	0.7
093 CHR CH (DISC).	1	815	1 113	2.4	5.1
097 CHR CHS&CHS CR	5	573	699*	1.5	3.2
123 CH GOD (ANDER)	2	63	189	0.4	0.9
127 CH GOD (CLEVE)	1	100	122*	0.3	0.6
151 L-D SAINTS....	1	NA	179	0.4	0.8
157 CH OF BRETHREN	3	627	765*	1.7	3.5
165 CH OF NAZARENE	3	255	441	1.0	2.0
167 CHS OF CHRIST.	4	395	500	1.1	2.3
175 CONGR CHR CHS.	1	221	270*	0.6	1.2
244 GRACE BRETHREN	2	676	825*	1.8	3.8
263 INT FOURSQ GOS	1	47	57*	0.1	0.3
281 LUTH CH AMER..	7	2 369	3 005	6.5	13.9
323 OLD ORD AMISH.	6	780	952*	2.1	4.4
329 OPEN BIBLE STD	1	78	150	0.3	0.7
403 SALVATION ARMY	1	86	140	0.3	0.6
419 SO BAPT CONV..	1	51	62*	0.1	0.3
443 UN C OF CHRIST	3	417	509*	1.1	2.4
449 UN METHODIST..	17	5 187	6 331*	13.7	29.3
453 UN PRES CH USA	5	1 135	1 385*	3.0	6.4
469 WELS..........	1	28	35	0.1	0.2
ASHTABULA	122	20 506	50 551*	48.5	100.0
019 AMER BAPT USA.	6	1 568	1 926*	1.8	3.8
053 ASSEMB OF GOD.	4	524	976	0.9	1.9
081 CATHOLIC......	13	NA	23 148	22.2	45.8
089 CHR & MISS AL.	2	168	262	0.3	0.5
093 CHR CH (DISC).	3	548	784	0.8	1.6
097 CHR CHS&CHS CR	6	793	974*	0.9	1.9
123 CH GOD (ANDER)	1	60	180	0.2	0.4
127 CH GOD (CLEVE)	4	102	125*	0.1	0.2
151 L-D SAINTS....	1	NA	325	0.3	0.6
165 CH OF NAZARENE	8	949	1 601	1.5	3.2
167 CHS OF CHRIST.	2	320	475	0.5	0.9
181 CONSRV CONGR..	1	118	145*	0.1	0.3
201 EVAN COV CH AM	1	93	114*	0.1	0.2
221 FREE METHODIST	3	67	372	0.4	0.7
263 INT FOURSQ GOS	1	66	81*	0.1	0.2
270 CONSRV JUDAISM	1	21	26*	–	0.1
281 LUTH CH AMER..	5	2 353	3 331	3.2	6.6
283 LUTH--MO SYNOD	2	630	789	0.8	1.6
349 PENT HOLINESS.	2	154	189*	0.2	0.4
353 CHR BRETHREN..	1	25	25	–	–
403 SALVATION ARMY	1	4	35	–	0.1
413 S.D.A.........	3	218	268*	0.3	0.5
419 SO BAPT CONV..	4	539	662*	0.6	1.3
443 UN C OF CHRIST	10	2 418	2 970*	2.8	5.9
449 UN METHODIST..	27	6 098	7 489*	7.2	14.8
453 UN PRES CH USA	10	2 670	3 279*	3.1	6.5
ATHENS	93	8 684	15 093*	26.8	100.0

NA— Not applicable   *Total adherents estimated from known number of communicant, confirmed, full members.   —Represents a percent less than 0.1.   Percentages may not total due to rounding.

Table 4. Churches and Church Membership by County and Denomination: 1980

County and Denomination	Number of churches	Communicant, confirmed, full members	Total adherents Number	Percent of total population	Percent of total adherents
019 AMER BAPT USA.	2	149	175*	0.3	1.2
053 ASSEMB OF GOD.	1	180	352	0.6	2.3
081 CATHOLIC......	7	NA	3 377	6.0	22.4
093 CHR CH (DISC).	7	1 044	1 506	2.7	10.0
097 CHR CHS&CHS CR	12	1 649	1 938*	3.4	12.8
123 CH GOD (ANDER)	2	69	207	0.4	1.4
151 L-D SAINTS....	1	NA	142	0.3	0.9
165 CH OF NAZARENE	6	389	825	1.5	5.5
167 CHS OF CHRIST.	3	190	240	0.4	1.6
193 EPISCOPAL.....	2	311	413	0.7	2.7
221 FREE METHODIST	2	23	297	0.5	2.0
244 GRACE BRETHREN	1	66	78*	0.1	0.5
281 LUTH CH AMER..	1	212	287	0.5	1.9
403 SALVATION ARMY	1	45	133	0.2	0.9
413 S.D.A.........	1	50	59*	0.1	0.4
419 SO BAPT CONV..	2	273	321*	0.6	2.1
435 UNITARIAN-UNIV	1	38	45*	0.1	0.3
443 UN C OF CHRIST	2	9	11*	-	0.1
449 UN METHODIST..	34	3 040	3 574*	6.3	23.7
453 UN PRES CH USA	5	947	1 113*	2.0	7.4
AUGLAIZE	52	13 059	28 670*	67.4	100.0
019 AMER BAPT USA.	2	411	507*	1.2	1.8
029 AMER LUTH CH..	4	1 662	2 197	5.2	7.7
053 ASSEMB OF GOD.	1	42	312	0.7	1.1
081 CATHOLIC......	7	NA	11 333	26.6	39.5
089 CHR & MISS AL.	1	82	120	0.3	0.4
097 CHR CHS&CHS CR	3	281	347*	0.8	1.2
107 CHRISTIAN UN..	1	135	167	0.4	0.6
123 CH GOD (ANDER)	1	23	69	0.2	0.2
165 CH OF NAZARENE	4	530	1 331	3.1	4.6
226 FRIENDS-USA...	1	41	51*	0.1	0.2
281 LUTH CH AMER..	1	540	741	1.7	2.6
283 LUTH--MO SYNOD	1	126	152	0.4	0.5
419 SO BAPT CONV..	2	193	238*	0.6	0.8
443 UN C OF CHRIST	7	4 842	5 979*	14.1	20.9
449 UN METHODIST..	15	3 998	4 937*	11.6	17.2
453 UN PRES CH USA	1	153	189*	0.4	0.7
BELMONT	142	21 996	41 774*	50.6	100.0
019 AMER BAPT USA.	1	435	522*	0.6	1.2
029 AMER LUTH CH..	1	396	507	0.6	1.2
053 ASSEMB OF GOD.	3	345	513	0.6	1.2
081 CATHOLIC......	19	NA	13 989	16.9	33.5
089 CHR & MISS AL.	1	37	65	0.1	0.2
093 CHR CH (DISC).	4	873	1 401	1.7	3.4
097 CHR CHS&CHS CR	11	2 282	2 739*	3.3	6.6
123 CH GOD (ANDER)	1	150	450	0.5	1.1
165 CH OF NAZARENE	7	420	648	0.8	1.6
167 CHS OF CHRIST.	14	965	1 327	1.6	3.2
193 EPISCOPAL.....	2	206	290	0.4	0.7
226 FRIENDS-USA...	3	871	1 046*	1.3	2.5
263 INT FOURSQ GOS	1	8	10*	-	-
281 LUTH CH AMER..	3	877	1 251	1.5	3.0
285 MENNONITE CH..	1	40	48*	0.1	0.1
403 SALVATION ARMY	1	114	190	0.2	0.5
419 SO BAPT CONV..	2	239	287*	0.3	0.7
443 UN C OF CHRIST	2	444	533*	0.6	1.3
449 UN METHODIST..	42	8 418	10 105*	12.2	24.2
453 UN PRES CH USA	23	4 876	5 853*	7.1	14.0
BROWN	68	7 565	14 411*	45.1	100.0
029 AMER LUTH CH..	1	365	549	1.7	3.8
053 ASSEMB OF GOD.	1	19	32	0.1	0.2
081 CATHOLIC......	8	NA	4 000	12.5	27.8
093 CHR CH (DISC).	1	78	118	0.4	0.8
097 CHR CHS&CHS CR	12	2 900	3 603*	11.3	25.0
101 C.M.E........	1	133	165*	0.5	1.1
107 CHRISTIAN UN..	2	12	48	0.2	0.3
127 CH GOD (CLEVE)	2	94	117*	0.4	0.8
151 L-D SAINTS....	1	NA	470	1.5	3.3
165 CH OF NAZARENE	4	273	723	2.3	5.0
167 CHS OF CHRIST.	1	40	50	0.2	0.3
419 SO BAPT CONV..	6	891	1 107*	3.5	7.7
443 UN C OF CHRIST	6	260	323*	1.0	2.2
449 UN METHODIST..	16	1 797	2 233*	7.0	15.5
453 UN PRES CH USA	6	703	873*	2.7	6.1
BUTLER	217	53 449	109 534*	42.3	100.0
017 AMER BAPT ASSN	6	421	421	0.2	0.4
019 AMER BAPT USA.	4	3 423	4 168*	1.6	3.8
029 AMER LUTH CH..	4	1 880	2 390	0.9	2.2
053 ASSEMB OF GOD.	6	1 841	3 073	1.2	2.8
081 CATHOLIC......	17	NA	33 000	12.8	30.1
089 CHR & MISS AL.	1	264	284	0.1	0.3
093 CHR CH (DISC).	4	1 149	1 636	0.6	1.5
097 CHR CHS&CHS CR	6	558	680*	0.3	0.6
101 C.M.E........	2	488	594*	0.2	0.5
123 CH GOD (ANDER)	17	4 120	12 360	4.8	11.3
127 CH GOD (CLEVE)	15	3 228	3 931*	1.5	3.6
151 L-D SAINTS....	2	NA	957	0.4	0.9
157 CH OF BRETHREN	2	69	84*	-	0.1
165 CH OF NAZARENE	12	1 958	3 584	1.4	3.3
167 CHS OF CHRIST.	13	1 070	1 360	0.5	1.2
193 EPISCOPAL.....	3	1 465	1 899	0.7	1.7
208 EVAN LUTH ASSN	1	147	195	0.1	0.2
226 FRIENDS-USA...	1	15	18*	-	-
271 REFORM JUDAISM	1	120	146*	0.1	0.1
281 LUTH CH AMER..	3	626	865	0.3	0.8
283 LUTH--MO SYNOD	2	630	810	0.3	0.7
287 MENN GEN CONF.	1	133	173	0.1	0.2

County and Denomination	Number of churches	Communicant, confirmed, full members	Total adherents Number	Percent of total population	Percent of total adherents
291 MISSIONARY CH.	3	167	169	0.1	0.2
353 CHR BRETHREN..	1	50	80	-	0.1
403 SALVATION ARMY	2	449	1 124	0.4	1.0
413 S.D.A.........	3	297	362*	0.1	0.3
419 SO BAPT CONV..	39	11 186	13 622*	5.3	12.4
443 UN C OF CHRIST	7	2 489	3 031*	1.2	2.8
449 UN METHODIST..	25	9 182	11 182*	4.3	10.2
453 UN PRES CH USA	14	6 024	7 336*	2.8	6.7
CARROLL	53	6 297	10 165*	39.7	100.0
029 AMER LUTH CH..	3	571	790	3.1	7.8
053 ASSEMB OF GOD.	2	129	226	0.9	2.2
081 CATHOLIC......	5	NA	1 992	7.8	19.6
093 CHR CH (DISC).	1	164	323	1.3	3.2
097 CHR CHS&CHS CR	2	636	788*	3.1	7.8
165 CH OF NAZARENE	2	63	142	0.6	1.4
167 CHS OF CHRIST.	3	200	255	1.0	2.5
197 EVAN CH OF NA.	1	41	41	0.2	0.4
263 INT FOURSQ GOS	1	16	20*	0.1	0.2
281 LUTH CH AMER..	2	532	702	2.7	6.9
285 MENNONITE CH..	1	28	35*	0.1	0.3
413 S.D.A.........	2	158	196*	0.8	1.9
443 UN C OF CHRIST	1	25	31*	0.1	0.3
449 UN METHODIST..	19	2 680	3 319*	13.0	32.7
453 UN PRES CH USA	8	1 054	1 305*	5.1	12.8
CHAMPAIGN	50	7 357	11 862*	35.3	100.0
019 AMER BAPT USA.	6	1 203	1 472*	4.4	12.4
081 CATHOLIC......	4	NA	1 777	5.3	15.0
089 CHR & MISS AL.	1	0	14	-	0.1
097 CHR CHS&CHS CR	1	70	86*	0.3	0.7
123 CH GOD (ANDER)	3	284	852	2.5	7.2
127 CH GOD (CLEVE)	1	55	67*	0.2	0.6
165 CH OF NAZARENE	3	281	721	2.1	6.1
167 CHS OF CHRIST.	3	150	191	0.6	1.6
193 EPISCOPAL.....	2	253	312	0.9	2.6
221 FREE METHODIST	1	24	144	0.4	1.2
226 FRIENDS-USA...	3	126	154*	0.5	1.3
239 SWEDENBORGIAN.	1	60	73*	0.2	0.6
281 LUTH CH AMER..	3	409	540	1.6	4.6
285 MENNONITE CH..	2	223	273*	0.8	2.3
291 MISSIONARY CH.	1	69	106	0.3	0.9
419 SO BAPT CONV..	1	26	32*	0.1	0.3
443 UN C OF CHRIST	1	?	?	?	?
449 UN METHODIST..	11	3 500	4 284*	12.7	36.1
453 UN PRES CH USA	2	624	764*	2.3	6.4
CLARK	150	34 247	62 206*	41.4	100.0
019 AMER BAPT USA.	6	1 431	1 741*	1.2	2.8
029 AMER LUTH CH..	2	448	610	0.4	1.0
053 ASSEMB OF GOD.	2	217	442	0.3	0.7
075 BRETHREN IN CR	2	86	146	0.1	0.2
081 CATHOLIC......	7	NA	13 666	9.1	22.0
093 CHR CH (DISC).	3	339	451	0.3	0.7
097 CHR CHS&CHS CR	5	1 950	2 372*	1.6	3.8
101 C.M.E........	1	452	550*	0.4	0.9
121 CH GOD (ABR)..	2	195	237*	0.2	0.4
123 CH GOD (ANDER)	7	1 552	4 656	3.1	7.5
127 CH GOD (CLEVE)	2	110	134*	0.1	0.2
151 L-D SAINTS....	1	NA	398	0.3	0.6
157 CH OF BRETHREN	3	661	804*	0.5	1.3
165 CH OF NAZARENE	8	1 114	2 573	1.7	4.1
167 CHS OF CHRIST.	8	675	859	0.6	1.4
193 EPISCOPAL.....	1	449	974	0.6	1.6
226 FRIENDS-USA...	1	44	54*	-	0.1
263 INT FOURSQ GOS	1	53	64*	-	0.1
270 CONSRV JUDAISM	1	4	5*	-	-
271 REFORM JUDAISM	1	210	255*	0.2	0.4
281 LUTH CH AMER..	15	7 558	10 553	7.0	17.0
285 MENNONITE CH..	3	224	273*	0.2	0.4
291 MISSIONARY CH.	3	271	292	0.2	0.5
329 OPEN BIBLE STD	1	122	178	0.1	0.3
403 SALVATION ARMY	1	70	412	0.3	0.7
413 S.D.A.........	3	437	532*	0.4	0.9
419 SO BAPT CONV..	8	2 127	2 588*	1.7	4.2
443 UN C OF CHRIST	10	1 713	2 084*	1.4	3.4
449 UN METHODIST..	35	9 441	11 486*	7.6	18.5
453 UN PRES CH USA	6	2 251	2 738*	1.8	4.4
469 WELS.........	1	43	79	0.1	0.1
CLERMONT	127	21 304	41 742*	32.5	100.0
017 AMER BAPT ASSN	2	136	136	0.1	0.3
019 AMER BAPT USA.	1	444	557*	0.4	1.3
053 ASSEMB OF GOD.	5	723	1 094	0.9	2.6
081 CATHOLIC......	13	NA	13 888	10.8	33.3
097 CHR CHS&CHS CR	12	3 754	4 712*	3.7	11.3
123 CH GOD (ANDER)	1	35	105	0.1	0.3
127 CH GOD (CLEVE)	4	291	365*	0.3	0.9
157 CH OF BRETHREN	1	54	68*	0.1	0.2
165 CH OF NAZARENE	9	842	1 756	1.4	4.2
167 CHS OF CHRIST.	7	440	560	0.4	1.3
179 CONSRV BAPT...	4	1 235	1 550*	1.2	3.7
203 EVAN FREE CH..	1	129	162*	0.1	0.4
226 FRIENDS-USA...	1	152	191*	0.1	0.5
263 INT FOURSQ GOS	1	57	72*	0.1	0.2
281 LUTH CH AMER..	1	107	151	0.1	0.4
283 LUTH--MO SYNOD	1	252	455	0.4	1.1
349 PENT HOLINESS	1	63	79*	0.1	0.2
353 CHR BRETHREN..	1	30	55	-	0.1
403 SALVATION ARMY	1	16	40	-	0.1
413 S.D.A.........	1	188	236*	0.2	0.6

NA—Not applicable   *Total adherents estimated from known number of communicant, confirmed, full members.   —Represents a percent less than 0.1.   Percentages may not total due to rounding.

Table 4. Churches and Church Membership by County and Denomination: 1980

County and Denomination	Number of churches	Communicant, confirmed, full members	Total adherents Number	Percent of total population	Percent of total adherents
419 SO BAPT CONV..	19	3 970	4 983*	3.9	11.9
443 UN C OF CHRIST	3	102	128*	0.1	0.3
449 UN METHODIST..	32	6 913	8 678*	6.8	20.8
453 UN PRES CH USA	7	1 371	1 721*	1.3	4.1
CLINTON	62	10 130	15 803*	45.7	100.0
019 AMER BAPT USA.	2	362	443*	1.3	2.8
053 ASSEMB OF GOD.	1	84	135	0.4	0.9
081 CATHOLIC......	3	NA	2 444	7.1	15.5
093 CHR CH (DISC).	1	359	625	1.8	4.0
097 CHR CHS&CHS CR	9	3 054	3 740*	10.8	23.7
107 CHRISTIAN UN..	1	35	65	0.2	0.4
123 CH GOD (ANDER)	2	181	543	1.6	3.4
127 CH GOD (CLEVE)	3	118	144*	0.4	0.9
151 L-D SAINTS....	1	NA	157	0.5	1.0
165 CH OF NAZARENE	2	224	523	1.5	3.3
167 CHS OF CHRIST.	3	120	153	0.4	1.0
193 EPISCOPAL.....	1	42	53	0.2	0.3
226 FRIENDS-USA...	9	1 455	1 782*	5.1	11.3
281 LUTH CH AMER..	1	242	277	0.8	1.8
413 S.D.A.........	1	42	51*	0.1	0.3
419 SO BAPT CONV..	5	356	436*	1.3	2.8
443 UN C OF CHRIST	2	126	154*	0.4	1.0
449 UN METHODIST..	14	3 068	3 757*	10.9	23.8
453 UN PRES CH USA	1	262	321*	0.9	2.0
COLUMBIANA	154	32 702	59 614*	52.5	100.0
005 AME ZION......	2	120	144	0.1	0.2
017 AMER BAPT ASSN	1	100	100	0.1	0.2
019 AMER BAPT USA.	3	797	973*	0.9	1.6
029 AMER LUTH CH..	4	1 496	1 944	1.7	3.3
053 ASSEMB OF GOD.	6	486	883	0.8	1.5
057 BAPT GEN CONF.	2	68	83*	0.1	0.1
071 BRETHREN (ASH)	1	122	149*	0.1	0.2
081 CATHOLIC......	12	NA	16 128	14.2	27.1
093 CHR CH (DISC).	4	1 450	2 135	1.9	3.6
097 CHR CHS&CHS CR	15	3 602	4 396*	3.9	7.4
123 CH GOD (ANDER)	1	30	90	0.1	0.2
127 CH GOD (CLEVE)	1	37	45*	–	0.1
143 CG IN CR(MENN)	1	74	74	0.1	0.1
151 L-D SAINTS....	1	NA	553	0.5	0.9
157 CH OF BRETHREN	1	62	76*	0.1	0.1
165 CH OF NAZARENE	9	1 773	3 263	2.9	5.5
167 CHS OF CHRIST.	8	650	827	0.7	1.4
221 FREE METHODIST	4	223	831	0.7	1.4
226 FRIENDS-USA...	7	1 601	1 954*	1.7	3.3
271 REFORM JUDAISM	1	86	105*	0.1	0.2
281 LUTH CH AMER..	4	2 297	2 824	2.5	4.7
285 MENNONITE CH..	2	322	393*	0.3	0.7
287 MENN GEN CONF.	1	6	6	–	–
403 SALVATION ARMY	2	277	861	0.8	1.4
413 S.D.A.........	1	38	46*	–	0.1
419 SO BAPT CONV..	2	172	210*	0.2	0.4
443 UN C OF CHRIST	2	788	962*	0.8	1.6
449 UN METHODIST..	29	8 657	10 566*	9.3	17.7
453 UN PRES CH USA	27	7 368	8 993*	7.9	15.1
COSHOCTON	68	11 197	16 624*	46.1	100.0
019 AMER BAPT USA.	5	694	848*	2.4	5.1
029 AMER LUTH CH..	1	85	101	0.3	0.6
053 ASSEMB OF GOD.	1	63	132	0.4	0.8
081 CATHOLIC......	2	NA	2 368	6.6	14.2
093 CHR CH (DISC).	2	255	351	1.0	2.1
097 CHR CHS&CHS CR	2	150	183*	0.5	1.1
123 CH GOD (ANDER)	2	100	300	0.8	1.8
127 CH GOD (CLEVE)	1	46	56*	0.2	0.3
165 CH OF NAZARENE	4	524	809	2.2	4.9
167 CHS OF CHRIST.	5	360	458	1.3	2.8
281 LUTH CH AMER..	1	629	795	2.2	4.8
285 MENNONITE CH..	2	321	392*	1.1	2.4
323 OLD ORD AMISH.	3	390	476*	1.3	2.9
403 SALVATION ARMY	1	268	424	1.2	2.6
413 S.D.A.........	1	24	29*	0.1	0.2
419 SO BAPT CONV..	1	168	205*	0.6	1.2
443 UN C OF CHRIST	3	604	738*	2.0	4.4
449 UN METHODIST..	25	5 392	6 586*	18.3	39.6
453 UN PRES CH USA	6	1 124	1 373*	3.8	8.3
CRAWFORD	81	17 633	29 666*	59.2	100.0
019 AMER BAPT USA.	2	205	251*	0.5	0.8
029 AMER LUTH CH..	8	3 678	4 763	9.5	16.1
053 ASSEMB OF GOD.	2	132	286	0.6	1.0
081 CATHOLIC......	5	NA	6 611	13.2	22.3
089 CHR & MISS AL.	1	132	201	0.4	0.7
093 CHR CH (DISC).	1	240	315	0.6	1.1
097 CHR CHS&CHS CR	3	465	569*	1.1	1.9
127 CH GOD (CLEVE)	3	189	231*	0.5	0.8
165 CH OF NAZARENE	3	558	1 010	2.0	3.4
167 CHS OF CHRIST.	2	150	190	0.4	0.6
179 CONSRV BAPT...	1	180	220*	0.4	0.7
221 FREE METHODIST	1	79	249	0.5	0.8
244 GRACE BRETHREN	1	64	78*	0.2	0.3
263 INT FOURSQ GOS	1	61	75*	0.1	0.3
281 LUTH CH AMER..	8	2 253	3 077	6.1	10.4
329 OPEN BIBLE STD	2	106	225	0.4	0.8
403 SALVATION ARMY	1	96	240	0.5	0.8
413 S.D.A.........	1	93	114*	0.2	0.4
419 SO BAPT CONV..	2	647	792*	1.6	2.7
443 UN C OF CHRIST	6	1 915	2 345*	4.7	7.9
449 UN METHODIST..	24	5 512	6 749*	13.5	22.7
453 UN PRES CH USA	3	878	1 075*	2.1	3.6

County and Denomination	Number of churches	Communicant, confirmed, full members	Total adherents Number	Percent of total population	Percent of total adherents
CUYAHOGA	778	254 274	949 659*	63.4	100.0
005 AME ZION......	7	13 730	16 476	1.1	1.7
019 AMER BAPT USA.	34	22 533	26 813*	1.8	2.8
029 AMER LUTH CH..	17	9 661	13 097	0.9	1.4
039 AP CHR CH(NAZ)	2	149	177*	–	–
049 ARMEN AP CH AM	1	40	60	–	–
053 ASSEMB OF GOD.	17	2 733	4 982	0.3	0.5
057 BAPT GEN CONF.	3	271	322*	–	–
081 CATHOLIC......	161	NA	622 059	41.5	65.5
089 CHR & MISS AL.	5	337	849	0.1	0.1
093 CHR CH (DISC).	23	6 898	10 693	0.7	1.1
097 CHR CHS&CHS CR	5	636	757*	0.1	0.1
101 C.M.E.........	5	6 616	7 873*	0.5	0.8
105 CHRISTIAN REF.	3	430	635	–	0.1
121 CH GOD (ABR)..	2	90	107*	–	–
123 CH GOD (ANDER)	8	664	1 992	0.1	0.2
127 CH GOD (CLEVE)	11	1 512	1 799*	0.1	0.2
149 CH OF JC (BIC)	1	43	43	–	–
151 L-D SAINTS....	5	NA	1 747	0.1	0.2
157 CH OF BRETHREN	2	257	306*	–	–
165 CH OF NAZARENE	10	1 101	2 675	0.2	0.3
167 CHS OF CHRIST.	12	1 413	1 767	0.1	0.2
175 CONGR CHR CHS.	3	561	668*	–	0.1
193 EPISCOPAL.....	116	43 322	58 482	3.9	6.2
195 ESTONIAN ELC..	1	54	158	–	–
201 EVAN COV CH AM	2	388	462*	–	–
203 EVAN FREE CH..	1	34	40*	–	–
208 EVAN LUTH ASSN	5	3 616	5 123	0.3	0.5
220 FREE LUTHERAN.	1	30	40	–	–
221 FREE METHODIST	4	111	468	–	–
226 FRIENDS-USA...	4	467	556*	–	0.1
233 GEN CH NEW JER	1	30	36*	–	–
239 SWEDENBORGIAN.	1	60	71*	–	–
244 GRACE BRETHREN	1	39	46*	–	–
263 INT FOURSQ GOS	4	467	556*	–	0.1
270 CONSRV JUDAISM	5	2 694	3 206*	0.2	0.3
271 REFORM JUDAISM	9	12 772	15 198*	1.0	1.6
274 LAT EVAN LUTH.	1	788	937	0.1	0.1
281 LUTH CH AMER..	22	7 387	9 551	0.6	1.0
283 LUTH--MO SYNOD	45	21 243	27 613	1.8	2.9
285 MENNONITE CH..	3	435	518*	–	0.1
290 METRO COMM CHS	0	25	50	–	–
291 MISSIONARY CH.	3	177	251	–	–
313 N AM BAPT CONF	4	1 175	1 398*	0.1	0.1
353 CHR BRETHREN..	5	270	410	–	–
363 PRIMITIVE METH	1	35	42*	–	–
371 REF CH IN AM..	5	882	1 549	0.1	0.2
375 REF EPISCOPAL.	1	40	48*	–	–
395 ROMANIAN OR CH	1	1 680	1 999*	0.1	0.2
403 SALVATION ARMY	8	602	2 753	0.2	0.3
413 S.D.A.........	9	3 034	3 610*	0.2	0.4
419 SO BAPT CONV..	17	4 072	4 845*	0.3	0.5
431 UKRANIAN AMER.	1	100	130	–	–
435 UNITARIAN-UNIV	4	1 502	1 787*	0.1	0.2
443 UN C OF CHRIST	51	20 587	24 498*	1.6	2.6
449 UN METHODIST..	60	35 094	41 760*	2.8	4.4
453 UN PRES CH USA	44	21 367	25 426*	1.7	2.7
469 WELS..........	1	20	33	–	–
DARKE	86	14 877	26 385*	47.9	100.0
017 AMER BAPT ASSN	1	9	9	–	–
029 AMER LUTH CH..	7	1 496	1 937	3.5	7.3
053 ASSEMB OF GOD.	1	146	196	0.4	0.7
081 CATHOLIC......	5	NA	6 777	12.3	25.7
089 CHR & MISS AL.	1	143	253	0.5	1.0
097 CHR CHS&CHS CR	3	488	603*	1.1	2.3
123 CH GOD (ANDER)	1	330	990	1.8	3.8
127 CH GOD (CLEVE)	1	52	64*	0.1	0.2
157 CH OF BRETHREN	11	2 253	2 784*	5.1	10.6
165 CH OF NAZARENE	2	172	396	0.7	1.5
167 CHS OF CHRIST.	2	160	200	0.4	0.8
193 EPISCOPAL.....	1	126	280	0.5	1.1
281 LUTH CH AMER..	2	892	1 162	2.1	4.4
291 MISSIONARY CH.	2	213	314	0.6	1.2
329 OPEN BIBLE STD	1	75	135	0.2	0.5
419 SO BAPT CONV..	4	478	591*	1.1	2.2
435 UNITARIAN-UNIV	1	77	95*	0.2	0.4
443 UN C OF CHRIST	10	2 167	2 678*	4.9	10.1
449 UN METHODIST..	27	4 892	6 046*	11.0	22.9
453 UN PRES CH USA	3	708	875*	1.6	3.3
DEFIANCE	60	13 303	27 367*	68.4	100.0
019 AMER BAPT USA.	1	458	572*	1.4	2.1
029 AMER LUTH CH..	3	1 078	1 366	3.4	5.0
053 ASSEMB OF GOD.	2	113	410	1.0	1.5
081 CATHOLIC......	6	NA	9 071	22.7	33.1
093 CHR CH (DISC).	1	26	33	0.1	0.1
097 CHR CHS&CHS CR	5	960	1 199*	3.0	4.4
123 CH GOD (ANDER)	1	375	1 125	2.8	4.1
127 CH GOD (CLEVE)	1	38	47*	0.1	0.2
157 CH OF BRETHREN	2	233	291*	0.7	1.1
165 CH OF NAZARENE	2	179	488	1.2	1.8
167 CHS OF CHRIST.	2	100	127	0.3	0.5
215 EVAN METH CH..	1	33	41*	0.1	0.1
281 LUTH CH AMER..	2	1 078	1 455	3.6	5.3
283 LUTH--MO SYNOD	4	2 386	3 327	8.3	12.2
285 MENNONITE CH..	2	96	120*	0.3	0.4
291 MISSIONARY CH.	1	37	60	0.2	0.2
323 OLD ORD AMISH.	1	130	162*	0.4	0.6
329 OPEN BIBLE STD	1	21	25	0.1	0.1
413 S.D.A.........	2	60	75*	0.2	0.3
419 SO BAPT CONV..	3	613	766*	1.9	2.8

NA— Not applicable   *Total adherents estimated from known number of communicant, confirmed, full members.   —Represents a percent less than 0.1.   Percentages may not total due to rounding.

215

Table 4. Churches and Church Membership by County and Denomination: 1980

County and Denomination	Number of churches	Communicant, confirmed, full members	Total adherents		
			Number	Percent of total population	Percent of total adherents
443 UN C OF CHRIST	2	421	526*	1.3	1.9
449 UN METHODIST..	13	4 104	5 127*	12.8	18.7
453 UN PRES CH USA	2	764	954*	2.4	3.5
DELAWARE	53	9 057	14 509*	26.9	100.0
019 AMER BAPT USA.	4	926	1 129*	2.1	7.8
029 AMER LUTH CH.	1	484	605	1.1	4.2
053 ASSEMB OF GOD.	1	55	81	0.2	0.6
081 CATHOLIC......	2	NA	2 800	5.2	19.3
097 CHR CHS&CHS CR	3	230	280*	0.5	1.9
107 CHRISTIAN UN..	1	20	20	–	0.1
123 CH GOD (ANDER)	1	59	177	0.3	1.2
127 CH GOD (CLEVE)	2	68	83*	0.2	0.6
151 L-D SAINTS....	1	NA	242	0.4	1.7
165 CH OF NAZARENE	2	253	525	1.0	3.6
167 CHS OF CHRIST.	1	103	158	0.3	1.1
193 EPISCOPAL.....	1	142	221	0.4	1.5
226 FRIENDS-USA...	1	59	72*	0.1	0.5
244 GRACE BRETHREN	1	50	61*	0.1	0.4
285 MENNONITE CH..	1	29	35*	0.1	0.2
413 S.D.A.........	2	115	140*	0.3	1.0
419 SO BAPT CONV..	2	293	357*	0.7	2.5
443 UN C OF CHRIST	2	458	558*	1.0	3.8
449 UN METHODIST..	17	4 280	5 218*	9.7	36.0
453 UN PRES CH USA	7	1 433	1 747*	3.2	12.0
ERIE	71	17 252	45 533*	57.2	100.0
005 AME ZION......	1	85	102	0.1	0.2
019 AMER BAPT USA.	1	141	172*	0.2	0.4
029 AMER LUTH CH..	8	5 176	7 090	8.9	15.6
053 ASSEMB OF GOD.	3	578	1 021	1.3	2.2
081 CATHOLIC......	7	NA	22 705	28.5	49.9
089 CHR & MISS AL.	3	90	185	0.2	0.4
097 CHR CHS&CHS CR	3	438	534*	0.7	1.2
101 C.M.E.........	2	535	652*	0.8	1.4
123 CH GOD (ANDER)	1	28	84	0.1	0.2
127 CH GOD (CLEVE)	1	122	149*	0.2	0.3
151 L-D SAINTS....	1	NA	320	0.4	0.7
165 CH OF NAZARENE	2	210	445	0.6	1.0
167 CHS OF CHRIST.	5	300	382	0.5	0.8
226 FRIENDS-USA...	1	46	56*	0.1	0.1
263 INT FOURSQ GOS	1	116	141*	0.2	0.3
271 REFORM JUDAISM	1	100	122*	0.2	0.3
403 SALVATION ARMY	1	46	112	0.1	0.2
413 S.D.A.........	1	38	46*	0.1	0.1
419 SO BAPT CONV..	3	1 420	1 730*	2.2	3.8
435 UNITARIAN-UNIV	1	22	27*	–	0.1
443 UN C OF CHRIST	12	4 272	5 206*	6.5	11.4
449 UN METHODIST..	9	2 452	2 988*	3.8	6.6
453 UN PRES CH USA	3	1 037	1 264*	1.6	2.8
FAIRFIELD	103	20 947	37 290*	39.8	100.0
029 AMER LUTH CH..	7	1 828	2 446	2.6	6.6
053 ASSEMB OF GOD.	2	45	106	0.1	0.3
081 CATHOLIC......	7	NA	9 619	10.3	25.8
097 CHR CHS&CHS CR	4	1 512	1 872*	2.0	5.0
107 CHRISTIAN UN..	1	76	125	0.1	0.3
123 CH GOD (ANDER)	1	80	240	0.3	0.6
127 CH GOD (CLEVE)	1	186	230*	0.2	0.6
151 L-D SAINTS....	1	NA	542	0.6	1.5
165 CH OF NAZARENE	3	358	684	0.7	1.8
167 CHS OF CHRIST.	4	238	352	0.4	0.9
179 CONSRV BAPT...	1	30	37*		0.1
193 EPISCOPAL.....	1	273	358	0.4	1.0
281 LUTH CH AMER..	9	1 511	2 126	2.3	5.7
283 LUTH--MO SYNOD	3	916	1 153	1.2	3.1
329 OPEN BIBLE STD	1	30	40	–	0.1
403 SALVATION ARMY	1	83	300	0.3	0.8
413 S.D.A.........	1	55	68*	0.1	0.2
419 SO BAPT CONV..	4	887	1 098*	1.2	2.9
443 UN C OF CHRIST	7	1 164	1 441*	1.5	3.9
449 UN METHODIST..	39	10 192	12 617*	13.5	33.8
453 UN PRES CH USA	5	1 483	1 836*	2.0	4.9
FAYETTE	32	6 457	9 100*	33.1	100.0
019 AMER BAPT USA.	2	763	935*	3.4	10.3
053 ASSEMB OF GOD.	1	52	104	0.4	1.1
081 CATHOLIC......	1	NA	1 003	3.7	11.0
097 CHR CHS&CHS CR	4	1 440	1 765*	6.4	19.4
123 CH GOD (ANDER)	2	70	210	0.8	2.3
127 CH GOD (CLEVE)	1	24	29*	0.1	0.3
165 CH OF NAZARENE	1	73	152	0.6	1.7
167 CHS OF CHRIST.	1	70	90	0.3	1.0
193 EPISCOPAL.....	1	189	191	0.7	2.1
281 LUTH CH AMER..	1	267	320	1.2	3.5
413 S.D.A.........	1	19	23*	0.1	0.3
419 SO BAPT CONV..	1	243	298*	1.1	3.3
449 UN METHODIST..	12	2 387	2 926*	10.7	32.2
453 UN PRES CH USA	3	860	1 054*	3.8	11.6
FRANKLIN	489	157 733	341 162*	39.3	100.0
001 ADVENT CHR CH.	1	48	58*	–	–
005 AME ZION......	3	2 076	2 638	0.3	0.8
019 AMER BAPT USA.	21	9 060	10 926*	1.3	3.2
029 AMER LUTH CH..	37	18 694	24 853	2.9	7.3
039 AP CHR CH(NAZ)	1	42	51*	–	–
053 ASSEMB OF GOD.	6	1 090	2 473	0.3	0.7
057 BAPT GEN CONF.	1	150	181*	–	0.1
071 BRETHREN (ASH)	1	30	36*	–	–
081 CATHOLIC......	70	NA	137 013	15.8	40.2

County and Denomination	Number of churches	Communicant, confirmed, full members	Total adherents		
			Number	Percent of total population	Percent of total adherents
083 CHRIST CATH CH	1	4	6	–	–
089 CHR & MISS AL.	5	545	861	0.1	0.3
093 CHR CH (DISC).	12	4 378	5 927	0.7	1.7
097 CHR CHS&CHS CR	24	7 710	9 298*	1.1	2.7
101 C.M.E.........	4	450	543*	0.1	0.2
105 CHRISTIAN REF.	1	116	212	–	0.1
107 CHRISTIAN UN..	1	30	30	–	–
121 CH GOD (ABR)..	2	63	76*	–	–
123 CH GOD (ANDER)	11	1 260	3 780	0.4	1.1
127 CH GOD (CLEVE)	10	1 829	2 206*	0.3	0.6
151 L-D SAINTS....	5	NA	2 552	0.3	0.7
165 CH OF NAZARENE	18	3 735	6 194	0.7	1.8
167 CHS OF CHRIST.	15	2 500	3 230	0.4	0.9
175 CONGR CHR CHS.	1	54	65*	–	–
193 EPISCOPAL.....	11	5 600	7 744	0.9	2.3
199 EVAN CONGR CH.	1	136	164*	–	–
201 EVAN COV CH AM	1	28	34*	–	–
208 EVAN LUTH ASSN	1	418	527	0.1	0.2
221 FREE METHODIST	2	189	672	0.1	0.2
226 FRIENDS-USA...	4	560	675*	0.1	0.2
244 GRACE BRETHREN	3	2 021	2 437*	0.3	0.7
270 CONSRV JUDAISM	1	300	362*		0.1
274 LAT EVAN LUTH.	1	121	131		
281 LUTH CH AMER..	9	3 904	5 322	0.6	1.6
283 LUTH--MO SYNOD	9	1 729	2 115	0.2	0.6
285 MENNONITE CH..	2	106	128*		
287 MENN GEN CONF.	1	95	145		
290 METRO COMM CHS	1	52	104	–	–
335 ORTH PRESB CH.	1	32	39*	–	–
371 REF CH IN AM..	1	180	449	0.1	0.1
381 REF PRES-EVAN.	1	28	34	–	–
403 SALVATION ARMY	3	360	624	0.1	0.2
413 S.D.A.........	8	1 911	2 305*	0.3	0.7
415 S-D BAPTIST GC	1	27	33*	–	–
419 SO BAPT CONV..	39	14 494	17 479*	2.0	5.1
435 UNITARIAN-UNIV	2	560	675*	0.1	0.2
443 UN C OF CHRIST	10	5 773	6 962*	0.8	2.0
449 UN METHODIST..	90	45 024	54 297*	6.2	15.9
453 UN PRES CH USA	34	19 278	23 248*	2.7	6.8
469 WELS..........	4	943	1 248	0.1	0.4
FULTON	73	13 380	25 833*	68.4	100.0
029 AMER LUTH CH..	4	1 378	1 763	4.7	6.8
053 ASSEMB OF GOD.	2	219	255	0.7	1.0
081 CATHOLIC......	6	NA	7 990	21.2	30.9
089 CHR & MISS AL.	1	75	188	0.5	0.7
093 CHR CH (DISC).	5	1 116	1 646	4.4	6.4
097 CHR CHS&CHS CR	3	633	788*	2.1	3.1
107 CHRISTIAN UN..	2	107	110	0.3	0.4
121 CH GOD (ABR)..	1	30	37*	0.1	0.1
123 CH GOD (ANDER)	1	160	480	1.3	1.9
127 CH GOD (CLEVE)	2	97	121*	0.3	0.5
143 CG IN CR(MENN)	1	7	7	–	–
151 L-D SAINTS....	1	NA	163	0.4	0.6
157 CH OF BRETHREN	1	88	110*	0.3	0.4
165 CH OF NAZARENE	6	278	579	1.5	2.2
213 EVAN MENN INC.	2	1 077	1 341*	3.6	5.2
283 LUTH--MO SYNOD	4	1 121	1 533	4.1	5.9
285 MENNONITE CH..	7	1 967	2 449*	6.5	9.5
291 MISSIONARY CH.	3	216	282	0.7	1.1
349 PENT HOLINESS.	1	36	45*	0.1	0.2
413 S.D.A.........	1	34	42*	0.1	0.2
419 SO BAPT CONV..	2	171	213*	0.6	0.8
435 UNITARIAN-UNIV	1	99	123*	0.3	0.5
443 UN C OF CHRIST	2	710	884*	2.3	3.4
449 UN METHODIST..	14	3 761	4 684*	12.4	18.1
GALLIA	42	4 826	7 321*	24.3	100.0
019 AMER BAPT USA.	5	805	981*	3.3	13.4
029 AMER LUTH CH..	1	64	83	0.3	1.1
053 ASSEMB OF GOD.	1	27	44	0.1	0.6
081 CATHOLIC......	1	NA	438	1.5	6.0
097 CHR CHS&CHS CR	1	350	426*	1.4	5.8
123 CH GOD (ANDER)	1	120	360	1.2	4.9
127 CH GOD (CLEVE)	1	54	66*	0.2	0.9
151 L-D SAINTS....	1	NA	198	0.7	2.7
165 CH OF NAZARENE	1	234	763	2.5	10.4
167 CHS OF CHRIST.	3	265	370	1.2	5.1
175 CONGR CHR CHS.	1	65	79*	0.3	1.1
193 EPISCOPAL.....	1	230	332	1.1	4.5
285 MENNONITE CH..	2	64	78*	0.3	1.1
419 SO BAPT CONV..	2	318	387*	1.3	5.3
449 UN METHODIST..	19	1 935	2 357*	7.8	32.2
453 UN PRES CH USA	1	295	359*	1.2	4.9
GEAUGA	91	13 286	32 662*	43.9	100.0
019 AMER BAPT USA.	1	318	396*	0.5	1.2
029 AMER LUTH CH..	1	235	292	0.4	0.9
053 ASSEMB OF GOD.	2	197	364	0.5	1.1
061 BEACHY AMISH..	1	48	60*	0.1	0.2
081 CATHOLIC......	9	NA	15 536	20.9	47.6
089 CHR & MISS AL.	2	56	95	0.1	0.3
093 CHR CH (DISC).	2	570	754	1.0	2.3
097 CHR CHS&CHS CR	3	525	653*	0.9	2.0
127 CH GOD (CLEVE)	2	49	61*	0.1	0.2
167 CHS OF CHRIST.	1	25	32	–	0.1
181 CONSRV CONGR.	1	225	280*	0.4	0.9
221 FREE METHODIST	1	10	180	0.2	0.6
281 LUTH CH AMER..	1	100	136	0.2	0.4
283 LUTH--MO SYNOD	3	766	1 179	1.6	3.6
285 MENNONITE CH..	3	223	277*	0.4	0.8
323 OLD ORD AMISH.	39	5 070	6 309*	8.5	19.3

NA—Not applicable   *Total adherents estimated from known number of communicant, confirmed, full members.   —Represents a percent less than 0.1.   Percentages may not total due to rounding.

Table 4. Churches and Church Membership by County and Denomination: 1980

County and Denomination	Number of churches	Communicant, confirmed, full members	Total adherents		
			Number	Percent of total population	Percent of total adherents
419 SO BAPT CONV..	2	345	429*	0.6	1.3
443 UN C OF CHRIST	9	2 208	2 747*	3.7	8.4
449 UN METHODIST..	6	1 558	1 939*	2.6	5.9
453 UN PRES CH USA	2	758	943*	1.3	2.9
GREENE	103	24 480	39 924*	30.8	100.0
019 AMER BAPT USA.	2	268	326*	0.3	0.8
029 AMER LUTH CH..	2	904	1 164	0.9	2.9
053 ASSEMB OF GOD.	2	102	213	0.2	0.5
081 CATHOLIC......	5	NA	6 666	5.1	16.7
093 CHR CH (DISC).	1	177	217	0.2	0.5
097 CHR CHS&CHS CR	8	2 646	3 221*	2.5	8.1
123 CH GOD (ANDER)	4	246	738	0.6	1.8
127 CH GOD (CLEVE)	3	477	581*	0.4	1.5
151 L-D SAINTS....	3	NA	872	0.7	2.2
157 CH OF BRETHREN	1	236	287*	0.2	0.7
165 CH OF NAZARENE	6	1 129	2 594	2.0	6.5
167 CHS OF CHRIST.	5	600	930	0.7	2.3
193 EPISCOPAL.....	2	396	597	0.5	1.5
226 FRIENDS-USA...	6	656	798*	0.6	2.0
281 LUTH CH AMER..	3	1 201	1 534	1.2	3.8
283 LUTH--MO SYNOD	1	347	539	0.4	1.4
291 MISSIONARY CH.	3	255	404	0.3	1.0
313 N AM BAPT CONF	1	90	110*	0.1	0.3
329 OPEN BIBLE STD	1	180	400	0.3	1.0
349 PENT HOLINESS.	1	15	18*	–	–
413 S.D.A.........	1	47	57*	–	0.1
419 SO BAPT CONV..	11	4 543	5 530*	4.3	13.9
435 UNITARIAN-UNIV	1	85	103*	0.1	0.3
443 UN C OF CHRIST	4	945	1 150*	0.9	2.9
449 UN METHODIST..	17	4 498	5 415*	4.2	13.6
453 UN PRES CH USA	9	4 486	5 460*	4.2	13.7
GUERNSEY	83	11 135	18 056*	43.0	100.0
001 ADVENT CHR CH.	1	42	51*	0.1	0.3
019 AMER BAPT USA.	6	679	832*	2.0	4.6
053 ASSEMB OF GOD.	2	354	676	1.6	3.7
061 BEACHY AMISH..	1	18	22*	0.1	0.1
081 CATHOLIC......	4	NA	3 523	8.4	19.5
093 CHR CH (DISC).	2	271	471	1.1	2.6
097 CHR CHS&CHS CR	2	120	147*	0.3	0.8
101 C.M.E.........	1	175	214*	0.5	1.2
123 CH GOD (ANDER)	1	55	165	0.4	0.9
127 CH GOD (CLEVE)	1	16	20*	–	0.1
165 CH OF NAZARENE	2	173	324	0.8	1.8
167 CHS OF CHRIST.	5	1 265	1 610	3.8	8.9
221 FREE METHODIST	2	68	246	0.6	1.4
263 INT FOURSQ GOS	1	116	142*	0.3	0.8
281 LUTH CH AMER..	3	480	582	1.4	3.2
283 LUTH--MO SYNOD	1	100	124	0.3	0.7
285 MENNONITE CH..	1	26	32*	0.1	0.2
323 OLD ORD AMISH.	1	130	159*	0.4	0.9
403 SALVATION ARMY	1	88	193	0.5	1.1
419 SO BAPT CONV..	1	257	315*	0.7	1.7
449 UN METHODIST..	33	4 796	5 874*	14.0	32.5
453 UN PRES CH USA	11	1 906	2 334*	5.6	12.9
HAMILTON	571	150 931	477 676*	54.7	100.0
005 AME ZION......	11	5 570	6 684	0.8	1.4
017 AMER BAPT ASSN	2	150	150	–	–
019 AMER BAPT USA.	19	8 320	10 030*	1.1	2.1
029 AMER LUTH CH..	9	2 721	3 683	0.4	0.8
053 ASSEMB OF GOD.	5	1 185	2 064	0.2	0.4
057 BAPT GEN CONF.	2	379	457*	0.1	0.1
075 BRETHREN IN CR	1	43	73	–	–
081 CATHOLIC......	103	NA	284 791	32.6	59.6
089 CHR & MISS AL.	4	185	348	–	0.1
093 CHR CH (DISC).	14	2 869	4 363	0.5	0.9
097 CHR CHS&CHS CR	32	11 659	14 032*	1.6	2.9
101 C.M.E.........	7	2 991	3 606*	0.4	0.8
105 CHRISTIAN REF.	1	42	42	–	–
123 CH GOD (ANDER)	12	1 266	3 798	0.4	0.8
127 CH GOD (CLEVE)	18	1 863	2 246*	0.3	0.5
151 L-D SAINTS....	5	NA	1 920	0.2	0.4
165 CH OF NAZARENE	20	2 361	4 601	0.5	1.0
167 CHS OF CHRIST.	18	1 915	2 560	0.3	0.5
179 CONSRV BAPT...	5	1 466	1 767*	0.2	0.4
193 EPISCOPAL.....	26	9 239	12 439	1.4	2.6
201 EVAN COV CH AM	1	42	51*	–	–
221 FREE METHODIST	1	5	9	–	–
226 FRIENDS-USA...	3	255	307*	–	0.1
239 SWEDENBORGIAN.	2	120	145*	–	–
263 INT FOURSQ GOS	1	62	75*	–	–
270 CONSRV JUDAISM	3	889	1 072*	0.1	0.2
271 REFORM JUDAISM	4	5 610	6 763*	0.8	1.4
281 LUTH CH AMER..	7	1 819	2 519	0.3	0.5
283 LUTH--MO SYNOD	13	4 058	5 370	0.6	1.1
285 MENNONITE CH..	3	86	104*	–	–
287 MENN GEN CONF.	1	17	23	–	–
290 METRO COMM CHS	1	110	220	–	–
329 OPEN BIBLE STD	1	20	50	–	–
353 CHR BRETHREN..	1	80	100	–	–
375 REF EPISCOPAL.	1	32	39*	–	–
381 REF PRES-EVAN.	1	89	131	–	–
395 ROMANIAN OR CH	1	545	657*	0.1	0.1
403 SALVATION ARMY	3	342	859	0.1	0.2
409 SEPARATE BAPT.	2	139	168*	–	–
413 S.D.A.........	3	1 552	1 871*	0.2	0.4
419 SO BAPT CONV..	43	12 471	15 035*	1.7	3.1
435 UNITARIAN-UNIV	5	712	858*	0.1	0.2
443 UN C OF CHRIST	31	11 145	13 436*	1.5	2.8
449 UN METHODIST..	73	31 879	38 433*	4.4	8.0

County and Denomination	Number of churches	Communicant, confirmed, full members	Total adherents		
			Number	Percent of total population	Percent of total adherents
453 UN PRES CH USA	51	24 534	29 578*	3.4	6.2
469 WELS..........	1	114	149	–	–
HANCOCK	77	18 725	32 259*	50.0	100.0
029 AMER LUTH CH..	2	836	1 130	1.7	3.5
053 ASSEMB OF GOD.	2	317	551	0.9	1.7
071 BRETHREN (ASH)	1	40	49*	0.1	0.2
081 CATHOLIC......	1	NA	7 037	10.9	21.8
089 CHR & MISS AL.	1	21	33	0.1	0.1
093 CHR CH (DISC).	1	207	341	0.5	1.1
097 CHR CHS&CHS CR	7	1 360	1 666*	2.6	5.2
123 CH GOD (ANDER)	1	315	945	1.5	2.9
127 CH GOD (CLEVE)	1	163	200*	0.3	0.6
151 L-D SAINTS....	1	NA	350	0.5	1.1
157 CH OF BRETHREN	2	76	93*	0.1	0.3
165 CH OF NAZARENE	3	197	444	0.7	1.4
167 CHS OF CHRIST.	1	60	85	0.1	0.3
199 EVAN CONGR CH.	1	106	130*	0.2	0.4
226 FRIENDS-USA...	1	41	50*	0.1	0.2
244 GRACE BRETHREN	1	61	75*	0.1	0.2
263 INT FOURSQ GOS	1	42	51*	0.1	0.2
281 LUTH CH AMER..	5	2 256	3 285	5.1	10.2
283 LUTH--MO SYNOD	1	256	370	0.6	1.1
403 SALVATION ARMY	1	103	270	0.4	0.8
413 S.D.A.........	1	69	85*	0.1	0.3
419 SO BAPT CONV..	1	220	270*	0.4	0.8
443 UN C OF CHRIST	1	126	154*	0.2	0.5
449 UN METHODIST..	32	8 960	10 977*	17.0	34.0
453 UN PRES CH USA	5	2 226	2 727*	4.2	8.5
469 WELS..........	2	667	891	1.4	2.8
HARDIN	66	10 000	14 772*	45.1	100.0
019 AMER BAPT USA.	3	528	643*	2.0	4.4
029 AMER LUTH CH..	1	295	366	1.1	2.5
053 ASSEMB OF GOD.	3	265	794	2.4	5.4
081 CATHOLIC......	2	NA	1 417	4.3	9.6
089 CHR & MISS AL.	1	44	64	0.2	0.4
093 CHR CH (DISC).	2	295	659	2.0	4.5
097 CHR CHS&CHS CR	7	880	1 071*	3.3	7.3
123 CH GOD (ANDER)	2	95	285	0.9	1.9
127 CH GOD (CLEVE)	1	?	?	?	?
165 CH OF NAZARENE	1	131	296	0.9	2.0
167 CHS OF CHRIST.	2	70	89	0.3	0.6
263 INT FOURSQ GOS	1	106	129*	0.4	0.9
281 LUTH CH AMER..	1	195	287	0.9	1.9
323 OLD ORD AMISH.	4	520	633*	1.9	4.3
419 SO BAPT CONV..	1	42	51*	0.2	0.3
443 UN C OF CHRIST	5	1 052	1 281*	3.9	8.7
449 UN METHODIST..	24	4 897	5 961*	18.2	40.4
453 UN PRES CH USA	4	498	606*	1.9	4.1
469 WELS..........	1	87	140	0.4	0.9
HARRISON	58	5 636	7 755*	42.7	100.0
053 ASSEMB OF GOD.	3	83	144	0.8	1.9
081 CATHOLIC......	5	NA	649	3.6	8.4
097 CHR CHS&CHS CR	4	535	652*	3.6	8.4
123 CH GOD (ANDER)	1	45	135	0.7	1.7
165 CH OF NAZARENE	4	107	222	1.2	2.9
167 CHS OF CHRIST.	3	210	267	1.5	3.4
281 LUTH CH AMER..	1	77	106	0.6	1.4
449 UN METHODIST..	26	3 096	3 773*	20.8	48.7
453 UN PRES CH USA	11	1 483	1 807*	10.0	23.3
HENRY	50	12 629	20 353*	71.7	100.0
029 AMER LUTH CH..	8	3 044	3 930	13.8	19.3
081 CATHOLIC......	5	NA	4 238	14.9	20.8
097 CHR CHS&CHS CR	1	140	172*	0.6	0.8
107 CHRISTIAN UN..	1	15	19	0.1	0.1
127 CH GOD (CLEVE)	1	17	21*	0.1	0.1
165 CH OF NAZARENE	2	60	112	0.4	0.6
167 CHS OF CHRIST.	1	20	25	0.1	0.1
281 LUTH CH AMER..	3	818	1 036	3.7	5.1
283 LUTH--MO SYNOD	9	3 900	5 117	18.0	25.1
413 S.D.A.........	1	29	36*	0.1	0.2
419 SO BAPT CONV..	1	211	260*	0.9	1.3
443 UN C OF CHRIST	2	719	885*	3.1	4.3
449 UN METHODIST..	13	3 158	3 889*	13.7	19.1
453 UN PRES CH USA	2	498	613*	2.2	3.0
HIGHLAND	79	8 969	12 139*	36.3	100.0
019 AMER BAPT USA.	3	870	1 067*	3.2	8.8
081 CATHOLIC......	2	NA	888	2.7	7.3
097 CHR CHS&CHS CR	17	2 363	2 899*	8.7	23.9
107 CHRISTIAN UN..	2	35	70	0.2	0.6
123 CH GOD (ANDER)	1	43	129	0.4	1.1
127 CH GOD (CLEVE)	2	86	105*	0.3	0.9
165 CH OF NAZARENE	2	186	386	1.2	3.2
167 CHS OF CHRIST.	3	190	250	0.7	2.1
193 EPISCOPAL.....	1	98	92	0.3	0.8
226 FRIENDS-USA...	5	450	552*	1.6	4.5
244 GRACE BRETHREN	1	38	47*	0.1	0.4
281 LUTH CH AMER..	1	213	261	0.8	2.2
291 MISSIONARY CH.	1	26	31	0.1	0.3
413 S.D.A.........	1	30	37*	0.1	0.3
419 SO BAPT CONV..	1	138	169*	0.5	1.4
443 UN C OF CHRIST	1	?	?	?	?
449 UN METHODIST..	28	3 337	4 094*	12.2	33.7
453 UN PRES CH USA	7	866	1 062*	3.2	8.7
HOCKING	54	5 550	8 425*	34.7	100.0

NA—Not applicable   *Total adherents estimated from known number of communicant, confirmed, full members.   —Represents a percent less than 0.1.   Percentages may not total due to rounding.

Table 4. Churches and Church Membership by County and Denomination: 1980

County and Denomination	Number of churches	Communicant, confirmed, full members	Total adherents			County and Denomination	Number of churches	Communicant, confirmed, full members	Total adherents		
			Number	Percent of total population	Percent of total adherents				Number	Percent of total population	Percent of total adherents
001 ADVENT CHR CH.	1	78	96*	0.4	1.1	KNOX	85	13 843	21 382*	46.2	100.0
029 AMER LUTH CH..	3	579	711	2.9	8.4						
081 CATHOLIC......	2	NA	1 180	4.9	14.0	001 ADVENT CHR CH.	2	123	148*	0.3	0.7
089 CHR & MISS AL.	1	29	46	0.2	0.5	019 AMER BAPT USA.	5	1 279	1 538*	3.3	7.2
093 CHR CH (DISC).	1	72	101	0.4	1.2	029 AMER LUTH CH..	3	635	842	1.8	3.9
097 CHR CHS&CHS CR	1	250	307*	1.3	3.6	053 ASSEMB OF GOD.	1	128	260	0.6	1.2
123 CH GOD (ANDER)	2	186	558	2.3	6.6	081 CATHOLIC......	4	NA	3 436	7.4	16.1
127 CH GOD (CLEVE)	1	35	43*	0.2	0.5	089 CHR & MISS AL.	1	80	80	0.2	0.4
165 CH OF NAZARENE	1	216	329	1.4	3.9	093 CHR CH (DISC).	1	501	1 005	2.2	4.7
167 CHS OF CHRIST.	1	26	32	0.1	0.4	097 CHR CHS&CHS CR	13	1 282	1 541*	3.3	7.2
193 EPISCOPAL.....	1	33	40	0.2	0.5	123 CH GOD (ANDER)	2	173	519	1.1	2.4
283 LUTH--MO SYNOD	1	100	138	0.6	1.6	127 CH GOD (CLEVE)	2	218	262*	0.6	1.2
285 MENNONITE CH..	2	78	96*	0.4	1.1	157 CH OF BRETHREN	2	222	267*	0.6	1.2
419 SO BAPT CONV..	1	315	387*	1.6	4.6	165 CH OF NAZARENE	3	808	1 150	2.5	5.4
449 UN METHODIST..	33	2 976	3 653*	15.0	43.4	167 CHS OF CHRIST.	3	275	328	0.7	1.5
453 UN PRES CH USA	2	577	708*	2.9	8.4	179 CONSRV BAPT...	1	75	90*	0.2	0.4
						244 GRACE BRETHREN	2	282	339*	0.7	1.6
HOLMES	108	14 276	19 177*	65.2	100.0	263 INT FOURSQ GOS	1	96	115*	0.2	0.5
						323 OLD ORD AMISH.	1	130	156*	0.3	0.7
019 AMER BAPT USA.	1	114	148*	0.5	0.8	403 SALVATION ARMY	1	151	428	0.9	2.0
061 BEACHY AMISH..	5	266	344*	1.2	1.8	413 S.D.A.........	4	839	1 009*	2.2	4.7
081 CATHOLIC......	4	NA	573	1.9	3.0	419 SO BAPT CONV..	1	78	94*	0.2	0.4
097 CHR CHS&CHS CR	7	1 917	2 482*	8.4	12.9	435 UNITARIAN-UNIV	1	12	14*	-	0.1
123 CH GOD (ANDER)	1	27	81	0.3	0.4	443 UN C OF CHRIST	1	358	430*	0.9	2.0
127 CH GOD (CLEVE)	2	36	47*	0.2	0.2	449 UN METHODIST..	26	5 068	6 093*	13.2	28.5
157 CH OF BRETHREN	1	102	132*	0.4	0.7	453 UN PRES CH USA	4	1 030	1 238*	2.7	5.8
165 CH OF NAZARENE	1	48	117	0.4	0.6						
167 CHS OF CHRIST.	2	175	220	0.7	1.1	LAKE	102	24 039	114 707*	53.9	100.0
221 FREE METHODIST	1	5	57	0.2	0.3						
281 LUTH CH AMER..	1	301	369	1.3	1.9	005 AME ZION......	1	225	300	0.1	0.3
283 LUTH--MO SYNOD	1	59	74	0.3	0.4	019 AMER BAPT USA.	6	998	1 218*	0.6	1.1
285 MENNONITE CH..	14	2 259	2 924*	9.9	15.2	029 AMER LUTH CH..	2	265	451	0.2	0.4
323 OLD ORD AMISH.	50	6 500	8 415*	28.6	43.9	053 ASSEMB OF GOD.	4	515	929	0.4	0.8
413 S.D.A.........	1	51	66*	0.2	0.3	057 BAPT GEN CONF.	1	115	140*	0.1	0.1
443 UN C OF CHRIST	6	993	1 286*	4.4	6.7	081 CATHOLIC......	15	NA	82 519	38.8	71.9
449 UN METHODIST..	7	1 039	1 345*	4.6	7.0	089 CHR & MISS AL.	2	148	339	0.2	0.3
453 UN PRES CH USA	3	384	497*	1.7	2.6	093 CHR CH (DISC).	4	637	1 116	0.5	1.0
						097 CHR CHS&CHS CR	2	578	705*	0.3	0.6
HURON	70	11 431	30 878*	56.5	100.0	101 C.M.E.........	1	155	189*	0.1	0.2
						123 CH GOD (ANDER)	1	89	267	0.1	0.2
019 AMER BAPT USA.	4	731	909*	1.7	2.9	127 CH GOD (CLEVE)	5	343	419*	0.2	0.4
029 AMER LUTH CH..	6	2 484	3 358	6.1	10.9	133 CH GOD(7TH)DEN	1	4	5*	-	-
053 ASSEMB OF GOD.	1	78	155	0.3	0.5	149 CH OF JC (BIC)	1	34	34	-	-
081 CATHOLIC......	10	NA	15 702	28.8	50.9	151 L-D SAINTS....	1	NA	363	0.2	0.3
089 CHR & MISS AL.	3	278	754	1.4	2.4	157 CH OF BRETHREN	1	236	288*	0.1	0.3
093 CHR CH (DISC).	1	58	89	0.2	0.3	163 CH OF LUTH BR.	1	29	57	-	-
097 CHR CHS&CHS CR	2	116	144*	0.3	0.5	165 CH OF NAZARENE	3	303	795	0.4	0.7
105 CHRISTIAN REF.	1	232	342	0.6	1.1	167 CHS OF CHRIST.	4	322	432	0.2	0.4
127 CH GOD (CLEVE)	3	311	387*	0.7	1.3	175 CONGR CHR CHS.	1	27	33*	-	-
165 CH OF NAZARENE	3	190	308	0.6	1.0	271 REFORM JUDAISM	1	150	183*	0.1	0.2
167 CHS OF CHRIST.	3	100	127	0.2	0.4	281 LUTH CH AMER..	4	1 640	2 400	1.1	2.1
263 INT FOURSQ GOS	1	57	71*	0.1	0.2	283 LUTH--MO SYNOD	8	3 060	4 079	1.9	3.6
403 SALVATION ARMY	1	58	148	0.3	0.5	353 CHR BRETHREN..	2	65	120	0.1	0.1
413 S.D.A.........	2	105	131*	0.2	0.4	403 SALVATION ARMY	1	122	248	0.1	0.2
419 SO BAPT CONV..	4	539	671*	1.2	2.2	413 S.D.A.........	1	144	176*	0.1	0.2
435 UNITARIAN-UNIV	1	20	25*	-	0.1	419 SO BAPT CONV..	5	1 729	2 110*	1.0	1.8
443 UN C OF CHRIST	6	1 121	1 395*	2.6	4.5	435 UNITARIAN-UNIV	1	205	250*	0.1	0.2
449 UN METHODIST..	15	4 121	5 127*	9.4	16.6	443 UN C OF CHRIST	9	3 105	3 790*	1.8	3.3
453 UN PRES CH USA	3	832	1 035*	1.9	3.4	449 UN METHODIST..	11	8 520	10 398*	4.9	9.1
						453 UN PRES CH USA	1	215	262*	0.1	0.2
JACKSON	50	6 484	9 070*	29.6	100.0	469 WELS..........	1	61	92	-	0.1
019 AMER BAPT USA.	4	1 151	1 415*	4.6	15.6	LAWRENCE	68	9 118	14 659*	23.0	100.0
053 ASSEMB OF GOD.	1	11	35	0.1	0.4						
081 CATHOLIC......	2	NA	815	2.7	9.0	019 AMER BAPT USA.	3	1 314	1 620*	2.5	11.1
093 CHR CH (DISC).	2	437	572	1.9	6.3	029 AMER LUTH CH..	1	186	228	0.4	1.6
097 CHR CHS&CHS CR	1	50	61*	0.2	0.7	081 CATHOLIC......	4	NA	2 798	4.4	19.1
127 CH GOD (CLEVE)	2	127	156*	0.5	1.7	097 CHR CHS&CHS CR	2	1 697	2 092*	3.3	14.3
165 CH OF NAZARENE	2	225	454	1.5	5.0	127 CH GOD (CLEVE)	3	94	116*	0.2	0.8
167 CHS OF CHRIST.	4	92	158	0.5	1.7	165 CH OF NAZARENE	10	946	1 803	2.8	12.3
281 LUTH CH AMER..	1	94	120	0.4	1.3	167 CHS OF CHRIST.	9	767	908	1.4	6.2
285 MENNONITE CH..	1	43	53*	0.2	0.6	193 EPISCOPAL.....	1	80	120	0.2	0.8
349 PENT HOLINESS.	2	90	111*	0.4	1.2	285 MENNONITE CH..	2	65	80*	0.1	0.5
413 S.D.A.........	1	54	66*	0.2	0.7	357 PRESB CH US...	1	67	83*	0.1	0.6
419 SO BAPT CONV..	2	362	445*	1.5	4.9	419 SO BAPT CONV..	2	420	518*	0.8	3.5
449 UN METHODIST..	18	2 864	3 522*	11.5	38.8	449 UN METHODIST..	29	3 233	3 986*	6.2	27.2
453 UN PRES CH USA	7	884	1 087*	3.6	12.0	453 UN PRES CH USA	1	249	307*	0.5	2.1
JEFFERSON	142	19 813	46 296*	50.6	100.0	LICKING	150	29 898	49 051*	40.5	100.0
001 ADVENT CHR CH.	1	39	47*	0.1	0.1	019 AMER BAPT USA.	12	2 551	3 109*	2.6	6.3
019 AMER BAPT USA.	2	319	382*	0.4	0.8	029 AMER LUTH CH..	1	162	245	0.2	0.5
029 AMER LUTH CH..	1	95	147	0.2	0.3	053 ASSEMB OF GOD.	3	182	312	0.3	0.6
053 ASSEMB OF GOD.	5	272	894	1.0	1.9	061 BEACHY AMISH..	1	31	38*	-	0.1
081 CATHOLIC......	31	NA	20 765	22.7	44.9	071 BRETHREN (ASH)	1	65	79*	0.1	0.2
093 CHR CH (DISC).	3	456	685	0.7	1.5	081 CATHOLIC......	9	NA	10 114	8.4	20.6
097 CHR CHS&CHS CR	9	2 511	3 010*	3.3	6.5	089 CHR & MISS AL.	1	38	153	0.1	0.3
101 C.M.E.........	1	160	192*	0.2	0.4	093 CHR CH (DISC).	3	922	1 578	1.3	3.2
123 CH GOD (ANDER)	3	232	696	0.8	1.5	097 CHR CHS&CHS CR	15	2 622	3 196*	2.6	6.5
151 L-D SAINTS....	1	NA	131	0.1	0.3	107 CHRISTIAN UN..	7	393	517	0.4	1.1
165 CH OF NAZARENE	8	621	1 012	1.1	2.2	123 CH GOD (ANDER)	2	80	240	0.2	0.5
167 CHS OF CHRIST.	3	250	315	0.3	0.7	127 CH GOD (CLEVE)	2	152	185*	0.2	0.4
226 FRIENDS-USA...	4	335	402*	0.4	0.9	151 L-D SAINTS....	1	NA	404	0.3	0.8
270 CONSRV JUDAISM	1	66	79*	0.1	0.2	165 CH OF NAZARENE	7	675	1 317	1.1	2.7
271 REFORM JUDAISM	1	194	233*	0.3	0.5	167 CHS OF CHRIST.	5	440	560	0.5	1.1
281 LUTH CH AMER..	1	367	405	0.4	0.9	193 EPISCOPAL.....	2	716	1 009	0.8	2.1
283 LUTH--MO SYNOD	1	197	249	0.3	0.5	221 FREE METHODIST	1	26	87	0.1	0.2
353 CHR BRETHREN..	1	25	25	-	0.1	244 GRACE BRETHREN	1	80	98*	0.1	0.2
403 SALVATION ARMY	1	68	318	0.3	0.7	263 INT FOURSQ GOS	1	62	76*	0.1	0.2
413 S.D.A.........	2	82	98*	0.1	0.2	271 REFORM JUDAISM	1	64	78*	0.1	0.2
419 SO BAPT CONV..	1	80	96*	0.1	0.2	281 LUTH CH AMER..	6	2 051	2 864	2.4	5.8
443 UN C OF CHRIST	1	547	656*	0.7	1.4	283 LUTH--MO SYNOD	2	462	627	0.5	1.3
449 UN METHODIST..	39	8 060	9 661*	10.6	20.9	323 OLD ORD AMISH.	2	260	317*	0.3	0.6
453 UN PRES CH USA	21	4 837	5 798*	6.3	12.5	403 SALVATION ARMY	1	79	169	0.1	0.3
						413 S.D.A.........	2	237	289*	0.2	0.6

NA—Not applicable   *Total adherents estimated from known number of communicant, confirmed, full members.   —Represents a percent less than 0.1.   Percentages may not total due to rounding.

Table 4. Churches and Church Membership by County and Denomination: 1980

County and Denomination	Number of churches	Communicant, confirmed, full members	Total adherents		
			Number	Percent of total population	Percent of total adherents
419 SO BAPT CONV..	8	1 891	2 305*	1.9	4.7
435 UNITARIAN-UNIV	1	46	56*		0.1
443 UN C OF CHRIST	4	1 145	1 396*	1.2	2.8
449 UN METHODIST..	37	10 187	12 417*	10.3	25.3
453 UN PRES CH USA	12	4 279	5 216*	4.3	10.6
LOGAN	73	11 035	17 633*	45.0	100.0
019 AMER BAPT USA.	2	131	161*	0.4	0.9
071 BRETHREN (ASH)	1	152	187*	0.5	1.1
081 CATHOLIC......	2	NA	2 555	6.5	14.5
093 CHR CH (DISC).	1	575	725	1.9	4.1
097 CHR CHS&CHS CR	6	607	745*	1.9	4.2
107 CHRISTIAN UN..	1	53	85	0.2	0.5
123 CH GOD (ANDER)	3	514	1 542	3.9	8.7
127 CH GOD (CLEVE)	1	45	55*	0.1	0.3
151 L-D SAINTS....	1	NA	167	0.4	0.9
157 CH OF BRETHREN	2	268	329*	0.8	1.9
165 CH OF NAZARENE	4	244	659	1.7	3.7
167 CHS OF CHRIST.	2	70	89	0.2	0.5
226 FRIENDS-USA...	4	178	218*	0.6	1.2
281 LUTH CH AMER..	4	847	1 064	2.7	6.0
285 MENNONITE CH..	2	466	572*	1.5	3.2
291 MISSIONARY CH.	1	12	29	0.1	0.2
323 OLD ORD AMISH.	1	130	160*	0.4	0.9
329 OPEN BIBLE STD	1	30	55	0.1	0.3
383 REF PRES OF NA	1	29	33	0.1	0.2
413 S.D.A........	3	117	144*	0.4	0.8
419 SO BAPT CONV..	1	451	553*	1.4	3.1
443 UN C OF CHRIST	1	261	320*	0.8	1.8
449 UN METHODIST..	22	4 484	5 503*	14.1	31.2
453 UN PRES CH USA	6	1 371	1 683*	4.3	9.5
LORAIN	186	41 138	152 662*	55.5	100.0
005 AME ZION......	1	350	445	0.2	0.3
019 AMER BAPT USA.	6	1 051	1 303*	0.5	0.9
029 AMER LUTH CH..	2	526	706	0.3	0.5
053 ASSEMB OF GOD.	7	986	1 798	0.7	1.2
057 BAPT GEN CONF.	1	195	242*	0.1	0.2
081 CATHOLIC......	37	NA	98 397	35.8	64.5
089 CHR & MISS AL.	2	66	113	–	0.1
093 CHR CH (DISC).	4	941	1 834	0.7	1.2
097 CHR CHS&CHS CR	2	140	174*	0.1	0.1
121 CH GOD (ABR)..	1	72	89*	–	0.1
123 CH GOD (ANDER)	1	85	255	0.1	0.2
127 CH GOD (CLEVE)	8	844	1 046*	0.4	0.7
133 CH GOD(7TH)DEN	1	15	19*	–	–
149 CH OF JC (BIC)	1	59	52	–	–
151 L-D SAINTS....	1	NA	468	0.2	0.3
157 CH OF BRETHREN	1	60	74*	–	–
165 CH OF NAZARENE	6	488	890	0.3	0.6
167 CHS OF CHRIST.	6	625	840	0.3	0.6
226 FRIENDS-USA...	1	8	10*	–	–
244 GRACE BRETHREN	1	94	117*	–	0.1
263 INT FOURSQ GOS	1	378	469*	0.2	0.3
270 CONSRV JUDAISM	2	294	364*	0.1	0.2
281 LUTH CH AMER..	7	1 899	2 501	0.9	1.6
283 LUTH--MO SYNOD	12	3 881	5 193	1.9	3.4
349 PENT HOLINESS.	1	49	61*	–	–
353 CHR BRETHREN..	3	75	75	–	–
403 SALVATION ARMY	2	244	771	0.3	0.5
413 S.D.A........	3	133	165*	0.1	0.1
419 SO BAPT CONV..	13	6 872	8 519*	3.1	5.6
435 UNITARIAN-UNIV	1	20	25*	–	–
443 UN C OF CHRIST	24	10 738	13 312*	4.8	8.7
449 UN METHODIST..	25	9 452	11 718*	4.3	7.7
453 UN PRES CH USA	2	498	617*	0.2	0.4
LUCAS	268	83 209	250 414*	53.1	100.0
005 AME ZION......	1	2 239	2 578	0.5	1.0
019 AMER BAPT USA.	11	3 497	4 259*	0.9	1.7
029 AMER LUTH CH..	16	10 944	15 845	3.4	6.3
053 ASSEMB OF GOD.	2	370	616	0.1	0.2
059 BAPT MISS ASSN	1	80	97*	–	–
081 CATHOLIC......	50	NA	137 347	29.1	54.8
089 CHR & MISS AL.	3	766	1 398	0.3	0.6
093 CHR CH (DISC).	5	1 230	1 453	0.3	0.6
097 CHR CHS&CHS CR	7	2 064	2 514*	0.5	1.0
123 CH GOD (ANDER)	7	1 247	3 741	0.8	1.5
127 CH GOD (CLEVE)	4	586	714*	0.2	0.3
151 L-D SAINTS....	2	NA	822	0.2	0.3
157 CH OF BRETHREN	1	206	251*	0.1	0.1
165 CH OF NAZARENE	6	684	1 066	0.2	0.4
167 CHS OF CHRIST.	8	1 640	2 069	0.4	0.8
175 CONGR CHR CHS.	3	1 171	1 426*	0.3	0.6
179 CONSRV BAPT...	1	100	122*	–	–
221 FREE METHODIST	4	172	1 167	0.2	0.5
244 GRACE BRETHREN	1	26	32*	–	–
263 INT FOURSQ GOS	3	140	171*	–	0.1
270 CONSRV JUDAISM	1	711	866*	0.2	0.3
271 REFORM JUDAISM	1	1 432	1 744*	0.4	0.7
281 LUTH CH AMER..	23	16 741	23 967	5.1	9.6
283 LUTH--MO SYNOD	10	3 224	4 367	0.9	1.7
285 MENNONITE CH..	1	55	67*	–	–
290 METRO COMM CHS	0	25	50	–	–
291 MISSIONARY CH.	1	38	47	–	–
313 N AM BAPT CONF	1	95	116*	–	–
329 OPEN BIBLE STD	2	130	140	–	0.1
349 PENT HOLINESS.	4	330	402*	0.1	0.2
403 SALVATION ARMY	1	155	630	0.1	0.3
413 S.D.A........	3	691	842*	0.2	0.3
419 SO BAPT CONV..	13	3 111	3 789*	0.8	1.5
435 UNITARIAN-UNIV	1	567	691*	0.1	0.3
443 UN C OF CHRIST	15	5 349	6 514*	1.4	2.6
449 UN METHODIST..	39	16 943	20 635*	4.4	8.2
453 UN PRES CH USA	11	5 387	6 561*	1.4	2.6
469 WELS..........	5	1 063	1 298	0.3	0.5
MADISON	48	8 965	13 767*	41.7	100.0
019 AMER BAPT USA.	1	214	262*	0.8	1.9
029 AMER LUTH CH..	1	272	349	1.1	2.5
061 BEACHY AMISH..	3	232	284*	0.9	2.1
081 CATHOLIC......	5	NA	2 143	6.5	15.6
097 CHR CHS&CHS CR	2	166	203*	0.6	1.5
123 CH GOD (ANDER)	1	20	60	0.2	0.4
165 CH OF NAZARENE	3	306	833	2.5	6.1
167 CHS OF CHRIST.	1	25	40	0.1	0.3
193 EPISCOPAL.....	1	105	132	0.4	1.0
281 LUTH CH AMER..	1	572	820	2.5	6.0
285 MENNONITE CH..	4	547	670*	2.0	4.9
323 OLD ORD AMISH.	1	130	159*	0.5	1.2
419 SO BAPT CONV..	2	560	686*	2.1	5.0
443 UN C OF CHRIST	2	342	419*	1.3	3.0
449 UN METHODIST..	16	4 257	5 216*	15.8	37.9
453 UN PRES CH USA	4	1 217	1 491*	4.5	10.8
MAHONING	229	55 003	191 961*	66.3	100.0
005 AME ZION......	2	1 097	1 524	0.5	0.8
019 AMER BAPT USA.	8	2 859	3 431*	1.2	1.8
029 AMER LUTH CH..	7	2 921	3 658	1.3	1.9
053 ASSEMB OF GOD.	8	1 450	2 211	0.8	1.2
057 BAPT GEN CONF.	5	1 084	1 301*	0.4	0.7
081 CATHOLIC......	47	NA	122 008	42.1	63.6
089 CHR & MISS AL.	1	46	76		
093 CHR CH (DISC).	7	1 348	2 077	0.7	1.1
097 CHR CHS&CHS CR	9	2 430	2 917*	1.0	1.5
101 C.M.E.........	1	590	708*	0.2	0.4
123 CH GOD (ANDER)	3	183	549	0.2	0.3
127 CH GOD (CLEVE)	3	251	301*	0.1	0.2
149 CH OF JC (BIC)	1	86	83		
157 CH OF BRETHREN	3	529	635*	0.2	0.3
165 CH OF NAZARENE	6	692	1 041	0.4	0.5
167 CHS OF CHRIST.	7	516	759	0.3	0.4
181 CONSRV CONGR..	1	230	276*	0.1	0.1
199 EVAN CONGR CH.	1	105	126*	–	0.1
201 EVAN COV CH AM	1	563	676*	0.2	0.4
221 FREE METHODIST	3	162	747	0.3	0.4
226 FRIENDS-USA...	5	657	789*	0.3	0.4
263 INT FOURSQ GOS	1	10	12*	–	–
270 CONSRV JUDAISM	2	539	647*	0.2	0.3
271 REFORM JUDAISM	1	1 472	1 767*	0.6	0.9
281 LUTH CH AMER..	16	5 501	6 951	2.4	3.6
283 LUTH--MO SYNOD	6	1 688	2 200	0.8	1.1
285 MENNONITE CH..	5	291	349*	0.1	0.2
329 OPEN BIBLE STD	1	75	150	0.1	0.1
363 PRIMITIVE METH	2	220	264*	0.1	0.1
381 REF PRES-EVAN.	2	234	291	0.1	0.2
403 SALVATION ARMY	1	197	1 057	0.4	0.6
413 S.D.A........	3	552	663*	0.2	0.3
419 SO BAPT CONV..	5	713	856*	0.3	0.4
435 UNITARIAN-UNIV	1	150	180*	0.1	0.1
443 UN C OF CHRIST	10	3 903	4 685*	1.6	2.4
449 UN METHODIST..	21	10 414	12 499*	4.3	6.5
453 UN PRES CH USA	23	11 245	13 497*	4.7	7.0
MARION	67	18 121	29 491*	43.4	100.0
019 AMER BAPT USA.	7	2 144	2 632*	3.9	8.9
029 AMER LUTH CH..	6	3 333	4 762	7.0	16.1
053 ASSEMB OF GOD.	1	53	156	0.2	0.5
081 CATHOLIC......	4	NA	5 668	8.3	19.2
089 CHR & MISS AL.	1	126	240	0.4	0.8
093 CHR CH (DISC).	1	343	548	0.8	1.9
097 CHR CHS&CHS CR	3	712	874*	1.3	3.0
123 CH GOD (ANDER)	1	55	165	0.2	0.6
127 CH GOD (CLEVE)	2	257	315*	0.5	1.1
151 L-D SAINTS....	1	NA	238	0.4	0.8
157 CH OF BRETHREN	1	118	145*	0.2	0.5
165 CH OF NAZARENE	3	669	950	1.4	3.2
167 CHS OF CHRIST.	1	210	265	0.4	0.9
197 EVAN CH OF NA.	1	31	31	–	0.1
201 EVAN COV CH AM	1	55	68*	0.1	0.2
263 INT FOURSQ GOS	1	48	59*	0.1	0.2
271 REFORM JUDAISM	1	80	98*	0.1	0.3
281 LUTH CH AMER..	1	394	511	0.8	1.7
403 SALVATION ARMY	1	198	356	0.5	1.2
413 S.D.A........	1	91	112*	0.2	0.4
443 UN C OF CHRIST	5	1 015	1 246*	1.8	4.2
449 UN METHODIST..	20	6 880	8 445*	12.4	28.6
453 UN PRES CH USA	3	1 309	1 607*	2.4	5.4
MEDINA	94	18 665	56 007*	49.5	100.0
001 ADVENT CHR CH.	1	37	46*	–	0.1
019 AMER BAPT USA.	2	228	285*	0.3	0.5
029 AMER LUTH CH..	4	1 081	1 458	1.3	2.6
039 AP CHR CH(NAZ)	1	35	44*	–	0.1
053 ASSEMB OF GOD.	3	343	565	0.5	1.0
071 BRETHREN (ASH)	1	?	?	?	?
081 CATHOLIC......	13	NA	30 675	27.1	54.8
089 CHR & MISS AL.	2	222	532	0.5	0.9
093 CHR CH (DISC).	4	1 049	1 732	1.5	3.1
097 CHR CHS&CHS CR	1	100	125*	0.1	0.2
127 CH GOD (CLEVE)	2	51	64*	0.1	0.1
151 L-D SAINTS....	1	NA	212	0.2	0.4
157 CH OF BRETHREN	1	74	93*	0.1	0.2

NA—Not applicable   *Total adherents estimated from known number of communicant, confirmed, full members.   —Represents a percent less than 0.1   Percentages may not total due to rounding.

Table 4. Churches and Church Membership by County and Denomination: 1980

County and Denomination	Number of churches	Communicant, confirmed, full members	Total adherents Number	Percent of total population	Percent of total adherents
165 CH OF NAZARENE	3	372	546	0.5	1.0
167 CHS OF CHRIST.	3	269	377	0.3	0.7
226 FRIENDS—USA...	1	57	71*	0.1	0.1
244 GRACE BRETHREN	1	178	223*	0.2	0.4
281 LUTH CH AMER..	5	2 615	3 506	3.1	6.3
283 LUTH—MO SYNOD	3	1 261	1 909	1.7	3.4
285 MENNONITE CH..	1	100	125*	0.1	0.2
287 MENN GEN CONF.	1	152	188	0.2	0.3
323 OLD ORD AMISH.	3	390	488*	0.4	0.9
371 REF CH IN AM..	1	116	234	0.2	0.4
403 SALVATION ARMY	1	58	148	0.1	0.3
413 S.D.A.........	1	65	81*	0.1	0.1
419 SO BAPT CONV..	5	751	940*	0.8	1.7
435 UNITARIAN-UNIV	1	39	49*	—	0.1
443 UN C OF CHRIST	9	3 164	3 960*	3.5	7.1
449 UN METHODIST..	18	5 729	7 170*	6.3	12.8
453 UN PRES CH USA	1	129	161*	0.1	0.3
MEIGS	**74**	**5 534**	**7 801***	**33.0**	**100.0**
019 AMER BAPT USA.	4	953	1 166*	4.9	14.9
029 AMER LUTH CH..	2	157	219	0.9	2.8
081 CATHOLIC......	2	NA	262	1.1	3.4
093 CHR CH (DISC).	2	118	182	0.8	2.3
097 CHR CHS&CHS CR	12	1 182	1 446*	6.1	18.5
123 CH GOD (ANDER)	1	40	120	0.5	1.5
127 CH GOD (CLEVE)	2	47	58*	0.2	0.7
165 CH OF NAZARENE	6	296	628	2.7	8.1
167 CHS OF CHRIST.	7	250	318	1.3	4.1
175 CONGR CHR CHS.	1	285	349*	1.5	4.5
193 EPISCOPAL.....	1	69	113	0.5	1.4
221 FREE METHODIST	2	63	402	1.7	5.2
413 S.D.A.........	1	23	28*	0.1	0.4
419 SO BAPT CONV..	1	63	77*	0.3	1.0
449 UN METHODIST..	27	1 801	2 204*	9.3	28.3
453 UN PRES CH USA	3	187	229*	1.0	2.9
MERCER	**61**	**7 083**	**27 582***	**72.0**	**100.0**
019 AMER BAPT USA.	1	34	42*	0.1	0.2
029 AMER LUTH CH..	6	1 675	2 137	5.6	7.7
053 ASSEMB OF GOD.	1	64	83	0.2	0.3
081 CATHOLIC......	20	NA	18 222	47.5	66.1
097 CHR CHS&CHS CR	3	330	412*	1.1	1.5
123 CH GOD (ANDER)	1	92	276	0.7	1.0
157 CH OF BRETHREN	1	60	75*	0.2	0.3
165 CH OF NAZARENE	2	374	747	1.9	2.7
167 CHS OF CHRIST.	1	30	38	0.1	0.1
215 EVAN METH CH..	1	22	27*	0.1	0.1
226 FRIENDS—USA...	3	36	45*	0.1	0.2
291 MISSIONARY CH.	1	158	224	0.6	0.8
419 SO BAPT CONV..	1	77	96*	0.3	0.3
443 UN C OF CHRIST	3	596	744*	1.9	2.7
449 UN METHODIST..	14	3 196	3 991*	10.4	14.5
453 UN PRES CH USA	2	339	423*	1.1	1.5
MIAMI	**100**	**23 178**	**38 515***	**42.6**	**100.0**
019 AMER BAPT USA.	5	2 234	2 738*	3.0	7.1
029 AMER LUTH CH..	1	341	468	0.5	1.2
053 ASSEMB OF GOD.	2	129	260	0.3	0.7
071 BRETHREN (ASH)	1	208	255*	0.3	0.7
075 BRETHREN IN CR	3	129	219	0.2	0.6
081 CATHOLIC......	7	NA	8 222	9.1	21.3
089 CHR & MISS AL.	1	12	12	—	—
093 CHR CH (DISC).	1	76	117	0.1	0.3
097 CHR CHS&CHS CR	3	350	429*	0.5	1.1
121 CH GOD (ABR)..	3	251	308*	0.3	0.8
123 CH GOD (ANDER)	3	221	663	0.7	1.7
127 CH GOD (CLEVE)	1	59	72*	0.1	0.2
151 L-D SAINTS....	1	NA	373	0.4	1.0
157 CH OF BRETHREN	9	2 005	2 457*	2.7	6.4
165 CH OF NAZARENE	4	601	1 296	1.4	3.4
167 CHS OF CHRIST.	2	244	371	0.4	1.0
193 EPISCOPAL.....	2	550	705	0.8	1.8
226 FRIENDS—USA...	2	359	440*	0.5	1.1
244 GRACE BRETHREN	2	136	167*	0.2	0.4
271 REFORM JUDAISM	1	48	59*	0.1	0.2
281 LUTH CH AMER..	7	2 389	3 044	3.4	7.9
291 MISSIONARY CH.	2	184	178	0.2	0.5
329 OPEN BIBLE STD	2	140	200	0.2	0.5
403 SALVATION ARMY	1	88	236	0.3	0.6
413 S.D.A.........	1	70	86*	0.1	0.2
419 SO BAPT CONV..	4	975	1 195*	1.3	3.1
443 UN C OF CHRIST	12	4 484	5 495*	6.1	14.3
449 UN METHODIST..	13	5 497	6 737*	7.5	17.5
453 UN PRES CH USA	4	1 398	1 713*	1.9	4.4
MONROE	**76**	**6 478**	**8 493***	**48.9**	**100.0**
019 AMER BAPT USA.	3	130	159*	0.9	1.9
081 CATHOLIC......	1	NA	212	1.2	2.5
097 CHR CHS&CHS CR	3	450	552*	3.2	6.5
105 CHRISTIAN REF.	1	83	144	0.8	1.7
107 CHRISTIAN UN..	1	5	10	0.1	0.1
123 CH GOD (ANDER)	1	26	78	0.4	0.9
165 CH OF NAZARENE	1	48	81	0.5	1.0
167 CHS OF CHRIST.	30	1 850	2 355	13.5	27.7
221 FREE METHODIST	1	32	177	1.0	2.1
323 OLD ORD AMISH.	2	260	319*	1.8	3.8
419 SO BAPT CONV..	2	635	778*	4.5	9.2
443 UN C OF CHRIST	5	929	1 139*	6.6	13.4
449 UN METHODIST..	22	1 836	2 251*	13.0	26.5
453 UN PRES CH USA	3	194	238*	1.4	2.8

County and Denomination	Number of churches	Communicant, confirmed, full members	Total adherents Number	Percent of total population	Percent of total adherents
MONTGOMERY	**413**	**127 671**	**245 914***	**43.0**	**100.0**
005 AME ZION......	2	662	950	0.2	0.4
017 AMER BAPT ASSN	4	168	168	—	0.1
019 AMER BAPT USA.	17	6 411	7 751*	1.4	3.2
029 AMER LUTH CH..	15	5 578	7 270	1.3	3.0
053 ASSEMB OF GOD.	8	2 394	3 857	0.7	1.6
071 BRETHREN (ASH)	2	691	835*	0.1	0.3
075 BRETHREN IN CR	3	129	219	—	0.1
081 CATHOLIC......	35	NA	78 333	13.7	31.9
089 CHR & MISS AL.	4	513	1 345	0.2	0.5
093 CHR CH (DISC).	5	1 611	2 026	0.4	0.8
097 CHR CHS&CHS CR	8	763	922*	0.2	0.4
101 C.M.E.........	4	4 877	5 896*	1.0	2.4
105 CHRISTIAN REF.	1	35	55	—	—
107 CHRISTIAN UN..	1	22	22	—	—
121 CH GOD (ABR)..	1	52	63*	—	—
123 CH GOD (ANDER)	12	2 361	7 083	1.2	2.9
127 CH GOD (CLEVE)	22	2 270	2 745*	0.5	1.1
151 L-D SAINTS....	4	NA	1 564	0.3	0.6
157 CH OF BRETHREN	11	2 782	3 364*	0.6	1.4
165 CH OF NAZARENE	21	2 940	5 484	1.0	2.2
167 CHS OF CHRIST.	21	2 800	3 565	0.6	1.4
179 CONSRV BAPT...	1	65	79*	—	—
193 EPISCOPAL.....	7	3 133	4 581	0.8	1.9
201 EVAN COV CH AM	1	50	60*	—	—
221 FREE METHODIST	1	12	90	—	—
226 FRIENDS—USA...	3	551	666*	0.1	0.3
244 GRACE BRETHREN	12	2 002	2 420*	0.4	1.0
263 INT FOURSQ GOS	1	250	302*	0.1	0.1
270 CONSRV JUDAISM	1	56	68*	—	—
271 REFORM JUDAISM	2	2 022	2 445*	0.4	1.0
274 LAT EVAN LUTH.	1	100	120	—	—
281 LUTH CH AMER..	18	7 994	10 241	1.8	4.2
283 LUTH—MO SYNOD	4	1 166	1 671	0.3	0.7
290 METRO COMM CHS	1	28	56	—	—
291 MISSIONARY CH.	3	208	264	—	0.1
313 N AM BAPT CONF	1	262	317*	0.1	0.1
329 OPEN BIBLE STD	7	810	1 345	0.2	0.5
335 ORTH PRESB CH.	1	22	27*	—	—
349 PENT HOLINESS.	2	100	121*	—	—
353 CHR BRETHREN..	1	60	100	—	—
403 SALVATION ARMY	2	213	957	0.2	0.4
413 S.D.A.........	6	2 310	2 793*	0.5	1.1
419 SO BAPT CONV..	38	21 618	26 137*	4.6	10.6
435 UNITARIAN-UNIV	3	255	308*	0.1	0.1
443 UN C OF CHRIST	23	8 926	10 792*	1.9	4.4
449 UN METHODIST..	57	30 020	36 295*	6.3	14.8
453 UN PRES CH USA	15	8 356	10 103*	1.8	4.1
469 WELS..........	1	23	39	—	—
MORGAN	**42**	**4 839**	**7 429***	**52.2**	**100.0**
029 AMER LUTH CH..	2	1 065	1 503	10.6	20.2
061 BEACHY AMISH..	1	38	47*	0.3	0.6
081 CATHOLIC......	5	NA	1 110	7.8	14.9
093 CHR CH (DISC).	1	66	76	0.5	1.0
097 CHR CHS&CHS CR	4	834	1 025*	7.2	13.8
165 CH OF NAZARENE	2	122	267	1.9	3.6
167 CHS OF CHRIST.	5	360	460	3.2	6.2
221 FREE METHODIST	1	3	45	0.3	0.6
226 FRIENDS—USA...	1	33	41*	0.3	0.6
281 LUTH CH AMER..	1	50	67	0.5	0.9
323 OLD ORD AMISH.	1	130	160*	1.1	2.2
419 SO BAPT CONV..	1	244	300*	2.1	4.0
449 UN METHODIST..	15	1 618	1 989*	14.0	26.8
453 UN PRES CH USA	2	276	339*	2.4	4.6
MORROW	**45**	**6 407**	**8 820***	**33.3**	**100.0**
001 ADVENT CHR CH.	2	147	183*	0.7	2.1
019 AMER BAPT USA.	3	678	846*	3.2	9.6
029 AMER LUTH CH..	1	293	410	1.5	4.6
081 CATHOLIC......	1	NA	350	1.3	4.0
097 CHR CHS&CHS CR	2	605	755*	2.9	8.6
127 CH GOD (CLEVE)	1	28	35*	0.1	0.4
165 CH OF NAZARENE	3	338	855	3.2	9.7
226 FRIENDS—USA...	2	299	373*	1.4	4.2
281 LUTH CH AMER..	1	80	99	0.4	1.1
285 MENNONITE CH..	2	109	136*	0.5	1.5
413 S.D.A.........	3	206	257*	1.0	2.9
449 UN METHODIST..	22	3 267	4 076*	15.4	46.2
453 UN PRES CH USA	2	357	445*	1.7	5.0
MUSKINGUM	**119**	**22 716**	**39 934***	**47.9**	**100.0**
019 AMER BAPT USA.	8	1 378	1 687*	2.0	4.2
029 AMER LUTH CH..	1	273	354	0.4	0.9
053 ASSEMB OF GOD.	2	168	482	0.6	1.2
081 CATHOLIC......	8	NA	9 640	11.6	24.1
083 CHRIST CATH CH	1	12	16	—	—
089 CHR & MISS AL.	2	58	126	0.2	0.3
093 CHR CH (DISC).	1	610	912	1.1	2.3
097 CHR CHS&CHS CR	2	500	612*	0.7	1.5
123 CH GOD (ANDER)	2	97	291	0.3	0.7
151 L-D SAINTS....	2	NA	542	0.7	1.4
157 CH OF BRETHREN	1	104	127*	0.2	0.3
165 CH OF NAZARENE	5	590	972	1.2	2.4
167 CHS OF CHRIST.	7	620	790	0.9	2.0
179 CONSRV BAPT...	1	20	24*	—	0.1
193 EPISCOPAL.....	1	444	462	0.6	1.2
221 FREE METHODIST	3	203	693	0.8	1.7
270 CONSRV JUDAISM	1	45	55*	0.1	0.1
281 LUTH CH AMER..	6	1 663	2 398	2.9	6.0
283 LUTH—MO SYNOD	1	918	1 200	1.4	3.0

NA—Not applicable   *Total adherents estimated from known number of communicant, confirmed, full members.   —Represents a percent less than 0.1.   Percentages may not total due to rounding.

Table 4. Churches and Church Membership by County and Denomination: 1980

County and Denomination	Number of churches	Communicant, confirmed, full members	Total adherents Number	Percent of total population	Percent of total adherents
285 MENNONITE CH..	1	24	29*	–	0.1
403 SALVATION ARMY	1	113	309	0.4	0.8
413 S.D.A.	1	137	168*	0.2	0.4
419 SO BAPT CONV..	1	241	295*	0.4	0.7
443 UN C OF CHRIST	1	495	606*	0.7	1.5
449 UN METHODIST..	40	10 726	13 132*	15.8	32.9
453 UN PRES CH USA	19	3 277	4 012*	4.8	10.0
NOBLE	42	2 986	5 381*	47.6	100.0
081 CATHOLIC......	5	NA	1 324	11.7	24.6
097 CHR CHS&CHS CR	1	400	491*	4.3	9.1
165 CH OF NAZARENE	1	58	175	1.5	3.3
167 CHS OF CHRIST.	7	655	833	7.4	15.5
179 CONSRV BAPT...	1	123	151*	1.3	2.8
221 FREE METHODIST	3	71	336	3.0	6.2
281 LUTH CH AMER..	1	106	140	1.2	2.6
419 SO BAPT CONV..	1	120	147*	1.3	2.7
449 UN METHODIST..	20	1 257	1 543*	13.6	28.7
453 UN PRES CH USA	2	196	241*	2.1	4.5
OTTAWA	46	11 980	23 791*	59.4	100.0
029 AMER LUTH CH..	12	5 375	7 496	18.7	31.5
081 CATHOLIC......	6	NA	7 900	19.7	33.2
089 CHR & MISS AL.	2	56	109	0.3	0.5
093 CHR CH (DISC).	2	135	266	0.7	1.1
123 CH GOD (ANDER)	1	64	192	0.5	0.8
127 CH GOD (CLEVE)	2	50	61*	0.2	0.3
165 CH OF NAZARENE	1	31	148	0.4	0.6
167 CHS OF CHRIST.	1	100	120	0.3	0.5
283 LUTH--MO SYNOD	1	350	427	1.1	1.8
419 SO BAPT CONV..	3	478	581*	1.4	2.4
443 UN C OF CHRIST	6	2 284	2 776*	6.9	11.7
449 UN METHODIST..	8	3 000	3 646*	9.1	15.3
453 UN PRES CH USA	1	57	69*	0.2	0.3
PAULDING	40	4 983	10 725*	50.3	100.0
017 AMER BAPT ASSN	1	28	28	0.1	0.3
029 AMER LUTH CH..	2	271	336	1.6	3.1
081 CATHOLIC......	5	NA	3 493	16.4	32.6
093 CHR CH (DISC).	1	327	557	2.6	5.2
097 CHR CHS&CHS CR	3	570	716*	3.4	6.7
123 CH GOD (ANDER)	4	186	558	2.6	5.2
165 CH OF NAZARENE	3	308	827	3.9	7.7
167 CHS OF CHRIST.	1	50	64	0.3	0.6
281 LUTH CH AMER..	1	406	530	2.5	4.9
283 LUTH--MO SYNOD	1	155	248	1.2	2.3
443 UN C OF CHRIST	1	114	143*	0.7	1.3
449 UN METHODIST..	14	2 194	2 755*	12.9	25.7
453 UN PRES CH USA	3	374	470*	2.2	4.4
PERRY	70	6 791	13 486*	43.5	100.0
019 AMER BAPT USA.	3	428	533*	1.7	4.0
029 AMER LUTH CH..	6	1 135	1 514	4.9	11.2
061 BEACHY AMISH..	1	17	21*	0.1	0.2
081 CATHOLIC......	10	NA	4 428	14.3	32.8
093 CHR CH (DISC).	2	204	335	1.1	2.5
097 CHR CHS&CHS CR	1	58	72*	0.2	0.5
107 CHRISTIAN UN..	2	27	106	0.3	0.8
123 CH GOD (ANDER)	1	44	132	0.4	1.0
157 CH OF BRETHREN	1	153	191*	0.6	1.4
165 CH OF NAZARENE	1	153	303	1.0	2.2
167 CHS OF CHRIST.	6	250	330	1.1	2.4
221 FREE METHODIST	2	75	231	0.7	1.7
419 SO BAPT CONV..	1	48	60*	0.2	0.4
443 UN C OF CHRIST	3	316	394*	1.3	2.9
449 UN METHODIST..	28	3 741	4 659*	15.0	34.5
453 UN PRES CH USA	2	142	177*	0.6	1.3
PICKAWAY	47	9 569	13 662*	31.3	100.0
029 AMER LUTH CH..	4	1 294	1 712	3.9	12.5
081 CATHOLIC......	1	NA	1 420	3.3	10.4
097 CHR CHS&CHS CR	2	363	445*	1.0	3.3
127 CH GOD (CLEVE)	1	98	120*	0.3	0.9
157 CH OF BRETHREN	1	74	91*	0.2	0.7
165 CH OF NAZARENE	3	417	786	1.8	5.8
167 CHS OF CHRIST.	1	159	257	0.6	1.9
193 EPISCOPAL.....	1	200	295	0.7	2.2
281 LUTH CH AMER..	1	117	141	0.3	1.0
419 SO BAPT CONV..	3	989	1 213*	2.8	8.9
449 UN METHODIST..	28	5 260	6 449*	14.8	47.2
453 UN PRES CH USA	1	598	733*	1.7	5.4
PIKE	35	3 468	4 848*	21.3	100.0
081 CATHOLIC......	2	NA	495	2.2	10.2
097 CHR CHS&CHS CR	2	203	250*	1.1	5.2
107 CHRISTIAN UN..	8	207	229	1.0	4.7
127 CH GOD (CLEVE)	1	59	73*	0.3	1.5
165 CH OF NAZARENE	1	40	135	0.6	2.8
167 CHS OF CHRIST.	3	253	327	1.4	6.7
283 LUTH--MO SYNOD	1	48	58	0.3	1.2
285 MENNONITE CH..	1	41	51*	0.2	1.1
323 OLD ORD AMISH.	2	260	321*	1.4	6.6
413 S.D.A.	1	33	41*	0.2	0.8
419 SO BAPT CONV..	2	663	818*	3.6	16.9
443 UN C OF CHRIST	1	33	41*	0.2	0.8
449 UN METHODIST..	9	1 178	1 454*	6.4	30.0
453 UN PRES CH USA	1	450	555*	2.4	11.4
PORTAGE	88	16 374	41 441*	30.5	100.0

County and Denomination	Number of churches	Communicant, confirmed, full members	Total adherents Number	Percent of total population	Percent of total adherents
019 AMER BAPT USA.	1	152	185*	0.1	0.4
029 AMER LUTH CH..	1	337	482	0.4	1.2
053 ASSEMB OF GOD.	4	587	1 378	1.0	3.3
081 CATHOLIC......	10	NA	18 747	13.8	45.2
089 CHR & MISS AL.	2	198	378	0.3	0.9
093 CHR CH (DISC).	6	1 551	2 189	1.6	5.3
123 CH GOD (ANDER)	4	257	771	0.6	1.9
127 CH GOD (CLEVE)	3	148	180*	0.1	0.4
149 CH OF JC (BIC)	1	14	14	–	–
151 L-D SAINTS....	1	NA	353	0.3	0.9
157 CH OF BRETHREN	1	205	250*	0.2	0.6
165 CH OF NAZARENE	4	412	895	0.7	2.2
167 CHS OF CHRIST.	4	422	593	0.4	1.4
203 EVAN FREE CH..	1	342	416*	0.3	1.0
221 FREE METHODIST	1	18	45	–	0.1
226 FRIENDS-USA...	1	99	121*	0.1	0.3
281 LUTH CH AMER..	2	682	949	0.7	2.3
283 LUTH--MO SYNOD	3	864	1 211	0.9	2.9
285 MENNONITE CH..	1	138	168*	0.1	0.4
353 CHR BRETHREN..	1	10	15	–	–
363 PRIMITIVE METH	1	144	175*	0.1	0.4
413 S.D.A.	1	111	135*	0.1	0.3
419 SO BAPT CONV..	5	460	560*	0.4	1.4
435 UNITARIAN-UNIV	1	56	68*	0.1	0.2
443 UN C OF CHRIST	8	2 839	3 457*	2.5	8.3
449 UN METHODIST..	18	6 086	7 411*	5.5	17.9
453 UN PRES CH USA	1	242	295*	0.2	0.7
PREBLE	67	10 630	15 473*	40.5	100.0
017 AMER BAPT ASSN	1	35	35	0.1	0.2
029 AMER LUTH CH..	3	1 111	1 318	3.4	8.5
053 ASSEMB OF GOD.	1	30	50	0.1	0.3
071 BRETHREN (ASH)	2	299	367*	1.0	2.4
081 CATHOLIC......	3	NA	1 444	3.8	9.3
097 CHR CHS&CHS CR	3	358	440*	1.2	2.8
123 CH GOD (ANDER)	3	450	1 350	3.5	8.7
127 CH GOD (CLEVE)	3	258	317*	0.8	2.0
157 CH OF BRETHREN	4	800	983*	2.6	6.4
165 CH OF NAZARENE	1	66	145	0.4	0.9
167 CHS OF CHRIST.	2	110	140	0.4	0.9
226 FRIENDS-USA...	1	104	128*	0.3	0.8
244 GRACE BRETHREN	2	66	81*	0.2	0.5
281 LUTH CH AMER..	3	925	1 278	3.3	8.3
419 SO BAPT CONV..	8	1 911	2 349*	6.1	15.2
435 UNITARIAN-UNIV	1	62	76*	0.2	0.5
443 UN C OF CHRIST	6	1 017	1 250*	3.3	8.1
449 UN METHODIST..	14	2 388	2 935*	7.7	19.0
453 UN PRES CH USA	6	640	787*	2.1	5.1
PUTNAM	50	5 505	27 354*	82.9	100.0
029 AMER LUTH CH..	2	138	198	0.6	0.7
081 CATHOLIC......	13	NA	20 368	61.7	74.5
093 CHR CH (DISC).	1	125	192	0.6	0.7
097 CHR CHS&CHS CR	1	35	44*	0.1	0.2
107 CHRISTIAN UN..	1	18	18	0.1	0.1
123 CH GOD (ANDER)	1	35	105	0.3	0.4
157 CH OF BRETHREN	1	137	172*	0.5	0.6
165 CH OF NAZARENE	1	63	150	0.5	0.5
167 CHS OF CHRIST.	1	40	50	0.2	0.2
221 FREE METHODIST	1	11	33	0.1	0.1
281 LUTH CH AMER..	1	252	309	0.9	1.1
285 MENNONITE CH..	1	30	38*	0.1	0.1
287 MENN GEN CONF.	2	637	717	2.2	2.6
291 MISSIONARY CH.	2	171	168	0.5	0.6
443 UN C OF CHRIST	2	482	606*	1.8	2.2
449 UN METHODIST..	16	3 051	3 834*	11.6	14.0
453 UN PRES CH USA	2	280	352*	1.1	1.3
RICHLAND	120	31 436	58 499*	44.6	100.0
005 AME ZION......	1	155	186	0.1	0.3
019 AMER BAPT USA.	5	1 333	1 625*	1.2	2.8
039 AP CHR CH(NAZ)	2	444	541*	0.4	0.9
053 ASSEMB OF GOD.	1	306	440	0.3	0.8
057 BAPT GEN CONF.	1	47	57*	–	0.1
071 BRETHREN (ASH)	1	65	79*	0.1	0.1
081 CATHOLIC......	5	NA	15 854	12.1	27.1
089 CHR & MISS AL.	3	699	1 140	0.9	1.9
093 CHR CH (DISC).	4	1 333	2 077	1.6	3.6
097 CHR CHS&CHS CR	4	439	535*	0.4	0.9
123 CH GOD (ANDER)	3	447	1 341	1.0	2.3
127 CH GOD (CLEVE)	4	302	368*	0.3	0.6
151 L-D SAINTS....	1	NA	622	0.5	1.1
157 CH OF BRETHREN	4	232	283*	0.2	0.5
165 CH OF NAZARENE	4	437	1 004	0.8	1.7
167 CHS OF CHRIST.	6	350	445	0.3	0.8
175 CONGR CHR CHS.	2	1 420	1 731*	1.3	3.0
179 CONSRV BAPT...	1	110	134*	0.1	0.2
197 EVAN CH OF NA.	1	34	34	–	0.1
199 EVAN CONGR CH.	1	64	78*	0.1	0.1
221 FREE METHODIST	1	172	417	0.3	0.7
226 FRIENDS-USA...	1	25	30*	–	0.1
244 GRACE BRETHREN	3	733	893*	0.7	1.5
263 INT FOURSQ GOS	2	239	291*	0.2	0.5
270 CONSRV JUDAISM	1	65	79*	0.1	0.1
271 REFORM JUDAISM	1	32	39*	–	0.1
281 LUTH CH AMER..	18	9 938	13 163	10.0	22.5
283 LUTH--MO SYNOD	1	127	186	0.1	0.3
329 OPEN BIBLE STD	3	327	630	0.5	1.1
353 CHR BRETHREN..	2	100	175	0.1	0.3
403 SALVATION ARMY	1	127	210	0.2	0.4
413 S.D.A.	1	153	186*	0.1	0.3
419 SO BAPT CONV..	5	720	877*	0.7	1.5

NA—Not applicable   *Total adherents estimated from known number of communicant, confirmed, full members.   —Represents a percent less than 0.1.   Percentages may not total due to rounding.

221

Table 4. Churches and Church Membership by County and Denomination: 1980

County and Denomination	Number of churches	Communicant, confirmed, full members	Total adherents Number	Percent of total population	Percent of total adherents
443 UN C OF CHRIST	4	1 583	1 929*	1.5	3.3
449 UN METHODIST..	17	6 656	8 112*	6.2	13.9
453 UN PRES CH USA	7	2 222	2 708*	2.1	4.6
ROSS	81	12 312	19 379*	29.8	100.0
019 AMER BAPT USA.	1	1 160	1 408*	2.2	7.3
053 ASSEMB OF GOD.	1	42	85	0.1	0.4
081 CATHOLIC......	4	NA	3 384	5.2	17.5
093 CHR CH (DISC).	1	145	217	0.3	1.1
097 CHR CHS&CHS CR	3	626	760*	1.2	3.9
107 CHRISTIAN UN..	6	241	313	0.5	1.6
123 CH GOD (ANDER)	2	133	399	0.6	2.1
127 CH GOD (CLEVE)	2	161	195*	0.3	1.0
151 L-D SAINTS....	1	NA	250	0.4	1.3
157 CH OF BRETHREN	1	70	85*	0.1	0.4
165 CH OF NAZARENE	2	315	648	1.0	3.3
167 CHS OF CHRIST.	3	160	245	0.4	1.3
193 EPISCOPAL.....	1	473	551	0.8	2.8
226 FRIENDS-USA...	2	16	19*	-	0.1
281 LUTH CH AMER..	1	406	516	0.8	2.7
283 LUTH--MO SYNOD	1	90	129	0.2	0.7
403 SALVATION ARMY	1	113	271	0.4	1.4
413 S.D.A........	1	66	80*	0.1	0.4
419 SO BAPT CONV..	2	389	472*	0.7	2.4
435 UNITARIAN-UNIV	1	29	35*	0.1	0.2
443 UN C OF CHRIST	3	578	701*	1.1	3.6
449 UN METHODIST..	33	5 432	6 593*	10.1	34.0
453 UN PRES CH USA	8	1 667	2 023*	3.1	10.4
SANDUSKY	75	17 305	37 320*	59.0	100.0
029 AMER LUTH CH..	10	6 143	8 153	12.9	21.8
053 ASSEMB OF GOD.	4	340	579	0.9	1.6
071 BRETHREN (ASH)	1	48	59*	0.1	0.2
081 CATHOLIC......	7	NA	14 946	23.6	40.0
089 CHR & MISS AL.	1	55	82	0.1	0.2
093 CHR CH (DISC).	2	180	297	0.5	0.8
097 CHR CHS&CHS CR	1	100	124*	0.2	0.3
123 CH GOD (ANDER)	1	35	105	0.2	0.3
127 CH GOD (CLEVE)	3	56	69*	0.1	0.2
165 CH OF NAZARENE	3	175	312	0.5	0.8
167 CHS OF CHRIST.	5	300	382	0.6	1.0
244 GRACE BRETHREN	2	300	371*	0.6	1.0
270 CONSRV JUDAISM	1	14	17*	-	-
281 LUTH CH AMER..	1	283	362	0.6	1.0
291 MISSIONARY CH.	1	124	140	0.2	0.4
313 N AM BAPT CONF	1	157	194*	0.3	0.5
353 CHR BRETHREN..	1	25	25	-	0.1
413 S.D.A........	2	63	78*	0.1	0.2
419 SO BAPT CONV..	4	1 192	1 475*	2.3	4.0
443 UN C OF CHRIST	4	995	1 232*	1.9	3.3
449 UN METHODIST..	17	5 758	7 127*	11.3	19.1
453 UN PRES CH USA	3	962	1 191*	1.9	3.2
SCIOTO	101	13 621	22 651*	26.8	100.0
019 AMER BAPT USA.	1	413	506*	0.6	2.2
029 AMER LUTH CH..	2	398	499	0.6	2.2
053 ASSEMB OF GOD.	1	40	125	0.1	0.6
081 CATHOLIC......	9	NA	3 815	4.5	16.8
093 CHR CH (DISC).	1	416	1 014	1.2	4.5
097 CHR CHS&CHS CR	9	2 104	2 576*	3.0	11.4
107 CHRISTIAN UN..	2	69	86	0.1	0.4
123 CH GOD (ANDER)	2	195	585	0.7	2.6
127 CH GOD (CLEVE)	4	482	590*	0.7	2.6
151 L-D SAINTS....	1	NA	249	0.3	1.1
165 CH OF NAZARENE	11	1 063	2 101	2.5	9.3
167 CHS OF CHRIST.	7	467	614	0.7	2.7
179 CONSRV BAPT...	1	50	61*	0.1	0.3
193 EPISCOPAL.....	1	181	257	0.3	1.1
271 REFORM JUDAISM	1	80	98*	0.1	0.4
403 SALVATION ARMY	1	95	211	0.2	0.9
413 S.D.A........	1	143	175*	0.2	0.8
419 SO BAPT CONV..	3	334	409*	0.5	1.8
443 UN C OF CHRIST	1	392	480*	0.6	2.1
449 UN METHODIST..	39	5 623	6 883*	8.1	30.4
453 UN PRES CH USA	3	1 076	1 317*	1.6	5.8
SENECA	75	14 465	43 513*	70.3	100.0
019 AMER BAPT USA.	2	288	356*	0.6	0.8
029 AMER LUTH CH..	3	1 257	1 643	2.7	3.8
053 ASSEMB OF GOD.	2	220	510	0.8	1.2
081 CATHOLIC......	14	NA	24 663	39.8	56.7
089 CHR & MISS AL.	1	36	72	0.1	0.2
093 CHR CH (DISC).	2	231	369	0.6	0.8
097 CHR CHS&CHS CR	1	150	185*	0.3	0.4
123 CH GOD (ANDER)	1	12	36	0.1	0.1
151 L-D SAINTS....	1	NA	115	0.2	0.3
157 CH OF BRETHREN	1	122	151*	0.2	0.3
165 CH OF NAZARENE	2	554	798	1.3	1.8
167 CHS OF CHRIST.	1	35	50	0.1	0.1
263 INT FOURSQ GOS	1	103	127*	0.2	0.3
281 LUTH CH AMER..	1	942	1 301	2.1	3.0
283 LUTH--MO SYNOD	1	106	166	0.3	0.4
403 SALVATION ARMY	1	96	230	0.4	0.5
413 S.D.A........	1	16	20*	-	-
443 UN C OF CHRIST	14	3 551	4 387*	7.1	10.1
449 UN METHODIST..	22	5 871	7 253*	11.7	16.7
453 UN PRES CH USA	3	875	1 081*	1.7	2.5
SHELBY	51	10 025	25 280*	58.7	100.0
019 AMER BAPT USA.	3	430	538*	1.2	2.1
029 AMER LUTH CH..	6	2 788	3 639	8.4	14.4
053 ASSEMB OF GOD.	1	61	95	0.2	0.4
081 CATHOLIC......	8	NA	11 888	27.6	47.0
093 CHR CH (DISC).	1	291	684	1.6	2.7
097 CHR CHS&CHS CR	2	123	154*	0.4	0.6
123 CH GOD (ANDER)	1	95	285	0.7	1.1
127 CH GOD (CLEVE)	1	214	268*	0.6	1.1
157 CH OF BRETHREN	1	125	156*	0.4	0.6
165 CH OF NAZARENE	1	119	189	0.4	0.7
167 CHS OF CHRIST.	1	10	13	-	0.1
283 LUTH--MO SYNOD	1	88	135	0.3	0.5
291 MISSIONARY CH.	1	57	65	0.2	0.3
403 SALVATION ARMY	1	52	205	0.5	0.8
413 S.D.A........	1	8	10*	-	-
419 SO BAPT CONV..	4	602	753*	1.7	3.0
443 UN C OF CHRIST	4	1 204	1 505*	3.5	6.0
449 UN METHODIST..	12	3 337	4 172*	9.7	16.5
453 UN PRES CH USA	1	421	526*	1.2	2.1
STARK	296	89 229	182 656*	48.2	100.0
005 AME ZION......	1	394	488	0.1	0.3
019 AMER BAPT USA.	5	2 214	2 683*	0.7	1.5
029 AMER LUTH CH..	13	5 287	7 204	1.9	3.9
053 ASSEMB OF GOD.	7	870	1 687	0.4	0.9
061 BEACHY AMISH..	2	140	170*	-	0.1
071 BRETHREN (ASH)	4	428	519*	0.1	0.3
075 BRETHREN IN CR	3	129	219	0.1	0.1
081 CATHOLIC......	29	NA	66 224	17.5	36.3
089 CHR & MISS AL.	2	146	347	0.8	1.6
093 CHR CH (DISC).	4	2 350	2 933	0.8	1.6
097 CHR CHS&CHS CR	12	8 839	10 710*	2.8	5.9
101 C.M.E........	2	2 187	2 650*	0.7	1.5
123 CH GOD (ANDER)	8	1 203	3 609	1.0	2.0
127 CH GOD (CLEVE)	8	1 509	1 828*	0.5	1.0
151 L-D SAINTS....	2	NA	822	0.2	0.5
157 CH OF BRETHREN	10	1 480	1 793*	0.5	1.0
165 CH OF NAZARENE	11	1 816	3 407	0.9	1.9
167 CHS OF CHRIST.	13	2 139	3 394	0.9	1.9
179 CONSRV BAPT...	1	170	206*	0.1	0.1
199 EVAN CONGR CH.	1	97	118*	-	0.1
221 FREE METHODIST	1	90	381	0.1	0.2
226 FRIENDS-USA...	2	472	572*	0.2	0.3
244 GRACE BRETHREN	4	505	612*	0.2	0.3
263 INT FOURSQ GOS	2	172	208*	0.1	0.1
270 CONSRV JUDAISM	1	287	348*	0.1	0.2
271 REFORM JUDAISM	1	876	1 061*	0.3	0.6
274 LAT EVAN LUTH.	1	24	25	-	-
281 LUTH CH AMER..	14	5 436	7 142	1.9	3.9
283 LUTH--MO SYNOD	3	1 152	1 556	0.4	0.9
285 MENNONITE CH..	14	1 713	2 076*	0.5	1.1
290 METRO COMM CHS	0	20	40	-	-
323 OLD ORD AMISH.	3	390	473*	0.1	0.3
329 OPEN BIBLE STD	1	130	300	0.1	0.2
335 ORTH PRESB CH.	1	30	36*	-	-
353 CHR BRETHREN..	1	20	20	-	-
403 SALVATION ARMY	3	416	941	0.2	0.5
413 S.D.A........	3	359	435*	0.1	0.2
419 SO BAPT CONV..	4	110	133*	-	0.1
435 UNITARIAN-UNIV	1	28	34*	-	-
443 UN C OF CHRIST	26	12 808	15 519*	4.1	8.5
449 UN METHODIST..	58	24 027	29 112*	7.7	15.9
453 UN PRES CH USA	14	8 766	10 621*	2.8	5.8
SUMMIT	328	92 219	266 905*	50.9	100.0
005 AME ZION......	1	1 522	2 244	0.4	0.8
019 AMER BAPT USA.	13	5 315	6 386*	1.2	2.4
029 AMER LUTH CH..	4	1 394	1 721	0.3	0.6
039 AP CHR CH(NAZ)	5	399	479*	0.1	0.2
053 ASSEMB OF GOD.	7	1 579	2 752	0.5	1.0
057 BAPT GEN CONF.	1	133	160*	-	0.1
075 BRETHREN IN CR	1	43	73	-	-
081 CATHOLIC......	44	NA	143 958	27.4	53.9
089 CHR & MISS AL.	9	1 356	2 970	0.6	1.1
093 CHR CH (DISC).	15	4 750	6 357	1.2	2.4
097 CHR CHS&CHS CR	15	4 833	5 807*	1.1	2.2
101 C.M.E........	3	1 880	2 259*	0.4	0.8
105 CHRISTIAN REF.	1	74	121	-	-
123 CH GOD (ANDER)	10	2 055	6 165	1.2	2.3
127 CH GOD (CLEVE)	7	820	985*	0.2	0.4
151 L-D SAINTS....	2	NA	874	0.2	0.3
157 CH OF BRETHREN	3	688	827*	0.2	0.3
165 CH OF NAZARENE	15	2 213	3 860	0.7	1.4
167 CHS OF CHRIST.	15	1 791	2 254	0.4	0.8
179 CONSRV BAPT...	2	335	403*	0.1	0.2
199 EVAN CONGR CH.	5	639	768*	0.1	0.3
201 EVAN COV CH AM	2	186	223*	-	0.1
221 FREE METHODIST	1	75	441	0.1	0.2
226 FRIENDS-USA...	4	216	260*	-	0.1
244 GRACE BRETHREN	4	502	603*	0.1	0.2
263 INT FOURSQ GOS	2	351	422*	0.1	0.2
270 CONSRV JUDAISM	1	385	463*	0.1	0.2
271 REFORM JUDAISM	2	1 478	1 776*	0.3	0.7
281 LUTH CH AMER..	13	5 403	7 103	1.4	2.7
283 LUTH--MO SYNOD	11	4 612	6 500	1.2	2.4
285 MENNONITE CH..	1	35	42*	-	-
290 METRO COMM CHS	0	70	140	-	0.1
291 MISSIONARY CH.	1	?	?	?	?
329 OPEN BIBLE STD	1	45	100	-	-
353 CHR BRETHREN..	3	100	165	-	0.1
356 PRESB CH AMER.	1	109	126	-	-
403 SALVATION ARMY	3	382	1 280	0.2	0.5
413 S.D.A........	3	851	1 023*	0.2	0.4
419 SO BAPT CONV..	12	1 434	1 723*	0.3	0.6

NA—Not applicable   *Total adherents estimated from known number of communicant, confirmed, full members.   —Represents a percent less than 0.1.   Percentages may not total due to rounding.

Table 4. Churches and Church Membership by County and Denomination: 1980

County and Denomination	Number of churches	Communicant, confirmed, full members	Total adherents Number	Percent of total population	Percent of total adherents
435 UNITARIAN-UNIV	1	575	691*	0.1	0.3
443 UN C OF CHRIST	22	12 331	14 816*	2.8	5.6
449 UN METHODIST..	47	23 302	27 998*	5.3	10.5
453 UN PRES CH USA	14	7 893	9 484*	1.8	3.6
469 WELS.........	1	65	103	-	-
TRUMBULL	183	41 868	121 923*	50.4	100.0
019 AMER BAPT USA.	5	1 268	1 541*	0.6	1.3
029 AMER LUTH CH..	5	2 259	2 892	1.2	2.4
039 AP CHR CH(NAZ)	1	15	18*	-	-
053 ASSEMB OF GOD.	7	1 168	3 232	1.3	2.7
081 CATHOLIC......	22	NA	63 768	26.4	52.3
089 CHR & MISS AL.	3	265	372	0.2	0.3
093 CHR CH (DISC).	17	6 927	10 099	4.2	8.3
097 CHR CHS&CHS CR	3	1 335	1 623*	0.7	1.3
101 C.M.E.........	1	18	22*	-	-
123 CH GOD (ANDER)	5	643	1 929	0.8	1.6
127 CH GOD (CLEVE)	5	391	475*	0.2	0.4
149 CH OF JC (BIC)	2	79	75	-	0.1
151 L-D SAINTS....	2	NA	818	0.3	0.7
157 CH OF BRETHREN	1	81	98*	-	0.1
165 CH OF NAZARENE	11	1 393	2 592	1.1	2.1
167 CHS OF CHRIST.	4	435	554	0.2	0.5
175 CONGR CHR CHS.	1	78	95*	-	0.1
179 CONSRV BAPT...	1	72	88*	-	0.1
199 EVAN CONGR CH.	3	318	387*	0.2	0.3
221 FREE METHODIST	1	143	357	0.1	0.3
226 FRIENDS-USA...	1	20	24*	-	-
270 CONSRV JUDAISM	1	74	90*	-	0.1
281 LUTH CH AMER..	7	2 211	3 052	1.3	2.5
283 LUTH--MO SYNOD	1	170	220	0.1	0.2
285 MENNONITE CH..	1	27	33*	-	-
323 OLD ORD AMISH.	1	130	158*	0.1	0.1
353 CHR BRETHREN..	1	25	25	-	-
403 SALVATION ARMY	1	209	389	0.2	0.3
413 S.D.A.........	3	192	233*	0.1	0.2
419 SO BAPT CONV..	13	1 983	2 411*	1.0	2.0
435 UNITARIAN-UNIV	1	21	26*	-	-
443 UN C OF CHRIST	3	1 274	1 549*	0.6	1.3
449 UN METHODIST..	36	13 570	16 496*	6.8	13.5
453 UN PRES CH USA	12	5 021	6 104*	2.5	5.0
469 WELS.........	1	53	78	-	0.1
TUSCARAWAS	158	31 269	49 828*	58.9	100.0
005 AME ZION......	1	100	120	0.1	0.2
019 AMER BAPT USA.	2	278	337*	0.4	0.7
053 ASSEMB OF GOD.	3	227	441	0.5	0.9
061 BEACHY AMISH..	1	112	136*	0.2	0.3
081 CATHOLIC......	10	NA	9 343	11.0	18.8
089 CHR & MISS AL.	1	108	183	0.2	0.4
093 CHR CH (DISC).	2	801	1 110	1.3	2.2
097 CHR CHS&CHS CR	6	1 539	1 866*	2.2	3.7
123 CH GOD (ANDER)	3	186	558	0.7	1.1
127 CH GOD (CLEVE)	5	235	285*	0.3	0.6
151 L-D SAINTS....	1	NA	157	0.2	0.3
157 CH OF BRETHREN	2	188	228*	0.3	0.5
165 CH OF NAZARENE	7	1 113	1 829	2.2	3.7
167 CHS OF CHRIST.	9	715	910	1.1	1.8
221 FREE METHODIST	1	54	195	0.2	0.4
263 INT FOURSQ GOS	4	456	553*	0.7	1.1
281 LUTH CH AMER..	15	5 177	6 810	8.0	13.7
285 MENNONITE CH..	1	9	11*	-	-
287 MENN GEN CONF.	1	276	386	0.5	0.8
293 MORAV CH-NORTH	7	1 845	2 310	2.7	4.6
323 OLD ORD AMISH.	12	1 560	1 891*	2.2	3.8
353 CHR BRETHREN..	1	25	25	-	0.1
403 SALVATION ARMY	1	130	584	0.7	1.2
413 S.D.A.........	1	55	67*	0.1	0.1
419 SO BAPT CONV..	2	381	462*	0.5	0.9
443 UN C OF CHRIST	15	6 096	7 390*	8.7	14.8
449 UN METHODIST..	39	8 426	10 214*	12.1	20.5
453 UN PRES CH USA	5	1 177	1 427*	1.7	2.9
UNION	40	7 925	11 430*	38.7	100.0
019 AMER BAPT USA.	3	469	577*	2.0	5.0
029 AMER LUTH CH..	1	954	1 397	4.7	12.2
053 ASSEMB OF GOD.	1	14	30	0.1	0.3
081 CATHOLIC......	3	NA	1 007	3.4	8.8
097 CHR CHS&CHS CR	1	75	92*	0.3	0.8
123 CH GOD (ANDER)	1	35	105	0.4	0.9
127 CH GOD (CLEVE)	1	45	55*	0.2	0.5
165 CH OF NAZARENE	1	100	257	0.9	2.2
167 CHS OF CHRIST.	3	234	316	1.1	2.8
226 FRIENDS-USA...	1	73	90*	0.3	0.8
244 GRACE BRETHREN	1	21	26*	0.1	0.2
263 INT FOURSQ GOS	1	24	30*	0.1	0.3
281 LUTH CH AMER..	1	153	254	0.9	2.2
283 LUTH--MO SYNOD	2	1 291	1 736	5.9	15.2
419 SO BAPT CONV..	1	109	134*	0.5	1.2
443 UN C OF CHRIST	1	165	203*	0.7	1.8
449 UN METHODIST..	16	3 403	4 186*	14.2	36.6
453 UN PRES CH USA	1	760	935*	3.2	8.2
VAN WERT	48	9 475	14 479*	47.5	100.0
053 ASSEMB OF GOD.	2	183	401	1.3	2.8
081 CATHOLIC......	1	NA	2 348	7.7	16.2
097 CHR CHS&CHS CR	1	195	238*	0.8	1.6
107 CHRISTIAN UN..	1	50	50	0.2	0.3
123 CH GOD (ANDER)	1	36	108	0.4	0.7
165 CH OF NAZARENE	1	132	284	0.9	2.0
167 CHS OF CHRIST.	1	30	38	0.1	0.3
226 FRIENDS-USA...	3	518	633*	2.1	4.4
281 LUTH CH AMER..	4	1 180	1 496	4.9	10.3
283 LUTH--MO SYNOD	4	1 035	1 415	4.6	9.8
285 MENNONITE CH..	1	25	31*	0.1	0.2
413 S.D.A.........	1	19	23*	0.1	0.2
419 SO BAPT CONV..	1	86	105*	0.3	0.7
443 UN C OF CHRIST	2	513	626*	2.1	4.3
449 UN METHODIST..	18	4 154	5 072*	16.7	35.0
453 UN PRES CH USA	4	1 319	1 611*	5.3	11.1
VINTON	25	1 294	2 006*	17.3	100.0
081 CATHOLIC......	1	NA	142	1.2	7.1
093 CHR CH (DISC).	3	206	415	3.6	20.7
107 CHRISTIAN UN..	1	26	28	0.2	1.4
165 CH OF NAZARENE	2	106	215	1.9	10.7
167 CHS OF CHRIST.	1	20	32	0.3	1.6
193 EPISCOPAL.....	1	12	29	0.3	1.4
419 SO BAPT CONV..	1	141	175*	1.5	8.7
449 UN METHODIST..	13	665	824*	7.1	41.1
453 UN PRES CH USA	2	118	146*	1.3	7.3
WARREN	103	19 740	30 047*	30.3	100.0
019 AMER BAPT USA.	4	1 398	1 724*	1.7	5.7
053 ASSEMB OF GOD.	1	29	36	-	0.1
081 CATHOLIC......	5	NA	3 666	3.7	12.2
089 CHR & MISS AL.	1	101	176	0.2	0.6
097 CHR CHS&CHS CR	8	1 329	1 639*	1.7	5.5
123 CH GOD (ANDER)	9	788	2 364	2.4	7.9
127 CH GOD (CLEVE)	7	652	804*	0.8	2.7
165 CH OF NAZARENE	5	548	942	0.9	3.1
167 CHS OF CHRIST.	5	280	356	0.4	1.2
179 CONSRV BAPT...	1	125	154*	0.2	0.5
193 EPISCOPAL.....	2	121	269	0.3	0.9
226 FRIENDS-USA...	1	121	149*	0.2	0.5
281 LUTH CH AMER..	3	474	683	0.7	2.3
329 OPEN BIBLE STD	1	285	450	0.5	1.5
419 SO BAPT CONV..	16	5 922	7 303*	7.4	24.3
443 UN C OF CHRIST	6	595	734*	0.7	2.4
449 UN METHODIST..	18	4 233	5 220*	5.3	17.4
453 UN PRES CH USA	10	2 739	3 378*	3.4	11.2
WASHINGTON	115	16 539	25 806*	40.2	100.0
019 AMER BAPT USA.	10	2 791	3 409*	5.3	13.2
053 ASSEMB OF GOD.	1	56	94	0.1	0.4
081 CATHOLIC......	6	NA	4 811	7.5	18.6
093 CHR CH (DISC).	1	134	186	0.3	0.7
097 CHR CHS&CHS CR	5	893	1 091*	1.7	4.2
107 CHRISTIAN UN..	2	20	24	-	0.1
127 CH GOD (CLEVE)	2	174	213*	0.3	0.8
151 L-D SAINTS....	1	NA	109	0.2	0.4
165 CH OF NAZARENE	4	509	1 123	1.7	4.4
167 CHS OF CHRIST.	15	1 853	2 259	3.5	8.8
175 CONGR CHR CHS.	1	221	270*	0.4	1.0
193 EPISCOPAL.....	1	245	312	0.5	1.2
281 LUTH CH AMER..	1	502	645	1.0	2.5
403 SALVATION ARMY	1	80	192	0.3	0.7
413 S.D.A.........	2	67	82*	0.1	0.3
419 SO BAPT CONV..	2	324	396*	0.6	1.5
435 UNITARIAN-UNIV	2	92	112*	0.2	0.4
443 UN C OF CHRIST	10	1 392	1 700*	2.6	6.6
449 UN METHODIST..	41	5 829	7 120*	11.1	27.6
453 UN PRES CH USA	7	1 357	1 658*	2.6	6.4
WAYNE	157	33 311	51 040*	52.4	100.0
019 AMER BAPT USA.	1	57	70*	0.1	0.1
029 AMER LUTH CH..	2	339	504	0.5	1.0
053 ASSEMB OF GOD.	2	203	531	0.5	1.0
071 BRETHREN (ASH)	1	302	372*	0.4	0.7
081 CATHOLIC......	5	NA	7 611	7.8	14.9
089 CHR & MISS AL.	2	365	652	0.7	1.3
093 CHR CH (DISC).	2	1 036	1 635	1.7	3.2
097 CHR CHS&CHS CR	5	1 493	1 840*	1.9	3.6
123 CH GOD (ANDER)	3	201	603	0.6	1.2
127 CH GOD (CLEVE)	1	115	142*	0.1	0.3
143 CG IN CR(MENN)	1	100	100	0.1	0.2
151 L-D SAINTS....	1	NA	167	0.2	0.3
157 CH OF BRETHREN	5	857	1 056*	1.1	2.1
165 CH OF NAZARENE	5	455	1 098	1.1	2.2
167 CHS OF CHRIST.	4	300	382	0.4	0.7
226 FRIENDS-USA...	1	37	46*	-	0.1
244 GRACE BRETHREN	3	1 049	1 293*	1.3	2.5
263 INT FOURSQ GOS	1	332	409*	0.4	0.8
270 CONSRV JUDAISM	1	47	58*	0.1	0.1
281 LUTH CH AMER..	9	2 902	3 904	4.0	7.6
283 LUTH--MO SYNOD	1	76	99	0.1	0.2
285 MENNONITE CH..	15	3 004	3 703*	3.8	7.3
287 MENN GEN CONF.	2	645	858	0.9	1.7
323 OLD ORD AMISH.	31	4 030	4 967*	5.1	9.7
413 S.D.A.........	1	93	115*	0.1	0.2
419 SO BAPT CONV..	5	1 230	1 516*	1.6	3.0
435 UNITARIAN-UNIV	1	23	28*	-	0.1
443 UN C OF CHRIST	8	3 174	3 912*	4.0	7.7
449 UN METHODIST..	28	7 398	9 119*	9.4	17.9
453 UN PRES CH USA	10	3 448	4 250*	4.4	8.3
WILLIAMS	60	11 110	19 199*	52.8	100.0
029 AMER LUTH CH..	3	1 088	1 517	4.2	7.9
053 ASSEMB OF GOD.	1	85	156	0.4	0.8
071 BRETHREN (ASH)	1	220	271*	0.7	1.4
081 CATHOLIC......	5	NA	4 387	12.1	22.9

NA—Not applicable *Total adherents estimated from known number of communicant, confirmed, full members. —Represents a percent less than 0.1. Percentages may not total due to rounding.

Table 4. Churches and Church Membership by County and Denomination: 1980

County and Denomination	Number of churches	Communicant, confirmed, full members	Total adherents		
			Number	Percent of total population	Percent of total adherents
089 CHR & MISS AL.	2	136	265	0.7	1.4
097 CHR CHS&CHS CR	5	1 525	1 878*	5.2	9.8
107 CHRISTIAN UN..	3	93	150	0.4	0.8
151 L-D SAINTS....	1	NA	146	0.4	0.8
157 CH OF BRETHREN	2	405	499*	1.4	2.6
165 CH OF NAZARENE	3	343	876	2.4	4.6
167 CHS OF CHRIST.	1	35	45	0.1	0.2
213 EVAN MENN INC.	1	130	160*	0.4	0.8
221 FREE METHODIST	1	19	162	0.4	0.8
281 LUTH CH AMER..	3	697	887	2.4	4.6
285 MENNONITE CH..	2	574	707*	1.9	3.7
413 S.D.A.........	1	19	23*	0.1	0.1
419 SO BAPT CONV..	3	236	291*	0.8	1.5
449 UN METHODIST..	16	4 389	5 405*	14.9	28.2
453 UN PRES CH USA	6	1 116	1 374*	3.8	7.2
WOOD	117	22 319	46 714*	43.5	100.0
019 AMER BAPT USA.	1	148	178*	0.2	0.4
029 AMER LUTH CH..	14	5 680	7 478	7.0	16.0
053 ASSEMB OF GOD.	2	340	595	0.6	1.3
081 CATHOLIC......	10	NA	17 612	16.4	37.7
089 CHR & MISS AL.	3	253	421	0.4	0.9
093 CHR CH (DISC).	4	774	1 143	1.1	2.4
097 CHR CHS&CHS CR	7	700	842*	0.8	1.8
123 CH GOD (ANDER)	1	31	93	0.1	0.2
127 CH GOD (CLEVE)	2	37	44*	–	0.1
133 CH GOD(7TH)DEN	1	29	35*	–	0.1
151 L-D SAINTS....	1	NA	187	0.2	0.4
157 CH OF BRETHREN	2	273	328*	0.3	0.7
165 CH OF NAZARENE	5	246	675	0.6	1.4
167 CHS OF CHRIST.	3	159	248	0.2	0.5
175 CONGR CHR CHS.	2	391	470*	0.4	1.0
244 GRACE BRETHREN	2	104	125*	0.1	0.3
263 INT FOURSQ GOS	1	30	36*	–	0.1
281 LUTH CH AMER..	3	2 133	2 825	2.6	6.0
283 LUTH--MO SYNOD	1	103	171	0.2	0.4
353 CHR BRETHREN..	1	150	300	0.3	0.6
413 S.D.A.........	1	32	38*	–	0.1
419 SO BAPT CONV..	2	368	442*	0.4	0.9
443 UN C OF CHRIST	2	400	481*	0.4	1.0
449 UN METHODIST..	37	7 968	9 579*	8.9	20.5
453 UN PRES CH USA	9	1 970	2 368*	2.2	5.1
WYANDOT	46	7 851	15 616*	68.9	100.0
019 AMER BAPT USA.	1	40	49*	0.2	0.3
029 AMER LUTH CH..	3	986	1 377	6.1	8.8
081 CATHOLIC......	5	NA	5 046	22.3	32.3
107 CHRISTIAN UN..	1	66	87	0.4	0.6
123 CH GOD (ANDER)	1	35	105	0.5	0.7
127 CH GOD (CLEVE)	1	6	7*	–	–
165 CH OF NAZARENE	2	184	648	2.9	4.1
167 CHS OF CHRIST.	3	100	127	0.6	0.8
281 LUTH CH AMER..	3	1 553	2 193	9.7	14.0
313 N AM BAPT CONF	1	79	97*	0.4	0.6
419 SO BAPT CONV..	1	117	143*	0.6	0.9
443 UN C OF CHRIST	3	921	1 128*	5.0	7.2
449 UN METHODIST..	19	3 460	4 237*	18.7	27.1
453 UN PRES CH USA	2	304	372*	1.6	2.4

OKLAHOMA

County and Denomination	Number of churches	Communicant, confirmed, full members	Total adherents		
			Number	Percent of total population	Percent of total adherents
THE STATE.....	5 329	1 294 314	1 754 071*	58.0	100.0
ADAIR	50	6 956	8 703*	46.9	100.0
017 AMER BAPT ASSN	1	66	66	0.4	0.8
053 ASSEMB OF GOD.	2	93	171	0.9	2.0
059 BAPT MISS ASSN	3	285	353*	1.9	4.1
123 CH GOD (ANDER)	1	11	33	0.2	0.4
167 CHS OF CHRIST.	8	700	891	4.8	10.2
349 PENT HOLINESS.	2	112	139*	0.7	1.6
381 REF PRES-EVAN.	1	38	42	0.2	0.5
413 S.D.A.........	1	19	24*	0.1	0.3
419 SO BAPT CONV..	25	4 953	6 142*	33.1	70.6
449 UN METHODIST..	5	669	830*	4.5	9.5
453 UN PRES CH USA	1	10	12*	0.1	0.1
ALFALFA	38	4 226	5 394*	76.2	100.0
053 ASSEMB OF GOD.	2	66	95	1.3	1.8
081 CATHOLIC......	2	NA	155	2.2	2.9
093 CHR CH (DISC).	5	736	961	13.6	17.8
097 CHR CHS&CHS CR	3	330	387*	5.5	7.2
107 CHRISTIAN UN..	1	36	54	0.8	1.0
143 CG IN CR(MENN)	1	44	44	0.6	0.8
157 CH OF BRETHREN	1	53	62*	0.9	1.1
165 CH OF NAZARENE	3	137	129	1.8	2.4
167 CHS OF CHRIST.	5	182	312	4.4	5.8
221 FREE METHODIST	1	37	138	1.9	2.6
226 FRIENDS-USA...	1	181	213*	3.0	3.9
283 LUTH--MO SYNOD	1	18	19	0.3	0.4

County and Denomination	Number of churches	Communicant, confirmed, full members	Total adherents		
			Number	Percent of total population	Percent of total adherents
313 N AM BAPT CONF	1	116	136*	1.9	2.5
419 SO BAPT CONV..	3	808	949*	13.4	17.6
443 UN C OF CHRIST	1	57	67*	0.9	1.2
449 UN METHODIST..	7	1 425	1 673*	23.6	31.0
ATOKA	51	6 515	8 159*	64.0	100.0
053 ASSEMB OF GOD.	3	108	205	1.6	2.5
059 BAPT MISS ASSN	2	225	271*	2.1	3.3
081 CATHOLIC......	1	NA	65	0.5	0.8
093 CHR CH (DISC).	1	50	54	0.4	0.7
101 C.M.E.........	1	13	16*	0.1	0.2
127 CH GOD (CLEVE)	1	?	?	?	?
133 CH GOD(7TH)DEN	1	16	19*	0.1	0.2
165 CH OF NAZARENE	1	39	101	0.8	1.2
167 CHS OF CHRIST.	6	500	635	5.0	7.8
185 CUMBER PRESB..	3	51	151	1.2	1.9
349 PENT HOLINESS.	4	196	236*	1.9	2.9
419 SO BAPT CONV..	20	4 939	5 951*	46.7	72.9
449 UN METHODIST..	5	339	408*	3.2	5.0
453 UN PRES CH USA	2	39	47*	0.4	0.6
BEAVER	28	3 420	4 396*	64.6	100.0
053 ASSEMB OF GOD.	1	29	37	0.5	0.8
081 CATHOLIC......	1	NA	23	0.3	0.5
097 CHR CHS&CHS CR	2	301	370*	5.4	8.4
123 CH GOD (ANDER)	1	49	147	2.2	3.3
165 CH OF NAZARENE	2	66	149	2.2	3.4
167 CHS OF CHRIST.	3	150	190	2.8	4.3
226 FRIENDS-USA...	1	125	154*	2.3	3.5
237 GC MENN BR CHS	1	104	128*	1.9	2.9
283 LUTH--MO SYNOD	1	32	40	0.6	0.9
287 MENN GEN CONF.	1	104	134	2.0	3.0
413 S.D.A.........	1	17	21*	0.3	0.5
419 SO BAPT CONV..	7	1 240	1 524*	22.4	34.7
449 UN METHODIST..	5	1 159	1 425*	20.9	32.4
453 UN PRES CH USA	1	44	54*	0.8	1.2
BECKHAM	50	9 562	13 549*	70.4	100.0
017 AMER BAPT ASSN	1	100	100	0.5	0.7
053 ASSEMB OF GOD.	4	255	572	3.0	4.2
059 BAPT MISS ASSN	1	52	63*	0.3	0.5
081 CATHOLIC......	2	NA	1 330	6.9	9.8
093 CHR CH (DISC).	2	406	511	2.7	3.8
097 CHR CHS&CHS CR	1	100	121*	0.6	0.9
123 CH GOD (ANDER)	1	130	390	2.0	2.9
165 CH OF NAZARENE	3	191	297	1.5	2.2
167 CHS OF CHRIST.	9	720	916	4.8	6.8
221 FREE METHODIST	1	5	24	0.1	0.2
283 LUTH--MO SYNOD	1	28	37	0.2	0.3
349 PENT HOLINESS.	1	18	22*	0.1	0.2
413 S.D.A.........	1	65	79*	0.4	0.6
419 SO BAPT CONV..	16	5 661	6 867*	35.7	50.7
449 UN METHODIST..	4	1 669	2 024*	10.5	14.9
453 UN PRES CH USA	2	162	196*	1.0	1.4
BLAINE	49	6 029	8 269*	61.5	100.0
017 AMER BAPT ASSN	1	100	100	0.7	1.2
019 AMER BAPT USA.	2	20	24*	0.2	0.3
053 ASSEMB OF GOD.	5	168	217	1.6	2.6
059 BAPT MISS ASSN	1	23	28*	0.2	0.3
081 CATHOLIC......	3	NA	512	3.8	6.2
093 CHR CH (DISC).	2	261	373	2.8	4.5
097 CHR CHS&CHS CR	3	600	729*	5.4	8.8
123 CH GOD (ANDER)	2	51	153	1.1	1.9
165 CH OF NAZARENE	2	127	418	3.1	5.1
167 CHS OF CHRIST.	4	202	263	2.0	3.2
221 FREE METHODIST	1	17	39	0.3	0.5
237 GC MENN BR CHS	1	60	73*	0.5	0.9
283 LUTH--MO SYNOD	1	124	155	1.2	1.9
287 MENN GEN CONF.	2	64	64	0.5	0.8
313 N AM BAPT CONF	1	141	171*	1.3	2.1
349 PENT HOLINESS.	1	22	27*	0.2	0.3
413 S.D.A.........	2	204	248*	1.8	3.0
419 SO BAPT CONV..	8	2 225	2 705*	20.1	32.7
443 UN C OF CHRIST	1	?	?	?	?
449 UN METHODIST..	6	1 620	1 970*	14.7	23.8
BRYAN	84	15 367	19 102*	62.6	100.0
017 AMER BAPT ASSN	1	100	100	0.3	0.5
053 ASSEMB OF GOD.	5	243	345	1.1	1.8
081 CATHOLIC......	1	NA	179	0.6	0.9
093 CHR CH (DISC).	1	302	517	1.7	2.7
097 CHR CHS&CHS CR	1	50	60*	0.2	0.3
123 CH GOD (ANDER)	1	14	42	0.1	0.2
151 L-D SAINTS....	1	NA	87	0.3	0.5
165 CH OF NAZARENE	3	302	496	1.6	2.6
167 CHS OF CHRIST.	14	1 252	1 557	5.1	8.2
193 EPISCOPAL.....	1	151	160	0.5	0.8
281 LUTH CH AMER..	1	107	151	0.5	0.8
349 PENT HOLINESS.	2	360	432*	1.4	2.3
357 PRESB CH US...	6	383	459*	1.5	2.4
413 S.D.A.........	1	54	65*	0.2	0.3
419 SO BAPT CONV..	35	10 379	12 449*	40.8	65.2
449 UN METHODIST..	10	1 670	2 003*	6.6	10.5
CADDO	118	19 147	25 180*	81.5	100.0
017 AMER BAPT ASSN	3	250	250	0.8	1.0
019 AMER BAPT USA.	3	175	213*	0.7	0.8
053 ASSEMB OF GOD.	8	386	692	2.2	2.7

NA—Not applicable   *Total adherents estimated from known number of communicant, confirmed, full members.   —Represents a percent less than 0.1.   Percentages may not total due to rounding.

Table 4. Churches and Church Membership by County and Denomination: 1980

County and Denomination	Number of churches	Communicant, confirmed, full members	Total adherents Number	Total adherents Percent of total population	Total adherents Percent of total adherents
081 CATHOLIC......	5	NA	566	1.8	2.2
089 CHR & MISS AL.	1	0	68	0.2	0.3
093 CHR CH (DISC).	5	558	839	2.7	3.3
097 CHR CHS&CHS CR	7	523	637*	2.1	2.5
127 CH GOD (CLEVE)	2	195	238*	0.8	0.9
151 L-D SAINTS....	1	NA	300	1.0	1.2
165 CH OF NAZARENE	3	208	660	2.1	2.6
167 CHS OF CHRIST.	11	900	1 150	3.7	4.6
208 EVAN LUTH ASSN	1	39	51	0.2	0.2
283 LUTH--MO SYNOD	2	119	142	0.5	0.6
287 MENN GEN CONF.	2	135	160	0.5	0.6
349 PENT HOLINESS.	11	586	714*	2.3	2.8
371 REF CH IN AM..	1	95	247	0.8	1.0
419 SO BAPT CONV..	24	9 737	11 866*	38.4	47.1
443 UN C OF CHRIST	1	76	93*	0.3	0.4
449 UN METHODIST..	26	5 084	6 195*	20.0	24.6
453 UN PRES CH USA	1	81	99*	0.3	0.4
CANADIAN	**72**	**16 642**	**24 267***	**43.0**	**100.0**
017 AMER BAPT ASSN	2	260	260	0.5	1.1
029 AMER LUTH CH..	1	219	374	0.7	1.5
053 ASSEMB OF GOD.	4	465	728	1.3	3.0
081 CATHOLIC......	4	NA	2 522	4.5	10.4
093 CHR CH (DISC).	5	991	1 447	2.6	6.0
097 CHR CHS&CHS CR	3	360	452*	0.8	1.9
101 C.M.E.........	1	37	46*	0.1	0.2
127 CH GOD (CLEVE)	1	29	36*	0.1	0.1
165 CH OF NAZARENE	8	576	1 101	2.0	4.5
167 CHS OF CHRIST.	8	880	1 120	2.0	4.6
193 EPISCOPAL.....	3	173	244	0.4	1.0
283 LUTH--MO SYNOD	3	777	1 023	1.8	4.2
349 PENT HOLINESS.	5	246	309*	0.5	1.3
353 CHR BRETHREN..	1	5	5	-	-
413 S.D.A.........	1	17	21*	-	0.1
419 SO BAPT CONV..	11	6 874	8 634*	15.3	35.6
443 UN C OF CHRIST	1	59	74*	0.1	0.3
449 UN METHODIST..	8	4 390	5 514*	9.8	22.7
453 UN PRES CH USA	2	284	357*	0.6	1.5
CARTER	**90**	**23 478**	**30 182***	**69.2**	**100.0**
001 ADVENT CHR CH.	1	?	?	?	?
017 AMER BAPT ASSN	4	471	471	1.1	1.6
053 ASSEMB OF GOD.	9	718	1 608	3.7	5.3
059 BAPT MISS ASSN	1	235	285*	0.7	0.9
081 CATHOLIC......	2	NA	518	1.2	1.7
089 CHR & MISS AL.	1	12	15	-	-
093 CHR CH (DISC).	2	422	568	1.3	1.9
097 CHR CHS&CHS CR	2	340	413*	0.9	1.4
101 C.M.E.........	1	50	61*	0.1	0.2
123 CH GOD (ANDER)	1	20	60	0.1	0.2
127 CH GOD (CLEVE)	1	21	25*	0.1	0.1
151 L-D SAINTS....	1	NA	183	0.4	0.6
165 CH OF NAZARENE	1	141	213	0.5	0.7
167 CHS OF CHRIST.	13	1 280	1 626	3.7	5.4
193 EPISCOPAL.....	1	300	414	0.9	1.4
271 REFORM JUDAISM	1	46	56*	0.1	0.2
283 LUTH--MO SYNOD	1	130	186	0.4	0.6
349 PENT HOLINESS.	6	340	413*	0.9	1.4
403 SALVATION ARMY	1	78	150	0.3	0.5
413 S.D.A.........	1	255	310*	0.7	1.0
419 SO BAPT CONV..	29	12 994	15 777*	36.2	52.3
449 UN METHODIST..	8	5 153	6 257*	14.3	20.7
453 UN PRES CH USA	2	472	573*	1.3	1.9
CHEROKEE	**54**	**8 914**	**11 583***	**37.7**	**100.0**
017 AMER BAPT ASSN	1	50	50	0.2	0.4
053 ASSEMB OF GOD.	2	170	359	1.2	3.1
081 CATHOLIC......	2	NA	81	0.3	0.7
093 CHR CH (DISC).	1	164	216	0.7	1.9
097 CHR CHS&CHS CR	2	139	169*	0.6	1.5
123 CH GOD (ANDER)	1	80	240	0.8	2.1
127 CH GOD (CLEVE)	1	27	33*	0.1	0.3
133 CH GOD(7TH)DEN	1	32	39*	0.1	0.3
151 L-D SAINTS....	1	NA	274	0.9	2.4
165 CH OF NAZARENE	1	58	103	0.3	0.9
167 CHS OF CHRIST.	7	650	825	2.7	7.1
193 EPISCOPAL.....	1	104	152	0.5	1.3
283 LUTH--MO SYNOD	1	64	85	0.3	0.7
349 PENT HOLINESS.	2	82	100*	0.3	0.9
413 S.D.A.........	1	100	121*	0.4	1.0
419 SO BAPT CONV..	21	5 420	6 582*	21.5	56.8
449 UN METHODIST..	6	1 509	1 832*	6.0	15.8
453 UN PRES CH USA	2	265	322*	1.0	2.8
CHOCTAW	**59**	**9 012**	**11 294***	**65.7**	**100.0**
017 AMER BAPT ASSN	2	82	82	0.5	0.7
053 ASSEMB OF GOD.	3	151	240	1.4	2.1
081 CATHOLIC......	2	NA	117	0.7	1.0
093 CHR CH (DISC).	1	149	170	1.0	1.5
101 C.M.E.........	1	33	40*	0.2	0.4
127 CH GOD (CLEVE)	2	103	126*	0.7	1.1
151 L-D SAINTS....	1	NA	49	0.3	0.4
165 CH OF NAZARENE	2	36	66	0.4	0.6
167 CHS OF CHRIST.	6	500	635	3.7	5.6
185 CUMBER PRESB..	1	6	24	0.1	0.2
193 EPISCOPAL.....	1	68	89	0.5	0.8
357 PRESB CH US...	1	96	118*	0.7	1.0
413 S.D.A.........	1	23	28*	0.2	0.2
419 SO BAPT CONV..	25	6 733	8 246*	47.9	73.0
449 UN METHODIST..	8	1 007	1 233*	7.2	10.9
453 UN PRES CH USA	2	25	31*	0.2	0.3
CIMARRON	**19**	**2 682**	**3 444***	**94.4**	**100.0**
053 ASSEMB OF GOD.	1	13	15	0.4	0.4
081 CATHOLIC......	1	NA	103	2.8	3.0
097 CHR CHS&CHS CR	1	150	182*	5.0	5.3
123 CH GOD (ANDER)	1	26	78	2.1	2.3
165 CH OF NAZARENE	1	23	37	1.0	1.1
167 CHS OF CHRIST.	3	260	330	9.0	9.6
283 LUTH--MO SYNOD	1	56	86	2.4	2.5
349 PENT HOLINESS.	1	35	42*	1.2	1.2
419 SO BAPT CONV..	4	1 230	1 492*	40.9	43.3
449 UN METHODIST..	5	889	1 079*	29.6	31.3
CLEVELAND	**99**	**35 943**	**50 185***	**37.7**	**100.0**
017 AMER BAPT ASSN	3	390	390	0.3	0.8
053 ASSEMB OF GOD.	4	206	266	0.2	0.5
059 BAPT MISS ASSN	2	701	854*	0.6	1.7
081 CATHOLIC......	4	NA	5 197	3.9	10.4
089 CHR & MISS AL.	1	0	18	-	-
093 CHR CH (DISC).	3	1 113	1 305	1.0	2.6
097 CHR CHS&CHS CR	3	1 199	1 460*	1.1	2.9
101 C.M.E.........	1	25	30*	-	0.1
123 CH GOD (ANDER)	1	52	156	0.1	0.3
127 CH GOD (CLEVE)	5	495	603*	0.5	1.2
151 L-D SAINTS....	1	NA	655	0.5	1.3
165 CH OF NAZARENE	6	513	870	0.7	1.7
167 CHS OF CHRIST.	10	2 406	3 062	2.3	6.1
193 EPISCOPAL.....	3	895	1 048	0.8	2.1
221 FREE METHODIST	1	23	99	0.1	0.2
283 LUTH--MO SYNOD	3	871	1 182	0.9	2.4
349 PENT HOLINESS.	3	217	264*	0.2	0.5
357 PRESB CH US...	1	128	156*	0.1	0.3
381 REF PRES-EVAN.	1	14	23	-	-
403 SALVATION ARMY	1	47	81	0.1	0.2
413 S.D.A.........	1	67	82*	0.1	0.2
419 SO BAPT CONV..	28	18 287	22 270*	16.7	44.4
435 UNITARIAN-UNIV	1	28	34*	-	0.1
449 UN METHODIST..	9	7 239	8 816*	6.6	17.6
453 UN PRES CH USA	2	955	1 163*	0.9	2.3
469 WELS..........	1	72	101	0.1	0.2
COAL	**27**	**2 630**	**3 416***	**56.5**	**100.0**
017 AMER BAPT ASSN	1	130	130	2.2	3.8
059 BAPT MISS ASSN	1	51	62*	1.0	1.8
081 CATHOLIC......	2	NA	163	2.7	4.8
165 CH OF NAZARENE	1	50	140	2.3	4.1
167 CHS OF CHRIST.	4	300	380	6.3	11.1
185 CUMBER PRESB..	1	10	30	0.5	0.9
193 EPISCOPAL.....	1	85	85	1.4	2.5
323 OLD ORD AMISH.	1	130	157*	2.6	4.6
349 PENT HOLINESS.	3	141	171*	2.8	5.0
357 PRESB CH US...	1	43	52*	0.9	1.5
413 S.D.A.........	1	49	59*	1.0	1.7
419 SO BAPT CONV..	6	1 058	1 281*	21.2	37.5
449 UN METHODIST..	4	583	706*	11.7	20.7
COMANCHE	**132**	**41 258**	**56 923***	**50.6**	**100.0**
017 AMER BAPT ASSN	2	209	209	0.2	0.4
019 AMER BAPT USA.	2	115	141*	0.1	0.2
053 ASSEMB OF GOD.	10	892	1 621	1.4	2.8
059 BAPT MISS ASSN	1	23	28*	-	-
081 CATHOLIC......	4	NA	4 024	3.6	7.1
093 CHR CH (DISC).	3	688	833	0.7	1.5
097 CHR CHS&CHS CR	4	843	1 035*	0.9	1.8
123 CH GOD (ANDER)	1	35	105	0.1	0.2
127 CH GOD (CLEVE)	7	788	968*	0.9	1.7
151 L-D SAINTS....	2	NA	998	0.9	1.8
165 CH OF NAZARENE	5	335	498	0.4	0.9
167 CHS OF CHRIST.	19	2 000	2 550	2.3	4.5
193 EPISCOPAL.....	2	560	689	0.6	1.2
237 GC MENN BR CHS	2	164	201*	0.2	0.4
281 LUTH CH AMER..	1	269	424	0.4	0.7
283 LUTH--MO SYNOD	2	394	548	0.5	1.0
349 PENT HOLINESS.	2	129	158*	0.1	0.3
357 PRESB CH US...	2	173	212*	0.2	0.4
371 REF CH IN AM..	1	69	171	0.2	0.3
403 SALVATION ARMY	1	148	468	0.4	0.8
413 S.D.A.........	1	190	233*	0.2	0.4
419 SO BAPT CONV..	34	24 816	30 472*	27.1	53.5
443 UN C OF CHRIST	1	174	214*	0.2	0.4
449 UN METHODIST..	20	7 567	9 292*	8.3	16.3
453 UN PRES CH USA	3	677	831*	0.7	1.5
COTTON	**27**	**4 926**	**6 148***	**83.8**	**100.0**
053 ASSEMB OF GOD.	2	75	156	2.1	2.5
081 CATHOLIC......	1	NA	150	2.0	2.4
093 CHR CH (DISC).	1	109	133	1.8	2.2
127 CH GOD (CLEVE)	1	71	86*	1.2	1.4
165 CH OF NAZARENE	2	95	86	1.2	1.4
167 CHS OF CHRIST.	3	230	290	4.0	4.7
419 SO BAPT CONV..	11	3 346	4 039*	55.0	65.7
449 UN METHODIST..	4	944	1 140*	15.5	18.5
453 UN PRES CH USA	2	56	68*	0.9	1.1
CRAIG	**40**	**7 848**	**10 115***	**67.4**	**100.0**
053 ASSEMB OF GOD.	4	203	335	2.2	3.3
081 CATHOLIC......	2	NA	391	2.6	3.9
093 CHR CH (DISC).	1	269	360	2.4	3.6
097 CHR CHS&CHS CR	3	895	1 066*	7.1	10.5
123 CH GOD (ANDER)	1	85	255	1.7	2.5

NA—Not applicable   *Total adherents estimated from known number of communicant, confirmed, full members.   —Represents a percent less than 0.1.   Percentages may not total due to rounding.

Table 4. Churches and Church Membership by County and Denomination: 1980

County and Denomination	Number of churches	Communicant, confirmed, full members	Total adherents		
			Number	Percent of total population	Percent of total adherents
127 CH GOD (CLEVE)	1	16	19*	0.1	0.2
165 CH OF NAZARENE	1	27	102	0.7	1.0
167 CHS OF CHRIST.	3	147	199	1.3	2.0
193 EPISCOPAL.....	1	89	99	0.7	1.0
263 INT FOURSQ GOS	2	259	309*	2.1	3.1
413 S.D.A........	1	43	51*	0.3	0.5
419 SO BAPT CONV..	15	4 144	4 938*	32.9	48.8
449 UN METHODIST..	4	1 498	1 785*	11.9	17.6
453 UN PRES CH USA	1	173	206*	1.4	2.0
CREEK	97	24 523	33 403*	56.4	100.0
001 ADVENT CHR CH.	1	30	37*	0.1	0.1
053 ASSEMB OF GOD.	9	861	1 357	2.3	4.1
059 BAPT MISS ASSN	2	168	207*	0.3	0.6
081 CATHOLIC......	4	NA	1 055	1.8	3.2
093 CHR CH (DISC).	4	295	402	0.7	1.2
097 CHR CHS&CHS CR	6	1 340	1 652*	2.8	4.9
101 C.M.E........	1	58	71*	0.1	0.2
123 CH GOD (ANDER)	6	722	2 166	3.7	6.5
151 L-D SAINTS....	1	NA	240	0.4	0.7
165 CH OF NAZARENE	4	590	969	1.6	2.9
167 CHS OF CHRIST.	10	1 225	1 560	2.6	4.7
193 EPISCOPAL.....	1	153	166	0.3	0.5
349 PENT HOLINESS.	2	130	160*	0.3	0.5
413 S.D.A........	3	334	412*	0.7	1.2
419 SO BAPT CONV..	29	14 466	17 832*	30.1	53.4
449 UN METHODIST..	12	3 501	4 316*	7.3	12.9
453 UN PRES CH USA	2	650	801*	1.4	2.4
CUSTER	71	13 926	18 078*	69.5	100.0
017 AMER BAPT ASSN	2	230	230	0.9	1.3
029 AMER LUTH CH..	1	246	296	1.1	1.6
053 ASSEMB OF GOD.	3	225	448	1.7	2.5
059 BAPT MISS ASSN	1	114	136*	0.5	0.8
061 BEACHY AMISH..	1	53	63*	0.2	0.3
075 BRETHREN IN CR	1	57	86	0.3	0.5
081 CATHOLIC......	3	NA	504	1.9	2.8
083 CHRIST CATH CH	1	10	14	0.1	0.1
093 CHR CH (DISC).	2	297	382	1.5	2.1
097 CHR CHS&CHS CR	4	578	692*	2.7	3.8
101 C.M.E........	1	7	8*	-	-
123 CH GOD (ANDER)	2	166	498	1.9	2.8
127 CH GOD (CLEVE)	1	?	?	?	?
143 CG IN CR(MENN)	1	15	15	0.1	0.1
151 L-D SAINTS....	1	NA	242	0.9	1.3
157 CH OF BRETHREN	1	51	61*	0.2	0.3
165 CH OF NAZARENE	3	71	108	0.4	0.6
167 CHS OF CHRIST.	6	860	1 131	4.4	6.3
181 CONSRV CONGR..	1	132	158*	0.6	0.9
185 CUMBER PRESB..	1	106	171	0.7	0.9
193 EPISCOPAL.....	2	83	104	0.4	0.6
237 GC MENN BR CHS	2	172	206*	0.8	1.1
283 LUTH--MO SYNOD	1	90	135	0.5	0.7
285 MENNONITE CH..	1	203	243*	0.9	1.3
287 MENN GEN CONF.	3	154	169	0.7	0.9
349 PENT HOLINESS.	2	56	67*	0.3	0.4
419 SO BAPT CONV..	9	6 437	7 705*	29.6	42.6
443 UN C OF CHRIST	1	13	16*	0.1	0.1
449 UN METHODIST..	11	3 360	4 022*	15.5	22.2
453 UN PRES CH USA	2	140	168*	0.6	0.9
DELAWARE	58	8 421	10 350*	43.2	100.0
017 AMER BAPT ASSN	1	30	30	0.1	0.3
029 AMER LUTH CH..	1	65	120	0.5	1.2
053 ASSEMB OF GOD.	4	220	349	1.5	3.4
059 BAPT MISS ASSN	2	166	199*	0.8	1.9
081 CATHOLIC......	1	NA	110	0.5	1.1
097 CHR CHS&CHS CR	3	770	924*	3.9	8.9
127 CH GOD (CLEVE)	1	57	68*	0.3	0.7
167 CHS OF CHRIST.	6	350	445	1.9	4.3
193 EPISCOPAL.....	1	63	63	0.3	0.6
208 EVAN LUTH ASSN	1	50	60	0.3	0.6
349 PENT HOLINESS.	1	15	18*	0.1	0.2
413 S.D.A........	1	116	139*	0.6	1.3
419 SO BAPT CONV..	29	5 446	6 537*	27.3	63.2
449 UN METHODIST..	6	1 073	1 288*	5.4	12.4
DEWEY	37	3 160	4 395*	74.2	100.0
053 ASSEMB OF GOD.	5	147	291	4.9	6.6
075 BRETHREN IN CR	1	57	86	1.5	2.0
081 CATHOLIC......	1	NA	36	0.6	0.8
093 CHR CH (DISC).	5	448	930	15.7	21.2
097 CHR CHS&CHS CR	5	324	389*	6.6	8.9
165 CH OF NAZARENE	3	104	195	3.3	4.4
167 CHS OF CHRIST.	3	126	133	2.2	3.0
226 FRIENDS-USA...	1	93	112*	1.9	2.5
287 MENN GEN CONF.	1	71	75	1.3	1.7
419 SO BAPT CONV..	5	996	1 195*	20.2	27.2
449 UN METHODIST..	7	794	953*	16.1	21.7
ELLIS	26	2 833	3 670*	65.6	100.0
053 ASSEMB OF GOD.	2	34	62	1.1	1.7
081 CATHOLIC......	1	NA	61	1.1	1.7
093 CHR CH (DISC).	2	114	154	2.8	4.2
097 CHR CHS&CHS CR	1	150	182*	3.3	5.0
123 CH GOD (ANDER)	2	40	120	2.1	3.3
165 CH OF NAZARENE	3	120	190	3.4	5.2
167 CHS OF CHRIST.	3	136	164	2.9	4.5
283 LUTH--MO SYNOD	1	73	104	1.9	2.8
313 N AM BAPT CONF	1	82	100*	1.8	2.7
413 S.D.A........	1	178	216*	3.9	5.9
419 SO BAPT CONV..	4	946	1 150*	20.6	31.3
449 UN METHODIST..	5	960	1 167*	20.9	31.8
GARFIELD	89	28 304	40 968*	65.2	100.0
029 AMER LUTH CH..	1	69	82	0.1	0.2
053 ASSEMB OF GOD.	8	749	1 538	2.4	3.8
081 CATHOLIC......	3	NA	3 767	6.0	9.2
093 CHR CH (DISC).	9	2 700	4 203	6.7	10.3
097 CHR CHS&CHS CR	3	1 415	1 713*	2.7	4.2
107 CHRISTIAN UN..	3	195	339	0.5	0.8
123 CH GOD (ANDER)	1	45	135	0.2	0.3
127 CH GOD (CLEVE)	2	42	51*	0.1	0.1
151 L-D SAINTS....	1	NA	467	0.7	1.1
157 CH OF BRETHREN	1	84	102*	0.2	0.2
165 CH OF NAZARENE	4	445	702	1.1	1.7
167 CHS OF CHRIST.	3	594	930	1.5	2.3
193 EPISCOPAL.....	2	547	613	1.0	1.5
221 FREE METHODIST	1	65	189	0.3	0.5
226 FRIENDS-USA...	1	58	70*	0.1	0.2
237 GC MENN BR CHS	1	360	436*	0.7	1.1
283 LUTH--MO SYNOD	8	2 602	3 331	5.3	8.1
287 MENN GEN CONF.	1	206	270	0.4	0.7
349 PENT HOLINESS.	2	334	404*	0.6	1.0
403 SALVATION ARMY	1	111	214	0.3	0.5
413 S.D.A........	2	174	211*	0.3	0.5
419 SO BAPT CONV..	14	9 124	11 048*	17.6	27.0
443 UN C OF CHRIST	2	135	163*	0.3	0.4
449 UN METHODIST..	14	7 145	8 652*	13.8	21.1
453 UN PRES CH USA	1	1 105	1 338*	2.1	3.3
GARVIN	73	16 408	20 401*	73.2	100.0
053 ASSEMB OF GOD.	5	234	549	2.0	2.7
059 BAPT MISS ASSN	6	751	902*	3.2	4.4
081 CATHOLIC......	2	NA	104	0.4	0.5
093 CHR CH (DISC).	2	297	486	1.7	2.4
097 CHR CHS&CHS CR	1	125	150*	0.5	0.7
123 CH GOD (ANDER)	1	41	123	0.4	0.6
127 CH GOD (CLEVE)	2	88	106*	0.4	0.5
165 CH OF NAZARENE	2	83	144	0.5	0.7
167 CHS OF CHRIST.	14	1 574	1 968*	7.1	9.6
193 EPISCOPAL.....	1	30	37	0.1	0.2
349 PENT HOLINESS.	2	296	355*	1.3	1.7
413 S.D.A........	1	27	32*	0.1	0.2
419 SO BAPT CONV..	22	9 684	11 629*	41.7	57.0
449 UN METHODIST..	9	2 902	3 485*	12.5	17.1
453 UN PRES CH USA	3	276	331*	1.2	1.6
GRADY	75	18 766	24 250*	61.4	100.0
053 ASSEMB OF GOD.	6	472	789	2.0	3.3
059 BAPT MISS ASSN	3	479	586*	1.5	2.4
081 CATHOLIC......	2	NA	604	1.5	2.5
093 CHR CH (DISC).	2	582	758	1.9	3.1
097 CHR CHS&CHS CR	2	255	312*	0.8	1.3
101 C.M.E........	1	?	?	?	?
127 CH GOD (CLEVE)	1	87	106*	0.3	0.4
143 CG IN CR(MENN)	1	193	193	0.5	0.8
151 L-D SAINTS....	1	NA	214	0.5	0.9
165 CH OF NAZARENE	2	98	175	0.4	0.7
167 CHS OF CHRIST.	11	1 346	1 762	4.5	7.3
193 EPISCOPAL.....	1	93	114	0.3	0.5
208 EVAN LUTH ASSN	1	81	117	0.3	0.5
283 LUTH--MO SYNOD	1	83	105	0.3	0.4
349 PENT HOLINESS.	4	204	249*	0.6	1.0
381 REF PRES-EVAN.	1	68	85	0.2	0.4
403 SALVATION ARMY	1	104	200	0.5	0.8
413 S.D.A........	1	47	57*	0.1	0.2
419 SO BAPT CONV..	21	10 996	13 448*	34.1	55.5
449 UN METHODIST..	11	3 353	4 101*	10.4	16.9
453 UN PRES CH USA	1	225	275*	0.7	1.1
GRANT	37	4 360	5 699*	87.4	100.0
053 ASSEMB OF GOD.	2	67	88	1.4	1.5
081 CATHOLIC......	3	NA	380	5.8	6.7
093 CHR CH (DISC).	6	774	1 047	16.1	18.4
097 CHR CHS&CHS CR	4	260	308*	4.7	5.4
165 CH OF NAZARENE	2	62	86	1.3	1.5
167 CHS OF CHRIST.	3	90	130	2.0	2.3
287 MENN GEN CONF.	2	137	138	2.1	2.4
419 SO BAPT CONV..	6	1 213	1 438*	22.1	25.2
443 UN C OF CHRIST	1	53	63*	1.0	1.1
449 UN METHODIST..	8	1 704	2 021*	31.0	35.5
GREER	33	5 477	6 694*	97.3	100.0
017 AMER BAPT ASSN	3	367	367	5.3	5.5
053 ASSEMB OF GOD.	4	153	258	3.8	3.9
081 CATHOLIC......	1	NA	225	3.3	3.4
093 CHR CH (DISC).	1	90	125	1.8	1.9
127 CH GOD (CLEVE)	1	62	72*	1.0	1.1
165 CH OF NAZARENE	1	42	43	0.6	0.6
167 CHS OF CHRIST.	7	550	700	10.2	10.5
283 LUTH--MO SYNOD	1	138	169	2.5	2.5
357 PRESB CH US...	1	95	110*	1.6	1.6
419 SO BAPT CONV..	7	3 068	3 565*	51.8	53.3
449 UN METHODIST..	6	912	1 060*	15.4	15.8
HARMON	23	3 694	4 595*	101.7	100.0
053 ASSEMB OF GOD.	1	42	84	1.9	1.8
081 CATHOLIC......	1	NA	35	0.8	0.8

NA—Not applicable   *Total adherents estimated from known number of communicant, confirmed, full members.   —Represents a percent less than 0.1.   Percentages may not total due to rounding.

Table 4. Churches and Church Membership by County and Denomination: 1980

County and Denomination	Number of churches	Communicant, confirmed, full members	Total adherents Number	Percent of total population	Percent of total adherents
165 CH OF NAZARENE	3	49	81	1.8	1.8
167 CHS OF CHRIST.	9	845	1 075	23.8	23.4
419 SO BAPT CONV..	7	2 312	2 783*	61.6	60.6
449 UN METHODIST..	2	446	537*	11.9	11.7
HARPER	17	3 015	3 852*	81.7	100.0
017 AMER BAPT ASSN	0	44	44	0.9	1.1
053 ASSEMB OF GOD.	2	114	176	3.7	4.6
081 CATHOLIC......	1	NA	32	0.7	0.8
093 CHR CH (DISC).	2	239	372	7.9	9.7
097 CHR CHS&CHS CR	1	150	178*	3.8	4.6
165 CH OF NAZARENE	2	60	153	3.2	4.0
167 CHS OF CHRIST.	2	65	95	2.0	2.5
283 LUTH--MO SYNOD	1	142	184	3.9	4.8
419 SO BAPT CONV..	3	1 250	1 487*	31.5	38.6
449 UN METHODIST..	3	951	1 131*	24.0	29.4
HASKELL	33	4 398	5 669*	51.5	100.0
017 AMER BAPT ASSN	1	130	130	1.2	2.3
053 ASSEMB OF GOD.	4	266	568	5.2	10.0
081 CATHOLIC......	2	NA	122	1.1	2.2
093 CHR CH (DISC).	1	47	56	0.5	1.0
097 CHR CHS&CHS CR	1	50	60*	0.5	1.1
167 CHS OF CHRIST.	4	215	274	2.5	4.8
349 PENT HOLINESS.	1	25	30*	0.3	0.5
419 SO BAPT CONV..	16	3 058	3 695*	33.6	65.2
449 UN METHODIST..	3	607	734*	6.7	12.9
HUGHES	68	8 446	10 688*	74.5	100.0
001 ADVENT CHR CH.	1	60	72*	0.5	0.7
017 AMER BAPT ASSN	3	450	450	3.1	4.2
053 ASSEMB OF GOD.	3	236	402	2.8	3.8
059 BAPT MISS ASSN	1	29	35*	0.2	0.3
081 CATHOLIC......	1	NA	67	0.5	0.6
093 CHR CH (DISC).	2	122	177	1.2	1.7
123 CH GOD (ANDER)	2	127	381	2.7	3.6
165 CH OF NAZARENE	3	255	479	3.3	4.5
167 CHS OF CHRIST.	12	850	1 080	7.5	10.1
193 EPISCOPAL.....	1	57	76	0.5	0.7
349 PENT HOLINESS.	5	245	292*	2.0	2.7
357 PRESB CH US...	1	21	25*	0.2	0.2
419 SO BAPT CONV..	21	4 588	5 474*	38.2	51.2
449 UN METHODIST..	12	1 406	1 678*	11.7	15.7
JACKSON	59	14 555	19 468*	64.1	100.0
017 AMER BAPT ASSN	1	130	130	0.4	0.7
053 ASSEMB OF GOD.	4	520	829	2.7	4.3
059 BAPT MISS ASSN	1	24	30*	0.1	0.2
081 CATHOLIC......	1	NA	700	2.3	3.6
093 CHR CH (DISC).	1	103	184	0.6	0.9
097 CHR CHS&CHS CR	1	30	37*	0.1	0.2
127 CH GOD (CLEVE)	1	26	32*	0.1	0.2
151 L-D SAINTS....	1	NA	328	1.1	1.7
165 CH OF NAZARENE	2	104	168	0.6	0.9
167 CHS OF CHRIST.	12	1 400	1 780	5.9	9.1
193 EPISCOPAL.....	1	162	235	0.8	1.2
283 LUTH--MO SYNOD	1	28	47	0.2	0.2
349 PENT HOLINESS.	5	169	209*	0.7	1.1
403 SALVATION ARMY	1	98	204	0.7	1.0
413 S.D.A.........	1	40	50*	0.2	0.3
419 SO BAPT CONV..	14	8 280	10 247*	33.8	52.6
449 UN METHODIST..	10	3 255	4 028*	13.3	20.7
453 UN PRES CH USA	1	186	230*	0.8	1.2
JEFFERSON	32	4 893	6 189*	75.6	100.0
017 AMER BAPT ASSN	3	435	435	5.3	7.0
053 ASSEMB OF GOD.	4	365	536	6.6	8.7
081 CATHOLIC......	2	NA	180	2.2	2.9
093 CHR CH (DISC).	1	43	54	0.7	0.9
165 CH OF NAZARENE	2	67	135	1.6	2.2
167 CHS OF CHRIST.	5	425	540	6.6	8.7
413 S.D.A.........	1	25	30*	0.4	0.5
419 SO BAPT CONV..	9	2 578	3 122*	38.2	50.4
449 UN METHODIST..	4	941	1 140*	13.9	18.4
453 UN PRES CH USA	1	14	17*	0.2	0.3
JOHNSTON	48	5 102	6 496*	62.7	100.0
053 ASSEMB OF GOD.	4	198	370	3.6	5.7
059 BAPT MISS ASSN	1	44	53*	0.5	0.8
081 CATHOLIC......	1	NA	35	0.3	0.5
093 CHR CH (DISC).	2	78	106	1.0	1.6
127 CH GOD (CLEVE)	3	99	120*	1.2	1.8
165 CH OF NAZARENE	2	210	374	3.6	5.8
167 CHS OF CHRIST.	8	334	428	4.1	6.6
349 PENT HOLINESS.	1	45	54*	0.5	0.8
357 PRESB CH US...	1	33	40*	0.4	0.6
413 S.D.A.........	1	47	57*	0.6	0.9
419 SO BAPT CONV..	15	3 307	4 003*	38.7	61.6
449 UN METHODIST..	8	641	776*	7.5	11.9
453 UN PRES CH USA	1	66	80*	0.8	1.2
KAY	93	27 564	38 532*	77.3	100.0
017 AMER BAPT ASSN	2	124	124	0.2	0.3
029 AMER LUTH CH..	1	43	63	0.1	0.2
053 ASSEMB OF GOD.	4	340	606	1.2	1.6
081 CATHOLIC......	4	NA	2 858	5.7	7.4
093 CHR CH (DISC).	9	3 554	5 351	10.7	13.9
097 CHR CHS&CHS CR	4	617	740*	1.5	1.9

County and Denomination	Number of churches	Communicant, confirmed, full members	Total adherents Number	Percent of total population	Percent of total adherents
101 C.M.E.........	1	70	84*	0.2	0.2
123 CH GOD (ANDER)	2	200	600	1.2	1.6
127 CH GOD (CLEVE)	1	3	4*	–	–
151 L-D SAINTS....	2	NA	436	0.9	1.1
165 CH OF NAZARENE	8	500	795	1.6	2.1
167 CHS OF CHRIST.	9	1 275	1 625	3.3	4.2
193 EPISCOPAL.....	2	464	540	1.1	1.4
221 FREE METHODIST	2	12	63	0.1	0.2
263 INT FOURSQ GOS	1	58	70*	0.1	0.2
271 REFORM JUDAISM	1	48	58*	0.1	0.2
283 LUTH--MO SYNOD	4	1 166	1 464	2.9	3.8
349 PENT HOLINESS.	2	139	167*	0.3	0.4
403 SALVATION ARMY	1	164	347	0.7	0.9
413 S.D.A.........	1	55	66*	0.1	0.2
419 SO BAPT CONV..	15	10 067	12 076*	24.2	31.3
449 UN METHODIST..	13	6 931	8 315*	16.7	21.6
453 UN PRES CH USA	4	1 734	2 080*	4.2	5.4
KINGFISHER	47	8 422	12 391*	87.3	100.0
053 ASSEMB OF GOD.	2	57	105	0.7	0.8
081 CATHOLIC......	4	NA	1 661	11.7	13.4
093 CHR CH (DISC).	6	1 078	1 491	10.5	12.0
097 CHR CHS&CHS CR	4	353	431*	3.0	3.5
107 CHRISTIAN UN..	1	49	103	0.7	0.8
165 CH OF NAZARENE	3	215	434	3.1	3.5
167 CHS OF CHRIST.	4	200	255	1.8	2.1
283 LUTH--MO SYNOD	1	230	290	2.0	2.3
313 N AM BAPT CONF	1	44	54*	0.4	0.4
349 PENT HOLINESS.	2	113	138*	1.0	1.1
419 SO BAPT CONV..	10	3 990	4 873*	34.3	39.3
443 UN C OF CHRIST	3	324	396*	2.8	3.2
449 UN METHODIST..	5	1 664	2 032*	14.3	16.4
453 UN PRES CH USA	1	105	128*	0.9	1.0
KIOWA	49	8 293	10 231*	80.5	100.0
017 AMER BAPT ASSN	3	430	430	3.4	4.2
019 AMER BAPT USA.	2	250	298*	2.3	2.9
029 AMER LUTH CH..	1	122	149	1.2	1.5
053 ASSEMB OF GOD.	4	46	99	0.8	1.0
081 CATHOLIC......	1	NA	236	1.9	2.3
093 CHR CH (DISC).	3	182	259	2.0	2.5
097 CHR CHS&CHS CR	2	148	176*	1.4	1.7
127 CH GOD (CLEVE)	1	12	14*	0.1	0.1
165 CH OF NAZARENE	2	37	112	0.9	1.1
167 CHS OF CHRIST.	7	500	635	5.0	6.2
226 FRIENDS-USA...	1	8	10*	0.1	0.1
283 LUTH--MO SYNOD	1	153	183	1.4	1.8
349 PENT HOLINESS.	3	89	106*	0.8	1.0
419 SO BAPT CONV..	9	4 994	5 949*	46.8	58.1
449 UN METHODIST..	8	1 227	1 462*	11.5	14.3
453 UN PRES CH USA	1	95	113*	0.9	1.1
LATIMER	33	4 071	5 237*	53.2	100.0
053 ASSEMB OF GOD.	4	165	301	3.1	5.7
081 CATHOLIC......	1	NA	173	1.8	3.3
097 CHR CHS&CHS CR	1	50	60*	0.6	1.1
165 CH OF NAZARENE	1	23	55	0.6	1.1
167 CHS OF CHRIST.	4	240	305	3.1	5.8
185 CUMBER PRESB..	1	10	22	0.2	0.4
419 SO BAPT CONV..	17	3 221	3 884*	39.5	74.2
449 UN METHODIST..	3	339	409*	4.2	7.8
453 UN PRES CH USA	1	23	28*	0.3	0.5
LE FLORE	128	16 904	22 273*	54.7	100.0
017 AMER BAPT ASSN	4	600	600	1.5	2.7
053 ASSEMB OF GOD.	21	1 273	2 147	5.3	9.6
081 CATHOLIC......	3	NA	638	1.6	2.9
093 CHR CH (DISC).	2	215	334	0.8	1.5
097 CHR CHS&CHS CR	6	390	477*	1.2	2.1
101 C.M.E.........	1	45	55*	0.1	0.2
133 CH GOD(7TH)DEN	1	11	13*	–	0.1
151 L-D SAINTS....	1	NA	87	0.2	0.4
165 CH OF NAZARENE	5	306	677	1.7	3.0
167 CHS OF CHRIST.	11	650	827	2.0	3.7
185 CUMBER PRESB..	1	33	56	0.1	0.3
193 EPISCOPAL.....	1	28	27	0.1	0.1
357 PRESB CH US...	1	21	26*	0.1	0.1
413 S.D.A.........	1	29	35*	0.1	0.2
419 SO BAPT CONV..	49	10 864	13 290*	32.7	59.7
449 UN METHODIST..	17	2 332	2 853*	7.0	12.8
453 UN PRES CH USA	3	107	131*	0.3	0.6
LINCOLN	77	10 762	14 431*	54.2	100.0
017 AMER BAPT ASSN	2	150	150	0.6	1.0
053 ASSEMB OF GOD.	10	576	1 124	4.2	7.8
081 CATHOLIC......	4	NA	540	2.0	3.7
093 CHR CH (DISC).	6	618	883	3.3	6.1
097 CHR CHS&CHS CR	6	519	635*	2.4	4.4
101 C.M.E.........	2	50	61*	0.2	0.4
107 CHRISTIAN UN..	1	60	90	0.3	0.6
165 CH OF NAZARENE	5	254	422	1.6	2.9
167 CHS OF CHRIST.	8	600	765	2.9	5.3
208 EVAN LUTH ASSN	1	131	187	0.7	1.3
221 FREE METHODIST	1	22	60	0.2	0.4
226 FRIENDS-USA...	1	116	142*	0.5	1.0
413 S.D.A.........	1	22	27*	0.1	0.2
419 SO BAPT CONV..	19	5 858	7 162*	26.9	49.6
449 UN METHODIST..	7	1 654	2 022*	7.6	14.0
453 UN PRES CH USA	3	132	161*	0.6	1.1

NA— Not applicable *Total adherents estimated from known number of communicant, confirmed, full members. —Represents a percent less than 0.1. Percentages may not total due to rounding.

Table 4. Churches and Church Membership by County and Denomination: 1980

County and Denomination	Number of churches	Communicant, confirmed, full members	Total adherents Number	Total adherents Percent of total population	Total adherents Percent of total adherents
LOGAN	51	5 115	7 295*	27.1	100.0
053 ASSEMB OF GOD.	3	190	268	1.0	3.7
081 CATHOLIC......	4	NA	606	2.3	8.3
093 CHR CH (DISC).	4	785	1 128	4.2	15.5
097 CHR CHS&CHS CR	3	270	328*	1.2	4.5
101 C.M.E.........	4	320	389*	1.4	5.3
127 CH GOD (CLEVE)	2	72	87*	0.3	1.2
165 CH OF NAZARENE	3	126	253	0.9	3.5
167 CHS OF CHRIST.	8	600	765	2.8	10.5
193 EPISCOPAL.....	2	203	241	0.9	3.3
221 FREE METHODIST	1	30	129	0.5	1.8
226 FRIENDS-USA...	1	51	62*	0.2	0.8
283 LUTH—MO SYNOD	1	216	309	1.1	4.2
353 CHR BRETHREN..	1	20	20	0.1	0.3
413 S.D.A.........	1	58	70*	0.3	1.0
419 SO BAPT CONV..	1	34	41*	0.2	0.6
443 UN C OF CHRIST	1	53	64*	0.2	0.9
449 UN METHODIST..	10	1 742	2 116*	7.9	29.0
453 UN PRES CH USA	1	345	419*	1.6	5.7
LOVE	24	4 162	5 119*	68.5	100.0
053 ASSEMB OF GOD.	1	27	59	0.8	1.2
093 CHR CH (DISC).	1	49	67	0.9	1.3
167 CHS OF CHRIST.	4	475	605	8.1	11.8
349 PENT HOLINESS.	4	160	194*	2.6	3.8
357 PRESB CH US...	1	33	40*	0.5	0.8
419 SO BAPT CONV..	10	2 873	3 492*	46.8	68.2
449 UN METHODIST..	3	545	662*	8.9	12.9
MC CLAIN	60	12 651	16 371*	80.7	100.0
053 ASSEMB OF GOD.	3	199	358	1.8	2.2
059 BAPT MISS ASSN	4	924	1 135*	5.6	6.9
081 CATHOLIC......	1	NA	494	2.4	3.0
093 CHR CH (DISC).	2	218	323	1.6	2.0
097 CHR CHS&CHS CR	7	2 113	2 595*	12.8	15.9
123 CH GOD (ANDER)	1	69	207	1.0	1.3
127 CH GOD (CLEVE)	2	61	75*	0.4	0.5
165 CH OF NAZARENE	1	31	33	0.2	0.2
167 CHS OF CHRIST.	11	1 200	1 527	7.5	9.3
237 GC MENN BR CHS	1	150	184*	0.9	1.1
349 PENT HOLINESS.	4	183	225*	1.1	1.4
419 SO BAPT CONV..	15	6 237	7 660*	37.8	46.8
449 UN METHODIST..	6	1 222	1 501*	7.4	9.2
453 UN PRES CH USA	2	44	54*	0.3	0.3
MC CURTAIN	122	12 552	16 332*	45.2	100.0
017 AMER BAPT ASSN	10	1 300	1 300	3.6	8.0
053 ASSEMB OF GOD.	13	836	1 502	4.2	9.2
059 BAPT MISS ASSN	2	398	497*	1.4	3.0
081 CATHOLIC......	2	NA	207	0.6	1.3
093 CHR CH (DISC).	2	119	183	0.5	1.1
097 CHR CHS&CHS CR	4	210	262*	0.7	1.6
101 C.M.E.........	4	124	155*	0.4	0.9
127 CH GOD (CLEVE)	5	205	256*	0.7	1.6
151 L-D SAINTS....	1	NA	75	0.2	0.5
165 CH OF NAZARENE	2	100	192	0.5	1.2
167 CHS OF CHRIST.	17	1 150	1 465	4.1	9.0
185 CUMBER PRESB..	5	100	233	0.6	1.4
193 EPISCOPAL.....	1	54	69	0.2	0.4
357 PRESB CH US...	4	312	390*	1.1	2.4
413 S.D.A.........	1	33	41*	0.1	0.3
419 SO BAPT CONV..	18	5 042	6 297*	17.4	38.6
449 UN METHODIST..	18	2 250	2 810*	7.8	17.2
453 UN PRES CH USA	13	319	398*	1.1	2.4
MC INTOSH	43	6 377	7 837*	50.6	100.0
053 ASSEMB OF GOD.	3	295	411	2.7	5.2
081 CATHOLIC......	1	NA	167	1.1	2.1
093 CHR CH (DISC).	1	22	29	0.2	0.4
097 CHR CHS&CHS CR	2	165	195*	1.3	2.5
165 CH OF NAZARENE	1	28	113	0.7	1.4
167 CHS OF CHRIST.	7	587	671	4.3	8.6
193 EPISCOPAL.....	1	33	46	0.3	0.6
349 PENT HOLINESS.	1	52	61*	0.4	0.8
419 SO BAPT CONV..	23	4 445	5 257*	33.9	67.1
449 UN METHODIST..	2	719	850*	5.5	10.8
453 UN PRES CH USA	1	31	37*	0.2	0.5
MAJOR	32	4 258	5 478*	62.4	100.0
053 ASSEMB OF GOD.	3	158	398	4.5	7.3
081 CATHOLIC......	1	NA	30	0.3	0.5
093 CHR CH (DISC).	3	373	446	5.1	8.1
097 CHR CHS&CHS CR	2	75	91*	1.0	1.7
107 CHRISTIAN UN..	1	63	76	0.9	1.4
133 CH GOD(7TH)DEN	1	20	24*	0.3	0.4
143 CG IN CR(MENN)	1	253	253	2.9	4.6
165 CH OF NAZARENE	4	225	438	5.0	8.0
167 CHS OF CHRIST.	2	104	143	1.6	2.6
237 GC MENN BR CHS	1	389	473*	5.4	8.6
287 MENN GEN CONF.	3	327	347	4.0	6.3
419 SO BAPT CONV..	5	1 159	1 408*	16.1	25.7
449 UN METHODIST..	4	1 061	1 289*	14.7	23.5
453 UN PRES CH USA	1	51	62*	0.7	1.1
MARSHALL	35	5 180	6 298*	59.7	100.0
017 AMER BAPT ASSN	1	95	95	0.9	1.5
053 ASSEMB OF GOD.	2	62	85	0.8	1.3
081 CATHOLIC......	1	NA	110	1.0	1.7
165 CH OF NAZARENE	2	86	106	1.0	1.7
167 CHS OF CHRIST.	7	685	872	8.3	13.8
349 PENT HOLINESS.	2	106	125*	1.2	2.0
357 PRESB CH US...	1	12	14*	0.1	0.2
413 S.D.A.........	1	26	31*	0.3	0.5
419 SO BAPT CONV..	14	2 943	3 482*	33.0	55.3
449 UN METHODIST..	4	1 165	1 378*	13.1	21.9
MAYES	82	12 797	17 626*	54.6	100.0
017 AMER BAPT ASSN	1	89	89	0.3	0.5
053 ASSEMB OF GOD.	10	546	966	3.0	5.5
081 CATHOLIC......	2	NA	721	2.2	4.1
093 CHR CH (DISC).	2	364	532	1.6	3.0
097 CHR CHS&CHS CR	4	291	356*	1.1	2.0
123 CH GOD (ANDER)	2	308	924	2.9	5.2
127 CH GOD (CLEVE)	3	189	231*	0.7	1.3
151 L-D SAINTS....	1	NA	176	0.5	1.0
165 CH OF NAZARENE	1	42	100	0.3	0.6
167 CHS OF CHRIST.	7	675	860	2.7	4.9
185 CUMBER PRESB..	1	50	112	0.3	0.6
193 EPISCOPAL.....	1	68	95	0.3	0.5
283 LUTH—MO SYNOD	2	202	253	0.8	1.4
285 MENNONITE CH..	2	191	234*	0.7	1.3
323 OLD ORD AMISH.	2	260	318*	1.0	1.8
349 PENT HOLINESS.	1	67	82*	0.3	0.5
413 S.D.A.........	2	192	235*	0.7	1.3
419 SO BAPT CONV..	25	6 915	8 467*	26.2	48.0
449 UN METHODIST..	11	2 165	2 651*	8.2	15.0
453 UN PRES CH USA	2	183	224*	0.7	1.3
MURRAY	34	6 229	7 877*	64.8	100.0
017 AMER BAPT ASSN	1	52	52	0.4	0.7
053 ASSEMB OF GOD.	4	220	487	4.0	6.2
081 CATHOLIC......	1	NA	90	0.7	1.1
093 CHR CH (DISC).	1	135	150	1.2	1.9
097 CHR CHS&CHS CR	1	125	152*	1.3	1.9
165 CH OF NAZARENE	1	32	69	0.6	0.9
167 CHS OF CHRIST.	5	440	541	4.5	6.9
283 LUTH—MO SYNOD	1	13	14	0.1	0.2
349 PENT HOLINESS.	2	168	204*	1.7	2.6
357 PRESB CH US...	1	74	90*	0.7	1.1
413 S.D.A.........	1	32	39*	0.3	0.5
419 SO BAPT CONV..	10	4 019	4 874*	40.1	61.9
449 UN METHODIST..	3	874	1 060*	8.7	13.5
453 UN PRES CH USA	2	45	55*	0.5	0.7
MUSKOGEE	131	33 170	42 973*	64.2	100.0
019 AMER BAPT USA.	1	64	78*	0.1	0.2
053 ASSEMB OF GOD.	14	1 831	2 524	3.8	5.9
059 BAPT MISS ASSN	1	132	161*	0.2	0.4
081 CATHOLIC......	4	NA	1 660	2.5	3.9
093 CHR CH (DISC).	2	215	276	0.4	0.6
097 CHR CHS&CHS CR	8	2 292	2 795*	4.2	6.5
101 C.M.E.........	1	210	256*	0.4	0.6
123 CH GOD (ANDER)	2	98	294	0.4	0.7
127 CH GOD (CLEVE)	2	132	161*	0.2	0.4
151 L-D SAINTS....	1	NA	263	0.4	0.6
165 CH OF NAZARENE	2	233	322	0.5	0.7
167 CHS OF CHRIST.	20	2 050	2 609	3.9	6.1
185 CUMBER PRESB..	1	34	34	0.1	0.1
193 EPISCOPAL.....	2	498	543	0.8	1.3
271 REFORM JUDAISM	1	30	37*	0.1	0.1
283 LUTH—MO SYNOD	2	333	463	0.7	1.1
349 PENT HOLINESS.	5	407	496*	0.7	1.2
403 SALVATION ARMY	1	122	140	0.2	0.3
413 S.D.A.........	2	301	367*	0.5	0.9
419 SO BAPT CONV..	38	16 319	19 899*	29.7	46.3
449 UN METHODIST..	17	6 871	8 378*	12.5	19.5
453 UN PRES CH USA	4	998	1 217*	1.8	2.8
NOBLE	34	5 107	7 316*	63.2	100.0
053 ASSEMB OF GOD.	4	123	230	2.0	3.1
081 CATHOLIC......	2	NA	710	6.1	9.7
093 CHR CH (DISC).	5	600	974	8.4	13.3
097 CHR CHS&CHS CR	1	50	60*	0.5	0.8
157 CH OF BRETHREN	1	56	68*	0.6	0.9
165 CH OF NAZARENE	1	67	144	1.2	2.0
167 CHS OF CHRIST.	1	138	176	1.5	2.4
193 EPISCOPAL.....	1	21	25	0.2	0.3
281 LUTH CH AMER..	1	153	192	1.7	2.6
283 LUTH—MO SYNOD	1	527	667	5.8	9.1
413 S.D.A.........	1	35	42*	0.4	0.6
419 SO BAPT CONV..	9	1 877	2 266*	19.6	31.0
449 UN METHODIST..	5	1 150	1 388*	12.0	19.0
453 UN PRES CH USA	1	310	374*	3.2	5.1
NOWATA	29	4 545	6 331*	55.1	100.0
053 ASSEMB OF GOD.	2	187	342	3.0	5.4
081 CATHOLIC......	1	NA	60	0.5	0.9
093 CHR CH (DISC).	1	135	210	1.8	3.3
097 CHR CHS&CHS CR	2	454	548*	4.8	8.7
123 CH GOD (ANDER)	4	297	891	7.8	14.1
165 CH OF NAZARENE	1	47	148	1.3	2.3
167 CHS OF CHRIST.	2	60	76	0.7	1.2
193 EPISCOPAL.....	1	19	15	0.1	0.2
349 PENT HOLINESS.	1	143	173*	1.5	2.7
413 S.D.A.........	1	59	71*	0.6	1.1
419 SO BAPT CONV..	6	1 983	2 395*	20.9	37.8
449 UN METHODIST..	6	1 061	1 281*	11.2	20.2
453 UN PRES CH USA	1	100	121*	1.1	1.9

NA—Not applicable   *Total adherents estimated from known number of communicant, confirmed, full members.   —Represents a percent less than 0.1.   Percentages may not total due to rounding.

Table 4. Churches and Church Membership by County and Denomination: 1980

County and Denomination	Number of churches	Communicant, confirmed, full members	Total adherents		
			Number	Percent of total population	Percent of total adherents
OKFUSKEE	34	4 656	5 850*	52.6	100.0
053 ASSEMB OF GOD.	3	162	302	2.7	5.2
081 CATHOLIC......	1	NA	62	0.6	1.1
093 CHR CH (DISC).	2	85	122	1.1	2.1
101 C.M.E.........	2	230	277*	2.5	4.7
123 CH GOD (ANDER)	2	40	120	1.1	2.1
165 CH OF NAZARENE	1	26	40	0.4	0.7
167 CHS OF CHRIST.	5	334	379	3.4	6.5
349 PENT HOLINESS.	1	59	71*	0.6	1.2
419 SO BAPT CONV.	10	2 967	3 571*	32.1	61.0
449 UN METHODIST..	6	734	883*	7.9	15.1
453 UN PRES CH USA	1	19	23*	0.2	0.4
OKLAHOMA	515	245 478	348 280*	61.2	100.0
001 ADVENT CHR CH.	2	48	58*	–	–
005 AME ZION......	2	542	733	0.1	0.2
017 AMER BAPT ASSN	12	1 560	1 560	0.3	0.4
029 AMER LUTH CH..	4	946	1 331	0.2	0.4
053 ASSEMB OF GOD.	43	6 617	12 016	2.1	3.5
059 BAPT MISS ASSN	5	1 143	1 384*	0.2	0.4
075 BRETHREN IN CR	1	57	86	–	–
081 CATHOLIC......	21	NA	32 987	5.8	9.5
089 CHR & MISS AL.	1	52	85	–	–
093 CHR CH (DISC).	25	11 121	16 630	2.9	4.8
097 CHR CHS&CHS CR	5	750	908*	0.2	0.3
101 C.M.E.........	7	2 991	3 621*	0.6	1.0
107 CHRISTIAN UN..	1	30	45	–	–
123 CH GOD (ANDER)	6	1 007	3 021	0.5	0.9
127 CH GOD (CLEVE)	5	227	275*	–	0.1
133 CH GOD(7TH)DEN	2	64	77*	–	–
151 L-D SAINTS....	8	NA	3 102	0.5	0.9
165 CH OF NAZARENE	38	8 523	14 056	2.5	4.0
167 CHS OF CHRIST.	52	12 788	16 277	2.9	4.7
175 CONGR CHR CHS.	2	469	568*	0.1	0.2
185 CUMBER PRESB..	1	99	172	–	–
193 EPISCOPAL.....	13	5 619	6 903	1.2	2.0
208 EVAN LUTH ASSN	3	388	546	0.1	0.2
221 FREE METHODIST	3	324	1 095	0.2	0.3
226 FRIENDS-USA...	2	139	168*	–	–
237 GC MENN BR CHS	2	126	153*	–	–
263 INT FOURSQ GOS	2	301	364*	0.1	0.1
270 CONSRV JUDAISM	1	231	280*	–	0.1
271 REFORM JUDAISM	1	772	935*	0.2	0.3
281 LUTH CH AMER..	4	1 165	1 521	0.3	0.4
283 LUTH--MO SYNOD	7	2 529	3 167	0.6	0.9
285 MENNONITE CH..	1	19	23*	–	–
287 MENN GEN CONF.	1	81	101	–	–
290 METRO COMM CHS	1	75	150	–	–
335 ORTH PRESB CH.	1	32	39*	–	–
349 PENT HOLINESS.	29	2 863	3 466*	0.6	1.0
353 CHR BRETHREN..	1	60	100	–	–
357 PRESB CH US...	6	2 318	2 806*	0.5	0.8
371 REF CH IN AM..	1	428	674	0.1	0.2
381 REF PRES-EVAN.	1	64	68	–	–
403 SALVATION ARMY	1	176	294	0.1	0.1
413 S.D.A.........	8	1 543	1 868*	0.3	0.5
419 SO BAPT CONV..	114	119 641	144 852*	25.5	41.6
431 UKRANIAN AMER.	1	80	120	–	–
435 UNITARIAN-UNIV	1	325	393*	0.1	0.1
443 UN C OF CHRIST	2	203	246*	–	0.1
449 UN METHODIST..	54	50 816	61 524*	10.8	17.7
453 UN PRES CH USA	10	5 954	7 209*	1.3	2.1
469 WELS..........	1	172	223	–	0.1
OKMULGEE	70	16 709	22 134*	56.5	100.0
005 AME ZION......	1	649	723	1.8	3.3
053 ASSEMB OF GOD.	8	672	1 229	3.1	5.6
081 CATHOLIC......	4	NA	1 184	3.0	5.3
093 CHR CH (DISC).	4	514	680	1.7	3.1
097 CHR CHS&CHS CR	1	225	271*	0.7	1.2
101 C.M.E.........	1	233	280*	0.7	1.3
123 CH GOD (ANDER)	1	39	117	0.3	0.5
127 CH GOD (CLEVE)	1	13	16*	–	0.1
151 L-D SAINTS....	1	NA	251	0.6	1.1
165 CH OF NAZARENE	2	428	679	1.7	3.1
167 CHS OF CHRIST.	7	666	704	1.8	3.2
193 EPISCOPAL.....	1	33	33	0.1	0.1
263 INT FOURSQ GOS	2	140	168*	0.4	0.8
283 LUTH--MO SYNOD	1	157	208	0.5	0.9
349 PENT HOLINESS.	4	278	334*	0.9	1.5
403 SALVATION ARMY	1	48	82	0.2	0.4
413 S.D.A.........	2	91	109*	0.3	0.5
419 SO BAPT CONV..	15	9 143	11 000*	28.1	49.7
449 UN METHODIST..	11	2 979	3 584*	9.2	16.2
453 UN PRES CH USA	2	401	482*	1.2	2.2
OSAGE	79	11 927	16 178*	41.1	100.0
053 ASSEMB OF GOD.	11	579	1 074	2.7	6.6
059 BAPT MISS ASSN	1	73	89*	0.2	0.6
081 CATHOLIC......	5	NA	1 020	2.6	6.3
093 CHR CH (DISC).	2	336	436	1.1	2.7
097 CHR CHS&CHS CR	4	515	627*	1.6	3.9
127 CH GOD (CLEVE)	7	376	458*	1.2	2.8
165 CH OF NAZARENE	5	243	514	1.3	3.2
167 CHS OF CHRIST.	5	225	291	0.7	1.8
193 EPISCOPAL.....	1	123	155	0.4	1.0
217 FIRE BAPTIZED.	1	13	16*	–	0.1
226 FRIENDS-USA...	1	56	68*	0.2	0.4
237 GC MENN BR CHS	1	145	177*	0.5	1.1
349 PENT HOLINESS.	6	301	366*	0.9	2.3
419 SO BAPT CONV..	17	6 936	8 444*	21.5	52.2

County and Denomination	Number of churches	Communicant, confirmed, full members	Total adherents		
			Number	Percent of total population	Percent of total adherents
449 UN METHODIST..	8	1 562	1 902*	4.8	11.8
453 UN PRES CH USA	4	444	541*	1.4	3.3
OTTAWA	83	18 127	23 101*	70.3	100.0
053 ASSEMB OF GOD.	17	1 303	1 729	5.3	7.5
081 CATHOLIC......	1	NA	569	1.7	2.5
093 CHR CH (DISC).	1	197	242	0.7	1.0
097 CHR CHS&CHS CR	10	1 956	2 359*	7.2	10.2
123 CH GOD (ANDER)	1	28	84	0.3	0.4
127 CH GOD (CLEVE)	1	13	16*	–	0.1
151 L-D SAINTS....	1	NA	171	0.5	0.7
165 CH OF NAZARENE	2	178	322	1.0	1.4
167 CHS OF CHRIST.	3	270	325	1.0	1.4
193 EPISCOPAL.....	1	142	259	0.8	1.1
217 FIRE BAPTIZED.	1	10	12*	–	0.1
226 FRIENDS-USA...	2	131	158*	0.5	0.7
283 LUTH--MO SYNOD	2	315	471	1.4	2.0
349 PENT HOLINESS.	1	20	24*	0.1	0.1
413 S.D.A.........	1	21	25*	0.1	0.1
419 SO BAPT CONV.	29	10 414	12 561*	38.2	54.4
449 UN METHODIST..	8	2 836	3 421*	10.4	14.8
453 UN PRES CH USA	1	293	353*	1.1	1.5
PAWNEE	40	7 103	9 219*	60.2	100.0
053 ASSEMB OF GOD.	4	246	340	2.2	3.7
081 CATHOLIC......	2	NA	194	1.3	2.1
093 CHR CH (DISC).	1	125	400	2.6	4.3
097 CHR CHS&CHS CR	2	643	780*	5.1	8.5
123 CH GOD (ANDER)	1	12	36	0.2	0.4
151 L-D SAINTS....	1	NA	100	0.7	1.1
165 CH OF NAZARENE	2	90	128	0.8	1.4
167 CHS OF CHRIST.	3	260	330	2.2	3.6
193 EPISCOPAL.....	3	487	553	3.6	6.0
349 PENT HOLINESS.	1	39	47*	0.3	0.5
413 S.D.A.........	2	37	45*	0.3	0.5
419 SO BAPT CONV.	12	4 354	5 283*	34.5	57.3
449 UN METHODIST..	6	810	983*	6.4	10.7
PAYNE	86	19 945	27 321*	43.8	100.0
001 ADVENT CHR CH.	1	70	81*	0.1	0.3
017 AMER BAPT ASSN	1	130	130	0.2	0.5
029 AMER LUTH CH..	1	94	121	0.2	0.4
053 ASSEMB OF GOD.	8	567	1 079	1.7	3.9
081 CATHOLIC......	3	NA	2 161	3.5	7.9
089 CHR & MISS AL.	1	50	120	0.2	0.4
093 CHR CH (DISC).	3	1 156	1 429	2.3	5.2
097 CHR CHS&CHS CR	8	958	1 110*	1.8	4.1
101 C.M.E.........	1	28	32*	0.1	0.1
123 CH GOD (ANDER)	4	190	570	0.9	2.1
127 CH GOD (CLEVE)	2	40	46*	0.1	0.2
151 L-D SAINTS....	3	NA	695	1.1	2.5
157 CH OF BRETHREN	1	170	197*	0.3	0.7
165 CH OF NAZARENE	3	302	504	0.8	1.8
167 CHS OF CHRIST.	5	1 065	1 355	2.2	5.0
193 EPISCOPAL.....	1	61	69	0.1	0.3
221 FREE METHODIST	1	22	105	0.2	0.4
226 FRIENDS-USA...	1	9	10*	–	–
281 LUTH CH AMER..	1	216	272	0.4	1.0
283 LUTH--MO SYNOD	3	357	433	0.7	1.6
349 PENT HOLINESS.	1	44	51*	0.1	0.2
403 SALVATION ARMY	2	66	125	0.2	0.5
413 S.D.A.........	4	94	109*	0.2	0.4
419 SO BAPT CONV..	14	7 606	8 812*	14.1	32.3
435 UNITARIAN-UNIV	1	56	65*	0.1	0.2
449 UN METHODIST..	10	5 244	6 076*	9.7	22.2
453 UN PRES CH USA	2	1 350	1 564*	2.5	5.7
PITTSBURG	100	19 322	25 573*	63.1	100.0
053 ASSEMB OF GOD.	8	473	958	2.4	3.7
059 BAPT MISS ASSN	1	120	144*	0.4	0.6
081 CATHOLIC......	4	NA	1 498	3.7	5.9
093 CHR CH (DISC).	2	271	387	1.0	1.5
097 CHR CHS&CHS CR	4	518	620*	1.5	2.4
123 CH GOD (ANDER)	1	15	45	0.1	0.2
127 CH GOD (CLEVE)	1	108	129*	0.3	0.5
133 CH GOD(7TH)DEN	3	30	36*	0.1	0.1
151 L-D SAINTS....	1	NA	237	0.6	0.9
165 CH OF NAZARENE	2	172	309	0.8	1.2
167 CHS OF CHRIST.	13	900	1 145	2.8	4.5
193 EPISCOPAL.....	1	112	122	0.3	0.5
283 LUTH--MO SYNOD	1	20	28	0.1	0.1
349 PENT HOLINESS.	3	146	175*	0.4	0.7
403 SALVATION ARMY	1	75	159	0.4	0.6
413 S.D.A.........	1	46	55*	0.1	0.2
419 SO BAPT CONV.	38	12 956	15 505*	38.3	60.6
449 UN METHODIST..	13	2 687	3 216*	7.9	12.6
453 UN PRES CH USA	2	673	805*	2.0	3.1
PONTOTOC	82	17 897	22 555*	69.2	100.0
017 AMER BAPT ASSN	2	150	150	0.5	0.7
053 ASSEMB OF GOD.	6	359	661	2.0	2.9
059 BAPT MISS ASSN	5	465	555*	1.7	2.5
081 CATHOLIC......	1	NA	416	1.3	1.8
093 CHR CH (DISC).	1	487	637	2.0	2.8
101 C.M.E.........	1	?	?	?	?
127 CH GOD (CLEVE)	2	138	165*	0.5	0.7
151 L-D SAINTS....	1	NA	182	0.6	0.8
165 CH OF NAZARENE	3	270	472	1.4	2.1
167 CHS OF CHRIST.	13	1 459	1 819	5.6	8.1
185 CUMBER PRESB..	1	80	178	0.5	0.8

NA—Not applicable   *Total adherents estimated from known number of communicant, confirmed, full members.   —Represents a percent less than 0.1.   Percentages may not total due to rounding.

Table 4. Churches and Church Membership by County and Denomination: 1980

County and Denomination	Number of churches	Communicant, confirmed, full members	Total adherents		
			Number	Percent of total population	Percent of total adherents
193 EPISCOPAL.....	1	262	301	0.9	1.3
283 LUTH--MO SYNOD	1	109	138	0.4	0.6
349 PENT HOLINESS.	9	869	1 037*	3.2	4.6
403 SALVATION ARMY	1	104	160	0.5	0.7
413 S.D.A.........	1	23	27*	0.1	0.1
419 SO BAPT CONV..	22	10 303	12 293*	37.7	54.5
449 UN METHODIST..	10	2 547	3 039*	9.3	13.5
453 UN PRES CH USA	1	272	325*	1.0	1.4
POTTAWATOMIE	102	25 809	34 340*	62.2	100.0
017 AMER BAPT ASSN	1	100	100	0.2	0.3
029 AMER LUTH CH..	1	344	455	0.8	1.3
053 ASSEMB OF GOD.	8	355	746	1.4	2.2
081 CATHOLIC......	5	NA	1 553	2.8	4.5
093 CHR CH (DISC).	2	425	597	1.1	1.7
097 CHR CHS&CHS CR	1	50	61*	0.1	0.2
101 C.M.E.........	1	78	95*	0.2	0.3
123 CH GOD (ANDER)	1	132	396	0.7	1.2
127 CH GOD (CLEVE)	3	223	270*	0.5	0.8
133 CH GOD(7TH)DEN	1	65	79*	0.1	0.2
151 L-D SAINTS....	1	NA	328	0.6	1.0
165 CH OF NAZARENE	3	260	664	1.2	1.9
167 CHS OF CHRIST.	17	1 050	1 335	2.4	3.9
193 EPISCOPAL.....	1	230	288	0.5	0.8
349 PENT HOLINESS.	1	78	95*	0.2	0.3
357 PRESB CH US...	1	59	71*	0.1	0.2
403 SALVATION ARMY	1	98	228	0.4	0.7
413 S.D.A.........	1	109	132*	0.2	0.4
419 SO BAPT CONV..	38	17 774	21 540*	39.0	62.7
449 UN METHODIST..	12	3 951	4 788*	8.7	13.9
453 UN PRES CH USA	2	428	519*	0.9	1.5
PUSHMATAHA	53	5 781	7 280*	61.8	100.0
017 AMER BAPT ASSN	2	350	350	3.0	4.8
053 ASSEMB OF GOD.	7	421	707	6.0	9.7
081 CATHOLIC......	1	NA	100	0.8	1.4
093 CHR CH (DISC).	1	60	72	0.6	1.0
097 CHR CHS&CHS CR	4	305	368*	3.1	5.1
151 L-D SAINTS....	1	NA	28	0.2	0.4
165 CH OF NAZARENE	1	42	93	0.8	1.3
167 CHS OF CHRIST.	5	430	516	4.4	7.1
193 EPISCOPAL.....	1	15	23	0.2	0.3
357 PRESB CH US...	1	53	64*	0.5	0.9
419 SO BAPT CONV..	16	3 100	3 745*	31.8	51.4
449 UN METHODIST..	12	968	1 169*	9.9	16.1
453 UN PRES CH USA	1	37	45*	0.4	0.6
ROGER MILLS	25	2 672	3 292*	68.6	100.0
053 ASSEMB OF GOD.	3	71	113	2.4	3.4
165 CH OF NAZARENE	2	?	?	?	?
167 CHS OF CHRIST.	6	240	305	6.4	9.3
349 PENT HOLINESS.	3	104	127*	2.6	3.9
419 SO BAPT CONV..	7	1 706	2 076*	43.3	63.1
449 UN METHODIST..	4	551	671*	14.0	20.4
ROGERS	75	16 045	21 757*	46.9	100.0
053 ASSEMB OF GOD.	8	980	1 448	3.1	6.7
059 BAPT MISS ASSN	1	82	102*	0.2	0.5
081 CATHOLIC......	1	NA	1 020	2.2	4.7
093 CHR CH (DISC).	2	418	538	1.2	2.5
097 CHR CHS&CHS CR	4	540	670*	1.4	3.1
123 CH GOD (ANDER)	1	60	180	0.4	0.8
127 CH GOD (CLEVE)	1	18	22*	–	0.1
133 CH GOD(7TH)DEN	1	46	57*	0.1	0.3
151 L-D SAINTS....	1	NA	238	0.5	1.1
165 CH OF NAZARENE	2	183	351	0.8	1.6
167 CHS OF CHRIST.	9	1 100	1 400	3.0	6.4
193 EPISCOPAL.....	1	130	151	0.3	0.7
208 EVAN LUTH ASSN	1	55	60	0.1	0.3
221 FREE METHODIST	1	18	78	0.2	0.4
263 INT FOURSQ GOS	1	8	10*	–	–
283 LUTH--MO SYNOD	2	272	309	0.8	1.7
287 MENN GEN CONF.	1	174	203	0.4	0.9
413 S.D.A.........	1	138	171*	0.4	0.8
419 SO BAPT CONV..	25	9 032	11 214*	24.1	51.5
449 UN METHODIST..	9	2 403	2 983*	6.4	13.7
453 UN PRES CH USA	2	388	482*	1.0	2.2
SEMINOLE	83	15 128	19 116*	69.6	100.0
005 AME ZION......	1	100	116	0.4	0.6
017 AMER BAPT ASSN	3	350	350	1.3	1.8
053 ASSEMB OF GOD.	9	546	1 061	3.9	5.6
081 CATHOLIC......	2	NA	103	0.4	0.5
093 CHR CH (DISC).	2	273	371	1.4	1.9
101 C.M.E.........	2	123	149*	0.5	0.8
123 CH GOD (ANDER)	3	159	477	1.7	2.5
127 CH GOD (CLEVE)	2	68	82*	0.3	0.4
165 CH OF NAZARENE	3	88	91	0.3	0.5
167 CHS OF CHRIST.	9	925	1 177	4.3	6.2
193 EPISCOPAL.....	1	52	65	0.2	0.3
349 PENT HOLINESS.	6	308	373*	1.4	2.0
357 PRESB CH US...	1	29	35*	0.1	0.2
413 S.D.A.........	1	40	48*	0.2	0.3
419 SO BAPT CONV..	23	9 251	11 207*	40.8	58.6
449 UN METHODIST..	10	2 547	3 085*	11.2	16.1
453 UN PRES CH USA	5	269	326*	1.2	1.7
SEQUOYAH	51	8 432	11 362*	37.0	100.0
017 AMER BAPT ASSN	4	520	520	1.7	4.6

County and Denomination	Number of churches	Communicant, confirmed, full members	Total adherents		
			Number	Percent of total population	Percent of total adherents
053 ASSEMB OF GOD.	8	892	1 386	4.5	12.2
059 BAPT MISS ASSN	1	117	145*	0.5	1.3
081 CATHOLIC......	1	NA	240	0.8	2.1
097 CHR CHS&CHS CR	1	125	155*	0.5	1.4
151 L-D SAINTS....	1	NA	211	0.7	1.9
165 CH OF NAZARENE	2	170	472	1.5	4.2
167 CHS OF CHRIST.	6	335	425	1.4	3.7
221 FREE METHODIST	1	31	90	0.3	0.8
413 S.D.A.........	1	99	122*	0.4	1.1
419 SO BAPT CONV..	18	4 784	5 915*	19.2	52.1
449 UN METHODIST..	6	1 259	1 557*	5.1	13.7
453 UN PRES CH USA	1	100	124*	0.4	1.1
STEPHENS	89	24 295	32 031*	73.8	100.0
017 AMER BAPT ASSN	6	1 714	1 714	3.9	5.4
053 ASSEMB OF GOD.	13	1 094	1 810	4.2	5.7
081 CATHOLIC......	2	NA	1 874	4.3	5.9
093 CHR CH (DISC).	2	786	1 013	2.3	3.2
097 CHR CHS&CHS CR	2	125	151*	0.3	0.5
101 C.M.E.........	1	90	109*	0.3	0.3
123 CH GOD (ANDER)	1	45	135	0.3	0.4
127 CH GOD (CLEVE)	2	107	129*	0.3	0.4
151 L-D SAINTS....	1	NA	169	0.4	0.5
165 CH OF NAZARENE	5	330	524	1.2	1.6
167 CHS OF CHRIST.	16	1 200	1 530	3.5	4.8
185 CUMBER PRESB..	2	154	253	0.6	0.8
193 EPISCOPAL.....	1	174	262	0.6	0.8
283 LUTH--MO SYNOD	1	140	179	0.4	0.6
357 PRESB CH US...	1	361	437*	1.0	1.4
413 S.D.A.........	1	38	46*	0.1	0.1
419 SO BAPT CONV..	24	13 942	16 864*	38.8	52.6
449 UN METHODIST..	8	3 995	4 832*	11.1	15.1
TEXAS	54	10 130	13 755*	77.6	100.0
053 ASSEMB OF GOD.	1	101	165	0.9	1.2
081 CATHOLIC......	2	NA	709	4.0	5.2
093 CHR CH (DISC).	3	501	604	3.4	4.4
097 CHR CHS&CHS CR	1	300	370*	2.1	2.7
123 CH GOD (ANDER)	3	87	261	1.5	1.9
151 L-D SAINTS....	1	NA	81	0.5	0.6
165 CH OF NAZARENE	3	271	511	2.9	3.7
167 CHS OF CHRIST.	9	925	1 177	6.6	8.6
193 EPISCOPAL.....	1	18	64	0.4	0.5
211 EVAN MENN BR..	1	103	134	0.8	1.0
237 GC MENN BR CHS	1	97	120*	0.7	0.9
263 INT FOURSQ GOS	1	176	217*	1.2	1.6
283 LUTH--MO SYNOD	3	461	592	3.3	4.3
349 PENT HOLINESS.	2	95	117*	0.7	0.9
413 S.D.A.........	2	70	86*	0.5	0.6
419 SO BAPT CONV..	10	3 498	4 317*	24.4	31.4
449 UN METHODIST..	9	3 116	3 846*	21.7	28.0
453 UN PRES CH USA	1	311	384*	2.2	2.8
TILLMAN	36	7 829	10 351*	83.5	100.0
053 ASSEMB OF GOD.	4	145	219	1.8	2.1
081 CATHOLIC......	3	NA	559	4.5	5.4
093 CHR CH (DISC).	2	106	250	2.0	2.4
165 CH OF NAZARENE	1	49	97	0.8	0.9
167 CHS OF CHRIST.	7	800	1 020	8.2	9.9
349 PENT HOLINESS.	1	38	46*	0.4	0.4
419 SO BAPT CONV..	11	5 321	6 489*	52.3	62.7
449 UN METHODIST..	5	1 228	1 498*	12.1	14.5
453 UN PRES CH USA	2	142	173*	1.4	1.7
TULSA	382	179 373	251 438*	53.4	100.0
005 AME ZION......	1	214	249	0.1	0.1
017 AMER BAPT ASSN	4	724	724	0.2	0.3
019 AMER BAPT USA.	2	900	1 090*	0.2	0.4
029 AMER LUTH CH..	1	565	756	0.2	0.3
053 ASSEMB OF GOD.	41	7 336	11 402	2.4	4.5
059 BAPT MISS ASSN	3	202	245*	0.1	0.1
081 CATHOLIC......	22	NA	24 167	5.1	9.6
093 CHR CH (DISC).	21	6 287	8 719	1.9	3.5
097 CHR CHS&CHS CR	22	6 425	7 779*	1.7	3.1
101 C.M.E.........	3	1 468	1 777*	0.4	0.7
123 CH GOD (ANDER)	5	613	1 839	0.4	0.7
127 CH GOD (CLEVE)	2	96	116*	–	–
133 CH GOD(7TH)DEN	1	28	34*	–	–
151 L-D SAINTS....	5	NA	2 051	0.4	0.8
165 CH OF NAZARENE	15	1 660	2 729	0.6	1.1
167 CHS OF CHRIST.	35	7 950	10 625	2.3	4.2
185 CUMBER PRESB..	2	176	283	0.1	0.1
193 EPISCOPAL.....	9	4 873	5 904	1.3	2.3
208 EVAN LUTH ASSN	1	229	376	0.1	0.1
217 FIRE BAPTIZED.	1	4	5*	–	–
221 FREE METHODIST	1	88	180	–	0.1
226 FRIENDS-USA...	2	206	249*	0.1	0.1
237 GC MENN BR CHS	1	273	331*	0.1	0.1
263 INT FOURSQ GOS	3	196	237*	0.1	0.1
270 CONSRV JUDAISM	1	324	392*	0.1	0.2
271 REFORM JUDAISM	1	1 040	1 259*	0.3	0.5
281 LUTH CH AMER..	3	1 005	1 503	0.3	0.6
283 LUTH--MO SYNOD	5	2 638	3 575	0.8	1.4
290 METRO COMM CHS	1	90	180	–	0.1
329 OPEN BIBLE STD	1	50	75	–	–
335 ORTH PRESB CH.	1	23	28*	–	–
349 PENT HOLINESS.	7	1 045	1 265*	0.3	0.5
353 CHR BRETHREN..	1	20	20	–	–
381 REF PRES-EVAN.	1	172	206	–	0.1
403 SALVATION ARMY	4	413	1 147	0.2	0.5
413 S.D.A.........	5	817	989*	0.2	0.4

NA--Not applicable   *Total adherents estimated from known number of communicant, confirmed, full members.   —Represents a percent less than 0.1.   Percentages may not total due to rounding.

Table 4. Churches and Church Membership by County and Denomination: 1980

County and Denomination	Number of churches	Communicant, confirmed, full members	Total adherents		
			Number	Percent of total population	Percent of total adherents
419 SO BAPT CONV..	85	77 649	94 014*	20.0	37.4
435 UNITARIAN-UNIV	2	1 225	1 483*	0.3	0.6
443 UN C OF CHRIST	1	224	271*	0.1	0.1
449 UN METHODIST..	45	41 072	49 728*	10.6	19.8
453 UN PRES CH USA	14	10 948	13 255*	2.8	5.3
469 WELS..........	1	105	181	-	0.1
WAGONER	43	7 497	10 102*	24.2	100.0
053 ASSEMB OF GOD.	3	263	547	1.3	5.4
081 CATHOLIC......	1	NA	250	0.6	2.5
093 CHR CH (DISC).	1	215	291	0.7	2.9
097 CHR CHS&CHS CR	2	361	456*	1.1	4.5
101 C.M.E.........	4	240	303*	0.7	3.0
127 CH GOD (CLEVE)	1	70	88*	0.2	0.9
151 L-D SAINTS....	1	NA	64	0.2	0.6
165 CH OF NAZARENE	2	126	232	0.6	2.3
167 CHS OF CHRIST.	5	300	380	0.9	3.8
193 EPISCOPAL.....	1	42	61	0.1	0.6
349 PENT HOLINESS.	2	210	265*	0.6	2.6
413 S.D.A.........	1	44	56*	0.1	0.6
419 SO BAPT CONV..	12	4 520	5 711*	13.7	56.5
449 UN METHODIST..	6	1 034	1 307*	3.1	12.9
453 UN PRES CH USA	1	72	91*	0.2	0.9
WASHINGTON	70	25 563	34 859*	72.5	100.0
017 AMER BAPT ASSN	4	359	359	0.7	1.0
053 ASSEMB OF GOD.	4	565	930	1.9	2.7
081 CATHOLIC......	3	NA	2 663	5.5	7.6
093 CHR CH (DISC).	2	716	896	1.9	2.6
097 CHR CHS&CHS CR	4	1 151	1 386*	2.9	4.0
123 CH GOD (ANDER)	1	105	315	0.7	0.9
127 CH GOD (CLEVE)	1	20	24*	-	0.1
151 L-D SAINTS....	2	NA	697	1.4	2.0
157 CH OF BRETHREN	1	21	25*	0.1	0.1
165 CH OF NAZARENE	3	510	623	1.3	1.8
167 CHS OF CHRIST.	5	1 060	1 306	2.7	3.7
193 EPISCOPAL.....	1	575	841	1.7	2.4
215 EVAN METH CH..	1	79	95*	0.2	0.3
217 FIRE BAPTIZED.	2	41	49*	0.1	0.1
226 FRIENDS-USA...	1	37	45*	0.1	0.1
283 LUTH--MO SYNOD	1	611	791	1.6	2.3
335 ORTH PRESB CH.	1	59	71*	0.1	0.2
349 PENT HOLINESS.	2	154	185*	0.4	0.5
403 SALVATION ARMY	1	182	292	0.6	0.8
413 S.D.A.........	1	138	166*	0.3	0.5
419 SO BAPT CONV..	18	10 555	12 712*	26.4	36.5
435 UNITARIAN-UNIV	1	20	24*	-	0.1
449 UN METHODIST..	8	6 373	7 676*	16.0	22.0
453 UN PRES CH USA	2	2 232	2 688*	5.6	7.7
WASHITA	40	7 746	9 520*	69.0	100.0
029 AMER LUTH CH..	1	228	284	2.1	3.0
053 ASSEMB OF GOD.	2	105	168	1.2	1.8
081 CATHOLIC......	1	NA	27	0.2	0.3
097 CHR CHS&CHS CR	1	12	15*	0.1	0.2
157 CH OF BRETHREN	1	26	31*	0.2	0.3
165 CH OF NAZARENE	1	?	?	?	?
167 CHS OF CHRIST.	10	973	1 124	8.1	11.8
185 CUMBER PRESB..	2	41	143	1.0	1.5
237 GC MENN BR CHS	2	585	709*	5.1	7.4
287 MENN GEN CONF.	1	157	213	1.5	2.2
313 N AM BAPT CONF	1	111	134*	1.0	1.4
349 PENT HOLINESS.	1	45	55*	0.4	0.6
419 SO BAPT CONV..	7	3 547	4 296*	31.1	45.1
449 UN METHODIST..	7	1 747	2 116*	15.3	22.2
453 UN PRES CH USA	2	169	205*	1.5	2.2
WOODS	35	5 486	7 432*	68.0	100.0
053 ASSEMB OF GOD.	2	125	296	2.7	4.0
081 CATHOLIC......	2	NA	275	2.5	3.7
093 CHR CH (DISC).	4	416	645	5.9	8.7
097 CHR CHS&CHS CR	1	67	78*	0.7	1.0
123 CH GOD (ANDER)	3	169	507	4.6	6.8
151 L-D SAINTS....	1	NA	63	0.6	0.8
165 CH OF NAZARENE	3	126	206	1.9	2.8
167 CHS OF CHRIST.	3	275	350	3.2	4.7
193 EPISCOPAL.....	1	74	80	0.7	1.1
226 FRIENDS-USA...	1	172	200*	1.8	2.7
283 LUTH--MO SYNOD	1	374	445	4.1	6.0
413 S.D.A.........	1	31	36*	0.3	0.5
419 SO BAPT CONV..	4	1 280	1 488*	13.6	20.0
443 UN C OF CHRIST	1	47	55*	0.5	0.7
449 UN METHODIST..	6	2 125	2 470*	22.6	33.2
453 UN PRES CH USA	1	205	238*	2.2	3.2
WOODWARD	35	8 369	12 103*	57.2	100.0
053 ASSEMB OF GOD.	4	537	935	4.4	7.7
081 CATHOLIC......	2	NA	492	2.3	4.1
093 CHR CH (DISC).	3	594	1 106	5.2	9.1
097 CHR CHS&CHS CR	2	124	154*	0.7	1.3
151 L-D SAINTS....	1	NA	140	0.7	1.2
165 CH OF NAZARENE	1	182	445	2.1	3.7
167 CHS OF CHRIST.	2	325	463	2.2	3.8
193 EPISCOPAL.....	1	68	107	0.5	0.9
221 FREE METHODIST	1	13	114	0.5	0.9
283 LUTH--MO SYNOD	1	188	279	1.3	2.3
413 S.D.A.........	1	57	71*	0.3	0.6
419 SO BAPT CONV..	7	3 330	4 134*	19.5	34.2
449 UN METHODIST..	8	2 726	3 384*	16.0	28.0
453 UN PRES CH USA	1	225	279*	1.3	2.3

County and Denomination	Number of churches	Communicant, confirmed, full members	Total adherents		
			Number	Percent of total population	Percent of total adherents
OREGON					
THE STATE.....	2 628	411 445	949 471*	36.1	100.0
BAKER	33	2 648	5 999*	37.2	100.0
029 AMER LUTH CH..	1	229	354	2.2	5.9
053 ASSEMB OF GOD.	3	150	231	1.4	3.9
081 CATHOLIC......	5	NA	1 149	7.1	19.2
097 CHR CHS&CHS CR	2	460	556*	3.4	9.3
123 CH GOD (ANDER)	1	74	222	1.4	3.7
151 L-D SAINTS....	3	NA	926	5.7	15.4
165 CH OF NAZARENE	2	139	357	2.2	6.0
167 CHS OF CHRIST.	2	34	50	0.3	0.8
179 CONSRV BAPT...	3	305	369*	2.3	6.2
193 EPISCOPAL.....	1	148	358	2.2	6.0
403 SALVATION ARMY	1	56	153	0.9	2.6
413 S.D.A.........	2	200	242*	1.5	4.0
419 SO BAPT CONV..	1	19	23*	0.1	0.4
449 UN METHODIST..	4	414	501*	3.1	8.4
453 UN PRES CH USA	2	420	508*	3.1	8.5
BENTON	54	10 851	21 172*	31.0	100.0
017 AMER BAPT ASSN	2	50	50	0.1	0.2
053 ASSEMB OF GOD.	3	425	865	1.3	4.1
063 BEREAN FUND CH	1	51	60*	0.1	0.3
081 CATHOLIC......	3	NA	5 426	8.0	25.6
089 CHR & MISS AL.	2	67	120	0.2	0.6
093 CHR CH (DISC).	1	511	561	0.8	2.6
097 CHR CHS&CHS CR	2	174	204*	0.3	1.0
105 CHRISTIAN REF.	1	30	46	0.1	0.2
127 CH GOD (CLEVE)	1	38	45*	0.1	0.2
151 L-D SAINTS....	5	NA	1 568	2.3	7.4
165 CH OF NAZARENE	2	210	492	0.7	2.3
167 CHS OF CHRIST.	4	247	311	0.5	1.5
179 CONSRV BAPT...	5	916	1 075*	1.6	5.1
193 EPISCOPAL.....	1	1 699	2 378	3.5	11.2
197 EVAN CH OF NA.	1	220	220	0.3	1.0
221 FREE METHODIST	1	31	201	0.3	0.9
226 FRIENDS-USA...	1	25	29*	-	0.1
263 INT FOURSQ GOS	1	150	176*	0.3	0.8
281 LUTH CH AMER..	1	1 076	1 465	2.1	6.9
283 LUTH--MO SYNOD	3	699	919	1.3	4.3
285 MENNONITE CH..	1	33	39*	0.1	0.2
353 CHR BRETHREN..	1	50	50	0.1	0.2
413 S.D.A.........	1	254	298*	0.4	1.4
419 SO BAPT CONV..	1	566	664*	1.0	3.1
435 UNITARIAN-UNIV	1	96	113*	0.2	0.5
443 UN C OF CHRIST	1	663	778*	1.1	3.7
449 UN METHODIST..	4	1 470	1 725*	2.5	8.1
453 UN PRES CH USA	2	1 050	1 232*	1.8	5.8
469 WELS..........	1	50	62	0.1	0.3
CLACKAMAS	183	32 180	67 708*	28.0	100.0
001 ADVENT CHR CH.	1	20	25*	-	-
017 AMER BAPT ASSN	1	99	99	-	0.1
019 AMER BAPT USA.	4	1 261	1 546*	0.6	2.3
029 AMER LUTH CH..	8	3 992	5 552	2.3	8.2
053 ASSEMB OF GOD.	11	895	1 869	0.8	2.8
057 BAPT GEN CONF.	1	100	123*	0.1	0.2
081 CATHOLIC......	11	NA	19 007	7.9	28.1
089 CHR & MISS AL.	3	147	349	0.1	0.5
093 CHR CH (DISC).	1	328	480	0.2	0.7
097 CHR CHS&CHS CR	15	3 224	3 951*	1.6	5.8
123 CH GOD (ANDER)	2	81	243	0.1	0.4
127 CH GOD (CLEVE)	1	?	?	?	?
151 L-D SAINTS....	14	NA	6 569	2.7	9.7
165 CH OF NAZARENE	5	854	1 321	0.5	2.0
167 CHS OF CHRIST.	6	650	825	0.3	1.2
175 CONGR CHR CHS.	1	214	262*	0.1	0.4
179 CONSRV BAPT...	15	3 000	3 677*	1.5	5.4
181 CONSRV CONGR..	1	17	21*	-	-
193 EPISCOPAL.....	7	3 114	4 065	1.7	6.0
197 EVAN CH OF NA.	6	891	891	0.4	1.3
201 EVAN COV CH AM	2	319	391*	0.2	0.6
203 EVAN FREE CH..	2	25	31*	-	-
215 EVAN METH CH..	1	11	13*	-	-
221 FREE METHODIST	2	40	219	0.1	0.3
226 FRIENDS-USA...	4	126	154*	0.1	0.2
263 INT FOURSQ GOS	4	336	412*	0.2	0.6
281 LUTH CH AMER..	2	400	640	0.3	0.9
283 LUTH--MO SYNOD	8	1 739	2 599	1.1	3.8
285 MENNONITE CH..	3	330	404*	0.2	0.6
287 MENN GEN CONF.	1	286	109	-	0.2
313 N AM BAPT CONF	2	134	164*	0.1	0.2
335 ORTH PRESB CH.	1	33	40*	-	0.1
353 CHR BRETHREN..	1	60	70	-	0.1
413 S.D.A.........	7	2 193	2 688*	1.1	4.0
419 SO BAPT CONV..	3	431	528*	0.2	0.8
435 UNITARIAN-UNIV	1	250	306*	0.1	0.5
443 UN C OF CHRIST	6	775	950*	0.4	1.4
449 UN METHODIST..	13	3 092	3 790*	1.6	5.6
453 UN PRES CH USA	8	2 713	3 325*	1.4	4.9
CLATSOP	44	4 477	8 368*	25.8	100.0
019 AMER BAPT USA.	1	108	129*	0.4	1.5
029 AMER LUTH CH..	1	453	656	2.0	7.8
045 APOSTOLIC LUTH	1	30	36*	0.1	0.4

NA—Not applicable   *Total adherents estimated from known number of communicant, confirmed, full members.

—Represents a percent less than 0.1.   Percentages may not total due to rounding.

Table 4. Churches and Church Membership by County and Denomination: 1980

County and Denomination	Number of churches	Communicant, confirmed, full members	Total adherents		
			Number	Percent of total population	Percent of total adherents
053 ASSEMB OF GOD.	5	228	398	1.2	4.8
081 CATHOLIC......	3	NA	1 833	5.6	21.9
089 CHR & MISS AL.	1	0	23	0.1	0.3
097 CHR CHS&CHS CR	3	290	347*	1.1	4.1
151 L-D SAINTS....	2	NA	662	2.0	7.9
165 CH OF NAZARENE	2	85	176	0.5	2.1
167 CHS OF CHRIST.	1	13	16	–	0.2
179 CONSRV BAPT...	4	332	397*	1.2	4.7
193 EPISCOPAL.....	3	426	501	1.5	6.0
220 FREE LUTHERAN.	1	125	160	0.5	1.9
226 FRIENDS-USA...	1	94	112*	0.3	1.3
263 INT FOURSQ GOS	2	75	90*	0.3	1.1
281 LUTH CH AMER..	3	1 048	1 417	4.4	16.9
283 LUTH--MO SYNOD	1	81	113	0.3	1.4
413 S.D.A.........	2	123	147*	0.5	1.8
443 UN C OF CHRIST	1	38	45*	0.1	0.5
449 UN METHODIST..	3	531	635*	2.0	7.6
453 UN PRES CH USA	3	397	475*	1.5	5.7
COLUMBIA	53	4 382	10 593*	29.7	100.0
017 AMER BAPT ASSN	1	100	100	0.3	0.9
045 APOSTOLIC LUTH	1	50	62*	0.2	0.6
053 ASSEMB OF GOD.	6	449	917	2.6	8.7
057 BAPT GEN CONF.	2	341	423*	1.2	4.0
081 CATHOLIC......	5	NA	2 400	6.7	22.7
093 CHR CH (DISC).	1	139	320	0.9	3.0
097 CHR CHS&CHS CR	2	121	150*	0.4	1.4
123 CH GOD (ANDER)	2	302	906	2.5	8.6
151 L-D SAINTS....	4	NA	1 423	4.0	13.4
165 CH OF NAZARENE	2	87	174	0.5	1.6
167 CHS OF CHRIST.	3	205	261	0.7	2.5
179 CONSRV BAPT...	4	356	441*	1.2	4.2
193 EPISCOPAL.....	2	136	216	0.6	2.0
197 EVAN CH OF NA.	1	82	82	0.2	0.8
221 FREE METHODIST	1	21	111	0.3	1.0
263 INT FOURSQ GOS	2	232	288*	0.8	2.7
281 LUTH CH AMER..	3	541	774	2.2	7.3
283 LUTH--MO SYNOD	2	225	312	0.9	2.9
413 S.D.A.........	3	215	266*	0.7	2.5
419 SO BAPT CONV..	1	103	128*	0.4	1.2
449 UN METHODIST..	3	442	548*	1.5	5.2
453 UN PRES CH USA	2	235	291*	0.8	2.7
COOS	82	8 248	16 674*	26.0	100.0
017 AMER BAPT ASSN	2	101	101	0.2	0.6
019 AMER BAPT USA.	2	335	407*	0.6	2.4
029 AMER LUTH CH..	2	319	453	0.7	2.7
053 ASSEMB OF GOD.	7	490	959	1.5	5.8
081 CATHOLIC......	6	NA	3 455	5.4	20.7
089 CHR & MISS AL.	1	32	92	0.1	0.6
093 CHR CH (DISC).	3	444	700	1.1	4.2
097 CHR CHS&CHS CR	5	610	741*	1.2	4.4
123 CH GOD (ANDER)	4	252	756	1.2	4.5
127 CH GOD (CLEVE)	3	167	203*	0.3	1.2
151 L-D SAINTS....	5	NA	1 547	2.4	9.3
157 CH OF BRETHREN	1	25	30*	–	0.2
165 CH OF NAZARENE	3	444	630	1.0	3.8
167 CHS OF CHRIST.	2	250	350	0.5	2.1
179 CONSRV BAPT...	5	341	414*	0.6	2.5
193 EPISCOPAL.....	5	802	956	1.5	5.7
221 FREE METHODIST	1	19	81	0.1	0.5
263 INT FOURSQ GOS	3	398	484*	0.8	2.9
281 LUTH CH AMER..	1	312	375	0.6	2.2
283 LUTH--MO SYNOD	2	279	370	0.6	2.2
329 OPEN BIBLE STD	2	74	205	0.3	1.2
403 SALVATION ARMY	1	54	327	0.5	2.0
413 S.D.A.........	4	656	797*	1.2	4.8
419 SO BAPT CONV..	3	372	452*	0.7	2.7
449 UN METHODIST..	4	814	989*	1.5	5.9
453 UN PRES CH USA	5	658	800*	1.2	4.8
CROOK	15	1 899	3 766*	28.8	100.0
029 AMER LUTH CH..	1	264	348	2.7	9.2
053 ASSEMB OF GOD.	1	98	223	1.7	5.9
081 CATHOLIC......	1	NA	531	4.1	14.1
097 CHR CHS&CHS CR	1	100	122*	0.9	3.2
123 CH GOD (ANDER)	1	31	93	0.7	2.5
127 CH GOD (CLEVE)	1	38	46*	0.4	1.2
151 L-D SAINTS....	1	NA	509	3.9	13.5
165 CH OF NAZARENE	1	137	343	2.6	9.1
167 CHS OF CHRIST.	1	125	159	1.2	4.2
179 CONSRV BAPT...	1	478	584*	4.5	15.5
193 EPISCOPAL.....	1	226	316	2.4	8.4
263 INT FOURSQ GOS	1	35	43*	0.3	1.1
413 S.D.A.........	1	71	87*	0.7	2.3
419 SO BAPT CONV..	1	224	274*	2.1	7.3
453 UN PRES CH USA	1	72	88*	0.7	2.3
CURRY	26	1 875	4 422*	26.0	100.0
019 AMER BAPT USA.	1	146	173*	1.0	3.9
029 AMER LUTH CH..	3	294	398	2.3	9.0
053 ASSEMB OF GOD.	4	293	521	3.1	11.8
081 CATHOLIC......	2	NA	1 510	8.9	34.1
097 CHR CHS&CHS CR	1	68	81*	0.5	1.8
151 L-D SAINTS....	2	NA	415	2.4	9.4
165 CH OF NAZARENE	1	30	83	0.5	1.9
167 CHS OF CHRIST.	2	95	123	0.7	2.8
179 CONSRV BAPT...	1	139	165*	1.0	3.7
193 EPISCOPAL.....	3	157	179	1.1	4.0
413 S.D.A.........	3	260	308*	1.8	7.0
419 SO BAPT CONV..	1	86	102*	0.6	2.3

County and Denomination	Number of churches	Communicant, confirmed, full members	Total adherents		
			Number	Percent of total population	Percent of total adherents
453 UN PRES CH USA	2	307	364*	2.1	8.2
DESCHUTES	64	8 145	17 029*	27.4	100.0
017 AMER BAPT ASSN	3	325	325	0.5	1.9
029 AMER LUTH CH..	3	757	1 018	1.6	6.0
053 ASSEMB OF GOD.	4	569	940	1.5	5.5
081 CATHOLIC......	3	NA	4 070	6.5	23.9
089 CHR & MISS AL.	1	34	58	0.1	0.3
093 CHR CH (DISC).	1	352	427	0.7	2.5
097 CHR CHS&CHS CR	5	666	815*	1.3	4.8
123 CH GOD (ANDER)	2	77	231	0.4	1.4
127 CH GOD (CLEVE)	1	36	44*	0.1	0.3
133 CH GOD(7TH)DEN	1	31	38*	0.1	0.2
151 L-D SAINTS....	5	NA	1 909	3.1	11.2
165 CH OF NAZARENE	1	219	419	0.7	2.5
167 CHS OF CHRIST.	4	295	375	0.6	2.2
179 CONSRV BAPT...	4	835	1 021*	1.6	6.0
193 EPISCOPAL.....	3	575	777	1.3	4.6
197 EVAN CH OF NA.	1	18	18	–	0.1
203 EVAN FREE CH..	1	27	33*	0.1	0.2
221 FREE METHODIST	2	103	456	0.7	2.7
263 INT FOURSQ GOS	4	305	373*	0.6	2.2
283 LUTH--MO SYNOD	2	412	602	1.0	3.5
335 ORTH PRESB CH.	1	49	60*	0.1	0.4
413 S.D.A.........	2	275	336*	0.5	2.0
419 SO BAPT CONV..	5	858	1 050*	1.7	6.2
435 UNITARIAN-UNIV	1	40	49*	0.1	0.3
449 UN METHODIST..	1	602	736*	1.2	4.3
453 UN PRES CH USA	2	609	745*	1.2	4.4
469 WELS..........	1	76	104	0.2	0.6
DOUGLAS	127	14 728	27 590*	29.4	100.0
017 AMER BAPT ASSN	5	319	319	0.3	1.2
019 AMER BAPT USA.	3	528	650*	0.7	2.4
053 ASSEMB OF GOD.	12	1 304	2 122	2.3	7.7
081 CATHOLIC......	6	NA	4 443	4.7	16.1
089 CHR & MISS AL.	1	27	44	–	0.2
093 CHR CH (DISC).	2	135	208	0.2	0.8
097 CHR CHS&CHS CR	12	1 528	1 882*	2.0	6.8
123 CH GOD (ANDER)	3	219	657	0.7	2.4
127 CH GOD (CLEVE)	3	162	200*	0.2	0.7
151 L-D SAINTS....	7	NA	2 596	2.8	9.4
165 CH OF NAZARENE	3	689	1 551	1.7	5.6
167 CHS OF CHRIST.	8	611	838	0.9	3.0
179 CONSRV BAPT...	5	862	1 062*	1.1	3.8
193 EPISCOPAL.....	5	530	770	0.8	2.8
203 EVAN FREE CH..	2	119	147*	0.2	0.5
209 EVAN LUTH SYN.	2	171	234	0.2	0.8
221 FREE METHODIST	2	91	315	0.3	1.1
263 INT FOURSQ GOS	3	233	287*	0.3	1.0
281 LUTH CH AMER..	1	641	1 009	1.1	3.7
283 LUTH--MO SYNOD	3	626	837	0.9	3.0
285 MENNONITE CH..	1	30	37*	–	0.1
291 MISSIONARY CH.	3	178	264	0.3	1.0
329 OPEN BIBLE STD	2	108	200	0.2	0.7
403 SALVATION ARMY	1	47	57	0.1	0.2
413 S.D.A.........	9	1 337	1 647*	1.8	6.0
419 SO BAPT CONV..	6	1 605	1 977*	2.1	7.2
449 UN METHODIST..	12	1 666	2 052*	2.2	7.4
453 UN PRES CH USA	5	962	1 185*	1.3	4.3
GILLIAM	9	350	713*	34.7	100.0
081 CATHOLIC......	2	NA	216	10.5	30.3
151 L-D SAINTS....	1	NA	43	2.1	6.0
165 CH OF NAZARENE	1	24	61	3.0	8.6
179 CONSRV BAPT...	2	70	84*	4.1	11.8
413 S.D.A.........	1	23	28*	1.4	3.9
443 UN C OF CHRIST	1	157	189*	9.2	26.5
449 UN METHODIST..	1	76	92*	4.5	12.9
GRANT	21	893	2 048*	24.9	100.0
053 ASSEMB OF GOD.	2	153	257	3.1	12.5
081 CATHOLIC......	4	NA	328	4.0	16.0
093 CHR CH (DISC).	1	49	58	0.7	2.8
151 L-D SAINTS....	1	NA	465	5.7	22.7
165 CH OF NAZARENE	1	59	108	1.3	5.3
167 CHS OF CHRIST.	1	27	27	0.3	1.3
179 CONSRV BAPT...	2	59	72*	0.9	3.5
193 EPISCOPAL.....	1	84	117	1.4	5.7
283 LUTH--MO SYNOD	1	142	226	2.8	11.0
413 S.D.A.........	2	101	123*	1.5	6.0
449 UN METHODIST..	2	164	200*	2.4	9.8
453 UN PRES CH USA	3	55	67*	0.8	3.3
HARNEY	14	858	2 595*	31.2	100.0
053 ASSEMB OF GOD.	1	64	105	1.3	4.0
081 CATHOLIC......	2	NA	1 008	12.1	38.8
093 CHR CH (DISC).	1	131	208	2.5	8.0
151 L-D SAINTS....	2	NA	391	4.7	15.1
165 CH OF NAZARENE	1	126	196	2.4	7.6
167 CHS OF CHRIST.	1	40	42	0.5	1.6
179 CONSRV BAPT...	1	155	192*	2.3	7.4
193 EPISCOPAL.....	1	67	98	1.2	3.8
263 INT FOURSQ GOS	1	47	58*	0.7	2.2
283 LUTH--MO SYNOD	1	45	71	0.9	2.7
413 S.D.A.........	1	31	38*	0.5	1.5
453 UN PRES CH USA	1	152	188*	2.3	7.2
HOOD RIVER	31	3 719	6 173*	39.0	100.0

NA—Not applicable   *Total adherents estimated from known number of communicant, confirmed, full members.   —Represents a percent less than 0.1.   Percentages may not total due to rounding.

Table 4. Churches and Church Membership by County and Denomination: 1980

County and Denomination	Number of churches	Communicant, confirmed, full members	Total adherents Number	Percent of total population	Percent of total adherents
017 AMER BAPT ASSN	1	25	25	0.2	0.4
053 ASSEMB OF GOD.	3	303	492	3.1	8.0
081 CATHOLIC......	1	NA	652	4.1	10.6
089 CHR & MISS AL.	1	97	163	1.0	2.6
093 CHR CH (DISC).	1	381	545	3.4	8.8
123 CH GOD (ANDER)	1	33	99	0.6	1.6
151 L-D SAINTS....	1	NA	556	3.5	9.0
165 CH OF NAZARENE	2	207	297	1.9	4.8
167 CHS OF CHRIST.	4	199	247	1.6	4.0
179 CONSRV BAPT...	1	188	229*	1.4	3.7
193 EPISCOPAL.....	1	354	494	3.1	8.0
263 INT FOURSQ GOS	1	?	?	?	?
281 LUTH CH AMER..	1	121	154	1.0	2.5
283 LUTH--MO SYNOD	2	154	202	1.3	3.3
413 S.D.A.........	1	187	228*	1.4	3.7
419 SO BAPT CONV..	3	643	783*	4.9	12.7
443 UN C OF CHRIST	2	361	440*	2.8	7.1
449 UN METHODIST..	3	363	442*	2.8	7.2
453 UN PRES CH USA	1	103	125*	0.8	2.0
JACKSON	**110**	**18 541**	**45 321***	**34.2**	**100.0**
001 ADVENT CHR CH.	1	48	58*	-	0.1
017 AMER BAPT ASSN	1	20	20	-	-
019 AMER BAPT USA.	2	974	1 176*	0.9	2.6
029 AMER LUTH CH..	1	353	504	0.4	1.1
053 ASSEMB OF GOD.	13	1 649	3 353	2.5	7.4
081 CATHOLIC......	6	NA	16 423	12.4	36.2
089 CHR & MISS AL.	3	216	401	0.3	0.9
093 CHR CH (DISC).	1	237	394	0.3	0.9
097 CHR CHS&CHS CR	7	737	890*	0.7	2.0
123 CH GOD (ANDER)	2	105	315	0.2	0.7
127 CH GOD (CLEVE)	1	48	58*	-	0.1
151 L-D SAINTS....	8	NA	3 426	2.6	7.6
165 CH OF NAZARENE	6	796	1 174	0.9	2.6
167 CHS OF CHRIST.	8	518	690	0.5	1.5
179 CONSRV BAPT...	4	2 154	2 601*	2.0	5.7
193 EPISCOPAL.....	4	1 006	1 365	1.0	3.0
217 FIRE BAPTIZED.	1	6	7*	-	-
221 FREE METHODIST	1	80	207	0.2	0.5
226 FRIENDS-USA...	2	460	555*	0.4	1.2
263 INT FOURSQ GOS	2	524	633*	0.5	1.4
271 REFORM JUDAISM	1	90	109*	0.1	0.2
281 LUTH CH AMER..	1	356	505	0.4	1.1
283 LUTH--MO SYNOD	4	798	1 091	0.8	2.4
329 OPEN BIBLE STD	2	844	1 276	1.0	2.8
403 SALVATION ARMY	1	155	402	0.3	0.9
413 S.D.A.........	6	1 574	1 901*	1.4	4.2
419 SO BAPT CONV..	6	1 157	1 397*	1.1	3.1
435 UNITARIAN-UNIV	1	86	104*	0.1	0.2
443 UN C OF CHRIST	2	383	462*	0.3	1.0
449 UN METHODIST..	5	1 201	1 450*	1.1	3.2
453 UN PRES CH USA	7	1 966	2 374*	1.8	5.2
JEFFERSON	**20**	**2 416**	**4 053***	**34.9**	**100.0**
017 AMER BAPT ASSN	1	23	23	0.2	0.6
029 AMER LUTH CH..	1	102	141	1.2	3.5
053 ASSEMB OF GOD.	1	117	140	1.2	3.5
081 CATHOLIC......	2	NA	568	4.9	14.0
093 CHR CH (DISC).	1	138	217	1.9	5.4
097 CHR CHS&CHS CR	1	140	175*	1.5	4.3
151 L-D SAINTS....	1	NA	255	2.2	6.3
165 CH OF NAZARENE	1	19	48	0.4	1.2
167 CHS OF CHRIST.	1	43	55	0.5	1.4
179 CONSRV BAPT...	1	160	200*	1.7	4.9
193 EPISCOPAL.....	1	84	105	0.9	2.6
221 FREE METHODIST	1	95	261	2.3	6.4
226 FRIENDS-USA...	1	102	127*	1.1	3.1
285 MENNONITE CH..	1	42	52*	0.4	1.3
413 S.D.A.........	1	101	126*	1.1	3.1
419 SO BAPT CONV..	2	918	1 146*	9.9	28.3
449 UN METHODIST..	1	315	393*	3.4	9.7
453 UN PRES CH USA	1	17	21*	0.2	0.5
JOSEPHINE	**48**	**7 338**	**15 612***	**26.5**	**100.0**
017 AMER BAPT ASSN	1	93	93	0.2	0.6
019 AMER BAPT USA.	3	1 187	1 438*	2.4	9.2
029 AMER LUTH CH..	1	211	272	0.5	1.7
053 ASSEMB OF GOD.	3	548	1 140	1.9	7.3
075 BRETHREN IN CR	1	76	85	0.1	0.5
081 CATHOLIC......	2	NA	3 892	6.6	24.9
089 CHR & MISS AL.	2	77	138	0.2	0.9
093 CHR CH (DISC).	1	325	345	0.6	2.2
097 CHR CHS&CHS CR	1	72	87*	0.1	0.6
123 CH GOD (ANDER)	1	43	129	0.2	0.8
127 CH GOD (CLEVE)	1	41	50*	0.1	0.3
133 CH GOD(7TH)DEN	1	9	11*	-	0.1
151 L-D SAINTS....	4	NA	1 933	3.3	12.4
157 CH OF BRETHREN	1	147	178*	0.3	1.1
165 CH OF NAZARENE	1	59	174	0.3	1.1
167 CHS OF CHRIST.	4	358	443	0.8	2.8
179 CONSRV BAPT...	2	140	170*	0.3	1.1
193 EPISCOPAL.....	2	386	480	0.8	3.1
221 FREE METHODIST	1	31	204	0.3	1.3
263 INT FOURSQ GOS	2	540	654*	1.1	4.2
283 LUTH--MO SYNOD	2	654	861	1.5	5.5
285 MENNONITE CH..	1	42	51*	0.1	0.3
335 ORTH PRESB CH.	1	43	52*	0.1	0.3
413 S.D.A.........	3	844	1 022*	1.7	6.5
419 SO BAPT CONV..	2	385	466*	0.8	3.0
449 UN METHODIST..	3	605	733*	1.2	4.7
453 UN PRES CH USA	1	422	511*	0.9	3.3
KLAMATH	**68**	**9 074**	**20 981***	**35.5**	**100.0**
017 AMER BAPT ASSN	1	131	131	0.2	0.6
029 AMER LUTH CH..	1	500	717	1.2	3.4
053 ASSEMB OF GOD.	8	519	1 202	2.0	5.7
081 CATHOLIC......	7	NA	5 995	10.1	28.6
089 CHR & MISS AL.	1	37	76	0.1	0.4
097 CHR CHS&CHS CR	4	1 013	1 244*	2.1	5.9
123 CH GOD (ANDER)	1	137	411	0.7	2.0
127 CH GOD (CLEVE)	1	?	?	?	?
151 L-D SAINTS....	6	NA	2 187	3.7	10.4
157 CH OF BRETHREN	1	45	55*	0.1	0.3
165 CH OF NAZARENE	1	110	141	0.2	0.7
167 CHS OF CHRIST.	3	183	314	0.5	1.5
179 CONSRV BAPT...	3	432	531*	0.9	2.5
193 EPISCOPAL.....	2	472	658	1.1	3.1
203 EVAN FREE CH..	1	16	20*	-	0.1
226 FRIENDS-USA...	1	64	79*	0.1	0.4
263 INT FOURSQ GOS	2	565	694*	1.2	3.3
281 LUTH CH AMER..	1	207	341	0.6	1.6
283 LUTH--MO SYNOD	1	341	452	0.8	2.2
329 OPEN BIBLE STD	3	376	750	1.3	3.6
403 SALVATION ARMY	1	36	204	0.3	1.0
413 S.D.A.........	1	340	418*	0.7	2.0
419 SO BAPT CONV..	4	1 910	2 346*	4.0	11.2
435 UNITARIAN-UNIV	1	25	31*	0.1	0.1
443 UN C OF CHRIST	1	55	68*	0.1	0.3
449 UN METHODIST..	6	631	775*	1.3	3.7
453 UN PRES CH USA	5	929	1 141*	1.9	5.4
LAKE	**20**	**886**	**2 374***	**31.5**	**100.0**
017 AMER BAPT ASSN	1	25	25	0.3	1.1
053 ASSEMB OF GOD.	1	76	175	2.3	7.4
081 CATHOLIC......	4	NA	858	11.4	36.1
127 CH GOD (CLEVE)	1	37	46*	0.6	1.9
151 L-D SAINTS....	1	NA	323	4.3	13.6
167 CHS OF CHRIST.	1	45	60	0.8	2.5
179 CONSRV BAPT...	1	83	102*	1.4	4.3
193 EPISCOPAL.....	2	43	54	0.7	2.3
263 INT FOURSQ GOS	1	65	80*	1.1	3.4
283 LUTH--MO SYNOD	1	80	112	1.5	4.7
329 OPEN BIBLE STD	1	35	50	0.7	2.1
413 S.D.A.........	1	50	62*	0.8	2.6
419 SO BAPT CONV..	1	108	133*	1.8	5.6
449 UN METHODIST..	2	83	102*	1.4	4.3
453 UN PRES CH USA	1	156	192*	2.5	8.1
LANE	**252**	**42 304**	**81 143***	**29.5**	**100.0**
017 AMER BAPT ASSN	1	101	101	-	0.1
019 AMER BAPT USA.	4	1 207	1 454*	0.5	1.8
029 AMER LUTH CH..	8	2 971	4 064	1.5	5.0
053 ASSEMB OF GOD.	21	3 567	8 009	2.9	9.9
057 BAPT GEN CONF.	1	44	53*	-	0.1
059 BAPT MISS ASSN	1	45	54*	-	0.1
081 CATHOLIC......	15	NA	14 740	5.4	18.2
089 CHR & MISS AL.	2	101	167	0.1	0.2
093 CHR CH (DISC).	9	1 738	3 265	1.2	4.0
097 CHR CHS&CHS CR	28	4 513	5 436*	2.0	6.7
101 C.M.E.........	1	153	184*	0.1	0.2
123 CH GOD (ANDER)	4	372	1 116	0.4	1.4
127 CH GOD (CLEVE)	5	184	222*	0.1	0.3
151 L-D SAINTS....	17	NA	6 696	2.4	8.3
157 CH OF BRETHREN	1	83	100*	-	0.1
163 CH OF LUTH BR.	1	56	65	-	0.1
165 CH OF NAZARENE	5	1 221	1 790	0.7	2.2
167 CHS OF CHRIST.	15	1 035	1 315	0.5	1.6
179 CONSRV BAPT...	16	3 296	3 970*	1.4	4.9
193 EPISCOPAL.....	7	2 004	2 695	1.0	3.3
197 EVAN CH OF NA.	6	782	782	0.3	1.0
201 EVAN COV CH AM	1	17	20*	-	-
217 FIRE BAPTIZED.	1	5	6*	-	-
220 FREE LUTHERAN.	1	140	170*	0.1	0.2
221 FREE METHODIST	3	264	963	0.3	1.2
226 FRIENDS-USA...	2	364	438*	0.2	0.5
237 GC MENN BR CHS	1	89	107*	-	0.1
263 INT FOURSQ GOS	6	2 249	2 709*	1.0	3.3
270 CONSRV JUDAISM	1	158	190*	0.1	0.2
281 LUTH CH AMER..	3	736	958	0.3	1.2
283 LUTH--MO SYNOD	8	1 977	2 893	1.1	3.6
285 MENNONITE CH..	1	34	41*	-	0.1
290 METRO COMM CHS	1	30	60	-	0.1
329 OPEN BIBLE STD	10	1 028	1 855	0.7	2.3
335 ORTH PRESB CH.	1	42	51*	-	0.1
349 PENT HOLINESS.	2	105	126*	-	0.2
353 CHR BRETHREN..	1	75	130	-	0.2
403 SALVATION ARMY	2	119	415	0.2	0.5
413 S.D.A.........	9	1 976	2 380*	0.9	2.9
419 SO BAPT CONV..	10	2 731	3 289*	1.2	4.1
435 UNITARIAN-UNIV	1	230	277*	0.1	0.3
443 UN C OF CHRIST	1	696	838*	0.3	1.0
449 UN METHODIST..	11	3 815	4 595*	1.7	5.7
453 UN PRES CH USA	6	1 863	2 244*	0.8	2.8
469 WELS..........	1	88	110	-	0.1
LINCOLN	**54**	**4 631**	**8 396***	**23.8**	**100.0**
017 AMER BAPT ASSN	1	50	50	0.1	0.6
019 AMER BAPT USA.	1	41	48*	0.1	0.6
053 ASSEMB OF GOD.	7	449	811	2.3	9.7
081 CATHOLIC......	5	NA	1 783	5.1	21.2
097 CHR CHS&CHS CR	5	500	588*	1.7	7.0
151 L-D SAINTS....	2	NA	588	1.7	7.0
165 CH OF NAZARENE	2	258	501	1.4	6.0

NA—Not applicable   *Total adherents estimated from known number of communicant, confirmed, full members.   —Represents a percent less than 0.1.   Percentages may not total due to rounding.

Table 4. Churches and Church Membership by County and Denomination: 1980

County and Denomination	Number of churches	Communicant, confirmed, full members	Total adherents		
			Number	Percent of total population	Percent of total adherents
167 CHS OF CHRIST.	2	70	89	0.3	1.1
179 CONSRV BAPT...	2	229	270*	0.8	3.2
193 EPISCOPAL....	4	346	426	1.2	5.1
197 EVAN CH OF NA.	1	82	82	0.2	1.0
215 EVAN METH CH..	1	19	22*	0.1	0.3
221 FREE METHODIST	1	17	51	0.1	0.6
263 INT FOURSQ GOS	2	326	384*	1.1	4.6
281 LUTH CH AMER..	1	196	276	0.8	3.3
283 LUTH--MO SYNOD	3	190	241	0.7	2.9
285 MENNONITE CH..	2	132	155*	0.4	1.8
413 S.D.A.........	3	299	352*	1.0	4.2
419 SO BAPT CONV..	3	398	468*	1.3	5.6
443 UN C OF CHRIST	1	204	240*	0.7	2.9
449 UN METHODIST..	1	198	233*	0.7	2.8
453 UN PRES CH USA	4	627	738*	2.1	8.8
LINN	123	17 424	30 625*	34.2	100.0
017 AMER BAPT ASSN	2	63	63	0.1	0.2
029 AMER LUTH CH..	4	938	1 225	1.4	4.0
053 ASSEMB OF GOD.	9	2 311	4 605	5.1	15.0
059 BAPT MISS ASSN	3	90	110*	0.1	0.4
081 CATHOLIC......	7	NA	3 990	4.5	13.0
089 CHR & MISS AL.	1	26	37	–	0.1
093 CHR CH (DISC).	3	727	982	1.1	3.2
097 CHR CHS&CHS CR	11	1 508	1 850*	2.1	6.0
123 CH GOD (ANDER)	3	229	687	0.8	2.2
127 CH GOD (CLEVE)	1	63	77*	0.1	0.3
133 CH GOD(7TH)DEN	1	139	171*	0.2	0.6
143 CG IN CR(MENN)	1	60	60	0.1	0.2
151 L-D SAINTS....	7	NA	2 123	2.4	6.9
165 CH OF NAZARENE	3	432	736	0.8	2.4
167 CHS OF CHRIST.	4	353	458	0.5	1.5
179 CONSRV BAPT...	9	2 113	2 592*	2.9	8.5
193 EPISCOPAL....	3	541	764	0.9	2.5
197 EVAN CH OF NA.	6	859	859	1.0	2.8
221 FREE METHODIST	3	177	771	0.9	2.5
244 GRACE BRETHREN	1	53	65*	0.1	0.2
263 INT FOURSQ GOS	2	21	26*	–	0.1
283 LUTH--MO SYNOD	3	725	956	1.1	3.1
285 MENNONITE CH..	11	1 243	1 525*	1.7	5.0
287 MENN GEN CONF.	1	186	186	0.2	0.6
291 MISSIONARY CH.	1	112	183	0.2	0.6
329 OPEN BIBLE STD	1	35	100	0.1	0.3
349 PENT HOLINESS.	1	12	15*	–	–
403 SALVATION ARMY	1	30	39	–	0.1
413 S.D.A.........	4	602	738*	0.8	2.4
419 SO BAPT CONV..	3	800	981*	1.1	3.2
443 UN C OF CHRIST	1	57	70*	0.1	0.2
449 UN METHODIST..	7	1 789	2 195*	2.5	7.2
453 UN PRES CH USA	5	1 130	1 386*	1.5	4.5
MALHEUR	49	4 476	11 638*	43.3	100.0
017 AMER BAPT ASSN	1	84	84	0.3	0.7
019 AMER BAPT USA.	1	520	647*	2.4	5.6
029 AMER LUTH CH..	2	121	157	0.6	1.3
053 ASSEMB OF GOD.	5	277	435	1.6	3.7
081 CATHOLIC......	7	NA	2 341	8.7	20.1
093 CHR CH (DISC).	1	282	318	1.2	2.7
097 CHR CHS&CHS CR	2	445	554*	2.1	4.8
151 L-D SAINTS....	8	NA	3 272	12.2	28.1
165 CH OF NAZARENE	4	536	929	3.5	8.0
167 CHS OF CHRIST.	1	100	127	0.5	1.1
179 CONSRV BAPT...	3	307	382*	1.4	3.3
193 EPISCOPAL....	3	325	503	1.9	4.3
226 FRIENDS-USA...	1	59	73*	0.3	0.6
281 LUTH CH AMER..	1	117	166	0.6	1.4
283 LUTH--MO SYNOD	1	265	358	1.3	3.1
413 S.D.A.........	1	73	91*	0.3	0.8
419 SO BAPT CONV..	1	36	45*	0.2	0.4
449 UN METHODIST..	4	690	859*	3.2	7.4
453 UN PRES CH USA	2	239	297*	1.1	2.6
MARION	199	37 408	116 361*	56.8	100.0
005 AME ZION......	1	102	119	0.1	0.1
017 AMER BAPT ASSN	1	58	58	–	–
019 AMER BAPT USA.	2	873	1 059*	0.5	0.9
029 AMER LUTH CH..	8	3 070	3 936	1.9	3.4
053 ASSEMB OF GOD.	14	2 924	6 317	3.1	5.4
075 BRETHREN IN CR	1	76	85	–	0.1
081 CATHOLIC......	18	NA	59 310	29.0	51.0
089 CHR & MISS AL.	4	799	1 640	0.8	1.4
093 CHR CH (DISC).	6	1 875	2 725	1.3	2.3
097 CHR CHS&CHS CR	11	1 032	1 252*	0.6	1.1
105 CHRISTIAN REF.	1	142	265	0.1	0.2
123 CH GOD (ANDER)	2	392	1 176	0.6	1.0
127 CH GOD (CLEVE)	9	304	369*	0.2	0.3
133 CH GOD(7TH)DEN	1	91	110*	0.1	0.1
151 L-D SAINTS....	17	NA	5 092	2.5	4.4
163 CH OF LUTH BR.	1	81	103	0.1	0.1
165 CH OF NAZARENE	6	1 688	2 381	1.2	2.0
167 CHS OF CHRIST.	6	488	670	0.3	0.6
175 CONGR CHR CHS.	1	7	8*	–	–
179 CONSRV BAPT...	11	3 469	4 210*	2.1	3.6
193 EPISCOPAL....	5	1 964	2 754	1.3	2.4
197 EVAN CH OF NA.	5	951	951	0.5	0.8
201 EVAN COV CH AM	1	145	176*	0.1	0.2
221 FREE METHODIST	3	242	846	0.4	0.7
226 FRIENDS-USA...	7	721	875*	0.4	0.8
237 GC MENN BR CHS	1	310	376*	0.2	0.3
263 INT FOURSQ GOS	4	837	1 016*	0.5	0.9
281 LUTH CH AMER..	3	1 841	2 501	1.2	2.1
283 LUTH--MO SYNOD	7	1 616	2 118	1.0	1.8

County and Denomination	Number of churches	Communicant, confirmed, full members	Total adherents		
			Number	Percent of total population	Percent of total adherents
285 MENNONITE CH..	3	252	306*	0.1	0.3
287 MENN GEN CONF.	1	226	340	0.2	0.3
290 METRO COMM CHS	1	25	50	–	–
313 N AM BAPT CONF	1	264	320*	0.2	0.3
329 OPEN BIBLE STD	1	70	95	–	0.1
349 PENT HOLINESS.	1	31	38*	–	–
353 CHR BRETHREN..	1	25	25	–	–
403 SALVATION ARMY	1	129	178	0.1	0.2
413 S.D.A.........	6	1 594	1 934*	0.9	1.7
419 SO BAPT CONV..	2	619	751*	0.4	0.6
435 UNITARIAN-UNIV	1	103	125*	0.1	0.1
443 UN C OF CHRIST	4	847	1 028*	0.5	0.9
449 UN METHODIST..	12	4 334	5 259*	2.6	4.5
453 UN PRES CH USA	6	2 687	3 261*	1.6	2.8
469 WELS..........	1	104	153	0.1	0.1
MORROW	18	1 033	2 079*	27.6	100.0
019 AMER BAPT USA.	1	20	25*	0.3	1.2
029 AMER LUTH CH..	2	185	239	3.2	11.5
053 ASSEMB OF GOD.	3	143	275	3.7	13.2
081 CATHOLIC......	2	NA	404	5.4	19.4
097 CHR CHS&CHS CR	2	145	180*	2.4	8.7
123 CH GOD (ANDER)	1	60	180	2.4	8.7
151 L-D SAINTS....	1	NA	117	1.6	5.6
165 CH OF NAZARENE	1	12	69	0.9	3.3
193 EPISCOPAL....	1	124	163	2.2	7.8
413 S.D.A.........	2	118	147*	2.0	7.1
443 UN C OF CHRIST	1	125	155*	2.1	7.5
449 UN METHODIST..	1	101	125*	1.7	6.0
MULTNOMAH	406	100 184	230 461*	41.0	100.0
001 ADVENT CHR CH.	1	80	94*	–	–
005 AME ZION......	2	368	399	0.1	0.2
019 AMER BAPT USA.	15	4 776	5 638*	1.0	2.4
029 AMER LUTH CH..	12	4 876	6 325	1.1	2.7
039 AP CHR CH(NAZ)	1	120	142*	–	0.1
045 APOSTOLIC LUTH	1	300	354*	0.1	0.2
053 ASSEMB OF GOD.	13	2 967	3 974	0.7	1.7
057 BAPT GEN CONF.	3	970	1 145*	0.2	0.5
081 CATHOLIC......	40	NA	91 142	16.2	39.5
089 CHR & MISS AL.	2	258	398	0.1	0.2
093 CHR CH (DISC).	4	1 612	2 928	0.5	1.3
097 CHR CHS&CHS CR	17	4 380	5 171*	0.9	2.2
101 C.M.E.........	1	1 000	1 181*	0.2	0.5
105 CHRISTIAN REF.	1	80	148	–	0.1
123 CH GOD (ANDER)	10	1 318	3 954	0.7	1.7
127 CH GOD (CLEVE)	3	426	503*	0.1	0.2
133 CH GOD(7TH)DEN	1	41	48*	–	–
151 L-D SAINTS....	20	NA	11 477	2.0	5.0
157 CH OF BRETHREN	1	95	112*	–	–
163 CH OF LUTH BR.	1	69	90	–	–
165 CH OF NAZARENE	9	2 018	3 209	0.6	1.4
167 CHS OF CHRIST.	10	1 098	1 397	0.2	0.6
179 CONSRV BAPT...	28	7 543	8 905*	1.6	3.9
181 CONSRV CONGR..	1		93*	–	–
193 EPISCOPAL....	15	5 770	8 083	1.4	3.5
195 ESTONIAN ELC..	1	52	160	–	0.1
197 EVAN CH OF NA.	9	1 540	1 540	0.3	0.7
201 EVAN COV CH AM	5	722	852*	0.2	0.4
203 EVAN FREE CH..	2	190	224*	–	0.1
215 EVAN METH CH..	2	156	184*	–	0.1
221 FREE METHODIST	7	343	1 116	0.2	0.5
226 FRIENDS-USA...	7	1 444	1 705*	0.3	0.7
239 SWEDENBORGIAN.	1	60	71*	–	–
244 GRACE BRETHREN	1	47	55*	–	–
263 INT FOURSQ GOS	4	4 478	5 287*	0.9	2.3
270 CONSRV JUDAISM	1	596	704*	0.1	0.3
271 REFORM JUDAISM	1	1 828	2 158*	0.4	0.9
274 LAT EVAN LUTH.	1	215	252	–	0.1
281 LUTH CH AMER..	12	4 359	5 953	1.1	2.6
283 LUTH--MO SYNOD	12	4 354	5 738	1.0	2.5
285 MENNONITE CH..	1	168	198*	–	0.1
287 MENN GEN CONF.	1	66	88	–	–
290 METRO COMM CHS	1	330	660	0.1	0.3
291 MISSIONARY CH.	2	71	101	–	–
313 N AM BAPT CONF	5	1 112	1 313*	0.2	0.6
329 OPEN BIBLE STD	4	485	680	0.1	0.3
335 ORTH PRESB CH.	1	160	189*	–	0.1
349 PENT HOLINESS.	1	49	58*	–	–
353 CHR BRETHREN..	5	520	800	0.1	0.3
403 SALVATION ARMY	3	355	521	0.1	0.2
413 S.D.A.........	13	5 443	6 426*	1.1	2.8
415 S-D BAPTIST GC	1	10	12*	–	–
419 SO BAPT CONV..	14	5 075	5 991*	1.1	2.6
435 UNITARIAN-UNIV	3	1 004	1 185*	0.2	0.5
443 UN C OF CHRIST	11	2 929	3 458*	0.6	1.5
449 UN METHODIST..	30	8 733	10 310*	1.8	4.5
453 UN PRES CH USA	30	12 659	14 945*	2.7	6.5
469 WELS..........	2	387	617	0.1	0.3
POLK	53	6 140	21 970*	48.6	100.0
029 AMER LUTH CH..	1	260	353	0.8	1.6
053 ASSEMB OF GOD.	3	496	839	1.9	3.8
081 CATHOLIC......	3	NA	12 900	28.5	58.7
089 CHR & MISS AL.	1	138	388	0.9	1.8
093 CHR CH (DISC).	1	320	419	0.9	1.9
097 CHR CHS&CHS CR	3	338	410*	0.9	1.9
123 CH GOD (ANDER)	1	13	39	0.1	0.2
127 CH GOD (CLEVE)	1	47	57*	0.1	0.3
151 L-D SAINTS....	2	NA	566	1.3	2.6
165 CH OF NAZARENE	2	117	227	0.5	1.0
167 CHS OF CHRIST.	2	135	172	0.4	0.8

NA—Not applicable   *Total adherents estimated from known number of communicant, confirmed, full members.   —Represents a percent less than 0.1.   Percentages may not total due to rounding.

Table 4. Churches and Church Membership by County and Denomination: 1980

County and Denomination	Number of churches	Communicant, confirmed, full members	Total adherents Number	Total adherents Percent of total population	Total adherents Percent of total adherents
179 CONSRV BAPT...	3	527	640*	1.4	2.9
193 EPISCOPAL.....	2	182	249	0.6	1.1
197 EVAN CH OF NA.	3	195	195	0.4	0.9
203 EVAN FREE CH..	1	18	22*	—	0.1
211 EVAN MENN BR..	2	574	746	1.7	3.4
221 FREE METHODIST	1	42	291	0.6	1.3
237 GC MENN BR CHS	1	123	149*	0.3	0.7
263 INT FOURSQ GOS	2	16	19*	—	0.1
283 LUTH--MO SYNOD	2	436	643	1.4	2.9
285 MENNONITE CH..	2	62	75*	0.2	0.3
287 MENN GEN CONF.	1	233	303	0.7	1.4
313 N AM BAPT CONF	1	395	480*	1.1	2.2
413 S.D.A.........	2	210	255*	0.6	1.2
419 SO BAPT CONV..	1	206	250*	0.6	1.1
435 UNITARIAN-UNIV	1	15	18*	—	0.1
449 UN METHODIST..	5	683	829*	1.8	3.8
453 UN PRES CH USA	2	359	436*	1.0	2.0
SHERMAN	9	616	878*	40.4	100.0
081 CATHOLIC......	2	NA	107	4.9	12.2
097 CHR CHS&CHS CR	1	30	37*	1.7	4.2
165 CH OF NAZARENE	1	4	22	1.0	2.5
179 CONSRV BAPT...	2	102	125*	5.8	14.2
419 SO BAPT CONV..	1	237	290*	13.4	33.0
449 UN METHODIST..	1	132	161*	7.4	18.3
453 UN PRES CH USA	1	111	136*	6.3	15.5
TILLAMOOK	31	2 992	5 619*	26.5	100.0
053 ASSEMB OF GOD.	3	190	285	1.3	5.1
081 CATHOLIC......	3	NA	1 405	6.6	25.0
097 CHR CHS&CHS CR	2	460	550*	2.6	9.8
151 L-D SAINTS....	1	NA	429	2.0	7.6
165 CH OF NAZARENE	2	308	490	2.3	8.7
167 CHS OF CHRIST.	2	103	131	0.6	2.3
179 CONSRV BAPT...	1	63	75*	0.4	1.3
193 EPISCOPAL.....	1	242	280	1.3	5.0
226 FRIENDS-USA...	1	39	47*	0.2	0.8
263 INT FOURSQ GOS	2	34	41*	0.2	0.7
281 LUTH CH AMER..	1	76	107	0.5	1.9
283 LUTH--MO SYNOD	1	176	225	1.1	4.0
413 S.D.A.........	2	222	265*	1.3	4.7
419 SO BAPT CONV..	2	130	155*	0.7	2.8
443 UN C OF CHRIST	1	250	299*	1.4	5.3
449 UN METHODIST..	4	589	704*	3.3	12.5
453 UN PRES CH USA	2	110	131*	0.6	2.3
UMATILLA	91	11 922	23 356*	39.7	100.0
019 AMER BAPT USA.	5	730	898*	1.5	3.8
029 AMER LUTH CH..	3	956	1 318	2.2	5.6
045 APOSTOLIC LUTH	1	25	31*	0.1	0.1
053 ASSEMB OF GOD.	9	656	1 291	2.2	5.5
081 CATHOLIC......	8	NA	3 611	6.1	15.5
093 CHR CH (DISC).	3	806	1 220	2.1	5.2
097 CHR CHS&CHS CR	3	858	1 056*	1.8	4.5
123 CH GOD (ANDER)	2	107	321	0.5	1.4
127 CH GOD (CLEVE)	3	122	150*	0.3	0.6
151 L-D SAINTS....	7	NA	2 855	4.9	12.2
157 CH OF BRETHREN	1	141	173*	0.3	0.7
165 CH OF NAZARENE	4	260	632	1.1	2.7
167 CHS OF CHRIST.	4	171	218	0.4	0.9
179 CONSRV BAPT...	6	497	612*	1.0	2.6
193 EPISCOPAL.....	3	837	1 380	2.3	5.9
221 FREE METHODIST	1	69	537	0.9	2.3
263 INT FOURSQ GOS	1	45	55*	0.1	0.2
283 LUTH--MO SYNOD	2	225	305	0.5	1.3
403 SALVATION ARMY	1	38	75	0.1	0.3
413 S.D.A.........	7	2 756	3 391*	5.8	14.5
419 SO BAPT CONV..	2	461	567*	1.0	2.4
443 UN C OF CHRIST	2	234	288*	0.5	1.2
449 UN METHODIST..	5	808	994*	1.7	4.3
453 UN PRES CH USA	8	1 120	1 378*	2.3	5.9
UNION	42	3 821	8 753*	36.6	100.0
029 AMER LUTH CH..	1	134	205	0.9	2.3
053 ASSEMB OF GOD.	4	198	320	1.3	3.7
081 CATHOLIC......	4	NA	1 246	5.2	14.2
093 CHR CH (DISC).	1	376	472	2.0	5.4
097 CHR CHS&CHS CR	2	115	141*	0.6	1.6
123 CH GOD (ANDER)	1	65	195	0.8	2.2
127 CH GOD (CLEVE)	1	20	25*	0.1	0.3
151 L-D SAINTS....	5	NA	2 226	9.3	25.4
165 CH OF NAZARENE	3	254	523	2.2	6.0
167 CHS OF CHRIST.	2	71	106	0.4	1.2
179 CONSRV BAPT...	4	701	862*	3.6	9.8
193 EPISCOPAL.....	1	280	389	1.6	4.4
215 EVAN METH CH..	1	25	31*	0.1	0.4
283 LUTH--MO SYNOD	1	102	150	0.6	1.7
329 OPEN BIBLE STD	1	25	80	0.3	0.9
403 SALVATION ARMY	1	48	52	0.2	0.6
413 S.D.A.........	3	309	380*	1.6	4.3
449 UN METHODIST..	5	782	961*	4.0	11.0
453 UN PRES CH USA	1	316	389*	1.6	4.4
WALLOWA	20	1 232	2 399*	33.0	100.0
053 ASSEMB OF GOD.	2	77	217	3.0	9.0
081 CATHOLIC......	2	NA	449	6.2	18.7
097 CHR CHS&CHS CR	3	325	392*	5.4	16.3
151 L-D SAINTS....	2	NA	335	4.6	14.0
165 CH OF NAZARENE	1	33	43	0.6	1.8
167 CHS OF CHRIST.	1	33	42	0.6	1.8
179 CONSRV BAPT...	2	169	204*	2.8	8.5
193 EPISCOPAL.....	1	42	54	0.7	2.3
283 LUTH--MO SYNOD	1	76	88	1.2	3.7
413 S.D.A.........	1	73	88*	1.2	3.7
443 UN C OF CHRIST	1	160	193*	2.7	8.0
449 UN METHODIST..	2	203	245*	3.4	10.2
453 UN PRES CH USA	1	41	49*	0.7	2.0
WASCO	33	3 835	7 650*	35.2	100.0
053 ASSEMB OF GOD.	2	113	245	1.1	3.2
081 CATHOLIC......	4	NA	1 784	8.2	23.3
093 CHR CH (DISC).	2	201	256	1.2	3.3
097 CHR CHS&CHS CR	2	350	427*	2.0	5.6
123 CH GOD (ANDER)	1	35	105	0.5	1.4
151 L-D SAINTS....	2	NA	734	3.4	9.6
165 CH OF NAZARENE	1	52	107	0.5	1.4
167 CHS OF CHRIST.	2	72	89	0.4	1.2
179 CONSRV BAPT...	3	365	445*	2.0	5.8
193 EPISCOPAL.....	1	289	439	2.0	5.7
197 EVAN CH OF NA.	2	154	154	0.7	2.0
263 INT FOURSQ GOS	1	54	66*	0.3	0.9
281 LUTH CH AMER..	1	482	648	3.0	8.5
283 LUTH--MO SYNOD	1	191	270	1.2	3.5
403 SALVATION ARMY	1	81	178	0.8	2.3
413 S.D.A.........	1	150	183*	0.8	2.4
419 SO BAPT CONV..	1	430	524*	2.4	6.8
443 UN C OF CHRIST	1	185	226*	1.0	3.0
449 UN METHODIST..	3	436	532*	2.4	7.0
453 UN PRES CH USA	1	195	238*	1.1	3.1
WASHINGTON	145	28 807	92 778*	37.8	100.0
017 AMER BAPT ASSN	1	25	25	—	—
019 AMER BAPT USA.	2	760	929*	0.4	1.0
029 AMER LUTH CH..	3	1 851	2 482	1.0	2.7
053 ASSEMB OF GOD.	8	1 185	2 004	0.8	2.2
057 BAPT GEN CONF.	1	51	62*	—	0.1
081 CATHOLIC......	13	NA	46 462	18.9	50.1
089 CHR & MISS AL.	1	30	47	—	0.1
093 CHR CH (DISC).	4	841	1 467	0.6	1.6
097 CHR CHS&CHS CR	5	1 582	1 934*	0.8	2.1
105 CHRISTIAN REF.	1	89	170	0.1	0.2
123 CH GOD (ANDER)	2	172	516	0.2	0.6
127 CH GOD (CLEVE)	1	51	62*	—	0.1
151 L-D SAINTS....	15	NA	8 019	3.3	8.6
165 CH OF NAZARENE	2	809	1 431	0.6	1.5
167 CHS OF CHRIST.	7	690	813	0.3	0.9
179 CONSRV BAPT...	9	1 500	1 834*	0.7	2.0
193 EPISCOPAL.....	5	2 392	2 967	1.2	3.2
197 EVAN CH OF NA.	2	263	263	0.1	0.3
221 FREE METHODIST	2	48	273	0.1	0.3
226 FRIENDS-USA...	2	269	329*	0.1	0.4
244 GRACE BRETHREN	1	103	126*	0.1	0.1
263 INT FOURSQ GOS	3	1 087	1 329*	0.5	1.4
281 LUTH CH AMER..	3	1 193	1 694	0.7	1.8
283 LUTH--MO SYNOD	9	3 917	5 329	2.2	5.7
313 N AM BAPT CONF	1	50	61*	—	0.1
329 OPEN BIBLE STD	1	35	50	—	0.1
349 PENT HOLINESS.	1	41	50*	—	0.1
353 CHR BRETHREN..	2	50	75	—	0.1
413 S.D.A.........	7	1 991	2 434*	1.0	2.6
419 SO BAPT CONV..	5	1 122	1 371*	0.6	1.5
443 UN C OF CHRIST	4	1 087	1 329*	0.5	1.4
449 UN METHODIST..	14	3 716	4 542*	1.9	4.9
453 UN PRES CH USA	7	1 683	2 057*	0.8	2.2
469 WELS.........	1	124	242	0.1	0.3
WHEELER	5	145	264*	17.4	100.0
053 ASSEMB OF GOD.	3	66	121	8.0	45.8
081 CATHOLIC......	1	NA	48	3.2	18.2
449 UN METHODIST..	1	79	95*	6.3	36.0
YAMHILL	76	10 967	21 910*	39.6	100.0
019 AMER BAPT USA.	2	931	1 140*	2.1	5.2
029 AMER LUTH CH..	1	267	345	0.6	1.6
053 ASSEMB OF GOD.	7	614	1 245	2.3	5.7
081 CATHOLIC......	5	NA	5 230	9.5	23.9
093 CHR CH (DISC).	1	144	221	0.4	1.0
097 CHR CHS&CHS CR	7	1 402	1 717*	3.1	7.8
123 CH GOD (ANDER)	1	74	222	0.4	1.0
151 L-D SAINTS....	5	NA	1 867	3.4	8.5
165 CH OF NAZARENE	3	487	738	1.3	3.4
167 CHS OF CHRIST.	2	290	333	0.6	1.5
179 CONSRV BAPT...	4	735	900*	1.6	4.1
193 EPISCOPAL.....	2	317	443	0.8	2.0
197 EVAN CH OF NA.	3	270	270	0.5	1.2
201 EVAN COV CH AM	1	50	61*	0.1	0.3
221 FREE METHODIST	3	245	717	1.3	3.3
226 FRIENDS-USA...	3	1 106	1 355*	2.4	6.2
263 INT FOURSQ GOS	1	?	?	?	?
281 LUTH CH AMER..	2	503	656	1.2	3.0
283 LUTH--MO SYNOD	2	336	456	0.8	2.1
285 MENNONITE CH..	3	220	269*	0.5	1.2
291 MISSIONARY CH.	1	0	60	0.1	0.3
329 OPEN BIBLE STD	1	90	130	0.2	0.6
335 ORTH PRESB CH.	1	21	26*	—	0.1
413 S.D.A.........	4	636	779*	1.4	3.6
419 SO BAPT CONV..	2	178	218*	0.4	1.0
449 UN METHODIST..	7	1 450	1 776*	3.2	8.1
453 UN PRES CH USA	2	601	736*	1.3	3.4

NA—Not applicable   *Total adherents estimated from known number of communicant, confirmed, full members.   —Represents a percent less than 0.1.   Percentages may not total due to rounding.

Table 4. Churches and Church Membership by County and Denomination: 1980

County and Denomination	Number of churches	Communicant, confirmed, full members	Total adherents		
			Number	Percent of total population	Percent of total adherents

PENNSYLVANIA

County and Denomination	Number of churches	Communicant, confirmed, full members	Number	Percent of total population	Percent of total adherents
THE STATE.....	12 386	2 604 959	7 231 834*	60.9	100.0
ADAMS	102	20 732	40 431*	59.2	100.0
005 AME ZION......	1	113	209	0.3	0.5
019 AMER BAPT USA.	2	231	279*	0.4	0.7
053 ASSEMB OF GOD.	2	305	597	0.9	1.5
075 BRETHREN IN CR	2	164	264	0.4	0.7
081 CATHOLIC.....	10	NA	13 184	19.3	32.6
123 CH GOD (ANDER)	1	184	552	0.8	1.4
127 CH GOD (CLEVE)	2	97	117*	0.2	0.3
151 L-D SAINTS....	2	NA	568	0.8	1.4
157 CH OF BRETHREN	3	572	692*	1.0	1.7
165 CH OF NAZARENE	1	47	77	0.1	0.2
167 CHS OF CHRIST.	1	24	37	0.1	0.1
179 CONSRV BAPT...	1	15	18*	–	–
193 EPISCOPAL.....	1	188	354	0.5	0.9
226 FRIENDS-USA...	1	27	33*	–	0.1
263 INT FOURSQ GOS	2	409	495*	0.7	1.2
281 LUTH CH AMER..	26	9 775	12 570	18.4	31.1
285 MENNONITE CH..	2	170	206*	0.3	0.5
287 MENN GEN CONF.	1	98	121	0.2	0.3
323 OLD ORD AMISH.	1	130	157*	0.2	0.4
413 S.D.A.........	2	118	143*	0.2	0.4
419 SO BAPT CONV..	1	553	669*	1.0	1.7
443 UN C OF CHRIST	16	3 815	4 616*	6.8	11.4
449 UN METHODIST..	18	2 715	3 285*	4.8	8.1
453 UN PRES CH USA	3	982	1 188*	1.7	2.9
ALLEGHENY	1 054	256 750	1 082 374*	74.6	100.0
005 AME ZION......	12	7 980	8 722	0.6	0.8
019 AMER BAPT USA.	41	10 773	12 609*	0.9	1.2
029 AMER LUTH CH..	33	10 252	13 237	0.9	1.2
053 ASSEMB OF GOD.	17	2 934	4 510	0.3	0.4
057 BAPT GEN CONF.	3	242	283*	–	–
071 BRETHREN (ASH)	1	89	104*	–	–
081 CATHOLIC.....	265	NA	761 066	52.5	70.3
089 CHR & MISS AL.	20	1 907	3 467	0.2	0.3
093 CHR CH (DISC).	6	990	1 401	0.1	0.1
097 CHR CHS&CHS CR	20	4 391	5 139*	0.4	0.5
101 C.M.E........	3	1 500	1 756*	0.1	0.2
123 CH GOD (ANDER)	5	560	1 680	0.1	0.2
127 CH GOD (CLEVE)	5	371	434*	–	–
149 CH OF JC (BIC)	4	147	162	–	–
151 L-D SAINTS....	5	NA	1 946	0.1	0.2
157 CH OF BRETHREN	4	674	789*	0.1	0.1
165 CH OF NAZARENE	11	948	1 779	0.1	0.2
167 CHS OF CHRIST.	8	498	757	0.1	0.1
175 CONGR CHR CHS.	7	1 125	1 317*	0.1	0.1
179 CONSRV BAPT...	5	525	614*	–	0.1
193 EPISCOPAL.....	40	11 747	15 971	1.1	1.5
201 EVAN COV CH AM	1	104	122*	–	–
203 EVAN FREE CH..	1	178	208*	–	–
208 EVAN LUTH ASSN	3	741	955	0.1	0.1
221 FREE METHODIST	5	247	1 248	0.1	0.1
226 FRIENDS-USA...	1	250	293*	–	–
233 GEN CH NEW JER	1	100	117*	–	–
239 SWEDENBORGIAN.	1	60	70*	–	–
244 GRACE BRETHREN	1	68	80*	–	–
270 CONSRV JUDAISM	7	2 514	2 942*	0.2	0.3
271 REFORM JUDAISM	6	6 538	7 652*	0.5	0.7
274 LAT EVAN LUTH.	1	52	53	–	–
281 LUTH CH AMER..	74	23 720	30 762	2.1	2.8
283 LUTH--MO SYNOD	31	7 082	8 888	0.6	0.8
285 MENNONITE CH..	1	23	27*	–	–
290 METRO COMM CHS	1	67	134	–	–
313 N AM BAPT CONF	3	385	451*	–	–
329 OPEN BIBLE STD	2	365	600	–	0.1
335 ORTH PRESB CH.	2	167	195*	–	–
353 CHR BRETHREN..	6	395	610	–	0.1
356 PRESB CH AMER.	3	177	248	–	–
363 PRIMITIVE METH	6	575	673*	–	0.1
381 REF PRES-EVAN.	1	363	459	–	–
383 REF PRES OF NA	4	195	257	–	–
403 SALVATION ARMY	10	847	7 456	0.5	0.7
413 S.D.A.........	4	1 230	1 440*	0.1	0.1
419 SO BAPT CONV..	6	1 454	1 702*	0.1	0.2
435 UNITARIAN-UNIV	5	707	827*	0.1	0.1
443 UN C OF CHRIST	26	4 707	5 509*	0.4	0.5
449 UN METHODIST..	133	59 118	69 192*	4.8	6.4
453 UN PRES CH USA	191	86 568	101 320*	7.0	9.4
469 WELS.........	2	100	141	–	–
ARMSTRONG	160	26 955	58 341*	75.0	100.0
019 AMER BAPT USA.	8	1 911	2 295*	3.0	3.9
053 ASSEMB OF GOD.	4	435	704	0.9	1.2
071 BRETHREN (ASH)	2	270	324*	0.4	0.6
081 CATHOLIC.....	20	NA	21 649	27.8	37.1
089 CHR & MISS AL.	1	18	60	0.1	0.1
101 C.M.E........	2	201	241*	0.3	0.4
123 CH GOD (ANDER)	6	830	2 490	3.2	4.3
127 CH GOD (CLEVE)	2	64	77*	0.1	0.1
151 L-D SAINTS....	1	NA	58	0.1	0.1
157 CH OF BRETHREN	3	562	675*	0.9	1.2
165 CH OF NAZARENE	1	124	262	0.3	0.4
167 CHS OF CHRIST.	1	36	40	0.1	0.1
193 EPISCOPAL.....	5	456	591	0.8	1.0

County and Denomination	Number of churches	Communicant, confirmed, full members	Number	Percent of total population	Percent of total adherents
221 FREE METHODIST	4	277	1 506	1.9	2.6
244 GRACE BRETHREN	2	404	485*	0.6	0.8
281 LUTH CH AMER..	27	7 936	10 515	13.5	18.0
323 OLD ORD AMISH.	1	130	156*	0.2	0.3
353 CHR BRETHREN..	1	25	25	–	–
381 REF PRES-EVAN.	1	67	86	0.1	0.1
403 SALVATION ARMY	2	175	451	0.6	0.8
413 S.D.A.........	2	78	94*	0.1	0.2
443 UN C OF CHRIST	6	868	1 042*	1.3	1.8
449 UN METHODIST..	31	5 116	6 143*	7.9	10.5
453 UN PRES CH USA	27	6 972	8 372*	10.8	14.4
BEAVER	208	42 181	130 975*	64.1	100.0
005 AME ZION......	1	438	544	0.3	0.4
019 AMER BAPT USA.	9	1 668	1 991*	1.0	1.5
029 AMER LUTH CH..	3	974	1 277	0.6	1.0
053 ASSEMB OF GOD.	5	247	601	0.3	0.5
081 CATHOLIC.....	32	NA	75 783	37.1	57.9
089 CHR & MISS AL.	9	828	1 632	0.8	1.2
093 CHR CH (DISC).	1	147	187	0.1	0.1
097 CHR CHS&CHS CR	1	325	388*	0.2	0.3
123 CH GOD (ANDER)	1	88	264	0.1	0.2
127 CH GOD (CLEVE)	2	83	99*	–	0.1
149 CH OF JC (BIC)	1	75	76	–	0.1
151 L-D SAINTS....	1	NA	347	0.2	0.3
165 CH OF NAZARENE	7	498	874	0.4	0.7
167 CHS OF CHRIST.	3	220	375	0.2	0.3
175 CONGR CHR CHS.	1	52	62*	–	–
193 EPISCOPAL.....	5	765	1 167	0.6	0.9
203 EVAN FREE CH..	1	45	54*	–	–
221 FREE METHODIST	6	344	1 704	0.8	1.3
270 CONSRV JUDAISM	2	161	192*	0.1	0.1
271 REFORM JUDAISM	1	44	53*	–	–
281 LUTH CH AMER..	21	6 866	8 954	4.4	6.8
283 LUTH--MO SYNOD	2	401	475	0.2	0.4
363 PRIMITIVE METH	1	110	131*	0.1	0.1
381 REF PRES-EVAN.	4	371	500	0.2	0.4
383 REF PRES OF NA	5	532	699	0.3	0.5
403 SALVATION ARMY	3	252	738	0.4	0.6
413 S.D.A.........	1	54	64*	–	–
419 SO BAPT CONV..	3	284	339*	0.2	0.3
449 UN METHODIST..	33	11 868	14 167*	6.9	10.8
453 UN PRES CH USA	43	14 441	17 238*	8.4	13.2
BEDFORD	142	18 181	25 374*	54.2	100.0
005 AME ZION......	1	137	153	0.3	0.6
053 ASSEMB OF GOD.	8	513	1 138	2.4	4.5
071 BRETHREN (ASH)	1	32	39*	0.1	0.2
075 BRETHREN IN CR	6	492	792	1.7	3.1
081 CATHOLIC.....	3	NA	2 041	4.4	8.0
089 CHR & MISS AL.	1	29	91	0.2	0.4
127 CH GOD (CLEVE)	3	629	767*	1.6	3.0
151 L-D SAINTS....	1	NA	83	0.2	0.3
157 CH OF BRETHREN	18	3 830	4 673*	10.0	18.4
165 CH OF NAZARENE	2	155	362	0.8	1.4
179 CONSRV BAPT...	1	15	18*	–	0.1
193 EPISCOPAL.....	1	119	147	0.3	0.6
226 FRIENDS-USA...	2	67	82*	0.2	0.3
244 GRACE BRETHREN	2	284	347*	0.7	1.4
281 LUTH CH AMER..	19	3 000	3 805	8.1	15.0
285 MENNONITE CH..	2	48	59*	0.1	0.2
287 MENN GEN CONF.	1	140	174	0.4	0.7
413 S.D.A.........	2	106	129*	0.3	0.5
415 S-D BAPTIST GC	1	52	63*	0.1	0.2
419 SO BAPT CONV..	1	187	228*	0.5	0.9
443 UN C OF CHRIST	25	3 007	3 669*	7.8	14.5
449 UN METHODIST..	39	4 863	5 933*	12.7	23.4
453 UN PRES CH USA	2	476	581*	1.2	2.3
BERKS	317	107 181	190 031*	60.8	100.0
019 AMER BAPT USA.	2	594	704*	0.2	0.4
053 ASSEMB OF GOD.	9	742	1 524	0.5	0.8
081 CATHOLIC.....	21	NA	53 107	17.0	27.9
089 CHR & MISS AL.	1	38	49	–	–
097 CHR CHS&CHS CR	2	97	115*	–	0.1
123 CH GOD (ANDER)	3	225	675	0.2	0.4
127 CH GOD (CLEVE)	4	350	415*	0.1	0.2
143 CG IN CR(MENN)	1	37	37	–	–
151 L-D SAINTS....	1	NA	565	0.2	0.3
157 CH OF BRETHREN	3	1 141	1 352*	0.4	0.7
165 CH OF NAZARENE	4	509	1 103	0.4	0.6
167 CHS OF CHRIST.	1	135	172	0.1	0.1
179 CONSRV BAPT...	2	400	474*	0.2	0.2
193 EPISCOPAL.....	7	2 282	2 949	0.9	1.6
199 EVAN CONGR CH.	21	3 734	4 424*	1.4	2.3
203 EVAN FREE CH..	2	136	161*	0.1	0.1
226 FRIENDS-USA...	2	119	141*	–	0.1
233 GEN CH NEW JER	1	35	41*	–	–
270 CONSRV JUDAISM	2	313	371*	0.1	0.2
271 REFORM JUDAISM	1	620	735*	0.2	0.4
281 LUTH CH AMER..	85	47 365	62 789	20.1	33.0
285 MENNONITE CH..	20	1 407	1 667*	0.5	0.9
287 MENN GEN CONF.	1	177	226	0.1	–
291 MISSIONARY CH.	1	43	85	–	–
293 MORAV CH-NORTH	1	230	325	0.1	0.2
353 CHR BRETHREN..	3	160	195	0.1	0.1
403 SALVATION ARMY	1	153	964	0.3	0.5
413 S.D.A.........	8	1 274	1 509*	0.5	0.8
419 SO BAPT CONV..	1	74	88*	–	–
435 UNITARIAN-UNIV	1	90	107*	–	0.1
443 UN C OF CHRIST	78	36 359	43 079*	13.8	22.7
449 UN METHODIST..	24	7 333	8 688*	2.8	4.6

NA—Not applicable   *Total adherents estimated from known number of communicant, confirmed, full members.   —Represents a percent less than 0.1.   Percentages may not total due to rounding.

236

Table 4. Churches and Church Membership by County and Denomination: 1980

County and Denomination	Number of churches	Communicant, confirmed, full members	Total adherents		
			Number	Percent of total population	Percent of total adherents
453 UN PRES CH USA	4	1 009	1 195*	0.4	0.6
BLAIR	190	38 075	81 881*	59.9	100.0
005 AME ZION......	1	165	266	0.2	0.3
019 AMER BAPT USA.	2	423	509*	0.4	0.6
053 ASSEMB OF GOD.	5	639	1 116	0.8	1.4
075 BRETHREN IN CR	4	328	528	0.4	0.6
081 CATHOLIC......	23	NA	33 320	24.4	40.7
089 CHR & MISS AL.	6	343	683	0.5	0.8
097 CHR CHS&CHS CR	1	500	602*	0.4	0.7
127 CH GOD (CLEVE)	3	448	540*	0.4	0.7
151 L-D SAINTS....	1	NA	336	0.2	0.4
157 CH OF BRETHREN	19	4 509	5 430*	4.0	6.6
167 CHS OF CHRIST.	1	72	93	0.1	0.1
179 CONSRV BAPT...	3	300	361*	0.3	0.4
193 EPISCOPAL.....	3	822	1 082	0.8	1.3
221 FREE METHODIST	1	29	195	0.1	0.2
244 GRACE BRETHREN	5	790	951*	0.7	1.2
270 CONSRV JUDAISM	1	200	241*	0.2	0.3
271 REFORM JUDAISM	1	234	282*	0.2	0.3
281 LUTH CH AMER..	26	9 613	12 524	9.2	15.3
285 MENNONITE CH..	3	145	175*	0.1	0.2
287 MENN GEN CONF.	2	77	98	0.1	0.1
291 MISSIONARY CH.	2	185	213	0.2	0.3
335 ORTH PRESB CH.	1	32	39*	-	-
353 CHR BRETHREN..	1	45	85	0.1	0.1
403 SALVATION ARMY	2	198	564	0.4	0.7
413 S.D.A.........	1	49	59*	-	0.1
419 SO BAPT CONV..	1	178	214*	0.2	0.3
443 UN C OF CHRIST	11	1 742	2 098*	1.5	2.6
449 UN METHODIST..	48	13 306	16 025*	11.7	19.6
453 UN PRES CH USA	11	2 678	3 225*	2.4	3.9
469 WELS..........	1	25	27	-	-
BRADFORD	117	15 197	28 507*	45.3	100.0
019 AMER BAPT USA.	12	1 827	2 245*	3.6	7.9
053 ASSEMB OF GOD.	1	75	125	0.2	0.4
081 CATHOLIC......	12	NA	8 743	13.9	30.7
089 CHR & MISS AL.	1	18	28	-	0.1
093 CHR CH (DISC).	5	725	1 194	1.9	4.2
097 CHR CHS&CHS CR	7	592	727*	1.2	2.6
123 CH GOD (ANDER)	1	110	330	0.5	1.2
151 L-D SAINTS....	1	NA	255	0.4	0.9
175 CONGR CHR CHS.	2	426	523*	0.8	1.8
179 CONSRV BAPT...	1	35	43*	0.1	0.2
193 EPISCOPAL.....	4	980	1 303	2.1	4.6
281 LUTH CH AMER..	2	760	1 069	1.7	3.7
285 MENNONITE CH..	1	24	29*	-	0.1
323 OLD ORD AMISH.	1	130	160*	0.3	0.6
403 SALVATION ARMY	1	55	136	0.2	0.5
413 S.D.A.........	2	108	133*	0.2	0.5
435 UNITARIAN-UNIV	3	78	96*	0.2	0.3
443 UN C OF CHRIST	5	334	410*	0.7	1.4
449 UN METHODIST..	43	6 674	8 199*	13.0	28.8
453 UN PRES CH USA	12	2 246	2 759*	4.4	9.7
BUCKS	274	73 141	271 613*	56.7	100.0
005 AME ZION......	1	170	179	-	0.1
019 AMER BAPT USA.	5	1 017	1 239*	0.3	0.5
053 ASSEMB OF GOD.	6	358	572	0.1	0.2
071 BRETHREN (ASH)	1	96	117*	-	-
075 BRETHREN IN CR	1	109	131	-	-
081 CATHOLIC......	39	NA	175 129	36.5	64.5
089 CHR & MISS AL.	3	123	236	-	0.1
093 CHR CH (DISC).	1	94	122	-	-
097 CHR CHS&CHS CR	2	113	138*	-	0.1
127 CH GOD (CLEVE)	3	143	174*	-	0.1
151 L-D SAINTS....	1	NA	408	0.1	0.2
157 CH OF BRETHREN	2	249	303*	0.1	0.1
165 CH OF NAZARENE	3	158	304	0.1	0.1
167 CHS OF CHRIST.	2	285	363	0.1	0.1
179 CONSRV BAPT...	6	1 115	1 358*	0.3	0.5
193 EPISCOPAL.....	18	5 513	7 823	1.6	2.9
208 EVAN FREE ASSN	1	214	282	0.1	0.1
226 FRIENDS-USA...	12	1 500	1 827*	0.4	0.7
270 CONSRV JUDAISM	3	524	638*	0.1	0.2
271 REFORM JUDAISM	2	810	987*	0.2	0.4
274 LAT EVAN LUTH.	1	227	236	-	0.1
281 LUTH CH AMER..	38	21 182	28 535	6.0	10.5
283 LUTH--MO SYNOD	3	1 098	1 817	0.4	0.7
285 MENNONITE CH..	15	2 297	2 798*	0.6	1.0
287 MENN GEN CONF.	8	1 477	2 108	0.4	0.8
293 MORAV CH-NORTH	1	76	91	-	-
313 N AM BAPT CONF	1	41	50*	-	-
335 ORTH PRESB CH.	1	118	144*	-	0.1
353 CHR BRETHREN..	4	385	570	0.1	0.2
363 PRIMITIVE METH	2	147	179*	-	0.1
371 REF CH IN AM..	6	2 113	3 751	0.8	1.4
375 REF EPISCOPAL.	2	140	171*	-	0.1
381 REF PRES-EVAN.	2	186	230	-	0.1
403 SALVATION ARMY	1	114	906	0.2	0.3
413 S.D.A.........	2	193	235*	-	0.1
419 SO BAPT CONV..	2	244	297*	0.1	0.1
435 UNITARIAN-UNIV	2	156	190*	-	0.1
443 UN C OF CHRIST	21	7 439	9 061*	1.9	3.3
449 UN METHODIST..	32	11 951	14 557*	3.0	5.4
453 UN PRES CH USA	19	10 966	13 357*	2.8	4.9
BUTLER	181	37 686	95 663*	64.7	100.0
019 AMER BAPT USA.	1	258	313*	0.2	0.3
029 AMER LUTH CH..	7	3 107	4 200	2.8	4.4

County and Denomination	Number of churches	Communicant, confirmed, full members	Total adherents		
			Number	Percent of total population	Percent of total adherents
053 ASSEMB OF GOD.	3	165	242	0.2	0.3
071 BRETHREN (ASH)	1	19	23*	-	-
081 CATHOLIC......	30	NA	45 474	30.7	47.5
089 CHR & MISS AL.	7	560	1 642	1.1	1.7
093 CHR CH (DISC).	1	80	128	0.1	0.1
097 CHR CHS&CHS CR	3	765	928*	0.6	1.0
123 CH GOD (ANDER)	1	654	1 962	1.3	2.1
151 L-D SAINTS....	2	NA	492	0.3	0.5
165 CH OF NAZARENE	4	230	409	0.3	0.4
167 CHS OF CHRIST.	2	98	142	0.1	0.1
193 EPISCOPAL.....	1	369	529	0.4	0.6
221 FREE METHODIST	4	107	591	0.4	0.6
270 CONSRV JUDAISM	1	78	95*	0.1	0.1
281 LUTH CH AMER..	16	5 449	7 158	4.8	7.5
283 LUTH--MO SYNOD	1	608	862	0.6	0.9
335 ORTH PRESB CH.	1	145	176*	0.1	0.2
353 CHR BRETHREN..	1	5	10	-	-
356 PRESB CH AMER.	2	653	794	0.5	0.8
381 REF PRES-EVAN.	1	52	79	0.1	0.1
383 REF PRES OF NA	1	27	27	-	-
403 SALVATION ARMY	1	167	155	0.1	0.2
413 S.D.A.........	1	55	67*	-	0.1
419 SO BAPT CONV..	1	263	319*	0.2	0.3
443 UN C OF CHRIST	7	2 477	3 006*	2.0	3.1
449 UN METHODIST..	31	8 170	9 914*	6.7	10.4
453 UN PRES CH USA	49	13 125	15 926*	10.8	16.6
CAMBRIA	258	40 225	155 130*	84.6	100.0
019 AMER BAPT USA.	5	882	1 060*	0.6	0.7
053 ASSEMB OF GOD.	5	441	757	0.4	0.5
071 BRETHREN (ASH)	5	584	702*	0.4	0.5
075 BRETHREN IN CR	1	82	132	0.1	0.1
081 CATHOLIC......	88	NA	103 998	56.7	67.0
089 CHR & MISS AL.	9	436	1 018	0.6	0.7
093 CHR CH (DISC).	3	514	654	0.4	0.4
123 CH GOD (ANDER)	3	142	426	0.2	0.3
127 CH GOD (CLEVE)	1	136	163*	0.1	0.1
151 L-D SAINTS....	2	NA	316	0.2	0.2
157 CH OF BRETHREN	11	3 337	4 010*	2.2	2.6
165 CH OF NAZARENE	5	320	542	0.3	0.3
167 CHS OF CHRIST.	1	50	64	-	-
193 EPISCOPAL.....	3	571	755	0.4	0.5
199 EVAN CONGR CH.	1	89	107*	0.1	0.1
244 GRACE BRETHREN	6	1 275	1 532*	0.8	1.0
271 REFORM JUDAISM	1	200	240*	0.1	0.2
281 LUTH CH AMER..	18	7 836	10 613	5.8	6.8
283 LUTH--MO SYNOD	1	130	138	0.1	0.1
285 MENNONITE CH..	2	103	124*	0.1	0.1
356 PRESB CH AMER.	1	76	108	0.1	0.1
403 SALVATION ARMY	1	90	116	0.1	0.1
413 S.D.A.........	1	73	88*	-	0.1
419 SO BAPT CONV..	1	170	204*	0.1	0.1
443 UN C OF CHRIST	10	1 886	2 266*	1.2	1.5
449 UN METHODIST..	61	17 273	20 756*	11.3	13.4
453 UN PRES CH USA	12	3 529	4 241*	2.3	2.7
CAMERON	13	1 615	3 709*	55.6	100.0
019 AMER BAPT USA.	1	313	375*	5.6	10.1
081 CATHOLIC......	2	NA	1 630	24.4	43.9
089 CHR & MISS AL.	2	67	162	2.4	4.4
193 EPISCOPAL.....	1	85	103	1.5	2.8
221 FREE METHODIST	1	23	87	1.3	2.3
281 LUTH CH AMER..	1	94	114	1.7	3.1
449 UN METHODIST..	4	784	940*	14.1	25.3
453 UN PRES CH USA	1	249	298*	4.5	8.0
CARBON	102	19 190	43 541*	81.7	100.0
019 AMER BAPT USA.	2	143	170*	0.3	0.4
081 CATHOLIC......	21	NA	19 145	35.9	44.0
123 CH GOD (ANDER)	1	20	60	0.1	0.1
151 L-D SAINTS....	1	NA	63	0.1	0.1
157 CH OF BRETHREN	1	60	71*	0.1	0.2
165 CH OF NAZARENE	1	38	62	0.1	0.1
167 CHS OF CHRIST.	1	75	94	0.2	0.2
193 EPISCOPAL.....	5	1 136	1 743	3.3	4.0
199 EVAN CONGR CH.	5	931	1 104*	2.1	2.5
203 EVAN FREE CH..	1	28	33*	0.1	0.1
281 LUTH CH AMER..	25	8 977	11 764	22.1	27.0
443 UN C OF CHRIST	21	5 673	6 730*	12.6	15.5
449 UN METHODIST..	14	1 494	1 772*	3.3	4.1
453 UN PRES CH USA	3	615	730*	1.4	1.7
CENTRE	160	30 411	53 007*	47.0	100.0
019 AMER BAPT USA.	4	975	1 131*	1.0	2.1
053 ASSEMB OF GOD.	3	326	665	0.6	1.3
057 BAPT GEN CONF.	1	159	184*	0.2	0.3
075 BRETHREN IN CR	3	246	396	0.4	0.7
081 CATHOLIC......	6	NA	14 818	13.1	28.0
089 CHR & MISS AL.	5	307	709	0.6	1.3
097 CHR CHS&CHS CR	3	781	906*	0.8	1.7
127 CH GOD (CLEVE)	3	234	271*	0.2	0.5
151 L-D SAINTS....	3	NA	478	0.4	0.9
157 CH OF BRETHREN	1	425	493*	0.4	0.9
165 CH OF NAZARENE	1	105	268	0.2	0.5
167 CHS OF CHRIST.	5	222	290	0.3	0.5
179 CONSRV BAPT...	1	150	174*	0.2	0.3
193 EPISCOPAL.....	5	2 377	3 018	2.7	5.7
203 EVAN FREE CH..	1	65	75*	0.1	0.1
221 FREE METHODIST	3	70	390	0.3	0.7
226 FRIENDS-USA...	1	169	196*	0.2	0.4
263 INT FOURSQ GOS	1	35	41*	-	0.1

NA—Not applicable   *Total adherents estimated from known number of communicant, confirmed, full members.   —Represents a percent less than 0.1.   Percentages may not total due to rounding.

237

Table 4. Churches and Church Membership by County and Denomination: 1980

County and Denomination	Number of churches	Communicant, confirmed, full members	Total adherents Number	Percent of total population	Percent of total adherents
281 LUTH CH AMER..	19	5 164	6 921	6.1	13.1
285 MENNONITE CH..	2	70	81*	0.1	0.2
290 METRO COMM CHS	1	15	30	–	0.1
323 OLD ORD AMISH.	5	650	754*	0.7	1.4
413 S.D.A.........	1	25	29*	–	0.1
419 SO BAPT CONV..	1	158	183*	0.2	0.3
435 UNITARIAN-UNIV	1	190	220*	0.2	0.4
443 UN C OF CHRIST	17	3 052	3 539*	3.1	6.7
449 UN METHODIST..	54	11 628	13 485*	12.0	25.4
453 UN PRES CH USA	9	2 813	3 262*	2.9	6.2
CHESTER	249	62 720	154 918*	48.9	100.0
005 AME ZION......	2	372	609	0.2	0.4
019 AMER BAPT USA.	20	6 459	7 806*	2.5	5.0
053 ASSEMB OF GOD.	6	630	1 271	0.4	0.8
081 CATHOLIC......	28	NA	75 528	23.9	48.8
089 CHR & MISS AL.	1	20	28	–	–
127 CH GOD (CLEVE)	2	224	271*	0.1	0.2
151 L-D SAINTS....	2	NA	600	0.2	0.4
157 CH OF BRETHREN	5	837	1 012*	0.3	0.7
165 CH OF NAZARENE	4	708	1 190	0.4	0.8
167 CHS OF CHRIST.	7	420	535	0.2	0.3
193 EPISCOPAL.....	15	6 891	8 539	2.7	5.5
203 EVAN FREE CH..	1	28	34*	–	–
226 FRIENDS-USA...	14	1 846	2 231*	0.7	1.4
263 INT FOURSQ GOS	1	98	118*	–	0.1
270 CONSRV JUDAISM	2	213	257*	0.1	0.2
281 LUTH CH AMER..	14	7 246	10 065	3.2	6.5
283 LUTH--MO SYNOD	1	277	399	0.1	0.3
285 MENNONITE CH..	18	1 209	1 461*	0.5	0.9
335 ORTH PRESB CH.	1	171	207*	0.1	0.1
349 PENT HOLINESS.	1	36	44*	–	–
353 CHR BRETHREN..	1	120	160	0.1	0.1
356 PRESB CH AMER.	2	137	190	0.1	0.1
363 PRIMITIVE METH	1	172	208*	0.1	0.1
381 REF PRES-EVAN.	1	96	110	–	0.1
403 SALVATION ARMY	1	59	410	0.1	0.3
413 S.D.A.........	2	179	216*	0.1	0.1
419 SO BAPT CONV..	2	381	460*	0.1	0.3
435 UNITARIAN-UNIV	2	497	601*	0.2	0.4
443 UN C OF CHRIST	12	2 688	3 249*	1.0	2.1
449 UN METHODIST..	43	14 545	17 578*	5.6	11.3
453 UN PRES CH USA	37	16 161	19 531*	6.2	12.6
CLARION	99	11 687	22 339*	51.5	100.0
019 AMER BAPT USA.	3	556	669*	1.5	3.0
029 AMER LUTH CH..	1	249	306	0.7	1.4
053 ASSEMB OF GOD.	2	159	280	0.6	1.3
081 CATHOLIC......	9	NA	6 769	15.6	30.3
089 CHR & MISS AL.	2	78	142	0.3	0.6
123 CH GOD (ANDER)	5	429	1 287	3.0	5.8
127 CH GOD (CLEVE)	1	48	58*	0.1	0.3
165 CH OF NAZARENE	5	297	590	1.4	2.6
179 CONSRV BAPT...	1	35	42*	0.1	0.2
193 EPISCOPAL.....	1	73	98	0.2	0.4
199 EVAN CONGR CH.	3	378	455*	1.0	2.0
221 FREE METHODIST	3	43	255	0.6	1.1
281 LUTH CH AMER..	7	1 115	1 478	3.4	6.6
323 OLD ORD AMISH.	1	130	156*	0.4	0.7
383 REF PRES OF NA	1	65	90	0.2	0.4
443 UN C OF CHRIST	6	708	852*	2.0	3.8
449 UN METHODIST..	34	4 865	5 853*	13.5	26.2
453 UN PRES CH USA	14	2 459	2 959*	6.8	13.2
CLEARFIELD	191	21 272	47 544*	56.9	100.0
019 AMER BAPT USA.	1	200	244*	0.3	0.5
053 ASSEMB OF GOD.	5	624	1 263	1.5	2.7
057 BAPT GEN CONF.	1	62	76*	0.1	0.2
081 CATHOLIC......	20	NA	18 713	22.4	39.4
089 CHR & MISS AL.	13	1 015	2 082	2.5	4.4
123 CH GOD (ANDER)	1	122	366	0.4	0.8
127 CH GOD (CLEVE)	1	18	22*	–	–
151 L-D SAINTS....	2	NA	77	0.1	0.2
157 CH OF BRETHREN	3	138	168*	0.2	0.4
165 CH OF NAZARENE	3	216	362	0.4	0.8
167 CHS OF CHRIST.	8	305	388	0.5	0.8
179 CONSRV BAPT...	1	80	98*	0.1	0.2
193 EPISCOPAL.....	5	447	675	0.8	1.4
197 EVAN CH OF NA.	2	206	206	0.2	0.4
201 EVAN COV CH AM	1	71	87*	0.1	0.2
203 EVAN FREE CH..	1	122	149*	0.2	0.3
221 FREE METHODIST	7	117	807	1.0	1.7
226 FRIENDS-USA...	1	93	113*	0.1	0.2
281 LUTH CH AMER..	12	3 303	4 184	5.0	8.8
283 LUTH--MO SYNOD	2	224	290	0.3	0.6
313 N AM BAPT CONF	1	105	128*	0.2	0.3
323 OLD ORD AMISH.	1	130	159*	0.2	0.3
363 PRIMITIVE METH	1	87	106*	0.1	0.2
403 SALVATION ARMY	2	151	389	0.5	0.8
413 S.D.A.........	1	23	28*	–	0.1
443 UN C OF CHRIST	5	473	577*	0.7	1.2
449 UN METHODIST..	76	10 693	13 046*	15.6	27.4
453 UN PRES CH USA	14	2 247	2 741*	3.3	5.8
CLINTON	76	11 895	19 936*	51.2	100.0
053 ASSEMB OF GOD.	2	74	189	0.5	0.9
075 BRETHREN IN CR	1	82	132	0.3	0.7
081 CATHOLIC......	3	NA	4 560	11.7	22.9
089 CHR & MISS AL.	4	62	123	0.3	0.6
097 CHR CHS&CHS CR	5	2 636	3 158*	8.1	15.8
151 L-D SAINTS....	1	NA	56	0.1	0.3
157 CH OF BRETHREN	1	89	107*	0.3	0.5
165 CH OF NAZARENE	1	21	26	0.1	0.1
167 CHS OF CHRIST.	4	140	205	0.5	1.0
193 EPISCOPAL.....	2	289	399	1.0	2.0
221 FREE METHODIST	2	63	339	0.9	1.7
271 REFORM JUDAISM	1	86	103*	0.3	0.5
281 LUTH CH AMER..	8	1 127	1 562	4.0	7.8
323 OLD ORD AMISH.	1	130	156*	0.4	0.8
403 SALVATION ARMY	1	167	519	1.3	2.6
413 S.D.A.........	1	29	35*	0.1	0.2
443 UN C OF CHRIST	4	778	932*	2.4	4.7
449 UN METHODIST..	31	5 449	6 529*	16.8	32.7
453 UN PRES CH USA	3	673	806*	2.1	4.0
COLUMBIA	115	22 218	40 227*	64.9	100.0
019 AMER BAPT USA.	2	597	708*	1.1	1.8
053 ASSEMB OF GOD.	4	554	1 024	1.7	2.5
081 CATHOLIC......	9	NA	12 460	20.1	31.0
093 CHR CH (DISC).	3	411	607	1.0	1.5
097 CHR CHS&CHS CR	6	1 767	2 095*	3.4	5.2
151 L-D SAINTS....	1	NA	194	0.3	0.5
165 CH OF NAZARENE	1	126	286	0.5	0.7
179 CONSRV BAPT...	1	65	77*	0.1	0.2
193 EPISCOPAL.....	3	520	732	1.2	1.8
281 LUTH CH AMER..	16	5 774	7 169	11.6	17.8
403 SALVATION ARMY	1	100	288	0.5	0.7
413 S.D.A.........	1	73	87*	0.1	0.2
435 UNITARIAN-UNIV	1	17	20*	–	–
443 UN C OF CHRIST	12	2 243	2 659*	4.3	6.6
449 UN METHODIST..	49	8 936	10 594*	17.1	26.3
453 UN PRES CH USA	5	1 035	1 227*	2.0	3.1
CRAWFORD	158	20 953	41 756*	47.0	100.0
019 AMER BAPT USA.	9	1 816	2 211*	2.5	5.3
053 ASSEMB OF GOD.	2	158	316	0.4	0.8
057 BAPT GEN CONF.	1	69	84*	0.1	0.2
081 CATHOLIC......	14	NA	13 212	14.9	31.6
089 CHR & MISS AL.	7	433	1 267	1.4	3.0
097 CHR CHS&CHS CR	3	925	1 126*	1.3	2.7
123 CH GOD (ANDER)	4	264	792	0.9	1.9
151 L-D SAINTS....	2	NA	245	0.3	0.6
165 CH OF NAZARENE	4	218	561	0.6	1.3
167 CHS OF CHRIST.	1	35	48	0.1	0.1
175 CONGR CHR CHS.	1	106	129*	0.1	0.3
193 EPISCOPAL.....	2	521	696	0.8	1.7
221 FREE METHODIST	5	165	921	1.0	2.2
226 FRIENDS-USA...	1	9	11*	–	–
281 LUTH CH AMER..	6	1 305	1 793	2.0	4.3
285 MENNONITE CH..	5	383	466*	0.5	1.1
323 OLD ORD AMISH.	10	1 300	1 583*	1.8	3.8
329 OPEN BIBLE STD	1	50	100	0.1	0.2
403 SALVATION ARMY	2	146	308	0.3	0.7
413 S.D.A.........	1	15	18*	–	–
435 UNITARIAN-UNIV	2	205	250*	0.3	0.6
443 UN C OF CHRIST	9	1 556	1 894*	2.1	4.5
449 UN METHODIST..	51	7 503	9 134*	10.3	21.9
453 UN PRES CH USA	14	3 771	4 591*	5.2	11.0
CUMBERLAND	181	56 113	91 671*	51.5	100.0
005 AME ZION......	3	447	765	0.4	0.8
019 AMER BAPT USA.	1	499	593*	0.3	0.6
053 ASSEMB OF GOD.	6	1 115	2 532	1.4	2.8
075 BRETHREN IN CR	9	738	1 188	0.7	1.3
081 CATHOLIC......	7	NA	19 161	10.8	20.9
089 CHR & MISS AL.	5	533	977	0.5	1.1
093 CHR CH (DISC).	1	288	453	0.3	0.5
123 CH GOD (ANDER)	1	67	201	0.1	0.2
127 CH GOD (CLEVE)	4	250	297*	0.2	0.3
151 L-D SAINTS....	2	NA	764	0.4	0.8
157 CH OF BRETHREN	7	1 486	1 765*	1.0	1.9
165 CH OF NAZARENE	3	324	551	0.3	0.6
167 CHS OF CHRIST.	4	319	444	0.2	0.5
179 CONSRV BAPT...	3	100	119*	0.1	0.1
193 EPISCOPAL.....	4	1 803	1 943	1.1	2.1
203 EVAN FREE CH..	1	129	153*	0.1	0.2
281 LUTH CH AMER..	29	16 035	21 084	11.8	23.0
285 MENNONITE CH..	6	320	380*	0.2	0.4
291 MISSIONARY CH.	1	29	30	–	–
323 OLD ORD AMISH.	2	260	309*	0.2	0.3
353 CHR BRETHREN..	1	20	20	–	–
381 REF PRES-EVAN.	1	84	134	0.1	0.1
403 SALVATION ARMY	1	162	866	0.5	0.9
413 S.D.A.........	1	85	101*	0.1	0.1
419 SO BAPT CONV..	2	742	881*	0.5	1.0
443 UN C OF CHRIST	9	2 645	3 141*	1.8	3.4
449 UN METHODIST..	56	21 208	25 188*	14.1	27.5
453 UN PRES CH USA	11	6 425	7 631*	4.3	8.3
DAUPHIN	256	68 833	125 011*	53.8	100.0
005 AME ZION......	2	531	733	0.3	0.6
019 AMER BAPT USA.	8	1 365	1 628*	0.7	1.3
053 ASSEMB OF GOD.	7	1 074	1 762	0.8	1.4
075 BRETHREN IN CR	4	436	524	0.2	0.4
081 CATHOLIC......	23	NA	37 488	16.1	30.0
089 CHR & MISS AL.	1	113	181	0.1	0.1
097 CHR CHS&CHS CR	2	83	99*	–	0.1
101 C.M.E.........	1	110	131*	0.1	0.1
123 CH GOD (ANDER)	2	173	519	0.2	0.4
127 CH GOD (CLEVE)	2	143	171*	0.1	0.1
151 L-D SAINTS....	2	NA	610	0.3	0.5
157 CH OF BRETHREN	6	1 996	2 381*	1.0	1.9

NA—Not applicable   *Total adherents estimated from known number of communicant, confirmed, full members.   —Represents a percent less than 0.1.   Percentages may not total due to rounding.

Table 4. Churches and Church Membership by County and Denomination: 1980

County and Denomination	Number of churches	Communicant, confirmed, full members	Total adherents Number	Percent of total population	Percent of total adherents
165 CH OF NAZARENE	2	163	307	0.1	0.2
167 CHS OF CHRIST.	4	67	109	–	0.1
193 EPISCOPAL.....	6	1 535	1 799	0.8	1.4
199 EVAN CONGR CH.	12	1 516	1 808*	0.8	1.4
203 EVAN FREE CH..	1	582	694*	0.3	0.6
226 FRIENDS-USA...	1	118	141*	0.1	0.1
244 GRACE BRETHREN	1	188	224*	0.1	0.2
263 INT FOURSQ GOS	1	29	35*	–	–
270 CONSRV JUDAISM	2	779	929*	0.4	0.7
271 REFORM JUDAISM	1	616	735*	0.3	0.6
281 LUTH CH AMER..	41	18 784	25 307	10.9	20.2
283 LUTH--MO SYNOD	1	158	185	0.1	0.1
285 MENNONITE CH..	8	360	429*	0.2	0.3
290 METRO COMM CHS	0	20	40	–	–
335 ORTH PRESB CH.	1	161	192*	0.1	0.2
353 CHR BRETHREN..	1	110	180	0.1	0.1
356 PRESB CH AMER.	1	19	24	–	–
381 REF PRES-EVAN.	1	19	21	–	–
403 SALVATION ARMY	1	57	768	0.3	0.6
413 S.D.A.........	4	540	644*	0.3	0.5
419 SO BAPT CONV..	3	606	723*	0.3	0.6
435 UNITARIAN-UNIV	1	227	271*	0.1	0.2
441 UN CHRISTIAN..	3	100	215	0.1	0.2
443 UN C OF CHRIST	21	6 627	7 904*	3.4	6.3
449 UN METHODIST..	66	22 933	27 352*	11.8	21.9
453 UN PRES CH USA	11	6 455	7 699*	3.3	6.2
469 WELS..........	1	40	49	–	–
DELAWARE	287	77 953	357 694*	64.4	100.0
005 AME ZION......	2	462	684	0.1	0.2
019 AMER BAPT USA.	22	5 137	6 065*	1.1	1.7
053 ASSEMB OF GOD.	1	51	100	–	–
081 CATHOLIC......	55	NA	258 353	46.5	72.2
089 CHR & MISS AL.	1	46	71	–	–
093 CHR CH (DISC).	1	110	123	–	–
097 CHR CHS&CHS CR	1	100	118*	–	–
101 C.M.E........	2	2 298	2 713*	0.5	0.8
105 CHRISTIAN REF.	1	81	139	–	–
123 CH GOD (ANDER)	1	18	54	–	–
127 CH GOD (CLEVE)	1	87	103*	–	–
151 L-D SAINTS....	2	NA	1 054	0.2	0.3
157 CH OF BRETHREN	1	118	139*	–	–
165 CH OF NAZARENE	3	335	590	0.1	0.2
167 CHS OF CHRIST.	4	139	177	–	–
179 CONSRV BAPT...	3	325	384*	0.1	0.1
193 EPISCOPAL.....	29	11 985	18 075	3.3	5.1
195 ESTONIAN ELC..	1	78	132	–	–
208 EVAN LUTH ASSN	1	224	263	–	0.1
226 FRIENDS-USA...	14	2 394	2 826*	0.5	0.8
270 CONSRV JUDAISM	6	1 017	1 201*	0.2	0.3
271 REFORM JUDAISM	1	600	708*	0.1	0.2
281 LUTH CH AMER..	22	9 657	12 695	2.3	3.5
283 LUTH--MO SYNOD	3	663	820	0.1	0.2
285 MENNONITE CH..	1	29	34*	–	–
335 ORTH PRESB CH.	1	37	44*	–	–
353 CHR BRETHREN..	3	185	180	–	0.1
375 REF EPISCOPAL.	2	303	358*	0.1	0.1
381 REF PRES-EVAN.	4	434	556	0.1	0.2
383 REF PRES OF NA	1	53	67	–	–
403 SALVATION ARMY	2	166	673	0.1	0.2
413 S.D.A.........	3	353	417*	0.1	0.1
419 SO BAPT CONV..	1	31	37*	–	–
435 UNITARIAN-UNIV	1	243	287*	0.1	0.1
443 UN C OF CHRIST	3	793	936*	0.2	0.3
449 UN METHODIST..	59	23 136	27 315*	4.9	7.6
453 UN PRES CH USA	28	16 265	19 203*	3.5	5.4
ELK	46	6 026	28 409*	74.1	100.0
019 AMER BAPT USA.	1	96	117*	0.3	0.4
053 ASSEMB OF GOD.	2	41	70	0.2	0.2
081 CATHOLIC......	11	NA	20 806	54.3	73.2
089 CHR & MISS AL.	2	60	219	0.6	0.8
097 CHR CHS&CHS CR	2	228	278*	0.7	1.0
165 CH OF NAZARENE	1	65	147	0.4	0.5
193 EPISCOPAL.....	3	449	464	1.2	1.6
201 EVAN COV CH AM	2	127	155*	0.4	0.5
281 LUTH CH AMER..	5	1 705	2 184	5.7	7.7
443 UN C OF CHRIST	1	457	557*	1.5	2.0
449 UN METHODIST..	12	2 055	2 506*	6.5	8.8
453 UN PRES CH USA	4	743	906*	2.4	3.2
ERIE	231	47 664	159 447*	57.0	100.0
001 ADVENT CHR CH.	1	39	47*	–	–
005 AME ZION......	1	450	523	0.2	0.3
019 AMER BAPT USA.	12	3 670	4 465*	1.6	2.8
039 AP CHR CH(NAZ)	1	33	40*	–	–
053 ASSEMB OF GOD.	5	715	1 080	0.4	0.7
081 CATHOLIC......	45	NA	92 078	32.9	57.7
089 CHR & MISS AL.	10	863	1 731	0.6	1.1
093 CHR CH (DISC).	1	120	188	0.1	0.1
097 CHR CHS&CHS CR	1	45	55*	–	–
123 CH GOD (ANDER)	4	305	915	0.3	0.6
127 CH GOD (CLEVE)	2	392	477*	0.2	0.3
149 CH OF JC (BIC)	1	15	15	–	–
151 L-D SAINTS....	3	NA	610	0.2	0.4
157 CH OF BRETHREN	1	176	214*	0.1	0.1
165 CH OF NAZARENE	6	629	1 126	0.4	0.7
167 CHS OF CHRIST.	1	94	129	–	0.1
193 EPISCOPAL.....	9	1 605	2 205	0.8	1.4
197 EVAN CH OF NA.	1	106	106	–	0.1
201 EVAN COV CH AM	1	119	145*	0.1	0.1
203 EVAN FREE CH..	1	36	44*	–	–

County and Denomination	Number of churches	Communicant, confirmed, full members	Total adherents Number	Percent of total population	Percent of total adherents
221 FREE METHODIST	5	169	612	0.2	0.4
233 GEN CH NEW JER	1	10	12*	–	–
263 INT FOURSQ GOS	1	12	15*	–	–
270 CONSRV JUDAISM	1	146	178*	0.1	0.1
271 REFORM JUDAISM	1	504	613*	0.2	0.4
281 LUTH CH AMER..	27	10 337	14 667	5.2	9.2
283 LUTH--MO SYNOD	4	976	1 405	0.5	0.9
285 MENNONITE CH..	1	170	207*	0.1	0.1
313 N AM BAPT CONF	1	66	80*	–	0.1
349 PENT HOLINESS.	1	79	96*	–	0.1
353 CHR BRETHREN..	1	50	100	–	0.1
356 PRESB CH AMER.	1	45	57	–	–
403 SALVATION ARMY	2	356	4 396	1.6	2.8
413 S.D.A.........	4	328	399*	0.1	0.3
419 SO BAPT CONV..	2	283	344*	0.1	0.2
435 UNITARIAN-UNIV	2	89	108*	–	0.1
443 UN C OF CHRIST	2	514	625*	0.2	0.4
449 UN METHODIST..	44	14 927	18 159*	6.5	11.4
453 UN PRES CH USA	23	9 191	11 181*	4.0	7.0
FAYETTE	241	32 958	101 642*	63.4	100.0
005 AME ZION......	1	258	503	0.3	0.5
019 AMER BAPT USA.	15	2 710	3 265*	2.0	3.2
053 ASSEMB OF GOD.	4	323	760	0.5	0.7
071 BRETHREN (ASH)	1	128	154*	0.1	0.2
075 BRETHREN IN CR	1	82	132	0.1	0.1
081 CATHOLIC......	45	NA	56 515	35.2	55.6
089 CHR & MISS AL.	5	287	712	0.4	0.7
093 CHR CH (DISC).	8	2 025	3 573	2.2	3.5
097 CHR CHS&CHS CR	8	1 302	1 569*	1.0	1.5
123 CH GOD (ANDER)	5	209	627	0.4	0.6
127 CH GOD (CLEVE)	4	306	369*	0.2	0.4
149 CH OF JC (BIC)	1	77	83	0.1	0.1
151 L-D SAINTS....	1	NA	152	0.1	0.1
157 CH OF BRETHREN	12	1 733	2 088*	1.3	2.1
165 CH OF NAZARENE	3	191	321	0.2	0.3
167 CHS OF CHRIST.	2	183	235	0.1	0.2
193 EPISCOPAL.....	3	352	497	0.3	0.5
197 EVAN CH OF NA.	3	363	363	0.2	0.4
221 FREE METHODIST	13	447	2 658	1.7	2.6
226 FRIENDS-USA...	1	13	16*	–	–
244 GRACE BRETHREN	1	284	342*	0.2	0.3
270 CONSRV JUDAISM	1	45	54*	–	0.1
271 REFORM JUDAISM	1	108	130*	0.1	0.1
281 LUTH CH AMER..	7	3 287	4 472	2.8	4.4
285 MENNONITE CH..	3	232	280*	0.2	0.3
363 PRIMITIVE METH	1	29	35*	–	–
403 SALVATION ARMY	2	192	299	0.2	0.3
413 S.D.A.........	2	135	163*	0.1	0.2
419 SO BAPT CONV..	1	131	158*	0.1	0.2
443 UN C OF CHRIST	1	61	73*	–	0.1
449 UN METHODIST..	57	11 156	13 442*	8.4	13.2
453 UN PRES CH USA	28	6 309	7 602*	4.7	7.5
FOREST	19	1 100	1 871*	36.9	100.0
029 AMER LUTH CH..	1	72	118	2.3	6.3
123 CH GOD (ANDER)	3	135	405	8.0	21.6
221 FREE METHODIST	6	25	318	6.3	17.0
449 UN METHODIST..	6	647	768*	15.1	41.0
453 UN PRES CH USA	3	221	262*	5.2	14.0
FRANKLIN	169	32 123	47 637*	41.9	100.0
005 AME ZION......	1	175	311	0.3	0.7
017 AMER BAPT ASSN	2	49	49	–	0.1
019 AMER BAPT USA.	1	104	126*	0.1	0.3
053 ASSEMB OF GOD.	10	973	1 872	1.6	3.9
061 BEACHY AMISH..	1	36	44*	–	0.1
071 BRETHREN (ASH)	1	105	127*	0.1	0.3
075 BRETHREN IN CR	10	820	1 320	1.2	2.8
081 CATHOLIC......	7	NA	6 713	5.9	14.1
089 CHR & MISS AL.	2	95	136	0.1	0.3
127 CH GOD (CLEVE)	4	454	549*	0.5	1.2
151 L-D SAINTS....	1	NA	519	0.5	1.1
157 CH OF BRETHREN	9	2 302	2 785*	2.5	5.8
167 CHS OF CHRIST.	1	10	13	–	–
193 EPISCOPAL.....	4	608	753	0.7	1.6
226 FRIENDS-USA...	1	24	29*	–	0.1
244 GRACE BRETHREN	2	295	357*	0.3	0.7
263 INT FOURSQ GOS	1	91	110*	0.1	0.2
270 CONSRV JUDAISM	1	55	67*	0.1	0.1
281 LUTH CH AMER..	21	6 793	8 521	7.5	17.9
285 MENNONITE CH..	17	1 443	1 746*	1.5	3.7
323 OLD ORD AMISH.	1	130	157*	0.1	0.3
353 CHR BRETHREN..	3	235	300	0.2	0.6
403 SALVATION ARMY	1	96	187	0.2	0.4
413 S.D.A.........	4	279	338*	0.3	0.7
419 SO BAPT CONV..	2	380	460*	0.4	1.0
443 UN C OF CHRIST	17	4 279	5 177*	4.6	10.9
449 UN METHODIST..	36	9 595	11 608*	10.2	24.4
453 UN PRES CH USA	8	2 697	3 263*	2.9	6.8
FULTON	46	3 942	5 156*	40.1	100.0
053 ASSEMB OF GOD.	1	34	100	0.8	1.9
081 CATHOLIC......	1	NA	190	1.5	3.7
127 CH GOD (CLEVE)	1	28	35*	0.3	0.7
157 CH OF BRETHREN	3	451	556*	4.3	10.8
165 CH OF NAZARENE	3	190	280	2.2	5.4
281 LUTH CH AMER..	3	537	665	5.2	12.9
285 MENNONITE CH..	3	78	96*	0.7	1.9
357 PRESB CH US...	1	143	176*	1.4	3.4
443 UN C OF CHRIST	9	825	1 017*	7.9	19.7

NA— Not applicable   *Total adherents estimated from known number of communicant, confirmed, full members.   —Represents a percent less than 0.1.   Percentages may not total due to rounding.

PENNSYLVANIA

Table 4. Churches and Church Membership by County and Denomination: 1980

County and Denomination	Number of churches	Communicant, confirmed, full members	Total adherents Number	Percent of total population	Percent of total adherents
449 UN METHODIST..	18	1 354	1 669*	13.0	32.4
453 UN PRES CH USA	3	302	372*	2.9	7.2
GREENE	103	11 827	20 739*	51.4	100.0
019 AMER BAPT USA.	13	2 198	2 683*	6.6	12.9
053 ASSEMB OF GOD.	3	253	570	1.4	2.7
071 BRETHREN (ASH)	1	6	7*	-	-
081 CATHOLIC.....	8	NA	5 276	13.1	25.4
093 CHR CH (DISC).	4	538	860	2.1	4.1
097 CHR CHS&CHS CR	5	871	1 063*	2.6	5.1
127 CH GOD (CLEVE)	2	326	398*	1.0	1.9
151 L-D SAINTS....	1	NA	97	0.2	0.5
165 CH OF NAZARENE	3	452	794	2.0	3.8
167 CHS OF CHRIST.	4	180	229	0.6	1.1
193 EPISCOPAL.....	1	51	63	0.2	0.3
221 FREE METHODIST	1	49	276	0.7	1.3
244 GRACE BRETHREN	1	111	135*	0.3	0.7
281 LUTH CH AMER..	1	145	182	0.5	0.9
291 MISSIONARY CH.	2	78	88	0.2	0.4
419 SO BAPT CONV..	1	248	303*	0.8	1.5
449 UN METHODIST..	43	4 380	5 346*	13.2	25.8
453 UN PRES CH USA	9	1 941	2 369*	5.9	11.4
HUNTINGDON	118	12 681	20 259*	47.9	100.0
019 AMER BAPT USA.	5	459	555*	1.3	2.7
053 ASSEMB OF GOD.	7	448	1 151	2.7	5.7
075 BRETHREN IN CR	2	164	264	0.6	1.3
081 CATHOLIC.....	4	NA	3 129	7.4	15.4
089 CHR & MISS AL.	3	329	702	1.7	3.5
123 CH GOD (ANDER)	1	100	300	0.7	1.5
127 CH GOD (CLEVE)	1	76	92*	0.2	0.5
151 L-D SAINTS....	1	NA	78	0.2	0.4
157 CH OF BRETHREN	8	1 059	1 280*	3.0	6.3
165 CH OF NAZARENE	4	318	619	1.5	3.1
167 CHS OF CHRIST.	2	31	43	0.1	0.2
193 EPISCOPAL.....	1	106	125	0.3	0.6
197 EVAN CH OF NA.	1	83	83	0.2	0.4
221 FREE METHODIST	1	21	120	0.3	0.6
281 LUTH CH AMER..	8	970	1 330*	3.1	6.6
285 MENNONITE CH..	1	79	95*	0.2	0.5
403 SALVATION ARMY	1	82	194	0.5	1.0
443 UN C OF CHRIST	4	668	807*	1.9	4.0
449 UN METHODIST..	49	5 908	7 141*	16.9	35.2
453 UN PRES CH USA	14	1 780	2 151*	5.1	10.6
INDIANA	174	22 811	45 677*	49.5	100.0
005 AME ZION......	2	358	430	0.5	0.9
019 AMER BAPT USA.	8	812	975*	1.1	2.1
053 ASSEMB OF GOD.	7	547	777	0.8	1.7
081 CATHOLIC.....	22	NA	15 798	17.1	34.6
089 CHR & MISS AL.	4	299	763	0.8	1.7
093 CHR CH (DISC).	2	243	447	0.5	1.0
097 CHR CHS&CHS CR	4	210	252*	0.3	0.6
123 CH GOD (ANDER)	4	153	459	0.5	1.0
127 CH GOD (CLEVE)	1	5	6*	-	-
151 L-D SAINTS....	2	NA	364	0.4	0.8
157 CH OF BRETHREN	5	606	728*	0.8	1.6
165 CH OF NAZARENE	2	225	467	0.5	1.0
167 CHS OF CHRIST.	6	350	445	0.5	1.0
179 CONSRV BAPT...	1	100	120*	0.1	0.3
193 EPISCOPAL.....	2	266	356	0.4	0.8
203 EVAN FREE CH..	1	91	109*	0.1	0.2
221 FREE METHODIST	4	83	468	0.5	1.0
244 GRACE BRETHREN	1	130	156*	0.2	0.3
281 LUTH CH AMER..	14	2 648	3 542*	3.8	7.8
323 OLD ORD AMISH.	5	650	781*	0.8	1.7
353 CHR BRETHREN..	1	20	20	-	-
403 SALVATION ARMY	1	124	331	0.4	0.7
413 S.D.A........	1	85	102*	0.1	0.2
419 SO BAPT CONV..	1	51	61*	0.1	0.1
435 UNITARIAN-UNIV	1	40	48*	0.1	0.1
443 UN C OF CHRIST	1	324	389*	0.4	0.9
449 UN METHODIST..	42	7 189	8 634*	9.4	18.9
453 UN PRES CH USA	29	7 202	8 649*	9.4	18.9
JEFFERSON	128	13 520	32 688*	67.7	100.0
019 AMER BAPT USA.	3	478	579*	1.2	1.8
053 ASSEMB OF GOD.	3	249	469	1.0	1.4
081 CATHOLIC.....	15	NA	14 574	30.2	44.6
089 CHR & MISS AL.	4	244	496	1.0	1.5
097 CHR CHS&CHS CR	2	170	206*	0.4	0.6
123 CH GOD (ANDER)	3	412	1 236	2.6	3.8
165 CH OF NAZARENE	3	131	300	0.6	0.9
167 CHS OF CHRIST.	4	200	255	0.5	0.8
179 CONSRV BAPT...	1	100	121*	0.3	0.4
193 EPISCOPAL.....	2	87	172	0.4	0.5
221 FREE METHODIST	4	50	318	0.7	1.0
281 LUTH CH AMER..	9	746	995*	2.1	3.0
283 LUTH--MO SYNOD	1	86	114	0.2	0.3
285 MENNONITE CH..	1	6	7*	-	-
323 OLD ORD AMISH.	1	130	157*	0.3	0.5
353 CHR BRETHREN..	1	10	20	-	0.1
403 SALVATION ARMY	1	64	134	0.3	0.4
413 S.D.A........	1	53	64*	0.1	0.2
443 UN C OF CHRIST	3	513	621*	1.3	1.9
449 UN METHODIST..	48	6 790	8 218*	17.0	25.1
453 UN PRES CH USA	18	3 001	3 632*	7.5	11.1
JUNIATA	64	9 070	11 559*	60.2	100.0
053 ASSEMB OF GOD.	2	106	158	0.8	1.4
075 BRETHREN IN CR	1	82	132	0.7	1.1
081 CATHOLIC......	1	NA	194	1.0	1.7
127 CH GOD (CLEVE)	2	53	65*	0.3	0.6
157 CH OF BRETHREN	3	356	434*	2.3	3.8
179 CONSRV BAPT...	2	150	183*	1.0	1.6
193 EPISCOPAL.....	1	?	?	?	?
281 LUTH CH AMER..	10	2 568	3 382	17.6	29.3
285 MENNONITE CH..	4	325	396*	2.1	3.4
323 OLD ORD AMISH.	2	260	317*	1.7	2.7
413 S.D.A.........	1	52	63*	0.3	0.5
443 UN C OF CHRIST	1	97	118*	0.6	1.0
449 UN METHODIST..	27	4 022	4 900*	25.5	42.4
453 UN PRES CH USA	7	999	1 217*	6.3	10.5
LACKAWANNA	220	30 396	173 103*	76.0	100.0
019 AMER BAPT USA.	20	3 459	4 078*	1.8	2.4
053 ASSEMB OF GOD.	9	788	1 376	0.6	0.8
081 CATHOLIC......	86	NA	135 496	59.5	78.3
089 CHR & MISS AL.	4	162	260	0.1	0.2
093 CHR CH (DISC).	2	199	301	0.1	0.2
123 CH GOD (ANDER)	1	41	123	0.1	0.1
151 L-D SAINTS....	1	NA	287	0.1	0.2
167 CHS OF CHRIST.	1	100	130	0.1	0.1
193 EPISCOPAL.....	7	1 882	2 601	1.1	1.5
221 FREE METHODIST	1	35	90	-	0.1
270 CONSRV JUDAISM	1	338	398*	0.2	0.2
271 REFORM JUDAISM	1	554	653*	0.3	0.4
281 LUTH CH AMER..	7	1 580	2 086	0.9	1.2
283 LUTH--MO SYNOD	3	911	1 140	0.5	0.7
329 OPEN BIBLE STD	1	50	75	-	-
363 PRIMITIVE METH	6	1 019	1 201*	0.5	0.7
375 REF EPISCOPAL.	1	110	130*	0.1	0.1
403 SALVATION ARMY	1	174	285	0.1	0.2
413 S.D.A.........	1	94	111*	-	0.1
435 UNITARIAN-UNIV	2	49	58*	-	-
443 UN C OF CHRIST	9	1 923	2 267*	1.0	1.3
449 UN METHODIST..	38	11 570	13 640*	6.0	7.9
453 UN PRES CH USA	17	5 358	6 317*	2.8	3.6
LANCASTER	516	127 109	202 711*	55.9	100.0
019 AMER BAPT USA.	2	766	929*	0.3	0.5
053 ASSEMB OF GOD.	10	1 869	3 224	0.9	1.6
061 BEACHY AMISH..	5	474	575*	0.2	0.3
075 BRETHREN IN CR	15	1 635	1 965	0.5	1.0
081 CATHOLIC......	21	NA	43 788	12.1	21.6
089 CHR & MISS AL.	3	242	334	0.1	0.2
097 CHR CHS&CHS CR	2	222	269*	0.1	0.1
127 CH GOD (CLEVE)	5	508	616*	0.2	0.3
151 L-D SAINTS....	1	NA	596	0.2	0.3
157 CH OF BRETHREN	20	8 156	9 887*	2.7	4.9
165 CH OF NAZARENE	4	503	964	0.3	0.5
167 CHS OF CHRIST.	1	130	165	-	0.1
179 CONSRV BAPT...	3	650	788*	0.2	0.4
193 EPISCOPAL.....	11	3 285	4 485	1.2	2.2
199 EVAN CONGR CH.	25	5 845	7 085*	2.0	3.5
203 EVAN FREE CH..	1	23	28*	-	-
226 FRIENDS-USA...	3	347	421*	0.1	0.2
244 GRACE BRETHREN	7	1 245	1 509*	0.4	0.7
263 INT FOURSQ GOS	1	53	64*	-	-
270 CONSRV JUDAISM	1	104	126*	-	0.1
271 REFORM JUDAISM	1	400	485*	0.1	0.2
281 LUTH CH AMER..	47	23 317	30 336	8.4	15.0
283 LUTH--MO SYNOD	2	446	541	0.1	0.3
285 MENNONITE CH..	100	14 447	17 513*	4.8	8.6
287 MENN GEN CONF.	4	779	1 041	0.3	0.5
293 MORAV CH-NORTH	2	1 462	1 755	0.5	0.9
323 OLD ORD AMISH.	63	8 190	9 928*	2.7	4.9
335 ORTH PRESB CH.	1	49	59*	-	-
353 CHR BRETHREN..	1	50	75	-	-
381 REF PRES-EVAN.	2	424	558	0.2	0.3
403 SALVATION ARMY	1	129	493	0.1	0.2
413 S.D.A.........	3	222	269*	0.1	0.1
419 SO BAPT CONV..	7	1 381	1 674*	0.5	0.8
435 UNITARIAN-UNIV	1	415	503*	0.1	0.2
441 UN CHRISTIAN..	1	41	67	-	-
443 UN C OF CHRIST	35	13 931	16 887*	4.7	8.3
449 UN METHODIST..	78	26 362	31 956*	8.8	15.8
453 UN PRES CH USA	17	8 228	9 974*	2.8	4.9
459 UNITED ZION CH	9	779	779	0.2	0.4
LAWRENCE	148	29 683	74 760*	69.8	100.0
005 AME ZION......	2	535	474	0.4	0.6
019 AMER BAPT USA.	4	841	1 003*	0.9	1.3
053 ASSEMB OF GOD.	6	619	1 007	0.9	1.3
057 BAPT GEN CONF.	2	875	1 043*	1.0	1.4
081 CATHOLIC......	18	NA	37 619	35.1	50.3
089 CHR & MISS AL.	9	619	1 019	1.0	1.4
093 CHR CH (DISC).	1	440	502	0.5	0.7
097 CHR CHS&CHS CR	6	971	1 158*	1.1	1.5
123 CH GOD (ANDER)	2	170	510	0.5	0.7
127 CH GOD (CLEVE)	2	111	132*	0.1	0.2
165 CH OF NAZARENE	2	213	399	0.4	0.5
167 CHS OF CHRIST.	1	47	72	0.1	0.1
193 EPISCOPAL.....	1	1 108	1 160	1.1	1.6
201 EVAN COV CH AM	1	93	111*	0.1	0.1
215 EVAN METH CH..	1	178	212*	0.2	0.3
221 FREE METHODIST	4	205	1 038	1.0	1.4
270 CONSRV JUDAISM	1	312	372*	0.3	0.5
271 REFORM JUDAISM	1	108	129*	0.1	0.2
281 LUTH CH AMER..	4	1 594	1 982	1.8	2.7
283 LUTH--MO SYNOD	1	210	253	0.2	0.3
323 OLD ORD AMISH.	11	1 430	1 705*	1.6	2.3

NA—Not applicable   *Total adherents estimated from known number of communicant, confirmed, full members.   —Represents a percent less than 0.1.   Percentages may not total due to rounding.

Table 4. Churches and Church Membership by County and Denomination: 1980

County and Denomination	Number of churches	Communicant, confirmed, full members	Total adherents Number	Percent of total population	Percent of total adherents
335 ORTH PRESB CH.	1	79	94*	0.1	0.1
349 PENT HOLINESS.	2	73	87*	0.1	0.1
356 PRESB CH AMER.	1	57	76	0.1	0.1
363 PRIMITIVE METH	1	67	80*	0.1	0.1
381 REF PRES-EVAN.	2	140	169	0.2	0.2
383 REF PRES OF NA	2	72	94	0.1	0.1
403 SALVATION ARMY	1	71	268	0.3	0.4
413 S.D.A.........	1	27	32*	-	-
443 UN C OF CHRIST	1	78	93*	0.1	0.1
449 UN METHODIST..	19	4 972	5 928*	5.5	7.9
453 UN PRES CH USA	38	13 368	15 939*	14.9	21.3
LEBANON	152	40 179	62 838*	57.2	100.0
053 ASSEMB OF GOD.	4	380	680	0.6	1.1
075 BRETHREN IN CR	2	218	262	0.2	0.4
081 CATHOLIC......	10	NA	12 727	11.6	20.3
089 CHR & MISS AL.	1	29	59	0.1	0.1
127 CH GOD (CLEVE)	1	200	240*	0.2	0.4
151 L-D SAINTS....	1	NA	266	0.2	0.4
157 CH OF BRETHREN	8	3 203	3 846*	3.5	6.1
167 CHS OF CHRIST.	1	30	42	-	0.1
193 EPISCOPAL.....	1	511	545	0.5	0.9
199 EVAN CONGR CH.	11	1 994	2 394*	2.2	3.8
244 GRACE BRETHREN	2	805	966*	0.9	1.5
263 INT FOURSQ GOS	1	32	38*	-	0.1
270 CONSRV JUDAISM	1	96	115*	0.1	0.2
281 LUTH CH AMER..	21	9 225	12 281	11.2	19.5
285 MENNONITE CH..	7	518	622*	0.6	1.0
293 MORAV CH-NORTH	1	290	385	0.4	0.6
323 OLD ORD AMISH.	3	390	468*	0.4	0.7
403 SALVATION ARMY	1	43	100	0.1	0.2
413 S.D.A.........	1	74	89*	0.1	0.1
419 SO BAPT CONV..	1	233	280*	0.3	0.4
441 UN CHRISTIAN..	7	287	506	0.5	0.8
443 UN C OF CHRIST	25	9 422	11 312*	10.3	18.0
449 UN METHODIST..	35	11 249	13 506*	12.3	21.5
453 UN PRES CH USA	2	793	952*	0.9	1.5
459 UNITED ZION CH	4	157	157	0.1	0.2
LEHIGH	216	82 170	175 856*	64.3	100.0
005 AME ZION......	1	272	290	0.1	0.2
019 AMER BAPT USA.	2	523	617*	0.2	0.4
053 ASSEMB OF GOD.	6	492	913	0.3	0.5
081 CATHOLIC......	28	NA	71 092	26.0	40.4
089 CHR & MISS AL.	3	173	316	0.1	0.2
097 CHR CHS&CHS CR	1	150	177*	0.1	0.1
127 CH GOD (CLEVE)	1	57	67*	-	-
151 L-D SAINTS....	1	NA	397	0.1	0.2
165 CH OF NAZARENE	2	342	547	0.2	0.3
167 CHS OF CHRIST.	1	121	190	0.1	0.1
179 CONSRV BAPT...	1	175	206*	0.1	0.1
193 EPISCOPAL.....	7	2 187	2 750	1.0	1.6
199 EVAN CONGR CH.	13	3 245	3 828*	1.4	2.2
203 EVAN FREE CH..	2	514	606*	0.2	0.3
221 FREE METHODIST	1	41	93	-	0.1
226 FRIENDS-USA...	1	117	138*	0.1	0.1
270 CONSRV JUDAISM	1	500	590*	0.2	0.3
271 REFORM JUDAISM	1	870	1 026*	0.4	0.6
281 LUTH CH AMER..	57	33 306	44 938	16.4	25.6
285 MENNONITE CH..	1	58	68*	-	-
287 MENN GEN CONF.	3	324	430	0.2	0.2
290 METRO COMM CHS	0	25	50	-	-
291 MISSIONARY CH.	2	13	34	-	-
293 MORAV CH-NORTH	6	2 066	2 668	1.0	1.5
353 CHR BRETHREN..	1	60	90	-	0.1
363 PRIMITIVE METH	1	88	104*	-	0.1
403 SALVATION ARMY	1	98	564	0.2	0.3
413 S.D.A.........	3	258	304*	0.1	0.2
419 SO BAPT CONV..	1	96	113*	-	0.1
431 UKRANIAN AMER.	1	560	840	0.3	0.5
435 UNITARIAN-UNIV	1	19	22*	-	-
443 UN C OF CHRIST	50	25 250	29 790*	10.9	16.9
449 UN METHODIST..	9	3 499	4 128*	1.5	2.3
453 UN PRES CH USA	6	6 671	7 870*	2.9	4.5
LUZERNE	386	53 814	258 338*	75.3	100.0
019 AMER BAPT USA.	15	2 126	2 503*	0.7	1.0
053 ASSEMB OF GOD.	13	953	1 625	0.5	0.6
075 BRETHREN IN CR	2	218	262	0.1	0.1
081 CATHOLIC......	132	NA	190 942	55.7	73.9
089 CHR & MISS AL.	7	250	399	0.1	0.2
093 CHR CH (DISC).	2	414	708	0.2	0.3
097 CHR CHS&CHS CR	4	1 078	1 269*	0.4	0.5
151 L-D SAINTS....	1	NA	223	0.1	0.1
167 CHS OF CHRIST.	3	155	250	0.1	0.1
175 CONGR CHR CHS.	4	745	877*	0.3	0.3
181 CONSRV CONGR..	1	169	199*	0.1	0.1
193 EPISCOPAL.....	12	2 904	3 996	1.2	1.5
199 EVAN CONGR CH.	1	109	128*	-	-
221 FREE METHODIST	4	127	681	0.2	0.3
226 FRIENDS-USA...	1	28	33*	-	-
270 CONSRV JUDAISM	2	772	909*	0.3	0.4
271 REFORM JUDAISM	2	680	801*	0.2	0.3
281 LUTH CH AMER..	26	9 256	11 938	3.5	4.6
283 LUTH--MO SYNOD	4	1 040	1 263	0.4	0.5
285 MENNONITE CH..	1	8	9*	-	-
363 PRIMITIVE METH	12	2 403	2 830*	0.8	1.1
403 SALVATION ARMY	3	349	1 124	0.3	0.4
413 S.D.A.........	3	188	221*	0.1	0.1
419 SO BAPT CONV..	2	484	570*	0.2	0.2
431 UKRANIAN AMER.	1	90	115	-	-
443 UN C OF CHRIST	24	4 452	5 242*	1.5	2.0
449 UN METHODIST..	76	18 524	21 812*	6.4	8.4
453 UN PRES CH USA	28	6 292	7 409*	2.2	2.9
LYCOMING	194	37 195	68 446*	57.8	100.0
005 AME ZION......	1	387	416	0.4	0.6
019 AMER BAPT USA.	12	2 494	3 008*	2.5	4.4
053 ASSEMB OF GOD.	4	709	2 186	1.8	3.2
075 BRETHREN IN CR	1	109	131	0.1	0.2
081 CATHOLIC......	13	NA	18 250	15.4	26.7
089 CHR & MISS AL.	5	328	641	0.5	0.9
093 CHR CH (DISC).	1	200	307	0.3	0.4
097 CHR CHS&CHS CR	4	529	638*	0.5	0.9
123 CH GOD (ANDER)	1	161	483	0.4	0.7
127 CH GOD (CLEVE)	1	14	17*	-	-
151 L-D SAINTS....	2	NA	345	0.3	0.5
165 CH OF NAZARENE	3	137	326	0.3	0.5
167 CHS OF CHRIST.	1	75	110	0.1	0.2
179 CONSRV BAPT...	3	75	90*	0.1	0.1
193 EPISCOPAL.....	8	1 791	2 462	2.1	3.6
221 FREE METHODIST	2	85	348	0.3	0.5
226 FRIENDS-USA...	4	226	273*	0.2	0.4
270 CONSRV JUDAISM	1	120	145*	0.1	0.2
271 REFORM JUDAISM	1	168	203*	0.2	0.3
281 LUTH CH AMER..	25	9 669	13 304	11.2	19.4
285 MENNONITE CH..	1	30	36*	-	0.1
323 OLD ORD AMISH.	1	130	157*	0.1	0.2
403 SALVATION ARMY	1	166	941	0.8	1.4
413 S.D.A.........	2	175	211*	0.2	0.3
419 SO BAPT CONV..	1	83	100*	0.1	0.1
435 UNITARIAN-UNIV	1	22	27*	-	-
443 UN C OF CHRIST	1	533	643*	0.5	0.9
449 UN METHODIST..	82	16 134	19 458*	16.4	28.4
453 UN PRES CH USA	11	2 645	3 190*	2.7	4.7
MC KEAN	98	13 404	29 682*	58.6	100.0
019 AMER BAPT USA.	3	863	1 047*	2.1	3.5
053 ASSEMB OF GOD.	1	90	80	0.2	0.3
081 CATHOLIC......	13	NA	11 104	21.9	37.4
089 CHR & MISS AL.	5	122	260	0.5	0.9
123 CH GOD (ANDER)	2	117	351	0.7	1.2
151 L-D SAINTS....	2	NA	160	0.3	0.5
165 CH OF NAZARENE	4	247	597	1.2	2.0
167 CHS OF CHRIST.	1	140	178	0.4	0.6
193 EPISCOPAL.....	6	738	956	1.9	3.2
197 EVAN CH OF NA.	6	385	385	0.8	1.3
201 EVAN COV CH AM	4	137	166*	0.3	0.6
221 FREE METHODIST	7	223	1 500	3.0	5.1
263 INT FOURSQ GOS	1	122	148*	0.3	0.5
271 REFORM JUDAISM	1	150	182*	0.4	0.6
281 LUTH CH AMER..	7	2 049	2 792	5.5	9.4
283 LUTH--MO SYNOD	1	194	277	0.5	0.9
285 MENNONITE CH..	1	55	67*	0.1	0.2
403 SALVATION ARMY	1	93	114	0.2	0.4
413 S.D.A.........	4	166	201*	0.4	0.7
419 SO BAPT CONV..	3	633	768*	1.5	2.6
449 UN METHODIST..	21	5 272	6 398*	12.6	21.6
453 UN PRES CH USA	4	1 608	1 951*	3.9	6.6
MERCER	157	38 104	81 113*	63.2	100.0
019 AMER BAPT USA.	8	2 041	2 436*	1.9	3.0
029 AMER LUTH CH..	1	359	441	0.3	0.5
039 AP CHR CH(NAZ)	1	9	11*	-	-
057 BAPT GEN CONF.	1	83	99*	0.1	0.1
061 BEACHY AMISH..	2	82	98*	0.1	0.1
081 CATHOLIC......	18	NA	33 299	26.0	41.1
089 CHR & MISS AL.	5	363	688	0.5	0.8
093 CHR CH (DISC).	2	504	763	0.6	0.9
097 CHR CHS&CHS CR	4	345	412*	0.3	0.5
101 C.M.E.........	1	20	24*	-	-
123 CH GOD (ANDER)	5	346	1 038	0.8	1.3
149 CH OF JC (BIC)	1	16	16	-	-
165 CH OF NAZARENE	5	429	878	0.7	1.1
167 CHS OF CHRIST.	2	177	279	0.2	0.3
193 EPISCOPAL.....	4	1 416	1 975	1.5	2.4
221 FREE METHODIST	2	87	246	0.2	0.3
271 REFORM JUDAISM	1	438	523*	0.4	0.6
281 LUTH CH AMER..	5	2 759	3 376	2.6	4.2
283 LUTH--MO SYNOD	1	375	435	0.3	0.5
323 OLD ORD AMISH.	2	260	310*	0.2	0.4
335 ORTH PRESB CH.	1	78	93*	0.1	0.1
349 PENT HOLINESS.	7	578	690*	0.5	0.9
381 REF PRES-EVAN.	1	?	?	?	?
403 SALVATION ARMY	2	236	631	0.5	0.8
413 S.D.A.........	1	49	58*	-	0.1
419 SO BAPT CONV..	2	234	279*	0.2	0.3
443 UN C OF CHRIST	6	2 659	3 174*	2.5	3.9
449 UN METHODIST..	33	11 409	13 619*	10.6	16.8
453 UN PRES CH USA	33	12 752	15 222*	11.9	18.8
MIFFLIN	106	19 575	27 300*	58.2	100.0
019 AMER BAPT USA.	2	618	750*	1.6	2.7
053 ASSEMB OF GOD.	1	137	495	1.1	1.8
061 BEACHY AMISH..	1	213	258*	0.6	0.9
075 BRETHREN IN CR	4	328	528	1.1	1.9
081 CATHOLIC......	3	NA	2 024	4.3	7.4
089 CHR & MISS AL.	6	569	979	2.1	3.6
127 CH GOD (CLEVE)	1	61	74*	0.2	0.3
143 CG IN CR(MENN)	1	100	100	0.2	0.4
151 L-D SAINTS....	1	NA	70	0.1	0.3
157 CH OF BRETHREN	7	1 323	1 605*	3.4	5.9
165 CH OF NAZARENE	1	29	47	0.1	0.2

NA—Not applicable   *Total adherents estimated from known number of communicant, confirmed, full members.   —Represents a percent less than 0.1.   Percentages may not total due to rounding.

Table 4. Churches and Church Membership by County and Denomination: 1980

County and Denomination	Number of churches	Communicant, confirmed, full members	Total adherents		
			Number	Percent of total population	Percent of total adherents
167 CHS OF CHRIST.	1	15	20	–	0.1
175 CONGR CHR CHS.	1	129	157*	0.3	0.6
179 CONSRV BAPT...	1	150	182*	0.4	0.7
193 EPISCOPAL.....	1	381	437	0.9	1.6
244 GRACE BRETHREN	1	26	32*	0.1	0.1
281 LUTH CH AMER..	10	3 325	4 627	9.9	16.9
285 MENNONITE CH..	8	1 405	1 705*	3.6	6.2
323 OLD ORD AMISH.	10	1 300	1 577*	3.4	5.8
329 OPEN BIBLE STD	1	10	30	0.1	0.1
353 CHR BRETHREN..	1	35	40	0.1	0.1
403 SALVATION ARMY	1	128	287	0.6	1.1
413 S.D.A.........	1	42	51*	0.1	0.2
419 SO BAPT CONV..	1	162	197*	0.4	0.7
443 UN C OF CHRIST	3	782	949*	2.0	3.5
449 UN METHODIST..	29	6 852	8 314*	17.7	30.5
453 UN PRES CH USA	8	1 455	1 765*	3.8	6.5
MONROE	79	14 960	30 235*	43.6	100.0
053 ASSEMB OF GOD.	1	113	140	0.2	0.5
081 CATHOLIC......	14	NA	10 702	15.4	35.4
089 CHR & MISS AL.	1	41	124	0.2	0.4
167 CHS OF CHRIST.	1	18	24	–	0.1
179 CONSRV BAPT...	1	150	178*	0.3	0.6
193 EPISCOPAL.....	2	439	595	0.9	2.0
199 EVAN CONGR CH.	1	128	152*	0.2	0.5
221 FREE METHODIST	1	6	63	0.1	0.2
270 CONSRV JUDAISM	1	78	93*	0.1	0.3
281 LUTH CH AMER..	11	4 232	5 776	8.3	19.1
283 LUTH--MO SYNOD	1	181	296	0.4	1.0
293 MORAV CH-NORTH	1	138	218	0.3	0.7
371 REF CH IN AM..	1	45	200	0.3	0.7
403 SALVATION ARMY	1	185	730	1.1	2.4
413 S.D.A.........	1	150	178*	0.3	0.6
443 UN C OF CHRIST	9	2 314	2 751*	4.0	9.1
449 UN METHODIST..	26	5 485	6 521*	9.4	21.6
453 UN PRES CH USA	5	1 257	1 494*	2.2	4.9
MONTGOMERY	430	148 591	398 535*	61.9	100.0
019 AMER BAPT USA.	34	10 356	12 225*	1.9	3.1
029 AMER LUTH CH..	1	110	140	–	–
053 ASSEMB OF GOD.	10	783	1 132	0.2	0.3
075 BRETHREN IN CR	3	327	393	0.1	0.1
081 CATHOLIC......	61	NA	209 341	32.5	52.5
089 CHR & MISS AL.	4	186	264	–	0.1
123 CH GOD (ANDER)	3	173	519	0.1	0.1
127 CH GOD (CLEVE)	2	76	90*	–	–
151 L-D SAINTS....	4	NA	1 274	0.2	0.3
157 CH OF BRETHREN	9	1 485	1 753*	0.3	0.4
165 CH OF NAZARENE	5	802	1 618	0.3	0.4
167 CHS OF CHRIST.	2	231	294	–	0.1
179 CONSRV BAPT...	2	450	531*	0.1	0.1
193 EPISCOPAL.....	36	16 011	21 777	3.4	5.5
199 EVAN CONGR CH.	8	1 136	1 341*	0.2	0.3
221 FREE METHODIST	1	38	168	–	–
226 FRIENDS--USA...	11	2 255	2 662*	0.4	0.7
233 GEN CH NEW JER	1	810	956*	0.1	0.2
244 GRACE BRETHREN	2	295	348*	0.1	0.1
270 CONSRV JUDAISM	11	4 311	5 089*	0.8	1.3
271 REFORM JUDAISM	5	6 978	8 237*	1.3	2.1
281 LUTH CH AMER..	49	37 013	50 862	7.9	12.8
283 LUTH--MO SYNOD	2	385	489	0.1	0.1
285 MENNONITE CH..	22	3 044	3 593*	0.6	0.9
287 MENN GEN CONF.	5	1 606	2 113	0.3	0.5
335 ORTH PRESB CH.	3	542	640*	0.1	0.2
353 CHR BRETHREN..	3	265	350	0.1	0.1
356 PRESB CH AMER.	2	136	161	–	–
363 PRIMITIVE METH	3	263	310*	–	0.1
371 REF CH IN AM..	1	402	585	0.1	0.1
375 REF EPISCOPAL.	2	322	380*	0.1	0.1
381 REF PRES-EVAN.	4	848	1 282	0.2	0.3
383 REF PRES OF NA	1	45	51	–	–
403 SALVATION ARMY	2	193	618	0.1	0.2
413 S.D.A.........	7	762	900*	0.1	0.2
419 SO BAPT CONV..	3	554	654*	0.1	0.2
435 UNITARIAN-UNIV	2	68	80*	–	–
443 UN C OF CHRIST	37	16 777	19 805*	3.1	5.0
449 UN METHODIST..	34	15 633	18 454*	2.9	4.6
453 UN PRES CH USA	32	22 865	26 991*	4.2	6.8
469 WELS..........	1	55	65	–	–
MONTOUR	31	6 286	10 646*	63.8	100.0
019 AMER BAPT USA.	1	110	131*	0.8	1.2
081 CATHOLIC......	1	NA	2 882	17.3	27.1
089 CHR & MISS AL.	1	13	43	0.3	0.4
165 CH OF NAZARENE	1	91	188	1.1	1.8
179 CONSRV BAPT...	1	250	297*	1.8	2.8
193 EPISCOPAL.....	1	177	201	1.2	1.9
281 LUTH CH AMER..	8	2 024	2 600	15.6	24.4
285 MENNONITE CH..	3	174	207*	1.2	1.9
323 OLD ORD AMISH.	2	260	309*	1.9	2.9
413 S.D.A.........	1	69	82*	0.5	0.8
443 UN C OF CHRIST	4	1 441	1 713*	10.3	16.1
449 UN METHODIST..	4	1 088	1 293*	7.8	12.1
453 UN PRES CH USA	3	589	700*	4.2	6.6
NORTHAMPTON	210	73 742	162 036*	71.9	100.0
005 AME ZION......	1	250	266	0.1	0.2
019 AMER BAPT USA.	4	867	1 028*	0.5	0.6
053 ASSEMB OF GOD.	6	380	733	0.3	0.5
081 CATHOLIC......	33	NA	68 653	30.5	42.4
151 L-D SAINTS....	1	NA	255	0.1	0.2

County and Denomination	Number of churches	Communicant, confirmed, full members	Total adherents		
			Number	Percent of total population	Percent of total adherents
165 CH OF NAZARENE	4	414	746	0.3	0.5
167 CHS OF CHRIST.	2	76	101	–	0.1
193 EPISCOPAL.....	5	2 958	4 086	1.8	2.5
199 EVAN CONGR CH.	6	1 524	1 808*	0.8	1.1
244 GRACE BRETHREN	1	140	166*	0.1	0.1
270 CONSRV JUDAISM	2	294	349*	0.2	0.2
271 REFORM JUDAISM	5	6 194	7 347*	3.3	4.5
281 LUTH CH AMER..	45	26 321	34 399	15.3	21.2
283 LUTH--MO SYNOD	2	687	807	0.4	0.5
285 MENNONITE CH..	3	257	305*	0.1	0.2
293 MORAV CH-NORTH	10	4 559	5 858	2.6	3.6
313 N AM BAPT CONF	1	336	399*	0.2	0.2
353 CHR BRETHREN..	1	80	120	0.1	0.1
371 REF CH IN AM..	1	143	350	0.2	0.2
383 REF PRES OF NA	1	3	4	–	–
403 SALVATION ARMY	3	228	1 009	0.4	0.6
413 S.D.A.........	2	122	145*	0.1	0.1
419 SO BAPT CONV..	1	115	136*	0.1	0.1
435 UNITARIAN-UNIV	1	230	273*	0.1	0.2
443 UN C OF CHRIST	37	17 583	20 855*	9.3	12.9
449 UN METHODIST..	24	7 461	8 849*	3.9	5.5
453 UN PRES CH USA	8	2 520	2 989*	1.3	1.8
NORTHUMBERLAND	168	32 266	73 570*	73.3	100.0
019 AMER BAPT USA.	4	680	809*	0.8	1.1
053 ASSEMB OF GOD.	4	243	393	0.4	0.5
081 CATHOLIC......	27	NA	32 093	32.0	43.6
089 CHR & MISS AL.	3	332	624	0.6	0.8
151 L-D SAINTS....	2	NA	381	0.4	0.5
165 CH OF NAZARENE	2	216	811	0.8	1.1
167 CHS OF CHRIST.	1	115	150	0.1	0.2
193 EPISCOPAL.....	6	489	722	0.7	1.0
199 EVAN CONGR CH.	5	951	1 132*	1.1	1.5
203 EVAN FREE CH..	1	70	83*	0.1	0.1
281 LUTH CH AMER..	36	11 913	15 556	15.5	21.1
285 MENNONITE CH..	1	63	75*	0.1	0.1
323 OLD ORD AMISH.	1	130	155*	0.2	0.2
363 PRIMITIVE METH	2	272	324*	0.3	0.4
403 SALVATION ARMY	3	348	694	0.7	0.9
413 S.D.A.........	1	42	50*	–	0.1
443 UN C OF CHRIST	23	5 145	6 122*	6.1	8.3
449 UN METHODIST..	37	9 174	10 917*	10.9	14.8
453 UN PRES CH USA	9	2 083	2 479*	2.5	3.4
PERRY	79	12 120	17 538*	49.1	100.0
053 ASSEMB OF GOD.	4	632	1 072	3.0	6.1
075 BRETHREN IN CR	3	246	396	1.1	2.3
081 CATHOLIC......	3	NA	1 328	3.7	7.6
127 CH GOD (CLEVE)	1	29	36*	0.1	0.2
157 CH OF BRETHREN	2	261	321*	0.9	1.8
167 CHS OF CHRIST.	1	8	14	–	0.1
179 CONSRV BAPT...	1	75	92*	0.3	0.5
193 EPISCOPAL.....	1	76	183	0.5	1.0
281 LUTH CH AMER..	15	3 469	5 090	14.3	29.0
323 OLD ORD AMISH.	1	130	160*	0.4	0.9
413 S.D.A.........	1	52	64*	0.2	0.4
443 UN C OF CHRIST	10	1 302	1 601*	4.5	9.1
449 UN METHODIST..	30	4 881	6 002*	16.8	34.2
453 UN PRES CH USA	6	959	1 179*	3.3	6.7
PHILADELPHIA	718	148 805	788 253*	46.7	100.0
005 AME ZION......	8	5 598	8 791	0.5	1.1
019 AMER BAPT USA.	64	22 139	26 350*	1.6	3.3
029 AMER LUTH CH..	2	591	793	–	0.1
049 ARMEN AP CH AM	1	600	1 200	0.1	0.2
053 ASSEMB OF GOD.	11	1 416	1 917	0.1	0.2
081 CATHOLIC......	150	NA	598 322	35.4	75.9
089 CHR & MISS AL.	5	188	338	–	–
093 CHR CH (DISC)	6	510	757	–	0.1
097 CHR CHS&CHS CR	1	50	60*	–	–
101 C.M.E.	5	3 981	4 738*	0.3	0.6
123 CH GOD (ANDER)	6	796	2 388	0.1	0.3
127 CH GOD (CLEVE)	7	278	331*	–	–
157 CH OF BRETHREN	3	135	161*	–	–
165 CH OF NAZARENE	2	157	215	–	–
167 CHS OF CHRIST.	6	363	462	–	0.1
175 CONGR CHR CHS.	1	237	282*	–	–
179 CONSRV BAPT...	5	600	714*	–	0.1
181 CONSRV CONGR..	2	130	155*	–	–
193 EPISCOPAL.....	71	24 976	30 668*	1.8	3.9
203 EVAN FREE CH..	1	39	46*	–	–
208 EVAN LUTH ASSN	1	311	434	–	0.1
226 FRIENDS--USA...	7	1 298	1 545*	0.1	0.2
239 SWEDENBORGIAN.	1	100	119*	–	–
244 GRACE BRETHREN	2	271	323*	–	–
270 CONSRV JUDAISM	19	4 214	5 015*	0.3	0.6
271 REFORM JUDAISM	1	480	571*	–	0.1
274 LAT EVAN LUTH.	2	361	400	–	0.1
281 LUTH CH AMER..	60	21 283	29 098	1.7	3.7
283 LUTH--MO SYNOD	7	1 130	1 647	0.1	0.2
285 MENNONITE CH..	7	190	226*	–	–
287 MENN GEN CONF.	2	66	71	–	–
290 METRO COMM CHS	1	100	200	–	–
293 MORAV CH-NORTH	2	300	393	–	–
313 N AM BAPT CONF	2	294	350*	–	–
335 ORTH PRESB CH.	3	187	223*	–	–
353 CHR BRETHREN..	7	620	775	–	0.1
363 PRIMITIVE METH	2	210	250*	–	–
371 REF CH IN AM..	1	164	245	–	–
375 REF EPISCOPAL.	9	726	864*	0.1	0.1
381 REF PRES-EVAN.	3	223	268	–	–
395 ROMANIAN OR CH	1	630	750*	–	0.1

NA—Not applicable   *Total adherents estimated from known number of communicant, confirmed, full members.   —Represents a percent less than 0.1.   Percentages may not total due to rounding.

242

Table 4. Churches and Church Membership by County and Denomination: 1980

County and Denomination	Number of churches	Communicant, confirmed, full members	Total adherents		
			Number	Percent of total population	Percent of total adherents
403 SALVATION ARMY	7	802	3 836	0.2	0.5
413 S.D.A.........	10	2 898	3 449*	0.2	0.4
419 SO BAPT CONV..	12	1 576	1 876*	0.1	0.2
423 SYRIAN ANTIOCH	1	400	476*	–	0.1
435 UNITARIAN-UNIV	3	738	878*	0.1	0.1
443 UN C OF CHRIST	24	4 217	5 019*	0.3	0.6
449 UN METHODIST..	89	22 184	26 403*	1.6	3.3
453 UN PRES CH USA	75	20 048	23 861*	1.4	3.0
PIKE	23	1 966	5 482*	30.0	100.0
019 AMER BAPT USA.	1	128	150*	0.8	2.7
029 AMER LUTH CH..	2	135	178	1.0	3.2
053 ASSEMB OF GOD.	1	45	65	0.4	1.2
081 CATHOLIC......	7	NA	3 070	16.8	56.0
193 EPISCOPAL.....	1	144	218	1.2	4.0
203 EVAN FREE CH..	1	45	53*	0.3	1.0
281 LUTH CH AMER..	3	331	413	2.3	7.5
449 UN METHODIST..	6	1 019	1 195*	6.5	21.8
453 UN PRES CH USA	1	119	140*	0.8	2.6
POTTER	47	3 132	6 275*	35.4	100.0
019 AMER BAPT USA.	4	313	386*	2.2	6.2
081 CATHOLIC......	6	NA	1 701	9.6	27.1
089 CHR & MISS AL.	4	204	447	2.5	7.1
193 EPISCOPAL.....	2	175	236	1.3	3.8
221 FREE METHODIST	4	84	519	2.9	8.3
281 LUTH CH AMER..	3	346	509	2.9	8.1
285 MENNONITE CH..	1	32	39*	0.2	0.6
413 S.D.A.........	1	98	121*	0.7	1.9
415 S-D BAPTIST GC	1	66	81*	0.5	1.3
449 UN METHODIST..	19	1 493	1 840*	10.4	29.3
453 UN PRES CH USA	2	321	396*	2.2	6.3
SCHUYLKILL	291	47 665	144 892*	90.2	100.0
019 AMER BAPT USA.	7	475	562*	0.3	0.4
053 ASSEMB OF GOD.	1	26	30	–	–
061 BEACHY AMISH..	1	23	27*	–	–
075 BRETHREN IN CR	2	218	262	0.2	0.2
081 CATHOLIC......	79	NA	85 024	52.9	58.7
151 L-D SAINTS....	1	NA	121	0.1	0.1
157 CH OF BRETHREN	1	368	435*	0.3	0.3
165 CH OF NAZARENE	3	207	387	0.2	0.3
175 CONGR CHR CHS.	1	123	145*	0.1	0.1
193 EPISCOPAL.....	4	1 016	1 352	0.8	0.9
199 EVAN CONGR CH.	16	2 885	3 411*	2.1	2.4
203 EVAN FREE CH..	1	46	54*	–	–
226 FRIENDS-USA...	1	50	59*	–	–
244 GRACE BRETHREN	1	37	44*	–	–
263 INT FOURSQ GOS	2	306	362*	0.2	0.2
270 CONSRV JUDAISM	1	90	106*	0.1	0.1
281 LUTH CH AMER..	49	18 230	24 126	15.0	16.7
285 MENNONITE CH..	4	87	103*	0.1	0.1
363 PRIMITIVE METH	7	1 031	1 219*	0.8	0.8
403 SALVATION ARMY	2	284	860	0.5	0.6
413 S.D.A.........	2	44	52*	–	–
443 UN C OF CHRIST	50	13 242	15 656*	9.7	10.8
449 UN METHODIST..	50	7 961	9 412*	5.9	6.5
453 UN PRES CH USA	5	916	1 083*	0.7	0.7
SNYDER	75	12 456	17 035*	50.7	100.0
053 ASSEMB OF GOD.	1	19	31	0.1	0.2
061 BEACHY AMISH..	1	31	37*	0.1	0.2
065 BETHEL M ASSN.	1	150	181*	0.5	1.1
075 BRETHREN IN CR	1	82	132	0.4	0.8
081 CATHOLIC......	1	NA	1 004	3.0	5.9
157 CH OF BRETHREN	1	24	29*	0.1	0.2
165 CH OF NAZARENE	1	159	376	1.1	2.2
179 CONSRV BAPT...	2	65	78*	0.2	0.5
281 LUTH CH AMER..	19	5 062	6 893	20.5	40.5
285 MENNONITE CH..	6	317	382*	1.1	2.2
323 OLD ORD AMISH.	3	390	470*	1.4	2.8
443 UN C OF CHRIST	11	2 415	2 911*	8.7	17.1
449 UN METHODIST..	27	3 742	4 511*	13.4	26.5
SOMERSET	204	31 851	56 257*	69.2	100.0
019 AMER BAPT USA.	2	160	194*	0.2	0.3
053 ASSEMB OF GOD.	6	299	680	0.8	1.2
061 BEACHY AMISH..	1	170	206*	0.3	0.4
071 BRETHREN (ASH)	2	482	584*	0.7	1.0
081 CATHOLIC......	23	NA	15 551	19.1	27.6
089 CHR & MISS AL.	6	349	658	0.8	1.2
097 CHR CHS&CHS CR	5	1 042	1 262*	1.6	2.2
127 CH GOD (CLEVE)	8	661	800*	1.0	1.4
151 L-D SAINTS....	1	NA	50	0.1	0.1
157 CH OF BRETHREN	25	4 961	6 007*	7.4	10.7
165 CH OF NAZARENE	4	393	695	0.9	1.2
167 CHS OF CHRIST.	1	62	115	0.1	0.2
193 EPISCOPAL.....	1	103	146	0.2	0.3
244 GRACE BRETHREN	7	892	1 080*	1.3	1.9
281 LUTH CH AMER..	42	11 010	14 579	17.9	25.9
283 LUTH--MO SYNOD	2	113	146	0.2	0.3
285 MENNONITE CH..	8	1 105	1 338*	1.6	2.4
323 OLD ORD AMISH.	3	390	472*	0.6	0.8
413 S.D.A.........	1	24	29*	–	0.1
443 UN C OF CHRIST	17	3 256	3 942*	4.9	7.0
449 UN METHODIST..	36	5 855	7 089*	8.7	12.6
453 UN PRES CH USA	3	524	634*	0.8	1.1
SULLIVAN	21	1 439	3 446*	54.3	100.0

County and Denomination	Number of churches	Communicant, confirmed, full members	Total adherents		
			Number	Percent of total population	Percent of total adherents
019 AMER BAPT USA.	1	20	24*	0.4	0.7
053 ASSEM OF GOD.	1	27	56	0.9	1.6
081 CATHOLIC......	5	NA	1 663	26.2	48.3
281 LUTH CH AMER..	1	492	640	10.1	18.6
285 MENNONITE CH..	2	42	50*	0.8	1.5
443 UN C OF CHRIST	1	61	72*	1.1	2.1
449 UN METHODIST..	10	797	941*	14.8	27.3
SUSQUEHANNA	81	7 307	18 216*	48.1	100.0
005 AME ZION......	1	159	182	0.5	1.0
019 AMER BAPT USA.	4	435	532*	1.4	2.9
053 ASSEMB OF GOD.	2	59	100	0.3	0.5
081 CATHOLIC......	17	NA	8 893	23.5	48.8
089 CHR & MISS AL.	2	49	112	0.3	0.6
151 L-D SAINTS....	1	NA	92	0.2	0.5
193 EPISCOPAL.....	5	557	911	2.4	5.0
283 LUTH--MO SYNOD	1	215	261	0.7	1.4
285 MENNONITE CH..	2	82	100*	0.3	0.5
413 S.D.A.........	1	41	50*	0.1	0.3
435 UNITARIAN-UNIV	1	68	83*	0.2	0.5
443 UN C OF CHRIST	1	271	331*	0.9	1.8
449 UN METHODIST..	36	4 551	5 566*	14.7	30.6
453 UN PRES CH USA	7	820	1 003*	2.6	5.5
TIOGA	97	9 105	16 536*	40.4	100.0
019 AMER BAPT USA.	10	1 593	1 942*	4.7	11.7
053 ASSEMB OF GOD.	4	324	689	1.7	4.2
075 BRETHREN IN CR	1	82	132	0.3	0.8
081 CATHOLIC......	10	NA	4 022	9.8	24.3
089 CHR & MISS AL.	4	102	176	0.4	1.1
093 CHR CH (DISC).	5	554	823	2.0	5.0
151 L-D SAINTS....	1	NA	123	0.3	0.7
193 EPISCOPAL.....	5	534	769	1.9	4.7
221 FREE METHODIST	2	69	603	1.5	3.6
281 LUTH CH AMER..	5	248	418	1.0	2.5
283 LUTH--MO SYNOD	1	140	185	0.5	1.1
285 MENNONITE CH..	3	85	104*	0.3	0.6
413 S.D.A.........	2	157	191*	0.5	1.2
443 UN C OF CHRIST	1	50	61*	0.1	0.4
449 UN METHODIST..	36	4 138	5 044*	12.3	30.5
453 UN PRES CH USA	7	1 029	1 254*	3.1	7.6
UNION	61	10 714	14 314*	43.5	100.0
019 AMER BAPT USA.	3	640	761*	2.3	5.3
053 ASSEMB OF GOD.	1	64	138	0.4	1.0
061 BEACHY AMISH..	2	109	130*	0.4	0.9
081 CATHOLIC......	1	NA	985	3.0	6.9
089 CHR & MISS AL.	1	64	143	0.4	1.0
097 CHR CHS&CHS CR	2	259	308*	0.9	2.2
143 CG IN CR(MENN)	1	34	34	0.1	0.2
157 CH OF BRETHREN	1	164	195*	0.6	1.4
165 CH OF NAZARENE	1	317	436	1.3	3.0
193 EPISCOPAL.....	1	201	246	0.7	1.7
226 FRIENDS-USA...	1	19	23*	0.1	0.2
263 INT FOURSQ GOS	1	127	151*	0.5	1.1
281 LUTH CH AMER..	10	3 753	4 865	14.8	34.0
285 MENNONITE CH..	4	192	228*	0.7	1.6
335 ORTH PRESB CH.	1	24	29*	0.1	0.2
435 UNITARIAN-UNIV	1	15	18*	0.1	0.1
443 UN C OF CHRIST	9	1 737	2 064*	6.3	14.4
449 UN METHODIST..	17	2 439	2 899*	8.8	20.3
453 UN PRES CH USA	3	556	661*	2.0	4.6
VENANGO	115	17 623	35 841*	55.6	100.0
019 AMER BAPT USA.	4	774	937*	1.5	2.6
029 AMER LUTH CH..	2	991	1 540	2.4	4.3
053 ASSEMB OF GOD.	1	28	50	0.1	0.1
081 CATHOLIC......	8	NA	11 544	17.9	32.2
089 CHR & MISS AL.	2	130	287	0.4	0.8
093 CHR CH (DISC).	1	32	49	0.1	0.1
123 CH GOD (ANDER)	5	397	1 191	1.8	3.3
151 L-D SAINTS....	1	NA	246	0.4	0.7
165 CH OF NAZARENE	2	347	692	1.1	1.9
167 CHS OF CHRIST.	1	30	50	0.1	0.1
193 EPISCOPAL.....	2	639	791	1.2	2.2
197 EVAN CH OF NA.	1	121	121	0.2	0.3
199 EVAN CONGR CH.	2	96	116*	0.2	0.3
221 FREE METHODIST	8	278	1 182	1.8	3.3
281 LUTH CH AMER..	4	606	800	1.2	2.2
283 LUTH--MO SYNOD	1	359	463	0.7	1.3
403 SALVATION ARMY	2	192	529	0.8	1.5
413 S.D.A.........	1	56	68*	0.1	0.2
435 UNITARIAN-UNIV	1	10	12*	–	–
443 UN C OF CHRIST	1	35	42*	0.1	0.1
449 UN METHODIST..	47	9 040	10 941*	17.0	30.5
453 UN PRES CH USA	18	3 462	4 190*	6.5	11.7
WARREN	79	13 047	27 037*	57.0	100.0
019 AMER BAPT USA.	1	328	397*	0.8	1.5
053 ASSEMB OF GOD.	1	56	97	0.2	0.4
057 BAPT GEN CONF.	2	247	299*	0.6	1.1
081 CATHOLIC......	9	NA	9 695	20.4	35.9
089 CHR & MISS AL.	2	53	161	0.3	0.6
123 CH GOD (ANDER)	1	101	303	0.6	1.1
127 CH GOD (CLEVE)	1	35	42*	0.1	0.2
151 L-D SAINTS....	1	NA	164	0.3	0.6
165 CH OF NAZARENE	1	370	544	1.1	2.0
167 CHS OF CHRIST.	1	60	76	0.2	0.3
175 CONGR CHR CHS.	2	168	203*	0.4	0.8
181 CONSRV CONGR..	1	26	31*	0.1	0.1

NA—Not applicable   *Total adherents estimated from known number of communicant, confirmed, full members.   —Represents a percent less than 0.1.   Percentages may not total due to rounding.

Table 4. Churches and Church Membership by County and Denomination: 1980

County and Denomination	Number of churches	Communicant, confirmed, full members	Total adherents		
			Number	Percent of total population	Percent of total adherents
193 EPISCOPAL.....	2	576	742	1.6	2.7
197 EVAN CH OF NA.	1	162	162	0.3	0.6
201 EVAN COV CH AM	4	231	280*	0.6	1.0
221 FREE METHODIST	6	163	828	1.7	3.1
281 LUTH CH AMER..	7	2 460	3 262	6.9	12.1
323 OLD ORD AMISH	1	130	157*	0.3	0.6
403 SALVATION ARMY	1	92	170	0.4	0.6
413 S.D.A.........	1	49	59*	0.1	0.2
419 SO BAPT CONV..	1	51	62*	0.1	0.2
443 UN C OF CHRIST	2	388	469*	1.0	1.7
449 UN METHODIST..	24	5 478	6 628*	14.0	24.5
453 UN PRES CH USA	6	1 823	2 206*	4.6	8.2
WASHINGTON	259	49 472	130 983*	60.3	100.0
005 AME ZION......	2	88	158	0.1	0.1
019 AMER BAPT USA.	11	2 542	3 027*	1.4	2.3
029 AMER LUTH CH..	1	183	263	0.1	0.2
053 ASSEMB OF GOD.	3	1 031	1 240	0.6	0.9
057 BAPT GEN CONF.	1	89	106*	–	0.1
071 BRETHREN (ASH)	1	102	121*	0.1	0.1
081 CATHOLIC......	42	NA	68 186	31.4	52.1
089 CHR & MISS AL.	4	435	765	0.4	0.6
093 CHR CH (DISC).	11	2 608	3 922	1.8	3.0
097 CHR CHS&CHS CR	10	1 948	2 320*	1.1	1.8
105 CHRISTIAN REF.	1	62	92	–	0.1
123 CH GOD (ANDER)	1	25	75	–	0.1
149 CH OF JC (BIC)	2	171	186	0.1	0.1
151 L-D SAINTS....	2	NA	549	0.3	0.4
157 CH OF BRETHREN	1	73	87*	–	0.1
165 CH OF NAZARENE	9	816	1 859	0.9	1.4
167 CHS OF CHRIST.	5	415	529	0.2	0.4
179 CONSRV BAPT...	3	175	208*	0.1	0.2
193 EPISCOPAL.....	6	1 794	2 770	1.3	2.1
208 EVAN LUTH ASSN	1	158	195	0.1	0.1
221 FREE METHODIST	2	102	396	0.2	0.3
244 GRACE BRETHREN	1	143	170*	0.1	0.1
270 CONSRV JUDAISM	1	111	132*	0.1	0.1
271 REFORM JUDAISM	1	150	179*	0.1	0.1
281 LUTH CH AMER..	8	2 886	3 589	1.7	2.7
283 LUTH--MO SYNOD	1	30	43	–	–
353 CHR BRETHREN..	5	145	180	0.1	0.1
356 PRESB CH AMER.	1	281	385	0.2	0.3
381 REF PRES-EVAN.	1	37	39	–	–
403 SALVATION ARMY	1	66	142	0.1	0.1
413 S.D.A.........	2	130	155*	0.1	0.1
419 SO BAPT CONV..	4	771	918*	0.4	0.7
443 UN C OF CHRIST	1	24	29*	–	–
449 UN METHODIST..	52	13 589	16 184*	7.5	12.4
453 UN PRES CH USA	61	18 292	21 784*	10.0	16.6
WAYNE	78	7 840	19 863*	56.4	100.0
019 AMER BAPT USA.	7	706	855*	2.4	4.3
053 ASSEMB OF GOD.	2	327	666	1.9	3.4
081 CATHOLIC......	17	NA	9 372	26.6	47.2
151 L-D SAINTS....	1	NA	85	0.2	0.4
167 CHS OF CHRIST.	1	7	7	–	–
193 EPISCOPAL.....	3	365	473	1.3	2.4
221 FREE METHODIST	2	123	642	1.8	3.2
271 REFORM JUDAISM	1	88	107*	0.3	0.5
281 LUTH CH AMER..	3	1 163	1 540	4.4	7.8
293 MORAV CH-NORTH	1	160	182	0.5	0.9
413 S.D.A.........	2	40	48*	0.1	0.2
449 UN METHODIST..	33	4 169	5 048*	14.3	25.4
453 UN PRES CH USA	5	692	838*	2.4	4.2
WESTMORELAND	410	92 226	273 770*	69.8	100.0
005 AME ZION......	1	313	366	0.1	0.1
019 AMER BAPT USA.	11	3 100	3 703*	0.9	1.4
053 ASSEMB OF GOD.	9	1 433	2 797	0.7	1.0
057 BAPT GEN CONF.	1	46	55*	–	–
071 BRETHREN (ASH)	2	137	164*	–	0.1
081 CATHOLIC......	82	NA	155 183	39.6	56.7
089 CHR & MISS AL.	12	717	1 225	0.3	0.4
093 CHR CH (DISC).	3	492	759	0.2	0.3
097 CHR CHS&CHS CR	8	2 349	2 806*	0.7	1.0
123 CH GOD (ANDER)	3	217	651	0.2	0.2
127 CH GOD (CLEVE)	2	65	78*	–	–
149 CH OF JC (BIC)	1	27	27	–	–
151 L-D SAINTS....	2	NA	432	0.1	0.2
157 CH OF BRETHREN	4	1 567	1 872*	0.5	0.7
165 CH OF NAZARENE	6	521	1 288	0.3	0.5
167 CHS OF CHRIST.	4	222	280	0.1	0.1
179 CONSRV BAPT...	2	75	90*	–	–
193 EPISCOPAL.....	6	1 396	2 023	0.5	0.7
221 FREE METHODIST	8	233	804	0.2	0.3
270 CONSRV JUDAISM	2	67	80*	–	–
271 REFORM JUDAISM	1	218	260*	0.1	0.1
281 LUTH CH AMER..	51	20 700	28 133	7.2	10.3
283 LUTH--MO SYNOD	4	753	1 059	0.3	0.4
291 MISSIONARY CH.	1	31	68	–	–
313 N AM BAPT CONF	1	220	263*	0.1	0.1
329 OPEN BIBLE STD	1	30	75	–	–
349 PENT HOLINESS	5	314	375*	0.1	0.1
353 CHR BRETHREN..	1	70	115	–	–
356 PRESB CH AMER.	1	14	29	–	–
363 PRIMITIVE METH	3	290	346*	0.1	0.1
381 REF PRES-EVAN.	2	169	234	0.1	0.1
383 REF PRES OF NA	2	118	175	–	0.1
403 SALVATION ARMY	5	395	1 144	0.3	0.4
413 S.D.A.........	1	78	93*	–	–
419 SO BAPT CONV..	1	210	251*	0.1	0.1
435 UNITARIAN-UNIV	1	57	68*	–	–

County and Denomination	Number of churches	Communicant, confirmed, full members	Total adherents		
			Number	Percent of total population	Percent of total adherents
443 UN C OF CHRIST	27	6 845	8 177*	2.1	3.0
449 UN METHODIST..	80	27 845	33 262*	8.5	12.1
453 UN PRES CH USA	52	20 752	24 789*	6.3	9.1
469 WELS..........	1	140	171	–	0.1
WYOMING	41	4 935	11 182*	42.3	100.0
019 AMER BAPT USA.	2	291	362*	1.4	3.2
053 ASSEMB OF GOD.	3	212	378	1.4	3.4
081 CATHOLIC......	6	NA	4 344	16.4	38.8
151 L-D SAINTS....	1	NA	125	0.5	1.1
193 EPISCOPAL.....	2	193	423	1.6	3.8
221 FREE METHODIST	2	40	219	0.8	2.0
226 FRIENDS-USA...	1	28	35*	0.1	0.3
281 LUTH CH AMER..	1	110	220	0.8	2.0
283 LUTH--MO SYNOD	1	137	199	0.7	1.8
413 S.D.A.........	2	96	119*	0.5	1.1
449 UN METHODIST..	18	3 416	4 246*	16.1	38.0
453 UN PRES CH USA	2	412	512*	1.9	4.6
YORK	367	110 896	178 988*	57.2	100.0
005 AME ZION......	2	1 364	1 616	0.5	0.9
019 AMER BAPT USA.	1	457	551*	0.2	0.3
053 ASSEMB OF GOD.	19	1 779	3 720	1.2	2.1
057 BAPT GEN CONF.	1	116	140*	–	0.1
075 BRETHREN IN CR	7	574	924	0.3	0.5
081 CATHOLIC......	12	NA	30 941	9.9	17.3
089 CHR & MISS AL.	6	873	1 606	0.5	0.9
127 CH GOD (CLEVE)	3	154	186*	0.1	0.1
151 L-D SAINTS....	2	NA	687	0.2	0.4
157 CH OF BRETHREN	14	4 275	5 154*	1.6	2.9
165 CH OF NAZARENE	5	688	1 499	0.5	0.8
167 CHS OF CHRIST.	3	215	334	0.1	0.2
179 CONSRV BAPT...	1	135	163*	0.1	0.1
193 EPISCOPAL.....	4	1 783	2 176	0.7	1.2
197 EVAN CH OF NA.	1	108	108	–	0.1
199 EVAN CONGR CH.	3	889	1 072*	0.3	0.6
203 EVAN FREE CH..	1	41	49*	–	–
226 FRIENDS-USA...	2	38	46*	–	–
244 GRACE BRETHREN	3	318	383*	0.1	0.2
263 INT FOURSQ GOS	2	276	333*	0.1	0.2
270 CONSRV JUDAISM	2	180	217*	0.1	0.1
271 REFORM JUDAISM	1	410	494*	0.2	0.3
281 LUTH CH AMER..	80	35 930	47 687*	15.2	26.6
283 LUTH--MO SYNOD	3	1 318	1 699	0.5	0.9
285 MENNONITE CH..	10	577	696*	0.2	0.4
291 MISSIONARY CH.	3	132	188	0.1	0.1
293 MORAV CH-NORTH	2	478	626	0.2	0.3
335 ORTH PRESB CH.	1	79	95*	–	0.1
353 CHR BRETHREN..	1	50	100	–	0.1
403 SALVATION ARMY	1	151	6 165	2.0	3.4
413 S.D.A.........	2	262	316*	0.1	0.2
419 SO BAPT CONV..	7	1 121	1 352*	0.4	0.8
435 UNITARIAN-UNIV	1	79	95*	–	0.1
443 UN C OF CHRIST	48	19 933	24 032*	7.7	13.4
449 UN METHODIST..	96	29 954	36 113*	11.5	20.2
453 UN PRES CH USA	17	6 159	7 425*	2.4	4.1

RHODE ISLAND

County and Denomination	Number of churches	Communicant, confirmed, full members	Total adherents		
			Number	Percent of total population	Percent of total adherents
THE STATE.....	498	88 129	715 569*	75.5	100.0
BRISTOL	30	5 415	39 429*	84.0	100.0
019 AMER BAPT USA.	2	329	389*	0.8	1.0
053 ASSEMB OF GOD.	1	36	75	0.2	0.2
057 BAPT GEN CONF.	1	213	252*	0.5	0.6
081 CATHOLIC......	12	NA	32 285	68.8	81.9
193 EPISCOPAL.....	5	2 600	3 760	8.0	9.5
271 REFORM JUDAISM	1	220	260*	0.6	0.7
281 LUTH CH AMER..	1	325	401	0.9	1.0
353 CHR BRETHREN..	1	20	30	0.1	0.1
443 UN C OF CHRIST	2	826	977*	2.1	2.5
449 UN METHODIST..	2	384	454*	1.0	1.2
453 UN PRES CH USA	2	462	546*	1.2	1.4
KENT	72	13 453	113 032*	73.3	100.0
001 ADVENT CHR CH.	1	135	162*	0.1	0.1
019 AMER BAPT USA.	13	3 416	4 093*	2.7	3.6
053 ASSEMB OF GOD.	2	160	355	0.2	0.3
081 CATHOLIC......	25	NA	94 878	61.5	83.9
089 CHR & MISS AL.	1	0	30	–	–
123 CH GOD (ANDER)	1	5	15	–	–
167 CHS OF CHRIST.	1	45	57	–	0.1
175 CONGR CHR CHS.	1	185	222*	0.1	0.2
193 EPISCOPAL.....	8	4 597	6 966	4.5	6.2
201 EVAN COV CH AM	2	70	84*	–	0.1
281 LUTH CH AMER..	4	1 799	2 428	1.6	2.1
353 CHR BRETHREN..	2	105	225	0.1	0.2
435 UNITARIAN-UNIV	2	234	280*	0.2	0.2
443 UN C OF CHRIST	2	208	249*	0.2	0.2

NA—Not applicable   *Total adherents estimated from known number of communicant, confirmed, full members.   —Represents a percent less than 0.1.   Percentages may not total due to rounding.

Table 4. Churches and Church Membership by County and Denomination: 1980

County and Denomination	Number of churches	Communicant, confirmed, full members	Total adherents		
			Number	Percent of total population	Percent of total adherents
449 UN METHODIST..	6	1 830	2 192*	1.4	1.9
453 UN PRES CH USA	1	664	796*	0.5	0.7
NEWPORT	48	6 814	52 141*	64.1	100.0
019 AMER BAPT USA.	7	1 375	1 653*	2.0	3.2
053 ASSEMB OF GOD.	1	41	80	0.1	0.2
081 CATHOLIC......	15	NA	42 648	52.4	81.8
151 L-D SAINTS....	1	NA	256	0.3	0.5
165 CH OF NAZARENE	1	34	39	–	0.1
167 CHS OF CHRIST.	1	37	47	0.1	0.1
193 EPISCOPAL.....	10	2 892	4 238	5.2	8.1
226 FRIENDS-USA...	2	111	133*	0.2	0.3
270 CONSRV JUDAISM	1	79	95*	0.1	0.2
281 LUTH CH AMER..	1	324	550	0.7	1.1
363 PRIMITIVE METH	1	83	100*	0.1	0.2
403 SALVATION ARMY	1	98	210	0.3	0.4
419 SO BAPT CONV..	1	354	426*	0.5	0.8
435 UNITARIAN-UNIV	1	140	168*	0.2	0.3
449 UN METHODIST..	3	773	929*	1.1	1.8
453 UN PRES CH USA	1	473	569*	0.7	1.1
PROVIDENCE	279	51 449	467 751*	81.9	100.0
001 ADVENT CHR CH.	2	223	263*	–	0.1
005 AME ZION......	2	330	495	0.1	0.1
019 AMER BAPT USA.	42	12 510	14 750*	2.6	3.2
049 ARMEN AP CH AM	1	350	950	0.2	0.2
053 ASSEMB OF GOD.	3	254	528	0.1	0.1
081 CATHOLIC......	105	NA	402 991	70.5	86.2
097 CHR CHS&CHS CR	1	21	25*	–	–
123 CH GOD (ANDER)	1	40	120	–	–
127 CH GOD (CLEVE)	5	205	242*	–	0.1
151 L-D SAINTS....	1	NA	586	0.1	0.1
163 CH OF LUTH BR.	1	38	65	–	–
165 CH OF NAZARENE	4	208	346	0.1	0.1
167 CHS OF CHRIST.	1	60	76	–	–
175 CONGR CHR CHS.	1	35	41*	–	–
181 CONSRV CONGR..	1	234	276*	–	0.1
193 EPISCOPAL.....	35	16 191	20 812	3.6	4.4
201 EVAN COV CH AM	3	479	565*	0.1	0.1
226 FRIENDS-USA...	2	258	304*	0.1	0.1
270 CONSRV JUDAISM	6	1 687	1 989*	0.3	0.4
271 REFORM JUDAISM	2	2 470	2 912*	0.5	0.6
281 LUTH CH AMER..	4	1 405	1 634	0.3	0.3
283 LUTH--MO SYNOD	2	786	975	0.2	0.2
290 METRO COMM CHS	1	57	114	–	–
353 CHR BRETHREN..	1	25	25	–	–
363 PRIMITIVE METH	3	316	373*	0.1	0.1
403 SALVATION ARMY	2	339	1 031	0.2	0.2
413 S.D.A.........	4	456	538*	0.1	0.1
419 SO BAPT CONV..	1	132	156*	–	–
423 SYRIAN ANTIOCH	1	800	943*	0.2	0.2
435 UNITARIAN-UNIV	5	830	979*	0.2	0.2
443 UN C OF CHRIST	19	6 153	7 255*	1.3	1.6
449 UN METHODIST..	11	3 834	4 520*	0.8	1.0
453 UN PRES CH USA	5	683	805*	0.1	0.2
469 WELS..........	1	40	67	–	–
WASHINGTON	69	10 998	43 216*	46.3	100.0
001 ADVENT CHR CH.	2	98	118*	0.1	0.3
019 AMER BAPT USA.	15	2 747	3 298*	3.5	7.6
053 ASSEMB OF GOD.	2	78	145	0.2	0.3
081 CATHOLIC......	17	NA	30 105	32.3	69.7
083 CHRIST CATH CH	2	67	86	0.1	0.2
123 CH GOD (ANDER)	1	88	264	0.3	0.6
127 CH GOD (CLEVE)	1	12	14*	–	–
151 L-D SAINTS....	1	NA	209	0.2	0.5
165 CH OF NAZARENE	1	12	11	–	–
167 CHS OF CHRIST.	1	14	18	–	–
193 EPISCOPAL.....	9	4 717	5 101	5.5	11.8
226 FRIENDS-USA...	1	31	37*	–	0.1
281 LUTH CH AMER..	1	154	216	0.2	0.5
283 LUTH--MO SYNOD	1	186	240	0.3	0.6
413 S.D.A.........	1	35	42*	–	0.1
415 S-D BAPTIST GC	3	395	474*	0.5	1.1
419 SO BAPT CONV..	2	361	433*	0.5	1.0
443 UN C OF CHRIST	3	1 180	1 417*	1.5	3.3
449 UN METHODIST..	3	485	582*	0.6	1.3
453 UN PRES CH USA	2	338	406*	0.4	0.9

SOUTH CAROLINA

County and Denomination	Number of churches	Communicant, confirmed, full members	Total adherents		
			Number	Percent of total population	Percent of total adherents
THE STATE.....	4 994	1 235 786	1 605 231*	51.5	100.0
ABBEVILLE	59	11 411	14 008*	61.9	100.0
055 AS REF PRES CH	3	460	522	2.3	3.7
061 BEACHY AMISH..	1	72	88*	0.4	0.6
081 CATHOLIC......	1	NA	138	0.6	1.0
101 C.M.E........	2	243	296*	1.3	2.1
127 CH GOD (CLEVE)	2	230	280*	1.2	2.0

County and Denomination	Number of churches	Communicant, confirmed, full members	Total adherents		
			Number	Percent of total population	Percent of total adherents
167 CHS OF CHRIST.	1	50	64	0.3	0.5
177 CONGR HOL CH..	1	85	104*	0.5	0.7
193 EPISCOPAL.....	1	108	114	0.5	0.8
285 MENNONITE CH..	1	101	123*	0.5	0.9
349 PENT HOLINESS.	4	492	600*	2.7	4.3
356 PRESB CH AMER.	3	407	508	2.2	3.6
357 PRESB CH US...	8	965	1 176*	5.2	8.4
419 SO BAPT CONV..	19	6 416	7 822*	34.6	55.8
449 UN METHODIST..	10	1 705	2 079*	9.2	14.8
453 UN PRES CH USA	2	77	94*	0.4	0.7
AIKEN	169	44 816	58 917*	55.8	100.0
017 AMER BAPT ASSN	1	19	19	–	–
053 ASSEMB OF GOD.	2	138	187	0.2	0.3
081 CATHOLIC......	4	NA	2 901	2.7	4.9
093 CHR CH (DISC).	5	412	573	0.5	1.0
101 C.M.E........	1	145	178*	0.2	0.3
123 CH GOD (ANDER)	4	136	408	0.4	0.7
127 CH GOD (CLEVE)	12	1 073	1 318*	1.2	2.2
151 L-D SAINTS....	1	NA	249	0.2	0.4
165 CH OF NAZARENE	3	338	601	0.6	1.0
167 CHS OF CHRIST.	9	500	635	0.6	1.1
177 CONGR HOL CH..	2	96	118*	0.1	0.2
193 EPISCOPAL.....	5	1 397	1 715	1.6	2.9
244 GRACE BRETHREN	1	58	71*	0.1	0.1
281 LUTH CH AMER..	4	1 374	1 780	1.7	3.0
283 LUTH--MO SYNOD	1	138	165	0.2	0.3
349 PENT HOLINESS.	9	478	587*	0.6	1.0
353 CHR BRETHREN..	2	90	105	0.1	0.2
356 PRESB CH AMER.	1	49	52	–	0.1
357 PRESB CH US...	3	2 369	2 911*	2.8	4.9
403 SALVATION ARMY	1	105	214	0.2	0.4
413 S.D.A.........	1	58	71*	0.1	0.1
419 SO BAPT CONV..	76	29 128	35 791*	33.9	60.7
421 SO METHODIST..	2	81	116	0.1	0.2
449 UN METHODIST..	19	6 634	8 152*	7.7	13.8
ALLENDALE	29	4 877	6 203*	58.0	100.0
081 CATHOLIC......	1	NA	33	0.3	0.5
093 CHR CH (DISC).	2	133	190	1.8	3.1
101 C.M.E........	4	1 054	1 323*	12.4	21.3
127 CH GOD (CLEVE)	1	35	44*	0.4	0.7
193 EPISCOPAL.....	1	55	102	1.0	1.6
281 LUTH CH AMER..	2	155	187	1.7	3.0
357 PRESB CH US...	1	69	87*	0.8	1.4
419 SO BAPT CONV..	10	2 197	2 757*	25.8	44.4
449 UN METHODIST..	7	1 179	1 480*	13.8	23.9
ANDERSON	210	63 207	79 470*	59.6	100.0
053 ASSEMB OF GOD.	5	621	778	0.6	1.0
055 AS REF PRES CH	3	388	434	0.3	0.5
081 CATHOLIC......	2	NA	1 183	0.9	1.5
089 CHR & MISS AL.	1	0	15	–	–
097 CHR CHS&CHS CR	1	50	61*	–	0.1
101 C.M.E........	4	1 262	1 538*	1.2	1.9
121 CH GOD (ABR)..	1	225	274*	0.2	0.3
127 CH GOD (CLEVE)	19	3 464	4 223*	3.2	5.3
151 L-D SAINTS....	1	NA	224	0.2	0.3
167 CHS OF CHRIST.	2	70	175	0.1	0.2
193 EPISCOPAL.....	1	421	558	0.4	0.7
244 GRACE BRETHREN	1	36	44*	–	0.1
281 LUTH CH AMER..	1	319	394	0.3	0.5
285 MENNONITE CH..	2	62	76*	0.1	0.1
349 PENT HOLINESS.	9	1 470	1 792*	1.3	2.3
353 CHR BRETHREN..	1	20	20	–	–
357 PRESB CH US...	19	3 630	4 425*	3.3	5.6
381 REF PRES-EVAN.	1	131	157	0.1	0.2
403 SALVATION ARMY	1	123	1 030	0.8	1.3
413 S.D.A.........	2	139	169*	0.1	0.2
419 SO BAPT CONV..	90	43 545	53 085*	39.8	66.8
449 UN METHODIST..	42	7 161	8 730*	6.6	11.0
453 UN PRES CH USA	1	70	85*	0.1	0.1
BAMBERG	57	7 398	9 581*	52.9	100.0
081 CATHOLIC......	0	NA	15	0.1	0.2
093 CHR CH (DISC).	3	333	555	3.1	5.8
127 CH GOD (CLEVE)	4	97	120*	0.7	1.3
151 L-D SAINTS....	1	NA	197	1.1	2.1
165 CH OF NAZARENE	1	108	230	1.3	2.4
167 CHS OF CHRIST.	1	30	38	0.2	0.4
193 EPISCOPAL.....	2	132	172	0.9	1.8
281 LUTH CH AMER..	2	131	146	0.8	1.5
349 PENT HOLINESS.	1	80	99*	0.5	1.0
357 PRESB CH US...	2	114	140*	0.8	1.5
419 SO BAPT CONV..	15	3 467	4 273*	23.6	44.6
421 SO METHODIST..	1	31	53	0.3	0.6
449 UN METHODIST..	24	2 875	3 543*	19.6	37.0
BARNWELL	53	8 830	11 306*	56.9	100.0
053 ASSEMB OF GOD.	1	39	42	0.2	0.4
061 BEACHY AMISH..	1	60	75*	0.4	0.7
081 CATHOLIC......	2	NA	195	1.0	1.7
097 CHR CHS&CHS CR	1	170	214*	1.1	1.9
101 C.M.E........	1	163	205*	1.0	1.8
123 CH GOD (ANDER)	1	14	42	0.2	0.4
127 CH GOD (CLEVE)	3	200	251*	1.3	2.2
167 CHS OF CHRIST.	3	120	153	0.8	1.4
193 EPISCOPAL.....	2	146	182	0.9	1.6
285 MENNONITE CH..	1	29	36*	0.2	0.3
349 PENT HOLINESS.	6	265	333*	1.7	2.9

NA—Not applicable   *Total adherents estimated from known number of communicant, confirmed, full members.   —Represents a percent less than 0.1.   Percentages may not total due to rounding.

Table 4. Churches and Church Membership by County and Denomination: 1980

County and Denomination	Number of churches	Communicant, confirmed, full members	Total adherents Number	Percent of total population	Percent of total adherents
357 PRESB CH US...	3	359	451*	2.3	4.0
419 SO BAPT CONV..	22	6 419	8 071*	40.6	71.4
421 SO METHODIST..	2	105	124	0.6	1.1
449 UN METHODIST..	4	741	932*	4.7	8.2
BEAUFORT	49	11 907	16 990*	26.0	100.0
053 ASSEMB OF GOD.	1	199	489	0.7	2.9
081 CATHOLIC......	4	NA	2 133	3.3	12.6
093 CHR CH (DISC).	4	337	408	0.6	2.4
097 CHR CHS&CHS CR	1	60	72*	0.1	0.4
127 CH GOD (CLEVE)	1	108	130*	0.2	0.8
151 L-D SAINTS....	2	NA	307	0.5	1.8
165 CH OF NAZARENE	1	45	90	0.1	0.5
167 CHS OF CHRIST.	2	50	64	0.1	0.4
193 EPISCOPAL.....	3	1 831	2 021	3.1	11.9
270 CONSRV JUDAISM	1	35	42*	0.1	0.2
281 LUTH CH AMER..	2	372	536	0.8	3.2
349 PENT HOLINESS.	2	75	90*	0.1	0.5
353 CHR BRETHREN..	2	30	30	-	0.2
357 PRESB CH US...	2	1 192	1 438*	2.2	8.5
403 SALVATION ARMY	1	34	44	0.1	0.3
413 S.D.A.........	1	38	46*	0.1	0.3
419 SO BAPT CONV..	9	5 474	6 604*	10.1	38.9
435 UNITARIAN-UNIV	1	23	28*	-	0.2
449 UN METHODIST..	8	1 994	2 406*	3.7	14.2
453 UN PRES CH USA	1	10	12*	-	0.1
BERKELEY	133	20 032	28 476*	30.1	100.0
081 CATHOLIC......	5	NA	1 841	1.9	6.5
093 CHR CH (DISC).	10	718	952	1.0	3.3
097 CHR CHS&CHS CR	4	568	724*	0.8	2.5
127 CH GOD (CLEVE)	3	237	302*	0.3	1.1
151 L-D SAINTS....	2	NA	760	0.8	2.7
165 CH OF NAZARENE	2	148	257	0.3	0.9
167 CHS OF CHRIST.	1	30	40	-	0.1
193 EPISCOPAL.....	5	416	610	0.6	2.1
281 LUTH CH AMER..	3	557	871	0.9	3.1
349 PENT HOLINESS.	20	967	1 232*	1.3	4.3
357 PRESB CH US...	4	784	999*	1.1	3.5
375 REF EPISCOPAL.	16	1 310	1 669*	1.8	5.9
413 S.D.A.........	1	13	17*	-	0.1
419 SO BAPT CONV..	22	9 122	11 624*	12.3	40.8
449 UN METHODIST..	35	5 162	6 578*	6.9	23.1
CALHOUN	24	3 311	4 214*	34.5	100.0
053 ASSEMB OF GOD.	1	39	84	0.7	2.0
081 CATHOLIC......	0	NA	40	0.3	0.9
123 CH GOD (ANDER)	1	28	84	0.7	2.0
193 EPISCOPAL.....	1	120	162	1.3	3.8
281 LUTH CH AMER..	5	448	545	4.5	12.9
357 PRESB CH US...	1	101	125*	1.0	3.0
419 SO BAPT CONV..	6	1 454	1 796*	14.7	42.6
421 SO METHODIST..	1	79	91	0.7	2.2
449 UN METHODIST..	8	1 042	1 287*	10.5	30.5
CHARLESTON	242	83 469	118 894*	42.9	100.0
001 ADVENT CHR CH.	1	53	64*	-	0.1
053 ASSEMB OF GOD.	5	794	1 136	0.4	1.0
055 AS REF PRES CH	1	18	20	-	-
081 CATHOLIC......	18	NA	14 952	5.4	12.6
089 CHR & MISS AL.	1	33	70	-	0.1
093 CHR CH (DISC).	2	448	633	0.2	0.5
097 CHR CHS&CHS CR	1	136	164*	0.1	0.1
101 C.M.E.	2	808	975*	0.4	0.8
123 CH GOD (ANDER)	2	80	240	0.1	0.2
127 CH GOD (CLEVE)	6	687	829*	0.3	0.7
151 L-D SAINTS....	3	NA	1 310	0.5	1.1
165 CH OF NAZARENE	4	505	729	0.3	0.6
167 CHS OF CHRIST.	5	1 142	1 472	0.5	1.2
193 EPISCOPAL.....	26	9 505	11 987	4.3	10.1
270 CONSRV JUDAISM	1	257	310*	0.1	0.3
271 REFORM JUDAISM	1	508	613*	0.2	0.5
281 LUTH CH AMER..	15	5 559	7 329	2.6	6.2
283 LUTH--MO SYNOD	1	311	422	0.2	0.4
349 PENT HOLINESS.	10	779	940*	0.3	0.8
353 CHR BRETHREN..	4	115	180	0.1	0.2
357 PRESB CH US...	14	5 128	6 187*	2.2	5.2
375 REF EPISCOPAL.	12	1 001	1 208*	0.4	1.0
381 REF PRES-EVAN.	2	120	151	0.1	0.1
403 SALVATION ARMY	1	186	256	0.1	0.2
413 S.D.A.........	3	510	615*	0.2	0.5
419 SO BAPT CONV..	51	37 178	44 858*	16.2	37.7
421 SO METHODIST..	3	312	375	0.1	0.3
435 UNITARIAN-UNIV	1	93	112*	-	0.1
443 UN C OF CHRIST	2	234	282*	0.1	0.2
449 UN METHODIST..	33	14 812	17 872*	6.4	15.0
453 UN PRES CH USA	11	2 157	2 603*	0.9	2.2
CHEROKEE	89	24 203	30 579*	74.6	100.0
005 AME ZION......	2	493	606	1.5	2.0
053 ASSEMB OF GOD.	1	27	52	0.1	0.2
055 AS REF PRES CH	1	111	122	0.3	0.4
081 CATHOLIC......	1	NA	174	0.4	0.6
101 C.M.E.	3	1 656	2 043*	5.0	6.7
127 CH GOD (CLEVE)	5	532	656*	1.6	2.1
151 L-D SAINTS....	1	NA	455	1.1	1.5
167 CHS OF CHRIST.	2	50	64	0.2	0.2
193 EPISCOPAL.....	1	88	128	0.3	0.4
263 INT FOURSQ GOS	1	93	115*	0.3	0.4
281 LUTH CH AMER..	1	89	126	0.3	0.4

County and Denomination	Number of churches	Communicant, confirmed, full members	Total adherents Number	Percent of total population	Percent of total adherents
356 PRESB CH AMER.	2	163	181	0.4	0.6
357 PRESB CH US...	1	410	506*	1.2	1.7
403 SALVATION ARMY	1	121	219	0.5	0.7
419 SO BAPT CONV..	56	18 887	23 302*	56.9	76.2
449 UN METHODIST..	8	1 423	1 756*	4.3	5.7
453 UN PRES CH USA	2	60	74*	0.2	0.2
CHESTER	99	21 436	25 039*	83.1	100.0
005 AME ZION......	25	8 672	9 090	30.2	36.3
053 ASSEMB OF GOD.	2	108	139	0.5	0.6
055 AS REF PRES CH	6	739	837	2.8	3.3
081 CATHOLIC......	2	NA	112	0.4	0.4
127 CH GOD (CLEVE)	5	547	674*	2.2	2.7
165 CH OF NAZARENE	2	340	614	2.0	2.5
167 CHS OF CHRIST.	1	20	38	0.1	0.2
193 EPISCOPAL.....	2	107	127	0.4	0.5
263 INT FOURSQ GOS	1	21	26*	0.1	0.1
281 LUTH CH AMER..	1	51	65	0.2	0.3
349 PENT HOLINESS.	1	39	48*	0.2	0.2
356 PRESB CH AMER.	2	262	299	1.0	1.2
357 PRESB CH US...	13	1 357	1 671*	5.5	6.7
419 SO BAPT CONV..	17	6 492	7 996*	26.5	31.9
449 UN METHODIST..	16	2 532	3 119*	10.3	12.5
453 UN PRES CH USA	3	149	184*	0.6	0.7
CHESTERFIELD	132	25 283	31 208*	81.8	100.0
005 AME ZION......	13	7 098	8 501	22.3	27.2
053 ASSEMB OF GOD.	1	21	26	0.1	0.1
081 CATHOLIC......	1	NA	141	0.4	0.5
127 CH GOD (CLEVE)	4	261	323*	0.8	1.0
165 CH OF NAZARENE	1	55	87	0.2	0.3
167 CHS OF CHRIST.	1	22	22	0.1	0.1
177 CONGR HOL CH..	1	86	107*	0.3	0.3
193 EPISCOPAL.....	1	190	245	0.6	0.8
349 PENT HOLINESS.	1	50	62*	0.2	0.2
356 PRESB CH AMER.	1	104	135	0.4	0.4
357 PRESB CH US...	10	975	1 208*	3.2	3.9
419 SO BAPT CONV..	58	11 108	13 764*	36.1	44.1
421 SO METHODIST..	1	40	53	0.1	0.2
449 UN METHODIST..	35	5 040	6 245*	16.4	20.0
453 UN PRES CH USA	3	233	289*	0.8	0.9
CLARENDON	43	6 960	8 678*	31.6	100.0
081 CATHOLIC......	1	NA	85	0.3	1.0
123 CH GOD (ANDER)	1	8	24	0.1	0.3
127 CH GOD (CLEVE)	3	99	123*	0.4	1.4
193 EPISCOPAL.....	1	102	134	0.5	1.5
349 PENT HOLINESS.	4	288	358*	1.3	4.1
356 PRESB CH AMER.	3	393	434	1.6	5.0
357 PRESB CH US...	3	519	645*	2.3	7.4
413 S.D.A.........	1	?	?	?	?
419 SO BAPT CONV..	11	2 898	3 599*	13.1	41.5
421 SO METHODIST..	2	251	293	1.1	3.4
449 UN METHODIST..	9	1 662	2 064*	7.5	23.8
453 UN PRES CH USA	4	740	919*	3.3	10.6
COLLETON	94	14 360	18 309*	57.8	100.0
001 ADVENT CHR CH.	4	475	587*	1.9	3.2
053 ASSEMB OF GOD.	1	16	25	0.1	0.1
081 CATHOLIC......	2	NA	348	1.1	1.9
093 CHR CH (DISC).	4	288	424	1.3	2.3
097 CHR CHS&CHS CR	3	313	387*	1.2	2.1
101 C.M.E.	5	1 537	1 901*	6.0	10.4
127 CH GOD (CLEVE)	1	133	164*	0.5	0.9
151 L-D SAINTS....	1	NA	131	0.4	0.7
167 CHS OF CHRIST.	1	20	25	0.1	0.1
193 EPISCOPAL.....	2	245	309	1.0	1.7
263 INT FOURSQ GOS	1	49	61*	0.2	0.3
281 LUTH CH AMER..	1	134	159	0.5	0.9
349 PENT HOLINESS.	3	145	179*	0.6	1.0
357 PRESB CH US...	1	193	239*	0.8	1.3
419 SO BAPT CONV..	26	6 498	8 037*	25.4	43.9
421 SO METHODIST..	1	23	26	0.1	0.1
449 UN METHODIST..	35	4 092	5 061*	16.0	27.6
453 UN PRES CH USA	2	199	246*	0.8	1.3
DARLINGTON	93	20 262	28 011*	44.7	100.0
001 ADVENT CHR CH.	1	56	70*	0.1	0.2
053 ASSEMB OF GOD.	1	103	309	0.5	1.1
081 CATHOLIC......	3	NA	336	0.5	1.2
123 CH GOD (ANDER)	6	587	1 761	2.8	6.3
127 CH GOD (CLEVE)	5	336	419*	0.7	1.5
151 L-D SAINTS....	3	NA	760	1.2	2.7
165 CH OF NAZARENE	2	190	400	0.6	1.4
177 CONGR HOL CH..	2	57	71*	0.1	0.3
193 EPISCOPAL.....	2	403	677	1.1	2.4
281 LUTH CH AMER..	1	96	143	0.2	0.5
349 PENT HOLINESS.	6	402	502*	0.8	1.8
353 CHR BRETHREN..	1	50	100	0.2	0.4
357 PRESB CH US...	5	1 171	1 462*	2.3	5.2
413 S.D.A.........	1	39	49*	0.1	0.2
419 SO BAPT CONV..	27	11 084	13 835*	22.1	49.4
421 SO METHODIST..	3	181	243	0.4	0.9
449 UN METHODIST..	23	5 491	6 854*	10.9	24.5
453 UN PRES CH USA	1	16	20*	-	0.1
DILLON	62	11 469	14 723*	47.4	100.0
053 ASSEMB OF GOD.	1	29	62	0.2	0.4
081 CATHOLIC......	1	NA	149	0.5	1.0

NA—Not applicable   *Total adherents estimated from known number of communicant, confirmed, full members.   —Represents a percent less than 0.1.   Percentages may not total due to rounding.

Table 4. Churches and Church Membership by County and Denomination: 1980

County and Denomination	Number of churches	Communicant, confirmed, full members	Total adherents Number	Percent of total population	Percent of total adherents
127 CH GOD (CLEVE)	7	859	1 090*	3.5	7.4
167 CHS OF CHRIST.	1	20	25	0.1	0.2
177 CONGR HOL CH..	1	172	218*	0.7	1.5
193 EPISCOPAL.....	1	59	70	0.2	0.5
349 PENT HOLINESS.	5	292	371*	1.2	2.5
357 PRESB CH US...	9	905	1 149*	3.7	7.8
419 SO BAPT CONV..	22	7 124	9 041*	29.1	61.4
421 SO METHODIST..	2	110	138	0.4	0.9
449 UN METHODIST..	12	1 899	2 410*	7.8	16.4
DORCHESTER	**94**	**20 164**	**28 135***	**48.3**	**100.0**
005 AME ZION......	1	183	233	0.4	0.8
017 AMER BAPT ASSN	2	82	82	0.1	0.3
053 ASSEMB OF GOD.	1	46	58	0.1	0.2
081 CATHOLIC......	1	NA	2 026	3.5	7.2
093 CHR CH (DISC).	7	434	618	1.1	2.2
097 CHR CHS&CHS CR	2	85	107*	0.2	0.4
123 CH GOD (ANDER)	2	210	630	1.1	2.2
127 CH GOD (CLEVE)	3	152	191*	0.3	0.7
165 CH OF NAZARENE	1	59	112	0.2	0.4
167 CHS OF CHRIST.	2	185	235	0.4	0.8
193 EPISCOPAL.....	2	1 079	1 475	2.5	5.2
215 EVAN METH CH..	1	22	28*	-	0.1
281 LUTH CH AMER..	1	462	698	1.2	2.5
283 LUTH--MO SYNOD	1	97	150	0.3	0.5
349 PENT HOLINESS.	4	128	161*	0.3	0.6
357 PRESB CH US...	2	819	1 031*	1.8	3.7
375 REF EPISCOPAL.	1	8	10*	-	-
413 S.D.A.........	1	34	43*	0.1	0.2
419 SO BAPT CONV..	16	7 088	8 918*	15.3	31.7
421 SO METHODIST..	4	295	375	0.6	1.3
449 UN METHODIST..	38	8 668	10 906*	18.7	38.8
469 WELS..........	1	28	48	0.1	0.2
EDGEFIELD	**33**	**5 005**	**7 762***	**44.3**	**100.0**
081 CATHOLIC......	2	NA	1 544	8.8	19.9
101 C.M.E.........	1	30	37*	0.2	0.5
127 CH GOD (CLEVE)	2	124	154*	0.9	2.0
177 CONGR HOL CH..	1	42	52*	0.3	0.7
193 EPISCOPAL.....	1	252	302	1.7	3.9
281 LUTH CH AMER..	1	89	111	0.6	1.4
349 PENT HOLINESS.	1	60	75*	0.4	1.0
357 PRESB CH US...	3	138	172*	1.0	2.2
413 S.D.A.........	1	14	17*	0.1	0.2
419 SO BAPT CONV..	15	3 379	4 206*	24.0	54.2
449 UN METHODIST..	5	877	1 092*	6.2	14.1
FAIRFIELD	**55**	**7 336**	**9 823***	**47.5**	**100.0**
005 AME ZION......	7	733	999	4.8	10.2
055 AS REF PRES CH	2	242	258	1.2	2.6
081 CATHOLIC......	1	NA	40	0.2	0.4
123 CH GOD (ANDER)	1	15	45	0.2	0.5
127 CH GOD (CLEVE)	2	226	280*	1.4	2.9
151 L-D SAINTS....	2	NA	481	2.3	4.9
165 CH OF NAZARENE	1	188	446	2.2	4.5
167 CHS OF CHRIST.	1	23	38	0.2	0.4
193 EPISCOPAL.....	3	252	295	1.4	3.0
349 PENT HOLINESS.	1	115	143*	0.7	1.5
356 PRESB CH AMER.	3	412	433	2.1	4.4
357 PRESB CH US...	4	553	686*	3.3	7.0
419 SO BAPT CONV..	13	2 921	3 624*	17.5	36.9
449 UN METHODIST..	9	1 340	1 663*	8.0	16.9
453 UN PRES CH USA	5	316	392*	1.9	4.0
FLORENCE	**175**	**37 552**	**49 554***	**45.0**	**100.0**
053 ASSEMB OF GOD.	3	209	276	0.3	0.6
081 CATHOLIC......	4	NA	1 732	1.6	3.5
097 CHR CHS&CHS CR	1	40	50*	-	0.1
123 CH GOD (ANDER)	3	179	537	0.5	1.1
127 CH GOD (CLEVE)	11	838	1 042*	0.9	2.1
151 L-D SAINTS....	1	NA	368	0.3	0.7
165 CH OF NAZARENE	1	54	98	0.1	0.2
167 CHS OF CHRIST.	5	230	293	0.3	0.6
193 EPISCOPAL.....	3	976	1 415	1.3	2.9
271 REFORM JUDAISM	1	148	184*	0.2	0.4
281 LUTH CH AMER..	1	346	447	0.4	0.9
283 LUTH--MO SYNOD	1	67	80	0.1	0.2
349 PENT HOLINESS.	32	2 401	2 985*	2.7	6.0
353 CHR BRETHREN..	2	210	250	0.2	0.5
357 PRESB CH US...	11	2 832	3 521*	3.2	7.1
381 REF PRES-EVAN.	1	14	26	-	0.1
403 SALVATION ARMY	1	100	259	0.2	0.5
413 S.D.A.........	2	251	312*	0.3	0.6
419 SO BAPT CONV..	41	17 294	21 500*	19.5	43.4
421 SO METHODIST..	5	244	356	0.3	0.7
449 UN METHODIST..	45	11 119	13 823*	12.5	27.9
GEORGETOWN	**81**	**11 151**	**14 906***	**35.1**	**100.0**
053 ASSEMB OF GOD.	2	155	309	0.7	2.1
081 CATHOLIC......	4	NA	511	1.2	3.4
123 CH GOD (ANDER)	3	22	66	0.2	0.4
127 CH GOD (CLEVE)	4	265	334*	0.8	2.2
151 L-D SAINTS....	1	NA	77	0.2	0.5
165 CH OF NAZARENE	1	85	198	0.5	1.3
167 CHS OF CHRIST.	3	184	234	0.6	1.6
193 EPISCOPAL.....	6	1 102	1 382	3.3	9.3
271 REFORM JUDAISM	1	48	60*	0.1	0.4
281 LUTH CH AMER..	1	182	247	0.6	1.7
349 PENT HOLINESS.	15	1 257	1 584*	3.7	10.6
356 PRESB CH AMER.	1	104	134	0.3	0.9
357 PRESB CH US...	4	718	905*	2.1	6.1
419 SO BAPT CONV.	18	4 872	6 140*	14.5	41.2
421 SO METHODIST..	1	4	12	-	0.1
449 UN METHODIST..	16	2 153	2 713*	6.4	18.2
GREENVILLE	**361**	**132 199**	**170 113***	**59.1**	**100.0**
017 AMER BAPT ASSN	2	185	185	0.1	0.1
053 ASSEMB OF GOD.	14	1 292	2 004	0.7	1.2
055 AS REF PRES CH	2	732	823	0.3	0.5
081 CATHOLIC......	6	NA	7 048	2.4	4.1
089 CHR & MISS AL.	1	25	59	-	-
093 CHR CH (DISC).	1	66	81	-	-
097 CHR CHS&CHS CR	2	175	212*	0.1	0.1
101 C.M.E........	3	2 223	2 689*	0.9	1.6
121 CH GOD (ABR)..	1	30	36*	-	-
123 CH GOD (ANDER)	3	121	363	0.1	0.2
127 CH GOD (CLEVE)	26	3 781	4 574*	1.6	2.7
151 L-D SAINTS....	2	NA	952	0.3	0.6
157 CH OF BRETHREN	1	97	117*	-	0.1
165 CH OF NAZARENE	2	165	264	0.1	0.2
167 CHS OF CHRIST.	11	1 096	1 320	0.5	0.8
193 EPISCOPAL.....	9	4 881	6 523	2.3	3.8
270 CONSRV JUDAISM	1	70	85*	-	-
271 REFORM JUDAISM	1	180	218*	0.1	0.1
281 LUTH CH AMER..	5	1 966	2 609	0.9	1.5
283 LUTH--MO SYNOD	1	200	252	0.1	0.1
349 PENT HOLINESS.	15	1 418	1 715*	0.6	1.0
353 CHR BRETHREN..	2	85	125	-	0.1
356 PRESB CH AMER.	5	1 102	1 223	0.4	0.7
357 PRESB CH US...	16	7 171	8 675*	3.0	5.1
381 REF PRES-EVAN.	4	1 290	1 487	0.5	0.9
403 SALVATION ARMY	1	175	1 056	0.4	0.6
413 S.D.A.........	2	453	548*	0.2	0.3
419 SO BAPT CONV..	154	85 056	102 898*	35.7	60.5
421 SO METHODIST..	1	80	94	-	0.1
435 UNITARIAN-UNIV	1	90	109*	-	0.1
449 UN METHODIST..	64	17 933	21 695*	7.5	12.8
453 UN PRES CH USA	2	61	74*	-	-
GREENWOOD	**95**	**26 425**	**32 664***	**56.5**	**100.0**
017 AMER BAPT ASSN	1	35	35	0.1	0.1
053 ASSEMB OF GOD.	1	219	206	0.4	0.6
055 AS REF PRES CH	1	244	292	0.5	0.9
081 CATHOLIC......	1	NA	400	0.7	1.2
097 CHR CHS&CHS CR	1	35	43*	0.1	0.1
101 C.M.E........	2	485	590*	1.0	1.8
123 CH GOD (ANDER)	1	10	30	0.1	0.1
127 CH GOD (CLEVE)	9	1 035	1 258*	2.2	3.9
151 L-D SAINTS....	1	NA	137	0.2	0.4
167 CHS OF CHRIST.	1	79	114	0.2	0.3
193 EPISCOPAL.....	1	454	479	0.8	1.5
281 LUTH CH AMER..	1	343	446	0.8	1.4
349 PENT HOLINESS.	10	965	1 173*	2.0	3.6
356 PRESB CH AMER.	1	98	99	0.2	0.3
357 PRESB CH US...	5	1 462	1 777*	3.1	5.4
403 SALVATION ARMY	1	72	189	0.3	0.6
413 S.D.A.........	1	32	39*	0.1	0.1
419 SO BAPT CONV..	30	14 237	17 309*	29.9	53.0
449 UN METHODIST..	26	6 620	8 048*	13.9	24.6
HAMPTON	**57**	**7 884**	**10 319***	**56.8**	**100.0**
081 CATHOLIC......	1	NA	76	0.4	0.7
093 CHR CH (DISC).	8	656	915	5.0	8.9
097 CHR CHS&CHS CR	1	140	176*	1.0	1.7
101 C.M.E........	4	1 198	1 503*	8.3	14.6
123 CH GOD (ANDER)	1	36	108	0.6	1.0
127 CH GOD (CLEVE)	3	87	109*	0.6	1.1
151 L-D SAINTS....	1	NA	109	0.6	1.1
165 CH OF NAZARENE	1	75	154	0.8	1.5
193 EPISCOPAL.....	3	66	108	0.6	1.0
349 PENT HOLINESS.	1	26	33*	0.2	0.3
357 PRESB CH US...	3	203	255*	1.4	2.5
419 SO BAPT CONV..	19	4 449	5 583*	30.7	54.1
449 UN METHODIST..	11	948	1 190*	6.6	11.5
HORRY	**168**	**35 458**	**45 270***	**44.6**	**100.0**
053 ASSEMB OF GOD.	3	186	254	0.3	0.6
081 CATHOLIC......	5	NA	1 188	1.2	2.6
089 CHR & MISS AL.	1	55	100	0.1	0.2
123 CH GOD (ANDER)	1	48	144	0.1	0.3
127 CH GOD (CLEVE)	5	475	582*	0.6	1.3
151 L-D SAINTS....	1	NA	347	0.3	0.8
165 CH OF NAZARENE	1	74	106	0.1	0.2
167 CHS OF CHRIST.	2	175	223	0.2	0.5
193 EPISCOPAL.....	4	1 167	1 367	1.3	3.0
281 LUTH CH AMER..	3	637	807	0.8	1.8
283 LUTH--MO SYNOD	1	101	132	0.1	0.3
347 PENT FW BAPT..	1	35	43*	-	0.1
349 PENT HOLINESS.	8	733	898*	0.9	2.0
353 CHR BRETHREN..	2	80	150	0.1	0.3
356 PRESB CH AMER.	1	26	26	-	0.1
357 PRESB CH US...	7	1 537	1 883*	1.9	4.2
381 REF PRES-EVAN.	1	64	80	0.1	0.2
403 SALVATION ARMY	1	52	146	0.1	0.3
413 S.D.A.........	2	78	96*	0.1	0.2
419 SO BAPT CONV..	88	23 025	28 204*	27.8	62.3
421 SO METHODIST..	3	108	162	0.2	0.4
449 UN METHODIST..	29	6 802	8 332*	8.2	18.4
JASPER	**24**	**3 768**	**5 077***	**35.0**	**100.0**

NA— Not applicable   *Total adherents estimated from known number of communicant, confirmed, full members.   —Represents a percent less than 0.1.   Percentages may not total due to rounding.

Table 4. Churches and Church Membership by County and Denomination: 1980

County and Denomination	Number of churches	Communicant, confirmed, full members	Total adherents Number	Percent of total population	Percent of total adherents
001 ADVENT CHR CH.	1	88	111*	0.8	2.2
053 ASSEMB OF GOD.	1	237	286	2.0	5.6
081 CATHOLIC......	2	NA	95	0.7	1.9
127 CH GOD (CLEVE)	1	53	67*	0.5	1.3
151 L-D SAINTS....	1	NA	229	1.6	4.5
193 EPISCOPAL.....	1	115	146	1.0	2.9
413 S.D.A.........	1	38	48*	0.3	0.9
419 SO BAPT CONV..	11	2 587	3 273*	22.6	64.5
449 UN METHODIST..	5	650	822*	5.7	16.2
KERSHAW	100	19 964	26 017*	66.7	100.0
005 AME ZION......	7	783	1 049	2.7	4.0
053 ASSEMB OF GOD.	1	42	79	0.2	0.3
081 CATHOLIC......	1	NA	505	1.3	1.9
123 CH GOD (ANDER)	2	186	558	1.4	2.1
127 CH GOD (CLEVE)	5	369	454*	1.2	1.7
151 L-D SAINTS....	1	NA	339	0.9	1.3
165 CH OF NAZARENE	1	121	257	0.7	1.0
167 CHS OF CHRIST.	4	110	140	0.4	0.5
193 EPISCOPAL.....	1	658	873	2.2	3.4
281 LUTH CH AMER..	1	157	190	0.5	0.7
349 PENT HOLINESS.	3	250	307*	0.8	1.2
357 PRESB CH US...	5	1 053	1 295*	3.3	5.0
413 S.D.A.........	1	85	105*	0.3	0.4
419 SO BAPT CONV..	38	11 804	14 515*	37.2	55.8
421 SO METHODIST..	2	22	34	0.1	0.1
449 UN METHODIST..	25	4 241	5 215*	13.4	20.0
453 UN PRES CH USA	2	83	102*	0.3	0.4
LANCASTER	121	36 553	45 086*	84.5	100.0
005 AME ZION......	22	11 413	13 679	25.6	30.3
053 ASSEMB OF GOD.	1	67	145	0.3	0.3
055 AS REF PRES CH	5	1 152	1 315	2.5	2.9
081 CATHOLIC......	1	NA	326	0.6	0.7
127 CH GOD (CLEVE)	3	303	374*	0.7	0.8
165 CH OF NAZARENE	1	54	137	0.3	0.3
167 CHS OF CHRIST.	1	40	49	0.1	0.1
193 EPISCOPAL.....	1	150	220	0.4	0.5
281 LUTH CH AMER..	1	203	278	0.5	0.6
349 PENT HOLINESS.	4	389	480*	0.9	1.1
356 PRESB CH AMER.	1	36	36	0.1	0.1
357 PRESB CH US...	9	1 301	1 604*	3.0	3.6
413 S.D.A.........	1	17	21*	-	-
419 SO BAPT CONV..	53	17 324	21 362*	40.0	47.4
449 UN METHODIST..	16	4 059	5 005*	9.4	11.1
453 UN PRES CH USA	1	45	55*	0.1	0.1
LAURENS	120	23 977	29 300*	56.1	100.0
053 ASSEMB OF GOD.	4	370	475	0.9	1.6
055 AS REF PRES CH	2	245	296	0.6	1.0
081 CATHOLIC......	2	NA	111	0.2	0.4
123 CH GOD (ANDER)	1	25	75	0.1	0.3
127 CH GOD (CLEVE)	7	728	882*	1.7	3.0
151 L-D SAINTS....	1	NA	36	0.1	0.1
165 CH OF NAZARENE	1	49	78	0.1	0.3
167 CHS OF CHRIST.	2	63	102	0.2	0.3
193 EPISCOPAL.....	2	173	216	0.4	0.7
281 LUTH CH AMER..	2	295	382	0.7	1.3
349 PENT HOLINESS.	5	485	588*	1.1	2.0
356 PRESB CH AMER.	3	260	260	0.5	0.9
357 PRESB CH US...	18	2 413	2 925*	5.6	10.0
413 S.D.A.........	1	54	65*	0.1	0.2
419 SO BAPT CONV..	45	14 451	17 515*	33.5	59.8
421 SO METHODIST..	1	63	79	0.2	0.3
449 UN METHODIST..	22	4 256	5 158*	9.9	17.6
453 UN PRES CH USA	1	47	57*	0.1	0.2
LEE	43	5 268	6 755*	35.7	100.0
001 ADVENT CHR CH.	1	194	243*	1.3	3.6
081 CATHOLIC......	0	NA	1	-	-
089 CHR & MISS AL.	1	55	73	0.4	1.1
123 CH GOD (ANDER)	1	41	123	0.6	1.8
127 CH GOD (CLEVE)	1	53	66*	0.3	1.0
165 CH OF NAZARENE	2	132	230	1.2	3.4
357 PRESB CH US...	5	417	522*	2.8	7.7
419 SO BAPT CONV..	12	2 023	2 533*	13.4	37.5
421 SO METHODIST..	1	30	55	0.3	0.8
449 UN METHODIST..	16	2 101	2 631*	13.9	38.9
453 UN PRES CH USA	3	222	278*	1.5	4.1
LEXINGTON	184	54 218	71 922*	51.2	100.0
005 AME ZION......	1	197	235	0.2	0.3
053 ASSEMB OF GOD.	4	585	858	0.6	1.2
055 AS REF PRES CH	2	82	100	0.1	0.1
081 CATHOLIC......	4	NA	2 588	1.8	3.6
089 CHR & MISS AL.	1	122	222	0.2	0.3
101 C.M.E.........	8	1 768	2 181*	1.6	3.0
127 CH GOD (CLEVE)	6	295	364*	0.3	0.5
151 L-D SAINTS....	2	NA	1 047	0.7	1.5
164 CH LUTH CONF..	1	246	344	0.2	0.5
165 CH OF NAZARENE	5	490	821	0.6	1.1
167 CHS OF CHRIST.	3	377	411	0.3	0.6
193 EPISCOPAL.....	4	786	1 243	0.9	1.7
281 LUTH CH AMER..	37	12 327	15 822	11.3	22.0
283 LUTH--MO SYNOD	2	309	446	0.3	0.6
349 PENT HOLINESS.	5	251	310*	0.2	0.4
356 PRESB CH AMER.	1	131	149	0.1	0.2
357 PRESB CH US...	4	1 399	1 726*	1.2	2.4
413 S.D.A.........	2	516	637*	0.5	0.9
419 SO BAPT CONV..	60	23 792	29 352*	20.9	40.8
421 SO METHODIST..	4	179	265	0.2	0.4
449 UN METHODIST..	27	10 327	12 740*	9.1	17.7
469 WELS.........	1	39	61	-	0.1
MC CORMICK	22	2 424	2 990*	38.3	100.0
055 AS REF PRES CH	5	238	242	3.1	8.1
081 CATHOLIC......	1	NA	32	0.4	1.1
127 CH GOD (CLEVE)	1	39	48*	0.6	1.6
349 PENT HOLINESS.	1	20	25*	0.3	0.8
357 PRESB CH US...	1	23	29*	0.4	1.0
375 REF EPISCOPAL.	1	33	41*	0.5	1.4
419 SO BAPT CONV..	8	1 315	1 634*	21.0	54.6
449 UN METHODIST..	4	756	939*	12.0	31.4
MARION	50	10 121	13 033*	38.1	100.0
081 CATHOLIC......	1	NA	114	0.3	0.9
127 CH GOD (CLEVE)	5	408	513*	1.5	3.9
151 L-D SAINTS....	1	NA	147	0.4	1.1
177 CONGR HOL CH..	1	10	13*	-	0.1
193 EPISCOPAL.....	1	83	89	0.3	0.7
349 PENT HOLINESS.	3	148	186*	0.5	1.4
357 PRESB CH US...	2	490	616*	1.8	4.7
413 S.D.A.........	1	63	79*	0.2	0.6
419 SO BAPT CONV..	15	5 763	7 240*	21.2	55.6
421 SO METHODIST..	5	229	359	1.1	2.8
449 UN METHODIST..	15	2 927	3 677*	10.8	28.2
MARLBORO	78	13 129	16 855*	53.3	100.0
005 AME ZION......	9	3 702	4 568	14.4	27.1
081 CATHOLIC......	1	NA	137	0.4	0.8
123 CH GOD (ANDER)	1	20	60	0.2	0.4
127 CH GOD (CLEVE)	4	389	489*	1.5	2.9
151 L-D SAINTS....	1	NA	147	0.5	0.9
165 CH OF NAZARENE	2	276	471	1.5	2.8
167 CHS OF CHRIST.	1	21	27	0.1	0.2
177 CONGR HOL CH..	1	10	13*	-	0.1
193 EPISCOPAL.....	1	186	230	0.7	1.4
349 PENT HOLINESS.	2	305	383*	1.2	2.3
357 PRESB CH US...	6	555	697*	2.2	4.1
419 SO BAPT CONV..	12	3 065	3 852*	12.2	22.9
449 UN METHODIST..	37	4 600	5 781*	18.3	34.3
NEWBERRY	85	16 044	19 840*	63.8	100.0
005 AME ZION......	4	456	691	2.2	3.5
053 ASSEMB OF GOD.	1	48	55	0.2	0.3
055 AS REF PRES CH	2	339	397	1.3	2.0
081 CATHOLIC......	1	NA	94	0.3	0.5
097 CHR CHS&CHS CR	1	140	168*	0.5	0.8
123 CH GOD (ANDER)	1	32	96	0.3	0.5
127 CH GOD (CLEVE)	3	206	248*	0.8	1.2
151 L-D SAINTS....	1	NA	69	0.2	0.3
167 CHS OF CHRIST.	1	24	41	0.1	0.2
193 EPISCOPAL.....	1	151	184	0.6	0.9
281 LUTH CH AMER..	25	6 134	7 543	24.2	38.0
349 PENT HOLINESS.	4	295	355*	1.1	1.8
357 PRESB CH US...	6	801	964*	3.1	4.9
419 SO BAPT CONV..	14	3 325	4 002*	12.9	20.2
421 SO METHODIST..	2	62	82	0.3	0.4
435 UNITARIAN-UNIV	1	38	46*	0.1	0.2
449 UN METHODIST..	16	3 878	4 667*	15.0	23.5
453 UN PRES CH USA	1	115	138*	0.4	0.7
OCONEE	112	22 196	27 458*	56.5	100.0
053 ASSEMB OF GOD.	1	23	31	0.1	0.1
081 CATHOLIC......	1	NA	150	0.3	0.5
127 CH GOD (CLEVE)	15	1 352	1 651*	3.4	6.0
151 L-D SAINTS....	1	NA	188	0.4	0.7
165 CH OF NAZARENE	1	37	88	0.2	0.3
167 CHS OF CHRIST.	2	80	102	0.2	0.4
193 EPISCOPAL.....	1	179	180	0.4	0.7
281 LUTH CH AMER..	1	346	422	0.9	1.5
349 PENT HOLINESS.	1	23	28*	0.1	0.1
357 PRESB CH US...	6	872	1 065*	2.2	3.9
413 S.D.A.........	2	123	150*	0.3	0.5
419 SO BAPT CONV..	63	17 284	21 108*	43.4	76.9
421 SO METHODIST..	1	59	59	0.1	0.2
449 UN METHODIST..	16	1 831	2 236*	4.6	8.1
ORANGEBURG	148	30 018	38 434*	46.7	100.0
053 ASSEMB OF GOD.	1	85	161	0.2	0.4
081 CATHOLIC......	3	NA	817	1.0	2.1
093 CHR CH (DISC).	2	564	800	1.0	2.1
097 CHR CHS&CHS CR	1	125	154*	0.2	0.4
123 CH GOD (ANDER)	2	23	69	0.1	0.2
127 CH GOD (CLEVE)	7	480	592*	0.7	1.5
133 CH GOD(7TH)DEN	2	11	14*	-	-
151 L-D SAINTS....	2	NA	249	0.3	0.6
165 CH OF NAZARENE	3	232	377	0.5	1.0
167 CHS OF CHRIST.	2	48	61	0.1	0.2
193 EPISCOPAL.....	3	692	921	1.1	2.4
281 LUTH CH AMER..	2	782	932	1.1	2.4
349 PENT HOLINESS.	5	314	387*	0.5	1.0
357 PRESB CH US...	1	659	813*	1.0	2.1
403 SALVATION ARMY	1	108	210	0.3	0.5
413 S.D.A.........	2	228	281*	0.3	0.7
419 SO BAPT CONV..	39	11 923	14 700*	17.9	38.2
421 SO METHODIST..	7	881	1 036	1.3	2.7
449 UN METHODIST..	62	12 740	15 708*	19.1	40.9
453 UN PRES CH USA	1	123	152*	0.2	0.4

NA—Not applicable   *Total adherents estimated from known number of communicant, confirmed, full members.   —Represents a percent less than 0.1.   Percentages may not total due to rounding.

Table 4. Churches and Church Membership by County and Denomination: 1980

County and Denomination	Number of churches	Communicant, confirmed, full members	Total adherents		
			Number	Percent of total population	Percent of total adherents
PICKENS	124	32 635	40 204*	50.7	100.0
053 ASSEMB OF GOD.	2	140	175	0.2	0.4
081 CATHOLIC......	3	NA	1 020	1.3	2.5
089 CHR & MISS AL.	1	0	12	–	–
127 CH GOD (CLEVE)	13	1 383	1 654*	2.1	4.1
167 CHS OF CHRIST.	4	135	172	0.2	0.4
193 EPISCOPAL.....	2	682	820	1.0	2.0
281 LUTH CH AMER..	2	342	526	0.7	1.3
349 PENT HOLINESS.	1	90	108*	0.1	0.3
357 PRESB CH US...	5	1 469	1 757*	2.2	4.4
419 SO BAPT CONV..	63	23 526	28 138*	35.5	70.0
435 UNITARIAN-UNIV	1	35	42*	0.1	0.1
449 UN METHODIST..	27	4 833	5 780*	7.3	14.4
RICHLAND	210	83 531	110 337*	41.2	100.0
005 AME ZION......	2	800	1 283	0.5	1.2
053 ASSEMB OF GOD.	3	524	675	0.3	0.6
055 AS REF PRES CH	2	738	839	0.3	0.8
081 CATHOLIC......	7	NA	6 280	2.3	5.7
093 CHR CH (DISC).	1	274	324	0.1	0.3
097 CHR CHS&CHS CR	2	215	257*	0.1	0.2
101 C.M.E.........	5	2 275	2 718*	1.0	2.5
123 CH GOD (ANDER)	5	667	2 001	0.7	1.8
127 CH GOD (CLEVE)	10	658	786*	0.3	0.7
133 CH GOD(7TH)DEN	1	1	1*	–	–
151 L-D SAINTS....	4	NA	1 410	0.5	1.3
165 CH OF NAZARENE	3	435	748	0.3	0.7
167 CHS OF CHRIST.	7	600	860	0.3	0.8
177 CONGR HOL CH..	1	32	38*	–	–
193 EPISCOPAL.....	12	6 383	8 224	3.1	7.5
226 FRIENDS-USA...	1	16	19*	–	–
270 CONSRV JUDAISM	1	271	324*	0.1	0.3
271 REFORM JUDAISM	1	490	585*	0.2	0.5
281 LUTH CH AMER..	19	8 141	10 046	3.8	9.1
283 LUTH--MO SYNOD	2	235	326	0.1	0.3
285 MENNONITE CH..	1	6	7*	–	–
290 METRO COMM CHS	1	35	70	–	0.1
349 PENT HOLINESS.	13	1 051	1 256*	0.5	1.1
353 CHR BRETHREN..	1	45	65	–	0.1
356 PRESB CH AMER.	3	1 678	1 885	0.7	1.7
357 PRESB CH US...	14	8 542	10 206*	3.8	9.2
403 SALVATION ARMY	1	118	205	0.1	0.2
413 S.D.A.........	2	238	284*	0.1	0.3
419 SO BAPT CONV..	46	32 369	38 674*	14.4	35.1
421 SO METHODIST..	2	118	137	0.1	0.1
435 UNITARIAN-UNIV	1	119	142*	0.1	0.1
449 UN METHODIST..	34	16 183	19 335*	7.2	17.5
453 UN PRES CH USA	2	274	327*	0.1	0.3
SALUDA	52	7 885	9 872*	61.1	100.0
001 ADVENT CHR CH.	1	77	95*	0.6	1.0
081 CATHOLIC......	1	NA	192	1.2	1.9
101 C.M.E.........	4	611	750*	4.6	7.6
127 CH GOD (CLEVE)	2	81	99*	0.6	1.0
177 CONGR HOL CH..	1	44	54*	0.3	0.5
193 EPISCOPAL.....	1	116	196	1.2	2.0
281 LUTH CH AMER..	7	842	977	6.0	9.9
349 PENT HOLINESS.	8	520	639*	4.0	6.5
357 PRESB CH US...	1	75	92*	0.6	0.9
419 SO BAPT CONV..	15	3 538	4 345*	26.9	44.0
449 UN METHODIST..	11	1 981	2 433*	15.1	24.6
SPARTANBURG	310	99 293	127 266*	63.1	100.0
005 AME ZION......	6	1 120	1 451	0.7	1.1
053 ASSEMB OF GOD.	5	1 099	1 647	0.8	1.3
055 AS REF PRES CH	3	282	329	0.2	0.3
081 CATHOLIC......	3	NA	3 851	1.9	3.0
089 CHR & MISS AL.	1	33	99	–	0.1
097 CHR CHS&CHS CR	1	44	53*	–	–
101 C.M.E.........	7	1 757	2 133*	1.1	1.7
123 CH GOD (ANDER)	1	240	720	0.4	0.6
127 CH GOD (CLEVE)	20	1 931	2 344*	1.2	1.8
151 L-D SAINTS....	1	NA	475	0.2	0.4
165 CH OF NAZARENE	2	103	148	0.1	0.1
167 CHS OF CHRIST.	6	593	776	0.4	0.6
193 EPISCOPAL.....	5	1 775	2 210	1.1	1.7
215 EVAN METH CH..	1	170	206*	0.1	0.2
270 CONSRV JUDAISM	1	56	68*	–	0.1
281 LUTH CH AMER..	3	998	1 318	0.7	1.0
283 LUTH--MO SYNOD	1	112	173	0.1	0.1
349 PENT HOLINESS.	5	215	261*	0.1	0.2
353 CHR BRETHREN..	2	45	70	–	0.1
356 PRESB CH AMER.	8	882	986	0.5	0.8
357 PRESB CH US...	13	4 638	5 630*	2.8	4.4
381 REF PRES-EVAN.	1	105	136	0.1	0.1
403 SALVATION ARMY	1	92	1 419	0.7	1.1
413 S.D.A.........	2	360	437*	0.2	0.3
419 SO BAPT CONV..	134	66 325	80 517*	39.9	63.3
435 UNITARIAN-UNIV	1	35	42*	–	–
449 UN METHODIST..	73	16 169	19 629*	9.7	15.4
453 UN PRES CH USA	3	114	138*	0.1	0.1
SUMTER	110	26 839	36 448*	41.3	100.0
001 ADVENT CHR CH.	1	30	37*	–	0.1
005 AME ZION......	1	150	225	0.3	0.6
053 ASSEMB OF GOD.	4	269	354	0.4	1.0
055 AS REF PRES CH	1	124	165	0.2	0.5
081 CATHOLIC......	2	NA	1 068	1.2	2.9
097 CHR CHS&CHS CR	1	75	94*	0.1	0.3
123 CH GOD (ANDER)	2	184	552	0.6	1.5
127 CH GOD (CLEVE)	2	173	216*	0.2	0.6
151 L-D SAINTS....	2	NA	641	0.7	1.8
165 CH OF NAZARENE	3	579	1 267	1.4	3.5
167 CHS OF CHRIST.	2	175	223	0.3	0.6
193 EPISCOPAL.....	6	951	1 141	1.3	3.1
271 REFORM JUDAISM	1	156	195*	0.2	0.5
281 LUTH CH AMER..	1	399	543	0.6	1.5
349 PENT HOLINESS.	4	389	486*	0.6	1.3
356 PRESB CH AMER.	1	73	99	0.1	0.3
357 PRESB CH US...	12	2 041	2 549*	2.9	7.0
403 SALVATION ARMY	1	98	391	0.4	1.1
413 S.D.A.........	2	221	276*	0.3	0.8
419 SO BAPT CONV..	27	11 389	14 225*	16.1	39.0
421 SO METHODIST..	2	149	192	0.2	0.5
449 UN METHODIST..	27	7 762	9 695*	11.0	26.6
453 UN PRES CH USA	5	1 452	1 814*	2.1	5.0
UNION	73	17 542	21 569*	70.1	100.0
005 AME ZION......	6	761	995	3.2	4.6
017 AMER BAPT ASSN	3	215	215	0.7	1.0
053 ASSEMB OF GOD.	1	10	18	0.1	0.1
081 CATHOLIC......	1	NA	100	0.3	0.5
127 CH GOD (CLEVE)	3	259	314*	1.0	1.5
151 L-D SAINTS....	1	NA	66	0.2	0.3
167 CHS OF CHRIST.	2	100	127	0.4	0.6
193 EPISCOPAL.....	1	65	69	0.2	0.3
281 LUTH CH AMER..	1	57	65	0.2	0.3
357 PRESB CH US...	8	838	1 017*	3.3	4.7
403 SALVATION ARMY	1	82	200	0.7	0.9
413 S.D.A.........	1	85	103*	0.3	0.5
419 SO BAPT CONV..	26	11 131	13 502*	43.9	62.6
449 UN METHODIST..	18	3 939	4 778*	15.5	22.2
WILLIAMSBURG	85	11 830	15 190*	39.7	100.0
005 AME ZION......	1	202	235	0.6	1.5
053 ASSEMB OF GOD.	2	74	138	0.4	0.9
081 CATHOLIC......	1	NA	204	0.5	1.3
127 CH GOD (CLEVE)	5	462	588*	1.5	3.9
165 CH OF NAZARENE	1	19	23	0.1	0.2
167 CHS OF CHRIST.	1	20	25	0.1	0.2
193 EPISCOPAL.....	1	101	122	0.3	0.8
270 CONSRV JUDAISM	1	25	32*	0.1	0.2
349 PENT HOLINESS.	12	760	967*	2.5	6.4
356 PRESB CH AMER.	4	440	456	1.2	3.0
357 PRESB CH US...	5	1 035	1 317*	3.4	8.7
413 S.D.A.........	3	149	190*	0.5	1.3
419 SO BAPT CONV..	14	3 050	3 881*	10.2	25.5
421 SO METHODIST..	1	23	51	0.1	0.3
449 UN METHODIST..	33	5 470	6 961*	18.2	45.8
YORK	187	52 146	68 426*	64.1	100.0
005 AME ZION......	25	8 878	11 504	10.8	16.8
017 AMER BAPT ASSN	1	9	9	–	–
053 ASSEMB OF GOD.	3	584	975	0.9	1.4
055 AS REF PRES CH	11	2 550	2 787	2.6	4.1
081 CATHOLIC......	3	NA	2 001	1.9	2.9
097 CHR CHS&CHS CR	1	66	81*	0.1	0.1
127 CH GOD (CLEVE)	11	2 006	2 463*	2.3	3.6
151 L-D SAINTS....	2	NA	599	0.6	0.9
165 CH OF NAZARENE	7	985	2 158	2.0	3.2
167 CHS OF CHRIST.	2	209	292	0.3	0.4
193 EPISCOPAL.....	2	545	857	0.8	1.3
263 INT FOURSQ GOS	2	105	129*	0.1	0.2
281 LUTH CH AMER..	2	447	632	0.6	0.9
349 PENT HOLINESS.	1	95	117*	0.1	0.2
356 PRESB CH AMER.	7	1 667	1 995	1.9	2.9
357 PRESB CH US...	21	5 405	6 637*	6.2	9.7
403 SALVATION ARMY	1	95	193	0.2	0.3
413 S.D.A.........	1	29	36*	–	0.1
419 SO BAPT CONV..	48	18 850	23 147*	21.7	33.8
449 UN METHODIST..	34	9 445	11 598*	10.9	16.9
453 UN PRES CH USA	2	176	216*	0.2	0.3

SOUTH DAKOTA

County and Denomination	Number of churches	Communicant, confirmed, full members	Total adherents		
			Number	Percent of total population	Percent of total adherents
THE STATE.....	1 710	245 267	462 277*	67.0	100.0
AURORA	13	1 461	3 122*	86.1	100.0
029 AMER LUTH CH..	2	443	592	16.3	19.0
081 CATHOLIC......	3	NA	1 177	32.4	37.7
283 LUTH--MO SYNOD	2	384	469	12.9	15.0
371 REF CH IN AM..	1	170	321	8.8	10.3
449 UN METHODIST..	4	427	518*	14.3	16.6
453 UN PRES CH USA	1	37	45*	1.2	1.4
BEADLE	38	8 435	14 067*	73.3	100.0
019 AMER BAPT USA.	1	400	481*	2.5	3.4
029 AMER LUTH CH..	3	1 601	2 288	11.9	16.3

NA—Not applicable   *Total adherents estimated from known number of communicant, confirmed, full members.   —Represents a percent less than 0.1.   Percentages may not total due to rounding.

Table 4. Churches and Church Membership by County and Denomination: 1980

County and Denomination	Number of churches	Communicant, confirmed, full members	Total adherents		
			Number	Percent of total population	Percent of total adherents
053 ASSEMB OF GOD.	1	224	350	1.8	2.5
081 CATHOLIC......	4	NA	3 050	15.9	21.7
089 CHR & MISS AL.	1	150	220	1.1	1.6
097 CHR CHS&CHS CR	1	174	209*	1.1	1.5
151 L-D SAINTS....	1	NA	131	0.7	0.9
165 CH OF NAZARENE	1	39	72	0.4	0.5
167 CHS OF CHRIST.	1	11	15	0.1	0.1
193 EPISCOPAL.....	1	160	223	1.2	1.6
237 GC MENN BR CHS	2	361	434*	2.3	3.1
283 LUTH--MO SYNOD	4	1 413	1 794	9.3	12.8
287 MENN GEN CONF.	1	140	189	1.0	1.3
291 MISSIONARY CH.	1	23	28	0.1	0.2
403 SALVATION ARMY	1	100	195	1.0	1.4
413 S.D.A........	1	56	67*	0.3	0.5
419 SO BAPT CONV..	2	289	348*	1.8	2.5
443 UN C OF CHRIST	1	375	451*	2.3	3.2
449 UN METHODIST..	5	1 842	2 216*	11.5	15.8
453 UN PRES CH USA	4	1 043	1 255*	6.5	8.9
469 WELS.........	1	34	51	0.3	0.4
BENNETT	14	734	1 192*	36.8	100.0
081 CATHOLIC......	3	NA	381	11.8	32.0
151 L-D SAINTS....	1	NA	?	?	?
193 EPISCOPAL.....	6	438	442	13.7	37.1
413 S.D.A........	1	25	32*	1.0	2.7
453 UN PRES CH USA	2	179	226*	7.0	19.0
469 WELS.........	1	92	111	3.4	9.3
BON HOMME	27	3 547	7 576*	94.0	100.0
029 AMER LUTH CH..	1	334	430	5.3	5.7
057 BAPT GEN CONF.	1	40	48*	0.6	0.6
081 CATHOLIC......	5	NA	3 075	38.2	40.6
193 EPISCOPAL.....	3	15	17	0.2	0.2
283 LUTH--MO SYNOD	4	557	715	8.9	9.4
287 MENN GEN CONF.	1	78	93	1.2	1.2
313 N AM BAPT CONF	3	494	588*	7.3	7.8
371 REF CH IN AM..	1	350	610	7.6	8.1
443 UN C OF CHRIST	2	698	831*	10.3	11.0
449 UN METHODIST..	2	365	435*	5.4	5.7
453 UN PRES CH USA	4	616	734*	9.1	9.7
BROOKINGS	43	9 067	14 020*	57.6	100.0
019 AMER BAPT USA.	1	174	204*	0.8	1.5
029 AMER LUTH CH..	6	3 931	5 116	21.0	36.5
053 ASSEMB OF GOD.	1	113	189	0.8	1.3
057 BAPT GEN CONF.	1	95	112*	0.5	0.8
081 CATHOLIC......	4	NA	2 016	8.3	14.4
097 CHR CHS&CHS CR	3	124	146*	0.6	1.0
105 CHRISTIAN REF.	1	211	334	1.4	2.4
123 CH GOD (ANDER)	1	170	510	2.1	3.6
151 L-D SAINTS....	1	NA	169	0.7	1.2
167 CHS OF CHRIST.	1	36	47	0.2	0.3
193 EPISCOPAL.....	1	124	152	0.6	1.1
209 EVAN LUTH SYN.	1	17	17	0.1	0.1
281 LUTH CH AMER..	1	67	77	0.3	0.5
283 LUTH--MO SYNOD	3	702	897	3.7	6.4
329 OPEN BIBLE STD	1	85	120	0.5	0.9
335 ORTH PRESB CH.	1	88	103*	0.4	0.7
371 REF CH IN AM..	2	198	280	1.2	2.0
419 SO BAPT CONV..	1	37	43*	0.2	0.3
435 UNITARIAN-UNIV	1	14	16*	0.1	0.1
443 UN C OF CHRIST	1	124	146*	0.6	1.0
449 UN METHODIST..	6	1 897	2 228*	9.2	15.9
453 UN PRES CH USA	2	572	672*	2.8	4.8
469 WELS.........	2	288	426	1.8	3.0
BROWN	58	13 729	26 399*	71.4	100.0
019 AMER BAPT USA.	1	773	935*	2.5	3.5
029 AMER LUTH CH..	10	4 518	6 047	16.4	22.9
053 ASSEMB OF GOD.	1	245	492	1.3	1.9
057 BAPT GEN CONF.	1	?	?	?	?
081 CATHOLIC......	5	NA	8 207	22.2	31.1
089 CHR & MISS AL.	1	78	157	0.4	0.6
097 CHR CHS&CHS CR	1	29	35*	0.1	0.1
151 L-D SAINTS....	1	NA	143	0.4	0.5
163 CH OF LUTH BR.	1	10	24	0.1	0.1
164 CH LUTH CONF.	2	37	60	0.2	0.2
165 CH OF NAZARENE	1	28	58	0.2	0.2
167 CHS OF CHRIST.	1	45	62	0.2	0.2
193 EPISCOPAL.....	1	237	317	0.9	1.2
220 FREE LUTHERAN.	1	25	30	0.1	0.1
263 INT FOURSQ GOS	1	?	?	?	?
270 CONSRV JUDAISM	1	8	10*	-	-
281 LUTH CH AMER..	1	77	98	0.3	0.4
283 LUTH--MO SYNOD	8	2 722	3 728	10.1	14.1
313 N AM BAPT CONF	1	207	250*	0.7	0.9
403 SALVATION ARMY	1	135	183	0.5	0.7
413 S.D.A........	1	108	131*	0.4	0.5
419 SO BAPT CONV..	1	14	17*	-	0.1
443 UN C OF CHRIST	4	1 024	1 239*	3.4	4.7
449 UN METHODIST..	7	2 365	2 862*	7.7	10.8
453 UN PRES CH USA	3	700	847*	2.3	3.2
469 WELS.........	1	344	467	1.3	1.8
BRULE	13	1 420	3 866*	73.7	100.0
029 AMER LUTH CH..	1	120	167	3.2	4.3
053 ASSEMB OF GOD.	1	22	52	1.0	1.3
057 BAPT GEN CONF.	1	98	121*	2.3	3.1
081 CATHOLIC......	3	NA	2 030	38.7	52.5
193 EPISCOPAL.....	1	41	45	0.9	1.2

County and Denomination	Number of churches	Communicant, confirmed, full members	Total adherents		
			Number	Percent of total population	Percent of total adherents
220 FREE LUTHERAN.	2	100	130	2.5	3.4
283 LUTH--MO SYNOD	1	430	569	10.8	14.7
443 UN C OF CHRIST	1	507	626*	11.9	16.2
449 UN METHODIST..	1	62	77*	1.5	2.0
453 UN PRES CH USA	1	40	49*	0.9	1.3
BUFFALO	6	232	727*	40.5	100.0
081 CATHOLIC......	1	NA	489	27.2	67.3
151 L-D SAINTS....	1	NA	?	?	?
193 EPISCOPAL.....	3	196	189	10.5	26.0
453 UN PRES CH USA	1	36	49*	2.7	6.7
BUTTE	16	2 080	3 396*	40.6	100.0
019 AMER BAPT USA.	1	306	376*	4.5	11.1
029 AMER LUTH CH..	3	551	796	9.5	23.4
053 ASSEMB OF GOD.	1	66	119	1.4	3.5
081 CATHOLIC......	2	NA	471	5.6	13.9
151 L-D SAINTS....	1	NA	178	2.1	5.2
193 EPISCOPAL.....	1	70	109	1.3	3.2
226 FRIENDS-USA...	1	25	31*	0.4	0.9
263 INT FOURSQ GOS	1	61	75*	0.9	2.2
329 OPEN BIBLE STD	1	60	85	1.0	2.5
413 S.D.A........	1	60	74*	0.9	2.2
443 UN C OF CHRIST	1	562	690*	8.2	20.3
449 UN METHODIST..	1	319	392*	4.7	11.5
CAMPBELL	12	1 149	1 801*	80.3	100.0
029 AMER LUTH CH..	3	447	535	23.9	29.7
053 ASSEMB OF GOD.	1	29	45	2.0	2.5
081 CATHOLIC......	1	NA	433	19.3	24.0
127 CH GOD (CLEVE)	1	5	6*	0.3	0.3
313 N AM BAPT CONF	1	231	273*	12.2	15.2
443 UN C OF CHRIST	1	28	33*	1.5	1.8
449 UN METHODIST..	2	53	63*	2.8	3.5
453 UN PRES CH USA	1	234	276*	12.3	15.3
469 WELS.........	1	122	137	6.1	7.6
CHARLES MIX	35	2 859	7 288*	75.3	100.0
029 AMER LUTH CH..	3	515	703	7.3	9.6
053 ASSEMB OF GOD.	1	10	15	0.2	0.2
057 BAPT GEN CONF.	1	45	56*	0.6	0.8
081 CATHOLIC......	7	NA	3 090	31.9	42.4
089 CHR & MISS AL.	1	25	35	0.4	0.5
105 CHRISTIAN REF.	1	378	591	6.1	8.1
151 L-D SAINTS....	1	NA	44	0.5	0.6
163 CH OF LUTH BR.	1	47	79	0.8	1.1
193 EPISCOPAL.....	5	75	326	3.4	4.5
283 LUTH--MO SYNOD	2	365	483	5.0	6.6
371 REF CH IN AM..	1	158	310	3.2	4.3
413 S.D.A........	1	42	53*	0.5	0.7
443 UN C OF CHRIST	1	50	63*	0.7	0.9
449 UN METHODIST..	2	526	658*	6.8	9.0
453 UN PRES CH USA	6	609	762*	7.9	10.5
469 WELS.........	1	14	20	0.2	0.3
CLARK	25	2 902	4 169*	85.2	100.0
029 AMER LUTH CH..	8	1 346	1 724	35.2	41.4
053 ASSEMB OF GOD.	1	51	101	2.1	2.4
081 CATHOLIC......	2	NA	488	10.0	11.7
371 REF CH IN AM..	1	106	141	2.9	3.4
419 SO BAPT CONV..	2	56	67*	1.4	1.6
443 UN C OF CHRIST	2	183	220*	4.5	5.3
449 UN METHODIST..	3	624	751*	15.3	18.0
453 UN PRES CH USA	2	144	173*	3.5	4.1
469 WELS.........	4	392	504	10.3	12.1
CLAY	26	3 418	6 326*	48.2	100.0
019 AMER BAPT USA.	2	154	180*	1.4	2.8
029 AMER LUTH CH..	5	1 387	1 902	14.5	30.1
053 ASSEMB OF GOD.	1	148	225	1.7	3.6
081 CATHOLIC......	2	NA	1 900	14.5	30.0
089 CHR & MISS AL.	1	42	54	0.4	0.9
105 CHRISTIAN REF.	1	26	42	0.3	0.7
165 CH OF NAZARENE	1	37	84	0.6	1.3
167 CHS OF CHRIST.	1	9	13	0.1	0.2
193 EPISCOPAL.....	1	129	135	1.0	2.1
281 LUTH CH AMER..	2	396	485	3.7	7.7
283 LUTH--MO SYNOD	1	147	203	1.5	3.2
435 UNITARIAN-UNIV	1	10	12*	0.1	0.2
443 UN C OF CHRIST	2	326	381*	2.9	6.0
449 UN METHODIST..	5	607	710*	5.4	11.2
CODINGTON	36	8 368	16 151*	77.3	100.0
019 AMER BAPT USA.	1	263	322*	1.5	2.0
029 AMER LUTH CH..	5	3 033	3 932	18.8	24.3
045 APOSTOLIC LUTH	1	50	61*	0.3	0.4
053 ASSEMB OF GOD.	1	77	125	0.6	0.8
081 CATHOLIC......	7	NA	5 490	26.3	34.0
089 CHR & MISS AL.	1	38	61	0.3	0.4
097 CHR CHS&CHS CR	1	25	31*	0.1	0.2
164 CH LUTH CONF..	1	118	142	0.7	0.9
167 CHS OF CHRIST.	1	78	109	0.5	0.7
193 EPISCOPAL.....	1	198	200	1.0	1.2
220 FREE LUTHERAN.	1	175	211	1.0	1.3
263 INT FOURSQ GOS	1	68	83*	0.4	0.5
283 LUTH--MO SYNOD	1	271	369	1.8	2.3
403 SALVATION ARMY	1	117	157	0.8	1.0
413 S.D.A........	1	94	115*	0.6	0.7

NA—Not applicable   *Total adherents estimated from known number of communicant, confirmed, full members.   —Represents a percent less than 0.1.   Percentages may not total due to rounding.

Table 4. Churches and Church Membership by County and Denomination: 1980

County and Denomination	Number of churches	Communicant, confirmed, full members	Total adherents Number	Percent of total population	Percent of total adherents
419 SO BAPT CONV..	1	81	99*	0.5	0.6
443 UN C OF CHRIST	2	561	687*	3.3	4.3
449 UN METHODIST..	3	1 394	1 708*	8.2	10.6
469 WELS..........	5	1 727	2 249	10.8	13.9
CORSON	33	1 737	3 944*	75.9	100.0
029 AMER LUTH CH..	3	434	554	10.7	14.0
081 CATHOLIC......	7	NA	1 312	25.3	33.3
089 CHR & MISS AL.	1	0	9	0.2	0.2
127 CH GOD (CLEVE)	1	17	22*	0.4	0.6
151 L-D SAINTS....	4	NA	?	?	?
193 EPISCOPAL.....	6	566	1 122	21.6	28.4
313 N AM BAPT CONF	2	104	134*	2.6	3.4
443 UN C OF CHRIST	4	349	450*	8.7	11.4
453 UN PRES CH USA	2	117	151*	2.9	3.8
469 WELS..........	3	150	190	3.7	4.8
CUSTER	15	1 117	1 897*	31.6	100.0
019 AMER BAPT USA.	1	25	30*	0.5	1.6
029 AMER LUTH CH..	2	204	311	5.2	16.4
063 BEREAN FUND CH	1	43	52*	0.9	2.7
081 CATHOLIC......	2	NA	460	7.7	24.2
193 EPISCOPAL.....	2	46	56	0.9	3.0
283 LUTH--MO SYNOD	1	238	301	5.0	15.9
329 OPEN BIBLE STD	1	60	80	1.3	4.2
413 S.D.A.........	1	58	70*	1.2	3.7
419 SO BAPT CONV..	1	19	23*	0.4	1.2
443 UN C OF CHRIST	2	390	473*	7.9	24.9
449 UN METHODIST..	1	34	41*	0.7	2.2
DAVISON	30	6 436	14 052*	78.9	100.0
019 AMER BAPT USA.	1	109	132*	0.7	0.9
029 AMER LUTH CH..	4	2 238	2 951	16.6	21.0
053 ASSEMB OF GOD.	1	53	111	0.6	0.8
057 BAPT GEN CONF.	1	42	51*	0.3	0.4
081 CATHOLIC......	4	NA	5 465	30.7	38.9
097 CHR CHS&CHS CR	1	24	29*	0.2	0.2
127 CH GOD (CLEVE)	1	7	8*	-	0.1
151 L-D SAINTS....	1	NA	82	0.5	0.6
165 CH OF NAZARENE	1	192	382	2.1	2.7
167 CHS OF CHRIST.	1	26	33	0.2	0.2
193 EPISCOPAL.....	1	210	268	1.5	1.9
281 LUTH CH AMER..	1	189	243	1.4	1.7
283 LUTH--MO SYNOD	2	773	981	5.5	7.0
371 REF CH IN AM..	1	163	301	1.7	2.1
403 SALVATION ARMY	1	93	187	1.0	1.3
413 S.D.A.........	1	11	13*	0.1	0.1
419 SO BAPT CONV..	1	78	94*	0.5	0.7
443 UN C OF CHRIST	1	346	419*	2.4	3.0
449 UN METHODIST..	3	1 551	1 879*	10.5	13.4
453 UN PRES CH USA	1	260	315*	1.8	2.2
469 WELS..........	1	71	108	0.6	0.8
DAY	33	3 546	6 936*	85.3	100.0
019 AMER BAPT USA.	1	28	34*	0.4	0.5
029 AMER LUTH CH..	11	1 895	2 384	29.3	34.4
053 ASSEMB OF GOD.	1	24	24	0.3	0.3
081 CATHOLIC......	6	NA	2 431	29.9	35.0
089 CHR & MISS AL.	1	14	34	0.4	0.5
193 EPISCOPAL.....	2	188	301	3.7	4.3
220 FREE LUTHERAN.	2	96	120	1.5	1.7
281 LUTH CH AMER..	1	397	504	6.2	7.3
283 LUTH--MO SYNOD	2	296	369	4.5	5.3
419 SO BAPT CONV..	1	57	69*	0.8	1.0
443 UN C OF CHRIST	1	73	88*	1.1	1.3
449 UN METHODIST..	3	440	532*	6.5	7.7
453 UN PRES CH USA	1	38	46*	0.6	0.7
DEUEL	22	3 224	4 583*	86.7	100.0
019 AMER BAPT USA.	2	62	75*	1.4	1.6
029 AMER LUTH CH..	7	1 633	2 044	38.6	44.6
081 CATHOLIC......	2	NA	523	9.9	11.4
105 CHRISTIAN REF.	1	107	159	3.0	3.5
163 CH OF LUTH BR.	2	90	100	1.9	2.2
371 REF CH IN AM..	1	42	67	1.3	1.5
443 UN C OF CHRIST	1	132	160*	3.0	3.5
449 UN METHODIST..	2	475	577*	10.9	12.6
453 UN PRES CH USA	1	66	80*	1.5	1.7
469 WELS..........	3	617	798	15.1	17.4
DEWEY	27	1 531	3 238*	60.3	100.0
019 AMER BAPT USA.	1	191	249*	4.6	7.7
029 AMER LUTH CH..	2	261	352	6.6	10.9
081 CATHOLIC......	6	NA	1 008	18.8	31.1
127 CH GOD (CLEVE)	2	32	42*	0.8	1.3
193 EPISCOPAL.....	6	305	617	11.5	19.1
220 FREE LUTHERAN.	1	40	55	1.0	1.7
313 N AM BAPT CONF	1	68	89*	1.7	2.7
369 PROT REF CHS..	1	16	25	0.5	0.8
419 SO BAPT CONV..	1	79	103*	1.9	3.2
443 UN C OF CHRIST	3	307	400*	7.5	12.4
449 UN METHODIST..	1	98	128*	2.4	4.0
469 WELS..........	2	134	170	3.2	5.3
DOUGLAS	18	2 931	4 546*	108.7	100.0
029 AMER LUTH CH..	5	752	991	23.7	21.8
081 CATHOLIC......	1	NA	462	11.0	10.2
105 CHRISTIAN REF.	3	634	951	22.7	20.9

County and Denomination	Number of churches	Communicant, confirmed, full members	Total adherents Number	Percent of total population	Percent of total adherents
283 LUTH--MO SYNOD	3	640	827	19.8	18.2
371 REF CH IN AM..	3	457	765	18.3	16.8
443 UN C OF CHRIST	2	395	485*	11.6	10.7
449 UN METHODIST..	1	53	65*	1.6	1.4
EDMUNDS	19	2 165	4 627*	89.7	100.0
019 AMER BAPT USA.	1	174	213*	4.1	4.6
029 AMER LUTH CH..	2	620	769	14.9	16.6
081 CATHOLIC......	4	NA	1 939	37.6	41.9
164 CH LUTH CONF..	2	205	269	5.2	5.8
283 LUTH--MO SYNOD	1	128	167	3.2	3.6
413 S.D.A.........	1	90	110*	2.1	2.4
443 UN C OF CHRIST	3	272	333*	6.5	7.2
449 UN METHODIST..	1	101	124*	2.4	2.7
453 UN PRES CH USA	2	94	115*	2.2	2.5
469 WELS..........	2	481	588	11.4	12.7
FALL RIVER	30	2 173	4 178*	49.5	100.0
019 AMER BAPT USA.	1	85	103*	1.2	2.5
029 AMER LUTH CH..	2	364	506	6.0	12.1
053 ASSEMB OF GOD.	2	75	200	2.4	4.8
081 CATHOLIC......	4	NA	1 173	13.9	28.1
097 CHR CHS&CHS CR	2	140	169*	2.0	4.0
127 CH GOD (CLEVE)	1	12	15*	0.2	0.4
151 L-D SAINTS....	1	NA	174	2.1	4.2
167 CHS OF CHRIST.	2	8	10	0.1	0.2
193 EPISCOPAL.....	1	164	171	2.0	4.1
283 LUTH--MO SYNOD	1	341	458	5.4	11.0
329 OPEN BIBLE STD	1	20	30	0.4	0.7
413 S.D.A.........	1	53	64*	0.8	1.5
419 SO BAPT CONV..	2	155	188*	2.2	4.5
443 UN C OF CHRIST	1	89	108*	1.3	2.6
449 UN METHODIST..	6	520	629*	7.5	15.1
453 UN PRES CH USA	1	115	139*	1.6	3.3
469 WELS..........	1	32	41	0.5	1.0
FAULK	17	1 461	3 013*	90.6	100.0
029 AMER LUTH CH..	2	173	242	7.3	8.0
081 CATHOLIC......	4	NA	1 200	36.1	39.8
164 CH LUTH CONF..	1	36	44	1.3	1.5
283 LUTH--MO SYNOD	3	294	370	11.1	12.3
443 UN C OF CHRIST	1	39	47*	1.4	1.6
449 UN METHODIST..	6	919	1 110*	33.4	36.8
GRANT	28	4 343	7 824*	86.8	100.0
029 AMER LUTH CH..	3	1 164	1 591	17.7	20.3
053 ASSEMB OF GOD.	1	43	55	0.6	0.7
057 BAPT GEN CONF.	4	170	210*	2.3	2.7
081 CATHOLIC......	3	NA	2 159	24.0	27.6
193 EPISCOPAL.....	1	34	44	0.5	0.6
201 EVAN COV CH AM	2	137	169*	1.9	2.2
203 EVAN FREE CH..	1	17	21*	0.2	0.3
281 LUTH CH AMER..	2	244	301	3.3	3.8
283 LUTH--MO SYNOD	3	1 283	1 732	19.2	22.1
443 UN C OF CHRIST	1	82	101*	1.1	1.3
449 UN METHODIST..	5	1 054	1 303*	14.5	16.7
453 UN PRES CH USA	1	55	68*	0.8	0.9
469 WELS..........	1	60	70	0.8	0.9
GREGORY	30	2 447	4 320*	71.8	100.0
019 AMER BAPT USA.	5	392	477*	7.9	11.0
053 ASSEMB OF GOD.	2	83	171	2.8	4.0
063 BEREAN FUND CH	1	20	24*	0.4	0.6
081 CATHOLIC......	4	NA	1 159	19.3	26.8
193 EPISCOPAL.....	3	102	223	3.7	5.2
283 LUTH--MO SYNOD	3	558	656	10.9	15.2
443 UN C OF CHRIST	3	321	390*	6.5	9.0
449 UN METHODIST..	4	442	537*	8.9	12.4
453 UN PRES CH USA	1	25	30*	0.5	0.7
469 WELS..........	4	504	653	10.9	15.1
HAAKON	17	904	1 924*	68.9	100.0
019 AMER BAPT USA.	1	20	25*	0.9	1.3
029 AMER LUTH CH..	4	370	496	17.8	25.8
081 CATHOLIC......	3	NA	695	24.9	36.1
193 EPISCOPAL.....	1	16	25	0.9	1.3
203 EVAN FREE CH..	2	34	43*	1.5	2.2
283 LUTH--MO SYNOD	2	205	289	10.3	15.0
329 OPEN BIBLE STD	1	70	110	3.9	5.7
449 UN METHODIST..	2	120	153*	5.5	8.0
453 UN PRES CH USA	1	69	88*	3.1	4.6
HAMLIN	22	2 671	4 144*	78.8	100.0
029 AMER LUTH CH..	6	1 327	1 695	32.2	40.9
045 APOSTOLIC LUTH	1	20	24*	0.5	0.6
057 BAPT GEN CONF.	1	48	58*	1.1	1.4
081 CATHOLIC......	3	NA	708	13.5	17.1
164 CH LUTH CONF..	1	28	30	0.6	0.7
201 EVAN COV CH AM	1	78	95*	1.8	2.3
281 LUTH CH AMER..	1	288	381	7.2	9.2
371 REF CH IN AM..	2	118	213	4.0	5.1
443 UN C OF CHRIST	2	214	260*	4.9	6.3
453 UN PRES CH USA	1	277	337*	6.4	8.1
469 WELS..........	3	273	343	6.5	8.3
HAND	13	1 348	3 453*	69.8	100.0
029 AMER LUTH CH..	1	420	553	11.2	16.0

NA—Not applicable   *Total adherents estimated from known number of communicant, confirmed, full members.   —Represents a percent less than 0.1.   Percentages may not total due to rounding.

Table 4. Churches and Church Membership by County and Denomination: 1980

County and Denomination	Number of churches	Communicant, confirmed, full members	Total adherents		
			Number	Percent of total population	Percent of total adherents
053 ASSEMB OF GOD.	1	36	60	1.2	1.7
081 CATHOLIC......	4	NA	1 665	33.6	48.2
165 CH OF NAZARENE	1	43	146	3.0	4.2
285 MENNONITE CH..	1	14	17*	0.3	0.5
443 UN C OF CHRIST	1	?	?	?	?
449 UN METHODIST..	2	406	492*	9.9	14.2
453 UN PRES CH USA	2	429	520*	10.5	15.1
HANSON	12	1 165	2 385*	69.8	100.0
081 CATHOLIC......	3	NA	912	26.7	38.2
165 CH OF NAZARENE	1	0	35	1.0	1.5
237 GC MENN BR CHS	1	167	209*	6.1	8.8
283 LUTH--MO SYNOD	2	245	286	8.4	12.0
313 N AM BAPT CONF	2	436	546*	16.0	22.9
449 UN METHODIST..	2	205	257*	7.5	10.8
453 UN PRES CH USA	1	112	140*	4.1	5.9
HARDING	15	428	882*	51.9	100.0
029 AMER LUTH CH..	3	233	306	18.0	34.7
053 ASSEMB OF GOD.	1	10	18	1.1	2.0
081 CATHOLIC......	6	NA	298	17.5	33.8
220 FREE LUTHERAN.	1	75	125	7.4	14.2
281 LUTH CH AMER..	1	14	18	1.1	2.0
443 UN C OF CHRIST	1	55	67*	3.9	7.6
449 UN METHODIST..	2	41	50*	2.9	5.7
HUGHES	31	5 065	8 727*	61.4	100.0
019 AMER BAPT USA.	1	432	537*	3.8	6.2
029 AMER LUTH CH..	1	1 004	1 390	9.8	15.9
053 ASSEMB OF GOD.	1	48	100	0.7	1.1
081 CATHOLIC......	3	NA	1 790	12.6	20.5
097 CHR CHS&CHS CR	1	90	112*	0.8	1.3
151 L-D SAINTS....	2	NA	168	1.2	1.9
164 CH LUTH CONF..	1	11	13	0.1	0.1
165 CH OF NAZARENE	1	18	40	0.3	0.5
167 CHS OF CHRIST.	2	88	117	0.8	1.3
193 EPISCOPAL.....	1	147	217	1.5	2.5
263 INT FOURSQ GOS	1	17	21*	0.1	0.2
281 LUTH CH AMER..	1	160	290	2.0	3.3
283 LUTH--MO SYNOD	3	748	1 037	7.3	11.9
329 OPEN BIBLE STD	2	35	50	0.4	0.6
413 S.D.A.........	2	289	359*	2.5	4.1
419 SO BAPT CONV..	2	122	152*	1.1	1.7
443 UN C OF CHRIST	1	407	506*	3.6	5.8
449 UN METHODIST..	3	1 193	1 484*	10.4	17.0
453 UN PRES CH USA	1	187	233*	1.6	2.7
469 WELS..........	1	69	111	0.8	1.3
HUTCHINSON	27	5 016	8 304*	88.8	100.0
029 AMER LUTH CH..	5	1 053	1 299	13.9	15.6
081 CATHOLIC......	3	NA	2 145	22.9	25.8
105 CHRISTIAN REF.	2	328	409	4.4	4.9
283 LUTH--MO SYNOD	6	1 208	1 474	15.8	17.8
287 MENN GEN CONF.	2	603	769	8.2	9.3
291 MISSIONARY CH.	1	91	137	1.5	1.6
313 N AM BAPT CONF	1	110	131*	1.4	1.6
443 UN C OF CHRIST	5	1 374	1 642*	17.6	19.8
449 UN METHODIST..	2	249	298*	3.2	3.6
HYDE	6	751	1 623*	78.4	100.0
029 AMER LUTH CH..	1	449	563	27.2	34.7
081 CATHOLIC......	2	NA	650	31.4	40.0
089 CHR & MISS AL.	1	29	78	3.8	4.8
097 CHR CHS&CHS CR	1	20	24*	1.2	1.5
449 UN METHODIST..	1	253	308*	14.9	19.0
JACKSON	14	764	1 511*	44.0	100.0
029 AMER LUTH CH..	2	175	270	7.9	17.9
081 CATHOLIC......	3	NA	443	12.9	29.3
193 EPISCOPAL.....	3	189	283	8.2	18.7
283 LUTH--MO SYNOD	1	72	89	2.6	5.9
443 UN C OF CHRIST	1	?	?	?	?
453 UN PRES CH USA	4	328	426*	12.4	28.2
JERAULD	13	1 373	2 102*	71.8	100.0
029 AMER LUTH CH..	1	334	435	14.9	20.7
081 CATHOLIC......	2	NA	330	11.3	15.7
221 FREE METHODIST	1	41	117	4.0	5.6
226 FRIENDS-USA...	1	4	5*	0.2	0.2
283 LUTH--MO SYNOD	1	111	141	4.8	6.7
313 N AM BAPT CONF	1	96	117*	4.0	5.6
443 UN C OF CHRIST	3	379	461*	15.7	21.9
449 UN METHODIST..	3	408	496*	16.9	23.6
JONES	7	551	817*	55.8	100.0
081 CATHOLIC......	2	NA	100	6.8	12.2
283 LUTH--MO SYNOD	2	192	257	17.6	31.5
371 REF CH IN AM..	1	28	57	3.9	7.0
449 UN METHODIST..	2	331	403*	27.5	49.3
KINGSBURY	32	4 016	6 205*	92.9	100.0
029 AMER LUTH CH..	8	2 477	3 183	47.7	51.3
053 ASSEMB OF GOD.	1	13	27	0.4	0.4
081 CATHOLIC......	4	NA	1 127	16.9	18.2
089 CHR & MISS AL.	1	41	106	1.6	1.7
097 CHR CHS&CHS CR	1	30	36*	0.5	0.6

County and Denomination	Number of churches	Communicant, confirmed, full members	Total adherents		
			Number	Percent of total population	Percent of total adherents
143 CG IN CR(MENN)	1	73	73	1.1	1.2
193 EPISCOPAL.....	1	18	21	0.3	0.3
201 EVAN COV CH AM	1	14	17*	0.3	0.3
281 LUTH CH AMER..	1	36	43	0.6	0.7
283 LUTH--MO SYNOD	1	47	57	0.9	0.9
335 ORTH PRESB CH.	2	53	63*	0.9	1.0
419 SO BAPT CONV..	1	42	50*	0.7	0.8
443 UN C OF CHRIST	3	413	494*	7.4	8.0
449 UN METHODIST..	5	680	813*	12.2	13.1
453 UN PRES CH USA	1	79	95*	1.4	1.5
LAKE	25	4 606	7 857*	73.3	100.0
019 AMER BAPT USA.	1	125	149*	1.4	1.9
029 AMER LUTH CH..	6	2 274	2 957	27.6	37.6
053 ASSEMB OF GOD.	1	36	85	0.8	1.1
081 CATHOLIC......	2	NA	1 940	18.1	24.7
151 L-D SAINTS....	1	NA	48	0.4	0.6
165 CH OF NAZARENE	1	58	65	0.6	0.8
167 CHS OF CHRIST.	1	14	18	0.2	0.2
193 EPISCOPAL.....	1	69	73	0.7	0.9
283 LUTH--MO SYNOD	3	621	828	7.7	10.5
313 N AM BAPT CONF	1	260	311*	2.9	4.0
329 OPEN BIBLE STD	1	50	70	0.7	0.9
413 S.D.A.........	1	49	59*	0.6	0.8
443 UN C OF CHRIST	1	133	159*	1.5	2.0
449 UN METHODIST..	2	654	781*	7.3	9.9
453 UN PRES CH USA	2	263	314*	2.9	4.0
LAWRENCE	31	4 579	8 458*	46.1	100.0
019 AMER BAPT USA.	1	157	189*	1.0	2.2
029 AMER LUTH CH..	2	869	1 278	7.0	15.1
053 ASSEMB OF GOD.	2	152	235	1.3	2.8
081 CATHOLIC......	3	NA	2 443	13.3	28.9
165 CH OF NAZARENE	1	35	50	0.3	0.6
167 CHS OF CHRIST.	2	15	22	0.1	0.3
193 EPISCOPAL.....	3	477	637	3.5	7.5
221 FREE METHODIST	1	1	12	0.1	0.1
263 INT FOURSQ GOS	1	102	123*	0.7	1.5
281 LUTH CH AMER..	2	316	444	2.4	5.2
283 LUTH--MO SYNOD	2	493	656	3.6	7.8
313 N AM BAPT CONF	1	108	130*	0.7	1.5
413 S.D.A.........	1	123	148*	0.8	1.7
443 UN C OF CHRIST	2	350	421*	2.3	5.0
449 UN METHODIST..	4	1 081	1 300*	7.1	15.4
453 UN PRES CH USA	2	244	293*	1.6	3.5
469 WELS..........	1	56	77	0.4	0.9
LINCOLN	27	5 669	8 625*	61.9	100.0
029 AMER LUTH CH..	13	3 792	5 113	36.7	59.3
081 CATHOLIC......	4	NA	1 009	7.2	11.7
181 CONSRV CONGR..	1	9	11*	0.1	0.1
371 REF CH IN AM..	3	481	775	5.6	9.0
443 UN C OF CHRIST	1	96	119*	0.9	1.4
449 UN METHODIST..	3	729	902*	6.5	10.5
453 UN PRES CH USA	2	562	696*	5.0	8.1
LYMAN	17	1 131	2 272*	58.8	100.0
029 AMER LUTH CH..	3	410	531	13.7	23.4
053 ASSEMB OF GOD.	1	5	50	1.3	2.2
081 CATHOLIC......	4	NA	597	15.5	26.3
193 EPISCOPAL.....	4	148	361	9.3	15.9
283 LUTH--MO SYNOD	2	216	285	7.4	12.5
449 UN METHODIST..	3	352	448*	11.6	19.7
MC COOK	24	2 835	5 836*	90.6	100.0
029 AMER LUTH CH..	4	800	1 032	16.0	17.7
057 BAPT GEN CONF.	2	360	437*	6.8	7.5
081 CATHOLIC......	4	NA	2 317	36.0	39.7
097 CHR CHS&CHS CR	1	50	61*	0.9	1.0
165 CH OF NAZARENE	1	25	28	0.4	0.5
201 EVAN COV CH AM	1	40	49*	0.8	0.8
281 LUTH CH AMER..	1	235	284	4.4	4.9
283 LUTH--MO SYNOD	3	627	780	12.1	13.4
335 ORTH PRESB CH.	1	49	60*	0.9	1.0
449 UN METHODIST..	3	304	369*	5.7	6.3
453 UN PRES CH USA	3	345	419*	6.5	7.2
MC PHERSON	13	2 545	3 551*	88.2	100.0
029 AMER LUTH CH..	3	1 403	1 660	41.2	46.7
081 CATHOLIC......	2	NA	532	13.2	15.0
133 CH GOD(7TH)DEN	1	47	56*	1.4	1.6
283 LUTH--MO SYNOD	1	162	200	5.0	5.6
313 N AM BAPT CONF	2	273	323*	8.0	9.1
413 S.D.A.........	1	30	35*	0.9	1.0
443 UN C OF CHRIST	1	257	304*	7.5	8.6
449 UN METHODIST..	2	373	441*	11.0	12.4
MARSHALL	25	3 223	5 065*	93.7	100.0
029 AMER LUTH CH..	7	1 782	2 234	41.3	44.1
053 ASSEMB OF GOD.	1	26	56	1.0	1.1
081 CATHOLIC......	4	NA	997	18.4	19.7
193 EPISCOPAL.....	1	28	11	0.2	0.2
203 EVAN FREE CH..	1	43	52*	1.0	1.0
220 FREE LUTHERAN.	1	39	40	0.7	0.8
281 LUTH CH AMER..	1	102	123	2.3	2.4
283 LUTH--MO SYNOD	1	212	289	5.3	5.7
371 REF CH IN AM..	1	58	139	2.6	2.7
449 UN METHODIST..	2	254	306*	5.7	6.0

NA—Not applicable   *Total adherents estimated from known number of communicant, confirmed, full members.   —Represents a percent less than 0.1.   Percentages may not total due to rounding.

252

Table 4. Churches and Church Membership by County and Denomination: 1980

County and Denomination	Number of churches	Communicant, confirmed, full members	Total adherents		
			Number	Percent of total population	Percent of total adherents
453 UN PRES CH USA	5	679	818*	15.1	16.2
MEADE	36	2 807	5 771*	27.9	100.0
019 AMER BAPT USA.	2	67	84*	0.4	1.5
029 AMER LUTH CH..	2	614	855	4.1	14.8
053 ASSEMB OF GOD.	1	59	150	0.7	2.6
081 CATHOLIC......	10	NA	1 910	9.2	33.1
097 CHR CHS&CHS CR	1	65	82*	0.4	1.4
127 CH GOD (CLEVE)	1	30	38*	0.2	0.7
151 L-D SAINTS....	1	NA	132	0.6	2.3
167 CHS OF CHRIST.	2	110	128	0.6	2.2
193 EPISCOPAL.....	1	95	129	0.6	2.2
220 FREE LUTHERAN.	1	64	83	0.4	1.4
329 OPEN BIBLE STD	1	65	85	0.4	1.5
419 SO BAPT CONV..	4	331	417*	2.0	7.2
443 UN C OF CHRIST	2	97	122*	0.6	2.1
449 UN METHODIST..	3	623	785*	3.8	13.6
453 UN PRES CH USA	2	433	546*	2.6	9.5
469 WELS.........	2	154	225	1.1	3.9
MELLETTE	17	552	1 261*	56.1	100.0
019 AMER BAPT USA.	1	9	12*	0.5	1.0
053 ASSEMB OF GOD.	2	36	115	5.1	9.1
081 CATHOLIC......	3	NA	339	15.1	26.9
151 L-D SAINTS....	1	NA	?	?	?
164 CH LUTH CONF..	1	53	78	3.5	6.2
165 CH OF NAZARENE	1	20	139	6.2	11.0
193 EPISCOPAL.....	3	82	130	5.8	10.3
283 LUTH--MO SYNOD	1	114	144	6.4	11.4
413 S.D.A.........	1	15	19*	0.8	1.5
443 UN C OF CHRIST	1	62	79*	3.5	6.3
449 UN METHODIST..	1	145	186*	8.3	14.8
469 WELS.........	1	16	20	0.9	1.6
MINER	17	1 627	3 344*	89.4	100.0
029 AMER LUTH CH..	2	449	601	16.1	18.0
081 CATHOLIC......	3	NA	1 288	34.4	38.5
097 CHR CHS&CHS CR	1	50	60*	1.6	1.8
165 CH OF NAZARENE	1	26	36	1.0	1.1
193 EPISCOPAL.....	1	6	8	0.2	0.2
281 LUTH CH AMER..	1	208	242	6.5	7.2
283 LUTH--MO SYNOD	1	351	465	12.4	13.9
443 UN C OF CHRIST	3	155	186*	5.0	5.6
449 UN METHODIST..	2	266	319*	8.5	9.5
453 UN PRES CH USA	2	116	139*	3.7	4.2
MINNEHAHA	125	40 379	74 688*	68.2	100.0
019 AMER BAPT USA.	6	2 191	2 662*	2.4	3.6
029 AMER LUTH CH..	27	17 994	23 722	21.7	31.8
053 ASSEMB OF GOD.	2	529	859	0.8	1.2
057 BAPT GEN CONF.	2	1 080	1 312*	1.2	1.8
081 CATHOLIC......	13	NA	20 490	18.7	27.4
089 CHR & MISS AL.	1	30	110	0.1	0.1
093 CHR CH (DISC).	1	368	597	0.5	0.8
097 CHR CHS&CHS CR	1	60	73*	0.1	0.1
105 CHRISTIAN REF.	3	637	1 103	1.0	1.5
123 CH GOD (ANDER)	1	25	75	0.1	0.1
127 CH GOD (CLEVE)	1	36	44*	-	0.1
151 L-D SAINTS....	1	NA	432	0.4	0.6
165 CH OF NAZARENE	1	67	93	0.1	0.1
167 CHS OF CHRIST.	1	75	95	0.1	0.1
193 EPISCOPAL.....	4	925	1 141	1.0	1.5
201 EVAN COV CH AM	2	144	175*	0.2	0.2
203 EVAN FREE CH..	1	65	79*	0.1	0.1
209 EVAN LUTH SYN.	1	118	150	0.1	0.2
221 FREE METHODIST	1	37	123	0.1	0.2
271 REFORM JUDAISM	1	130	158*	0.1	0.2
281 LUTH CH AMER..	4	1 547	2 056	1.9	2.8
283 LUTH--MO SYNOD	7	2 972	3 863	3.5	5.2
285 MENNONITE CH..	1	16	19*	-	-
287 MENN GEN CONF.	2	58	112	0.1	0.1
290 METRO COMM CHS	1	15	30	-	-
313 N AM BAPT CONF	2	381	463*	0.4	0.6
329 OPEN BIBLE STD	3	435	630	0.6	0.8
371 REF CH IN AM..	5	981	1 794	1.6	2.4
403 SALVATION ARMY	1	131	804	0.7	1.1
413 S.D.A.........	1	235	286*	0.3	0.4
419 SO BAPT CONV..	2	267	324*	0.3	0.4
435 UNITARIAN-UNIV	1	50	61*	0.1	0.1
443 UN C OF CHRIST	5	1 494	1 815*	1.7	2.4
449 UN METHODIST..	12	5 107	6 205*	5.7	8.3
453 UN PRES CH USA	5	1 881	2 286*	2.1	3.1
469 WELS.........	2	298	447	0.4	0.6
MOODY	18	2 811	4 708*	70.4	100.0
019 AMER BAPT USA.	1	136	168*	2.5	3.6
029 AMER LUTH CH..	5	1 435	1 866	27.9	39.6
081 CATHOLIC......	2	NA	1 133	16.9	24.1
167 CHS OF CHRIST.	1	6	8	0.1	0.2
193 EPISCOPAL.....	1	46	54	0.8	1.1
283 LUTH--MO SYNOD	1	69	88	1.3	1.9
449 UN METHODIST..	4	645	794*	11.9	16.9
453 UN PRES CH USA	2	393	484*	7.2	10.3
469 WELS.........	1	81	113	1.7	2.4
PENNINGTON	75	17 817	36 120*	51.5	100.0
019 AMER BAPT USA.	2	621	763*	1.1	2.1
029 AMER LUTH CH..	5	4 038	5 488	7.8	15.2
053 ASSEMB OF GOD.	3	388	626	0.9	1.7
081 CATHOLIC......	10	NA	11 692	16.7	32.4
097 CHR CHS&CHS CR	1	380	467*	0.7	1.3
105 CHRISTIAN REF.	1	73	139	0.2	0.4
123 CH GOD (ANDER)	1	20	60	0.1	0.2
127 CH GOD (CLEVE)	1	58	71*	0.1	0.2
151 L-D SAINTS....	2	NA	889	1.3	2.5
165 CH OF NAZARENE	1	70	101	0.1	0.3
167 CHS OF CHRIST.	3	156	214	0.3	0.6
193 EPISCOPAL.....	3	889	1 165	1.7	3.2
203 EVAN FREE CH..	4	135	166*	0.2	0.5
221 FREE METHODIST	1	53	141	0.2	0.4
237 GC MENN BR CHS	1	40	49*	0.1	0.1
263 INT FOURSQ GOS	1	58	71*	0.1	0.2
271 REFORM JUDAISM	1	38	47*	0.1	0.1
283 LUTH--MO SYNOD	6	2 165	2 909	4.1	8.1
290 METRO COMM CHS	0	10	20	-	0.1
313 N AM BAPT CONF	1	176	216*	0.3	0.6
329 OPEN BIBLE STD	1	400	600	0.9	1.7
403 SALVATION ARMY	1	129	430	0.6	1.2
413 S.D.A.........	1	339	417*	0.6	1.2
419 SO BAPT CONV..	5	1 763	2 167*	3.1	6.0
443 UN C OF CHRIST	5	1 125	1 383*	2.0	3.8
449 UN METHODIST..	10	2 897	3 561*	5.1	9.9
453 UN PRES CH USA	3	1 406	1 728*	2.5	4.8
469 WELS.........	1	390	540	0.8	1.5
PERKINS	26	1 975	3 322*	70.7	100.0
029 AMER LUTH CH..	7	886	1 122	23.9	33.8
081 CATHOLIC......	4	NA	815	17.3	24.5
105 CHRISTIAN REF.	1	55	87	1.9	2.6
127 CH GOD (CLEVE)	2	176	212*	4.5	6.4
151 L-D SAINTS....	1	NA	?	?	?
164 CH LUTH CONF..	1	132	194	4.1	5.8
193 EPISCOPAL.....	1	24	24	0.5	0.7
313 N AM BAPT CONF	1	54	65*	1.4	2.0
381 REF PRES-EVAN.	1	64	84	1.8	2.5
413 S.D.A.........	2	52	63*	1.3	1.9
449 UN METHODIST..	1	26	31*	0.7	0.9
453 UN PRES CH USA	3	430	518*	11.0	15.6
469 WELS.........	1	76	107	2.3	3.2
POTTER	12	1 140	3 330*	90.6	100.0
081 CATHOLIC......	3	NA	1 905	51.9	57.2
127 CH GOD (CLEVE)	1	37	45*	1.2	1.4
151 L-D SAINTS....	1	NA	?	?	?
193 EPISCOPAL.....	1	65	67	1.8	2.0
237 GC MENN BR CHS	1	51	62*	1.7	1.9
283 LUTH--MO SYNOD	2	484	633	17.2	19.0
449 UN METHODIST..	2	483	591*	16.1	17.7
469 WELS.........	1	20	27	0.7	0.8
ROBERTS	41	5 084	8 886*	81.4	100.0
029 AMER LUTH CH..	7	2 620	3 253	29.8	36.6
053 ASSEMB OF GOD.	3	216	495	4.5	5.6
081 CATHOLIC......	4	NA	2 068	19.0	23.3
089 CHR & MISS AL.	2	45	59	0.5	0.7
151 L-D SAINTS....	1	NA	64	0.6	0.7
165 CH OF NAZARENE	1	6	0	-	-
167 CHS OF CHRIST.	1	10	15	0.1	0.2
193 EPISCOPAL.....	4	318	554	5.1	6.2
220 FREE LUTHERAN.	2	185	235	2.2	2.6
221 FREE METHODIST	1	5	16	0.1	0.2
281 LUTH CH AMER..	3	245	319	2.9	3.6
283 LUTH--MO SYNOD	4	669	859	7.9	9.7
313 N AM BAPT CONF	1	78	97*	0.9	1.1
449 UN METHODIST..	2	42	52*	0.5	0.6
453 UN PRES CH USA	5	645	800*	7.3	9.0
SANBORN	14	982	2 423*	75.4	100.0
029 AMER LUTH CH..	4	546	681	21.2	28.1
081 CATHOLIC......	3	NA	1 221	38.0	50.4
283 LUTH--MO SYNOD	1	101	120	3.7	5.0
443 UN C OF CHRIST	2	122	146*	4.5	6.0
449 UN METHODIST..	3	173	207*	6.4	8.5
453 UN PRES CH USA	1	40	48*	1.5	2.0
SHANNON	51	1 369	7 113*	62.8	100.0
081 CATHOLIC......	14	NA	4 840	42.7	68.0
123 CH GOD (ANDER)	1	10	30	0.3	0.4
151 L-D SAINTS....	1	NA	?	?	?
193 EPISCOPAL.....	26	892	1 608	14.2	22.6
237 GC MENN BR CHS	2	50	69*	0.6	1.0
413 S.D.A.........	1	46	63*	0.6	0.9
419 SO BAPT CONV..	1	50	69*	0.6	1.0
453 UN PRES CH USA	4	203	279*	2.5	3.9
469 WELS.........	1	118	155	1.4	2.2
SPINK	31	3 551	6 502*	70.7	100.0
029 AMER LUTH CH..	2	563	748	8.1	11.5
053 ASSEMB OF GOD.	1	24	41	0.4	0.6
081 CATHOLIC......	7	NA	2 103	22.9	32.3
089 CHR & MISS AL.	1	19	54	0.6	0.8
237 GC MENN BR CHS	1	139	167*	1.8	2.6
283 LUTH--MO SYNOD	3	494	607	6.6	9.3
287 MENN GEN CONF.	1	236	292	3.2	4.5
413 S.D.A.........	1	62	74*	0.8	1.1
443 UN C OF CHRIST	6	753	903*	9.8	13.9
449 UN METHODIST..	7	1 225	1 470*	16.0	22.6
453 UN PRES CH USA	1	36	43*	0.5	0.7

NA—Not applicable   *Total adherents estimated from known number of communicant, confirmed, full members.   —Represents a percent less than 0.1.   Percentages may not total due to rounding.

Table 4. Churches and Church Membership by County and Denomination: 1980

County and Denomination	Number of churches	Communicant, confirmed, full members	Total adherents		
			Number	Percent of total population	Percent of total adherents
STANLEY	5	167	425*	16.8	100.0
029 AMER LUTH CH..	1	54	66	2.6	15.5
081 CATHOLIC......	1	NA	209	8.3	49.2
193 EPISCOPAL.....	2	60	83	3.3	19.5
443 UN C OF CHRIST	1	53	67*	2.6	15.8
SULLY	10	774	1 314*	66.0	100.0
081 CATHOLIC......	2	NA	350	17.6	26.6
237 GC MENN BR CHS	1	94	115*	5.8	8.8
283 LUTH--MO SYNOD	2	206	258	13.0	19.6
329 OPEN BIBLE STD	1	21	35	1.8	2.7
419 SO BAPT CONV..	1	25	31*	1.6	2.4
449 UN METHODIST..	2	286	351*	17.6	26.7
453 UN PRES CH USA	1	142	174*	8.7	13.2
TODD	24	577	3 800*	51.9	100.0
053 ASSEMB OF GOD.	1	19	70	1.0	1.8
081 CATHOLIC......	8	NA	2 933	40.0	77.2
151 L-D SAINTS....	2	NA	?	?	?
164 CH LUTH CONF..	1	19	31	0.4	0.8
193 EPISCOPAL.....	9	329	480	6.6	12.6
443 UN C OF CHRIST	1	?	?	?	?
449 UN METHODIST..	1	63	85*	1.2	2.2
469 WELS.........	1	147	201	2.7	5.3
TRIPP	27	2 190	4 503*	62.0	100.0
019 AMER BAPT USA.	3	182	225*	3.1	5.0
053 ASSEMB OF GOD.	1	66	95	1.3	2.1
081 CATHOLIC......	4	NA	1 417	19.5	31.5
093 CHR CH (DISC).	1	91	140	1.9	3.1
164 CH LUTH CONF..	1	67	95	1.3	2.1
165 CH OF NAZARENE	1	55	179	2.5	4.0
193 EPISCOPAL.....	2	265	420	5.8	9.3
283 LUTH--MO SYNOD	3	223	284	3.9	6.3
335 ORTH PRESB CH.	2	97	120*	1.7	2.7
443 UN C OF CHRIST	2	25	31*	0.4	0.7
449 UN METHODIST..	2	473	584*	8.0	13.0
453 UN PRES CH USA	1	57	70*	1.0	1.6
469 WELS.........	4	589	843	11.6	18.7
TURNER	45	6 723	10 006*	108.1	100.0
019 AMER BAPT USA.	3	354	423*	4.6	4.2
029 AMER LUTH CH..	7	1 883	2 376	25.7	23.7
053 ASSEMB OF GOD.	1	16	31	0.3	0.3
081 CATHOLIC......	4	NA	1 180	12.7	11.8
105 CHRISTIAN REF.	1	52	69	0.7	0.7
123 CH GOD (ANDER)	1	145	435	4.7	4.3
165 CH OF NAZARENE	1	29	41	0.4	0.4
211 EVAN MENN BR..	1	131	170	1.8	1.7
237 GC MENN BR CHS	1	125	149*	1.6	1.5
281 LUTH CH AMER..	1	199	229	2.5	2.3
283 LUTH--MO SYNOD	4	431	523	5.7	5.2
287 MENN GEN CONF.	4	1 243	1 557	16.8	15.6
313 N AM BAPT CONF	1	223	267*	2.9	2.7
371 REF CH IN AM..	4	493	885	9.6	8.8
413 S.D.A.........	1	69	82*	0.9	0.8
443 UN C OF CHRIST	1	157	188*	2.0	1.9
449 UN METHODIST..	4	407	486*	5.3	4.9
453 UN PRES CH USA	5	766	915*	9.9	9.1
UNION	22	3 890	7 299*	66.7	100.0
029 AMER LUTH CH..	6	1 826	2 388	21.8	32.7
057 BAPT GEN CONF.	3	411	509*	4.7	7.0
081 CATHOLIC......	4	NA	2 360	21.6	32.3
201 EVAN COV CH AM	1	66	82*	0.7	1.1
203 EVAN FREE CH..	1	102	126*	1.2	1.7
281 LUTH CH AMER..	1	421	526	4.8	7.2
283 LUTH--MO SYNOD	1	237	283	2.6	3.9
443 UN C OF CHRIST	3	497	616*	5.6	8.4
449 UN METHODIST..	2	330	409*	3.7	5.6
WALWORTH	26	3 821	6 077*	86.7	100.0
019 AMER BAPT USA.	1	196	237*	3.4	3.9
029 AMER LUTH CH..	4	1 783	2 219	31.7	36.5
053 ASSEMB OF GOD.	1	34	74	1.1	1.2
081 CATHOLIC......	2	NA	1 306	18.6	21.5
127 CH GOD (CLEVE)	1	51	62*	0.9	1.0
151 L-D SAINTS....	1	NA	?	?	?
181 CONSRV CONGR..	1	31	38*	0.5	0.6
193 EPISCOPAL.....	1	45	72	1.0	1.2
313 N AM BAPT CONF	1	27	33*	0.5	0.5
413 S.D.A.........	1	57	69*	1.0	1.1
419 SO BAPT CONV..	1	53	64*	0.9	1.1
443 UN C OF CHRIST	5	728	881*	12.6	14.5
449 UN METHODIST..	3	354	429*	6.1	7.1
469 WELS.........	3	462	593	8.5	9.8
YANKTON	31	5 341	12 604*	66.5	100.0
019 AMER BAPT USA.	1	58	70*	0.4	0.6
029 AMER LUTH CH..	8	2 241	2 845	15.0	22.6
053 ASSEMB OF GOD.	1	47	125	0.7	1.0
057 BAPT GEN CONF.	1	198	239*	1.3	1.9
081 CATHOLIC......	4	NA	5 600	29.5	44.4
151 L-D SAINTS....	1	NA	136	0.7	1.1
165 CH OF NAZARENE	1	37	96	0.5	0.8
167 CHS OF CHRIST.	1	46	59	0.3	0.5
193 EPISCOPAL.....	1	170	209	1.1	1.7

County and Denomination	Number of churches	Communicant, confirmed, full members	Total adherents		
			Number	Percent of total population	Percent of total adherents
221 FREE METHODIST	1	21	42	0.2	0.3
283 LUTH--MO SYNOD	2	758	981	5.2	7.8
371 REF CH IN AM..	1	138	204	1.1	1.6
413 S.D.A.........	1	59	71*	0.4	0.6
419 SO BAPT CONV..	1	57	69*	0.4	0.5
443 UN C OF CHRIST	3	750	906*	4.8	7.2
449 UN METHODIST..	2	700	845*	4.5	6.7
469 WELS.........	1	61	107	0.6	0.8
ZIEBACH	22	538	1 782*	77.2	100.0
081 CATHOLIC......	6	NA	942	40.8	52.9
127 CH GOD (CLEVE)	1	20	27*	1.2	1.5
151 L-D SAINTS....	3	NA	?	?	?
193 EPISCOPAL.....	8	253	466	20.2	26.2
263 INT FOURSQ GOS	1	?	?	?	?
443 UN C OF CHRIST	2	222	295*	12.8	16.6
469 WELS.........	1	43	52	2.3	2.9

TENNESSEE

County and Denomination	Number of churches	Communicant, confirmed, full members	Total adherents		
			Number	Percent of total population	Percent of total adherents
THE STATE.....	8 529	1 911 978	2 492 387*	54.3	100.0
ANDERSON	118	36 520	47 556*	70.6	100.0
005 AME ZION......	1	270	360	0.5	0.8
053 ASSEMB OF GOD.	4	103	146	0.2	0.3
081 CATHOLIC......	3	NA	3 206	4.8	6.7
089 CHR & MISS AL.	1	96	166	0.2	0.3
093 CHR CH (DISC).	1	148	248	0.4	0.5
097 CHR CHS&CHS CR	2	224	269*	0.4	0.6
123 CH GOD (ANDER)	1	8	24	-	0.1
127 CH GOD (CLEVE)	1	114	137*	0.2	0.3
151 L-D SAINTS....	1	NA	316	0.5	0.7
165 CH OF NAZARENE	1	118	130	0.2	0.3
167 CHS OF CHRIST.	9	989	1 158	1.7	2.4
185 CUMBER PRESB..	1	137	171	0.3	0.4
193 EPISCOPAL.....	2	889	998	1.5	2.1
270 CONSRV JUDAISM	1	78	94*	0.1	0.2
281 LUTH CH AMER..	1	484	609	0.9	1.3
283 LUTH--MO SYNOD	1	328	439	0.7	0.9
357 PRESB CH US...	1	240	288*	0.4	0.6
419 SO BAPT CONV..	66	25 858	31 065*	46.1	65.3
435 UNITARIAN-UNIV	1	225	270*	0.4	0.6
449 UN METHODIST..	18	5 820	6 992*	10.4	14.7
453 UN PRES CH USA	1	391	470*	0.7	1.0
BEDFORD	86	12 050	15 461*	55.4	100.0
053 ASSEMB OF GOD.	1	38	68	0.2	0.4
081 CATHOLIC......	1	NA	233	0.8	1.5
093 CHR CH (DISC).	1	364	504	1.8	3.3
123 CH GOD (ANDER)	1	45	135	0.5	0.9
127 CH GOD (CLEVE)	3	120	146*	0.5	0.9
151 L-D SAINTS....	1	NA	45	0.2	0.3
165 CH OF NAZARENE	4	233	404	1.4	2.6
167 CHS OF CHRIST.	20	1 863	2 480	8.9	16.0
185 CUMBER PRESB..	3	38	79	0.3	0.5
193 EPISCOPAL.....	1	129	142	0.5	0.9
281 LUTH CH AMER..	3	165	207	0.7	1.3
353 CHR BRETHREN..	1	40	75	0.3	0.5
357 PRESB CH US...	2	448	544*	1.9	3.5
419 SO BAPT CONV..	17	5 103	6 193*	22.2	40.1
421 SO METHODIST..	1	47	59	0.2	0.4
449 UN METHODIST..	25	3 371	4 091*	14.7	26.5
453 UN PRES CH USA	1	46	56*	0.2	0.4
BENTON	46	5 278	6 620*	44.4	100.0
081 CATHOLIC......	1	NA	210	1.4	3.2
101 C.M.E.........	1	88	105*	0.7	1.6
165 CH OF NAZARENE	1	84	91	0.6	1.4
167 CHS OF CHRIST.	9	695	883	5.9	13.3
185 CUMBER PRESB..	1	72	132	0.9	2.0
323 OLD ORD AMISH.	1	130	156*	1.0	2.4
419 SO BAPT CONV..	11	2 327	2 788*	18.7	42.1
449 UN METHODIST..	20	1 864	2 233*	15.0	33.7
453 UN PRES CH USA	1	18	22*	0.1	0.3
BLEDSOE	31	2 554	3 142*	33.2	100.0
127 CH GOD (CLEVE)	8	394	475*	5.0	15.1
167 CHS OF CHRIST.	12	900	1 146	12.1	36.5
413 S.D.A.........	1	43	52*	0.5	1.7
419 SO BAPT CONV..	4	661	798*	8.4	25.4
449 UN METHODIST..	6	556	671*	7.1	21.4
BLOUNT	145	41 660	51 316*	66.0	100.0
005 AME ZION......	4	1 775	2 130	2.7	4.2
053 ASSEMB OF GOD.	2	116	141	0.2	0.3
081 CATHOLIC......	2	NA	650	0.8	1.3
097 CHR CHS&CHS CR	4	756	908*	1.2	1.8

NA—Not applicable   *Total adherents estimated from known number of communicant, confirmed, full members.   —Represents a percent less than 0.1.   Percentages may not total due to rounding.

Table 4. Churches and Church Membership by County and Denomination: 1980

County and Denomination	Number of churches	Communicant, confirmed, full members	Total adherents Number	Percent of total population	Percent of total adherents
123 CH GOD (ANDER)	1	50	150	0.2	0.3
127 CH GOD (CLEVE)	8	770	924*	1.2	1.8
151 L-D SAINTS....	1	NA	247	0.3	0.5
165 CH OF NAZARENE	2	127	280	0.4	0.5
167 CHS OF CHRIST.	4	575	732	0.9	1.4
185 CUMBER PRESB..	1	84	177	0.2	0.3
193 EPISCOPAL.....	1	437	561	0.7	1.1
226 FRIENDS-USA...	2	223	268*	0.3	0.5
281 LUTH CH AMER..	1	239	315	0.4	0.6
356 PRESB CH AMER.	1	92	111	0.1	0.2
413 S.D.A.........	1	82	98*	0.1	0.2
419 SO BAPT CONV..	80	28 224	33 887*	43.6	66.0
449 UN METHODIST..	22	6 468	7 766*	10.0	15.1
453 UN PRES CH USA	8	1 642	1 971*	2.5	3.8
BRADLEY	120	29 192	37 162*	55.0	100.0
017 AMER BAPT ASSN	1	160	160	0.2	0.4
053 ASSEMB OF GOD.	1	51	124	0.2	0.3
059 BAPT MISS ASSN	2	181	222*	0.3	0.6
081 CATHOLIC......	1	NA	995	1.5	2.7
093 CHR CH (DISC).	1	98	156	0.2	0.4
097 CHR CHS&CHS CR	2	131	161*	0.2	0.4
127 CH GOD (CLEVE)	21	4 535	5 569*	8.2	15.0
151 L-D SAINTS....	1	NA	107	0.2	0.3
165 CH OF NAZARENE	1	69	69	0.1	0.2
167 CHS OF CHRIST.	5	475	605	0.9	1.6
185 CUMBER PRESB..	3	92	148	0.2	0.4
193 EPISCOPAL.....	1	550	770	1.1	2.1
283 LUTH--MO SYNOD	1	190	251	0.4	0.7
357 PRESB CH US...	2	319	392*	0.6	1.1
413 S.D.A.........	2	435	534*	0.8	1.4
419 SO BAPT CONV..	54	17 717	21 755*	32.2	58.5
449 UN METHODIST..	21	4 189	5 144*	7.6	13.8
CAMPBELL	67	13 349	16 657*	47.8	100.0
005 AME ZION......	1	65	78	0.2	0.5
053 ASSEMB OF GOD.	1	14	13	—	0.1
081 CATHOLIC......	1	NA	62	0.2	0.4
093 CHR CH (DISC).	1	22	34	0.1	0.2
097 CHR CHS&CHS CR	1	20	25*	0.1	0.2
127 CH GOD (CLEVE)	7	699	859*	2.5	5.2
151 L-D SAINTS....	1	NA	181	0.5	1.1
167 CHS OF CHRIST.	2	136	170	0.5	1.0
357 PRESB CH US...	2	98	120*	0.3	0.7
413 S.D.A.........	1	110	135*	0.4	0.8
419 SO BAPT CONV..	42	10 833	13 318*	38.2	80.0
449 UN METHODIST..	7	1 352	1 662*	4.8	10.0
CANNON	40	4 178	5 201*	50.8	100.0
127 CH GOD (CLEVE)	2	105	127*	1.2	2.4
165 CH OF NAZARENE	1	24	17	0.2	0.3
167 CHS OF CHRIST.	21	1 718	2 174	21.2	41.8
221 FREE METHODIST	1	39	114	1.1	2.2
357 PRESB CH US...	1	13	16*	0.2	0.3
413 S.D.A.........	1	103	124*	1.2	2.4
419 SO BAPT CONV..	8	1 720	2 078*	20.3	40.0
449 UN METHODIST..	5	456	551*	5.4	10.6
CARROLL	82	12 597	15 456*	54.6	100.0
053 ASSEMB OF GOD.	2	139	215	0.8	1.4
101 C.M.E.........	1	503	605*	2.1	3.9
167 CHS OF CHRIST.	19	1 890	2 320	8.2	15.0
185 CUMBER PRESB..	10	534	862	3.0	5.6
323 OLD ORD AMISH.	1	130	156*	0.6	1.0
357 PRESB CH US...	1	11	13*	—	0.1
413 S.D.A.........	2	129	155*	0.5	1.0
419 SO BAPT CONV..	21	6 349	7 630*	27.0	49.4
449 UN METHODIST..	22	2 768	3 327*	11.8	21.5
453 UN PRES CH USA	3	144	173*	0.6	1.1
CARTER	91	21 943	26 770*	53.3	100.0
005 AME ZION......	1	290	348	0.7	1.3
053 ASSEMB OF GOD.	1	78	110	0.2	0.4
081 CATHOLIC......	1	NA	35	0.1	0.1
097 CHR CHS&CHS CR	19	4 272	5 133*	10.2	19.2
123 CH GOD (ANDER)	2	130	390	0.8	1.5
127 CH GOD (CLEVE)	5	302	363*	0.7	1.4
165 CH OF NAZARENE	1	77	135	0.3	0.5
167 CHS OF CHRIST.	4	355	452	0.9	1.7
193 EPISCOPAL.....	1	45	89	0.2	0.3
283 LUTH--MO SYNOD	1	112	153	0.3	0.6
357 PRESB CH US...	4	333	400*	0.8	1.5
413 S.D.A.........	1	32	38*	0.1	0.1
419 SO BAPT CONV..	40	14 139	16 988*	33.8	63.5
449 UN METHODIST..	9	1 599	1 921*	3.8	7.2
453 UN PRES CH USA	1	179	215*	0.4	0.8
CHEATHAM	40	4 793	6 292*	29.1	100.0
017 AMER BAPT ASSN	1	160	160	0.7	2.5
053 ASSEMB OF GOD.	1	75	150	0.7	2.4
081 CATHOLIC......	1	NA	216	1.0	3.4
165 CH OF NAZARENE	3	158	261	1.2	4.1
167 CHS OF CHRIST.	18	1 765	2 245	10.4	35.7
413 S.D.A.........	1	54	67*	0.3	1.1
419 SO BAPT CONV..	3	900	1 113*	5.1	17.7
449 UN METHODIST..	12	1 681	2 080*	9.6	33.1
CHESTER	38	5 600	6 978*	54.8	100.0

County and Denomination	Number of churches	Communicant, confirmed, full members	Total adherents Number	Percent of total population	Percent of total adherents
053 ASSEMB OF GOD.	1	85	155	1.2	2.2
093 CHR CH (DISC).	1	49	75	0.6	1.1
097 CHR CHS&CHS CR	1	40	48*	0.4	0.7
101 C.M.E.........	5	747	893*	7.0	12.8
127 CH GOD (CLEVE)	1	53	63*	0.5	0.9
167 CHS OF CHRIST.	8	1 179	1 584	12.4	22.7
185 CUMBER PRESB..	1	93	152	1.2	2.2
419 SO BAPT CONV..	11	2 373	2 836*	22.3	40.6
449 UN METHODIST..	9	981	1 172*	9.2	16.8
CLAIBORNE	103	14 462	17 836*	72.5	100.0
053 ASSEMB OF GOD.	1	23	50	0.2	0.3
097 CHR CHS&CHS CR	2	102	125*	0.5	0.7
151 L-D SAINTS....	1	NA	79	0.3	0.4
167 CHS OF CHRIST.	2	95	130	0.5	0.7
283 LUTH--MO SYNOD	1	25	33	0.1	0.2
419 SO BAPT CONV..	83	12 986	15 911*	64.7	89.2
449 UN METHODIST..	13	1 231	1 508*	6.1	8.5
CLAY	28	2 186	2 778*	36.2	100.0
123 CH GOD (ANDER)	1	50	150	2.0	5.4
167 CHS OF CHRIST.	23	1 777	2 195	28.6	79.0
413 S.D.A.........	1	18	22*	0.3	0.8
419 SO BAPT CONV..	1	175	211*	2.7	7.6
449 UN METHODIST..	2	166	200*	2.6	7.2
COCKE	82	12 356	15 487*	53.8	100.0
005 AME ZION......	3	438	584	2.0	3.8
081 CATHOLIC......	1	NA	75	0.3	0.5
089 CHR & MISS AL.	1	39	39	0.1	0.3
097 CHR CHS&CHS CR	4	480	584*	2.0	3.8
123 CH GOD (ANDER)	2	125	375	1.3	2.4
127 CH GOD (CLEVE)	6	615	749*	2.6	4.8
151 L-D SAINTS....	1	NA	53	0.2	0.3
165 CH OF NAZARENE	1	27	80	0.3	0.5
167 CHS OF CHRIST.	3	160	203	0.7	1.3
193 EPISCOPAL.....	1	49	106	0.4	0.7
281 LUTH CH AMER..	3	536	603	2.1	3.9
357 PRESB CH US...	1	131	159*	0.6	1.0
413 S.D.A.........	1	47	57*	0.2	0.4
419 SO BAPT CONV..	39	8 201	9 984*	34.7	64.5
449 UN METHODIST..	14	1 499	1 825*	6.3	11.8
453 UN PRES CH USA	1	9	11*	—	0.1
COFFEE	82	13 707	19 172*	50.0	100.0
017 AMER BAPT ASSN	1	50	50	0.1	0.3
053 ASSEMB OF GOD.	2	68	115	0.3	0.6
081 CATHOLIC......	1	NA	1 200	3.1	6.3
093 CHR CH (DISC).	1	463	565	1.5	2.9
123 CH GOD (ANDER)	1	35	105	0.3	0.5
127 CH GOD (CLEVE)	1	78	95*	0.2	0.5
151 L-D SAINTS....	1	NA	171	0.4	0.9
165 CH OF NAZARENE	5	255	567	1.5	3.0
167 CHS OF CHRIST.	28	2 246	3 430	9.0	17.9
185 CUMBER PRESB..	2	130	192	0.5	1.0
193 EPISCOPAL.....	2	321	404	1.1	2.1
281 LUTH CH AMER..	1	553	730	1.9	3.8
283 LUTH--MO SYNOD	1	128	177	0.5	0.9
357 PRESB CH US...	1	100	121*	0.3	0.6
413 S.D.A.........	1	71	86*	0.2	0.4
419 SO BAPT CONV..	13	5 378	6 520*	17.0	34.0
435 UNITARIAN-UNIV	1	20	24*	0.1	0.1
449 UN METHODIST..	18	3 509	4 254*	11.1	22.2
453 UN PRES CH USA	1	302	366*	1.0	1.9
CROCKETT	55	9 391	11 670*	78.1	100.0
053 ASSEMB OF GOD.	2	117	168	1.1	1.4
093 CHR CH (DISC).	2	219	269	1.8	2.3
097 CHR CHS&CHS CR	2	225	271*	1.8	2.3
101 C.M.E.........	4	575	692*	4.6	5.9
127 CH GOD (CLEVE)	2	111	134*	0.9	1.1
167 CHS OF CHRIST.	12	1 055	1 343	9.0	11.5
185 CUMBER PRESB..	1	38	67	0.4	0.6
193 EPISCOPAL.....	1	1 072	1 526	10.2	13.1
419 SO BAPT CONV..	13	3 864	4 653*	31.1	39.9
449 UN METHODIST..	16	2 115	2 547*	17.0	21.8
CUMBERLAND	68	8 723	11 336*	39.5	100.0
053 ASSEMB OF GOD.	1	29	65	0.2	0.6
061 BEACHY AMISH..	1	17	21*	0.1	0.2
081 CATHOLIC......	2	NA	262	0.9	2.3
093 CHR CH (DISC).	1	393	604	2.1	5.3
097 CHR CHS&CHS CR	1	60	73*	0.3	0.6
127 CH GOD (CLEVE)	3	235	287*	1.0	2.5
151 L-D SAINTS....	1	NA	177	0.6	1.6
165 CH OF NAZARENE	2	125	201	0.7	1.8
167 CHS OF CHRIST.	12	1 083	1 378	4.8	12.2
193 EPISCOPAL.....	1	47	52	0.2	0.5
283 LUTH--MO SYNOD	1	55	63	0.2	0.6
413 S.D.A.........	1	92	112*	0.4	1.0
419 SO BAPT CONV..	26	4 587	5 600*	19.5	49.4
443 UN C OF CHRIST	3	369	450*	1.6	4.0
449 UN METHODIST..	9	1 476	1 802*	6.3	15.9
453 UN PRES CH USA	3	155	189*	0.7	1.7
DAVIDSON	470	188 754	256 032*	53.6	100.0
005 AME ZION......	1	175	210	—	0.1
017 AMER BAPT ASSN	5	1 000	1 000	0.2	0.4

NA—Not applicable   *Total adherents estimated from known number of communicant, confirmed, full members.   —Represents a percent less than 0.1.   Percentages may not total due to rounding.

Table 4. Churches and Church Membership by County and Denomination: 1980

County and Denomination	Number of churches	Communicant, confirmed, full members	Total adherents Number	Percent of total population	Percent of total adherents
019 AMER BAPT USA.	2	1 925	2 282*	0.5	0.9
029 AMER LUTH CH..	1	208	275	0.1	0.1
053 ASSEMB OF GOD.	13	1 469	1 987	0.4	0.8
081 CATHOLIC.....	16	NA	21 229	4.4	8.3
093 CHR CH (DISC).	9	2 746	3 591	0.8	1.4
097 CHR CHS&CHS CR	4	577	684*	0.1	0.3
101 C.M.E.	6	7 188	8 521*	1.8	3.3
123 CH GOD (ANDER)	3	181	543	0.1	0.2
127 CH GOD (CLEVE)	4	719	852*	0.2	0.3
133 CH GOD(7TH)DEN	1	8	9*	–	–
151 L-D SAINTS....	2	NA	873	0.2	0.3
165 CH OF NAZARENE	31	4 989	7 202	1.5	2.8
167 CHS OF CHRIST.	112	30 932	41 857	8.8	16.3
185 CUMBER PRESB..	13	2 595	4 645	1.0	1.8
193 EPISCOPAL.....	12	4 789	6 495	1.4	2.5
221 FREE METHODIST	1	11	81	–	–
226 FRIENDS-USA...	1	42	50*	–	–
263 INT FOURSQ GOS	1	29	34*	–	–
270 CONSRV JUDAISM	1	366	434*	0.1	0.2
271 REFORM JUDAISM	1	1 406	1 667*	0.3	0.7
281 LUTH CH AMER..	5	1 568	2 104	0.4	0.8
283 LUTH--MO SYNOD	4	714	965	0.2	0.4
290 METRO COMM CHS	1	75	150	–	0.1
349 PENT HOLINESS.	1	19	23*	–	0.1
353 CHR BRETHREN..	2	150	185	–	0.1
357 PRESB CH US...	18	8 701	10 314*	2.2	4.0
403 SALVATION ARMY	2	130	197	–	0.1
413 S.D.A.	10	3 361	3 984*	0.8	1.6
419 SO BAPT CONV.	96	75 040	88 952*	18.6	34.7
421 SO METHODIST..	6	763	895	0.2	0.3
435 UNITARIAN-UNIV	1	215	255*	0.1	0.1
443 UN C OF CHRIST	4	367	435*	0.1	0.2
449 UN METHODIST..	74	35 239	41 772*	8.7	16.3
453 UN PRES CH USA	5	980	1 162*	0.2	0.5
469 WELS..........	1	77	118	–	–
DECATUR	44	4 721	5 887*	54.2	100.0
053 ASSEMB OF GOD.	1	238	354	3.3	6.0
081 CATHOLIC......	2	NA	23	0.2	0.4
167 CHS OF CHRIST.	4	385	495	4.6	8.4
185 CUMBER PRESB..	4	86	170	1.6	2.9
193 EPISCOPAL.....	1	592	739	6.8	12.6
413 S.D.A.	1	59	71*	0.7	1.2
419 SO BAPT CONV.	19	2 184	2 622*	24.2	44.5
449 UN METHODIST..	12	1 177	1 413*	13.0	24.0
DE KALB	53	6 076	7 485*	55.1	100.0
075 BRETHREN IN CR	1	43	73	0.5	1.0
127 CH GOD (CLEVE)	2	176	213*	1.6	2.8
165 CH OF NAZARENE	1	25	32	0.2	0.4
167 CHS OF CHRIST.	6	350	445	3.3	5.9
185 CUMBER PRESB..	2	134	260	1.9	3.5
413 S.D.A.	1	26	31*	0.2	0.4
419 SO BAPT CONV..	20	3 582	4 329*	31.9	57.8
449 UN METHODIST..	19	1 690	2 042*	15.0	27.3
453 UN PRES CH USA	1	50	60*	0.4	0.8
DICKSON	82	9 231	12 956*	43.1	100.0
053 ASSEMB OF GOD.	1	55	100	0.3	0.8
081 CATHOLIC......	1	NA	400	1.3	3.1
151 L-D SAINTS....	1	NA	95	0.3	0.7
165 CH OF NAZARENE	2	169	350	1.2	2.7
167 CHS OF CHRIST.	32	3 130	4 736	15.8	36.6
185 CUMBER PRESB..	4	248	396	1.3	3.1
193 EPISCOPAL.....	1	59	77	0.3	0.6
349 PENT HOLINESS.	1	10	12*	–	0.1
413 S.D.A.	1	71	87*	0.3	0.7
419 SO BAPT CONV.	11	2 510	3 065*	10.2	23.7
449 UN METHODIST..	24	2 791	3 408*	11.3	26.3
453 UN PRES CH USA	3	188	230*	0.8	1.8
DYER	104	18 243	23 264*	67.1	100.0
053 ASSEMB OF GOD.	6	520	1 139	3.3	4.9
081 CATHOLIC......	1	NA	257	0.7	1.1
097 CHR CHS&CHS CR	2	359	437*	1.3	1.9
101 C.M.E.	5	1 488	1 812*	5.2	7.8
127 CH GOD (CLEVE)	3	373	454*	1.3	2.0
165 CH OF NAZARENE	1	44	97	0.3	0.4
167 CHS OF CHRIST.	21	1 879	2 393	6.9	10.3
185 CUMBER PRESB..	9	701	998	2.9	4.3
193 EPISCOPAL.....	1	129	148	0.4	0.6
215 EVAN METH CH..	1	35	43*	0.1	0.2
283 LUTH--MO SYNOD	1	22	29	0.1	0.1
357 PRESB CH US...	1	177	216*	0.6	0.9
413 S.D.A.	1	75	91*	0.3	0.4
419 SO BAPT CONV.	28	9 162	11 157*	32.2	48.0
449 UN METHODIST..	21	3 201	3 898*	11.2	16.8
453 UN PRES CH USA	2	78	95*	0.3	0.4
FAYETTE	75	13 132	16 777*	66.3	100.0
017 AMER BAPT ASSN	1	50	50	0.2	0.3
053 ASSEMB OF GOD.	1	32	65	0.3	0.4
061 BEACHY AMISH..	1	?	?	?	?
081 CATHOLIC......	1	NA	133	0.5	0.8
093 CHR CH (DISC).	2	90	195	0.8	1.2
101 C.M.E.	17	6 555	8 193*	32.4	48.8
127 CH GOD (CLEVE)	2	65	81*	0.3	0.5
165 CH OF NAZARENE	1	17	41	0.2	0.2
167 CHS OF CHRIST.	6	335	495	2.0	3.0
185 CUMBER PRESB..	3	63	122	0.5	0.7

County and Denomination	Number of churches	Communicant, confirmed, full members	Total adherents Number	Percent of total population	Percent of total adherents
193 EPISCOPAL.....	2	24	26	0.1	0.2
357 PRESB CH US...	3	283	354*	1.4	2.1
413 S.D.A.	1	20	25*	0.1	0.1
419 SO BAPT CONV.	17	4 197	5 246*	20.7	31.3
449 UN METHODIST..	17	1 401	1 751*	6.9	10.4
FENTRESS	27	3 600	4 794*	32.3	100.0
127 CH GOD (CLEVE)	3	80	99*	0.7	2.1
151 L-D SAINTS....	1	NA	197	1.3	4.1
165 CH OF NAZARENE	2	106	268	1.8	5.6
167 CHS OF CHRIST.	2	250	319	2.2	6.7
409 SEPARATE BAPT.	2	334	413*	2.8	8.6
419 SO BAPT CONV.	7	1 554	1 921*	13.0	40.1
449 UN METHODIST..	9	1 162	1 436*	9.7	30.0
453 UN PRES CH USA	1	114	141*	1.0	2.9
FRANKLIN	89	12 410	19 486*	60.9	100.0
053 ASSEMB OF GOD.	1	15	50	0.2	0.3
081 CATHOLIC......	3	NA	3 360	10.5	17.2
127 CH GOD (CLEVE)	5	269	326*	1.0	1.7
165 CH OF NAZARENE	8	552	1 033	3.2	5.3
167 CHS OF CHRIST.	20	1 835	2 335	7.3	12.0
185 CUMBER PRESB..	9	789	1 394	4.4	7.2
193 EPISCOPAL.....	5	729	1 013	3.2	5.2
226 FRIENDS-USA...	1	6	7*	–	–
357 PRESB CH US...	1	68	83*	0.3	0.4
419 SO BAPT CONV.	22	5 681	6 893*	21.6	35.4
443 UN C OF CHRIST	1	105	127*	0.4	0.7
449 UN METHODIST..	11	2 304	2 796*	8.7	14.3
453 UN PRES CH USA	2	57	69*	0.2	0.4
GIBSON	156	30 160	37 819*	76.5	100.0
053 ASSEMB OF GOD.	6	652	1 257	2.5	3.3
081 CATHOLIC......	2	NA	505	1.0	1.3
093 CHR CH (DISC).	1	242	342	0.7	0.9
097 CHR CHS&CHS CR	1	160	192*	0.4	0.5
101 C.M.E.	15	3 499	4 205*	8.5	11.1
127 CH GOD (CLEVE)	2	123	148*	0.3	0.4
167 CHS OF CHRIST.	29	2 833	3 521	7.1	9.3
185 CUMBER PRESB..	12	1 134	1 784	3.6	4.7
193 EPISCOPAL.....	1	52	68	0.1	0.2
357 PRESB CH US...	3	341	410*	0.8	1.1
419 SO BAPT CONV.	51	15 891	19 098*	38.6	50.5
449 UN METHODIST..	30	4 959	5 960*	12.0	15.8
453 UN PRES CH USA	3	274	329*	0.7	0.9
GILES	93	11 027	13 757*	55.9	100.0
081 CATHOLIC......	1	NA	152	0.6	1.1
123 CH GOD (ANDER)	2	68	204	0.8	1.5
127 CH GOD (CLEVE)	1	67	81*	0.3	0.6
167 CHS OF CHRIST.	26	2 103	2 676	10.9	19.5
185 CUMBER PRESB..	4	90	139	0.6	1.0
193 EPISCOPAL.....	1	85	126	0.5	0.9
357 PRESB CH US...	6	315	380*	1.5	2.8
413 S.D.A.	2	54	65*	0.3	0.5
419 SO BAPT CONV..	21	4 701	5 664*	23.0	41.2
449 UN METHODIST..	29	3 544	4 270*	17.3	31.0
GRAINGER	61	10 503	12 857*	76.8	100.0
157 CH OF BRETHREN	1	24	29*	0.2	0.2
167 CHS OF CHRIST.	1	35	45	0.3	0.4
226 FRIENDS-USA...	1	29	35*	0.2	0.3
357 PRESB CH US...	1	8	10*	0.1	0.1
419 SO BAPT CONV..	47	9 650	11 811*	70.5	91.9
449 UN METHODIST..	10	757	927*	5.5	7.2
GREENE	137	19 328	26 499*	48.7	100.0
005 AME ZION......	2	408	544	1.0	2.1
053 ASSEMB OF GOD.	1	42	180	0.3	0.7
081 CATHOLIC......	1	NA	408	0.7	1.5
097 CHR CHS&CHS CR	2	649	783*	1.4	3.0
123 CH GOD (ANDER)	6	1 100	3 300	6.1	12.5
127 CH GOD (CLEVE)	3	182	220*	0.4	0.8
151 L-D SAINTS....	1	NA	?	?	?
157 CH OF BRETHREN	1	120	145*	0.3	0.5
165 CH OF NAZARENE	1	37	128	0.2	0.5
167 CHS OF CHRIST.	3	215	327	0.6	1.2
185 CUMBER PRESB..	11	947	1 658	3.0	6.3
193 EPISCOPAL.....	1	189	224	0.4	0.8
221 FREE METHODIST	1	7	33	0.1	0.1
281 LUTH CH AMER..	4	941	1 087	2.0	4.1
283 LUTH--MO SYNOD	1	44	47	0.1	0.2
349 PENT HOLINESS.	2	100	121*	0.2	0.5
356 PRESB CH AMER.	1	89	89	0.2	0.3
357 PRESB CH US...	2	62	75*	0.1	0.3
413 S.D.A.	2	427	515*	0.9	1.9
419 SO BAPT CONV.	21	5 458	6 586*	12.1	24.9
449 UN METHODIST..	61	7 473	9 018*	16.6	34.0
453 UN PRES CH USA	9	838	1 011*	1.9	3.8
GRUNDY	45	3 409	4 705*	34.1	100.0
127 CH GOD (CLEVE)	4	242	304*	2.2	6.5
151 L-D SAINTS....	1	NA	252	1.8	5.4
165 CH OF NAZARENE	2	102	195	1.4	4.1
167 CHS OF CHRIST.	15	1 000	1 273	9.2	27.1
185 CUMBER PRESB..	1	4	27	0.2	0.6
193 EPISCOPAL.....	3	194	285*	2.1	6.1
353 CHR BRETHREN..	1	35	65	0.5	1.4

NA– Not applicable   *Total adherents estimated from known number of communicant, confirmed, full members.   –Represents a percent less than 0.1.   Percentages may not total due to rounding.

Table 4. Churches and Church Membership by County and Denomination: 1980

County and Denomination	Number of churches	Communicant, confirmed, full members	Total adherents		
			Number	Percent of total population	Percent of total adherents
413 S.D.A.........	2	188	236*	1.7	5.0
419 SO BAPT CONV..	6	768	966*	7.0	20.5
449 UN METHODIST..	10	876	1 102*	8.0	23.4
HAMBLEN	81	23 007	29 186*	59.2	100.0
053 ASSEMB OF GOD.	2	97	133	0.3	0.5
081 CATHOLIC......	1	NA	725	1.5	2.5
097 CHR CHS&CHS CR	2	325	397*	0.8	1.4
123 CH GOD (ANDER)	1	200	600	1.2	2.1
127 CH GOD (CLEVE)	2	279	341*	0.7	1.2
151 L-D SAINTS....	1	NA	191	0.4	0.7
165 CH OF NAZARENE	1	36	69	0.1	0.2
167 CHS OF CHRIST.	1	190	242	0.5	0.8
185 CUMBER PRESB..	1	58	76	0.2	0.3
193 EPISCOPAL.....	1	420	256	0.5	0.9
281 LUTH CH AMER..	1	150	178	0.4	0.6
283 LUTH--MO SYNOD	1	84	113	0.2	0.4
357 PRESB CH US...	2	786	960*	1.9	3.3
413 S.D.A.........	2	125	153*	0.3	0.5
419 SO BAPT CONV..	42	16 558	20 232*	41.0	69.3
449 UN METHODIST..	18	3 520	4 301*	8.7	14.7
453 UN PRES CH USA	2	179	219*	0.4	0.8
HAMILTON	336	114 109	150 319*	52.2	100.0
001 ADVENT CHR CH.	1	64	77*	–	0.1
005 AME ZION......	5	1 201	1 802	0.6	1.2
053 ASSEMB OF GOD.	5	728	868	0.3	0.6
081 CATHOLIC......	5	NA	8 245	2.9	5.5
089 CHR & MISS AL.	1	271	281	0.1	0.2
093 CHR CH (DISC).	3	716	1 043	0.4	0.7
097 CHR CHS&CHS CR	2	668	806*	0.3	0.5
101 C.M.E.........	3	3 029	3 654*	1.3	2.4
123 CH GOD (ANDER)	5	230	690	0.2	0.5
127 CH GOD (CLEVE)	41	5 454	6 579*	2.3	4.4
133 CH GOD(7TH)DEN	1	21	25*	–	–
151 L-D SAINTS....	2	NA	604	0.2	0.4
165 CH OF NAZARENE	8	1 436	2 181	0.8	1.5
167 CHS OF CHRIST.	40	5 309	6 690	2.3	4.5
185 CUMBER PRESB..	6	1 380	2 239	0.8	1.5
193 EPISCOPAL.....	9	3 684	4 951	1.7	3.3
215 EVAN METH CH..	1	84	101*	–	0.1
226 FRIENDS-USA...	1	9	11*	–	–
270 CONSRV JUDAISM	1	276	333*	0.1	0.2
271 REFORM JUDAISM	1	442	533*	0.2	0.4
281 LUTH CH AMER..	2	974	1 314	0.5	0.9
283 LUTH--MO SYNOD	4	853	1 603	0.6	1.1
290 METRO COMM CHS	0	27	54	–	–
335 ORTH PRESB CH.	1	30	36*	–	–
356 PRESB CH AMER.	6	2 847	2 962	1.0	2.0
357 PRESB CH US...	12	5 355	6 459*	2.2	4.3
381 REF PRES-EVAN.	2	280	399	0.1	0.3
403 SALVATION ARMY	2	259	1 116	0.4	0.7
413 S.D.A.........	12	4 869	5 873*	2.0	3.9
419 SO BAPT CONV..	98	51 364	61 957*	21.5	41.2
421 SO METHODIST..	1	64	73	–	–
435 UNITARIAN-UNIV	1	125	151*	0.1	0.1
443 UN C OF CHRIST	2	418	504*	0.2	0.3
449 UN METHODIST..	47	20 705	24 975*	8.7	16.6
453 UN PRES CH USA	5	937	1 130*	0.4	0.8
HANCOCK	43	7 032	8 575*	124.5	100.0
201 EVAN COV CH AM	1	29	35*	0.5	0.4
419 SO BAPT CONV..	37	6 678	8 144*	118.3	95.0
449 UN METHODIST..	3	289	352*	5.1	4.1
453 UN PRES CH USA	2	36	44*	0.6	0.5
HARDEMAN	70	11 391	14 277*	59.8	100.0
017 AMER BAPT ASSN	1	160	160	0.7	1.1
053 ASSEMB OF GOD.	1	19	31	0.1	0.2
081 CATHOLIC......	1	NA	111	0.5	0.8
101 C.M.E.........	5	1 650	2 038*	8.5	14.3
127 CH GOD (CLEVE)	1	28	35*	0.1	0.2
167 CHS OF CHRIST.	10	740	948	4.0	6.6
185 CUMBER PRESB..	4	121	237	1.0	1.7
193 EPISCOPAL.....	1	54	69	0.3	0.5
357 PRESB CH US...	1	28	35*	0.1	0.2
419 SO BAPT CONV..	33	7 245	8 950*	37.5	62.7
449 UN METHODIST..	12	1 346	1 663*	7.0	11.6
HARDIN	65	8 795	11 202*	50.3	100.0
053 ASSEMB OF GOD.	4	284	500	2.2	4.5
081 CATHOLIC......	2	NA	160	0.7	1.4
101 C.M.E.........	1	750	912*	4.1	8.1
123 CH GOD (ANDER)	1	24	72	0.3	0.6
127 CH GOD (CLEVE)	1	35	43*	0.2	0.4
165 CH OF NAZARENE	1	20	29	0.1	0.3
167 CHS OF CHRIST.	9	1 023	1 254	5.6	11.2
185 CUMBER PRESB..	4	421	646	2.9	5.8
263 INT FOURSQ GOS	3	199	242*	1.1	2.2
413 S.D.A.........	1	165	201*	0.9	1.8
419 SO BAPT CONV..	16	3 555	4 323*	19.4	38.6
449 UN METHODIST..	21	2 295	2 791*	12.5	24.9
453 UN PRES CH USA	1	24	29*	0.1	0.3
HAWKINS	123	20 757	25 686*	58.7	100.0
005 AME ZION......	1	212	324	0.7	1.3
081 CATHOLIC......	1	NA	126	0.3	0.5
097 CHR CHS&CHS CR	5	280	342*	0.8	1.3
123 CH GOD (ANDER)	1	50	150	0.3	0.6
127 CH GOD (CLEVE)	5	404	494*	1.1	1.9
157 CH OF BRETHREN	3	84	103*	0.2	0.4
165 CH OF NAZARENE	1	47	91	0.2	0.4
167 CHS OF CHRIST.	2	156	179	0.4	0.7
185 CUMBER PRESB..	2	31	45	0.1	0.2
357 PRESB CH US...	4	498	609*	1.4	2.4
419 SO BAPT CONV..	70	15 554	19 554*	44.7	76.1
449 UN METHODIST..	26	2 968	3 629*	8.3	14.1
453 UN PRES CH USA	2	33	40*	0.1	0.2
HAYWOOD	53	10 242	12 943*	63.7	100.0
053 ASSEMB OF GOD.	2	204	307	1.5	2.4
081 CATHOLIC......	1	NA	105	0.5	0.8
097 CHR CHS&CHS CR	1	34	42*	0.2	0.3
101 C.M.E.........	8	2 737	3 413*	16.8	26.4
127 CH GOD (CLEVE)	1	45	56*	0.3	0.4
167 CHS OF CHRIST.	5	358	460	2.3	3.6
193 EPISCOPAL.....	1	34	43	0.2	0.3
271 REFORM JUDAISM	1	20	25*	0.1	0.2
357 PRESB CH US...	3	287	358*	1.8	2.8
413 S.D.A.........	1	17	21*	0.1	0.2
419 SO BAPT CONV..	15	4 521	5 638*	27.7	43.6
449 UN METHODIST..	14	1 985	2 475*	12.2	19.1
HENDERSON	61	7 707	9 645*	45.1	100.0
053 ASSEMB OF GOD.	1	28	40	0.2	0.4
081 CATHOLIC......	1	NA	81	0.4	0.8
127 CH GOD (CLEVE)	1	72	88*	0.4	0.9
167 CHS OF CHRIST.	17	1 280	1 619	7.6	16.8
185 CUMBER PRESB..	4	269	445	2.1	4.6
357 PRESB CH US...	1	17	21*	0.1	0.2
419 SO BAPT CONV..	22	4 635	5 640*	26.4	58.5
449 UN METHODIST..	14	1 406	1 711*	8.0	17.7
HENRY	90	16 003	19 795*	69.1	100.0
053 ASSEMB OF GOD.	1	58	110	0.4	0.6
061 BEACHY AMISH..	1	106	127*	0.4	0.6
081 CATHOLIC......	1	NA	600	2.1	3.0
093 CHR CH (DISC).	1	278	305	1.1	1.5
101 C.M.E.........	3	1 325	1 583*	5.5	8.0
127 CH GOD (CLEVE)	1	11	13*	–	0.1
151 L-D SAINTS....	1	NA	75	0.3	0.4
165 CH OF NAZARENE	1	99	133	0.5	0.7
167 CHS OF CHRIST.	19	2 349	2 737	9.6	13.8
185 CUMBER PRESB..	3	66	98	0.3	0.5
193 EPISCOPAL.....	1	102	146	0.5	0.7
283 LUTH--MO SYNOD	1	97	114	0.4	0.6
323 OLD ORD AMISH.	1	130	155*	0.5	0.8
413 S.D.A.........	1	82	98*	0.3	0.5
419 SO BAPT CONV..	28	8 211	9 810*	34.2	49.6
421 SO METHODIST..	1	16	19	0.1	0.1
449 UN METHODIST..	24	2 884	3 446*	12.0	17.4
453 UN PRES CH USA	1	189	226*	0.8	1.1
HICKMAN	64	5 545	6 988*	46.1	100.0
053 ASSEMB OF GOD.	1	22	46	0.3	0.7
165 CH OF NAZARENE	1	22	40	0.3	0.6
167 CHS OF CHRIST.	40	3 148	4 047	26.7	57.9
185 CUMBER PRESB..	2	40	65	0.4	0.9
413 S.D.A.........	1	8	10*	0.1	0.1
419 SO BAPT CONV..	9	1 353	1 632*	10.8	23.4
449 UN METHODIST..	10	952	1 148*	7.6	16.4
HOUSTON	28	2 505	3 511*	51.1	100.0
053 ASSEMB OF GOD.	1	29	31	0.5	0.9
101 C.M.E.........	2	381	464*	6.8	13.2
127 CH GOD (CLEVE)	1	35	43*	0.6	1.2
165 CH OF NAZARENE	2	223	348	5.1	9.9
167 CHS OF CHRIST.	2	82	195	2.8	5.6
185 CUMBER PRESB..	5	291	648	9.4	18.5
349 PENT HOLINESS.	2	161	196*	2.9	5.6
419 SO BAPT CONV..	4	424	516*	7.5	14.7
449 UN METHODIST..	9	879	1 070*	15.6	30.5
HUMPHREYS	55	5 988	8 355*	52.4	100.0
053 ASSEMB OF GOD.	2	62	84	0.5	1.0
081 CATHOLIC......	1	NA	440	2.8	5.3
151 L-D SAINTS....	1	NA	124	0.8	1.5
165 CH OF NAZARENE	2	121	261	1.6	3.1
167 CHS OF CHRIST.	15	1 686	2 280	14.3	27.3
185 CUMBER PRESB..	6	315	509	3.2	6.1
193 EPISCOPAL.....	1	80	89	0.6	1.1
349 PENT HOLINESS.	4	152	186*	1.2	2.2
419 SO BAPT CONV..	8	1 884	2 311*	14.5	27.7
421 SO METHODIST..	1	15	18	0.1	0.2
449 UN METHODIST..	13	1 620	1 988*	12.5	23.8
453 UN PRES CH USA	1	53	65*	0.4	0.8
JACKSON	54	2 758	3 530*	37.6	100.0
053 ASSEMB OF GOD.	1	23	40	0.4	1.1
167 CHS OF CHRIST.	40	1 800	2 291	24.4	64.9
221 FREE METHODIST	1	12	87	0.9	2.5
419 SO BAPT CONV..	3	361	435*	4.6	12.3
449 UN METHODIST..	8	559	673*	7.2	19.1
453 UN PRES CH USA	1	3	4*	–	0.1
JEFFERSON	87	16 247	19 612*	62.7	100.0

NA—Not applicable   *Total adherents estimated from known number of communicant, confirmed, full members.   —Represents a percent less than 0.1.   Percentages may not total due to rounding.

257

Table 4. Churches and Church Membership by County and Denomination: 1980

County and Denomination	Number of churches	Communicant, confirmed, full members	Total adherents Number	Percent of total population	Percent of total adherents
053 ASSEMB OF GOD.	1	22	30	0.1	0.2
097 CHR CHS&CHS CR	1	135	162*	0.5	0.8
123 CH GOD (ANDER)	2	32	96	0.3	0.5
127 CH GOD (CLEVE)	7	442	529*	1.7	2.7
157 CH OF BRETHREN	1	96	115*	0.4	0.6
167 CHS OF CHRIST.	1	90	115	0.4	0.6
185 CUMBER PRESB..	2	44	144	0.5	0.7
357 PRESB CH US...	2	382	457*	1.5	2.3
419 SO BAPT CONV..	38	11 430	13 685*	43.7	69.8
449 UN METHODIST..	25	3 345	4 005*	12.8	20.4
453 UN PRES CH USA	7	229	274*	0.9	1.4
JOHNSON	45	7 517	9 201*	66.9	100.0
097 CHR CHS&CHS CR	8	1 026	1 253*	9.1	13.6
167 CHS OF CHRIST.	6	425	542	3.9	5.9
285 MENNONITE CH..	1	38	46*	0.3	0.5
357 PRESB CH US...	3	129	158*	1.1	1.7
413 S.D.A.....	1	32	39*	0.3	0.4
419 SO BAPT CONV..	19	4 907	5 991*	43.6	65.1
449 UN METHODIST..	7	960	1 172*	8.5	12.7
KNOX	417	161 995	202 838*	63.4	100.0
005 AME ZION......	12	7 955	9 211	2.9	4.5
029 AMER LUTH CH..	1	46	81	-	-
053 ASSEMB OF GOD.	10	435	634	0.2	0.3
059 BAPT MISS ASSN	4	572	679*	0.2	0.3
081 CATHOLIC......	5	NA	8 460	2.6	4.2
089 CHR & MISS AL.	1	0	20	-	-
093 CHR CH (DISC).	3	875	1 025	0.3	0.5
097 CHR CHS&CHS CR	9	1 251	1 485*	0.5	0.7
101 C.M.E.	2	806	956*	0.3	0.5
123 CH GOD (ANDER)	1	62	186	0.1	0.1
127 CH GOD (CLEVE)	16	1 590	1 887*	0.6	0.9
151 L-D SAINTS....	3	NA	923	0.3	0.5
157 CH OF BRETHREN	1	50	59*	-	-
165 CH OF NAZARENE	4	231	330	0.1	0.2
167 CHS OF CHRIST.	17	2 560	3 343	1.0	1.6
185 CUMBER PRESB..	6	925	1 819	0.6	0.9
193 EPISCOPAL.....	6	2 392	2 664	0.8	1.3
208 EVAN LUTH ASSN	1	101	121	-	0.1
226 FRIENDS-USA...	2	96	114*	-	0.1
270 CONSRV JUDAISM	1	200	237*	0.1	0.1
271 REFORM JUDAISM	1	388	460*	0.1	0.2
281 LUTH CH AMER..	6	1 577	2 053	0.6	1.0
283 LUTH--MO SYNOD	3	598	748	0.2	0.4
285 MENNONITE CH..	2	81	96*	-	-
290 METRO COMM CHS	1	25	50	-	-
349 PENT HOLINESS.	1	34	40*	-	-
356 PRESB CH AMER.	2	351	370	0.1	0.2
357 PRESB CH US...	18	6 383	7 575*	2.4	3.7
403 SALVATION ARMY	1	140	237	0.1	0.1
413 S.D.A.........	4	821	974*	0.3	0.5
419 SO BAPT CONV..	181	100 932	119 776*	37.5	59.1
421 SO METHODIST..	1	12	18	-	-
435 UNITARIAN-UNIV	1	432	513*	0.2	0.3
443 UN C OF CHRIST	1	166	197*	0.1	0.1
449 UN METHODIST..	72	26 026	30 885*	9.7	15.2
453 UN PRES CH USA	16	3 842	4 559*	1.4	2.2
469 WELS.........	1	40	53	-	-
LAKE	22	3 834	4 779*	64.1	100.0
101 C.M.E........	1	142	174*	2.3	3.6
127 CH GOD (CLEVE)	2	70	86*	1.2	1.8
167 CHS OF CHRIST.	5	470	656	8.8	13.7
357 PRESB CH US...	1	45	55*	0.7	1.2
419 SO BAPT CONV..	9	2 455	3 009*	40.4	63.0
449 UN METHODIST..	4	652	799*	10.7	16.7
LAUDERDALE	71	10 660	13 360*	54.4	100.0
053 ASSEMB OF GOD.	8	450	745	3.0	5.6
081 CATHOLIC......	1	NA	45	0.2	0.3
093 CHR CH (DISC).	1	88	135	0.5	1.0
101 C.M.E........	5	906	1 110*	4.5	8.3
127 CH GOD (CLEVE)	2	157	192*	0.8	1.4
167 CHS OF CHRIST.	8	312	403	1.6	3.0
185 CUMBER PRESB..	3	71	104	0.4	0.8
357 PRESB CH US...	1	88	108*	0.4	0.8
419 SO BAPT CONV..	23	6 013	7 364*	30.0	55.1
449 UN METHODIST..	19	2 575	3 154*	12.8	23.6
LAWRENCE	129	16 136	22 065*	64.7	100.0
053 ASSEMB OF GOD.	1	27	48	0.1	0.2
081 CATHOLIC......	3	NA	1 641	4.8	7.4
127 CH GOD (CLEVE)	7	343	419*	1.2	1.9
151 L-D SAINTS....	1	NA	239	0.7	1.1
165 CH OF NAZARENE	4	215	278	0.8	1.3
167 CHS OF CHRIST.	36	3 333	4 295	12.6	19.5
185 CUMBER PRESB..	5	521	864	2.5	3.9
323 OLD ORD AMISH.	3	390	476*	1.4	2.2
357 PRESB CH US...	1	60	73*	0.2	0.3
413 S.D.A.........	1	204	249*	0.7	1.1
419 SO BAPT CONV..	34	7 762	9 477*	27.8	43.0
449 UN METHODIST..	33	3 281	4 006*	11.7	18.2
LEWIS	30	2 799	3 615*	37.3	100.0
053 ASSEMB OF GOD.	1	36	62	0.6	1.7
127 CH GOD (CLEVE)	1	21	26*	0.3	0.7
167 CHS OF CHRIST.	15	1 500	1 909	19.7	52.8
185 CUMBER PRESB..	1	73	153	1.6	4.2
419 SO BAPT CONV..	6	660	827*	8.5	22.9
449 UN METHODIST..	6	509	638*	6.6	17.6
LINCOLN	100	13 510	17 320*	65.4	100.0
053 ASSEMB OF GOD.	2	115	148	0.6	0.9
055 AS REF PRES CH	3	504	534	2.0	3.1
081 CATHOLIC......	1	NA	148	0.6	0.9
123 CH GOD (ANDER)	2	95	285	1.1	1.6
151 L-D SAINTS....	1	NA	128	0.5	0.7
165 CH OF NAZARENE	1	85	187	0.7	1.1
167 CHS OF CHRIST.	33	2 415	3 074	11.6	17.7
185 CUMBER PRESB..	10	700	1 277	4.8	7.4
193 EPISCOPAL.....	1	77	108	0.4	0.6
357 PRESB CH US...	4	318	382*	1.4	2.2
413 S.D.A.	1	60	72*	0.3	0.4
419 SO BAPT CONV..	27	7 375	8 856*	33.4	51.1
449 UN METHODIST..	14	1 766	2 121*	8.0	12.2
LOUDON	77	16 779	20 540*	71.9	100.0
005 AME ZION......	3	474	632	2.2	3.1
081 CATHOLIC......	1	NA	91	0.3	0.4
123 CH GOD (ANDER)	1	27	81	0.3	0.4
127 CH GOD (CLEVE)	11	1 121	1 345*	4.7	6.5
165 CH OF NAZARENE	3	106	223	0.8	1.1
167 CHS OF CHRIST.	2	125	159	0.6	0.8
185 CUMBER PRESB..	4	250	390	1.4	1.9
193 EPISCOPAL.....	1	110	138	0.5	0.7
357 PRESB CH US...	1	72	86*	0.3	0.4
413 S.D.A.........	1	51	61*	0.2	0.3
419 SO BAPT CONV..	34	12 065	14 480*	50.7	70.5
449 UN METHODIST..	13	2 183	2 620*	9.2	12.8
453 UN PRES CH USA	2	195	234*	0.8	1.1
MC MINN	128	26 279	33 065*	79.0	100.0
005 AME ZION......	9	970	1 070	2.6	3.2
081 CATHOLIC......	1	NA	221	0.5	0.7
097 CHR CHS&CHS CR	2	163	198*	0.5	0.6
123 CH GOD (ANDER)	6	433	1 299	3.1	3.9
127 CH GOD (CLEVE)	5	492	599*	1.4	1.8
151 L-D SAINTS....	1	NA	97	0.2	0.3
165 CH OF NAZARENE	1	34	75	0.2	0.2
167 CHS OF CHRIST.	12	1 200	1 527	3.6	4.6
193 EPISCOPAL.....	1	221	228	0.5	0.7
283 LUTH--MO SYNOD	1	56	96	0.2	0.3
357 PRESB CH US...	2	334	407*	1.0	1.2
413 S.D.A.........	1	87	106*	0.3	0.3
419 SO BAPT CONV..	64	18 482	22 506*	53.7	68.1
449 UN METHODIST..	21	3 744	4 559*	10.9	13.8
453 UN PRES CH USA	1	63	77*	0.2	0.2
MC NAIRY	80	9 774	12 436*	55.2	100.0
053 ASSEMB OF GOD.	1	4	4	-	0.7
081 CATHOLIC......	1	NA	81	0.4	0.7
097 CHR CHS&CHS CR	4	388	469*	2.1	3.8
101 C.M.E........	1	83	100*	0.4	0.8
127 CH GOD (CLEVE)	2	91	110*	0.5	0.9
165 CH OF NAZARENE	1	12	36	0.2	0.3
167 CHS OF CHRIST.	17	1 616	2 281	10.1	18.3
185 CUMBER PRESB..	5	286	530	2.4	4.3
357 PRESB CH US...	3	143	173*	0.8	1.4
419 SO BAPT CONV..	25	5 337	6 457*	28.7	51.9
449 UN METHODIST..	17	1 543	1 867*	8.3	15.0
453 UN PRES CH USA	3	271	328*	1.5	2.6
MACON	19	1 851	2 310*	14.7	100.0
053 ASSEMB OF GOD.	1	30	75	0.5	3.2
127 CH GOD (CLEVE)	2	69	84*	0.5	3.6
167 CHS OF CHRIST.	7	985	1 220	7.8	52.8
419 SO BAPT CONV..	3	374	454*	2.9	19.7
449 UN METHODIST..	6	393	477*	3.0	20.6
MADISON	119	42 364	53 763*	72.1	100.0
053 ASSEMB OF GOD.	3	239	395	0.5	0.7
081 CATHOLIC......	1	NA	1 387	1.9	2.6
089 CHR & MISS AL.	1	0	55	0.1	0.1
093 CHR CH (DISC).	1	54	79	0.1	0.1
097 CHR CHS&CHS CR	1	450	547*	0.7	1.0
101 C.M.E........	11	9 479	11 518*	15.5	21.4
123 CH GOD (ANDER)	1	12	36	-	0.1
127 CH GOD (CLEVE)	4	293	356*	0.5	0.7
151 L-D SAINTS....	1	NA	258	0.3	0.5
165 CH OF NAZARENE	1	87	132	0.2	0.2
167 CHS OF CHRIST.	11	2 200	2 833	3.8	5.3
185 CUMBER PRESB..	5	416	670	0.9	1.2
271 REFORM JUDAISM	1	102	124*	0.2	0.2
283 LUTH--MO SYNOD	1	203	320	0.4	0.6
356 PRESB CH AMER.	1	34	39	0.1	0.1
357 PRESB CH US...	4	744	904*	1.2	1.7
403 SALVATION ARMY	1	95	148	0.2	0.3
413 S.D.A.........	2	226	275*	0.4	0.5
419 SO BAPT CONV..	40	20 265	24 625*	33.0	45.8
421 SO METHODIST..	1	117	133	0.2	0.2
449 UN METHODIST..	27	7 348	8 929*	12.0	16.6
MARION	69	7 922	10 229*	41.9	100.0
081 CATHOLIC......	1	NA	76	0.3	0.7
127 CH GOD (CLEVE)	13	913	1 122*	4.6	11.0
165 CH OF NAZARENE	2	85	150	0.6	1.5

NA— Not applicable *Total adherents estimated from known number of communicant, confirmed, full members. —Represents a percent less than 0.1. Percentages may not total due to rounding.

Table 4. Churches and Church Membership by County and Denomination: 1980

County and Denomination	Number of churches	Communicant, confirmed, full members	Total adherents		
			Number	Percent of total population	Percent of total adherents
167 CHS OF CHRIST.	9	625	795	3.3	7.8
185 CUMBER PRESB..	8	392	689	2.8	6.7
193 EPISCOPAL.....	2	553	820	3.4	8.0
413 S.D.A.........	2	149	183*	0.7	1.8
419 SO BAPT CONV..	15	3 712	4 560*	18.7	44.6
449 UN METHODIST..	17	1 493	1 834*	7.5	17.9
MARSHALL	63	8 594	10 917*	55.4	100.0
053 ASSEMB OF GOD.	2	62	115	0.6	1.1
081 CATHOLIC......	1	NA	115	0.6	1.1
123 CH GOD (ANDER)	1	40	120	0.6	1.1
127 CH GOD (CLEVE)	2	103	124*	0.6	1.1
151 L-D SAINTS....	1	NA	31	0.2	0.3
165 CH OF NAZARENE	1	82	110	0.6	1.0
167 CHS OF CHRIST.	23	2 725	3 460	17.6	31.7
185 CUMBER PRESB..	2	93	220	1.1	2.0
357 PRESB CH US...	4	403	486*	2.5	4.5
419 SO BAPT CONV..	8	3 003	3 623*	18.4	33.2
449 UN METHODIST..	18	2 083	2 513*	12.8	23.0
MAURY	141	18 855	24 232*	47.4	100.0
053 ASSEMB OF GOD.	1	82	150	0.3	0.6
055 AS REF PRES CH	1	27	31	0.1	0.1
081 CATHOLIC......	1	NA	370	0.7	1.5
093 CHR CH (DISC).	1	284	311	0.6	1.3
127 CH GOD (CLEVE)	2	117	141*	0.3	0.6
151 L-D SAINTS....	1	NA	260	0.5	1.1
165 CH OF NAZARENE	8	415	588	1.2	2.4
167 CHS OF CHRIST.	54	5 700	7 124	13.9	29.4
185 CUMBER PRESB..	11	664	1 229	2.4	5.1
193 EPISCOPAL.....	2	377	512	1.0	2.1
283 LUTH--MO SYNOD	1	93	133	0.3	0.5
356 PRESB CH AMER.	1	181	206	0.4	0.9
357 PRESB CH US...	4	607	733*	1.4	3.0
413 S.D.A.........	1	49	59*	0.1	0.2
419 SO BAPT CONV..	23	5 764	6 959*	13.6	28.7
449 UN METHODIST..	26	4 257	5 139*	10.1	21.2
453 UN PRES CH USA	3	238	287*	0.6	1.2
MEIGS	28	3 289	4 097*	55.1	100.0
053 ASSEMB OF GOD.	1	45	80	1.1	2.0
167 CHS OF CHRIST.	1	30	38	0.5	0.9
413 S.D.A.........	2	134	166*	2.2	4.1
419 SO BAPT CONV..	14	2 505	3 101*	41.7	75.7
449 UN METHODIST..	10	575	712*	9.6	17.4
MONROE	109	18 009	22 401*	78.1	100.0
005 AME ZION......	1	150	225	0.8	1.0
053 ASSEMB OF GOD.	1	140	175	0.6	0.8
097 CHR CHS&CHS CR	1	80	98*	0.3	0.4
123 CH GOD (ANDER)	1	60	180	0.6	0.8
127 CH GOD (CLEVE)	6	411	505*	1.8	2.3
165 CH OF NAZARENE	2	68	142	0.5	0.6
167 CHS OF CHRIST.	2	75	95	0.3	0.4
185 CUMBER PRESB..	2	40	77	0.3	0.3
226 FRIENDS--USA..	3	162	199*	0.7	0.9
281 LUTH CH AMER..	1	35	45	0.2	0.2
357 PRESB CH US...	8	862	1 059*	3.7	4.7
419 SO BAPT CONV..	64	14 033	17 245*	60.1	77.0
421 SO METHODIST..	1	5	35	0.1	0.2
443 UN C OF CHRIST	1	104	128*	0.4	0.6
449 UN METHODIST..	14	1 751	2 152*	7.5	9.6
453 UN PRES CH USA	1	33	41*	0.1	0.2
MONTGOMERY	99	25 154	35 649*	42.8	100.0
005 AME ZION......	1	111	161	0.2	0.5
053 ASSEMB OF GOD.	2	394	731	0.9	2.1
081 CATHOLIC......	1	NA	3 000	3.6	8.4
093 CHR CH (DISC).	1	313	432	0.5	1.2
097 CHR CHS&CHS CR	1	45	55*	0.1	0.2
101 C.M.E.........	2	931	1 133*	1.4	3.2
123 CH GOD (ANDER)	1	37	111	0.1	0.3
127 CH GOD (CLEVE)	1	238	290*	0.3	0.8
151 L-D SAINTS....	2	NA	660	0.8	1.9
165 CH OF NAZARENE	5	638	943	1.1	2.6
167 CHS OF CHRIST.	11	1 547	2 270	2.7	6.4
185 CUMBER PRESB..	5	649	1 176	1.4	3.3
193 EPISCOPAL.....	2	365	398	0.5	1.1
283 LUTH--MO SYNOD	1	324	481	0.6	1.3
357 PRESB CH US...	2	724	881*	1.1	2.5
413 S.D.A.........	1	118	144*	0.2	0.4
419 SO BAPT CONV..	28	11 333	13 793*	16.5	38.7
449 UN METHODIST..	32	7 387	8 990*	10.8	25.2
MOORE	16	1 543	1 909*	42.3	100.0
127 CH GOD (CLEVE)	1	20	25*	0.6	1.3
167 CHS OF CHRIST.	6	537	673	14.9	35.3
419 SO BAPT CONV..	2	297	365*	8.1	19.1
449 UN METHODIST..	7	689	846*	18.8	44.3
MORGAN	35	5 771	7 310*	44.0	100.0
081 CATHOLIC......	1	NA	45	0.3	0.6
165 CH OF NAZARENE	2	63	221	1.3	3.0
167 CHS OF CHRIST.	1	70	113	0.7	1.5
185 CUMBER PRESB..	1	29	29	0.2	0.4
193 EPISCOPAL.....	1	12	38	0.2	0.5
283 LUTH--MO SYNOD	2	296	347	2.1	4.7
409 SEPARATE BAPT.	1	23	28*	0.2	0.4

County and Denomination	Number of churches	Communicant, confirmed, full members	Total adherents		
			Number	Percent of total population	Percent of total adherents
413 S.D.A.........	2	217	267*	1.6	3.7
419 SO BAPT CONV..	18	4 805	5 907*	35.6	80.8
449 UN METHODIST..	4	213	262*	1.6	3.6
453 UN PRES CH USA	2	43	53*	0.3	0.7
OBION	115	16 973	21 589*	65.9	100.0
053 ASSEMB OF GOD.	6	494	667	2.0	3.1
055 AS REF PRES CH	2	62	62	0.2	0.3
081 CATHOLIC......	1	NA	445	1.4	2.1
093 CHR CH (DISC).	1	171	263	0.8	1.2
097 CHR CHS&CHS CR	2	216	263*	0.8	1.2
101 C.M.E.........	2	322	392*	1.2	1.8
123 CH GOD (ANDER)	1	33	99	0.3	0.5
127 CH GOD (CLEVE)	4	285	347*	1.1	1.6
165 CH OF NAZARENE	1	12	0	-	-
167 CHS OF CHRIST.	26	2 102	2 724	8.3	12.6
185 CUMBER PRESB..	16	906	1 276	3.9	5.9
193 EPISCOPAL.....	1	124	141	0.4	0.7
283 LUTH--MO SYNOD	1	82	107	0.3	0.5
357 PRESB CH US...	1	68	83*	0.3	0.4
413 S.D.A.........	1	7	9*	-	-
419 SO BAPT CONV..	23	8 916	10 850*	33.1	50.3
449 UN METHODIST..	26	3 173	3 861*	11.8	17.9
OVERTON	57	6 826	8 549*	48.6	100.0
053 ASSEMB OF GOD.	2	97	146	0.8	1.7
093 CHR CH (DISC).	5	437	553	3.1	6.5
123 CH GOD (ANDER)	1	51	153	0.9	1.8
127 CH GOD (CLEVE)	1	14	17*	0.1	0.2
167 CHS OF CHRIST.	15	1 450	1 845	10.5	21.6
185 CUMBER PRESB..	2	44	81	0.5	0.9
419 SO BAPT CONV..	14	2 805	3 410*	19.4	39.9
449 UN METHODIST..	16	1 891	2 299*	13.1	26.9
453 UN PRES CH USA	1	37	45*	0.3	0.5
PERRY	25	2 201	2 929*	47.9	100.0
097 CHR CHS&CHS CR	1	260	313*	5.1	10.7
127 CH GOD (CLEVE)	1	18	22*	0.4	0.8
151 L-D SAINTS....	1	NA	234	3.8	8.0
167 CHS OF CHRIST.	9	656	835	13.7	28.5
413 S.D.A.........	1	25	30*	0.5	1.0
419 SO BAPT CONV..	3	466	561*	9.2	19.2
449 UN METHODIST..	9	776	934*	15.3	31.9
PICKETT	10	1 325	1 664*	38.2	100.0
093 CHR CH (DISC).	2	113	189	4.3	11.4
097 CHR CHS&CHS CR	2	318	387*	8.9	23.3
167 CHS OF CHRIST.	1	25	32	0.7	1.9
419 SO BAPT CONV..	3	645	784*	18.0	47.1
449 UN METHODIST..	2	224	272*	6.2	16.3
POLK	63	10 340	12 949*	95.2	100.0
081 CATHOLIC......	1	NA	140	1.0	1.1
127 CH GOD (CLEVE)	5	275	340*	2.5	2.6
167 CHS OF CHRIST.	5	250	318	2.3	2.5
193 EPISCOPAL.....	1	39	62	0.5	0.5
357 PRESB CH US...	1	114	141*	1.0	1.1
419 SO BAPT CONV..	45	9 003	11 133*	81.8	86.0
449 UN METHODIST..	5	659	815*	6.0	6.3
PUTNAM	109	17 432	22 971*	48.3	100.0
053 ASSEMB OF GOD.	3	176	330	0.7	1.4
081 CATHOLIC......	3	NA	785	1.6	3.4
097 CHR CHS&CHS CR	1	125	148*	0.3	0.6
123 CH GOD (ANDER)	3	218	654	1.4	2.8
127 CH GOD (CLEVE)	7	340	403*	0.8	1.8
143 CG IN CR(MENN)	1	20	20	-	0.1
151 L-D SAINTS....	1	NA	359	0.8	1.6
165 CH OF NAZARENE	2	228	361	0.8	1.6
167 CHS OF CHRIST.	28	3 486	4 479	9.4	19.5
185 CUMBER PRESB..	5	312	519	1.1	2.3
193 EPISCOPAL.....	1	234	328	0.7	1.4
283 LUTH--MO SYNOD	1	158	217	0.5	0.9
357 PRESB CH US...	2	65	77*	0.2	0.3
413 S.D.A.........	1	74	88*	0.2	0.4
419 SO BAPT CONV..	30	8 559	10 134*	21.3	44.1
449 UN METHODIST..	15	3 024	3 580*	7.5	15.6
453 UN PRES CH USA	5	413	489*	1.0	2.1
RHEA	60	8 745	10 922*	45.1	100.0
081 CATHOLIC......	1	NA	153	0.6	1.4
127 CH GOD (CLEVE)	10	838	1 030*	4.3	9.4
133 CH GOD(7TH)DEN	1	12	15*	0.1	0.1
167 CHS OF CHRIST.	4	259	339	1.4	3.1
263 INT FOURSQ GOS	2	418	514*	2.1	4.7
349 PENT HOLINESS.	1	22	27*	0.1	0.2
413 S.D.A.........	4	388	477*	2.0	4.4
419 SO BAPT CONV..	21	4 892	6 012*	24.8	55.0
449 UN METHODIST..	15	1 829	2 248*	9.3	20.6
453 UN PRES CH USA	1	87	107*	0.4	1.0
ROANE	88	22 225	27 834*	57.5	100.0
081 CATHOLIC......	2	NA	346	0.7	1.2
093 CHR CH (DISC).	1	361	519	1.1	1.9
097 CHR CHS&CHS CR	5	690	838*	1.7	3.0
127 CH GOD (CLEVE)	4	353	429*	0.9	1.5
151 L-D SAINTS....	1	NA	192	0.4	0.7

NA—Not applicable   *Total adherents estimated from known number of communicant, confirmed, full members.   —Represents a percent less than 0.1.   Percentages may not total due to rounding.

Table 4. Churches and Church Membership by County and Denomination: 1980

County and Denomination	Number of churches	Communicant, confirmed, full members	Total adherents Number	Percent of total population	Percent of total adherents
165 CH OF NAZARENE	1	13	40	0.1	0.1
167 CHS OF CHRIST.	5	567	763	1.6	2.7
185 CUMBER PRESB..	2	87	197	0.4	0.7
193 EPISCOPAL.....	1	219	243	0.5	0.9
221 FREE METHODIST	1	6	57	0.1	0.2
263 INT FOURSQ GOS	1	209	254*	0.5	0.9
283 LUTH--MO SYNOD	1	141	204	0.4	0.7
356 PRESB CH AMER.	1	142	142	0.3	0.5
413 S.D.A.........	2	56	68*	0.1	0.2
419 SO BAPT CONV..	39	16 085	19 538*	40.3	70.2
449 UN METHODIST..	18	2 742	3 331*	6.9	12.0
453 UN PRES CH USA	3	554	673*	1.4	2.4
ROBERTSON	84	17 956	22 554*	60.9	100.0
053 ASSEMB OF GOD.	2	112	173	0.5	0.8
081 CATHOLIC......	2	NA	286	0.8	1.3
093 CHR CH (DISC).	1	100	140	0.4	0.6
101 C.M.E.........	2	671	820*	2.2	3.6
127 CH GOD (CLEVE)	1	?	?	?	?
165 CH OF NAZARENE	1	93	125	0.3	0.6
167 CHS OF CHRIST.	13	1 988	2 531	6.8	11.2
185 CUMBER PRESB..	3	198	407	1.1	1.8
413 S.D.A.........	4	425	519*	1.4	2.3
419 SO BAPT CONV..	27	10 863	13 270*	35.8	58.8
449 UN METHODIST..	26	3 280	4 007*	10.8	17.8
453 UN PRES CH USA	2	226	276*	0.7	1.2
RUTHERFORD	147	27 354	36 262*	43.1	100.0
053 ASSEMB OF GOD.	2	85	167	0.2	0.5
081 CATHOLIC......	1	NA	1 450	1.7	4.0
093 CHR CH (DISC).	1	284	410	0.5	1.1
097 CHR CHS&CHS CR	1	16	19*	-	0.1
101 C.M.E.........	1	268	326*	0.4	0.9
123 CH GOD (ANDER)	3	193	579	0.7	1.6
127 CH GOD (CLEVE)	2	136	165*	0.2	0.5
151 L-D SAINTS....	1	NA	181	0.2	0.5
165 CH OF NAZARENE	2	141	224	0.3	0.6
167 CHS OF CHRIST.	46	6 525	8 305	9.9	22.9
185 CUMBER PRESB..	7	450	847	1.0	2.3
193 EPISCOPAL.....	1	257	324	0.4	0.9
221 FREE METHODIST	1	67	222	0.3	0.6
281 LUTH CH AMER..	1	176	236	0.3	0.7
283 LUTH--MO SYNOD	1	146	200	0.2	0.6
357 PRESB CH US...	6	831	1 009*	1.2	2.8
413 S.D.A.........	2	82	100*	0.1	0.3
419 SO BAPT CONV..	39	12 729	15 462*	18.4	42.6
421 SO METHODIST..	1	16	20	-	0.1
435 UNITARIAN-UNIV	1	12	15*	-	-
449 UN METHODIST..	25	4 865	5 910*	7.0	16.3
453 UN PRES CH USA	2	75	91*	0.1	0.3
SCOTT	36	6 876	8 813*	45.8	100.0
081 CATHOLIC......	2	NA	144	0.7	1.6
127 CH GOD (CLEVE)	1	105	132*	0.7	1.5
167 CHS OF CHRIST.	2	140	180	0.9	2.0
409 SEPARATE BAPT.	2	156	197*	1.0	2.2
419 SO BAPT CONV..	23	6 092	7 677*	39.9	87.1
443 UN C OF CHRIST	3	52	66*	0.3	0.7
449 UN METHODIST..	2	261	329*	1.7	3.7
453 UN PRES CH USA	1	70	88*	0.5	1.0
SEQUATCHIE	20	2 908	3 610*	42.0	100.0
127 CH GOD (CLEVE)	3	246	304*	3.5	8.4
167 CHS OF CHRIST.	6	400	509	5.9	14.1
413 S.D.A.........	1	126	156*	1.8	4.3
419 SO BAPT CONV..	7	1 623	2 007*	23.3	55.6
449 UN METHODIST..	3	513	634*	7.4	17.6
SEVIER	101	21 031	25 711*	62.1	100.0
081 CATHOLIC......	1	NA	310	0.7	1.2
097 CHR CHS&CHS CR	3	225	272*	0.7	1.1
127 CH GOD (CLEVE)	4	584	706*	1.7	2.7
167 CHS OF CHRIST.	3	150	191	0.5	0.7
193 EPISCOPAL.....	1	189	212	0.5	0.8
281 LUTH CH AMER..	1	85	92	0.2	0.4
357 PRESB CH US...	2	127	153*	0.4	0.6
419 SO BAPT CONV..	62	16 371	19 786*	47.8	77.0
449 UN METHODIST..	23	3 133	3 787*	9.1	14.7
453 UN PRES CH USA	1	167	202*	0.5	0.8
SHELBY	521	268 283	374 335*	48.2	100.0
001 ADVENT CHR CH.	1	56	69*	-	-
005 AME ZION......	6	1 076	1 176	0.2	0.3
017 AMER BAPT ASSN	7	2 500	2 500	0.3	0.7
019 AMER BAPT USA.	4	2 290	2 802*	0.4	0.7
029 AMER LUTH CH..	4	711	937	0.1	0.3
053 ASSEMB OF GOD.	14	6 027	6 014	0.8	1.6
055 AS REF PRES CH	3	484	556	0.1	0.1
059 BAPT MISS ASSN	4	716	876*	0.1	0.2
065 BETHEL M ASSN.	1	200	245*	-	0.1
081 CATHOLIC......	28	NA	41 233	5.3	11.0
089 CHR & MISS AL.	1	115	180	-	-
093 CHR CH (DISC).	17	5 166	6 466	0.8	1.7
097 CHR CHS&CHS CR	6	1 197	1 465*	0.2	0.4
101 C.M.E.........	30	27 047	33 096*	4.3	8.8
123 CH GOD (ANDER)	4	258	774	0.1	0.2
127 CH GOD (CLEVE)	11	1 357	1 660*	0.2	0.4
151 L-D SAINTS....	5	NA	2 265	0.3	0.6
165 CH OF NAZARENE	12	907	2 032	0.3	0.5
167 CHS OF CHRIST.	58	15 907	20 247	2.6	5.4
185 CUMBER PRESB..	14	1 582	2 916	0.4	0.8
193 EPISCOPAL.....	20	9 676	12 430	1.6	3.3
215 EVAN METH CH...	2	323	395*	0.1	0.1
226 FRIENDS-USA...	1	10	12*	-	-
270 CONSRV JUDAISM	1	162	198*	-	0.1
271 REFORM JUDAISM	1	2 868	3 509*	0.5	0.9
281 LUTH CH AMER..	4	926	1 190	0.2	0.3
283 LUTH--MO SYNOD	10	2 656	3 720	0.5	1.0
285 MENNONITE CH..	1	?	?	?	?
290 METRO COMM CHS	1	25	50	-	-
349 PENT HOLINESS.	7	749	917*	0.1	0.2
353 CHR BRETHREN..	1	60	50	-	-
356 PRESB CH AMER.	1	55	61	-	-
357 PRESB CH US...	28	13 881	16 985*	2.2	4.5
381 REF PRES-EVAN.	1	127	152	-	-
403 SALVATION ARMY	2	250	449	0.1	0.1
413 S.D.A.........	8	1 953	2 390*	0.3	0.6
419 SO BAPT CONV..	117	124 725	152 617*	19.6	40.8
421 SO METHODIST..	2	130	161	-	-
435 UNITARIAN-UNIV	2	382	467*	0.1	0.1
443 UN C OF CHRIST	2	227	278*	-	0.1
449 UN METHODIST..	71	40 825	49 955*	6.4	13.3
453 UN PRES CH USA	7	618	756*	0.1	0.2
469 WELS..........	1	59	84	-	-
SMITH	43	4 522	5 664*	37.9	100.0
093 CHR CH (DISC).	1	24	32	0.2	0.6
127 CH GOD (CLEVE)	2	146	175*	1.2	3.1
165 CH OF NAZARENE	2	98	282	1.9	5.0
167 CHS OF CHRIST.	6	505	640	4.3	11.3
185 CUMBER PRESB..	2	103	145	1.0	2.6
419 SO BAPT CONV..	12	2 004	2 409*	16.1	42.5
421 SO METHODIST..	1	56	75	0.5	1.3
449 UN METHODIST..	17	1 586	1 906*	12.8	33.7
STEWART	51	4 742	6 148*	71.0	100.0
053 ASSEMB OF GOD.	1	21	37	0.4	0.6
093 CHR CH (DISC).	1	91	144	1.7	2.3
101 C.M.E.........	1	143	170*	2.0	2.8
123 CH GOD (ANDER)	4	193	579	6.7	9.4
165 CH OF NAZARENE	2	102	179	2.1	2.9
167 CHS OF CHRIST.	9	451	571	6.6	9.3
185 CUMBER PRESB..	1	47	68	0.8	1.1
419 SO BAPT CONV..	14	1 946	2 318*	26.8	37.7
449 UN METHODIST..	18	1 748	2 082*	24.0	33.9
SULLIVAN	192	57 450	72 222*	50.2	100.0
005 AME ZION......	3	1 305	1 740	1.2	2.4
053 ASSEMB OF GOD.	7	557	955	0.7	1.3
081 CATHOLIC......	1	NA	1 534	1.1	2.1
097 CHR CHS&CHS CR	18	4 556	5 491*	3.8	7.6
123 CH GOD (ANDER)	2	305	915	0.6	1.3
127 CH GOD (CLEVE)	2	193	233*	0.2	0.3
151 L-D SAINTS....	3	NA	?	?	?
157 CH OF BRETHREN	3	220	265*	0.2	0.4
165 CH OF NAZARENE	3	138	288	0.2	0.4
167 CHS OF CHRIST.	3	430	604	0.4	0.8
193 EPISCOPAL.....	4	798	1 149	0.8	1.6
271 REFORM JUDAISM	1	110	133*	0.1	0.2
281 LUTH CH AMER..	5	1 167	1 469	1.0	2.0
283 LUTH--MO SYNOD	2	184	242	0.2	0.3
349 PENT HOLINESS.	1	53	64*	-	0.1
356 PRESB CH AMER.	6	680	808	0.6	1.1
357 PRESB CH US...	21	5 431	6 545*	4.5	9.1
381 REF PRES-EVAN.	1	57	59	-	0.1
403 SALVATION ARMY	2	273	328	0.2	0.5
413 S.D.A.........	2	192	231*	0.2	0.3
415 S-D BAPTIST GC	1	15	18*	-	-
419 SO BAPT CONV..	47	25 313	30 505*	21.2	42.2
435 UNITARIAN-UNIV	1	70	84*	0.1	0.1
449 UN METHODIST..	50	15 119	18 220*	12.7	25.2
453 UN PRES CH USA	3	284	342*	0.2	0.5
SUMNER	114	26 328	36 086*	42.1	100.0
053 ASSEMB OF GOD.	3	328	760	0.9	2.1
081 CATHOLIC......	2	NA	2 061	2.4	5.7
093 CHR CH (DISC).	1	145	159	0.2	0.4
097 CHR CHS&CHS CR	1	800	989*	1.2	2.7
101 C.M.E.........	2	321	397*	0.5	1.1
127 CH GOD (CLEVE)	2	109	135*	0.2	0.4
151 L-D SAINTS....	2	NA	317	0.4	0.9
165 CH OF NAZARENE	4	439	795	0.9	2.2
167 CHS OF CHRIST.	31	4 850	6 185	7.2	17.1
185 CUMBER PRESB..	3	226	390	0.5	1.1
193 EPISCOPAL.....	2	369	495	0.6	1.4
221 FREE METHODIST	1	44	231	0.3	0.6
281 LUTH CH AMER..	1	327	456	0.5	1.3
357 PRESB CH US...	3	820	1 014*	1.2	2.8
413 S.D.A.........	4	583	721*	0.8	2.0
419 SO BAPT CONV..	27	11 869	14 677*	17.1	40.7
449 UN METHODIST..	22	5 029	6 219*	7.2	17.2
453 UN PRES CH USA	2	69	85*	0.1	0.2
TIPTON	91	15 722	20 010*	61.1	100.0
017 AMER BAPT ASSN	1	160	160	0.5	0.8
053 ASSEMB OF GOD.	11	903	1 365	4.2	6.8
055 AS REF PRES CH	4	663	712*	2.2	3.6
059 BAPT MISS ASSN	1	48	60*	0.2	0.3
081 CATHOLIC......	1	NA	93	0.3	0.5

NA—Not applicable   *Total adherents estimated from known number of communicant, confirmed, full members.   —Represents a percent less than 0.1.   Percentages may not total due to rounding.

Table 4. Churches and Church Membership by County and Denomination: 1980

County and Denomination	Number of churches	Communicant, confirmed, full members	Total adherents Number	Percent of total population	Percent of total adherents
097 CHR CHS&CHS CR	2	211	262*	0.8	1.3
101 C.M.E.	9	2 758	3 431*	10.5	17.1
165 CH OF NAZARENE	2	68	154	0.5	0.8
167 CHS OF CHRIST.	7	692	842	2.6	4.2
185 CUMBER PRESB.	3	272	451	1.4	2.3
193 EPISCOPAL	4	133	269	0.8	1.3
215 EVAN METH CH.	1	63	78*	0.2	0.4
353 CHR BRETHREN.	1	25	25	0.1	0.1
356 PRESB CH AMER.	1	11	23	0.1	0.1
357 PRESB CH US...	4	406	505*	1.5	2.5
419 SO BAPT CONV..	17	6 294	7 830*	23.9	39.1
449 UN METHODIST..	20	2 891	3 596*	11.0	18.0
453 UN PRES CH USA	2	124	15*	0.5	0.8
TROUSDALE	14	1 269	1 707*	27.8	100.0
167 CHS OF CHRIST.	5	295	448	7.3	26.2
185 CUMBER PRESB.	2	34	126	2.1	7.4
419 SO BAPT CONV..	2	566	682*	11.1	40.0
449 UN METHODIST..	5	374	451*	7.3	26.4
UNICOI	35	7 451	9 023*	55.1	100.0
053 ASSEMB OF GOD.	1	41	42	0.3	0.5
097 CHR CHS&CHS CR	5	939	1 125*	6.9	12.5
123 CH GOD (ANDER)	1	25	75	0.5	0.8
127 CH GOD (CLEVE)	2	164	197*	1.2	2.2
157 CH OF BRETHREN	1	56	67*	0.4	0.7
165 CH OF NAZARENE	1	14	61	0.4	0.7
167 CHS OF CHRIST.	2	165	210	1.3	2.3
349 PENT HOLINESS.	1	138	165*	1.0	1.8
419 SO BAPT CONV..	14	4 579	5 487*	33.5	60.8
449 UN METHODIST..	4	954	1 143*	7.0	12.7
453 UN PRES CH USA	3	376	451*	2.8	5.0
UNION	23	3 422	4 222*	36.1	100.0
053 ASSEMB OF GOD.	1	75	90	0.8	2.1
167 CHS OF CHRIST.	1	15	28	0.2	0.7
419 SO BAPT CONV..	17	3 076	3 789*	32.4	89.7
449 UN METHODIST..	4	256	315*	2.7	7.5
VAN BUREN	20	1 911	2 410*	51.0	100.0
127 CH GOD (CLEVE)	3	130	162*	3.4	6.7
167 CHS OF CHRIST.	12	1 200	1 525	32.3	63.3
413 S.D.A.	1	24	30*	0.6	1.2
419 SO BAPT CONV..	4	557	693*	14.7	28.8
WARREN	98	13 105	17 142*	52.5	100.0
053 ASSEMB OF GOD.	3	119	215	0.7	1.3
075 BRETHREN IN CR	1	43	73	0.2	0.4
081 CATHOLIC	1	NA	221	0.7	1.3
123 CH GOD (ANDER)	1	47	141	0.4	0.8
127 CH GOD (CLEVE)	3	434	529*	1.6	3.1
133 CH GOD(7TH)DEN	1	6	7*	-	-
151 L-D SAINTS....	1	NA	215	0.7	1.3
165 CH OF NAZARENE	1	24	52	0.2	0.3
167 CHS OF CHRIST.	42	5 600	7 130	21.8	41.6
185 CUMBER PRESB.	8	288	441	1.4	2.6
193 EPISCOPAL	1	80	137	0.4	0.8
221 FREE METHODIST	1	28	117	0.4	0.7
283 LUTH--MO SYNOD	1	55	89	0.3	0.5
357 PRESB CH US...	1	71	87*	0.3	0.5
413 S.D.A.	1	91	111*	0.3	0.6
419 SO BAPT CONV..	15	4 486	5 466*	16.7	31.9
449 UN METHODIST..	15	1 598	1 947*	6.0	11.4
453 UN PRES CH USA	1	135	164*	0.5	1.0
WASHINGTON	166	36 552	46 907*	52.8	100.0
005 AME ZION	3	858	1 144	1.3	2.4
053 ASSEMB OF GOD.	2	106	204	0.2	0.4
081 CATHOLIC	1	NA	1 965	2.2	4.2
089 CHR & MISS AL.	1	34	51	0.1	0.1
093 CHR CH (DISC).	2	224	261	0.3	0.6
097 CHR CHS&CHS CR	20	4 394	5 260*	5.9	11.2
123 CH GOD (ANDER)	3	333	999	1.1	2.1
127 CH GOD (CLEVE)	5	368	441*	0.5	0.9
151 L-D SAINTS....	1	NA	?	?	?
157 CH OF BRETHREN	11	775	928*	1.0	2.0
165 CH OF NAZARENE	2	138	174	0.2	0.4
167 CHS OF CHRIST.	7	577	774	0.9	1.7
185 CUMBER PRESB.	3	134	261	0.3	0.6
193 EPISCOPAL	1	493	608	0.7	1.3
221 FREE METHODIST	1	12	60	0.1	0.1
244 GRACE BRETHREN	3	208	249*	0.3	0.5
281 LUTH CH AMER..	2	295	432	0.5	0.9
283 LUTH--MO SYNOD	1	241	266	0.3	0.6
356 PRESB CH AMER.	3	257	320	0.4	0.7
357 PRESB CH US...	7	1 722	2 061*	2.3	4.4
403 SALVATION ARMY	2	212	316	0.4	0.7
413 S.D.A.	1	155	186*	0.2	0.4
419 SO BAPT CONV..	48	15 875	19 004*	21.4	40.5
449 UN METHODIST..	32	8 508	10 185*	11.5	21.7
453 UN PRES CH USA	4	633	758*	0.9	1.6
WAYNE	60	5 488	6 875*	49.3	100.0
093 CHR CH (DISC).	1	52	76	0.5	1.1
127 CH GOD (CLEVE)	4	140	171*	1.2	2.5
151 L-D SAINTS....	1	NA	79	0.6	1.1
165 CH OF NAZARENE	1	27	31	0.2	0.5
167 CHS OF CHRIST.	16	1 500	1 900	13.6	27.6
185 CUMBER PRESB.	1	62	83	0.6	1.2
349 PENT HOLINESS.	1	24	29*	0.2	0.4
419 SO BAPT CONV..	19	2 658	3 252*	23.3	47.3
449 UN METHODIST..	15	979	1 198*	8.6	17.4
453 UN PRES CH USA	1	46	56*	0.4	0.8
WEAKLEY	128	18 710	23 153*	70.4	100.0
053 ASSEMB OF GOD.	4	146	250	0.8	1.1
081 CATHOLIC	1	NA	573	1.7	2.5
093 CHR CH (DISC).	2	94	144	0.4	0.6
097 CHR CHS&CHS CR	1	30	35*	0.1	0.2
101 C.M.E.	4	374	441*	1.3	1.9
127 CH GOD (CLEVE)	1	16	19*	0.1	0.1
167 CHS OF CHRIST.	22	2 118	2 708	8.2	11.7
185 CUMBER PRESB.	12	492	760	2.3	3.3
193 EPISCOPAL	1	62	87	0.3	0.4
349 PENT HOLINESS.	1	21	25*	0.1	0.1
357 PRESB CH US...	1	60	71*	0.2	0.3
419 SO BAPT CONV..	46	12 126	14 300*	43.5	61.8
449 UN METHODIST..	29	3 038	3 583*	10.9	15.5
453 UN PRES CH USA	3	133	157*	0.5	0.7
WHITE	71	7 510	9 228*	47.2	100.0
053 ASSEMB OF GOD.	1	19	22	0.1	0.2
075 BRETHREN IN CR	1	43	73	0.4	0.8
093 CHR CH (DISC).	1	83	128	0.7	1.4
127 CH GOD (CLEVE)	8	625	754*	3.9	8.2
165 CH OF NAZARENE	2	144	300	1.5	3.3
167 CHS OF CHRIST.	23	1 958	2 343	12.0	25.4
185 CUMBER PRESB.	1	30	47	0.2	0.5
413 S.D.A.	1	99	119*	0.6	1.3
419 SO BAPT CONV..	12	2 710	3 271*	16.7	35.4
449 UN METHODIST..	17	1 596	1 926*	9.8	20.9
453 UN PRES CH USA	4	203	245*	1.3	2.7
WILLIAMSON	101	18 361	26 556*	45.7	100.0
081 CATHOLIC	2	NA	2 893	5.0	10.9
089 CHR & MISS AL.	1	39	107	0.2	0.4
127 CH GOD (CLEVE)	1	21	26*	-	0.1
151 L-D SAINTS....	1	NA	277	0.5	1.0
165 CH OF NAZARENE	3	145	245	0.4	0.9
167 CHS OF CHRIST.	36	5 360	6 821	11.7	25.7
185 CUMBER PRESB.	6	400	709	1.2	2.7
193 EPISCOPAL	1	487	622	1.1	2.3
281 LUTH CH AMER.	1	135	233	0.4	0.9
357 PRESB CH US...	5	960	1 188*	2.0	4.5
413 S.D.A.	2	47	58*	0.1	0.2
419 SO BAPT CONV..	16	4 974	6 156*	10.6	23.2
421 SO METHODIST..	3	70	138	0.2	0.5
449 UN METHODIST..	23	5 723	7 083*	12.2	26.7
WILSON	121	23 106	29 474*	52.6	100.0
053 ASSEMB OF GOD.	2	92	203	0.4	0.7
081 CATHOLIC	1	NA	400	0.7	1.4
097 CHR CHS&CHS CR	1	35	43*	0.1	0.1
101 C.M.E.	4	1 122	1 379*	2.5	4.7
123 CH GOD (ANDER)	1	35	105	0.2	0.4
127 CH GOD (CLEVE)	3	239	294*	0.5	1.0
165 CH OF NAZARENE	3	208	460	0.8	1.6
167 CHS OF CHRIST.	36	3 835	4 881	8.7	16.6
185 CUMBER PRESB.	8	361	576	1.0	2.0
193 EPISCOPAL	1	93	127	0.2	0.4
357 PRESB CH US...	2	60	74*	0.1	0.3
419 SO BAPT CONV..	33	13 516	16 617*	29.6	56.4
449 UN METHODIST..	25	3 166	3 892*	6.9	13.2
453 UN PRES CH USA	1	344	423*	0.8	1.4

TEXAS

County and Denomination	Number of churches	Communicant, confirmed, full members	Total adherents Number	Percent of total population	Percent of total adherents
THE STATE.....	16 111	4 311 259	7 781 967*	54.7	100.0
ANDERSON	94	16 713	22 239*	57.9	100.0
017 AMER BAPT ASSN	9	745	745	1.9	3.3
053 ASSEMB OF GOD.	8	489	707	1.8	3.2
059 BAPT MISS ASSN	5	1 048	1 256*	3.3	5.6
081 CATHOLIC	1	NA	1 857	4.8	8.4
093 CHR CH (DISC).	6	522	881	2.3	4.0
097 CHR CHS&CHS CR	2	150	180*	0.5	0.8
101 C.M.E.	1	?	?	?	?
165 CH OF NAZARENE	1	39	47	0.1	0.2
167 CHS OF CHRIST.	13	1 000	1 273	3.3	5.7
193 EPISCOPAL	1	486	581	1.5	2.6
283 LUTH--MO SYNOD	1	206	272	0.7	1.2
353 CHR BRETHREN.	1	25	50	0.1	0.2
357 PRESB CH US...	2	235	282*	0.7	1.3
413 S.D.A.	1	74	89*	0.2	0.4
419 SO BAPT CONV..	24	8 836	10 593*	27.6	47.6
449 UN METHODIST..	16	2 625	3 147*	8.2	14.2

NA—Not applicable   *Total adherents estimated from known number of communicant, confirmed, full members.   —Represents a percent less than 0.1.   Percentages may not total due to rounding.

Table 4. Churches and Church Membership by County and Denomination: 1980

County and Denomination	Number of churches	Communicant, confirmed, full members	Total adherents Number	Percent of total population	Percent of total adherents
453 UN PRES CH USA	2	233	279*	0.7	1.3
ANDREWS	22	6 214	8 565*	64.3	100.0
017 AMER BAPT ASSN	1	150	150	1.1	1.8
053 ASSEMB OF GOD.	4	311	644	4.8	7.5
081 CATHOLIC......	1	NA	480	3.6	5.6
093 CHR CH (DISC).	1	20	30	0.2	0.4
097 CHR CHS&CHS CR	1	53	67*	0.5	0.8
127 CH GOD (CLEVE)	1	77	97*	0.7	1.1
165 CH OF NAZARENE	1	27	53	0.4	0.6
167 CHS OF CHRIST.	3	425	540	4.1	6.3
193 EPISCOPAL.....	1	41	41	0.3	0.5
283 LUTH--MO SYNOD	1	115	146	1.1	1.7
357 PRESB CH US...	1	131	166*	1.2	1.9
419 SO BAPT CONV..	4	3 946	4 990*	37.5	58.3
449 UN METHODIST..	2	918	1 161*	8.7	13.6
ANGELINA	117	27 858	38 142*	59.4	100.0
017 AMER BAPT ASSN	9	1 167	1 167	1.8	3.1
053 ASSEMB OF GOD.	9	1 169	1 808	2.8	4.7
059 BAPT MISS ASSN	21	3 509	4 370*	6.8	11.5
081 CATHOLIC......	2	NA	2 650	4.1	6.9
093 CHR CH (DISC).	1	510	894	1.4	2.3
101 C.M.E.	6	914	1 138*	1.8	3.0
123 CH GOD (ANDER)	1	28	84	0.1	0.2
127 CH GOD (CLEVE)	1	60	75*	0.1	0.2
151 L-D SAINTS....	1	NA	220	0.3	0.6
165 CH OF NAZARENE	2	241	371	0.6	1.0
167 CHS OF CHRIST.	18	1 545	1 965	3.1	5.2
193 EPISCOPAL.....	1	392	509	0.8	1.3
283 LUTH--MO SYNOD	1	212	273	0.4	0.7
357 PRESB CH US...	1	290	361*	0.6	0.9
403 SALVATION ARMY	1	69	148	0.2	0.4
413 S.D.A.........	1	71	88*	0.1	0.2
419 SO BAPT CONV..	31	14 552	18 124*	28.2	47.5
449 UN METHODIST..	10	3 129	3 897*	6.1	10.2
ARANSAS	17	3 426	7 005*	49.1	100.0
053 ASSEMB OF GOD.	2	107	179	1.3	2.6
081 CATHOLIC......	1	NA	2 530	17.7	36.1
123 CH GOD (ANDER)	1	20	60	0.4	0.9
151 L-D SAINTS....	1	NA	71	0.5	1.0
167 CHS OF CHRIST.	2	232	274	1.9	3.9
193 EPISCOPAL.....	1	151	360	2.5	5.1
283 LUTH--MO SYNOD	1	109	132	0.9	1.9
357 PRESB CH US...	1	394	477*	3.3	6.8
419 SO BAPT CONV..	6	1 999	2 421*	17.0	34.6
449 UN METHODIST..	1	414	501*	3.5	7.2
ARCHER	24	3 478	5 501*	75.7	100.0
053 ASSEMB OF GOD.	3	69	104	1.4	1.9
081 CATHOLIC......	3	NA	1 251	17.2	22.7
093 CHR CH (DISC).	1	40	60	0.8	1.1
101 C.M.E.	2	438	530*	7.3	9.6
167 CHS OF CHRIST.	3	175	223	3.1	4.1
413 S.D.A.........	1	122	148*	2.0	2.7
419 SO BAPT CONV..	6	2 212	2 675*	36.8	48.6
449 UN METHODIST..	5	422	510*	7.0	9.3
ARMSTRONG	8	1 177	1 521*	76.3	100.0
081 CATHOLIC......	0	NA	100	5.0	6.6
093 CHR CH (DISC).	1	22	31	1.6	2.0
167 CHS OF CHRIST.	1	50	64	3.2	4.2
419 SO BAPT CONV..	4	685	822*	41.2	54.0
449 UN METHODIST..	2	420	504*	25.3	33.1
ATASCOSA	45	5 660	18 175*	72.5	100.0
029 AMER LUTH CH..	1	307	385	1.5	2.1
053 ASSEMB OF GOD.	3	162	235	0.9	1.3
081 CATHOLIC......	11	NA	10 965	43.8	60.3
151 L-D SAINTS....	1	NA	44	0.2	0.2
167 CHS OF CHRIST.	7	600	765	3.1	4.2
193 EPISCOPAL.....	1	105	139	0.6	0.8
357 PRESB CH US...	1	98	123*	0.5	0.7
419 SO BAPT CONV..	13	3 241	4 076*	16.3	22.4
449 UN METHODIST..	7	1 147	1 443*	5.8	7.9
AUSTIN	34	5 624	9 004*	50.8	100.0
029 AMER LUTH CH..	5	1 813	2 150	12.1	23.9
081 CATHOLIC......	5	NA	2 181	12.3	24.2
151 L-D SAINTS....	1	NA	48	0.3	0.5
167 CHS OF CHRIST.	3	156	220	1.2	2.4
193 EPISCOPAL.....	2	247	295	1.7	3.3
226 FRIENDS-USA...	1	30	36*	0.2	0.4
283 LUTH--MO SYNOD	2	623	738	4.2	8.2
419 SO BAPT CONV..	3	1 206	1 460*	8.2	16.2
449 UN METHODIST..	12	1 549	1 876*	10.6	20.8
BAILEY	24	4 272	7 232*	88.5	100.0
053 ASSEMB OF GOD.	2	238	333	4.1	4.6
059 BAPT MISS ASSN	1	168	210*	2.6	2.9
081 CATHOLIC......	1	NA	1 800	22.0	24.9
093 CHR CH (DISC).	1	46	86	1.1	1.2
165 CH OF NAZARENE	1	12	34	0.4	0.5
167 CHS OF CHRIST.	4	425	540	6.6	7.5
419 SO BAPT CONV..	10	2 595	3 244*	39.7	44.9
449 UN METHODIST..	4	788	985*	12.1	13.6
BANDERA	15	2 049	3 319*	46.9	100.0
029 AMER LUTH CH..	1	134	195	2.8	5.9
081 CATHOLIC......	3	NA	858	12.1	25.9
167 CHS OF CHRIST.	3	150	190	2.7	5.7
193 EPISCOPAL.....	1	69	90	1.3	2.7
419 SO BAPT CONV..	4	1 169	1 369*	19.3	41.2
449 UN METHODIST..	3	527	617*	8.7	18.6
BASTROP	55	7 001	9 381*	37.9	100.0
029 AMER LUTH CH..	5	708	870	3.5	9.3
053 ASSEMB OF GOD.	7	215	260	1.1	2.8
081 CATHOLIC......	6	NA	690	2.8	7.4
093 CHR CH (DISC).	3	117	175	0.7	1.9
097 CHR CHS&CHS CR	1	50	61*	0.2	0.7
165 CH OF NAZARENE	1	11	26	0.1	0.3
167 CHS OF CHRIST.	8	550	700	2.8	7.5
193 EPISCOPAL.....	1	108	212	0.9	2.3
203 EVAN FREE CH..	1	40	49*	0.2	0.5
283 LUTH--MO SYNOD	2	356	450	1.8	4.8
357 PRESB CH US...	1	68	83*	0.3	0.9
413 S.D.A.........	2	176	214*	0.9	2.3
419 SO BAPT CONV..	10	3 179	3 862*	15.6	41.2
449 UN METHODIST..	6	1 319	1 603*	6.5	17.1
453 UN PRES CH USA	1	104	126*	0.5	1.3
BAYLOR	18	3 243	4 374*	88.9	100.0
053 ASSEMB OF GOD.	2	191	171	3.5	3.9
081 CATHOLIC......	2	NA	569	11.6	13.0
093 CHR CH (DISC).	1	72	95	1.9	2.2
127 CH GOD (CLEVE)	1	33	39*	0.8	0.9
167 CHS OF CHRIST.	4	200	255	5.2	5.8
283 LUTH--MO SYNOD	1	31	40	0.8	0.9
357 PRESB CH US...	1	53	63*	1.3	1.4
419 SO BAPT CONV..	4	2 011	2 372*	48.2	54.2
449 UN METHODIST..	1	599	707*	14.4	16.2
453 UN PRES CH USA	1	53	63*	1.3	1.4
BEE	45	5 702	15 748*	60.5	100.0
029 AMER LUTH CH..	2	291	371	1.4	2.4
053 ASSEMB OF GOD.	2	85	120	0.5	0.8
081 CATHOLIC......	5	NA	8 295	31.9	52.7
093 CHR CH (DISC).	2	114	131	0.5	0.8
151 L-D SAINTS....	1	NA	186	0.7	1.2
165 CH OF NAZARENE	1	69	192	0.7	1.2
167 CHS OF CHRIST.	7	550	700	2.7	4.4
193 EPISCOPAL.....	1	168	199	0.8	1.3
357 PRESB CH US...	1	380	477*	1.8	3.0
413 S.D.A.........	1	70	88*	0.3	0.6
419 SO BAPT CONV..	16	2 961	3 716*	14.3	23.6
443 UN C OF CHRIST	1	39	49*	0.2	0.3
449 UN METHODIST..	5	975	1 224*	4.7	7.8
BELL	154	42 763	64 117*	40.6	100.0
017 AMER BAPT ASSN	1	40	40	–	0.1
029 AMER LUTH CH..	3	1 350	1 621	1.0	2.5
053 ASSEMB OF GOD.	7	768	1 149	0.7	1.8
059 BAPT MISS ASSN	1	82	101*	0.1	0.2
081 CATHOLIC......	6	NA	9 802	6.2	15.3
093 CHR CH (DISC).	8	1 163	1 476	0.9	2.3
097 CHR CHS&CHS CR	2	65	80*	0.1	0.1
127 CH GOD (CLEVE)	3	162	199*	0.1	0.3
151 L-D SAINTS....	3	NA	796	0.5	1.2
165 CH OF NAZARENE	5	538	1 176	0.7	1.8
167 CHS OF CHRIST.	22	2 500	3 180	2.0	5.0
193 EPISCOPAL.....	4	1 047	1 297	0.8	2.0
283 LUTH--MO SYNOD	3	882	1 160	0.7	1.8
357 PRESB CH US...	5	923	1 135*	0.7	1.8
413 S.D.A.........	2	226	278*	0.2	0.4
419 SO BAPT CONV..	49	25 638	31 537*	20.0	49.2
435 UNITARIAN-UNIV	1	20	25*	–	–
449 UN METHODIST..	23	6 745	8 297*	5.3	12.9
453 UN PRES CH USA	5	549	675*	0.4	1.1
469 WELS..........	1	65	93	0.1	0.1
BEXAR	514	166 475	591 177*	59.8	100.0
017 AMER BAPT ASSN	3	100	100	–	–
019 AMER BAPT USA.	3	2 560	3 180*	0.3	0.5
029 AMER LUTH CH..	17	9 603	11 880	1.2	2.0
053 ASSEMB OF GOD.	37	4 265	5 803	0.6	1.0
059 BAPT MISS ASSN	3	927	1 152*	0.1	0.2
081 CATHOLIC......	98	NA	373 484	37.8	63.2
089 CHR & MISS AL.	2	50	106	–	–
093 CHR CH (DISC).	10	3 237	5 218	0.5	0.9
097 CHR CHS&CHS CR	9	1 791	2 225*	0.2	0.4
101 C.M.E.	1	380	472*	–	0.1
123 CH GOD (ANDER)	5	341	1 023	0.1	0.2
127 CH GOD (CLEVE)	11	758	942*	0.1	0.2
133 CH GOD(7TH)DEN	1	105	130*	–	–
151 L-D SAINTS....	11	NA	5 125	0.5	0.9
165 CH OF NAZARENE	13	945	2 020	0.2	0.3
167 CHS OF CHRIST.	42	6 171	8 873	0.9	1.5
185 CUMBER PRESB..	2	125	352	–	0.1
193 EPISCOPAL.....	19	11 530	13 891	1.4	2.3
203 EVAN FREE CH..	2	278	345*	–	0.1
209 EVAN LUTH SYN.	1	39	64	–	–
221 FREE METHODIST	2	81	240	–	–
226 FRIENDS-USA...	2	113	140*	–	–
263 INT FOURSQ GOS	1	113	140*	–	–
270 CONSRV JUDAISM	1	524	651*	0.1	0.1

NA— Not applicable *Total adherents estimated from known number of communicant, confirmed, full members. —Represents a percent less than 0.1. Percentages may not total due to rounding.

Table 4. Churches and Church Membership by County and Denomination: 1980

County and Denomination	Number of churches	Communicant, confirmed, full members	Total adherents		
			Number	Percent of total population	Percent of total adherents
271 REFORM JUDAISM	2	1 730	2 149*	0.2	0.4
281 LUTH CH AMER..	8	2 502	3 420	0.3	0.6
283 LUTH--MO SYNOD	11	5 970	7 715	0.8	1.3
290 METRO COMM CHS	1	73	146	–	–
335 ORTH PRESB CH.	1	89	111*	–	–
349 PENT HOLINESS.	1	39	48*	–	–
353 CHR BRETHREN..	3	65	85	–	–
357 PRESB CH US...	23	5 478	6 805*	0.7	1.2
403 SALVATION ARMY	1	172	1 044	0.1	0.2
413 S.D.A.........	6	1 033	1 283*	0.1	0.2
419 SO BAPT CONV..	93	73 131	90 851*	9.2	15.4
435 UNITARIAN-UNIV	1	361	448*	–	0.1
443 UN C OF CHRIST	2	570	708*	0.1	0.1
449 UN METHODIST..	54	29 010	36 039*	3.6	6.1
453 UN PRES CH USA	10	2 128	2 644*	0.3	0.4
469 WELS.........	1	88	125	–	–
BLANCO	15	2 111	3 286*	70.2	100.0
029 AMER LUTH CH..	2	413	554	11.8	16.9
053 ASSEMB OF GOD.	2	40	51	1.1	1.6
081 CATHOLIC......	1	NA	689	14.7	21.0
093 CHR CH (DISC).	1	39	60	1.3	1.8
167 CHS OF CHRIST.	3	125	159	3.4	4.8
193 EPISCOPAL.....	1	54	65	1.4	2.0
419 SO BAPT CONV..	2	817	969*	20.7	29.5
449 UN METHODIST..	3	623	739*	15.8	22.5
BORDEN	6	369	513*	59.7	100.0
081 CATHOLIC......	0	NA	75	8.7	14.6
167 CHS OF CHRIST.	2	60	70	8.1	13.6
185 CUMBER PRESB..	1	59	59	6.9	11.5
419 SO BAPT CONV..	2	196	242*	28.2	47.2
449 UN METHODIST..	1	54	67*	7.8	13.1
BOSQUE	53	8 681	10 388*	77.5	100.0
029 AMER LUTH CH..	4	1 258	1 482	11.1	14.3
053 ASSEMB OF GOD.	1	17	35	0.3	0.3
081 CATHOLIC......	2	NA	157	1.2	1.5
093 CHR CH (DISC).	1	8	12	0.1	0.1
167 CHS OF CHRIST.	9	665	846	6.3	8.1
193 EPISCOPAL.....	1	21	37	0.3	0.4
283 LUTH--MO SYNOD	1	185	230	1.7	2.2
357 PRESB CH US...	1	40	47*	0.4	0.5
419 SO BAPT CONV..	18	4 337	5 042*	37.6	48.5
443 UN C OF CHRIST	1	194	226*	1.7	2.2
449 UN METHODIST..	12	1 872	2 176*	16.2	20.9
453 UN PRES CH USA	2	84	98*	0.7	0.9
BOWIE	145	37 949	48 152*	63.9	100.0
017 AMER BAPT ASSN	9	1 787	1 787	2.4	3.7
029 AMER LUTH CH..	1	153	190	0.3	0.4
053 ASSEMB OF GOD.	8	696	1 106	1.5	2.3
059 BAPT MISS ASSN	3	622	762*	1.0	1.6
081 CATHOLIC......	2	NA	1 588	2.1	3.3
093 CHR CH (DISC).	2	774	928	1.2	1.9
097 CHR CHS&CHS CR	4	760	931*	1.2	1.9
101 C.M.E........	12	1 628	1 994*	2.6	4.1
123 CH GOD (ANDER)	1	18	54	0.1	0.1
127 CH GOD (CLEVE)	3	114	140*	0.2	0.3
151 L-D SAINTS....	1	NA	443	0.6	0.9
165 CH OF NAZARENE	2	490	561	0.7	1.2
167 CHS OF CHRIST.	17	2 249	2 665	3.5	5.5
193 EPISCOPAL.....	3	1 352	1 477	2.0	3.1
215 EVAN METH CH..	1	47	58*	0.1	0.1
263 INT FOURSQ GOS	1	199	244*	0.3	0.5
271 REFORM JUDAISM	1	82	100*	0.1	0.2
283 LUTH--MO SYNOD	1	261	350	0.5	0.7
357 PRESB CH US...	5	504	617*	0.8	1.3
403 SALVATION ARMY	1	67	131	0.2	0.3
413 S.D.A.........	1	123	151*	0.2	0.3
419 SO BAPT CONV..	40	19 390	23 750*	31.5	49.3
449 UN METHODIST..	21	6 123	7 500*	10.0	15.6
453 UN PRES CH USA	5	510	625*	0.8	1.3
BRAZORIA	161	50 243	86 358*	50.9	100.0
017 AMER BAPT ASSN	4	900	900	0.5	1.0
029 AMER LUTH CH..	5	1 153	1 528	0.9	1.8
053 ASSEMB OF GOD.	14	1 660	3 027	1.8	3.5
059 BAPT MISS ASSN	1	25	31*	–	–
081 CATHOLIC......	14	NA	21 854	12.9	25.3
093 CHR CH (DISC).	5	527	718	0.4	0.8
101 C.M.E........	1	50	62*	–	0.1
123 CH GOD (ANDER)	1	20	60	–	0.1
127 CH GOD (CLEVE)	1	89	110*	0.1	0.1
151 L-D SAINTS....	3	NA	1 030	0.6	1.2
165 CH OF NAZARENE	5	301	491	0.3	0.6
167 CHS OF CHRIST.	23	2 850	3 775	2.2	4.4
193 EPISCOPAL.....	4	1 805	1 897	1.1	2.2
226 FRIENDS-USA...	1	22	27*	–	–
281 LUTH CH AMER..	1	354	508	0.3	0.6
283 LUTH--MO SYNOD	3	425	577	0.3	0.7
349 PENT HOLINESS.	1	98	121*	0.1	0.1
357 PRESB CH US...	10	2 214	2 744*	1.6	3.2
403 SALVATION ARMY	1	50	162	0.1	0.2
413 S.D.A.........	1	29	36*	–	–
419 SO BAPT CONV..	41	28 098	34 829*	20.5	40.3
449 UN METHODIST..	20	9 543	11 829*	7.0	13.7
469 WELS.........	1	30	42	–	–
BRAZOS	69	23 281	35 636*	38.1	100.0
017 AMER BAPT ASSN	1	50	50	0.1	0.1
029 AMER LUTH CH..	2	729	968	1.0	2.7
053 ASSEMB OF GOD.	6	588	748	0.8	2.1
059 BAPT MISS ASSN	1	356	418*	0.4	1.2
081 CATHOLIC......	4	NA	6 991	7.5	19.6
093 CHR CH (DISC).	1	329	530	0.6	1.5
097 CHR CHS&CHS CR	1	100	117*	0.1	0.3
151 L-D SAINTS....	2	NA	751	0.8	2.1
165 CH OF NAZARENE	1	63	109	0.1	0.3
167 CHS OF CHRIST.	5	1 300	1 655	1.8	4.6
193 EPISCOPAL.....	2	810	997	1.1	2.8
203 EVAN FREE CH..	1	69	81*	0.1	0.2
271 REFORM JUDAISM	1	84	99*	0.1	0.3
283 LUTH--MO SYNOD	2	619	772	0.8	2.2
349 PENT HOLINESS.	1	27	32*	–	0.1
356 PRESB CH AMER.	1	68	102	0.1	0.3
357 PRESB CH US...	2	1 045	1 226*	1.3	3.4
413 S.D.A.........	1	39	46*	–	0.1
419 SO BAPT CONV..	19	11 993	14 066*	15.0	39.5
435 UNITARIAN-UNIV	1	74	87*	0.1	0.2
443 UN C OF CHRIST	3	499	585*	0.6	1.6
449 UN METHODIST..	11	4 439	5 206*	5.6	14.6
BREWSTER	18	1 733	4 114*	54.3	100.0
053 ASSEMB OF GOD.	3	40	74	1.0	1.8
081 CATHOLIC......	3	NA	1 910	25.2	46.4
093 CHR CH (DISC).	1	102	157	2.1	3.8
151 L-D SAINTS....	1	NA	71	0.9	1.7
165 CH OF NAZARENE	1	1	0	–	–
167 CHS OF CHRIST.	2	125	138	1.8	3.4
193 EPISCOPAL.....	1	21	33	0.4	0.8
419 SO BAPT CONV..	3	830	995*	13.1	24.2
449 UN METHODIST..	2	473	567*	7.5	13.8
453 UN PRES CH USA	1	141	169*	2.2	4.1
BRISCOE	9	1 712	2 312*	89.6	100.0
053 ASSEMB OF GOD.	1	?	?	?	?
081 CATHOLIC......	1	NA	200	7.8	8.7
167 CHS OF CHRIST.	3	325	414	16.1	17.9
419 SO BAPT CONV..	2	1 070	1 310*	50.8	56.7
449 UN METHODIST..	2	317	388*	15.0	16.8
BROOKS	17	1 299	6 694*	79.4	100.0
053 ASSEMB OF GOD.	2	86	109	1.3	1.6
081 CATHOLIC......	4	NA	5 000	59.3	74.7
123 CH GOD (ANDER)	1	42	126	1.5	1.9
157 CH OF BRETHREN	1	36	45*	0.5	0.7
167 CHS OF CHRIST.	1	50	62	0.7	0.9
193 EPISCOPAL.....	1	11	14	0.2	0.2
349 PENT HOLINESS.	1	23	29*	0.3	0.4
357 PRESB CH US...	2	131	163*	1.9	2.4
413 S.D.A.........	1	47	59*	0.7	0.9
419 SO BAPT CONV..	1	633	788*	9.3	11.8
449 UN METHODIST..	2	240	299*	3.5	4.5
BROWN	65	16 470	22 989*	69.5	100.0
053 ASSEMB OF GOD.	2	112	227	0.7	1.0
081 CATHOLIC......	1	NA	2 500	7.6	10.9
093 CHR CH (DISC).	1	391	519	1.6	2.3
151 L-D SAINTS....	1	NA	213	0.6	0.9
165 CH OF NAZARENE	2	98	123	0.4	0.5
167 CHS OF CHRIST.	14	1 530	2 072	6.3	9.0
193 EPISCOPAL.....	2	402	503	1.5	2.2
283 LUTH--MO SYNOD	1	180	259	0.8	1.1
357 PRESB CH US...	1	188	226*	0.7	1.0
413 S.D.A.........	1	51	61*	0.2	0.3
419 SO BAPT CONV..	28	10 924	13 161*	39.8	57.2
449 UN METHODIST..	10	2 397	2 888*	8.7	12.6
453 UN PRES CH USA	1	197	237*	0.7	1.0
BURLESON	31	3 369	5 419*	44.0	100.0
029 AMER LUTH CH..	4	551	668	5.4	12.3
053 ASSEMB OF GOD.	3	126	145	1.2	2.7
081 CATHOLIC......	3	NA	1 230	10.0	22.7
093 CHR CH (DISC).	1	48	74	0.6	1.4
123 CH GOD (ANDER)	1	55	165	1.3	3.0
167 CHS OF CHRIST.	3	200	255	2.1	4.7
283 LUTH--MO SYNOD	1	22	23	0.2	0.4
357 PRESB CH US...	2	55	66*	0.5	1.2
419 SO BAPT CONV..	9	1 560	1 885*	15.3	34.8
443 UN C OF CHRIST	1	136	164*	1.3	3.0
449 UN METHODIST..	3	616	744*	6.0	13.7
BURNET	47	8 050	10 329*	58.0	100.0
017 AMER BAPT ASSN	1	20	20	0.1	0.2
029 AMER LUTH CH..	2	271	328	1.8	3.2
053 ASSEMB OF GOD.	3	243	343	1.9	3.3
081 CATHOLIC......	3	NA	620	3.5	6.0
093 CHR CH (DISC).	4	243	309	1.7	3.0
167 CHS OF CHRIST.	12	1 200	1 525	8.6	14.8
185 CUMBER PRESB..	1	118	165	0.9	1.6
193 EPISCOPAL.....	1	223	244	1.4	2.4
357 PRESB CH US...	2	285	337*	1.9	3.3
413 S.D.A.........	1	29	34*	0.2	0.3
419 SO BAPT CONV..	12	4 339	5 129*	28.8	49.7
449 UN METHODIST..	5	1 079	1 275*	7.2	12.3
CALDWELL	47	6 550	10 559*	44.7	100.0

NA—Not applicable *Total adherents estimated from known number of communicant, confirmed, full members. —Represents a percent less than 0.1. Percentages may not total due to rounding.

Table 4. Churches and Church Membership by County and Denomination: 1980

County and Denomination	Number of churches	Communicant, confirmed, full members	Total adherents Number	Percent of total population	Percent of total adherents
017 AMER BAPT ASSN	1	12	12	0.1	0.1
029 AMER LUTH CH..	2	183	221	0.9	2.1
053 ASSEMB OF GOD.	1	118	182	0.8	1.7
081 CATHOLIC......	3	NA	2 471	10.5	23.4
093 CHR CH (DISC).	2	200	314	1.3	3.0
127 CH GOD (CLEVE)	1	36	44*	0.2	0.4
165 CH OF NAZARENE	2	?	?	?	?
167 CHS OF CHRIST.	4	400	510	2.2	4.8
193 EPISCOPAL.....	2	174	238	1.0	2.3
357 PRESB CH US...	3	205	248*	1.0	2.3
413 S.D.A.........	1	13	16*	0.1	0.2
419 SO BAPT CONV..	13	3 579	4 331*	18.3	41.0
443 UN C OF CHRIST	2	210	254*	1.1	2.4
449 UN METHODIST..	10	1 420	1 718*	7.3	16.3
CALHOUN	**30**	**5 829**	**18 846***	**96.3**	**100.0**
053 ASSEMB OF GOD.	5	432	436	2.2	2.3
081 CATHOLIC......	4	NA	11 574	59.1	61.4
093 CHR CH (DISC).	1	40	62	0.3	0.3
151 L-D SAINTS....	1	NA	61	0.3	0.3
167 CHS OF CHRIST.	5	380	500	2.6	2.7
193 EPISCOPAL.....	1	182	209	1.1	1.1
281 LUTH CH AMER..	2	558	740	3.8	3.9
357 PRESB CH US...	1	206	256*	1.3	1.4
419 SO BAPT CONV..	6	3 059	3 800*	19.4	20.2
449 UN METHODIST..	3	916	1 138*	5.8	6.0
453 UN PRES CH USA	1	56	70*	0.4	0.4
CALLAHAN	**31**	**5 368**	**6 505***	**59.2**	**100.0**
053 ASSEMB OF GOD.	2	29	69	0.6	1.1
059 BAPT MISS ASSN	1	80	96*	0.9	1.5
081 CATHOLIC......	2	NA	?	?	?
127 CH GOD (CLEVE)	1	21	25*	0.2	0.4
167 CHS OF CHRIST.	8	600	765	7.0	11.8
215 EVAN METH CH..	1	40	48*	0.4	0.7
357 PRESB CH US...	2	46	55*	0.5	0.8
419 SO BAPT CONV..	8	3 656	4 375*	39.8	67.3
449 UN METHODIST..	4	850	1 017*	9.3	15.6
453 UN PRES CH USA	2	46	55*	0.5	0.8
CAMERON	**161**	**26 821**	**151 254***	**72.1**	**100.0**
017 AMER BAPT ASSN	1	75	75	-	-
053 ASSEMB OF GOD.	13	1 454	2 001	1.0	1.3
081 CATHOLIC......	35	NA	114 608	54.7	75.8
089 CHR & MISS AL.	3	45	75	-	-
093 CHR CH (DISC).	3	455	599	0.3	0.4
097 CHR CHS&CHS CR	3	405	525*	0.3	0.3
121 CH GOD (ABR)..	1	32	42*	-	-
123 CH GOD (ANDER)	1	30	90	-	0.1
127 CH GOD (CLEVE)	5	76	99*	-	0.1
151 L-D SAINTS....	2	NA	1 141	0.5	0.8
165 CH OF NAZARENE	5	383	770	0.4	0.5
167 CHS OF CHRIST.	14	1 250	1 590	0.8	1.1
193 EPISCOPAL.....	5	1 538	2 357	1.1	1.6
197 EVAN CH OF NA.	1	46	46	-	-
271 REFORM JUDAISM	1	200	259*	0.1	0.2
281 LUTH CH AMER..	2	303	359	0.2	0.2
283 LUTH--MO SYNOD	5	959	1 198	0.6	0.8
285 MENNONITE CH..	1	59	77*	-	0.1
349 PENT HOLINESS.	8	460	597*	0.3	0.4
357 PRESB CH US...	9	1 829	2 373*	1.1	1.6
403 SALVATION ARMY	1	76	127	0.1	0.1
413 S.D.A.........	4	233	302*	0.1	0.2
419 SO BAPT CONV..	26	13 151	17 063*	8.1	11.3
435 UNITARIAN-UNIV	1	20	26*	-	-
449 UN METHODIST..	11	3 742	4 855*	2.3	3.2
CAMP	**41**	**5 865**	**7 437***	**80.2**	**100.0**
017 AMER BAPT ASSN	3	169	169	1.8	2.3
053 ASSEMB OF GOD.	1	58	65	1.1	1.4
059 BAPT MISS ASSN	7	923	1 126*	12.1	15.1
101 C.M.E........	8	1 464	1 787*	19.3	24.0
127 CH GOD (CLEVE)	1	30	37*	0.4	0.5
151 L-D SAINTS....	1	NA	242	2.6	3.3
165 CH OF NAZARENE	1	47	100	1.1	1.3
167 CHS OF CHRIST.	5	278	339	3.7	4.6
185 CUMBER PRESB..	1	14	23	0.2	0.3
193 EPISCOPAL.....	1	105	120	1.3	1.6
357 PRESB CH US...	1	7	9*	0.1	0.1
419 SO BAPT CONV..	8	2 180	2 660*	28.7	35.8
449 UN METHODIST..	2	575	702*	7.6	9.4
453 UN PRES CH USA	1	15	18*	0.2	0.2
CARSON	**20**	**4 040**	**5 964***	**89.4**	**100.0**
053 ASSEMB OF GOD.	3	111	120	1.8	2.0
081 CATHOLIC......	3	NA	1 000	15.0	16.8
093 CHR CH (DISC).	1	180	221	3.3	3.7
167 CHS OF CHRIST.	4	200	255	3.8	4.3
349 PENT HOLINESS.	1	53	65*	1.0	1.1
419 SO BAPT CONV..	5	2 525	3 108*	46.6	52.1
449 UN METHODIST..	3	971	1 195*	17.9	20.0
CASS	**105**	**18 870**	**23 198***	**78.8**	**100.0**
017 AMER BAPT ASSN	15	1 639	1 639	5.6	7.1
053 ASSEMB OF GOD.	4	208	300	1.0	1.3
081 CATHOLIC......	1	NA	165	0.6	0.7
097 CHR CHS&CHS CR	1	45	55*	0.2	0.2
101 C.M.E........	12	2 620	3 204*	10.9	13.8
123 CH GOD (ANDER)	1	35	105	0.4	0.5
151 L-D SAINTS....	1	NA	227	0.8	1.0
165 CH OF NAZARENE	1	145	154	0.5	0.7
167 CHS OF CHRIST.	7	500	635	2.2	2.7
193 EPISCOPAL.....	1	55	55	0.2	0.2
357 PRESB CH US...	1	27	33*	0.1	0.1
413 S.D.A.........	2	125	153*	0.5	0.7
419 SO BAPT CONV..	39	10 691	13 075*	44.4	56.4
421 SO METHODIST..	1	25	28	0.1	0.1
449 UN METHODIST..	17	2 729	3 338*	11.3	14.4
453 UN PRES CH USA	1	26	32*	0.1	0.1
CASTRO	**22**	**4 293**	**8 620***	**81.7**	**100.0**
053 ASSEMB OF GOD.	1	45	83	0.8	1.0
081 CATHOLIC......	3	NA	3 000	28.4	34.8
097 CHR CHS&CHS CR	1	54	71*	0.7	0.8
165 CH OF NAZARENE	1	15	25	0.2	0.3
167 CHS OF CHRIST.	4	500	635	6.0	7.4
349 PENT HOLINESS.	1	32	42*	0.4	0.5
357 PRESB CH US...	1	290	379*	3.6	4.4
419 SO BAPT CONV..	7	2 595	3 390*	32.1	39.3
449 UN METHODIST..	2	736	961*	9.1	11.1
453 UN PRES CH USA	1	26	34*	0.3	0.4
CHAMBERS	**27**	**5 747**	**9 418***	**50.8**	**100.0**
053 ASSEMB OF GOD.	2	154	276	1.5	2.9
081 CATHOLIC......	2	NA	2 084	11.2	22.1
167 CHS OF CHRIST.	6	450	575	3.1	6.1
193 EPISCOPAL.....	1	56	62	0.3	0.7
283 LUTH--MO SYNOD	1	134	192	1.0	2.0
419 SO BAPT CONV..	9	3 475	4 370*	23.6	46.4
449 UN METHODIST..	6	1 478	1 859*	10.0	19.7
CHEROKEE	**131**	**21 377**	**26 048***	**68.3**	**100.0**
017 AMER BAPT ASSN	11	2 064	2 064	5.4	7.9
019 AMER BAPT USA.	1	380	458*	1.2	1.8
053 ASSEMB OF GOD.	10	441	664	1.7	2.5
059 BAPT MISS ASSN	19	4 457	5 373*	14.1	20.6
081 CATHOLIC......	1	NA	525	1.4	2.0
093 CHR CH (DISC).	4	356	438	1.1	1.7
101 C.M.E........	17	2 118	2 553*	6.7	9.8
127 CH GOD (CLEVE)	1	28	34*	0.1	0.1
165 CH OF NAZARENE	3	221	346	0.9	1.3
167 CHS OF CHRIST.	12	1 100	1 210	3.2	4.6
185 CUMBER PRESB..	2	12	38	0.1	0.1
193 EPISCOPAL.....	2	86	138	0.4	0.5
215 EVAN METH CH..	1	143	172*	0.5	0.7
283 LUTH--MO SYNOD	1	45	69	0.2	0.3
357 PRESB CH US...	2	181	218*	0.6	0.8
413 S.D.A.........	1	107	129*	0.3	0.5
419 SO BAPT CONV..	19	6 480	7 812*	20.5	30.0
449 UN METHODIST..	22	2 973	3 584*	9.4	13.8
453 UN PRES CH USA	2	185	223*	0.6	0.9
CHILDRESS	**20**	**3 647**	**5 430***	**78.1**	**100.0**
053 ASSEMB OF GOD.	1	81	115	1.7	2.1
059 BAPT MISS ASSN	1	130	155*	2.2	2.9
081 CATHOLIC......	1	NA	900	12.9	16.6
093 CHR CH (DISC).	1	94	182	2.6	3.4
101 C.M.E........	1	25	30*	0.4	0.6
127 CH GOD (CLEVE)	1	?	?	?	?
151 L-D SAINTS....	1	NA	68	1.0	1.3
165 CH OF NAZARENE	1	14	29	0.4	0.5
167 CHS OF CHRIST.	2	100	127	1.8	2.3
357 PRESB CH US...	1	48	57*	0.8	1.0
419 SO BAPT CONV..	5	2 359	2 817*	40.5	51.9
449 UN METHODIST..	3	748	893*	12.8	16.4
453 UN PRES CH USA	1	48	57*	0.8	1.0
CLAY	**30**	**5 265**	**6 467***	**67.5**	**100.0**
053 ASSEMB OF GOD.	2	29	53	0.6	0.8
081 CATHOLIC......	1	NA	125	1.3	1.9
093 CHR CH (DISC).	1	61	85	0.9	1.3
127 CH GOD (CLEVE)	1	123	146*	1.5	2.3
167 CHS OF CHRIST.	5	420	535	5.6	8.3
193 EPISCOPAL.....	1	31	43	0.4	0.7
419 SO BAPT CONV..	12	3 780	4 502*	47.0	69.6
449 UN METHODIST..	7	821	978*	10.2	15.1
COCHRAN	**13**	**2 651**	**4 280***	**88.7**	**100.0**
053 ASSEMB OF GOD.	3	104	149	3.1	3.5
059 BAPT MISS ASSN	1	403	511*	10.6	11.9
081 CATHOLIC......	1	NA	900	18.7	21.0
167 CHS OF CHRIST.	3	200	255	5.3	6.0
419 SO BAPT CONV..	3	1 490	1 889*	39.2	44.1
449 UN METHODIST..	2	454	576*	11.9	13.5
COKE	**18**	**2 070**	**2 471***	**77.3**	**100.0**
053 ASSEMB OF GOD.	1	10	16	0.5	0.6
059 BAPT MISS ASSN	1	213	249*	7.8	10.1
081 CATHOLIC......	2	NA	?	?	?
127 CH GOD (CLEVE)	1	10	12*	0.4	0.5
167 CHS OF CHRIST.	6	450	575	18.0	23.3
419 SO BAPT CONV..	4	959	1 119*	35.0	45.3
449 UN METHODIST..	2	428	500*	15.6	20.2
COLEMAN	**52**	**6 029**	**8 199***	**78.5**	**100.0**
053 ASSEMB OF GOD.	2	62	98	0.9	1.2

NA—Not applicable   *Total adherents estimated from known number of communicant, confirmed, full members.   —Represents a percent less than 0.1.   Percentages may not total due to rounding.

Table 4. Churches and Church Membership by County and Denomination: 1980

County and Denomination	Number of churches	Communicant, confirmed, full members	Total adherents		
			Number	Percent of total population	Percent of total adherents
059 BAPT MISS ASSN	1	148	175*	1.7	2.1
081 CATHOLIC......	1	NA	800	7.7	9.8
093 CHR CH (DISC).	2	123	169	1.6	2.1
123 CH GOD (ANDER)	1	10	30	0.3	0.4
165 CH OF NAZARENE	1	33	35	0.3	0.4
167 CHS OF CHRIST.	7	545	697	6.7	8.5
185 CUMBER PRESB..	1	2	4	–	–
193 EPISCOPAL.....	1	65	110	1.1	1.3
353 CHR BRETHREN..	1	150	300	2.9	3.7
357 PRESB CH US...	2	98	116*	1.1	1.4
413 S.D.A.........	1	54	64*	0.6	0.8
419 SO BAPT CONV..	17	3 476	4 108*	39.4	50.1
449 UN METHODIST..	12	1 165	1 377*	13.2	16.8
453 UN PRES CH USA	2	98	116*	1.1	1.4
COLLIN	**171**	**41 593**	**64 915***	**44.9**	**100.0**
017 AMER BAPT ASSN	1	250	250	0.2	0.4
019 AMER BAPT USA.	1	75	95*	0.1	0.1
053 ASSEMB OF GOD.	10	900	1 144	0.8	1.8
059 BAPT MISS ASSN	1	177	225*	0.2	0.3
081 CATHOLIC......	5	NA	10 170	7.0	15.7
093 CHR CH (DISC).	14	1 898	2 543	1.8	3.9
097 CHR CHS&CHS CR	5	967	1 229*	0.9	1.9
101 C.M.E.........	1	492	626*	0.4	1.0
127 CH GOD (CLEVE)	6	232	295*	0.2	0.5
151 L-D SAINTS....	3	NA	1 196	0.8	1.8
165 CH OF NAZARENE	2	128	244	0.2	0.4
167 CHS OF CHRIST.	19	2 491	3 171	2.2	4.9
193 EPISCOPAL.....	4	1 089	1 609	1.1	2.5
203 EVAN FREE CH..	1	38	48*	–	0.1
281 LUTH CH AMER..	1	483	758	0.5	1.2
283 LUTH--MO SYNOD	2	473	706	0.5	1.1
353 CHR BRETHREN..	1	40	100	0.1	0.2
357 PRESB CH US...	9	673	856*	0.6	1.3
419 SO BAPT CONV..	52	23 105	29 375*	20.3	45.3
449 UN METHODIST..	24	7 408	9 418*	6.5	14.5
453 UN PRES CH USA	9	674	857*	0.6	1.3
COLLINGSWORTH	**18**	**2 712**	**3 769***	**81.1**	**100.0**
053 ASSEMB OF GOD.	1	43	36	0.8	1.0
081 CATHOLIC......	1	NA	500	10.8	13.3
097 CHR CHS&CHS CR	1	85	103*	2.2	2.7
101 C.M.E.........	1	15	18*	0.4	0.5
165 CH OF NAZARENE	2	148	152	3.3	4.0
167 CHS OF CHRIST.	6	420	535	11.5	14.2
419 SO BAPT CONV..	4	1 476	1 789*	38.5	47.5
449 UN METHODIST..	2	525	636*	13.7	16.9
COLORADO	**46**	**5 296**	**12 455***	**66.2**	**100.0**
029 AMER LUTH CH..	5	1 219	1 425	7.6	11.4
053 ASSEMB OF GOD.	4	53	90	0.5	0.7
081 CATHOLIC......	7	NA	5 999	31.9	48.2
123 CH GOD (ANDER)	1	8	24	0.1	0.2
165 CH OF NAZARENE	1	39	50	0.3	0.4
167 CHS OF CHRIST.	5	250	320	1.7	2.6
193 EPISCOPAL.....	1	125	214	1.1	1.7
357 PRESB CH US...	1	106	128*	0.7	1.0
419 SO BAPT CONV..	9	1 879	2 260*	12.0	18.1
443 UN C OF CHRIST	2	378	455*	2.4	3.7
449 UN METHODIST..	10	1 239	1 490*	7.9	12.0
COMAL	**34**	**9 571**	**22 236***	**61.0**	**100.0**
029 AMER LUTH CH..	2	1 618	2 059	5.6	9.3
053 ASSEMB OF GOD.	2	99	159	0.4	0.7
081 CATHOLIC......	7	NA	10 006	27.5	45.0
097 CHR CHS&CHS CR	1	100	120*	0.3	0.5
151 L-D SAINTS....	1	NA	263	0.7	1.2
165 CH OF NAZARENE	1	24	45	0.1	0.2
167 CHS OF CHRIST.	2	378	481	1.3	2.2
193 EPISCOPAL.....	1	302	597	1.6	2.7
203 EVAN FREE CH..	1	15	18*	–	0.1
263 INT FOURSQ GOS	1	8	10*	–	–
283 LUTH--MO SYNOD	1	352	451	1.2	2.0
349 PENT HOLINESS.	1	49	59*	0.2	0.3
357 PRESB CH US...	2	369	444*	1.2	2.0
419 SO BAPT CONV..	7	2 859	3 438*	9.4	15.5
443 UN C OF CHRIST	2	2 076	2 496*	6.8	11.2
449 UN METHODIST..	2	1 322	1 590*	4.4	7.2
COMANCHE	**50**	**6 433**	**7 970***	**63.2**	**100.0**
029 AMER LUTH CH..	1	53	75	0.6	0.9
053 ASSEMB OF GOD.	1	92	161	1.3	2.0
081 CATHOLIC......	2	NA	205	1.6	2.6
093 CHR CH (DISC).	1	39	64	0.5	0.8
097 CHR CHS&CHS CR	1	40	47*	0.4	0.6
167 CHS OF CHRIST.	10	660	840	6.7	10.5
193 EPISCOPAL.....	1	32	37	0.3	0.5
357 PRESB CH US...	1	22	26*	0.2	0.3
419 SO BAPT CONV..	23	4 260	5 051*	40.0	63.4
449 UN METHODIST..	8	1 213	1 438*	11.4	18.0
453 UN PRES CH USA	1	22	26*	0.2	0.3
CONCHO	**17**	**1 282**	**1 534***	**52.6**	**100.0**
081 CATHOLIC......	3	NA	?	?	?
093 CHR CH (DISC).	1	13	20	0.7	1.3
167 CHS OF CHRIST.	4	179	207	7.1	13.5
283 LUTH--MO SYNOD	2	151	171	5.9	11.1
419 SO BAPT CONV..	4	724	876*	30.1	57.1
449 UN METHODIST..	3	215	260*	8.9	16.9
COOKE	**61**	**11 212**	**17 365***	**62.8**	**100.0**
017 AMER BAPT ASSN	3	275	275	1.0	1.6
053 ASSEMB OF GOD.	2	153	218	0.8	1.3
081 CATHOLIC......	5	NA	3 595	13.0	20.7
093 CHR CH (DISC).	1	187	334	1.2	1.9
101 C.M.E.........	1	300	362*	1.3	2.1
127 CH GOD (CLEVE)	1	21	25*	0.1	0.1
151 L-D SAINTS....	1	NA	126	0.5	0.7
165 CH OF NAZARENE	3	111	134	0.5	0.8
167 CHS OF CHRIST.	9	1 200	1 467	5.3	8.4
193 EPISCOPAL.....	1	107	136	0.5	0.8
283 LUTH--MO SYNOD	1	67	85	0.3	0.5
357 PRESB CH US...	1	129	156*	0.6	0.9
381 REF PRES-EVAN.	1	256	296	1.1	1.7
413 S.D.A.........	2	68	82*	0.3	0.5
419 SO BAPT CONV..	20	6 449	7 791*	28.2	44.9
449 UN METHODIST..	8	1 761	2 128*	7.7	12.3
453 UN PRES CH USA	1	128	155*	0.6	0.9
CORYELL	**68**	**13 111**	**16 986***	**29.9**	**100.0**
029 AMER LUTH CH..	1	184	213	0.4	1.3
053 ASSEMB OF GOD.	2	82	140	0.2	0.8
081 CATHOLIC......	2	NA	500	0.9	2.9
093 CHR CH (DISC).	2	64	99	0.2	0.6
121 CH GOD (ABR)	1	38	46*	0.1	0.3
151 L-D SAINTS....	2	NA	381	0.7	2.2
167 CHS OF CHRIST.	11	900	1 145	2.0	6.7
283 LUTH--MO SYNOD	4	629	823	1.4	4.8
357 PRESB CH US...	1	109	133*	0.2	0.8
419 SO BAPT CONV..	29	8 778	10 676*	18.8	62.9
449 UN METHODIST..	11	2 128	2 588*	4.6	15.2
453 UN PRES CH USA	2	199	242*	0.4	1.4
COTTLE	**13**	**2 098**	**2 986***	**101.3**	**100.0**
053 ASSEMB OF GOD.	2	52	85	2.9	2.8
059 BAPT MISS ASSN	1	326	391*	13.3	13.1
081 CATHOLIC......	1	NA	400	13.6	13.4
093 CHR CH (DISC).	1	102	149	5.1	5.0
167 CHS OF CHRIST.	4	250	318	10.8	10.6
419 SO BAPT CONV..	2	1 049	1 260*	42.8	42.2
449 UN METHODIST..	2	319	383*	13.0	12.8
CRANE	**7**	**1 987**	**2 860***	**62.2**	**100.0**
053 ASSEMB OF GOD.	1	32	55	1.2	1.9
081 CATHOLIC......	1	NA	305	6.6	10.7
097 CHR CHS&CHS CR	1	250	318*	6.9	11.1
167 CHS OF CHRIST.	2	215	287	6.2	10.0
419 SO BAPT CONV..	1	1 156	1 470*	32.0	51.4
449 UN METHODIST..	1	334	425*	9.2	14.9
CROCKETT	**9**	**1 660**	**4 296***	**93.2**	**100.0**
053 ASSEMB OF GOD.	1	64	101	2.2	2.4
081 CATHOLIC......	1	NA	2 180	47.3	50.7
167 CHS OF CHRIST.	2	125	159	3.5	3.7
283 LUTH--MO SYNOD	1	25	34	0.7	0.8
419 SO BAPT CONV..	3	1 019	1 284*	27.9	29.9
449 UN METHODIST..	1	427	538*	11.7	12.5
CROSBY	**20**	**4 556**	**8 241***	**93.0**	**100.0**
053 ASSEMB OF GOD.	2	63	92	1.0	1.1
081 CATHOLIC......	3	NA	2 500	28.2	30.3
167 CHS OF CHRIST.	6	400	510	5.8	6.2
419 SO BAPT CONV..	6	3 120	3 917*	44.2	47.5
449 UN METHODIST..	3	973	1 222*	13.8	14.8
CULBERSON	**11**	**989**	**3 299***	**99.5**	**100.0**
081 CATHOLIC......	2	NA	2 000	60.3	60.6
165 CH OF NAZARENE	2	6	22	0.7	0.7
167 CHS OF CHRIST.	2	100	127	3.8	3.8
193 EPISCOPAL.....	1	21	28	0.8	0.8
413 S.D.A.........	1	23	30*	0.9	0.9
419 SO BAPT CONV..	1	561	730*	22.0	22.1
449 UN METHODIST..	2	278	362*	10.9	11.0
DALLAM	**20**	**4 532**	**7 491***	**114.7**	**100.0**
053 ASSEMB OF GOD.	1	35	48	0.7	0.6
081 CATHOLIC......	2	NA	1 800	27.6	24.0
097 CHR CHS&CHS CR	1	525	659*	10.1	8.8
143 CG IN CR(MENN)	2	93	93	1.4	1.2
167 CHS OF CHRIST.	4	300	382	5.8	5.1
193 EPISCOPAL.....	1	114	145	2.2	1.9
283 LUTH--MO SYNOD	1	73	105	1.6	1.4
357 PRESB CH US...	1	60	75*	1.1	1.0
413 S.D.A.........	1	51	64*	1.0	0.9
419 SO BAPT CONV..	3	2 550	3 202*	49.0	42.7
449 UN METHODIST..	2	672	844*	12.9	11.3
453 UN PRES CH USA	1	59	74*	1.1	1.0
DALLAS	**984**	**507 120**	**769 821***	**49.5**	**100.0**
005 AME ZION......	3	955	1 088	0.1	0.1
017 AMER BAPT ASSN	10	2 510	2 510	0.2	0.3
019 AMER BAPT USA.	38	10 463	12 762*	0.8	1.7
029 AMER LUTH CH..	8	3 165	4 170	0.3	0.5
053 ASSEMB OF GOD.	86	18 436	23 284	1.5	3.0
059 BAPT MISS ASSN	41	14 600	17 808*	1.1	2.3
081 CATHOLIC......	37	NA	130 507	8.4	17.0

NA—Not applicable *Total adherents estimated from known number of communicant, confirmed, full members. —Represents a percent less than 0.1. Percentages may not total due to rounding.

Table 4. Churches and Church Membership by County and Denomination: 1980

County and Denomination	Number of churches	Communicant, confirmed, full members	Total adherents		
			Number	Percent of total population	Percent of total adherents
089 CHR & MISS AL.	1	36	66	–	–
093 CHR CH (DISC).	41	14 008	22 208	1.4	2.9
097 CHR CHS&CHS CR	9	900	1 098*	0.1	0.1
101 C.M.E.........	18	11 345	13 838*	0.9	1.8
105 CHRISTIAN REF.	1	50	76	–	–
123 CH GOD (ANDER)	2	224	672	–	0.1
127 CH GOD (CLEVE)	17	1 616	1 971*	0.1	0.3
133 CH GOD(7TH)DEN	2	48	59*	–	–
149 CH OF JC (BIC)	1	13	13	–	–
151 L-D SAINTS....	13	NA	6 708	0.4	0.9
165 CH OF NAZARENE	15	2 792	3 654	0.2	0.5
167 CHS OF CHRIST.	118	30 090	38 300	2.5	5.0
177 CONGR HOL CH..	1	35	43*	–	–
185 CUMBER PRESB..	1	209	384	–	–
193 EPISCOPAL.....	39	19 965	26 024	1.7	3.4
203 EVAN FREE CH..	1	67	82*	–	–
208 EVAN LUTH ASSN	3	567	819	0.1	0.1
209 EVAN LUTH SYN.	1	0	93	–	–
215 EVAN METH CH..	3	616	751*	–	0.1
221 FREE METHODIST	3	138	378	–	–
263 INT FOURSQ GOS	5	774	944*	0.1	0.1
270 CONSRV JUDAISM	2	1 113	1 358*	0.1	0.2
271 REFORM JUDAISM	2	5 334	6 506*	0.4	0.8
281 LUTH CH AMER..	13	3 949	5 227	0.3	0.7
283 LUTH--MO SYNOD	15	6 693	8 600	0.6	1.1
285 MENNONITE CH..	1	20	24*	–	–
290 METRO COMM CHS	1	400	800	0.1	0.1
313 N AM BAPT CONF	1	61	74*	–	–
349 PENT HOLINESS.	3	213	260*	–	–
353 CHR BRETHREN..	8	625	1 055	0.1	0.1
356 PRESB CH AMER.	3	229	239	–	–
357 PRESB CH US...	47	13 545	16 521*	1.1	2.1
381 REF PRES-EVAN.	1	69	120	–	–
403 SALVATION ARMY	4	611	3 126	0.2	0.4
413 S.D.A.........	10	2 325	2 836*	0.2	0.4
419 SO BAPT CONV..	195	228 493	278 703*	17.9	36.2
421 SO METHODIST..	1	67	96	–	–
423 SYRIAN ANTIOCH	2	800	976*	0.1	0.1
435 UNITARIAN-UNIV	4	998	1 217*	0.1	0.2
443 UN C OF CHRIST	4	1 580	1 927*	0.1	0.3
449 UN METHODIST..	99	92 541	112 876*	7.3	14.7
453 UN PRES CH USA	47	13 456	16 413*	1.1	2.1
469 WELS..........	3	376	557	–	0.1
DAWSON	46	9 386	14 975*	92.5	100.0
017 AMER BAPT ASSN	2	81	81	0.5	0.5
053 ASSEMB OF GOD.	3	229	371	2.3	2.5
059 BAPT MISS ASSN	2	513	643*	4.0	4.3
081 CATHOLIC......	2	NA	3 000	18.5	20.0
093 CHR CH (DISC).	1	105	150	0.9	1.0
101 C.M.E.........	1	45	56*	0.3	0.4
127 CH GOD (CLEVE)	1	23	29*	0.2	0.2
165 CH OF NAZARENE	2	183	380	2.3	2.5
167 CHS OF CHRIST.	9	715	874	5.4	5.8
193 EPISCOPAL.....	1	18	18	0.1	0.1
263 INT FOURSQ GOS	1	159	199*	1.2	1.3
283 LUTH--MO SYNOD	1	134	177	1.1	1.2
357 PRESB CH US...	1	114	143*	0.9	1.0
419 SO BAPT CONV..	13	5 701	7 142*	44.1	47.7
449 UN METHODIST..	5	1 252	1 569*	9.7	10.5
453 UN PRES CH USA	1	114	143*	0.9	1.0
DEAF SMITH	28	7 309	15 619*	73.8	100.0
053 ASSEMB OF GOD.	2	154	275	1.3	1.8
081 CATHOLIC......	2	NA	5 900	27.9	37.8
093 CHR CH (DISC).	1	385	430	2.0	2.8
127 CH GOD (CLEVE)	1	?	?	?	?
151 L-D SAINTS....	1	NA	164	0.8	1.1
165 CH OF NAZARENE	1	120	255	1.2	1.6
167 CHS OF CHRIST.	4	545	695	3.3	4.4
193 EPISCOPAL.....	1	126	162	0.8	1.0
283 LUTH--MO SYNOD	1	85	116	0.5	0.7
357 PRESB CH US...	1	167	216*	1.0	1.4
413 S.D.A.........	1	56	72*	0.3	0.5
419 SO BAPT CONV..	8	3 984	5 152*	24.3	33.0
449 UN METHODIST..	3	1 520	1 966*	9.3	12.6
453 UN PRES CH USA	1	167	216*	1.0	1.4
DELTA	27	3 366	4 026*	83.2	100.0
053 ASSEMB OF GOD.	1	63	94	1.9	2.3
059 BAPT MISS ASSN	1	25	30*	0.6	0.7
093 CHR CH (DISC).	1	15	23	0.5	0.6
101 C.M.E.........	3	188	222*	4.6	5.5
165 CH OF NAZARENE	1	19	19	0.4	0.5
167 CHS OF CHRIST.	4	250	320	6.6	7.9
357 PRESB CH US...	1	9	11*	0.2	0.3
419 SO BAPT CONV..	8	1 955	2 312*	47.8	57.4
449 UN METHODIST..	6	834	986*	20.4	24.5
453 UN PRES CH USA	1	8	9*	0.2	0.2
DENTON	155	34 839	53 692*	37.5	100.0
017 AMER BAPT ASSN	4	343	343	0.2	0.6
019 AMER BAPT USA.	1	220	270*	0.2	0.5
053 ASSEMB OF GOD.	11	635	927	0.6	1.7
059 BAPT MISS ASSN	1	212	260*	0.2	0.5
081 CATHOLIC......	6	NA	9 237	6.5	17.2
093 CHR CH (DISC).	4	652	845	0.6	1.6
097 CHR CHS&CHS CR	3	271	333*	0.2	0.6
101 C.M.E.........	2	423	520*	0.4	1.0
127 CH GOD (CLEVE)	2	127	156*	0.1	0.3
151 L-D SAINTS....	3	NA	1 163	0.8	2.2

County and Denomination	Number of churches	Communicant, confirmed, full members	Total adherents		
			Number	Percent of total population	Percent of total adherents
165 CH OF NAZARENE	4	263	338	0.2	0.6
167 CHS OF CHRIST.	25	2 725	3 470	2.4	6.5
175 CONGR CHR CHS.	1	70	86*	0.1	0.2
185 CUMBER PRESB..	1	97	196	0.1	0.4
193 EPISCOPAL.....	3	686	850	0.6	1.6
281 LUTH CH AMER..	1	126	180	0.1	0.3
283 LUTH--MO SYNOD	2	622	895	0.6	1.7
357 PRESB CH US...	6	900	1 106*	0.8	2.1
413 S.D.A.........	1	49	60*	–	0.1
419 SO BAPT CONV..	42	18 019	22 136*	15.5	41.2
421 SO METHODIST..	1	29	38	–	0.1
435 UNITARIAN-UNIV	1	30	37*	–	0.1
443 UN C OF CHRIST	1	75	92*	0.1	0.2
449 UN METHODIST..	23	7 365	9 048*	6.3	16.9
453 UN PRES CH USA	6	900	1 106*	0.8	2.1
DE WITT	37	6 277	12 776*	67.6	100.0
029 AMER LUTH CH..	6	1 893	2 148	11.4	16.8
053 ASSEMB OF GOD.	1	56	85	0.4	0.7
081 CATHOLIC......	8	NA	5 283	27.9	41.4
167 CHS OF CHRIST.	2	125	159	0.8	1.2
193 EPISCOPAL.....	1	117	158	0.8	1.2
281 LUTH CH AMER..	2	1 547	1 904	10.1	14.9
357 PRESB CH US...	2	281	336*	1.8	2.6
419 SO BAPT CONV..	9	1 749	2 094*	11.1	16.4
449 UN METHODIST..	6	509	609*	3.2	4.8
DICKENS	19	2 449	3 396*	96.0	100.0
053 ASSEMB OF GOD.	1	25	36	1.0	1.1
059 BAPT MISS ASSN	1	81	98*	2.8	2.9
081 CATHOLIC......	1	NA	400	11.3	11.8
093 CHR CH (DISC).	1	26	34	1.0	1.0
165 CH OF NAZARENE	1	11	20	0.6	0.6
167 CHS OF CHRIST.	7	350	445	12.6	13.1
419 SO BAPT CONV..	4	1 479	1 787*	50.5	52.6
449 UN METHODIST..	3	477	576*	16.3	17.0
DIMMIT	15	1 354	9 863*	86.8	100.0
053 ASSEMB OF GOD.	2	77	115	1.0	1.2
081 CATHOLIC......	3	NA	8 082	71.1	81.9
167 CHS OF CHRIST.	1	40	50	0.4	0.5
193 EPISCOPAL.....	1	51	76	0.7	0.8
349 PENT HOLINESS.	1	25	32*	0.3	0.3
357 PRESB CH US...	1	10	13*	0.1	0.1
413 S.D.A.........	1	16	21*	0.2	0.2
419 SO BAPT CONV..	2	831	1 079*	9.5	10.9
449 UN METHODIST..	3	304	395*	3.5	4.0
DONLEY	16	2 347	2 955*	72.5	100.0
053 ASSEMB OF GOD.	1	52	104	2.6	3.5
081 CATHOLIC......	1	NA	100	2.5	3.4
097 CHR CHS&CHS CR	1	70	82*	2.0	2.8
165 CH OF NAZARENE	1	31	46	1.1	1.6
167 CHS OF CHRIST.	3	200	275	6.7	9.3
193 EPISCOPAL.....	1	84	106	2.6	3.6
357 PRESB CH US...	1	42	49*	1.2	1.7
419 SO BAPT CONV..	4	1 325	1 556*	38.2	52.7
449 UN METHODIST..	2	501	588*	14.4	19.9
453 UN PRES CH USA	1	42	49*	1.2	1.7
DUVAL	16	1 448	4 160*	33.2	100.0
053 ASSEMB OF GOD.	1	41	89	0.7	2.1
081 CATHOLIC......	6	NA	2 280	18.2	54.8
127 CH GOD (CLEVE)	1	10	13*	0.1	0.3
167 CHS OF CHRIST.	1	33	56	0.4	1.3
419 SO BAPT CONV..	4	1 179	1 488*	11.9	35.8
449 UN METHODIST..	3	185	234*	1.9	5.6
EASTLAND	70	11 824	14 672*	75.3	100.0
053 ASSEMB OF GOD.	2	52	73	0.4	0.5
081 CATHOLIC......	4	NA	430	2.2	2.9
093 CHR CH (DISC).	2	278	377	1.9	2.6
123 CH GOD (ANDER)	1	39	117	0.6	0.8
127 CH GOD (CLEVE)	2	93	109*	0.6	0.7
151 L-D SAINTS....	1	NA	68	0.3	0.5
165 CH OF NAZARENE	1	96	112	0.6	0.8
167 CHS OF CHRIST.	19	1 500	1 900	9.8	12.9
193 EPISCOPAL.....	1	35	50	0.3	0.3
215 EVAN METH CH..	1	46	54*	0.3	0.4
283 LUTH--MO SYNOD	1	204	263	1.4	1.8
357 PRESB CH US...	2	65	76*	0.4	0.5
419 SO BAPT CONV..	22	7 740	9 077*	46.6	61.9
449 UN METHODIST..	8	1 614	1 893*	9.7	12.9
453 UN PRES CH USA	2	62	73*	0.4	0.5
ECTOR	96	40 496	70 385*	61.0	100.0
017 AMER BAPT ASSN	3	797	797	0.7	1.1
029 AMER LUTH CH..	2	1 156	1 409	1.2	2.0
053 ASSEMB OF GOD.	9	1 245	1 996	1.7	2.8
059 BAPT MISS ASSN	3	806	1 000*	0.9	1.4
081 CATHOLIC......	6	NA	17 818	15.4	25.3
093 CHR CH (DISC).	2	543	921	0.8	1.3
097 CHR CHS&CHS CR	3	900	1 117*	1.0	1.6
101 C.M.E.........	1	155	192*	0.2	0.3
123 CH GOD (ANDER)	1	144	432	0.4	0.6
127 CH GOD (CLEVE)	2	180	223*	0.2	0.3
151 L-D SAINTS....	2	NA	681	0.6	1.0
165 CH OF NAZARENE	4	402	787	0.7	1.1

NA—Not applicable   *Total adherents estimated from known number of communicant, confirmed, full members.   —Represents a percent less than 0.1.   Percentages may not total due to rounding.

Table 4. Churches and Church Membership by County and Denomination: 1980

County and Denomination	Number of churches	Communicant, confirmed, full members	Total adherents		
			Number	Percent of total population	Percent of total adherents
167 CHS OF CHRIST.	17	3 322	4 270	3.7	6.1
185 CUMBER PRESB..	1	247	477	0.4	0.7
193 EPISCOPAL.....	1	681	953	0.8	1.4
215 EVAN METH CH..	1	73	91*	0.1	0.1
263 INT FOURSQ GOS	1	161	200*	0.2	0.3
283 LUTH--MO SYNOD	1	464	635	0.6	0.9
349 PENT HOLINESS	1	50	62*	0.1	0.1
357 PRESB CH US...	3	1 509	1 873*	1.6	2.7
403 SALVATION ARMY	1	83	226	0.2	0.3
413 S.D.A.........	1	44	55*	–	0.1
419 SO BAPT CONV..	22	21 969	27 264*	23.6	38.7
435 UNITARIAN-UNIV	1	30	37*	–	0.1
449 UN METHODIST..	7	5 535	6 869*	6.0	9.8
EDWARDS	9	662	1 573*	77.4	100.0
081 CATHOLIC......	1	NA	735	36.2	46.7
167 CHS OF CHRIST.	2	100	127	6.2	8.1
357 PRESB CH US...	1	63	80*	3.9	5.1
419 SO BAPT CONV..	2	363	459*	22.6	29.2
449 UN METHODIST..	3	136	172*	8.5	10.9
ELLIS	123	24 380	36 197*	60.6	100.0
053 ASSEMB OF GOD.	16	1 091	1 777	3.0	4.9
059 BAPT MISS ASSN	14	4 669	5 762*	9.6	15.9
081 CATHOLIC......	4	NA	5 420	9.1	15.0
093 CHR CH (DISC).	6	444	641	1.1	1.8
101 C.M.E........	1	203	251*	0.4	0.7
127 CH GOD (CLEVE)	1	78	96*	0.2	0.3
151 L-D SAINTS....	1	NA	112	0.2	0.3
165 CH OF NAZARENE	1	26	35	0.1	0.1
167 CHS OF CHRIST.	18	2 024	2 558	4.3	7.1
185 CUMBER PRESB..	1	127	157	0.4	0.4
193 EPISCOPAL.....	2	241	264	0.4	0.7
283 LUTH--MO SYNOD	1	134	189	0.3	0.5
357 PRESB CH US...	7	427	527*	0.9	1.5
413 S.D.A.........	1	43	53*	0.1	0.1
419 SO BAPT CONV..	16	9 510	11 736*	19.6	32.4
449 UN METHODIST..	26	4 933	6 088*	10.2	16.8
453 UN PRES CH USA	7	430	531*	0.9	1.5
EL PASO	236	53 511	205 221*	42.8	100.0
017 AMER BAPT ASSN	1	50	50	–	–
029 AMER LUTH CH..	1	341	474	0.1	0.2
053 ASSEMB OF GOD.	13	1 487	2 062	0.4	1.0
059 BAPT MISS ASSN	1	61	77*	–	–
081 CATHOLIC......	64	NA	131 742	27.5	64.2
089 CHR & MISS AL.	1	12	47	–	–
093 CHR CH (DISC).	7	1 753	2 236	0.5	1.1
097 CHR CHS&CHS CR	4	280	356*	0.1	0.2
101 C.M.E........	1	153	194*	–	0.1
105 CHRISTIAN REF.	1	40	60	–	–
123 CH GOD (ANDER)	1	60	180	–	0.1
127 CH GOD (CLEVE)	2	41	52*	–	–
133 CH GOD(7TH)DEN	1	83	105*	–	0.1
151 L-D SAINTS....	13	NA	4 606	1.0	2.2
165 CH OF NAZARENE	8	865	1 244	0.3	0.6
167 CHS OF CHRIST.	12	1 725	2 189	0.5	1.1
175 CONGR CHR CHS.	1	63	80*	–	–
193 EPISCOPAL.....	7	3 301	4 462	0.9	2.2
215 EVAN METH CH..	1	16	20*	–	–
263 INT FOURSQ GOS	2	348	442*	0.1	0.2
270 CONSRV JUDAISM	1	282	358*	0.1	0.2
271 REFORM JUDAISM	1	900	1 143*	0.2	0.6
281 LUTH CH AMER..	4	776	1 072	0.2	0.5
283 LUTH--MO SYNOD	4	1 007	1 346	0.3	0.7
290 METRO COMM CHS	0	15	30	–	–
349 PENT HOLINESS	3	117	149*	–	0.1
353 CHR BRETHREN..	2	65	100	–	–
357 PRESB CH US...	5	930	1 181*	0.2	0.6
403 SALVATION ARMY	2	214	217	–	0.1
413 S.D.A.........	3	624	793*	0.2	0.4
419 SO BAPT CONV..	37	23 624	30 006*	6.3	14.6
435 UNITARIAN-UNIV	1	101	128*	–	0.1
443 UN C OF CHRIST	2	210	267*	0.1	0.1
449 UN METHODIST..	21	11 812	15 002*	3.1	7.3
453 UN PRES CH USA	6	1 942	2 466*	0.5	1.2
469 WELS..........	2	211	285	0.1	0.1
ERATH	60	12 091	15 964*	70.8	100.0
053 ASSEMB OF GOD.	3	70	139	0.6	0.9
081 CATHOLIC......	2	NA	1 348	6.0	8.4
093 CHR CH (DISC).	2	257	332	1.5	2.1
101 C.M.E........	1	98	115*	0.5	0.7
127 CH GOD (CLEVE)	1	29	34*	0.2	0.2
151 L-D SAINTS....	1	NA	95	0.4	0.6
165 CH OF NAZARENE	1	72	85	0.4	0.5
167 CHS OF CHRIST.	10	1 600	2 035	9.0	12.7
193 EPISCOPAL.....	2	148	218	1.0	1.4
283 LUTH--MO SYNOD	1	119	154	0.7	1.0
357 PRESB CH US...	1	62	73*	0.3	0.5
419 SO BAPT CONV..	24	7 592	8 931*	39.6	55.9
449 UN METHODIST..	10	1 982	2 332*	10.3	14.6
453 UN PRES CH USA	1	62	73*	0.3	0.5
FALLS	53	8 206	11 901*	66.3	100.0
029 AMER LUTH CH..	1	290	339	1.9	2.8
053 ASSEMB OF GOD.	2	188	239	1.3	2.0
081 CATHOLIC......	2	NA	2 010	11.2	16.9
093 CHR CH (DISC).	1	42	65	0.4	0.5
167 CHS OF CHRIST.	6	400	510	2.8	4.3
193 EPISCOPAL.....	1	110	171	1.0	1.4
283 LUTH--MO SYNOD	3	571	713	4.0	6.0
357 PRESB CH US...	2	106	126*	0.7	1.1
419 SO BAPT CONV..	18	4 416	5 251*	29.3	44.1
443 UN C OF CHRIST	2	274	326*	1.8	2.7
449 UN METHODIST..	13	1 702	2 024*	11.3	17.0
453 UN PRES CH USA	2	107	127*	0.7	1.1
FANNIN	117	14 459	17 586*	72.4	100.0
053 ASSEMB OF GOD.	5	114	157	0.6	0.9
081 CATHOLIC......	1	NA	162	0.7	0.9
093 CHR CH (DISC).	6	457	643	2.6	3.7
101 C.M.E........	4	618	731*	3.0	4.2
127 CH GOD (CLEVE)	3	212	251*	1.0	1.4
151 L-D SAINTS....	1	NA	38	0.2	0.2
165 CH OF NAZARENE	1	135	159	0.7	0.9
167 CHS OF CHRIST.	25	1 500	1 910	7.9	10.9
193 EPISCOPAL.....	2	58	89	0.4	0.5
283 LUTH--MO SYNOD	2	73	95	0.4	0.5
357 PRESB CH US...	4	151	191*	0.7	1.0
419 SO BAPT CONV..	35	8 655	10 233*	42.1	58.2
449 UN METHODIST..	24	2 336	2 762*	11.4	15.7
453 UN PRES CH USA	4	150	177*	0.7	1.0
FAYETTE	56	6 064	15 066*	80.0	100.0
029 AMER LUTH CH..	10	2 226	2 576	13.7	17.1
053 ASSEMB OF GOD.	2	69	97	0.5	0.6
081 CATHOLIC......	16	NA	7 920	42.1	52.6
167 CHS OF CHRIST.	3	250	320	1.7	2.1
193 EPISCOPAL.....	1	116	158	0.8	1.0
281 LUTH CH AMER..	1	207	241	1.3	1.6
283 LUTH--MO SYNOD	4	1 153	1 360	7.2	9.0
357 PRESB CH US...	1	171	200*	1.1	1.3
413 S.D.A.........	1	21	25*	0.1	0.2
419 SO BAPT CONV..	5	972	1 139*	6.0	7.6
443 UN C OF CHRIST	1	133	156*	0.8	1.0
449 UN METHODIST..	11	746	874*	4.6	5.8
FISHER	23	3 662	5 379*	91.3	100.0
053 ASSEMB OF GOD.	1	18	31	0.5	0.6
081 CATHOLIC......	3	NA	950	16.1	17.7
165 CH OF NAZARENE	1	28	40	0.7	0.7
167 CHS OF CHRIST.	2	150	190	3.2	3.5
263 INT FOURSQ GOS	1	15	18*	0.3	0.3
419 SO BAPT CONV..	11	2 869	3 450*	58.6	64.1
449 UN METHODIST..	4	582	700*	11.9	13.0
FLOYD	28	6 005	8 997*	91.5	100.0
029 AMER LUTH CH..	1	83	94	1.0	1.0
053 ASSEMB OF GOD.	5	257	389	4.0	4.3
081 CATHOLIC......	2	NA	1 400	14.2	15.6
093 CHR CH (DISC).	1	72	105	1.1	1.2
101 C.M.E........	1	40	50*	0.5	0.6
165 CH OF NAZARENE	1	36	44	0.4	0.5
167 CHS OF CHRIST.	5	650	825	8.4	9.2
419 SO BAPT CONV..	9	3 846	4 812*	48.9	53.5
449 UN METHODIST..	3	1 021	1 278*	13.0	14.2
FOARD	10	1 498	1 878*	87.0	100.0
053 ASSEMB OF GOD.	1	48	114	5.3	6.1
081 CATHOLIC......	1	NA	35	1.6	1.9
097 CHR CHS&CHS CR	1	125	148*	6.9	7.9
167 CHS OF CHRIST.	2	119	153	7.1	8.1
419 SO BAPT CONV..	3	815	965*	44.7	51.4
449 UN METHODIST..	2	391	463*	21.5	24.7
FORT BEND	86	18 191	49 336*	37.7	100.0
017 AMER BAPT ASSN	1	50	50	–	0.1
029 AMER LUTH CH..	4	746	997	0.8	2.0
053 ASSEMB OF GOD.	7	724	826	0.6	1.7
081 CATHOLIC......	8	NA	25 410	19.4	51.5
093 CHR CH (DISC).	1	95	109	0.1	0.2
097 CHR CHS&CHS CR	1	125	160*	0.1	0.3
123 CH GOD (ANDER)	4	129	387	0.3	0.8
127 CH GOD (CLEVE)	11	594	758*	0.6	1.5
133 CH GOD(7TH)DEN	1	3	4*	–	–
151 L-D SAINTS....	2	NA	381	0.3	0.8
167 CHS OF CHRIST.	7	1 010	1 230	0.9	2.5
193 EPISCOPAL.....	3	655	935	0.7	1.9
281 LUTH CH AMER..	1	215	347	0.3	0.7
283 LUTH--MO SYNOD	2	540	758	0.6	1.5
357 PRESB CH US...	1	556	710*	0.5	1.4
413 S.D.A.........	2	55	70*	0.1	0.1
419 SO BAPT CONV..	12	6 050	7 723*	5.9	15.7
443 UN C OF CHRIST	3	1 283	1 638*	1.3	3.3
449 UN METHODIST..	12	4 752	6 066*	4.6	12.3
453 UN PRES CH USA	3	609	777*	0.6	1.6
FRANKLIN	27	4 033	4 848*	70.3	100.0
053 ASSEMB OF GOD.	1	91	104	1.5	2.1
059 BAPT MISS ASSN	2	463	557*	8.1	11.5
093 CHR CH (DISC).	1	26	29	0.4	0.6
101 C.M.E........	4	316	380*	5.5	7.8
127 CH GOD (CLEVE)	1	35	42*	0.6	0.9
165 CH OF NAZARENE	1	14	7	0.1	0.1
167 CHS OF CHRIST.	3	175	225	3.3	4.6
419 SO BAPT CONV..	11	2 440	2 935*	42.6	60.5
449 UN METHODIST..	3	473	569*	8.3	11.7

NA—Not applicable   *Total adherents estimated from known number of communicant, confirmed, full members.   —Represents a percent less than 0.1.   Percentages may not total due to rounding.

TEXAS

Table 4. Churches and Church Membership by County and Denomination: 1980

County and Denomination	Number of churches	Communicant, confirmed, full members	Total adherents Number	Percent of total population	Percent of total adherents
FREESTONE	52	6 557	8 175*	55.1	100.0
053 ASSEMB OF GOD.	4	222	268	1.8	3.3
059 BAPT MISS ASSN	10	1 600	1 941*	13.1	23.7
081 CATHOLIC......	2	NA	200	1.3	2.4
167 CHS OF CHRIST.	6	275	350	2.4	4.3
283 LUTH--MO SYNOD	1	25	35	0.2	0.4
357 PRESB CH US...	4	88	107*	0.7	1.3
419 SO BAPT CONV..	7	2 692	3 266*	22.0	40.0
449 UN METHODIST..	14	1 566	1 900*	12.8	23.2
453 UN PRES CH USA	4	89	108*	0.7	1.3
FRIO	25	3 063	8 271*	60.0	100.0
053 ASSEMB OF GOD.	3	102	124	0.9	1.5
081 CATHOLIC......	5	NA	4 320	31.3	52.2
093 CHR CH (DISC).	1	14	22	0.2	0.3
167 CHS OF CHRIST.	4	200	225	1.6	2.7
193 EPISCOPAL.....	1	5	9	0.1	0.1
283 LUTH--MO SYNOD	1	59	71	0.5	0.9
419 SO BAPT CONV..	4	1 662	2 168*	15.7	26.2
449 UN METHODIST..	5	986	1 286*	9.3	15.5
453 UN PRES CH USA	1	35	46*	0.3	0.6
GAINES	28	6 086	8 808*	67.0	100.0
017 AMER BAPT ASSN	1	125	125	1.0	1.4
053 ASSEMB OF GOD.	4	318	592	4.5	6.7
059 BAPT MISS ASSN	1	72	92*	0.7	1.0
081 CATHOLIC......	2	NA	800	6.1	9.1
093 CHR CH (DISC).	1	59	61	0.5	0.7
127 CH GOD (CLEVE)	1	92	117*	0.9	1.3
151 L-D SAINTS....	1	NA	103	0.8	1.2
165 CH OF NAZARENE	1	31	50	0.4	0.6
167 CHS OF CHRIST.	7	500	635	4.8	7.2
357 PRESB CH US...	1	192	245*	1.9	2.8
419 SO BAPT CONV..	6	4 081	5 203*	39.6	59.1
449 UN METHODIST..	2	616	785*	6.0	8.9
GALVESTON	163	48 267	94 943*	48.5	100.0
017 AMER BAPT ASSN	6	1 050	1 050	0.5	1.1
029 AMER LUTH CH..	6	2 468	3 180	1.6	3.3
053 ASSEMB OF GOD.	14	905	1 254	0.6	1.3
081 CATHOLIC......	15	NA	32 948	16.8	34.7
093 CHR CH (DISC).	4	642	866	0.4	0.9
097 CHR CHS&CHS CR	1	200	245*	0.1	0.3
101 C.M.E.........	2	1 058	1 293*	0.7	1.4
123 CH GOD (ANDER)	2	48	144	0.1	0.2
127 CH GOD (CLEVE)	1	45	55*	—	0.1
151 L-D SAINTS....	3	NA	1 320	0.7	1.4
165 CH OF NAZARENE	4	261	423	0.2	0.4
167 CHS OF CHRIST.	17	1 566	2 218	1.1	2.3
193 EPISCOPAL.....	10	3 989	5 725	2.9	6.0
226 FRIENDS-USA...	4	933	1 141*	0.6	1.2
270 CONSRV JUDAISM	1	140	171*	0.1	0.2
271 REFORM JUDAISM	1	396	484*	0.2	0.5
281 LUTH CH AMER..	1	140	173	0.1	0.2
283 LUTH--MO SYNOD	3	1 269	1 621	0.8	1.7
290 METRO COMM CHS	1	30	60	—	0.1
349 PENT HOLINESS.	3	134	164*	0.1	0.2
357 PRESB CH US...	7	1 781	2 177*	1.1	2.3
403 SALVATION ARMY	1	61	148	0.1	0.2
413 S.D.A.........	2	69	84*	—	0.1
419 SO BAPT CONV..	30	21 529	26 320*	13.4	27.7
435 UNITARIAN-UNIV	1	64	78*	—	0.1
449 UN METHODIST..	23	9 489	11 601*	5.9	12.2
GARZA	21	2 495	3 472*	65.1	100.0
053 ASSEMB OF GOD.	1	18	31	0.6	0.9
081 CATHOLIC......	1	NA	300	5.6	8.6
093 CHR CH (DISC).	1	106	156	2.9	4.5
165 CH OF NAZARENE	1	80	110	2.1	3.2
167 CHS OF CHRIST.	4	300	398	7.5	11.5
283 LUTH--MO SYNOD	1	17	19	0.4	0.5
357 PRESB CH US...	1	49	61*	1.1	1.8
419 SO BAPT CONV..	8	1 482	1 845*	34.6	53.1
449 UN METHODIST..	2	394	491*	9.2	14.1
453 UN PRES CH USA	1	49	61*	1.1	1.8
GILLESPIE	22	5 702	10 251*	75.8	100.0
029 AMER LUTH CH..	8	3 513	4 172	30.8	40.7
053 ASSEMB OF GOD.	1	36	53	0.4	0.5
081 CATHOLIC......	3	NA	3 431	25.4	33.5
167 CHS OF CHRIST.	1	50	64	0.5	0.6
193 EPISCOPAL.....	1	137	212	1.6	2.1
203 EVAN FREE CH..	1	42	50*	0.4	0.5
357 PRESB CH US...	1	110	130*	1.0	1.3
413 S.D.A.........	1	19	22*	0.2	0.2
419 SO BAPT CONV..	2	780	920*	6.8	9.0
449 UN METHODIST..	2	960	1 132*	8.4	11.0
453 UN PRES CH USA	1	55	65*	0.5	0.6
GLASSCOCK	4	275	895*	68.6	100.0
081 CATHOLIC......	1	NA	540	41.4	60.3
167 CHS OF CHRIST.	1	40	50	3.8	5.6
419 SO BAPT CONV..	1	164	213*	16.3	23.8
449 UN METHODIST..	1	71	92*	7.1	10.3
GOLIAD	18	1 502	3 416*	65.8	100.0
081 CATHOLIC......	5	NA	1 600	30.8	46.8
167 CHS OF CHRIST.	1	35	45	0.9	1.3
193 EPISCOPAL.....	1	50	58	1.1	1.7
281 LUTH CH AMER..	4	727	868	16.7	25.4
357 PRESB CH US...	1	92	113*	2.2	3.3
419 SO BAPT CONV..	2	347	425*	8.2	12.4
449 UN METHODIST..	4	251	307*	5.9	9.0
GONZALES	44	6 124	11 338*	67.2	100.0
029 AMER LUTH CH..	1	305	400	2.4	3.5
053 ASSEMB OF GOD.	2	58	78	0.5	0.7
081 CATHOLIC......	5	NA	3 805	22.5	33.6
167 CHS OF CHRIST.	2	100	127	0.8	1.1
193 EPISCOPAL.....	1	99	127	0.8	1.1
357 PRESB CH US...	1	206	252*	1.5	2.2
419 SO BAPT CONV..	16	3 644	4 456*	26.4	39.3
449 UN METHODIST..	14	1 674	2 047*	12.1	18.1
453 UN PRES CH USA	2	38	46*	0.3	0.4
GRAY	47	15 548	21 074*	79.9	100.0
017 AMER BAPT ASSN	1	25	25	0.1	0.1
053 ASSEMB OF GOD.	4	382	573	2.2	2.7
081 CATHOLIC......	1	NA	1 500	5.7	7.1
093 CHR CH (DISC).	1	730	880	3.3	4.2
097 CHR CHS&CHS CR	1	120	145*	0.5	0.7
101 C.M.E.........	2	335	406*	1.5	1.9
127 CH GOD (CLEVE)	1	163	197*	0.7	0.9
151 L-D SAINTS....	1	NA	245	0.9	1.2
157 CH OF BRETHREN	1	102	124*	0.5	0.6
165 CH OF NAZARENE	1	87	130	0.5	0.6
167 CHS OF CHRIST.	8	1 335	1 854	7.0	8.8
193 EPISCOPAL.....	1	276	351	1.3	1.7
263 INT FOURSQ GOS	1	58	70*	0.3	0.3
283 LUTH--MO SYNOD	1	171	247	0.9	1.2
349 PENT HOLINESS.	4	170	206*	0.8	1.0
357 PRESB CH US...	1	190	230*	0.9	1.1
403 SALVATION ARMY	1	65	160	0.6	0.8
413 S.D.A.........	1	27	33*	0.1	0.2
419 SO BAPT CONV..	9	8 959	10 849*	41.1	51.5
449 UN METHODIST..	5	2 163	2 619*	9.9	12.4
453 UN PRES CH USA	1	190	230*	0.9	1.1
GRAYSON	195	47 292	60 802*	67.7	100.0
017 AMER BAPT ASSN	13	2 286	2 286	2.5	3.8
019 AMER BAPT USA.	1	44	53*	0.1	0.1
029 AMER LUTH CH..	1	163	208	0.2	0.3
053 ASSEMB OF GOD.	11	1 552	2 367	2.6	3.9
059 BAPT MISS ASSN	1	82	98*	0.1	0.2
081 CATHOLIC......	2	NA	2 335	2.6	3.8
093 CHR CH (DISC).	6	929	1 324	1.5	2.2
097 CHR CHS&CHS CR	1	20	24*	—	—
101 C.M.E.........	8	1 251	1 498*	1.7	2.5
127 CH GOD (CLEVE)	3	193	231*	0.3	0.4
151 L-D SAINTS....	2	NA	279	0.3	0.5
165 CH OF NAZARENE	3	371	591	0.7	1.0
167 CHS OF CHRIST.	33	3 760	4 655	5.2	7.7
185 CUMBER PRESB..	2	38	94	0.1	0.2
193 EPISCOPAL.....	2	626	915	1.0	1.5
271 REFORM JUDAISM	1	74	89*	0.1	0.1
283 LUTH--MO SYNOD	1	200	260	0.3	0.4
349 PENT HOLINESS.	1	15	18*	—	—
357 PRESB CH US...	9	916	1 097*	1.2	1.8
403 SALVATION ARMY	2	111	866	1.0	1.4
413 S.D.A.........	1	108	129*	0.1	0.2
419 SO BAPT CONV..	51	27 351	32 759*	36.5	53.9
449 UN METHODIST..	31	6 286	7 529*	8.4	12.4
453 UN PRES CH USA	9	916	1 097*	1.2	1.8
GREGG	141	46 097	60 552*	60.9	100.0
017 AMER BAPT ASSN	6	1 627	1 627	1.6	2.7
029 AMER LUTH CH..	1	265	346	0.3	0.6
053 ASSEMB OF GOD.	12	1 147	1 569	1.6	2.6
059 BAPT MISS ASSN	4	935	1 143*	1.1	1.9
081 CATHOLIC......	3	NA	2 440	2.4	4.0
089 CHR & MISS AL.	2	282	705	0.7	1.2
093 CHR CH (DISC).	7	1 653	2 387	2.4	3.9
097 CHR CHS&CHS CR	1	100	122*	0.1	0.2
101 C.M.E.........	9	2 222	2 717*	2.7	4.5
123 CH GOD (ANDER)	3	275	825	0.8	1.4
127 CH GOD (CLEVE)	2	198	242*	0.2	0.4
133 CH GOD(7TH)DEN	1	3	4*	—	—
165 CH OF NAZARENE	4	422	582	0.6	1.0
167 CHS OF CHRIST.	17	2 800	3 565	3.6	5.9
185 CUMBER PRESB..	4	763	1 293	1.3	2.1
193 EPISCOPAL.....	4	1 138	1 548	1.6	2.6
203 EVAN FREE CH..	1	61	75*	0.1	0.1
244 GRACE BRETHREN	1	13	16*	—	—
263 INT FOURSQ GOS	1	15	18*	—	—
271 REFORM JUDAISM	1	100	122*	0.1	0.2
283 LUTH--MO SYNOD	2	246	316	0.3	0.5
353 CHR BRETHREN..	1	50	65	0.1	0.1
357 PRESB CH US...	6	786	961*	1.0	1.6
403 SALVATION ARMY	1	110	137	0.1	0.2
413 S.D.A.........	1	133	163*	0.2	0.3
419 SO BAPT CONV..	26	22 605	27 639*	27.8	45.6
449 UN METHODIST..	14	7 358	8 997*	9.0	14.9
453 UN PRES CH USA	6	790	966*	1.0	1.6
GRIMES	51	5 198	9 490*	69.9	100.0
005 AME ZION......	1	25	33	0.2	0.3
053 ASSEMB OF GOD.	2	35	76	0.6	0.8

NA—Not applicable   *Total adherents estimated from known number of communicant, confirmed, full members.   —Represents a percent less than 0.1.   Percentages may not total due to rounding.

Table 4. Churches and Church Membership by County and Denomination: 1980

County and Denomination	Number of churches	Communicant, confirmed, full members	Total adherents		
			Number	Percent of total population	Percent of total adherents
059 BAPT MISS ASSN	5	310	378*	2.8	4.0
081 CATHOLIC......	5	NA	3 086	22.7	32.5
167 CHS OF CHRIST.	4	200	255	1.9	2.7
193 EPISCOPAL.....	1	68	101	0.7	1.1
283 LUTH--MO SYNOD	3	728	886	6.5	9.3
357 PRESB CH US...	1	182	222*	1.6	2.3
413 S.D.A.........	1	46	56*	0.4	0.6
419 SO BAPT CONV..	12	2 472	3 016*	22.2	31.8
449 UN METHODIST..	15	1 099	1 341*	9.9	14.1
453 UN PRES CH USA	1	33	40*	0.3	0.4
GUADALUPE	44	11 302	23 433*	50.2	100.0
017 AMER BAPT ASSN	1	25	25	0.1	0.1
029 AMER LUTH CH..	4	2 754	3 446	7.4	14.7
053 ASSEMB OF GOD.	3	184	254	0.5	1.1
081 CATHOLIC......	4	NA	9 414	20.2	40.2
097 CHR CHS&CHS CR	1	35	43*	0.1	0.2
151 L-D SAINTS....	1	NA	61	0.1	0.3
167 CHS OF CHRIST.	2	60	76	0.2	0.3
193 EPISCOPAL.....	1	354	468	1.0	2.0
283 LUTH--MO SYNOD	2	329	407	0.9	1.7
313 N AM BAPT CONF	1	16	20*	–	0.1
349 PENT HOLINESS	1	43	53*	0.1	0.2
357 PRESB CH US...	1	158	193*	0.4	0.8
413 S.D.A.........	1	69	84*	0.2	0.4
419 SO BAPT CONV..	10	3 413	4 170*	8.9	17.8
443 UN C OF CHRIST	4	1 801	2 201*	4.7	9.4
449 UN METHODIST..	7	2 061	2 518*	5.4	10.7
HALE	71	21 371	32 055*	85.3	100.0
053 ASSEMB OF GOD.	6	487	656	1.7	2.0
059 BAPT MISS ASSN	1	62	78*	0.2	0.2
081 CATHOLIC......	5	NA	5 000	13.3	15.6
093 CHR CH (DISC).	1	280	401	1.1	1.3
101 C.M.E.........	1	115	144*	0.4	0.4
127 CH GOD (CLEVE)	1	70	88*	0.2	0.3
151 L-D SAINTS....	1	NA	111	0.3	0.3
165 CH OF NAZARENE	5	392	551	1.5	1.7
167 CHS OF CHRIST.	13	2 104	2 572	6.8	8.0
193 EPISCOPAL.....	1	183	222	0.6	0.7
263 INT FOURSQ GOS	1	107	134*	0.4	0.4
283 LUTH--MO SYNOD	1	299	377	1.0	1.2
357 PRESB CH US...	2	274	344*	0.9	1.1
403 SALVATION ARMY	1	63	144	0.4	0.4
413 S.D.A.........	1	29	36*	0.1	0.1
419 SO BAPT CONV..	19	13 002	16 302*	43.4	50.9
449 UN METHODIST..	9	3 631	4 553*	12.1	14.2
453 UN PRES CH USA	2	273	342*	0.9	1.1
HALL	24	4 060	5 419*	96.9	100.0
053 ASSEMB OF GOD.	3	63	81	1.4	1.5
081 CATHOLIC......	2	NA	500	8.9	9.2
097 CHR CHS&CHS CR	1	140	168*	3.0	3.1
127 CH GOD (CLEVE)	1	35	42*	0.8	0.8
167 CHS OF CHRIST.	5	480	610	10.9	11.3
357 PRESB CH US...	1	13	16*	0.3	0.3
419 SO BAPT CONV..	6	2 586	3 109*	55.6	57.4
449 UN METHODIST..	4	729	876*	15.7	16.2
453 UN PRES CH USA	1	14	17*	0.3	0.3
HAMILTON	38	4 865	5 989*	72.2	100.0
029 AMER LUTH CH..	2	221	274	3.3	4.6
053 ASSEMB OF GOD.	1	17	32	0.4	0.5
081 CATHOLIC......	1	NA	208	2.5	3.5
093 CHR CH (DISC).	1	14	22	0.3	0.4
167 CHS OF CHRIST.	8	600	765	9.2	12.8
193 EPISCOPAL.....	1	17	41	0.5	0.7
283 LUTH--MO SYNOD	2	558	654	7.9	10.9
357 PRESB CH US...	1	50	58*	0.7	1.0
419 SO BAPT CONV..	15	2 314	2 688*	32.4	44.9
449 UN METHODIST..	5	1 024	1 189*	14.3	19.9
453 UN PRES CH USA	1	50	58*	0.7	1.0
HANSFORD	15	3 560	4 837*	77.9	100.0
029 AMER LUTH CH..	1	157	191	3.1	3.9
053 ASSEMB OF GOD.	1	40	68	1.1	1.4
081 CATHOLIC......	1	NA	400	6.4	8.3
093 CHR CH (DISC).	2	246	340	5.5	7.0
167 CHS OF CHRIST.	2	341	400	6.4	8.3
357 PRESB CH US...	1	26	32*	0.5	0.7
413 S.D.A.........	1	18	22*	0.4	0.5
419 SO BAPT CONV..	3	1 625	2 013*	32.4	41.6
449 UN METHODIST..	2	1 081	1 339*	21.6	27.7
453 UN PRES CH USA	1	26	32*	0.5	0.7
HARDEMAN	22	4 101	4 997*	78.5	100.0
017 AMER BAPT ASSN	1	25	25	0.4	0.5
053 ASSEMB OF GOD.	1	46	75	1.2	1.5
081 CATHOLIC......	1	NA	115	1.8	2.3
093 CHR CH (DISC).	1	123	164	2.6	3.3
101 C.M.E.........	1	58	70*	1.1	1.4
165 CH OF NAZARENE	2	84	79	1.2	1.6
167 CHS OF CHRIST.	5	615	695	10.9	13.9
193 EPISCOPAL.....	1	26	26	0.4	0.5
357 PRESB CH US...	1	26	31*	0.5	0.6
419 SO BAPT CONV..	4	2 176	2 611*	41.0	52.3
449 UN METHODIST..	3	895	1 074*	16.9	21.5
453 UN PRES CH USA	1	27	32*	0.5	0.6

County and Denomination	Number of churches	Communicant, confirmed, full members	Total adherents		
			Number	Percent of total population	Percent of total adherents
HARDIN	62	14 834	20 990*	51.5	100.0
017 AMER BAPT ASSN	1	125	125	0.3	0.6
029 AMER LUTH CH..	1	75	111	0.3	0.5
053 ASSEMB OF GOD.	12	982	1 122	2.8	5.3
059 BAPT MISS ASSN	1	143	178*	0.4	0.8
081 CATHOLIC......	3	NA	2 174	5.3	10.4
093 CHR CH (DISC).	1	53	60	0.1	0.3
097 CHR CHS&CHS CR	1	100	125*	0.3	0.6
127 CH GOD (CLEVE)	1	101	126*	0.3	0.6
151 L-D SAINTS....	1	NA	460	1.1	2.2
167 CHS OF CHRIST.	6	400	510	1.3	2.4
193 EPISCOPAL.....	1	156	172	0.4	0.8
357 PRESB CH US...	1	138	172*	0.4	0.8
419 SO BAPT CONV..	24	10 682	13 313*	32.7	63.4
449 UN METHODIST..	8	1 879	2 342*	5.8	11.2
HARRIS	1 105	544 995	1 027 768*	42.7	100.0
005 AME ZION......	1	320	371		–
017 AMER BAPT ASSN	20	3 704	3 704	0.2	0.4
019 AMER BAPT USA.	4	1 810	2 230*	0.1	0.2
029 AMER LUTH CH..	16	8 579	11 080	0.5	1.1
053 ASSEMB OF GOD.	86	16 386	22 785	0.9	2.2
059 BAPT MISS ASSN	20	5 264	6 485*	0.3	0.6
081 CATHOLIC......	90	NA	328 243	13.6	31.9
089 CHR & MISS AL.	4	276	523		0.1
093 CHR CH (DISC).	22	6 955	10 018	0.4	1.0
097 CHR CHS&CHS CR	14	2 606	3 211*	0.1	0.3
101 C.M.E.........	18	8 505	10 478*	0.4	1.0
105 CHRISTIAN REF.	1	15	29	–	–
123 CH GOD (ANDER)	12	2 010	6 030	0.3	0.6
127 CH GOD (CLEVE)	7	529	652*		0.1
133 CH GOD(7TH)DEN	3	172	212*	–	–
151 L-D SAINTS....	23	NA	10 362	0.4	1.0
164 CH LUTH CONF..	1	78	114	–	–
165 CH OF NAZARENE	23	2 749	5 068	0.2	0.5
167 CHS OF CHRIST.	127	24 400	31 055	1.3	3.0
175 CONGR CHR CHS.	1	500	616*		0.1
185 CUMBER PRESB..	1	153	318	–	–
193 EPISCOPAL.....	43	31 738	40 103	1.7	3.9
203 EVAN FREE CH..	1	60	74*	–	–
221 FREE METHODIST	1	30	39	–	–
226 FRIENDS-USA...	1	83	102*	–	–
263 INT FOURSQ GOS	1	38	47*	–	–
270 CONSRV JUDAISM	5	3 656	4 504*	0.2	0.4
271 REFORM JUDAISM	3	6 052	7 456*	0.3	0.7
281 LUTH CH AMER..	16	4 278	5 896	0.2	0.6
283 LUTH--MO SYNOD	49	24 020	32 194	1.3	3.1
285 MENNONITE CH..	1	58	71*	–	–
287 MENN GEN CONF.	1	60	84	–	–
290 METRO COMM CHS	1	321	642	–	0.1
313 N AM BAPT CONF	2	182	224*	–	–
349 PENT HOLINESS.	5	184	227*	–	–
353 CHR BRETHREN..	5	380	885	–	0.1
356 PRESB CH AMER.	5	351	443	–	–
357 PRESB CH US...	36	21 979	27 078*	1.1	2.6
369 PROT REF CHS..	1	10	26	–	–
403 SALVATION ARMY	4	266	2 778	0.1	0.3
413 S.D.A.........	10	2 382	2 935*	0.1	0.3
415 S-D BAPTIST GC	1	12	15*	–	–
419 SO BAPT CONV..	246	244 518	301 246*	12.5	29.3
435 UNITARIAN-UNIV	5	1 154	1 422*	0.1	0.1
443 UN C OF CHRIST	11	3 095	3 813*	0.2	0.4
449 UN METHODIST..	135	108 792	134 032*	5.6	13.0
453 UN PRES CH USA	19	5 904	7 274*	0.3	0.7
469 WELS..........	3	381	574	–	0.1
HARRISON	115	23 333	30 921*	59.2	100.0
017 AMER BAPT ASSN	2	283	283	0.5	0.9
019 AMER BAPT USA.	1	80	98*	0.2	0.3
053 ASSEMB OF GOD.	4	247	323	0.6	1.0
059 BAPT MISS ASSN	3	255	314*	0.6	1.0
081 CATHOLIC......	1	NA	930	1.8	3.0
093 CHR CH (DISC).	3	319	465	0.9	1.5
101 C.M.E.........	14	2 143	2 638*	5.0	8.5
127 CH GOD (CLEVE)	1	?	?	?	?
151 L-D SAINTS....	3	NA	1 114	2.1	3.6
165 CH OF NAZARENE	2	133	145	0.3	0.5
167 CHS OF CHRIST.	9	1 000	1 273	2.4	4.1
185 CUMBER PRESB..	2	243	434	0.8	1.4
193 EPISCOPAL.....	2	480	552	1.1	1.8
281 LUTH CH AMER..	1	51	70	0.1	0.2
357 PRESB CH US...	3	217	267*	0.5	0.9
413 S.D.A.........	2	72	89*	0.2	0.3
419 SO BAPT CONV..	36	13 754	16 932*	32.4	54.8
421 SO METHODIST..	1	47	59	0.1	0.2
449 UN METHODIST..	22	3 791	4 667*	8.9	15.1
453 UN PRES CH USA	3	218	268*	0.5	0.9
HARTLEY	7	1 007	1 343*	33.7	100.0
081 CATHOLIC......	0	NA	100	2.5	7.4
165 CH OF NAZARENE	1	57	60	1.5	4.5
167 CHS OF CHRIST.	1	30	38	1.0	2.8
419 SO BAPT CONV..	2	433	539*	13.5	40.1
449 UN METHODIST..	3	487	606*	15.2	45.1
HASKELL	36	6 613	7 901*	102.3	100.0
029 AMER LUTH CH..	2	349	414	5.4	5.2
053 ASSEMB OF GOD.	1	63	104	1.3	1.3
059 BAPT MISS ASSN	2	169	201*	2.6	2.5
081 CATHOLIC......	1	NA	?	?	?

NA—Not applicable   *Total adherents estimated from known number of communicant, confirmed, full members.   —Represents a percent less than 0.1.   Percentages may not total due to rounding.

Table 4. Churches and Church Membership by County and Denomination: 1980

County and Denomination	Number of churches	Communicant, confirmed, full members	Total adherents		
			Number	Percent of total population	Percent of total adherents
093 CHR CH (DISC).	1	15	23	0.3	0.3
097 CHR CHS&CHS CR	1	96	114*	1.5	1.4
127 CH GOD (CLEVE)	2	42	50*	0.6	0.6
167 CHS OF CHRIST.	4	455	544	7.0	6.9
263 INT FOURSQ GOS	2	137	163*	2.1	2.1
357 PRESB CH US...	2	59	70*	0.9	0.9
419 SO BAPT CONV..	10	4 440	5 281*	68.4	66.8
449 UN METHODIST..	6	730	868*	11.2	11.0
453 UN PRES CH USA	2	58	69*	0.9	0.9
HAYS	44	10 817	17 186*	42.3	100.0
029 AMER LUTH CH..	1	342	438	1.1	2.5
053 ASSEMB OF GOD.	3	116	140	0.3	0.8
081 CATHOLIC......	4	NA	3 920	9.7	22.8
093 CHR CH (DISC).	1	175	425	1.0	2.5
151 L-D SAINTS....	1	NA	182	0.4	1.1
165 CH OF NAZARENE	1	?	?	?	?
167 CHS OF CHRIST.	4	400	510	1.3	3.0
193 EPISCOPAL.....	1	368	456	1.1	2.7
283 LUTH--MO SYNOD	1	106	134	0.3	0.8
349 PENT HOLINESS.	1	23	27*	0.1	0.2
357 PRESB CH US...	2	362	427*	1.1	2.5
413 S.D.A.........	1	94	111*	0.3	0.6
419 SO BAPT CONV..	13	6 815	8 038*	19.8	46.8
443 UN C OF CHRIST	2	198	234*	0.6	1.4
449 UN METHODIST..	8	1 818	2 144*	5.3	12.5
HEMPHILL	11	1 791	2 676*	50.5	100.0
053 ASSEMB OF GOD.	1	100	234	4.4	8.7
081 CATHOLIC......	1	NA	250	4.7	9.3
097 CHR CHS&CHS CR	1	250	314*	5.9	11.7
165 CH OF NAZARENE	1	7	21	0.4	0.8
167 CHS OF CHRIST.	1	168	265	5.0	9.9
357 PRESB CH US...	1	86	108*	2.0	4.0
419 SO BAPT CONV..	2	676	850*	16.0	31.8
449 UN METHODIST..	2	418	526*	9.9	19.7
453 UN PRES CH USA	1	86	108*	2.0	4.0
HENDERSON	100	16 973	21 188*	49.7	100.0
017 AMER BAPT ASSN	2	101	101	0.2	0.5
053 ASSEMB OF GOD.	9	928	1 308	3.1	6.2
059 BAPT MISS ASSN	13	2 481	2 959*	6.9	14.0
081 CATHOLIC......	2	NA	464	1.1	2.2
093 CHR CH (DISC).	2	258	338	0.8	1.6
101 C.M.E.........	10	1 453	1 733*	4.1	8.2
123 CH GOD (ANDER)	1	14	42	0.1	0.2
151 L-D SAINTS....	1	NA	150	0.4	0.7
165 CH OF NAZARENE	1	21	34	0.1	0.2
167 CHS OF CHRIST.	12	850	1 080	2.5	5.1
185 CUMBER PRESB..	1	12	22	0.1	0.1
193 EPISCOPAL.....	1	73	102	0.2	0.5
283 LUTH--MO SYNOD	1	125	146	0.3	0.7
357 PRESB CH US...	1	142	169*	0.4	0.8
413 S.D.A.........	1	56	67*	0.2	0.3
419 SO BAPT CONV..	24	7 654	9 128*	21.4	43.1
449 UN METHODIST..	17	2 664	3 177*	7.5	15.0
453 UN PRES CH USA	1	141	168*	0.4	0.8
HIDALGO	211	31 510	188 894*	66.7	100.0
017 AMER BAPT ASSN	4	200	200	0.1	0.1
029 AMER LUTH CH..	5	664	926	0.3	0.5
053 ASSEMB OF GOD.	12	991	1 704	0.6	0.9
059 BAPT MISS ASSN	1	75	98*	–	0.1
075 BRETHREN IN CR	1	57	86	–	–
081 CATHOLIC......	50	NA	144 710	51.1	76.6
089 CHR & MISS AL.	4	206	324	0.1	0.2
093 CHR CH (DISC).	7	1 064	1 522	0.5	0.8
097 CHR CHS&CHS CR	3	461	601*	0.2	0.3
123 CH GOD (ANDER)	1	32	96	–	0.1
127 CH GOD (CLEVE)	1	28	37*	–	–
133 CH GOD(7TH)DEN	1	28	37*	–	–
151 L-D SAINTS....	3	NA	1 870	0.7	1.0
165 CH OF NAZARENE	8	350	804	0.3	0.4
167 CHS OF CHRIST.	14	1 062	1 386	0.5	0.7
193 EPISCOPAL.....	4	1 000	1 328	0.5	0.7
199 EVAN CONGR CH.	1	38	50*	–	–
201 EVAN COV CH AM	1	59	77*	–	–
221 FREE METHODIST	1	22	81	–	–
237 GC MENN BR CHS	6	217	283*	0.1	0.1
263 INT FOURSQ GOS	2	258	336*	0.1	0.2
271 REFORM JUDAISM	1	224	292*	0.1	0.2
281 LUTH CH AMER..	1	170	203	0.1	0.1
283 LUTH--MO SYNOD	4	1 232	1 682	0.6	0.9
313 N AM BAPT CONF	2	73	95*	–	0.1
349 PENT HOLINESS.	7	412	537*	0.2	0.3
357 PRESB CH US...	10	1 749	2 280*	0.8	1.2
403 SALVATION ARMY	1	105	221	0.1	0.1
413 S.D.A.........	7	783	1 021*	0.4	0.5
419 SO BAPT CONV..	25	12 278	16 009*	5.7	8.5
435 UNITARIAN-UNIV	1	17	22*	–	–
449 UN METHODIST..	21	7 620	9 935*	3.5	5.3
469 WELS..........	1	35	41	–	–
HILL	84	11 559	15 375*	61.4	100.0
017 AMER BAPT ASSN	3	765	765	3.1	5.0
029 AMER LUTH CH..	1	96	119	0.5	0.8
053 ASSEMB OF GOD.	2	82	156	0.6	1.0
059 BAPT MISS ASSN	2	419	498*	2.0	3.2
081 CATHOLIC......	3	NA	1 523	6.1	9.9
093 CHR CH (DISC).	1	88	93	0.4	0.6

County and Denomination	Number of churches	Communicant, confirmed, full members	Total adherents		
			Number	Percent of total population	Percent of total adherents
123 CH GOD (ANDER)	1	22	66	0.3	0.4
165 CH OF NAZARENE	2	136	215	0.9	1.4
167 CHS OF CHRIST.	13	839	1 068	4.3	6.9
185 CUMBER PRESB..	4	71	129	0.5	0.8
193 EPISCOPAL.....	2	82	95	0.4	0.6
283 LUTH--MO SYNOD	3	501	597	2.4	3.9
357 PRESB CH US...	3	209	248*	1.0	1.6
413 S.D.A.........	2	76	90*	0.4	0.6
419 SO BAPT CONV..	27	6 463	7 664*	30.7	49.9
449 UN METHODIST..	11	1 467	1 742*	7.0	11.3
453 UN PRES CH USA	3	208	247*	1.0	1.6
469 WELS..........	1	35	50	0.2	0.3
HOCKLEY	51	11 989	16 962*	73.0	100.0
017 AMER BAPT ASSN	1	77	77	0.3	0.5
029 AMER LUTH CH..	1	60	72	0.3	0.4
053 ASSEMB OF GOD.	4	255	376	1.6	2.2
059 BAPT MISS ASSN	3	1 117	1 407*	6.1	8.3
081 CATHOLIC......	1	NA	1 800	7.7	10.6
093 CHR CH (DISC).	1	175	210	0.9	1.2
127 CH GOD (CLEVE)	2	64	81*	0.3	0.5
165 CH OF NAZARENE	2	102	135	0.6	0.8
167 CHS OF CHRIST.	13	1 330	1 695	7.3	10.0
193 EPISCOPAL.....	1	87	125	0.5	0.7
263 INT FOURSQ GOS	1	196	247*	1.1	1.5
357 PRESB CH US...	1	84	106*	0.5	0.6
419 SO BAPT CONV..	12	6 922	8 717*	37.5	51.4
449 UN METHODIST..	5	1 435	1 807*	7.8	10.7
453 UN PRES CH USA	1	85	107*	0.5	0.6
HOOD	32	5 826	7 354*	41.5	100.0
053 ASSEMB OF GOD.	3	166	201	1.1	2.7
081 CATHOLIC......	1	NA	300	1.7	4.1
093 CHR CH (DISC).	1	95	103	0.6	1.4
127 CH GOD (CLEVE)	1	22	26*	0.1	0.4
151 L-D SAINTS....	1	NA	78	0.4	1.1
165 CH OF NAZARENE	1	41	68	0.4	0.9
167 CHS OF CHRIST.	5	275	350	2.0	4.8
283 LUTH--MO SYNOD	1	120	157	0.9	2.1
357 PRESB CH US...	1	34	40*	0.2	0.5
413 S.D.A.........	1	32	38*	0.2	0.5
419 SO BAPT CONV..	11	3 674	4 368*	24.7	59.4
449 UN METHODIST..	4	1 333	1 585*	8.9	21.6
453 UN PRES CH USA	1	34	40*	0.2	0.5
HOPKINS	96	14 070	17 635*	69.8	100.0
017 AMER BAPT ASSN	1	160	160	0.6	0.9
053 ASSEMB OF GOD.	5	175	232	0.9	1.3
059 BAPT MISS ASSN	13	1 886	2 282*	9.0	12.9
081 CATHOLIC......	1	NA	365	1.4	2.1
093 CHR CH (DISC).	1	425	529	2.1	3.0
097 CHR CHS&CHS CR	1	85	103*	0.4	0.6
101 C.M.E.........	2	371	449*	1.8	2.5
127 CH GOD (CLEVE)	1	116	140*	0.6	0.8
151 L-D SAINTS....	1	NA	57	0.2	0.3
165 CH OF NAZARENE	1	102	184	0.7	1.0
167 CHS OF CHRIST.	16	1 600	2 035	8.1	11.5
185 CUMBER PRESB..	1	6	13	0.1	0.1
193 EPISCOPAL.....	1	80	102	0.4	0.6
283 LUTH--MO SYNOD	1	64	95	0.4	0.5
357 PRESB CH US...	3	97	117*	0.5	0.7
413 S.D.A.........	1	35	42*	0.2	0.2
419 SO BAPT CONV..	22	6 019	7 283*	28.8	41.3
449 UN METHODIST..	21	2 749	3 326*	13.2	18.9
453 UN PRES CH USA	3	100	121*	0.5	0.7
HOUSTON	70	8 961	10 883*	48.8	100.0
017 AMER BAPT ASSN	7	350	350	1.6	3.2
053 ASSEMB OF GOD.	3	153	229	1.0	2.1
059 BAPT MISS ASSN	4	701	825*	3.7	7.6
081 CATHOLIC......	2	NA	265	1.2	2.4
093 CHR CH (DISC).	3	166	204	0.9	1.9
101 C.M.E.........	3	381	449*	2.0	4.1
127 CH GOD (CLEVE)	1	73	86*	0.4	0.8
165 CH OF NAZARENE	1	22	29	0.1	0.3
167 CHS OF CHRIST.	10	760	965	4.3	8.9
357 PRESB CH US...	2	151	178*	0.8	1.6
419 SO BAPT CONV..	21	4 779	5 626*	25.2	51.7
449 UN METHODIST..	13	1 425	1 677*	7.5	15.4
HOWARD	68	16 996	27 113*	81.8	100.0
017 AMER BAPT ASSN	1	25	25	0.1	0.1
053 ASSEMB OF GOD.	4	280	352	1.1	1.3
081 CATHOLIC......	4	NA	5 646	17.0	20.8
093 CHR CH (DISC).	1	233	313	0.9	1.2
097 CHR CHS&CHS CR	1	50	61*	0.2	0.2
123 CH GOD (ANDER)	2	120	360	1.1	1.3
127 CH GOD (CLEVE)	1	177	215*	0.6	0.8
151 L-D SAINTS....	1	NA	207	0.6	0.8
165 CH OF NAZARENE	1	167	288	0.9	1.1
167 CHS OF CHRIST.	17	1 800	2 290	6.9	8.4
193 EPISCOPAL.....	1	197	281	0.8	1.0
263 INT FOURSQ GOS	1	43	52*	0.2	0.2
283 LUTH--MO SYNOD	1	224	294	0.9	1.1
357 PRESB CH US...	2	564	686*	2.1	2.5
403 SALVATION ARMY	1	78	190	0.6	0.7
413 S.D.A.........	1	37	45*	0.1	0.2
419 SO BAPT CONV..	23	10 976	13 346*	40.3	49.2
449 UN METHODIST..	5	2 025	2 462*	7.4	9.1

NA—Not applicable   *Total adherents estimated from known number of communicant, confirmed, full members.   —Represents a percent less than 0.1.   Percentages may not total due to rounding.

Table 4. Churches and Church Membership by County and Denomination: 1980

County and Denomination	Number of churches	Communicant, confirmed, full members	Total adherents Number	Total adherents Percent of total population	Percent of total adherents
HUDSPETH	12	694	2 518*	92.3	100.0
053 ASSEMB OF GOD.	1	18	44	1.6	1.7
081 CATHOLIC......	2	NA	1 600	58.7	63.5
167 CHS OF CHRIST.	2	100	127	4.7	5.0
226 FRIENDS-USA...	1	6	8*	0.3	0.3
419 SO BAPT CONV..	3	456	591*	21.7	23.5
449 UN METHODIST..	3	114	148*	5.4	5.9
HUNT	131	26 165	33 142*	60.0	100.0
017 AMER BAPT ASSN	1	96	96	0.2	0.3
053 ASSEMB OF GOD.	9	570	823	1.5	2.5
059 BAPT MISS ASSN	3	241	289*	0.5	0.9
081 CATHOLIC......	2	NA	936	1.7	2.8
093 CHR CH (DISC).	7	765	1 087	2.0	3.3
101 C.M.E.........	7	1 451	1 742*	3.2	5.3
127 CH GOD (CLEVE)	1	79	95*	0.2	0.3
151 L-D SAINTS....	1	NA	194	0.4	0.6
165 CH OF NAZARENE	3	203	322	0.6	1.0
167 CHS OF CHRIST.	20	2 200	2 800	5.1	8.4
193 EPISCOPAL.....	2	268	389	0.7	1.2
281 LUTH CH AMER..	1	138	195	0.4	0.6
283 LUTH--MO SYNOD	1	115	135	0.2	0.4
356 PRESB CH AMER.	1	35	44	0.1	0.1
357 PRESB CH US...	3	384	461*	0.8	1.4
403 SALVATION ARMY	1	46	37	0.1	0.1
413 S.D.A.........	1	76	91*	0.2	0.3
419 SO BAPT CONV..	44	14 676	17 617*	31.9	53.2
449 UN METHODIST..	20	4 439	5 329*	9.6	16.1
453 UN PRES CH USA	3	383	460*	0.8	1.4
HUTCHINSON	47	13 879	19 344*	73.5	100.0
017 AMER BAPT ASSN	1	105	105	0.4	0.5
053 ASSEMB OF GOD.	3	278	412	1.6	2.1
081 CATHOLIC......	2	NA	1 500	5.7	7.8
093 CHR CH (DISC).	3	460	1 022	3.9	5.3
097 CHR CHS&CHS CR	1	50	61*	0.2	0.3
127 CH GOD (CLEVE)	1	101	123*	0.5	0.6
151 L-D SAINTS....	1	NA	189	0.7	1.0
165 CH OF NAZARENE	4	216	306	1.2	1.6
167 CHS OF CHRIST.	7	1 284	1 684	6.4	8.7
193 EPISCOPAL.....	1	139	194	0.7	1.0
283 LUTH--MO SYNOD	1	322	429	1.6	2.2
349 PENT HOLINESS	2	77	94*	0.4	0.5
357 PRESB CH US...	1	149	181*	0.7	0.9
403 SALVATION ARMY	1	38	86	0.3	0.4
413 S.D.A.........	1	22	27*	0.1	0.1
419 SO BAPT CONV..	10	8 229	10 003*	38.0	51.7
449 UN METHODIST..	6	2 260	2 747*	10.4	14.2
453 UN PRES CH USA	1	149	181*	0.7	0.9
IRION	6	602	737*	53.2	100.0
081 CATHOLIC......	1	NA	?	?	?
093 CHR CH (DISC).	1	17	22	1.6	3.0
167 CHS OF CHRIST.	1	45	57	4.1	7.7
419 SO BAPT CONV..	1	356	434*	31.3	58.9
449 UN METHODIST..	2	184	224*	16.2	30.4
JACK	35	4 206	5 277*	71.2	100.0
001 ADVENT CHR CH.	1	18	22*	0.3	0.4
053 ASSEMB OF GOD.	4	216	343	4.6	6.5
059 BAPT MISS ASSN	1	50	60*	0.8	1.1
081 CATHOLIC......	1	NA	101	1.4	1.9
093 CHR CH (DISC).	1	100	134	1.8	2.5
101 C.M.E.........	1	13	16*	0.2	0.3
167 CHS OF CHRIST.	7	400	510	6.9	9.7
357 PRESB CH US...	1	31	37*	0.5	0.7
419 SO BAPT CONV..	12	2 737	3 285*	44.3	62.3
449 UN METHODIST..	5	610	732*	9.9	13.9
453 UN PRES CH USA	1	31	37*	0.5	0.7
JACKSON	34	4 875	8 599*	64.4	100.0
029 AMER LUTH CH..	1	278	355	2.7	4.1
053 ASSEMB OF GOD.	1	22	37	0.3	0.4
081 CATHOLIC......	4	NA	2 523	18.9	29.3
093 CHR CH (DISC).	1	34	52	0.4	0.6
167 CHS OF CHRIST.	6	375	475	3.6	5.5
193 EPISCOPAL.....	1	30	62	0.5	0.7
283 LUTH--MO SYNOD	1	190	256	1.9	3.0
357 PRESB CH US...	2	187	228*	1.7	2.7
419 SO BAPT CONV..	9	2 637	3 219*	24.1	37.4
449 UN METHODIST..	7	1 036	1 265*	9.5	14.7
469 WELS,.........	1	86	127	1.0	1.5
JASPER	78	14 733	18 827*	61.2	100.0
017 AMER BAPT ASSN	12	1 071	1 071	3.5	5.7
053 ASSEMB OF GOD.	5	396	470	1.5	2.5
059 BAPT MISS ASSN	10	1 156	1 427*	4.6	7.6
081 CATHOLIC......	3	NA	644	2.1	3.4
101 C.M.E.........	6	639	789*	2.6	4.2
151 L-D SAINTS....	2	NA	230	0.7	1.2
165 CH OF NAZARENE	2	111	139	0.5	0.7
167 CHS OF CHRIST.	6	753	1 000	3.2	5.3
193 EPISCOPAL.....	1	153	156	0.5	0.8
283 LUTH--MO SYNOD	1	53	58	0.2	0.3
419 SO BAPT CONV..	20	8 528	10 530*	34.2	55.9
449 UN METHODIST..	9	1 817	2 244*	7.3	11.9
453 UN PRES CH USA	1	56	69*	0.2	0.4
JEFF DAVIS	9	1 730	2 246*	136.4	100.0
081 CATHOLIC......	2	NA	120	7.3	5.3
097 CHR CHS&CHS CR	1	50	61*	3.7	2.7
101 C.M.E.........	2	1 285	1 578*	95.8	70.3
167 CHS OF CHRIST.	1	35	45	2.7	2.0
419 SO BAPT CONV..	1	203	249*	15.1	11.1
449 UN METHODIST..	1	71	87*	5.3	3.9
453 UN PRES CH USA	1	86	106*	6.4	4.7
JEFFERSON	222	85 727	171 181*	68.2	100.0
017 AMER BAPT ASSN	4	630	630	0.3	0.4
019 AMER BAPT USA.	1	150	182*	0.1	0.1
029 AMER LUTH CH..	2	866	1 082	0.4	0.6
053 ASSEMB OF GOD.	11	2 231	3 002	1.2	1.8
059 BAPT MISS ASSN	7	2 890	3 505*	1.4	2.0
081 CATHOLIC......	28	NA	63 850	25.4	37.3
093 CHR CH (DISC).	5	1 241	1 547	0.6	0.9
097 CHR CHS&CHS CR	3	463	561*	0.2	0.3
123 CH GOD (ANDER)	3	364	1 092	0.4	0.6
127 CH GOD (CLEVE)	1	39	47*	–	–
151 L-D SAINTS....	2	NA	1 009	0.4	0.6
165 CH OF NAZARENE	9	579	1 095	0.4	0.6
167 CHS OF CHRIST.	28	3 000	3 800	1.5	2.2
193 EPISCOPAL.....	5	3 318	4 488	1.8	2.6
215 EVAN METH CH..	1	23	28*	–	–
271 REFORM JUDAISM	2	428	519*	0.2	0.3
283 LUTH--MO SYNOD	7	2 061	2 643	1.1	1.5
353 CHR BRETHREN..	1	20	20	–	–
357 PRESB CH US...	6	2 416	2 930*	1.2	1.7
403 SALVATION ARMY	2	223	576	0.2	0.3
413 S.D.A.........	3	265	321*	0.1	0.2
419 SO BAPT CONV..	57	44 437	53 890*	21.5	31.5
421 SO METHODIST..	1	49	68	–	–
435 UNITARIAN-UNIV	1	112	136*	0.1	0.1
443 UN C OF CHRIST	2	165	200*	0.1	0.1
449 UN METHODIST..	28	18 779	22 774*	9.1	13.3
453 UN PRES CH USA	2	978	1 186*	0.5	0.7
JIM HOGG	13	461	4 453*	86.2	100.0
081 CATHOLIC......	6	NA	3 856	74.6	86.6
167 CHS OF CHRIST.	3	21	26	0.5	0.6
193 EPISCOPAL.....	1	35	57	1.1	1.3
419 SO BAPT CONV..	1	253	321*	6.2	7.2
449 UN METHODIST..	2	152	193*	3.7	4.3
JIM WELLS	43	7 039	21 305*	58.4	100.0
029 AMER LUTH CH..	2	698	845	2.3	4.0
053 ASSEMB OF GOD.	2	154	172	0.5	0.8
081 CATHOLIC......	11	NA	12 057	33.0	56.6
093 CHR CH (DISC).	1	94	109	0.3	0.5
151 L-D SAINTS....	1	NA	336	0.9	1.6
165 CH OF NAZARENE	1	?	?	?	?
167 CHS OF CHRIST.	5	360	460	1.3	2.2
193 EPISCOPAL.....	1	191	302	0.8	1.4
283 LUTH--MO SYNOD	2	110	141	0.4	0.7
285 MENNONITE CH..	2	86	109*	0.3	0.5
357 PRESB CH US...	2	257	326*	0.9	1.5
413 S.D.A.........	2	52	66*	0.2	0.3
419 SO BAPT CONV..	6	3 737	4 735*	13.0	22.2
443 UN C OF CHRIST	1	173	219*	0.6	1.0
449 UN METHODIST..	4	1 127	1 428*	3.9	6.7
JOHNSON	106	30 737	39 096*	57.8	100.0
053 ASSEMB OF GOD.	10	964	1 290	1.9	3.3
059 BAPT MISS ASSN	1	33	41*	0.1	0.1
081 CATHOLIC......	1	NA	525	0.8	1.3
093 CHR CH (DISC).	2	305	434	0.6	1.1
101 C.M.E.........	1	253	311*	0.5	0.8
127 CH GOD (CLEVE)	4	546	671*	1.0	1.7
151 L-D SAINTS....	1	NA	317	0.5	0.8
165 CH OF NAZARENE	2	90	108	0.2	0.3
167 CHS OF CHRIST.	15	2 775	3 530	5.2	9.0
185 CUMBER PRESB..	1	128	174	0.3	0.4
193 EPISCOPAL.....	3	269	442	0.7	1.1
283 LUTH--MO SYNOD	2	243	350	0.5	0.9
357 PRESB CH US...	2	262	322*	0.5	0.8
413 S.D.A.........	8	3 062	3 765*	5.6	9.6
419 SO BAPT CONV..	34	16 770	20 622*	30.5	52.7
449 UN METHODIST..	18	4 820	5 927*	8.8	15.2
453 UN PRES CH USA	1	217	267*	0.4	0.7
JONES	57	9 613	14 715*	85.2	100.0
029 AMER LUTH CH..	1	76	95	0.6	0.6
053 ASSEMB OF GOD.	5	326	443	2.6	3.0
059 BAPT MISS ASSN	2	426	516*	3.0	3.5
081 CATHOLIC......	3	NA	3 000	17.4	20.4
101 C.M.E.........	1	?	?	?	?
165 CH OF NAZARENE	1	151	184	1.1	1.3
167 CHS OF CHRIST.	13	625	800	4.6	5.4
263 INT FOURSQ GOS	2	130	157*	0.9	1.1
281 LUTH CH AMER..	1	282	327	1.9	2.2
357 PRESB CH US...	2	73	88*	0.5	0.6
419 SO BAPT CONV..	18	6 148	7 440*	43.1	50.6
449 UN METHODIST..	6	1 304	1 578*	9.1	10.7
453 UN PRES CH USA	2	72	87*	0.5	0.6
KARNES	37	3 665	11 868*	87.3	100.0
029 AMER LUTH CH..	2	387	488	3.6	4.1

NA— Not applicable   *Total adherents estimated from known number of communicant, confirmed, full members.   —Represents a percent less than 0.1.   Percentages may not total due to rounding.

Table 4. Churches and Church Membership by County and Denomination: 1980

County and Denomination	Number of churches	Communicant, confirmed, full members	Total adherents		
			Number	Percent of total population	Percent of total adherents
053 ASSEMB OF GOD.	2	68	80	0.6	0.7
081 CATHOLIC......	9	NA	7 286	53.6	61.4
151 L-D SAINTS....	1	NA	66	0.5	0.6
167 CHS OF CHRIST.	5	155	197	1.4	1.7
193 EPISCOPAL.....	1	33	40	0.3	0.3
281 LUTH CH AMER..	2	304	362	2.7	3.1
357 PRESB CH US...	1	133	164*	1.2	1.4
419 SO BAPT CONV..	9	1 884	2 321*	17.1	19.6
449 UN METHODIST..	5	701	864*	6.4	7.3
KAUFMAN	88	17 583	23 088*	59.2	100.0
017 AMER BAPT ASSN	1	25	25	0.1	0.1
053 ASSEMB OF GOD.	6	527	855	2.2	3.7
059 BAPT MISS ASSN	12	2 079	2 538*	6.5	11.0
081 CATHOLIC......	3	NA	1 191	3.1	5.2
093 CHR CH (DISC).	2	361	492	1.3	2.1
097 CHR CHS&CHS CR	1	965	1 178*	3.0	5.1
101 C.M.E.........	2	175	214*	0.5	0.9
165 CH OF NAZARENE	1	39	80	0.2	0.3
167 CHS OF CHRIST.	16	1 950	2 480	6.4	10.7
185 CUMBER PRESB..	1	9	16	–	0.1
193 EPISCOPAL.....	3	208	294	0.8	1.3
357 PRESB CH US...	5	173	211*	0.5	0.9
413 S.D.A.........	1	45	55*	0.1	0.2
419 SO BAPT CONV..	17	8 335	10 173*	26.1	44.1
449 UN METHODIST..	12	2 519	3 075*	7.9	13.3
453 UN PRES CH USA	5	173	211*	0.5	0.9
KENDALL	15	2 797	5 514*	51.8	100.0
029 AMER LUTH CH..	2	707	896	8.4	16.2
081 CATHOLIC......	3	NA	1 900	17.9	34.5
151 L-D SAINTS....	1	NA	118	1.1	2.1
167 CHS OF CHRIST.	1	140	270	2.5	4.9
193 EPISCOPAL.....	2	265	304	2.9	5.5
419 SO BAPT CONV..	3	835	1 004*	9.4	18.2
449 UN METHODIST..	2	725	872*	8.2	15.8
453 UN PRES CH USA	1	125	150*	1.4	2.7
KENEDY	2	0	483	89.0	100.0
081 CATHOLIC......	2	NA	483	89.0	100.0
KENT	6	655	846*	73.9	100.0
053 ASSEMB OF GOD.	1	45	79	6.9	9.3
081 CATHOLIC......	1	NA	50	4.4	5.9
167 CHS OF CHRIST.	2	125	153	13.4	18.1
419 SO BAPT CONV..	1	344	400*	34.9	47.3
449 UN METHODIST..	1	141	164*	14.3	19.4
KERR	33	9 264	14 134*	49.1	100.0
029 AMER LUTH CH..	1	581	730	2.5	5.2
053 ASSEMB OF GOD.	2	208	384	1.3	2.7
081 CATHOLIC......	2	NA	2 700	9.4	19.1
093 CHR CH (DISC).	2	309	365	1.3	2.6
123 CH GOD (ANDER)	1	36	108	0.4	0.8
151 L-D SAINTS....	1	NA	194	0.7	1.4
165 CH OF NAZARENE	1	50	120	0.4	0.8
167 CHS OF CHRIST.	3	300	380	1.3	2.7
193 EPISCOPAL.....	1	610	727	2.5	5.1
283 LUTH--MO SYNOD	1	340	452	1.6	3.2
357 PRESB CH US...	1	883	1 031*	3.6	7.3
413 S.D.A.........	2	58	68*	0.2	0.5
419 SO BAPT CONV..	8	4 121	4 811*	16.7	34.0
435 UNITARIAN-UNIV	1	20	23*	0.1	0.2
449 UN METHODIST..	5	1 682	1 964*	6.8	13.9
453 UN PRES CH USA	1	66	77*	0.3	0.5
KIMBLE	12	1 939	2 608*	64.2	100.0
029 AMER LUTH CH..	1	33	37	0.9	1.4
081 CATHOLIC......	1	NA	280	6.9	10.7
167 CHS OF CHRIST.	4	310	370	9.1	14.2
193 EPISCOPAL.....	1	73	99	2.4	3.8
357 PRESB CH US...	1	185	221*	5.4	8.5
419 SO BAPT CONV..	2	1 036	1 240*	30.5	47.5
449 UN METHODIST..	2	302	361*	8.9	13.8
KING	3	128	212*	49.9	100.0
081 CATHOLIC......	0	NA	50	11.8	23.6
419 SO BAPT CONV..	2	110	139*	32.7	65.6
449 UN METHODIST..	1	18	23*	5.4	10.8
KINNEY	7	330	1 509*	66.2	100.0
081 CATHOLIC......	2	NA	1 080	47.4	71.6
167 CHS OF CHRIST.	1	35	45	2.0	3.0
193 EPISCOPAL.....	1	32	59	2.6	3.9
419 SO BAPT CONV..	2	191	236*	10.4	15.6
449 UN METHODIST..	1	72	89*	3.9	5.9
KLEBERG	36	7 141	21 531*	64.5	100.0
029 AMER LUTH CH..	1	143	178	0.5	0.8
053 ASSEMB OF GOD.	2	283	425	1.3	2.0
081 CATHOLIC......	8	NA	12 191	36.5	56.6
093 CHR CH (DISC).	1	226	252	0.8	1.2
151 L-D SAINTS....	1	NA	278	0.8	1.3
165 CH OF NAZARENE	2	53	151	0.5	0.7
167 CHS OF CHRIST.	1	350	480	1.4	2.2
193 EPISCOPAL.....	1	281	338	1.0	1.6

County and Denomination	Number of churches	Communicant, confirmed, full members	Total adherents		
			Number	Percent of total population	Percent of total adherents
237 GC MENN BR CHS	1	35	44*	0.1	0.2
283 LUTH--MO SYNOD	1	230	305	0.9	1.4
349 PENT HOLINESS.	2	65	81*	0.2	0.4
357 PRESB CH US...	2	271	337*	1.0	1.6
413 S.D.A.........	1	15	19*	0.1	0.1
419 SO BAPT CONV..	7	3 944	4 904*	14.7	22.8
449 UN METHODIST..	5	1 245	1 548*	4.6	7.2
KNOX	32	3 984	5 597*	105.0	100.0
053 ASSEMB OF GOD.	1	41	47	0.9	0.8
081 CATHOLIC......	2	NA	708	13.3	12.6
093 CHR CH (DISC).	2	74	114	2.1	2.0
097 CHR CHS&CHS CR	1	90	107*	2.0	1.9
101 C.M.E.........	1	12	14*	0.3	0.3
151 L-D SAINTS....	1	NA	61	1.1	1.1
167 CHS OF CHRIST.	8	600	765	14.4	13.7
263 INT FOURSQ GOS	1	115	137*	2.6	2.4
419 SO BAPT CONV..	9	2 324	2 775*	52.1	49.6
449 UN METHODIST..	6	728	869*	16.3	15.5
LAMAR	104	19 436	24 452*	58.0	100.0
017 AMER BAPT ASSN	2	360	360	0.9	1.5
053 ASSEMB OF GOD.	7	594	756	1.8	3.1
059 BAPT MISS ASSN	1	110	134*	0.3	0.5
081 CATHOLIC......	1	NA	516	1.2	2.1
093 CHR CH (DISC).	5	697	922	2.2	3.8
101 C.M.E.........	1	200	243*	0.6	1.0
127 CH GOD (CLEVE)	3	512	623*	1.5	2.5
143 CG IN CR(MENN)	1	51	51	0.1	0.2
151 L-D SAINTS....	1	NA	197	0.5	0.8
165 CH OF NAZARENE	2	132	178	0.4	0.7
167 CHS OF CHRIST.	15	1 125	1 430	3.4	5.8
193 EPISCOPAL.....	1	242	276	0.7	1.1
283 LUTH--MO SYNOD	1	129	178	0.4	0.7
356 PRESB CH AMER.	1	75	82	0.2	0.3
357 PRESB CH US...	4	307	373*	0.9	1.5
403 SALVATION ARMY	1	101	137	0.3	0.6
413 S.D.A.........	1	44	53*	0.1	0.2
419 SO BAPT CONV..	32	11 233	13 658*	32.4	55.9
449 UN METHODIST..	20	3 218	3 913*	9.3	16.0
453 UN PRES CH USA	4	306	372*	0.9	1.5
LAMB	44	9 202	13 471*	72.2	100.0
029 AMER LUTH CH..	1	59	72	0.4	0.5
053 ASSEMB OF GOD.	3	103	105	0.6	0.8
059 BAPT MISS ASSN	2	165	206*	1.1	1.5
081 CATHOLIC......	3	NA	2 000	10.7	14.8
093 CHR CH (DISC).	1	25	45	0.2	0.3
165 CH OF NAZARENE	2	66	75	0.4	0.6
167 CHS OF CHRIST.	9	675	860	4.6	6.4
283 LUTH--MO SYNOD	1	105	126	0.7	0.9
357 PRESB CH US...	1	51	64*	0.3	0.5
413 S.D.A.........	1	16	20*	0.1	0.1
419 SO BAPT CONV..	13	6 120	7 632*	40.9	56.7
449 UN METHODIST..	6	1 766	2 202*	11.8	16.3
453 UN PRES CH USA	1	51	64*	0.3	0.5
LAMPASAS	27	4 650	6 471*	53.9	100.0
053 ASSEMB OF GOD.	1	40	100	0.8	1.5
081 CATHOLIC......	2	NA	550	4.6	8.5
093 CHR CH (DISC).	1	102	164	1.4	2.5
151 L-D SAINTS....	1	NA	106	0.9	1.6
167 CHS OF CHRIST.	5	675	855	7.1	13.2
193 EPISCOPAL.....	1	111	174	1.4	2.7
283 LUTH--MO SYNOD	1	87	114	0.9	1.8
419 SO BAPT CONV..	10	2 629	3 188*	26.6	49.3
449 UN METHODIST..	3	734	890*	7.4	13.8
453 UN PRES CH USA	2	272	330*	2.7	5.1
LA SALLE	15	1 055	4 777*	86.6	100.0
081 CATHOLIC......	3	NA	3 435	62.3	71.9
133 CH GOD(7TH)DEN	1	17	22*	0.4	0.5
167 CHS OF CHRIST.	2	100	127	2.3	2.7
193 EPISCOPAL.....	1	15	22	0.4	0.5
357 PRESB CH US...	2	66	84*	1.5	1.8
419 SO BAPT CONV..	4	596	756*	13.7	15.8
449 UN METHODIST..	2	261	331*	6.0	6.9
LAVACA	43	4 062	15 343*	80.7	100.0
029 AMER LUTH CH..	4	579	680	3.6	4.4
053 ASSEMB OF GOD.	1	60	62	0.3	0.4
081 CATHOLIC......	9	NA	10 516	55.3	68.5
093 CHR CH (DISC).	1	10	15	0.1	0.1
123 CH GOD (ANDER)	1	18	54	0.3	0.4
167 CHS OF CHRIST.	5	250	320	1.7	2.1
193 EPISCOPAL.....	2	57	58	0.3	0.4
271 REFORM JUDAISM	1	46	55*	0.3	0.4
281 LUTH CH AMER..	1	622	704	3.7	4.6
357 PRESB CH US...	1	40	48*	0.3	0.3
419 SO BAPT CONV..	10	1 484	1 765*	9.3	11.5
449 UN METHODIST..	7	896	1 066*	5.6	6.9
LEE	30	5 383	7 154*	65.3	100.0
029 AMER LUTH CH..	2	740	911	8.3	12.7
053 ASSEMB OF GOD.	1	66	62	0.6	0.9
081 CATHOLIC......	2	NA	600	5.5	8.4
093 CHR CH (DISC).	1	37	47	0.4	0.7
097 CHR CHS&CHS CR	1	100	120*	1.1	1.7

NA— Not applicable   *Total adherents estimated from known number of communicant, confirmed, full members.   —Represents a percent less than 0.1.   Percentages may not total due to rounding.

Table 4. Churches and Church Membership by County and Denomination: 1980

County and Denomination	Number of churches	Communicant, confirmed, full members	Total adherents Number	Percent of total population	Percent of total adherents
123 CH GOD (ANDER)	1	10	30	0.3	0.4
167 CHS OF CHRIST.	4	160	204	1.9	2.9
283 LUTH--MO SYNOD	8	2 529	3 084	28.2	43.1
357 PRESB CH US...	1	52	63*	0.6	0.9
419 SO BAPT CONV..	6	1 177	1 417*	12.9	19.8
449 UN METHODIST..	3	512	616*	5.6	8.6
LEON	52	4 789	5 839*	60.9	100.0
053 ASSEMB OF GOD.	5	181	263	2.7	4.5
059 BAPT MISS ASSN	14	1 009	1 199*	12.5	20.5
081 CATHOLIC......	1	NA	57	0.6	1.0
093 CHR CH (DISC).	1	32	38	0.4	0.7
127 CH GOD (CLEVE)	1	53	63*	0.7	1.1
167 CHS OF CHRIST.	6	310	395	4.1	6.8
283 LUTH--MO SYNOD	1	42	68	0.7	1.2
419 SO BAPT CONV..	7	2 043	2 427*	25.3	41.6
449 UN METHODIST..	16	1 119	1 329*	13.9	22.8
LIBERTY	91	18 238	26 709*	56.7	100.0
017 AMER BAPT ASSN	6	352	352	0.7	1.3
029 AMER LUTH CH..	1	67	102	0.2	0.4
053 ASSEMB OF GOD.	16	1 089	1 528	3.2	5.7
059 BAPT MISS ASSN	4	645	800*	1.7	3.0
081 CATHOLIC......	6	NA	3 307	7.0	12.4
093 CHR CH (DISC).	2	51	79	0.2	0.3
101 C.M.E........	1	50	62*	0.1	0.2
151 L-D SAINTS....	2	NA	642	1.4	2.4
167 CHS OF CHRIST.	9	600	765	1.6	2.9
193 EPISCOPAL.....	1	164	173	0.4	0.6
283 LUTH--MO SYNOD	1	130	190	0.4	0.7
357 PRESB CH US...	2	90	112*	0.2	0.4
419 SO BAPT CONV..	30	12 476	15 468*	32.8	57.9
449 UN METHODIST..	10	2 524	3 129*	6.6	11.7
LIMESTONE	52	8 671	10 756*	53.2	100.0
017 AMER BAPT ASSN	1	150	150	0.7	1.4
053 ASSEMB OF GOD.	4	171	257	1.3	2.4
059 BAPT MISS ASSN	3	278	330*	1.6	3.1
081 CATHOLIC......	1	NA	360	1.8	3.3
093 CHR CH (DISC).	1	72	116	0.6	1.1
167 CHS OF CHRIST.	11	952	1 178	5.8	11.0
193 EPISCOPAL.....	1	36	49	0.2	0.5
357 PRESB CH US...	3	105	125*	0.6	1.2
419 SO BAPT CONV..	16	5 006	5 937*	29.4	55.2
449 UN METHODIST..	8	1 797	2 131*	10.5	19.8
453 UN PRES CH USA	3	104	123*	0.6	1.1
LIPSCOMB	18	2 154	2 747*	72.9	100.0
081 CATHOLIC......	1	NA	50	1.3	1.8
097 CHR CHS&CHS CR	1	150	186*	4.9	6.8
165 CH OF NAZARENE	1	33	65	1.7	2.4
167 CHS OF CHRIST.	3	150	190	5.0	6.9
181 CONSRV CONGR..	1	74	92*	2.4	3.3
226 FRIENDS-USA...	1	139	172*	4.6	6.3
281 LUTH CH AMER..	1	178	222	5.9	8.1
419 SO BAPT CONV..	5	698	864*	22.9	31.5
449 UN METHODIST..	4	732	906*	24.1	33.0
LIVE OAK	24	2 447	5 019*	52.2	100.0
053 ASSEMB OF GOD.	1	98	94	1.0	1.9
081 CATHOLIC......	4	NA	2 022	21.0	40.3
133 CH GOD(7TH)DEN	1	11	14*	0.1	0.3
167 CHS OF CHRIST.	5	215	275	2.9	5.5
193 EPISCOPAL.....	1	67	73	0.8	1.5
281 LUTH CH AMER..	2	232	307	3.2	6.1
283 LUTH--MO SYNOD	1	37	37	0.4	0.7
419 SO BAPT CONV..	6	1 242	1 527*	15.9	30.4
449 UN METHODIST..	3	545	670*	7.0	13.3
LLANO	27	3 668	5 039*	49.7	100.0
029 AMER LUTH CH..	2	265	332	3.3	6.6
053 ASSEMB OF GOD.	1	65	156	1.5	3.1
081 CATHOLIC......	3	NA	751	7.4	14.9
093 CHR CH (DISC).	1	83	110	1.1	2.2
167 CHS OF CHRIST.	8	460	585	5.8	11.6
193 EPISCOPAL.....	1	126	122	1.2	2.4
357 PRESB CH US...	1	39	44*	0.4	0.9
419 SO BAPT CONV..	6	2 111	2 359*	23.3	46.8
449 UN METHODIST..	4	519	580*	5.7	11.5
LOVING	0	0	0	–	–
LUBBOCK	199	81 892	127 013*	60.0	100.0
017 AMER BAPT ASSN	2	322	322	0.2	0.3
029 AMER LUTH CH..	3	538	659	0.3	0.5
053 ASSEMB OF GOD.	17	1 180	1 845	0.9	1.5
059 BAPT MISS ASSN	8	2 898	3 537*	1.7	2.8
081 CATHOLIC......	12	NA	24 225	11.4	19.1
093 CHR CH (DISC).	5	2 219	2 632	1.2	2.1
097 CHR CHS&CHS CR	2	285	348*	0.2	0.3
101 C.M.E........	1	260	317*	0.1	0.2
123 CH GOD (ANDER)	1	130	390	0.2	0.3
127 CH GOD (CLEVE)	4	231	282*	0.1	0.2
133 CH GOD(7TH)DEN	2	15	18*	–	–
151 L-D SAINTS....	3	NA	1 107	0.5	0.9
165 CH OF NAZARENE	5	530	725	0.3	0.6
167 CHS OF CHRIST.	31	11 069	14 336	6.8	11.3
185 CUMBER PRESB..	1	631	729	0.3	0.6

County and Denomination	Number of churches	Communicant, confirmed, full members	Total adherents Number	Percent of total population	Percent of total adherents
193 EPISCOPAL.....	5	1 483	1 853	0.9	1.5
215 EVAN METH CH..	1	69	84*	–	0.1
263 INT FOURSQ GOS	4	662	808*	0.4	0.6
271 REFORM JUDAISM	1	160	195*	0.1	0.2
281 LUTH CH AMER..	1	187	265	0.1	0.2
283 LUTH--MO SYNOD	3	843	1 139	0.5	0.9
290 METRO COMM CHS	1	25	50	–	–
349 PENT HOLINESS.	3	111	135*	0.1	0.1
353 CHR BRETHREN..	1	35	80	–	0.1
357 PRESB CH US...	6	1 072	1 308*	0.6	1.0
403 SALVATION ARMY	1	187	356	0.2	0.3
413 S.D.A.........	2	190	232*	0.1	0.2
419 SO BAPT CONV..	45	40 956	49 985*	23.6	39.4
435 UNITARIAN-UNIV	1	95	116*	0.1	0.1
443 UN C OF CHRIST	1	22	27*	–	–
449 UN METHODIST..	19	14 327	17 485*	8.3	13.8
453 UN PRES CH USA	6	1 074	1 311*	0.6	1.0
469 WELS..........	1	86	112	0.1	0.1
LYNN	27	4 896	7 168*	83.3	100.0
029 AMER LUTH CH..	1	110	124	1.4	1.7
053 ASSEMB OF GOD.	1	41	92	1.1	1.3
081 CATHOLIC......	3	NA	1 000	11.6	14.0
101 C.M.E........	1	18	23*	0.3	0.3
165 CH OF NAZARENE	1	52	63	0.7	0.9
167 CHS OF CHRIST.	6	360	460	5.3	6.4
283 LUTH--MO SYNOD	1	169	217	2.5	3.0
419 SO BAPT CONV..	8	3 303	4 134*	48.0	57.7
449 UN METHODIST..	5	843	1 055*	12.3	14.7
MC CULLOCH	32	3 708	5 149*	58.9	100.0
053 ASSEMB OF GOD.	1	?	?	?	?
081 CATHOLIC......	2	NA	629	7.2	12.2
093 CHR CH (DISC).	2	288	391	4.5	7.6
165 CH OF NAZARENE	1	?	?	?	?
167 CHS OF CHRIST.	7	550	660	7.6	12.8
193 EPISCOPAL.....	1	98	171	2.0	3.3
203 EVAN FREE CH..	1	12	14*	0.2	0.3
283 LUTH--MO SYNOD	1	69	69	0.8	1.3
419 SO BAPT CONV..	10	1 980	2 362*	27.0	45.9
449 UN METHODIST..	5	614	733*	8.4	14.2
453 UN PRES CH USA	1	101	120*	1.4	2.3
MC LENNAN	229	80 995	133 771*	78.3	100.0
017 AMER BAPT ASSN	1	123	123	0.1	0.1
029 AMER LUTH CH..	4	1 400	1 738	1.0	1.3
053 ASSEMB OF GOD.	13	2 064	2 768	1.6	2.1
059 BAPT MISS ASSN	2	246	296*	0.2	0.2
081 CATHOLIC......	10	NA	33 870	19.8	25.3
089 CHR & MISS AL.	1	41	64	–	–
093 CHR CH (DISC).	6	887	1 182	0.7	0.9
097 CHR CHS&CHS CR	1	50	60*	–	–
101 C.M.E........	1	215	259*	0.2	0.2
123 CH GOD (ANDER)	1	22	66	–	–
127 CH GOD (CLEVE)	1	14	17*	–	–
151 L-D SAINTS....	1	NA	569	0.3	0.4
165 CH OF NAZARENE	4	407	699	0.4	0.5
167 CHS OF CHRIST.	26	3 143	4 000	2.3	3.0
193 EPISCOPAL.....	4	1 932	2 424	1.4	1.8
270 CONSRV JUDAISM	1	108	130*	0.1	0.1
271 REFORM JUDAISM	1	354	426*	0.2	0.3
281 LUTH CH AMER..	1	292	383	0.2	0.3
283 LUTH--MO SYNOD	5	1 281	2 352	1.4	1.8
313 N AM BAPT CONF	2	263	316*	0.2	0.2
353 CHR BRETHREN..	1	50	75	–	0.1
357 PRESB CH US...	6	679	817*	0.5	0.6
403 SALVATION ARMY	1	135	208	0.1	0.2
413 S.D.A.........	2	159	191*	0.1	0.1
419 SO BAPT CONV..	71	49 489	59 521*	34.9	44.5
435 UNITARIAN-UNIV	1	28	34*	–	–
443 UN C OF CHRIST	6	836	1 005*	0.6	0.8
449 UN METHODIST..	49	16 096	19 359*	11.3	14.5
453 UN PRES CH USA	6	681	819*	0.5	0.6
MC MULLEN	3	142	317*	40.2	100.0
081 CATHOLIC......	1	NA	150	19.0	47.3
419 SO BAPT CONV..	2	142	167*	21.2	52.7
MADISON	26	3 812	4 977*	46.7	100.0
053 ASSEMB OF GOD.	2	83	114	1.1	2.3
059 BAPT MISS ASSN	2	128	149*	1.4	3.0
081 CATHOLIC......	1	NA	330	3.1	6.6
151 L-D SAINTS....	1	NA	120	1.1	2.4
167 CHS OF CHRIST.	8	500	636	6.0	12.8
283 LUTH--MO SYNOD	1	98	122	1.1	2.5
419 SO BAPT CONV..	5	2 131	2 488*	23.4	50.0
449 UN METHODIST..	6	872	1 018*	9.6	20.5
MARION	37	4 191	5 221*	50.4	100.0
053 ASSEMB OF GOD.	1	36	31	0.3	0.6
081 CATHOLIC......	1	NA	175	1.7	3.4
093 CHR CH (DISC).	1	40	62	0.6	1.2
101 C.M.E........	1	63	76*	0.7	1.5
165 CH OF NAZARENE	1	25	33	0.3	0.6
167 CHS OF CHRIST.	2	150	190	1.8	3.6
185 CUMBER PRESB..	1	11	12	0.1	0.2
193 EPISCOPAL.....	1	82	89	0.9	1.7
413 S.D.A.........	4	454	546*	5.3	10.5
419 SO BAPT CONV..	9	2 291	2 757*	26.6	52.8

NA— Not applicable   *Total adherents estimated from known number of communicant, confirmed, full members.   —Represents a percent less than 0.1.   Percentages may not total due to rounding.

Table 4. Churches and Church Membership by County and Denomination: 1980

County and Denomination	Number of churches	Communicant, confirmed, full members	Total adherents Number	Percent of total population	Percent of total adherents
449 UN METHODIST..	15	1 039	1 250*	12.1	23.9
MARTIN	13	1 713	3 882*	82.9	100.0
053 ASSEMB OF GOD.	1	35	44	0.9	1.1
081 CATHOLIC......	2	NA	1 700	36.3	43.8
127 CH GOD (CLEVE)	1	10	13*	0.3	0.3
167 CHS OF CHRIST.	3	260	365	7.8	9.4
419 SO BAPT CONV..	5	1 019	1 274*	27.2	32.8
449 UN METHODIST..	1	389	486*	10.4	12.5
MASON	14	2 020	2 837*	77.0	100.0
029 AMER LUTH CH..	1	443	538	14.6	19.0
053 ASSEMB OF GOD.	1	17	24	0.7	0.8
081 CATHOLIC......	1	NA	400	10.9	14.1
093 CHR CH (DISC).	1	29	44	1.2	1.6
167 CHS OF CHRIST.	3	265	340	9.2	12.0
419 SO BAPT CONV..	1	490	577*	15.7	20.3
449 UN METHODIST..	6	776	914*	24.8	32.2
MATAGORDA	55	10 801	21 315*	56.3	100.0
029 AMER LUTH CH..	1	265	353	0.9	1.7
053 ASSEMB OF GOD.	2	120	162	0.4	0.8
081 CATHOLIC......	6	NA	7 376	19.5	34.6
093 CHR CH (DISC).	4	768	1 100	2.9	5.2
151 L-D SAINTS....	1	NA	284	0.8	1.3
165 CH OF NAZARENE	2	77	98	0.3	0.5
167 CHS OF CHRIST.	7	735	935	2.5	4.4
193 EPISCOPAL.....	3	408	535	1.4	2.5
283 LUTH--MO SYNOD	1	31	41	0.1	0.2
357 PRESB CH US...	5	689	856*	2.3	4.0
419 SO BAPT CONV..	15	5 746	7 138*	18.9	33.5
449 UN METHODIST..	8	1 962	2 437*	6.4	11.4
MAVERICK	21	1 336	16 446*	52.4	100.0
053 ASSEMB OF GOD.	3	325	420	1.3	2.6
081 CATHOLIC......	6	NA	14 431	46.0	87.7
097 CHR CHS&CHS CR	1	22	29*	0.1	0.2
151 L-D SAINTS....	1	NA	328	1.0	2.0
167 CHS OF CHRIST.	2	100	127	0.4	0.8
193 EPISCOPAL.....	1	211	216	0.7	1.3
413 S.D.A........	1	11	15*	—	0.1
419 SO BAPT CONV..	3	435	574*	1.8	3.5
449 UN METHODIST..	3	232	306*	1.0	1.9
MEDINA	36	5 226	18 459*	79.7	100.0
029 AMER LUTH CH..	3	865	1 032	4.5	5.6
053 ASSEMB OF GOD.	1	22	40	0.2	0.2
081 CATHOLIC......	8	NA	11 983	51.7	64.9
093 CHR CH (DISC).	1	26	41	0.2	0.2
097 CHR CHS&CHS CR	1	50	62*	0.3	0.3
127 CH GOD (CLEVE)	1	16	20*	0.1	0.1
167 CHS OF CHRIST.	3	200	255	1.1	1.4
193 EPISCOPAL.....	1	39	53	0.2	0.3
283 LUTH--MO SYNOD	1	60	77	0.3	0.4
357 PRESB CH US...	1	26	32*	0.1	0.2
413 S.D.A........	1	48	60*	0.3	0.3
419 SO BAPT CONV..	10	2 820	3 497*	15.1	18.9
449 UN METHODIST..	4	1 054	1 307*	5.6	7.1
MENARD	13	1 105	1 685*	71.8	100.0
081 CATHOLIC......	2	NA	310	13.2	18.4
167 CHS OF CHRIST.	4	200	255	10.9	15.1
193 EPISCOPAL.....	2	74	130	5.5	7.7
283 LUTH--MO SYNOD	1	45	54	2.3	3.2
413 S.D.A........	1	50	60*	2.6	3.6
419 SO BAPT CONV..	1	514	612*	26.1	36.3
449 UN METHODIST..	1	196	233*	9.9	13.8
453 UN PRES CH USA	1	26	31*	1.3	1.8
MIDLAND	69	32 470	46 374*	56.1	100.0
017 AMER BAPT ASSN	1	205	205	0.2	0.4
029 AMER LUTH CH..	1	439	547	0.7	1.2
053 ASSEMB OF GOD.	4	396	616	0.7	1.3
059 BAPT MISS ASSN	1	307	377*	0.5	0.8
081 CATHOLIC......	2	NA	5 577	6.7	12.0
089 CHR & MISS AL.	1	34	54	0.1	0.1
093 CHR CH (DISC).	2	1 209	1 419	1.7	3.1
097 CHR CHS&CHS CR	1	200	246*	0.3	0.5
101 C.M.E.........	1	270	332*	0.4	0.7
127 CH GOD (CLEVE)	1	111	136*	0.2	0.3
133 CH GOD(7TH)DEN	1	7	9*	—	—
151 L-D SAINTS....	2	NA	662	0.8	1.4
165 CH OF NAZARENE	2	129	162	0.2	0.3
167 CHS OF CHRIST.	11	3 450	4 201	5.1	9.1
193 EPISCOPAL.....	2	1 490	1 878	2.3	4.0
221 FREE METHODIST	2	55	195	0.2	0.4
226 FRIENDS-USA...	1	7	9*	—	—
263 INT FOURSQ GOS	1	170	209*	0.3	0.5
281 LUTH CH AMER..	1	97	130	0.2	0.3
283 LUTH--MO SYNOD	1	520	656	0.8	1.4
349 PENT HOLINESS.	1	28	34*	—	0.1
357 PRESB CH US...	3	2 134	2 623*	3.2	5.7
403 SALVATION ARMY	1	71	113	0.1	0.2
413 S.D.A........	1	73	90*	0.1	0.2
419 SO BAPT CONV..	15	15 531	19 089*	23.1	41.2
435 UNITARIAN-UNIV	1	26	32*	—	0.1
449 UN METHODIST..	7	5 323	6 542*	7.9	14.1
453 UN PRES CH USA	1	188	231*	0.3	0.5

County and Denomination	Number of churches	Communicant, confirmed, full members	Total adherents Number	Percent of total population	Percent of total adherents
MILAM	75	9 040	14 295*	62.9	100.0
017 AMER BAPT ASSN	1	25	25	0.1	0.2
029 AMER LUTH CH..	4	904	1 088	4.8	7.6
053 ASSEMB OF GOD.	4	143	213	0.9	1.5
081 CATHOLIC......	4	NA	2 830	12.4	19.8
093 CHR CH (DISC).	5	273	524	2.3	3.7
097 CHR CHS&CHS CR	2	217	265*	1.2	1.9
165 CH OF NAZARENE	1	25	32	0.1	0.2
167 CHS OF CHRIST.	11	636	859	3.8	6.0
193 EPISCOPAL.....	2	83	121	0.5	0.8
283 LUTH--MO SYNOD	2	567	809	3.6	5.7
357 PRESB CH US...	3	137	167*	0.7	1.2
419 SO BAPT CONV..	20	4 436	5 416*	23.8	37.9
443 UN C OF CHRIST	1	132	161*	0.7	1.1
449 UN METHODIST..	12	1 326	1 619*	7.1	11.3
453 UN PRES CH USA	3	136	166*	0.7	1.2
MILLS	23	3 088	3 828*	85.5	100.0
029 AMER LUTH CH..	1	282	323	7.2	8.4
053 ASSEMB OF GOD.	1	96	75	1.7	2.0
081 CATHOLIC......	1	NA	220	4.9	5.7
121 CH GOD (ABR)..	1	16	19*	0.4	0.5
167 CHS OF CHRIST.	8	460	585	13.1	15.3
419 SO BAPT CONV..	7	1 655	1 931*	43.1	50.4
449 UN METHODIST..	4	579	675*	15.1	17.6
MITCHELL	28	4 649	7 369*	81.1	100.0
017 AMER BAPT ASSN	1	25	25	0.3	0.3
053 ASSEMB OF GOD.	2	57	88	1.0	1.2
059 BAPT MISS ASSN	1	23	28*	0.3	0.4
081 CATHOLIC......	2	NA	1 625	17.9	22.1
093 CHR CH (DISC).	1	66	102	1.1	1.4
101 C.M.E.........	1	123	150*	1.7	2.0
167 CHS OF CHRIST.	5	350	445	4.9	6.0
193 EPISCOPAL.....	1	55	74	0.8	1.0
357 PRESB CH US...	1	37	45*	0.5	0.6
419 SO BAPT CONV..	7	3 070	3 756*	41.3	51.0
449 UN METHODIST..	5	807	987*	10.9	13.4
453 UN PRES CH USA	1	36	44*	0.5	0.6
MONTAGUE	58	8 222	10 286*	59.1	100.0
053 ASSEMB OF GOD.	4	239	367	2.1	3.6
059 BAPT MISS ASSN	3	136	161*	0.9	1.6
081 CATHOLIC......	3	NA	265	1.5	2.6
093 CHR CH (DISC).	3	257	338	1.9	3.3
157 CH OF BRETHREN	1	98	116*	0.7	1.1
165 CH OF NAZARENE	2	88	152	0.9	1.5
167 CHS OF CHRIST.	11	925	1 175	6.7	11.4
193 EPISCOPAL.....	1	58	89	0.5	0.9
283 LUTH--MO SYNOD	1	111	140	0.8	1.4
357 PRESB CH US...	3	66	78*	0.4	0.8
413 S.D.A........	1	10	12*	0.1	0.1
419 SO BAPT CONV..	14	4 903	5 815*	33.4	56.5
449 UN METHODIST..	8	1 264	1 499*	8.6	14.6
453 UN PRES CH USA	3	67	79*	0.5	0.8
MONTGOMERY	112	31 680	47 338*	36.8	100.0
005 AME ZION......	1	82	138	0.1	0.3
017 AMER BAPT ASSN	2	148	148	0.1	0.3
029 AMER LUTH CH..	1	105	156	0.1	0.3
053 ASSEMB OF GOD.	14	1 209	1 647	1.3	3.5
059 BAPT MISS ASSN	10	2 019	2 534*	2.0	5.4
081 CATHOLIC......	3	NA	6 280	4.9	13.3
093 CHR CH (DISC).	1	280	369	0.3	0.8
101 C.M.E.........	1	53	67*	0.1	0.1
123 CH GOD (ANDER)	1	55	165	0.1	0.3
127 CH GOD (CLEVE)	1	52	65*	0.1	0.1
133 CH GOD(7TH)DEN	1	84	105*	0.1	0.2
151 L-D SAINTS....	2	NA	858	0.7	1.8
165 CH OF NAZARENE	1	164	180	0.1	0.4
167 CHS OF CHRIST.	15	1 875	2 385	1.9	5.0
193 EPISCOPAL.....	2	977	1 197	0.9	2.5
281 LUTH CH AMER..	1	309	446	0.3	0.9
283 LUTH--MO SYNOD	3	614	909	0.7	1.9
357 PRESB CH US...	1	861	1 081*	0.8	2.3
413 S.D.A........	2	117	147*	0.1	0.3
419 SO BAPT CONV..	33	17 921	22 493*	17.5	47.5
443 UN C OF CHRIST	2	334	419*	0.3	0.9
449 UN METHODIST..	14	4 421	5 549*	4.3	11.7
MOORE	31	6 776	10 914*	65.8	100.0
053 ASSEMB OF GOD.	4	435	669	4.0	6.1
081 CATHOLIC......	3	NA	1 900	11.5	17.4
093 CHR CH (DISC).	1	177	249	1.5	2.3
097 CHR CHS&CHS CR	1	75	95*	0.6	0.9
127 CH GOD (CLEVE)	1	21	27*	0.2	0.2
151 L-D SAINTS....	1	NA	153	0.9	1.4
165 CH OF NAZARENE	1	85	182	1.1	1.7
167 CHS OF CHRIST.	5	520	660	4.0	6.0
193 EPISCOPAL.....	1	20	54	0.3	0.5
263 INT FOURSQ GOS	1	10	13*	0.1	0.1
283 LUTH--MO SYNOD	1	146	207	1.2	1.9
349 PENT HOLINESS.	1	38	48*	0.3	0.4
357 PRESB CH US...	1	115	146*	0.9	1.3
419 SO BAPT CONV..	4	3 845	4 876*	29.4	44.7
449 UN METHODIST..	4	1 174	1 489*	9.0	13.6
453 UN PRES CH USA	1	115	146*	0.9	1.3
MORRIS	40	7 056	8 890*	60.8	100.0

NA—Not applicable   *Total adherents estimated from known number of communicant, confirmed, full members.   —Represents a percent less than 0.1.   Percentages may not total due to rounding.

274

Table 4. Churches and Church Membership by County and Denomination: 1980

County and Denomination	Number of churches	Communicant, confirmed, full members	Total adherents Number	Total adherents Percent of total population	Total adherents Percent of total adherents
017 AMER BAPT ASSN	5	1 162	1 162	7.9	13.1
029 AMER LUTH CH..	1	55	84	0.6	0.9
053 ASSEMB OF GOD.	3	194	331	2.3	3.7
059 BAPT MISS ASSN	1	56	69*	0.5	0.8
081 CATHOLIC......	1	NA	280	1.9	3.1
093 CHR CH (DISC).	2	185	284	1.9	3.2
097 CHR CHS&CHS CR	2	87	107*	0.7	1.2
101 C.M.E.	2	406	498*	3.4	5.6
167 CHS OF CHRIST.	7	400	510	3.5	5.7
185 CUMBER PRESB..	1	31	65	0.4	0.7
193 EPISCOPAL.....	1	26	35	0.2	0.4
419 SO BAPT CONV..	8	3 265	4 006*	27.4	45.1
449 UN METHODIST..	6	1 189	1 459*	10.0	16.4
MOTLEY	15	1 532	2 043*	104.8	100.0
053 ASSEMB OF GOD.	2	85	118	6.1	5.8
059 BAPT MISS ASSN	1	40	47*	2.4	2.3
081 CATHOLIC......	1	NA	200	10.3	9.8
167 CHS OF CHRIST.	4	200	255	13.1	12.5
419 SO BAPT CONV..	4	904	1 066*	54.7	52.2
449 UN METHODIST..	3	303	357*	18.3	17.5
NACOGDOCHES	105	19 013	24 208*	51.7	100.0
017 AMER BAPT ASSN	2	396	396	0.8	1.6
053 ASSEMB OF GOD.	2	187	271	0.6	1.1
059 BAPT MISS ASSN	20	2 221	2 634*	5.6	10.9
081 CATHOLIC......	3	NA	975	2.1	4.0
093 CHR CH (DISC).	1	274	314	0.7	1.3
101 C.M.E.	19	2 495	2 959*	6.3	12.2
123 CH GOD (ANDER)	1	50	150	0.3	0.6
151 L-D SAINTS....	1	NA	217	0.5	0.9
165 CH OF NAZARENE	1	270	508	1.1	2.1
167 CHS OF CHRIST.	15	1 300	1 655	3.5	6.8
193 EPISCOPAL.....	1	437	602	1.3	2.5
221 FREE METHODIST	1	7	12	-	-
283 LUTH--MO SYNOD	1	121	167	0.4	0.7
413 S.D.A.	1	72	85*	0.2	0.4
419 SO BAPT CONV..	19	8 506	10 088*	21.6	41.7
435 UNITARIAN-UNIV	1	20	24*	0.1	0.1
449 UN METHODIST..	13	2 335	2 769*	5.9	11.4
453 UN PRES CH USA	3	322	382*	0.8	1.6
NAVARRO	88	18 479	23 561*	66.7	100.0
017 AMER BAPT ASSN	9	873	873	2.5	3.7
053 ASSEMB OF GOD.	3	184	232	0.7	1.0
059 BAPT MISS ASSN	9	1 155	1 390*	3.9	5.9
081 CATHOLIC......	1	NA	855	2.4	3.6
093 CHR CH (DISC).	3	221	307	0.9	1.3
101 C.M.E.	1	140	168*	0.5	0.7
127 CH GOD (CLEVE)	1	56	67*	0.2	0.3
151 L-D SAINTS....	1	NA	141	0.4	0.6
165 CH OF NAZARENE	1	32	87	0.2	0.4
167 CHS OF CHRIST.	8	1 250	1 590	4.5	6.7
185 CUMBER PRESB..	1	6	17	-	0.1
193 EPISCOPAL.....	1	295	562	1.6	2.4
271 REFORM JUDAISM	1	76	91*	0.3	0.4
283 LUTH--MO SYNOD	1	61	74	0.2	0.3
357 PRESB CH US...	2	263	316*	0.9	1.3
403 SALVATION ARMY	1	73	196	0.6	0.8
413 S.D.A.	2	42	51*	0.1	0.2
419 SO BAPT CONV..	21	9 642	11 600*	32.8	49.2
449 UN METHODIST..	19	3 847	4 628*	13.1	19.6
453 UN PRES CH USA	2	263	316*	0.9	1.3
NEWTON	36	4 643	6 038*	45.6	100.0
017 AMER BAPT ASSN	2	240	240	1.8	4.0
053 ASSEMB OF GOD.	2	81	120	0.9	2.0
059 BAPT MISS ASSN	1	112	140*	1.1	2.3
101 C.M.E.	10	939	1 173*	8.9	19.4
123 CH GOD (ANDER)	3	157	471	3.6	7.8
167 CHS OF CHRIST.	5	160	205	1.5	3.4
419 SO BAPT CONV..	7	2 449	3 046*	23.0	50.4
449 UN METHODIST..	6	515	643*	4.9	10.6
NOLAN	41	10 046	14 534*	83.7	100.0
029 AMER LUTH CH..	1	149	186	1.1	1.3
053 ASSEMB OF GOD.	2	312	322	1.9	2.2
059 BAPT MISS ASSN	1	120	147*	0.8	1.0
081 CATHOLIC......	3	NA	2 100	12.1	14.4
093 CHR CH (DISC).	1	208	257	1.5	1.8
123 CH GOD (ANDER)	1	9	27	0.2	0.2
127 CH GOD (CLEVE)	1	89	109*	0.6	0.7
151 L-D SAINTS....	1	NA	68	0.4	0.5
165 CH OF NAZARENE	1	23	29	0.2	0.2
167 CHS OF CHRIST.	7	1 060	1 350	7.8	9.3
193 EPISCOPAL.....	1	88	125	0.7	0.9
215 EVAN METH CH..	1	62	76*	0.4	0.5
263 INT FOURSQ GOS	1	30	37*	0.2	0.3
283 LUTH--MO SYNOD	1	96	135	0.8	0.9
357 PRESB CH US...	1	125	153*	0.9	1.1
413 S.D.A.	1	10	12*	0.1	0.1
419 SO BAPT CONV..	10	6 050	7 420*	42.7	51.1
449 UN METHODIST..	5	1 490	1 828*	10.5	12.6
453 UN PRES CH USA	1	125	153*	0.9	1.1
NUECES	202	62 484	149 583*	55.8	100.0
017 AMER BAPT ASSN	2	50	50	-	-
029 AMER LUTH CH..	5	1 690	2 186	0.8	1.5
053 ASSEMB OF GOD.	10	2 197	2 599	1.0	1.7
081 CATHOLIC......	31	NA	68 178	25.4	45.6
093 CHR CH (DISC).	7	1 414	2 164	0.8	1.4
097 CHR CHS&CHS CR	2	65	81*	-	0.1
123 CH GOD (ANDER)	3	204	612	0.2	0.4
127 CH GOD (CLEVE)	1	30	38*	-	-
133 CH GOD(7TH)DEN	1	22	28*	-	-
151 L-D SAINTS....	4	NA	1 295	0.5	0.9
164 CH LUTH CONF..	1	57	67	-	-
165 CH OF NAZARENE	5	376	463	0.2	0.3
167 CHS OF CHRIST.	24	2 900	3 691	1.4	2.5
193 EPISCOPAL.....	7	2 882	3 730	1.4	2.5
203 EVAN FREE CH..	1	66	83*	-	0.1
221 FREE METHODIST	1	36	135	0.1	0.1
263 INT FOURSQ GOS	1	22	28*	-	-
270 CONSRV JUDAISM	1	41	51*	-	-
271 REFORM JUDAISM	1	400	501*	0.2	0.3
281 LUTH CH AMER..	1	411	514	0.2	0.3
283 LUTH--MO SYNOD	5	1 655	2 282	0.9	1.5
285 MENNONITE CH..	2	94	118*	-	0.1
349 PENT HOLINESS.	3	211	264*	0.1	0.2
357 PRESB CH US...	11	3 091	3 870*	1.4	2.6
403 SALVATION ARMY	1	98	850	0.3	0.6
413 S.D.A.	3	284	356*	0.1	0.2
419 SO BAPT CONV..	47	34 342	42 995*	16.0	28.7
435 UNITARIAN-UNIV	1	44	55*	-	-
443 UN C OF CHRIST	2	130	163*	0.1	0.1
449 UN METHODIST..	17	9 619	12 043*	4.5	8.1
469 WELS.	1	53	93	-	0.1
OCHILTREE	20	3 905	5 647*	58.9	100.0
053 ASSEMB OF GOD.	2	116	200	2.1	3.5
081 CATHOLIC......	1	NA	600	6.3	10.6
093 CHR CH (DISC).	1	321	454	4.7	8.0
097 CHR CHS&CHS CR	1	50	62*	0.6	1.1
127 CH GOD (CLEVE)	1	80	99*	1.0	1.8
151 L-D SAINTS....	1	NA	74	0.8	1.3
157 CH OF BRETHREN	1	74	92*	1.0	1.6
165 CH OF NAZARENE	1	99	106	1.1	1.9
167 CHS OF CHRIST.	2	215	285	3.0	5.0
193 EPISCOPAL.....	1	10	17	0.2	0.3
283 LUTH--MO SYNOD	1	47	60	0.6	1.1
285 MENNONITE CH..	1	81	101*	1.1	1.8
357 PRESB CH US...	1	61	76*	0.8	1.3
419 SO BAPT CONV..	3	1 729	2 150*	22.4	38.1
449 UN METHODIST..	1	961	1 195*	12.5	21.2
453 UN PRES CH USA	1	61	76*	0.8	1.3
OLDHAM	10	1 382	2 238*	98.0	100.0
081 CATHOLIC......	1	NA	500	21.9	22.3
167 CHS OF CHRIST.	3	170	215	9.4	9.6
419 SO BAPT CONV..	2	639	803*	35.2	35.9
449 UN METHODIST..	4	573	720*	31.5	32.2
ORANGE	91	32 584	53 480*	63.8	100.0
017 AMER BAPT ASSN	2	180	180	0.2	0.3
029 AMER LUTH CH..	2	288	400	0.5	0.7
053 ASSEMB OF GOD.	8	964	1 315	1.6	2.5
059 BAPT MISS ASSN	5	1 256	1 565*	1.9	2.9
081 CATHOLIC......	7	NA	11 095	13.2	20.7
093 CHR CH (DISC).	3	412	613	0.7	1.1
097 CHR CHS&CHS CR	4	390	486*	0.6	0.9
101 C.M.E.	3	551	686*	0.8	1.3
123 CH GOD (ANDER)	1	73	219	0.3	0.4
127 CH GOD (CLEVE)	2	91	113*	0.1	0.2
151 L-D SAINTS....	3	NA	1 270	1.5	2.4
165 CH OF NAZARENE	2	231	367	0.4	0.7
167 CHS OF CHRIST.	9	950	1 265	1.5	2.4
193 EPISCOPAL.....	1	281	341	0.4	0.6
283 LUTH--MO SYNOD	1	168	249	0.3	0.5
357 PRESB CH US...	3	736	917*	1.1	1.7
403 SALVATION ARMY	1	120	144	0.2	0.3
413 S.D.A.	2	104	130*	0.2	0.2
419 SO BAPT CONV..	25	21 443	26 711*	31.9	49.9
449 UN METHODIST..	7	4 346	5 414*	6.5	10.1
PALO PINTO	66	11 109	15 524*	64.5	100.0
053 ASSEMB OF GOD.	3	165	234	1.0	1.5
059 BAPT MISS ASSN	3	435	524*	2.2	3.4
081 CATHOLIC......	5	NA	1 900	7.9	12.2
093 CHR CH (DISC).	2	182	284	1.2	1.8
101 C.M.E.	2	203	244*	1.0	1.6
127 CH GOD (CLEVE)	1	170	205*	0.9	1.3
165 CH OF NAZARENE	1	61	146	0.6	0.9
167 CHS OF CHRIST.	10	800	1 020	4.2	6.6
193 EPISCOPAL.....	2	151	191	0.8	1.2
283 LUTH--MO SYNOD	1	125	163	0.7	1.0
356 PRESB CH AMER.	1	25	25	0.1	0.2
357 PRESB CH US...	2	113	136*	0.6	0.9
413 S.D.A.	1	62	75*	0.3	0.5
419 SO BAPT CONV..	22	7 063	8 506*	35.4	54.8
449 UN METHODIST..	8	1 440	1 734*	7.2	11.2
453 UN PRES CH USA	2	114	137*	0.6	0.9
PANOLA	69	9 429	11 436*	55.2	100.0
017 AMER BAPT ASSN	13	1 374	1 374	6.6	12.0
053 ASSEMB OF GOD.	2	149	172	0.8	1.5
059 BAPT MISS ASSN	11	1 873	2 278*	11.0	19.9
081 CATHOLIC......	1	NA	257	1.2	2.2
097 CHR CHS&CHS CR	1	180	219*	1.1	1.9
101 C.M.E.	4	636	774*	3.7	6.8

NA— Not applicable   *Total adherents estimated from known number of communicant, confirmed, full members.   —Represents a percent less than 0.1.   Percentages may not total due to rounding.

TEXAS

Table 4. Churches and Church Membership by County and Denomination: 1980

County and Denomination	Number of churches	Communicant, confirmed, full members	Total adherents Number	Percent of total population	Percent of total adherents
165 CH OF NAZARENE	1	22	22	0.1	0.2
167 CHS OF CHRIST.	5	304	387	1.9	3.4
193 EPISCOPAL.	1	68	87	0.4	0.8
357 PRESB CH US...	2	55	67*	0.3	0.6
419 SO BAPT CONV..	14	2 789	3 392*	16.4	29.7
449 UN METHODIST..	12	1 925	2 341*	11.3	20.5
453 UN PRES CH USA	2	54	66*	0.3	0.6
PARKER	91	18 488	23 491*	52.7	100.0
053 ASSEMB OF GOD.	5	420	516	1.2	2.2
059 BAPT MISS ASSN	3	409	497*	1.1	2.1
081 CATHOLIC......	1	NA	575	1.3	2.4
093 CHR CH (DISC).	1	270	340	0.8	1.4
101 C.M.E.........	2	126	153*	0.3	0.7
127 CH GOD (CLEVE)	2	191	232*	0.5	1.0
151 L-D SAINTS....	1	NA	276	0.6	1.2
165 CH OF NAZARENE	1	20	12	-	0.1
167 CHS OF CHRIST.	17	1 850	2 355	5.3	10.0
185 CUMBER PRESB..	1	11	21	-	0.1
193 EPISCOPAL.	1	125	169	0.4	0.7
283 LUTH--MO SYNOD	1	96	150	0.3	0.6
357 PRESB CH US...	1	187	227*	0.5	1.0
413 S.D.A.........	1	48	58*	0.1	0.2
419 SO BAPT CONV..	38	11 519	14 001*	31.4	59.6
449 UN METHODIST..	14	3 030	3 683*	8.3	15.7
453 UN PRES CH USA	1	186	226*	0.5	1.0
PARMER	27	6 219	9 473*	85.8	100.0
053 ASSEMB OF GOD.	2	73	92	0.8	1.0
059 BAPT MISS ASSN	1	53	68*	0.6	0.7
081 CATHOLIC......	2	NA	1 500	13.6	15.8
167 CHS OF CHRIST.	6	575	732	6.6	7.7
283 LUTH--MO SYNOD	3	173	240	2.2	2.5
349 PENT HOLINESS	1	29	37*	0.3	0.4
419 SO BAPT CONV..	6	4 018	5 143*	46.6	54.3
443 UN C OF CHRIST	1	83	106*	1.0	1.1
449 UN METHODIST..	5	1 215	1 555*	14.1	16.4
PECOS	31	4 818	10 902*	74.6	100.0
053 ASSEMB OF GOD.	3	156	190	1.3	1.7
081 CATHOLIC......	6	NA	4 657	31.9	42.7
093 CHR CH (DISC).	2	423	540	3.7	5.0
097 CHR CHS&CHS CR	1	90	115*	0.8	1.1
151 L-D SAINTS....	1	NA	63	0.4	0.6
165 CH OF NAZARENE	1	?	?	?	?
167 CHS OF CHRIST.	4	498	657	4.5	6.0
193 EPISCOPAL.	1	11	18	0.1	0.2
283 LUTH--MO SYNOD	1	61	79	0.5	0.7
357 PRESB CH US...	1	240	307*	2.1	2.8
419 SO BAPT CONV..	7	2 302	2 948*	20.2	27.0
449 UN METHODIST..	3	1 037	1 328*	9.1	12.2
POLK	59	9 141	11 642*	47.7	100.0
017 AMER BAPT ASSN	1	50	50	0.2	0.4
053 ASSEMB OF GOD.	7	542	651	2.7	5.6
059 BAPT MISS ASSN	16	2 685	3 267*	13.4	28.1
081 CATHOLIC......	1	NA	400	1.6	3.4
151 L-D SAINTS....	1	NA	69	0.3	0.6
167 CHS OF CHRIST.	6	449	584	2.4	5.0
193 EPISCOPAL.	1	69	102	0.4	0.9
283 LUTH--MO SYNOD	1	123	164	0.7	1.4
357 PRESB CH US...	2	280	341*	1.4	2.9
419 SO BAPT CONV..	13	3 794	4 616*	18.9	39.6
449 UN METHODIST..	10	1 149	1 398*	5.7	12.0
POTTER	117	59 551	87 524*	88.7	100.0
017 AMER BAPT ASSN	3	505	505	0.5	0.6
053 ASSEMB OF GOD.	7	1 015	1 434	1.5	1.6
059 BAPT MISS ASSN	2	250	306*	0.3	0.3
081 CATHOLIC......	8	NA	13 000	13.2	14.9
093 CHR CH (DISC).	4	1 858	2 300	2.3	2.6
097 CHR CHS&CHS CR	6	3 195	3 911*	4.0	4.5
101 C.M.E.........	2	450	551*	0.6	0.6
123 CH GOD (ANDER)	1	60	180	0.2	0.2
151 L-D SAINTS....	2	NA	852	0.9	1.0
165 CH OF NAZARENE	5	807	1 205	1.2	1.4
167 CHS OF CHRIST.	19	3 750	4 773	4.8	5.5
193 EPISCOPAL.	2	1 643	1 975	2.0	2.3
263 INT FOURSQ GOS	2	420	514*	0.5	0.6
271 REFORM JUDAISM	1	194	237*	0.2	0.3
283 LUTH--MO SYNOD	3	959	1 341	1.4	1.5
290 METRO COMM CHS	0	20	40	-	-
349 PENT HOLINESS	3	272	333*	0.3	0.4
357 PRESB CH US...	3	1 577	1 930*	2.0	2.2
403 SALVATION ARMY	1	156	215	0.2	0.2
413 S.D.A.........	4	642	786*	0.8	0.9
419 SO BAPT CONV..	24	31 651	38 741*	39.3	44.3
435 UNITARIAN-UNIV	1	50	61*	0.1	0.1
449 UN METHODIST..	10	8 246	10 093*	10.2	11.5
453 UN PRES CH USA	4	1 831	2 241*	2.3	2.6
PRESIDIO	16	1 037	4 047*	78.0	100.0
081 CATHOLIC......	7	NA	2 751	53.0	68.0
093 CHR CH (DISC).	1	45	57	1.1	1.4
167 CHS OF CHRIST.	1	30	38	0.7	0.9
193 EPISCOPAL.	1	53	53	1.0	1.3
419 SO BAPT CONV..	2	539	681*	13.1	16.8
449 UN METHODIST..	3	321	405*	7.8	10.0
453 UN PRES CH USA	1	49	62*	1.2	1.5

County and Denomination	Number of churches	Communicant, confirmed, full members	Total adherents Number	Percent of total population	Percent of total adherents
RAINS	22	2 924	3 476*	71.8	100.0
017 AMER BAPT ASSN	2	50	50	1.0	1.4
053 ASSEMB OF GOD.	3	132	156	3.2	4.5
059 BAPT MISS ASSN	1	103	122*	2.5	3.5
127 CH GOD (CLEVE)	2	131	156*	3.2	4.5
167 CHS OF CHRIST.	3	150	190	3.9	5.5
419 SO BAPT CONV..	8	1 428	1 697*	35.1	48.8
449 UN METHODIST..	3	930	1 105*	22.8	31.8
RANDALL	43	19 583	28 428*	37.9	100.0
017 AMER BAPT ASSN	1	182	182	0.2	0.6
029 AMER LUTH CH..	1	490	687	0.9	2.4
053 ASSEMB OF GOD.	2	298	427	0.6	1.5
059 BAPT MISS ASSN	2	575	702*	0.9	2.5
081 CATHOLIC......	4	NA	4 000	5.3	14.1
093 CHR CH (DISC).	1	179	196	0.3	0.7
097 CHR CHS&CHS CR	1	35	43*	0.1	0.2
127 CH GOD (CLEVE)	2	208	254*	0.3	0.9
151 L-D SAINTS....	1	NA	123	0.2	0.4
165 CH OF NAZARENE	2	66	194	0.3	0.7
167 CHS OF CHRIST.	6	1 855	2 361	3.1	8.3
193 EPISCOPAL.	2	109	185	0.2	0.7
237 GC MENN BR CHS	1	56	68*	0.1	0.2
283 LUTH--MO SYNOD	1	146	216	0.3	0.8
357 PRESB CH US...	2	433	529*	0.7	1.9
419 SO BAPT CONV..	9	11 072	13 523*	18.0	47.6
449 UN METHODIST..	4	3 694	4 512*	6.0	15.9
453 UN PRES CH USA	1	185	226*	0.3	0.8
REAGAN	9	1 385	2 669*	64.5	100.0
053 ASSEMB OF GOD.	1	45	62	1.5	2.3
081 CATHOLIC......	1	NA	865	20.9	32.4
093 CHR CH (DISC).	1	12	12	0.3	0.4
167 CHS OF CHRIST.	1	35	45	1.1	1.7
419 SO BAPT CONV..	3	971	1 265*	30.6	47.4
449 UN METHODIST..	1	300	391*	9.5	14.6
453 UN PRES CH USA	1	22	29*	0.7	1.1
REAL	9	1 136	1 791*	72.5	100.0
081 CATHOLIC......	2	NA	400	16.2	22.3
167 CHS OF CHRIST.	2	80	102	4.1	5.7
419 SO BAPT CONV..	3	930	1 135*	46.0	63.4
449 UN METHODIST..	2	126	154*	6.2	8.6
RED RIVER	67	8 833	10 699*	66.4	100.0
017 AMER BAPT ASSN	8	1 495	1 495	9.3	14.0
053 ASSEMB OF GOD.	3	151	233	1.4	2.2
081 CATHOLIC......	1	NA	97	0.6	0.9
093 CHR CH (DISC).	2	55	85	0.5	0.8
097 CHR CHS&CHS CR	1	50	60*	0.4	0.6
101 C.M.E.........	1	145	175*	1.1	1.6
127 CH GOD (CLEVE)	1	13	16*	0.1	0.1
151 L-D SAINTS....	1	NA	62	0.4	0.6
167 CHS OF CHRIST.	11	650	825	5.1	7.7
185 CUMBER PRESB..	2	86	175	1.1	1.6
193 EPISCOPAL.	1	12	17	0.1	0.2
283 LUTH--MO SYNOD	1	59	74	0.5	0.7
357 PRESB CH US...	3	143	173*	1.1	1.6
419 SO BAPT CONV..	12	3 977	4 801*	29.8	44.9
449 UN METHODIST..	16	1 854	2 238*	13.9	20.9
453 UN PRES CH USA	3	143	173*	1.1	1.6
REEVES	37	4 555	11 809*	74.7	100.0
053 ASSEMB OF GOD.	1	37	83	0.5	0.7
059 BAPT MISS ASSN	1	36	46*	0.3	0.4
081 CATHOLIC......	7	NA	5 735	36.3	48.6
093 CHR CH (DISC).	1	273	338	2.1	2.9
101 C.M.E.........	1	28	36*	0.2	0.3
151 L-D SAINTS....	1	NA	156	1.0	1.3
165 CH OF NAZARENE	1	20	45	0.3	0.4
167 CHS OF CHRIST.	7	350	445	2.8	3.8
193 EPISCOPAL.	1	72	90	0.6	0.8
283 LUTH--MO SYNOD	1	75	104	0.7	0.9
357 PRESB CH US...	1	138	178*	1.1	1.5
413 S.D.A.........	2	92	119*	0.8	1.0
419 SO BAPT CONV..	8	2 762	3 566*	22.6	30.2
449 UN METHODIST..	4	672	868*	5.5	7.4
REFUGIO	30	3 171	6 887*	74.1	100.0
029 AMER LUTH CH..	1	196	240	2.6	3.5
053 ASSEMB OF GOD.	1	22	33	0.4	0.5
081 CATHOLIC......	8	NA	2 955	31.8	42.9
123 CH GOD (ANDER)	1	13	39	0.4	0.6
167 CHS OF CHRIST.	1	184	235	2.5	3.4
193 EPISCOPAL.	1	50	56	0.6	0.8
281 LUTH CH AMER..	1	46	52	0.6	0.8
283 LUTH--MO SYNOD	1	28	40	0.4	0.6
357 PRESB CH US...	3	210	258*	2.8	3.7
419 SO BAPT CONV..	5	1 869	2 299*	24.7	33.4
443 UN C OF CHRIST	1	83	102*	1.1	1.5
449 UN METHODIST..	3	470	578*	6.2	8.4
ROBERTS	4	708	981*	82.6	100.0
081 CATHOLIC......	0	NA	100	8.4	10.2
093 CHR CH (DISC).	1	86	98	8.3	10.0
167 CHS OF CHRIST.	1	70	89	7.5	9.1
419 SO BAPT CONV..	1	350	440*	37.1	44.9

NA—Not applicable   *Total adherents estimated from known number of communicant, confirmed, full members.   —Represents a percent less than 0.1.   Percentages may not total due to rounding.

Table 4. Churches and Church Membership by County and Denomination: 1980

County and Denomination	Number of churches	Communicant, confirmed, full members	Total adherents Number	Percent of total population	Percent of total adherents
449 UN METHODIST..	1	202	254*	21.4	25.9
ROBERTSON	41	4 789	6 660*	45.5	100.0
053 ASSEMB OF GOD.	2	72	88	0.6	1.3
081 CATHOLIC......	3	NA	780	5.3	11.7
167 CHS OF CHRIST.	9	500	635	4.3	9.5
193 EPISCOPAL.....	1	27	45	0.3	0.7
357 PRESB CH US...	1	19	23*	0.2	0.3
419 SO BAPT CONV..	15	3 418	4 170*	28.5	62.6
449 UN METHODIST..	10	753	919*	6.3	13.8
ROCKWALL	25	4 819	6 893*	47.4	100.0
017 AMER BAPT ASSN	1	125	125	0.9	1.8
053 ASSEMB OF GOD.	2	126	189	1.3	2.7
059 BAPT MISS ASSN	1	178	220*	1.5	3.2
081 CATHOLIC......	1	NA	560	3.9	8.1
093 CHR CH (DISC).	2	138	199	1.4	2.9
167 CHS OF CHRIST.	3	150	190	1.3	2.8
193 EPISCOPAL.....	1	141	150	1.0	2.2
221 FREE METHODIST	1	82	450	3.1	6.5
283 LUTH--MO SYNOD	1	144	194	1.3	2.8
357 PRESB CH US...	2	89	110*	0.8	1.6
419 SO BAPT CONV..	4	2 395	2 960*	20.4	42.9
449 UN METHODIST..	4	1 165	1 440*	9.9	20.9
453 UN PRES CH USA	2	86	106*	0.7	1.5
RUNNELS	49	6 420	11 044*	93.0	100.0
029 AMER LUTH CH..	1	251	300	2.5	2.7
053 ASSEMB OF GOD.	2	64	146	1.2	1.3
081 CATHOLIC......	6	NA	3 090	26.0	28.0
093 CHR CH (DISC).	1	123	161	1.4	1.5
123 CH GOD (ANDER)	1	13	39	0.3	0.4
165 CH OF NAZARENE	1	23	36	0.3	0.3
167 CHS OF CHRIST.	10	640	789	6.6	7.1
193 EPISCOPAL.....	1	19	33	0.3	0.3
263 INT FOURSQ GOS	1	18	22*	0.2	0.2
281 LUTH CH AMER..	1	145	170	1.4	1.5
283 LUTH--MO SYNOD	1	10	60	0.5	0.5
357 PRESB CH US...	1	213	258*	2.2	2.3
419 SO BAPT CONV..	13	3 672	4 451*	37.5	40.3
443 UN C OF CHRIST	1	63	76*	0.6	0.7
449 UN METHODIST..	8	1 166	1 413*	11.9	12.8
RUSK	111	18 822	22 864*	55.3	100.0
017 AMER BAPT ASSN	15	3 131	3 131	7.6	13.7
053 ASSEMB OF GOD.	7	327	472	1.1	2.1
059 BAPT MISS ASSN	6	615	747*	1.8	3.3
081 CATHOLIC......	1	NA	294	0.7	1.3
093 CHR CH (DISC).	5	342	432	1.0	1.9
101 C.M.E.........	6	402	488*	1.2	2.1
127 CH GOD (CLEVE)	1	22	27*	0.1	0.1
151 L-D SAINTS....	1	NA	173	0.4	0.8
165 CH OF NAZARENE	2	74	127	0.3	0.6
167 CHS OF CHRIST.	9	840	1 070	2.6	4.7
185 CUMBER PRESB..	1	42	68	0.2	0.3
193 EPISCOPAL.....	1	106	145	0.4	0.6
357 PRESB CH US...	4	162	197*	0.5	0.9
413 S.D.A.........	1	12	15*	–	0.1
419 SO BAPT CONV..	27	9 672	11 744*	28.4	51.4
449 UN METHODIST..	20	2 912	3 536*	8.5	15.5
453 UN PRES CH USA	4	163	198*	0.5	0.9
SABINE	41	3 736	4 742*	54.5	100.0
017 AMER BAPT ASSN	4	242	242	2.8	5.1
053 ASSEMB OF GOD.	2	31	52	0.6	1.1
059 BAPT MISS ASSN	1	504	600*	6.9	12.7
081 CATHOLIC......	1	NA	104	1.2	2.2
101 C.M.E.........	2	170	203*	2.3	4.3
123 CH GOD (ANDER)	3	98	294	3.4	6.2
165 CH OF NAZARENE	1	?	?	?	?
167 CHS OF CHRIST.	4	160	204	2.3	4.3
221 FREE METHODIST	1	36	69	0.8	1.5
283 LUTH--MO SYNOD	1	12	16	0.2	0.3
419 SO BAPT CONV..	7	1 802	2 147*	24.7	45.3
449 UN METHODIST..	14	681	811*	9.3	17.1
SAN AUGUSTINE	22	3 167	3 869*	44.0	100.0
017 AMER BAPT ASSN	2	254	254	2.9	6.6
053 ASSEMB OF GOD.	1	83	104	1.2	2.7
059 BAPT MISS ASSN	2	327	393*	4.5	10.2
081 CATHOLIC......	1	NA	61	0.7	1.6
101 C.M.E.........	2	311	374*	4.3	9.7
123 CH GOD (ANDER)	1	15	45	0.5	1.2
167 CHS OF CHRIST.	3	150	190	2.2	4.9
193 EPISCOPAL.....	1	24	41	0.5	1.1
357 PRESB CH US...	1	84	101*	1.1	2.6
419 SO BAPT CONV..	6	1 531	1 840*	20.9	47.6
449 UN METHODIST..	2	388	466*	5.3	12.0
SAN JACINTO	29	3 127	3 783*	33.1	100.0
017 AMER BAPT ASSN	2	242	242	2.1	6.4
053 ASSEMB OF GOD.	2	145	174	1.5	4.6
059 BAPT MISS ASSN	4	401	492*	4.3	13.0
167 CHS OF CHRIST.	2	100	127	1.1	3.4
357 PRESB CH US...	1	57	70*	0.6	1.9
419 SO BAPT CONV..	10	1 764	2 165*	18.9	57.2
449 UN METHODIST..	8	418	513*	4.5	13.6

County and Denomination	Number of churches	Communicant, confirmed, full members	Total adherents Number	Percent of total population	Percent of total adherents
SAN PATRICIO	84	12 777	35 834*	61.8	100.0
029 AMER LUTH CH..	3	359	451	0.8	1.3
053 ASSEMB OF GOD.	7	295	400	0.7	1.1
059 BAPT MISS ASSN	1	469	599*	1.0	1.7
081 CATHOLIC......	14	NA	19 243	33.2	53.7
093 CHR CH (DISC).	3	195	288	0.5	0.8
097 CHR CHS&CHS CR	2	150	192*	0.3	0.5
127 CH GOD (CLEVE)	1	28	36*	0.1	0.1
151 L-D SAINTS....	2	NA	171	0.3	0.5
165 CH OF NAZARENE	2	81	123	0.2	0.3
167 CHS OF CHRIST.	13	650	825	1.4	2.3
193 EPISCOPAL.....	3	238	320	0.6	0.9
281 LUTH CH AMER..	1	204	282	0.5	0.8
283 LUTH--MO SYNOD	2	110	137	0.2	0.4
285 MENNONITE CH..	2	166	212*	0.4	0.6
349 PENT HOLINESS.	2	64	82*	0.1	0.2
357 PRESB CH US...	5	533	681*	1.2	1.9
419 SO BAPT CONV..	13	6 941	8 863*	15.3	24.7
449 UN METHODIST..	8	2 294	2 929*	5.0	8.2
SAN SABA	24	3 078	4 064*	71.4	100.0
053 ASSEMB OF GOD.	1	44	52	0.9	1.3
081 CATHOLIC......	1	NA	251	4.4	6.2
093 CHR CH (DISC).	1	25	79	1.4	1.9
167 CHS OF CHRIST.	7	440	560	9.8	13.8
193 EPISCOPAL.....	1	29	35	0.6	0.9
357 PRESB CH US...	2	220	267*	4.7	6.6
419 SO BAPT CONV..	9	1 925	2 340*	41.1	57.6
449 UN METHODIST..	2	395	480*	8.4	11.8
SCHLEICHER	9	1 047	1 758*	62.3	100.0
081 CATHOLIC......	1	NA	450	16.0	25.6
093 CHR CH (DISC).	1	13	30	1.1	1.7
167 CHS OF CHRIST.	2	80	102	3.6	5.8
193 EPISCOPAL.....	1	14	15	0.5	0.9
357 PRESB CH US...	1	88	109*	3.9	6.2
419 SO BAPT CONV..	2	613	757*	26.8	43.1
449 UN METHODIST..	1	239	295*	10.5	16.8
SCURRY	48	9 864	15 042*	82.7	100.0
017 AMER BAPT ASSN	2	845	845	4.6	5.6
053 ASSEMB OF GOD.	4	213	303	1.7	2.0
059 BAPT MISS ASSN	1	199	245*	1.3	1.6
081 CATHOLIC......	3	NA	2 850	15.7	18.9
093 CHR CH (DISC).	1	125	207	1.1	1.4
123 CH GOD (ANDER)	1	35	105	0.6	0.7
127 CH GOD (CLEVE)	1	63	78*	0.4	0.5
165 CH OF NAZARENE	1	47	45	0.2	0.3
167 CHS OF CHRIST.	10	1 279	1 613	8.9	10.7
193 EPISCOPAL.....	1	36	54	0.3	0.4
281 LUTH CH AMER..	1	97	155	0.9	1.0
357 PRESB CH US...	1	58	72*	0.4	0.5
419 SO BAPT CONV..	12	5 451	6 723*	37.0	44.7
449 UN METHODIST..	8	1 358	1 675*	9.2	11.1
453 UN PRES CH USA	1	58	72*	0.4	0.5
SHACKELFORD	17	2 236	2 822*	72.1	100.0
053 ASSEMB OF GOD.	1	28	104	2.7	3.7
081 CATHOLIC......	1	NA	15	0.4	0.5
093 CHR CH (DISC).	2	112	142	3.6	5.0
101 C.M.E.........	1	38	46*	1.2	1.6
167 CHS OF CHRIST.	3	150	190	4.9	6.7
193 EPISCOPAL.....	1	12	12	0.3	0.4
283 LUTH--MO SYNOD	1	103	143	3.7	5.1
357 PRESB CH US...	1	51	62*	1.6	2.2
419 SO BAPT CONV..	3	1 330	1 609*	41.1	57.0
449 UN METHODIST..	2	361	437*	11.2	15.5
453 UN PRES CH USA	1	51	62*	1.6	2.2
SHELBY	97	12 895	15 372*	66.6	100.0
017 AMER BAPT ASSN	25	2 629	2 629	11.4	17.1
053 ASSEMB OF GOD.	4	366	567	2.5	3.7
059 BAPT MISS ASSN	9	1 474	1 783*	7.7	11.6
081 CATHOLIC......	1	NA	130	0.6	0.8
093 CHR CH (DISC).	3	188	239	1.0	1.6
097 CHR CHS&CHS CR	3	605	732*	3.2	4.8
101 C.M.E.........	8	1 279	1 547*	6.7	10.1
165 CH OF NAZARENE	1	24	32	0.1	0.2
167 CHS OF CHRIST.	10	500	635	2.8	4.1
193 EPISCOPAL.....	1	54	92	0.4	0.6
357 PRESB CH US...	2	47	57*	0.2	0.4
419 SO BAPT CONV..	13	4 154	5 024*	21.8	32.7
449 UN METHODIST..	15	1 528	1 848*	8.0	12.0
453 UN PRES CH USA	2	47	57*	0.2	0.4
SHERMAN	8	1 608	2 298*	72.4	100.0
053 ASSEMB OF GOD.	1	46	77	2.4	3.4
081 CATHOLIC......	1	NA	300	9.5	13.1
093 CHR CH (DISC).	1	176	219	6.9	9.5
167 CHS OF CHRIST.	1	100	127	4.0	5.5
419 SO BAPT CONV..	1	793	971*	30.6	42.3
449 UN METHODIST..	3	493	604*	19.0	26.3
SMITH	191	60 117	80 118*	62.4	100.0
017 AMER BAPT ASSN	4	395	395	0.3	0.5
019 AMER BAPT USA.	1	150	183*	0.1	0.2
053 ASSEMB OF GOD.	23	2 090	3 100	2.4	3.9

NA— Not applicable   *Total adherents estimated from known number of communicant, confirmed, full members.   —Represents a percent less than 0.1.   Percentages may not total due to rounding.

Table 4. Churches and Church Membership by County and Denomination: 1980

County and Denomination	Number of churches	Communicant, confirmed, full members	Total adherents Number	Percent of total population	Percent of total adherents
059 BAPT MISS ASSN	12	1 526	1 865*	1.5	2.3
081 CATHOLIC......	1	NA	5 300	4.1	6.6
093 CHR CH (DISC).	3	1 202	1 507	1.2	1.9
097 CHR CHS&CHS CR	1	75	92*	0.1	0.1
101 C.M.E.........	14	4 554	5 564*	4.3	6.9
123 CH GOD (ANDER)	1	60	180	0.1	0.2
127 CH GOD (CLEVE)	3	224	274*	0.2	0.3
151 L-D SAINTS....	1	NA	493	0.4	0.6
165 CH OF NAZARENE	4	412	547	0.4	0.7
167 CHS OF CHRIST.	21	3 125	3 975	3.1	5.0
193 EPISCOPAL.....	3	1 103	1 274	1.0	1.6
226 FRIENDS-USA...	1	28	34*	–	–
270 CONSRV JUDAISM	1	58	71*	0.1	0.1
271 REFORM JUDAISM	1	162	198*	0.2	0.2
281 LUTH CH AMER..	1	158	195	0.2	0.2
283 LUTH--MO SYNOD	1	422	552	0.4	0.7
356 PRESB CH AMER.	2	487	541	0.4	0.7
357 PRESB CH US...	4	653	798*	0.6	1.0
403 SALVATION ARMY	1	107	285	0.2	0.4
413 S.D.A.........	2	219	268*	0.2	0.3
419 SO BAPT CONV..	55	32 365	39 546*	30.8	49.4
435 UNITARIAN-UNIV	1	20	24*	–	–
449 UN METHODIST..	25	9 870	12 060*	9.4	15.1
453 UN PRES CH USA	4	652	797*	0.6	1.0
SOMERVELL	**10**	**1 715**	**2 170***	**52.2**	**100.0**
053 ASSEMB OF GOD.	1	39	62	1.5	2.9
081 CATHOLIC......	1	NA	46	1.1	2.1
167 CHS OF CHRIST.	2	100	127	3.1	5.9
419 SO BAPT CONV..	5	1 277	1 568*	37.7	72.3
449 UN METHODIST..	1	299	367*	8.8	16.9
STARR	**20**	**920**	**39 154***	**143.6**	**100.0**
053 ASSEMB OF GOD.	1	81	162	0.6	0.4
081 CATHOLIC......	12	NA	37 737	138.4	96.4
151 L-D SAINTS....	1	NA	150	0.6	0.4
237 GC MENN BR CHS	1	50	66*	0.2	0.2
313 N AM BAPT CONF	1	78	103*	0.4	0.3
419 SO BAPT CONV..	3	494	650*	2.4	1.7
449 UN METHODIST..	1	217	286*	1.0	0.7
STEPHENS	**25**	**4 145**	**5 805***	**58.5**	**100.0**
053 ASSEMB OF GOD.	1	36	61	0.6	1.1
059 BAPT MISS ASSN	1	25	30*	0.3	0.5
081 CATHOLIC......	1	NA	700	7.1	12.1
093 CHR CH (DISC).	1	268	317	3.2	5.5
101 C.M.E.........	2	150	182*	1.8	3.1
127 CH GOD (CLEVE)	1	53	64*	0.6	1.1
165 CH OF NAZARENE	1	20	49	0.5	0.8
167 CHS OF CHRIST.	2	463	589	5.9	10.1
193 EPISCOPAL.....	1	132	185	1.9	3.2
357 PRESB CH US...	1	72	87*	0.9	1.5
413 S.D.A.........	1	32	39*	0.4	0.7
419 SO BAPT CONV..	7	2 146	2 597*	26.2	44.7
449 UN METHODIST..	4	676	818*	8.2	14.1
453 UN PRES CH USA	1	72	87*	0.9	1.5
STERLING	**5**	**638**	**796***	**66.0**	**100.0**
081 CATHOLIC......	1	NA	?	?	?
167 CHS OF CHRIST.	1	50	64	5.3	8.0
357 PRESB CH US...	1	40	50*	4.1	6.3
419 SO BAPT CONV..	1	361	449*	37.2	56.4
449 UN METHODIST..	1	187	233*	19.3	29.3
STONEWALL	**9**	**1 200**	**1 431***	**59.5**	**100.0**
059 BAPT MISS ASSN	1	132	156*	6.5	10.9
081 CATHOLIC......	1	NA	?	?	?
101 C.M.E.........	1	13	15*	0.6	1.0
167 CHS OF CHRIST.	3	130	165	6.9	11.5
419 SO BAPT CONV..	2	776	919*	38.2	64.2
449 UN METHODIST..	1	149	176*	7.3	12.3
SUTTON	**10**	**1 089**	**3 154***	**61.5**	**100.0**
053 ASSEMB OF GOD.	1	24	22	0.4	0.7
081 CATHOLIC......	1	NA	1 695	33.0	53.7
151 L-D SAINTS....	1	NA	40	0.8	1.3
167 CHS OF CHRIST.	1	35	45	0.9	1.4
193 EPISCOPAL.....	1	88	155	3.0	4.9
283 LUTH--MO SYNOD	1	23	32	0.6	1.0
357 PRESB CH US...	1	83	105*	2.0	3.3
419 SO BAPT CONV..	2	510	647*	12.6	20.5
449 UN METHODIST..	1	326	413*	8.1	13.1
SWISHER	**29**	**5 464**	**7 627***	**78.4**	**100.0**
053 ASSEMB OF GOD.	2	54	63	0.6	0.8
059 BAPT MISS ASSN	1	69	86*	0.9	1.1
081 CATHOLIC......	2	NA	800	8.2	10.5
093 CHR CH (DISC).	1	15	26	0.3	0.3
127 CH GOD (CLEVE)	1	36	45*	0.5	0.6
167 CHS OF CHRIST.	6	500	635	6.5	8.3
283 LUTH--MO SYNOD	1	43	51	0.5	0.7
357 PRESB CH US...	2	130	162*	1.7	2.1
419 SO BAPT CONV..	6	3 357	4 187*	43.1	54.9
449 UN METHODIST..	5	1 132	1 412*	14.5	18.5
453 UN PRES CH USA	2	128	160*	1.6	2.1
TARRANT	**638**	**299 415**	**429 742***	**49.9**	**100.0**

County and Denomination	Number of churches	Communicant, confirmed, full members	Total adherents Number	Percent of total population	Percent of total adherents
001 ADVENT CHR CH.	2	236	287*	–	0.1
005 AME ZION......	1	370	465	0.1	0.1
017 AMER BAPT ASSN	5	548	548	0.1	0.1
019 AMER BAPT USA.	5	1 580	1 924*	0.2	0.4
029 AMER LUTH CH..	5	1 951	2 544	0.3	0.6
053 ASSEMB OF GOD.	64	10 461	11 948	1.4	2.8
059 BAPT MISS ASSN	15	3 194	3 889*	0.5	0.9
081 CATHOLIC......	29	NA	57 457	6.7	13.4
089 CHR & MISS AL.	2	88	119	–	–
093 CHR CH (DISC).	23	9 710	13 653	1.6	3.2
097 CHR CHS&CHS CR	6	698	850*	0.1	0.2
101 C.M.E.........	6	4 371	5 322*	0.6	1.2
123 CH GOD (ANDER)	2	120	360	–	0.1
127 CH GOD (CLEVE)	6	685	834*	0.1	0.2
151 L-D SAINTS....	9	NA	3 574	0.4	0.8
165 CH OF NAZARENE	14	1 524	2 425	0.3	0.6
167 CHS OF CHRIST.	83	22 406	27 464	3.2	6.4
185 CUMBER PRESB..	6	819	1 255	0.1	0.3
193 EPISCOPAL.....	20	9 986	12 623	1.5	2.9
215 EVAN METH CH..	2	305	371*	–	0.1
221 FREE METHODIST	1	30	75	–	–
226 FRIENDS-USA...	1	77	94*	–	–
263 INT FOURSQ GOS	2	305	371*	–	0.1
270 CONSRV JUDAISM	1	?	?	?	?
271 REFORM JUDAISM	1	770	938*	0.1	0.2
281 LUTH CH AMER..	8	1 493	2 103	0.2	0.5
283 LUTH--MO SYNOD	10	4 697	6 439	0.7	1.5
290 METRO COMM CHS	1	45	90	–	–
349 PENT HOLINESS.	2	66	80*	–	–
353 CHR BRETHREN..	3	85	150	–	–
356 PRESB CH AMER.	1	39	67	–	–
357 PRESB CH US...	26	5 790	7 050*	0.8	1.6
381 REF PRES-EVAN.	1	30	38	–	–
403 SALVATION ARMY	1	202	439	0.1	0.1
413 S.D.A.........	10	1 435	1 747*	0.2	0.4
415 S-D BAPTIST GC	1	6	7*	–	–
419 SO BAPT CONV..	158	152 606	185 809*	21.6	43.2
435 UNITARIAN-UNIV	3	183	223*	–	0.1
443 UN C OF CHRIST	2	548	667*	0.1	0.2
449 UN METHODIST..	73	56 016	68 204*	7.9	15.9
453 UN PRES CH USA	26	5 819	7 085*	0.8	1.6
469 WELS..........	1	121	154	–	–
TAYLOR	**146**	**52 326**	**72 508***	**65.4**	**100.0**
017 AMER BAPT ASSN	1	154	154	0.1	0.2
029 AMER LUTH CH..	1	478	657	0.6	0.9
053 ASSEMB OF GOD.	7	609	918	0.8	1.3
059 BAPT MISS ASSN	2	159	193*	0.2	0.3
081 CATHOLIC......	4	NA	6 918	6.2	9.5
093 CHR CH (DISC).	2	888	1 377	1.2	1.9
097 CHR CHS&CHS CR	1	30	36*	–	–
101 C.M.E.........	1	565	685*	0.6	0.9
123 CH GOD (ANDER)	1	15	45	–	0.1
127 CH GOD (CLEVE)	2	123	149*	0.1	0.2
151 L-D SAINTS....	2	NA	601	0.5	0.8
165 CH OF NAZARENE	4	356	584	0.5	0.8
167 CHS OF CHRIST.	37	9 518	11 959	10.8	16.5
193 EPISCOPAL.....	2	1 342	1 864	1.7	2.6
215 EVAN METH CH..	1	159	193*	0.2	0.3
221 FREE METHODIST	2	27	75	0.1	0.1
263 INT FOURSQ GOS	3	285	346*	0.3	0.5
271 REFORM JUDAISM	1	40	49*	–	0.1
283 LUTH--MO SYNOD	2	564	680	0.6	0.9
335 ORTH PRESB CH.	1	155	188*	0.2	0.3
357 PRESB CH US...	3	549	666*	0.6	0.9
403 SALVATION ARMY	1	152	309	0.3	0.4
413 S.D.A.........	1	89	108*	0.1	0.1
419 SO BAPT CONV..	38	27 614	33 497*	30.2	46.2
435 UNITARIAN-UNIV	1	12	15*	–	–
449 UN METHODIST..	22	7 893	9 575*	8.6	13.2
453 UN PRES CH USA	3	550	667*	0.6	0.9
TERRELL	**7**	**626**	**1 478***	**92.7**	**100.0**
081 CATHOLIC......	1	NA	700	43.9	47.4
167 CHS OF CHRIST.	1	60	75	4.7	5.1
357 PRESB CH US...	1	105	130*	8.2	8.8
419 SO BAPT CONV..	1	255	317*	19.9	21.4
449 UN METHODIST..	3	206	256*	16.1	17.3
TERRY	**35**	**6 824**	**10 791***	**74.0**	**100.0**
053 ASSEMB OF GOD.	3	189	349	2.4	3.2
081 CATHOLIC......	1	NA	2 000	13.7	18.5
093 CHR CH (DISC).	1	191	220	1.5	2.0
127 CH GOD (CLEVE)	2	116	146*	1.0	1.4
151 L-D SAINTS....	1	NA	69	0.5	0.6
165 CH OF NAZARENE	1	46	67	0.5	0.6
167 CHS OF CHRIST.	6	950	1 210	8.3	11.2
193 EPISCOPAL.....	1	57	74	0.5	0.7
263 INT FOURSQ GOS	2	375	473*	3.2	4.4
357 PRESB CH US...	1	65	82*	0.6	0.8
419 SO BAPT CONV..	10	3 848	4 855*	33.3	45.0
449 UN METHODIST..	5	923	1 165*	8.0	10.8
453 UN PRES CH USA	1	64	81*	0.6	0.8
THROCKMORTON	**19**	**2 061**	**2 574***	**125.4**	**100.0**
053 ASSEMB OF GOD.	1	16	20	1.0	0.8
081 CATHOLIC......	1	NA	100	4.9	3.9
093 CHR CH (DISC).	2	46	71	3.5	2.8
167 CHS OF CHRIST.	6	350	445	21.7	17.3
357 PRESB CH US...	1	8	9*	0.4	0.3
419 SO BAPT CONV..	4	1 395	1 640*	79.9	63.7

NA—Not applicable   *Total adherents estimated from known number of communicant, confirmed, full members.   —Represents a percent less than 0.1.   Percentages may not total due to rounding.

Table 4. Churches and Church Membership by County and Denomination: 1980

County and Denomination	Number of churches	Communicant, confirmed, full members	Total adherents		
			Number	Percent of total population	Percent of total adherents
449 UN METHODIST..	3	238	280*	13.6	10.9
453 UN PRES CH USA	1	8	9*	0.4	0.3
TITUS	64	11 078	13 664*	63.7	100.0
017 AMER BAPT ASSN	16	1 655	1 655	7.7	12.1
053 ASSEMB OF GOD.	3	205	331	1.5	2.4
059 BAPT MISS ASSN	2	1 078	1 319*	6.2	9.7
081 CATHOLIC......	1	NA	312	1.5	2.3
093 CHR CH (DISC).	2	156	196	0.9	1.4
101 C.M.E........	1	305	373*	1.7	2.7
127 CH GOD (CLEVE)	1	20	24*	0.1	0.2
165 CH OF NAZARENE	1	90	160	0.7	1.2
167 CHS OF CHRIST.	14	1 230	1 550	7.2	11.3
193 EPISCOPAL.....	1	53	54	0.3	0.4
283 LUTH--MO SYNOD	1	?	?	?	?
357 PRESB CH US..	2	156	191*	0.9	1.4
413 S.D.A.........	1	50	61*	0.3	0.4
419 SO BAPT CONV..	11	4 676	5 720*	26.7	41.9
449 UN METHODIST...	5	1 248	1 527*	7.1	11.2
453 UN PRES CH USA	2	156	191*	0.9	1.4
TOM GREEN	92	28 224	45 680*	53.9	100.0
017 AMER BAPT ASSN	1	30	30		0.1
029 AMER LUTH CH..	1	340	450	0.5	1.0
053 ASSEMB OF GOD.	9	833	1 136	1.3	2.5
059 BAPT MISS ASSN	1	84	101*	0.1	0.2
081 CATHOLIC......	9	NA	10 235	12.1	22.4
093 CHR CH (DISC).	3	733	1 120	1.3	2.5
097 CHR CHS&CHS CR	1	15	18*	–	–
101 C.M.E........	1	120	145*	0.2	0.3
123 CH GOD (ANDER)	1	30	90	0.1	0.2
127 CH GOD (CLEVE)	1	30	36*		0.1
151 L-D SAINTS....	1	NA	492	0.6	1.1
165 CH OF NAZARENE	2	169	243	0.3	0.5
167 CHS OF CHRIST.	13	2 250	2 865	3.4	6.3
193 EPISCOPAL.....	2	749	912	1.1	2.0
263 INT FOURSQ GOS	2	231	279*	0.3	0.6
281 LUTH CH AMER..	1	126	154	0.2	0.3
283 LUTH--MO SYNOD	1	608	857	1.0	1.9
357 PRESB CH US...	2	1 202	1 451*	1.7	3.2
403 SALVATION ARMY	1	138	279	0.3	0.6
413 S.D.A.........	2	201	243*	0.3	0.5
419 SO BAPT CONV..	20	15 941	19 240*	22.7	42.1
435 UNITARIAN-UNIV	1	24	29*		0.1
449 UN METHODIST..	13	3 791	4 576*	5.4	10.0
453 UN PRES CH USA	3	579	699*	0.8	1.5
TRAVIS	266	100 162	194 194*	46.3	100.0
017 AMER BAPT ASSN	1	35	35	–	–
019 AMER BAPT USA.	1	100	120*	–	0.1
029 AMER LUTH CH..	7	4 666	5 964	1.4	3.1
053 ASSEMB OF GOD.	19	1 979	2 816	0.7	1.5
059 BAPT MISS ASSN	1	175	209*	–	0.1
081 CATHOLIC......	18	NA	69 018	16.5	35.5
089 CHR & MISS AL.	1	55	105	–	0.1
093 CHR CH (DISC).	8	2 023	2 820	0.7	1.5
097 CHR CHS&CHS CR	2	475	568*	0.1	0.3
123 CH GOD (ANDER)	1	52	156	–	0.1
127 CH GOD (CLEVE)	3	96	115*	–	0.1
133 CH GOD(7TH)DEN	1	17	20*	–	–
151 L-D SAINTS....	4	NA	2 125	0.5	1.1
164 LUTH CONF....	1	12	20	–	–
165 CH OF NAZARENE	3	553	807	0.2	0.4
167 CHS OF CHRIST.	37	4 950	6 300	1.5	3.2
177 CONGR HOL CH..	1	25	30*	–	–
185 CUMBER PRESB..	4	727	1 436	0.3	0.7
193 EPISCOPAL.....	12	7 208	8 437	2.0	4.3
203 EVAN FREE CH..	2	323	386*	0.1	0.2
208 EVAN LUTH ASSN	1	90	106	–	0.1
226 FRIENDS-USA...	1	87	104*	–	0.1
263 INT FOURSQ GOS	1	10	12*	–	–
270 CONSRV JUDAISM	1	148	177*	–	0.1
271 REFORM JUDAISM	1	630	753*	0.2	0.4
281 LUTH CH AMER..	9	2 486	3 110	0.7	1.6
283 LUTH--MO SYNOD	12	4 868	6 442	1.5	3.3
290 METRO COMM CHS	1	75	150	–	0.1
313 N AM BAPT CONF	1	39	47*	–	–
349 PENT HOLINESS.	4	179	214*	0.1	0.1
353 CHR BRETHREN..	4	425	555	0.1	0.3
357 PRESB CH US...	11	4 577	5 473*	1.3	2.8
403 SALVATION ARMY	1	140	274	0.1	0.1
413 S.D.A.........	1	277	331*	0.1	0.2
419 SO BAPT CONV..	53	45 445	54 339*	13.0	28.0
435 UNITARIAN-UNIV	1	312	373*	0.1	0.2
443 UN C OF CHRIST	3	479	573*	0.1	0.3
449 UN METHODIST..	27	15 110	18 067*	4.3	9.3
453 UN PRES CH USA	5	1 194	1 428*	0.3	0.7
469 WELS..........	1	120	179	–	0.1
TRINITY	32	3 911	4 712*	49.9	100.0
053 ASSEMB OF GOD.	3	127	155	1.6	3.3
101 C.M.E........	2	83	99*	1.0	2.1
127 CH GOD (CLEVE)	1	76	91*	1.0	1.9
167 CHS OF CHRIST.	9	500	635	6.7	13.5
357 PRESB CH US...	1	18	21*	0.2	0.4
419 SO BAPT CONV..	12	2 620	3 129*	33.1	66.4
449 UN METHODIST..	4	487	582*	6.2	12.4
TYLER	58	7 882	10 195*	62.8	100.0
017 AMER BAPT ASSN	1	90	90	0.6	0.9

County and Denomination	Number of churches	Communicant, confirmed, full members	Total adherents		
			Number	Percent of total population	Percent of total adherents
053 ASSEMB OF GOD.	8	416	551	3.4	5.4
059 BAPT MISS ASSN	2	45	55*	0.3	0.5
081 CATHOLIC......	1	NA	400	2.5	3.9
093 CHR CH (DISC).	1	78	120	0.7	1.2
101 C.M.E........	1	45	55*	0.3	0.5
151 L-D SAINTS....	2	NA	149	0.9	1.5
167 CHS OF CHRIST.	7	420	535	3.3	5.2
413 S.D.A.........	1	28	34*	0.2	0.3
419 SO BAPT CONV..	30	6 155	7 472*	46.1	73.3
449 UN METHODIST..	4	605	734*	4.5	7.2
UPSHUR	83	13 235	17 340*	60.6	100.0
017 AMER BAPT ASSN	1	45	45	0.2	0.2
053 ASSEMB OF GOD.	3	157	212	0.7	1.2
059 BAPT MISS ASSN	20	3 372	4 144*	14.5	23.9
093 CHR CH (DISC).	1	42	49	0.2	0.3
101 C.M.E........	6	836	1 027*	3.6	5.9
127 CH GOD (CLEVE)	2	67	82*	0.3	0.5
151 L-D SAINTS....	2	NA	1 041	3.6	6.0
165 CH OF NAZARENE	1	55	41	0.1	0.2
167 CHS OF CHRIST.	16	1 200	1 530	5.4	8.8
419 SO BAPT CONV..	20	5 949	7 311*	25.6	42.2
449 UN METHODIST..	11	1 512	1 858*	6.5	10.7
UPTON	18	2 534	3 642*	78.8	100.0
053 ASSEMB OF GOD.	3	52	94	2.0	2.6
081 CATHOLIC......	3	NA	400	8.7	11.0
093 CHR CH (DISC).	1	38	54	1.2	1.5
167 CHS OF CHRIST.	2	115	150	3.2	4.1
283 LUTH--MO SYNOD	1	27	30	0.6	0.8
419 SO BAPT CONV..	4	1 864	2 360*	51.1	64.8
449 UN METHODIST..	3	425	538*	11.6	14.8
453 UN PRES CH USA	1	13	16*	0.3	0.4
UVALDE	38	6 106	14 380*	64.1	100.0
029 AMER LUTH CH..	1	216	252	1.1	1.8
053 ASSEMB OF GOD.	2	198	296	1.3	2.1
081 CATHOLIC......	3	NA	6 443	28.7	44.8
089 CHR & MISS AL.	1	35	51	0.2	0.4
093 CHR CH (DISC).	1	139	214	1.0	1.5
097 CHR CHS&CHS CR	1	125	158*	0.7	1.1
151 L-D SAINTS....	1	NA	251	1.1	1.7
165 CH OF NAZARENE	1	44	65	0.3	0.5
167 CHS OF CHRIST.	9	600	764	3.4	5.3
193 EPISCOPAL.....	1	362	338	1.5	2.4
221 FREE METHODIST	1	5	24	0.1	0.2
283 LUTH--MO SYNOD	1	130	160	0.7	1.1
357 PRESB CH US...	1	212	267*	1.2	1.9
413 S.D.A.........	1	18	23*	0.1	0.2
419 SO BAPT CONV..	8	2 815	3 551*	15.8	24.7
449 UN METHODIST..	5	1 207	1 523*	6.8	10.6
VAL VERDE	25	5 312	21 360*	59.5	100.0
053 ASSEMB OF GOD.	3	490	733	2.0	3.4
081 CATHOLIC......	4	NA	13 874	38.6	65.0
093 CHR CH (DISC).	1	110	200	0.6	0.9
151 L-D SAINTS....	1	NA	424	1.2	2.0
165 CH OF NAZARENE	1	31	86	0.2	0.4
167 CHS OF CHRIST.	3	175	225	0.6	1.1
193 EPISCOPAL.....	1	306	411	1.1	1.9
283 LUTH--MO SYNOD	1	157	190	0.5	0.9
357 PRESB CH US...	1	235	303*	0.8	1.4
413 S.D.A.........	1	46	59*	0.2	0.3
419 SO BAPT CONV..	5	2 777	3 584*	10.0	16.8
449 UN METHODIST..	3	985	1 271*	3.5	6.0
VAN ZANDT	108	16 753	20 427*	65.0	100.0
017 AMER BAPT ASSN	1	67	67	0.2	0.3
029 AMER LUTH CH..	1	85	106	0.3	0.5
053 ASSEMB OF GOD.	6	489	692	2.2	3.4
059 BAPT MISS ASSN	22	2 764	3 313*	10.5	16.2
093 CHR CH (DISC).	1	4	14	–	0.1
101 C.M.E........	7	1 513	1 814*	5.8	8.9
127 CH GOD (CLEVE)	2	189	227*	0.7	1.1
151 L-D SAINTS....	1	NA	162	0.5	0.8
165 CH OF NAZARENE	3	178	202	0.6	1.0
167 CHS OF CHRIST.	19	1 200	1 525	4.9	7.5
215 EVAN METH CH..	1	40	48*	0.2	0.2
357 PRESB CH US...	3	74	89*	0.3	0.4
419 SO BAPT CONV..	22	7 854	9 415*	30.0	46.1
449 UN METHODIST..	16	2 223	2 665*	8.5	13.0
453 UN PRES CH USA	3	73	88*	0.3	0.4
VICTORIA	64	16 486	43 850*	63.7	100.0
029 AMER LUTH CH..	3	1 560	2 030	3.0	4.6
053 ASSEMB OF GOD.	3	273	424	0.6	1.0
081 CATHOLIC......	10	NA	22 516	32.7	51.3
093 CHR CH (DISC).	1	71	314	0.5	0.7
097 CHR CHS&CHS CR	1	20	25*	–	0.1
123 CH GOD (ANDER)	1	12	36	0.1	0.1
127 CH GOD (CLEVE)	1	54	67*	0.1	0.2
151 L-D SAINTS....	1	NA	318	0.5	0.7
165 CH OF NAZARENE	1	53	80	0.1	0.2
167 CHS OF CHRIST.	10	1 102	1 510	2.2	3.4
193 EPISCOPAL.....	2	643	767	1.1	1.7
271 REFORM JUDAISM	1	76	95*	0.1	0.2
281 LUTH CH AMER..	4	2 145	2 579	3.7	5.9
283 LUTH--MO SYNOD	1	279	340	0.5	0.8
357 PRESB CH US...	3	1 068	1 331*	1.9	3.0

NA—Not applicable   *Total adherents estimated from known number of communicant, confirmed, full members.   —Represents a percent less than 0.1.   Percentages may not total due to rounding.

Table 4. Churches and Church Membership by County and Denomination: 1980

County and Denomination	Number of churches	Communicant, confirmed, full members	Total adherents Number	Percent of total population	Percent of total adherents
403 SALVATION ARMY	1	17	57	0.1	0.1
413 S.D.A.........	1	29	36*	0.1	0.1
419 SO BAPT CONV..	11	6 687	8 336*	12.1	19.0
435 UNITARIAN-UNIV	1	23	29*	-	0.1
449 UN METHODIST..	7	2 374	2 960*	4.3	6.8
WALKER	**41**	**10 760**	**14 517***	**34.7**	**100.0**
017 AMER BAPT ASSN	3	190	190	0.5	1.3
053 ASSEMB OF GOD.	1	621	1 040	2.5	7.2
059 BAPT MISS ASSN	1	118	135*	0.3	0.9
081 CATHOLIC......	2	NA	1 502	3.6	10.3
123 CH GOD (ANDER)	1	7	21	0.1	0.1
151 L-D SAINTS....	1	NA	219	0.5	1.5
167 CHS OF CHRIST.	4	600	765	1.8	5.3
193 EPISCOPAL.....	1	344	443	1.1	3.1
283 LUTH--MO SYNOD	1	219	307	0.7	2.1
357 PRESB CH US...	1	385	440*	1.1	3.0
413 S.D.A.........	1	36	41*	0.1	0.3
419 SO BAPT CONV..	12	6 280	7 175*	17.2	49.4
449 UN METHODIST..	12	1 960	2 239*	5.4	15.4
WALLER	**37**	**4 929**	**7 495***	**37.9**	**100.0**
029 AMER LUTH CH..	2	347	440	2.2	5.9
081 CATHOLIC......	3	NA	1 551	7.8	20.7
093 CHR CH (DISC).	1	131	144	0.7	1.9
167 CHS OF CHRIST.	6	400	510	2.6	6.8
193 EPISCOPAL.....	2	233	292	1.5	3.9
215 EVAN METH CH..	1	47	56*	0.3	0.7
283 LUTH--MO SYNOD	1	137	147	0.7	2.0
413 S.D.A.........	1	40	48*	0.2	0.6
419 SO BAPT CONV..	8	2 406	2 883*	14.6	38.5
449 UN METHODIST..	12	1 188	1 424*	7.2	19.0
WARD	**32**	**6 255**	**10 003***	**71.6**	**100.0**
053 ASSEMB OF GOD.	1	148	115	0.8	1.1
081 CATHOLIC......	2	NA	2 100	15.0	21.0
093 CHR CH (DISC).	2	83	107	0.8	1.1
097 CHR CHS&CHS CR	1	75	94*	0.7	0.9
151 L-D SAINTS....	1	NA	102	0.7	1.0
165 CH OF NAZARENE	1	20	27	0.2	0.3
167 CHS OF CHRIST.	7	475	600	4.3	6.0
193 EPISCOPAL.....	1	73	75	0.5	0.7
283 LUTH--MO SYNOD	1	59	93	0.7	0.9
357 PRESB CH US...	1	46	58*	0.4	0.6
419 SO BAPT CONV..	9	4 207	5 288*	37.8	52.9
449 UN METHODIST..	4	899	1 130*	8.1	11.3
453 UN PRES CH USA	1	170	214*	1.5	2.1
WASHINGTON	**34**	**9 460**	**13 717***	**62.4**	**100.0**
029 AMER LUTH CH..	12	4 813	5 745	26.1	41.9
053 ASSEMB OF GOD.	1	68	110	0.5	0.8
081 CATHOLIC......	3	NA	2 185	9.9	15.9
093 CHR CH (DISC).	2	114	160	0.7	1.2
123 CH GOD (ANDER)	1	50	150	0.7	1.1
167 CHS OF CHRIST.	1	200	255	1.2	1.9
193 EPISCOPAL.....	1	235	297	1.4	2.2
283 LUTH--MO SYNOD	2	1 060	1 342	6.1	9.8
313 N AM BAPT CONF	1	86	102*	0.5	0.7
357 PRESB CH US...	1	156	186*	0.8	1.4
419 SO BAPT CONV..	4	1 125	1 338*	6.1	9.8
443 UN C OF CHRIST	3	761	905*	4.1	6.6
449 UN METHODIST..	2	792	942*	4.3	6.9
WEBB	**47**	**3 784**	**57 570***	**58.0**	**100.0**
053 ASSEMB OF GOD.	5	741	888	0.9	1.5
081 CATHOLIC......	16	NA	51 959	52.3	90.3
093 CHR CH (DISC).	1	131	169	0.2	0.3
127 CH GOD (CLEVE)	1	50	65*	0.1	0.1
151 L-D SAINTS....	2	NA	678	0.7	1.2
165 CH OF NAZARENE	2	37	136	0.1	0.2
167 CHS OF CHRIST.	3	115	172	0.2	0.3
193 EPISCOPAL.....	1	294	276	0.3	0.5
221 FREE METHODIST	1	15	84	0.1	0.1
270 CONSRV JUDAISM	1	66	86*	0.1	0.1
271 REFORM JUDAISM	1	50	65*	0.1	0.1
357 PRESB CH US...	2	132	172*	0.2	0.3
403 SALVATION ARMY	1	83	119	0.1	0.2
413 S.D.A.........	1	89	116*	0.1	0.2
419 SO BAPT CONV..	5	1 441	1 880*	1.9	3.3
449 UN METHODIST..	4	540	705*	0.7	1.2
WHARTON	**64**	**9 811**	**29 371***	**73.0**	**100.0**
019 AMER BAPT USA.	1	175	215*	0.5	0.7
029 AMER LUTH CH..	3	755	950	2.4	3.2
053 ASSEMB OF GOD.	5	224	338	0.8	1.2
081 CATHOLIC......	12	NA	16 941	42.1	57.7
093 CHR CH (DISC).	2	128	191	0.5	0.7
123 CH GOD (ANDER)	2	88	264	0.7	0.9
143 CG IN CR(MENN)	1	63	63	0.2	0.2
151 L-D SAINTS....	1	NA	75	0.2	0.3
167 CHS OF CHRIST.	5	600	765	1.9	2.6
193 EPISCOPAL.....	1	119	135	0.3	0.5
281 LUTH CH AMER..	2	371	436	1.1	1.5
283 LUTH--MO SYNOD	1	282	371	0.9	1.3
357 PRESB CH US...	3	402	495*	1.2	1.7
413 S.D.A.........	1	21	26*	0.1	0.1
419 SO BAPT CONV..	11	3 833	4 720*	11.7	16.1
449 UN METHODIST..	13	2 750	3 386*	8.4	11.5

County and Denomination	Number of churches	Communicant, confirmed, full members	Total adherents Number	Percent of total population	Percent of total adherents
WHEELER	**29**	**4 565**	**5 989***	**83.9**	**100.0**
001 ADVENT CHR CH.	1	45	55*	0.8	0.9
017 AMER BAPT ASSN	2	89	89	1.2	1.5
053 ASSEMB OF GOD.	2	41	78	1.1	1.3
081 CATHOLIC......	1	NA	400	5.6	6.7
097 CHR CHS&CHS CR	1	15	18*	0.3	0.3
127 CH GOD (CLEVE)	1	11	13*	0.2	0.2
165 CH OF NAZARENE	2	45	60	0.8	1.0
167 CHS OF CHRIST.	3	400	510	7.1	8.5
193 EPISCOPAL.....	1	12	12	0.2	0.2
283 LUTH--MO SYNOD	1	103	131	1.8	2.2
419 SO BAPT CONV..	7	2 902	3 518*	49.3	58.7
421 SO METHODIST..	1	12	26	0.4	0.4
449 UN METHODIST..	6	890	1 079*	15.1	18.0
WICHITA	**133**	**53 236**	**75 811***	**62.6**	**100.0**
017 AMER BAPT ASSN	2	174	174	0.1	0.2
029 AMER LUTH CH..	1	289	373	0.3	0.5
053 ASSEMB OF GOD.	14	1 554	2 476	2.0	3.3
081 CATHOLIC......	5	NA	8 738	7.2	11.5
093 CHR CH (DISC).	6	1 559	2 023	1.7	2.7
097 CHR CHS&CHS CR	1	164	197*	0.2	0.3
123 CH GOD (ANDER)	1	30	90	0.1	0.1
127 CH GOD (CLEVE)	5	641	771*	0.6	1.0
151 L-D SAINTS....	1	NA	726	0.6	1.0
165 CH OF NAZARENE	4	423	749	0.6	1.0
167 CHS OF CHRIST.	17	3 811	5 433	4.5	7.2
193 EPISCOPAL.....	4	766	1 056	0.9	1.4
263 INT FOURSQ GOS	1	236	284*	0.2	0.4
271 REFORM JUDAISM	1	30	36*	-	-
281 LUTH CH AMER..	1	194	271	0.2	0.4
283 LUTH--MO SYNOD	5	1 180	1 551	1.3	2.0
357 PRESB CH US...	6	1 120	1 347*	1.1	1.8
403 SALVATION ARMY	1	91	215	0.2	0.3
413 S.D.A.........	1	11	13*	-	-
419 SO BAPT CONV..	34	31 391	37 767*	31.2	49.8
449 UN METHODIST..	15	8 437	10 151*	8.4	13.4
453 UN PRES CH USA	6	1 121	1 349*	1.1	1.8
469 WELS..........	1	14	21	-	-
WILBARGER	**38**	**10 258**	**13 191***	**82.8**	**100.0**
053 ASSEMB OF GOD.	2	146	341	2.1	2.6
059 BAPT MISS ASSN	1	35	42*	0.3	0.3
081 CATHOLIC......	1	NA	700	4.4	5.3
093 CHR CH (DISC).	1	190	234	1.5	1.8
101 C.M.E.........	1	88	106*	0.7	0.8
127 CH GOD (CLEVE)	1	91	109*	0.7	0.8
165 CH OF NAZARENE	1	17	23	0.1	0.2
167 CHS OF CHRIST.	9	962	1 140	7.2	8.6
193 EPISCOPAL.....	1	72	80	0.5	0.6
281 LUTH CH AMER..	1	144	190	1.2	1.4
283 LUTH--MO SYNOD	3	769	942	5.9	7.1
357 PRESB CH US...	1	122	146*	0.9	1.1
413 S.D.A.........	1	19	23*	0.1	0.2
419 SO BAPT CONV..	10	6 248	7 491*	47.0	56.8
449 UN METHODIST..	3	1 233	1 478*	9.3	11.2
453 UN PRES CH USA	1	122	146*	0.9	1.1
WILLACY	**30**	**3 084**	**24 661***	**141.0**	**100.0**
053 ASSEMB OF GOD.	2	200	206	1.2	0.8
081 CATHOLIC......	7	NA	20 601	117.8	83.5
093 CHR CH (DISC).	1	51	78	0.4	0.3
151 L-D SAINTS....	1	NA	83	0.5	0.3
165 CH OF NAZARENE	1	?	?	?	?
167 CHS OF CHRIST.	4	250	320	1.8	1.3
193 EPISCOPAL.....	1	25	37	0.2	0.2
263 INT FOURSQ GOS	1	26	34*	0.2	0.1
281 LUTH CH AMER..	1	136	168	1.0	0.7
283 LUTH--MO SYNOD	1	156	229	1.3	0.9
349 PENT HOLINESS.	1	46	60*	0.3	0.2
357 PRESB CH US...	1	48	62*	0.4	0.3
413 S.D.A.........	1	43	56*	0.3	0.2
419 SO BAPT CONV..	4	1 368	1 774*	10.1	7.2
449 UN METHODIST..	3	735	953*	5.4	3.9
WILLIAMSON	**102**	**20 567**	**30 312***	**39.6**	**100.0**
029 AMER LUTH CH..	9	2 638	3 330	4.4	11.0
053 ASSEMB OF GOD.	9	475	677	0.9	2.2
059 BAPT MISS ASSN	1	212	266*	0.3	0.9
081 CATHOLIC......	7	NA	4 210	5.5	13.9
093 CHR CH (DISC).	3	84	130	0.2	0.4
097 CHR CHS&CHS CR	2	150	188*	0.2	0.6
127 CH GOD (CLEVE)	1	16	20*	-	0.1
167 CHS OF CHRIST.	12	1 490	1 895	2.5	6.3
185 CUMBER PRESB..	1	12	12	-	-
193 EPISCOPAL.....	3	297	445	0.6	1.5
203 EVAN FREE CH..	1	71	89*	0.1	0.3
281 LUTH CH AMER..	2	751	984	1.3	3.2
283 LUTH--MO SYNOD	4	1 228	1 599	2.1	5.3
357 PRESB CH US...	4	559	700*	0.9	2.3
413 S.D.A.........	2	29	36*	-	0.1
419 SO BAPT CONV..	20	8 115	10 168*	13.3	33.5
443 UN C OF CHRIST	1	329	412*	0.5	1.4
449 UN METHODIST..	20	4 111	5 151*	6.7	17.0
WILSON	**30**	**3 609**	**10 910***	**65.1**	**100.0**
029 AMER LUTH CH..	4	938	1 154	6.9	10.6
053 ASSEMB OF GOD.	2	221	275	1.6	2.5
081 CATHOLIC......	6	NA	6 417	38.3	58.8

NA—Not applicable   *Total adherents estimated from known number of communicant, confirmed, full members.   —Represents a percent less than 0.1.   Percentages may not total due to rounding.

Table 4. Churches and Church Membership by County and Denomination: 1980

County and Denomination	Number of churches	Communicant, confirmed, full members	Total adherents		
			Number	Percent of total population	Percent of total adherents
133 CH GOD(7TH)DEN	1	16	20*	0.1	0.2
151 L-D SAINTS....	1	NA	19	0.1	0.2
167 CHS OF CHRIST.	4	200	255	1.5	2.3
419 SO BAPT CONV..	7	1 435	1 779*	10.6	16.3
449 UN METHODIST..	5	799	991*	5.9	9.1
WINKLER	**22**	**5 214**	**8 544***	**85.9**	**100.0**
053 ASSEMB OF GOD.	2	178	202	2.0	2.4
081 CATHOLIC......	2	NA	1 961	19.7	23.0
093 CHR CH (DISC).	1	25	45	0.5	0.5
097 CHR CHS&CHS CR	2	150	189*	1.9	2.2
127 CH GOD (CLEVE)	1	23	29*	0.3	0.3
165 CH OF NAZARENE	1	27	54	0.5	0.6
167 CHS OF CHRIST.	4	500	635	6.4	7.4
193 EPISCOPAL.....	1	39	54	0.5	0.6
283 LUTH—MO SYNOD	1	73	92	0.9	1.1
419 SO BAPT CONV..	5	3 522	4 431*	44.6	51.9
449 UN METHODIST..	2	677	852*	8.6	10.0
WISE	**81**	**11 106**	**14 277***	**53.7**	**100.0**
053 ASSEMB OF GOD.	8	423	562	2.1	3.9
081 CATHOLIC......	2	NA	419	1.6	2.9
093 CHR CH (DISC).	2	39	88	0.3	0.6
127 CH GOD (CLEVE)	1	9	11*	–	0.1
151 L-D SAINTS....	1	NA	141	0.5	1.0
165 CH OF NAZARENE	1	15	30	0.1	0.2
167 CHS OF CHRIST.	18	1 065	1 355	5.1	9.5
185 CUMBER PRESB..	1	36	64	0.2	0.4
193 EPISCOPAL.....	2	53	63	0.2	0.4
283 LUTH—MO SYNOD	2	101	140	0.5	1.0
357 PRESB CH US...	1	41	50*	0.2	0.4
419 SO BAPT CONV..	29	7 287	8 873*	33.4	62.1
449 UN METHODIST..	12	1 997	2 432*	9.2	17.0
453 UN PRES CH USA	1	40	49*	0.2	0.3
WOOD	**82**	**13 962**	**16 965***	**68.7**	**100.0**
053 ASSEMB OF GOD.	6	359	435	1.8	2.6
059 BAPT MISS ASSN	24	3 383	4 019*	16.3	23.7
081 CATHOLIC......	1	NA	202	0.8	1.2
093 CHR CH (DISC).	4	328	443	1.8	2.6
101 C.M.E.........	1	220	261*	1.1	1.5
165 CH OF NAZARENE	1	34	74	0.3	0.4
167 CHS OF CHRIST.	9	500	635	2.6	3.7
185 CUMBER PRESB..	1	15	41	0.2	0.2
193 EPISCOPAL.....	1	119	157	0.6	0.9
357 PRESB CH US...	1	32	38*	0.2	0.2
413 S.D.A.........	1	25	30*	0.1	0.2
419 SO BAPT CONV..	14	6 337	7 529*	30.5	44.4
449 UN METHODIST..	17	2 578	3 063*	12.4	18.1
453 UN PRES CH USA	1	32	38*	0.2	0.2
YOAKUM	**16**	**4 384**	**6 725***	**81.0**	**100.0**
053 ASSEMB OF GOD.	3	140	227	2.7	3.4
081 CATHOLIC......	2	NA	1 100	13.3	16.4
097 CHR CHS&CHS CR	1	35	44*	0.5	0.7
101 C.M.E.........	1	643	816*	9.8	12.1
127 CH GOD (CLEVE)	1	60	76*	0.9	1.1
165 CH OF NAZARENE	1	45	71	0.9	1.1
167 CHS OF CHRIST.	2	100	127	1.5	1.9
419 SO BAPT CONV..	3	2 738	3 474*	41.9	51.7
449 UN METHODIST..	2	623	790*	9.5	11.7
YOUNG	**58**	**10 879**	**13 874***	**73.0**	**100.0**
053 ASSEMB OF GOD.	3	353	565	3.0	4.1
081 CATHOLIC......	2	NA	300	1.6	2.2
093 CHR CH (DISC).	3	138	217	1.1	1.6
127 CH GOD (CLEVE)	3	341	410*	2.2	3.0
151 L-D SAINTS....	1	NA	83	0.4	0.6
165 CH OF NAZARENE	1	38	102	0.5	0.7
167 CHS OF CHRIST.	14	1 131	1 440	7.6	10.4
185 CUMBER PRESB..	1	109	165	0.9	1.2
193 EPISCOPAL.....	2	145	194	1.0	1.4
283 LUTH—MO SYNOD	2	274	350	1.8	2.5
357 PRESB CH US...	1	183	220*	1.2	1.6
413 S.D.A.........	1	17	20*	0.1	0.1
419 SO BAPT CONV..	14	5 671	6 825*	35.9	49.2
449 UN METHODIST..	9	2 296	2 763*	14.5	19.9
453 UN PRES CH USA	1	183	220*	1.2	1.6
ZAPATA	**10**	**435**	**3 058***	**46.1**	**100.0**
081 CATHOLIC......	4	NA	2 500	37.7	81.8
151 L-D SAINTS....	1	NA	14	0.2	0.5
167 CHS OF CHRIST.	2	108	135	2.0	4.4
283 LUTH—MO SYNOD	1	23	26	0.4	0.9
419 SO BAPT CONV..	1	251	316*	4.8	10.3
449 UN METHODIST..	1	53	67*	1.0	2.2
ZAVALA	**22**	**1 586**	**9 407***	**80.6**	**100.0**
053 ASSEMB OF GOD.	2	131	354	3.0	3.8
081 CATHOLIC......	3	NA	7 150	61.3	76.0
097 CHR CHS&CHS CR	1	25	33*	0.3	0.4
133 CH GOD(7TH)DEN	1	13	17*	0.1	0.2
165 CH OF NAZARENE	1	?	?	?	?
167 CHS OF CHRIST.	3	175	225	1.9	2.4
283 LUTH—MO SYNOD	1	54	71	0.6	0.8
357 PRESB CH US...	1	25	33*	0.3	0.4
413 S.D.A.........	1	3	4*	–	–
419 SO BAPT CONV..	5	883	1 157*	9.9	12.3

County and Denomination	Number of churches	Communicant, confirmed, full members	Total adherents		
			Number	Percent of total population	Percent of total adherents
449 UN METHODIST..	3	277	363*	3.1	3.9

UTAH

County and Denomination	Number of churches	Communicant, confirmed, full members	Total adherents		
			Number	Percent of total population	Percent of total adherents
THE STATE.....	2 422	39 496	1 098 578*	75.2	100.0
BEAVER	**12**	**56**	**3 529***	**80.6**	**100.0**
081 CATHOLIC......	1	NA	35	0.8	1.0
151 L-D SAINTS....	8	NA	3 422	78.2	97.0
413 S.D.A.........	1	11	14*	0.3	0.4
419 SO BAPT CONV..	1	17	22*	0.5	0.6
449 UN METHODIST..	1	28	36*	0.8	1.0
BOX ELDER	**70**	**1 033**	**28 131***	**84.7**	**100.0**
053 ASSEMB OF GOD.	1	17	17	0.1	0.1
081 CATHOLIC......	2	NA	1 000	3.0	3.6
105 CHRISTIAN REF.	1	29	58	0.2	0.2
151 L-D SAINTS....	59	NA	25 711	77.4	91.4
167 CHS OF CHRIST.	1	18	23	0.1	0.1
193 EPISCOPAL.....	1	94	122	0.4	0.4
281 LUTH CH AMER..	1	142	239	0.7	0.8
419 SO BAPT CONV..	1	377	494*	1.5	1.8
449 UN METHODIST..	2	134	176*	0.5	0.6
453 UN PRES CH USA	1	222	291*	0.9	1.0
CACHE	**125**	**993**	**47 282***	**82.7**	**100.0**
053 ASSEMB OF GOD.	1	24	26	–	0.1
081 CATHOLIC......	1	NA	1 072	1.9	2.3
151 L-D SAINTS....	116	NA	44 958	78.6	95.1
167 CHS OF CHRIST.	1	28	38	0.1	0.1
193 EPISCOPAL.....	1	135	158	0.3	0.3
226 FRIENDS—USA...	1	26	33*	0.1	0.1
283 LUTH—MO SYNOD	1	88	109	0.2	0.2
419 SO BAPT CONV..	2	295	379*	0.7	0.8
453 UN PRES CH USA	1	397	509*	0.9	1.1
CARBON	**35**	**951**	**15 243***	**68.7**	**100.0**
053 ASSEMB OF GOD.	3	95	149	0.7	1.0
081 CATHOLIC......	5	NA	4 130	18.6	27.1
089 CHR & MISS AL.	2	74	111	0.5	0.7
151 L-D SAINTS....	18	NA	9 817	44.3	64.4
167 CHS OF CHRIST.	1	33	84	0.4	0.6
193 EPISCOPAL.....	2	66	74	0.3	0.5
413 S.D.A.........	1	28	36*	0.2	0.2
419 SO BAPT CONV..	2	428	550*	2.5	3.6
449 UN METHODIST..	1	227	292*	1.3	1.9
DAGGETT	**3**	**0**	**462**	**60.1**	**100.0**
081 CATHOLIC......	1	NA	20	2.6	4.3
151 L-D SAINTS....	2	NA	442	57.5	95.7
DAVIS	**207**	**3 449**	**107 922***	**73.6**	**100.0**
019 AMER BAPT USA.	3	793	1 056*	0.7	1.0
053 ASSEMB OF GOD.	1	99	190	0.1	0.2
081 CATHOLIC......	2	NA	6 425	4.4	6.0
151 L-D SAINTS....	188	NA	96 714	66.0	89.6
165 CH OF NAZARENE	1	20	35	–	–
167 CHS OF CHRIST.	2	139	232	0.2	0.2
179 CONSRV BAPT...	1	121	161*	0.1	0.1
193 EPISCOPAL.....	2	204	307	0.2	0.3
283 LUTH—MO SYNOD	2	510	720	0.5	0.7
419 SO BAPT CONV..	4	950	1 265*	0.9	1.2
443 UN C OF CHRIST	1	613	817*	0.6	0.8
DUCHESNE	**21**	**362**	**10 141***	**80.7**	**100.0**
053 ASSEMB OF GOD.	1	43	100	0.8	1.0
081 CATHOLIC......	1	NA	350	2.8	3.5
151 L-D SAINTS....	16	NA	9 260	73.7	91.3
419 SO BAPT CONV..	2	298	403*	3.2	4.0
453 UN PRES CH USA	1	21	28*	0.2	0.3
EMERY	**15**	**44**	**7 913**	**69.1**	**100.0**
053 ASSEMB OF GOD.	1	36	50	0.4	0.6
081 CATHOLIC......	1	NA	21	0.2	0.3
151 L-D SAINTS....	12	NA	7 828	68.4	98.9
193 EPISCOPAL.....	1	8	14	0.1	0.2
GARFIELD	**11**	**0**	**3 054**	**83.1**	**100.0**
081 CATHOLIC......	1	NA	15	0.4	0.5
151 L-D SAINTS....	10	NA	3 039	82.7	99.5
GRAND	**15**	**892**	**4 083***	**49.5**	**100.0**
019 AMER BAPT USA.	1	402	515*	6.2	12.6

NA—Not applicable   *Total adherents estimated from known number of communicant, confirmed, full members.   —Represents a percent less than 0.1.   Percentages may not total due to rounding.

281

Table 4. Churches and Church Membership by County and Denomination: 1980

County and Denomination	Number of churches	Communicant, confirmed, full members	Total adherents		
			Number	Percent of total population	Percent of total adherents
053 ASSEMB OF GOD.	1	47	100	1.2	2.4
081 CATHOLIC......	1	NA	416	5.0	10.2
151 L-D SAINTS....	6	NA	2 357	28.6	57.7
167 CHS OF CHRIST.	1	8	8	0.1	0.2
193 EPISCOPAL.....	1	109	247	3.0	6.0
283 LUTH--MO SYNOD	1	21	49	0.6	1.2
413 S.D.A.........	2	82	105*	1.3	2.6
419 SO BAPT CONV..	1	223	286*	3.5	7.0
IRON	39	264	13 673*	78.8	100.0
081 CATHOLIC......	1	NA	175	1.0	1.3
151 L-D SAINTS....	33	NA	13 103	75.5	95.8
167 CHS OF CHRIST.	1	17	39	0.2	0.3
193 EPISCOPAL.....	1	9	41	0.2	0.3
283 LUTH--MO SYNOD	1	51	70	0.4	0.5
419 SO BAPT CONV..	1	122	160*	0.9	1.2
453 UN PRES CH USA	1	65	85*	0.5	0.6
JUAB	10	46	4 907*	88.7	100.0
081 CATHOLIC......	1	NA	104	1.9	2.1
151 L-D SAINTS....	8	NA	4 742	85.8	96.6
449 UN METHODIST..	1	46	61*	1.1	1.2
KANE	12	33	3 100*	77.0	100.0
081 CATHOLIC......	1	NA	90	2.2	2.9
151 L-D SAINTS....	9	NA	2 967	73.7	95.7
179 CONSRV BAPT...	1	19	25*	0.6	0.8
419 SO BAPT CONV..	1	14	18*	0.4	0.6
MILLARD	27	21	7 310*	81.5	100.0
081 CATHOLIC......	1	NA	27	0.3	0.4
151 L-D SAINTS....	25	NA	7 255	80.9	99.2
453 UN PRES CH USA	1	21	28*	0.3	0.4
MORGAN	11	0	5 948	121.0	100.0
081 CATHOLIC......	1	NA	1 607	32.7	27.0
151 L-D SAINTS....	10	NA	4 341	88.3	73.0
PIUTE	3	0	921	69.3	100.0
081 CATHOLIC......	0	NA	5	0.4	0.5
151 L-D SAINTS....	3	NA	916	68.9	99.5
RICH	5	0	1 699	80.9	100.0
081 CATHOLIC......	0	NA	8	0.4	0.5
151 L-D SAINTS....	5	NA	1 691	80.5	99.5
SALT LAKE	833	19 701	439 433*	71.0	100.0
019 AMER BAPT USA.	4	1 064	1 370*	0.2	0.3
029 AMER LUTH CH..	3	816	1 281	0.2	0.3
053 ASSEMB OF GOD.	5	677	1 202	0.2	0.3
081 CATHOLIC......	16	NA	31 801	5.1	7.2
089 CHR & MISS AL.	1	90	165	—	—
093 CHR CH (DISC)	2	330	444	0.1	0.1
097 CHR CHS&CHS CR	2	515	663*	0.1	0.2
105 CHRISTIAN REF.	3	209	364	0.1	0.1
127 CH GOD (CLEVE)	1	7	9*	—	—
151 L-D SAINTS....	739	NA	381 008	61.5	86.7
165 CH OF NAZARENE	2	125	190	—	0.1
167 CHS OF CHRIST.	2	180	235	—	0.1
175 CONGR CHR CHS.	1	351	452*	0.1	0.1
179 CONSRV BAPT...	1	76	98*	—	—
193 EPISCOPAL.....	5	1 969	2 711	0.4	0.6
203 EVAN FREE CH..	1	122	157*	—	—
226 FRIENDS-USA...	1	15	19*	—	—
270 CONSRV JUDAISM	1	100	129*	—	—
271 REFORM JUDAISM	1	790	1 017*	0.2	0.2
281 LUTH CH AMER..	3	1 032	1 418	0.2	0.3
283 LUTH--MO SYNOD	3	1 419	2 041	0.3	0.5
290 METRO COMM CHS	1	25	50	—	—
403 SALVATION ARMY	1	110	128	—	—
413 S.D.A.........	3	438	564*	0.1	0.1
419 SO BAPT CONV..	14	2 666	3 434*	0.6	0.8
435 UNITARIAN-UNIV	1	315	406*	0.1	0.1
443 UN C OF CHRIST	2	392	505*	0.1	0.1
449 UN METHODIST..	6	2 867	3 693*	0.6	0.8
453 UN PRES CH USA	7	2 943	3 790*	0.6	0.9
469 WELS..........	1	58	89	—	—
SAN JUAN	27	431	5 891*	48.1	100.0
053 ASSEMB OF GOD.	1	59	48	0.4	0.8
081 CATHOLIC......	2	NA	160	1.3	2.7
151 L-D SAINTS....	17	NA	5 125	41.8	87.0
167 CHS OF CHRIST.	2	35	96	0.8	1.6
193 EPISCOPAL.....	1	8	9	0.1	0.2
413 S.D.A.........	1	223	307*	2.5	5.2
419 SO BAPT CONV..	3	106	146*	1.2	2.5
SANPETE	34	98	12 768*	87.3	100.0
081 CATHOLIC......	1	NA	40	0.3	0.3
151 L-D SAINTS....	32	NA	12 599	86.2	98.7
453 UN PRES CH USA	1	98	129*	0.9	1.0
SEVIER	33	280	12 980*	88.1	100.0
053 ASSEMB OF GOD.	1	14	66	0.4	0.5
081 CATHOLIC......	1	NA	100	0.7	0.8
151 L-D SAINTS....	28	NA	12 459	84.6	96.0
283 LUTH--MO SYNOD	1	28	42	0.3	0.3
419 SO BAPT CONV..	1	205	270*	1.8	2.1
453 UN PRES CH USA	1	33	43*	0.3	0.3
SUMMIT	17	19	6 459*	63.3	100.0
081 CATHOLIC......	1	NA	405	4.0	6.3
151 L-D SAINTS....	15	NA	6 030	59.1	93.4
179 CONSRV BAPT...	1	19	24*	0.2	0.4
TOOELE	42	662	18 324*	70.4	100.0
053 ASSEMB OF GOD.	1	43	103	0.4	0.6
081 CATHOLIC......	1	NA	2 292	8.8	12.5
151 L-D SAINTS....	34	NA	15 141	58.2	82.6
167 CHS OF CHRIST.	1	25	31	0.1	0.2
193 EPISCOPAL.....	1	64	64	0.2	0.3
283 LUTH--MO SYNOD	1	85	108	0.4	0.6
419 SO BAPT CONV..	2	251	330*	1.3	1.8
449 UN METHODIST..	1	194	255*	1.0	1.4
UINTAH	41	1 241	14 158*	69.0	100.0
017 AMER BAPT ASSN	1	25	25	0.1	0.2
053 ASSEMB OF GOD.	1	12	39	0.2	0.3
057 BAPT GEN CONF.	1	180	241*	1.2	1.7
081 CATHOLIC......	1	NA	580	2.8	4.1
097 CHR CHS&CHS CR	1	25	33*	0.2	0.2
151 L-D SAINTS....	29	NA	11 915	58.1	84.2
167 CHS OF CHRIST.	1	35	65	0.3	0.5
193 EPISCOPAL.....	2	114	109	0.5	0.8
283 LUTH--MO SYNOD	1	123	179	0.9	1.3
419 SO BAPT CONV..	2	635	849*	4.1	6.0
443 UN C OF CHRIST	1	92	123*	0.6	0.9
UTAH	478	1 795	188 669*	86.5	100.0
053 ASSEMB OF GOD.	2	200	296	0.1	0.2
081 CATHOLIC......	3	NA	1 900	0.9	1.0
127 CH GOD (CLEVE)	1	13	17*	—	—
151 L-D SAINTS....	459	NA	184 282	84.5	97.7
165 CH OF NAZARENE	1	25	55	—	—
167 CHS OF CHRIST.	2	38	53	—	—
193 EPISCOPAL.....	1	114	142	0.1	0.1
203 EVAN FREE CH..	1	68	89*	—	—
283 LUTH--MO SYNOD	1	201	344	0.2	0.2
413 S.D.A.........	1	135	177*	0.1	0.1
419 SO BAPT CONV..	2	442	580*	0.3	0.3
443 UN C OF CHRIST	2	376	494*	0.2	0.3
453 UN PRES CH USA	2	183	240*	0.1	0.1
WASATCH	16	0	6 818	80.0	100.0
081 CATHOLIC......	1	NA	45	0.5	0.7
151 L-D SAINTS....	15	NA	6 773	79.5	99.3
WASHINGTON	57	268	19 969*	76.6	100.0
019 AMER BAPT USA.	1	79	103*	0.4	0.5
053 ASSEMB OF GOD.	1	15	26	0.1	0.1
081 CATHOLIC......	1	NA	160	0.6	0.8
151 L-D SAINTS....	52	NA	19 452	74.6	97.4
413 S.D.A.........	1	34	45*	0.2	0.2
419 SO BAPT CONV..	1	140	183*	0.7	0.9
WAYNE	8	0	1 642	85.9	100.0
081 CATHOLIC......	0	NA	5	0.3	0.3
151 L-D SAINTS....	8	NA	1 637	85.7	99.7
WEBER	215	6 857	106 149*	73.4	100.0
019 AMER BAPT USA.	1	421	536*	0.4	0.5
029 AMER LUTH CH..	1	146	204	0.1	0.2
053 ASSEMB OF GOD.	3	237	408	0.3	0.4
081 CATHOLIC......	4	NA	6 856	4.7	6.5
093 CHR CH (DISC)	1	249	288	0.2	0.3
097 CHR CHS&CHS CR	2	126	160*	0.1	0.2
105 CHRISTIAN REF.	1	53	105	0.1	0.1
127 CH GOD (CLEVE)	2	60	76*	0.1	0.1
151 L-D SAINTS....	179	NA	90 086	62.3	84.9
165 CH OF NAZARENE	1	49	127	0.1	0.1
167 CHS OF CHRIST.	1	32	38	—	—
179 CONSRV BAPT...	1	245	312*	0.2	0.3
193 EPISCOPAL.....	1	413	492	0.3	0.5
281 LUTH CH AMER..	2	658	1 007	0.7	0.9
283 LUTH--MO SYNOD	1	556	818	0.6	0.8
403 SALVATION ARMY	1	97	162	0.1	0.2
413 S.D.A.........	1	210	267*	0.2	0.3
419 SO BAPT CONV..	5	746	950*	0.7	0.9
443 UN C OF CHRIST	2	173	220*	0.2	0.2
449 UN METHODIST..	2	1 130	1 438*	1.0	1.4
453 UN PRES CH USA	3	1 256	1 599*	1.1	1.5

NA—Not applicable   *Total adherents estimated from known number of communicant, confirmed, full members.   —Represents a percent less than 0.1.   Percentages may not total due to rounding.

Table 4. Churches and Church Membership by County and Denomination: 1980

County and Denomination	Number of churches	Communicant, confirmed, full members	Total adherents Number	Percent of total population	Percent of total adherents
VERMONT					
THE STATE.....	716	68 523	244 730*	47.8	100.0
ADDISON	43	3 723	12 749*	43.4	100.0
019 AMER BAPT USA.	6	560	683*	2.3	5.4
053 ASSEMB OF GOD.	2	47	79	0.3	0.6
081 CATHOLIC......	7	NA	7 642	26.0	59.9
105 CHRISTIAN REF.	1	168	320	1.1	2.5
151 L-D SAINTS....	1	NA	153	0.5	1.2
165 CH OF NAZARENE	1	54	132	0.4	1.0
193 EPISCOPAL.....	2	267	537	1.8	4.2
226 FRIENDS-USA...	3	52	63*	0.2	0.5
413 S.D.A.........	1	33	40*	0.1	0.3
443 UN C OF CHRIST	8	1 106	1 349*	4.6	10.6
449 UN METHODIST..	11	1 436	1 751*	6.0	13.7
BENNINGTON	44	4 549	16 401*	49.2	100.0
019 AMER BAPT USA.	5	943	1 137*	3.4	6.9
029 AMER LUTH CH..	1	32	56	0.2	0.3
053 ASSEMB OF GOD.	1	67	210	0.6	1.3
081 CATHOLIC......	10	NA	10 121	30.4	61.7
089 CHR & MISS AL.	2	59	104	0.3	0.6
097 CHR CHS&CHS CR	1	50	60*	0.2	0.4
123 CH GOD (ANDER)	1	18	54	0.2	0.3
151 L-D SAINTS....	1	NA	109	0.3	0.7
167 CHS OF CHRIST.	1	50	64	0.2	0.4
175 CONGR CHR CHS.	2	133	168*	0.5	1.0
193 EPISCOPAL.....	3	842	1 486	4.5	9.1
226 FRIENDS-USA...	1	32	39*	0.1	0.2
413 S.D.A.........	1	80	96*	0.3	0.6
435 UNITARIAN-UNIV	1	15	18*	0.1	0.1
443 UN C OF CHRIST	5	822	991*	3.0	6.0
449 UN METHODIST..	8	1 406	1 696*	5.1	10.3
CALEDONIA	50	4 252	11 271*	43.7	100.0
019 AMER BAPT USA.	6	597	729*	2.8	6.5
053 ASSEMB OF GOD.	1	37	58	0.2	0.5
081 CATHOLIC......	5	NA	5 759	22.3	51.1
151 L-D SAINTS....	1	NA	276	1.1	2.4
165 CH OF NAZARENE	1	11	29	0.1	0.3
193 EPISCOPAL.....	3	206	275	1.1	2.4
353 CHR BRETHREN..	1	25	25	0.1	0.2
413 S.D.A.........	1	66	81*	0.3	0.7
435 UNITARIAN-UNIV	2	50	61*	0.2	0.5
443 UN C OF CHRIST	14	1 327	1 619*	6.3	14.4
449 UN METHODIST..	10	1 617	1 973*	7.6	17.5
453 UN PRES CH USA	5	316	386*	1.5	3.4
CHITTENDEN	82	12 214	65 533*	56.7	100.0
019 AMER BAPT USA.	5	1 232	1 479*	1.3	2.3
029 AMER LUTH CH..	1	92	152	0.1	0.2
053 ASSEMB OF GOD.	1	256	588	0.5	0.9
081 CATHOLIC......	20	NA	49 365	42.7	75.3
089 CHR & MISS AL.	3	319	512	0.4	0.8
151 L-D SAINTS....	1	NA	384	0.3	0.6
165 CH OF NAZARENE	1	81	155	0.1	0.2
167 CHS OF CHRIST.	5	220	280	0.2	0.4
193 EPISCOPAL.....	6	1 513	2 161	1.9	3.3
221 FREE METHODIST	1	33	123	0.1	0.2
226 FRIENDS-USA...	1	50	60*	0.1	0.1
270 CONSRV JUDAISM	1	365	438*	0.4	0.7
271 REFORM JUDAISM	1	132	159*	0.1	0.2
281 LUTH CH AMER..	1	136	229	0.2	0.3
283 LUTH--MO SYNOD	1	243	301	0.3	0.5
335 ORTH PRESB CH.	1	28	34*	-	0.1
403 SALVATION ARMY	1	56	159	0.1	0.2
413 S.D.A.........	1	48	58*	0.1	0.1
419 SO BAPT CONV..	1	92	110*	0.1	0.2
435 UNITARIAN-UNIV	1	251	301*	0.3	0.5
443 UN C OF CHRIST	14	3 661	4 360*	3.8	6.7
449 UN METHODIST..	13	3 369	4 045*	3.5	6.2
453 UN PRES CH USA	1	67	80*	0.1	0.1
ESSEX	18	607	2 315*	36.7	100.0
081 CATHOLIC......	5	NA	1 562	24.7	67.5
193 EPISCOPAL.....	3	93	121	1.9	5.2
244 GRACE BRETHREN	1	38	47*	0.7	2.0
443 UN C OF CHRIST	3	138	170*	2.7	7.3
449 UN METHODIST..	6	338	415*	6.6	17.9
FRANKLIN	53	4 063	22 144*	63.7	100.0
019 AMER BAPT USA.	5	631	785*	2.3	3.5
053 ASSEMB OF GOD.	2	42	68	0.2	0.3
081 CATHOLIC......	16	NA	16 981	48.8	76.7
165 CH OF NAZARENE	1	52	86	0.2	0.4
193 EPISCOPAL.....	5	339	493	1.4	2.2
413 S.D.A.........	1	20	25*	0.1	0.1
443 UN C OF CHRIST	6	394	490*	1.4	2.2
449 UN METHODIST..	17	2 585	3 216*	9.2	14.5
GRAND ISLE	12	520	3 449*	74.8	100.0
081 CATHOLIC......	5	NA	2 802	60.7	81.2
193 EPISCOPAL.....	1	11	23	0.5	0.7

County and Denomination	Number of churches	Communicant, confirmed, full members	Total adherents Number	Percent of total population	Percent of total adherents
443 UN C OF CHRIST	2	208	255*	5.5	7.4
449 UN METHODIST..	4	301	369*	8.0	10.7
LAMOILLE	31	2 069	5 942*	35.4	100.0
001 ADVENT CHR CH.	2	110	134*	0.8	2.3
053 ASSEMB OF GOD.	1	30	46	0.3	0.8
081 CATHOLIC......	6	NA	3 224	19.2	54.3
151 L-D SAINTS....	1	NA	72	0.4	1.2
165 CH OF NAZARENE	3	145	264	1.6	4.4
193 EPISCOPAL.....	2	126	182	1.1	3.1
413 S.D.A.........	1	44	54*	0.3	0.9
443 UN C OF CHRIST	9	797	971*	5.8	16.3
449 UN METHODIST..	6	817	995*	5.9	16.7
ORANGE	53	3 511	6 743*	29.7	100.0
019 AMER BAPT USA.	3	354	435*	1.9	6.5
081 CATHOLIC......	9	NA	2 368	10.4	35.1
089 CHR & MISS AL.	3	101	138	0.6	2.0
193 EPISCOPAL.....	2	128	205	0.9	3.0
203 EVAN FREE CH..	1	75	92*	0.4	1.4
244 GRACE BRETHREN	1	37	45*	0.2	0.7
413 S.D.A.........	2	59	72*	0.3	1.1
419 SO BAPT CONV..	2	130	160*	0.7	2.4
435 UNITARIAN-UNIV	1	42	52*	0.2	0.8
443 UN C OF CHRIST	18	1 798	2 209*	9.7	32.8
449 UN METHODIST..	10	734	902*	4.0	13.4
453 UN PRES CH USA	1	53	65*	0.3	1.0
ORLEANS	53	3 231	11 534*	49.2	100.0
001 ADVENT CHR CH.	2	50	62*	0.3	0.5
019 AMER BAPT USA.	3	309	382*	1.6	3.3
053 ASSEMB OF GOD.	1	27	62	0.3	0.5
081 CATHOLIC......	10	NA	7 455	31.8	64.6
127 CH GOD (CLEVE)	1	19	23*	0.1	0.2
165 CH OF NAZARENE	2	88	144	0.6	1.2
167 CHS OF CHRIST.	1	15	19	0.1	0.2
193 EPISCOPAL.....	2	191	261	1.1	2.3
413 S.D.A.........	1	18	22*	0.1	0.2
435 UNITARIAN-UNIV	1	40	49*	0.2	0.4
443 UN C OF CHRIST	17	1 277	1 577*	6.7	13.7
449 UN METHODIST..	11	1 115	1 377*	5.9	11.9
453 UN PRES CH USA	1	82	101*	0.4	0.9
RUTLAND	71	7 847	29 350*	50.3	100.0
001 ADVENT CHR CH.	1	72	86*	0.1	0.3
019 AMER BAPT USA.	8	1 281	1 535*	2.6	5.2
053 ASSEMB OF GOD.	1	83	190	0.3	0.6
081 CATHOLIC......	21	NA	19 618	33.6	66.8
089 CHR & MISS AL.	1	44	74	0.1	0.3
097 CHR CHS&CHS CR	2	74	89*	0.2	0.3
151 L-D SAINTS....	1	NA	138	0.2	0.5
167 CHS OF CHRIST.	1	15	19	-	0.1
175 CONGR CHR CHS.	1	81	97*	0.2	0.3
193 EPISCOPAL.....	7	1 416	1 633	2.8	5.6
201 EVAN COV CH AM	1	5	6*	-	-
270 CONSRV JUDAISM	1	75	90*	0.2	0.3
281 LUTH CH AMER..	2	432	585	1.0	2.0
403 SALVATION ARMY	1	52	136	0.2	0.5
413 S.D.A.........	1	59	71*	0.1	0.2
443 UN C OF CHRIST	8	1 823	2 185*	3.7	7.4
449 UN METHODIST..	12	2 265	2 714*	4.7	9.2
453 UN PRES CH USA	1	70	84*	0.1	0.3
WASHINGTON	66	8 128	26 313*	50.2	100.0
019 AMER BAPT USA.	4	479	578*	1.1	2.2
053 ASSEMB OF GOD.	1	73	150	0.3	0.6
081 CATHOLIC......	13	NA	16 066	30.7	61.1
089 CHR & MISS AL.	1	17	17	-	0.1
151 L-D SAINTS....	1	NA	297	0.6	1.1
167 CHS OF CHRIST.	2	119	151	0.3	0.6
193 EPISCOPAL.....	3	754	923	1.8	3.5
208 EVAN LUTH ASSN	1	38	56	0.1	0.2
226 FRIENDS-USA...	1	39	47*	0.1	0.2
403 SALVATION ARMY	1	42	106	0.2	0.4
413 S.D.A.........	1	86	104*	0.2	0.4
419 SO BAPT CONV..	1	78	94*	0.2	0.4
435 UNITARIAN-UNIV	4	486	586*	1.1	2.2
443 UN C OF CHRIST	13	2 108	2 543*	4.9	9.7
449 UN METHODIST..	17	3 423	4 129*	7.9	15.7
453 UN PRES CH USA	2	386	466*	0.9	1.8
WINDHAM	65	5 797	12 817*	34.7	100.0
001 ADVENT CHR CH.	1	106	128*	0.3	1.0
019 AMER BAPT USA.	17	1 557	1 873*	5.1	14.6
053 ASSEMB OF GOD.	1	48	72	0.2	0.6
081 CATHOLIC......	10	NA	5 714	15.5	44.6
089 CHR & MISS AL.	1	31	55	0.1	0.4
097 CHR CHS&CHS CR	1	23	28*	0.1	0.2
167 CHS OF CHRIST.	1	21	34	0.1	0.3
193 EPISCOPAL.....	2	638	828	2.2	6.5
201 EVAN COV CH AM	1	5	6*	-	-
226 FRIENDS-USA...	1	19	23*	0.1	0.2
281 LUTH CH AMER..	1	205	275	0.7	2.1
413 S.D.A.........	2	110	132*	0.4	1.0
435 UNITARIAN-UNIV	1	150	180*	0.5	1.4
443 UN C OF CHRIST	20	2 574	3 096*	8.4	24.2
449 UN METHODIST..	4	310	373*	1.0	2.9
WINDSOR	75	8 012	18 169*	35.6	100.0

NA—Not applicable   *Total adherents estimated from known number of communicant, confirmed, full members.   —Represents a percent less than 0.1.   Percentages may not total due to rounding.

Table 4. Churches and Church Membership by County and Denomination: 1980

County and Denomination	Number of churches	Communicant, confirmed, full members	Total adherents		
			Number	Percent of total population	Percent of total adherents
001 ADVENT CHR CH.	1	107	128*	0.3	0.7
019 AMER BAPT USA.	5	1 071	1 286*	2.5	7.1
053 ASSEMB OF GOD.	3	93	184	0.4	1.0
081 CATHOLIC......	8	NA	7 919	15.5	43.6
151 L-D SAINTS....	1	NA	295	0.6	1.6
167 CHS OF CHRIST.	2	260	328	0.6	1.8
193 EPISCOPAL.....	8	898	1 327	2.6	7.3
203 EVAN FREE CH..	1	155	186*	0.4	1.0
226 FRIENDS-USA...	1	15	18*	–	0.1
285 MENNONITE CH..	3	129	155*	0.3	0.9
419 SO BAPT CONV..	2	114	137*	0.3	0.8
435 UNITARIAN-UNIV	6	389	467*	0.9	2.6
443 UN C OF CHRIST	20	2 708	3 251*	6.4	17.9
449 UN METHODIST..	14	2 073	2 488*	4.9	13.7

VIRGINIA

County and Denomination	Number of churches	Communicant, confirmed, full members	Total adherents		
			Number	Percent of total population	Percent of total adherents
THE STATE.....	6 496	1 548 865	2 232 913*	41.8	100.0
ACCOMACK	88	13 071	15 987*	51.1	100.0
053 ASSEMB OF GOD.	1	40	65	0.2	0.4
081 CATHOLIC......	2	NA	320	1.0	2.0
093 CHR CH (DISC).	3	131	202	0.6	1.3
123 CH GOD (ANDER)	1	8	24	0.1	0.2
167 CHS OF CHRIST.	1	25	35	0.1	0.2
193 EPISCOPAL.....	4	551	615	2.0	3.8
357 PRESB CH US...	5	286	342*	1.1	2.1
419 SO BAPT CONV..	17	3 645	4 358*	13.9	27.3
449 UN METHODIST..	54	8 385	10 026*	32.1	62.7
ALBEMARLE-CHARLOTTES	108	30 287	39 952*	41.7	100.0
019 AMER BAPT USA.	2	1 270	1 475*	1.5	3.7
053 ASSEMB OF GOD.	1	80	112	0.1	0.3
081 CATHOLIC......	3	NA	3 309	3.5	8.3
089 CHR & MISS AL.	1	92	136	0.1	0.3
093 CHR CH (DISC).	2	183	334	0.3	0.8
097 CHR CHS&CHS CR	9	2 048	2 378*	2.5	6.0
127 CH GOD (CLEVE)	3	215	250*	0.3	0.6
151 L-D SAINTS....	1	NA	659	0.7	1.6
157 CH OF BRETHREN	4	439	510*	0.5	1.3
165 CH OF NAZARENE	1	132	280	0.3	0.7
167 CHS OF CHRIST.	1	140	167	0.2	0.4
193 EPISCOPAL.....	14	3 580	4 373	4.6	10.9
226 FRIENDS-USA...	1	33	38*	–	0.1
271 REFORM JUDAISM	1	226	262*	0.3	0.7
281 LUTH CH AMER..	1	433	614	0.6	1.5
283 LUTH--MO SYNOD	1	171	190	0.2	0.5
285 MENNONITE CH..	1	63	73*	0.1	0.2
349 PENT HOLINESS.	1	49	57*	0.1	0.1
356 PRESB CH AMER.	1	219	258	0.3	0.6
357 PRESB CH US...	8	3 126	3 630*	3.8	9.1
403 SALVATION ARMY	1	169	388	0.4	1.0
413 S.D.A.........	3	161	187*	0.2	0.5
419 SO BAPT CONV..	26	11 046	12 826*	13.4	32.1
435 UNITARIAN-UNIV	2	208	242*	0.3	0.6
449 UN METHODIST..	19	6 204	7 204*	7.5	18.0
ALLEGHANY-CLF FR-COV	65	12 849	16 470*	57.9	100.0
001 ADVENT CHR CH.	2	422	506*	1.8	3.1
019 AMER BAPT USA.	2	605	725*	2.5	4.4
053 ASSEMB OF GOD.	2	110	194	0.7	1.2
055 AS REF PRES CH	2	454	507	1.8	3.1
081 CATHOLIC......	2	NA	422	1.5	2.6
093 CHR CH (DISC).	3	409	659	2.3	4.0
097 CHR CHS&CHS CR	1	125	150*	0.5	0.9
127 CH GOD (CLEVE)	2	33	40*	0.1	0.2
151 L-D SAINTS....	1	NA	248	0.9	1.5
157 CH OF BRETHREN	2	120	144*	0.5	0.9
165 CH OF NAZARENE	1	74	147	0.5	0.9
167 CHS OF CHRIST.	1	80	100	0.4	0.6
193 EPISCOPAL.....	2	189	309	1.1	1.9
244 GRACE BRETHREN	1	194	232*	0.8	1.4
281 LUTH CH AMER..	1	29	40	0.1	0.2
353 CHR BRETHREN..	1	10	10	–	0.1
357 PRESB CH US...	11	2 423	2 904*	10.2	17.6
403 SALVATION ARMY	1	68	141	0.5	0.9
413 S.D.A.........	1	19	23*	0.1	0.1
419 SO BAPT CONV..	7	2 583	3 095*	10.9	18.8
449 UN METHODIST..	19	4 902	5 874*	20.7	35.7
AMELIA	26	2 340	3 028*	36.0	100.0
053 ASSEMB OF GOD.	1	39	51	0.6	1.7
081 CATHOLIC......	1	NA	171	2.0	5.6
093 CHR CH (DISC).	1	35	54	0.6	1.8
127 CH GOD (CLEVE)	1	52	63*	0.7	2.1
193 EPISCOPAL.....	1	55	76	0.9	2.5
283 LUTH--MO SYNOD	1	31	34	0.4	1.1
285 MENNONITE CH..	1	70	85*	1.0	2.8
357 PRESB CH US...	4	298	361*	4.3	11.9

County and Denomination	Number of churches	Communicant, confirmed, full members	Total adherents		
			Number	Percent of total population	Percent of total adherents
419 SO BAPT CONV..	6	968	1 173*	14.0	38.7
449 UN METHODIST..	7	657	796*	9.5	26.3
453 UN PRES CH USA	2	135	164*	2.0	5.4
AMHERST	47	8 952	10 986*	37.7	100.0
093 CHR CH (DISC).	2	294	466	1.6	4.2
097 CHR CHS&CHS CR	1	505	607*	2.1	5.5
127 CH GOD (CLEVE)	1	48	58*	0.2	0.5
157 CH OF BRETHREN	1	95	114*	0.4	1.0
193 EPISCOPAL.....	4	257	420	1.4	3.8
349 PENT HOLINESS.	1	30	36*	0.1	0.3
356 PRESB CH AMER.	1	59	78	0.3	0.7
357 PRESB CH US...	4	523	628*	2.2	5.7
419 SO BAPT CONV..	14	3 790	4 553*	15.6	41.4
449 UN METHODIST..	18	3 351	4 026*	13.8	36.6
APPOMATTOX	32	5 842	7 187*	60.0	100.0
081 CATHOLIC......	1	NA	?	?	?
127 CH GOD (CLEVE)	1	43	52*	0.4	0.7
193 EPISCOPAL.....	2	141	264	2.2	3.7
349 PENT HOLINESS.	1	64	78*	0.7	1.1
357 PRESB CH US...	4	243	295*	2.5	4.1
413 S.D.A.........	1	40	44*	0.4	0.7
419 SO BAPT CONV..	14	3 720	4 517*	37.7	62.8
449 UN METHODIST..	8	1 591	1 932*	16.1	26.9
ARLINGTON-ALEXANDRIA	153	64 832	125 179*	48.9	100.0
005 AME ZION......	3	1 548	1 662	0.6	1.3
019 AMER BAPT USA.	1	700	790*	0.3	0.6
029 AMER LUTH CH..	2	1 155	1 718	0.7	1.4
053 ASSEMB OF GOD.	3	882	1 484	0.6	1.2
081 CATHOLIC......	14	NA	46 061	18.0	36.8
089 CHR & MISS AL.	1	94	229	0.1	0.2
093 CHR CH (DISC).	3	568	839	0.3	0.7
101 C.M.E.........	1	525	593*	0.2	0.5
123 CH GOD (ANDER)	2	55	165	0.1	0.1
127 CH GOD (CLEVE)	3	403	455*	0.2	0.4
151 L-D SAINTS....	4	NA	1 705	0.7	1.4
157 CH OF BRETHREN	1	342	386*	0.2	0.3
165 CH OF NAZARENE	4	533	1 159	0.5	0.9
167 CHS OF CHRIST.	1	305	400	0.2	0.3
193 EPISCOPAL.....	17	8 950	11 743	4.6	9.4
221 FREE METHODIST	1	48	186	0.1	0.1
226 FRIENDS-USA...	1	58	65*	–	0.1
244 GRACE BRETHREN	1	88	99*	–	0.1
270 CONSRV JUDAISM	2	578	653*	0.3	0.5
271 REFORM JUDAISM	1	1 200	1 355*	0.5	1.1
281 LUTH CH AMER..	2	1 023	1 186	0.5	0.9
283 LUTH--MO SYNOD	2	907	1 149	0.4	0.9
290 METRO COMM CHS	0	35	70	–	0.1
353 CHR BRETHREN..	1	50	60	–	0.1
357 PRESB CH US...	15	5 721	6 458*	2.5	5.2
403 SALVATION ARMY	2	270	713	0.3	0.6
413 S.D.A.........	3	354	400*	0.2	0.3
419 SO BAPT CONV..	31	20 259	22 871*	8.9	18.3
435 UNITARIAN-UNIV	2	1 009	1 139*	0.4	0.9
443 UN C OF CHRIST	1	146	165*	0.1	0.1
449 UN METHODIST..	21	15 853	17 897*	7.0	14.3
453 UN PRES CH USA	7	1 173	1 324*	0.5	1.1
AUGUSTA-STAUN-WAYNES	190	41 951	53 717*	59.1	100.0
001 ADVENT CHR CH.	2	162	193*	0.2	0.4
019 AMER BAPT USA.	2	65	77*	0.1	0.1
053 ASSEMB OF GOD.	1	123	357	0.4	0.7
055 AS REF PRES CH	2	522	616	0.7	1.1
061 BEACHY AMISH..	2	172	205*	0.2	0.4
081 CATHOLIC......	2	NA	1 981	2.2	3.7
089 CHR & MISS AL.	1	26	31	–	0.1
097 CHR CHS&CHS CR	6	1 112	1 323*	1.5	2.5
123 CH GOD (ANDER)	1	70	210	0.2	0.4
127 CH GOD (CLEVE)	6	315	375*	0.4	0.7
151 L-D SAINTS....	1	NA	463	0.5	0.9
157 CH OF BRETHREN	17	4 064	4 834*	5.3	9.0
165 CH OF NAZARENE	4	337	585	0.6	1.1
167 CHS OF CHRIST.	2	282	401	0.4	0.7
193 EPISCOPAL.....	4	1 130	1 362	1.5	2.5
221 FREE METHODIST	1	126	546	0.6	1.0
263 INT FOURSQ GOS	2	253	301*	0.3	0.6
271 REFORM JUDAISM	1	66	79*	0.1	0.1
281 LUTH CH AMER..	13	2 828	3 510	3.9	6.5
283 LUTH--MO SYNOD	1	301	393	0.4	0.7
285 MENNONITE CH..	7	712	847*	0.9	1.6
323 OLD ORD AMISH.	1	130	155*	0.2	0.3
349 PENT HOLINESS.	4	141	168*	0.2	0.3
353 CHR BRETHREN..	1	50	55	0.1	0.1
356 PRESB CH AMER.	1	47	58	0.1	0.1
357 PRESB CH US...	25	8 333	9 912*	10.9	18.5
403 SALVATION ARMY	2	270	516	0.6	1.0
413 S.D.A.........	3	679	808*	0.9	1.5
419 SO BAPT CONV..	18	6 796	8 084*	8.9	15.0
435 UNITARIAN-UNIV	1	38	45*	–	0.1
443 UN C OF CHRIST	2	280	333*	0.4	0.6
449 UN METHODIST..	54	12 521	14 894*	16.4	27.7
BATH	25	2 431	3 021*	51.6	100.0
001 ADVENT CHR CH.	2	127	151*	2.6	5.0
081 CATHOLIC......	1	NA	120	2.0	4.0
157 CH OF BRETHREN	1	112	133*	2.3	4.4
193 EPISCOPAL.....	1	91	117	2.0	3.9
349 PENT HOLINESS.	1	80	95*	1.6	3.1

NA—Not applicable *Total adherents estimated from known number of communicant, confirmed, full members. —Represents a percent less than 0.1. Percentages may not total due to rounding.

Table 4. Churches and Church Membership by County and Denomination: 1980

County and Denomination	Number of churches	Communicant, confirmed, full members	Total adherents		
			Number	Percent of total population	Percent of total adherents
357 PRESB CH US...	5	541	644*	11.0	21.3
419 SO BAPT CONV..	4	478	569*	9.7	18.8
449 UN METHODIST..	10	1 002	1 192*	20.3	39.5
BEDFORD-BEDFORD CITY	93	15 532	22 329*	54.6	100.0
019 AMER BAPT USA.	1	35	42*	0.1	0.2
081 CATHOLIC......	3	NA	3 362	8.2	15.1
093 CHR CH (DISC).	1	255	380	0.9	1.7
123 CH GOD (ANDER)	2	18	54	0.1	0.2
127 CH GOD (CLEVE)	1	76	91*	0.2	0.4
151 L-D SAINTS....	1	NA	88	0.2	0.4
157 CH OF BRETHREN	3	432	520*	1.3	2.3
167 CHS OF CHRIST.	1	27	37	0.1	0.2
193 EPISCOPAL.....	3	434	599	1.5	2.7
349 PENT HOLINESS.	3	313	377*	0.9	1.7
357 PRESB CH US...	7	648	780*	1.9	3.5
419 SO BAPT CONV..	31	8 315	10 007*	24.5	44.8
449 UN METHODIST..	36	4 979	5 992*	14.6	26.8
BLAND	42	2 740	3 303*	52.0	100.0
093 CHR CH (DISC).	2	94	145	2.3	4.4
097 CHR CHS&CHS CR	2	78	93*	1.5	2.8
127 CH GOD (CLEVE)	3	173	207*	3.3	6.3
281 LUTH CH AMER..	3	84	94	1.5	2.8
349 PENT HOLINESS.	1	39	47*	0.7	1.4
357 PRESB CH US...	2	77	92*	1.4	2.8
413 S.D.A.........	1	9	11*	0.2	0.3
419 SO BAPT CONV..	4	367	439*	6.9	13.3
449 UN METHODIST..	24	1 819	2 175*	34.3	65.8
BOTETOURT	55	8 691	10 512*	45.2	100.0
001 ADVENT CHR CH.	1	196	236*	1.0	2.2
053 ASSEMB OF GOD.	1	39	68	0.3	0.6
157 CH OF BRETHREN	8	1 562	1 884*	8.1	17.9
167 CHS OF CHRIST.	1	20	25	0.1	0.2
193 EPISCOPAL.....	2	218	268	1.2	2.5
244 GRACE BRETHREN	1	40	48*	0.2	0.5
281 LUTH CH AMER..	4	405	493	2.1	4.7
357 PRESB CH US...	5	431	520*	2.2	4.9
381 REF PRES-EVAN.	1	?	?	?	?
419 SO BAPT CONV..	17	4 139	4 991*	21.4	47.5
449 UN METHODIST..	14	1 641	1 979*	8.5	18.8
BRUNSWICK	44	5 905	7 349*	47.0	100.0
053 ASSEMB OF GOD.	3	185	278	1.8	3.8
081 CATHOLIC......	1	NA	17	0.1	0.2
093 CHR CH (DISC).	3	196	319	2.0	4.3
097 CHR CHS&CHS CR	1	475	575*	3.7	7.8
101 C.M.E.........	2	225	272*	1.7	3.7
193 EPISCOPAL.....	6	463	613	3.9	8.3
357 PRESB CH US...	2	178	215*	1.4	2.9
419 SO BAPT CONV..	7	1 307	1 581*	10.1	21.5
443 UN C OF CHRIST	1	65	79*	0.5	1.1
449 UN METHODIST..	18	2 811	3 400*	21.8	46.3
BUCHANAN	34	4 572	5 838*	15.4	100.0
081 CATHOLIC......	1	NA	68	0.2	1.2
097 CHR CHS&CHS CR	8	1 694	2 138*	5.6	36.6
127 CH GOD (CLEVE)	2	56	71*	0.2	1.2
167 CHS OF CHRIST.	4	100	125	0.3	2.1
357 PRESB CH US...	6	369	466*	1.2	8.0
419 SO BAPT CONV..	7	1 697	2 142*	5.6	36.7
449 UN METHODIST..	6	656	828*	2.2	14.2
BUCKINGHAM	39	4 858	5 975*	50.8	100.0
061 BEACHY AMISH..	1	24	29*	0.2	0.5
081 CATHOLIC......	1	NA	43	0.4	0.7
097 CHR CHS&CHS CR	1	175	213*	1.8	3.6
165 CH OF NAZARENE	1	39	67	0.6	1.1
357 PRESB CH US...	4	217	264*	2.2	4.4
419 SO BAPT CONV..	18	3 068	3 734*	31.8	62.5
449 UN METHODIST..	13	1 335	1 625*	13.8	27.2
CAMPBELL-LYNCHBURG	144	44 009	57 695*	51.4	100.0
019 AMER BAPT USA.	2	660	791*	0.7	1.4
053 ASSEMB OF GOD.	3	240	299	0.3	0.5
075 BRETHREN IN CR	1	109	131	0.1	0.2
081 CATHOLIC......	1	NA	3 207	2.9	5.6
093 CHR CH (DISC).	6	2 808	3 829	3.4	6.6
097 CHR CHS&CHS CR	2	194	233*	0.2	0.4
101 C.M.E.........	1	403	483*	0.4	0.8
123 CH GOD (ANDER)	2	102	306	0.3	0.5
127 CH GOD (CLEVE)	2	155	186*	0.2	0.3
151 L-D SAINTS....	1	NA	508	0.5	0.9
157 CH OF BRETHREN	2	138	165*	0.1	0.3
165 CH OF NAZARENE	1	108	162	0.1	0.3
167 CHS OF CHRIST.	1	118	171	0.2	0.3
193 EPISCOPAL.....	6	2 188	2 913	2.6	5.0
263 INT FOURSQ GOS	1	?	?	?	?
271 REFORM JUDAISM	1	200	240*	0.2	0.4
281 LUTH CH AMER..	2	677	897	0.8	1.6
283 LUTH--MO SYNOD	1	133	174	0.2	0.3
285 MENNONITE CH..	1	84	101*	0.1	0.2
335 ORTH PRESB CH.	1	34	41*	–	0.1
357 PRESB CH US...	14	4 366	5 233*	4.7	9.1
403 SALVATION ARMY	1	96	240	0.2	0.4
413 S.D.A.........	3	342	410*	0.4	0.7
419 SO BAPT CONV..	38	17 174	20 583*	18.4	35.7

County and Denomination	Number of churches	Communicant, confirmed, full members	Total adherents		
			Number	Percent of total population	Percent of total adherents
421 SO METHODIST..	1	71	82	0.1	0.1
435 UNITARIAN-UNIV	1	52	62*	0.1	0.1
443 UN C OF CHRIST	1	15	18*	–	–
449 UN METHODIST..	47	13 542	16 230*	14.5	28.1
CAROLINE	25	4 361	5 520*	30.8	100.0
081 CATHOLIC......	1	NA	144	0.8	2.6
093 CHR CH (DISC).	1	20	30	0.2	0.5
097 CHR CHS&CHS CR	1	50	62*	0.3	1.1
127 CH GOD (CLEVE)	1	?	?	?	?
193 EPISCOPAL.....	2	126	160	0.9	2.9
419 SO BAPT CONV..	11	3 243	3 990*	22.3	72.3
449 UN METHODIST..	8	922	1 134*	6.3	20.5
CARROLL-GALAX CITY	87	12 236	15 286*	45.2	100.0
053 ASSEMB OF GOD.	1	21	42	0.1	0.3
075 BRETHREN IN CR	1	109	131	0.4	0.9
081 CATHOLIC......	1	NA	128	0.4	0.8
093 CHR CH (DISC).	8	607	1 060	3.1	6.9
097 CHR CHS&CHS CR	1	225	269*	0.8	1.8
101 C.M.E.........	1	75	90*	0.3	0.6
127 CH GOD (CLEVE)	6	704	841*	2.5	5.5
151 L-D SAINTS....	1	NA	138	0.4	0.9
157 CH OF BRETHREN	3	352	421*	1.2	2.8
165 CH OF NAZARENE	1	12	54	0.2	0.4
167 CHS OF CHRIST.	4	545	695	2.1	4.5
193 EPISCOPAL.....	1	26	24	0.1	0.2
247 HOLINESS CH...	1	100	100	0.3	0.7
281 LUTH CH AMER..	1	213	243	0.7	1.6
295 MORÁV CH-SOUTH	3	196	237	0.7	1.6
349 PENT HOLINESS.	1	25	30*	0.1	0.2
357 PRESB CH US...	6	552	659*	2.0	4.3
413 S.D.A.........	1	126	151*	0.4	1.0
419 SO BAPT CONV..	25	5 770	6 893*	20.4	45.1
443 UN C OF CHRIST	2	91	109*	0.3	0.7
449 UN METHODIST..	18	2 487	2 971*	8.8	19.4
CHARLES CITY	6	1 895	2 412*	36.0	100.0
193 EPISCOPAL.....	1	142	268	4.0	11.1
357 PRESB CH US...	1	26	32*	0.5	1.3
419 SO BAPT CONV..	3	1 562	1 910*	28.5	79.2
449 UN METHODIST..	1	165	202*	3.0	8.4
CHARLOTTE	45	5 917	7 394*	60.3	100.0
093 CHR CH (DISC).	1	73	132	1.1	1.8
097 CHR CHS&CHS CR	2	600	731*	6.0	9.9
151 L-D SAINTS....	1	NA	144	1.2	1.9
193 EPISCOPAL.....	1	17	17	0.1	0.2
215 EVAN METH CH..	1	30	37*	0.3	0.5
357 PRESB CH US...	13	642	782*	6.4	10.6
419 SO BAPT CONV..	13	2 835	3 455*	28.2	46.7
449 UN METHODIST..	12	1 671	2 036*	16.6	27.5
453 UN PRES CH USA	1	49	60*	0.5	0.8
CHESTERFIELD	81	23 504	35 845*	25.4	100.0
005 AME ZION......	1	135	155	0.1	0.4
019 AMER BAPT USA.	2	397	493*	0.3	1.4
029 AMER LUTH CH..	2	394	504	0.4	1.4
053 ASSEMB OF GOD.	5	383	785	0.6	2.2
081 CATHOLIC......	4	NA	4 891	3.5	13.6
089 CHR & MISS AL.	2	145	245	0.2	0.7
097 CHR CHS&CHS CR	1	69	86*	0.1	0.2
127 CH GOD (CLEVE)	1	42	52*	–	0.1
151 L-D SAINTS....	2	NA	763	0.5	2.1
167 CHS OF CHRIST.	2	104	134	0.1	0.4
193 EPISCOPAL.....	8	2 565	3 604	2.5	10.1
281 LUTH CH AMER..	1	71	108	0.1	0.3
283 LUTH--MO SYNOD	2	719	1 049	0.7	2.9
349 PENT HOLINESS.	6	1 113	1 383*	1.0	3.9
353 CHR BRETHREN..	2	90	155	0.1	0.4
356 CHR REF AMER..	1	148	148	0.1	0.4
357 PRESB CH US...	5	1 429	1 776*	1.3	5.0
419 SO BAPT CONV..	14	6 614	8 221*	5.8	22.9
449 UN METHODIST..	19	8 940	11 112*	7.9	31.0
453 UN PRES CH USA	1	146	181*	0.1	0.5
CLARKE	19	2 901	3 676*	36.9	100.0
019 AMER BAPT USA.	1	120	144*	1.4	3.9
193 EPISCOPAL.....	4	355	625	6.3	17.0
357 PRESB CH US...	2	222	266*	2.7	7.2
419 SO BAPT CONV..	4	949	1 137*	11.4	30.9
449 UN METHODIST..	8	1 255	1 504*	15.1	40.9
CRAIG	17	1 414	1 834*	46.5	100.0
053 ASSEMB OF GOD.	1	51	102	2.6	5.6
093 CHR CH (DISC).	5	117	250	6.3	13.6
097 CHR CHS&CHS CR	5	609	724*	18.3	39.5
419 SO BAPT CONV..	1	98	117*	3.0	6.4
449 UN METHODIST..	5	539	641*	16.2	35.0
CULPEPER	39	6 707	9 468*	41.9	100.0
053 ASSEMB OF GOD.	2	150	316	1.4	3.3
081 CATHOLIC......	1	NA	694	3.1	7.3
097 CHR CHS&CHS CR	1	25	30*	0.1	0.3
127 CH GOD (CLEVE)	1	21	26*	0.1	0.3
151 L-D SAINTS....	1	NA	115	0.5	1.2
165 CH OF NAZARENE	1	22	0	–	–

NA—Not applicable   *Total adherents estimated from known number of communicant, confirmed, full members.   —Represents a percent less than 0.1.   Percentages may not total due to rounding.

Table 4. Churches and Church Membership by County and Denomination: 1980

County and Denomination	Number of churches	Communicant, confirmed, full members	Total adherents Number	Percent of total population	Percent of total adherents
167 CHS OF CHRIST.	1	67	85	0.4	0.9
193 EPISCOPAL.....	3	453	788	3.5	8.3
221 FREE METHODIST	1	29	114	0.5	1.2
281 LUTH CH AMER..	1	148	218	1.0	2.3
353 CHR BRETHREN..	1	50	95	0.4	1.0
357 PRESB CH US...	3	520	633*	2.8	6.7
413 S.D.A.........	2	89	108*	0.5	1.1
419 SO BAPT CONV..	13	3 490	4 247*	18.8	44.9
449 UN METHODIST..	7	1 643	1 999*	8.8	21.1
CUMBERLAND	18	1 607	2 046*	26.0	100.0
053 ASSEMB OF GOD.	1	40	87	1.1	4.3
193 EPISCOPAL.....	1	32	72	0.9	3.5
357 PRESB CH US...	3	248	305*	3.9	14.9
419 SO BAPT CONV..	7	801	985*	12.5	48.1
449 UN METHODIST..	6	486	597*	7.6	29.2
DICKENSON	20	1 712	2 175*	11.0	100.0
005 AME ZION......	1	28	43	0.2	2.0
081 CATHOLIC......	1	NA	63	0.3	2.9
097 CHR CHS&CHS CR	3	130	162*	0.8	7.4
157 CH OF BRETHREN	2	196	244*	1.2	11.2
167 CHS OF CHRIST.	3	100	125	0.6	5.7
356 PRESB CH AMER.	1	169	181	0.9	8.3
419 SO BAPT CONV..	4	767	956*	4.8	44.0
449 UN METHODIST..	4	322	401*	2.0	18.4
DINWIDDIE-COL HT-PET	91	26 494	34 589*	43.1	100.0
005 AME ZION......	2	523	637	0.8	1.8
019 AMER BAPT USA.	3	2 059	2 465*	3.1	7.1
053 ASSEMB OF GOD.	1	188	298	0.4	0.9
081 CATHOLIC......	3	NA	2 072	2.6	6.0
093 CHR CH (DISC).	3	443	561	0.7	1.6
097 CHR CHS&CHS CR	1	65	78*	0.1	0.2
101 C.M.E.........	1	50	60*	0.1	0.2
127 CH GOD (CLEVE)	2	45	54*	0.1	0.2
151 L-D SAINTS....	1	NA	360	0.4	1.0
165 CH OF NAZARENE	1	62	87	0.1	0.3
167 CHS OF CHRIST.	4	701	891	1.1	2.6
193 EPISCOPAL.....	8	1 019	1 417*	1.8	4.1
270 CONSRV JUDAISM	1	108	129*	0.2	0.4
281 LUTH CH AMER..	1	275	402	0.5	1.2
356 PRESB CH AMER.	1	188	194	0.2	0.6
357 PRESB CH US...	8	1 456	1 743*	2.2	5.0
403 SALVATION ARMY	1	71	106	0.1	0.3
413 S.D.A.........	3	422	505*	0.6	1.5
419 SO BAPT CONV..	23	10 944	13 102*	16.3	37.9
449 UN METHODIST..	23	7 875	9 428*	11.8	27.3
ESSEX	18	3 080	3 988*	45.0	100.0
081 CATHOLIC......	1	NA	108	1.2	2.7
093 CHR CH (DISC).	1	168	252	2.8	6.3
127 CH GOD (CLEVE)	1	32	38*	0.4	1.0
151 L-D SAINTS....	1	NA	124	1.4	3.1
193 EPISCOPAL.....	4	479	585	6.6	14.7
413 S.D.A.........	1	188	226*	2.5	5.7
419 SO BAPT CONV..	7	1 759	2 110*	23.8	52.9
449 UN METHODIST..	2	454	545*	6.1	13.7
FAIRFAX-FAIRFX-FL CH	275	103 326	222 060*	35.5	100.0
019 AMER BAPT USA.	4	910	1 102*	0.2	0.5
029 AMER LUTH CH..	8	4 723	6 649	1.1	3.0
053 ASSEMB OF GOD.	8	1 179	2 375	0.4	1.1
057 BAPT GEN CONF.	1	65	79*	-	-
081 CATHOLIC......	24	NA	84 806	13.6	38.2
089 CHR & MISS AL.	2	135	265	-	0.1
093 CHR CH (DISC).	6	1 483	2 229	0.4	1.0
097 CHR CHS&CHS CR	6	775	939*	0.2	0.4
105 CHRISTIAN REF.	1	68	117	-	0.1
121 CH GOD (ABR)..	1	34	41*	-	-
123 CH GOD (ANDER)	2	100	300	-	0.1
127 CH GOD (CLEVE)	3	104	126*	-	0.1
151 L-D SAINTS....	10	NA	4 792	0.8	2.2
157 CH OF BRETHREN	2	495	600*	0.1	0.3
165 CH OF NAZARENE	2	147	185	-	0.1
167 CHS OF CHRIST.	7	1 135	1 642	0.3	0.7
193 EPISCOPAL.....	23	13 871	19 967*	3.2	9.0
201 EVAN COV CH AM	1	39	47*	-	-
203 EVAN FREE CH..	1	170	206*	-	0.1
226 FRIENDS-USA...	1	201	243*	-	0.1
270 CONSRV JUDAISM	1	453	549*	0.1	0.2
271 REFORM JUDAISM	2	992	1 202*	0.2	0.5
281 LUTH CH AMER..	9	3 947	5 352	0.9	2.4
283 LUTH--MO SYNOD	6	2 931	4 003	0.6	1.8
285 MENNONITE CH..	1	20	24*	-	-
290 METRO COMM CHS	0	35	70	-	-
329 OPEN BIBLE STD	1	30	60	-	-
335 ORTH PRESB CH.	1	129	156*	-	0.1
347 PENT FW BAPT..	1	50	61*	-	-
349 PENT HOLINESS.	1	32	39*	-	-
356 PRESB CH AMER.	2	166	190	-	0.1
357 PRESB CH US...	17	2 439	2 954*	0.5	1.3
381 REF PRES-EVAN.	3	587	789	0.1	0.4
403 SALVATION ARMY	1	77	132	-	0.1
413 S.D.A.........	2	451	546*	0.1	0.2
419 SO BAPT CONV..	27	17 977	21 774*	3.5	9.8
435 UNITARIAN-UNIV	2	562	681*	0.1	0.3
443 UN C OF CHRIST	5	2 258	2 735*	0.4	1.2
449 UN METHODIST..	52	37 194	45 049*	7.2	20.3
453 UN PRES CH USA	27	7 129	8 635*	1.4	3.9

County and Denomination	Number of churches	Communicant, confirmed, full members	Total adherents Number	Percent of total population	Percent of total adherents
469 WELS.........	1	233	349	0.1	0.2
FAUQUIER	69	9 393	13 668*	38.1	100.0
053 ASSEMB OF GOD.	4	285	423	1.2	3.1
061 BEACHY AMISH..	2	83	101*	0.3	0.7
081 CATHOLIC......	1	NA	1 493	4.2	10.9
127 CH GOD (CLEVE)	1	16	19*	0.1	0.1
149 CH OF JC (BIC)	1	36	37	0.1	0.3
151 L-D SAINTS....	1	NA	294	0.8	2.2
157 CH OF BRETHREN	1	132	161*	0.4	1.2
165 CH OF NAZARENE	2	78	182	0.5	1.3
167 CHS OF CHRIST.	1	100	175	0.5	1.3
193 EPISCOPAL.....	9	1 495	2 001	5.6	14.6
281 LUTH CH AMER..	1	196	289	0.8	2.1
357 PRESB CH US...	4	194	236*	0.7	1.7
413 S.D.A.........	1	54	66*	0.2	0.5
419 SO BAPT CONV..	16	3 854	4 695*	13.1	34.4
449 UN METHODIST..	20	2 677	3 261*	9.1	23.9
453 UN PRES CH USA	4	193	235*	0.7	1.7
FLOYD	37	3 682	4 449*	38.5	100.0
093 CHR CH (DISC).	2	64	98	0.8	2.2
157 CH OF BRETHREN	11	1 557	1 856*	16.1	41.7
165 CH OF NAZARENE	1	47	85	0.7	1.9
167 CHS OF CHRIST.	1	50	65	0.6	1.5
244 GRACE BRETHREN	1	30	36*	0.3	0.8
281 LUTH CH AMER..	2	116	143	1.2	3.2
349 PENT HOLINESS.	2	85	101*	0.9	2.3
357 PRESB CH US...	3	216	257*	2.2	5.8
419 SO BAPT CONV..	3	575	685*	5.9	15.4
449 UN METHODIST..	11	942	1 123*	9.7	25.2
FLUVANNA	25	4 257	5 285*	51.6	100.0
081 CATHOLIC......	1	NA	87	0.8	1.6
193 EPISCOPAL.....	2	129	194	1.9	3.7
357 PRESB CH US...	1	57	69*	0.7	1.3
419 SO BAPT CONV..	12	2 957	3 585*	35.0	67.8
449 UN METHODIST..	9	1 114	1 350*	13.2	25.5
FRANKLIN	83	12 005	15 013*	42.0	100.0
019 AMER BAPT USA.	3	244	293*	0.8	2.0
053 ASSEMB OF GOD.	4	268	468	1.3	3.1
075 BRETHREN IN CR	1	109	131	0.4	0.9
093 CHR CH (DISC).	4	623	1 031	2.9	6.9
097 CHR CHS&CHS CR	3	290	348*	1.0	2.3
123 CH GOD (ANDER)	1	34	102	0.3	0.7
127 CH GOD (CLEVE)	2	58	70*	0.2	0.5
151 L-D SAINTS....	1	NA	73	0.2	0.5
157 CH OF BRETHREN	13	2 099	2 516*	7.0	16.8
165 CH OF NAZARENE	1	12	56	0.2	0.4
193 EPISCOPAL.....	2	171	210	0.6	1.4
208 EVAN LUTH ASSN	1	39	50	0.1	0.3
244 GRACE BRETHREN	1	48	58*	0.2	0.4
353 CHR BRETHREN..	1	10	15	-	0.1
357 PRESB CH US...	2	209	251*	0.7	1.7
419 SO BAPT CONV..	19	4 409	5 286*	14.8	35.2
449 UN METHODIST..	24	3 382	4 055*	11.3	27.0
FREDERICK-WINCHESTER	99	17 736	25 065*	46.1	100.0
019 AMER BAPT USA.	1	191	230*	0.4	0.9
053 ASSEMB OF GOD.	7	767	1 050	1.9	4.2
081 CATHOLIC......	1	NA	2 644	4.9	10.5
093 CHR CH (DISC).	4	356	526	1.0	2.1
097 CHR CHS&CHS CR	3	456	550*	1.0	2.2
101 C.M.E.........	2	68	82*	0.2	0.3
127 CH GOD (CLEVE)	1	50	60*	0.1	0.2
151 L-D SAINTS....	1	NA	353	0.6	1.4
157 CH OF BRETHREN	4	519	625*	1.1	2.5
165 CH OF NAZARENE	1	109	141	0.3	0.6
167 CHS OF CHRIST.	2	160	205	0.4	0.8
193 EPISCOPAL.....	1	496	778	1.4	3.1
226 FRIENDS-USA...	1	28	34*	0.1	0.1
244 GRACE BRETHREN	1	498	600*	1.1	2.4
271 REFORM JUDAISM	1	78	94*	0.2	0.4
281 LUTH CH AMER..	7	1 512	2 017	3.7	8.0
290 METRO COMM CHS	0	20	40	0.1	0.2
349 PENT HOLINESS.	1	48	58*	0.1	0.2
356 PRESB CH AMER.	1	0	3	-	-
357 PRESB CH US...	10	2 366	2 851*	5.2	11.4
403 SALVATION ARMY	1	68	139	0.3	0.6
413 S.D.A.........	1	132	159*	0.3	0.6
419 SO BAPT CONV..	3	1 762	2 123*	3.9	8.5
435 UNITARIAN-UNIV	1	21	25*	-	0.1
443 UN C OF CHRIST	2	323	389*	0.7	1.6
449 UN METHODIST..	41	7 708	9 289*	17.1	37.1
GILES	65	7 127	10 113*	56.8	100.0
053 ASSEMB OF GOD.	1	26	102	0.6	1.0
081 CATHOLIC......	1	NA	224	1.3	2.2
093 CHR CH (DISC).	8	765	1 343	7.5	13.3
097 CHR CHS&CHS CR	2	276	333*	1.9	3.3
123 CH GOD (ANDER)	2	115	345	1.9	3.4
127 CH GOD (CLEVE)	2	193	233*	1.3	2.3
151 L-D SAINTS....	2	NA	570	3.2	5.6
167 CHS OF CHRIST.	3	100	125	0.7	1.2
193 EPISCOPAL.....	1	76	108	0.6	1.1
281 LUTH CH AMER..	2	81	106	0.6	1.0
349 PENT HOLINESS.	4	275	331*	1.9	3.3
357 PRESB CH US...	3	265	319*	1.8	3.2

NA—Not applicable   *Total adherents estimated from known number of communicant, confirmed, full members.   —Represents a percent less than 0.1.   Percentages may not total due to rounding.

Table 4. Churches and Church Membership by County and Denomination: 1980

County and Denomination	Number of churches	Communicant, confirmed, full members	Total adherents		
			Number	Percent of total population	Percent of total adherents
413 S.D.A.........	1	29	35*	0.2	0.3
419 SO BAPT CONV..	8	1 565	1 887*	10.6	18.7
449 UN METHODIST..	24	3 361	4 052*	22.8	40.1
GLOUCESTER	28	6 757	8 788*	43.7	100.0
019 AMER BAPT USA.	1	75	90*	0.4	1.0
053 ASSEMB OF GOD.	1	27	61	0.3	0.7
081 CATHOLIC......	1	NA	404	2.0	4.6
097 CHR CHS&CHS CR	1	28	34*	0.2	0.4
151 L-D SAINTS....	1	NA	70	0.3	0.8
167 CHS OF CHRIST.	1	43	57	0.3	0.6
193 EPISCOPAL.....	2	527	782	3.9	8.9
226 FRIENDS-USA...	1	45	54*	0.3	0.6
357 PRESB CH US...	3	556	669*	3.3	7.6
419 SO BAPT CONV..	8	3 439	4 139*	20.6	47.1
449 UN METHODIST..	8	2 017	2 428*	12.1	27.6
GOOCHLAND	19	3 365	4 508*	38.3	100.0
081 CATHOLIC......	1	NA	96	0.8	2.1
093 CHR CH (DISC).	4	412	827	7.0	18.3
193 EPISCOPAL.....	1	78	161	1.4	3.6
357 PRESB CH US...	2	84	100*	0.9	2.2
419 SO BAPT CONV..	8	2 156	2 568*	21.8	57.0
449 UN METHODIST..	3	635	756*	6.4	16.8
GRAYSON	72	8 102	9 656*	58.2	100.0
097 CHR CHS&CHS CR	1	40	48*	0.3	0.5
127 CH GOD (CLEVE)	1	14	17*	0.1	0.2
167 CHS OF CHRIST.	1	80	100	0.6	1.0
226 FRIENDS-USA...	4	96	114*	0.7	1.2
247 HOLINESS CH...	1	70	70	0.4	0.7
281 LUTH CH AMER..	1	44	69	0.4	0.7
349 PENT HOLINESS.	1	107	127*	0.8	1.3
357 PRESB CH US...	1	250	298*	1.8	3.1
419 SO BAPT CONV..	23	3 126	3 722*	22.5	38.5
449 UN METHODIST..	38	4 275	5 091*	30.7	52.7
GREENE	20	1 998	2 475*	32.5	100.0
061 BEACHY AMISH..	1	19	23*	0.3	0.9
127 CH GOD (CLEVE)	1	12	15*	0.2	0.6
157 CH OF BRETHREN	1	179	219*	2.9	8.8
193 EPISCOPAL.....	1	70	114	1.5	4.6
285 MENNONITE CH..	2	69	85*	1.1	3.4
413 S.D.A.........	1	24	29*	0.4	1.2
419 SO BAPT CONV..	5	851	1 042*	13.7	42.1
443 UN C OF CHRIST	1	85	104*	1.4	4.2
449 UN METHODIST..	7	689	844*	11.1	34.1
GREENSVILLE-EMPORIA	29	5 528	7 200*	45.7	100.0
053 ASSEMB OF GOD.	1	61	81	0.5	1.1
081 CATHOLIC......	1	NA	215	1.4	3.0
093 CHR CH (DISC).	1	20	31	0.2	0.4
097 CHR CHS&CHS CR	1	32	39*	0.2	0.5
123 CH GOD (ANDER)	1	60	180	1.1	2.5
127 CH GOD (CLEVE)	1	?	?	?	?
193 EPISCOPAL.....	3	284	400	2.5	5.6
283 LUTH--MO SYNOD	1	129	171	1.1	2.4
357 PRESB CH US...	2	212	261*	1.7	3.6
419 SO BAPT CONV..	9	3 000	3 693*	23.5	51.3
449 UN METHODIST..	8	1 730	2 129*	13.5	29.6
HALIFAX-SOUTH BOSTON	91	18 566	22 566*	60.2	100.0
053 ASSEMB OF GOD.	1	89	99	0.3	0.4
081 CATHOLIC......	1	NA	104	0.3	0.5
101 C.M.E.........	12	1 808	2 184*	5.8	9.7
127 CH GOD (CLEVE)	1	208	251*	0.7	1.1
167 CHS OF CHRIST.	1	29	39	0.1	0.2
193 EPISCOPAL.....	5	403	525	1.4	2.3
285 MENNONITE CH..	1	33	40*	0.1	0.2
357 PRESB CH US...	8	815	985*	2.6	4.4
413 S.D.A.........	3	110	133*	0.4	0.6
419 SO BAPT CONV..	33	10 505	12 690*	33.8	56.2
443 UN C OF CHRIST	5	952	1 150*	3.1	5.1
449 UN METHODIST..	19	3 568	4 310*	11.5	19.1
453 UN PRES CH USA	1	46	56*	0.1	0.2
HAMPTON CITY	67	28 462	40 603*	33.1	100.0
019 AMER BAPT USA.	2	800	970*	0.8	2.4
029 AMER LUTH CH..	1	118	165	0.1	0.4
053 ASSEMB OF GOD.	2	483	987	0.8	2.4
059 BAPT MISS ASSN	1	569	690*	0.6	1.7
081 CATHOLIC......	3	NA	4 526	3.7	11.1
093 CHR CH (DISC).	2	470	733	0.6	1.8
097 CHR CHS&CHS CR	3	934	1 132*	0.9	2.8
127 CH GOD (CLEVE)	2	206	250*	0.2	0.6
133 CH GOD(7TH)DEN	1	5	6*	–	–
151 L-D SAINTS....	1	NA	406	0.3	1.0
165 CH OF NAZARENE	1	210	317	0.3	0.8
193 EPISCOPAL.....	4	1 878	2 584	2.1	6.4
270 CONSRV JUDAISM	1	135	164*	0.1	0.4
281 LUTH CH AMER..	2	484	707	0.6	1.7
283 LUTH--MO SYNOD	1	357	464	0.4	1.1
349 PENT HOLINESS.	1	276	335*	0.3	0.8
357 PRESB CH US...	5	1 661	2 013*	1.6	5.0
381 REF PRES-EVAN.	1	65	94	0.1	0.2
403 SALVATION ARMY	1	94	163	0.1	0.4
419 SO BAPT CONV..	16	11 933	14 463*	11.8	35.6
443 UN C OF CHRIST	2	684	829*	0.7	2.0

County and Denomination	Number of churches	Communicant, confirmed, full members	Total adherents		
			Number	Percent of total population	Percent of total adherents
449 UN METHODIST..	14	7 100	8 605*	7.0	21.2
HANOVER	67	18 134	24 187*	48.0	100.0
001 ADVENT CHR CH.	2	274	331*	0.7	1.4
019 AMER BAPT USA.	2	200	241*	0.5	1.0
053 ASSEMB OF GOD.	1	148	235	0.5	1.0
081 CATHOLIC......	2	NA	1 167	2.3	4.8
093 CHR CH (DISC).	5	766	1 217	2.4	5.0
097 CHR CHS&CHS CR	4	799	964*	1.9	4.0
123 CH GOD (ANDER)	1	8	24	–	0.1
127 CH GOD (CLEVE)	1	131	158*	0.3	0.7
151 L-D SAINTS....	1	NA	156	0.3	0.6
193 EPISCOPAL.....	8	1 128	1 929	3.8	8.0
226 FRIENDS-USA...	1	161	194*	0.4	0.8
281 LUTH CH AMER..	1	128	186	0.4	0.8
283 LUTH--MO SYNOD	1	94	139	0.3	0.6
349 PENT HOLINESS.	1	50	60*	0.1	0.2
357 PRESB CH US...	6	927	1 118*	2.2	4.6
419 SO BAPT CONV..	15	9 210	11 110*	22.0	45.9
449 UN METHODIST..	15	4 110	4 958*	9.8	20.5
HENRICO-RICHMOND CTY	301	154 121	212 503*	53.1	100.0
005 AME ZION......	16	1 785	2 633	0.7	1.2
019 AMER BAPT USA.	22	13 224	15 577*	3.9	7.3
039 AP CHR CH(NAZ)	1	44	52*	–	–
053 ASSEMB OF GOD.	3	562	828	0.2	0.4
081 CATHOLIC......	13	NA	22 606	5.7	10.6
089 CHR & MISS AL.	1	78	123	–	0.1
093 CHR CH (DISC).	10	2 425	3 749	0.9	1.8
097 CHR CHS&CHS CR	11	1 661	1 957*	0.5	0.9
101 C.M.E.........	2	665	783*	0.2	0.4
123 CH GOD (ANDER)	2	117	351	0.1	0.2
127 CH GOD (CLEVE)	3	576	679*	0.2	0.3
151 L-D SAINTS....	4	NA	1 954	0.5	0.9
157 CH OF BRETHREN	1	148	174*	–	0.1
165 CH OF NAZARENE	4	747	2 072	0.5	1.0
167 CHS OF CHRIST.	5	601	818	0.2	0.4
193 EPISCOPAL.....	24	14 955	20 166	5.0	9.5
226 FRIENDS-USA...	1	60	71*	–	–
244 GRACE BRETHREN	1	70	82*	–	–
270 CONSRV JUDAISM	1	679	800*	0.2	0.4
271 REFORM JUDAISM	2	1 446	1 703*	0.4	0.8
281 LUTH CH AMER..	5	2 333	2 971	0.7	1.4
283 LUTH--MO SYNOD	5	1 315	1 648	0.4	0.8
285 MENNONITE CH..	1	55	65*	–	–
290 METRO COMM CHS	1	30	60	–	–
349 PENT HOLINESS.	1	208	245*	0.1	0.1
356 PRESB CH AMER.	1	55	57	–	–
357 PRESB CH US...	30	13 556	15 968*	4.0	7.5
381 REF PRES-EVAN.	1	160	210	0.1	0.1
403 SALVATION ARMY	1	97	465	0.1	0.2
413 S.D.A.........	3	1 169	1 377*	0.3	0.6
419 SO BAPT CONV..	79	66 433	78 255*	19.6	36.8
443 UN C OF CHRIST	2	737	868*	0.2	0.4
449 UN METHODIST..	44	28 130	33 136*	8.3	15.6
HENRY-MARTINSVILLE	100	24 356	31 034*	40.9	100.0
053 ASSEMB OF GOD.	3	243	394	0.5	1.3
081 CATHOLIC......	1	NA	611	0.8	2.0
093 CHR CH (DISC).	15	2 265	3 227	4.3	10.4
097 CHR CHS&CHS CR	7	2 000	2 412*	3.2	7.8
123 CH GOD (ANDER)	1	50	150	0.2	0.5
127 CH GOD (CLEVE)	3	382	461*	0.6	1.5
151 L-D SAINTS....	1	NA	194	0.3	0.6
157 CH OF BRETHREN	4	856	1 032*	1.4	3.3
165 CH OF NAZARENE	1	48	162	0.2	0.5
167 CHS OF CHRIST.	7	354	468	0.6	1.5
193 EPISCOPAL.....	2	500	600	0.8	1.9
226 FRIENDS-USA...	1	119	143*	0.2	0.5
271 REFORM JUDAISM	1	80	96*	0.1	0.3
281 LUTH CH AMER..	1	163	193	0.3	0.6
357 PRESB CH US...	3	948	1 143*	1.5	3.7
403 SALVATION ARMY	1	20	60	0.1	0.2
413 S.D.A.........	2	71	86*	0.1	0.3
419 SO BAPT CONV..	29	12 415	14 970*	19.7	48.2
449 UN METHODIST..	14	3 723	4 489*	5.9	14.5
453 UN PRES CH USA	3	119	143*	0.2	0.5
HIGHLAND	21	1 575	1 854*	63.1	100.0
001 ADVENT CHR CH.	1	77	91*	3.1	4.9
157 CH OF BRETHREN	2	70	83*	2.8	4.5
353 CHR BRETHREN..	1	20	20	0.7	1.1
357 PRESB CH US...	5	280	330*	11.2	17.8
413 S.D.A.........	1	23	27*	0.9	1.5
449 UN METHODIST..	11	1 105	1 303*	44.4	70.3
ISLE OF WIGHT	29	5 919	7 201*	33.3	100.0
017 AMER BAPT ASSN	1	20	20	0.1	0.3
053 ASSEMB OF GOD.	2	173	262	1.2	3.6
097 CHR CHS&CHS CR	1	75	91*	0.4	1.3
167 CHS OF CHRIST.	1	25	32	0.1	0.4
193 EPISCOPAL.....	1	212	233	1.1	3.2
226 FRIENDS-USA...	3	239	290*	1.3	4.0
357 PRESB CH US...	1	71	86*	0.4	1.2
419 SO BAPT CONV..	7	2 685	3 255*	15.1	45.2
443 UN C OF CHRIST	6	857	1 039*	4.8	14.4
449 UN METHODIST..	6	1 562	1 893*	8.8	26.3
JAMES CITY-WILLIAMS	27	7 872	11 369*	34.8	100.0

NA—Not applicable   *Total adherents estimated from known number of communicant, confirmed, full members.   —Represents a percent less than 0.1.   Percentages may not total due to rounding.

Table 4. Churches and Church Membership by County and Denomination: 1980

County and Denomination	Number of churches	Communicant, confirmed, full members	Total adherents — Number	Percent of total population	Percent of total adherents
053 ASSEMB OF GOD.	1	36	45	0.1	0.4
081 CATHOLIC......	1	NA	1 742	5.3	15.3
093 CHR CH (DISC).	1	170	320	1.0	2.8
097 CHR CHS&CHS CR	1	150	174*	0.5	1.5
151 L-D SAINTS....	1	NA	213	0.7	1.9
165 CH OF NAZARENE	1	68	152	0.5	1.3
167 CHS OF CHRIST.	1	120	148	0.5	1.3
193 EPISCOPAL.....	3	1 269	1 417	4.3	12.5
281 LUTH CH AMER..	2	641	869	2.7	7.6
285 MENNONITE CH..	1	31	36*	0.1	0.3
335 ORTH PRESB CH.	1	55	64*	0.2	0.6
349 PENT HOLINESS.	1	62	72*	0.2	0.6
357 PRESB CH US...	2	889	1 032*	3.2	9.1
419 SO BAPT CONV..	6	2 441	2 833*	8.7	24.9
435 UNITARIAN-UNIV	1	35	41*	0.1	0.4
449 UN METHODIST..	3	1 905	2 211*	6.8	19.4
KING AND QUEEN	**16**	**2 195**	**2 730***	**45.7**	**100.0**
053 ASSEMB OF GOD.	1	46	77	1.3	2.8
093 CHR CH (DISC).	1	100	183	3.1	6.7
193 EPISCOPAL.....	1	16	25	0.4	0.9
419 SO BAPT CONV..	9	1 627	1 957*	32.8	71.7
449 UN METHODIST..	4	406	488*	8.2	17.9
KING GEORGE	**15**	**4 543**	**5 946***	**56.4**	**100.0**
081 CATHOLIC......	1	NA	298	2.8	5.0
193 EPISCOPAL.....	3	294	348	3.3	5.9
283 LUTH--MO SYNOD	1	111	157	1.5	2.6
419 SO BAPT CONV..	6	2 310	2 871*	27.2	48.3
449 UN METHODIST..	4	1 828	2 272*	21.5	38.2
KING WILLIAM	**23**	**3 820**	**5 402***	**57.9**	**100.0**
019 AMER BAPT USA.	1	100	122*	1.3	2.3
081 CATHOLIC......	1	NA	585	6.3	10.8
093 CHR CH (DISC).	2	227	367	3.9	6.8
097 CHR CHS&CHS CR	1	60	73*	0.8	1.4
193 EPISCOPAL.....	3	292	434	4.7	8.0
357 PRESB CH US...	2	111	135*	1.4	2.5
419 SO BAPT CONV..	9	2 211	2 690*	28.8	49.8
449 UN METHODIST..	4	819	996*	10.7	18.4
LANCASTER	**25**	**4 607**	**5 738***	**56.6**	**100.0**
053 ASSEMB OF GOD.	1	7	9	0.1	0.2
081 CATHOLIC......	1	NA	350	3.5	6.1
151 L-D SAINTS....	1	NA	33	0.3	0.6
193 EPISCOPAL.....	3	634	744	7.3	13.0
357 PRESB CH US...	2	336	390*	3.9	6.8
413 S.D.A........	1	54	63*	0.6	1.1
419 SO BAPT CONV..	9	2 140	2 483*	24.5	43.3
449 UN METHODIST..	7	1 436	1 666*	16.4	29.0
LEE	**91**	**11 136**	**13 785***	**53.1**	**100.0**
005 AME ZION......	1	85	124	0.5	0.9
053 ASSEMB OF GOD.	2	37	48	0.2	0.3
081 CATHOLIC......	1	NA	38	0.1	0.3
093 CHR CH (DISC).	1	20	31	0.1	0.2
097 CHR CHS&CHS CR	8	598	736*	2.8	5.3
127 CH GOD (CLEVE)	4	156	192*	0.7	1.4
165 CH OF NAZARENE	1	13	32	0.1	0.2
167 CHS OF CHRIST.	1	25	32	0.1	0.2
201 EVAN COV CH AM	2	81	100*	0.4	0.7
357 PRESB CH US...	1	44	54*	0.2	0.4
419 SO BAPT CONV..	39	7 178	8 831*	34.0	64.1
449 UN METHODIST..	30	2 899	3 567*	13.7	25.9
LOUDOUN	**84**	**11 768**	**22 344***	**38.9**	**100.0**
029 AMER LUTH CH..	1	89	154	0.3	0.7
053 ASSEMB OF GOD.	3	175	354	0.6	1.6
081 CATHOLIC......	4	NA	5 837	10.2	26.1
097 CHR CHS&CHS CR	1	65	81*	0.1	0.4
127 CH GOD (CLEVE)	1	28	35*	0.1	0.2
151 L-D SAINTS....	2	NA	741	1.3	3.3
165 CH OF NAZARENE	3	183	471	0.8	2.1
167 CHS OF CHRIST.	1	25	60	0.1	0.3
193 EPISCOPAL.....	6	952	1 660	2.9	7.4
226 FRIENDS-USA...	1	142	177*	0.3	0.8
281 LUTH CH AMER..	3	688	1 044	1.8	4.7
335 ORTH PRESB CH.	1	101	126*	0.2	0.6
357 PRESB CH US...	6	417	519*	0.9	2.3
413 S.D.A........	1	69	86*	0.1	0.4
419 SO BAPT CONV..	13	3 896	4 851*	8.4	21.7
443 UN C OF CHRIST	1	87	108*	0.2	0.5
449 UN METHODIST..	30	4 431	5 517*	9.6	24.7
453 UN PRES CH USA	6	420	523*	0.9	2.3
LOUISA	**46**	**6 011**	**7 806***	**43.8**	**100.0**
053 ASSEMB OF GOD.	1	50	47	0.3	0.6
081 CATHOLIC......	1	NA	128	0.7	1.6
093 CHR CH (DISC).	9	714	1 218	6.8	15.6
097 CHR CHS&CHS CR	2	450	544*	3.1	7.0
157 CH OF BRETHREN	1	25	30*	0.2	0.4
193 EPISCOPAL.....	3	232	353	2.0	4.5
357 PRESB CH US...	3	120	145*	0.8	1.9
419 SO BAPT CONV..	16	3 134	3 787*	21.2	48.5
435 UNITARIAN-UNIV	1	55	66*	0.4	0.8
449 UN METHODIST..	9	1 231	1 488*	8.3	19.1
LUNENBERG	**33**	**4 898**	**6 421***	**53.0**	**100.0**
081 CATHOLIC......	1	NA	?	?	?
093 CHR CH (DISC).	7	1 090	1 667	13.7	26.0
097 CHR CHS&CHS CR	2	160	192*	1.6	3.0
127 CH GOD (CLEVE)	1	57	69*	0.6	1.1
165 CH OF NAZARENE	1	194	345	2.8	5.4
193 EPISCOPAL.....	3	114	150	1.2	2.3
283 LUTH--MO SYNOD	1	48	82	0.7	1.3
353 CHR BRETHREN..	1	35	70	0.6	1.1
357 PRESB CH US...	2	138	166*	1.4	2.6
419 SO BAPT CONV..	7	1 779	2 138*	17.6	33.3
449 UN METHODIST..	7	1 283	1 542*	12.7	24.0
MADISON	**25**	**3 187**	**4 091***	**40.0**	**100.0**
061 BEACHY AMISH..	1	71	86*	0.8	2.1
081 CATHOLIC......	1	NA	123	1.2	3.0
093 CHR CH (DISC).	2	148	221	2.2	5.4
157 CH OF BRETHREN	1	59	71*	0.7	1.7
165 CH OF NAZARENE	1	37	88	0.9	2.2
281 LUTH CH AMER..	2	305	407	4.0	9.9
357 PRESB CH US...	1	66	80*	0.8	2.0
419 SO BAPT CONV..	6	1 163	1 402*	13.7	34.3
449 UN METHODIST..	10	1 338	1 613*	15.8	39.4
MATHEWS	**21**	**3 697**	**4 553***	**56.9**	**100.0**
093 CHR CH (DISC).	2	131	198	2.5	4.3
165 CH OF NAZARENE	1	57	130	1.6	2.9
193 EPISCOPAL.....	1	245	443	5.5	9.7
226 FRIENDS-USA...	2	94	109*	1.4	2.4
419 SO BAPT CONV..	5	1 192	1 381*	17.3	30.3
449 UN METHODIST..	10	1 978	2 292*	28.7	50.3
MECKLENBURG	**74**	**12 108**	**14 836***	**50.4**	**100.0**
081 CATHOLIC......	2	NA	217	0.7	1.5
093 CHR CH (DISC).	1	58	88	0.3	0.6
097 CHR CHS&CHS CR	1	100	120*	0.4	0.8
127 CH GOD (CLEVE)	2	122	147*	0.5	1.0
167 CHS OF CHRIST.	1	22	25	0.1	0.2
193 EPISCOPAL.....	10	504	648	2.2	4.4
349 PENT HOLINESS.	1	31	37*	0.1	0.2
357 PRESB CH US...	4	224	269*	0.9	1.8
419 SO BAPT CONV..	24	6 676	8 028*	27.3	54.1
443 UN C OF CHRIST	3	370	445*	1.5	3.0
449 UN METHODIST..	22	3 854	4 635*	15.7	31.2
453 UN PRES CH USA	3	147	177*	0.6	1.2
MIDDLESEX	**15**	**3 358**	**3 988***	**51.7**	**100.0**
093 CHR CH (DISC).	1	150	273	3.5	6.8
193 EPISCOPAL.....	1	215	248	3.2	6.2
419 SO BAPT CONV..	6	1 642	1 902*	24.6	47.7
449 UN METHODIST..	7	1 351	1 565*	20.3	39.2
MONTGOMERY-RADFORD	**100**	**19 070**	**25 054***	**32.6**	**100.0**
053 ASSEMB OF GOD.	1	13	23	—	0.1
081 CATHOLIC......	2	NA	1 380	1.8	5.5
093 CHR CH (DISC).	5	730	1 077	1.4	4.3
097 CHR CHS&CHS CR	4	740	852*	1.1	3.4
123 CH GOD (ANDER)	4	206	618	0.8	2.5
127 CH GOD (CLEVE)	8	895	1 031*	1.3	4.1
151 L-D SAINTS....	1	NA	529	0.7	2.1
157 CH OF BRETHREN	1	326	375*	0.5	1.5
167 CHS OF CHRIST.	4	475	605	0.8	2.4
177 CONGR HOL CH..	2	21	24*	—	0.1
193 EPISCOPAL.....	3	911	1 414	1.8	5.6
244 GRACE BRETHREN	2	168	193*	0.3	0.8
281 LUTH CH AMER..	5	752	1 003	1.3	4.0
349 PENT HOLINESS.	12	1 132	1 304*	1.7	5.2
357 PRESB CH US...	6	1 966	2 264*	3.0	9.0
381 REF PRES-EVAN.	1	?	?	?	?
413 S.D.A........	1	63	73*	0.1	0.3
419 SO BAPT CONV..	11	4 681	5 390*	7.0	21.5
435 UNITARIAN-UNIV	1	65	75*	0.1	0.3
449 UN METHODIST..	26	5 926	6 824*	8.9	27.2
NELSON	**43**	**6 564**	**8 277***	**67.8**	**100.0**
081 CATHOLIC......	1	NA	41	0.3	0.5
093 CHR CH (DISC).	4	204	640	5.2	7.7
157 CH OF BRETHREN	1	109	130*	1.1	1.6
167 CHS OF CHRIST.	1	60	70	0.6	0.8
193 EPISCOPAL.....	3	194	229	1.9	2.8
285 MENNONITE CH..	1	23	27*	0.2	0.3
349 PENT HOLINESS.	2	64	76*	0.6	0.9
357 PRESB CH US...	3	236	282*	2.3	3.4
419 SO BAPT CONV..	18	4 252	5 082*	41.6	61.4
449 UN METHODIST..	9	1 422	1 700*	13.9	20.5
NEW KENT	**10**	**1 785**	**2 295***	**26.1**	**100.0**
193 EPISCOPAL.....	1	154	301	3.4	13.1
357 PRESB CH US...	1	166	203*	2.3	8.8
419 SO BAPT CONV..	5	1 020	1 247*	14.2	54.3
449 UN METHODIST..	3	445	544*	6.2	23.7
NEWPORT NEWS CITY	**90**	**43 255**	**60 511***	**41.8**	**100.0**
005 AME ZION......	3	2 244	2 454	1.7	4.1
019 AMER BAPT USA.	3	1 285	1 561*	1.1	2.6
053 ASSEMB OF GOD.	3	454	877	0.6	1.4
081 CATHOLIC......	3	NA	6 092	4.2	10.1
089 CHR & MISS AL.	1	10	15	—	-

NA—Not applicable   *Total adherents estimated from known number of communicant, confirmed, full members.   —Represents a percent less than 0.1.   Percentages may not total due to rounding.

Table 4. Churches and Church Membership by County and Denomination: 1980

County and Denomination	Number of churches	Communicant, confirmed, full members	Total adherents — Number	Total adherents — Percent of total population	Total adherents — Percent of total adherents
093 CHR CH (DISC).	1	210	432	0.3	0.7
097 CHR CHS&CHS CR	4	2 975	3 614*	2.5	6.0
123 CH GOD (ANDER)	3	211	633	0.4	1.0
127 CH GOD (CLEVE)	4	523	635*	0.4	1.0
151 L-D SAINTS....	2	NA	856	0.6	1.4
157 CH OF BRETHREN	1	200	243*	0.2	0.4
165 CH OF NAZARENE	1	92	145	0.1	0.2
167 CHS OF CHRIST.	3	392	498	0.3	0.8
193 EPISCOPAL.....	6	2 304	3 099	2.1	5.1
271 REFORM JUDAISM	1	316	384*	0.3	0.6
281 LUTH CH AMER..	2	901	1 119	0.8	1.8
283 LUTH--MO SYNOD	1	237	307	0.2	0.5
285 MENNONITE CH..	4	472	573*	0.4	0.9
290 METRO COMM CHS	1	25	50	–	0.1
349 PENT HOLINESS.	1	57	69*	–	0.1
357 PRESB CH US...	7	3 395	4 124*	2.8	6.8
403 SALVATION ARMY	1	100	113	0.1	0.2
413 S.D.A.........	1	287	349*	0.2	0.6
419 SO BAPT CONV..	17	17 326	21 047*	14.5	34.8
435 UNITARIAN-UNIV	1	62	75*	0.1	0.1
443 UN C OF CHRIST	4	1 106	1 343*	0.9	2.2
449 UN METHODIST..	10	7 715	9 372*	6.5	15.5
453 UN PRES CH USA	1	356	432*	0.3	0.7
NORFOLK-CHESAP-PORTS	318	129 182	177 329*	36.5	100.0
005 AME ZION......	13	13 745	14 252	2.9	8.0
019 AMER BAPT USA.	14	6 612	7 975*	1.6	4.5
029 AMER LUTH CH..	1	161	217	–	0.1
053 ASSEMB OF GOD.	6	761	1 365	0.3	0.8
081 CATHOLIC......	13	NA	16 308	3.4	9.2
089 CHR & MISS AL.	2	607	1 507	0.3	0.8
093 CHR CH (DISC).	15	1 616	2 724	0.6	1.5
097 CHR CHS&CHS CR	16	2 678	3 230*	0.7	1.8
101 C.M.E.........	1	2 000	2 412*	0.5	1.4
123 CH GOD (ANDER)	2	142	426	0.1	0.2
127 CH GOD (CLEVE)	9	910	1 098*	0.2	0.6
151 L-D SAINTS....	4	NA	2 071	0.4	1.2
165 CH OF NAZARENE	3	269	420	0.1	0.2
167 CHS OF CHRIST.	5	598	778	0.2	0.4
193 EPISCOPAL.....	18	7 769	10 697	2.2	6.0
270 CONSRV JUDAISM	3	997	1 202*	0.2	0.7
271 REFORM JUDAISM	2	1 302	1 570*	0.3	0.9
281 LUTH CH AMER..	8	2 523	3 551	0.7	2.0
283 LUTH--MO SYNOD	4	1 104	1 516	0.3	0.9
285 MENNONITE CH..	3	257	310*	0.1	0.2
290 METRO COMM CHS	1	30	60	–	–
347 PENT FW BAPT..	3	300	362*	0.1	0.2
349 PENT HOLINESS.	9	1 032	1 245*	0.3	0.7
356 PRESB CH AMER.	1	292	377	0.1	0.2
357 PRESB CH US...	25	7 109	8 574*	1.8	4.8
381 REF PRES-EVAN.	1	101	123	–	0.1
403 SALVATION ARMY	2	286	1 317	0.3	0.7
413 S.D.A.........	4	891	1 075*	0.2	0.6
419 SO BAPT CONV..	67	49 014	59 116*	12.2	33.3
435 UNITARIAN-UNIV	1	110	133*	–	0.1
443 UN C OF CHRIST	15	2 566	3 095*	0.6	1.7
449 UN METHODIST..	44	23 072	27 827*	5.7	15.7
453 UN PRES CH USA	3	328	396*	0.1	0.2
NORTHAMPTON	24	4 192	5 332*	36.5	100.0
053 ASSEMB OF GOD.	1	29	43	0.3	0.8
081 CATHOLIC......	1	NA	194	1.3	3.6
093 CHR CH (DISC).	2	25	54	0.4	1.0
123 CH GOD (ANDER)	1	31	93	0.6	1.7
193 EPISCOPAL.....	3	203	261	1.8	4.9
283 LUTH--MO SYNOD	1	52	77	0.5	1.4
357 PRESB CH US...	2	223	267*	1.8	5.0
419 SO BAPT CONV..	6	1 740	2 082*	14.2	39.0
449 UN METHODIST..	7	1 889	2 261*	15.5	42.4
NORTHUMBERLAND	24	4 541	5 440*	55.4	100.0
123 CH GOD (ANDER)	1	82	246	2.5	4.5
193 EPISCOPAL.....	3	276	354	3.6	6.5
419 SO BAPT CONV..	8	1 950	2 256*	23.0	41.5
449 UN METHODIST..	12	2 233	2 584*	26.3	47.5
NOTTOWAY	37	5 139	6 709*	45.7	100.0
005 AME ZION......	4	177	289	2.0	4.3
053 ASSEMB OF GOD.	1	28	99	0.7	1.5
081 CATHOLIC......	1	NA	?	?	?
093 CHR CH (DISC).	2	306	489	3.3	7.3
097 CHR CHS&CHS CR	4	158	189*	1.3	2.8
127 CH GOD (CLEVE)	1	41	49*	0.3	0.7
151 L-D SAINTS....	1	NA	188	1.3	2.8
165 CH OF NAZARENE	1	40	76	0.5	1.1
167 CHS OF CHRIST.	1	20	25	0.2	0.4
193 EPISCOPAL.....	2	161	273	1.9	4.1
357 PRESB CH US...	3	474	567*	3.9	8.5
413 S.D.A.........	1	37	44*	0.3	0.7
419 SO BAPT CONV..	3	1 534	1 834*	12.5	27.3
449 UN METHODIST..	11	2 113	2 527*	17.2	37.7
453 UN PRES CH USA	1	50	60*	0.4	0.9
ORANGE	40	7 370	9 542*	53.5	100.0
053 ASSEMB OF GOD.	1	90	173	1.0	1.8
081 CATHOLIC......	2	NA	468	2.6	4.9
093 CHR CH (DISC).	2	115	211	1.2	2.2
097 CHR CHS&CHS CR	3	556	672*	3.8	7.0
127 CH GOD (CLEVE)	1	43	52*	0.3	0.5
193 EPISCOPAL.....	2	312	403	2.3	4.2
281 LUTH CH AMER..	1	58	76	0.4	0.8
349 PENT HOLINESS.	4	172	208*	1.2	2.2
357 PRESB CH US...	3	453	547*	3.1	5.7
413 S.D.A.........	1	26	31*	0.2	0.3
419 SO BAPT CONV..	13	4 249	5 135*	28.8	53.8
449 UN METHODIST..	7	1 296	1 566*	8.8	16.4
PAGE	53	7 743	9 827*	50.7	100.0
019 AMER BAPT USA.	3	180	217*	1.1	2.2
053 ASSEMB OF GOD.	3	134	234	1.2	2.4
081 CATHOLIC......	1	NA	145	0.7	1.5
093 CHR CH (DISC).	3	676	907	4.7	9.2
097 CHR CHS&CHS CR	2	325	391*	2.0	4.0
157 CH OF BRETHREN	6	997	1 200*	6.2	12.2
167 CHS OF CHRIST.	1	30	38	0.2	0.4
193 EPISCOPAL.....	3	165	364	1.9	3.7
281 LUTH CH AMER..	9	1 144	1 407	7.3	14.3
285 MENNONITE CH..	2	60	72*	0.4	0.7
349 PENT HOLINESS.	1	10	12*	0.1	0.1
413 S.D.A.........	2	283	341*	1.8	3.5
419 SO BAPT CONV..	4	1 075	1 294*	6.7	13.2
443 UN C OF CHRIST	3	415	499*	2.6	5.1
449 UN METHODIST..	10	2 249	2 706*	13.9	27.5
PATRICK	41	4 139	5 039*	28.7	100.0
081 CATHOLIC......	1	NA	?	?	?
093 CHR CH (DISC).	4	210	298	1.7	5.9
127 CH GOD (CLEVE)	1	36	43*	0.2	0.9
157 CH OF BRETHREN	2	249	300*	1.7	6.0
167 CHS OF CHRIST.	2	45	57	0.3	1.1
357 PRESB CH US...	7	339	409*	2.3	8.1
413 S.D.A.........	1	28	34*	0.2	0.7
419 SO BAPT CONV..	12	2 048	2 470*	14.0	49.0
449 UN METHODIST..	11	1 184	1 428*	8.1	28.3
PITTSYLVANIA-DANVILL	165	38 100	47 435*	42.4	100.0
005 AME ZION......	1	195	258	0.2	0.5
053 ASSEMB OF GOD.	2	78	150	0.1	0.3
081 CATHOLIC......	1	NA	758	0.7	1.6
093 CHR CH (DISC).	8	692	1 002	0.9	2.1
097 CHR CHS&CHS CR	12	1 509	1 804*	1.6	3.8
127 CH GOD (CLEVE)	4	657	785*	0.7	1.7
151 L-D SAINTS....	2	NA	513	0.5	1.1
157 CH OF BRETHREN	3	350	418*	0.4	0.9
165 CH OF NAZARENE	1	102	220	0.2	0.5
167 CHS OF CHRIST.	1	70	118	0.1	0.2
193 EPISCOPAL.....	6	807	1 074	1.0	2.3
215 EVAN METH CH..	1	313	374*	0.3	0.8
226 FRIENDS-USA...	2	99	118*	0.1	0.2
271 REFORM JUDAISM	1	90	108*	0.1	0.2
281 LUTH CH AMER..	1	382	502	0.4	1.1
283 LUTH--MO SYNOD	1	143	198	0.2	0.4
357 PRESB CH US...	11	1 870	2 235*	2.0	4.7
403 SALVATION ARMY	1	66	135	0.1	0.3
413 S.D.A.........	2	182	218*	0.2	0.5
419 SO BAPT CONV..	60	20 828	24 893*	22.3	52.5
449 UN METHODIST..	42	9 522	11 381*	10.2	24.0
453 UN PRES CH USA	2	145	173*	0.2	0.4
POWHATAN	19	3 046	3 773*	28.9	100.0
081 CATHOLIC......	1	NA	113	0.9	3.0
127 CH GOD (CLEVE)	1	40	48*	0.4	1.3
167 CHS OF CHRIST.	1	40	60	0.5	1.6
193 EPISCOPAL.....	3	495	581	4.4	15.4
285 MENNONITE CH..	1	56	67*	0.5	1.8
357 PRESB CH US...	2	104	125*	1.0	3.3
419 SO BAPT CONV..	7	1 900	2 285*	17.5	60.6
449 UN METHODIST..	3	411	494*	3.8	13.1
PRINCE EDWARD	36	5 426	6 731*	40.9	100.0
081 CATHOLIC......	1	NA	200	1.2	3.0
093 CHR CH (DISC).	2	261	401	2.4	6.0
097 CHR CHS&CHS CR	3	240	283*	1.7	4.2
127 CH GOD (CLEVE)	1	35	41*	0.2	0.6
193 EPISCOPAL.....	1	192	238	1.4	3.5
283 LUTH--MO SYNOD	2	142	196	1.2	2.9
357 PRESB CH US...	9	942	1 111*	6.8	16.5
413 S.D.A.........	1	39	46*	0.3	0.7
419 SO BAPT CONV..	10	2 329	2 746*	16.7	40.8
449 UN METHODIST..	6	1 246	1 469*	8.9	21.8
PRINCE GEORGE-HOPEWE	48	10 991	13 801*	28.1	100.0
081 CATHOLIC......	1	NA	?	?	?
093 CHR CH (DISC).	1	339	465	0.9	3.4
097 CHR CHS&CHS CR	1	62	76*	0.2	0.6
127 CH GOD (CLEVE)	2	278	339*	0.7	2.5
151 L-D SAINTS....	1	NA	285	0.6	2.1
157 CH OF BRETHREN	1	101	123*	0.3	0.9
165 CH OF NAZARENE	1	118	261	0.5	1.9
167 CHS OF CHRIST.	2	400	509	1.0	3.7
181 CONSRV CONGR..	1	77	94*	0.2	0.7
193 EPISCOPAL.....	3	387	645	1.3	4.7
226 FRIENDS-USA...	1	50	61*	0.1	0.4
283 LUTH--MO SYNOD	1	385	460	0.9	3.3
349 PENT HOLINESS.	2	345	421*	0.9	3.1
356 PRESB CH AMER.	3	1 430	1 495	3.0	10.8
357 PRESB CH US...	5	766	935*	1.9	6.8
413 S.D.A.........	2	202	247*	0.5	1.8
419 SO BAPT CONV..	7	3 530	4 308*	8.8	31.2

NA—Not applicable   *Total adherents estimated from known number of communicant, confirmed, full members.   —Represents a percent less than 0.1.   Percentages may not total due to rounding.

Table 4. Churches and Church Membership by County and Denomination: 1980

County and Denomination	Number of churches	Communicant, confirmed, full members	Total adherents		
			Number	Percent of total population	Percent of total adherents
443 UN C OF CHRIST	3	273	333*	0.7	2.4
449 UN METHODIST..	9	2 145	2 618*	5.3	19.0
453 UN PRES CH USA	1	103	126*	0.3	0.9
PRINCE WILLIAM-MANAS	100	25 971	58 816*	35.3	100.0
017 AMER BAPT ASSN	2	356	356	0.2	0.6
029 AMER LUTH CH..	1	364	584	0.4	1.0
053 ASSEMB OF GOD.	6	932	1 764	1.1	3.0
081 CATHOLIC......	7	NA	20 937	12.6	35.6
089 CHR & MISS AL.	1	20	50		0.1
093 CHR CH (DISC).	1	85	123	0.1	0.2
097 CHR CHS&CHS CR	1	140	179*	0.1	0.3
127 CH GOD (CLEVE)	5	443	566*	0.3	1.0
151 L-D SAINTS....	4	NA	1 855	1.1	3.2
157 CH OF BRETHREN	3	695	887*	0.5	1.5
165 CH OF NAZARENE	2	199	301	0.2	0.5
167 CHS OF CHRIST.	5	420	721	0.4	1.2
193 EPISCOPAL.....	6	1 540	3 387	2.0	5.8
203 EVAN FREE CH..	1	84	107*	0.1	0.2
271 REFORM JUDAISM	1	40	51*		0.1
281 LUTH CH AMER..	4	1 381	2 187	1.3	3.7
283 LUTH--MO SYNOD	2	534	762	0.5	1.3
347 PENT FW BAPT..	1	44	56*		0.1
349 PENT HOLINESS.	4	208	266*	0.2	0.5
353 CHR BRETHREN..	1	40	75		0.1
356 PRESB CH AMER.	2	30	37		0.1
357 PRESB CH US...	5	742	947*	0.6	1.6
403 SALVATION ARMY	1	57	123	0.1	0.2
413 S.D.A.........	2	221	282*	0.2	0.5
419 SO BAPT CONV..	14	9 202	11 750*	7.1	20.0
449 UN METHODIST..	14	7 518	9 600*	5.8	16.3
453 UN PRES CH USA	4	676	863*	0.5	1.5
PULASKI	71	10 656	15 132*	43.0	100.0
053 ASSEMB OF GOD.	1	39	149	0.4	1.0
075 BRETHREN IN CR	1	109	131	0.4	0.9
081 CATHOLIC......	1	NA	1 551	4.4	10.2
093 CHR CH (DISC).	6	557	840	2.4	5.6
097 CHR CHS&CHS CR	3	380	464*	1.3	3.1
127 CH GOD (CLEVE)	5	909	1 109*	3.1	7.3
165 CH OF NAZARENE	1	56	93	0.3	0.6
167 CHS OF CHRIST.	3	110	140	0.4	0.9
193 EPISCOPAL.....	1	162	281	0.8	1.9
281 LUTH CH AMER..	1	246	301	0.9	2.0
349 PENT HOLINESS.	8	609	743*	2.1	4.9
356 PRESB CH AMER.	2	161	171	0.5	1.1
357 PRESB CH US...	7	1 304	1 591*	4.5	10.5
403 SALVATION ARMY	1	107	363	1.0	2.4
413 S.D.A.........	1	73	89*	0.3	0.6
419 SO BAPT CONV..	5	1 893	2 309*	6.6	15.3
449 UN METHODIST..	24	3 941	4 807*	13.6	31.8
RAPPAHANNOCK	17	2 031	2 450*	40.2	100.0
053 ASSEMB OF GOD.	1	17	36	0.6	1.5
193 EPISCOPAL.....	1	132	177	2.9	7.2
413 S.D.A.........	1	18	21*	0.3	0.9
419 SO BAPT CONV..	9	1 275	1 516*	24.9	61.9
449 UN METHODIST..	5	589	700*	11.5	28.6
RICHMOND	22	4 790	7 159*	103.0	100.0
081 CATHOLIC......	1	NA	1 350	19.4	18.9
127 CH GOD (CLEVE)	1	52	62*	0.9	0.9
193 EPISCOPAL.....	3	1 402	1 806	26.0	25.2
353 CHR BRETHREN..	1	40	40	0.6	0.6
357 PRESB CH US...	1	144	170*	2.4	2.4
413 S.D.A.........	1	46	54*	0.8	0.8
419 SO BAPT CONV..	8	2 018	2 389*	34.4	33.4
435 UNITARIAN-UNIV	1	424	502*	7.2	7.0
449 UN METHODIST..	5	664	786*	11.3	11.0
ROANOKE-ROANOKE-SALM	206	81 952	108 036*	54.7	100.0
005 AME ZION......	1	378	431	0.2	0.4
019 AMER BAPT USA.	3	1 025	1 217*	0.6	1.1
053 ASSEMB OF GOD.	5	407	667	0.3	0.6
055 AS REF PRES CH	1	69	79		0.1
075 BRETHREN IN CR	1	109	131	0.1	0.1
081 CATHOLIC......	5	NA	5 995	3.0	5.5
089 CHR & MISS AL.	1	48	81		0.1
093 CHR CH (DISC).	9	2 362	3 906	2.0	3.6
097 CHR CHS&CHS CR	7	2 020	2 399*	1.2	2.2
123 CH GOD (ANDER)	5	465	1 395	0.7	1.3
127 CH GOD (CLEVE)	6	581	690*	0.3	0.6
151 L-D SAINTS....	3	NA	1 484	0.8	1.4
157 CH OF BRETHREN	15	3 930	4 668*	2.4	4.3
165 CH OF NAZARENE	5	980	1 624	0.8	1.5
167 CHS OF CHRIST.	6	450	575	0.3	0.5
177 CONGR HOL CH..	1	29	34*		
193 EPISCOPAL.....	5	2 941	3 647	1.8	3.4
215 EVAN METH CH..	1	91	108*	0.1	0.1
226 FRIENDS-USA...	1	33	39*		
244 GRACE BRETHREN	7	872	1 036*	0.5	1.0
263 INT FOURSQ GOS	1	632	751*	0.4	0.7
270 CONSRV JUDAISM	1	100	119*	0.1	0.1
271 REFORM JUDAISM	1	250	297*	0.2	0.3
281 LUTH CH AMER..	9	3 475	4 204	2.1	3.9
283 LUTH--MO SYNOD	1	151	187	0.1	0.2
335 ORTH PRESB CH.	1	10	12*		
349 PENT HOLINESS.	4	726	862*	0.4	0.8
353 CHR BRETHREN..	1	100	175	0.1	0.2
356 PRESB CH AMER.	1	421	421	0.2	0.4

County and Denomination	Number of churches	Communicant, confirmed, full members	Total adherents		
			Number	Percent of total population	Percent of total adherents
357 PRESB CH US...	13	6 275	7 453*	3.8	6.9
381 REF PRES-EVAN.	1	55	72		0.1
403 SALVATION ARMY	1	144	539	0.3	0.5
413 S.D.A.........	3	494	587*	0.3	0.5
419 SO BAPT CONV..	48	35 619	42 305*	21.4	39.2
435 UNITARIAN-UNIV	1	151	179*	0.1	0.2
449 UN METHODIST..	30	16 463	19 553*	9.9	18.1
453 UN PRES CH USA	1	96	114*	0.1	0.1
ROCKBRIDGE-BN VS-LEX	74	12 701	15 967*	50.0	100.0
001 ADVENT CHR CH.	2	92	108*	0.3	0.7
055 AS REF PRES CH	5	1 116	1 223	3.8	7.7
081 CATHOLIC......	1	NA	418	1.3	2.6
151 L-D SAINTS....	1	NA	413	1.3	2.6
157 CH OF BRETHREN	2	459	540*	1.7	3.4
167 CHS OF CHRIST.	1	80	100	0.3	0.6
193 EPISCOPAL.....	4	703	973	3.0	6.1
215 EVAN METH CH..	1	24	28*	0.1	0.2
244 GRACE BRETHREN	1	611	719*	2.3	4.5
281 LUTH CH AMER..	3	321	505	1.6	3.2
349 PENT HOLINESS.	8	886	1 042*	3.3	6.5
356 PRESB CH AMER.	1	22	29	0.1	0.2
357 PRESB CH US...	16	3 219	3 786*	11.9	23.7
381 REF PRES-EVAN.	1	46	60	0.2	0.4
413 S.D.A.........	1	119	140*	0.4	0.9
419 SO BAPT CONV..	9	2 706	3 182*	10.0	19.9
449 UN METHODIST..	17	2 297	2 701*	8.5	16.9
ROCKINGHAM-HARRISON	159	28 895	36 666*	47.8	100.0
029 AMER LUTH CH..	1	162	196	0.3	0.5
053 ASSEMB OF GOD.	1	56	108	0.1	0.3
071 BRETHREN (ASH)	2	209	246*	0.3	0.7
081 CATHOLIC......	1	NA	1 329	1.7	3.6
097 CHR CHS&CHS CR	3	185	218*	0.3	0.6
127 CH GOD (CLEVE)	3	280	330*	0.4	0.9
151 L-D SAINTS....	1	NA	378	0.5	1.0
157 CH OF BRETHREN	24	5 866	6 913*	9.0	18.9
165 CH OF NAZARENE	3	337	677	0.9	1.8
167 CHS OF CHRIST.	2	71	99	0.1	0.3
193 EPISCOPAL.....	2	578	871	1.1	2.4
226 FRIENDS-USA...	1	9	11*		
271 REFORM JUDAISM	1	128	151*	0.2	0.4
281 LUTH CH AMER..	6	1 250	1 587	2.1	4.3
285 MENNONITE CH..	32	3 377	3 980*	5.2	10.9
335 ORTH PRESB CH.	1	26	31*		0.1
357 PRESB CH US...	8	2 538	2 991*	3.9	8.2
403 SALVATION ARMY	1	138	400	0.5	1.1
413 S.D.A.........	2	110	130*	0.2	0.4
419 SO BAPT CONV..	7	1 743	2 054*	2.7	5.6
421 CH OF BRETHREN	1	28	54	0.1	0.1
443 UN C OF CHRIST	15	1 656	1 952*	2.5	5.3
449 UN METHODIST..	41	10 148	11 960*	15.6	32.6
RUSSELL	59	5 685	7 161*	22.5	100.0
005 AME ZION......	2	483	541	1.7	7.6
053 ASSEMB OF GOD.	1	83	204	0.6	2.8
081 CATHOLIC......	2	NA	127	0.4	1.8
093 CHR CH (DISC).	1	35	50	0.2	0.7
097 CHR CHS&CHS CR	1	100	123*	0.4	1.7
127 CH GOD (CLEVE)	4	176	216*	0.7	3.0
167 CHS OF CHRIST.	3	160	204	0.6	2.8
357 PRESB CH US...	2	130	159*	0.5	2.2
419 SO BAPT CONV..	24	2 904	3 559*	11.2	49.7
449 UN METHODIST..	19	1 614	1 978*	6.2	27.6
SCOTT	55	5 637	6 904*	27.5	100.0
053 ASSEMB OF GOD.	1	42	82	0.3	1.2
081 CATHOLIC......	1	NA	77	0.3	1.1
127 CH GOD (CLEVE)	3	30	36*	0.1	0.5
167 CHS OF CHRIST.	1	65	85	0.3	1.2
357 PRESB CH US...	1	80	96*	0.4	1.4
419 SO BAPT CONV..	17	2 539	3 058*	12.2	44.3
449 UN METHODIST..	31	2 881	3 470*	13.8	50.3
SHENANDOAH	100	14 252	18 395*	66.7	100.0
029 AMER LUTH CH..	2	62	73	0.3	0.4
053 ASSEMB OF GOD.	1	29	26	0.1	0.1
071 BRETHREN (ASH)	3	302	359*	1.3	2.0
081 CATHOLIC......	2	NA	202	0.7	1.1
093 CHR CH (DISC).	8	981	1 891	6.9	10.3
121 CH GOD (ABR)..	2	84	100*	0.4	0.5
151 L-D SAINTS....	1	NA	81	0.3	0.4
157 CH OF BRETHREN	9	1 972	2 341*	8.5	12.7
165 CH OF NAZARENE	1	40	126	0.5	0.7
167 CHS OF CHRIST.	1	20	25	0.1	0.1
193 EPISCOPAL.....	3	173	222	0.8	1.2
244 GRACE BRETHREN	1	102	121*	0.4	0.7
281 LUTH CH AMER..	25	4 567	5 798	21.0	31.5
285 MENNONITE CH..	2	115	137*	0.5	0.7
357 PRESB CH US...	3	473	562*	2.0	3.1
413 S.D.A.........	1	364	432*	1.6	2.3
419 SO BAPT CONV..	1	199	236*	0.9	1.3
443 UN C OF CHRIST	12	1 023	1 215*	4.4	6.6
449 UN METHODIST..	22	3 746	4 448*	16.1	24.2
SMYTH	85	11 313	14 933*	44.8	100.0
005 AME ZION......	1	185	202	0.6	1.4
053 ASSEMB OF GOD.	1	16	35	0.1	0.2
081 CATHOLIC......	1	NA	183	0.5	1.2

NA—Not applicable   *Total adherents estimated from known number of communicant, confirmed, full members.   —Represents a percent less than 0.1.   Percentages may not total due to rounding.

Table 4. Churches and Church Membership by County and Denomination: 1980

County and Denomination	Number of churches	Communicant, confirmed, full members	Total adherents		
			Number	Percent of total population	Percent of total adherents
093 CHR CH (DISC).	1	71	121	0.4	0.8
097 CHR CHS&CHS CR	4	325	390*	1.2	2.6
123 CH GOD (ANDER)	7	518	1 554	4.7	10.4
127 CH GOD (CLEVE)	2	167	200*	0.6	1.3
151 L-D SAINTS....	1	NA	?	?	?
157 CH OF BRETHREN	2	115	138*	0.4	0.9
165 CH OF NAZARENE	3	105	337	1.0	2.3
167 CHS OF CHRIST.	2	46	63	0.2	0.4
193 EPISCOPAL.....	1	133	186	0.6	1.2
281 LUTH CH AMER..	5	743	863	2.6	5.8
349 PENT HOLINESS.	2	69	83*	0.2	0.6
353 CHR BRETHREN..	1	25	25	0.1	0.2
356 PRESB CH AMER.	1	47	53	0.2	0.4
357 PRESB CH US...	5	539	647*	1.9	4.3
413 S.D.A.........	1	48	58*	0.2	0.4
419 SO BAPT CONV..	16	4 235	5 083*	15.2	34.0
449 UN METHODIST..	28	3 926	4 712*	14.1	31.6
SOUTHAMPTON-FRANKLIN	**55**	**11 793**	**16 842***	**64.7**	**100.0**
005 AME ZION......	7	1 611	4 018	15.4	23.9
081 CATHOLIC......	1	NA	325	1.2	1.9
123 CH GOD (ANDER)	1	26	78	0.3	0.5
127 CH GOD (CLEVE)	2	121	145*	0.6	0.9
151 L-D SAINTS....	1	NA	225	0.9	1.3
193 EPISCOPAL.....	2	357	490	1.9	2.9
226 FRIENDS-USA...	1	109	130*	0.5	0.8
283 LUTH--MO SYNOD	1	34	34	0.1	0.2
357 PRESB CH US...	1	136	163*	0.6	1.0
419 SO BAPT CONV..	17	5 265	6 293*	24.2	37.4
443 UN C OF CHRIST	6	1 426	1 704*	6.5	10.1
449 UN METHODIST..	15	2 708	3 237*	12.4	19.2
SPOTSYLVANIA-FREDERI	**55**	**15 572**	**25 468***	**51.2**	**100.0**
019 AMER BAPT USA.	1	110	136*	0.3	0.5
081 CATHOLIC......	1	NA	4 249	8.5	16.7
093 CHR CH (DISC).	2	358	593	1.2	2.3
097 CHR CHS&CHS CR	1	20	25*	0.1	0.1
127 CH GOD (CLEVE)	1	46	57*	0.1	0.2
151 L-D SAINTS....	2	NA	652	1.3	2.6
165 CH OF NAZARENE	1	55	130	0.3	0.5
167 CHS OF CHRIST.	1	120	160	0.3	0.6
193 EPISCOPAL.....	3	1 007	2 095	4.2	8.2
271 REFORM JUDAISM	1	120	148*	0.3	0.6
281 LUTH CH AMER..	1	380	563	1.1	2.2
283 LUTH--MO SYNOD	1	29	51	0.1	0.2
349 PENT HOLINESS.	1	32	39*	0.1	0.2
357 PRESB CH US...	1	550	678*	1.4	2.7
403 SALVATION ARMY	1	105	312	0.6	1.2
413 S.D.A.........	1	198	244*	0.5	1.0
419 SO BAPT CONV..	27	11 075	13 651*	27.4	53.6
435 UNITARIAN-UNIV	1	38	47*	0.1	0.2
449 UN METHODIST..	7	1 329	1 638*	3.3	6.4
STAFFORD	**24**	**6 641**	**9 474***	**23.4**	**100.0**
053 ASSEMB OF GOD.	2	208	383	0.9	4.0
081 CATHOLIC......	1	NA	984	2.4	10.4
127 CH GOD (CLEVE)	1	105	131*	0.3	1.4
167 CHS OF CHRIST.	1	20	25	0.1	0.3
193 EPISCOPAL.....	1	456	577	1.4	6.1
281 LUTH CH AMER..	1	141	248	0.6	2.6
357 PRESB CH US...	1	157	196*	0.5	2.1
419 SO BAPT CONV..	8	4 073	5 082*	12.6	53.6
449 UN METHODIST..	8	1 481	1 848*	4.6	19.5
SUFFOLK CITY	**60**	**15 673**	**19 882***	**41.8**	**100.0**
005 AME ZION......	3	388	589	1.2	3.0
053 ASSEMB OF GOD.	3	108	192	0.4	1.0
081 CATHOLIC......	1	NA	282	0.6	1.4
093 CHR CH (DISC).	1	7	27	0.1	0.1
105 CHRISTIAN REF.	1	72	122	0.3	0.6
127 CH GOD (CLEVE)	2	135	164*	0.3	0.8
165 CH OF NAZARENE	1	45	99	0.2	0.5
167 CHS OF CHRIST.	1	40	90	0.2	0.5
193 EPISCOPAL.....	4	545	745	1.6	3.7
226 FRIENDS-USA...	1	86	105*	0.2	0.5
357 PRESB CH US...	1	172	209*	0.4	1.1
381 REF PRES-EVAN.	1	104	121	0.3	0.6
403 SALVATION ARMY	1	52	217	0.5	1.1
413 S.D.A.........	1	53	64*	0.1	0.3
419 SO BAPT CONV..	11	5 617	6 828*	14.3	34.3
443 UN C OF CHRIST	15	5 004	6 083*	12.8	30.6
449 UN METHODIST..	12	3 245	3 945*	8.3	19.8
SURRY	**15**	**1 485**	**1 855***	**30.7**	**100.0**
053 ASSEMB OF GOD.	1	39	102	1.7	5.5
193 EPISCOPAL.....	2	78	93	1.5	5.0
419 SO BAPT CONV..	5	693	841*	13.9	45.3
443 UN C OF CHRIST	1	27	33*	0.5	1.8
449 UN METHODIST..	6	648	786*	13.0	42.4
SUSSEX	**21**	**3 215**	**3 946***	**36.3**	**100.0**
081 CATHOLIC......	1	NA	55	0.5	1.4
193 EPISCOPAL.....	1	36	39	1.0	1.0
413 S.D.A.........	1	85	103*	0.9	2.6
419 SO BAPT CONV..	7	1 568	1 900*	17.5	48.2
443 UN C OF CHRIST	4	269	326*	3.0	8.3
449 UN METHODIST..	7	1 257	1 523*	14.0	38.6
TAZEWELL	**125**	**14 219**	**19 169***	**38.0**	**100.0**

County and Denomination	Number of churches	Communicant, confirmed, full members	Total adherents		
			Number	Percent of total population	Percent of total adherents
001 ADVENT CHR CH.	4	180	222*	0.4	1.2
005 AME ZION......	1	161	187	0.4	1.0
053 ASSEMB OF GOD.	11	900	1 840	3.6	9.6
081 CATHOLIC......	2	NA	188	0.4	1.0
089 CHR & MISS AL.	1	59	109	0.2	0.6
093 CHR CH (DISC).	8	891	1 366	2.7	7.1
097 CHR CHS&CHS CR	10	1 120	1 380*	2.7	7.2
123 CH GOD (ANDER)	4	189	567	1.1	3.0
127 CH GOD (CLEVE)	10	809	997*	2.0	5.2
151 L-D SAINTS....	1	NA	119	0.2	0.6
167 CHS OF CHRIST.	3	160	204	0.4	1.1
193 EPISCOPAL.....	4	224	250	0.5	1.3
281 LUTH CH AMER..	1	40	50	0.1	0.3
349 PENT HOLINESS.	3	247	304*	0.6	1.6
357 PRESB CH US...	9	1 320	1 627*	3.2	8.5
413 S.D.A.........	2	48	59*	0.1	0.3
419 SO BAPT CONV..	10	2 333	2 875*	5.7	15.0
449 UN METHODIST..	41	5 538	6 825*	13.5	35.6
VIRGINIA BEACH CITY	**116**	**41 976**	**76 611***	**29.2**	**100.0**
019 AMER BAPT USA.	1	650	801*	0.3	1.0
053 ASSEMB OF GOD.	2	405	944	0.4	1.2
061 BEACHY AMISH..	1	44	54*	-	0.1
081 CATHOLIC......	8	NA	21 362	8.1	27.9
093 CHR CH (DISC).	3	474	687	0.3	0.9
097 CHR CHS&CHS CR	5	1 160	1 429*	0.5	1.9
123 CH GOD (ANDER)	2	72	216	0.1	0.3
127 CH GOD (CLEVE)	3	300	370*	0.1	0.5
151 L-D SAINTS....	2	NA	1 114	0.4	1.5
157 CH OF BRETHREN	1	198	244*	0.1	0.3
165 CH OF NAZARENE	2	570	608	0.2	0.8
167 CHS OF CHRIST.	2	250	320	0.1	0.4
193 EPISCOPAL.....	9	4 224	6 663	2.5	8.7
221 FREE METHODIST	1	6	8	-	-
226 FRIENDS-USA...	2	178	219*	0.1	0.3
244 GRACE BRETHREN	1	108	133*	0.1	0.2
270 CONSRV JUDAISM	2	127	156*	0.1	0.2
281 LUTH CH AMER..	4	1 295	1 775	0.7	2.3
283 LUTH--MO SYNOD	2	605	849	0.3	1.1
285 MENNONITE CH..	1	32	39*	-	0.1
349 PENT HOLINESS.	2	83	102*	-	0.1
353 CHR BRETHREN..	1	30	50	-	0.1
356 PRESB CH AMER.	2	122	190	0.1	0.2
357 PRESB CH US...	11	4 795	5 907*	2.3	7.7
419 SO BAPT CONV..	18	14 581	17 962*	6.9	23.4
443 UN C OF CHRIST	5	944	1 163*	0.4	1.5
449 UN METHODIST..	22	10 632	13 098*	5.0	17.1
469 WELS..........	1	91	148	0.1	0.2
WARREN	**39**	**6 673**	**9 282***	**43.8**	**100.0**
053 ASSEMB OF GOD.	3	456	948	4.5	10.2
081 CATHOLIC......	1	NA	634	3.0	6.8
097 CHR CHS&CHS CR	4	295	354*	1.7	3.8
101 C.M.E.........	1	123	148*	0.7	1.6
121 CH GOD (ABR)..	2	102	123*	0.6	1.3
127 CH GOD (CLEVE)	1	33	40*	0.2	0.4
151 L-D SAINTS....	1	NA	210	1.0	2.3
157 CH OF BRETHREN	1	163	196*	0.9	2.1
167 CHS OF CHRIST.	1	65	80	0.4	0.9
193 EPISCOPAL.....	1	299	356	1.7	3.8
281 LUTH CH AMER..	1	241	288	1.4	3.1
357 PRESB CH US...	3	488	586*	2.8	6.3
403 SALVATION ARMY	1	99	141	0.7	1.5
413 S.D.A.........	2	104	125*	0.6	1.3
419 SO BAPT CONV..	5	1 861	2 236*	10.5	24.1
449 UN METHODIST..	11	2 344	2 817*	13.3	30.3
WASHINGTON-BRISTOL	**141**	**27 372**	**34 811***	**53.1**	**100.0**
005 AME ZION......	2	470	573	0.9	1.6
053 ASSEMB OF GOD.	4	370	712	1.1	2.0
081 CATHOLIC......	2	NA	1 363	2.1	3.9
093 CHR CH (DISC).	1	334	514	0.8	1.5
097 CHR CHS&CHS CR	10	980	1 175*	1.8	3.4
123 CH GOD (ANDER)	3	152	456	0.7	1.3
127 CH GOD (CLEVE)	5	382	458*	0.7	1.3
165 CH OF NAZARENE	2	104	102	0.2	0.3
167 CHS OF CHRIST.	7	570	725	1.1	2.1
193 EPISCOPAL.....	2	759	845	1.3	2.4
281 LUTH CH AMER..	3	243	330	0.5	0.9
349 PENT HOLINESS.	2	109	131*	0.2	0.4
356 PRESB CH AMER.	5	340	376	0.6	1.1
357 PRESB CH US...	15	2 351	2 819*	4.3	8.1
413 S.D.A.........	1	92	110*	0.2	0.3
419 SO BAPT CONV..	31	11 293	13 542*	20.7	38.9
449 UN METHODIST..	46	8 823	10 580*	16.1	30.4
WESTMORELAND	**25**	**4 404**	**6 032***	**43.0**	**100.0**
053 ASSEMB OF GOD.	1	97	128	0.9	2.1
081 CATHOLIC......	2	NA	440	3.1	7.3
093 CHR CH (DISC).	1	80	140	1.0	2.3
193 EPISCOPAL.....	5	522	896	6.4	14.9
419 SO BAPT CONV..	6	1 727	2 064*	14.7	34.2
449 UN METHODIST..	10	1 978	2 364*	16.8	39.2
WISE-NORTON CITY	**71**	**10 660**	**14 347***	**29.5**	**100.0**
005 AME ZION......	2	650	728	1.5	5.1
053 ASSEMB OF GOD.	4	461	977	2.0	6.8
081 CATHOLIC......	3	NA	365	0.8	2.5
093 CHR CH (DISC).	1	100	156	0.3	1.1
097 CHR CHS&CHS CR	3	345	425*	0.9	3.0

NA—Not applicable   *Total adherents estimated from known number of communicant, confirmed, full members.   —Represents a percent less than 0.1.   Percentages may not total due to rounding.

Table 4. Churches and Church Membership by County and Denomination: 1980

County and Denomination	Number of churches	Communicant, confirmed, full members	Total adherents Number	Percent of total population	Percent of total adherents
123 CH GOD (ANDER)	3	261	783	1.6	5.5
127 CH GOD (CLEVE)	5	199	245*	0.5	1.7
151 L-D SAINTS....	1	NA	?	?	?
167 CHS OF CHRIST.	5	250	320	0.7	2.2
193 EPISCOPAL.....	3	201	259	0.5	1.8
356 PRESB CH AMER.	2	92	98	0.2	0.7
357 PRESB CH US...	7	413	509*	1.0	3.5
419 SO BAPT CONV..	13	4 241	5 230*	10.8	36.5
449 UN METHODIST..	18	3 410	4 206*	8.7	29.3
453 UN PRES CH USA	1	37	46*	0.1	0.3
WYTHE	**87**	**10 204**	**12 980***	**50.9**	**100.0**
053 ASSEMB OF GOD.	2	135	253	1.0	1.9
081 CATHOLIC......	1	NA	178	0.7	1.4
093 CHR CH (DISC).	3	217	395	1.5	3.0
097 CHR CHS&CHS CR	1	50	61*	0.2	0.5
123 CH GOD (ANDER)	1	75	225	0.9	1.7
127 CH GOD (CLEVE)	5	312	378*	1.5	2.9
167 CHS OF CHRIST.	3	100	125	0.5	1.0
193 EPISCOPAL.....	1	265	383	1.5	3.0
281 LUTH CH AMER..	9	1 213	1 494	5.9	11.5
349 PENT HOLINESS.	16	1 424	1 724*	6.8	13.3
357 PRESB CH US...	4	506	613*	2.4	4.7
413 S.D.A.........	1	149	180*	0.7	1.4
419 SO BAPT CONV..	3	901	1 091*	4.3	8.4
449 UN METHODIST..	37	4 857	5 880*	23.0	45.3
YORK	**23**	**10 253**	**13 502***	**30.6**	**100.0**
053 ASSEMB OF GOD.	1	65	99	0.2	0.7
081 CATHOLIC......	1	NA	614	1.4	4.5
093 CHR CH (DISC).	1	185	200	0.5	1.5
097 CHR CHS&CHS CR	1	84	104*	0.2	0.8
193 EPISCOPAL.....	1	297	630	1.4	4.7
226 FRIENDS-USA...	1	138	170*	0.4	1.3
281 LUTH CH AMER..	1	252	359	0.8	2.7
349 PENT HOLINESS.	1	28	35*	0.1	0.3
353 CHR BRETHREN..	1	125	100	0.2	0.7
357 PRESB CH US...	1	588	725*	1.6	5.4
413 S.D.A.........	2	253	312*	0.7	2.3
419 SO BAPT CONV..	5	3 499	4 313*	9.8	31.9
449 UN METHODIST..	6	4 739	5 841*	13.2	43.3

WASHINGTON

County and Denomination	Number of churches	Communicant, confirmed, full members	Total adherents Number	Percent of total population	Percent of total adherents
THE STATE.....	3 381	584 461	1 280 918*	31.0	100.0
ADAMS	**33**	**3 443**	**7 173***	**54.1**	**100.0**
029 AMER LUTH CH..	3	801	1 037	7.8	14.5
053 ASSEMB OF GOD.	4	251	547	4.1	7.6
081 CATHOLIC......	4	NA	1 270	9.6	17.7
093 CHR CH (DISC).	1	110	140	1.1	2.0
151 L-D SAINTS....	3	NA	1 092	8.2	15.2
165 CH OF NAZARENE	2	142	384	2.9	5.4
167 CHS OF CHRIST.	1	28	36	0.3	0.5
193 EPISCOPAL.....	1	20	36	0.3	0.5
283 LUTH--MO SYNOD	1	80	121	0.9	1.7
287 MENN GEN CONF.	1	169	188	1.4	2.6
353 CHR BRETHREN..	1	25	25	0.2	0.3
413 S.D.A.........	2	92	116*	0.9	1.6
419 SO BAPT CONV..	1	221	279*	2.1	3.9
443 UN C OF CHRIST	3	498	630*	4.7	8.8
449 UN METHODIST..	3	563	712*	5.4	9.9
453 UN PRES CH USA	2	443	560*	4.2	7.8
ASOTIN	**17**	**1 932**	**5 130***	**30.5**	**100.0**
001 ADVENT CHR CH.	1	16	20*	0.1	0.4
029 AMER LUTH CH..	1	461	610	3.6	11.9
053 ASSEMB OF GOD.	2	65	162	1.0	3.2
081 CATHOLIC......	1	NA	2 320	13.8	45.2
093 CHR CH (DISC).	1	208	253	1.5	4.9
123 CH GOD (ANDER)	1	108	324	1.9	6.3
164 CH LUTH CONF..	1	66	79	0.5	1.5
165 CH OF NAZARENE	1	36	95	0.6	1.9
167 CHS OF CHRIST.	1	35	45	0.3	0.9
221 FREE METHODIST	1	14	93	0.6	1.8
263 INT FOURSQ GOS	1	12	15*	0.1	0.3
413 S.D.A.........	1	158	193*	1.1	3.8
419 SO BAPT CONV..	1	128	157*	0.9	3.1
449 UN METHODIST..	3	625	764*	4.5	14.9
BENTON	**96**	**18 607**	**48 723***	**44.5**	**100.0**
019 AMER BAPT USA.	3	556	689*	0.6	1.4
029 AMER LUTH CH..	3	1 742	2 336	2.1	4.8
039 AP CHR CH(NAZ)	1	35	43*	-	0.1
053 ASSEMB OF GOD.	5	919	1 167	1.1	2.4
059 BAPT MISS ASSN	1	21	26*	-	0.1
081 CATHOLIC......	4	NA	18 016	16.5	37.0
089 CHR & MISS AL.	1	125	235	0.2	0.5

County and Denomination	Number of churches	Communicant, confirmed, full members	Total adherents Number	Percent of total population	Percent of total adherents
093 CHR CH (DISC).	4	567	910	0.8	1.9
097 CHR CHS&CHS CR	1	55	68*	0.1	0.1
105 CHRISTIAN REF.	1	101	152	0.1	0.3
123 CH GOD (ANDER)	1	135	405	0.4	0.8
127 CH GOD (CLEVE)	2	126	156*	0.3	0.3
151 L-D SAINTS....	15	NA	6 598	6.0	13.5
163 CH OF LUTH BR.	1	22	47	-	0.1
165 CH OF NAZARENE	4	547	809	0.7	1.7
167 CHS OF CHRIST.	6	500	636	0.6	1.3
179 CONSRV BAPT...	1	286	355*	0.3	0.7
193 EPISCOPAL.....	3	1 164	1 380	1.3	2.8
201 EVAN COV CH AM	1	42	52*	-	0.1
221 FREE METHODIST	1	18	57	0.1	0.1
244 GRACE BRETHREN	1	38	47*	-	0.1
281 LUTH CH AMER..	2	236	358	0.3	0.7
283 LUTH--MO SYNOD	4	1 023	1 339	1.2	2.7
413 S.D.A.........	3	483	599*	0.5	1.2
419 SO BAPT CONV..	7	3 429	4 251*	3.9	8.7
435 UNITARIAN-UNIV	1	35	43*	-	0.1
443 UN C OF CHRIST	1	59	73*	0.1	0.1
449 UN METHODIST..	9	4 197	5 203*	4.8	10.7
453 UN PRES CH USA	8	2 067	2 563*	2.3	5.3
469 WELS..........	1	79	110	0.1	0.2
CHELAN	**63**	**11 088**	**19 343***	**42.9**	**100.0**
017 AMER BAPT ASSN	1	51	51	0.1	0.3
019 AMER BAPT USA.	2	683	813*	1.8	4.2
029 AMER LUTH CH..	5	1 197	1 646	3.7	8.5
053 ASSEMB OF GOD.	5	362	629	1.4	3.3
081 CATHOLIC......	4	NA	3 440	7.6	17.8
089 CHR & MISS AL.	1	80	130	0.3	0.7
093 CHR CH (DISC).	3	445	717	1.6	3.7
121 CH GOD (ABR).	2	135	161*	0.4	0.8
123 CH GOD (ANDER)	1	90	270	0.6	1.4
127 CH GOD (CLEVE)	1	46	55*	0.1	0.3
151 L-D SAINTS....	3	NA	671	1.5	3.5
157 CH OF BRETHREN	2	619	737*	1.6	3.8
165 CH OF NAZARENE	3	363	577	1.3	3.0
167 CHS OF CHRIST.	4	265	358	0.8	1.9
193 EPISCOPAL.....	3	824	1 192	2.6	6.2
197 EVAN CH OF NA.	1	110	110	0.2	0.6
221 FREE METHODIST	1	267	1 131	2.5	5.8
226 FRIENDS-USA...	2	119	142*	0.3	0.7
283 LUTH--MO SYNOD	1	317	361	0.8	1.9
403 SALVATION ARMY	1	102	181	0.4	0.9
413 S.D.A.........	3	170	202*	0.4	1.0
419 SO BAPT CONV..	4	978	1 165*	2.6	6.0
443 UN C OF CHRIST	1	99	118*	0.3	0.6
449 UN METHODIST..	6	2 532	3 016*	6.7	15.6
453 UN PRES CH USA	3	1 234	1 470*	3.3	7.6
CLALLAM	**48**	**6 444**	**15 067***	**29.2**	**100.0**
019 AMER BAPT USA.	1	275	332*	0.6	2.2
029 AMER LUTH CH..	2	991	1 316	2.5	8.7
053 ASSEMB OF GOD.	6	639	1 226	2.4	8.1
081 CATHOLIC......	4	NA	4 857	9.4	32.2
089 CHR & MISS AL.	2	82	215	0.4	1.4
093 CHR CH (DISC).	1	69	98	0.2	0.7
123 CH GOD (ANDER)	2	121	363	0.7	2.4
127 CH GOD (CLEVE)	1	24	29*	0.1	0.2
151 L-D SAINTS....	3	NA	1 225	2.4	8.1
165 CH OF NAZARENE	1	55	159	0.3	1.1
167 CHS OF CHRIST.	3	113	139	0.3	0.9
193 EPISCOPAL.....	2	707	872	1.7	5.8
217 FIRE BAPTIZED.	1	9	11*	-	0.1
221 FREE METHODIST	1	24	84	0.2	0.6
226 FRIENDS-USA...	1	65	79*	0.2	0.5
283 LUTH--MO SYNOD	3	640	819	1.6	5.4
403 SALVATION ARMY	1	55	131	0.3	0.9
413 S.D.A.........	3	350	423*	0.8	2.8
419 SO BAPT CONV..	2	412	498*	1.0	3.3
435 UNITARIAN-UNIV	1	67	81*	0.2	0.5
443 UN C OF CHRIST	1	89	108*	0.2	0.7
449 UN METHODIST..	2	1 022	1 235*	2.4	8.2
453 UN PRES CH USA	4	635	767*	1.5	5.1
CLARK	**137**	**27 200**	**56 662***	**29.5**	**100.0**
005 AME ZION......	1	288	355	0.2	0.6
019 AMER BAPT USA.	2	216	268*	0.1	0.5
029 AMER LUTH CH..	6	2 185	2 941	1.5	5.2
045 APOSTOLIC LUTH	1	600	745*	0.4	1.3
053 ASSEMB OF GOD.	5	906	1 580	0.8	2.8
057 BAPT GEN CONF.	1	229	284*	0.1	0.5
081 CATHOLIC......	11	NA	13 468	7.0	23.8
093 CHR CH (DISC).	3	827	1 318	0.7	2.3
097 CHR CHS&CHS CR	3	547	679*	0.4	1.2
105 CHRISTIAN REF.	1	84	153	0.1	0.3
123 CH GOD (ANDER)	4	701	2 103	1.1	3.7
127 CH GOD (CLEVE)	1	94	117*	0.1	0.2
151 L-D SAINTS....	10	NA	5 147	2.7	9.1
163 CH OF LUTH BR.	1	42	102	0.1	0.2
165 CH OF NAZARENE	9	1 690	3 065	1.6	5.4
167 CHS OF CHRIST.	4	670	848	0.4	1.5
179 CONSRV BAPT...	9	1 355	1 683*	0.9	3.0
193 EPISCOPAL.....	4	684	1 030	0.5	1.8
197 EVAN CH OF NA.	3	391	391	0.2	0.7
203 EVAN FREE CH..	6	458	569*	0.3	1.0
215 EVAN METH CH..	1	48	60*	-	0.1
220 FREE LUTHERAN.	1	15	20	-	-
221 FREE METHODIST	1	23	96	-	0.2
226 FRIENDS-USA...	4	547	679*	0.4	1.2
263 INT FOURSQ GOS	2	413	513*	0.3	0.9

NA—Not applicable *Total adherents estimated from known number of communicant, confirmed, full members. —Represents a percent less than 0.1. Percentages may not total due to rounding.

Table 4. Churches and Church Membership by County and Denomination: 1980

County and Denomination	Number of churches	Communicant, confirmed, full members	Total adherents Number	Percent of total population	Percent of total adherents
281 LUTH CH AMER..	5	1 990	2 747	1.4	4.8
283 LUTH--MO SYNOD	4	1 681	2 522	1.3	4.5
291 MISSIONARY CH.	1	0	26	-	-
329 OPEN BIBLE STD	2	90	115	0.1	0.2
403 SALVATION ARMY	1	127	237	0.1	0.4
413 S.D.A.........	7	2 276	2 827*	1.5	5.0
419 SO BAPT CONV..	5	1 596	1 982*	1.0	3.5
435 UNITARIAN-UNIV	1	45	56*	-	0.1
443 UN C OF CHRIST	1	367	456*	0.2	0.8
449 UN METHODIST..	11	3 642	4 524*	2.4	8.0
453 UN PRES CH USA	4	2 251	2 796*	1.5	4.9
469 WELS.........	1	122	160	0.1	0.3
COLUMBIA	13	774	1 544*	38.1	100.0
053 ASSEMB OF GOD.	1	60	150	3.7	9.7
081 CATHOLIC......	2	NA	315	7.8	20.4
097 CHR CHS&CHS CR	1	30	36*	0.9	2.3
151 L-D SAINTS....	1	NA	160	3.9	10.4
165 CH OF NAZARENE	1	25	42	1.0	2.7
179 CONSRV BAPT...	1	84	101*	2.5	6.5
193 EPISCOPAL.....	1	31	55	1.4	3.6
283 LUTH--MO SYNOD	1	116	171	4.2	11.1
413 S.D.A.........	2	99	119*	2.9	7.7
443 UN C OF CHRIST	1	136	163*	4.0	10.6
449 UN METHODIST..	1	193	232*	5.7	15.0
COWLITZ	73	14 373	26 623*	33.5	100.0
017 AMER BAPT ASSN	1	26	26	-	0.1
019 AMER BAPT USA.	2	989	1 218*	1.5	4.6
029 AMER LUTH CH..	3	1 202	1 615	2.0	6.1
045 APOSTOLIC LUTH	1	30	37*	-	0.1
053 ASSEMB OF GOD.	7	1 194	1 880	2.4	7.1
081 CATHOLIC......	3	NA	4 279	5.4	16.1
089 CHR & MISS AL.	1	54	87	0.1	0.3
093 CHR CH (DISC).	3	784	1 114	1.4	4.2
097 CHR CHS&CHS CR	3	330	406*	0.5	1.5
123 CH GOD (ANDER)	1	66	198	0.2	0.7
127 CH GOD (CLEVE)	3	272	335*	0.4	1.3
151 L-D SAINTS....	5	NA	2 846	3.6	10.7
163 CH OF LUTH BR.	1	42	119	0.1	0.4
165 CH OF NAZARENE	5	550	1 249	1.6	4.7
167 CHS OF CHRIST.	2	256	308	0.4	1.2
179 CONSRV BAPT...	3	192	236*	0.3	0.9
193 EPISCOPAL.....	1	584	700	0.9	2.6
203 EVAN FREE CH..	1	36	44*	0.1	0.2
221 FREE METHODIST	1	22	60	0.1	0.2
226 FRIENDS-USA...	1	106	130*	0.2	0.5
263 INT FOURSQ GOS	1	124	153*	0.2	0.6
274 LAT EVAN LUTH.	1	39	43	0.1	0.2
281 LUTH CH AMER..	3	1 520	2 059	2.6	7.7
283 LUTH--MO SYNOD	1	470	657	0.8	2.5
329 OPEN BIBLE STD	1	80	120	0.2	0.5
403 SALVATION ARMY	1	68	133	0.2	0.5
413 S.D.A.........	3	528	650*	0.8	2.4
419 SO BAPT CONV..	7	2 902	3 573*	4.5	13.4
449 UN METHODIST..	4	1 263	1 555*	2.0	5.8
453 UN PRES CH USA	3	644	793*	1.0	3.0
DOUGLAS	31	2 881	5 582*	25.2	100.0
019 AMER BAPT USA.	1	35	43*	0.2	0.8
029 AMER LUTH CH..	1	207	262	1.2	4.7
053 ASSEMB OF GOD.	3	99	164	0.7	2.9
081 CATHOLIC......	5	NA	829	3.7	14.9
093 CHR CH (DISC).	2	44	75	0.3	1.3
123 CH GOD (ANDER)	1	58	174	0.8	3.1
127 CH GOD (CLEVE)	1	131	161*	0.7	2.9
151 L-D SAINTS....	2	NA	960	4.3	17.2
165 CH OF NAZARENE	1	19	46	0.2	0.8
167 CHS OF CHRIST.	1	200	265	1.2	4.7
193 EPISCOPAL.....	1	14	17	0.1	0.3
283 LUTH--MO SYNOD	1	220	303	1.4	5.4
413 S.D.A.........	2	633	777*	3.5	13.9
419 SO BAPT CONV..	1	541	664*	3.0	11.9
449 UN METHODIST..	3	315	387*	1.7	6.9
453 UN PRES CH USA	3	279	343*	1.5	6.1
469 WELS.........	2	86	112	0.5	2.0
FERRY	11	218	900*	15.5	100.0
053 ASSEMB OF GOD.	1	8	11	0.2	1.2
081 CATHOLIC......	3	NA	420	7.2	46.7
151 L-D SAINTS....	1	NA	108	1.9	12.0
165 CH OF NAZARENE	1	29	92	1.6	10.2
193 EPISCOPAL.....	1	14	10	0.2	1.1
283 LUTH--MO SYNOD	1	50	113	1.9	12.6
413 S.D.A.........	1	41	51*	0.9	5.7
453 UN PRES CH USA	2	76	95*	1.6	10.6
FRANKLIN	47	6 159	15 578*	44.5	100.0
017 AMER BAPT ASSN	1	34	34	0.1	0.2
019 AMER BAPT USA.	2	295	373*	1.1	2.4
029 AMER LUTH CH..	3	535	710	2.0	4.6
053 ASSEMB OF GOD.	5	542	917	2.6	5.9
081 CATHOLIC......	3	NA	4 520	12.9	29.0
097 CHR CHS&CHS CR	1	497	629*	1.8	4.0
101 C.M.E.........	1	293	371*	1.1	2.4
127 CH GOD (CLEVE)	2	178	225*	0.6	1.4
151 L-D SAINTS....	7	NA	2 547	7.3	16.3
165 CH OF NAZARENE	2	302	601	1.7	3.9
167 CHS OF CHRIST.	2	192	282	0.8	1.8
193 EPISCOPAL.....	1	211	359	1.0	2.3

County and Denomination	Number of churches	Communicant, confirmed, full members	Total adherents Number	Percent of total population	Percent of total adherents
197 EVAN CH OF NA.	1	18	18	0.1	0.1
263 INT FOURSQ GOS	1	50	63*	0.2	0.4
283 LUTH--MO SYNOD	2	223	308	0.9	2.0
285 MENNONITE CH..	1	64	81*	0.2	0.5
353 CHR BRETHREN..	1	20	20	0.1	0.1
403 SALVATION ARMY	1	46	156	0.4	1.0
413 S.D.A.........	1	451	571*	1.6	3.7
419 SO BAPT CONV..	2	755	955*	2.7	6.1
443 UN C OF CHRIST	2	430	544*	1.6	3.5
449 UN METHODIST..	4	913	1 155*	3.3	7.4
453 UN PRES CH USA	1	110	139*	0.4	0.9
GARFIELD	9	1 322	2 135*	86.5	100.0
053 ASSEMB OF GOD.	1	34	50	2.0	2.3
081 CATHOLIC......	1	NA	409	16.6	19.2
097 CHR CHS&CHS CR	1	222	268*	10.9	12.6
165 CH OF NAZARENE	1	91	151	6.1	7.1
193 EPISCOPAL.....	1	98	198	8.0	9.3
283 LUTH--MO SYNOD	1	23	28	1.1	1.3
413 S.D.A.........	1	24	29*	1.2	1.4
449 UN METHODIST..	1	428	517*	20.9	24.2
453 UN PRES CH USA	1	402	485*	19.7	22.7
GRANT	96	7 229	20 136*	41.5	100.0
019 AMER BAPT USA.	1	33	41*	0.1	0.2
029 AMER LUTH CH..	5	1 008	1 346	2.8	6.7
053 ASSEMB OF GOD.	11	680	1 122	2.3	5.6
057 BAPT GEN CONF.	1	241	301*	0.6	1.5
081 CATHOLIC......	8	NA	5 305	10.9	26.3
089 CHR & MISS AL.	1	24	74	0.2	0.4
093 CHR CH (DISC).	2	100	152	0.3	0.8
105 CHRISTIAN REF.	1	84	152	0.3	0.8
123 CH GOD (ANDER)	1	25	75	0.2	0.4
127 CH GOD (CLEVE)	1	24	30*	0.1	0.1
151 L-D SAINTS....	13	NA	4 517	9.3	22.4
165 CH OF NAZARENE	5	350	752	1.5	3.7
167 CHS OF CHRIST.	4	178	224	0.5	1.1
179 CONSRV BAPT...	2	175	218*	0.4	1.1
193 EPISCOPAL.....	3	194	347	0.7	1.7
203 EVAN FREE CH..	1	47	59*	0.1	0.3
215 EVAN METH CH..	2	88	110*	0.2	0.5
221 FREE METHODIST	2	103	354	0.7	1.8
226 FRIENDS-USA...	1	49	61*	0.1	0.3
283 LUTH--MO SYNOD	6	696	974	2.0	4.8
287 MENN GEN CONF.	1	50	75	0.2	0.4
291 MISSIONARY CH.	1	31	45	0.1	0.2
349 PENT HOLINESS.	1	34	42*	0.1	0.2
413 S.D.A.........	4	411	513*	1.1	2.5
419 SO BAPT CONV..	5	414	516*	1.1	2.6
443 UN C OF CHRIST	2	277	345*	0.7	1.7
449 UN METHODIST..	5	1 097	1 368*	2.8	6.8
453 UN PRES CH USA	6	816	1 018*	2.1	5.1
GRAYS HARBOR	79	8 444	16 981*	25.6	100.0
019 AMER BAPT USA.	3	671	817*	1.2	4.8
029 AMER LUTH CH..	4	857	1 211	1.8	7.1
053 ASSEMB OF GOD.	10	533	1 184	1.8	7.0
057 BAPT GEN CONF.	3	451	549*	0.8	3.2
081 CATHOLIC......	7	NA	3 380	5.1	19.9
089 CHR & MISS AL.	4	110	219	0.3	1.3
093 CHR CH (DISC).	1	147	246	0.4	1.4
097 CHR CHS&CHS CR	1	95	116*	0.2	0.7
123 CH GOD (ANDER)	3	222	666	1.0	3.9
127 CH GOD (CLEVE)	1	2	2*	-	-
151 L-D SAINTS....	4	NA	1 430	2.2	8.4
165 CH OF NAZARENE	1	53	134	0.2	0.8
167 CHS OF CHRIST.	1	80	110	0.2	0.6
179 CONSRV BAPT...	1	35	43*	0.1	0.3
193 EPISCOPAL.....	4	341	607	0.9	3.6
201 EVAN COV CH AM	1	67	82*	0.1	0.5
221 FREE METHODIST	1	24	126	0.2	0.7
271 REFORM JUDAISM	1	20	24*	-	0.1
281 LUTH CH AMER..	3	467	649	1.0	3.8
283 LUTH--MO SYNOD	1	429	649	1.0	3.8
329 OPEN BIBLE STD	1	184	250	0.4	1.5
349 PENT HOLINESS.	1	23	28*	-	0.2
353 CHR BRETHREN..	1	45	100	0.2	0.6
403 SALVATION ARMY	1	91	103	0.2	0.6
413 S.D.A.........	3	265	322*	0.5	1.9
419 SO BAPT CONV..	3	367	447*	0.7	2.6
443 UN C OF CHRIST	1	40	49*	0.1	0.3
449 UN METHODIST..	8	1 787	2 175*	3.3	12.8
453 UN PRES CH USA	5	1 038	1 263*	1.9	7.4
ISLAND	34	5 432	10 978*	24.9	100.0
019 AMER BAPT USA.	1	180	219*	0.5	2.0
029 AMER LUTH CH..	4	1 021	1 300	3.0	11.8
053 ASSEMB OF GOD.	2	146	271	0.6	2.5
081 CATHOLIC......	4	NA	2 332	5.3	21.2
089 CHR & MISS AL.	1	103	341	0.8	3.1
105 CHRISTIAN REF.	1	177	244	0.6	2.2
151 L-D SAINTS....	4	NA	1 223	2.8	11.1
165 CH OF NAZARENE	1	155	193	0.4	1.8
167 CHS OF CHRIST.	2	100	161	0.4	1.5
193 EPISCOPAL.....	3	536	788	1.8	7.2
221 FREE METHODIST	1	29	135	0.3	1.2
263 INT FOURSQ GOS	1	46	56*	0.1	0.5
283 LUTH--MO SYNOD	1	198	287	0.7	2.6
371 REF CH IN AM..	1	497	699	1.6	6.4
413 S.D.A.........	2	81	98*	0.2	0.9
419 SO BAPT CONV..	1	804	978*	2.2	8.9

NA—Not applicable   *Total adherents estimated from known number of communicant, confirmed, full members.   —Represents a percent less than 0.1.   Percentages may not total due to rounding.

Table 4. Churches and Church Membership by County and Denomination: 1980

County and Denomination	Number of churches	Communicant, confirmed, full members	Total adherents		
			Number	Percent of total population	Percent of total adherents
449 UN METHODIST..	3	1 176	1 430*	3.2	13.0
453 UN PRES CH USA	1	183	223*	0.5	2.0
JEFFERSON	18	1 781	3 439*	21.5	100.0
019 AMER BAPT USA.	1	280	333*	2.1	9.7
029 AMER LUTH CH..	1	120	171	1.1	5.0
053 ASSEMB OF GOD.	2	125	192	1.2	5.6
081 CATHOLIC......	1	NA	850	5.3	24.7
151 L-D SAINTS....	1	NA	292	1.8	8.5
165 CH OF NAZARENE	1	19	52	0.3	1.5
167 CHS OF CHRIST.	1	47	62	0.4	1.8
193 EPISCOPAL.....	1	138	237	1.5	6.9
203 EVAN FREE CH..	1	42	50*	0.3	1.5
215 EVAN METH CH..	1	6	7*	–	0.2
413 S.D.A.........	2	83	99*	0.6	2.9
419 SO BAPT CONV..	1	140	166*	1.0	4.8
449 UN METHODIST..	2	426	506*	3.2	14.7
453 UN PRES CH USA	2	355	422*	2.6	12.3
KING	733	174 027	378 536*	29.8	100.0
001 ADVENT CHR CH.	1	152	180*	–	–
005 AME ZION......	2	389	415	–	0.1
017 AMER BAPT ASSN	1	32	32	–	–
019 AMER BAPT USA.	39	11 330	13 389*	1.1	3.5
029 AMER LUTH CH..	41	18 643	25 799	2.0	6.8
045 APOSTOLIC LUTH	1	300	355*	–	0.1
053 ASSEMB OF GOD.	40	7 803	13 477	1.1	3.6
057 BAPT GEN CONF.	13	2 621	3 097*	0.2	0.8
081 CATHOLIC......	60	NA	121 614	9.6	32.1
089 CHR & MISS AL.	11	1 350	2 359	0.2	0.6
093 CHR CH (DISC).	13	2 878	4 150	0.3	1.1
097 CHR CHS&CHS CR	14	4 518	5 339*	0.4	1.4
101 C.M.E.........	2	685	809*	0.1	0.2
105 CHRISTIAN REF.	3	567	951	0.1	0.3
123 CH GOD (ANDER)	9	584	1 752	0.1	0.5
127 CH GOD (CLEVE)	7	218	258*	–	0.1
133 CH GOD(7TH)DEN	2	23	27*	–	–
151 L-D SAINTS....	52	NA	25 671	2.0	6.8
157 CH OF BRETHREN	3	464	548*	–	0.1
163 CH OF LUTH BR.	2	281	504	–	0.1
164 CH LUTH CONF..	1	90	133	–	–
165 CH OF NAZARENE	20	2 938	4 111	0.3	1.1
167 CHS OF CHRIST.	21	2 817	3 674	0.3	1.0
175 CONGR CHR CHS.	1	76	90*	–	–
179 CONSRV BAPT...	7	1 083	1 280*	0.1	0.3
193 EPISCOPAL.....	35	15 182	21 398	1.7	5.7
195 ESTONIAN ELC..	1	88	250	–	0.1
197 EVAN CH OF NA.	4	503	503	–	0.1
201 EVAN COV CH AM	11	2 175	2 570*	0.2	0.7
203 EVAN FREE CH..	7	495	585*	–	0.2
215 EVAN METH CH..	1	80	95*	–	–
220 FREE LUTHERAN.	1	145	225	–	0.1
221 FREE METHODIST	14	2 245	5 952	0.5	1.6
226 FRIENDS-USA...	4	607	717*	0.1	0.2
233 GEN CH NEW JER	1	60	71*	–	–
237 GC MENN BR CHS	1	33	39*	–	–
239 SWEDENBORGIAN.	1	60	71*	–	–
244 GRACE BRETHREN	1	133	157*	–	–
263 INT FOURSQ GOS	4	270	319*	–	0.1
270 CONSRV JUDAISM	2	608	718*	0.1	0.1
271 REFORM JUDAISM	2	3 666	4 332*	0.3	1.1
274 LAT EVAN LUTH.	1	458	549	–	0.1
281 LUTH CH AMER..	28	11 373	15 922	1.3	4.2
283 LUTH--MO SYNOD	27	9 112	12 969	1.0	3.4
287 MENN GEN CONF.	1	79	103	–	–
290 METRO COMM CHS	1	167	300	–	0.1
313 N AM BAPT CONF	3	315	372*	–	0.1
329 OPEN BIBLE STD	3	760	1 010	0.1	0.3
349 PENT HOLINESS.	2	57	67*	–	–
353 CHR BRETHREN..	5	610	840	0.1	0.2
356 PRESB CH AMER.	2	608	640	0.1	0.2
371 REF CH IN AM..	1	353	620	–	0.2
381 REF PRES-EVAN.	3	270	354	–	0.1
383 REF PRES OF NA	1	70	94	–	–
403 SALVATION ARMY	4	440	1 893	0.1	0.5
413 S.D.A.........	17	4 281	5 059*	0.4	1.3
415 S-D BAPT GC ..	1	70	83*	–	–
419 SO BAPT CONV..	31	8 135	9 613*	0.8	2.5
435 UNITARIAN-UNIV	7	1 058	1 250*	0.1	0.3
443 UN C OF CHRIST	32	7 855	9 282*	0.7	2.5
449 UN METHODIST..	47	20 290	23 977*	1.9	6.3
453 UN PRES CH USA	55	20 905	24 704*	1.9	6.5
469 WELS..........	5	569	819	0.1	0.2
KITSAP	99	17 652	41 051*	28.0	100.0
001 ADVENT CHR CH.	1	62	76*	0.1	0.2
017 AMER BAPT ASSN	1	77	77	0.1	0.2
019 AMER BAPT USA.	6	1 273	1 554*	1.1	3.8
029 AMER LUTH CH..	7	3 422	4 636	3.2	11.3
053 ASSEMB OF GOD.	9	1 413	2 854	1.9	7.0
057 BAPT GEN CONF.	2	488	596*	0.4	1.5
081 CATHOLIC......	7	NA	12 943	8.8	31.5
089 CHR & MISS AL.	3	267	481	0.3	1.2
093 CHR CH (DISC).	2	323	475	0.3	1.2
097 CHR CHS&CHS CR	2	170	208*	0.1	0.5
123 CH GOD (ANDER)	1	67	201	0.1	0.5
127 CH GOD (CLEVE)	1	23	28*	–	0.1
151 L-D SAINTS....	8	NA	3 837	2.6	9.3
165 CH OF NAZARENE	3	348	834	0.6	2.0
167 CHS OF CHRIST.	5	357	504	0.3	1.2
179 CONSRV BAPT...	1	40	49*	–	0.1
193 EPISCOPAL.....	4	1 809	2 087	1.4	5.1

County and Denomination	Number of churches	Communicant, confirmed, full members	Total adherents		
			Number	Percent of total population	Percent of total adherents
201 EVAN COV CH AM	1	126	154*	0.1	0.4
203 EVAN FREE CH..	1	119	145*	0.1	0.4
209 EVAN LUTH SYN.	1	222	302	0.2	0.7
221 FREE METHODIST	1	62	174	0.1	0.4
237 GC MENN BR CHS	1	85	104*	0.1	0.3
263 INT FOURSQ GOS	1	123	150*	0.1	0.4
281 LUTH CH AMER..	4	1 054	1 464	1.0	3.6
283 LUTH--MO SYNOD	2	845	1 036	0.7	2.5
353 CHR BRETHREN..	1	35	70	–	0.2
381 REF PRES-EVAN.	1	37	42	–	0.1
403 SALVATION ARMY	1	93	188	0.1	0.5
413 S.D.A.........	3	485	592*	0.4	1.4
419 SO BAPT CONV..	5	985	1 203*	0.8	2.9
435 UNITARIAN-UNIV	2	47	57*	–	0.1
443 UN C OF CHRIST	1	178	217*	0.1	0.5
449 UN METHODIST..	7	2 495	3 046*	2.1	7.4
453 UN PRES CH USA	2	407	497*	0.3	1.2
469 WELS..........	1	115	170	0.1	0.4
KITTITAS	38	3 208	7 022*	28.2	100.0
019 AMER BAPT USA.	3	188	221*	0.9	3.1
029 AMER LUTH CH..	1	299	383	1.5	5.5
053 ASSEMB OF GOD.	3	140	328	1.3	4.7
081 CATHOLIC......	3	NA	1 745	7.0	24.9
089 CHR & MISS AL.	2	139	305	1.2	4.3
093 CHR CH (DISC).	1	175	225	0.9	3.2
097 CHR CHS&CHS CR	2	156	183*	0.7	2.6
123 CH GOD (ANDER)	1	35	105	0.4	1.5
127 CH GOD (CLEVE)	1	?	?	?	?
151 L-D SAINTS....	3	NA	766	3.1	10.9
165 CH OF NAZARENE	2	119	221	0.9	3.1
167 CHS OF CHRIST.	1	100	127	0.5	1.8
179 CONSRV BAPT...	1	56	66*	0.3	0.9
193 EPISCOPAL.....	3	309	568	2.3	8.1
221 FREE METHODIST	1	32	51	0.2	0.7
413 S.D.A.........	2	101	118*	0.5	1.7
419 SO BAPT CONV..	1	320	375*	1.5	5.3
435 UNITARIAN-UNIV	1	12	14*	0.1	0.2
449 UN METHODIST..	1	424	497*	2.0	7.1
453 UN PRES CH USA	3	521	611*	2.5	8.7
469 WELS..........	2	82	113	0.5	1.6
KLICKITAT	33	2 343	4 815*	30.4	100.0
019 AMER BAPT USA.	1	329	406*	2.6	8.4
045 APOSTOLIC LUTH	1	30	37*	0.2	0.8
053 ASSEMB OF GOD.	4	133	260	1.6	5.4
081 CATHOLIC......	2	NA	780	4.9	16.2
097 CHR CHS&CHS CR	1	50	62*	0.4	1.3
123 CH GOD (ANDER)	1	57	171	1.1	3.6
151 L-D SAINTS....	3	NA	802	5.1	16.7
165 CH OF NAZARENE	2	100	238	1.5	4.9
167 CHS OF CHRIST.	1	30	38	0.2	0.8
244 GRACE BRETHREN	1	28	35*	0.2	0.7
281 LUTH CH AMER..	1	138	176	1.1	3.7
283 LUTH--MO SYNOD	2	226	302	1.9	6.3
413 S.D.A.........	3	243	300*	1.9	6.2
419 SO BAPT CONV..	4	157	194*	1.2	4.0
443 UN C OF CHRIST	1	99	122*	0.8	2.5
449 UN METHODIST..	3	555	685*	4.3	14.2
453 UN PRES CH USA	2	168	207*	1.3	4.3
LEWIS	88	9 259	18 577*	33.6	100.0
019 AMER BAPT USA.	3	524	644*	1.2	3.5
029 AMER LUTH CH..	1	244	345	0.6	1.9
053 ASSEMB OF GOD.	16	1 205	2 340	4.2	12.6
081 CATHOLIC......	10	NA	3 657	6.6	19.7
089 CHR & MISS AL.	1	56	86	0.2	0.5
093 CHR CH (DISC).	2	466	717	1.3	3.9
097 CHR CHS&CHS CR	2	470	578*	1.0	3.1
123 CH GOD (ANDER)	3	127	381	0.7	2.1
127 CH GOD (CLEVE)	1	45	55*	0.1	0.3
151 L-D SAINTS....	4	NA	1 633	3.0	8.8
157 CH OF BRETHREN	2	162	199*	0.4	1.1
165 CH OF NAZARENE	2	292	576	1.0	3.1
167 CHS OF CHRIST.	2	108	165	0.3	0.9
179 CONSRV BAPT...	3	349	429*	0.8	2.3
193 EPISCOPAL.....	2	325	362	0.7	1.9
197 EVAN CH OF NA.	2	71	71	0.1	0.4
201 EVAN COV CH AM	1	30	37*	0.1	0.2
203 EVAN FREE CH..	1	66	81*	0.1	0.4
221 FREE METHODIST	1	70	219	0.4	1.2
263 INT FOURSQ GOS	2	139	171*	0.3	0.9
281 LUTH CH AMER..	3	743	1 029	1.9	5.5
283 LUTH--MO SYNOD	1	241	344	0.6	1.9
329 OPEN BIBLE STD	1	60	90	0.2	0.5
353 CHR BRETHREN..	1	60	100	0.2	0.5
403 SALVATION ARMY	1	49	141	0.3	0.8
413 S.D.A.........	5	619	761*	1.4	4.1
419 SO BAPT CONV..	2	296	364*	0.7	2.0
449 UN METHODIST..	7	1 560	1 918*	3.5	10.3
453 UN PRES CH USA	6	882	1 084*	2.0	5.8
LINCOLN	33	3 514	5 210*	54.2	100.0
029 AMER LUTH CH..	7	1 211	1 553	16.2	29.8
053 ASSEMB OF GOD.	1	68	119	1.2	2.3
081 CATHOLIC......	6	NA	845	8.8	16.2
093 CHR CH (DISC).	1	139	178	1.9	3.4
165 CH OF NAZARENE	1	42	42	0.4	0.8
263 INT FOURSQ GOS	1	?	?	?	?
283 LUTH--MO SYNOD	1	161	194	2.0	3.7
313 N AM BAPT CONF	1	32	39*	0.4	0.7

NA—Not applicable   *Total adherents estimated from known number of communicant, confirmed, full members.   —Represents a percent less than 0.1.   Percentages may not total due to rounding.

Table 4. Churches and Church Membership by County and Denomination: 1980

County and Denomination	Number of churches	Communicant, confirmed, full members	Total adherents Number	Percent of total population	Percent of total adherents
353 CHR BRETHREN..	1	25	25	0.3	0.5
443 UN C OF CHRIST	4	815	983*	10.2	18.9
449 UN METHODIST..	5	440	531*	5.5	10.2
453 UN PRES CH USA	4	581	701*	7.3	13.5
MASON	**22**	**3 434**	**7 034***	**22.6**	**100.0**
019 AMER BAPT USA.	1	341	409*	1.3	5.8
029 AMER LUTH CH..	2	583	892	2.9	12.7
053 ASSEMB OF GOD.	3	276	520	1.7	7.4
081 CATHOLIC......	1	NA	1 495	4.8	21.3
097 CHR CHS&CHS CR	1	172	206*	0.7	2.9
127 CH GOD (CLEVE)	1	62	74*	0.2	1.1
151 L-D SAINTS....	1	NA	818	2.6	11.6
165 CH OF NAZARENE	1	45	118	0.4	1.7
179 CONSRV BAPT...	1	532	638*	2.0	9.1
193 EPISCOPAL.....	3	315	476	1.5	6.8
263 INT FOURSQ GOS	1	66	79*	0.3	1.1
283 LUTH--MO SYNOD	1	184	286	0.9	4.1
353 CHR BRETHREN..	1	25	25	0.1	0.4
413 S.D.A........	1	167	200*	0.6	2.8
419 SO BAPT CONV..	2	126	151*	0.5	2.1
449 UN METHODIST..	1	540	647*	2.1	9.2
OKANOGAN	**61**	**4 107**	**9 811***	**32.0**	**100.0**
017 AMER BAPT ASSN	1	48	48	0.2	0.5
019 AMER BAPT USA.	1	83	102*	0.3	1.0
053 ASSEMB OF GOD.	5	292	589	1.9	6.0
057 BAPT GEN CONF.	3	167	205*	0.7	2.1
081 CATHOLIC.....	9	NA	2 530	8.3	25.8
151 L-D SAINTS....	5	NA	979	3.2	10.0
157 CH OF BRETHREN	2	294	362*	1.2	3.7
167 CHS OF CHRIST.	3	168	225	0.7	2.3
193 EPISCOPAL.....	4	330	461	1.5	4.7
215 EVAN METH CH..	1	52	64*	0.2	0.7
221 FREE METHODIST	3	200	1 182	3.9	12.0
283 LUTH--MO SYNOD	4	368	478	1.6	4.9
353 CHR BRETHREN..	1	25	25	0.1	0.3
413 S.D.A........	4	409	503*	1.6	5.1
419 SO BAPT CONV..	1	151	186*	0.6	1.9
443 UN C OF CHRIST	1	106	130*	0.4	1.3
449 UN METHODIST..	9	860	1 058*	3.5	10.8
453 UN PRES CH USA	2	427	525*	1.7	5.4
469 WELS.........	2	127	159	0.5	1.6
PACIFIC	**30**	**2 153**	**3 808***	**22.1**	**100.0**
019 AMER BAPT USA.	1	359	426*	2.5	11.2
029 AMER LUTH CH..	3	365	485	2.8	12.7
053 ASSEMB OF GOD.	3	282	406	2.4	10.7
081 CATHOLIC......	2	NA	645	3.7	16.9
151 L-D SAINTS....	2	NA	405	2.3	10.6
165 CH OF NAZARENE	1	25	60	0.3	1.6
179 CONSRV BAPT...	2	120	142*	0.8	3.7
193 EPISCOPAL.....	2	137	216	1.3	5.7
201 EVAN COV CH AM	1	51	61*	0.4	1.6
283 LUTH--MO SYNOD	1	36	41	0.2	1.1
353 CHR BRETHREN..	1	20	20	0.1	0.5
413 S.D.A........	2	63	75*	0.4	2.0
443 UN C OF CHRIST	1	64	76*	0.4	2.0
449 UN METHODIST..	6	361	429*	2.5	11.3
453 UN PRES CH USA	2	270	321*	1.9	8.4
PEND OREILLE	**20**	**1 184**	**2 415***	**28.1**	**100.0**
019 AMER BAPT USA.	1	48	59*	0.7	2.4
029 AMER LUTH CH..	1	275	359	4.2	14.9
053 ASSEMB OF GOD.	3	129	363	4.2	15.0
081 CATHOLIC......	5	NA	516	6.0	21.4
151 L-D SAINTS....	1	NA	144	1.7	6.0
165 CH OF NAZARENE	1	42	110	1.3	4.6
167 CHS OF CHRIST.	1	20	25	0.3	1.0
287 MENN GEN CONF.	1	61	86	1.0	3.6
413 S.D.A........	3	211	261*	3.0	10.8
419 SO BAPT CONV..	1	122	151*	1.8	6.3
443 UN C OF CHRIST	2	276	341*	4.0	14.1
PIERCE	**296**	**61 920**	**132 797***	**27.3**	**100.0**
017 AMER BAPT ASSN	2	115	115	–	0.1
019 AMER BAPT USA.	15	4 550	5 524*	1.1	4.2
029 AMER LUTH CH..	18	8 753	12 285	2.5	9.3
053 ASSEMB OF GOD.	19	3 301	6 148	1.3	4.6
057 BAPT GEN CONF.	4	1 204	1 462*	0.3	1.1
059 BAPT MISS ASSN	1	30	36*	–	–
081 CATHOLIC......	24	NA	39 460	8.1	29.7
089 CHR & MISS AL.	1	170	270	0.1	0.2
093 CHR CH (DISC).	8	1 328	1 820	0.4	1.4
097 CHR CHS&CHS CR	8	1 070	1 299*	0.3	1.0
101 C.M.E........	1	188	228*	–	0.2
105 CHRISTIAN REF.	1	156	270	0.1	0.2
123 CH GOD (ANDER)	3	385	1 155	0.2	0.9
127 CH GOD (CLEVE)	3	204	248*	0.1	0.2
133 CH GOD(7TH)DEN	1	18	22*	–	–
151 L-D SAINTS....	23	NA	10 537	2.2	7.9
157 CH OF BRETHREN	1	60	73*	–	0.1
163 CH OF LUTH BR.	1	31	79	–	0.1
165 CH OF NAZARENE	7	921	1 633	0.3	1.2
167 CHS OF CHRIST.	11	1 085	1 380	0.3	1.0
175 CONGR CHR CHS.	1	466	566*	0.1	0.4
179 CONSRV BAPT...	3	618	750*	0.2	0.6
193 EPISCOPAL.....	9	3 483	3 812	0.8	2.9
201 EVAN COV CH AM	3	529	642*	0.1	0.5
203 EVAN FREE CH..	4	203	246*	0.1	0.2
209 EVAN LUTH SYN.	2	441	619	0.1	0.5
221 FREE METHODIST	4	201	852	0.2	0.6
226 FRIENDS-USA...	4	303	368*	0.1	0.3
263 INT FOURSQ GOS	1	90	109*	–	0.1
271 REFORM JUDAISM	1	472	573*	0.1	0.4
274 LAT EVAN LUTH.	1	206	233	–	0.2
281 LUTH CH AMER..	10	2 685	3 671	0.8	2.8
283 LUTH--MO SYNOD	9	4 340	6 560	1.4	4.9
290 METRO COMM CHS	1	20	40	–	–
291 MISSIONARY CH.	1	48	60	–	–
313 N AM BAPT CONF	3	758	920*	0.2	0.7
329 OPEN BIBLE STD	5	693	1 045	0.2	0.8
349 PENT HOLINESS	1	28	34*	–	–
381 REF PRES-EVAN.	1	82	96	–	0.1
403 SALVATION ARMY	1	166	175	–	0.1
413 S.D.A........	7	1 343	1 631*	0.3	1.2
419 SO BAPT CONV..	9	4 043	4 909*	1.0	3.7
435 UNITARIAN-UNIV	1	168	204*	–	0.2
443 UN C OF CHRIST	7	655	795*	0.2	0.6
449 UN METHODIST..	25	8 430	10 235*	2.1	7.7
453 UN PRES CH USA	28	7 565	9 185*	1.9	6.9
469 WELS.........	2	315	423	0.1	0.3
SAN JUAN	**8**	**450**	**1 134***	**14.5**	**100.0**
029 AMER LUTH CH..	1	42	60	0.8	5.3
081 CATHOLIC......	1	NA	400	5.1	35.3
151 L-D SAINTS....	1	NA	131	1.7	11.6
179 CONSRV BAPT...	1	27	32*	0.4	2.8
193 EPISCOPAL.....	2	155	247	3.2	21.8
413 S.D.A........	1	34	40*	0.5	3.5
453 UN PRES CH USA	1	192	224*	2.9	19.8
SKAGIT	**83**	**12 790**	**22 985***	**35.8**	**100.0**
019 AMER BAPT USA.	4	838	1 012*	1.6	4.4
029 AMER LUTH CH..	6	2 098	2 796	4.4	12.2
053 ASSEMB OF GOD.	5	858	1 441	2.2	6.3
057 BAPT GEN CONF.	1	438	529*	0.8	2.3
081 CATHOLIC......	6	NA	4 340	6.8	18.9
089 CHR & MISS AL.	1	63	133	0.2	0.6
093 CHR CH (DISC).	2	308	397	0.6	1.7
097 CHR CHS&CHS CR	4	807	974*	1.5	4.2
105 CHRISTIAN REF.	2	320	597	0.9	2.6
127 CH GOD (CLEVE)	2	32	39*	0.1	0.2
151 L-D SAINTS....	3	NA	1 387	2.2	6.0
163 CH OF LUTH BR.	1	23	42	0.1	0.2
165 CH OF NAZARENE	3	185	323	0.5	1.4
167 CHS OF CHRIST.	4	300	380	0.6	1.7
179 CONSRV BAPT...	1	100	121*	0.2	0.5
193 EPISCOPAL.....	3	406	550	0.9	2.4
201 EVAN COV CH AM	2	201	243*	0.4	1.1
209 EVAN LUTH SYN.	1	0	27	–	0.1
221 FREE METHODIST	4	138	624	1.0	2.7
263 INT FOURSQ GOS	2	196	237*	0.4	1.0
281 LUTH CH AMER..	2	866	1 128	1.8	4.9
283 LUTH--MO SYNOD	1	517	721	1.1	3.1
403 SALVATION ARMY	1	60	70	0.1	0.3
413 S.D.A........	2	303	366*	0.6	1.6
419 SO BAPT CONV..	4	777	938*	1.5	4.1
435 UNITARIAN-UNIV	2	32	39*	0.1	0.2
443 UN C OF CHRIST	2	76	92*	0.1	0.4
449 UN METHODIST..	8	2 158	2 606*	4.1	11.3
453 UN PRES CH USA	4	690	833*	1.3	3.6
SKAMANIA	**9**	**536**	**1 062***	**13.4**	**100.0**
081 CATHOLIC......	1	NA	238	3.0	22.4
165 CH OF NAZARENE	2	69	210	2.7	19.8
179 CONSRV BAPT...	1	45	56*	0.7	5.3
281 LUTH CH AMER..	1	77	130	1.6	12.2
329 OPEN BIBLE STD	1	120	150	1.9	14.1
413 S.D.A........	1	56	69*	0.9	6.5
449 UN METHODIST..	1	154	190*	2.4	17.9
453 UN PRES CH USA	1	15	19*	0.2	1.8
SNOHOMISH	**216**	**36 846**	**80 261***	**23.8**	**100.0**
017 AMER BAPT ASSN	1	26	26	–	–
019 AMER BAPT USA.	10	2 280	2 793*	0.8	3.5
029 AMER LUTH CH..	15	6 078	8 265	2.5	10.3
053 ASSEMB OF GOD.	16	2 129	4 132	1.2	5.1
057 BAPT GEN CONF.	5	759	930*	0.3	1.2
081 CATHOLIC......	15	NA	20 853	6.2	26.0
089 CHR & MISS AL.	7	430	766	0.2	1.0
093 CHR CH (DISC).	1	133	178	0.1	0.2
097 CHR CHS&CHS CR	5	484	593*	0.2	0.7
105 CHRISTIAN REF.	4	520	837	0.2	1.0
123 CH GOD (ANDER)	4	205	615	0.2	0.8
127 CH GOD (CLEVE)	1	28	34*	–	–
151 L-D SAINTS....	13	NA	7 515	2.2	9.4
163 CH OF LUTH BR.	3	432	928	0.3	1.2
165 CH OF NAZARENE	7	542	1 073	0.3	1.3
167 CHS OF CHRIST.	4	477	628	0.2	0.8
175 CONGR CHR CHS.	1	153	187*	0.1	0.2
179 CONSRV BAPT...	4	720	882*	0.3	1.1
193 EPISCOPAL.....	7	1 766	2 430	0.7	3.0
201 EVAN COV CH AM	4	446	546*	0.2	0.7
203 EVAN FREE CH..	2	47	58*	–	0.1
220 FREE LUTHERAN.	2	293	355	0.1	0.4
221 FREE METHODIST	5	698	1 815	0.5	2.3
263 INT FOURSQ GOS	2	248	304*	0.1	0.4
281 LUTH CH AMER..	6	1 862	2 935	0.9	3.7
283 LUTH--MO SYNOD	10	2 722	3 807	1.1	4.7
313 N AM BAPT CONF	3	251	307*	0.1	0.4

NA—Not applicable   *Total adherents estimated from known number of communicant, confirmed, full members.   —Represents a percent less than 0.1.   Percentages may not total due to rounding.

Table 4. Churches and Church Membership by County and Denomination: 1980

County and Denomination	Number of churches	Communicant, confirmed, full members	Total adherents Number	Percent of total population	Percent of total adherents
329 OPEN BIBLE STD	3	365	530	0.2	0.7
335 ORTH PRESB CH.	1	46	56*	-	0.1
353 CHR BRETHREN..	1	35	50	-	0.1
371 REF CH IN AM..	2	138	329	0.1	0.4
381 REF PRES-EVAN.	3	291	411	0.1	0.5
403 SALVATION ARMY	1	100	199	0.1	0.2
413 S.D.A.........	9	1 356	1 661*	0.5	2.1
419 SO BAPT CONV..	12	2 029	2 486*	0.7	3.1
435 UNITARIAN-UNIV	2	239	293*	0.1	0.4
443 UN C OF CHRIST	4	529	648*	0.2	0.8
449 UN METHODIST..	12	5 628	6 895*	2.0	8.6
453 UN PRES CH USA	8	2 266	2 776*	0.8	3.5
469 WELS.........	1	95	135	-	0.2
SPOKANE	**255**	**50 209**	**125 407***	**36.7**	**100.0**
017 AMER BAPT ASSN	2	75	75	-	0.1
019 AMER BAPT USA.	9	1 424	1 727*	0.5	1.4
029 AMER LUTH CH..	13	4 729	6 527	1.9	5.2
053 ASSEMB OF GOD.	10	1 946	3 487	1.0	2.8
057 BAPT GEN CONF.	2	220	267*	0.1	0.2
081 CATHOLIC......	26	NA	47 001	13.7	37.5
089 CHR & MISS AL.	3	243	377	0.1	0.3
093 CHR CH (DISC).	10	1 762	3 054	0.9	2.4
097 CHR CHS&CHS CR	4	557	676*	0.2	0.5
101 C.M.E.........	1	28	34*	-	-
105 CHRISTIAN REF.	1	61	140	-	0.1
123 CH GOD (ANDER)	3	249	747	0.2	0.6
127 CH GOD (CLEVE)	2	77	93*	-	0.1
133 CH GOD(7TH)DEN	1	26	32*	-	-
151 L-D SAINTS....	19	NA	9 937	2.9	7.9
164 CH LUTH CONF..	2	351	521	0.2	0.4
165 CH OF NAZARENE	9	1 635	2 802	0.8	2.2
167 CHS OF CHRIST.	8	900	1 145	0.3	0.9
175 CONGR CHR CHS.	2	309	375*	0.1	0.3
179 CONSRV BAPT...	6	1 854	2 249*	0.7	1.8
193 EPISCOPAL.....	9	3 906	5 321	1.6	4.2
197 EVAN CH OF NA.	3	260	260	0.1	0.2
201 EVAN COV CH AM	2	236	286*	0.1	0.2
203 EVAN FREE CH..	2	103	125*	-	0.1
220 FREE LUTHERAN.	1	20	28	-	-
221 FREE METHODIST	3	284	879	0.3	0.7
226 FRIENDS-USA...	1	95	115*	-	0.1
244 GRACE BRETHREN	1	43	52*	-	-
263 INT FOURSQ GOS	5	574	696*	0.2	0.6
270 CONSRV JUDAISM	1	150	182*	0.1	0.1
281 LUTH CH AMER..	9	3 793	5 216	1.5	4.2
283 LUTH--MO SYNOD	8	2 642	3 823	1.1	3.0
290 METRO COMM CHS	0	15	30	-	-
313 N AM BAPT CONF	1	77	93*	-	0.1
329 OPEN BIBLE STD	2	496	800	0.2	0.6
349 PENT HOLINESS.	1	30	36*	-	-
353 CHR BRETHREN..	2	50	50	-	-
403 SALVATION ARMY	1	204	906	0.3	0.7
413 S.D.A.........	10	2 408	2 921*	0.9	2.3
419 SO BAPT CONV..	15	3 825	4 640*	1.4	3.7
435 UNITARIAN-UNIV	1	314	381*	0.1	0.3
443 UN C OF CHRIST	9	1 473	1 787*	0.5	1.4
449 UN METHODIST..	19	5 641	6 843*	2.0	5.5
453 UN PRES CH USA	15	6 970	8 455*	2.5	6.7
469 WELS.........	1	154	216	0.1	0.2
STEVENS	**44**	**2 707**	**7 429***	**25.6**	**100.0**
029 AMER LUTH CH..	2	386	540	1.9	7.3
053 ASSEMB OF GOD.	8	538	1 458	5.0	19.6
081 CATHOLIC......	11	NA	1 994	6.9	26.8
093 CHR CH (DISC).	1	147	226	0.8	3.0
097 CHR CHS&CHS CR	1	50	63*	0.2	0.8
123 CH GOD (ANDER)	1	100	300	1.0	4.0
151 L-D SAINTS....	2	NA	722	2.5	9.7
165 CH OF NAZARENE	1	76	114	0.4	1.5
167 CHS OF CHRIST.	1	88	112	0.4	1.5
193 EPISCOPAL.....	1	86	112	0.4	1.5
221 FREE METHODIST	2	111	372	1.3	5.0
353 CHR BRETHREN..	1	25	25	0.1	0.3
413 S.D.A.........	3	272	344*	1.2	4.6
419 SO BAPT CONV..	1	80	101*	0.3	1.4
443 UN C OF CHRIST	3	329	416*	1.4	5.6
449 UN METHODIST..	1	352	445*	1.5	6.0
453 UN PRES CH USA	3	67	85*	0.3	1.1
THURSTON	**77**	**16 304**	**35 288***	**28.4**	**100.0**
017 AMER BAPT ASSN	1	37	37	-	0.1
019 AMER BAPT USA.	2	558	682*	0.5	1.9
029 AMER LUTH CH..	1	722	1 134	0.9	3.2
053 ASSEMB OF GOD.	7	1 867	2 885	2.3	8.2
057 BAPT GEN CONF.	1	221	270*	0.2	0.8
081 CATHOLIC......	4	NA	9 825	7.9	27.8
089 CHR & MISS AL.	1	105	158	0.1	0.4
093 CHR CH (DISC).	2	506	811	0.7	2.3
097 CHR CHS&CHS CR	1	105	128*	0.1	0.4
105 CHRISTIAN REF.	1	72	152	0.1	0.4
123 CH GOD (ANDER)	2	430	1 290	1.0	3.7
127 CH GOD (CLEVE)	2	69	84*	0.1	0.2
151 L-D SAINTS....	5	NA	2 650	2.1	7.5
157 CH OF BRETHREN	1	190	232*	0.2	0.7
163 CH OF LUTH BR.	1	63	178	0.1	0.5
165 CH OF NAZARENE	1	238	462	0.4	1.3
167 CHS OF CHRIST.	2	152	226	0.2	0.6
179 CONSRV BAPT...	6	975	1 192*	1.0	3.4
193 EPISCOPAL.....	1	1 246	1 510	1.2	4.3
201 EVAN COV CH AM	1	99	121*	0.1	0.3
203 EVAN FREE CH..	1	107	131*	0.1	0.4

County and Denomination	Number of churches	Communicant, confirmed, full members	Total adherents Number	Percent of total population	Percent of total adherents
209 EVAN LUTH SYN.	1	62	116	0.1	0.3
221 FREE METHODIST	1	52	210	0.2	0.6
263 INT FOURSQ GOS	1	314	384*	0.3	1.1
281 LUTH CH AMER..	5	1 967	2 604	2.1	7.4
283 LUTH--MO SYNOD	2	856	1 250	1.0	3.5
329 OPEN BIBLE STD	1	30	50	-	0.1
349 PENT HOLINESS.	2	62	76*	0.1	0.2
403 SALVATION ARMY	1	82	183	0.1	0.5
413 S.D.A.........	3	600	734*	0.6	2.1
419 SO BAPT CONV..	3	733	896*	0.7	2.5
435 UNITARIAN-UNIV	1	50	61*	-	0.2
443 UN C OF CHRIST	2	304	372*	0.3	1.1
449 UN METHODIST..	6	2 257	2 760*	2.2	7.8
453 UN PRES CH USA	4	1 163	1 422*	1.1	4.0
469 WELS.........	1	10	12	-	-
WAHKIAKUM	**9**	**356**	**780***	**20.4**	**100.0**
029 AMER LUTH CH..	1	53	106	2.8	13.6
045 APOSTOLIC LUTH	1	30	37*	1.0	4.7
053 ASSEMB OF GOD.	1	86	140	3.7	17.9
081 CATHOLIC......	1	NA	122	3.2	15.6
151 L-D SAINTS....	1	NA	145	3.8	18.6
413 S.D.A.........	1	22	27*	0.7	3.5
443 UN C OF CHRIST	1	66	81*	2.1	10.4
449 UN METHODIST..	2	99	122*	3.2	15.6
WALLA WALLA	**45**	**11 933**	**22 690***	**47.8**	**100.0**
019 AMER BAPT USA.	1	500	594*	1.3	2.6
029 AMER LUTH CH..	2	687	907	1.9	4.0
053 ASSEMB OF GOD.	2	377	728	1.5	3.2
059 BAPT MISS ASSN	1	87	103*	0.2	0.5
081 CATHOLIC......	4	NA	5 600	11.8	24.7
089 CHR & MISS AL.	1	53	101	0.2	0.4
093 CHR CH (DISC).	2	582	627	1.3	2.8
123 CH GOD (ANDER)	1	588	1 764	3.7	7.8
133 CH GOD(7TH)DEN	1	39	46*	0.1	0.2
151 L-D SAINTS....	3	NA	1 270	2.7	5.6
165 CH OF NAZARENE	3	483	494	1.0	2.2
167 CHS OF CHRIST.	2	120	182	0.4	0.8
179 CONSRV BAPT...	1	120	143*	0.3	0.6
193 EPISCOPAL.....	1	646	826	1.7	3.6
221 FREE METHODIST	2	46	156	0.3	0.7
263 INT FOURSQ GOS	1	21	25*	0.1	0.1
283 LUTH--MO SYNOD	1	218	307	0.6	1.4
290 METRO COMM CHS	0	20	40	0.1	0.2
403 SALVATION ARMY	1	103	172	0.4	0.8
413 S.D.A.........	7	4 163	4 946*	10.4	21.8
419 SO BAPT CONV..	1	257	305*	0.6	1.3
443 UN C OF CHRIST	1	457	543*	1.1	2.4
449 UN METHODIST..	2	1 459	1 733*	3.7	7.6
453 UN PRES CH USA	4	907	1 078*	2.3	4.8
WHATCOM	**112**	**16 964**	**31 441***	**29.5**	**100.0**
001 ADVENT CHR CH.	3	400	481*	0.5	1.5
019 AMER BAPT USA.	4	628	755*	0.7	2.4
029 AMER LUTH CH..	6	1 666	2 326	2.2	7.4
053 ASSEMB OF GOD.	7	1 336	2 398	2.2	7.6
057 BAPT GEN CONF.	3	602	724*	0.7	2.3
081 CATHOLIC......	8	NA	4 911	4.6	15.6
089 CHR & MISS AL.	2	91	175	0.2	0.6
093 CHR CH (DISC).	1	310	370	0.3	1.2
097 CHR CHS&CHS CR	1	54	65*	0.1	0.2
105 CHRISTIAN REF.	12	2 603	4 497	4.2	14.3
123 CH GOD (ANDER)	1	60	180	0.2	0.6
127 CH GOD (CLEVE)	1	5	6*	-	-
151 L-D SAINTS....	3	NA	1 993	1.9	6.3
163 CH OF LUTH BR.	1	121	214	0.2	0.7
165 CH OF NAZARENE	4	166	344	0.3	1.1
167 CHS OF CHRIST.	2	198	291	0.3	0.9
179 CONSRV BAPT...	1	41	49*	-	0.2
193 EPISCOPAL.....	2	841	968	0.9	3.1
201 EVAN COV CH AM	1	131	158*	0.1	0.5
220 FREE LUTHERAN.	1	170	215	0.2	0.7
221 FREE METHODIST	1	114	318	0.3	1.0
237 GC MENN BR CHS	2	210	253*	0.2	0.8
263 INT FOURSQ GOS	1	8	10*	-	-
281 LUTH CH AMER..	5	1 005	1 387	1.3	4.4
283 LUTH--MO SYNOD	3	686	913	0.9	2.9
287 MENN GEN CONF.	1	90	143	0.1	0.5
291 MISSIONARY CH.	1	24	30	-	0.1
329 OPEN BIBLE STD	1	60	90	0.1	0.3
353 CHR BRETHREN..	2	40	70	0.1	0.2
369 PROT REF CHS..	1	82	190	0.2	0.6
371 REF CH IN AM..	3	709	1 490	1.4	4.7
381 REF PRES-EVAN.	1	53	58	0.1	0.2
403 SALVATION ARMY	1	121	150	0.1	0.5
413 S.D.A.........	3	457	550*	0.5	1.7
419 SO BAPT CONV..	3	200	241*	0.2	0.8
435 UNITARIAN-UNIV	1	82	99*	0.1	0.3
443 UN C OF CHRIST	4	742	892*	0.8	2.8
449 UN METHODIST..	7	1 816	2 184*	2.0	6.9
453 UN PRES CH USA	6	1 042	1 253*	1.2	4.0
WHITMAN	**67**	**6 506**	**15 413***	**38.4**	**100.0**
019 AMER BAPT USA.	5	635	725*	1.8	4.7
029 AMER LUTH CH..	5	907	1 206	3.0	7.8
053 ASSEMB OF GOD.	4	290	431	1.1	2.8
081 CATHOLIC......	12	NA	6 414	16.0	41.6
089 CHR & MISS AL.	1	16	26	0.1	0.2
093 CHR CH (DISC).	4	399	649	1.6	4.2
097 CHR CHS&CHS CR	2	190	217*	0.5	1.4

NA — Not applicable   *Total adherents estimated from known number of communicant, confirmed, full members.   —Represents a percent less than 0.1.   Percentages may not total due to rounding.

Table 4. Churches and Church Membership by County and Denomination: 1980

County and Denomination	Number of churches	Communicant, confirmed, full members	Total adherents		
			Number	Percent of total population	Percent of total adherents
151 L-D SAINTS....	3	NA	923	2.3	6.0
165 CH OF NAZARENE	4	221	399	1.0	2.6
167 CHS OF CHRIST.	1	30	38	0.1	0.2
193 EPISCOPAL.....	3	264	293	0.7	1.9
203 EVAN FREE CH..	1	54	62*	0.2	0.4
283 LUTH--MO SYNOD	1	141	182	0.5	1.2
313 N AM BAPT CONF	1	300	343*	0.9	2.2
413 S.D.A.........	3	213	243*	0.6	1.6
419 SO BAPT CONV..	1	121	138*	0.3	0.9
443 UN C OF CHRIST	5	546	624*	1.6	4.0
449 UN METHODIST..	8	1 610	1 839*	4.6	11.9
453 UN PRES CH USA	2	542	619*	1.5	4.0
469 WELS.........	1	27	42	0.1	0.3
YAKIMA	198	28 732	69 958*	40.6	100.0
019 AMER BAPT USA.	6	1 400	1 725*	1.0	2.5
029 AMER LUTH CH..	3	346	449	0.3	0.6
053 ASSEMB OF GOD.	20	1 907	3 835	2.2	5.5
059 BAPT MISS ASSN	4	137	169*	0.1	0.2
081 CATHOLIC......	16	NA	26 085	15.1	37.3
089 CHR & MISS AL.	1	42	112	0.1	0.2
093 CHR CH (DISC).	9	1 507	2 230	1.3	3.2
097 CHR CHS&CHS CR	6	285	351*	0.2	0.5
105 CHRISTIAN REF.	3	303	566	0.3	0.8
123 CH GOD (ANDER)	4	461	1 383	0.8	2.0
127 CH GOD (CLEVE)	5	290	357*	0.2	0.5
151 L-D SAINTS....	11	NA	3 992	2.3	5.7
157 CH OF BRETHREN	1	37	46*	–	0.1
165 CH OF NAZARENE	11	1 462	2 497	1.4	3.6
167 CHS OF CHRIST.	6	550	700	0.4	1.0
179 CONSRV BAPT...	4	653	805*	0.5	1.2
193 EPISCOPAL.....	5	1 400	1 889	1.1	2.7
197 EVAN CH OF NA.	2	302	302	0.2	0.4
201 EVAN COV CH AM	3	377	465*	0.3	0.7
221 FREE METHODIST	3	176	465	0.3	0.7
244 GRACE BRETHREN	6	826	1 018*	0.6	1.5
263 INT FOURSQ GOS	1	?	?	?	?
281 LUTH CH AMER..	3	1 398	1 889	1.1	2.7
283 LUTH--MO SYNOD	5	1 678	2 261	1.3	3.2
291 MISSIONARY CH.	3	176	190	0.1	0.3
349 PENT HOLINESS.	2	309	381*	0.2	0.5
353 CHR BRETHREN..	6	335	410	0.2	0.6
371 REF CH IN AM..	1	124	182	0.1	0.3
403 SALVATION ARMY	1	101	187	0.1	0.3
413 S.D.A.........	9	1 701	2 096*	1.2	3.0
419 SO BAPT CONV..	11	2 259	2 784*	1.6	4.0
435 UNITARIAN-UNIV	1	91	112*	0.1	0.2
443 UN C OF CHRIST	2	231	285*	0.2	0.4
449 UN METHODIST..	11	3 810	4 695*	2.7	6.7
453 UN PRES CH USA	10	3 491	4 302*	2.5	6.1
469 WELS..........	3	567	743	0.4	1.1

WEST VIRGINIA

County and Denomination	Number of churches	Communicant, confirmed, full members	Total adherents		
			Number	Percent of total population	Percent of total adherents
THE STATE.....	4 159	509 754	774 064*	39.7	100.0
BARBOUR	68	4 623	6 286*	37.8	100.0
019 AMER BAPT USA.	7	1 034	1 258*	7.6	20.0
081 CATHOLIC......	5	NA	395	2.4	6.3
097 CHR CHS&CHS CR	1	22	27*	0.2	0.4
157 CH OF BRETHREN	3	103	125*	0.8	2.0
165 CH OF NAZARENE	3	142	423	2.5	6.7
167 CHS OF CHRIST.	6	365	465	2.8	7.4
193 EPISCOPAL.....	1	25	26	0.2	0.4
357 PRESB CH US...	2	93	113*	0.7	1.8
449 UN METHODIST..	40	2 839	3 454*	20.8	54.9
BERKELEY	80	15 333	22 270*	47.6	100.0
017 AMER BAPT ASSN	4	156	156	0.3	0.7
019 AMER BAPT USA.	1	85	104*	0.2	0.5
053 ASSEMB OF GOD.	5	573	991	2.1	4.4
081 CATHOLIC......	1	NA	2 692	5.8	12.1
093 CHR CH (DISC).	1	296	560	1.2	2.5
097 CHR CHS&CHS CR	5	1 107	1 353*	2.9	6.1
123 CH GOD (ANDER)	1	4	12	–	0.1
151 L-D SAINTS....	1	NA	410	0.9	1.8
157 CH OF BRETHREN	4	706	863*	1.8	3.9
165 CH OF NAZARENE	1	58	108	0.2	0.5
167 CHS OF CHRIST.	1	125	155	0.3	0.7
193 EPISCOPAL.....	2	727	732	1.6	3.3
244 GRACE BRETHREN	1	193	236*	0.5	1.1
263 INT FOURSQ GOS	1	50	61*	0.1	0.3
271 REFORM JUDAISM	1	30	37*	0.1	0.2
281 LUTH CH AMER..	2	1 033	1 274	2.7	5.7
356 PRESB CH AMER.	1	175	241	0.5	1.1
357 PRESB CH US...	10	1 119	1 368*	2.9	6.1
403 SALVATION ARMY	1	82	143	0.3	0.6
413 S.D.A.........	2	265	324*	0.7	1.5
419 SO BAPT CONV..	4	1 475	1 803*	3.9	8.1
443 UN C OF CHRIST	1	418	511*	1.1	2.3

County and Denomination	Number of churches	Communicant, confirmed, full members	Total adherents		
			Number	Percent of total population	Percent of total adherents
449 UN METHODIST..	29	6 656	8 136*	17.4	36.5
BOONE	63	5 263	7 355*	24.2	100.0
001 ADVENT CHR CH.	1	15	19*	0.1	0.3
019 AMER BAPT USA.	9	2 256	2 835*	9.3	38.5
053 ASSEMB OF GOD.	1	38	100	0.3	1.4
081 CATHOLIC......	2	NA	208	0.7	2.8
093 CHR CH (DISC).	1	38	58	0.2	0.8
123 CH GOD (ANDER)	1	58	174	0.6	2.4
127 CH GOD (CLEVE)	8	404	508*	1.7	6.9
165 CH OF NAZARENE	4	127	419	1.4	5.7
167 CHS OF CHRIST.	18	1 004	1 371	4.5	18.6
357 PRESB CH US...	1	41	52*	0.2	0.7
449 UN METHODIST..	13	1 126	1 415*	4.6	19.2
453 UN PRES CH USA	4	156	196*	0.6	2.7
BRAXTON	63	3 596	4 583*	33.0	100.0
019 AMER BAPT USA.	13	1 515	1 837*	13.2	40.1
081 CATHOLIC......	1	NA	91	0.7	2.0
127 CH GOD (CLEVE)	1	13	16*	0.1	0.3
151 L-D SAINTS....	1	NA	116	0.8	2.5
167 CHS OF CHRIST.	1	27	48	0.3	1.0
357 PRESB CH US...	1	43	52*	0.4	1.1
413 S.D.A.........	1	52	63*	0.5	1.4
449 UN METHODIST..	44	1 946	2 360*	17.0	51.5
BROOKE	46	6 737	14 365*	46.2	100.0
019 AMER BAPT USA.	1	205	247*	0.8	1.7
081 CATHOLIC......	4	NA	4 719	15.2	32.9
093 CHR CH (DISC).	4	390	648	2.1	4.5
097 CHR CHS&CHS CR	4	1 465	1 767*	5.7	12.3
123 CH GOD (ANDER)	4	140	420	1.3	2.9
127 CH GOD (CLEVE)	4	346	417*	1.3	2.9
165 CH OF NAZARENE	6	805	1 369	4.4	9.5
167 CHS OF CHRIST.	2	200	250	0.8	1.7
193 EPISCOPAL.....	4	394	684	2.2	4.8
221 FREE METHODIST	2	131	606	1.9	4.2
403 SALVATION ARMY	1	82	127	0.4	0.9
449 UN METHODIST..	6	1 462	1 764*	5.7	12.3
453 UN PRES CH USA	3	811	978*	3.1	6.8
CABELL	126	33 428	47 647*	44.6	100.0
019 AMER BAPT USA.	28	11 853	14 134*	13.2	29.7
029 AMER LUTH CH..	1	298	380	0.4	0.8
053 ASSEMB OF GOD.	1	110	178	0.2	0.4
081 CATHOLIC......	5	NA	5 006	4.7	10.5
093 CHR CH (DISC).	2	901	1 144	1.1	2.4
097 CHR CHS&CHS CR	8	1 345	1 604*	1.5	3.4
123 CH GOD (ANDER)	5	438	1 314	1.2	2.8
127 CH GOD (CLEVE)	4	556	663*	0.6	1.4
151 L-D SAINTS....	1	NA	638	0.6	1.3
165 CH OF NAZARENE	3	650	1 193	1.1	2.5
167 CHS OF CHRIST.	7	735	819	0.8	1.7
193 EPISCOPAL.....	4	1 730	2 463	2.3	5.2
221 FREE METHODIST	3	57	294	0.3	0.6
270 CONSRV JUDAISM	1	56	67*	0.1	0.1
271 REFORM JUDAISM	1	330	393*	0.4	0.8
281 LUTH CH AMER..	1	633	868	0.8	1.8
283 LUTH--MO SYNOD	1	57	75	0.1	0.2
349 PENT HOLINESS.	1	22	26*	–	0.1
357 PRESB CH US...	8	3 057	3 645*	3.4	7.7
403 SALVATION ARMY	1	78	196	0.2	0.4
413 S.D.A.........	2	169	202*	0.2	0.4
419 SO BAPT CONV..	2	335	399*	0.4	0.8
435 UNITARIAN-UNIV	1	8	10*	–	–
443 UN C OF CHRIST	1	158	188*	0.2	0.4
449 UN METHODIST..	34	9 852	11 748*	11.0	24.7
CALHOUN	32	2 386	2 982*	36.1	100.0
019 AMER BAPT USA.	7	1 461	1 781*	21.6	59.7
081 CATHOLIC......	1	NA	60	0.7	2.0
167 CHS OF CHRIST.	2	42	65	0.8	2.2
449 UN METHODIST..	22	883	1 076*	13.0	36.1
CLAY	34	2 409	3 288*	29.2	100.0
001 ADVENT CHR CH.	3	102	128*	1.1	3.9
019 AMER BAPT USA.	14	1 803	2 269*	20.1	69.0
081 CATHOLIC......	1	NA	66	0.6	2.0
123 CH GOD (ANDER)	1	25	75	0.7	2.3
165 CH OF NAZARENE	2	77	244	2.2	7.4
449 UN METHODIST..	13	402	506*	4.5	15.4
DODDRIDGE	37	2 398	3 038*	40.9	100.0
019 AMER BAPT USA.	9	983	1 208*	16.3	39.8
081 CATHOLIC......	2	NA	70	0.9	2.3
093 CHR CH (DISC).	1	30	46	0.6	1.5
097 CHR CHS&CHS CR	3	185	227*	3.1	7.5
127 CH GOD (CLEVE)	2	49	60*	0.8	2.0
167 CHS OF CHRIST.	1	30	38	0.5	1.3
281 LUTH CH AMER..	1	71	99	1.3	3.3
415 S-D BAPTIST GC	1	24	29*	0.4	1.0
449 UN METHODIST..	17	1 026	1 261*	17.0	41.5
FAYETTE	139	13 196	19 431*	33.6	100.0
001 ADVENT CHR CH.	2	44	54*	0.1	0.3
017 AMER BAPT ASSN	1	50	50	0.1	0.3

NA— Not applicable   *Total adherents estimated from known number of communicant, confirmed, full members.   —Represents a percent less than 0.1.   Percentages may not total due to rounding.

Table 4. Churches and Church Membership by County and Denomination: 1980

County and Denomination	Number of churches	Communicant, confirmed, full members	Total adherents		
			Number	Percent of total population	Percent of total adherents
019 AMER BAPT USA.	42	6 409	7 854*	13.6	40.4
053 ASSEMB OF GOD.	4	149	273	0.5	1.4
071 BRETHREN (ASH)	2	171	210*	0.4	1.1
081 CATHOLIC.	5	NA	1 675	2.9	8.6
093 CHR CH (DISC).	1	77	102	0.2	0.5
097 CHR CHS&CHS CR	2	85	104*	0.2	0.5
123 CH GOD (ANDER)	13	703	2 109	3.6	10.9
127 CH GOD (CLEVE)	7	430	527*	0.9	2.7
157 CH OF BRETHREN	2	121	148*	0.3	0.8
165 CH OF NAZARENE	1	225	408	0.7	2.1
167 CHS OF CHRIST.	4	123	177	0.3	0.9
193 EPISCOPAL.	3	239	385	0.7	2.0
349 PENT HOLINESS.	2	81	99*	0.2	0.5
357 PRESB CH US...	9	901	1 104*	1.9	5.7
413 S.D.A.	1	20	25*	–	0.1
419 SO BAPT CONV..	1	293	359*	0.6	1.8
449 UN METHODIST..	37	3 075	3 768*	6.5	19.4
GILMER	**32**	**1 846**	**2 351***	**28.2**	**100.0**
019 AMER BAPT USA.	4	708	850*	10.2	36.2
081 CATHOLIC.	2	NA	108	1.3	4.6
127 CH GOD (CLEVE)	1	23	28*	0.3	1.2
157 CH OF BRETHREN	1	21	25*	0.3	1.1
167 CHS OF CHRIST.	3	88	126	1.5	5.4
193 EPISCOPAL.	1	12	21	0.3	0.9
357 PRESB CH US...	1	67	80*	1.0	3.4
413 S.D.A.	1	23	28*	0.3	1.2
449 UN METHODIST..	18	904	1 085*	13.0	46.2
GRANT	**44**	**4 332**	**6 007***	**58.8**	**100.0**
019 AMER BAPT USA.	6	557	684*	6.7	11.4
029 AMER LUTH CH..	1	83	100	1.0	1.7
053 ASSEMB OF GOD.	3	431	716	7.0	11.9
075 BRETHREN IN CR	1	82	132	1.3	2.2
081 CATHOLIC.	1	NA	126	1.2	2.1
093 CHR CH (DISC).	1	25	38	0.4	0.6
127 CH GOD (CLEVE)	2	160	196*	1.9	3.3
151 L-D SAINTS....	1	NA	340	3.3	5.7
157 CH OF BRETHREN	8	1 083	1 329*	13.0	22.1
167 CHS OF CHRIST.	1	26	33	0.3	0.5
357 PRESB CH US...	2	357	438*	4.3	7.3
449 UN METHODIST..	17	1 528	1 875*	18.4	31.2
GREENBRIER	**128**	**13 397**	**17 719***	**47.0**	**100.0**
017 AMER BAPT ASSN	1	30	30	0.1	0.2
019 AMER BAPT USA.	26	4 416	5 345*	14.2	30.2
053 ASSEMB OF GOD.	1	20	40	0.1	0.2
055 AS REF PRES CH	1	114	129	0.3	0.7
081 CATHOLIC.	5	NA	705	1.9	4.0
097 CHR CHS&CHS CR	1	241	292*	0.8	1.6
123 CH GOD (ANDER)	4	124	372	1.0	2.1
127 CH GOD (CLEVE)	8	554	671*	1.8	3.8
151 L-D SAINTS....	1	NA	280	0.7	1.6
157 CH OF BRETHREN	1	34	41*	0.1	0.2
165 CH OF NAZARENE	2	101	252	0.7	1.4
167 CHS OF CHRIST.	3	100	127	0.3	0.7
193 EPISCOPAL.	4	265	462	1.2	2.6
329 OPEN BIBLE STD	1	34	60	0.2	0.3
349 PENT HOLINESS.	7	452	547*	1.5	3.1
357 PRESB CH US...	11	1 684	2 038*	5.4	11.5
413 S.D.A.	2	71	86*	0.2	0.5
419 SO BAPT CONV..	3	756	915*	2.4	5.2
449 UN METHODIST..	46	4 401	5 327*	14.1	30.1
HAMPSHIRE	**67**	**5 139**	**7 245***	**48.7**	**100.0**
019 AMER BAPT USA.	6	489	600*	4.0	8.3
029 AMER LUTH CH..	1	193	260	1.7	3.6
053 ASSEMB OF GOD.	5	315	682	4.6	9.4
081 CATHOLIC.	1	NA	260	1.7	3.6
093 CHR CH (DISC).	4	259	395	2.7	5.5
097 CHR CHS&CHS CR	6	515	632*	4.3	8.7
127 CH GOD (CLEVE)	1	50	61*	0.4	0.8
151 L-D SAINTS....	1	NA	139	0.9	1.9
157 CH OF BRETHREN	4	490	601*	4.0	8.3
165 CH OF NAZARENE	1	72	163	1.1	2.2
167 CHS OF CHRIST.	1	35	45	0.3	0.6
193 EPISCOPAL.	1	75	117	0.8	1.6
281 LUTH CH AMER..	2	116	184	1.2	2.5
357 PRESB CH US...	5	377	463*	3.1	6.4
443 UN C OF CHRIST	1	104	128*	0.9	1.8
449 UN METHODIST..	27	2 049	2 515*	16.9	34.7
HANCOCK	**50**	**9 727**	**27 211***	**67.3**	**100.0**
019 AMER BAPT USA.	2	1 148	1 389*	3.4	5.1
029 AMER LUTH CH..	2	460	610	1.5	2.2
081 CATHOLIC.	6	NA	13 070	32.3	48.0
089 CHR & MISS AL.	1	65	205	0.5	0.8
093 CHR CH (DISC).	1	345	550	1.4	2.0
097 CHR CHS&CHS CR	5	1 000	1 210*	3.0	4.4
127 CH GOD (CLEVE)	1	25	30*	0.1	0.1
165 CH OF NAZARENE	5	784	2 083	5.2	7.7
167 CHS OF CHRIST.	4	888	1 290	3.2	4.7
193 EPISCOPAL.	1	43	51	0.1	0.2
221 FREE METHODIST	3	106	714	1.8	2.6
403 SALVATION ARMY	1	173	337	0.8	1.2
413 S.D.A.	1	34	41*	0.1	0.2
419 SO BAPT CONV..	2	322	389*	1.0	1.4
449 UN METHODIST..	8	2 409	2 914*	7.2	10.7
453 UN PRES CH USA	7	1 925	2 328*	5.8	8.6

County and Denomination	Number of churches	Communicant, confirmed, full members	Total adherents		
			Number	Percent of total population	Percent of total adherents
HARDY	**42**	**3 936**	**4 925***	**49.1**	**100.0**
029 AMER LUTH CH..	1	17	18	0.2	0.4
053 ASSEMB OF GOD.	4	228	417	4.2	8.5
071 BRETHREN (ASH)	1	70	84*	0.8	1.7
081 CATHOLIC.	0	NA	32	0.3	0.6
097 CHR CHS&CHS CR	1	65	78*	0.8	1.6
127 CH GOD (CLEVE)	1	?	?	?	?
157 CH OF BRETHREN	8	1 045	1 257*	12.5	25.5
167 CHS OF CHRIST.	1	80	89	0.9	1.8
193 EPISCOPAL.	1	13	15	0.1	0.3
281 LUTH CH AMER..	1	126	179	1.8	3.6
285 MENNONITE CH..	2	60	72*	0.7	1.5
357 PRESB CH US...	3	301	362*	3.6	7.4
419 SO BAPT CONV..	1	32	38*	0.4	0.8
449 UN METHODIST..	17	1 899	2 284*	22.8	46.4
HARRISON	**144**	**22 502**	**35 744***	**46.0**	**100.0**
019 AMER BAPT USA.	33	7 171	8 644*	11.1	24.2
053 ASSEMB OF GOD.	1	125	150	0.2	0.4
081 CATHOLIC.	10	NA	7 933	10.2	22.2
089 CHR & MISS AL.	1	75	107	0.1	0.3
093 CHR CH (DISC).	3	281	404	0.5	1.1
101 C.M.E.	2	108	130*	0.2	0.4
123 CH GOD (ANDER)	2	51	153	0.2	0.4
127 CH GOD (CLEVE)	3	275	331*	0.4	0.9
151 L-D SAINTS....	1	NA	273	0.4	0.8
165 CH OF NAZARENE	1	87	192	0.2	0.5
167 CHS OF CHRIST.	7	555	667*	0.9	1.9
193 EPISCOPAL.	2	616	772	1.0	2.2
270 CONSRV JUDAISM	1	526	634*	0.8	1.8
281 LUTH CH AMER..	1	444	577	0.7	1.6
403 SALVATION ARMY	1	109	217	0.3	0.6
413 S.D.A.	1	191	230*	0.3	0.6
415 S-D BAPTIST GC	2	266	321*	0.4	0.9
419 SO BAPT CONV..	2	215	259*	0.3	0.7
449 UN METHODIST..	66	10 425	12 566*	16.2	35.2
453 UN PRES CH USA	4	982	1 184*	1.5	3.3
JACKSON	**70**	**5 362**	**7 594***	**29.4**	**100.0**
019 AMER BAPT USA.	9	1 123	1 372*	5.3	18.1
053 ASSEMB OF GOD.	1	12	23	0.1	0.3
081 CATHOLIC.	1	NA	532	2.1	7.0
093 CHR CH (DISC).	1	40	54	0.2	0.7
097 CHR CHS&CHS CR	1	92	112*	0.4	1.5
127 CH GOD (CLEVE)	2	90	110*	0.4	1.4
151 L-D SAINTS....	1	NA	168	0.7	2.2
165 CH OF NAZARENE	2	158	513	2.0	6.8
167 CHS OF CHRIST.	5	330	413	1.6	5.4
193 EPISCOPAL.	2	151	195	0.8	2.6
281 LUTH CH AMER..	1	81	93	0.4	1.2
357 PRESB CH US...	1	93	114*	0.4	1.5
359 PRIM AD CHR CH	1	28	28	0.1	0.4
419 SO BAPT CONV..	1	187	229*	0.9	3.0
449 UN METHODIST..	40	2 865	3 501*	13.6	46.1
453 UN PRES CH USA	1	112	137*	0.5	1.8
JEFFERSON	**62**	**8 374**	**11 738***	**38.7**	**100.0**
017 AMER BAPT ASSN	1	43	43	0.1	0.4
019 AMER BAPT USA.	4	310	379*	1.3	3.2
053 ASSEMB OF GOD.	5	393	664	2.2	5.7
081 CATHOLIC.	3	NA	811	2.7	6.9
097 CHR CHS&CHS CR	1	30	37*	0.1	0.3
127 CH GOD (CLEVE)	1	83	101*	0.3	0.9
157 CH OF BRETHREN	1	134	164*	0.5	1.4
193 EPISCOPAL.	8	1 240	1 898	6.3	16.2
281 LUTH CH AMER..	4	816	1 133	3.7	9.7
357 PRESB CH US...	5	792	968*	3.2	8.2
413 S.D.A.	1	84	103*	0.3	0.9
419 SO BAPT CONV..	4	1 121	1 370*	4.5	11.7
443 UN C OF CHRIST	2	137	167*	0.6	1.4
449 UN METHODIST..	22	3 191	3 900*	12.9	33.2
KANAWHA	**334**	**61 359**	**91 894***	**39.7**	**100.0**
001 ADVENT CHR CH.	16	1 009	1 208*	0.5	1.3
005 AME ZION.	2	54	106	–	0.1
019 AMER BAPT USA.	45	18 415	22 048*	9.5	24.0
029 AMER LUTH CH..	2	602	805	0.3	0.9
053 ASSEMB OF GOD.	6	375	661	0.3	0.7
081 CATHOLIC.	10	NA	9 338	4.0	10.2
089 CHR & MISS AL.	1	27	39	–	–
093 CHR CH (DISC).	4	651	1 167	0.5	1.3
097 CHR CHS&CHS CR	6	725	868*	0.4	0.9
123 CH GOD (ANDER)	24	1 576	4 728*	2.0	5.1
127 CH GOD (CLEVE)	11	585	700*	0.3	0.8
151 L-D SAINTS....	2	NA	904	0.4	1.0
165 CH OF NAZARENE	33	4 148	8 406	3.6	9.1
167 CHS OF CHRIST.	25	1 735	2 501	1.1	2.7
193 EPISCOPAL.	12	2 219	3 273	1.4	3.6
271 REFORM JUDAISM	1	350	419*	0.2	0.5
281 LUTH CH AMER..	2	646	813	0.4	0.9
283 LUTH--MO SYNOD	1	153	207	0.1	0.2
290 METRO COMM CHS	0	10	20	–	–
349 PENT HOLINESS.	3	111	133*	0.1	0.1
356 PRESB CH AMER.	5	451	489	0.2	0.5
357 PRESB CH US...	32	8 157	9 766*	4.2	10.6
359 PRIM AD CHR CH	8	497	497	0.2	0.5
381 REF PRES-EVAN.	1	?	?	?	?
403 SALVATION ARMY	2	128	367	0.2	0.4
413 S.D.A.	2	414	496*	0.2	0.5
419 SO BAPT CONV..	8	1 891	2 264*	1.0	2.5

NA—Not applicable   *Total adherents estimated from known number of communicant, confirmed, full members.   —Represents a percent less than 0.1.   Percentages may not total due to rounding.

Table 4. Churches and Church Membership by County and Denomination: 1980

County and Denomination	Number of churches	Communicant, confirmed, full members	Total adherents		
			Number	Percent of total population	Percent of total adherents
435 UNITARIAN-UNIV	1	47	56*	–	0.1
449 UN METHODIST..	68	15 844	18 970*	8.2	20.6
453 UN PRES CH USA	1	539	645*	0.3	0.7
LEWIS	**55**	**4 914**	**7 084***	**37.7**	**100.0**
019 AMER BAPT USA.	9	1 362	1 644*	8.7	23.2
053 ASSEMB OF GOD.	1	49	135	0.7	1.9
081 CATHOLIC......	3	NA	1 003	5.3	14.2
123 CH GOD (ANDER)	1	50	150	0.8	2.1
127 CH GOD (CLEVE)	1	52	63*	0.3	0.9
167 CHS OF CHRIST.	1	45	72	0.4	1.0
193 EPISCOPAL.....	1	247	265	1.4	3.7
419 SO BAPT CONV..	1	197	238*	1.3	3.4
449 UN METHODIST..	36	2 847	3 436*	18.3	48.5
453 UN PRES CH USA	1	65	78*	0.4	1.1
LINCOLN	**47**	**4 220**	**5 887***	**24.9**	**100.0**
019 AMER BAPT USA.	19	2 675	3 353*	14.2	57.0
053 ASSEMB OF GOD.	1	65	134	0.6	2.3
081 CATHOLIC......	1	NA	26	0.1	0.4
123 CH GOD (ANDER)	1	75	225	1.0	3.8
127 CH GOD (CLEVE)	2	76	95*	0.4	1.6
165 CH OF NAZARENE	1	13	41	0.2	0.7
167 CHS OF CHRIST.	10	576	1 085	4.6	18.4
419 SO BAPT CONV..	1	28	35*	0.1	0.6
449 UN METHODIST..	11	712	893*	3.8	15.2
LOGAN	**67**	**5 905**	**9 165***	**18.1**	**100.0**
019 AMER BAPT USA.	10	1 269	1 596*	3.1	17.4
053 ASSEMB OF GOD.	1	59	100	0.2	1.1
081 CATHOLIC......	4	NA	810	1.6	8.8
093 CHR CH (DISC).	4	358	532	1.0	5.8
097 CHR CHS&CHS CR	3	250	314*	0.6	3.4
123 CH GOD (ANDER)	1	19	57	0.1	0.6
127 CH GOD (CLEVE)	15	1 250	1 572*	3.1	17.2
151 L-D SAINTS....	1	NA	222	0.4	2.4
165 CH OF NAZARENE	2	304	737	1.5	8.0
167 CHS OF CHRIST.	8	445	566	1.1	6.2
193 EPISCOPAL.....	1	62	89	0.2	1.0
271 REFORM JUDAISM	1	22	28*	0.1	0.3
357 PRESB CH US...	2	359	451*	0.9	4.9
403 SALVATION ARMY	1	49	257	0.5	2.8
413 S.D.A.........	1	20	25*	–	0.3
419 SO BAPT CONV..	1	55	69*	0.1	0.8
449 UN METHODIST..	11	1 384	1 740*	3.4	19.0
MC DOWELL	**115**	**7 546**	**11 789***	**23.6**	**100.0**
001 ADVENT CHR CH.	4	148	187*	0.4	1.6
005 AME ZION......	5	816	931	1.9	7.9
019 AMER BAPT USA.	7	1 165	1 472*	2.9	12.5
053 ASSEMB OF GOD.	3	92	198	0.4	1.7
081 CATHOLIC......	5	NA	1 406	2.8	11.9
089 CHR & MISS AL.	1	2	11	–	0.1
093 CHR CH (DISC).	2	64	99	0.2	0.8
097 CHR CHS&CHS CR	3	200	253*	0.5	2.1
123 CH GOD (ANDER)	4	195	585	1.2	5.0
127 CH GOD (CLEVE)	15	1 080	1 365*	2.7	11.6
151 L-D SAINTS....	1	NA	385	0.8	3.3
165 CH OF NAZARENE	1	44	54	0.1	0.5
167 CHS OF CHRIST.	2	50	65	0.1	0.6
193 EPISCOPAL.....	3	126	148	0.3	1.3
247 HOLINESS CH...	2	80	80	0.2	0.7
271 REFORM JUDAISM	1	16	20*	–	0.2
349 PENT HOLINESS.	8	536	677*	1.4	5.7
357 PRESB CH US...	2	197	249*	0.5	2.1
403 SALVATION ARMY	1	74	242	0.5	2.1
413 S.D.A.........	2	52	66*	0.1	0.6
419 SO BAPT CONV..	3	214	270*	0.5	2.3
449 UN METHODIST..	39	2 378	3 005*	6.0	25.5
453 UN PRES CH USA	1	17	21*	–	0.2
MARION	**152**	**18 425**	**32 649***	**49.6**	**100.0**
019 AMER BAPT USA.	17	4 068	4 885*	7.4	15.0
053 ASSEMB OF GOD.	2	332	690	1.0	2.1
081 CATHOLIC......	12	NA	8 311	12.6	25.5
089 CHR & MISS AL.	1	78	128	0.2	0.4
093 CHR CH (DISC).	3	303	640	1.0	2.0
123 CH GOD (ANDER)	2	21	63	0.1	0.2
127 CH GOD (CLEVE)	3	128	154*	0.2	0.5
151 L-D SAINTS....	1	NA	451	0.7	1.4
157 CH OF BRETHREN	1	40	48*	0.1	0.1
165 CH OF NAZARENE	3	450	1 037	1.6	3.2
167 CHS OF CHRIST.	15	1 560	1 880	2.9	5.8
193 EPISCOPAL.....	1	334	389	0.6	1.2
221 FREE METHODIST	4	118	627	1.0	1.9
271 REFORM JUDAISM	1	46	55*	0.1	0.2
281 LUTH CH AMER..	1	452	567	0.9	1.7
329 OPEN BIBLE STD	1	57	80	0.1	0.2
403 SALVATION ARMY	2	119	253	0.4	0.8
413 S.D.A.........	1	47	56*	0.1	0.2
419 SO BAPT CONV..	1	214	257*	0.4	0.8
449 UN METHODIST..	77	8 992	10 798*	16.4	33.1
453 UN PRES CH USA	3	1 066	1 280*	1.9	3.9
MARSHALL	**62**	**9 727**	**17 703***	**42.5**	**100.0**
019 AMER BAPT USA.	2	1 291	1 573*	3.8	8.9
029 AMER LUTH CH..	1	106	156	0.4	0.9
071 BRETHREN (ASH)	1	34	41*	0.1	0.2
081 CATHOLIC......	6	NA	4 653	11.2	26.3

County and Denomination	Number of churches	Communicant, confirmed, full members	Total adherents		
			Number	Percent of total population	Percent of total adherents
093 CHR CH (DISC).	6	1 197	1 735	4.2	9.8
097 CHR CHS&CHS CR	1	50	61*	0.1	0.3
123 CH GOD (ANDER)	2	122	366	0.9	2.1
127 CH GOD (CLEVE)	2	188	229*	0.6	1.3
151 L-D SAINTS....	1	NA	332	0.8	1.9
165 CH OF NAZARENE	2	212	440	1.1	2.5
167 CHS OF CHRIST.	7	949	1 242	3.0	7.0
193 EPISCOPAL.....	1	214	297	0.7	1.7
281 LUTH CH AMER..	1	91	120	0.3	0.7
403 SALVATION ARMY	1	58	104	0.2	0.6
419 SO BAPT CONV..	1	246	300*	0.7	1.7
435 UNITARIAN-UNIV	1	24	29*	0.1	0.2
449 UN METHODIST..	20	4 195	5 111*	12.3	28.9
453 UN PRES CH USA	6	750	914*	2.2	5.2
MASON	**73**	**7 285**	**9 789***	**36.2**	**100.0**
001 ADVENT CHR CH.	2	66	81*	0.3	0.8
019 AMER BAPT USA.	10	1 702	2 083*	7.7	21.3
053 ASSEMB OF GOD.	1	19	50	0.2	0.5
081 CATHOLIC......	2	NA	417	1.5	4.3
123 CH GOD (ANDER)	2	156	468	1.7	4.8
127 CH GOD (CLEVE)	1	20	24*	0.1	0.2
165 CH OF NAZARENE	1	228	480	1.8	4.9
167 CHS OF CHRIST.	5	412	459	1.7	4.7
193 EPISCOPAL.....	2	183	210	0.8	2.1
281 LUTH CH AMER..	4	266	341	1.3	3.5
353 CHR BRETHREN..	1	20	20	0.1	0.2
357 PRESB CH US...	1	254	311*	1.1	3.2
413 S.D.A.........	1	18	22*	0.1	0.2
419 SO BAPT CONV..	2	90	110*	0.4	1.1
449 UN METHODIST..	38	3 851	4 713*	17.4	48.1
MERCER	**147**	**25 140**	**34 119***	**46.1**	**100.0**
001 ADVENT CHR CH.	1	126	153*	0.2	0.4
005 AME ZION......	2	406	452	0.6	1.3
019 AMER BAPT USA.	8	532	647*	0.9	1.9
053 ASSEMB OF GOD.	3	128	264	0.4	0.8
081 CATHOLIC......	3	NA	1 569	2.1	4.6
093 CHR CH (DISC).	8	1 187	1 727	2.3	5.1
097 CHR CHS&CHS CR	13	1 567	1 907*	2.6	5.6
123 CH GOD (ANDER)	5	400	1 200	1.6	3.5
127 CH GOD (CLEVE)	8	1 104	1 344*	1.8	3.9
151 L-D SAINTS....	1	NA	317	0.4	0.9
157 CH OF BRETHREN	3	188	229*	0.3	0.7
165 CH OF NAZARENE	3	283	513	0.7	0.8
167 CHS OF CHRIST.	2	201	285	0.4	0.8
193 EPISCOPAL.....	2	491	619	0.8	1.8
221 FREE METHODIST	1	31	258	0.3	0.8
271 REFORM JUDAISM	1	122	148*	0.2	0.4
281 LUTH CH AMER..	1	298	366	0.5	1.1
349 PENT HOLINESS.	11	936	1 139*	1.5	3.3
353 CHR BRETHREN..	1	20	20	–	0.1
356 PRESB CH AMER.	1	?	?	?	?
357 PRESB CH US...	7	1 667	2 029*	2.7	5.9
403 SALVATION ARMY	2	171	334	0.5	1.0
413 S.D.A.........	1	167	203*	0.3	0.6
419 SO BAPT CONV..	22	7 577	9 222*	12.5	27.0
449 UN METHODIST..	37	7 538	9 174*	12.4	26.9
MINERAL	**67**	**8 998**	**12 567***	**46.1**	**100.0**
053 ASSEMB OF GOD.	9	454	1 105	4.1	8.8
081 CATHOLIC......	2	NA	797	2.9	6.3
097 CHR CHS&CHS CR	1	50	61*	0.2	0.5
127 CH GOD (CLEVE)	3	348	426*	1.6	3.4
151 L-D SAINTS....	1	NA	164	0.6	1.3
157 CH OF BRETHREN	7	1 022	1 251*	4.6	10.0
165 CH OF NAZARENE	1	?	?	?	?
167 CHS OF CHRIST.	1	14	20	0.1	0.2
193 EPISCOPAL.....	1	65	79	0.3	0.6
281 LUTH CH AMER..	1	281	386	1.4	3.1
349 PENT HOLINESS.	3	154	188*	0.7	1.5
357 PRESB CH US...	5	671	821*	3.0	6.5
419 SO BAPT CONV..	2	615	753*	2.8	6.0
449 UN METHODIST..	30	5 324	6 516*	23.9	51.9
MINGO	**54**	**5 810**	**7 895***	**21.1**	**100.0**
019 AMER BAPT USA.	5	1 030	1 311*	3.5	16.6
053 ASSEMB OF GOD.	3	194	319	0.9	4.0
081 CATHOLIC......	1	NA	240	0.6	3.0
093 CHR CH (DISC).	7	339	521	1.4	6.6
097 CHR CHS&CHS CR	4	429	546*	1.5	6.9
127 CH GOD (CLEVE)	14	988	1 258*	3.4	15.9
167 CHS OF CHRIST.	6	340	450	1.2	5.7
193 EPISCOPAL.....	1	151	160	0.4	2.0
271 REFORM JUDAISM	1	34	43*	0.1	0.5
357 PRESB CH US...	2	278	354*	0.9	4.5
403 SALVATION ARMY	1	42	167	0.4	2.1
413 S.D.A.........	1	12	15*	–	0.2
419 SO BAPT CONV..	3	1 244	1 583*	4.2	20.1
449 UN METHODIST..	5	729	928*	2.5	11.8
MONONGALIA	**111**	**12 732**	**23 632***	**31.5**	**100.0**
019 AMER BAPT USA.	9	1 589	1 862*	2.5	7.9
053 ASSEMB OF GOD.	4	218	346	0.5	1.5
081 CATHOLIC......	7	NA	6 572	8.8	27.8
089 CHR & MISS AL.	1	242	792	1.1	3.4
093 CHR CH (DISC).	3	263	647	0.9	2.7
097 CHR CHS&CHS CR	1	40	47*	0.1	0.2
123 CH GOD (ANDER)	1	27	81	0.1	0.3
127 CH GOD (CLEVE)	2	127	149*	0.2	0.6

NA— Not applicable   *Total adherents estimated from known number of communicant, confirmed, full members.   —Represents a percent less than 0.1.   Percentages may not total due to rounding.

Table 4. Churches and Church Membership by County and Denomination: 1980

County and Denomination	Number of churches	Communicant, confirmed, full members	Total adherents Number	Percent of total population	Percent of total adherents
151 L-D SAINTS....	1	NA	416	0.6	1.8
157 CH OF BRETHREN	1	124	145*	0.2	0.6
165 CH OF NAZARENE	2	197	419	0.6	1.8
167 CHS OF CHRIST.	5	455	551	0.7	2.3
193 EPISCOPAL......	2	397	480	0.6	2.0
221 FREE METHODIST	3	72	351	0.5	1.5
226 FRIENDS-USA...	1	6	7*	-	-
281 LUTH CH AMER..	1	372	501	0.7	2.1
290 METRO COMM CHS	1	25	50	0.1	0.2
403 SALVATION ARMY	1	114	300	0.4	1.3
413 S.D.A.........	1	80	94*	0.1	0.4
419 SO BAPT CONV..	1	349	409*	0.5	1.7
435 UNITARIAN-UNIV	1	36	42*	0.1	0.2
443 UN C OF CHRIST	1	15	18*	-	0.1
449 UN METHODIST..	56	6 953	8 145*	10.9	34.5
453 UN PRES CH USA	5	1 031	1 208*	1.6	5.1
MONROE	**60**	**4 820**	**6 042***	**46.9**	**100.0**
019 AMER BAPT USA.	14	1 483	1 805*	14.0	29.9
055 AS REF PRES CH	1	81	86	0.7	1.4
061 BEACHY AMISH..	1	29	35*	0.3	0.6
081 CATHOLIC......	1	NA	75	0.6	1.2
093 CHR CH (DISC).	1	28	35	0.3	0.6
097 CHR CHS&CHS CR	4	555	675*	5.2	11.2
127 CH GOD (CLEVE)	1	33	40*	0.3	0.7
157 CH OF BRETHREN	1	146	178*	1.4	2.9
165 CH OF NAZARENE	3	199	361	2.8	6.0
193 EPISCOPAL.....	1	34	36	0.3	0.6
349 PENT HOLINESS.	2	94	114*	0.9	1.9
357 PRESB CH US...	6	447	544*	4.2	9.0
449 UN METHODIST..	24	1 691	2 058*	16.0	34.1
MORGAN	**39**	**3 161**	**4 396***	**41.0**	**100.0**
053 ASSEMB OF GOD.	2	114	199	1.9	4.5
081 CATHOLIC......	2	NA	287	2.7	6.5
093 CHR CH (DISC).	1	108	166	1.5	3.8
097 CHR CHS&CHS CR	1	80	97*	0.9	2.2
127 CH GOD (CLEVE)	1	20	24*	0.2	0.5
165 CH OF NAZARENE	1	8	25	0.2	0.6
167 CHS OF CHRIST.	4	160	197	1.8	4.5
193 EPISCOPAL.....	1	79	131	1.2	3.0
353 CHR BRETHREN..	1	60	200	1.9	4.5
357 PRESB CH US...	2	260	315*	2.9	7.2
419 SO BAPT CONV..	1	238	289*	2.7	6.6
449 UN METHODIST..	22	2 034	2 466*	23.0	56.1
NICHOLAS	**88**	**9 141**	**12 370***	**44.0**	**100.0**
017 AMER BAPT ASSN	2	150	150	0.5	1.2
019 AMER BAPT USA.	24	4 929	6 134*	21.8	49.6
053 ASSEMB OF GOD.	1	113	130	0.5	1.1
081 CATHOLIC......	2	NA	415	1.5	3.4
097 CHR CHS&CHS CR	2	190	236*	0.8	1.9
123 CH GOD (ANDER)	2	205	615	2.2	5.0
127 CH GOD (CLEVE)	4	177	220*	0.8	1.8
165 CH OF NAZARENE	4	141	457	1.6	3.7
167 CHS OF CHRIST.	2	115	147	0.5	1.2
193 EPISCOPAL.....	1	82	83	0.3	0.7
357 PRESB CH US...	2	199	248*	0.9	2.0
413 S.D.A.........	1	40	50*	0.2	0.4
419 SO BAPT CONV..	1	77	96*	0.3	0.8
449 UN METHODIST..	40	2 723	3 389*	12.0	27.4
OHIO	**82**	**16 153**	**38 382***	**62.5**	**100.0**
019 AMER BAPT USA.	1	488	575*	0.9	1.5
029 AMER LUTH CH..	2	943	1 258	2.0	3.3
053 ASSEMB OF GOD.	2	109	230	0.4	0.6
081 CATHOLIC......	15	NA	17 605	28.7	45.9
089 CHR & MISS AL.	2	156	262	0.4	0.7
093 CHR CH (DISC).	2	450	783	1.3	2.0
097 CHR CHS&CHS CR	4	690	814*	1.3	2.1
123 CH GOD (ANDER)	3	169	507	0.8	1.3
127 CH GOD (CLEVE)	1	53	62*	0.1	0.2
165 CH OF NAZARENE	2	44	86	0.1	0.2
167 CHS OF CHRIST.	2	449	576	0.9	1.5
193 EPISCOPAL......	5	1 243	1 679	2.7	4.4
271 REFORM JUDAISM	1	300	354*	0.6	0.9
281 LUTH CH AMER..	6	1 757	2 331	3.8	6.1
290 METRO COMM CHS	0	10	20	-	0.1
403 SALVATION ARMY	1	127	433	0.7	1.1
413 S.D.A.........	1	104	123*	0.2	0.3
435 UNITARIAN-UNIV	1	35	41*	0.1	0.1
443 UN C OF CHRIST	3	656	774*	1.3	2.0
449 UN METHODIST..	20	5 253	6 194*	10.1	16.1
453 UN PRES CH USA	8	3 117	3 675*	6.0	9.6
PENDLETON	**54**	**3 424**	**4 675***	**59.1**	**100.0**
029 AMER LUTH CH..	6	587	776	9.8	16.6
053 ASSEMB OF GOD.	2	40	61	0.8	1.3
081 CATHOLIC......	1	NA	78	1.0	1.7
093 CHR CH (DISC).	1	34	52	0.7	1.1
097 CHR CHS&CHS CR	1	78	94*	1.2	2.0
123 CH GOD (ANDER)	1	3	9	0.1	0.2
127 CH GOD (CLEVE)	1	51	61*	0.8	1.3
151 L-D SAINTS....	1	NA	230	2.9	4.9
157 CH OF BRETHREN	10	518	624*	7.9	13.3
167 CHS OF CHRIST.	1	23	29	0.4	0.6
221 FREE METHODIST	1	56	210	2.7	4.5
285 MENNONITE CH..	3	92	111*	1.4	2.4
357 PRESB CH US...	5	375	452*	5.7	9.7
413 S.D.A.........	1	20	24*	0.3	0.5

County and Denomination	Number of churches	Communicant, confirmed, full members	Total adherents Number	Percent of total population	Percent of total adherents
419 SO BAPT CONV..	1	91	110*	1.4	2.4
449 UN METHODIST..	18	1 456	1 754*	22.2	37.5
PLEASANTS	**27**	**3 252**	**4 235***	**51.4**	**100.0**
019 AMER BAPT USA.	3	962	1 180*	14.3	27.9
081 CATHOLIC......	1	NA	220	2.7	5.2
165 CH OF NAZARENE	1	54	82	1.0	1.9
167 CHS OF CHRIST.	8	818	977	11.9	23.1
193 EPISCOPAL.....	1	83	139	1.7	3.3
449 UN METHODIST..	12	1 157	1 419*	17.2	33.5
453 UN PRES CH USA	1	178	218*	2.6	5.1
POCAHONTAS	**51**	**2 452**	**3 112***	**31.4**	**100.0**
001 ADVENT CHR CH.	1	12	14*	0.1	0.4
029 AMER LUTH CH..	1	22	30	0.3	1.0
081 CATHOLIC......	2	NA	63	0.6	2.0
127 CH GOD (CLEVE)	1	53	64*	0.6	2.1
157 CH OF BRETHREN	2	263	316*	3.2	10.2
165 CH OF NAZARENE	2	100	205	2.1	6.6
167 CHS OF CHRIST.	1	14	25	0.3	0.8
193 EPISCOPAL.....	1	30	42	0.4	1.3
285 MENNONITE CH..	1	18	22*	0.2	0.7
357 PRESB CH US...	8	511	614*	6.2	19.7
419 SO BAPT CONV..	1	120	144*	1.5	4.6
449 UN METHODIST..	30	1 309	1 573*	15.9	50.5
PRESTON	**109**	**7 407**	**11 081***	**36.4**	**100.0**
019 AMER BAPT USA.	8	972	1 201*	3.9	10.8
053 ASSEMB OF GOD.	3	119	210	0.7	1.9
071 BRETHREN (ASH)	1	12	15*	-	0.1
081 CATHOLIC......	7	NA	1 094	3.6	9.9
151 L-D SAINTS....	1	NA	339	1.1	3.1
157 CH OF BRETHREN	6	624	771*	2.5	7.0
165 CH OF NAZARENE	3	239	489	1.6	4.4
167 CHS OF CHRIST.	2	75	100	0.3	0.9
193 EPISCOPAL.....	1	75	82	0.3	0.7
221 FREE METHODIST	1	22	132	0.4	1.2
281 LUTH CH AMER..	5	248	334	1.1	3.0
353 CHR BRETHREN..	1	30	150	0.5	1.4
449 UN METHODIST..	67	4 702	5 807*	19.1	52.4
453 UN PRES CH USA	3	289	357*	1.2	3.2
PUTNAM	**52**	**6 876**	**9 212***	**24.1**	**100.0**
019 AMER BAPT USA.	11	3 681	4 536*	11.9	49.2
053 ASSEMB OF GOD.	1	70	120	0.3	1.3
081 CATHOLIC......	1	NA	93	0.2	1.0
093 CHR CH (DISC).	1	17	26	0.1	0.3
123 CH GOD (ANDER)	4	190	570	1.5	6.2
127 CH GOD (CLEVE)	2	96	118*	0.3	1.3
165 CH OF NAZARENE	4	261	506	1.3	5.5
167 CHS OF CHRIST.	6	494	673	1.8	7.3
193 EPISCOPAL.....	1	108	160	0.4	1.7
203 EVAN FREE CH..	1	53	65*	0.2	0.7
356 PRESB CH AMER.	1	17	17	-	0.2
357 PRESB CH US...	5	344	424*	1.1	4.6
419 SO BAPT CONV..	1	42	52*	0.1	0.6
449 UN METHODIST..	13	1 503	1 852*	4.9	20.1
RALEIGH	**123**	**20 081**	**28 874***	**33.3**	**100.0**
001 ADVENT CHR CH.	2	29	36*	-	0.1
019 AMER BAPT USA.	32	8 593	10 616*	12.2	36.8
053 ASSEMB OF GOD.	4	756	1 825	2.1	6.3
081 CATHOLIC......	1	NA	2 254	2.6	7.8
093 CHR CH (DISC).	3	1 000	1 134	1.3	3.9
097 CHR CHS&CHS CR	3	450	556*	0.6	1.9
123 CH GOD (ANDER)	3	214	642	0.7	2.2
127 CH GOD (CLEVE)	17	1 526	1 885*	2.2	6.5
151 L-D SAINTS....	1	NA	289	0.3	1.0
157 CH OF BRETHREN	1	201	248*	0.3	0.9
165 CH OF NAZARENE	1	112	202	0.2	0.7
167 CHS OF CHRIST.	8	355	497	0.6	1.7
193 EPISCOPAL.....	2	488	658	0.8	2.3
221 FREE METHODIST	1	24	117	0.1	0.4
271 REFORM JUDAISM	1	48	59*	0.1	0.2
281 LUTH CH AMER..	1	165	251	0.3	0.9
349 PENT HOLINESS.	5	175	216*	0.2	0.7
357 PRESB CH US...	2	828	1 023*	1.2	3.5
403 SALVATION ARMY	1	57	114	0.1	0.4
413 S.D.A.........	2	119	147*	0.2	0.5
419 SO BAPT CONV..	5	1 913	2 363*	2.7	8.2
435 UNITARIAN-UNIV	1	14	17*	-	0.1
449 UN METHODIST..	20	2 819	3 483*	4.0	12.1
453 UN PRES CH USA	5	172	212*	0.2	0.7
469 WELS..........	1	23	30	-	0.1
RANDOLPH	**73**	**6 484**	**9 920***	**34.5**	**100.0**
019 AMER BAPT USA.	3	506	611*	2.1	6.2
053 ASSEMB OF GOD.	4	201	363	1.3	3.7
081 CATHOLIC......	4	NA	1 336	4.6	13.5
097 CHR CHS&CHS CR	2	251	303*	1.1	3.1
127 CH GOD (CLEVE)	4	347	419*	1.5	4.2
151 L-D SAINTS....	1	NA	437	1.5	4.4
157 CH OF BRETHREN	3	212	256*	0.9	2.6
165 CH OF NAZARENE	1	213	341	1.2	3.4
167 CHS OF CHRIST.	1	106	160	0.6	1.6
193 EPISCOPAL.....	1	110	205	0.7	2.1
281 LUTH CH AMER..	1	178	221	0.8	2.2
285 MENNONITE CH..	3	129	156*	0.5	1.6
357 PRESB CH US...	11	880	1 063*	3.7	10.7

NA—Not applicable   *Total adherents estimated from known number of communicant, confirmed, full members.   —Represents a percent less than 0.1.   Percentages may not total due to rounding.

Table 4. Churches and Church Membership by County and Denomination: 1980

County and Denomination	Number of churches	Communicant, confirmed, full members	Total adherents Number	Percent of total population	Percent of total adherents
413 S.D.A.........	1	53	64*	0.2	0.6
419 SO BAPT CONV..	1	107	129*	0.4	1.3
449 UN METHODIST..	32	3 191	3 856*	13.4	38.9
RITCHIE	57	3 652	4 612*	40.3	100.0
019 AMER BAPT USA.	10	961	1 170*	10.2	25.4
081 CATHOLIC......	3	NA	128	1.1	2.8
127 CH GOD (CLEVE)	3	190	231*	2.0	5.0
167 CHS OF CHRIST.	8	519	671	5.9	14.5
415 S-D BAPTIST GC	1	24	29*	0.3	0.6
449 UN METHODIST..	31	1 921	2 338*	20.4	50.7
453 UN PRES CH USA	1	37	45*	0.4	1.0
ROANE	66	4 086	5 351*	33.5	100.0
001 ADVENT CHR CH.	8	318	387*	2.4	7.2
019 AMER BAPT USA.	24	2 031	2 471*	15.5	46.2
053 ASSEMB OF GOD.	1	14	30	0.2	0.6
081 CATHOLIC......	1	NA	146	0.9	2.7
165 CH OF NAZARENE	2	208	472	3.0	8.8
167 CHS OF CHRIST.	2	72	93	0.6	1.7
357 PRESB CH US...	1	49	60*	0.4	1.1
359 PRIM AD CHR CH	1	17	17	0.1	0.3
413 S.D.A.........	1	44	54*	0.3	1.0
419 SO BAPT CONV..	1	140	170*	1.1	3.2
449 UN METHODIST..	24	1 193	1 451*	9.1	27.1
SUMMERS	40	3 698	4 766*	30.0	100.0
019 AMER BAPT USA.	11	1 990	2 395*	15.1	50.3
081 CATHOLIC......	1	NA	164	1.0	3.4
097 CHR CHS&CHS CR	2	160	193*	1.2	4.0
127 CH GOD (CLEVE)	1	16	19*	0.1	0.4
165 CH OF NAZARENE	1	26	80	0.5	1.7
167 CHS OF CHRIST.	3	115	155	1.0	3.3
193 EPISCOPAL.....	1	50	57	0.4	1.2
353 CHR BRETHREN..	1	50	150	0.9	3.1
357 PRESB CH US...	2	145	174*	1.1	3.7
449 UN METHODIST..	17	1 146	1 379*	8.7	28.9
TAYLOR	40	5 124	7 404*	44.6	100.0
019 AMER BAPT USA.	8	1 713	2 090*	12.6	28.2
053 ASSEMB OF GOD.	2	104	191	1.2	2.6
081 CATHOLIC......	2	NA	660	4.0	8.9
093 CHR CH (DISC).	1	104	145	0.9	2.0
127 CH GOD (CLEVE)	1	30	37*	0.2	0.5
157 CH OF BRETHREN	1	40	49*	0.3	0.7
165 CH OF NAZARENE	2	128	455	2.7	6.1
167 CHS OF CHRIST.	1	125	145	0.9	2.0
193 EPISCOPAL.....	1	49	65	0.4	0.9
244 GRACE BRETHREN	1	122	149*	0.9	2.0
281 LUTH CH AMER..	1	96	117	0.7	1.6
403 SALVATION ARMY	1	108	245	1.5	3.3
413 S.D.A.........	1	36	44*	0.3	0.6
449 UN METHODIST..	16	2 405	2 934*	17.7	39.6
453 UN PRES CH USA	1	64	78*	0.5	1.1
TUCKER	37	2 496	3 567*	41.1	100.0
019 AMER BAPT USA.	1	383	464*	5.3	13.0
053 ASSEMB OF GOD.	1	42	76	0.9	2.1
081 CATHOLIC......	3	NA	417	4.8	11.7
127 CH GOD (CLEVE)	4	164	199*	2.3	5.6
157 CH OF BRETHREN	1	17	21*	0.2	0.6
165 CH OF NAZARENE	1	110	124	1.4	3.5
167 CHS OF CHRIST.	1	30	38	0.4	1.1
221 FREE METHODIST	1	20	120	1.4	3.4
281 LUTH CH AMER..	1	69	95	1.1	2.7
357 PRESB CH US...	3	190	230*	2.7	6.4
413 S.D.A.........	1	36	44*	0.5	1.2
449 UN METHODIST..	19	1 435	1 739*	20.0	48.8
TYLER	49	5 274	6 963*	61.5	100.0
019 AMER BAPT USA.	3	506	623*	5.5	8.9
081 CATHOLIC......	2	NA	175	1.5	2.5
093 CHR CH (DISC)	1	55	85	0.8	1.2
097 CHR CHS&CHS CR	3	200	246*	2.2	3.5
127 CH GOD (CLEVE)	1	26	32*	0.3	0.5
165 CH OF NAZARENE	1	60	218	1.9	3.1
167 CHS OF CHRIST.	13	2 790	3 551*	31.4	51.0
193 EPISCOPAL.....	1	103	144	1.3	2.1
449 UN METHODIST..	23	1 345	1 656*	14.6	23.8
453 UN PRES CH USA	1	189	233*	2.1	3.3
UPSHUR	82	5 397	7 322*	31.3	100.0
019 AMER BAPT USA.	8	782	952*	4.1	13.0
053 ASSEMB OF GOD.	1	32	51	0.2	0.7
081 CATHOLIC......	1	NA	380	1.6	5.2
089 CHR & MISS AL.	1	49	88	0.4	1.2
097 CHR CHS&CHS CR	1	30	37*	0.2	0.5
127 CH GOD (CLEVE)	1	56	68*	0.3	0.9
151 L-D SAINTS....	1	NA	237	1.0	3.2
165 CH OF NAZARENE	1	57	149	0.6	2.0
167 CHS OF CHRIST.	3	100	119	0.5	1.6
193 EPISCOPAL.....	1	72	107	0.5	1.5
413 S.D.A.........	1	73	89*	0.4	1.2
449 UN METHODIST..	60	4 040	4 916*	21.0	67.1
453 UN PRES CH USA	2	106	129*	0.6	1.8
WAYNE	64	10 097	12 646*	27.5	100.0

County and Denomination	Number of churches	Communicant, confirmed, full members	Total adherents Number	Percent of total population	Percent of total adherents
019 AMER BAPT USA.	21	3 888	4 792*	10.4	37.9
081 CATHOLIC......	1	NA	35	0.1	0.3
093 CHR CH (DISC).	4	512	671	1.5	5.3
123 CH GOD (ANDER)	1	65	195	0.4	1.5
127 CH GOD (CLEVE)	6	316	389*	0.8	3.1
167 CHS OF CHRIST.	8	785	979	2.1	7.7
175 CONGR CHR CHS.	1	63	78*	0.2	0.6
357 PRESB CH US...	2	168	207*	0.4	1.6
419 SO BAPT CONV..	3	2 348	2 894*	6.3	22.9
449 UN METHODIST..	17	1 952	2 406*	5.2	19.0
WEBSTER	39	2 378	3 227*	26.4	100.0
001 ADVENT CHR CH.	1	7	9*	0.1	0.3
019 AMER BAPT USA.	7	1 234	1 544*	12.6	47.8
081 CATHOLIC......	2	NA	120	1.0	3.7
097 CHR CHS&CHS CR	1	30	38*	0.3	1.2
151 L-D SAINTS....	1	NA	131	1.1	4.1
167 CHS OF CHRIST.	1	25	33	0.3	1.0
193 EPISCOPAL.....	1	6	5	–	0.2
357 PRESB CH US...	1	112	140*	1.1	4.3
419 SO BAPT CONV..	1	114	143*	1.2	4.4
449 UN METHODIST..	23	850	1 064*	8.7	33.0
WETZEL	74	7 194	11 374*	52.0	100.0
019 AMER BAPT USA.	3	474	583*	2.7	5.1
081 CATHOLIC......	3	NA	1 123	5.1	9.9
093 CHR CH (DISC).	4	453	879	4.0	7.7
097 CHR CHS&CHS CR	5	1 015	1 249*	5.7	11.0
123 CH GOD (ANDER)	3	165	495	2.3	4.4
127 CH GOD (CLEVE)	2	132	162*	0.7	1.4
151 L-D SAINTS....	1	NA	322	1.5	2.8
165 CH OF NAZARENE	2	276	638	2.9	5.6
167 CHS OF CHRIST.	24	1 337	1 793	8.2	15.8
193 EPISCOPAL.....	1	119	142	0.6	1.2
281 LUTH CH AMER..	1	86	127	0.6	1.1
419 SO BAPT CONV..	1	121	149*	0.7	1.3
449 UN METHODIST..	22	2 752	3 387*	15.5	29.8
453 UN PRES CH USA	2	264	325*	1.5	2.9
WIRT	30	1 791	2 229*	45.3	100.0
019 AMER BAPT USA.	10	851	1 040*	21.1	46.7
081 CATHOLIC......	1	NA	29	0.6	1.3
165 CH OF NAZARENE	1	32	52	1.1	2.3
167 CHS OF CHRIST.	2	53	63	1.3	2.8
449 UN METHODIST..	15	830	1 014*	20.6	45.5
453 UN PRES CH USA	1	25	31*	0.6	1.4
WOOD	148	32 390	46 696*	49.9	100.0
019 AMER BAPT USA.	23	8 994	10 924*	11.7	23.4
053 ASSEMB OF GOD.	2	182	460	0.5	1.0
081 CATHOLIC......	4	NA	4 535	4.8	9.7
089 CHR & MISS AL.	1	26	53	0.1	0.1
093 CHR CH (DISC).	2	378	541	0.6	1.2
097 CHR CHS&CHS CR	2	146	177*	0.2	0.4
123 CH GOD (ANDER)	1	115	345	0.4	0.7
127 CH GOD (CLEVE)	4	465	565*	0.6	1.2
133 CH GOD(7TH)DEN	1	1	1*	–	–
151 L-D SAINTS....	1	NA	475	0.5	1.0
165 CH OF NAZARENE	5	845	1 703	1.8	3.6
167 CHS OF CHRIST.	19	2 820	4 022	4.3	8.6
193 EPISCOPAL.....	3	989	1 526	1.6	3.3
215 EVAN METH CH..	2	182	221*	0.2	0.5
244 GRACE BRETHREN	1	96	117*	0.1	0.3
271 REFORM JUDAISM	1	110	134*	0.1	0.3
281 LUTH CH AMER..	2	1 156	1 424	1.5	3.0
283 LUTH--MO SYNOD	1	258	363	0.4	0.8
349 PENT HOLINESS.	1	29	35*	–	0.1
403 SALVATION ARMY	1	163	328	0.4	0.7
413 S.D.A.........	2	321	390*	0.4	0.8
419 SO BAPT CONV..	2	779	946*	1.0	2.0
449 UN METHODIST..	61	12 447	15 118*	16.1	32.4
453 UN PRES CH USA	6	1 888	2 293*	2.4	4.9
WYOMING	64	6 881	9 656*	26.8	100.0
001 ADVENT CHR CH.	1	73	93*	0.3	1.0
019 AMER BAPT USA.	26	4 058	5 156*	14.3	53.4
081 CATHOLIC......	2	NA	213	0.6	2.2
093 CHR CH (DISC).	1	22	66	0.2	0.7
123 CH GOD (ANDER)	3	260	780	2.2	8.1
127 CH GOD (CLEVE)	8	597	759*	2.1	7.9
165 CH OF NAZARENE	1	190	399	1.1	4.1
167 CHS OF CHRIST.	2	54	76	0.2	0.8
349 PENT HOLINESS.	1	178	226*	0.6	2.3
353 CHR BRETHREN..	1	30	85	0.2	0.9
357 PRESB CH US...	3	209	266*	0.7	2.8
419 SO BAPT CONV..	1	90	114*	0.3	1.2
449 UN METHODIST..	14	1 120	1 423*	4.0	14.7

NA—Not applicable   *Total adherents estimated from known number of communicant, confirmed, full members.   —Represents a percent less than 0.1.   Percentages may not total due to rounding.

Table 4. Churches and Church Membership by County and Denomination: 1980

County and Denomination	Number of churches	Communicant, confirmed, full members	Total adherents Number	Percent of total population	Percent of total adherents
WISCONSIN					
THE STATE.....	4 698	1 138 006	3 038 209*	64.6	100.0
ADAMS	15	1 378	3 500*	26.0	100.0
029 AMER LUTH CH..	3	680	928	6.9	26.5
053 ASSEMB OF GOD.	1	89	200	1.5	5.7
081 CATHOLIC.....	2	NA	1 600	11.9	45.7
175 CONGR CHR CHS.	1	99	117*	0.9	3.3
283 LUTH--MO SYNOD	2	293	400	3.0	11.4
419 SO BAPT CONV..	1	35	41*	0.3	1.2
443 UN C OF CHRIST	3	70	82*	0.6	2.3
449 UN METHODIST..	2	112	132*	1.0	3.8
ASHLAND	34	4 489	12 793*	76.2	100.0
029 AMER LUTH CH..	1	315	420	2.5	3.3
053 ASSEMB OF GOD.	2	93	191	1.1	1.5
057 BAPT GEN CONF.	1	268	324*	1.9	2.5
081 CATHOLIC.....	11	NA	6 574	39.2	51.4
151 L-D SAINTS....	1	NA	48	0.3	0.4
167 CHS OF CHRIST.	1	15	22	0.1	0.2
193 EPISCOPAL.....	1	126	171	1.0	1.3
201 EVAN COV CH AM	1	45	54*	0.3	0.4
209 EVAN LUTH SYN.	1	71	106	0.6	0.8
281 LUTH CH AMER..	1	745	1 160	6.9	9.1
283 LUTH--MO SYNOD	5	1 802	2 505	14.9	19.6
413 S.D.A.........	1	54	65*	0.4	0.5
443 UN C OF CHRIST	3	287	347*	2.1	2.7
449 UN METHODIST..	3	261	315*	1.9	2.5
453 UN PRES CH USA	1	407	491*	2.9	3.8
BARRON	75	13 724	24 973*	64.5	100.0
001 ADVENT CHR CH.	1	56	68*	0.2	0.3
029 AMER LUTH CH..	15	5 775	7 485	19.3	30.0
053 ASSEMB OF GOD.	2	213	320	0.8	1.3
057 BAPT GEN CONF.	1	67	82*	0.2	0.3
081 CATHOLIC.....	11	NA	7 184	18.5	28.8
123 CH GOD (ANDER)	1	40	120	0.3	0.5
143 CG IN CR(MENN)	2	227	227	0.6	0.9
151 L-D SAINTS....	1	NA	177	0.5	0.7
157 CH OF BRETHREN	1	26	32*	0.1	0.1
193 EPISCOPAL.....	3	92	135	0.3	0.5
201 EVAN COV CH AM	1	111	135*	0.3	0.5
203 EVAN FREE CH..	1	75	91*	0.2	0.4
220 FREE LUTHERAN	1	115	175	0.5	0.7
221 FREE METHODIST	1	25	36	0.1	0.1
263 INT FOURSQ GOS	1	96	117*	0.3	0.5
281 LUTH CH AMER..	4	831	1 089	2.8	4.4
283 LUTH--MO SYNOD	9	2 545	3 273	8.5	13.1
323 OLD ORD AMISH.	2	260	316*	0.8	1.3
367 PROT CONF (WI)	1	10	20	0.1	0.1
395 ROMANIAN OR CH	1	25	30*	0.1	0.1
413 S.D.A.........	2	136	165*	0.4	0.7
449 UN METHODIST..	8	2 137	2 600*	6.7	10.4
453 UN PRES CH USA	1	375	456*	1.2	1.8
469 WELS..........	4	487	640	1.7	2.6
BAYFIELD	40	2 835	6 900*	49.9	100.0
029 AMER LUTH CH..	4	839	1 085	7.8	15.7
053 ASSEMB OF GOD.	3	65	92	0.7	1.3
057 BAPT GEN CONF.	3	263	318*	2.3	4.6
081 CATHOLIC.....	13	NA	3 312	24.0	48.0
089 CHR & MISS AL.	1	59	94	0.7	1.4
193 EPISCOPAL.....	1	19	9	0.1	0.1
203 EVAN FREE CH..	1	45	54*	0.4	0.8
220 FREE LUTHERAN	3	269	323	2.3	4.7
281 LUTH CH AMER..	3	477	628	4.5	9.1
283 LUTH--MO SYNOD	1	194	252	1.8	3.7
413 S.D.A.........	1	23	28*	0.2	0.4
443 UN C OF CHRIST	2	166	201*	1.5	2.9
449 UN METHODIST..	2	185	224*	1.6	3.2
453 UN PRES CH USA	2	231	280*	2.0	4.1
BROWN	116	28 854	132 085*	75.4	100.0
019 AMER BAPT USA.	1	280	344*	0.2	0.3
029 AMER LUTH CH..	10	7 953	10 710	6.1	8.1
053 ASSEMB OF GOD.	2	399	850	0.5	0.6
057 BAPT GEN CONF.	1	326	401*	0.2	0.3
081 CATHOLIC.....	40	NA	91 974	52.5	69.6
089 CHR & MISS AL.	1	66	141	0.1	0.1
097 CHR CHS&CHS CR	1	125	154*	0.1	0.1
151 L-D SAINTS....	1	NA	337	0.2	0.3
165 CH OF NAZARENE	1	56	115	0.1	0.1
167 CHS OF CHRIST.	3	110	140	0.1	0.1
175 CONGR CHR CHS.	1	514	632*	0.4	0.5
193 EPISCOPAL.....	6	1 815	2 562*	1.5	1.9
226 FRIENDS-USA...	1	18	22*	-	-
270 CONSRV JUDAISM	1	100	123*	0.1	0.1
281 LUTH CH AMER..	3	958	1 408	0.8	1.1
283 LUTH--MO SYNOD	9	4 439	6 175	3.5	4.7
293 MORAV CH-NORTH	2	663	851	0.5	0.6
335 ORTH PRESB CH.	1	62	76*	-	0.1
403 SALVATION ARMY	1	125	1 349	0.8	1.0
413 S.D.A.........	1	359	441*	0.3	0.3
419 SO BAPT CONV..	1	236	290*	0.2	0.2
435 UNITARIAN-UNIV	1	21	26*	-	-
443 UN C OF CHRIST	3	1 219	1 498*	0.9	1.1
449 UN METHODIST..	8	3 754	4 613*	2.6	3.5
453 UN PRES CH USA	6	1 831	2 250*	1.3	1.7
469 WELS..........	10	3 425	4 603	2.6	3.5
BUFFALO	30	5 616	10 042*	70.2	100.0
029 AMER LUTH CH..	7	2 292	2 900	20.3	28.9
057 BAPT GEN CONF.	1	10	12*	0.1	0.1
081 CATHOLIC.....	4	NA	2 910	20.3	29.0
167 CHS OF CHRIST.	1	25	37	0.3	0.4
283 LUTH--MO SYNOD	4	1 053	1 449	10.1	14.4
413 S.D.A.........	1	54	66*	0.5	0.7
443 UN C OF CHRIST	3	552	672*	4.7	6.7
449 UN METHODIST..	4	644	784*	5.5	7.8
469 WELS..........	5	986	1 212	8.5	12.1
BURNETT	27	2 913	4 728*	38.3	100.0
029 AMER LUTH CH..	3	636	795	6.4	16.8
053 ASSEMB OF GOD.	1	69	110	0.9	2.3
057 BAPT GEN CONF.	4	605	727*	5.9	15.4
081 CATHOLIC.....	4	NA	958	7.8	20.3
089 CHR & MISS AL.	1	18	41	0.3	0.9
201 EVAN COV CH AM	2	128	154*	1.2	3.3
203 EVAN FREE CH..	2	55	66*	0.5	1.4
281 LUTH CH AMER..	3	712	1 033	8.4	21.8
283 LUTH--MO SYNOD	2	218	277	2.2	5.9
449 UN METHODIST..	5	472	567*	4.6	12.0
CALUMET	34	5 131	19 566*	63.4	100.0
053 ASSEMB OF GOD.	1	72	171	0.6	0.9
081 CATHOLIC.....	13	NA	12 856	41.6	65.7
089 CHR & MISS AL.	1	39	71	0.2	0.4
163 CH OF LUTH BR.	1	34	56	0.2	0.3
193 EPISCOPAL.....	1	32	38	0.1	0.2
283 LUTH--MO SYNOD	6	1 909	2 573	8.3	13.2
443 UN C OF CHRIST	4	1 341	1 674*	5.4	8.6
449 UN METHODIST..	4	681	850*	2.8	4.3
453 UN PRES CH USA	1	32	40*	0.1	0.2
469 WELS..........	2	991	1 237	4.0	6.3
CHIPPEWA	70	10 866	32 731*	63.3	100.0
029 AMER LUTH CH..	11	4 216	5 940	11.5	18.1
053 ASSEMB OF GOD.	2	109	231	0.4	0.7
057 BAPT GEN CONF.	1	36	45*	0.1	0.1
081 CATHOLIC.....	16	NA	18 290	35.4	55.9
097 CHR CHS&CHS CR	4	264	327*	0.6	1.0
127 CH GOD (CLEVE)	1	11	14*	-	-
133 CH GOD(7TH)DEN	1	21	26*	0.1	0.1
157 CH OF BRETHREN	2	198	245*	0.5	0.7
167 CHS OF CHRIST.	1	10	15	-	-
179 CONSRV BAPT...	2	150	186*	0.4	0.6
193 EPISCOPAL.....	2	259	264	0.5	0.8
203 EVAN FREE CH..	1	42	52*	0.1	0.2
209 EVAN LUTH SYN.	1	125	161	0.3	0.5
283 LUTH--MO SYNOD	5	1 768	2 358	4.6	7.2
353 CHR BRETHREN..	1	20	20	-	0.1
413 S.D.A.........	1	29	36*	0.1	0.1
415 S-D BAPTIST GC	1	87	108*	0.2	0.3
443 UN C OF CHRIST	1	75	93*	0.2	0.3
449 UN METHODIST..	9	1 744	2 161*	4.2	6.6
453 UN PRES CH USA	3	537	665*	1.3	2.0
469 WELS..........	4	1 165	1 494	2.9	4.6
CLARK	69	10 003	24 362*	74.0	100.0
029 AMER LUTH CH..	7	1 922	2 578	7.8	10.6
053 ASSEMB OF GOD.	3	136	255	0.8	1.0
081 CATHOLIC.....	12	NA	10 940	33.2	44.9
089 CHR & MISS AL.	2	90	226	0.7	0.9
151 L-D SAINTS....	1	NA	83	0.3	0.3
179 CONSRV BAPT...	1	75	93*	0.3	0.4
193 EPISCOPAL.....	1	72	86	0.3	0.4
203 EVAN FREE CH..	1	17	21*	0.1	0.1
221 FREE METHODIST	1	25	96	0.3	0.4
281 LUTH CH AMER..	3	484	692	2.1	2.8
283 LUTH--MO SYNOD	12	3 449	4 577	13.9	18.8
285 MENNONITE CH..	1	34	42*	0.1	0.2
323 OLD ORD AMISH.	1	130	161*	0.5	0.7
413 S.D.A.........	1	28	35*	0.1	0.1
443 UN C OF CHRIST	7	1 329	1 644*	5.0	6.7
449 UN METHODIST..	12	1 265	1 565*	4.8	6.4
469 WELS..........	3	947	1 268	3.9	5.2
COLUMBIA	74	18 097	34 990*	81.0	100.0
019 AMER BAPT USA.	4	457	554*	1.3	1.6
029 AMER LUTH CH..	6	2 449	3 223	7.5	9.2
053 ASSEMB OF GOD.	3	260	464	1.1	1.3
081 CATHOLIC.....	9	NA	11 321	26.2	32.4
105 CHRISTIAN REF.	2	489	837	1.9	2.4
165 CH OF NAZARENE	1	41	95	0.2	0.3
175 CONGR CHR CHS.	1	45	55*	0.1	0.2
179 CONSRV BAPT...	1	65	79*	0.2	0.2
181 CONSRV CONGR..	1	44	53*	0.1	0.2
193 EPISCOPAL.....	1	71	83	0.2	0.2
203 EVAN FREE CH..	1	50	61*	0.1	0.2
209 EVAN LUTH SYN.	1	185	240	0.6	0.7
281 LUTH CH AMER..	3	1 308	1 789	4.1	5.1
283 LUTH--MO SYNOD	3	2 463	3 335	7.7	9.5
353 CHR BRETHREN..	1	20	20	-	0.1
369 PROT REF CHS..	1	61	121	0.3	0.3

NA—Not applicable   *Total adherents estimated from known number of communicant, confirmed, full members.   —Represents a percent less than 0.1.   Percentages may not total due to rounding.

Table 4. Churches and Church Membership by County and Denomination: 1980

County and Denomination	Number of churches	Communicant, confirmed, full members	Total adherents		
			Number	Percent of total population	Percent of total adherents
371 REF CH IN AM..	2	602	961	2.2	2.7
413 S.D.A.........	2	299	363*	0.8	1.0
443 UN C OF CHRIST	3	614	745*	1.7	2.1
449 UN METHODIST..	10	2 695	3 270*	7.6	9.3
453 UN PRES CH USA	10	2 165	2 627*	6.1	7.5
469 WELS.........	8	3 714	4 694	10.9	13.4
CRAWFORD	32	3 488	11 127*	67.2	100.0
029 AMER LUTH CH..	7	1 999	2 727	16.5	24.5
081 CATHOLIC......	8	NA	6 550	39.6	58.9
097 CHR CHS&CHS CR	2	200	246*	1.5	2.2
127 CH GOD (CLEVE)	1	77	95*	0.6	0.9
175 CONGR CHR CHS.	1	63	77*	0.5	0.7
193 EPISCOPAL.....	1	63	81	0.5	0.7
203 EVAN FREE CH..	1	45	55*	0.3	0.5
413 S.D.A.........	1	14	17*	0.1	0.2
443 UN C OF CHRIST	1	51	63*	0.4	0.6
449 UN METHODIST..	8	893	1 097*	6.6	9.9
469 WELS.........	1	83	119	0.7	1.1
DANE	214	70 575	176 944*	54.7	100.0
001 ADVENT CHR CH.	1	?	?	?	?
019 AMER BAPT USA.	3	1 181	1 400*	0.4	0.8
029 AMER LUTH CH..	40	29 339	40 084	12.4	22.7
053 ASSEMB OF GOD.	4	309	570	0.2	0.3
057 BAPT GEN CONF.	1	38	45*	–	–
081 CATHOLIC......	38	NA	84 575	26.1	47.8
097 CHR CHS&CHS CR	4	359	426*	0.1	0.2
105 CHRISTIAN REF.	1	159	276	0.1	0.2
123 CH GOD (ANDER)	1	41	123	–	0.1
127 CH GOD (CLEVE)	1	11	13*	–	–
151 L-D SAINTS....	3	NA	1 110	0.3	0.6
164 CH LUTH CONF..	2	58	76	–	–
165 CH OF NAZARENE	1	155	254	0.1	0.1
167 CHS OF CHRIST.	1	85	130	–	0.1
175 CONGR CHR CHS.	1	368	436*	0.1	0.2
179 CONSRV BAPT...	2	400	474*	0.1	0.3
193 EPISCOPAL.....	6	1 921	2 245	0.7	1.3
201 EVAN COV CH AM	1	80	95*	–	0.1
203 EVAN FREE CH..	5	400	474*	0.1	0.3
209 EVAN LUTH SYN.	4	2 092	2 666	0.8	1.5
221 FREE METHODIST	1	53	165	0.1	0.1
226 FRIENDS-USA...	1	167	198*	0.1	0.1
270 CONSRV JUDAISM	1	191	226*	0.1	0.1
271 REFORM JUDAISM	1	920	1 091*	0.3	0.6
281 LUTH CH AMER..	9	5 150	6 748	2.1	3.8
283 LUTH--MO SYNOD	9	3 674	4 710	1.5	2.7
285 MENNONITE CH..	1	?	?	?	?
290 METRO COMM CHS	0	15	30	–	–
293 MORAV CH-NORTH	4	992	1 286	0.4	0.7
353 CHR BRETHREN..	3	65	85	–	–
363 PRIMITIVE METH	1	123	146*	–	0.1
371 REF CH IN AM..	1	84	173	0.1	0.1
403 SALVATION ARMY	1	145	270	0.1	0.2
413 S.D.A.........	2	667	791*	0.2	0.4
419 SO BAPT CONV..	3	739	876*	0.3	0.5
435 UNITARIAN-UNIV	2	677	803*	0.2	0.5
443 UN C OF CHRIST	15	5 360	6 355*	2.0	3.6
449 UN METHODIST..	22	8 181	9 700*	3.0	5.5
453 UN PRES CH USA	9	3 722	4 413*	1.4	2.5
469 WELS.........	8	2 654	3 406	1.1	1.9
DODGE	99	27 581	50 307*	67.3	100.0
019 AMER BAPT USA.	1	135	165*	0.2	0.3
029 AMER LUTH CH..	10	5 356	6 837	9.1	13.6
053 ASSEMB OF GOD.	2	387	575	0.8	1.1
081 CATHOLIC......	18	NA	14 479	19.4	28.8
089 CHR & MISS AL.	1	30	67	0.1	0.1
105 CHRISTIAN REF.	1	66	129	0.2	0.3
167 CHS OF CHRIST.	1	50	75	0.1	0.1
193 EPISCOPAL.....	3	300	374	0.5	0.7
221 FREE METHODIST	1	30	105	0.1	0.2
281 LUTH CH AMER..	2	865	1 158	1.5	2.3
283 LUTH--MO SYNOD	13	5 599	7 189	9.6	14.3
371 REF CH IN AM..	4	1 806	2 821	3.8	5.6
413 S.D.A.........	1	70	85*	0.1	0.2
443 UN C OF CHRIST	5	1 016	1 239*	1.7	2.5
449 UN METHODIST..	8	2 458	2 996*	4.0	6.0
453 UN PRES CH USA	4	864	1 053*	1.4	2.1
469 WELS.........	24	8 549	10 960	14.7	21.8
DOOR	50	7 990	15 775*	63.0	100.0
029 AMER LUTH CH..	7	1 511	1 980	7.9	12.6
053 ASSEMB OF GOD.	1	101	250	1.0	1.6
057 BAPT GEN CONF.	3	439	529*	2.1	3.4
081 CATHOLIC......	12	NA	5 639	22.5	35.7
193 EPISCOPAL.....	3	100	115	0.5	0.7
203 EVAN FREE CH..	1	33	40*	0.2	0.3
226 FRIENDS-USA...	1	58	70*	0.3	0.4
281 LUTH CH AMER..	2	416	553	2.2	3.5
283 LUTH--MO SYNOD	2	415	560	2.2	3.5
293 MORAV CH-NORTH	3	938	1 114	4.5	7.1
353 CHR BRETHREN..	1	20	20	0.1	0.1
367 PROT CONF (WI)	1	20	30	0.1	0.2
413 S.D.A.........	2	37	45*	0.2	0.3
443 UN C OF CHRIST	1	262	316*	1.3	2.0
449 UN METHODIST..	4	807	973*	3.9	6.2
469 WELS.........	6	2 833	3 541	14.1	22.4
DOUGLAS	56	8 191	21 561*	48.5	100.0
019 AMER BAPT USA.	1	50	60*	0.1	0.3
029 AMER LUTH CH..	5	1 939	2 739	6.2	12.7
053 ASSEMB OF GOD.	2	163	329	0.7	1.5
057 BAPT GEN CONF.	3	419	505*	1.1	2.3
081 CATHOLIC......	15	NA	10 188	22.9	47.3
089 CHR & MISS AL.	1	50	140	0.3	0.6
163 CH OF LUTH BR.	1	14	45	0.1	0.2
181 CONSRV CONGR..	1	164	198*	0.4	0.9
193 EPISCOPAL.....	1	128	240	0.5	1.1
201 EVAN COV CH AM	4	168	203*	0.5	0.9
270 CONSRV JUDAISM	1	52	63*	0.1	0.3
281 LUTH CH AMER..	4	2 210	3 146	7.1	14.6
283 LUTH--MO SYNOD	2	612	791	1.8	3.7
403 SALVATION ARMY	1	196	471	1.1	2.2
413 S.D.A.........	1	49	59*	0.1	0.3
449 UN METHODIST..	3	625	754*	1.7	3.5
453 UN PRES CH USA	10	1 352	1 630*	3.7	7.6
DUNN	55	11 577	19 371*	56.5	100.0
029 AMER LUTH CH..	17	6 751	8 884	25.9	45.9
053 ASSEMB OF GOD.	1	55	94	0.3	0.5
081 CATHOLIC......	5	NA	4 140	12.1	21.4
089 CHR & MISS AL.	1	103	318	0.9	1.6
121 CH GOD (ABR)..	1	25	30*	0.1	0.2
123 CH GOD (ANDER)	1	9	27	0.1	0.1
163 CH OF LUTH BR.	1	21	76	0.2	0.4
165 CH OF NAZARENE	3	141	236	0.7	1.2
193 EPISCOPAL.....	1	95	127	0.4	0.7
220 FREE LUTHERAN.	1	130	150	0.4	0.8
226 FRIENDS-USA...	1	15	18*	0.1	0.1
283 LUTH--MO SYNOD	3	571	744	2.2	3.8
413 S.D.A.........	1	48	57*	0.2	0.3
419 SO BAPT CONV..	1	39	47*	0.1	0.2
443 UN C OF CHRIST	1	213	254*	0.7	1.3
449 UN METHODIST..	12	1 994	2 380*	6.9	12.3
469 WELS.........	4	1 367	1 789	5.2	9.2
EAU CLAIRE	82	27 536	49 937*	63.4	100.0
019 AMER BAPT USA.	3	455	544*	0.7	1.1
029 AMER LUTH CH..	12	12 456	16 078	20.4	32.2
053 ASSEMB OF GOD.	3	281	584	0.7	1.2
057 BAPT GEN CONF.	2	344	411*	0.5	0.8
081 CATHOLIC......	10	NA	13 800	17.5	27.6
097 CHR CHS&CHS CR	1	115	137*	0.2	0.3
151 L-D SAINTS....	1	NA	361	0.5	0.7
163 CH OF LUTH BR.	1	208	333	0.4	0.7
164 CH LUTH CONF..	1	238	336	0.4	0.7
165 CH OF NAZARENE	1	84	194	0.2	0.4
167 CHS OF CHRIST.	1	22	28	–	0.1
179 CONSRV BAPT...	1	175	209*	0.3	0.4
193 EPISCOPAL.....	2	589	840	1.1	1.7
201 EVAN COV CH AM	1	17	20*	–	–
203 EVAN FREE CH..	1	15	18*	–	–
209 EVAN LUTH SYN.	3	856	1 186	1.5	2.4
270 CONSRV JUDAISM	1	23	27*	–	0.1
281 LUTH CH AMER..	1	297	390	0.5	0.8
283 LUTH--MO SYNOD	14	5 975	7 887	10.0	15.8
285 MENNONITE CH..	1	23	27*	–	0.1
323 OLD ORD AMISH.	1	130	155*	0.2	0.3
353 CHR BRETHREN..	1	20	20	–	–
403 SALVATION ARMY	1	104	186	0.2	0.4
413 S.D.A.........	1	145	173*	0.2	0.3
435 UNITARIAN-UNIV	2	59	71*	0.1	0.1
443 UN C OF CHRIST	4	1 382	1 652*	2.1	3.3
449 UN METHODIST..	7	2 767	3 308*	4.2	6.6
453 UN PRES CH USA	2	536	641*	0.8	1.3
469 WELS.........	2	220	321	0.4	0.6
FLORENCE	9	362	1 611*	38.6	100.0
057 BAPT GEN CONF.	1	52	63*	1.5	3.9
081 CATHOLIC......	3	NA	1 167	28.0	72.4
201 EVAN COV CH AM	1	10	12*	0.3	0.7
281 LUTH CH AMER..	1	43	44	1.1	2.7
453 UN PRES CH USA	1	96	117*	2.8	7.3
469 WELS.........	2	161	208	5.0	12.9
FOND DU LAC	94	23 379	67 987*	76.4	100.0
019 AMER BAPT USA.	3	447	547*	0.6	0.8
029 AMER LUTH CH..	6	4 047	5 359	6.0	7.9
053 ASSEMB OF GOD.	4	267	434	0.5	0.6
081 CATHOLIC......	27	NA	36 702	41.3	54.0
105 CHRISTIAN REF.	3	621	1 076	1.2	1.6
127 CH GOD (CLEVE)	1	25	31*	–	–
164 CH LUTH CONF..	1	385	477	0.5	0.7
167 CHS OF CHRIST.	1	20	30	–	–
193 EPISCOPAL.....	3	1 079	1 519	1.7	2.2
274 LAT EVAN LUTH.	1	84	84	0.1	0.1
281 LUTH CH AMER..	1	848	1 095	1.2	1.6
283 LUTH--MO SYNOD	4	1 564	2 259	2.5	3.3
371 REF CH IN AM..	2	619	1 037	1.2	1.5
403 SALVATION ARMY	1	110	557	0.6	0.8
413 S.D.A.........	1	43	53*	0.1	0.1
443 UN C OF CHRIST	9	4 156	5 085*	5.7	7.5
449 UN METHODIST..	11	2 766	3 384*	3.8	5.0
453 UN PRES CH USA	1	821	1 005*	1.1	1.5
469 WELS.........	14	5 477	7 253	8.2	10.7
FOREST	19	1 278	4 494*	49.7	100.0
081 CATHOLIC......	6	NA	2 869	31.7	63.8
127 CH GOD (CLEVE)	1	46	56*	0.6	1.2

NA— Not applicable   *Total adherents estimated from known number of communicant, confirmed, full members.   —Represents a percent less than 0.1.   Percentages may not total due to rounding.

Table 4. Churches and Church Membership by County and Denomination: 1980

County and Denomination	Number of churches	Communicant, confirmed, full members	Total adherents Number	Percent of total population	Percent of total adherents
165 CH OF NAZARENE	1	35	91	1.0	2.0
181 CONSRV CONGR..	1	73	89*	1.0	2.0
283 LUTH--MO SYNOD	2	247	327	3.6	7.3
413 S.D.A.......	1	29	35*	0.4	0.8
449 UN METHODIST..	2	252	307*	3.4	6.8
453 UN PRES CH USA	2	181	220*	2.4	4.9
469 WELS..........	3	415	500	5.5	11.1
GRANT	84	11 079	41 761*	80.7	100.0
019 AMER BAPT USA.	1	15	18*	-	-
029 AMER LUTH CH..	5	2 332	3 036	5.9	7.3
053 ASSEMB OF GOD.	2	96	146	0.3	0.3
081 CATHOLIC......	19	NA	27 436	53.0	65.7
097 CHR CHS&CHS CR	1	20	24*	-	0.1
165 CH OF NAZARENE	1	10	31	0.1	0.1
167 CHS OF CHRIST.	1	35	45	0.1	0.1
175 CONGR CHR CHS.	1	100	122*	0.2	0.3
179 CONSRV BAPT...	1	40	49*	0.1	0.1
181 CONSRV CONGR..	1	103	125*	0.2	0.3
193 EPISCOPAL.....	2	48	70	0.1	0.2
203 EVAN FREE CH..	2	80	97*	0.2	0.2
220 FREE LUTHERAN.	2	151	204	0.4	0.5
221 FREE METHODIST	2	108	333	0.6	0.8
281 LUTH CH AMER..	5	1 218	1 786	3.5	4.3
283 LUTH--MO SYNOD	1	159	210	0.4	0.5
285 MENNONITE CH..	1	51	62*	0.1	0.1
363 PRIMITIVE METH	2	165	201*	0.4	0.5
413 S.D.A.........	1	59	72*	0.1	0.2
443 UN C OF CHRIST	8	1 287	1 567*	3.0	3.8
449 UN METHODIST..	20	4 371	5 323*	10.3	12.7
453 UN PRES CH USA	3	386	470*	0.9	1.1
469 WELS..........	2	245	334	0.6	0.8
GREEN	39	9 993	17 553*	58.5	100.0
019 AMER BAPT USA.	4	366	448*	1.5	2.6
029 AMER LUTH CH..	7	1 518	2 129	7.1	12.1
053 ASSEMB OF GOD.	1	109	265	0.9	1.5
081 CATHOLIC......	4	NA	4 438	14.8	25.3
165 CH OF NAZARENE	2	86	151	0.5	0.9
167 CHS OF CHRIST.	1	35	45	0.1	0.3
193 EPISCOPAL.....	1	16	36	0.1	0.2
281 LUTH CH AMER..	1	921	1 490	5.0	8.5
323 OLD ORD AMISH.	1	130	159*	0.5	0.9
443 UN C OF CHRIST	6	3 761	4 603*	15.3	26.2
449 UN METHODIST..	8	2 607	3 190*	10.6	18.2
453 UN PRES CH USA	1	160	196*	0.7	1.1
469 WELS..........	2	284	403	1.3	2.3
GREEN LAKE	28	5 899	15 520*	84.5	100.0
029 AMER LUTH CH..	1	708	941	5.1	6.1
053 ASSEMB OF GOD.	1	57	100	0.5	0.6
081 CATHOLIC......	7	NA	7 796	42.4	50.2
164 CH LUTH CONF..	1	212	300	1.6	1.9
175 CONGR CHR CHS.	1	103	124*	0.7	0.8
283 LUTH--MO SYNOD	1	762	1 081	5.9	7.0
443 UN C OF CHRIST	2	272	328*	1.8	2.1
449 UN METHODIST..	5	1 097	1 324*	7.2	8.5
453 UN PRES CH USA	1	14	17*	0.1	0.1
469 WELS..........	8	2 674	3 509	19.1	22.6
IOWA	46	4 913	13 313*	67.2	100.0
019 AMER BAPT USA.	1	58	71*	0.4	0.5
029 AMER LUTH CH..	9	2 065	2 665	13.5	20.0
053 ASSEMB OF GOD.	1	39	60	0.3	0.5
081 CATHOLIC......	11	NA	7 097	35.8	53.3
193 EPISCOPAL.....	1	65	92	0.5	0.7
203 EVAN FREE CH..	1	33	41*	0.2	0.3
283 LUTH--MO SYNOD	1	109	155	0.8	1.2
363 PRIMITIVE METH	3	97	119*	0.6	0.9
443 UN C OF CHRIST	3	747	920*	4.6	6.9
449 UN METHODIST..	13	1 523	1 875*	9.5	14.1
453 UN PRES CH USA	2	177	218*	1.1	1.6
IRON	16	872	3 945*	58.6	100.0
081 CATHOLIC......	7	NA	2 843	42.2	72.1
165 CH OF NAZARENE	1	26	72	1.1	1.8
283 LUTH--MO SYNOD	2	353	450	6.7	11.4
285 MENNONITE CH..	1	9	11*	0.2	0.3
449 UN METHODIST..	1	150	177*	2.6	4.5
453 UN PRES CH USA	2	192	226*	3.4	5.7
469 WELS..........	2	142	166	2.5	4.2
JACKSON	34	5 627	8 958*	53.2	100.0
029 AMER LUTH CH..	8	2 960	3 885	23.1	43.4
053 ASSEMB OF GOD.	2	205	370	2.2	4.1
057 BAPT GEN CONF.	1	43	52*	0.3	0.6
081 CATHOLIC......	5	NA	1 620	9.6	18.1
097 CHR CHS&CHS CR	1	41	50*	0.3	0.6
164 CH LUTH CONF..	1	70	91*	0.5	1.0
167 CHS OF CHRIST.	1	40	50	0.3	0.6
283 LUTH--MO SYNOD	3	457	560	3.3	6.3
367 PROT CONF (WI)	1	200	300	1.8	3.3
443 UN C OF CHRIST	2	101	123*	0.7	1.4
449 UN METHODIST..	7	1 309	1 594*	9.5	17.8
453 UN PRES CH USA	1	170	207*	1.2	2.3
469 WELS..........	1	31	56	0.3	0.6
JEFFERSON	70	25 856	51 246*	77.5	100.0
001 ADVENT CHR CH.	1	69	84*	0.1	0.2
019 AMER BAPT USA.	1	130	158*	0.2	0.3
029 AMER LUTH CH..	6	3 087	4 128	6.2	8.1
053 ASSEMB OF GOD.	1	124	250	0.4	0.5
081 CATHOLIC......	10	NA	17 715	26.8	34.6
167 CHS OF CHRIST.	2	33	60	0.1	0.1
179 CONSRV BAPT...	1	75	91*	0.1	0.2
193 EPISCOPAL.....	2	279	368	0.6	0.7
281 LUTH CH AMER..	3	2 596	3 502	5.3	6.8
283 LUTH--MO SYNOD	4	1 313	1 700	2.6	3.3
293 MORAV CH-NORTH	4	1 531	1 911	2.9	3.7
313 N AM BAPT CONF	1	106	128*	0.2	0.2
413 S.D.A.........	2	71	86*	0.1	0.2
443 UN C OF CHRIST	4	1 557	1 887*	2.9	3.7
449 UN METHODIST..	12	3 109	3 769*	5.7	7.4
469 WELS..........	16	11 776	15 409	23.3	30.1
JUNEAU	40	5 764	13 029*	61.9	100.0
019 AMER BAPT USA.	1	120	146*	1.1	1.1
029 AMER LUTH CH..	8	1 857	2 562	12.2	19.7
053 ASSEMB OF GOD.	2	43	92	0.4	0.7
057 BAPT GEN CONF.	1	69	84*	0.4	0.6
081 CATHOLIC......	10	NA	5 390	25.6	41.4
165 CH OF NAZARENE	1	76	188	0.9	1.4
179 CONSRV BAPT...	1	75	91*	0.4	0.7
193 EPISCOPAL.....	1	36	61	0.3	0.5
283 LUTH--MO SYNOD	3	356	464	2.2	3.6
449 UN METHODIST..	6	1 420	1 732*	8.2	13.3
453 UN PRES CH USA	1	82	100*	0.5	0.8
469 WELS..........	5	1 630	2 119	10.1	16.3
KENOSHA	79	19 289	68 691*	55.8	100.0
019 AMER BAPT USA.	2	305	370*	0.3	0.5
029 AMER LUTH CH..	3	2 057	2 987	2.4	4.3
053 ASSEMB OF GOD.	1	400	700	0.6	1.0
057 BAPT GEN CONF.	1	355	431*	0.4	0.6
081 CATHOLIC......	17	NA	43 183	35.1	62.9
097 CHR CHS&CHS CR	1	325	395*	0.3	0.6
105 CHRISTIAN REF.	1	134	217	0.2	0.3
123 CH GOD (ANDER)	1	79	237	0.2	0.3
127 CH GOD (CLEVE)	3	192	233*	0.2	0.3
151 L-D SAINTS....	1	NA	419	0.3	0.6
165 CH OF NAZARENE	1	92	192	0.2	0.3
167 CHS OF CHRIST.	3	150	190	0.2	0.3
175 CONGR CHR CHS.	2	1 080	1 311*	1.1	1.9
193 EPISCOPAL.....	2	647	891	0.7	1.3
203 EVAN FREE CH..	1	236	287*	0.2	0.4
263 INT FOURSQ GOS	1	115	140*	0.1	0.2
271 REFORM JUDAISM	1	224	272*	0.2	0.4
281 LUTH CH AMER..	5	3 838	4 920	4.0	7.2
283 LUTH--MO SYNOD	2	373	546	0.4	0.8
313 N AM BAPT CONF	1	162	197*	0.2	0.3
403 SALVATION ARMY	1	147	178	0.1	0.3
413 S.D.A.........	1	32	39*	-	0.1
419 SO BAPT CONV..	5	845	1 026*	0.8	1.5
443 UN C OF CHRIST	2	368	447*	0.4	0.7
449 UN METHODIST..	10	2 793	3 391*	2.8	4.9
453 UN PRES CH USA	1	411	499*	0.4	0.7
469 WELS..........	9	3 929	4 993	4.1	7.3
KEWAUNEE	30	3 722	16 572*	84.8	100.0
053 ASSEMB OF GOD.	1	38	50	0.3	0.3
081 CATHOLIC......	17	NA	11 835	60.6	71.4
167 CHS OF CHRIST.	1	4	5	-	-
175 CONGR CHR CHS.	1	367	452*	2.3	2.7
193 EPISCOPAL.....	1	66	84	0.4	0.5
283 LUTH--MO SYNOD	3	1 016	1 362	7.0	8.2
353 CHR BRETHREN..	1	30	65	0.3	0.4
449 UN METHODIST..	2	217	267*	1.4	1.6
469 WELS..........	3	1 984	2 452	12.5	14.8
LA CROSSE	71	25 507	59 007*	64.8	100.0
019 AMER BAPT USA.	2	175	208*	0.2	0.4
029 AMER LUTH CH..	13	8 857	11 807	13.0	20.0
053 ASSEMB OF GOD.	1	175	300	0.3	0.5
081 CATHOLIC......	12	NA	25 750	28.3	43.6
097 CHR CHS&CHS CR	3	349	416*	0.5	0.7
105 CHRISTIAN REF.	1	41	71	0.1	0.1
151 L-D SAINTS....	1	NA	356	0.4	0.6
164 CH LUTH CONF..	1	33	41	-	0.1
165 CH OF NAZARENE	1	35	98	0.1	0.2
167 CHS OF CHRIST.	1	60	76	0.1	0.1
193 EPISCOPAL.....	1	363	573	0.6	1.0
203 EVAN FREE CH..	2	288	343*	0.4	0.6
281 LUTH CH AMER..	2	2 073	2 768	3.0	4.7
283 LUTH--MO SYNOD	1	341	474	0.5	0.8
313 N AM BAPT CONF	1	89	106*	0.1	0.2
353 CHR BRETHREN..	1	40	90	0.1	0.2
367 PROT CONF (WI)	1	300	400	0.4	0.7
403 SALVATION ARMY	1	109	212	0.2	0.4
413 S.D.A.........	1	120	143*	0.2	0.2
419 SO BAPT CONV..	1	119	142*	0.2	0.2
435 UNITARIAN-UNIV	1	40	48*	0.1	0.1
443 UN C OF CHRIST	3	1 204	1 434*	1.6	2.4
449 UN METHODIST..	4	2 909	3 466*	3.8	5.9
453 UN PRES CH USA	6	1 727	2 058*	2.3	3.5
469 WELS..........	9	6 060	7 627	8.4	12.9
LAFAYETTE	43	5 412	14 090*	80.9	100.0
019 AMER BAPT USA.	1	189	232*	1.3	1.6

NA—Not applicable   *Total adherents estimated from known number of communicant, confirmed, full members.   —Represents a percent less than 0.1.   Percentages may not total due to rounding.

304

Table 4. Churches and Church Membership by County and Denomination: 1980

County and Denomination	Number of churches	Communicant, confirmed, full members	Total adherents Number	Percent of total population	Percent of total adherents
029 AMER LUTH CH..	9	2 384	3 078	17.7	21.8
081 CATHOLIC......	13	NA	7 304	41.9	51.8
193 EPISCOPAL.....	1	6	6	–	–
203 EVAN FREE CH..	1	19	23*	0.1	0.2
281 LUTH CH AMER..	1	404	486	2.8	3.4
363 PRIMITIVE METH	5	279	343*	2.0	2.4
443 UN C OF CHRIST	2	450	553*	3.2	3.9
449 UN METHODIST..	10	1 681	2 065*	11.9	14.7
LANGLADE	**33**	**4 649**	**14 809***	**74.1**	**100.0**
019 AMER BAPT USA.	1	154	188*	0.9	1.3
053 ASSEMB OF GOD.	2	157	350	1.8	2.4
081 CATHOLIC......	9	NA	8 626	43.2	58.2
127 CH GOD (CLEVE)	1	28	34*	0.2	0.2
151 L-D SAINTS....	1	NA	58	0.3	0.4
165 CH OF NAZARENE	1	30	79	0.4	0.5
167 CHS OF CHRIST.	1	20	25	0.1	0.2
193 EPISCOPAL.....	1	72	99	0.5	0.7
281 LUTH CH AMER..	3	640	830	4.2	5.6
283 LUTH--MO SYNOD	6	2 641	3 412	17.1	23.0
413 S.D.A.........	1	41	50*	0.3	0.3
443 UN C OF CHRIST	3	508	619*	3.1	4.2
449 UN METHODIST..	1	310	378*	1.9	2.6
453 UN PRES CH USA	1	30	37*	0.2	0.2
469 WELS.........	1	18	24	0.1	0.2
LINCOLN	**39**	**10 787**	**19 963***	**75.9**	**100.0**
029 AMER LUTH CH..	3	1 931	2 534	9.6	12.7
053 ASSEMB OF GOD.	2	314	465	1.8	2.3
057 BAPT GEN CONF.	1	26	32*	0.1	0.2
081 CATHOLIC......	6	NA	6 108	23.2	30.6
167 CHS OF CHRIST.	1	7	8	–	–
193 EPISCOPAL.....	2	60	72	0.3	0.4
201 EVAN COV CH AM	2	32	39*	0.1	0.2
281 LUTH CH AMER..	2	138	174	0.7	0.9
283 LUTH--MO SYNOD	8	5 539	7 183	27.3	36.0
381 REF PRES-EVAN.	1	70	99	0.4	0.5
413 S.D.A.........	2	100	121*	0.5	0.6
443 UN C OF CHRIST	2	1 488	1 805*	6.9	9.0
449 UN METHODIST..	3	624	757*	2.9	3.8
453 UN PRES CH USA	2	239	290*	1.1	1.5
469 WELS.........	2	219	276	1.0	1.4
MANITOWOC	**78**	**19 061**	**64 213***	**77.4**	**100.0**
019 AMER BAPT USA.	1	90	109*	0.1	0.2
029 AMER LUTH CH..	3	2 774	3 739	4.5	5.8
053 ASSEMB OF GOD.	1	83	140	0.2	0.2
081 CATHOLIC......	27	NA	39 593	47.7	61.7
167 CHS OF CHRIST.	1	30	38	–	0.1
193 EPISCOPAL.....	1	192	222	0.3	0.3
203 EVAN FREE CH..	1	78	95*	0.1	0.1
281 LUTH CH AMER..	1	356	488	0.6	0.8
283 LUTH--MO SYNOD	2	919	1 214	1.5	1.9
313 N AM BAPT CONF	1	90	109*	0.1	0.2
367 PROT CONF (WI)	1	52	80	0.1	0.1
403 SALVATION ARMY	1	128	382	0.5	0.6
413 S.D.A.........	1	16	19*	–	–
419 SO BAPT CONV..	1	79	96*	0.1	0.1
443 UN C OF CHRIST	8	2 552	3 104*	3.7	4.8
449 UN METHODIST..	6	1 468	1 786*	2.2	2.8
453 UN PRES CH USA	3	1 027	1 249*	1.5	1.9
469 WELS.........	18	9 127	11 750	14.2	18.3
MARATHON	**111**	**31 091**	**84 254***	**75.7**	**100.0**
029 AMER LUTH CH..	16	7 245	9 693	8.7	11.5
053 ASSEMB OF GOD.	3	303	678	0.6	0.8
057 BAPT GEN CONF.	1	64	79*	0.1	0.1
081 CATHOLIC......	26	NA	43 250	38.9	51.3
127 CH GOD (CLEVE)	1	97	120*	0.1	0.1
151 L-D SAINTS....	1	NA	192	0.2	0.2
165 CH OF NAZARENE	1	72	110	0.1	0.1
167 CHS OF CHRIST.	1	45	65	0.1	0.1
193 EPISCOPAL.....	2	430	492	0.4	0.6
208 EVAN LUTH ASSN	1	1 961	2 437	2.2	2.9
209 EVAN LUTH SYN.	1	108	137	0.1	0.2
226 FRIENDS-USA...	1	5	6*	–	–
263 INT FOURSQ GOS	1	166	205*	0.2	0.2
271 REFORM JUDAISM	1	150	185*	0.2	0.2
283 LUTH--MO SYNOD	16	7 995	10 599*	9.5	12.5
313 N AM BAPT CONF	1	438	540*	0.5	0.6
371 REF CH IN AM..	1	256	416	0.4	0.5
403 SALVATION ARMY	1	112	270	0.2	0.3
413 S.D.A.........	1	112	138*	0.1	0.2
419 SO BAPT CONV..	1	176	217*	0.2	0.3
435 UNITARIAN-UNIV	1	334	412*	0.4	0.5
443 UN C OF CHRIST	5	2 816	3 472*	3.1	4.1
449 UN METHODIST..	6	2 144	2 643*	2.4	3.1
453 UN PRES CH USA	4	1 871	2 307*	2.1	2.7
469 WELS.........	17	4 191	5 631	5.1	6.7
MARINETTE	**59**	**8 816**	**24 518***	**62.4**	**100.0**
029 AMER LUTH CH..	4	779	1 031	2.6	4.2
053 ASSEMB OF GOD.	5	368	636	1.6	2.6
057 BAPT GEN CONF.	2	148	180*	0.5	0.7
081 CATHOLIC......	14	NA	13 075	33.3	53.3
167 CHS OF CHRIST.	1	25	32	0.1	0.1
193 EPISCOPAL.....	2	221	240	0.6	1.0
201 EVAN COV CH AM	2	133	162*	0.4	0.7
209 EVAN LUTH SYN.	1	315	394	1.0	1.6
263 INT FOURSQ GOS	1	39	47*	0.1	0.2
281 LUTH CH AMER..	4	1 589	2 001	5.1	8.2
283 LUTH--MO SYNOD	1	173	264	0.7	1.1
313 N AM BAPT CONF	1	163	198*	0.5	0.8
403 SALVATION ARMY	1	90	164	0.4	0.7
413 S.D.A.........	1	57	69*	0.2	0.3
443 UN C OF CHRIST	2	161	196*	0.5	0.8
449 UN METHODIST..	5	1 132	1 375*	3.5	5.6
453 UN PRES CH USA	6	888	1 079*	2.7	4.4
469 WELS.........	6	2 535	3 375	8.6	13.8
MARQUETTE	**27**	**3 584**	**7 070***	**60.6**	**100.0**
029 AMER LUTH CH..	2	252	323	2.8	4.6
081 CATHOLIC......	5	NA	2 694	23.1	38.1
283 LUTH--MO SYNOD	8	1 435	1 729	14.8	24.5
413 S.D.A.........	1	35	42*	0.4	0.6
443 UN C OF CHRIST	1	82	98*	0.8	1.4
449 UN METHODIST..	5	706	847*	7.3	12.0
453 UN PRES CH USA	3	320	384*	3.3	5.4
469 WELS.........	2	754	953	8.2	13.5
MENOMINEE	**4**	**25**	**1 791**	**53.1**	**100.0**
053 ASSEMB OF GOD.	1	25	35	1.0	2.0
081 CATHOLIC......	3	NA	1 756	52.1	98.0
MILWAUKEE	**469**	**163 161**	**557 864***	**57.8**	**100.0**
019 AMER BAPT USA.	18	4 831	5 783*	0.6	1.0
029 AMER LUTH CH..	21	14 874	19 457	2.0	3.5
053 ASSEMB OF GOD.	14	2 076	3 453	0.4	0.6
057 BAPT GEN CONF.	3	172	206*	–	–
081 CATHOLIC......	111	NA	349 091	36.2	62.6
089 CHR & MISS AL.	1	147	257	–	–
093 CHR CH (DISC).	1	163	187	–	–
097 CHR CHS&CHS CR	1	129	154*	–	–
101 C.M.E........	5	4 551	5 448*	0.6	1.0
123 CH GOD (ANDER)	4	362	1 086	0.1	0.2
127 CH GOD (CLEVE)	4	173	207*	–	–
164 CH LUTH CONF..	1	76	114	–	–
165 CH OF NAZARENE	2	188	237	–	–
167 CHS OF CHRIST.	8	635	810	0.1	0.1
175 CONGR CHR CHS.	4	4 117	4 928*	0.5	0.9
179 CONSRV BAPT...	1	65	78*	–	–
181 CONSRV CONGR..	1	82	98*	–	–
193 EPISCOPAL.....	16	5 326	6 432	0.7	1.2
197 EVAN CH OF NA.	1	37	37	–	–
201 EVAN COV CH AM	1	93	111*	–	–
203 EVAN FREE CH..	2	164	196*	–	–
208 EVAN LUTH ASSN	3	1 829	2 260	0.2	0.4
226 FRIENDS-USA...	1	50	60*	–	–
263 INT FOURSQ GOS	1	63	75*	–	–
270 CONSRV JUDAISM	3	1 025	1 227*	0.1	0.2
271 REFORM JUDAISM	3	4 782	5 724*	0.6	1.0
274 LAT EVAN LUTH.	3	849	979	0.1	0.2
281 LUTH CH AMER..	32	18 286	23 829	2.5	4.3
283 LUTH--MO SYNOD	47	35 937	45 526	4.7	8.2
287 MENN GEN CONF.	1	21	36	–	–
290 METRO COMM CHS	1	50	100	–	–
313 N AM BAPT CONF	3	648	776*	0.1	0.1
353 CHR BRETHREN..	4	230	320	–	0.1
367 PROT CONF (WI)	1	10	20	–	–
371 REF CH IN AM..	2	450	783	0.1	0.1
403 SALVATION ARMY	3	564	3 331	0.3	0.6
413 S.D.A.........	4	1 362	1 630*	0.2	0.3
419 SO BAPT CONV..	18	4 342	5 198*	0.5	0.9
435 UNITARIAN-UNIV	2	415	497*	0.1	0.1
443 UN C OF CHRIST	20	7 225	8 649*	0.9	1.6
449 UN METHODIST..	27	12 294	14 717*	1.5	2.6
453 UN PRES CH USA	21	7 713	9 233*	1.0	1.7
469 WELS.........	49	26 755	34 524	3.6	6.2
MONROE	**58**	**10 160**	**21 546***	**61.4**	**100.0**
019 AMER BAPT USA.	1	175	214*	0.6	1.0
029 AMER LUTH CH..	7	2 814	3 705	10.6	17.2
053 ASSEMB OF GOD.	3	231	443	1.3	2.1
081 CATHOLIC......	9	NA	8 140	23.2	37.8
123 CH GOD (ANDER)	1	20	60	0.2	0.3
151 L-D SAINTS....	1	NA	125	0.4	0.6
165 CH OF NAZARENE	1	?	?	?	?
167 CHS OF CHRIST.	2	90	115	0.3	0.5
181 CONSRV CONGR..	1	45	55*	0.2	0.3
193 EPISCOPAL.....	2	151	228	0.7	1.1
203 EVAN FREE CH..	1	24	29*	0.1	0.1
323 OLD ORD AMISH.	2	260	318*	0.9	1.5
353 CHR BRETHREN..	1	20	20	0.1	0.1
413 S.D.A.........	3	141	173*	0.5	0.8
419 SO BAPT CONV..	1	30	37*	0.1	0.2
443 UN C OF CHRIST	2	603	739*	2.1	3.4
449 UN METHODIST..	8	1 740	2 131*	6.1	9.9
469 WELS.|.......	12	3 816	5 014	14.3	23.3
OCONTO	**56**	**7 701**	**20 076***	**69.4**	**100.0**
029 AMER LUTH CH..	8	2 799	3 625	12.5	18.1
053 ASSEMB OF GOD.	1	93	119	0.4	0.6
081 CATHOLIC......	14	NA	10 138	35.0	50.5
089 CHR & MISS AL.	3	98	290	1.0	1.4
097 CHR CHS&CHS CR	2	132	161*	0.6	0.8
193 EPISCOPAL.....	1	51	103	0.4	0.5
283 LUTH--MO SYNOD	10	2 207	2 778	9.6	13.8
353 CHR BRETHREN..	1	20	20	0.1	0.1
413 S.D.A.........	3	134	164*	0.6	0.8
449 UN METHODIST..	7	1 239	1 515*	5.2	7.5

NA—Not applicable   *Total adherents estimated from known number of communicant, confirmed, full members.   —Represents a percent less than 0.1.   Percentages may not total due to rounding.

Table 4. Churches and Church Membership by County and Denomination: 1980

County and Denomination	Number of churches	Communicant, confirmed, full members	Total adherents Number	Percent of total population	Percent of total adherents
453 UN PRES CH USA	2	391	478*	1.7	2.4
469 WELS.........	4	537	685	2.4	3.4
ONEIDA	34	8 254	17 939*	57.5	100.0
019 AMER BAPT USA.	1	125	149*	0.5	0.8
029 AMER LUTH CH..	2	1 772	2 450	7.8	13.7
053 ASSEMB OF GOD.	1	44	95	0.3	0.5
057 BAPT GEN CONF.	1	91	109*	0.3	0.6
081 CATHOLIC......	9	NA	7 264	23.3	40.5
151 L-D SAINTS....	1	NA	?	?	?
167 CHS OF CHRIST.	1	26	44	0.1	0.2
193 EPISCOPAL.....	2	399	444	1.4	2.5
263 INT FOURSQ GOS	1	293	350*	1.1	2.0
281 LUTH CH AMER..	1	303	408	1.3	2.3
283 LUTH--MO SYNOD	3	841	1 156	3.7	6.4
413 S.D.A.........	2	234	280*	0.9	1.6
443 UN C OF CHRIST	3	1 058	1 264*	4.0	7.0
449 UN METHODIST..	2	1 098	1 312*	4.2	7.3
469 WELS.........	4	1 970	2 614	8.4	14.6
OUTAGAMIE	100	31 964	105 042*	81.6	100.0
019 AMER BAPT USA.	2	152	188*	0.1	0.2
029 AMER LUTH CH..	6	6 581	9 044	7.0	8.6
053 ASSEMB OF GOD.	5	561	921	0.7	0.9
057 BAPT GEN CONF.	1	53	65*	0.1	0.1
081 CATHOLIC......	29	NA	61 891	48.1	58.9
089 CHR & MISS AL.	1	93	154	0.1	0.1
105 CHRISTIAN REF.	1	16	16	-	-
151 L-D SAINTS....	1	NA	285	0.2	0.3
165 CH OF NAZARENE	1	73	179	0.1	0.2
167 CHS OF CHRIST.	1	113	144	0.1	0.1
181 CONSRV CONGR..	1	111	137*	0.1	0.1
193 EPISCOPAL.....	1	480	640	0.5	0.6
270 CONSRV JUDAISM	1	109	135*	0.1	0.1
281 LUTH CH AMER..	2	2 497	3 743	2.9	3.6
283 LUTH--MO SYNOD	5	3 492	4 805	3.7	4.6
293 MORAV CH-NORTH	1	168	209	0.2	0.2
367 PROT CONF (WI)	1	150	200	0.2	0.2
403 SALVATION ARMY	1	67	169	0.1	0.2
413 S.D.A.........	1	122	151*	0.1	0.1
419 SO BAPT CONV..	1	150	185*	0.1	0.2
435 UNITARIAN-UNIV	1	28	35*	-	-
443 UN C OF CHRIST	6	2 815	3 473*	2.7	3.3
449 UN METHODIST..	10	3 423	4 223*	3.3	4.0
453 UN PRES CH USA	2	653	806*	0.6	0.8
469 WELS.........	18	10 057	13 245	10.3	12.6
OZAUKEE	52	17 061	49 457*	73.8	100.0
005 AME ZION......	1	164	221	0.3	0.4
019 AMER BAPT USA.	1	121	149*	0.2	0.3
029 AMER LUTH CH..	7	3 646	4 775	7.1	9.7
053 ASSEMB OF GOD.	1	85	155	0.2	0.3
081 CATHOLIC......	12	NA	27 482	41.0	55.6
089 CHR & MISS AL.	1	0	66	0.1	0.1
165 CH OF NAZARENE	1	11	32	-	0.1
193 EPISCOPAL.....	2	366	444	0.7	0.9
281 LUTH CH AMER..	3	1 033	1 281	1.9	2.6
283 LUTH--MO SYNOD	7	5 971	7 782	11.6	15.7
435 UNITARIAN-UNIV	1	122	150*	0.2	0.3
443 UN C OF CHRIST	5	1 202	1 475*	2.2	3.0
449 UN METHODIST..	3	1 238	1 519*	2.3	3.1
453 UN PRES CH USA	1	1 376	1 689*	2.5	3.4
469 WELS.........	6	1 726	2 237	3.3	4.5
PEPIN	18	1 931	5 700*	76.2	100.0
029 AMER LUTH CH..	3	626	852	11.4	14.9
081 CATHOLIC......	3	NA	3 240	43.3	56.8
157 CH OF BRETHREN	1	30	37*	0.5	0.6
201 EVAN COV CH AM	2	144	176*	2.4	3.1
203 EVAN FREE CH..	1	23	28*	0.4	0.5
281 LUTH CH AMER..	1	250	306	4.1	5.4
283 LUTH--MO SYNOD	1	153	204	2.7	3.6
293 MORAV CH-NORTH	1	39	41	0.5	0.7
413 S.D.A.........	1	34	42*	0.6	0.7
443 UN C OF CHRIST	1	52	64*	0.9	1.1
449 UN METHODIST..	3	580	710*	9.5	12.5
PIERCE	53	8 395	17 045*	54.7	100.0
029 AMER LUTH CH..	11	3 600	4 983	16.0	29.2
053 ASSEMB OF GOD.	1	47	120	0.4	0.7
057 BAPT GEN CONF.	1	10	12*	-	0.1
081 CATHOLIC......	9	NA	5 990	19.2	35.1
181 CONSRV CONGR..	1	138	168*	0.5	1.0
193 EPISCOPAL.....	2	93	117	0.4	0.7
201 EVAN COV CH AM	3	360	437*	1.4	2.6
203 EVAN FREE CH..	1	81	98*	0.3	0.6
281 LUTH CH AMER..	2	247	388	1.2	2.3
283 LUTH--MO SYNOD	2	305	424	1.4	2.5
443 UN C OF CHRIST	4	1 150	1 397*	4.5	8.2
449 UN METHODIST..	11	1 652	2 007*	6.4	11.8
453 UN PRES CH USA	3	276	335*	1.1	2.0
469 WELS.........	2	436	569	1.8	3.3
POLK	82	12 182	19 978*	61.8	100.0
029 AMER LUTH CH..	19	3 926	5 273	16.3	26.4
053 ASSEMB OF GOD.	1	55	100	0.3	0.5
057 BAPT GEN CONF.	2	225	275*	0.9	1.4
081 CATHOLIC......	9	NA	3 779	11.7	18.9
089 CHR & MISS AL.	3	214	455	1.4	2.3

County and Denomination	Number of churches	Communicant, confirmed, full members	Total adherents Number	Percent of total population	Percent of total adherents
165 CH OF NAZARENE	1	80	241	0.7	1.2
167 CHS OF CHRIST.	1	64	95	0.3	0.5
179 CONSRV BAPT...	2	80	98*	0.3	0.5
193 EPISCOPAL.....	1	55	78	0.2	0.4
201 EVAN COV CH AM	1	142	174*	0.5	0.9
203 EVAN FREE CH..	3	111	136*	0.4	0.7
220 FREE LUTHERAN.	2	42	62	0.2	0.3
281 LUTH CH AMER..	12	3 104	4 046	12.5	20.3
283 LUTH--MO SYNOD	4	700	904	2.8	4.5
413 S.D.A.........	2	155	190*	0.6	1.0
443 UN C OF CHRIST	1	331	405*	1.3	2.0
449 UN METHODIST..	12	1 294	1 583*	4.9	7.9
469 WELS.........	6	1 604	2 084	6.4	10.4
PORTAGE	54	7 624	41 375*	72.1	100.0
019 AMER BAPT USA.	3	352	426*	0.7	1.0
029 AMER LUTH CH..	5	2 094	2 968	5.2	7.2
053 ASSEMB OF GOD.	1	141	349	0.6	0.8
081 CATHOLIC......	18	NA	31 020	54.0	75.0
151 L-D SAINTS....	1	NA	148	0.3	0.4
167 CHS OF CHRIST.	1	54	71	0.1	0.2
193 EPISCOPAL.....	2	182	217	0.4	0.5
203 EVAN FREE CH..	1	95	115*	0.2	0.3
209 EVAN LUTH SYN.	1	42	48	0.1	0.1
283 LUTH--MO SYNOD	5	2 357	3 163	5.5	7.6
323 OLD ORD AMISH.	2	260	315*	0.5	0.8
413 S.D.A.........	3	142	172*	0.3	0.4
435 UNITARIAN-UNIV	1	32	39*	0.1	0.1
443 UN C OF CHRIST	1	80	97*	0.2	0.2
449 UN METHODIST..	6	1 246	1 508*	2.6	3.6
453 UN PRES CH USA	1	414	501*	0.9	1.2
469 WELS.........	1	133	218	0.4	0.5
PRICE	31	4 039	9 962*	63.1	100.0
029 AMER LUTH CH..	1	120	167	1.1	1.7
053 ASSEMB OF GOD.	1	54	143	0.9	1.4
057 BAPT GEN CONF.	4	442	539*	3.4	5.4
081 CATHOLIC......	6	NA	4 790	30.3	48.1
193 EPISCOPAL.....	2	27	41	0.3	0.4
201 EVAN COV CH AM	1	49	60*	0.4	0.6
281 LUTH CH AMER..	4	1 028	1 277	8.1	12.8
283 LUTH--MO SYNOD	4	1 383	1 794	11.4	18.0
413 S.D.A.........	1	27	33*	0.2	0.3
443 UN C OF CHRIST	2	417	509*	3.2	5.1
449 UN METHODIST..	3	266	324*	2.1	3.3
453 UN PRES CH USA	1	173	211*	1.3	2.1
469 WELS.........	1	53	74	0.5	0.7
RACINE	121	35 638	100 341*	58.0	100.0
019 AMER BAPT USA.	2	607	744*	0.4	0.7
029 AMER LUTH CH..	11	7 840	10 590	6.1	10.6
049 ARMEN AP CH AM	1	100	200	0.1	0.2
053 ASSEMB OF GOD.	2	299	438	0.3	0.4
081 CATHOLIC......	24	NA	52 380	30.3	52.2
097 CHR CHS&CHS CR	1	38	47*	-	0.1
101 C.M.E.........	1	68	83*	-	0.1
105 CHRISTIAN REF.	1	262	441	0.3	0.4
123 CH GOD (ANDER)	3	233	699	0.4	0.7
127 CH GOD (CLEVE)	2	89	109*	0.1	0.1
165 CH OF NAZARENE	3	250	213	0.1	0.2
167 CHS OF CHRIST.	2	150	190	0.1	0.2
175 CONGR CHR CHS.	1	399	489*	0.3	0.5
193 EPISCOPAL.....	5	986	1 399	0.8	1.4
203 EVAN FREE CH..	2	39	48*	-	-
270 CONSRV JUDAISM	1	125	153*	0.1	0.2
281 LUTH CH AMER..	8	5 827	7 881	4.6	7.9
283 LUTH--MO SYNOD	13	6 629	9 403	5.4	9.4
313 N AM BAPT CONF	1	301	369*	0.2	0.4
329 OPEN BIBLE STD	1	70	100	0.1	0.1
371 REF CH IN AM..	1	121	193	0.1	0.2
403 SALVATION ARMY	1	97	314	0.2	0.3
413 S.D.A.........	2	265	325*	0.2	0.3
419 SO BAPT CONV..	3	448	549*	0.3	0.5
435 UNITARIAN-UNIV	1	214	262*	0.2	0.3
443 UN C OF CHRIST	5	1 147	1 406*	0.8	1.4
449 UN METHODIST..	14	4 673	5 730*	3.3	5.7
453 UN PRES CH USA	1	1 537	1 885*	1.1	1.9
469 WELS.........	6	2 824	3 701	2.1	3.7
RICHLAND	33	3 693	8 030*	45.9	100.0
019 AMER BAPT USA.	2	179	217*	1.2	2.7
029 AMER LUTH CH..	3	844	1 180	6.8	14.7
053 ASSEMB OF GOD.	1	67	106	0.6	1.3
081 CATHOLIC......	5	NA	3 030	17.3	37.7
097 CHR CHS&CHS CR	1	200	243*	1.4	3.0
165 CH OF NAZARENE	1	113	265	1.5	3.3
167 CHS OF CHRIST.	1	25	32	0.2	0.4
175 CONGR CHR CHS.	1	114	138*	0.8	1.7
179 CONSRV BAPT...	1	40	49*	0.3	0.6
193 EPISCOPAL.....	1	32	44	0.3	0.5
221 FREE METHODIST	1	108	330	1.9	4.1
283 LUTH--MO SYNOD	2	181	225	1.3	2.8
285 MENNONITE CH..	1	19	23*	0.1	0.3
413 S.D.A.........	1	93	113*	0.6	1.4
449 UN METHODIST..	10	1 431	1 735*	9.9	21.6
453 UN PRES CH USA	1	247	300*	1.7	3.7
ROCK	131	44 553	89 722*	64.4	100.0
001 ADVENT CHR CH.	1	81	99*	0.1	0.1
019 AMER BAPT USA.	6	2 136	2 617*	1.9	2.9

Table 4. Churches and Church Membership by County and Denomination: 1980

County and Denomination	Number of churches	Communicant, confirmed, full members	Total adherents Number	Percent of total population	Percent of total adherents
029 AMER LUTH CH..	15	12 482	17 272	12.4	19.3
053 ASSEMB OF GOD.	2	333	550	0.4	0.6
057 BAPT GEN CONF.	2	102	125*	0.1	0.1
081 CATHOLIC......	13	NA	30 225	21.7	33.7
089 CHR & MISS AL.	1	79	154	0.1	0.2
093 CHR CH (DISC).	1	168	218	0.2	0.2
097 CHR CHS&CHS CR	4	1 050	1 286*	0.9	1.4
101 C.M.E.........	1	604	740*	0.5	0.8
127 CH GOD (CLEVE)	2	38	47*	–	0.1
151 L-D SAINTS....	1	NA	363	0.3	0.4
165 CH OF NAZARENE	1	115	234	0.2	0.3
167 CHS OF CHRIST.	1	100	127	0.1	0.1
175 CONGR CHR CHS.	5	1 910	2 340*	1.7	2.6
193 EPISCOPAL.....	2	714	903	0.6	1.0
201 EVAN COV CH AM	1	217	266*	0.2	0.3
203 EVAN FREE CH..	1	83	102*	0.1	0.1
221 FREE METHODIST	2	175	549	0.4	0.6
226 FRIENDS-USA...	1	11	13*	–	–
263 INT FOURSQ GOS	1	126	154*	0.1	0.2
271 REFORM JUDAISM	1	60	74*	0.1	0.1
281 LUTH CH AMER..	3	1 917	2 653	1.9	3.0
283 LUTH--MO SYNOD	11	7 186	9 534	6.8	10.6
323 OLD ORD AMISH.	2	260	319*	0.2	0.4
329 OPEN BIBLE STD	1	70	150	0.1	0.2
335 ORTH PRESB CH.	1	47	58*	–	0.1
371 REF CH IN AM..	1	165	305	0.2	0.3
403 SALVATION ARMY	2	321	824	0.6	0.9
413 S.D.A.........	4	380	466*	0.3	0.5
415 S-D BAPTIST GC	2	527	646*	0.5	0.7
419 SO BAPT CONV..	3	356	436*	0.3	0.5
443 UN C OF CHRIST	6	1 841	2 255*	1.6	2.5
449 UN METHODIST..	20	7 598	9 308*	6.7	10.4
453 UN PRES CH USA	6	1 936	2 372*	1.7	2.6
469 WELS.........	4	1 365	1 938	1.4	2.2
RUSK	**36**	**3 881**	**9 268***	**59.5**	**100.0**
029 AMER LUTH CH..	5	1 201	1 570	10.1	16.9
053 ASSEMB OF GOD.	1	61	150	1.0	1.6
057 BAPT GEN CONF.	1	48	59*	0.4	0.6
081 CATHOLIC......	11	NA	4 230	27.1	45.6
097 CHR CHS&CHS CR	2	734	900*	5.8	9.7
283 LUTH--MO SYNOD	2	837	1 132	7.3	12.2
285 MENNONITE CH..	4	187	229*	1.5	2.5
413 S.D.A.........	1	51	63*	0.4	0.7
443 UN C OF CHRIST	3	287	352*	2.3	3.8
449 UN METHODIST..	6	475	583*	3.7	6.3
ST CROIX	**54**	**12 434**	**28 550***	**65.1**	**100.0**
019 AMER BAPT USA.	1	191	237*	0.5	0.8
029 AMER LUTH CH..	13	6 353	8 715	19.9	30.5
053 ASSEMB OF GOD.	2	108	156	0.4	0.5
057 BAPT GEN CONF.	1	24	30*	0.1	0.1
081 CATHOLIC......	8	NA	11 229	25.6	39.3
105 CHRISTIAN REF.	1	143	202	0.5	0.7
179 CONSRV BAPT...	1	75	93*	0.2	0.3
193 EPISCOPAL.....	2	157	221	0.5	0.8
201 EVAN COV CH AM	2	49	61*	0.1	0.2
281 LUTH CH AMER..	1	256	371	0.8	1.3
283 LUTH--MO SYNOD	4	1 252	2 268	5.2	7.9
371 REF CH IN AM..	1	381	621	1.4	2.2
443 UN C OF CHRIST	2	356	441*	1.0	1.5
449 UN METHODIST..	8	1 767	2 190*	5.0	7.7
453 UN PRES CH USA	2	703	871*	2.0	3.1
469 WELS.........	5	619	844	1.9	3.0
SAUK	**70**	**15 040**	**34 130***	**78.5**	**100.0**
001 ADVENT CHR CH.	2	243	296*	0.7	0.9
019 AMER BAPT USA.	1	55	67*	0.2	0.2
029 AMER LUTH CH..	7	3 140	4 159	9.6	12.2
053 ASSEMB OF GOD.	1	116	222	0.5	0.7
081 CATHOLIC......	9	NA	14 654	33.7	42.9
123 CH GOD (ANDER)	2	180	540	1.2	1.6
151 L-D SAINTS....	1	NA	82	0.2	0.2
165 CH OF NAZARENE	1	75	136	0.3	0.4
175 CONGR CHR CHS.	1	106	129*	0.3	0.4
179 CONSRV BAPT...	1	75	91*	0.2	0.3
193 EPISCOPAL.....	2	291	340	0.8	1.0
209 EVAN LUTH SYN.	1	118	136	0.3	0.4
226 FRIENDS-USA...	1	106	129*	0.3	0.4
281 LUTH CH AMER..	1	611	789	1.8	2.3
283 LUTH--MO SYNOD	6	2 006	2 557	5.9	7.5
313 N AM BAPT CONF	2	130	158*	0.4	0.5
413 S.D.A.........	1	83	101*	0.2	0.3
419 SO BAPT CONV..	1	66	80*	0.2	0.2
435 UNITARIAN-UNIV	1	42	51*	0.1	0.1
443 UN C OF CHRIST	2	601	731*	1.7	2.1
449 UN METHODIST..	14	3 307	4 024*	9.3	11.8
453 UN PRES CH USA	3	740	900*	2.1	2.6
469 WELS.........	8	2 949	3 758	8.6	11.0
SAWYER	**28**	**2 221**	**5 832***	**45.4**	**100.0**
029 AMER LUTH CH..	3	880	1 158	9.0	19.9
053 ASSEMB OF GOD.	1	23	30	0.2	0.5
057 BAPT GEN CONF.	1	17	21*	0.2	0.4
081 CATHOLIC......	8	NA	2 995	23.3	51.4
175 CONGR CHR CHS.	1	380	458*	3.6	7.9
193 EPISCOPAL.....	1	122	131	1.0	2.2
203 EVAN FREE CH..	2	46	55*	0.4	0.9
281 LUTH CH AMER..	2	215	296	2.3	5.1
283 LUTH--MO SYNOD	1	237	325	2.5	5.6
285 MENNONITE CH..	1	24	29*	0.2	0.5
413 S.D.A.........	1	19	23*	0.2	0.4
443 UN C OF CHRIST	1	16	19*	0.1	0.3
449 UN METHODIST..	1	37	45*	0.4	0.8
453 UN PRES CH USA	4	205	247*	1.9	4.2
SHAWANO	**79**	**15 639**	**27 939***	**77.8**	**100.0**
029 AMER LUTH CH..	16	3 475	4 451	12.4	15.9
053 ASSEMB OF GOD.	2	150	273	0.8	1.0
057 BAPT GEN CONF.	1	41	50*	0.1	0.2
081 CATHOLIC......	13	NA	7 940	22.1	28.4
151 L-D SAINTS....	2	NA	341	0.9	1.2
165 CH OF NAZARENE	1	119	192	0.5	0.7
193 EPISCOPAL.....	1	60	67	0.2	0.2
209 EVAN LUTH SYN.	1	150	172	0.5	0.6
283 LUTH--MO SYNOD	25	8 866	11 053	30.8	39.6
335 ORTH PRESB CH.	1	66	81*	0.2	0.3
413 S.D.A.........	1	18	22*	0.1	0.1
419 SO BAPT CONV..	1	46	56*	0.2	0.2
443 UN C OF CHRIST	3	837	1 021*	2.8	3.7
449 UN METHODIST..	7	905	1 104*	3.1	4.0
453 UN PRES CH USA	1	242	295*	0.8	1.1
469 WELS.........	3	664	821	2.3	2.9
SHEBOYGAN	**117**	**38 606**	**79 242***	**78.5**	**100.0**
019 AMER BAPT USA.	2	173	210*	0.2	0.3
029 AMER LUTH CH..	4	1 357	1 797	1.8	2.3
053 ASSEMB OF GOD.	1	91	200	0.2	0.3
075 BRETHREN IN CR	1	43	73	0.1	0.1
081 CATHOLIC......	18	NA	29 212	28.9	36.9
089 CHR & MISS AL.	1	51	51	0.1	0.1
105 CHRISTIAN REF.	3	1 088	1 624	1.6	2.0
123 CH GOD (ANDER)	1	15	45	–	0.1
127 CH GOD (CLEVE)	1	5	6*	–	–
151 L-D SAINTS....	1	NA	150	0.1	0.2
165 CH OF NAZARENE	1	38	31	–	–
167 CHS OF CHRIST.	2	100	125	0.1	0.2
181 CONSRV CONGR..	1	114	138*	0.1	0.2
193 EPISCOPAL.....	3	633	679	0.7	0.9
203 EVAN FREE CH..	1	27	33*	–	–
281 LUTH CH AMER..	2	1 536	2 147	2.1	2.7
283 LUTH--MO SYNOD	25	16 560	21 285	21.1	26.9
313 N AM BAPT CONF	1	103	125*	0.1	0.2
335 ORTH PRESB CH.	2	773	939*	0.9	1.2
349 PENT HOLINESS.	1	28	34*	–	–
353 CHR BRETHREN..	1	60	100	0.1	0.1
371 REF CH IN AM..	8	3 404	4 959	4.9	6.3
403 SALVATION ARMY	1	116	194	0.2	0.2
413 S.D.A.........	1	85	103*	0.1	0.1
419 SO BAPT CONV..	1	59	72*	0.1	0.1
443 UN C OF CHRIST	20	7 845	9 529*	9.4	12.0
449 UN METHODIST..	7	2 715	3 298*	3.3	4.2
453 UN PRES CH USA	3	798	969*	1.0	1.2
469 WELS.........	3	789	1 114	1.1	1.4
TAYLOR	**33**	**4 922**	**12 201***	**64.8**	**100.0**
029 AMER LUTH CH..	2	337	459	2.4	3.8
057 BAPT GEN CONF.	1	186	231*	1.2	1.9
081 CATHOLIC......	9	NA	5 850	31.1	47.9
281 LUTH CH AMER..	2	441	557	3.0	4.6
283 LUTH--MO SYNOD	3	607	845	4.5	6.9
323 OLD ORD AMISH.	4	520	645*	3.4	5.3
443 UN C OF CHRIST	1	213	264*	1.4	2.2
449 UN METHODIST..	2	250	310*	1.6	2.5
453 UN PRES CH USA	4	255	316*	1.7	2.6
469 WELS.........	5	2 113	2 724	14.5	22.3
TREMPEALEAU	**49**	**10 654**	**21 788***	**83.3**	**100.0**
029 AMER LUTH CH..	26	9 188	11 514	44.0	52.8
053 ASSEMB OF GOD.	2	50	99	0.4	0.5
081 CATHOLIC......	10	NA	8 410	32.2	38.6
165 CH OF NAZARENE	1	14	25	0.1	0.1
179 CONSRV BAPT...	2	130	159*	0.6	0.7
283 LUTH--MO SYNOD	1	121	150	0.6	0.7
323 OLD ORD AMISH.	1	130	159*	0.6	0.7
443 UN C OF CHRIST	1	331	404*	1.5	1.9
449 UN METHODIST..	3	272	332*	1.3	1.5
453 UN PRES CH USA	1	377	460*	1.8	2.1
469 WELS.........	1	41	76	0.3	0.3
VERNON	**66**	**11 763**	**17 787***	**69.4**	**100.0**
019 AMER BAPT USA.	1	139	168*	0.7	0.9
029 AMER LUTH CH..	23	6 994	9 014	35.2	50.7
053 ASSEMB OF GOD.	1	38	58	0.2	0.3
081 CATHOLIC......	8	NA	2 780	10.8	15.6
089 CHR & MISS AL.	1	18	33	0.1	0.2
097 CHR CHS&CHS CR	3	375	452*	1.8	2.5
163 CH OF LUTH BR.	1	68	119	0.5	0.7
164 CH LUTH CONF..	1	39	50	0.2	0.3
165 CH OF NAZARENE	1	47	52	0.2	0.3
167 CHS OF CHRIST.	1	30	38	0.1	0.2
181 CONSRV CONGR..	1	453	546*	2.1	3.1
221 FREE METHODIST	1	32	123	0.5	0.7
323 OLD ORD AMISH.	4	520	627*	2.4	3.5
413 S.D.A.........	1	18	22*	0.1	0.1
449 UN METHODIST..	12	1 610	1 941*	7.6	10.9
469 WELS.........	6	1 382	1 764	6.9	9.9
VILAS	**28**	**2 884**	**6 073***	**36.7**	**100.0**
053 ASSEMB OF GOD.	1	60	88	0.5	1.4

NA—Not applicable   *Total adherents estimated from known number of communicant, confirmed, full members.   —Represents a percent less than 0.1.   Percentages may not total due to rounding.

307

Table 4. Churches and Church Membership by County and Denomination: 1980

County and Denomination	Number of churches	Communicant, confirmed, full members	Total adherents		
			Number	Percent of total population	Percent of total adherents
081 CATHOLIC......	7	NA	2 566	15.5	42.3
165 CH OF NAZARENE	2	39	94	0.6	1.5
193 EPISCOPAL.....	1	96	119	0.7	2.0
201 EVAN COV CH AM	1	174	205*	1.2	3.4
203 EVAN FREE CH..	3	97	114*	0.7	1.9
281 LUTH CH AMER..	2	424	527	3.2	8.7
283 LUTH--MO SYNOD	3	737	886	5.4	14.6
443 UN C OF CHRIST	4	602	709*	4.3	11.7
453 UN PRES CH USA	2	146	172*	1.0	2.8
469 WELS..........	2	509	593	3.6	9.8
WALWORTH	76	15 931	33 452*	46.8	100.0
019 AMER BAPT USA.	8	1 344	1 609*	2.3	4.8
029 AMER LUTH CH..	4	1 759	2 316	3.2	6.9
053 ASSEMB OF GOD.	3	167	304	0.4	0.9
057 BAPT GEN CONF.	1	30	36*	0.1	0.1
081 CATHOLIC......	10	NA	12 990	18.2	38.8
105 CHRISTIAN REF.	1	340	642	0.9	1.9
193 EPISCOPAL.....	4	449	643	0.9	1.9
203 EVAN FREE CH..	1	33	40*	0.1	0.1
281 LUTH CH AMER..	7	2 730	3 461	4.8	10.3
283 LUTH--MO SYNOD	5	1 622	2 269	3.2	6.8
371 REF CH IN AM..	1	37	154	0.2	0.5
413 S.D.A.........	1	41	49*	0.1	0.1
435 UNITARIAN-UNIV	1	20	24*	–	0.1
443 UN C OF CHRIST	10	2 449	2 932*	4.1	8.8
449 UN METHODIST..	13	2 558	3 062*	4.3	9.2
453 UN PRES CH USA	1	227	272*	0.4	0.8
469 WELS..........	5	2 125	2 649	3.7	7.9
WASHBURN	28	2 859	5 765*	43.8	100.0
029 AMER LUTH CH..	4	987	1 316	10.0	22.8
053 ASSEMB OF GOD.	1	32	69	0.5	1.2
081 CATHOLIC......	7	NA	1 801	13.7	31.2
089 CHR & MISS AL.	2	45	190	1.4	3.3
165 CH OF NAZARENE	2	85	217	1.6	3.8
193 EPISCOPAL.....	3	135	165	1.3	2.9
281 LUTH CH AMER..	1	324	429	3.3	7.4
283 LUTH--MO SYNOD	2	412	559	4.2	9.7
413 S.D.A.........	1	23	28*	0.2	0.5
443 UN C OF CHRIST	1	69	84*	0.6	1.5
449 UN METHODIST..	4	747	907*	6.9	15.7
WASHINGTON	69	17 598	55 508*	65.4	100.0
029 AMER LUTH CH..	3	1 390	1 890	2.2	3.4
053 ASSEMB OF GOD.	1	190	350	0.4	0.6
081 CATHOLIC......	21	NA	31 162	36.7	56.1
127 CH GOD (CLEVE)	1	41	51*	0.1	0.1
151 L-D SAINTS....	1	NA	350	0.4	0.6
165 CH OF NAZARENE	1	17	63	0.1	0.1
167 CHS OF CHRIST.	1	37	59	0.1	0.1
175 CONGR CHR CHS.	1	58	73*	0.1	0.1
193 EPISCOPAL.....	2	271	389	0.5	0.7
209 EVAN LUTH SYN.	1	240	314	0.4	0.6
281 LUTH CH AMER..	4	2 401	3 558	4.2	6.4
283 LUTH--MO SYNOD	4	2 942	4 112	4.8	7.4
443 UN C OF CHRIST	13	2 915	3 644*	4.3	6.6
449 UN METHODIST..	4	1 996	2 495*	2.9	4.5
453 UN PRES CH USA	1	41	51*	0.1	0.1
469 WELS..........	10	5 059	6 947	8.2	12.5
WAUKESHA	175	56 929	188 733*	67.3	100.0
019 AMER BAPT USA.	4	899	1 108*	0.4	0.6
029 AMER LUTH CH..	13	8 041	10 992	3.9	5.8
053 ASSEMB OF GOD.	3	952	1 525	0.5	0.8
057 BAPT GEN CONF.	1	10	12*	–	–
081 CATHOLIC......	29	NA	110 761	39.5	58.7
089 CHR & MISS AL.	1	134	295	0.1	0.2
093 CHR CH (DISC).	1	50	69	–	–
097 CHR CHS&CHS CR	2	197	243*	0.1	0.1
105 CHRISTIAN REF.	1	183	316	0.1	0.2
127 CH GOD (CLEVE)	2	43	53*	–	–
151 L-D SAINTS....	4	NA	2 280	0.8	1.2
165 CH OF NAZARENE	2	104	201	0.1	0.1
167 CHS OF CHRIST.	1	95	140	–	0.1
175 CONGR CHR CHS.	3	484	596*	0.2	0.3
179 CONSRV BAPT...	1	50	62*	–	–
193 EPISCOPAL.....	11	2 367	3 142	1.1	1.7
203 EVAN FREE CH..	3	120	148*	0.1	0.1
208 EVAN LUTH ASSN	1	636	932	0.3	0.5
209 EVAN LUTH SYN.	1	340	433	0.2	0.2
221 FREE METHODIST	1	115	222	0.1	0.1
281 LUTH CH AMER..	14	7 741	10 859	3.9	5.8
283 LUTH--MO SYNOD	14	10 031	13 143	4.7	7.0
285 MENNONITE CH..	1	19	23*	–	–
313 N AM BAPT CONF	1	262	323*	0.1	0.2
335 ORTH PRESB CH.	1	100	123*	–	0.1
371 REF CH IN AM..	1	139	249	0.1	0.1
403 SALVATION ARMY	1	93	160	0.1	0.1
413 S.D.A.........	1	98	121*	–	0.1
419 SO BAPT CONV..	1	96	118*	–	0.1
435 UNITARIAN-UNIV	2	317	391*	0.1	0.2
443 UN C OF CHRIST	12	4 731	5 829*	2.1	3.1
449 UN METHODIST..	13	5 963	7 347*	2.6	3.9
453 UN PRES CH USA	12	3 241	3 993*	1.4	2.1
469 WELS..........	16	9 278	12 524	4.5	6.6
WAUPACA	64	21 195	35 366*	82.6	100.0
029 AMER LUTH CH..	16	7 432	10 018	23.4	28.3
053 ASSEMB OF GOD.	2	206	283	0.7	0.8

County and Denomination	Number of churches	Communicant, confirmed, full members	Total adherents		
			Number	Percent of total population	Percent of total adherents
081 CATHOLIC......	7	NA	7 755	18.1	21.9
123 CH GOD (ANDER)	1	20	60	0.1	0.2
167 CHS OF CHRIST.	2	75	95	0.2	0.3
193 EPISCOPAL.....	2	185	224	0.5	0.6
203 EVAN FREE CH..	1	49	59*	0.1	0.2
209 EVAN LUTH SYN.	2	154	223	0.5	0.6
281 LUTH CH AMER..	1	311	411	1.0	1.2
283 LUTH--MO SYNOD	9	4 531	5 753	13.4	16.3
413 S.D.A.........	2	38	46*	0.1	0.1
443 UN C OF CHRIST	4	738	895*	2.1	2.5
449 UN METHODIST..	9	2 137	2 592*	6.1	7.3
453 UN PRES CH USA	1	189	229*	0.5	0.6
469 WELS..........	5	5 130	6 723	15.7	19.0
WAUSHARA	39	5 447	9 677*	52.2	100.0
019 AMER BAPT USA.	2	138	166*	0.9	1.7
029 AMER LUTH CH..	6	1 374	1 972	10.6	20.4
053 ASSEMB OF GOD.	2	158	251	1.4	2.6
081 CATHOLIC......	4	NA	2 538	13.7	26.2
175 CONGR CHR CHS.	1	27	32*	0.2	0.3
193 EPISCOPAL.....	1	90	137	0.7	1.4
221 FREE METHODIST	1	10	48	0.3	0.5
283 LUTH--MO SYNOD	8	1 496	1 888	10.2	19.5
413 S.D.A.........	2	97	117*	0.6	1.2
443 UN C OF CHRIST	2	211	254*	1.4	2.6
449 UN METHODIST..	7	1 276	1 534*	8.3	15.9
453 UN PRES CH USA	1	92	111*	0.6	1.1
469 WELS..........	2	478	629	3.4	6.5
WINNEBAGO	91	37 053	83 096*	63.1	100.0
019 AMER BAPT USA.	4	441	527*	0.4	0.6
029 AMER LUTH CH..	10	9 629	13 090	9.9	15.8
053 ASSEMB OF GOD.	4	266	472	0.4	0.6
081 CATHOLIC......	13	NA	35 197	26.7	42.4
097 CHR CHS&CHS CR	1	75	90*	0.1	0.1
127 CH GOD (CLEVE)	1	12	14*	–	–
151 L-D SAINTS....	1	NA	132	0.1	0.2
164 CH LUTH CONF..	1	14	22	–	–
165 CH OF NAZARENE	1	19	11	–	–
167 CHS OF CHRIST.	2	67	108	0.1	0.1
181 CONSRV CONGR..	1	254	304*	0.2	0.4
193 EPISCOPAL.....	2	1 516	1 950	1.5	2.3
226 FRIENDS-USA...	1	13	16*	–	–
271 REFORM JUDAISM	1	90	108*	0.1	0.1
281 LUTH CH AMER..	6	4 639	6 153	4.7	7.4
283 LUTH--MO SYNOD	6	3 653	4 806	3.6	5.8
403 SALVATION ARMY	1	90	103	0.1	0.1
413 S.D.A.........	1	27	32*	–	–
435 UNITARIAN-UNIV	1	10	12*	–	–
443 UN C OF CHRIST	5	2 494	2 983*	2.3	3.6
449 UN METHODIST..	8	3 437	4 111*	3.1	4.9
453 UN PRES CH USA	5	2 377	2 843*	2.2	3.4
469 WELS..........	15	7 930	10 012	7.6	12.0
WOOD	79	18 785	53 638*	73.7	100.0
019 AMER BAPT USA.	1	153	188*	0.3	0.4
029 AMER LUTH CH..	2	1 151	1 529	2.1	2.9
053 ASSEMB OF GOD.	2	326	556	0.8	1.0
057 BAPT GEN CONF.	1	69	85*	0.1	0.2
081 CATHOLIC......	22	NA	28 750	39.5	53.6
089 CHR & MISS AL.	1	79	79	0.1	0.1
105 CHRISTIAN REF.	1	88	131	0.2	0.2
151 L-D SAINTS....	1	NA	258	0.4	0.5
165 CH OF NAZARENE	1	27	57	0.1	0.1
167 CHS OF CHRIST.	3	150	190	0.3	0.4
193 EPISCOPAL.....	2	387	452	0.6	0.8
203 EVAN FREE CH..	2	167	205*	0.3	0.4
274 LAT EVAN LUTH.	1	35	36	–	0.1
281 LUTH CH AMER..	2	983	1 354	1.9	2.5
283 LUTH--MO SYNOD	13	8 185	10 950	15.0	20.4
293 MORAV CH-NORTH	5	967	1 210	1.7	2.3
371 REF CH IN AM..	1	131	237	0.3	0.4
413 S.D.A.........	3	347	426*	0.6	0.8
435 UNITARIAN-UNIV	1	26	32*	–	0.1
443 UN C OF CHRIST	6	1 643	2 015*	2.8	3.8
449 UN METHODIST..	4	1 682	2 063*	2.8	3.8
453 UN PRES CH USA	2	667	818*	1.1	1.5
469 WELS..........	2	1 522	2 017	2.8	3.8

WYOMING

County and Denomination	Number of churches	Communicant, confirmed, full members	Total adherents		
			Number	Percent of total population	Percent of total adherents
THE STATE.....	628	77 189	207 484*	44.1	100.0
ALBANY	29	4 684	10 984*	37.8	100.0
019 AMER BAPT USA.	1	474	558*	1.9	5.1
053 ASSEMB OF GOD.	3	104	195	0.7	1.8
081 CATHOLIC......	3	NA	3 760	12.9	34.2
093 CHR CH (DISC).	1	179	275	0.9	2.5
151 L-D SAINTS....	4	NA	1 159	4.0	10.6

NA—Not applicable   *Total adherents estimated from known number of communicant, confirmed, full members.   —Represents a percent less than 0.1.   Percentages may not total due to rounding.

Table 4. Churches and Church Membership by County and Denomination: 1980

County and Denomination	Number of churches	Communicant, confirmed, full members	Total adherents		
			Number	Percent of total population	Percent of total adherents
165 CH OF NAZARENE	1	53	106	0.4	1.0
167 CHS OF CHRIST.	1	95	175	0.6	1.6
179 CONSRV BAPT...	1	535	630*	2.2	5.7
193 EPISCOPAL.....	2	393	583	2.0	5.3
281 LUTH CH AMER..	1	346	476	1.6	4.3
283 LUTH--MO SYNOD	2	410	595	2.0	5.4
403 SALVATION ARMY	1	53	67	0.2	0.6
413 S.D.A.........	1	185	218*	0.8	2.0
419 SO BAPT CONV..	3	435	512*	1.8	4.7
435 UNITARIAN-UNIV	1	40	47*	0.2	0.4
443 UN C OF CHRIST	1	145	171*	0.6	1.6
449 UN METHODIST..	1	642	756*	2.6	6.9
453 UN PRES CH USA	1	595	701*	2.4	6.4
BIG HORN	**30**	**1 327**	**8 116***	**68.2**	**100.0**
019 AMER BAPT USA.	2	95	119*	1.0	1.5
053 ASSEMB OF GOD.	2	28	67	0.6	0.8
081 CATHOLIC......	3	NA	2 486	20.9	30.6
089 CHR & MISS AL.	1	19	45	0.4	0.6
151 L-D SAINTS....	8	NA	3 779	31.8	46.6
165 CH OF NAZARENE	1	18	25	0.2	0.3
167 CHS OF CHRIST.	1	8	16	0.1	0.2
193 EPISCOPAL.....	2	93	191	1.6	2.4
283 LUTH--MO SYNOD	3	505	684	5.7	8.4
413 S.D.A.........	1	30	38*	0.3	0.5
419 SO BAPT CONV..	1	141	177*	1.5	2.2
449 UN METHODIST..	4	303	380*	3.2	4.7
453 UN PRES CH USA	1	87	109*	0.9	1.3
CAMPBELL	**19**	**3 515**	**7 569***	**31.1**	**100.0**
017 AMER BAPT ASSN	1	50	50	0.2	0.7
019 AMER BAPT USA.	1	172	220*	0.9	2.9
029 AMER LUTH CH..	1	172	278	1.1	3.7
053 ASSEMB OF GOD.	2	241	502	2.1	6.6
081 CATHOLIC......	1	NA	1 840	7.6	24.3
097 CHR CHS&CHS CR	1	375	480*	2.0	6.3
151 L-D SAINTS....	3	NA	708	2.9	9.4
167 CHS OF CHRIST.	1	135	187	0.8	2.5
193 EPISCOPAL.....	2	140	298	1.2	3.9
283 LUTH--MO SYNOD	1	447	700	2.9	9.2
329 OPEN BIBLE STD	1	450	600	2.5	7.9
413 S.D.A.........	1	83	106*	0.4	1.4
419 SO BAPT CONV..	1	300	384*	1.6	5.1
449 UN METHODIST..	1	77	99*	0.4	1.3
453 UN PRES CH USA	1	873	1 117*	4.6	14.8
CARBON	**41**	**2 716**	**10 510***	**48.0**	**100.0**
019 AMER BAPT USA.	1	254	319*	1.5	3.0
053 ASSEMB OF GOD.	5	251	419	1.9	4.0
081 CATHOLIC......	5	NA	5 425	24.8	51.6
089 CHR & MISS AL.	1	2	22	0.1	0.2
151 L-D SAINTS....	6	NA	1 262	5.8	12.0
165 CH OF NAZARENE	1	32	107	0.5	1.0
167 CHS OF CHRIST.	1	52	92	0.4	0.9
193 EPISCOPAL.....	5	491	722	3.3	6.9
283 LUTH--MO SYNOD	4	300	465	2.1	4.4
413 S.D.A.........	1	68	85*	0.4	0.8
419 SO BAPT CONV..	5	397	499*	2.3	4.7
449 UN METHODIST..	3	388	488*	2.2	4.6
453 UN PRES CH USA	3	481	605*	2.8	5.8
CONVERSE	**20**	**1 744**	**3 838***	**27.3**	**100.0**
019 AMER BAPT USA.	2	376	483*	3.4	12.6
053 ASSEMB OF GOD.	2	58	122	0.9	3.2
081 CATHOLIC......	3	NA	936	6.7	24.4
097 CHR CHS&CHS CR	3	96	123*	0.9	3.2
151 L-D SAINTS....	2	NA	522	3.7	13.6
193 EPISCOPAL.....	2	215	338	2.4	8.8
283 LUTH--MO SYNOD	2	157	232	1.6	6.0
419 SO BAPT CONV..	2	299	384*	2.7	10.0
443 UN C OF CHRIST	1	182	234*	1.7	6.1
449 UN METHODIST..	1	361	464*	3.3	12.1
CROOK	**15**	**841**	**1 599***	**30.1**	**100.0**
019 AMER BAPT USA.	1	168	210*	4.0	13.1
053 ASSEMB OF GOD.	3	44	71	1.3	4.4
081 CATHOLIC......	3	NA	400	7.5	25.0
151 L-D SAINTS....	1	NA	76	1.4	4.8
167 CHS OF CHRIST.	1	20	38	0.7	2.4
193 EPISCOPAL.....	1	103	145	2.7	9.1
283 LUTH--MO SYNOD	2	198	274	5.2	17.1
413 S.D.A.........	1	52	65*	1.2	4.1
449 UN METHODIST..	1	157	196*	3.7	12.3
453 UN PRES CH USA	1	99	124*	2.3	7.8
FREMONT	**59**	**6 123**	**17 499***	**43.5**	**100.0**
019 AMER BAPT USA.	1	218	273*	0.7	1.6
029 AMER LUTH CH..	2	413	655	1.6	3.7
053 ASSEMB OF GOD.	3	111	204	0.5	1.2
081 CATHOLIC......	8	NA	5 175	12.9	29.6
089 CHR & MISS AL.	1	30	80	0.2	0.5
097 CHR CHS&CHS CR	2	95	119*	0.3	0.7
151 L-D SAINTS....	8	NA	2 719	6.8	15.5
165 CH OF NAZARENE	3	254	469	1.2	2.7
167 CHS OF CHRIST.	4	154	224	0.6	1.3
179 CONSRV BAPT...	1	535	669*	1.7	3.8
193 EPISCOPAL.....	7	1 131	2 802	7.0	16.0
263 INT FOURSQ GOS	1	?	?	?	?
283 LUTH--MO SYNOD	5	772	1 084	2.7	6.2
353 CHR BRETHREN..	1	20	20	–	0.1
381 REF PRES-EVAN.	1	49	78	0.2	0.4
413 S.D.A.........	2	170	213*	0.5	1.2
419 SO BAPT CONV..	3	635	794*	2.0	4.5
449 UN METHODIST..	4	1 266	1 583*	3.9	9.0
453 UN PRES CH USA	2	270	338*	0.8	1.9
GOSHEN	**22**	**3 449**	**5 539***	**46.0**	**100.0**
019 AMER BAPT USA.	1	262	318*	2.6	5.7
053 ASSEMB OF GOD.	2	48	75	0.6	1.4
057 BAPT GEN CONF.	3	340	413*	3.4	7.5
063 BEREAN FUND CH	1	55	67*	0.6	1.2
081 CATHOLIC......	2	NA	1 000	8.3	18.1
097 CHR CHS&CHS CR	2	58	70*	0.6	1.3
151 L-D SAINTS....	1	NA	235	2.0	4.2
165 CH OF NAZARENE	1	27	51	0.4	0.9
193 EPISCOPAL.....	1	143	230	1.9	4.2
283 LUTH--MO SYNOD	1	352	454	3.8	8.2
413 S.D.A.........	1	130	158*	1.3	2.9
443 UN C OF CHRIST	1	375	455*	3.8	8.2
449 UN METHODIST..	1	552	670*	5.6	12.1
453 UN PRES CH USA	4	1 107	1 343*	11.2	24.2
HOT SPRINGS	**11**	**1 057**	**2 327***	**40.8**	**100.0**
019 AMER BAPT USA.	1	390	474*	8.3	20.4
053 ASSEMB OF GOD.	1	45	77	1.3	3.3
081 CATHOLIC......	1	NA	475	8.3	20.4
151 L-D SAINTS....	1	NA	332	5.8	14.3
167 CHS OF CHRIST.	1	45	60	1.1	2.6
193 EPISCOPAL.....	1	129	329	5.8	14.1
263 INT FOURSQ GOS	1	?	?	?	?
283 LUTH--MO SYNOD	1	155	223	3.9	9.6
413 S.D.A.........	1	24	29*	0.5	1.2
449 UN METHODIST..	1	146	178*	3.1	7.6
453 UN PRES CH USA	1	123	150*	2.6	6.4
JOHNSON	**11**	**1 133**	**2 555***	**38.1**	**100.0**
053 ASSEMB OF GOD.	1	48	48	0.7	1.9
081 CATHOLIC......	1	NA	900	13.4	35.2
151 L-D SAINTS....	1	NA	139	2.1	5.4
167 CHS OF CHRIST.	1	12	26	0.4	1.0
193 EPISCOPAL.....	1	354	520	7.8	20.4
281 LUTH CH AMER..	1	176	239	3.6	9.4
283 LUTH--MO SYNOD	1	69	99	1.5	3.9
413 S.D.A.........	1	90	111*	1.7	4.3
443 UN C OF CHRIST	1	184	227*	3.4	8.9
449 UN METHODIST..	2	200	246*	3.7	9.6
LARAMIE	**69**	**15 523**	**33 445***	**48.7**	**100.0**
017 AMER BAPT ASSN	1	50	50	0.1	0.1
019 AMER BAPT USA.	3	1 838	2 253*	3.3	6.7
029 AMER LUTH CH..	1	313	468	0.7	1.4
053 ASSEMB OF GOD.	5	370	702	1.0	2.1
057 BAPT GEN CONF.	2	320	392*	0.6	1.2
063 BEREAN FUND CH	1	74	91*	0.1	0.3
071 BRETHREN (ASH)	1	40	49*	0.1	0.1
081 CATHOLIC......	7	NA	11 185	16.3	33.4
089 CHR & MISS AL.	1	53	100	0.1	0.3
093 CHR CH (DISC).	1	552	707	1.0	2.1
097 CHR CHS&CHS CR	1	150	184*	0.3	0.6
127 CH GOD (CLEVE)	1	78	96*	0.1	0.3
151 L-D SAINTS....	5	NA	2 190	3.2	6.5
164 CH LUTH CONF..	1	77	110	0.2	0.3
165 CH OF NAZARENE	2	202	409	0.6	1.2
167 CHS OF CHRIST.	2	320	560	0.8	1.7
175 CONGR CHR CHS.	1	1 400	1 716*	2.5	5.1
193 EPISCOPAL.....	2	1 235	1 396	2.0	4.2
201 EVAN COV CH AM	1	41	50*	0.1	0.1
221 FREE METHODIST	1	11	90	0.1	0.3
244 GRACE BRETHREN	1	12	15*	–	–
263 INT FOURSQ GOS	1	?	?	?	?
281 LUTH CH AMER..	2	835	1 110	1.6	3.3
283 LUTH--MO SYNOD	4	1 362	1 824	2.7	5.5
290 METRO COMM CHS	0	20	40	0.1	0.1
329 OPEN BIBLE STD	1	85	148	0.2	0.4
335 ORTH PRESB CH.	1	24	29*	–	0.1
403 SALVATION ARMY	1	113	175	0.3	0.5
413 S.D.A.........	2	175	214*	0.3	0.6
419 SO BAPT CONV..	3	1 832	2 245*	3.3	6.7
435 UNITARIAN-UNIV	1	24	29*	–	0.1
443 UN C OF CHRIST	1	180	221*	0.3	0.7
449 UN METHODIST..	7	2 303	2 822*	4.1	8.4
453 UN PRES CH USA	3	1 373	1 683*	2.5	5.0
469 WELS..........	1	61	92	0.1	0.3
LINCOLN	**28**	**388**	**8 586***	**70.5**	**100.0**
053 ASSEMB OF GOD.	1	33	52	0.4	0.6
081 CATHOLIC......	2	NA	985	8.1	11.5
151 L-D SAINTS....	17	NA	6 974	57.3	81.2
167 CHS OF CHRIST.	1	6	8	0.1	0.1
193 EPISCOPAL.....	2	49	162	1.3	1.9
203 EVAN FREE CH..	1	23	30*	0.2	0.3
283 LUTH--MO SYNOD	1	139	194	1.6	2.3
419 SO BAPT CONV..	2	62	81*	0.7	0.9
449 UN METHODIST..	1	76	100	0.8	1.2
NATRONA	**54**	**12 241**	**30 316***	**42.2**	**100.0**
019 AMER BAPT USA.	3	618	763*	1.1	2.5
029 AMER LUTH CH..	2	1 098	1 562	2.2	5.2

NA— Not applicable
*Total adherents estimated from known number of communicant, confirmed, full members.
—Represents a percent less than 0.1.
Percentages may not total due to rounding.

Table 4. Churches and Church Membership by County and Denomination: 1980

County and Denomination	Number of churches	Communicant, confirmed, full members	Total adherents Number	Percent of total population	Percent of total adherents
053 ASSEMB OF GOD.	3	307	547	0.8	1.8
081 CATHOLIC......	4	NA	11 305	15.7	37.3
093 CHR CH (DISC).	1	593	633	0.9	2.1
097 CHR CHS&CHS CR	4	332	410*	0.6	1.4
123 CH GOD (ANDER)	2	190	570	0.8	1.9
127 CH GOD (CLEVE)	1	154	190*	0.3	0.6
151 L-D SAINTS....	6	NA	2 677	3.7	8.8
165 CH OF NAZARENE	1	251	437	0.6	1.4
167 CHS OF CHRIST.	3	180	230	0.3	0.8
179 CONSRV BAPT...	1	535	660*	0.9	2.2
193 EPISCOPAL.....	3	635	952	1.3	3.1
203 EVAN FREE CH..	1	51	63*	0.1	0.2
263 INT FOURSQ GOS	1	42	52*	0.1	0.2
281 LUTH CH AMER..	1	435	594	0.8	2.0
283 LUTH--MO SYNOD	2	898	1 281	1.8	4.2
329 OPEN BIBLE STD	2	85	145	0.2	0.5
403 SALVATION ARMY	1	58	115	0.2	0.4
413 S.D.A.........	1	297	366*	0.5	1.2
419 SO BAPT CONV..	4	2 267	2 797*	3.9	9.2
443 UN C OF CHRIST	1	132	163*	0.2	0.5
449 UN METHODIST..	3	1 906	2 352*	3.3	7.8
453 UN PRES CH USA	3	1 177	1 452*	2.0	4.8
NIOBRARA	11	683	1 171*	40.0	100.0
019 AMER BAPT USA.	1	119	143*	4.9	12.2
081 CATHOLIC......	1	NA	223	7.6	19.0
089 CHR & MISS AL.	2	40	74	2.5	6.3
097 CHR CHS&CHS CR	1	35	42*	1.4	3.6
151 L-D SAINTS....	1	NA	52	1.8	4.4
193 EPISCOPAL.....	1	53	67	2.3	5.7
283 LUTH--MO SYNOD	1	148	196	6.7	16.7
329 OPEN BIBLE STD	1	40	75	2.6	6.4
413 S.D.A.........	1	32	39*	1.3	3.3
443 UN C OF CHRIST	1	216	260*	8.9	22.2
PARK	37	5 404	11 424*	52.8	100.0
029 AMER LUTH CH..	2	468	722	3.3	6.3
053 ASSEMB OF GOD.	2	103	210	1.0	1.8
081 CATHOLIC......	3	NA	2 058	9.5	18.0
089 CHR & MISS AL.	1	56	86	0.4	0.8
097 CHR CHS&CHS CR	1	25	31*	0.1	0.3
123 CH GOD (ANDER)	2	57	171	0.8	1.5
151 L-D SAINTS....	7	NA	2 251	10.4	19.7
165 CH OF NAZARENE	2	107	139	0.6	1.2
167 CHS OF CHRIST.	2	64	79	0.4	0.7
179 CONSRV BAPT...	2	1 070	1 311*	6.1	11.5
193 EPISCOPAL.....	3	414	558	2.6	4.9
283 LUTH--MO SYNOD	2	398	572	2.6	5.0
413 S.D.A.........	1	116	142*	0.7	1.2
419 SO BAPT CONV..	3	418	512*	2.4	4.5
449 UN METHODIST..	2	928	1 137*	5.3	10.0
453 UN PRES CH USA	2	1 180	1 445*	6.7	12.6
PLATTE	18	1 509	3 122*	26.1	100.0
029 AMER LUTH CH..	1	123	202	1.7	6.5
053 ASSEMB OF GOD.	1	29	60	0.5	1.9
063 BEREAN FUND CH	1	10	12*	0.1	0.4
081 CATHOLIC......	4	NA	1 122	9.4	35.9
097 CHR CHS&CHS CR	1	150	186*	1.6	6.0
165 CH OF NAZARENE	1	37	62	0.5	2.0
193 EPISCOPAL.....	3	223	294	2.5	9.4
283 LUTH--MO SYNOD	1	179	244	2.0	7.8
419 SO BAPT CONV..	1	191	237*	2.0	7.6
443 UN C OF CHRIST	1	170	211*	1.8	6.8
449 UN METHODIST..	2	268	332*	2.8	10.6
453 UN PRES CH USA	1	129	160*	1.3	5.1
SHERIDAN	29	5 009	10 462*	41.8	100.0
053 ASSEMB OF GOD.	1	83	124	0.5	1.2
081 CATHOLIC......	5	NA	2 800	11.2	26.8
089 CHR & MISS AL.	1	8	32	0.1	0.3
093 CHR CH (DISC).	1	287	466	1.9	4.5
097 CHR CHS&CHS CR	1	45	55*	0.2	0.5
151 L-D SAINTS....	3	NA	869	3.5	8.3
165 CH OF NAZARENE	1	47	58	0.2	0.6
167 CHS OF CHRIST.	1	35	60	0.2	0.6
175 CONGR CHR CHS.	1	123	150*	0.6	1.4
179 CONSRV BAPT...	1	535	654*	2.6	6.3
193 EPISCOPAL.....	1	955	1 440	5.7	13.8
263 INT FOURSQ GOS	1	97	119	0.5	1.1
281 LUTH CH AMER..	1	483	720	2.9	6.9
283 LUTH--MO SYNOD	1	426	534	2.1	5.1
329 OPEN BIBLE STD	1	100	200	0.8	1.9
353 CHR BRETHREN..	1	20	20	0.1	0.2
403 SALVATION ARMY	1	53	67	0.3	0.6
413 S.D.A.........	1	177	217*	0.9	2.1
419 SO BAPT CONV..	1	77	94*	0.4	0.9
443 UN C OF CHRIST	1	241	295*	1.2	2.8
449 UN METHODIST..	2	695	850*	3.4	8.1
453 UN PRES CH USA	1	522	638*	2.5	6.1
SUBLETTE	12	524	1 980*	43.5	100.0
053 ASSEMB OF GOD.	1	15	17	0.4	0.9
081 CATHOLIC......	2	NA	600	13.2	30.3
151 L-D SAINTS....	2	NA	655	14.4	33.1
175 CONGR CHR CHS.	1	128	160*	3.5	8.1
193 EPISCOPAL.....	2	159	243	5.3	12.3
283 LUTH--MO SYNOD	1	81	129	2.8	6.5
413 S.D.A.........	1	13	16*	0.4	0.8
419 SO BAPT CONV..	1	32	40*	0.9	2.0
443 UN C OF CHRIST	1	96	120*	2.6	6.1
SWEETWATER	42	3 467	17 752*	42.5	100.0
019 AMER BAPT USA.	2	234	299*	0.7	1.7
053 ASSEMB OF GOD.	3	120	290	0.7	1.6
081 CATHOLIC......	4	NA	7 140	17.1	40.2
097 CHR CHS&CHS CR	1	44	56*	0.1	0.3
151 L-D SAINTS....	12	NA	5 604	13.4	31.6
165 CH OF NAZARENE	2	71	195	0.5	1.1
167 CHS OF CHRIST.	3	104	175	0.4	1.0
193 EPISCOPAL.....	3	486	817	2.0	4.6
203 EVAN FREE CH..	1	55	70*	0.2	0.4
281 LUTH CH AMER..	1	117	187	0.4	1.1
283 LUTH--MO SYNOD	2	335	488	1.2	2.7
413 S.D.A.........	1	80	102*	0.2	0.6
419 SO BAPT CONV..	4	771	986*	2.4	5.6
443 UN C OF CHRIST	2	841	1 076*	2.6	6.1
449 UN METHODIST..	1	209	267*	0.6	1.5
TETON	10	546	2 707*	28.9	100.0
019 AMER BAPT USA.	1	220	260*	2.8	9.6
053 ASSEMB OF GOD.	1	15	29	0.3	1.1
081 CATHOLIC......	2	NA	500	5.3	18.5
151 L-D SAINTS....	3	NA	1 402	15.0	51.8
167 CHS OF CHRIST.	1	40	45	0.5	1.7
193 EPISCOPAL.....	1	153	321	3.4	11.9
283 LUTH--MO SYNOD	1	118	150	1.6	5.5
UINTA	24	696	7 384*	56.7	100.0
019 AMER BAPT USA.	1	55	71*	0.5	1.0
081 CATHOLIC......	3	NA	800	6.1	10.8
151 L-D SAINTS....	12	NA	5 658	43.5	76.6
165 CH OF NAZARENE	1	?	?	?	?
167 CHS OF CHRIST.	1	6	8	0.1	0.1
193 EPISCOPAL.....	1	121	179	1.4	2.4
413 S.D.A.........	1	36	47*	0.4	0.6
419 SO BAPT CONV..	2	301	391*	3.0	5.3
453 UN PRES CH USA	2	177	230*	1.8	3.1
WASHAKIE	22	3 121	5 914*	62.3	100.0
019 AMER BAPT USA.	1	336	420*	4.4	7.1
029 AMER LUTH CH..	1	141	210	2.2	3.6
053 ASSEMB OF GOD.	3	186	263	2.8	4.4
081 CATHOLIC......	1	NA	750	7.9	12.7
097 CHR CHS&CHS CR	1	75	94*	1.0	1.6
123 CH GOD (ANDER)	1	82	246	2.6	4.2
151 L-D SAINTS....	3	NA	914	9.6	15.5
165 CH OF NAZARENE	1	27	62	0.7	1.0
167 CHS OF CHRIST.	1	85	125	1.3	2.1
193 EPISCOPAL.....	1	220	351	3.7	5.9
283 LUTH--MO SYNOD	1	160	218	2.3	3.7
413 S.D.A.........	2	99	124*	1.3	2.1
419 SO BAPT CONV..	1	425	531*	5.6	9.0
443 UN C OF CHRIST	1	350	437*	4.6	7.4
449 UN METHODIST..	2	799	999*	10.5	16.9
453 UN PRES CH USA	1	136	170*	1.8	2.9
WESTON	15	1 489	2 685*	37.8	100.0
029 AMER LUTH CH..	1	170	277	3.9	10.3
053 ASSEMB OF GOD.	2	124	220	3.1	8.2
057 BAPT GEN CONF.	1	85	106*	1.5	3.9
081 CATHOLIC......	1	NA	450	6.3	16.8
097 CHR CHS&CHS CR	1	30	37*	0.5	1.4
123 CH GOD (ANDER)	1	10	30	0.4	1.1
151 L-D SAINTS....	1	NA	191	2.7	7.1
193 EPISCOPAL.....	2	65	119	1.7	4.4
413 S.D.A.........	2	93	116*	1.6	4.3
419 SO BAPT CONV..	1	166	207*	2.9	7.7
449 UN METHODIST..	2	746	932*	13.1	34.7

NA—Not applicable   *Total adherents estimated from known number of communicant, confirmed, full members.   —Represents a percent less than 0.1.   Percentages may not total due to rounding.

Appendices

Appendix A

DESCRIPTIVE DEFINITIONS OF CHURCHES AND CHURCH MEMBERSHIP

[The word "communicants" in the table below refers to "communicant, confirmed, full members."]

001   Advent Christian Church
      Churches: officially organized congregations.
      Communicants: baptized believers, active and inactive.

005   African Methodist Episcopal Zion Church
      Churches: individual congregations.
      Communicants: regular members with full membership status.
      Adherents: probationary, baptized children, full members.

017   American Baptist Association
      Churches: regularly organized churches and mission points.
      Communicants: those baptized into each church or mission and reported, plus members added by letter or statement.

019   American Baptist Churches in the U.S.A.
      Churches: all congregations cooperating with ABC/USA.
      Communicants: the total membership reported by each congregation (using the Baptist definition of members as baptized believers), plus the judiciary estimated membership for any non-reporting churches.

029   American Lutheran Church, The
      Churches: member congregations on the congregational roster of the ALC.
      Communicants: confirmed members.
      Adherents: baptized members.

049   Armenian Apostolic Church of America (Eastern Prelacy)
      Communicants: dues paying members.
      Adherents: dues paying members, plus non-paying members.

053   Assemblies of God
      Churches: local congregations who are in full fellowship with a district council of the Assemblies of God. Does not include independent churches served by an Assemblies of God minister or branch churches under the auspices of another local assembly.

      Communicants: persons who have been approved for membership by the local church. Requirements for membership may vary slightly from church to church. Usual criteria for acceptance as a member is a testimony of faith in Christ as personal Saviour, baptism in water, a consistent moral life, and committment to support the church in attendance, finance, and personal involvement in its ministries. This figure may include some children under 12; however, it would be a very slight number.
      Adherents: the instruction letter accompanying the Annual Church Ministries Report form sent to the local churches defined adherents as "The total number of persons who consider your church their church home or to whom your church regularly ministers whether they are members or not. Count all ages including children." If a church reported fewer adherents than their membership, Sunday morning average attendance, or Sunday school enrollment, the computer used the higher figure in tabulating adherents.

055   Associate Reformed Presbyterian Church (General Synod)
      Churches: a congregation is a company of Christians, with their children, associated together according to the Scriptures for worship and work in the name of Christ, subscribing to a form of church government, and choosing and ordaining some to perform selected ministries.
      Communicants: the communicant church member is one who has been baptized, who has made public his profession of faith in Jesus Christ and who has submitted his life to his lordship and to the ministry of the Church.
      Adherents: includes communicant members and those children of believers who have not yet made public their profession of faith.

057   Baptist General Conference
      Churches: the 696 churches have been officially accepted by the Conference in session at annual meetings.
      Communicants: all members counted have joined the local church through baptism or transfer of letters.

059   Baptist Missionary Association of America
      Churches: organized churches, mission churches not included.
      Communicants: baptized members.

071   Brethren Church (Ashland, Ohio)
      Churches: congregations that have voted to unite with our conference and have been approved for organization by the district conference.
      Communicants: must profess faith in Jesus Christ as Lord, the Son of God, repent and be baptized by

immersion, and be confirmed by the laying on of hands.

083 Christ Catholic Church
Churches: organized congregations.
Communicants: must be confirmed and communing regularly.
Adherents: baptized or baptized and confirmed.

089 Christian and Missionary Alliance, The
Churches: local congregations of believers meeting under the guidance of a pastor who has been recognized as being associated with the Christian and Missionary Alliance.
Communicants: persons formally received into membership of a local congregation.
Adherents: total adherents includes members plus those persons who regularly attend and support the local congregation.

093 Christian Church (Disciples of Christ)
Churches: a congregation which meets regularly for worship, and which is listed in our denominational *Year Book and Directory.*
Communicants: the term we use is participating member. A participating member is one who exercises a continuing interest in one or more of the following ways: attendance, giving, activity, and spiritual concern for the fellowship of the congregation regardless of the place of residence.
Adherents: includes both participating members, as defined above; and non-participating members, which is defined as a member who exercises no interest in the fellowship of the congregation, regardless of place of residence. Note: membership in the Christian Church (Disciples of Christ) does not include children below the level of 10-12 years of age.

097 Christian Churches and Churches of Christ
Churches: an organized congregation of Christians that is recorded in the *Directory of the Ministry of the Christian Churches/Churches of Christ* and meeting at one location.
Communicants: baptized believers in Christ who have been officially added to the membership rolls of a church.

105 Christian Reformed Church
Churches: organized and unorganized.
Communicants: professing members.
Adherents: professing and baptized members.

107 Christian Union
Churches: buildings with regular services.
Adherents: total membership of active members plus non-active, but are still on the church rolls.

133 Church of God (Seventh Day), Denver, Colorado, The
Churches: an assembly of 10 or more members with enough qualified personnel for office of elder and deacon.
Communicants: one who has been baptized by immersion and officially taken out membership in the Church of God.

149 Church of Jesus Christ, The (Bickertonites)
Churches: established missions or branches consisting of a minimum of 2 members of the priesthood.
Communicants: baptized members over the age of 13 taking communion.
Adherents: baptized members who are not active members and taking communion. This does not include children and regular participants.

163 Church of the Lutheran Brethren of America
Churches: all member congregations, home mission churches, and independent churches served by Lutheran Brethren pastors.
Communicants: members with full membership status.
Adherents: communicant and non-communicant (i.e., confirmed and/or baptized members).

165 Church of the Nazarene
Churches: local groups organized according to the Nazarene bylaws.
Communicants: full members.
Adherents: total Sunday School enrollment.

167 Churches of Christ
Churches: autonomous congregations of the Restoration movement which do not use instrumental music in worship.
Communicants: baptized believers who are attached to local congregations, nearly all of whom are active in church attendance (Churches of Christ usually keep clean church rolls).
Adherents: unbaptized persons (mostly under age of 12 and children of members) who participate regularly in local church activities.

181 Conservative Congregational Christian Conference
Churches: CCCC member churches in each county.
Communicants: Full members. These represent our only records.

185 Cumberland Presbyterian Church
Churches: organized congregations in the U.S. and organized fellowships with intent of becoming organized congregations in the U.S.
Communicants: confessing members, active in a parish, including U.S. clergy which number 689.
Adherents: confessing members, active and inactive, baptized children, and clergy in the U.S.

193 Episcopal Church, The
Churches: parishes (self supported) and missions (diocesan supported).
Communicants: those who have been confirmed and who are active and in good standing in the parish.
Adherents: all baptized persons, including children, who are active and in good standing in the parish.

197 Evangelical Church of North America, The
Churches: only those formally organized.
Communicants: only have one class of members.

199 Evangelical Congregational Church
Communicants: E. C. Church records only full members.

201 Evangelical Covenant Church of America, The
Churches: organized congregations.
Communicants: regular members with full membership status.

203 Evangelical Free Church of America, The
Churches: those autonomous, legally incorporated congregations which are listed in the official yearbook of the denomination.
Communicants: those persons holding full membership on the rolls of our churches.

208 Evangelical Lutheran Churches, Association of
Churches: congregations of believers gathered around word and sacraments.
Communicants: communicant members.
Adherents: baptized members.

209 Evangelical Lutheran Synod
Churches: all congregations, preaching stations, or missions served by pastors of our affiliation.
Communicants: those who have been accepted as communicant members of our congregations.
Adherents: all those who are under the spiritual care of our pastors.

211 Evangelical Mennonite Brethren Conference
Churches: self-administering congregations.
Communicants: baptized members.
Adherents: regular attendants.

213 Evangelical Mennonite Church, Inc.
Churches: organized congregations with resident pastors.
Communicants: believers' (not infant) baptism necessary to membership. Formal reception into membership.

217 Fire Baptized Holiness Church, (Wesleyan), The
Churches: where worship services are held at least twice a week. They are recognized by the General Church.
Communicants: individuals agreeing to adhere to our doctrine and pay an annual fee.

221 Free Methodist Church of North America
Churches: local congregations with charter from Free Methodist denomination.
Communicants: full members (adults 16 and over) in good standing with membership status in a chartered Free Methodist society (church).
Adherents: all members, full, junior and preparatory and all regular participants not holding membership. Totals were derived by multiplying two recorded figures: (1) member families, and (2) non-member families by the approximate U.S. average family size (approx. 3 members per family used as a base for our purposes).

226 Friends
Churches: Friends Monthly or Preparatory Meetings.
Communicants: Friends are those persons who belong to a Friends Monthly or Preparatory Meeting.

237 General Conference of Mennonite Brethren Churches
Churches: independent congregations of believers desiring affiliation with Mennonite Brethren Conference.
Communicants: baptized believers who desire to affiliate with Mennonite Brethren Churches.

239 General Convention of the New Jerusalem in the U.S.A. "The Swedenborgian Church"
Churches: parishes with buildings for worship and educational programs, i.e. Sunday schools, Bible classes, doctrinal studies, etc.
Communicants: confirmed or full members reported only.

247 Holiness Church of God, Inc., The
Churches: it is a rule of the *Yearbook* that leaders bring or mail the reports of their churches to the annual assembly.
Communicants: as stated in letter reported.
Adherents: more or less from last reporting date.

263 International Church of the Foursquare Gospel
Churches: meeting places in each county.
Communicants: full members.

270 Conservative Judaism
Churches: conservative synagogues which are members of United Synagogues of America.
Communicants: individual adult members.

274 Latvian Evangelical Lutheran Church in America, The
Adherents: confirmed and baptized.

281 Lutheran Church in America
Churches: all congregations that have been officially received by a Synod. Does not include missions in process of formation.
Communicants: persons Grade 7 and above who have been confirmed.
Adherents: all confirmed persons, plus all children baptized but not yet confirmed.

283 Lutheran Church-Missouri Synod, The
Churches: total stations, including organized congregations, and mission stations.
Communicants: confirmed members—persons who have completed confirmation instructions and the rite of confirmation.
Adherents: baptized members; includes all persons (including children/infants) having received the rite of baptism whether or not they have also been confirmed.

285 Mennonite Church
Churches: congregations.
Communicants: members with full membership status.

287 Mennonite Church, The General Conference
Churches: full members of the General Conference Mennonite Church.
Communicants: full members of the local church.
Adherents: full members plus children.

290 Metropolitan Community Churches, Universal Fellowship of
Churches: congregations recognized by the UFMCC and listed in our *Directory,* under the governance of the UFMCC bylaws.
Communicants: those listed on the official rolls, as required by the UFMCC bylaws.
Adherents: those who attend a local UFMCC church or who were members but moved to a location where there is no church; those who subscribe to our publications. Since we have rather a high commitment for membership, our average collective Sunday attendance in some cases more than doubles membership.

291 Missionary Church, The
Churches: organized body of believers.
Communicants: those making confession of faith for the first time, or transferring their membership from another church.
Adherents: total church worship service attendance.

293 Moravian Church in America (Unitas Fratrum), Northern Province
Churches: organized congregations.
Communicants: communicant membership.
Adherents: includes baptized children and others associated with the congregation.

295 Moravian Church in America (Unitas Fratrum), Southern Province
Adherents: non-communicants and children. Non-communicants are baptized children of communicant members. They remain non-communicants until they

become communicant members of a Moravian congregation or some other denomination or forfeit this privilege by misconduct in later years or failure to contribute to the financial support of the church. Unbaptized children of members and children under care of the church until their 16th year shall be listed as children of the church.

313 North American Baptist Conference
Churches: an organized body of baptized believers who have been duly constituted as a Baptist church and received into one of the 21 associations of the North American Baptist Conference.
Communicants: any individual who has received Jesus Christ as Savior and Lord, been baptized by immersion and requested membership in a given local church.

329 Open Bible Standard Churches, Inc.
Churches: Actual.
Communicants: average Sunday morning attendance. In our case, membership is not representative. Membership totals approximately one-third to one-half of attendance in most churches.
Adherents: Church constituency, i.e. those who consider our church "their church," includes shut-ins, etc.

335 Orthodox Presbyterian Church, The
Churches: organized congregations with a particular membership.
Communicants: persons who have made a credible profession of faith to ruling body in the local church.

347 Pentecostal Free Will Baptist Church, Inc., The
Churches: fully established indigenous churches.
Communicants: people who are members in good standing in one of the churches as specified above.

357 Presbyterian Church in the United States
Churches: organized churches (local congregations). No chapels or unorganized churches included.
Communicants: "Communing members are those who have made a profession of faith in Christ, have been baptized, and have been admitted by the session to the Lord's table. They are entitled to all the rights and privileges of the church, including the right to participate in the sacrament of the Lord's supper, the right to present children for baptism and the right to take part in meetings of the congregation of which they are members in good standing." *Book of Church Order,* PCUS 1979-1980, 7-1.

363 Primitive Methodist Church, U.S.A.
Communicants: Adult and junior.

367 The Protes'tant Conference of the Wisconsin Synod
Churches: congregations which meet weekly for divine worship. Typical Lutheran congregations.
Communicants: members who have professed themselves Lutheran Christians and take an active role in congregational life (attending services, partaking of Lord's supper, financial support).
Adherents: Above definition plus all baptized (but not yet confirmed) children, those less than about 14 years old.

371 Reformed Church in America
Churches: a formally organized body under the supervision of a classis.
Communicants: active communicants.
Adherents: total baptized membership plus those who participate in the life of the church but are not members.

403 Salvation Army, The
Churches: total number of neighborhood corps—community centers.
Communicants: full members: (four categories)—junior soldiers, senior soldiers, recruits, adherents.
Adherents: total constituent membership (unduplicated count)

413 Seventh-day Adventists
Churches: number of churches.
Communicants: church membership.

415 Seventh Day Baptist General Conference
Churches: locally constituted body officially recognized by the Seventh Day Baptist General Conference.
Communicants: baptized persons accepted for membership by local church.

419 Southern Baptist Convention
Churches: churches cooperating with the Southern Baptist Convention.
Communicants: membership totals reported by churches.

421 The Southern Methodist Church
Churches: body of members who must regularly meet for worship services and carry the function of a church.
Communicants: those who have professed a belief in Christ, have been baptized and received into membership.
Adherents: includes members of families who are members and attend, and other visitors who attend regularly.

435 Unitarian Universalist Association
Churches: societies belonging to the Unitarian Universalist Association, includes both fellowships and churches.
Communicants: defined by local society.

443 United Church of Christ
Churches: A UCC is a congregation that has been accepted into membership in the UCC by an association of the UCC.
Communicants: membership as reported by each local church on the UCC local church Yearbook report. Although no definition of membership is given on the Yearbook report, churches generally report only active resident members.

449 United Methodist Church, The
Churches: "The local church is a connectional society of persons who have professed their faith in Christ, have been baptized, have assumed the vows of membership in The United Methodist Church, and are associated in fellowship as a local United Methodist church in order that they may hear the Word of God, receive the Sacraments, and carry forward the work which Christ has committed to his Church. Such a society of believers, being within The United Methodist Church and subject to its Discipline, is also an inherent part of the Church Universal, which is composed of all who accept Jesus Christ as Lord and Savior, and which in the Apostles' Creed we declare to be the holy catholic Church." *Book of Discipline 1980,* par. 203.
Communicants: "The membership of a local United Methodist church shall include all baptized persons who have come into membership by confession of faith or transfer and whose names have not been removed from the membership rolls by reason of death, transfer, withdrawal, or removal for cause." *Book of Discipline 1980,* par. 209.

453 United Presbyterian Church in the USA, The
Churches: a building or congregation organized by the authority of a presbytery of the United Presbyterian Church of the USA and under the state laws where applicable.
Communicants: active member: a person who has made a profession of faith in Christ, who has been baptized, who has been received into membership of the church and who is in the church's work and worship.

469 Wisconsin Evangelical Lutheran Synod
Churches: local parishes or congregations.
Communicants: those eligible for communion are those who have been confirmed.
Adherents: communicants plus non-communicants, or total baptized members.

Appendix B

DENOMINATIONAL COMMENTS ON THE CMS FORMULA FOR ESTIMATING TOTAL ADHERENTS

001 Advent Christian Church
I agree with your process.

019 American Baptist Churches in the U.S.A
We accept your procedure.

061 Beachy Amish Mennonite Churches
Perhaps this method of computing would be more accurate if also some allowance were made for persons not attending any church.

065 Bethel Ministerial Association, Inc.
Appears to be the best way.

071 Brethren Church (Ashland, Ohio)
Fine.

097 Christian Churches and Churches of Christ
Statistically, the method is sound. Since we can only deal with this in a statistical manner for our purposes, I agree with the method.

101 Christian Methodist Episcopal Church
I have no objections to the procedure as described.

127 Church of God (Cleveland, Tennessee)
o.k.

157 Church of the Brethren
No suggestions.

177 Congregational Holiness Church
This is probably the best way to estimate.

181 Conservative Congregational Christian Conference
We would have no alternate suggestion.

199 Evangelical Congregational Church
If you compute according to your program, this figure will not be our reporting figure.

201 Evangelical Covenant Church of America, The
Estimation by staff is acceptable to us.

203 Evangelical Free Church of America, The
You may either use the procedure you have proposed, or just double the figure given for full members. Membership rolls in the Free Church do not usually include children, but only persons 18 years of age and older.

213 Evangelical Mennonite Church, Inc.
o.k.

217 Fire Baptized Holiness Church (Wesleyan), The
Your proposal to estimate total adherents is good.

237 General Conference of Mennonite Brethren Churches
Your suggested way would fit well with our membership procedures.

263 International Church of the Foursquare Gospel
This seems to be a logical plan for estimating total adherents.

270 Conservative Judaism
I would suggest using 18 years or under rather than 13 years.

285 Mennonite Church
Your projected procedure is acceptable.

313 North American Baptist Conference
We suggest you go ahead and estimate the adherents the way you have described.

335 Orthodox Presbyterian Church, The
Method proposed is appropriate.

347 Pentecostal Free Will Baptist Church, Inc., The
The described procedure is fair and adequate.

349 Pentecostal Holiness Church, Inc.
The number that attend our Sunday Schools.

357 Presbyterian Church in the United States
No suggestions.

375 Reformed Episcopal Church
Average estimated factor: multiply by one and one-third (based on consideration of Sunday School figures—non adult, and regular non-communicant supporters).

395 Romanian Orthodox Church in America, The
Acceptable.

415 Seventh Day Baptist General Conference
Described method is acceptable.

435 Unitarian Universalist Association
No suggestions.

443 United Church of Christ
The adjustment formula for communions not supplying data on total adherents is probably as appropriate as any, although it does probably overestimate the number of UCC adherents. We know from our studies that our membership is older than the population as a whole and that our members' fertility rates are low.

449   United Methodist Church, The
       (1) Appears to assume that children under 13 will be adherents in the same proportion as adults—a questionable assumption. (2) Affords no way of estimating adult adherents.

453   United Presbyterian Church in the U.S.A., The
       As good as any.

Appendix C

VIRGINIA INDEPENDENT CITY/COUNTY COMBINATIONS

Independent City	County	Abbreviation
Alexandria city *with*	Arlington	Arlington-Alexandria
Bedford city *with*	Bedford	Bedford-Bedford City
Bristol city *with*	Washington	Washington-Bristol
Buena Vista city *with*	Rockbridge	Rockbridge-Bn Vs-Lex
Charlottesville city *with*	Albemarle	Albemarle-Charlottes
Clifton Forge city *with*	Alleghany	Alleghany-Clf Fr-Cov
Colonial Heights city *with*	Dinwiddie	Dinwiddie-Col Ht-Pet
Covington city *with*	Alleghany	Alleghany-Clf-Fr-Cov
Danville city *with*	Pittsylvania	Pittsylvania-Danvill
Emporia city *with*	Greensville	Greensville-Emporia
Fairfax city *with*	Fairfax	Fairfax-Fairfx-Fl Ch
Falls Church city *with*	Fairfax	Fairfax-Fairfx-Fl Ch
Franklin city *with*	Southampton	Southampton-Franklin
Fredericksburg city *with*	Spotsylvania	Spotsylvania-Frederi
Galax city *with*	Carroll	Carroll-Galax City
Harrisonburg city *with*	Rockingham	Rockingham-Harrison
Hopewell city *with*	Prince George	Prince George-Hopewe
Lexington city *with*	Rockbridge	Rockbridge-Bn Vs-Lex
Lynchburg city *with*	Campbell	Campbell-Lynchburg
Manassas city *with*	Prince William	Prince William-Manassas
Manassas Park city *with*	Prince William	Prince William-Manassas
Martinsville city *with*	Henry	Henry-Martinsville
Norton city *with*	Wise	Wise-Norton City
Petersburg city *with*	Dinwiddie	Dinwiddie-Col Ht-Pet
Poquoson city *with*	York	York-Poquoson City
Radford city *with*	Montgomery	Montgomery-Radford
Richmond city *with*	Henrico	Henrico-Richmond
Roanoke city *with*	Roanoke	Roanoke-Roanoke-Salm
Salem city *with*	Roanoke	Roanoke-Roanoke-Salm
South Boston city *with*	Halifax	Halifax-South Boston
Staunton city *with*	Augusta	Augusta-Staun-Waynes
Waynesboro city *with*	Augusta	Augusta-Staun-Waynes
Williamsburg city *with*	James City	James City-Williams
Winchester city *with*	Frederick	Frederick-Winchester

The only exceptions to the above pattern occur in the case of Independent Cities which have annexed their parent counties. These are usually treated as separate "city-county" combinations and will be treated as such in the membership study.

Independent City	Name
Hampton city	Hampton City
Newport News city	Newport News City
Norfolk city	Norfolk-Chesap-Ports
Chesapeake city	
Portsmouth city	
Suffolk city	Suffolk City (formerly Nansemond County)
Virginia Beach city	Virginia Beach City

Appendix D

ALASKA COUNTY-EQUIVALENTS

1980	1970
Aleutian Islands	Part of Aleutian Islands
Anchorage	No change
Bethel	Part of Kuskokwim added
Bristol Bay (Borough)	No change
Dillingham	Bristol Bay Division. Part of Aleutian Islands added
Fairbanks North Star	Fairbanks
Haines	Part of Haines
Juneau	No change
Kenai Peninsula	Kenai-Cook Inlet and Seward
Ketchikan Gateway	Ketchikan
Kobuk	Parts of Kobuk and Nome
Kodiak Island	Kodiak
Matanuska-Susitna	No change
Nome	Part of Nome
North Slope	Parts of Barrow-North Slope, Kobuk and Upper Yukon
Prince of Wales-Outer Ketchikan	Prince of Wales and Outer Ketchikan
Sitka	Part of Sitka
Skagway-Yakutat-Angoon	Angoon, Skagway-Yakutat and parts of Haines and Wrangell-Petersburg
Southeast Fairbanks	Parts of Southeast Fairbanks and Upper Yukon
Valdez-Cordova	Cordova-McCarthy, Valdez-Chitina-Whittier and part of Southeast Fairbanks
Wade Hampton	Wade Hampton and part of Nome
Wrangell-Petersburg	Parts of Wrangell-Petersburg and Sitka
Yukon-Koyukuk	Yukon-Koyukuk and parts of Kuskokwim and Upper Yukon

Appendix E

SELF-ASSESSMENT OF REPORTING PROCEDURES

[An asterisk indicates that the group also supplied forms that were used in gathering the data. Those groups that supplied forms but did not comment on the accuracy of their reporting procedures are listed at the end.]

001   Advent Christian Church
      Better than 95 percent.

005   African Methodist Episcopal Zion Church
      Report is dependent upon yearly statistical report blanks submitted to each annual conference by pastors. Impossible to determine degree of accuracy.

017   American Baptist Association
      Estimates were made only when printed associational minutes were not available.

019 American Baptist Churches in the U.S.A.
We have succeeded in securing a membership figure for every church listed in our current roster, with the exception of the Alabama church noted in our print-out. Considerable effort has been expended to insure accuracy in these reports.

*029 American Lutheran Church, The
These statistics are based on current reports from 96.72 percent of the congregations whose membership is 97.75 percent of the total membership. The latest available baptized and confirmed membership figures were used for those congregations that did not submit current reports.

*053 Assemblies of God
Our total figures vary from those supplied to the *Yearbook of American Churches* because we count Puerto Rico and the Virgin Islands as an integral part of our General Council of the Assemblies of God in the United States. Also, the figures are non-comparable without figures released district by district for two reasons. First a number of our districts are multi-state or only part of a state. Also we have 8 non-geographic ethnic districts. The Hispanic, German, and Italian churches are added into their respective county and state in this report. These nongeographical ethnic districts represent some 8 per cent of our churches and constituency.

*059 Baptist Missionary Association of America
Data taken from churches reporting to local and district associations at the end of the church year. Minutes of these associations are collected and memberships are taken from those minutes for each church. Also, Baptist News Service mails each church a questionnaire and receives the same information.

061 Beachy Amish Mennonite Churches
Forms are mailed annually to a leader of each congregation to be filled in, indicating any change of leadership or number of members.

071 Brethren Church (Ashland, Ohio)
Information is sent from local church and tabulated for district and national reports.

075 Brethren In Christ Church
Our estimates are accepted as having general validity.

*081 Catholic Church
Figures are probably low.

097 Christian Churches and Churches of Christ
We used the most up to date statistics available at the time our research was done. These figures were from 1978-79. In a few cases we estimated membership where none was furnished for churches that were listed in the *Directory of The Ministry of Christian Churches/Churches of Christ.* Our procedure was based on the premise that the great majority of churches not reporting were small. In counties with a large population the small church had approximately 50 members. In counties with a small population the small churches had 25 members. These two figures were based on random contacts with small churches. Since only a few churches did not report their membership, we have determined our figures to be within 3 per cent accurate for the statistics that were available. When a city was listed in two counties of a state, the first county listed was credited with the churches and their membership. Our reference source was *Webster's New Geographical Dictionary,* published in 1972.

*105 Christian Reformed Church
They should be very accurate.

107 Christian Union
Some churches cooperated very well, but others did not; Arkansas and South Missouri very poorly. Others not reporting: Ohio 5, North Missouri 2, Iowa 2. I took information from other sources. I would say this report is 95 per cent correct.

133 Church of God (Seventh Day), Denver, Colorado, The
Isolated members were undoubtedly missed since the census was conducted at sabbath morning assembly.

149 Church of Jesus Christ, The (Bickertonites)
Accurate within plus or minus 0.02 per cent.

*165 Church of The Nazarene
Our procedures have been well established and our polity assures 100 per cent of local churches participating.

*167 Churches of Christ
Over one year of active solicitation by letter, visitation and phone calls has, in my opinion, produced a fairly accurate picture of the Churches of Christ. Totals are well below popular estimates, but these figures are realistic. No good census has been done on Churches of Christ since 1926.

177 Congregational Holiness Church
Taken from 1979 minutes of the 18th general conference.

179 Conservative Baptist Association of America
Our state directors who assisted us in this study misunderstood the directions, and figures were quite incomplete. However, I did add the number of adherents, as properly listed from 28 churches and divided them by 28. I came up with about 32 per cent of the average membership as determining those who are adherents. We did not total each state.

*181 Conservative Congregational Christian Conference
We record the information sent annually from our member churches; 15 per cent carry over old information.

*193 Episcopal Church, The
Each parish is required to report annually. Maximum error in a diocese would be a possible undercount of 1 per cent. The national totals are reliable (plus or minus 0.5 per cent).

195 Estonian Evangelical Lutheran Church
Pretty accurate.

197 Evangelical Church of North America, The
Reporting dates differ in some of our units, thus making for some slight discrepancy if individual county totals were to be added. The total given is as accurate as possible, as of the end of 1980.

*201 Evangelical Covenant Church of America, The
A high degree of accuracy has been achieved through the use of the attached annual statistical report form procedure.

*213 Evangelical Mennonite Church, Inc.
Each church is to fill out forms annually. We get full cooperation (with some repeated reminders).

217 Fire Baptized Holiness Church, (Wesleyan), The
Membership is updated annually and forwarded to the general secretary.

220 Free Lutheran Congregations, The Association of
Information secured from annual statistical reports sent by each congregation.

*221 Free Methodist Church of North America
For your general information, we have not, in the past, required churches to report the county in which they were located. Because of the number of small country churches in some states, considerable research was required to ascertain proper county position. I noticed that this caused a few differences in the position of a few churches when compared to their position reported in the 1971 church membership study you conducted. In future report forms, the county of each church will be required, thus alleviating the need for such long, time consuming research. My apologies for the delay in the transmittal of this information.

226 Friends
There is about 3 per cent difference in this report and material which we compiled in this office in April 1981 a year later. For this report we requested membership statistics from each Yearly Meeting office of the Society of Friends in USA, May 1980. Membership is defined in different ways. Some Monthly Meetings include children. Not all Meetings returned information and we did not always know the county location.

*237 General Conference of Mennonite Brethren Churches
We consider all our reporting procedures quite accurate in the area of membership. We are however dependent upon records and information submitted by the local church.

263 International Church of The Foursquare Gospel
The reporting procedures seem to be adequate.

270 Conservative Judaism
Our statistics are based on a yearly dues reporting form furnished by each member synagogue. We are totally dependent on the accuracy of their figures.

*274 Latvian Evangelical Lutheran Church In America, The
Quite accurate.

*281 Lutheran Church In America
The possibility exists for congregations to do an annual cleaning of membership rolls. However there is no churchwide uniformity in the performing of such a function. Other than that the statistics are quite adequate.

*287 Mennonite Church, The General Conference
Not all of the churches reported their membership this year. In that case, last year's figure was used if available. Some churches also do not report children, so that total adherents figure is low.

*290 Metropolitan Community Churches, Universal Fellowship of
Since we are small our figures are accurate. Each church reports its attendance and membership monthly.

291 Missionary Church, The
Based on reports submitted by churches and district offices.

293 Moravian Church In America (Unitas Fratrum), Northern Province
Statistics are accurate as of December 31, 1979. Where statistics were lacking, 1978 statistics were used.

*313 North American Baptist Conference
Of the 254 churches listed, 27 did not send in reports this year. Therefore, we used the figures we had from 1978.

323 Old Order Amish Church
There is no accurate way of determining membership of the Old Order Amish. All we use is the *Almanac's* Minister's List and to my knowledge it is about all we have that contains all the church districts.

*329 Open Bible Standard Churches, Inc.
Should be very accurate as they were obtained for us by our district superintendents.

335 Orthodox Presbyterian Church, The
Some counties not reported by churches. Best information used to determine missing counties.

347 Pentecostal Free Will Baptist Church, Inc., The
These statistics are reported to us by the officials of the local church and may be considered facts.

349 Pentecostal Holiness Church, Inc.
I took the churches recorded and located them in their proper county.

353 Christian Brethren
50 per cent of churches provided data. For the remainder, home office and field personnel provided data.

*357 Presbyterian Church In The United States
The membership figures are taken directly from our statistical files on the computer. The accuracy of the county report breaks down at the point of dividing members between our denomination and the other denominations. Our actual membership on Dec. 31, 1979 was 852,711.

367 The Protes'tant Conference of The Wisconsin Synod
Interviewed pastors of various congregations at annual conference.

*371 Reformed Church In America
Very accurate.

403 Salvation Army, The
Number of churches and full members 100 per cent accurate. Total adherents accurate to within 1-2 per cent.

413 Seventh-day Adventists
Each quarter begins with the closing membership of the previous quarter. Then the baptisms and letters of transfer into the church are added and the letters of transfer out to another church and the missing, deaths, apostasies are subtracted. This makes the total for that quarter. This is very accurate.

415 Seventh Day Baptist General Conference
Since Seventh Day Baptists are autonomous we are dependent upon their record keeping methods which may include inactive or non resident members.

*443 United Church of Christ
Our studies indicate that local church membership reporting is pretty good as church membership

statistics go. The vast majority of our churches report that they have a regular procedure for reviewing their membership rolls and most include in their reports only active resident members.

*453 United Presbyterian Church In The U.S.A., The
We believe that our figures are quite accurate. They are edited using figures supplied by the individual churches by using the previous year's ending figure, plus gains and minus losses to equal active members.

*469 Wisconsin Evangelical Lutheran Synod
Our pastors follow instructions pretty well, out of 1127, only 6 failed to report; figures for them were used from previous year. Figures requested and received are through December 31, 1979.

GROUPS WHO SUPPLIED FORMS USED TO COLLECT THE DATA, BUT WHO DID NOT COMMENT ON THE ACCURACY OF THEIR REPORTING PROCEDURES: 063 Berean Fundamental Church; 089 Christian and Missionary Alliance; 157 Church of the Brethren; 163 Church of the Lutheran Brethren of America; 185 Cumberland Presbyterian Church; 203 Evangelical Free Church of America; 295 Moravian Church in America (Unitas Fratrum), Southern Province; 356 Presbyterian Church in America; 359 Primitive Advent Christian Church; 363 Primitive Methodist Church, U.S.A.; 375 Reformed Episcopal Church; 419 Southern Baptist Convention; 435 Unitarian Universalist Association.

Appendix F

COMMENTS ON DUAL AFFILIATION OF CONGREGATIONS

019 American Baptist Churches in the U.S.A.
Of the reported churches, 773 are also affiliated with one or more other denominations: Baptist General Conference, Christian Church (Disciples of Christ), Church of the Brethren, North American Baptist General Conference, National Baptist Convention of America, National Baptist Convention U.S.A., Inc., Progressive National Baptist Convention, Reformed Church in America, Southern Baptist Convention, Episcopal Church, United Church of Christ, The United Methodist Church, United Presbyterian Church in the U.S.A.

055 Associate Reformed Presbyterian Church (General Synod)
One church, Presbyterian Church U.S.

057 Baptist General Conference
Only two, which are affiliated with American Baptist Churches U.S.A.

071 Brethren Church (Ashland, Ohio)
We have two congregations who maintain relations with the Grace Brethren Church (Winona Lake). It involves about 25 members in total.

075 Brethren In Christ Church
Only one church in the Atlantic Regional Conference.

093 Christian Church (Disciples of Christ)
We do not have complete records, but we estimate at least 20-25 churches have dual affiliation. This would involve federated and community churches, as well as others which could be affiliated with one or more denominations, such as Methodist, UCC, Presbyterian, Baptist, Church of the Brethren, etc.

157 Church of the Brethren
Yes, with Baptists.

163 Church of The Lutheran Brethren of America
Possibly only two congregations maintain affiliation with another denomination, but continue to use Lutheran Brethren pastors in their pulpits.

175 Congregational Christian Churches, Nat'l Association of
Not Significant.

179 Conservative Baptist Association of America
Minimal.

181 Conservative Congregational Christian Conference
One CCCC church belongs to the UCC. One other church belongs to the National Association of Congregational Churches.

185 Cumberland Presbyterian Church
We have a few congregations which are union or tri-union congregations with the PCUS and/or UPCUSA. But our membership figures report only one-third or one-half, as the case may be.

195 Estonian Evangelical Lutheran Church
Some affiliations are with LCA and Missouri synod.

208 Evangelical Lutheran Churches, Association of
About seven congregations. Four have dual membership in the LC-MS, one in the ALC and two with LCA.

237 General Conference of Mennonite Brethren Churches
Only two or three congregations are involved.

270 Conservative Judaism
A very few are also affiliated with the Union of American Hebrew Congregations.

274 Latvian Evangelical Lutheran Church in America, The
Churches of dual affiliation have been excluded. They would have belonged to LCA or ALC.

283 Lutheran Church—Missouri Synod, The
Less than one per cent of LC-MS congregations would possibly claim affiliation with the Association of Evangelical Lutheran Churches.

287 Mennonite Church, The General Conference
31 churches involved.

293 Moravian Church In America (Unitas Fratrum), Northern Province
Only in terms of sharing pastoral leadership.

313 North American Baptist Conference
One church in Brookfield, Wisconsin, American Baptist Churches.

357 Presbyterian Church In the United States
Of the 978,447 membership shown on page 54 of the PCUS computer printout, 251,371 are also members of other denominations—UPCUSA, United Methodists, Associate Reformed Presbyterian, Cumberland Presbyterian, United Church of Christ. [NOTE. With PCUS approval, the CMS staff subtracted from the PCUS original report one-half the total membership of those PCUS churches which are dually affiliated with the UPCUSA.]

371 Reformed Church In America
Very limited, with UPUSA and United Church of Christ.

419 Southern Baptist Convention
Many of our churches in the District of Columbia state convention are affiliated with the American Baptists. These churches are located both in DC and Maryland.

435 Unitarian Universalist Association
About 40 churches have dual affiliation, either federated churches or tied in with Congregational, Methodists, Baptists or Quakers.

443 United Church of Christ
Between five and ten per cent of our congregations maintain relations with a variety of Protestant communions.

449 United Methodist Church, The
Federated churches are instructed to report only their United Methodist membership to this office.

453 United Presbyterian Church In The U.S.A., The
Yes. On our listing the churches are indicated with a (U) to the right of the membership figure. That total should be doubled for the total membership of the church. The total listed membership is our denomination's portion of the total. The denomination that is affiliated with us is the Presbyterian Church in the U.S.

Appendix G

INSTRUMENTS FOR GATHERING THE DATA

Initial Invitation

Dear Friend,

We are writing to you at the suggestion of Constant Jacquet, editor of the *Yearbook of American Churches*. This is a cordial invitation to your denomination to participate in the 1980 update of the Church Membership Study. This study is a unique gathering of information which has the potential of meeting various needs of the institutional Church, the religious community at large, and religious and academic researchers. As a compilation of statistics from many religious bodies, it is an important planning and analytical tool. From its data we learn about our own and other communions in geographical, historical and comparative perspective. It is an important resource for documenting our challenge to evangelize the unchurched. Finally, it is the statistical foundation upon which much research is constructed, beneficial to religious and academic communities.

Denominations are asked to furnish 1979 county data on number of churches and members, by SEPTEMBER, 1980. Details are on the enclosed green sheet.

We will, of course, furnish complimentary copies of the study's printed publications to all participating communions.

A flyer about the study is enclosed. If you need more information, please let me know. In the meantime, PLEASE INDICATE YOUR WILLINGNESS TO PARTICIPATE IN THE STUDY BY RETURNING THE BLUE MEMORANDUM in the self-addressed envelope. We hope to hear from you soon.

Sincerely,

Rev. Bernard Quinn
Liaison for Data Collection

Memorandum of Participation—Form F

1. DENOMINATION:
2. CONTACT PERSON FOR DATA:
Name:
Address:
Title:
Phone:
3. EXPECTED DATE OF TRANSMITTAL:
The Committee is asking that statistics be sent to us no later than September 30, 1980. We hope to receive data for your statistical year that ends anytime during 1979; earlier data may be reported only if that is all that is available by September, 1980.

Please indicate the approximate date on which we might expect to receive the statistics in our office.
4. FORM OF TRANSMITTAL. Please check one:
_____ We plan to furnish the data by means of our own print-out, etc.
_____ Please send us Form C, containing a list of counties by state.
5. DATA AVAILABLE. Please check one:
_____ We are able to furnish county data on (1) number of churches, (2) number of communicant-confirmed-full members, and (3) number of total adherents.
_____ We are able to furnish county data on (1) and (2) only.

SIGNED: DATE:

Instructions for Reporting Denominational Data—Form A

DATA REQUESTED

For each state and county of the United States, we are requesting three items of information:
1. the number of CHURCHES: local parishes or congregations;
2. the number of COMMUNICANT, CONFIRMED, FULL MEMBERS: regular members with full membership status; and
3. (if available), the number of TOTAL ADHERENTS: all members, including full members, their children and the estimated number of other regular participants who are not considered as communicant, confirmed or full members, for example, the "baptized," "those not confirmed," "those not eligible for communion," and the like.

Procedure. Data may be reported on the State-County List (Form C) furnished by us, or, if more convenient, on your own computer print-out or list of comparable format. Please complete the Transmittal Sheet (Form B), which will be useful for determining the comparability of statistics reported by the various religious bodies.

DATE OF STATISTICS

We are asking that statistics be reported to us by the month of September, 1980. We hope to receive data for your *statistical year that ends anytime during 1979;* report earlier data only if that is all that is available by September, 1980.

SPECIAL PROBLEMS

DATA ON TOTAL ADHERENTS NOT AVAILABLE

It is our hope that denominations reporting full members will also be able to furnish data on total adherents. If they are unable to do so, the total adherents will be estimated by the staff of the Church Membership Study as follows: the total county population will be divided by the total county population less children 13 years of age and under, and the resulting figure will be multiplied by the communicant, confirmed or full members. In the published report, an asterisk will indicate that total adherents were estimated through use of this procedure.

If you will not be furnishing data on total adherents, please complete Item 5 on the Transmittal Sheet.

REPORTING COUNTY OF MEMBERSHIP VERSUS COUNTY OF RESIDENCE

Ideally, we hope to count church members in their county of residence instead of the county in which they hold membership or participate in a church. We realize,however, that many denominations count members in their county of membership or participation rather than in their county of residence. For the record, please state your policy on this by completing Item 6 on the Transmittal Sheet.

DUAL AFFILIATION OF LOCAL CHURCHES

Some local churches maintain affiliation with two denominations. If this is true of local churches in your denomination, please complete Item 7 on the Transmittal Sheet.

ALASKA

The data of the U.S. Census for Alaska has been classified by "census divisions." Since Alaska has no counties, the census divisions serve as county equivalents for statistical reporting purposes. A list of census divisions follows: [See *Appendix D.*]

VIRGINIA

In Virginia there are 38 "Independent Cities" which are legally separate from the counties of that state. Most denominations probably still record churches by location within the counties from which the cities have separated. For this reason we request that the data of your denomination be so organized as to record the data of the following Independent Cities with the counties indicated: [See *Appendix C.*]

Transmittal Sheet for Denominational Data—Form B

1. DENOMINATION:

   Name:
   Code: Abbreviation:
   Denominational Contact Person: (Name, Title, Address, Phone)

2. DATE OF STATISTICS REPORTED:

3. UNITED STATES TOTALS:
   Churches:
   Communicant, Confirmed or Full Members:
   Total Adherents (if Available):

4. DEFINITIONS ACTUALLY EMPLOYED IN REPORTING DATA:
   Churches:
   Communicant, Confirmed or Full Members:
   Total Adherents:

5. IF TOTAL ADHERENTS ARE NOT REPORTED:
   Please comment on the procedure described in the Instruction Sheet whereby we propose to estimate the total adherents. Is this the best way? Would you offer any suggestions?

6. COUNTY OF MEMBERSHIP VERSUS COUNTY OF RESIDENCE
   For the record, please state your general policy on reporting church members: by county of membership and/or by county of residence?

7. DUAL AFFILIATION OF LOCAL CHURCHES
   Do any local congregations of your denomination maintain affiliation with another denomination as well? If "yes," please indicate the general extent of this practice and the denomination(s) involved.

8. COMMENTS ON ACCURACY OF REPORTING PROCEDURES
   (Attach additional sheets if needed.)

NOTE. It would be greatly appreciated if you could attach to this Transmittal Sheet sample copies of forms used for gathering local data.

SIGNED: DATE:

State-County Form for Reporting Statistics—Form C

CHURCH MEMBERSHIP STUDY 1980

GROUP _____ PAGE _1_

STATE: ALABAMA

County	Number of Churches 1	Communicant, Confirmed, Full Members 2	Total Adherents 3
Autauga	_____	_____	_____
Baldwin	_____	_____	_____
Barbour	_____	_____	_____
Bibb	_____	_____	_____
Blount	_____	_____	_____
Bullock	_____	_____	_____
Butler	_____	_____	_____
Calhoun	_____	_____	_____
Chambers	_____	_____	_____
Cherokee	_____	_____	_____
Chilton	_____	_____	_____
Choctaw	_____	_____	_____
Clarke	_____	_____	_____
Clay	_____	_____	_____
Cleburne	_____	_____	_____
Coffee	_____	_____	_____
Colbert	_____	_____	_____
Conecuh	_____	_____	_____
Coosa	_____	_____	_____
Covington	_____	_____	_____
Crenshaw	_____	_____	_____
Cullman	_____	_____	_____
Dale	_____	_____	_____
Dallas	_____	_____	_____
De Kalb	_____	_____	_____
Elmore	_____	_____	_____